Glencoe Literature
Reading with Purpose

Course 1

Program Consultants

Jeffrey D. Wilhelm, PhD

Douglas Fisher, PhD

Kathleen A. Hinchman, PhD

David G. O'Brien, PhD

Taffy Raphael, PhD

Cynthia Hynd Shanahan, EdD

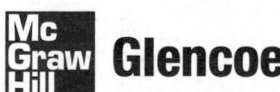

McGraw Hill **Glencoe**

New York, New York   Columbus, Ohio   Chicago, Illinois   Peoria, Illinois   Woodland Hills, California

Acknowledgments

Grateful acknowledgment is given authors, publishers, photographers, museums, and agents for permission to reprint the following copyrighted material. Every effort has been made to determine copyright owners. In case of any omissions, the Publisher will be pleased to make suitable acknowledgments in future editions.

Acknowledgments continued on page R83.

Glencoe

The *McGraw-Hill* Companies

Send all inquiries to:
Glencoe/McGraw-Hill
8787 Orion Place
Columbus, OH 43240-4027

ISBN-13 (student edition): 978-0-07-845476-9
ISBN-10 (student edition): 0-07-845476-X
ISBN-13 (teacher wraparound edition): 978-0-07-845487-5
ISBN-10 (teacher wraparound edition): 0-07-845487-5

Printed in the United States of America.

2 3 4 5 6 7 8 9 079/111 12 11 10 09 08 07 06

Senior Program Consultants

Jeffrey D. Wilhelm, PhD Jeffrey Wilhelm is Professor of English Education at Boise State University. He specializes in reading and adolescent literacy and does research on ways to engage readers and writers. A middle and high school teacher for thirteen years, Wilhelm is author or coauthor of eleven books, including the award-winning works *You Gotta BE the Book* and *Reading Don't Fix No Chevys.*

Douglas Fisher, PhD Douglas Fisher is Professor of Language and Literacy Education at San Diego State University. He is also Director of the award-winning City Heights Educational Pilot, a project for improving urban adolescent literacy. Fisher has published many articles on reading and literacy and has co-authored *Improving Adolescent Literacy: Strategies that Work.*

Program Consultants

Kathleen A. Hinchman, PhD Kathleen Hinchman is Professor and Chair, Reading and Language Arts Center, School of Education, Syracuse University. A former middle school English and reading teacher, Hinchman researches social perspectives toward literacy. She is coauthor of three books on reading and literacy, including *Principled Practices of a Literate America: A Framework for Literacy and Learning in the Upper Grades.*

David G. O'Brien, PhD David O'Brien is Professor of Literacy Education at the University of Minnesota and a former classroom teacher. O'Brien's research explores reading in content areas as well as ways to motivate learners to engage in school-based literacy tasks. He is conducting studies on the use of technology-based literacy, using computers and related technology.

Taffy Raphael, PhD Taffy Raphael is Professor of Literacy Education at the University of Illinois at Chicago (UIC). She does literacy research on upper elementary and middle school students and has coauthored several books, including *Book Club: A Literature-Based Curriculum* and *Book Club for Middle School.* She has received the International Reading Association (IRA) Outstanding Educator Award and is in the IRA Hall of Fame.

Cynthia Hynd Shanahan, EdD Cynthia Hynd Shanahan is Professor in the Reading, Writing, and Literacy program at the University of Illinois at Chicago (UIC). She is also a consultant with the Center for Literacy at UIC. Hynd Shanahan has been a classroom teacher and has taught reading instruction to elementary-level through college-level teachers. She has authored a chapter in the book *Engaged Reading,* edited by John T. Guthrie and Donna Alverman.

Advisory Board

Special Consultants

FOLDABLE **Dinah Zike, MEd** Dinah Zike was a classroom teacher and a consultant for many years before she began to develop Foldables™—a variety of easily created graphic organizers. Zike has written and developed more than 150 supplemental books and materials used in classrooms worldwide. Her *Big Book of Books and Activities* won the Teacher's Choice Award.

Mary A. Avalos, PhD Mary Avalos is Assistant Professor and Director of the TESOL Graduate Program at the University of Miami, Coral Gables, Florida. Her contributions to TESOL books include "No Two Learners Are Alike: Readers with Linguistic and Cultural Differences," in *Reading Assessment and Instruction for All Learners,* by J. S. Schrum (ed.) Avalos is a frequent presenter at reading and TESOL conferences.

Glencoe National Reading and Language Arts Advisory Council

Wanda J. Blanchett, PhD
Associate Dean for Academic
    Affairs and Associate Professor
    of Exceptional Education
School of Education
University of Wisconsin-Milwaukee
Milwaukee, Wisconsin

William G. Brozo, PhD
Professor of Literacy
Graduate School of Education,
    College of Education and
    Human Development
George Mason University
Fairfax, Virginia

Nancy Drew, EdD
LaPointe Educational Consultants
Corpus Christi, Texas 78411

Susan Floria-Ruane, EdD
Professor, College of Education
Michigan State University
East Lansing, Michigan

Nancy Frey, PhD
Associate Professor of Literacy in
    Teacher Education
School of Teacher Education
San Diego State University
San Diego, California

Kimberly Lawless, PhD
Associate Professor
Curriculum, Instruction and
    Evaluation
College of Education
University of Illinois at Chicago
Chicago, Illinois

Sharon Fontenot O'Neal, PhD
Associate Professor
Texas State University
San Marcos, Texas

William Ray, MA
Lincoln-Sudbury Regional High
    School
Sudbury, Massachusetts

Victoria Gentry Ridgeway, PhD
Associate Professor
Reading Education
Clemson University
Clemson, South Carolina

Janet Saito-Furukawa, MEd
Literacy Coach
Washington Irving Middle School
Los Angeles, California

Bonnie Valdes, MEd
Independent Reading Consultant
CRISS Master Trainer
Largo, Florida

Teacher Reviewers

The following teachers contributed to the review of *Glencoe Literature*.

Bridget M. Agnew
St. Michael School
Chicago, IL

Monica Anzaldua Araiza
Dr. Juliet V. Garcia Middle School
Brownsville, TX

Katherine R. Baer
Howard County Public Schools
Ellicott City, MD

Tanya Baxter
Roald Amundsen High School
Chicago, IL

Danielle R. Brain
Thomas R. Proctor Senior High School
Utica, NY

Yolanda Conder
Owasso Mid-High School
Owasso, OK

Gwenn De Mauriac
The Wiscasset Schools
Wiscasset, ME

Courtney Doan
Bloomington High School
Bloomington, IL

Susan M. Griffin
Edison Preparatory School
Tulsa, OK

Cindi Davis Harris
Helix Charter High School
La Mesa, CA

Joseph F. Hutchinson
Toledo Public Schools
Toledo, OH

Ginger Jordan
Florien High School
Florien, LA

Dianne Konkel
Cypress Lake Middle School
Fort Myers, FL

Melanie A. LaFleur
Many High School
Many, LA

Patricia Lee
Radnor Middle School
Wayne, PA

Linda Copley Lemons
Cleveland High School
Cleveland, TN

Heather S. Lewis
Waverly Middle School
Lansing, MI

Sandra C. Lott
Aiken Optional School
Alexandria, LA

Connie M. Malacarne
O'Fallon Township High School
O'Fallon, IL

Lori Howton Means
Edward A. Fulton Junior High School
O'Fallon, IL

Claire C. Meitl
Howard County Public Schools
Ellicott City, MD

Patricia P. Mitcham
Mohawk High School (Retired)
New Castle, PA

Lisa Morefield
South-Western Career Academy
Grove City, OH

Kevin M. Morrison
Hazelwood East High School
St. Louis, MO

Jenine M. Pokorak
School Without Walls Senior
High School, Washington, D.C.

Susan Winslow Putnam
Butler High School
Matthews, NC

Paul C. Putnoki
Torrington Middle School
Torrington, CT

Stephanie L. Robin
N. P. Moss Middle School
Lafayette, LA

Ann C. Ryan
Lindenwold High School
Lindenwold, NJ

Pamela Schoen
Hopkins High School
Minnetonka, MN

Megan Schumacher
Friends' Central School
Wynnewood, PA

Fareeda J. Shabazz
Paul Revere Elementary School
Chicago, IL

Molly Steinlage
Brookpark Middle School
Grove City, OH

Barry Stevenson
Garnet Valley Middle School
Glen Mills, PA

Paul Stevenson
Edison Preparatory School
Tulsa, OK

Jane Thompson Rae
Cab Calloway High School of the Arts
Wilmington, DE

Kathy Thompson
Owasso Mid-High School
Owasso, OK

Teacher Wraparound Edition Overview

Research-Based Classroom Solution

Instructional Planning

Book Overview

UNIT 1   Why Read? 1

Genre Focus:	Informational Media
Reading Skills:	Setting a Purpose for Reading, Skimming and Scanning, Understanding Graphics, Identifying Main Idea and Supporting Details
Text and Literary Elements:	Text Features, Titles and Subheads, Process, Author's Purpose
Writing Product:	Summary
English Language Coach:	Word References, Multiple-Meaning Words
Grammar:	Parts of Speech, Verbs

UNIT 2   What Brings Out the Best in You? 114

Genre Focus:	Biography/Autobiography
Reading Skills:	Activating Prior Knowledge, Connecting, Predicting, Questioning
Literary Elements:	Narrator, Point of View, Chronological Order, Tone
Writing Product:	Autobiographical Narrative
English Language Coach:	Synonyms, Antonyms, Negating Prefixes, Word Choice
Grammar:	Nouns, Pronouns

UNIT 3   What's Fair and What's Not? 252

Genre Focus:	Persuasive Writing
Reading Skills:	Distinguishing Fact and Opinion, Clarifying, Inferring, Identifying Problems and Solutions
Literary Elements:	Author's Style, Bias, Argument, Mood
Writing Product:	Persuasive Essay
English Language Coach:	Denotation/Connotation, Synonyms and Shades of Meaning, Semantic Slanting
Grammar:	Adjectives, Adverbs, Other Parts of Speech

UNIT 4   What Makes You Who You Are? 370

Genre Focus:	Poetry
Reading Skills:	Visualizing, Responding, Interpreting, Monitoring Comprehension
Literary Elements:	Poetic Features, Sound Devices, Rhythm, Rhyme, and Meter, Figurative Language
Writing Product:	Poetry
English Language Coach:	Context Clues, Definition and Restatement, Comparison and Contrast, Examples
Grammar:	Sentences, Fragments, Subject/Predicate, Direct and Indirect Objects

Reference Section

Contents

UNIT 2

 What Brings Out
the Best in You? 114

Genre Focus: Biography/Autobiography

Reading Skills Focus
Activating Prior Knowledge
Connecting
Predicting
Questioning

Vocabulary Skills
Synonyms
Antonyms
Negating Prefixes
Word Choice

Literary Elements
Narrator
Point of View
Tone
Chronological Order

Grammar
Nouns
Pronouns

UNIT 3

Genre Focus: Persuasive Writing

Reading Skills Focus
Distinguishing Fact and Opinion
Clarifying
Inferring
Identifying Problems and
   Solutions

Vocabulary Skills
Denotation/Connotation
Synonyms and Shades
   of Meaning
Semantic Slanting

Literary Elements
Author's Style
Bias
Argument
Mood

Grammar
Adjectives
Adverbs
Other Parts
   of Speech

UNIT 4

The BIG Question What Makes You Who You Are? 370

Genre Focus: Poetry

Reading Skills Focus
Visualizing
Responding
Interpreting
Monitoring Comprehension

Literary Elements
Poetic Features
Sound Devices
Rhythm, Rhyme, and Meter
Figurative Language

Vocabulary Skills
Context Clues
(Definition and Restatement,
    Comparison and Contrast,
    Examples)

Grammar
Sentences
Fragments
Subject/Predicate
Direct and Indirect
    Objects

UNIT 5

How Should You Deal with Bullies? 480

Genre Focus: Short Story

Reading Skills Focus
Drawing Conclusions
Understanding Cause and Effect
Identifying Sequence
Paraphrasing and Summarizing

Vocabulary Skills
Base Words   Prefixes
Suffixes   Roots

Literary Elements
Dialogue
Conflict
Plot
Characterization

Grammar
Phrases
Independent and Dependent Clauses
Commas

UNIT 6

 What Makes a Hero? 614

Genre Focus: Folktale, Fantasy, and Myth

Reading Skills Focus
Activating Prior
  Knowledge
Clarifying
Comparing
  and Contrasting
Predicting

Vocabulary Skills
Compound Words
Borrowed Words
Word Histories

Literary Elements
Hero
Cultural Context
Theme
Setting

Grammar
Capitalization
Sentence Combining
Run-on Sentences
Commas in Sentences

UNIT 7

 What Can We Learn from Our Mistakes? . . 772

Genre Focus: Historical Fiction and Nonfiction

Reading Skills Focus
Synthesizing
Identifying Main Idea and
   Supporting Details
Evaluating
Inferring

Vocabulary Skills
Base Words and Roots
Latin Roots
Greek Roots
Anglo-Saxon Origins

Literary Elements
Symbol
Narrator
Description
Time Order/Sequence

Grammar
Subject-Verb
   Agreement

UNIT 8

 What Makes a Friend? 926

Genre Focus: Drama

Reading Skills Focus
Visualizing
Clarifying
Skimming and Scanning
Predicting

Literary Elements
Act and Scene
Characterization
Stage Directions
Sensory Imagery

Vocabulary Skills
Dialect and Slang
Clipped Words
Literal/Figurative Meanings
Idioms

Grammar
Hyphens
Semicolons
Colons
Quotation Marks

Selections by Genre

Fiction

Poetry

Drama

Folktales

Graphic Stories and Cartoons

Personal Essays

Biography, Autobiography, Memoirs, Letters

Informational Texts

Historical Documents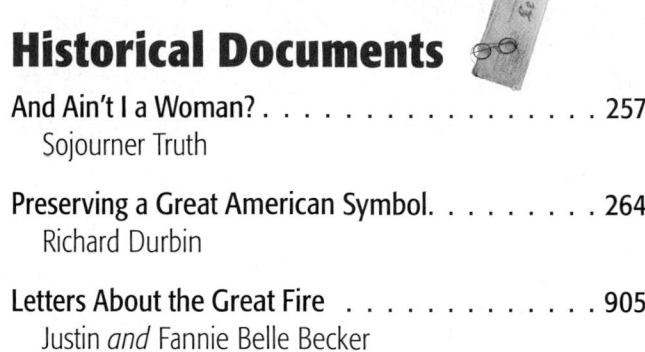

Functional Texts

Skills Features

Comparing Literature

VOCABULARY SKILLS

English Language Coach

WRITING SKILLS

Writing Products

Writing Traits

GRAMMAR SKILLS

LISTENING, SPEAKING, AND VIEWING

Philosophy Statement

By Jeffrey D. Wilhelm, Ph.D.

The middle school series, *Reading with Purpose*, is a unique and powerful program designed to engage your students in reading a variety of texts. The program is an integrated, inquiry-oriented approach based on the latest research in motivation, general and literacy education, and cognitive science.

Motivation

Motivating students is the greatest challenge facing teachers today, particularly when it comes to reading and writing. The seminal research of John Guthrie (2002), my own research on adolescent boys and literacy development (Smith and Wilhelm, 2002, 2006), and various national reports and reviews (e.g., Hidi and Harackiewicz, 2000) confirm this challenge. (Editor's note: Wilhelm's research won the NCTE Russell Award for Distinguished Research in English Education.)

When Michael Smith and I undertook our study on the literacy habits of adolescent and teenage males, we found that before students would engage with a literary text, they had to understand the purpose for reading such a text. Students are also more inclined to engage with a text if they are assured to receive the necessary assistance to successfully comprehend the material. The research of Czikszentmihalyi (1990), Gee (2003), and others indicate *Reading with Purpose* is designed first and foremost to meet these motivational prerequisites for engagement and learning.

Inquiry

Inquiry is the most powerful instructional tool to engage students' interest in reading and discovery. George Hillocks (see 1995, 1999) famously argued that all reading and writing are forms of inquiry, and therefore most effectively taught and learned through an inquiry process. In our own research (Smith and Wilhelm, 2002, 2006), we found that inquiry met all the conditions of "flow" sought by our student informants.

Essential Questions

An inquiry-oriented program has many positive effects. First, it organizes instruction around an "essential question" (also known as a big or guiding question). This question must be personally relevant and socially significant to the student. The question must connect students to problems they confront in both the textual material and their own lives.

An essential question makes learning "matter" as students relate to and form individual answers to the question. Inquiry-based learning also provides what is known as "curricular coherence" and "curricular integration" (Jacobs, 1989; Wiggins and McTighe, 2003; see Applebee, Burroughs, Stevens, 2000, and Caskey, 2006 for nice reviews of the importance of coherence and integration to learning).

Curricular coherence is achieved by focusing both conceptual and procedural instruction around the essential question. *Reading with Purpose* presents stories, poems, and informational texts all in the same unit. Although the genres in a particular workshop may vary, every selection is unified by the essential question. By reading selections chosen in service to an essential question, students are exposed to different perspectives they may consider when formulating their own views on a central theme.

Big Understandings

Students using an inquiry approach are more likely to read with purpose and motivation. Students learn major conceptual understandings to apply both to their lives and future reading and writing. The work of John Dewey and Ralph Tyler in the 1930s and '40s (e.g., Tyler, 1949) demonstrates that students quickly forget material presented in information-driven instruction. The hands-on inquiry approach results in central understandings much more likely to be remembered and transferred to new situations.

Strategic Reading and Writing

Curricular integration also includes problem solving, speaking, and listening skills. Inquiry-based learning connects those skills to the student's reading and writing assignments. This approach allows many skills to be taught under one unifying theme—the essential question. Many researchers, including myself (see Wilhelm, Baker, and Dube-Hackett, 2001) have explored how reading and writing are two sides of the same coin. For example, writing a narrative requires the same conventions, declarative knowledge, and strategic knowledge as reading a narrative: what a writer must "code" into a narrative or argument must also be "decoded" and interpreted by the reader of that text. Simply put, teaching the reading and writing techniques of particular genre structures simultaneously makes learning more efficient.

Contextualized Skill and Strategy Development

Reading with Purpose pays special attention to the development of a student "tool box" through the context of unit inquiries. The "tool box" is a concept promoted by socio-cultural psychology and current cognitive science (e.g., Wertsch, 1998). Each unit works step-by-step and activity-by-activity to develop conceptual and strategic tools that are important to exploring, discussing, writing about, and ultimately understanding the knowledge base related to the essential question. Students are given explicit knowledge of and repeated practice with the strategies that are necessary to read and write texts to explore and understand the question. Since particular genres are often particularly powerful for addressing certain topics, *Reading with Purpose* focuses on particular genres in each unit. In this way, strategies are developed to meet a purpose in a meaningful context. The work on "situated cognition" (see Brown, Collins, DuGuid, 1989)

shows that "situations co-produce knowledge." With a meaningful purpose, students are motivated to read, develop strategic knowledge, and learn which concepts to concentrate on and remember.

Differentiated Instruction

All classroom teachers understand that their students bring different interests, needs, and abilities to class. It is absolutely necessary to differentiate instruction to meet students in their various "zones of proximal development," the motivational or cognitive zones in which students become motivated to do something that they would not attempt on their own (Wilhelm, 2006).

Differentiated instruction allows students to read texts that are geared to their interests and abilities. Teachers have the flexibility to engage students in particular strategies, work individually or in small groups, and still be part of the common classroom project of pursuing the essential question. With inquiry-based learning, differences become assets and resources; those who read different texts and learn skills at varying levels offer unique contributions to the group's understanding (Wilhelm, 2006). That is why *Reading with Purpose* includes popular culture resources, selections of young adult literature, and canonical texts that can be used with individual students or small groups. We have also recommended various selections and activities to pursue with different students in order to maximize the power of differentiation.

Works Cited

Applebee, A. N., Burroughs, R., and Stevens, A. S. 2000. "Shaping Conversations: A Study of Continuity and Coherence in High School Literature Curricula." *Research in the Teaching of English*, 34: 396–429.

Brown, J., Collins, A., and DuGuid, P. 1989. "Situated Cognition and the Culture of Learning." *Educational Researcher*, 18, 32–42.

Caskey, M. 2006. "The Evidence for Core Curriculum—Past and Present." *Middle School Journal*, (47)3, 48-54.

Csikszentmihalyi, Mihalyi. 1990 *Flow: The psychology of optimal experience*. New York: Harper and Row.

Gee, James. 2003. *What Video Games Have to Teach Us About Learning and Literacy*. New York: Palgrave Macmillan.

Guthrie, J. 2002. "Classroom contexts for engaged reading: An Overview." http://www.cori.umd.edu/Research/Papers/Classroom.htm.

Hidi, S., & Harackiewicz, J. M. 2000. "Motivating the academically unmotivated: A critical issue for the 21st century." *Review of Educational Research*, 70, 151-180.

Hillocks, G. 1995. *Teaching Writing as Reflective Practice*. New York: Teachers College Press.

Hillocks, G. 1999. *Ways of Teaching/Ways of Learning*. New York: Teachers College Press.

Jacobs, Heidi Hayes. 1989. *Interdisciplinary Curriculum: Design and Implementation*. Washington DC: ASCD.

Smith, Michael W. and Wilhelm, Jeffrey D. 2006. *Going with the Flow: How to engage boys (and girls) in their literacy learning*. Portsmouth, NH: Heinemann.

Smith, Michael W. and Wilhelm, Jeffrey D. 2002. *Reading Don't Fix No Chevys: Literacy in the lives of young men*. Portsmouth, NH: Heinemann.

Tyler, R. 1949. *Basic principles of curriculum and instruction*. Chicago: University of Chicago Press.

Wertsch, J. 1998. *Mind as action*. New York: Oxford University Press.

Wiggins, Grant and McTighe, Jay. 2003. *Understanding by Design*. Washington DC: ASCD.

Wilhelm, J. D., Baker, T. and Dube-Hackett, J. 2001. *Strategic Reading*. Portsmouth, NH: Heinemann.

Wilhelm, Jeffrey D. 2006. *Inquiring Minds Learn to Read and Write: Inquiry, Questioning and Discussion Strategies to Improve Reading and Writing*. New York: Scholastic.

The *Reading Next* Report

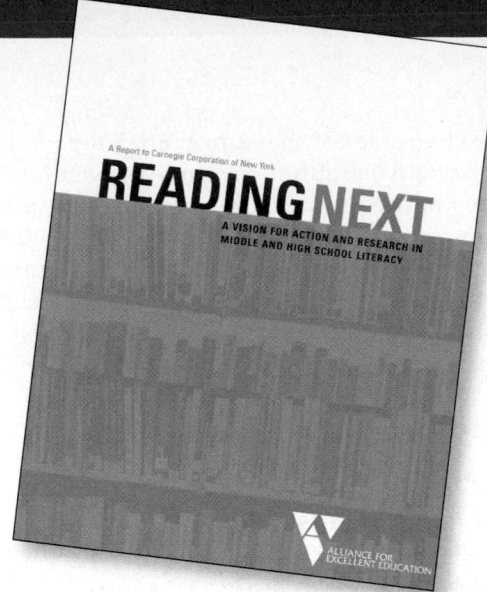

What Is It?

In 2004, the Carnegie Corporation released *Reading Next—A Vision for Action and Research in Middle and High School Literacy: A Report from Carnegie Corporation of New York*. Authored by Harvard researchers Gina Biancarosa and Dr. Catherine Snow, and published by the Alliance for Excellent Education in Washington, D.C., the report responds to the growing literacy crisis among middle and high school students.

The statistics bear out the severity of the problem. In the United States today, more than 8 million students in grades 4–12 lack the ability to read proficiently (U.S. DOE, 2003). Every day, more than 3,000 students drop out of high school (Alliance for Excellent Education, 2003)—largely because they lack the literacy skills to keep up (Kamil, 2003; Snow and Biancarosa, 2003). Only 70 percent of high school students graduate on time, and fewer than 60 percent of all African American and Latino students get their diplomas (Greene, 2002). Clearly, these numbers paint a picture of a system in crisis.

The driving force behind the *Reading Next* report is simple. Students who lack literacy skills face serious disadvantages in almost every aspect of their lives—at school, at work, and in the community. Research indicates that most middle and high school readers can decode. Many of these readers, however, are unable to conceptualize what they read or to connect new words and ideas to those they already know. Unable to comprehend the various texts they encounter, these students quickly fall behind.

The *Reading Next* report draws attention to this problem and seeks to dispel the outdated notion that struggling and reluctant middle and high school readers are unable to benefit from literacy instruction. Instead, the report asserts, these students can and *do* benefit—significantly—from literacy instruction. Educators and other interested parties should then work hard to develop effective literacy programs for struggling middle and high school students.

Why Is It Important?

The report identifies fifteen characteristics of an effective literacy program. The first nine characteristics, or recommendations, are instructional—ideas and activities that teachers can implement. The remaining six are infrastructural—ideas and activities that can be realized at the school-wide level, or in the student's home or community.

According to the report, effective literacy programs for struggling readers share the following **instructional** components:

1. **Direct, explicit comprehension instruction,** or teaching core reading strategies.
2. **Effective instructional principles embedded in content,** or teaching students to use reading skills in all content areas.
3. **Motivation and self-directed learning,** or motivating students to read (now *and* after graduation), and to become independent, lifelong learners.
4. **Text-based collaborative learning,** or teaching students to interact with one another vis-à-vis using a variety of texts.
5. **Strategic tutoring,** or giving students intense, individualized instruction when necessary.
6. **Diverse texts,** or using texts whose genre, topic, and level of difficulty vary.
7. **Intensive writing,** or offering instruction that relates to the writing tasks students will perform at the high school level and beyond.
8. **A technology component,** or using technology as a tool for and topic of literacy instruction.
9. **Ongoing formative assessment of students,** or conducting frequent, informal assessments of student progress under current instructional practices.

The report also notes that effective literacy programs share the following **infrastructural** components:

10. **Extended time for literacy,** or offering two to four hours of interdisciplinary (cross-classroom and cross-content area) literacy instruction per day.
11. **Professional development,** or offering long-term and ongoing support for teachers.
12. **Ongoing summative assessment of students and programs,** or evaluating students and educators in order to build accountability and improve systems.

13. **Teacher teams,** or forming interdisciplinary groups that discuss and are accountable for students' progress.

14. **Leadership,** or the execution of program goals by teachers and principals who understand their students and their reading and writing curriculum.

15. **A comprehensive and coordinated literacy program,** or the formation of a literacy program that draws strength from various disciplines, departments, and community organizations.

Reading with Purpose and the *Reading Next* Report

The *Reading Next* report recommends nine instructional improvements, and the *Reading with Purpose* program equips teachers to implement all of them—when, where, and how they choose. Developed with these improvements in mind, this program helps teachers help students in the ways that matter most.

The *Reading Next* Report recommends:	*Reading with Purpose* features:
direct, explicit comprehension instruction	**Genre Focus:** highlights 4 reading skills and 4 literary elements **Reading Workshops: Skill Lesson**—explicit instruction on one reading skill **Reading Selections**—vocabulary instruction and review, side notes that provide explicit reading skill instruction and practice
effective instructional principles embedded in content	**Reading, Writing, Comparing Literature and Reading Across Texts Workshops:** inquiry-based instruction using the Workshop approach; teach-model-practice-assess mode of instruction
motivation and self-directed learning	**Big Questions:** Inquiry-based instruction **Unit Challenges:** choice of activities **Learner's Notebooks and Foldables:** record individual's thoughts and learning
text-based collaborative learning	**Workshop Approach:** emphasis on collaboration **Partner Talk, Think-Pair-Share, Small-Group Discussion, and Whole-Class Discussion:** activities that emphasize collaboration **Unit Challenge:** includes a suggested group activity
strategic tutoring	**Partner Talk and Think-Pair-Share:** students work one-on-one with one another, and/or with an instructor **Reading and Writing Workshops:** opportunity to work in small mentoring groups
diverse texts	**Genre Focus:** one per unit **Diverse reading selections:** fiction, nonfiction, informational text **Reading on Your Own:** suggested readings at the end of each unit
intensive writing	**Writing Workshop:** a two-part writing project in every unit; teaches students to write within the focus genre **Reading Workshops:** students encounter numerous writing activities, including the **Write to Learn** prompt
a technology component	Examples include **glencoe.online,** the **Student Works CD-ROM,** and the **Skill Level Up! CD-ROM**
ongoing formative assessment of students	**After You Read:** assessment and skills review following each reading selection **Test Practice:** skills and strategies assessment **Ancillary Assessment materials: Selection Quick Checks, Assessment by Objectives, Examview Pro Assessment Suite, Selection and Unit Assessments**

Inquiry-Based Instruction

By Jeffrey D. Wilhelm, Ph.D.

As educators, we often fail to establish the relevance of what we teach. For example, the boys in my *Reading Don't Fix No Chevys* study (Smith and Wilhelm, 2002) felt that what they learned in school was completely separate from, and not useful in, "real" life. In short, they wanted the type of education that MIT physicist Jerrold Zaccharias championed—one that raises, as Zaccharias put it, "questions worth arguing about."

How, then, do we use "hands-on/minds-on" modes of instruction to help students ask and answer worthwhile questions? The research is in, and it points toward inquiry. Shown to improve student engagement, attitude, achievement, and learning in a variety of areas, inquiry approaches eclipse other modes of simple information transmission—and best help students do the work that matters.

What Is Inquiry?

Inquiry is the problem-oriented exploration of questions that drive and organize disciplines. Through inquiry, students learn essential concepts and strategies for applying those concepts in the real world. They engage the same problems and questions that real practitioners of a given discipline engage, and therefore learn to think, read, and write like experts in that area.

Discovering information is part of true inquiry, *but it is only the first step.* Inquirers must then interpret that information and shape it into knowledge. Human beings want to make meanings, not just receive them—or, as James Britton famously remarked, "Being told is the opposite of finding out."

To this end, research shows that inquiry approaches—active, discussion-based, and supported by a purposeful curriculum—focus on HOW to do something, and WHY to do it (Applebee, 1996; Hillocks, 1995, 1999, 2002; Applebee, Langer, Nystrand, and Gamoran, 2003; Nystrand, 1997). However, teacher-centered approaches—often lecture, memorization, and test-based—focus simply on WHAT to do (see Rogoff, Matusov, White, 1996).

Literacy researcher George Hillocks argues that reading and writing are forms of inquiry and are best taught, and learned, in that context. His research findings support that argument. According to Hillocks, inquiry approaches had the most powerful effects on student engagement, learning, and achievement (see Hillocks, 1995, 1999, 2002).

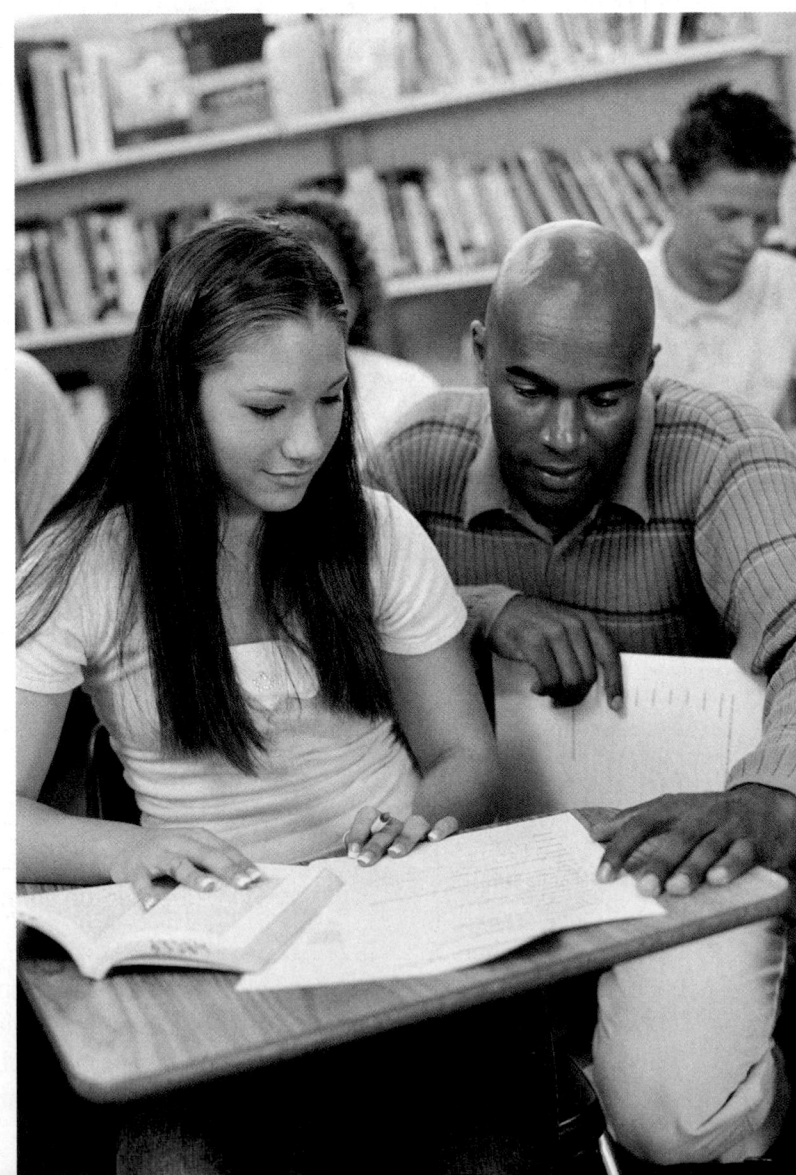

How Is Inquiry Applied in *Reading with Purpose?*

Motivation My research (Smith and Wilhelm, 2002, 2006; Wilhelm and Friedemann, 1998) has shown that the inquiry approach, organized around essential questions, increases student engagement. Because it is organized around Big Questions, the instruction in *Reading with Purpose* makes learning matter to students in very immediate ways.

Meaningful Context In *Reading with Purpose,* the reading, writing, and language activities are organized around real issues that students face in their own lives. When students practice a skill or create a writing product, they are also learning to ask and think through important real-life questions.

Schema Theory Modern cognitive science explains that people learn by either assimilating new data into existing patterns, or "schema," or by changing schema to accommodate new data. In *Reading with Purpose,* units are organized so that students develop their schema text-by-text and activity-by-activity. Doing this allows students to build their schema about the inquiry question and to develop key reading and writing tools. This gives students a coherent learning experience, where each activity better equips them for the next.

Curricular Coherence and Integration Inquiry teaching uses what Applebee, Burroughs, and Stevens (2000) call an *integrated* curriculum, or a curriculum that helps students build a set of skills that they apply with increasing sophistication across a range of activities. The integrated curriculum helps students achieve a range of objectives (Wiggins and McTighe, 1998). For example, students address the socially significant Big Question as developing readers and writers. They also encounter grammar in the context of the literary selections—and their own writing—so that the lessons they learn are situated and meaningful. In *Reading with Purpose,* reading and writing are integrated as forms of inquiry taught in an inquiring context. Use this exciting approach and watch your students begin to ask—and answer—the questions that matter most.

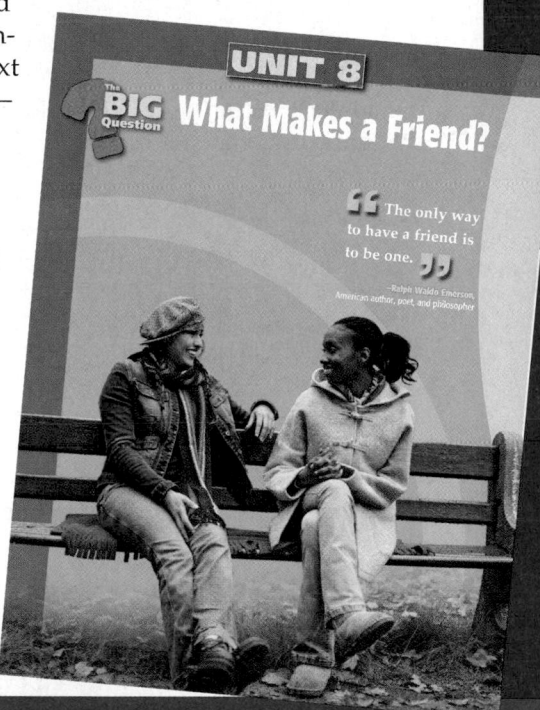

Works Cited

Applebee, A. N., Burroughs, R., and Stevens, A.S. 2000. "Shaping Conversation: A Study of Continuity and Coherence in High School Literature Curricula." *Research in the Teaching of English,* 34: 396–429.

Applebee, A.N. 1996. *Curriculum as conversation: Transforming traditions of teaching and learning.* Chicago: University of Chicago Press.

Applebee, A., Langer, J., Nystrand, M. and Gamoran, A. 2003. "Discussion-Based Approaches to Developing Understanding: Classroom Instruction and Student Performance in Middle and High School English." *American Educational Research Journal,* Fall.

Hillocks, G., Jr. 1995. *Teaching Writing as Reflective Practice.* New York: Teachers College Press.

Hillocks, G., Jr. 1999. *Ways of Thinking, Ways of Teaching.* New York: Teachers College Press.

Hillocks, G., Jr. 2002. *The Testing Trap.* New York: Teachers College Press.

Smith, M. W., and Wilhelm. J. 2002. *Reading Don't Fix No Chevys: Literacy in the Lives of Young Men.* Portsmouth, NH: Heinemann.

Smith, M. W. and Wilhelm, J. 2006. *Going with the Flow: Making literacy learning in school more like life.* Portsmouth, NH: Heinemann.

Soder, R. 1999. "When Words Find Their Meaning: Renewal versus Reform." *Phi Delta Kappan.* April, 568–570.

Wiggins, G., and McTighe, J. 1998. *Understanding by Design.* Alexandria, VA: ASCD.

Wilhelm, J. 2003. *Reading IS Seeing.* New York: Scholastic.

Wilhelm, J., and Friedemann, P. 1998. *Hyperlearning: Where Inquiry, Projects and Technology Meet.* York, ME: Stenhouse.

The Workshop Approach

By Douglas Fisher, Ph.D.

While there are a number of ways to provide this instruction, the reading and writing workshops are particularly effective, and therefore hold promise for all students (e.g., Fletcher & Portalupi, 2001; Serafini, 2001).

A Workshop Defined

Workshops are about collaboration and creation. In the classroom, the workshop is a philosophy; it is also a way to organize instructional time. For example, reading and writing workshops provide time for students to respond to texts they have read and to write about their ideas (Atwell, 1987; Calkins, 1986). These workshops also allow students to assume more responsibility for literacy tasks and to become independent learners. In this way, the workshop model provides a context for students to build skills and perfect their craft.

The Evidence Base

As Lausé (2004) noted, the implementation of a workshop approach to teaching reading and writing inspires students to become lifelong readers. According to Lausé's data, it creates faster, more competent readers; it also creates students who enjoy reading (and do read) more.

Taylor and Nesheim (2000/2001) used the workshop model to engage their "high-risk" students in literacy instruction. As they note, the "readers' workshop project prompted students to engage as readers and to experiment with new views of reading" (p. 317). Similarly, Williams (2001) noted that "a workshop format and strategy instruction helped struggling middle school readers connect with books, the teacher, and one another" (p. 588).

The workshop model has also been shown to improve writing achievement (Fisher & Frey, 2003), the use of multiple forms of media (Labbo, 2004), performance on tests (Shelton & Fu, 2004; Santman, 2002), problem solving skills (Christensen, 1990), and the expectations of teachers (Graves, 2004).

A Guiding Philosophy

Simply telling students what they should know will not ensure that they read better and read more. As teachers, we must model, scaffold, guide, and support learning. Current research suggests that the "gradual release of responsibility" model is an effective way to organize instruction (Fisher & Frey, 2003; Pearson & Fielding, 1991). In this model, the teacher moves from assuming "all the

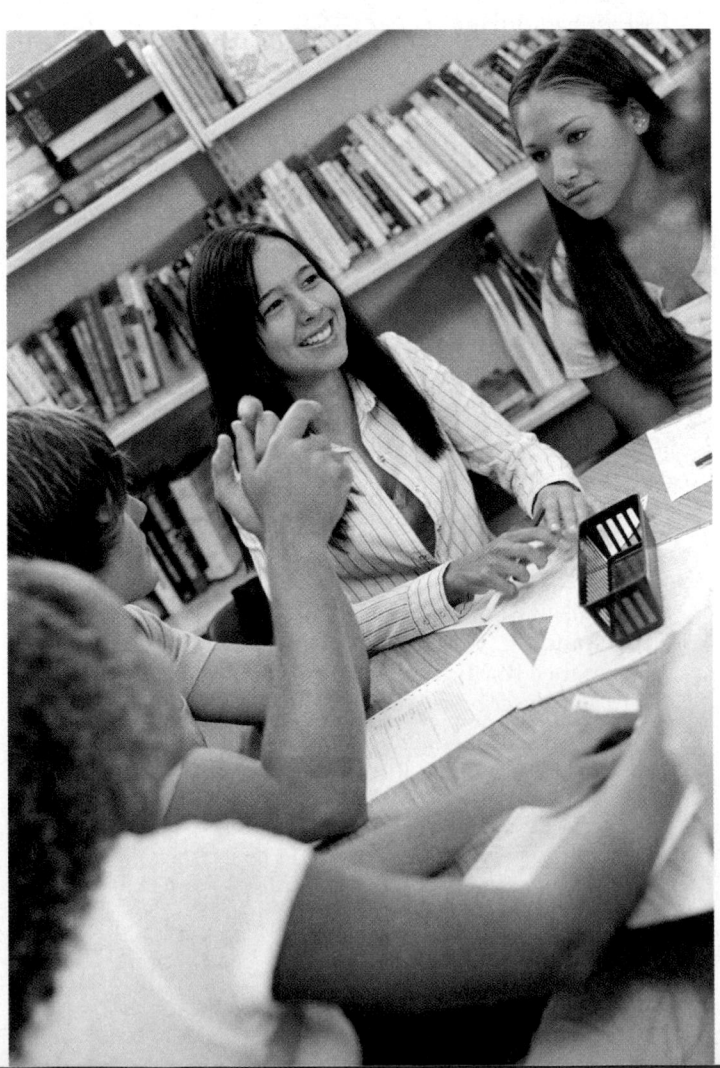

responsibility for performing a task . . . to a situation in which the students assume all of the responsibility" (Duke & Pearson, 2002, p. 211). This gradual release may occur over a day, a week, or a term. In *Reading with Purpose,* reading workshops are designed to encourage this gradual release of responsibility.

Components of the Workshop

To facilitate the gradual release of responsibility, the workshop moves students through phases of extensive teacher support and guided instruction, allowing them to become more independent learners. This model includes the following components:

- **A focus lesson** allows teachers to model a skill, strategy, or writing technique. Some strategies include read and think alouds, shared reading and writing activities, and language-based approaches. In *Reading with Purpose,* every Reading Workshop begins with a Skill Lesson that introduces that unit's reading skill.

- **Guided instruction** gives students an opportunity to practice the skills, strategies, and techniques introduced during the focus lesson under the teacher's close supervision. It provides a

scaffold between teacher modeling and student independence. Some strategies include guided reading, guided writing, writing models, and choral reading. In *Reading with Purpose,* reading selections are accompanied by notes that guide students' use of the unit's skills while they read.

- **Collaborative learning** encourages peer work to help students become more competent readers and writers. It also allows students to assist and coach one another. Some strategies include learning centers, paired reading, and reciprocal teaching. In *Reading with Purpose,* Partner Talk activities occur throughout the book.

- **Independent reading and writing** provides time for students to apply skills and strategies practiced during focus lessons, guided instruction, and collaborative learning to their own reading and writing. Independent learning need not be completed in solitary silence; it should, however, give each student a chance to apply new skills and strategies to his or her own work. Teachers may also use this time to conference with students individually. In *Reading with Purpose,* each unit ends with suggested readings to help students further explore the Big Question on their own.

Works Cited

Atwell, N. 1987. *In the middle: Writing, reading, and learning with adolescents.* Portsmouth, NH: Heinemann.

Calkins, L. M. 1986. *The art of teaching writing.* Portsmouth, NH: Heinemann.

Christensen, A. W. 1990. "Problem solving our way through writers' workshop." *The Reading Teacher,* 44, 357–358.

Duke, N. K., & Pearson, P. D. 2002. "Effective practices for developing reading comprehension." In A. Farstrup & J. Samuels (Eds.), *What research has to say about reading instruction* (3rd ed.). Newark, DE: International Reading Association.

Fisher, D., & Frey, N. 2003. "Writing instruction for struggling adolescent readers: A gradual release model." *Journal of Adolescent and Adult Literacy,* 46, 396–405.

Fletcher, R., & Portalupi, J. 2001. *Writing workshop: The essential guide.* Portsmouth, NH: Heinemann.

Frey, N., & Fisher, D. 2006. *Language arts workshop: Purposeful reading and writing instruction.* Upper Saddle River, NJ: Merrill Education.

Graves, D. 2004. "What I've learned from teachers of writing." *Language Arts,* 82(2), 88–94.

Labbo, L. D. 2004. "From writing workshop to multimedia workshop." *Language Arts,* 82(2), 119.

Lausé, J. 2004. "Using reading workshop to inspire lifelong readers." *English Journal,* 93(5), 24–30.

Pearson, P. D., & Fielding, L. 1991. "Comprehension instruction." In R. Barr, M. L. Kamil, P. Mosenthal, & P. D. Pearson (Eds.), *Handbook of reading research* (Vol. II), (pp. 815–860). Mahwah, NJ: Erlbaum.

Santman, D. 2002. "Teaching to the test? Test preparation in the reading workshop." *Language Arts,* 79(3), 203–211.

Serafini, F. 2001. *The reading workshop: Creating space for readers.* Portsmouth, NH: Heinemann.

Shelton, N. R., & Fu, D. 2004. "Creating space for teaching writing and for test preparation." *Language Arts,* 82(2), 120–128.

Taylor, S. V., & Nesheim. D. W. 2000/2001. "Making literacy real for 'high-risk' adolescent emerging readers: An innovative application of readers' workshop." *Journal of Adolescent & Adult Literacy,* 44, 308–318.

Williams, M. 2001. "Making connections: A workshop for adolescents who struggle with reading." *Journal of Adolescent & Adult Literacy,* 44, 588–602.

Differentiated Instruction

By Douglas Fisher, Ph.D.

Today's classroom contains students from a variety of backgrounds and with a variety of learning styles, strengths, and challenges. With careful planning, you can address the needs of all students in the literature classroom, using *Glencoe Literature: Reading with Purpose.* The basis for this planning is differentiated learning.

Differentiated Instruction Is a Key to Access

To differentiate instruction, teachers must acknowledge students' differences in background knowledge, current reading, writing, and English language skills, learning styles and preferences, interests, and needs, and they must react accordingly. There are a number of general guidelines for differentiating instruction:

- **Link assessment with instruction.** Assessments should occur before, during, and after instruction to ensure that the curriculum is aligned with what students do and do not know. Using assessments in this way allows you to plan instruction for whole groups, small groups, and individual students.

- **Clarify key concepts and generalizations.** Students need to know what is essential and how this information can be used in their future learning. In addition, students need to develop a sense of the **Big Questions,** which focus on life issues students need to think about in each unit in *Reading with Purpose.*

- **Emphasize critical and creative thinking.** The content, process, and products used or assigned in the classroom should require that students think about what they are learning. While some students may require support, additional motivation, varied tasks, materials, or equipment, the overall focus on critical and creative thinking allows for all students to participate in the lesson.

- **Include teacher- and student-selected tasks.** A differentiated classroom includes both teacher- and student-selected activities and tasks. At some points in the lesson, the teacher must provide instruction and assign learning activities. In other parts of the lesson, students should be provided choices in how they engage with the content. This balance increases motivation, engagement, and learning.

Supporting Individual Students

The vast majority of students will thrive in a classroom based on differentiated instruction. However, wise teachers recognize that no single option will work for all students and that there may be students who require unique systems of support to be successful.

Tips for Instruction

The following tips for instruction can support your efforts to help all students reach their maximum potential.

- Survey students to discover their individual differences. Use interest inventories of their unique talents so you can encourage contributions in the classroom.

- Be a model for respecting others. Adolescents crave social acceptance. The student with learning differences is especially sensitive to correction and criticism, particularly when it comes from a teacher. Your behavior will set the tone for how students treat one another.

- Expand opportunities for success. Provide a variety of instructional activities that reinforce skills and concepts.

- Establish measurable objectives and decide how you can best help students who meet them.

- Celebrate successes, and make note of and praise "work in progress."

- Keep it simple. Point out problem areas if doing so can help a student effect change. Avoid overwhelming students with too many goals at one time.

- Assign cooperative group projects that challenge all students to contribute to solving a problem or creating a product.

How Do I Reach Students with Learning Disabilities?

- Provide support and structure. Clearly specify rules, assignments, and responsibilities.

- Practice skills frequently. Use games and drills to help maintain student interest.

- Incorporate many modalities into the learning process. Provide opportunities to say, hear, write, read, and act out important concepts and information.

- Link new skills and concepts to those already mastered.

- If possible, allow students to record answers on audiotape.
- Allow extra time to complete assessments and assignments.
- Let students demonstrate proficiency with alternative presentations, including oral reports, role plays, art projects, and musical presentations.
- Provide outlines, notes, or tape recordings of lecture material.
- Pair students with peer helpers, and provide class time for pair interaction.

How Do I Reach English Language Learners?
- Remember, students' ability to speak English does not reflect their academic abilities.
- Try to incorporate the students' cultural experience into your instruction. The help of a bilingual aide may be effective.
- Avoid any references in your instruction that could be construed as cultural stereotypes.
- Preteach important vocabulary and concepts.
- Encourage students to preview text before they begin reading, noting headings.
- Remind students not to ignore graphic organizers, photographs, and maps since there is much information in these visuals.
- Use artifacts and photographs whenever possible to build background knowledge and understanding. An example of this would be coins in a foreign currency or a raw cotton ball to reinforce its importance in history.

How Do I Reach Gifted Students?
- Make arrangements for students to take selected subjects early and to work on independent projects.
- Ask "what if" questions to develop high-level thinking skills. Establish an environment safe for risk taking in your classroom.
- Emphasize concepts, theories, ideas, relationships, and generalizations about the content.
- Promote interest in the past by inviting students to make connections to the present.
- Let students express themselves in alternate ways such as creative writing, acting, debates, simulations, drawing, or music.
- Provide students with a catalog of helpful resources, listing such things as agencies that provide free and inexpensive materials, appropriate community services and programs, and community experts who might be called upon to speak to your students.
- Assign extension projects that allow students to solve real-life problems related to their communities.

References

Fisher, D. 2005. "The missing link: Standards, assessment, and instruction." *Voices from the Middle*, 13(2), 8–11.

McTighe, J., Seif, E., Wiggins, G. 2004. "You can teach for meaning." *Educational Leadership*, 62(1), 26–30.

Pfaum, S. W., & Bishop, P. A. 2004. "Student perceptions of reading engagement: Learning from the Learners." *Journal of Adolescent and Adult Literacy*, 48(3), 202–213.

Tomlinson, C. A., & McTighe, J. 2006. *Integrating differentiated instructions & understanding by design: Connecting content and kids.* Alexandria, VA: Association for Supervision and Curriculum Development.

Question Answer Relationship (QAR)

by Taffy Raphael, Ph.D.

What Is It?

QAR provides a framework that offers teachers a straightforward approach for reading comprehension instruction. QAR can serve as a reasonable starting point for addressing four problems that stand in the way of moving all students to high levels of literacy:

- a shared language to make visible the processes underlying reading and listening comprehension

- a framework for organizing questioning activities and comprehension instruction

- accessible and straightforward reform for literacy instruction oriented toward higher level thinking

- preparing students for high-stakes testing without undermining a strong focus on higher level thinking

Two decades ago, research showed that QAR could reliably improve students' comprehension (Raphael & McKinney, 1983; Raphael & Pearson, 1985; Raphael & Wonnacott, 1985). In the two decades since, literacy educators in a broad range of settings have demonstrated its practical value and shared their experiences in professional journals (e.g., Mesmer & Hutchins, 2002), textbooks (e.g., Leu & Kinzer, 2003; Reutzel & Cooper, 2004; Roe, Smith, & Burns, 2005; Vacca et al., 2003), and on the World Wide Web (e.g., gallery.carnegiefoundation.org/yhutchinson and www.smsd.org/schools/diemer/).

Why Is It Important?

Promoting high levels of literacy for all children is a core responsibility for today's teachers. With increasing accountability at the district, state, and national levels, teachers are often judged on the basis of how well their students perform on mandated, high-stakes tests.

But what does it mean to achieve high levels of literacy? Recent national panels and current reviews detailing what it means to comprehend text help inform us about current policies and future trends (e.g., Pressley, 2002; Snow, 2002; Sweet & Snow, 2003). For example, the RAND report (Snow), commissioned by the U.S. Department of Education, identifies literacy proficiency as reached when a reader can read a variety of materials with ease and interest, can read for varying purposes, and can read with comprehension even when the material is neither easy to understand nor intrinsically interesting. Proficient readers are capable of acquiring new knowledge and understanding new concepts, are capable of applying textual information appropriately, and are capable of being engaged in the reading process and reflecting on what is being read. This same view is reflected in the current National Assessment of Educational Progress (NAEP; Donahue, Daane, & Grigg, 2003), the only federally funded large-scale testing program in the United States, and the framework for the NAEP 2009 reading assessment (National Assessment Governing Board, 2004) pushes the definition for proficiency even further. For example, students will be expected to read comfortably across genres within fiction, nonfiction, procedural texts, and poetry. They will be required to successfully answer questions, 70 to 80 percent of which call for the integration, interpretation, critique, and evaluation of texts read independently.

Traditional questions that simply require readers to locate and recall information will constitute only a third to a fourth of the questions that students will face. Over half of the higher level questions will require students to provide a short or extended written response rather than simply to select from multiple-choice options. To be judged as proficient in reading fiction, students must demonstrate that they can think deeply about, and write in response to, questions that address themes, lessons, elements of plot, and multiple points of view. The kind of strategic knowledge assessed on national and state tests, now and in the future, is central to the achievement of high levels of literacy.

How Do I Do It?

The vocabulary of QAR—**In the Book, In My Head, Right There, Think & Search, Author & Me,** and **On My Own**—gives teachers and students a language for talking about the largely invisible processes that constitute listening and reading comprehension across grades and subject areas.

Teachers know the value of modeling and thinking aloud to make visible the thought processes involved in higher levels of thinking, but it can be frustrating trying to convey complex ideas without a shared vocabulary. Thus, QAR first and foremost provides teachers and students with a much-needed common language. Introduce students to the basic principle underlying QAR: that generating and answering questions draws on two core sources of information. These sources are the texts that we read and our background knowledge and experiences or, in the language of QAR, information that is **In the Book** or **In My Head,** respectively.

Teachers should use QAR language as they emphasize the importance of both sources of information. Furthermore, teachers should use QAR language to help students learn to use strategies effectively. For example, explain how skimming or scanning might lead to details for an **In the Book** QAR (a typical locate/recall strategy) or how using clues from the title and chapter headings can point to relevant background knowledge for answering an **In My Head** QAR (a relatively simple interpret/integrate/infer task).

Introduce students to the language of QAR by analyzing the differences between questions with answer sources in the book and those where the answer source is in students' own heads. Shorter texts work quite effectively for characterizing basic differences between these two information sources, but as students become

more experienced with QARs, this simple distinction is not sufficient to capture the range of strategies used to answer and generate questions related to text. Build on **In the Book** and **In My Head** by introducing the four core QARs. Once students are confidently and accurately identifying **In the Book** QARs, introduce its subcategories, **Right There** and **Think & Search.** Similarly, when students are confident and accurate with **In My Head** QARs, introduce its subcategories, **Author & Me** and **On My Own** (see chart below for definitions of each).

Readers functioning at high levels of literacy use strategies in combination and apply different approaches to strategic thinking, depending on the genre or difficulty of the texts. Understanding how strategies interrelate can be quite abstract for students faced with the need to apply several strategies, as well as quite demanding for teachers in terms of providing effective instruction. QAR provides a framework that students can use to link strategies at appropriate points in the reading cycle. Understanding and control of strategies learned helps readers engage in the high levels of literacy for which they are accountable in their day-to-day classroom literacy activities and in high-stakes assessments at the district, state, and national levels.

In the Book

Right There

The answer is in one place in the text. Words from the question and words that answer the question are often in the same sentence.

Sample Comprehension Strategies:

Skimming and Scanning

Note-taking

Context Clues

Think & Search

The answer is in the text. Readers need to put together different parts of the text to find the answer. The answer can be within a paragraph, across paragraphs, or even across chapters and books.

Sample Comprehension Strategies:

Summarizing

Compare and Contrast

Making Simple Inferences

Clarifying

Figurative Language

In My Head

On My Own

The answer is not in the text. Readers need to use their own ideas and experiences to answer the question.

Sample Comprehension Strategies:

Activating Prior Knowledge

Connecting

Author & Me

The answer is not in the text. To answer the question, readers need to think about how the text and what they already know fit together.

Sample Comprehension Strategies:

Predicting

Visualizing

Making Simple and Complex Inferences

Distinguishing Fact and Opinion

Making Text-to-Self Connections

English Language Learners

by Mary A. Avalos, Ph.D.

English language learners (ELLs) are a growing population in our schools. During the 2000–2001 academic year, more than 4.5 million English language learners were enrolled in U.S. public schools (McREL, 2003). The growth of culturally and linguistically diverse populations is expected to continue. Immigrants come to the United States for various reasons—some to escape political or economic oppression, others to seek higher wages or secure a higher standard of living for their families. Although shifting demographics have a greater impact on certain regions of the United States, all teachers should be prepared to teach all students.

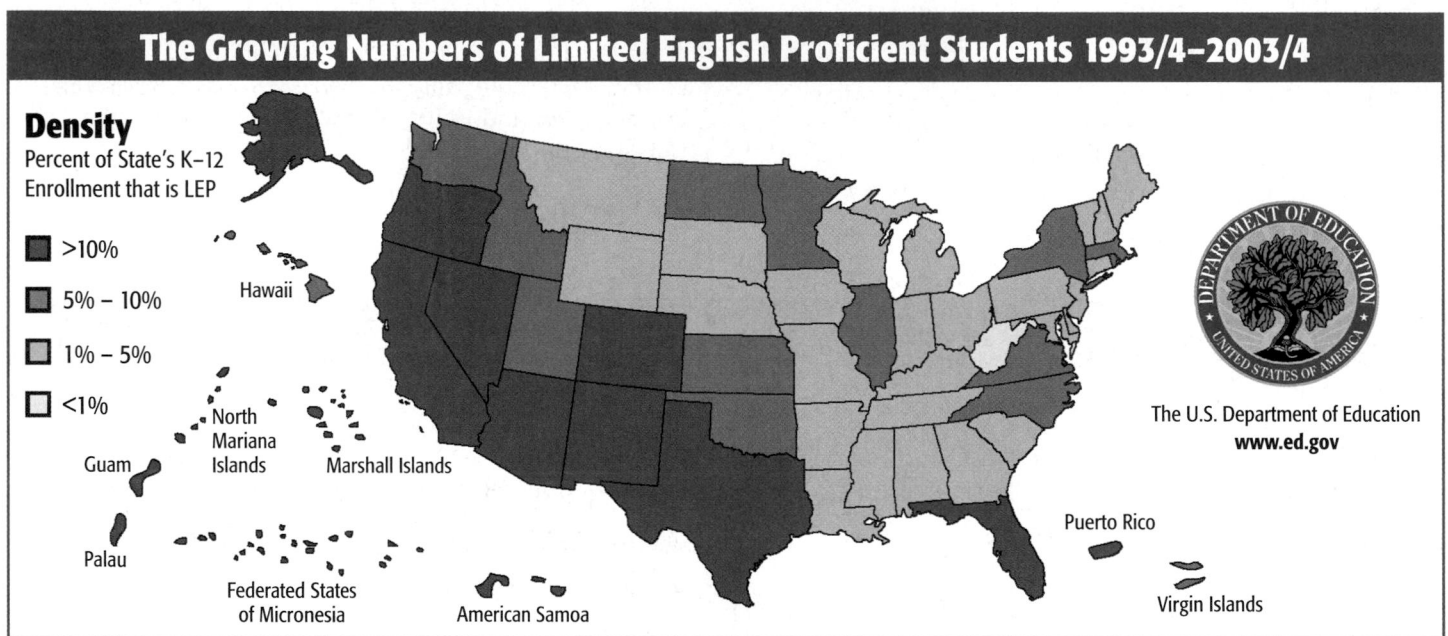

The Growing Numbers of Limited English Proficient Students 1993/4–2003/4

Density
Percent of State's K–12 Enrollment that is LEP

- >10%
- 5% – 10%
- 1% – 5%
- <1%

Hawaii

North Mariana Islands

Guam

Marshall Islands

Palau

Federated States of Micronesia

American Samoa

Puerto Rico

Virgin Islands

The U.S. Department of Education
www.ed.gov

Meeting the Challenge

English language learners are challenged by having to learn content while simultaneously learning to read, write, and speak a new language. English language learners' literacy proficiency in their first language, or **L1,** will impact their literacy acquisition of a second language, or **L2** (Au, 1993; Cummins, 2003; Hudelson, 1984; Snow, 1990), particularly if the L1 is similar to the L2.

English language learners make an easier transition between L1 and L2 if both languages share a similar writing system.

Writing System	Example
Alphabetic	English, French, Spanish, Italian
Syllabic	Cherokee
Logographic	Chinese

To provide effective instruction, build upon what English language learners know about language and literacy knowledge. Also consider English language learners' cultural differences, such as celebration and mourning rituals, child-rearing practices, and favorite foods. Try to incorporate the students' cultural experience into your teaching.

Gauging Levels of Language Proficiency

A common misconception exists that once English language learners are able to converse using everyday language, they are ready to proceed to mainstream instruction with little or no support. In reality, there are three levels of language proficiency as labeled by Cummins (2003).

Level of Language Proficiency	Example
Basic Interpersonal Conversation Skills (BICS)	ability to talk about daily activities, make requests, and retell a personal story or event
Discrete Language Skills	knowledge of phonological awareness, grammar rules, or conventions of writing in the learner's first language
Cognitive Academic Language Proficiency (CALP)	ability to read and understand technical or subject area texts with low frequency words of Latin or Greek origin

By learning about language acquisition processes, teachers can better meet the needs of English language learners.

Glencoe Literature: Reading with Purpose helps English language learners develop higher levels of language proficiency by:

1. Analyzing the reading selections to facilitate comprehension of low frequency vocabulary, as well as identified vocabulary words for study.
2. Prompting students to activate prior knowledge before/while reading to make connections between the reader and the text.
3. Integrating literary elements throughout the selections to provide meaningful prompts in context.
4. Setting objectives to ensure that all students receive high quality, standards-based instruction.
5. Contextualizing writing, grammar, and spelling instruction throughout the program.

All of these aids increase teacher awareness of text- and reader-based features as teachers instruct English language learners. This approach to instruction, in turn, better meets the unique needs of English language learners as they learn content and language together.

Works Cited

Au, K. H. 1993. *Literacy instruction in multicultural settings.* Orlando, FL: Harcourt Brace College Publishers.

Cummins, J. 2003. "Reading and the bilingual student: Fact and friction." In G. G. Garcia's (Ed.), *English learners: Reaching the highest level of English literacy.* Newark, DE: International Reading Association.

Hudelson, S. 1984. "Kan yu ret an rayt en ingles: Children become literate in English as a second language." *TESOL Quarterly,* 18, 221–238.

McREL. Fall, 2003. "English language learners and the No Child Left Behind Act." *Changing Schools: A Newsletter from the Central Region Educational Laboratory. Aurora, CO: Mid-continent Research for Education and Learning.* Retrieved from the Internet on February 17, 2006: http://www.mcrel.org/PDF/ChangingSchools/5032NL_CSfall2003.pdf#search='percentage%20of%20English%20language%20learners%20in%20U.S.%20schools

Snow, C. E. 1990. "Rationales for native language instruction in the education of language minority children. Evidence from research." In A. Padilla, H. Fairchild, & C. Valadez (Eds.), *Bilingual education: Issues and strategies*, pp. 60–74. Newbury Park, CA: Sage.

Digital Technology

by David G. O'Brien, Ph.D.

Students' Digital Lives

By cultivating an awareness of the issues below, teachers can help students connect the literacy practices they learn in school to their busy lives outside the classroom.

- **New Literacies** In the digital age, many students are fluent in new languages, or literacies—for example, those of instant messaging, text messaging, and blogging.

- **Increased Media Use** Kids and teens spend an average of six hours per day using media (Kaiser Family Foundation, 2005).

- **Internet as Reference Text** An increasing number of young people use the Internet as their primary reference text for everything, including school assignments.

- **Closing the Gap** The digital divide—long cited in the argument against technology-based learning in schools—is slowly closing. More students from all socioeconomic levels are gaining access to technology at home and in the community.

Using Technology to Teach

New technologies—and the media they make available—appeal to a variety of learners. These technologies can help motivate students to engage in reading, writing, and the use of other literacies, including traditional, school-based literacies and multiple texts (O'Brien, 2001, 2003). As you incorporate technology into your classroom, use the tips below.

Connect print text to digital text. Look for Web sites that support kids' reading. An emerging body of research shows that engagement with online texts can motivate struggling readers to read print texts as well (O'Brien, 2001; 2003, in press).

- In *Reading with Purpose*, the Literature Online feature encourages readers to research topics and authors by linking to a provided Web site. These sorts of intertextual links help motivate struggling, disengaged readers who are often tired of typical textbook formats—even when those books are interesting and accessible. For example, a selection in *Reading with Purpose* on skateboarder Tony Hawk (Unit 2's *Tony Hawk: Chairman of the Board*) can be augmented by using print and media texts from Tony Hawk's official Web site.

Connect print to other print media.

Texts from popular genres (e.g., cartoons, illustrations, and graphic novels) motivate all learners. They also provide struggling learners, or those learners who lose attention easily when presented with traditional formats, a way to access and understand the lesson.

- In *Reading with Purpose,* cartoons are used to introduce reading skills, highlighting those skills' relevance in new and emerging literacies. Students can also engage the wide variety of reading selections culled from the literature most familiar to them—Web sites, magazines, graphic novels, and cartoons.

Utilize other digital resources to enhance reading.

As educators, we want to connect digital texts to traditional ones; we do not, however, want to replace all print texts with digital ones. To foster this connection, though, we must be aware that digital media use is on the rise among middle school students. Also, we cannot ignore the extent to which digital media motivates and engages struggling readers, or readers who have disengaged from more typical reading tasks in school.

- *Reading with Purpose* offers an array of digital products that help students relate to what they read and acquire more skills. One such product is Skill Level Up!^{TM}, a computer game that helps students practice and master reading skills in a context with which many are probably familiar. Another product, StudentWorks, gives students a digitized work center wherein they can access many *Reading with Purpose* resources. Finally, the Web site glencoe.com provides a wealth of resources for digitally savvy students to use and enjoy.

Works Cited

Beach, R. 2000. "Critical Issues: Reading and responding to literature at the level of activity." *Journal of Literacy Research,* 32 (2), 237–251.

Beach, R. & O'Brien, D. (in press). "Teaching popular culture texts in the classroom." In D. Leu, J. Coiro, M. Knobel, & C. Lankshear (Eds.) *Handbook of research on new literacies.* Mahwah, NJ: Lawrence Erlbaum Associates.

Kaiser Family Foundation. March, 2005. "Generation M: Media in the Lives of 8–18 Year-olds."

O'Brien, D. G. 2001. "At-risk adolescents: Redefining competence through the multiliteracies of intermediality, visual arts, and representation." *Reading Online,* 4(11). Available http://www.readingonline.org/newliteracies/lit_index.asp?HREF=/newliteracies/obrien/index.html

O'Brien, D. G. 2003. "Juxtaposing traditional and intermedial literacies to redefine the competence of struggling adolescents." *Reading Online,* 6(7). Available: http://www.readingonline.org/newliteracies/lit_index.asp?HREF=obrien2/

O'Brien, D. G. (in press). "Struggling Adolescents' Engagement in Multimediating: Countering the Institutional Construction of Incompetence." In D. E. Alvermann, S. F. Phelps, D. R. Waff, K. A. Hinchman, & D. W. Moore (Eds) (2nd Ed.), *Reconceptualizing the literacies in adolescents' lives.* Mahwah, NJ: Erlbaum Associates.

Rushkoff, D. 1999. *Playing the future: What we can learn from digital kids.* New York: Riverhead.

Sefton-Green, J. (1998). "Introduction: Being Young in the Digital Age." In J. Sefton-Green (Ed.), *Digital Diversions: Youth Culture in the Age of Multimedia* (pp. 1–20). London: UCL Press Limited.

Project CRISS

By Carol M. Santa, Ph.D.

CRISS stands for CReating Independence through Student-owned Strategies. It is a staff development program that I created in collaboration with middle and high school teachers in Kalispell, Montana.

The CRISS Philosophy

Project CRISS is more than a collection of learning strategies. Its underlying power rests not on the individual strategies, but on the teaching philosophy behind them. This philosophy integrates work from cognitive psychology, social learning theory, and neurological research about how the brain learns. It incorporates these overlapping principles:

Background knowledge and purposeful reading are powerful determinants of reading comprehension.

Readers are far more likely to learn new information when they have some previous knowledge before they read or listen.

More Than Simply Reading We warn students not to simply begin reading. We also remind them to preview the assignment and think about their goals for reading. We ask students, *"What might you already know about the topic? What questions do you have about the topic?"*

KWLH One proven CRISS strategy for helping students activate prior knowledge is to develop a **KWHL** chart (**K**now, **W**ant to learn, **L**earned, **H**ow to learn more). Students can work together to generate a KWHL chart based on the model below. They can generate questions about what they want to learn, and then, after completing the reading assignment, they can list the new information they have learned and how they can learn more.

K	W	L	H
What I **KNOW**	What I **WANT** to find out	What I **LEARNED**	**HOW** I can learn more

Reading Goals *"Don't ignore your purposes for reading. Take time to think about them before delving into your reading."* We also suggest ways to make sure your students have clear goals for their reading. Each selection preview in *Glencoe Literature: Reading with Purpose* lists reading strategies and sets reading purposes.

Good readers have an intuitive understanding of the author's craft.

When students know how authors craft their writing, they can more readily understand and remember what they read. Good readers will analyze the author's style of presentation as they read. They might ask themselves, "What is this author doing to help me learn key concepts? How does the writer lead me from one idea to the next?"

Effective learners are actively involved when they listen and read.

We learn best when we act on the information presented. We can do this by using a variety of organizing activities that require us to write, talk, and transform the information we are absorbing.

Students need many opportunities to talk with one another about what they are learning.

We focus on how to get students to lead their own discussions about a topic. We want them to understand that it is their discussing, their oral grappling with meaning that leads to deeper understanding.

Competent readers know several ways to organize information for learning.

We show students different ways to organize information. They can take notes, underline selectively, develop concept maps, and summarize ideas in charts.

Students deserve opportunities to write about what they are learning.

Writing lets us figure out what we know and what we still need to know. The Writing Workshops in *Glencoe Literature: Reading with Purpose* guide students to explore various topics and communicate the information and impressions they have discovered.

Teaching involves explanation and modeling.

Students learn to think strategically when we use these processes as part of our instruction. Our demonstrations are especially critical for struggling readers. Most have never been taught how to learn. We have to show them how.

Take Center Stage When you introduce a new strategy, take center stage: show, tell, model, demonstrate, and explain the skill and how it is used by effective readers. As students learn to use the strategy, gradually release responsibility to them.

Systematic Approach Project CRISS is a valuable basis for instruction. It provides a systematic approach for using what we now know about teaching and learning. The following chart lists questions we need to continually ask ourselves while we are teaching. Use this chart to monitor your efforts to incorporate CRISS principles into your teaching.

CRISS Principles	The CRISS Philosophy	Yes	No	Somewhat
Background knowledge	• Did I assist students in thinking about what they already knew about the topic before beginning the unit? • Did I develop necessary concepts before students read?			
Purpose setting	• Did my students have a clear purpose about what they were going to learn before beginning the lesson?			
Author's craft	• Can my students use the author's style of presentation to facilitate their understanding?			
Active involvement	• Were my students engaged in the topic? • Did I help students become actively involved in their learning?			
Discussion	• Did my students have opportunities to talk about what they were learning?			
Organization	• Did my students organize information in a variety of ways?			
Writing	• Did my students write about what they were learning?			
Teacher modeling	• Did I do enough teacher modeling of learning strategies so that students could begin doing them on their own?			

Jamestown Education: Support for All Readers

Jamestown Education has been helping *all* readers become *better* readers for more than 35 years. Jamestown provides research-based products that are flexible enough to allow for a variety of learning styles and interests. At the same time, they are appropriate for both the reading levels and age levels of all adolescent readers.

Jamestown Literature: An Adapted Reader

- Grade Levels 6–10
- Reading Levels 4–8
- Instructional Support:
  This series provides grade-specific collections of literature adapted to lower reading levels. These alternative versions of canon literature offer an additional opportunity to differentiate instruction. Look for references to *Jamestown Literature: An Adapted Reader* in this edition. These references mean you can find the same selection in both *Glencoe Literature: Reading with Purpose* and *Jamestown Literature*.

In the Spotlight™

- Reading Levels 2–10
- Instructional Support:
  This eight-book series will provide your students with engaging and motivating biographies to read while building their reading skills and vocabulary development. In each graduated unit, students are guided before, during, and after reading, with comprehension, skill, and vocabulary reinforcement, as well as writing exercises.

Timed Readings Plus in Science, Timed Readings Plus, Timed Readings in Literature

- Reading Levels 4–13+
- Instructional Support:
  Each series (ten books in each) will help your students increase reading rate, fluency, and comprehension. The fiction and nonfiction passages of uniform length are designed for systematic classroom practice to prepare students for standardized tests.

Reading Fluency

- Reading Levels 1–10
- Instructional Support:
This ten-book series will help your students read smoothly, accurately, and expressively. Students work in pairs to provide immediate feedback and self-assessment. Author Camille Blachowicz states that "the ability to read fluently is highly correlated with many other measures of reading competence."

Jamestown Reading Improvement

- Reading Levels 4–10
- Instructional Support:
Authored by renowned reading expert Edward Fry, this eight-book series focuses on helping build your students' comprehension, vocabulary, and study skills. Repeated practice with targeted exercises ensures mastery of valuable reading skills.

Critical Reading Series

- Reading Levels 2–8
- Instructional Support:
This 27-book high-interest series, written at three reading spans, encourages reluctant readers to build a love for nonfiction while focusing on critical reading skills. Topics that include *Fateful Journeys*, *Weird Science*, and *Heroes* draw students in and provide ample opportunities to master important skills found on standardized tests.

Jamestown Reading Navigator

This online and print-based intervention program is built upon the latest research in adolescent literacy cited in *Reading Next*. The program is available to students 24 hours a day from anywhere they can connect to the Web. Here are the key objectives of the online version.

- Increase student achievement through direct, explicit instruction in comprehension strategies and modeling of good reading practices.
- Motivate and engage reluctant readers with a student-directed, self-paced learning environment enriched with interactive activities and media.
- Provide teachers with a formative and summative assessment to help track student progress and make instructional decisions.

Teaching Students from Impoverished Backgrounds

by Ruby K. Payne, Ph.D.

Poverty is not just an economic condition; often, it's also an intellectual condition. That's because students who live in places where resources are few—either at home or at school—are less likely to achieve their academic potential. *Reading with Purpose* is designed to help struggling students build vocabulary, develop reading skills, and bridge cultural gaps to connect meaningfully with what they read.

Many of the students to whom this series is geared lack adequate vocabulary skills. Research indicates that a child whose caregivers are welfare-dependent hears about 10 million words in a given two-year time frame. Within that same time frame, however, a child whose caregivers are educated professionals hears about 30 million words (Betty Hart and Todd Risley). This research also shows that a three-year-old from a professional household has a larger vocabulary than an adult from a welfare-dependent one.

Lev Vygotsky's research tells us that vocabulary is stored and used vis-à-vis schema, or networks of thoughts. That is, we make sense of new ideas in relationship to old ones and are more likely to remember words and concepts that are proximal to the things we know and care about. Margaret McKeown's work shows that vocabulary is best learned in a non-threatening environment, a few words at a time. This is important, as Maria Montano-Harmon's work tells us that the longer children exist in poverty, the less "formal" diction and syntax they know.

Built upon this and other research, *Reading with Purpose* equips kids to learn new words organically and at a moderate pace. Vocabulary exercises are not *just* exercises; instead, vocabulary activities extend and deepen students' knowledge of what they are already reading. In this way, these books invite students to use and expand their own schema, one manageable step at a time.

Research also shows that many students from impoverished backgrounds lack the ability to think critically about what they read. They don't know how to set a purpose for reading or how to evaluate, draw conclusions about, or summarize the work they're assigned. Many struggle to form and understand questions. Question-making is an important cognitive skill, as it allows us to assess our knowledge (or lack thereof). It is also a reading skill, though, as questioning facilitates connection to and comprehension of the texts that we encounter.

Reading with Purpose teaches students how to ask the questions that matter. It also gives students focused instruction in other reading skills they need. In that vein, this series' Reading, Comparing Literature, and Reading Across Texts Workshops encourage students to become confident, inquisitive, and independent learners by allowing them to practice—and master—proven strategies.

Other research indicates that, for many students from impoverished backgrounds, there exists a significant gap between the culture of home and the culture of school. For example, if a student's home culture is not print-rich, or values oral traditions over written ones, he or she may struggle in school. If a student's home culture is reactive—but his or her classroom culture is proactive—then he or she may struggle in school. Finally, if a student's home culture says that asking questions or discussing ideas openly is rude or disrespectful, then he or she may (and probably will) struggle in school.

This series demonstrates sensitivity toward these and other cultural differences. It utilizes work by men and women of varying ages, races, and ethnicities. The Unit Challenge feature encourages students to begin each unit with an end project in mind; this strategy helps unfocused students become proactive, productive learners. The Analyzing Cartoons feature appeals to visual learners, as do the graphic story selections. The Reading on Your Own feature gives an eager reader the place to begin his or her own reading adventure.

In the United States today, 13 million children live in poverty. Most of them live in urban areas. As educators, we must strive to reach these learners before it is too late. *Reading with Purpose* seeks to do just that, providing these students with the tools they need for learning success.

Guide to Text Readability

Throughout the teacher materials in your **Teacher Wraparound Edition,** you will encounter DRP readability measures assigned to the reading selections in *Reading with Purpose.* You will also find readability scores based on the Lexile Framework® for Reading and the Dale-Chall Readability Formula. You can use these scores to select reading materials that are suitable for your entire class, or individual students.

Degrees of Reading Power® (DRP)

DRP values indicate the readability of prose text. The higher the value, the more difficult the text. The scale ranges from 1 to 100; commonly encountered English text tends to fall somewhere between 25 and 85. Although middle school texts have an average difficulty of 56 and high school texts have an average difficulty of 62, no single readability level is appropriate for each grade level. Rather, a typical classroom has materials with a range of readability levels available for use—some intended for less-proficient readers, some for average readers, and some for stronger readers. The following chart shows the average DRP readability range for materials widely available for use at each grade. Some materials you might use, however, will certainly fall outside the range for your particular grade.

Grade	DRP Readability Ranges
6	51–61
7	52–62
8	53–64
9	53–65
10	51–68
11	56–67
12	57–68

The Lexile® Framework

A lexile measure assigned to a text is the specific number that describes the reading demands of the text. The typical Lexile Scale ranges from 200 to 1700 Lexiles. As with the DRP measures, there is not a direct translation from a specific Lexile measure to a specific grade level. Within any classroom, there will be a range of readers and a range of materials to be read. The levels shown on the following chart indicate the approximate range of Lexile scores for 50 percent of the materials found in a typical grade-level classroom. For example, the middle half of the instructional materials typically found in a sixth-grade classroom range in difficulty from about 850L to 1050L.

Grade	Text Measures (from Lexile Framework Map)
6	850L to 1050L
7	950L to 1075L
8	1000L to 1100L
9	1050L to 1150L
10	1100L to 1200L
11 and 12	1100L to 1300L

Dale-Chall Readability Formula

The Dale-Chall Formula is based on the average sentence length and the number of unfamiliar words in a passage. The idea behind this formula is that readers typically find it easier to read, process, and recall a passage if the words and sentences are familiar and grade appropriate. The Dale-Chall Formula assesses the difficulty of a passage by computing two different values from the text. The first measure is the average number of words per sentence. The second measure is the percentage of words in the passage not found on the grade appropriate Dale Word List. The following chart shows the average Dale-Chall readability scores for grades 5 through 12.

Grade	DRP Readability Ranges
5–6	5.0 to 5.9
7–8	6.0 to 6.9
9–10	7.0 to 7.9
11–12	8.0 to 8.9

* Degrees of Reading Power, DRP, and TASA are registered trademarks of Touchstone Applied Science Associates, Inc. (TASA). Lexile is a registered trademark of MetaMetrics, Inc.

Scope and Sequence

The following charts provide an overview of the scope and sequence for *Reading with Purpose*, Grade 6. A more detailed Skills Scope and Sequence can be found on the interleaf pages preceding each unit.

● = focused instruction
● = review

Skills	UNIT 1	UNIT 2	UNIT 3	UNIT 4	UNIT 5	UNIT 6	UNIT 7	UNIT 8
Reading Skills								
Activate prior knowledge	●	●	●	●	●	●	●	●
Analyze	●	●	●	●	●	●	●	●
Clarify			●			●	●	●
Compare and contrast	●	●	●	●	●	●	●	●
Connect	●	●	●	●	●	●	●	●
Determine main idea and supporting details	●	●	●				●	
Distinguish fact and opinion			●				●	
Draw conclusions					●		●	
Evaluate						●	●	●
Identify author's purpose	●		●		●		●	
Identify sequence		●	●		●		●	
Infer			●		●		●	
Interpret				●		●	●	
Monitor comprehension				●			●	
Paraphrase and summarize	●				●			
Predict		●			●	●	●	●
Question		●		●		●		
Respond				●			●	
Review								
Set a purpose for reading	●	●	●	●	●	●	●	●
Skim and scan	●							●
Synthesize							●	
Take notes								
Understand cause and effect					●	●		
Understand persuasive techniques			●					
Understand text structure	●		●			●	●	
Use text features	●							
Visualize				●	●			●

T54

Skills	UNIT 1	UNIT 2	UNIT 3	UNIT 4	UNIT 5	UNIT 6	UNIT 7	UNIT 8
Literary Elements								
Bias			●				●	
Character					●			●
Conflict		●			●			
Cultural Context						●		
Dialect								●
Dialogue					●			
Figurative language				●				
Hero						●		
Mood				●				
Narrator		●					●	
Poetic Features				●				
Plot					●		●	
Point of view		●	●	●				●
Repetition				●				
Rhyme, rhythm, and meter				●				
Scene								●
Sensory details				●				●
Setting						●		●
Sound devices				●				
Stage directions								●
Stereotypes				●	●			
Style			●					
Symbolism							●	
Theme						●		
Tone		●						
Text Elements								
Author's craft	●		●					
Author's purpose	●		●		●		●	
Description and Imagery							●	●
Photos and illustrations	●	●	●	●	●	●	●	●
Titles and heads	●				●			
Understanding graphics	●							

Scope and Sequence

● = focused instruction   ● = review

Skills	UNIT 1	UNIT 2	UNIT 3	UNIT 4	UNIT 5	UNIT 6	UNIT 7	UNIT 8
Literary Genres								
Biography/Autobiography		●						
Folktale, Fantasy, and Myths						●		
Historical Fiction and Nonfiction								
Informational media	●						●	●
Persuasive writing			●					
Poetry				●				
Drama								●
Short story					●			
Vocabulary Skills								
Acronyms								●
Roots and base words					●		●	
Borrowed words						●		
Compound words						●		
Context clues				●				
Denotation/editorial connotation			●					
Dialect and dialogue					●			●
Figurative use of language				●				●
Idioms								●
Multiple-meaning words	●							
Prefixes and suffixes		●			●			
Structural analysis						●	●	
Synonyms and antonyms		●	●					●
Writing Skills • Writing Products								
Summary	●							
Autobiographical narrative		●						
Short fictional story					●			
Speech								●
Persuasive Essay			●					
Fable						●		
Personal narrative							●	
Poem				●				

● = focused instruction ● = review

Skills	UNIT 1	UNIT 2	UNIT 3	UNIT 4	UNIT 5	UNIT 6	UNIT 7	UNIT 8
Writing Skills • Writing Process								
Drafting	●	●	●	●	●	●	●	●
Editing	●	●	●	●	●	●	●	●
Presenting/publishing	●	●	●	●	●	●	●	●
Prewriting	●	●	●	●	●	●	●	●
Proofreading	●	●	●	●	●	●	●	●
Revising	●	●	●	●	●	●	●	●
Writing Skills • Writing Traits								
Conventions		●						
Ideas	●							
Organization					●			
Presentation								●
Sentence fluency and variety			●					
Voice						●	●	
Word choice				●				
Writing Skills • Grammar								
Articles			●					
Phrases, clauses, and sentences				●	●	●		●
Parts of speech	●	●	●	●	●	●	●	
Phrases					●			
Punctuation				●	●	●		●
Subjects and predicates				●				
Subject-verb agreement							●	
Listening, Speaking, and Viewing								
Active listening and group discussion	●	●	●	●	●	●	●	●
Oral presentations			●		●	●	●	●
Oral reading			●	●	●	●	●	
Persuasive techniques			●					
Storytelling					●	●		
Using visuals	●	●	●	●	●	●	●	●
Viewing art, cartoons, and photographs	●	●	●	●	●	●	●	●

To Teachers:

Welcome to the Teacher Wraparound Edition of *Glencoe Literature: Reading with Purpose.* We have created this teacher edition based on input from experienced teachers and educational consultants. Teaching suggestions, additional resources, and leveled activities for differentiated instruction are all labeled and "wrapped" around the student text for your convenience.

Planning the Unit

Planning pages appear at the beginning of each unit.

Unit Preview Tells you about the Big Question and genre focus found in the unit

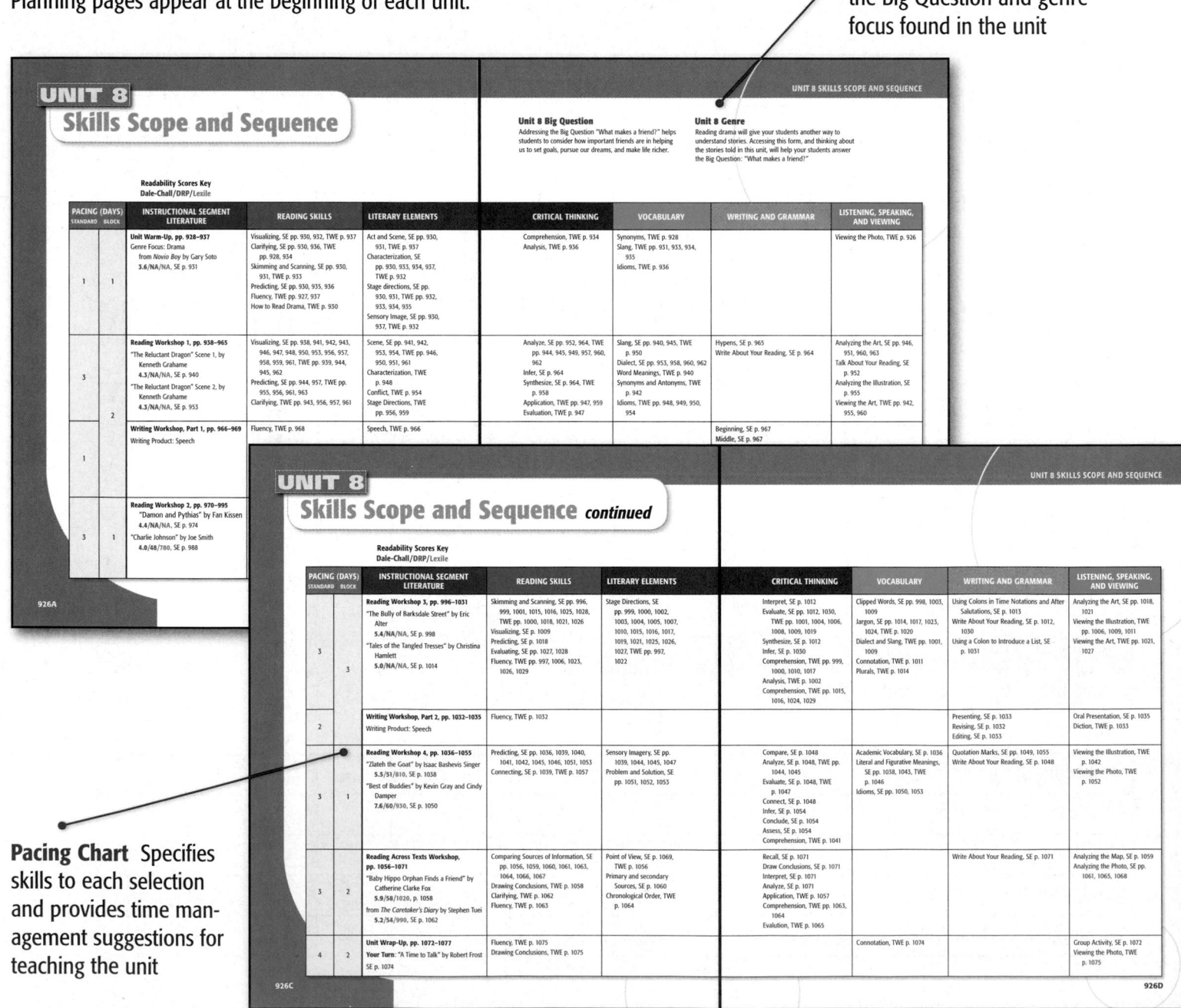

Pacing Chart Specifies skills to each selection and provides time management suggestions for teaching the unit

Teaching the Unit

Objectives Lists the main teaching goals of the unit

BQ Focus Information about the connections and importance of the unit Big Question

Reading Preview Background about the skills and selections taught in the unit and how to use the material to help students answer the Big Question

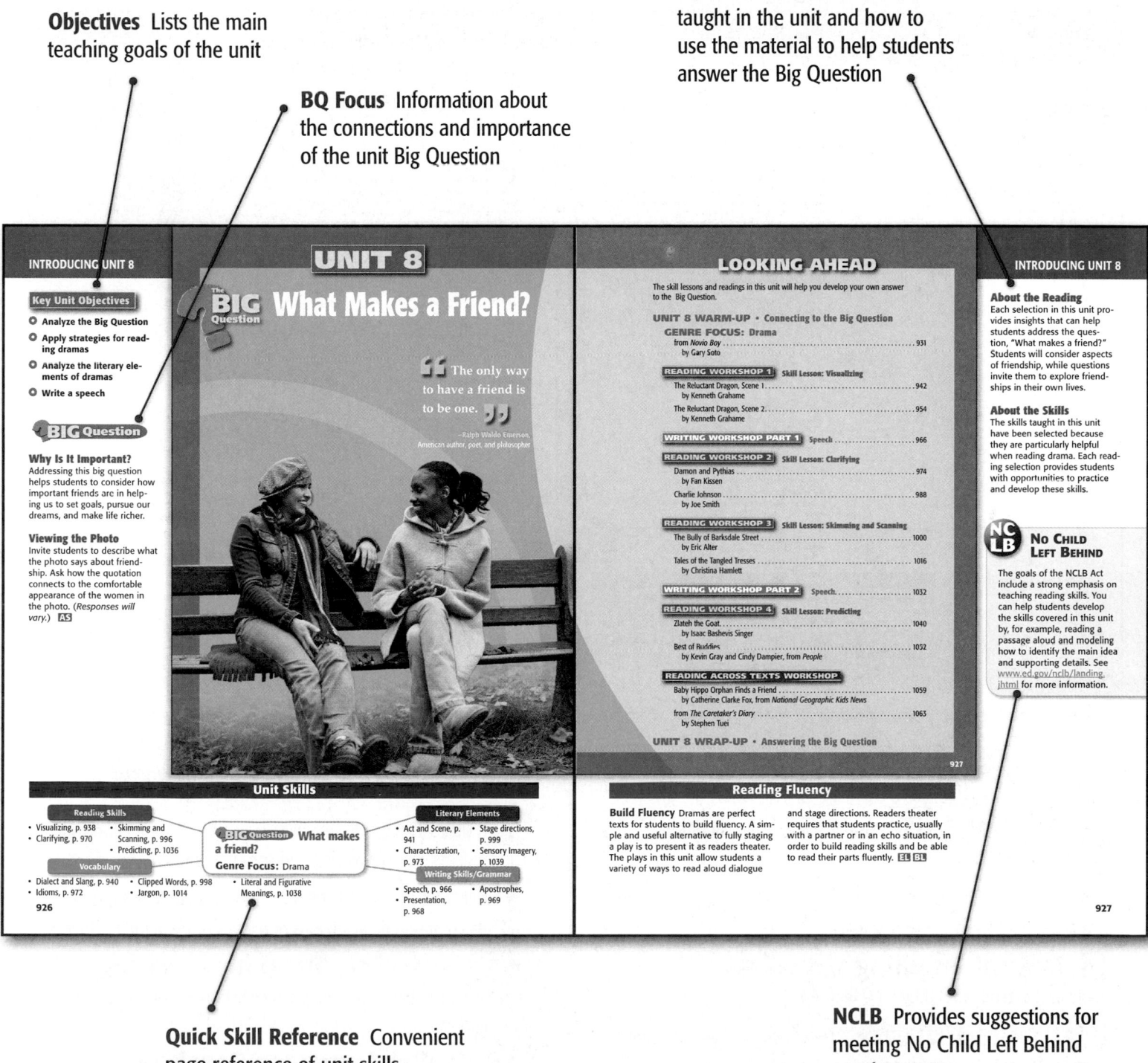

INTRODUCING UNIT 8

Key Unit Objectives

Analyze the Big Question

Apply strategies for reading dramas

Analyze the literary elements of dramas

Write a speech

BIG Question

Why Is It Important?
Addressing this big question helps students to consider how important friends are in helping us to set goals, pursue our dreams, and make life richer.

Viewing the Photo
Invite students to describe what the photo says about friendship. Ask how the quotation connects to the comfortable appearance of the women in the photo. (*Responses will vary.*) **AS**

UNIT 8

BIG Question — What Makes a Friend?

" The only way to have a friend is to be one. "

–Ralph Waldo Emerson, American author, poet, and philosopher

LOOKING AHEAD

The skill lessons and readings in this unit will help you develop your own answer to the Big Question.

UNIT 8 WARM-UP • Connecting to the Big Question
GENRE FOCUS: Drama

UNIT 8 WRAP-UP • Answering the Big Question

927

INTRODUCING UNIT 8

About the Reading
Each selection in this unit provides insights that can help students address the question, "What makes a friend?" Students will consider aspects of friendship, while questions invite them to explore friendships in their own lives.

About the Skills
The skills taught in this unit have been selected because they are particularly helpful when reading drama. Each reading selection provides students with opportunities to practice and develop these skills.

NCLB — NO CHILD LEFT BEHIND

The goals of the NCLB Act include a strong emphasis on teaching reading skills. You can help students develop the skills covered in this unit by, for example, reading a passage aloud and modeling how to identify the main idea and supporting details. See www.ed.gov/nclb/landing.jhtml for more information.

Unit Skills

Reading Skills
- Visualizing, p. 938
- Clarifying, p. 970
- Skimming and Scanning, p. 996
- Predicting, p. 1036

BIG Question What makes a friend?
Genre Focus: Drama

Literary Elements
- Act and Scene, p. 941
- Characterization, p. 973
- Stage directions, p. 999
- Sensory Imagery, p. 1039

Vocabulary
- Dialect and Slang, p. 940
- Idioms, p. 972
- Clipped Words, p. 998
- Jargon, p. 1014
- Literal and Figurative Meanings, p. 1038

Writing Skills/Grammar
- Speech, p. 966
- Presentation, p. 968
- Apostrophes, p. 969

926

Reading Fluency

Build Fluency Dramas are perfect texts for students to build fluency. A simple and useful alternative to fully staging a play is to present it as readers theater. The plays in this unit allow students a variety of ways to read aloud dialogue and stage directions. Readers theater requires that students practice, usually with a partner or in an echo situation, in order to build reading skills and be able to read their parts fluently. **EL BL**

927

Quick Skill Reference Convenient page reference of unit skills

NCLB Provides suggestions for meeting No Child Left Behind requirements

Understanding the Brackets and Letters

Letters The letters on the reduced student edition page identify the type of skill or activity. See the key below to learn about the different types of skills and activities.

Brackets Brackets on the reduced student edition page correspond to teaching the skills and activities. The brackets show you exactly where to teach the skills and activities for each workshop.

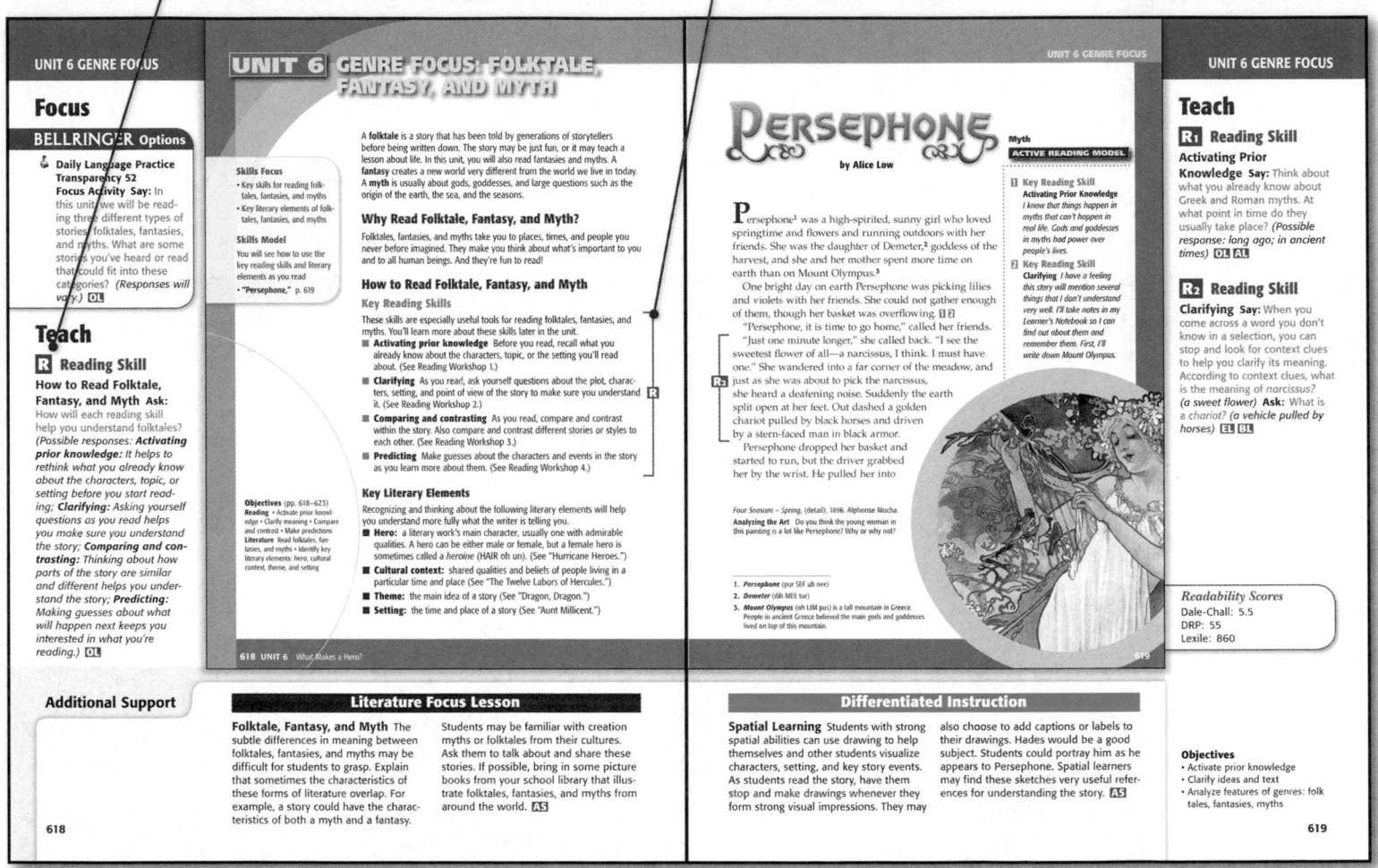

Teacher Wraparound Edition Key

R **Reading Skill** These activities help you teach reading skills and vocabulary.

V **Vocabulary** These activities help students comprehend words and incorporate into reading.

C **Critical Thinking** These strategies help students apply and extend what they have learned.

BQ **BIG Question** These activities and questions prompt students to prepare to answer the Big Question.

E **Text Element** These activities help students recognize and understand the use of text elements.

W **Writing** These activities provide writing opportunities to help students practice writing and comprehend text.

L **Literary Element** These activities and questions help students comprehend selections and learn more about each genre.

LSV **Listening, Speaking, Viewing** These activities help students practice listening, speaking, and viewing skills.

EL **English Language Coach** These skills help English language learners as well as students who need additional reading support.

Activity Leveling

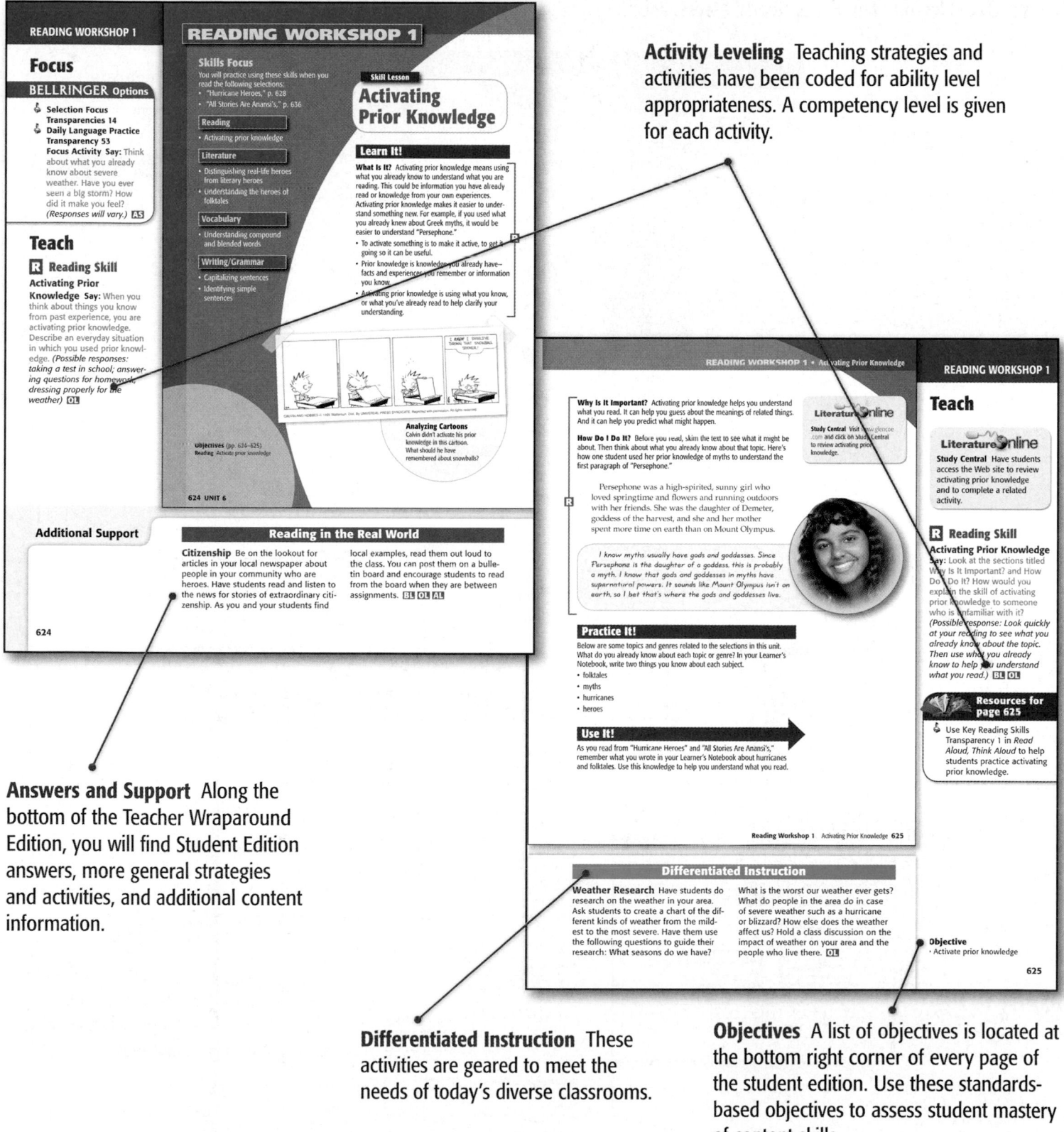

Activity Leveling Teaching strategies and activities have been coded for ability level appropriateness. A competency level is given for each activity.

Answers and Support Along the bottom of the Teacher Wraparound Edition, you will find Student Edition answers, more general strategies and activities, and additional content information.

Differentiated Instruction These activities are geared to meet the needs of today's diverse classrooms.

Objectives A list of objectives is located at the bottom right corner of every page of the student edition. Use these standards-based objectives to assess student mastery of content skills.

Workshop Structure

The instructions in each workshop in *Reading with Purpose* is presented in a structured lesson plan: Focus, Teach, Assess, and Close.

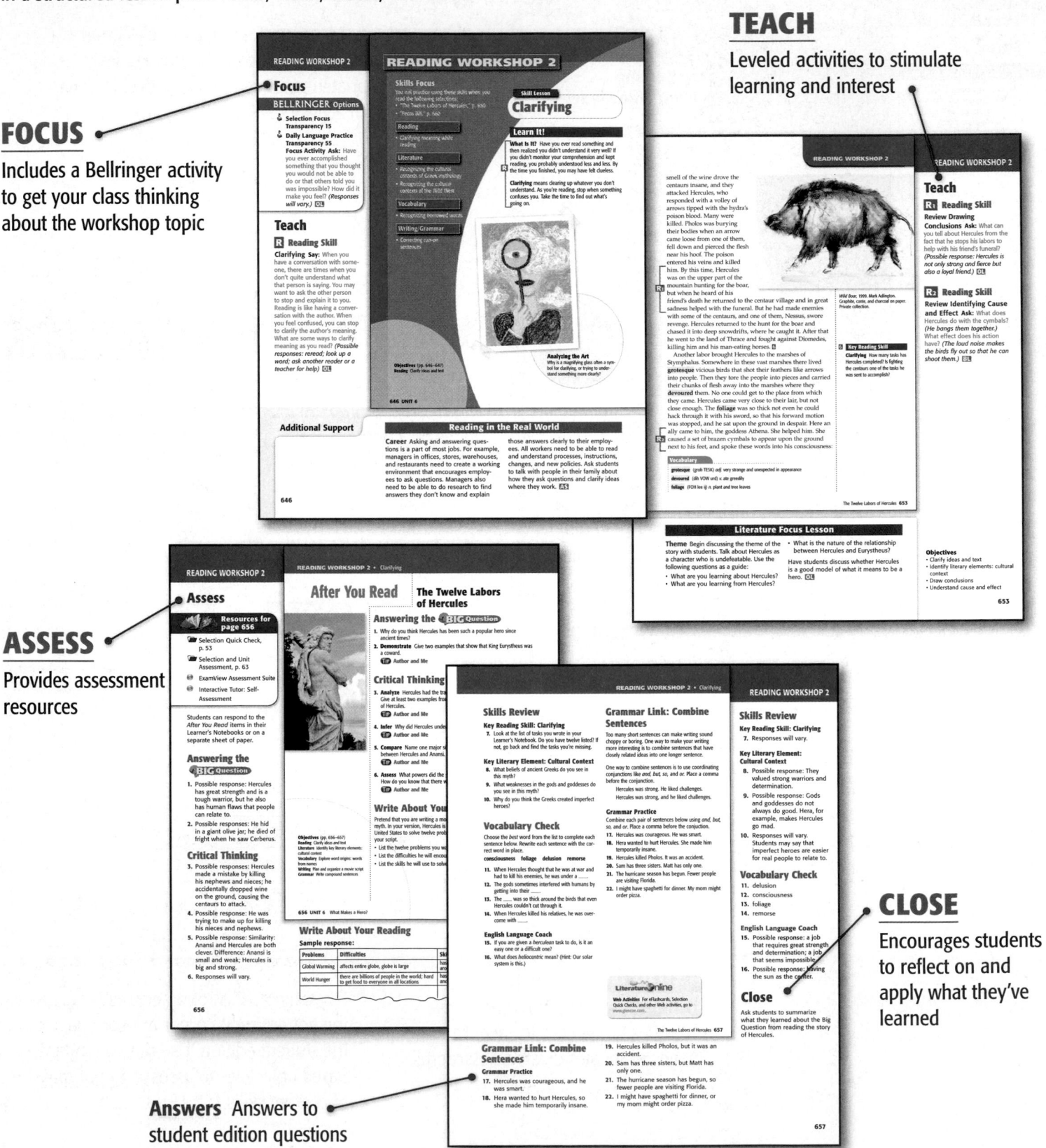

TEACH

Leveled activities to stimulate learning and interest

FOCUS

Includes a Bellringer activity to get your class thinking about the workshop topic

ASSESS

Provides assessment resources

CLOSE

Encourages students to reflect on and apply what they've learned

Answers Answers to student edition questions

Resources and Support

For every unit the teacher wraparound edition includes a page of additional teaching resources and online support for both you and your students.

Fast File A list of blackline master practice and activity sheets available in the Unit Resources booklets

Assessments Use these resources to track and assess your student's reading and writing skills in the classroom or online.

ELL Unit resources for engaging English Language Learners.

Tech Support A list of online and CD-ROM-based resources available for students and teachers

Teaching the Selection

Each selection in the student edition is preceded by a "Before Your Read" page that prepares students for the vocabulary and themes of the selection. Reading selections are followed by an "After You Read" section where students can respond and connect to the selection.

Author Information Provides additional information about the author or selection

Resource Guide Directs you to additional Glencoe material developed to enhance and assess students' comprehension of the selection

Skills Reinforcement Opportunities to reinforce the key Reading Skills and Literary Elements found throughout the selection

Readability Scores Dale-Chall, DRP, and Lexile readability scores are provided for every selection.

Teaching Informational Text

The wide range of informational texts and functional documents in *Glencoe Literature: Reading with Purpose* broadens student reading to include more than poetry, stories, and plays.

InTime Articles from the **TIME** family of magazines deliver insight and facts on timely issues and topics related to the Big Question.

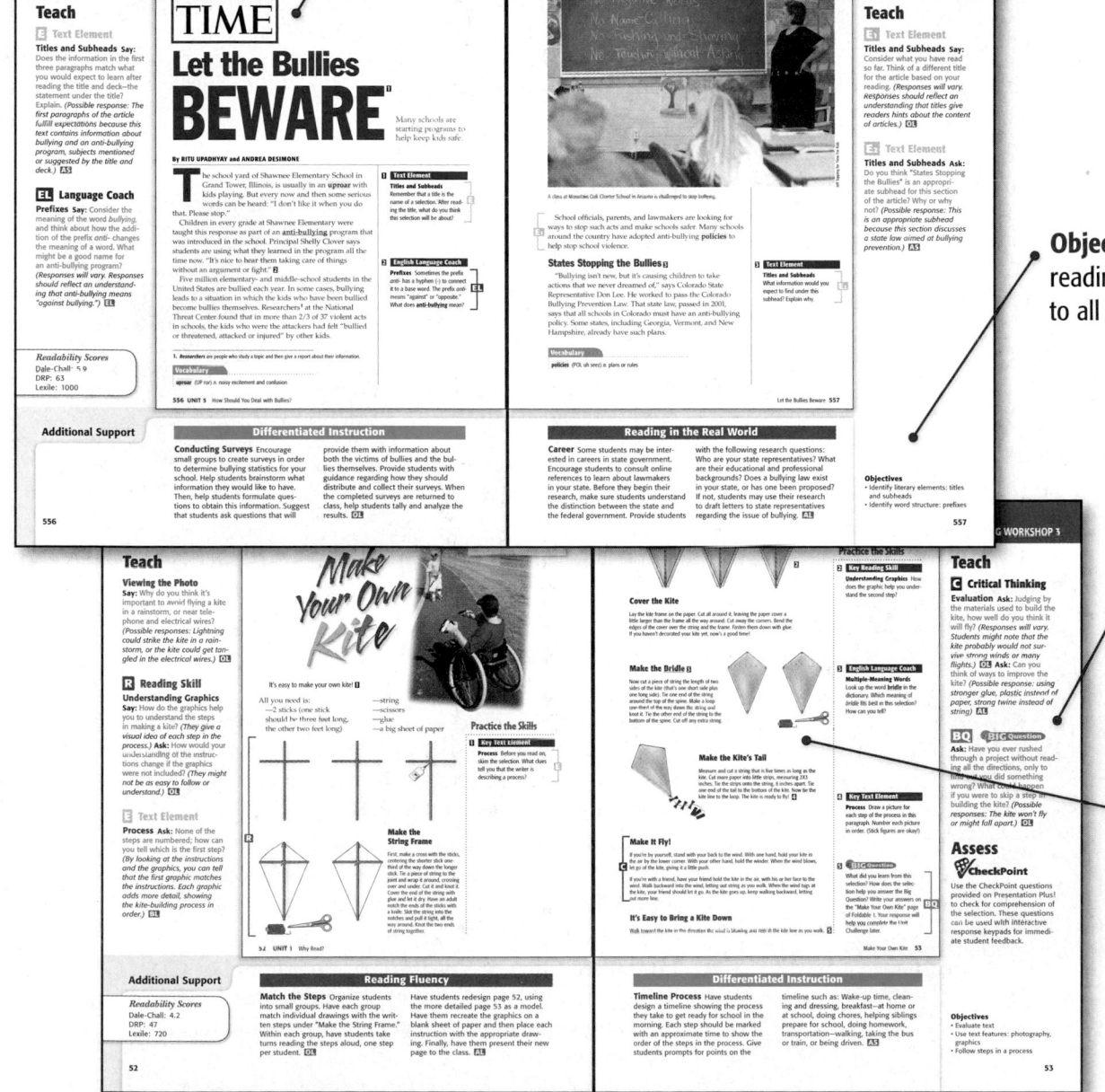

Objectives Standards-based reading objectives are correlated to all nonfiction selections.

BQ Connection Teaching suggestions and questions to help students connect the article to the unit Big Question

Functional Documents *Reading with Purpose* fulfills state standards requirements for reading and comprehending functional documents that students encounter outside the classroom.

Classroom Resources

Unit Resources

Fast File Booklets

These blackline master booklets provide all the teaching materials you need to reinforce the content in each unit of *Glencoe Literature: Reading with Purpose.* Worksheets in each booklet focus on the following:

- Unit Warm-Up
- The Big Question Foldables
- The Big Question: Home-School Connection (English and Spanish versions)
- Unit Challenge: Planner and Rubrics
- Literary Analysis
- Active Reading Graphic Organizers
- Comparing Literature Graphic Organizers
- Spelling and Handwriting Practice
- Academic Vocabulary Review
- Unit Vocabulary Review
- English Language Coach Review
- Grammar Practice
- Writing Workshop Graphic Organizers
- Key Reading Skills
- Viewing and Representing
- Listening and Speaking

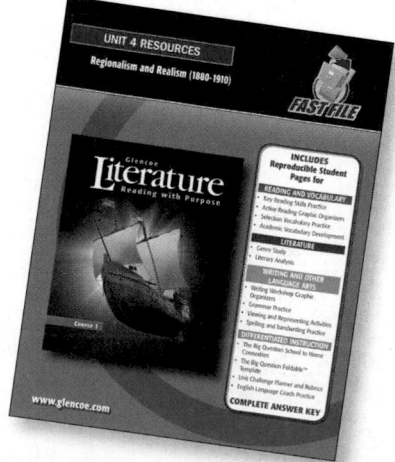

Literature and Reading

Active Learning and Note Taking Guides

This set of consumable workbooks provides structured outline support for students to use before, during, and after reading, helping them focus on key concepts and information. Activities include interactive exercises on literary elements and vocabulary for writing about literature. To meet the needs of all your students, the workbooks are offered in four versions:

- **Active Learning and Note Taking Guide (Grade Level)**
- **Active Learning and Note Taking Guide: Enriched**
- **Active Learning and Note Taking Guide: Adapted**
- **Active Learning and Note Taking Guide: ELL**

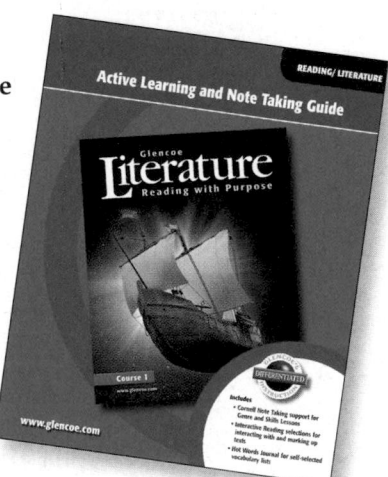

Glencoe Literature Library

This collection of 120 hardcover books helps you encourage your students to read independently. Choose from novels, novellas, plays, and nonfiction. Each book includes related readings from a broad range of genres. Support your teaching with these technology products:

- **Literature Library ExamView Suite Assessment CD-ROM** allows you to create customized tests for all the literary works included in the Literature Library collection.
- **Literature Library Vocabulary Puzzlemaker CD** helps you and your students create word puzzles based on vocabulary selected from the Literature Library collection.

Glencoe Backpack Reader

These portable collections of stories, poems, essays, and plays offer students additional reading for skills practice and personal enjoyment. The leveled selections promote gradual release of responsibility and increase students' confidence in reading and literature.

inTIME Magazine

These high-interest collections of articles drawn from issues of *TIME* magazine and other Time, Inc., publications help students develop reading strategies that interact with informational text. The *inTIME* magazines are available in both English and Spanish and include teacher guides.

Literature Launchers: Prereading Videos/DVD

These short, lively video segments on DVD introduce each unit in *Glencoe Literature: Reading with Purpose.*

Literature Classics CD

This software brings more than 1,100 additional literature selections—accessible by author, title, date, genre, and big idea—to your classroom. Genre Focus Lesson Plans and blackline masters are also provided.

Writing

Real Success in Writing: Research and Reports

These blackline masters reinforce and extend the coverage of research presented in the student edition.

Writing Constructed Responses

This sourcebook with blackline masters help students respond effectively to short essay questions.

Differentiated Instruction

Leveled Vocabulary Development

These blackline masters provide practice on selection vocabulary words. The booklet is offered in four versions:

- **Leveled Vocabulary Development: (Grade Level)**
- **Leveled Vocabulary Development: Enriched**
- **Leveled Vocabulary Development: Adapted**
- **Leveled Vocabulary Development: English Language Learner**

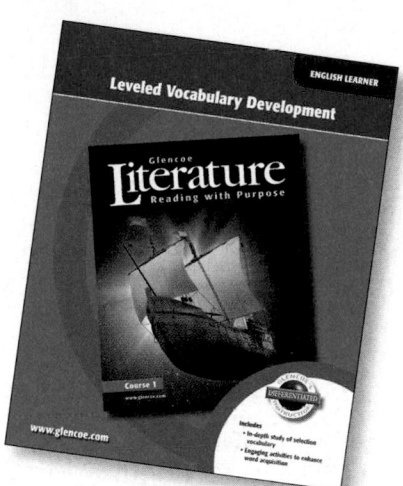

Vocabulary Puzzlemaker

This software lets you or your students create word puzzles based on selection vocabulary.

Listening Library Audio CD-ROM (English and Spanish)

This audio collection offers engaging readings of selections in English and Spanish.

Skill Level Up!™: A Language Arts Game

This CD-ROM game motivates students to practice and master language arts skills covered in *Glencoe Literature: Reading with Purpose* and frequently assessed on standardized tests. Students have fun and you receive valuable skills-based performance data by individual or class.

Glencoe BookLink 3 CD-ROM

Use the *Glencoe BookLink 3* CD-ROM, a database of more than 26,700 titles, to create customized reading lists for your students. Search for award-winning titles and for books on several state-recommended reading lists.

Assessment

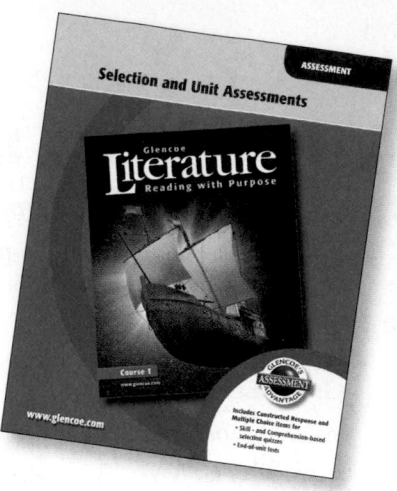

Selection and Unit Assessments

This assessment tool contains comprehensive tests and answer keys for all selections and units.

Selection Quick Check

These short-answer questions serve as a quick way to assess students' basic comprehension of a selection (Spanish and English)

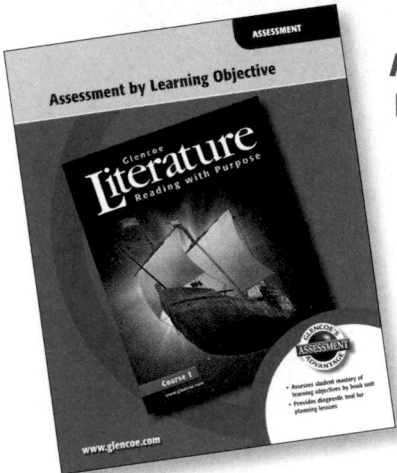

Assessment by Learning Objective

These booklets help you assess learning objectives related to reading strategy, literary element, genre, or literary period or movement.

Rubrics for Assessing Student Writing, Listening, and Speaking

This booklet provides you with rubrics to use for all Writing Workshop products as well as for key listening and speaking activities.

Standardized Test Preparation and Practice

These materials feature exercises and activities that get students ready for standardized exams.

Technology Resources

StudentWorks™ Plus CD-ROM

StudentWorks™ Plus contains the Student Edition (PDF) with selection audio; student workbooks (PDF); Student Presentation Builder (provides Unit-based multimedia projects, PowerPoint tutorial, and PowerPoint presentation template); and Daily Assignments and a Grade Log that allows students to organize their assignments and track their own progress.

Online Student Edition (MHLN)

Showcasing the interactive versions of McGraw-Hill textbooks, mhln.com offers the same content as the printed text, with multimedia-enhanced content. Games, interactivities, and other items are correlated directly to each page.

TeacherWorks™ Plus CD-ROM

TeacherWorks™ Plus contains a suite of easy-to-use and effective tools designed to help you manage daily activities, access all textbook materials, and utilize resources on the Internet. Included are daily lesson plans and a block schedule guide.

ExamViewPro® Assessment Suite

With the Test Generator you can quickly create customized unit- or selection-based assessments in a snap! Use the unit exams or the selection-specific exams provided in both English and Spanish on this CD-ROM, or create your own questions.

Presentation Plus! CD-ROM

This multimedia application enables teachers to present dynamic lessons for every unit and selection in Glencoe Literature. The PowerPoint multimedia presentations can be edited and customized for teacher lesson planning.

Skill Level Up!™: A Language Arts Game

This CD-ROM game motivates students to practice and master language arts skills covered in *Glencoe Literature: Reading with Purpose* and frequently assessed on standardized tests. Students have fun and you receive valuable skills-based performance data by individual or class.

Vocabulary Puzzlemaker

This software lets you or your students create word puzzles based on selection vocabulary.

Literature Classics CD-ROM

This software brings more than 1,100 additional literature selections—accessible by author, title, date, genre, and big idea—to your classroom. Genre Focus Lesson Plans and blackline masters are also provided.

Literature Library ExamView Assessment Suite CD-ROM

This software allows you to create customized tests for all the literary works included in the Literature Library collection.

Literature Library Vocabulary Puzzlemaker CD-ROM

This software helps you and your students create word puzzles based on vocabulary selected from the Literature Library collection.

Literature Launchers: Prereading Videos/DVD

These short, lively video segments on DVD introduce each unit in *Glencoe Literature: Reading with Purpose*.

Listening Library Audio CD-ROM (English and Spanish)

This audio collection offers engaging readings of selections in English and Spanish.

Glencoe BookLink 3 CD-ROM

Use the *Glencoe BookLink 3* CD-ROM, a database of more than 26,700 titles, to create customized reading lists for your students. Search for award-winning titles and for books on several state-recommended reading lists.

Glencoe Online Essay Grader

Improve student writing and save time with Glencoe's Online Essay Grader, powered by SkillWriter™. Glencoe's Online Essay Grader will score your students' writing assignments and provide individualized feedback automatically.

Transparencies

- **Read Aloud, Think Aloud** model active reading.
- **Bellringer Options Transparencies** include warm-up exercises to engage student interest or provide a quick review of previously taught activities.
- **Literary Analysis Transparencies** help reinforce or reteach literary elements that are the focus of each lesson.
- **Grammar and Writing Workshop Transparencies** help reinforce the skills taught in the grammar and writing workshops in the student edition.
- **Fine Art Transparencies** enhance a strong humanities approach to literature and help students analyze visual representations of literary concepts and characters. These transparencies are an excellent source of writing prompts.

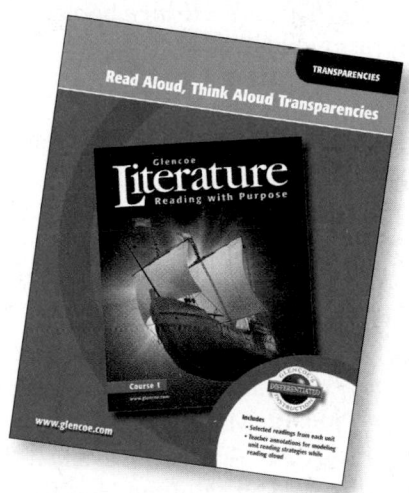

Internet Resources (www.glencoe.com)

For online resources that support the instruction in *Glencoe Literature: Reading with Purpose*, students and teachers can visit our Web site at **www.glencoe.com**. Students will find additional learning, practice, and assessment opportunities.

Glencoe Resources for Independent Reading

Glencoe Literature Library

This collection of hardcover books includes full-length novels, novellas, plays, and works of nonfiction. Each *Glencoe Literature Library* volume consists of at least one complete extended-length reading accompanied by several related readings from a broad range of genres, such as short stories, poems, essays, or informational articles. In addition, a separate **Study Guide** for each *Glencoe Literature Library* book provides teaching notes and reproducible activity pages for students. Students may also find these activity pages on the **Glencoe Web site http://www.glencoe.com.**

Across Five Aprils by Irene Hunt **DRP 59**

The Adventures of Tom Sawyer by Mark Twain **DRP 55**

Anne Frank Remembered: The Story of the Woman Who Helped to Hide the Frank Family by Miep Gies and Alison Leslie Gold **DRP 57**

Bearstone by Will Hobbs **DRP 51**

Bridge to Terabithia by Katherine Paterson **DRP 50**

The Call of the Wild by Jack London **DRP 62**

Cezanne Pinto by Mary Stoltz **DRP 54**

A Christmas Carol by Charles Dickens **DRP 60**

The Clay Marble by Minfong Ho **DRP 49**

Dandelion Wine by Ray Bradbury **DRP 56**

Dogsong by Gary Paulsen **DRP 51**

Dragonwings by Lawrence Yep **DRP 54**

The Friends by Rosa Guy **DRP 51**

A Gathering of Days: A New England Girl's Journal 1830–1832 by Joan W. Blos **DRP 56**

The Glory Field by Walter Dean Myers **DRP 51**

Hatchet by Gary Paulsen **DRP 54**

High Elk's Treasure by Virginia Driving Hawk Sneve

Homecoming by Cynthia Voigt **DRP 48**

The House of Dies Drear by Virginia Hamilton **DRP 49**

I, Juan de Pareja by Elizabeth Borton de Treviño **DRP 58**

Island of the Blue Dolphins by Scott O'Dell **DRP 53**

Jacob Have I Loved by Katherine Paterson **DRP 52**

Johnny Tremain by Esther Forbes **DRP 55**

Journey to Jo'burg by Beverly Naidoo **DRP 50**

Julie of the Wolves by Jean Craighead George **DRP 55**

Letters from a Slave Girl by Mary E. Lyons **DRP 51**

Letters from Rifka by Karen Hesse **DRP 49**

Little Women by Louisa May Alcott **DRP 60**

Lupita Mañana by Patricia Beatty **DRP 53**

Missing May by Cynthia Rylant **DRP 53**

Mrs. Frisby and the Rats of NIMH by Robert O'Brien **DRP 52**

Number the Stars by Lois Lowry **DRP 52**

The Pigman by Paul Zindel **DRP 55**

Shabanu: Daughter of the Wind by Suzanne Fisher Staples **DRP 54**

Shiloh by Phyllis Reynolds Naylor **DRP 50**

The Slave Dancer by Paula Fox **DRP 55**

So Far from the Bamboo Grove by Yoko Kawashima Watkins **DRP 50**

Sounder by William H. Armstrong **DRP 53, CRL 9**

The Summer of the Swans by Betsy Byars **DRP 50**

Taking Sides by Gary Soto **DRP 52**

There's a Girl in My Hammerlock by Jerry Spinelli **DRP 46**

Treasure Island by Robert Louis Stevenson **DRP 56**

The True Confessions of Charlotte Doyle by Avi **DRP 52**

Tuck Everlasting by Natalie Babbitt **DRP 56**

The View from Saturday by E.L. Konigsburg **DRP 53**

Walk Two Moons by Sharon Creech **DRP 49**

Where the Red Fern Grows by Wilson Rawls **DRP 47**

Winter Thunder and *The Christmas of the Phonograph Records* by Mari Sandoz

The Witch of Blackbird Pond by Elizabeth George Speare **DRP 57**

A Wrinkle in Time by Madeleine L'Engle **DRP 51**

Glencoe Backpack Reader

These portable collections of stories, poems, essays, and plays offer students additional reading for skills practice and personal enjoyment. The selections promote gradual release reading and increase students' confidence in reading and literature. Find teacher resources for Backpack Reader on Teacher Works Plus or glencoe.com.

inTIME magazine

This lively collection of articles drawn from issues of TIME helps students develop the skills they need to interact with informational text in a meaningful way. Each of the news stories, feature articles, reviews, profiles, and essays in the magazines connects to an author, reading selection, or Big Question in *Glencoe Literature: Reading with Purpose.* The magazines are available in both English and Spanish editions. In addition, a separate **Teacher Guide,** including lessons and reproducible student worksheets designed to develop students' reading and critical thinking skills, accompanies each magazine.

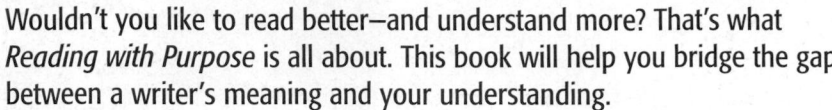

Wouldn't you like to read better—and understand more? That's what *Reading with Purpose* is all about. This book will help you bridge the gap between a writer's meaning and your understanding.

The next few pages will show you some of the ways *Reading with Purpose* can help you read, think, and write better.

Consultant's Note

People read for enjoyment, to help themselves think, to solve problems, and to get work done. Their reading is often organized around "inquiry" questions. These questions help them explore how what they learn can help make a difference in the real world.

—Jeff Wilhelm

What's In it for You?

Every unit in *Reading with Purpose* is built around a **Big Question,** a question that you will want to think about, talk about, maybe even argue about, and finally answer. The unit's reading selections will help you come up with your answers.

Organization

Each unit contains:

- A **Unit Warm-Up** that introduces the unit's Big Question
- Four **Reading Workshops,** each one containing reading selections that will help you think about the Big Question
  - **Literature** such as short stories, poems, plays, and biographies
  - **Informational texts** such as nonfiction, newspaper and magazine articles, reference books, and manuals
  - **Functional documents** such as signs, schedules, labels, and instructions
- A two-part **Writing Workshop** to help you put your ideas about the Big Question into writing
- A **Comparing Workshop** that will give you a chance to compare different pieces of writing
- A **Unit Wrap-Up** where you'll answer the Big Question.

Reading and Thinking

Here are some of the ways **Reading with Purpose** will help you develop your reading and thinking skills.

Skills and Strategies The skills you need to become a better reader are related to the standards that state and local school districts test you on. We call these *objectives.*

Consultant's Note

Standards tell what you are expected to do or learn—the learning objectives. They help teachers plan lessons and select reading and writing tasks. In addition, standards ensure that the content taught at one school will be similar to the content at other schools in the state. The standards also help you figure out what will be on tests. Standards help you figure out what you need to learn to do well in school!

—Doug Fisher

Margin Notes These notes will help you with a difficult passage, point out an important development, model a skill, or ask a question to get you thinking about what you are reading.

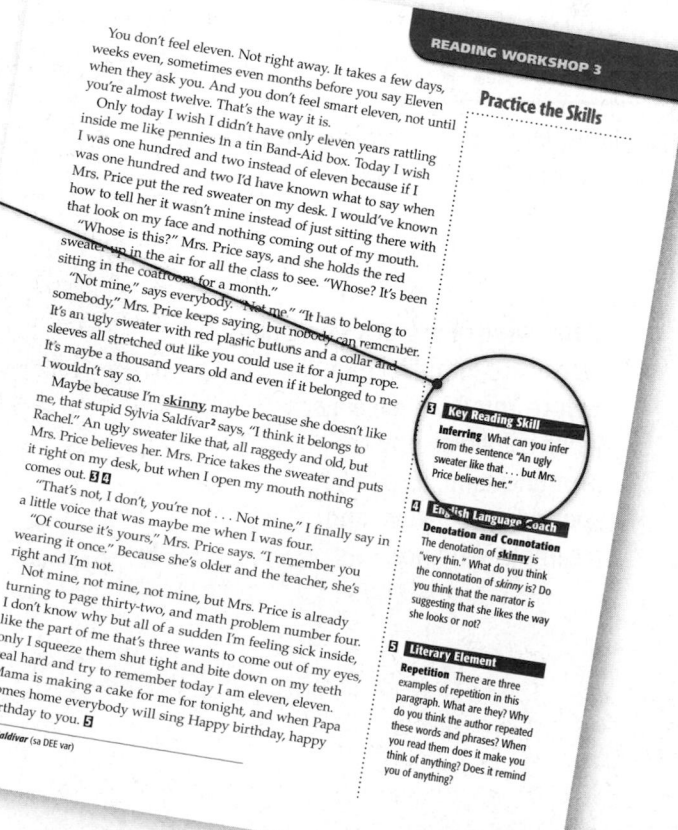

READING WORKSHOP 3 • Inferring

Before You Read
Eleven

Sandra Cisneros

Meet the Author
Sandra Cisneros lives in San Antonio, Texas. She often writes about Latino children living in the United States. "Eleven," Cisneros said, "was my story except . . . it didn't happen at eleven (I was nine), . . . But I did cry. . . . Why did they pick me out? Because I was the one that looked like I belonged to something that shabby?" See page R2 of the Author Files in the *Luck* of the book for more on Sandra Cisneros.

Literature Online
Author Search For more about Sandra Cisneros, go to www.glencoe.com.

Objectives (pp. 306–311)
Reading Make inferences • Make connections from text to self
Literature Identify literary elements: repetition • Understand effects of repetition
Vocabulary Understand denotation and connotation • Identify uses of connotation: meaning in semantic slanting

306 UNIT 3 What's Fair and What's Not?

English Language Coach
Denotation and Connotation As you know, some words have a connotation—an extra meaning suggested by a word.

Some words have a positive connotation. For example, *slender* can suggest an appearance that is more attractive than *thin*. Some words have a negative connotation. For example, *cheap* often suggests something more negative than *inexpensive.*

Positive	Negative
young	childish
plump	fat
daring	reckless

Many connotations are neither positive nor negative. They're just feelings or ideas we associate with certain words. For example, the word *warrior* suggests an extra meaning that *soldier* doesn't have. It makes us think of a brave and mighty fighter from the past.

The words in this web are ways of *looking*, but each word has a different connotation. For example, when someone *stares* at you, it can be upsetting.

gaze — look — stare — observe — glance

Partner Talk With a partner, talk about what each word says about ways of looking.

You don't feel eleven. Not right away. It takes a few days, weeks even, sometimes even months before you say Eleven when they ask you. And you don't feel smart eleven, not until you're almost twelve. That's the way it is.

Only today I wish I didn't have only eleven years rattling inside me like pennies In a tin Band-Aid box. Today I wish I was one hundred and two instead of eleven because if I was one hundred and two I'd have known what to say when Mrs. Price put the red sweater on my desk. I would've known how to tell her it wasn't mine instead of just sitting there with that look on my face and nothing coming out of my mouth.

"Whose is this?" Mrs. Price says, and she holds the red sweater up in the air for all the class to see. "Whose? It's been sitting in the coatroom for a month."

"Not mine," says everybody. "Not me." "It has to belong to somebody," Mrs. Price keeps saying, but nobody can remember. It's an ugly sweater with red plastic buttons and a collar and sleeves all stretched out like you could use it for a jump rope. It's maybe a thousand years old and even if it belonged to me I wouldn't say so.

Maybe because I'm *skinny,* maybe because she doesn't like me, that stupid Sylvia Saldívar[2] says, "I think it belongs to Rachel." An ugly sweater like that, all raggedy and old, but Mrs. Price believes her. Mrs. Price takes the sweater and puts it right on my desk, but when I open my mouth nothing comes out. **3 4**

"That's not, I don't, you're not . . . Not mine," I finally say in a little voice that was maybe me when I was four.

"Of course it's yours," Mrs. Price says. "I remember you wearing it once." Because she's older and the teacher, she's right and I'm not.

Not mine, not mine, not mine, but Mrs. Price is already turning to page thirty-two, and math problem number four. I don't know why but all of a sudden I'm feeling sick inside, like the part of me that's three wants to come out of my eyes, only I squeeze them shut tight and bite down on my teeth real hard and try to remember today I am eleven, eleven. Mama is making a cake for me for tonight, and when Papa comes home everybody will sing Happy birthday, happy birthday to you. **5**

2. *Saldívar* (sa DEE var)

Practice the Skills

3 Key Reading Skill
Inferring What can you infer from the sentence "An ugly sweater like that . . . but Mrs. Price believes her."

4 English Language Coach
Denotation and Connotation The denotation of *skinny* is "very thin." What do you think the connotation of *skinny* is? Do you think that the narrator is suggesting that she likes the way she looks or not?

5 Literary Element
Repetition There are three examples of repetition in this paragraph. What are they? Why do you think the author repeated these words and phrases? When you read them does it make you think of anything? Does it remind you of anything?

Question and Answer Relationship

Four types of questions are used on standardized tests:

1. **Right There Questions** The answer is "right there" on the page.

2. **Think and Search Questions** The answers to these questions are on the page (or pages), but you'll need to use information from different parts of the text.

3. **Author and Me Questions** Information from the text may help, but you'll put it together with your own ideas to answer a question.

4. **On My Own Questions** Answers do not come from the text. You'll base your answer on what you know.

Knowing how to deal with such questions can help improve your test scores. At the end of most Workshops is a set of questions. In the first two units, each question is followed by a tip to help you answer. For example:

- What promise does Victor make to himself about this school year?

  TIP **Right There** You will find the answer in the story.

Vocabulary

Vocabulary Words may be difficult or new to you, but they're useful words.

Vocabulary Preview Vocabulary words are introduced on the Before You Read page. Each word is followed by its pronunciation, its part of speech, a definition, and a sample sentence.

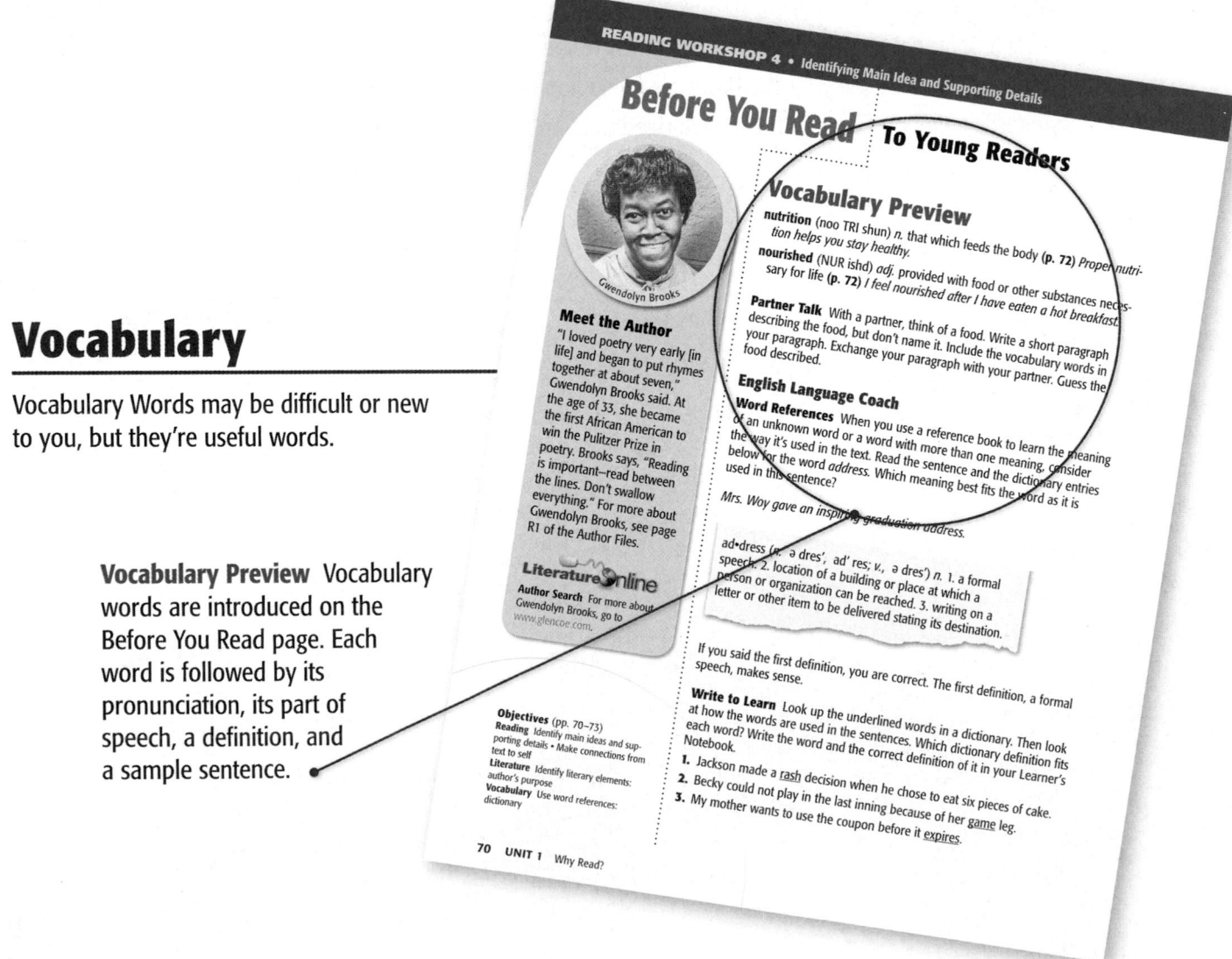

READING WORKSHOP 4 • Identifying Main Idea and Supporting Details

Before You Read

To Young Readers

Meet the Author
"I loved poetry very early [in life] and began to put rhymes together at about seven," Gwendolyn Brooks said. At the age of 33, she became the first African American to win the Pulitzer Prize in poetry. Brooks says, "Reading is important—read between the lines. Don't swallow everything." For more about Gwendolyn Brooks, see page R1 of the Author Files.

Gwendolyn Brooks

Literature Online
Author Search For more about Gwendolyn Brooks, go to www.glencoe.com.

Objectives (pp. 70–73)
Reading Identify main ideas and supporting details • Make connections from text to self
Literature Identify literary elements: author's purpose
Vocabulary Use word references: dictionary

Vocabulary Preview

nutrition (noo TRI shun) *n.* that which feeds the body **(p. 72)** Proper nutrition helps you stay healthy.

nourished (NUR ishd) *adj.* provided with food or other substances necessary for life **(p. 72)** I feel nourished after I have eaten a hot breakfast.

Partner Talk With a partner, think of a food. Write a short paragraph describing the food, but don't name it. Include the vocabulary words in your paragraph. Exchange your paragraph with your partner. Guess the food described.

English Language Coach

Word References When you use a reference book to learn the meaning of an unknown word or a word with more than one meaning, consider the way it's used in the text. Read the sentence and the dictionary entries below for the word *address*. Which meaning best fits the word as it is used in this sentence?

Mrs. Woy gave an inspiring graduation address.

ad•dress (ʔ dres', ad' res; *v.*, ʔ dres') *n.* 1. a formal speech. 2. location of a building or place at which a person or organization can be reached. 3. writing on a letter or other item to be delivered stating its destination.

If you said the first definition, you are correct. The first definition, a formal speech, makes sense.

Write to Learn Look up the underlined words in a dictionary. Then look at how the words are used in the sentences. Which dictionary definition fits each word? Write the word and the correct definition of it in your Learner's Notebook.

1. Jackson made a <u>rash</u> decision when he chose to eat six pieces of cake.
2. Becky could not play in the last inning because of her <u>game</u> leg.
3. My mother wants to use the coupon before it <u>expires</u>.

70   UNIT 1   Why Read?

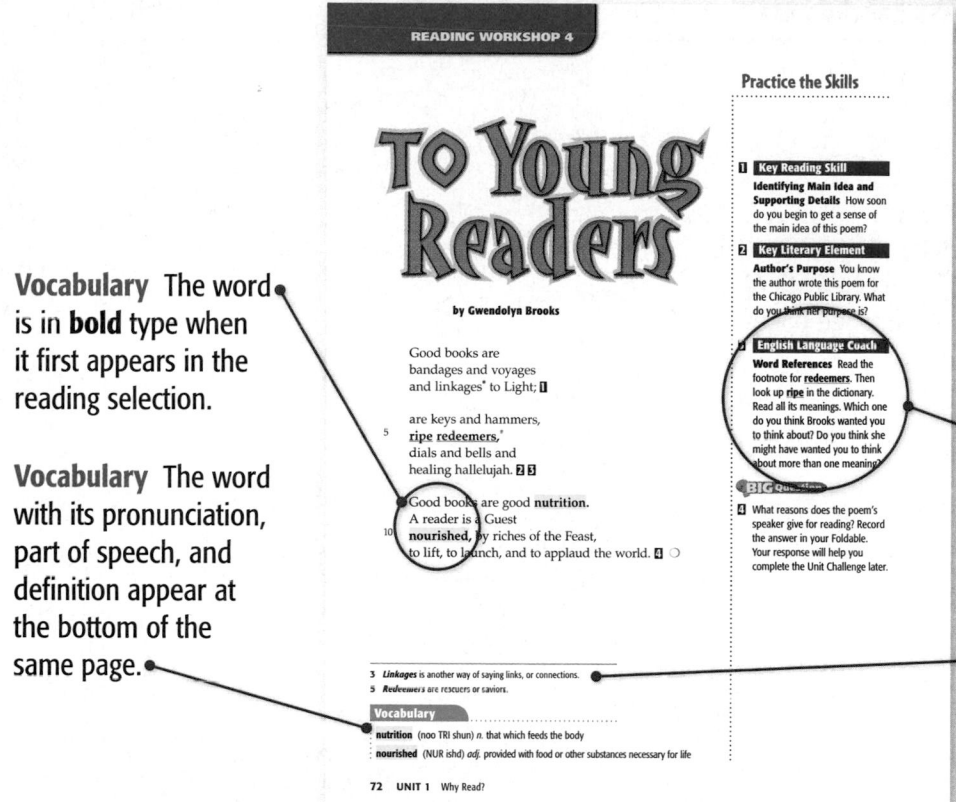

Vocabulary The word is in **bold** type when it first appears in the reading selection.

Vocabulary The word with its pronunciation, part of speech, and definition appear at the bottom of the same page.

English Language Coach These notes help students whose first language is not English. For example, they help explain multiple meaning words and also idioms—phrases that mean something other than what their individual words mean.

Footnotes Selection footnotes explain words or phrases that you may not know to help you understand the story.

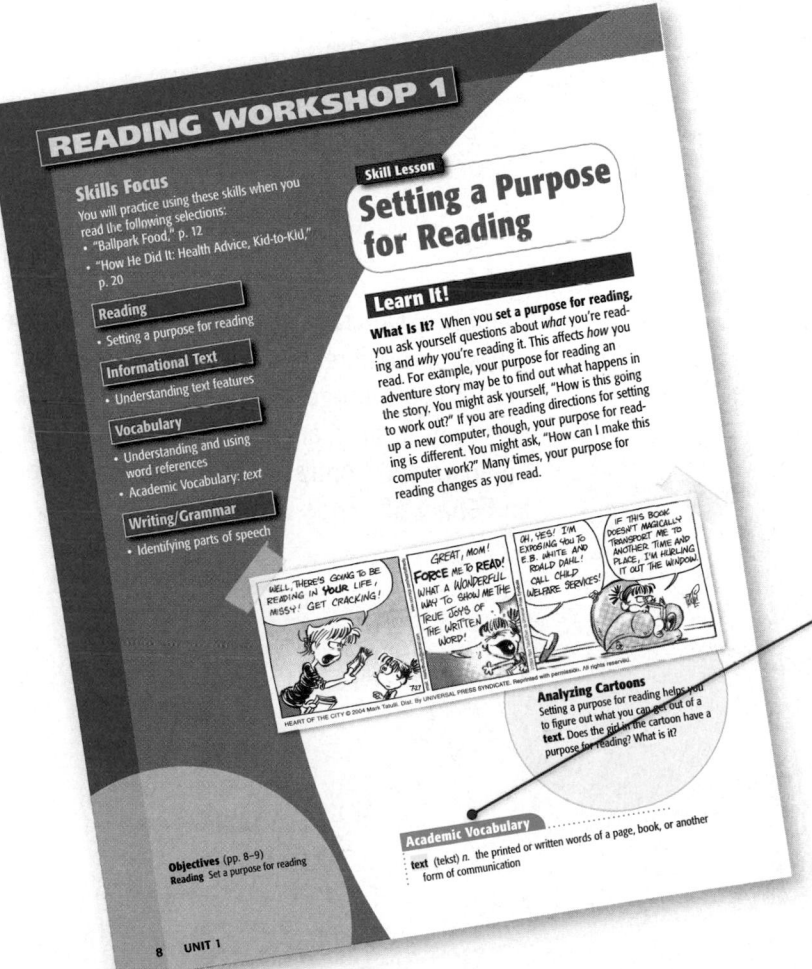

Academic Vocabulary These are words you come across in your school work—in science, math, or social studies books as well as this book. The academic words are treated the same as regular vocabulary words.

Organizing Information

Foldables For every unit, you'll be shown how to make a *Foldable* that will help you keep track of your thoughts about the Big Question. See pages R8–R9 for more about Foldables.

You and the Big Question
The question of what's fair or unfair comes up in many situations. As you read the selections in this unit, think about how you would answer the Big Question.

Literature Online
Big Question Link to Web resources to further explore the Big Question at www.glencoe.com.

Plan for the Unit Challenge
At the end of the unit, you'll use notes from all your reading to complete the Unit Challenge.

You'll choose one of the following activities:
A. TV Call-In Show With members of your group, you'll write questions and answers about what's fair and what's not for a television call-in show that your group will present.
B. A Rap or Song You'll write a rap or song about something you feel is unfair and what you think can be done about it.
• Start thinking about which activity you'd like to do so that you can focus your thoughts as you go through the unit.
• In your Learner's Notebook, write your thoughts about the activity you'd like to do.
• Each time you make notes about the Big Question, think about how your ideas will help you complete the Unit Challenge activity you chose.

Keep Track of Your Ideas
FOLDABLES Study Organizer

As you read, you'll make notes about the Big Question. Later, you'll use these notes to complete the Unit Challenge. See pages R8–R9 for help with making Foldable 3. This diagram shows how it should look.

1. Use this Foldable for the selections in this unit. Label the stapled edge with the unit number and the Big Question.
2. Label each flap with a selection title. (See page 253 for titles.)
3. Open each flap. Label the top of the inside page **My Purpose for Reading.** You will write your purpose for reading the selection below this label.
4. Halfway down the inside page, write the label **The Big Question.** You'll write your thoughts about the Big Question below this label.

Preserving a Great American Symbol

Warm-Up **255**

Before You Read Eleven

Sandra Cisneros

Meet the Author
Sandra Cisneros lives in San Antonio, Texas. She often writes about Latino children living in the United States. "Eleven," Cisneros said, "was my story except . . . it didn't happen at eleven (I was nine), . . . But I did cry. . . . Why did they pick me out? Because I was the one that looked like I belonged to something that shabby?" See page R2 of the Author Files in the back of the book for more on Sandra Cisneros.

Literature Online
Author Search For more about Sandra Cisneros, go to www.glencoe.com.

English Language Coach
Denotation and Connotation As you know, some words have a connotation—an extra meaning suggested by a word.

Some words have a positive connotation. For example, *slender* can suggest an appearance that is more attractive than *thin.* Some words have a negative connotation. For example, *cheap* often suggests something more negative than *inexpensive.*

Positive	Negative
young	childish
plump	fat
daring	reckless

Many connotations are neither positive nor negative. For example, the word *warrior* or ideas we associate with certain words. It makes us think of a suggests an extra meaning that *soldier* doesn't have. It makes us think of a brave and mighty fighter from the past.

The words in this web are ways of *looking,* but each word has a different connotation. For example, when someone *stares* at you, it can be upsetting.

stare
gaze
look
glance
observe

Partner Talk With a partner, talk about what each word says about ways of looking.

Objectives (pp. 306–311)
Reading Make inferences • Make connections from text to self
Literature Identify literary elements: repetition • Understand effects of repetition
Vocabulary Understand denotation and connotation • Identify uses of connotative meaning in semantic slanting

306 UNIT 3 What's Fair and What's Not?

Writing

In the selections on *Reading with Purpose,* you'll read many examples of excellent writing. And you'll explore what makes those pieces of writing so good.

Here are some other ways *Reading with Purpose* will help you become a better writer.

Writing to Learn As you learn new skills, you will sometimes complete a short writing assignment that will help you practice or think about your new skill.

Test Preparation and Practice

Following each unit, you will be tested on the literature, reading, and vocabulary skills you learned. This simulated standardized test will give you the practice you need to succeed while providing an assessment of how you have met the unit objectives.

Foldables™

by Dinah Zike, MEd, Creator of Foldables™

 Foldables™, are three-dimensional interactive graphic organizers for taking notes and organizing your ideas. They're also fun! You will fold paper, cut tabs, write, and manipulate what you have made in order to organize information; review skills, concepts, and strategies; and assess your learning.

Using Dinah Zike's Foldables in Reading and Literature Classes

Use Foldables before, during, and after reading selections in *Glencoe Literature: Reading With Purpose.*

■ **Before you read:** Your unit Foldable will help you to focus on your purpose for reading by reminding you about the Big Question.

■ **During reading:** Your unit Foldable will help you to stay focused and engaged. You will track key ideas and your thoughts about each selection and how it helps you answer the Big Question. It will also encourage you to use higher level thinking skills in approaching text.

■ **After reading:** Your Foldable will help you to review your thoughts from your reading and to analyze, interpret, and evaluate various aspects of the Big Question. Your Foldable notes will also help you with your unit challenge. They also stimulate rich group discussions and inquiry.

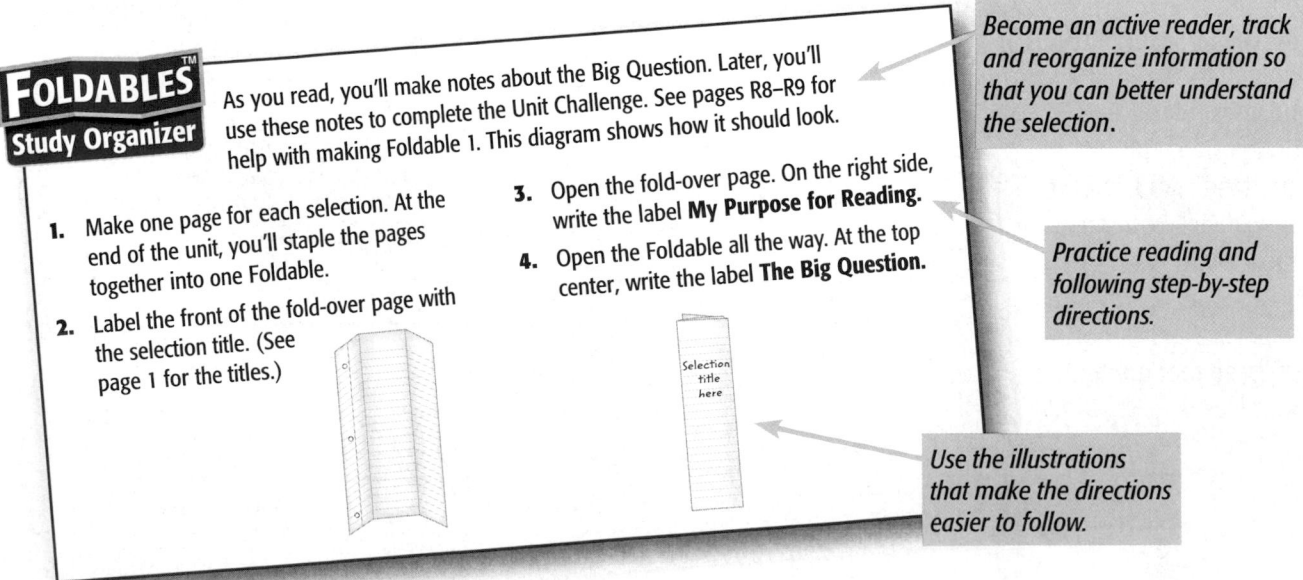

As you read, you'll make notes about the Big Question. Later, you'll use these notes to complete the Unit Challenge. See pages R8–R9 for help with making Foldable 1. This diagram shows how it should look.

1. Make one page for each selection. At the end of the unit, you'll staple the pages together into one Foldable.

2. Label the front of the fold-over page with the selection title. (See page 1 for the titles.)

3. Open the fold-over page. On the right side, write the label **My Purpose for Reading.**

4. Open the Foldable all the way. At the top center, write the label **The Big Question.**

Become an active reader, track and reorganize information so that you can better understand the selection.

Practice reading and following step-by-step directions.

Use the illustrations that make the directions easier to follow.

Scavenger Hunt

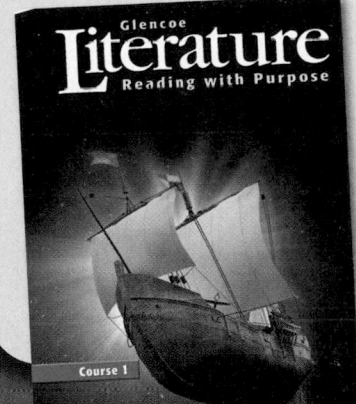

Reading with Purpose has a lot of information, excitement, and entertainment. This Scavenger Hunt will help you explore the book. You'll learn how to find what you need quickly. There are ten questions in your scavenger hunt. All the answers are in this book. Write your answers in your Learner's Notebook.

1. How many units are there in the book?

2. How many types of Workshops are in a unit and what are their names?

3. What is the genre focus of Unit 6?

4. How many short stories are in Unit 3?

5. Where can you find a list of all the poems in this book?

6. What's the fastest way to find a particular short story in the book?

7. Where in this book can you quickly find the correct pronunciation of the word *anesthetist?*

8. Where could you most quickly find the difference between a simile and a metaphor?

9. Where can you look for the answer to a question about grammar?

10. Name two places in the book where you can find biographical information about a writer.

After you answer all the questions, meet with a small group to compare answers.

READING HANDBOOK

You don't read a news article the way you read a novel. You read a news article mainly for information; you read a novel mainly for fun. To get the most out of your reading, you need to choose the right reading strategy to fit the reason you're reading. This handbook focuses on skills and strategies that can help you understand what you read.

Identifying Words and Building Vocabulary

What do you do when you come across a word you don't know as you read? Do you skip over the word and keep reading? If you're reading for fun or entertainment, you might. And that's just fine. But if you're reading for information, an unfamiliar word may get in the way of your understanding. When that happens, try the following strategies to figure out how to say the word and what it means. These strategies will help you better understand what you read. They will also help you increase the vocabulary you use in everyday speaking and reading.

Reading Unfamiliar Words

Sounding the Word Out

One way to figure out how to say a new word is to sound it out, syllable by syllable. Look carefully at the word's beginning, middle, and ending. Inside the new word, do you see a word you already know how to pronounce? What vowels are in the syllables? Use the following tips when sounding out new words.

▶ **Ask Yourself**

- What letters make up the beginning sound or beginning syllable of the word?

   Example: In the word *coagulate*, co- rhymes with so.

- What sounds do the letters in the middle part of the word make?

   Example: In the word *coagulate*, the syllable ag has the same sound as the *ag* in bag, and the syllable *u* is pronounced like the letter u.

- What letters make up the ending sound or syllable?

   Example: In the word *coagulate, late* is a familiar word you already know how to pronounce.

- Now try pronouncing the whole word: *co ag u late.*

Using Word Parts

Looking closely at the parts of a word is another way to learn it. By studying word parts—the root or base word, prefixes, and suffixes—you may discover more than just how to pronounce a word. You may also find clues to the word's meaning.

- **Roots and Base Words** The main part of a word is called its **root.** When the root is a complete word, it may be called the **base word.** Many roots in English come from an old form of English called Anglo-Saxon. You probably know many of these roots already. For example, *endearing* and *remarkable* have the familiar words dear and mark as their roots. Other roots come from Greek and Latin.

You may not be as familiar with them. For example, the word *spectator* contains the Latin root *spec*, which means "to look at." You can see that root in the word *spectator*, "one who looks."

When you come across a new word, check whether you recognize its root or base word. It can help you pronounce the word and figure out its meaning.

- **Prefixes** A prefix is a word part that can be added to the beginning of a root or base word to change the word's meaning. For example,

  the prefix *semi-* means "half" or "partial," so *semicircle* means "half a circle"

  un- means "not," so *unhappy* means "not happy"

- **Suffixes** A suffix is a word part that can be added to the end of a root or base word to change the word's meaning. Adding a suffix to a word can also change that word from one part of speech to another. For example,

  the word *joy* (which is a noun) becomes an adjective when the suffix *-ful* (meaning "full of") is added. *Joyful* means "full of joy"

Determining a Word's Meaning

Using Syntax

Languages have rules and patterns for the way words are arranged in sentences. The way a sentence is organized is called the **syntax** of the sentence. If English is your first language, you have known this pattern since you started talking in sentences. If you're learning English now, you may find the syntax is different from the patterns you know in your first language.

In a simple sentence in English, someone or something (the **subject**) does something (the **predicate** or **verb**) to or with another person or thing (the **object**).

Sometimes adjectives, adverbs, and phrases are added to spice up the sentence.

▶ Check It Out

Knowing about syntax can help you figure out the meaning of an unfamiliar word. Just look at how syntax can help you figure out the following nonsense sentence.

The blizzy kwarkles sminched the flerky broogs.

Your experience with English syntax tells you that the action word, or verb, in this sentence is *sminched.*

Who did the *sminching?* The *kwarkles.*
What kind of *kwarkles* were they? *Blizzy.*
Whom did they *sminch?* The *broogs.*
What kind of *broogs* were they? *Flerky.*

Even though you don't know the meaning of the words in the nonsense sentence, you can make some sense of the entire sentence by studying its syntax.

Using Context Clues

You can often figure out the meaning of an unfamiliar word by looking at its context (the words and sentences that surround it).

▶ Do It!

To learn new words as you read, follow these steps for using context clues.

1. Look before and after the unfamiliar word for
   - a definition or a synonym (another word that means the same as the unfamiliar word)

     Some outdoor plants need to be **insulated,** or shielded, against cold weather.

   - a general topic associated with the word

     The painter brushed **primer** on the walls before the first coat of paint.

   - a clue to what the word is similar to or different from

     Like a spinning top, the dancer **pirouetted** gracefully.

   - an action or a description that has something to do with the word

     The cook used a **spatula** to flip the pancakes.

2. Connect what you already know with what the author has written.

3. Predict a possible meaning.

4. Use the meaning in the sentence.

5. Try again if your guess does not make sense.

Using reference materials

Dictionaries and other reference sources can help you learn new words. Check out these reference sources:

- A **dictionary** gives the pronunciation and the meaning or meanings of a word. Some dictionaries also give other forms of words, their parts of speech, and synonyms. You might also find the historical background of a word, such as its Greek, Latin, or Anglo-Saxon origins.

- A **glossary** is a word list that appears at the end of a book or other written work. It includes only words that are in that work. Like dictionaries, glossaries have the pronunciation and definitions of words. However, the definitions in a glossary give just enough information to help you understand the words as they are used in that work.

- A **thesaurus** lists groups of words that have the same, or almost the same, meaning. Words with similar meanings are called **synonyms.** Seeing the synonyms of words can help you build your vocabulary.

Understanding Denotation and Connotation

Words can have two types of meaning.

Denotation is the literal meaning, the meaning you find in dictionaries.

Connotation is a meaning or feeling that people connect with the word.

For example, you may say that flowers have a *fragrance* but that garbage has a *stench.* Both words mean "smell," but *fragrance* has a pleasant connotation, while *stench* has a very unpleasant one. As you read, it's important to think about the connotation of a word to completely understand what a writer is saying.

Recognizing Word Meanings Across Subjects

Have you ever learned a new word in one class and then noticed it in your reading for other subjects? The word may not mean exactly the same thing in each class. But you can use what you know about the word's meaning to help you understand what it means in a different subject area.

Look at the following example from three subjects:

Social Studies: One major **product** manufactured in the South is cotton cloth. (something manufactured by a company)

Math: After you multiply those two numbers, explain how you arrived at the **product.** (the result of multiplying two numbers)

Science: One **product** of photosynthesis is oxygen. (the result of a chemical reaction)

In all three subject areas, a product is the result of something.

▶ Practice It!

1. Write each word below in your Learner's Notebook. Then underline the familiar word or root inside it. (Notice that the end of the familiar word or root may change in spelling a little when a suiffix is added to it.)

a. configuration **d.** perspective

b. contemporary **e.** invaluable

c. reformation

2. Try to pronounce each of the words. Then check your pronunciation against the pronunciation given in the Glossary at the back of this book.

3. The following sentences can all be completed by the same word or form of the word. Use context clues to find the missing word. Write the word in your Learner's Notebook.

 a. I took the ____ to the photo shop to have a large print made.

 b. Protons are positive; electrons are ____.

 c. You always think ____; can't you think positively for a change?

Reading Fluently

Reading fluently is reading easily. When you read fluently, your brain recognizes each word so you can read without skipping or tripping over words. If you're a fluent reader, you can concentrate on the ideas in your reading because you don't have to worry about what each word means or how to say it.

To develop reading fluency. . .

• **Read often!** The more, the better. Reading often will help you develop a good sight vocabulary—the ability to quickly recognize words.

• **Practice reading aloud.** Believe it or not, reading aloud does help you become a better silent reader.

 – Begin by reading aloud a short, interesting passage that is easy for you.

 – Reread the same passage aloud at least three times or until your reading sounds smooth. Make your reading sound like you are speaking to a friend.

 – Then move on to a longer passage or a slightly more difficult one.

▶ Practice It!
Practice reading the paragraph under the following heading. After you think you can read it fluently—without errors or unnecessary pauses—read it aloud to a partner. Ask your partner to comment on your fluency.

Reading for a Reason

Why are you reading that paperback mystery? What do you hope to get from your science textbook? And are you going to read either of these books in the same way that you read a restaurant menu?

The point is, you read for different reasons. The reason you're reading something helps you decide on the reading strategies you use with a text. In other words, how you read will depend on why you're reading.

Knowing Your Reason for Reading

In school and in life, you'll have many reasons for reading, and those reasons will lead you to a wide range of materials. For example,

- **To learn and understand new information,** you might read news magazines, textbooks, news on the Internet, books about your favorite pastime, encyclopedia articles, primary and secondary sources for a school report, instructions on how to use a calling card or directions for a standardized test.

- **To find specific information,** you might look at the sports section for the score of last night's game, a notice on where to register for a field trip, weather reports, bank statements, or television listings.

- **To be entertained,** you might read your favorite magazine, e-mails or letters from friends, the Sunday comics, or even novels, short stories, plays, or poems!

Adjusting How Fast You Read

How quickly or how carefully you should read a text depends on your purpose for reading it. Think about your purpose and choose a strategy that works best. Try out these strategies:

- **Scanning** means quickly running your eyes over the material, looking for **key words** or **phrases** that point to the information you're looking for. Scan when you need to find a particular piece or type of information. For example, you might scan a newspaper for movie show times or an encyclopedia article for facts to include in a research report.

- **Skimming** means quickly reading a piece of writing **to find its main idea** or to **get a general overview** of it. For example, you might skim the sports section of the daily newspaper to find out how your favorite teams are doing. Or you might skim a chapter in your science book to prepare for a test.

- **Careful reading** involves **reading slowly and paying attention** with a purpose in mind. Read carefully when you're learning new concepts, following complicated directions, or preparing to explain information to someone else. You definitely should read carefully when you're studying a textbook to prepare for class.

But you might also use this strategy when you're reading a mystery story and don't want to miss any details. Below are some tips you can use to help you read more carefully.

– **Take breaks** when you need them. There's no point in reading when you're sleepy. And if you're reading on the computer, give your eyes a break about every fifteen minutes by focusing on something more distant than your monitor screen.

– **Take notes** as you read. Write in your book if it's OK or use a notebook or sticky notes on the pages. Your notes may be just words or phrases that will jog your memory when you need to review. If you use a notebook, write page numbers from the book in the margin of your notes. That way you can quickly find the original material later if you need it.

– **Make graphic organizers** to help you organize the information from your reading. These can sort out ideas, clear up difficult passages, and help you remember important points. For example, **webs** can show a main idea and supporting details. A **flowchart** can help you keep track of events in a sequence. A **Venn diagram,** made up of overlapping circles, can help you organize how two characters, ideas, or events are alike and different.

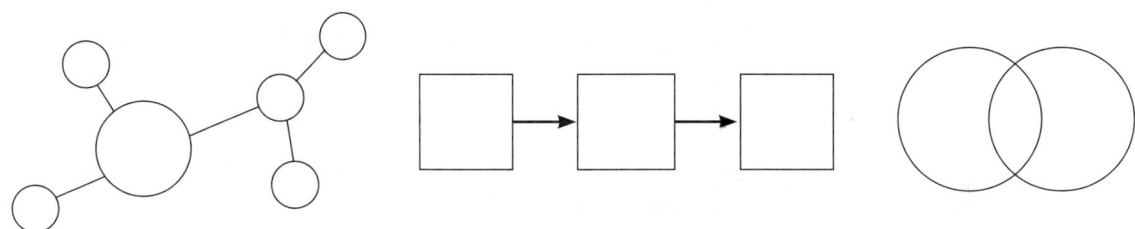

– **Review material** before stopping. Even a short review will help you remember what you've read. Try rereading difficult passages. They will be much easier to understand the second time.

▶ Practice It!

1. In your Learner's Notebook, write whether you would **skim, scan,** or **read carefully** in each of the following cases.

   a. a short story for your English class

   b. the school newspaper for your team's score in last week's game

   c. reviewing a chapter for tomorrow's social studies test

   d. a science book to find if it has information about nuclear waste

   e. to decide which stories and articles to read in a magazine

Becoming Engaged

In reading, *engagement* means relating to what you're reading in a way that makes it meaningful to you. It means finding links between the text and your own life. As you begin to read something, be ready to become engaged with the text. Then as you read, react to the text and relate it to your own experience. Your reading will be much more interesting, and you'll find it easier to understand and remember what you read.

Connect

You will become more involved with your reading and remember events, characters, and ideas better if you relate what you're reading to your own life. Connecting is finding the links between what you read and your own experience.

▶ **Ask Yourself**

- Have I been to places similar to the **setting** described by this writer?

- What **experiences** have I had that compare or contrast with what I am reading?

- What **opinions** do I already have about this topic?

- What **characters** from life or literature remind me of the characters or narrator in the selection?

Respond

Enjoy what you read and make it your own by responding to what's going on in the text. Think about and express what you like or don't like, what you find boring or interesting. What surprises you, entertains you, scares you, makes you angry, makes you sad, or makes you laugh out loud? The relationship between you and what you're reading is personal, so react in a personal way.

Understanding What You Read

Reading without understanding is like trying to drive a car on an empty gas tank. You can go through all the motions, but you won't get anywhere! Skilled readers adopt a number of strategies before, during, and after reading to make sure they understand what they read.

Previewing

If you were making a preview for a movie, you would want to let your audience know what the movie is like. When you preview a piece of writing, you're treating yourself like that movie audience. You're trying to get an idea about that piece of writing. If you know what to expect before reading, you will have an easier time understanding ideas and relationships. Follow these steps to preview your reading assignments.

▶ Do It!

1. **Look** at the title and any illustrations that are included.

2. **Read** the headings, subheadings, and anything in bold letters.

3. **Skim** over the passage to see how it is organized. Is it divided into many parts? Is it a long poem or short story? Don't forget to look at the graphics—pictures, maps, or diagrams.

4. **Set a purpose** for your reading. Are you reading to learn something new? Are you reading to find specific information?

Activating Prior Knowledge

Believe it or not, you already know quite a bit about what you're going to read. You don't know the plot or the information, of course, but keep in mind that you bring knowledge and unique personal experience to a selection. Drawing on your own background is called **activating prior knowledge,** and it can help you create meaning in what you read. Ask yourself, What do I already know about this topic? What do I know about related topics?

Predicting

You don't need a crystal ball to make **predictions** when you read. The predictions don't even have to be accurate! What's important is that you get involved in your reading from the moment you turn to page one. Take educated guesses before and during your reading about what might happen in the story. Follow these steps:

1. Use your prior knowledge and the information you gathered in your preview to predict what you will learn or what might happen in a selection. Will the hero ever get home? Did the butler do it?

2. As you read on, you may find that your prediction was way off base. Don't worry. Just adjust your predictions and go on reading.

3. Afterwards, check to see how accurate your predictions were. You don't have to keep score. By getting yourself involved in a narrative, you always end up a winner.

Visualizing

Creating pictures in your mind as you read—called visualizing—is a powerful aid to understanding. As you read, set up a movie theater in your imagination.

- Imagine what a character looks like.
- Picture the setting—city streets, the desert, or the surface of the Moon.
- Picture the steps in a process or the evidence that an author wants you to consider. If you can visualize what you read, selections will be more vivid, and you'll recall them better later on.

Identifying Sequence

When you discover the logical order of events or ideas, you are identifying sequence. Look for clues and signal words that will help you find the way information is organized.

Are you reading a story that takes place in chronological, or time, order? Do you need to understand step-by-step directions? Are you reading a persuasive speech with the reasons listed in order of importance? You'll understand and remember the information better when you know the organization the author has used.

Determining the Main Idea

When you look for the main idea of a selection, you look for the most important idea. The examples, reasons, or details that further explain the main idea are called supporting details.

Some main ideas are clearly stated within a passage—often in the first sentence of a paragraph, or sometimes in the last sentence of a passage.

Other times, an author doesn't directly state the main idea but provides details that help readers figure out what the main idea is.

▶ Ask Yourself

- What is each sentence about?
- Is there one sentence that tells about the whole passage or that is more important than the others?
- What main idea do the supporting details point out?

Questioning

Keep up a conversation with yourself as you read by **asking questions** about the text. Feel free to question anything!

- Ask about the importance of the information you're reading.
- Ask how one event relates to another or why a character acts a certain way.
- Ask yourself if you understand what you just read.
- As you answer your own questions, you're making sure that you understand what's going on.

Clarifying

Clear up, or **clarify,** confusing or difficult passages as you read. When you realize you don't understand something, try these techniques to help you clarify the ideas.

- Reread the confusing parts slowly and carefully.
- Diagram relationships between ideas.
- Look up unfamiliar words.
- Simply "talk out" the part to yourself.

Then read the passage once more. The second time through is often much easier and more informative.

Reviewing

You probably **review** in school every day in one class or another. You review what you learned the day before so the ideas stick in your mind. Reviewing when you read does the same thing.

Take time now and then to pause and review what you've read. Think about the main ideas and reorganize them for yourself so you can recall them later. Filling in study aids such as graphic organizers, notes, or outlines can help you review.

Monitoring Your Comprehension

Who's checking up on you when you read? You are! There's no teacher standing by to ask questions or to make sure that you're paying attention. As a reader, you are both the teacher and the student. It's up to you to make sure you accomplish a reader's most important task: understanding the material. As you read, check your understanding by using the following strategies.

- **Summarize** what you read by pausing from time to time and telling yourself the main ideas of what you've just read. When you summarize, include only the main ideas of a selection and only the useful supporting details. Answer the questions *Who? What? Where? When? Why?* and *How?* Summarizing tests your comprehension by encouraging you to clarify key points in your own words.

- **Paraphrase** Sometimes you read something that you "sort of" understand, but not quite. Use **paraphrasing** as a test to see whether you really got the point. Paraphrasing is retelling something in your own words. So shut the book and try putting what you've just read into your own words. If you can't explain it clearly, you should probably have another look at the text.

▶ **Practice It!**
Here are some strategies good readers use to understand a text. In your Learner's Notebook, tell which way is shown by each statement below.

connect   respond   predict   monitor comprehension
visualize   question   clarify   preview

1. I'm sure the doctor's going to be the main character in this story.

2. Why would this smart character make a dumb remark like that?

3. This woman reminds me of my mother when she's really mad.

4. This is a difficult passage. I'd better read it again and also look up the word malefactor in the dictionary.

5. Let's see if I've got this plot straight. So far, Greg's crazy about Donna, but she's hooked on Jesse, who seems interested in Sheila, who is Greg's date for the dance. And Dana's out to mess up everybody.

Thinking Critically About Your Reading

You've engaged with the text and used helpful reading strategies to understand what you've read. But is that all there is to it? Not always. Sometimes it's important to think more deeply about what you've read so that you can get the most out of what the author says. These critical thinking skills will help you go beyond what the words say and get at the important messages of your reading.

Interpreting

When you listen to your best friend talk, you don't just hear the words he or she says. You also watch your friend, listen to the tone of voice, and use what you already know about that person to put meaning to the words. In doing so, you are making meaning from what your friend says by using what you understand. You are interpreting what your friend says.

Readers do the same thing when they interpret as they read. Interpreting is more than just understanding the facts or story line you read. It's asking yourself, What's the writer really saying here? and then using what you know about the world to help answer that question. When you interpret as you read, you come to a much better understanding of the work.

Inferring

You may not realize it, but you infer, or make inferences, every day. Here's an example:

> You run to the bus stop a little later than usual. There's no one there. "I've missed the bus," you say to yourself. You may be wrong, but that's the way our minds work. We look at the evidence (you're late; no one's there) and come to a conclusion (you've missed the bus).

When you read, you go through exactly the same process because writers don't always directly state what they want you to understand. By providing clues and interesting details, they suggest certain information. Whenever you combine those clues with your own background and knowledge, you are making an inference.

Drawing Conclusions

Skillful readers are always drawing conclusions, or figuring out much more than an author says directly. The process is a little like a detective solving a mystery. You combine information and evidence that the author provides to come up with a statement about the topic, about a character, or about anything else in the work. Drawing conclusions helps you find connections between ideas and events and helps you have a better understanding of what you're reading.

Analyzing

Analyzing, or looking at separate parts of something to understand the entire piece, is a way to think critically about written work.

- In analyzing **fiction,** for example, you might look at the characters' values, events in the plot, and the author's style to figure out the story's theme.

- In analyzing persuasive **nonfiction**, you might look at the writer's reasons to see if they actually support the main point of the argument.

- In analyzing **informational text,** you might look at how the ideas are organized to see what's most important.

Distinguishing Fact from Opinion

Distinguishing between fact and opinion is one of the most important reading skills you can learn.

A **fact** is a statement that can be proved with supporting information.

An **opinion,** on the other hand, is what a writer believes on the basis of his or her personal viewpoint. An opinion is something that cannot be proved.

As you examine information, always ask yourself, Is this a fact or an opinion?

Don't think that opinions are always bad. Very often they are just what you want. You read editorials and essays for their authors' opinions. Reviews of movies, and CDs can help you decide whether to spend your time and money on something. It's when opinions are based on faulty reasoning or prejudice or when they are stated as facts that they become troublesome.

For example, look at the following examples of fact and opinion.

> Fact: California produces fruits and other agricultural products.

> Opinion: California is a wonderful place for a vacation.

You could prove that fruits and other agricultural products are grown in California. It's a fact. However, not everyone might agree that California is a great vacation site. That's someone's opinion.

Evaluating

When you form an opinion or make a judgment about something you're reading, you are **evaluating.**

If you're reading **informational texts** or something on the Internet, it's important to evaluate how qualified the author is to write about the topic and how reliable the information that's presented is. Ask yourself whether

- the author seems biased.
- the information is one-sided.
- the argument presented is logical.

If you're reading **fiction,** evaluate the author's style or ask yourself questions such as

- Is this character interesting or dull?
- Are the events in the plot believable or realistic?
- Does the author's message make sense?

Synthesizing

When you **synthesize,** you combine ideas (maybe even from different sources) to come up with something new. It may be a new understanding of an important idea or a new way of combining and presenting information.

Many readers enjoy taking ideas from their reading and combining them with what they already know to come to new understandings. For example, you might

1. Read a manual on coaching soccer

2. Combine what you learn from that reading with your own experiences playing soccer

3. Add what you know about coaches you've had

4. Come up with a winning plan for coaching your sister's soccer team this spring.

Understanding Text Structure

Writers organize each piece of their writing in a specific way for a specific purpose. That pattern of organization is called **text structure.** When you know the text structure of a selection, you'll find it easier to locate and recall an author's ideas. Here are four ways that writers organize text, along with some signal words and phrases containing clues to help you identify their methods.

Comparison and Contrast

Comparison-and-contrast structure shows the similarities and differences between people, things, and ideas. When writers use comparison-and-contrast structure, often they want to show you how things that seem alike are different or how things that seem different are alike.

- **Signal words and phrases:** similarly, more, less, on the one hand, on the other hand, in contrast to, but, however

  Example: That day had been the best and worst of her life. **On the one hand,** the tornado had destroyed her home. **On the other hand,** she and her family were safe. Her face was full of cuts and bruises, **but** she smiled at the little girl on her lap.

Cause and Effect

Just about everything that happens in life is the cause or the effect of some other event or action. Sometimes what happens is pretty minor: You don't look when you're pouring milk (cause); you spill milk on the table (effect). Sometimes it's a little more serious: You don't look at your math book before the big test (cause); you mess up on the test (effect).

Writers use cause-and-effect structure to explore the reasons for something happening and to examine the results of previous events. A scientist might explain why the rain falls. A sports writer might explain why a team is doing badly. A historian might tell us why an empire rose and fell. Cause-and-effect structure is all about explaining things.

- **Signal words and phrases:** so, because, as a result, therefore, for the following reasons

  Example: The blizzard raged for twelve hours. **Because** of the heavy snow, the streets were clogged within an hour of being plowed. **As a result,** the city was at a standstill. Of course, we had no school that day, **so** we went sledding!

Problem and Solution

How did scientists overcome the difficulty of getting a person to the Moon? How can our team win the pennant this year? How will I brush my teeth when I've forgotten my toothpaste? These questions may be very different in importance, but they have one thing in common: each identifies a problem and asks how to solve it. Problems and solutions are part of what makes life interesting.

By organizing their texts around that important question-word *how,* writers state the problem and suggest a solution. Sometimes they suggest many solutions. Of course, it's for you to decide if they're right.

- **Signal words and phrases:** how, help, problem, obstruction, overcome, difficulty, need, attempt, have to, must

    Example: A major **difficulty** in learning to drive a car with a standard shift is starting on hills. Students **need** to practice starting slowly and smoothly on a level surface before they graduate to slopes. Observing an experienced driver perform the maneuver will also **help.**

Sequence

Consider these requests: Tell us what happened at the picnic. Describe your favorite CD cover. Identify the causes of the Civil War. Three very different instructions, aren't they? Well, yes and no. They are certainly about different subjects. But they all involve sequence, the order in which thoughts are arranged. Take a look at three common forms of sequencing.

- **Chronological order** refers to the order in which events take place. First you wake up; next you have breakfast; then you go to school. Those events don't make much sense in any other order. Whether you are explaining how to wash the car, giving directions to a friend's house, or telling your favorite joke, the world would be a confusing place if people didn't organize their ideas in chronological order. Look for signal words such as *first, next, then, later,* and *finally.*

- **Spatial order** describes the order of things in space. For example, take a look at this description of an ice cream sundae:

    At the bottom of the dish are two scoops of vanilla. The scoops are covered with fudge and topped with whipped cream and a cherry.

    Your eyes follow the sundae from the bottom to the top. Spatial order is important in descriptive writing because it helps you as a reader to see an image the way the author does. Signal words include *above, below, behind, left, right,* and *next to.*

- **Order of importance** is going from most important to least important or the other way around. For example, a typical news article has a most-to-least-important structure. Readers who don't have the time to read the entire article can at least learn the main idea by reading the first few paragraphs. Signal words include *principal, central, important,* and *fundamental.*

Reading for Research

An important part of doing research is knowing how to get information from a wide variety of sources. The following skills will help you when you have a research assignment for a class or when you want information about a topic outside of school.

Reading Text Features

Researching a topic is not only about asking questions. It's about finding answers. Textbooks, references, magazines, and other sources provide a variety of text features to help you find those answers quickly and efficiently.

- Tables of contents Look at the table of contents first to see whether a resource offers information you need.

- Indexes An index is an alphabetical listing of significant topics covered in a book. It is found in the back of a book.

- Headings and subheadings Headings often tell you what information is going to follow in the text you're reading. Subheadings allow you to narrow your search for information even further.

- Graphic features Photos, diagrams, maps, charts, graphs, and other graphic features can communicate large amounts of information at a glance. They usually include captions that explain what they show.

Interpreting Graphic Aids

When you're researching a topic, be sure to read and interpret the graphic aids you find. **Graphic aids** explain information visually. When reading graphic aids, read the title first to see if you're likely to find information you want.

- **Reading a map** Maps are flat representations of land. A **compass rose** shows you directions—north, south, east, and west. A **legend,** or **key,** explains the map's symbols. A **scale** shows you how distances shown on the map relate to the actual distances.

- **Reading a graph** A graph shows you how two or more things relate. Graphs can use circles, dots, bars, or lines. For example, on the weather part of a TV newscast you might see a weather graph that predicts how the temperatures for the next five days will rise or fall.

- **Reading a table** A table groups numbers or facts and puts them into categories so you can compare what is in each category. The facts are organized in rows and columns. Find the row that has the category you're looking for. Then read across to the column that has the information you need.

Organizing Information

When researching a topic, you can't stop after you've read your sources of information. You also have to make sense of that information, organize it, and put it all together in ways that will help you explain it to someone else. Here are some ways of doing just that.

- **Record** information from your research and keep track of your resources on note cards.

- **Summarize** information before you write it on a note card. That way you'll have the main ideas in your own words.

- **Outline** ideas so you can see how subtopics and supporting information will fit under a main idea.

- **Make a table or graph** to compare items or categories of information.

Skills Scope and Sequence

Readability Scores Key
Dale-Chall/DRP/Lexile

PACING (DAYS)		INSTRUCTIONAL SEGMENT LITERATURE	READING SKILLS	LITERARY ELEMENTS
STANDARD	BLOCK			
1	1	**Unit Warm-Up, pp. 2–7** Genre Focus: "Animal Attraction" by Sally S. Stich **3.9/49/710**, p. 6	Setting a Purpose for Reading, SE p. 6 Skimming and Scanning, SE p. 6, TWE p. 5 Main Idea and Supporting Details, SE p. 6 Understanding Graphics, SE p. 7	Titles, SE p. 6 Process, SE p. 7, TWE p. 5 Author's Purpose, SE p. 7
3	2	**Reading Workshop 1, pp. 8–29** "Ballpark Food" **4.9/58/1040**, p. 12 "How He Did It: Health Advice, Kid-to-Kid" by Amy Bertrand **6.7/61/910**, p. 20	Setting a Purpose for Reading, SE pp. 8, 9, 11, 12, 15, 17, 19, 21, 25 Fluency, TWE p. 8	Text Features, SE pp. 11, 12, 13, 15, 17, 19, 20 TWE pp. 14, 21
1		**Writing Workshop, Part 1, pp. 26–29** Writing Product: Summary	Skimming and Scanning, TWE p. 26	
3	1	**Reading Workshop 2, pp. 30–47** "Messaging Mania" by Kathryn R. Hoffman **8.1/59/1020**, p. 34 "The Real Magic of Harry Potter" by Nancy Gibbs **4.6/55/940**, p. 42	Skimming and Scanning, SE pp. 30, 31, 33, 34, 41, 42, 44, 47, TWE p. 35	Titles and Subheads, pp. 33, 34, 41, 42, 45, 47
3	1	**Reading Workshop 3, pp. 48–63** "Make Your Own Kite" **4.2/47/720** from *Bone*, "The Great Cow Race" by Jeff Smith **6.5/N/A/280**	Understanding Graphics, SE pp. 48, 49, 51, 55, 57, 58, 61, 63, TWE pp. 52, 59, 60	Process, SE pp. 51, 52, 53, 55, 57, 60, 63

Unit 1 Big Question

"The question, "Why Read?" is designed to help students consider their own reasons for reading and see why others read. In this unit, students will read a variety of selections that will give them ideas about why people read and make them think about why *they* read."

Unit 1 Genre

Many of the selections in this unit are informational media, which provide knowledge. These selections will also help students answer the big question: Why Read? Use these informational media to help students learn how reading can help them get the information they need.

CRITICAL THINKING	VOCABULARY	WRITING AND GRAMMAR	LISTENING, SPEAKING, AND VIEWING
Application, TWE p. 4	Word References, TWE p. 6		
Evaluation, SE p. 24, TWE pp. 14, 22, 23 Analysis, TWE p. 15 Analyze, SE p. 16 Apply, SE pp. 16, 24 Comprehension, TWE p. 21 Infer, SE p. 24	Academic Vocabulary, SE p. 8 Picture It, TWE p. 10 Word References, SE pp. 10, 18, 20, TWE p. 12 Context Clues, TWE p. 13	Parts of Speech, SE p. 17, TWE p. 10 Nouns and Verbs, SE p. 25 Write About Your Reading, SE p. 24	Talk About Your Reading, SE p. 16 Viewing the Photo, TWE pp. 13, 21 Viewing the Graphic, TWE p. 22
		Prewriting, SE p. 26 Applying Good Writing Traits: Ideas, p. 27 Main Idea and Supporting Details, TWE p. 27 Summary, TWE p. 28 Verbs, SE p. 29 Linking Verbs, TWE p. 29	Clarity Check, TWE p. 28
Analyze, SE p. 46, TWE p. 35 Compare and Contrast, SE pp. 38, 46 Infer, SE p. 38 Evaluate, SE pp. 38, 46, TWE pp. 43, 44 Interpret, SE p. 46	Multiple-Meaning Words, SE pp. 32, 40, 43, TWE p. 36 Word Webs, TWE p. 32 Sentences, TWE p. 40	Main and Helping Verbs, SE p. 39 Present and Present Progressive Tenses, p. 47 Write About Your Reading, SE p. 46	Analyzing the Graphic, SE p. 37 Talk About Your Reading, SE p. 38 Viewing the Photo, TWE p. 43
Evaluation, SE p. 54, 62, TWE p. 53 Infer, SE pp. 54, 62 Analyze, TWE p. 59 Draw Conclusions, SE p. 62	Academic Vocabulary, SE pp. 48, 55 Multiple-Meaning Words, SE pp. 50, 56, 59 Slang, TWE p. 58 Abbreviations, TWE p. 60	Present, Past, and Future Verb Tenses, SE p. 55 Write About Your Reading, SE pp. 54, 62 Verb Tenses, SE p. 63	Viewing the Photo, TWE p. 52

Skills Scope and Sequence *continued*

Readability Scores Key
Dale-Chall/DRP/Lexile

PACING (DAYS)		INSTRUCTIONAL SEGMENT LITERATURE	READING SKILLS	LITERARY ELEMENTS
STANDARD	BLOCK			
2	1	**Writing Workshop, Part 2, pp. 64–67** Writing Product: Summary		
3	1	**Reading Workshop 4, pp. 68–83** "To Young Readers" by Gwendolyn Brooks **N/A** "Why Books Are Dangerous" by Neil Gaiman **5.9/55/1090**, p. 78	Identifying Main Idea and Supporting Details, SE pp. 68, 69 Main Idea, TWE p. 68 Skimming and Scanning, TWE p. 69 Main Idea Supporting Details, SE pp. 71, 72, 75, 77, 78, 81 Building Fluency, TWE p. 81	Author's Purpose, SE pp. 71, 72, 75, 77, 80, TWE p. 79 Metaphor, SE p. 73
3	2	**Comparing Literature Workshop, pp. 84–99** "The Southpaw" by Judith Viorst **4.2/49/640**, p. 88 "Concha" by Mary Helen Ponce **6.9/53/860**, p. 93	Build Fluency, TWE p. 91	Author's Purpose, SE pp. 88, 90, 93, 94, 96, 97, TWE pp. 85, 89, 91 Process, TWE p. 93 Setting, TWE p. 94
4	2	**Unit Wrap-Up, pp. 100–101** **Your Turn, pp. 102–107** "The Scribe" by Kristin Hunter Tattany **5.3/47/690**	Review Skimming and Scanning, TWE p. 102 Review Setting a Purpose for Reading, TWE p. 103 Story Mapping, TWE p. 103 Identifying Main Idea and Supporting Details, TWE p. 106 Author's Purpose, TWE p. 107	Figurative Language, TWE p. 105

CRITICAL THINKING	VOCABULARY	WRITING AND GRAMMAR	LISTENING, SPEAKING, AND VIEWING
Analysis, TWE p. 66 Evaluating Messages, TWE p. 67		Writing a Summary: Editing and Revising, SE pp. 64–66 Summary, TWE p. 64 Comparing and Contrasting, TWE p. 65 Main Idea, TWE p. 66	Getting Information from Visuals, SE p. 67 Advertising Technique, TWE p. 67
Application, TWE p. 71 Comprehension, SE p. 73, TWE pp. 72, 80 Evaluate, SE p. 74 Apply, SE p. 74 Analyze, SE pp. 74, 82 Analysis, TWE p. 81 Connect, SE p. 82 Infer, SE p. 82	Word References, SE pp. 70, 72, 76, TWE p. 71 Word Associations, TWE p. 70 Time-Order Words, TWE, p. 80	Personal Response, TWE p. 73 Write About Your Reading, SE pp. 74, 82 Irregular Verbs, SE p. 75	Viewing the Painting, SE p. 73 Viewing the Photo, TWE p. 79
Application, TWE p. 87 Evaluation, TWE pp. 89, 90 Comprehension, TWE p. 90 Analysis, TWE pp. 95, 96 Analyze, SE p. 99 Interpret, SE p. 99 Contrast, SE p. 99	Word References, SE pp. 86, 89, 92, 94, 95, 97, TWE p. 88 Using Context, TWE p. 86 Sentences, TWE p. 92 Idioms, TWE p. 92 Multiple Meanings, TWE p. 94	Writing a News Article, TWE p. 89 Writing Song Lyrics, p. 95 Compare the Literature, SE p. 99	Viewing the Illustration, TWE p. 89 Viewing the Photograph, TWE p. 93
Comprehension, TWE pp. 103, 105 Analysis, TWE pp. 104, 107	Word References, TWE p. 104 Figurative Language, TWE p. 105 Multiple-Meaning Words, TWE pp. 105, 106		Viewing the Painting, TWE p. 104 Analyzing the Photo, TWE p. 107

Reading with Purpose offers a comprehensive package of tools to optimize student learning and the teaching experience. Each resource has been designed to assist students in specific areas and to offer instructional support for teachers. While all of these areas are covered in the core textbook, some students may need extra practice or additional help in specific areas. The resource package is designed so that you, the teacher, can choose which items will best assist your students. You may also use these resources as homework assignments and for assessment purposes. The following are resources recommended for use with Unit 1.

Keys for Unit Resources

- 📁 Blackline Master
- 📕 Workbook
- 📖 Supplemental Text
- 💿 CD-ROM
- 🔒 DVD
- 🎨 Transparency
- 💻 Web-based
- 📁 Fast File

Essential Instructional Support

FAST FILE UNIT 1 RESOURCES

Reading and Literature

- Academic Vocabulary Review
- Big Question: School to Home
- The Big Question Foldable
- Unit Challenge: Planner and Rubrics
- Comparing Literature Graphic Organizer
- Key Reading Skills
- Active Reading Graphic Organizers
- Literary Analysis
- Unit Vocabulary Review

Writing, Grammar, and Spelling

- Spelling and Handwriting Practice
- Grammar Practice
- Writing Workshop Graphic Organizer

Listening, Speaking, and Viewing

- Viewing and Representing
- Listening and Speaking

English Language Learners

- English Language Coach Review

DIFFERENTIATED INSTRUCTION

- 📁 Leveled Vocabulary Development
- 💿 Skills Level Up!™ A Language Arts Game
- 💿 Listening Library CD
- 💿 BookLink 3
- 💿 Literature Library Vocabulary Puzzlemaker
- 💿 Vocabulary Puzzlemaker

ASSESSMENT — GLENCOE'S ASSESSMENT ADVANTAGE

- 📁 Selection and Unit Assessments
- 📁 Selection Quick Checks
- 📁 Assessment by Learning Objectives
- 📁 Rubrics for Assessing Student Writing, Listening, and Speaking
- 💻 Glencoe Online Essay Grader
- 💿 Interactive Tutor: Self-Assessment
- 💿 ExamView Assessment Suite
- 💿 Literature Library ExamView Assessment Suite

Additional Instructional Support

WRITING, GRAMMAR, AND SPELLING

- Real Success in Writing: Research and Reports
- Writing Constructed Responses Sourcebook
- Spelling Power eWorkbook
- Grammar & Composition Handbook
- Grammar and Language Workbook
- Revising with Style eWorkbook

READING AND LITERATURE

- Active Learning and Note Taking Guide
- inTime Magazines
- Backpack Reader Volume 1
- Literature Library
- Literature Launchers Pre-Reading Videos DVD
- Literature Classics

TRANSPARENCIES

- Read Aloud, Think Aloud
- Literary and Text Analysis Transparencies
- Bellringer Options Transparencies
- Grammar and Writing Workshop Transparencies
- Fine Arts Transparencies

TECHNOLOGY

- TeacherWorks Plus
- StudentWorks Plus
- BookLink 3
- Skill Level Up!
- ExamView Assessment Suite
- Interactive Tutor Self-Assessment
- Listening Library CD
- Spanish Listening Library CD
- Literature Classics
- Literature Launchers Pre-Reading Videos DVD
- Literature Library ExamView Assessment Suite
- Vocabulary Puzzlemaker
- Literature Library Vocabulary Puzzlemaker
- glencoe.com
- Online Student Edition
- Presentation Plus!
- Glencoe Online Essay Grading

ENGLISH LANGUAGE LEARNER

- English Language Coach
- Fluency Practice and Assessment
- inTime Magazines (Spanish)
- Spanish Listening Library CD

PROFESSIONAL DEVELOPMENT

- Professional Development Package

Additional Glencoe Resources

Dinah Zike's Foldables

Foldables are three-dimensional, interactive graphic organizers that help students practice basic writing skills, review key vocabulary terms, and answer Big Questions. Every unit contains a foldable activity. You can find the pattern and directions for the Unit 1 Foldable in the Unit 1 Resources Fast Files booklet. You can use the foldables as they are presented or modify them to suit the needs of your students. More information about foldables for Unit 1 can be found on page R8.

Glencoe Literature Library

This collection of hardcover books includes full-length novels, novellas, plays, and works of nonfiction. Each volume consists of at least one complete extended-length reading accompanied by several related readings from a broad range of genres. A separate Study Guide for each Glencoe Literature Library book provides teaching notes and reproducible activity pages for students.

Glencoe Literature Library titles that complement this unit include:
A Gathering of Days, by Joan W. Blos
Letters from a Slave Girl, by Mary E. Lyons
Letters from Rifka, by Karen Hesse

For a wealth of online resources that support the instruction in Unit 1 of *Glencoe Literature: Reading with Purpose,* students and teachers can visit our Web site at www.glencoe.com. Students will find additional learning, practice, and assessment opportunities such as these, which are noted in the student text:

- **Big Question Overview**
- **Study Central**
- **Author Search**
- **Writing Models**
- **Interactive Literary Elements Handbook**
- **Web Activities**

Teachers will find planning and instructional tools that include the following:

- **Book Lesson Plans**
- **Teacher Forum**
- **Professional Development**
- **Web Activities Lesson Plans (with answers to student activities)**

Go to www.glencoe.com to see the entire selection of Reading with Purpose online resources.

Use the Glencoe BookLink 3 CD-ROM, a database of more than 26,700 titles, to create customized reading lists for your students.

- Search for award-winning titles, (e.g., Newbery Award winners, Coretta Scott King Award winners, and Caldecott Medal winners) and for books on several state-recommended reading lists.
- Find Degrees of Reading Power™ (DRP) and Lexile™ readability scores for all selections.
- Organize reading lists by students' reading level, author, genre, theme, or area of interest.
- Get a brief summary of each selection.

You can find recommended leveled readings for this unit with Reading on Your Own (see page 108).

Glencoe's **Presentation Plus!**, a multimedia teaching tool, lets you present dynamic lessons that will engage your students. Using Microsoft PowerPoint,® you can customize the presentations to create your own personalized lessons. Use **CheckPoint** questions with interactive response keypads to get immediate student feedback during lessons, to increase student participation, and to assess student comprehension.

A lively collection of articles drawn from issues of the TIME family of magazines helps students develop the skills they need to interact with informational text in a meaningful way. Each of the news stories, feature articles, reviews, profiles, and essays in the magazine connect to an author, work, or theme in *Glencoe Literature: Reading with Purpose.* Articles for Unit 1 are found in Volume A. See the *inTIME* Teacher's Guide for specific connections to each unit and for reproducible student worksheets designed to develop students' reading and critical thinking skills.

Literature Launchers

Set the scene with Glencoe's Literature Launchers, engaging video segments that introduce each unit's genre focus. Each video brings the genre to life, relating it to your students' worlds.

Insert the Glencoe Literature Launchers Pre-Reading Videos DVD into your DVD player. Select the Unit 1 Launcher from the menu to introduce the genre and Big Question for this unit.

Online Essay Grader

Use Glencoe's Online Essay Grader to score your students' writing and to provide individualized feedback to each student automatically.

You and your students can visit www.glencoe.com to link to the essay grader. *Students* can enter their essays and receive feedback on demand. *You* can manage demographic data, assign tests and generate individual student and aggregated reports. The essay grader can help you

- Save time with automatic scoring and individualized feedback.
- Supplement in-class writing instruction using guided writing practice.
- Get reports for individual students or for special populations.
- Track student improvement over time.

REAL Success: Reading Excellence at All Levels

Glencoe now provides all of your students with the tools they need to become better, more enthusiastic readers. The REAL Success suite of reading and language arts products encourages reading excellence by meeting the needs of students at all levels. Glencoe products that can be used in conjunction with Unit 1 include the following:

- Jamestown Literature: An Adapted Reader
- Jamestown *Reading Fluency*
- Jamestown *Critical Reading Series, In the Line of Duty*
- *Vocabulary Builder*
- *The Glencoe Reader, Course 1*

To order these products, call Glencoe at 1-800-USA-READ.

Teacher Wraparound Edition Key

Level Appropriate Code

AS = Activities for all students

AL = Activities for students working above grade level

OL = Activities for students working at grade level

BL = Activities for students working below grade level

EL = Activities for English language learners

Teacher Wraparound Prompts

R Reading Skill These activities help you teach reading comprehension skills.

V Vocabulary These activities help students comprehend words and incorporate them into their reading and writing.

C Critical Thinking These strategies help students apply and extend what they have learned.

BQ BIG Question These activities and questions prompt students to prepare to answer the Big Question.

W Writing These activities provide writing opportunities to help students practice writing and comprehend text.

L Literary Element These activities and questions help students comprehend selections and learn more about each genre.

E Text Element These activities help students comprehend text elements.

LSV Listening, Speaking, Viewing These activities help students practice listening, speaking, and viewing skills.

EL English Language Coach These skills help English language learners as well as students who need additional reading support.

From an Author

Doug Fisher

Preparing Students to Read Informational Media

Start with an illustration Students enjoy looking at illustrations and graphics, often in the form of graphic novels and cartoons. Start the class by sharing a current political cartoon or photograph. Invite students to discuss the graphic with a partner—what do they see? What does it mean? This type of partner conversation builds interest in the topic as well as background information about the topic. Describe the ways in which informational media uses illustrations. For example, newspaper and magazine articles often have photographs or illustrations. Ask students to discuss the purposes of photographs and illustrations in informational media—why are they there? What do they do? How do they help the reader?

Activate background knowledge Informational media often relates to the current events in our lives. Ask students about the current events being covered in magazines and newspapers. How are those stories being reported? Whose perspective is shared in these types of articles? Preview the selections in this unit by inviting students to skim the table of contents. Ask them to note the types of topics being discussed—ballpark foods, obesity, instant messaging, etc. Ask students what they already know about these topics and what they'd like to know about these topics.

Teacher to Teacher

Linda I. Rodriguez
Weis Middle School
Texas City, Texas

The newspaper is a valuable instrument in the classroom because there is a reality to newspapers that forces students to confront possibilities in their own lives that they may think they can ignore in fiction. When studying newspaper and other informational media, I bring in a number of newspaper articles and let each student select an article that represents a challenge he or she is interested in reading about. We discuss how students might face these challenges, focusing on their strengths and creativity. I like to include inspirational stories of real people who have faced and overcome challenges and have students apply their personal experiences to the situations in the stories. I ask, "What would you do if you were the person in this newspaper story?" We discuss the ways newspapers and other written media connect our lives to the lives of others and how reading about these stories impacts our lives.

Teacher Chatroom

Using Informational Media

 What is informational media and why is it important?

 This genre focuses on the types of texts used to inform—and teach—people about topics important in their lives. It extends traditional nonfiction texts to include a wide range of media outlets that can be used to provide people with accurate information. Informational media is important as it is one of the primary ways that people receive information in the world. For example, we read newspapers, magazines, and the Internet to find out the answers to our questions and to understand the events of the world. In fact, informational media is one of the most common types of texts adults read. Middle school students need to know how to read for information and how to evaluate the information they read.

 Are students interested in informational media?

 Very much so. In fact, there is evidence that reluctant readers and many male students prefer informational media and texts. The difficulty with this type of text is the background knowledge that is assumed by some authors. For example, in the selection "Gymnasts in Pain," the author assumes his readers know what gymnasts do. To help students understand this text, which many of them will find fascinating, you may want to focus on key ideas before sharing the text. Building background and front-loading information is always a good idea as it helps students make connections between what they already know and what they will learn.

 How are informational media texts organized?

 There are a number of structures that authors of informational media texts use. In many newspaper articles, for example, the key ideas are presented toward the beginning of the article and details are presented in the paragraphs that follow. This is for ease of editing when a paragraph needs to be cut. Magazine articles often use descriptive structures that allow a reader to develop a deeper sense of the content based on the reading. Of course, all of the informational text structures can be used, including problem/solution, cause/effect, and temporal/sequence. Helping readers understand the structure of the text facilitates their comprehension of the content.

UNIT 1

Why Read?

"The only way to do all the things you'd like to do is to read."

–Tom Clancy
action and adventure novelist

Key Unit Objectives

- ● **Answer the Big Question**
- ● **Analyze the text and literary elements of informational media**
- ● **Apply strategies for reading informational media**
- ● **Write summaries**

Why Is It Important?

Reflecting on this big question helps students identify the uses and pleasures of reading.

Viewing the Illustration

Tell students to read the quote and share what they think it means. Then ask them how they think the picture relates to the quote. *(Possible responses: Reading takes you to many different places and shows you different ways to do things; in the illustration, the girl is reading one book and has another on her desk; her reading has probably taken her somewhere away from her desk.)* **OL**

Unit Skills

Reading Skills
- Setting a Purpose for Reading, p. 8
- Skimming and Scanning, p. 30
- Understanding Graphics, p. 48
- Identifying Main Idea p. 68

BIG Question Why read?
Genre Focus: Informational Media

Key Elements
- Text Features, p. 11
- Titles and Subheads, p. 33
- Process, p. 51
- Author's Purpose, p. 71

Vocabulary
- Word References, p. 10
- Multiple-meaning Words, p. 32

Writing Skills/Grammar
- Summary, p. 26
- Ideas, p. 27
- Verbs, p. 29

LOOKING AHEAD

The skill lessons and readings in this unit will help you develop your own answer to the Big Question.

UNIT 1 WRAP-UP • **Answering the Big Question**

1

About the Reading
Each selection in this unit provides insights that can help students address the question, "Why read?" Students consider their own reasons for reading and see why others read.

About the Skills
The skills taught in this unit have been selected because they are particularly helpful when reading the featured genre—informational media. Each reading selection provides students with opportunities to practice and develop these skills.

No Child Left Behind

The NCLB Teacher's Toolkit says, "Improving the reading skills of children is a top priority for leaders at all levels. . . ." Modeling the skills covered in this unit will aid students' development. For example, read aloud a passage from a selection and illustrate how to find the main idea and supporting details.

Reading Fluency

Reading Along To develop fluency, students should hear good models. First, have students read along silently as you read aloud from one of the selections in this unit. Then, organize students into small groups. Have each student take a turn reading several lines from the same passage. Remind students to take the time to self-correct as they read. Students should continue reading the passage until their fluency improves. **EL BL**

Focus

BELLRINGER Options

- **Literature Launcher**
- **Daily Skills Practice 1**
Focus Activity Ask: What types of information can you obtain by reading? *(Responses will vary.)* **AS** On the board, begin a web diagram with a center circle labeled "Reading for Information." Complete the web with student responses.

Teach

BQ1 **BIG Question**

To help students connect to the Big Question, ask them to list ways they use reading every day. Have them compare their lists with a partner's, and then use these prompts:

- Find something on your list that is not on your partner's.
- Explain why that item is important to you. **AS**

BQ2 **BIG Question**

- Have students read the profiles and look at the pictures of Kennedy and Dominic.
- Have students choose partners and then role-play the parts of Kennedy and Dominic to explain why they read. **OL**

Additional Support

Connecting to The BIG Question Why Read?

Reading helps you learn about the world and your place in it. How do you find out where the bus stops, what time a movie starts, or where the movie is showing? You find out by reading. In this unit, you'll learn how reading can help you get the information you need. **BQ1**

Real Kids and the Big Question

KENNEDY'S best friend, Ashley, is moving to another state next month. They don't want distance to change their friendship. However, Kennedy knows it's going to be hard to keep in touch. She thinks instant messaging and e-mailing will help her stay connected to her friend. How do you think Kennedy might answer the question, "Why read?"

DOMINIC'S aunt and uncle have asked him to babysit for their young twins two days a week. Dominic is used to baby-sitting, but he has never helped with twins. He is worried about how to keep them entertained, so he checked out some library books to read to the twins before their naps. How do you think Dominic might answer the question, "Why read?"

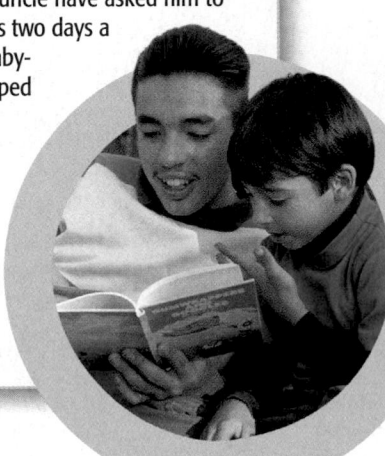

Warm-Up Activity

Think about the reasons that Kennedy and Dominic read. With a partner, discuss how reading helps Kennedy and Dominic. Write a paragraph telling how each person might answer the Big Question.

Reading in the Real World

Career Like Dominic, students may find their first work opportunities with family members or neighbors. As they grow older, they may be required to fill out job applications. Such documents ask for specific pieces of information. They may include formal language and big words, and they may present items indirectly. Job applications do have a logical structure to help applicants find, follow, and understand the instructions. Provide students with a basic job application to read and discuss their questions. **AS**

You and the Big Question

We read for many reasons. Reading different selections will give you ideas about why people read. You will also think about why *you* read.

Plan for the Unit Challenge

At the end of the unit, you'll use notes from all your reading to complete the Unit Challenge. The Challenge will help you explore your answer to the Big Question!

You'll choose one of the following activities:

A. Comic Strip You'll work with classmates to create a comic strip about a reading superhero who fights illiteracy, which means not knowing how to read.

B. Conduct Interviews You'll interview friends and family members to find out what they read and why they read it.

• Start thinking about which activity you'd like to do so that you can focus your thoughts as you go through the unit.

• In your Learner's Notebook, write about which you like better—working by yourself or working with other students. That may help you decide which activity you'd like to do.

• Remember to take notes about possible answers to the Big Question. Your notes will help you complete the Unit Challenge activity you choose.

Keep Track of Your Ideas

As you read, you'll make notes about the Big Question. Later, you'll use these notes to complete the Unit Challenge. See pages R8–R9 for help with making Foldable 1. This diagram shows how it should look.

1. Use this Foldable for the selections in this unit. Label each page with a selection title. (See page 1 for titles.) You should be able to see all the titles without opening the Foldable.

2. Below each title, write **My Purpose for Reading.** You'll write your purpose for reading the selection below this label.

3. A third of the way down on the page, write the label **The Big Question.** You'll write your thoughts about the Big Question below this label.

> from The Great Cow Race
> Make Your Own Kite
> The Real Magic of Harry Potter
> Messaging Mania
> How He Did It
> Ballpark Food
>
> Unit 1
> Why Read?

Teach

Big Question Have students access the Web site for English and Spanish summaries and annotated links to related Web resources.

For each selection they read, students will enter notes about how that selection applies to the Big Question. For details about using Dinah Zike's Foldables, see page R8—R9.

Assess/Close

Review the list of reasons for reading that students brainstormed. Ask students how they think answering the Big Question might help them improve their reading skills.

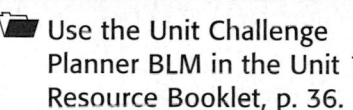

Resources for page 3

📁 Use the Unit Challenge Planner BLM in the Unit 1 Resource Booklet, p. 36.

📁 Use the Foldable BLM in the Unit 1 Resource Booklet, p. 7.

Reading in the Real World

Citizenship In a democracy, citizens have many responsibilities. Responsible citizens read newspapers and magazines and check news on the Internet to get information about important issues and events. Before voting, well-informed citizens learn which candidates for government office share their ideas. Some citizens take part in candidates' election campaigns. Lead a discussion about a politician. Ask students where they might find information about this politician's agenda. Discuss whether students support this politician and their reasons for supporting or not supporting the politician. **OL**

Objectives
• Activate prior knowledge
• Make connections from text to self
• Use text features: photographs

In the sidebar, near "Literature Online":

Big Question Link to Web resources to further explore the Big Question at www.glencoe.com.

Focus

BELLRINGER Options

✍ **Daily Language Practice Transparency 2**
Focus Activity Say: Think of the different kinds of information you need every day, such as an after-school activity schedule or a homework schedule. Where can you find that information? (*Responses will vary.*) **AS**

Teach

C Critical Thinking

Application Say: Describe specific information that you can find in a newspaper, a magazine, a Web site, and an advertisement. (*Possible responses:* **newspaper:** *news about current events, sports scores, movie times;* **magazine:** *fitness tips, political commentaries;* **Web site:** *facts for a research report, homework help;* **advertisement:** *sale prices at a local store, product descriptions*) **OL**

UNIT 1 GENRE FOCUS: INFORMATIONAL MEDIA

Skills Focus
• Key skills for reading informational media
• Key text and literary elements of informational media

Skills Model
You will see how to use the key reading skills and text and literary elements as you read
• *"Animal Attraction,"* p. 6

Objectives (pp. 4–7)
Reading Set a purpose for reading • Skim and scan text • Identify main ideas and supporting details • Use graphics
Informational Text Use text features: title, subtitle, deck, subheads • Identify text structure: steps in a process
Literature Identify literary elements: author's purpose

The term **informational media** (MEE dee uh) might be new to you. (**Media** is the plural for **medium.**) But you probably use some form of media every day. Media are ways of communicating with large groups. Media that provide information are called **informational media.** The newspaper on your doorstep, the television in your living room, the radio in the car, the Web sites you visit on the computer, and the advertisements you find in magazines, newspapers, and on billboards are forms of media. **C**

• **Television** is the most popular medium. At least ninety-nine percent of households own at least one television set. The average American watches more than four hours of TV each day.

• Before television, **radio** was the most popular medium. Radio was first broadcast in 1920. From its start, radio carried sports, news, and musical programming. This format is still used by most radio stations today.

• The **newspaper** is a form of print media. Besides news, people read the paper for the comics, advice columns, recipes, sports news, and ads.

• **News articles** found in magazines and newspapers provide information about particular topics, issues, or events.

• The **Internet** is a vast system of computer networks connected to one another around the world. The Internet provides a wide variety of information at your fingertips.

• **Web pages** are the basic units of the Internet. The main purpose of Web pages is to provide information, entertainment, or advertising. These electronic pages contain text, pictures, animation, and movies.

• A **Web site** is a collection of pages grouped together to organize the information offered by the person, company, or group that owns it. For example, your favorite musical performer or actor probably has a Web site. Many companies and organizations have Web sites, where you can learn more about them.

• **Advertising** is the use of media—such as television, newspapers, and radio—to promote a product or service. The aim of advertising is to get the reader, viewer, or listener to buy or use a certain product or service.

Additional Support

English Language Coach

Plurals Remind students that a plural noun names more than one person, place, thing, or idea. The plurals of most nouns in English are formed by adding -*s* or -*es*. Plurals formed by adding an -*a* are unusual in English. The singular word *medium* comes from Latin. *Media* is its plural. *Data* is another plural that English takes from Latin. In Latin, *data* is the plural of *datum*. The singular form *datum* is not used in English. Give students a list of singular nouns. Have them work in groups to form the plural of each of the nouns. **EL BL**

Why Read Informational Media?

You need practical information every day. Whether you want to find out about the weather or your favorite team's stats, you can often get the facts through informational media. You can read informational media to

- get the latest news
- learn how to make or do something
- find information for a school report

How to Read Informational Media

Key Reading Skills

These reading skills are especially useful tools for reading and understanding informational media. You'll see these skills modeled in the Active Reading Model on pages 6–7, and you'll learn more about them later in this unit.

- **Setting a purpose for reading** Before you read, decide *why* you are reading. (See Reading Workshop 1.)

- **Skimming and scanning** Get a rough idea of what a selection is about by scanning to look for key words and phrases. To skim, read through something quickly to find its main idea or get a general overview. (See Reading Workshop 2.)

- **Understanding graphics** Use the information from graphics to locate and analyze information. (See Reading Workshop 3.)

- **Identifying main idea and supporting details** As you read, find the most important idea in a paragraph or selection. Also find the details that support the most important idea. (See Reading Workshop 4.)

Key Text and Literary Elements

Recognizing and thinking about the following elements will help you understand the text more fully.

- **Text features:** titles, subtitles, and decks (See "Ball Park Food.")

- **Titles:** large or dark type that introduces text and grabs the reader's attention **Subheads:** smaller titles that introduce parts of the text (See "The Magic of Harry Potter.")

- **Process:** the way things need to happen in order to get a certain result (See "Make Your Own Kite.")

- **Author's purpose:** the writer's goal in a particular work, which may be to entertain, inform, persuade, or express emotions (See "To Young Readers.")

Teach

R Reading Skill

Skimming and Scanning Say: Skimming gives readers a general picture of a text, and scanning helps readers locate specific information in a text. Suppose you've created a Web page about yourself. What could someone learn about you by skimming the page? What key words or phrases might help someone scanning the page find facts about you? *(Responses will vary.)* **OL**

E Text Element

Process Say: A process is a series of actions or steps that are followed to make or do something. Is there a process you would like to know more about? Where would you look for information about it? *(Responses will vary.)* **AS**

Literature Focus Lesson

Text Features Explain to students that the text features of informational media will vary. For example:

- A Web page often has a menu at the top or side to help readers navigate the site. Highlighted or underlined words and phrases serve as links to other pages or sites.

- The title of a magazine or newspaper article is usually a headline. Below that headline, there is often a subtitle known as the deck.

Ask students to look at a magazine, newspaper, or Web page, and identify the features mentioned. **AS**

Objectives

- Analyze features of genres: informational media
- Follow steps in a process
- Identify word structure: plurals

Teach

EL Language Coach

Word References

Organize the class into two groups. Give one group a dictionary and the other a thesaurus. Have both groups look up the word *attraction*.

- Have the dictionary group write a definition of *attraction* in their own words.

- Have the thesaurus group write a sentence using an appropriate synonym for *attraction* as it is used in the title. *(Responses will vary.)* **EL BL OL**

R Reading Skill

Identifying Main Idea and Supporting Details Ask:

What is the main idea of the selection? *(Possible response: Scientists think that pets may help keep their owners healthy.)*
Say: Find two details that support the main idea of the selection. *(Possible responses: Levels of "good" chemicals in the body rise when people are around pets. In nursing homes that keep pets, fewer people stay in bed all day.)* **OL**

Readability Scores
Dale-Chall: 3.9
DRP: 49
Lexile: 710

TIME

Animal Attraction EL

Sure, pets provide lots of pleasure. But now scientists think they might help people live longer, too. **1 2 3**

By SALLY S. STICH

The notes in the side columns model how to use the skills and elements you read about on page 5.

Informational Media
ACTIVE READING MODEL

When her father died, Karen Wright was very worried. Her mother, Violet, was 72 years old. "Mom had always been full of energy and enthusiasm," says Wright. "But after Dad died, she didn't take care of herself and got sick a lot." Wright's mother didn't feel that she had much to live for—except a dog named Buddy. "I never paid much attention to Buddy when my husband was alive," says Violet. "But suddenly he depended on me for his survival."

Most people agree that a pet adds joy to a person's life. This can be more true after a loved one dies. Scientists are now finding that having a pet may keep its owner healthy. And good health may add years to a person's life. **4**

Scientists have been looking at the tie between pets and health for years. In 1990, a study was done with people age 65 and older. It showed that pet owners went to the doctor less than people without pets. Do pets make people happier? Do they help people live on their own longer? Are people able to handle their everyday lives better? Alan Beck is the head of the Center for the Human-Animal Bond. Beck says that if the answer to these questions is yes, then having pets may be a good idea.

Can pets also help people live longer? Rebecca Johnson did a study to find out. Johnson teaches nurses how to care for older people. She shared the findings of her study at a meeting about Pets and the Aging. Her study shows that having pets may cause people to age more slowly.

1 Key Text Element
Titles and Decks *The title tells me that the article is going to be about animals. The deck tells that pets might help people live longer.*

2 Key Reading Skill
Setting a Purpose for Reading *How can pets help people live longer? My purpose for reading is to find the answer.*

3 Key Reading Skill
Skimming and Scanning *As I skimmed this article, I saw that it's about how pets add joy and good health to people's lives. I scanned for the word dog and learned that some people have robotic dogs!*

4 Key Reading Skill
Identifying Main Idea and Supporting Details *The main idea is that scientists think animals can help people live longer. Let's see what details the article provides to support that idea.* **R**

Additional Support

Reading in the Real World

Citizenship Have students conduct research on the Internet or at the library to find out more about pet therapy. Tell students to answer these questions:

- What kind of training is necessary for workers, volunteers, and pets?

- How does pet therapy affect different people?

- What groups or individuals in the students' communities provide pet therapy?

Have students present their findings to the rest of the class. **OL**

ACTIVE READING MODEL

The human body makes many chemicals. Some of the chemicals make people feel good. Others make people feel bad. In Johnson's study, levels of the "good" chemicals rose when people were around pets. Levels of the "bad" chemicals went down. The good chemicals seemed to slow the aging of cells. If this is true, maybe people should spend more time with their pets. Then the levels of good chemicals will go up. People might feel better and age more slowly. They might even live longer. **5**

Having pets may also be good for people in nursing homes. In a study of five nursing homes with pets, 25% fewer people stayed in bed all day. And sores caused by being in bed were down 57%. Having pets around was good for the workers too. They missed work 48% less than before the pets came.

Of course, you could be allergic to pets. Or you may not want to take care of a pet. Never fear. A robotic, or computer, pet may be just the thing for you. Scientists are testing computer pets, like the robotic dog AIBO.[1] They want to see if computer pets can help people the way real dogs do. **6**

Will a robotic pet take the place of the pet pal snuggling with you on the sofa? Something tells us that the furry couch potato lying next to you has little to worry about.

—Updated 2005, from *TIME*, October 20, 2003

---

1. **AIBO** is a robotic dog made by a major electronics company. It is programmed to react to directions from its owner.

Partner Talk With a partner, talk about the different reasons someone may have for reading this article.

Study Central Visit www.glencoe.com and click on Study Central to review informational text.

5 Key Text Element
Process *If you have a pet, your body makes "good" chemicals. What's the next step? The good chemicals rise, the "bad" chemicals go down, and you age more slowly.*

6 Key Literary Element
Author's Purpose *I think that the author's main purpose is to inform readers about the positive effects of pets on people's health.*

7 Key Reading Skill
Understanding Graphics *The picture is kind of funny. But it also helps me understand the article. The man is relaxing with his cat. He's smiling. I'll bet his "good chemicals" are rising!*

Edwin Frothingham

Genre Focus: Informational Media   **7**

Teach

E Text Element

Process Say: Writers often use signal words to show steps or actions. Words such as *first, next, then,* and *finally* signal time order. *So, because, as a result, when,* and *then* point to causes and effects. What signal words are used to show the cause and effect of humans interacting with pets in the first paragraph on this page? (*Possible response:* when *and* then*) **OL**

L Literary Element

Author's Purpose Say: Explain what would lead you to conclude that the author's purpose in this selection is to inform. (*Possible response: The author discusses different studies addressing the connection between pets and good health and then gives results and statistics from the studies.*) **AL**

Literature Online
Study Central Have students access the Web site to review informational text and to complete a related activity.

Differentiated Instruction

Use Graphic Organizers Draw a simple cause-and-effect diagram on the board, such as the one on the right. Help students comprehend the effects of pets on people's health by working as a class to complete the diagram. **EL BL**

Cause	Cause/Effect	Effect
People are around pets.	Levels of "good" chemicals go up.	Aging of cells slows down.

Objectives
- Use word references
- Identify main idea and supporting details
- Follow steps in a process
- Identify author's purpose

Setting a Purpose for Reading

Objective covered in this workshop:
• Set a purpose for reading

Teaching Students to Set a Purpose for Reading

Why Is It Important?
• Reading is more interesting and more likely to be recalled when there is a clear purpose.
• It provides a focus for the reader and allows the reader to monitor that he or she is getting what is needed from the reading.
• Good readers read for a variety of reasons, and they know *why* they're reading a specific piece.

How to Help Students Get It
• A purpose can be set by the reader or by someone else. For students who are purposeless readers, they need support to learn about setting purpose.
• Show students the sports pages of the local newspaper. Ask them why they might read this section of the paper. Then show them the For Sale ads. Ask them why they might read these ads. Proceed through the newspaper, generating different purposes for different parts.
• Ask students to make a list of things they'd like to know more about—an interest inventory. For one of the items on this list, ask them to write a purpose statement. Help students find independent reading materials related to their topic and purpose.

Reading to Answer the Big Question

Ball Park Foods
A *Consumer Reports for Kids* article makes the argument that ballpark food is costly in many ways. Readers are encouraged to consider price and nutrition as they learn that getting information through careful reading of advertisements enables them to make good choices.

How He Did It
When a sixth-grade student realizes that there is lack of information about childhood obesity that is specifically directed toward children, he develops his own kid-friendly Web site. Robert Kohn begins this project for a language arts class assignment that required students to combine research with action steps. In addition to finding inspiration from Robert's accomplishments, students will read practical advice on how to make healthful lifestyle choices.

Workshop Resources

PACING (DAYS)		LESSON	STUDENT MATERIALS	TEACHER RESOURCES
STANDARD	BLOCK			
1	1/2	Key Skill Lesson: Setting a Purpose for Reading	🐾 Key Reading Skills Practice, p. 9 🐾 English Language Coach Review, p. 42	📖 Bellringer Options Transparencies –Daily Language Practice 3 📖 Read Aloud, Think Aloud Transparencies –Key Reading Skills 22 ⊙ Presentation Plus!
1	1	"Ball Park Foods"	💻 Glencoe Online 🐾 Unit Vocabulary Review, p. 40 🐾 Academic Vocabulary Review, p. 43 📁 English Language Coach 🐾 Active Reading Graphic Organizer, p. 11 🐾 Literary Analysis, p. 10 ⊙ StudentWorks Plus™ 💻 Online Student Edition ⊙ Literature Classics 📁 Selection and Unit Assessments, p. 1	📖 Literary and Text Analysis Transparencies S3 💻 Puzzlemaker ⊙ Skill Level Up!™ A Language Arts Game 💻 BookLink 3 📓 Assessment by Learning Objective (Diagnostic and Formative) ⊙ Interactive Tutor: Self-Assessment ⊙ TeacherWorks Plus™
1		"How He Did It"	💻 Glencoe Online 🐾 Unit Vocabulary Review, p. 40 🐾 Academic Vocabulary Review, p. 43 📁 English Language Coach 🐾 Active Reading Graphic Organizer, p. 13 🐾 Literary Analysis, p. 10 ⊙ StudentWorks Plus™ 💻 Online Student Edition ⊙ Literature Classics 📁 Selection and Unit Assessments, p. 2	📖 Literary and Text Analysis Transparencies S3 💻 Puzzlemaker ⊙ Skill Level Up!™ A Language Arts Game 💻 BookLink 3 📓 Assessment by Learning Objective (Diagnostic and Formative) ⊙ Interactive Tutor: Self-Assessment ⊙ TeacherWorks Plus™

Keys for Unit Resource

📁 Blackline Master
📓 Workbook
📖 Supplemental Text
⊙ CD-ROM
💿 DVD
📖 Transparency
💻 Web-based
🐾 Fast File

Level Appropriate Code

AS = Activities for all students
AL = Activities for students working above grade level
OL = Activities for students working at grade level
BL = Activities for students working below grade level
EL = Activities for English language learners

Focus

BELLRINGER Options

✎ **Daily Language Practice Transparency 3**
Focus Activity Ask: What did you read this week because you had to? What did you read because you wanted to? *(Responses will vary.)*

Teach

R Reading Skill

Setting a Purpose for Reading Say: In your Learner's Notebooks, make a two-column chart. In the first column, list what you have read in the last few days. In the second column, list your purposes for reading the items in the first column. Remember that you may have more than one purpose for reading a piece of text. *(Responses will vary.)* **OL**

V Vocabulary

Academic Vocabulary Say: Read the definition of *text* at the bottom of page 8. Then name several different kinds of texts. *(Possible responses: newspapers, magazine articles, short stories, novels, advertisements, instructions)* **OL**

Skills Focus

You will practice using these skills when you read the following selections:
• "Ballpark Food," p. 12
• "How He Did It: Health Advice, Kid-to-Kid," p. 20

Reading

• Setting a purpose for reading

Informational Text

• Understanding text features

Vocabulary

• Understanding and using word references
• Academic Vocabulary: *text*

Writing/Grammar

• Identifying parts of speech

Objectives (pp. 8–9)
Reading Set a purpose for reading

8 UNIT 1

Skill Lesson

Setting a Purpose for Reading

Learn It!

What Is It? When you **set a purpose for reading,** you ask yourself questions about *what* you're reading and *why* you're reading it. This affects *how* you read. For example, your purpose for reading an adventure story may be to find out what happens in the story. You might ask yourself, "How is this going to work out?" If you are reading directions for setting up a new computer, though, your purpose for reading is different. You might ask, "How can I make this computer work?" Many times, your purpose for reading changes as you read. **R**

Analyzing Cartoons
Setting a purpose for reading helps you to figure out what you can get out of a **text.** Does the girl in the cartoon have a purpose for reading? What is it?

Academic Vocabulary

text (tekst) *n.* the printed or written words of a page, book, or another form of communication **V**

Additional Support

Reading Fluency

Build Fluency Have students read the cartoon aloud with a partner. One student should take the part of the mother, and the other student should take the part of the daughter. First have pairs read for understanding. Then tell them to pay close attention to punctuation marks and words in darker type and to read with appropriate expression. Students should then practice reading their parts smoothly. When students can read their parts with both understanding and expression, they should switch parts and repeat the exercise. **EL BL**

Why Is It Important? It always helps to know why you're doing something! Also, setting a purpose for reading helps you choose the way to read something. For example, if you have to define certain words for a science worksheet, your purpose for reading a chapter in your science book is to find the meanings of those words. So you look quickly through the chapter, searching for those words. When you find one, you slow down and read carefully to find out what it means.

Study Central Visit www.glencoe. com and click on Study Central to review setting a purpose for reading.

How Do I Do It? Before you start to read, think about what might be interesting or what you might need to learn from the selection. What questions come into your mind? Write these questions down. They are your purpose for reading. After reading the title and deck of "Animal Attraction," this is how one student set her purpose for reading.

Animal Attraction
Sure, pets provide lots of pleasure. But now scientists think they might help people live longer, too.

> It looks like this is about pets, but I had no idea pets could help people live longer. I've never heard of anything like that, and it doesn't make sense to me. How can pets do this? I want to find out how a pet can help someone live longer, so I'll read to find out. That's my purpose for reading.

Practice It!

The title of the first selection is "Ballpark Food." Look over the headings, questions, and pictures and use them to set a purpose for reading. In your Learner's Notebook, write your purpose for reading.

Use It!

"Ballpark Food" starts with some multiple choice questions. As you read make notes in your Learner's Notebook of what *you* think are the right answers. Does this activity change your purpose for reading? That's okay! It means that you are thinking and learning as you read! Just write any new purpose in your Learner's Notebook.

Teach

Study Central Have students access the Web site to review setting a purpose for reading and to complete a related activity.

R Reading Skill

Setting a Purpose for Reading Say: It's important to read carefully when your purpose is to learn something new or to find specific information. Why might you read carefully when your purpose is to enjoy a story? *(Possible responses: to make sure that I don't miss any details and that I can follow the story line; to appreciate an author's style of writing; to find meaning in the story)* **OL**

Resources for page 9

📁 Use Key Reading Skills Transparency 22 in *Read Aloud, Think Aloud* to help students practice Setting a Purpose for Reading.

Differentiated Instruction

Asking Questions Explain to students that previewing text features, such as titles, headings, and pictures, and asking questions help readers set a purpose for reading. Suggest that students use the title and headings of each selection to form questions before reading. For example, a student previewing the selection "Animal Attraction" might ask, "What is 'animal attraction'?" Then his or her purpose for reading might be to find information in the selection to answer that question. Remind students that they can begin their questions with *when, where, why, what, who,* or *how.* **BL OL**

Objectives
• Set a purpose for reading
• Ask questions
• Learn and use new vocabulary

9

Teach

More About the Authors

The Snack Squad published the results of their research about ballpark food in the form of a quiz on the *Consumer Reports for Kids Online* Web site. This Web site features contributions by kids on a variety of topics having to do with money, products, and consumerism. It is written for readers who are ages eight and older.

V Vocabulary

Picture It Say: In your Learner's Notebooks, draw a picture for each of the vocabulary words. Then add a caption that includes the word, its pronunciation, its meaning, and a sentence that uses the word to describe the picture. *(Responses will vary. Students should demonstrate that they understand the correct meaning and usage of the words.)* As you learn additional vocabulary words, you may add them to your picture dictionary **AS**

Before You Read | Ballpark Food

Meet the Authors

A group of thirty-six kids, who call themselves the Snack Squad, decided to gather information about foods sold at baseball parks. The Snack Squad wanted to know if it was cheaper and healthier to bring your own food than to eat the food sold at the ballparks. They also wanted to know what effect the advertisements in the ballparks had on food sales. They put all the information into the quiz you are about to read. Find out what they learned as you read and take the quiz.

Objectives (pp. 10–15)
Reading Set a purpose for reading
Informational Text Use text features: title, subtitle, deck
Vocabulary Use word references: dictionary, glossary

Vocabulary Preview

vendors (VEN durz) *n.* people who sell products or services **(p. 14)** *Vendors sell food, clothes, and other items during a game.*

ushers (USH urz) *n.* people who help others find their seats in a theater or stadium **(p. 15)** *The ushers took us to our seats in row twelve.*

Partner Talk Discuss the vocabulary words with a partner.

1. **Vendors** Have you ever bought something from a vendor, like food at an amusement park or a t-shirt at a sporting event? Did you pay too much for it, or was the price fair? Talk about what you bought, where you bought it, and why. What are some other items vendors might sell?

2. **Ushers** Talk about three places you might see an usher.

English Language Coach

Word References Sometimes you will see a new word or a word you recognize used in a new way. Don't panic! Use a dictionary or a glossary to help you find the word's meaning.

* A dictionary can show you a word's definition, how to pronounce the word, and its part of speech.

* You can also learn the word's root (the history of where it comes from). Look at this dictionary entry.

---

sale \sāl\ *n.* [Old English *sala* act of selling.] **1.** transfer of ownership from one party to another in exchange for money: *the sale of a house.* **2.** selling goods at a reduced price: *an end-of-the-season sale.* **3. for sale.** available for purchase. **4. on sale.** offered at a reduced price: *to buy pants on sale.*

---

* A glossary is similar to a dictionary, but it appears at the back of a book and shows the meanings of words that appear in that book. See the glossary in this book that begins on p. R54.

Write to Learn Look in the glossary on p. R54 and choose a word. Write its meaning and its part of speech. Then write a sentence using the word you chose.

Additional Support

English Language Coach

Parts of Speech Explain to students that when they see a new word or a word used in a new way, it is helpful to decide how the word is being used, or its part of speech. Then, if they need to, they can look in a dictionary to find the correct meaning for that part of speech.

Write the following sentences on the board and have volunteers tell how the word *fancy* is used in each sentence.

1. I have always had a *fancy* for cats. (*noun*)

2. I bought a *fancy* collar with a bell. (*adjective*) **EL OL**

Skills Preview

Key Reading Skill: Setting a Purpose for Reading

There are many purposes for reading, and there may be several different reasons for reading one selection. You've already written one purpose for reading "Ballpark Food." It might be to learn

• why ballpark food costs so much
• who gets the money from the food sales

Write to Learn Pick one of these questions and write the answers as you read. The answer won't always be in one place.

• Which is cheaper, food bought from a grocery store or a ballpark? How do you know?
• Why do you think there are so many ads in a ball-park? Explain.

Key Text Element: Text Features

When you're looking at a page of informational text, you hardly ever see a big block of words that all look alike. Instead, you see titles printed big and other words in italics. You may see bullets—those dots like big periods that come before one of a series of things. These are all **text features,** which are special ways of presenting information. They make what you're reading easier to understand.

The title of an article can be important when you are setting a purpose to read. It may give you an idea of what the article is about or just make it sound interesting.

In "Ballpark Food," the text is set as questions and answers, with numbers and boldface (dark) text to make the material look more interesting and make it easier to read. While you're reading, ask yourself whether this text feature works.

Partner Talk With a partner, find text features that appear in "Ballpark Food." How do they hint at what the text is about? Does a graphic make the text more clear?

Get Ready to Read

Connect to the Reading

Have you ever felt as though you paid too much for something? As you read, think about where your money goes when you buy items at a ballpark.

Write to Learn In your Learner's Notebook, write about how you decide which items are worth buying and how you save money for those items.

Build Background

The Snack Squad asked questions about the high price of ballpark food and found some interesting answers.

Set Purposes for Reading

BIG Question One answer to "Why read?" is "To get information." Read "Ballpark Food" to discover where your money goes at the ballpark and how you can save some of it.

Set Your Own Purpose What else would you like to learn from the selection to help you answer the Big Question? Write your own purpose on the "Ballpark Food" page of Foldable 1.

Literature Online

Interactive Literary Elements Handbook
To review or learn more about the literary elements, go to www.glencoe.com.

Keep Moving

Use these skills as you read the following selection.

Teach

E **Text Element**

Text Features Say: Text features—such as titles and graphics—should help readers understand the selection. Titles are usually short and catchy so they can grab the readers' attention. Look at page 12. What is the title of this selec-tion? *(Ballpark Food)* **BL Ask:** How does the graphic help you understand what the selec-tion will be about? *(Possible response: The graphic shows foods sold at baseball parks and a baseball so the story will probably be about these foods.)* **OL**

Literature Online

Interactive Literary Elements Handbook Have students access the Web site to improve their understanding of text features.

Literature Focus Lesson

Text Features Have students copy this chart in their Learner's Notebooks and use it to make notes on text features in the selection "Ballpark Food." **AS**

Text Features	Description
Title	
Headings	
Graphics	
Photographs	
Other features (name) _____	

Objectives

• Use text features
• Learn and use new vocabulary
• Identify parts of speech

11

Teach

EL Language Coach

Word References Sports terms in the selection may be unfamiliar to some students. Have students use a dictionary to find the meaning of *major league* and *ballpark*.
Ask: What sport do these two words refer to? (*Students should indicate the words have something to do with baseball.*) EL

E Text Element

Text Features Say: The quiz on this page is a kind of text feature that's often used in magazines and newspapers, and on Web pages. Why do you think a writer would begin an article by having the readers take a quiz? (*Possible responses: to get readers interested; to let readers see what they know and don't know about a subject*) OL

Readability Scores
Dale-Chall: 4.9
DRP: 58
Lexile: 1040

Consumer Reports 4 Kids

Do you have major-league complaints about the high price of ballpark food? **1** EL

Take this quiz to see if you can guess what our 36-kid Snack Squad discovered when they visited baseball parks to buy and test their food.

1. **How did the price of hot dogs, soda, and peanuts at the ballpark compare to their price at a food store?**
   A. The food cost twice as much at the ballpark.
   B. It cost three to seven times more at the ballpark.
   C. Ballpark and food store prices were the same.

2. **Say you paid $2.50 for this hot dog at a ballpark. How much of that covers the cost of the hot dog and bun?**
   A. 10¢   D. $1.50
   B. 50¢   E. $2
   C. $1

3. **Will most baseball parks let you bring in your own food?**
   A. Yes   B. No

4. **How many ads do you think our Snack Squad spotted in the ballparks they visited? 2**
   A. None   B. Just a few   C. Dozens

12 UNIT 1 Why Read?

Practice the Skills

1 Key Text Element

Text Features What can you find out about the topic of this selection from the title? Does it help you set your purpose for reading?

2 Key Reading Skill

Setting a Purpose for Reading Look at the questions on this page. What purpose could you set for reading this part of the selection?

Additional Support

Reading in the Real World

College The quiz in the selection, like many standardized tests students will take, consists of multiple-choice questions. Provide these tips for answering multiple-choice questions:

• Read each question carefully.

• Read all of the answers carefully.

• Use all the information given to you to answer the question. Also, think about what you know from your own experience.

• Eliminate answer choices that you *know* are wrong. Then choose the remaining answer that makes the most sense. **AS**

ANSWERS **3** **E**

1. **B!** Hot dogs, soda, and peanuts cost three to seven times more at the ballpark than at a store!

You almost need a major-league salary to afford ballpark **EL** food! The hot dogs, soda, and peanuts our Snack Squad bought cost three to seven times more than their local food stores charged. In Ohio, for example, $7.50 bought a hot dog, 24-ounce soda, and bag of about 90 peanuts at the Cincinnati Reds stadium. But that same $7.50 would buy five hot dogs, 190 ounces of soda, and about 380 peanuts at a grocery store!

Practice the Skills

3 **Key Text Element**

Text Features This text feature tells me that this is the answer key. I see that the correct answer to the first question is **B**.

Analyzing the Photo This ballpark vendor is tossing a bag of peanuts to a customer. Look closely. How much do they cost? Is that more or less than at a store?

Ballpark Food **13**

Teach

E Text Element

Text Features **Say:** Look at the heading on this page. What does it tell you about the items numbered 1–4 here and on the next two pages? *(Possible response: The numbered items on these pages are answers to the questions on the quiz.)* **BL**

EL Language Coach

Context Clues **Ask:** What does *major-league* mean in the phrases *major-league complaints* and *major-league salary*? *(Possible response: big)* **OL**

Viewing the Photo

Ask: What does the photo tell you about how food is sold at ballparks? *(Possible response: Vendors carry foods around the stands to sell to people.)* **BL** What you do think the man in the photo is saying? *(Possible response: He's telling people what he's selling.)* **OL**

Differentiated Instruction

Doing the Math Have students use the information provided in the answer to question 1 to calculate the cost of a hot dog, a 24-ounce soda, and a bag of peanuts at a store if the items were three times less and seven times less than the ballpark prices. Copy the chart on the board and demonstrate the math in each column so students can verify their answers. **AL**

Hot Dog, 24-Ounce Soda, Bag of Peanuts		
Cost at Ballpark	Cost at Store: three times less	Cost at Store: seven times less
$7.50	$2.50 3)$7.50	$1.07 7)$7.50

Objectives
- Use word references
- Use context clues to determine meaning
- Use text features

Teach

E Text Element

Text Features Say: The graphic gives information about the amount and weight of similarly priced bags of peanuts at the ballpark and at the store. Use this information to compare what you get at the store with what you get at the ballpark. *(Possible responses: For the same price, you get more than four times more peanuts at the store than you do at the ballpark; at the ballpark, you get a quarter of the peanuts you get at the store.)* **AL**

C Critical Thinking

Evaluation Ask: Who makes more from the sale of a hot dog at the ballpark—the food service workers or the concession company? *(the food service workers)* **OL Ask:** Who do you think should make the most from food sales at the ballpark? Why? *(Possible responses: the food service workers because they do the hardest work; the concession company because it has to buy the food items)* **AL**

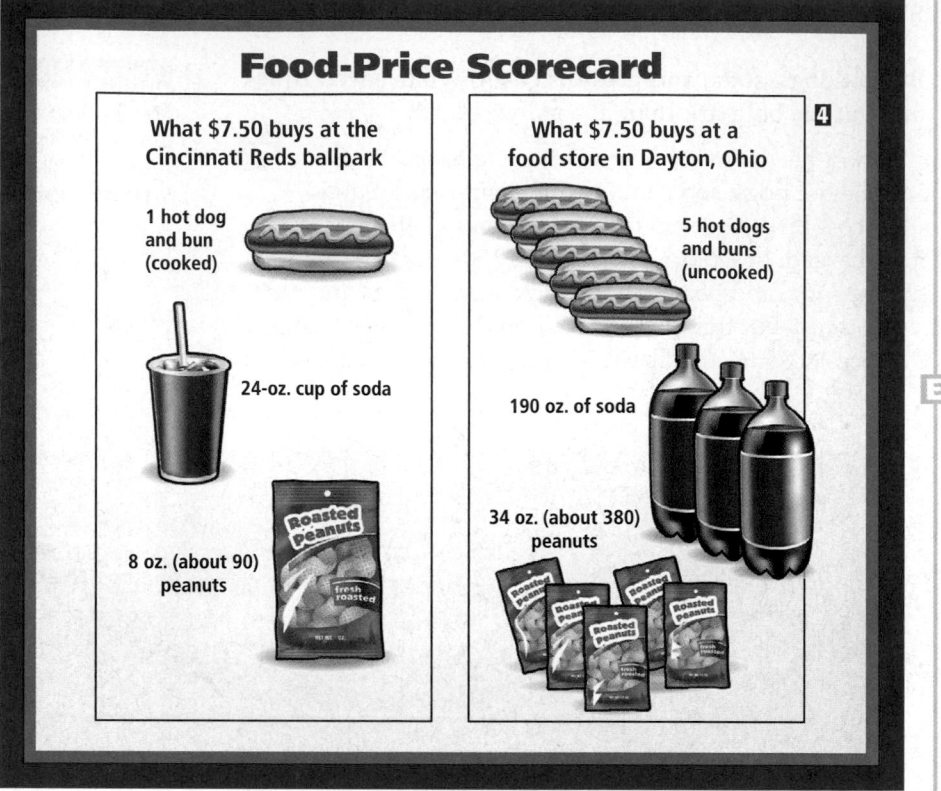

Food-Price Scorecard

What $7.50 buys at the Cincinnati Reds ballpark

1 hot dog and bun (cooked)

24-oz. cup of soda

8 oz. (about 90) peanuts

What $7.50 buys at a food store in Dayton, Ohio 4

5 hot dogs and buns (uncooked)

190 oz. of soda

34 oz. (about 380) peanuts

E

Analyzing the Graphic Complete this sentence to summarize what you learn from the "Food-Price Scorecard": The next time I go to the ballpark, I'll be sure to . . .

2. B! Of the $2.50 you pay for a hot dog at a ballpark, only 50¢ goes for the cost of the hot dog and bun!

If the hot dog and bun and all the fixings only cost the concession companies (food-sellers) 50¢, where does the other $2 go? Wages for **vendors** who sell the hot dogs come to 50¢. The concession **company** takes 25¢ as a profit, and 25¢ covers cleaning, phones, and other costs. The biggest chunk of that hog-dog price ($1.00) goes to the baseball team and stadium owners! 5

Vocabulary

vendors (VEN durz) *n.* people who sell products or services

14 **UNIT 1** Why Read?

Practice the Skills

4 Key Text Element

Text Features Do you think the question and answer form of the text helps you understand the material better? Why or why not?

5 English Language Coach

Word References Some words have more than one meaning. You can find all the meanings for a word in a dictionary. What are two meanings for the word **company**?

Additional Support

Reading Fluency

Question and Answer To build fluency have students practice reading aloud the quiz questions and answers. Have students work with a partner, taking turns posing as the moderator and contestant on a quiz show. The moderator should practice reading each question and its possible answers clearly. The contestant should respond by reading the correct answer and its explanation smoothly. When they can read and respond fluently, then they should switch roles and begin the activity again. **EL BL**

Hot dog and bun
50¢

Team and stadium owners
$1.00

Food-service workers
50¢

Concession company
25¢

Cleaning supplies, telephones and other costs
25¢

Analyzing the Graphic Who gets the greatest amount of the money you spend on a hot dog at the ballpark? How much do they get for each hot dog?

3. **A! Yes, most ballparks will let you bring in your own food.**

Visual Vocabulary
Turnstiles are posts that allow only one person at a time to pass through an entrance on foot.

Nearly all major-league stadiums say they'll let fans bring food from home. When our Snack Squad brought their own food, some were stopped at the turnstiles and asked to open their packs. "They were just looking for cans," reported Peter, 11. **Ushers** have the right to inspect bags and take away glass bottles, cans, thermoses, and other items that could be thrown onto the field. Juice boxes and plastic bottles are usually okay. In the end, *none* of our testers had their food taken away.

4. **C! Snack Squad kids spotted dozens of ads in the ballparks they visited.**

Kids spotted ads on their scorecards, ticket stubs, and seatbacks. They saw ads on lighting towers and at the concession stands. According to Tess, the sneakiest ads at the Oakland Coliseum were on the big-screen TV. "Right after replays, when everyone's attention was on the big screen, they showed commercials," she said. **6 7** ○

Vocabulary
ushers (USH urz) *n.* people who help others find their seats in a theater or stadium

Practice the Skills

6 Key Reading Skill

Setting a Purpose for Reading Suppose your purpose for reading this article was to answer the question "Can I bring my own food to a ballpark?" How would that change *how* you read the selection? Write your answer in your Learner's Notebook.

BIG Question

7 Why might a baseball fan want to read this selection? How does this help you answer the Big Question? Write your answer on the "Ballpark Food" page of Foldable 1. Your response will help you answer the Unit Challenge later. **BQ**

Teach

C Critical Thinking

Analysis Ask: Why do people buy food at the ballpark when they know it's cheaper to buy it at the store? *(Possible responses: They don't have time to stop at the store; it's more convenient to buy the food at the ballpark; they can get cold drinks and freshly cooked hot dogs at the ballpark; they think they are not allowed to bring their own food.)* **OL**

BQ

Ask: What new or especially interesting information did you learn from reading this selection? *(Possible responses: You can bring your own food to most ballparks; teams and stadium owners make a lot of money from food sales at ballparks.)* **OL**

Assess

✓CheckPoint

Use the CheckPoint questions provided on Presentation Plus! to check for comprehension of the selection. These questions can be used with interactive response keypads for immediate student feedback.

English Language Coach

Comparative and Superlative Adjectives *Sneakiest* is the superlative form of the adjective *sneaky*. *Sneakier* is the comparative form. Explain that the comparative form compares one person or thing with another while the superlative form compares one person or thing with several others. For adjectives with one syllable, and some adjectives with two syllables, add *-er* to form the comparative and *-est* to form the superlative. Also note that the *y* in adjectives such as *sneaky* changes to *i* when the comparative and superlative of these adjectives are formed. Have students practice forming comparatives and superlatives of *big*. **EL**

Objectives
• Use text features
• Analyze text
• Evaluate text
• Use modifiers: comparative and superlative adjectives

15

Assess

Resources for page 16

📁 Selection Quick Check, p. 1

📁 Selection and Unit Assessment, p. 1

⊕ ExamView Assessment Suite

⊕ Interactive Tutor: Self-Assessment

Students can respond to the *After You Read* items in their Learner's Notebooks or on a separate sheet of paper.

Answering the
BIG Question

1. Responses will vary.
2. Ballpark food is expensive.
3. You see commercials.

Critical Thinking

4. Possible response: Money from food sales goes to workers, concession companies, supplies and services, and the team and stadium owners.

5. Possible response: Owners don't want people throwing things on the field that could hurt someone.

6. Possible response: People might bring their own food because they will know that they are allowed to do so and that it will save them money.

After You Read | Ballpark Food

Answering the BIG Question

1. Think about the article you just read. Explain why you would–or would not–recommend this article to a friend.

2. **Recall** What problem with ballpark food does the writer mention in the first paragraph?
   Tip **Right There** You will find the answer in the text.

3. **Recall** At the Oakland Coliseum, what do you see after replays on the big-screen TV?
   Tip **Right There** You will find the answer in the text.

Critical Thinking

4. **Analyze** Why does food cost so much more at a ballpark than at a store?
   Tip **Author and Me** You will find clues in the text, but you must also use the information in your head.

5. **Analyze** Why don't stadium owners want people to bring in bottles, cans, or thermoses?
   Tip **Author and Me** You will find clues in the text, but you must also use the information in your head.

6. **Apply** How might reading this selection be helpful to someone who is going to a ballpark?
   Tip **On My Own** Answer from your own experiences.

Talk About Your Reading

Discuss this article with a partner. Think about these topics as you discuss "Ballpark Food":

• Which text features did you find the most helpful and why?

• Pick out one passage in the text that is *surprising,* another passage that is *important,* and finally, pick out something you will *remember* from the reading and be able to use outside of class. Discuss these passages with your partner.

• Share your purpose for reading with your partner, and talk about something in "Ballpark Food" that you'd like to learn more about.

Objectives (pp. 16–17)
Reading Set a purpose for reading
Informational Text Use text features: title, subtitle, deck
Vocabulary Use word references: dictionary, glossary
Grammar Identify parts of speech

Talk About Your Reading

Possible responses:

• The graphics were the most helpful because they made it easier to compare spending at the ballpark and at the store. They also showed where the profits from food sales go and who benefits most from the high prices of ballpark food.

• The most surprising passage compares what you can buy with $7.50 at a store with what you get for the same price at a ballpark; the most important passage explains the huge profit from ballpark food and who gets most of it; I'll remember that I can bring my own food to most ballparks.

• Responses will vary.

Skills Review

Key Reading Skill: Setting a Purpose for Reading

7. Look at the purpose (or purposes) for reading that you wrote in your Learner's Notebook. Did your purpose for reading change? Why or why not? Explain your answer in your Learner's Notebook.

Key Text Element: Text Features

8. Do you think it was a good idea for the writers to use a multiple-choice quiz at the beginning of "Ballpark Food?" Explain.

9. Why did the writers use sentences in dark type at the beginning of each answer?

10. Which text feature did you find most helpful? Explain.

Vocabulary Check

In your Learner's Notebook, use your own words to write the meaning of each vocabulary word.

11. **vendors**

12. **ushers**

13. **Academic Vocabulary** Which part of a newspaper article is the text?

14. **English Language Coach** Use a dictionary to find two meanings for the word *bill.* Then write two sentences, each using the word *bill* in a different way.

Web Activities For eFlashcards, Selection Quick Checks, and other Web activities, go to www.glencoe.com.

Grammar Link: Parts of Speech

Words can be organized into eight groups called **parts of speech.** Each part of speech describes what a particular kind of word does. Here's an overview of the eight parts:

What is it?	What does it do?
Noun	names a person, a place, or a thing
Verb	shows action or state of being
Pronoun	takes the place of a noun
Adjective	tells which one, what kind, how many
Adverb	tells how, when, where, how much
Preposition	helps show space, time, position
Conjunction	connects words or groups of words
Interjection	expresses feeling

In many cases you'll need to see a word in a sentence before you can know what part of speech it is.

In the first sentence below, for example, *phone* works as a verb. In the second sentence, *phone* works as a noun. In the third sentence, *phone* works as an adjective.

- **Verb: Phone** Jody and ask if she's coming with us.
  (*Phone* shows action.)
- **Noun:** We bought a new **phone** and gave Max the old one.
  (*Phone* names a thing.)
- **Adjective:** They had a **phone** conversation six days ago.
  (*Phone* describes the conversation.)

Grammar Practice

Write two sentences for each word listed below. In the first sentence, use the word as a verb. In the second sentence, use the word as a noun. Label the word *noun* or *verb.*

show   surprise   roll

Ballpark Food   **17**

Skills Review

Key Reading Skill: Setting a Purpose for Reading

7. Possible response: When I looked at the title and the picture, my purpose for reading was to find out why ballpark food is so expensive. When I started taking the quiz, my purpose for reading changed because I wanted to find out whether my answers were correct.

Key Text Element: Text Features

8. Possible response: Yes, the quiz grabs readers' interest and gets them involved in the selection.

9. Possible response: Readers can choose to read only the sentences in dark type for quick answers. If they want more information, they can continue reading.

10. Possible response: the scorecard because it shows how much more food $7.50 will buy at a store

Vocabulary Check

11. Possible response: people who sell things

12. Possible response: people who show you to your seat

13. **Academic Vocabulary** Possible response: all of the printed or written words of the article

14. **English Language Coach** Possible responses: The bill showed what we needed to pay. Congress will write a bill to limit the cost of ballpark food.

Grammar Link: Parts of Speech

Grammar Practice

Sample responses:
Show me what you bought. (*verb*)
We met them after the show. (*noun*)

He surprised them with a gift. (*verb*)
The surprise was a new puppy. (*noun*)

The ball rolled into the street. (*verb*)
She put butter on the roll. (*noun*)

Close

Ask students to summarize what they learned from reading "Ballpark Food" to help them answer the Big Question.

Teach

More About the Author

Amy Bertrand not only writes about health and fitness but also runs marathons and has a black belt in karate. A graduate of the University of Missouri-Columbia, Bertrand wrote news, sports, and feature stories for the *St. Louis Post-Dispatch* before starting its Health and Fitness section. She also shares fitness tips on a regular TV show in the St. Louis area.

EL Language Coach

Word References Say: A thesaurus is a useful tool for expanding vocabulary and making writing more descriptive. Thesauruses are available online and in word-processing software, as well as in book form. Write a paragraph that describes a person, place, or thing. Be sure to use vivid descriptions in your writing. Then use a thesaurus to find synonyms for at least five words in your paragraph. *(Responses will vary.)* **AS**

Before You Read

How He Did It: Health Advice, Kid-to-Kid

Meet the Author

Amy Bertrand is the Health and Fitness Editor for the *St. Louis Post-Dispatch* newspaper.

Author Search For more about Amy Bertrand, go to www.glencoe.com.

Objectives (pp. 18–23)
Reading Set a purpose for reading
Informational Text Use text features: title, subtitle, deck
Vocabulary Use word references: thesaurus

Vocabulary Preview

obesity (oh BEE si tee) *n.* condition of being extremely overweight **(p. 20)** *Obesity is a serious health problem.*

advisory (ad VY zuh ree) *adj.* having the power to give advice **(p. 21)** *The school formed an advisory group to recommend a change in the dress code.*

administrator (ad MIN i stray tur) *n.* person who manages or directs **(p. 21)** *The administrator makes sure that all work is done on time.*

calories (KAL uh reez) *n.* units used to measure the energy supplied by food **(p. 22)** *Some foods have more calories than others.*

ultimate (UL tuh mut) *adj.* greatest; most important **(p. 22)** *My ultimate hope is that the Web site helps someone who has questions.*

Partner Talk Give your partner a clue to one of the words above (for example, "it is a health problem"). Have your partner name the vocabulary word without looking at the book. Take turns until you both know the words and their definitions.

English Language Coach

Word References A thesaurus is a dictionary of synonyms, or words with similar meanings. A thesaurus can be helpful when you are unsure of a word's meaning, or if you are looking for words with similar meanings.

Look at this thesaurus entry for the word *lively*.

> **lively** *adjective*
> 1. very brisk, alert, and high-spirited:
> *a lively personality*
> **Syns:** animated, bouncy, peppy

Partner Talk With a partner, use a thesaurus to find at least two words with similar meanings to each underlined word.

1. She will <u>walk</u> to the store.
2. It was a <u>hot</u> day.
3. I <u>admire</u> that singer.

18 UNIT 1 Why Read?

Additional Support

Author Search To expand students' appreciation of Amy Bertrand, have them access the Web site for additional information and resources.

Differentiated Instruction

Pronouncing Unfamiliar Words The Vocabulary Preview includes the correct pronunciation for each vocabulary word. Guide students in pronouncing the words as indicated. Explain that they can also sound out an unfamiliar word if no pronunciation is given. Tell students to divide the word into syllables, sounding out each one. They can then put all the sounds together to say the whole word. Have students practice sounding out these words: *cardio, council, dietitian.* **EL** **BL**

Skills Preview

Key Reading Skill: Setting a Purpose for Reading

"How He Did It: Health Advice, Kid-to-Kid" is about a boy who is concerned about overweight kids and creates a Web site to help them stay fit. Why would you want to read this article? Maybe you have questions about fitness or a healthy diet. Maybe you have a similar idea that might help others.

Write to Learn Write your purpose for reading in your Learner's Notebook.

Key Text Element: Text Features

Titles can have a lot of information in them or just a little. They can catch your attention and make you want to read.

- If You Traveled on the Underground Railroad
- Green Eggs and Ham
- Here, There and Everywhere: My Life Recording the Music of the Beatles

The first title gives you a good idea of what the book is about. The second one suggests that the book will be funny. (You hope!) The last title doesn't tell you much, but it has a **subtitle** that does. A subtitle usually comes after a colon and adds more information to the title.

Another text feature that gives more information is a **deck.** A deck is a sentence or two that tells you about something you are going to read.

Write to Learn Find a text feature that you found helpful. Write a short paragraph telling how it helped you understand what you were reading.

Interactive Literary Elements Handbook
To review or learn more about the literary elements, go to www.glencoe.com.

Get Ready to Read

Connect to the Reading

Name an important project you've done. Maybe you had to do a project for science, math, or language arts class. What kinds of text features did you include in your project? Explain.

Partner Talk With a partner, make a list of projects that you think might be interesting for kids your age to do.

Build Background

In this article you'll learn how a boy named Robert starts a little project that turns into a big help for overweight kids.

- Body fat is important for good health, but too much body fat can lead to health problems.
- When the body stores too much fat, it can result in obesity.
- Obesity can lead to health problems such as high blood pressure and heart disease.
- Health officials are worried that obesity is an epidemic, or a rapidly spreading disease.
- Robert's Web site, which is no longer online, encouraged kids to make good decisions about diet and exercise.

Set Purposes for Reading

BIG Question Read the selection "How He Did It: Health Advice, Kid-to-Kid" to find out about how you can make healthy choices.

Set Your Own Purpose What else would you like to learn from the article to help you answer the Big Question? Remember that you can have more than one purpose. Write your own purpose on the "How He Did It: Health Advice, Kid-to-Kid" page of Foldable 1.

Keep Moving

Use these skills as you read the following selection.

Teach

R Reading Skill

Setting a Purpose for Reading Say: All types of writing have a main purpose, or goal. The purpose of fiction is to tell a story. Nonfiction tells about real people, places, and events. The informational text found in newspapers, magazines, and many Web sites is a type of nonfiction. The main purpose of informational text is to inform readers about a topic. Name something you have read that was meant to inform. *(Possible response: "Ballpark Food")* Name something that you have read that was meant to inform, entertain, or persuade. *(Possible responses: a newspaper editorial; a movie review)* **AS**

Literature Online

Interactive Literary Elements Handbook Have students access the Web site to improve their understanding of text features.

Literature Focus Lesson

Text Features While titles and subtitles are made up of phrases or sentences that include important information, graphics give readers information through a visual format. They help readers make sense of what the text is saying, and they are also used to make reading more interesting. Graphics such as timelines, maps, and tables usually appear in history and social studies textbooks. Have students read a short article with a graphic. Invite them to discuss what information that graphic adds to the article. **OL**

Objectives
- Use word references
- Set a purpose for reading
- Use text features

Teach

E **Text Element**

Text Features Say: This newspaper article has text features that are found in most kinds of informational text. What text features are included on the first page of the article? *(Possible responses: title or headline, subtitle or deck, art or picture)* **BL** What do you think is the purpose of each text feature? *(Possible responses: The title sparks interest; the subtitle tells more about the article's topic; the art suggests activities related to the topic.)* **OL**

Readability Scores
Dale-Chall: 6.7
DRP: 61
Lexile: 910

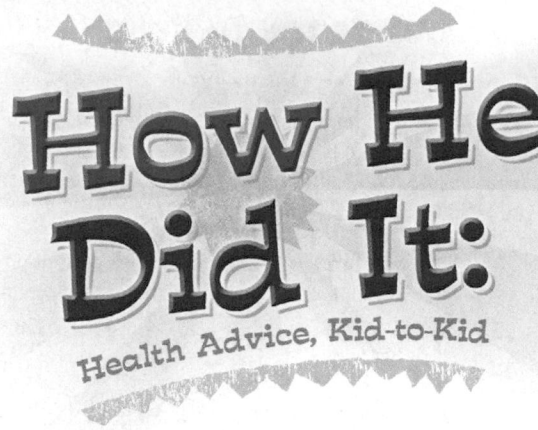

How He Did It:

Health Advice, Kid-to-Kid

by Amy Bertrand

Sixth-grader's Web site helps other children stay fit. **1**

Ever since Robert Kohn can remember, his parents have stressed the importance of healthy eating and exercise.

"I think I've heard about it forever," he says.

That education led to a remarkable project by Robert, a sixth-grader. For a school project, he wrote a research paper on childhood **obesity**, then created an advisory council on it, which in turn led to a Web site, created especially for use by children.

Robert's not known for being big into team sports at school, says his mom, Dee Dee, but he still values the importance of working out. He plays golf and tennis and works out about two days a week in a gym, lifting weights and "focusing on cardio[1] right now," he says.

He's never had a weight problem, but knows kids who have.

"It's a huge problem," he says.

That's why he wanted to **tackle** it for his school project. **2**

---

1. **Cardio** is short for *cardiovascular,* meaning of the heart and blood vessels. Exercise that increases heart rate is often referred to as *cardio.*

Vocabulary . . . .

obesity (oh BEE si tee) *n.* condition of being extremely overweight

20 UNIT 1 Why Read?

Practice the Skills

1 **Key Text Element**

Text Features Read the subtitle and the deck, which is right below the writer's name. Do they give you information that might help you set a purpose for reading?

2 **English Language Coach**

Word References What does it mean to **tackle** a problem? Use a dictionary to find the meaning of *tackle* that is used here.

Additional Support

English Language Coach

Word Meanings Doctors often have a technical definition for a medical term. In the case of *obesity,* doctors don't all agree on an exact definition. Most say that it is the condition of being twenty percent or more above one's ideal body weight. Doctors also agree that the main causes of obesity are eating too many calories and exercising too little.

Word Forms The word *obesity* is the noun form of the adjective *obese. Obesity* means "the condition of being extremely overweight." Many adjectives become nouns when you add *-ity.* Have students identify the "other" form of each of these words: *able, activity, captive, equal, falsity, negativity, scarcity.* **AS**

The project:

In his language arts class, students were required to come up with a topic that would be used in a three-pronged,[2] yearlong project. The first part of the project was to write a research paper; the second part was to come up with an action plan; and the third portion was to get someone to take action.

Robert began by reading books and searching the Web. He found quite a bit of information on the topic, but not much of it was directed at children.

So, he put together an **advisory** council on the subject, which included teachers, a dietitian,[3] a hospital **administrator** and a chef. They met a couple of times and helped Robert cultivate information[4] for his next big project: creating a Web site just for kids. **3**

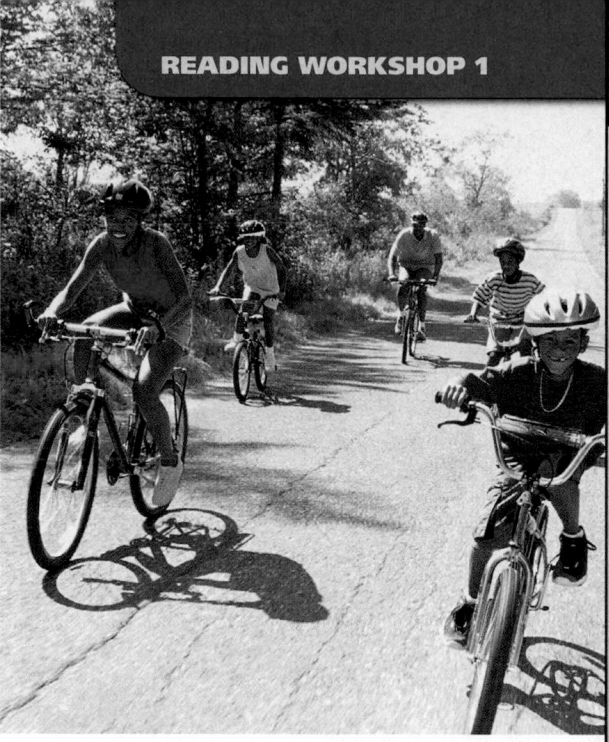

Analyzing the Photo Do you think that this would be a good picture to appear on Robert's Web site? Why or why not?

The Web site:

What resulted was **www.healthychoicesforkids.com.**

Robert gathered all of the information he wanted to include, then sketched out what he wanted each page of the Web site to look like, along with the words to go on it. A professional designed the Web site for him, and the result is a kid-friendly site with kid-friendly graphics. It's easy to navigate and written in a language kids can easily understand.

---

2. **Three-pronged** means that the project has three parts.
3. A **dietitian** is an expert in planning meals or diets.
4. When someone **cultivates information,** he or she prepares and organizes it in a way that is clear and easy to follow.

Vocabulary

advisory (ad VY zuh ree) *adj.* having the power to give advice

administrator (ad MIN i stray tur) *n.* person who manages or directs

Practice the Skills

3 **Key Reading Skill**

Setting a Purpose for Reading Has your purpose for reading changed now that you've started to read the article? Think about your original purpose, and then think of a second purpose for reading.

How He Did It **21**

Text Features Ask: What are the article's subheads? *(The project, The Web site, and The action plan)* **BL** What is the purpose of the subheads? *(to divide the article into sections)* **OL** What do the subheads tell you about Robert's project? *(Possible response: It went through several stages, starting as a school project, then developing into a Web site, and finally becoming a plan for action.)* **AL**

C **Critical Thinking**

Comprehension Ask: How did Robert get the idea to create a Web site to help kids stay fit? *(Possible response: He searched the Web but couldn't find information for kids on the topic.)* **OL**

Viewing the Photo
Ask: Why do you think this photograph is included in the article? *(Possible responses: to show that biking is a good way to keep fit; to show that doing something outdoors is a good way to stay healthy)* **OL**

Reading in the Real World

College Students should begin developing the research skills needed to write college papers. One of the first research steps is to find information about a topic. The library houses excellent resources. Students can find computers there with access to the Internet. Most libraries have an online catalog that lists all their holdings according to subject, title, or author. These materials include books, reference works, magazines and journals, newspapers, videotapes, audiotapes, and CDs. Have students browse the library's catalogue to find three titles pertaining to health and fitness. **OL** Challenge students to list three different kinds of sources. **AL**

Objectives
• Use text features
• Monitor comprehension
• Clarify word meanings

Teach

R Reading Skill

Setting a Purpose for Reading Say: If your purpose for reading is mainly to find out about the Web site that Robert created, you might scan the article for that information. What key words or phrases in the article point to the information you want? *(the subhead "The Web site" and the URL, or address, of the site)* OL

C Critical Thinking

Evaluation Ask: What do you think about Robert's action plan? Compare and contrast what you would have done to what Robert did. *(Responses will vary.)* Why do you think Robert wants lawmakers to take over his Web site eventually? *(Possible response: He believes that lawmakers have the power to reach and educate more people than he can.)*

BQ BIG Question

Ask: Why might Robert's Web site be helpful to those who want to lose weight? *(Possible response: People who want to lose weight will learn how to make better food choices and how many calories they can burn doing different activities.)* AS

Topics on the site include:

- How do I know if I'm overweight?
- What are the risks of being overweight?
- Portion sizes.
- Making healthy choices while dining out.
- How many **calories** do I burn during common activities?

"I'm hoping other kids get educated about obesity: What it is, the risks of being obese, how to get in better shape," Robert says. ▨

Analyzing the Graphic According to this food pyramid, what is one food *you* should eat more of for better health?

The action plan:

Robert's strong views on the subject took him to his next step: writing lawmakers.

"In my research I found HB 81,[5] a bill about having exercise and healthy foods at public schools," Robert says.

So he wrote the supporters of that bill, and though he's still waiting for confirmation, he's been asked to speak about his findings. C

"I think I'll tell them why I think childhood obesity is such a huge problem, how horrible obesity is and how many people are suffering," he says. "It can cause diseases like cancer, heart disease, high blood pressure."

His **ultimate** goal is to have the lawmakers take over his Web site. "I want to see what they can do." ▤ ○

---

5. *HB 81* means "House Bill 81," a proposed law on which Congress has been asked to vote.

Vocabulary

calories (KAL uh reez) *n.* units used to measure the energy supplied by food

ultimate (UL tuh mut) *adj.* greatest; most important

Practice the Skills

▨ **BIG Question**
What information could you read on Robert's Web site that might help you or someone you know? R

▤ **BIG Question**
Write three things that you learned from reading this article. Write your answer on the "How He Did It" page of Foldable 1. Your response will help you complete the Unit Challenge later. BQ

Additional Support

Differentiated Instruction

Interpreting Graphics Guide students in reading and interpreting the Activity Pyramid. Point out how the graphic is structured with activities for every day as the base of the pyramid, activities to be done less frequently in the middle, and little or no activity at the peak. Call on students to read aloud the explanatory text for the various labels on the pyramid. Model the pronunciation of less familiar words. EL BL OL

The Activity Pyramid

The Peak
Add daily activity to break up periods of sitting. Cut down on
- Watching TV
- Playing computer games
- Sitting for more than 30 minutes at a time

Leisure Activities
Do leisure activities a couple of times each week to add balance to your weekly Activity Pyramid. Leisure activities are low-level activities that don't expend as much energy as recreational activities. Examples include
- Badminton
- Frisbee

Flexibility and Strength
Flexibility exercises help improve or maintain muscle flexibility. Strength exercises help improve muscle strength if they are done two or three times per week. Flexibility examples include
- Gymnastics
- Stretching

Strength examples include
- Weight Machine
- Hand Weights

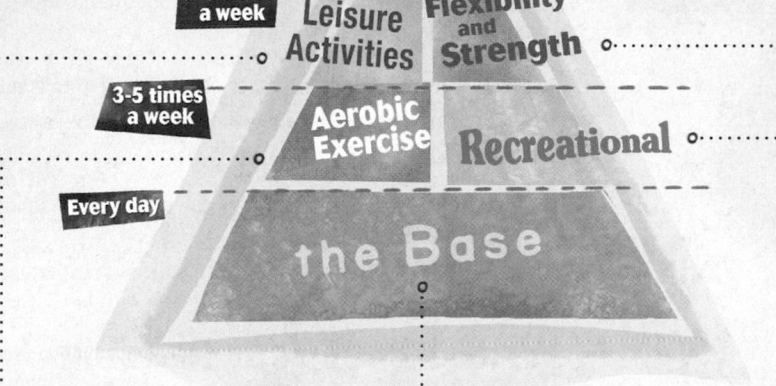

Cut Down On
the Peak
2-3 times a week
Leisure Activities
Flexibility and Strength
3-5 times a week
Aerobic Exercise
Recreational
Every day
the Base

Aerobic Exercise
Aerobic exercise—best for your heart—means moving continuously for 20 minutes or more. Examples include
- Running/Jogging
- Jumping Rope
- In-Line Skating

The Base
It's important for everyone to add as many steps as possible to each day. The goal is to try to get 30 minutes of activity every day. Activities at this level include
- Taking the stairs
- Walking or Biking

Recreational Activities
Recreational activities will also improve your health. It's fun to try these sports. Examples include
- Volleyball
- Racquetball
- Karate

How He Did It **23**

Teach

Viewing the Graphic
Say: Look at the graphic and read the labels. What do the colors on the graphic show? *(different activities)* **BL** Why do you think each activity is marked by a color? *(Possible response: That makes it easier to see which stripe in the pyramid represents a particular activity.)* **OL**

Assess

CheckPoint

Use the CheckPoint questions provided on Presentation Plus! to check for comprehension of the selection. These questions can be used with interactive response keypads for immediate student feedback.

Reading in the Real World

Citizenship Robert is a citizen of the state of Missouri. HB 81 is a bill before the Missouri House of Representatives. To become a law in the state of Missouri, the bill must be passed by both the state House of Representatives and the state Senate and be signed by the governor of Missouri. Challenge students to find out what the current standing of HB 81 is. Students may look for this information online at www.house.mo.gov. **OL** **AL**

Objectives
- Set a purpose for reading
- Use text features: graphics
- Evaluate text

Assess

Resources for page 24

📁 Selection Quick Check, p. 2

📁 Selection and Unit Assessment, p. 2

🌐 ExamView Assessment Suite

🌐 Interactive Tutor: Self-Assessment

Students can respond to the *After You Read* items in their Learner's Notebooks or on a separate sheet of paper.

Answering the

BIG Question

1. Responses will vary. Possible responses: to learn how to do something or to get information

2. He was concerned about childhood obesity.

3. oils

Critical Thinking

4. Responses will vary. Students' menus should include more grains, vegetables, milk, and fruits than meat, beans, and oils in the approximate proportions shown in the food pyramid.

5. Responses will vary. Students may say that Robert did not know how to do all that he needed to do. As a result, he sought help from experts.

6. Responses will vary.

After You Read

How He Did It: Health Advice, Kid-to-Kid

Answering the BIG Question

1. Why do people read articles like "How He Did It"?

2. **Recall** How did Robert choose his topic for his school project?

   Tip **Right There** You will find this information in the article.

3. **Recall** According to the food pyramid, what foods should you eat the least?

   Tip **Right There** You will find this information in the article.

Critical Thinking

4. **Apply** Plan a menu for tomorrow's meals that meets the food pyramid guidelines.

   Tip **Author and Me** You will find clues in the article, but you must also use the information in your head.

5. **Infer** Why did Robert ask other people for help to create his Web site?

   Tip **Author and Me** You will find clues in the article, but you must also use the information in your head.

6. **Evaluate** Should the government be involved in helping people decide what to eat? Explain.

   Tip **On Your Own** Answer from your own experiences.

Write About Your Reading

Think about a Web site you'd like to design to help people. The front page, or home page, of a Web site is what you see when you go to the site. Create the home page of your Web site on a blank piece of paper. Your home page should include the answers to these questions:

• What will the site be about; what is your purpose or goal?

• Who will it help?

• How will it help people?

• What will you call your Web site, and where will the title be?

• What kind of graphics will you have, and where will they be?

Think about other Web sites you have seen.

Objectives (pp. 24–25)
Reading Set a purpose for reading
Grammar Identify parts of speech: action verbs

24 UNIT 1 Why Read?

Write About Your Reading

Responses will vary. Students should cover all the bulleted items in designing their home page.

Skills Review

Key Reading Skill: Setting a Purpose for Reading

7. Review the sentence you wrote about your purpose for reading. Now write why your purpose stayed the same or why it changed as you read "How He Did It."

Key Text Element: Text Features

8. Look again at the Activity Pyramid. Do you think this is a good title for it? Explain your answer.

9. Think about the title and subtitle of this article, "How He Did It: Health Advice, Kid-to-Kid." Which part gives you more information? Explain your answer.

Vocabulary Check

In your Learner's Notebook write the words matched with their correct definition below. Then write a sentence for each word.

administrator   advisory
obesity   calories
ultimate

10. condition of being overweight

11. given the power to inform or give opinions

12. person who manages or directs

13. units used to measure the energy supplied by food

14. greatest; most important

15. **English Language Coach** What is the meaning of the word *wages*? Use a thesaurus to find two words that have a meaning similar to that of *wages*.

Web Activities For eFlashcards, Selection Quick Checks, and other Web activities, go to www.glencoe.com.

Grammar Link: Action Verbs

A verb is a word that shows an action or a state of being. **Action verbs** show what someone or something does.

Many action verbs are easy to spot, but some are not. To find an action verb, look for what something or someone *does*. In the following paragraph, all of the words in italics are physical or mental actions.

Ginny *walks* to school. Harvey *runs* to catch up. Leo *jumps* onto the sidewalk. Harvey and Ginny *leap* in surprise. At school, Ginny *reads* her textbook, Harvey *writes* a report, and Leo *dreams* about the weekend.

Some action verbs might be less obvious. Some action verbs show what someone or something is *thinking* or *feeling*.

Tania *cares* about all living things, but she really *loves* cats and dogs. She *wants* a kitten, but her mom *dislikes* pets.

Grammar Practice

Underline the action verbs in the following sentences.

16. Aisha and Frank share a seat on the bus.

17. During the game, Lisa twisted her ankle.

18. Grandpa plants a new crop of peppers every year.

19. I respect Quinn's talent as a singer.

Writing Application

Look at your Web site design page and circle all the action verbs you can find.

Skills Review

Key Reading Skill: Setting a Purpose for Reading

7. Possible response: My purpose stayed the same because the article answered most of the questions I had before reading.

Key Text Element: Text Features

8. six

9. grains; oils

Vocabulary Check

Sample responses:

10. obesity; Childhood obesity is a serious problem.

11. advisory; The advisory group made many helpful suggestions.

12. administrator; The hospital administrator shared tips for staying healthy.

13. calories; You won't burn many calories watching TV.

14 ultimate; Her ultimate concern is the safety of her children.

15. **English Language Coach** Possible responses: Wages are pay for work; *salary* and *earnings*

Close

Ask students to write in their Learner's Notebooks what they learned from Robert's story about the Big Question.

Grammar Link: Action Verbs

Grammar Practice

16. share

17. twisted

18. plants

19. respect

Summary

Objectives covered in this workshop:
• **Writing** Write a summary indentifying main idea and details

Teaching Students to Write a Summary

Why Is It Important?

• Writing a summary of a selection will help students retain information better and understand concepts more easily.

• Discerning the main idea and supporting details in a text will improve students' organizational skills in their own writing.

• Summarizing is a skill that can be applied to any kind of writing, fiction or nonfiction.

• Editing for focus is very important for summaries; building this skill will help students keep writing focused when they create longer products.

How to Help Students Get It

• Talk about examples of summaries in real life. For example, abstracts in the library, video game reviews that summarize all the levels of play, the news "blurbs" that lead into the full length coverage of a story, or the plot summaries on the backs of movies.

• Lead the class through the construction of a summary, using a text they are all familiar with, such as a fairy tale.

• Ask students to answer the following questions about the story they choose to summarize: Who, What, When, Where, Why, How?

• Discuss the importance of including references; the summary is not meant to replace the original document, but must help readers find the original document.

• Some students may benefit from hearing their summaries read aloud, or reading aloud to a peer. This "fresh take" on the material can help a student separate important main ideas from supporting details.

The Writing Trait: Ideas

Recognition of the seven Traits of Good Writing is especially helpful to students as they revise their writing. See the chart on the next page for descriptions of each trait and brief checklists students can use as they revise their work.

The Writing Workshops of each unit focus on one trait. Introduce and discuss all seven traits in Writing Workshop 1 of Unit 1, and then have students focus on the Unit 1 trait (see chart) in Writing Workshop 2. Although each unit focuses on one trait, you might want to occasionally review all seven.

Writing Trait	Student Checklist
Ideas: the message or the theme and the details that develop it	• Does the title suggest the theme of the composition? • Does the composition focus on a single narrow topic? • Is the thesis, or main idea, clearly stated? • Do well-chosen details elaborate the main idea?
Organization: the arrangement of main points and supporting details	• Are the beginning, middle, and end clearly linked? • Is the order of ideas easy to follow? • Does the introduction capture readers' attention? • Do sentences and paragraphs flow from one to the next in a way that makes sense? • Does the conclusion wrap up the composition?
Voice: a writer's unique way of using tone and style	• Does the writing sound interesting when read aloud? • Does the writing show what the writer thinks about the topic? • Does the writing sound like the writer—or does it sound like the writer is imitating someone else?
Word Choice: the vocabulary a writer uses to convey meaning	• Does the writer use lively verbs to show action? • Does the writer use vivid words to create word pictures in the readers' minds? • Does the writer use precise words to explain his or her ideas simply and clearly?
Sentence Fluency: the smooth rhythm and flow of sentences that vary in length and style	• Do sentences vary in length and structure? • Do transition words and phrases show connections between ideas and sentences? • Does parallelism help balance and unify related ideas?
Conventions: correct spelling, grammar, usage, and mechanics	• Are all words spelled correctly? • Are all proper nouns—as well as the first word of every sentence—capitalized? • Is the composition free of sentence fragments and run-on sentences? • Are punctuation marks—such as apostrophes, commas, and end marks—inserted in the right places?
Presentation: the way words and design elements look on a page	Appearance matters, so encourage students to make their compositions inviting to read. Handwritten papers should be neat and legible. If a word processor is used, the text should be double spaced and the font should be readable. Encourage students to also use other design elements—such as boldfaced headings, bulleted lists, pictures, and charts—to make their papers attractive and inviting.

Unit Focus

Workshop Resources

PACING (DAYS) STANDARD	BLOCK	LESSON	STUDENT MATERIALS	TEACHER RESOURCES
1	1/2	Writing Workshop Part 1: Prewriting and Drafting	• Writing Workshop Graphic Organizer, p. 15 • Grammar Practice, p. 16 • Spelling and Handwriting Practice, p. 45 • Grammar and Composition Handbook, p 101 • Real Success in Writing: Research and Reports	• TeacherWorks Plus™ • Presentation Plus! • Rubrics for Assessing Student Writing, Listening, and Speaking, p. 11 • Grammar and Writing Workshop Transparencies 1–2
2	1	Writing Workshop Part 2: Editing, Revising, and Presenting	• Interactive Grammar and Language Workbook • Grammar and Composition Handbook, p. 101 • Listening and Speaking, p. 28 • Viewing and Representing, p. 29	• Grammar and Writing Workshop Transparencies 17–18

Focus

Summary
Prewriting and Drafting

BELLRINGER Options

Daily Language Practice Transparency 4
Focus Activity Ask: What did you do yesterday? *(Responses will vary.)* What you just shared is a summary. Next you'll write a summary of a selection in this unit. As you prepare, think of why a reader would read the selection.

Teach

R Reading Skill

Skimming and Scanning Say: Scan the selections listed under *Get Ready to Write.* Find words and phrases that give clues to each selection's main idea. Which selection will you summarize? Explain your choice. *(Responses will vary.)* **AS**

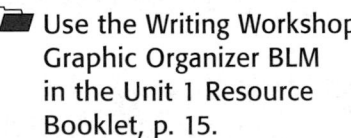
Resources for page 26

📁 Use the Writing Workshop Graphic Organizer BLM in the Unit 1 Resource Booklet, p. 15.

 Use the Grammar and Writing Workshop Transparencies 1–2.

ASSIGNMENT Write a summary

Purpose: Summarize main ideas and important details

Audience: You, your teacher, and some classmates

Writing Rubric

As you work through this assignment, you should

- write a summary of a selection you've read
- state the main idea in your own words
- correctly use linking verbs
- include important details
- leave out minor details
- correctly use linking verbs

See page 66 in Part 2 for a model of a summary.

Objectives (pp. 26–29)
Writing Use the writing process: prewriting, drafting • Paraphrase and summarize text: main ideas and supporting details
Grammar Identify parts of speech: linking verbs

Writing a summary of a selection in this unit will help you answer the Unit 1 Big Question: Why Read?

What Is It? A summary is a short piece of writing that retells the main idea and important details of a story or an event in your own words.

Prewriting
Get Ready to Write

In this workshop you'll write a summary about one of these selections:
- "Animal Attraction"
- "How He Did It: Health Advice, Kid-to-Kid"

Gather Ideas

After you choose the selection you want to summarize, read that selection again. As you reread, answer these questions in your Learner's Notebook:
- What is the selection's main, or most important, idea?
- Who or what is this selection about?
- What are the most important details?
- What happens in this selection?

Drafting
Start Writing!

It's time to start your summary. Whether you feel ready or not, get your pencil out and start writing!

Get It on Paper

These tips can help you start your summary:
- Look at the notes you made about the main points of the selection.
- Write the main idea in your own words.
- Write details that will help readers understand the main idea.
- Use your own words—don't copy what the author wrote.

Additional Support

Differentiated Instruction

Organizing Ideas Some students may have trouble organizing ideas into a structured paragraph. These students may have more success if they first write each idea on a separate note card. Tell students to arrange and rearrange the note cards until they are satisfied with the order of ideas. Then they can use these ideas in the final order as a basis for their summaries. **OL**

Applying Good Writing Traits

Ideas

One of the best things about writing is that you get to share your ideas with other people. The ideas you share when you write may be yours, or they may belong to someone else like a friend, a family member, an author, or an expert on the topic you are writing about.

What Are Ideas?

Ideas are the important points a writer or speaker expresses.

- In nonfiction, the most important idea is called the **main idea.** The main idea is what you want readers to remember the most from your writing.
- In fiction, the main idea is called the **theme.**
- An **important detail** explains a lot about the main idea or the theme.
- A less important detail is called a **minor detail.**

Why Are They Important?

- People write for the purpose of sharing ideas.
- The main idea tells the reader what the rest of the writing will be about.

How Do I Do It?

1. **Main Idea** Write the main idea in one simple sentence.
2. **Important Detail** Write another sentence that explains the main idea.
3. **Minor Detail** Include a specific detail that relates to the important detail.

Analyzing Cartoons Imagine that the person in this cartoon is a writer. What do the light bulbs represent? What size light bulbs does the writer want to catch?

In the example below, Damon writes about his day. Notice that he includes a main idea, an important detail, and a minor detail.

Today I had a really good day (**main idea**). *I got an A on the French quiz* (**important detail**) *that I studied really hard for* (**minor detail**). *After school, my basketball team won our game* (**important detail**). *The team we played was really tough* (**minor detail**).

When you write a summary, find the author's main idea and important details. Include the main idea and the most important details in your summary. Remember that summaries are short retellings of an original work, so don't include the minor details.

Write to Learn Write a paragraph about a good day that you had recently. This will be your main idea. Include important details that tell your

Teach

W Writing

Main Idea and Supporting Details Share the following paragraph from Nancy Gibbs's article with students. Ask them to identify the main idea and any major details in the paragraph.

As in real life, Harry's world is exciting but not perfect. (*main idea*) Wizards have worries and egos and worn-out robes that they are embarrassed to wear. (*major detail*) Even in Harry's magical world, there's no spell that fills a person's head with knowledge. (*major detail*) The best Hermione can do in Book 3 is the Time Turner, which gives her more hours to study. Learning takes time for characters in a book as well as for real-life humans. (*major detail*)

Then have students label the paragraphs in their responses to the *Write to Learn* activity in the same way. **OL**

Reading in the Real World

College Explain that most college courses require students to write research papers. To do so, students need to read a variety of texts to support their main arguments. They also summarize these texts in their own words in order to remember the content and to include the ideas within their research papers. Ask students what idea in the selection they have chosen to summarize could be used for a research paper. For example, "The Real Magic of Harry Potter" could be used for a research paper about magic in young adult fiction. **OL AL**

Objectives
- Write a summary
- Include main idea and supporting details
- Distinguish between major and minor detail
- Review skimming and scanning

Teach

W Writing

Summary Say: An article or an essay will contain main ideas and major and minor details. What should be included in a summary? *(Possible response: A summary should include only the main ideas and the major details.)* Remember that each major detail in your summary must support the main idea. **OL**

Assess

Have students exchange drafts of their summaries with a partner and critique each other's work. Did the partner include all the main ideas? Did the partner include all important details? Did the partner include any unnecessary details? After a few minutes, tell each student to assess his or her partner's feedback, make any needed revisions, and save the revised draft for later use. **AL**

Literature Online

Writing Models Have students access the Web site for an additional and interactive Writing Workshop-based student model.

Literature Online

Writing Models For models and other writing activities, go to www.glencoe.com.

Writing Tip ▶

Authors write for many reasons:
- to persuade
- to explain
- to inform
- to entertain

Knowing why the author is writing will help you find the main idea to include in your summary.

Writing Tip ▶

Summaries include the main idea and the most important details. Remove any extra or unnecessary information from your summary.

Writing Tip ▶

Paraphrase by briefly retelling what you just read. Paraphrasing helps you understand and remember the selection.

Building Your Draft

Form

Your summary should be written in paragraph form. A paragraph is a series of sentences that are all about the same topic. When you write a summary, the topic of the paragraph is the main idea of the selection that you are summarizing.

Structure

- Begin by writing the main idea in a clear and simple sentence.
- Reread the original selection and then write three sentences that are related to the main idea.
- Put these sentences together to form a paragraph.
- You can begin your paragraph with the main idea, or you can end your paragraph with the main idea.

Main Idea	**OR**	Sentence About Main Idea
↓		↓
Sentence About Main Idea		Sentence About Main Idea
↓		↓
Sentence About Main Idea		Sentence About Main Idea
↓		↓
Sentence About Main Idea		**Main Idea**

W

Read the summary below. One of the sentences in this summary does not support the main idea. Can you find it?

"How He Did It: Health Advice, Kid-to-Kid" is an informational article about a nutrition Web site. The site was created by a boy named Robert Kohn as part of a school project. Robert's school is in Weston, New Jersey. Robert uses the site to help kids make healthy choices about diet and exercise.

Style

As you write your summary, keep in mind these two tips:

1. Write the main idea and supporting sentences in your own words. Using the author's words is copying, not summarizing. You will remember the selection better if you summarize in your own words.

2. Summaries do not include your own opinions or thoughts. Stick to the important details of the selection when you write a summary.

Go for It! Use the information in this workshop to continue your draft. Don't worry about spelling and grammar for now—just get your draft on paper!

Additional Support

Differentiated Instruction

Clarity Check Tell students that they are going to help each other with their writing. Divide students into small groups. Have students in each group take turns reading their summaries aloud. Each listener should write down what he or she thinks is the reader's main idea. When each person has had a turn read-

ing, students should take turns sharing the main ideas they identified. If there is confusion about a main idea, the student should consider rewording or revising for clarity. Encourage students to provide constructive criticism and possible solutions to each writer's problems. **BL OL**

Grammar Link

Linking Verbs

What Are They?

Not every sentence is about doing, thinking, or feeling. Some are just about the way things *are.* So not every verb is an action verb. Some verbs show a **state of being**. These are **linking verbs**.

Why Are They Important?

We use linking verbs all the time. They connect a person, place, or thing with a word that *describes* it or *tells what it is.*

The Linking Verb *To Be* The most common linking verb is the verb *to be.* Here are some forms of the *to be* verb:

> *is, am, are, was, were, been*

• The food **is** spicy.

The verb *is* links *food* to *spicy. Spicy* describes *the food.*

• The trees in the park **were** all maples.

The verb *were* links *the trees* to *maples. Maples* names the kind of *trees.*

Other Linking Verbs Here are some other common linking verbs:

seem, look, feel, become, appear, grow, turn, taste, feel, smell, sound

• Chandra **turns** thirteen today.

The verb *turns* links *Chandra* and *thirteen. Thirteen* describes *Chandra.*

• At her party, Elli **seemed** shy.

The verb *seemed* links *Elli* to *shy. Shy* describes *Elli.*

How Do I Use Them?

Warning, Warning, Warning! Some words can be used as either action verbs or linking verbs. The job a verb does in the sentence makes it an action verb or a linking verb.

• Maria **looks** for music on the Internet.

Here the verb *looks* is an action. Maria is doing something.

• Maria **looks** pretty in that picture.

Here the verb *looks* connects *Maria* and *pretty.*

There's an easy test to tell whether a verb is a linking verb. Try replacing the verb with a form of the verb *to be.* If the sentence still makes sense, you're dealing with a linking verb.

• Maria **is** music on the Internet. (No! This use of *looks* is not a linking verb.)

• Maria **is** pretty in that picture. (Yes! This use of *looks* is a linking verb.)

Grammar Practice Copy the following sentences and underline the linking verb (or verbs) in each. If there are no linking verbs in a sentence, write an "N" next to it.

1. They seem serious about their work.
2. Food at ballparks is expensive, but it tastes good.
3. Ferdinand smells the flower.
4. The pitcher on the baseball team looked nervous.

Writing Application Underline all of the linking verbs in your summary.

Looking Ahead

That's all for now! Keep the writing you've done so far to use in Part 2 of this Writing Workshop.

Teach

Grammar Link Say: List several linking verbs. *(Possible responses: be and all its forms, seem, feel)* Now use each verb in a sentence of your own. *(Responses will vary.)* **OL**

Grammar Practice

1. seem
2. is
3. (no linking verbs)
4. looked

English Language Coach

Linking Verbs To help students understand linking verbs, focus on *to be.* Remind students that this is an irregular verb and review its various forms if necessary. Point out that *be* can link a subject with a noun, pronoun, or adjective. It links the subject to another noun that tells what the subject is in this example: *Mia* **is** my *cousin.* In the next example, it links the subject to an adjective that tells what the subject is like: *Mia* **is** *smart.* To show that other linking verbs can take the place of *be,* give these examples: *Mia* **seems** *happy. Mia* **looks** *happy.* **EL**

Objectives

• Write a summary
• Include main ideas and supporting details
• Distinguish between major and minor details
• Identify and use action and linking verbs

29

Skimming and Scanning

**Objective covered in
this workshop:**
• Skim and scan to preview
and analyze texts

Teaching Students to Skim and Scan

Why Is It Important?

• Skimming and scanning are very useful tools when readers need to find information quickly.

• Skimming includes reviewing the selection to get an idea of what it is about.

• Skimming is helpful when students need to find out whether or not a document contains the information they are searching for.

• Scanning is glancing over a selection to find specific information, such as the time a bus leaves from a certain station.

How to Help Students Get It

• Tell students that they already use these skills

• While skimming, students should read headlines, headings, captions, and part of the first paragraph to get an overview of the piece.

• While scanning, students should look for key words that would help them.

• Before skimming and scanning, make sure students know what they are looking for.

Reading to Answer the Big Question

Messaging Mania

Instant messaging is explained and evaluated in this *TIME for Kids* article. The author addresses issues such as the effects of informal IM spelling and slang on students' writing. Readers will be challenged to consider the pros and cons of communication through reading and writing online in place of face-to-face conversations.

The Magic of Harry Potter by Nancy Gibbs

The popularity of the Harry Potter books and characters is discussed in this *TIME* article. Gibbs, Maurice Sendak, and several young readers offer reasons for the large number of enthusiastic fans of the Harry Potter series.

Workshop Resources

PACING (DAYS) STANDARD	BLOCK	LESSON	STUDENT MATERIALS	TEACHER RESOURCES
1	1	Key Skill Lesson: Skimming and Scanning	👤 Key Reading Skills Practice, p. 16 👤 English Language Coach Review, p. 42	🖋 Bellringer Options Transparencies –Daily Language Pratice 5 🖋 Read Aloud, Think Aloud Transparencies –Key Reading Skills 23 –Read alound, Think Aloud 1–3 💿 Presentation Plus!
2	2–3	"Messaging Mania"	💻 Glencoe Online 👤 Unit Vocabulary Review, p. 40 👤 Academic Vocabulary Review, p. 43 📂 English Language Coach 👤 Active Reading Graphic Organizer, p. 19 👤 Text Analysis, p. 18 💿 StudentWorks Plus™ 💻 Online Student Edition 💿 Literature Classics 📂 Selection and Unit Assessments, p. 3	🖋 Literary and Text Analysis Transparencies 55 💻 Puzzlemaker 💿 Skill Level Up!™ A Language Arts Game 💻 BookLink 3 📙 Assessment by Learning Objective (Diagnostic and Formative) 💿 Interactive Tutor: Self-Assessment 💿 TeacherWorks Plus™
2		"The Magic of Harry Potter"	💻 Glencoe Online 👤 Unit Vocabulary Review, p. 40 👤 Academic Vocabulary Review, p. 43 📂 English Language Coach 👤 Active Reading Graphic Organizer, p. 21 👤 Text Analysis, p. 18 💿 StudentWorks Plus™ 💻 Online Student Edition 💿 Literature Classics 📂 Selection and Unit Assessments, p. 4	🖋 Read Aloud, Think Aloud Transparencies –Read Aloud, Think Aloud 4–9 🖋 Literary and Text Analysis Transparencies 55 💻 Puzzlemaker 💿 Skill Level Up!™ A Language Arts Game 💻 BookLink 3 📙 Assessment by Learning Objective (Diagnostic and Formative) 💿 Interactive Tutor: Self-Assessment 💿 TeacherWorks Plus™

Keys for Unit Resource

📂 Blackline Master   🔒 DVD

📙 Workbook   🖋 Transparency

📖 Supplemental Text   💻 Web-based

💿 CD-ROM   👤 Fast File

Level Appropriate Code

AS = Activities for all students

AL = Activities for students working above grade level

OL = Activities for students working at grade level

BL = Activities for students working below grade level

EL = Activities for English language learners

Focus

READING WORKSHOP 2

BELLRINGER Options

📖 **Daily Language Practice Transparency 5**
Focus Activity Say: Name some items that you might read over quickly. Why would you concentrate less on these items than on others? *(Responses will vary. Students may suggest food packages to determine ingredients, calories, or fat content; or CD jackets to locate favored selections.)* **AS**

Teach

R Reading Skill

Skimming and Scanning Ask: What is the difference between skimming and scanning? *(A reader skims to find the general idea of a text and scans to locate specific information.)* **Ask:** When might you skim a book or a story? When might you scan it? *(Possible responses: Skimming: to determine whether a book is a good reference to use for a report; Scanning: to find information that will answer a study question)* **OL**

Skills Focus

You will practice using these skills when you read the following selections:
• "Messaging Mania," p. 34
• "The Real Magic of Harry Potter," p. 42

Reading
• Skimming and scanning

Informational Text
• Using titles and subheads

Vocabulary
• Understanding multiple-meaning words in context

Writing/Grammar
• Using main and helping verbs
• Using present and present progressive tenses

Objectives (pp. 30–31)
Reading Skim and scan text

Skill Lesson

Skimming and Scanning

Learn It!

What Are They? To get information fast, try **skimming** and **scanning.** Skimming means quickly reading a piece of writing to get a *general idea* of what it's about. Scanning means looking for *key words* or *phrases,* usually ones you already know. For example, you would skim a newspaper article to find out what it is about. You would scan a newspaper article to see if it mentions your favorite musician.

• Skim to get the general idea of a text.
• Scan to look for specific words and information.
• Skimming and scanning are quick ways to get information, and they save time when you have a lot of reading to do.

ASSIGNMENT:
MOBY DICK
PG. 1 - 200

GLASBERGEN

"I don't like to give a lot of homework over the weekend, so just read every other word."
1998 Randy Glasbergen

Analyzing Cartoons
Moby Dick is the name of a famous American novel. Why wouldn't reading every other word be a good way to skim the novel?

Additional Support

English Language Coach

Building Background Students may be unfamiliar with Herman Melville's classic novel *Moby Dick.* The story centers around a conflict between Captain Ahab and a white whale called Moby Dick, who is responsible for the loss of Ahab's leg. The paperback version is typically more than 600 pages. Ask students why they think Randy Glasbergen chose *Moby Dick* rather than another novel for his cartoon. Discuss with them how the length of the novel makes it appropriate for use in a joke about reading every other word. Then have students name other books that would also work in this cartoon. **AS**

Why Are They Important? Skimming and scanning can help you save time, and who doesn't like to save time? When you skim, you can find out if a text is something you want or need to read without having to read the text carefully. When you scan a text, you can quickly find a section or part of a text that has the information you need.

How Do I Do Them? There are many ways to skim a text. Usually, you read only the title, any subheads, and the beginning of each paragraph. When you scan, you keep in mind the words or phrases you are looking for, then you run your eyes over the text to see if you can see them. Here is what one student noticed when using these skills to research a report on the Cinco de Mayo (SEENK oh day MY oh) celebration in Mexico.

Study Central Visit www.glencoe. com and click on Study Central to review skimming and scanning.

Mexican Culture

Celebrations Throughout the year, Mexicans enjoy several special celebrations called fiestas (fee EHS tuhs). National holidays include Independence Day (September 16) and Cinco de Mayo (May 5). Cinco de Mayo celebrates the day in 1862 that Mexicans defeated an invading French army in battle.

When I skimmed the passage, I saw the words <u>Mexican Culture</u> and <u>Celebrations</u> in dark print; that must be what this section is about. When I scanned the paragraph, I saw the words <u>Cinco de Mayo</u>, so I know this has information I need.

Practice It!

Skim and scan the article "Messaging Mania." Here, *mania* means a feeling of excitement over the trend of instant messaging. Skim the entire selection to find out what the article is about, and then scan for the word *parents.*

Use It!

Copy this list of questions in your Learner's Notebook. Write answers to the questions as you skim and scan "Messaging Mania."
- What do the subheads tell you?
- What does the first paragraph tell you?
- What is the selection about?
- What do some parents think about the subject?

Teach

Study Central Have students access the Web site to review skimming and scanning and to complete a related activity.

R Reading Skill

Skimming and Scanning Ask: How is reading for specific information different from reading for pleasure? *(Responses will vary. Students may say that reading for specific information or for school subjects requires readers to learn, retain, and use information. Reading for pleasure requires only that readers enjoy the text.)* **Ask:** With which kind of reading are you more likely to use skimming and scanning? Explain. *(Possible response: Reading for information requires skimming and scanning because students are held accountable for finding, knowing, and using specific information.)* **OL**

Resources for page 31

📖 Use Key Reading Skills Transparency 23 in *Read Aloud, Think Aloud* to help students practice skimming and scanning.

Reading in the Real World

Career Tell students that many jobs require skimming and scanning. An insurance agent, for example, often has to scan files to identify the proper policy. A doctor or a nurse scans a chart for a patient's blood pressure and symptoms. A server in a restaurant scans a list of the daily specials to tell customers what they can order. Have students ask their parents or guardians how they use skimming and scanning in their jobs. Make a class list of careers and invite students to compare how skimming and scanning are used on these jobs every day. **AS**

Objectives
- Skim and scan text
- Analyze text features: cartoons

Teach

More About the Author

One of Kathryn R. Hoffman's favorite classes in school was a history class in which she got to dress like a historical figure and reenact history. She enjoys writing on the subway because she finds unusual people to observe. She likes being a writer because she is "able to reach out to a lot of people at once."

V Vocabulary

Word Webs Say: One way to learn and remember multiple-meaning vocabulary words is to make word webs. On an index card, write a word in the center of a web. In the connecting circles, write the multiple meanings of the word. If necessary, use a dictionary for help. *(Responses will vary.)* **OL** **EL**

Before You Read Messaging Mania

Meet the Author

Kathryn R. Hoffman enjoys being a writer. She says, "I like the idea of being able to reach out to a lot of people at once." Hoffman has always loved to read. Reading inspired her to start writing. Hoffman writes best in her journal. She says, "It's like talking to a good friend who won't criticize anything I say."

Author Search For more about Kathryn R. Hoffman, go to www.glencoe.com.

Objectives (pp. 32–37)
Reading Skim and scan text • Make connections from text to self
Informational Text Use text features: title, subheads
Vocabulary Use context clues: multiple meanings

Vocabulary Preview

formal (FOR mul) *adj.* proper, following rules **(p. 34)** *Many kids speak formal English at school, but when they're with friends they speak in a more relaxed way.*

monitor (MAHN ih tur) *v.* to check or watch **(p. 36)** *Many parents monitor their children's use of the computer.*

Write to Learn Write the vocabulary word that each clue describes:
- You might do this if you want to follow the wins and losses of your favorite team.
- This describes the clothes you would wear to go to a wedding or some other special occasion.

English Language Coach

Multiple-Meaning Words Many words you already know have more than one meaning. The context, or other words in the sentence and paragraph, can help you find the correct meaning. Look at these two words in dark type and some of their meanings.

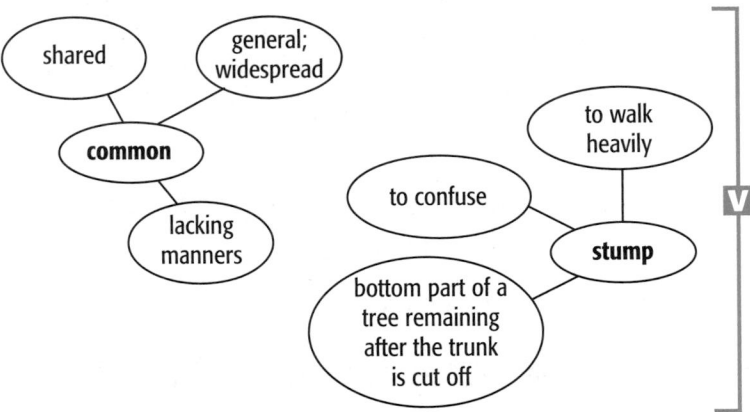

Partner Talk With a partner, read these sentences. Which definition of the underlined word makes sense in each sentence? Which words help you figure out the correct meanings? Talk it over with your partner.

1. His cousin was very <u>common</u>; he talked with food in his mouth.
2. We tried to <u>stump</u> Juan with hard questions, but he always knew the answers.

Additional Support

Author Search To expand students' appreciation of Kathryn R. Hoffman, have them access the Web site for additional information and resources.

Literature Focus Lesson

Abbreviated Communication Put students in pairs. Tell each student to write a brief note and exchange it with his or her partner. Remind students to exercise respect in their writing. Instruct students to use abbreviated slang, referring them to page 37 for ideas. Then have students discuss whether or not they were able to understand the notes from their partners and why. Lead students in a discussion about how instant messaging has affected the English language. **OL**

Skills Preview

Key Reading Skill: Skimming and Scanning

Before you read the selection, get a general idea of what it's about by skimming the title, the subheads, and parts of paragraphs and the text. Then, scan the text to find specific information about kinds of instant-messaging software, parents and IM, and IM slang.

Write to Learn After scanning the article, write down two companies that offer instant messaging software. Also, write down three examples of IM slang and their meanings.

Key Text Element: Titles and Subheads

A *title* is the name of a selection. *Subheads* emphasize parts of a selection and spark interest. To grab your attention, subheads are darker or a larger size than the rest of the text. Titles and subheads help you find and use information. Sometimes they show the important points of a selection. Use these tips to help you understand and use titles and subheads:

- Read the title and think about it.
  What does the title tell me about the subject of the selection?

- Read the subheads.
  What do the subheads tell me about the subject of the selection? What do they tell me about how the selection is organized?

- Think about how the title and subheads grab your attention.
  Do the title and subheads make me want to read this selection? Why or why not?

Partner Talk With a partner, talk about types of writing that use titles and subheads. Write at least three of these sources in your Learner's Notebook. Explain how titles and subheads help you find or understand information that you read in these sources.

Get Ready to Read

Connect to the Reading

Think about the ways you stay in touch with friends. Do you get together? Do you call each other? Do you send e-mails or instant messages to one another?

Whole Class Talk about ways to communicate with friends. List different ways you can stay in touch. Find out which ways your classmates use most or like best.

Build Background

Instant messaging is popular, but it's not new.

- Instant messaging is communicating over the Internet by two or more people typing messages that they receive instantly.
- People at colleges and universities started instant messaging in the 1980s and 1990s.
- After a program allowing most computer users to instant message came out in 1996, the Internet became a place for anyone to hold a conversation.

Set Purposes for Reading

BIG Question Read "Messaging Mania" to answer the Big Question "Why read?"

Set Your Own Purpose What else would you like to learn from the selection to help you answer the Big Question? Write your own purpose on the "Messaging Mania" page of Foldable 1.

Interactive Literary Elements Handbook
To review or learn more about the literary elements, go to www.glencoe.com.

Keep Moving

Use these skills as you read the following selection.

Messaging Mania   **33**

Teach

R Reading Skill

Skimming and Scanning **Say:** Skim the article that begins on page 34. What is the article about? *(instant messaging)* **Say:** Now scan the article. What are some different kinds of IM software? *(Yahoo, MSN, and AOL)* **Ask:** What do most parents think about IM? *(Possible response: They worry that IM takes kids' focus away from other activities.)* **Ask:** Why do people who instant message use abbreviations and slang? *(They save time and computer space.)* **OL**

Literature Online

Interactive Literary Elements Handbook Have students access the Web site to improve their understanding of titles and subheads.

Objectives
- Skim and scan text

Teach

INFORMATIONAL TEXT
MAGAZINE
TIME for Kids

E Text Element

Titles and Subheads Ask:
What do the title and the subheads suggest about the writer's attitude toward the subject? *(Responses will vary. Students may suggest that the writer's attitude toward the subject will be lighthearted.)* **OL**

R Reading Skill

Skimming and Scanning
Say: Scan the article. Do you think it will address instant messaging in a positive or negative way? Explain. *(Possible response: The titles, subheads, and graphics suggest that the article will address instant messaging in a positive way.)* **OL**

Messaging Mania

by Kathryn R. Hoffman

1 **2**

Think fast! Translate this conversation into **formal** English: "Wass^?" "N2M, U?" "JC." "G2G. BFN." Stumped?[1] The dictionary won't help you, but our handy guide will (*see page 37*).

If you figured it out right away, you are probably among the 60% of kids online who use instant messaging, or IM. Yahoo, MSN and AOL offer software that allows users to have real-time[2] conversations in pop-up text windows online. Instant messages are typed so fast that users don't slow down to capitalize, add periods and commas or spell out words. As a result, new word abbreviations and IM slang[3] are being invented faster than a high-speed Internet connection.

KEYBOARD NATION

An instant-messaging "chat" usually lasts more than half an hour, is between three or more people and often includes friends from different areas. More than one in three IM users say they use it every day, according to the Pew Internet and American Life Project. Nearly half of all online teens believe that the Internet has made their friendships better. It's a quick, easy way to keep in touch. **3**

---

1. **Stumped** means confused about something.
2. **Yahoo, MSN** (Microsoft Network), and **AOL** (America Online) are companies that provide **software,** or computer programs, for instant messaging. The programs allow for **real-time** text conversations, or typed messages on a computer screen that show up as the typing comes in.
3. **Abbreviations** (uh bree vee AY shuns) are letters or groups of letters that stand for longer words or phrases, such as ASAP for "as soon as possible." **Slang** is a relaxed language that people use in conversation.

Vocabulary ....

formal (FOR mul) *adj.* proper, following rules

34 UNIT 1 Why Read?

Practice the Skills

1 Key Text Element

Titles and Subheads What does the title tell you about this selection? What do you learn from the subheads? **E**

2 Key Reading Skill

Skimming and Scanning Skim the text to get a "big picture" of the selection. What does it look like this article is about? **R**

3 Key Reading Skill

Skimming and Scanning Scan the first three paragraphs to find out about teens and instant messaging. How do many teens feel about IM?

Readability Scores
Dale-Chall: 8.1
DRP: 59
Lexile: 1020

Additional Support

Reading Fluency

IM Slang Provide students with a paragraph of text written in instant messaging slang to read aloud. After students have finished reading the paragraph, lead them in a discussion regarding how the use of instant messaging slang affected their fluency. Were they able to read quickly? Did they stumble over words? Was their phrasing correct? If the slang caused fluency problems, ask students to speculate why. **EL** **OL**

Steven Mintz, 13, prefers messaging to the phone "because I can talk to more people at once." Chatting online is also a good way to keep up with friends who live far away. Kids don't have to worry about running up the telephone bill.

WRONG MESSAGE?

R Instant messaging is not always a friendship builder. Sometimes, kids use it to air[4] angry or hurt feelings. Such kids aren't necessarily trying to be mean. Often, it's just easier to say something online than in person. Oliver Davies, 11, of Palo Alto, California, says that with IM, "I can express my emotions more easily, without having the guilt of saying it face-to-face."

Many parents and teachers thinks kids' instant messaging habits are taking away from more important things. Julia Long of Bellingham, Washington, says that when her son Taylor, 13, "is waiting for a beep,[5] it's hard (for him) to stay focused on homework or any kind of family activity."

---

4. When you *air* feelings, you express them or make them known to other people.
5. *Waiting for a beep* means waiting for the sound that means you have an instant message.

Analyzing the Graphic The article says, "Instant messaging is not always a friendship builder." Does this graphic support that idea? Explain.

Messaging Mania **35**

Teach

R **Reading Skill**

Skimming and Scanning Say: Skim the page. What are some reasons that people use instant messaging? *(People use instant messaging to communicate with more than one person at a time or to say things that they're not comfortable saying in person.)* **OL**

Viewing the Graphic

Ask: Who did not get invited to Jenny's party? *(Katie, GoodGirl109, or the girl on the left)* What detail does that girl give to support the idea that Jenny should have invited her? *(Jenny was invited to all of Katie's parties.)* **BL** **OL** Say: The problem between the other girls creates a problem for SupaStar. What would you have said in this chat if you were in her place? *(Possible responses: I would have said the same things. I would have told Jenny to explain and apologize to Katie.)* **AL**

C **Critical Thinking**

Analysis Ask: What are some of the pros and cons of instant messaging? *(Responses will vary. Students may say that an advantage is the ability to communicate quickly and that a disadvantage is less face-to-face interaction among people.)* **AL**

Differentiated Instruction

Internet Safety Brochures Lead a discussion about Internet safety. Begin by listing tips on the board. Then, have small groups continue the activity by creating Internet safety brochures. Tell students to use titles, subheads, and graphics to organize the information. **OL** Have students use the brochures to create an Internet safety exhibit in the school library or in a hallway display case. **AL**

Objectives
• Skim and scan text
• Use text features: graphics, titles and subheads
• Analyze text

Teach

EL Language Coach

Multiple-Meaning

Words Say: Using the context, replace the word *note* with synonyms that make sense. *(Responses will vary. Students may suggest* say point out, observe, *or* document.*)* **EL OL**

BQ BIG Question

Ask: Why do you read instant messages? *(Responses will vary. Students may say that they read instant messages to gain information about their friends' thoughts, feelings, or lives.)* **AS**

Teachers get upset when Internet slang and emoticons,[6] such as "u" and "r" and "wuz," show up in kids' writing.

Kids' safety is also a concern. Staying connected is fine, but an online friendship with a stranger is not. Many parents **monitor** IM'ing, either by limiting time online or by keeping the computer in a **common** area. **4**

I.M. NOT SO BAD

Researchers who study kids and the Internet say instant messaging isn't getting in the way of real life. They note that new technology often triggers[7] old, exaggerated fears. "It's similar to what was said in the 1980s about video games and in the '60s about television," says Nalini Kotamraju, an expert on how kids use technology to communicate. "There was this worry that kids would do nothing else." **EL**

Even parents and teachers who don't like IM have to admit that at least kids are writing. And their typing skills are improving. Is it at the expense of[8] proper English? Not so long as kids learn the difference between formal and conversational English,[9] says Naomi Baron, professor of linguistics[10] at American University in Washington, D.C.

"Language has always changed, and it always will," Baron said. "It must change as the things we do and things we encounter change."

Wat a relief! G2G. L8R. **5** ○

---

6. *Emoticons* are groups of keyboard characters that are supposed to look like facial expressions. People use them to express feelings when typing.

7. *Trigger* means to start something.

8. When something is done *at the expense of* something else, one thing is given up for the other.

9. *Conversational English* is the relaxed language you speak with friends or family members.

10. *Linguistics* (ling GWIS tiks) is the study of language and how people speak.

Vocabulary

monitor (MAHN ih tur) *v.* to check or watch

EMOTICONS

:-)	happy
:-(	sad
:-|	no feelings
:-D	very happy
:-P	tongue out
:-&	tongue twisted
;-)	wink
:-$	mouth shut, "not tellin'"
:'(	crying
:-O	surprised

Analyzing the Graphic Which emoticon on this graphic best describes how you feel as you read this article? Explain your answer.

Practice the Skills

4 **English Language Coach**

Multiple-Meaning Words Use the other words in a sentence or paragraph to help you figure out the meaning of a word with more than one meaning. Which meaning for the word **common** makes the most sense here?

5 **BIG Question**

On the "Messaging Mania" page of Foldable 1, explain how instant messaging relates to the Big Question. Your answer will help you complete the Unit Challenge later. **BQ**

Additional Support

English Language Coach

Multiple-Meaning Words Write several multiple-meaning words on index cards. Suggested words include *kind, last, like, rest, press, present, pen, yard,* and *fan.* Divide students into two teams. Each team will take turns drawing a card. The team will then be given time to create a sentence using two different meanings of the word drawn. Give students this example before they begin:

My father is a big fan of ceiling fans.

Allow students to write silly sentences, but remind them that the meanings of the words must be accurate. **EL BL**

The Graphic (Instant Messaging conversations)

ShoppingDiva01

hey!

hey julia! wass^???

nm, u???

n2m either jc...doing homework BLAH!

o i c...> so what'd u think of rebecca's party saturday???

it wuz rly fun. i had a sleepover with anna afterwards

o thats coool! hold on brb

hey julia, sara, mike sup???

sup jake???

SoccerQueen89

nm jc u???

jc too, except POS right now!!!

back...sry i had to check with my mom to see when American Idol was coming on

ooooo i'm soooo excited for that!

hey mike y were u limping today? did u hurt urslf???

MrPopular5000

no, he split his pants LOL!!!

hey thats not funny dude u promised u wouldnt tell

sry dude>...> ROFL!!!!

o well 2 immature for me, i g2g buh-bye

signed off at 6:21:46PM

Dean MacAdam

HiTeckerrr

Analyzing the Graphic
Which of these IM conversations do you think is the most interesting? Which is the funniest? Which is most like one you might be part of? Explain your answers.

Get the Message!

bfn: bye for now	**nm:** not much	**sry:** sorry
brb: be right back	**n2m:** not too much	**sup, wass^:** What's up?
g2g: got to go	**oic:** Oh, I see	**ur:** your
jc: just chillin'	**pos:** parents over shoulder	**wat:** what
l8r: later	**rly:** really	**wuz:** was
lol: laugh out loud	**rofl:** rolling on the floor laughing	

C

—Updated 2005, from *TIME FOR KIDS*, May 2, 2003

Messaging Mania **37**

Teach

C Critical Thinking

Application Ask: What other Internet abbreviations or slang do you use? *(Responses will vary. Students may suggest the following: ADN = any day now; AFAIK = as far as I know; BBL= be back later; BTW = by the way; CUL8R= see you later; FAQ=frequently asked questions.)* **OL Say:** Use what you've learned in this article to create an Instant Messaging dictionary in your Learner's Notebooks. **AS**

Assess

✓CheckPoint

Use the Checkpoint questions provided on Presentation Plus! to check for comprehension of the selection. These questions can be used with interactive response keypads for immediate student feedback.

Differentiated Instruction

Chatting About Issues Have students review the sample messaging sessions on this page. Draw students' attention to how little content each message contains. Challenge students to use Internet slang to write personal stories or to communicate their opinions about a complex issue, such as school uniforms or snack foods in schools. Discuss how the use of Internet slang facilitates or impedes real communication. **AL**

Objectives
- Apply information
- Understand multiple-meaning words

Assess

Resources for page 38

📁 Selection Quick Check, p. 3

📁 Selection and Unit Assessment, p. 3

💿 ExamView Assessment Suite

💿 Interactive Tutor: Self-Assessment

Students can respond to the *After You Read* items in their Learner's Notebooks or on a separate sheet of paper.

Answering the
BIG Question

1. Responses will vary. Students might cite the warning about chatting with strangers.

2. Students can communicate with more than one person at a time, and they do not incur long distance charges.

3. Problems include taking attention away from schoolwork and family time, transferring IM language to schoolwork, and chatting with potentially dangerous strangers.

Critical Thinking

4. **(a)** TV and video games sparked a fear that kids would do nothing else. **(b)** Fears about instant messaging are similar.

5. Possible response: IM'ing will likely lead to new words or spellings.

6. Responses will vary. Students may say that IM'ing makes communication easy.

After You Read | Messaging Mania

> Shhh, don't tell her I'm here.

Dean MacAdam

Answering the BIG Question

1. What is the most useful thing you learned from reading "Messaging Mania"? How do you think you will use this information?

2. **Recall** What are two reasons kids like instant messaging better than talking on the phone?
   Tip **Right There** You will find the answer in the article.

3. **Summarize** What are some problems with instant messaging?
   Tip **Think and Search** The answer is in the article, but the details are not all in one place.

Critical Thinking

4. **Compare and Contrast** The article lists two other forms of technology that caused "exaggerated fears" in the past. **(a)** What were they? **(b)** Compare those fears with fears of instant messaging today.
   Tip **Author and Me** You must use information from the article and your own thoughts.

5. **Infer** What effect do you think instant messaging will have on the English language?
   Tip **Author and Me** You must use information from the article and your own thoughts.

6. **Evaluate** Does instant messaging help or hurt friendships? Explain.
   Tip **On My Own** Answer from your own experiences.

Talk About Your Reading

Internet slang and abbreviations are common online, but we also use slang in our everyday conversations. With a partner, talk about slang that you use in conversation with friends and family.

- Make a list of three terms or phrases that you use in conversational, or slang, English, and talk about what they mean in formal, or proper, English.
- For example, does *chillin'* mean that you're relaxing?
- Talk about why it is a good idea to separate slang from formal English at school.

Objectives (pp. 38–39)
Reading Skim and scan text
Informational Text Use text features: title, subheads
Vocabulary Use context clues: multiple meanings
Grammar Identify parts of speech: main and helping verbs, present and present progressive tenses

38 UNIT 1 Why Read?

Talk About Your Reading

Responses will vary. Students should note that language choices must be tailored to the task and to the audience.

Skills Review

Key Reading Skill: Skimming and Scanning

7. How did skimming the article at the beginning help you learn what it was about in general? How did scanning the article help you find specific information about instant messaging?

Key Text Element: Titles and Subheads

8. The title of the selection is "Messaging Mania." What does the title suggest about instant messaging?

9. What did you learn about the main points of the article from the subheads in the selection?

10. Why are titles and subheads helpful in a magazine article?

Vocabulary Check

In the following sentences, fill in the blank with the correct vocabulary word from below.

formal   monitor

11. Many teachers ____ their classes during tests.

12. Most people wear ____ clothes to the prom.

13. **English Language Coach** In your own words, write a short definition for each multiple-meaning word in bold. Use the context of the sentence for help.

   • He's the **kind** of person who is **kind**.
   • She works at a **bank** on the **bank** of a river.

Web Activities For eFlashcards, Selection Quick Checks, and other Web activities, go to www.glencoe.com.

Grammar Link: Main and Helping Verbs

• A **verb** is a word that shows action or a state of being.
• A **helping verb** is a verb that helps the main verb tell about an action or make a statement.

In these sentences, the verb is bold, and the helping verb or verbs are underlined.

Juan <u>is</u> **acting** in a play tonight.
Our class <u>will</u> **study** global warming.
Emilio <u>had been</u> **yelling** all day.
You <u>should have</u> **tried** harder.
No one <u>could have</u> **been** nicer to me.

• A **verb phrase** is one or more helping verbs followed by a main verb. In each sentence above, the underlined and bold words form a verb phrase.

Grammar Practice

Rewrite each sentence below, circle the main verb, and underline the helping verb or verbs.

14. The Internet club will meet after school.

15. Carol had been watching the basketball game.

16. Tiffany has helped her brother often.

17. Both girls are riding red bicycles.

18. The children should be listening to the story.

Writing Application Look back at the list you made of terms or phrases you use in conversational, or slang, English. Use each one in a sentence with a helping verb and a main verb.

Skills Review

Key Reading Skill: Skimming and Scanning

7. Responses will vary.

Key Text Element: Titles and Subheads

8. Possible response: The title suggests that people are crazy about IM'ing.

9. Possible response: The subheads reinforce the idea of IM's popularity, suggest the problems, and suggest a defense.

10. Possible response: Titles and subheads help readers understand text organization and main ideas.

Vocabulary Check

Possible responses:

11. monitor

12. formal

13. **kind:** type; concerned about others
    bank: financial institution; land along a lake or river

Close

Ask students to summarize what they learned to help them answer the Big Question.

Grammar Link: Main and Helping Verbs

Grammar Practice

14. The Internet club <u>will</u> (meet) after school.

15. Carol <u>had been</u> (watching) the basketball game.

16. Tiffany <u>has</u> (helped) her brother often.

17. Both girls <u>are</u> (riding) red bicycles.

18. The children <u>should be</u> (listening) to the story.

More About the Author

Nancy Gibbs studied history and politics at Yale and Oxford Universities. In 1996, she became *Time* magazine's chief political writer. She went on to write about the presidential elections in 1996 and 2000 and covered the impeachment of President Clinton in 1998.

V Vocabulary

Sentences Say: One way to learn and remember vocabulary words is to write sentences. On the front of an index card, write a vocabulary word. On the back of the index card, write a sentence that illustrates the meaning of the word. *(Responses will vary.)* **EL** **OL**

Before You Read

The Real Magic of Harry Potter

Meet the Author

Nancy Gibbs has been writing for *TIME* magazine for twenty years. Almost 100 of her stories have appeared in *TIME*. Gibbs writes about all types of interesting people, events, and issues. She reported for *TIME* on the events of September 11, 2001. When writing about heroes, she noted, "On a normal day, we value heroism because it is uncommon. On September 11, we valued heroism because it was everywhere."

Literature Online

Author Search For more about Nancy Gibbs, go to www.glencoe.com.

Objectives (pp. 40–45)
Reading Skim and scan text • Make connections from text to self
Informational Text Use text features: title, subheads
Vocabulary Use context clues: multiple meanings

Vocabulary Preview

brilliant (BRIL yuhnt) *adj.* having or showing great ability or talent **(p. 43)** *He was a brilliant soccer player who always scored goals.*

familiar (FUH mil yur) *adj.* commonly seen, heard, or experienced; well-known **(p. 43)** *The words were familiar, but I couldn't remember the name of the song.*

resourceful (rih SORS ful) *adj.* able to deal with new or difficult situations **(p. 44)** *She is a resourceful artist who could make a work of art out of a pile of junk.*

Write to Learn In your Learner's Notebook, write a description of a person you know. Think of a friend or family member. Use at least two of the vocabulary words in your description.

English Language Coach

Multiple-Meaning Words You know that many words have more than one meaning. You can use other words in the sentence or paragraph to find out which meaning is being used. As you read "The Real Magic of Harry Potter," watch for these words. Use context clues to choose the correct meaning.

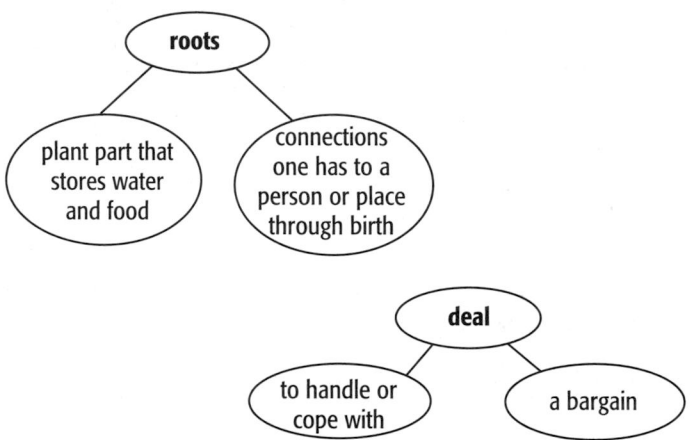

Work with a Partner Work with a partner to write sentences showing the different meanings of *roots* and *deal.* One of you should take the word *roots;* the other should take the word *deal.* Trade work with your partner and identify the meaning in each sentence.

Additional Support

Literature Online

Author Search To expand students' appreciation of Nancy Gibbs, have them access the Web site for additional information and resources.

Literature Focus Lesson

Character Identification Gibbs suggests that readers love the Harry Potter series because they identify with the characters. Provide students with Gibbs's descriptions of the characters:

Harry: ordinary, small, fast, brave, black hair, glasses, breaks rules

Ron: sweet, hardworking, generous, loyal, unsure of himself

Hermione: smart, resourceful, tough, loves to read, stubborn

Ask students which character they are most like and why. **OL** Provide students with this sentence starter: *I am most like [character's name] because ____.* **BL**

Skills Preview

Key Reading Skill: Skimming and Scanning

Skimming and scanning make a good pair. You skim an article to get the big idea. You scan it to find specific information.

- When you skim, look at the title and subheads. Read the beginnings of paragraphs and quickly look over the entire text.
- When you scan, look for key words and phrases that have to do with the information you need.

Whole Class Discussion Point to the title and subheads in the selection. Discuss what the subject of the article might be. Brainstorm a short list of topics connected with the subject that you'd like to know more about. List key words that might lead you to that information in the article.

Key Text Element: Titles and Subheads

Titles and subheads make you curious, help you find information, and hint at what a selection is about. These tips will help you use titles and subheads.

- What hints does the title of the article give you about the subject of the article?
- If the title poses a question, there's a good chance you'll find an answer to the question in the text.
- What do you learn about the article from the deck?
- What do the subheads tell you about the article?

Partner Talk "The Real Magic of Harry Potter" has two subheads.

- Wild About Harry
- Bridging the Gap

With a partner, pick one of the subheads. Talk about what the subhead means and what main points it might touch on, and think of a question it might answer.

Interactive Literary Elements Handbook
To review or learn more about the literary elements, go to www.glencoe.com.

Get Ready to Read

Connect to the Reading

Do you have a favorite video game, TV show, book, or movie? Why do you like it?

Write to Learn If you were going to write a book that most kids could relate to, what would the book be about? Explain.

Build Background

You will learn from the article that people of all ages are fans of the Harry Potter books. There are now six books in the series.

- The author of the books, J. K. Rowling, first thought of the character Harry Potter in 1990 while riding on a train.
- It took Rowling a few years to write the first Harry Potter book. She was busy with a small child and had time to write only while her child slept.
- *Harry Potter and the Half-Blood Prince,* the sixth book in the series, was published July 16, 2005.

Set Purposes for Reading

BIG Question Read the selection the "Real Magic of Harry Potter" to find out why kids like to read the Harry Potter books.

Set Your Own Purpose What else would you like to learn from the article to help you answer the Big Question? Write your own purpose on the "Real Magic of Harry Potter" page of Foldable 1.

Keep Moving

Use these skills as you read the following selection.

The Real Magic of Harry Potter **41**

Teach

R Reading Skill

Skimming and Scanning **Ask:** Based on the title, what do you think the article is about? *(Responses will vary. Students might say that Harry is a magician but the title could refer to the books' popularity.)* **OL**

E Text Element

Titles and Subheads **Ask:** In the subheads, what do "wild about" and "bridging the gap" mean? *(Possible responses: Wild means "enthusiastic or excited." Bridging the gap means "connecting two things.")* **OL** **AL**

Literature Online

Interactive Literary Elements Handbook Have students access the Web site to improve their understanding of titles and subheads.

Differentiated Instruction

Build More Background Although many students are familiar with the Harry Potter series, some students may not have read all the books. Ask students what they already know about Harry Potter and his adventures. Record this prior knowledge on the board. Then, ask students to create three more bullet points for the *Build Background* section on this page. Suggest that students consult Internet sites during their research. **EL** **OL**

Objectives
- Skim and scan text
- Use text features: titles and subheads
- Learn and use new vocabulary

Teach

E Text Element

Titles and Subheads **Say:** The text below a title that is not part of the article is called the *deck*. What does this deck include? *(Possible response: The deck states the writer's research question as well as its answer.)* **OL** **Say:** One purpose of a deck is to get the reader interested in reading the article. Is this deck successful in achieving this purpose? Explain. *(Responses will vary. Some students may think that this deck orients the reader in a helpful way whereas others may feel they have no reason to read the article because they already have the answer to the writer's initial question.)* **AL**

R Reading Skill

Skimming and Scanning **Ask:** What is one way to find answers to the questions posed in the Student Edition? *(Students might scan the article looking for key words and phrases such as* magic, Harry Potter, *or* gap.*)* **BL**

Readability Scores
Dale-Chall: 4.6
DRP: 55
Lexile: 940

Glynis Sweeny

TIME

The Real Magic of HARRY POTTER

Why are kids around the world so eager for each installment[1] of a story about a boy wizard? Some kids say it's because they see themselves in him. **1** **2**

By NANCY GIBBS

It is hard not to believe in magic when you think about what J. K. Rowling has done. The author of the Harry Potter books has written the most popular children's series ever. Through more than 250 million copies of her books, Rowling speaks to kids in 200 countries—from China to the United States and points in between—in 61 languages and in Braille.[2]

It's probably no surprise to Rowling's fans that many children buy the books with their own money. Or that they wear out flashlight batteries reading the books after lights-out. And, no surprise here, even readers who dislike thick books have read Harry Potter not once or twice but a dozen times. For many fans, the books are far better than watching TV or staring at a computer screen.

When the fifth book in the series, *Harry Potter and the Order of the Phoenix,* was published in June 2003, it created a lot of excitement. There were Potter parties complete with owls,

---

1. An *installment* is a part of a story that is published separately.
2. *Braille* (brayl) is a system of printing for people without sight. It is "read" by running your fingers over raised dots on a page or surface.

1 **Key Text Element**

Titles and Subheads Read the title and the deck. Which tells you more about the subject of the article? What does it tell you? **E**

2 **Key Reading Skill**

Skimming and Scanning Skim the entire article to get an idea of what it's about. What questions do you have after skimming? What key words and phrases would you use to scan the article for answers to these questions? **R**

Additional Support

Reading in the Real World

Citizenship Suggest that students ask adults about books that were popular during their childhood. Provide students with the following interview questions:

• When you were growing up, what book or series was popular with students?

• Why do you think this book or series was so popular?

• How does the popularity of this book or series compare with the Harry Potter craze today?

Ask students to use their results to draw conclusions about the interests of kids in the past versus the interests of kids today. **AL** cloaks, and butterbeer.[3] Kids wore their Potter pajamas. They even wanted to sleep in a "cupboard under the stairs," as Harry is forced to do by his creepy adopted family on Privet Drive. Some families ordered two or three books so that everyone could read the book at the same time. At close to 900 pages, *Harry Potter and the Order of the Phoenix* is the longest children's book there is. It was the best seller online only two hours after it was possible for computer users to order copies of it.

Other children's authors are fans of Rowling, too. "I think Rowling's a terrific writer," says Maurice Sendak, the award-winning author and illustrator of children's books. "She's a ripper-offer,[4] like me. She has taken from some of the best English literature and cooked up her own stew. It's **brilliant**."

Wild About Harry

So why all the fuss about Harry Potter? There were already lots of books with unicorns and wizards in them before Harry came along. And there were certainly lots of books about orphans searching for their **roots** and young people coming of age. **3** **EL**

What makes Rowling's books different? Simply put, readers say, she gets everything right. Rowling writes as though she knows what it's like to be 13 years old. She knows how it feels to be nervous or shocked at discovering what you can do if you try. Through her books, Rowling talks to kids as though they know as much as—or more than—she does about the things that matter. Many readers say they like the characters she has created, Harry above all, not because he is fantastic but because he is **familiar**. **C**

Unlike big and all-powerful superheroes, Harry has the look of an ordinary guy but the heart of a hero. He is small but fast, and his slogan might be "The wand is mightier than the sword."

---

3. **Butterbeer** is a fictional drink from the Harry Potter books.
4. When Sendak says that Rowling is a **ripper-offer**, he means that she borrows ideas from other works of literature.

Vocabulary

brilliant (BRIL yuhnt) *adj.* having or showing ability or talent

familiar (FUH mil yur) *adj.* commonly seen, heard, or experienced; well-known

---

3 **English Language Coach**

Multiple-Meaning Words
Review the meanings of the word **roots** on page 40. Use the context around the word *roots* to determine the right definition in this sentence.

GERMANY Children at a Stuttgart library dress up as Harry, his friends, and some dragons.

Gottfried Stoppel

The Real Magic of Harry Potter **43**

Teach

EL Language Coach

Multiple-Meaning Words Say: Read the sentence that contains the word *roots*. Identify what it means in this context. Then replace it with a synonym. *(Responses will vary. Students may suggest* heritage, past, *or* family history.*)* **EL**

C Critical Thinking

Evaluation Say: Many parents and teachers say that it is difficult to get students to read. Why are students willing to read Harry Potter books when they will not read others? *(Responses will vary. Students may suggest that they connect with the Harry Potter books in ways that they do not with others.)* **AS**

Viewing the Photo

Ask: How does this photo demonstrate the way that readers identify with the characters in *Harry Potter?* *(Responses will vary. Students may note that some readers identify with the characters so much that they show it by dressing like them.)* **OL**

Differentiated Instruction

Mythology Research Maurice Sendak praises Rowling for borrowing from other literature. Tell students that one body of literature from which Rowling borrows is Greek mythology. Give students the following list of references from the Harry Potter series: Three-headed beast (Cerberus); lightning bolt (Zeus); Hermione; Minerva; and Riddle of the Sphinx. Have students use the Internet or library resources to identify each reference. **AL**

Objectives
- Evaluate text
- Skim and scan text
- Understand multiple-meaning words
- Use text features: photography, titles and subheads

Teach

R Reading Skill

Skimming and Scanning Ask: What key words or phrases will you look for to find information about Hermione and Ron? *(Responses will vary. Students may suggest the following words or phrases: Hermione, Ron, Granger, Weasley, or best friends.)* **OL**

C Critical Thinking

Evaluation Say: Name one research strategy that Gibbs used to gain information about the popularity of the Harry Potter books. *(She interviewed young fans of the series.)* **OL**
Ask: Was this strategy an effective means of gathering information? *(Responses will vary. Students may say that it was an effective means because the popularity of the books is based on the tastes and opinions of individual readers.)* **AL**

"He's kind of like me," says Alex Heggen, 12, of Des Moines, Iowa, who sees some of himself in Harry and hopes to find more of Harry in himself. "He's just brave sometimes. . . . I've got black hair, I wear glasses, we're about the same height. . . . Wearing glasses and having braces—getting picked on is just your life. You have to deal with it."

Kids say that the friendship between Harry, Ron, and Hermione shows that Rowling understands how young people deal with one another. "She gets almost everything right," says Ligia Mizhquiri, 12, of Chicago, Illinois. "What happens [at Harry's school] happens to us. Some of us are popular. Some of us are not. Some of us get bullied. Some of us are bullies."

Harry's friendship with his buddy Ron is so familiar to kids that when word got out that a character would die in Book 4, children wrote to Rowling and begged her not to kill off Ron. They were afraid it would be the way it often is in the movies—the sweet best friend is the one who dies.

And Hermione is more than "the smart one." She's **resourceful** and at times she can be the toughest of the three. "Hermione ignores a lot," says Ellis O'Connor, 10, of Evanston, Illinois. "Ignoring while people are teasing is very, very important, because if you don't ignore them, they'll get on your nerves more, and it will be worse."

Kids who are teased because they don't have cool clothes can connect with Ron Weasley and his large family. "If you took all three [Harry, Ron, and Hermione] and put them into a blender, you'd get me," says Ryan Gepperth, 12, of Chicago. "I like to try new things, like Harry. I love reading, like Hermione. And I have problems of my own, like Ron. Ron gets made fun of a lot because he has a lot of brothers and sisters and he comes from a poor family. The other kids don't like him because of that."

The Weasleys *are* poor, but they also are hardworking, loving, and generous. Mrs. Weasley can cast a spell to make dirty dishes clean themselves, but she can't create money out of thin air to buy new appliances for the kitchen. That's the kind of family many Potter readers can understand.

SCOTLAND Fans young and old await Rowling's arrival aboard a recreated Hogwarts Express in Edinburgh.

4 Key Reading Skill

Skimming and Scanning Skim the article to find out more information about Hermione and Ron. What did you learn? **R**

Vocabulary

resourceful (rih SORS ful) *adj.* able to deal with new or difficult situations

---

Additional Support

Reading in the Real World

Career Point out to students that each reader quoted on this page mentions that characters in the Harry Potter books are bullied. Tell students to imagine that they write an advice column for a newspaper and that a reader has written for advice on how to deal with bullying. Ask students to respond with their best advice. Provide students with several examples of newspaper advice columns to use as models. Invite volunteers to share their responses aloud with the class. **OL**

Bridging the Gap [5]

Rowling creates a bridge for kids that connects Harry's world to their own. And the two worlds are very similar. The author knows the real world is "a bit spooky," she says. "I sleep at the top of the house (like Ron), and when it's stormy, I keep waking up wondering what creaked. . . . You see, I'm not as brave as Harry. If you told me there was a gigantic snake wandering around at night where I was living, I'd hide under the bedclothes and let someone else sort it out." [E]

Rowling has created a world in which a boy can fly on a broom, talk to snakes, and grow gills like a fish. But he also has a hard time dealing with his sadness about his dead parents. "She mixes the real-life struggles in with the imaginary, magic struggles," says Casey Brewer, 15, of Longwood, Florida. "Harry and his friends have to think through [problems] in life the same as they have to think through a [problem] that's a three-headed dog. It's, like, inspirational." [5]

As in real life, Harry's world is exciting but not perfect. Wizards have worries and egos[6] and worn-out robes that they are embarrassed to wear. Even in Harry's magical world, there's no spell that fills a person's head with knowledge. The best Hermione can do in Book 3 is the Time Turner, which gives her more hours to study. Learning takes time for characters in a book as well as for real-life humans.

Harry is capable of jealousy and of not caring for others. He breaks rules and doesn't always tell grown-ups everything they'd like to know. He gets into trouble. ("If he didn't, you wouldn't have all those pages to read," notes Zack Ferleger, 12, of Encino, California.) Hermione may be smart, but she can be stubborn. Ron is loyal but unsure of himself.

Rowling loves her characters and invites her readers to love them, too. But the author doesn't love Harry, Ron, and Hermione only for their good qualities. She also loves them for the mistakes and the blemishes[7] that make them just like real kids—and real adults. [6] ○

—Updated 2005, from *TIME*, June 13, 2003

---

5. Something *inspirational* (in spuh RAY shun ul) gives you hope.
6. *Egos* (EE gohs) are people's sense or feeling of self.
7. *Blemishes* (BLEM ish es) are flaws or marks that keep things from being perfect.

FRANCE Reading *Harry Potter et la Coupe de Feu* seems like more fun if you have the right accessories.

Pitchal Frederic/Corbis/Sygma

[5] Key Text Element

Titles and Subheads Subheads divide the text of this article into sections. What is the main idea of each section?

[6] BIG Question

On the "Harry Potter" page of Foldable 1, write three reasons to read a Harry Potter book. Think about why other kids said they enjoyed reading about Harry and his friends. Your response will help you complete the Unit Challenge later. [BQ]

The Real Magic of Harry Potter **45**

Teach

[E] Text Element

Titles and Subheads Say: Remember that the main idea of a section is often stated at the beginning or end of the first paragraph. What is the main idea of the text that follows the subhead *Bridging the Gap*? *(The Harry Potter books serve as a bridge between the very similar worlds of Harry Potter and the readers.)* **OL**

BQ BIG Question

Ask: According to Gibbs's article, what is the main reason that readers enjoy the Harry Potter books? *(Readers see themselves in the characters.)* What are two other reasons that readers enjoy the books? *(Responses will vary. Students may say that Harry, Ron, and Hermione are role models for readers or that the characters make common mistakes and face everyday problems.)* **OL**

✓ CheckPoint

Use the CheckPoint questions provided on Presentation Plus! to check for comprehension of the selection. These questions can be used with interactive response keypads for immediate student feedback.

Differentiated Instruction

Good Book Recipes Have students think about their favorite books or stories. Have them list three things they like about the books. Then, divide students into small groups. Have students share their lists with the group. Instruct students to create a "Recipe for Success" by listing all the things that make their books good. The elements that students find most important will be given the largest quantities in the recipe. For example, *2 cups of believable characters* might be part of the recipe. Invite groups to share and compare their recipes as a class. **OL**

Objectives
• Evaluate text
• Skim and scan text
• Use text features: titles and subheads

Assess

Resources for page 46

📁 Selection Quick Check, p. 4

📁 Selection and Unit Assessment, p. 4

💿 ExamView Assessment Suite

💿 Interactive Tutor: Self-Assessment

Students can respond to the *After You Read* items in their Learner's Notebooks or on a separate sheet of paper.

Answering the BIG Question

1. Responses will vary. Students may say that the familiar and magical qualities of the characters are appealing.
2. J. K. Rowling is the author of the Harry Potter novels.
3. Possible response: Both young people and adults read the Harry Potter novels.

Critical Thinking

4. Possible response: The footnote says that he means that she borrows ideas from other literature.
5. Possible response: Young readers see themselves in the characters.
6. Possible responses: **(a)** Harry Potter's world contains real problems such as poverty and bullying. **(b)** It also contains magical potions and creatures.
7. Responses will vary. Students might prefer Harry to a superhero because he is more like them.

46

After You Read | The Real Magic of Harry Potter

Glynis Sweeny

Answering the BIG Question

1. What did you learn about the Harry Potter books that might make you interested in reading them?
2. **Recall** Who is J. K. Rowling?
   Tip **Right There** You will find the answer in the article.
3. **Summarize** Who reads the Harry Potter books?
   Tip **Author and Me** Answer from the information in the article and from your own experience.

Critical Thinking

4. **Interpret** What does Maurice Sendak mean on page 43 when he calls Rowling a "ripper-offer"? How do you know?
   Tip **Author and Me** Answer using clues from the article and your own thoughts.
5. **Analyze** What makes the Harry Potter books so popular among kids?
   Tip **Author and Me** Answer from the information in the article and from your own thoughts.
6. **Compare and Contrast** **(a)** How is Harry Potter's world like the real world? **(b)** How is it different from the real world?
   Tip **Author and Me** Answer using clues from the article and from your own thoughts.
7. **Evaluate** Would you rather read a book about a superhero or about a hero like Harry Potter? Explain.
   Tip **On My Own** Answer from your own experiences.

Objectives (pp. 46–47)
Reading Skim and scan text
Informational Text Use text features: title, subheads
Vocabulary Use context clues: multiple meanings
Grammar Identify parts of speech: present and progressive tenses

Write About Your Reading

Imagine that you are going to interview a fan of the Harry Potter books. Write a list of seven questions about the books to ask the reader. Skim the article to get ideas for questions, but also think of questions that weren't covered in the article.

Write About Your Reading

Possible response:
1) Who is your favorite character?
2) Why do you like this character?
3) How do you go about reading the novels?
4) What question would you like to ask J. K. Rowling?
5) Which is your favorite book?
6) Why is this your favorite book?
7) How do you hope that the series will end?

Skills Review

Key Reading Skill: Skimming and Scanning

8. Think about how skimming and scanning helped you understand and find information in the article. What general idea did you get by skimming the article? What specific information did you find by scanning?

Key Text Element: Titles and Subheads

9. What hints did the title "The Real Magic of Harry Potter" give you about the article?

10. What important information did the subheads give you?

11. Did the subheads tell you much about the sections of the article? Suggest two new subhead titles that would tell more about each section of the article.

Reviewing Skills: Setting a Purpose for Reading

12. What purpose do you think adults might have for reading the Harry Potter books?

Vocabulary Check

Copy the sentences below. Mark each sentence with a *T* or an *F* to show whether it is true or false.

13. Izzy can't play a note, so he's a brilliant musician.

14. A resourceful person can often get out of a difficult situation.

15. Icebergs are a familiar sight in Florida.

16. **English Language Coach** Write the word *cool* in the center of a word web. Use a dictionary to find the different meanings of *cool* and add them to your web. On page 44, read the first sentence of paragraph 5. What does *cool* mean here?

Grammar Link: Present and Present Progressive Tenses

Verbs change to tell when an action or state of being occurred. These different forms are called **verb tenses**.

The **present tense** may be used to talk about something that is happening now.

• The bus **is** late.

• We **need** help over here!

More often, the present tense is used to talk about actions that happen regularly, to describe something, or to state a general truth.

• Nate **plays** basketball. (happens regularly)

• Tia **has** long hair. (description)

• French people **speak** French. (general truth)

Usually, to show that something is happening at this very minute, you use the **present progressive tense**. To do so, use a form of the helping verb *be* and add *-ing* to the end of the main verb.

• I **am playing** the violin.

• You **are playing** the violin.

Grammar Practice

Copy each sentence below, filling in the correct verb or verb phrase. Use the verb shown before the sentence. Use the *form* of that verb that will communicate the fact given after the sentence.

17. (ride) Ed and Lily ___ the bus. (They regularly do.)

18. (walk) Joe ___ home. (He's doing this now.)

19. (write) She ___ poetry. (She's doing this now.)

20. (work) He ___ at the park. (He regularly does.)

Web Activities For eFlashcards, Selection Quick Checks, and other Web activities, go to www.glencoe.com.

Skills Review

Key Reading Skill: Skimming and Scanning

8. Responses will vary.

Key Text Element: Titles and Subheads

9. Responses will vary. Students may say that the word *Real* suggests that the writer looks at the books in a new or different way.

10. Responses will vary. Students may say that the subheads suggest that the article will be about the popularity of the novels.

11. Responses will vary. Possible alternatives are *Harry's Fans* and *Finding Magic in the Real World.*

Reviewing Skill: Setting a Purpose for Reading

12. Responses will vary.

Vocabulary Check

13. F

14. T

15. F

16. **English Language Coach** Word webs will vary. Students may say that the word *cool* refers to something modern and trendy.

Close

Ask students to summarize what they learned about the Big Question from reading the article.

Grammar Link: Present and Present Progressive Tenses

Grammar Practice

17. ride

18. is walking

19. is writing

20. works

Understanding Graphics

Objective covered in this workshop:
• Use graphics to understand reading

Helping Students Understand Graphics

Why Is It Important?

• Graphic aids such as maps, graphs, charts, and tables help students see information at a glance and show how multiple pieces of information relate to each other.

• Graphic organizers help students visualize what they read so they can sort ideas out, clear up difficult passages, and remember important ideas in a selection. According to some research, visual and graphic aids can improve retention by up to 38 percent.

• A picture or diagram can make a confusing description of a process much easier for people to understand. Graphic aids are also good for presenting numeric or technical information in a clear, concise, engaging way. Maps, charts, graphs, tables, and images help organize information, make it more understandable, and bring it to life.

How to Help Students Get It

• Look in a current newspaper or newsmagazine to find an example of a chart, graph, or table. Explain the graphic aid to the class and briefly analyze the information presented.

• Give students a variety of informational articles that contain charts, graphs, or diagrams. Using one of the articles as an example, model how to preview informational articles. Read aloud the title of an article, the subheads, and the titles of the graphics. Review with the class how to read graphic presentations. Then make a prediction about the content of the article, explaining how you arrived at your prediction. Have students read the article to verify your predictions.

• Remind students to skim graphic presentations when they preview informational text in order to make predictions about content.

Reading to Answer the Big Question

Make Your Own Kite
Instructions and illustrations from an Internet site teach students to construct, decorate, and fly kites.

from *Bone, The Great Cow Race* by Jeff Smith
In this excerpt from a graphic novel, a character named Bone wants to tell a beautiful girl he likes her, but he's afraid that she will focus on his funny looks. He is persuaded to write to her so that she will not be looking at him when she reads his romantic message. Ironically, what he tells her is that she has a secret admirer who is short, bald, and has a big nose.

Workshop Resources

PACING (DAYS) STANDARD	BLOCK	LESSON	STUDENT MATERIALS	TEACHER RESOURCES
1	1/2	Key Skill Lesson: Understanding Graphics	👤 Key Reading Skills Practice, p. 22 👤 English Language Coach Review, p. 42	👆 Bellringer Options Transparencies Daily Language Practice 6 👆 Read Aloud, Think Aloud Transparencies Key Reading Skills 27 💿 Presentation Plus!
1	1	"Make Your Own Kite"	💻 Glencoe Online 👤 Unit Vocabulary Review, p. 40 👤 Academic Vocabulary Review, p. 43 📁 English Language Coach 👤 Active Reading Graphic Organizer, p. 24 👤 Literary Analysis, p. 23 💿 StudentWorks Plus™ 💻 Online Student Edition 💿 Literature Classics 📁 Selection and Unit Assessments, p. 5	👆 Literary and Text Analysis Transparencies 40 💻 Puzzlemaker 💿 Skill Level Up!™ A Language Arts Game 💻 BookLink 3 ▦ Assessment by Learning Objective (Diagnostic and Formative) 💿 Interactive Tutor: Self-Assessment 💿 TeacherWorks Plus™
1		from *Bone, The Great Cow Race*	💻 Glencoe Online 👤 Unit Vocabulary Review, p. 40 👤 Academic Vocabulary Review, p. 43 📁 English Language Coach 👤 Active Reading Graphic Organizer, p. 26 👤 Literary Analysis, p. 23 💿 StudentWorks Plus™ 💻 Online Student Edition 💿 Literature Classics 📁 Selection and Unit Assessments, p. 6	👆 Literary and Text Analysis Transparencies 40 💻 Puzzlemaker 💿 Skill Level Up!™ A Language Arts Game 💻 BookLink 3 ▦ Assessment by Learning Objective (Diagnostic and Formative) 💿 Interactive Tutor: Self-Assessment 💿 TeacherWorks Plus™

Keys for Unit Resource

📁 Blackline Master	💾 DVD
▦ Workbook	👆 Transparency
📖 Supplemental Text	💻 Web-based
💿 CD-ROM	👤 Fast File

Level Appropriate Code

AS = Activities for all students

AL = Activities for students working above grade level

OL = Activities for students working at grade level

BL = Activities for students working below grade level

EL = Activities for English language learners

Focus

BELLRINGER Options

✒ **Daily Language Practice Transparency 6**
Focus Activity Say: Explain this saying: "A picture is worth a thousand words." *(Responses will vary. Students might say an image can make us understand something faster and more easily than words can.)*

Teach

R Reading Skill

Understanding Graphics
Ask: What textbooks, besides this one, use graphics? *(Possible responses: math, science, social studies)* What kinds of graphics are used? *(Possible responses: photos, charts, maps, tables, graphs)* **AS**

Skills Focus

You will practice using these skills when you read the following selections:
• "Make Your Own Kite," p. 52
• from *The Great Cow Race*, p. 58

Reading

• Understanding graphics

Informational Text

• Identifying steps in a process

Vocabulary

• Understanding multiple-meaning words in context
• Academic Vocabulary: *process*

Writing/Grammar

• Using verb tenses correctly

Objectives (pp. 48–49)
Reading Use graphics to understand reading

48   UNIT 1

Skill Lesson

Understanding Graphics

Learn It!

What Is It? The term **graphics** refers to pictures, drawings, maps, charts, tables, and graphs that present information to readers. Photographs, pictures, and art in books, magazines, and newspapers are graphics.

• Graphics get the reader's attention and direct the reader to particular information.
• Graphics add to the reader's understanding of information in a text.
• Graphics arrange information so that it's easy to read at a glance.

R

CLOSE TO HOME ⓟ 2005 John McPherson. Reprinted with permission of UNIVERSAL PRESS SYNDICATE. All rights reserved.

Analyzing Cartoons
Look at the graphic on the wall in this cartoon. Who do you think created this graphic? Explain. What information are the children getting from the graphic?

Additional Support

Reading in the Real World

Career Tell students that video games are made up of graphics. Some people make a living writing plot lines for video games. Fantasy, science fiction, and script writers all have an advantage when it comes to working in the gaming industry. These writers think about many of the things a fiction writer considers: plot, setting, and character development.

Some Web sites post video game writing jobs regularly. Have students do research to find out what it takes to become a professional game writer: What skills would be necessary for this career? What web sites can they find that list work for writers? **OL** Challenge students to write their own video game plot and present it to the class. **AL**

Why Is It Important? It's not *always* true that a picture is worth a thousand words. But many things are easier to show than to tell. They may also be easier to understand. Graphics often give a great deal of information at a glance.

How Do I Do It? Look at the picture and the words together. On a graphic, the few words are used to explain or label what the picture shows you. Sometimes, there are also lines and arrows that point from the words to the parts of the graphic they explain. Here's how one student used a graphic to learn about the cost of food at a ballpark.

Literature Online
Study Central Visit www.glencoe.com and click on Study Central to review graphics.

R

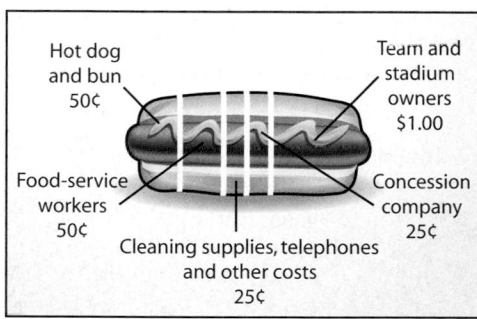

Hot dog and bun 50¢

Team and stadium owners $1.00

Food-service workers 50¢

Concession company 25¢

Cleaning supplies, telephones and other costs 25¢

When I buy a hot dog, who gets the money? Where does the money go? This graphic really explains the answer, and it's easy to follow. The lines connecting the picture to the words show me where the money ends up.

Practice It!

Below are some questions you will learn answers to in "Make Your Own Kite." A graphic will help you answer each question. In your Learner's Notebook, try to write answers and draw pictures to answer these questions before you read. You may not know the answer to all these questions yet.

- What does a kite's frame look like?
- How do you make the *bridle* for a kite?
- What is the *tail* of a kite?
- How do you make a kite fly?

Use It!

As you read "Make Your Own Kite," think about the answers you wrote. Rewrite your answers and draw new pictures if necessary.

Teach

Literature Online
Study Central Have students access the Web site to review understanding graphics and to complete a related activity.

R Reading Skill

Understanding Graphics
Say: Graphics are everywhere. A stop sign tells you to stop your car—that's a graphic. Think about your trip to school this morning. What graphics did you see on the way? *(Responses will vary. Students may say they noticed a variety of traffic signs, billboards, or advertisements.)* **AS**
Say: A graphic can contain a lot of information in one image. Look at the hot dog graphic. It tells you how the money you spend on a hot dog at the ballpark is distributed. What can you learn from this graphic? *(Responses will vary. Students may point out that you can tell who gets the most money and who gets the least money.)* **AS**

Resources for page 49

- Use Key Reading Skills Transparency 27 in *Read Aloud, Think Aloud* to help students practice understanding graphics.

Literature Focus Lesson

How-To Process Have students brainstorm about something they do well, such as playing a sport, painting, playing an instrument, acting, or writing poetry. Ask them to write their own step-by-step "How-To" process. As they write, tell them to imagine that their audience is someone from another planet—who has no knowledge of their subject. Therefore, they should include as many details as possible. Ask them to number each step. **OL** Have students limit the process to no more than five steps, and include their own graphics or drawings to illustrate the steps. **AL**

Objectives
- Use text features: graphics
- Follow steps in a process
- Learn and use new vocabulary

Teach

More About the Author

Technical writers put complex information into terms that are easy to understand. They might write instructions explaining how to program your DVD player or how to assemble a piece of furniture. They write manuals, catalogs, and assembly instructions. They might even oversee the preparation of graphics such as illustrations, photographs, diagrams, and charts. In 2004 about 50,000 Americans were employed as technical writers.

V Vocabulary

Sentences Say: Write one sentence for each meaning of the words *order* and *tip.* Read the sentences to your partner and have your partner determine which definition best fits each sentence. *(Responses will vary.)* **AS**

Before You Read : Make Your Own Kite

Technical writers write and sometimes design schedules, instructions, manuals, maps, and other important materials. Very few technical writers are famous. You usually don't see their names in print. Yet we all read the work of these specialized writers. They help us learn how to do and to make many things.

Objectives (pp. 50–53)
Reading Use graphics • Make connections from text to self
Informational Text Identify text structure: steps in a process
Vocabulary Use context clues: multiple meanings

Vocabulary Preview

English Language Coach

Multiple-Meaning Words Sometimes you'll see a word you know, but it doesn't make sense in the sentence. That may be because you do not know all the meanings of the word.

Many words have multiple meanings. Often you can figure out the meaning that's being used by using clues from other words in the sentence or paragraph.

Look at the words below and some of their meanings.

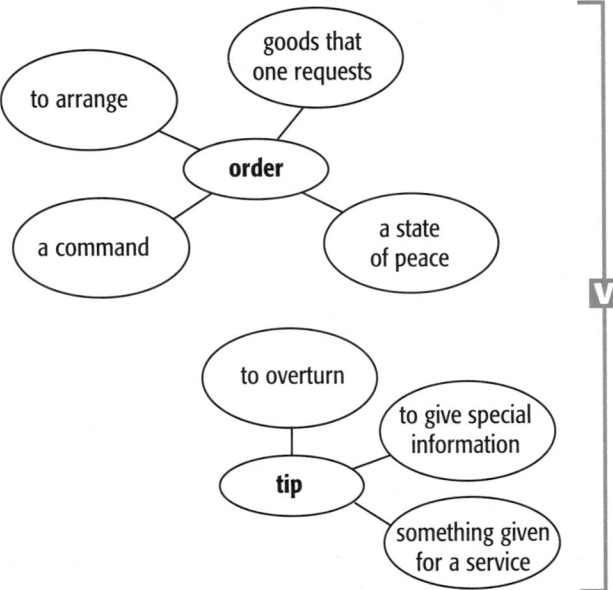

Partner Talk With a partner, discuss the meanings of the words *tip* and *order* in the following sentences.

1. Mr. Jones enjoyed his meal, so he left the waiter a <u>tip</u>.
2. Is your lunch <u>order</u> ready?
3. If you <u>tip</u> the boat, we're going to get wet.
4. The soldiers followed the general's <u>order</u>.
5. After the disaster, the police called for law and <u>order</u>.

Additional Support

English Language Coach

Understanding Multiple-Meaning Words Context clues are words that help you understand an unfamiliar word. A context clue is usually in the same sentence or same paragraph as the word you don't know. Using context clues can help you understand the definition of a multiple-meaning word.

Have students use a dictionary to make word maps, like those on this page, for these words:

- pepper *(a spice; a fruit; to sprinkle; to hit repeatedly)*
- horn *(an antler; a musical instrument; a noise-making device; a phone)*
- anchor *(a weight for holding a ship or object in place; a newscaster)* **EL OL**

Skills Preview

Key Reading Skill: Understanding Graphics

Before you read, think about the importance of graphics in your life. Have you ever

- followed signs and arrows to go somewhere?
- found information from a graph or chart?

R

Partner Talk With a partner, discuss two graphics you have each used in the past week. Explain what you learned from each graphic.

Key Text Element: Process

The events in a story are usually told in the order in which they happened. That's called time order. The organization of an article or a set of directions may be the order in which things *need* to happen in order to get a certain result. That's called a **process**. Seeing the structure of a process makes it much easier to understand what you're reading.

E

As you read, use these tips to help you recognize and understand process.

- Locate what the writer wants you to do or to make.
  Does the writer want you to understand an idea or an object?

- Look for a specific order or organization.
  How does the writer structure information? Does the writer use words such as first, next, now, *and* finally?

- Look for graphic aids, such as pictures, bullets, numbers, or bold type.
  Does the writer use graphics to walk you through a series of steps or groups of information?

Write to Learn Write a step-by-step process of one thing you do every day.

Academic Vocabulary

process (PRAH ses) *n.* a series of steps to follow in making or doing something

Get Ready to Read

Connect to the Reading

Have you ever tried to put something new together? Maybe you bought a game and needed to figure out how to play it. Or maybe you followed the directions for cooking a frozen pizza. You probably use processes to learn how to do things all the time!

Write to Learn Quickwrite for five minutes about a time you used directions. What did you learn? How did the directions help you?

Build Background

The selection you are going to read is about kites.

- There are many different kinds of kites. Most kites are simple wooden frames covered with paper or cloth and attached to a long line.
- Many people believe that a Chinese man named Mo Zi invented the kite more than 2,000 years ago. He got the idea for the kite after watching hawks fly through the sky.

Set Purposes for Reading

BIG Question Read "Make Your Own Kite" to learn how you can use graphics to build something.

Set Your Own Purpose What would you like to learn from the selection to help you answer the Big Question? Write your own purpose on the "Make Your Own Kite" page of Foldable 1.

Literature Online

Interactive Literary Elements Handbook
To review or learn more about the literary elements, go to www.glencoe.com.

Keep Moving

Use these skills as you read the following selection.

Make Your Own Kite **51**

Teach

R Reading Skill

Understanding Graphics
Ask: What kinds of graphics are here in school, not counting those in books? *(Responses will vary. Students might list sign-up sheets, athletic schedules, attendance charts, and murals.)* **AS**

E Text Element

Process Say: Most people have a process for getting ready for work or school. Each person's process is different, but all processes include steps. What steps do you take to get ready for school? *(Responses will vary.)* **AS**

V Vocabulary

Academic Vocabulary Ask: If you learn a process for solving a math problem, what do you learn? *(Possible response: I learned the steps I take to solve it.)* **AS**

Literature Online

Interactive Literary Elements Handbook Have students access the Web site to improve their understanding of process.

Differentiated Instruction

Kite Art The art of decorating a kite has a rich history. Over time, kites have been used to ward off evil, deliver messages, represent the gods, raise banners, catch fish, spy on enemies, send radio signals, and even measure the weather. The way a kite is decorated often has a lot to do with the kite's purpose. Have students think about how they'd like to design a kite. First tell them to think about the purpose, because that may help to determine the kite's colors and graphics. Ask them to design and color a kite on a blank sheet of paper and to write a paragraph about the kite's purpose and why they designed it as they did. **AS**

Objectives
- Use text features: graphics
- Follow steps in a process
- Understand multiple-meaning words
- Learn and use new vocabulary

Teach

Viewing the Photo

Say: Why do you think it's important to avoid flying a kite in a rainstorm, or near telephone and electrical wires? *(Possible responses: Lightning could strike the kite in a rainstorm, or the kite could get tangled in the electrical wires.)* **OL**

R Reading Skill

Understanding Graphics

Say: How do the graphics help you to understand the steps in making a kite? *(They give a visual idea of each step in the process.)* **Ask:** How would your understanding of the instructions change if the graphics were not included? *(They might not be as easy to follow or understand.)* **OL**

E Text Element

Process Ask: None of the steps are numbered; how can you tell which is the first step? *(By looking at the instructions and the graphics, you can tell that the first graphic matches the instructions. Each graphic adds more detail, showing the kite-building process in order.)* **BL**

INFORMATIONAL TEXT
WEB SITE

Make Your Own Kite

It's easy to make your own kite! **1**

All you need is:
- —2 sticks (one stick should be three feet long, the other two feet long)
- —string
- —scissors
- —glue
- —a big sheet of paper

Make the String Frame

First, make a cross with the sticks, centering the shorter stick one-third of the way down the longer stick. Tie a piece of string to the joint and wrap it around, crossing over and under. Cut it and knot it. Cover the end of the string with glue and let it dry. Have an adult notch the ends of the sticks with a knife. Slot the string into the notches and pull it tight, all the way around. Knot the two ends of string together.

Practice the Skills

1 Key Text Element

Process Before you read on, skim the selection. What clues tell you that the writer is describing a process?

Additional Support

Readability Scores
Dale-Chall: 4.2
DRP: 47
Lexile: 720

Reading Fluency

Match the Steps Organize students into small groups. Have each group match individual drawings with the written steps under "Make the String Frame." Within each group, have students take turns reading the steps aloud, one step per student. **OL**

Have students redesign page 52, using the more detailed page 53 as a model. Have them recreate the graphics on a blank sheet of paper and then place each instruction with the appropriate drawing. Finally, have them present their new page to the class. **AL**

Cover the Kite

Lay the kite frame on the paper. Cut all around it, leaving the paper cover a little larger than the frame all the way around. Cut away the corners. Bend the edges of the cover over the string and the frame. Fasten them down with glue. If you haven't decorated your kite yet, now's a good time!

Make the Bridle **3**

Now cut a piece of string the length of two sides of the kite (that's one short side plus one long side). Tie one end of the string around the top of the spine. Make a loop one-third of the way down the string and knot it. Tie the other end of the string to the bottom of the spine. Cut off any extra string.

Make the Kite's Tail

Measure and cut a string that is five times as long as the kite. Cut more paper into little strips, measuring 2X3 inches. Tie the strips onto the string, 8 inches apart. Tie one end of the tail to the bottom of the kite. Now tie the kite line to the loop. The kite is ready to fly! **4**

Make It Fly!

C

If you're by yourself, stand with your back to the wind. With one hand, hold your kite in the air by the lower corner. With your other hand, hold the winder. When the wind blows, let go of the kite, giving it a little push.

If you're with a friend, have your friend hold the kite in the air, with his or her face to the wind. Walk backward into the wind, letting out string as you walk. When the wind tugs at the kite, your friend should let it go. As the kite goes up, keep walking backward, letting out more line.

It's Easy to Bring a Kite Down

Walk toward the kite in the direction the wind is blowing and reel in the kite line as you walk. **5**

Practice the Skills

2 **Key Reading Skill**

Understanding Graphics How does the graphic help you understand the second step?

3 **English Language Coach**

Multiple-Meaning Words Look up the word **bridle** in the dictionary. Which meaning of *bridle* fits best in this selection? How can you tell?

4 **Key Text Element**

Process Draw a picture for each step of the process in this paragraph. Number each picture in order. (Stick figures are okay!)

5 **BIG Question**

What did you learn from this selection? How does the selection help you answer the Big Question? Write your answers on the "Make Your Own Kite" page of Foldable 1. Your response will help you complete the Unit Challenge later. **BQ**

Teach

C Critical Thinking

Evaluation Ask: Judging by the materials used to build the kite, how well do you think it will fly? *(Responses will vary. Students might note that the kite probably would not survive strong winds or many flights.)* **OL** **Ask:** Can you think of ways to improve the kite? *(Possible response: using stronger glue, plastic instead of paper, strong twine instead of string)* **AL**

BQ **BIG Question**

Ask: Have you ever rushed through a project without reading all the directions, only to find out you did something wrong? What could happen if you were to skip a step in building the kite? *(Possible responses: The kite won't fly or might fall apart.)* **OL**

Assess
CheckPoint

Use the CheckPoint questions provided on Presentation Plus! to check for comprehension of the selection. These questions can be used with interactive response keypads for immediate student feedback.

Differentiated Instruction

Timeline Process Have students design a timeline showing the process they take to get ready for school in the morning. Each step should be marked with an approximate time to show the order of the steps in the process. Give students prompts for points on the timeline such as: Wake-up time, cleaning and dressing, breakfast—at home or at school, doing chores, helping siblings prepare for school, doing homework, transportation—walking, taking the bus or train, or being driven. **AS**

Objectives
• Evaluate text
• Use text features: photography, graphics
• Follow steps in a process

Assess

 Resources for page 54

📁 Selection Quick Check, p. 5

📁 Selection and Unit Assessment, p. 5

⚪ ExamView Assessment Suite

⚪ Interactive Tutor: Self-Assessment

Students can respond to the *After You Read* items in their Learner's Notebooks or on a separate sheet of paper.

Answering the BIG Question

1. Directions tell you how to do something correctly. By reading the directions, you are likely to save time because you'll probably do the task right.

2. Have an adult notch the ends of the stick with a knife.

3. You should stand with your back to the wind.

Critical Thinking

4. Possible response: You should fly the kite in an open space, such as an athletic field, a track, or a beach. The selection mentions you'll need wind, so an open space (without trees to block the wind and tangle the kite) would be ideal.

5. Answers will vary. Possible response: It looks easy to make, but it probably won't fly very well. The instructions and graphics are helpful, but the materials are weak.

54

After You Read   Make Your Own Kite

Answering the BIG Question

1. Why is it important to read directions? What can they help you do?

2. **Recall** What do you do after you cover the end of the string with glue and let it dry?

   Tip **Right There** You will find the answer in the selection.

3. If you fly your kite by yourself, how should you stand?

   Tip **Right There** You will find the answer in the selection.

Critical Thinking

4. **Infer** Where should you fly a kite? What clues from the selection tell you?

   Tip **Author and Me** You will find clues in the selection, but you must also use the information in your head.

5. **Evaluate** The writer says, "It's easy to make your own kite!" After reading the selection, do you agree with the writer? Use details from the selection to explain your answer.

   Tip **Author and Me** You will find clues in the selection, but you must also use the information in your head.

Write About Your Reading

Write a Letter If you wanted to make a kite, would the selection help you build it successfully? Write a brief letter to the writer about how the directions were helpful or how they could be improved. Remember to include details. Use the following questions to get started.

• Overall, are the directions helpful? Why or why not?

• What is good about the directions?

• Which part of the directions would most help you make your kite?

• Which part of the directions confuse you?

• What would you change about the directions?

• What steps would you add to the directions?

Objectives (pp. 54–55)
Reading Use graphics
Informational Text Identify text structure: steps in a process
Vocabulary Use context clues: multiple meanings
Writing Write a letter to provide information
Grammar Identify parts of speech: past and past progressive tenses

54   UNIT 1 Why Read?

Write About Your Reading

Possible Response:

To whom it may concern,

Recently, my friends tried to build a kite with your instructions. The directions were very detailed, and the step-by-step process made them easy to follow. The graphics were the best part. They helped me to see each step. None of it was confusing, but I wondered why the materials were so weak. If you could change anything, I think you should use stronger materials. I stretched a plastic garbage bag (instead of the paper) across the kite's frame, and my kite lasted longer than everyone else's!

Skills Review

Key Reading Skill: Understanding Graphics

6. How do the graphics in this selection help you better understand the process of building a kite? Do you think you could build a kite if the writer had not included graphics?

7. Which graphic most helps you "see" what to do? Why?

Key Text Element: Process

8. What words in the text help you recognize that the writer is describing a process?

9. Summarize the process of building a kite in five or six steps. Use the subheads if you need help.

Vocabulary Check

10. Academic Vocabulary A process is a series of ____ that you follow when you make or do something.

English Language Coach You saw the word *frame* in the selection. Look at the word and some of its meanings below. Then rewrite the sentences and match each meaning of *frame* to a sentence.

frame
- **a.** the skeleton of a human or animal body
- **b.** a construction that gives shape or strength
- **c.** an open structure that holds a picture, mirror, etc.
- **d.** to create false evidence against someone

11. Before you add walls, you must build the <u>frame</u> of the house.

12. He needs very long pants because of his tall <u>frame</u>.

13. The burglar tried to <u>frame</u> me for his crime.

14. I put the photo in a <u>frame</u>.

Web Activities For eFlashcards, Selection Quick Checks, and other Web activities, go to www.glencoe.com.

Grammar Link: Past and Past Progressive Tenses

The **past tense** of a verb shows an action or state of being that has already happened. Usually, you form the past tense by adding -ed to the end of the verb.

- It **rained** hard last night.
- As a child, Mom **played** tennis.

There is more than one way to talk about the past. You may want to talk about continuing action. To show that something was still going on at the time you're talking about, use the **past progressive tense**. To do this, use the helping verb *was* or *were* and add -ing to the main verb.

In the sentences below, the helping verb is underlined and the main verb is bold.

- We <u>were</u> **watching** TV together.
- While I <u>was</u> **sleeping**, the rain started.
- Fran <u>was</u> **cooking** dinner, while her brothers <u>were</u> **cleaning** the house.
- They <u>were</u> **eating** when the phone rang.

Grammar Practice

Copy the sentences below on a separate sheet of paper. Underline all the verbs or verb phrases in each sentence. Look for both the past tense and the past progressive!

15. I was practicing all afternoon.

16. Cara was swimming while Marsha was walking on the track.

17. Jon and Milly bought books at the mall while they were shopping.

18. The cookies were baking when Les arrived.

Writing Application Look back over the letter you wrote. Check to make sure that you used the past and past progressive tenses correctly.

Skills Review

Key Reading Skill: Understanding Graphics

6. Possible responses: The graphics help me to "see" each step of the process, and to understand new terms, like "bridle." It would probably be harder to build the kite without the graphics.

7. Responses will vary. Possible response: The graphic with the picture of the bridle was the most helpful because I didn't know that word.

Key Text Element: Process

8. The writer uses words like "First" and "Now." The writer lets me know when my kite is done, by adding "The kite is ready to fly!"

9. 1. Make the string frame, 2. Cover the kite with paper, 3. Make the bridle, 4. Make the kite's tail, 5. Tie on the kite line.

Vocabulary Check

10. Academic Vocabulary: steps

English Language Coach

11. b

12. a

13. d

14. c

Grammar Link: Past and Past Progressive Tenses

Grammar Practice

15. was practicing

16. was swimming

17. bought

18. were baking

Close

Ask students to summarize what they learned from reading "Make Your Own Kite" to answer the Big Question.

Teach

More About the Author

Jeff Smith learned about cartooning by watching cartoons and reading comic books. He started his own company to publish his well-known *Bone* series. Against tough odds, Smith stuck to his vision of combining quality art with creative story lines to come up with books that are at the forefront of the comic book industry. His hard work paid off. Smith has won numerous awards, and his work is published in at least thirteen languages.

EL Language Coach

Multiple-Meaning Words

Say: If you don't see any context clues to help you understand a multiple-meaning word, a dictionary will help you find all of its meanings. Look at the chart on this page. Using it as a model, make a chart with the following multiple-meaning words: *activity, gum, strain.* *(Responses will vary, but should model the context of the chart on page 56.)* **AS**

Before You Read : from *The Great Cow Race*

Meet the Author

Jeff Smith was born and raised in the American Midwest. He wrote comic strips for Ohio State University's student newspaper for four years. In 1991 he started his own company, Cartoon Books. Smith's work has been published in thirteen languages, and he received an Eisner Award for *The Great Cow Race* in 1994.

Literature Online

Author Search For more about Jeff Smith, go to www.glencoe.com.

Objectives (pp. 56–61)
Reading Use graphics • Make connections from text to self
Informational Text Identify text structure: steps in a process
Vocabulary Use context clues: multiple meanings

Vocabulary Preview

English Language Coach

Multiple-Meaning Words When you run into a word with more than one meaning, the first step is to look for clues to its meaning in the sentences around it. But sometimes the meaning used may be unfamiliar to you. In that case, you also need to look in a dictionary. Then you can try the different meanings to see which one makes sense in the sentence. Look at the examples in the chart.

Sentence	Multiple Meanings of Word	Context Definition
I took the dog for a walk in the <u>park</u>.	a piece of ground kept in a city for recreation; an enclosed arena or stadium used for games; a space occupied by vehicles	a piece of ground kept in a city for recreation
She <u>delivered</u> the puppies from the thief's clutches.	to send to an intended destination; to set free; to assist in giving birth	to set free
Miles needed a new <u>reed</u> for his saxophone.	tall grasses with slender, jointed stems that grow in wet areas; a person or thing too weak to rely on; a thin wood or plastic tongue that vibrates against the mouthpiece of a wind instrument causing sound when blown upon	a thin wood or plastic tongue that vibrates against the mouthpiece of a wind instrument causing sound when blown upon

Write to Learn Look up the following words in a dictionary. In your Learner's Notebook, write the multiple meanings of the words. Then write a paragraph for one of the words using several of its meanings.

1. cook

2. pass

3. reflect

Additional Support

Literature Online

Author Search To expand students' appreciation of Jeff Smith, have them access the Web site for additional information and resources.

Differentiated Instruction

Making Storyboards Graphic novels combine text and images. Most graphic novels start in the form of a storyboard. Have students make a one-page storyboard of a process of their choice. Each panel should contain an illustration and a (written) step in the process. The process should be simple enough to fit on one page, for example, making a sandwich, planting a flower, or feeding a pet. **OL** Students can work with a partner—one as the writer, the other as the illustrator—to draw and color the panels. They should make copies, distribute them, and present their process to the class. **EL BL**

Skills Preview

Key Reading Skill: Understanding Graphics

Graphics, such as charts, graphs, time lines, and pictures, give you information at a glance and explain something visually. Graphics are especially important in graphic novels, cartoons, and comic strips. These all have little text, so writers use graphics to share information with readers. Keep the following questions in mind as you read the selection:

- How do the graphics share the characters' emotions?
- What information do the graphics give you that the text does not?

Write to Learn Pick a school subject that you have seen graphics in, and write about how graphics help you to understand that subject (a time line in a history class, for example). How does the graphic help you to understand the subject?

Key Text Element: Process

To understand a **process**, you need to be able to see and follow the steps. Writers use clues to help you, including time words (such as *next* and *finally*), numbers, and graphics. As you read, you can use the tips below to help you recognize the steps in a process and understand what you're reading.

- Sometimes a process will use words like *first, then, after, next,* and *finally* to show when to complete the different steps in the process.

  How do these steps show you the end of one step and the beginning of another?

- Sometimes a process is numbered.

  Do you see numbers indicating the order of the steps?

- Some processes have graphics or pictures to explain the steps visually.

  How can a graphic be helpful when you are learning a process?

Write to Learn Think of a process you go through every day. In your Learner's Notebook, number and list all of the steps. Circle any steps that might be hard for someone else to understand. Make notes next to those steps about ways to explain them clearly.

Get Ready to Read

Connect to the Reading

Have you ever admired someone, but didn't know how to express yourself? Did you call them on the phone, have a friend tell them, write a letter, or say something in person? What kind of advice would you give a friend in that situation?

Write to Learn In your Learner's Notebook, write about how you would approach someone you admire. Would you write a letter or a poem, call the person on the phone, write a song, or draw a picture? Explain why your choice is the best way to impress the person you admire.

Build Background

The selection that you are about to read is a passage from the graphic novel *The Great Cow Race. The Great Cow Race* is the second novel in a series called *Bone.* It is about the adventures of the Bone cousins: Fone Bone, Phoney Bone, and Smiley Bone.

- A graphic novel is a long, illustrated story.
- Graphic novels are growing in popularity in the United States. In 2003 graphic novels had more than $120 million in sales.

Set Purposes for Reading

BIG Question Read *The Great Cow Race* to find out why you should read the letters people write you.

Set Your Own Purpose What else would you like to learn from the selection to help you answer the Big Question? Write your own purpose on the "Great Cow Race" page of Foldable 1.

Interactive Literary Elements Handbook
To review or learn more about the literary elements, go to www.glencoe.com.

Keep Moving

Use these skills as you read the following selection.

from *The Great Cow Race* **57**

Teach

R Reading Skill

Understanding Graphics

Ask: What are some of the similarities and differences between a story with illustrations, and one without them? *(Possible similarities: Both have words, a plot, characters, and a setting. Possible differences: An illustrated story might have fewer words and might require less imagination from the reader.)* **AS**

E Text Element

Process Say: With a graphic story, you might wonder which to do first—read the words or look at the pictures. The easiest process for reading a graphic story is to do both at once. Read the text and view the drawing in one frame, or box, at a time. **AS**

Interactive Literary Elements Handbook Have students access the Web site to improve their understanding of process.

Reading in the Real World

Career Sometimes, a comic book writer is not the illustrator. Jeff Smith *both* writes and draws the *Bone* series. Tell interested students to research careers in either the illustration or the writing world of comic books, graphic novels, or comic strips.

Some questions they could start with are: What companies publish graphic novels? What kind of education do you need to be a comic book writer or illustrator? Are there contests for art and/or stories in this field? **AS**

Objectives

- Use text features: graphics
- Follow steps in a process
- Understand multiple-meaning words

Teach

R Reading Skill

Understanding Graphics Say: In a graphic story, it's important to look at characters' expressions to understand their thoughts and feelings. Notice how Bone's expression changes in each frame. How do you think Bone feels in the first frame when he's reading? *(He looks like he's concentrating.)* **Ask:** How does he feel in the second frame when he sees Ted? *(He looks happy to see Ted.)* **Ask:** How does he feel in the fourth frame when the heart is above his head? *(He looks thoughtful or troubled.)* **AS**

EL Language Coach

Slang Say: Bone and Ted speak loose, conversational English called slang. You might speak slang with your friends but speak a different way when you give a report in school. What do you think Bone means when he says, "Whatcha been up to?" *(What have you been doing?)* **Ask:** What does Ted mean when he asks, "Why don't ya jes **tell** Thorn that ya **likes** her—" *(Why don't you just tell Thorn that you like her—)* **EL**

Practice the Skills

1 **Key Reading Skill**

Understanding Graphics Look at the first graphic. One piece of information you learn from the graphic is that Bone is in a forest. What other information does the graphic give you that the text does not?

2 **BIG Question**

You can see that Bone is in the woods reading. What might be his purpose for reading? Your response will help you complete the Unit Challenge.

3 **Key Reading Skill**

Understanding Graphics The fourth picture, or frame, contains no words at all. What does the graphic tell you about Bone's thoughts? How do you know this?

from The Great Cow Race

From BONE ®: THE GREAT COW RACE by Jeff Smith. Copyright © 2005, 1993, 1992 by Jeff Smith. Published by Graphix, an imprint of Scholastic Inc. Reprinted by permission.

Additional Support

Readability Scores
Dale-Chall: 6.5
DRP: N/A
Lexile: 280

Reading Fluency

Graphic Story Theater Organize students into groups of three, and assign each group three reading parts: Bone, Ted, and a narrator (to read Bone's letter). Tell students to read their parts in the loose, conversational way Bone and Ted speak. Have them gesture and mimic the characters' expressions and behavior. **AS** Tell students to memorize their lines and have the groups present their skits (in costume, if they wish) to the class. **AL**

Practice the Skills

4 **English Language Coach**

Multiple-Meaning Words You'd probably say that a joke is **funny** because it makes you laugh. But notice how *funny* is used here. Can you find the clue to the meaning of *funny* in Ted's reply to Bone? If not, check a dictionary.

from *The Great Cow Race* **59**

Teach

C Critical Thinking

Analyze **Say:** Bone is concerned about the way he looks. Is it fair to judge people by the way they look? *(Responses will vary.)* **Ask:** What positive qualities does Bone have? *(Possible response: He seems friendly, creative, funny, and devoted.)* **AS**

R Reading Skill

Understanding Graphics
Say: The way words are written in a graphic story helps you to understand the way characters feel almost as much as their expressions do. Look at the darker printed words. Some words such as "NOW YER TALKIN'!" or "YOUR LIPS IS LIKE SWOLLEN POOLS . . ." are in larger print. Why do you think some words are written in different print? *(Possible responses: Those words are stressed for different reasons. Sometimes they stress a word or phrase. Other times they show an emotion, such as excitement.)* **AS**

English Language Coach

Slang Translation Tell students to make two columns. In the first column have them make a list of all the slang terms and phrases used by Ted and Bone. In the second column they should translate the phrases. For instance, Ted's statement, "You writes a real rowzer of a rhyme, see?" might be translated as, "You should write a moving poem." In some cases, students might have to translate entire sentences; in other cases, just a word. **AS**

Objectives
• Use text features: graphics
• Analyze text
• Understand slang

Teach

R Reading Skill

Understanding Graphics

Say: The *Bone* series was originally illustrated in black and white. Imagine this graphic story in black and white. How do you think color affects the illustrations? *(Responses will vary.)* **OL**

EL Language Coach

Abbreviations Say: An abbreviation is a shortened form of a word or group of words. People often use abbreviations in personal letters, e-mails, and instant messages. In Bone's love letter, "xxxooo" means "hugs and kisses." (It's often written as "xoxo.") Write the following on the board: SWAK, WBS, TMI, LLL Do you know these abbreviations? *(Sealed with a Kiss, Write Back Soon, Too Much Information, Longer Letter Later)* **AS**

Practice the Skills

5 Key Text Element

Process Bone is actually going through a *writing process.* Look back through the graphics, and find the beginning of Bone's writing process. How do you know when his process begins; how do you know when it ends? Is most of the process shown with pictures or words? How many steps are in Bone's process?

EL

Additional Support

Reading in the Real World

Citizenship Writing to political representatives is a good way for students to use their letter-writing skills. Ask them to think of issues that concern them and the representatives (local, state, or federal) to whom they wish to write. Tell students to research their topics, focus on specifics, and draft their letters. Have them exchange drafts and make final changes. Tell students to find the addresses of the people they're writing to. (E-mails are fine and likely to get quicker responses.) Invite students who get responses to read their letters and the responses to the class. **AL**

Practice the Skills

6 Key Reading Skill

Understanding Graphics In the last graphic, Bone's letter is sitting on a stump. What do you think that means? Why do you think that graphic is so much larger than all the others?

7 BIG Question

What would you do if you were walking through the woods and saw a letter sitting on a stump? What might your reasons be for reading the letter? **BQ** Write your answer on "The Great Cow Race" page of Foldable 1. Your response will help you complete the Unit Challenge later.

from *The Great Cow Race* **61**

Teach

BQ **BIG Question**

Say: At the beginning of the story, Bone is reading a novel titled *Moby Dick.* A novel is a long fictional story that deals with imaginary events and characters. What are some purposes for reading fiction? *(Possible responses: for fun or entertainment; to discover something new)* **OL**

Assess

✓CheckPoint

Use the CheckPoint questions provided on Presentation Plus! to check for comprehension of the selection. These questions can be used with interactive response keypads for immediate student feedback.

Differentiated Instruction

Write the Ending The last panel is mysterious. One way to solve the mystery is to encourage students to read the series. Another way is to have them write their own endings. Tell them to think about these questions as they get started: Where did Bone go? Why did he leave his backpack behind? Did he leave in a hurry? Why did he leave his letter? Who will find it? Will Thorn ever learn that Bone likes her? **OL** Have students turn their endings into storyboards, complete with Bone and his friends. **AL**

Objectives
- Use text features: graphics
- Identify acronyms and abbreviations

61

Assess

Resources for page 62

- 📁 Selection Quick Check, p. 6
- 📁 Selection and Unit Assessment, p. 6
- 🌐 ExamView Assessment Suite
- 🌐 Interactive Tutor: Self-Assessment

Students can respond to the *After You Read* items in their Learner's Notebooks or on separate sheets of paper.

Answering the
BIG Question

1. Possible response: Two purposes for reading graphic novels are: to be entertained and to learn.

2. Bone is writing his poem to Thorn.

3. Ted says that since Bone looks so "doofy," a poem is his only hope of impressing Thorn.

Critical Thinking

4. Possible response: Ted seems to think that Bone cannot write a good poem. After encouraging Bone to write the poem, Ted immediately gives him suggestions about what to write.

5. Responses will vary: I don't think Bone gives Thorn the letter because it has been left on the stump. Maybe Thorn, or someone else, will find it.

6. Responses will vary: I think it's a good idea, but it's a waste of time if you don't sign the poem. It's better to tell the person face-to-face.

62

After You Read   from *The Great Cow Race*

Answering the BIG Question

1. What are two reasons for reading graphic novels?
2. **Recall** To whom is Bone writing his poem?
   Tip **Right There** You will find the answer in the text.
3. **Recall** Why does Ted suggest that Bone write a poem?
   Tip **Right There** You will find the answer in the text.

Critical Thinking

4. **Infer** Does Ted think Bone has the ability to write a love poem? Use details from the text to support your answer.
   Tip **Author and Me** You will find clues in the story, but you must also use the information in your head.

5. **Draw Conclusions** What do you think happens at the end of the story?
   Tip **Author and Me** You will find clues in the story, but you must also use the information in your head.

6. **Evaluate** Do you think writing a love poem is a good way to show someone that you like him or her?
   Tip **On My Own** You must use the information in your head.

Write About Your Reading

Design your own "graphic novel" explaining a process. Look back at the activity on page 57 in which you explained and numbered a process. Use the process you explained or choose another one. Give each step its own graphic (draw boxes, use text, and maybe even create your own character—like Bone—to help explain the steps). If you have time, add color. You don't have to be a perfect artist—use stick figures or simple shapes if you want.

Objectives (pp. 62–63)
Reading Use graphics • Make connections from text to self
Informational Text Identify text structure: steps in a process
Vocabulary Use context clues: multiple meanings
Writing Design a graphic novel
Grammar Identify parts of speech: present perfect and past perfect verb tenses

62   UNIT 1   Why Read?

Write About Your Reading
Responses will vary.

Skills Review

Key Reading Skill:
Understanding Graphics

7. The graphics show Bone's different expressions. How do these expressions reveal what Bone is thinking or feeling? Give examples from the story.

Key Text Element: Process

8. How many steps are there in Bone's writing process? What is each step?

Vocabulary Check

9. English Language Coach Look back at the word *sweeps* in the tenth frame of the story. In your Learner's Notebook, write two sentences with different meanings for that word. Use a dictionary to look up the meanings of *sweep* if necessary.

Grammar Link: Present Perfect and Past Perfect Tenses

Another tense to use while talking about the past is the **present perfect tense**. To form it, use the helping verb *have* or *has* and what is called the "past participle" of the main verb. (For most verbs, the past participle is the same as the past tense.)

You can use this tense to talk about something that happened but only if *when* it happened isn't important. Don't use it to talk about a specific time.

- Right: I **painted** my house.
- Right: I **have painted** my house.
- Wrong: I **have painted** my house in May.

You can use this tense with *never* or *already*, because they don't refer to a particular time.

- Right: I **have** already **painted** my house.
- Right: I **have** never **painted** my house.

You *must* use this tense to talk about something that happened and is still happening.

- Wrong: I **collected** stamps since last year.
- Right: I **have collected** stamps since last year.

To talk about something that happened (or didn't happen) before something else, you can use the **past perfect tense**. To form it, use the helping verb *had* and the past participle of the main verb.

- Hilda **had mowed** the lawn before the rain started.
- Hilda **had** never **mowed** the lawn until Ruth showed her how.

Don't use this tense to talk about only one event. Use it only if you're talking about something that happened before something else.

- Wrong: This morning, Dad **had poured** my juice.
- Right: Before I got up, Dad **had poured** my juice.

Grammar Practice

Write the numbers from 10 to 15 on a separate sheet of paper. Next to each, write *C* if the sentence is correct. If it's incorrect, write it correctly.

10. I have never missed a day of school.

11. When Martha was six, she has learned to read.

12. Since July, Chaz played better.

13. Every year, tulips have bloomed in our yard.

14. Last summer, we have traveled to Mexico.

15. When we got there, Sam had not arrived.

Writing Application Look back at your writing assignment. Check to see if you wrote correctly about things that happened in the past. If you made any mistakes, correct them.

Web Activities For eFlashcards, Selection Quick Checks, and other Web activities, go to www.glencoe.com.

Skills Review

Key Reading Skill:
Understanding Graphics

7. Possible responses: Since there are fewer words, Bone's facial expressions help to share his thoughts and feelings with the reader. When he writes the letter his face changes a little bit in each picture—at first he looks thoughtful, and at the end he smiles, as if he is satisfied with his work.

Key Text Element: Process

8. There are at least three steps: 1. He gathers pencil and paper. 2. He thinks about what to write. 3. He writes and signs the letter.

Vocabulary Check

English Language Coach

9. Possible responses: Jocelyn hastily *sweeps* the back porch. He always *sweeps* the ladies off of their feet when he sings.

Close

Ask students to think about the Big Question, and explain why reading letters can be important.

Grammar Link: Present Perfect and Past Perfect

Grammar Practice

10. C

11. When Martha was six, she learned to read.

12. Since July, Chaz has played better.

13. C

14. Last summer, we traveled to Mexico.

15. C

Web Activities Have students access the Web site for interactive activities that will help them assess their understanding of the selection.

Focus

Summary
Revising, Editing, and Presenting

BELLRINGER Options

- **Daily Language Practice Transparency 7**
Focus Activity Share the following statement by writer Ellen Hunnicut:
Sometimes [writing] seems to be all revision. And the longer I write, the more I revise—and it's never completely right. **Ask:** Do you agree or disagree with the quotation? Explain. *(Responses will vary.)*

ASSIGNMENT Write a summary

Purpose: Summarize main ideas and important details

Audience: You, your teacher, and some classmates

In Writing Workshop Part 1, you drafted a summary about one selection from the beginning of the unit. You may not remember what these selections were about, and that's okay. Read the draft of your summary to refresh your memory. Then reread the original selection. Think about how well your summary reflects the original selection.

Revising
Make It Better

In this workshop, you'll work on a few skills to improve your draft. This part of the writing process is called revising, and it is your chance to make your writing look and sound just right. As you revise, you will use the tips in this workshop to turn your draft into a final product.

W

Teach

W Writing

Summary Say: Quotations can make a summary more interesting to read. Choose a sentence from the selection that is memorable *and* supports a main idea. It might be a funny sentence or one that makes you think. Include this sentence as a quotation in your summary. *(Give students a quick lesson on capitalization and punctuation in quotations. See the Grammar Links on pages 1049 and 1055.)* **AS**

Revising Rubric

Your revised summary should have

- a main idea stated in your own words
- important details from the selection
- no unrelated information
- all words spelled correctly
- verbs used correctly

Objectives (pp. 64–67)
Writing Use the writing process: paraphrasing and summarizing • Revise a draft to include: main ideas and supporting details • Compare summary to original • Edit writing for: grammar, spelling, punctuation • Present writing
Grammar Use verbs
Listening, Speaking, and Viewing Use visuals in presentation • Listen actively

Check for Main Idea Read your summary again and ask yourself these questions: Have I included the author's main idea? Have I included the most important details?

If you answered *no* to one or both of these questions, go back and correct your summary.

Check for Coherence When all of the sentences in the paragraph fit together just right, the writing is coherent. That means that it holds together and makes sense. Here is one way to make your writing more coherent:

- Write events in the order that they happened: this is called **chronological order.**

Chronological Order	Not Chronological Order
Robert was given a homework assignment.	Robert decided that childhood obesity was a good topic.
He talked about the assignment with his parents.	Robert researched topics for his assignment.
Robert decided that childhood obesity was a good topic.	Robert was given a homework assignment.

- Start your sentences with linking words and phrases. These are called **transitions.** Some transitions can help you write in chronological order. Try using the words *first, in the beginning, next, finally,* or *last.*

Additional Support

Differentiated Instruction

Track Ideas Students need to be sure to include the selection's main ideas in their summaries. Suggest that they use a chart like this one to track ideas and details as they reread their selections. After filling in the chart, they should add to their summaries any important ideas and details they missed. **OL**

Main Idea and Details	
in Selection	in Summary

Editing

Finish It Up

After you finish writing, it's time to edit your work for grammar, usage, mechanics, and spelling. Read your summary one sentence at a time and use the **Editing Checklist** to look for errors.

Literature Online

Writing Models For models and other writing activities, go to www.glencoe.com.

Teach

W Writing

Students could compare and contrast their summaries with the original selections in a Venn diagram. The sample text below compares the Active Writing Model on page 66 with the selection on pages 12-15. **OL**

Editing Checklist

☑ All words are spelled correctly.

☑ Every sentence has a verb.

☑ All verbs agree with their subjects.

☑ Verb tenses are correct.

Compare Your Summary with the Original

Before you say that your summary is finished, compare it with the original selection. Read the entire selection and ask yourself the following questions about your summary:

• Have I created a shorter version of the original?

• Have I included the author's main idea?

• Have I clearly written what this selection is about?

• Have I left the minor details out of my summary?

You should have answered *yes* to all of the questions, but if you didn't, there is still time to go back and make changes to your summary.

◀ **Writing Tip**

One of the most important parts of editing is making sure that all words are spelled correctly. Even if you use a spellchecker on your computer, look up words you're not sure about in a dictionary.

Main ideas: high prices; high number of ads
Details: who did the study; quotations; specific prices; bringing food in; where ads appeared

question-answer format; graphics; specific prices

paragraph format; shorter and more general; no graphics

Publishing and Presenting

Show It Off

Now that your summary is finished, print it out or write a new copy that is easy for you to read.

• Find a partner who has summarized a different selection.

• Take turns reading your summaries aloud.

• After your partner reads his or her summary, tell the writer interesting sentences, phrases, or words that you heard in the summary.

Listen for these parts of your classmate's summary:

• Main idea

• Important details

• Extra information

After school, ask a family member to read your summary. See if the person can identify the main idea and topic sentences.

◀ **Writing Tip**

If you are handwriting your final draft, try to use your best handwriting. Take your time. Erase your mistakes instead of crossing them out.

Resources for page 65

📁 Use the BLM in the Unit 1 Resource Booklet, pp. 28–29.

🖱 Use the Grammar and Writing Workshop Transparencies 17–18

Reading Fluency

Read Aloud Hearing their own voices can help students develop reading fluency. Invite struggling readers to read their summaries to you. If they can't read quickly and smoothly, what slows them down? Is it an inability to recognize words? Address any issues with writing, grammar, and punctuation that might cause reading problems. If necessary, read part of the summary aloud yourself, and then have students try again. Your assessment will help you with curricular decisions for each student. **BL**

Objectives

• Write a summary

• Identify main ideas and supporting details

• Revise summary

• Edit writing for spelling errors

• Compare and contrast

Teach

W Writing

Main Idea Ask: Do the first two sentences tell the main idea of "Ballpark Food"? *(yes)* Why is it good to begin the summary with the main idea? *(Possible response: It lets readers know right away what the summary will be about.)* **AS**

C Critical Thinking

Analysis Ask: What is implied about the stadium owners by the article and its summary? *(Possible response: The stadium owners are taking advantage of the fans.)* **OL Ask:** Why does the writer include the partial quotation about the "sneakiest ads"? *(Possible response: The word* sneakiest *helps convey this idea.)* **AL**

Literature Online

Writing Models Have students access the Web site for an additional and interactive Writing Workshop-based student model.

Active Writing Model

Writer's Model

Summary of "Ballpark Food"
By Sharice Johnson

The student wrote the main idea of the original selection in her own words.

Thirty-six kids investigated the high price of food at baseball parks. The kids found that ballpark food costs three to seven times more than the same food at the grocery store. Most of the profits of high-priced stadium food go to the athletes and the stadium owners.

This is an important detail that supports the main idea.

The kids concluded, "You almost need a major-league salary to afford ballpark food!"

The writer uses a transition, *the kids concluded,* to begin this sentence.

One way to avoid high prices at the ballpark is to bring your own food. Most stadiums let you do this, but ushers have the right to check inside bags and take away items that could be thrown onto the field.

This paragraph begins with an important detail from the article.

The kids also collected information about advertisements found at ballparks. They found ads on just about everything, including concession stands. One fan named Tess believed that the "sneakiest ads" followed the replays on the big-screen television because everyone in the stadium watches the replays.

This sentence supports the important detail.

Additional Support

Reading in the Real World

College Students who plan to further their education will attend lectures, or classes in which a teacher gives a speech about a topic. Students will be responsible for taking notes during the lectures. Explain that when students take notes they write the main ideas and major details about a topic. These main ideas and details can be combined to create a summary. Students can review these summaries to prepare for tests and essays. Invite students to share their note-taking experiences from your class or other classes. **AL**

Listening, Speaking, and Viewing

Getting Information from Visuals

What Are Visuals?

Visuals are the images or pictures that you see in various forms of mass communication such as television, the Internet, and magazines. When you look at visuals in media, you make a judgment of what you see—either you like it, or you don't. How you respond to a picture of a sleeping kitten is different from how you respond to a picture of a roaring tiger.

Why Are Visuals Important?

Pictures are powerful. They appeal to our minds, our feelings, and our imaginations. Looking at a picture carefully can help you notice more details and get more information. You may also see things that entertain you or make you laugh.

At the same time, learning to look at a picture carefully can help you make up your own mind about things. Otherwise, a picture may make you think things that are not true.

How Do I Do It?

Here are some ways to evaluate visuals:

- Look at all the parts of the picture. If there are people, look at their expressions. Look at how they are standing or sitting. If a picture shows an activity, imagine the movement it shows.
- Look at the colors in a picture. If they are dark, they may make you feel sad, even if what the picture shows is not particularly sad. A dark picture of a person may make you like that person less.
- Think about what the picture suggests. Suppose an article is about crime, and the picture shows a young person. Does that suggest that young people are the worst criminals or that lots of young people are criminals? Do the facts in the article back up what the picture or pictures suggest?

View to Learn Analyze the advertisement on this page. With a partner, answer these questions:

- What is the purpose of this advertisement?
- Does the visual in this advertisement affect the viewers' feelings in a positive or negative way? How?

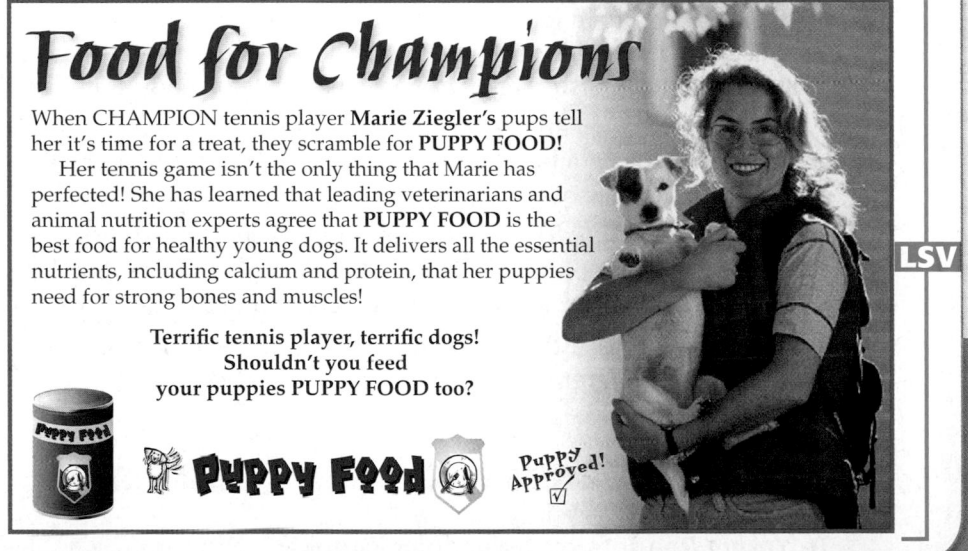

Food for Champions

When CHAMPION tennis player **Marie Ziegler's** pups tell her it's time for a treat, they scramble for **PUPPY FOOD!**

Her tennis game isn't the only thing that Marie has perfected! She has learned that leading veterinarians and animal nutrition experts agree that **PUPPY FOOD** is the best food for healthy young dogs. It delivers all the essential nutrients, including calcium and protein, that her puppies need for strong bones and muscles!

Terrific tennis player, terrific dogs!
Shouldn't you feed
your puppies PUPPY FOOD too?

PUPPY FOOD

Puppy Approved! ☑

LSV

Teach

LSV Active Listening

Advertising Technique Say: The *Food for Champions* ad is a testimonial—an ad in which a famous person claims to use the advertised product. The product makers hope that consumers will buy their product because the famous person uses it. Is this an effective ad? Explain. *(Responses will vary. Students might criticize the ad by noting that there's no connection between dog food and tennis.)* **OL** Ask: What is the unstated message of the *Puppy Food* ad? *(Possible response: Consumers will be champions if they feed their pets* Puppy Food.*)* **AL**

Assess

Organize students into groups based on which article they chose to summarize. Have students take turns reading their summaries in their groups. When they finish, they should discuss the similarities and differences between their summaries.

Differentiated Instruction

Evaluating Messages Discuss with students the target audiences of specific advertisements. For example, you might mention an ad for food or an ad for shoes. Explain that every ad aims to attract a specific group of people. Point out to students that the actors in commercials are often selected to represent the target audience for the product. Sometimes such actors present an ideal view of the person who might buy the product. Invite students to identify and discuss ads that specifically target them. They might list the range of products that target their age group and the techniques the advertisers use. **AS**

Objectives
- Identify main ideas and supporting details
- Analyze text
- Identify advertising techniques
- Use text features: visuals

67

Main Idea and Supporting Details

Objectives covered in this workshop:
• Identify main idea and supporting details
• Distinguish between significant and minor details

Helping Students Determine the Main Idea and Supporting Details

Why Is It Important?

• Understanding the main ideas in a selection helps students comprehend the material better.

• Supporting details help point readers to the main ideas.

• Readers can use the details they identify to visualize what is happening in the story, which will improve comprehension.

• When students can clearly distinguish main ideas from supporting details, they will also become better writers. They will better understand the need to add ideas that explain, corroborate, and enhance their main ideas.

How to Help Students Get It

• Ask students where they think that they might find the key idea of a selection. The main idea is often presented as the topic sentence in informational text, but it's usually not included in a creative attention-getting introduction. It's also rare to have the main idea clearly stated in fiction.

• Ask students to review a text from a previous unit, focusing on the author's use of details. They should make a list of the words the author uses to convey his or her ideas. Remembering to notice details will help students to learn to incorporate them into their own writing.

• Discuss the types of details that an author can use, including facts, statistics, anecdotes, adjectives, dialogue, and rich descriptions.

• Ask students to use the details from a text to create visual images, which will help them determine main ideas.

Reading to Answer the Big Question

To Young Readers by Gwendolyn Brooks
Gwendolyn Brooks's poem uses a variety of inviting images to describe what books can do and be for young readers.

Why Books Are Dangerous by Neil Gaiman
This short story is an amusing first-person account of the experiences of an avid reader. Gaiman recounts the consequences he suffered after reading "dangerous" books while he was a student at a boarding school in England.

Workshop Resources

PACING (DAYS)		LESSON	STUDENT MATERIALS	TEACHER RESOURCES
STANDARD	BLOCK			

1	1/2	Key Skill Lesson: Determining the Main Idea and Supporting Details	🐾 Key Reading Skills Practice, p. 30
			🐾 English Language Coach, Review, p. 42
				🖌 Bellringer Options Transparencies
				  –Daily Language Practice 8
				  –Selection Focus 1
				🖌 Read Aloud, Think Aloud Transparencies
				  –Key reading Skills 6
				💿 Presentation Plus!

1	1	"To Young Readers"	💻 Glencoe Online 🐾 Unit Vocabulary Review, p. 40 🐾 Academic Vocabulary Review, p. 43 📁 English Language Coach 🐾 Active Reading Graphic Organizer, p. 32 🐾 Literary Analysis, p. 31 💿 StudentWorks Plus™ 💻 Online Student Edition 💿 Literature Classics 📁 Selection and Unit Assessments, p. 7	🖌 Literary and Text Analysis Transparencies 3 💻 Puzzlemaker 💿 Skill Level Up!™ A Language Arts Game 💻 BookLink 3 📖 Assessment by Learning Objective (Diagnostic and Formative) 💿 Interactive Tutor: Self-Assessment 💿 TeacherWorks Plus™
1		"Why Books are Dangerous"	💻 Glencoe Online 🐾 Unit Vocabulary Review, p. 40 🐾 Academic Vocabulary Review, p. 43 📁 English Language Coach 🐾 Active Reading Graphic Organizer, p. 34 🐾 Literary Analysis, p. 31 💿 StudentWorks Plus™ 💻 Online Student Edition 💿 Literature Classics 📁 Selection and Unit Assessments, p. 8	🖌 Literary and Text Analysis Transparencies 3 💻 Puzzlemaker 📖 Skill Level Up!™ A Language Arts Game 💻 BookLink 3 📖 Assessment by Learning Objective (Diagnostic and Formative) 💿 Interactive Tutor: Self-Assessment 💿 TeacherWorks Plus™

Keys for Unit Resource

📁 Blackline Master   🔒 DVD

📖 Workbook   🖌 Transparency

📖 Supplemental Text   💻 Web-based

💿 CD-ROM   🐾 Fast File

Level Appropriate Code

AS = Activities for all students

AL = Activities for students working above grade level

OL = Activities for students working at grade level

BL = Activities for students working below grade level

EL = Activities for English language learners

Focus

BELLRINGER Options

✍ **Daily Language Practice Transparency 8**
Focus Activity Say: Think of a fairy tale or legend. What are some details that support the main idea of that fairy tale? *(Possible response: In "Cinderella," the main idea is the magical change of a young woman into a princess. Supporting details include her fairy godmother, glass slipper, and marriage to the prince.)* **AS**

Teach

R Reading Skill

Identifying Main Idea and Supporting Details Ask: What is the main idea of the illustration on this page? What details support that idea? *(Possible response: The people all have light bulbs above their heads. Light bulbs often symbolize ideas. The main idea of the illustration is that everyone has an idea in mind.)* **AL**

READING WORKSHOP 4

Skills Focus

You will practice using these skills when you read the following selections:
- "To Young Readers," p. 72
- "Why Books Are Dangerous," p. 78

Reading

- Identifying main idea and supporting details

Literature

- Determining the author's purpose

Vocabulary

- Using word references to determine the meaning of unknown or multiple-meaning words

Writing/Grammar

- Identifying and using irregular verbs

Objectives (pp. 68–69)
Reading Identify main ideas and supporting details

Skill Lesson

Identifying Main Idea and Supporting Details

Learn It!

What Is It? The **main idea** is the most important idea in a paragraph or an article. In many paragraphs, a topic sentence states the main idea. The other sentences add **supporting details.** Other times the main idea is not clearly stated, and the reader needs to figure out the main idea that connects the supporting details. If you can't find a topic sentence, try to state the main idea in your own words.

Analyzing Illustrations
What is going on in this picture? Keep in mind that light bulbs stand for ideas.
- What is the man in the middle of the picture doing?
- Who has "the best idea" in this picture? Explain why you think so.

Additional Support

Literature Focus Lesson

Main Idea Write the following sentences on the board: *Dogs give lots of love. Dogs guard a house. Dogs provide hours of fun. Dogs are great pets.* Have students identify the sentence in the group that states the main idea. **BL**

Then write these sentences on the board: *Reading helps you use your imagination. Reading is fun. Reading is more challenging than watching TV.* Ask students to provide a main idea that is supported by these details. **OL**

Why Is It Important? Finding the main idea helps you

- understand what the author is trying to say
- understand and recall information better
- form your own opinions and ideas as you read

How Do I Do It? A writer may tell you the main idea at the beginning of an article or paragraph. "People should plant more trees," for example. This idea is followed by details that support it. If the main idea isn't stated, you need to figure out what it is. Look for clues as you read. Does the writer go back to one idea again and again? Do most of the details seem to be about one thing? When you finish reading, try to finish this sentence: "This writer believes . . ." Here's how one student found the main idea in "Animal Attraction."

> Most people agree that a pet adds joy to its owner's life. A pet can give a person's life meaning. And this can be more true after the death of a loved one. Scientists are now finding that pets may also keep their owners healthy.

This paragraph is about people and pets. I think the main idea is that owning a pet is good because every sentence talks about some way in which pets help people.

Study Central Visit www.glencoe. com and click on Study Central to review main idea and supporting details.

Practice It!

In your Learner's Notebook, practice finding the main idea and supporting details for the opening lines of "To Young Readers." You can ask yourself these questions to help find the main idea and supporting details.

- What are these lines about, and what do I already know about this topic?
- Is there one idea that all of the lines in the poem relate to?
- What main idea do the supporting details point out?

Good books are / bandages and voyages / and linkages to Light;

Use It!

As you read "To Young Readers" and "Why Books Are Dangerous," remember to use these questions to help you find the main idea and supporting details of a text. Write the questions out in your Learner's Notebook ahead of time, and answer them as you read the selection.

Teach

Study Central Have students access the Web site to review identifying main idea and supporting details and to complete a related activity.

Reading Skill

Review Skimming and Scanning Say: Look at the *How Do I Do It?* section. Scan the section to find two questions that can help you find the main idea of a paragraph. *(Does the writer go back to one idea again and again? Do most of the details seem to be about one thing?)* **BL Say:** Skim the material to learn where in a paragraph the main idea can sometimes be found. *(Possible response: Sometimes the main idea can be found in a topic sentence.)* **OL**

Resources for page 69

📁 Use Key Reading Skills Transparency 6 in *Read Aloud, Think Aloud* to help students practice identifying main idea and supporting details.

Differentiated Instruction

Main Idea and Supporting Details Have students work in small groups. Give each group four note cards. Ask students to think of a favorite summer activity and write a sentence identifying the activity on one note card. Then ask them to write details about this activity on the remaining note cards. When students have finished, ask them to arrange the note cards in random order on their desks. Then have student groups look at one another's arrangements and identify the main idea from each set of note cards. **OL**

Objectives
- Identify main ideas and supporting details
- Skim and scan text

Teach

More About the Author

Gwendolyn Brooks was the first African American woman to serve as poetry consultant to the Library of Congress. She considered her visits to local schools the most important aspect of her job. Brooks was later named poet laureate of Illinois. She encouraged poets there by sponsoring literary awards ceremonies. At these ceremonies, she provided prizes that she paid for herself.

V Vocabulary

Word Associations Say: In your Learner's Notebooks, list foods that have associations with your vocabulary words. Create two columns and label one *Healthful* and the other *Unhealthful.* Write as many foods as you can think of that belong in each column. You may want to check a thesaurus to find synonyms for the words *nutrition* and *nourished.* (Responses will vary.) **OL**

Before You Read : To Young Readers

Gwendolyn Brooks

Meet the Author

"I loved poetry very early [in life] and began to put rhymes together at about seven," Gwendolyn Brooks said. At the age of 33, she became the first African American to win the Pulitzer Prize in poetry. Brooks says, "Reading is important—read between the lines. Don't swallow everything." For more about Gwendolyn Brooks, see page R1 of the Author Files.

Author Search For more about Gwendolyn Brooks, go to www.glencoe.com.

Objectives (pp. 70–73)
Reading Identify main ideas and supporting details • Make connections from text to self
Literature Identify literary elements: author's purpose
Vocabulary Use word references: dictionary

Vocabulary Preview

nutrition (noo TRI shun) *n.* that which feeds the body **(p. 72)** *Proper nutrition helps you stay healthy.*

nourished (NUR ishd) *adj.* provided with food or other substances necessary for life **(p. 72)** *I feel nourished after I have eaten a hot breakfast.*

Partner Talk With a partner, think of a food. Write a short paragraph describing the food, but don't name it. Include the vocabulary words in your paragraph. Exchange your paragraph with your partner. Guess the food described.

English Language Coach

Word References When you use a reference book to learn the meaning of an unknown word or a word with more than one meaning, consider the way it's used in the text. Read the sentence and the dictionary entries below for the word *address.* Which meaning best fits the word as it is used in this sentence?

Mrs. Woy gave an inspiring graduation address.

ad•dress (*n.* ə dres', ad' res; *v.,* ə dres') *n.* 1. a formal speech. 2. location of a building or place at which a person or organization can be reached. 3. writing on a letter or other item to be delivered stating its destination.

If you said the first definition, you are correct. The first definition, a formal speech, makes sense.

Write to Learn Look up the underlined words in a dictionary. Then look at how the words are used in the sentences. Which dictionary definition fits each word? Write the word and the correct definition of it in your Learner's Notebook.

1. Jackson made a <u>rash</u> decision when he chose to eat six pieces of cake.

2. Becky could not play in the last inning because of her <u>game</u> leg.

3. My mother wants to use the coupon before it <u>expires</u>.

Additional Support

Author Search To expand students' appreciation of Gwendolyn Brooks, have them access the Web site for additional information and resources.

Literature Focus Lesson

Poetry Gwendolyn Brooks's poetry includes a number of styles, including free verse and sonnets. She once called her style a "folksy narrative." Ask students to think of a piece of advice that they might give to younger readers. Have them write the advice in a friendly, "folksy" tone. When they have finished, have students turn their advice into a poem. They can recopy their advice, inserting line breaks to emphasize important words or ideas, or they might change the order of the words or ideas to make it more like poetry. They should give their advice a title that reflects the subject. Ask students to share their poems and discuss how they wrote them. **OL AL**

Skills Preview

Key Reading Skill: Identifying Main Idea and Supporting Details

As you read the poem, look for the main idea. Remember that the main idea in poetry is often not stated directly. To find the main idea

- ask yourself what the poem is about
- use the details to determine the main idea

Write to Learn In your Learner's Notebook, list the things that Brooks compares good books to. What do these items have in common? Use your answer to determine the main idea.

Key Literary Element: Author's Purpose

There are many different purposes for writing. There are, however, four main ones: to entertain, inform, persuade, or express emotions. Of course, most of the time, an author has more than one purpose. To understand the author's purpose, ask yourself some questions as you read.

- What is the genre? This can give you an idea about the author's purpose. For example, short stories are often written to entertain, and editorials are often written to persuade.
- Who is the intended audience? That is, who is supposed to be reading the material?
- What words were chosen? An author who uses a lot of emotional or strong words may be trying to persuade you of something.

Interactive Literary Elements Handbook
To review or learn more about the literary elements, go to www.glencoe.com.

Get Ready to Read

Connect to the Reading

Brooks says, "Good books are good nutrition." She means that books are like healthy food; they strengthen her. What hobby do you have that feeds you? Sports? Dancing? Painting? Video games?

Write to Learn Complete the line *To Young ____*. Finish the line with *Football Players, Dancers, Painters, Gamers,* or some other audience. Then write what you would say to people who are just beginning to enjoy your favorite hobby.

Build Background

Gwendolyn Brooks lived most of her life in Chicago and was Poet Laureate of Illinois. Her poetry often showed the impact of urban, or city, life.

- Brooks taught classes and held poetry contests for young people.
- The classes and contests were ways to help inner-city children see "the poetry" in their lives.
- "To Young Readers" was written for the Chicago Public Library.

Set Purposes for Reading

BIG Question Read "To Young Readers" to discover reasons that people read.

Set Your Own Purpose What else would you like to learn from the poem to help you answer the Big Question? Write your own purpose on the "To Young Readers" page of Foldable 1.

Keep Moving

Use these skills as you read the following selection.

Teach

L Literary Element

Author's Purpose Say: Some kinds of writing have specific purposes. For example, the articles on a newspaper's front page are meant to inform readers, but the paper's editorials attempt to persuade. What purposes might a poem have? *(Possible responses: to tell a story, to entertain, to describe, to express a feeling)* **OL**

C Critical Thinking

Application Say: Think about your favorite book. How did that book give you "good nutrition"? *(Responses will vary. Students may say that books like the Harry Potter series made them feel as if they could do anything.)* **AS**

Interactive Literary Elements Handbook Have students access the Web site to improve their understanding of author's purpose.

English Language Coach

Word References Have students practice using a thesaurus and dictionary to discern the differences in denotation and connotation between synonyms. Have them look up the word *journey.* Ask them the following questions:

1. How many synonyms are given?

2. What is the difference between taking a *voyage* and going on an *excursion?*

3. Which sounds more exciting: taking a *trip* or going on a *cruise?* Explain.

Have students discuss their answers as a class. **EL BL**

Objectives
- Identify author's purpose
- Use word references
- Apply information
- Learn and use new vocabulary
- Analyze features of genres: poetry

Teach

C Critical Thinking

Comprehension Ask: What does the poet mean when she says that books are bandages? *(Possible response: A book can help heal us when we feel hurt.)* How can books be voyages? *(Possible response: Books can describe faraway places.)* **OL Ask:** How do you think that books can be "linkages to Light"? *(Possible response: Books can help readers find knowledge and truth.)* **AL**

R Reading Skill

Main Idea and Supporting Details Ask: What main message does the author give about books? *(Possible response: She loves books and thinks they are necessary for helping young people to heal and to grow.)* **Say:** Identify two details that support her message. *(Responses should include details listed in the poem.)* **OL**

BQ BIG Question

Ask: How can reading a book be good for you? *(Possible response: Books can give information, provide entertainment, or explain how to accomplish a task.)* **OL**

To Young Readers

by Gwendolyn Brooks

Good books are
bandages and voyages
and linkages* to Light; **C 1**

5 are keys and hammers,
ripe redeemers,*
dials and bells and
healing hallelujah. **2 3**

Good books are good **nutrition.**
A reader is a Guest
10 **nourished,** by riches of the Feast,
to lift, to launch, and to applaud the world. **4**

R

---

3 *Linkages* is another way of saying links, or connections.

5 *Redeemers* are rescuers or saviors.

Vocabulary

nutrition (noo TRI shun) *n.* that which feeds the body

nourished (NUR ishd) *adj.* provided with food or other substances necessary for life

72 UNIT 1 Why Read?

Practice the Skills

1 Key Reading Skill

Identifying Main Idea and Supporting Details How soon do you begin to get a sense of the main idea of this poem?

2 Key Literary Element

Author's Purpose You know the author wrote this poem for the Chicago Public Library. What do you think her purpose is?

3 English Language Coach

Word References Read the footnote for **redeemers**. Then look up **ripe** in the dictionary. Read all its meanings. Which one do you think Brooks wanted you to think about? Do you think she might have wanted you to think about more than one meaning?

BIG Question

4 What reasons does the poem's speaker give for reading? Record the answer in your Foldable. Your response will help you complete the Unit Challenge later. **BQ**

Additional Support

Literature Focus Lesson

Metaphor Tell students that a metaphor compares or equates things in a fresh way. Poets often use metaphor because they can say a lot in just a few words. For example, with the lines "Good books are bandages and voyages," Brooks says that books can help people heal and take them to various places within their imagination. Have students identify three more metaphors within the poem. Then ask students to explain what Brooks means by each metaphor. **OL**

Teach

Viewing the Art

Ask: What are the people doing in the painting? *(They are reading books.)* **BL** How do you think the people feel about those books? *(Possible response: They seem very interested in reading the books.)* **OL**

Ask: Which description from the poem do you think the people in the picture would use to describe good books? Explain your answer. *(Responses will vary.)* **AS**

Assess

 CheckPoint

Use the Checkpoint questions provided on Presentation Plus! to check for comprehension of the selection. These questions can be used with interactive response keypads for immediate student feedback.

The Library, 1960. Jacob Lawrence. Tempera, 60.9 x 75.8 cm. National Museum of American Art, Washington, DC.

Analyzing the Art Does this painting help you understand Brooks's poem? Explain your answer.

To Young Readers **73**

Differentiated Instruction

Personal Response Read the quotation below from the work of historian Barbara Tuchman.

Books are the carriers of civilization. Without books, history is silent, literature dumb, science crippled, thought and speculation at a standstill.

Have students complete a five-minute freewrite about this quotation. Then have students share their responses. Lead a discussion about how this quotation relates to the painting by Jacob Lawrence. **AL**

Objectives
- Identify main ideas and supporting details
- Find meaning in art
- Monitor comprehension
- Identify literary devices: metaphor

Assess

Resources for page 74

📁 Selection Quick Check, p. 7

📁 Selection Test and Unit Assessment, p. 7

⊙ ExamView Assessment Suite

⊙ Interactive Tutor: Self-Assessment

Students can respond to the *After You Read* items in their Learner's Notebooks or on a separate sheet of paper.

Answering the

BIG Question

1. Possible response: People read to learn about distant places, to gain other forms of knowledge, or to be healed.

2. Books are compared to bandages, voyages, to knowledge or Light, keys, hammers, redeemers, dials, bells, healing hallelujah, and a feast.

3. The author suggests that a reader should "lift, launch, and applaud the world."

Critical Thinking

4. Possible response: *Light, Guest,* and *Feast* can hold religious or spiritual meanings. By capitalizing these words, Brooks suggests that reading is a spiritual experience.

5. Some students may say that reading is difficult; others may say that it is escape or entertainment.

6. Responses will vary. Students should support their opinions with their own experiences.

74

After You Read | To Young Readers

Answering the **BIG Question**

1. What does this poem tell you about why people read?

2. **Recall** The author compares books to many things. Name five of these things.

   Tip **Right There** You will find the answer in the poem.

3. **Recall** What does the author suggest that a reader should do for the world?

   Tip **Right There** You will find the answer in the poem.

Critical Thinking

4. **Analyze** Why do you think Brooks capitalizes the words *Light, Guest,* and *Feast*?

   Tip **Author and Me** You will find clues in the poem, but you must also use information in your head.

5. **Evaluate** Does the poem leave out anything important about reading? If so, what is it?

   Tip **On My Own** Answer from your own experiences.

6. **Apply** Do you agree with Brooks about the power of reading? Explain.

   Tip **On My Own** Answer from your own experiences.

Write About Your Reading

Choose just one of the things Brooks says a book can be.

> bandage   voyage   linkage   key
> hammer   redeemer   dial   bell
> hallelujah   nutrition

Write a short essay, two or three paragraphs long, about how a book could be one of these things. If you can, use a book you have read as an example. Begin with a sentence that states your main idea. For example, "A book can be a hammer." Then give details that support and explain that idea.

Objectives (pp. 74–75)
Reading Identify main ideas and supporting details
Literature Identify literary elements: author's purpose
Vocabulary Use word references: dictionary
Writing Write a short essay • Respond to literature
Grammar Identify parts of speech: future verb tense

74   UNIT 1   Why Read?

Write About Your Reading

Students' essays should be two or three paragraphs long and should explain or describe how a book can be one of the metaphors in the poem. Paragraphs should include a sentence stating the main idea. Other sentences should consist of details that support the main idea.

Skills Review

Key Reading Skill: Identifying Main Idea and Supporting Details

7. How well did the poem's details support the main idea? Give examples from the poem to support your answer.

Key Literary Element: Author's Purpose

8. Which of these helped you most in determining the author's purpose—the author's word choices, the audience she was writing for, or the way the poem was organized? Explain.

9. Did the author achieve her purpose? Explain.

Vocabulary Check

Fit each vocabulary word into the correct sentence. Then explain why the word does not fit into the other sentence.

10. nutrition

Proper ____ gives children necessary vitamins and minerals.

Carlos was worried about the ____ of the painting.

11. nourished

By the time we finally got to the restaurant, I was ____.

I felt ____ after the large meal.

English Language Coach Match the correct meaning with the underlined word in each group of sentences.

12. Go change for gym.

13. Get the correct change when you pay.

14. My mom suggested a change in attitude.

   a. *n.* coins or money returned

   b. *v.* to put on different clothing

   c. *n.* the act of becoming different

15. Draw a picture of your new bike.

16. When neither team scored, we called it a draw.

17. Draw close to hear his secret.

   a. *n.* undecided game or contest; tie

   b. *v.* make lines with a pencil or pen

   c. *v.* move toward someone or something

Grammar Link: Future Tense

When you want to talk about an action that will happen in the future, there are two ways to do it. You can use the word *will* as a helping verb and the present tense of the main verb.

• I **will wash** the dishes later.

You can also use *going to* with *am*, *is*, or *are* along with the present tense of the main verb.

• I **am going to wash** the dishes later.

You can use *not* or *never* with either of these phrases.

• I **will** never **wash** the dishes.

• I **am** never **going to wash** the dishes.

Grammar Practice

In your Learner's Notebook, write a sentence about a future action you will take. Use *will*. Then rewrite the sentence, using *am going to*.

Writing Application Look back at the essay you wrote about what a book can be. Underline any verb phrases you used to talk about the future.

Web Activities For eFlashcards, Selection Quick Checks, and other Web activities, go to www.glencoe.com.

Grammar Link: Future Tense

Grammar Practice

Responses will vary. Students' sentences should demonstrate their knowledge of forming the future tense with helping verbs and main verbs.

Close

Ask students to summarize what they learned from Gwendolyn Brooks's poem to help them answer the Big Question.

Skills Review

Key Reading Skill: Identifying Main Idea and Supporting Details

7. Possible response: The details support the main idea well. For example, describing books as bandages shows the healing power of books. This detail supports the main idea that books benefit people.

Key Literary Element: Author's Purpose

8. Possible response: Analyzing the word choice gave the most insight into the author's purpose.

9. Responses will vary. Students should provide support from the poem for their opinions.

Vocabulary Check

10. Proper nutrition gives children necessary vitamins and minerals. *Nutrition* does not fit into the second sentence because a painting is not alive, so nutrition does not apply to it.

11. I felt nourished after the large meal. *Nourished* does not fit into the first sentence because people who take a long time to get to a restaurant are famished, not nourished.

English Language Coach

12. b   **15.** b

13. a   **16.** a

14. c   **17.** c

Teach

More About the Author

British author Neil Gaiman's work draws on a number of different sources, including mythology, fairy tales, history, and popular culture. He says that he read everything as a child and was a "cheerfully undiscerning reader." One of his favorite books was *Alice in Wonderland*, which he reread a number of times. "There are things Lewis Carroll did in *Alice* that are etched onto my circuitry," Gaiman says.

EL Language Coach

Word References Say: Write in English three sentences about your native land. Include at least three words from your first language to add interest and color to your writing. Write the words from your first language, provide a pronunciation key, and then write a definition in English for each word. *(Responses will vary.)* EL

Before You Read

Neil Gaiman

Meet the Author

Neil Gaiman is best known for his graphic novels, or long-form comic books with high-quality story lines and artwork. As a boy, Gaiman says that he was a "bookie kid . . . one of those kids who had books on them." He admits to becoming "very grumpy at school when they'd tell us that we couldn't read comics, because 'if you read comics, you will not read OTHER THINGS.'" Gaiman proved his teachers wrong. He read comics as well as the entire children's library.

Literature Online

Author Search For more about Neil Gaiman, go to www.glencoe.com.

Objectives (pp. 76–81)
Reading Identify main ideas and supporting details • Make connections from text to self
Literature Identify literary elements: author's purpose
Vocabulary Use word references: dictionary

Why Books Are Dangerous

Vocabulary Preview

confiscated (KAHN fuh skayt id) *v.* took someone's property by authority **(p. 79)** *The headmaster probably confiscated books from other students.*

interrogated (in TAIR uh gayt id) *v.* asked questions harshly or in great detail **(p. 79)** *The spy was nervous when interrogated by the police.*

fragments (FRAG munts) *n.* small pieces that are broken off **(p. 81)** *The glass broke into fragments when it hit the floor.*

sarcastic (sar KAS tik) *adj.* describes sharp or bitter words that are meant to hurt or make fun of someone **(p. 81)** *The bully made sarcastic comments about my clothes.*

Guess What? With a partner, role-play the words *confiscated, interrogated,* and *sarcastic.* Perform one of your role plays for another pair of classmates. Have them guess the vocabulary word you are acting out.

English Language Coach

Word References We speak the same language and use most of the same words as people in England, but some of those words have different meanings. Someone from England would understand the first sentence in each pair of sentences below. You may not. Use a dictionary to look up the words that seem to have a different meaning in England. **EL**

The lorry on the side of the road had an open bonnet and boot.
The truck on the side of the road had an open hood and trunk.

The baby in the pram needs a dummy and a clean nappy.
The baby in the buggy needs a pacifier and a clean diaper.

Try to match each term from England in the left column to one of the meanings from the United States in the right column. Use a dictionary to help you.

Word used in England	Word used in U.S.
fringe	french fries
biscuit	bangs
torch	flashlight
chips	cookie

Additional Support

Literature Online

Author Search To expand students' appreciation of Neil Gaiman, have them access the Web site for additional information and resources.

Literature Focus Lesson

Autobiographical Essays In "Why Books Are Dangerous," Neil Gaiman writes an autobiographical account of his childhood reading experiences. Autobiographical essays are told in the first person. They are not expected to be objective or balanced. Instead, they reveal the author's perspective, which includes his or her biases, joys, and fears.

Tell students to think of an incident that had a big impact on them. Then, have students write a short autobiographical essay about that incident. Remind students to include their own feelings and observations in their descriptions. Invite volunteers to share their writing with the class. **AS**

Skills Preview

Key Reading Skill: Identifying Main Idea and Supporting Details

To determine which supporting details are important and which are not, find the main idea of the paragraph or the passage. Then, for each detail, ask yourself this question:

- Does the reader need this detail to understand the main idea?

  If you answer yes, then the detail is important. If the answer is no, then it's a minor detail.

  It may be important to the main idea to know that the character ordered a pizza, but it's probably not really necessary to know that it was a pepperoni pizza.

Write to Learn In your Learner's Notebook, make a two-column chart. When you read "Why Books Are Dangerous," record the main ideas in the first column. Record the supporting details in the second column.

Key Literary Element: Author's Purpose

The author's purpose shows up in many ways, from word choices to how the writing is organized. You decide whether the author is informing the reader, entertaining, expressing an opinion, or trying to convince you, the reader, to agree.

These tips will help you determine the author's purpose when you read the selection:

- Look carefully at what the author is telling you. Decide whether the author really means what he or she says.

  Does Gaiman really believe that books are dangerous? Explain.

- Think about why the author might say the opposite of what he or she means.

  If Gaiman does not believe that books are dangerous, why would he say that they are? How does he really feel about books?

- Consider the reason for the author's writing.

  Why does the author want to share this particular incident from his life? Does he want to teach or entertain the reader?

Get Ready to Read

Connect to the Reading

Have you ever been in trouble in school or at home? Why were you in trouble? Did you learn something, good or bad, from that experience?

Freewrite Write a short paragraph about a time that you were in trouble at home or school. What did you do? What was the consequence? Did you believe that the consequence was fair?

Build Background

This short story takes place at a boys' school in the 1970s in the south of England. Discipline was very tough at such schools.

Set Purposes for Reading

BIG Question Read the selection "Why Books Are Dangerous" to discover reasons why people read.

Set Your Own Purpose What else would you like to learn from the essay to help you answer the Big Question? Write your own purpose on the "Why Books Are Dangerous" page of Foldable 1.

Interactive Literary Elements Handbook To review or learn more about the literary elements, go to www.glencoe.com.

Keep Moving

Use these skills as you read the following selection.

Teach

R Reading Skill

Identifying Main Idea and Supporting Details **Say:** *Supporting details make writing more interesting. Would you remember a character who eats a pizza topped with garlic, pineapple, and anchovies? Why? (Possible response: Yes, because the combination of toppings is so unusual.)* **OL**

C Critical Thinking

Application **Ask:** *What new activity or food have you tried or would you like to try because of something you read? (Responses will vary.)* **AS**

Interactive Literary Elements Handbook Have students access the Web site to improve their understanding of author's purpose.

English Language Coach

Word References On the board, copy the words and sentences shown on the right. Explain that the underlined words have different meanings in the United States than they do in England. Ask students to replace each underlined word with the word Americans would use. **EL** **OL**

soccer   sweater   vacation

1. William's sister gave him a <u>jumper</u> for his birthday.

2. After exams, we will go on <u>holiday</u> to the mountains.

3. Our school's <u>football</u> team won the city tournament.

Objectives

- Use word references
- Analyze features of genres: autobiographical essays
- Identify main ideas and supporting details
- Apply information

Teach

R Reading Skill

Identifying Main Idea and Supporting Details **Say:** Look at the list in the third sentence of this paragraph. What is the purpose of this list? *(Possible response: The list of different kinds of stories functions as a detail that supports the main idea that the author liked to read anything.)* **OL**

Readability Scores
Dale-Chall: 5.9
DRP: 55
Lexile: 1090

Why Books Are Dangerous

by Neil Gaiman

When I was a boy, I was almost always carrying a book. It might not have been obvious. Paperbacks were fairly easy to slip into pockets, after all. My father would frisk[1] me for books before family weddings or funerals; otherwise he knew that, while other people were being bored, I'd be sitting comfortably, probably under a table, off in my own world, reading.

I liked books. I did not yet suspect that books were dangerous. I didn't care what the books were about, as long as they had a story of some kind—spy stories, horror stories, SF or fantasy, histories, adventures, tales. I'd read true-life stories about people who caught spies or captured rare animals for zoos or people who hunted down man-eating tigers. I also was very fond of detectives and the books they came in. These were, I think, looking back on it, all very sensible things for a boy to like, and not the least bit dangerous. **1**

The headmaster of my school in the south of England, a pipe-smoking, gruff gentleman who was famous for his precise and painful use of the slipper[2] on boys who were sent

---

1. To search for something by running the hands over the clothing and through the pockets is to **frisk** the person.

2. A teacher who is famous for his **use of the slipper** is one well-known for using a slipper or other type of shoe to spank students.

78 UNIT 1 Why Read?

Practice the Skills

1 Key Reading Skill

Identifying Main Idea and Supporting Details Reread the second paragraph. What is the main idea of this paragraph? Where in the paragraph do you see the main idea? Name one important detail that supports this main idea.

Additional Support

Differentiated Instruction

Building Background Neil Gaiman attended what is called a public school in England. These English public schools are the equivalent to American private schools. They are open to the general public, but they charge fees because they are not supported by government money. The author attended Whitgift School, a secondary school that was founded in 1596 by the Archbishop of Canterbury. Have students visit the school's Web site to find out more about the school Gaiman attended or conduct additional research to learn more about the author and his works. **AS**

to him for misbehaving, once **confiscated** a book from me. It was called *And to my nephew Albert I leave the island what I won off Fatty Hagen in a poker game,* and it had a photograph of a naked lady on the cover, which was why it was confiscated. This seemed particularly unfair, as in the early 1970s, most books seemed to have naked ladies on the covers, which, at least in the case of *And to my nephew Albert . . .* political comedy, had little or nothing to do with what was going on inside the book. I was **interrogated** by the **headmaster** and was given the book back at the end of term, with a warning to watch what I read. He didn't use the slipper, though. Not that time. **2**

Vocabulary

confiscated (KAHN fuh skayt id) *v.* took someone's property by authority

interrogated (in TAIR uh gayt id) *v.* asked questions harshly or in great detail

Practice the Skills

2 **English Language Coach**

Word Reference Use a dictionary to find the meaning of the word **headmaster.** What is a more common American word that has the same meaning as *headmaster?*

Neil Gaiman went to a school in the south of England. The school was run by a *headmaster,* and academic standards were very high. Students had to wear uniforms, as the students do in this present-day photo.

Analyzing the Photo Based on the picture, what feelings do you get about the students at this school? Do they seem happy? Explain your answers.

Why Books Are Dangerous **79**

Reading in the Real World

Citizenship The author's headmaster gives him a warning to watch what he reads. Have students learn more about censorship by finding out about banned books. Every September the American Library Association (ALA) celebrates Banned Books Week. Have students use online resources to learn more about Banned Books Week and how the ALA celebrates the freedom to read and write. Invite students to share their findings with the class. **AL**

Teach

L Literary Element

Author's Purpose Ask: What does the author want readers to think of his school experience? *(Possible response: The author wants readers to think that his school is strict.)* **OL** How do the vocabulary words *confiscated* and *interrogated* contribute to the author's purpose? *(Possible response: Confiscated and* interrogated *sound like words that could be used by the police. The word choices show that discipline at the author's school is rigid.)* **AL**

Viewing the Photo

Ask: What do you notice about the students' clothes in the photo? *(The students are wearing uniforms.)* **BL** What might the students' clothes indicate about the school they attend? *(Possible response: The school maintains a dress code to ensure traditional or uniform behavior. Freedom of expression might not be encouraged.)* **AL**

Objectives
- Identify author's purpose
- Use text features: photographs
- Identify main ideas and supporting details

79

Teach

L Literary Element

Author's Purpose Say: Look at the title of the book the author claims is dangerous. What kind of book do you think it is? *(The book claims to tell about "Jolly Interesting Things" for boys. It must be an activity book for children.)* Why do you think the author includes the title of this book in his essay? *(Possible response: Students might say that the title is funny and doesn't sound at all like a "dangerous" book.)* OL

C Critical Thinking

Comprehension Say: What has the author learned from his "dangerous" book? *(He has learned to make dyes from common garden vegetables. He has also learned to make toffee.)* BL How do you think the author feels about his experience with this book? *(Possible response: The author is unaffected by his shirt-dyeing disaster and pleased that he has mastered making a treat that is both tasty and messy.)* OL

Obviously the headmaster understood the dangers of books. He was trying to tell me something. I didn't listen. Eventually I started to read the dangerous books.

The really dangerous books had titles like *1001 Jolly Interesting Things a Boy Can Do*. You could make dyes from common garden vegetables. It explained it all. **3** L

I read the article on making dyes from common garden vegetables, and then I boiled a beetroot and soaked a white school shirt in the beet water, and turned it a purply sort of red. I decided that I wouldn't be caught dead wearing it. Then I put it in the washing, and it turned all the shirts and socks and underwear it was washed with a rather startling shade of pink.

I had not learned my lesson. The next thing I found was the toffee[3] recipe. C

I learned that if I melted some butter in a saucepan, and then added sugar and golden syrup and a tablespoon of water, and I heated it all together and got it very hot (but didn't burn it), and dripped drops of the boiling liquid into a glass of cold water, when the drops went solid, it was done. Then I'd pour it out onto a greased pie-pan, and let it set hard.

I was so proud. I'd made a golden-clear, buttery toffee. Pure sugar, with a little fat. It tasted amazing. Chewing it was a battle between the toffee and my teeth. Sometimes my teeth would win, sometimes the toffee would prove the victor and pull out a filling, or deal with a loose tooth.

This went on for several months.

I was, I think, in a math lesson. I'd put a fist-sized lump of the toffee into my pocket, where it had melted, slowly, to the shape of my leg. And I had forgotten about it. I also had a handkerchief in the pocket.

"You. Boy," said the teacher. "Gaiman. You're sniveling,[4] boy. Blow your nose."

I said, "Yes, sir," and pulled the handkerchief from the pocket. It came out, and as it did so, a large lump of toffee that was stuck to the handkerchief sailed out across the room and hit the tiled floor.

Visual Vocabulary
Beetroot is a beet grown for its edible red root.

---

3. **Toffee** is a kind of hard, caramel candy.
4. Someone who is **sniveling** has a runny nose.

Practice the Skills

3 **Key Literary Element**

Author's Purpose Do you believe that Gaiman really wants to show you that books are dangerous? Or does he have some other purpose? Explain.

Additional Support

Differentiated Instruction

Time Order Words Help English language learners trace the sequence of events regarding the author's "dangerous" book. Point out time order words and phrases on page 80 such as *eventually,* *then, next,* and *for several months.* Have students use the words to help them complete a sequence-of-events chart for this part of the selection. EL

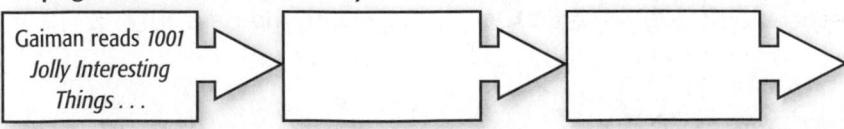

Gaiman reads *1001 Jolly Interesting Things . . .*

The Scholar, Saturday Evening Post Cover, June 26, 1926. Norman Rockwell.

Analyzing the Art This painting shows an English schoolboy and a headmaster. Do you think the artist meant for this picture to be funny? Do you think the picture *is* funny? Explain your answers.

It shattered when it hit the floor, like glass, into several hundred sharp-edged **fragments.**

I spent the rest of the lesson on my knees, picking up the sticky-sharp bits of toffee from the floor, while the teacher, convinced that I had done this on purpose to be funny (as if I'd waste a huge lump of toffee on a joke), made **sarcastic** comments. And, at the end of the lesson, I was sent to the headmaster with a note explaining what I'd done.

The headmaster read the note, puffed on his pipe, then walked slowly to the cupboard at the back of his study and, opening it, produced a large tartan[5] slipper.

That was the day I discovered that books were dangerous. At least, books that suggested you do something. . . . **4 5 6** ○

---

5. **Tartan** refers to a piece of plaid cloth or clothing.

Vocabulary

fragments (FRAG munts) *n.* small pieces that are broken off

sarcastic (sar KAS tik) *adj.* describes sharp or bitter words that are meant to hurt or make fun of someone

Practice the Skills

4 Key Reading Skill

Identifying Main Idea and Supporting Details Think of the title and the last two sentences. What did the author do? What happened as a result? What is the main idea of the entire essay?

5 Key Reading Skill

Identifying Main Idea and Supporting Details What is one important detail that supports the main idea of the article? What is one unimportant, minor detail?

6 BIG Question

How would Gaiman answer the question, "Why read?" Record your answer on the "Why Books Are Dangerous" page of Foldable 1. Your response will help you complete the Unit Challenge later. **BQ**

Why Books Are Dangerous **81**

Teach

C Critical Thinking

Analysis Ask: Why does the author's toffee make the teacher so angry? *(Possible response: The teacher thinks the author has tried to make a joke and is purposefully disrupting the class.)* **BL**

BQ **BIG Question**

Ask: Where do you get ideas when you are looking for new things to do? *(Possible responses: friends, magazines, books)* **BL** How does the author's interest in reading keep him active? *(Possible response: The author applies what he reads and tries new activities.)* **AS**

Assess

CheckPoint

Use the CheckPoint questions provided on Presentation Plus! to check for comprehension of the selection. These questions can be used with interactive response keypads for immediate student feedback.

Reading Fluency

Building Fluency Ask students to discuss what makes the selection humorous. Have students work in pairs, taking turns reading aloud one page at a time. During the first reading, have students note words, phrases, or incidents that the author uses for humorous effect. In the second reading, have students use appropriate tone and effective pauses to communicate and accentuate this humor. Have students offer each other feedback. Partners should practice until they can read the selection smoothly and with emotion. **AS**

Objectives
• Identify author's purpose
• Monitor comprehension
• Analyze text
• Understand sequence: time order words

Assess

Resources for page 82

📁 Selection Quick Check, p. 8

📁 Selection Test and Assessment, p. 8

💿 ExamView Assessment Suite

💿 Interactive Tutor: Self-Assessment

Students can respond to the *After You Read* items in their Learner's Notebooks or on a separate sheet of paper.

Answering the

1. Possible response: The essay shows that people read to learn about different topics.

2. Gaiman boils a beetroot and soaks a white shirt in the beet water. Then he puts the shirt into the laundry, and it turns his other clothes pink.

3. Gaiman drops the toffee onto the floor during math class. The teacher gets angry when the toffee shatters into many pieces.

Critical Thinking

4. Possible response: Yes, because some books teach children experiments that can be troublesome to adults.

5. Responses will vary. Students should support their responses with details from the text.

6. Responses will vary. Students may say they tried a new food or a new game after reading about it.

After You Read | Why Books Are Dangerous

Answering the BIG Question

1. What have you learned from this essay about why people read?

2. **Recall** How does Gaiman turn his shirt, socks, and underwear pink?
   Tip **Right There** You will find the answer in the essay.

3. **Recall** How does toffee get Gaiman into trouble?
   Tip **Right There** You will find the answer in the essay.

Critical Thinking

4. **Analyze** Would Gaiman's father and headmaster think books are dangerous? Why?
   Tip **Think and Search** You will find this information in the essay, but you will have to look for it.

5. **Infer** Do you think that Gaiman stopped reading after getting into trouble? Explain.
   Tip **Author and Me** Answer using clues from the selection and from your own experiences.

6. **Connect** What is one interesting thing you learned to do from reading a book that you chose to read?
   Tip **On Your Own** Answer from your own experiences.

Write About Your Reading

Suppose that you are Gaiman. If you could speak to the headmaster without fear of punishment, what would you say? Write a letter to the headmaster. Tell him what you think and try to persuade him to agree with your point of view.

• Would you argue that everyone was overreacting? How so?
• Would you feel you were in the wrong and apologize? Why or why not?
• Would you blame the book? What for?
• Would you say that more kids should read books? Why or why not?

Objectives (pp. 82–83)
Reading Identify main ideas and supporting details • Make connections from text to self
Literature Identify literary elements: author's purpose
Vocabulary Use word references: dictionary
Writing Respond to literature
Grammar Identify parts of speech: irregular verbs

82 UNIT 1 Why Read?

Write About Your Reading

Possible response:
Dear Headmaster,
I respect your school, and I don't intentionally disrupt class. However, I love to read and learn about new things. I think that the school should encourage students to read all sorts of books because we can learn from many different sources. I don't think there are any bad or dangerous books—just interesting ones!
—*Neil*

Skills Review

Key Reading Skill: Identifying Main Idea and Supporting Details

7. How did sorting important details from less important details help you determine the main idea of the article?

Key Literary Element: Author's Purpose

8. Did determining the main idea of the article help you learn the author's purpose? Explain.

9. Did the title give any clues to the author's purpose? Explain.

Reviewing Skills: Skimming and Scanning

10. Why is it helpful to skim or scan text before reading?

Vocabulary Check

Complete the following sentences with the correct vocabulary word.

> **interrogated   confiscated**
> **fragments   sarcastic**

11. The teacher ___ the girl's bubble gum.

12. The guard ___ the prisoner.

13. Her friend's ___ comment made Emily cry.

14. The plate broke into ___ when it hit the floor.

15. English Language Coach What word meanings or cultural references from England did you find difficult to understand when you read "Why Books Are Dangerous"? Which new words or references did you most enjoy discovering?

Literature Online

Web Activities For eFlashcards, Selection Quick Checks, and other Web activities, go to www.glencoe.com.

Grammar Link: Irregular Verbs

All verbs have "principal parts" that are used to form the various tenses. Most verbs are **regular**. Their parts look like this:

Regular Verbs			
Base	**Present Participle**	**Past**	**Past Participle**
walk	walking	walked	walked

So you would say, "I walk to school. I am walking today. I walked yesterday. I have walked every day."

Some verbs are **irregular**. The past and past participle are not formed by simply adding *-ed* to the base form. Also, the past participle for some irregular verbs is different from the past. Here are a few examples:

Irregular Verbs		
Base	**Past**	**Past Participle**
bring	brought	brought
leave	left	left
win	won	won
begin	began	begun
go	went	gone
know	knew	known
run	ran	run
see	saw	seen
speak	spoke	spoken

Grammar Practice

Choose three verbs from the chart of irregular verbs. Write three sentences for each one, using the base form, the past form, and the past participle.

Writing Application Look at the letter that you wrote. Do you recognize any irregular verbs in your writing? If so, circle the verbs. If not, add sentences that contain the past or past participle of irregular verbs.

Skills Review

Key Reading Skill: Identifying Main Idea and Supporting Details

7. Possible response: Eliminating some details meant less information to deal with, making it easier to find the main idea.

Key Literary Element: Author's Purpose

8. Possible response: The main idea that books inspire readers helped me see that the author's purpose was to encourage reading and exploration.

9. Responses will vary. Students may say that the use of the word *dangerous* made them think that the author's purpose was to warn them about books, not encourage them to read.

Reviewing Skill: Skimming and Scanning

10. Possible response: Skimming and scanning help in setting a purpose for reading and finding information quickly.

Vocabulary Check

11. confiscated

12. interrogated

13. sarcastic

14. fragments

15. English Language Coach Responses will vary. Students may say that they didn't understand the use of the slipper or the concept of a dangerous book.

Grammar Link: Irregular Verbs

Grammar Practice

Possible responses: Base form: Delia wants to <u>win</u> the writing contest.; Past form: Vidar <u>ran</u> after the school bus.; Past participle form: I have <u>left</u> your lunch on the counter.

Close

Ask students to explain what made dangerous books interesting to Neil Gaiman and why he loved reading so much.

Author's Purpose

Objectives covered in this workshop:
• Find similarities and differences across texts
• Identify author's purpose

Teaching Students to Compare Author's Purpose

Why Is It Important?

• Comparing authors' purposes helps students to read critically; they will look for satire, factual information, propaganda, irrational logic, symbolism, etc.

• Comparing authors' purposes from different genres, points of view, structures, and writing styles helps students make connections from text to text.

• Identifying an author's purpose and perspective will enable students to tell the difference between the topic and how the author feels about the topic.

• Identifying an author's purpose and perspective will also help students form their own opinions about a topic.

How to Help Students Get It

• Suggest that students ask the following questions as they read: Does the title of the selection give any clues as to the author's purpose? Is the author's purpose clearly stated? Does the selection provide information, entertain, express the author's thoughts and feelings, or attempt to convince the reader of something?

• When comparing authors' purposes in multiple selections, ask the students to consider each author's intended audience.

• Remind students that an author's purpose is his or her reason for writing about a topic. An author's perspective is the way he or she looks at or feels about the topic.

• Tell students that they can look for clues in the text, such as the author's word choices and how he or she organized the writing, to help them identify the author's purpose and perspective.

Reading to Answer the Big Question

The Southpaw by Judith Viorst
A boy and a girl write amusing letters back and forth after he refuses to let her play on his all-boys baseball team. In the end, her letters not only get her on the team, but negotiate spots for four other girls.

Concha by Mary Helen Ponce
The author shares memories of her childhood in the barrio. Siblings and friends make toys from natural materials like berries, mud, and grass. They have battles and contests with insects as they look for challenges and ways to prove their bravery.

Workshop Resources

PACING (DAYS)		LESSON	STUDENT MATERIALS	TEACHER RESOURCES
STANDARD	BLOCK			
1	1	Comparing Literature: Theme	🔨 English Language Coach, Review, p. 42	🔨 Bellringer Options Transparencies –Daily Language Practice 9 –Selection Focus 2 💿 Presentation Plus!
1	1	"The Southpaw"	💻 Glencoe Online 🔨 Unit Vocabulary Review, p. 40 🔨 Academic Vocabulary Review, p. 43 📁 English Language Coach 🔨 Comparing Literature Graphic Organizer, p. 35 💿 StudentWorks Plus™ 💻 Online Student Edition 💿 Literature Classics	💻 Puzzlemaker 💿 Skill Level Up!™ A Language Arts Game 💻 BookLink 3 📓 Assessment by Learning Objective (Diagnostic and Formative) 💿 Interactive Tutor: Self-Assessment 💿 TeacherWorks Plus™ 💿 ExamView Assessment Suite
1		"Concha"	💻 Glencoe Online 🔨 Selection Vocabulary Development 🔨 Academic Vocabulary Development 📁 English Language Coach 🔨 Active Reading Graphic Organizer 🔨 Literary Analysis 💿 StudentWorks Plus™ 💻 Online Student Edition 💿 Literature Classics	💻 Puzzlemaker 💿 Skill Level Up!™ A Language Arts Game 💻 BookLink 3 📓 Assessment by Learning Objective (Diagnostic and Formative) 💿 Interactive Tutor: Self-Assessment 💿 TeacherWorks Plus™ 💿 ExamView Assessment Suite

Keys for Unit Resource

- 📁 Blackline Master
- 📓 Workbook
- 📖 Supplemental Text
- 💿 CD-ROM
- 💿 DVD
- 🔨 Transparency
- 💻 Web-based
- 🔨 Fast File

Level Appropriate Code

- **AS** = Activities for all students
- **AL** = Activities for students working above grade level
- **OL** = Activities for students working at grade level
- **BL** = Activities for students working below grade level
- **EL** = Activities for English language learners

Focus

- 🖢 **Selection Focus Transparencies 2**
- 🖢 **Daily Language Practice Transparency 10**
Focus Activity Write the following on the board: How would you compare two restaurants? List the features you would use to compare the two and make a chart. You might start out with something like this:

	Restaurant 1	Restaurant 2
Price		
Quality of Food		
Service		

Teach

L Literary Element

Author's Purpose Ask: What are the four main reasons authors write? *(to entertain, to persuade, to explain, to describe)* **Ask:** What reasons might an author have for writing a story? *(to entertain)* **BL**

The Southpaw & Concha

by Judith Viorst   *by* Mary Helen Ponce

Skills Focus

You will use these skills as you read and compare the following selections:
- "The Southpaw," p. 88
- "Concha," p. 93

Reading
- Comparing and contrasting

Literature
- Identifying author's purpose

Writing
- Writing to compare and contrast

Objectives (pp. 84–85)
Literature Identify literary elements: author's purpose • Compare and contrast: literature
Writing Write a response to literature: compare and contrast

Comparing is nothing new to you. You compare things every day. When you choose between two jackets, you compare how they look on you and their warmth. When you talk about movies with a friend, you might compare how funny or exciting they are. You compare all kinds of things, including literature. Comparing is thinking about how two things are *alike* and how they are *different*.

How to Compare Literature: Author's Purpose

Before you compare two things, you need to figure out what you're going to base your comparison on. When you compare "The Southpaw" and "Concha" you'll compare the **authors' purposes** for writing the stories. Often, a writer will have more than one purpose. Use the clues below to help you figure out an author's purposes.

If a work	Its purpose is usually
• tells a story or is funny	• to *entertain*
• tells why to do something	• to *persuade*
• gives facts or tells steps	• to *explain*
• describes something the writer cares about	• to *express emotion*

As you read, look for clues that might tell you the *authors' purposes* for these stories.

Additional Support

Literature Focus Lesson

Author's Purpose Remind students that asking questions as they read helps clarify the text and the author's purpose. Students can use the following questions to determine the author's purpose:

- How does the author's word choice get his or her point across?
- Who is the author's intended audience?
- What response do you think the author expects from the reader? **OL**

Get Ready to Compare

In a short story one of the author's purposes is usually to entertain. While you're reading a story, try to figure out *how* the author is trying to entertain you. Some of the ways an author will entertain readers are through

- Humor–funny stories
- Excitement–adventure, science fiction, horror stories
- Mystery–suspense stories, science fiction stories
- Connection–poems and stories

To figure out an author's purpose, take notes in a chart like the one below. For example, if you read a horror story about how pollution causes house flies to grow very large and attack people, you might make a chart like this:

Author's Purpose

Entertain	Persuade	Inform or Explain	Express Emotion
Excitement: The way the flies attack people is scary.	Pollution causes the problem. The author wants us to do something to stop pollution.	There is a lot of detail about how pollution can ruin our environment.	The author expresses anger and fear about the effects of pollution.

Making Your Comparison

Before you start reading, make a chart like the one below in your Learner's Notebook for each of the stories. Then, as you read each story, fill in the chart with clues you find about the author's purpose. You won't fill in every square for each story.

Author's Purpose–(Name of Story)

Entertain (Humor, Excitement, Mystery, Connection)	Persuade	Inform or Explain	Express Emotion

After you've finished, you'll use your notes to compare the authors' purposes for writing these stories.

Teach

L Literary Element

Author's Purpose Have students list books or stories they have read that show the different ways a writer can entertain an audience: humor, excitement, mystery, and connection. Tell students to write their responses in their Learner's Notebooks. Then, have students share their responses with the class. (*Responses will vary.*) **AS**

Assess/Close

Say: Write a recommendation for one of the stories you listed. Your recommendation should explain how the author achieved his or her purpose. **AS** Have a few students read their recommendations aloud and discuss how the authors achieved their purposes. **AL**

Resources for page 85

 Use the Comparing Literature Graphic Organizer BLM in the Unit 1 Resource Booklet, p. 35.

Differentiated Instruction

Creating Charts Direct students' attention to the bulleted lists on page 84. Have students copy the lists in their notebooks, leaving room for a third column. Tell students to label that column Type of Writing. Then, work with students to identify a type of writing that fits each description. For example, the third column of the first row, "tells a story or is funny," could be filled in with "novel, short story, comic book." Continue to work with students to complete the rest of the column. Have students consider the genre of each work as they attempt to identify the author's purpose. **AS**

Objectives
- Compare and contrast
- Identify author's purpose

85

Teach

More About the Author

Judith Viorst has often found material for writing in problems faced by her three sons. Viorst says, "Four of the books . . . I consciously sat down and wrote because one child or another of mine had a problem. . . . I hoped it might help my boys to laugh at their problems."

V Vocabulary

Using Context Say: You can often determine the meanings of unknown words by paying attention to their contexts. If you see an unfamiliar word, look at the other words in the sentence or at the surrounding sentences. You might find clues to the word's meaning. Check your guesses by looking in a dictionary. **BL** **EL**

Before You Read : The Southpaw

Judith Viorst

Meet the Author

Born in Newark, New Jersey, in 1931, Judith Viorst (vyorst) knew that she wanted to be a writer in the second grade. Many of her poems, short stories, and novels have presented humorous views of her family life. "The Southpaw" was published in 1974. See page R7 of the Author Files for more on Judith Viorst.

Author Resources For more about Judith Viorst, go to www.glencoe.com.

Objectives (pp. 86–91)
Literature Identify literary elements: author's purpose • Compare and contrast: literature
Vocabulary Use word references: dictionary

Vocabulary Preview

former (FOR mer) *adj.* earlier; coming before in time **(p. 88)** *Mr. Judson, my former baseball coach, sent me a letter.*

cavities (KAV ih teez) *n.* hollow spaces in a tooth caused by decay **(p. 88)** *The dentist found two cavities in my tooth.*

laughingstock (LAF ing stahk) *n.* a person or thing that is made fun of **(p. 89)** *Alphonse became the laughingstock of the class when he almost ate the gerbil's food.*

English Language Coach

Word References Imagine that you've just started reading this selection when you come across a word you've never seen before. Luckily, you don't have to go too far to find its meaning. The bold, or darker, type tells you to look at the bottom of the page for a definition. But what if the word isn't defined on the page? You can look up the word in a dictionary but you will still have a decision to make.

Look at these dictionary entries for the words *formative, former,* and *formerly.*

> **for • ma • tive** (fôr′ mə tiv) *adj.* giving or capable of giving form.
>
> **for • mer** (fôr′ mər) *adj.* 1. being first (of two mentioned or understood). 2. belonging to, being of, or occurring in the past; previous; earlier.
>
> **for • mer • ly** (fôr′ mər lē) *adv.* in time past; once; previously.

As you can see, *former* has two definitions. Which definition you use depends on how the word is used in a sentence.

- As you read "The Southpaw," use a dictionary to look up any words that you don't understand.
- Write the words and their definitions in your Learner's Notebook.

Additional Support

Author Search To expand students' appreciation of Judith Viorst, have them access the Web site for additional information and resources.

English Language Coach

Word References Review the main parts of a dictionary entry, using the entry for *former* as an example. Identify the following parts of the entry:

- Pronunciation: the letters and symbols that show how the word is said
- Part of speech: the abbreviation that shows how the word is used

- Definition: the word's meaning or meanings

Have students look up *formative* and identify each part of the dictionary entry as you list it. **EL** **BL**

Get Ready to Read

Connect to the Reading

In "The Southpaw," the story is told in an exchange of notes between two former friends, Richard and Janet. Has a disagreement ever caused you to lose a friend? How did you feel? Were you able to make up?

Partner Talk With a partner, talk about an argument you had with a friend and how you handled it.

Build Background

A story written in the form of an exchange of letters is called an epistolary (ee PIS toh lare ee) story. In "The Southpaw," two friends—a boy and a girl—argue by letter whether or not girls can play on the team.

- *Southpaw* is a baseball term for a left-handed pitcher.

- A batting average indicates how often a batter gets a hit. A batting average higher than .300 is very good.

- The nine positions in baseball are pitcher, catcher, first base, second base, third base, shortstop, left field, center field, and right field.

- Pitcher is a difficult position to play. Often, the best athlete on a team is selected to pitch.

- Vassar College created the first women's baseball team in 1866.

- Early women players wore high-button shoes, high necklines, long skirts, and long sleeves.

- Amelia Bloomer created loose women's pants called "bloomers." The female baseball players who wore these pants were called "Bloomer Girls."

- Women were first paid to play baseball in 1875.

- During World War II, the All-American Girls Baseball League (AAGBL) was formed. The AAGBL continued for twelve years.

- Girls were not allowed to play Little League baseball until 1974. This story was published that year.

- In 1994, a group of women formed a team called the Colorado Silver Bullets.

- The American Women's Baseball Federation (AWBF) was founded to help promote women's baseball teams. Since 1992 the AWBF has organized regional and national tournaments, giving girls and women opportunities to play organized baseball.

Set Purposes for Reading

BIG Question Read the selection to learn how reading helped two friends settle a problem.

Set Your Own Purpose What would you like to learn from this selection to help you answer the Big Question? Write your own purpose on the "Southpaw" page of Foldable 1.

The Southpaw **87**

Teach

C Critical Thinking

Application Ask: Girls haven't always had the same opportunities as boys to play sports. Do you think girls should be allowed to play on teams with boys? (*Responses will vary. Students may say that as long as a girl is willing to play her best for a boys' team, she should be allowed to participate.*) **OL**

Literature Focus Lesson

Stories in Letters Judith Viorst tells the story of "The Southpaw" using an exchange of letters. Students may not be familiar with this style of storytelling, but it has a long history. Familiarize students with the general format of a letter. Label the salutation, body, closing, and signature. Have each student write a friendly letter to a partner. Explain to students that in "The Southpaw," the main characters write letters back and forth to each other and that this exchange tells the story. **BL** Suggest that students visit the library or the Internet to find other examples of stories that are told in the form of letters. **OL**

Objectives
- Use word references
- Use context clues
- Apply information
- Analyze features of genres: short story

87

Teach

L Literary Element

Author's Purpose Say: An author chooses a particular format and style for a reason. Why do you think Viorst chose to write the story in the form of letters? *(Responses will vary.)*
Ask: How might the story seem different if it were not told in such a unique way? Explain. *(Responses will vary. Some may say that this format makes the story unique and therefore fun to read. A different format may make the story seem less entertaining.)* **OL**

EL Language Coach

Word References Have students look for any unfamiliar words on the page. Tell the students to write those words in their Learner's Notebooks. Then have students look up the words in a dictionary. Suggest that students keep a running list of unfamiliar words and definitions to refer to as they read. **EL BL**

Readability Scores
Dale-Chall: 4.2
DRP: 49
Lexile: 640

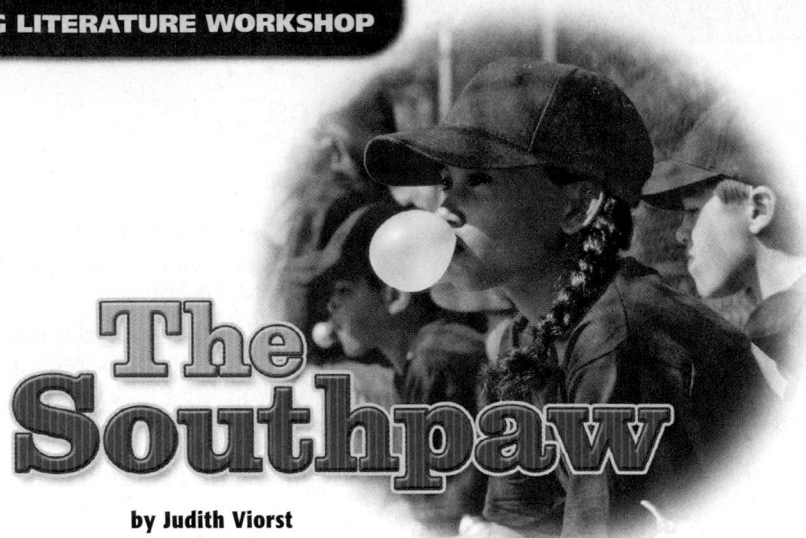

The Southpaw
by Judith Viorst

Dear Richard,
    Don't invite me to your birthday party because I'm not coming. And give back the Disneyland sweatshirt I said you could wear. If I'm not good enough to play on your team, I'm not good enough to be friends with.
        Your **former** friend,
        Janet
P.S. I hope when you go to the dentist he finds twenty **cavities.** **1**

Dear Janet,
    Here is your stupid Disneyland sweatshirt, if that's how you're going to be. I want my comic books now—finished or not. No girl has ever played on the Mapes Street baseball team, and as long as I'm captain, no girl ever will.
        Your former friend,
        Richard
P.S. I hope when you go for your checkup you need a tetanus[1] shot. **2**

---

1. **Tetanus** (TET un us) is a serious disease that people can get when bacteria get into a wound. A doctor gives a person a tetanus shot to keep her from getting tetanus.

Vocabulary
former (FOR mer) *adj.* from the past

cavities (CAV ih teez) *n.* hollow spaces in a tooth caused by decay

88 UNIT 1 Why Read?

Practice the Skills

1 Comparing Literature

Author's Purpose In this selection, the author uses letters from Richard and Janet to tell the story. Why do you think the author does this? Does it make the story more entertaining? How do the letters support the author's purpose? In your Author's Purpose chart, write "use of letters" under the author's purpose that you selected. **L**

2 Comparing Literature

Author's Purpose This letter shows you how Richard feels about having girls on a baseball team. Do you think the author agrees with Richard? Do you think the author might be trying to persuade or convince readers of something? If so, write a note in the *Persuade* box of the Author's Purpose chart.

Additional Support

Reading in the Real World

Citizenship Ask students to suggest pursuits other than sports, such as business and politics, in which the ability of women to participate has been questioned. List students' responses on the board. Have students conduct Internet research to learn about women's contributions in the fields they listed. Each student should pick a field and find an example of a notable woman in it. The student should identify the woman and write a paragraph describing her contributions to the field. Allow time for students to share their paragraphs with the rest of the class. **OL AL**

Dear Richard,

I'm changing my goldfish's name from Richard to Stanley. Don't count on my vote for class president next year. Just because I'm a member of the ballet club doesn't mean I'm not a terrific ballplayer.

Your former friend,
Janet

P.S. I see you lost your first game, 28–0.

L

Dear Janet,

I'm not saving any more seats for you on the bus. For all I care you can stand the whole way to school. Why don't you forget about baseball and learn something nice like knitting?

Your former friend,
Richard

P.S. Wait until Wednesday.

Dear Richard,

My father said I could call someone to go with us for a ride and hot-fudge sundaes. In case you didn't notice, I didn't call you.

Your former friend,
Janet

P.S. I see you lost your second game, 34-0.

Dear Janet,

Remember when I took the laces out of my blue-and-white sneakers and gave them to you? I want them back.

Your former friend,
Richard

P.S. Wait until Friday.

C

Dear Richard,

Congratulations on your unbroken record. Eight straight losses, wow! I understand you're the **laughingstock** of New Jersey. **3**

Your former friend,
Janet

P.S. Why don't you and your team forget about baseball and learn something nice like knitting maybe.

Vocabulary

laughingstock (LAF ing STAHK) *n.* a person or thing that is made fun of

Meeting on the Mound, © 1994 Stretar.
Analyzing the Art Do you think the artist meant for this picture to be serious or funny? Explain your answer.

Practice the Skills

3 | **English Language Coach**

Word References Use a thesaurus or dictionary to find a word or phrase that means about the same as **laughingstock**. Then test the word or phrase by reading it instead of *laughingstock* in Janet's letter.

The Southpaw **89**

Teach

Viewing the Art
Ask: How does this artwork help illustrate the story? *(Responses will vary. Some may say that it serves as a general illustration of how young people look playing baseball. Other may say the manager's small size adds to the humor of the story.)* **AS**

L Literary Element

Author's Purpose Ask: Why does the author include the P.S. notes? *(Possible response: to add humor.)* **Ask:** Why does the author include the detail about "something nice like knitting"? *(Possible response: She wants to show how sexist Richard is being by suggesting that Janet do a "girl's" activity, such as knitting, instead of a "boy's," such as baseball.)* **OL**

C Critical Thinking

Evaluation Say: Richard and Janet are responding to each other's actions. Do you think their responses are reasonable? *(Possible response: No. Each response is an exaggerated reaction to the previous action.)* **AS**

Differentiated Instruction

Writing a News Article Ask students to imagine that they are news reporters writing about the dispute between Janet and Richard. Ask students to separate the facts from the emotional content of the letters by considering the following:

• What is the basis (or cause) of the dispute?

• What reasons do Janet and Richard have for their positions?

Ask students to write a brief article based on the facts of the story. Suggest that they prepare by making notes in a chart with columns labeled *Facts* and *Feelings*. Invite students to share their news stories with the class. **AL**

Objectives
• Identify author's purpose
• Use word references
• Find meaning in art
• Evaluate text

Teach

C1 Critical Thinking

Evaluation Say: Read footnote number 2 at the bottom of this page. What does Richard mean when he suggests that Janet is kicking him "when he's down"? *(Possible response: Richard's team has lost eight games in a row, so Janet's mocking congratulations are like kicking someone who's already been beaten to the ground.)* **OL Ask:** Do you think Janet is being mean to Richard? Explain. *(Responses will vary.)* **AL**

C2 Critical Thinking

Comprehension Ask: Why do you think Richard stops signing his letters to Janet as "Your former friend"? *(Possible response: He wants her to join the team.)* **AL**

C1
Dear Janet,
    Here's the silver horseback-riding trophy that you gave me. I don't think I want to keep it anymore.
        Your former friend,
        Richard
P.S. I didn't think you'd be the kind who'd kick a man when he's down.[2]

Dear Richard,
    I wasn't kicking exactly. I was kicking back.
        Your former friend,
        Janet
P.S. In case you were wondering, my batting average is .345.

Dear Janet,
    Alfie is having his tonsils[3] out tomorrow. We might be able to let you catch next week. **4**
        Richard

Dear Richard,
    I pitch.
        Janet

Dear Janet,
    Joel is moving to Kansas and Danny sprained his wrist. How about a permanent place in the outfield?
        Richard

C2

Dear Richard,
    I pitch.
        Janet

Dear Janet,
    Ronnie caught the chicken pox and Leo broke his toe and Elwood has these stupid violin lessons. I'll give you first base, and that's my final offer.
        Richard

---

2. If you **kick a man when he's down,** you are being mean to someone who has already had bad things happen to him.

3. **Tonsils** are small organs in the throat near the back of the mouth. Sometimes doctors perform surgery to remove them.

Practice the Skills

4 Comparing Literature

Author's Purpose Richard is starting to change his mind about letting girls play on the team. Why is he changing his mind? Does this tell you anything about one of the author's purposes for this story? If so, write a note in your chart.

Additional Support

Differentiated Instruction

Role-Playing To help students improve their understanding of each character's point of view, have them role-play. Divide students into groups of four or five. Each group should select one student to be Richard and one to be Janet.

The other students should develop questions to ask either Janet or Richard. The students playing the characters should answer questions as they think Janet and Richard would. **OL AL**

Dear Richard,
   Susan Reilly plays first base, Marilyn Jackson catches, Ethel Kahn plays center field, I pitch. It's a package deal.[5]
   Janet

P.S. Sorry about your 12-game losing streak.

Dear Janet,
   Please! Not Marilyn Jackson.
   Richard

Dear Richard,
   Nobody ever said that I was unreasonable. How about Lizzie Martindale instead?
   Janet

Dear Janet,
   At least could you call your goldfish Richard again? 5
Your friend,
   Richard ○

---

5. A *package deal* is an offer that includes several items. Whoever agrees to the deal must take all of the items.

Practice the Skills

5 **BIG Question**
Did you enjoy reading "The Southpaw"? Explain why or why not. Write your answer on the "Southpaw" page of Foldable 1. Your response will help you complete the Unit Challenge later.

Analyzing the Photo Does the story you've just read change your thoughts about this photograph? Why or why not?

The Southpaw **91**

Teach

L Literary Element

Author's Purpose Ask: What does the resolution of the story suggest about one of Viorst's purposes for writing "The Southpaw"? *(Possible response: One of the author's purposes is to describe how people involved in a disagreement can learn to compromise.)* **OL**

BQ BIG Question
Ask: What answer do you think Janet and Richard would give to the question "Why read?" *(Possible response: Reading allowed the characters to not have to speak face-to-face when they were upset.)* **OL**

Reading Fluency

Build Fluency Have students practice reading the last page of "The Southpaw" aloud with a partner. Each student should take the role of one of the main characters. Ask students to read the passage aloud several times until they can smoothly read all the sentences with feeling and understanding. Tell students to aim at making their reading sound as fluid and natural as if they were talking to one another. **AS**

Objectives
• Evaluate text
• Identify author's purpose
• Monitor comprehension

Teach

More About the Author

Mary Helen Ponce's interest in reading began when she was a child. One of her sisters gave her a subscription to the Book of the Month Club. Ponce became a full-time homemaker shortly after graduating from high school and getting married. After her youngest child began attending school, she started work on her bachelor's degree. In addition to literary writing, she has published scholarly articles in journals.

V Vocabulary

Sentences Say: Using new vocabulary words in context can help you remember their meanings. In your Learner's Notebook, write a sentence for each of the words found in the Vocabulary Preview. *(Responses will vary.)* **AS**

Before You Read : Concha

Mary Helen Ponce

Meet the Author

Mary Helen Ponce (POHN say) grew up in a Mexican American community in California. She says, "We feared few things in the barrio [*neighborhood*]. We knew everyone; everyone knew us. We belonged." Mary Helen Ponce was born in 1938. "Concha" was published in 1988.

Author Resources For more about Mary Helen Ponce, go to www.glencoe.com.

Objectives (pp. 92–97)
Literature Identify literary elements: author's purpose • Compare and contrast: literature
Vocabulary Use word references: dictionary

Vocabulary Preview

amassed (uh MAST) *v.* piled up, collected, or gathered a great quantity of something **(p. 93)** *Joey amassed a huge pile of berries to shoot.*

pelted (PELT id) *v.* struck over and over again **(p. 94)** *The kids pelted each other with peas from their pea shooters.*

treacherous (TRECH ur us) *adj.* dangerous and unpredictable **(p. 95)** *Ants and bees can be treacherous.*

feat (feet) *n.* an act that shows skill, strength, or courage **(p. 96)** *Standing still while a wasp walks on you is quite a feat.*

incident (IN suh dunt) *n.* an event or situation **(p. 97)** *They all remembered the incident in which Concha got stung.*

English Language Coach

Word References In this book, a lot of words are defined in footnotes. A footnote tells you what a word or phrase means as it's used in the text. You can look up any other confusing words in a dictionary. Another useful word reference is a **thesaurus**. It lists words that mean the same, or almost the same, as the word you have looked up. A thesaurus may also list words that mean the opposite.

Get Ready to Read

Connect to the Reading

What were your favorite outdoor games when you were younger? Did you ever make up games? Were any of them dangerous or risky?

Build Background

- This story takes place in California during the 1940s.
- Stinging red ants are common in some areas of California.
- Kick-the-can, kickball, and red rover are all children's games.

Set Purposes for Reading

BIG Question Read to find out what kinds of games the children played and how Concha became a champion of one game.

Set Your Own Purpose What else would you like to learn from the selection that might help you answer the Big Question? Write your own purpose on the "Concha" page of Foldable 1.

Additional Support

Author Search To expand students' appreciation of Mary Helen Ponce, have them access the Web site for additional information and resources.

English Language Coach

Idioms Ask Spanish-speaking students to explain the Spanish expressions and phrases in "Concha." Ask them to give the literal translations of the Spanish words and to tell when expressions such as *ujule* and *ya vamonos* may be used in real-life situations. Organize students into groups and have them practice using the Spanish expressions and phrases. **EL**

Concha

by Mary Helen Ponce

While growing up in the small barrio[1] of Pacoima,[2] my younger brother Joey and I were left alone to find ways *para divertirnos*,[3] to keep ourselves busy—and out of our mother's way. One way in which we whiled away long summer days was by making pea shooters. These were made from a hollow reed which we first cleaned with a piece of wire. We then collected berries from *los pirules*,[4] the pepper trees that lined our driveway. Once we **amassed** enough dry berries we put them in our mouths and spat them out at each other through the pea shooter. **1**

---

1. A *barrio* is a neighborhood of Spanish-speaking people.
2. *Pacoima* (PAW koh EE maw) is a community in Los Angeles, California.
3. *Para divertirnos* (PAH rah dee vair TEER nohs) means "to amuse ourselves" in Spanish, or, as the speaker in the story says, "to keep ourselves busy."
4. *Los pirules* (lohs pee ROO lays) is Spanish for "the pepper trees."

Vocabulary

amassed (uh MAST) *v.* piled up, collected, or gathered a great quantity of something

Practice the Skills

1 **Comparing Literature**

Author's Purpose Start taking notes in the "Concha" chart you made in your Learner's Notebook. Does the first paragraph give clues about the author's purpose in writing this story? Does the author seem to want to entertain, persuade, inform, or express her feelings? **L**

Concha **93**

Teach

Viewing the Photo
Ask: What emotions do you see on the face of the child in this photograph? *(The child looks excited and happy.)* **BL**
Ask: On the basis of the photograph, what do you expect the story will be about? *(Possible response: The story will most likely be about children doing something fun and exciting.)* **OL**

L Literary Element

Author's Purpose Ask: What kinds of details does the narrator give about the games kids played? *(The narrator describes in detail how they made pea shooters, including the materials used and the process of making them.)* **BL Ask:** What does the description indicate about the author's purpose for writing this story? *(Possible response: The author is trying to document in detail the world of her childhood, and in the process she describes, informs, and entertains.)* **OL**

Readability Scores
Dale-Chall: 6.9
DRP: 53
Lexile: 860

Differentiated Instruction

Sequence Chart In the first paragraph of "Concha," Mary Helen Ponce describes the process of making pea shooters. Her description is a good example of a process analysis, a step-by-step description of how to do something. Ask students to identify the words that show the order in which the steps take place. *(first, then, once)* Have students create a sequence chart that shows the order of the steps. **BL** Then ask students to consider a process that they know how to do, such as making a sandwich. Have students create a sequence chart that shows the process. **OL AL**

Objectives
• Identify author's purpose
• Learn and use new vocabulary
• Understand idioms
• Use text features: photographs

Teach

EL Language Coach

Multiple-Meaning Words
Say: Use a dictionary to find another possible meaning for the word *pelt*. *(Possible response: The skin of an animal with the fur still on it.)* **EL OL**

L Literary Element

Author's Purpose Say:
An author's word choice can often give clues to his or her purpose for writing. Pay attention to words such as *pelted* and *slumped*. What do these descriptive words suggest about the author's purpose? *(Responses will vary. Students may suggest that the author's purpose is to describe and to entertain.)* **OL AL**

The berries had a terrible taste—they were even said to be poison! I was most careful not to swallow them. We selected only the hard, firm peas. The soft ones, we knew, would get mushy, crumble in our mouths and force us to gag—and lose a fight. During an important battle a short pause could spell defeat.[5] Oftentimes while playing with Joey I watched closely. When he appeared to gag I dashed back to the pepper tree to load up on ammunition. I **pelted** him without mercy until he begged me to stop. **EL**

"No more. Ya no," Joey cried as he bent over to spit berries. "No more!"

"Ha, ha I got you now." I spat berries at Joey until, exhausted, we called a **truce** and slumped onto a wooden bench. **2 3**

In fall our game came to a halt—the trees dried up; the berries fell to the ground. This was a sign for us to begin other games.

Our games were seasonal. During early spring we made whistles from the long blades of grass that grew in the open field behind our house. In winter we made dams, forts and canals from the soft mud that was our street. We tied burnt matchsticks together with string. These were our men. We positioned them along the forts (camouflaged with small branches). We also played kick the can, but our most challenging game was playing with red ants.

---

5. When you say something *could spell defeat,* you mean that it could result in defeat.

Vocabulary

pelted (PELT id) *v.* struck over and over again **EL**

Red ants are also known as fire ants because their painful stings can cause blisters, and even death.

Practice the Skills

2 Comparing Literature

Author's Purpose These paragraphs tell more about the peashooter fights. What details hint at the author's purpose? Write them in your chart. **L**

3 English Language Coach

Word References Work with a classmate. Use a dictionary to find the meaning of **truce** while your partner uses a thesaurus. Compare your findings.

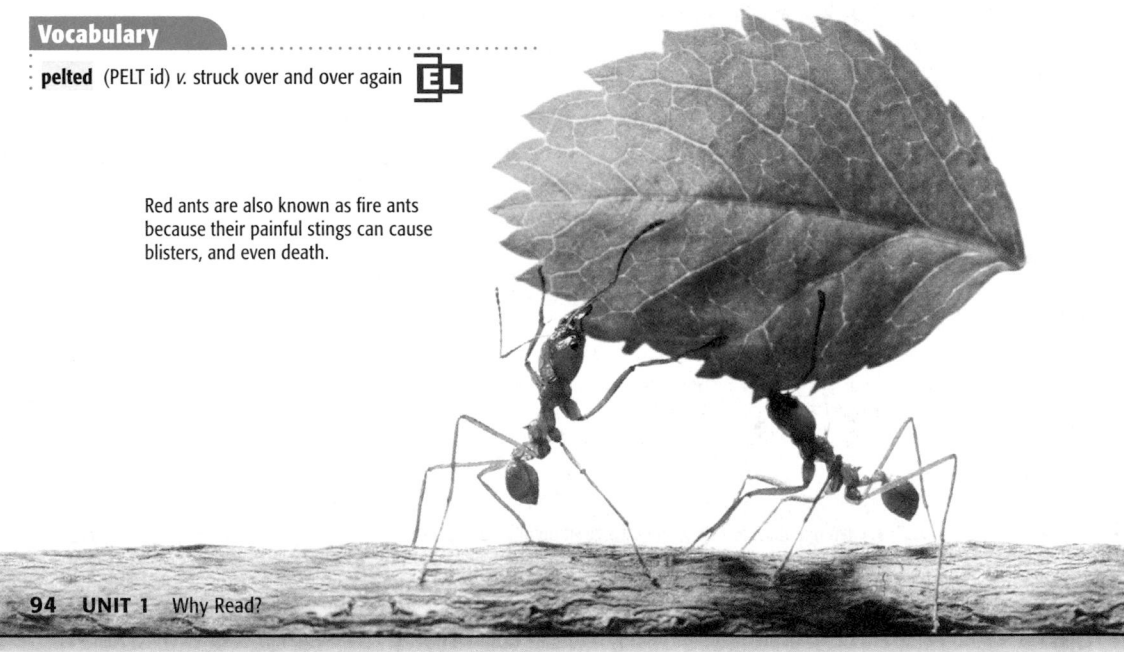

Additional Support

Literature Focus Lesson

Setting One of Mary Helen Ponce's primary purposes in writing "Concha" is to evoke a sense of a particular time and place. First have students use an atlas to locate Pacoima, California. Then ask students to write a short description of the setting of "Concha," using as many different sensory details as they can.

Finally ask students to rewrite the major events of "Concha" set in their own neighborhood. Have them think about what changes would be necessary and what parts of the story would remain the same. When they are finished, have them share their stories with the class. **OL AL**

The ants were of the common variety: red, round and **treacherous.** They invaded our yard and the *llano*[6] every summer. We always knew where ants could be found, *donde habia hormigas.*[7] We liked to build mud and grass forts smack in the middle of ant territory. The ants were the enemy, the matchstickmen the heroes, or good guys.

Playing with ants was a real challenge! While placing our men in battle positions we timed it so as not to get bitten. We delighted in beating the ants at their own game.

Sometimes we got really brave and picked up ants with a stick, then twirled the stick around until the ants got dizzy-drunk (or so we thought)—and fell to the ground. We made ridges of dirt and pushed the ants inside, covered them with dirt and made bets as to how long it would take them to dig their way out.

Concha, my best friend and neighbor, was quite **timid** at school. She avoided all rough games such as kickball and Red Rover. When it came to playing with ants however, Concha held first place for bravery. She could stand with her feet atop an anthill for the longest time! We stood trembling as ants crawled up our shoes, then quickly stomped our feet to scare them off. But Concha never lost her nerve. **4**

One time we decided to have an ant contest. The prize was a candy bar—a Sugar Daddy sucker. We first found an anthill, lined up, then took turns standing beside the anthill while the juicy red ants climbed over our shoes. We dared not move—but when the first ant moved towards our ankles we stomped away, our Oxfords making swirls of dust that allowed us to **retreat** to the sidelines. But not Concha. She remained in place as big red ants crept up her shoes. One, five, ten! We stood and counted, holding our breath as the ants continued to climb. Fifteen, twenty! Twenty ants were crawling over Concha! **5**

---

6. *Llano* (YAH noh) is the Spanish word for "flat ground."

7. *Donde habia hormigos* (DOHN day ah BEE ah or MEE gohs) means "where ants lived."

Vocabulary

treacherous (TRECH ur us) *adj.* dangerous and unpredictable

La Nina del Chupetin. Graciela Genoves (b. 1962). Zurbaran Galeria, Buenos Aires, Argentina.

Analyzing the Art What feeling do you get from this picture? Is it similar to the feeling you get from reading the story? Explain.

Practice the Skills

C

4 English Language Coach

Word References Do you know any other words for **timid**? List them in your Learner's Notebook. Then look up *timid* in a thesaurus. List any new synonyms (words that mean the same thing) you find there.

5 English Language Coach

Word References Look up **retreat** in a dictionary. What did everyone except Concha do?

Concha **95**

Teach

EL Language Coach

Word References Say: Look up the word *treacherous* in a thesaurus. What words have similar meanings? Share your findings with a partner. *(Possible responses: unsafe, risky, hazardous, dangerous)* **OL**

C Critical Thinking

Analysis Ask: Why is Concha so determined to stand on the hill? *(Possible response: She wants to prove that she is not so timid.)* **OL AL**

Differentiated Instruction

Writing Song Lyrics Divide students into small groups. Ask students to select a scene from the story. Each group should then select a song with which they are familiar. Students should replace the existing lyrics of the song with lyrics that describe the scene. The lyrics could describe the action and what the characters are feeling. Ask each group to write lyrics for at least one verse and a refrain. Groups can rehearse their new lyrics and then perform their songs for the class. **AS**

Objectives
• Analyze text
• Identify author's purpose
• Use word references
• Understand multiple-meaning words
• Identify literary elements: setting

Teach

C Critical Thinking

Analysis Say: Mundo says "in a hushed voice" that Concha isn't scared. What does this suggest about how Mundo feels at that moment? *(Possible response: Mundo is impressed and frightened by Concha's behavior.)* **OL** **Ask:** Why do you think Mundo then adds to Beto, "I mean for a girl"? *(Possible response: Feeling impressed by Concha makes him embarrassed, so he tries to diminish her bravery.)* **AL**

L Literary Element

Author's Purpose Say: When Concha gets bitten by the ants, the other children discuss what might happen to both her and the ants. Do you learn more about how Concha feels or how the other children feel? *(Ponce focuses more on the reaction of the other children.)* **OL** **Ask:** What does this scene suggest about the author's purpose? *(Possible response: Ponce's purpose may be to describe and to entertain.)* **AL**

"*Ujule,*[8] she sure ain't scared," cried Mundo in a hushed voice. "*No le tiene miedo a las hormigas.*"[9]

"Uhhhhh," answered Beto, his eyes wide.

". . . I mean for a girl," added Mundo as he poked Beto in the ribs. We knew Beto liked Concha—and always came to her rescue.

We stood and counted ants. We were so caught up in this **feat** that we failed to notice the twenty-first ant that climbed up the back of Concha's sock . . . and bit her!

"Ay, ay, ay," screeched Concha.

"Gosh, she's gonna die," cried an alarmed Virgie as she helped stomp out ants. "She's gonna die!"

"She's too stupid to die," laughed Mundo, busy brushing ants off his feet. "She's too stupid."

"But sometimes people die when ants bite them," insisted Virgie, her face pale. "They gets real sick."

"The ants will probably die," Mundo snickered, holding his stomach and laughing loudly. "Ah, ha, ha."

"Gosh you're mean," said a shocked Virgie, hands on hips. "You are so mean."

"Yeah, but I ain't stupid." **G**

"Come on you guys, let's get her to the *mangera,*"[10] Beto cried as he reached out to Concha who by now had decided she would live. "Come on, let's take her to the faucet."

We held Concha by the waist as she hobbled[11] to the water faucet. Her cries were now mere[12] whimpers as no grownup had come out to investigate. From experience we knew that if a first cry did not bring someone to our aid we should stop crying—or go home.

Children's Games, 1959. Rufino Tamayo. Oil on canvas. The Metropolitan Museum of Art, New York.

Analyzing the Art Does this picture look to you like children playing games? Explain why or why not.

---

8. ***Ujule*** (oo HOO lay) is a Spanish exclamation that means something like "Oh my!" or "Wow!"
9. ***No le tiene miedo*** (noh lay TYEH nay mee AY doh) *a las hormigas* means "She's not afraid of the ants."
10. ***Mangera*** (mahn HAY raw) is Spanish for "faucet."
11. ***Hobbled*** means "walked with a limp."
12. ***Mere*** is another word for "only" or "nothing more than."

Vocabulary

feat (feet) *n.* an act that shows skill, strength, or courage

Practice the Skills

G Comparing Literature

Author's Purpose Reread the page up to this point. What clues do you see about the author's purpose? Look especially at the sentences "She's too stupid to die" and "The ants will probably die." Based on those sentences, is the author trying to entertain, to persuade, to explain, or to express feelings? Explain your answer.

Additional Support

English Language Coach

Word References Students can play games to practice using the dictionary and thesaurus. Students can compete individually or in teams.

Dueling Definitions Player 1 chooses a vocabulary word from the story, writes down its dictionary definition, and then writes down an incorrect definition that he or she has made up. Player 2 must decide which is the correct meaning.

Name That Word Player 1 selects a vocabulary word from the story and then identifies synonyms for that word from a thesaurus. After each synonym is revealed, Player 2 gets to guess the vocabulary word. **EL OL**

We helped Concha to the faucet, turned it on and began to mix water with dirt. We knew the best remedy for insect bites was *lodo*.[13] We applied mud to all bug stings to stop the swelling. Mud was especially good for wasp stings, the yellowjackets we so feared—and from which we ran away at top speed. Whenever bees came close we stood still until they flew away, but there were no set rules on how to get rid of *avispas*.[14] We hit out at them, and tried to scare them off but the yellowjackets were fierce! In desperation[15] we flung dirt at them, screamed and ran home.

Visual Vocabulary
Jacks is a game in which the object is to pick up a number of small, six-pointed metal pieces while bouncing and catching a small rubber ball with the same hand.

Not long after the ant **incident** Concha decided she was not about to run when a huge wasp broke up our game of jacks. She stood still, so still the wasp remained on her dark head for what seemed like hours. We stood and watched, thinking perhaps the wasp had mistaken Concha's curly hair for a bush! We watched—and waited.

"*Ujule*, she sure is brave," exclaimed Virgie as she sucked on a popsicle. "She sure is brave."

"She's stupid," grunted Mundo, trying to be **indifferent**. "She's just a big show-off who thinks she's so big." **7**

"So are you," began Virgie, backing off. "So are you."

"Yeah? Ya wanna make something outta it?"

"Let's go," interrupted Beto in his soft voice. "*Ya vamonos*."[16] He smiled at Concha—who smiled back.

In time the wasp flew away. Concha immediately began to brag about how a "real big wasp" sat on her hair for hours. She never mentioned the ant contest—nor the twenty-first ant that led her to *el lodo*. **8 9** ○

---

13. *Lodo* (LOH doh) means "mud."
14. *Avispas* (ah VEES pahs) are wasps.
15. When you do something *in desperation,* you have usually run out of ideas about what to do.
16. *Ya vamonos* (yah VAH moh nohs) means "Let's go."

Vocabulary

incident (IN suh dunt) *n.* an event or situation

Practice the Skills

7 English Language Coach

Word References Do you know what **indifferent** means? Look up this word in a dictionary or thesaurus. Then explain its meaning to a partner.

8 Comparing Literature

Author's Purpose The selection ends with a story about Concha and a huge wasp. Talk with a partner about the story. Discuss its effect on you. Did you enjoy it? In your chart, add any details from the end of the story that give clues about the author's purpose.

BIG Question

9 What kinds of books or magazines do you think the kids in this story might have liked to read? Write your answer on the "Concha" page of Foldable 1. Your response will help you complete the Unit Challenge later.

Concha **97**

Teach

EL Language Coach

Word References Say: Mundo tries to act indifferent when the wasp lands on Concha's head. Use a thesaurus to find two words that have similar meanings to *indifferent*. *(Possible responses: uninterested, uncaring, cool)* **Say:** Then write two sentences in your Learner's Notebooks that use the new words correctly. *(Responses will vary.)* **EL BL**

L Literary Element

Author's Purpose Say: Think about how Ponce describes Concha's encounters with the ants and the wasp. How does she use these descriptions to entertain the reader? *(She uses suspense to entertain the reader; we don't know what will happen to Concha.)* **OL Ask:** How does she use these descriptions to make a point? *(Possible response: Concha's behavior shows that social embarrassment can be scarier than physical injury.)* **AL**

BQ BIG Question

Ask: Why would you read a story like "Concha"? *(Possible response: to be entertained, or to learn more about life for children in a different geographical location or era)* **AS**

Literature Focus Lesson

Cross-Cultural Literature The characters in "Concha" belong to a bilingual community. Mary Helen Ponce emphasizes this fact by including several Spanish words and phrases within her story. Ask students to prepare charts showing the Spanish words and phrases along with their English translations.

Then ask students to consider why the author uses Spanish vocabulary in her writing. Have students think about the following questions:

• What effect does the use of Spanish have on Spanish-speaking readers?

• What effect does it have on non-Spanish-speaking readers? **AS**

Objectives
• Identify author's purpose
• Analyze text
• Use word references

Assess

Resources for page 98

📁 Selection QuickCheck, pp. 9–10

🌐 Exam View Assessment Suite

🌐 Interactive Tutor: Self-Assessment

Vocabulary Check

The Southpaw

1. cavity
2. former

Concha

3. pelted
4. feat
5. treacherous
6. amassed
7. incident
8. amassed
9. incident
10. feat
11. treacherous
12. pelted

After You Read

The Southpaw & Concha

Vocabulary Check

Write the answers to the following twelve questions on a separate sheet of paper. For the first two items below, write the word from the list that best fits each meaning.

The Southpaw

former   cavity

1. a hollow space in a tooth, caused by decay ____
2. something from the past ____

Concha

For items 3–7, write the word from the list that means most nearly the same as the words below.

amassed   pelted   treacherous   feat   incident

3. attacked ____
4. remarkable accomplishment ____
5. unsafe ____
6. gathered together ____
7. event ____

Now complete each sentence with one of the vocabulary words from "Concha."

8. Mary and Joey ____ as many dry berries as they could.
9. The author writes about what she calls "the ant ____."
10. Counting all those ants was quite a ____.
11. Mary feared the ants. They seemed ____.
12. Mary ____ her brother with dry berries.

Objectives (pp. 98–99)
Reading Evaluate text
Literature Identify literary elements: author's purpose • Compare and contrast: literature
Vocabulary Use word references: dictionary
Writing Write a response to literature: compare and contrast

98   UNIT 1   Why Read?

---

17. "The Southpaw"

Entertain	Persuade	Inform/Explain	Describe
uses vivid vocabulary for humor	shows that girls can be strong athletes	explains the situation between Richard and Janet	
uses letter format to encourage identification with characters			

Reading/Critical Thinking

On a separate sheet of paper, answer the following questions.

The Southpaw

13. **Analyze** Richard didn't want Janet to pitch, even after he realized that she could help his team. Why do you think he resisted? Was it only because she was a girl? Explain.

    Tip **On My Own** You must use what you know from your own experience.

14. **Analyze** When do Richard and Janet start trying to understand each other? Which note shows the change?

    Tip **Author and Me** You will find clues in the story, but you'll also need to use information in your head.

Concha

15. **Interpret** Why do you think Concha and her friends find the ants so fascinating?

    Tip **Author and Me** You will find clues in the story, but you'll also need to use information in your head.

16. **Contrast** What does the author show about Concha by contrasting the way she acts at school with the way she deals with ants?

    Tip **Author and Me** You will find clues in the story, but you'll also need to use information in your head.

Writing: Compare the Literature

Use Your Notes

17. Follow these steps to help you compare the author's purposes in "The Southpaw" with the author's purposes in "Concha."

Step 1: Look at the notes you wrote in your Author's Purpose charts. Based on your notes, write down what you think the *author's purpose* or *purposes* for "The Southpaw" are. Remember, the author might have more than one purpose.

Step 2: Look at your notes for "Concha." Write down what you think the *author's purpose* or *purposes* were for that story.

Get It on Paper

At the beginning of this lesson, you saw a list of several methods that authors use to entertain readers. These methods included

humor   excitement   mystery   connection

To compare "The Southpaw" and "Concha" and evaluate how well each author carried out her purpose, answer these questions in your Learner's Notebook.

18. For both of these stories, one of the *author's purposes* was to entertain. Which of the above methods did the author of "The Southpaw" use to entertain? Using details from your chart, describe at least one way the author used this method to entertain her readers.

19. What method or methods did the author of "Concha" use to entertain you? Using details from your chart, describe at least one way the author used this method.

20. Look at your charts. Do you feel that either or both of these authors had a second purpose for writing? If so, explain what those purposes were, and why you think that was the author's purpose.

21. Use your author's purpose charts and your answers to questions 17–19 to help you answer this question: Which author, do you think, was more successful in achieving her purposes? Give details from your notes to support your opinion.

BIG Question

22. Why do you think people might want to read stories like "The Southpaw" and "Concha"?

Reading/Critical Thinking

The Southpaw

13. Possible response: He wanted to control his team.

14. Possible response: They start trying to understand each other when Richard begins losing his team. The turning point comes when he says, "We might be able to let you catch next week."

Concha

15. Possible responses: The ants are alive, unpredictable, and dangerous.

16. Possible response: She stands on the anthill to prove that she is not as timid as she seems.

Writing: Compare the Literature

Use Your Notes (See sample chart)

17. Possible responses: Step 1: to entertain; Step 2: A secondary purpose for "The Southpaw" is to persuade. A secondary purpose for "Concha" is to describe.

Get It On Paper

18–21. Responses will vary.

22. Responses will vary.

Close

Hold a class discussion based on students' responses to question 22.

17. "Concha"

Entertain	Persuade	Inform/Explain	Describe
suspenseful descriptions of Concha's interactions with insects		explains what the children did to pass their time	detailed descriptions of the children's games
Lifelike characters, like Mundo and Concha, remind readers of their own friends			

The Unit Challenge

Focus

BELLRINGER Options

🖐 **Daily Language Practice Transparency 10**
Focus Activity Ask: What new reasons for reading did you discover in this unit? Which selections suggested these ideas? *(Responses will vary.)*

Invite students to share their comments with the class. Use the responses to emphasize the uses and the importance of reading for people of all ages.

Teach

Group Activity: Comic Strip

- Have students select one member of the group to record the group's ideas.

- Provide examples of comic strips to help students visualize the assignment. Explain that comics focus on both humorous and serious topics.

- Suggest that students who have a talent for drawing create the final pictures.

Assess/Close

Group Activity

Say: Think about what your comic strip says about reading. Then, in one sentence, tell why reading is important. *(Students may share their statements orally or write them in their Learner's Notebooks.)* **AS**

100

UNIT 1 WRAP-UP

Answering The BIG Question — Why Read?

You've just read several different selections, and you thought about why people read. Now use what you've learned to do the Unit Challenge.

The Unit Challenge

Choose Activity A or Activity B and follow the directions for that activity.

A. Group Activity: Comic Strip

You and three friends have been asked to create a comic strip to tell why reading is important. A comic strip is a short sequence of cartoon drawings that tell a story.

1. **Discuss the Assignment** First brainstorm with your group to come up with a list of answers to the question *Why Read?* Use the notes on your Foldable. Discuss all the reasons why you read. Do you read to be entertained, to pass the time, to visit other worlds, or to learn how to do something?

2. **Get Started** Think about some of the comic strips that you've read. Remember that a comic strip uses a sequence of comic drawings to tell a story. Use the reasons you listed to brainstorm a story line for your comic strip that would fit into four or five frames.

3. **Make a Storyboard** A storyboard is a rough draft of what your comic strip will look like. It shows what the characters will look like and what you think they will say to each other. Keep working on your storyboard until you all agree on the story line.

4. **Create the Comic** Draw your comic strip on a clean sheet of paper. Color in the drawings, and have a group member check all the spelling and grammar.

5. **Present Your Comic Strip** Now it's time to present your comic strip to the class. Choose one member of the group to read your comic strip to the class. Hang it in the classroom.

Storyboard

Description	Description
Description	Description

B. Solo Activity: Conduct Interviews

Why people read does not have to be a mystery. All you need to do is ask! Interview three friends or family members to find out why they read.

1. **Gather Information** Before conducting your interview, use the notes from your Foldable to prepare a list of questions. Also include this question:
   - What have you read lately?

Use a chart like the one below to record the answers.

2. **Summarize What You Find** Write a paragraph for each person you interviewed. Summarize what each person says. Ask your sources if you may use their names in your report. If not, you might refer to the people you interviewed as Subject A, Subject B, and so on. Write a paragraph drawing a conclusion about all the people you interviewed. You might learn, for example, that older people read more books than magazines. You might also learn that your friends read more magazines than newspapers.

3. **Present Your Findings** Make sure your paragraphs are neat and easy to read. Check your spelling. Then hand in your detective's report.

Question Row	Subject A	Subject B	Subject C
What have you read lately?	a teen magazine	the Sunday comics	school books
How does this help you?	Reading helps me keep up with fashions. I learn what's cool to wear.		

Teach

Solo Activity: Conduct Interviews

- Encourage students to choose friends or family members of different ages as their interviewees.
- Students may brainstorm additional interview questions in their Learner's Notebooks.
- Have students make a draft of the chart in their Learner's Notebooks and then make a larger copy of it on a separate sheet of paper for use in the interview process.
- Students may wish to record basic information about their subjects, such as age and gender.
- Suggest that students include a row in the chart for a quote from each person about why reading is important to him or her.
- Tell students to include two or three general statements about their findings.

Assess/Close

Solo Activity

Write on the board: What new ideas about reading did you get from interviewing others? Which ideas will you put into practice in your own life? How? *(Have students respond to the questions in their Learner's Notebooks.)* **AS**

Objectives
- Create a comic strip
- Conduct an interview

Focus

Vocabulary Preview

List the following words on the board and review their definitions before students begin reading.

- loitering
- veteran
- nuisance
- substantiate
- immunization
- scribe

Build Background

The story describes a neighborhood in which few people use bank accounts. People who do not have bank accounts often pay high fees for check-cashing services.

Teach

R Reading Skill

Review Skimming and Scanning Say: Skim the story to find clues about its content. Based on those clues, what do you think the story will be about? *(Responses will vary. Students might say it's about a person who writes something or that it's about what happens at a check-cashing service.)* **OL**

Readability Scores
Dale-Chall: 5.3
DRP: 47
Lexile: 690

Your Turn: Read and Apply Skills

Meet the Author

At the age of 14, Kristin Hunter began writing for the *Pittsburgh Courier.* Her writings include novels, short stories, poems, and magazine articles for young adults and children. She has received numerous awards, including the Children's Prize of the Council on Interracial Books for Children, the Lewis Carroll Shelf Award for *Soul Brothers and Sister Lou,* and the *Chicago Tribune* Book World Prize for *Guests in the Promised Land.* See page R3 of the Author Files for more on Kristin Hunter.

Literature Online

Author Search For more about Kristin Hunter, go to www.glencoe.com.

the Scribe

by Kristin Hunter

We been living in the apartment over the Silver Dollar Check Cashing Service five years. But I never had any reason to go in there till two days ago, when Mom had to go to the Wash-a-Mat and asked me to get some change.

And man! Are those people who come in there in some bad shape.

Old man Silver and old man Dollar, who own the place, have signs tacked up everywhere:

NO LOUNGING, NO LOITERING[1]
THIS IS NOT A WAITING ROOM
and
MINIMUM CHECK CASHING FEE, 50¢
and
LETTERS ADDRESSED, 50¢
and
LETTERS READ, 75¢
and
LETTERS WRITTEN, ONE DOLLAR

R

---

1. *Loitering* (LOY tur ing) is staying around without a purpose.

Additional Support

Literature Online

Author Search To expand students' appreciation of Kristin Hunter, have them access the Web site for additional information and resources.

Literature Focus Lesson

Summary James, the narrator of this story, is a young African American boy. He notices that a local check-cashing business takes advantage of illiteracy in his neighborhood. Since James is a strong reader and writer, he offers to provide his services to his neighbors for free. But a policeman tells him that he must have a license to compete with the check cashers. James then organizes a trip to a bank to help neighbors avoid expensive check-cashing fees. Only one woman makes the whole trip with him, but her example inspires James to continue his fight to improve his community's situation. **OL**

And everybody who comes in there to cash a check gets their picture taken like they're some kind of criminal.

After I got my change, I stood around for a while digging the action. First comes an old lady with some kind of long form to fill out. The mean old man behind the counter points to the "One Dollar" sign. She nods. So he starts to fill it out for her.

"Name?"

"Muskogee Marie Lawson."

"SPELL it!" he hollers.

"M, m, u, s—well, I don't exactly know, sir."

"I'll put down 'Marie,' then. Age?"

"Sixty-three my last birthday."

"Date of birth?"

"March twenty-third"—a pause—"I think, 1900."

"Look, Marie," he says, which makes me mad, hearing him first-name a dignified old gray-haired lady like that, "if you'd been born in 1900, you'd be seventy-two. Either I put that down, or I put 1910." **C**

"Whatever you think best, sir," she says timidly.

Analyzing the Photo This store might look like the Silver Dollar Check Cashing Service. What words would you use to describe the way the store looks?

He sighs, rolls his eyes to the ceiling, and bangs his fist on the form angrily. Then he fills out the rest.

"One dollar," he says when he's finished. She pays like she's grateful to him for taking the trouble.

Next is a man with a cane, a veteran[2] who has to let the government know he moved. He wants old man Silver to do this for him, but he doesn't want him to know he can't do it himself.

"My eyes are kind of bad, sir. Will you fill this thing out for me? Tell them I moved from 121 South 15th Street to 203 North Decatur Street."

Old man Silver doesn't blink an eye. Just fills out the form, and charges the crippled man a dollar.

And it goes on like that. People who can't read or write or count their change. People who don't know how to pay their gas bills, don't know how to fill out forms, don't know how to address envelopes. And old man Silver and old man Dollar cleaning up on all of them. It's pitiful. It's disgusting. Makes me so mad I want to yell. **R**

And I do, but mostly at Mom. "Mom, did you know there are hundreds of people in this city who can't read and write?"

Mom isn't upset. She's a wise woman. "Of course, James," she says. "A lot of the older people around here haven't had your advantages. They came from down South, and they had to quit school very young to go to work.

"In the old days, nobody cared whether our people got an education. They were only interested in getting the crops in." She sighed. "Sometimes I think they *still* don't

2. A **veteran** (VEH tuh run) is someone who has served in the armed services.

Teach

C Critical Thinking

Comprehension Ask: In what year does the story take place? How can you tell? *(The story must take place in 1972 because the man tells Ms. Lawson that she would be seventy-two if she were born in 1900.)* **AL**

R Reading Skill

Review Setting a Purpose for Reading Ask: What is your purpose for reading this selection? *(Possible responses: to learn what a scribe does; to learn about the lives of people living in a city; to be entertained)* **AS**

Differentiated Instruction

Story Mapping To help students better comprehend and remember this story, suggest they complete a story map. In their Learner's Notebooks, they should write the title of the story at the top of the page. Then they should list the major characters they encounter as they read. They should include a summary of the plot, either in paragraph form or in a sequence-of-events chart. Finally, they should record the theme, or main idea, of the selection. Tell students to refer to their story maps as needed. **BL**

Objectives
• Skim and scan text
• Set a purpose for reading
• Monitor comprehension
• Learn and use new vocabulary

Teach

Viewing the Art

Ask: What does the painting on this page show? *(Possible response: A scribe and two other people. He is writing something.)* **AS** **Ask:** How does the scribe in the painting differ from those in the check-cashing place in the story? *(Possible response: The scribe in the painting seems to be treating his customers politely. The men in the check-cashing place are rude to their customers.)* **OL**

EL Language Coach

Word References Say: Use a thesaurus to look up the word *ancient.* What words share a similar meaning? *(Possible response: old, antique, prehistoric)* **EL** **BL**

C Critical Thinking

Analysis Ask: Why does the old woman tell James that her glasses are broken? *(She is embarrassed to admit that she can't read.)* **Ask:** Why does James keep quiet? *(Possible response: He understands what she really means and doesn't want to make her feel bad.)* **OL**

The Arab Scribe, Cairo. John Frederick Lewis, (1805–1876). Private Collection.

care. If we hadn't gotten you into that good school, you might not be able to read so well either. A lot of boys and girls your age can't, you know."

"But that's awful!" I say. "How do they expect us to make it in a big city? You can't even cross the streets if you can't read the 'Walk' and 'Don't Walk' signs."

"It's hard," Mom says, "but the important thing to remember is it's no disgrace. There was a time in history when nobody could read or write except a special class of people."

And Mom takes down her Bible. She has three Bible study certificates and is always giving me lessons from Bible history. I don't exactly go for all the stuff she believes in, but sometimes it *is* interesting.

"In ancient times," she says, "no one **EL** could read or write except a special class of people known as scribes.³ It was their job to write down the laws given by the rabbis

and the judges.⁴ No one else could do it.

"Jesus criticized the scribes," she goes on, "because they were so proud of themselves. But he needed them to write down his teachings."

"Man," I said when she finished, "that's something."

My mind was working double time. I'm the best reader and writer in our class. Also it was summertime. I had nothing much to do except go to the park or hang around the library and read till my eyeballs were ready to fall out, and I was tired of doing both.

So the next morning, after my parents went to work, I took Mom's card table and a folding chair down to the sidewalk. I lettered a sign with a Magic Marker, and I was in business. My sign said:

PUBLIC SCRIBE—ALL SERVICES FREE

I set my table up in front of the Silver Dollar and waited for business. Only one thing bothered me. If the people couldn't read, how would they know what I was there for?

But five minutes had hardly passed when an old lady stopped and asked me to read her grandson's letter. She explained that she **C** had just broken her glasses. I knew she was fibbing, but I kept quiet.

I read the grandson's letter. It said he was having a fine time in California but was a

---

3. ***Scribes*** were educated people who served as copyists, editors, and teachers.

4. ***The rabbis and the judges*** were the teachers and rulers of the ancient Hebrews.

Additional Support

Reading in the Real World

Citizenship The narrator in "The Scribe" decides to help his neighborhood by reading and writing for illiterate people. Have students brainstorm ways that they could help their neighborhood or community. They could do something as simple as picking up trash along their block or complete a bigger project, such as helping to plant new trees in their neighborhood park. Write students' ideas on the board. Have students then write up a plan for implementing their ideas. Suggest that students follow through with the plan, possibly as a class project. **AS**

little short. He would send her some money as soon as he made another payday. I handed the letter back to her.

"Thank you, son," she said, and gave me a quarter.

I handed that back to her too.

The word got around. By noontime I had a whole crowd of customers around my table. I was kept busy writing letters, addressing envelopes, filling out forms, and explaining official-looking letters that scared people half to death.

I didn't blame them. The language in some of those letters—"Establish whether your disability is one-fourth, one-third, one-half, or total, and substantiate[5] in paragraph 3 (b) below"—would upset anybody. I mean, why can't the government write English like everybody else?

Most of my customers were old, but there were a few young ones too. Like the girl who had gotten a letter about her baby from the Health Service and didn't know what "immunization"[6] meant.

At noontime one old lady brought me some iced tea and a peach, and another gave me some fried chicken wings. I was really having a good time when the shade of all the people standing around me suddenly vanished. The sun hit me like a ton of hot bricks.

Only one long shadow fell across my table. The shadow of a tall, heavy, blue-eyed cop. In our neighborhood, when they see a cop, people scatter. That was why the back of my neck was burning.

"What are you trying to do here, sonny?" the cop asks.

"Help people out," I tell him calmly, though my knees are knocking together under the table.

"Well, you know," he says, "Mr. Silver and Mr. Dollar have been in business a long time on this corner. They are very respected men in this neighborhood. Are you trying to run them out of business?"

"I'm not charging anybody," I pointed out.

"That," the cop says, "is exactly what they don't like. Mr. Silver says he is glad to have some help with the letter writing. Mr. Dollar says it's only a nuisance[7] to them anyway and takes up too much time. But if you don't charge for your services, it's unfair competition."

Well, why not? I thought. After all, I could use a little profit.

"All right," I tell him. "I'll charge a quarter."

"Then it is my duty to warn you," the cop says, "that it's against the law to conduct a business without a license. The first time you accept a fee, I'll close you up and run you off this corner."

He really had me there. What did I know about licenses? I'm only thirteen, after all. Suddenly I didn't feel like the big black businessman anymore. I felt like a little kid who wanted to holler for his mother. But she was at work, and so was Daddy.

"I'll leave," I said, and did, with all the cool I could muster. But inside I was burning up, and not from the sun.

One little old lady hollered "You big bully!" and shook her umbrella at the cop. But the rest of those people were so beaten down they didn't say anything. Just

---

5. When you **substantiate** something, you give evidence to prove a claim.

6. An **immunization** (im yuh nuh ZAY shun) is medicine given to protect against disease.

7. A **nuisance** (NOO sunts) is something that is annoying or unpleasant.

Teach

C Critical Thinking

Comprehension Ask: What is the main point of the interaction between James and the policeman? *(In response to complaints from the owners of the Silver Dollar, the policeman confronts James about his "illegal" business.)* **Ask:** How does the policeman stop James? *(He says James cannot operate for free and cannot charge fees without a business license.)* **AS**

EL Language Coach

Multiple-Meaning Words

Say: The policeman tells James that he needs a license. The word *license* has multiple meanings. Use a dictionary to discover which definition is the correct meaning of the word on this page. *(a document that gives official permission)* **EL**

English Language Coach

Figurative Language Explain to English language learners that figurative language is meant to spark readers' imaginations. However, English learners often find figurative language difficult to understand because it includes idiomatic sayings and unusual comparisons. Explain that Mr. Silver and Mr. Dollar are not the men's real names. These names refer to their business and their greed. Direct students to the third full paragraph on the page, which describes "letters that scared people half to death." Ask students what they think this means. Have students continue to record figurative language in their notebooks along with a "translation" of its meaning. **EL**

Objectives

• Analyze text
• Monitor comprehension
• Use word references
• Understand multiple-meaning words
• Find meaning in art
• Identify literary devices: figurative language

105

Teach

R Reading Skill

Identifying Main Idea and Supporting Details Ask:
What is the main idea of the conversation James has with his mom and dad? *(Possible response: Even though having a bank account is free, many of the people in the neighborhood are afraid to open one.)*
Say: Identify a detail that supports this main idea. *(Possible response: James's mom says that some of the people remember the Depression when the banks closed and the people couldn't get their money out.)* **OL**

EL Language Coach

Multiple-Meaning Words
Say: Use a dictionary or thesaurus to find different meanings of the word *interest*. *(Possible responses: a charge for borrowed money; concern; the profit earned on investments)* **Ask:** Based on the context, what meaning of *interest* is used here? *(the profit earned on investments)* **EL**

---

shuffled back on inside to give Mr. Silver and Mr. Dollar their hard-earned money like they always did.

I was so mad I didn't know what to do with myself that afternoon. I couldn't watch TV. It was all soap operas anyway, and they seemed dumber than ever. The library didn't appeal to me either. It's not air-conditioned, and the day was hot and muggy.

Finally I went to the park and threw stones at the swans in the lake. I was careful not to hit them, but they made good targets because they were so fat and white. Then after a while the sun got lower. I kind of cooled off and came to my senses. They were just big, dumb, beautiful birds and not my enemies. I threw them some crumbs from my sandwich and went home.

"Daddy," I asked that night, "how come you and Mom never cash checks downstairs in the Silver Dollar?"

"Because," he said, "we have an account at the bank, where they cash our checks free."

"Well, why doesn't everybody do that?" I wanted to know.

"Because some people want all their money right away," he said. "The bank insists that you leave them a minimum balance."

"How much?" I asked him.

"Only five dollars."

"But that five dollars still belongs to you after you leave it there?"

"Sure," he says. "And if it's in a savings account, it earns interest."

"So why can't people see they lose money when they *pay* to have their checks cashed?"

"A lot of *our* people," Mom said, "are scared of banks, period. Some of them remember the Depression,[8] when all the banks closed and the people couldn't get their money out. And others think banks are only for white people. They think they'll be insulted, or maybe even arrested, if they go in there."

Wow. The more I learned, the more pitiful it was. "Are there any black people working at our bank?"

"There didn't used to be," Mom said, "but now they have Mr. Lovejoy and Mrs. Adams. You know Mrs. Adams, she's nice. She has a daughter your age."

"Hmmm," I said, and shut up before my folks started to wonder why I was asking all those questions.

The next morning, when the Silver Dollar opened, I was right there. I hung around near the door, pretending to read a copy of *Jet* magazine.

"Psst," I said to each person who came in. "I know where you can cash checks *free*."

It wasn't easy convincing them. A man blinked his red eyes at me like he didn't believe he had heard right. A carpenter with tools hanging all around his belt said he was on his lunch hour and didn't have time. And a big fat lady with two shopping bags pushed past me and almost knocked me down, she was in such a hurry to give Mr. Silver and Mr. Dollar her money.

But finally I had a little group who were interested. It wasn't much. Just three people. Two men—one young, one old—and the little old lady who'd asked me to read her the letter from California. Seemed the

---

8. The *Depression*, or Great Depression, was a period of high unemployment from 1929 through the 1930s.

Additional Support

Differentiated Instruction

Illustrations James worries that the people he wants to reach won't realize what he's offering because they can't read. Ask students how James could use a graphic presentation to show the services he offers. Divide students into small groups. Have each group design a poster for James's reading and writing service. Students should combine an illustration with a brief slogan. Remind students that viewers who can't read the slogan must still be able to understand the poster. Have the groups display their posters in the classroom. **BL OL**

grandson had made his payday and sent her a money order.

"How far is this place?" asked the young man.

"Not far. Just six blocks," I told him.

"Aw shoot. I ain't walking all that way just to save fifty cents."

So then I only had two. I was careful not to tell them where we were going. When we finally got to the Establishment Trust National Bank, I said, "This is the place."

"I ain't goin' in there," said the old man. "No sir. Not me. You ain't gettin' me in *there*." And he walked away quickly, going back in the direction where we had come.

To tell the truth, the bank did look kind of scary. It was a big building with tall white marble pillars. A lot of Brink's armored trucks and Cadillacs were parked out front. Uniformed guards walked back and forth inside with guns. It might as well have a "Colored Keep Out" sign.

Whereas the Silver Dollar is small and dark and funky and dirty. It has trash on the floors and tape across the broken windows.

I looked at the little old lady. She smiled back bravely. "Well, we've come this far, son," she said. "Let's not turn back now."

So I took her inside. Fortunately Mrs. Adams's window was near the front.

"Hi, James," she said.

"I've brought you a customer," I told her.

Mrs. Adams took the old lady to a desk to fill out some forms. They were gone a long time, but finally they came back.

Analyzing the Photo In what way do you think this bank teller might be helping the man in the picture?

"Now, when you have more business with the bank, Mrs. Franklin, just bring it to me," Mrs. Adams said.

"I'll do that," the old lady said. She held out her shiny new bankbook. "Son, do me a favor and read that to me."

"Mrs. Minnie Franklin," I read aloud. "July 9, 1972. Thirty-seven dollars."

"That sounds real nice," Mrs. Franklin said. "I guess now I have a bankbook, I'll have to get me some glasses."

Mrs. Adams winked at me over the old lady's head, and I winked back.

"Do you want me to walk you home?" I asked Mrs. Franklin.

"No thank you, son," she said. "I can cross streets by myself all right. I know red from green."

And then she winked at both of us, letting us know she knew what was happening.

"Son," she went on, "don't ever be afraid to try a thing just because you've never done it before. I took a bus up here from Alabama by myself forty-four years ago. I ain't thought once about going back. But I've stayed too long in one neighborhood since I've been in this city. Now I think I'll go out and take a look at *this* part of town."

Then she was gone. But she had really started me thinking. If an old lady like that wasn't afraid to go in a bank and open an account for the first time in her life, why should I be afraid to go up to City Hall and apply for a license?

Wonder how much they charge you to be a scribe? ○

Teach

C Critical Thinking

Analysis Ask: Why does Mrs. Franklin refuse James's offer to walk her home? *(Possible response: She wants to explore a new neighborhood.)* **OL Ask:** What lesson does James learn from Mrs. Franklin? *(Possible response: He learns from Mrs. Franklin's example not to fear trying new things.)* **AL**

L Literary Element

Author's Purpose Ask: What do you think Kristin Hunter's purpose is for writing the story? *(Possible response: to entertain readers while inspiring them to fight against injustice in their communities)* **AS**

Reading in the Real World

Career Some students might be interested in learning how to advertise services to the community. Organize students into small groups. Have each group create a commercial for the Establishment Trust National Bank. The commercials should appeal to the people in James's neighborhood. Encourage students to be creative. They might sing a jingle, write a catchy slogan, or have a celebrity endorse the bank. Groups should plan and develop their commercial ideas and then rehearse their commercials. Allow time for each group to perform before the class. **OL AL**

Objectives
• Identify author's purpose
• Analyze text
• Understand multiple-meaning words
• Identify main ideas and supporting details

107

Fiction

Tell students that they have many reasons to read fictional accounts of people from different backgrounds. Fictional stories can be entertaining, and they can also teach them about new cultures.

Ask students to share an example of a fictional story they've already read that was particularly entertaining or that taught them something interesting. They may name fictional stories from this unit or ones they have read independently.

UNIT 1

Reading on Your Own

To read more about the Big Question, choose one of these books from your school or local library. Work on your reading skills by choosing books that challenge you.

Fiction

The House of Dies Drear
by Virginia Hamilton

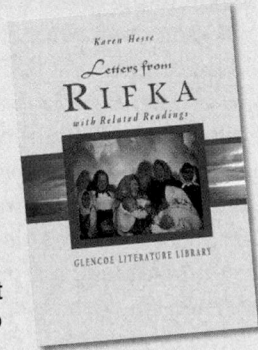

When Thomas moves into a new (haunted?) house, he decides to do some sleuthing. Soon, he discovers that his new home was once a stop on the Underground Railroad. Exploring the dark passageways in and under the building, Thomas moves closer to the truth about his Civil War–era home . . . and into harm's way, as well.

The Firebringer and Other Great Stories: Fifty-five Legends That Live Forever
by Louis Untermeyer

This anthology is packed with retold tales from cultures near and far. Read one or two or ten of the legends in Untermeyer's book—but make sure you're ready to travel. Like all great story collections, *The Firebringer* will transport you to places you've never been!

Letters from Rifka
by Karen Hesse

Twelve-year-old Rifka's journey from the Ukraine to the U.S. is anything but easy, and she has to keep her wits about her to survive. Read about how she survives typhus, ringworm, and the high seas in her fearless quest for a new and better life.

I, Juan de Pareja
by Elizabeth Borton de Trevino

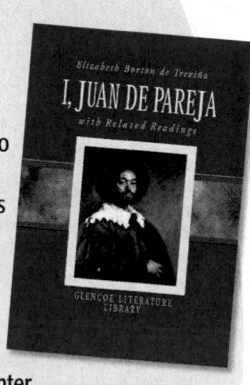

Juan de Pareja was a painter's servant; he was also an artist himself. Despite the fact that sixteenth-century Spanish law prohibited slaves from making art, de Pareja became an accomplished painter.

Additional Support

Differentiated Instruction

BOOKLINK Use the Glencoe BookLink CD-ROM to create customized reading lists to help students answer the Big Question. Suggestions for Unit 1:
Grade 4: *Pirate's Promise* by Clyde Robert Bulla

Grade 5: *Trouble Will Find You* by Joan M. Lexau
Grade 6: *Hostage* by Edward Myers
Grade 7: *The Thirteen Clocks* by James Thurber
Grade 8: *Walker of Time* by Helen Hughes Vick

Nonfiction

A Strong Right Arm: The Story of Mamie "Peanut" Johnson
by Michelle Y. Green

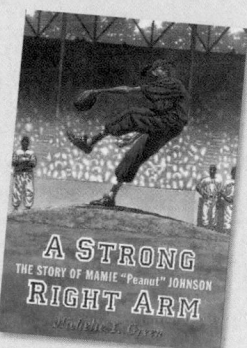

One of the first women to play professional baseball, Mamie "Peanut" Johnson was a pitcher with the Negro League's Indianapolis Clowns from 1953–1955. This biography details the struggles and triumphs that defined her—as a ball player and as a person.

Shipwreck at the Bottom of the World: The Extraordinary True Story of Shackleton and the Endurance
by Jennifer Armstrong

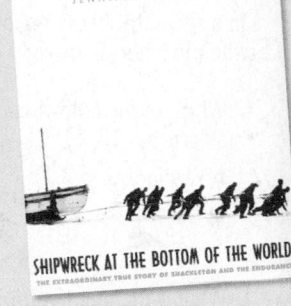

Shipwrecked in Antarctica, Shackleton and his crew of 27 survived a brutal winter and walked over 600 miles to the deserted Elephant Island. Leaving 22 men behind and sailing 800 miles in a tiny open boat, Shackleton and five others made it to civilization . . . then led a rescue party to retrieve those left behind.

Top Secret: A Handbook of Codes, Ciphers, and Secret Writing
by Paul B. Janeczko

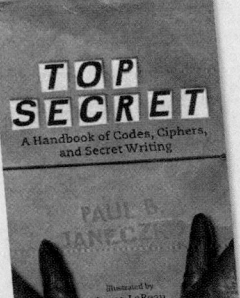

Want to learn how to write in code, or how to pen a note in invisible ink? If so, this guide to the secrets of the super-secret is a must-read for you!

The Life and Death of Crazy Horse
by Russell Freedman

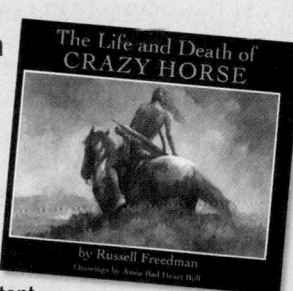

Crazy Horse was a shy young man, but he grew up to be a fierce Sioux warrior. Believing nothing was more important than freedom, he led the fight to save his people's hunting grounds—and their entire way of life.

Nonfiction
Tell students that the books on this page are all nonfiction books. They tell true stories about real people. These books give detailed accounts of the lives of their subjects.

Autobiographies and Biographies
Remind students that an autobiography is the story of a person's life told by that person. A biography is a story of a person's life told by a different person. Reading autobiographies and biographies can provide students with new insights into people's lives.

About the Subjects
Invite students to share their prior knowledge about any of the subjects of the books listed in the student edition. Then ask students to share why they might want to read one of these books.

Test-Taking Tip

TIP When students must answer multiple-choice questions, they should use the following strategy:

- First answer each question that you are absolutely certain about.
- If you're not certain about the answer to a question, skip it for now.
- When you've answered all the questions you're sure about, return to the ones you're not sure about.

Standardized Test Practice

Part 1: Text and Literary Elements

1. B
2. C
3. D
4. A
5. C

Test Practice

Part 1: Text and Literary Elements

On a separate sheet of paper, write the numbers 1–5. Next to each number, write the letter of the right answer for that question.

1. Which of the following is most likely to involve a "process"?

   A. a diary   **C.** an index

   B. a recipe   **D.** an advertisement

2. What is the main purpose of the graphics in an article or a passage?

   A. to break up the text

   B. to give a clue to the content

   C. to present information visually

   D. to provide a purpose for reading

Use the following passage to answer questions 3–5.

Interesting Beginnings: Where Words Came From

Boycott In the middle of the 19th century, a man named Captain Charles Boycott controlled the use of a large piece of Irish land owned by an Englishman. The rent he charged those who farmed the land was high, and he refused to lower it. The farmers decided to refuse to have anything to do with him, and stores and other local businesses joined in. Soon, Boycott was unable to buy food because no one would sell to him. He could not hire workers because no one would work for him. He even had difficulty getting his mail delivered. It didn't take long before he gave up and fled back to England. This is where we got the word *boycott,* meaning "to refuse to deal with a person or business as a sign of disapproval or to force a change in behavior or attitude."

---

3. The text features in this passage suggest that it will be about

   A. Captain Charles Boycott's life

   B. the history of the word *boycott*

   C. what makes boycotts successful

   D. where all English words came from

4. It is most likely that the author's *main* purpose in writing this passage was to

   A. inform   **C.** persuade

   B. entertain   **D.** express emotion

5. In the passage, the phrase "Where Words Came From" is an example of a

   A. deck   **C.** subtitle

   B. head   **D.** subhead

Objectives (pp. 110–111)
Reading Set a purpose for reading • Identify main ideas and supporting details • Skim and scan text • Use graphics
Informational Text Use text features: title, subtitle, deck, subheads • Identify text structure: steps in a process
Literature Identify literary elements: author's purpose

Part 2: Reading Skills

On a separate sheet of paper, write the numbers 1–4. Next to each number, write the letter of the right answer for that question. Use the passage and graphic below to answer questions 1 and 2.

Does it really matter if you graduate from high school? In terms of making a living, it matters a great deal! In 1950, about half of all Americans graduated from high school. By 1985, this had risen to just over 85%, where it has remained. The increase is mainly due to the fact that American businesses have changed. They depend more and more on skilled workers.

Today, for most jobs, having a high school diploma is considered absolutely necessary. Anyone who has not graduated from high school is likely to end up earning very low wages—if he or she can find a job at all. Most high-paying jobs require education or training beyond high school, which is not available to high school dropouts.

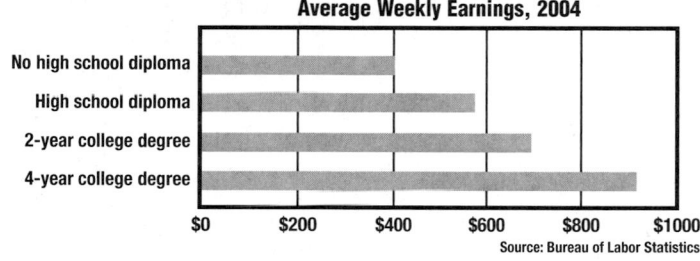

Average Weekly Earnings, 2004

Source: Bureau of Labor Statistics

1. Which of the following best states the main idea of the passage and graphic?

   A. American businesses have changed over time.

   B. Education has a large effect on earned income.

   C. People should celebrate high school graduations.

   D. More people graduate from high school now than in the past.

2. In 2004, having a high school diploma increased a worker's weekly wages by about

   A. $25   C. $100

   B. $50   D. $175

3. Suppose that your purpose for reading an article is to locate information. Which of the following would probably be *most* helpful as a first step?

   A. scanning the article

   B. finding the main idea

   C. looking up unfamiliar words

   D. studying the graphics in the article

4. Which of the following is *most* likely to determine whether you skim an article or whether you read it carefully, word for word?

   A. your purpose for reading it

   B. how many illustrations it has

   C. how difficult it is to understand

   D. the author's purpose for writing it

Part 2: Reading Skills

1. B

2. D

3. D

4. A

Resources for pages 110–113

Use these resources to review, assess, or reteach the unit: Active Learning, Note Taking Guide, Selection and Unit Assessment, ExamView Assessment Suite, and Skill Level Up™ A Language Arts Game.

Literature Online

Unit Assessment Have students access the Web site to prepare for the Unit 1 test.

Test-Taking Tip

TIP It can't be stressed often enough: Read the directions carefully and be sure that you answer the question you are asked. If you're asked to choose the answer that fills a blank, be sure to say the sentence to yourself with your choice in the blank.

Part 3: Vocabulary Skills

1. C
2. B
3. D
4. A
5. B
6. C
7. B
8. A

Part 3: Vocabulary Skills

On a separate sheet of paper, write the numbers 1–8. Next to each number, write the letter of the right answer for that question.

For questions 1–5, write the letter of the word or phrase that means about the same as the underlined word.

1. to <u>encounter</u> a problem
   - **A.** avoid
   - **B.** expect
   - **C.** run into
   - **D.** be afraid of

2. a <u>treacherous</u> journey
   - **A.** long
   - **B.** risky
   - **C.** boring
   - **D.** exciting

3. to <u>monitor</u> an activity
   - **A.** enjoy
   - **B.** hear about
   - **C.** take part in
   - **D.** keep an eye on

4. was <u>nourished</u> by
   - **A.** fed
   - **B.** lit up
   - **C.** surprised
   - **D.** entertained

5. had <u>interrogated</u> them
   - **A.** met
   - **B.** questioned
   - **C.** made fun of
   - **D.** run away from

6. Choose the multiple-meaning word that best fits in both of the sentences.

   Be sure to ___ your answers.
   Dad used a ___ to pay the bill.
   - **A.** fix
   - **B.** pen
   - **C.** check
   - **D.** change

7. Choose the multiple-meaning word that fits in both of the sentences.

   Turn ___ and then go two blocks.
   Think about what is the ___ thing to do.
   - **A.** left
   - **B.** right
   - **C.** smart
   - **D.** around

8. "Ballpark Food" says, "The hot dogs, soda, and peanuts our snack squad bought cost three to seven times more than their local food stores <u>charged</u>." In which sentence below does *charged* have the same meaning?
   - **A.** The babysitter <u>charged</u> $4 an hour.
   - **B.** I yelled when the bull <u>charged</u> right at me.
   - **C.** Has anyone been <u>charged</u> with the crime?
   - **D.** She didn't have enough cash, so she <u>charged</u> her purchase.

Objectives (pp. 112–113)
Vocabulary Use word references: dictionary • Use context clues: multiple meanings
Grammar Identify parts of speech: main, helping, action verbs; verb tenses

Part 4: Writing Skills

On a separate sheet of paper, write the numbers 1–8. Next to each number, write the letter of the right answer for that question.

---

1. In which sentence is *light* used as an adjective?
   - **A.** Turn on the light.
   - **B.** Is that package light?
   - **C.** Let's light the candles.
   - **D.** The porch light has burned out.

2. In which sentence is *iron* used as a verb?
   - **A.** The iron is hot!
   - **B.** We put up an iron railing.
   - **C.** Hurry up and iron your shirt.
   - **D.** Did they find iron in the mine?

3. What word in the sentence below is a helping verb?

   I saw Andy and waved while I was looking for Jim.

   - **A.** saw
   - **B.** waved
   - **C.** was
   - **D.** looking

4. Which of the following verbs is "irregular"?
   - **A.** see
   - **B.** watch
   - **C.** allow
   - **D.** remember

5. In which sentence is *taste* a linking verb?
   - **A.** Just taste the soup.
   - **B.** The potatoes taste good.
   - **C.** Some people have good taste.
   - **D.** I just want a little taste of your dessert.

6. Which verb or verb phrase belongs in the blank in the sentence below?

   Next month, we ___ to Ohio.

   - **A.** travels
   - **B.** traveled
   - **C.** traveling
   - **D.** will travel

7. Which sentence should you use to mean that Lucy's action happens regularly?
   - **A.** Lucy uses my book.
   - **B.** Lucy used my book.
   - **C.** Lucy had used my book.
   - **D.** Lucy was using my book.

8. Which sentence is written correctly?
   - **A.** We winned the game.
   - **B.** They spoken in loud voices.
   - **C.** She has grown two inches this summer.
   - **D.** The boys had knew each other for a long time.

Part 4: Writing Skills

1. B
2. C
3. C
4. A
5. B
6. D
7. A
8. C

Skills Scope and Sequence

Readability Scores Key
Dale-Chall/DRP/Lexile

PACING (DAYS)		INSTRUCTIONAL SEGMENT LITERATURE	READING SKILLS	LITERARY ELEMENTS
STANDARD	BLOCK			
1	1	**Unit Opener, pp. 114–115** **Unit Warm-Up, pp. 116–125** Genre Focus: "Madam C.J. Walker" by Jim Haskins **5.8/58/1080**, p. 119	Build Fluency, TWE p. 115 Connecting, SE p. 121, TWE p. 116 How to Read a Biography or an Autobiography, TWE p. 118 Activating Prior Knowledge, SE p. 119 Questioning, SE pp. 120, 121, TWE p. 119 Predicting, SE pp. 121, 122	Narrator, SE p. 123, TWE p. 118 Chronological Order, SE p. 125, TWE p. 120 Point of View, SE p. 124, TWE p. 121 Character, SE p. 124
3	2	**Reading Workshop 1, pp. 126–141** "The Jacket" by Gary Soto **4.6/54/1030**, p. 130 "The World Is Not a Pleasant Place to Be" by Nikki Giovanni **N/A**	Activating Prior Knowledge, SE pp. 126, 129, 130, 132, 137, 138, 139, 141, TWE p. 134 Setting a Purpose for Reading, SE p. 130 Visualizing, TWE p. 130 Comparison Chart, TWE p. 134 Build Fluency, TWE p. 139	Using Text Features, TWE p. 131 Narrator, SE pp. 129, 131, 134, 137, TWE p. 130 Simile and Metaphor, TWE p. 132 Elements of Autobiography, TWE p. 133 Personification, TWE p. 135 Speaker, SE pp. 138, 139, 141 Free Verse, TWE p. 138
1		**Writing Workshop, Part 1, pp. 142–145** Writing Product: Autobiographical Narrative		Autobiographical Narrative, TWE p. 142
3	1	**Reading Workshop 2, pp. 146–163** "Satchel Paige" by Bill Littlefield **6.4/58/1130**, p. 150 "Song for a Surf-Rider" by Sara Van Alstyne Allen **N/A**	Connecting, SE pp. 146, 147, 149, 151, 159, 160, 161, 163, TWE p. 157 Activating Prior Knowledge, TWE p. 147	Point of View, SE pp. 149, 150, 152, 153, 159, 160, 161, 163, TWE p. 154 Character, TWE p. 150 Tone, TWE p. 154 Extended Metaphor, TWE p. 160

Unit 2 Big Question

The question, "What brings out the best in you?" is designed to help students recognize their individual strengths and their potential to achieve excellence. In this unit, students will see a variety of aspects of character and growth to use as a springboard for their own personal reflections.

Unit 2 Genre

Many of the selections in this unit are biography, the story of a person's life written by another person, or autobiography, a biography in which the author tells his or her own story. These selections will also help students answer the big question: "What brings out the best in you?" Use these informational media to help students learn what happened to bring out the best in real people.

CRITICAL THINKING	VOCABULARY	WRITING AND GRAMMAR	LISTENING, SPEAKING, AND VIEWING
Analysis, TWE pp. 120, 124	Negating Prefixes, TWE p. 122 Language from the Past, TWE p. 122		Visual Clues, TWE p. 117 Viewing the Photo, TWE pp. 122, 125 Viewing the Illustration, TWE p. 123
Infer, SE pp. 136, 140 Conclude, SE p. 136 Analyze, SE pp. 136, 140 Evaluation, TWE p. 139 Evaluate, SE p. 140	Academic Vocabulary, SE p. 126 Synonyms, SE pp. 128, 132, TWE pp. 129, 131, 139 Vocabulary File, TWE p. 128	Applying Good Writing Traits: Conventions, SE p. 144 Write About Your Reading, SE pp. 136, 140 Nouns, SE p. 137 Pronouns, SE p. 141	Viewing the Art, TWE pp. 131, 133
		Prewriting, SE p. 142 Mind Map, TWE p. 142 Conventions, SE p. 144 Nouns, SE p. 145	
Synthesis, TWE p. 155 Analyze, SE p. 158 Predict, SE p. 158 Infer, SE p. 162 Evaluate, SE p. 162 Draw Conclusions, SE p. 162	Jargon, TWE p. 155 Vocabulary File, TWE p. 160 Sentences, TWE p. 148 Antonyms, SE pp. 148, 152, TWE p. 156 Positive and Negative Connotations, TWE p. 157	Write About Your Reading, SE pp. 158, 162 Pronoun Antecedents, SE p. 159 Indefinite Pronouns, SE p. 163	Class Discussion, TWE p. 147 Viewing the Photo, TWE p. 150

Readability Scores Key
Dale-Chall/DRP/Lexile

PACING (DAYS)		INSTRUCTIONAL SEGMENT LITERATURE	READING SKILLS	LITERARY ELEMENTS
STANDARD	BLOCK			

3	3	**Reading Workshop 3, pp. 164–183**
		
		"Eleanor Roosevelt" by William Jay Jacobs
		6.5/58/960, p. 168
		
		"In Eleanor Roosevelt's Time"
		5.8/N/A/N/A, p. 180
			Predicting, SE pp. 164, 165, 173, 174, 177, 181, 183, TWE pp. 167, 168
			Connecting, SE p. 169
			Main Idea, TWE p. 173
				Time Order Words,
				    TWE p. 165
				Chronological Order,
				    SE p. 169, 172, 177, 179,
				    183, TWE pp. 167, 168,
				    170, 171, 180
				Characterization Chart,
				    TWE p. 169
				Time Lines, TWE p. 178

1		**Writing Workshop, Part 2, pp. 184–187** Writing Product: Autobiographical Narrative		Chronological Order, SE p. 186

3	1	**Reading Workshop 4, pp. 188–207**
		"Gentleman of the Pool" by Alice Park
		    6.1/58/920, p. 192
		"Primary Lessons" by Judith Ortiz Cofer
		    5.9/57/1060, p. 198
			Questioning, SE pp. 188, 189, 191, 192,
			    195, 197, 198, 201, 202, 205, 207,
			    TWE p. 203
			Connecting, SE p. 199, TWE p. 192
				Tone, SE pp. 191, 193, 195,
				    197, 199, 200, 202, 207,
				    TWE pp. 199, 200
				Author's Purpose,
				    TWE p. 198
				Dialogue, TWE p. 199
				Comparison Chart, TWE
				    p. 200

3	2	**Comparing Literature Workshop,
		pp. 208–235**
		
		from *The Pigman & Me* by Paul Zindel
		    5.6/51/830, p. 211
		"The Goodness of Matt Kaizer" by Avi
		    5.2/46/620, p. 221
			Asking Questions, TWE p. 208
			Build Fluency, TWE pp. 214, 222
			Predicting, TWE p. 227
				Character, SE pp. 208,
				    211–217, 219, 221–228,
				    230, 231, TWE pp. 209,
				    218
				Point of View, SE p. 218
				Figurative Language,
				    TWE p. 218
				Plot, TWE pp. 211, 219, 230
				Theme, TWE p. 221
				Narrator, TWE p. 233, 239,
				    241

4	2	**Unit Wrap-Up, pp. 236–237** **Your Turn, pp. 238–245** "Ta-Na-E-Ka" by Mary Whitebird **5.9/55/720**, p. 238	Predicting, TWE pp. 241, 244 Connecting, TWE pp. 243, 245 Compare and Contrast, TWE p. 243	Autobiography, TWE p. 241 Character, TWE p. 245 Chronological Order p. 240

CRITICAL THINKING	VOCABULARY	WRITING AND GRAMMAR	LISTENING, SPEAKING, AND VIEWING
Analysis, TWE p. 173 Evaluation, TWE p. 174 Infer, SE pp. 176, 182 Evaluate, SE p. 176 Analyze, SE pp. 176, 182 Application, TWE p. 179 Evaluating Graphic Organizers, TWE p. 179 Draw Conclusions, SE p. 182	Using Vocabulary, TWE p. 166 Negating Prefixes, TWE p. 166 Prefixes, SE pp. 178, 181	Reflexive Pronouns, SE p. 177 Write About Your Reading, SE p. 182 Intensive Pronouns, SE p. 183 Research Essay, TWE p. 174	Viewing the Photo, TWE p. 168 Using Images to Understand Text, TWE p. 171 Talk About Your Reading, SE p. 176 Interpreting Images, TWE p. 181
			Group Discussion and Active Listening, SE p. 187
Infer, SE p. 194 Support, SE p. 194 Synthesis, TWE pp. 197, 202 Comprehension, TWE p. 201 Analysis, TWE p. 204	Synonyms, SE p. 193, TWE p. 190 Word References, TWE p. 190 Vocabulary File, TWE p. 196 Word Choice, SE p. 196 Multiple-Meaning Words, TWE p. 201 Pronouns, SE p. 202	Pronoun Case, SE p. 195 Write About Your Reading, SE p. 206 Pronoun Usage, SE p. 207	Viewing the Photo, TWE pp. 192, 198, 203 Talk About Your Reading, SE p. 194 Analyzing the Art, TWE p. 200 Diagrams, TWE p. 203
Analysis, TWE pp. 212, 217, 222, 230 Infer, SE p. 234 Character Analysis, TWE p. 224 Synthesis, TWE p. 229 Comprehension, TWE pp. 225, 232 Irony, TWE p. 228 Describe, SE p. 235	Synonyms, TWE p. 210 Regional Expressions, TWE p. 213 Antonyms, SE p. 227, TWE p. 229 Word Choice, TWE p. 216 Hyperbole, TWE p. 216 Word Play, TWE p. 220 Synonyms and Antonyms, SE p. 220	Creative Writing, TWE p. 210 Adaptation, TWE p. 227	Viewing the Photo, TWE pp. 211, 214, 226 Illustrating Character Change, TWE p. 232
	Synonyms, TWE p. 239	Small Group Research Activity, TWE p. 240	Visualizing, TWE p. 242

Reading with Purpose offers a comprehensive package of tools to optimize student learning and the teaching experience. Each resource has been designed to assist students in specific areas and to offer instructional support for teachers. While all of these areas are covered in the core textbook, some students may need extra practice or additional help in specific areas. The resource package is designed so that you, the teacher, can choose which items will best assist your students. You may also use these resources as homework assignments and for assessment purposes. The following are resources recommended for use with Unit 2.

Keys for Unit Resources

- 📁 Blackline Master
- 📗 Workbook
- 📖 Supplemental Text
- 💿 CD-ROM
- 💾 DVD
- 🔥 Transparency
- 💻 Web-based
- ⚙ Fast File

Essential Instructional Support

FAST FILE UNIT 2 RESOURCES

Reading and Literature
- Academic Vocabulary Review
- Big Question: School to Home
- The Big Question Foldable
- Unit Challenge: Planner and Rubrics
- Comparing Literature Graphic Organizer
- Key Reading Skills
- Active Reading Graphic Organizers
- Literary Analysis
- Unit Vocabulary Review

Writing, Grammar, and Spelling
- Spelling and Handwriting Practice
- Grammar Practice
- Writing Workshop Graphic Organizer

Listening, Speaking, and Viewing
- Viewing and Representing
- Listening and Speaking

English Language Learners
- English Language Coach Review

DIFFERENTIATED INSTRUCTION

- 📁 Leveled Vocabulary Development
- 💿 Skill Level Up!™ A Language Arts Game
- 💿 Listening Library CD
- 💿 BookLink 3
- 💿 Literature Library Vocabulary Puzzlemaker
- 💿 Vocabulary Puzzlemaker

ASSESSMENT
GLENCOE'S ASSESSMENT ADVANTAGE

- 📁 Selection and Unit Assessments
- 📁 Selection Quick Checks
- 📁 Assessment by Learning Objectives
- 📁 Rubrics for Assessing Student Writing, Listening, and Speaking
- 💻 Glencoe Online Essay Grader
- 💿 Interactive Tutor: Self-Assessment
- 💿 ExamView Assessment Suite
- 💿 Literature Library ExamView Assessment Suite

Additional Instructional Support

WRITING, GRAMMAR, AND SPELLING

- Real Success in Writing: Research and Reports
- Writing Constructed Responses
- Spelling Power eWorkbook
- Grammar & Composition Handbook
- Grammar and Language Workbook
- Revising with Style eWorkbook

READING AND LITERATURE

- Active Learning and Note Taking Guide
- inTime Magazines
- Backpack Reader Volume 1
- Literature Library
- Literature Launchers Pre-Reading Videos DVD
- Literature Classics

TRANSPARENCIES

- Read Aloud, Think Aloud Transparencies
- Literary and Text Analysis Transparencies
- Bellringer Options Transparencies
- Grammar and Writing Workshop Transparencies
- Fine Art Transparencies

TECHNOLOGY

- TeacherWorks Plus™
- StudentWorks Plus™
- BookLink 3
- Skill Level Up!
- ExamView Assessment Suite
- Interactive Tutor: Self-Assessment
- Listening Library CD
- Spanish Listening Library CD
- Literature Classics
- Literature Launchers Pre-Reading Videos DVD
- Literature Library ExamView Assessment Suite
- Vocabulary Puzzlemaker
- Literature Library Vocabulary Puzzlemaker
- glencoe.com
- Online Student Edition
- Presentation Plus!
- Glencoe Online Essay Grader

ENGLISH LANGUAGE LEARNER

- English Language Coach
- Fluency Practice and Assessment
- inTime Magazines (Spanish)
- Spanish Listening Library CD

PROFESSIONAL DEVELOPMENT

- Professional Development Package

Additional Glencoe Resources

Dinah Zike's Foldables

Foldables are three-dimensional, interactive graphic organizers that help students practice basic writing skills, review key vocabulary terms, and answer Big Questions. Every unit contains a foldable activity. You can find the pattern and directions for the Unit 2 Foldable in the Unit 2 Resources Fast Files booklet. You can use the foldables as they are presented or modify them to suit the needs of your students. More information about foldables for Unit 2 can be found on page R8.

Unit
Big Question

Glencoe Literature Library

This collection of hardcover books includes full-length novels, novellas, plays, and works of nonfiction. Each volume consists of at least one complete extended-length reading accompanied by several related readings from a broad range of genres. A separate Study Guide for each Glencoe Literature Library book provides teaching notes and reproducible activity pages for students.

Glencoe Literature Library titles that complement this unit include:
> ***Bearstone,*** by Will Hobbs
> ***Hatchet,*** by Gary Paulsen
> ***Island of the Blue Dolphins,*** by Scott O'Dell

For a wealth of online resources that support the instruction in Unit 2 of *Glencoe Literature: Reading with Purpose,* students and teachers can visit our Web site at www.glencoe.com. Students will find additional learning, practice, and assessment opportunities such as these, which are noted in the student text:

- **Big Question Overview**
- **Study Central**
- **Author Search**
- **Writing Models**
- **Interactive Literary Elements Handbook**
- **Web Activities**

Teachers will find planning and instructional tools that include the following:

- **Book Lesson Plans**
- **Teacher Forum**
- **Professional Development**
- **Web Activities Lesson Plans (with answers to student activities)**

Go to www.glencoe.com to see the entire selection of Reading with Purpose online resources.

Reading List Generator CD-ROM

Use the Glencoe BookLink 3 CD-ROM, a database of more than 26,700 titles, to *create customized reading lists* for your students.

- Search for award-winning titles, (e.g., Newbery Award winners, Coretta Scott King Award winners, and Caldecott Medal winners) and for books on several state-recommended reading lists.
- Find Degrees of Reading Power™ (DRP) and Lexile™ readability scores for all selections.
- Organize reading lists by students' reading level, author, genre, theme, or area of interest.
- Get a brief summary of each selection.

You can find recommended leveled readings for this unit with Reading on Your Own (see page 246).

Glencoe's **Presentation Plus!**, a multimedia teaching tool, lets you present dynamic lessons that will engage your students. Using Microsoft PowerPoint,® you can customize the presentations to create your own personalized lessons. Use **CheckPoint** questions with interactive response keypads to get immediate student feedback during lessons, to increase student participation, and to assess student comprehension.

A lively collection of articles drawn from issues of the TIME family of magazines helps students develop the skills they need to interact with informational text in a meaningful way. Each of the news stories, feature articles, reviews, profiles, and essays in the magazine connect to an author, work, or theme in *Glencoe Literature: Reading with Purpose.* Articles for Unit 2 are found in Volume A. See the *inTIME* Teacher's Guide for specific connections to each unit and for reproducible student worksheets designed to develop students' reading and critical thinking skills.

Literature Launchers

Set the scene with Glencoe's Literature Launchers, engaging video segments that introduce each unit's genre focus. Each video brings the genre to life, relating it to your students' worlds.

Insert the Glencoe Literature Launchers Pre-Reading Videos DVD into your DVD player. Select the Unit 2 Launcher from the menu to introduce the genre and Big Question for this unit.

Online Essay Grader

Use Glencoe's Online Essay Grader to score your students' writing and to provide individualized feedback to each student automatically.

You and your students can visit www.glencoe.com to link to the essay grader. *Students* can enter their essays and receive feedback on demand. *You* can manage demographic data, assign tests, and generate individual student and aggregated reports. The essay grader can help you

- Save time with automatic scoring and individualized feedback.
- Supplement in-class writing instruction using guided writing practice.
- Get reports for individual students or for special populations.
- Track student improvement over time.

REAL Success: Reading Excellence at All Levels

Glencoe now provides all of your students with the tools they need to become better, more enthusiastic readers. The REAL Success suite of reading and language arts products encourages reading excellence by meeting the needs of students at all levels. Glencoe products that can be used in conjunction with Unit 2 include the following:

- Jamestown Literature: An Adapted Reader
- Jamestown *Reading Fluency*
- Jamestown *Critical Reading Series, In the Line of Duty*
- *Vocabulary Builder*
- *The Glencoe Reader, Course 1*

To order these products, call Glencoe at 1-800-USA-READ.

Teacher Wraparound Edition Key

Level Appropriate Code

AS = Activities for all students

AL = Activities for students working above grade level

OL = Activities for students working at grade level

BL = Activities for students working below grade level

EL = Activities for English language learners

Teacher Wraparound Prompts

R **Reading Skill** These activities help you teach reading comprehension skills.

V **Vocabulary** These activities help students comprehend words and incorporate them into their reading and writing.

C **Critical Thinking** These strategies help students apply and extend what they have learned.

BQ **BIG Question** These activities and questions prompt students to prepare to answer the Big Question.

W **Writing** These activities provide writing opportunities to help students practice writing and comprehend text.

L **Literary Element** These activities and questions help students comprehend selections and learn more about each genre.

E **Text Element** These activities help students comprehend text elements.

LSV **Listening, Speaking, Viewing** These activities help students practice listening, speaking, and viewing skills.

EL **English Language Coach** These skills help English language learners as well as students who need additional reading support.

Doug Fisher

From an Author

Preparing Students to Read Biographies

Tap into prior knowledge. Quick writes are frequently used in English classrooms at the introduction of a new reading to tap into prior knowledge and reader-related experiences, as well as to initiate a reading/writing connection. The choice of text is crucial, too. Reading multicultural literature can build confidence in fledgling second language readers and writers. When students relate to good literature on a personal level, they discover a purpose for reading and response, and begin to find their writer's voice. Before reading *The Circuit: Stories From the Life of a Migrant Child* by Francisco Jimenez (1997), the students in Rita ElWardi's ESL class participated in a number of anticipatory activities focused on thought-provoking questions related to a quick write designed to accomplish these objectives.

Make personal connections. In order to establish a personal connection with the character and the central conflict in the story, students were asked to write about a moment they remembered well; a moment when they had to say good-bye. Because English language learners need structured support in writing, Ms. ElWardi created a list of guiding questions to help even the most reluctant writers begin to recount such an experience. She reminded her students that these questions are there to provoke thought and should not all be answered. To introduce this activity, she recounted an unforgettable moment when she also had to leave a place and a group of friends. Using the questions as her guide, she modeled how these questions could structure a response. Her questions included:

- Where and when did this take place?
- Who was with you and why?
- Why did you have to leave this place or say good-bye to this person?

Teacher to Teacher

Shelly Evans
Marshall, MA

Using Personal Stories

What do I do when I want the undivided attention of my students? I tell a personal story, like the time I went to a dance with a boy and never danced or the time I had to apologize to my entire gym class because I got into an argument with my best friend. When I begin to tell a personal story, the students sit up straight; they make eye contact, and they raise their hands to ask questions. By sharing my stories, I build bridges that connect with the stories of my students; I become more than a teacher to my students, I become a real person who experiences many of the same feelings as they do. While using this unit on biographies, help students see that these selections are personal stories about people.

Teacher Chat Room

Using Biographies

 How do I make biographies interesting to middle schoolers?

 Author Doug Fisher says students need to feel some type of connection to biographical subjects in order to want to read about the subject. To help students connect to subjects, try these strategies:

- Help students recall facts they know about the subjects (activating prior knowledge).

- Choose biographies of people students already know.

- Choose biographies based around subjects students know (some students may not know who Satchel Paige is but they may know something about baseball).

- Choose biographies that share details from the person's life as a teenager. Students love reading and hearing stories about how life was when someone was their age.

 If the biographical subject is foreign to students, how can I make students interested in the subject?

 Author Jeff Wilhelm says in order to help students connect to foreign subjects, you need to dig into the story and find things that students already know. This is often referred to as

building background. For instance, readers of "Satchel Paige" may not know anything about the Negro Leagues. The Build Background section helps to explain what went on at this time in history. Activities in the Before You Read section help students think about how they would feel if they were excluded from activities because of other people's prejudices. The Meet the Author section gives insight into who the writer is and why he chose to write about a baseball player. All of these features will prompt your students to read the biographical story of Satchel Paige.

 What language and structures do writers of biographies use, and how can readers use these elements in their own writing?

 Author Cyndie Hynd Shanahan says writers often use time order, point of view, and narration to convey their stories in biographies. In this unit, we point out literary elements and help students learn to identify them and think about how they influence the story. In the Writing Workshops and in the assessment section after each selection, students will have a chance to practice writing using some of the elements they've read.

Key Unit Objectives

- Answer the Big Question
- Analyze the literary elements of biography and autobiography
- Apply strategies for reading biography and autobiography
- Write autobiographical narratives

BIG Question

Why Is It Important?
Addressing this big question encourages students to recognize their individual strengths and their potential to achieve excellence.

Viewing the Photo
Use the photograph on this page to discuss how overcoming a disability can bring out the best in someone. You may want to have students share any personal stories they have about themselves or someone they know.
Ask: How do you think the boy in this picture was able to achieve his goal? (Responses will vary.) **AS Ask:** How do you think the quote applies to achieving goals? (Responses will vary.) **AL**

UNIT 2

The BIG Question: What Brings Out the Best in You?

> " Friends laugh at your silliest jokes, put up with your worst moves, go along with your craziest ideas, and always see the best in you. "
>
> — Unknown

Unit Skills

Reading Skills
- Activating Prior Knowledge, p. 126
- Connecting, p. 146
- Predicting, p. 164
- Questioning, p. 188

Vocabulary
- Synonyms and Antonyms, pp. 128, 148
- Prefixes, p. 166
- Word Choice, p. 190

BIG Question What brings out the best in you?

Genre Focus: Biography and Autobiography

Literary Elements
- Narrator, p. 129
- Point of view, p. 149
- Chronological Order, p. 167
- Tone, p. 191

Writing Skills/Grammar
- Autobiographical Narrative, pp. 142, 184
- Revising, Editing, p. 184

114

LOOKING AHEAD

The skill lessons and readings in this unit will help you develop your own answer to the Big Question.

UNIT 2 WRAP-UP • Answering the Big Question

About the Reading

The selections in this unit allow students to see how the autobiography authors and biography subjects became the best that they could be. As students study these examples, they will contemplate the Big Question as it applies to them: "What brings out the best in you?" Students will see a variety of aspects of character and growth to use as a springboard for their own personal reflections.

About the Skills

The skills taught in this unit are appropriate for teaching the genres of biography and autobiography. Students will have the opportunity to activate their prior knowledge about specific subjects and connect their own experiences to those of the authors whose works they will read. They will be given the opportunity to question the text and predict outcomes based on clues and their own existing experience.

NO CHILD LEFT BEHIND

The goals of the NCLB act include a strong emphasis on developing reading skills. Help students develop stronger reading skills by modeling the strategies taught in this unit. For example, read aloud a passage from a selection and illustrate how to activate prior knowledge.

Reading Fluency

Build Fluency To build and monitor students' fluency, begin by reading one of the unit selections aloud. Have students take turns reading parts of the selection aloud to you and the class. Tell students that as the unit progresses they should continue their practice of reading aloud. You might allow students class time to work with partners to practice reading aloud the various selections in the unit. At the end of the unit, have students revisit the selection you read aloud and take turns reading it aloud to you and the class. Performance should indicate improvement over time. **AS**

Focus

BELLRINGER Options

- **Literature Launcher**
- **Daily Language Transparency 11**
  Focus Activity Write on the board: Runners improve their skills by tracking their personal best times. What helps you to do your best? *(Responses will vary.)* **OL**

Teach

R Reading Skill

Connecting To help students connect their experiences to the Big Question, ask them to write several sentences in their Learner's Notebooks about what brings out the best in them. Provide the following questions as prompts:

- What does "personal best" mean to you?
- Describe someone or something that made it possible for you to achieve your personal best. **OL**

BQ BIG Question

- Have students read the profiles of Jordan and Bettina.
- Have students discuss the questions at the end of the profiles with a partner.

UNIT 2 WARM-UP

Connecting to The BIG Question What Brings Out the Best in You?

R Every day you have different kinds of experiences. How you respond to these experiences shows what type of person you are. Sometimes you might act bravely. Other times you might show kindness. Think about who or what has helped to bring out the best in you.

Real Kids and the Big Question

JORDAN is one of the smartest students at school. Jordan's friend Guy asked Jordan to help him improve his reading skills. Because of Jordan's help, Guy is more confident when he has to read aloud in class. Do you think helping his friend brings out the best in Jordan? Why or why not? **BQ**

BETTINA sings in a city choir. The choir is planning a trip to Mexico. Bettina's parents told her that she would have to pay for the trip. Bettina has been walking dogs, cutting grass, and babysitting for almost a year to earn enough money. How can working to pay her own way bring out the best in Bettina?

Warm-Up Activity

As a class, discuss the things that you think bring out the best in people. Talk about how helping friends and neighbors can bring out the best in a person. Then tell the class about an experience that brought out your best.

Additional Support

Reading in the Real World

Career Invite students to think of jobs that Jordan and Bettina might enjoy. Point out that the activities they enjoy can be an important clue in helping them find satisfying jobs.

- Ask students to identify their own personal strengths that they could use in a job.

- Provide resources for exploring careers, such as biographies about people in different professions, the *Occupational Outlook Handbook,* or age-appropriate career sites on the Internet. **AS**

You and the Big Question

Reading about experiences that brought out the best in others can help you recognize what might bring out the best in you.

Plan for the Unit Challenge

At the end of the unit, you'll use notes from all your reading to complete the Unit Challenge, which will explore your answer to the Big Question.

You will choose one of the following activities:

A. Magazine Article Work with a group to write an article telling others how they can bring out the best in themselves.

B. Your Interview Prepare for an interview by answering a list of questions.

• Start thinking about which activity you'd like to do so that you can narrow your focus as you read each selection.

• In your Learner's Notebook, write your thoughts about the activity you'd like to do.

• Each time you make notes about the Big Question, think about how your ideas will help you with the Unit Challenge activity you chose.

Big Question Link to Web resources to further explore the Big Question at www.glencoe.com.

As you read, you'll make notes about the Big Question. Later, you'll use these notes to complete the Unit Challenge. See pages R8–R9 for help with making each Unit 2 Foldable. This diagram shows how each should look.

1. Make one Foldable for each workshop. Keep all of your Foldables for the unit in your Foldables folder.

2. On the bottom fold of your Foldable, write the workshop number and the Big Question.

3. Write the titles of the selections in the workshop on the front of the flaps— one title on each flap. (See page 115 for the titles.)

4. Open the flaps. At the very top of each flap, write **My Purpose for Reading.** Below each crease, write **The Big Question.**

The Jacket | The World Is Not a Pleasant Place to Be

Reading Workshop 1
What Brings Out the Best in You?

Teach

Big Question Have students access the Web site for English and Spanish summaries and annotated links to related Web resources.

BQ **BIG Question**

Have students write their initial response to the Big Question in their Learner's Notebooks. **OL**

FOLDABLES
Study Organizer

For each selection they read, students will enter notes about how that selection applies to the Big Question. For details about using Foldables, see pages R8–R9.

Assess/Close

Ask students to share their thoughts about why looking for an answer to the Big Question might be important to them.

 Resources for page 117

📁 Use the Unit Challenge Planner BLM in the Unit 2 Resource Booklet, p. 35.

📁 Use the Foldable BLM in the Unit 2 Resource Booklet, p. 7.

Differentiated Instruction

Visual Clues Draw students' attention to the photographs of Jordan and Bettina. Discuss how the photographs illustrate or complement the text. Ask students to think about the visual clues provided by the pictures. These clues can provide a context that helps clarify the meaning of the paragraphs. Encourage students to find photographs that express their ideas about what it means to do their personal best. Have them paste the images into their Learner's Notebooks to illustrate their entries about this Big Question. **BL EL**

Objectives
• Make connections from text to self
• Use text features: photographs

117

Focus

BELLRINGER Options

✍ **Daily Language Practice Transparency 12**
Focus Activity Say: Think of someone you find interesting or inspiring. What could you learn from a story about that person? *(Responses will vary.)* **OL**

Teach

R Reading Skill

How to Read a Biography or an Autobiography

Ask: Why do you think each reading skill is helpful for understanding biographies and autobiographies? *(Possible responses: **Activating prior knowledge:** Using what you already know about a subject can help you understand what you are reading. **Connecting:** Linking your own experiences to a story might help you understand what the subject is feeling or experiencing. **Predicting:** Sometimes you can figure out some things about a story by guessing what might happen next. **Questioning** will help you make sure you understand what you're reading.)* **OL**

A **biography** is the story of a person's life, written by another person. Biographies tell about real people, real times, and real events. Reading biographies is a great way to find out what brought out the best in a real person. An **autobiography** is a biography in which the author tells his or her own story.

Skills Focus
• Key skills for reading biography and autobiography
• Key literary elements of biography and autobiography

Skills Model
You will see how to use the key reading skills and elements as you read
• *Madam C. J. Walker,* p. 119

Objectives (pp. 118–125)
Reading Activate prior knowledge • Make connections from text to self • Make predictions • Ask questions
Literature Identify literary elements: narrator, point of view, chronological order, tone

Why Read Biography and Autobiography?

Reading about the lives of real people can be interesting. You'll learn about
• people from other cultures and other times in history
• what happened to bring out the best in other people

How to Read Biography and Autobiography

Key Reading Skills

These key reading skills are especially useful tools for reading and understanding biography and autobiography. You'll see these skills modeled in the Active Reading Model on pages 119–125, and you'll learn more about them later in this unit.

R ■ **Activating prior knowledge** As you read, use what you know to help you understand the subject, the story, the main character, or the setting. (See Reading Workshop 1.)

■ **Connecting** Link what you are reading to your own experiences. (See Reading Workshop 2.)

■ **Predicting** Based on what you know and have read, guess what will happen next in the selection. (See Reading Workshop 3.)

■ **Questioning** Check your understanding as you read by asking yourself questions about the text. (See Reading Workshop 4.)

Key Literary Elements

Recognizing and thinking about the following literary elements will help you understand a text more fully.
■ **Narrator:** the voice telling the story (See "The Jacket.")
■ **Point of view:** the person through whose eyes you see the story (See "Satchel Paige.")
■ **Chronological order:** the order in which events in a story happen (See "Eleanor Roosevelt.")
■ **Tone:** the attitude of the author (See "Gentleman of the Pool.")

Additional Support

Literature Focus Lesson

Narrator Explain to students that the main difference between a biography and an autobiography is the point of view of the narrator. While the author of an autobiography knows firsthand what has happened in his or her life and why he or she did the things he or she did, the author of a biography must rely on his or her interpretation of facts. Therefore, the opinions and biases of the biographer can affect the way the subject of the biography is portrayed. Ask students to write about how biographies of them written by friends, relatives, or teachers would differ from autobiographies they would write about themselves. **AL**

Madam C.J. Walker

by Jim Haskins

The notes in the side columns model how to use the skills and elements you read about on page 118.

Biography

ACTIVE READING MODEL

1 Key Reading Skill
Connecting *I would like to earn a million dollars! I wonder how Madam C. J. Walker did it!*

R2 Madam C. J. Walker was the first American woman to earn a million dollars. There were American women millionaires before her time, but they had inherited their wealth, either from their husbands or from their families. Madam Walker was the first woman to earn her fortune by setting up her own business and proving that women could be financially independent of men. The company she started in the early years of this century is still in operation today. **1**

This photo of Madam Walker was taken around 1914. It was widely used in Walker Company advertisements. This portrait was also used on a 1998 commemorative postage stamp.

Madam C. J. Walker

119

Reading in the Real World

Citizenship Many students know someone in their family or community who has become "the best" at something through determination and hard work rather than luck. Lead a discussion about what these people accomplished and what obstacles they overcame to accomplish what they did. Be sure not to limit the discussion just to individuals who are involved in sports, politics, or the performing arts. You might also ask students to write short biographical narratives about family or community members who have excelled. **AL**

Teach

R1 Reading Skill

Activating Prior Knowledge
Ask: What does it take to start and run a successful business? *(Students may identify qualities such as being a self-starter, working hard, developing a saleable product, providing good service, or having a good reputation.)* **OL Ask:** Do you think the qualities needed for success are the same for both men and women? *(Responses may vary depending on how much discrimination students believe women face.)* **AL**

R2 Reading Skill

Questioning Ask: What questions about Madam Walker are answered on the first page of the selection? *(Possible responses: Why is she important? How did she make a million dollars?)* **OL**

Readability Scores
Dale-Chall: 5.8
DRP: 58
Lexile: 1080

Objectives
- Identify literary elements: narrator
- Activate prior knowledge
- Make connections between text and self
- Ask questions
- Analyze features of genres: biography and autobiography

119

Teach

L Literary Element

Chronological Order Draw a sequence-of-events chart on the board. Work with the class to fill in the chart with the details of Sarah Breedlove's history found on pages 120–121. Write in the first box, "At six, Sarah began working in the cotton fields." End the chart with, "Sarah's hair began falling out." Have students identify the main events in between. *(Responses should include: Her parents died by the time she was eleven. She moved in with her sister. They moved to Vicksburg. Sarah married McWilliams. Lelia was born in 1885. McWilliams was murdered. Sarah and Lelia moved to St. Louis. Sarah enrolled Lelia in public school.)* **AS**

C Critical Thinking

Analysis Say: Read note number 4 at the bottom of this page. Why do you think the author makes a note to tell the reader that there is not documentation to prove how McWilliams died? *(Possible response: The author wants the reader to know that the information is not proven because it could be controversial.)* **AL**

Madam C. J. Walker was born Sarah Breedlove on December 23, 1867. She grew up in the South under very racist conditions. Her parents, Owen and Minerva Breedlove, had been slaves until President Abraham Lincoln's Emancipation Proclamation and the Union victory in the Civil War had freed the slaves.

After the war, few provisions[1] were made to help former slaves become independent. They did not receive money to help them get started in their new lives. They were uneducated, they had few skills except the ability to grow crops, and many were unaware of what freedom meant. Like the majority of former slaves, the Breedloves remained on the Burney family plantation in Delta, Louisiana. They had little choice but to stay on the same land where they had been slaves, only now they were sharecroppers. **2**

The Breedloves sharecropped cotton. Like her brothers and sisters, Sarah was working in the cotton fields by the time she was six. By the time she was eleven, both her parents were dead, and she moved in with her older sister, Louvenia. A few years later, they moved across the river to Vicksburg, Mississippi.

Sarah married a man named McWilliams to get away from her sister's household. At that time, conditions in the South for blacks were actually worse than they had been during slavery. This was the time when Jim Crow laws were passed, segregating[2] southern blacks from whites in nearly every area of life. It was the time when white supremacy groups like the Ku Klux Klan achieved their greatest power, and lynchings[3] of blacks were common.

Sarah and her husband lived with the terror of being black as best they could. In 1885 their daughter, Lelia, was born, and her parents dreamed of making a better life for their little girl. Then, when Lelia was two, McWilliams was killed by a lynch mob.[4]

2 Key Reading Skill
Questioning *What are sharecroppers? I better look up the meaning of the word in a dictionary, in case it appears later in the text.*

L

---

1. Here **provisions** (pruh VIZH unz) are arrangements made for the future.
2. **Segregating** means "separating or setting apart."
3. **Lynchings** are acts of killing by a mob, without a trial or other legal action.
4. **McWilliams . . . mob.** No documentation actually proves that he died this way. **C**

Additional Support

 Leveled Reading An adapted version of this selection (4th grade readability) is available on page 230 of *Jamestown Literature: An Adapted Reader* for Grade 6.

Differentiated Instruction

Historical Context Divide students into small groups. Have groups record what they know about Jim Crow laws, the South after slavery, and sharecropping. Ask each group to write three unanswered questions about these topics. Then have groups exchange questions. Allow students to use classroom and library resources to answer the questions. When groups finish, lead a class discussion about these topics and how they impacted Madam Walker and other blacks at the time. **AL**

ACTIVE READING MODEL

Sarah was a widow at the age of twenty, and the sole support of a two-year-old daughter. She took in laundry to earn a living and was determined to leave the South. With Lelia, she made her way up the Mississippi River and settled in St. Louis, where she worked fourteen hours a day doing other people's laundry. She enrolled Lelia in the St. Louis public schools and was pleased that her daughter would get the education that had been denied to her. But she wanted more for her daughter and for herself. **3**

Not long after they moved to St. Louis, Sarah McWilliams realized that her hair was falling out. She did not know why, but it is likely that the practice of braiding her hair too tightly was part of the cause. At the time, few hair-care products were available for black women. For years she tried every hair-care product available. But nothing worked. **4**

Then one night she had a dream. As she told the story many years later, in her dream "a black man appeared to me and told me what to mix up for my hair. Some of the remedy was grown in Africa, but I sent for it, mixed it, put it on my scalp, and in a few weeks my hair was coming in faster than it had ever fallen out." Sarah never publicly revealed[5] the formula of her mixture.

Sarah's friends remarked on what a full and healthy head of hair she had, and she gave some of her mixture to them. It worked on them, too, so she decided to sell it. She later said that she started her "Hair Grower" business with an investment of $1.50.

She had not been in business long when she received word that a brother who lived in Denver, Colorado, had died, leaving a wife and daughters. Sarah decided to go to Denver to live with her sister-in-law and nieces.

Wonderful Hair Grower was the most popular product made by Madam Walker's Company. It was released in 1906.

3 Key Reading Skill
Activating Prior Knowledge *I know that St. Louis is a big city in the Midwest. It is farther north than Vicksburg, Mississippi. The North was less racist than the South. I bet that's why Sarah moved north.*

4 Key Reading Skill
Predicting *Sarah had a problem. Her hair was falling out! Maybe Sarah will invent her own hair-care product.*

5. *Revealed* means "showed or made known."

Genre Focus: Biography **121**

Teach

R1 Reading Skill

Connecting Say: Think of a time when you wanted something that wasn't easy to achieve. Based on that experience, how do you think Sarah might have felt when she moved to St. Louis? *(Responses may vary. Students may say that Sarah might have felt new hope and determination, but she might also have been frightened, grief-stricken, discouraged, lonely, or tired.)* **AS**

R2 Reading Skill

Questioning Say: Good writers anticipate readers' questions and try to answer them. What question would you expect readers to have after reading the description of Sarah's dream? *(Possible response: What was in her formula?)* **Ask:** How does the writer answer that question? *(Sarah never revealed the ingredients.)* **AS**

Literature Focus Lesson

Point of View Help students distinguish first- and third-person points of view:

• **first person:** The narrator is involved in and is part of the story. The narrator will frequently use the words *I* or *we*. Autobiography is told from the first-person point of view.

• **third person:** The narrator is not part of the story. The narrator does not use *I* to describe the events of the story. Biography is told from the third-person point of view.

Discuss with students how the point of view of this selection would be different if it were an autobiography. **AS**

Objectives
• Identify literary elements: point of view
• Make connections between text and self
• Ask questions
• Understand sequence: chronological order
• Analyze text

121

Teach

Viewing the Photo

Say: Photographs can be primary sources, or first-hand information, about the past. Historians study photographs for clues about how people lived and thought. What details in the photograph might provide clues about Madame Walker's life and personality? *(Possible responses: beauty supply store and beauty school in the background; Madam Walker's name on the sign; women wearing caps and gowns)* **OL Ask:** What conclusions could be drawn from these details? *(Possible responses: Madam Walker owned and ran the beauty school and supply store; Madam Walker valued education.)* **AL**

EL Language Coach

Negating Prefixes Write *possible* on the board. Then write *im-* in front of it.
Ask: How does adding *im-* change the meaning of *possible*? *(It turns it into the opposite.)* **OL** Have students practice adding *im-* to words like *mature, mobile, perfect, personal,* and *polite*. Ask students to think of other prefixes that change words into their opposites, such as *un-, in-,* and *ir-*. **EL**

Additional Support

In Denver, Sarah began to sell her special haircare product and did well. But she realized she needed to advertise to get more customers. Six months after arriving in Denver, she married C. J. Walker, a newspaperman who knew a lot about selling by mail order. With his help, she began to advertise her product, first in black newspapers across the state and later in black newspapers nationwide, and to make more money.

But soon her marriage was in trouble. As Sarah Walker later said of her husband, "I had business disagreements with him, for when we began to make ten dollars a day, he thought that amount was enough and that I should be satisfied. But I was convinced that my hair preparations would fill a longfelt want, and when we found it impossible to agree, due to his narrowness of vision, I embarked in business for myself." **5**

5 Key Reading Skill
Predicting *Based on what I know about Sarah, I predict that her business will be successful because she is smart and works hard.*

1939 graduates of the St. Louis Walker Beauty School. "I got my start by giving myself a start." Madam C. J. Walker

---

English Language Coach

Language From the Past Tell students that quotations from Sarah Walker contain some words that are not often used today. One example is *longfelt.* Breaking the word into two parts—*long* and *felt*—makes it easier to understand. In this case, the word means *continuing.*

Another way to improve comprehension is to paraphrase. Work with students to identify key phrases, such as "impossible to agree" and "narrowness of vision." Ask students to state the meaning of each phrase. Work with students to paraphrase the entire quotation. **EL**

ACTIVE READING MODEL

In addition to helping her learn about advertising, her marriage gave Sarah Breedlove McWilliams Walker the name she would use for the rest of her life—Madam C. J. Walker. The "Madam" part was an affectation,[6] but Sarah liked the way it sounded. She thought it would be good for her business. By 1906 her business was so well that she was able to stop doing laundry for a living and devote all her time to her hair-care company.

Madam Walker was very proud of being a woman, and she was convinced that she could make it in the business world without the help of men. Almost from the start she determined that her business would be run by women. In 1906 she put her twenty-one-year-old daughter, Lelia, in charge of her growing mail-order business.

L Madam Walker realized that the normal outlets for her products—white department stores and pharmacies—were not open to her. These stores would not stock black products because they did not want black customers. In addition to advertising, mostly in black newspapers, Madam Walker had to depend on the institutions in the black communities, the black churches, and the black women's clubs. **6**

Madam Walker's lectures on hair culture were widely attended. She was an excellent speaker and a commanding woman, nearly six feet tall, who was always beautifully dressed and coiffed.[7] She made a lasting impression wherever she went.

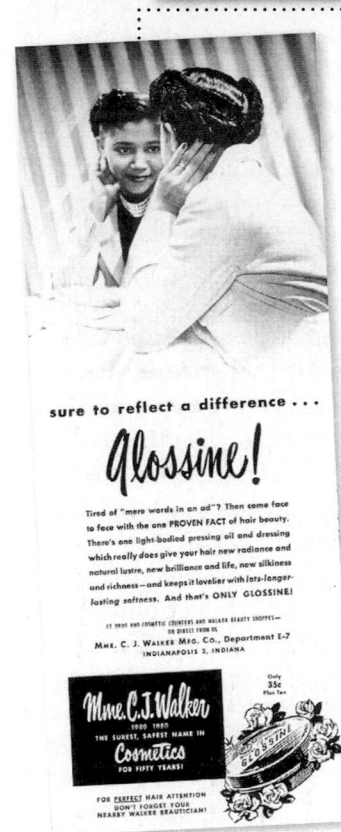

Advertisements like this were placed in newspapers around the country.

6 **Key Literary Element**
Narrator *Someone other than Madam Walker is telling this story. The person telling Madam Walker's story seems to admire her.*

6. An *affectation* (af ek TAY shun) is a fake way of acting.
7. *Coiffed* (kwafd) means "styled," especially hair.

Genre Focus: Biography **123**

Teach

L Literary Element

Narrator Say: The narrator describes the discrimination Madam Walker faced. Is this description objective or biased? *(Possible response: The author gives historical facts and avoids judgmental words like prejudiced or mean.)* **OL** **Ask:** Why do you think the author lets readers draw their own conclusions? *(Possible response: to keep the focus on Madam Walker instead of on a controversial issue)* **AL**

Viewing the Illustration

Ask: What does the advertisement shown on this page tell you about Madam Walker's success? *(Possible response: The fact that the ad was shown in newspapers around the country indicates that her company was very successful.)* **OL**

Differentiated Instruction

Using a Chart Encourage students to discuss the fact that people deal with difficult situations more effectively when they have input and support from people they know and trust. Have small groups create a three-column chart to outline plans for dealing with a situation or decision they may have to face, such as starting in a new school or helping a friend in need. **OL**

Situation	Issues	Consultants

Objectives
• Identify literary elements: narrator
• Identify word structure: prefixes
• Clarify word meanings
• Use text features: photographs

123

Teach

C Critical Thinking

Analysis Say: Reread the paragraph beginning, "Although she lacked. . . ." What can you determine about Madam Walker based on this description? *(Possible response: She was not egotistical or too proud. She did what she needed to do to succeed.)* **OL**

L Literary Element

Character Say: Character traits can be inferred from the way the author describes a character. List three words or phrases to describe Madam Walker. *(Possible responses: hardworking, ambitious, practical)* **BL**

*Madam C.J. Walker's daughter changed her name from Lelia to A'Lelia later in her life.

Although she lacked the formal education that most of these women had, Madam Walker never felt ashamed of her shortcomings[8] in that area. She taught herself as much as she could and was not afraid to ask someone to define a word she did not know or explain something she did not understand. **C**

Madam Walker also wanted black women to go into business. Why should they toil over hot laundry tubs and clean white people's houses when they could be in business for themselves? Helping other black women also helped the Walker Company, and with this goal in mind Madam Walker recruited[9] and trained scores of women to use and sell Walker products. Many of them set up salons in their own homes. Others traveled door-to-door selling Walker products and demonstrating the Walker System. Madam Walker insisted that her agents sign contracts promising to abide by her strict standards of personal hygiene[10]—long before various states passed similar laws for workers in the cosmetics field. By 1910 the Walker Company had trained around 5,000 black female agents, not just in the United States but in England, France, Italy, and the West Indies. The company itself was taking in $1,000 a day, seven days a week. **7 8**

That same year, Madam Walker's travels took her to Indianapolis, Indiana, a city that impressed her so much that she decided to move her headquarters there.

Madam Walker did not have much of a private life. She spent her time thinking of new ways to increase her business. The friends she had were people who could help her. **L**

Madam Walker's daughter A'Lelia Walker getting a manicure at the Walker Beauty School in New York City.*

7 Key Literary Element
Point of View *The narrator calls Madam Walker by name and uses the pronoun "her." This is third-person point of view.*

8 Key Literary Element
Tone *The author says a lot of good things about Madam Walker. The tone is admiring.*

---

8. **Shortcomings** are weaknesses.
9. **Recruited** means "hired or engaged the services of."
10. **Hygiene** (HI jeen) is cleanliness and sanitary practices.

Additional Support

Reading in the Real World

Career Madam Walker built her own career around her hair-care products. Lead a discussion with students about what it is like to own one's own business. Have students think about the responsibilities that would come with such a situation. Then ask students to identify careers they might like and how they might become their own bosses. Have students use the Internet to learn what is necessary to start up such businesses. **AL**

By 1917 the years of traveling and overwork began to take their toll on her. She developed high blood pressure, and in 1918 her doctors warned her that she had to slow down. She died quietly of kidney failure resulting from hypertension in May 1919. **9**

In her will, Madam Walker left the bulk of her estate and the business to her daughter A'Lelia. But she also provided generously for a variety of educational institutions run by black women. She established a trust fund for an industrial and mission school in West Africa and provided bequests[11] to Negro orphanages, old people's homes, and Negro YWCA branches. In addition, she made bequests to many friends and employees.

Also in her will, Madam Walker insisted that the Madam C. J. Walker Company always be headed by a woman, and her wishes were carried out. Her daughter, A'Lelia, became president of the company after her death and presided at the dedication of the new company headquarters in Indianapolis in 1927, fulfilling a long-held dream of her mother's. ○

---

11. **Bequests** (bih KWESTS) are things handed down or passed on.

9 Key Literary Element
Chronological Order
Dates, such as 1917 and 1919, help me know the sequence of events.

L

In 1917 Madam Walker moved into this mansion, where she lived until her death in 1919. The house has thirty or more rooms and was decorated with valuable statues, tapestries, and paintings.

Teach

L Literary Element

Chronological Order **Say:** The author describes several events at the end of Madam Walker's life. How does the author show the order in which they happened? *(Possible responses: gives dates; provides clue words; describes events in the order in which they happened)* **OL**

Viewing the Photo

Ask: How does this photograph illustrate Madam Walker's success? *(Possible response: The large group of people in front of her house look very tiny. That indicates the house was huge and therefore very expensive. She was very wealthy at the time of her death.)* **OL**

Differentiated Instruction

Class Discussion When Madam Walker developed her hair growth formula, she did more than solve a personal problem. She built a business and used some of the profits to help her community. Ask students to identify the legacy left by Madam Walker and how she contributed to society. Students may mention specific bequests, such as those to old people's homes and orphanages; they may also note that she helped other women set up their own businesses and was a pioneer who proved that women could overcome discrimination and manage a successful company. **OL** Ask students to identify other businesses that have contributed to society. **AL**

Objectives
- Analyze text
- Interpret and analyze character
- Understand sequence: chronological order
- Use text features: photographs

125

Activating Prior Knowledge

**Objectives covered in
this workshop:**
• Activate prior knowledge
before reading
• Make connections from text
to self

Teaching Students to Activate Prior Knowledge

Why Is It Important?

• Teaching students to activate prior knowledge helps them use their experience and knowledge to better understand a selection.

• Research has proven that activating prior knowledge increases comprehension.

• Students who activate prior knowledge are better readers.

How to Help Students Get It

• Emphasize that reading is an interactive process; the author and the reader both participate.

• Reading is interactive when you combine your experiences and knowledge and combine it with the words in the text to produce meaning.

• Emphasizing that your students have unique experiences and knowledge helps them feel empowered when reading selections.

• Regardless of how foreign the subject may seem to students, helping them activate prior knowledge on even minor points in the selection can give them the confidence and interest they need to gain meaning from a selection.

Reading to Answer the Big Question

The Jacket by Gary Soto
Gary Soto reminisces about his unhappy middle school years. The author paints a picture of poverty characterized by an ugly jacket "the color of day-old guacamole" and shares what having to wear it brought out in him.

The World Is Not a Pleasant Place to Be by Nikki Giovanni
In this poem, the speaker uses examples from nature to describe feelings of loneliness and longing for a connection with someone.

Workshop Resources

PACING (DAYS) STANDARD	BLOCK	LESSON	STUDENT MATERIALS	TEACHER RESOURCES
1	1/2	Key Skill Lesson: Activating Prior Knowledge	🖺 Key Reading Skills Practice, p. 9 🖺 English Language Coach Review, p. 41	🖎 Bellringer Options Transparencies Daily Language Practice 13 🖎 Read Aloud, Think Aloud Transparencies Key Reading Skills 1 💿 Presentation Plus!
1	1	from *The Jacket*	💻 Glencoe Online 🖺 Unit Vocabulary Review, p. 39 🖺 Academic Vocabulary Review, p. 42 📂 English Language Coach 🖺 Active Reading Graphic Organizer, p. 11 🖺 Literary Analysis, p. 10 💿 StudentWorks Plus™ 💻 Online Student Edition 💿 Literature Classics 📂 Selection and Unit Assessments, p. 13	🖎 Literary and Text Analysis Transparencies 32 💻 Puzzlemaker 💿 Skill Level Up!™ A Language Arts Game 💻 BookLink 3 📓 Assessment by Learning Objective (Diagnostic and Formative) 💿 Interactive Tutor: Self-Assessment 💿 TeacherWorks Plus™
1		"The World is Not a Pleasant Place to Be"	💻 Glencoe Online 🖺 Unit Vocabulary Review, p. 39 🖺 Academic Vocabulary Review, p. 42 📂 English Language Coach 🖺 Active Reading Graphic Organizer, p. 13 🖺 Literary Analysis, p. 10 💿 StudentWorks Plus™ 💻 Online Student Edition 💿 Literature Classics 📂 Selection and Unit Assessments, p. 14	🖎 Literary and Text Analysis Transparencies 32 💻 Puzzlemaker 💿 Skill Level Up!™ A Language Arts Game 💻 BookLink 3 📓 Assessment by Learning Objective (Diagnostic and Formative) 💿 Interactive Tutor: Self-Assessment 💿 TeacherWorks Plus™

Keys for Unit Resource

- 📂 Blackline Master
- 📓 Workbook
- 📖 Supplemental Text
- 💿 CD-ROM
- 🔒 DVD
- 🖎 Transparency
- 💻 Web-based
- 🖺 Fast File

Level Appropriate Code

- **AS** = Activities for all students
- **AL** = Activities for students working above grade level
- **OL** = Activities for students working at grade level
- **BL** = Activities for students working below grade level
- **EL** = Activities for English language learners

Focus

BELLRINGER Options

✎ **Daily Language Practice Transparency 13**
Focus Activity Ask: What brings out the best in you? Consider what helps people rise to the occasion and be their best selves. *(Responses will vary.)* **AS**

Teach

R Reading Skill

Activating Prior Knowledge

Say: You activate prior knowledge every day when you use something you already know. Give an example of activating prior knowledge from your day today. *(Possible response: taking another route to school because you remembered the sidewalk construction on your usual route)* **AS**

V Vocabulary

Academic Vocabulary

Say: Look at the word *prior* at the bottom of page 126. What does it mean to have prior experience? *(to already have experience in something)*
Ask: What are prior plans? *(plans you already had)* **OL**

READING WORKSHOP 1

Skills Focus

You will practice using these skills when you read the following selections:
- "The Jacket," p. 130
- "The World Is Not a Pleasant Place to Be," p. 139

Reading
- Activating prior knowledge

Literature
- Identifying the narrator in what you read
- Recognizing the effect of the narrator on the story

Vocabulary
- Using synonyms
- Academic Vocabulary: *prior*

Writing/Grammar
- Properly using nouns and pronouns

Objectives (pp. 126–127)
Reading Activate prior knowledge

Skill Lesson

Activating Prior Knowledge

Learn It!

What Is It? Activating **prior knowledge** means using what you already know. You should do this every time you read. It helps you understand what you're reading about. Can you imagine reading a story about a bicycle race if you had never seen or even heard of a bicycle? It would be very hard to understand. But when you read a story about a bicycle race, the image of a bicycle might pop into your head. You have activated your prior knowledge!

Analyzing Cartoons
What prior knowledge should Calvin activate the next time he comes through the door? Why?

CALVIN AND HOBBES © 1987 Watterson. Dist. By UNIVERSAL PRESS SYNDICATE. Reprinted with permission. All rights reserved.

V **Academic Vocabulary**
prior (PRY er) *adj.* earlier; coming before

English Language Coach

Building Background Bill Watterson created *Calvin and Hobbes* in 1985. Calvin is a six-year-old boy. Hobbes is a stuffed tiger—except when he and Calvin are the only characters in the frame. Then Hobbes comes to life. Much of the humor comes from Hobbes's antics. Readers have prior knowledge of Hobbes's behavior, so they are able to predict what will happen in the cartoons. Provide students with several Calvin and Hobbes cartoons and then lead a discussion about how prior knowledge applies to them. **EL**

Additional Support

Why Is It Important? Activating prior knowledge helps you understand what you read and makes reading more useful and more fun. For example, if a story takes place in New York City, you think about everything you have ever heard and learned about the city to help you understand what the author is describing.

How Do I Do It? Before you read, skim the title and text. Look at the pictures. Think about what you already know about the topic. Here's how one student used his prior knowledge when reading an article on downhill mountain bike racing.

Study Central Visit www.glencoe.com and click on Study Central to review activating prior knowledge.

> R Thick pads shield their chests, hips, arms, and legs. The special gloves they wear have padding on each finger. On their heads, they display space-age helmets designed to protect the face as well as the head. These are the daredevils known as downhill mountain bike racers.

> *I've never seen mountain bike helmets, but I have seen bike helmets. The ones I've seen don't cover your face, though. I know some motorcycle helmets do. Maybe mountain bike helmets look more like motorcycle helmets.*

Practice It!

Below are some of the feelings that the narrator of "The Jacket" experiences. In your Learner's Notebook, describe a time that you felt these emotions. What caused those feelings? What was it like? What did you do?

- anger
- embarrassment
- sadness
- loneliness

Use It!

As you read "The Jacket," remember what you wrote about the above emotions. Activate your prior knowledge about those feelings to help you understand what you read.

Teach

Study Central Have students access the Web site to review activating prior knowledge and to complete a related activity.

R Reading Skill

Activating Prior Knowledge
Say: Read the sample paragraph in the "How Do I Do It?" section. Then, connect your own prior knowledge to the text. What do you know about bicycle riding and racing? *(Responses will vary.)* **OL**

Resources for page 127

Use Key Reading Skills Transparency 7 in *Read Aloud, Think Aloud* to help students practice Activating Prior Knowledge.

Reading in the Real World

Career One key workplace competency, according to the Secretary's Commission on Achieving Necessary Skills, is acquiring and using information. Ask students to give examples of skills that adults they know have had to learn on the job. Discuss how activating prior knowledge could help people keep up with changes in the workplace. For example, people who have worked in sales can apply their prior knowledge and skills to marketing a new product. Have interested students do library or Internet research to find out more about the jobs discussed. **AS**

Objectives
- Activate prior knowledge
- Learn and use new vocabulary

127

Teach

More About the Author

"Writing is my one talent," says Gary Soto. "There are a lot of people who never discover what their talent is. . . . I am very lucky to have found mine." Soto published several books of poetry and a book of auto-biographical stories before he tried writing fiction. In his stories, Soto says, he tries to recreate the friends and Mexican American neighborhood of his early years. "I wrote, rewrote, and rewrote the rewrite, so that my friends would jump up and down on the page."

V Vocabulary

Vocabulary File Say: One way to learn and remember vocabulary words is to keep a vocabulary file. Write each word on a 3" x 5" index card. Include the pronunciation, the meaning, and a sentence that gives you an example of how to use the word. **BL EL**

Before You Read : The Jacket

Gary Soto

Meet the Author

Gary Soto was born in Fresno, California, in 1952. His parents, although born in America, were of Mexican heritage. Soto uses his poems and stories to tell about his experiences as a boy growing up. Many of his stories focus on issues that deal with being Latino in America. See page R6 of the Author Files for more on Gary Soto.

Author Search For more about Gary Soto, go to www.glencoe .com.

Objectives (pp. 128–135)
Reading Activate prior knowledge
• Make connections from text to self
Literature Identify literary elements: narrator
Vocabulary Identify synonyms

Vocabulary Preview

vinyl (VY nul) *adj.* made of vinyl, which is a tough, shiny plastic **(p. 130)** *That vinyl chair looks very similar to a leather chair.*

profile (PROH fyl) *n.* a side view **(p. 131)** *You could tell he had a small nose when he stood sideways and you saw his profile.*

mope (mohp) *v.* to be gloomy or in low spirits **(p. 134)** *When it rains I mope around the house and wish the sun would come out.*

Write to Learn Answer each question about the vocabulary words.

1. Would vinyl be more useful for making a belt or for making a shirt? Why?
2. Why would a photograph of someone in profile be a good way to get an idea of their facial features?
3. What is something that might cause you to mope? Write a sentence about a time that you moped.

English Language Coach

Synonyms Synonyms are words that have the same or similar meanings. For example, the words *taunt* and *insult* are synonyms, but they have slightly different meanings. A *taunt* is a kind of *insult* that mocks someone.

• It is rare for synonyms to mean exactly the same thing.
• There are almost always small differences between synonyms. These differences may be important.
• The best way to find a synonym for a word is to use a thesaurus, a dictionary of synonyms.

Write to Learn In your Learner's Notebook, answer each question by thinking about the meanings of the synonyms. If you need help, look up the definitions of the words in a dictionary.

1. Which word best describes a baby's first steps—*walking, tottering,* or *marching*?
2. What word is better for describing loud construction in the street—*racket* or *sound*?
3. If you just scored a 100% on your science test, would you feel *content, satisfied,* or *thrilled*?

128 UNIT 2   What Brings Out the Best in You?

Additional Support

Author Search To expand students' appreciation of Gary Soto, have them access the Web site for additional information and resources.

Literature Focus Lesson

Autobiography Gary Soto has many reasons for writing about growing up in Fresno, California. He says that he began writing about his childhood because "it was a time that I could only call back by writing about it." He also wanted young Latinos to see themselves on the pages of his books and develop pride in their heritage. Share Soto's reasons for writing "The Jacket" with students and discuss how they relate to the Big Question. **OL**

Skills Preview

Key Reading Skill: Activating Prior Knowledge

Before you read the story, think about what you know about

- being a fifth or sixth grader
- getting new clothes
- feeling like an outsider

R **Write to Learn** Pick one of the topics above and, in your Learner's Notebook, write a brief paragraph about that topic. Why did you choose that topic? What do you already know about the topic? What experiences have you had that come to mind?

Key Literary Element: Narrator

L The person telling a story is the **narrator.** When you read a story, you feel the hopes and disappointments with the narrator as he or she describes them. The narrator of a *biography* is someone other than the person being written about. The narrator of an *autobiography* is the author. In this selection from Gary Soto's autobiography, Soto is the narrator. As you read, use these tips to help you learn about the narrator:

- An autobiography gives only one side of what happened—the author's side. Think about the details that the author provides.

  Do you think that being a fifth or sixth grader affected how Soto felt about his new jacket?

- Decide if you trust the narrator as a storyteller.

  Does he exaggerate details? Does he seem honest or dishonest?

Partner Talk How do you know when a narrator is trustworthy? Take turns with your partner telling a story about something that happened to you on your way to school. Keep it short, but exaggerate one detail. Let your partner try to pick out the detail you exaggerated in the story.

Get Ready to Read

Connect to the Reading

As you read "The Jacket," think about how the narrator felt when he wore his new jacket. Compare his feelings to the way you might have felt.

Class Talk Talk about clothes at your school. How are clothing trends started? If you have a dress code at school, do kids ever try to push the limits of the dress code? Explain.

Build Background

"The Jacket" is about the narrator's life as a fifth- and sixth-grader, a time when he didn't quite fit in and was growing out of his clothes fast.

- Soto's family is of Mexican heritage, and he grew up in California.
- Soto often draws upon experiences from his youth in his writing.

Set Purposes for Reading

BIG Question Read the "The Jacket" to find out how looking back on an event can bring out the best in you.

Set Your Own Purpose What else would you like to learn from the story to help you answer the Big Question? Write your purpose on "The Jacket" part of the Workshop 1 Foldable.

Literature Online

Interactive Literary Elements Handbook
To review or learn more about the literary elements, go to www.glencoe.com.

Keep Moving

Use these skills as you read the following selection.

Teach

R **Reading Skill**

Activating Prior Knowledge
Say: The topics you wrote about are the same as those described by the writer of "The Jacket." How will remembering your feelings help you better understand this selection? *(Students may say that recalling their feelings will help them empathize with Soto.)* **AS**

L **Literary Element**

Narrator Ask: Can you believe everything the narrator of a story tells you? Discuss what would make you trust or distrust the narrator of an autobiography. *(Possible answers: trust—firsthand account, neutral language; distrust—bias, embarrassing details omitted or exaggerated)* **OL**

English Language Coach

Synonyms Write on the board: *happy, jacket, mean, old.* Tell students to write sentences of their own using these words. Then have students identify synonyms of the words, such as *joyful, coat, nasty,* and *aged.* Allow them to use a thesaurus to do so. If necessary, coach students on how to use a thesaurus.

When students have listed their synonyms, have them write new sentences using the synonyms. Tell students they will encounter the listed words in the story they are about to read. Suggest that they keep their writing in their Learner's Notebooks to clarify meaning when necessary. **EL** **BL**

Objectives

- Activate prior knowledge
- Identify and analyze narrator
- Identify and use synonyms
- Learn and use new vocabulary

129

Teach

R Reading Skill

Review Setting a Purpose for Reading **Say:** To help set a purpose for reading "The Jacket," think about what you have learned from other autobiographies you have read. *(Possible responses: I learned about the life and experiences of a famous person; I realized that other people feel like I sometimes do.)* **OL** **Ask:** What do you think you can learn from "The Jacket"? *(Responses will vary.)* **AS**

L Literary Element

Narrator **Ask:** What do you learn about the narrator from the first paragraph of the story? *(Possible response: He is telling a story from his past. He is likely one of the guys that would stand "against a greasy wall" at a dance because he says his "clothes have failed [him].")* **AS**

Readability Scores
Dale-Chall: 4.6
DRP: 54
Lexile: 1030

The Jacket

by Gary Soto

My clothes have failed me. I remember the green coat that I wore in fifth and sixth grades when you either danced like a champ or pressed yourself against a greasy wall, bitter as a penny toward the happy couples. **1**

When I needed a new jacket and my mother asked what kind I wanted, I described something like bikers wear: black leather and silver studs with enough belts to hold down a small town. We were in the kitchen, steam on the windows from her cooking. She listened so long while stirring dinner that I thought she understood for sure the kind I wanted. The next day when I got home from school, I discovered draped on my bedpost a jacket the color of day-old guacamole. I threw my books on the bed and approached the jacket slowly, as if it were a stranger whose hand I had to shake. I touched the **vinyl** sleeve, the collar, and peeked at the mustard-colored lining. **2**

From the kitchen mother yelled that my jacket was in the closet. I closed the door to her voice and pulled at the rack of clothes in the closet, hoping the jacket on the bedpost wasn't

Vocabulary

vinyl (VY nul) *adj.* made of vinyl, which is a tough, shiny plastic

130 UNIT 2 What Brings Out the Best in You?

Practice the Skills

1 Reviewing Skills

Setting a Purpose for Reading This story is an autobiography. It's about a boy in sixth grade. What purpose could you set for reading an autobiographical story like "The Jacket"? **R**

2 Key Reading Skill

Activating Prior Knowledge The narrator has mentioned
- a jacket "like bikers wear,"
- "the color of day-old guacamole,"
- "mustard-colored"

Did your prior knowledge help you understand these terms or anything else in the first two paragraphs? Explain.

Additional Support

Reading Fluency

Visualizing Begin by reading passages from the story and asking students to listen with their eyes closed. Read the passages in which Soto tries the jacket on (page 131). Encourage students to visualize the scene as they listen. After reading, have students discuss what they pictured in detail. Encourage them to describe the jacket, the setting, and the expressions on the narrator's face. **BL**

for me but my mean brother. No luck. I gave up. From my bed, I stared at the jacket. I wanted to cry because it was so ugly and so big that I knew I'd have to wear it a long time. I was a small kid, thin as a young tree, and it would be years before I'd have a new one. I stared at the jacket, like an enemy, thinking bad things before I took off my old jacket whose sleeves climbed halfway to my elbow. **3**

I put the big jacket on.

I zipped it up and down several times, and rolled the cuffs up so they didn't cover my hands. I put my hands in the pockets and flapped the jacket like a bird's wings. I stood in front of the mirror, full face, then **profile**, and then looked over my shoulder as if someone had called me. I sat on the bed, stood against the bed, and combed my hair to see what I would look like doing something natural. I looked ugly. I threw it on my brother's bed and looked at it for a long time before I slipped it on and went out to the backyard, smiling a "thank you" to my mom as I passed her in the kitchen. With my hands in my pockets I kicked a ball against the fence, and then climbed it to sit looking into the alley. I hurled orange peels at the mouth of an open garbage can and when the peels were gone I watched the white puffs of my breath thin to nothing.

I jumped down, hands in my pockets, and in the backyard on my knees I teased my dog, Brownie, by swooping my arms while making bird calls. He jumped at me and missed.

Analyzing the Art How does this picture help you understand how the narrator felt about the green jacket? Explain, using details from the story.

Vocabulary

profile (PROH fyl) *n.* a side view

Practice the Skills

3 Key Literary Element

Narrator In the opening paragraphs you can already begin to hear the narrator's "voice." He seems disappointed. What do you think of the narrator at this point? Explain.

The Jacket **131**

Teach

EL Language Coach

Synonyms Say: Synonyms are different words that have nearly the same meaning. In the first paragraph, the author describes the jacket as *ugly* and *big*. What are some synonyms for these words? *(Possible responses: unattractive, huge)* **Say:** Consult a thesaurus to identify two more synonyms for each word. *(Responses will vary.)* **OL**

Viewing the Art

Ask: How would you feel about wearing this jacket? *(Responses will vary.)* **Ask:** How does this jacket compare to the one in the story? *(Responses will vary.)* **Say:** As you read, keep in mind descriptions from the story that help you visualize the jacket. **AS**

Objectives
• Set a purpose for reading
• Identify and analyze narrator
• Identify and use synonyms
• Visualize
• Find meaning in art

Teach

R Reading Skill

Activating Prior Knowledge
Ask: Have you ever thought people were talking about you when they really weren't? Why might the narrator have believed everyone was talking about him? *(Possible response: He was so self-conscious about the jacket that he thought everyone else was noticing it, too.)* **OL**

EL Language Coach

Synonyms Ask: How is a friendly country different from a friendly person? *(Possible response: A friendly country is an ally, while a friendly person is willing to get to know other people.)* **OL**

He jumped again and again, until a tooth sunk deep, ripping an L-shaped tear on my left sleeve. I pushed Brownie away to study the tear as I would a cut on my arm. There was no blood, only a few loose pieces of fuzz. Dumb dog, I thought, and pushed him away hard when he tried to bite again. I got up from my knees and went to my bedroom to sit with my jacket on my lap, with the lights out.

That was the first afternoon with my new jacket. The next day I wore it to sixth grade and got a D on a math quiz. During the morning recess Frankie T., the playground terrorist, pushed me to the ground and told me to stay there until recess was over. My best friend, Steve Negrete, ate an apple while looking at me, and the girls turned away to whisper on the monkey bars. The teachers were no help: they looked my way and talked about how foolish I looked in my new jacket. I saw their heads bob with laughter, their hands half-covering their mouths. **4**

Even though it was cold, I took off the jacket during lunch and played kickball in a thin shirt, my arms feeling like Braille from goose bumps. But when I returned to class I slipped the jacket on and shivered until I was warm. I sat on my hands, heating them up, while my teeth chattered like a cup of crooked dice. Finally warm, I slid out of the jacket but a few minutes later put it back on when the fire bell rang. We paraded out into the yard where we, the sixth graders, walked past all the other grades to stand against the back fence. Everybody saw me. Although they didn't say out loud, "Man, that's ugly," I heard the buzz-buzz of gossip and even laughter that I knew was meant for me.

And so I went, in my guacamole-colored jacket. So embarrassed, so hurt, I couldn't even do my homework. I received Cs on quizzes, and forgot the state capitals and the rivers of South America, our friendly neighbor. Even the girls who had been **friendly** blew away like loose flowers to follow the boys in neat jackets. **5**

I wore that thing for three years until the sleeves grew short and my forearms stuck out like the necks of turtles. All during that time no love came to me—no little dark girl in a Sunday dress she wore on Monday. At lunchtime I stayed with the ugly boys who leaned against the chainlink fence and looked around with propellers of grass spinning in our

Practice the Skills

4 Key Reading Skill

Activating Prior Knowledge
Think about what a teacher's job is all about. Do you think the teachers are really talking about how the narrator looks in his jacket? Why or why not?

5 English Language Coach

Synonyms What are some synonyms for **friendly**? If the author had used the word *helpful* or the word *kind*, would the meaning of the sentence have changed? Why or why not? **EL**

Additional Support

Literature Focus Lesson

Simile and Metaphor Tell students that authors use simile and metaphor to add color and life to writing. Read the first sentence of the third paragraph of the selection on page 132, beginning "Even though it was cold. . . ." Identify the simile in which he compares his arms to Braille. Have students discuss how the simile helps them visualize the situation. Then have them find other examples of simile and metaphor on this page. *(Possible responses: "like a cup of crooked dice"; "like loose flowers"; "like the necks of turtles"; "propellers of grass")* **OL AL**

mouths. We saw girls walk by alone, saw couples, hand in hand, their heads like bookends pressing air together. We saw them and spun our propellers so fast our faces were blurs. **6**

I blame that jacket for those bad years. I blame my mother for her bad taste and her cheap ways. It was a sad time for the heart. With a friend I spent my sixth-grade year in a tree in the alley, waiting for something good to happen to me in that jacket, which had become the ugly brother who tagged along wherever I went. And it was about that time that I began to grow. My chest puffed up with muscle and, strangely, a few more ribs. Even my hands, those fleshy hammers, showed bravely through the cuffs, the fingers already hardening for the coming fights. But that L-shaped rip on the left sleeve got bigger, bits of stuffing coughed out from its wound after a

Practice the Skills

6 **Key Literary Element**

Narrator Now that you've read more of the story, what do you think of the narrator? Do you trust him? Is he honest? Does he exaggerate?

Analyzing the Art Which boy in this picture is the narrator? How do you know? Where do you think the green jacket might be?

The Jacket **133**

Teach

Viewing the Art

Ask: What scene from the narrative does this artwork illustrate? *(Responses may vary. Students might mention that it shows the narrator during recess.)* **BL** **OL**

C Critical Thinking

Evaluation **Say:** Describe the narrator. Do you trust the narrator's account of events? Why or why not? Find sentences in the story to support your opinions. *(Responses will vary.)* **OL** **AL**

English Language Coach

Elements of Autobiography Bring in pictures of famous people from magazines. Choose one to post on the board. Ask students to suggest ideas for an autobiography of the person in the picture. Students may need to conduct some research on the person in order to determine some of these elements. **BL**

Have students work in groups that include English language learners as well as English-proficient students. Ask each group to choose a picture and repeat the class activity for that picture. Suggest that each group present its work to the class in poster form—as an ad for an autobiographical book or movie. **AS**

Objectives
- Activate prior knowledge
- Identify and use synonyms
- Evaluate text
- Identify literary devices: simile and metaphor
- Find meaning in art

Teach

L Literary Element

Narrator Say: Describe how the narrator is feeling at this moment. *(Possible responses: frustration, anger, insignificance)* **OL**

R Reading Skill

Activating Prior Knowledge

Say: Look again at the last sentence. What comes to mind when you read that the jacket "breathed over my shoulder"? *(Possible response: someone closely watching me and making me nervous)* **Ask:** How do your experiences help you understand how Soto felt about the jacket? *(Possible response: It seems like the jacket makes him feel uncomfortable. I know how that feels. He wishes it would go away.)* **OL**

BQ ⟨BIG Question⟩

Ask: How do you think Gary Soto would answer the question, "Do clothes bring out the best in people?" *(Responses will vary. Students should support their ideas with material from the text.)* **AS**

---

hard day of play. I finally Scotch-taped it closed, but in rain or cold weather the tape peeled off like a scab and more stuffing fell out until that sleeve shriveled into a palsied[1] arm. That winter the elbows began to crack and whole chunks of green began to fall off. I showed the cracks to my mother, who always seemed to be at the stove with steamed-up glasses, and she said that there were children in Mexico who would love that jacket. I told her that this was America and yelled that Debbie, my sister, didn't have a jacket like mine. I ran outside, ready to cry, and climbed the tree by the alley to think bad thoughts and watch my breath puff white and disappear. **7**

But whole pieces still casually flew off my jacket when I played hard, read quietly, or took vicious spelling tests at school. When it became so spotted that my brother began to call me "camouflage," I flung it over the fence into the alley. Later, however, I swiped the jacket off the ground and went inside to drape it across my lap and **mope**.

I was called to dinner: steam silvered my mother's glasses as she said grace; my brother and sister with their heads bowed made ugly faces at their glasses of powdered milk. I gagged too, but eagerly ate big rips of buttered tortilla that held scooped-up beans. Finished, I went outside with my jacket across my arm. It was a cold sky. The faces of clouds were piled up, hurting. I climbed the fence, jumping down with a grunt. I started up the alley and soon slipped into my jacket, that green ugly brother who breathed over my shoulder that day and ever since. **8** ○

---

1. **palsied** (PAWL zeed) means "withered by disease."

Vocabulary

mope (mohp) *v.* to be gloomy or in low spirits

134 UNIT 2 What Brings Out the Best in You?

Practice the Skills

7 Key Literary Element

Narrator Can you "hear" the narrator's voice in this paragraph? Explain. What words would you use to describe the way the narrator is feeling? **L**

8 ✓BIG Question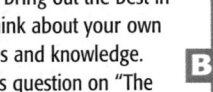

Do clothes bring out the best in people? Think about your own experiences and knowledge. Answer this question on "The Jacket" part of the Workshop 1 Foldable. **BQ**

Additional Support

Differentiated Instruction

Comparison Chart Ask students whether they can relate to how upset the narrator gets about his jacket. Discuss how he handles his frustration. Point out that yelling at his mother does not work, but taking some time to calm down by going outside does. Have students work in small groups to complete a chart about the two ways the narrator has of dealing with frustration, listing *Ways That Work* in one column and *Ways That Don't Work* in the other. **OL**

Teach

Viewing the Art

Ask: How well does this picture reflect what happens in the final paragraph of "The Jacket"? *(Responses will vary).* **AS**

Ask: What would you add or take away to make this picture fit the final paragraph? *(Responses will vary).* **OL**

Say: Draw a picture to reflect how you think the narrator felt about his jacket. **AS**

Assess

CheckPoint

Use the CheckPoint questions provided on Presentation Plus! to check for comprehension of the selection. These questions can be used with interactive response keypads for immediate student feedback.

Analyzing the Art What details from the story's final paragraph do you see in this picture?

The Jacket **135**

Literature Focus Lesson

Personification Soto says his jacket "breathed over [his] shoulder." Personification is a form of figurative language that gives human qualities to animals or inanimate objects. Ask students to find another example of personification in the last paragraph *("the faces of clouds were piled up, hurting")*. Discuss what effect Soto achieves by personifying the clouds and his jacket. **AS**

Objectives
• Activate prior knowledge
• Identify literary devices: personification
• Identify and analyze narrator
• Find meaning in art

Assess

Resources for page 136

📁 Selection Quick Check, p. 11

📁 Selection and Unit Assessment, p. 13

💿 ExamView Assessment Suite

💿 Interactive Tutor: Self-Assessment

Students can respond to the *After You Read* items in their Learner's Notebooks or on a separate sheet of paper.

Answering the

1. Responses will vary.

2. The narrator, Gary Soto

3. The sleeves of his old jacket "climbed halfway to my elbow" and the weather was cold.

Critical Thinking

4. Possible response: He was so disappointed that he wanted to cry. He had hoped for a leather jacket "like bikers wear," but he received a cheap, ugly, vinyl one.

5. Possible response: He wore the jacket to keep warm and because it was the only one he would have for a long time.

6. Possible response: Even though he hated the jacket, he "thanked" his mother for it.

7. Possible response: At first, the narrator hates the jacket and blames it for "those bad years." He comes to think of it as an "ugly brother" and carries the memory of the jacket (and the insecurities it symbolizes) into adulthood.

136

After You Read | The Jacket

Answering the BIG Question

1. Do you think the narrator's new coat brings out the best in him? Why or why not?

2. **Recall** Who is this story mostly about?
   TIP **Right There** You will find the answer in the story.

3. **Summarize** What does the narrator's new jacket look like?
   TIP **Think and Search** The answer is in the story, but the details are not in one place.

Critical Thinking

4. **Infer** How does the narrator feel when he sees his new green jacket? Why do you think he feels this way?
   TIP **Author and Me** You will find clues in the story, but you must also use the information in your head.

5. **Conclude** Why does the narrator wear the jacket even though he hates it?
   TIP **Think and Search** The answer is in the story, but the details are not in one place.

6. **Infer** How can you tell the narrator cares about his mother's feelings?
   TIP **Author and Me** You will find clues in the story, but you must also use the information in your head.

7. **Analyze** Do you think the narrator's attitude toward the jacket changes by the end of the story? Explain.
   TIP **Author and Me** You will find clues in the story, but you must also use the information in your head.

Objectives (pp. 136–137)
Reading Activate prior knowledge • Make connections from text to self
Literature Identify literary elements: narrator
Vocabulary Identify synonyms
Grammar Identify parts of speech: common and proper nouns

Talk About Your Reading

The writer Mark Twain said that "Clothes make the man." What do you think that means? Think about what you just read, and consider the big question. Think about your own experiences and discuss the quote with the class. Answer these questions:

- Do you think the narrator of "The Jacket" would agree that "Clothes make the man" or not?
- Do you ever feel pressure to fit in by dressing a certain way? Explain.
- Do your clothes make you who you are?

Write About Your Reading

Possible response:
At first, the narrator believed that "clothes make the man." He felt foolish in the ugly green jacket. His shame made it hard for him to concentrate in school. He blamed all of his troubles on the jacket. However, as he began to grow, the jacket no longer fit. His old image of himself no longer fit either. At the end of the story, he begins to realize that the most important thing is not how he looks, but who he is.

Skills Review

Key Reading Skill: Activating Prior Knowledge

8. What prior knowledge did you have that most helped you understand this selection?

9. How did the activities on page 129 help you read and understand this selection? Rank the activities in order of helpfulness, with 1 being the most helpful and 3 the least helpful. Explain your rankings.
   • Talking about clothing trends
   • Previewing the reading skill
   • Reading the facts in Build Background

Key Literary Element: Narrator

10. Describe the narrator. Is he suspenseful, funny, serious? Use a line from the text to back up your opinion.

11. How might the story be different if Soto's mother narrated "The Jacket"?

12. Do you think time has changed the way the narrator feels about his green jacket? Explain.

Reviewing Skills: Setting a Purpose for Reading

13. If you recommended this story to someone, what would you tell them is a good purpose for reading "The Jacket"?

Vocabulary Check

In your own words write a definition for each vocabulary word. Next write a sentence for each word.

14. vinyl

15. profile

16. mope

17. **Academic Vocabulary** What *prior* knowledge would you need to use the Internet?

18. **English Language Coach** What three words would you use to describe the narrator of this story? What are their synonyms?

Grammar Link: Nouns

A **noun** names a person, place, thing, or idea.

• A **common noun** names *any* person, place, thing, or idea.

• A **proper noun** names a *particular* person, place, thing, or idea. Proper nouns always begin with a capital letter.

Common Nouns	Proper Nouns
city	Los Angeles
actor	Johnny Depp
school	Wilson Middle School
baseball team	Chicago White Sox

Grammar Practice

Rewrite each sentence, circle both common and proper nouns, then write a **C** above each *common noun* and a **P** above each *proper noun*.

19. Bart and Trent went to a movie.

20. In Washington D.C., the class visited several monuments.

21. Our family will have a picnic at Lincoln Park this weekend.

Now write three sentences of your own using both common and proper nouns. For each sentence you write, circle the nouns, and write a **C** above each *common noun* and a **P** above each *proper noun*.

Literature Online

Web Activities For eFlashcards, Selection Quick Checks, and other Web activities, go to www.glencoe.com.

The Jacket **137**

Grammar Link: Nouns

Grammar Practice

19. (Bart) and (Trent) went to a (movie.)
    P   P   C

20. In (Washington, D.C.,) the class
         P
    visited several (monuments.)
                     C

21. Our family will have a (picnic) at
                            C
    (Lincoln Park) this (weekend.)
     P   C

Additional sentences will vary.

Close

Have students relate what they learned from the selection about the Big Question.

Skills Review

Key Reading Skill: Activating Prior Knowledge

8. Responses will vary.

9. Responses will vary. Students should provide reasons for their rankings.

Key Literary Element: Narrator

10. Responses will vary. Students should use the text to support their responses.

11. Possible response: Soto's mother would probably explain why she bought the jacket or talk about how she feels about her son and his struggle.

12. Students should explain their opinions.

Reviewing Skills: Setting a Purpose for Reading

13. Possible response: to find out about Gary Soto or growing up Latino

Vocabulary Check

Sentences and definitions will vary.

14. plastic

15. side view

16. sulk

17. **Academic Vocabulary** Possible response: Name of the subject you want to research; alphabetical order; where to find the encyclopedia

18. **English Language Coach** Responses will vary.

Teach

More About the Author

When young writers ask Nikki Giovanni for advice, they might be surprised by her answer: "The main thing is . . . you have to read." Giovanni says she reads something every day, even if it's a cookbook. When she reads, she learns, and that gives her ideas for her writing. Giovanni has written about everything from racism to love, but she doesn't worry about what other people think of her topics. "If you know what you're talking about, or if you feel that you do, the reader will believe you."

R Reading Skill

Activating Prior Knowledge

Ask: What is most important to you? What makes the world a pleasant place for you and why? *(Responses will vary.)* **AS**

Before You Read : The World Is Not a Pleasant Place to Be

Yolande Cornelia "Nikki" Giovanni, Jr.

Meet the Author

Yolande Cornelia "Nikki" Giovanni, Jr., was born in 1943 in Knoxville, Tennessee. She is a poet, writer, and educator. Giovanni is one of the most widely read American poets. She takes pride in being "a Black American, a daughter, a mother, a professor of English." Giovanni is committed to the fight for civil rights and equality. See page R3 of the Author Files for more on Nikki Giovanni.

Literature Online

Author Search For more about Nikki Giovanni, go to www.glencoe.com.

Objectives (pp. 138–139)
Reading Activate prior knowledge
• Make connections from text to self
Literature Identify literary elements: speaker

Skills Preview

Key Reading Skill: Activating Prior Knowledge

Before you read the poem, think about how you feel when you're alone. How do you feel when you're with your family and friends? **R**

Write to Learn Write a short paragraph about what you think makes the world a pleasant place to be.

Literary Element: Speaker

In a poem, the narrator is called the speaker. The **speaker** is the voice that communicates the poem's ideas, actions, descriptions, and feelings. As you read "The World Is Not a Pleasant Place to Be," pay special attention to the thoughts and emotions that the speaker expresses.
• Try to get a feeling for what the speaker is like.
  How would you describe this speaker to a friend?

Get Ready to Read

Connect to the Reading

The speaker in this poem expresses feelings of loneliness through images of a river and the ocean. What everyday objects or scenes in life and nature make you think about loneliness?

Build Background

Nikki Giovanni began writing in the 1960s, a time of great social change. Many of her poems focus on social and political issues. In her later poetry she writes about personal subjects such as family, love, and loneliness. This poem comes from Giovanni's book of poems, *My House*.

Set Purposes for Reading

BIG Question Read the poem "The World Is Not a Pleasant Place to Be" to learn about what the speaker feels brings out the best in people.

Set Your Own Purpose What else would you like to learn from the poem to help you answer the Big Question? Write your own purpose on the "The World" part of the Workshop 1 Foldable.

Keep Moving

Use these skills as you read the following selection.

Additional Support

Literature Online

Author Search To expand students' appreciation of Nikki Giovanni, have them access the Web site for additional information and resources.

Literature Focus Lesson

Free Verse Poems with no rhyming words or formal rhythm are called free verse. Line breaks are determined by meaning and speech patterns. "You know what the trick is?" explains Giovanni. "You read it on a human breath." Ask for volunteers to read Giovanni's poem aloud. Notice the effect of pausing in different places. **OL**

Have students rewrite a prose passage as if it were free verse. Compare versions and discuss how students decided where to break the lines. **AL**

The World Is Not a Pleasant Place to Be

by Nikki Giovanni

the world is not a pleasant place
to be without
someone to hold and be held by **1**

a river would stop
5 its flow if only
a stream were there
to receive it   **C**

an ocean would never laugh
if clouds weren't there
10 to kiss her tears **2**

the world is not
a pleasant place to be without
someone **3** ○

Practice the Skills

1 Key Reading Skill

Activating Prior Knowledge
Think about your experiences
with family, friends, or even pets.
Would the world be less pleasant
without them in your life?

2 Literary Element

Speaker The speaker has specific ideas about what makes the
world "pleasant." Do you agree
with the speaker?

3

What does the speaker say
makes the world a better place?
Do you agree or disagree? Write
your answer on "The World" part
of the Workshop 1 Foldable. **BQ**

The World Is Not a Pleasant Place to Be **139**

Teach

C Critical Thinking

**Evaluation Ask: How would
you summarize the meaning
of this poem in a sentence or
two?** *(Possible answer: Feeling
lonely takes the joy out of life.)*
**Is the summary as moving as
the poem? Why or why not?**
(Responses will vary.) **AL**

EL Language Coach

Synonyms Have students
read the third stanza aloud,
substituting synonyms for the
word *laugh*. Discuss how each
synonym changes the meaning
of the poem. **EL**

BQ BIG Question

Before students discuss the
Big Question, remind them
that they are entitled to agree
or disagree with the narrator.
Encourage them to use examples from the poem and their
own experience to support their
opinions. **OL**

Assess

CheckPoint

Use the CheckPoint questions
provided on Presentation Plus!
to check for comprehension of
the selection. These questions
can be used with interactive
response keypads for immediate student feedback.

Objectives
• Activate prior knowledge
• Identify and use synonyms
• Recognize distinctive features of
  poetry
• Evaluate text

Reading Fluency

Build Fluency Have students meet
with a partner in a quiet place. Ask them
to take turns reading stanzas from "The
World Is Not a Pleasant Place to Be." Tell
students to read aloud the first stanza.
Then, like an echo, their partner should
read aloud the same stanza. Have them
continue reading each stanza of the
poem this way. Tell students to practice
reading the lines smoothly with expression and understanding. Finally, students
should take a turn reading aloud the
entire poem from beginning to end. **AS**

139

Assess

Resources for page 140

📁 Selection Quick Check, p. 12

📁 Selection and Unit Assessment, p. 14

💿 ExamView Assessment Suite

💿 Interactive Tutor: Self-Assessment

Students can respond to the *After You Read* items in their Learner's Notebooks or on a separate sheet of paper.

Answering the

1. Responses will vary.

2. Responses will vary, but they should include some mention of how loneliness or being connected to others affects people.

3. Responses will vary. Students should identify the lines about the river, stream, ocean, or clouds.

Critical Thinking

4. Responses will vary. Students are likely to note that the repetition of "not a pleasant place" and images like "tears" suggest loneliness.

5. Responses will vary. Students should provide reasons for their opinions.

6. Responses will vary. Students might note that negation and repetition are forms of emphasis.

After You Read

The World Is Not a Pleasant Place to Be

Answering the BIG Question

1. Who brings out the best in you? How?

2. **Summarize** What is this poem about?

   Tip Think and Search The answer is in the poem, but the details are not in one place.

3. **Identify** Write two lines from the poem that use images from nature.

   Tip Think and Search The answer is in the poem, but the details are not in one place.

Critical Thinking

4. **Infer** Think about the feelings expressed in the poem. How do you think the author felt when she wrote this poem?

   Tip Author and Me You will find clues in the poem, but you must also use the information in your head.

5. **Evaluate** Do you agree with the speaker about what is important in life, or can you think of more important things in life? Explain.

   Tip Author and Me You will find clues in the poem, but you must also use the information in your head.

6. **Analyze** Why do you think the author starts and ends the poem using the phrase "the world is not a pleasant place to be"? That phrase is also the title. Explain why you think the author repeated that phrase so often.

   Tip Author and Me You will find clues in the poem, but you must also use the information in your head.

Write About Your Reading

Use the poem "The World Is Not a Pleasant Place to Be" as a model to write your own poem about what makes the world a good and pleasant place.

- Choose a speaker. Will the speaker be you or someone else?

- What feelings do you want to express: happiness, sadness, loneliness, frustration? What words will help you express those feelings?

- Make sure that your poem has four stanzas, like "The World Is Not a Pleasant Place to Be." Stanzas are sections of a poem and are similar to paragraphs.

Objectives (pp. 140–141)
Reading Activate prior knowledge • Make connections from text to self
Literature Identify literary elements: speaker
Grammar Identify parts of speech: subject and object pronouns
Writing Respond to literature: write a poem

140 UNIT 2 What Brings Out the Best in You?

Write About Your Reading

Possible response:
the world is a pleasant place
to be with a challenge that's just the
right size

climbers head to the top of a mountain
if the top can be seen

singers try for the high
notes once the low tones are secure

the world is a pleasant place
to be with a challenge

Skills Review

Key Reading Skill: Activating Prior Knowledge

7. Do the images from nature in the poem help you understand the speaker's feelings? Why or why not?

Literary Element: Speaker

8. Do the words the speaker uses help you understand the way the speaker feels? Why or why not?

9. Do you think the speaker and author are the same person in this poem? Explain.

10. In what ways do you think the speaker is like you? In what ways do you think the speaker is different?

Vocabulary Check

11. Academic Vocabulary What *prior* knowledge do you think the author of this poem had to help her write this poem about the world?

12. English Language Coach List three synonyms for the word *pleasant*. If you want to, use a thesaurus. Why do you think the poet chose the word *pleasant* instead of one of its synonyms?

13. English Language Coach The words *river* and *stream* are synonyms. Use a dictionary to discover the slightly different meanings of the words.

Grammar Link: Pronouns

A **pronoun** is a word that takes the place of one or more nouns. Pronouns make reading easier. For example, look at the sentence below. It doesn't use any pronouns.

Ben let Ben's sister borrow Ben's bike so Ben's sister could ride to Ben and Ben's sister's school.

Now look at the sentence with pronouns.

Ben let **his** sister borrow **his** bike so **she** could ride to **their** school.

What pronoun you use depends on how and when you use it in a sentence. Some pronouns replace nouns that are the **subject** of a sentence. Other pronouns replace nouns that are the **object** of a sentence. (You will learn more about subjects and objects in Unit 4.)

Subject pronouns: *I, you, he, she, it, we, they*
Object pronouns: *me, you, him, her, us, them*

Grammar Practice

Rewrite each sentence below replacing each underlined word or group of words with the correct **subject pronoun**.

14. <u>Queen Latifah</u> is a movie star.

15. After ice-skating, <u>Jenny and Juan</u> had hot chocolate.

16. The movie was scary, but <u>Sumi and I</u> watched <u>the movie</u> anyway.

Rewrite each sentence below replacing each underlined word or group of words with the correct **object pronoun**.

17. Have you seen <u>Jamal and Derek</u>?

18. Mr. Yoshida drove <u>Alex and Kaori</u> to the dance.

19. Emily told <u>Luz</u> a joke.

Writing Application Choose one stanza in your poem with a noun, or group of nouns, that you could change into a pronoun. Rewrite that stanza with the noun, or group of nouns, changed to a pronoun.

Web Activities For eFlashcards, Selection Quick Checks, and other Web activities, go to www.glencoe.com.

Skills Review

Key Reading Skill: Activating Prior Knowledge

7. Possible response: The images from nature show how everything needs something else to be complete.

Key Literary Element: Speaker

8. Students may note that the speaker uses words with strong sense appeal and emotional connotations.

9. Students may conclude that the author seems to be speaking directly.

Reviewing Skills: Connecting

10. Responses will vary.

11. Academic Vocabulary The author had to know about parts of nature such as rivers, streams, oceans, and clouds, and feelings like laughter, connectedness, and loneliness.

12. English Language Coach Answers will vary but may include words like *nice, positive, good*. Possible response: The poet chose the word *pleasant* because it feels removed and formal.

13. A river is a large stream of water.

Grammar Link: Pronouns

Grammar Practice

14. She is a movie star.

15. After ice-skating, they had hot chocolate.

16. The movie was scary, but we watched it anyway.

17. Have you seen them?

18. Mr. Yoshida drove them to the dance.

19. Emily told her a joke.

Close

Hold a class discussion based on students' answers to question 13.

Autobiographical Narrative

UNIT 2

**Objectives covered in
this workshop:**
• **Writing** Write autobiography
using the writing process;
revise writing for word
choice, tone, and style
• **Grammar** Use adjectives
and adverbs to enhance
writing

Teaching Students to Write an Autobiographical Narrative

Why Is It Important?

• Autobiographical narrative provides students with practice writing in the first person point of view.

• Students will enjoy writing about something they really know: their own lives.

• Writing in their own voices will help students hone their understanding of tone and word choice.

How to Help Students Get It

• Remind students to use the language that comes naturally to them; this will help them develop their writing "voice."

• Encourage students to start small. The prewriting process will be easier if they do not take on too much material at once.

• Remind the class to use "I" and "me" in their writing, and to talk about a goal of their own.

• Ask: "Did you include a beginning, middle, and end?"

• Ask: "Could a friend identify you as the person in this story without seeing who wrote it?"

The Writing Process

This is a good opportunity to review with students the process that good writers often follow.

• Prewriting: gathering facts and ideas and narrowing down your topic

• Drafting: getting your thoughts on paper; writing your first draft

• Revising: rereading and adding, deleting, or rearranging ideas; finalizing your ideas in writing

• Editing: checking spelling, grammar, and punctuation

• Presenting: your final product—a paper, speech, or presentation

Traits of Good Writing	
Ideas	the message or the theme and the details that develop it
Voice	a writer's unique way of using tone and style Have students use the following checklist when checking their compositions: • Does your writing sound interesting when you read it aloud? • Does your writing show what you think about your topic? • Does your writing sound like you—or does it sound like you're imitating someone else?
Organization	the arrangement of main points and supporting details
Word Choice	the vocabulary a writer uses to convey meaning
Sentence Fluency	the smooth rhythm and flow of sentences that vary in length and style
Conventions	• Are all words spelled correctly? • Are all proper nouns – as well as the first word of every sentence – capitalized? • Is the composition free of sentence fragments? • Is the composition free of run-on sentences? • Are punctuation marks – such as apostrophes, commas, and end marks – inserted in the right places? correct spelling, grammar, usage, and mechanics
Presentation	the way words and design elements look on a page

Unit Focus (marker beside Voice row)

Workshop Resources

Pacing (days) Standard	Pacing (days) Block	Lesson	Student Materials	Teacher Resources
1	1/2	Writing Workshop Part 1: Prewriting and Drafting	🖊 Writing Workshop Graphic Organizer, p. 15 🖊 Spelling and Handwriting Practice, p. 44 💻 Spelling Power eWorkbook 🔵 Interactive Grammar and Language Workbook 📖 Grammar and Composition Handbook, p. 81	🔵 TeacherWorks Plus™ 🔵 Presentation Plus! 📁 Rubrics for Assessing Student Writing, Listening, and Speaking, p. 13
			📁 Real Success in Writing: Research and Reports 📁 Writing Constructed Responses	✊ Grammar and Writing Workshop Transparencies 9–10
2	1	Writing Workshop Part 2: Editing, Revising, and Presenting	🔵 Interactive Grammar and Language Workbook 📖 Grammar and Composition Handbook, p. 81	✊ Grammar and Writing Workshop Transparencies 19–20
			🖊 Listening and Speaking, p. 27 🖊 Viewing and Representing, p. 28	🔵 Interactive Grammar and Language Workbook
			📁 Real Success in Writing: Research and Reports 📁 Writing Constructed Responses	📁 Rubrics for Assessing Student Writing, Listening, and Speaking, p. 13

Focus

- **Daily Language Practice Transparency 14**
  Focus Activity Say: Briefly summarize an interesting incident in your life. Include where it happened and who was there. You will write about a personal incident in this Writing Workshop.

Teach

L Literary Element

Autobiographical Narrative
Ask: What is the difference between a biography and an autobiography? *(A biography is about someone else's life; an autobiography is about the writer's life.)* **Say:** A narrative is simply a story. What types of writings are narratives? *(Possible responses: novels, autobiographies, folktales)* **OL**

Resources for page 142

- Use the Writing Workshop Graphic Organizer BLM in the Unit 2 Resource Booklet, p. 15.

- Use the Grammar and Writing Workshop Transparencies 9–10.

WRITING WORKSHOP PART 1

Autobiographical Narrative
Prewriting and Drafting

ASSIGNMENT Write an autobiographical narrative
Purpose: Share a story about a friend who brought out the best in you
Audience: You, your teacher, and your classmates

Writing Rubric

As you work through this Writing Workshop, you will
- write about an important friendship
- tell a story in your own words
- write details and descriptions
- use chronological order
- use nouns correctly

See page 186 in Part 2 for a model of an autobiographical narrative.

Objectives (pp. 142–145)
Writing Use the writing process: autobiographical narrative • Use literary elements: details, chronological order, conventions of language
Grammar Use nouns: common, proper, abstract, collective

Writing an autobiographical narrative will help you think about the Unit 2 Big Question: What brings out the best in you?

| Autobiography: When you write about your life or an event in your life, you write autobiography. | + | Narrative: Any story, real or imagined, is a narrative. | = | Autobiographical Narrative: When you write or tell a story that is about your life, you are creating an autobiographical narrative. **L** |

Prewriting
Get Ready to Write

In this Writing Workshop you are going to write about a time in your life when a friend helped you do something that you thought was impossible.

Gather Ideas and Choose a Topic

In your Learner's Notebook make a list of important friends in your life. Next to each name on your list, write a memorable experience you shared with that friend that made you better or stronger. Next, choose the friend and the experience you'd like to write an autobiographical narrative about.

Drafting
Start Writing!

For about five or ten minutes, freewrite about your friend and the experience. Try to remember the order in which the events took place. Write descriptions, details, feelings, or whatever else comes to mind.

Additional Support

Writing Models Have students access the Web site for an additional and interactive Writing Workshop-based student model.

Differentiated Instruction

Mind Map Offer students the option of starting their autobiographical incident by making a mind map. Draw an example of a mind map on the board. Have interested students create a mind map of their autobiographical incident. Ask them to share their mind maps with a partner when they have completed them. **AS**

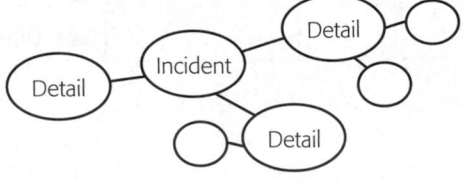

Get It on Paper

Autobiographical narratives are usually about a special event in the writer's life. In this narrative, the special event is a time when a friend brought out the best in you. Make sure that your draft tells the reader how this event was special to you.

Sort Through the Details

Choose only the details that are important to the story. Do this so your reader won't get confused by unimportant information. Read the example below and pick out the detail that the writer should leave out of this narrative.

> *Last year, I ran for fifth grade class president. Fifth grade was really fun because Pablo and I were in the same homeroom and lunch period. Pablo gave me the idea to run for class president. On the day of the election, I had to give a speech in front of the entire grade about why I would make a good class president. As I was waiting for my turn to speak, I became really nervous. My stomach felt like it was tied in knots and my hands got sweaty. I started thinking that I didn't want to be class president anymore.*

What detail is not necessary and can be deleted from this narrative?

Put the Story in Order

As you write, you need to make sure that the events of your narrative are in a particular order. Chronological, or time, order is a good way to organize an autobiographical narrative. Just write events in the order that they happened: first, second, third, and so on. Begin some sentences with words like *then* and *next* to help readers follow your story. Read the passage below for an example of chronological order.

> *Pablo helped me with all of the election preparations. First, we made posters to hang in the fifth grade hallway. Then, we made buttons with my name on them for our classmates to wear. Finally, on the night before the election, we baked cookies to pass out at school the next day.*

Writing Models For models and other writing activities, go to www.glencoe.com.

Writing Tip

Remember that autobiographical narratives are written in the first-person point of view. That means you should use words like *I* and *me* to refer to yourself.

Writing Tip

Stay focused on the story that you are telling. Make a list of the important events you want to write about and stick to those events in your narrative.

Writing Tip

Keep your readers interested by including details about how you felt at certain points throughout the narrative.

Teach

W Writing

Narrative Techniques Say: There are different ways to start your narrative. For example, you can start with someone doing something (action), saying or thinking about something (reaction), or characters talking about someone (dialogue). **AS**

Read aloud the following examples and ask students to identify the technique used by each writer. **OL**

Once upon a midnight dreary, while I pondered, weak and weary,

Over many a quaint and curious volume of forgotten lore—

While I nodded, nearly napping, suddenly there came a tapping,

As of someone gently rapping, rapping at my chamber door.
—Edgar Allan Poe *(action)*

WHEN I was a boy, there was but one permanent ambition among my comrades in our village on the west bank of the Mississippi River. That was, to be a steamboatman.
—Mark Twain *(reaction)*

"Ready?"
"Ready."
"Now?"
"Soon."
—Ray Bradbury *(dialogue)*

Objectives

- Use the writing process: autobiographical narrative
- Respond to literature: narrative
- Analyze features for genres: biography and autobiography

Literature Focus Lesson

Autobiography The more familiar students become with the genre of autobiography, the more models they have for this writing assignment. You might want to send students to the library to gather examples of autobiographies. They could photocopy excerpts or bring the books to class. You might even choose to show a small portion of an autobiographical film or read parts of an autobiography by a famous person. Ask students to choose short excerpts from the examples they find to share with the rest of the class. Discuss with students what parts of the autobiographies are interesting to them and why. **OL**

Teach

C Critical Thinking

Comprehension Have students reread number 4. **Ask:** Are there other words that spell-check won't catch? *(Possible response: there, their, and they're)* What do these words have in common? *(they sound alike but have different meanings)* **OL Ask:** These kinds of words are called homonyms. What are some ways to proof words like these? *(Students may say that they could use the find-and-replace feature to search for a word such as* weather *and check to see if they should have used* whether *instead.)* **AL**

Applying Good Writing Traits

Conventions

Writers have a common set of rules. It's not terrible to break the rules, but you have to know the rules in order to play the game.

What Are Conventions?

Conventions are the rules of language—spelling, capitalization, punctuation, grammar, usage, and paragraphing.

Why Are Conventions Important?

When you follow the rules of language, your writing is easy for others to read. Readers can pay attention to your message and your unique ideas instead of trying to figure out what you meant to say.

You can play around with conventions for a specific effect. For example, you may misspell a word or break a grammar rule to show how a character speaks. However, your writing must show strong control of conventions so readers know you're breaking the rules on purpose and for good reasons.

How Do I Use Conventions in My Writing?

- Read your paper slowly. Focus on seeing the words as they appear on the page.
- Look for one kind of error at a time.

1. Look for grammatical errors. Reading your paper aloud may help you find them.
2. Check to make sure you have punctuation and capital letters in all the right places.
3. Check that your paragraphs begin in the right places and that the first line of each paragraph is indented.
4. Circle any words you need to check for spelling and then look them up in a dictionary. If you use a computer, you can use the spell-check feature, but don't trust it completely. If you accidentally typed *here* but meant to type *hear*, the spell-check feature won't notice the mistake.

Write to Learn Read over your draft carefully. Follow the steps above to find and correct errors in conventions.

C

ADAM @ 1999 HOME © by UNIVERSAL PRESS SYNDICATE. Reprinted with permission. All rights reserved.

Analyzing Cartoons
Here, *fundamentals* means "the most important skills." What is Clint's problem? How are the fundamentals in a sport like the conventions in writing?

Additional Support

Differentiated Instruction

Using Graphic Organizers Work with students to eliminate unessential details from the passage in the "Sort Through the Details" section on page 143. Draw a large circle on the board and write *running for class president* in the center. Have students look for details in the story. As they identify details, ask if each detail is related to the main idea. If it is, draw a smaller circle, connect it to the main idea circle, and add the detail. If it is not, omit it. Then ask students to rewrite the passage on their own using the graphic organizer to help them include important details and to leave out unnecessary details. **AS**

Grammar Link

Nouns

A **noun** names a person, place, or thing. Using a variety of nouns is an important part of good writing.

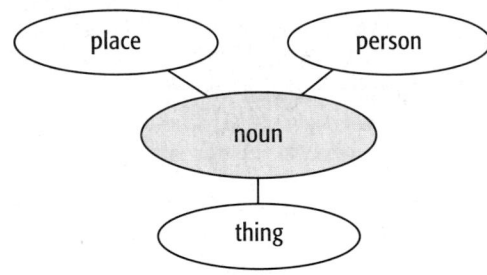

Look at the three underlined nouns in the following sentence.

Ramon sent a letter to Mexico.

What Are the Different Types of Nouns?

A *common noun* is the name of a general person, place, or thing.

• The boys are playing baseball.

A *proper noun* is the name of a specific person, place, or thing. Proper nouns are capitalized.

• Tom and Jarrod are playing for the Yankees.

An *abstract noun* refers to something that is an idea, emotion, or feeling, rather than something that you can touch.

• The teacher expressed joy when she read the students' reports.

A *collective noun* refers to a group of people or things.

• The family took a walk every Saturday.

How Can I Use Nouns Correctly in My Autobiographical Narrative?

Read your autobiographical narrative. Circle all the nouns you find.

Step 1: Review all sentences that have common nouns that are NOT abstract or collective.

• Is it the right noun for that sentence?

• Should it be singular or plural?

Step 2: Review all sentences that have abstract nouns.

• Is it the right noun for that sentence?

• Should it be singular or plural?

Step 3: Review all sentences that have collective nouns.

• Is it the right noun for that sentence?

Step 4: Review all sentences that have proper nouns.

• Is it the right noun for that sentence?

• Is it capitalized?

Step 5: See if there are any nouns that you have not already fixed.

As you continue writing your autobiographical narrative, correctly use a variety of nouns to keep your reader interested in your story.

Looking Ahead

Keep the writing you did here. In Part 2 you will add the finishing touches.

Reading Fluency

Reading and Writing Some students might find that they can analyze their drafts better if they read them aloud. Allow these students to work with a partner for this step in revision. Students should take turns reading their own drafts to their partners. Then they should discuss the content of their narratives with their partners, including their point of view and chronological order. Encourage students to use the rubric from page 142 as a guideline for discussing their drafts. **OL**

Teach

Grammar Link

Ask: What is the difference between a common noun and a proper noun? *(A common noun is a general name for a person, place, or thing, and it is not capitalized. A proper noun names a specific person, place, or thing, and it begins with a capital letter.)* **OL**

Write the following words on the board and have students determine whether they are proper or common nouns. **BL** **EL**

• United States *(proper)*

• school *(common)*

• July *(Proper)*

• mother *(common)*

Assess

Have students exchange their drafts with a partner and answer each of the following questions about their partner's autobiography: What is best about this story? What would you change? What should the writer do more of? Then have students use the answers to these questions to make a plan for revision.

Objectives

• Use Standard English grammar, usage, and mechanics

• Use the writing process: autobiographical narrative

• Apply comprehension skills

• Identify and use various kinds of nouns

Connecting

Objective covered in this workshop:
• Connect text to self

Teaching Students to Connect to Text

Why Is It Important?

• There are many kinds of connections: self to world, self to text, world to text, text to text, self to world, and connections within the text.

• Seeing simple and complex implied relationships is essential to understanding an implied main idea or theme.

• Connecting to the reading helps to pique student interest and enhances comprehension.

How to Help Students Get It

• Before, during, and after reading, have students recall events, situations, and emotions they have experienced that can help them connect to the reading.

• Remind students to recall selections they have read, movies they have seen, or other sources that would help them connect the world to the text. Students do not always have to personally experience an event to make a connection. They often "experience" events through people they know or through situations they have read about or viewed through other media.

Reading to Answer the Big Question

In Workshop 2 of Unit 2, readers will find selections that discuss sports, nature, and the human character. These will help students to generate their own answers to the Big Question: **What brings out the best in you?**

Satchel Paige by Bill Littlefield
This biographical sketch of baseball great Satchel Paige chronicles his twenty years playing in the Negro leagues and his career with the Cleveland Indians. It demonstrates how Paige's response to racial discrimination brought out the best in him. In addition to his athletic accomplishments, Paige's talent, hard work, dignity, and gracious spirit are evident throughout this account.

Song for a Surf-Rider by Sara Van Alstyne Allen
The speaker uses vivid images of a horse and horseback riding to describe the beauty and excitement of the sea and surfing in this nine-stanza poem.

Workshop Resources

Pacing (days)		Lesson	Student Materials	Teacher Resources
Standard	**Block**			
1	1/2	Key Skill Lesson: Connecting	👤 Key Reading Skills Practice, p. 16 👤 English Language Coach Review, p. 41	✎ Bellringer Options Transparencies –Daily Language Practice 15 –Selection Focus 3 ✎ Read Aloud, Think Aloud Transparencies Read Aloud, Think Aloud 10–19 –Key Reading Skills 5 💿 Presentation Plus!
1	1	"Satchel Paige"	💻 Glencoe Online 👤 Unit Vocabulary Review, p. 39 👤 Academic Vocabulary Review, p. 42 📁 English Language Coach 👤 Active Reading Graphic Organizer, p. 18 👤 Literary Analysis, p. 17 💿 StudentWorks Plus™ 💻 Online Student Edition 💿 Literature Classics 📁 Selection and Unit Assessments, p. 15	✎ Literary and Text Analysis Transparencies 39 💻 Puzzlemaker 💿 Skill Level Up!™ A Language Arts Game 💻 BookLink 3 📖 Assessment by Learning Objective (Diagnostic and Formative) 💿 Interactive Tutor: Self-Assessment 💿 TeacherWorks Plus™
1		"Song for a Surf-Rider"	💻 Glencoe Online 👤 Unit Vocabulary Review, p. 39 👤 Academic Vocabulary Review, p. 42 📁 English Language Coach 👤 Active Reading Graphic Organizer, p.20 👤 Literary Analysis, p. 17 💿 StudentWorks Plus™ 💻 Online Student Edition 💿 Literature Classics 📁 Selection and Unit Assessments, p. 16	✎ Literary and Text Analysis Transparencies 39 💻 Puzzlemaker 💿 Skill Level Up!™ A Language Arts Game 💻 BookLink 3 📖 Assessment by Learning Objective (Diagnostic and Formative) 💿 Interactive Tutor: Self-Assessment 💿 TeacherWorks Plus™

Keys for Unit Resource

📁	Blackline Master	🔒	DVD
📓	Workbook	✎	Transparency
📖	Supplemental Text	💻	Web-based
💿	CD-ROM	👤	Fast File

Level Appropriate Code

AS = Activities for all students

AL = Activities for students working above grade level

OL = Activities for students working at grade level

BL = Activities for students working below grade level

EL = Activities for English language learners

Focus

BELLRINGER Options

- **Selection Focus Transparency 3**
- **Daily Language Practice Transparency 5**
Focus Activity Ask: How does it feel to be treated unfairly? List some words that describe how this feels. *(Possible responses: terrible, discouraging, sad, frustrating)* **AS**

Teach

R Reading Skill

Connecting Say: Think of a time when you and someone you know read the same book and had very different reactions to it. Why might that be? *(Responses will vary.)* **OL** Readers often find it easy to connect with a book if they have had experiences with people, events, or settings similar to those in the selection. What are some ways that you have connected with books about experiences that at first seemed very different from your own? *(Responses will vary.)* **AL**

READING WORKSHOP 2

Skills Focus

You will practice using these skills when you read the following selections:
- "Satchel Paige," p. 150
- "Song for a Surf-Rider," p. 161

Reading

- Connecting to the text

Literature

- Identifying the author's point of view

Vocabulary

- Using antonyms

Writing/Grammar

- Identifying pronouns and their antecedents correctly
- Identifying indefinite pronouns

Objectives (pp. 146–147)
Reading Make connections from text to self

Skill Lesson

Connecting

Learn It!

What Is It? Connecting means linking what you read to events in your own life or to other selections you've read.

When you connect to what you read, you
R • compare the characters to yourself, people you know, and people you have read about.
- compare the setting to places you have been to or places you have learned about.
- relate the events to emotions and events in your own life.

Analyzing the Art
Does this artwork show what it's like to *connect* with another person's (or a writer's) thinking? Explain your answer.

Additional Support

Reading in the Real World

Citizenship Stories of determination are all around us—at home and in our communities. Invite students (alone or in pairs) to interview family members, friends, or neighbors about a time when they showed great determination to succeed. Students may be surprised at the obstacles and challenges ordinary people around them have overcome. Encourage students to share these stories orally or by writing newspaper articles about the information they uncover. Compile the stories into a class newsletter to share with other classes. **AS**

Why Is It Important? You'll be more involved in your reading and able to recall information and ideas better by connecting events, emotions, and characters to your own life.

Study Central Visit www.glencoe.com and click on Study Central to review connecting.

R **How Do I Do It?** Ask yourself:
• Do I know someone like this?
• Have I ever felt this way?
• What else have I read that is like this selection?

Here's how one reader connected to a paragraph in Jim Haskins's biography of Madam C. J. Walker.

> Then one night she had a dream. As she told the story many years later, in her dream "a black man appeared to me and told me what to mix up for my hair. Some of the remedy was grown in Africa, but I sent for it, mixed it, put it on my scalp, and in a few weeks my hair was coming in faster than it had ever fallen out."

I once had a dream about a project for a science fair. I did the project I dreamed about and won a ribbon. I know that dreams sometimes help us solve problems that we are thinking about when we are awake. Sarah's dream helped her solve her problem about losing her hair, just like my dream helped me with my science project.

Practice It!

Below are some experiences that happened to Satchel Paige, the main character in the selection you are about to read. Think about how you might connect to each experience.
• being treated unfairly because of his race
• doing what he loved to do, but under very hard circumstances
• being recognized for his talents

Use It!

As you read "Satchel Paige," practice connecting to the text. Compare what you know and have experienced with what you read about in the selection. Write the connections you make in your Learner's Notebook.

Teach

Study Central Have students access the Web site to review connecting and to complete a related activity.

R Reading Skill

Review Activating Prior Knowledge Say: Part of connecting to the text is activating your prior knowledge and accessing past experience, like you did in Reading Workshop 1. Connecting takes it a step further. Now you must relate your experience and knowledge to the text and determine how they are connected. **OL**

Resources for page 147

✍ Use Key Reading Skills Transparency 5 in *Read Aloud, Think Aloud, Unit 2* to help students practice connecting.

Differentiated Instruction

Class Discussion Discuss with students how filmmakers use camera angle to control perspective. Ask students questions like: If you were filming a horror movie, how might you film a monster to make it seem large? (Possible responses: close up; from below) How might you make the hero seem to be in danger? (Possible response: shoot from above to make him or her seem isolated and tiny) Then ask students to think about how writers use perspective. They may think about how writers omit information, state their opinions, or use tone to convey their attitude towards a subject. Have students keep this in mind as they read the selections. **OL**

Objectives
• Make connections from text to self
• Activate prior knowledge

147

Teach

More About the Author

"People like to tell their stories to folks inclined to listen, and I'm one of those folks." So says Bill Littlefield, radio host, teacher, and author. In his book *Champions: Stories of Ten Remarkable Athletes*, Littlefield emphasizes the courage shown by players who had to overcome such difficult problems as discrimination, poverty, and physical handicaps. Littlefield is a professor at Curry College in Milton, Massachusetts, and the host and writer for a weekly sports show on public radio. He has won five broadcast awards from the Associated Press.

V Vocabulary

Sentences Say: Writing the vocabulary words in sentences can help you remember their meaning. After you've heard your classmates' sentences, write one sentence for each word in your Learner's Notebooks. Choose a sentence other than the sentence you made up. *(Responses will vary.)* **AS**

Before You Read · Satchel Paige

Bill Littlefield

Meet the Author

Bill Littlefield writes sports stories. His stories show young readers why it is important to focus on goals and work hard to reach them. Littlefield says, "As a writer, I've invented the stories of fictional characters, recounted the tales of old baseball scouts and young ballplayers, and retold for young readers the stories of great athletes."

Literature Online

Author Search For more about Bill Littlefield, go to www.glencoe.com.

Objectives (pp. 148–157)
Reading Make connections from text to self
Literature Identify literary elements: point of view
Vocabulary Identify antonyms

Vocabulary Preview

potential (puh TEN shul) *adj.* capable of being; possible **(p. 152)** *Satchel Paige was a potential superstar in Major League Baseball.*

confrontations (kon frun TAY shunz) *n.* unpleasant face-to-face meetings **(p. 154)** *The new baseball player had some confrontations with the coach.*

prejudice (PREJ uh dis) *n.* an opinion that is formed unfairly **(p. 154)** *When Satchel was on the field people cheered, yet they showed their prejudice against him when he was off the field.*

exploits (EK sploytz) *n.* brave acts or deeds **(p. 156)** *The woman who saved the little boy from drowning in the river did not brag about her exploits.*

Class Talk As a class, take turns defining the words and using them in sentences.

English Language Coach

Antonyms Antonyms are words that have opposite meanings. You can use antonyms to help you tell how two things are different, such as *it's cold outside, but hot inside*. Knowing antonyms can help you understand the meanings of other words and help you increase your vocabulary.

Look at the following chart. In the left-hand column, you will see words from the selection "Satchel Paige." In the right-hand column, you will see the antonyms of those words.

Selection Words	Antonyms
narrow	wide
late	early
triumph	failure

Partner Talk In your Learner's Notebook, rewrite the sentences below using the antonym of each underlined word. With a partner, discuss how the meaning of the sentences changed.

1. Satchel slung a pole across his <u>narrow</u> shoulders to hang the bags.

2. Satchel Paige was inducted into the Baseball Hall of Fame <u>late</u> in his life.

3. Satchel Paige had many baseball <u>triumphs</u>.

Additional Support

Literature Online

Author Search To expand students' appreciation of Bill Littlefield, have them access the Web site for additional information and resources.

Differentiated Instruction

Building Background Satchel Paige and the story of African American baseball players may be unfamiliar to students. Invite students to research baseball's history and the racism African American players endured in the beginnings of their careers in the major leagues and the hardships that led up to the induction of Jackie Robinson as the first African American major league player. Suggest that students use both the Internet and the library as sources of information. Have students present their findings to the class. **AL**

Skills Preview

Key Reading Skill: Connecting

As you read, connect your personal experiences with what you read. Think about

- the ways you are like the people in a selection.
- how the events are like experiences you may have had.

Key Literary Element: Point of View

Point of view is the relationship of the writer or narrator to the story. A story may be told by someone in the story. The storyteller refers to himself or herself as *I*, and the reader sees everything through that person's eyes. This is the *first-person point of view.* All autobiographies are written this way. Many novels and short stories also use first-person point of view.

At other times, a story is told by someone outside the story, someone who is not part of what happens. This is called *third-person point of view.* All biographies are written this way, and most magazine and news articles are, too. Many novels and short stories also use third-person point of view.

As you read, use this tip to help you identify the point of view:

- Pay attention to who is telling the story. Is the story-teller a character or person in the story or not?

Write to Learn In your Learner's Notebook, name a story that uses third-person point of view and one that uses first-person. Explain how you know which point of view is used in each.

Get Ready to Read

Connect to the Reading

Think about how it feels to be treated unfairly. Satchel Paige probably felt that it was unfair that he was not allowed to play in the major leagues because he was African American. As you read Satchel's story, think about how you would feel if you were kept from doing the one thing you love to do, even though you're as good as everyone else—or better.

Freewrite Write about something you love and how you would feel about not being able to participate due to other people's prejudices.

Build Background

This biography of Satchel Paige describes his love and talent for baseball as a child, how he got started playing pro baseball, and the challenges he faced as an African American player.

- Before 1947, African American baseball players were not allowed to play in Major League Baseball. They could only play in the Negro Leagues.
- Jackie Robinson became the first African American Major League Baseball player when he signed with the Brooklyn Dodgers in 1947.

Set Purposes for Reading

Read this selection to find out what brought out the best in Satchel Paige as he faced prejudice.

Set Your Own Purpose What else would you like to learn from the selection to help you answer the Big Question? Write your own purpose on the "Satchel Paige" part of the Workshop 2 Foldable.

Literature Online

Interactive Literary Elements Handbook
To review or learn more about the literary elements, go to www.glencoe.com.

Keep Moving

Use these skills as you read the following selection.

Satchel Paige **149**

Teach

L Literary Element

Point of View Divide students into pairs. Have them describe their day so far to their partner. When students finish, point out that they have used the first-person point of view to give their descriptions. Then tell them to retell their narratives, changing the point of view to third person. **OL**

R Reading Skill

Connecting Say: At the beginning of this workshop, you listed some words that expressed how it feels to be treated unfairly. Remember a time when you weren't treated fairly. How did you react? What can you do about a situation that is unfair? *(Responses will vary.)* **AS**

Reading in the Real World

College Students who are planning to further their education need to develop academic research skills. Challenge students to create an exhibit to introduce people to the Negro Leagues. Students who are interested in baseball statistics might prepare a spreadsheet or poster highlighting some key figures. Others might create an illustrated timeline or a photo exhibit with captions. **OL** Those who enjoy research might prepare an annotated bibliography. **AL**

Objectives
- Make connections from text to self
- Identify and analyze author's point of view
- Learn and use new vocabulary

149

Teach

Viewing the Photo

Ask: What does this photo of Satchel Paige tell you about how he feels about playing baseball? *(Possible response: He looks like he really enjoys it.)* **AS**

L Literary Element

Point of View Ask: How would the paragraph be different if it were written from the first-person point of view? *(Possible response: It would likely focus more on the way Satchel Paige feels as he approaches the pitcher's mound than on the way he looks and the crowd's reaction.)* **OL**

Readability Scores
Dale-Chall: 6.4
DRP: 58
Lexile: 1130

Satchel Paige

by Bill Littlefield

Practice the Skills

Late in the afternoon of July 9, 1948, Leroy "Satchel" Paige began the long walk from the bullpen to the mound at Cleveland's Municipal Stadium. He didn't hurry. He never hurried. As he said himself, he "kept the juices flowing by jangling gently" as he moved. The crowd roared its appreciation. This was the fellow they'd come to see. **1**

When Satchel finally reached the mound, Cleveland manager Lou Boudreau took the ball from starting pitcher Bob Lemon, who would eventually be voted into the Hall of Fame but had tired that day, and gave it to Paige. Probably he said something like, "Shut 'em down, Satchel." Whatever he said, Paige had no doubt heard the words a thousand times. Though he was a rookie with the Indians that year, no pitcher in the history of baseball had ever been more thoroughly prepared for a job. He kicked at the rubber, looked in for the sign, and got set to throw. In a moment, twenty-odd years later than it should have happened, Satchel Paige would deliver his first pitch in the big leagues.

1   Key Literary Element

Point of View What point of view is this selection told through? What pronoun gives you a clue? **L**

150 UNIT 2   What Brings Out the Best in You?

Additional Support

Literature Focus Lesson

Character Write on the board: *what the character says; what the character does and thinks; how the character looks;* and *how others react to the character.* Tell students that these are the four methods of characterization. Ask students to find examples of each method in the selection. **OL** Challenge students to evaluate the author's skill. Ask them to use examples from the text to explain to what extent Littlefield gives readers a sense of what Satchel Paige is like. **AL**

Visual Vocabulary
A *satchel* is a type of suitcase.

The tall, skinny kid named Leroy Paige became Satchel Paige one day at the railroad station in Mobile, Alabama. He was carrying bags for the folks getting on and off the trains, earning all the nickels and dimes he could to help feed his ten brothers and sisters. Eventually it occurred to him that if he slung a pole across his narrow shoulders and hung the bags, or satchels, on the ends of the pole, he could carry for more people at once and collect more nickels and dimes. It worked, but it looked a little funny. "You look like some kind of ol' satchel tree," one of his friends told him, and the nickname stuck. **2**

Even in those days, before he was a teenager, Satchel Paige could throw hard and accurately. Years later, Paige swore that when his mother would send him out into the yard to get a chicken for dinner, he would brain the bird[1] with a rock. "I used to kill *flying* birds with rocks, too," he said. "Most people need shotguns to do what I did with rocks."

It was not a talent that would go unnoticed for long. He was pitching for the semipro[2] Mobile Tigers before he was eighteen . . . or maybe before he was sixteen, or before he was twelve. There is some confusion about exactly when Satchel Paige was born, and Satchel never did much to clarify the matter. But there never has been any confusion about whether he could pitch. His first steady job in baseball was with the Chattanooga Black Lookouts. He was paid fifty dollars a month. In the seasons that followed he would also pitch for the Birmingham Black Barons, the Nashville Elite Giants, the

---

1. To **brain the bird** means to "hit it in the head."
2. To be **semipro** means the team member is only paid to play part-time and may have another full-time job.

Practice the Skills

2 Key Reading Skill

Connecting Have you ever had a nickname? Who gave it to you? How did you get it?

R

Satchel Paige and his teammates on the Pittsburgh Crawfords pose as the champions of the Negro National League in 1935.

Satchel Paige **151**

Reading Fluency

Sequence of Events Explain that biographies are usually written in chronological order. However, authors sometimes interrupt the sequence of events to give readers background information. The author goes back to Satchel Paige's childhood on this page. Ask students to point out the time order words the author uses to help readers keep track of when things happened. Possible responses might include "even in those days, before he was a teenager," and "in the seasons that followed." **OL**

Teach

C Critical Thinking

Analysis Ask: How does Leroy Paige get the name Satchel? (He carried a lot of bags for travelers so a friend said he looked like a "satchel tree.") **BL Ask:** Do you think this is a good nickname? Explain. (Answers will vary.) **AS**

R Reading Skill

Connecting Ask: What are you especially good at? (Responses will vary.) How does it feel to be good at something? (Possible response: It makes me feel good about myself and gives me self-confidence.) **AS Ask:** How are your feelings similar to Satchel's? (Possible response: When the author quotes Satchel, he shows that Satchel is proud of his ability to throw.) **OL**

Viewing the Photo

Say: This is a photo of the Pittsburgh Crawfords baseball club in 1935. What do you see when you look at this picture? How is it different from pictures of professional sports teams today? (Possible responses: I see a line of African American men in front of a bus. Pictures of teams today show all different races, and teams rarely ride buses anymore.) **OL**

Objectives
• Identify and analyze author's point of view
• Make connections from text to self
• Analyze text
• Use text features: photographs
• Interpret and analyze character

151

Teach

R Reading Skill

Connecting Ask: Have you ever been ready to play a game or participate in another activity only to find out that it was canceled? If so, how did you feel? (Responses will vary.) How do you think Satchel Paige and his teammates felt when they were not able to play games? (Possible responses: disappointed, sad, angry) OL

EL Language Coach

Antonyms Review the antonyms for *appreciative* and *healthier* that students wrote in their Learner's Notebooks. *(Possible responses: appreciative—ungrateful; healthier—sicker.)* If students chose different antonyms, suggest that they include all responses in their notebooks for future reference. **AS**

Baltimore Black Sox, the Pittsburgh Crawfords, and the Kansas City Monarchs, among other teams.

If those names are not as familiar sounding as those of the New York Yankees, the Los Angeles Dodgers, or the Boston Red Sox, it's because they were all clubs in the Negro leagues, not the major leagues. Today the presence of black baseball players in the big leagues is taken for granted. Hank Aaron is the greatest of the home run hitters, and Rickey Henderson has stolen more bases than any other big leaguer. But before 1947, neither of them would have had the opportunity to do what they have done. Until Brooklyn Dodger general manager Branch Rickey signed Jackie Robinson, black players had no choice but to play for one of the all-black teams, and making that choice, they faced hardships no major-leaguer today could imagine.

Players in the Negro leagues crowded into broken-down cars and bumped over rutted[3] roads to makeshift[4] ball fields with lights so bad that every pitch was a **potential** weapon. Then they drove all night for an afternoon game three hundred miles away. On good days they played before big, **appreciative** crowds in parks they'd rented from the major league teams in Chicago, New York, or Pittsburgh. On bad days they learned that the team they were playing for was too broke to finish the season, and they would have to look **R** for a **healthier** team that could use them, or else find a factory job. **3**

It took talent, hard work, and a sense of humor to survive in the Negro leagues, and Satchel Paige had a lot of all three. But he didn't just survive. He prospered. Everybody knows about the fastball, the curve, and the slider. But Satchel threw a "bee" ball, which, he said, "would always *be* where I wanted it to *be*." He featured a trouble ball, which, of course, gave the hitters a lot of trouble. Even the few who could see it couldn't hit it. Sometimes he'd come at them with his hesitation pitch, a delivery so mysterious that the man at the plate would sometimes swing before the ball left Satchel's hand.

---

3. A road that's been well-worn by wheels or travel is **rutted.**

4. *Makeshift* means "a temporary substitute."

Vocabulary

potential (puh TEN shul) *adj*. capable of being; possible

Practice the Skills

3 English Language Coach

Antonyms Find the words *appreciative* and *healthier* in this paragraph. Do you know what they mean? List these words in your Learner's Notebook. Then write the antonym for each word. Use a dictionary if you need help. **EL**

Additional Support

Reading in the Real World

Citizenship Students who are good at geography, or those who need extra help learning about cities in the United States may enjoy finding the cities of the teams Satchel Paige played for. Give students copies of a map of the United States. Have them find the cities of the teams Satchel Paige played for that are listed on pages 151–152. They can draw baseballs or other symbols on the map to show particular cities. You may wish to compile students' maps in a classroom display. **EL BL**

Nor was pitching his sole triumph. Early in his career Satchel Paige began building a reputation as a storyteller, a spinner of tall tales as well as shutouts. He particularly liked to recall an occasion upon which he was asked to come on in relief of a pitcher who'd left men on first and third with nobody out. "It was a tight situation," Satchel would say.

We only had a one-run lead, and that was looking mighty slim. But I had an idea. When I left the bench, I stuck a baseball in my pocket, so when the manager gave me the game ball on the mound, I had two. I went into my stretch just like usual. Then I threw one ball to first and the other to third. It was a good pick-off move, you see, and it fooled the batter, too. He swung, even though there was no ball to swing at. Those boys at first and third were both out, of course, and the umpire[5] called strike three on the batter, so that was it for the inning. It's always good to save your strength when you can. **4**

Major-leaguers today make enough money so that they don't have to work over the winter, but it hasn't always been so. Big-leaguers and Negro-leaguers alike used to make extra money after their regular seasons ended by putting together makeshift teams and playing each other wherever they could draw a paying crowd. This practice was called barnstorming, and Satchel Paige was the world champion at it. For thirty years, from 1929 to 1958, he played baseball summer and winter. When it was too cold to play in the Negro league cities, he played in Cuba, Mexico, and the Dominican Republic. In Venezuela he battled a boa constrictor in the outfield, or so he said, and in Ciudad Trujillo[6] he dodged the machine-gun fire of fans who'd bet on the losing team.

---

5. An *umpire* is the official in a baseball game. The umpire makes sure the players follow the rules.
6. *Cuidad Trujillo* (SEE yoo dahd troo HEE oh) is the Spanish name for a city in northwestern Venezuela.

The first successful Negro Baseball League was started in 1920. The Negro Leagues played eleven World Series and created their own All-Star game that became the biggest black sports attraction in the country. This picture shows players of the Negro Leagues.

Practice the Skills

4 Key Literary Element

Point of View Here Satchel Paige is telling a story. Is he the main subject of his own story? How do you know? What point of view is he using? How do you know? **L**

Satchel Paige **153**

Teach

L Literary Element

Point of View Ask: Why do you think the author included a story in Satchel Paige's own words? *(Possible responses: to add variety; to give a sense of what the ballplayer is like; to show that Paige is a good storyteller; to increase credibility by using a primary source)* **OL**

R Reading Skill

Review Identifying Main Idea Say: The author contrasts the money major league players make today to what players in the Big Leagues and Negro Leagues used to make. How does that contrast help you find the main idea of the paragraph? *(Possible response: The main idea isn't directly stated, but the contrast leads readers to conclude that baseball players were not well-paid.)* **OL**

Differentiated Instruction

Using Graphic Organizers Draw the graphic organizer below on the board. Work with students to find examples of Satchel's talent, hard work, and sense of humor. Then record the examples in the appropriate boxes. **OL** Work with students to find more examples and develop each detail box into a paragraph. **AL**

Main Idea: Satchel Paige had the qualities needed to succeed

↓

Talent:

Hard work:

Sense of humor:

Objectives
• Identify and analyze author's point of view
• Identify main ideas and supporting details
• Identify and use antonyms
• Make connections from text to self

Teach

L Literary Element

Point of View Ask: How does the third-person narrator feel about the way Satchel Paige was treated? *(He is angered about the prejudice Satchel faced and believes he deserved much better.)* **Ask:** How does the third-person narrator feel about Satchel's talent? What evidence from the text supports your answer? *(Possible response: He feels that Satchel was extremely talented and deserved a place in the big leagues much sooner than he got one. The narrator's quotations from other famous and talented baseball players support this idea.)* **AS**

BQ BIG Question

Ask: What do you think brought out the best in Satchel Paige? *(Responses will vary.)* **AS**

Throughout the early years of these adventures, the years of Satchel's prime, he often barnstormed against the best white ballplayers of his day. St. Louis Cardinal great Dizzy Dean once told him, "You're a better pitcher than I ever hope to be." Paige beat Bob Feller and struck out Babe Ruth. And when Joe DiMaggio, considered by some the most multi-talented ballplayer ever, beat out an infield hit against Paige in 1936, DiMaggio turned to his teammates and said, "Now I know I can make it with the Yankees. I finally got a hit off of ol' Satch."

L Everywhere these **confrontations** took place, Satchel Paige would hear the same thing: "If only you were white, you'd be a star in the big leagues." The fault, of course, was not with Satchel. The fault and the shame were with major league baseball, which stubbornly, stupidly clung to the same **prejudice** that characterized many institutions in the United States besides baseball. Prejudice has not yet disappeared from the game. Black players are far less likely than their white counterparts[7] to be hired as managers or general managers. But today's black players can thank Robinson, Paige, and a handful of other pioneers for the opportunities they enjoy. **5**

BQ Though the color line prevented Satchel Paige from pitching in the company his talent and hard work should have earned for him, he was not bitter or defeated. Ignorant white fans would sometimes taunt him, but he kept their insults in perspective. "Some of them would call you names," he said of his early years on the road, "but most of them would cheer you." Years later he worked to shrug off the pain caused by the restaurants that would not serve him, the

Bob Feller (Hall of Fame pitcher for the Cleveland Indians) and Satchel Paige in 1948, the year the Indians won the World Series

Practice the Skills

5 Reviewing Skills

Identifying Main Idea and Supporting Details What is the main idea of this paragraph? What details support the main idea?

---

7. Here, *counterparts* refers to people who hold similar positions.

Vocabulary

confrontations (kon frun TAY shunz) *n.* unpleasant face-to-face meetings

prejudice (PREJ uh dis) *n.* an opinion that is formed unfairly

Additional Support

Literature Focus Lesson

Tone: Tone is an author's attitude towards a subject. One way to find the tone is to look at the descriptive words an author uses. Review the student page above. Ask students to list words that tell them how the author feels about prejudice. *(Possible responses: shame, stubbornly, stupidly)* The author says,

"Prejudice has not yet disappeared from the game." Have students discuss whether they think he believes that it should disappear. Students should use evidence from the text, such as the "color line" reference to support their answers. **OL** hotels that would not rent him a room, the fans who would roar for his bee ball but would not acknowledge him on the street the next day. "Fans all holler the same at a ball game," he would say, as if the racists[8] and the racist system had never touched him at all.

When he finally got the chance to become the first black pitcher in the American League at age forty-two (or forty-six, or forty-eight), he made the most of it. On that first day in Cleveland, Satchel Paige did the job he'd never doubted he could do. First he smiled for all the photographers. Then he told the butterflies in his stomach to leave off their flapping around. Then he shut down the St. Louis Browns for two innings before being lifted for a pinch hitter.

And still there were doubters. "Sure," they said to each other the next day when they read the sports section. "The old man could work two innings against the Browns. Who couldn't?"

But Satchel Paige fooled 'em, as he'd been fooling hitters for twenty-five years and more. He won a game in relief six days later, his first major league win. Then on August 3 he started a game against the Washington Senators before 72,000 people. Paige went seven innings and won. In his next two starts he threw shutouts against the Chicago White Sox, and through the waning[9] months of that summer, his only complaint was that he was "a little tired from underwork." The routine on the major league level must have been pretty leisurely for a fellow who'd previously pitched four or five times a week.

Satchel Paige finished the 1948 season with six wins and only one loss. He'd allowed the opposing teams an average of just over two runs a game. Paige was named Rookie of the Year, an honor he might well have achieved twenty years earlier if he'd had the chance. The sports-writers of the day

Satchel Paige played in his first Major League game on July 9, 1948, at age 42.

8. *Racists* are people who believe that one race is better than another.
9. Here, *waning* means "nearing the end of it."

Satchel Paige **155**

Teach

EL Language Coach

Jargon Say: Each profession has its own jargon, just as baseball does. For example, *shut down,* and *pinch hitter* are examples of baseball jargon. Do you see any more unfamiliar jargon in this story? *(Responses will vary.)* **Say:** Use a dictionary or a baseball reference to look up and identify the meaning of unfamiliar jargon. **AS**

C Critical Thinking

Synthesis Ask: Are there any athletes today that remind you of Satchel Paige? If so, who are they and how are they like Paige? *(Responses will vary.)* Do you think athletes like Satchel Paige make a difference in the world? Why or why not? *(Responses will vary.)* Lead a group discussion about Satchel Paige and other athletes like him and the effect they have on society. **OL AL**

Reading in the Real World

Citizenship The author says, ". . . today's black players can thank Robinson, Paige, and a handful of other pioneers for the opportunities they enjoy." Ask students to share how they think Satchel Paige helped other black players. *(Possible responses: He was an outstanding athlete who proved that stereotypes about black players were wrong. He never let racism drag him down or provoke him. He worked to get other black players recognized.)* Discuss whether Paige still serves as a good role model today. **OL**

Objectives
• Identify and analyze author's point of view
• Identify and use antonyms
• Clarify word meanings
• Synthesize information

Teach

BQ **BIG Question**

Ask: What words or phrases describe the attitude Satchel Paige shows by saying, "Ain't no other way to take them"? *(Possible responses: patient, uncomplaining, tolerant, resigned, making the best of a bad situation)* Write students' responses on the board. Have students rank the responses, using 1 for the word or phrase that best expresses Paige's attitude. Tally the rankings and identify the top three words and/or phrases. **Ask:** What do these words and phrases show about Satchel Paige? *(Possible response: They show how he accepted others' ignorance without a fight because he was so confident in himself and his own abilities. He did not need outside approval.)* **OL** **AL**

---

agreed that without Satchel's contribution, the Indians, who won the pennant, would have finished second at best. Many of the writers were dismayed when Satchel appeared for only two-thirds of an inning in the World Series that fall. Paige, too, was disappointed that the manager hadn't chosen to use him more, but he was calm in the face of what others might have considered an insult. The writers told him, "You sure take things good." Satchel smiled and said, "Ain't no other way to take them." **BQ**

Satchel Paige outlasted the rule that said he couldn't play in the big leagues because he was black. Then he made fools of the people who said he couldn't get major league hitters out because he was too old. But his big league numbers over several years—twenty-eight wins and thirty-two saves—don't begin to tell the story of Paige's unparalleled[10] career. Playing for teams that no longer exist in leagues that came and went with the seasons, Satchel Paige pitched in some 2,500 baseball games. Nobody has ever pitched in more. And he had such fun at it. Sometimes he'd accept offers to pitch in two cities on the same day. He'd strike out the side for three innings in one game, then fold his long legs into his car and race down the road toward the next ballpark. If the police could catch him, they would stop him for speeding. But when they recognized him, as often as not they'd escort him to the second game with sirens howling, well aware that there might be a riot in the park if Satchel Paige didn't show up as advertised. Once he'd arrived, he'd instruct his infielders and outfielders to sit down for an inning, then he'd strike out the side again.

For his talent, his energy, and his showmanship, Satchel Paige was the most famous of the Negro league players, but when he got some measure of recognition in the majors, he urged the writers to remember that there had been lots of other great ballplayers in those Negro league games. He named them, and he told their stories. He made their **exploits** alive and real for generations of fans who'd never have known. **6**

---

10. If something is ***unparalleled,*** nothing is equal to it or better than it.

Vocabulary

exploits (EK sploytz) *n.* brave acts or deeds

Practice the Skills

6 **BIG Question**

In this paragraph, how does Satchel Paige show that he is the best person that he can be? Write your answer on the "Satchel Paige" part of the Workshop 2 Foldable. Your answer will help you with the Unit Challenge later.

Additional Support

Differentiated Instruction

Research Some students might be interested in researching the Baseball Hall of Fame. Invite students to use the library or Internet to find more information about the organization. Suggest that students investigate the ratio of white to African American players who have been inducted. You might also have students locate the years the African American players were accepted into the Hall of Fame. Allow students time to share their findings with the rest of the class. **AL**

In 1971, the Baseball Hall of Fame in Cooperstown, New York, inducted[11] Satchel Paige. The action was part of the Hall's attempt to remedy baseball's shame, the color line. The idea was to honor Paige and some of the other great Negro league players like Josh Gibson and Cool Papa Bell, however late that honor might come. Satchel Paige could have rejected that gesture. He could have told the baseball establishment that what it was doing was too little, too late. But when the time came for Satchel Paige to speak to the crowd gathered in front of the Hall of Fame to celebrate his triumphs, he told the people, "I am the proudest man on the face of the earth today." **7**

Satchel Paige was the first Negro League star elected to the National Baseball Hall of Fame.

Satchel Paige, whose autobiography was entitled *Maybe I'll Pitch Forever,* died in Kansas City in 1982. He left behind a legend as large as that of anyone who ever played the game, as well as a long list of achievements celebrated in story and song—and in at least one fine poem, by Samuel Allen:

To Satch

Sometimes I feel like I will *never* stop
Just go on forever
Till one fine mornin'
I'm gonna reach up and grab me a handfulla stars
Swing out my long lean leg
And whip three hot strikes burnin' down the heavens
And look over at God and say
How about that! ○

Practice the Skills

7 Key Reading Skill

Connecting How would you feel if you were finally recognized for your work after years of being snubbed? How would you act? **R**

---

11. When players are **inducted** into the Hall of Fame, they are honored by being admitted into this special group.

Satchel Paige **157**

Teach

R Reading Skill

Connecting After students describe how they would react to belated recognition, have them compare their reactions to Satchel Paige's response to being inducted into the Baseball Hall of Fame. **Ask:** Do you think his behavior was something to be proud of? Why? *(Possible response: Yes, he accepted the praise of the league because he honored the sport and the other African American players who had been snubbed.)* **OL**

Assess

CheckPoint

Use the CheckPoint questions provided on Presentation Plus! to check for comprehension of the selection. These questions can be used with interactive response keypads for immediate student feedback.

English Language Coach

Positive and Negative Connotations Work with students to make a list of adjectives that describe Satchel Paige such as *talented, energetic, entertaining, famous,* and *generous.* First, direct their attention to the paragraph beginning "For his talent . . ." on page 156. Then, make a two-column chart, headed Positive and Negative. Write students' suggestions for positive adjectives that describe Paige in the first column. To complete the chart, ask students to suggest antonyms to the words in the Positive column. **EL**

Objectives
- Identify and use antonyms
- Make connections from text to self
- Distinguish positive and negative connotations

Assess

Resources for page 158

📁 Selection Quick Check, p. 13

📁 Selection and Unit Assessment, p. 15

💿 ExamView Assessment Suite

💿 Interactive Tutor: Self-Assessment

Students can respond to the *After You Read* items in their Learner's Notebooks or on a separate sheet of paper.

Answering the

1. Responses will vary.

2. Baseball was segregated until 1947.

3. Paige was hired for $50 per month. Players barn-stormed—played extra games in the off-season.

Critical Thinking

4. Possible response: African Americans could not play in the big leagues until Jackie Robinson broke the color line.

5. Possible response: Today he would have a good salary and not have to wait to play in the major leagues.

6. Responses will vary. Students may note that Paige was talented, hardworking, energetic, entertaining, proud of his skill, unprejudiced, and able to rise above discrimination.

After You Read · Satchel Paige

Answering the BIG Question

1. After reading "Satchel Paige," why do you think it is important for people to be the best they can be? Support your answer with details from the selection.

2. **Recall** Why wasn't Satchel Paige allowed to play in the major leagues?
   Tip **Right There** You will find the answer in the text.

3. **Summarize** How much did some players in the Negro Leagues earn per month? What else did they do to make a living?
   Tip **Think and Search** The answers are in the text, but the details are not all in one place.

Critical Thinking

4. **Analyze** Why were the Negro Leagues created?
   Tip **Author and Me** You will find clues in the text, but you must also use the information in your head.

5. **Predict** If Satchel Paige was a young baseball player today, how would his life be different?
   Tip **Author and Me** You will find clues in the text, but you must also use the information in your head.

6. **Evaluate** What kind of person do you think Satchel Paige was? How can you tell? Support your answer with details from the selection.
   Tip **Author and Me** You will find clues in the text, but you must also use the information in your head.

Write About Your Reading

Pretend you are Satchel Paige. Write a letter to the commissioner of baseball telling why you should be allowed in the major leagues.
As you write, remember

• your letter should have a salutation, a body, and a closing
• each paragraph in your letter should be indented
• each paragraph should contain a main idea and supporting details

Objectives (pp. 158–159)
Reading Make connections from text to self
Literature Identify literary elements: point of view
Writing Write a letter: persuasive
Grammar Identify parts of speech: pronoun antecedents

Write About Your Reading

Possible response:
December 28, 1936
Dear Commissioner:
   I love playing baseball, and I'm good at it. I can fool a batter into swinging at the ball before I've even thrown it. Joe DiMaggio once said, "Now I know I can make it with the Yankees. I finally got a hit off of ol' Satch."
   The Negro Leagues are full of other good players who'd like a chance to make it in the majors. Please judge us by our ability instead of the color of our skin.
Sincerely,
Satchel Paige

Skills Review

Key Reading Skill: Connecting

7. What would you have done if you wanted to play on a team but were not allowed to because of the color of your skin? What would you do to make the situation better?

8. How did the activities on page 149 help you connect with Satchel Paige and his story? Rank the activities in order of helpfulness, with 1 being the most helpful. Explain your rankings.
   - Using the advice in **Key Reading Skill: Connecting**
   - Doing the **Freewrite** in **Connect to the Reading**
   - Reading the facts in **Build Background**
   - **Set Purposes for Reading**

Key Literary Element: Point of View

9. What is point of view?

10. Is the selection "Satchel Paige" told mostly in first-person or third-person point of view?

11. Who tells the story—the main character, Satchel Paige, or a narrator outside the story?

Reviewing Skills: Identifying Main Idea and Supporting Details

12. In your opinion, what is the main idea of the selection "Satchel Paige"? Support your answer with details from the selection.

Vocabulary Check

Rewrite each sentence below, replacing the underlined word or phrase with the correct vocabulary word.

prejudice exploits confrontations potential

13. Satchel Paige reached his full <u>capability</u>.

14. <u>Unfair opinions</u> kept a lot of talented players out of the major leagues.

15. There were many <u>unpleasant meetings</u> on the ball field between black and white players.

16. Satchel Paige told stories about the <u>brave deeds</u> of other ball players.

17. **English Language Coach** Find and write down an antonym for each of the following words:

   throw   hard   triumph   shame   familiar

Grammar Link: Pronoun Antecedents

The noun or group of words that a pronoun refers to is called its *antecedent*.

Satchel Paige showed that **he** was a talented pitcher.

| antecedent | | pronoun |

When you use a pronoun, be sure that it refers to its antecedent clearly. Read the following sentence.

Mark competed against David for the starting lineup. ***He*** *waited to see who won.*

The second sentence is not clear because the word *he* could refer to either Mark or David.

Clear pronoun antecedents make sure readers know to whom or what each pronoun refers.

Grammar Practice

Write the antecedent of the underlined pronoun.

18. I brought my baseball cards to school. I wanted to show <u>them</u> to my friends.

19. I also play on a Little League team. <u>It</u> is in first place.

Writing Application Look back at your Write About Your Reading assignment. Make sure your antecedents are clear.

Web Activities For eFlashcards, Selection Quick Checks, and other Web activities, go to www.glencoe.com.

Satchel Paige **159**

Skills Review

Key Reading Skill: Connecting

7. Responses will vary.

8. Responses will vary.

Key Literary Element: Point of View

9. Point of view is the perspective from which a story is told (first or third person).

10. It is told in third person.

11. The story is told by a narrator.

Reviewing Skills: Identifying Main Idea

12. Responses will vary.

Vocabulary Check

13. potential
14. Prejudice
15. confrontations
16. exploits

Close

Ask students to summarize what they learned from the selection to help them answer the Big Question.

Web Activities Have students access the Web site for interactive activities that will help them assess their understanding of the selection.

17. **English Language Coach**
    Possible responses:
    throw (catch)
    hard (soft)
    triumph (failure)
    shame (pride)
    familiar (exotic)

Grammar Link: Pronoun Antecedents

Grammar Practice

18. baseball cards
19. team

Teach

More About the Author

Sara Van Alstyne Allen apparently published a few short stories in pulp fiction magazines during the 1930s. Her poem "One Ocean" was published in *The Nation* Jan. 21, 1961 (Vol 192, Issue 3). Her book *The Season's Name* was published in 1968 by Golden Quill Press. She was one of the poets included in an anthology by Steuben Glass, in which glass designers interpreted poems in crystal.

V Vocabulary

Vocabulary File **Say:** Copy the vocabulary words and their definitions in your Learner's Notebooks. Include an original sentence that shows how to use each word properly. *(Responses will vary.)* **OL** English language learners might also include the pronunciation keys in their notebooks. **EL**

Before You Read Song for a Surf-Rider

Meet the Author

In the 1930s four of Sara Van Alstyne Allen's poems appeared in *Street & Smith's Love Story* magazine. Her poem "Vine in Early Spring" was published in *Poetry* magazine in 1941. *The Season's Name*, her book of poems, was published by Golden Quill Press in 1968. In the poem "Song for a Surf-Rider," Sara Van Alstyne Allen uses some very striking figurative language when she compares the sea to a horse—and surfing to horseback riding.

Author Search For more about Sara Van Alstyne Allen, go to www .glencoe.com.

Objectives (pp. 160–161)
Reading Make connections from text to self
Literature Identify literary elements: point of view

Vocabulary Preview

mane (mayn) *n.* the long, thick hair on an animal's neck or head **(p. 161)** *Jewel braided her horse's mane with ribbon.*

emerald (EM ur uld) *adj.* brightly or richly green **(p. 161)** *The emerald ocean was beautiful under the orange sunset.*

quivers (KWIV urz) *v.* to shake or move with a slight trembling motion **(p. 161)** *Knowing we would soon surf on the Pacific Ocean made us quiver with excitement.*

Key Reading Skill: Connecting

Read the poem and connect your personal experiences with those of the speaker. Think about what you know about surfing and horses.

Key Literary Element: Point of View

Point of view is the speaker's relationship to the story or poem. Poets can use the first-person point of view if they are telling about themselves, such as "As I was going to St. Ives I met a man with seven wives." The third-person point of view is used in poems like "Jack and Jill."

Get Ready to Read

Connect to the Reading

The speaker loves surfing and compares it with horse-riding. What do you love to do? What would you compare it to in a poem?

Build Background

Surfing, or surfboarding, is the sport of riding on a wave while standing or lying on a surfboard. It's a popular sport all over the world.

Set Purposes for Reading

Read the poem "Song for a Surf-Rider" to find out if surfing helps the speaker be the best that he or she can be.

Set Your Own Purpose What else would you like to learn from this poem to help you answer the Big Question? Write your own purpose on the "Song for a Surf-Rider" part of the Workshop 2 Foldable.

Keep Moving ➡

Use these skills as you read the following selection.

Additional Support

Author Search To expand students' appreciation of Sara Van Alstyne Allen, have them access the Web site for additional information and resources.

Literature Focus Lesson

Extended Metaphor Explain to students that a metaphor is a comparison between two seemingly unlike things. Often the author speaks of one thing as if it were another. Tell students that an extended metaphor is one that lasts throughout a work, such as a poem or speech. Have students identify the extended metaphor in "Song for a Surf-Rider." *(Allen talks about the sea as if it were a horse.)* Have students take a few moments and analyze the poem line by line, identifying the details that are used to support the larger metaphor. *(mane of foam; waves crashing as hoofbeats; the ceaseless waves as a mighty heart)* Remind students that some metaphors are implied, not directly stated. **OL**

Song for a Surf-Rider

by Sara Van Alstyne Allen

I ride the horse that is the sea.
His **mane** of foam flows wild and free.
His eyes flash with an **emerald** fire.
His mighty heart will never tire.
5 His hoofbeats echo on the sand.
He **quivers** as I raise my hand.
We race together, the sea and I,
Under the watching summer sky
To where the magic islands lie. **1 2 3** ○

Vocabulary

mane (mayn) *n.* the long, thick hair on an animal's neck or head

emerald (EM ur uld) *adj.* brightly or richly green

quiver (KWIV urz) *v.* to shake or move with a slight trembling motion

Practice the Skills

1 Key Reading Skill

Connecting Have you ever gone swimming in an ocean, lake, or at the beach? What was it like? **R**

2 Key Literary Element

Point of View Who or what is the speaker talking about? From what point of view is the poem written? **L**

3 BIG Question

What do you think brings out the best in the speaker? Explain your answer on the "Song for a Surf-Rider" part of the Workshop 2 Foldable. **BQ**

Song for a Surf-Rider **161**

Teach

R Reading Skill

Connecting Ask: What do you think the person in the photograph is seeing, smelling, hearing, and feeling? *(Possible response: the smell of the ocean, the taste of saltwater, the waves crashing on the shore, the sun in the sky)* **AS**

L Literary Element

Point of View BL Ask: What relationship does the speaker describe? *(his or her relationship with the sea)* **OL**

BQ BIG Question

Ask: What word suggests that the narrator finds a challenge in the sea? *(race)* When the challenge is met, what happens? *("we race together . . . To where the magic islands lie")* **OL**

Assess

CheckPoint

Use the CheckPoint questions provided on Presentation Plus! to check for comprehension of the selection. These questions can be used with interactive response key pads for immediate student feedback.

Differentiated Instruction

Small Group Project:
Animation Have students work in groups to plan an animated version of "Song for a Surf-Rider." Different groups might develop concept sketches that show how the horse and/or waves, the narrator, and the background might look. Students could also identify actors who would make good narrators and suggest appropriate music and sound effects. Have students share their sketches and sound ideas with the class. Students with an interest in animation might want to create storyboards or a multimedia presentation based on the poem. **AL**

Objectives
• Make connections from text to self
• Identify and analyze author's point of view
• Recognize distinctive features of poetry
• Learn and use new vocabulary

161

Assess

Resources for page 162

📁 Selection Quick Check, p. 14

📁 Selection and Unit Assessment, p. 16

💿 ExamView Assessment Suite

💿 Interactive Tutor: Self-Assessment

Students can respond to the *After You Read* items in their Learner's Notebooks or on a separate sheet of paper.

Answering the
BIG Question

1. Responses will vary.
2. The speaker is describing the sea.
3. The narrator races with the sea.

Critical Thinking

4. Possible response: The sound of the waves echoes like hoofbeats.
5. Responses will vary. Students may mention that the energy of the tides renews itself after every ebb.
6. Possible response: The speaker will always feel connected to the sea.

After You Read   Song for a Surf-Rider

Answering the BIG Question

1. The ocean seems to bring out the best in the poem's speaker. Have you ever felt so connected to something that it brought out the best in you? Explain.

2. **Recall** What is the speaker describing?
   Tip **Right There** You will find the answer in the poem.

3. **Recall** Who or what does the speaker race with?
   Tip **Right There** You will find the answer in the poem.

Critical Thinking

4. **Infer** What is really making the sound of "hoofbeats"?
   Tip **Author and Me** You will find clues in the poem, but you must also use the information in your head.

5. **Draw Conclusions** Why will the "horse"—the sea—never tire?
   Tip **On My Own** Answer from your own experiences.

6. **Evaluate** Do you think the speaker will ever tire of surfing? Explain.
   Tip **Author and Me** You will find clues in the poem, but you must also use the information in your head.

Write About Your Reading

The speaker helps us understand how free she feels on a surfboard by making it seem like riding a horse. Horses and surfing have little in common, but the poem helps us to link the two.

Think about your favorite activity and something that seems very different from that, such as playing basketball and flying. Write a poem that describes the connection you make between your favorite activity and something different.

What do you see? What do you hear? How do you feel?

Use descriptive words that help your poem's reader to experience the things you are writing about. Your poem does not have to rhyme.

Objectives (pp. 162–163)
Reading Make connections from text to self
Literature Identify literary elements: point of view
Writing Write a poem • Use literary elements: imagery, sensory details
Grammar Identify parts of speech: indefinite pronouns

162 UNIT 2 What Brings Out the Best in You?

Write About Your Reading

Possible response:

Writing as Sumo Wrestling

I gather myself as if I were going into the ring to meet an opponent twice my size, massive with stored fat from meals of sumo wrestler stew, hard-eyed, hunkered down, waiting for the slightest error that allows him to send me sprawling to the mat.

I am nervous, yet confident, for I have gathered my thoughts and polished my weapons: my synonyms, my pronouns, my periods and semicolons. If my subject starts to defeat me, I can still win. I can rewrite the wrestler and change the ending.

Skills Review

Key Reading Skill: Connecting

7. Did writing a poem about your favorite activity help you to connect to the selection? Why or why not?

Key Literary Element: Point of View

8. *His* and *he* refer to whom or what in the poem?

9. From what point of view is the poem written?

Vocabulary Check

Copy the sentences onto a separate sheet of paper and complete with the correct vocabulary word below.

mane   emerald   quiver

10. The lion's long and heavy ___ framed its face.

11. To tremble is also to ___.

12. The ___ grass looked beautiful after the rain.

13. **English Language Coach** In your Learner's Notebook, write sentences that correctly use the antonym for each of these words: *wild*, *never*, and *together*.

Grammar Link: Indefinite Pronouns

An *indefinite pronoun* is a pronoun that does not refer to a particular person, place, or thing.

Does **anyone** know the poem "Song for a Surf-Rider"?

Most indefinite pronouns are either singular or plural.

Singular: another, anybody, anyone, anything, each, either, everybody, everyone, everything, much, neither, nobody, no one, nothing, one, somebody, someone, something

Plural: both, few, many, others, several

Some indefinite pronouns can be singular or plural:

all, any, most, none, some

Often, an indefinite pronoun will be the subject of a sentence. The verb must agree with the indefinite pronoun in number.

Everyone likes the poem. [singular]

Many enjoy reading it aloud. [plural]

All of poetry uses sound to convey a message. [singular]

We read many poems. **All** are very interesting. [plural]

Grammar Practice

Write each sentence, using the verb in parentheses that correctly agrees with the indefinite pronoun. Underline each indefinite pronoun and write whether it is *singular* or *plural*.

14. Some (have, has) important skills that help them be the best they can be.

15. One of them (is, are) Dwain, who knows how to fix bikes.

16. Others (is, are) very happy for Dwain.

17. Anything (is, are) possible if you have the right attitude.

18. No one (think, thinks) that Dwain will have any trouble finding a summer job.

19. Everyone (want, wants) to do well in life.

Writing Application Look back at the poem you wrote. Check to see if you have used the correct verbs with any indefinite pronouns you used.

Web Activities For eFlashcards, Selection Quick Checks, and other Web activities, go to www.glencoe.com.

Skills Review

Key Reading Skill: Connecting

7. Responses will vary.

Key Literary Element: Point of View

8. *His* and *he* refer to "the horse that is the sea."

9. The poem is written in the first person.

Vocabulary Check

10. The lion's long and heavy <u>mane</u> framed its face.

11. To tremble is also to <u>quiver</u>.

12. The <u>emerald</u> grass looked beautiful after the rain.

13. **English Language Coach** Responses will vary. Possible antonyms: wild/tame; never/always; together/apart

Close

The two selections in this workshop are very different in content and form. Discuss the similarities and differences between these selections with the whole class.

Web Activities Have students access the Web site for interactive activities that will help them assess their understanding of the selection.

Grammar Link: Indefinite Pronouns

Grammar Practice

14. <u>Some</u> **have** important skills that help them be the best they can be; plural

15. <u>One</u> of them **is** Dwain, who knows how to fix bikes; singular

16. <u>Others</u> **are** very happy for Dwain; plural

17. <u>Anything</u> **is** possible if you have the right attitude; singular

18. <u>No one</u> **thinks** that Dwain will have any trouble finding a summer job; singular

19. <u>Everyone</u> **wants** to do well in life; singular

Predicting

Objective covered in this workshop:
• Make predictions about reading

Teaching Students How to Predict

Why Is It Important?

• Predicting helps readers monitor comprehension when they compare what they had expected to read to what they have actually read.

• Predicting engages students more actively with the texts they are reading.

• Predicting is a familiar skill that serves as a model of the way using reading strategies can enhance comprehension.

How to Help Students Get It

• Point out that reading is an interactive process involving both the reader and the author.

• Emphasize that using background knowledge (including what they have already read in the text) to make a prediction is one way to become more engaged with what they are reading.

• Predicting is one way to make inferences. To make a prediction, readers have to think about what is already read, recall what they know about the relevant events or information, and compose an idea of what will happen next.

Reading to Answer the Big Question

By telling the story of Eleanor Roosevelt's life through prose and graphics, and showing the events and ideas that helped her achieve greatness, the reading selections in Workshop 3 of Unit 2 will help your students think about answers to the Big Question: **What brings out the best in you?**

Eleanor Roosevelt by William Jay Jacobs

This biography of Eleanor Roosevelt illustrates her determination to be strong and to help others despite a difficult childhood and the adversity she later faced. Students will learn about Roosevelt's many accomplishments before, during, and after her years as First Lady. They will read about specific situations and challenges that brought out the best in her.

Eleanor Roosevelt's Life

A timeline illustrates the sequence of personal milestones in the life of Eleanor Roosevelt interspersed with national and international events from her era. Recognition of her accomplishments in the context of concurrent historical events will help students understand and appreciate their significance.

Workshop Resources

Pacing (Days)		Lesson	Student Materials	Teacher Resources
Standard	**Block**			
1	1/2	Key Skill Lesson: Predicting	📖 Key Reading Skills Practice, p. 22 📖 English Language Coach Review, p. 41	🖋 Bellringer Options Transparencies –Daily Language Practice 16 🖋 Read Aloud, Think Aloud Transparencies –Key Reading Skills 17 💿 Presentation Plus!
1	1	"Eleanor Roosevelt"	💻 Glencoe Online 📖 Unit Vocabulary Review, p. 39 📖 Academic Vocabulary Review, p. 42 📁 English Language Coach 📖 Active Reading Graphic Organizer, p. 24 📖 Literary Analysis, p. 23 💿 StudentWorks Plus™ 💻 Online Student Edition 💿 Literature Classics 📁 Selection and Unit Assessments, p. 17	💻 Puzzlemaker 💿 Skill Level Up!™ A Language Arts Game 💻 BookLink 3 📓 Assessment by Learning Objective (Diagnostic and Formative) 💿 Interactive Tutor: Self-Assessment 💿 TeacherWorks Plus™
1		"Eleanor Roosevelt's Life"	💻 Glencoe Online 📖 Unit Vocabulary Review, p. 39 📖 Academic Vocabulary Review, p. 42 📁 English Language Coach 📖 Active Reading Graphic Organizer, p. 26 📖 Literary Analysis, p. 23 💿 StudentWorks Plus™ 💻 Online Student Edition 💿 Literature Classics 📁 Selection and Unit Assessments, p. 18	💻 Puzzlemaker 💿 Skill Level Up!™ A Language Arts Game 💻 BookLink 3 📓 Assessment by Learning Objective (Diagnostic and Formative) 💿 Interactive Tutor: Self-Assessment 💿 TeacherWorks Plus™

Keys for Unit Resource

📁 Blackline Master 📀 DVD
📓 Workbook 🖋 Transparency
📖 Supplemental Text 💻 Web-based
💿 CD-ROM 📖 Fast File

Level Appropriate Code

AS = Activities for all students
AL = Activities for students working above grade level
OL = Activities for students working at grade level
BL = Activities for students working below grade level
EL = Activities for English language learners

Focus

BELLRINGER Options

Daily Language Practice Transparency 16 Focus Activity Say: Eleanor Roosevelt said, "We gain strength, and courage, and confidence by each experience in which we really stop to look fear in the face. . . . We must do that which we think we cannot." Based on this quotation, what kind of person do you expect Eleanor Roosevelt to be? *(Possible responses: courageous, fearless, intelligent, wise)* **AS**

Teach

R Reading Skill

Predicting Say: If a story begins "Once upon a time," what kind of story do you think it will be? *(a fairy tale)* **BL** How does being able to predict what kind of story you're going to read help you? *(Possible response: Doing so lets you know what to expect and how to approach the text to get the most out of your reading.)* **OL**

READING WORKSHOP 3

Skills Focus

You will practice using these skills when you read the following selections:
- "Eleanor Roosevelt," p. 168
- "In Eleanor Roosevelt's Time," p. 180

Reading
- Making predictions about reading

Literature
- Recognizing and understanding chronological order

Vocabulary
- Using prefixes

Writing/Grammar
- Using reflexive pronouns
- Using intensive pronouns

Objectives (pp. 164–165)
Reading Make predictions

Predicting

Learn It!

What Is It? Predicting means making good guesses about what will happen next. When you predict, you
- are involved in your reading
- think about what you already know
- look for clues from the writer about upcoming events

R In a mystery book, you would try to solve the mystery. In a biography, you might use information about the person's childhood to predict what might happen later on in life.

- As you read, you will find more information. Pay attention to details. You will probably need to change your predictions.
- When you have finished reading, see if your predictions were correct.

KAT SAID THAT SHE PLAYED PENALTY KICKS SO WELL BECAUSE SHE COULD ANTICIPATE WHERE THE KICK WAS GOING AND THEN COMMIT TO IT.

UNGH!

I THINK I COMMITTED TOO SOON.

© 2002 Bill Hinds, Dist. By Universal Press Syndicate

Analyzing Cartoons
The soccer player predicted where the ball would be kicked. What was wrong with her prediction? Think of a situation where you made a bad prediction because you didn't have enough information.

Additional Support

Differentiated Instruction

Building Background Bill Hinds is a sports cartoonist. *Cleats* began when an editor asked him to draw a strip about the rapidly growing sport of soccer. Hinds's children were learning to play, which may be why the artist says the strip "is not just about soccer. It's about the relationship between parents and kids seen through organized sports." Hinds also draws two other award-winning strips about sports: *Buzz Beamer*, which he calls "wacky, immature kid humor," and *Tank McNamara*, which is satirical. Have students visit the library or use the Internet to find examples of other sports cartoons to share with the class. **AS**

Why Is It Important? Making predictions keeps you thinking while you read so that you become more active as a reader. It gives you a purpose for reading and makes reading more interesting.

R **How Do I Do It?** Before you read, look at the title and any introductions or pictures. Then skim the selection. Use your prior knowledge and what you learned from your preview of the selection to predict the main ideas. While you are reading, continue to make and revise predictions as you gather new information.

Here is how one student made predictions as she read the following part of the *Madam C. J. Walker* selection.

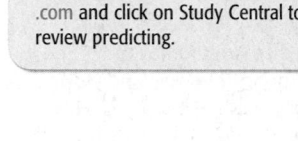

Study Central Visit www.glencoe.com and click on Study Central to review predicting.

Not long after they moved to St. Louis, Sarah McWilliams realized that her hair was falling out. . . . At the time, few hair-care products were available for black women. For years she tried every hair-care product available. But nothing worked. . . . Then one night she had a dream.

I know from the introduction to the selection that Sarah made a million dollars. I also know that people can get rich by starting businesses. I predict that Sarah's dream was about a new hair care product that would become very successful.

Practice It!

Read the title and the first three paragraphs of the selection "Eleanor Roosevelt." In your Learner's Notebook, predict what the selection will be about and what you think you will learn from it.

Look at "In Eleanor Roosevelt's Time." In your Learner's Notebook, predict what kind of additional information you will learn from the time line.

Use It!

After you read the first paragraph of each page of "Eleanor Roosevelt," make a prediction in your Learner's Notebook about what might happen later in the selection. If you learn something that causes you to change your mind about that prediction, write a new one. Continue making and checking predictions throughout the story.

Teach

Study Central Have students access the Web site to review predicting and to complete a related activity.

R Reading Skill

Predicting Say: Predicting requires you to locate clues in the text and use those clues to form educated guesses about events to come or about a work's content. Predictions should be made throughout the reading of a passage. What are some ways to make predictions? *(Students may mention that they should stop periodically to analyze the clues they have encountered and then make predictions. When they read further, they should then stop to verify the predictions they already made.)* **OL**

Resources for page 165

📁 Use Key Reading Skills Transparency 17 in *Read Aloud, Think Aloud* to help students practice predicting.

Literature Focus Lesson

Time Order Words Write the words *first, second,* and *next* on the board. Work with students to develop instructions for a familiar task, such as responding to a fire alarm. After the final step is written, ask students what word they could use to introduce this step. *(finally, last)* Then ask them to think about what would happen if someone did the steps out of order. *(The procedure wouldn't be performed properly.)* Have students explain the importance of time order words. **BL**

Objectives
• Make predictions
• Understand sequence: time order words

165

Teach

More About the Author

William Jay Jacobs had a sign hanging over his desk at Darien High School that identified the intended audience for his books: "a very special audience: young people searching for models, trying to understand themselves." He worked at that high school, where he was known as "Dr. J," from 1975 through 1993. During his time there, he and several students traveled together to China. The trip promoted good relations between America and China.

V Vocabulary

Using Vocabulary After students have completed the Partner Talk activity, challenge them to use the vocabulary words in sentences of their own. Have them write their sentences in their Learner's Notebooks. *(Responses will vary.)* OL

Before You Read : Eleanor Roosevelt

Meet the Author

William Jay Jacobs wrote many biographies of American heroes and stories about American history for children and young adults. His research and writing are very important to him. His parents were immigrants who chose to come to America. Jacobs says, "America to me is more than just a place of residence. It is a passion."

Literature Online

Author Search For more about William Jay Jacobs, go to www.glencoe.com.

Objectives (pp. 166–175)
Reading Make predictions • Make connections from text to self
Literature Identify literary elements: chronological order
Vocabulary Use prefixes

Vocabulary Preview

self-discipline (self DIS uh plin) *n.* control over your behavior in order to improve yourself **(p. 170)** *It took self-discipline for Eleanor Roosevelt to do exercises and take cold showers every day.*

prominent (PROM uh nunt) *adj.* well-known **(p. 171)** *Eleanor Roosevelt was a prominent person.*

slums (slumz) *n.* parts of cities where poor people live in crowded, run-down buildings **(p. 173)** *The slums in many large cities are being rebuilt.*

migrant (MY grunt) *adj.* moving from place-to-place **(p. 173)** *Mrs. Roosevelt was concerned about the suffering of migrant farm workers who were poorly paid.*

Partner Talk Choose the vocabulary word that best fits the blank in each sentence below. Then take turns reading the completed sentences with a partner.

1. George Washington, Abraham Lincoln, and Franklin D. Roosevelt were ___ American presidents.

2. Eleanor Roosevelt cared about poor people who lived in ___.

3. The ___ workers worked in the south in the winter and in the north in the summer.

4. It took ___ for Eleanor Roosevelt to do what it took to be successful as a student and athlete.

English Language Coach

Prefixes Prefixes are word parts placed at the beginning of root or base words. Prefixes change the meaning of a word. The prefix *un-* means "not" or "do the opposite of." This prefix changes the meaning of a word to its antonym, a word that means the opposite.

Word	Prefix	Antonym
happy	un-	unhappy
complete	in-	incomplete

Partner Talk Work with a partner to make a list of six words that begin with the prefixes *un-* or *in-*. Take turns telling the meaning of the words. If you get a definition from a dictionary, explain it in your own words.

Additional Support

Literature Online

Author Search To expand students' appreciation of William Jay Jacobs, have them access the Web site for additional information and resources.

English Language Coach

Negating Prefixes Explain to students that several prefixes, in addition to *un-* and *in-*, mean "not" or "the opposite of." Write the following prefixes on the board: *il-, ir-, im-*. Ask students to volunteer words that use these prefixes. *(Possible responses: illegal, illogical, irrelevant, irresponsible, impolite, impossible)* OL Allow students to use dictionaries if they have difficulty coming up with words. Tell students some of the rules for using these prefixes: for example, use *il-* before *l, ir-* before *r, im-* before *m* or *p.* EL BL

Skills Preview

Key Reading Skill: Predicting

As you read about Eleanor Roosevelt, make predictions about

- how she was affected by the experience of an unhappy childhood.
- how her life changed when her husband became president of the United States.
- what she did after her husband died.

R **Class Talk** Brainstorm a list of predictions about what you will learn about Eleanor Roosevelt as you read this selection. Write the ideas on the board.

Key Literary Element: Chronological Order

L **Chronological order** refers to the time order in which events take place. Whether you are giving instructions on how to bake a cake or giving directions to your school, the information has to be put in a certain order so it will make sense. Some terms most often used to show chronological order are dates and times, such as *December 4, 1921, in the 1950s,* or *Tuesday afternoon,* and signal words, such as *first, next, then, later,* and *finally.*

Write to Learn Make a list of important events that have happened in your own life. Then write a paragraph about them. Put the events in chronological order, using both dates and signal words to show the reader the order in which they happened.

Interactive Literary Elements Handbook
To review or learn more about the literary elements, go to www.glencoe.com.

Get Ready to Read

Connect to the Reading

Eleanor Roosevelt enjoyed helping other people. As you read her biography, think about things that you do to help others. Think about the problems in our country that concerned Eleanor and the problems that concern you.

Class Talk Discuss ways in which young people today can volunteer to help other people in your community. (Think about groups and events which help the environment, serve the poor, tutor students, assist the elderly, or welcome newcomers.)

Build Background

Eleanor Roosevelt was a pioneer in many areas. She was the first president's wife to

- speak in front of a national convention.
- write a national newspaper column.
- become a radio commentator.
- hold regular press conferences.

When Eleanor's husband, President Franklin D. Roosevelt, was paralyzed by polio, she traveled around the United States to gather firsthand knowledge and speak for him.

Set Purposes for Reading

BIG Question Read "Eleanor Roosevelt" to find out what brought out the best in her.

Set Your Own Purpose What else would you like to learn from the selection to help you answer the Big Question? Write your own purpose on the "Eleanor Roosevelt" part of the Workshop 3 Foldable.

Keep Moving

Use these skills as you read the following selection.

Eleanor Roosevelt **167**

Teach

R Reading Skill

Predicting After students complete the Class Talk activity, have them write the three predictions they think are most likely to be correct in their Learner's Notebooks. Then have students list the clues they used to make those predictions. *(Responses will vary.)* **BL** **OL**

L Literary Element

Chronological Order **Say:** *Think about your life. What important dates come to mind? (Responses will vary.)* **Ask:** *If you were to write an autobiography, how would you order these dates? Why? (Students may say that they would write about things in the order that they occurred to make it easier for readers to follow the flow of events.)* **OL**

Reading in the Real World

College As students move into higher grades, they will be expected to locate and use primary sources. Eleanor Roosevelt wrote letters, speeches, newspaper columns, and a book. She also gave interviews. Have students visit the library or use the Internet to find at least two of Eleanor Roosevelt's works. Have students bring copies of the primary sources to the class to share with other students. Discuss how researching and viewing these primary sources affected students' ideas about Eleanor Roosevelt. **AL**

Objectives

- Make predictions
- Understand sequence: chronological order
- Identify and use prefixes
- Learn and use new vocabulary

Teach

Viewing the Photo

Ask: When you look at the photograph of Eleanor Roosevelt, what do you notice? What does her expression say to you? *(Possible responses: She is dressed conservatively; she looks kind of happy but more serious, like she is thinking.)* **OL**

Ask: How does seeing a photograph of Eleanor Roosevelt influence how you read her story? *(Possible response: It makes visualizing events easier for me because I can see her clearly.)* **AL**

R Reading Skill

Predicting Ask: Why do you think the author didn't begin by writing "Anna Eleanor Roosevelt was born on October 11, 1884"? *(Possible responses: The author wanted to show why readers should care about Eleanor Roosevelt first.)* **OL Ask:** After reading the introduction, have you changed your predictions about what you will learn about Eleanor Roosevelt? *(Responses will vary.)* **AS**

Readability Scores
Dale-Chall: 6.5
DRP: 58
Lexile: 960

Eleanor & Roosevelt

by William Jay Jacobs

Eleanor Roosevelt was the wife of President Franklin Delano Roosevelt. But Eleanor was much more than just a president's wife, an echo of her husband's career.

Sad and lonely as a child, Eleanor was called "Granny" by her mother because of her seriousness. People teased her about her looks and called her the "ugly duckling." . . .

Yet despite all of the disappointments, the bitterness, the misery she experienced, Eleanor Roosevelt refused to give up. Instead she turned her unhappiness and pain to strength. She devoted her life to helping others. Today she is remembered as one of America's greatest women.

Almost from the day of her birth, October 11, 1884, people noticed that she was an unattractive child. As she grew older, she could not help but notice her mother's extraordinary beauty, as well as the beauty of her aunts and cousins. Eleanor was plain looking, ordinary, even, as some called her, homely. For a time she had to wear a bulky brace on her back to straighten her crooked spine. **1**

When Eleanor was born, her parents had wanted a boy. They were scarcely able to hide their disappointment. Later, with the arrival of two boys, Elliott and Hall, Eleanor watched her mother hold the boys on her lap and lovingly stroke their hair, while for Eleanor there seemed only coolness, distance.

168 UNIT 2 What Brings Out the Best in You?

Practice the Skills

1 **Key Reading Skill**

Predicting Based on the information so far, what do you think Eleanor Roosevelt might be like as an adult? Do you predict that she turned out to be a confident person?

Additional Support

Literature Focus Lesson

Chronological Order Draw a time line on the board with these categories: *childhood, adulthood,* and *today.* Ask students where these sentences would be placed on the time line: "People teased her . . ." *(childhood);* ". . . she turned her unhappiness and pain to strength" *(adulthood);* "Today she is remembered . . ." *(today).* Have students identify the time order clues they used to place the sentences on the time line. *(Possible responses: "Sad and lonely as a child," "devoted her life," "today")* **AS**

Feeling <u>unwanted</u>, Eleanor became shy and withdrawn. She also developed many fears. She was afraid of the dark, afraid of animals, afraid of other children, afraid of being scolded, afraid of strangers, afraid that people would not like her. She was a frightened, lonely little girl. **2**

The one joy in the early years of her life was her father, who always seemed to care for her, love her. He used to dance with her, to pick her up and throw her into the air while she laughed and laughed. He called her "little golden hair" or "darling little Nell."

The next year, when Eleanor was eight, her mother, the beautiful Anna, died. Afterward her brother Elliott suddenly caught diphtheria[1] and he, too, died. Eleanor and her baby brother, Hall, were taken to live with their grandmother in Manhattan.

A few months later another tragedy struck. Elliott Roosevelt, Eleanor's father, also died. Within eighteen months Eleanor had lost her mother, a brother, and her dear father.

Few things in life came easily for Eleanor, but the first few years after her father's death proved exceptionally hard. Grandmother Hall's dark and gloomy townhouse had no place for children to play. The family ate meals in silence. Every morning Eleanor and Hall were expected to take cold baths for their health. Eleanor had to work at better posture by walking with her arms behind her back, clamped over a walking stick.

Instead of making new friends, Eleanor often sat alone in her room and read. For many months after her father's death she pretended that he was still alive. She made him the hero of stories she wrote for school. Sometimes, alone and unhappy, she just cried.

Just before Eleanor turned fifteen, Grandmother Hall decided to send her to boarding school in England. The school she chose was Allenswood, a private academy[2] for girls located on the outskirts of London.

It was at Allenswood that Eleanor, still thinking of herself as an "ugly duckling," first dared to believe that one day she might be able to become a swan. **3**

---

1. **Diphtheria** is a disease that is easily spread from one person to another.
2. An **academy** is a school.

Eleanor Roosevelt **169**

Practice the Skills

2 **English Language Coach**

Prefixes Use your knowledge of prefixes to understand what <u>unwanted</u> means in this paragraph.

3 **Key Literary Element**

Chronological Order In what order did these events occur?
- Death of Eleanor's father
- Eleanor sent to Allenswood
- Eleanor sent to live with her Grandmother

Eleanor with her father, Elliott Roosevelt April 30, 1889

Teach

R Reading Skill

Review Connecting Ask: How does the author help you understand why Eleanor Roosevelt was unhappy as a child? *(Possible responses: He explains why she felt unwanted, using adjectives like* frightened *and* lonely, *and describes the losses she suffered; he gives examples of how she acted after her father's death.)* **OL** Ask: Which of these techniques made it easiest for you to connect to Eleanor Roosevelt's experience? *(Answers will vary.)* **AL**

L Literary Element

Chronological Order Have students identify the place(s) in the text where they found the answers to the side note question. *(Students may mention that the deaths are described sequentially in the paragraph beginning "The next year. . ." and listed in order in the summary sentence, "Within eighteen months Eleanor had lost her mother, a brother, and her dear father.")* **OL** **AL**

Differentiated Instruction

Characterization Chart Draw a chart on the board with three columns, headed *Character's Thoughts, Character's Actions,* and *Other Characters' Reactions.* Have students find examples of each type of characterization on pages 168–169. *(Possible responses: Character's Thoughts—felt unwanted;* *Character's Actions—made up stories about her father; Other Characters' Reactions—her parents were disappointed that she was a girl.)* **BL** **OL** Ask students to explain whether or not they think the author makes Eleanor Roosevelt's personality "come alive." *(Responses will vary.)* **AL**

Objectives
- Make predictions
- Make connections from text to self
- Understand sequence: chronological order
- Use text features: photographs

Teach

BQ **BIG Question**

Ask: What do you think brought out the best in Eleanor Roosevelt during her time at Allenswood? *(Possible responses: physical exercise, self-discipline, joining a team)* **OL** **Ask: How do you think her time there helped her to be the best she could be in the future?** *(Possible response: She learned she could change herself and make her life better, helping her get what she wants out of life.)* **AL**

L Literary Element

Chronological Order **Say: Identify at least three words or phrases from this page that indicate chronological order.** *(Possible responses: Every day; In 1902; Shortly after her return)* **AS**

At Allenswood she worked to toughen herself physically. Every day she did exercises in the morning and took a cold shower. Although she did not like competitive team sports, as a matter of **self-discipline** she tried out for field hockey. Not only did she make the team but, because she played so hard, also won the respect of her teammates. **4**

Eleanor was growing up, and the joy of young womanhood had begun to transform her personality.

In 1902, nearly eighteen years old, she left Allenswood, not returning for her fourth year there. Grandmother Hall insisted that, instead, she must be introduced to society as a debutante—to go to dances and parties and begin to take her place in the social world with other wealthy young women.

Eleanor, as always, did as she was told. She went to all of the parties and dances. But she also began working with poor children at the Rivington Street Settlement House on New York's Lower East Side. She taught the girls gymnastic exercises. She took children to museums and to musical performances. She tried to get the parents interested in politics in order to get better schools and cleaner, safer streets.

Meanwhile Eleanor's life reached a turning point. She fell in love! The young man was her fifth cousin, Franklin Delano Roosevelt.

Eleanor and Franklin had known each other since childhood. Shortly after her return from Allenswood, they had met by chance on a train. They talked and almost at once realized how much they liked each other.

For a time they met secretly. Then they attended parties together. Franklin—tall, strong, handsome—saw her as a person he could trust. He knew that she would not try to dominate him.

Vocabulary

self-discipline (self DIS uh plin) *n.* control over your behavior in order to improve yourself

170 UNIT 2 What Brings Out the Best in You?

Practice the Skills

Eleanor as a young girl with her horse. She described her self-conscious age in her autobiography, *This is My Story:* "I was tall, very thin, and very shy."

4 **BIG Question**

How did getting involved in exercise and sports at Allenswood bring out the best in Eleanor?

Additional Support

English Language Coach

Context Clues Explain to students that one way to determine the meaning of an unfamiliar word is to use context clues, which are other words or phrases around the unfamiliar word. Direct students to the word *debutante*. Model how to use clues to determine meaning: *What's a debutante? Let's see, it's someone who's "introduced to society."*

That involves going to dances and parties and other social events. Suggest that students verify definitions using a dictionary. Challenge them to stop when they encounter unfamiliar words and use context clues to determine meaning. Have students keep a log of the words in their Learner's Notebooks. **EL** **OL**

On March 17, 1905, Eleanor and Franklin were married. In May 1906 the couple's first child was born. During the next nine years Eleanor gave birth to five more babies, one of whom died in infancy. Still timid, shy, afraid of making mistakes, she found herself so busy that there was little time to think of her own drawbacks.

Meanwhile Franklin's career in politics advanced rapidly. In 1910 he was elected to the New York State Senate. In 1913 President Wilson appointed him Assistant Secretary of the Navy—a powerful position in the national government, which required the **L** Roosevelts to move to Washington, D.C.

In 1917 the United States entered World War I as an active combatant. Like many socially **prominent** women, Eleanor threw herself into the war effort. Sometimes she worked fifteen and sixteen hours a day. She made sandwiches for soldiers passing through the nation's capital. She knitted sweaters. She used Franklin's influence to get the Red Cross to build a recreation room for soldiers who had been shell-shocked in combat. . . .

In the summer of 1921 disaster struck the Roosevelt family. While on vacation Franklin suddenly fell ill with infantile paralysis—polio—the horrible disease that each year used to kill or cripple thousands of children, and many adults as well. When Franklin became a victim of polio, nobody knew what caused the disease or how to cure it.

Franklin lived, but the lower part of his body remained paralyzed. For the rest of his life he never again had the use of his legs. He had to be lifted and carried from place to place. He had to wear heavy steel braces from his waist to the heels of his shoes. **5**

His mother, as well as many of his advisers, urged him to give up politics, to live the life of a country gentleman on the Roosevelt estate at Hyde Park, New York. This time, Eleanor, calm and strong, stood up for her ideas. She argued that he should not be treated like a sick person, tucked away in the country, inactive, just waiting for death to come.

Vocabulary

prominent (PROM uh nunt) *adj.* well-known

Practice the Skills

FDR and Eleanor with their children, Elliot, James, Franklin Jr., John, and Anna, circa 1915

5 Key Reading Skill

Predicting You know that Franklin Roosevelt became president in spite of his paralysis. Predict what this selection will tell you about how that happened. Write your prediction in your Learner's Notebook.

Eleanor Roosevelt **171**

Teach

L Literary Element

Chronological Order Say: There are a lot of dates on this page. Draw a timeline in your Learner's Notebooks, starting with the date the Roosevelts married and ending with the year Franklin Roosevelt became ill. Make sure that you include a brief description of each event. *(Possible responses: 1905: Eleanor and Franklin Roosevelt get married; 1906: Their first child is born; 1910: Franklin Roosevelt elected to the New York state Senate; 1913: Franklin Roosevelt becomes Assistant Secretary of the Navy; 1917: Eleanor Roosevelt joins in the war effort; 1921: Franklin Roosevelt is diagnosed with polio)* **AS Say:** Discuss the importance of each date to Eleanor's biography. *(Responses may vary.)* **AL**

Differentiated Instruction

Using Images to Understand Text Direct students to the Visual Vocabulary at the top of the next page. Ask them when would be a good time to look at this image. *(Possible responses: when you read the word braces; after* *reading the paragraph; when skimming the article before you start to read)* **OL** Guide students to understand that good readers look at images whenever they are helpful, often moving back and forth between the images and the text. **BL**

Objectives

- Use text features: photographs
- Understand sequence: chrono-logical order
- Use context clues to determine word meaning

Teach

L Literary Element

Chronological Order **Ask:** What time order clues did you use to identify events that happened *before* and *after* FDR got polio? *(Students may mention that the dates served as clues for them.)* **BL** **Ask:** What directly preceded Eleanor's dropping out of the "fashionable" society and joining the world of reform? *(Her work with the WTUL)* **OL**

R Reading Skill

Predicting **Ask:** What condition was the nation in when FDR took the presidency? *(It was in a deep depression.)* **BL** **Ask:** How do you think FDR will handle the situation? *(Responses will vary. Students may say that talking with Eleanor and her friends helped prepare him to deal with the situation.)* **Ask:** What do you think Eleanor will contribute to the situation? *(Responses will vary. Students may say that Eleanor was already prepared to work with the poor because of her past experiences.)* **OL** **Say:** Remember to stop to verify your predictions after you have read further. **AS**

Visual Vocabulary
A **brace** is a device used to support part of the body.

Franklin agreed. Slowly he recovered his health. His energy returned. In 1928 he was elected governor of New York. Then, just four years later, he was elected president of the United States.

Meanwhile Eleanor had changed. To keep Franklin in the public eye while he was recovering, she had gotten involved in politics herself. It was, she thought, her "duty." From childhood she had been taught "to do the thing that has to be done, the way it has to be done, when it has to be done." **6**

After becoming interested in the problems of working women, she gave time to the Women's Trade Union League (WTUL). It was through the WTUL that she met a group of remarkable women—women doing exciting work that made a difference in the world. They taught Eleanor about life in the slums. They awakened her hopes that something could be done to improve the condition of the poor. She dropped out of the "fashionable" society of her wealthy friends and joined the world of reform—social change.

For hours at a time Eleanor and her reformer friends talked with Franklin. They showed him the need for new laws: laws to get children out of the factories and into schools; laws to cut down the long hours that women worked; laws to get fair wages for all workers.

By the time that Franklin was sworn in as president, the nation was facing its deepest depression. One out of every four Americans was out of work, out of hope. At mealtimes people stood in lines in front of soup kitchens for something to eat. Mrs. Roosevelt herself knew of once-prosperous families who found themselves reduced to eating stale bread from thrift shops or traveling to parts of town where they were not known to beg for money from house to house.

172 UNIT 2 What Brings Out the Best in You?

Practice the Skills

6 **Key Literary Element**

Chronological Order When did Franklin Roosevelt become ill with polio? Name one important thing that happened *before* he got polio and one important thing that happened *after* he got polio. **L**

Eleanor Roosevelt and FDR on election night, 1932

Additional Support

Literature Focus Lesson

Turning Point Tell students that the plot in a fiction story has a turning point, or climax. Before the turning point, the action rises to reach the moment when a decision must be made and things change. After the turning point, things go in the other direction and issues are often resolved. Tell students that nonfiction often mirrors this pattern. Explain that Eleanor Roosevelt's time at Allenswood was a turning point for her. Work with students to make a list of how things were for Eleanor Roosevelt before Allenswood and another list for how things were after. **OL**

Eleanor worked in the charity kitchens, ladling out soup. She visited **slums**. She crisscrossed the country learning about the suffering of coal miners, shipyard workers, **migrant** farm workers, students, housewives—Americans caught up in the paralysis of the Great Depression. Since Franklin himself remained crippled, she became his eyes and ears, informing him of what the American people were really thinking and feeling. Eleanor also was the president's conscience, personally urging on him some of the most compassionate, forward-looking laws of his presidency.

She lectured widely, wrote a regularly syndicated[3] newspaper column, "My Day," and spoke frequently on the radio. She fought for equal pay for women in industry. Like no other First Lady up to that time, she became a link between the president and the American public.

Above all she fought against racial and religious prejudice. When Eleanor learned that the DAR (Daughters of the American Revolution) would not allow the great black singer Marian Anderson to perform in their auditorium in Washington, D.C., she resigned from the organization. Then she arranged to have Miss Anderson sing in front of the Lincoln Memorial.

Similarly, when she entered a hall where, as often happened in those days, blacks and whites were seated in separate sections, she made it a point to sit with the blacks. Her example marked an important step in making the rights of blacks a matter of national priority.[4] **7**

On December 7, 1941, Japanese forces launched a surprise attack on the American naval base at Pearl Harbor, Hawaii. The United States entered World War II, fighting not only against Japan but against the brutal dictators who then controlled Germany and Italy. **8**

---

3. When an article is *syndicated*, it is sold to different newspapers to be printed.

4. A *priority* is something that needs to be done first.

Vocabulary

slums (slumz) *n.* parts of cities where poor people live in crowded, run-down buildings

migrant (MY grunt) *adj.* moving from place-to-place

Practice the Skills

First Lady Eleanor Roosevelt, on the cover of *TIME* magazine, April 17, 1939

7 **BIG Question**
How did fighting against racial prejudice bring out the best in Eleanor Roosevelt?

8 **Key Reading Skill**
Predicting From everything you have read about Eleanor Roosevelt, what do you think she might have done when America went to war? **R**

Eleanor Roosevelt **173**

Teach

C Critical Thinking

Analysis **Ask:** What effect did FDR's illness have on Eleanor? (*Possible responses: She became stronger; she argued for what she wanted; she got involved in politics.*) **OL**
Ask: What did the change in her cause her to do in the world? (*Possible responses: She helped poor people; she helped change the politics of the country by educating her husband.*) **AL**

R Reading Skill

Predicting Have students verify the predictions they made by comparing them to the paragraph beginning "Eleanor helped. . . ." on the following page. Invite students to make adjustments as necessary. **AS**

Differentiated Instruction

Main Idea Web Work with students to make a main idea web. Draw a large circle and write *Eleanor Roosevelt Is a Social Activist* in the center. Ask students to identify details that support this idea. Add the details they suggest to the chart in smaller circles connected to the main idea circle. (*Possible responses: met reformers through WTUL; left fashionable society; suggested better laws; visited slums; worked in soup kitchens; kept president in touch with poor people*) Invite students to use a main idea web to organize their ideas whenever they find a text confusing. **OL**

Objectives
• Make predictions
• Understand sequence: chronological order
• Analyze text
• Identify literary elements: turning point

173

Teach

C Critical Thinking

Evaluation Ask: Do you think that Eleanor's work during the war and with the United Nations was effective? Explain. *(Responses will vary. Students are likely to say it was effective based on comments about people's reactions to her and events that occurred because of her work.)* **AL**

R Reading Skill

Predicting Ask students to explain the reasoning behind their predictions about what Eleanor would do after her husband's death. *(Responses will vary based on their predictions.)* **AS**

Eleanor helped the Red Cross raise money. She gave blood, sold war bonds. But she also did the unexpected. In 1943, for example, she visited barracks and hospitals on islands throughout the South Pacific. When she visited a hospital, she stopped at every bed. To each soldier she said something special, something that a mother might say. Often, after she left, even battle-hardened men had tears in their eyes. Admiral Nimitz, who originally thought such visits would be a nuisance, became one of her strongest admirers. Nobody else, he said, had done so much to help raise the spirits of the men.

By spring 1945 the end of the war in Europe seemed near. Then, on April 12, a phone call brought Eleanor the news that Franklin Roosevelt, who had gone to Warm Springs, Georgia, for a rest, was dead. **9**

With Franklin dead, Eleanor Roosevelt might have dropped out of the public eye, might have been remembered in the history books only as a footnote to the president's program of social reforms. Instead she found new strengths within herself, new ways to live a useful, interesting life—and to help others. Now, moreover, her successes were her own, not the result of being the president's wife.

In December 1945 President Harry S. Truman invited her to be one of the American delegates going to London to begin the work of the United Nations. Eleanor hesitated, but the president insisted. He said that the nation needed her; it was her duty. After that Eleanor agreed.

In the beginning some of her fellow delegates from the United States considered her unqualified for the position, but after seeing her in action, they changed their minds.

Mrs. Roosevelt helped draft the United Nations Declaration of Human Rights. The Soviets wanted the declaration to list the duties people owed to their countries. Eleanor insisted that the United Nations should stand for individual freedom—the rights of people to free speech, freedom of religion, and such human needs as health care and education. In December 1948, with the Soviet Union and its allies refusing to vote, the Declaration of Human Rights won approval of the UN General Assembly by a vote of forty-eight to zero.

Practice the Skills

9 Key Reading Skill

Predicting After Franklin Roosevelt died, many people thought that Mrs. Roosevelt would retire from public service. What do you predict she will do? Why? **R**

Eleanor Roosevelt holds a poster of the Universal Declaration of Human Rights. This document was adopted by the United Nations General Assembly on December 10, 1948, in honor of Human Rights Day.

174 UNIT 2 What Brings Out the Best in You?

Additional Support

Literature Focus Lesson

Research Essay Have each student write a list of three questions about Eleanor Roosevelt that are not answered in the text. Then have each student choose one question as a starting point for research. For example, "What kind of work did she do for the U.N. besides help draft the Declaration of Human Rights?" or "What did Eleanor do for the Red Cross?" or "What was her relationship with her husband like?" Invite students to use the library or the Internet to search for information. Tell them to write short essays in answer to their own questions. Remind students to include a list of their sources of information. **AL**

Even after retiring from her post at the UN, Mrs. Roosevelt continued to travel. In places around the world she dined with presidents and kings. But she also visited tenement slums in Bombay, India; factories in Yugoslavia; farms in Lebanon and Israel.

Everywhere she met people who were eager to greet her. Although as a child she had been brought up to be formal and distant, she had grown to feel at ease with people. They wanted to touch her, to hug her, to kiss her.

Eleanor's doctor had been telling her to slow down, but that was hard for her. She continued to write her newspaper column, "My Day," and to appear on television. She still began working at seven-thirty in the morning and often continued until well past midnight. Not only did she write and speak, she taught special needs children and raised money for health care of the poor.

As author Clare Boothe Luce put it, "Mrs. Roosevelt has done more good deeds on a bigger scale for a longer time than any woman who ever appeared on our public scene. No woman has ever so comforted the distressed or so distressed the comfortable."

Gradually, however, she was forced to withdraw from some of her activities, to spend more time at home.

On November 7, 1962, at the age of seventy-eight, Eleanor died in her sleep. She was buried in the rose garden at Hyde Park, alongside her husband.

Adlai Stevenson, the American ambassador to the United Nations, remembered her as "the First Lady of the World," as the person—male or female—most effective in working for the cause of human rights. As Stevenson declared, "She would rather light a candle than curse the darkness."

And perhaps, in sum, that is what the struggle for human rights is all about. **10** ○

Eleanor Roosevelt, Chair of Human Rights Committee, United Nations, 1950

Eleanor Roosevelt arrives at a U.S. Navy yard in Pearl Harbor, September 22, 1943

Practice the Skills

10 **BIG Question**

What do you think brought out the best in Eleanor Roosevelt? Name three events in her life that you believe affected her the most. Write your answer on the "Eleanor Roosevelt" part of the Workshop 3 Foldable. Your response will help you answer the Unit Challenge. **BQ**

Eleanor Roosevelt **175**

Reading in the Real World

Citizenship Remind students that "separate but equal" facilities for blacks and whites were legal in the United States until the 1960s. Many prejudiced people believed that blacks were inferior to whites. Discuss why Eleanor Roosevelt's public stand against discrimination was so influential. *(Possible responses: As First Lady, she held a highly visible, respected position. She had the power to effect change. She was not afraid to do what she thought was right.)* **AS**

Objectives
• Make predictions
• Evaluate text

Assess

Resources for page 176

📁 Selection Quick Check, p. 15

📁 Selection and Unit Assessment, p. 17

💿 ExamView Assessment Suite

💿 Interactive Tutor: Self-Assessment

Students can respond to the *After You Read* items in their Learner's Notebooks or on a separate sheet of paper.

Answering the

1. Possible response: Eleanor developed strength and self-discipline and learned that hard work earned respect.

2. Possible response: Eleanor's childhood was unhappy for many reasons. People teased Eleanor about her looks. Her mother was cold toward her but loving toward her brothers. She lost her mother, her father, and a brother.

3. Polio paralyzed Franklin Roosevelt.

Critical Thinking

4. Responses will vary. Students should give examples that show the author's positive attitude towards his subject.

5. Possible response: Yes, because of her reform efforts and her public stand against discrimination.

6. Responses will vary.

176

After You Read Eleanor Roosevelt

Answering the BIG Question

1. Do you think that Eleanor Roosevelt's experience at boarding school brought out the best in her? Why or why not?

2. **Summary** In your Learner's Notebook, write a paragraph about Eleanor's unhappy childhood. Explain at least three reasons why her childhood was unhappy.

   TIP Think and Search The answer is in the text, but the details are not all in one place.

3. **Recall** What caused Franklin Roosevelt to become paralyzed?

   TIP Right There You will find the answer in the text.

Critical Thinking

4. **Infer** How do you think the author feels about Eleanor Roosevelt? How can you tell?

   TIP Author and Me Answer from information in the selection and from your own thoughts.

5. **Evaluate** Was Eleanor Roosevelt a good role model for future First Ladies? Why or why not?

   TIP Author and Me Answer from information in the selection and from your own thoughts.

6. **Analyze** Eleanor Roosevelt went through many hard times. What did you notice about how she faced the challenges in her life?

   TIP Author and Me Answer from information in the selection and from your own thoughts.

Talk About Your Reading

In a group, talk about whether it was harder for Eleanor Roosevelt to overcome her lack of confidence in order to speak in public and help her husband or for Franklin Roosevelt to get elected president in spite of his physical disability. Use information from the story and your own life experience to think of the challenges each of them faced.

Objectives (pp. 176–177)
Reading Make predictions • Make connections from text to self
Literature Identify literary elements: chronological order
Vocabulary Use prefixes
Grammar Identify parts of speech: reflexive pronouns

Talk About Your Reading
Possible response:
The country has been going through hard times.
Twenty-five percent of workers have lost their jobs.
Women work all day in the factories.
Children work in factories instead of learning to read.
Some people don't have enough to eat without soup kitchens.
We need better pay for factory workers.
We need to end child labor so that the next generation can learn the skills needed to support themselves and their families.
Everyone must have a chance to get a good job and prosper.

Skills Review

Key Reading Skill: Predicting

7. What did you predict you would learn about Eleanor Roosevelt from this selection? Explain how you made your predictions and whether your predictions were correct.

Key Literary Element: Chronological Order

8. Did Eleanor go to boarding school before or after her father died?

9. Put the following events in chronological order:
   - The United States entered World War II.
   - The Japanese forces launched a surprise attack at Pearl Harbor.
   - Eleanor Roosevelt visited hospitals in the South Pacific.

10. Did Eleanor become the American delegate to the United Nations before or after Franklin D. Roosevelt died?

Vocabulary Check

self-discipline   prominent   migrant   slum

Answer *true* or *false* to each statement.

11. Eleanor Roosevelt continued to be a **prominent** woman even after the president died.

12. A rich person would probably have lived in a **slum** during Roosevelt's time.

13. Eleanor Roosevelt loved field hockey so much that it did not require any **self-discipline** for her to practice hard.

14. **Migrant** workers had a difficult time during the depression.

15. **English Language Coach** Rewrite the following sentences, replacing the two underlined words with one word beginning with the prefix *-in* or *-un*.
   - Why is Chandra <u>not lucky</u> today?
   - Cerise didn't apply for the job, because she thought she was <u>not qualified.</u>

Grammar Link: Reflexive Pronouns

You know that a pronoun takes the place of a noun or, sometimes, another pronoun. So every pronoun refers back to another noun or pronoun. But **reflexive pronouns** refer back in a special way. We use reflexive pronouns anytime a pronoun that is *not possessive* refers back to the subject of the sentence. We say "I stopped my swing," but it's wrong to say "I stopped me." Instead, we say "I stopped myself." The stopped one *reflects* the stopper, so we use a reflexive pronoun.

- The cat cleaned itself.
- Juan bought himself a soccer ball.
- Jasmine walked home by herself.

Singular Reflexive Pronouns	Plural Reflexive Pronouns
myself yourself himself, herself, itself	ourselves yourselves themselves

Grammar Practice

Choose the correct reflexive pronoun to complete each sentence below. Rewrite each sentence with the correct word in place. The subjects *I, We,* and *Jin* will give you clues to help you choose the correct reflexive pronoun.

16. I gave ____ a present for my birthday.

17. We found ____ on the wrong bus.

18. Jin told ____ that he should not eat another donut.

Literature Online

Web Activities For eFlashcards, Selection Quick Checks, and other Web activities, go to www.glencoe.com.

Eleanor Roosevelt **177**

Skills Review

Key Reading Skill: Predicting

7. Responses will vary depending on the accuracy of predictions.

Key Literary Element: Chronological Order

8. Eleanor went to boarding school after her father's death.

9. Japan attacks Pearl Harbor; the U.S. enters WWII; Eleanor visits hospitals.

10. Eleanor became a U.N. delegate after Franklin's death.

Vocabulary Check

11. True

12. False

13. False

14. True

15. **English Language Coach**
   - Why is Chandra unlucky today?
   - Cerise didn't apply for the job, because she thought she was unqualified.

Grammar Link: Reflexive Pronouns

Grammar Practice

16. I gave <u>myself</u> a present for my birthday.

17. We found <u>ourselves</u> on the wrong bus.

18. Jin told <u>himself</u> that he should not eat another donut.

Close

Ask students what they learned from Eleanor Roosevelt about what brings out the best in a person.

Teach

More About Biography Writers

A biography is a true story written by an author about the life of another person. The writer researches the person's life by conducting interviews and by reading letters, books, and diaries. A good biography makes its subject come alive for readers. A biography may cover a person's entire life, or it may focus on one period of time.

EL Language Coach

Prefixes Write the prefixes *non-* and *dis-* on the board. Have students volunteer words that have these prefixes, such as *nonsense* or *disinterest*. If necessary, allow students to consult dictionaries for words. *(Responses will vary.)* **AS**

Before You Read

Meet the Author

Biographers are authors who write the story of another's person life. Many biographers write about the events that happened in a person's life in chronological order. A time line is a great way for a biographer to begin writing about a person's life. The biographer can use the time line to decide which dates and events to highlight in a biography.

Objectives (pp. 178–181)
Reading Make predictions • Make connections from text to self
Literature Identify literary elements: chronological order
Vocabulary Use prefixes

In Eleanor Roosevelt's Time

Vocabulary Preview

Congress (KONG gris) *n.* the part of the United States government that makes laws **(p. 180)** *Congress passed a new law yesterday.*

seminary (SEM ih nair ee) *n.* a school for advanced education **(p. 180)** *The girls learned about history in the seminary.*

appointed (uh POIN tid) *v.* selected or named for an office or position **(p. 180)** *The president appointed Supreme Court justices.*

morale (muh RAL) *n.* the state of a person's mind and spirit **(p. 181)** *The cheerleaders gave a special cheer to boost the football team's morale.*

Class Talk Discuss the meaning of each vocabulary word. Practice using each word in a sentence.

English Language Coach

Prefixes You already know that a negative prefix can change a word into its antonym. Another important prefix is *re-*. It means "again" or "back," and it is attached to verbs and nouns made from verbs. If you see the word *rebuild,* you can figure out that it means "to build again" or "build back." Look at these other words and see whether you can figure out what they mean.

readjust   reboot   redecorate   reinvest   reorder

Sometimes, to make a word easier to read or to prevent confusion with another word, there may be a hyphen between a prefix and the word it has been added to. For example, we write *re-sort* to mean "to sort again" because there is already an English word spelled *resort,* meaning a place to go for vacation.

Individual Activity Write a short paragraph using all of the words below.

reappear   re-create   rewrite

EL

Additional Support

Literature Focus Lesson

Time Lines Tell students that the time line they are about to see shows two types of events: important events in Eleanor Roosevelt's personal life and important events in history. Work with students to identify Internet and library resources with information about some of the events on the time line. Have students look for additional images to add to the events that do not have photos included with them on the time line. **OL**

Skills Preview

Key Reading Skill: Predicting

Since you've just read a story about Eleanor Roosevelt, you have a lot of knowledge you can use to make predictions about the selection you are about to read. The following time line gives important events in Eleanor Roosevelt's life and things that were accomplished during her husband's time in office. It also shows some other events that happened in the world during Eleanor's lifetime.

Class Talk Discuss the kind of person Eleanor Roosevelt was and try to predict the kinds of activities she would have been involved in during her life. Make notes in your Learner's Notebook.

Key Literary Element: Chronological Order

Chronological order refers to the order in which events take place. "In Eleanor Roosevelt's Time" shows important dates and events in chronological order.

Write to Learn

- Draw a horizontal line across a new page in your Learner's Notebook.
- Under the line on the left end, write the year you were born.
- Under the line on the right end, write the year it is now.
- *Above* the line, list five important events from your life.
- *Under* the events, write the years when they happened. Keep them in chronological order.

Interactive Literary Elements Handbook
To review or learn more about the literary elements, go to www.glencoe.com.

Get Ready to Read

Connect to the Reading

As a child, Eleanor Roosevelt was very shy. She decided to set some goals to become more confident. Think about goals you have set so you would feel better about yourself. If you have never set any goals to improve your feelings about yourself, set one now.

Freewrite Answer the following questions about one goal:

- Why did I choose that goal?
- What actions would I have to take to reach it?
- How much time should I give myself to reach it?
- Who or what could encourage and help me to reach it?

Build Background

- When Eleanor Roosevelt was born, women did not have the right to vote in the United States.
- During her lifetime, women were fighting for equal rights in the home and in the workplace.
- During her lifetime, there were two world wars and other tragic events.
- During her lifetime, segregation of races was common and organizations were allowed to reject people because of their race.

Set Purposes for Reading

BIG Question Read the time line to better understand the events in Eleanor Roosevelt's life that brought out the best in her.

Set Your Own Purpose What else would you like to learn from the time line to help you answer the Big Question? Write your own purpose on the "In Eleanor Roosevelt's Time" part of the Workshop 3 Foldable.

➤ Keep Moving

Use these skills as you read the following selection.

In Eleanor Roosevelt's Time **179**

Teach

L Literary Element

Chronological Order Tell students that the word *chronological* comes from the Greek word for time: *chronos.* Have students use a dictionary to find other words related to *chronological.* (Possible responses: chronology, chronicle, chronic) **BL** **OL**

C Critical Thinking

Application After students write their goals, ask them to share quotations or stories about people who inspire them to be their best. (Responses will vary.) **AS**

Interactive Literary Elements Handbook Have students access the Web site to improve their understanding of chronological order.

Differentiated Instruction

Evaluating Graphic Organizers

Discuss the advantages and disadvantages of time lines with students. Some advantages might be that they give a quick overview, give a sense of historical context, and show how events are related. Disadvantages might be that readers have to come up with their own connections and that descriptive details are omitted. Ask students if they can think of other types of information that are easier to read when displayed in a graphic like a chart or a table. Possible responses may include statistics, some types of instructions, and calendars. **OL**

Objectives

- Make predictions
- Understand sequence: chronological order
- Make connections between text and self

Teach

L Literary Element

Chronological Order Say: This time line shows that the first important event in Eleanor's life is marrying Franklin. After reading the first selection in this workshop, what do you think were important events in Eleanor's life *before* she married Franklin? *(Possible responses: the death of her family members; her time at Allenswood)* **OL**

In Eleanor Roosevelt's Time

1905 March 17: Eleanor marries Franklin D. Roosevelt in New York.

1920 **Congress** passes the Nineteenth Amendment[2] granting women the right to vote.

1917 The United States enters World War I.

1939 DAR denies Marian Anderson the right to sing in their concert hall. Eleanor arranges to hold Anderson's concert on the steps of the Lincoln Memorial.

1932 Franklin D. Roosevelt is elected president of the United States.

1900   1910   1920   1930   1940

1912 Eleanor attends her first Democratic Party Convention.[1]

1926 Eleanor helps purchase Todhunter School, a girls **seminary**, where she teaches history and government.

1928 Eleanor is **appointed** Director of Women's Activities for the Democratic Party; FDR is elected governor of New York.

1933 Frances Perkins becomes Secretary of Labor, the first woman cabinet member in U.S. history.

1936 FDR runs for and wins re-election. With Eleanor's help, African American Mary McLeod Bethune is appointed director of Negro Affairs in the National Youth Administration (NYA).

1938 Congress passes a law banning child labor.

1941 December 7: The U.S. enters the war in Europe.

1. The **Democratic Party Convention** is a meeting for people who are part of the Democratic political party.
2. The **Nineteenth Amendment** is the 19th change to the Constitution of the United States.

Vocabulary

Congress (KONG gris) *n.* the part of the United States government that makes laws

seminary (SEM ih nair ee) *n.* a school for advanced education

appointed (uh POIN tid) *v.* selected or named for an office or position

180 UNIT 2 What Brings Out the Best in You?

Additional Support

Reading in the Real World

Citizenship Eleanor Roosevelt had strong beliefs and values, which she expressed in her speeches and writings. Have students compile a collection of their favorite quotations of Eleanor Roosevelt. Quotations are available online and in dictionaries of quotations. You might ask students to present each quotation, explain when and where Roosevelt said/wrote it (if known), and comment on what the quotation means to them. **OL** **AL**

Practice the Skills

1 Key Reading Skill

Predicting In 1952 Eleanor resigned from the United Nations. Do you predict that she stopped being involved with politics and social issues after that? Why or why not? **R**

2 English Language Coach

Prefixes What does the word **reappoints** mean? Use your knowledge of prefixes to help you.

3 Key Literary Element

Chronological Order Which of the events happened first?

- The U.S. entered World War II
- Eleanor Roosevelt attended her first Democratic Party Convention
- Eleanor Roosevelt was elected head of the United Nations Human Rights commission

4 BIG Question

What is one experience that brought out the best in Eleanor Roosevelt? Write your answer on the "In Eleanor Roosevelt's Time" part of the Workshop 3 Foldable. Your response will help you complete the Unit Challenge later. **BQ**

1943 Eleanor tours the South Pacific to boost the soldiers' **morale**.

1945 Eleanor influences the Army Nurse Corps to open its membership to black women; she joins the NAACP board of directors.

April 12: Franklin Delano Roosevelt dies.
September 2: Japan surrenders to the Allies, World War II ends.

1957 Congress passes a law making it a federal crime to prevent an African American from voting.

1961 John F. Kennedy **reappoints** Eleanor to the United Nations and appoints her as chair of the President's Commission on the Status of Women.

1950 1960 1970

1948 Eleanor's leadership leads to passage of the Universal Declaration of Human Rights.

1954 The *Brown v. Board of Education* decision outlaws segregation in public schools.

1952 Eleanor resigns from the United Nations. **1**

1962 November 7: Eleanor dies at the age of seventy-eight of tuberculosis.[3]

2 3 4

1946 Eleanor is elected as head of the United Nations Human Rights commission.

---

3. *Tuberculosis* is a deadly lung disease that is easily spread from one person to another.

Vocabulary

morale (muh RAL) *n.* the state of a person's mind and spirit

In Eleanor Roosevelt's Time **181**

Teach

R Reading Skill

Predicting Discuss students' predictions. Have students share the clues they used to form their predictions. **AS**

BQ BIG Question

Have students explain their choice of the person or experience they thought brought out the best in Eleanor Roosevelt. **AS**

Assess

CheckPoint

Use the CheckPoint questions provided on Presentation Plus! to check for comprehension of the selection. These questions can be used with interactive response keypads for immediate student feedback.

Differentiated Instruction

Interpreting Images Discuss with students how the images help them understand the time line. Tell students that historians use such images as primary sources, treating details shown in photographs as clues to the past. Model how students can look for and interpret details in one of the images. *(e.g., she wore a very formal wedding dress, so she must have had a traditional wedding.)* Then have students work with partners to identify clues in another image. Have students share their findings with the rest of the class. **AL**

Objectives
- Make predictions
- Understand sequence: chronological order
- Identify and use prefixes

Assess

📁 Selection Quick Check, p. 16

📁 Selection and Unit Assessment, p. 18

💿 ExamView Assessment Suite

💿 Interactive Tutor: Self-Assessment

Students can respond to the *After You Read* items in their Learner's Notebooks or on a separate sheet of paper.

Answering the

1. Responses will vary.
2. 1932
3. Twelve years

Critical Thinking

4. Possible response: Eleanor was an effective speaker who worked hard for women's rights and to end injustice.
5. Possible response: Eleanor believed in equality and had the courage to act on her convictions.
6. Responses will vary. Students should supply reasons for their choices.

After You Read | In Eleanor Roosevelt's Time

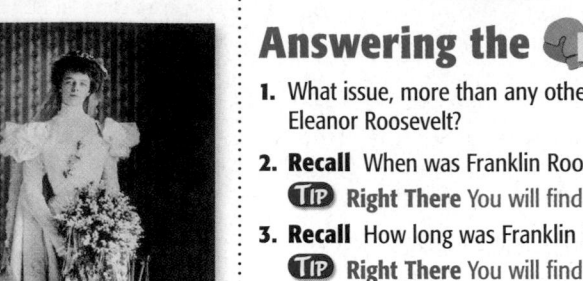

Answering the BIG Question

1. What issue, more than any other, do you believe brought out the best in Eleanor Roosevelt?

2. **Recall** When was Franklin Roosevelt first elected president?
   TIP **Right There** You will find the answer in the text.

3. **Recall** How long was Franklin Roosevelt president?
   TIP **Right There** You will find the answer in the text.

Critical Thinking

4. **Analyze** Look closely at the events that occurred during Franklin Roosevelt's time in office. How do you think Eleanor may have influenced him?
   TIP **Author and Me** You will find information in the text, but you must also use the information in your head.

5. **Draw Conclusions** What kind of person do you think Eleanor Roosevelt was?
   TIP **Author and Me** You will find information in the text, but you must also use the information in your head.

6. **Interpret** How might Eleanor Roosevelt have affected the future of human rights?
   TIP **Author and Me** You will find information in the text, but you must also use the information in your head.

Write About Your Reading

The time line tells the important events in Eleanor Roosevelt's life. It also includes some national events that had an impact on her, such as World War II. Think about some of the important things that have happened in the country during your lifetime. Add those events to the time line in your Learner's Notebook. Also add events in your school, community, country, and around the world which have affected your life.

Objectives (pp. 182–183)
Reading Make predictions • Make connections from text to self
Literature Identify literary elements: chronological order
Vocabulary Use prefixes
Writing Respond to literature: time line
Grammar Identify parts of speech: intensive pronouns

182 UNIT 2 What Brings Out the Best in You?

Write About Your Reading

Responses will vary but may include the attacks on the World Trade Center, the wars in Afghanistan and Iraq, Hurricane Katrina, and the mapping of the human genome.

Skills Review

Key Reading Skill: Predicting

7. Look back at the predictions you wrote in your Learner's Notebook. Did they help you to stay focused and involved with the text? Why or why not?

8. Were your predictions right about the kinds of activities Eleanor would be involved in?

Key Literary Element: Chronological Order

9. Name one event that happened before Franklin D. Roosevelt became president and one event that happened afterward.

10. How many years did Eleanor spend in the United Nations the first time she served?

11. How many years passed from when Eleanor Roosevelt resigned from the United Nations until she was reappointed by President Kennedy?

Vocabulary Check

seminary   appointed   morale

Write the vocabulary word that each clue describes.

12. It will probably be good if the team wins a lot of games.

13. Students go here to study.

14. One way a person is picked for a position.

15. **English Language Coach** The word *comparable* means *similar to others.* The word *incomparable* means *outstanding* or *beyond comparison*. Name three things Eleanor Roosevelt did that show she was incomparable.

Grammar Link: Intensive Pronouns

A pronoun is a word that takes the place of a noun, a group of words acting as a noun, or another pronoun. **Intensive pronouns** are a lot like reflexive pronouns. They also end with *-self* or *-selves*. They are used to draw special attention to a noun or a pronoun already named. If they are removed, the meaning of the sentence will be the same.

• Yolanda *herself* repaired the engine.

• Yolanda repaired the engine *herself*.

In both sentences, the word *herself* draws special attention back to Yolanda.

Singular Intensive Pronouns	Plural Intensive Pronouns
myself yourself himself, herself, itself	ourselves yourselves themselves

Grammar Practice

Choose the correct intensive pronoun to complete each sentence below. Rewrite each sentence with the correct word in place.

16. Lakisha designed the computer game ___.

17. The trumpet player ___ wrote his music.

18. James ___ taught the dog to jump through a hoop.

Writing Application Look back at your writing assignment. Add an intensive pronoun to a note on your time line. (*I myself played a solo. I went to New York myself.*) Make sure you use the pronoun correctly.

Web Activities For eFlashcards, Selection Quick Checks, and other Web activities, go to www.glencoe.com.

In Eleanor Roosevelt's Time **183**

Skills Review

Key Reading Skill: Predicting

7. Responses will vary.

8. Responses will vary.

Key Literary Element: Chronological Order

9. Responses will vary. Events should be before and after 1932.

10. Six years

11. Eleanor was reappointed in 1961, nine years after she resigned.

Vocabulary Check

12. morale

13. seminary

14. appointed

15. **English Language Coach** Responses will vary but should either reflect Eleanor Roosevelt's unique accomplishments or show that she was *not* incomparable.

Close

Hold a class discussion based on student responses to question 15.

Grammar Link: Intensive Pronouns

Grammar Practice

16. Lakisha designed the computer game <u>herself.</u>

17. The trumpet player <u>himself</u> wrote his music.

18. James <u>himself</u> taught the dog to jump through a hoop.

Web Activities Have students access the Web site for interactive activities that will help them assess their understanding of the selection.

Focus

Focus

BELLRINGER Options

- **Daily Language Practice Transparency 17**
  Focus Activity Say: Now, you'll revise your narrative. What are some ways you can improve your first draft? *(Possible responses: checking grammar and spelling, looking for more descriptive adjectives, or deleting unnecessary information)*

Teach

 Writing

Revising Say: When you revise your writing, check for one element, or strategy, at a time. For example, the first time you read through your narrative, make sure you used enough details to answer readers' questions. The second time, make sure that you clearly described the setting. **OL**

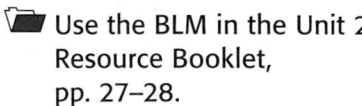 **Resources for page 184**

- Use the BLM in the Unit 2 Resource Booklet, pp. 27–28.
- Use the Grammar and Writing Workshop Transparencies 19–20.

ASSIGNMENT: Write an autobiographical narrative

Purpose: Share a story about a friend who brought out the best in you

Audience: You, your teacher, and your classmates

Revising Rubric

Your revised autobiographical narrative should have
- first-person point of view
- events told in chronological order
- well-chosen details and elaborations
- no spelling or grammatical errors
- nouns and pronouns used correctly

Objectives (pp. 184–187)
Writing Use the writing process: autobiographical narrative • Revise a draft to include: main ideas and supporting details, audience • Edit writing for: grammar, spelling, punctuation • Present writing
Grammar Use nouns and pronouns
Listening, Speaking, and Viewing Participate in a group discussion • Listen actively

---

WRITING WORKSHOP PART 2

Autobiographical Narrative
Revising, Editing, and Presenting

In Part 1 of the Writing Workshop, you wrote the first draft of your autobiographical narrative. In Part 2 of the Writing Workshop, you will revise and edit your work and share it with your classmates.

Revising

Make It Better

The best way to start revising is to reread your draft and underline the places where you think your writing sounds awkward. Cross out sentences that you think are unnecessary and write notes about information you'd like to add.

Consider the Audience

Read the questions below and write the answers in your Learner's Notebook.
- What do you want your readers to know about your friend?
- What about this friend brought out the best in you?
- What did you learn about yourself from this experience?

Reread your draft and make sure that the answers you wrote can be found in your narrative. Now is the time to add the information you forgot to include in your first draft.

Check the Details

As you revise, write more details in the places where your autobiography needs further explanation or more details.

One of the most important details in a narrative is the setting, or where the story takes place. Find the setting in your draft and add to the description of that place. Can't find the setting in your draft? Now is the time to add one!

Setting	More Details
Pablo and I ate lunch in the **cafeteria.**	The cafeteria smelled like fish sticks, and I had trouble hearing Pablo over the noise of all the other students.
Lucy and I were at the **shopping mall** after school.	Lucy and I were sitting in the food court at the mall. The neon sign for Pita Palace flashed behind Lucy's head.

Additional Support

Literature Focus Lesson

First-person Point of View Remind students that their narratives should tell events from the first-person point of view. In other words, they should tell the story from their own perspectives. Help students practice writing in the first person by having them rewrite the following sentences in first person, as if they were the subjects in the sentences.

1. She gave herself the day off.
2. He was a hero to his friends.
3. She took her brother to the mall in her new car.
4. He finished the test all by himself.
5. She spent her allowance on clothes and books. **EL BL**

Partner Talk The best way to find out where you should add more details is by asking a friend. Read your story out loud to a partner. Ask these questions when you are finished:

- What parts of my autobiography need more details?
- What else would you like to know about my friend?

Writing Models For models and other writing activities, go to www.glencoe.com.

Editing
Finish It Up

Now it's time to put the finishing touches on your autobiographical narrative. A careful editing job shows your readers that you care about your work and don't want them distracted by any errors. During the editing process you should check spelling and grammar, and follow the Proofreading Checklist that is below.

Proofreading Checklist

☑ Proper nouns are capitalized correctly.
☑ Pronouns are in the correct form and agree with their antecedents.
☑ All words are spelled correctly.
☑ All sentences are complete.

Presenting
Show It Off

Write or type a final version of your autobiographical narrative.

Add illustrations or fancy title lettering to make your paper really stand out. You may also cut images from magazines or download images from your computer.

Make a class binder called *How We Became the Best We Can Be* to compile the autobiographies of your entire class. Use a three-hole puncher to punch holes in your paper and then add your work to the class binder.

Read your autobiographical narrative to the class. Listen as everyone reads his or her narrative. Talk about any common experiences that you have with your friends and how they bring out the best in you.

▶ **Writing Tip**

Remember that some nouns have different endings when they become plural. Singular nouns that end in a consonant and *y* get an *ies* ending when they become plural (*story/stories*).

▶ **Writing Tip**

If your autobiographical narrative is written on a computer, use your spell checker, but also check it manually. Spell checkers only tell you if the word you used is not a word. They won't tell you if you used the wrong form of a word (for example: there, their, and they're). If you're unsure of the spelling, look it up in a dictionary.

▶ **Writing Tip**

Don't let messy handwriting get in the way of your story! Make your final draft easy to read by using your best handwriting or a word processor.

Teach

W Writing

Elaboration Give students practice with elaboration by asking them to add descriptive details to these sentences.

1 My mother says my room is a mess. *(Sample response: She complains about the smell of dirty clothes, the socks hanging off the lamp, and the shoes strewn across the floor.)*

2 The old house looked scary. *(Sample response: It was abandoned decades ago. The porch was falling off, and the windows were all broken. If you listened carefully, you could hear the house groan in the wind.)* **OL**

Assess

Have students exchange their papers and use the proofreading checklist to critique one another's work. Have students make last-minute changes to their own work and then add their papers to the class binder.

Differentiated Instruction

Creative Writing Encourage students to use the following techniques to add flair to their writing:

- Vary the length and type of sentences to create rhythm in your narrative. Do not start all sentences with a subject followed by a predicate. Mix up the form of your sentences.

- Use metaphors or similes, comparisons of unlike things, to bring your writing to life.

- Try appealing to all five senses in your narrative—sight, sound, taste, touch, and smell. This will help your reader really experience your story. **AS**

Objectives
- Revise writing for key elements, style, and word choice
- Use first-person point of view
- Write an autobiographical narrative
- Use elaboration

185

Teach

L Literary Element

Chronological Order Ask students to skim the model to find examples of time order clues. *(Possible responses: Late last August, First, Then, Next)* **BL**

C Critical Thinking

Evaluation Ask: What do you think of this Writer's Model? *(Responses will vary.)* **Say:** In a small group, create a brief evaluation of the model. Keep your comments constructive and helpful, and be specific. For example, if you think the author needs to add more detail, tell what details you would like to read. When you're finished, have a group representative present your evaluation to the class. *(Responses will vary. Students should be able to support their arguments constructively.)* **OL Say:** Use your suggestions to write a second draft of this model. **AL**

Writer's Model

The Election
By Oscar Mendez

Late last August, I was walking home from playing soccer with my friend Pablo. "Our school needs a fifth grade soccer team," I told Pablo.

"You should run for fifth grade class president," said Pablo. "Then you could set one up."

"Who'd want me for president?" I asked, shocked at the idea.

"You always do your best in sports and in school," said Pablo. "Maybe you're not a big shot, but that means you're not stuck up. You're friendly to everybody. Those are the things we need in a class president."

"I don't know," I stalled. "Running for president will be so much work, and I already have trumpet practice and all the homework we get."

"I'll help you," said Pablo.

I did run, and Pablo helped me. First, we made posters to hang in the fifth grade hallway. Then, we made soccer ball shaped buttons with my name on them. Next, Pablo helped me write a speech about why I'd make a good class president.

On the day of the election, I had to give my speech in front of the whole fifth grade. When I got to the microphone, I promised my classmates that if they elected me, I'd start a fifth grade soccer team and promote any other worthwhile project that anyone suggested to me.

For the rest of the day, Pablo and I nervously waited for the election results. When it was finally announced that I was fifth grade class president, we gave each other high fives.

"Come on over on Saturday," I told Pablo. "My dad'll take us to a soccer game!"

"Sure," said Pablo, "but right now you go ask Coach Simpson how you can start our new fifth grade soccer team!"

The author uses the proper conventions for writing and punctuating dialogue. Dialogue makes the story more interesting to read.

L Several events happen in this paragraph. The writer uses chronological order to organize the events.

The author includes the emotions he remembers feeling at the time.

Specific details help the reader visualize the characters and the scene.

C

Additional Support

Literature Focus Lesson

Autobiographies Remind students that people write autobiographies for many reasons, such as to tell the story of their lives or to help people who are facing similar problems. Encourage students to think about the purpose of their autobiographies by asking, "What do I want my readers to learn?" As students edit their narratives, remind them to keep this question in mind: "Have I given my readers enough information?" Encourage students to share their narratives with classmates and have them explain what they learned from reading each other's narratives. **OL**

Listening, Speaking, and Viewing

Active Listening in a Group Discussion

Just as you need skills to play football or write a story, you also need skills to be a good listener and an effective speaker.

What Is It?

Have you ever sat in a class discussion just thinking about what you're going to say next? Or looking out the window and wondering if practice was going to get rained out? If so, you may have heard what was being said, but you weren't actively listening. Active listening involves paying attention to the person speaking, thinking about what's being said, and asking yourself questions about whether you understand and agree with what's being said. Hearing is something that happens. Listening is something you do.

Why Is It Important?

Group discussions are good ways to learn things you don't know, but they are even better for something else. They help you explore what you think about things. You share your ideas. Then, if you really listen to what others have to say, you may change your ideas or add to them. Your listening can lead you to think about things in different ways.

How Do I Do It?

Follow these tips to be an active listener:

- Clear your mind of other thoughts and distractions.
- Look at the speaker and focus on the words he or she is saying.
- Connect what you hear to your own knowledge and experience.
- Identify the main ideas.
- If you don't understand something, raise your hand and ask a question.
- Let your own ideas grow as you listen to others. Don't only focus on your own point of view.
- Try to be open to different ideas and points of view, even if you don't agree with them at first.

Speak to Learn Follow these tips for participating in a group discussion about the Big Question:

- Form a group of three or more students. **LSV**
- Discuss activities in your lives that bring out the best in you.
- Ask your group members questions about the activities they mention. **BQ**
- Be respectful of your group members by not interrupting when they are speaking and responding appropriately to their questions.

Teach

LSV Listening, Speaking and Viewing

Asking Questions Say: As you listen to the other members of your group talk about what brings out the best in them, think of one follow-up question you could ask them. Asking follow-up questions shows you have been listening and helps you make sure you've understood what you've heard. *(Responses will vary.)* **BL** **EL**

Close

BQ **BIG Question**

Say: Think of one thing you've learned from your discussion with your classmates that can help you answer the Big Question. Write your thoughts in your Learner's Notebooks. *(Responses will vary.)* **AS**

Differentiated Instruction

Discussion Techniques Some students may have a difficult time staying focused during a group discussion. Encourage these students to try the following techniques for focusing to help them focus during a discussion:
Repeat what you hear: Silently repeat the main points of what another group member has said. Then write them down.
Be an active participant: If you speak often, it will be easier for you to stay focused on the topic at hand.
Put away books and other distractions: Make sure your desk is clear of anything that might distract you from the conversation. **BL**

Objectives

- Understand sequence: chronological order
- Evaluate autobiographical narratives
- Listen actively
- Participate in group discussion
- Edit for spelling, punctuation, and grammar

Questioning

Objective covered in this workshop:
• Ask questions

Teaching Students Questioning

Why Is It important?

• Questioning strategies help students monitor their comprehension.

• Questioning strategies are fundamental to engaging in inquiry.

• Questioning strategies are central to peer-led discussion.

• Questioning strategies are essential for students to demonstrate what they have learned in a variety of assessment settings.

How to Help Students Get It

• Make sure that students understand the relationship between questions asked and the source(s) of information for answering the question.

• Tell students that information can be found in their own background knowledge and experiences as well as in the texts they read.

• Emphasize to students that different types of questions are asked before, during and after reading.

• Teach students strategies that will align well with particular types of questions (e.g., skimming and scanning in response to questions that ask for important text details; making inferences in response to questions that ask them to fill in gaps or read between the lines). Model these strategies for students.

Reading to Answer the Big Question

By telling the stories of people and what they overcome when the best is brought out in them, the selections in Workshop 4 of Unit 2 will help your students devise their own answers to the Big Question: **What brings out the best in you?**

Gentleman of the Pool by Alice Park
An *InTime* article explains why swimmer Michael Phelps is a winner both a in and out of the pool. Students will learn how the Olympics brings out the best of Phelps' character, demonstrated by his team spirit and good sportsmanship, as he wins eight Olympic medals.

Primary Lessons by Judith Ortiz Cofer
Judith Ortiz Cofer relates a childhood story. When Judith and her family move back to Puerto Rico after living in the U.S., she is treated with favoritism because she has lived in New York and can speak English. Striving to understand the prejudice she observes brings out the best in Judith.

Workshop Resources

Pacing (days) Standard	Pacing (days) Block	Lesson	Student Materials	Teacher Resources
1	1/2	Key Skill Lesson: Questioning	• Key Reading Skills Practice, p. 29 • English Language Coach Review, p. 41	• Bellringer Options Transparencies –Daily Language Practice 18 • Read Aloud, Think Aloud Transparencies –Key Reading Skills 19 • Presentation Plus!
1	1	"Gentleman of the Pool"	• Glencoe Online • Unit Vocabulary Review, p. 39 • Academic Vocabulary Review, p. 42 • English Language Coach • Active Reading Graphic Organizer, p. 31 • Literary Analysis, p. 30 • StudentWorks Plus™ • Online Student Edition • Literature Classics • Selection and Unit Assessments, p. 19	• Literary and Text Analysis Transparencies 56 • Puzzlemaker • Skill Level Up!™ A Language Arts Game • BookLink 3 • Assessment by Learning Objective (Diagnostic and Formative) • Interactive Tutor: Self-Assessment • TeacherWorks Plus™
1		"Primary Lessons"	• Glencoe Online • Unit Vocabulary Review, p. 39 • Academic Vocabulary Review, p. 42 • English Language Coach • Active Reading Graphic Organizer, p. 33 • Literary Analysis, p. 30 • StudentWorks Plus™ • Online Student Edition • Literature Classics • Selection and Unit Assessments, p. 20	• Bellringers Option Transparencies –Selection Focus 4 • Literary and Text Analysis Transparencies 56 • Puzzlemaker • Skill Level Up!™ A Language Arts Game • BookLink 3 • Assessment by Learning Objective (Diagnostic and Formative) • Interactive Tutor: Self-Assessment • TeacherWorks Plus™

Keys for Unit Resource

- Blackline Master
- Workbook
- Supplemental Text
- CD-ROM
- DVD
- Transparency
- Web-based
- Fast File

Level Appropriate Code

AS = Activities for all students

AL = Activities for students working above grade level

OL = Activities for students working at grade level

BL = Activities for students working below grade level

EL = Activities for English language learners

Focus

BELLRINGER Options

- 📖 **Selection Focus Transparency 4**

- 📖 **Daily Language Transparency 18 Focus Activity Say:** Claude Levi-Strauss said: "The wise man doesn't give the right answers; he poses the right questions." Explain why you agree or disagree with this statement. *(Responses will vary.)* **OL**

Teach

R Reading Skill

Questioning Say: Asking questions is one of the best ways to learn about someone or something. Why do you think we sometimes find it hard to ask questions? *(Possible responses: We're afraid to look stupid; we don't want to offend other people by asking the wrong question; it's not cool to look too interested.)* **Ask:** What would make it easier for you to ask questions as you read? *(Possible responses: keeping a list; talking about my reading with someone)* **OL**

Additional Support

Skills Focus

You will practice using these skills when you read the following selections:
- "Gentleman of the Pool," p. 192
- "Primary Lessons," p. 198

Reading
- Asking questions

Literature
- Understanding tone

Vocabulary
- Understanding word choice

Writing/Grammar
- Understanding pronoun case and usage

Objectives
(pp. 188–189)
Reading Ask questions

188 UNIT 2

Skill Lesson

Questioning

Learn It!

What Is It? Reading is like having a conversation between the author and the reader. You don't get to tell the author what you're thinking, but you can ask questions in your head. Then you read to find out the answers. That's the way the best readers always read.

They ask questions that help them
R
- use their own knowledge.
- make predictions.
- grasp the meaning.
- figure out the author's purpose.
- find specific information.
- understand and remember events and characters.
- wonder about "big" ideas.

Analyzing Cartoons
What did the bird ask itself? Do you think it considered the answer to its own question?

© Patrick McDonnell. Reprinted with permission of King Features Syndicate.

Differentiated Instruction

Building Background Patrick McDonnell describes Earl as "one lovable pup" who enjoys belly rubs. His best friend, Mooch, is "the curious cat who lives next door." The artist gets many of his ideas from his own dog, Earl, and his cat Meemow. He also finds inspiration from Charles Schultz's *Snoopy.* Since he began drawing the strip in 1994, McDonnell has educated readers about seal hunts, animal shelters, endangered tigers, chained-up animals, and other animal welfare issues. Have students search the library or Internet for other examples of McDonnell's work and share their findings with the class. **AL**

Why Is It Important? Asking questions makes you an active reader. It helps you really think about what you're reading. When you do that, you remember more. You also understand more and get new ideas that will help you in school and in your life.

How Do I Do It? Begin asking questions even before you read. Ask yourself what you already know about the subject. Then ask what you expect or hope to learn from reading. While you're reading, don't let anything slip past you. If the author mentions something you haven't heard of before, ask yourself questions. Then look to see if the author tells you the answers. If there's a word you don't know, ask whether there are any clues that will help you understand it. If there's a mystery, ask how it will be solved. After you've finished, ask what the main idea of the selection was and whether you agree with that idea.

While a student was reading "Madam C. J. Walker," he asked questions:

> Sarah was a widow at the age of twenty, and the sole support of a two-year-old daughter. She took in laundry to earn a living and was determined to leave the South. With Lelia, she made her way up the Mississippi River and settled in St. Louis, where she worked fourteen hours a day doing other people's laundry.

> *Before I read the paragraph, I asked myself who and what this was about. As I read this paragraph, I asked myself why it was important for Sarah to leave the South. After I read the paragraph, I asked myself why this information was important to the selection.*

Practice It!

In your Learner's Notebook, write the following questions. Then write a question of your own.

Who is this selection about? Who else is important?

Use It!

As you read "Gentleman of the Pool" and "Primary Lessons," come up with more questions about the selections. Add them to your Learner's Notebook and answer the questions as you read.

Reading in the Real World

College Write the words *Who, What, When, Where, Why,* and *How* on the board. Ask students to pick a topic they are currently studying. Work with them to generate questions about their topic, beginning with the 5 *W*s and an *H*. Have students share their questions in small groups. Have them discuss how this list of questions can help them study, understand what they read, or prepare for research. **AS**

Teach

R Reading Skill

Questioning Say: Look at the *Why Is It Important?* section. What main idea about questioning does the writer want you to learn? *(Questioning helps you understand things and identify ideas that are important. Skilled readers ask questions and look for answers as they read.)* **OL**

Resources for page 189

📁 Use Key Reading Skills Transparency 19 in *Read Aloud, Think Aloud* to help students practice questioning.

Objectives
• Ask questions
• Analyze text features

189

Teach

More About the Author

Alice Park earned a master of science in journalism from Boston University. She has used her training to report on topics ranging from how much Americans need to worry about SARS to whether elite athletes can push themselves too hard. Park has appeared on network news shows and panels to talk about the latest developments in science and health research.

EL Language Coach

Synonyms Say: Synonyms rarely mean exactly the same thing. Almost always, there are small but important differences between their meanings. For example, *cheap* and *inexpensive* are synonyms. However, something that is "cheap" often is not well made. Something that is "inexpensive" can be well made without costing a lot. Which word is better for describing a time you bruised your knee—*mishap* or *disaster*? *(mishap)* **OL** **Ask:** How would you compliment a friend's new outfit—*admiringly* or *reverently*? *(admiringly)* **AL**

Before You Read Gentleman of the Pool

Meet the Author

Alice Park is a senior science reporter with *TIME* magazine. Since 1993, she has reported on health and medicine, including articles on AIDS, cancer, and Alzheimer's disease. At Harvard Medical School, Ms. Park designed a program to help doctors understand the latest research on AIDS.

Literature Online

Author Search For more about Alice Park, go to www.glencoe.com.

Objectives (pp. 190–193)
Reading Ask questions • Make connections from text to self
Literature Identify literary elements: tone
Vocabulary Identify synonyms • Make word choices

Vocabulary Preview

goal (gohl) *n.* something that you aim for **(p. 192)** *Michael had a goal to win at least one gold medal.*

ambitions (am BISH unz) *n.* strong desires to succeed **(p. 193)** *The members of the swim team had a lot of different ambitions, but all of them wanted to win.*

victory (VIK tur ee) *n.* the win in a contest or battle **(p. 193)** *The team celebrated their victory after the swimming competition.*

Partner Activity

- Write each vocabulary word on a strip of paper.
- Fold the strips so you cannot see the words.
- Take turns picking a strip.
- Use each word you pick in a sentence.
- Refold the strips, and choose again. This time tell what the word means.

English Language Coach

Word Choice Using just the *right* word is called good **word choice.** Sometimes there are plenty of words you *could* use, but one is often better than the rest. Choosing the right word is important, and a good writer has the ability to strengthen descriptions and give details with this skill. One way to determine which word is the best is to think about synonyms by using a thesaurus. Keep in mind that the best word isn't *always* a synonym. Picking the *best* word is all about understanding what you want to say and making it as clear as possible. **EL**

Write to Learn In your Learner's Notebook rewrite each sentence. Pick one of the words in parentheses to replace the word in dark print. You might notice that more than one word will work, but only one word is the *best* word. If you are unsure about the meaning of any words, use a dictionary.

1. Andre has a **large** baseball card collection. (massive, bulky, excessive)
2. Chandra, a **talented** writer, always wins the school poetry slam. (excellent, gifted, genius)
3. It was a close election, but Marq was **defeated** when he ran for student council. (obliterated, unsuccessful, trounced)

Additional Support

Literature Online

Author Search To expand students' appreciation of Alice Park, have them access the Web site for additional information and resources.

English Language Coach

Word References Students may have had little practice in using a thesaurus or a synonym finder. Explain that a thesaurus such as Roget's may group related words into categories with numbered subdivisions. This type of thesaurus also includes an index to individual words. A synonym finder, on the other hand, arranges word entries alphabetically with a list of synonyms for each word. Give students practice by having them look up synonyms for *propel, tremulous, muffle,* and *indignant. (Possible responses: propel—push; tremulous—trembling; muffle—silence; indignant—outraged)* **EL** **BL**

Skills Preview

Key Reading Skill: Questioning

As you read "Gentleman of the Pool," have a conversation with yourself by asking and trying to answer questions. You might ask yourself questions like these:

- Why does the author call Michael Phelps a gentleman?
- How is he a winner "out of the pool"?

Write to Learn As you read, write your questions and answers in your Learner's Notebook.

Key Literary Element: Tone

"Don't use that tone of voice with me!" You've probably heard that, particularly if you were being rude or unpleasant. It's easy to pick up on someone's tone of voice. But how do you figure out the tone of someone's writing?

The **tone** of a piece of writing is the attitude of the author. Since the author doesn't have an actual voice, he or she chooses particular words and phrases. They show how the author feels about the subject of the writing. Some words that describe tone are *respectful, admiring, angry, bored, amused,* and *hurt.*

- Carrie had a wide range of knowledge.
- Carrie was a know-it-all.

It's pretty easy to tell what the authors of these sentences think about Carrie, isn't it?

Partner Talk Exchange sentences that have a clear tone. Then rewrite the sentences so that they express a different attitude.

Interactive Literary Elements Handbook
To review or learn more about the literary elements, go to www.glencoe.com.

Get Ready to Read

Connect to the Reading

Michael Phelps loves to swim. Think about sports, games, or other group activities that you like to participate in or watch. Think about the winning teams you know of.

Class Talk Discuss what makes a person a good team player.

Build Background

- The Olympics Games are athletic competitions which began over 2700 years ago and lasted almost 1200 years. They were held in Olympia, Greece, in the summer every four years. Just like today, many of the best athletes became famous and were treated like celebrities for the rest of their lives.
- The modern Olympic Games began in 1896 in Athens, Greece.
- The Games are held in cities around the world. The number of athletes, participating countries, and events has increased over the years.
- All Olympic events are still held every four years. However, since 1996, winter events (like skiing) and summer events (like swimming) are held in different cities two years apart.

Set Purposes for Reading

BIG Question Read the biography "Gentleman of the Pool" to find out what brought out the best in Michael Phelps.

Set Your Own Purpose What else would you like to learn from the story to help you answer the Big Question? Write your own purpose on the "Gentleman of the Pool" part of the Workshop 4 Foldable.

Keep Moving

Use these skills as you read the following selection.

Gentleman of the Pool **191**

Teach

Key Literary Element: Tone

Ask: What circumstance would cause a person to use the following tones? Give an example of something someone might say in each tone.
- stern
- cheerful
- admiringly
- apologetic
(Responses will vary.)

C Critical Thinking

Analysis Ask: How can swimming be both an individual and a team sport? *(Students may mention that an individual swimmer can be a good team player.)* **AS**

Interactive Literary Elements Handbook Have students access the Web site to improve their understanding of character.

Reading in the Real World

Citizenship Athletes are often considered role models. Ask students to name athletes whom they admire. Encourage them to name competitors from several different sports. Then work with students to identify characteristics these athletes have in common. Ask students what makes the athletes they admire good role models. Encourage students to support their answers with examples. **AS**

Objectives
- Ask questions
- Identify and use synonyms
- Interpret and analyze tone
- Analyze text
- Use word references: thesaurus

READING WORKSHOP 4

Teach

Viewing the Photo

Say: What can you learn about Michael Phelps from the photograph? *(Possible responses: He won gold at the 2004 Olympics. His victory made him proud and happy.)* **AS**

R Reading Skill

Review Connecting

Say: Think of people in the world, such as scientists, authors, athletes, and political activists, who are respected for different kinds of accomplishments. What qualities do you think are the most important for these people to have and be known for by others? *(Responses will vary.)* **Ask:** Whom do you admire? What qualities do you possess that that person also possesses? *(Responses will vary.)* **AS**

Readability Scores
Dale-Chall: 6.1
DRP: 58
Lexile: 920

TIME

Gentleman of the POOL

R Michael Phelps didn't beat the Olympic gold medal record at the 2004 Games. But the young swimmer left no doubt. He is a winner in—and out of—the pool.

By ALICE PARK

Mike Blake/ Reuters/NewsCom

OLYMPIC WINNER Michael Phelps is all smiles as he shows off one of the six gold medals he won at the 2004 Olympic Games in Athens, Greece.

During the 2004 Olympics in Athens, Greece, the world expected record-breaking success from swimmer Michael Phelps. The 19-year-old American was favored to win the most gold medals ever at a single Olympics. To reach that **goal**, Phelps would have needed to win 8 gold medals. That number would beat the record held by U.S. swimmer Mark Spitz, who had won 7 gold medals at the 1972 Olympics in Munich, Germany. **1**

Phelps's swimming meets were the most popular events of the first week of the Games. Fans streamed into the Olympic Aquatic Centre. TV ratings hit the roof.[1] Phelps chose to swim in the 200-meter freestyle on day three. The teenage swimmer knew he was not favored to win. But that didn't keep him from reaching for a personal goal.

---

1. If the television ratings *hit the roof,* a lot of people watched the Olympics on TV.

Vocabulary

goal (gohl) *n.* something that you aim for

1 Key Reading Skill

Questioning At this point, you might ask *why* Michael Phelps was favored to win so many medals.

Additional Support

Differentiated Instruction

Asking Questions Invite students to share the questions they asked themselves as they read the first page. You might model the process by reading the first sentence aloud and saying, "*Record-breaking success. What records did people expect Phelps to break? Oh, here's* the answer—they thought he might beat Mark Spitz's record of seven gold medals." Then ask students to read the next paragraph and share their questions. *(Possible response: What was the personal goal Phelps reached for?)* **BL**

Instead of giving in to doubt and fear, Phelps raced stroke for stroke against Olympic medal winners Ian Thorpe of Australia and Pieter van den Hoogenband of the Netherlands. Phelps came in third place, winning a bronze medal. That third-place win ended the race for the record 8 gold medals that the world had been watching for.

For Phelps, there was more to the Olympics than earning gold medals. The 200-meter bronze medal was proof that he could compete with the world's best—and enjoy it. "Racing the two greatest freestylers of all time in an Olympic final— it's fun," Phelps said after the race. "I had fun out there."

Phelps had gone to Athens as a star attraction. While there, he also became known as a sportsman. After the 200-meter freestyle, the teenage swimmer continued to work toward his goals. But he also cared about the **ambitions** and feelings of his teammates. Phelps wanted to share the fun of the Games. **2** So he gave up his spot in a medley relay[2] to teammate Ian Crocker. Earlier in the week, Crocker had cost the U.S. team the gold medal in another event. "He wasn't feeling too well [then], and I was willing to give him a chance to step up," says Phelps. "It was the right thing to do." **3**

By the end of the Games in Athens, Phelps had won 8 medals (6 gold medals and 2 bronze). That matched the record for the most medals earned at an Olympics. Building on Phelps's powerful swimming, the U.S. team had achieved its own **victory.** It swam to a world-record win in the medley relay. Phelps's winning effort had paid off for everyone. The young swimmer was an all-around winner. **4** **5**

—From *TIME*, August 30, 2004

2. A *medley relay* has four swimmers working together with each athlete swimming a different stroke in his or her part of the competition.

Vocabulary

ambitions (am BISH unz) *n.* strong desires to succeed

victory (VIK tur ee) *n.* the win in a contest or battle

---

2 | **English Language Coach**

Word Choice Michael Phelps cared about the *ambitions* of his teammates. Synonyms for *ambitions* are *aims*, *goals*, and *hopes*. **EL** Which of those words would you choose to replace the word *ambitions* here? Why?

3 | **Key Reading Skill**

Questioning Phelps wanted to share the fun of the Olympic Games. What question could you ask about that?

4 | **Key Literary Element**

Tone How would you describe the author's tone in this article? Can you tell what her attitude is toward Michael Phelps?

5 | **BIG Question**

What brought out the best in Phelps as a sportsman? Write your answer on the "Gentleman of the Pool" part of the Workshop 4 Foldable. **BQ**

Gentleman of the Pool **193**

Teach

EL Language Coach

Word Choice Say: *Ambitions* connotes a desire for recognition. Which of the suggested replacements do you think best expresses that desire? *(Responses will vary.)* **OL**

BQ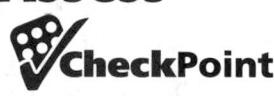

Ask: What challenges did Phelps face at the 2004 Olympics? *(Possible responses: the pressure of Olympic-level competition and his standards of sportsmanship)* **BL**
Ask: Which challenges were set by someone else? Which did Phelps set himself? *(Responses will vary.)* **OL**

Assess

✔CheckPoint

Use the CheckPoint questions provided on Presentation Plus! to check for comprehension of the selection. These questions can be used with interactive response keypads for immediate student feedback.

Reading in the Real World

College Conducting independent research is an important skill. Have students make a list of their unanswered questions about Michael Phelps. Brainstorm various resources they could use to answer these questions, including print and Internet resources and local experts, such as sports reporters or swimming coaches. Have a small group research each question. Require students to provide a source for each answer. **AS**

Objectives
- Make connections from text to self
- Ask questions
- Interpret and analyze character
- Identify and use synonyms
- Use text features: photographs

Assess

Resources for page 194

📁 Selection Quick Check, p. 17

📁 Selection and Unit Assessment, p. 19

💿 ExamView Assessment Suite

💿 Interactive Tutor: Self-Assessment

Students can respond to the *After You Read* items in their Learner's Notebooks or on a separate sheet of paper.

Answering the

1. Possible responses: rising to the challenge of Olympic competition, achieving a personal goal, or putting his teammate before himself

2. 200-meter freestyle (bronze medal); 100- and 200-meter butterfly (gold); 200- and 400-meter individual medley (gold); 400-meter freestyle (bronze); or 800-meter free relay (gold)

3. Michael tried to beat Mark Spitz's record.

Critical Thinking

4. Possible response: Fans hoped to see Michael win eight gold medals.

5. Possible response: Michael wanted to test himself and have fun.

6. Possible response: The quote "I had fun out there" suggests that Michael was not disappointed.

194

After You Read | Gentleman of the Pool

Answering the 🐟BIG Question

1. What brought out the best in Michael Phelps at the Olympic Games in Athens?

2. **Recall** What is one of the swimming events in which Michael competed at the Olympics? Which medals did he win?

   TIP **Right There** You will find the answer in the text.

3. **Recall** Whose record did Michael try to beat?

   TIP **Right There** You will find the answer in the text.

Critical Thinking

4. **Infer** Why were the swimming meets in which Michael Phelps competed the most popular events of the first week of the Olympic Games?

   TIP **Author and Me** You will find clues in the text, but you must also use the information in your head.

5. **Infer** Why did Michael choose to swim in the 200-meter freestyle even though he was not favored to win?

   TIP **Author and Me** You will find clues in the text, but you must also use the information in your head.

6. **Support** What fact from this selection supports the conclusion that Michael was not upset when he won the bronze medal for the 200-meter freestyle?

   TIP **Author and Me** You will find clues in the text, but you must also use the information in your head.

Talk About Your Reading

Michael Phelps gave up his place in a medley relay to his teammate Ian Crocker. What if the team had lost with Crocker? Get together with a partner to discuss whether Phelps giving his place to Crocker was a good idea or not. One of you will list reasons why it was a good idea and one of you will list reasons why it was a bad idea. Discuss the ideas on your lists and see if you come to the same conclusion in the end.

Objectives (pp. 194–195)
Reading Ask questions
Literature Identify literary elements: tone
Vocabulary Identify synonyms • Make word choices
Grammar Identify parts of speech: subject pronouns

194 UNIT 2 What Brings Out the Best in You?

Talk About Your Reading

Responses will vary. Students might give some of these reasons in support of their opinions about whether Phelps should have given up his place in the relay to Crocker.

Reasons Crocker should have raced:
- Crocker got another chance to help the team.
- He helped the U.S. team set a world record.
- Phelps had already earned a medal.

Reasons Phelps should have raced:
- He had qualified.
- He might have gotten more endorsements.
- Many think he is the best swimmer in history.

Skills Review

Key Reading Skill: Questioning

7. What questions did you ask yourself as you read this selection? How did asking yourself questions help you as a reader?

Key Literary Element: Tone

8. Which of the following words would you choose to describe the tone of this article about Michael Phelps?
admiring
playful
disappointed
jealous
sympathetic

9. Do you think a writer could use the same facts and a different tone? Do you think he or she could you make you feel differently about Michael Phelps? Explain your answer.

Vocabulary Check

goal   ambition   victory

10. In your Learner's Notebook, write two to four sentences about Michael Phelps using all three vocabulary words above. (You can use more than one word in a sentence.)

11. English Language Coach Pick three sentences from the selection. Copy the sentences in your Learner's Notebook. Choose one word in each sentence to replace with a synonym. Rewrite the sentences with that word.

Grammar Link: Subject Pronouns

You already know that sometimes it is correct to use *she* or *I* and sometimes it is correct to use *her* or *me*. The problem is knowing when to use which.

The subject of a sentence is who or what the sentence is about. A pronoun used as a subject must be one of the "subject pronouns."

Singular subject pronouns: I, you, he, she, it
Plural subject pronouns: We, you, they

It's easy to use subject pronouns correctly when the subject is one person. You would never say "Me ate breakfast" or "Her ran a mile." You must also use subject pronouns when the subject is more than one person.

• Wrong: Him and Joan tied for first place.
• Wrong: Joan and him tied for first place.
• Right: He and Joan tied for first place.

If you wonder what the correct subject is, get rid of the extra person (or people) in your mind.

Grammar Practice

Choose a pronoun to complete each sentence below. Rewrite each sentence with an appropriate pronoun in place. (There might be more than one correct answer.)

12. ____ and Lucy played catch.
13. The director chose Jarrod and ____ to play the lead roles.
14. ____ and Una asked my mother for cookies.

Skills Review

Key Reading Skill: Questioning

7. Responses will vary.

8. admiring

9. Responses will vary

Vocabulary Check

10. Responses will vary. Students should demonstrate knowledge of the vocabulary words' meanings in their sentences.

11. English Language Coach Responses will vary. Students should demonstrate their understanding of word meanings and word choices.

Close

Ask students to summarize what they learned about how to answer the Big Question from Michael Phelps's story.

Web Activities For eFlashcards, Selection Quick Checks, and other Web activities, go to www.glencoe.com.

Gentleman of the Pool **195**

Grammar Link: Pronoun Case

Grammar Practice
Possible responses

12. <u>She</u> and Lucy played catch.
13. The director chose Jarrod and <u>me</u> to play the lead roles.
14. <u>He</u> and Una asked my mother for cookies.

Teach

More About the Author

When Judith Ortiz Cofer's father was at sea serving in the U.S. Navy, her family lived in Puerto Rico. At other times, they lived in Paterson, New Jersey. *Silent Dancing: A Partial Remembrance of a Puerto Rican Childhood* was published in 1990.

V Vocabulary

Vocabulary File Say: The best way to learn new vocabulary is to use new words in your own writing. Now that you have written sentences using the words, try your hand at using the words in organized writing. In your Learner's Notebooks, write a paragraph about an experience you had as a child. Use at least four of the seven words in your paragraph. *(Responses will vary.)* **OL**

Before You Read : Primary Lessons

Judith Ortiz Cofer

Meet the Author

Judith Ortiz Cofer wrote about things that happened to her when she was a child. Through her writing, she shows her readers ways to adapt to new places and new cultures. She once wrote that memories come into her poems and stories "like time-travelers popping up with a message for me." See page R2 of the Author Files for more on Judith Ortiz Cofer.

Author Search For more about Judith Ortiz Cofer, go to www.glencoe.com.

Objectives (pp. 196–205)
Reading Ask questions • Make connections from text to self
Literature Identify literary elements: tone
Vocabulary Identify synonyms • Make word choices

Vocabulary Preview

emerged (ih MERJD) *v.* came out; past tense of *emerge* **(p. 198)** *The students emerged from their classrooms when the bell rang.*

chaos (KAY ahs) *n.* total confusion and disorder **(p. 198)** *Many children getting ready at the same time resulted in chaos.*

defiance (dih FY uns) *n.* bold resistance to authority **(p. 199)** *She showed defiance when she argued with her mother about going to school.*

indifference (in DIF fur uns) *n.* a lack of feeling or concern **(p. 200)** *Judith showed indifference to her friend's wishes.*

yearning (YUR ning) *n.* wanting something badly; past participle of *yearn* **(p. 201)** *Judith felt a yearning to stay at her grandmother's familiar house.*

unmindful (un MYND ful) *adj.* not aware **(p. 204)** *Judith was unmindful of the prejudice shown toward Lorenzo.*

relish (REL ish) *v.* to enjoy **(p. 204)** *If Lorenzo was asked to host the PTA show, he would relish the opportunity.*

Partner Talk Discuss the meaning of each word. Work together to create a sentence for each word. Write your sentences in your Learner's Notebook.

English Language Coach

Word Choice Good **word choice** is using just the *right* word. Choosing the right word will help you give the best descriptions and details. Sometimes there are plenty of words to choose from, but usually there is one that really stands out. One way to determine which word is the best is to use a thesaurus. To pick the best word, think about what you want to say and make it as clear as possible.

Write to Learn Choose one of the five situations below and think about ways to describe the scene using good word choice. First, make a list of vivid words and phrases that come to mind. Next, use those words and phrases in a paragraph describing the scene.
- a busy playground
- a sinking pirate ship
- harsh weather or environment
- a treasure hunt in the jungle
- an active animal indoors or outdoors

196 UNIT 2 What Brings Out the Best in You?

Additional Support

Author Search To expand students' appreciation of Judith Ortiz Cofer, have them access the Web site for additional information and resources.

Differentiated Instruction

Building Background In 1917, Puerto Ricans became United States citizens. In 1952, Puerto Rico became a commonwealth of the United States. Today, it is associated with the United States, but it has an independent government. Puerto Ricans share most of the rights and duties of U.S. citizens, but they do not pay federal income tax and do not vote in national elections unless they live on the mainland. Puerto Ricans debate whether the island should remain a commonwealth, become independent, or become the fifty-first U.S. state. Have students research the issue of Puerto Rican statehood and give short presentations about what they learn. **AL**

Skills Preview

Key Reading Skill: Questioning

As you read, it's important to ask yourself questions about the text. Look for the answers as you read. If you have questions that have not been answered when you are done reading, review the text. See if there is information you overlooked that will answer those questions.

Class Talk Brainstorm a list of questions you would ask someone to find out what brings out the best in him or her. Write the questions on the board.

Key Literary Element: Tone

The **tone** of a piece of writing shows you the author's attitude toward the subject. And it can change. It can be different in one part of the article or story than it is in another part. That's one of the ways an author leads readers to change their feelings about something.

It's important to remember, though, that the **tone** is the author's attitude, not the main character's or any other character's attitude. An author could even have an amused tone while one of the characters was very angry.

In an autobiographical story, the author may have a different attitude when writing about an event than he or she did while the event was happening. The author may be angry about something he or she was confused about twenty years before.

Group Discussion Talk in a group about things you feel differently about now than you did when they happened. Try to find examples in your own lives. Then ask why you feel differently. What caused the change in your attitude? What would your tone be now if you were writing about one of those events?

Interactive Literary Elements Handbook
To review or learn more about the literary elements, go to www.glencoe.com.

Get Ready to Read

Connect to the Reading

You learn a lot of different things at school, such as multiplying or writing reports. You also learn more real-life lessons, like how to get along with other people or how to be a dependable person. Think about the real-life lessons you have learned in school.

Write to Learn In your Learner's Notebook, list the three most important life lessons you have learned in school.

Build Background

Puerto Rico is a Caribbean island. The Taíno Indians were the first people to live there. In 1493 the explorer Christopher Columbus claimed the island for Spain. In 1899 America took it over after winning the Spanish-American War.

- Puerto Rico is about the size of the state of Delaware and has a population of about four million people.
- In 1917 Puerto Ricans were granted U.S. citizenship.
- Puerto Rico has two official languages: Spanish and English.

Set Purposes for Reading

BIG Question Read "Primary Lessons" to find out what brought out the best in Judith Ortiz Cofer.

Set Your Own Purpose What else would you like to learn from the story to help you answer the Big Question? Write your own purpose on the "Primary Lessons" part of the Workshop 4 Foldable.

Keep Moving

Use these skills as you read the following selection.

Primary Lessons **197**

Teach

L Literary Element

Tone Say: Begin to think about key events in your own life that occurred during or before grade school. Does one event stick out in your mind as being particularly meaningful? *(Responses will vary.)* **Say:** Try to recall your feelings and attitude about the event. Perhaps at the time you felt very strongly about what was happening. Do you still feel strongly about it, or has your attitude about it changed? If you were going to write about the event, what tone would you use? *(Responses will vary.)* **OL AL**

C Critical Thinking

Synthesis Say: Based on the real-life lessons you have learned, create slogans that express your lessons, such as "Play fair" or "Don't give up." *(Responses will vary.)* **AS**

Interactive Literary Elements Handbook Have students access the Web site to improve their understanding of character.

English Language Coach

Spanish Language This is a good opportunity for Spanish-speaking students to take leadership roles by translating Spanish words and concepts. Ask students to locate Spanish words and phrases in the text. Write the words on the board and invite Spanish-speaking students to translate them into English. If necessary, invite English-speaking students to write them in a way that reflects more common English usage. Encourage students to ask their classmates questions to clarify word meanings. **EL OL**

Objectives
- Ask questions
- Identify literary elements: tone
- Learn and use new vocabulary
- Synthesize text

Teach

Viewing the Photo

Say: Describe what you see in this photo. *(A group of young children running toward a truck. It looks like it takes place in a warm climate.)* **BL** **Ask:** Can you explain what the words in the picture mean? *(Free Reading for Everyone. Library on Wheels Number 3.)* **EL** If your class does not have Spanish speakers, provide the above translation for students.

R Reading Skill

Questioning Say: When something in the text triggers a question, the answer might not be given immediately. Instead, you may have to keep the question in mind as you read, especially if the author wants to build suspense, or you may need to jot it down. You might also have to review what you've already read. For example, reread the first paragraph to answer the question, Why are schools color-coded? *(to identify them as government property)* **BL**

Readability Scores
Dale-Chall: 5.9
DRP: 57
Lexile: 1060

Primary LESSONS

by Judith Ortiz Cofer

My mother walked me to my first day at school at La Escuela Segundo Ruiz Belvis, named after the Puerto Rican patriot born in our town. I remember yellow cement with green trim. All the classrooms had been painted these colors to identify them as government property. This was true all over the Island.

Everything was color-coded, including the children, who wore uniforms from first through twelfth grade. We were a midget army in white and brown, led by the hand to our battleground. From practically every house in our barrio[1] **emerged** a crisply ironed uniform inhabited by the wild creatures we had become over a summer of running wild in the sun. **1**

At my grandmother's house where we were staying until my father returned to Brooklyn Yard in New York and sent for us, it had been complete **chaos,** with several children to get ready for school. My mother had pulled my hair harder than usual while braiding it, and I had dissolved into a pool of total self-pity. I wanted to stay home with her and *Mamà*, to continue listening to stories in the late afternoon, to drink *café con leche*[2] with them, and to play rough games with my many cousins. I wanted to continue living the dream of summer

---

1. A *barrio* (BAH ree oh) is a neighborhood where Hispanic people live.
2. *Café con leche* (KAH fay con LAY chay) is coffee with milk in it.

Vocabulary

emerged (ih MERJD) *v.* came out

chaos (KAY ahs) *n.* total confusion and disorder

198 UNIT 2 What Brings Out the Best in You?

Practice the Skills

1 **Key Reading Skill**

Questioning What question could you ask about the color-coding in the school? **R**

Additional Support

Literature Focus Lesson

Author's Purpose Tell students that authors have many reasons for writing autobiographies. Sometimes they want to tell about the main events of their lives. Sometimes they want to express their ideas about things that are important to them. Ask students to listen as you read aloud the passage located in the middle of the third full paragraph on the following page. It begins, "I had spent my early childhood. . . ." Ask students how they think the author's experience of living in two cultures will influence her autobiography. **AS**

afternoons in Puerto Rico, and if I could not have that, then I wanted to go back to Paterson, New Jersey, back to where I imagined our apartment waited, peaceful and cool for the three of us to return to our former lives. Our gypsy lifestyle had convinced me, at age six, that one part of life stops and waits for you while you live another for a while—and if you don't like the present, you can always return to the past. Buttoning me into my stiff blouse while I tried to squirm away from her, my mother tried to explain to me that I was a big girl now and should try to understand that, like all the other children my age, I had to go to school. **2**

"What about him?" I yelled pointing at my brother who was lounging on the tile floor of our bedroom in his pajamas, playing quietly with a toy car.

"He's too young to go to school, you know that. Now stay still." My mother pinned me between her thighs to button my skirt, as she had learned to do from *Mamà*, from whose grip it was impossible to escape.

"It's not fair, it's not fair. I can't go to school here. I don't speak Spanish." It was my final argument, and it failed miserably because I was shouting my **defiance** in the language I claimed not to speak. Only I knew what I meant by saying in Spanish that I did not speak Spanish. I had spent my early childhood in the U.S. where I lived in a bubble created by my Puerto Rican parents in a home where two cultures and languages became one. I learned to listen to the English from the television with one ear while I heard my mother and father speaking in Spanish with the other. I thought I was an ordinary American kid—like the children on the shows I watched—and that everyone's parents spoke a secret second language at home. When we came to Puerto Rico right before I started first grade, I switched easily to Spanish. It was the language of fun, of summertime games. But school—that was a different matter.

I made one last desperate attempt to make my mother see reason: "Father will be very angry. You know that he wants us to speak good English." My mother, of course, ignored me as she dressed my little brother in his playclothes. I could not

Practice the Skills

2 | **Reviewing Skills**

Connecting Have you ever felt sorry for yourself? Why or why not? **R**

The author, Judith Ortiz Cofer, as a child

Vocabulary

defiance (dih FY uns) *n.* bold resistance to authority

Primary Lessons **199**

Teach

R Reading Skill

Review Connecting Ask: If you were in the author's situation, how would you have reacted? *(Responses will vary.)* How does thinking about your reaction help you understand how the author felt? *(Possible response: I remember how I felt the first day of kindergarten. I was so upset that I cried. This memory helps me understand how the author feels.)* **AS**

L Literary Element

Character Ask: What do you learn about the narrator's character as a child based on her reaction to dressing for and going to school? *(Possible responses: She cherished her freedom. She feared going to school. She didn't like the confinements of the uniform.)* **OL** The narrator is an adult reflecting back on her experience as a child. Do you think the adult narrator is sympathetic to herself as a little girl? Explain. *(Possible responses: She is sympathetic. Her description of her fear and her desperation to stay home are told in a way that is both kind and humorous. She helps the reader truly understand how she felt.)* **AL**

Reading Fluency

Dialogue Remind students that dialogue is a conversation between two people. Ask one student to read Judith's words and have another take her mother's part. Instruct them to read only the words in quotation marks as the other students listen. Ask students to suppose that they are helping a director make pages 198–199 into a movie. How do they handle the narrator's thoughts? *(Possible responses: try to convey them with facial expressions and body movements; include a voice-over with the author's narration)* **OL AL**

Objectives

- Ask questions
- Make connections from text to self
- Identify literary elements: tone
- Use text features: photographs
- Identify author's purpose

199

Teach

L Literary Element

Tone Ask: How does Ortiz describe having to go to school? How did it make her feel? *(Possible response: She says she will no longer be able to play games and she'll have to be silent. She also will have to control her "wild imagination." She feels "locked into" and a loss of freedom. She says that this causes her anxiety.)* **AL**

Analyzing the Art

Say: How would you describe this painting? Does it help you visualize the setting of this story? Explain. *(Responses will vary.)* **OL**

believe her **indifference** to my father's wishes. She was usually so careful about our safety and the many other areas that he was forever reminding her about in his letters. But I was right, and she knew it.

Our father spoke to us in English as much as possible, and he corrected my pronunciation constantly—not "jes" but "y-es." Y-es, sir. How could she send me to school to learn Spanish when we would be returning to Paterson in just a few months? **3**

But, of course, what I feared was not language, but loss of freedom. At school there would be no playing, no stories, only lessons. It would not matter if I did not understand a word, and I would not be allowed to make up my own definitions. I would have to learn silence. I would have to keep my wild imagination in check. Feeling locked into my stiffly starched uniform, I only sensed all this. I guess most children can intuit³ their loss of childhood's freedom on that

3. When you *intuit* (in TOO it) something, no one teaches or explains it to you; you just know it.

Vocabulary

indifference (in DIF fur uns) *n.* a lack of feeling or concern

Practice the Skills

3 Key Literary Element

Tone How does the young Judith Ortiz feel in this part of the story? What is her attitude toward going to school? What attitude does the older Judith Ortiz Cofer, the author, have toward her younger self?

L

El Sol Asombre, 1989. Rafael Ferrer (b. 1933). Puerto Rico (Spanish descent). Oil on canvas, 60 x 72 in. The Butler Institute of American Art, Youngstown, OH.

Analyzing the Art In this painting, Puerto Rican artist Rafael Ferrer shows the brilliant light and striking colors of the Caribbean islands. Does Ortiz Cofer write about Puerto Rico's beautiful scenery in this story? Why or why not?

200 UNIT 2 What Brings Out the Best in You?

Additional Support

Differentiated Instruction

Comparison Chart The paragraph about "loss of freedom" contrasts "childhood's freedom" to school. Draw a two-column chart on the board. Ask students to reread the paragraph beginning "But, of course . . ." and find items related to freedom. *(playing, stories, making up my own definitions, imagination, playground)* Place these items on one side of the chart. Place items related to school on the other side. *(no playing, no stories, lessons, silence, controlling imagination, feeling locked in, stiff, starched, loss of childhood's freedom)* Ask students why they think the author develops the comparison at such length. Then ask if they agree with her comparison. **OL**

first day of school. It is separation anxiety[4] too, but mother is just the guardian of the "playground" of our early childhood.

The sight of my cousins in similar straits[5] comforted me. We were marched down the hill of our barrio where *Mamà's* robin-egg-blue house stood at the top. I must have glanced back at it with **yearning**. *Mamà's* house—a place built for children—where anything that could be broken had already been broken by my grandmother's early batch of offspring (they ranged in age from my mother's oldest sisters to my uncle who was six months older than me). Her house had long since been made child-proof. It had been a perfect **C** summer place. And now it was September—the cruelest month for a child.

La Mrs., as all the teachers were called, waited for her class of first-graders at the door of the yellow and green classroom. She too wore a uniform: it was a blue skirt and a white blouse. This teacher wore black high heels with her "standard issue." I remember this detail because when we were all seated in rows she called on one little girl and pointed to the back of the room where there were shelves. She told the girl to bring her a shoebox from the bottom shelf. Then, when the box had been placed in her hands, she did something unusual. She had the little girl kneel at her feet and take the pointy high heels off her feet and replace them with a pair of satin slippers from the shoebox. She told the group that every one of us would have a chance to do this if we behaved in her class. Though confused about the prize, I soon felt caught up in the competition to bring *La Mrs.* her slippers in the morning. Children fought over the privilege. **4**

Our first lesson was English. In Puerto Rico, every child has to take twelve years of English to graduate from school. It is the law. In my parents' schooldays, all subjects were taught in English. The U.S. Department of Education had specified that as U.S. territory, the Island had to be "Americanized," and to accomplish this task, it was necessary for the Spanish

---

4. **Separation anxiety** is the fear that some people feel when they are away from their loved ones.

5. **Straits** means "difficult positions."

Vocabulary

yearning (YUR ning) *n.* wanting something badly

Practice the Skills

4 | **Key Reading Skill**

Questioning What question would you ask yourself about the children changing the teacher's shoes?

R

Teach

C Critical Thinking

Comprehension Ask: What does the author mean when she says September is "the cruelest month for a child"? *(Possible response: She means that it is horrible for children because they have to start school and say good-bye to the freedoms of summer.)* **Ask:** Do you agree with her evaluation of September? *(Responses will vary.)* **AS**

R Reading Skill

Questioning Invite students to share their questions. Discuss how the questions might help them understand the selection. For example, "Would I have wanted to change the teacher's shoes?" helps students connect. "Why did the teacher do this?" helps students understand how important status was to the teacher. **OL**

English Language Coach

Multiple-Meaning Words Point out that the word *primary* in the title can have multiple meanings. It can refer to the early grades in school, but it can also mean "basic" or "most important." Ask students to explain in what ways what Judith learned about status could be called a "primary lesson." *(Possible response: On a literal level, Judith learned the lesson she describes in first grade; figuratively, she learned basic truths about her culture and the importance of status.)* **AL**

Objectives
- Identify literary elements: tone
- Ask questions
- Understand multiple-meaning words
- Monitor comprehension
- Find meaning in art

Teach

R Reading Skill

Questioning Say: Review the questions you have previously recorded. Have you encountered answers to any of those questions in the text? *(Responses will vary.)* Record any answers you have encountered. **AS**

C Critical Thinking

Synthesis Ask: What would you do if you could not understand your teacher's instructions? *(Possible response: I wouldn't want to look like I didn't know what I was doing, so I would just imitate what others were doing or saying.)* **AS**

---

language to be replaced in one generation through the teaching of English in all schools. My father began his school day by saluting the flag of the United States and singing "America" and "The Star-Spangled Banner" by rote,[6] without understanding a word of what he was saying. The logic behind this system was that, though the children did not understand the English words, they would remember the rhythms. Even the games the teacher's manuals required them to play became absurd adaptations. "Here We Go Round the Mulberry Bush" became "Here We Go Round the Mango Tree." I have heard about the confusion caused by the use of a primer[7] in which the sounds of animals were featured. The children were forced to accept that a rooster says *cockadoodledoo*, when they knew perfectly well from hearing their own roosters each morning that in Puerto Rico a rooster says *cocorocó*. Even the vocabulary of their pets was changed; there are still family stories circulating about the bewilderment of a first-grader coming home to try to teach his dog to speak in English. The policy of assimilation by immersion[8] failed on the Island. Teachers adhered to it on paper, substituting their own materials for the texts, and no one took their English home. In due time, the program was minimized[9] to the one class in English per day that I encountered when I took my seat in *La Mrs.'s* first-grade class. **5 6**

Catching us all by surprise, she stood very straight and tall in front of us and began to sing in English: "Pollito—Chicken, Gallina—Hen, Làpiz—Pencil, Y Pluma—Pen."

C "Repeat after me, children: Pollito—Chicken," she commanded in her heavily accented English that only I understood, being the only child in the room who had ever been exposed to the language. But I too remained silent. No use making waves, or showing off. Patiently *La Mrs.* sang her song and gestured for us to join in. At some point it must have dawned on the class that this silly routine was likely to

---

6. If you do a thing by **rote,** you do it from memory without thinking about it.

7. A **primer** is a textbook that children use to learn to read.

8. **The policy of assimilation by immersion** is the method of teaching English by having all school work done in English in the hope that students will start using English as their first language.

9. **Minimized** (MIN ih myzd) means "cut back."

202 UNIT 2 What Brings Out the Best in You?

Practice the Skills

5 Key Literary Element

Tone What attitude does the author have toward the attempts to replace Spanish with English? How would you describe the tone of this section?

6 English Language Coach

Word Choice What words in this paragraph help you understand the author's tone?

Additional Support

Reading in the Real World

Citizenship Show students how they might evaluate the effect of the U.S. policy on teaching English in Puerto Rico. Tell students that when the U.S. government tried to replace Spanish with English, the children were confused because their families still spoke Spanish.

Learning English could help people get better jobs in the United States. Ask students what they think would happen to Puerto Rican culture if everyone spoke English. The author says the policy failed. Ask students to explain whether or not they agree. **AL** go on all day if we did not "repeat after her." It was not her fault that she had to follow the rule in her teacher's manual stating that she must teach English *in* English, and that she must not translate, but must repeat her lesson in English until the children "begin to respond" more or less "unconsciously." This was one of the vestiges of the regimen followed by her predecessors in the last generation. To this day I can recite "Pollito—Chicken" mindlessly, never once pausing to visualize chicks, hens, pencils, or pens. **7**

I soon found myself crowned "teacher's pet" without much effort on my part. I was a privileged child in her eyes simply because I lived in "Nueva York," and because my father was in the Navy. His name was an old one in our pueblo, associated with once-upon-a-time landed people and long-gone money. Status is judged by unique standards in a culture where, by definition, everyone is a second-class citizen. Remembrance of past glory is as good as titles and money. Old families living in decrepit old houses rank over factory workers living in modern comfort in cement boxes— all the same. The professions raise a person out of the dreaded "sameness" into a niche of status, so that teachers, nurses, and everyone who went to school for a job were given the honorifics of *El Míster* or *La Mrs.* by the common folks, people who were likely to be making more money in American factories than the poorly paid educators and government workers.

My first impression of the hierarchy[10] began with my teacher's shoe-changing ceremony and the exaggerated respect she received from our parents. *La Mrs.* was always right, and adults scrambled to meet her requirements. She wanted all our schoolbooks covered in the brown paper now

---

10. A ***hierarchy*** (HY ur ar kee) is a ranking of people or things based on certain standards.

Analyzing the Photo The author says that she was the "teacher's pet," or the teacher's favorite student. Who do you think might be the "teacher's pet" in this photo? Explain your answer.

Practice the Skills

7 | **Key Reading Skill**

Questioning Ask yourself whether this reciting was a good way to learn. Does the author think it was good?

Primary Lessons **203**

Teach

Viewing the Photo
Ask: How does this photo help you visualize the text? *(Possible response: The photo helps me visualize the classroom setting from the author's childhood. It helps me imagine the events more clearly.)* **OL**

R Reading Skill

Questioning Ask students to identify any sentences they find unclear or confusing. Work with them to generate questions that would help them better understand the passage. **BL OL EL**

Differentiated Instruction

Diagrams Have students work with partners to visually represent the hierarchy of relationships in the community the author describes. After the diagrams are completed, invite students who used different formats (such as pyramids, writing the people at the top in larger letters and those at the bottom in smaller letters, or other creative approaches) to explain why they organized their diagrams as they did. **AL**

Objectives
- Ask questions
- Identify literary elements: tone
- Identify and use pronouns
- Synthesize text
- Use text features: photographs

203

Teach

C Critical Thinking

Analysis Ask: What similarity does the narrator note between herself and Lorenzo? *(They were both the teacher's pets.)* What difference does she note? *(She didn't have to work for the teacher's affection, but Lorenzo did.)* **OL Ask:** What does the narrator realize this means? *(Possible response: She realizes that wealth and status are privileged.)* **AL**

used for paperbags (used at that time by the grocer to wrap meats and other foods). That first week of school the grocer was swamped with requests for paper which he gave away to the women. That week and the next, he wrapped produce in newspapers. All school projects became family projects. It was considered disrespectful at *Mamà's* house to do homework in privacy. Between the hours when we came home from school and dinner time, the table was shared by all of us working together with the women hovering in the background. The teachers communicated directly with the mothers, and it was a matriarchy[11] of far-reaching power and influence. **8**

C There was a black boy in my first-grade classroom who was also the teacher's pet but for a different reason than I: I did not have to do anything to win her favor; he would do anything to win a smile. He was as black as the cauldron that *Mamà* used for cooking stew and his hair was curled into tight little balls on his head—*pasitas*, like little raisins glued to his skull, my mother had said. There had been some talk at *Mamà's* house about this boy; Lorenzo was his name. I later gathered that he was the grandson of my father's nanny. Lorenzo lived with Teresa, his grandmother, having been left in her care when his mother took off for "Los Nueva Yores" shortly after his birth. And they were poor. Everyone could see that his pants were too big for him—hand-me-downs—and his shoe soles were as thin as paper. Lorenzo seemed **unmindful** of the giggles he caused when he jumped up to erase the board for *La Mrs.* and his baggy pants rode down to his thin hips as he strained up to get every stray mark. He seemed to **relish** playing the little clown when she asked him to come to the front of the room and sing his phonetic version of "o-bootifool, forpashios-keeis" leading the class in our incomprehensible tribute to the American flag. He was a bright, loving child, with a talent for song and mimicry[12] that

---

11. A *matriarchy* (MA tree ar kee) is a form of rule where women have most of the power.
12. *Mimicry* (MIH mih kree) is the act of mimicking, or copying, someone.

Vocabulary

unmindful (un MYND ful) *adj.* not aware
relish (REL ish) *v.* to enjoy

Practice the Skills

8 Key Reading Skill

Questioning What questions would you ask yourself to help understand this paragraph better?

Additional Support

Literature Focus Lesson

Character Ask students to explain how the author makes Lorenzo's character come to life. Discuss how she describes his appearance, clothes, mannerisms, and personality and explains how others react to him. Then have students use the descriptions the author provides as guidelines for drawing a picture of Lorenzo. Invite students to share their pictures with the rest of the class. **BL OL**

everyone commented on. He should have been chosen to host the PTA show that year instead of me. **9**

At recess one day, I came back to the empty classroom to get something, my cup? My nickel for a drink from the kioskman? I don't remember. But I remember the conversation my teacher was having with another teacher. I remember because it concerned me, and because I memorized it so that I could ask my mother to explain what it meant.

"He is a funny *negrito*, and, like a parrot, he can repeat anything you teach him. But his *mamà* must not have the money to buy him a suit."

"I kept Rafaelito's First Communion suit; I bet Lorenzo could fit in it. It's white with a bow-tie," the other teacher said.

"But, Marisa," laughed my teacher, "in that suit, Lorenzo would look like a fly drowned in a glass of milk."

Both women laughed. They had not seen me crouched at the back of the room, digging into my schoolbag. My name came up then.

"What about the Ortiz girl? They have money."

"I'll talk to her mother today. The superintendent, *El Americano* from San Juan, is coming down for the show. How about if we have her say her lines in both Spanish and English." **10**

Visual Vocabulary
Women and girls used to wear *crinoline petticoats,* stiff underskirts that made dresses or skirts stand out.

The conversation ends there for me. My mother took me to Mayagüez and bought me a frilly pink dress and two crinoline petticoats to wear underneath so that I looked like a pink and white parachute with toothpick legs sticking out. I learned my lines, "Padres, maestros, Mr. Leonard, bienvenidos/Parents, teachers, Mr. Leonard, welcome . . ." My first public appearance. I took no pleasure in it. The words were formal and empty. I had simply memorized them. My dress pinched me at the neck and arms, and made me itch all over. **11**

I had asked my mother what it meant to be a "mosca en un vaso de leche," a fly in a glass of milk. She had laughed at the image, explaining that it meant being "different," but it wasn't something I needed to worry about. **12** ○

Primary Lessons **205**

Practice the Skills

9 **Key Reading Skill**

Questioning Ask yourself why Lorenzo was not chosen to host the PTA show. Look for an answer in the rest of the story.

10 **Key Literary Element**

Tone Carefully read the last seven paragraphs again. Can you tell what the author thinks about the teachers and the way they talked about Lorenzo? If you're not sure, keep reading to find out. **L**

11 **Key Reading Skill**

Questioning Did you ask a question about the importance of the lessons Judith learned in school? If you didn't write a question about the importance of what Judith learned, write one in your Learner's Notebook. Be sure to answer your question. **R**

12 **BIG Question**

A struggle often brings out the best in a person. What does Judith struggle with in this story? Do you think it brings out the best in her? Explain your answer on the "Primary Lesson" part of the Workshop 4 Foldable.

Teach

C Critical Thinking

Analysis Ask: What do you learn about the teachers from the way they are talking about their students? *(Possible response: They are very concerned about the school looking good, and they value wealth and status over achievement.)* **AL**

R Reading Skill

Questioning Ask: Do you think you are better at asking questions now than when you started this unit? What kinds of things have you learned about asking questions as you read? How has questioning helped improve your understanding? *(Responses will vary.)* **AS**

Assess

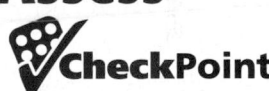
CheckPoint

Use the CheckPoint questions provided on Presentation Plus! to check for comprehension of the selection. These questions can be used with interactive response keypads for immediate student feedback.

Reading in the Real World

Citizenship There are issues of status and prejudice in every culture. Cofer recognized these issues in Puerto Rico, partly because she was new to the culture. Ask students to think about what it means to be "a second-class citizen" in our culture and what might be done to make sure people are treated equally. Divide students into small groups and allow them time to discuss their responses to the above questions. Invite groups to share the main points of their discussions with the rest of the class. **AS**

Objectives
• Identify literary elements: tone
• Ask questions
• Analyze text

Assess

Resources for page 206

📁 Selection Quick Check, p. 18

📁 Selection and Unit Assessment, p. 20

💿 ExamView Assessment Suite

💿 Interactive Tutor: Self-Assessment

Students can respond to the *After You Read* items in their Learner's Notebooks or on a separate sheet of paper.

Answering the

1. Responses will vary.
2. Yellow cement with green trim marked the school as government property.
3. Her hair was braided, and she wore a brown and white uniform.

Critical Thinking

4. Possible response: Judith's father was a Navy officer who encouraged his children to speak good English and whose word was law in his household.
5. Possible response: Educators who require uniforms often believe they encourage good behavior and make differences between rich and poor children less obvious.
6. Possible response: Judith spoke English and had more opportunities than people who lived on the island.

After You Read | Primary Lessons

Answering the BIG Question

1. Do you think the school brought out the best in either Judith or Lorenzo? Explain.
2. **Recall** How did Judith know the school was government property?
   Tip **Right There** You will find the answer in the text.
3. **Describe** What did Judith look like when she was ready for school?
   Tip **Think and Search** The answer is in the text, but the details are not all in one place.

Critical Thinking

4. **Infer** What kind of person was Judith's father? How can you tell?
   Tip **Author and Me** You will find clues in the text, but you must also use the information in your head.
5. **Explain** Why do you think the children were required to wear uniforms?
   Tip **Author and Me** You will find clues in the text, but you must also use the information in your head.
6. **Draw Conclusions** Why did the fact that Judith had lived in New York cause her to be considered a privileged child?
   Tip **Author and Me** You will find clues in the text, but you must also use the information in your head.

Write About Your Reading

Use what you learned from "Primary Lessons" to complete this **RAFT** assignment. Scan the story if you need to find particular details or events you don't remember clearly.

Objectives (pp. 206–207)
Reading Ask questions • Make connections from text to self
Literature Identify literary elements: tone
Vocabulary Identify synonyms • Make word choices
Writing Write a response to literature
Grammar Identify parts of speech: object pronouns

R Your role is a school inspector.
A Your audience is the school board.
F Your form is a three-paragraph report.
T Your topic is whether the children of Puerto Rico should have been forced to speak only English in school. Give examples to support your position.

206 UNIT 2 What Brings Out the Best in You?

Write About Your Reading

Responses will vary. Check students' responses for examples from the story.

Skills Review

Key Reading Skill: Questioning

7. How did you use questioning to help you understand this story? List the three questions you wrote that most helped you.

Key Literary Element: Tone

8. How would you describe the overall tone of "Primary Lessons"? Look at the words below and see if any of them fit. Or choose your own words.

angry   critical   gentle   heartbroken   anxious

9. What would you write about in an angry tone? Explain your answer.

Reviewing Skills: Connecting

10. Have you ever felt different at school? What was that experience like for you? If you have never felt different at school, why do you think that is?

Vocabulary Check

chaos   yearning   defiance

Write *True* or *False* for each statement below.

11. There was **chaos** in grandmother's house when all the children got ready for school.

12. Judith was **yearning** to go to school in Puerto Rico.

13. Judith showed **defiance** to her teacher, *La Mrs.*

14. **English Language Coach** Copy three sentences from the selection into your Learner's Notebook. Choose one word in each sentence to replace with a synonym. Rewrite the sentences with that word.

Literature Online

Web Activities For eFlashcards, Selection Quick Checks, and other Web activities, go to www.glencoe.com.

Grammar Link: Object Pronouns

You'll learn about objects later on in this book. Then the term *object pronouns* will make more sense. For now, you need to know one thing: object pronouns are the personal pronouns that aren't used as subjects.

Singular object pronouns: me, you, him, her, it
Plural object pronouns: us, you, them

It's easy to use object pronouns correctly when you're talking about one person. You would never say "The ball hit I" or "I really like she." You must also use object pronouns when the object is more than one person.

• Wrong: Keira made Patsy and I lunch.
• Wrong: She argued with he and Greg.
• Right: Jerry laughed at Gary and him.

If you wonder what the correct pronoun is, get rid of the extra person (or people) in your mind.

• Yuri liked Will and (she, her).

You would never say "Yuri liked she," so you would use *her* in this sentence.

Grammar Practice

Choose a pronoun to complete each sentence below. Rewrite each sentence with an appropriate pronoun in place.

15. Lauren took ____ to the store on the island.

16. La Mrs. started singing and asked Judith and ____ to join in.

17. The teachers respected Judith and ____.

Writing Application Look back at your writing assignment. Check to see that you used all pronouns correctly.

Skills Review

Key Reading Skill: Questioning

7. Responses will vary.

Key Literary Element: Tone

8. Possible response: The tone is gentle, even though she is learning an important lesson about how people view race, wealth, and status.

9. Responses will vary.

Reviewing Skills: Connecting

10. Responses will vary.

Vocabulary Check

11. True
12. False
13. False
14. **English Language Coach** Responses will vary. Students should demonstrate a clear understanding of word meaning and word choice.

Close

Ask students what they learned about the Big Question from reading "Primary Lessons".

Grammar Link: Pronoun Usage

Grammar Practice

15. Lauren took me went to the store on the island.

16. La Mrs. started singing and asked Judith and <u>them</u> to join in.

17. The teachers respected Judith and <u>him</u>.

Comparing Characters

Objectives covered in this workshop:
• Understand and evaluate author's use of characterization
• Connect, compare, and contrast characters across texts

Comparing Literature: Characters

Why Is It Important?

• Understanding characters is integral to comprehending stories and other selections. Understanding and comparing characters in texts will also help students think about how they relate to the characters.

• Understanding and comparing characters in texts will help students learn how to understand and compare real people in the media and in their lives.

• Students will be able to learn lessons from characters' words and actions when they perceive and compare them.

How to Help Students Get It

• Read one or more selections with rich character description. Choose two or three characters to compare. Together with your students, create a Venn diagram that compares several relevant characteristics.

• Model identifying and comparing characters in texts by doing a Think Aloud with your students. Choose two selections. As you read the first selection, comment when you come across significant descriptions, actions, thoughts, words, interactions, and responses to a character. Discuss what those elements reveal about the characters. As you progress, shift the responsibility for recognizing attributes of the characters to the students. When you read the second selection, ask students to help you compare the characters in the two selections.

Reading to Answer the Big Question

The two selections in the Comparing Literature Workshop of Unit 2 describe different situations in which external events lead to the main character discovering something about himself. As they read, your students will think about their own answers to the Big Question: **What brings out the best in you?**

The Pigman and Me by Paul Zindel
In this excerpt from a memoir, Zindel describes a conflict he faces in his first week at a new school. He is given lots of advice from Nonno (grandfather) Frankie, some of it good and some of it unhelpful, but all very creative. Figuring out how to solve the conflict without hurting or being hurt by his opponent brings out the best in Paul.

The Goodness of Matt Kaizer by Avi
Matt Kaizer is the unruly son of a wise minister who has faith that his son will eventually change for the better. Matt is determined to maintain his bad reputation, but reluctantly gives it up when he gets involved with Mr. Bataky, a dying man with a truly wicked past who considers Matt his angel. Matt's friends regret the sad sight of "a bad kid going good."

Workshop Resources

PACING (DAYS) STANDARD	BLOCK	LESSON	STUDENT MATERIALS	TEACHER RESOURCES
1	1	Comparing Literature: Setting	🔥 English Language Coach Review, p. 41	🔥 Bellringer Options Transparencies –Daily Language Practice 19 💿 Presentation Plus!
1	1	"The Pigman and Me"	💻 Glencoe Online 🔥 Unit Vocabulary Review, p. 39 🔥 Academic Vocabulary Review, p. 42 📁 English Language Coach 🔥 Comparing Literature Graphic Organizer, p. 34 💿 StudentWorks Plus™ 💻 Online Student Edition 💿 Literature Classics	💻 Puzzlemaker 💿 Skill Level Up!™ A Language Arts Game 💻 BookLink 3 📘 Assessment by Learning Objective (Diagnostic and Formative) 💿 Interactive Tutor: Self-Assessment 💿 TeacherWorks Plus™ 💿 ExamView Assessment Suite
1		"The Goodness of Matt Kaizer"	💻 Glencoe Online 🔥 Unit Vocabulary Review, p. 39 🔥 Academic Vocabulary Review, p. 42 📁 English Language Coach 🔥 Comparing Literature Graphic Organizer, p. 34 💿 StudentWorks Plus™ 💻 Online Student Edition 💿 Literature Classics	💻 Puzzlemaker 💿 Skill Level Up!™ A Language Arts Game 💻 BookLink 3 📘 Assessment by Learning Objective (Diagnostic and Formative) 💿 Interactive Tutor: Self-Assessment 💿 TeacherWorks Plus™ 💿 ExamView Assessment Suite

Keys for Unit Resource

- 📁 Blackline Master
- 📘 Workbook
- 📖 Supplemental Text
- 💿 CD-ROM
- 💾 DVD
- 🔥 Transparency
- 💻 Web-based
- 🔥 Fast File

Level Appropriate Code

- **AS** = Activities for all students
- **AL** = Activities for students working above grade level
- **OL** = Activities for students working at grade level
- **BL** = Activities for students working below grade level
- **EL** = Activities for English language learners

from
The Pigman & Me

by Paul Zindel

& The Goodness of Matt Kaizer

by Avi

Focus

BELLRINGER Options

Daily Language Practice Transparency 19

Focus Activity Draw a Venn diagram on the board. Label one circle *Cats* and the other *Dogs*. Label the overlap *Similarities*. Then have students list traits for each. Begin by saying, "They have fur" and listing it in the overlap. Encourage students to identify at least three characteristics for each part of the diagram. **AS**

Teach

L Literary Element

Character Say: One way to understand characters is to pay attention to how they meet challenges. Can you think of some examples of characters that you have read about who have overcome obstacles or solved problems? *(Responses will vary.)* **OL**

What You'll Learn

• How to compare two pieces of literature
• How to analyze characters

Skills Focus

You will practice using these skills when you read the following selections:
• from *The Pigman & Me*, p. 211
• "The Goodness of Matt Kaizer," p. 221

Point of Comparison

• Character

Purpose

• To compare characters in two texts

Objectives (pp. 208–209)
Literature Identify literary elements: character • Compare and contrast: literature

208 UNIT 2

How is a dinosaur like a bird? How are they different? To answer these questions, you have to compare the characteristics that you know about each. For example, you might compare when they lived, how big they are (or were), and whether they had feathers. Whether you are comparing two animals, two movies, or two books, the skills you use are the same.

How to Compare Literature: Character

You can't compare every single detail in two stories. It would take too much time, and most of the details wouldn't be important. You need to think about the characteristics of the selections that are most important. When you compare the excerpt from *The Pigman & Me* and "The Goodness of Matt Kaizer," you will look closely at the *main character* in each selection. One is a real person and the other is fictional, but you can use the same methods to look at both of them.

As you read, look for details and clues that tell you what the main character is like. Think of words that you might use to describe the character—like *brave, scared, confident, cruel, greedy, thoughtful,* or *funny*. To find details about the character, look at:

• the things a character says and does
• the things that other characters think and say about a particular character
• the way other characters react to a particular character
• the author's description of the character

L

Additional Support

Differentiated Instruction

Asking Questions Remind students that questioning helps them clarify their understanding of a text as they read. Provide them with the following prompts to analyze characters.

• What kind of person is the character?

• Why does the character act this way?
• How does the character try to solve problems?
• How does the character change?
• What does the character learn? **AS**

Get Ready to Compare

Before you compare the main characters in the excerpt from *The Pigman & Me* and "The Goodness of Matt Kaizer," you need to analyze and understand those characters. One good way to analyze a character is to make notes about the clues you find that reveal things about the character. Then write down what each clue tells you about the character. Sometimes you'll find out that a character changes during the selection. Early in the selection a clue might tell you that a character is mean to other people. Later in the selection, though, you might find clues that tell you the character has changed—he's nice to other people.

Here's how one student filled out a character chart for a story about a boy named Antoine.

Character Chart For Antoine

Clue	What it tells me about Antoine
Antoine looked away when Elise looked at him.	Antoine was either shy or he liked Elise.
Antoine could speak to his friend Jenny but not to Elise.	He wanted Elise to be his girlfriend, but he didn't have confidence.
Antoine hated to look in the mirror.	He thought he was not attractive. He didn't have confidence.
After the contest, he spoke to Elise.	He gained confidence after the contest.

Use Your Comparison

In the excerpt from *The Pigman & Me*, the main character is named Paul. Before you start reading this selection, make a chart like the one above. The columns should have the headings "Clues" and "What it tells me about Paul." Fill in the chart as you read.

After you finish the selection, make a similar chart for the character Matt in "The Goodness of Matt Kaizer." When you've finished both charts, compare the two main characters to see which character changed the most.

Comparing Literature Workshop 209

Teach

L Literary Element

Character Say: Read the beginning of the excerpt from *The Pigman & Me*. List any clues to Paul's character in your chart. *(Possible responses: nervous, new, ready to defend himself, accident-prone, not usually violent)* **AS**

Assess/Close

Have students choose a picture from a magazine and use it to create a character. Ask them to write a caption for the picture that gives the character a name, a hometown, and a problem to solve. Tell students to list three words that describe the character. **BL OL**

Resources for page 209

 Use the Comparing Literature Graphic Organizer BLM in the Unit 2 Resource Booklet, p. 34.

Literature Focus Lesson

Types of Characters Introduce students to words used to describe characters. *Flat* characters have only one trait. *Round* characters have many traits; they are like real people. *Static* characters don't change; *dynamic* characters do. Work with students to think of examples of each type of character.

Give the following examples to begin: flat-Cinderella's ugly stepsisters; round-Cinderella; static-fairy godmother; dynamic-prince who falls in love with Cinderella. Have students think of characters from other folktales that can fit into these categories. **OL**

Objectives
• Compare and contrast character across texts
• Interpret and analyze character
• Ask questions

209

Teach

More About the Author

Paul Zindel was a high school chemistry and physics teacher before he became a writer. He noticed that most of the books written for young adults "had no connection to the young people I knew." So he started writing about "the continuous battle to get through the years between twelve and twenty." Eventually he decided that he could do most for young people as a writer, so he left teaching. Besides writing numerous young adult novels, Zindel won a Pulitzer Prize for the play *The Effect of Gamma Rays on Man-in-the-Moon Marigolds.*

V   Vocabulary

Synonyms Tell students to identify at least two synonyms for each of the vocabulary words. If necessary, provide a thesaurus. Encourage students to use synonyms with which they are familiar to help them remember the new words. *(Responses will vary.)* **AS**

Before You Read *from* The Pigman & Me

Paul Zindel

Meet the Author

Paul Zindel is the author of realistic books for adults, children, and teenagers. His stories teach the lessons that he learned while growing up. Many of his characters and stories are based on his own experiences. One of his most popular novels, *The Pigman & Me,* is an autobiographical book about Zindel's life growing up in Staten Island, New York. See page R7 of the Author Files for more on Paul Zindel.

Literature Online

Author Search For more about Paul Zindel, go to www.glencoe .com.

Objectives (pp. 210–219)
Literature Identify literary elements: character • Make connections from text to self • Compare and contrast: literature

Vocabulary Preview

paranoid (PAIR uh noyd) *adj.* feeling like everyone is against you **(p. 211)** *Grace was so paranoid that we couldn't even joke with her anymore.*

observant (ub ZER vunt) *adj.* good at noticing details **(p. 216)** *I wasn't observant enough to notice the stain on my shirt.*

vicious (VISH us) *adj.* mean and cruel **(p. 216)** *Eldon's vicious dog kept everyone away from his house.*

decent (DEE sunt) *adj.* kind or thoughtful **(p. 219)** *Even though some kids were afraid of her, Mrs. Wren was decent to me.*

Get Ready to Read

Connect to the Reading

Have you ever felt like an outsider? Why? What did you do to make yourself feel better?

Build Background

This excerpt from *The Pigman & Me* takes place during Paul's first week at a new school. Paul lives with his sister Betty and his mother. The other kids mentioned in the selection are friends and neighbors of Paul. Paul's family is of Italian heritage.

- *Nonno* means "grandfather" in Italian.
- Nonno Frankie is an older man who is a friend of Paul's family.
- Nonno Frankie tells Paul about Sicilian combat tactics. Sicily is an island off the coast of Italy.

Set Purposes for Reading

BIG Question   Read to find out if anyone in this story has an experience that brings out the best in him or her.

Set Your Own Purpose What else would you like to learn from the story to help you answer the Big Question? Write your own purpose on "The Pigman & Me" part of the Comparing Literature Workshop Foldable.

Additional Support

Literature Online

Author Search To expand students' appreciation of Paul Zindel, have them access the Web site for additional information and activities.

Differentiated Instruction

Creative Writing Tell students to review their answers to the Connect to the Reading questions. Then, challenge them to write short stories based on their answers. Encourage students to consider how they want to portray themselves. Also, have them consider how to portray their feelings through their actions and reactions. When students finish their stories, invite them to trade papers with partners. Partners can provide constructive comments for revisions. When students have finished revisions, have them put their stories in a class binder to share with others. **AL**

from
The Pigman & Me

by Paul Zindel

When trouble came to me, it didn't involve anybody I thought it would. It involved the nice, normal, smart boy by the name of John Quinn. Life does that to us a lot. Just when we think something awful's going to happen one way, it throws you a curve and the something awful happens another way. This happened on the first Friday, during gym period, when we were allowed to play games in the school yard. A boy by the name of Richard Cahill, who lived near an old linoleum factory, asked me if I'd like to play paddle ball with him, and I said, "Yes." Some of the kids played softball, some played warball, and there were a few other games where you could sign out equipment and do what you wanted. What I didn't know was that you were allowed to sign out the paddles for only fifteen minutes per period so more kids could get a chance to use them. I just didn't happen to know that little rule, and Richard Cahill didn't think to tell me about it. Richard was getting a drink from the water fountain when John Quinn came up to me and told me I had to give him my paddle. ∎

"No," I said, being a little **paranoid** about being the new kid and thinking everyone was going to try to take advantage of me.

Vocabulary

paranoid (PAIR uh noyd) *adj.* feeling like everyone is against you

Practice the Skills

1 | **Comparing Literature**

Character This paragraph describes how Paul feels when he starts going to a new school. Think about what it tells you about Paul. Is he nervous or calm? Is he afraid or unafraid? In your Character Chart, write what Paul says or does that gives you a clue to his character. Now write what the clue tells you about Paul in the second column.

from *The Pigman & Me* **211**

Teach

Viewing the Photo
Ask: What is pictured? *(an apple tree in a field)* **BL** In this story, the main character and his family's elderly friend have a conversation about a special tree. When you encounter the dialogue, pay attention. It is a clue to Paul's character. **AS**

L Literary Element

Character Ask: What techniques does the author use to characterize himself as a child? *(Possible response: He reflects on the situation, describes what he knew and didn't know, and explains how he felt.)* **OL**

Readability Scores
Dale-Chall: 5.6
DRP: 51
Lexile: 830

Literature Focus Lesson

Reversals Paul says, "Just when we think something awful's going to happen one way, [life] throws you a curve and the something awful happens another way." Such reversals, or unexpected changes, are one way authors keep readers interested in their stories. Ask students if they have ever found this to be true in their own lives. Then have them write about a time that something like this has happened. Ask volunteers to share their narratives with the class. **AS**

Objectives
• Interpret and analyze character
• Identify and use synonyms
• Use text features: photographs
• Learn and use new vocabulary

Teach

L Literary Element

Character Ask: What does Paul's shock suggest about whether or not he intended to hurt John? Was his apology sincere? *(Responses will vary. Students may suggest that his shock indicates that he was sincere.)* **OL AL**

C Critical Thinking

Analysis Ask: What does the beginning of the sentence, "I was expecting him to notice right off the bat that I was white with fear," tell you about Paul? *(Possible response: He is really worried about John's planned revenge.)* **OL Ask:** What does it imply about his relationship with Nonno Frankie? *(Possible response: They must be close if Paul thinks Nonno Frankie can discern his fear from just looking at him sitting in a tree.)* **AL**

"Look, you have to give it to me," John Quinn insisted. That was when I did something beserk. I was so wound up and frightened that I didn't think, and I struck out at him with my right fist. I had forgotten I was holding the paddle, and it smacked into his face, giving him an instant black eye. John was shocked. I was shocked. Richard Cahill came running back and he was shocked. **2**

"What's going on here?" Mr. Trellis, the gym teacher, growled.

"He hit me with the paddle," John moaned, holding his eye. He was red as a beet, as Little Frankfurter, Conehead, Moose, and lots of the others gathered around.

"He tried to take the paddle away from me!" I complained.

"His time was up," John said.

Mr. Trellis set me wise to the rules as he took John over to a supply locker and pulled out a first-aid kit.

"I'm sorry," I said, over and over again.

Then the bell rang, and all John Quinn whispered to me was that he was going to get even. He didn't say it like a nasty rotten kid, just more like an all-American boy who knew he'd have to regain his dignity about having to walk around school with a black eye. Before the end of school, Jennifer came running up to me in the halls and told me John Quinn had announced to everyone he was going to exact revenge on me after school on Monday. That was the note of disaster my first week at school ended on, and I was terrified because I didn't know how to fight. I had never even been in a fight. What had happened was all an accident. It really was.

When Nonno Frankie arrived on Saturday morning, he found me sitting in the apple tree alone. Mom had told him it was O.K. to walk around the whole yard now, as long as he didn't do any diggings or mutilations other than weed-pulling on her side. I was expecting him to notice right off the bat that I was white with fear, but instead he stood looking at the carvings Jennifer and I had made in the trunk of the tree. I thought he was just intensely curious about what "ESCAPE! PAUL & JENNIFER!" meant. Of course, the twins,

Practice the Skills

2 Comparing Literature

Character How does Paul feel after he hits Richard? Write your clue in the Clues column on your chart. In the second column, write what the clue tells you about Paul. **L**

Apple Tree, 1912. Gustav Klimt. On deposit at the Oesterreichische Galerie, Vienna, Austria. Private Collection.

Additional Support

Reading in the Real World

Citizenship Paul got into a conflict with John. Discuss whether the way he responded was the best way to try to resolve the situation. If your school has an anti-bullying or conflict resolution program, help students apply the principles taught in these programs to the incident between Paul and John. If your school doesn't, suggest rules that would be good to apply to this situation and others like it. Have students discuss their ideas in small groups and present them to the class. Then have students develop a classroom conflict resolution program as a class. **AS**

being such copycats, had already added their names so the full carving away of the bark now read, "ESCAPE! PAUL & JENNIFER! & NICKY & JOEY!" And the letters circled halfway around the tree.

"You're killing it," Nonno Frankie said sadly.

"What?" I jumped down to his side.

"The tree will die if you cut any more."

I thought he was kidding, because all we had done was carve off the outer pieces of bark. We hadn't carved deep into the tree, not into the heart of the tree. The tree was too important to us. It was the most crucial place to me and Jennifer, and the last thing we'd want to do was hurt it.

"The heart of a tree isn't deep inside of it. Its heart and blood are on the outside, just under the bark," Nonno Frankie explained. "That's the living part of a tree. If you carve in a circle all around the trunk, it's like slitting its throat. The water and juices and life of the tree can't move up from the roots!" I knew about the living layer of a tree, but I didn't know exposing it would kill the whole tree. I just never thought about it, or I figured trees patched themselves up.

"Now it can feed itself from only half its trunk," Nonno Frankie explained. "You must not cut any more."

"I won't," I promised. Then I felt worse than ever. Not only was I scheduled to get beat up by John Quinn after school on Monday. I was also a near tree-killer. Nonno Frankie finally looked closely at me. **3**

"Your first week at school wasn't all juicy meatballs?" he asked.

That was all he had to say, and I spilled out each and every horrifying detail. Nonno Frankie let me babble on and on. He looked as if he understood exactly how I felt and wasn't going to call me stupid or demented or a big yellow coward. When I didn't have another word left in me, I just shut up and stared down at the ground.

"Stab nail at ill Italian bats!" Nonno Frankie finally said.

"What?"

He repeated the weird sentence and asked me what was special about it. I guessed, "It reads the same backward as forward?"[1]

---

1. Words, phrases, or sentences that are spelled the same way backwards and forwards (not counting spaces and punctuation) are called **palindromes.**

Practice the Skills

3 **Comparing Literature**

Character How does Paul feel after he learns what carving the tree could do to it? What does his reaction tell you about his character? Write this clue and what it tells you in your Character Chart. **L**

from *The Pigman & Me* **213**

Teach

L **Literary Element**

Character **Say:** At first, Paul doesn't take Nonno Frankie's warning about killing the tree seriously. Why is this? *(He doesn't see how cutting the bark could hurt the tree.)* **Ask:** What changes Paul's mind? *(Nonno Frankie explains how carving the bark could kill a tree.)* **BL** **Ask:** How does Nonno Frankie's explanation change Paul's feelings? *(Possible response: He feels guilty for being a "near tree-killer.")* **OL** **Ask:** Compare Paul's reaction to hitting John and his reaction to hurting the tree. Does the conversation about the tree confirm or change your first impressions of Paul? *(Responses will vary.)* **AL**

Literature Focus Lesson

Regional Expressions Explain that writers sometimes have characters use words and expressions characteristic of people who live in a certain region. Ask students to find examples that show Nonno Frankie's Italian heritage. *(using* Nonno *for "grandfather"; "your first week at school wasn't all juicy meatballs?"; "stab nail at ill Italian bats!")* Discuss what these examples add to the story. *(local color; humor; help to better understand characters)* **AS**

Objectives
• Analyze text
• Interpret and analyze character
• Identify and analyze expressions

Teach

L Literary Element

Character **Say:** Describe Nonno Frankie's character. *(Possible response: He is a smart and funny man. He obviously is in touch with Paul's feelings and wants to help.)* **OL**

Ask: What do you learn about Nonno Frankie from his description of "Sicilian combat tactics"? *(Possible response: He values intelligence and survival over saving face. He does not want Paul to fear bullies.)* **AL**

Viewing the Photo

Ask: How does the picture relate to the text? *(The picture shows a plane taking off, like the one Paul and Nonno Frankie hear.)* **BL**

"Right! Ho! Ho! Ho! See, you learn! You remember things I teach you. So today I will teach you how to fight, and you will smack this John Quinn around like floured pizza dough."

"But I can't fight."

"I'll show you Sicilian combat tactics."[2]

"Like what?"

"Everything about Italian fighting. It has to do with your mind and body. Things you have to know so you don't have to be afraid of bullies. Street smarts my father taught me. Like 'Never miss a good chance to shut up!'" **4**

VAROOOOOOOOOOM!

A plane took off over our heads. We walked out beyond the yard to the great field overlooking the airport.

Nonno Frankie suddenly let out a yell. *"Aaeeeeeyaaaayeeeeeh!"* It was so blood-curdlingly weird, I decided to wait until he felt like explaining it.

"Aaeeeeeyaaaayeeeeeh!" he bellowed again. "It's good to be

---

2. The word **Sicilian** refers to Sicily, an island off the coast of Italy. **Sicilian combat tactics** are ways of fighting.

Practice the Skills

4 **Comparing Literature**

Character Nonno Frankie claims that his father taught him street smarts like, "Never miss a good chance to shut up!" What can you guess about Nonno Frankie's father from this advice? **L**

Analyzing the Photo What word does the author use to help readers "hear" the sound that this plane makes?

Additional Support

Reading Fluency

Build Fluency Point out that much of the story consists of a dialogue between Paul and Nonno Frankie. Ask for two volunteers to read the first part of the conversation aloud, beginning with "Stab nail . . ." on page 213 and ending with ". . . shut up!" on page 214. After students have finished, explain that one way to read dialogue is to imagine how each character's voice sounds. Ask students how they think Nonno Frankie might sound and what Paul's voice might be like. Then have students read again, taking on the personas of the given characters. **AS**

able to yell like Tarzan!" he said. "This confuses your enemy, and you can also yell it if you have to retreat. You run away roaring and everyone thinks you at least have guts! It confuses everybody!"

"Is that all I need to know?" I asked, now more afraid than ever of facing John Quinn in front of all the kids.

"No. Tonight I will cut your hair."

"Cut it?"

"Yes. It's too long!"

"It is?"

"Ah," Nonno Frankie said, "you'd be surprised how many kids lose fights because of their hair. Alexander the Great always ordered his entire army to shave their heads. Long hair makes it easy for an enemy to grab it and cut off your head."[3]

"John Quinn just wants to beat me up!"

"You can never be too sure. This boy might have the spirit of Genghis Khan!"[4]

"Who was Genghis Khan?"

"Who? He once killed two million enemies in one hour. Some of them he killed with yo-yos." [5]

"Yo-yos?"

"See, these are the things you need to know. The yo-yo was first invented as a weapon. Of course, they were as heavy as steel pipes and had long rope cords, but they were still yo-yos!"

"I didn't know that," I admitted. [6]

"That's why I'm telling you. You should always ask about the rules when you go to a new place."

"I didn't think there'd be a time limit on handball paddles."

"That's why you must ask."

"I can't ask everything," I complained.

"Then you *read*. You need to know all the rules wherever you go. Did you know it's illegal to hunt camels in Arizona?"

"No."

"See? These are little facts you pick up from books and teachers and parents as you grow older. Some facts and rules

---

3. *Alexander the Great* was a Greek soldier-king who built a huge empire more than 2300 years ago that included parts of three continents.

4. *Genghis Kahn* was an Asian soldier-emperor who conquered much of Asia and built an enormous empire between the years 1185 and 1226.

Practice the Skills

5 | Comparing Literature

Character How would you describe Nonno Frankie? List three interesting or unusual things that he says or does. Then explain what these "clues" tell you about Nonno Frankie. **L1**

6 | Comparing Literature

Character Do you think Paul believes Nonno Frankie's statement that yo-yos were used as weapons by Genghis Khan? Does Paul's response to the statement tell you anything about him? If so, make a note of it in your Character Chart. **L2**

from *The Pigman & Me* 215

Teach

L1 Literary Element

Character Ask: If you were making this story into a movie, whom would you choose to play Nonno Frankie? Why do you think this actor fits the part? *(Responses will vary.)* **OL**

L2 Literary Element

Character Say: Decide whether Nonno Frankie is trying to give Paul factual information about yo-yos or whether he is exaggerating to make a point. What makes you think so? *(Possible response: It seems like he is trying to make a point, which is to let Paul know that he doesn't need to be afraid of a bully.)* **OL**

Differentiated Instruction

Fact Checking Just because something appears in print doesn't mean it is true. Sometimes common sense tells readers something can't be true. Ask students if they think anything Nonno Frankie says about yo-yos is exaggerated. Then ask them if they think he gives an accurate history of the yo-yo. Discuss how students could check the facts. Have students follow through on their fact checking. Invite them to share their findings with the class. Students may discover that yo-yos were used to hunt animals and attack enemies in the Philippines, but the Mongols preferred bows and arrows, battle axes, and curved swords. **BL OL**

Objectives
• Interpret and analyze character
• Use text features: photographs

215

Teach

EL Language Coach

Word Choice Say:
Sometimes substituting a word with its synonym can affect the word's meaning. For example, "this vicious John Quinn" sounds scarier than "this mean John Quinn." Using a thesaurus, find other words that have the same connotations as vicious. *(Possible responses: savage or fierce)* **EL** **BL**

L Literary Element

Character Ask: How does the narrator describe John Quinn in the first paragraph of the story? *("nice, normal, smart boy")* **BL**
Ask: Why doesn't Paul think John is "vicious"? *(Possible responses: John was responding to an unprovoked attack. Paul is fair-minded.)* **OL**

---

come in handy, some don't. You've got to be **observant**. Did you know that Mickey Mouse has only *four* fingers on each hand?"

"No."

"All you have to do is look. And rules change! You've got to remember that. In ancient Rome, my ancestors worshipped a god who ruled over mildew. Nobody does anymore, but it's an interesting thing to know. You have to be connected to the past and present and future. At NBC, when they put in a new cookie-cutting machine, I had to have an open mind. I had to prepare and draw upon everything I knew so that I didn't get hurt." **7**

Nonno Frankie must have seen my mouth was open so wide a baseball could have flown into my throat and choked me to death. He stopped at the highest point in the rise of land above the airport. "I can see you want some meat and potatoes. You want to know exactly how to beat this **vicious** John Quinn."

"He's not vicious." **8**

"Make believe he is. It'll give you more energy for the fight. When he comes at you, don't underestimate the power of negative thinking! You must have only positive thoughts in your heart that you're going to cripple this monster. Stick a piece of garlic in your pocket for good luck. A woman my mother knew in Palermo did this, and she was able to fight off a dozen three-foot-tall muscular Greeks who landed and

Visual Vocabulary
A *Portuguese man-of-war* is a jelly-like animal that lives in the ocean and has long, stinging tentacles.

tried to eat her. You think this is not true, but half her town saw it. The Greeks all had rough skin and wore backpacks and one-piece clothes. You have to go with what you feel in your heart. One of my teachers in Sicily believed the Portuguese man-of-war jellyfish originally came from England. He felt that in his heart, and he eventually proved it. He later went on to be awarded a government grant to study tourist swooning sickness in Florence."

Vocabulary

observant (ub ZER vunt) *adj.* good at noticing details

vicious (VISH us) *adj.* mean and cruel

Practice the Skills

7 **Comparing Literature**

Character Why did Nonno Frankie have to have an open mind when they put in a new machine where he worked? What did his determination to learn to use it safely say about his character?

8 **Comparing Literature**

Character When Nonno Frankie calls John Quinn "vicious," Paul defends John. What does this tell you about Paul's sense of fairness? Write the clue and what it tells you in your Character Chart. **L** **EL**

Additional Support

English Language Coach

Hyperbole Paul and Nonno Frankie both exaggerate. Paul's mouth isn't just open, it's "open so wide a baseball could have flown" in. This kind of exaggeration is called *hyperbole*. Ask students to find other examples of hyperbole. *(Possible responses: Nonno Frankie's curses, Paul's acting as though he'd "received a death blow")* Discuss what hyperbole adds to the story. *(Possible responses: humor, vivid description)* **EL** **OL**

216

"But how do I hold my hands to fight? How do I hold my fists?" I wanted to know.

"Like *this*!" Nonno Frankie demonstrated, taking a boxing stance with his left foot and fist forward.

"And then I just swing my right fist forward as hard as I can?"

"No. First you curse him."

"*Curse* him?"

"Yes, you curse this John Quinn. You tell him, 'May your left ear wither and fall into your right pocket!' And you tell him he looks like a fugitive from a brain gang! And tell him he has a face like a mattress! And that an espresso coffee cup would fit on his head like a sombrero. And then you just give him the big Sicilian surprise!" **9**

"What?"

"You *kick* him in the shins!"

By the time Monday morning came, I was a nervous wreck. Nonno Frankie had gone back to New York the night before, but had left me a special bowl of pasta and steamed octopus that he said I should eat for breakfast so I'd have "gusto" for combat. I had asked him not to discuss my upcoming bout with my mother or sister, and Betty didn't say anything so I assumed she hadn't heard about it.

Jennifer had offered to get one of her older brothers to protect me, and, if I wanted, she was willing to tell Miss Haines so she could stop anything from happening. I told her, "No." I thought there was a chance John Quinn would have even forgotten the whole incident and wouldn't make good on his revenge threat. Nevertheless, my mind was numb with fear all day at school. In every class I went to, it seemed there were a dozen different kids coming over to me and telling me they heard John Quinn was going to beat me up after school.

At 3 P.M. sharp, the bell rang.

All the kids started to leave school.

I dawdled.[5]

---

5. To *dawdle* is to take more time than needed.

Practice the Skills

9 ▎**Comparing Literature**

Character What do you think is the purpose for the curses? What do they tell you about Nonno Frankie's personality? Write this clue and what it tells you in your Character Chart. **C**

Analyzing the Art Does this picture remind you of the advice that Nonno Frankie gives to Paul? Explain why or why not.

from *The Pigman & Me* **217**

Teach

C Critical Thinking

Analysis Say: Why do you think Nonno Frankie teaches Paul how to fight instead of telling him fighting is wrong? *(Possible responses: Paul needs to know how to defend himself. In some cultures fighting is acceptable.)* **Ask:** Do you think Nonno Frankie's techniques will work? Why or why not? *(Responses will vary.)* **OL**

Literature Focus Lesson

Suspense Direct students to the paragraph beginning "By the time Monday morning came . . ." Ask them why they think the author takes so long to build up to the fight. Help students identify techniques the author uses to build suspense as they continue to read the story, such as the description of Paul's feelings and of the faces of the "mob" (page 218). **OL** Ask students if they can find places where the author changes the pace to match what Paul is experiencing. *(Possible responses: slows with Paul's dawdling; speeds up as Paul walks to meet John)* **AL**

Objectives
• Interpret and analyze character
• Identify and use synonyms
• Identify hyperbole
• Identify literary elements: suspense

Teach

L1 Literary Element

Character **Say:** There are many possible answers to the question about why Paul doesn't run. However, his response is somewhat unexpected. Why? *(Some students may mention that Paul does not look forward to the fight like some people might—he has already described himself as "numb with fear" about the whole thing.)* **AL**

L2 Literary Element

Character **Ask:** What do Jennifer's actions and reactions say about her character? *(Possible response: She is reasonable. She is not violent.)* **Ask:** What do they say about her relationship with Paul? *(Possible response: She cares about him and doesn't want to see him hurt.)* **OL** **AL**

I cleaned my desk and took time packing up my books. Jennifer was at my side as we left the main exit of the building. There, across the street in a field behind Ronkewitz's Candy Store, was a crowd of about 300 kids standing around like a big undulating[6] horseshoe, with John Quinn standing at the center bend glaring at me.

"You could *run*," Jennifer suggested, tossing her hair all to the left side of her face. She looked much more than pretty now. She looked loyal to the bone.

"No," I said. I just walked forward toward my fate, with the blood in my temples pounding so hard I thought I was going to pass out. Moose and Leon and Mike and Conehead and Little Frankfurter were sprinkled out in front of me, goading[7] me forward. I didn't even hear what they said. I saw only their faces distorted in ecstasy and expectation. They looked like the mob I had seen in a sixteenth-century etching where folks in London had bought tickets to watch bulldogs attacking water buffalo. **10**

John stood with his black eye, and his fists up.

I stopped a few feet from him and put my fists up. A lot of kids in the crowd started to shout, "Kill him, Johnny!" but I may have imagined that part.

L2 John came closer. He started to dance on his feet like all father-trained fighters do. I danced, too, as best I could. The crowd began to scream for blood. Jennifer kept shouting, "Hey, there's no need to fight! You don't have to fight, guys!"

But John came in for the kill. He was close enough now so any punch he threw could hit me. All I thought of was Nonno Frankie, but I couldn't remember half of what he told me and I didn't think any of it would work anyway.

"Aaeeeeeyaaaayeeeeeh!" I suddenly screamed at John. He stopped in his tracks and the crowd froze in amazed silence. Instantly, I brought back my right foot, and shot it forward to kick John in his left shin. The crowd was shocked, and booed me with mass condemnation for my Sicilian fighting

Borders & Boundaries, 2002. Diana Ong. Computer graphics.

Practice the Skills

10 **Comparing Literature**

Character Why do you think Paul says "No" when Jennifer suggests that he run? Could he have more than one reason? Does this tell you anything about his character? If so, write your clue and what it tells you in your Character Chart. **L1**

---

6. *Undulating* means "moving back and forth or up and down like a wave."

7. If you *goad* someone, you push him or her into doing something they don't want to do.

Additional Support

English Language Coach

Figurative Language Explain to students that figurative language is often used to paint lively pictures with words. Draw students' attention to the last sentence of the paragraph labeled 10. Explain that the author uses a simile here to compare the crowd of students to a historical mob. By doing so, he creates a picture of a savage crowd waiting to witness death of some sort. Ask students to discuss the effects of the phrases *for blood* and *in for the kill* used later on the page. Lead students to see that these exaggerations help paint the picture of Paul's fear. In other words, things seem that bad to him, when in fact this is a relatively mild schoolyard fight. **EL** **BL**

technique. I missed John's shin, and kicked vainly again. He threw a punch at me. It barely touched me, but I was so busy kicking, I tripped myself and fell down. The crowd cheered. I realized everyone including John thought his punch had floored me. I decided to go along with it. I groveled in the dirt for a few moments, and then stood up slowly holding my head as though I'd received a death blow. John put his fists down. He was satisfied justice had been done and his black eye had been avenged. He turned to leave, but Moose wasn't happy. **11**

"Hey, ya didn't punch him enough," Moose complained to John.

"It's over," John said, like the **decent** kid he was.

"No, it's not," Moose yelled, and the crowd began to call for more blood. Now it was Moose coming toward me, and I figured I was dead meat. He came closer and closer. Jennifer shouted for him to stop and threatened to pull his eyeballs out, but he kept coming. And that was when something amazing happened. I was aware of a figure taller than me, running, charging. The figure had long blond hair, and it struck Moose from behind. I could see it was a girl and she had her hands right around Moose's neck, choking him. When she let him go, she threw him about ten feet, accidentally tearing off a religious medal from around his neck. Everyone stopped dead in their tracks, and I could see my savior was my sister. **12**

"If any of you tries to hurt my brother again, I'll rip your guts out," she announced.

Moose was not happy. Conehead and Little Frankfurter were not happy. But the crowd broke up fast and everyone headed home. I guess that was the first day everybody learned that if nothing else, the Zindel kids stick together. As for Nonno Frankie's Sicilian fighting technique, I came to realize he was ahead of his time. In fact, these days it's called karate.[8] **13** ○

---

8. **Karate** is a form of self-defense that uses kicks and punches.

Vocabulary

decent (DEE sunt) *adj.* kind or thoughtful

Practice the Skills

11 | **Comparing Literature**

Character Paul acted like he was hurt even though he wasn't. Why did he do that? What do you think was more important to him than winning the fight? Does this add anything to your view of Paul's character? If so, put it in your Character Chart. **L1**

12 | **Comparing Literature**

Character This paragraph describes how Paul's sister helps him. What does the description tell you about Paul's relationship with his sister? Make a note of this relationship in your Character Chart.

13 | **BIG Question**

In this story, did anything bring out the best in Paul? Explain. Did the fight bring out the best in anyone else? Explain. Write your answer on "The Pigman & Me" part of the Comparing Literature Workshop Foldable. Your answer will help you complete the Unit Challenge later. **BQ**

from *The Pigman & Me* **219**

Teach

L1 **Literary Element**

Character **Say:** Paul acted like he was hurt. Was that a smart way for him to get out of a fight he didn't want to have, or should he have kept fighting? *(Responses will vary.)* **BL** **OL**

L2 **Literary Element**

Character **Ask:** Does anything in the last paragraph help you answer the question about Paul's relationship with his sister? *(Possible response: "[T]he Zindel kids stick together.")* **Ask:** Can you find another clue to their relationship? *(Paul calls his sister "my savior.")* **BL** **OL**

BQ

Ask: Do you believe a fight can ever bring out the best in someone? Explain. *(Responses will vary.)* **AS**

Assess

✓**CheckPoint**

Use the CheckPoint questions provided on Presentation Plus! to check for comprehension of the selection. These questions can be used with interactive response keypads for immediate student feedback.

Literature Focus Lesson

Plot Twists Readers might expect the climax, or decisive moment, to be when John put his fists down. However, Zindel has a surprise in store: Moose starts to attack Paul. In yet another surprise, Paul's sister enters the fight. Only then does Zindel provide a final resolution of the conflict. Discuss whether students find the ending satisfying, or whether they would have preferred a different ending to the story. **AS**

Objectives
• Interpret and analyze character
• Identify literary elements: plot twists
• Understand figurative language

219

Teach

More About the Author

Avi is an award-winning author, but the first versions of his books are a mess. He has dysgraphia, which means that his first drafts are filled with misspellings and reversed letters. He remembers that in school he "was perceived as being sloppy and erratic, and not paying attention." However, he liked what he wrote, so he kept writing more stories. Now he has published more than thirty books. When asked which of them is his favorite, he says, "The next one."

Vocabulary

Word Play To familiarize students with the vocabulary words, have them make crossword puzzles in which the vocabulary words are the answers. Tell students to be creative in forming clues. When they finish, have them trade papers with partners and complete the puzzles. **AS**

Before You Read | The Goodness of Matt Kaizer

Meet the Author

When Avi was a child in Brooklyn, New York, he had a lot of trouble with writing. He misspelled words and reversed letters. He even failed many of his courses in high school. But he did not give up writing. Today Avi is one of the most popular writers of books for young people. See page R1 of the Author Files for more on Avi.

Literature Online

Author Search For more about Avi, go to www.glencoe.com.

Objectives (pp. 220–233)
Literature Identify literary elements: character • Make connections from text to self • Compare and contrast: literature
Vocabulary Identify synonyms and antonyms

Vocabulary Preview

taunt (tawnt) *v.* to try to anger someone by teasing him or her **(p. 222)** *Don't taunt me about my haircut.*

retreat (rih TREET) *v.* to move backward, away from a situation **(p. 225)** *If it's too dangerous, we'll retreat.*

gloomy (GLOO mee) *adj.* dull, dark, and depressing **(p. 226)** *The closed curtains made the room look really gloomy.*

reputation (rep yuh TAY shun) *n.* character as judged by other people **(p. 230)** *Matt was concerned about his reputation.*

English Language Coach

Synonyms and Antonyms Good writers use a lot of different words in their writing. To practice learning the synonyms and antonyms of a word, create a word web like the one below that has *goodness* in the inner circle. Fill in the synonyms and antonyms in the outer circles.

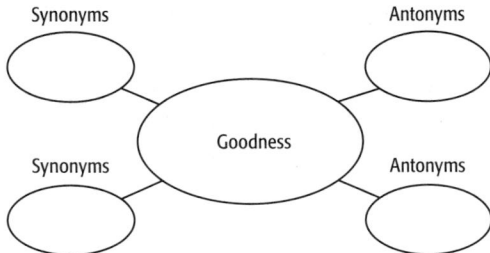

Get Ready to Read

Connect to the Reading

How would you feel if you tried to do something that was bad or cruel, but other people thought that what you did was good or kind?

Set Purposes for Reading

BIG Question Read to find out how Mr. Bataky brings out the best in Matt and how Matt brings out the best in Mr. Bataky.

Set Your Own Purpose What else would you like to learn from the story to help you answer the Big Question? Write your own purpose on "The Goodness of Matt Kaizer" part of the Comparing Literature Workshop Foldable.

220 UNIT 2 What Brings Out the Best in You?

Additional Support

Literature Online

Author Search To expand students' appreciation of Avi, have them access the Web site for additional information and resources.

English Language Coach

Synonyms and Antonyms After students complete their word webs, remind them that synonyms often have slightly different meanings. For example, one synonym for *goodness* is *honesty;* its antonym is *deceit.* Another synonym is *kind-heartedness;* its antonym is *cold-heartedness.* Lead students to see that *cold-heartedness* and *deceit* are not synonyms, as they would expect. Work with students to make up sentences that illustrate the different meanings among the words in their webs. **EL OL**

The Goodness of Matt Kaizer

by Avi

P eople are always saying, "Nothing's worse than when a kid goes bad." Well, let me tell you, going good isn't all that great either. Tell you what I mean.

Back in sixth grade there was a bunch of us who liked nothing better than doing bad stuff. I don't know why. We just liked doing it. And the baddest of the bad was Matt Kaizer. **1**

Matt was a tall, thin kid with long, light blond hair that reached his shoulders. He was twelve years old—like I was. His eyes were pale blue and his skin was a vanilla cream that never—no matter the season—seemed to darken, except with dirt. What with the way he looked—so pale and all—plus the fact that he was into wearing extra large blank white T-shirts that reached his knees, we called him "Spirit."

Now, there are two important things you need to know about Matt Kaizer. The first was that as far as he was concerned there was nothing good about him at all. Nothing. The second thing was that his father was a minister.

Our gang—I'm Marley, and then there was Chuck, Todd, and Nick—loved the fact that Matt was so bad and his father a minister. You know, we were always daring him to do bad

Practice the Skills

1 | **Comparing Literature**

Character Create a Character Chart for Matt like the one you made for Paul. As you read, fill in clues to Matt's character. Then write a note for each clue that explains what you learned about Matt from that clue.

Teach

L1 Literary Element

Character **Ask:** What tone does the narrator use? *(He uses a friendly, informal tone.)* **OL** **Ask:** Do you think the narrator is an adult or a kid? Why? *(Possible response: He seems like a kid because of his informal tone and the way he speaks in sentence fragments.)* **AL**

L2 Literary Element

Character **Ask:** How does the author signal that he's giving important clues to Matt's character? *(Possible response: The narrator says, "there are two important things you need to know about Matt Kaizer.")* **OL** **AL**

Readability Scores
Dale-Chall: 5.2
DRP: 46
Lexile: 620

Literature Focus Lesson

Theme A theme is an idea expressed in a literary work. For example, the idea that families stick together is important in *The Pigman & Me.* Avi explores how people react to others' expectations. Ask students what people might expect of Matt as a minister's son. Do his reac- tions to those expectations seem believ- able? *(Possible response: He is rebelling against an unspoken expectation that he is supposed to be perfect.)* As students continue to read, have them pay atten- tion to how Matt reacts to other people's expectations. **AS**

Objectives
- Make connections from text to self
- Interpret and analyze character
- Understand synonyms and antonyms
- Identify literary elements: theme
- Learn and use new vocabulary

221

Teach

L Literary Element

Character **Ask:** If Matt Kaizer went to school with you, would you want to be his friend? Why or why not? *(Responses will vary.)* **Ask:** Do you think Matt is really bad? Explain. *(Possible response: He seems ornery, but he doesn't seem like a bad person. He is just trying too hard to be bad.)* **OL**

C Critical Thinking

Analysis **Ask:** How would you compare Matt with his father? *(Reverend Kaizer is a good man. Matt is bad. They are exact opposites.)* **BL** **Ask:** Why do you think Matt tries so hard to be bad? *(Possible response: He doesn't want to be like his father.)* **OL** **Ask:** Do you think that Matt's rebellion is typical? Explain. *(Possible response: He is rebelling against his father and the expectations of the community. It seems that he has it harder because more is expected from a minister's son.)* **AL**

things. "Hey, minister's kid!" we'd **taunt**. "Dare you to . . ." and we'd challenge him to do something, you know, really gross. Thing is, we could always count on Matt—who wanted to show he wasn't good—to take a dare.

For instance: Say there was some dead animal out on the road. We'd all run to Matt and say, "Dare you to pick it up."

Matt would look at it—up close and personal—or more than likely poke it with a stick, then pick it up and fling it at one of us.

Disgusting stories? Someone would tell one and then say, "Dare you to tell it to Mary Beth Bataky"—the class slug—and Matt would tell it to her—better than anyone else, too.

TV and movies? The more blood and gore there was, the more Matt ate it up—if you know what I mean. MTV, cop shows, all that bad stuff, nothing was too gross for him.

And it didn't take just dares to get Matt going. No, Matt would do stuff on his own. If anyone blew a toot—even in class—he would bellow, "Who cut the cheese?" He could belch whenever he wanted to, and did, a lot. Spitballs, booger flicking, wedgie yanking, it was all wicked fun for Matt. No way was he going to be good! Not in front of us. **2**

Now, his father, the minister, "Rev. Kaizer" we called him, wasn't bad. In fact just the opposite. The guy was easygoing, always dressed decently, and as far as I knew, never raised his voice or acted any way than what he was, a nice man, a good man. Sure, he talked a little funny, like he was reading from a book, but that was all.

C Did Matt and his father get along? In a way. For example, once I was with Matt after he did something bad—I think he blew his nose on someone's lunch. Rev. Kaizer had learned about it. Instead of getting mad he just gazed at Matt, shook his head, and said, "Matt, I do believe there's goodness in everyone. That goes for you too. Someday you'll find your own goodness. And when you do you'll be free."

Vocabulary

taunt (tawnt) *v.* to try to anger someone by teasing him or her

222 UNIT 2 What Brings Out the Best in You?

Practice the Skills

2 **Comparing Literature**

Character These paragraphs give you several clues about Matt's character. For example, they tell you how Matt acted around other people, and how Matt wanted to act. In your Character Chart, write at least two clues you found to Matt's character in these paragraphs. Then write notes about what you learned from these clues. **L**

Analyzing the Photo In what ways does the boy in this photo fit the description of Matt Kaizer?

Additional Support

Reading Fluency

Build Fluency The conversational tone of the narrator provides students with a perfect opportunity to practice reading as they naturally speak. Point out to students that the narrator is especially animated, so they should use their tone of voice, pace, and rhythm to emphasize this quality. Divide students into pairs and have them take turns reading aloud. Suggest that they read the same paragraphs and discuss whose rendition sounded more relaxed and realistic. **AS**

"I'm not good," Matt insisted.

"Well, I think you are," his father said, patiently.

Matt grinned. "Long as my friends dare me to do bad things, I'll do 'em."

"Never refuse a dare?" his father asked, sadly.

"Never," Matt said with pride.

Rev. Kaizer sighed, pressed his hands together, and looked toward heaven.

So there we were, a bunch of us who knew we were bad and that it was doing bad things that held us together. And the baddest of the bad, like I said, was Matt—the Spirit—Kaizer. But then . . . oh, man, I'll tell you what happened.

One day after school we were hanging out in the playground. The five of us were just sitting around telling disgusting stories, when suddenly Chuck said, "Hey, hear about Mary Beth Bataky?"

"What about her?" Matt asked.

"Her old man's dying."

Right away Matt was interested. "Really?"

"It's true, man," Chuck insisted. "He's just about had it."

"How come?" I asked.

"Don't know," said Chuck. "He's sick. So sick they sent him home from the hospital. That's why Mary Beth is out. She's waiting for him to die."

"Cool," said Matt. **3**

Now, Mary Beth was one small straw of a sad slug. She had this bitsy face with pale eyes and two gray lines for lips all framed in a pair of frizzy braids. Her arms were thin and always crossed over her chest, which was usually bundled in a brown sweater. The only bits of color on her were her fingernails, which, though chewed, were spotted with bright red nail polish—chipped.

So when we heard what was going on with Mary Beth and her father, we guys eyed one another, almost knowing what was going to happen next. But, I admit, it was me who said, "Hey, Spirit, I dare you to go and see him."

Matt pushed the blond hair out of his face and looked at us with those pale blue, cool-as-ice eyes of his.

"Or maybe," Todd said, "you're too chicken, being as you're a minister's kid and all."

Practice the Skills

3 ▮ **Comparing Literature**

Character Think about how Matt reacts when he learns that the father of one of the kids in his class is dying. Write down how he reacts in the clues column of your Character Chart. Is Matt just being cool? Or is he being cruel? Write down what this clue tells you in your chart. **L**

The Goodness of Matt Kaizer **223**

Teach

EL Language Coach

Synonyms Say: List several synonyms for the word *bad*, which is used repeatedly to describe Matt and the gang. *(Possible responses: awful, horrible, terrible, rotten)* Allow students to use a thesaurus if necessary. **EL**

L Literary Element

Character Say: Sometimes people are deliberately cruel, and sometimes they don't realize how their words or actions affect others. Is Matt being cruel or is he just trying to live up to others' image of him? *(Responses will vary.)* Fill in your charts with your opinions about Matt's actions. **AS**

Literature Focus Lesson

Round Characters Remind students that round characters undergo a change through the conflict posed in the story. Matt's self-image is that he is "the baddest of the bad." The conversation with his father suggests that there's a difference between Matt's self-image and who he really is. Remind students that one way authors develop character is by showing what the character thinks. Suggest that they watch for changes in the way Matt thinks about himself. Tell students to consider whether they think Matt is a round character. **OL**

Objectives
• Interpret and analyze character
• Understand and use synonyms
• Analyze text

Teach

L₁ Literary Element

Character If students have difficulty deciding what taking the dare shows about Matt's character, suggest that they find other places where Matt or the narrator has mentioned dares. **BL**

L₂ Literary Element

Character Say: Avi uses two methods of characterization to show how the narrator feels: what Marley says (*"Made me really uncomfortable"*) and what others say (*"You scared?";* *"you're too good!"*). What do these statements tell you about the character? *(Students may say that he feels uncomfortable and scared about visiting Mary Beth's father with Matt.)* **BL OL**

That did it. Course it did. No way Matt could resist a dare. He got up, casual like. "I'll do it," he said. "Who's coming with me?" **4**

To my disgust the other guys backed off. But I accepted. Well, actually, I really didn't think he'd do it.

But then, soon as we started off, I began to feel a little nervous. "Matt," I warned. "I think Mary Beth is very religious."

"Don't worry. I know about all that stuff."

"Yeah, but what would your father say?"

"I don't care," he bragged. "Anyway, I'm not going to do anything except look. It'll be neat. Like a horror movie. Maybe I can even touch the guy. A dying body is supposed to be colder than ice."

That was Matt. Always taking up the dare and going you one worse.

The more he talked the sorrier I was we had dared him to go. Made me really uncomfortable. Which I think he noticed, because he said, "What's the matter, Marley? You scared or something?" **5**

"Just seems . . ."

"I know," he taunted, "you're too good!" He belched loudly to make his point that he wasn't. "See you later, dude." He started off.

I ran after him. "Do you know where she lives?"

"Follow me."

"They might not let you see him," I warned.

He pulled out some coins. "I'm going to buy some flowers and bring them to him. That's what my mother did when my aunt was sick." He stuffed his mouth full of bubble gum and began blowing and popping.

Mary Beth's house was a wooden three-decker[1] with a front porch. Next to the front door were three bell buttons with plastic name labels. The Batakys lived on the first floor.

By the time Matt and I got there he had two wilted carnations in his hand. One was dyed blue, the other green. The flower store guy had sold them for ten cents each.

"You know," I said in a whisper, as we stood before the door, "her father might already be dead."

---

1. A *three-decker* house is a house with three floors, or levels.

Practice the Skills

4 Comparing Literature

Character Think about why people take dares. Is it for the adventure? Are they proving something to themselves or to others? In your chart, write that Matt took the dare to see Mary Beth's father. Then write down what this tells you about Matt. **L₁**

5 Comparing Literature

Character How does the narrator, Marley, feel now that he has to go with Matt to see Mary Beth's father? Does this tell you anything about the character of the narrator? Why do you think he agrees to go? **L₂**

Additional Support

Differentiated Instruction

Character Analysis One way to understand a character is to put yourself in the character's shoes. Authors sometimes let us get inside a character's head by describing what a character is thinking. If we aren't told what a character is thinking, we can imagine it. Ask students to describe what Marley and Matt might be thinking as they go to the Batakys' house. *(Possible responses: Marley: I never thought I'd have to go. I hope Mrs. Bataky won't be mad at us. Matt: I took the dare, and I've got to go through with it.)* **OL**

"Cool," Matt replied, blowing another bubble, while cleaning out an ear with a pinky and inspecting the earwax carefully before smearing it on his shirt. "Did you know your fingernails still grow when you're dead? Same for your hair. I mean, how many really dead people can you get to see?" he said and rang the Bataky's bell.

From far off inside there was a buzzing sound.

I was trying to get the nerve to leave when the door opened a crack. Mary Beth—pale eyes rimmed with red—peeked out. There were tears on her cheeks and her lips were crusty. Her small hands—with their spots of red fingernail polish—were trembling.

"Oh, hi," she said, her voice small and tense.

I felt tight with embarrassment.

Matt spoke out loudly. "Hi, Mary Beth. We heard your old man was dying."

"Yes, he is," Mary Beth murmured. With one hand on the doorknob it was pretty clear she wanted to **retreat** as fast as possible. "He's delirious."²

"Delirious?" Matt said. "What's that?"

"Sort of . . . crazy."

"Oh . . . wow, sweet!" he said, giving me a nudge of appreciation. Then he held up the blue and green carnations, popped his gum, and said, "I wanted to bring him these." **6**

Mary Beth stared at the flowers, but didn't move to take them. All she said was, "My mother's at St. Mary's, praying."

Now I really wanted to get out of there. But Matt said, "How about if I gave these to your father?" He held up the flowers again. "Personally."

"My mother said he may die any moment," Mary Beth informed us.

"I know," Matt said. "So I'd really like to see him before he does."

Mary Beth gazed at him. "He's so sick," she said, "he's not up to visiting."

"Yeah," Matt pressed, "but, you see, the whole class elected me to come and bring these flowers."

---

2. A **delirious** person is confused, has problems speaking, and sees things that aren't there.

Vocabulary

retreat (rih TREET) *v.* to move backward, away from a situation

Practice the Skills

6 Comparing Literature

Character When Matt learns that Mary Beth's father is delirious, he says "Oh. . . wow, sweet!" Do you feel this is the right thing to say to Mary Beth? In your Character Chart, write down what Matt says and what this tells you about him.

The Goodness of Matt Kaizer **225**

Teach

L Literary Element

Character Ask: What clues tell you how Mary Beth feels about her father's condition? *(She's been crying, her hands are trembling, and her voice is "small and tense.")* **BL Ask:** Does Matt's response show any awareness of Mary Beth's feelings? Why do you think he responds this way to her? *(Possible responses: He is mean or just ignorant. He is putting up a front to cover his real feelings of fear.)* **OL**

C Critical Thinking

Comprehension Ask: What is Mary Beth trying to do when she tells the boys that her father is delirious, that her mother is at church praying, and that her father may die any minute? *(Possible response: She is trying to get the boys to leave, possibly by scaring them with the horrid details of her father's condition.)* **AL**

Literature Focus Lesson

Foils A *foil* is a character used to emphasize the traits of the main character by contrast. Ask students to contrast Matt's reaction to Mr. Bataky's condition to the reactions of Mary Beth and Marley. *(Possible response: Mary Beth is grieving. Marley is "embarrassed." Matt is curious about death and preoccupied with being cool.)* Then ask students to describe how this contrast affects their impression of Matt. *(Possible response: It makes it even more obvious that he is trying too hard to be cool.)* **OL AL**

Objectives
• Interpret and analyze character
• Monitor comprehension

Teach

Viewing the Photo

Ask: How does the girl in the photo seem to feel? *(Possible response: She seems upset or, at the very least, introspective.)*
Ask: What makes you think so? *(Her eyes are downcast. She has a serious look on her face.)* **OL**

L Literary Element

Character If students can think of more than one possible meaning for the clue they wrote in their Character Charts, discuss how they can decide which meaning is best. As they read, they will find other clues to support the best meaning. They may also find evidence that one possible meaning doesn't fit the story. **BL**

Analyzing the Photo Based on what you know about Mary Beth, does the girl in this photo look like her? Describe the expression on her face.

His lie worked. "Oh," Mary Beth murmured, and she pulled the door open. "Well, I suppose . . ." **7**

We stepped into a small entrance way. A low-watt bulb dangled over our heads from a wire. Shoes, boots, and broken umbrellas lay in a plastic milk crate.

Mary Beth shut the outside door then pushed open an inner one that led to her apartment. It was **gloomy** and stank of medicine.

Matt bopped me on the arm. "Who cut the cheese!" he said with a grin. I looked around at him. He popped another bubble.

"Down this way," Mary Beth whispered.

We walked down a long hallway. Two pictures were on the walls. They were painted on black velvet. One was a scene of a mountain with snow on it and the sun shining on a stag with antlers. The second picture was of a little girl praying by her bed. Fuzzy gold light streamed in on her from a window.

At the end of the hall was a closed door. Mary Beth halted. "He's in here," she whispered. "He's really sick," she warned

7 | **Comparing Literature**

Character Matt makes up a lie about why he came to see Mary Beth's father. Why doesn't he just tell her the truth? In your chart, write down this clue. Then write down what this tells you about Matt. **L**

Vocabulary

gloomy (GLOO mee) *adj.* dull, dark, and depressing

Additional Support

Literature Focus Lesson

Character Sometimes villains are so evil that readers hate and detest them. Other characters do bad things, but readers understand their motives and may be inclined to feel for them. Discuss whether students feel sympathy for Matt when he lies to Mary Beth. Some may not like him and feel that he shows no awareness of her feelings; others may think he just doesn't know any better. Ask students if they think the author sees Matt as a sympathetic character and how they know. Discuss why, even though Matt often acts like a jerk, the narrator looks up to him, his father believes the best of him, and the story is fashioned to give him the opportunity to change. **AS**

again. "And he doesn't notice anyone. You really sure you want to see him?"

"You bet," Matt said with enthusiasm. 🛚

"I mean, he won't say hello or anything," Mary Beth said in her low voice. "He just lies there with his eyes open. I don't even know if he sees anything."

"Does he have running sores?" Matt asked.

I almost gagged.

"Running *what*?" Mary Beth asked.

"You know, wounds."

"It's his liver," Mary Beth explained sadly, while turning the door handle and opening the door. "The doctor said it was all his bad life and drinking."

Dark as the hall had been, her father's room was darker. The air was heavy and really stank. A large bed took up most of the space. On one side of the bed was a small chest of drawers. On top of the chest was a lit candle and a glass of water into which a pair of false teeth had been dropped. On the other side of the bed was a wooden chair. Another burning candle was on that.

On the bed—beneath a brown blanket—lay Mr. Bataky. He was stretched out on his back perfectly straight, like a log. His head and narrow chest were propped up on a pile of four pillows with pictures of flowers on them. At the base of the bed his toes poked up from under the blanket. He was clothed in pajamas dotted with different colored hearts. His hands—looking like a bunch of knuckles—were linked over his chest. His poorly shaven face—yellow in color—was thin. With his cheeks sunken, his nose seemed enormous. His thin hair was uncombed. His breathing was drawn out, almost whistling, and collapsed into throat gargles—as if he were choking.

Worst of all, his eyes were open but he was just staring up, like he was waiting for something to happen in heaven.

Mary Beth stepped to one side of the bed. Matt stood at the foot, with me peering over his shoulder. We stared at the dying man. He really looked bad. Awful.

"I don't think he'll live long," Mary Beth murmured, her sad voice breaking, her tears dripping.

Matt lifted the blue and green carnations. "Mr. Bataky," he shouted, "I brought you some flowers to cheer you up." 🟟

Practice the Skills

🛚 English Language Coach

Synonyms and Antonyms
What does the word *enthusiasm* mean in this sentence? Name a word that means about the same as *enthusiasm*. How would the tone of Matt's voice change if he said "You bet" with the opposite of enthusiasm?

🟟 Comparing Literature

Character Why does Matt speak to Mr. Bataky? Is it just to keep up the lie that he told to Mary Beth? Does Matt's comment tell you anything about how he feels at this point? If so, write down this clue and what it means in your Character Chart. **L**

The Goodness of Matt Kaizer **227**

Teach

R Reading Skill

Predicting Say: You have just read a description of Mr. Bataky who is dying from "all his bad life and drinking." What effect do you think meeting him will have on Matt? *(Possible response: Meeting Mr. Bataky is going to make Matt rethink wanting to be bad.)* **OL AL**

L Literary Element

Character Ask: How is Mr. Bataky characterized? *(through descriptions of him from other characters)* **Ask:** What kind of person was he? *(He is reported to have been a bad person.)* **Ask:** What is the result of his being a bad person? *(He is dying as a direct result of his behavior.)* **OL Ask:** How do you think this will affect Matt? *(Possible response: Maybe it will affect Matt's decision to prove he is bad.)* **AL**

Differentiated Instruction

Adaptation Tell students to adapt this scene or another scene from the story into a play. Divide students into small groups. Some students should be in charge of writing the dialogue. Others should describe the setting. Others should write the stage directions for the characters. When students finish their adaptations, have them perform a read-through for the class. You might provide practice time before their performances. When all groups finish, discuss the differences and similarities in interpretations. **AL**

Objectives
• Interpret and analyze character
• Make predictions
• Use text features: photographs

Teach

L1 Literary Element

Character Guide students to see that Matt's attempt at cheering Mr. Bataky up suggests that he is not completely sure of himself and his actions. **BL**
Ask: What does the description, "Matt . . . froze" tell you about him? *(He is terrified.)* **OL**

L2 Literary Element

Character **Ask:** How does Marley react when Mr. Bataky reaches for Matt? *(He is frightened.)* **Ask:** How does Matt look when he leaves the house? *(He is pale.)* **Ask:** Could Matt have been frightened? What else might he have been feeling? *(Responses will vary.)* **BL** **OL**

"His hearing isn't good," Mary Beth said apologetically.

Matt looked about for a place to put the flowers, saw the glass with the teeth near Mr. Bataky's head, and moved to put them into the water. In the flickering candlelight, Matt's pale skin, his long blond hair, seemed to glow.

Now, just as Matt came up to the head of the bed, Mr. Bataky's eyes shifted. They seemed to fasten on Matt. The old man gave a start, made a convulsive³ twitch as his eyes positively bulged. Matt, caught in the look, froze.

"It's . . . it's . . . an *angel* . . ." Mr. Bataky said in a low, rasping⁴ voice. "An angel . . . from heaven has come to save me."

Matt lifted his hand—the one that held the carnations—and tried to place them in the glass of water. Before he could, Mr. Bataky made an unexpected jerk with one of his knobby hands and took hold of Matt's arm. Matt was so surprised he dropped the flowers.

"Father!" Mary Beth cried.

"Thank . . . you . . . for coming, Angel," Mr. Bataky rasped.

"No . . . really," Matt stammered, "I'm not—"

"Yes, you're an angel," Mr. Bataky whispered. His eyes—full of tears—were hot with joy.

Matt turned red. "No, I'm not . . ."

"Please," Mr. Bataky cried out with amazing energy. "I don't want to die bad." Tears gushed down his hollow cheeks. "You got to help me. Talk to me. Bless me."

Matt, speechless for once, gawked at the man.

With considerable effort he managed to pry Mr. Bataky's fingers from his arm. Soon as he did he bolted from the room.

"Don't abandon me!" Mr. Bataky begged, somehow managing to lift himself up and extend his arms toward the doorway. "Don't!"

Frightened, I hurried out after Matt.

My buddy was waiting outside, breathing hard. His normally pale face was paler than ever. As we walked away he didn't say anything. **10**

Now, according to Matt—he told us all this later—what happened was that night Rev. Kaizer called him into his study.

---

3. When someone is *convulsive*, the person cannot control his or her muscle movements.

4. A *rasping* voice sounds like someone has almost lost his or her voice.

228 UNIT 2 What Brings Out the Best in You?

Practice the Skills

10 **Comparing Literature**

Character Why is Matt quiet as he walks away from the Batakys' house? Write this clue in your character chart, then try to figure out what it tells you about Matt. **L2**

Additional Support

Literature Focus Lesson

Irony One form of irony is the difference between what is expected and what actually happens. Ask students to identify the irony in the situation described on this page of the story.

Discuss how Matt visits Mr. Bataky because he wants to look bad; ironically, however, Mr. Bataky thinks he's an angel. Suggest that students look for other examples of irony as they read. **AL**

"Matt, please sit down."

Matt, thinking he was going to get a lecture about visiting Mary Beth's house, sat.

His father said, "Matt, I think it's quite wonderful what you've done, going to the home of your classmate's dying father to comfort him."

"What do you mean?" Matt asked.

Rev. Kaizer smiled sweetly. "A woman by the name of Mrs. Bataky called me. She said her husband was very ill. Dying. She said you—I gather you go to school with her daughter—came to visit him today. Apparently her husband thought you were an . . . angel. It's the first real sign of life her poor husband has shown in three days. And now, Matt, he's quite desperate to see the angel—you—again."

"It's not true," Matt rapped out.

"Now, Matt," his father said, "I found the woman's story difficult to believe, too. 'Madam,' I said to her, 'are you quite certain you're talking about *my* son? And are you truly saying your husband really thought he was . . . an angel?'

"And she said, 'Rev. Kaizer—you being a minister I can say it—my husband led a bad, sinful life. But there's something about your son that's making him want to talk about it. Sort of like a confession.[5] Know what I'm saying? I mean, it would do him a lot of good. What I'm asking is, could you get your son to come again? I'm really scared my husband will get worse if he doesn't.'

"Matt," said Rev. Kaizer, "I'm proud of you. I think it would be a fine thing if you visited him again."

"I'm not an angel," Matt replied in a sulky[6] voice.

---

5. In a **confession**, a person tells the things he or she has done wrong and asks for forgiveness.

6. A **sulky** voice sounds moody and unhappy.

Analyzing the Art Which two characters in the story might this picture show? How do you know?

TRUMAN

The Goodness of Matt Kaizer **229**

Teach

C Critical Thinking

Synthesis Help students synthesize the clues in the text that lead up to Mr. Bataky mistaking Matt for an angel. Have students read the description of Matt's appearance on the first page of the selection. Remind students that Matt's nickname is *Spirit*, another term for an angel. Tell students that these are examples of the author's use of foreshadowing, or preparing readers for events to come. **Ask:** What other events do you think are foreshadowed in the story? *(Possible response: Matt's revealing his goodness is foreshadowed by his father's belief in him and Matt's desperate resistance to being good.)* **AL**

English Language Coach

Antonyms Remind students that the prefix *un-* negates the meaning of a root word. Ask students to use that knowledge to find an antonym for *sulky*. Direct students to footnote 6 for a definition of *sulky*. Point out that the definition uses synonyms to define the term. Draw students' attention to the synonym *unhappy*. Then, ask them to identify an antonym of *sulky*. *(happy)* **EL**

Objectives
• Interpret and analyze character
• Identify and use antonyms
• Identify literary elements: irony
• Synthesize text

229

Teach

L Literary Element

Character Ask: Were you surprised when Matt agreed to go back to see Mr. Bataky? Why or why not? *(Possible response: Matt prides himself on never refusing a dare, so I am not surprised he goes.)* **OL**

C Critical Thinking

Analysis Ask: How is Matt's behavior different now than it was at the beginning of the story? *(He is loud and obnoxious at the beginning of the story. He would say anything for a laugh. Now he is completely quiet.)* **OL** **Ask:** What do you think is happening to him? *(Possible response: He is undergoing a change because of his exposure to Mr. Bataky. In some ways, he is growing up.)* **AL**

"I never said you were an angel," his father said. "But as I've told you many times, there is goodness inside you as there is in everyone. And now you are in the fortunate position of being able to help this sinful man."

"I don't want to."

"Son, here is a sick man who needs to unburden himself of the unhappy things he's done. I know your **reputation**. Are you fearful of hearing what Mr. Bataky has to say for himself?"

"I don't want to."

Rev. Kaizer sat back in his chair, folded his hands over his stomach, smiled gently, and said, "I dare you to go back and listen to Mr. Bataky. I dare you to do goodness."

Alarmed, Matt looked up. "But . . ."

"Or are you, being a minister's son, afraid to?"

Matt shifted uncomfortably in his seat and tried to avoid his father's steady gaze.

Rev. Kaizer offered up a faint smile. "Matt, I thought you never refused a dare."

Matt squirmed. Then he said, "I'll go." **11**

Anyway, that's the way Matt explained it all. And as he said to me sadly, "What choice did I have? He dared me."

We all saw then that Matt was in a bad place.

So the next day when Matt went to visit Mr. Bataky, the bunch of us—me, Chuck, Todd, and Nick—tagged along. We all wanted to see what Matt would do. We figured it *had* to be gross.

Mary Beth opened the door. I think she was surprised to see all of us. But she looked at Matt with hope. "Thank you for coming," she said in her tissue paper voice. "He's waiting for you."

Matt gave us an imploring[7] look. There was nothing we could do. He disappeared inside. We waited outside.

Half an hour later, when he emerged, there was a ton of worry in his eyes. We waited him out, hoping he'd say something ghastly. Didn't say a word.

Carnations and Clematis in a Crystal Vase, 1882. Edouard Manet. Oil on canvas, 56 x 35.5 cm. Musee d'Orsay, Paris.

Practice the Skills

11 **Comparing Literature**

Character Matt doesn't want to go back to see Mr. Bataky. But when his father dares him to go, he agrees to return. What does this tell you about Matt? In your Character Chart, write this clue and what it means. **L**

---

7. If you give an *imploring* look, you are begging for something.

Vocabulary

reputation (rep yuh TAY shun) *n.* character as judged by other people

Additional Support

Literature Focus Lesson

Plot Early in the story, Avi lets readers know what to expect if Matt Kaizer is offered a dare—he'll accept. Discuss with students how this consistency is important to the plot. Explain to students that Matt's father dares him to be good; therefore, Matt feels he has no choice but to visit Mr. Bataky. Much like the clues that the author provides about Matt becoming an "angel," this character trait also foreshadows a situation that will compromise Matt in the end. **OL**

Two blocks from Mary Beth's house I couldn't hold back. "Okay, Matt," I said. "What's happening?"

Matt stopped walking. "He really thinks I'm a good angel." **12**

"How come?" Nick asked.

"I don't know." There was puzzlement in Matt's voice. "He thinks I'm there to give him a second chance at living."

"I don't get it," Todd said.

Matt said, "He thinks, you know, if he tells me all his bad stuff, he'll get better."

We walked on in silence. Then I said—easy like, "He tell you anything, you know . . . really bad?"

Matt nodded.

"Oooo, that's so cool," Nick crowed, figuring Matt would—as he always did—pass it on. "Like what?"

Instead of answering, Matt remained silent. Finally, he said, "Not good."

"Come on!" we cried. "Tell us!"

"He dared me to forgive him. To give him a second chance."

"Forgive him for what?" I asked.

"All the stuff he's done."

"Like what?"

"He said he was talking to me . . . in confidence."

"What's that mean?"

"Angels can't tell secrets." **13**

"You going to believe that?" Todd asked after a bit of silence.

Matt stopped walking again. "But . . . what," he stammered. "What . . . if it's true?"

"What if *what's* true?" I asked.

"What if I'm really good inside?"

"No way," we all assured him.

"But he thinks so," Matt said with real trouble in his voice. "And my father is always saying that too."

"Do *you* think so?" Chuck asked.

Matt got a flushed look in his eyes. Then he said, "If it is true, it'll be the grossest thing ever."

"Hey, maybe it's just a phase,"[8] I suggested, hopefully. "You know, something you'll grow out of."

---

8. Everyone goes through different *phases*, or stages, in life.

Practice the Skills

12 | **Comparing Literature**

Character Matt is worried because Mr. Bataky thinks he is a "good angel." Why do you think this worries Matt? Doesn't it sound like a joke that Matt would usually enjoy? Write this clue and what it tells you about Matt in your Character Chart. **L1**

13 | **Comparing Literature**

Character At the beginning of the story, Matt likes to say and do gross things. But after Mr. Bataky thinks that Matt is an angel, Matt won't tell the boys any of the bad things Mr. Bataky has done. Why not? Write this clue and what you think it means in your Character Chart. **L2**

The Goodness of Matt Kaizer **231**

Teach

L1 Literary Element

Character Ask: Why do you think Matt takes Mr. Bataky's belief that he is an angel seriously? *(Possible responses: Mr. Bataky is dying. He is in emotional distress. Matt respects his confidence. Matt is compassionate. Matt lives up to Mr. Bataky's expectations of him.)* **OL**

L2 Literary Element

Character Say: Matt doesn't tell his friends what Mr. Bataky talks about when they are together. How does this show that Matt is good? *(Possible response: He does the right thing even though his friends want him to tell the secrets he's learned in confidence.)* **OL**

Reading in the Real World

Citizenship The dilemmas—or moral choices—characters face in books can help readers make similar choices in real life. One way to make such decisions is to consider the possible consequences, good and bad. Ask students why they think Matt is keeping Mr. Bataky's secrets. Discuss with students that it appears that Matt believes if he keeps the secrets Mr. Bataky will get better. Matt suddenly seems to want to be good and trustworthy. Then ask students to think about how Matt's behavior might inspire others. Discuss how it might make someone consider doing a good deed for a family in need, or that it might make someone think about how his or her words affect another person. **OL**

Objectives
• Interpret and analyze character
• Analyze text
• Identify literary elements: plot

231

Teach

L1 Literary Element

Character Ask: Why is Matt so troubled by the idea that he might be good? *(Possible response: His self-image is built on the idea that he is bad; changing your self-image is hard.)* **OL**

C Critical Thinking

Comprehension Ask: What do you think causes Matt to change so much? *(Possible responses: Matt changes because somebody is counting on his goodness. Matt changes because he doesn't want to get sick as a result of being bad.)* **OL** **AL**

L2 Literary Element

Character Ask: How does Matt's external change relate to his internal change? *(Possible response: The more good he does, the more clean-cut he becomes. Within a week, he goes from being a grubby, unkempt kid to wearing white without a smudge.)* **AL**

Matt gave a shake to his head that suggested he was really seriously confused. **14**

Anyway, every afternoon that week, Matt went to see Mr. Bataky. Each time we went with him. For support. We felt we owed him that, though really, we were hoping we'd get to hear some of the bad stuff. But I think we were getting more and more upset, too. See, Matt was changing. Each time he came out of the sick man's room, he looked more and more haggard.[9] And silent.

"What did he say this time?" someone would finally ask.

"Really bad," he'd say.

"Worse than before?"

"Much worse."

We'd go on for a bit, not saying anything. Then the pleading would erupt. "Come on! Tell us! What'd he say?"

"Can't."

"Why?"

"I told you: He thinks I'm an angel," Matt said and visibly shuddered. "Angels can't tell secrets."

C As the week progressed, Matt began to look different from before. He wasn't so grubby. His clothes weren't torn. Things went so fast that by Friday morning, when he came to school, he was actually wearing a tie! Even his hair was cut short and combed. It was awful.

"What's the matter with Matt?" we kept asking one another.

"I think he's beginning to think he really is an angel," was the only explanation I could give.

L Finally, on Friday afternoon, when Matt came out of Mary Beth's house, he sat on the front steps, utterly beat. By that time he was dressed all in white: white shirt, pale tie, white pants, and even white sneakers. Not one smudge on him. I'm telling you, it was eerie. Nothing missing but wings.

"What's up?" I asked.

"The doctor told Mr. Bataky he's better."

"You cured him!" cried Nick. "Cool! That mean you don't have to visit him again?"

"Right." But Matt just sat there looking as sad as Mary Beth ever did.

---

9. A thin, tired, and worried person looks *haggard.*

232 UNIT 2 What Brings Out the Best in You?

14 **Comparing Literature**

Character At the beginning of the story, Matt believed he was bad. Now what does he believe? **L1** Write this clue and what it means in your Character Chart.

Additional Support

Differentiated Instruction

Illustrating Character Change Ask students to sketch Matt as he was before he started visiting Mary Beth's father and as he was on the day he learned Mr. Bataky was recovering. Invite students to share their illustrations with the rest of the class. Discuss why Avi emphasizes the change in Matt's appearance. *(Possible response: The change in Matt's outward appearance shows how he has changed inside.)* **BL**

"What's the matter?" I asked.

"I've been sitting and listening to that guy talk and talk about all the things he's done. I mean, I used to think I was bad. But, you know what?"

"What?"

"I'm not bad. No way. Not compared to him. I even tried to tell him of some of the things I've done."

"What did he say?"

"He laughed. Said I was only a young angel. Which was the reason I didn't have wings."

Matt stared down at the ground for a long time. We waited patiently. Finally he looked up. There were tears trickling down his pale face.

"I have to face it," he said, turning to look at us, his pals, with real grief[10] in his eyes. "The more I heard that stuff Mr. Bataky did, the more I knew that deep down, inside, I'm just a good kid. I mean, what am I going to do? Don't you see, I'm just like my father said. I'm *good*."

You can't believe how miserable he looked. All we could do was sit there and pity him. I mean, just to look at him we knew there weren't going to be any more wicked grins, belches, leers,[11] sly winks, wedgies, or flying boogers.

Life went on, but with Matt going angel on us, our gang couldn't hold together. We were finished. Busted.

So I'm here to tell you, when a guy turns good, hey, it's rough. **15** ○

The Sick Spaniard. Edvard Munch (1863–1944). National Gallery, Oslo, Norway.

---

10. *Grief* is deep sadness.
11. When you give a *leer,* you give someone a nasty look as if you know something bad.

Practice the Skills

15 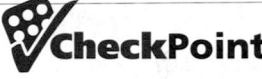 **BIG Question**

What brings out the goodness in Matt Kaizer? What makes Mr. Bataky get better? Write your answers on the "Goodness of Matt Kaizer" part of the Comparing Literature Workshop Foldable. Your answer will help you answer the Unit Challenge later. **BQ**

The Goodness of Matt Kaizer **233**

Teach

BQ **BIG Question**

After students answer the Big Question side note, ask them to think about people in their lives who have changed. Lead a class discussion about how people change, heal from illness, or heal after bad things happen to them. **AS**

Assess

✓CheckPoint

Use the CheckPoint questions provided on Presentation Plus! to check for comprehension of the selection. These questions can be used with interactive response keypads for immediate student feedback.

Literature Focus Lesson

Narrator Avi ends the story with Matt's realization that "deep down, inside, I'm just a good kid." However, the narrator gives several hints about what happens next. Have students write in their Learner's Notebooks a brief paragraph describing what they predict will happen next. Remind students to use evidence from the text. Then have students share their predictions with the class. (Some may say that Matt will stop trying to prove he's bad, that the gang will break up, or even that Matt will go back to being bad.) **OL**

Objectives
• Interpret and analyze character
• Monitor comprehension
• Identify and analyze narrator

233

Assess

Vocabulary Check

From **The Pigman & Me**

1. decent
2. paranoid
3. vicious
4. observant

The Goodness of Matt Kaizer

5. retreat
6. reputation
7. taunt
8. gloomy

Reading/Critical Thinking

From **The Pigman & Me**

9. Possible response: Nonno Frankie taught Paul respect for nature, curiosity, and how to stand up for himself.

10. Possible response: Paul learned that some people have a thirst for violence, that quick-wittedness could divert trouble, and that his sister would protect him. He never wanted to fight, so he might be more careful to avoid provoking conflict.

After You Read

from The Pigman & Me & *The Goodness of* Matt Kaizer

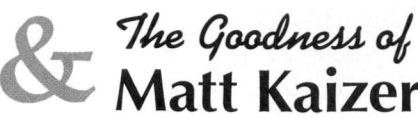

Vocabulary Check

For items 1 to 8, copy the definitions listed below into your Learner's Notebook. Then write the word next to the correct definition.

from The Pigman & Me

paranoid   observant   vicious   decent

1. kind or thoughtful: ____
2. feeling like everyone is against you: ____
3. mean and cruel: ____
4. good at noticing things: ____

The Goodness of Matt Kaizer

taunt   retreat   gloomy   reputation

5. to move backward, away from a situation: ____
6. your character as judged by other people: ____
7. to try to anger someone by teasing him or her: ____
8. dull, dark, and depressing: ____

Reading/Critical Thinking

On a separate sheet of paper, answer the following questions.

from The Pigman & Me

9. **Infer** What important life lessons do you think Nonno Frankie taught Paul?

   TIP **Author and Me** You will find clues in the text, but you must also use the information in your head.

10. **Infer** What do you think Paul learned from the fight with John Quinn? Do you think he will act differently after the fight? Why or why not?

Objectives (pp. 234–235)
Literature Identify literary elements: character • Compare and contrast: literature
Writing Write a response to literature: character, diagram

The Goodness of Matt Kaizer

11. Matt looks like an angel, which makes Mr. Bataky's mistake plausible.

12. Possible response: At the beginning Matt is determined to be bad, accepting every dare and behaving outrageously. By the end, he recognizes that he is good at heart.

Tip Author and Me You will find clues in the text, but you must also use the information in your head.

The Goodness of Matt Kaizer

11. Analyze Why is Matt's appearance important to the plot of this story?

Tip Author and Me You will find clues in the text, but you must also use the information in your head.

12. Describe How does Matt change from the beginning of the story to the end?

Tip Author and Me You will find clues in the text, but you must also use the information in your head.

Writing: Compare the Literature

Use Your Notes

13. Follow these steps to use your Character Charts to compare the main characters in these two selections.

Step 1: Review the Character Charts you completed for these two selections.

Step 2: In the two charts, circle ways in which Paul and Matt were completely different at the beginnings of both stories. You'll need to look carefully. You may not have used the exact same words to describe Paul and Matt.

Step 3: Now find ways in which Paul and Matt were similar by the end of the story. Put a star beside those similarities.

Step 4: In your Learner's Notebook, draw a diagram like the one at the top of the next column to show how Paul and Matt were similar and different at the beginning of the story. In the overlapping center section of the circles, list the traits that Paul and Matt have in common **at the beginning of the story.** On the left side list only traits that describe Paul. On the right side list only traits that describe Matt.

Beginning

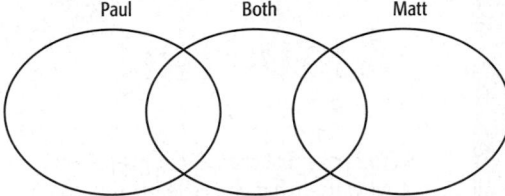

Paul   Both   Matt

Step 5: Now draw another diagram to show how Paul and Matt were similar and different *at the end of the story.* Title this diagram *Ending.* In the center circle list the traits that Paul and Matt have in common at the end of the stories. On the left side list only traits that describe Paul. On the right side list only traits that describe Matt.

Step 6: Examine your two diagrams. They show how the boys changed during the course of the stories, and they show how the boys were similar and different at the beginnings and ends of the stories.

Get It on Paper

Answer the following questions on a separate sheet of paper.

14. How were Paul and Matt different at the beginnings of the two stories? Write details from your Character Charts to support your statements.

15. How were Paul and Matt similar at the end of the two stories? Write details from your Character Charts to support your statements.

16. At the end of "The Goodness of Matt Kaizer," how has Matt changed? Give at least one detail that shows what he was like at the beginning of the story and one detail that shows what he was like at the end of the story.

17. At the end of the selection from *The Pigman & Me,* how has Paul changed? Support your statement with two details from the selection. If you don't think he has changed, give two details that show that he is the same.

18. Choose either Paul or Matt and explain why the character became the best that he could be.

Writing: Compare the Literature

11. Responses will vary.

12. Responses will vary.

Get It On Paper

14. Possible response: Matt looked for trouble, while Paul tried to avoid it.

15. Possible response: Paul and Matt chose to do the right thing.

16. Possible response: At the beginning, Matt was always ready to do something gross, but by the end, he had "gone angel."

17. Possible response: Paul has overcome his fear and has made a place for himself at his new school by accepting the consequences of his rash act.

BQ **BIG Question**

18. Responses will vary, depending on which character students chose.

Close

Ask students to summarize what they learned about the Big Question by comparing the characters in *The Pigman & Me* and "The Goodness of Matt Kaizer."

Use Your Notes

13. Completed responses will differ. Possible response:

new kid, gentle, not a leader, accepts Nonno Frankie's advice, wants to avoid trouble, takes responsibility for his mistakes, overcomes his fear, learns that his family sticks together

can talk and think fast, able to influence people, has a trusted adult who believes in him, does the right thing, shows compassion, meets people's expectations

looks like an angel, wants to be bad, is a leader, never refuses a dare, resists his father's advice, looks for trouble, discovers he's good, keeps a confidence despite peer pressure, stops trying to be bad

The Unit Challenge

Focus

Daily Language Practice Transparency 20 Focus Activity Ask: In your mind, which of the characters we've read about in this unit stands out as someone who brought out the best in himself or herself? Why?

The discussion will remind students of the selections they've read, which will help them begin the group activity or the solo activity.

Teach

Group Activity: Magazine Article

- Have at least one person take notes as you discuss the questions in step 1.

- Make sure the group is on step 3 by the middle of the class period to allow enough time to write the article.

- Have someone write the final draft of the article neatly or type it on a computer.

- Make each student responsible for reading the article to check it for mistakes.

Assess/Close

Group Activity

Ask: How can you use the advice you've given in your article to bring out the best in yourself? *(Suggest that students write their answers in their Learner's Notebooks.)* **AS**

236

UNIT 2 WRAP-UP

Answering The BIG Question — What Brings Out the Best in You?

You have just read about people who answered the Big Question: What brings out the best in you? Now use what you've learned to complete the Unit Challenge.

The Unit Challenge

Choose Activity A or Activity B and follow the directions for that activity.

A. Group Activity: Magazine Article

Look at the notes on your Foldables about what brings out the best in people. Think about what brings out the best in you. It could be music, sports, writing, helping a friend, or even reading. You'll use what you think has brought out your best to advise others.

- You and a group of friends will write an article for a teen magazine called "Bringing Out the Best in Yourself."

1. **Discuss the Assignment** As a group think about and discuss these questions:
   - What is something in which you do your best?
   - What makes you do your best?
   - What advice would you give to someone who wanted to be the best at what you like to do?

   Write down your answers. Then have each group member decide on something that they think brings out their best.

2. **Create Your Article** According to what each group member decides brings out his or her best, each group member will write an article telling other sixth graders how they can also bring out their best in that area.

3. **Write Your Article** As you begin writing your article, these tips may be helpful.
   - Look over the answers to the questions that you wrote.
   - Use key words and phrases from the answers to the questions that you wrote to begin your article.
   - Work together to use the words and phrases in a paragraph that explains what you did to bring out the best in what you like to do.
   - Review the paragraph to make sure it makes sense.

4. **Present Your Article**
   - Make sure the article is clear and has no mistakes, such as misspelled words.
   - With your teacher and the other groups in your class, use the finished articles to create an issue of the "Bringing Out the Best in Yourself" magazine.

B. Solo Activity: Your Interview

You see and hear people being interviewed on the television and radio all the time: now it's your turn to be interviewed.

1. Think about the Assignment You are being interviewed to find out what brings out the best in you. Create a web diagram like the one below and include those things that you like to do that you think bring out the best in you.

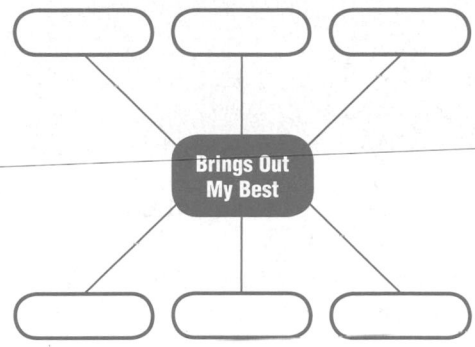

2. Write Interview Questions When you decide what brings out your best, write three or four questions that you think an interviewer would ask about what brings out your best. Use the notes on your Foldables.

If you want, make a list like the one below.

INTERVIEW QUESTIONS
1. What qualities do people need to bring out their best?

2. Who has helped bring out the best in you? How did they help?

3. How does what you like to do bring out your best?

4. What advice would you give to people about how to bring out their best?

3. Answer the Questions Now that you've written your questions, think of how you would answer them. Jot down some possible answers.

4. "Publish" Your Interview Write a final draft of your interview that includes the questions and your answers. Be sure to include details about the people and events that have helped bring out your best. Check your final draft for grammar and spelling, and post your interview in the classroom for other students to read.

Teach

Solo Activity: Give an Interview

- Have students decide what they want to talk about in their interview.
- If students have trouble thinking of a subject, ask them to think of things they are good at or challenges that they enjoy meeting.
- Suggest that they look at the list of questions for Activity A, step 1, to determine a topic.
- Encourage students to use the words *Who, What, When, Where, Why,* and *How* to develop their list of questions.
- Have students review their questions to be sure that the idea of bringing out their best is covered.
- Have students write their list of questions and responses in their Learner's Notebooks.
- Work with students to schedule a time to be interviewed.

Assess/Close

Solo Activity
After giving their interviews, have students ask their interviewers what they learned about the Big Question: What brings out the best in you?

Objectives
- Write a magazine article
- Design and conduct an interview

237

Focus

Vocabulary Preview

List the following words on the board:

- acculturated
- endurance
- heritage
- liberation
- originator
- reservation

Review their definitions before students begin reading.

Build Background

This story is about the Ta-Na-E-Ka tradition of the Kaw, or Kansa Indians. Both names mean "people of the south wind." Originally the Kaw lived along the lower Kansas River, where they hunted buffalo. In 1873, the government moved the Kaw to Indian Territory (present-day Oklahoma).

Teach

L Literary Element

Character **Ask:** What do you learn about Amos Deer Leg, the narrator's grandfather. *(Possible responses: devoted to tradition; wears handmade moccasins; keeps his hair in braids; speaks English and Sioux)* BL OL

Readability Scores
Dale-Chall: 5.9
DRP: 55
Lexile: 720

Your Turn: Read and Apply Skills

Meet the Author

Mary Whitebird is a member of the Kaw or Kansa Nation, also known as the "wind people." The names Kaw and Kansa are from early French traders and both were used. The Kaw/Kansa originally lived in central Kansas along the Kansas and Saline Rivers. They hunted buffalo and farmed. They lived in villages consisting of dome-shaped lodges. See page R7 of the Author Files for more on Mary Whitebird.

Literature Online

Author Search For more about Mary Whitebird, go to www .glencoe.com.

by Mary Whitebird

As my birthday drew closer, I had awful nightmares about it. I was reaching the age at which all Kaw Indians had to participate in Ta-Na-E-Ka.

Well, not all Kaws. Many of the younger families on the reservation were beginning to give up the old customs. But my grandfather, Amos Deer Leg, was devoted to tradition. He still wore handmade beaded moccasins instead of shoes and kept his iron-gray hair in tight braids. He could speak English, but he spoke it only with white men. With his family he used a Sioux dialect.[1]

Grandfather was one of the last living Indians (he died in 1953, when he was eighty-one) who actually fought against the U.S. Cavalry. Not only did he fight, he was wounded in a skirmish at Rose Creek—a famous encounter in which the celebrated Kaw chief Flat Nose lost his life. At the time, my grandfather was only eleven years old.

Eleven was a magic word among the Kaws. It was the time of Ta-Na-E-Ka, the "flowering of adulthood." It was the age,

---

1. The *Sioux dialect* is a language spoken by some Native Americans of the Great Plains.

Additional Support

Literature Online

Author Search To expand students' appreciation of Mary Whitebird, have them access the Web site for additional information and resources.

Literature Focus Lesson

Summary In this autobiography, Mary Whitebird tells the story of her Ta-Na-E-Ka experience. According to custom, Kaw children go alone into the wilderness on Ta-Na-E-Ka when they turn eleven. Mary dreaded the endurance ritual and found a creative way to make it through her Ta-Na-E-Ka by spending it at a restaurant. The owner let her work for food and sleep there. As she told him about Kaw traditions, Mary learned to appreciate her heritage. OL my grandfather informed us hundreds of times, "when a boy could prove himself to be a warrior and a girl took the first steps to womanhood."

"I don't want to be a warrior," my cousin Roger Deer Leg, confided to me. "I'm going to become an accountant."

"None of the other tribes make girls go through the endurance ritual," I complained to my mother.

"It won't be as bad as you think, Mary," my mother said, ignoring my protests. "Once you've gone through it, you'll certainly never forget it. You'll be proud."

I even complained to my teacher, Mrs. Richardson, feeling that, as a white woman, she would side with me.

She didn't. "All of us have rituals of one kind or another," Mrs. Richardson said. "And look at it this way: How many girls have the opportunity to compete on equal terms with boys? Don't look down on your heritage."

Heritage, indeed! I had no intention of living on a reservation for the rest of my life. I was a good student. I loved school. My fantasies were about knights in armor and fair ladies in flowing gowns, being saved from dragons. It never once occurred to me that being an Indian was exciting.

But I've always thought that the Kaw were the originators of the women's liberation movement. No other Indian tribe—and I've spent half a lifetime researching the subject—treated women more "equally" than the Kaw. Unlike most

of the sub-tribes of the Sioux Nation, the Kaw allowed men and women to eat together. And hundreds of years before we were "acculturated,"[2] a Kaw woman had the right to refuse a prospective husband even if her father arranged the match.

The wisest women (generally wisdom was equated with age) often sat in tribal councils. Furthermore, most Kaw legends revolve around "Good Woman," a kind of supersquaw, a Joan of Arc[3] of the high plains. Good Woman led Kaw warriors into battle after battle, from which they always seemed to emerge victorious.

And girls as well as boys were required to undergo Ta-Na-E-Ka. The actual ceremony varied from tribe to tribe, but since the Indians' life on the plains was dedicated to survival, Ta-Na-E-Ka was a test of survival.

"Endurance is the loftiest virtue[4] of the Indian," my grandfather explained. "To survive, we must endure. When I was a boy, Ta-Na-E-Ka was more than the mere symbol it is now. We were painted white with the juice of a sacred herb and sent naked into the wilderness without so much as a knife. We couldn't return until the white had worn off. It wouldn't wash off. It took almost 18 days, and during that time we had to stay alive, trapping food, eating insects and roots and berries, and watching out for enemies. And we did have enemies—both the white soldiers and the Omaha warriors, who were always trying to capture Kaw boys and girls undergoing

---

2. A group that is **acculturated** is forced to adopt another people's culture, in this case the culture of the European Americans.

3. **Joan of Arc** was a French heroine in the early 1400s.

4. The **loftiest virtue** is the most noble quality.

Teach

EL Language Coach

Synonyms Say: The narrator uses three phrases that mean the same thing as Ta-Na-E-Ka. Find these phrases. *("flowering of adulthood," "endurance ritual," "test of survival")* **Ask:** How do they help you understand what Ta-Na-E-Ka means? *(Possible response: The synonyms help describe it as a rite of passage into adulthood and a test of strength and courage.)* **OL**

L Literary Element

Narrator Ask: How does the narrator feel about going through the Ta-Na-E-Ka? Contrast her attitude with that of Mrs. Richardson. *(Possible response: She dreads the ordeal and doesn't see why she has to go through with it; her teacher says the ritual is an important part of her heritage, especially because both girls and boys participate.)* **OL Ask:** Do you find anything ironic in the difference between the way the narrator views her heritage and the way Mrs. Richardson views it? *(Possible response: The narrator doesn't seem to value her heritage, but Mrs. Richardson, who is not a member of the tribe, appreciates its uniqueness.)* **AL**

Reading in the Real World

Citizenship The narrator gives several details to support the idea that the Kaw treated women equally. Ask students to identify details that support this idea. Discuss with them that Kaw women could refuse an arranged marriage; the wisest women sat in tribal councils; Good Woman, who led warriors into battle, was an important figure in legend; and both girls and boys underwent the survival test. Have students conduct library or Internet research about other ways the Kaw were, as the narrator puts it, "the originators of the women's liberation movement." Have them share the information with the class. **OL**

Objectives

• Identify and use synonyms
• Clarify word meanings
• Identify and analyze narrator
• Interpret and analyze character

Teach

L1 Literary Element

Chronological Order

Ask: When does the story take place? *(1947)* **BL** Why is the difference between the time when Grandfather underwent the survival test and the time when the narrator underwent it important? *(Possible response: Grandfather followed the old ways, which helped the Kaw survive on the Plains; the narrator must survive in a more developed and urban world.)* **AL**

L2 Literary Element

Character Ask: Do you feel the same way that the narrator does about eating grasshoppers? *(Responses will vary.)* **AS** What does her idea to borrow money from Mrs. Richardson show about the narrator? *(Possible responses: she's a problem-solver; she's willing to bend the rules; she isn't afraid to ask for help from others; she's resourceful.)* **OL**

Sea-buckthorn berries are nutritious, but very unpleasant to eat raw.

their endurance test. It was an exciting time."

"What happened if you couldn't make it?" Roger asked. He was born only three days after I was, and we were being trained for Ta-Na-E-Ka together. I was happy to know he was frightened, too.

"Many didn't return," Grandfather said. "Only the strongest and shrewdest. Mothers were not allowed to weep over those who didn't return. If a Kaw couldn't survive, he or she wasn't worth weeping over. It was our way."

"What a lot of hooey," Roger whispered. "I'd give anything to get out of it."

"I don't see how we have any choice," I replied.

Roger gave my arm a little squeeze. "Well, it's only five days."

Five days! Maybe it was better than being painted white and sent out naked for eighteen days. But not much better.

We were to be sent, barefoot and in bathing suits, into the woods. Even our very traditional parents put their foot down when Grandfather suggested we go naked. For five days we'd have to live off the land, keeping warm as best we could, getting food where we could. It was May, but on the northernmost reaches of the Missouri River the days were still chilly and the nights were fiercely cold.

Grandfather was in charge of the month's training for Ta-Na-E-Ka. One day he caught a grasshopper and demonstrated how to pull its legs and wings off in one flick of the fingers and how to swallow it.

I felt sick, and Roger turned green. "It's a darn good thing it's 1947," I told Roger teasingly. "You'd make a terrible warrior." Roger just grimaced.

I knew one thing. This particular Kaw Indian girl wasn't going to swallow a grasshopper no matter how hungry she got. And then I had an idea. Why hadn't I thought of it before? It would have saved nights of bad dreams about squooshy grasshoppers.

I headed straight for my teacher's house. "Mrs. Richardson," I said, "would you lend me five dollars?"

"Five dollars!" she exclaimed. "What for?"

"You remember the ceremony I talked about?"

"Ta-Na-E-Ka. Of course. Your parents have written me and asked me to excuse you from school so you can participate in it."

Additional Support

Differentiated Instruction

Small Group Research Activity The narrator was supposed to spend five days in the woods, without any food and where the nights got very cold. Ask students to identify dangers they would face if they spent five days and nights out in the open. Then have them work in small groups to research survival tips and write a question-and-answer guide to help people survive in their area. **OL AL**

"Well, I need some things for the ceremony," I replied, in a half-truth. "I don't want to ask my parents for the money."

"It's not a crime to borrow money, Mary. But how can you pay it back?"

"I'll baby-sit for you ten times."

"That's more than fair," she said, going to her purse and handing me a crisp, new five-dollar bill. I'd never had that much money at once.

"I'm happy to know the money's going to be put to a good use," Mrs. Richardson said.

A few days later the ritual began with a long speech from my grandfather about how we had reached the age of decision, how we now had to fend for ourselves and prove that we could survive the most horrendous of ordeals.[5] All the friends and relatives who had gathered at our house for dinner made jokes about their own Ta-Na-E-Ka experiences. They all advised us to fill up now, since for the next five days we'd be gorging[6] ourselves on crickets. Neither Roger nor I was very hungry. "I'll probably laugh about this when I'm an accountant," Roger said, trembling.

"Are you trembling?" I asked.

"What do you think?"

"I'm happy to know boys tremble, too," I said.

At six the next morning, we kissed our parents and went off to the woods. "Which side do you want?" Roger asked. According to the rules, Roger and I would stake out "territories" in separate areas of the woods, and we weren't to communicate during the entire ordeal. "I'll go toward the river, if it's

okay with you," I said.

"Sure," Roger answered. "What difference does it make?"

To me, it made a lot of difference. There was a marina a few miles up the river, and there were boats moored there. At least, I hoped so. I figured that a boat was a better place to sleep than under a pile of leaves.

"Why do you keep holding your head?" Roger asked.

"Oh, nothing. Just nervous," I told him. Actually, I was afraid I'd lose the five-dollar bill, which I had tucked into my hair with a bobby pin. As we came to a fork in the trail, Roger shook my hand. "Good luck, Mary."

"N'ko-n'ta," I said. It was the Kaw word for "courage."

The sun was shining and it was warm, but my bare feet began to hurt immediately. I spied one of the berry bushes Grandfather had told us about. "You're lucky," he had said. "The berries are ripe in the spring, and they are delicious and nourishing." They were orange and fat, and I popped one into my mouth.

Argh! I spat it out. It was awful and bitter, and even grasshoppers were probably better tasting, although I never intended to find out.

I sat down to rest my feet. A rabbit hopped out from under the berry bush. He nuzzled the berry I'd spat out and ate it. He picked another one and ate that, too. He liked them. He looked at me, twitching his nose. I watched a red-headed woodpecker bore into an elm tree, and I caught a glimpse of a civet cat[7] waddling through some twigs. All of a sudden I realized I was

---

5. An *ordeal* is a difficult or painful experience.
6. If you are *gorging* yourself, you are stuffing yourself with food.

7. A *civet cat* is a spotted skunk.

Teach

L Literary Element

Narrator Ask: Why do you think the narrator includes Grandfather's speech? *(Possible responses: to show the importance of the ritual; to build suspense by suggesting that the ordeal would be "horrendous")* **OL Ask: Why do you think she also mentions that her other relatives made jokes about their own experiences?** *(Possible response: Possibly to show that although her relatives took the ritual seriously, they felt that the children were capable of fending for themselves and wanted to ease their fears before the "ordeal" began.)* **AL**

R Reading Skill

Predicting Ask: What do you think the narrator plans to do with the five-dollar bill she has hidden in her hair? *(Responses will vary.)* **AS**

Literature Focus Lesson

Autobiography This selection is an autobiographical narrative, similar to the ones students wrote for the Writing Workshop in this unit. Have them analyze this selection using the following questions. For each item, have them provide evidence from the story.

Did the author:
• write about a goal she once had?
• use first-person point of view?
• use her own voice?
• describe the setting so that you could visualize it?
• arrange events in a logical order? **AS**

Objectives
• Understand sequence: chronological order
• Interpret and analyze character
• Identify and analyze narrator
• Make predictions
• Analyze features of genres: autobiography

241

Teach

L1 Literary Element

Character Say: The narrator originally planned to sleep in a boat. What does she do when she doesn't find one? *(goes into Ernie's restaurant)* **BL**
Ask: What does this show about her character? *(Possible response: She's adaptable and resourceful.)* **OL** **AL**

no longer frightened. Ta-Na-E-Ka might be more fun than I'd anticipated. I got up and headed toward the marina.

"Not one boat," I said to myself dejectedly.[8] But the restaurant on the shore, "Ernie's Riverside," was open. I walked in, feeling silly in my bathing suit. The man at the counter was big and tough-looking. He wore a sweatshirt with the words "Fort Sheridan, 1944," and he had only three fingers on one of his hands. He asked me what I wanted.

"A hamburger and a milkshake," I said, holding the five-dollar bill in my hand so he'd know I had money.

"That's a pretty heavy breakfast, honey," he murmured.

---

8. To react **dejectedly** is to respond in a depressed manner.

"That's what I always have for breakfast," I lied.

"Forty-five cents," he said, bringing me the food. (Back in 1947, hamburgers were twenty-five cents and milkshakes were twenty cents.) "Delicious," I thought. "Better'n grasshoppers—and Grandfather never once mentioned that I couldn't eat hamburgers."

While I was eating, I had a grand idea. Why not sleep in the restaurant? I went to the ladies room and made sure the window was unlocked. Then I went back outside and played along the riverbank, watching the water birds and trying to identify each one. I planned to look for a beaver dam the next day.

A diner (DY nuhr) is a small restaurant built to look like the dining car of a train.

Additional Support

Differentiated Instruction

Visualizing Ask students whether the photograph on the page matches their mental image of Ernie's restaurant. Ask them to think about what clues in the story might have been used to select this particular photograph. *(Possible response: night light, reference to the counter)* Then ask students if they think the photograph matches the way the narrator might be feeling when she spends the night alone. Students may suggest that the photograph looks dark and empty, possibly scary. **AS**

The restaurant closed at sunset, and I watched the three-fingered man drive away. Then I climbed in the unlocked window. There was a night light on, so I didn't turn on any lights. But there was a radio on the counter. I turned it on to a music program. It was warm in the restaurant, and I was hungry. I helped myself to a glass of milk and a piece of pie, intending to keep a list of what I'd eaten so I could leave money. I also planned to get up early, sneak out through the window, and head for the woods before the three-fingered man returned. I turned off the radio, wrapped myself in the man's apron, and in spite of the hardness of the floor, fell asleep.

"What the heck are you doing here, kid?" It was the man's voice.

It was morning. I'd overslept. I was scared.

"Hold it, kid. I just wanna know what you're doing here. You lost? You must be from the reservation. Your folks must be worried sick about you. Do they have a phone?"

"Yes, yes," I answered. "But don't call them."

I was shivering. The man, who told me his name was Ernie, made me a cup of hot chocolate while I explained about Ta-Na-E-Ka.

"Darnedest thing I ever heard," he said, when I was through. "Lived next to the reservation all my life and this is the first I've heard of Ta-Na whatever-you-call-it." He looked at me, all goose bumps in my bathing suit. "Pretty silly thing to do to a kid," he muttered.

That was just what I'd been thinking for months, but when Ernie said it, I became

Analyzing the Photo Do you think this is the way Mary's grandfather pictured her surviving Ta-Na-E-Ka? Explain.

Teach

L1 Literary Element

Character Ask: What does the narrator's plan to keep a record of the food she takes show about her? *(Possible responses: She's honest; she considers the consequences of her actions.)* **OL**

L2 Literary Element

Character Say: What does Ernie's reaction to finding the narrator show about his character? *(Possible response: Ernie looks tough, but he is concerned about the narrator's safety and is willing to help her out.)* **OL**

R Reading Skill

Connecting Ask: Were you surprised by the way the narrator reacted to Ernie's comment? *(Responses will vary.)* **AS** How does Ernie's comment help Mary appreciate her heritage? *(Possible response: When Ernie—an outsider—criticizes the tradition, Mary starts to defend it. In the process, she begins to understand and value her warrior heritage.)* **OL**

Reading Fluency

Compare and Contrast Some students may improve their reading fluency by creating a compare-and-contrast chart. Work with students to make a two-column chart, with one column headed *What Mary Expected Ta-Na-E-Ka to Be Like* and another headed *What It Was Actually Like.* Possible details for the first column might include: alone in the woods, eating grasshoppers and berries, cold, scary; Possible details in the second column might include: warm, well-fed, enjoying wildlife, new friend, fun. **BL OL**

Objectives
• Make connections from text to self
• Interpret and analyze character
• Visualize

243

Teach

R Reading Skill

Predicting Say: **What do you think will happen when Mary goes home after Ta-Na-E-Ka?** (Possible responses: Her grandfather will be angry at her for staying at the restaurant; Mary will lie about what she did during the ritual; her grandfather will be proud of her for finding a creative way to survive the ritual.) **OL**

angry. "No, it isn't silly. It's a custom of the Kaw. We've been doing this for hundreds of years. My mother and my grandfather and everybody in my family went through this ceremony. It's why the Kaw are great warriors."

"Okay, great warrior," Ernie chuckled, "suit yourself. And, if you want to stick around, it's okay with me." Ernie went to the broom closet and tossed me a bundle. "That's the lost-and-found closet," he said. "Stuff people left on boats. Maybe there's something to keep you warm."

The sweater fitted loosely, but it felt good. I felt good. And I'd found a new friend. Most important, I was surviving Ta-Na-E-Ka.

R My grandfather had said the experience would be filled with adventure, and I was having my fill. And Grandfather had never said we couldn't accept hospitality.[9]

I stayed at Ernie's Riverside for the entire period. In the mornings I went into the woods and watched the animals and picked flowers for each of the tables in Ernie's. I had never felt better. I was up early enough to watch the sun rise on the Missouri, and I went to bed after it set. I ate everything I wanted— insisting that Ernie take all my money for the food. "I'll keep this in trust for you, Mary," Ernie promised, "in case you are ever desperate for five dollars." (He did, too, but that's another story.)

I was sorry when the five days were over. I'd enjoyed every minute with Ernie. He taught me how to make Western omelets and to make Chili Ernie Style (still one of my favorite dishes). And I told Ernie all about the legends of the Kaw. I hadn't realized I knew so much about my people.

But Ta-Na-E-Ka was over, and as I approached my house, at about nine-thirty in the evening, I became nervous all over again. What if Grandfather asked me about the berries and the grasshoppers? And my feet were hardly cut. I hadn't lost a pound and my hair was combed.

"They'll be so happy to see me," I told myself hopefully, "that they won't ask too many questions."

I opened the door. My grandfather was in the front room. He was wearing the ceremonial beaded deerskin shirt which had belonged to *his* grandfather. "*N'g'da'ma,*" he said. "Welcome back."

I embraced my parents warmly, letting go only when I saw my cousin Roger sprawled

Analyzing the Photo Does this grasshopper look delicious to you?

---

9. *Hospitality* is the kindness that people extend to their guests.

Additional Support

Reading in the Real World

Citizenship Mary learns to value her heritage, but she also proves that she can adapt to living in a world that is not designed for Native Americans. Invite students who have had to make similar choices to speak to the class about how to keep traditions alive while adapting to American culture. **AS**

on the couch. His eyes were red and swollen. He'd lost weight. His feet were an unsightly mass of blood and blisters, and he was moaning: "I made it, see. I made it. I'm a warrior. A warrior."

My grandfather looked at me strangely. I was clean, obviously well-fed, and radiantly healthy. My parents got the message. My uncle and aunt gazed at me with hostility.

Finally my grandfather asked, "What did you eat to keep you so well?"

I sucked in my breath and blurted out the truth: "Hamburgers and milkshakes."

"Hamburgers!" my grandfather growled.

"Milkshakes!" Roger moaned.

"You didn't say we had to eat grasshoppers," I said sheepishly.

"Tell us all about your Ta-Na-E-Ka," my grandfather commanded.

I told them everything, from borrowing the five dollars, to Ernie's kindness, to observing the beaver.

"That's not what I trained you for," my grandfather said sadly.

I stood up. "Grandfather, I learned that Ta-Na-E-Ka is important. I didn't think so during training. I was scared stiff of it. I handled it my way. And I learned I had nothing to be afraid of. There's no reason in 1947 to eat grasshoppers when you can eat a hamburger."

I was inwardly shocked at my own audacity.[10] But I liked it. "Grandfather, I'll bet you never ate one of those rotten berries yourself."

Grandfather laughed! He laughed aloud! My mother and father and aunt and uncle were all dumbfounded. Grandfather never laughed. Never.

"Those berries—they are terrible," Grandfather admitted. "I could never swallow them. I found a dead deer on the first day of my Ta-Na-E-Ka—shot by a soldier, probably—and he kept my belly full for the entire period of the test!"

Grandfather stopped laughing. "We should send you out again," he said.

I looked at Roger. "You're pretty smart, Mary," Roger groaned. "I'd never have thought of what you did."

"Accountants just have to be good at arithmetic," I said comfortingly. "I'm terrible at arithmetic."

Roger tried to smile but couldn't. My grandfather called me to him. "You should have done what your cousin did. But I think you are more alert to what is happening to our people today than we are. I think you would have passed the test under any circumstances, in any time. Somehow, you know how to exist in a world that wasn't made for Indians. I don't think you're going to have any trouble surviving."

Grandfather wasn't entirely right. But I'll tell about that another time. ○

---

10. **Audacity** is the act of being bold.

Literature Focus Lesson

Characterization One way that authors develop characters is by showing other characters' reactions to them. Ask students to describe how the other characters react when Mary returns. *(parents: puzzled; Roger's parents: hostile; Roger: admiring; grandfather: disappointed, then accepting)* **BL**

Then ask students how these reactions help them understand what Mary has accomplished. *(Possible response: Mary has fulfilled the traditional requirement in a nontraditional way and is able to persuade her grandfather to recognize her as a survivor.)* **OL** **AL**

Teach

L Literary Element

Character Ask: How does the narrator persuade her grandfather that she has truly passed her survival test? *(Possible responses: She explains why she did what she did; she points out the need to adapt old ways to modern times; she demonstrates resourcefulness.)* **OL**
Ask: What does this tell you about the kind of person the narrator is? *(Students may say that she is resourceful and determined, and she will probably be able to handle further situations creatively as well.)* **AL**

R Reading Skill

Connecting Ask: If you were in Grandfather's position, what would you have said to Mary? *(Responses will vary. Some students may agree with Mary's grandfather and some may not.)* **Ask:** What do you think it takes to be a warrior in today's world? *(Answers will vary.)* **OL**

Assess

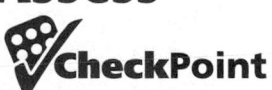
CheckPoint

Use the CheckPoint questions provided on Presentation Plus! to check for comprehension of the selection. These questions can be used with interactive response keypads for immediate student feedback.

Objectives
- Make connections to the text
- Interpret and analyze character
- Make predictions

245

UNIT 2
Reading on Your Own

To read more about the Big Question, choose one of these books from your school or local library. Work on your reading skills by choosing books that are challenging to you.

Fiction

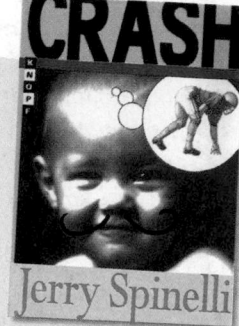

Crash
by Jerry Spinelli

Seventh-grader Crash Coogan is a bully. He's aggressive, mean, and smug . . . until an unlikely friendship makes him realize a thing or two about the way he treats others. Read Crash's story to find out what—and who—he comes to care about, after all.

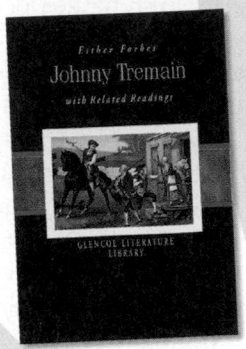

Johnny Tremain
by Esther Forbes

A compelling historical drama, this book chronicles the events leading up to the 1776 signing of the Declaration of Independence. Read this classic story of one young boy's journey to adulthood, and let history come to life.

Cezanne Pinto
by Mary Stolz

This fictional memoir follows Cezanne from Virginia to Canada and back down to Texas. In Texas, Cezanne becomes a cowboy, finds a home, and begins a family of his own. Read this book to learn more about Cezanne's journeys—journeys that take him out on the road and deep inside himself, too.

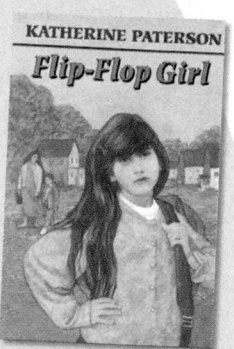

Flip-Flop Girl
by Katherine Paterson

After her father dies, Vinnie and her family move to a small town to live with Vinnie's grandmother. Things aren't going well when Vinnie makes a new friend at school—someone who is also an outsider. Read to find out how Vinnie's friendship helps her and her family get past their grief and come together again.

Additional Support

Differentiated Instruction

Nonfiction

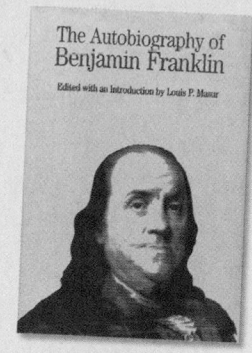

The Autobiography of Benjamin Franklin
by Benjamin Franklin

Originally, Franklin wrote this work, or "family history," as an encouragement for his son. Franklin's account of his own rise from penniless printer's apprentice to a place of world renown, however, is a "rags-to-riches" story everyone can enjoy.

Ellington Is Not a Street
by Ntozake Shange

Told as an illustrated poem, this account brings to life the language and music of a bygone era. Using biographical sketches of men like Paul Robeson and Duke Ellington, *Ellington Is Not a Street* depicts an important part of African American history—and some of the great men who made it.

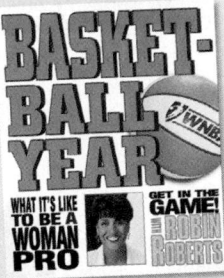

Basketball Year: What It's Like to Be a Woman Pro
by Robin Roberts

Eight women from the Women's National Basketball Association discuss their jobs, their lives, and the elite level at which they compete. Read to learn more about how these amazing women have turned their passion into a paycheck—and are having a ball, too.

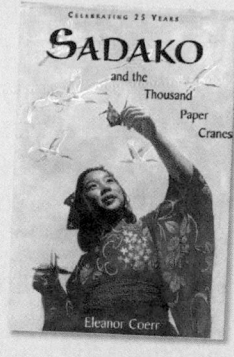

Sadako and the Thousand Paper Cranes
by Eleanor Coerr

Sadako is her school's track star when she is diagnosed with leukemia. Then she remembers a Japanese legend that says the gods will grant the wish of any sick person who folds a thousand paper cranes. Sadako sets to work—folding cranes and searching for the courage to face what lies ahead.

Nonfiction

Share with students that the books on this page are all nonfiction books. They give detailed accounts of the lives of real people.

Autobiographies

Ask: Can you tell if these are biographies or autobiographies by reading the title, viewing the cover, and knowing the name of the author? *(Yes. If the name of the subject is also the name of the author, the book is an autobiography.* **OL**

About the Subjects

Invite students to share their knowledge about the subjects on this page. What do students expect to find out in these biographies and autobiographies? *(Responses will vary.)* **AS**

Test-Taking Tips

TIP Tell the students that it is often a good idea to read the questions they will have to answer *before* they actually read the passages. It isn't necessary to read the question choices, but by reading the questions, they will be able to focus their reading on finding the answers that they will have to give later.

TIP Remind students to refer back to the passage to find evidence for their answers when they begin to answer the questions. Students need only to refer back to the passage to find clues in the text to help them with their responses.

Standardized Test Practice

Part 1: Literary Elements

1. B
2. C
3. C
4. A
5. B

Test Practice

Part 1: Literary Elements

On a separate sheet of paper, write the numbers 1–5. Next to each number, write the letter of the right answer for that question.

Each of the following passages is from a different short story about the same people. Use these passages to answer questions 1–4.

from Story 1: Scotty has called me "Ram Man" instead of Ramon ever since I accidentally knocked him down one day. He thinks it's funny. I don't, but it doesn't upset me. I mean, what difference does it make, really?

from Story 2: Whenever Scotty got angry, the other boys took a step back, as if he had a disease they didn't want to catch. Ramon would try to calm him down because Scotty's temper scared him, scared him down to his bones.

from Story 3: I know I've got a temper. I wish I could control it and be all laid back, but things are always ticking me off, you know? Ramon's always telling me, "Take it easy, Scott, my man!" I wish I could.

from Story 4: My firstborn, Sonya, is always in a sunny mood and has been since the moment she was born. My second, Scotty, has never heard the word *no* without having a tantrum.

Objectives (pp. 248–249)
Reading Ask questions • Make connections from text to self • Make predictions • Activate prior knowledge
Literature Identify literary elements: narrator, point of view, chronological order, tone

1. Which story is written from the third-person point of view?
   - **A.** Story 1
   - **B.** Story 2
   - **C.** Story 3
   - **D.** Story 4

2. Which story is *sure* to reveal Scotty's thoughts and feelings?
   - **A.** Story 1
   - **B.** Story 2
   - **C.** Story 3
   - **D.** Story 4

3. Who is the narrator in Story 4?
   - **A.** Scotty himself
   - **B.** a friend of Scotty's
   - **C.** Scotty's mother or father
   - **D.** someone outside the story

4. Which of the following best describes the tone of Story 2?
   - **A.** angry
   - **B.** serious
   - **C.** proud
   - **D.** playful

Use the following passage to answer question 5.

Before raising her hand, Kavitha checked her notes. After writing Kavitha's answer on the chalkboard, the teacher praised her for getting it right.

5. Which event occurred first?
   - **A.** Kavitha raised her hand.
   - **B.** Kavitha checked her notes.
   - **C.** The teacher wrote down Kavitha's answer.
   - **D.** The teacher praised Kavitha.

Part 2: Reading Skills

On a separate sheet of paper, write the numbers 1–4. Next to numbers 1–3, write the letter of the right answer for that question. Next to number 4, write your answer to the final question.

1. As you read, what is the main purpose of asking yourself questions and trying to answer them?

   A. to remain interested in the material

   B. to prove that the material is hard to read

   C. to check your understanding of the material

   D. to remind yourself that you don't know as much as the author

The following passage is from the beginning of a short story. Use it to answer questions 2 and 3.

Erika liked to run whether she was in a hurry to get some place or not. She liked the rhythm of the movement and the sound of her feet hitting the ground. She liked the feel of the wind on her face and the warmth that flowed through her muscles. She just liked running. She was good at it, too.

On the first day of sixth grade, Erika was surprised to see a notice posted in the gym. "Franklin Middle School Track Team Try-Outs," it said. "Wednesday, September 10, immediately after school behind the gym. See the coach, Mr. Seward, for details."

2. After reading this passage, it is **most** reasonable to predict that Erika will

   A. be chosen for the track team.

   B. try out for the team but not make it.

   C. decide she doesn't have time for track.

   D. ask Mr. Seward if she can help coach the team.

3. Which statement might be made by a reader who was "making a connection" to this passage?

   A. I wonder why Erika was surprised to see the notice.

   B. I'll bet Erika is the most important character in this story.

   C. Erika's probably getting faster and stronger as time goes on.

   D. Running makes me feel warm, too, and I know why she likes it.

4. What does it mean to "activate prior knowledge"? Why is it a good idea to do this when you are reading?

  Resources for pages 248–250

Use these resources to review, assess, or reteach the Unit: Active Learning, Note Taking Guide, Selection and Unit Assessments, ExamView Assessment Suite, and Skill Level Up!™ A Language Arts Game.

Part 2: Reading Skills

1. C

2. A

3. D

4. *Possible response:* Activating prior knowledge means thinking about what I already know about the subject. This helps me connect to the reading, and synthesize new ideas.

Test-Taking Tip

TIP Remind students to read each question carefully and to make sure they understand what the question is asking before looking for the answer.

Part 3: Vocabulary Skills

1. B
2. D
3. A
4. C
5. D
6. C
7. A
8. D
9. B
10. B

Part 3: Vocabulary Skills

On a separate sheet of paper, write the numbers 1–10. Next to each number, write the letter of the right answer for that question.

Write the letter of the word or phrase that means about the same as the underlined word.

1. to quiver with anger

  A. yell   **C.** respond

  B. shake   **D.** make a plan

2. to show their indifference

  A. similarity   **C.** high hopes

  B. worried feeling   **D.** lack of interest

3. when they emerged

  A. came out   **C.** fell down

  B. joined together   **D.** shared ideas

4. a gloomy day

  A. busy   **C.** dull and dark

  B. surprising   **D.** extremely hot

5. to mope all day

  A. try hard   **C.** show fear

  B. be foolish   **D.** act unhappy

Objectives (pp. 250–251)
Vocabulary Identify synonyms and antonyms
Grammar Identify parts of speech: nouns, pronouns

Choose the correct answer for each question.

6. Which pair of words are synonyms?

  A. no / know

  B. high / low

  C. big / large

  D. penny / dime

7. Which pair of words are antonyms?

  A. left / right

  B. begin / start

  C. small / tiny

  D. friend / neighbor

8. Which word can be made into its antonym by adding the prefix in-?

  A. door   **C.** come

  B. crease   **D.** correct

9. Which prefix, when added to all of the words below, would make them into their antonyms?

  happy   broken   cooked

  A. in-   **C.** dis-

  B. un-   **D.** non-

10. Which synonym for *hard* could be used to replace it in the following sentence?

  "The test was so hard that most of us failed it."

  A. firm   **C.** powerful

  B. difficult   **D.** unbreakable

Part 4: Writing Skills

On a separate sheet of paper, write the numbers 1–8. Next to each number, write the letter of the right answer for that question.

1. Which of the following words is a common noun?

   A. January   **C.** India

   B. Mary   **D.** house

2. Which of the following is a collective noun?

   A. herd   **C.** stamp

   B. meeting   **D.** togetherness

3. Which of the following is an abstract noun?

   A. book   **C.** sorrow

   B. piano   **D.** raindrop

4. Which noun in the following sentence is a proper noun that should be capitalized?

   When we arrived in the city of denver, we got off the bus and took a cab to my uncle's house.

   A. city   **C.** bus

   B. denver   **D.** uncle

5. In which sentence is a pronoun used incorrectly?

   A. Chiyo and I are going.

   B. Himself did all the work.

   C. Mike told Dan and me the score.

   D. The teacher gave everyone a paper.

6. In which sentence is the word *run* used as a noun?

   A. Cars won't <u>run</u> without gas.

   B. Laura can <u>run</u> faster than Richard.

   C. Would you <u>run</u> to the store for me?

   D. If we get one more <u>run</u>, we'll win the game.

7. Which pronoun in the following passage has an unclear antecedent?

   Joan called Melissa to talk about <u>her</u> birthday party. After a while, Joan looked at the clock. <u>She</u> could hardly believe what <u>it</u> said. <u>They</u> had been talking for an hour!

   A. her   **C.** it

   B. She   **D.** They

8. Which of the following sentences uses pronouns correctly?

   A. Both he and his brother were tall.

   B. Both his brother and him were tall.

   C. Both him and his brother were tall.

   D. Both his brother and himself were tall.

Part 4: Writing Skills

1. C

2. A

3. C

4. B

5. B

6. D

7. A

8. A

UNIT 3
Skills Scope and Sequence

Readability Scores Key
Dale-Chall/DRP/Lexile

PACING (DAYS)		INSTRUCTIONAL SEGMENT LITERATURE	READING SKILLS	LITERARY ELEMENTS
STANDARD	BLOCK			
1	1	**Unit Warm-Up, pp. 252–259** Genre Focus: "And Ain't I a Woman" by Sojourner Truth **4.2/48/690**, p. 257	Distinguishing Fact and Opinion, SE p. 257 Inferring, SE p. 258 Clarifying, SE p. 259 Identifying Problem and Solution, SE p. 259 Fluency, TWE p. 253 Connecting, TWE p. 254	Stereotypes, SE p. 257, TWE p. 256 Style, SE p. 257 Bias, TWE p. 257 Tone, SE p. 259 Mood, SE p. 259
3	2	**Reading Workshop 1, pp. 260–277** "Preserving a Great American Symbol," by Richard Durbin **9.4/62/1010**, p. 264 "Looking for America," by Elizabeth Partridge **3.7/55/860**, p. 270	Distinguishing Fact and Opinion, SE pp. 260, 261, 263, 264, 265, 269, 270, 273 Determining Main Idea, SE p. 264 Connecting, TWE p. 263 Fluency, TWE pp. 264, 275	Style, SE pp. 263, 265, 269, 271, 273, 275 Onomatopoeia and Personfication, TWE p. 265 Point of View, TWE p. 273
1		**Writing Workshop, Part 1, pp. 278–281** Writing Product: Persuasive Essay		Rhythm, TWE p. 280
3	1	**Reading Workshop 2, pp. 282–297** Two Advertisements **5.3/NA/620**, p. 286 "Stray" by Cynthia Rylant **4.6/49/780**, p. 292	Clarifying, SE pp. 282, 283, 285, 286 Point of View, SE pp. 287, 291, 292 Activating Prior Knowledge, SE p. 294 Fluency, TWE p. 292	Bias, SE pp. 285, 286, 287 Point of View, SE pp. 291, 293, 294
3	3	**Reading Workshop 3, pp. 298–313** "Dressed for Success" by Melanie Bertotto **4.6/64/970**, p. 302 "Eleven" by Sandra Cisneros **4.2/52/1090**, p. 308	Inferring, SE pp. 298, 299, 301, 302, 307–310 Connecting, SE p. 308, TWE p. 301	Argument, SE pp. 301, 303 Repetition, SE pp. 307, 309, 310 Similes, TWE p. 306

Unit 3 Big Question

The question, "What's fair and what's not?" is designed to help students assess life situations and develop strategies to cope with adversity. In this unit, students will read a variety of selections with inspiring characters and situations.

Unit 3 Genre

Many of the selections in this unit are persuasive texts. These selections will also help students answer the big question: "What's fair and what's not?" Use these persuasive texts to help students learn to evaluate ideas about what's fair and what's not.

CRITICAL THINKING	VOCABULARY	WRITING AND GRAMMAR	LISTENING, SPEAKING, AND VIEWING
	Connotation, TWE p. 258 Dialect, TWE p. 258		Analyzing the Art, SE p. 258
Infer, SE pp. 266, 276 Analyze, SE pp. 266, 276 Evaluate, SE p. 266 Comprehension, TWE p. 269 Analysis, TWE pp. 272, 273	Academic Vocabulary, SE p. 260 Word Origins, TWE p. 260 Denotation and Connotation, SE pp. 262, 265, 268, 274 Idioms, TWE p. 264 Negative Prefixes, TWE p. 274	Adjectives, SE p. 267 Write About Your Reading, SE p. 276 Adverbs, SE p. 277	Talk About Your Reading, SE p. 266 Viewing the Art, TWE pp. 270 Viewing the Photo, SE p. 271
		Prewriting, SE pp. 278, 279 Plan, SE p. 279 Applying Good Writing Traits: Sentence Fluency, SE p. 280 Adjectives and Adverbs, SE p. 281	
Draw Conclusions, SE p. 288 Infer, SE pp. 288, 296 Evaluate, SE p. 288, TWE p. 294 Synthesize, SE p. 296 Application, TWE p. 293	Academic Vocabulary, SE p. 282 Denotation and Connotation, SE pp. 284, 290, 292, TWE p. 293	Write About Your Reading, SE pp. 288, 296 Comparative and Superlative Adjectives, SE pp. 289, 297	Viewing the Photo, TWE p. 286, SE p. 293, 295
Synthesize, SE p. 304 Infer, SE pp. 304, 312 Evaluate, SE p. 304 Connect, SE p. 312	Academic Vocabulary, SE p. 298 Semantic Slanting, TWE p. 307 Homonyms, TWE p. 302 Descriptive Words, TWE p. 309	Demonstratives, SE p. 305 Write About Your Reading, SE p. 312 Articles, SE p. 313	Talk About Your Reading, SE p. 304 Viewing the Art, SE p. 311 Listening and Speaking, TWE pp. 303, 311

Readability Scores Key
Dale-Chall/DRP/Lexile

PACING (DAYS)		INSTRUCTIONAL SEGMENT LITERATURE	READING SKILLS	LITERARY ELEMENTS
STANDARD	BLOCK			
2	cont'd	Writing Workshop, Part 2, pp. 314–317 Writing Product: Persuasive Essay		
3	1	**Reading Workshop 4, pp. 318–335** from *50 Simple Things Kids Can Do to Save the Earth,* by The EarthWorks Group **3.4/51/810**, SE p. 322 "Greyling" by Jane Yolen **3.1/50/880**, SE p. 328	Identifying Problem and Solution, SE pp. 318, 319, 321, 322, 323, 327, 330, 332, 333 Activating Prior Knowledge, SE p. 328 Inferring, TWE p. 319 Connecting, TWE p. 321 Using Text Structure, TWE p. 322 Build Fluency, TWE p. 328 Questioning, TWE p. 329 Predicting, TWE p. 331	Mood, SE pp. 321, 322, 327, 329, 331 Rhetoric, TWE p. 320 Moral, TWE p. 332
3	2	**Comparing Literature Workshop, pp. 336–355** "The Scholarship Jacket" by Marta Salinas **6.1/54/790**, p. 339 "The Circuit" by Francisco Jimenez **4.2/50/730**, p. 347	Comparing and Contrasting, TWE p. 337 Identifying Problem and Solution, TWE pp. 340, 342, 352 Build Fluency, TWE pp. 340, 349 Clarifying, TWE pp. 341, 349 Inferring, TWE pp. 341, 348	Conflict, SE pp. 336, 337, 339, 340, 341, 342, 344, 345, 347, 348, 349, 350, 352, 353 Descriptive Language, TWE p. 336 Narrator, TWE pp. 339, 347 Dialogue, TWE p. 341 Point of View, TWE p. 350 Character, TWE p. 353
4	2	**Unit Wrap-Up, pp. 356–357**		

CRITICAL THINKING	VOCABULARY	WRITING AND GRAMMAR	LISTENING, SPEAKING, AND VIEWING
	Word Choices, TWE p. 314 Multiple-Meaning Words, TWE p. 316	Writing a Persuasive Essay: Revising, Editing, and Presenting, SE pp. 314–316	Effective Speaking, SE p. 317
Infer, SE pp. 324, 334 Draw Conclusions, SE pp. 324, 334 Evaluate, SE p. 324 Interpret, SE p. 334	Semantic Slanting, SE pp. 320, 323, 326, 329, 330 Compound Words, TWE p. 323	Write About Your Reading, SE pp. 324, 334 Prepositions, SE p. 325 Interjections, SE p. 335	Viewing the Photo, SE pp. 323, 332 Viewing the Art, SE p. 331
Comprehension, TWE pp. 342, 347, 351			Viewing the Painting, SE p. 343 Viewing the Photo, SE p. 345 Viewing the Art, SE pp. 348, 349

Reading with Purpose offers a comprehensive package of tools to optimize student learning and the teaching experience. Each resource has been designed to assist students in specific areas and to offer instructional support for teachers. While all of these areas are covered in the core textbook, some students may need extra practice or additional help in specific areas. The resource package is designed so that you, the teacher, can choose which items will best assist your students. You may also use these resources as homework assignments and for assessment purposes. The following are resources recommended for use with Unit 3.

Keys for Unit Resources

- 📂 Blackline Master
- 📗 Workbook
- 📖 Supplemental Text
- 💿 CD-ROM
- 💾 DVD
- 🖌 Transparency
- 💻 Web-based
- ⚒ Fast File

Essential Instructional Support

FAST FILE — UNIT 3 RESOURCES

Reading and Literature
- Academic Vocabulary Review
- Big Question: School to Home
- The Big Question Foldable
- Unit Challenge: Planner and Rubrics
- Comparing Literature Graphic Organizer
- Key Reading Skills
- Active Reading Graphic Organizers
- Literary Analysis
- Unit Vocabulary Review

Writing, Grammar, and Spelling
- Spelling and Handwriting Practice
- Grammar Practice
- Writing Workshop Graphic Organizer

Listening, Speaking, and Viewing
- Viewing and Representing
- Listening and Speaking

English Language Learners
- English Language Coach Review

DIFFERENTIATED INSTRUCTION

- 📂 Leveled Vocabulary Development
- 💿 Skill Level Up!™ A Language Arts Game
- 💿 Listening Library CD
- 💿 BookLink 3
- 💿 Literature Library Vocabulary Puzzlemaker
- 💿 Vocabulary Puzzlemaker

ASSESSMENT — GLENCOE'S ASSESSMENT ADVANTAGE

- 📂 Selection and Unit Assessments
- 📂 Selection Quick Checks
- 📂 Assessment by Learning Objectives
- 📂 Rubrics for Assessing Student Writing, Listening, and Speaking
- 💻 Glencoe Online Essay Grader
- 💿 Interactive Tutor: Self-Assessment
- 💿 ExamView Assessment Suite
- 💿 Literature Library ExamView Assessment Suite

Additional Instructional Support

WRITING, GRAMMAR, AND SPELLING

- Real Success in Writing: Research and Reports
- Writing Constructed Responses
- Spelling Power eWorkbook
- Grammar & Composition Handbook
- Grammar and Language Workbook
- Revising with Style eWorkbook

READING AND LITERATURE

- Active Learning and Note Taking Guide
- inTime Magazines
- Backpack Reader Volume 1
- Literature Library
- Literature Launchers Pre-Reading Videos DVD
- Literature Classics

TRANSPARENCIES

- Read Aloud, Think Aloud Transparencies
- Literary and Text Analysis Transparencies
- Bellringer Options Transparencies
- Grammar and Writing Workshop Transparencies
- Fine Art Transparencies

TECHNOLOGY

- TeacherWorks Plus™
- StudentWorks Plus™
- BookLink 3
- Skill Level Up!™ A Language Arts Game
- ExamView Assessment Suite
- Interactive Tutor: Self-Assessment
- Listening Library CD
- Spanish Listening Library CD
- Literature Classics
- Literature Launchers Pre-Reading Videos DVD
- Literature Library ExamView Assessment Suite
- Vocabulary Puzzlemaker
- Literature Library Vocabulary Puzzlemaker
- glencoe.com
- Online Student Edition
- Presentation Plus!
- Glencoe Online Essay Grader

ENGLISH LANGUAGE LEARNER

- English Language Coach
- Fluency Practice and Assessment
- inTime Magazines (Spanish)
- Spanish Listening Library CD

PROFESSIONAL DEVELOPMENT

- Professional Development Package

Additional Glencoe Resources

Dinah Zike's Foldables

Foldables are three-dimensional, interactive graphic organizers that help students practice basic writing skills, review key vocabulary terms, and answer Big Questions. Every unit contains a foldable activity. You can find the pattern and directions for the Unit 3 Foldable in the Unit 3 Resources Fast Files booklet. You can use the foldables as they are presented or modify them to suit the needs of your students. More information about foldables for Unit 3 can be found on pages R8–R9.

Glencoe Literature Library

This collection of hardcover books includes full-length novels, novellas, plays, and works of nonfiction. Each volume consists of at least one complete extended-length reading accompanied by several related readings from a broad range of genres. A separate Study Guide for each Glencoe Literature Library book provides teaching notes and reproducible activity pages for students.

Glencoe Literature Library titles that complement this unit include:
> **The Clay Marble,** by Minfong Ho
> **Journey to Jo'burg: A South African Story,**
>   by Beverley Naidoo
> **Shiloh,** by Phyllis Reynolds Naylor

For a wealth of online resources that support the instruction in Unit 3 of *Glencoe Literature: Reading with Purpose,* students and teachers can visit our Web site at www.glencoe.com. Students will find additional learning, practice, and assessment opportunities such as these, which are noted in the student text:

- **Big Question Overview**
- **Study Central**
- **Author Search**
- **Writing Models**
- **Interactive Literary Elements Handbook**
- **Web Activities**

Teachers will find planning and instructional tools that include the following:

- **Book Lesson Plans**
- **Teacher Forum**
- **Professional Development**
- **Web Activities Lesson Plans (with answers to student activities)**

Go to www.glencoe.com to see the entire selection of Reading with Purpose online resources.

 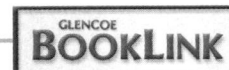

Use the Glencoe **BookLink 3** CD-ROM, a database of more than 26,700 titles, to *create customized reading lists* for your students.

- Search for award-winning titles, (e.g., Newbery Award winners, Coretta Scott King Award winners, and Caldecott Medal winners) and for books on several state-recommended reading lists.
- Find Degrees of Reading Power™ (DRP) and Lexile™ readability scores for all selections.
- Organize reading lists by students' reading level, author, genre, theme, or area of interest.
- Get a brief summary of each selection.

You can find recommended leveled readings for this unit with Reading on Your Own (see page 364).

Glencoe's **Presentation Plus!**, a multimedia teaching tool, lets you present dynamic lessons that will engage your students. Using Microsoft PowerPoint,® you can customize the presentations to create your own personalized lessons. Use **CheckPoint** questions with interactive response keypads to get immediate student feedback during lessons, to increase student participation, and to assess student comprehension.

A lively collection of articles drawn from issues of the TIME family of magazines helps students develop the skills they need to interact with informational text in a meaningful way. Each of the news stories, feature articles, reviews, profiles, and essays in the magazine connect to an author, work, or theme in *Glencoe Literature: Reading with Purpose.* Articles for Unit 3 are found in Volume A. See the *inTIME* Teacher's Guide for specific connections to each unit and for reproducible student worksheets designed to develop students' reading and critical thinking skills.

Literature Launchers

Set the scene with Glencoe's **Literature Launchers,** engaging video segments that introduce each unit's genre focus. Each video brings the genre to life, relating it to your students' worlds.

Insert the Glencoe Literature Launchers Pre-Reading Videos DVD into your DVD player. Select the Unit 3 Launcher from the menu to introduce the genre and Big Question for this unit.

Online Essay Grader

Use Glencoe's **Online Essay Grader** to score your students' writing and to provide individualized feedback to each student automatically.

You and your students can visit www.glencoe.com to link to the essay grader. *Students* can enter their essays and receive feedback on demand. *You* can manage demographic data, assign tests and generate individual student and aggregated reports. The essay grader can help you

- Save time with automatic scoring and individualized feedback.
- Supplement in-class writing instruction using guided writing practice.
- Get reports for individual students or for special populations.
- Track student improvement over time.

 REAL Success: Reading Excellence at All Levels

Glencoe now provides all of your students with the tools they need to become better, more enthusiastic readers. The REAL Success suite of reading and language arts products encourages reading excellence by meeting the needs of students at all levels. Glencoe products that can be used in conjunction with Unit 3 include the following:

- Jamestown Literature: An Adapted Reader
- Jamestown *Reading Fluency*
- Jamestown *Critical Reading Series, In the Line of Duty*
- *Vocabulary Builder*
- *The Glencoe Reader, Course 1*

To order these products, call Glencoe at 1-800-USA-READ.

Teacher Wraparound Edition Key

Level Appropriate Code

AS = Activities for all students

AL = Activities for students working above grade level

OL = Activities for students working at grade level

BL = Activities for students working below grade level

EL = Activities for English language learners

Teacher Wraparound Prompts

R **Reading Skill** These activities help you teach reading comprehension skills.

V **Vocabulary** These activities help students comprehend words and incorporate them into their reading and writing.

C **Critical Thinking** These strategies help students apply and extend what they have learned.

BQ **BIG Question** These activities and questions prompt students to prepare to answer the Big Question.

W **Writing** These activities provide writing opportunities to help students practice writing and comprehend text.

L **Literary Element** These activities and questions help students comprehend selections and learn more about each genre.

E **Text Element** These activities help students comprehend text elements.

LSV **Listening, Speaking, Viewing** These activities help students practice listening, speaking, and viewing skills.

EL **English Language Coach** These skills help English language learners as well as students who need additional reading support.

From an Author

Helping Students Read Persuasive Text

Emphasize the importance of understanding persuasive text. Students are bombarded with persuasive messages in their everyday lives, and at some point these messages influence their actions, if they are persuasive enough. If students are to think critically about what they read, we need to ensure that the purposes for reading include making up one's mind. If students understand they have the ability to make up their own minds, they will be more likely to become engaged in assessing the messages they receive from television, radio, magazines, newspapers, the Internet, billboards, and so on.

Explain how to analyze persuasive text. A first step is for students to think about what they currently believe about a topic. Then they must read with a critical eye. Readers who engage in critical reading of text read both inside and outside of the text. That is, they read and evaluate the message itself, but they also evaluate the author's qualifications, pay attention to where the message appears (in an editorial or in a textbook, for example), when the message appears (in the 1950s or yesterday), and to whom the message was written. Wineburg (1991) calls these elements *sourcing (who wrote the message, where did it come from, what sources were used)* and *contextualization (when was it writ-*

Cynthia Shanahan

ten and for whom; what about the context influenced the message). In addition, Wineburg discusses *corroboration (comparing and contrasting the message with other messages on the same topic).* When a reader engages in sourcing, contextualization, and corroboration, he is evaluating the trustworthiness of the information. Using these elements also influences how he interprets the text. Reading both inside and outside the text helps readers make up their minds.

Teacher to Teacher

Bridget Agnew
St. Michael School
Chicago, IL

"That's not fair!" Because young adolescents are so aware of justice issues, we as middle school teachers often hear this complaint. This unit draws upon the students' natural sense of fairness, so it is easy to engage them in the theme. I start by simply writing the question on the board. Then I read the Big Question aloud ("What's fair and what's not?") and ask the students to do a free-write about the topic. While they are writing, I make my own list on the board to model some sample answers. After the students have finished writing, I ask for a few to share their answers with the class. If the response is particularly enthusiastic, I ask the students to share a few of their responses with a neighbor. Later in the unit, when the students are ready to begin drafting their persuasive writing pieces, they can use the writing, the discussion, and the enthusiasm from the opening lesson to inspire their work.

Teacher Chat Room

Using Persuasive Text

 How do I make persuasive text interesting to students?

 Most students will be interested in persuasive text that deals with subjects they are interested in. Scan various media to find examples of persuasive text or have students look for as many persuasive messages that they can find in one day. Then, as a class, discuss how these texts are persuasive, how the writer makes his or her argument, and how students are influenced by the text.

 What should I teach my students about persuasive text?

 First, teach students how to read the text to find the persuasive message. We cover this in Reading Workshop 1 of this unit, where we show students how to understand persuasive techniques. Next, we recommend teaching students how to distinguish between fact and opinion. Students need to know when something is substantiated with evidence and proof and when something is simply someone's thoughts or ideas.

Questioning information and ideas is another skill that is useful when reading persuasive text. Encourage students to become engaged with what they read by considering what they would like to know about the issues presented in the text. Remind them of the basic inquiry questions Who, What, When, Where, How and Why. If they can't find answers to their questions in the text, direct them to other resources in the library and on the Internet. To ensure that students have a clear understanding of a text, especially when complex ideas are presented, remind them to review and clarify as they read.

 What can I do to help students understand the language that writers of persuasive text use?

 Careful use of language is an important way for writers of persuasive text to convey their messages. Explain to students why identifying semantic slanting is important to evaluating a persuasive text. Share examples of semantic slanting used in texts students encounter every day, such as advertisements and news or magazine articles, or the language used in television commercials. Discuss how the semantic slanting in the text leaves a positive or negative impression. Divide students into two groups and have each come up with language that uses semantic slanting to support opposite ideas.

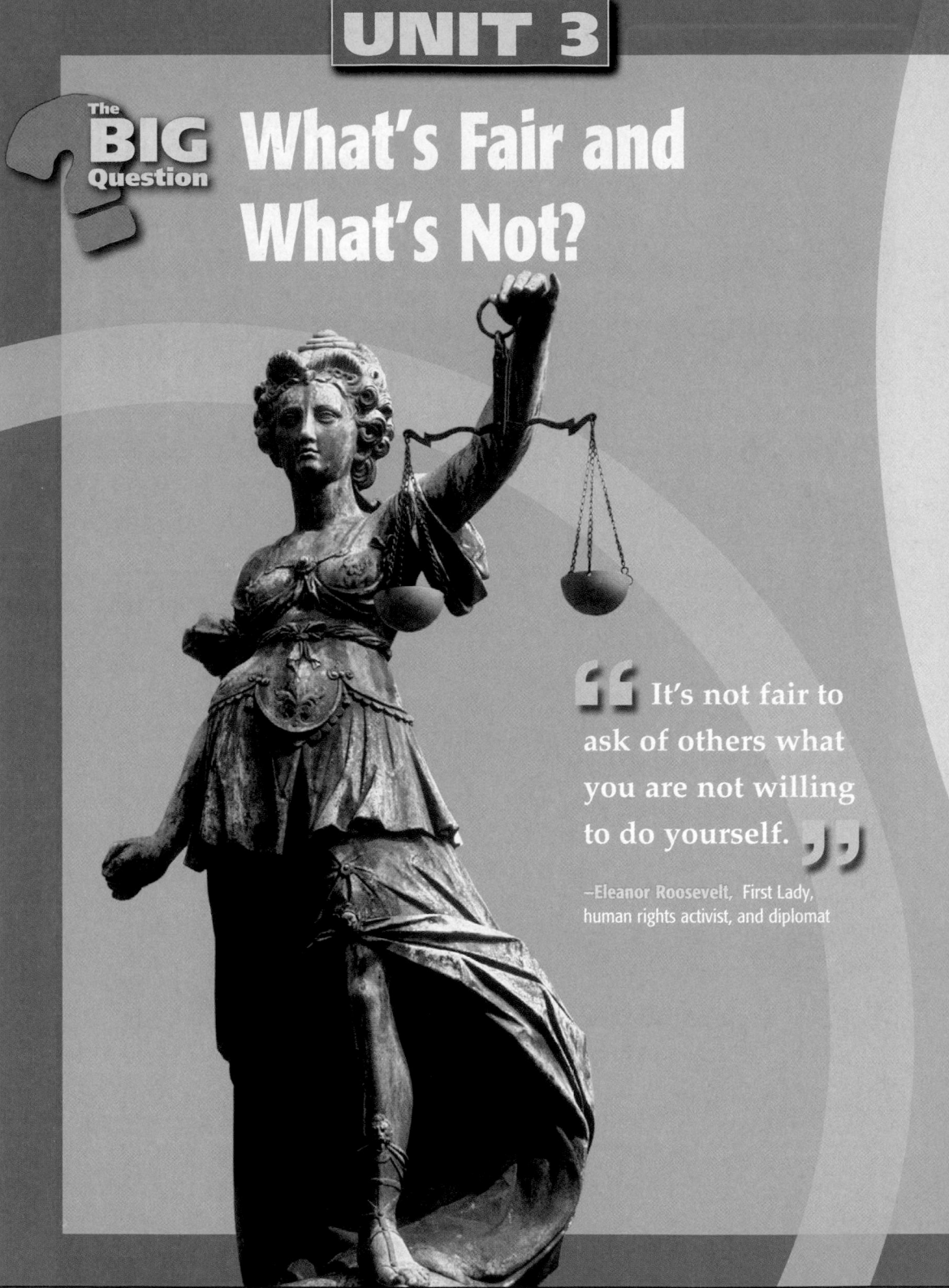

The BIG Question What's Fair and What's Not?

BIG Question

Why Is It Important?
Examining this big question helps students recognize situations that are unfair and develop appropriate strategies for dealing with similar situations in their own lives.

Analyzing the Quote
Say: As wife of President Franklin D. Roosevelt, Eleanor Roosevelt was the First Lady of the United States. Do you agree with her statement that it's not fair to ask other people to do what you won't do yourself? *(Possible response: I agree with her. I wouldn't ask someone else to do something I didn't want to do.)* **AS**

> **❝** It's not fair to ask of others what you are not willing to do yourself. **❞**
>
> –Eleanor Roosevelt, First Lady, human rights activist, and diplomat

Unit Skills

Reading Skills

- Distinguishing Fact and Opinion, p. 260
- Clarifying, p. 282
- Inferring, p. 298
- Identifying Problem and Solution, p. 318

BIG Question What's fair and what's not?

Genre Focus: Persuasive Writing

Literary Elements

- Style, p. 263
- Bias, p. 285
- Argument, p. 301
- Repetition, p. 307
- Mood, p. 321, 327

Vocabulary

- Hyperbole, p. 262
- Denotation and Connotation, p. 290

Writing Skills/Grammar

- Persuasive Essay, pp. 278 and 314
- Adjectives and Adverbs, p. 281

LOOKING AHEAD

The skill lessons and readings in this unit will help you develop your own answer to the Big Question.

UNIT 3 WRAP-UP • **Answering the Big Question**

253

About the Reading

Each selection in this unit provides insights that can help students address the question, "What's fair and what's not?" Students consider different aspects of the question and see how other people deal with unfair situations.

About the Skills

The skills taught in this unit have been selected because they are particularly helpful when reading the featured genre—persuasive writing. Each reading selection provides students with opportunities to practice and develop these skills.

NO CHILD LEFT BEHIND

One way to improve reading skills and comprehension is to encourage students to use a graphic organizer as they read. When students are asked to distinguish fact and opinion in Workshop 1, for example, you might model using a T-chart to help distinguish between the two.

Telling the Difference Between Fact and Opinion	
Fact	Opinion

Reading Fluency

Charting Progress Have students keep a log of their progress. Give them a worksheet with the following chart on which they can note words or phrases that present particular problems for them while they are reading. Encourage students to look up the meaning and pronunciation of these words, and have them make notes on their worksheets. **EL** **BL**

Word or Phrase	Pronunciation	Meaning
adapt	*uh dapt*	*change*

Focus

💾 **Literature Launcher DVD**

🖨 **Daily Language Practice Transparency 21**
Focus Activity Ask: What does the word *fair* mean to you? *(Responses will vary. Possible responses: according to the rules; not favoring one person over another; right; equal)*

Teach

R **Reading Skill**

Review Connecting
Say: Think of a time when you or someone else said, "That's not fair!" Write about the experience in your Learner's Notebooks. Tell where and when the situation took place, who was involved, and what wasn't fair. *(Responses will vary.)* **AS**

BQ **BIG Question**

• Call on volunteers to read the profiles aloud.

• Have students form small groups to discuss what they would do if they were Jodi or Hector. **OL**

UNIT 3 WARM-UP

Connecting to ❓ The BIG Question — What's Fair and What's Not?

R You've seen it happen. Or maybe it has happened to you. Someone is treated differently from others. Somebody gets to do something you don't. A decision or rule doesn't make sense. What do you do when you think something's unfair? In this unit, you'll read about people in various situations that they thought were unfair. You'll learn how they felt and how they reacted.

Real Kids and the Big Question

JODI knows that any player who misses three soccer practices is off the team. Because Jodi has to walk her little brother home after school, she has already missed two practices. If she misses another practice, she can't play on the soccer team. What advice would you give Jodi? **BQ**

HECTOR heard students laughing in the cafeteria. When he walked into the cafeteria, he realized that they were laughing at his new neighbor, Stella. Whenever she got close to a table, suddenly there was no room to sit there. Hector remembered what it was like to be the new kid. What would you do if you were Hector?

Warm-Up Activity
In a small group, talk about how you would feel and what you would do if you were Jodi or Hector. Then tell about a situation you experienced that was unfair. Describe how you felt and what you did.

Additional Support

Differentiated Instruction

Perform a Skit Invite each group to dramatize Jodi's or Hector's situation. Tell group members to work together to develop the story line of the drama. Students should identify characters and decide what each will say or do. Suggest that group members choose a note taker to record the characters' lines and actions in a simple script. Students may then choose the characters they will play and use the script to practice their lines. Have the groups perform their skits for the rest of the class. Allow time for discussion after each skit. **BL EL OL**

You and the Big Question

The question of what's fair or unfair comes up in many situations. As you read the selections in this unit, think about how you would answer the Big Question.

Literature Online

Big Question Link to Web resources to further explore the Big Question at www.glencoe.com.

Plan for the Unit Challenge

At the end of the unit, you'll use notes from all your reading to complete the Unit Challenge.

You'll choose one of the following activities:

A. TV Call-In Show With members of your group, you'll write questions and answers about what's fair and what's not for a television call-in show that your group will present.

B. A Rap or Song You'll write a rap or song about something you feel is unfair and what you think can be done about it.

- Start thinking about which activity you'd like to do so that you can focus your thoughts as you go through the unit.
- In your Learner's Notebook, write your thoughts about the activity you'd like to do.
- Each time you make notes about the Big Question, think about how your ideas will help you complete the Unit Challenge activity you chose.

Keep Track of Your Ideas

FOLDABLES™
Study Organizer

As you read, you'll make notes about the Big Question. Later, you'll use these notes to complete the Unit Challenge. See pages R8–R9 for help with making Foldable 3. This diagram shows how it should look.

1. Use this Foldable for the selections in this unit. Label the stapled edge with the unit number and the Big Question.

2. Label each flap with a selection title. (See page 253 for titles.)

3. Open each flap. Label the top of the inside page **My Purpose for Reading.** You will write your purpose for reading the selection below this label.

4. Halfway down the inside page, write the label **The Big Question.** You'll write your thoughts about the Big Question below this label.

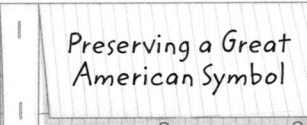
Preserving a Great American Symbol

Teach

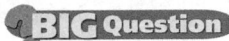
BQ **BIG Question**

Say: Think about what's fair and what's not, and give an example of each. *(Responses will vary.)* **OL**

FOLDABLES™
Study Organizer

For each selection they read, students will enter notes about how that selection applies to the Big Question. For details about using Dinah Zike's Foldables, see page R8–R9.

Assess/Close

Ask students if they have ever been unsure about what's fair and what's not. Tell them that they will find answers to the Big Question as they read the selections in this unit.

Resources for page 255

📁 Use the Unit Challenge Planner BLM in the Unit 3 Resource Booklet, p. 35.

📁 Use the Foldable BLM in the Unit 3 Resource Booklet, p. 7.

Reading in the Real World

Citizenship Basic rights of citizens of the United States are described in the first ten amendments of the Constitution of the United States, known as the Bill of Rights. These rights help ensure that all people are treated fairly. All three branches of the government play a part in protecting citizens' constitutional rights. The legislative branch makes laws to protect people's rights, the judicial branch makes sure the laws agree with what the Constitution says, and the executive branch enforces the laws. Emphasize that citizens also have a responsibility to protect each other's rights. Ask students what citizens can do when they see others treated unfairly. **OL AL**

Objectives

- Make connections from text to self
- Participate in a group discussion

Focus

BELLRINGER Options

 Daily Language Practice Transparency 22
Focus Activity Say:
Describe a TV or radio commercial that you like. What do you like about it? Does it convince you that you need to have the product? If so, what persuades you? *(Responses will vary.)* **AS**

Teach

R Reading Skill

How to Read Persuasive Writing Ask: Which of the reading skills do you think you will find most useful in understanding persuasive writing? Why? *(Possible response: Distinguishing fact and opinion, because persuasive writing includes a writer's thoughts, feelings, or point of view; I will need to be able to separate opinions and feelings from fact to make sense of what I'm reading and to decide whether I agree with it.)* **OL**

Skills Focus
• Key skills for reading and persuasive writing
• Key literary elements of persuasive writing

Skills Model
You will see how to use the key reading skills and literary elements as you read
• "And Ain't I a Woman?" p. 257

Objectives (pp. 256–259)
Reading Distinguish fact and opinion • Monitor comprehension: clarify • Make inferences • Identify problems and solutions
Literature Identify literary elements: style, author's bias, argument, mood

---

UNIT 3 GENRE FOCUS: PERSUASIVE WRITING

In **persuasive writing,** a writer tries to persuade the reader to share a certain point of view or take a particular action. Persuasive writing can take many forms, including speeches, editorials, billboards, and advertisements.

Why Read Persuasive Writing?

Discovering what makes effective persuasive writing is a great way to develop your thinking skills. You'll learn how an author feels about a subject, how you feel about a subject, and what you think is fair and what's not fair.

How to Read Persuasive Writing

R Key Reading Skills

These key reading skills are useful tools for reading and understanding persuasive writing. You'll see them modeled in the Active Reading Model on pages 257–259, and you'll learn more about them in this unit.

■ **Distinguishing fact and opinion** A fact can be proved. An opinion is different; it's what someone thinks or feels about something. Learn to tell them apart. (See Reading Workshop 1.)

■ **Clarifying** Figure out confusing words, phrases, or ideas by using the text and other resources. (See Reading Workshop 2.)

■ **Inferring** Figure out information the author doesn't give you by using what he or she does give you and your own knowledge and experience. (See Reading Workshop 3.)

■ **Identifying problems and solutions** Learn to spot problems and solutions presented by the author. (See Reading Workshop 4.)

Key Literary Elements

Recognizing and thinking about the following literary elements will help you understand more fully what the author is telling you.

■ **Style:** a form of expression in writing, just as in music and fashion (See "Preserving a Great American Symbol.")

■ **Bias:** being for or against something or a preference for one side of an argument (See "Two Advertisements.")

■ **Argument:** the case a writer presents for or against something (See "Dressed for Success?")

■ **Mood:** the feeling that writing creates in the reader (See "from 50 Things Kids Can Do to Save the Earth.")

Additional Support

Literature Focus Lesson

Stereotypes A stereotype is an overly simple or general view of a particular group. Stereotypes can be negative or positive. Tell students that characters in literature and on TV can be stereotypes. These characters are often called "flat" because they have only one or two characteristics and aren't like fully developed, real people. In a book or TV show about a high school, for example, there might be a "geek," a "jock," and a "brain." The "geek" character might do everything a stereotyped "geek" does and nothing else. Invite students to share some characters from books or TV that they believe are examples of stereotypes. **OL AL**

And Ain't I a Woman?

by Sojourner Truth

The notes in the side columns model how to use the skills and elements you read about on page 256.

Personal and Persuasive Text
ACTIVE READING MODEL

Address to the Ohio Women's Rights Convention, 1851

L
R

That man over there says that women need to be helped into carriages, and lifted over ditches, and to have the best place everywhere. Nobody ever helps me into carriages, or over mud-puddles, or gives me any best place! And ain't I a woman? Look at me! Look at my arm. I have ploughed and planted, and gathered into barns, and no man could head[1] me! And ain't I a woman? I could work as much and eat as much as a man—when I could get it—and bear the lash as well! And ain't I a woman? I have borne thirteen children, and seen them most all sold off to slavery, and when I cried out with my mother's grief, none but Jesus heard me! And ain't I a woman? **1** **2** **3**

_____
1. In this speech, **head** means "to do something better than someone else."

1 Key Literary Element
Argument *I can see that Truth is giving very effective examples to back up her argument that women are equal to men.*

2 Key Reading Skill
Distinguishing Fact and Opinion *The number of children that a person has is a matter of fact, not opinion.*

3 Key Literary Element
Style *Repeating the question "And ain't I a woman?" reminds me of preaching. I think Truth has kind of a "preaching" style.*

Genre Focus: Persuasive Writing **257**

Teach

L Literary Element

Bias Ask: Who has a bias against women, according to Sojourner Truth? *(the man who says that women aren't able to do various simple things on their own)* **OL**

R Reading Skill

Distinguishing Fact and Opinion Help students distinguish fact and opinion.

- A fact can be proved true.
- An opinion is what someone believes to be true.

Ask: In the sentence that begins "I have ploughed," which statements are fact and which are opinion? *(Possible response: Truth's statements about ploughing and planting and gathering into barns are facts; her statement that no man could do these things better than she could is an opinion.)* **OL**

Readability Scores
Dale-Chall: 4.2
DRP: 48
Lexile: 690

Reading in the Real World

Citizenship Born into slavery as Isabella Baumfree in 1797, Sojourner Truth worked for many brutal masters. She escaped in 1827, changed her name, and traveled throughout the northeastern United States, speaking out against slavery and for women's rights. Truth was over six feet tall so she got attention wherever she went. Although she could not read or write, Truth was a compelling speaker. "And Ain't I a Woman?" is her best-known speech. Delivered in 1851 at a women's rights convention in Akron, Ohio, it was later published by Frances Gage. Have students consider why Truth would have been a convincing speaker on the issues of women's rights and slavery. **OL** **AL**

Objectives
- Recognize author's bias
- Distinguish fact from opinion
- Identify literary elements: stereotype
- Understand persuasive techniques

257

Teach

R Reading Skill

Inferring Ask: What leads you to infer that Truth doesn't think intellect has anything to do with equal rights? *(Possible response: She asks what intellect has to do with women's rights or Negroes' rights.)* **BL**

EL Language Coach

Denotation and Connotation Say: Words with similar meanings are called synonyms. While their meanings might be close, their connotations, or the feelings connected with them, can be different.

- Write these synonyms for *mean* on the board: *nasty, cruel, unkind.*

Ask: What feeling or special meaning do you connect with each synonym of *mean*? *(Responses will vary. Students might note that the word "cruel" makes them think of a really brutal person, while the word "unkind" makes them think of someone who is careless but not cruel.)* **EL OL**

Then they talk about this thing in the head; what's this they call it? [Intellect,[2] someone whispers.] That's it, honey. What's that got to do with women's rights or Negroes rights? If my cup won't hold but a pint, and yours holds a quart, wouldn't you be mean not to let me have my little half-measure full? **4 5**

2. A person's ***intellect*** (IN tuh lekt) is his or her intelligence

In *Sojourner Truth I Fought for the Rights of Women as Well as Blacks,* 1947. Elizabeth Catlett. Linocut. 15 x 22.5 cm. Private Collection.

Analyzing the Art Sojourner Truth looks very *determined* in this picture. What other qualities does she seem to have, based on this picture? Explain your answer.

ACTIVE READING MODEL

4 Key Literary Element
Bias *Truth obviously prefers one side of the argument about women's rights. So, her speech is biased in favor of women's rights.*

5 Key Reading Skill
Inferring *Truth doesn't say it directly, but I think that she means what's in a person's head, or intellect, doesn't have anything to do with having equal rights.* **R**

Additional Support

English Language Coach

Understanding Dialect Sojourner Truth uses a particular dialect—a nonstandard form of English spoken by people who live in a specific region or who belong to a specific group. Have students read the speech aloud to get a feel for the dialect. They should listen to the rhythm of the words and see if they can guess the meaning of unfamiliar phrases. If the dialect makes some sentences difficult for students to understand, help them rewrite the sentences in standard English. **EL**

ACTIVE READING MODEL

This photograph was taken in Belton, South Carolina, in 1899. These women did not have the right to vote, and their husbands and sons were denied their legal rights, too.

L

Then that little man in black there, he says women can't have as much rights as men, 'cause Christ wasn't a woman! Where did your Christ come from? Where did your Christ come from? From God and a woman! Man had nothing to do with Him. **6**

R

If the first woman God ever made was strong enough to turn the world upside down all alone, these women together ought to be able to turn it back, and get it right side up again! And now they is asking to do it, the men better let them.

Obliged[3] to you for hearing me, and now old Sojourner ain't got nothing more to say. **7** **8** ○

_____

3. **Obliged** (uh BLYJD) is another word for "grateful."

Whole-Class Discussion Give some examples of common stereotypes. Talk about how bias leads to forming stereotypes about people.

Write to Learn Write in your journal an example of persuasive writing or speaking that you have read or heard recently. Did it persuade you to change your thoughts or to do something? Explain your answer.

Literature Online

Study Central Visit www.glencoe.com and click on Study Central to review persuasive writing.

6 Key Reading Skill
Clarifying *I'll have to read this paragraph again more slowly. I didn't get what Truth was saying.*

7 Key Reading Skill
Identifying Problems and Solutions *According to Truth, the problem is that women don't have the same rights as men. The solution is for men to give women equal rights.*

8 Key Literary Element
Mood *Reading this makes me feel sad about what Truth went through but also respectful of her. I'll bet the people who heard her give the speech felt like working hard for women's rights.*

Teach

L Literary Element

Style Ask: What question does Truth repeat? *(She repeats the question "Where did your Christ come from?")* **BL**
Ask: Why might Truth repeat the question? *(Possible responses: to get her point across, to emphasize ideas)* **OL**

R Reading Skill

Clarifying Students may need help understanding the second paragraph on page 259. **Say:** Truth is referring to the Biblical story of Adam and Eve in the second paragraph. According to the Bible, God banished Adam and Eve from their perfect garden because Eve ate a piece of forbidden fruit. Now that you know this, reread the paragraph. What point is Truth making? *(Possible response: She makes the point that if one women, Eve, had the power to change the world for the worse, then all the women at the meeting have the power to change it for the better.)* **AL**

Literature Online

Study Central Have students access the Web site to review persuasive writing and to complete a related activity.

Literature Focus Lesson

Tone Tone expresses to readers or listeners the writer's or speaker's feelings and attitude toward his or her subject. An informative article on women's rights might have an objective tone, whereas a persuasive speech on the topic, such as Sojourner Truth's, would have a persuasive tone. Factors that contribute to tone are elements such as repetition and questioning, word choice, details, and images. Ask students to identify the words, details, and images that give Truth's speech its persuasive, forceful tone. **OL**

Objectives
• Make inferences
• Understand connotation
• Identify author's style
• Clarify ideas and text
• Identify literary elements: tone
• Understand dialect

Distinguishing Fact and Opinion

**Objective covered in
this workshop:**
• Distinguish between fact
  and opinion in various texts

Teaching Students to Distinguish Fact and Opinion

Why Is It Important?

• Students will learn how to tell the difference between statements that can be proven—or *facts*—and those that someone believes are true—*opinions*.

• When students read, they'll come across writers who try to convince them of their beliefs. If they can tell the difference between facts and opinions, they will be able to make up their own minds.

• As students learn how to recognize opinions, they'll be able to judge whether or not they should believe what they've heard or read. They will also learn that they can disagree with an opinion.

How to Help Students Get It

• Tell students to look at the title of the selection first. Sometimes the title can express an opinion about a topic.

• As they read, remind students to think about which parts of the selection are convincing. Then ask them to try to determine if those parts are facts or opinions.

• Remind students that sometimes a good persuasive argument is a balance between a writer's opinions and the facts used to support those opinions.

Reading to Answer the Big Question

In Workshop 1 of Unit 3, readers will encounter different visions of America, and different definitions of what is right. As they read, they will be prompted to answer the Big Question: **What's fair and what's not?**

Preserving a Great American Symbol by Richard Durbin
Congressman Richard Durbin's satirical speech demonstrates his love for baseball. Though his tone is humorous and several statements are greatly exaggerated, it is evident that Durbin believes it would be unfair to Americans to lose their baseball traditions.

Looking for America by Elizabeth Partridge
Elizabeth Partridge chronicles a cross country trip she took with her family in 1963. In a home in the South, she observes overt discrimination for the first time. Partridge portrays the bewilderment, sadness, and helplessness she feels in the face of rules and laws that seem unfair and senseless to her.

Workshop Resources

Pacing (days) Standard	Block	Lesson	Student Materials	Teacher Resources
1	1/2	Key Skill Lesson: Distinguishing Fact and Opinion	🪨 Key Reading Skills Practice, p. 9 🪨 English Language Coach Review, p. 41	🖌 Bellringer Options Transparencies –Daily Language Practice 23 🖌 Read Aloud, Think Aloud Transparencies –Key Reading Skills 7 💿 Presentation Plus!
1	1	"Preserving a Great American Symbol"	💻 Glencoe Online 🪨 Unit Vocabulary Review, p. 39 🪨 Academic Vocabulary Review, p. 42 📁 English Language Coach 🪨 Active Reading Graphic Organizer, p. 11 🪨 Literary Analysis, p. 10 💿 StudentWorks Plus™ 💻 Online Student Edition 💿 Literature Classics 📁 Selection and Unit Assessments, p. 25	🖌 Literary and Text Analysis Transparencies 50 💻 Puzzlemaker 💿 Skill Level Up!™ A Language Arts Game 💻 BookLink 3 📕 Assessment by Learning Objective (Diagnostic and Formative) 💿 Interactive Tutor: Self-Assessment 💿 TeacherWorks Plus™
1		"Looking for America"	💻 Glencoe Online 🪨 Unit Vocabulary Review, p. 39 🪨 Academic Vocabulary Review, p. 42 📁 English Language Coach 🪨 Active Reading Graphic Organizer 🪨 Literary Analysis, p. 10 💿 StudentWorks Plus™ 💻 Online Student Edition 💿 Literature Classics 📁 Selection and Unit Assessments, p. 26	🖌 Literary and Text Analysis Transparencies 50 💻 Puzzlemaker 💿 Skill Level Up!™ A Language Arts Game 💻 BookLink 3 📕 Assessment by Learning Objective (Diagnostic and Formative) 💿 Interactive Tutor: Self-Assessment 💿 TeacherWorks Plus™

Keys for Unit Resource

📁 Blackline Master   🔒 DVD

📕 Workbook   🖌 Transparency

📖 Supplemental Text   💻 Web-based

💿 CD-ROM   🪨 Fast File

Level Appropriate Code

AS = Activities for all students

AL = Activities for students working above grade level

OL = Activities for students working at grade level

BL = Activities for students working below grade level

EL = Activities for English language learners

Focus

BELLRINGER Options

✍ **Daily Language Practice Transparency 23 Focus Activity** Have students write two facts about themselves in their Learner's Notebooks. Then tell them to write two opinions. Suggest that students start their opinion statements with *I think, I believe,* or *In my opinion.* *(Responses will vary.)* **AS**

Teach

R Reading Skill

Distinguishing Fact and Opinion Ask students to describe the difference between a fact and an opinion. *(Possible response: A fact is something that can be proven. An opinion is what someone believes to be true.)* **OL**

V Vocabulary

Academic Vocabulary
Say: Write a sentence using the word *distinguish.* *(Check students' sentences to make sure they understand the meaning of the word.)* **AS**

READING WORKSHOP 1

Skills Focus

You will practice using these skills when you read the following selections:
• "Preserving a Great American Symbol," p. 264
• "Looking for America," p. 270

Reading

• Distinguishing fact and opinion

Literature

• Identifying an author's style
• Explaining how style affects the reader

Vocabulary

• Understanding hyperbole
• Academic Vocabulary: *distinguish*

Writing/Grammar

• Identifying and using adjectives and adverbs

Objectives (pp. 260–261)
Reading Distinguish fact from opinion

Skill Lesson

Distinguishing Fact and Opinion

Learn It!

What Is It? A **fact** is something that can be proved. An **opinion** is what someone believes is true. Opinions are based on feelings and experiences; they cannot be proved. When deciding whether to believe what a writer has written, you'll have to **distinguish** *fact from opinion.* Writers can support their opinions with facts, but an opinion is something that cannot be proved.

R

Fact: Beijing is the capital of China.

Opinion: China is the best place to vacation.

You could prove that Beijing is the capital of China. It's a fact. But not everyone would agree that China is the best place for a vacation. That's someone's opinion.

Analyzing Cartoons
Is the larger dog presenting a fact or an opinion? How do you know? How does the smaller dog feel about this bit of information?

V Academic Vocabulary

distinguish (dih STING gwish) *v.* to know the difference between, tell apart

---

Additional Support

English Language Coach

Word Origins To enhance students' understanding of the meaning of the Academic Vocabulary word, explain that the English word *distinguish* can be traced back to the Latin word *distinguere,* which means "to separate." Also point out that the Latin prefix *dis-* means "apart." Thus *distinguish* means "to separate or tell apart." Reinforce students' grasp of the meaning of *distinguish* by asking them to name other things besides fact and opinion that someone might distinguish between. **OL**

R **Why Is It Important?** As you read, ask yourself, *Is this a fact or an opinion?* Opinions can be useful, but sometimes opinions are based on prejudice or feelings you don't share. Before you accept something as true, you need to find out if it's *fact* or *opinion*.

How Do I Do It? To tell fact from opinion, ask: *Can this be proved?*

- *What is the source of the statement?* The source is where the information came from. An encyclopedia is one trustworthy source.
- *Is the author an expert on the subject?* An expert on that topic would usually know a lot of proven facts about it.
- *Are there numbers or dates with the statement?* Numbers and dates could prove the time, the place, how much, or how many.

Take a look at how one student distinguished between facts and opinions in a newspaper article about a supposed UFO sighting.

Literature Online

Study Central Visit www.glencoe.com and click on Study Central to review distinguishing fact and opinion.

> Recorded calls to the station-house indicate that the policeman radioed in the sighting on April 4, 1997 at 2:48 AM. "You're not going to believe this," he said, "But *I think* I saw a UFO! The engine died on my car, and the radio started going haywire! All of the sudden I saw red, white, and green lights flashing from behind the trees!" Weather reports prove that there were no thunderstorms that evening, but the policeman was near a swamp. Sometimes, people mistake swamp gas for a UFO.

> *They have a recording of the policeman with the date and time saying that he saw a UFO, so I know he saw something. It's a fact that he called in on his radio; that can be proven. But I wonder what he saw? He said he thinks he saw a UFO, but that doesn't make it a fact—just an opinion.*

Practice It!

Look at articles in a newspaper. Find a sentence that tells a fact and a sentence that tells an opinion. Copy the examples in your Learner's Notebook. Explain why you think the example is a fact or an opinion.

Use It!

Remember what you've learned about facts and opinions as you read "Preserving a Great American Symbol."

Teach

Literature Online

Study Central Have students access the Web site to review distinguishing fact and opinion and to complete a related activity.

R Reading Skill

Distinguishing Fact and Opinion Emphasize that when examining a piece of information, it is important to determine whether it is a fact or an opinion. **Say:** Opinions aren't always bad. Sometimes they're just what you're looking for. What kinds of texts do you read for opinions? *(Possible responses: editorials, essays, and reviews)* **OL Ask:** How might you use opinions that you get from reading reviews? *(Possible response: Reviews of books, movies, video games, and CDs help me to decide how to spend my time and money.)* **AL**

Resources for page 261

📁 Use Key Reading Skills Transparency 7 in *Read Aloud, Think Aloud* to help students practice distinguishing fact and opinion.

Reading in the Real World

Citizenship Tell students that learning to distinguish fact and opinion will help them when they search online. Anyone can post just about anything online, and there's no one to check if information is fact, opinion, or just plain false. Provide these tips for identifying reliable sources on the Web.

- Look for Web sites with *.edu*, *.gov*, or *.org* in their domain name.
- Check to see whether the Web site has links to other trustworthy sites.
- Beware of Web sites that include many opinions or ideas from only one side of an issue. **OL**

Objectives

- Distinguish fact from opinion
- Learn and use new vocabulary
- Explore word origins

Teach

More About the Author

Richard Durbin has been a member of the U.S. Senate since 1997. In 2004, other Democrats in the Senate elected him Assistant Minority Leader, or Democratic Whip. This is the second highest Democratic leadership position. Issues of concern to Senator Durbin include health care, protection of consumers, and gun safety. Durbin is also a strong supporter of farmers in Illinois and in the rest of the nation.

V Vocabulary

Word Webs To expand their understanding of the vocabulary, have students create a word web for each vocabulary word.

• Tell students to write the word in the center circle of the web. Then ask students to write two synonyms for the word around the center circle.

• Students may use a dictionary or thesaurus as an aid.

• Have students compare their webs with a partner's. **EL** **BL** **OL**

Before You Read

Richard Durbin

Meet the Author

Richard Durbin has been a member of Congress since 1983. Today he represents the people of Illinois in the United States Senate. Senator Durbin makes many speeches. Most are about more serious issues than saving the baseball bat. Education, for instance, is an issue Durbin takes very seriously. He sees education as "the key to opportunity."

Literature Online

Author Search For more about Richard Durbin, go to www.glencoe.com.

Objectives (pp. 262–265)
Reading Distinguish fact and opinion
• Make connections from text to self
Literature Identify literary elements: style, symbol, hyperbole
Vocabulary Understanding hyperbole

Preserving a Great American Symbol

Vocabulary Preview

condemn (kun DEM) *v.* to express a strong feeling against something **(p. 264)** *Don't condemn a person for making a bad choice.*

endure (en DUR) *v.* to put up with **(p. 264)** *When Emilio moved from Florida to New York he found the winters hard to endure.*

indignities (in DIG nuh teez) *n.* insulting treatment **(p. 264)** *The new members had to suffer many indignities before they were accepted into the club.*

forsake (for SAYK) *v.* to give up something or someone **(p. 265)** *When Y-Ming became famous, she refused to forsake her old friends.*

Fill in the Blank Write a sentence for each word. Put a blank in each sentence where the word should appear. Trade sentences with a partner. Then fill in the blanks in each other's sentences with the correct words.

English Language Coach

Hyperbole "When I lost my new scarf, I almost died!" Have you ever said anything like that? Did you really mean your life was in danger? Of course not. You were exaggerating. That kind of extreme exaggeration is called **hyperbole**. People may use it to express strong feelings or to emphasize a point. Sometimes, people use it to be funny. Hyperbole uses exaggerated words and exaggerated comparisons. As a reader, you're expected to understand that it is not the exact truth.

Partner Work Read the sentences below to each other. Then discuss which ones you think use hyperbole. Talk about what your reasons are.

1. I'm so tired I could sleep for a year.
2. You could put his common sense in a thimble and have room left over for the Great Lakes.
3. When I lost my homework, I was quite worried.
4. Bella has told that same joke a million times.
5. Cafeteria workers faced a tragedy today when they ran out of tortilla chips.

Additional Support

Literature Online

Author Search To expand students' appreciation of Richard Durbin, have them access the Web site for additional resources.

English Language Coach

Connotation Write the following word chains on the board: weep-sob-blubber-wail; walk-stroll-march-toddle; think-brainstorm-daydream-consider; write-scribble-record-jot. Point to each word in the chains and ask students to explain what thoughts, feelings, or images they associate with the word.

Invite students to act out what the word suggests to them. Encourage partners to use a thesaurus or dictionary to create other word chains in their Learner's Notebooks and write their ideas about the connotations of the words they've listed. **EL** **BL** **OL**

Skills Preview

Key Reading Skill:
Distinguishing Fact and Opinion

Sometimes it's difficult to tell a fact from an opinion, especially when the writer is being funny. After all, most humor is not written for the purpose of giving information. And yet, sometimes a writer uses humor to make a point. Then, facts may be scattered in among the jokes and exaggerations.

As you read "Preserving a Great American Symbol," look for statements that can be proved. Ask yourself whether these facts help support the writer's opinions.

Write to Learn In your Learner's Notebook, write one way in which you can tell facts and opinions apart.

Key Literary Element: Style

You probably know all about **style** when it comes to fashion and music. You might dress in a certain style or like a particular style of music. Style is just a particular way of doing something. A writer's style is his or her own way of putting words and sentences together.

One style of writing is sometimes called "mock seriousness." (*Mock* means "pretend, not real.") The writer chooses a subject that isn't very important and writes about it as if it were. There is usually some hyperbole in the mock serious style. This style can be very funny. It can also help the author make a point.

Partner Talk With a partner choose an unimportant subject. Then work together to make up a mock serious sentence about it.

Get Ready to Read

Connect to the Reading

A symbol is an object that stands for a big idea. For example, a lion is often a symbol for courage. People often have strong feelings about symbols, such as the flag and even wooden baseball bats. What symbol has special meaning for you? Why is it important to you?

Whole-Class Discussion Name a symbol that means something special to you. Explain its meaning, and talk about its importance. How would you feel without it?

Build Background

In this selection, Richard Durbin argues that the wooden baseball bat is a part of the baseball tradition that must be saved.

- Baseball is often called our "national pastime" because so many Americans enjoy the sport.
- Professional baseball players must use wooden bats. Aluminum bats are not allowed.
- Wooden bats are made either from one piece of wood or from layers of wood that are pressed together.

Set Purposes for Reading

BIG Question Read the selection "Preserving a Great American Symbol" to find out why Richard Durbin thinks replacing wooden bats with metal ones would harm the tradition of baseball.

Set Your Own Purpose What else would you like to learn from the reading to help you answer the Big Question? Write your purpose on the "Preserving a Great American Symbol" page of Foldable 3.

Literature Online

Interactive Literary Elements Handbook To review or learn more about the literary elements, go to www.glencoe.com.

Keep Moving

Use these skills as you read the following selection.

Preserving a Great American Symbol **263**

Teach

L Literary Element

Style Say: An author's style is sometimes described as formal or informal. Which style do you suppose Richard Durbin uses in his speech to Congress—formal or informal? Explain your answer. *(Possible response: formal, because he is speaking to a government body)* **OL**

C Critical Thinking

Comprehension Say: The 13 stripes on the American flag represent the 13 original colonies, and the 50 stars represent the 50 states. Name another common symbol, and tell what it represents. *(Possible response: A dove represents peace.)* **OL**

Literature Online

Interactive Literary Elements Handbook Have students access the Web site to improve their understanding of style.

Literature Focus Lesson

Style Have students review the selections in Units 1 and 2 to identify an author whose style they especially liked. Tell students to read aloud a passage from the selection, paying attention to the writer's choice of words and to the rhythm of the writing (sentence length and arrangement). After reading, students should tell what they like about how the writer uses language. Use the questions on page 263 under "Style" to help guide the conversation. **OL**

Objectives
- Distinguish fact from opinion
- Identify author's style
- Make connections from text to self
- Understand connotation
- Learn and use new vocabulary

263

Teach

L Literary Element

Style Say: Durbin's choice of words helps create a formal style. Which words add to the formality of his speech? *(Possible responses: words and phrases such as* condemn, desecration, endure, *and* indignities*)* **OL** **AL**

EL Language Coach

Idioms Some students may not understand the idiom "leave well enough alone." Explain that an idiom is a word or phrase that has special meaning different from the ordinary meaning of the word or words.
Say: Use context clues to figure out the meaning of the idiom and then explain its meaning in your own words. *(Possible response: Let something stay as it is because it does not need to be improved.)* **EL**

Readability Scores
Dale-Chall: 9.4
DRP: 62
Lexile: 1010

★★★★ *Preserving a* ★★★★
Great American Symbol

by Richard Durbin

Mr. Speaker, I rise to **condemn** the desecration[1] of a great American symbol. No, I am not referring to flagburning; I am referring to the baseball bat. **1**

    Several experts tell us that the wooden baseball bat is doomed to extinction, that major league baseball players will soon be standing at home plate with aluminum bats in their hands.

    Baseball fans have been forced to **endure** countless **indignities** by those who just cannot leave well enough alone: designated hitters,[2] plastic grass, uniforms that look like pajamas, chicken clowns dancing on the base lines, and,

---

1. A **desecration** is an act that shows disrespect for something sacred.
2. A **designated hitter** bats in place of the pitcher.

Vocabulary

condemn (kun DEM) *v.* to express a strong feeling against something

endure (en DUR) *v.* to put up with

indignities (in DIG nuh teez) *n.* insulting treatment

264 UNIT 3 What's Fair and What's Not?

Practice the Skills

1 Key Literary Element

Style Look at the footnote for *desecration* at the bottom of the page. Do you think this word is usually used for things a lot more important than a baseball bat? What clue does that give you about the style of this selection?

Additional Support

Reading Fluency

Build Fluency Encourage students to read aloud Durbin's entire speech or a passage from it. First, have students practice reading the selection aloud on their own. Students should reread the selection several times until they can smoothly read all the sentences expressively.

Instruct students to look up the pronunciation and meaning of any words they do not know. Encourage them to make their reading sound like natural speech. When students are ready, have them take turns reading the speech or a passage aloud to a small group. **EL** **BL** of course, the most heinous sacrilege,[3] lights in Wrigley Field.[4] **2 3**

Are we willing to hear the <u>crack</u> of a bat replaced by the dinky <u>ping</u>? Are we ready to see the Louisville Slugger[5] replaced by the aluminum ping dinger? Is nothing sacred?

Please do not tell me that wooden bats are too expensive, when players who cannot hit their weight are being paid more money than the President of the United States.

Please do not try to sell me on the notion that these metal clubs will make better hitters.

What will be next? Teflon[6] baseballs? Radar-enhanced gloves? I ask you.

I do not want to hear about saving trees. Any tree in America would gladly give its life for the glory of a day at home plate. **4**

I do not know if it will take a constitutional amendment to keep our baseball traditions alive, but if we **forsake** the great Americana of broken-bat singles and pine tar,[7] we will have certainly lost our way as a nation. **5** ○

---

3. A **heinous sacrilege** is the act of misusing something that is sacred in an unusually shocking way. Here the statement is meant to be dramatic.

4. Chicago's **Wrigley Field** is one of the oldest baseball fields in the United States. No night games were played there until 1988, when the field finally got lights.

5. The wooden baseball bat known as the **Louisville Slugger** was first made in Louisville, Kentucky, in 1884. Today it is the official bat of major league baseball.

6. **Teflon** is the name for a tough, waxy material that is very hard to damage.

7. **Americana** includes anything that has something to do with American culture. When a batter breaks a bat while hitting but gets safely to first base, the play is called a **broken-bat single. Pine tar** is a sticky substance that batters use to get a tight grip on a wooden bat.

Vocabulary

forsake (for SAYK) v. to give up something or someone

Practice the Skills

2 Key Reading Skill

Distinguishing Fact and Opinion Is it a fact that fans of baseball have to put up with the things listed in this paragraph? Is it a fact that these things are **indignities**, or insulting treatment? Explain. **BQ**

3 BIG Question

Durbin thinks that a change from wooden to metal bats would be unfair to baseball fans. What other changes in the sport does he think have been unfair to fans? Record your answers on the "Preserving a Great American Symbol" page of Foldable 3. These notes will help you complete the Unit Challenge later.

4 Key Literary Element

Style What is there about this paragraph that might be thought of as mock serious in style?

5 English Language Coach

Hyperbole What example or examples of hyperbole can you find in this paragraph?

Preserving a Great American Symbol **265**

Teach

BQ **BIG Question**

Ask: Why might metal bats and other changes in baseball be unfair to fans? (*Possible response: Traditions, such as the wooden baseball bat, are one of the things baseball fans like about the sport, and no one has asked them whether they want changes.*) **AL**

R Reading Skill

Distinguishing Fact and Opinion Point out that opinions often include strong language and very broad, or general, statements. When stating an opinion, for example, a person might use the word *should* or *must* or state something with great confidence.
Ask: What suggests that the last sentence is an opinion, not a fact? (*Possible response: It cannot be proved; Durbin uses the word* certainly *to emphasize what he thinks.*) **OL**

Literature Focus Lesson

Onomatopoeia and Personification Tell students that Durbin uses two literary elements in his speech that add to his unique style:

• **Onomatopoeia** is the use of a word or phrase that imitates the sound it represents. Ask students to find two examples of onomatopoeia in the speech. (*crack, ping*)

• **Personification** is applying human characteristics to animals or things. Have students find an example of personification in the speech. ("*Any tree in America would gladly give its life for the glory of a day at home plate.*") **AL**

Objectives

• Identify author's style
• Distinguish fact from opinion
• Understand connotation
• Identify literary elements: style, symbol, hyperbole
• Understand idioms

Assess

Resources for page 266

- Selection Quick Check, p. 21
- Selection and Unit Assessment, p. 25
- ExamView Assessment Suite
- Interactive Tutor: Self-Assessment

Students can respond to the *After You Read* items in their Learner's Notebooks or on a separate sheet of paper.

Answering the

BIG Question

1. Responses will vary.
2. Possible responses: designated hitters, plastic grass, uniforms that look like pajamas, chicken clowns dancing on the base lines, and lights in Wrigley Field
3. lights in Wrigley Field
4. Wooden bats are a baseball tradition; the crack of a wooden bat sounds better than the dinky ping of a metal bat.

Critical Thinking

5. Possible response: Yes, his speech indicates he knows a lot about baseball and loves the sport.
6. Possible response: He mentions an amendment and the nation losing its way.
7. Responses will vary.

After You Read

Preserving a Great American Symbol

Answering the BIG Question

1. Do you agree with the author that changing from wooden bats to metal bats would be unfair to baseball fans? Explain.
2. **Recall** Name three things that the writer says baseball fans have been forced to endure.
   Tip Right There
3. **Recall** What does Durbin call "the most heinous sacrilege"?
   Tip Right There
4. **Summarize** What are some of the reasons Durbin prefers wooden bats to aluminum?
   Tip Think and Search

Critical Thinking

5. **Infer** Do you think Richard Durbin is a baseball fan? Explain.
   Tip Author and Me
6. **Analyze** Which details in the final paragraph show that this speech is not meant to be serious?
   Tip Author and Me
7. **Evaluate** What effect do you think this speech had on its audience?
   Tip On My Own

Talk About Your Reading

Think about these statements in Durbin's speech:

I do not want to hear about saving trees. Any tree in America would gladly give its life for the glory of a day at home plate.

This is Durbin's *opinion.* How would you feel if you were the tree? With a partner, take turns making your own speech, but pretend that you are the tree. Include facts and opinions of your own. Before you begin, take a few moments to jot down at least three points you'd like to make in your speech. Do you think it would be fair to be turned into a baseball bat? Would you favor aluminum bats instead, or is Durbin right? Would you "gladly" give your life "for the glory of a day at home plate"?

Objectives (pp. 266–267)
Reading Distinguish fact and opinion
Literature Identify literary elements: style, hyperbole
Grammar Identify parts of speech: adjectives

Talk About Your Reading

Possible response:
I'm a tree, and I'd like to respond. What happened to concern for the environment? Sure, trees can be replanted, but it takes years for us to grow tall, and once a tree is cut down, that's the end of its life. Why would any tree give up many years of a good life in the forest for one day in a baseball stadium? Who cares about baseball? Besides, no one asks us if we want to be cut down. It just isn't fair. I'm in favor of switching to aluminum bats. After all, we trees are living things.

Skills Review

Key Reading Skill: Distinguishing Fact and Opinion

8. In your Learner's Notebook, answer the following questions about the selection.
   - What was the subject of the speech?
   - What was the speaker's opinion on the subject?
   - What facts did he use to support his opinion?

Key Literary Element: Style

9. Write down two words or phrases that you think might be "mock serious" in the selection. Explain why you think they are.

10. Do you think the big words in the selection help make it funny? Explain why or why not.

11. Do you think the style of the selection helped the author make his point? Why or why not?

Vocabulary Check

Look over the vocabulary words from the story:

condemn   endure   indignities   forsake

Then come up with as many answers as you can to these questions. Write the questions and the answers on a separate sheet of paper. You may be "mock serious" if you like.

12. What would you **condemn**?

13. What do you have to **endure**?

14. What **indignities** have you suffered in your life?

15. Who or what would you never **forsake**?

16. **Academic Vocabulary** Which pair of things below might be difficult to **distinguish** from each other? Explain the reason for your choice.

      apple and orange
      glass and plate
      moth and butterfly

17. **English Language Coach** What makes the sentence below an example of hyperbole? What point is the writer making?

      The bell rang, shattering our ear drums.

Grammar Link: Adjectives

As you know, different kinds of words do different jobs in a sentence. Words that are used to describe nouns or pronouns are **adjectives**. Adjectives answer these questions:

- What kind?
- Which one?
- How many

The adjectives in the sentences below are in bold type. The nouns they describe are underlined.

Deb found a **young** <u>squirrel</u> under a tree. (*What kind?*)
She fed it with **this** <u>bottle</u>. (*Which one?*)
Careful <u>treatment</u> helped the **lonely** <u>squirrel</u>.
(*What kind? What kind?*)
Deb has helped **several** <u>animals</u>. (*How many?*)

Sometimes a word that you think of as a noun does the job of an adjective. Then, the word is an adjective.

Deb found a **baby** squirrel under an **oak** tree.

Most adjectives come right before the noun they describe. Some come after a linking verb. As you learned before, a linking verb shows a condition or state of being.

The <u>tornado</u> was **huge** and **dark**.
Suddenly, the <u>sky</u> looked **green**.

Grammar Practice

Copy the sentences below on another sheet of paper. Underline each adjective.

18. Bees gather a sweet liquid from flowers.

19. One bee may visit five hundred flowers in one trip.

20. Each flower has powder called pollen that is yellow.

21. Pollen gets on the busy bee.

22. She leaves some powder on another flower.

Literature Online

Web Activities For eFlashcards, Selection Quick Checks, and other Web activities, go to www.glencoe.com.

Preserving a Great American Symbol   **267**

Grammar Link: Adjectives

Grammar Practice

18. Bees gather a <u>sweet</u> liquid from flowers.

19. <u>One</u> bee may visit <u>five hundred</u> flowers in <u>one</u> trip.

20. <u>Each</u> flower has powder called pollen that is <u>yellow</u>.

21. Pollen gets on the <u>busy</u> bee.

22. She leaves <u>some</u> powder on <u>another</u> flower.

Close

Ask students what they learned from this selection to answer the Big Question.

Skills Review

Key Reading Skill: Distinguishing Fact and Opinion

8. **Subject:** replacing wooden bats with metal bats
   Speaker's opinion: Wooden bats should be saved.
   Support: He does not use facts. He supports his opinion with other opinions.

Key Literary Element: Style

9. Possible responses: "doomed to extinction," "Is nothing sacred?" "we will have lost our way"

10. Responses will vary.

11. Possible response: Yes, he persuades by using a humorous style. He also creates humor by using serious words to discuss a light topic.

Vocabulary Check

Sample responses:

12. an evil person

13. doing chores

14. having to wash the garbage cans

15. my dedication to playing the guitar

16. **Academic Vocabulary** A moth and a butterfly are very similar so one might not be able to distinguish between the two.

17. **English Language Coach** Possible response: A loud bell couldn't shatter ear drums; the writer is saying the bell was very loud.

Teach

More About the Author

One of five children, Elizabeth Partridge grew up in the San Francisco area. She says that her family's summer trips often lasted into October or November, "which never seemed to bother my parents much. They would just call the school in late September and ask them to save places for all of us." In addition to writing children's books, including picture books, biographies, and historical fiction, Partridge is a doctor of Chinese medicine and an acupuncturist. She lives in San Francisco with her husband and children.

V Vocabulary

Using New Vocabulary

Challenge students to include all four vocabulary words into one sentence. *(Possible response: The architect beckoned for his assistant to help buffet the attacking cicadas.)* **OL**

Before You Read · Looking for America

Meet the Author

Elizabeth Partridge grew up in a large family. During the summers, her family often traveled across the country in an old Cadillac limousine, usually not returning until after school had started. As a writer, Partridge believes that it is important to "offer our young adults examples of critical listeners and critical thinkers. We need . . . to let them know that they, too, can have a voice."

Author Search For more about Elizabeth Partridge, go to www.glencoe.com.

Objectives (pp. 268–275)
Reading Distinguish fact and opinion
• Make connections from text to self
Literature Identify literary elements: style
Vocabulary Understand word choice

268 UNIT 3 What's Fair and What's Not?

Vocabulary Preview

architect (AR kuh tekt) *n.* a person who designs buildings **(p. 271)** *The architect designed a famous house made of glass.*

cicadas (sih KAY duz) *n.* large insects, also called locusts; males make a shrill buzzing sound **(p. 271)** *You could hear cicadas buzzing in the trees.*

beckoned (BEK und) *v.* moved the head or hand to make a sign to approach or come nearer; form of the verb *beckon* **(p. 272)** *Her mother beckoned her to the table.*

buffet (BUF it) *v.* to strike with force **(p. 275)** *The strong wind will buffet the kids as they walk to school.*

Write to Learn Write the vocabulary word that each clue describes.
• This describes what a storm can do to the branches of a tree.
• If you did this, a waiter would come take your order.
• This person might draw plans for a skyscraper.
• You might see these (and hear them) in the summertime.

English Language Coach

Word Choice You might sometimes wonder why writers use uncommon words instead of the plainest, simplest ones. There's often a good reason. Maybe he or she writes, "Suki ambled by." Why? Well, *ambled* is a really good verb. It doesn't just mean "walked." It means "walked in a slow, easy way, usually without an important goal."

Even if you know the definition of a word a writer chooses to use, sometimes you need to think about it. In "Looking for America," Elizabeth Partridge says, "[In] Yellowstone, we were drenched by Old Faithful." She doesn't say "got wet" because that's not what she means. She means that they were soaked, wet clear through, dripping.

Partner Work With a partner, look up one of the verbs below. If possible, use more than one dictionary. (Make sure you look for the *verb* definition.) Find out all you can. Then talk about why a writer might choose to use it.

sprawl   zigzag   shepherd

Additional Support

Literature Online

Author Search To expand students' appreciation of Elizabeth Partridge, have them access the Web site for additional information and resources.

Literature Focus Lesson

Personal Narrative Elizabeth Partridge's story "Looking for America" is an example of a personal narrative. In this genre authors write about their experiences and explore thoughts and feelings about things that matter to them. Personal narratives might be entries in a private diary, notes kept in a school journal, or published essays. Some personal narratives are meant for the writer alone; others are written for a wider audience. Have students generate ideas for personal narratives of their own. Ask students to think of ideas and experiences they have had and to list as many of them as they can recall. **OL**

Skills Preview

Key Reading Skill: Distinguishing Fact and Opinion

As you read "Looking for America," think about facts you already know about segregation, or the separation of races, in America's history. For example, it is a fact that African Americans and whites were separated in the South at the time Partridge had the experience she writes about. Think about the *opinions* that led to racial separation.

Group Talk In a small group, discuss this question: How can unfair opinions lead to the unfair treatment of people?

Key Literary Element: Style

Style is personal. You dress a certain way, and you like certain colors. Style is what makes one writer's work unlike the work of any other. Style is made up of all the ways the writer uses language to express feelings and attitudes. Use these tips to help you learn about Elizabeth Partridge's style in "Looking for America."

- *What kind of language does the author use and how is memory part of the author's style?*
- *What are the sentence patterns? How important are conversations to the selection?*
- *How does the author feel about this subject?*

Write to Learn Authors have their own style; so do you! What kind of style do you have when you tell a story? Do you use humor when you tell a story? Are you serious? Do you use facts or opinions? Are you dramatic? Do you exaggerate details or stretch the truth? In your Learner's Notebook, write about your storytelling style.

Literature Online

Interactive Literary Elements Handbook
To review or learn more about the literary elements, go to www.glencoe.com.

Get Ready to Read

Connect to the Reading

As a little girl, Elizabeth Partridge saw that laws were not the same for everyone. What reasons did people give for making unfair rules and laws? Were those reasons based on facts or opinions? Can you think of any rules or laws we have now that we will say were unfair one day?

Partner Talk With a partner, talk about a time when it seemed as though one set of rules applied to you and another set of rules applied to others. Was this fair treatment? Is it ever fair to have different rules for different people?

Build Background

The events in Elizabeth Partridge's essay take place in the summer of 1963 in Atlanta, Georgia.

- In the American South at that time, laws kept African Americans segregated—or separated—from whites. These laws were known as Jim Crow laws.
- It was against the law for African Americans and whites to eat at the same restaurants, sit together on buses or trains, or go to school together.
- It was also against the law for African Americans to use bathrooms or drinking fountains labeled "Whites Only." Bathrooms or drinking fountains for African Americans were not always available.

Set Purposes for Reading

BIG Question Read the essay "Looking for America" to find out what Elizabeth Partridge learned about fairness.

Set Your Own Purpose What else would you like to learn from the story to help you answer the Big Question? Write your own purpose on the "Looking for America" page of Foldable 3.

Keep Moving

Use these skills as you read the following selection.

Teach

L Literary Element

Style Point out that dialogue is an important part of the author's style in this selection. Explain that dialogue is conversation between characters in a story. **Ask:** Why do you think a writer might include dialogue in a story? (*Possible response: to make the characters seem more real. A character's own words may explain a story event better than a narrator's description would.*) **OL**

C Critical Thinking

Comprehension Ask: Do you think it's fair to have different rules for different people? Write a response in your Learner's Notebooks, telling what you think and why. (*Responses will vary.*) **OL**

Literature Online

Interactive Literary Elements Handbook Have students access the Web site to improve their understanding of style.

Reading in the Real World

Citizenship Tell students that in the 1950s and 1960s, many Americans participated in protests to end the unfair practice of segregation. In 1955, Rosa Parks refused to give up her seat on a public bus in Montgomery, Alabama, to a white person. She was arrested, and her action sparked a wave of political activity that came to be called the Civil Rights movement. (Civil rights are rights that every person has as a citizen.) Have small groups research key events in the Civil Rights movement, such as sit-ins at Woolworths lunch counters, integration of public schools in Little Rock, Arkansas, and the 1963 March on Washington. Ask groups to share their findings with the class. **OL** **AL**

Objectives

- Identify literary elements: style
- Make connections from text to self
- Understand word choice
- Distinguish fact from opinion

269

Teach

Viewing the Art

Say: You've read that people stared at the author's family because of the color of the Cadillac and how the kids lay on a mattress while traveling. What else does this illustration tell you about why people might have stared? *(Possible response: The author's family brought a lot of things with them on their trip.)* **BL**

R Reading Skill

Distinguish Fact and Opinion Have students determine people's opinion of the author's family and her own opinion of her family's trip.
Ask: What did people think of the author's family? How do you know? *(People thought they were strange. People stared at the family, and their mouths dropped open.)* **AL Ask:** What was the author's opinion of her family's trip? *(She hated being stared at.)* **OL**

Readability Scores
Dale-Chall: 3.7
DRP: 55
Lexile: 860

Looking for America

by Elizabeth Partridge

What I hated most was how people stared at us. I didn't mind so much while we were driving, and I would see people's mouths drop open as we flew by. But I hated it when we pulled into a campground or a gas station. As soon as my father rolled down the window, someone would stick his head in, look us over, and ask, "Where're you folks from?"

"California," my dad would say. They'd nod, like that explained it.

But it didn't, of course. It didn't begin to explain why our family was driving across the country in the summer of 1963, in an old Cadillac limousine painted a bright, metallic gold. The five of us kids didn't sit tidily in a row like regular kids but instead were sprawled on a double bed mattress that my dad had spread across the back. My parents called it "looking for America." I thought it was more like being looked *at* by America. **1**

270 UNIT 3 What's Fair and What's Not?

Practice the Skills

1 **Key Literary Element**
Style Do most stories begin like this? Do you feel as though someone just started talking to you? That's a clue to the artist's style.

Additional Support

Differentiated Instruction

Fact and Opinion Clues Tell students who are having difficulty distinguishing fact and opinion to look for signal words and other clues that point to each type of statement.

• Statements that tell thoughts or feelings are statements of opinion. *("What I hated most . . .")*

• Descriptive words—*beautiful, terrible, wonderful, impressive*—usually indicate opinions.

• Statements that tell what someone did or said are usually facts (although they might include an opinion of what the person did or said). **BL**

270

My dad was a freelance photographer,[1] and to fund our trip he'd arranged to photograph buildings and parks all over the United States. We ranged in age from my seventeen-year-old sister, Joan, to baby Aaron. I was eleven, smack in the middle of the pack, with my brother Josh three years older and my sister Meg two years younger.

We threaded our way through national and state parks, zigzagging toward New York City. In the Southwest we climbed rickety wooden ladders up a cliff into old Pueblo Indian houses; in Yellowstone we were drenched by Old Faithful;[2] in Kansas we rolled out of bed at five A.M. to watch a farmer milk his cows. **2**

"Look at it!" my father would say, throwing his arms out. "Just look at it all." With off-the-cuff comments[3] by my father, and more thoughtful views from my mother, we took in the rhythms and lives of other Americans. "We're lucky to be alive," my father said. "Right now, right here!"

By late August we had made it to New York, camped our way down the Great Smoky Mountains,[4] and were headed for Atlanta, Georgia.

An **architect** my father knew, Mr. McNeeley, had designed his own house in Atlanta. We were invited to stay while my father photographed the house. I was excited—after weeks of smoky fires and pit toilets, we were going to stay in a real house. Maybe they'd even have a TV in their rumpus room[5] and we could spread out on a comfortable couch and watch something like *The Wonderful World of Disney*.

We hit the Deep South just as a hot spell struck. The air was thick and steamy and smelled like mildew. The buzz of **cicadas** filled my ears.

---

1. A *freelance photographer* is a photographer who works on his or her own for many different employers.
2. The *Pueblo Indians* are a group of Native Americans living mainly in New Mexico and Arizona. *Yellowstone* is a park in Wyoming, Idaho, and Montana; it is famous for a hot spring known as *Old Faithful* that sprays water and steam from the ground.
3. To make an *off-the-cuff comment* is to say something without thinking carefully about it.
4. The *Great Smoky Mountains* are mountains on the border between North Carolina and Tennessee.
5. A *rumpus room* is a play room or family room.

Vocabulary

architect (AR kuh tekt) *n.* a person who designs buildings

cicadas (sih KAY duz) *n.* large insects also called locusts; males make a buzzing sound

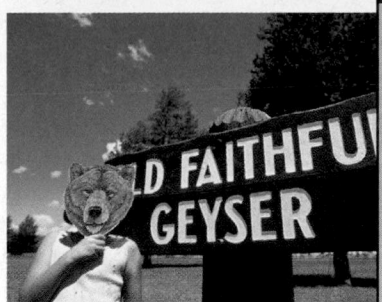

Analyzing the Photo Read the second paragraph on this page and footnote 2. What place does this photo show? What is a geyser?

Practice the Skills

2 **English Language Coach**

Word Choice Think about the verbs the author uses in this paragraph—*threaded, zigzagging, drenched,* and *rolled.* Think about why she chose those particular verbs.

Teach

R Reading Skill

Distinguishing Fact and Opinion Ask: Are the details in the first paragraph on this page facts or opinions? *(They are facts about the author's family and their vacation.)* **OL**

L Literary Element

Style Say: The writer uses vivid words to describe the trip—*rickety, drenched,* and *rolled out of bed.* How does her style of describing the trip let you know how she feels about the trip? *(Possible response: The words suggest she is not having a good time. They climb rickety ladders, get drenched, and have to get up early in the morning.)* **AL**

Differentiated Instruction

Map Skills To help students visualize the zigzag route of the trip, have them work in small groups to create a map that shows the family's itinerary. First have students use a map or an atlas to locate places the author's family visited. Then tell students to plot those places on an outline map of the United States and connect them to show the family's general route from coast to coast. Remind students that the family began the trip in California. **OL** **EL**

Objectives

• Distinguish fact from opinion
• Identify literary elements: style
• Use text features: photographs

271

Teach

L Literary Element

Style Say: When writers choose words to describe something, they often appeal to the five senses—hearing, sight, touch, taste, and smell. Which senses does the author appeal to when she describes the McNeeley's house? *(She appeals to the senses of sight, "shiny clean surfaces," touch, "huge, fluffy towels," and smell, "sweet-smelling soap.")* **AL**

C Critical Thinking

Analysis Ask: Why does the author say that her family doesn't fit in with the McNeeleys? *(The McNeeleys live in a beautiful home that includes everything anyone could want; the author's family left their home in a car filled with all kinds of things and has been camping out all across America.)* **OL**

My mother insisted we stop for the night at a campground outside of Atlanta, so we could clean up. After dinner she handed out towels and shepherded us into the public showers, a squat cement building with huge spiders in the corners and black beetles scuttling across the wet floors. Washing my hair, I discovered a big knotted tangle in the back, but it hurt too much when I tried to brush it out so I just left it. At least my hair was clean.

Late the next morning when we arrived at the McNeeleys', I saw that my mother had been right to tidy us up. Their new house was perfect. Every surface was shiny clean, nothing out of place. Built around a courtyard filled with plants, floor to ceiling glass windows let a dappled[6] green light into every room. Antique Persian rugs[7] covered the smooth cement floors, and modern sculptures made of glass and ceramic perched on back-lit shelves. There wasn't a rumpus room in sight. Mrs. McNeeley wore bright red lipstick and white slacks with a crisp linen blouse. I was painfully aware of the big snarl in my hair.

Mrs. McNeeley showed my sisters and me into a guest room with its own bathroom loaded with huge, fluffy towels and sweet-smelling soap, then left us, saying she needed to speak with the cook about lunch arrangements.

I stood on one foot and stared out into the courtyard. Our mother was right to be concerned: we didn't fit in. "How long do you think we're staying here?" I asked Meg nervously. **3**

At lunchtime my mother **beckoned** me to take the chair next to Aaron. A tall black woman wearing a starched apron came in through a swinging door. She carried a casserole with a heavy silver spoon laid across the top.

"Thank you, Annie," said Mrs. McNeeley. I stared at my mother, frozen. What were we supposed to do

Visual Vocabulary
A *casserole* is a baked food with many types of ingredients inside.

___

6. Something *dappled* is marked with spots or patches of color.

7. *Antique Persian rugs* are rugs made in an early period of Iran's history. The rugs are very expensive.

Vocabulary

beckoned (BEK und) *v.* moved the head or hand to make a sign to approach or come nearer

272 UNIT 3 What's Fair and What's Not?

Practice the Skills

3 Reviewing Skills

Connecting Have you ever been in a situation in which you weren't sure how to act? In your Learner's Notebook, explain what happened. **C**

Additional Support

Differentiated Instruction

Illustrating the Story Invite students to distinguish between the living situations of the author's family and the McNeeleys by creating two illustrations. The first illustration should show the McNeeleys' house. The second should show the author's family and their Cadillac at a campsite. Students should base their illustrations on details provided in the story and provide captions that explain the images. Post the illustrations in the classroom. **EL BL OL**

now? Did we dip the spoon in the casserole and serve ourselves? Did we get served? Annie stood next to my mother, the casserole in her outstretched arms. My mother looked uncomfortable and busied herself with tucking a napkin into the neck of Aaron's shirt. My stomach twisted. Even my mother wasn't sure what to do. **4**

"Please," said Mrs. McNeeley to my mother, "help yourself."

When Annie stood next to me I just looked at her helplessly, afraid I would spill casserole all over my lap from the big silver spoon. She winked at me so quickly I wasn't sure she had, and put a spoonful of casserole on my plate.

After lunch my father started shooting interiors[8] of the house. The rest of us were shepherded to the courtyard. My mother and Mrs. McNeeley sat under a big umbrella, and Annie brought out a pitcher of iced tea and tall glasses full of clinking ice cubes.

Meg and I played hopscotch on the flagstones, while Joan challenged Josh to a game of rummy.[9] Aaron sat and banged on a metal pail. The heat fell down on us, heavy and moist, and the whiny buzz of the cicadas set my teeth on edge. Aaron smashed his hand under the pail and started screaming. Suddenly my head felt like it was exploding with noise and heat and an anxious worry.

C I had to get away from my sisters and brothers, away from Mrs. McNeeley sitting stiffly with a tight smile. I slipped inside, crossed the dining room, and bolted through the swinging door, right into the kitchen. Annie stood with her back to me, working at the sink. **5**

"Yes, Ma'am?" she said, turning around. "Oh," she said, surprised to see me. I stood awkwardly, ready to dash out again. Maybe I wasn't allowed in the kitchen. The cook tipped her head toward a small pine table.

"Sit, honey," she said. I tried to ease graciously into the chair but managed to knock my funny bone on the edge of the table and let out a yelp.

"You must be growing," the cook said. "Skinny as all get out, and don't know where your body's at."

I didn't want to tell her I was always banging myself on something. She put two sugar cookies and a tall, cold glass

---

8. If a photographer is **shooting interiors,** he or she is taking pictures inside.
9. **Flagstones** are paving stones, and **rummy** is a card game for two or more players.

Practice the Skills

4 **Key Literary Element**

Style Here the author asks many questions. How are the questions a part of her style? Do they make you feel as if you know her and what she's feeling?

5 **English Language Coach**

Word Choice Look at the verbs in the second sentence of this paragraph—*slipped, crossed,* and *bolted*. How do they describe the narrator's trip from the backyard to the kitchen?

Teach

R Reading Skill

Distinguishing Fact and Opinion Students will have formed opinions of various characters by this point in the story. Have students use the chart below to record their opinions of characters and details from the story that led them to form their opinions.

Character	My Opinion	Story Details

- Invite students to share their opinions of characters in the story in a class discussion. Have students add to their charts as the story progresses. **OL**

C Critical Thinking

Analysis **Ask:** Why do you think the author has to get away from her sisters and brothers and Mrs. McNeeley? *(Possible responses: She doesn't know how to act in the situation; she feels that something is wrong and can't keep pretending that everything is fine.)* **AL**

Literature Focus Lesson

First-Person Point of View Remind students that this selection is a personal narrative told from the point of view of the author. In a first-person narrative, all information about the story's characters and events comes from the narrator. Readers must determine how the narrator's experience influences the story.

- What affects the narrator's description of Mrs. McNeeley? *(the narrator's feeling of awkwardness in the situation)*
- If Mrs. McNeeley were telling the story, how might she describe the scene? *(Possible response: She might tell how the people in the Partridge family seem very uncomfortable.)* **AL**

Objectives

- Distinguish fact from opinion
- Identify literary elements: style
- Analyze text

273

Teach

EL Language Coach

Word Choice Say: The writer uses uncommon verbs that are vivid and descriptive. Look at paragraphs three and four in which the author is drinking from the drinking fountain. Try to rewrite these paragraphs using different verbs. How does your word choice change the meaning of the paragraph? *(Responses will vary.)* **OL**

R Reading Skill

Distinguishing Fact and Opinion Point out that the Jim Crow laws, or segregation laws, in the South were based on opinions, not facts, about African Americans. They represented prejudice, not reason. **Ask:** Why are laws based on people's prejudices unfair? *(Possible response: Those laws favor one group over another instead of protecting the rights of all groups.)* **OL**

of milk in front of me. As I ate, I watched her wash the lunch dishes. Steam rose from the sink, and moisture beaded up on her forehead. When she finished she filled a quart-size canning jar with cold water and drank. I was grateful for her quiet company.

When Aaron woke up from his nap we walked to a nearby city park. Though the sun was low, the air still felt like we were walking in a huge oven, with more heat radiating[10] up from the cement. My mother sat on a bench next to the sandbox and plunked Aaron down in the sand.

EL I spotted a drinking fountain and ran over, guzzling the water in great big gulps. Meg thumped into my back.

"My turn!" she said. I clung tight to the faucet and jabbed backward at her with my elbows until my stomach was full.

When I stood up, water slid down my neck and under my shirt. Over the fountain was a sign I hadn't noticed: "Whites Only."

"Mom," I yelled back across the playground. "What does 'Whites Only' mean?"

My mother flung her hand out. "Sh. . . ." she said. "Come over here."

I stood next to my mother, who leaned in close. "Negroes aren't allowed to drink from the same fountains as whites in the South, or use the same bathrooms."

I stared at my mother, disbelieving.

"Are those rules?"

R "More than rules," she said sadly. "Laws."

I walked all around the playground, but I didn't see any other drinking fountain. **6**

The next morning as my parents were packing the car, I slipped back into the kitchen.

"We're leaving," I said to Annie.

"I know, honey," she said. "You have a good trip now, you hear?"

The breakfast dishes were sitting in the rack drying, carrots and potatoes lay on the counter, next to her half-full jar of water. I wanted to ask Annie what she did when she got

---

10. Here ***radiating*** means that the heat was coming up from the sidewalk.

274 UNIT 3 What's Fair and What's Not?

Practice the Skills

6 ▌**Key Reading Skill**

Distinguishing Fact and Opinion Is what the narrator's mother tells her here a fact or an opinion? Could what she says be proved?

Additional Support

English Language Coach

Negative Prefixes Write the word *dis-believing* on the board and ask students to define it. If necessary, prompt them with the clue that the prefix *dis-* in the word means "not." Challenge students to name other words with the prefix *dis-*.

(Some examples are dislike, dishonest, *and* dissatisfy.*)* Explain that the following prefixes can also mean "not": *in-, non-, un-.* Have students identify words with these prefixes that have a negative meaning. **EL OL**

thirsty at the park. But it seemed like too big a question. I searched for something I could ask, something that was small and not tangled up.

"Why do you drink from a jar?" I blurted out.

She looked at me, considering. Her eyes were full of a lot of things I couldn't read.

"I get mighty thirsty," she finally said. "Those glasses aren't big enough for me."

I didn't understand. She was by the sink all day where she could easily refill her glass.

I heard my father call out, "Let's go!" and I spun out of the kitchen through the swinging door. We drove away from the house of clean rooms and dappled green light and extra-good behavior. Away from the park and kitchen and rules—laws—I didn't understand.

In no time we were out on the highway, my father whistling with the joy of being back on the open road. I leaned over the front seat and asked my mother, "Why did Annie drink out of a jar?"

My mother didn't look at me but spoke softly to her hands resting in her lap. "She probably wasn't allowed to drink from the glasses the family used."

I lay back on the mattress and thought about that. The cook prepared all their food, washing, peeling, chopping, and serving. She set the table, touching every dish. Why couldn't she drink out of their glasses?

My mother must have felt me thinking behind her, because she turned around and said gently, "Some things just don't make sense." **7**

She turned back, discomfort settling on her shoulders like an old sorrow. It was all too big, too complicated, even for her.

I still didn't understand. Why would everyone go along with something that didn't make any sense? I rolled down my window and let the hot air **buffet** my face, hoping it would blow away some of the helplessness I felt. ○

U.S. Highway 1, Number 5, 1962. Allan D'Arcangelo. Gift of Mr. and Mrs. Herbert Fischbach. The Museum of Modern Art, New York.

Analyzing the Art Study this painting. Does it help you understand why Elizabeth's father was "whistling with the joy of being back on the open road"? Explain your answer.

Practice the Skills

7 **BIG Question**

Do you agree with the author's mother that "Some things just don't make sense," when it comes to what's fair and what's not? Explain. Are there ways to change things that are unfair? Write your answers on the "Looking for America" page of Foldable 3. Your response will help you complete the Unit Challenge later. **BQ**

Looking for America **275**

Teach

BQ **BIG Question**

Ask: What do you think the author's mother means when she says, "Some things just don't make sense"? (*Possible response: She means that things like prejudice and unfair laws can't be explained because there's no good reason for them.*) **AL** **Say:** Describe an unfair situation that didn't make sense to you. What happened? What was unfair about it? What didn't you understand about it? (*Responses will vary.*) **BL**

Assess

CheckPoint

Use the CheckPoint questions provided on Presentation Plus! to check comprehension of the selection. These questions can be used with interactive response keypads for immediate student feedback.

Reading Fluency

Build Fluency Have each student choose a partner and read aloud a passage from the story, alternating paragraphs or other sections as appropriate. If the passage includes dialogue, have students choose parts. Tell partners to meet in a quiet place to practice reading the passage aloud several times until they can read it smoothly and with expression. Students should take cues from the description of the characters and other details in the text about how to deliver dialogue, if any. Partners who wish to volunteer might read their passage aloud for the whole class. **BL** **OL**

Objectives
- Distinguish fact from opinion
- Synthesize text
- Understand word choice

Assess

Resources for page 276

📁 Selection Quick Check, p. 22

📁 Selection and Unit Assessment, p. 26

💿 ExamView Assessment Suite

💿 Interactive Tutor: Self-Assessment

Students can respond to the *After You Read* items in their Learner's Notebooks or on a separate sheet of paper.

Answering the BIG Question

1. Possible response: I might have told Mrs. McNeeley she was unfair to Annie.

2. Annie puts a spoonful of casserole on the narrator's plate because the narrator is afraid of serving herself.

3. Possible response: Yellowstone, Kansas, and New York City

Critical Thinking

4. Possible response: The McNeeleys' house is perfect, she feels out of place, and she isn't sure how to behave.

5. Possible response: a) She wants to ask Annie what she does when she gets thirsty at the park. b) It seems like too big a question to ask.

6. Possible response: She feels helpless because she has seen an unfair situation that doesn't make sense. She is confused and does not know what to do.

276

After You Read | Looking for America

Answering the BIG Question

1. If you were the narrator, how would you respond to the unfair situation that Annie faced?

2. **Recall** How does Annie help the narrator at lunch?
   Tip Right There

3. **Recall** List three places the narrator visited that summer.
   Tip Think and Search

Critical Thinking

4. **Infer** Why is the narrator uncomfortable at the McNeeleys' house?
   Tip Author and Me

5. **Infer** a) What question does the narrator want to ask Annie? b) Why doesn't she ask this question?
   Tip Author and Me

6. **Analyze** At the end of the essay, why does the narrator feel helpless?
   Tip Author and Me

Write About Your Reading

Suppose that you are the narrator. Write two postcards. Write the first postcard to a friend. Describe an event from the beginning of the trip, such as the trip through New York City or the scene at Old Faithful. Then write a second postcard to the same person after the visit to the McNeeleys'.

Objectives (pp. 276–277)
Reading Distinguish fact and opinion • Make connections from text to self
Literature Identify literary elements: style
Vocabulary Understand word choice
Grammar Identify parts of speech: adverbs
Writing Respond to literature: postcard

276 UNIT 3 What's Fair and What's Not?

Write About Your Reading

Possible first postcard
Hi Jane,
We finally got to New York. It's noisy and crowded, but we're having a good time. We've seen lots of interesting people and tall buildings.
Elizabeth

Possible second postcard
Dear Jane,
I was glad to leave Atlanta yesterday. A lot of the public places are segregated.
Elizabeth

Skills Review

Key Reading Skill: Distinguishing Fact and Opinion

7. Which of the following statements from the story are statements of opinion?
   - "We're lucky to be alive."
   - "Their new house was perfect."
   - "Aaron smashed his hand under the pail and started screaming."
   - "But it seemed like too big a question."

8. List three things mentioned in the story that are statements of facts.

Key Literary Element: Style

9. How would you describe the author's style in "Looking for America"? You can choose one or more of the words below or use your own.

   | formal | chatty | personal | dramatic |
   | colorful | simple | funny | complicated |

Reviewing Skills: Connecting

10. The narrator is upset by the way Annie is treated by the McNeeleys. Describe a time when you saw a person being treated unfairly. How did you feel?

Vocabulary Check

Which of these sentences using vocabulary words makes sense? Which do not?

11. We sat in the shade of the **cicada.**
12. She **beckoned** me to come over.
13. The waves began to **buffet** the boat.
14. The bus broke down, so we called an **architect.**
15. **Academic Vocabulary** What are two things that you find it difficult to distinguish between?
16. **English Language Coach** Rewrite the following sentence with a more descriptive verb. Use a thesaurus if necessary.
    - I drove into the door of the garage.

Grammar Link: Adverbs

Adverbs describe verbs by giving information that answers *how, when,* or *where* questions. The adverbs in the sentences below are in bold type. The words they describe are underlined.

- She <u>spoke</u> **quietly.** (*How?*)
- He <u>jogged</u> **yesterday.** (*When?*)
- They <u>danced</u> **there.** (*Where?*)

Another job adverbs have is to describe adjectives.

- She was **very** <u>tired</u>.
- The sky was **pale** <u>blue</u>.

Adverbs also describe other adverbs.

- We'll arrive **late** <u>tomorrow</u>.
- I **absolutely** <u>never</u> do that.

Many adverbs end in *-ly,* especially those that answer the question *How?*

Grammar Practice

Rewrite each sentence. Circle each adverb. (Hint: Look for the types of words adverbs *can* describe, and see if they *are* described.) The number after each sentence tells how many adverbs you should find.

17. Suzanne and Joel danced gracefully. (1)
18. We gradually stopped taking the bus. (1)
19. Geoff reads very quickly. (2)
20. The car is bright red, and it runs well. (2)
21. He was barely awake and yawned deeply. (2)

Writing Application Look back at the postcards you wrote. See if you can add adverbs to describe any of your verbs.

Web Activities For eFlashcards, Selection Quick Checks, and other Web activities, go to www.glencoe.com.

Looking for America **277**

Skills Review

Key Reading Skill: Distinguishing Fact and Opinion

7. We're lucky to be alive.

   Their new house was perfect.

   But it seemed like too big a question.

8. Responses will vary.

Key Literary Element: Style

9. Possible responses: funny, dramatic

Reviewing Skills: Activate Prior Knowledge

10. Responses will vary.

Vocabulary Check

11. does not make sense
12. makes sense
13. makes sense
14. does not make sense
15. **Academic Vocabulary** Possible response: lizards and geckos
16. **English Language Coach** I rammed into the door of the garage.

Grammar Link: Adverbs

Grammar Practice

17. Suzanne and Joel danced the waltz (gracefully.)
18. They (gradually) stopped taking the bus (together.)
19. Geoff reads (faster) than Brandon.
20. The TV was (downstairs.)
21. She (almost)(always) studied (there.)
22. He was (barely) awake when the phone rang.

Close

Ask students whether or not reading this selection helped them look at the Big Question in a new way.

Persuasive Essay

Objectives covered in this workshop:
- **Writing** Write persuasively using the writing process; revise writing for word choice, tone, and style
- **Grammar** Use adjectives and adverbs to enhance writing

Teaching Students to Write a Persuasive Essay

Why Is It important?

- The power to persuade is important in many kinds of writing.
- Exploring bias in persuasive essays will show students how to choose words carefully.
- Students will use facts to create supporting arguments for their essays. This will help them practice discerning between opinion and fact, making them more critical readers.
- Writing persuasive essays will help students be more aware of the ways they are influenced by the media.
- Making precise and intentional word choices will increase students' powers of persuasion.

How to Help Students Get It

- Discuss possible audiences with students. Depending on the topic they choose, they may want to write as though addressing their peers, their family, the school administration, or a broader audience.
- Remind students to consider their audiences as they write. Suggest questions such as: "What are my readers' views on this issue?" "What reasoning might make sense to them, considering their views?" "What are my readers' personal concerns?" "What emotional appeals might touch their concerns?" Define emotional appeal for your students. Readers of a persuasive essay should feel that the topic discussed has some personal meaning for them, or that they have some stake in the matter at hand.
- Remind students that strong feelings can lead to strong arguments: choosing a topic they're interested in will strengthen their papers, but using emotionally loaded terminology may not.
- Have students think about their own credibility: why should their audiences believe them? This will help them generate good support for their arguments.
- Ask students to remember times they've been talked into or talked out of doing or buying something. Ask: "What made you change your mind?" "What persuasive techniques worked?" "What kind of persuasion did you see right through, or ignore?"
- Talk with your students about preempting the opposition. Ask: "What arguments might be brought against your persuasive essay? How would you respond?" Have students use that to strengthen their writing.
- Ask students to consider the selections in Unit 3, and choose one or two opinions expressed in the text. Ask: "Were those opinions backed up with proof? Did the author make you agree with them?"

Traits of Good Writing	Student Checklist
Ideas	the message or the theme and the details that develop it
Organization	the arrangement of main points and supporting details
Voice	a writer's unique way of using tone and style
Word Choice	the vocabulary a writer uses to convey meaning
Sentence Fluency: the smooth rhythm and flow of sentences that vary in length and style	• Do sentences vary in length and structure? • Do transition words and phrases show connections between ideas and sentences? • Does parallelism help balance and unify related ideas?
Conventions	correct spelling, grammar, usage, and mechanics
Presentation	the way words and design elements look on a page

Unit Focus ▶ (pointing to the Sentence Fluency row)

Workshop Resources

PACING (DAYS) STANDARD	BLOCK	LESSON	STUDENT MATERIALS	TEACHER RESOURCES
1	1/2	Writing Workshop Part 1: Prewriting and Drafting	📓 Writing Workshop Graphic Organizer, p. 14 📓 Grammar Practice, p. 15 📓 Spelling and Handwriting Practice, p. 44 💻 Spelling Power eWorkbook 💿 Interactive Grammar and Language Workbook 📖 Grammar and Composition Handbook, p. 164 📁 Real Success in Writing: Research and Reports 📁 Writing Constructed Responses	💿 TeacherWorks Plus™ 💿 Presentation Plus! 📁 Rubrics for Assessing Student Writing, Listening, and Speaking, p. 16 📄 Grammar and Writing Workshop Transparencies 5–6
2	1	Writing Workshop Part 2: Editing, Revising, and Presenting	💿 Interactive Grammar and Language Workbook 📖 Grammar and Composition Handbook, p. 164 📁 Real Success in Writing: Research and Reports 📁 Writing Constructed Responses 📓 Listening and Speaking, p. 27 📓 Viewing and Representing, p. 28	📄 Grammar and Writing Workshop Transparencies 21–22 💿 Interactive Grammar and Language Workbook 📁 Rubrics for Assessing Student Writing, Listening, and Speaking, p. 16

Focus

- **Daily Language Practice Transparency 24**
  Focus Activity Say: Tell about a time when you tried to persuade someone to do something. How did you go about trying to convince that person? Were you successful? Why or why not? *(Responses will vary.)*

Teach

W **Writing**

Freewriting If students have difficulty focusing on a topic, remind them that freewriting lets them get their thoughts down on paper quickly.
Say: If you get stuck, keep writing even if you have to repeat words or phrases. One idea can lead to other ideas until a good topic presents itself. **OL**

Resources for page 278

- 📁 Use the Writing Workshop Graphic Organizer BLM in the Unit 3 Resource Booklet, p. 14.

- Use the Grammar and Writing Workshop Transparencies 5–6.

ASSIGNMENT Write a persuasive essay
Purpose: Write an essay that argues either *for* or *against* a specific issue
Audience: You, your teacher, and classmates

Writing Rubric

As you work through this assignment, you should

- write your opinion about a topic
- include evidence to support your opinion
- write a five paragraph essay that includes an introduction, a body, and a conclusion
- address arguments that oppose your own views

See page 316 in Part 2 for a model of a persuasive essay.

Objectives (pp. 278–281)
Reading Use the writing process: prewriting, drafting • Write persuasively • Include main ideas and supporting details • Write with fluency and clarity
Grammar Understand function of modifiers • Identify parts of speech: adjectives, adverbs

---

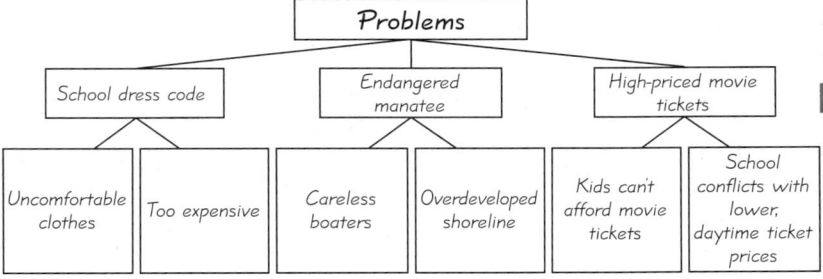

Persuasive Essay
Prewriting and Drafting

An effort to persuade someone usually involves arguing *for* or *against* something. In this workshop, you will identify a problem you think is unfair and persuade your readers to take action.

Prewriting
Get Ready to Write

You should choose a topic that you are already familiar with and have strong feelings about.

- What problem do I care most about?
- Can I think of a possible solution?
- What about this problem is unfair?

Choose a Topic

Explore different topics by making an idea tree like the one below. Choose a problem from your idea tree to be the subject of your persuasive essay.

```
                    Problems
        ┌──────────────┼──────────────┐
  School dress code  Endangered    High-priced movie
                      manatee          tickets
     ┌────┴────┐    ┌────┴────┐     ┌────┴────┐
Uncomfortable  Too  Careless  Overdeveloped  Kids can't   School
  clothes   expensive boaters   shoreline   afford movie conflicts with
                                              tickets      lower,
                                                         daytime ticket
                                                            prices
```

Take a Stand

Now that you have chosen a problem, think about what makes it unfair. In your Learner's Notebook, freewrite a short paragraph describing your problem and why you think it is unfair.

I think having a dress code at school is unfair. Students should be able to express themselves through the clothes they choose to wear. No two students look alike, so why should we have to dress alike?

Additional Support

English Language Coach

Learning English Encourage English language learners to discuss some of the problems faced by people who do not speak English. Brainstorm ways in which communities could become more receptive to people who are learning English. Invite students to think of possible solutions, and help them focus their solutions. Ask students to share their problems and solutions with the class. **EL**

Consider Other Views

When you write persuasively, you should be prepared for people who do not agree with you. In your Learner's Notebook, make a pro and con chart to determine how others may argue against your position.

Position: End the school dress code	
Pros + :	**Cons − :**
Jeans and sneakers are more comfortable	Students focus more on school and less on clothing
Dress code clothing is too expensive	Students learn how to dress for a job
Students get to express their individuality	Nice clothing will increase self-esteem

Make a Plan

- Your essay should be divided into five paragraphs: the introduction, three main paragraphs, and the conclusion.
- Pick three reasons from your "pros" list to write about; these are your main points.
- Provide facts, examples, and reasons to support your position.

> **Introduction:** The school dress code is unfair because it requires students to wear clothing that is uncomfortable and expensive.
>
> **Main Point I.** Dressy clothes are uncomfortable
>
> Evidence A. Girls should be allowed to wear jeans instead of skirts, especially in cold weather
>
>   B. Sneakers are more supportive than dress shoes.
>
> **Main Point II.** Dress clothes are expensive
>
> Evidence A. Many students have families living on tight budgets
>
>   B. Jeans and sneakers cost less than dress pants and shoes
>
> **Main Point III.** Increase self esteem
>
> Evidence A. Students should be allowed to express themselves
>
>   B. Students have more self respect when they choose their own clothes
>
> **Conclusion:** A dress code does not help students focus on learning. Students are capable of choosing both comfortable and appropriate school clothes.

Drafting
Start Writing!

By now your views about this topic are clear and you are ready to start persuading. Begin by stating your topic and why you think it is unfair. Keep your Learner's Notebook nearby and follow your plan.

◄ **Writing Tip**

Prewriting Each main point should be developed in a separate paragraph. The strongest point of the argument should be either first or last.

◄ **Writing Tip**

Drafting Get your reader's attention by using a real life example in your introduction, *"Last week Jimmy Albert sprained his ankle during morning recess. The sprain was caused by playing basketball in dress shoes that did not have enough support for such activities . . ."*

Writing Models For models and other writing activities, go to www.glencoe.com.

Teach

Writing Models Have students access the Web site for an additional and interactive Writing Workshop-based student model.

W1 Writing

Pros and Cons Say: As you try to think of pros and cons for your topic, think of people who might agree with your idea and people who might disagree with it. Then ask yourself: Why would this person agree? Why would this person disagree? This will help you get more pros and cons for your argument. **OL** You may also want to read articles on both sides of your issue to get more ideas. **AL**

W2 Writing

Persuasive Writing
Say: The goal of persuasive writing is to persuade readers to share a certain point of view or take a particular action. Where have you seen examples of persuasion? *(Possible responses: almost everywhere—advertisements, newspapers, magazines, speeches, posters, television, parents, friends, teachers)* **OL**

Differentiated Instruction

Using a Chart Tell students that one way to build an argument is to list reasons to support their opinions. The next step is to gather evidence to support their reasons. Draw a chart like this on on the board and have students fill in one of their own.

Type	Definition	Example
Fact	something that can be proven	Plants need food and water.
Statistic	fact expressed in numbers	95 percent of the teachers own plants.
Example	particular instance	

Objectives
- Write persuasively
- Create a graphic organizer
- Include main ideas and supporting details
- Understand function of modifiers
- Write with fluency and clarity

Teach

W Writing

Fluency Say: Find a quiet place to read your draft to a partner. Ask your partner to point out places that flow smoothly and places that need transitions. As you read, look for these places, too, and then go back and add transitions where needed. Use the chart to help you. **OL**

Assess

Have students read over their draft. Ask them to note whether they stated their position clearly and included three reasons, supported by facts or evidence, for their position. Have students save their draft for later use. Tell them that in Writing Workshop 2, they will revise their draft and present it to the class.

Applying Good Writing Traits

Sentence Fluency

Have you ever put on your favorite pants, your favorite shirt, your favorite sweater and your favorites shoes . . . and realized the outfit looked terrible? Each piece was just fine, but they didn't work together. Sentences can be just like that.

What Is Sentence Fluency?

Fluency is a fancy word for flow. When you're writing, your sentences should flow. Your writing should help the reader go from one sentence to the next to the next. Here are some problems to watch out for:

- short, choppy sentences
- long, rambling sentences
- confusing word order
- sentences that don't lead to the next one

Why Is Sentence Fluency Important?

Fluent sentences make your writing easier to understand and more enjoyable to read. Which example below is fluent and which is not?

A. There are lots of holes in my backyard. My dog Skippy likes to dig. Skippy is a terrier. Terriers are known for digging in the ground. My dad gets angry at Skippy for digging holes in the ground.

B. My dog Skippy likes to dig. As a result, there are lots of holes in my backyard. Even though Skippy is a terrier, a type of dog known for digging, my dad gets angry at him.

How Do I Do It?

Transitions help. Transitions are words or phrases that connect ideas from one sentence to another. In the example above, the writer used the transitions *as a result* to link two sentences about the same topic.

Transitions can also link ideas in the same sentence. *Even though* connects the dog to the father's anger.

Use this transition chart to improve sentence fluency.

Sentence Type	Transition Words and Phrases
Locate Students cheered **inside** the gymnasium.	*above, below, beside, in the distance, around the corner, underneath, inside*
Sequence We waited and waited. **Finally** my sister arrived at the restaurant.	*first, next, when, later, finally, meanwhile, then, after*
Importance **More importantly,** she brought the birthday cake.	*First, most importantly, mainly, primarily, above all*
Compare Skippy digs holes **just like** the terrier down the street.	*also, like, just as, just like, similarly, similar to*
Contrast **However,** Skippy's holes are much deeper.	*But, even so, however, unlike*

Write to Learn Use transitions to make these sentences more fluent.

1. Sal and I rode our bikes to the park. We played soccer and went home.

2. Marcia plays the harmonica well. Her sister does not.

3. Skippy plays in the yard, runs through the house, jumps on my neighbor, digs a hole, eats dinner, and goes to sleep.

Additional Support

English Language Coach

Rhythm Tell students to read their papers to themselves. In this way, they can hear the rhythm of their writing. Ask them to evaluate how their writing sounds. Explain that if their writing sounds choppy, chances are the ideas are not presented clearly. Transitions can help connect ideas more smoothly. Explain that if their writing sounds dull, then students may want to try to vary sentence length. Many short sentences in a row can sound choppy, and many long sentences can sound tedious. **EL** **BL**

Grammar Link

Adjectives and Adverbs

What Are Adjectives and Adverbs?

Remember, you can tell what part of speech a word is by what it *does* in the sentence. One word can be many different parts of speech.

Adjectives and adverbs do similar things. They are both **modifiers**. They modify, or tell more about, other words. As you know, **adjectives** modify nouns or pronouns. **Adverbs** modify verbs, adjectives, or other adverbs.

Adjectives may come before or after the word they modify. *He's a <u>nice</u> boy, <u>sweet</u> and <u>friendly</u>.* When a linking verb is used, the adjective comes afterwards.

- The music was <u>loud</u> and <u>clear</u>. (*Was* is a linking verb. *Loud* and *clear* describe the music.)
- bullet>This sandwich tastes <u>salty</u>. (*Tastes* is a linking verb. *Salty* describes the sandwich.)

It is easy to tell if a word is acting as an adverb if it comes right after the verb or if it ends in *-ly*.

- The child waited <u>patiently</u>. (*Patiently* tells *how* the child waited. It modifies the verb.)

But not all adverbs are so easy to spot!

- Bob <u>never</u> pets strange dogs. (*Never* tells *when* Bob pets strange dogs. It modifies the verb.)
- I shop <u>here</u> for clothes. (*Here* tells *where* I shop. It modifies the verb.)
- The <u>unusually</u> ugly cat was sleeping. (*Unusually* modifies the adjective *ugly*.)
- She talks <u>too</u> loudly. (*Too* modifies the adverb *loudly*.)

Warning! Warning! Warning! Beware of words that look like verbs! Sometimes a word that you think is a verb might really be a modifier (or even a noun).

- That <u>smiling</u> man is my Uncle Albert. (Even though *smiling* can be a verb, here it is an adjective describing *man*.)

Why Are Adjectives and Adverbs Important?

Adjectives and adverbs combined make your writing more interesting.

How Do I Use Adjectives and Adverbs?

Use an adjective to tell more about a person, a place, a thing, or an idea. Use an adverb to tell how, when, or where things are done.

Grammar Practice

Copy the sentences. Then underline the adjectives and circle the adverbs.

Every player is waiting eagerly.

The final game will start soon.

The bright red uniforms are very colorful.

Our excellent band will play loudly and well.

Writing Application Review your draft to see if you should add any modifiers to make your writing more clear and interesting.

Looking Ahead

Keeping the writing you did here. In Part 2, you'll learn how to turn it into a solid, persuasive essay.

Teach

Grammar Link

Adjectives and Adverbs

Give students additional practice in identifying adjectives and adverbs. Write the following sentences on the board. (*Correct answers are underlined.*)

Have students point out the adjectives in sentences 1–3.

1. The <u>friendly</u> boy met us at home.
2. The toddler wore a <u>bright</u> tunic.
3. Henry likes <u>blue</u> jeans.

Have students point out the adverbs in sentences 4–6.

4. May spoke <u>politely</u> to her teacher.
5. Chuck ate his dinner <u>speedily</u>.
6. The ballerinas danced <u>gracefully</u>. **BL OL**

Grammar Practice

<u>Every</u>, (eagerly)
<u>final</u>, (soon)
bright, <u>red</u>, (very)
<u>excellent</u>, loudly, (well)

Differentiated Instruction

Using Adjectives and Adverbs in Writing Tell students that using adjectives and adverbs can help them create vivid pictures for their readers. Have students read over their drafts and underline three or four sentences where they could add an adjective, an adverb, or both. Have students revise their sentences, and ask volunteers to read their new sentences aloud to the class. Encourage class members to identify the adjectives or adverbs in the volunteers' sentences. Have students continue to look for places to add adjectives and adverbs as they turn their drafts into final persuasive essays. **EL OL**

Objectives
- Write with fluency and clarity
- Understand function of modifiers
- Identify parts of speech: adjectives and adverbs

281

Objective covered in this workshop:
• Clarify difficult or confusing text

Teaching Students How to Clarify

Why Is It Important?

• Clarifying helps students clear up difficult portions of text.

• Students often need to clarify one idea before they can grasp another idea in a selection.

• When students gain clarifying skills, they become better readers and have more confidence in reading new passages.

How to Help Students Get It

• Tell students to reread sections that are not clear.

• Advise them to stop to clarify ideas before they get too far into a confusing text.

• Encourage students to use dictionaries to look up unfamiliar words and to enter the definitions in their Learner's Notebooks, so they can review them.

• Emphasize the importance of context clues. What else is being said in the paragraph? Can this information help clarify the confusing part?

• Encourage students to practice several of the other reading strategies they have learned to clarify information. Questioning, responding, connecting, and activating prior knowledge can be particularly helpful when clarifying.

Reading to Answer the Big Question

Two Advertisements

A 1951 ad for a car and a contemporary ad for a juice box offer students the opportunity to analyze and compare bias, connotation, and other persuasive elements in the advertisements.

Stray by Cynthia Rylant

In this short story, a girl named Doris Lacey finds a lost puppy. Doris wants to persuade her parents to keep it, but knows that it would be unfair to insist because the added expense of a pet would cause financial hardship. In the end, her father decides that it is worth the sacrifice it will take to save the puppy and bring happiness to his daughter.

Workshop Resources

Pacing (days)		Lesson	Student Materials	Teacher Resources
Standard	**Block**			
1	1/2	Key Skill Lesson: Clarifying	▪ Key Reading Skills Practice, p. 16 ▪ English Language Coach Review, p. 41	▪ Bellringer Options Transparencies –Daily Language Practice 25 ▪ Read Aloud, Think Aloud Transparencies –Key Reading Skills 3 ▪ Presentation Plus!
1	1	Two Advertisements	▪ Literary Analysis Transparencies ▪ Glencoe Online ▪ Unit Vocabulary Review, p. 39 ▪ Academic Vocabulary Review, p. 42 ▪ English Language Coach ▪ Active Reading Graphic Organizer, p. 18 ▪ StudentWorks Plus™ ▪ Online Student Edition ▪ Literature Classics ▪ Selection and Unit Assessments, p. 27	▪ Literary and Text Analysis Transparencies 4 ▪ Puzzlemaker ▪ Skill Level Up!™ A Language Arts Game ▪ BookLink 3 ▪ Assessment by Learning Objective (Diagnostic and Formative) ▪ Interactive Tutor: Self-Assessment ▪ TeacherWorks Plus™
1		"Stray"	▪ Glencoe Online ▪ Unit Vocabulary Review, p. 39 ▪ Academic Vocabulary Review, p. 42 ▪ English Language Coach ▪ Active Reading Graphic Organizer, p. 20 ▪ Literary Analysis, p. 17 ▪ StudentWorks Plus™ ▪ Online Student Edition ▪ Literature Classics ▪ Selection and Unit Assessments, p. 28	▪ Literary and Text Analysis Transparencies 39 ▪ Puzzlemaker ▪ Skill Level Up!™ A Language Arts Game ▪ BookLink 3 ▪ Assessment by Learning Objective (Diagnostic and Formative) ▪ Interactive Tutor: Self-Assessment ▪ TeacherWorks Plus™

Keys for Unit Resource

▪ Blackline Master
▪ Workbook
▪ Supplemental Text
▪ CD-ROM
▪ DVD
▪ Transparency
▪ Web-based
▪ Fast File

Level Appropriate Code

AS = Activities for all students
AL = Activities for students working above grade level
OL = Activities for students working at grade level
BL = Activities for students working below grade level
EL = Activities for English language learners

Focus

BELLRINGER Options

✏ **Daily Language Practice Transparency 25**
Focus Activity Say: Have you ever had to make an important decision for someone? How did you decide what was fair? Explain. *(Responses will vary.)* **OL**

Teach

R Reading Skill

Clarifying Say: When might you want to clarify what someone says to you? *(Possible response: If the doctor gives me instructions about medicine, I'd want to be sure they were clear.)* **OL**

READING WORKSHOP 2

Skills Focus

You will practice using these skills when you read the following selections:
• "Two Advertisements," p. 286
• "Stray," p. 292

Reading

• Clarifying

Literature

• Identifying author's bias
• Identifying point of view

Vocabulary

• Identifying semantic slanting
• Understanding denotation and connotation

Writing/Grammar

• Comparative and superlative adjectives
• Comparative and superlative adverbs

Objectives (pp. 282–283)
Reading Monitor comprehension: clarify

Skill Lesson

Clarifying

Learn It!

What Is It? As you know by now, you can learn skills that will help you better understand what you read. One of these skills is **clarifying**. That means "making things clear." When you're reading, you sometimes come to a word, a sentence, or a paragraph that you don't really understand. When you stop and try to figure it out, you're clarifying. Not all readers do that, but really good readers do.

R

Why Is It Important? Authors often build ideas one on another. If you don't clear up a confusing passage, you may not understand main ideas or information that comes later.

© Patrick McDonnell. Reprinted with Permission of King Features Syndicate.

Analyzing Cartoons

When the crab said, "Let's do lunch," what did he mean? How could he *clarify* what he said?

Additional Support

English Language Coach

Building Background Readers of this strip might be familiar with one of the characters known as Crabby. Crabby spends most of his time whining and complaining about various mundane occurrences and events. In this particular strip, Crabby has a run-in with a pelican. Some English language learners may not recognize the "symbols" in the cartoon as a slew of curses or complaints. **EL** Ask students if they think Crabby's response to the pelican's actions was fair or not. Have them explain their responses and describe a time when they might have been misunderstood. **AS**

How Do I Do It? Go back and read a confusing section slowly. Look up words you don't know, and read any footnotes. Ask questions about what you don't understand. Sometimes you may want to read on to see if further information helps you clarify.

Here is how one student clarified a hard section from his science book.

> The earth's surface seems solid and stable. The outer layer of our planet, however, is split into large pieces called *plates*. Plates are like pieces of a puzzle—an enormous jigsaw puzzle in which the pieces slowly move together, apart, and past one another. Where the edges of the plates bump together, as they do in the region around Mexico, earthquakes can occur.

Literature Online

Study Central Visit www.glencoe. com and click on Study Central to review clarifying.

> *It looks like the main point of this paragraph is about how the moving plates cause earthquakes in Mexico, but I'm not sure I understand this part about the plates. It's clearer when the author compares the moving plates to moving jigsaw puzzle pieces. That makes more sense to me. I think I'll read it again and look up the word "enormous."*

Practice It!

In your Learner's Notebook, write down the point that Richard Durbin is making in this sentence from "Preserving a Great American Symbol."

Please do not tell me that wooden bats are too expensive, when players who cannot hit their weight are being paid more money than the President of the United States.

Use It!

Use the following questions to help you clarify hard sections of a text.
- Do I understand all the words?
- Is there some information missing?
- Is there a chance that this will make more sense to me if I read on further?

Teach

Literature Online

Study Central Have students access the Web site to review clarifying and to complete a related activity.

R Reading Skill

Clarifying Say: Review the *How Do I Do It?* section. List the different ways to clarify a confusing section of text. *(Responses should include rereading the confusing section slowly, looking up unfamiliar words, reading footnotes, asking questions, and reading on for further information.)* **BL**

Say: In your Learner's Notebooks, ask questions that will help you clarify the text in the *Practice It!* section. *(Responses will vary.)* **OL**

Resources for page 283

📁 Use Key Reading Skills Transparency 3 in *Read Aloud, Think Aloud* to help students practice clarifying.

Differentiated Instruction

Web Graphic Organizers Graphic organizers can help students organize what they are reading so they can sort out ideas, clear up difficult passages, and remember important ideas in a selection. Draw the following web on the board and explain to students how it will help them keep track of the main idea and supporting details of a selection.

Objectives
- Clarify ideas and text
- Learn and use new vocabulary words

283

Teach

More about the Author

Manufacturers do research to develop products they wish to sell. Advertising agencies often suggest product names that will appeal to the people most likely to buy the products. First, agencies learn all about a product—how it looks, what gadgets or innovations it has, how it makes people feel—before thinking up names to suggest to the manufacturer. Considering all of the new products, it's amazing that agencies continue to think of new, clever names!

V Vocabulary

Vocabulary File Say: One way to learn and remember the vocabulary words is to keep a vocabulary file. In your Learner's Notebooks, write each word, including its pronunciation, definition, and a sentence that gives you an example of how to use the word. Refer to your file each time the vocabulary words appear in the selections. **AS**

Before You Read · Two Advertisements

Reading an Advertisement

"Buying this product will make you a happier person!" That's the idea behind a lot of advertisements, or ads. This method is called an **emotional appeal.** Advertisers use emotional appeals to persuade you to buy things. Would any of these appeals persuade you to buy a product?

- Your friends will feel jealous.
- You will get a feeling of well-being.
- This product is made better than similar products.
- This product will give you the energy to keep up with your busy schedule.
- This product contributes to better health.

Think about these appeals as you read the two advertisements on pages 286–287.

Objectives (pp. 284–287)
Reading Monitor comprehension: clarify • Make connections from text to self
Literature Identify literary elements: author's bias
Vocabulary Identify semantic slanting

284 UNIT 3 What's Fair or What's Not?

Vocabulary Preview

envy (EN vee) *n.* jealousy; desire to have something someone else has **(p. 286)** *Kori's new sweater filled Maria with envy.*

well-being (wel BEE ing) *n.* good physical and mental condition **(p. 286)** *Torrance had a feeling of well-being after his workout at the gym.*

nutrition (noo TRISH un) *n.* the food needed for life and health **(p. 287)** *Fresh fruit is a good source of nutrition.*

unique (yoo NEEK) *adj.* having no like or equal **(p. 287)** *You are a unique person.*

Write to Learn Use each vocabulary word in a sentence.

English Language Coach

Semantic Slanting "Semantic" means the study of words. "Slant" means to present a certain view in order to favor one side over another. Semantic slanting means using words so only one side of an argument or issue is presented favorably. Positive things are said about one side, and negative words are used against the other.

Here's Carlos's argument for why the family should get a dog.

Why We Should Get a Dog
Dogs make the best pets. They're loyal, they protect the house, and they do what you tell them. Cats, on the other hand, are unfriendly, lazy, and they never come when you call them.

Carlos's words *for* dogs	Carlos's words *against* cats
loyal	unfriendly
protect	lazy
do what you tell them	never come when you call them

Did Carlos say anything good about having a cat as a pet? He presented only his view of the issue and carefully chose his words. Be sure you recognize semantic slanting when you hear it and try to hear both sides.

Write to Learn Write two short paragraphs about hip hop or rock music. Give one a positive semantic slant and the other a negative slant.

Additional Support

English Language Coach

Connotation Remind students that the denotation of a word is its dictionary definition, while its connotation is certain feelings associated with the word. Two words may have similar denotations, but very different connotations. For example, *sobbing* suggests pitiful crying, while *blubbering* suggests foolish, crying.

Have students use the information given about connotations to answer the following question:

- The word *industrious* suggests being active in a careful and steady way. Both a bird building a nest and a puppy playing with a ball are busy. Which one is industrious? *(the bird)* **EL OL**

Skills Preview

Key Reading Skill: Clarifying

If you read something that doesn't make sense, take a minute to clarify. Clarifying is clearing up confusing or difficult passages. To clarify an advertisement, make sure you understand not only the words, but also any illustrations and the writer's purpose. Ask yourself these questions.

- What is the purpose of this ad?
- What is the ad trying to persuade me to do, and how is it trying to do that?
- What emotions does the ad appeal to? How are words and images used for that purpose?

Key Literary Element: Bias

A **bias** is a tendency to be in favor of something or against it. Use these tips to find each writer's bias as you read "Two Advertisements."

- Think about the writer's purpose.
  Is the author trying to persuade, entertain, inform?
- Think about the writer's opinions.
  How many sides of the story does the writer give—more than one? Or do you just see the writer's side?
  Does the writer use facts to prove points?
- Pay attention to word choice.
  How do the writer's words make you feel about the subject?

Partner Talk Remember that bias is a tendency for or against something. Think about a conversation you've had recently in which one person showed a bias, or favoritism. Tell your partner about that conversation. What was the person's bias? How were you able to recognize that bias?

Interactive Literary Elements Handbook
To review or learn more about the literary elements, go to www.glencoe.com.

Get Ready to Read

Connect to the Reading

Have you ever wanted people to be jealous of you and wish they had what you have? Have you ever been particularly proud of something you owned? Could someone get you to do something or buy something by telling you it would give you that feeling?

Write to Learn Think about your answers to the questions above. Jot down your thoughts on a separate piece of paper.

Build Background

Advertisers use certain writing "tricks" to get their messages across. Understanding advertisers' tricks helps readers make better choices about what they believe and what they buy.

The car advertisement you will read, uses a "picture of success."

- It shows smiling, well-dressed, successful-looking people using the product.
- The message is that you will also be smiling, well dressed, and successful if you use the product.

Set Purposes for Reading

BIG Question Read "Two Advertisements" to decide whether these ads use fair methods to get readers to buy their products.

Set Your Own Purpose What else would you like to learn from the reading to help you answer the Big Question? Write your purpose on the "Two Advertisements" page of Foldable 3.

Keep Moving

Use these skills as you read the following selections.

Two Advertisements **285**

Teach

R Reading Skill

Clarifying Ask: How might readers clarify terms they don't recognize in an advertisement? *(Possible response: They could use reference books, such as dictionaries and encyclopedias, to get information that will help them understand the selection; they could look at images.)* **BL** **EL**

L Literary Element

Bias Ask: Do you think it is fair for advertisers to show favoritism in their ads? *(Responses will vary. Some students may say that it is an advertiser's job to persuade people to buy a product and to make the product sound as positive and vital to individual happiness as possible.)* **OL** **AL**

Interactive Literary Elements Handbook Have students access the Web site to improve their understanding of bias.

Reading in the Real World

Careers Students interested in advertising or marketing may benefit from learning how an ad agency coordinates all aspects of a product promotion. Invite the manager of an ad agency into the classroom, take students to an agency to observe the various jobs people do, or have them conduct Internet or library research. Help students brainstorm a product and work with classmates—as an agency—to promote the product, from design and copywriting to sales, graphics, and media. **OL**

Objectives
- Learn and use new vocabulary
- Monitor comprehension: clarify
- Recognize author's bias
- Understand semantic slanting

285

Teach

Viewing the Photo

Ask: How does the photo help to illustrate the advertisement on this page? *(Possible response: The photo shows people smiling in front of a large, expensive-looking house. The ad seems to be saying that the car will make the buyers happy and successful.)* **OL**

R Reading Skill

Clarifying Ask: What did you use to clarify words you did not understand in this advertisement? *(the footnotes and Vocabulary section)* **EL** **BL**

EL Language Coach

Semantic Slanting

Ask: What does it mean to have a "look of envy"? *(Possible response: someone who looks jealous or eager to have something.)* **Ask:** According to the advertisement, why would the neighbors have a "look of envy" if they saw you drive home in a new Packard? *(Possible response: They would be jealous and want one too.)*

Two Advertisements

New 1951 Packard Convertible—one of nine all-new models

Pride of Possession[1] is Standard Equipment ▮

How can we put a price tag on your neighbors' look of **envy** . . . or on your own feeling of **well-being** . . . as you drive your new 1951 Packard home for the first time?

We can't, of course. So—*Pride of Possession is Standard Equipment.*

Like the exclusiveness[2] of Packard beauty—and the years–ahead superiority[3] of Packard engineering[4]—you can't buy a new 1951 Packard without it. And you never can match it—no matter how much you may be willing to pay—*in any other car!* ▮ ▮

It's more than a car . . . it's a

PACKARD

ASK THE MAN WHO OWNS ONE

---

1. Here, *possession* (puh ZEH shun) means ownership—the state of having or owning something.
2. *Exclusiveness* (eks KLOO suv niss) is the quality of belonging only to a small group.
3. *Superiority* (suh PEER ee OHR uh tee) is the quality of being better than others.
4. *Engineering* (en juh NEER ing) is the planning, building, and workmanship involved in creating a product.

Vocabulary

envy (EN vee) *n.* jealousy; desire to have something that someone else has

well-being (wel BEE ing) *n.* good physical and mental condition

Practice the Skills

▮ Key Literary Element

Bias Does every advertisement writer have a bias in favor of the product? Do you expect to see all the facts in an advertisement? What words in the ad show the writer's bias? List them in your Learner's Notebook.

▮ Key Reading Skill

Clarifying As you read, ask yourself questions to help you clarify the claims made in the ad.

In your Learner's Notebook, write a question of your own about one of the claims in this ad.

▮ English Language Coach

Semantic Slanting What examples of semantic slanting can you find in this advertisement? Explain why you think they are semantic slanting.

Additional Support

Differentiated Instruction

Illustrations Discuss with students the time period from which the Packard advertisement is from. Then have students use what they read on the page to create their own updated illustration for the advertisement. You may wish to have them look through current magazines or Web sites for ideas. Allow students to create their illustrations using whatever materials they are most comfortable with. When students are finished, have them display their illustrations in the classroom for other students to see. **AS**

Classes and tests. 4
Practices and meetings.
Chores and homework. 5

Who has time for nutrition?

YOU DO.

JIFFY JUICE has the vitamins and minerals to help keep up with your busy schedule and a unique shape that makes it easy to take with you. So now you have NO EXCUSES. 6

For nutrition that's ready when you are, drink **JIFFY JUICE.**

Vocabulary

nutrition (noo TRISH un) *n.* the food needed for life and health

unique (yoo NEEK) *adj.* having no like or equal

Practice the Skills

4 Key Literary Element

Bias What words or phrases in this ad show the writer's bias? List them in your Learner's Notebook.

5 Key Reading Skill

Clarifying Reread these first three lines. What do the lines tell you about the audience the ad is aimed at? What is the writer saying with these three lines? Why do you think the writer used fragments rather than complete sentences?

6 BIG Question

Each ad uses emotional appeals. The writer of the car ad uses words like *pride of possession, envy,* and *superiority.* The writer of the juice ad says things like, *So now you have no excuses.* Is it fair that writers use emotional appeals to persuade readers to buy products? Why or why not? Write your response on the "Two Advertisements" page of Foldable 3. Your response will help you complete the Unit Challenge later.

Two Advertisements **287**

Teach

EL Language Coach

Semantic Slanting

Say: Advertisers carefully present their products in very positive ways that will hopefully persuade the consumer to buy them. What positive words are used in this ad to attract consumers? Explain why the words are effective selling tools. *(Possible response: It's called "Jiffy" and the ad says it has a lot of vitamins and minerals. People can drink it fast and get a lot of nutritional vitamins.)* EL OL

BQ BIG Question

Ask: Do you think the writers of these advertisements represented the products fairly? Why or why not? How would you change the ads? *(Responses will vary.)* AS

Assess

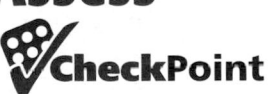CheckPoint

Use the CheckPoint Questions provided on Presentation Plus! to check for comprehension of the selections. These questions can be used with interactive response keypads for immediate student feedback.

Literature Focus Lesson

Author's Purpose Remind students that all writers have a purpose or goal they want to achieve in their writing. Writers present factual information when they wish to inform. When writers want to describe something, they present sensory details. Writers who want to entertain may tell a story, and writers who hope to persuade readers to believe something present ideas to influence readers. Discuss with students the purpose of writing advertisements. Have students identify the persuasive techniques used in each ad. Then have students rewrite the ads in their own words. EL OL

Objectives
• Monitor comprehension: clarify
• Understand semantic slanting
• Recognize author's bias
• Identify author's purpose

Assess

Students can respond to the *After You Read* items in their Learner's Notebooks or on separate sheets of paper.

Answering the

1. Responses will vary. Some students may say that emotional appeals are unfair because they are a way of tricking people into doing or purchasing things they may not normally do or want.

2. a new 1951 Packard Convertible

3. Possible response: Jiffy Juice is a quick and easy way for busy people to get vital nutrition.

Critical Thinking

4. Responses will vary. Students should support their responses with information from the text.

5. Possible response: The car ad is aimed at people who purchase items as status symbols.

6. Responses will vary. Students may say that the juice ad works better because it shows people a way to fit nutrition into their hectic schedules.

288

After You Read   Two Advertisements

New 1951 Packard Convertible—one of nine all-new models

Pride of Possession' is Standard Equipment

How can we put a price tag on your neighbors' look of envy . . . or on your own feeling of well-being . . . as you drive your new 1951 Packard home . . . the first ti...

Like the exclusiveness of Packard beauty—and the years- ahead superiority of Packard engineering—you ? buy ...... 1951 Packard

Answering the 🗨️BIG Question

1. Do you think it's fair to use emotional appeals to win arguments or sell things? Why or why not?

2. **Recall** What kind of car is the first ad trying to sell?
   Tip **Right There**

3. **Summarize** According to the Jiffy Juice ad, why should you drink Jiffy Juice?
   Tip **Think and Search**

Critical Thinking

4. **Draw Conclusions** Would you buy Jiffy Juice? Why or why not?
   Tip **Author and Me**

5. **Infer** What audience do you think the car ad is aimed at? Explain your answer.
   Tip **Author and Me**

6. **Evaluate** Which of the two ads works better to make the product seem appealing? Explain.
   Tip **On My Own**

Write About Your Reading

Think about a product you own or would like to own. Using the ads you've just read as models, write a one-page ad for that product. In your ad, be sure to
- tell what the product is and what it does
- tell readers why they should buy the product
- use emotional appeals to persuade readers to buy the product

If you need help, look through magazines to see some other ads and use those as models.

288 UNIT 3   What's Fair and What's Not?

Write About Your Reading

Responses will vary. Students should make sure they respond to all three bullet points in their ads.

Skills Review

Key Reading Skill: Clarifying

7. In your Learner's Notebook, write at least one method you used to clarify a section of "Two Advertisements."

Key Literary Element: Bias

8. Give an example of how the writer's word choice reveals bias in favor of the 1951 Packard.

9. Do the writers' emotional appeals make you feel a bias for or against either product? Explain.

10. The Packard ad is more than half a century old. In what ways are today's car ads similar to the 1951 ad?

11. Since you are a kid, do you feel that you relate to the Jiffy Juice ad? Does that mean you have a bias? Explain.

Vocabulary Check

Answer the following questions about the vocabulary words.

> envy   well-being   nutrition   unique

12. Would you rather have a feeling of **envy** or of **well-being**?

13. Are things made in a factory usually **unique**?

14. Does good **nutrition** help you have a feeling of **well-being**?

15. **English Language Coach** Both ads put a positive slant on their product. For each ad, list one way it uses semantic slanting.

Web Activities For eFlashcards, Selection Quick Checks, and other Web activities, go to www.glencoe.com.

Grammar Link: Comparative and Superlative Adjectives

Use the **comparative** (kum PAIR uh tiv) form of an adjective to compare two persons, places, things, or ideas.

- Most adjectives of one syllable are made into the comparative by adding -er to the adjective.
  *Joan is **older** than Elizabeth.*

- Most adjectives with more than one syllable add *more* or *less* before the word.
  *This week was **less exciting** than last week.*

Use the **superlative** (soo PUR luh tiv) form of an adjective to compare more than two persons, places, things, or ideas.

- Most adjectives of one syllable are made into the superlative by adding -est to the adjective.
  *Aaron is the **youngest** of the five children.*

- Most adjectives with more than one syllable add *most* or *least* before the word.
  *Who is the **most helpful** person you know?*

- Do not use both the -er/-est ending and *more/less* or *most/least* together in a sentence.
  WRONG: *He was the **most smartest** student in the class.*

  RIGHT: *He was the **smartest** student in the class.*

Grammar Practice

Rewrite each sentence below, choosing the correct form of the adjective in parentheses.

16. The Partridges were the (most unusual/more unusual) of all the families on their street.

17. Hayden was (faster/fastest) than Mitchell.

18. Elizabeth was (more tired/most tired) than Meg.

19. Dawson's car was (more nicer/nicer) than the car we rented.

Two Advertisements **289**

Skills Review

Key Reading Skill: Clarifying

7. Possible responses: rereading, asking questions, consulting a dictionary

Key Literary Element: Bias

8. Possible response: The writer uses words like "feeling of well-being," and "years-ahead superiority."

9. Responses will vary. Some students may say that the language is too over-the-top and makes them feel biased against the car and/ or the juice.

10. Possible response: Car ads today still try to get people to think that certain cars have the most high-tech advances.

11. Responses will vary. Some students may say that they identify with the ad because their lives are busy, plus some may find juice drinks more appealing than cars or any other status symbols.

Vocabulary Check

12. well-being

13. No

14. Yes

15. **English Language Coach** The first ad stresses that the person who buys a Packard will be the "envy" of the neighbors. The second ad emphasizes the nutrition one will get from drinking the juice.

Grammar Link: Comparative and Superlative Adjectives

16. The Partridges were the <u>most</u> unusual of all the families on their street.

17. Hayden was <u>faster</u> than Mitchell.

18. Elizabeth was <u>more tired</u> than Meg.

19. Dawson's car <u>was nicer</u> than the car we rented.

Close

Ask students to summarize what they learned from reading the selections to answer the Big Question.

Teach

More About the Author

Cynthia Rylant loves animals, so readers will find many of them in her stories. One of her favorite pastimes is taking long, quiet walks with her dogs Martha Jane and Leia. Rylant claims that walking with her dogs helps her writing. She says that such activities allow one to relax and appreciate life, leaving time to "cook up interesting stuff in your head."

V Vocabulary

Word Webs Say: One way to remember the meaning of words is to explore the feelings that you associate with a word. On an index card, draw a web diagram. Write a vocabulary word such as *timidly* in the center of the web. Then write the feelings that you associate with this word in the radiating circles. **OL EL**

Before You Read Stray

Cynthia Rylant

Meet the Author

When Cynthia Rylant was four years old, her parents separated. She went to live with her grandparents in West Virginia. She lived with them for nearly four years, and her experiences from that time are an important part of the stories she tells. Rylant writes to make the world a better place, saying, "Every person is able to add beauty." See page R5 of the Author Files in the back of the book for more on Cynthia Rylant.

Literature Online

Author Search For more about Cynthia Rylant, go to www.glencoe.com.

Objectives (pp. 290–295)
Reading Clarify ideas and text • Make connections from text to self
Literature Identify narrator
• Understand point of view
Vocabulary Understand denotation and connotation

Vocabulary Preview

abandoned (uh BAN dund) *v.* given up or left behind; form of the verb *abandon* **(p. 292)** *Their plan to go camping was abandoned once it started to rain.*

timidly (TIM ud lee) *adv.* fearfully **(p. 292)** *The child was shy, and she entered the playground timidly.*

grudgingly (GRUJ ing lee) *adv.* unhappily, unwillingly **(p. 293)** *Chloe didn't want to sit beside Amy on the bus, but she did it grudgingly.*

distress (dis TRES) *n.* pain or suffering **(p. 294)** *It caused her distress to see a pet without a home.*

Group Work With a few other students, make up a very short story about an old, empty house. Use all the vocabulary words in it.

English Language Coach

Denotation and Connotation All words have a **denotation** (dee noh TAY shun), a meaning found in the dictionary. Many words also have a **connotation** (kawn noh TAY shun), which is a feeling associated with that word.

Look at the words *house* and *home,* for example. They have the same dictionary meaning, or denotation. But the word *home* also has a connotation.

• **Denotation** for *house* and *home:* A place where people live
• **Connotation** for *home:* A familiar place where people feel safe and comfortable

Think-Pair-Share Each of the words below has a strong connotation. Copy each word and write down some notes about what it suggests to you. Then share the words and connotations with a partner. Do your connotations match?

family   chef   rat

Additional Support

Literature Online

Author Search To expand students' appreciation of Cynthia Rylant, have them access the Web site for additional information and resources.

Differentiated Instruction

Classroom Display Tell students that sometimes people, animals, or things come into people's lives unexpectedly. Perhaps an unexpected encounter led to a friendship, or an animal befriended them. Ask a student or a group of two or three students to create a large treasure chest from construction paper and tack it to a bulletin board. Invite students to write about times when unexpected treasures came into their lives. Invite volunteers to share their writing with the class. Have students cut symbolic shapes from construction paper on which to mat their writing. Then add the matted writing to the class treasure chest. **AS**

Skills Preview

Key Reading Skill: Clarifying

Before you read "Stray," plan your strategy for clarifying confusing sections. Be sure to

- reread confusing sections slowly and carefully
- look up unfamiliar words
- ask yourself questions about what you don't understand

Write to Learn As you read "Stray," list any unfamiliar words that make the selection hard to understand. Also, list any questions you ask yourself to help clarify what you read.

Literary Element: Point of View

As you know, in **first-person point of view,** a narrator who is "I" tells the story. The reader knows only what that narrator actually sees, hears, thinks, or feels. In **third-person point of view,** the narrator is not named and is not a character in the story. That narrator is outside the story, not involved in it.

There are two major kinds of third-person point of view.

- Many stories are written from a point of view called **third-person limited.** In this type of narration, the writer doesn't use an "I" narrator, but he or she limits the story to what the main character sees, hears, thinks, and feels.
- A few stories use a point of view called **third-person omniscient.** In these stories, the narrator reveals what many or all of the characters see, hear, think, and feel.

As you read "Stray," notice what the narrator reveals to you, the reader. See if you can tell what point of view the story is being told from.

Think-Pair-Share Think about stories you see on TV and in movies. What point of view is used? What would a movie be like if it showed things from just one character's point of view? Discuss with a classmate how a movie like that might work.

Get Ready to Read

Connect to the Reading

Have you ever deeply wanted something, even though there were plenty of good reasons against it? As you read "Stray," think about what Doris wants. Think about why her parents want something different. What would you do if you were in Doris's situation?

Partner Talk With a partner, talk about a time when you did not get something you wanted. What was it? Why didn't you get it? How did you react?

Build Background

- Animal shelters—often called *pounds*—take in 6 to 8 million dogs and cats each year.
- These shelters try to find new homes for many of the animals, but some cats and dogs cannot be adopted. They may be too sick, they may have behavior problems, or there may just not be enought people willing to adopt them.

Set Purposes for Reading

BIG Question Read "Stray" to find out how one family struggles to make a fair decision about a stray animal.

Set Your Own Purpose What else would you like to learn from the reading to help you answer the Big Question? Write your purpose on the "Stray" page of Foldable 3.

Interactive Literary Elements Handbook
To review or learn more about the literary elements, go to www.glencoe.com.

Keep Moving

Use these skills as you read the following selection.

Stray **291**

Teach

R Reading Skill

Clarify Say: In your Learner's Notebooks, draw a four-column chart. In the first column, list unfamiliar words that you encounter as you read "Stray." In the second column, write the definition of each word. In the third column, record any questions that you have about the story. In the fourth column, write responses to your questions. *(Responses will vary.)* **OL**

L Literary Element

Point of View Say: In your Learner's Notebooks, write about an episode in your life, but try writing about it from the third-person point of view. Remember that the narrator is outside the story, not a character in the story. How might your stories be different if they were told from the first-person point of view? *(Responses will vary.)* **OL**

Interactive Literary Elements Handbook Have students access the Web site to improve their understanding of bias.

Reading in the Real World

Career Discuss with students the following tasks that animal control workers do:

- Use nets, nooses, and tranquilizers to take animals away from poor environments.
- Euthanize sick, unwanted, or injured animals.
- Give animals food, water, and shelter.
- Lead public awareness campaigns regarding animal safety and care. **BL**

Ask students if they think the tasks are fair to the animals. Have them explain their reasoning. **AL**

Objectives
- Clarify ideas and text
- Recognize author's point of view
- Learn and use new vocabulary

Teach

R Reading Skill

Clarifying Say: "Snowdrifts swallowed up automobiles" is an example of personification. How does this literary technique help the writer tell you how deep the snow is? *(Possible response: It helps me visualize that the snow is so deep, the automobiles are buried beneath it.)* **OL**

EL Language Coach

Denotation and Connotation Ask: What are some synonyms for the verb *trudged?* *(Possible response: plodded, hiked, marched, trekked)* **EL Ask:** What connotation does *trudged* have in this sentence? *(Possible response: The snow probably made it difficult to walk, so it means that Doris had to walk sort of slowly and heavily through the yard.)* **OL**

Readability Scores
Dale-Chall: 4.6
DRP: 49
Lexile: 780

Stray
by Cynthia Rylant

In January, a puppy **wandered** onto the property of Mr. Amos Lacey and his wife, Maggie and their daughter, Doris. Icicles hung three feet or more from the eaves[1] of houses, snowdrifts swallowed up automobiles, and the birds were so fluffed up they looked comic. **1 2**

The puppy had been **abandoned,** and it made its way down the road toward the Laceys' small house, its tail between its legs, shivering.

Doris, whose school had been called off because of the snow, was out shoveling the cinder-block front steps when she spotted the pup on the road. She set down the shovel.

"Hey! Come on!" she called.

The puppy stopped in the road, wagging its tail **timidly,** trembling with shyness and cold.

EL Doris trudged through the yard, went up the shoveled drive and met the dog.

"Come on, pooch."

"Where did *that* come from?" Mrs. Lacey asked as soon as Doris put the dog down in the kitchen.

---

1. **Eaves** (eevz) are the lower edges of roofs.

Vocabulary

abandoned (uh BAN dund) *v.* given up or left behind

timidly (TIM ud lee) *adv.* fearfully

292 UNIT 3 What's Fair and What's Not?

Practice the Skills

1 English Language Coach

Denotation and Connotation The puppy **wandered** into the Laceys' yard. Why do you suppose the author used the word *wandered* instead of *walked* or *strolled?*

2 Key Reading Skill

Clarifying The first paragraph describes a snowy January day. Think about the statement that "snowdrifts swallowed up automobiles, and the birds were so fluffed up they looked comic." What does the author mean? How could you clarify those words? **R**

Additional Support

Reading Fluency

Tone Remind students that tone is the speaker's attitude toward a subject. Point out Mrs. Lacey's line "Where did *that* come from?" Discuss how the line should be delivered. Ask student pairs to practice delivering the line in different tones by first deciding how the speaker feels about the dog and then creating a tone that conveys the speaker's attitude. Have students experiment with several attitudes. Then ask students to do the same with Doris's lines on this page. Invite students to deliver the lines to the class in different ways. Ask the class to identify the tone of each delivery. **AS**

Mr. Lacey was at the table, cleaning his fingernails with his pocketknife. The snow was keeping him home from his job at the warehouse.

"I don't know where it came from," he said mildly, "but I know for sure where it's going."

Doris hugged the puppy hard against her. She said nothing.

Because the roads would be too bad for travel for many days, Mr. Lacey couldn't get out to take the puppy to the pound in the city right away. He agreed to let it sleep in the basement, while Mrs. Lacey **grudgingly** let Doris feed it table scraps. The woman was sensitive about throwing out food.

By the looks of it, Doris figured the puppy was about six months old and on its way to being a big dog. She thought it might have some shepherd in it.

Four days passed and the puppy did not complain. It never cried in the night or howled at the wind. It didn't tear up everything in the basement. It wouldn't even follow Doris up the basement steps unless it was invited.

It was a good dog.

Several times Doris had opened the door in the kitchen that led to the basement, and the puppy had been there, all stretched out, on the top step. Doris knew it had wanted some company and that it had lain against the door, listening to the talk in the kitchen, smelling the food, being a part of things. It always wagged its tail, eyes all sleepy, when she found it there. **3**

Even after a week had gone by, Doris didn't name the dog. She knew her parents wouldn't let her keep it, that her father made so little money any pets were out of the question, and that the pup would definitely go to the pound when the weather cleared. **4**

Still, she tried talking to them about the dog at dinner one night.

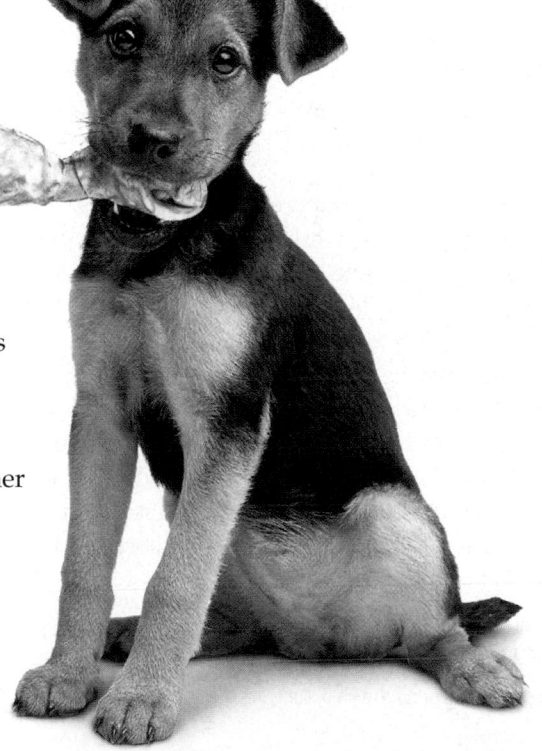

Practice the Skills

3 ▸ **Literary Element**

Point of View What do you know about the point of view of the story so far? Is the narrator first-person or third-person? Is the narrator a character in the story? **L**

4 ▸ **BIG Question**

Why do Mr. and Mrs. Lacey want to get rid of the dog? Do you think getting rid of the dog is fair? Write your answers on the "Stray" page of Foldable 3. Your response will help you complete the Unit Challenge later. **BQ**

Analyzing the Photo Would you keep this puppy if you found it abandoned in the snow? Why or why not?

Vocabulary

grudgingly (GRUJ ing lee) *adv.* unhappily, unwillingly

Stray **293**

Teach

L Literary Element

Point of View Ask: How did you determine that the story is told from the third-person point of view? *(Possible response: The narrator never says "I" and refers to the characters as Mr. and Mrs. Lacey, Doris, she.)* **OL**

BQ ▸ BIG Question

Say: Think about the needs of the dog and the needs of the family. What is fair in this situation? *(Responses will vary. Students may say that if the family cannot afford the dog, then it isn't fair to keep it. However, some might say the family should try to find a good home for the dog rather than taking it to the pound.)* **AS**

C Critical Thinking

Application Ask: What would you do if you were in Doris's place? *(Responses will vary. Some students may say that they would not act differently. Other students may say that they would protest more strongly.)* **OL**

English Language Coach

Connotations of Names Emphasize that Doris does not name the dog because naming something establishes a connection with it. Ask students to work with partners or in small groups to discuss their own names or the names of parents, siblings, pets, or objects they may have named. Suggest that students address these questions:

- Who is the person, pet, or object?
- What is the relationship to you?
- Who decided on the name?
- What does the name mean, both literally and personally?
- Why was it chosen?
- If you could rename yourself or your pet, what name would you choose? Why? **AS**

Objectives
- Clarify ideas and text
- Recognize author's point of view
- Understand connotation
- Respond to literature: application

Teach

L Literary Element

Point of View Ask: We get information about how Doris and her parents feel about the dog, but how does the narrator feel about the dog? *(Possible response: We don't know how the narrator feels because the story is told from the third-person point of view.)* **OL**

C Critical Thinking

Evaluation Say: What does Mrs. Lacey mean when she tells Doris to act more grown-up? *(Possible response: She means that Doris's show of emotion and her disappointment over losing the dog aren't adult behavior.)* **OL Ask:** Is Mrs. Lacey correct about what adult behavior is? *(Responses will vary. Students may speculate about the value of hiding one's feelings.)* **AL**

"She's a good dog, isn't she?" Doris said, hoping one of them would agree with her.

Her parents glanced at each other and went on eating.

"She's not much trouble," Doris added. "I like her." She smiled at them, but they continued to ignore her.

"I figure she's real smart," Doris said to her mother. "I could teach her things."

Mrs. Lacey just shook her head and stuffed a forkful of sweet potato in her mouth. Doris fell silent, praying the weather would never clear.

But on Saturday, nine days after the dog had arrived, the sun was shining and the roads were plowed. Mr. Lacey opened up the trunk of his car and came into the house.

C Doris was sitting alone in the living room, hugging a pillow and rocking back and forth on the edge of a chair. She was trying not to cry but she was not strong enough. Her face was wet and red, her eyes full of **distress.**

Mrs. Lacey looked into the room from the doorway.

"Mama," Doris said in a small voice. "Please."

Mrs. Lacy shook her head.

"You know we can't afford a dog, Doris. You try to act more grown-up about this." **5**

Doris pressed her face into the pillow.

Outside, she heard the trunk of the car slam shut, one of the doors open and close, the old engine cough and choke and finally start up.

"Daddy," she whispered. "Please."

She heard the car travel down the road, and though it was early afternoon, she could do nothing but go to her bed. She cried herself to sleep, and her dreams were full of searching and searching for things lost.

It was nearly night when she finally woke up. Lying there, like stone, still exhausted, she wondered if she would ever in her life have anything. She stared at the wall for a while. **6**

But she started feeling hungry, and she knew she'd have to make herself get out of bed and eat some dinner. She wanted not to go into the kitchen, past the basement door. She wanted not to face her parents.

Vocabulary
distress (dis TRES) *n.* pain or suffering

Practice the Skills

5 Literary Element

Point of View Have you noticed more about the narrator? Does the narrator reveal what Doris feels and thinks? Does the narrator reveal what Mr. and Mrs. Lacey feel and think? **L**

6 Reviewing Skills

Connecting How do you think Doris feels about not keeping the puppy? Think of a time you wanted something like a pet, clothes, or a bike, but knew you couldn't have it. Why couldn't you have it? How did you feel?

Additional Support

Differentiated Instruction

Dream Journals Doris's dreams are connected to an event in her life. Invite students to keep dream journals for a week or more. Tell students to keep a pen and paper next to their beds and to record their dreams immediately after waking. When students have made several entries, have them bring their journals to class. Ask students to think about what happened during the day preceding each dream as well as what they might have been thinking about before falling asleep. Ask students to explain the connections or lack of connections between their waking and sleeping selves. **AL**

But she rose up heavily.

Her parents were sitting at the table, dinner over, drinking coffee. They looked at her when she came in, but she kept her head down. No one spoke.

Doris made herself a glass of powdered milk and drank it all down. Then she picked up a cold biscuit and started out of the room.

"You'd better feed that mutt before it dies of starvation," Mr. Lacey said.

Doris turned around.

"What?"

"I said, you'd better feed your dog. I figure it's looking for you."

Doris put her hand to her mouth.

"You didn't take her?" she asked.

"Oh, I took her all right," her father answered. "Worst-looking place I've ever seen. Ten dogs to a cage. Smell was enough to knock you down. And they give an animal six days to live. Then they kill it with some kind of a shot."

Doris stared at her father.

"I wouldn't leave an *ant* in that place," he said. "So I brought the dog back."

Mrs. Lacey was smiling at him and shaking her head as if she would never, ever, understand him.

Mr. Lacey sipped his coffee.

"Well," he said, "are you going to feed it or not?" **7** ○

Practice the Skills

7 **BIG** Question

Do you think Mr. Lacey makes a fair decision in the end? Do you think the reason he gives for keeping the dog is the *only* reason he decides to let the dog stay? Write your response on the "Stray" page of Foldable 3. Your response will help you complete the Unit Challenge later.

BQ

Analyzing the Photo Does this picture fit in well with the ending of the story? Why or why not?

Stray **295**

Reading in the Real World

Citizenship Ask students to brainstorm the reasons that people have pets. Then ask students to prepare a list of tips for Doris about how to take care of her new pet. Have them find out information at the library or online about the following topics:

• Establishing a schedule for feeding, watering, brushing, and exercise.

• Creating an area in which the dog can walk.

• Housebreaking the dog and teaching it to follow basic commands.

• Making an appointment with a veterinarian for a checkup and vaccinations. **AS**

Objectives
• Evaluate text
• Recognize author's point of view

Assess

Resources for page 296

📁 Selection Quick Check, p. 24

📁 Selection and Unit Assessment, p. 28

⊙ ExamView Assessment Suite

⊙ Interactive Tutor: Self-Assessment

Students can respond to the *After You Read* items in their Learner's Notebooks or on a separate sheet of paper.

Answering the
BIG Question

1. Responses will vary. Students should cite examples from the text.

2. The Laceys were homebound because of the snow.

3. Possible response: The dog's behavior, as well as Doris's evaluation of it, lets the reader know that the stray is a good dog.

Critical Thinking

4. Responses will vary. Students may say that the author wants the reader to view the parents as Doris does.

5. Possible response: a) naming the dog would establish a deeper connection between Doris and the dog. b) It would be even more difficult for her to let the dog go.

6. Some students may say that Doris didn't want them to be disappointed with her.

After You Read Stray

Answering the BIG Question

1. Do you think people sometimes feel forced to do things that seem unfair because they have no choice? Explain. Use the situation in "Stray" as an example.

2. **Recall** Why did Doris's parents let the dog stay at first?
   Tip Right There

3. **Summarize** How do you know that the stray is a friendly, good dog?
   Tip Think and Search

Critical Thinking

4. **Infer** Do you think the author wants readers to like Mr. and Mrs. Lacey? Explain.
   Tip Author and Me

5. **Infer** a) Why doesn't Doris name the dog when it arrives?
   b) How would naming the dog change Doris's feelings about it?
   Tip Author and Me

6. **Synthesize** At the end of the story, why doesn't Doris want to face her parents?
   Tip Author and Me

Write About Your Reading

Make a comparison chart to show how Mr. Lacey felt at the beginning of the story, and how he felt at the end. Explain his reasons at the beginning, and explain what changed his feelings. Use quotes and examples from the story.

Objectives (pp. 296–297)
Reading Monitor comprehension: clarify • Make connections from text to self
Literature Identify narrator
• Understand point of view
Vocabulary Understand denotation and connotation
Writing Make a comparison chart
Grammar Identify parts of speech: comparative and superlative adverbs
• Use comparative and superlative adverbs correctly

Mr. Lacey

BEGINNING:	END:
How did he feel about the stray in the beginning?	*How* did he feel about the stray by the end of the story?
Use a quote:	Use a quote:
Why did he feel this way?	*Why* did his feelings change?
Give an example or a quote:	Give an example or a quote:

Write About Your Reading

Possible response:
BEGINNING:
At the beginning of the story, Mr. Lacey felt negative toward the dog: "I don't know where it came from . . . but I know for sure where it's going."

He felt this way because the family couldn't afford a pet: "her father made so little money any pets were out of the question."
END:
At the end of the story, Mr. Lacey decides to keep the dog: "I brought the dog back."

His opinion changed because of the poor conditions at the pound: "I wouldn't leave an *ant* in that place."

Skills Review

Key Reading Skill: Clarifying

7. Did you need to use your clarifying strategies to understand any parts of this story? Explain.

Literary Element: Point of View

8. Was the narrator of this story a first-person narrator or a third-person narrator? How could you tell?

9. Was the information you received limited to the experiences of one character? If so, which one?

Reviewing Skills: Connecting

10. When you were reading "Stray," were you able to understand Doris's feelings? Had you ever felt any of the things she felt? Explain.

Vocabulary Check

Write a sentence that answers each of the following questions. Use the vocabulary word in your answer.

11. What is one thing you do **grudgingly?**

12. What is one place you might enter **timidly?**

13. What would you feel like if you were **abandoned** by your friends?

14. What is one thing that might cause you **distress?**

15. **English Language Coach** For each word below write its denotation and its connotation.

    exhausted   trudged   mutt

Web Activities For eFlashcards, Selection Quick Checks, and other Web activities, go to www.glencoe.com.

Grammar Link: Comparative and Superlative Adverbs

- Use the **comparative** form of an adverb to compare <u>two actions.</u> For one-syllable adverbs, form the comparative by adding -er to the end of the word. Use the word *more* or *less* before adverbs that end in -ly:

  *The dog ran **faster** than Doris.*

  *The stray dog behaved **more timidly** than the other dog.*

- Use the **superlative** form of an adverb to compare <u>more than</u> two actions. For short adverbs, form the superlative by adding -est. Use the word *most* or *least* for adverbs that end in -ly:

  *Of all the dogs at the pound, the black one barked **loudest.***

  *The toy varieties of poodles are my **least** favorite.*

- Do not use both the -er/-est ending and *more/less* or *most/least.*

Grammar Practice

Rewrite each sentence below, choosing the correct form of the adverb in parentheses.

16. By afternoon, the snow began to pile up (most quickly/more quickly) than it did in the morning.

17. On Saturday, Doris got up (earlier/more earlier) than usual.

18. Mr. Lacey acted (more calmly/most calmly) than Doris.

19. Doris waited (more patiently, most patiently) than her mother.

Writing Application Look back at your comparison chart and make sure you used adverbs correctly. Circle comparative adverbs and underline any superlative adverbs.

Stray **297**

Skills Review

Key Reading Skill: Clarifying

7. Possible response: Yes, rereading, asking questions, and consulting a dictionary helped me clarify.

Key Literary Element: Bias

8. third-person narrator; the narrator reveals information about what all of the characters think.

9. No, there is information about several <u>characters.</u>

Reviewing Skills: Connecting

10. Responses will vary.

Vocabulary Check

11. chores

12. a courtroom

13. sad

14. losing my backpack

15. **English Language Coach**
    Exhausted, tired, extremely tired

    Trudged, plodded, walked slowly

    Mutt, dog, mangy dog

Grammar Link: Comparative and Superlative Adverbs

Grammar Practice

16. By afternoon, the snow began to pile up <u>more quickly</u> than it did in the morning.

17. On Saturday Doris got up <u>earlier</u> than usual.

18. Mr. Lacey acted <u>more calmly</u> than Doris.

19. Doris waited <u>more patiently</u> than her mother.

Close

Ask students to discuss what's fair and unfair from two points of view.

Inferring

Objective covered in this workshop:
• Make inferences about contexts, events, characters, and settings

Teaching Students to Make Inferences

Why Is It Important?

• Inferences depend on seeing connections that are not articulated.

• Most writers do not come out and say everything a character thinks; readers need to make inferences to fully comprehend what is being communicated.

• Students who make inferences successfully understand characters better and are better able to identify themes.

How to Help Students Get It

• Tell students to always pay attention to everything a writer tells them through a character's actions as well as words.

• Help students notice descriptions, dialogue, events, and relationships.

• Encourage students to ask themselves: "Why does the author tell me this? What does this suggest about this character or situation?"

• To build their confidence in making inferences while reading, remind students that they already make many inferences in everyday life. (This workshop provides several examples of how we make inferences.)

Reading to Answer the Big Question

By tackling the clothing question, how people perceive themselves and others based on clothing appearances, the selections in Workshop 3 of Unit 3 will lead your students to generate their own answers to the Big Question: **What's fair and what's not?**

Dressed for Success? by Melanie Bertotto
Pros and cons of requiring school uniforms are discussed in this *TIME* article. Students, administrators, and lawyers present persuasive arguments about what students should and should not be required or allowed to wear to school.

Eleven by Sandra Cisneros
On Rachel's eleventh birthday, she is faced with a frustrating and difficult situation at school. She is declared the owner of an ugly smelly sweater and forced to wear it in class. Her inability to cope with the unfair situation makes Rachel wish that she was turning one hundred and two instead of eleven.

Workshop Resources

PACING (DAYS)		LESSON	STUDENT MATERIALS	TEACHER RESOURCES
STANDARD	BLOCK			
1	1/2	Key Skill Lesson: Inferring	🔨 Key Reading Skills Practice, p. 21 🔨 English Language Coach Review, p. 41	🔥 Bellringer Options Transparencies –Daily Language Practice 26 🔥 Read Aloud, Think Aloud Transparencies –Key Reading Skills 13 💿 Presentation Plus!
1		"Dressed for Success?"	💻 Glencoe Online 🔨 Unit Vocabulary Review, p. 39 🔨 Academic Vocabulary Review, p. 42 📁 English Language Coach 🔨 Active Reading Graphic Organizer, p. 23 🔨 Literary Analysis, p. 22 💿 StudentWorks Plus™ 💻 Online Student Edition 💿 Literature Classics 📁 Selection and Unit Assessments, p. 29	💻 Puzzlemaker 💿 Skill Level Up!™ A Language Arts Game 💻 BookLink 3 📗 Assessment by Learning Objective (Diagnostic and Formative) 💿 Interactive Tutor: Self-Assessment 💿 TeacherWorks Plus™
1	1	"Eleven"	💻 Glencoe Online 🔨 Unit Vocabulary Review, p. 39 🔨 Academic Vocabulary Review, p. 42 📁 English Language Coach 🔨 Active Reading Graphic Organizer, p. 23 💿 StudentWorks Plus™ 💻 Online Student Edition 💿 Literature Classics 📁 Selection and Unit Assessments, p. 30	🔥 Bellringer Options Transparencies –Selection Focus 5 🔥 Read Aloud, Think Aloud Transparencies –Read Aloud, Think Aloud 20–24 🔥 Literary and Text Analysis Transparencies 42 💻 Puzzlemaker 💿 Skill Level Up!™ A Language Arts Game 💻 BookLink 3 📗 Assessment by Learning Objective (Diagnostic and Formative) 💿 Interactive Tutor: Self-Assessment 💿 TeacherWorks Plus™

Keys for Unit Resource

- 📁 Blackline Master
- 📗 Workbook
- 📖 Supplemental Text
- 💿 CD-ROM
- 📀 DVD
- 🔥 Transparency
- 💻 Web-based
- 🔨 Fast File

Level Appropriate Code

- **AS** = Activities for all students
- **AL** = Activities for students working above grade level
- **OL** = Activities for students working at grade level
- **BL** = Activities for students working below grade level
- **EL** = Activities for English language learners

Focus

BELLRINGER Options

- **Selection Focus Transparency 5**
- **Daily Language Practice Transparency 26**
Focus Activity Say: Have you ever used a person's tone of voice or facial expression to figure out something? Explain how you used them to figure out the secret. *(Students may explain how they used information around them to make inferences.)* **OL**

Teach

R Reading Skill

Inferring Ask: If you know that your sister loves dogs, and someone has left a book about dogs in the kitchen, whose book would you guess it is? Why? *(Possible response: my sister's because I know she loves dogs)* **OL**

V Vocabulary

Academic Vocabulary Ask: What is another way of saying, "I *infer* from the look on your face that you won the game"? *(Possible responses: I can tell . . .; I guess . . .; I figure . . .)* **OL**

Additional Support

298

Skills Focus

You will practice using these skills when you read the following selections:
- "Dressed for Success?" p. 302
- "Eleven," p. 308

Reading
- Making inferences

Literature
- Understanding elements of argument
- Recognizing repetition

Vocabulary
- Identifying balanced language
- Academic Vocabulary: *infer*

Writing/Grammar
- Identifying demonstratives
- Identifying articles

Objectives (pp. 298–299)
Reading Make inferences

298 UNIT 3

Inferring

Learn It!

What Is It? When you **infer**, you use your knowledge, reasoning, and experiences to guess what a writer does not come right out and say.

Without realizing it, you make inferences every day. For example, you arrive at the bus stop a little later than usual. No one is there. You say to yourself, "I've missed the bus." You may be wrong, but you've used the evidence (you're late; no one's there) to make an inference (you've missed the bus).

Many times in a piece of writing the author does not come right out and say every little thing about every character or event. To really understand what is going on, you have to make inferences.

Calvin and Hobbes © 1990 Watterson. Distributed by UNIVERSAL PRESS SYNDICATE. Reprinted with permission. All rights reserved.

Analyzing Cartoons
What happens in the first two panels of this cartoon? In the next two panels, Calvin makes an inference. Do you agree with his inference? Why or why not?

Academic Vocabulary

V **infer** (in FUR) *v.* to use reason and experience to figure out what an author does not say directly

---

English Language Coach

Building Background Help students understand the cartoon by telling them the comic strip "Calvin and Hobbes" is about the life of a curious, mischievous little boy and his stuffed tiger. Ask them the following questions to help them get the joke:

- Who is Calvin talking to?
- What does Calvin ask his father?
- How does the father respond?
- What leads Calvin to guess that his father just wants to get rid of him?
- Do you think Calvin's inference is right? Why or why not?

Point out to students that Calvin's father confirms his inference by continuing to read his book and by telling Calvin to go show his mother. **EL OL**

Why Is It Important? Making inferences will help you to find meaning in what you read. Inferring helps you understand characters, find the theme of a selection, and stay involved with what you are reading.

How Do I Do It? Inferring uses many of the skills you have learned in the previous units, such as activating prior knowledge, connecting, and predicting. In order to make inferences, pay attention to details. They give you the clues you need. But be careful. Making inferences does *not* mean guessing without thinking! Here's how one student used inferring to understand the passage below:

R

> Everything was all set—the balloons, the presents and the cake. Darla nervously glanced out the window. Things must go as planned! Darla had worked for weeks on the details for the party, everything from the colors to the strawberry filling in the cake. She hoped her brother would get this one thing right—picking their grandmother up from the station. "Please let him do this!" thought Darla. "I knew I should have gone myself!"

> *This must be an important party since it's taken Darla weeks to plan it and she's nervous. I think she doesn't trust her brother. He's probably messed up before.*

Literature Online

Study Central Visit www.glencoe.com and click on Study Central to review inferring.

Practice It!

You can often tell when a person is upset by how he or she acts and what he or she says . . . or doesn't say.

> *Grandmother said the taxi driver was very nice. Darla fumed for the rest of the party.*

What can we infer here? Remember who was supposed to pick up Grandmother. What probably happened?

Use It!

As you read "Dressed for Success?" and "Eleven," notice the clues the authors provide. In your Learner's Notebook, use these clues to make inferences.

Teach

Literature Online

Study Central Have students access the Web site to review inferring and to complete a related activity.

R Reading Skill

Inferring Say: Read the sample passage in the *How Do I Do It?* section. Pay attention to the details in this passage. Notice that Darla is nervous and that she has planned the party for weeks. She is also worried that her grandmother may not make it to the party. What do these details tell you about the party? *(Possible response: The party is important to Darla.)* **OL**
Say: Although the author does not say that this is an important event for Darla, a reader can *infer* from these details that the event is important to her.

Resources for page 299

📁 Use Key Reading Skills Transparency 13 in *Read Aloud, Think Aloud* to help students practice Inferring.

Reading in the Real World

Career Explain to students that jobs involving dealing with the public often require workers to be sensitive to people's needs. In these jobs, people must often make inferences based on the clues they see in a situation. For example, a sick person might be able to describe the way he or she feels but probably could not say exactly what is wrong. A doctor must infer, or figure out, why a patient is sick by using the information that the person provides. Have students interview people whose jobs require them to meet the public. Students should prepare questions about the workers' interactions with the public and how they make inferences to help meet people's needs. **AL**

Objectives
• Make inferences
• Learn and use new vocabulary

299

Teach

More About the Author

In her spare time, Melanie Bertotto conducts scientific experiments in her room. She loves pets, especially her dog, cat, and hermit crab. In fact, one of her goals is to become the host of a wildlife show. Bertotto hopes someday to report on what happens behind the scenes of a Broadway play and at the Ringling Brothers and Barnum and Bailey Circus.

V Vocabulary

Say: One way to learn and remember the vocabulary words is to form mental pictures. For example, think about the image that comes to mind when you hear the word *discipline*. You might think of a young man or woman dressed in a uniform, standing up straight, and paying attention. Try this technique with each of the vocabulary words and have a friend or family member test you later on the word's meaning. **OL**

Before You Read | Dressed for Success?

Meet the Writer

Melanie Bertotto was born in 1992 and is on the 2004–2005 team of kid reporters for *TIME FOR KIDS*. Bertotto's other stories are "Book Review: Wolf Brother Chronicles of Ancient Darkness" and "Meet Ming-Na, Voice of Mulan."

As you read "Dressed for Success?" you'll notice that the writer interviewed several people for the article, including a school principal, a student, a deputy superintendent, and a lawyer. Interviewing different people is one way that journalists present different viewpoints on a topic.

Literature Online

Author Resources For more on Melanie Bertotto, go to www.glencoe.com.

Objectives (pp. 300–303)
Reading Make inferences • Make connections from text to self
Literature Understand characteristics of argument
Vocabulary Identify balanced language

Vocabulary Preview

adopt (uh DOPT) *v.* to accept and put into effect **(p. 303)** *Our middle school will adopt a student dress code for the new school year.*

discipline (DIS uh plin) *n.* self-control; the obeying of rules **(p. 303)** *Supporters claim that uniforms and dress codes improve discipline and increase student achievement.*

individuality (in duh vij oo AL uh tee) *n.* the combined qualities or characteristics that make one person or thing different from another **(p. 303)** *Some people argue that dress codes take away from a student's individuality.*

Write to Learn Write the vocabulary word that each clue describes:
- A strict teacher might believe in this.
- A person might wear unusual clothes to express this.
- Members of a city council would vote to decide whether to do this to a new law.

English Language Coach

Balanced Language In persuasive writing, the way the writer makes his or her argument is very important. You have learned how writers use semantic slanting and hyperbole. In addition, they may make *generalizations*, which are broad statements about a large group. "Snakes are dangerous" and "Big cars use a lot of gas" are both generalizations—true in many, but not all, cases.

However, other writers will be very careful *not* to make generalizations or to exaggerate. They remind the reader that they are simply giving *their* view. These writers try to use **balanced language.** Recognizing the use of balanced language will help you decide if you want to be persuaded, and whether you can believe what the writer is saying. To see if a writer is using balanced language look for words such as *I think, in my opinion, probably, possibly, generally, many, some, often,* and *sometimes.*

Partner Up Together, rewrite the statement below, adding at least two of the words listed above. Then discuss whether this changes your opinion of the statement.

Individuality is less important than discipline. Dress codes will give students the discipline they need.

Additional Support

Literature Online

Author Search To expand students' knowledge of Melanie Bertotto, have them access the Web site for additional information and resources.

Literature Focus Lesson

Sources in News Articles Discuss with students the way journalists use quotations from sources to support the main points in an article. Before writing an article, journalists find the most appropriate or qualified sources to talk to about a particular subject. When they write their article, they illustrate a point by quoting some or all of what those sources have said. Tell students to imagine that they've been asked to write an article discussing the pros and cons of school uniforms at their school. Encourage them to think about which sources they would quote in their articles to cover both sides of the issue. Then have them read to see which sources Bertotto quotes. **OL**

Skills Preview

Key Reading Skill: Inferring

Writers don't always say what they want you to know. Sometimes they give clues. Details in a piece of writing can help the reader infer, or figure out, information that is not stated directly. As you read "Dressed for Success?" you will probably need to make inferences. Think about what you know about the writers' arguments and whether they have stated those things directly.

Write to Learn Write down what you are inferring in your Learner's Notebook.

Key Literary Element: Argument

In writing, an **argument** is the reason or reasons a writer uses to support his or her opinion. Let's say your teacher wants you to learn some new spelling tricks, and you ask why. Your teacher might say, "You aren't doing well in spelling. You need to get better. These tricks have helped lots of other students spell better. They're easy to learn and will help you. Then you'll pass the tests and get better grades in English." Those are good reasons, and using them makes a good argument for learning the spelling tricks!

The article "Dressed for Success?" presents the reader with two arguments—one on each side of the issue of dress codes and school uniforms. By doing so, it provides a fair and balanced view of the subject. As you read, look at the arguments presented in favor of and against dress codes and uniforms. Do the deputy superintendent and the lawyer give good reasons for their views?

Write to Learn Imagine that you need to create an argument for or against the use of uniforms at your school. Make a list of reasons that you would use to support your opinion.

Get Ready to Read

Connect to the Reading

This article talks about the pros and cons of uniforms and dress codes in public schools. Does your school have a dress code or require uniforms? What do you think about this? If your school does not have a dress code, do you think it would be a good idea?

Partner Talk With a partner, discuss whether school dress codes or uniforms are a good idea.

Build Background

- Most schools have some type of dress code, and many are now requiring uniforms.
- The American Civil Liberties Union (ACLU) is a group of lawyers who act to protect the rights of people in the United States.
- The ACLU has been involved in a number of famous "test cases," or cases that test whether certain laws are against the Constitution. For example, ACLU lawyers helped end school segregation in the 1950s.

Set Purposes for Reading

BIG Question Read the selection "Dressed for Success?" to think about whether dress codes are fair.

Set Your Own Purpose What else would you like to learn from the article to help you answer the Big Question? Write your own purpose on the "Dressed for Success" page of Foldable 3.

Interactive Literary Elements Handbook To review or learn more about the literary elements, go to www.glencoe.com.

Keep Moving

Use these skills as you read the following selection.

Teach

L Literary Element

Argument Ask: Have you had to convince someone to do something or let you do something? Perhaps you've tried to convince someone to give you something or go somewhere with you. What were the reasons you gave in your argument? *(Responses will vary.)* **OL Ask:** Did you use balanced language in your argument? If so, what words did you use? *(Responses will vary.)* **AL**

C Critical Thinking

Evaluation Say: Think of one possible pro and one possible con of wearing a uniform to school. *(Possible response: Pro: I wouldn't have to choose a new outfit every day. Con: I couldn't wear my fun new clothes to school.)* **OL**

Interactive Literary Elements Handbook Have students access the Web site to improve their understanding of stereotype and bias.

Reading in the Real World

Career Explain to students that Melanie Bertotto is a journalist, someone who writes about issues and events for a magazine or newspaper. Point out that one goal of a journalist is to present all of the information about a topic in a fair and unbiased manner. Explain that while some journalists may report on current events, others may choose to write about a number of topics, including music, theater, art, and sports. If some students are interested in a career in journalism, ask a journalist from a local newspaper to visit the class and answer questions about his or her career. **OL AL**

Objectives
- Make inferences
- Understand arguments
- Make connections from text to self
- Learn and use new vocabulary

301

Teach

L Literary Element

Argument Ask: What is Leah Hawthorn's argument against wearing school uniforms? *(Possible response: She claims that wearing whatever she likes helps her do good work in school. She feels that the less worried students are about their looks, the more focused they will be in their schoolwork.)* **OL**

R Reading Skill

Inferring Ask: What can you infer about students' performance in school once they were required to wear uniforms? Explain. *(Possible response: They did better in school because more of them attended school.)*

Readability Scores
Dale-Chall: 4.6
DRP: 64
Lexile: 970

TIME
Dressed for Success?

What should students wear to class?

By MELANIE BERTOTTO

At my school in Lemoyne, Pennsylvania, Principal Joseph Gargiulo follows the latest styles. But his interest has nothing to do with a love of fashion. He is just trying to back up Lemoyne Middle School's dress code.

Lemoyne does not let students wear flip-flops and pajama pants. "Pajamas are for sleeping in," says Gargiulo. "School is a student's job. You don't go to your job in pajamas."

Seventh-grader Leah Hawthorn disagrees. She says that wearing whatever she likes helps her do good work at school. "You worry less about how you look," she says. "So you are more focused on what you're doing in class."

Pennsylvania is one of 28 states that has given school districts[1] the power to decide what students can wear to class. Many who are in charge of education believe that dress codes are good for students. They point to places such as the Long Beach Unified School District in California to prove it. In 1994, that school district became the first public school system to order elementary and middle school students to wear uniforms. Soon after, the school district found that fewer students had been absent and fewer had been put out of school than before. **1**

---

1. A **school district** is an area of public schools that are managed together.

1 Key Reading Skill

Inferring Remember that inferring is using reasoning to figure out what a writer doesn't say outright. When this school district made students wear uniforms, fewer students were absent and fewer students were put out of school. What inference can you make from this statement? **R**

Additional Support

English Language Coach

Homonyms Tell students that homonyms are words that sound the same but have different spellings and meanings. Write the words *principal* and *principle* on the board, along with their definitions. (A *principal* is *the head of a school;* a *principle* is *a basic truth, law, or standard.*) Suggest the following pneumonic device: "The *principal* is your *pal*." Ask students whether they can think of any more homonyms. (*Examples include* ant *and* aunt; blue *and* blew; cell *and* sell.) Have students keep a "homonyms list" to help them remember the correct spellings and meanings. **EL OL**

Some people say that dress codes and uniforms go against the right of freedom of expression. The American Civil Liberties Union (ACLU) has filed lawsuits for parents and students who say that school dress codes are unfair.

—From *TIME FOR KIDS*, February 4, 2005

Should schools be able to tell students what to wear?

Dorothy Harper *was the deputy of the Long Beach Unified School District.*

YES! Dress codes can play a major role in helping schools fulfill one of their [main] responsibilities: keeping students safe. Dress codes help schools [set] standards of behavior. This results in safe and orderly classrooms. Most important, dress codes require that all students be held accountable for maintaining a school climate that encourages learning. Schools that successfully **adopt** dress codes are generally safer, have more positive climates, and have a stronger sense of school pride. That's a lot to gain without having to give up much at all. **2**

Allen Lichtenstein *is an ACLU lawyer in Nevada.*

NO! The Supreme Court has said that students do not leave their constitutional rights at the schoolhouse door. Yet some schools' dress codes restrict students' freedom of expression. Supporters claim that uniforms and dress codes improve **discipline** and increase student achievement. But there is little evidence to support this. Codes stifle **individuality.** While no one supports allowing clothing that is dangerous, disruptive, or too revealing, many codes go too far. America has always prided itself on the individual's right to self-expression. That respect should extend to student clothing. **3 4**

Vocabulary

adopt (uh DOPT) *v.* to accept and put into effect

discipline (DIS uh plin) *n.* self-control; the obeying of rules

individuality (in duh vij oo AL uh tee) *n.* the combined qualities or characteristics that make one person or thing different from another

---

2 English Language Coach

Balanced Language Why do you think Dorothy Harper uses such words and phrases as "generally" and "more positive"? How would her argument have changed if she used "always" instead of "generally"? What if she had used "most positive" instead of "more positive"? Would that change what you thought of her argument?

3 Key Literary Element

Argument Have the writers stated their arguments? If so, which sentence in each half of the boxed section states that writer's main argument?

4 BIG Question

Is it fair for schools to decide what students wear to school? Record your answer on the "Dressed for Success" page of Foldable 3. Your response will help you complete the Unit Challenge later. **BQ**

Dressed for Success? **303**

Teach

L Literary Element

Argument Ask: Does the lawyer admit that it is acceptable to place some limits on what students can wear? Does this make his argument seem less convincing? Explain. *(Possible response: No. By admitting that there should be some limits, he shows that he thinks student safety and well-being are important.)* **AL**

BQ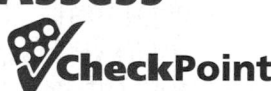

Say: A dress code may force many students to buy new clothes. Is it fair to ask students to buy new clothes that match the school's dress code? *(Responses will vary. Some students may say that some dress codes allow students to wear clothes that they already own or that students will have to buy new school clothes at some point anyway.)* **OL**

Assess

CheckPoint

Use the CheckPoint questions provided on Presentation Plus! to check for comprehension of the selection. These questions can be used with interactive response keypads for immediate student feeback.

Differentiated Instruction

Debate Hold a debate about school uniforms and dress codes. Organize two teams, one *for* and one *against*. Have students on each team come up with three questions for the other team and then submit their questions to you, the moderator. In the debate, ask each team a question and give a volunteer two minutes to answer. After a team has answered, give the other team a chance to argue its position. If students are engaged, allow the debate to go back and forth. Otherwise, proceed to the next question. **OL AL**

Objectives
• Make inferences
• Understand arguments
• Understand homonyms

303

Assess

Resources for page 304

📁 Selection Quick Check, p. 25

📁 Selection and Unit Assessment, p. 29

⊙ ExamView Assessment Suite

⊙ Interactive Tutor: Self-Assessment

Students can respond to the *After You Read* items in their Learner's Notebooks or on a separate sheet of paper.

Answering the

1. Students should support their opinions with information from the article or ideas discussed in class.

2. Dorothy Harper believes that dress codes keep students safe, set standards of behavior, and promote positive learning environments.

3. Leah Hawthorn says that she is able to be more focused and do better work when she can wear whatever she likes.

Critical Thinking

4. Students may say that a dress code could eliminate violence or misconduct associated with clothing.

5. Students may say schools will lose the sense of individuality and diversity among their students.

6. Responses will vary. Some students will see clothing as a means of self-expression because each student makes choices about what to wear.

304

After You Read · Dressed for Success?

Answering the **BIG Question**

1. After reading this article, are you for or against school dress codes or uniforms? Do you feel dress codes are fair to students?

2. **Recall** What does Leah Hawthorn say about how clothing affects schoolwork?

   Tip Right There

3. **Summarize** What does Dorothy Harper say about dress codes?

   Tip Think and Search

Critical Thinking

4. **Synthesize** Why might a dress code affect school attendance and suspensions?

   Tip On My Own

5. **Infer** Harper says that schools have more to gain than give up in regard to dress codes. What would schools be giving up if they adopted a dress code?

   Tip On My Own

6. **Evaluate** Is student clothing a form of self-expression? Explain.

   Tip On My Own

Talk About Your Reading

Suppose that your local school district is thinking about making students wear uniforms. Based on the arguments in "Dressed for Success?" discuss whether or not you agree or disagree with this decision, and explain your reasoning. For help, use a graphic organizer like the one below.

Objectives (pp. 304–305)
Reading Make inferences
Literature Understand characteristics of argument
Vocabulary Identify balanced language
Grammar Identify parts of speech: demonstrative adjectives, demonstrative pronouns

Should students wear uniforms?	
Agree Reasons:	**Disagree** Reasons:

304 UNIT 3 What's Fair and What's Not?

Talk About Your Reading

Possible response:
Agree. Reasons: School uniforms will keep students safe, encourage them to follow the rules, and keep their focus on learning.
Disagree. Reasons: School uniforms will take away students' rights to express themselves creatively; students will look alike and lose their sense of individuality.

Skills Review

Key Reading Skill: Inferring

7. When Dorothy Harper writes that a school's major responsibility is keeping students safe, can you infer anything about her experiences with schools?

Key Literary Element: Argument

8. Which writer (Harper or Lichtenstein) do you think makes a better argument? Why?

Vocabulary Check

9. Fill in the blanks with the correct vocabulary words.

   adopt   individuality   discipline

   Our school has strict ___ and rules.

   Last school year, our school decided to ___ a dress code.

   Some kids feel it stifles their ___, but I don't mind the dress code.

10. **Academic Vocabulary** Your friend tells you that the drama club meeting starts at 7:00. When you arrive, no one is there. What can you *infer* from this?

11. **English Language Coach** Review "Dressed for Success?" and find words or phrases that are examples of balanced language. Write down two sentences from the article that contain such words and underline the example or examples of balanced language in each.

Web Activities For eFlashcards, Selection Quick Checks, and other Web activities, go to www.glencoe.com.

Grammar Link: Demonstratives

The words *this, that, these,* and *those* are called **demonstratives.** They "demonstrate," or point out, people, places, or things.

- *This* and *these* point out people or things near to you. *That* and *those* point out people or things at a distance from you.
- *This* and *that* are singular demonstratives. Each refers to one thing. *These* and *those* are plural demonstratives. Each refers to more than one thing.

Demonstrative adjectives *This, that, these,* and *those* are called demonstrative adjectives when they describe nouns. They are followed by nouns.

- **That** bridge is unusual. (*That* describes bridge.)
- Look at **those** DVD players. (*Those* describes DVD players.)

Demonstrative pronouns *This, that, these,* and *those* are called demonstrative pronouns when they take the place of nouns and point out something.

- **This** is a glass dome. (*This* takes the place of the noun *dome* and points it out.)
- **Those** are large windows. (*Those* takes the place of the noun *windows* and points them out.)

Grammar Practice

Identify whether each demonstrative is an adjective or a pronoun.

12. **That** skirt does not follow the dress code.
13. **This** is mine.
14. **These** shirts are acceptable, but **those** are not.

Write the correct demonstrative adjective below.

15. (This, These) coats are the latest style.
16. (This, These) picture shows proper clothes to wear at school.
17. (This, That) girl down the hall wrote an editorial in favor of a dress code.
18. (This, That) leaflet I'm holding tells about the school dress code.

Dressed for Success? **305**

Skills Review

Key Lesson Skill: Inferring

7. Possible response: She has had to deal with safety issues in school before.

Key Literary Element: Argument

8. Responses will vary.

Vocabulary Check

9. discipline; adopt; individuality

10. **Academic Vocabulary** Sample response: You can infer that your friend gave you the wrong time or that the meeting has been canceled.

11. **English Language Coach** Possible responses: Schools that successfully adopt dress codes are <u>generally</u> safer, have more positive climates, and have a stronger sense of school pride.

   <u>Some</u> people say that dress codes and uniforms go against the right of freedom of expression.

Grammar Link: Demonstratives

Grammar Practice

12. adjective
13. pronoun
14. pronoun
15. These
16. This
17. That
18. This

Close

Ask students to summarize what they learned about fairness from reading "Dressed for Success?"

Teach

More About the Author

Sandra Cisneros was born in Chicago, Illinois. She was the only daughter in a family of seven children. She says her brothers' influence made her feel as if she had "seven fathers." Her writing draws on her experience as a Mexican American woman, which she says gives her writing *sabor* (flavor) and *picante* (spice).

EL Language Coach

Denotation and Connotation Say: When you are learning new vocabulary, labeling each descriptive word as positive or negative can help you learn what each word means and how it should be used. As you read "Eleven," note in your Learner's Notebooks the descriptive words Rachel uses. Put a plus sign (+) next to each positive word and a minus sign (−) next to each negative word. **EL** **OL**

Before You Read | Eleven

Sandra Cisneros

Meet the Author

Sandra Cisneros lives in San Antonio, Texas. She often writes about Latino children living in the United States. "Eleven," Cisneros said, "was my story except . . . it didn't happen at eleven (I was nine), . . . But I did cry. . . . Why did they pick me out? Because I was the one that looked like I belonged to something that shabby?" See page R2 of the Author Files in the back of the book for more on Sandra Cisneros.

Author Search For more about Sandra Cisneros, go to www.glencoe.com.

Objectives (pp. 306–311)
Reading Make inferences • Make connections from text to self
Literature Identify literary elements: repetition • Understand effects of repetition
Vocabulary Understand denotation and connotation • Identify uses of connotative meaning in semantic slanting

English Language Coach

Denotation and Connotation As you know, some words have a connotation—an extra meaning suggested by a word.

Some words have a positive connotation. For example, *slender* can suggest an appearance that is more attractive than *thin*. Some words have a negative connotation. For example, *cheap* often suggests something more negative than *inexpensive*.

Positive	Negative
young	childish
plump	fat
daring	reckless

Many connotations are neither positive nor negative. They're just feelings or ideas we associate with certain words. For example, the word *warrior* suggests an extra meaning that *soldier* doesn't have. It makes us think of a brave and mighty fighter from the past.

The words in this web are ways of *looking,* but each word has a different connotation. For example, when someone *stares* at you, it can be upsetting.

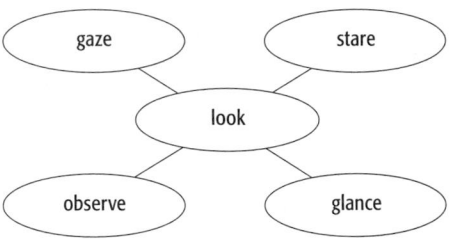

Partner Talk With a partner, talk about what each word says about ways of looking.

EL

Additional Support

Author Search To expand students' appreciation of Sandra Cisneros, have them access the Web site for additional information and resources.

Literature Focus Lesson

Similes Tell students that Rachel, the narrator of "Eleven," uses similes to help her describe what it is like to grow older. A simile is a comparison of unlike things that is introduced by *like* or *as*. Share the following similes from the story, and help students explain how the things are all like the way Rachel says as you grow older. Then, have students evaluate the similes: Do the similes help them understand what Rachel means about growing older?

• the way you grow old is . . .
  like an onion
  like the rings inside a tree trunk
  like little wooden dolls that fit one inside the other **OL**

Skills Preview

Key Reading Skill: Inferring

Sometimes people don't always say what they're thinking. It can be the same way in a story. Everything about a character isn't always stated. You'll see this in "Eleven." When you learn to draw inferences, reading becomes more interesting. You're more involved in the story. You will dig deeper into the characters and the plot.

Quick Write In your Learner's Notebook, write about a time—either at school, home, or elsewhere—when you kept your true feelings to yourself. What did you show outwardly and what did you hold inside you?

Literary Element: Repetition

Repetition is the frequent use of words or phrases in a story or poem for emphasis. A writer may use repetition to emphasize an idea or a feeling. For example, in the book "Millions of Cats" by Wanda Gag, the phrase *"hundreds of cats, thousands of cats, millions and billions and trillions of cats"* is repeated throughout the book.

As you read "Eleven," use these tips to help you understand repetition:

- Watch for the words and phrases that are repeated in the story.
  What do these particular words or phrases have to do with the story? What do they mean to the character?

- Pay attention to when repetition shows up in the story.
  What is going on in the story when you see the words and phrases? What is the character going through and feeling at that point?

- Pay attention to the sound or rhythm of the repeated words.
  How do they make you feel? Do they remind you of anything?

Get Ready to Read

Connect to the Reading

Have you ever been afraid to speak up for yourself? Have you ever been embarrassed in front of the whole class? As you read "Eleven," think of what you might do if these things happened to you.

Write to Learn Write about a time when you should have stood up for yourself, but you didn't. To help you organize your thoughts use the bullets below:

- What happened:
- What I did:
- What the result was:
- What I should have done:
- What would have been the result:

Set Purposes for Reading

BIG Question Read "Eleven" to find out if what happens to Rachel is fair or not.

Set Your Own Purpose What else would you like to learn from the selection to help you answer the Big Question? Write your own purpose on the "Eleven" page of Foldable 3.

Interactive Literary Elements Handbook
To review or learn more about the literary elements, go to www.glencoe.com.

Keep Moving

Use these skills as you read the following selection.

Teach

R Reading Skill

Inferring Say: Say your best friend has just tried out for a sports team. She comes up to you, looks at her feet, and then bursts into tears. What would you infer without her saying a word? What clues would you have used? *(Possible responses: You could infer she did not make the team. You would have used her body language and her tears to help you infer this.)* OL

L Literary Element

Repetition Say: Suppose your big brother told you three times to meet him by the gym at 3 o'clock. Why might he have repeated this information? *(Possible response: He doesn't want you to forget it.)* OL

Interactive Literary Elements Handbook Have students access the Web site to improve their understanding of repetition.

English Language Coach

Semantic Slanting To help students better understand the use of semantic slanting, point out that advertisements often feature this technique. Share a newspaper or magazine ad with the class, noting that the terms used to describe the advertised product are positive. Conversely, any description of competitors' products is likely negative. Tell students to design their own magazine ads, using semantic slanting that favors their product over competitors' products. **EL BL**

Objectives
- Make inferences
- Identify literary elements: repetition
- Identify literary devices: similes
- Understand denotation and connotation

Teach

R1 Reading Skill

Inferring Ask: What does Rachel tell her mother when her mother needs to cry? *(that maybe she's feeling three)* **BL**
Ask: What can you infer about how Rachel feels about her mother? *(I can infer that Rachel cares deeply for her mother and wants to comfort her mother when she is sad.)* **AL**

R2 Reading Skill

Review Connecting
Ask: Why do you think that older children are expected to cry less often than younger children? *(Possible responses: Older children are supposed to be able to control their emotions and find other ways to cope with their problems.)* **OL Ask:** Do you think that expectations for older children are always fair? Explain. *(Responses will vary.)* **AS**

Readability Scores
Dale-Chall: 4.2
DRP: 52
Lexile: 1090

Eleven

by Sandra Cisneros

What they don't understand about birthdays and what they never tell you is that when you're eleven, you're also ten, and nine, and eight, and seven, and six, and five, and four, and three, and two, and one. And when you wake up on your eleventh birthday you expect to feel eleven, but you don't. You open your eyes and everything's just like yesterday, only it's today. And you don't feel eleven at all. You feel like you're still ten. And you are—underneath the year that makes you eleven. **1**

R1 ⌐ Like some days you might say something stupid, and that's the part of you that's still ten. Or maybe some days you might need to sit on your mama's lap because you're scared, and that's the part of you that's five. And maybe one day when you're all grown up maybe you will need to cry like if you're three, and that's okay. That's what I tell Mama when she's sad and needs to cry. Maybe she's feeling three. **2**

Because the way you grow old is kind of like an onion or like the rings inside a tree trunk[1] or like my little wooden dolls that fit one inside the other, each year inside the next one. That's how being eleven years old is.

---

1. If something is *like the rings inside a tree trunk*, it has layers that show its age. Each ring in a tree trunk is a layer of wood added during a single growth period.

308 UNIT 3 What's Fair and What's Not?

Practice the Skills

1 Key Reading Skill

Inferring The narrator explains that "underneath" eleven you are also ten, nine, eight, and so on. She also says that you expect to feel different when you wake up on your birthday, but you don't. How do you think the narrator feels when she wakes up on her eleventh birthday?

2 Reviewing Skills

Connecting Can you think of a time when you were expected to act your age, but you wanted to act as though you were younger? **R2** Do you agree or disagree with the narrator's thoughts about age? Explain.

Additional Support

 Leveled Reading An adapted version of this selection (4th grade readability) is available on page 92 of **Jamestown Adapted Literature** for Grade 6.

Differentiated Instruction

Illustrating Have students draw a picture to illustrate this story. Encourage students to look for details in the text, such as the color and description of the sweater, to help guide them as they draw. Students might like to add their own details, such as how they imagine Mrs. Price might look, as they draw. Students should share their pictures with the class, explaining what aspect of the story they have illustrated. **EL BL OL**

You don't feel eleven. Not right away. It takes a few days, weeks even, sometimes even months before you say Eleven when they ask you. And you don't feel smart eleven, not until you're almost twelve. That's the way it is.

Only today I wish I didn't have only eleven years rattling inside me like pennies in a tin Band-Aid box. Today I wish I was one hundred and two instead of eleven because if I was one hundred and two I'd have known what to say when Mrs. Price put the red sweater on my desk. I would've known how to tell her it wasn't mine instead of just sitting there with that look on my face and nothing coming out of my mouth.

"Whose is this?" Mrs. Price says, and she holds the red sweater up in the air for all the class to see. "Whose? It's been sitting in the coatroom for a month."

"Not mine," says everybody. "Not me." "It has to belong to somebody," Mrs. Price keeps saying, but nobody can remember. It's an ugly sweater with red plastic buttons and a collar and sleeves all stretched out like you could use it for a jump rope. It's maybe a thousand years old and even if it belonged to me I wouldn't say so.

Maybe because I'm **skinny**, maybe because she doesn't like me, that stupid Sylvia Saldívar[2] says, "I think it belongs to Rachel." An ugly sweater like that, all raggedy and old, but Mrs. Price believes her. Mrs. Price takes the sweater and puts it right on my desk, but when I open my mouth nothing comes out. **3 4**

"That's not, I don't, you're not . . . Not mine," I finally say in a little voice that was maybe me when I was four.

"Of course it's yours," Mrs. Price says. "I remember you wearing it once." Because she's older and the teacher, she's right and I'm not.

Not mine, not mine, not mine, but Mrs. Price is already turning to page thirty-two, and math problem number four. I don't know why but all of a sudden I'm feeling sick inside, like the part of me that's three wants to come out of my eyes, only I squeeze them shut tight and bite down on my teeth real hard and try to remember today I am eleven, eleven. Mama is making a cake for me for tonight, and when Papa comes home everybody will sing Happy birthday, happy birthday to you. **5**

_____
2. *Saldívar* (sa DEE var)

Practice the Skills

3 **Key Reading Skill**

Inferring What can you infer from the sentence "An ugly sweater like that . . . but Mrs. Price believes her."

4 **English Language Coach**

Denotation and Connotation The denotation of **skinny** is "very thin." What do you think the connotation of *skinny* is? Do you think that the narrator is suggesting that she likes the way she looks or not?

5 **Literary Element**

Repetition There are three examples of repetition in this paragraph. What are they? Why do you think the author repeated these words and phrases? When you read them does it make you think of anything? Does it remind you of anything?

Teach

R **Reading Skill**

Inferring Ask: Why do you think Rachel has trouble correcting her teacher? (*Possible response: Rachel may be afraid of making her teacher angry. She may also be worried that it would seem disrespectful to argue with her teacher.*) **OL**

L1 **Literary Element**

Repetition Say: Why do you think Rachel repeats the phrase "not mine" so many times? (*Possible response: The repetition shows how much she wants people to know that the sweater is not hers.*) **BL**

L2 **Literary Element**

Repetition Say: "Happy birthday" is usually a kind greeting from a friend or loved one. Why does Rachel repeat this phrase to herself on her birthday? (*Possible response: Rachel repeats "happy birthday" to distract herself from her unhappiness. She wants to be excited about her party in the evening.*) **AL**

English Language Coach

Descriptive Words Students may not be familiar with the words Rachel uses to describe the sweater she dislikes so much. Invite students to use dictionaries and other resources to familiarize themselves with these terms. After students have found definitions for the words, ask them to write two sentences describing the sweater in their own words.

- ugly
- red plastic buttons
- collar
- sleeves all stretched out
- raggedy **BL** **EL**

Objectives
- Make inferences
- Identify literary elements: repetition
- Make connections from text to self

Teach

R1 Reading Skill

Inferring **Ask:** Why do you think Rachel is so upset when the teacher forces her to wear the sweater? *(Possible response: Rachel thinks that the sweater is ugly, and she doesn't want the other students to think that she would own such an ugly sweater.)* **OL**

R2 Reading Skill

Inferring **Ask:** Do you think the teacher understands what Rachel is feeling? Why or why not? *(Possible response: The teacher seems busy with her class and does not understand why Rachel would refuse to take the sweater.)* **AL**

But when the sick feeling goes away and I open my eyes, the red sweater's still sitting there like a big red mountain. I move the red sweater to the corner of my desk with my ruler. I move my pencil and books and eraser as far from it as possible. I even move my chair a little to the right. Not mine, not mine, not mine.

In my head I'm thinking how long till lunchtime, how long till I can take the red sweater and throw it over the schoolyard fence, or leave it hanging on a parking meter, or bunch it up into a little ball and toss it in the alley. Except when math period ends Mrs. Price says loud and in front of everybody, "Now, Rachel, that's enough," because she sees I've shoved the red sweater to the tippy-tip corner of my desk and it's hanging all over the edge like a waterfall, but I don't care.

"Rachel," Mrs. Price says. She says it like she's getting mad. "You put that sweater on right now and no more nonsense."

"But it's not—"

"Now!" Mrs. Price says.

R1 This is when I wish I wasn't eleven, because all the years inside of me—ten, nine, eight, seven, six, five, four, three, two, and one—are pushing at the back of my eyes when I put one arm through one sleeve of the sweater that smells like cottage cheese, and then the other arm through the other and stand there with my arms apart like if the sweater hurts me and it does, all itchy and full of germs that aren't even mine. **6**

R2 That's when everything I've been holding in since this morning, since when Mrs. Price put the sweater on my desk, finally lets go, and all of a sudden I'm crying in front of everybody. I wish I was invisible but I'm not. I'm eleven and it's my birthday today and I'm crying like I'm three in front of everybody. I put my head down on the desk and bury my face in my stupid clown-sweater arms. My face all hot and spit coming out of my mouth because I can't stop the little animal noises from coming out of me, until there aren't any more tears left in my eyes, and it's just my body shaking like when you have the hiccups, and my whole head hurts like when you drink milk too fast.

Practice the Skills

6 | **Literary Element**

Repetition What is the repetition here in this paragraph? Why do you think the writer decided to reemphasize the ages again? How is Rachel feeling right now?

Additional Support

English Language Coach

Long Sentences Direct students to reread the second-to-last paragraph on page 310 (the one that starts "This is when I wish I wasn't eleven . . . "). Point out that this paragraph is a single long sentence. Have students work in pairs to rewrite this sentence as several shorter sentences. Tell them that they may add or eliminate words to make the sentences flow more smoothly. Ask volunteers to present their sentences to the class. As a class, discuss which form students prefer and brainstorm possible reasons why the author expresses the character's thoughts in such a long sentence. **EL BL**

R I wish I was invisible but I'm not.

But the worst part is right before the bell rings for lunch. That stupid Phyllis Lopez, who is even dumber than Sylvia Saldívar, says she remembers the red sweater is hers! I take it off right away and give it to her, only Mrs. Price pretends like everything's okay.

Today I'm eleven. There's a cake Mama's making for tonight, and when Papa comes home from work we'll eat it. There'll be candles and presents and everybody will sing Happy birthday, happy birthday to you, Rachel, only it's too late.

I'm eleven today. I'm eleven, ten, nine, eight, seven, six, five, four, three, two, and one, but I wish I was one hundred and two. I wish I was anything but eleven, because I want today to be far away already, far away like a runaway balloon, like a tiny *o* in the sky, so tiny-tiny you have to close your eyes to see it. **7** ○

Analyzing the Art Do you think this painting expresses the narrator's feelings in the story's last sentence? Explain your answer.

Practice the Skills

7

What would Rachel say about what's fair and what's not? Record your response on the "Eleven" page of Foldable 3. Your answer will help you complete the Unit Challenge later. **BQ**

Eleven **311**

Teach

R Reading Skill

Inferring Ask: Why do you think Rachel wishes she were "invisible"? *(Possible responses: Rachel is unhappy and embarrassed. She doesn't want people to see her crying.)* **BL**

BQ **BIG Question**

Ask: Do you think that Rachel's teacher treated her fairly? Why or why not? *(Possible response: She did not treat Rachel fairly. She should have apologized after she learned the sweater was not hers.)* **OL**

Assess

CheckPoint

Use the CheckPoint questions provided on Presentation Plus! to check for comprehension of the selection. These questions can be used with interactive response keypads for immediate student feedback.

Differentiated Instruction

Role Playing In "Eleven," a misunderstanding between Rachel and her teacher leads to Rachel feeling miserable on her birthday. Have students form pairs and imagine they are Rachel, and Mrs. Price has just put the sweater on their desk. Tell them to write a script in which Rachel politely explains her point of view and Mrs. Price responds. Have partners present their scripts to the class. Encourage classmates to provide constructive feedback. Does Rachel do a good job of defending herself? Does Mrs. Price's response seem realistic? **OL**

Objectives
• Make inferences
• Identify literary elements: repetition

311

Assess

Resources for page 312

📁 Selection Quick Check, p. 26

📁 Selection and Unit Assessment, p. 30

💿 Exam View Assessment Suite

💿 Interactive Tutor: Self-Assessment

Students can respond to the *After You Read* items in their Learner's Notebooks or on a separate sheet of paper.

Answering the BIG Question

1. Responses will vary. Students may say that the teacher should listen to Rachel. Other students may say that Rachel does not voice her objection strongly enough.

2. The teacher believes another student who says that the sweater belongs to Rachel.

3. The teacher makes Rachel put on the ugly sweater.

Critical Thinking

4. Rachel thinks the sweater is dirty and ugly, and she doesn't want to touch it.

5. Possible response: Rachel is so upset that her birthday seems ruined, but her family will probably make her feel better. If I were her, getting to be the center of my family's attention would make me feel better after such a bad day.

312

After You Read : Eleven

Answering the BIG Question

1. Do you think that Rachel is treated fairly? Explain.

2. **Recall** Why does the teacher think the red sweater belongs to Rachel?
   TIP Right There

3. **Recall** What does the teacher make Rachel do?
   TIP Right There

Critical Thinking

4. **Infer** Why does Rachel move the sweater to the edge of her desk with a ruler and move her belongings away from the sweater?
   TIP Author and Me

5. **Connect** Early in the story, the narrator says that a birthday party at home later should make her feel better. Do you think it will? Would it make you feel better if you were in her situation?
   TIP Author and Me

Write About Your Reading

Use the RAFT system to write about "Eleven." A RAFT assignment provides four details:

R is for your *role* as a writer—who or what you must pretend to be as you write.

A stands for your *audience*—the person or group who will read what you write.

F means *format*—the form for your writing, such as a letter or a speech.

T means *topic*—what your writing should be about.

Role: Write as if you were Mrs. Price, Sylvia Saldívar, or Phyllis Lopez.

Audience: Write to yourself.

Format: A journal entry

Topic: Rewrite what happened about the sweater from your point of view (first-person). Remember that when you use the first-person point of view, the narrator is speaking and using the pronoun *I*.

Objectives (pp. 312–313)
Reading Make inferences • Make connections from text to self
Literature Identify literary elements: repetition • Understand effects of repetition
Vocabulary Understand denotation and connotation
Writing Use the RAFT system: respond to literature
Grammar Identify parts of speech: definite and indefinite articles

Write About Your Reading

Possible response:

Dear Journal,
Today I pulled a trick on Rachel. Mrs. Price found Phyllis's old, ugly sweater in the closet. I told Mrs. Price it belonged to Rachel! Rachel always wears such pretty clothes, so it serves her right. But then Rachel started to cry, and I felt really sorry for her. I didn't know how to make it better. I didn't realize it was her birthday, or I wouldn't have teased her. Phyllis and I decided that tomorrow we'll try to be a little nicer to Rachel. We're going to tell her that we're sorry about messing up her birthday.
—Sylvia

Skills Review

Key Reading Skill: Inferring

6. On page 309 Rachel says "the part of me that's three wants to come out of my eyes . . ." What can you infer is happening to Rachel?

7. At the end of the story Mrs. Price "pretends like everything is okay." What can you infer about what Rachel wanted Mrs. Price to do?

Literary Element: Repetition

8. Rachel believes that people are made up of every age they have ever been. She thinks, "when you're eleven, you're also ten, and nine, and eight, and seven, and six, and five, and four, and three, and two, and one." What does the repetition of ages tell you about Rachel?

9. Find another example of repetition in "Eleven." Tell what that example adds to the story.

Reviewing Skills: Connecting

10. Do you agree that your younger ages still live inside of you? Explain.

Vocabulary Check

11. Academic Vocabulary You see your friend after his or her basketball game. He or she looks sad and angry. What can you infer about the results of the game?

12. English Language Coach The denotation of *snake* is "a scaly, legless reptile." Its connotation might involve something sneaky or wicked. In your Learner's Notebook write the denotation of *kitten.* Then write its connotation.

Literature Online

Web Activities For eFlashcards, Selection Quick Checks, and other Web activities, go to www.glencoe.com.

Grammar Link: Articles

The words *a, an,* and *the* make up a special group of adjectives called **articles.**

- *A* and *an* are called **indefinite** articles. They refer to any one item of a group of people, places, things, or ideas.

  *She bought **a** ticket.*

- Use *a* before words that begin with a consonant sound.

  a pilot   **a** space ship

- Use *an* before words that begin with a vowel sound.

  an hour   **an** astronaut

- *The* is a **definite** article. It indicates that the noun is a specific person, place, or thing.

  *She liked **the** movie.*

  *Neil Armstrong was **the** first man to walk on **the** moon.*

Grammar Practice

On a separate sheet of paper, tell whether the bolded articles are indefinite or definite.

13. The way you grow old is like **an** onion.

14. The hat's been left in **the** coatroom for **a** month.

15. The red sweater's still sitting there, like **a** big red mountain.

16. Your smile is **the** part of you that I like best.

Now write each word or group of words with the correct indefinite article—*a* or *an.*

17. birthday

18. onion

19. tree trunk

20. wooden doll

21. ugly sweater

22. eraser

Writing Application Look back at the RAFT assignment you wrote. Make sure that the definite and indefinite articles you used are correct.

Eleven **313**

Skills Review

Key Reading Skill: Inferring

6. Possible response: She wants to cry like a 3-year-old might.

7. Possible response: Rachel wanted Mrs. Price to tell the class that the sweater did not belong to Rachel.

Literary Element: Repetition

8. Possible response: The repetition of ages shows that Rachel feels different ages at different times in her life.

9. Rachel repeats that her mother has made her a cake and that her family will eat it together. The repetition emphasizes her parents' love and concern for her.

Reviewing Skills: Connecting

10. Responses will vary.

Vocabulary Check

11. Academic Vocabulary Possible response: that his or her team lost the game

12. English Language Coach Sample responses: baby, sweet

Close

Ask students to summarize what they thought was unfair about Rachel's situation and what could have been done to make it fairer.

Grammar Link: Articles

Grammar Practice

13. *the*: definite; *an*: indefinite

14. *the*: definite; *a*: indefinite

15. *the*: definite; *a*: indefinite

16. *the*: definite

17. a birthday

18. an onion

19. a tree trunk

20. a wooden doll

21. an ugly sweater

22. an eraser

Focus

BELLRINGER Options

- **Daily Language Transparency 27 Focus Activity Ask:** How is persuasive writing different from other forms of writing that you have done? *(Responses will vary.)* **OL**

Teach

W Writing

Word Choice Say: As you revise your persuasive essay, use the following tips:

- Aim for strong words and phrases that grab your readers' attention.
- Choose words that represent your feelings and viewpoint.
- Look up synonyms for words that best express the exact meaning you want. **OL**

Resources for page 314

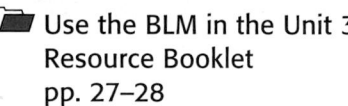

- Use the BLM in the Unit 3 Resource Booklet pp. 27–28
- Use the Grammar and Writing Workshop Transparencies 21–22

ASSIGNMENT Write a persuasive essay

Purpose: Write an essay that argues either for or against a specific issue and persuade others to agree with you

Audience: You, your teacher, and classmates

Revising Rubric

Your revised essay should have

- evidence to support your opinion
- responses to possible counterarguments
- five paragraphs that include an introduction, a body, and a conclusion
- transitions to improve sentence fluency
- adjectives and adverbs used correctly

Objectives (pp. 314–317)
Writing Write persuasively • Revise writing for key elements, style, and word choice • Present writing
Listening, Speaking, and Viewing Speak effectively • Use persuasive techniques

---

Persuasive Essay
Revising, Editing, and Presenting

You've already chosen a topic, organized your ideas, and written the first draft of your essay. Great work! Now it's time to revise your draft and share your work with an audience.

Revising
Make It Better

Revising is your chance to make changes to your writing. You may need to write more in places where your draft seems unclear. Or, you may need to delete parts of your draft that repeat or are unnecessary.

Check Your Draft

Read over your draft and add missing information. The questions below will help you decide what to revise.

- Does the introduction explain the unfair situation?
- Is your position stated clearly?
- Does the body of your essay have three main paragraphs?
- Does each paragraph include a main point about why the topic is unfair?
- Does each paragraph have evidence to support your main points?
- Is your evidence in the best and most persuasive order?

You probably answered "no" to some of the questions. That's okay! Drafts are not supposed to be perfect. You may need to think of more evidence to support your main points or write a stronger introduction to interest readers. Go back and make the necessary improvements to your essay.

Say It Like You Mean It

Your persuasive essay should be about an issue that you feel strongly about. Use words that express your emotions or personal views. Use detailed arguments. If your readers feel that you really know and care about the issue, they will be more willing to listen to your argument. Consider these examples.

W

> *Following a dress code makes students feel like robots. After a few weeks we get tired of seeing the same colors and outfits every day.*

Additional Support

Differentiated Instruction

Visual Aids Students may want to include visual aids to support their argument. This will give students an opportunity to express their ideas in a different format. Students could create bumper stickers, collages, a picture or painting, a personally decorated T-shirt, or a poster. Students should present their visual aids to the class when they present their essays. **AL**

> Students should not have to wear the same clothes.
> Following a dress code is a bad idea.

The first example is more persuasive because it is more descriptive. It lets the reader know not only that the writer thinks that dress codes are a bad idea but also *why* they are a bad idea. The use of descriptions such as "feel like robots" puts some emotion into the writing as well.

Editing
Finish It Up

Now you are ready to edit your persuasive essay. Read your essay and look for errors in grammar, punctuation, and usage. Follow the editing checklist to spot your errors.

Editing Checklist

☑ All sentences end with correct punctuation.
☑ Each paragraph begins on a new line.
☑ All names are capitalized.
☑ Commas and apostrophes are used correctly.
☑ Spelling is correct.

Finally, take one last look at the language of your essay. Does the writing sound like you really *mean* what you're saying? Could you add an adjective or adverb to make a sentence stronger? Double check that you used the most persuasive language and chose the most effective words.

Presenting
Show It Off

Read your essay to a small group of classmates. As you read, make sure to vary the volume and pitch of your voice to emphasize the main points of your essay. You have spent a lot of time writing your essay, now is your chance to persuade a real audience. Read with enthusiasm to show your classmates that you really care about this topic.

Literature Online
Writing Models For models and other writing activities, go to www.glencoe.com.

◄ Writing Tip
Proofreading Make sure that you have used the correct forms of superlative and comparative adjectives and adverbs. **W1**

◄ Writing Tip
Proofreading The normal way to form an adverb is to add -*ly,* as in *commonly, slowly,* or *nervously.* However, there are exceptions: If the word already ends -*ll,* just add -*y* (for example, *fully*). **W2**

◄ Writing Tip
Spelling Break long words into small parts to help you remember how they are spelled. For example, you could break the following words:
busi/ness
to/mor/row

Teach

Literature Online
Writing Models Have students access the Web site for an additional interactive Writing Workshop-based student model.

W1 Writing

Proofreading Say: The best way to proofread your work is to check for one kind of error at a time. For example, you might first check to make sure that you have clearly expressed your thoughts and feelings. On a second read, you might make sure all sentences are complete. This way, you will be able to focus on one thing at a time. **OL**

W2 Writing

Proofreading Say: Think about the language you used. Have you used the most persuasive language and chosen the most effective words? Will your words grab readers' attention and hold it? **AS**

Reading Fluency

Reading Models To develop fluency, students need models. Ask volunteers who have problems with fluency to listen to you read their persuasive essays aloud. Then, choose several sentences from each student's essay, read each sentence aloud, and ask the student to repeat the sentence back to you, mimicking your speed, tone, and phrasing. Next, invite the student to read the entire essay aloud to you. Assess each student's fluency by noting the problems the student is still having. Use this session to identify each student's fluency needs. **EL BL**

Objectives
• Write persuasively
• Use persuasive techniques
• Revise writing for key elements, style, and word choice

Teach

W1 Writing

Persuasive Writing

Ask: How does the introduction grab readers' attention? *(Possible response: The first sentence is shocking—a boy had to go to the emergency room. It also mentions that he is a fellow student, so readers will be particularly interested in finding out what made him have to go to the emergency room.)* **OL**

W2 Writing

Evaluate: Ask: Do you agree with the writer's last reason for the dress code being unfair? Explain. *(Responses will vary.)* **BL** Do you think ending with an emotional appeal helps persuade readers? Explain. *(Responses will vary.)* **OL**

Assess

Have students tell what they learned about persuading others.

Active Writing Model

Writer's Model

W1 The introduction grabs the reader's attention.

The writer states the issue and proposes a solution.

The writer responds to counterarguments to help convince readers the dress code is unfair.

The writer provides evidence to support a point.

This transition word increases the fluency of the essay.

This transition phrase links two sentences about the same topic. Transition phrases make writing more fluent.

Ending the essay with an emotional appeal helps persuade readers to agree with the writer's argument.

> The Hope Middle School dress code caused student Jimmy Albert to spend his Friday night at the emergency room. Jimmy sprained his ankle playing basketball during afternoon recess. His sprain was caused because the dress shoes he was wearing did not provide enough support for basic recess activities. Jimmy's injury is one of several reasons why it is unfair for students to have to follow a dress code. I suggest the school dress code be changed to allow jeans and sneakers.
>
> According to our principal, the dress code prevents distractions and helps students focus on learning. I disagree. Dressy clothes are distracting because the pants are itchy and dress shoes cause our feet to hurt. As a result, uncomfortable clothes actually distract students from schoolwork.
>
> The second reason the dress code is unfair is because dress clothes are expensive. Many families at our school live on a tight budget and don't have money to invest on clothes that are only worn at school. This expense is unfair to parents who are struggling to make ends meet and students who can't afford to buy other clothes. Blue jeans are a practical alternative because they don't wear out quickly and they are easy to clean.
>
> Finally, wearing a uniform makes students feel like robots. After a few weeks we get tired of seeing the same outfits and colors every day. Students should be allowed to express themselves through the clothes they choose to wear. In fact, making students conform to a dress code shows disrespect for the student's ability to make decisions. **W2**
>
> A dress code does not help students focus on learning. Students like Jimmy shouldn't have to worry about hurting themselves during recess. I propose allowing jeans and sneakers to be part of the school dress code immediately, before another student gets hurt.

Additional Support

English Language Coach

Multiple-Meaning Words Tell students that the word *code* has a couple of different meanings. It can mean a system of rules of conduct, such as a moral code, a code of ethics, or, as it is used in the essay, a dress code. It is also a system of communication in which sounds, light flashes, or other signals represent numbers, letters, or words to send by telegraph. Have students search through their essays to find words that have multiple meanings. As a class, create a list of these words and encourage students to write the words and all of their definitions. **EL BL**

Listening, Speaking, and Viewing

Effective Speaking

You don't always persuade other people in writing. Sometimes you have to persuade using your voice and body language. Effective speaking is an important part of sharing your ideas and opinions with others.

What Is Effective Speaking?

Effective speaking is being able to communicate your thoughts and ideas clearly through the spoken word.

Why Is Effective Speaking Important?

Sometimes you have to speak for more important reasons, like giving directions, explaining a process, or making a speech. In these situations, it is important that you express yourself to your listeners as clearly as possible. Effective speakers use more than just their voice to express themselves—they also use their eyes, arms, hands, and feet.

How Do I Do It?

To practice effective speaking, choose a passage or paragraph from a Unit 3 reading selection and read it aloud to your classmates.

Once you have chosen a passage, read it silently to yourself. Then follow the tips below for reading it aloud to a small group.

1. Voice

- Speak loudly enough to be heard easily by the rest of your group.
- Speak clearly so that each word you say is distinct.
- Keep a steady tempo—don't speak too slowly or too fast.
- Match the tone of your voice to the tone of your passage.

2. Face

- Keep your head up! Look at your audience, and move your eyes from person to person.
- Use facial expressions. Smile, raise an eyebrow, or roll your eyes to express emotions that are conveyed in your speech.

3. Body

- Make gestures with your hands and arms to help describe what you are saying. Words like *huge* and *tiny,* and phrases like *over there, I have an idea,* and *come here* can easily include a gesture.
- Keep your audience's attention by standing up and acting out parts of your passage as you speak.

Don't forget to practice your reading a few times before presenting it to your group—the more you practice, the better you will sound! **LSV**

Analyzing the Photo
What does the "thumbs up" gesture mean? What might you be speaking about when you use this gesture?

Teach

LSV Listening, Speaking, and Viewing

Preparing to Speak Say: As you prepare your presentation, answer the following questions:

- What is the tone of the passage? What attitude do I need to communicate to my audience?
- How can I use my voice and my body to communicate this attitude?
- What is the theme or message of the passage?
- How can I use my voice and my body to communicate this message?

After you answer these questions, mark a copy of the passage as a script for presentation, including notes about how you will use your voice, facial expressions, and gestures. **OL**

Assess/Close

Lead students in a discussion about the effect of voice, expressions, and gestures on speaking. How do these elements help a speaker communicate a message? How do these elements affect the audience?

Reading in the Real World

Citizenship Invite groups of students to use the information on this page to create rubrics for effective speaking. Provide students with a sample rubric to use as a model. Then, show students a video of a famous speech, such as Martin Luther King Jr.'s *I Have a Dream* speech or a presidential speech. Have students use their rubrics to evaluate the speech. What does the speaker do well? What advice do the students have for improving the speaker's delivery? Then, give students time to practice reading their passages aloud with partners. Encourage students to use their rubrics to provide their partners with constructive feedback. **OL**

Objectives

- Practice and use effective speaking techniques
- Analyze persuasive writing
- Use context clues: multiple-meaning words
- Use appropriate expressions and gestures

Identifying Problems and Solutions

Objectives covered in this workshop:
• Analyze and evaluate problem and solution text structure
• Explain how setting influences problem and solution

Teaching Students to Identify Problems and Solutions

Why Is It Important?

• Many informational texts are written around common text structures (cause-effect, sequence, description, and problem-solution); teaching students to identify the structure helps them comprehend the text.

• Problem-solution text structure is one of the most common structures found in scientific, technical, and social sciences texts, so students with a strong grasp of this structure will realize an improved ability to read across the curriculum.

How to Help Students Get It

• Emphasize the importance of understanding text structure in comprehending texts; review the common structures with a focus on problem-solution.

• Give text previews in which you use talk-alouds to alert student to headings, key phrases, or illustrations in a sample of text that gives clues that it is a problem-solution format.

• Provide guided practice in which students can skim and scan various texts—for example, photocopies of text pages, and mark problems with one notation and solutions with another (underlining in color; using notion marks like "P" [problem] and "S" [solution]).

Reading to Answer the Big Question

from **50 Simple Things Kids Can Do to Save the Earth** by the EarthWorks Group
This excerpt focuses on recycling paper. The authors explain why they believe it is fair to expect students to recycle and suggest many practical ideas on how to do it.

Greyling by Jane Yolen
A fisherman and his wife long for children. One day the fisherman brings home a stranded seal pup that turns out to be a selchie—a seal in water and a human on land. Years later the selchie child they have named Greyling goes into the sea to save the fisherman from drowning. When he does not come back, the couple must decide whether or not it is fair for him to stay in the sea.

Workshop Resources

PACING (DAYS)		LESSON	STUDENT MATERIALS	TEACHER RESOURCES
STANDARD	BLOCK			
1	1/2	Key Skill Lesson: Identifying Problem and Solution	🐾 Key Reading Skills Practice, p. 29 🐾 English Language Coach, p. 41	🖐 Bellringer Options Transparencies –Daily Language Practice 28 🖐 Read Aloud, Think Aloud Transparencies –Key Reading Skills 11 ⊙ Presentation Plus!
1	1	from *50 Simple Things Kids Can Do to Save the Earth*	💻 Glencoe Online 🐾 Unit Vocabulary Review, p. 39 🐾 Academic Vocabulary Review, p. 42 📁 English Language Coach 🐾 Active Reading Graphic Organizer, p. 31 🐾 Literary Analysis, p. 30 ⊙ StudentWorks Plus™ 💻 Online Student Edition ⊙ Literature Classics 📁 Selection and Unit Assessments, p. 31	🖐 Literary and Text Analysis Transparencies 31 💻 Puzzlemaker ⊙ Skill Level Up!™ A Language Arts Game 💻 BookLink 3 📕 Assessment by Learning Objective (Diagnostic and Formative) ⊙ Interactive Tutor: Self-Assessment ⊙ TeacherWorks Plus™
1		"Greyling"	💻 Glencoe Online 🐾 Unit Vocabulary Review, p. 39 🐾 Academic Vocabulary Review, p. 42 📁 English Language Coach 🐾 Active Reading Graphic Organizer, p. 33 🐾 Literary Analysis, p. 30 ⊙ StudentWorks Plus™ 💻 Online Student Edition ⊙ Literature Classics 📁 Selection and Unit Assessments, p. 32	🖐 Literary and Text Analysis Transparencies 31 💻 Puzzlemaker ⊙ Skill Level Up!™ A Language Arts Game 💻 BookLink 3 📕 Assessment by Learning Objective (Diagnostic and Formative) ⊙ Interactive Tutor: Self-Assessment ⊙ TeacherWorks Plus™

Keys for Unit Resource

📁 Blackline Master   🔘 DVD

📕 Workbook   🖐 Transparency

📖 Supplemental Text   💻 Web-based

⊙ CD-ROM   🐾 Fast File

Level Appropriate Code

AS = Activities for all students

AL = Activities for students working above grade level

OL = Activities for students working at grade level

BL = Activities for students working below grade level

EL = Activities for English language learners

Focus

BELLRINGER Options

📌 **Daily Language Practice Transparency 28**
Focus Activity Ask: When was the last time you had a hard time solving a problem? What was the problem? How did it work out in the end? Were you happy about the solution? Write for five minutes in your journals describing the problem, its solution, your role in the solution, and your feelings about it. *(Responses will vary.)* **AS**

Teach

R Reading Skill

Identifying Problems and Solutions Say: Every day you encounter problems, from little ones to big ones. Each problem has a variety of possible solutions. It is your job to figure out which is the best solution. Review your journal writing for the Bellringer Focus Activity. List one other way that your problem could have been solved. When you read literature, you should identify the problem presented in the text and then think of how you would solve it. Compare your ideas to the ones the author presents in the text. **OL**

Skills Focus

You will practice using these skills when you read the following selections:
- "from *50 Simple Things Kids Can Do to Save the Earth*," p. 322
- "Greyling," p. 328

Reading

- Identifying problems and solutions

Literature

- Understanding mood

Vocabulary

- Understanding synonyms and shades of meaning

Writing/Grammar

- Identifying prepositions
- Identifying interjections

Objectives (pp. 318–319)
Reading Identify problems and solutions

Skill Lesson

Identifying Problems and Solutions

Learn It!

What Is It? What will happen to Richelle who is sick and can't keep up with her homework? How will Safa make friends in a new school where no one speaks her language? How will Sean get home if his bike has a flat tire? What will Dippy, the Talking Dog, do when she is attacked by an angry ostrich? Problems make stories interesting. Some problems are very serious and some may be humorous. When **R** identifying **problems and solutions** in a text, you need to figure out what the obstacles or conflicts are and how they are overcome. Authors may use words such as *need, attempt, help, problem,* or *obstruction* when they write about

- fights, disagreements, or arguments.
- challenges or obstacles.
- questions or mysteries.

CALVIN AND HOBBES © 1993 Watterson. Dist. By UNIVERSAL PRESS SYNDICATE. Reprinted with permission. All rights reserved.

Analyzing Cartoons
Do you think that Calvin has found a good solution to his problem? Explain.

Additional Support

English Language Coach

Vocabulary and Concept Write on the board: *conflict, fight, resolve, disagreement, overcome, argument, challenge, obstacle, solve, work out,* and *obstruction.* Have students draw a two-column chart in their vocabulary notebooks. Tell them to label the first column *Problem* and the second *Solution.* Then, have them work with partners to place the words on the board into the appropriate columns. Finally, have students discuss the meanings of each of the words, clarifying the subtle differences in denotation and connotation. Challenge students to use each word in an original sentence. **EL**

Why Is It Important? Finding the problems and solutions in a selection will help you understand what's happening and why. If you know that a story is about a girl searching for her missing parents, you'll know which events are key parts of the story. Understanding problems and solutions may even help you solve your own problems.

How Do I Do It? As you read, ask questions to help identify the main problems. For instance, you might ask, "What challenge does the narrator face?" or "What are these characters arguing about?" Then you can pick out the parts of the story that move these problems toward their solutions. Also, notice how story elements such as setting and characters affect problems and their solutions.

Here's how a student looked at the problem/solution structure in "Stray."

> Even after a week had gone by, Doris didn't name the dog. She knew her parents wouldn't let her keep it, that her father made so little money any pets were out of the question, and that the pup would definitely go to the pound when the weather cleared.

> *I can see the problem. Doris is attached to the stray dog, but she knows that she can't keep it unless she convinces her parents to let it stay. I'll read on to find out what she did. I'll also think about whether her solution could be used for any problems that I have.*

Practice It!

As you read "from *50 Simple Things Kids Can Do to Save the Earth*" and "Greyling," look closely to pick out important problems or conflicts. Ask yourself, "What are these problems about? What is causing them?" Then pay attention to the solutions.

Use It!

Make notes as you answer these questions, and refer to them later.

- What is the problem or conflict?
- Who is involved?
- What is the cause of the problem or conflict?
- What solutions are tried?
- What is the final outcome?

Teach

R Reading Skill

Review Inferring Say: Look at the excerpt of the selection on the student page. Notice that the author does not directly state the problem that the character experiences, namely that she wants to keep the puppy but knows she will not be allowed to keep it. The author implies that the character wants to keep the puppy. In order to understand this implication, you must read between the lines, or make inferences. Doing so will help you identify problems that are not directly stated within a text. What problem is implied by the title "50 Simple Things Kids Can Do to Save the Earth"? *(The Earth is in danger.)* **OL AL**

Resources for page 319

 Use Key Reading Skills Transparency 11 in *Read Aloud, Think Aloud* to help students practice identifying problem and solution.

Reading in the Real World

Career Explain to students that many careers require that a person be an excellent problem solver. For example, a doctor must analyze the symptoms of a patient, determine the problem that is causing the symptoms, and then consider the possible solutions. Finally she or he will need to try the solution that seems to be the best. If that solution does not work, another must be tried until the problem is solved. Other careers require the same kind of skills, only in a different setting. Tell students to consider a career that interests them and to write a paragraph explaining why they would need problem-solving skills to perform the job. **OL AL**

Objectives
- Identify problem and solution
- Make inferences

Teach

More About the Authors

The EarthWorks Group's first book was well received. The excerpt printed here is taken from the first book. They followed up that publication with several others, including *The Next Step: 50 More Things You Can Do to Save the Earth, 50 Simple Things Businesses Can Do to Save the Earth,* and *Kid Heroes of the Environment,* to name a few. Students might be interested in obtaining copies of the EarthWorks Group's *Student Environmental Action Guide* to learn how to set up a recycling program within their school and their community.

EL Language Coach

Synonyms and Word Choice **Ask:** What words would you use to persuade someone to buy a certain brand of sneakers? *(Possible response: quick, sleek, stylish, comfortable)* **AS**

Before You Read : from *50 Simple Things Kids Can Do to Save the Earth*

The EarthWorks Group is dedicated to helping to save the environment. Here's what one EarthWorks member says about the book *50 Simple Things Kids Can Do to Save the Earth:*

"I guess a lot of kids don't really think they can make a difference in saving the Earth. They think they don't have the power.

"But they're wrong.

"Kids have a lot of power. . . . This book is full of things you can do to help protect our planet. A lot of them are fun. Some take work. Some give you a chance to teach your parents, instead of the other way around. But all of them will show you that you can make a difference. And that is the power to save the Earth."

Objectives (pp. 320–323)
Reading Identify problems and solutions
Literature Identify literary elements: mood
Vocabulary Understand synonyms: shades of meaning

English Language Coach

Synonyms and Word Choice As you know, writers carefully choose the words they will use. Sometimes a writer uses a certain word because of its connotation. Sometimes, though, it's a matter of choosing among synonyms to get the exact right word.

Because synonyms rarely mean exactly the same thing, it matters which one a writer chooses. There is a difference between *frightened* and *terrified*. There is a difference between *run* and *scamper*. The differences may be small, but they're important.

Choosing just the right word is especially important in persuasive writing. The following choices all involve the use of synonyms:

• Would you choose a health bar described as *chewy* or one described as *leathery*?

• Would you rather walk on *a gloomy trail* or *a shady path*?

• Would you prefer to be *greeted by a fragrance* or *met by an odor*?

The words below in dark type are all synonyms for *eat*. Although they have similar meanings, the differences are important.

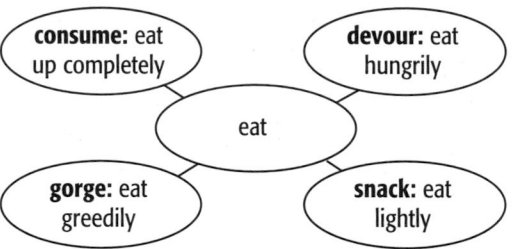

consume: eat up completely

devour: eat hungrily

eat

gorge: eat greedily

snack: eat lightly

Word Webs Make your own word webs, like the one above, for any two of the following words. (You do not need to include the definitions.) Use a dictionary or thesaurus if you need help.

• fear
• beautiful
• laugh
• difficult
• run
• say

EL

Additional Support

Literature Focus Lesson

Rhetoric In order to effectively persuade an audience, authors may use a variety of rhetorical devices. Semantic slanting is one such device. If you look closely, you can often tell how an author feels about the subject by the words used. Many times, the negative side of an argument is not mentioned. This is a form of rhetoric, too. It allows the author to persuade someone without addressing the downfalls of his or her ideas. Think of a persuasive article or speech you have read or heard. Then, explain what kinds of rhetoric the author uses. What devices are used to persuade readers? Write a paragraph describing the rhetorical devices in your chosen piece. **AL**

Skills Preview

Key Reading Skill: Identifying Problems and Solutions

R1 Think about a TV show you've seen in which the main character had a problem. Think about

- what the problem was and what caused it
- what actions were taken to solve it
- what the solution was

Key Literary Element: Mood

The **mood** of a piece of writing is the feeling it creates in the reader. We often talk about the mood created by a story or play, but nonfiction writing can also have a mood. A newspaper article might create a mood of sympathy or anger or even joy. A letter to the editor can make a reader feel determined or, perhaps, amused.

Persuasive writing always involves an attempt to make the reader react. In good persuasive writing, the attempt is often successful, and the reaction may well involve emotions of one sort or another.

As you read, use these tips to help you understand the selection's mood.

- Pay attention to the feelings you get as you read.

  Do you have an emotional reaction to what you're reading? Do you feel, for example, hopeless or encouraged?

- Is the writer trying to make you feel a particular way? Is this successful?

  Does the author try to reach out to you as a reader, to get you to react?

L **Partner Talk** Think about something you've read that excited you, surprised you, made you laugh, or affected you in some other noticeable way. Tell your partner about what you read and how you reacted.

Get Ready to Read

Connect to the Reading

How do you feel about forests and trees? Do they make you feel peaceful and happy? Do you think they are beautiful? Or do you not think about them much at all?

Partner Talk Talk about whether you think it's important to save the trees and forests of the Earth.

Build Background

This selection is from *50 Simple Things Kids Can Do to Save the Earth.*

- The selection is about **recycling** paper products. Recycling is the process of using waste materials, or trash, to make new objects.
- More than 500,000 trees are cut down every year just to create the paper for newspapers.
- Today about half of the used paper in this country is sent for recycling.

Set Purposes for Reading

BIG Question Read "50 Simple Things Kids Can Do to Save the Earth" to find out whether or not it's fair for people to waste paper.

Set Your Own Purpose What else would you like to learn from the reading to help you answer the Big Question? Write your own purpose on the "50 Simple Things" page of Foldable 3.

Literature Online

Interactive Literary Elements Handbook
To review or learn more about the literary elements, go to www.glencoe.com.

Keep Moving

Use these skills as you read the following selection.

from *50 Simple Things Kids Can Do to Save the Earth* **321**

Teach

R1 Reading Skill

Identifying Problems and Solutions **Say:** Most writing purposes can be structured around the problem-and-solution organization. For example, an author writing to entertain might tell a story about a character who faces a big problem and overcomes the problem by the end of the story. How might this text structure be used when the author's purpose is to persuade? *(Possible response: The author could explain a problem and try to convince readers to adopt his or her solution.)* **OL**

L Literary Element

Mood **Say:** After you've shared how the selection made you feel, think about the mood of the selection. Do you think the author created the mood he or she intended to create? Explain. *(Responses will vary.)* **AL**

Differentiated Instruction

Building Background Challenge students to learn more about recycling or waste production as it relates to paper. Students should choose a specific question to research, such as *How much paper is thrown away each year?* or *How can recycling paper help save the forests?* Make sure students choose a question

that is focused and can be answered within one page. Have students use the Internet and the library to answer their questions. Students might also be interested in examining the local recycling facilities and services. Allow students time to present their findings to the class as you proceed through the lesson. **AL**

Objectives

- Understand synonyms: shades of meaning
- Identify literary elements: mood
- Identify problem and solution
- Make connections between text and self

Teach

L Literary Element

Mood Ask: How does the author create an encouraging and hopeful mood? *(Possible response: The author uses positive language, such as "we can make that happen—there is a way.")* **OL**

R Reading Skill

Identifying Problems and Solutions Ask: What solution does the writer present in the fourth bulleted item under *Did You Know?* *(Recycling paper will cut down on the number of trees used to make it.)* **AS**
Ask: What is the purpose of the last bulleted item on this page? *(It describes how paper is recycled.)* **AS**

Readability Scores
Dale-Chall: 3.4
DRP: 51
Lexile: 810

from 50 Simple Things Kids Can Do to Save the Earth

by The EarthWorks Group

Take a Guess.
If you stacked up all the paper an average American uses in a year, the pile would be as tall as . . .
A) A car B) An elephant's eye C) A two-story house

It takes years for a tree to grow enough to be made into paper. And it takes many forests to make all the paper we use . . . and throw away.

Wouldn't it be great if old paper could be turned back into new paper? Then we'd have more trees and a greener world.

We can make that happen—there *is* a way. We can recycle our paper.

Does that really work? You bet! **1**

Did You Know?

- Americans use millions of tons of paper every year.
- To make all that paper, we use more than a *billion* trees! **2**
- How much is that? The paper that four people use in a year weighs as much as a big car.
- If everyone in the U.S. recycled their newspapers (including the comics), we'd save hundreds of thousands of trees every week.
- How is paper recycled? It's shredded and mashed into a glop called pulp, which is then turned back into paper.

Answer: C. Believe it or not, as high as a two-story house!

Practice the Skills

1 Key Literary Element
Mood What mood is created by these opening paragraphs? **L**

2 Key Reading Skill
Identifying Problems and Solutions What problem is the writer presenting here? Write the problem on your problem-and-solution chart. **R**

Additional Support

Differentiated Instruction

Using Text Structure Point out to students that this text is presented in the form of a bulleted list. Ask students: Why do you think the writer organized the text this way? Do you think it makes it easier to read or harder? Why? Have students work in small groups to rewrite the *Did You Know?* information in paragraph form. When groups finish their paragraphs, have representatives from each group read the paragraphs to the rest of the class. Discuss how the bulleted list makes the main ideas perfectly clear and gets directly to the point. **OL**

What You Can Do

- You can recycle all kinds of paper—cereal boxes, note paper, bags, newspaper, and so on. **3**
- To start recycling in your house, first find a place where you can put a pile of newspapers and a box for collecting other types of paper.
- Whenever you empty a cereal box, or get ready to toss out a piece of paper, put it in the box instead of the garbage. If you get a newspaper at your house, stack it neatly on the pile every day.
- Don't put shiny paper or paper with plastic attached to it in your box—you can't recycle that stuff.
- Ask a parent to find out where the nearest recycling center is. Maybe your neighborhood has a curbside recycling program. That would really make it easy!
- Every week or two, tie the newspapers into small bundles and take them (and other paper) to the recycling center or put them on the curb for pickup.
- **Extra Tip:** Don't use just one side of a piece of paper—use the other side for scrap paper. That's recycling, too. **4 5** ○

Analyzing the Photo Study the photo. What ideas does it give you about ways to conserve paper at home? Explain.

Practice the Skills

3 Key Reading Skill

Identifying Problems and Solutions The writer proposes one *big* solution—recycling. Write that on your problem-and-solution chart. Continue reading to find out what *smaller* solutions the writer suggests to help kids recycle paper. Write at least three of those on your chart also. **R**

4 English Language Coach

Synonyms and Word Choice The word *recycle* is familiar to most people. What about its synonym, *reuse*? Does it have a different connotation than *recycle*?

5 BIG Question

Do you think it's fair to expect people to follow the writer's suggestion and try to save the world's trees? Or do you think it's too much trouble? Explain your answer on the "50 Simple Things" page of Foldable 3. Your answer will help you complete the Unit Challenge later. **BQ**

from *50 Simple Things Kids Can Do to Save the Earth* **323**

Teach

R Reading Skill

Identifying Problems and Solutions Say: Other forms of pollution also cause environmental problems. Identify one problem and propose three solutions. *(Possible response: Using cars that burn a lot of gasoline hurts the air and the earth. People could use public transportation, car pool, or ride bicycles instead.)* **OL AL**

BQ BIG Question

Ask: What is *fair?* Why would recycling be considered treating the Earth *fairly?* *(Being "fair" means being just or reasonable. Recycling is fair because it saves the resources the Earth provides for us.)* **OL AL**

CheckPoint

Use the CheckPoint questions provided on Presentation Plus! to check for comprehension of the selection. These questions can be used with interactive response keypads for immediate student feedback.

English Language Coach

Compound Words Tell students that compound words are words that are made up of two or more smaller words. Direct students' attention to the first bulleted item. Challenge them to identify the compound word used in that sentence. *(newspaper)* Ask them to identify the two words that make up the compound. *(news and paper)* Then ask students to use the two separate words to define the compound word. *(a paper that has the news printed on it)* Have students identify at least three more compound words from this selection, tell what smaller words make up the compound, and then define the compound word based on the meanings of the smaller words. **EL OL**

Objectives
- Identify problem and solution
- Identify literary elements: tone
- Identify compound words

Assess

Students can respond to the *After You Read* items in their Learner's Notebooks or on a separate sheet of paper.

Answering the

1. Responses will vary. Students should support their responses with information from the selection.

2. It takes more than a billion trees.

3. The writer wants readers to recycle in order to save the trees and the Earth.

Critical Thinking

4. Possible response: Yes, the writer does suggest kids take charge. Specific instructions are given for kids to organize and execute paper recycling.

5. Possible response: We should recycle paper because it will help save the trees, which provide the air we breathe.

6. Possible response: The "writer" is the Earthworks Group, which is dedicated to saving the environment. Therefore, the writer seems qualified. The bias is towards recycling and helping save the planet.

After You Read | from *50 Simple Things Kids Can Do to Save the Earth*

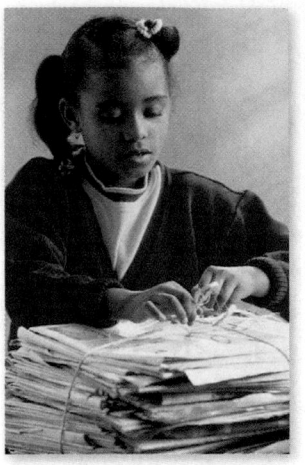

Answering the **BIG Question**

1. The writer of this selection creates a cheerful, "can-do" mood about recycling, partly by telling only about easy ways to recycle. Do you think this writer is being fair in using these methods to get kids to recycle? Why or why not?

2. **Recall** How many trees does it take to make all the paper that Americans use in a year?
   Tip Right There

3. **Summarize** What does the writer want readers to do, and why?
   Tip Think and Search

Critical Thinking

4. **Infer** Do you think this writer is suggesting that kids should "take charge" of recycling in their families? Explain.
   Tip Author and Me

5. **Draw Conclusions** Imagine that you have decided to ask your family to start recycling paper. Based on this selection, what one main reason would you give them to recycle?
   Tip Author and Me

6. **Evaluate** Does this writer seem qualified to write about this subject? Does the writer show a bias, or favoritism, toward one opinion or another? Explain your answers.
   Tip On My Own

Write About Your Reading

Imagine that you want to start a paper recycling program at your school. Using the selection as a model, create a bulleted list of at least five activities students can do at school as part of the recycling program.

If you need help thinking of activities, review the bulleted list under "What You Can Do" in the selection and write your list so the activities can apply to your school.

Objectives (pp. 324–325)
Reading Identify problems and solutions
Literature Identify literary elements: mood
Vocabulary Understand synonyms: shades of meaning
Writing Write a list
Grammar Identify parts of speech: prepositions, prepositional phrases

---

Write About Your Reading

Possible response:
Recycle That Paper

- Instead of putting paper in the trash, keep it for scrap paper.
- Look for the paper recycling bins in the hallway. Don't just use the nearest trash can for the paper you throw away.
- When you finish a notebook, tear the paper off the spiral and put it in the recycling bin.
- If you don't recycle newspapers at home, bring them in once a week for our newspaper collection day.
- Use a small piece of paper to write notes. Save larger pieces for more writing.

Skills Review

Key Reading Skill: Identifying Problems and Solutions

7. Do you think the solutions that the writer suggests can really solve the problem? Explain your answer.

Key Literary Element: Mood

8. Describe the mood of this selection.

9. How does the writer create a mood in the selection?

10. It would certainly be possible to create a mood of hopelessness while writing about the environment. Why do you think this writer might have wanted to avoid creating that mood?

11. **English Language Coach** All the words below are synonyms for the word *walks*. Think about which one best communicates the kind of walking suggested by each sentence. Then copy the sentences and fill in the blanks.

totters struts trudges strolls creeps

- Roger is so stuck-up, he ___ like a rooster!
- The silent tiger ___ through the jungle.
- Tired after a hard day, Peter ___ home.
- I watch the baby as she ___ a few steps before losing her balance.
- Every summer evening, Mr. Hu ___ around the neighborhood to relax.

Literature Online

Web Activities For eFlashcards, Selection Quick Checks, and other Web activities, go to www.glencoe.com.

Grammar Link: Prepositions

- A **preposition** is a word that shows the relationship of a noun or pronoun to some other word in the sentence.
- Prepositions include the following: *about, above, among, before, behind, below, between, by, in, into, near, of, to, through, under.*

The troll hid <u>under</u> the bridge.

The preposition *under* shows the relationship between *troll* and *bridge*.

- A preposition is always part of a **prepositional phrase**. A prepositional phrase begins with a preposition and ends with a noun or pronoun.

Preposition

Ramona left the recycling bag on the sidewalk.

Prepositional phrase

Preposition

The boy with my brother is our new next-door neighbor.

Prepositional phrase

Grammar Practice

Underline the preposition in each of the following sentences.

12. Aggie tucked the coupon into her tablet.

13. The leader of the band waved her baton.

14. Nobody on her street used house numbers.

15. The bat bounced in the dirt.

16. The ball sailed over the fence.

Writing Application Look back at the list of recycling activities you wrote. Add one prepositional phrase to a sentence on your list.

from 50 Simple Things Kids Can Do to Save the Earth **325**

Skills Review

Key Reading Skill: Identifying Problem and Solution

7. Possible response: The solutions seem plausible if recycling facilities are nearby and available.

Key Literary Element: Mood

8. Possible response: The mood is positive and encouraging.

9. Possible response: The writer gives helpful tips.

10. Possible response: The writer is trying to encourage kids to help save the earth; the writer doesn't want to scare kids or make them feel hopeless about the future.

11. **English Language Coach**

struts

creeps

trudges

totters

strolls

Close

Ask students to summarize what they learned from this selection to answer the Big Question.

Grammar Link: Prepositions

Grammar Practice

12. Aggie tucked the coupon <u>into</u> her tablet.

13. The leader <u>of</u> the band waved her baton.

14. Nobody <u>on</u> her street used house numbers.

15. The bat bounced <u>in</u> the dirt.

16. The ball sailed <u>over</u> the fence.

Teach

More About the Author

Jane Yolen has written over 250 children's books. She says she has written so many she has "lost count." The author was born in New York and spent most of her childhood there. Her father enlisted during World War II and had to go to Europe to fight in the war. She, her mother, and her younger brother Stevie stayed in Virginia while her father was away. Jane was always a good student, but she had to work hard for her grades. She initially saw herself as a poet, but she found her biggest success as a children's story writer. Jane has three children of her own and several grandchildren.

V Vocabulary

Vocabulary File Say: Copy the words and their definitions in your Vocabulary notebooks. Write a sentence of your own that shows how each word should be used. **OL** Tell English learners to include pronunciations in their Vocabulary files if necessary. **EL**

Before You Read : Greyling

Jane Yolen

Meet the Author

Born in 1939, Jane Yolen is an author, songwriter, teacher, and storyteller. She has become well known for her fairy tales and folktales. "I don't care whether the story is real or fantastical. I tell the story that needs to be told," she says. See page R7 of the Author Files for more on Jane Yolen.

Author Search For more about Jane Yolen, go to www.glencoe.com.

Objectives (pp. 326–333)
Reading Identify problems and solutions
• Make connections from text to self
Literature Identify literary elements: mood
Vocabulary Understand synonyms: shades of meaning

Vocabulary Preview

grief (greef) *n.* unhappiness or suffering, often about the loss of something **(p. 329)** *The death of the fisherman would add to his wife's grief.*

stranded (STRAN did) *adj.* left helpless in a difficult place **(p. 329)** *The seal was stranded on a sandbar.*

sheared (sheerd) *v.* cut off sharply; form of the verb *shear* **(p. 329)** *The cliffs sheared off into the sea.*

kin (kin) *n.* family or relatives **(p. 329)** *The seal pup was not old enough to find its kin.*

tended (TEN did) *v.* cared for; kept in working order; form of the verb *tend* **(p. 330)** *Greyling tended his father's boat.*

Write to Learn Write a short paragraph that correctly uses all of the vocabulary words.

English Language Coach

Synonyms and Word Choice Synonyms are words that have the same–or similar *but not the same*–meanings. The right word can help you create a clear picture in your mind. By paying attention to synonyms, you can clearly imagine what a character is like or how an author feels about a topic. Compare these two sentences:

Jamal *hung up* the phone.
Jamal *slammed down* the phone.

• The words *hung up* and *slammed down* describe the same action, but *slammed down* lets you know how Jamal felt.

Synonym Chart Copy the chart in your Learner's Notebook. For each word, write a synonym that has a more precise meaning. Next to each synonym, write the feeling or idea that the word creates.

	Synonym	Feeling or Idea
walk		
huge		
pretty		
difficult		

Additional Support

Author Search To expand students' appreciation of Jane Yolen, have them access the Web site for additional information and resources.

Literature Focus Lesson

Folktales Tell students that folktales are literally tales of the people. They are often handed down from generation to generation. To prepare students to read this genre, review some of the common elements of folktales: magic used, teaches a moral or lesson, usually set in a faraway land or place, characters face a challenge. Tell students to be prepared to encounter many of these elements as they read the selection. When they finish the selection, have them return to this list to identify which elements "Greyling" includes. **OL** **AL**

Skills Preview

Key Reading Skill: Identifying Problems and Solutions

Before you read the story, think about the following:

- Have you ever put off dealing with a problem you knew you'd have to solve eventually?
- Why didn't you want to solve this problem right away?
- How did you feel when you finally solved the problem?

Write to Learn Write your answers to these questions in your Learner's Notebook. Think about these responses as you read the story.

Key Literary Element: Mood

The feeling or atmosphere created in a story is called the **mood**. Word choice, settings, and characters all help create mood. Think about how these different descriptions create different moods:

> *"It was a dark and stormy night."*
> *"It was a beautiful evening of cool rain."*

As you read "Greyling,"

- Think about how the story is making you feel.
- What details in the story are helping to create the mood?
- Does the mood stay the same?

Partner Talk Talk about the scariest or saddest books you ever read. List some ways in which the author set the mood in one of those books.

Interactive Literary Elements Handbook
To review or learn more about the literary elements, go to www.glencoe.com.

Get Ready to Read

Connect to the Reading

You probably have felt at times that it's hard to be fair. Maybe something that you did made one friend happy, but upset another friend. The characters in this story find themselves in a similar situation and have to make tough decisions. As you read "Greyling," think about what you would do in their places.

Small Groups In small groups, talk about fair and unfair solutions to the following problem:

Your parents told you that you can invite two friends to go to a concert for your birthday. Four of your friends have told you that they love the band that is playing and hope you will chose them to go with you.

Build Background

This story tells of a fisherman and his wife who take in a selchie (SELL kee) that the fisherman finds stranded on a sandbar. The selchie grows up to become a young man named Greyling.

- A selchie is an imaginary creature often described in Celtic myths. Selchies live as seals in the ocean and as humans on land.
- Seals are mammals that live in the ocean and have fins or flippers instead of feet.

Set Purposes for Reading

BIG Question Read "Greyling" to find out more about how people respond to situations that seem unfair.

Set Your Own Purpose What else would you like to learn from the story to help you answer the Big Question? Write your own purpose on the "Greyling" page of Foldable 3.

> **Keep Moving** →
>
> Use these skills as you read the following selection.

Greyling **327**

Teach

L Literary Element

Mood Say: Just about everybody has a day when he or she is in a bad or good mood. How do you act when you are in a bad mood? *(Possible responses: grouchy, frowning, being short with people or angry)* Explain to students that their moods are similar to the mood of a text. **Say:** If the mood of a text is lighthearted, the characters will often act like they are in a good mood. The author uses description, word choice, and dialogue to create mood. What kind of setting would create a scary mood for a story? *(Possible response: a dark, stormy night)* Lead students to see how each element of the story contributes to the creation of the story's mood. **AS**

Interactive Literary Elements Handbook Have students access the Web site to improve their understanding of mood.

English Language Coach

Cultural Exchange Tell students the story they are about to read includes an element of Celtic folklore, the selchie. (See Build Background on the student page for information.) Explain that each culture has its own mythology and folklore. For example, many American Indians have the Coyote trickster in their folklore. Anansi, a trickster spider, populates African folklore. Have students identify a character from their culture's mythology or folklore and explain the role the character plays within that folklore. Allow students time to meet in small groups and share their cultural knowledge with their group mates. They might even bring in stories featuring the character to share with their groups. **EL OL**

Objectives
- Identify literary elements: mood
- Learn and use new vocabulary
- Identify problems and solutions
- Understand synonyms: shades of meaning

327

READING WORKSHOP 4

Teach

R1 Reading Skill

Review Activating Prior Knowledge Remind students of the Literature Focus Activity from page 326. **Ask:** What other characteristics do such stories possess? *(Students should list the elements discussed on page 326.)* **AS**

R2 Reading Skill

Identifying Problems and Solutions Say: The author immediately sets up the problem in the first two paragraphs. What is the problem? *(The fisherman and his wife want a child but do not have one.)* **Ask:** How does the wife react to this problem? *(She cries and rocks the empty cradle. She also complains that she has no baby.)* **OL Ask:** Do you think the fisherman's boat and nets are a good substitute for a baby, as the wife implies? Explain. *(Possible response: They give him something to do, but they don't take away his yearning for a child. The last sentence in the first paragraph states that they both want a child.)* **AL**

Readability Scores
Dale-Chall: 3.1
DRP: 50
Lexile: 880

GREYLING

by Jane Yolen

R2 Once on a time when wishes were aplenty,[1] a fisherman and his wife lived by the side of the sea. All that they ate came out of the sea. Their **hut** was covered with the finest mosses that kept them cool in the summer and warm in the winter. And there was nothing they needed or wanted except a child. **1 2**

Each morning, when the moon touched down behind the water and the sun rose up behind the plains, the wife would say to the fisherman, "You have your boat and your nets and your lines. But I have no baby to hold in my arms." And again, in the evening, it was the same. She would weep and wail and rock the cradle that stood by the hearth.[2] But year in and year out the cradle stayed empty.

---

1. When something is *aplenty,* a large amount of it can be found.
2. A *hearth* is the area in front of a fireplace.

328 UNIT 3 What's Fair and What's Not?

Practice the Skills

1 Reviewing Skills

Activating Prior Knowledge
You have probably read many stories that begin with the similar words "Once upon a time." What do you know about stories that begin with these words? **R1**

2 English Language Coach

Synonyms and Word Choice
What kind of house is a **hut**? Why might the writer have used this word instead of one of its synonyms, such as *shack* or *cottage*?

Additional Support

Reading Fluency

Building Reading Fluency Tell students that reading fluently takes practice and skill. Divide students into small groups and have them perform a choral reading of this selection. Each student should read two paragraphs and then the next student should take over. Remind students to speak clearly, keep an appropriate pace, pause with the indicated punctuation, and use tone and volume to add interest to the text. Also tell students to stop and self-correct as needed. As groups present their choral readings, walk around the classroom to monitor students' fluency. **AS**

Now the fisherman was also sad that they had no child. But he kept his sorrow to himself so that his wife would not know his **grief** and thus double her own. Indeed, he would leave the hut each morning with a breath of song and return each night with a whistle on his lips. His nets were full but his heart was empty, yet he never told his wife. **3**

One sunny day, when the beach was a tan thread spun between sea and plain, the fisherman as usual went down to his boat. But this day he found a small grey seal **stranded** on the sandbar, crying for its own.

The fisherman looked up the beach and down. He looked in front of him and behind. And he looked to the town on the great grey cliffs that **sheared** off into the sea. But there were no other seals in sight.

So he shrugged his shoulders and took off his shirt. Then he dipped it into the water and wrapped the seal pup carefully in its folds.

"You have no father and you have no mother," he said. "And I have no child. So you shall come home with me."

And the fisherman did no fishing that day but brought the seal pup, wrapped in his shirt, straight home to his wife.

When she saw him coming home early with no shirt on, the fisherman's wife ran out of the hut, fear riding in her heart. Then she looked wonderingly at the bundle which he held in his arms.

"It's nothing," he said, "but a seal pup I found stranded in the shallows and longing³ for its own. I thought we could give it love and care until it is old enough to seek its **kin**."

The fisherman's wife nodded and took the bundle. Then she uncovered the wrapping and gave a loud cry. "Nothing!" she said. "You call this nothing?"

The fisherman looked. Instead of a seal lying in the folds, there was a strange child with great grey eyes and silvery grey hair, smiling up at him.

---

3. *Longing* for something means really wanting it.

Vocabulary

grief (greef) *n.* unhappiness or suffering, often about the loss of something

stranded (STRAN did) *adj.* left helpless in a difficult place

sheared (sheerd) *v.* cut off sharply

kin (kin) *n.* family or relatives

Practice the Skills

3 Key Literary Element

Mood To figure out the mood, look at the words that the writer uses. In this paragraph, the writer uses the words *sad, sorrow, grief,* and *empty.* What mood do those words create?

Greyling **329**

Teach

L Literary Element

Mood Say: How does the word choice add to the mood? *(It helps create the solemn mood that surrounds the fisherman and his wife.)* **Ask:** What do you think the lack of names for the fisherman and his wife contributes to the story? *(Possible response: Their namelessness could show that they represent anyone who has wanted a child desperately and has not been able to have one.)* **AL**

R Reading Skill

Identifying Problems and Solutions Ask: What problem and solution are stated in the fifth paragraph on the page? *(Problem: The seal has no parents and the fisherman has no child and wants one. Solution: The fisherman will take the seal home and raise him.)* **AS**

Differentiated Instruction

Questioning Tell students that one way to better understand a text is to stop periodically to ask questions about the text. If students don't understand a passage, they should stop and jot down their questions. Then, they can reread to find the answer or read on to find the answer. Explain that they might question the meanings of words or of figurative language, such as idioms or metaphors. They might also need to clarify an event in the plot. Have students stop at the end of this page and record any questions they have about the text. Then have them reread to see if they can locate answers. If they do, have them record their answers. If not, they should read further to find answers in the remainder of the text. **BL EL**

Objectives
• Identify literary elements: mood
• Identify problems and solutions
• Activate prior knowledge

Teach

BQ BIG Question

Ask: Why does the wife decide she will never let the boy return to the sea? *(He will become a seal and leave her.)* **Ask:** Why does the man agree even though he thinks it is unfair? *(He wants his wife to be happy and will do almost anything to make her happy.)* **OL**

R Reading Skill

Identifying Problems and Solutions Ask: What problem is introduced in the last paragraph on this page? *(A huge storm blows in and floods the beach.)* **Ask:** What do you think will happen to the fisherman? *(He will likely be stuck on his boat during the dangerous storm.)* **OL**

The fisherman wrung his hands. "It is a selchie," he cried. "I have heard of them. They are men upon the land and seals in the sea. I thought it was but a tale."

"Then he shall remain a man upon the land," said the fisherman's wife, clasping the child in her arms, "for I shall never let him return to the sea."

"Never," agreed the fisherman, for he knew how his wife had wanted a child. And in his secret heart, he wanted one, too. Yet he felt, somehow, it was wrong. **4**

"We shall call him Greyling," said the fisherman's wife, "for his eyes and hair are the color of a storm-coming sky. Greyling, though he has brought sunlight into our home."

And though they still lived by the side of the water in a hut covered with mosses that kept them warm in the winter and cool in the summer, the boy Greyling was never allowed into the sea.

He grew from a child to a **lad**. **5** He grew from a lad to a young man. He gathered driftwood for his mother's hearth and searched the tide pools for shells for her mantel.[4] He mended his father's nets and **tended** his father's boat. But though he often stood by the shore or high in the town on the great grey cliffs, looking and longing and grieving in his heart for what he did not really know, he never went into the sea. **6**

Then one wind-wailing morning just fifteen years from the day that Greyling had been found, a great storm blew up suddenly in the North. It was such a storm as had never been seen before: the sky turned nearly black and even the fish had trouble swimming. The wind pushed huge waves onto the shore. The waters gobbled up the little hut on the beach. And Greyling and the fisherman's wife were forced to flee to the town high on the great grey cliffs. There they looked down at the roiling, boiling,[5] sea. Far from shore they spied the fisherman's boat, its sails flapping like the wings of

---

4. A *mantel* is a shelf above a fireplace.
5. *Roiling* and *boiling* mean "bubbling" and "churning."

Vocabulary

tended (TEN did) *v.* cared for; kept in working order

330 UNIT 3 What's Fair and What's Not?

Practice the Skills

4 BIG Question

Do you think that keeping the selchie was fair when the fisherman had a feeling that it was wrong? Explain your answer. **BQ**

5 English Language Coach

Synonyms and Word Choice What does the word **lad** mean or suggest to you? Why do you think the author used that word instead of *boy*?

6 Key Reading Skill

Identifying Problems and Solutions What problem does Greyling face as he grows up? Think about possible solutions. **R**

Additional Support

Differentiated Instruction

Illustrations Tell students that often folktales and fairy tales are accompanied by illustrations. Have those students who enjoy drawing illustrate one or two scenes from the text. Help students choose particularly poignant scenes, such as the fisherman finding the seal, the fisherman showing the selchie to his wife and her look of surprise, or the fisherman stuck in the boat in the middle of the storm. When students finish their drawings, post them on the class bulletin board for the entire class to view and enjoy. **BL**

a wounded gull. And clinging to the broken mast[6] was the fisherman himself, sinking deeper with every wave. **7**

The fisherman's wife gave a terrible cry, "Will no one save him?" she called to the people of the town who had gathered on the edge of the cliff. "Will no one save my own dear husband who is all of life to me?"

But the townsmen looked away. There was no man there who dared risk his life in that sea, even to save a drowning soul.

"Will no one at all save him?" she cried out again.

"Let the boy go," said one old man, pointing at Greyling with his stick. "He looks strong enough."

But the fisherman's wife clasped Greyling in her arms and held his ears with her hands. She did not want him to go into the sea. She was afraid he would never return.

"Will no one save my own dear heart?" cried the fisherman's wife for a third and last time.

---

6. The **mast** of a ship is the tall pole to which the sail ties.

Practice the Skills

7 **Key Literary Element**

Mood A key event such as a storm often adds mood to a story. What mood does the author create with this storm?

Analyzing the Art How does this picture make you feel? Does it create a mood? If it does, does that mood match the mood of the story? Explain your answer.

Sunset Over the Sea, 1887. George Inness. Oil on panel, 22 1/16 x 36 1/8 in. Brooklyn Museum of Art, NY.

Greyling **331**

Teach

L Literary Element

Mood Ask: How does the repetition of the wife's words "Will no one save him?" affect the mood? *(Possible response: The repetition of this question adds to the suspense that is building.)* **Ask:** Why won't the men in the village help the fisherman? *(They are afraid of drowning themselves.)* **OL**

R Reading Skill

Review Predicting Ask: What do you think will happen next in the story? Why? *(Possible response: Based on the events so far and on the man's suggestion that Greyling should go save his father, I predict that Greyling will jump into the sea and save his father from the storm.)* **AS**

Viewing the Art

Ask: How well do you think this illustration shows what is happening in the selection? Explain your answer. *(Responses will vary.)* **OL**

Reading in the Real World

Career Tell students that some people make a career out of saving people in trouble in the sea. The members of the U.S. Coast Guard often risk their lives to save fishermen and others who have been trapped in the ocean or whose boats have sunk because of foul weather. Challenge students to research the qualifications needed to join the Coast Guard along with the duties expected of Coast Guard members while on the job. Students should focus on the jobs of those who learn to rescue stranded boats and their crews. Have students compile one- to two-page reports about their findings. Invite them to share the information with the rest of the class. **AL**

Objectives
• Identify problems and solutions
• Identify literary elements: mood
• Make predictions
• Use text features: illustrations

331

Teach

L Literary Element

Mood Ask: How does the dialogue of the villagers add to the mood? *(Possible response: It adds a sense of dread and hopelessness to the story.)* **AS**
Ask: What response does the mood create in you as a reader? *(Possible response: It makes me feel the worry of the mother and involves me in the suspense of the story. I want to know what will happen to Greyling.)* **OL AL**

R Reading Skill

Identifying Problems and Solutions Draw students' attention to the text on page 330 that describes Greyling as "looking and longing and grieving in his heart for what he did not really know." Point out that the reader knows what he is grieving for, and have students name it. *(He is grieving for the lost part of himself, the seal that must return to the ocean.)* **OL**
Then have students answer the question in the side column on page 332.

But shaking their heads, the people of the town edged to their houses and shut their doors and locked their windows and set their backs to the ocean and their faces to the fires that glowed in every hearth.

"I will save him, Mother," cried Greyling, "or die as I try."

And before she could tell him no, he broke from her grasp and dived from the top of the great cliffs, down, down, down into the tumbling sea.

"He will surely sink," whispered the women as they ran from their warm fires to watch.

"He will certainly drown," called the men as they took down their spyglasses[7] from the shelves.

They gathered on the cliffs and watched the boy dive down into the sea.

As Greyling disappeared beneath the waves, little fingers of foam tore at his clothes. They snatched his shirt and his pants and his shoes and sent them bubbling away to the shore. And as Greyling went deeper beneath the waves, even his skin seemed to slough off[8] till he swam, free at last, in the sleek grey coat of a great grey seal.

The selchie had returned to the sea. **8**

_____

7. **Spyglasses** are objects that help people see things that are far away.
8. To **slough off** is to shed or get rid of something.

Practice the Skills

8   Key Reading Skill

Identifying Problems and Solutions How is the storm a solution to Greyling's problem? **R**

Analyzing the Photo Do you think this is what Greyling looks like at the end of the story? Explain your answer using details from the selection.

Additional Support

Literature Focus Lesson

Moral Explain to students that a moral is a lesson to be learned from a story. Remind students of the wife's reaction when she and her husband discovered the boy was a selchie. *(She said she would never let him go back to the sea.)* Then, lead students to see that the wife is forced to let the boy go when he finally grows old enough to take care of himself. In doing so, the wife is rewarded with the gift of her husband's survival. Have students state the moral of the story based on all these clues. *(Possible response: You cannot hold onto a thing or person you love forever or If you love something, set it free. It will return to you.)* **OL AL**

But the people of the town did not see this. All they saw was the diving boy disappearing under the waves and then, farther out, a large seal swimming toward the boat that wallowed[9] in the sea. The sleek grey seal, with no effort at all, eased the fisherman to the shore though the waves were wild and bright with foam. And then, with a final salute, it turned its back on the land and headed joyously out to sea.

The fisherman's wife hurried down to the sand. And behind her followed the people of the town. They searched up the beach and down, but they did not find the boy.

"A brave son," said the men when they found his shirt, for they thought he was certainly drowned.

"A very brave son," said the women when they found his shoes, for they thought him lost for sure.

"Has he really gone?" asked the fisherman's wife of her husband when at last they were alone.

"Yes, quite gone," the fisherman said to her. "Gone where his heart calls, gone to the great wide sea. And though my heart grieves at his leaving, it tells me this way is best."

The fisherman's wife sighed. And then she cried. But at last she agreed that, perhaps, it was best. "For he is both man and seal," she said. "And though we cared for him for a while, now he must care for himself." And she never cried again. So once more they live alone by the side of the sea in a new little hut which was covered with mosses to keep them warm in the winter and cool in the summer. **9**

Yet, once a year, a great grey seal is seen at night near the fisherman's home. And the people in town talk of it, and wonder. But seals do come to the shore and men do go to the sea; and so the townfolk do not dwell upon it very long.

But it is no ordinary seal. It is Greyling himself come home—come to tell his parents tales of the lands that lie far beyond the waters, and to sing them songs of the wonders that lie far beneath the sea. **10** ○

_____

9. **Wallowed** means "tossed or rolled about in something."

Practice the Skills

9 BIG Question

Was it fair of the fisherman and his wife to keep Greyling from the sea? Why or why not? Write your answer on the "Greyling" page of Foldable 3. Your response will help you answer the Unit Challenge later. **BQ**

10 Key Reading Skill

Identifying Problems and Solutions Not every solution to a problem has a happy ending. How is the main problem in "Greyling" finally solved? Do you think this is the best solution? **R**

Greyling **333**

Teach

BQ BIG Question

Ask: How do the final responses of the wife and husband show their fairness? *(Possible response: They realize that they took care of the boy long enough and needed to let him return to the sea. They understand that they had to release him in order to show their love for him.)* **OL**

R Reading Skill

Identifying Problems and Solutions Ask: What problems were presented in this story? Think of each of the characters as you answer. *(The husband and the wife wanted a child and did not have one. Greyling yearned for something he did not understand. The fisherman was caught in a bad storm. No one would dive in to help him. The wife did not want to let Greyling ever go back to the sea.)* **Ask:** Do you think the solutions to these problems were satisfying? Explain. *(Responses will vary.)* **AS**

CheckPoint

Use the CheckPoint questions provided on Presentation Plus! to check for comprehension of the selection. These questions can be used with interactive response keypads for immediate student feedback.

Differentiated Instruction

Levels of Meaning Tell students that most literary pieces have different levels of meaning. For example, "Greyling" is a story about a selchie who is rescued by a fisherman and raised by him and his wife. This is the surface, or literal, level of meaning. However, there are underlying meanings presented in this text, as in most others. Ask students how a deeper meaning could be extracted from this story. If students need prompting, ask them: How could this story relate to that of an ordinary teenager? Help students see that the deeper meaning of the story is about a young boy's coming of age and separating from his parents. It also explores the mother's wanting to keep her child and having to let him grow up and live on his own. **AL**

Objectives
• Identify literary elements: mood
• Identify problems and solutions
• Identify literary elements: moral

333

Assess

Resources for page 334

📁 Selection Quick Check, p. 28

📁 Selection and Unit Assessment, p. 32

💿 ExamView Assessment Suite

💿 Interactive Tutor: Self-Assessment

Students can respond to the *After You Read* items in their Learner's Notebooks or on separate sheets of paper.

Answering the

1. Possible response: Their keeping him out of the sea was motivated by their love for him; however, it was not fair to keep him from the sea for so long.

2. He thought he was bringing home a seal pup.

3. He lives with the fisherman and his wife in a small hut. His life seems quiet and happy, but he longs for something he cannot identify.

Critical Thinking

4. Responses will vary.

5. Possible response: He is a loving husband and a good person.

6. Possible response: Greyling was missing the sea but did not know why he felt that way.

7. Possible response: She realized that it was necessary for Greyling to return to the sea and accepted that fact while remembering his childhood with fondness.

334

After You Read : Greyling

Answering the BIG Question

1. Was it fair for Greyling's parents to keep him out of the sea? Explain.

2. **Recall** What did the fisherman think he was bringing home at the beginning of the story?
   TIP Right There

3. **Summarize** What is Greyling's life like as a young boy? Write your answer in your own words.
   TIP Think and Search

Critical Thinking

4. **Contrast** How was Greyling's childhood different from your own?
   TIP Author and Me

5. **Draw Conclusions** After reading about his actions in the story, what kind of person do you think the fisherman is?
   TIP Author and Me

6. **Interpret** What does the author mean by saying that Greyling "grieved in his heart for what he did not really know"?
   TIP Author and Me

7. **Infer** Why do you think the fisherman's wife cried once after losing Greyling and then never cried again?
   TIP Author and Me

Write About Your Reading

What do you think of the author's solution to Greyling's problem? Can you think of a different ending for the story? Write a new ending from the point at which Greyling dives into the sea.

- Include details and description when you tell what happens.
- Include dialogue with quotation marks and characters' names to show who is speaking.

Objectives (pp. 334–335)
Reading Identify problems and solutions
Literature Identify literary elements: mood
Vocabulary Understand synonyms: shades of meaning
Writing Respond to literature: write a story ending
Grammar Identify parts of speech: interjections

Write About Your Reading

Students' endings should work with the plot flow of the story. Students should be sure to include dialogue and vivid description in their new endings.

Skills Review

Key Reading Skill: Identifying Problems and Solutions

8. Think about your own experiences with problems and solutions as you answer the questions below.
   - What is Greyling's main problem?
   - How do Greyling's parents react when his problem is finally solved?

Key Literary Element: Mood

9. How would you describe the overall mood of the story? Explain your answer.

10. Does the mood of the story help you better understand it? Would you have enjoyed the story more if the mood were different?

Reviewing Skills: Activating Prior Knowledge

11. What did you already know about seals before you read the story? How would having seen a live seal help the reader understand Greyling?

Vocabulary Check

Choose the best word from the list to match each definition below. Rewrite the correct words and definitions on a separate sheet of paper.

sheared   grief   stranded   kin   tended

12. ___ left helpless in a difficult place
13. ___ cared for; kept in working order
14. ___ cut off sharply
15. ___ family or relatives
16. ___ unhappiness or suffering, often about the loss of something
17. **English Language Coach** The word *gobble* can mean "eat." It means something a little different than just "eat," however, and it has a strong connotation! Think of three other synonyms for *eat*. Make sure each means or suggests something a little different, and use each in a sentence.

Grammar Link: Interjections

- An **interjection** is a word or phrase that shows feeling, such as surprise, or attracts attention. An interjection often appears before the beginning of a sentence.
  Hooray! We won!
  Oh, thank you.
  Hey, watch it!
- Sometimes an interjection stands by itself.
  Ouch!
  Yikes!
- An exclamation point follows an interjection that shows very strong feeling. A comma appears after an interjection that isn't as strong.
  Wow! You won the spelling bee!
  Yes, you may go to the concert.

Grammar Practice

Rewrite each of the following sentences, using one of these interjections to show your feelings.

hey   wow   uh-oh   oops

18. Watch where you're going.
19. I didn't study enough for the test.
20. You got an A on that test.
21. Maria broke the vase.

Writing Application Add two interjections that show how the characters felt in the new ending you wrote for "Greyling."

Web Activities For eFlashcards, Selection Quick Checks, and other Web activities, go to www.glencoe.com.

Greyling **335**

Skills Review

Key Reading Skill: Identifying Problem and Solution

8. Possible response: He misses the sea. They accept his return to the sea as a necessity and go on with their lives as before.

Key Literary Element: Mood

9. Possible response: The mood is often sad, desperate, and suspenseful. The story ends, however, with a mood of acceptance and calmness.

10. Responses will vary.

Reviewing Skills: Activating Prior Knowledge

11. Responses will vary.

Vocabulary Check

12. stranded
13. tended
14. sheared
15. kin
16. grief
17. **English Language Coach** Possible responses: I devoured the steak; we munched on popcorn during the movie; the toddler chewed his food carefully.

Close

Ask students to summarize what they learned from reading "Greyling" that helped them answer the Big Question.

Grammar Link: Interjections

Grammar Practice

18. Hey! Watch where you're going.
19. Uh-oh, I didn't study enough for the test.
20. Wow! You got an A on that test.
21. Oops! Maria broke the vase.

Web Activities Have students access the Web site for interactive activities that will help them assess their understanding of the selection.

Conflict

Objectives covered in this workshop:
• Identify tone and mood
• Compare and contrast tone and mood across texts

Teaching Students to Compare Conflict

Why Is It Important?

• Recognizing the different types of conflict and how they affect each other will help students identify aspects of plot and character.

• Students will benefit from connecting events that occur externally in a story to the internal workings of characters. This skill will help them become more analytic thinkers.

• Students who master the difference between external and internal conflict will be more skilled writers and better readers of fiction and nonfiction. Close examination of conflict and its sources can lead to better understanding of people and situations outside the classroom as well.

How to Help Students Get It

• Ask: "What are some of the physical problems the writers describe encountering?" Things you can see or hear or feel, things outside yourself, are external.

• Ask: "What are some of the mental difficulties they describe going through?" When you disagree with yourself, or cannot choose between mutually exclusive goals or values, you are experiencing internal conflict.

• Clarify that conflict does not refer to small matters that can be resolved easily. In literature, conflict is used to mean something with high stakes; either a character must change (internal) or the world itself must change around the character (external) to resolve the conflict.

• Encourage students to connect to the readings: Thinking about times when they experienced a conflict with another person or situation will help them to identify external conflict in the reading. Likewise, remembering a time when they wanted two mutually exclusive things might help them identify internal conflict.

Reading to Answer the Big Question

Scholarship Jacket by Marta Salinas
A small Texas school has a tradition of awarding a special scholarship jacket to the student with the best grades over eight years. One year the school board decides to require payment for the jacket so they may award it to a girl whose father is a prominent citizen. A Mexican-American girl named Martha deserves to win, but her grandpa refuses to pay for the jacket because he believes that the situation is unfair. The principal must decide what to do.

The Circuit by Francisco Jimenez
Panchito is a young migrant worker who moves with his family from farm to farm harvesting crops. Because his family needs him to work, he is rarely able to attend school. It seems even more unfair when, just as Panchito finally develops a relationship with a sympathetic teacher who helps and encourages him, the family moves again.

Workshop Resources

PACING (DAYS)		LESSON	STUDENT MATERIALS	TEACHER RESOURCES
STANDARD	BLOCK			
1	1	Comparing Literature: Conflict	🔬 English Language Coach Review, p. 41	🔬 Bellringer Options Transparencies –Daily Language Practice 29 –Selection Focus 6 🔬 Read Aloud, Think Aloud Transparencies –Read Aloud, Think Aloud 25–32 💿 Presentation Plus!
1	1	"Scholarship Jacket"	💻 Glencoe Online 🔬 Unit Vocabulary Review, p. 39 🔬 Academic Vocabulary Review, p. 42 📁 English Language Coach 🔬 Comparing Literature Graphic Organizer, p. 34 🔬 Literary Analysis 💿 StudentWorks Plus™ 💻 Online Student Edition 💿 Literature Classics	💻 Puzzlemaker 💿 Skill Level Up!™ A Language Arts Game 💻 BookLink 3 📄 Assessment by Learning Objective (Diagnostic and Formative) 💿 Interactive Tutor: Self-Assessment 💿 TeacherWorks Plus™ 💿 ExamView Assessment Suite
1		"The Circuit"	💻 Glencoe Online 🔬 Unit Vocabulary Review, p. 39 🔬 Academic Vocabulary Review, p. 42 📁 English Language Coach 🔬 Comparing Literature Graphic Organizer, p. 34 🔬 Literary Analysis 💿 StudentWorks Plus™ 💻 Online Student Edition 💿 Literature Classics	💻 Puzzlemaker 💿 Skill Level Up!™ A Language Arts Game 💻 BookLink 3 📄 Assessment by Learning Objective (Diagnostic and Formative) 💿 Interactive Tutor: Self-Assessment 💿 TeacherWorks Plus™ 💿 ExamView Assessment Suite

Keys for Unit Resource

📁 Blackline Master   📀 DVD

📄 Workbook   🔥 Transparency

📖 Supplemental Text   💻 Web-based

💿 CD-ROM   🔬 Fast File

Level Appropriate Code

AS = Activities for all students

AL = Activities for students working above grade level

OL = Activities for students working at grade level

BL = Activities for students working below grade level

EL = Activities for English language learners

Focus

BELLRINGER Options

- **Selection Focus Transparency 6**
- **Daily Language Practice Transparency 29**
Focus Activity Say: Think about a problem you've recently had. It probably involved a conflict between you and something, someone else, or yourself. Write a sentence describing your conflict and whether it was between you, someone else, or something. *(Responses will vary.)* **AS**

Teach

L Literary Elements

Conflict Say: Think about the conflict in one of the selections you've read in this unit. Who was the conflict between? Was it an external conflict or an internal conflict? *(Responses will vary.)* **OL**

The Scholarship Jacket & The Circuit

by Marta Salinas

by Francisco Jiménez

What You'll Learn

- How to compare two pieces of literature
- How to identify external and internal conflict

What You'll Read

- "The Scholarship Jacket," p. 339
- "The Circuit," p. 347

Point of Comparison

- Conflict

Purpose

- To compare conflict in two texts

Objectives (pp. 336–337)
Reading Compare and contrast across texts: conflict
Literature Identify literary elements: external conflict, internal conflict

336 UNIT 3

Whenever you've decided between two outfits or sandwiches or solutions to a problem, you've had to make comparisons. You can make comparisons in literature, too. Comparing the similarities and differences in two stories can help you understand both stories better.

How to Compare Literature: Conflict

In the next two selections you will look at the similarities and differences between the **conflicts** in two stories.

In life or in literature, a **conflict** is a struggle between two people or forces or feelings. Most stories contain a conflict, and usually more than one. Conflict is the gas that keeps the engine of the story running. It makes stories interesting because you ask the question, "Who or what will win?"

There are two main types of conflict:

External conflict

- conflict between two people, such as a race or an election or a difference of opinion
- conflict between a person and nature, in the form of storms or animals and so forth
- conflict between a person and society, such as a struggle to be yourself while fitting in with the community you live in

Internal conflict

- a conflict within a person, such as having to make a difficult choice

---

Additional Support

Literature Focus Lesson

Descriptive Language Explain that descriptive language directly contributes to tone and mood. Show students a picture of a farmhouse that looks slightly run down. Write on the board: 1. *The old, run-down house creaked and moaned at every step I took. I couldn't imagine living in this dump.* 2. *The quaint house showed its history in beautiful wooden floors. Its charm immediately drew me in. I couldn't believe I was lucky enough to live there.* Point out that both items describe the same house. Have students identify descriptive language used in each. Then ask students how the descriptive language set up tone and mood. **AS**

Get Ready to Compare

To figure out the **conflicts** in a story, pay attention to whether someone is happy or unhappy. (Happy people generally are not in conflict with something or someone.) Remember that one story can have many conflicts and many different kinds of conflict.

When you think about a story's conflicts, remember these terms:

- **Forces** are not living things, but they create conflicts. They are problems such as poverty or prejudice or the weather.
- **Obstacles** are any problems that make it hard for a person to get what he or she wants. They can be physical, such as a fence or ocean, or not physical, such as fear or ignorance.

L

Use Your Comparison

To help yourself find and keep track of the conflicts in the two stories you are about to read, use conflict charts like the one below.

Conflict Chart "The Scholarship Jacket"	
Who is the main character?	
Who does he or she have problems (conflicts) with?	
What forces is he or she in conflict with?	
Is there an obstacle to overcome? What is it?	
What internal conflicts does he or she have?	
Do other characters have similar conflicts?	
Is the main character's main conflict resolved? How?	

Now copy and fill in the conflict chart for each story you'll read in this workshop.

Teach

L Literary Elements

Conflict Ask: What forces could create a conflict between an 8th grade Mexican American student and the principal of a school? *(Possible responses: racism or prejudice)* **OL**

Ask: What obstacles might an 8th grade Mexican American student face in school? *(Possible responses: learning to speak English, understanding American traditions)* **AL**

Assess/Close

Say: Write a short paragraph about the conflict in one of your favorite stories. Discuss whether the conflict is external, internal, or both. Share what forces and obstacles are involved in the conflict. **OL**

Resources for page 337

Use the Comparing Literature Graphic Organizer BLM in the Unit 3 Resource Booklet, p. 34.

Differentiated Instruction

Practice Comparing and Contrasting Draw a Venn diagram. Explain to students that this diagram will help them organize their comparisons and contrasts. Help students compare and contrast two basic things, such as apples and oranges or cats and dogs. First, have students identify all the characteristics of the first subject in a list.

Then, have them identify the characteristics of the second. Finally, have them compare their lists and decide which characteristics are similar. List these in the overlap of the Venn diagram. List the individual characteristics in their appropriate sections. Tell students they can use this technique to compare elements of a text. **OL**

Objectives

- Identify literary elements: external conflict, internal conflict
- Compare and contrast across texts: conflict

337

Teach

More About the Author

Marta Salinas has also published her writing in the anthology *Nosotras: Latino Literature Today.* She is published in *Nosotras* with authors such as Anna Castillo, Pat Mora, and Judith Ortiz-Cofer, to name a few. Salinas has also written and collaborated on several tourist guides for Argentina and Buenos Aires. For the most part, her tourist guides are written in Spanish, her native language.

R Reading Skill

Review Connecting

Say: Think about a situation in which you were treated unfairly. How did you feel? How did you react? *(Responses will vary.)* **AS**

Say: Use these feelings to connect to the main character in "The Scholarship Jacket." **OL**

Before You Read : The Scholarship Jacket

Meet the Author

Marta Salinas is the author of many short stories. Her short story "The Scholarship Jacket" was first published in *Cuentos Chicanos: A Short Story Anthology.* "Cuentos Chicanos" means "stories by Americans of Mexican descent." Her work has also appeared in the *Los Angeles Herald Examiner* and in *California Living* magazine.

Literature Online

Author Search For more about Marta Salinas, go to www.glencoe.com.

Vocabulary Preview

coincidence (koh IN sih dens) *n.* a situation in which two events that seem unrelated accidentally occur at the same time **(p. 341)** *It was a lucky coincidence when we both won tickets for the same show.*

dismay (dis MAY) *n.* a feeling of disappointment or unpleasant surprise **(p. 341)** *She felt dismay that the room was such a mess.*

muster (MUS tur) *v.* to find and gather together; collect **(p. 342)** *We'll need to muster our courage to face the champions in this game.*

withdrawn (with DRAWN) *adj.* shy, quiet, or unsociable **(p. 344)** *He seemed unusually withdrawn at the dance.*

vile (vyl) *adj.* very bad; unpleasant; foul **(p. 344)** *A vile odor leaked from the lunch bag they found in the closet.*

Get Ready to Read

Connect to the Reading

How would you feel if you were in a contest and the rules were changed just so someone else could win? How would you feel if the rules were changed so *you* could win?

Build Background

- This story takes place in a small town in Texas.
- The word *valedictorian* comes from the Latin word *valedicere,* which means "to say farewell." The valedictorian has gotten the highest grades in the class and often gives a speech at the graduation.

Set Purposes for Reading

BIG Question Read to find out how the main character dealt with an unfair situation.

Set Your Own Purpose What else would you like to learn from the story to help you answer the Big Question? Write your own purpose on "The Scholarship Jacket" page of Foldable 3.

Objectives (pp. 338–345)
Reading Compare and contrast across texts: conflict • Make connections from text to self
Literature Identify literary elements: external conflict, internal conflict

---

Additional Support

Author Search To expand students' appreciation of Marta Salinas, have them access the Web site for additional information and resources.

Reading in the Real World

Citizenship Tell students that part of being an upstanding citizen includes recognizing, respecting, and supporting equal rights for all people, regardless of their ethnicity or socioeconomic status. Some people have dedicated their lives to fighting for the rights of oppressed people whether the oppression is due to their political beliefs, ethnicity, gender, or poverty. Major historical figures, such as Ghandi, Martin Luther King Jr., and Elizabeth Cady Stanton, are good examples of such citizens. Have students choose a historical figure to research and write a one-page description of his or her contribution to relieving the oppression of a certain group of people. Have students consider which characters stand up to the oppressors in the story. **OL** **AL**

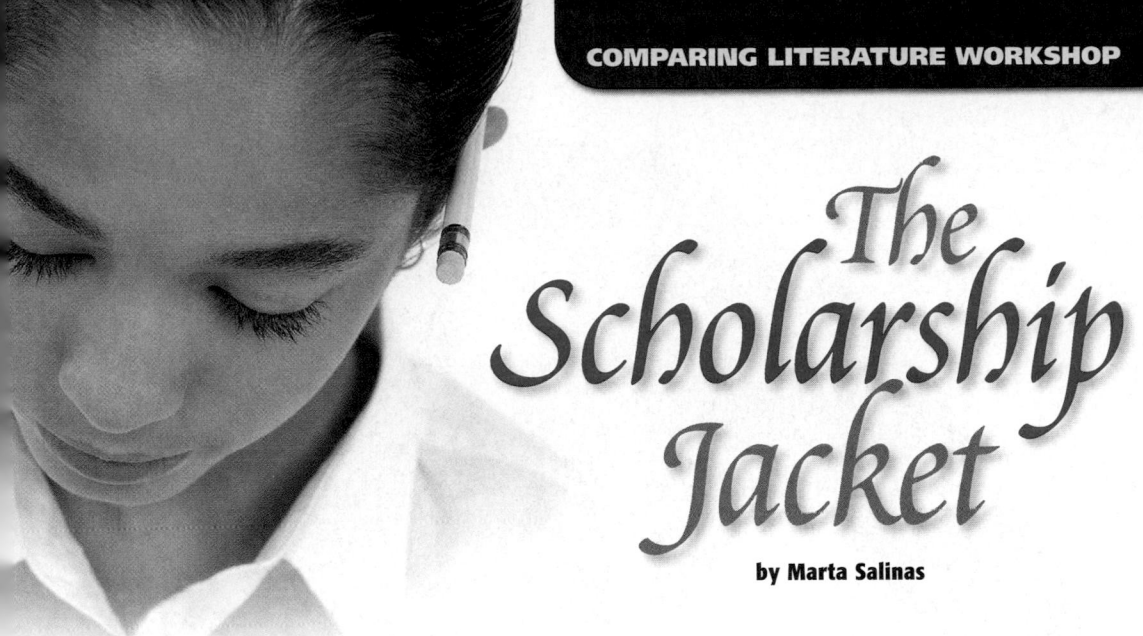

The Scholarship Jacket

by Marta Salinas

Teach

L Literary Element

Review Narrator Ask: Who is the narrator of the story? *(An adult looking back at her life as a fourteen-year-old girl)* What do you know about her? *(Possible responses: Her father is a farm laborer. She has seven brothers and sisters. She is raised by her grandparents because her parents can't afford to feed all of their children.)* **AS**

BQ BIG Question

Ask: How might the situation described be remedied in a fair way? *(Responses will vary.)* **AS**

The small Texas school that I attended carried out a tradition every year during the eighth grade graduation; a beautiful gold and green jacket, the school colors, was awarded to the class valedictorian, the student who had maintained the highest grades for eight years. The scholarship jacket had a big gold S on the left front side and the winner's name was written in gold letters on the pocket.

My oldest sister Rosie had won the jacket a few years back and I fully expected to win also. I was fourteen and in the eighth grade. I had been a straight A student since the first grade, and the last year I had looked forward to owning that jacket. My father was a farm laborer who couldn't earn enough money to feed eight children, so when I was six I was given to my grandparents to raise. We couldn't participate in sports at school because there were registration fees, uniform costs, and trips out of town; so even though we were quite agile and athletic, there would never be a sports school jacket for us. This one, the scholarship jacket, was our only chance. **1**

In May, close to graduation, spring fever struck, and no one paid any attention in class; instead we stared out the windows and at each other, wanting to speed up the last few weeks of school. I despaired every time I looked in the mirror. Pencil

Practice the Skills

1 **BIG Question**

Because the narrator's family was poor, she couldn't participate in sports at school. Do you feel this is fair or not? Explain your answer. **BQ**

The Scholarship Jacket **339**

Readability Scores
Dale-Chall: 6.1
DRP: 54
Lexile: 790

Differentiated Instruction

Character Web Tell students one way to better understand a story is to analyze its main character. Draw a web diagram on the board. In the center circle write *main character*. Then, draw several outlying circles. Ask the class to identify things they know about the narrator so far.

Record students' responses in the outlying circles. Then, ask students to discuss how the narrator seems to feel about all these details. Stop at the end of each page and add information to the chart as you read the story. **OL**

Objectives

• Identify and analyze narrator
• Identify literary elements: external conflict, internal conflict
• Make connections from text to self

Teach

Identifying Problems and Solutions Ask: What problem is introduced on this page? *(When the narrator returns to her classroom to get her shorts, she hears two teachers arguing about her. She doesn't want to eavesdrop, but she also doesn't want to get in trouble with the P.E. teacher.)* **AS** How do you think she will solve this problem? *(Possible response: She will hide until the teachers leave then quickly grab her shorts and return to P.E. class.)* **OL**

L **Literary Elements**

Conflict Say: The narrator discovers a conflict between two people. Who is having an external conflict on this page? *(Mr. Schmidt and Mr. Boone)* **OL**

thin, not a curve anywhere, I was called "Beanpole" and "String Bean" and I knew that's what I looked like.

A flat chest, no hips, and a brain, that's what I had. That really isn't much for a fourteen-year-old to work with, I thought, as I absentmindedly wandered from my history class to the gym. Another hour of sweating in basketball and displaying my toothpick legs was coming up. Then I remembered my P.E. shorts were still in a bag under my desk where I'd forgotten them. I had to walk all the way back and get them. Coach Thompson was a real bear if anyone wasn't dressed for P.E. She had said I was a good forward and once she even tried to talk Grandma into letting me join the team. Grandma, of course, said no. **2**

R
L
I was almost back at my classroom's door when I heard angry voices and arguing. I stopped. I didn't mean to eavesdrop; I just hesitated, not knowing what to do. I needed those shorts and I was going to be late, but I didn't want to interrupt an argument between my teachers. I recognized the voices: Mr. Schmidt, my history teacher, and Mr. Boone, my math teacher. They seemed to be arguing about me. I couldn't believe it. I still remember the shock that rooted me flat against the wall as if I were trying to blend in with the graffiti written there.

340 UNIT 3 What's Fair and What's Not?

Practice the Skills

2 **Comparing Literature**

Conflict Who is the main character? Are there any forces or people stopping her from doing something? If so, write this down in your conflict chart.

Additional Support

Reading Fluency

Building Fluency Tell students that the informal language and the perspective of a fourteen-year-old in this selection give them a perfect opportunity to build fluency. Divide students into groups. Have them discuss how they talk to friends or family members. Then, have them take turns reading the selection, using the informal tone of the narrator. Tell them to pretend they are telling a story to their friends or family members. Each student should read several paragraphs. Tell students to stop and self-correct if necessary. If a student gets stuck, he or she should ask a group member for help with pronunciation. **AS**

"I refuse to do it! I don't care who her father is, her grades don't even begin to compare to Martha's. I won't lie or falsify records. Martha[1] has a straight A plus average and you know it." That was Mr. Schmidt and he sounded very angry. Mr. Boone's voice sounded calm and quiet.

"Look, Joann's father is not only on the Board, he owns the only store in town; we could say it was a close tie and—"

The pounding in my ears drowned out the rest of the words, only a word here and there filtered through. ". . . Martha is Mexican. . . . resign. . . . won't do it. . . ." Mr. Schmidt came rushing out, and luckily for me went down the opposite way toward the auditorium, so he didn't see me. Shaking, I waited a few minutes and then went in and grabbed my bag and fled from the room. Mr. Boone looked up when I came in but didn't say anything. To this day I don't remember if I got in trouble in P.E. for being late or how I made it through the rest of the afternoon. I went home very sad and cried into my pillow that night so grandmother wouldn't hear me. It seemed a cruel **coincidence** that I had overheard that conversation. **3**

The next day when the principal called me into his office, I knew what it would be about. He looked uncomfortable and unhappy. I decided I wasn't going to make it any easier for him so I looked him straight in the eye. He looked away and fidgeted with the papers on his desk.

"Martha," he said, "there's been a change in policy this year regarding the scholarship jacket. As you know, it has always been free." He cleared his throat and continued. "This year the Board decided to charge fifteen dollars—which still won't cover the complete cost of the jacket."

I stared at him in shock and a small sound of **dismay** escaped my throat. I hadn't expected this. He still avoided looking in my eyes. **4**

"So if you are unable to pay the fifteen dollars for the jacket, it will be given to the next one in line." **5**

---

1. The main character is called **"Martha"** at school and "Marta" at home. Martha is an English version of the main character's Spanish name.

Vocabulary

coincidence (koh IN sih dens) *n.* a situation in which two events that seem unrelated accidentally occur at the same time

dismay (dis MAY) *n.* a feeling of disappointment or unpleasant surprise

---

Practice the Skills

3 | Comparing Literature

Conflict What conflict has been introduced to the story in the last few paragraphs? Add it to your conflict chart.

4 | Comparing Literature

Conflict Do you think the principal has an internal conflict? If so, add it to your conflict chart. Is Martha faced with a new conflict? If so, add it to your conflict chart.

5 | BIG Question

In your opinion, why did the board change the rules for winning the scholarship jacket? Do you believe that changing the rules was fair? Write your answers in your Learner's Notebook.

The Scholarship Jacket **341**

Teach

R1 | Reading Skill

Review Clarifying Ask: What are the two teachers arguing about? *(who should get the scholarship jacket.)* **Ask:** Who do you think is right in the argument? *(Most students will say Mr. Schmidt because he wants to give the jacket based on performance.)* **AS Ask:** Why is Mr. Schmidt so upset? *(Possible response: because of the unfairness of the situation)* **OL AL**

R2 | Reading Skill

Review Inferring Ask: Why doesn't Martha remember whether she got in trouble for being late for P.E.? *(Possible response: She is so upset about hearing the argument and about the possibility of not getting the jacket that she cannot remember.)* **Ask:** Why does the principal avoid looking in Martha's eyes? *(Possible response: He is ashamed of what he is doing.)* **OL AL**

BQ | BIG Question

Ask: Do you think changing the rules is fair or unfair? Explain. *(Possible response: It is unfair because it is meant to keep the poor student from getting the prize.)* **AS**

Literature Focus Lesson

Dialogue Divide students into groups of three. Tell students that one student will play the role of Martha while the other two will play the roles of the teachers. Have students prepare for their acting by rereading the scene in the story where Martha overhears the teachers arguing. Tell students to imagine they are making a movie of the scene. Then, have them jot down the dialogue they will speak based on the discussion Martha overhears. Allow students time to practice the scene. Then have them present the scenes to the class. Discuss how students' reproductions are similar and how they differ. **OL**

Objectives
• Identify literary elements: external conflict, internal conflict
• Identify problems and solutions
• Clarify ideas and text
• Make inferences

Teach

C Critical Thinking

Comprehension Ask: Why does Martha cry all the way home? *(Possible response: She knows that her grandfather does not have the money for the jacket. She wants the jacket and expects not to get it.)* **AS**

R Reading Skill

Review Identifying Problems and Solutions

Ask: What is Martha's problem? *(Possible response: She needs fifteen dollars to get the scholarship jacket she wants so badly.)* **Ask:** What is her only solution to the problem? *(Possible response: The only solution is to ask her grandfather for the money.)* **AS**

Standing with all the dignity I could **muster,** I said, "I'll speak to my grandfather about it, sir, and let you know tomorrow." I cried on the walk home from the bus stop. The dirt road was a quarter of a mile from the highway, so by the time I got home, my eyes were red and puffy.

"Where's Grandpa?" I asked Grandma, looking down at the floor so she wouldn't ask me why I'd been crying. She was sewing on a quilt and didn't look up.

"I think he's out back working in the bean field."

I went outside and looked out at the fields. There he was. I could see him walking between the rows, his body bent over the little plants, hoe in hand. I walked slowly out to him, trying to think how I could best ask him for the money. There was a cool breeze blowing and a sweet smell of mesquite in the air, but I didn't appreciate it. I kicked at a dirt clod. I wanted that jacket so much. It was more than just being a valedictorian and giving a little thank you speech for the jacket on graduation night. It represented eight years of hard work and expectation. I knew I had to be honest with Grandpa; it was my only chance. He saw me and looked up.

Visual Vocabulary
Mesquite (mes KEET) is a small, thorny tree. Its pleasant-smelling wood is a favorite barbecue fuel in the Southwest.

He waited for me to speak. I cleared my throat nervously and clasped my hands behind my back so he wouldn't see them shaking. "Grandpa, I have a big favor to ask you," I said in Spanish, the only language he knew. He still waited silently. I tried again. "Grandpa, this year the principal said the scholarship jacket is not going to be free. It's going to cost fifteen dollars and I have to take the money in tomorrow, otherwise it'll be given to someone else." The last words came out in an eager rush. Grandpa straightened up tiredly and leaned his chin on the hoe handle. He looked out over the field that was filled with the tiny green bean plants. I waited, desperately hoping he'd say I could have the money. **6**

He turned to me and asked quietly, "What does a scholarship jacket mean?"

Vocabulary
muster (MUS tur) *v.* to find and gather together; collect

Practice the Skills

6 **Comparing Literature**

Conflict Is Martha facing a new conflict now? If so, add it to your conflict chart.

Additional Support

English Language Coach

Vocabulary In order to fully understand a text, students must understand the meanings of the words that make up the text. Suggest that students jot down unfamiliar words as they encounter them in the text. After reading a few paragraphs, students should then stop to determine the meanings of the unfamiliar words. When students identify the meanings, they should record them in vocabulary notebooks. Finally, they should reread the paragraphs that include the now familiar words to make sure they understand what is happening and how the characters feel. **EL BL**

I answered quickly; maybe there was a chance. "It means you've earned it by having the highest grades for eight years and that's why they're giving it to you." Too late I realized the significance of my words. Grandpa knew that I understood it was not a matter of money. It wasn't that. He went back to hoeing the weeds that sprang up between the delicate little bean plants. It was a time consuming job; sometimes the small shoots were right next to each other. Finally he spoke again.

"Then if you pay for it, Marta, it's not a scholarship jacket, is it? Tell your principal I will not pay the fifteen dollars."

I walked back to the house and locked myself in the bathroom for a long time. I was angry with grandfather even though I knew he was right, and I was angry with the Board, whoever they were. Why did they have to change the rules just when it was my turn to win the jacket? **7**

Practice the Skills

7 🗨 **BIG Question**

Martha was angry with her grandfather for refusing to pay the fifteen dollars, but she still believed he was right. Why did she feel he was right? Do you feel he was being fair or unfair to Martha? Explain.

New Mexico Peon, 1942. Ernest L. Blumenschein. Oil on canvas, 40 x 25 in. Gerald Peters Gallery, Santa Fe.

Analyzing the Painting Does the person in the painting remind you of anyone in the story? Explain.

The Scholarship Jacket **343**

Teach

BQ 🗨 **BIG Question**

Ask: What does Martha mean when she says, "Too late I realized the significance of my words"? *(Possible response: She means she realizes that she just gave a reason to not pay for the jacket. She is upset because she has ruined her chance to get the jacket. She is also upset because she realizes how unfair the situation truly is.)* **OL**

Ask: Why is Grandpa's refusal "not a matter of money"? *(He refuses not because he doesn't have the money but because he will not participate in the unfairness of the situation.)* **AL**

L Literary Elements

Review Mood Ask: How would you describe the mood of the story at this point? *(Possible responses: desperate, frustrated, angry)* **OL**

Viewing the Art

Ask: How does this painting help you visualize Martha's grandfather? Explain. *(Responses will vary.)* **AS**

Reading in the Real World

Citizenship Invite students to imagine they are Martha's best friend and they just found out about Martha's situation. They are angry about the way Martha is being treated and want to do something about it. Ask them to write a letter to the editor of Martha's school newspaper. In their letters, remind them to include a description of the situation, their opinion about the people's actions, their relationship to Martha, and their ideas about how to solve the problem. If necessary, read a few letters to the editor from a local paper to help students structure their letters. When they have finished writing their letters, post them on the bulletin board. **OL**

Objectives
- Identify literary elements: external conflict, internal conflict
- Identify problems and solutions
- Make inferences
- Use comprehension skills
- Use text features: illustration

Teach

BQ

Ask: What does the principal realize when Martha tells him why her grandfather won't pay? *(Possible response: He realizes that Martha and her family understand the real reasons Martha is not getting the jacket.)* What does the principal realize when Martha says to give the jacket to Joann? *(He realizes she has overheard a conversation about giving the jacket to the other girl.)* **OL**

L Literary Elements

Conflict Ask: What force do you think is causing the main conflict in this story? *(Possible response: racism, favoritism)* **OL**

It was a very sad and **withdrawn** girl who dragged into the principal's office the next day. This time he did look me in the eyes.

"What did your grandfather say?"

I sat very straight in my chair.

"He said to tell you he won't pay the fifteen dollars."

The principal muttered something I couldn't understand under his breath, and walked over to the window. He stood looking out at something outside. He looked bigger than usual when he stood up; he was a tall gaunt[3] man with gray hair, and I watched the back of his head while I waited for him to speak.

"Why?" he finally asked. "Your grandfather has the money. Doesn't he own a small bean farm?" **8**

I looked at him, forcing my eyes to stay dry. "He said if I had to pay for it, then it wouldn't be a scholarship jacket," I said and stood up to leave. "I guess you'll just have to give it to Joann." I hadn't meant to say that; it had just slipped out. I was almost to the door when he stopped me.

"Martha—wait."

I turned and looked at him, waiting. What did he want now? I could feel my heart pounding. Something bitter and **vile** tasting was coming up in my mouth; I was afraid I was going to be sick. I didn't need any sympathy speeches. He sighed loudly and went back to his big desk. He looked at me, biting his lip, as if thinking.

"Okay. We'll make an exception in your case. I'll tell the Board, you'll get your jacket." **9**

I could hardly believe it. I spoke in a trembling rush. "Oh, thank you sir!" Suddenly I felt great. I didn't know about adrenalin[4] in those days, but I knew something was pumping through me, making me feel as tall as the sky. I wanted to yell, jump, run the mile, do something. I ran out so I could cry in the hall where there was no one to see me. At the end of the day, Mr. Schmidt winked at me and said, "I hear you're getting a scholarship jacket this year."

---

3. A **gaunt** person is thin and bony.
4. **Adrenalin** (uh DREN uh lin) is a chemical released into the blood in times of stress or excitement. It increases the body's energy.

Vocabulary

withdrawn (with DRAWN) *adj.* shy, reserved, or unsociable

vile (vyl) *adj.* very bad; unpleasant; foul

Practice the Skills

8 **BIG Question**

How do you think the principal felt when Martha told him her grandfather refused to pay for the jacket? Do you think he wanted the other girl to get the jacket? Do you think the principal felt he was being fair? Explain why or why not. **BQ**

9 **Comparing Literature**

Conflict Is Martha's conflict resolved? If so, how? Is the principal's conflict resolved? If so, how?

Additional Support

Differentiated Instruction

Connecting Have students think about a time when they wanted something badly. Ask students how they felt about what they wanted. How did they go about getting it? How did the situation turn out? Have students write a short description of the situation and emphasize the feelings they had as they went through the process of trying to get what they wanted. Remind them to make sure to include how the situation turned out and how they felt about it. Then, in small groups, have them discuss how their feelings compare to Martha's. **BL**

His face looked as happy and innocent as a baby's, but I knew better. Without answering I gave him a quick hug and ran to the bus. I cried on the walk home again, but this time because I was so happy. I couldn't wait to tell Grandpa and ran straight to the field. I joined him in the row where he was working and without saying anything I crouched down and started pulling up the weeds with my hands. Grandpa worked alongside me for a few minutes, but he didn't ask what had happened. After I had a little pile of weeds between the rows, I stood up and faced him.

"The principal said he's making an exception for me, Grandpa, and I'm getting the jacket after all. That's after I told him what you said."

Grandpa didn't say anything, he just gave me a pat on the shoulder and a smile. He pulled out the crumpled red handkerchief that he always carried in his back pocket and wiped the sweat off his forehead.

"Better go see if your grandmother needs any help with supper."

I gave him a big grin. He didn't fool me. I skipped and ran back to the house whistling some silly tune. **10** ○

Analyzing the Photo How do you think the girl in this picture is feeling? Explain your answer.

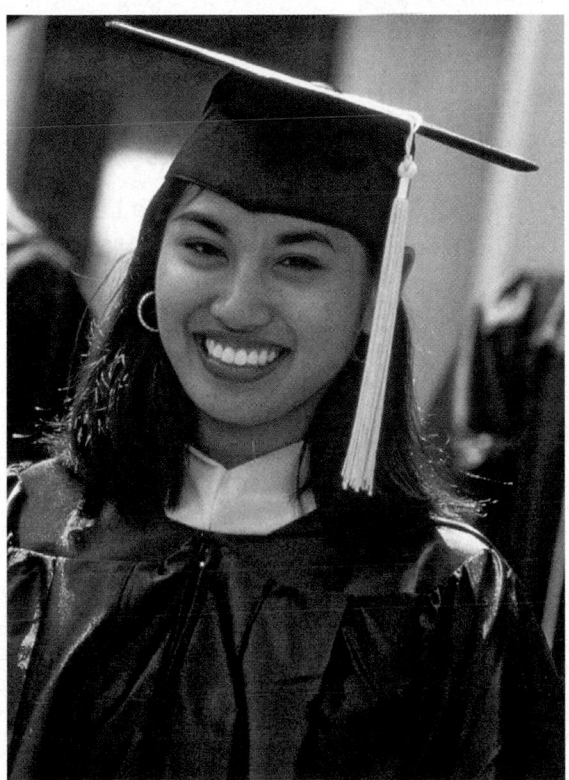

The Scholarship Jacket **345**

Practice the Skills

10

For Martha to win the jacket, the principal had to bend or break the new rule that the school board had made. When is it fair to break a rule? Record your answer on "The Scholarship Jacket" page of Foldable 3. Your response will help you complete the Unit Challenge later.

BQ

Teach

BQ **BIG Question**

Ask: Do you think the outcome of the story is fair? Why or why not? *(Possible response: The outcome is fair because Martha receives the jacket that she deserves based on her performance in her classes.)* **AS**

Viewing the Photo

Ask: How does this photo illustrate the tone and mood of the outcome of the story? *(Responses will vary.)* **OL**

✓ CheckPoint

Use the CheckPoint questions provided on Presentation Plus! to check for comprehension of the selection. These questions can be used with interactive response keypads for immediate student feedback.

Reading in the Real World

Career Remind students that the story is set in a small town in Texas. The narrator's grandfather is a bean farmer. Have students use the Internet and the library to learn more about the setting of the story. Students should research the elements of the lives of such small farmers in Texas. They should discuss how weather affects the harvest and the farmers' incomes. Have students present their findings to the class. Then, lead a class discussion in which students connect the lifestyle described to the setting of this story. **AL**

Objectives
• Identify literary elements: external conflict, internal conflict
• Use text features: photograph

345

Teach

More About the Author

In one of his short stories, Jiménez describes his family's illegal border crossing from Mexico to the United States: "On both sides of the fence were armed guards in green uniforms. Papa . . . explained that we had to cross the fence . . . without being seen by these men. If we succeeded, we would enter los Estados Unidos." After they arrived, a woman took them to the San Joaquin Valley to find work as migrant farmers. The life they found was challenging. They moved constantly and lived in shacks with no electricity or running water. Jiménez began working at the age of six.

V Vocabulary

Incorporating Vocabulary

Say: Review the new vocabulary words. Then, in your Learner's Notebooks write a short paragraph using at least three of the words correctly. *(Responses will vary.)* **AS**

Before You Read : The Circuit

Francisco Jiménez

Meet the Author

Born in Mexico, Francisco Jiménez came to the United States when he was four years old. At the age of six, he became a farm laborer like others in his family. Jiménez is now a professor of literature at Santa Clara University in California, and the author of many books and stories. "The Circuit" is based on journal notes that Jiménez wrote while in college. See page R4 of the Author Files for more on Francisco Jiménez.

Author Search For more about Francisco Jiménez, go to www.glencoe.com.

Objectives (pp. 346–353)
Reading Compare and contrast across texts: conflict
Literature Identify literary elements: external conflict, internal conflict

Vocabulary Preview

sharecropper (SHAIR krop ur) *n.* a farmer who works land owned by someone else and shares the crop or the money from its sale with the landowner **(p. 347)** *The sharecropper worked thirteen hours a day during the harvest.*

acquired (uh KWY urd) *v.* obtained, got, received; form of the verb *acquire* **(p. 349)** *He acquired the old car from another farmer.*

drone (drohn) *n.* steady, low, humming sound **(p. 351)** *I could hear the drone of the truck engine across the field.*

instinctively (in STINK tiv lee) *adv.* in a way that comes naturally, without thinking **(p. 351)** *Jerome instinctively ducked as the bee flew toward his face.*

savoring (SAY vur ing) *v.* taking great delight in; form of the verb *savor* **(p. 352)** *We were still savoring the chicken when my father brought in the pie.*

hesitantly (HEZ uh tunt lee) *adv.* in a way that shows uncertainty or fear **(p. 353)** *We boarded the battered old bus hesitantly.*

Get Ready to Read

Connect to the Reading

Think about something that you really want or have wanted. Is anything keeping you from getting this thing? How much control do you have over this obstacle? In "The Circuit," the narrator faces obstacles that keep him from what he wants.

Build Background

Migrant workers travel from farm to farm to pick vegetables and fruit.

- They follow the harvest, moving to another farm after each type of crop is harvested.
- Traveling from farm to farm is sometimes called traveling "the circuit."

Set Purposes for Reading

BIG Question Read to learn about what's fair and what's not.

Set Your Own Purpose What else would you like to learn from the story to help you answer the Big Question? Write your own purpose on "The Circuit" page of Foldable 3.

Additional Support

Author Search To expand students' appreciation of Francisco Jiménez, have them access the Web site for additional information and resources.

Differentiated Instruction

Building Background Tell students that the story they are about to read is based on the author's life. Explain that the author and thousands of other illegal immigrants worked as migrant farm laborers. The wages were meager and their living conditions were substandard. One man in particular is known for his contribution to improving working conditions for the migrant farmers: Cesar Chavez. Have students conduct research on Chavez, using the library or the Internet. Students should identify what Chavez has done to improve the lives of thousands of people. Invite students to share their findings with the rest of the class. **AL**

The Circuit

by Francisco Jiménez

It was that time of year again. Ito,[1] the strawberry **sharecropper,** did not smile. It was natural. The peak of the strawberry season was over and the last few days the workers, most of them *braceros,*[2] were not picking as many boxes as they had during the months of June and July.

As the last days of August disappeared, so did the number of braceros. Sunday, only one—the best picker—came to work. I liked him. Sometimes we talked during our half-hour lunch break. That is how I found out he was from Jalisco,[3] the same state in Mexico my family was from. That Sunday was the last time I saw him.

When the sun had tired and sunk behind the mountains, Ito signaled us that it was time to go home. *"Ya esora,"*[4] he yelled in his broken Spanish. Those were the words I waited for twelve hours a day, every day, seven days a week, week after week. And the thought of not hearing them again saddened me. ∎

---

1. *Ito* (EE toh)
2. *Braceros* (brah SAY rohs) are Mexican farm laborers.
3. *Jalisco* (hah LEES koh)
4. *Ya esora* Ito is trying to say *"Ya es hora"* (yah es OH rah), which means "It is time."

Vocabulary

sharecropper (SHAIR krop ur) *n.* a farmer who works land owned by someone else and shares the crop or the money from its sale with the landowner

Practice the Skills

1 **Comparing Literature**

Conflict Who is the main character? Do you know a name? If not, write "narrator" in your conflict chart.

The Circuit **347**

Teach

L Literary Element

Review Narrator Ask: Who is the narrator of the story? *(He is a Mexican who is a farm laborer.)* What do you learn about him on this page? *(Possible response: He has been working as a strawberry picker. He works twelve hours a day, seven days a week.)* **OL**

C Critical Thinking

Comprehension Ask: How does the narrator feel about Ito leaving the strawberry fields? *(He is sad to leave.)* **OL**

Readability Scores
Dale-Chall: 4.2
DRP: 50
Lexile: 730

English Language Coach

Spanish Translators If you have Spanish-speaking students in your class, give them a chance to assist English-speaking students. Spanish speakers can practice their English by explaining the meanings of Spanish words and phrases within the story. They can also help English speakers with pronunciations of the Spanish words and phrases. Suggest that all students make a Spanish-to-English dictionary in their Learner's Notebooks. They can use this dictionary as a reference as they read the selection. **EL**

Objectives

• Identify and analyze narrator
• Learn and use new vocabulary

Teach

L Literary Elements

Conflict Ask: Is the conflict you entered on your chart an internal conflict or an external conflict? Explain. *(Responses will vary.)* **OL**

R Reading Skill

Review Inferring Ask: What kind of person is Papa? Use the clues in the text to arrive at your answer. *(Possible response: He is a hard worker, a proud man, and a careful and conscientious spender. He does his best to take care of his family.)* **OL**

Viewing the Art

Ask: How does this painting help you visualize the life of a migrant farm worker? *(Responses will vary.)* **AS**

As we drove home Papa did not say a word. With both hands on the wheel, he stared at the dirt road. My older brother, Roberto, was also silent. He leaned his head back and closed his eyes. Once in a while he cleared from his throat the dust that blew in from outside.

Yes, it was that time of year. When I opened the front door to the shack, I stopped. Everything we owned was neatly packed in cardboard boxes. Suddenly I felt even more the weight of hours, days, weeks, and months of work. I sat down on a box. The thought of having to move to Fresno[5] and knowing what was in store for me there brought tears to my eyes.

That night I could not sleep. I lay in bed thinking about how much I hated this move. **2**

A little before five o'clock in the morning, Papa woke everyone up. A few minutes later, the yelling and screaming of my little brothers and sisters, for whom the move was a great adventure, broke the silence of dawn. Shortly, the barking of the dogs accompanied them.

While we packed the breakfast dishes, Papa went outside to start the "Carcanchita."[6] That was the name Papa gave his old '38 black Plymouth. He bought it in a used-car lot in Santa Rosa in the winter of 1949. Papa was very proud of his little jalopy. He had a right to be proud of it. He spent a lot of time looking at other cars before buying this one. When he finally chose the "Carcanchita," he checked it thoroughly before driving it out of the car lot. He examined every inch of the car. He listened to the motor, tilting his head from side to side like a parrot, trying to detect any noises that spelled car trouble. After being satisfied with the looks and sounds of the car, Papa then insisted on knowing who the original owner was. He never did find out from the car salesman, but he

---

5. **Fresno** is a city in one of California's main farming regions.
6. **Carcanchita** (kar kahn CHEE tah)

Practice the Skills

2 | **Comparing Literature**

Conflict Has a conflict been introduced to the story yet? If so, enter it into the right place on your conflict chart. **L**

Trabajadores, 1950. Castera Bazile. Oil on canvas, 27 x 19 1/2 in. Private collection.

Analyzing the Art *Trabajadores* (trah hah bah DOHR ays) means "workers" in Spanish. Do you think it is the beginning or the end of the workers' day?

Additional Support

Differentiated Instruction

Illustration Have students illustrate a scene from the story. Students might illustrate the narrator leaving the strawberry field for the last time, or his coming home and finding the boxes packed, or the family piling into the old car. Tell students to search for clues in the text about the way the characters might look and act, as well as the expressions they might make. Students might use pencil, pen and ink, watercolors, or acrylic paints to draw their illustrations. Invite students to hang their illustrations on the class bulletin board for the entire class to enjoy. **AS**

Teach

bought the car anyway. Papa figured the original owner must have been an important man because behind the rear seat of the car he found a blue necktie.

Papa parked the car out in front and left the motor running. *"Listo,"*[7] he yelled. Without saying a word, Roberto and I began to carry the boxes out to the car. Roberto carried the two big boxes and I carried the two smaller ones. Papa then threw the mattress on top of the car roof and tied it with ropes to the front and rear bumpers. **3**

Everything was packed except Mama's pot. It was an old large galvanized pot she had picked up at an army surplus store in Santa María the year I was born. The pot had many dents and nicks, and the more dents and nicks it **acquired** the more Mama liked it. *"Mi olla,"*[8] she used to say proudly.

R I held the front door open as Mama carefully carried out her pot by both handles, making sure not to spill the cooked beans. When she got to the car, Papa reached out to help her with it. Roberto opened the rear car door and Papa gently placed it on the floor behind the front seat. All of us then climbed in. Papa sighed, wiped the sweat off his forehead with his sleeve, and said wearily: *"Es todo."*[9]

As we drove away, I felt a lump in my throat. I turned around and looked at our little shack for the last time

Despedida, 1941. Hector Poleo. Oil on linen, 60 x 50 cm. Private collection.

Analyzing the Art *Despedida* (dehs pay DEE dah) means "departure" in Spanish. Does the mood of the painting remind you of anything in the story? Explain.

---

7. *Listo* (LEES toh) means "Ready."

8. Mama's favorite *olla* (OH yah) is a *galvanized* (GAL vun yzd) *pot,* an iron pot with a thin coat of zinc. She got it at an *army surplus store,* which sells goods no longer needed by the U.S. military.

9. *Es todo* (es TOH doh) means "That's everything."

Viewing the Art

Ask: How does the painting capture the mood of the narrator as he and his family prepare to move yet again? *(Responses will vary.)* **OL**

R Reading Skill

Review Clarifying

Ask: What has happened so far in the story? *(Possible response: Strawberry season has ended, and the characters must move. They have packed their things, have put them in the car, and are driving away to find more work.)* **BL**

Practice the Skills

3 **BIG Question**

Is it fair that the narrator and his family have to move? Is it fair that Roberto had to carry two bigger boxes? Explain why or why not.

The Circuit **349**

Reading Fluency

Building Fluency Tell students that reading a selection fluently is comprised of more than pronouncing all the words correctly. Fluent reading should bring a text to life for the listeners. Read aloud a section of the story for students. Use your voice to express the tone and mood of the story. For example, the reader's tone should match the narrator's tone. Assign a passage to each student. Have him or her practice reading aloud, using their voices to express tone and mood and to bring life to the story. Then, host a choral reading with the entire class. **AS**

Objectives

• Make inferences
• Use text features
• Clarify ideas and text

Teach

L1 Literary Elements

Conflict Ask: What force is creating the conflict in these paragraphs? *(Possible response: poverty)* **Ask:** What obstacles does the family have to overcome? *(Papa not being able to speak English and not having work.)* **Ask:** How does the family overcome the obstacles? *(Mama speaks English and they travel to another place for work.)* **OL**

L2 Literary Element

Review Point of View

Say: Reread the narrator's description of his first day at work. How does having a first-person narrator affect your reaction to the text? *(Possible response: It helps me really understand how the character feels because he describes it directly from his own experience.)* **OL**

At sunset we drove into a labor camp near Fresno. Since Papa did not speak English, Mama asked the camp foreman if he needed any more workers. "We don't need no more," said the foreman, scratching his head. "Check with Sullivan down the road. Can't miss him. He lives in a big white house with a fence around it."

When we got there, Mama walked up to the house. She went through a white gate, past a row of rose bushes, up the stairs to the front door. She rang the doorbell. The porch light went on and a tall husky man came out. They exchanged a few words. After the man went in, Mama clasped her hands and hurried back to the car. "We have work! Mr. Sullivan said we can stay there the whole season," she said, gasping and pointing to an old garage near the stables. **4**

The garage was worn out by the years. It had no windows. The walls, eaten by termites, strained to support the roof full of holes. The dirt floor, populated by earth worms, looked like a gray road map.

Visual Vocabulary
This lamp can burn *kerosene*, a liquid fuel made from petroleum.

That night, by the light of a kerosene lamp, we unpacked and cleaned our new home. Roberto swept away the loose dirt, leaving the hard ground. Papa plugged the holes in the walls with old newspapers and tin can tops. Mama fed my little brothers and sisters. Papa and Roberto then brought in the mattress and placed it on the far corner of the garage. "Mama, you and the little ones sleep on the mattress. Roberto, Panchito, and I will sleep outside under the trees," Papa said.

Early next morning Mr. Sullivan showed us where his crop was, and after breakfast, Papa, Roberto, and I headed for the vineyard to pick.

Around nine o'clock the temperature had risen to almost one hundred degrees.

I was completely soaked in sweat and my mouth felt as if I had been chewing on a handkerchief. I walked over to the end of the row, picked up the jug of water we had brought, and began drinking. "Don't drink too much; you'll get sick," Roberto shouted. No sooner had he said that than I felt sick to my stomach. I dropped to my knees and let the jug roll off my hands. I remained motionless with my eyes glued on the hot

350 UNIT 3 What's Fair and What's Not?

Practice the Skills

4 Comparing Literature

Conflict What conflict was introduced in the first paragraph on this page and resolved in the second? Add this conflict to your conflict chart. What does this tell you about the life of the narrator?

Additional Support

English Language Coach

Visual Vocabulary Draw students' attention to the Visual Vocabulary feature on the student page. Explain that one way to cement knowledge of a new word is to associate it with an actual object. Viewing an object can help students recall what a word means. Invite students to create their own Visual Vocabulary dictionaries. Students should record unfamiliar words from the selection. Provide students with access to old magazines or newspapers so they can cut out photos of the words they list. Also, you might allow them to print images from the computer or Internet for their Visual Vocabulary dictionaries. **AS** Point out that not all words represent concrete objects, so words like *early*, *late*, and *after* cannot be depicted visually. **EL**

sandy ground. All I could hear was the **drone** of insects. Slowly I began to recover. I poured water over my face and neck and watched the dirty water run down my arms to the ground.

I still felt a little dizzy when we took a break to eat lunch. It was past two o'clock and we sat underneath a large walnut tree that was on the side of the road. While we ate, Papa jotted down the number of boxes we had picked. Roberto drew designs on the ground with a stick. Suddenly I noticed Papa's face turn pale as he looked down the road. "Here comes the school bus," he whispered loudly in alarm. **Instinctively,** Roberto and I ran and hid in the vineyards. We did not want to get in trouble for not going to school. The neatly dressed boys about my age got off. They carried books under their arms. After they crossed the street, the bus drove away. Roberto and I came out from hiding and joined Papa. *"Tienen que tener cuidado,"*[10] he warned us. "You have to be careful." **5 6**

After lunch we went back to work. The sun kept beating down. The buzzing insects, the wet sweat, and the hot dry dust made the afternoon seem to last forever. Finally the mountains around the valley reached out and swallowed the sun. Within an hour it was too dark to continue picking. The vines blanketed the grapes, making it difficult to see the bunches. *"Vámonos,"*[11] said Papa, signaling to us that it was time to quit work. Papa then took out a pencil and began to figure out how much we had earned our first day. He wrote down numbers, crossed some out, wrote down some more. *"Quince,"*[12] he murmured.

When we arrived home, we took a cold shower underneath a water-hose. We then sat down to eat dinner around some wooden crates that served as a table. Mama had cooked a special meal for us. We had rice and tortillas with *carne con chile,*[13] my favorite dish.

---

10. *Tienen que tener cuidado* (TYEH nen kay tay NAIR kwee DAH doh)
11. *Vámonos* (VAh moh nohs) means "Let's go."
12. *Quince* (KEEN say) means "fifteen."
13. A *tortilla* (tor TEE yuh) is made from corn or wheat meal and baked on a griddle so that it resembles a very flat pancake. *Carne con chile* (KAR nay kohn CHEE lay) is meat cooked with red peppers and beans.

Vocabulary

drone (drohn) *n.* steady, low, humming sound

instinctively (in STINK tiv lee) *adv.* in a way that comes naturally, without thinking

Practice the Skills

5 | **Comparing Literature**

Conflict What conflict has been introduced in this paragraph? Make a note of it in your conflict chart.

6 | **BIG Question**

The boys have to hide so they won't get in trouble for not going to school. Why can't they go to school? Do you think it's fair that they can't go to school? How do you think the boys feel about it? Explain. **BQ**

The Circuit **351**

Teach

BQ **BIG Question**

Ask: How does the narrator's description of himself and his brother compare to the boys who get off the bus? *(Possible response: The narrator is hot and sick and dirty from all the work he has done before lunch. He is scared and hiding from the bus. The boys are "neatly dressed" and they "carried books under their arms.")* **BL**

Ask: How does this make you feel about the family's situation? *(Possible response: It is unfair that some children don't get to go to school because they are so poor.)* **AS**

C Critical Thinking

Comprehension Ask: How late do the narrator, his brother, and his father work? *(They work until it is too dark to see the grapes.)* **BL**

Reading in the Real World

Citizenship At the end of the student page, the narrator describes his favorite meal, a particularly Mexican dish. Tell students that every culture is associated with a particular style of cooking. For example, Jamaicans are known for jerk chicken and spicy foods. The Irish are known for kidney pies and potatoes. Indians make curries and dhal. Italians are known for their pasta. Have students identify one of their favorite "cultural" dishes. Students should describe the dish to the class and tell which culture it represents in their family. **OL**

Objectives
- Identify literary elements: external conflict, internal conflict
- Identify author's point of view
- Use comprehension skills

Teach

Ask: How does the narrator's brother feel as they eat breakfast? *(He is sad.)* Why is he sad? *(He doesn't get to go to school like the narrator.)* Why? *(He has to work in the cotton fields for the season.)* **AS Ask:** Why do you think the narrator gets to go to school now and his brother doesn't? *(Possible response: He is younger and can't work in the cotton fields yet. He needs more schooling to catch up with his older brother.)* **Ask:** Do you think it is fair that Roberto has to work longer? Why? *(Possible response: It isn't fair because all kids deserve to go to school instead of work.)* **OL AL**

R Reading Skill

Review Identifying Problems and Solutions

Ask: What problems are introduced in the last two paragraphs on the page? *(Possible response: At first, the narrator has a hard time remembering English so he can explain his situation to the principal. Then he is scared as he enters his new classroom and everyone looks at him.)* **OL**

The next morning I could hardly move. My body ached all over. I felt little control over my arms and legs. This feeling went on every morning for days until my muscles finally got used to the work.

BQ It was Monday, the first week of November. The grape season was over and I could now go to school. I woke up early that morning and lay in bed, looking at the stars and **savoring** the thought of not going to work and of starting sixth grade for the first time that year. Since I could not sleep, I decided to get up and join Papa and Roberto at breakfast. I sat at the table across from Roberto, but I kept my head down. I did not want to look up and face him. I knew he was sad. He was not going to school today. He was not going tomorrow, or next week, or next month. He would not go until the cotton season was over, and that was sometime in February. I rubbed my hands together and watched the dry, acid stained[14] skin fall to the floor in little rolls. **7**

When Papa and Roberto left for work, I felt relief. I walked to the top of a small grade next to the shack and watched the "Carcanchita" disappear in the distance in a cloud of dust.

Two hours later, around eight o'clock, I stood by the side of the road waiting for school bus number twenty. When it arrived I climbed in. Everyone was busy either talking or yelling. I sat in an empty seat in the back.

R When the bus stopped in front of the school, I felt very nervous. I looked out the bus window and saw boys and girls carrying books under their arms. I put my hands in my pant pockets and walked to the principal's office. When I entered I heard a woman's voice say: "May I help you?" I was startled. I had not heard English for months. For a few seconds I remained speechless. I looked at the lady who waited for an answer. My first instinct was to answer her in Spanish, but I held back. Finally, after struggling for English words, I managed to tell her that I wanted to enroll in the sixth grade. After answering many questions, I was led to the classroom.

Mr. Lema, the sixth grade teacher, greeted me and assigned me a desk. He then introduced me to the class. I was so nervous and scared at that moment when everyone's eyes were on me

---

14. The narrator's hands are *acid stained* by grapes.

Vocabulary

savoring (SAY vur ing) *v.* taking great delight in

7 Comparing Literature

Conflict What conflict has been solved for the narrator? What new conflict does he have? What about Roberto? Does he have a conflict? If so, what is it? Write your answers in your conflict chart.

Additional Support

Differentiated Instruction

Using Graphic Organizers Suggest that students use graphic organizers to help them better understand the story. Draw a story map on the board, including the headings *Title, Characters, Plot Summary*. Within the story map, students might find it useful to use graphics such as a sequence-of-events chart for the plot summary or a character web to further analyze the author's characterization. Provide students with a variety of graphic organizers and guide them in using the organizers to help them analyze the story. Invite students to work on their graphic organizers with partners or in small groups. **EL BL**

that I wished I were with Papa and Roberto picking cotton. After taking roll, Mr. Lema gave the class the assignment for the first hour. "The first thing we have to do this morning is finish reading the story we began yesterday," he said enthusiastically. He walked up to me, handed me an English book, and asked me to read. "We are on page 125," he said politely. When I heard this, I felt my blood rush to my head; I felt dizzy. "Would you like to read?" he asked **hesitantly.** I opened the book to page 125. My mouth was dry. My eyes began to water. I could not begin. "You can read later," Mr. Lema said understandingly.

For the rest of the reading period I kept getting angrier and angrier with myself. I should have read, I thought to myself. **8**

During recess I went into the restroom and opened my English book to page 125. I began to read in a low voice, pretending I was in class. There were many words I did not know. I closed the book and headed back to the classroom.

Mr. Lema was sitting at his desk correcting papers. When I entered he looked up at me and smiled. I felt better. I walked up to him and asked if he could help me with the new words. "Gladly," he said.

The rest of the month I spent my lunch hours working on English with Mr. Lema, my best friend at school.

One Friday during lunch hour Mr. Lema asked me to take a walk with him to the music room. "Do you like music?" he asked me as we entered the building.

"Yes, I like *corridos*,"[15] I answered. He then picked up a trumpet, blew on it, and handed it to me. The sound gave me goose bumps. I knew that sound. I had heard it in many *corridos*. "How would you like to learn how to play it?" he asked. He must have read my face because before I could answer, he added: "I'll teach you how to play it during our lunch hours."

That day I could hardly wait to get home to tell Papa and Mama the great news. As I got off the bus, my little brothers and sisters ran up to meet me. They were yelling and screaming. I thought they were happy to see me, but when I opened the door to our shack, I saw that everything we owned was neatly packed in cardboard boxes. **9 10** ○

---

15. **Corridos** (koh REE dohs) are songs, especially slow, romantic ones.

Vocabulary

hesitantly (HEZ uh tunt lee) *adv.* in a way that shows uncertainty or fear

Practice the Skills

8 | **Comparing Literature**

Conflict What conflicts does the narrator face when he goes to school? Are they external or internal conflicts, or both? Add them to your conflict chart.

9 | **Comparing Literature**

Conflict When the narrator opens the door to his home at the end of the story, what new conflict does he face? Does that tell you anything about the major conflict of this story? Do you think the conflict will be resolved? At the end of your conflict chart, make a few notes about this.

10 **BIG Question**

How do you think the main character of "The Circuit" would answer the Big Question about what is fair and what is not? Record your answer on "The Circuit" page of Foldable 3. Your response will help you complete the Unit Challenge later. **BQ**

The Circuit **353**

Teach

L Literary Elements

Conflict Ask: What is the conflict on this page? *(The narrator is afraid to read in front of the class.)* **OL Ask:** How does he resolve his conflict? *(He works on his English with his teacher at lunch.)*

BQ **BIG Question**

Ask: Do you think the story supports the saying "Life isn't fair"? Why or why not? *(Possible response: It does support the saying because the last thing that happens to the narrator is unfair. His hopes of having some childhood fun are dashed at the very end of the story.)* **OL AL**

CheckPoint

Use the CheckPoint questions provided on Presentation Plus! to check for comprehension of the selection. These questions can be used with interactive response keypads for immediate student feedback.

Literature Focus Lesson

Mood Explain to students that authors fashion their works to elicit emotional responses in their readers. Go through the last two paragraphs and analyze the word choice and the content. Point out that the narrator is finally showing joy and interest in something. Then, the author changes the mood immediately by describing the inside of the shack. The reader knows the narrator's response to such a scene because it was presented at the beginning of the text. Now the reaction is even more poignant because the narrator is excited about being a child instead of working in the fields. Have students write an alternate ending to the story in their Learner's Notebooks. **OL**

Objectives
- Identify problem and solution
- Identify literary elements: tone and mood
- Identify and analyze character

Assess

Vocabulary Check

The Scholarship Jacket

1. vile
2. coincidence
3. dismay
4. muster
5. withdrawn

The Circuit

6. drone
7. instinctively
8. hesitantly
9. sharecropper
10. acquired
11. savoring

Objectives (pp. 354–355)
Reading Compare and contrast across texts: conflict
Literature Identify literary elements: external conflict, internal conflict

After You Read

The Scholarship Jacket & The Circuit

Vocabulary Check

For items 1–11, choose the best vocabulary word from the list to fill each blank. Write your answers on a separate sheet of paper.

The Scholarship Jacket

coincidence   dismay   muster   withdrawn   vile

1. The sticky cough medicine caused me to wrinkle my nose because of its ___ taste.
2. I ran into my cousin twice in one day: once at the grocery store and once at the doctor's office. What a ___!
3. I felt ___ when I saw the amount of work we had to finish before dinner.
4. With all the courage that I could ___, I marched into the store and demanded that my money be returned.
5. On the boy's first day of school, he was shy and ___.

The Circuit

sharecropper   acquired   drone   instinctively   savoring   hesitantly

6. The ___ of the lawnmower woke me.
7. Most mother animals protect their babies ___ .
8. I knew that our neighbor wasn't very friendly, so I rang the doorbell ___.
9. The ___ gave the landowner part of the money he earned from crop sales.
10. I ___ some skill in carpentry when I worked in my uncle's shop.
11. I was ___ the taste of hot, cheesy pizza.

Reading/Critical Thinking

On a separate sheet of paper, answer the following questions.

BIG Question

12. Was Grandpa being fair when he said he wouldn't pay the fifteen dollars? Explain.

The Scholarship Jacket

13. Recall Why did Martha deserve to receive the scholarship jacket more than Joann?

Tip **Right There**

14. Recall What were Mr. Boone and Mr. Schmidt arguing about?

Tip **Think and Search**

15. Interpret What does Grandpa mean when he says, "If you pay for it, Marta, it's not a scholarship jacket, is it?"

Tip **Author and Me**

16. Infer Did the principal want Martha to receive the jacket?

Tip **Author and Me**

17. Evaluate Did you find this story realistic and believable? Explain why or why not.

Tip **On My Own**

The Circuit

18. Recall What does the narrator mean when he says in the first sentence, "It was that time of year again"?

Tip **Right There**

19. Interpret At the beginning of the story, how did the main character feel about moving to Fresno?

Tip **Author and Me**

20. Interpret Why do you think the narrator spent recess practicing his reading?

Tip **On My Own**

21. Interpret At the end of the story, how do you think the boy feels when he sees the packed boxes?

Tip **On My Own**

Writing: Compare the Literature

Use Your Notes

22. Follow these steps to use the notes in your Conflict charts to compare the conflicts in "The Scholarship Jacket" and "The Circuit."

Step 1: Look at your charts and make notes about what you think is the **main conflict** in each story.

Step 2: Write down the total number of conflicts in each story. Also, make notes about whether only the main character faced conflicts or if other characters in the story had conflicts as well.

Step 3: Look at the charts and make notes about the different kinds of conflicts in each story. Were there more external or internal conflicts? If there were external conflicts, make notes about what kind they were. Were they between two people? Were they between a person and a force outside the person?

Get It on Paper

To compare the conflicts in "The Scholarship Jacket" and "The Circuit," answer these questions on a separate sheet of paper.

23. Is the main conflict different or the same in the two stories? Explain your answer.

24. How many conflicts did you find in "The Scholarship Jacket"? What kind were they?

25. How many conflicts did you find in "The Circuit"? What kind were they?

26. Was the main conflict resolved in both stories? Did this affect the way you felt about each story?

Reading/Critical Thinking

BIG Question

12. Responses will vary.

The Scholarship Jacket

13. Martha had the best grades.

14. They argued about who should get the jacket.

15. Possible response: A scholarship jacket is an award, not something to buy.

16. Possible response: He did because he "made an exception" to the rule so she could have it.

17. Responses will vary.

The Circuit

18. He means it was time to move again.

19. Possible response: He didn't want to leave the strawberry farm.

20. Possible response: He wants to read English better.

21. Possible response: He feels dismay and disappointment.

Close

Review the Big Question and hold a class discussion about the fairness of the circumstances in both selections.

Writing: Compare the Literature

Use Your Notes

22. Completed charts will differ.

Get It On Paper

23. Possible response: different; the main conflict in "The Scholarship Jacket" is between the principal and Martha; the main conflict in "The Circuit" is between the narrator's family and poverty.

24. Responses will vary.

25. Responses will vary.

26. Possible response: the main conflict was resolved in "The Scholarship Jacket," but it was not resolved in "The Circuit."

355

The Unit Challenge

Focus

BELLRINGER Options

- **Selection Focus Transparency 8**
- **Daily Language Practice Transparency 30**
Focus Activity Ask: Which selections were about situations familiar to you? What did you learn about handling those situations?

Teach

Group Activity: TV Call-In Show

- If students have difficulty deciding which situations to feature on their show, suggest they choose those that young people would most identify with.

- Each student can write his or her own lines. Then, the group can organize and fine-tune the final script.

- Suggest that the show host ask for comments or questions and field them to the show's expert or participants as appropriate.

Assess/Close

Group Activity

Ask: What new understanding of the Big Question did you gain from the group activity? *(Have students write their responses in their Learner's Notebooks and then choose an insight to share with the rest of the class.)* **OL**

356

UNIT 3 WRAP-UP

Answering What's Fair and What's Not?

You've just read several different selections and you thought about what's fair and what's not. Now use what you've learned to do the Unit Challenge.

The Unit Challenge

Choose Activity A or Activity B and follow the directions for that activity.

A. Group Activity: TV Call-In Show

With five other students, imagine that you produce a TV show in which people call in with questions about a topic. The topic today is "What's fair and what's not?"

1. **Discuss the Assignment** Brainstorm with members of your group to come up with unfair situations. The notes you made on your Foldable will give you some ideas from the selections in the unit. Choose a member of the group to record the group's ideas. You can also share ideas from your own experience.

2. **Plan the Show** Discuss the ideas on the list. Choose three situations to feature on the show. Then decide what each group member will do.
   - Choose one member to act as the host.
   - Choose group members who will call the show with questions.
   - Choose another member to act as the show's expert, or person who answers the callers' questions.

3. **Write a Script** Work together to write a script for the show. When you write a script, you write down what the people who are participating will do and say.
   - Decide what the host will say about the topic at the beginning and end of the show.
   - For each caller, write a description of the situation and finish with a question about what is unfair in that situation.
   - Discuss how each situation should be resolved. Then write an answer for the expert to give to each caller's question.
   - Organize the script in the order in which the different parts will be used in the show. Each member of the group should have a copy of the final script.

4. **Practice the Show** As a group, practice reading your parts. Change the script as needed to clarify questions or answers and to help the show run more smoothly.

5. **Present the Show** Now you're ready to present your show to the class. At the end of the show, ask your audience to share their ideas about what's fair and what's not in the situations you presented.

B. Solo Activity: A Rap or Song

Musicians write raps and songs about things that they think are unfair. Think about a situation or issue that you think is unfair. You'll write a rap or song to get others to see the situation as you do.

1. **Choose Your Topic** Think about possible topics for your rap or song. Look through your Foldable notes for ideas. Think of experiences that you or someone close to you has had that seemed unfair. List all of your ideas in your Learner's Notebook.

2. **Select a Song** Think of a rap or song whose beat, rhyme pattern, or tune you like. You're going to use that rap or song's beat, rhyme pattern, or tune to write lyrics (words to a song) about a topic you think is unfair.

3. **Start Writing** Keep your audience in mind and the message you want them to understand. Write down the topic of your rap or song.

   - Tell the story of the topic you chose. Include your thoughts and feelings about it. Explain what is unfair and what should be done about it.

   - Make your words fit the same beat, rhyme pattern, or tune as the song or rap you chose.

   - If you are having trouble writing the story in song or rap form, don't worry! Just write the story in sentences first.

   - Think of a catchy title for your rap or song. Your title should draw attention to the topic and make people want to hear your message.

Rap or Song	
Topic:	
Title:	
Rap or song to pattern mine after:	
Lyrics:	

4. **Give It Some Shape** Now it's time to go back and revise your rap or song.

   - If you need to, read over your sentences and separate them into "lines." Now look at each line. Does it say what you want it to? Can you make it shorter and clearer? Can you change the last words of lines so that they rhyme?

   - Review your song or rap to make sure it makes sense.

5. **Say It!** When you are ready, present your rap or song to the members of your class. Discuss with your classmates whether or not they got your message about your subject, or if they agree or disagree.

Teach

Solo Activity: Tell It in a Rap or Song

- Suggest that students select a topic from their list by asking themselves, "Which topic do I feel most strongly about?"

- As a prewriting strategy, have students jot down in their Learner's Notebooks words, phrases, thoughts, and feelings that the topic brings to mind.

- Students may create their own beat, rhyme pattern, or tune.

- Suggest that students brainstorm lists of rhyming words in their Learner's Notebooks. Some students may find a rhyming dictionary useful.

- Tell students that many raps and songs include a refrain—a line or group of lines that is repeated. A refrain often emphasizes an important idea. Encourage students to use a refrain, if appropriate, in their rap or song to call attention to an important idea.

- Students may wish to photocopy and swap rap or song texts with one another.

Assess/Close

Solo Activity

Ask: Do you think a rap or song is a good format for expressing thoughts and feelings about the Big Question? Why or why not? *(Responses will vary.)* **AS**

Objectives
- Participate in a group activity
- Write a script
- Write and perform a rap or song
- Practice and use effective speaking techniques

357

Focus

Vocabulary Preview

List the following words on the board:

- compounded
- civilization
- muffled
- slackened
- immense
- suspended
- solemn

Review their definitions.

Build Background

This science fiction story is set on Venus.

- Venus is surrounded by thick, dense clouds of sulfuric acid that cause acid rain.
- In this story, humans live on Venus, where Bradbury imagines there is nearly constant rain.

Teach

R Reading Skill

Review Inferring Ask: Who is speaking the opening lines of the story? *(the children waiting to see the Sun)* **Ask:** How do you know this? *(The author describes the children in the first paragraph after the dialogue.)* **OL**

Readability Scores
Dale-Chall: 8.6
DRP: 51
Lexile: 950

Ray Bradbury

Meet the Author

Ray Bradbury was born in Illinois. He is best known for his science fiction and fantasy stories. He has published more than 30 books, including a collection of short stories, poems, essays, and plays. His most popular books include *The Martian Chronicles, Fahrenheit 451,* and *Something Wicked This Way Comes.* In his writing, Bradbury offers warnings against the dangers of uncontrolled technological development. Bradbury has won numerous awards for his science fiction writing. See page R1 of the Author Files for more on Ray Bradbury.

Literature Online

Author Search For more about Ray Bradbury, go to www.glencoe.com.

All Summer in a Day

by Ray Bradbury

"READY?"

"Ready."

"Now?"

"Soon."

"Do the scientists really know? Will it happen today, will it?"

"Look, look; see for yourself!"

The children pressed to each other like so many roses, so many weeds, intermixed, peering out for a look at the hidden sun.

It rained.

It had been raining for seven years; thousand upon thousands of days compounded and filled from one end to the other with rain, with the drum and gush of water, with the sweet crystal fall of showers and the concussion[1] of

R

---

1. Here, *concussion* refers to a violent shaking or pounding.

Additional Support

Literature Online

Author Search To expand students' appreciation of Ray Bradbury, have them access the Web site for additional information and resources.

Literature Focus Lesson

Summary The story is set in a colony of people from Earth who live on Venus. Once every seven years, the rain on Venus stops and the Sun comes out. A group of schoolchildren waits eagerly to see the Sun. The children do not accept Margot because she is a more recent arrival to Venus who remembers life on Earth without constant rain. Before the rain stops, the other children lock Margot in a closet. Then they enjoy the two hours of summer, playing outside in the sunshine. After the rain begins again, they remember Margot and let her out. **OL**

storms so heavy they were tidal waves come over the islands. A thousand forests had been crushed under the rain and grown up a thousand times to be crushed again. And this was the way life was forever on the planet Venus, and this was the schoolroom of the children of the rocket men and women who had come to a raining world to set up civilization and live out their lives.

"It's stopping, it's stopping!"

"Yes, yes!"

Margot stood apart from them, from these children who could never remember a time when there wasn't rain and rain and rain. They were all nine years old, and if there had been a day, seven years ago, when the sun came out for an hour and showed its face to the stunned world, they could not recall. Sometimes, at night, she heard them stir, in remembrance, and she knew they were dreaming and **R1** remembering gold or a yellow crayon or a coin large enough to buy the world with. She knew they thought they remembered a warmness, like a blushing in the face, in the body, in the arms and legs and trembling hands. But then they always awoke to the tatting drum, the endless shaking down of clear bead necklaces upon the roof, the walk, the gardens, the forests, and their dreams were gone.

All day yesterday they had read in class about the sun. About how like a lemon it

Analyzing the Photo How would you describe the feeling you get from this photo? Is it similar to the feeling you get from the story? Explain.

was, and how hot. And they had written small stories or essays or poems about it:

> I think the sun is a flower,
> That blooms for just one hour.

That was Margot's poem, read in a quiet voice in the still classroom while the rain was falling outside.

"Aw, you didn't write that!" protested one of the boys.

"I did," said Margot. "I *did*."

"William!" said the teacher.

But that was yesterday. Now the rain was slackening,[2] and the children were crushed **R2** in the great thick windows.

---

2. When the rain was *slackening*, it was beginning to stop.

Teach

R1 Reading Skill

Review Clarifying Say: The author states that the children remember "gold or a yellow crayon or a coin large enough to buy the world with." What is he describing? Skim the third full paragraph on page 359 to find the answer. *(the Sun)* **AL**

R2 Reading Skill

Review Inferring Ask: How do you think the children feel as the rain begins to slow down? *(Possible response: The children probably feel excited and impatient.)* **OL**

Differentiated Instruction

Illustrated Poems The children in "All Summer in a Day" don't remember ever seeing the Sun, but they write about it in school. Have students work in pairs to produce illustrated poems about the Sun. Tell partners to start by listing all the words they can think of to describe the Sun. Then have them use the words to write a short poem. Next, partners should create a painting or draw a picture to accompany their poem. Create a classroom display of the completed poems and pictures. **BL OL**

Objectives
- Identify literary elements: tone
- Clarify ideas and text
- Make Inferences
- Learn and use new vocabulary

359

Teach

C Critical Thinking

Analysis Say: Why don't the other children like Margot? *(She doesn't participate in their games. She remembers the Sun.)* BL

R1 Reading Skill

Review Distinguishing Fact and Opinion Ask: When the children say that Margot is lying, are they stating a fact or expressing an opinion? *(They are expressing an opinion. They cannot prove that she is lying.)* OL

R2 Reading Skill

Review Inferring Ask: Why might the children accuse Margot of lying about remembering the Sun? *(Possible response: They are jealous of her. They wish they could remember, too.)* OL

"Where's teacher?"

"She'll be back."

"She'd better hurry, we'll miss it!"

They turned on themselves, like a feverish wheel, all tumbling spokes.

Margot stood alone. She was a very frail girl who looked as if she had been lost in the rain for years and the rain had washed out the blue from her eyes and the red from her mouth and the yellow from her hair. She was an old photograph dusted from an album, whitened away, and if she spoke at all her voice would be a ghost. Now she stood, separate, staring at the rain and the loud wet world beyond the huge glass.

"What're *you* looking at?" said William. Margot said nothing.

"Speak when you're spoken to." He gave her a shove. But she did not move; rather she let herself be moved only by him and nothing else.

They edged away from her, they would not look at her. She felt them go away. And this was because she would play no games with them in the echoing tunnels of the underground city. If they tagged her and ran, she stood blinking after them and did not follow. When the class sang songs about happiness and life and games her lips barely moved. Only when they sang about the sun and the summer did her lips move as she watched the drenched windows.

And then, of course, the biggest crime of all was that she had come here only five years ago from Earth, and she remembered the sun and the way the sun was and the sky was when she was four in Ohio. And they, they had been on Venus all their lives, and they had been only two years old when

last the sun came out and had long since forgotten the color and heat of it and the way it really was. But Margot remembered.

"It's like a penny," she said once, eyes closed.

"No it's not!" the children cried.

"It's like a fire," she said, "in the stove."

"You're lying, you don't remember!" cried the children.

But she remembered and stood quietly apart from all of them and watched the patterning windows. And once, a month ago, she had refused to shower in the school shower rooms, had clutched her hands to her ears and over her head, screaming the water mustn't touch her head. So after that, dimly, dimly, she sensed it, she was different and they knew her difference and kept away.

Analyzing the Photo Does the person in this picture remind you of Margot in the story? Why or why not?

Additional Support

Literature Focus Lesson

Science Fiction "All Summer in a Day" is an example of science fiction. Writers of this genre use current scientific knowledge to imagine what the future may be like. Have students brainstorm a list of questions they could answer about the future in a science fiction story. In his

story, Bradbury answers the question, "What would it be like to live on a planet where it nearly always rains?" Students might ask questions like "What will cars be like in the future?" or "How will we shop in the year 2050?" Have students share their ideas with the class. EL BL

There was talk that her father and mother were taking her back to Earth next year; it seemed vital[3] to her that they do so, though it would mean the loss of thousands of dollars to her family. And so, the children hated her for all these reasons of big and little consequence.[4] They hated her pale snow face, her waiting silence, her thinness, and her possible future.

"Get away!" The boy gave her another push. "What're you waiting for?"

Then, for the first time, she turned and looked at him. And what she was waiting for was in her eyes.

"Well, don't wait around here!" cried the boy savagely. "You won't see nothing!"

Her lips moved.

"Nothing!" he cried. "It was all a joke, wasn't it?" He turned to the other children. "Nothing's happening today. *Is* it?"

They all blinked at him and then, understanding, laughed and shook their heads. "Nothing, nothing!"

"Oh, but," Margot whispered, her eyes helpless. "But this is the day, the scientists predict, they say, they *know*, the sun . . ."

"All a joke!" said the boy, and seized her roughly. "Hey, everyone, let's put her in a closet before teacher comes!"

"No," said Margot, falling back.

They surged[5] about her, caught her up and bore her, protesting, and then pleading, and then crying, back into a tunnel, a room, a closet, where they slammed and locked the door. They stood looking at the door and saw it tremble from her beating and

throwing herself against it. They heard her muffled cries. Then, smiling, they turned and went out and back down the tunnel, just as the teacher arrived.

"Ready, children?" She glanced at her watch.

"Yes!" said everyone.

"Are we all here?"

"Yes!"

The rain slackened still more.

They crowded to the huge door.

The rain stopped.

It was as if, in the midst of a film concerning an avalanche, a tornado, a hurricane, a volcanic eruption, something had, first, gone wrong with the sound apparatus,[6] thus muffling and finally cutting off all noise, all of the blasts and repercussions[7] and thunders, and then, second, ripped the film from the projector and inserted in its place a peaceful tropical slide which did not move or tremor. The world ground to a standstill. The silence was so immense and unbelievable that you felt your ears had been stuffed or you had lost your hearing altogether. The children put their hands to their ears. They stood apart. The door slid back and the smell of the silent, waiting world came in to them.

The sun came out.

It was the color of flaming bronze and it was very large. And the sky around it was a blazing blue tile color. And the jungle burned with sunlight as the children, released from their spell, rushed out, yelling, into the springtime.

---

3. Something that is *vital* is very important.

4. *Consequence* is importance.

5. When the children *surged,* they pushed or moved forward with a force like a wave.

6. An *apparatus* is something created or invented for a particular purpose.

7. *Repercussions* are echoes or vibrations.

Teach

R Reading Skill

Review Inferring Ask: How do you think Margot feels when the other children push her into the closet? *(terrified, desperate, alone, angry)* **BL**

L Literary Element

Mood Say: The children rush outside into the springtime. What is the mood of this scene? *(happy and excited)* **OL**

Reading in the Real World

Citizenship Although "All Summer in a Day" takes place in a remote, futuristic setting, the bullying situation it describes is similar to situations in the world today. Have students brainstorm responses to bullying. Have two students role-play an interaction between a bully and a victim. Other students can evaluate the choices made and suggest alternatives. Have students investigate the resources available within the school district to deal with bullying. Ask them to evaluate these resources and write a class letter to the school board suggesting improvements. **OL AL**

Objectives
- Distinguish fact from opinion
- Identify literary elements: mood
- Identify literary elements: bias
- Make inferences
- Analyze text

361

YOUR TURN

Teach

R Reading Skill

Review Inferring Ask: Why does the girl cry when she sees a raindrop on her palm? *(She understands that the period of sunlight is over; the rain is returning.)* **OL**

L Literary Element

Mood Say: While the children are playing outside, the narrator never mentions Margot. How is the mood of this scene affected by the knowledge that Margot is trapped in the closet? *(Even though the children are happy, there is a mood of anxiety and sadness because Margot is trapped.)* **AL**

"Now, don't go too far," called the teacher after them. "You've only two hours, you know. You wouldn't want to get caught out!"

But they were running and turning their faces up to the sky and feeling the sun on their cheeks like a warm iron; they were taking off their jackets and letting the sun burn their arms.

"Oh, it's better than the sun lamps, isn't it?"

"Much, much better!"

They stopped running and stood in the great jungle that covered Venus, that grew and never stopped growing, tumultuously,[8] even as you watched it. It was a nest of octopi, clustering up great arms of fleshlike weed, wavering, flowering in this brief spring. It was the color of rubber and ash, this jungle, from the many years without sun. It was the color of stones and white cheeses and ink, and it was the color of the moon.

Visual Vocabulary
Octopi is the plural form of octopus. An octopus is a sea creature that has eight arms.

The children lay out, laughing, on the jungle mattress, and heard it sigh and squeak under them, resilient[9] and alive. They ran among the trees, they slipped and fell, they pushed each other, they played hide-and-seek and tag, but most of all they squinted at the sun until tears ran down their faces, they put their hands up to that yellowness and that amazing blueness and breathed of the fresh, fresh air and listened and listened to the silence which suspended them in a blessed sea of no sound and no

motion. They looked at everything and savored everything. Then, wildly, like animals escaped from their caves, they ran and ran in shouting circles. They ran for an hour and did not stop running.

And then—

In the midst of their running one of the girls wailed.

Everyone stopped.

The girl, standing in the open, held out her hand.

"Oh, look, look," she said, trembling.

They came slowly to look at her opened palm.

In the center of it, cupped and huge, was a single raindrop.

She began to cry, looking at it.

They glanced quietly at the sky.

"Oh. Oh."

A few cold drops fell on their noses and their cheeks and their mouths. The sun faded behind a stir of mist. A wind blew cool around them. They turned and started to walk back toward the underground house, their hands at their sides, their smiles vanishing away.

A boom of thunder startled them and like leaves before a new hurricane, they tumbled upon each other and ran. Lightning struck ten miles away, five miles away, a mile, a half mile. The sky darkened into midnight in a flash.

They stood in the doorway of the underground for a moment until it was raining hard. Then they closed the door and heard the gigantic sound of the rain falling in tons and avalanches, everywhere and forever.

---

8. ***Tumultuously*** means "in a wildly excited or confused way."

9. Something that is ***resilient*** is capable of springing back into shape or position after being bent, stretched, or pressed together.

Additional Support

Differentiated Instruction

Act It Out Organize students into three groups. Assign each group a portion of the story: the beginning of the story until Margot is put in the closet; the period outside in the Sun; and the return of the rain and the release of Margot. Have each group act out its portion of the story, using gestures and facial expressions in addition to dialogue. Groups should keep in mind the emotions experienced by the characters. Give students the opportunity to rehearse their scenes before they perform them for the class. **OL**

Teach

Sunrise, 1887. George Inness.

R1 **Reading Skill**

Review Identifying Problems and Solutions
Ask: What problem do the children recognize after the rain starts again? *(Margot remains trapped in the closet.)* **BL**
Ask: Is there a satisfactory solution to this problem? Why or why not? *(Possible response: No. The chance to see the Sun has been taken from Margot.)* **AL**

R2 **Reading Skill**

Review Inferring **Ask:** Why can't the children look one another in the eye? *(They are ashamed of how they have treated Margot.)* **OL**

BQ **BIG Question**

Ask: What lesson does "All Summer in a Day" teach about the causes of unfairness? *(Possible response: The story shows that seeing someone as different and being jealous of that person can lead to unfair treatment.)* **AS**

R1

"Will it be seven more years?"
"Yes. Seven."
Then one of them gave a little cry.
"Margot!"
"What?"
"She's still in the closet where we locked her."
"Margot."

R2

They stood as if someone had driven them, like so many stakes, into the floor. They looked at each other and then looked away. They glanced out at the world that was raining now and raining and raining steadily. They could not meet each other's glances. Their faces were solemn and pale.

They looked at their hands and feet, their faces down.
"Margot."
One of the girls said, "Well . . . ?"
No one moved.
"Go on," whispered the girl.
They walked slowly down the hall in the sound of cold rain. They turned through the doorway to the room in the sound of the storm and thunder, lightning on their faces, blue and terrible. They walked over to **BQ** the closet door slowly and stood by it.
Behind the closet door was only silence.
They unlocked the door, even more slowly, and let Margot out. ○

Reading in the Real World

Citizenship Ask students to imagine that the events described in the story are being investigated by the school administration. Give students the option of taking the role of the teacher or of the boy who suggested putting Margot in the closet. Have students write a brief explanation of their actions in the voice of their chosen character. Students who take the role of the boy should explain why Margot was put into the closet and why she wasn't released before the class went outside. Students who take the role of the teacher should explain why a count or roll call wasn't taken to make sure that all students were present. The teacher should also account for failing to notice that Margot was missing. **AL**

Objectives
• Identify literary elements: mood
• Identify problem and solution
• Make inferences

Reading on Your Own

To read more about the Big Question, choose one of these books from your school or local library. Work on your reading skills by choosing books that challenge you.

Fiction

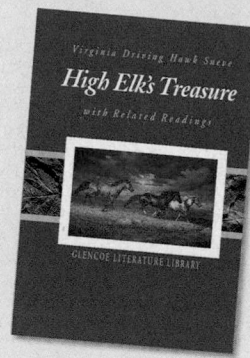

High Elk's Treasure
by Virginia Driving Hawk Sneve

Joe High Elk learns the importance of family and cultural heritage in this tale of exploration and adventure. Read for more details about Joe and the South Dakota reservation on which he lives.

The True Confessions of Charlotte Doyle
by Avi

The only passenger aboard an 1832 sailing ship, thirteen-year-old Charlotte must decide whether she will side with a tyrannical captain or a crew ready for mutiny. Dive right in to this tale of adventure on the high seas!

Lucy's Wish
by Joan Lowery Nixon

In 1886, Lucy is a ten-year-old orphan on the streets of New York. She finds hope when the Children's Aid Society sends her to a new home out West…but her new family is far from perfect.

The Cat Ate My Gymsuit
by Paula Danziger

At first, Marcy Lewis just wants to fit in. She is overweight and overlooked—convinced she'll never get asked out. Then Marcy stands up for one of her teachers, a woman whose courage and conviction Marcy admires. Read to find out what Marcy learns afterward about her own convictions.

Additional Support

Differentiated Instruction

 Use the Glencoe BookLink CD-ROM to create customized reading lists to help students answer the Big Question. Suggestions for Unit 3:

Grade 4: *How Many Spots Does a Leopard Have? and Other Tales* by Julius Lester

Grade 5: *Song of the Trees* by Mildred D. Taylor
Grade 6: *All My Life* by Gerda Weissmann Klein
Grade 7: *Journey to Jo'burg: A South African Story* by Beverly Naidoo
Grade 8: *After the War* by Carol Matas

Nonfiction

Oh, Freedom!: Kids Talk About the Civil Rights Movement with the People Who Made It Happen
by Casey King, Linda Barrett Osborne

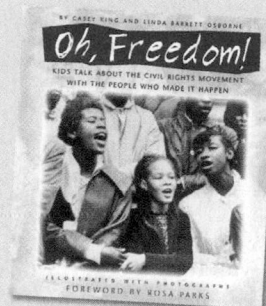

This collection of oral histories about the civil rights movement includes 31 interviews, all conducted by students. Don't miss these profiles in courage—read to find out more about real people's lives during and after segregation.

Words That Built a Nation: A Young Person's Collection of Historic American Documents
by Marilyn Miller

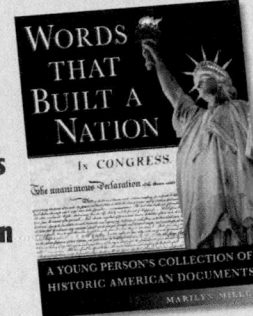

Discover for yourself the Declaration of Independence or the beauty of a Chief Joseph speech. Read this collection of 39 original documents and speeches to learn more about history, language, and the force of big ideas.

When I Was Your Age: Original Stories About Growing Up
Edited by Amy Ehrlich

This collection of stories by ten popular writers includes fiction and nonfiction. Read it to yourself, or read it aloud—either way, these short pieces about growing up will give you something to think about.

Beyond the Limits
by Stacy Allison and Peter Carlin

Stacy Allison sets out with three other climbers to scale Mt. Everest—something no other woman had yet succeeded in doing. Read to find out more about her amazing adventure.

Nonfiction

Ask students to explain the difference between fiction and nonfiction books. *(Nonfiction books describe the lives and actions of real people, while fiction books describe imaginary events.)* **OL**

Autobiographies

Ask: Is an autobiography guaranteed to give a more accurate picture of its subject than a biography? *(No. Someone writing their own story might have more direct access to information, but he or she will still have biases that affect how the story is told.)* **OL**

About the Subjects

Ask students to rank the books shown on this page according to how enthusiastic they are about the subjects. Compile the results on the board to find out which subjects are most interesting to the class as a whole.

Test-Taking Tips

TIP Point out that if students cannot answer one or more of the questions, they should proceed with the rest of the test. They can return to more difficult questions when they have completed all of the questions that they can answer easily.

TIP By reading the questions before they read the passage, students will find out that they have to look for the tone and choose details that support their answer.

Part 1: Literary Elements

1. C
2. C
3. C
4. Responses will vary.

Test Practice

Part 1: Literary Elements

On a separate sheet of paper, write the numbers 1–4. For the first three questions, write the letter of the correct answer next to the number for that question. Then, next to number 4, write your answers to the question.

1. What is the most important part of your writing "style"?
   A. whether you spell correctly
   B. whether you print or use cursive writing
   C. how you put words and sentences together
   D. how many reasons you give for your opinions

Use the following passage to answer question 2.

Rena's rowboat moved gently on the lake. The sun was warm on her face, and a slight breeze moved her hair. From the nearby shore came the faint rustle of chipmunks moving among the trees. A single, feathery cloud moved lazily, high in the blue sky.

2. The mood of this passage could best be described as
   A. sad   C. peaceful
   B. angry   D. enthusiastic

Objectives (pp. 366–367)
Literature Identify literary elements: style, bias, mood • Understand characteristics of argument
Reading Distinguish fact and opinion • Monitor comprehension: clarify • Make inferences • Identify problem and solution

Use the following passage to answer questions 3 and 4.

The child of today is the adult of tomorrow. What a scary thought! I mean, just think about today's kids! If they're inside, they're watching some junk on TV. They have no interest in the educational shows they could be watching. Or maybe they're "instant messaging" their pals, as if that was the only thing a computer could be used for. If they're outside, are they playing sports or doing something useful? Not a chance! They're spray painting slogans on a garage or crowding old people off the sidewalk. The whole time, of course, they're blasting idiotic pop music at an eardrum-cracking volume. Now, can you imagine what our country will be like when these people are *running* it?

3. Which of the following is something the writer has a negative bias about?
   A. television   C. pop music
   B. computers   D. old people

4. What makes the writer's argument a bad one? (Think about what you learned about such things as "support for a view," "generalizations," and "bias.")

Part 2: Reading Skills

On a separate sheet of paper, write the numbers 1–4. Next to numbers 1–3, write the letter of the right answer. Next to number 4, write your answer to the question.

---

1. Which of the following is often a helpful way to clarify confusing text?
   A. Reread it more carefully.
   B. Skip the parts that are unclear.
   C. Concentrate on the parts you understand.
   D. Ignore any words that are unfamiliar.

Read the following passage and answer the questions that follow it.

The bell rang, ending Mr. Wang's class, and the students raced for the door. Three who were trying to get through the doorway at the same time ended up on the floor. One boy hit his head hard enough to raise a large lump.

Mr. Wang began class the next day with an announcement. "I have new rules for this class," he said. He paused until the sound of groans died down. "The first requires everyone to form a single line in order to leave class. Do you understand?"

Fritz raised his hand. "Sure," he said. "When we want to leave class, we form a line." He stood up. "OK, everybody, let's line up and get out of here!"

Mr. Wang had to work hard not to laugh. "That's not funny, Fritz," he said sternly.

2. What can you infer from the students' response to the news that there would be new rules?
   A. They feared Mr. Wang.
   B. They were unhappy about it.
   C. They did not intend to obey the rules.
   D. They understood that rules were necessary.

3. Which of the following is a statement of opinion?
   A. The bell rang, ending Mr. Wang's class.
   B. One boy hit his head hard enough to raise a large lump.
   C. "I have new rules for this class."
   D. "That's not funny, Fritz."

4. What is the problem described in this passage, and what effort is made to solve it?

Literature Online

Unit Assessment To prepare for the Unit test, go to www.glencoe.com.

  Resources for pages 366–369

Use these resources to review, assess, or reteach the Unit: Active Learning Note Taking Guide, Selection and Unit Assessment, ExamView Assessment Suite, and Skill Level Up!™ A Language Arts Game.

Test-Taking Tips

TIP Tell students that when they're answering a multiple-choice question, they should begin by reading the question carefully. Next, they should read each possible response. If necessary, they should reread portions of the passage to look for the answer. Finally, they should choose the best response.

Part 2: Reading Skills

1. A
2. B
3. D
4. *Possible response:* The problem is that students are getting injured in their chaotic attempts to leave the classroom in a hurry. The proposed solution is that students will leave one at a time, in a line.

Part 3: Vocabulary Skills

1. B
2. A
3. C
4. D
5. D
6. A
7. D
8. C
9. A
10. C

Part 3: Vocabulary Skills

On a separate sheet of paper, write the numbers 1–10. Next to each number, write the letter of the correct answer for that question.

For questions 1–5, write the letter of the word or phrase that means about the same as the underlined word.

1. feelings of distress
- **A.** anger
- **B.** misery
- **C.** delight
- **D.** jealousy

2. to have to endure it
- **A.** bear
- **B.** finish
- **C.** leave
- **D.** correct

3. a vile remark
- **A.** loud
- **B.** funny
- **C.** horrible
- **D.** embarrassing

4. if we forsake them
- **A.** notice
- **B.** annoy
- **C.** enjoy
- **D.** desert

5. the child's individuality
- **A.** success
- **B.** loneliness
- **C.** shyness
- **D.** personality

6. Which of the following synonyms best communicates the idea that a wound is a really bad one?
- **A.** gash
- **B.** scrape
- **C.** cut
- **D.** scratch

7. Which of the following synonyms best communicates the idea of looking at something quickly and briefly?
- **A.** gaze
- **B.** watch
- **C.** view
- **D.** glance

8. Which of the following synonyms has the most negative connotation?
- **A.** funny
- **B.** amusing
- **C.** ridiculous
- **D.** humorous

9. Which description is an example of semantic slanting?
- **A.** The room was a cluttered mess.
- **B.** The room contained many objects.
- **C.** A large variety of things filled the entire room.
- **D.** There was a lot of furniture as well as other items in the room.

10. Which statement shows an awareness of the connotation of words?
- **A.** It's more *rectangular* than *square.*
- **B.** Do you call root beer *pop* or *soda?*
- **C.** I would say I'm *selective,* not *fussy.*
- **D.** That dog is really a *spaniel,* not a *terrier.*

Objectives (pp. 368–369)
Vocabulary Learn and use new vocabulary
• Identify semantic slanting • Understand connotation • Understand synonyms: shades of meaning
Grammar Identify parts of speech: adjectives, adverbs, demonstrative pronouns, prepositions, interjections

Part 4: Writing Skills

On a separate sheet of paper, write the numbers 1–8. Next to each number, write the letter of the correct answer for that question.

---

1. In the sentence below, which word is an adjective?

I heard a nervous voice loudly call my name.

A. nervous

B. voice

C. loudly

D. my

2. In the sentence below, which word is an adverb?

The whole family often goes to a nearby beach.

A. whole

B. often

C. goes

D. nearby

3. Which word or phrase best fills in the blank in the sentence below?

Ray responded ___ than I did.

A. happier

B. happily

C. happilier

D. more happily

4. In the sentence below, which word is an article?

Wow, that was such a good movie!

A. Wow

B. such

C. a

D. movie

5. Which word or phrase best fills in the blank in the sentence below?

Our pitcher is the ___ player on the team.

A. taller

B. tallest

C. most tall

D. most tallest

6. In which sentence is the demonstrative *that* used as a pronoun?

A. That was mean.

B. That dog is mine.

C. Is that movie any good?

D. Could I borrow that jacket?

7. In the sentence below, which word is a preposition?

If you like lakes, mountains, or both, you will like the view around the bend.

A. If

B. or

C. around

D. the

8. Which sentence contains an interjection?

A. Stop right there!

B. Gee, I thought so.

C. What a beautiful day!

D. Remember, Jake said he'd be late.

Part 4: Writing Skills

1. A

2. B

3. D

4. C

5. B

6. A

7. C

8. B

UNIT 4
Skills Scope and Sequence

Readability Scores Key
Dale-Chall/DRP/Lexile

PACING (DAYS)		INSTRUCTIONAL SEGMENT LITERATURE	READING SKILLS	LITERARY ELEMENTS
STANDARD	**BLOCK**			
1	1	**Unit Warm-Up, pp. 372–375** Genre Focus: "Whatif" by Shel Silverstein p. 375	Visualizing, SE pp. 374, 375, Interpreting, SE pp. 374, 375 Responding, SE p. 375 Monitoring Comprehension, SE p. 375 Fluency, TWE pp. 371, 375 Connecting, TWE p. 372	Figurative Language, SE p. 375 Form, SE p. 375 Sound Device, SE p. 375
3	2	**Reading Workshop 1, pp. 376–397** "My Father is a Simple Man" by Luis Omar Salinas p. 380 "The All-American Slurp" by Lensey Namioka **5.1/53/890**, p. 386	Visualizing, SE pp. 379, 380, 385, 387, 391, 394, TWE pp. 376, 377, 386, 389, 392, 395 Connecting, SE pp. 389, 392, TWE pp. 385, 393	Stanzas, SE p. 379 Poetic Features, SE pp. 379, 381, TWE p. 380 Stereotyping, SE pp. 385, 386, 390, 395
1		Writing Workshop, Part 1, pp. 398–401 Writing Product: Poem		Poetic Forms, TWE p. 398
3	1	**Reading Workshop 2, pp. 402–419** "Life Doesn't Frighten Me" by Maya Angelou p. 406 "Geraldine Moore the Poet" by Toni Cade Bambara **4.7/55/930**, p. 412	Responding, SE pp. 402, 405, 406, 407, 412, 413, 414, 417, TWE p. 403, 415, 416 Build Fluency, TWE p. 407 Drawing Conclusions, TWE p. 417 Review Visualizing, TWE p. 414	Rhyme, Rhythm and Meter, SE pp. 405, 407, TWE p. 406 Point of View, SE pp. 411, 415, TWE p. 412 Repetition, TWE p. 404 Theme, TWE p. 417
3	3	**Reading Workshop 3, pp. 420–435** "Same Song" by Pat Mora p. 424 "Flowers and Freckle Cream" by Elizabeth Ellis **6.4/54/1020**, p. 430	Interpreting, SE pp. 420, 423, 424, 425, 429, 431, 433, TWE p. 430 Connecting, SE p. 430, TWE pp. 423, 429 Responding, TWE p. 432	Sound Devices, SE pp. 423, 424 Point of View, SE pp. 429, 430, 432 Alliteration, TWE p. 423 Narrator, TWE p. 429

Unit 4 Big Question

The question, "What makes you who you are?" will prompt students to consider how they define themselves and others, what role influence and experience have in their lives, and how they form a sense of identity.

Unit 4 Genre

Many of the selections in this unit are poetry; these selections will help students learn to differentiate between prose and verse. All of the selections in the unit will stimulate students to take a broad view of literature and the way it connects to the Big Question: "What makes you who you are?"

CRITICAL THINKING	VOCABULARY	WRITING AND GRAMMAR	LISTENING, SPEAKING, AND VIEWING
			Viewing the Art, TWE p. 370
Infer, SE pp. 382, 396 Interpret, SE p. 382 Evaluate, SE pp. 382, 396, TWE p. 381 Synthesize, SE p. 396 Comprehension, TWE pp. 380, 384, 390, 394	Academic Vocabulary, SE p. 376 Context Clues, SE pp. 378, 380, 384, 388, 390, TWE pp. 379, 387, 391, 392	Write About Your Reading, SE p. 382, 396 Sentence Types, SE p. 383 End Punctuation, SE p. 397	Analyzing the Photo, SE pp. 388, 391, 394 Analyzing the Art, SE p. 392
	Synonyms, TWE p. 399	Applying Good Writing Traits: Word Choice, SE p. 400 Complete Sentences, SE p. 401 Descriptive Words, TWE p. 398 Choosing a Topic, TWE p. 399 "I Am" poem, TWE p. 399	
Infer, SE p. 408 Visualize, SE p. 408 Respond, SE pp. 408, 418 Evaluate, SE pp. 408, 418 Interpret, SE p. 418 Connect, SE p. 418 Comprehension, TWE pp. 413, 415	Academic Vocabulary, SE p. 402 Context Clues, SE pp. 404, 407, 410, 414, 416, TWE pp. 411, 413, 415	Fragments, SE pp. 409, 419 Write About Your Reading, SE p. 408, 418	Viewing the Art, TWE p. 416
Infer, SE pp. 426, 434 Analyze, SE p. 426 Synthesize, SE p. 434 Comprehension, TWE p. 420	Academic Vocabulary, SE p. 420 Context Clues, SE pp. 422, 425, 428, 430, TWE pp. 431, 432 Vocabulary, TWE p. 422 Prefixes, TWE p. 428 Idioms, TWE p. 433	Write About Your Reading, SE p. 426 Subjects and Predicates SE pp. 427, 435	Viewing the Cartoon, TWE p. 420 Analyzing the Art, SE p. 425 Analyzing the Photo, SE p. 433

Readability Scores Key
Dale-Chall/DRP/Lexile

PACING (DAYS)		INSTRUCTIONAL SEGMENT LITERATURE	READING SKILLS	LITERARY ELEMENTS
STANDARD	BLOCK			
2	cont'd	**Writing Workshop, Part 2, pp. 436–439** Writing Product: Poem		Figures of Speech, SE pp. 436, 437 Sensory Language, TWE p. 437 Figurative Language, TWE p. 438
3	1	**Reading Workshop 4, pp. 440–457** "The March of the Dead" by Robert Service p. 444 "Gene Scene" by Jordan Brown, from *Time for Kids* **8.9/59/790**, p. 452	Monitoring Comprehension, SE pp. 440, 443, 445, 449, 451, 453, TWE pp. 446, 447, 454 Questioning, SE p. 452 Interpreting, TWE p. 441 Visualizing, TWE pp. 444, 445 Fluency, TWE pp. 441, 447	Figurative Language, SE pp. 443, 445, 446, 451, 455, TWE p. 454 Theme, TWE p. 444 Soud Devices, TWE p. 445 Meter, Rhythm, and Rhyme, TWE, p. 454
3	2	**Comparing Literature Workshop, pp. 458–467** "maggie and milly and molly and may" by E. E. Cummings p. 461 "Daydreamers" by Eloise Greenfield p. 463	Monitoring Comprehension, TWE p. 463 Visualizing, TWE p. 461 Fluency, TWE p. 461 Connecting, TWE p. 462	Figurative Language, SE pp. 458, 459, 461, 463, 464 Meter, TWE p. 460 Rhythm, Rhyme, and Meter, TWE pp. 461, 463
4	2	**Unit Wrap-Up, pp. 468–469 Your Turn** "The Walrus and the Carpenter" by Lewis Carroll, pp. 470–473	Interpreting, TWE pp. 471, 473 Responding, TWE p. 473	Figurative Language, TWE pp. 470, 472 Sound Devices, TWE p. 471 Meter, Rhythm, and Rhyme, TWE p. 472

CRITICAL THINKING	VOCABULARY	WRITING AND GRAMMAR	LISTENING, SPEAKING, AND VIEWING
		Figurative Language, TWE p. 436 Rhythm, TWE p. 437 Editing, TWE p. 437	Reading Poetry Aloud, SE p. 439
Synthesize, SE p. 448 Infer, SE pp. 448, 456 Analyze, SE pp. 448, 456 Evaluate, SE p. 456	Context Clues, SE pp. 442, 446, 450, 453, 454, TWE pp. 440, 441, 455 Word Categories, TWE p. 442	Write About Your Reading, SE p. 448 Direct Objects, SE p. 449 Indirect Objects, SE p. 457	Talk About Your Reading, TWE p. 456 Viewing the Photos, TWE pp. 444, 452
	Word Associations, TWE p. 460 Context Clues, TWE p. 465	Compare the Literature, SE p. 467	Analyzing the Art, SE p. 464
			Viewing the Art, TWE p. 471

Reading with Purpose offers a comprehensive package of tools to optimize student learning and the teaching experience. Each resource has been designed to assist students in specific areas and to offer instructional support for teachers. While all of these areas are covered in the core textbook, some students may need extra practice or additional help in specific areas. The resource package is designed so that you, the teacher, can choose which items will best assist your students. You may also use these resources as homework assignments and for assessment purposes. The following are resources recommended for use with Unit 4.

Keys for Unit Resources

- 📁 Blackline Master
- 🗎 Workbook
- 📖 Supplemental Text
- 💿 CD-ROM
- 💿 DVD
- ♨ Transparency
- 💻 Web-based
- 🗄 Fast File

Essential Instructional Support

FAST FILE — UNIT 4 RESOURCES

Reading and Literature
- Academic Vocabulary Review
- Big Question: School to Home
- The Big Question Foldable
- Unit Challenge: Planner and Rubrics
- Comparing Literature Graphic Organizer
- Key Reading Skills
- Active Reading Graphic Organizers
- Literary Analysis
- Unit Vocabulary Review

Writing, Grammar, and Spelling
- Spelling and Handwriting Practice
- Grammar Practice
- Writing Workshop Graphic Organizer

Listening, Speaking, and Viewing
- Viewing and Representing
- Listening and Speaking

English Language Learners
- English Language Coach Review

DIFFERENTIATED INSTRUCTION

- 📁 Leveled Vocabulary Development
- 💿 Skill Level Up!™ A Language Arts Game
- 💿 Listening Library CD
- 💿 BookLink 3
- 💿 Literature Library Vocabulary Puzzlemaker
- 💿 Vocabulary Puzzlemaker

ASSESSMENT

GLENCOE'S ASSESSMENT ADVANTAGE

- 📁 Selection and Unit Assessments
- 📁 Selection Quick Checks
- 📁 Assessment by Learning Objectives
- 📁 Rubrics for Assessing Student Writing, Listening, and Speaking
- 💻 Glencoe Online Essay Grader
- 💿 Interactive Tutor: Self-Assessment
- 💿 ExamView Assessment Suite
- 💿 Literature Library ExamView Assessment Suite

Additional Instructional Support

WRITING, GRAMMAR, AND SPELLING

- Real Success in Writing: Research and Reports
- Writing Constructed Responses
- Spelling Power eWorkbook
- Grammar & Composition Handbook
- Grammar and Language Workbook
- Revising with Style eWorkbook

READING AND LITERATURE

- Active Learning and Note Taking Guide
- inTime Magazines
- Backpack Reader Volume 1
- Literature Library
- Literature Launchers Pre-Reading Videos DVD
- Literature Classics

TRANSPARENCIES

- Read Aloud, Think Aloud Transparencies
- Literary and Text Analysis Transparencies
- Bellringer Options Transparencies
- Grammar and Writing Workshop Transparencies
- Fine Art Transparencies

TECHNOLOGY

- TeacherWorks Plus™
- StudentWorks Plus™
- BookLink 3
- Skill Level Up!™ A Language Arts Game
- ExamView Assessment Suite
- Interactive Tutor: Self-Assessment
- Listening Library CD
- Spanish Listening Library CD
- Literature Classics
- Literature Launchers Pre-Reading Videos DVD
- Literature Library ExamView Assessment Suite
- Vocabulary Puzzlemaker
- Literature Library Vocabulary Puzzlemaker
- glencoe.com
- Online Student Edition
- Presentation Plus!
- Glencoe Online Essay Grader

ENGLISH LANGUAGE LEARNER

- English Language Coach
- Fluency Practice and Assessment
- inTime Magazines (Spanish)
- Spanish Listening Library CD

PROFESSIONAL DEVELOPMENT

- Professional Development Package

Additional Glencoe Resources

Dinah Zike's Foldables

Foldables are three-dimensional, interactive graphic organizers that help students practice basic writing skills, review key vocabulary terms, and answer Big Questions. Every unit contains a foldable activity. You can find the pattern and directions for the Unit 4 Foldable in the Unit 4 Resources Fast Files booklet. You can use the foldables as they are presented or modify them to suit the needs of your students. More information about foldables for Unit 4 can be found on pages R8–R9.

Unit
Big Question

Glencoe Literature Library

This collection of hardcover books includes full-length novels, novellas, plays, and works of nonfiction. Each volume consists of at least one complete extended-length reading accompanied by several related readings from a broad range of genres. A separate Study Guide for each Glencoe Literature Library book provides teaching notes and reproducible activity pages for students.

Glencoe Literature Library titles that complement this unit include:
Cezanne Pinto, by Mary Stolz
High Elk's Treasure, by Virginia Driving Hawk Sneve
Julie of the Wolves, by Jean Craighead George

For a wealth of online resources that support the instruction in Unit 4 of *Glencoe Literature: Reading with Purpose,* students and teachers can visit our Web site at www.glencoe.com. Students will find additional learning, practice, and assessment opportunities such as these, which are noted in the student text:

- **Big Question Overview**
- **Study Central**
- **Author Search**
- **Writing Models**
- **Interactive Literary Elements Handbook**
- **Web Activities**

Teachers will find planning and instructional tools that include the following:

- **Book Lesson Plans**
- **Teacher Forum**
- **Professional Development**
- **Web Activities Lesson Plans (with answers to student activities)**

Go to www.glencoe.com to see the entire selection of Reading with Purpose online resources.

Reading List Generator CD-ROM

Use the Glencoe **BookLink 3** CD-ROM, a database of more than 26,700 titles, to *create customized reading lists* for your students.

- Search for award-winning titles, (e.g., Newbery Award winners, Coretta Scott King Award winners, and Caldecott Medal winners) and for books on several state-recommended reading lists.
- Find Degrees of Reading Power™ (DRP) and Lexile™ readability scores for all selections.
- Organize reading lists by students' reading level, author, genre, theme, or area of interest.
- Get a brief summary of each selection.

You can find recommended leveled readings for this unit with Reading on Your Own (see page 474).

Glencoe's **Presentation Plus!**, a multimedia teaching tool, lets you present dynamic lessons that will engage your students. Using Microsoft PowerPoint,® you can customize the presentations to create your own personalized lessons. Use **CheckPoint** questions with interactive response keypads to get immediate student feedback during lessons, to increase student participation, and to assess student comprehension.

A lively collection of articles drawn from issues of the TIME family of magazines helps students develop the skills they need to interact with informational text in a meaningful way. Each of the news stories, feature articles, reviews, profiles, and essays in the magazine connect to an author, work, or theme in *Glencoe Literature: Reading with Purpose.* Articles for Unit 4 are found in Volume A. See the *inTIME* Teacher's Guide for specific connections to each unit and for reproducible student worksheets designed to develop students' reading and critical thinking skills.

Literature Launchers

Set the scene with Glencoe's Literature Launchers, engaging video segments that introduce each unit's genre focus. Each video brings the genre to life, relating it to your students' worlds.

Insert the Glencoe Literature Launchers Pre-Reading Videos DVD into your DVD player. Select the Unit 4 Launcher from the menu to introduce the genre and Big Question for this unit.

Online Essay Grader

Use Glencoe's Online Essay Grader to score your students' writing and to provide individualized feedback to each student automatically.

You and your students can visit www.glencoe.com to link to the essay grader. *Students* can enter their essays and receive feedback on demand. *You* can manage demographic data, assign tests and generate individual student and aggregated reports. The essay grader can help you

- Save time with automatic scoring and individualized feedback.
- Supplement in-class writing instruction using guided writing practice.
- Get reports for individual students or for special populations.
- Track student improvement over time.

REAL Success: Reading Excellence at All Levels

Glencoe now provides all of your students with the tools they need to become better, more enthusiastic readers. The REAL Success suite of reading and language arts products encourages reading excellence by meeting the needs of students at all levels. Glencoe products that can be used in conjunction with Unit 4 include the following:

- Jamestown Literature: An Adapted Reader
- Jamestown *Reading Fluency*
- Jamestown *Critical Reading Series, In the Line of Duty*
- *Vocabulary Builder*
- *The Glencoe Reader, Course 1*

To order these products, call Glencoe at 1-800-USA-READ.

Teacher Wraparound Edition Key

Level Appropriate Code

AS = Activities for all students

AL = Activities for students working above grade level

OL = Activities for students working at grade level

BL = Activities for students working below grade level

EL = Activities for English language learners

Teacher Wraparound Prompts

R **Reading Skill** These activities help you teach reading comprehension skills.

V **Vocabulary** These activities help students comprehend words and incorporate them into their reading and writing.

C **Critical Thinking** These strategies help students apply and extend what they have learned.

BQ **BIG Question** These activities and questions prompt students to prepare to answer the Big Question.

W **Writing** These activities provide writing opportunities to help students practice writing and comprehend text.

L **Literary Element** These activities and questions help students comprehend selections and learn more about each genre.

E **Text Element** These activities help students comprehend text elements.

LSV **Listening, Speaking, Viewing** These activities help students practice listening, speaking, and viewing skills.

EL **English Language Coach** These skills help English language learners as well as students who need additional reading support.

From an Author

Preparing Students to Read Poetry

Tap into students' knowledge of the genre To gain understanding of what students already know about the genre, teachers can ask students to brainstorm what they already know about poetry, perhaps drawing a web of students' ideas as they speak. Students may remember that sometimes poetry rhymes or has rhythm, that it's a way of expressing feelings, that wording matters, and that there are types of poetry. The teacher's web can show relationships among students' ideas about form, function, and word selection. Students can be invited to bring in favorite bits of poetry, perhaps including lyrics to favorite songs, raps, or jump rope rhymes as they engage in the reading and writing required in this unit.

Kathleen Hinchman

Make personal connections Generations of young people have ended up disliking poetry because teachers identified only some poetry interpretations or themes as correct. Instead of being the teacher who perpetuates such antipathy, ask students to share their interpretations first, building small group, and, then, whole class discussions from their ideas. To do this, teachers may find it helpful to invite a group of students to listen to or read from the same poem and to write about the poem—anything they wanted—for a few minutes after the reading. Invite students to tell one another something about what they wrote, choosing whether or not they actually want to share their quick write. This can be followed with a discussion of similarities and differences in students' responses, which can, in turn, lead into a discussion of interpretations—perhaps comparing students' responses to interpretations published in literary criticisms. Seeing how classmates bring prior knowledge to their interpretations of poetry can help students learn to discern themes with increasing acumen.

Teacher to Teacher

Gloria Dukes
Coastal Middle School
Savannah, Georgia

I introduce the theme "What Makes You Who You Are?" with Write Night, a special evening that brings parents and students together. Students take home questions to interview parents, such as: Who was there when I was born? Why did you choose this particular name for me? Who came to visit you at the hospital? That evening, parents bring in memorabilia from the child's birth, and together parents and children write about the experience in the form of a poem, a song, or a story. I encourage them to share in groups. Then I close the evening with reflective writing that answers questions like: What did you learn about one another that you might not have known? How did this experience change you? I put the reflective writing into an anthology and give a copy to every parent who attends.

Teacher Chat Room

Reading and Writing Poetry

 How can I make poetry interesting to middle school students?

 Middle grade students will like poetry more when they discover that their favorite lyrics or nursery rhymes are a kind of poetry, that their own first response is grounding for poetic interpretation, and, most importantly, that poetry represents a unique, intense way of representing important insights. To help students immerse themselves in different kinds of poetry:

- Bring stacks of a wide range of poetry to your classroom. Include poems ranging from the Shel Silverstein poetry students will remember from their elementary school reading to the Robert Frost poems appreciated by older readers.

- Invite students to work in inquiry groups, reading poetry to themselves and each other and finding poetry to share with the rest of the class in a daily "read aloud" that ends each day's inquiry.

- Students can bring in examples of poetry they find at home, in song lyrics, and on the Internet in youth poetry collections.

- Maintain an ongoing discussion, noting the reasons individuals find particular poems engaging. Tie this discussion to the study of poetry throughout history, noting variations in use and form represented by Homer, Chaucer, Shakespeare, and more contemporary poets.

 How can I help students to understand poetry from different historical periods?

 Invite students to team up and engage in brief inquiry about particular time periods during which poetry was written, noting historical events or issues of gender, race, or class that might have affected the ways in which individuals chose to represent ideas. Students can then read bits of poetry to see what they can discern of its meaning or historical content.

 What language and structures do poetry writers use, and how can students use these elements in their own writing?

 Teachers should explain that authors use poetic devices to come up with the concise representations that make poetry what it is. Students can learn that authors use such poetic devices to tell the stories in narrative poems or to make points in lyric poems. Teach figurative language and sound devices as they are needed to interpret particular poems, one or two at a time. Post these on a bulletin board or work wall for later reference. Conduct brief mini lessons during the writers workshop that refer back to examples in poetry that has been read. Invite students to draft bits of poetry using devices taught in these mini lessons.

UNIT 4

The BIG Question: What Makes You Who You Are?

Key Unit Objectives

- Answer the Big Question
- Identify, understand, and apply the unit's key reading skills
- Identify, understand, and apply the unit's key literary elements
- Write poems

BIG Question

Why Is It Important?
Addressing this big question helps students identify their positive qualities, their likes and dislikes, and the experiences and influences that have helped make them who they are.

Viewing the Art
Ask: What does it mean to "make the most of yourself"? *(Possible response: do your best)* **OL** Invite students to share how they think the art-work fits the quote. *(Possible response: By playing music, the violinist is making the most of her musical skills and gifts.)* **Ask:** How might you make the most of yourself? *(Possible responses: by trying hard in school, by caring for others, by focusing on my good features)* **AS**

"Make the most of yourself, for that is all there is of you.

–Ralph Waldo Emerson, American author, poet, and philosopher

Unit Skills

Reading Skills
- Visualizing, p. 376
- Responding, p. 402
- Interpreting, p. 420
- Monitoring Comprehension, p. 440

Vocabulary
- Context Clues, p. 378

BIG Question What makes you who you are?
Genre Focus: Poetry

Literary Elements
- Rhyme, Rhythm, and Meter, p. 405
- Figurative Language, p. 443

Writing Skills/Grammar
- Poetry, pp. 398, 436
- Word Choice, p. 400
- Complete Sentences, p. 401

LOOKING AHEAD

The skill lessons and readings in this unit will help you develop your own answer to the Big Question.

About the Reading
Each selection in this unit provides insights that can help students address the question, "What makes you who you are?" Students consider the influences, experiences, and characteristics that make up the identities of the people in the unit selections.

About the Skills
The skills taught in this unit have been selected because they are particularly helpful when reading poetry. Each reading selection provides students with opportunities to review and to continue practicing these skills.

NO CHILD LEFT BEHIND

One of the five key skills for reading success is the ability to understand and gain meaning from what is read, according to the *Report of the National Reading Panel* (2000). Monitoring comprehension, which is covered in this unit, will especially help students learn to gain meaning from their reading. Help students become proficient in monitoring their understanding as they read.

Reading Fluency

Reading Aloud Offer these tips for reading a poem out loud:

- Do not stop at the end of every line. Let punctuation marks tell you when and how long to pause. Pause a short time for commas, longer for periods.
- Read a poem silently several times to figure out its meaning. Find words or phrases to emphasize. When you read aloud, say those words louder or slower or in a higher or lower voice.
- Let the feeling of the poem tell you how quickly or slowly to read it.
EL **BL** **OL**

Focus

BELLRINGER Options

✍ **Daily Language Practice Transparency 31**

💿 **LIterature Launcher Focus Activity Write on the board:** Imagine designing an ID tag that would help someone identify you. What three adjectives would you have engraved on your tag? *(Responses will vary.)* **AS**

Teach

R Reading Skill

Review Connecting Say: Suppose you're writing a letter to an adult who hasn't seen you in five years. What would you tell the adult about who you are now? *(Responses will vary.)* **OL**

BQ **BIG Question**

• Have students read the profiles of Miles and Lan and look at their pictures.

• Assign a partner to each student and have partners discuss what influences who people are and what advice they would give to Miles and Lan. **AS**

Connecting to The BIG Question

What Makes You Who You Are?

R If there were another person who looked exactly like you, how would your family and friends know who was the real you? What is it about *you* that they would recognize? What interests do you have? What are your beliefs and values? All of these things—besides your good looks!—help to make you who you are.

Real Kids and the Big Question

MILES had gone away for the summer to visit his grandparents. When he returned home, Miles had grown at least two inches. Miles looked like a different person. Do you think that a summer away from home and growing two inches will change who Miles is? Why or why not?

BQ **LAN** moved to the United States from Vietnam when she was eight years old. Now she speaks English very well. She loves to cook and often helps her grandmother in the kitchen. Lan's class is having a picnic, and everyone will bring food to share. Lan is worried that the other students will not like the kind of food she and her grandmother prepare. What advice would you give her?

Partner Talk

With a partner, discuss what you would say to Miles or Lan. Then discuss with your partner what you think makes a person who he or she is. Is it interests, beliefs, culture, or a combination of all of these things?

Additional Support

Reading in the Real World

Citizenship There are more than 988,000 foreign-born Vietnamese living in the United States, making them the fifth largest immigrant population in the country. More than half of these people live in just two states: California and Texas. Adapting to the culture of their new American homeland can be a challenge for Vietnamese people, as it can be for all immigrants. Have student partners find two facts online or at the library about Vietnamese culture. Ask students to create charts showing in what ways Vietnamese and American cultures are similar and/or different. **OL**

You and the Big Question

Many things go into making you who you are. Reading the selections in this unit will give you a chance to think about some of them.

BQ Literature Online

Big Question Link to Web resources to further explore the Big Question at www.glencoe.com.

Plan for the Unit Challenge

At the end of the unit, you'll use notes from all your reading to complete the Unit Challenge.

You'll choose one of the following activities:

A. Who Am I? Play a game to see how much you know about your classmates.

B. Self-Portrait Collage Make a collage showing what helps to make you who you are.

- Start thinking about which activity you'd like to do so that you can focus your thinking as you go through the unit.

- In your Learner's Notebook, write your thoughts about which activity you'd like to do.

- Each time you make notes about the Big Question, think about how your ideas will help you with the Unit Challenge.

Keep Track of Your Ideas

As you read, you'll make notes about the Big Question. Later, you'll use these notes to complete the Unit Challenge. See pages R8–R9 for help with making Foldable 4. This diagram shows how it should look.

1. Use this Foldable for all selections in this unit.

2. On the front, write **Unit 4** and **What Makes You Who You Are?** Leave the other half of that folded page blank.

3. Across the top of each of the next folded pages, write a selection title. (See page 371 for titles.)

4. To the left of each crease, write **My Purpose for Reading.** Below this heading, you will write your purpose for reading each selection.

5. To the right of each crease, write **The Big Question.** Below this, you will write your thoughts about the Big Question.

Teach

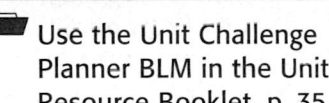

BQ **BIG Question**

Ask: What is the first thing that pops into your mind when you think about what makes you who you are? *(Responses will vary.)* **AS**

FOLDABLES™
Study Organizer

For each selection they read, students will enter notes about how that selection applies to the Big Question. For details about using Dinah Zike's Foldables, see pages R8–R9.

Assess/Close

Ask students to explain how thinking about the Big Question might make them better appreciate themselves and others.

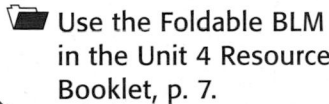

Resources for page 373

📁 Use the Unit Challenge Planner BLM in the Unit 4 Resource Booklet, p. 35.

📁 Use the Foldable BLM in the Unit 4 Resource Booklet, p. 7.

Differentiated Instruction

Creating Visuals Discuss with students how photographs and illustrations can help readers picture characters and concepts, give readers more information, or clarify what they read. Help students to understand that captions can often help readers interpret what they see. Encourage students to include magazine photos or brief sketches in their Learner's Notebooks to illustrate their ideas about who they are. Students might choose to include photographs of themselves or pictures of people, places, and events that have influenced them in some way. Have students write a brief caption for each image. **BL**

Objectives
- Activate prior knowledge
- Make connections from self to text

Focus

BELLRINGER Options

✍ **Daily Language Practice Transparency 32**

✍ **Selection Focus Transparency 9**
Focus Activity Say: Name two ways poems differ from other types of writing. *(Possible response: Poems are often shorter, and they sometimes rhyme.)* **AS**

Teach

R Reading Skill

How to Read Poetry Say: Some poems can be difficult to read at first. How might visualizing help you understand a poem? *(Possible response: Picturing elements in a poem might help me understand actions or descriptions.)* **Ask:** How might interpreting help you understand a poem about a new subject? *(Possible response: I can use what I know about the world to help me figure out the new subject.)* **OL**

Skills Focus
• Key skills for reading poetry
• Key literary elements of poetry

Skills Model
You will see how to use the key reading skills and literary elements as you read
• "Whatif," p. 375

Objectives (pp. 374–375)
Reading Visualize • Respond to literature • Interpret text • Monitor comprehension
Literature Identify features of poetry • Identify sound devices: rhyme, rhythm, meter, alliteration • Identify and interpret figurative language: simile, metaphor, personification

Poetry looks different from other kinds of literature. Poetry is written in **verse**—that is, in lines instead of running text. Many poems may be divided into groups of lines called **stanzas.** Stanzas function like paragraphs in a story. The following are types of poetry:
• **Narrative** poetry tells a story.
• **Lyric** poetry tells about the poet's feelings or emotions.
• **Free verse** has no fixed meter, rhyme, line length, or stanza arrangement.

Why Read Poetry?

A good poem sharpens all of your senses. It helps you see and hear things in a fresh, exciting way. In this unit, you'll learn how to:
• appreciate the use of rhythm and rhyme in poetry
• understand sensory language

How to Read Poetry

Key Reading Skills

These key reading skills are especially useful tools for reading and understanding poetry. You'll see these skills modeled in the Active Reading Model on page 375, and you'll learn more about them later in this unit.

■ **Visualizing** As you read, try to picture in your mind what the writer is describing. (See Reading Workshop 1.)

■ **Responding** Tell what you like, dislike, or find surprising or interesting about a selection. (See Reading Workshop 2.) **R**

■ **Interpreting** Use your own understanding of the world to decide what the events or ideas in a selection mean. (See Reading Workshop 3.)

■ **Monitoring comprehension** You may have to reread a passage to fully understand what a writer means (See Reading Workshop 4.)

Key Literary Elements

Recognizing and thinking about the following literary elements will help you understand more fully what the author is telling you.

■ **Poetic features:** the characteristics that make poetry different from prose (See "My Father Is a Simple Man.")

■ **Rhyme, rhythm, and meter:** the repetition of the end sounds of words and the pattern of beats and stresses (See "Life Doesn't Frighten Me.")

■ **Sound devices: Alliteration:** the repetition of the beginning sounds of words (See "Same Song.")

■ **Figurative language:** language used for descriptive effect, such as personification, simile, and metaphor (See "March of the Dead.")

Additional Support

Literature Focus Lesson

Point of View Pronouns can tell something about the speaker of a poem, or who is "telling" it. A poet might use

• first person *(I)* to make readers feel the narrator or speaker is sharing personal information

• second person *(you)* to make readers feel they are in the story or poem

• third person *(he, she, it)* to tell readers a story about characters that are not "you" or "I"

The most common points of view are first-person and third-person. **BL EL OL**

Whatif₁

by Shel Silverstein

Last night, while I lay thinking here,
Some Whatifs crawled inside my ear
And pranced and partied all night long
And sang their same old Whatif song: **2 3 4**
5 Whatif I'm dumb in school?
Whatif they've closed the swimming pool?
Whatif I get beat up?
Whatif there's poison in my cup?
Whatif I start to cry?
10 Whatif I get sick and die? **5**
Whatif I flunk that test?
Whatif green hair grows on my chest?
Whatif nobody likes me? **6**
Whatif a bolt of lightning strikes me?
15 Whatif I don't grow taller?
Whatif my head starts getting smaller?
Whatif the fish won't bite?
Whatif the wind tears up my kite?
Whatif they start a war?
20 Whatif my parents get divorced?
Whatif the bus is late?
Whatif my teeth don't grow in straight?
Whatif I tear my pants?
Whatif I never learn to dance?
25 Everything seems swell, and then
The nightmare Whatifs strike again! **7 8** ○

R1
R2
R3

Write to Learn If you wrote a poem about your nighttime thoughts, what exact words might you use to give readers a vivid picture of the thoughts that go through your mind?

 Study Central Visit www.glencoe.com and click on Study Central to review poetry.

1 Key Literary Element
Poetic Features *Even if I didn't know this was a poem, the way the lines look would tell me.*

2 Key Literary Element
Sound Devices: Alliteration *The repeated p in "pranced and partied" emphasizes these words.*

3 Key Reading Skill
Visualizing *I can imagine tiny, annoying animals jumping around.*

4 Key Literary Element
Figurative Language *The speaker describes worries and fears as if they are little creatures having a party in his head.*

5 Key Literary Element
Rhyme, Rhythm, and Meter *This poem has a regular way of rhyming and a strong rhythm, which make it fun to read.*

6 Key Reading Skill
Responding *I worry about things at bedtime, too!*

7 Key Reading Skill
Monitoring Comprehension *At first, I was confused about what Whatifs are. That didn't last long! I might reread this poem for fun, but not because I don't get it.*

8 Key Reading Skill
Interpreting *I think the poet is saying that everyone has "What if?" worries and that they're no big deal.*

Teach

R1 Reading Skill

Visualizing Ask: How does the poet help you picture the "Whatifs"? *(The poet describes them crawling inside the speaker's ear, prancing, partying, and singing.)* **BL**

R2 Reading Skill

Interpreting Ask: What are Whatifs? *(things that make the speaker worry)* **BL Ask:** How do the Whatifs make the speaker feel? *(Possible response: They make the speaker feel scared.)* **OL**

R3 Reading Skill

Monitoring Comprehension Say: Reread the last two lines of the poem. What do you learn about Whatifs from these lines? *(Possible response: They come back, even when things seem to be going fine.)* **OL**

English Language Coach

Build Fluency Some students may benefit from meeting with a partner in a quiet place to read the poem. Together both partners should read the first four lines. Then have students take turns reading the "Whatif" lines in the poem. Remind students that they should raise their tone of voice at the end of sentences that ask questions. Ask partners to read the last two lines together. Partners should discuss what they have read, volunteering insights that help both partners comprehend the poem. Encourage students to read with expression. **BL EL**

Objectives
• Interpret text
• Monitor comprehension
• Visualizing

**Objective covered in this
workshop:**
• Visualize

Teaching Students to Visualize

What Is It?
• Visualizing is creating a clear mental picture of something by using a writer's ideas or descriptions.
• Visualizing helps students better understand what the author is saying.
• Visualizing helps students remember what they have read by keeping them engaged with the material.

How to Help Students Get It
• Remind students to pay attention to each detail the writer uses to describe a character, the setting, etc.
• Tell students to constantly ask themselves as they read: What would this look like? How would this work?
• Some students may benefit from actually illustrating their visualizations. Encourage students to keep unlined paper near by when they are reading selections in this unit. When they feel the need to see a description more vividly, invite them to draw what they visualize.

Reading to Answer the Big Question

My Father Is a Simple Man by Luis Omar Salinas
The speaker of this poem is on a walk with his father who is portrayed as a simple but kind and wise man. He expects that he will learn from the father whatever there is to know about greatness.

The All-American Slurp by Lensey Namioka
The narrator of this short story relates the embarrassment she feels when her Chinese family makes mistakes while attempting to master American table manners. She becomes more comfortable with her status as a new American when she realizes that her American friends have similar difficulty learning Chinese etiquette.

Workshop Resources

PACING (DAYS) STANDARD	BLOCK	LESSON	STUDENT MATERIALS	TEACHER RESOURCES

1	½	Key Skill Lesson: Visualizing	🔏 Key Reading Skills Practice, p. 9
			🔏 English Language Coach Review, p. 41
				📖 Bellringer Options Transparencies
				  – Selection Focus Transparency 10
				  – Daily Language Practice 33
				📖 Read Aloud, Think Aloud Transparencies
				  – Key Reading Skills 30
				  – Read Aloud, Think Aloud 33–34
				💿 Presentation Plus!

1	1	"My Father is a Simple Man"	💻 Glencoe Online 🔏 Unit Vocabulary Review, p. 39 🔏 Academic Vocabulary Review, p. 42 📁 English Language Coach 🔏 Active Reading Graphic Organizer, p. 11 🔏 Literary Analysis, p. 10 💿 StudentWorks Plus™ 💻 Online Student Edition 💿 Literature Classics 📁 Selection and Unit Assessments, p. 37	📖 Literary and Text Analysis Transparencies 38 💻 Puzzlemaker 💿 Skill Level Up!™ A Language Arts Game 💻 BookLink 3 📗 Assessment by Learning Objective (Diagnostic and Formative) 💿 Interactive Tutor: Self-Assessment 💿 TeacherWorks Plus™
1		"The All-American Slurp"	💻 Glencoe Online 🔏 Unit Vocabulary Review, p. 39 🔏 Academic Vocabulary Review, p. 42 📁 English Language Coach 🔏 Active Reading Graphic Organizer, p. 13 💿 StudentWorks Plus™ 💻 Online Student Edition 💿 Literature Classics 📁 Selection and Unit Assessments, p. 38	📖 Literary and Text Analysis Transparencies 4 💻 Puzzlemaker 💿 Skill Level Up!™ A Language Arts Game 💻 BookLink 3 📗 Assessment by Learning Objective (Diagnostic and Formative) 💿 Interactive Tutor: Self-Assessment 💿 TeacherWorks Plus™

Keys for Unit Resource

📁 Blackline Master
📗 Workbook
📖 Supplemental Text
💿 CD-ROM
💾 DVD
📖 Transparency
💻 Web-based
🔏 Fast File

Level Appropriate Code

AS = Activities for all students
AL = Activities for students working above grade level
OL = Activities for students working at grade level
BL = Activities for students working below grade level
EL = Activities for English language learners

Focus

BELLRINGER Options

- **Selection Focus Transparency 10**
- **Daily Language Practice Transparency 33**
  Focus Activity Say: Think about someone who is a hero in your life. How has this person influenced you? *(Responses will vary.)* **AS**

Teach

R Reading Skill

Visualizing Ask: What is visualizing? *(picturing something in your mind)* **OL Say:** Visualize the following scenes, and tell what you see in your mind:

- a busy mall around the holidays *(Possible responses: crowds of shoppers, colorful decorations)*
- a park on a sunny day *(Possible responses: blue sky, bright grass, children playing)* **BL**

V Vocabulary

Academic Vocabulary Say: *Visualize* comes from the Latin word *visus*, meaning *sight*. Name other words that come from *visus*. *(Possible responses: visual, vision, vista)* **AL**

Skills Focus

You will practice these skills when you read these selections:
- "My Father Is a Simple Man," p. 380
- "The All-American Slurp," p. 386

Reading
- Visualizing

Literature
- Understanding poetic features

Vocabulary
- Using context clues that involve restatement
- Academic Vocabulary: *visualize*

Writing/Grammar
- Identifying and using different sentence types and end punctuation

Objectives (pp. 376–377)
Reading Visualize • Make connections from text to self

Skill Lesson

Visualizing

Learn It!

What Is It? When you **visualize**, you form pictures in your mind as you read. Visualizing means using your imagination to "see" the scenes that are described in words in a poem or story. When you read about a blue sky, you should "see" a clear blue sky in your mind. Visualizing helps you connect to what you're reading.

- To *visualize* something is to see it in your mind. The writer uses words that help you create pictures as you read.
- Poems create pictures in your mind that suggest different emotions and moods. Can you think of some words that suggest vivid pictures to you?

R

CALVIN AND HOBBES © 1988 Watterson. Dist. By UNIVERSAL PRESS SYNDICATE. Reprinted with permission. All rights reserved.

Analyzing Cartoons
What is Hobbes asking Calvin to visualize here? Why is Calvin so frightened?

Academic Vocabulary

visualize (VIH zhu ul eyez) *v.* to form a mental image or picture of **V**

Additional Support

English Language Coach

Building Background Tell students that, like fiction and nonfiction stories, cartoons can have many different purposes—to entertain readers, to teach readers about a subject, to persuade readers to think a certain way, or to bring up emotions, such as sadness or joy. Explain that although Calvin's adventures exist only in his imagination, Bill Watterson, creator of *Calvin and Hobbes*, often uses them to comment on serious world issues as well as to entertain. Ask students to tell the purpose of the cartoon on page 376. *(Possible responses: to entertain, to tell a funny story)* **EL BL**

Why Is It Important? Visualizing is one of the best ways to understand and remember information in fiction, nonfiction, and informational text. When you read, you try to visualize, or picture, something or someone that is described through words. This helps you to understand what the author is saying.

How Do I Do It? As you read, imagine that you are painting a picture. Read carefully, so that you will be able to include all the details. Imagine what the characters look like. Visualize the setting—a darkened room at night, a small-town street, a family's dinner table. If you are reading a poem or short story, imagine all the details the writer provides. **R**

As you read, jot down notes or make sketches of details that you can "see." Here are the notes that one student jotted down after reading Shel Silverstein's poem "Whatif."

Study Central Visit www.glencoe .com and click on Study Central to review visualizing.

> I could see the boy lying in bed at night thinking about all sorts of horrible stuff. I saw all of his worries—green hair on his chest, his head shrinking, his kite tearing apart. If I had to paint a picture of the scene, I'd do it by showing the little worry monsters going into his ear, filling up his head with awful things. I could make a great drawing of the scene!

Practice It!

Below are some images that are related to the selections that follow this Workshop. As you read each one, what do you see? In your Learner's Notebook, jot down notes or make a sketch about the things you visualize for each phrase.

- a father and son walking together
- a juicy orange cut in half
- a girl munching a stalk of celery
- a fancy restaurant

Use It!

As you read "My Father Is a Simple Man" and "The All-American Slurp," remember the notes you jotted down or the sketches you made to practice visualizing. When you find a detail that you can picture clearly, add it to your notes and sketches.

Teach

Study Central Have students access the Web site to review visualizing and to complete a related activity.

R Reading Skill

Visualizing Say: Setting adds a great deal to a story. How do you picture the setting of a scary story? *(Possible response: It would be dark, with just a little moonlight showing through clouds. There'd be an old, creepy-looking house on a hill.)* **BL Ask:** Why might your "picture" be different from the "pictures" of others in your classroom? *(Possible response: We might be frightened by different things.)* **OL**

Resources for page 377

Use Key Reading Skills Transparency 30 in *Read Aloud, Think Aloud* to help students practice visualizing.

Differentiated Instruction

Mental Pictures Ask students why some poems make them grin, shiver, yell, or sob. Explain that a really good word picture can make readers see or feel what is being described. On the board draw a vertical line. At the top of the left side, write THE POET'S WORDS. On the other side, write MADE ME SEE/FEEL. Then read parts of "Whatif" and have students suggest words and phrases to fill in the appropriate columns. Lines 1–3, 12, 16, and 18 might be especially fun for practicing visualization. **OL**

Objectives
- Visualize
- Interpret text
- Learn and use new vocabulary

377

Teach

More About the Author

Luis Omar Salinas has been called one of the most important Chicano poets writing today. While attending Fresno State College in California, he published *Crazy Gypsy,* his first book, which sold over 4,000 copies in a few months, a great accomplishment for a first-time writer. Later, he returned to teach poetry at Fresno. Salinas was honored in 1987 by being asked to read his poetry at the Library of Congress.

Vocabulary

Related Words Say: An easy way to figure out new words is to think of similar words. What words are similar to *scholar* and *pretense?* *(Possible responses: school, scholastic, scholarship; pretend)* **Ask:** How do these words help you with the vocabulary words? *(Possible response: A scholar must be someone who studies. A pretense must involve pretending or faking.)* **OL**

Before You Read

My Father Is a Simple Man

Meet the Author

Luis Omar Salinas is one of the founding fathers of Chicano poetry in America. Many of Salinas's poems show how he was shaped by his experiences as a Mexican American. Salinas once said that he deals with the real world by accepting the tragic and painful parts of life in order to "gain a vision that transcends this world in some way." See page R6 of the Author Files for more on Luis Omar Salinas.

Author Search For more about Luis Omar Salinas, go to www .glencoe.com.

Objectives (pp. 378–381)
Reading Visualize • Make connections from text to self
Literature Identify features of poetry: narrative and lyric poems, free verse
Vocabulary Use context clues: restatement

Vocabulary Preview

perpetual (pur PEH choo ul) *adj.* continuing forever **(p. 380)** *The Earth revolves around the sun in a perpetual cycle.*

scholar (SKOL ur) *n.* a person of great learning **(p. 381)** *Mr. Wilson is a great scholar who has earned many degrees.*

pretense (PREE tens) *n.* a false show or appearance, pretending **(p. 381)** *I was terrified, but I grinned with a pretense of bravery.*

fanfare (FAN fair) *n.* a very noticeable public display **(p. 381)** *When the mayor cut the ribbon for the new park, there was a lot of fanfare.*

I Write, You Write In a small group, take turns writing a sentence using the vocabulary words until each word is used. The goal is to write a paragraph that makes sense. Read the paragraph aloud. Were the words used correctly?

English Language Coach

Context Clues When you read a word you don't know, you can figure out its meaning by looking at context clues. **Context clues** are the other words in the sentence or paragraph that help you understand the word you don't know.

*My father walked in an **unhurried** way, moving **slowly** so he could enjoy the outdoors.*

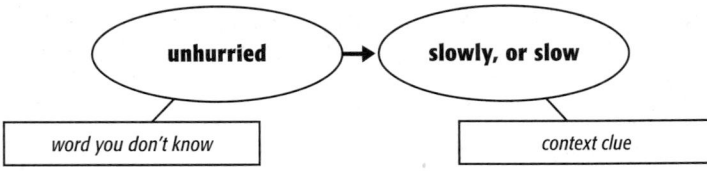

With this context clue, the meaning of *unhurried* is inside the sentence. *Unhurried* means "slow."

On Your Own Using context clues found inside the sentences, write the meaning of the words in dark type on a separate sheet of paper.

1. The Johnsons are a **simple** family; they're honest and ordinary.
2. Although they're quite **affluent,** having a lot of money doesn't change them.
3. The Johnsons are helpful to others. Any one who witnesses the Johnsons' acts of kindness or other good deeds can see how **benevolent** they are.

Additional Support

Author Search To expand students' appreciation of Luis Omar Salinas, have them access the Web site for additional information and resources.

Literature Focus Lesson

Speaker Explain to students that in poetry, the narrator, or person speaking, is called the speaker. The speaker might be the poet or a character the poet has created. Tell students to answer these questions about the speaker as they read "My Father Is a Simple Man":

- Who is the speaker?
- What are the speaker's ideas?
- Are there other characters in the poem? If so, who?

Have students tell how the poem might have been different if the speaker had been the father. **BL OL**

Skills Preview

Key Reading Skill: Visualizing

Words can tell a story or explain an idea. They can also give you the outlines and colors to paint pictures in your mind. But *you* have to supply the attention and the imagination. If a writer says, "The autumn leaves looked like splashes of bright paint," you have to pay attention to the words *splashes* and *bright paint*. Then you have to use your imagination to "see" splashes of bright paint in your mind.

Quickwrite Think about a special time you spent with a family member. In your Learner's Notebook, write about the pictures that form in your mind as you remember that time.

Key Literary Element: Poetic Features

A person who writes stories or essays may use several pages to get an idea across, but a poet might use only a few words. Poets choose words that appeal to the reader's emotions, senses, and imaginations. Poetry looks different from prose. The lines of a poem usually don't run all the way across the page. Instead, poets carefully decide how long each line will be, and each line adds something to the meaning of the poem.

Groups of lines are called **stanzas.** Stanzas are like paragraphs in a story. Each one contains a single idea or helps develop the poem's main idea.

There are many kinds of poems. Two broad categories are *narrative* and *lyric*. **Narrative** poems tell stories. They can be serious, or they can be funny. **Lyric** poems express thoughts and feelings. They present clear images.

Many poems have a regular "beat," or rhythm, and many poems contain rhyme. **Free verse** is poetry that has irregular rhythm and often doesn't rhyme. There's no regular pattern, and the rhythm can be like everyday speech or conversation. "My Father Is a Simple Man" is a poem written in free verse.

Get Ready to Read

Connect to the Reading

Think about the parents you know or have known. Think about your own parents and the parents of your friends. What can a parent do to make a child feel proud or safe? What can a parent do to make a child feel loved and happy? As you read "My Father Is a Simple Man," think about your own experience of what makes a good parent.

Small Group Discussion With a small group of classmates, talk about ways a parent can influence or shape a child. What are some helpful things the parent can do? What are good values—standards and ways of living—for a son or daughter to learn? Make a list of your ideas.

Set Purposes for Reading

 Read the selection "My Father Is a Simple Man" to find out how the speaker learned some important life lessons from his father—lessons that helped him become the person he is now.

Set Your Own Purpose What else would you like to learn from the selection to help you answer the Big Question? Write your own purpose on the "My Father Is a Simple Man" page of Foldable 4.

Interactive Literary Elements Handbook To review or learn more about the literary elements, go to www.glencoe.com.

Keep Moving

Use these skills as you read the following selection.

My Father Is a Simple Man **379**

Teach

R Reading Skill

Visualizing Say: When you visualize, you imagine the important details of a scene or event. Which were the most important details of the special time you spent with your family member? Which ones might you include in a poem? *(Responses will vary.)* **BL** **OL**

L Literary Element

Poetic Features Ask: Which form would a poet most likely choose if he or she wanted to

- share a feeling without worrying about line length, meter, and rhyme? *(free verse)*
- tell a long story? *(narrative)*
- express joy? *(lyric)* **OL**

Interactive Literary Elements Handbook Have students access the Web site to improve their understanding of poetic features.

English Language Coach

Using Context Clues Copy the chart below on the board and have students copy it in their Learner's Notebooks. Tell them a chart can be helpful when they come across unfamiliar words. Have students complete the chart, adding rows for the words *convince, healthy, education, punishing,* and *stranger*. **EL**

Word	It Might Mean	Context Clues	I Know It Means

Objectives
- Visualize
- Identify literary elements: poetic features
- Learn and use new vocabulary
- Use context clues

379

Teach

L Literary Element

Poetic Features Say: Read aloud the first four lines of the poem. What tells you the poem is free verse? *(Possible response: There is no rhyme and no set rhythm. It sounds like regular speech.)* **OL**

C Critical Thinking

Comprehension Say: In your own words, tell what the father says about death. *(Possible response: He says he's not afraid of it, but he won't do anything to make it come before its time.)* **AL**

My Father Is a Simple Man

by Luis Omar Salinas

I walk to town with my father
to buy a newspaper. He walks slower
than I do so I must slow up.
The street is filled with children. **1** **L**
5 We argue about the price
of pomegranates,* I convince
him it is the fruit of scholars.
He has taken me on this journey
and it's been lifelong.
10 He's sure I'll be healthy
so long as I eat more oranges,
and tells me the orange
has seeds and so is **perpetual**; **2**
and we too will come back
15 like the orange trees.
I ask him what he thinks
about death and he says
he will gladly face it when **C**
it comes but won't jump
20 out in front of a car.

---

6 A *pomegranate* is a pulpy golden-red fruit with many seeds.

Vocabulary

perpetual (pur PEH choo ul) *adj.* continuing forever

Practice the Skills

1 Key Reading Skill

Visualizing Create a picture in your mind of these two men walking down the street. As the poem goes on, add to that picture with details of what they see and what happens on their trip into town.

2 English Language Coach

Using context clues Look at the word **perpetual.** How does the next line help you figure out the meaning of *perpetual*?

Additional Support

Reading in the Real World

Citizenship The speaker in the poem says that he has learned a lot about life from his father. Have students ask people in their families to tell what important lesson about life they learned from a parent or guardian. Have students use the following questions as prompts:

• What kind of lesson did you learn?

• What were the important details of the situation?

• When did you use this lesson to help you in life?

• Would you pass the lesson along to your own children?

Encourage students to share their findings with the class. **AS**

I'd gladly give my life
for this man with a sixth
grade education, whose kindness
and patience are true . . .
25 The truth of it is, he's the **scholar**,
and when the bitter-hard reality
comes at me like a punishing
evil stranger, I can always
remember that here was a man
30 who was a worker and provider,
who learned the simple facts
in life and lived by them,
who held no **pretense**. 🞃
And when he leaves without
35 benefit of **fanfare** or applause
I shall have learned what little
there is about greatness. 🞄 ○

Vocabulary

scholar (SKOL ur) *n.* a person of great learning

pretense (PREE tens) *n.* a false show or appearance; pretending

fanfare (FAN fair) *n.* a very noticeable public display

Practice the Skills

3 Key Literary Element

Poetic Features Reread the poem. How would it be different if it were a short story?

4 🞄 BIG Question

Who helped the speaker become the person he is? How? Write your answer on the "My Father Is a Simple Man" page of Foldable 4. Your response will help you complete the Unit Challenge later.

My Father Is a Simple Man **381**

Teach

C Critical Thinking

Evaluation Ask: Do you think the poet does a good job of describing the father? Why or why not? *(Possible response: The poet does a good job of describing the father's beliefs, actions, and history. He doesn't describe how he looks, however.)* **AL**

BQ

Say: The speaker says that he has learned "what little there is about greatness." Who does he think is great? *(his father)* **BL** How might believing that his father is great influence the speaker? *(Possible response: He might try to be great in the same ways.)* **OL**

Assess

✓ CheckPoint

Use the CheckPoint questions provided on Presentation Plus! to check for comprehension of the selection. These questions can be used with interactive response keypads for immediate student feedback.

Differentiated Instruction

Creating Posters The speaker notes that his father "learned the simple facts in life and lived by them." Tell students that the book *All I Really Need to Know I Learned in Kindergarten* expresses this same idea—that there are simple truths we can use to live a good life. Have students form groups and make posters telling five simple truths by which everyone should live. Give them the following example: Being generous can bring great happiness. Encourage students to illustrate their posters. **OL AL**

Objectives
• Identify literary elements: poetic features
• Monitor comprehension
• Evaluate text

Assess

Resources for page 382

📁 Selection Quick Check, p. 31

📁 Selection and Unit Assessment, p. 37

💿 ExamView Assessment Suite

💿 Interactive Tutor: Self-Assessment

Students can respond to the *After You Read* items in their Learner's Notebooks or on a separate sheet of paper.

Answering the

BIG Question

1. Responses will vary but should include the idea that parents can be a great influence on their children.

2. a sixth-grade education

3. Responses will vary but may include kindness, patience, courage, and wisdom.

Critical Thinking

4. Possible response: He is elderly. He walks slowly and says he's not afraid to die.

5. Possible response: The father is a scholar because he has studied life. He knows the importance of patience, kindness, hard work, and providing for his family.

6. Possible response: The speaker thinks his father is great because he taught the speaker about life.

After You Read

My Father Is a Simple Man

Answering the **BIG** Question

1. What are your thoughts about what makes you who you are after reading "My Father Is a Simple Man"?

2. **Recall** What kind of education does the speaker's father have?
   TIP Right There

3. **Recall** What qualities does the father have?
   TIP Think and Search

Critical Thinking

4. **Infer** Is the speaker's father a young man or an older man? How do you know?
   TIP Author and Me

5. **Interpret** In what way do you suppose the speaker's father is a scholar? What has his father learned about life?
   TIP Author and Me

6. **Evaluate** In the speaker's eyes, what makes his father great?
   TIP Author and Me

Write About Your Reading

Use the RAFT system to write about "My Father Is a Simple Man." A RAFT assignment provides four details:

Role: Write as if you were a passerby who sees the father and son on the street

Audience: Write to a friend

Format: A paragraph

Topic: Describe the father and son from the poem as you see them, during their walk

Objectives (pp. 382–383)
Reading Visualize
Literature Identify poetic features: free verse
Vocabulary Use context clues: restatement
Writing Use the RAFT system: paragraph • Respond to literature
Grammar Identify sentence types: declarative, interrogative, exclamatory, imperative

Write About Your Reading

Sample response:

Yesterday, I saw an elderly man slowly walking and talking with a young man. They were talking about pomegranates and oranges! Because I was curious, I listened closely and figured out that the two men were father and son. The father was using oranges to teach his son about the cycle of life. I could tell by the kind way the father spoke, and the respectful way the son listened, that they loved each other a lot. Seeing them made my whole day brighter!

Skills Review

Key Reading Skill: Visualizing

7. How did visualizing help you read and understand the poem "My Father Is a Simple Man"? What pictures did you form in your mind as you read the poem? Which words from the poem created the most vivid pictures for you?

Key Literary Element: Poetic Features

8. When you were reading "My Father Is a Simple Man," did it seem like a poem to you even though it didn't rhyme? Explain your answer.

Vocabulary Check

Use your knowledge of the vocabulary words to decide whether each sentence is true or false.

9. There would probably be a great deal of **fanfare** if the president visited our town.

10. A **scholar** knows very little about any subject.

11. A **perpetual** motion machine would never stop.

12. You expect **pretense** from someone you think is a phony.

13. **Academic Vocabulary** Answer *true* or *false:* When you visualize something, you erase it.

14. **English Language Coach** Using context clues in the following sentence, figure out the meaning of the word *jovial.*

- Our neighbor is a **jovial** man, always cheerful and smiling.

Grammar Link: Sentence Types

A sentence is a group of words that expresses a complete thought. For example,
This is not a sentence: *The poet each morning.*
This is a sentence: *The poet writes each morning.*

Different types of sentences have different purposes. There are four main types of sentences:

- A **declarative** sentence makes a statement.
  The two men walk through town.

- An **interrogative** sentence asks a question.
  What is the price of pomegranates?

- An **exclamatory** sentence expresses a strong feeling.
  I love oranges!

- An **imperative** sentence gives a command or makes a request.
  Shut the window.

Grammar Practice

For each sentence, write in your Learner's Notebook whether it is declarative, interrogative, exclamatory, or imperative.

15. The children play on the sidewalk.

16. There is no one on earth like my father!

17. Tell me about the orange tree.

18. Are the pomegranates in season?

Writing Application Look back at the RAFT assignment you wrote.

- Make sure all your sentences express complete thoughts.

Literature Online

Web Activities For eFlashcards, Selection Quick Checks, and other Web activities, go to www.glencoe.com.

My Father Is a Simple Man **383**

Skills Review

Key Reading Skill: Visualizing

7. Possible response: I pictured the old man and his son walking and the bright oranges. The words *walks slower, orange, seeds,* and *orange trees* created the most vivid pictures for me.

Key Literary Element: Poetic Features

8. Possible response: Even though the lines don't rhyme, it still seemed like a poem. The lines are short, and there are separate stanzas that express a single idea.

Vocabulary Check

9. true

10. false

11. true

12. true

Academic Vocabulary

13. false

English Language Coach

14. cheerful

Close

Say: In your Learner's Notebooks, write down a list of the people in your life who have had the most influence on who you are.

Grammar Link: Sentence Types

Grammar Practice

15. declarative

16. exclamatory

17. imperative

18. interrogative

Literature Online

Web Activities Have students access the Web site for interactive activities that will help them assess their understanding of the selection.

Teach

More About the Author

Lensey Namioka's name shows the influence of parents and culture in her life. Her father, who developed an easier system of writing and reading Chinese, invented the name Lensey to celebrate his success. Her last name comes from her Japanese husband, who shares his name with a castle in his hometown.

C Critical Thinking

Comprehension Say: Reread the section on context clues. What is the context of a word? *(the words and sentences that surround it)* **Ask:** How can a context clue help you? *(It can help you guess the meaning of a word you aren't familiar with.)* **OL**

Before You Read : The All-American Slurp

Lensey Namioka

Meet the Author

Lensey Namioka was born in China in 1929. Her family moved often. Namioka came to the United States as a young adult and attended Radcliffe College. Namioka has said that her books draw heavily on her Chinese cultural heritage and on her husband's Japanese cultural heritage. See page R5 of the Author Files for more on Lensey Namioka.

Author Search For more about Lensey Namioka, go to www.glencoe.com.

Objectives (pp. 384–395)
Reading Visualize • Make connections from text to self
Literature Identify stereotyping
Vocabulary Use context clues: definition

Vocabulary Preview

disgraced (dis GRAYSD) *v.* brought shame upon; form of the verb *disgrace* **(p. 386)** *The child's rudeness disgraced his parents.*

lavishly (LAV ish lee) *adv.* in a way that provides much more than is needed **(p. 387)** *The bed was lavishly covered with pillows.*

spectacle (SPEK tih kul) *n.* something that attracts too much of the wrong kind of attention **(p. 388)** *He made a spectacle of himself by wearing an orange suit to the funeral.*

consumption (kun SUMP shun) *n.* eating, drinking, or using up **(p. 392)** *Our consumption of too much fast food is causing health problems.*

coping (KOHP ing) *v.* successfully dealing with something difficult; form of the verb *cope* **(p. 395)** *He's coping with having a broken leg.*

Write to Learn Create a sentence for each vocabulary word. Leave a blank where the word should go. Have a partner fill in the blanks.

English Language Coach: Using Context Clues

You can often guess the meaning of an unfamiliar word by looking at **context clues.** These are nearby words and phrases that provide hints to the word's meaning. Sometimes the meaning of an unfamiliar word may be **restated** in different words.

After the flood, we had to **disinfect** the basement. That is, we had to kill the germs.

disinfect	kill the germs

The context tells you that *disinfect* means "to kill the germs."

Get a Clue On a separate sheet of paper, write each word that appars in italic (slanted) type in the sentences below. Next to it, write the context clue that helps you find the meaning. Compare answers with a partner.
• Tony *hoodwinked* me. That is to say, he tricked me completely!
• My brother's behavior *mortified* me. In other words, I was horribly embarrassed.

Additional Support

Author Search To expand students' appreciation of Lensey Namioka, have them access the Web site for additional information and resources.

Literature Focus Lesson

Titles A title should pack a punch, with hints about the selection that make readers curious to find out more. Copy the following titles on the board. Ask students to suggest the topics of the selections, based on their titles.
• "Homework Horrors"
• "Rusty, the Canine Counselor"

• "What More Can Happen?"
• "The Valentine's Day Victor"
• "Marvelous Mom, Money Manager"

Then have students tell what the "All American-Slurp" might be about. After students read the story, have them evaluate the title. **OL**

Skills Preview

Key Reading Skill: Visualizing

Some writers don't give you much help when you visualize. The author of "The All-American Slurp" gives you a lot! In fact, it's the kind of story that a cartoonist would have fun illustrating. Instead, you need to illustrate it yourself—inside your mind. When the author says that her family "packed" themselves into a sofa, imagine four people jammed together on a sofa that barely holds them. Then, if you visualize what happens after that, it will be even funnier.

Literary Element: Stereotyping

This story talks about the customs of people from different backgrounds. It's interesting and funny, but while you're reading any story about different cultures, you should ask yourself: "Is this a real cultural difference or a **stereotype**?" A stereotype is a broad, general idea about a group. It is often an exaggeration. And it is never true of every member of the group. A writer who expresses such an idea is *stereotyping* the people he or she is describing.

You need to recognize stereotypes because they can limit the way you see people. "Boys like sports" might seem like an accurate statement. But if you don't realize it's a stereotype and not true of all boys, you will never understand real life.

Get Ready to Read

Connect to the Reading

Have you ever felt really different from everyone around you? Has your family ever embarrassed you? Think about these things as you read the story.

Interactive Literary Elements Handbook
To review or learn more about the literary elements, go to www.glencoe.com.

Small Group Discussion Discuss the good and bad parts of feeling different from other people.

Build Background

In the story "The All-American Slurp," a Chinese family and an American family share a meal at each other's homes. Food, manners, and dining situations cook up very funny scenes. Author Lensey Namioka drew on her Chinese American background to write this amusing story. Keep these facts in mind as you read:

- In traditional Chinese culture, people consider it polite to eat a little bit of everything instead of picking out only one or two favorite foods at a meal.
- Traditional Chinese meals usually offer a number of different dishes, but the foods are not mixed together on a single plate.

Partner Talk With a partner, make a list of some foods you enjoy that are difficult to eat neatly, such as corn on the cob, fried chicken, or spaghetti. How do you manage to eat these foods? What is the polite way to do this? Discuss any funny or embarrassing moments that have to do with handling a tricky food.

Set Purposes for Reading

BIG Question Read "The All-American Slurp" to find out how just being who they are causes funny situations for the narrator's family.

Set Your Own Purpose What else would you like to learn from the selection to help you answer the Big Question? Write your own purpose on the "All-American Slurp" page of Foldable 4.

Keep Moving

Use these skills as you read the following selection.

Teach

L Literary Element

Stereotyping Ask: Why is stereotyping hurtful to people? (Possible response: Stereotyping labels people and categorizes them.)

R Reading Skill

Review Connecting Say: Name a custom or habit you have that might seem odd to others. Do you recall how it started? (Responses will vary.) **AS**

Interactive Literary Elements Handbook Have students access the Web site to improve their understanding of narrators.

Differentiated Instruction

Using a Graphic Organizer Some students may benefit from using this organizer to identify the narrator and their feelings toward the narrator. Draw the organizer on the board and ask students to complete it as they read the selection. **EL** **BL**

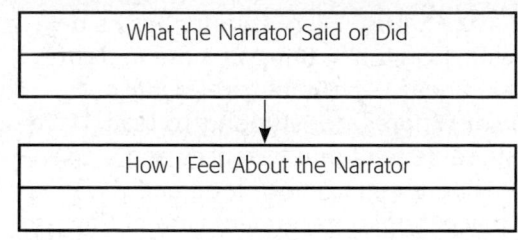

What the Narrator Said or Did

↓

How I Feel About the Narrator

Objectives
- Monitor comprehension
- Identify and analyze narrator
- Make connections from text to self

385

Teach

C Critical Thinking

Comprehension Ask: What do you learn about the narrator in the first paragraph? *(She has just moved to the U.S. from China; her family has different table manners than Americans.)* **BL Ask:** Do you agree with the narrator that doing something different, such as eating celery in an unusual way, disgraces a person? *(Responses will vary.)* **OL**

R Reading Skill

Visualizing Say: Picture the narrator and her family sitting in their neighbors' living room. From the narrator's description, how can you tell they are nervous? *(Possible response: They are sitting stiffly in a row, glancing at each other to figure out how to act.)* **BL**

Readability Scores
Dale-Chall: 5.1
DRP: 53
Lexile: 890

The All-American SLURP

by Lensey Namioka

The first time our family was invited out to dinner in America, we **disgraced** ourselves while eating celery. We had emigrated[1] to this country from China, and during our early days here, we had a hard time with American table manners. **C**

In China we never ate celery raw, or any other kind of vegetable raw. We always had to disinfect[2] the vegetables in boiling water first. When we were presented with our first relish tray, the raw celery caught us unprepared.

We had been invited to dinner by our neighbors, the Gleasons. After arriving at the house, we shook hands with our hosts and packed ourselves into a sofa. As our family of four sat stiffly in a row, my younger brother and I stole glances at our parents for a clue as to what to do next. **R**

Mrs. Gleason offered the relish tray to Mother. The tray looked pretty, with its tiny red radishes, curly sticks of carrots, and long, slender stalks of pale green celery. "Do try some of the celery, Mrs. Lin," she said. "It's from a local farmer, and it's sweet."

Mother picked up one of the green stalks, and Father followed suit. Then I picked up a stalk, and my brother did too. So there we sat, each with a stalk of celery in our right hand. **1**

---

1. A family who has **emigrated** has moved from one place or country to settle in another place.
2. When you **disinfect** something, you clean it to kill the germs on it.

Vocabulary

disgraced (dis GRAYSD) *v.* brought shame upon

Practice the Skills

1 Key Reading Skill

Visualizing Can you create a picture in your mind of the Lin family at this point?

Additional Support

Leveled Reading An adapted version of this selection (Grade 4 readability) is available on page 104 of **Jamestown Literature: An Adapted Reader** for Grade 6.

386

Reading in the Real World

Citizenship Every country has its own dining customs. Bring in a menu from a Chinese restaurant *(preferably one with pictures)* for students to read. Have students tell the differences and similarities between Chinese food and the food they eat. If some students are of Chinese descent, you may wish to have them tell how their food is different from what they might find at an American-style restaurant. Have students connect to the narrator's experience by providing chopsticks and instructing students in their use. **AS**

Mrs. Gleason kept smiling. "Would you like to try some of the dip, Mrs. Lin? It's my own recipe: sour cream and onion flakes, with a dash of Tabasco sauce."

Most Chinese don't care for dairy products, and in those days I wasn't even ready to drink fresh milk. Sour cream sounded perfectly revolting. Our family shook our heads in unison.[3] **EL**

Mrs. Gleason went off with the relish tray to the other guests, and we carefully watched to see what they did. Everyone seemed to eat the raw vegetables quite happily.

Mother took a bite of her celery. *Crunch*. "It's not bad!" she whispered.

Father took a bite of his celery. *Crunch*. "Yes, it is good," he said, looking surprised.

I took a bite, and then my brother. *Crunch, crunch*. It was more than good; it was delicious. Raw celery has a slight sparkle, a zingy taste that you don't get in cooked celery. When Mrs. Gleason came around with the relish tray, we each took another stalk of celery, except my brother. He took two.

There was only one problem: long strings ran through the length of the stalk, and they got caught in my teeth. When I help my mother in the kitchen, I always pull the strings out before slicing celery. I pulled the strings out of my stalk. *Z-z-zip, z-z-zip*. My brother followed suit. *Z-z-zip, z-z-zip, z-z-zip*. To my left, my parents were taking care of their own stalks. *Z-z-zip, z-z-zip, z-z-zip*. **2** **BQ**

Suddenly I realized that there was dead silence except for our zipping. Looking up, I saw that the eyes of everyone in the room were on our family. Mr. and Mrs. Gleason, their daughter Meg, who was my friend, and their neighbors the Badels—they were all staring at us as we busily pulled the strings of our celery. **C**

That wasn't the end of it. Mrs. Gleason announced that dinner was served and invited us to the dining table. It was **lavishly** covered with platters of food, but we couldn't see

---

3. When people speak or act in **unison,** they say or do the thing at the same moment.

Vocabulary

lavishly (LAV ish lee) *adv.* in a way that provides much more than is needed

---

2 **Key Reading Skill**

Visualizing Have you ever had celery stuck in your teeth? If so, maybe you can imagine what this scene must look like. The narrator describes a lot of things to help you visualize: sights, sounds, and even tastes. Visualizing is a good way to understand what is happening. When you think about the dinner, how do you picture it in your mind?

Teach

EL Language Coach

Using Context Clues **Ask:** What context clues help readers understand what *dairy* products are in the second paragraph on this page? *(milk, sour cream)* How about *relish* in the third paragraph? *(raw vegetables)* **BL**

BQ **BIG Question**

Ask: How have your parents and grandparents influenced the way you eat or prepare your food? *(Responses will vary.)* **AS**

C Critical Thinking

Analysis **Ask:** How do you think the narrator feels when she realizes everyone in the room is looking at her and her family? *(Possible response: She is probably embarrassed.)* **OL**

English Language Coach

Vivid Language Good writers like Namioka use vivid language, such as *crunch* and *zip*. Vivid words help readers feel, taste, smell, see, and hear the story. Copy this paragraph on the board. Have students replace underlined words with vivid, sensory language. **EL OL**

I can't believe I just did that! I <u>went</u> into the classroom just as the bell rang, <u>sat</u> down, <u>put</u> down my books, <u>looked</u> at the other kids in class, and <u>found out</u> I was in the wrong room. I feel <u>dumb</u>!

Objectives
• Identify literary elements: stereotyping
• Visualize
• Use context clues to determine word meaning

Teach

L Literary Element

Style Say: Look at the way the author describes the family returning to the couch. Remember, the words an author chooses, and the way he or she expresses ideas, are part of the author's style. Do you think Namioka's style in this description is humorous or serious? Explain. *(Possible response: Here, her style is humorous because she says the family returns to the couch so quickly that it's "as if they were being chased by enemy soldiers." This is a funny image.)* **OL**

Viewing the Photo

Say: Friends often look for things they have in common. What do the girls in the photo have in common? *(Possible response: They're both girls of about the same age, both have long hair, and both are smiling and enjoying a snack.)* **BL**

---

any chairs around the table. So we helpfully carried over some dining chairs and sat down. All the other guests just stood there.

Mrs. Gleason bent down and whispered to us, "This is a **buffet** dinner. You help yourselves to some food and eat it in the living room." **3**

Our family beat a retreat back to the sofa as if chased by enemy soldiers. For the rest of the evening, too mortified to go back to the dining table, I nursed[4] a bit of potato salad on my plate.

Next day Meg and I got on the school bus together. I wasn't sure how she would feel about me after the **spectacle** our family made at the party. But she was just the same as usual, and the only reference she made to the party was, "Hope you and your folks got enough to eat last night. You certainly didn't take very much. Mom never tries to figure out how much food to prepare. She just puts everything on the table and hopes for the best."

I began to relax. The Gleasons' dinner party wasn't so different from a Chinese meal after all. My mother also puts everything on the table and hopes for the best.

Meg was the first friend I had made after we came to America. I eventually got acquainted with a few other kids in school, but Meg was still the only real friend I had.

My brother didn't have any problems making friends. He spent all his time with some boys who were teaching him baseball, and in no time he could speak English much faster than I could—not better, but faster.

I worried more about making mistakes, and I spoke carefully, making sure I could say everything right before opening my mouth. At least I had a better accent than my parents, who never really got rid of their Chinese accent, even years later.

---

4. To *nurse* food or drink is to eat or drink it very slowly.

Vocabulary

spectacle (SPEK tih kul) *n.* something that attracts too much of the wrong kind of attention

388 UNIT 4 What Makes You Who You Are?

Practice the Skills

3 English Language Coach

Context Clues Look at the word **buffet** (buh FAY). What does it mean? You probably know it has to do with food because the word *dinner* is right next to it. What does the next sentence say you do? So a buffet is a dinner in which you serve yourself the food.

Analyzing the Photo Does this picture seem to reflect the friendship between the narrator and Meg? Why or why not?

Additional Support

Literature Focus Lesson

Point of View Tell students that how we interpret events is often influenced by who tells us about them. The narrator in this story describes in great detail what happened and how she felt at the dinner party. Have students tell the events of the party from Meg's point of view. How might Meg have seen things differently? How might her reactions have been different from the narrator's? **AL**

My parents had both studied English in school before coming to America, but what they had studied was mostly written English, not spoken.

Father's approach to English was a scientific one. Since Chinese verbs have no tense, he was fascinated by the way English verbs changed form according to whether they were in the present, past imperfect, perfect, pluperfect, future, or future perfect tense. He was always making diagrams of verbs and their inflections,[5] and he looked for opportunities to show off his mastery of the pluperfect and future perfect tenses, his two favorites. "I shall have finished my project by Monday," he would say smugly.

Mother's approach was to memorize lists of polite phrases that would cover all possible social situations. She was constantly muttering things like "I'm fine, thank you. And you?" Once she accidentally stepped on someone's foot, and hurriedly blurted, "Oh, that's quite all right!" Embarrassed by her slip, she resolved to do better next time. So when someone stepped on *her* foot, she cried, "You're welcome!" **4**

In our own different ways, we made progress in learning English. But I had another worry, and that was my appearance. My brother didn't have to worry, since Mother bought him blue jeans for school, and he dressed like all the other boys. But she insisted that girls had to wear skirts. By the time she saw that Meg and the other girls were wearing jeans, it was too late. My school clothes were bought already, and we didn't have money left to buy new outfits for me. We had too many other things to buy first, like furniture, pots, and pans.

The first time I visited Meg's house, she took me upstairs to her room, and I wound up trying on her clothes. We were pretty much the same size, since Meg was shorter and thinner than average. Maybe that's how we became friends in the first place. Wearing Meg's jeans and T-shirt, I looked at myself in the mirror. I could almost pass for an American— from the back, anyway. At least the kids in school wouldn't stop and stare at me in the hallways, which was what they did when they saw me in my white blouse and navy blue skirt that went a couple of inches below the knees. **5**

---

5. A word's *inflection*—or form and tense—changes depending on how it's used in a sentence.

Practice the Skills

4 Literary Element

Stereotyping Could either of these approaches to learning English lead someone to form a stereotype of Chinese people? Does getting to know the individuals through this story help keep those stereotypes from forming?

5 Reviewing Skills

Connecting The narrator tells about how kids in school stared at her when she wore a certain blouse and skirt. Think about a time when you felt like you weren't wearing the right clothes or shoes. How did you feel?

The All-American Slurp **389**

Teach

R Reading Skill

Visualizing **Ask:** How does the narrator help you visualize the mother's difficulties in learning English? *(Possible response: She tells about scenes in which her mother steps on someone's foot and then someone steps on her mother's foot. Imagining these scenes and her mother's inappropriate responses helped me understand how difficult learning a new language must be.)* **OL** **AL**

C Critical Thinking

Analysis **Ask:** Given what you know about the narrator, how do you think she feels about having to wear skirts to school? *(Possible responses: She is probably very embarrassed; She doesn't like to be different.)* **AL**

Reading in the Real World

Career Students who are interested in languages may enjoy learning more about the job of translators. Have students work in pairs to research the duties and job requirements of this career. To extend the activity, invite a translator to the classroom. Have students use what they learned in their research to interview the guest about the opportunities available in this field. **AL**

Objectives
- Identify literary elements: stereotyping
- Visualize
- Use text features: photographs
- Identify literary elements: Point of view

389

Teach

C Critical Thinking

Analysis Ask: What does the narrator want? *(She wants jeans.)* **BL** How does the narrator "work on" her mother to convince her to give her what she wants? *(She tells her that she must ride a boy's bike. Doing so while wearing a skirt shows her legs, which her mother disapproves of. This convinces her mother to buy her some jeans.)* **OL** What can you tell about the narrator from this story? *(You can tell she is clever and knows how to use her mother's concerns to get what she wants.)* **AL**

L Literary Element

Tone Point out how the author uses humor to convey serious ideas in these lines: "There was hope that the Lins might become a normal American family after all."

When Meg came to my house, I invited her to try on my Chinese dresses, the ones with a high collar and slits up the sides. Meg's eyes were bright as she looked at herself in the mirror. She struck several sultry poses, and we nearly fell over laughing.

The dinner party at the Gleasons' didn't stop my growing friendship with Meg. Things were getting better for me in other ways too. Mother finally bought me some jeans at the end of the month, when Father got his paycheck. She wasn't in any hurry about buying them at first, until I worked on her. This is what I did. Since we didn't have a car in those days, I often ran down to the neighborhood store to pick up things for her. The groceries cost less at a big supermarket, but the closest one was many blocks away. One day, when she ran out of flour, I offered to borrow a bike from our neighbor's son and buy a ten-pound bag of flour at the big supermarket. I mounted the boy's bike and waved to Mother. "I'll be back in five minutes!"

Before I started pedaling, I heard her voice behind me. "You can't go out in public like that! People can see all the way up to your thighs!"

"I'm sorry," I said innocently. "I thought you were in a hurry to get the flour." For dinner we were going to have pot-stickers (fried Chinese dumplings), and we needed a lot of flour. **6**

"Couldn't you borrow a girl's bicycle?" complained Mother. "That way your skirt won't be pushed up."

"There aren't too many of those around," I said. "Almost all the girls wear jeans while riding a bike, so they don't see any point buying a girl's bike."

We didn't eat pot-stickers that evening, and Mother was thoughtful. Next day we took the bus downtown and she bought me a pair of jeans. In the same week, my brother made the baseball team of his junior high school, Father started taking driving lessons, and Mother discovered rummage sales. We soon got all the furniture we needed, plus a dart board and a 1,000-piece jigsaw puzzle (fourteen hours later, we discovered that it was a 999-piece jigsaw puzzle). There was hope that the Lins might become a normal **L** American family after all. **7**

C

Practice the Skills

6 English Language Coach

Context Clues What are *pot stickers*? How does the author tell the reader what they are?

7 Literary Element

Stereotyping Think about what people mean when they refer to "a normal American family." Where does this kind of family live? How many children do they have? What is the father's job? What does the mother do? Is the idea of "the normal American family" a stereotype?

Additional Support

Differentiated Instruction

Comparison and Contrast

Chart Copy this chart on the board. Tell students the author provides many details to help you compare Chinese and American cultures. Copy this chart and work with a partner to complete it with four similar details from each culture. **EL BL**

Chinese	American

Visual Vocabulary
The headwaiter is wearing a formal suit with a jacket that has long panels in the back. The jacket is called *tails* because the panels look like the tail of a bird.

Then came our dinner at the Lakeview restaurant.

The Lakeview was an expensive restaurant, one of those places where a headwaiter dressed in tails conducted you to your seat, and the only light came from candles and flaming desserts. In one corner of the room a lady harpist played tinkling melodies. **8**

Father wanted to celebrate, because he had just been promoted. He worked for an electronics company, and after his English started improving, his superiors decided to appoint him to a position more suited to his training. The promotion not only brought a higher salary but was also a tremendous boost to his pride.

Up to then we had eaten only in Chinese restaurants. Although my brother and I were becoming fond of hamburgers, my parents didn't care much for western food, other than chow mein.[6]

But this was a special occasion, and Father asked his coworkers to recommend a really elegant restaurant. So there we were at the Lakeview, stumbling after the head-waiter in the murky dining room.

At our table we were handed our menus, and they were so big that to read mine I almost had to stand up again. But why bother? It was mostly in French, anyway. **R**

Father, being an engineer, was always systematic. He took out a pocket French dictionary. "They told me that most of the items would be in French, so I came prepared." He even had a pocket flashlight, the size of a marking pen. While Mother held the flashlight over the menu, he looked up the items that were in French. **C**

"*Pâté en croûte,*" he muttered. "Let's see . . . *pâté* is paste . . . *croûte* is crust . . . hmm . . . a paste in crust."

---

6. **Chow mein** is a Chinese American dish made of shredded fish or meat and vegetables, served with noodles or rice.

Practice the Skills

8 | **Key Reading Skill**

Visualizing Have you ever seen a fancy restaurant on television or in a movie? What did it look like? The narrator has given you details about this restaurant. Imagine a darkened room with candles on the tables. What does that look like? Picture the lady playing a harp. What details help you to visualize the setting?

Analyzing the Photo As you visualized the Lakeview restaurant, did it look like this picture? Explain.

Teach

R Reading Skill

Visualizing Ask: How does the author help you visualize the size of the menus? *(She describes them as so big she feels she almost has to stand up to read hers.)* **BL Ask:** How does this description help you picture the narrator as well? *(Possible response: It might mean that she is a short, small person.)* **OL**

C Critical Thinking

Analysis Ask: How does the speaker remind readers of her father's organized nature? *(She mentions that her father brought along a pocket dictionary to help him translate menu items from French to English. He also brought a small flashlight in case the restaurant was dark.)* **OL**

English Language Coach

Context Clues The speaker includes many details to help readers picture the elegant restaurant her father has chosen for the celebration. Ask students to volunteer the definition of *murky,* using context clues. Discuss how this word usually has negative connotations, usually associated with mystery or lack of cleanliness. Have students sketch the restaurant interior or the table at which the family is seated. Display the sketches in the classroom. **EL BL**

Objectives
• Monitor comprehension
• Visualize
• Identify literary elements: stereotyping
• Use context clues

Teach

EL Language Coach

Context Clues Say: Sometimes writers use made-up words. You can often use context clues to guess what these words mean. What does *shloop* mean? *(Shloop is the sound made when you slurp your soup.)* **EL Ask:** How might this word have been invented? *(Possible response: The author might have combined the hissing sound shl– with the word soup.)* **AL**

L Literary Element

Tone Say: Describe the tone of this passage. In order to do this, identify the author's attitude toward what is happening and the language she uses to describe events. *(Possible response: The author describes the event of her family slurping soup in public and the waiter's response to them with humor. She describes the sounds they make as so "hypnotizing" that neither the waiter nor the customer notices when wine is spilled all over the customer.)* **OL**

The waiter stood looking patient. I squirmed and died at least fifty times. **9**

At long last Father gave up. "Why don't we just order four complete dinners at random?" he suggested.

"Isn't that risky?" asked Mother. "The French eat some rather peculiar things, I've heard."

"A Chinese can eat anything a Frenchman can eat," Father declared.

The soup arrived in a plate. How do you get soup up from a plate? I glanced at the other diners, but the ones at the nearby tables were not on their soup course, while the more distant ones were invisible in the darkness.

Fortunately my parents had studied books on western etiquette[7] before they came to America. "Tilt your plate," whispered my mother. "It's easier to spoon the soup up that way."

She was right. Tilting the plate did the trick. But the etiquette book didn't say anything about what you did after the soup reached your lips. As any respectable Chinese knows, the correct way to eat your soup is to slurp. This helps to cool the liquid and prevent you from burning your lips. It also shows your appreciation.

We showed our appreciation. *Shloop*, went my father. *Shloop*, went my mother. *Shloop, shloop*, went my brother, who was the hungriest. **EL**

The lady harpist stopped playing to take a rest. And in the silence, our family's **consumption** of soup suddenly seemed unnaturally loud. You know how it sounds on a rocky beach when the tide goes out and the water drains from all those little pools? They go *shloop, shloop, shloop*. That was the Lin family, eating soup. **L**

At the next table a waiter was pouring wine. When a large *shloop* reached him, he froze. The bottle continued to pour, and red wine flooded the tabletop and into the lap of a customer. Even the customer didn't notice

---

7. ***Etiquette*** means the rules for manners or polite behavior, which vary in different places and cultures.

Vocabulary

consumption (kun SUMP shun) *n.* eating, drinking, or using up

392 UNIT 4 What Makes You Who You Are?

Practice the Skills

9 Reviewing Skill

Connecting Have you ever felt embarrassed by something you had no control over? How does the narrator seem to feel when her parents pull out a flashlight and a dictionary to try and understand the menu?

Analyzing the Art Does this picture help you "hear" the *schloop, schloop* sound that the narrator describes? Why or why not?

Additional Support

Differentiated Instruction

Etiquette Poster Many books on etiquette (manners) list formal rules of social behavior that are now outdated or ignored. Check out several different older etiquette books from the public library. Have students work in groups to identify four rules of etiquette that are observed today and four that are not. Ask them to discuss why some rules are no longer appropriate. Have groups prepare a poster that illustrates the old and new rules of etiquette. Invite students to present their posters to the class. **BL OL**

anything at first, being also hypnotized by the *shloop, shloop, shloop.*

It was too much. "I need to go to the toilet," I mumbled, jumping to my feet. A waiter, sensing my urgency, quickly directed me to the ladies' room.

I splashed cold water on my burning face, and as I dried myself with a paper towel, I stared into the mirror. In this perfumed ladies' room, with its pink-and-silver wallpaper and marbled sinks, I looked completely out of place. What was I doing here? What was our family doing in the Lakeview restaurant? In America?

The door to the ladies' room opened. A woman came in and glanced curiously at me. I retreated into one of the toilet cubicles and latched the door. **10**

Time passed—maybe half an hour, maybe an hour. Then I heard the door open again, and my mother's voice. "Are you in there? You're not sick, are you?"

There was real concern in her voice. A girl can't leave her family just because they slurp their soup. Besides, the toilet cubicle had a few drawbacks as a permanent residence. "I'm all right," I said, undoing the latch.

Mother didn't tell me how the rest of the dinner went, and I didn't want to know. In the weeks following, I managed to push the whole thing into the back of my mind, where it jumped out at me only a few times a day. Even now, I turn hot all over when I think of the Lakeview restaurant.

But by the time we had been in this country for three months, our family was definitely making progress toward becoming Americanized. I remember my parents' first PTA[8] meeting. Father wore a neat suit and tie, and Mother put on her first pair of high heels. She stumbled only once. They met my homeroom teacher and beamed as she told them that I would make honor roll soon at the rate I was going. Of course Chinese etiquette forced Father to say that I was a very stupid girl and Mother to protest that the teacher was showing favoritism toward me. But I could tell they were both very proud.

---

8. *PTA* stands for Parent Teacher Association.

Practice the Skills

10 Reviewing Skill

Connecting Have you ever felt this embarrassed? How long did it take you to get over it? (Or are you still not over it?)

Teach

R **Reading Skill**

Review Connecting Say: Think of an embarrassing situation you've experienced. How was your reaction to it similar to the narrator's? How was it different? *(Responses will vary.)* **EL OL**

L **Literary Element**

Review Narrator Say: The narrator says her parents' comments to the teacher reflect Chinese etiquette. How does the narrator feel about the comments? *(She accepts them because she knows why her parents say what they do.)* How would *you* feel if your parents said this to *your* teacher? *(Responses will vary.)* **EL BL OL**

Reading in the Real World

Citizenship Chinese culture is known for its many rules for etiquette. Have students choose one of the following subjects and research Chinese etiquette:

• gift giving
• greeting people
• dinner parties/entertainment
• compliments

Encourage students to share their findings with the class. Have them describe how these rules are different from ones in the United States. **AL**

Objectives
• Identify literary elements: stereotyping
• Make connections from text to self
• Use context clues
• Visualize

393

Teach

C Critical Thinking

Comprehension Say: The narrator says "Sometimes guests were too polite to help themselves and you had to serve them with more food." What does she mean? *(Possible response: She means that she has to encourage guests to take more food.)* **OL** Ask: What does this tell you about Chinese eating customs? *(Possible response: It is considered polite to take more food without being invited.)* **AL**

R Reading Skill

Visualizing Ask: How does the narrator help you visualize her amazement when she spies Meg's loaded plate? *(She says, "My eyes nearly popped out.")* **BL**

The day came when my parents announced that they wanted to give a dinner party. We had invited Chinese friends to eat with us before, but this dinner was going to be different. In addition to a Chinese-American family, we were going to invite the Gleasons.

"Gee, I can hardly wait to have dinner at your house," Meg said to me. "I just *love* Chinese food."

That was a relief. Mother was a good cook, but I wasn't sure if people who ate sour cream would also eat chicken gizzards stewed in soy sauce.

Mother decided not to take a chance with chicken gizzards. Since we had western guests, she set the table with large dinner plates, which we never used in Chinese meals. In fact we didn't use individual plates at all, but picked up food from the platters in the middle of the table and brought it directly to our rice bowls. Following the practice of Chinese-American restaurants, Mother also placed large serving spoons on the platters. **11**

The dinner started well. Mrs. Gleason exclaimed at the beautifully arranged dishes of food: the colorful candied fruit in the sweet-and-sour pork dish, the noodle-thin shreds of chicken meat stir-fried with tiny peas, and the glistening pink prawns in a ginger sauce.

At first I was too busy enjoying my food to notice how the guests were doing. But soon I remembered my duties. Sometimes guests were too polite to help themselves and you had to serve them with more food.

I glanced at Meg, to see if she needed more food, and my eyes nearly popped out at the sight of her plate. It was piled with food: the sweet-and-sour meat pushed right against the chicken shreds, and the chicken sauce ran into the prawns. She had been taking food from a second dish before she finished eating her helping from the first!

Visual Vocabulary
Prawns are large shrimp.

Horrified, I turned to look at Mrs. Gleason. She was dumping rice out of her bowl and putting it on her

394 UNIT 4 What Makes You Who You Are?

Practice the Skills

11 Key Reading Skill

Visualizing Think back to the dinner with celery at the Gleasons' house. How did you picture that dinner? Imagine the dinner with soup in the French restaurant. How did you picture that dinner? How are the details about the Chinese dinner different from the other dinners? Think about those different descriptions, and consider how visualizing helps you understand the story.

C

R

Analyzing the Photo How is this bowl of rice different from Meg's plate for the Chinese dinner? Explain your answer with details from the story.

Additional Support

394

Literature Focus Lesson

Conflict Tell students that conflict in a story is the struggle between opposing forces. In this story, the conflict is not an external conflict between two people. Rather, it is an internal conflict, one that occurs inside the narrator's mind. She struggles with adapting to life in a new culture and with her embarrassment when she makes mistakes. Ask students to describe how this conflict is resolved in the story. *(It is resolved when the narrator sees Meg's family making mistakes at her mother's party. She realizes that everyone makes mistakes in new situations.)* **AL**

dinner plate. Then she ladled prawns and gravy on top of the rice and mixed everything together, the way you mix sand, gravel, and cement to make concrete.

I couldn't bear to look any longer, and I turned to Mr. Gleason. He was chasing a pea around his plate. Several times he got it to the edge, but when he tried to pick it up with his chopsticks, it rolled back toward the center of the plate again. Finally he put down his chopsticks and picked up the pea with his fingers. He really did! A grown man! **R**

All of us, our family and the Chinese guests, stopped eating to watch the activities of the Gleasons. I wanted to giggle. Then I caught my mother's eyes on me. She frowned and shook her head slightly, and I understood the message: the Gleasons were not used to Chinese ways, and they were just **coping** the best they could. For some reason I thought of celery strings. **12**

When the main courses were finished, Mother brought out a platter of fruit. "I hope you weren't expecting a sweet dessert," she said. "Since the Chinese don't eat dessert, I didn't think to prepare any."

"Oh, I couldn't possibly eat dessert!" cried Mrs. Gleason. "I'm simply stuffed!"

Meg had different ideas. When the table was cleared, she announced that she and I were going for a walk. "I don't know about you, but I feel like dessert," she told me, when we were outside. "Come on, there's a Dairy Queen down the street. I could use a big chocolate milkshake!"

Although I didn't really want anything more to eat, I insisted on paying for the milkshakes. After all, I was still hostess.

Meg got her large chocolate milkshake and I had a small one. Even so, she was finishing hers while I was only half done. Toward the end she pulled hard on her straws and went *shloop, shloop*. **13**

"Do you always slurp when you eat a milkshake?" I asked, before I could stop myself.

Meg grinned. "Sure. All Americans slurp." ○

Vocabulary

coping (KOHP ing) *v.* successfully dealing with something difficult

Analyzing the Photo Do you think that you could drink this milkshake without making a slurping noise? Explain.

Practice the Skills

12 **Literary Element**

Stereotyping Based on this dinner, what kind of stereotype could the Lin family form of Americans? Could they think all Americans are crude and greedy? Would that be accurate and fair?

13

How do you think the narrator's family and culture are a part of what makes her who she is? Write your answer on the "All-American Slurp" page of Foldable 4. Your response will help you complete the Unit Challenge later. **BQ**

The All-American Slurp **395**

Teach

R Reading Skill

Visualizing Say: Visualize Mr. Gleason trying to eat his food. Describe it in your own words. *(Responses will vary.)* How is this scene similar to the scene at the restaurant? *(The scenes are similar because, in both, people stop to stare at what they consider unusual behavior.)* **OL**

BQ **BIG Question**

Ask: How do you think having Meg as a friend helps make the narrator who she is? *(Possible response: Meg does not judge the narrator or her family. Her friendship probably helps the narrator become more relaxed about making mistakes and being too critical of herself.)* **OL**

Assess

CheckPoint

Use the CheckPoint questions provided on Presentation Plus! to check for comprehension of the selection. These questions can be used with interactive response keypads for immediate student feedback.

Reading in the Real World

Citizenship The title, "The All-American Slurp," hints that American culture consists of specific things. Discuss the various aspects of culture, such as foods, language, entertainment, customs, religion, various forms of art, clothing, etc. Ask students what it means to be "All-American." Have students look through magazines and newspapers with partners and clip out words and pictures that show American culture. Students should use their clippings to create posters to present to the class. Discuss similarities and differences in their ideas of what is All-American. **EL BL OL**

Objectives
• Visualize
• Identify literary elements: conflict
• Monitor comprehension

395

Assess

Resources for page 396

📁 Selection Quick Check, p. 32

📁 Selection and Unit Assessment, p. 38

💿 ExamView Assessment Suite

💿 Interactive Tutor: Self-Assessment

Students can respond to the *After You Read* items in their Learner's Notebooks or on a separate sheet of paper.

Answering the

BIG Question

1. Possible response: Our family, friends, and culture help make us who we are.

2. They peel their celery and take chairs to the table.

3. She makes sure her mother sees that her thighs show when she wears a skirt to ride a boy's bike.

Critical Thinking

4. Possible response: She is embarrassed by her family's behavior.

5. Possible responses: Young people are more eager to learn new ways; older people have a harder time giving up familiar customs.

6. Responses will vary but could include that the family has learned more American ways but is also comfortable keeping some of their Chinese customs.

After You Read   The All-American Slurp

Answering the **BIG Question**

1. What are your thoughts about what makes us who we are after reading "The All-American Slurp"?

2. **Recall** What "mistakes" does the Lin family make at the Gleasons' dinner party?
   Tip Right There

3. **Recall** How does the narrator get her mother to buy her a pair of jeans?
   Tip Right There

Critical Thinking

4. **Infer** Why does the narrator run and hide in the elegant restaurant?
   Tip Author and Me

5. **Evaluate** Why do you think it was easier for the narrator to pick up American customs than for her parents?
   Tip Author and Me

6. **Synthesize** By the end of the story, how had the narrator and her family changed or become more comfortable with their American surroundings?
   Tip Think and Search

Write About Your Reading

Write to Learn Choose one of the following activities:

- Imagine that you are a member of the Lin family and are just getting used to life in America. Write a postcard to a friend in China, describing one way in which Chinese and American customs seem very different.

- Write a letter to the narrator, comparing some of your experiences with hers.

- Draw a cartoon strip that shows what happens at a dinner with the Lins and the Gleasons. Be sure to write captions for each picture (a sentence that tells what is going on in the picture) or some speech bubbles.

Objectives (pp. 396–397)
Reading Visualize • Make connections from text to self
Literature Identify stereotyping
Vocabulary Use context clues: definition
Writing Respond to literature
Grammar Use end punctuation correctly

396 UNIT 4 What Makes You Who You Are?

Write About Your Reading

Sample response:
Boy, do I know how you feel! Once I went to a fancy restaurant with a friend's family. I was doing fine until the waiter delivered my friend's dessert. It was on fire! I said, "Hey, Maria, your dessert's burning! Tell that guy to blow it out fast, or it'll be ruined!" Was I ever embarrassed when she said that Pineapple Flambé was French for *Flaming Pineapple.*
Your red-faced friend,
Greta

Skills Review

Key Reading Skill: Visualizing

7. Did visualizing parts of the story help you to understand what was happening and enjoy the story? Explain.

8. Imagine that you had to draw a scene from the story. What scene would it be? Describe the details from the story that help you to picture the scene.

Literary Element: Stereotyping

9. What did the Lin family and the Gleason family do that might keep them from forming stereotypes?

Reviewing Skills: Connecting

10. How did your own experiences or previous reading help you connect to the story? Use examples from the story to explain how you connected.

Vocabulary Check

Write the correct vocabulary word for each sentence.

**coping   lavishly   consumption
disgraced   spectacle**

11. The chef ____ praised the wonderful meal.

12. Owen's behavior caused him to make a ____ of himself.

13. Owen's family was embarrassed because he ____ them.

14. ____ with a difficult problem is hard.

15. My ____ of cookies doubled when I learned to bake them myself.

Literature Online

Web Activities For eFlashcards, Selection Quick Checks, and other Web activities, go to www.glencoe.com.

English Language Coach: Using Context Clues

16. Which words in the following sentence restate the meaning of the underlined word?

Eating buffet style was <u>alien</u>, or strange and unfamiliar, to the Lin family.

Grammar Link: End Punctuation

Different types of sentences have different purposes. The punctuation at the end of a sentence must match the purpose of the sentence.

- A **declarative** sentence simply makes a statement. It always ends with a period.
  Example: *She saw the bus go by.*

- An **interrogative** sentence asks a question. It always ends with a question mark.
  Example: *Are you ready to go?*

- An **exclamatory** sentence expresses a strong feeling. It ends with an exclamation point.
  Example: *I can't believe it!*

- An **imperative** sentence gives a command. It may end with a period or, if the command is forceful, an exclamation point.
  Examples: *Please hand me a glass. Don't drop it!*

Remember: The purpose of the sentence determines the end punctuation.

Grammar Practice

Add correct end punctuation to these sentences.

17. That makes me furious

18. We went to visit friends

19. Do you like dumplings

20. Celery is a vegetable

21. Stop slurping right this minute

Writing Application Look back at the writing activity you did in this part of the Workshop. Make sure you have used the right end punctuation for every sentence.

The All-American Slurp **397**

Skills Review

Key Reading Skill: Visualizing

7. Possible response: Visualizing the dinner scenes helped me see how they were alike.

8. Possible response: I'd draw the Lins slurping, the narrator looking embarrassed, and other people staring.

Key Literary Element: Stereotyping

9. They invited each others' family to dinner.

Reviewing Skills: Connecting

10. Possible response: At Thanksgiving last year, my uncle kept belching, so I know how the narrator felt at the restaurant.

Vocabulary Check

11. lavishly

12. spectacle

13. disgraced

14. Coping

15. consumption

English Language Coach: Using Context Clues

16. strange, unfamiliar

Grammar Link: End Punctuation

Grammar Practice
Possible responses:

17. That makes me furious!

18. We went to visit friends.

19. Do you like dumplings?

20. Celery is a vegetable.

21. Stop slurping right this minute!

Close

Have students write in their Learner's Notebooks about the influence of a family tradition.

Poem

**Objective covered in this
workshop:**
Writing Write a poem
using figurative language

Teaching Students to Write a Poem

Why Is It Important?

• Poetry provides a unique opportunity to indulge in play with language.

• Figurative language plays a large role in every communication, written or spoken. Writing a poem will expand students' awareness of the plethora of metaphors in their own verbal lives.

• Students may find it easier to appreciate or analyze poetry after they have created some of their own.

• Revision, the "re-seeing," is especially important to this genre. If the student's poem is short, each word in it must contribute greatly to the whole.

• Poetry can be a place for self-expression; academic, or purely personal aspects of a student's personality may be articulated through figurative language.

• Students may find that revision of all written work becomes clearer after applying the practice to something personally meaningful, like a "what makes me tick" poem.

How to Help Students Get It

• Review the definitions of verse and stanza with students.

• Share a few of your own favorite "bite-size" poems with the class. Read them aloud, have students read them silently or to each other, or post them in stations around the classroom.

• Consider transcribing the lyrics to some songs your students are familiar with. Seeing the terminology of poetry applied to familiar text may clarify the concepts, especially rhyme pattern and alliteration.

• Discuss some popular clichés, and identify them as metaphors and similes. (Sleep like a baby, faster than a locomotive, etc.)

• Provide students with access to a thesaurus, in print or online.

• Bring in a short sample of your own favorite author, and read aloud a section that exemplifies one of the literary concepts applicable to poetry.

• Review the definitions of mood and tone with students.

Traits of Good Writing	
Ideas	the message or the theme and the details that develop it
Voice	a writer's unique way of using tone and style
Organization	the arrangement of main points and supporting details
Word Choice: the vocabulary a writer uses to convey meaning	• Does the writer use lively verbs to show action? • Does the writer use vivid words to create word pictures in the readers' minds? • Does the writer use precise words to explain his or her ideas simply and clearly?
Sentence Fluency	the smooth rhythm and flow of sentences that vary in length and style
Conventions	correct spelling, grammar, usage, and mechanics
Presentation	the way words and design elements look on a page

Unit Focus (marked beside Word Choice row)

Workshop Resources

PACING (DAYS)		LESSON	STUDENT MATERIALS	TEACHER RESOURCES
STANDARD	**BLOCK**			
1	½	Writing Workshop Part 1: Prewriting and Drafting	👤 Writing Workshop Graphic Organizer, p. 14 👤 Grammar Practice, p. 15 👤 Spelling and Handwriting Practice, p. 44 💻 Spelling Power eWorkbook 🌐 Interactive Grammar and Language Workbook 📖 Grammar and Composition Handbook, p. 193 📁 Real Success in Writing: Research and Reports 📁 Writing Constructed Responses	💿 TeacherWorks Plus™ 💿 Presentation Plus! 📁 Rubrics for Assessing Student Writing, Listening, and Speaking, p. 24 📑 Grammar and Writing Workshop Transparencies 1–2
2	1	Writing Workshop Part 2: Editing, Revising, and Presenting	🌐 Interactive Grammar and Language Workbook 📖 Grammar and Composition Handbook. p. 193 📁 Real Success in Writing: Research and Reports 📁 Writing Constructed Responses 📁 Listening and Speaking, p. 27 📁 Viewing and Representing, p. 28	📑 Grammar and Writing Workshop Transparencies 23–24 🌐 Interactive Grammar and Language Workbook 📁 Rubrics for Assessing Student Writing, Listening, and Speaking, p. 24

Focus

- **Daily Language Practice Transparency 34**
  Focus Activity Tell: List five to ten words that tell something about you. Next to each word, write an explanation. You can use these words to help you write a poem about what makes you who you are.

Teach

W Writing

Descriptive Words Say: What descriptive words could you include in your poem that would help readers visualize you? *(Responses will vary.)* **AS**

L Literary Element

Poetic Forms Ask: What form of poetry is most like a song? *(lyric)* What form of poetry might you use if you wanted your poem to sound more like natural speech? *(free verse)* **OL AL**

ASSIGNMENT Write a poem

Purpose: To write a poem about what makes you who you are

Audience: You, your teacher, classmates, family, and friends

Writing Rubric

As you work through this writing assignment, you should

- think about what makes you who you are
- use poetic forms such as lines and stanzas
- choose words appropriate to your purpose and audience

See page 438 in Part 2 for a model of a poem.

Objectives (pp. 398–401)
Writing Use the writing process: prewrite, draft • Write a poem • Use literary elements: conventions of poetry, word choice
Grammar Identify complete sentences

Writing a poem will help you think about the Unit 4 Big Question: What makes you who you are?

Prewriting
Get Ready to Write

Writing a poem is like writing a song. Poets use rhythm and often use rhyme. They also use a lot fewer words than writers of fiction and nonfiction. Most importantly, poets use word images to describe emotions. In this Writing Workshop, you will learn how to express yourself using these poetic devices.

Gather Ideas

In your Learner's Notebook, write a short paragraph describing one of your personality traits.

> My name is Max, and I like to talk. Sometimes, talking gets me in trouble with my teacher or parents. The reason I talk so much is that I like to make people laugh. My mom says that I should be a comedian because I'm always making up jokes and cheering people up when they're feeling down.

Now, write a short paragraph about an activity that you enjoy (for example, soccer, reading, drawing, karate).

> I really like gymnastics. I practice at the gym three days a week after school. My coach is really cool, and right now we are working on back handsprings. I think gymnastics is a great sport for both boys and girls because it makes your body strong and flexible.

Additional Support

Differentiated Instruction

Supporting Details Draw the following chart on the board. Have students copy it in their Learner's Notebooks and use it to help them think of details for their poems. **BL EL OL**

To show that I am _____, I can write about ...	Details
things I like to do	
people I choose as friends	
how I act at home	

Choose a Topic

W1 Pick a characteristic about yourself, or an activity that is important to you, as the topic of your poem. On a fresh sheet of paper in your Learner's Notebook, write your name and topic on the first line. Make a list of words and phrases that come to mind when you think about that topic.

Literature Online

Writing Models For models and other writing activities, go to www.glencoe.com.

Max Jones	Talkative	Stephanie Carter	Gymnastics
Laughter		Balance Beam	
Voice		Competition	
My mother		Sprained ankle	
After school detention		Back handspring	

Drafting

Start Writing!

Pick an item from the list you made in your Learner's Notebook. On a single line of paper, write your feelings about this item. This can be the first line of your poem. Keep writing, using the ideas from your list.

Get It on Paper

W2 Poems are written in single lines of text. Many poems are divided into groups of lines called stanzas. Read the poem below. Notice that the verse is divided into four different stanzas. The bird's *key* is the highness or lowness of the notes in his song.

A Minor Bird
by Robert Frost

I have wished a bird would fly away,
And not sing by my house all day;

Have clapped my hands at him from the door
When it seemed as if I could bear no more.

The fault must partly have been in me.
The bird was not to blame for his key.

And of course there must be something wrong
In wanting to silence any song.

In your own poem, skip a line and start a new stanza when you begin a new idea or extend an idea further.

> **Writing Tip**
>
> Writing poetry is like drawing a picture with words. Describe little details to make your picture interesting. For example, instead of writing *My cat is soft,* write the details that make your cat *soft: My cat looks like a dust mop and feels like a down pillow.*

> **Writing Tip**
>
> Poetry doesn't require complete sentences or perfect punctuation. Don't worry about these things as you write your draft. Just get your main idea and feelings down on paper. You can experiment with punctuation and grammar later in the workshop.

English Language Coach

Synonyms Remind students that synonyms are words with similar meanings. When students write their poems, they should try to use vivid, precise words. Encourage students to use a thesaurus to find synonyms for regular words they use every day. For example, they might replace *happy* with a new and interesting word like *elated* or *blissful.* Tell students to check a dictionary to be sure the word they choose fits the context of the poem. **EL** **BL**

Teach

W1 Writing

Choosing a Topic **Say:** Look over the many words you've used to describe yourself. Choose one aspect of yourself to focus on in your poem. Which words will you use in your poem? Write a list. **AS**

W2 Writing

"I Am" Poem **Say:** If you're having a hard time structuring your poem, you might try writing an "I Am" poem. The first words of each line of your poem should be "I am" and should tell something important about you. For example, you might write "I am an athlete, proud and strong." **AS**

Resources for page 399

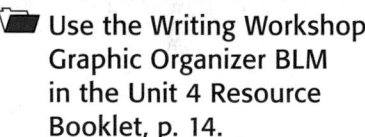

📁 Use the Writing Workshop Graphic Organizer BLM in the Unit 4 Resource Booklet, p. 14.

✒ Use the Grammar and Writing Workshop Transparencies 1–2.

Objectives
- Use the writing process: poem
- Recognize distinctive features of poetry
- Use descriptive language

399

Teach

W Writing

Word Choice Write the following pairs of words on the board:

- *food, salsa*
- *big, humongous*
- *disgusting, bad*

Ask: Which word in each pair is more precise and interesting? *(salsa, humongous, disgusting)* Why are these words effective? *(Possible response: because they are very specific and make it easy to picture the ideas they express)* **Ask:** What vivid words might you choose to replace the following? **OL** **AL**

- *nice*
- *sad*
- *walked*
- *beverage*

Applying Good Writing Traits

Word Choice

So many words and so little time! The English language has hundreds of thousands of words. How do you decide which ones to use?

What Is Word Choice?

Word choice is choosing words that make your writing clear, interesting, and easy to understand.

Why Is Word Choice Important?

Words that are thoughtfully chosen make readers remember your writing long after they have finished reading. Imagine that you spent hours cleaning your room. You dusted, vacuumed, and even cleaned under your bed! You call your parents to show off your hard work, and all they say is, "Good job." Is *good* the word that you were hoping for? Probably not. *Terrific, amazing,* or *incredible* all would have been better words for that situation. People who read your poetry want the same thing—descriptive words that are carefully chosen.

How Do I Use Word Choice in My Writing?

- Use lively verbs to show action. Try to replace boring verbs such as *do* and *make* with more exciting words such as *perform* and *create*.
- Use words that match your purpose. As you write, consider who your readers are. Try to use words that you know your readers use and will understand. For example, if you are writing a letter to your grandparents, you may use different words than if you were writing a letter to a friend.

Analyzing Cartoons
The boy's dad has just used the expression "super duper." What do you think that means? Would you ever use that expression when you talk to your friends or in your writing? Why or why not?

REAL LIFE ADVENTURES © 1997 GarLanco. Reprinted with permission of UNIVERSAL SYNDICATE. All right reserved.

- Add adjectives and adverbs to your writing. Instead of writing about *the shopping mall*, write about the <u>crowded</u> *shopping mall*.
- Instead of saying *the dog chased the ball*, explain that *the dog* <u>slowly</u> *chased the* <u>old, green, tennis</u> *ball*.

Write to Learn Activity Write a short review of the last movie you saw. Tell why you liked it or why you didn't like it and recommend whether your readers should see it or not. As you write, use adjectives, adverbs, and words that match your purpose and audience.

Additional Support

Differentiated Instruction

Actions Speak Louder Than Words Poets can use activities to describe who they are. Have students work with a partner to write about an activity that could be used in a poem to describe the following personality traits:

- competitive
- thoughtful
- honest
- selfish
- sensitive **OL** **AL**

Grammar Link: Complete Sentences

One thing all sentences have in common is that they must be complete.

What Is a Complete Sentence?

A complete sentence is a group of words that includes a

• subject

• verb

• complete thought

A sentence does not have to be long to be complete. These are all complete sentences:

> Cows moo.
> I am tired.
> Francine laughed.

Why Are Complete Sentences Important?

Your sentences must include a subject, a verb, and a complete thought to be understood by readers. Sentences that do not meet all three requirements are called sentence fragments. If your writing includes fragments, readers may not understand what you mean.

How Do I Write Complete Sentences?

Include a Subject
The subject of a sentence tells whom or what the sentence is about. It always includes a noun or pronoun.

My sister is thinking about moving to Greece.
Who is this sentence about? *My sister.*
My sister is the subject of this sentence.

Use a Verb
The verb part of a sentence expresses action or a state of being.
DeMarcus plans his birthday party.
What does DeMarcus do in this sentence? He *plans* his birthday party.
Plans is the verb of this sentence.
DeMarcus is twelve years old. *Is* links the subject with words that describe him.

Express a Complete Thought
Sometimes, it's not enough to just include a subject and a verb. You must not leave a reader hanging, wondering what else is supposed to be there.

Fragment: When Joey yelled.
Complete: I jumped when Joey yelled.
Complete: When Joey yelled, we came running.

Write to Learn Copy these sentences into your Learner's Notebook. Next to each, write "C" if it is a complete sentence. Write "F" if it is a sentence fragment.

1. Ryan went home.

2. Stopped to tie her shoes.

3. A dog with huge and muddy paws.

4. We saw Teresa at the game.

5. While he was playing the trumpet.

6. Slipped and fell all the way down the stairs.

Looking Ahead

Part 2 of this Writing Workshop is coming up later. Be sure to keep the writing you have done so far.

Write to Learn

1. Ryan went home. (C)

2. Stopped to tie her shoes. (F)

3. A dog with huge and muddy paws. (F)

4. We saw Teresa at the game. (C)

5. While he was playing the trumpet. (F)

6. Slipped and fell all the way down the stairs. (F)

Teach

Grammar Link

Complete Sentences Say:
Tell whether the following are complete sentences or fragments. If they are fragments, add a subject or verb to make them complete. *(Possible responses are provided.)* **OL**

1. Was running to the store. *(fragment: He was running to the store.)*

2. The campers found a perfect site. *(complete sentence)*

3. The pleasant doctor *(fragment: The pleasant doctor asked me about my sore knee.)*

4. The grapes are in the fridge. *(complete sentence)*

5. The carpet in the living room *(fragment; The carpet in the living room needed to be cleaned.)*

Assess

Have students check their poems for unintended fragments and make needed revisions.

Objectives

• Use word choice and figurative language to create meaning and tone

• Identify and use complete sentences and correct verb tense

401

Responding

**Objective covered in this
workshop:**
• Respond to the text

Teaching Students Responding

Why Is It Important?

• Responding helps students comprehend what they are reading.

• Responding teaches students to think critically by engaging with the text through their likes, dislikes, and reactions.

• Responding helps students enjoy reading more.

• When students enjoy their reading, they are better able to understand the benefits of reading and incorporate reading into their lives.

How to Help Students Get It

• Tell students that responding is reacting to their reading.

• Help them feel like their opinions matter. Let students know that their interpretations and prior knowledge are legitimate, and their responses based on these things are a part of reading.

• Remind them to always support their opinions with information from the text; if they dislike a selection, they must have a reason. Help them think about that reason and cite specific examples from the text to support their reactions.

Reading to Answer the Big Question

Life Doesn't Frighten Me by Maya Angelou
In this poem, the speaker describes scary things that she claims do not frighten her. Her refusal to allow herself to fear helps her to cope with life.

Geraldine Moore the Poet by Toni Cade Bambara
Geraldine Moore's mother is very ill and her father is gone. She and her sister have just been evicted from their apartment. When her teacher, Mrs. Scott, asks the class to write a poem expressing what it's like to be alive in "this glorious world," Geraldine says she can't and blurts out the realities of her world. Mrs. Scott writes Geraldine's words as lines of poetry and tells the class that it is the best poem they will ever read.

Workshop Resources

PACING (DAYS)		LESSON	STUDENT MATERIALS	TEACHER RESOURCES
STANDARD	BLOCK			
1	½	Key Skill Lesson: Responding	👤 Key Reading Skills Practice, p. 16 👤 English Language Coach Review, p. 41	📖 Bellringer Options Transparencies – Selection Focus Transparency 9 – Daily Language Practice 35 📖 Read Aloud, Think Aloud Transparencies – Key Reading Skills 20 💿 Presentation Plus!
1	1	"Life Doesn't Frighten Me"	💻 Glencoe Online 👤 Unit Vocabulary Review, p. 39 👤 Academic Vocabulary Review, p. 42 📁 English Language Coach 👤 Active Reading Graphic Organizer, p.18 👤 Literary Analysis, p. 17 💿 StudentWorks Plus™ 💻 Online Student Edition 💿 Literature Classics 📁 Selection and Unit Assessments, p. 39	📖 Literary and Text Analysis Transparencies 43 💻 Puzzlemaker 💿 Skill Level Up!™ A Language Arts Game 💻 BookLink 3 📒 Assessment by Learning Objective (Diagnostic and Formative) 💿 Interactive Tutor: Self-Assessment 💿 TeacherWorks Plus™
1		"Geraldine Moore the Poet"	💻 Glencoe Online 👤 Unit Vocabulary Review, p. 39 👤 Academic Vocabulary Review, p. 42 📁 English Language Coach 👤 Active Reading Graphic Organizer, p. 20 💿 StudentWorks Plus™ 💻 Online Student Edition 💿 Literature Classics 📁 Selection and Unit Assessments, p. 40	📖 Literary and Text Analysis Transparencies 39 💻 Puzzlemaker 💿 Skill Level Up!™ A Language Arts Game 💻 BookLink 3 📒 Assessment by Learning Objective (Diagnostic and Formative) 💿 Interactive Tutor: Self-Assessment 💿 TeacherWorks Plus™

Keys for Unit Resource

📁 Blackline Master 📀 DVD
📒 Workbook 📖 Transparency
📖 Supplemental Text 💻 Web-based
💿 CD-ROM 👤 Fast File

Level Appropriate Code

AS = Activities for all students
AL = Activities for students working above grade level
OL = Activities for students working at grade level
BL = Activities for students working below grade level
EL = Activities for English language learners

Focus

BELLRINGER Options

- **Selection Focus Transparency 9**
- **Daily Language Practice Transparency 35**
  Focus Activity Ask: What are some ways that people deal with fear, sadness, or other difficult feelings? *(Possible response: They might talk to a friend, write in a journal, or go for a long walk.)* **AS**

Teach

R Reading Skill

Responding Ask: What are some possible ways you might respond to a story or poem? *(Possible response: You might like or dislike it. You might feel sad or disappointed. You might be surprised by the ending.)* **BL Ask:** How might being asked to respond to what you read make you a better reader? *(Possible response: You might pay more attention to what you read if you know you have to respond to it.)* **AL**

Skills Focus

You will practice using these skills when you read the following selections:
- "Life Doesn't Frighten Me," p. 406
- "Geraldine Moore the Poet," p. 412

Reading

- Responding to what you read

Literature

- Identifying rhyme, rhythm, and meter

Vocabulary

- Using context clues that involve definitions
- Understanding idioms

Writing/Grammar

- Identifying sentence framents

Objectives (pp. 402–403)
Reading Respond to literature

Skill Lesson

Responding to What You Read

Learn It!

What Is It? When you read something you enjoy, you **respond** to what you read in a personal way. Reading becomes much more meaningful when you pay attention to

- what you like
- what you find surprising
- what you find interesting
- what the writer makes you feel

R

Analyzing Cartoons

Baldo says that an angry response is better than no response.
Do you believe that any response is better than none?

BALDO © 2004 Baldo Partnership. Dist. By UNIVERSAL PRESS SYNDICATE. Reprinted with permission. All rights reserved.

Additional Support

English Language Coach

Build Background Carlos Castellanos and Hector Cantu launched *Baldo* to show readers that "growing up Latino in the United States can be a great experience." In the strip, Baldo is a Hispanic American teen with a widowed father. Ask students to tell why a negative response from his father might be worse than a negative response from someone else. *(Possible responses: His father can punish him while others can't; he cares what his father thinks.)* **OL**

Why Is It Important? When you read actively and respond thoughtfully, you enjoy a selection more. You also learn and remember more from what you read. When you respond to a selection, you

- ask questions
- connect it to your own life
- may even argue with the author

How Do I Do It? As you read, think about how you feel about the story elements or ideas in a selection.

- What's your reaction to the characters in a story?
- What grabs your attention as you read?

Read the following excerpt from Shel Silverstein's poem, "Whatif."

> Whatif I get beat up?
> Whatif there's poison in my cup?
> Whatif I start to cry?
> Whatif I get sick and die?

Here is how one student responded to this poem:

> I read about someone wondering about being beat up or poisoned, crying, and getting sick and dying. I feel afraid of some of these things myself. I often worry that I might cry. I wonder whether any of the things in this poem happened to the speaker and what would I do if any of them happened to me.

Practice It!

Divide a page in your Learner's Notebook into three columns. Label the first one "I read . . ." Label the second one "I think/feel . . ." Label the third one, "I wonder . . ."
Use these to help you write your response to the lines above from "Whatif."

Use It!

As you read "Life Doesn't Frighten Me" and "Geraldine Moore the Poet," use the "I read" column to write down the words and phrases that trigger questions and feelings. Write your thoughts and feelings in the "I think/feel," column. List the questions that come to your mind in the "I wonder" column.

Literature Online

Study Central Visit www.glencoe.com and click on Study Central to review responding to what you read.

Teach

Literature Online

Study Central Have students access the Web site to review responding and to complete a related activity.

R Reading Skill

Responding Ask: According to the *Why Is It Important?* section, what three things can you do when you respond to a selection? *(ask questions, connect it to your own life, argue with the author)* **BL Say:** Use the "ask a question" and "make a connection" techniques to respond to "What if." *(Possible response: Ask a question: Why is the speaker so afraid? Make a connection: I get afraid sometimes when I think about starting high school.)* **OL**

Resources for page 403

Use Key Reading Skills Transparency 20 in *Read Aloud, Think Aloud* to help students practice responding.

Reading in the Real World

Careers Many people who work with others must be good at responding thoughtfully to what they see and hear.

- School counselors must listen carefully to students' concerns and respond appropriately.
- Doctors must listen to their patients and respond with correct diagnoses.

- Financial advisers must listen to their customers' life plans and give appropriate advice about investing money.

Have students think of other careers that require good responding skills. Tell them to explain their responses. **OL**

Objectives
- Respond to the text
- Make connections from text to self and from text to world

Teach

More About the Author

If it hadn't been for her good friends, Maya Angelou might never have started writing. After listening to her stories, Angelou's friends urged her to write about her childhood experiences in rural Arkansas with her grandmother and in St. Louis with her mother. Angelou's autobiography *I Know Why the Caged Bird Sings* tells the story of her life to age 16.

EL Language Coach

Context Clues Ask: What might be some benefits of using context clues, rather than dictionaries, to find out the meanings of words? *(Possible responses: You might not have access to a dictionary. Using a dictionary might be slower. You might remember more definitions by learning them through context clues.)* EL BL

Before You Read Life Doesn't Frighten Me

Maya Angelou

Meet the Author

Maya Angelou was born Marguerite Johnson on April 4, 1928. She became an accomplished actress, director, educator, poet, and author of twelve best-selling books. She once said, "I can be changed by what happens to me. But I refuse to be reduced by it." See page R1 of the Author Files for more on Maya Angelou.

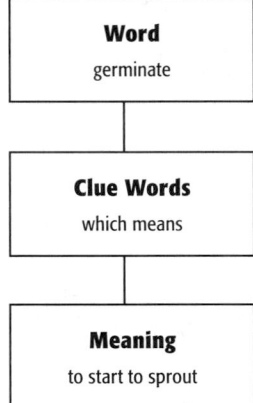

Author Search For more about Maya Angelou, go to www.glencoe.com.

Objectives (pp. 404–407)
Reading Respond to literature • Make connections from text to self
Literature Identify poetic features: rhyme, rhythm, meter
Vocabulary Use context clues: definition, restatement

Vocabulary Preview

Write to Learn A **phobia** (FO bee uh) is a deep fear or dread of something. With a partner, use a dictionary to find out what fear, or phobia, each of these words names: *zoophobia, agoraphobia, xenophobia, arachnophobia.*

English Language Coach

Context Clues The "context" of a word is the other words and sentences around it. The context of an unfamiliar word often contains clues to its meaning. Sometimes a word's context will actually define the word. Definitions are usually introduced with clue words. For example: "The plant has begun to germinate, which means that it is starting to sprout." Maybe you don't know what "germinate" means. Then you read the clue words "which means." These words tell you that "germinate" means "to start to sprout."

```
┌─────────────────────┐
│        Word         │
│     germinate       │
└─────────────────────┘
           │
┌─────────────────────┐
│     Clue Words      │
│    which means      │
└─────────────────────┘
           │
┌─────────────────────┐
│      Meaning        │
│   to start to sprout│
└─────────────────────┘
```

Other times, a word's context may provide another way of saying the same thing. For example, "We expected Luis to **bungle** the science experiment, but he didn't mess up a step."

On Your Own In your Learner's Notebook, write the meaning of the word *bungle* from the sentence above. List the context clues that helped you figure out the word's meaning.

EL

Additional Support

Author Search To expand students' appreciation of Maya Angelou, have them access the Web site for more information and resources.

Literature Focus Lesson

Repetition Tell students that poets use repetition to create rhythm and to emphasize important ideas. They might repeat a word, a phrase, or an entire sentence. Ask students to tell why Shel Silverstein repeats the word *Whatif* in his poem. Encourage them to see that the repetition emphasizes the speaker's worries. Tell students to look for words, phrases, or sentences that are repeated in Angelou's "Life Doesn't Frighten Me." OL

Skills Preview

Key Reading Skill: Responding

More than most kinds of writing, poetry asks you to respond. Poems don't spell everything out; they give you hints and clues. They often offer ideas that you "get" only if you make connections to your own feelings and experiences. As you read "Life Doesn't Frighten Me," ask yourself these questions:

• What would that look like?
• What does that make me think of?
• How would that make me feel?
• Does this word have more than one meaning? Should I think of both of them?

Key Literary Element: Rhyme, Rhythm, and Meter

A **rhyme** is made up of words whose sounds match, such as *sing* and *ring* or *money* and *honey*.

• Rhyme can occur at the end of lines or within a line.
• Rhymes form patterns that connect the lines of the poem.

Rhythm is the pattern of beats made by parts that are meant to be stressed (spoken with greater force) and the parts that are meant to be softer.

In this poem, the stressed syllables are underlined. You can see that the rhythm is very regular, which is not the case in all poems.

> The <u>mon</u>sters <u>of</u> the <u>night</u>
> Will <u>soon</u> <u>enough</u> be <u>gone</u>.
> They <u>disappear</u> at <u>sunrise</u>
> <u>In</u> the <u>first</u> faint <u>light</u> of <u>dawn</u>.

Meter is a predictable rhythm.

• To find the meter of a poem, read it aloud.
• As you read, listen for the pattern of stressed and unstressed syllables.

As you read "Life Doesn't Frighten Me," look for

• rhyming words
• rhythmic beats
• a steady meter

Get Ready to Read

Connect to the Reading

What used to scare you, but no longer does? What helped you get over your fear?

Write to Learn In your Learner's Notebook, create and fill in a chart like the one below.

Overcoming Fears	
Fear	How I Overcame It

Build Background

Most people experience one or more of the following fears at some point during their childhood:

• monsters
• the dark
• deep water

• getting lost
• doctors and shots
• thunderstorms

Set Purposes for Reading

 Read the poem "Life Doesn't Frighten Me" to understand what makes the speaker the person she is.

Set Your Own Purpose What else would you like to learn from the poem that may help you answer the Big Question? Write your own purpose on the "Life Doesn't Frighten Me" page of Foldable 4.

Literature Online

Interactive Literary Elements Handbook
To review or learn more about the literary elements, go to www.glencoe.com.

Keep Moving

Use these skills as you read the following selection.

Life Doesn't Frighten Me **405**

Teach

L1 Literary Element

Rhyme, Rhythm, and Meter Read students the following pairs of words. Have them determine which pairs rhyme and which ones do not.

• shape, ship
• battle, cattle
• grape, gripe
• move, approve

EL **BL**

L2 Literary Element

Rhyme, Rhythm, and Meter Say: Poetry isn't the only place you might find rhyme and rhythm. Where else might you find these elements? *(Possible responses: in songs, speeches, commercials)* **OL**

Interactive Literary Elements Handbook Have students access the Web site to improve their understanding of rhyme, rhythm, and meter.

Differentiated Instruction

Meter Tell students to try clapping as they read aloud "Life Doesn't Frighten Me" to get an idea of the meter, or regular rhythm, of the poem. Model for students by clapping as you read aloud the first stanza. Have students tell which lines have the same number of beats. **OL** For those who may have trouble with this activity, point out that lines 1, 2, 4, and 5 have the same number of beats, as do lines 3 and 6. **BL**

Objectives

• Identify literary devices: rhyme, rhythm, and meter
• Use context clues

Teach

L1 Literary Element

Rhyme, Rhythm, and Meter Ask: Which words in the first stanza are stressed? *(Possible response: shadows, wall, noises, hall, life, frighten, all, dogs, loud, ghosts, cloud)* **OL** Which words rhyme? *(wall, hall, all; loud, cloud)* **BL**

L2 Literary Element

Rhyme, Rhythm, and Meter Ask: Do *goose* and *loose* rhyme? *(yes)* Do *flame* and *pane* rhyme? *(Possible responses: Yes, they both have the long a sound; No, one ends with the m sound and the other with the n sound.)* **OL** *Flame* and *pane* are not an exact rhyme. Poets call this "near rhyme." **AS**

BQ **BIG Question**

Ask: How might fear influence who a person becomes? *(Responses will vary. Students might note that fear could get in the way of having exciting or new adventures.)* **AS**

Life Doesn't Frighten Me

by Maya Angelou

Fatima, 1994. Elizabeth Hodges. Acrylic.

Shadows on the wall
Noises down the hall
Life doesn't frighten me at all
Bad dogs barking loud
5 Big ghosts in a cloud
Life doesn't frighten me at all.

L1

Mean old Mother Goose*
Lions on the loose
They don't frighten me at all
10 Dragons breathing flame **1**
On my counterpane*
That doesn't frighten me at all

L2

Practice the Skills

1 | **Key Reading Skill**

Responding Notice how the poet uses examples of things many people fear, such as loose lions, fiery dragons, and ghosts. Were you ever afraid of any of these things?

BQ

7 ***Mother Goose*** is said to be the author of many English nursery rhymes, although people are not sure where the name comes from.

11 A ***counterpane*** is a bedspread or quilt.

406 UNIT 4 What Makes You Who You Are?

Additional Support

Differentiated Instruction

Illustrating the Poem Maya Angelou includes vivid images in this poem to help readers see the things that the speaker might fear. Have students choose several of the images and make "Life Doesn't Frighten Me" posters that illustrate the poem. Students may sketch their own pictures, clip them from magazines, or download public domain images from the Internet. Have students display their finished posters in the classroom. **AS**

I go boo
Make them shoo
15 I make fun
Way they run
I won't cry
So they fly
I just smile
20 They go wild
Life doesn't frighten me at all.

Tough guys in a fight
All alone at night
Life doesn't frighten me at all.

25 Panthers in the park
Strangers in the dark **2**
No, they don't frighten me at all.   **R**

That new classroom where
Boys all pull my hair
30 (**Kissy** little girls **3**
With their hair in curls)
They don't frighten me at all.

Don't show me frogs and snakes
And listen for my scream,
35 If I'm afraid at all
It's only in my dreams.

I've got a magic charm
That I keep up my sleeve, **4**
I can walk the ocean floor
40 And never have to breathe.

Life doesn't frighten me at all
Not at all
Not at all. **5**
Life doesn't frighten me at all. ○

Practice the Skills

2 Key Literary Element

Rhyme, Rhythm, and Meter What are some words in this poem that rhyme?

3 English Language Coach

Context Clues The word **kissy** is probably new to you. From the context, what do you think it means?

4 Key Reading Skill

Responding What do you think the speaker's magic charm could be? Why do you think she didn't tell you what it is?

5 BIG Question

Discuss with a partner what made the speaker want to look like a brave person. Write your answers on the "Life Doesn't Frighten Me" page of Foldable 4. Your response will help you complete the Unit Challenge later.   **BQ**

Life Doesn't Frighten Me **407**

Teach

R Reading Skill

Responding Ask: Do you think Angelou does a good job of choosing things that people are afraid of? *(Possible response: Yes, she does a good job. For example, many people are afraid in the dark, so "strangers in the dark" is an effective image in the poem.)* **AL**

BQ   BIG Question

Ask: How do you think the speaker might answer the question, "What makes us who we are?" *(Possible response: Being brave helps make us who we are.)* **OL**

Assess

✓ CheckPoint

Use the CheckPoint questions provided on Presentation Plus! to check for comprehension of the selection. These questions can be used with interactive response keypads for immediate student feedback.

Reading Fluency

Build Fluency First read the poem aloud to students, deliberately emphasizing the rhythm and rhyme pattern. Then have students choose partners and find a quiet place to read the poem aloud.

Partners should take turns reading the same stanzas aloud. Encourage students to practice until they are able to read the poem smoothly, with expression and understanding. **EL** **BL**

Objectives
• Identify and analyze sound devices: rhyme, rhythm, meter
• Respond to literature

407

Assess

Students can respond to the *After You Read* items in their Learner's Notebooks or on a separate sheet of paper.

Answering the

1. Responses will vary. Students might note that asking for help in a scary situation is a sign of bravery and honesty.

2. shadows and noises

3. in her dreams

4. Responses will vary.

Critical Thinking

5. Possible response: I think life does frighten her, because she needs a "magic charm" to protect her.

6. Responses will vary. Students might see the speaker rubbing her charm after waking from a bad dream.

7. Possible response: I would like to be brave, as would the speaker.

8. Possible response: The speaker is believable. Like many people, she has fears but wants to be brave.

408

After You Read | Life Doesn't Frighten Me

Answering the BIG Question

1. How does the way you respond to scary situations make you who you are?

2. What are the first two things that the poem's speaker mentions?
   TIP Right There

3. **Recall** According to the speaker, what is the only time she is afraid?
   TIP Right There

4. **Summarize** What are three fears that the speaker mentions in the poem?
   TIP Think and Search

Critical Thinking

5. **Infer** Does life frighten the speaker at all?
   TIP Author and Me

6. **Visualize** Picture the speaker using her magic charm. What do you see as you visualize that scene? Explain.
   TIP Author and Me

7. **Respond** Do you want to be like the speaker of this poem? Why or why not?
   TIP On My Own

8. **Evaluate** Is the speaker of this poem a believable character? Explain.
   TIP On My Own

Objectives (pp. 408–409)
Reading Respond to literature • Make connections from text to self
Literature Identify poetic features: rhyme, rhythm, meter
Vocabulary Use context clues: definition, restatement
Writing Respond to literature: personal letter
Grammar Identify sentence fragments

Write About Your Reading

Write a letter to the speaker in the poem.

• Tell her how you felt when you read her poem.

• Name something that you are afraid of.

• Tell her how you handle your fear.

Write About Your Reading

Sample response:

Dear Friend,

When I read your poem, I thought *I've felt the same way.* I was really scared about starting at a new middle school. I didn't know anyone because I'd just moved from a different state. Then I met Harry at my local swimming pool. He was the same age as me. He was very friendly, so I shared my fears about starting a new school with him. He introduced me to a bunch of new people, so my first day was a breeze. Everyone helped me out, showing me how to get to class and where the lockers were. It was great!

Your fearless friend,

Michael

Skills Review

Key Reading Skill: Responding

9. Poets want readers to react to their poetry. What do you think Angelou hoped this poem would cause you to think or feel?

10. The speaker of "Life Doesn't Frighten Me" first lists harmless things that young children fear. Then she lists things that might be real fears for older kids. Do you think that her statement "Life doesn't frighten me at all" is true?

Key Literary Element: Rhyme, Rhythm, and Meter

11. Would "Life Doesn't Frighten Me" be as much fun to read if it didn't rhyme? Why or why not?

12. Do you think this poem could become a song or a rap? Why or why not?

Vocabulary Check

English Language Coach: Context Clues

For each word in dark type, write the word's meaning and the clue words you used to figure out the meaning.

13. Lily is studying **calligraphy,** which is the art of fine handwriting.

14. Norman used a **template,** or pattern, for cutting the wood to build his mother a birdhouse.

15. I wish my mother would not **admonish** me in front of my friends. Being scolded is so embarrassing.

Grammar Link: Fragments

Many times, poets do not write in complete sentences. They may think that *fragments,* incomplete sentences, sound better. Maya Angelou uses both sentences and fragments in her poem. To spot sentences, remember that

- sentences have subjects and verbs. Fragments may be missing either a subject or a verb.
- subjects can be nouns (people, places, animals, things) or pronouns (*I, we, you, he, she, it, they*). A fragment may have no subject and look like this: *Cooked her favorite meal.*
- verbs are "action words'" (describing what the subject *does*) or "being words" (describing what the subject *is, was,* or *will be*). A fragment may have no verb and look like this: *All the students in the class.*

Remember: Use complete sentences for school assignments and business writing. Use fragments only in creative writing or in conversation with family and friends.

Grammar Practice

Identify which of the following are fragments and which are complete sentences. Remember, a sentence has both a subject and a verb.

16. Mean old Mother Goose.

17. Tough guys run away when they see me coming.

18. Life doesn't frighten me at all.

19. Not at all.

Writing Application Read the letter you wrote. Make sure your sentences are complete.

Web Activities For eFlashcards, Selection Quick Checks, and other Web activities, go to www.glencoe.com.

Life Doesn't Frighten Me **409**

Skills Review

Key Reading Skill: Responding

9. Possible response: I think Angelou wanted me to realize that most people get scared and that it's okay to be afraid sometimes.

10. Possible response: No, I think that many things scare the speaker.

Key Literary Element: Rhyme, Rhythm, and Meter

11. Possible response: I don't think this poem would be nearly as much fun to read if it didn't rhyme. The rhyme gives it rhythm and a beat, like a rap song.

12. Responses will vary.

Vocabulary Check

English Language Coach: Context Clues

Possible responses:

13. fancy lettering; *art of fine handwriting*

14. outline; *pattern*

15. tell off; *being scolded*

Close

Ask students to tell what they learned about overcoming fears from reading and responding to this poem.

Grammar Link: Fragments

Grammar Practice

16. fragment

17. complete sentence

18. complete sentence

19. fragment

Web Activities Have students access the Web site for interactive activities that will help them assess their understanding of the selection.

Teach

More About the Author

Like Toni Cade Bambara, many characters in her stories are women who actively work to help their communities and get satisfaction and strength from telling stories. During her life, Bambara helped fellow African Americans by supporting movements that improved urban living conditions and by creating television documentaries that revealed social and racial injustices.

EL Language Coach

Context Clues Tell students to look for definitions, restatements (phrases stated in a different way), antonyms (words with opposite meanings), and other context clues to help them guess the meaning of idioms. **EL OL**

Before You Read | Geraldine Moore the Poet

Toni Cade Bambara

Meet the Author

Toni Cade Bambara grew up in and near New York City. She was an author, college professor, and social activist. She wrote most of her work in the 1960s and 1970s. Toni Cade added "Bambara" to her name after she found the name on a sketchbook in her great-grandmother's trunk. See page R1 of the Author Files on Toni Cade Bambara.

Author Search For more about Toni Cade Bambara, go to www.glencoe.com.

Objectives (pp. 410–417)
Reading Respond to literature • Make connections from text to self
Literature Identify point of view: third-person limited, third-person omniscient
Vocabulary Use context clues to understand idioms

Vocabulary Preview

muttered (MUT urd) *v.* spoke quietly to complain or express anger; form of the verb *mutter* **(p. 412)** *He muttered because he was annoyed.*

minded (MYN did) *v.* took charge of; form of the verb *mind* **(p. 412)** *I minded my little brother for my Mom.*

shrugged (shruhgd) *v.* raised the shoulders to show doubt, lack of interest, or uncertainty; form of the verb *shrug* **(p. 412)** *Leon shrugged because he didn't care.*

manufacturing (man yoo FAK chur ing) *v.* making out of raw materials; form of the verb *manufacture* **(p. 415)** *The factory is manufacturing steel.*

moist (moyst) *adj.* just wet enough to notice **(p. 415)** *She noticed that her hair was moist from the steam.*

expressing (eks PRES ing) *n.* the act of making feelings or opinions known **(p. 416)** *Expressing how she felt about writing was difficult for Geraldine.*

whimper (WHIM pur) *n.* a soft cry **(p. 417)** *She gave a whimper of delight when she saw the new sweater.*

English Language Coach

Context Clues Some words in English are put together into idioms, or phrases with special meaning. You often have to use context clues to understand the meaning of these idioms. Read these sentences containing idioms. See if you can use the context to figure out what the idiom means. Write the meaning in your Learner's Notebook. **EL**

Idiom	Idiom in Context
Keep your chin up	This may be the third time you've taken the driver's test, but you have to keep your chin up.
Over the top	The boy just cleaned his room. Don't you think it was over the top to celebrate the clean room with a party?
Rise and shine	Get out of bed now; it's time to rise and shine.

Additional Support

Author Search To expand students' appreciation of Toni Cade Bambara, have them access the Web site for more information and resources.

English Language Coach

Context Clues Explain that idioms are phrases that use words to mean something other than their dictionary meaning. Have students use context clues to guess the meaning of these idioms that use the word *cake*:

• I finished my homework in no time. It was a piece of cake. *(easy task)*

• These popular CDs have been selling like hot cakes. *(really quickly)*

• Winning the game was great, but meeting our favorite athlete was the icing on the cake. *(something that makes a good thing even better)* **EL OL**

Skills Preview

Key Reading Skill: Responding

Responding to what you read may, at times, make you feel sad. Does that mean you should try not to respond? That's a difficult question, isn't it? Most of us would rather feel happy than sad. But sometimes, if we want to learn about and understand other people, we have to let ourselves feel things that may be painful. As you read "Geraldine Moore the Poet," try to imagine her life and her feelings, even if your response is to feel sad. Ask yourself some of these questions as you read.

- How would that feel?
- Would I be able to do that?
- How would I handle that?

Partner Talk Talk with a partner about reading sad stories or seeing sad movies. Do you think there's any reason to do it? Why do you think people create them?

Literary Element: Point of View

As you learned in Unit 3, when the narrator of a story is not a character in the story, the narration is called "third-person point of view." There are two main kinds of third-person point of view.

Third-person limited is called "limited" for a reason. What the narrator knows (and reveals) is limited to what one character can see, hear, or think.

Third-person omniscient is called "omniscient" because that word means "all-knowing." The narrator knows (and reveals) the knowledge and thoughts of many or all of the characters.

Interactive Literary Elements Handbook
To review or learn more about the literary elements, go to www.glencoe.com.

Get Ready to Read

Connect to the Reading

Think about how you feel when you come home from school.

- What would it be like if you didn't have a place to come home to?
- As you read this story, let yourself feel what the main character goes through.

Partner Talk Share with a partner how your home and family help to make you who you are.

- Who lives with you?
- What is your favorite thing to do at home?
- What responsibilities do you have at home?

Build Background

The number of Americans who have no place to live has risen in the last 25 years. There are many reasons why people find themselves homeless.

- It costs a great deal of money to buy or rent a home.
- Some cities do not have enough homes for people to buy or rent at prices they can afford.
- Sometimes people with low-paying jobs, or who lose their jobs, cannot get help to find a place to live.

Set Purposes for Reading

BIG Question Read "Geraldine Moore the Poet" to find out what experiences made Geraldine the person she is.

Set Your Own Purpose What else would you like to learn from the story to help you answer the Big Question? Write your own purpose on the "Geraldine Moore" page of Foldable 4.

Keep Moving

Use these skills as you read the following selection.

Geraldine Moore the Poet **411**

Teach

L Literary Element

Point of View Ask: Why is one type of third-person point of view described as *limited*? *(Possible response: because the narrator's knowledge is limited to the thoughts of just one character)* **OL**

R Reading Skill

Responding Say: Before you meet with your partner to discuss reading sad stories or seeing sad movies, make a list of some you are familiar with. **OL**

Interactive Literary Elements Handbook Have students access the Web site to improve their understanding of point of view.

Reading in the Real World

Citizenship To increase students' knowledge and understanding of homelessness, take them to the library. Ask students to work in pairs to answer one of these research questions:

- Who are the homeless?
- What causes homelessness?
- Who is helping the homeless?
- How can I help the homeless?

As a class, combine student research to prepare a presentation for other students in the school. **OL** **AL**

Objectives

- Identify and analyze point of view
- Use context clues

Teach

L Literary Element

Point of View **Ask:** Is this story told from a first-person or a third-person point of view? How do you know? *(Possible response: It's told from a third-person point of view. The narrator does not use "I"; instead, the narrator tells about Geraldine, the main character in the story, using the words* she *and* her.*)* **OL**

R Reading Skill

Responding **Ask:** What questions do you have so far about the story? *(Possible responses: Who is Mrs. Watson? How old is Geraldine?)* **BL**

Readability Scores
Dale-Chall: 4.7
DRP: 53
Lexile: 930

Geraldine Moore the Poet

by Toni Cade Bambara

Geraldine[1] paused at the corner to pull up her knee socks. The rubber bands she was using to hold them up made her legs itch. She dropped her books on the sidewalk while she gave a good scratch. But when she pulled the socks up again, two fingers poked right through the top of her left one.

"That stupid dog," she **muttered** to herself, grabbing at her books and crossing against traffic. "First he chews up my gym suit and gets me into trouble, and now my socks."

Geraldine shifted her books to the other hand and kept muttering angrily to herself about Mrs. Watson's dog, which she **minded** two days a week for a dollar. She passed the hot-dog man on the corner and waved. He **shrugged** as if to say business was very bad. **1**

Must be, she thought to herself. *Three guys before you had to pack up and forget it. Nobody's got hot-dog money around here.* **2**

Geraldine turned down her street, wondering what her sister Anita would have for her lunch. She was glad she didn't have to eat the free lunches in high school any more. She was

---

1. *Geraldine* (jehr uhl DEEN)

Vocabulary
muttered (MUT urd) *v.* spoke quietly to complain or express anger

minded (MYN did) *v.* took charge of

shrugged (shruhgd) *v.* raised the shoulders to show doubt, lack of interest, or uncertainty

412 UNIT 4 What Makes You Who You Are?

Practice the Skills

1 **Key Reading Skill**

Responding What's your response to Geraldine so far? Explain. **R**

2 **Reviewing Skill**

Drawing Conclusions Geraldine is wearing socks held up by rubber bands. For a dollar a week, she minds a dog that chews her clothes. She says that no one in her neighborhood has money to buy hot dogs. What can you conclude about Geraldine?

Additional Support

Differentiated Instruction

Understanding Characters Draw a web diagram on the board. Tell students that Bambara used certain words in the second paragraph to help readers see how upset Geraldine is. In the center circle write "Geraldine is angry." Ask students to find words and phrases in the paragraph that show Geraldine's anger. Fill in the outer circles with appropriate responses. Then, as students continue to read the story, have them use a web diagram to analyze Geraldine's feelings in another scene. **BL**

sick of the funny-looking tomato soup and the dried-out cheese sandwiches and those oranges that were more green than orange.

When Geraldine's mother first took sick and went away, Geraldine had been on her own except when Miss Gladys next door came in on Thursdays and cleaned the apartment and made a meat loaf so Geraldine could have dinner. But in those days Geraldine never quite managed to get breakfast for herself. So she'd sit through social studies class, scraping her feet to cover up the noise of her stomach growling.

Now Anita,[2] Geraldine's older sister, was living at home waiting for her husband to get out of the Army. She usually had something good for lunch—chicken and dumplings if she managed to get up in time, or baked ham from the night before and sweet-potato bread. But even if there was only a hot dog and some baked beans—sometimes just a TV dinner if those soap operas[3] kept Anita glued to the TV set— anything was better than the noisy school lunchroom where monitors[4] kept pushing you into a straight line or rushing you to the tables. Anything was better than that.

Geraldine was almost home when she stopped dead. Right outside her building was a pile of furniture and some boxes. That wasn't anything new. She had seen people get put out in the street before, but this time the ironing board looked familiar. And she recognized the big, ugly sofa standing on its arm, its under-belly showing the hole where Mrs. Watson's dog had gotten to it. **3**

Miss Gladys was sitting on the stoop,[5] and she looked up and took off her glasses. "Well, Gerry," she said slowly, wiping her glasses on the hem of her dress, "looks like you'll be staying with me for a while." She looked at the men carrying out a big box with an old doll sticking up over the edge. "Anita's upstairs. Go on up and get your lunch."

---

2. *Anita* (uh NEE tuh)

3. *Soap operas* are continuing stories on daytime TV. They usually involve very dramatic situations.

4. In the passage, *monitors* are students who do tasks for teachers or around the school.

5. In this case, a *stoop* is a porch, stairway entrance, or small platform at the door of a house or apartment building.

Analyzing the Art Does this look to you like it could be a picture of Geraldine Moore? Why or why not?

The Reader #1, 1999, Diana Ong (b.1940)

Practice the Skills

3 | **Key Reading Skill**

Responding What grabs your attention in this paragraph? Why?

Teach

R Reading Skill

Responding Ask: What thoughts and feelings did you have when you read that Geraldine was on her own before her sister moved back home? *(Possible responses: I felt sorry for her. I was surprised she would be left alone.)* **OL**

EL Language Coach

Context Clues Ask: What do you think the idiom "stopped dead" means? *(Possible response: It means stopped in surprise or stopped suddenly.)* **Ask:** What clues suggest the meaning? *(Geraldine sees familiar items in front of her building. She is probably shocked by this.)* **EL OL**

C Critical Thinking

Comprehension Ask: What is happening in the last paragraph on this page? *(Geraldine is watching as her things are being moved out of her apartment.)* **BL**

Literature Focus Lesson

Sensory Language Writers use sensory words (words that appeal to the five senses) to make readers feel all kinds of emotions. Have students read Bambara's description of the free lunches at school.

• What senses does the writer appeal to? *(sight, touch, and taste)*

• What feelings do the descriptions bring to mind? *(Possible response: feelings of disgust)*

Ask students to use words that appeal to sight, taste, and touch to write three sentences describing their own lunches. Have students share their sentences. **OL**

Objectives
• Respond to literature
• Use context clues
• Monitor comprehension
• Identify and analyze point of view
• Identify literary devices: sensory language

Teach

R1 Reading Skill

Review Visualizing Say: Geraldine's sister's face was twisted as she began to cry. How do you picture Anita's face from this description? *(Possible response: Her eyes are half-shut, her nose is wrinkled up, and her lips are tightly pressed together.)* **BL**

R2 Reading Skill

Responding Ask: What did you think and feel when you read about Geraldine adding up her expenses during math class? *(Possible response: I felt sorry for her. She had to worry about adult concerns when she should have been acting like a regular kid in school.)* **AS**

Geraldine stepped past the old woman and almost bumped into the superintendent.[6] He took off his cap to wipe away the sweat.

"Darn shame," he said to no one in particular. "Poor people sure got a hard row to hoe." **4**

"That's the truth," said Miss Gladys, standing up with her hands on her hips to watch the men set things on the sidewalk.

Upstairs, Geraldine went into the apartment and found Anita in the kitchen.

"I dunno, Gerry," Anita said. "I just don't know what we're going to do. But everything's going to be all right soon as Ma gets well." Anita's voice cracked as she set a bowl of soup before Geraldine.

"What's this?" Geraldine said.

"It's tomato soup, Gerry."

Geraldine was about to say something. But when she looked up at her big sister, she saw how Anita's face was getting all twisted as she began to cry. **5** **R1**

That afternoon, Mr. Stern, the geometry teacher, started drawing cubes and cylinders on the board. Geraldine sat at her desk adding up a column of figures in her notebook—the rent, the light and gas bills, a new gym suit, some socks. **R2**

Maybe they would move somewhere else, and she could have her own room. Geraldine turned the squares and triangles into little houses in the country.

"For your homework," Mr. Stern was saying with his back to the class, "set up your problems this way." He wrote GIVEN: in large letters, and then gave the formula[7] for the first problem. Then he wrote TO FIND: and listed three items they were to include in their answers.

---

6. A building ***superintendent*** (soo pur in TEN dint) is a person who is in charge of a building. A superintendent's job may include fixing broken things for people who live in the building, collecting rent, and cleaning.

7. A geometry ***formula*** (FOR myoo luh) is a rule students use to solve geometry problems.

414 UNIT 4 What Makes You Who You Are?

Practice the Skills

4 **English Language Coach**

Context Clues The superintendent says that "Poor people sure got a hard row to hoe." This expression is an *idiom*. Look up the word *hoe*. Look at the context of the sentence. What does the idiom tell how you about how the superintendent feels about Geraldine's situation?

5 **Key Reading Skill**

Responding How do you feel about the girls' future after seeing how Anita acts when she talks about Ma?

Chicago, Illinois: Public Art, 1978. Franklin McMahon. Polymer painting.

Analyzing the Art What feeling do you get when you look at this painting? Is it similar to the feeling you get from reading this story? Explain.

Additional Support

Reading in the Real World

Citizenship Many families create a budget—that is, they calculate their earnings and expenses and make sure they don't spend more than they earn. Help students brainstorm items in a household budget, such as rent, mortgage, utilities, food, transportation, etc. List their responses on the board. Have students suggest some reasons why families might have a budget. Some reasons may be to ensure they don't spend too much money, to save for future expenses, or to get out of debt. **OL**

Geraldine started to raise her hand to ask what all these squares and angles had to do with solving real problems, like the ones she had. Better not, she warned herself, and sat on her hands. *Your big mouth got you in trouble last term.*

In hygiene class,[8] Mrs. Potter kept saying that the body was a wonderful machine. Every time Geraldine looked up from her notebook, she would hear the same thing. "Right now your body is **manufacturing** all the proteins and tissues and energy you will need to get through tomorrow."

And Geraldine kept wondering, *How? How does my body know what it will need, when I don't even know what I'll need to get through tomorrow?*

As she headed down the hall to her next class, Geraldine remembered that she hadn't done the homework for English. Mrs. Scott had said to write a poem, and Geraldine had meant to do it at lunchtime. After all, there was nothing to it—a flower here, a raindrop there, moon, June, rose, nose. But the men carrying off the furniture had made her forget. 6

And now put away your books," Mrs. Scott was saying as Geraldine tried to scribble a poem quickly. "Today we can give King Arthur's knights a rest. Let's talk about poetry."

Mrs. Scott moved up and down the aisles, talking about her favorite poems and reciting a line now and then. She got very excited whenever she passed a desk and could pick up the homework from a student who had remembered to do the assignment.

"A poem is your own special way of saying what you feel and what you see," Mrs. Scott went on, her lips **moist**. It was her favorite subject.

"Some poets write about the light that . . . that . . . makes the world sunny," she said, passing Geraldine's desk. "Sometimes an idea takes the form of a picture—an image."

For almost half an hour, Mrs. Scott stood at the front of the room, reading poems and talking about the lives of the great poets. Geraldine drew more houses, and designs for curtains.

---

8. A **hygiene** (HEYE jeen) class is the same as a health class. Students learn how to get and stay healthy.

Vocabulary

manufacturing (man yoo FAK chur ing) *v.* making out of raw materials

moist (moyst) *adj.* just wet enough to notice

Geraldine Moore the Poet **415**

Practice the Skills

6 Literary Element

Point of View Is this story told from a **third-person limited point of view** or a **third-person omniscient point of view** (showing the thoughts of several characters)? Why do you think Bambara chose to use this point of view?

Teach

EL Language Coach

Context Clues Say: Use context clues to guess the meaning of the idiom "there was nothing to it." *(Geraldine was going to write her poem at lunchtime, so she obviously thinks writing a poem is easy. "There was nothing to it" probably means "It was not a difficult task.")* EL OL

R Reading Skill

Responding Say: When Geraldine thinks of poetry, she thinks of flowers and raindrops. How does this compare to your view of poetry? *(Possible response: I think that poetry can be about any subject. It doesn't have to be about pretty things.)* OL

C Critical Thinking

Comprehension Ask: Why didn't Geraldine write her poem at lunchtime? *(The men carrying off her furniture made her forget about her assignment.)* BL

Differentiated Instruction

Build Background Geraldine could be suffering from major depression. She shows several of the symptoms: persistent sadness or irritability; boredom; difficulty concentrating; and feelings of worthlessness or inappropriate guilt. She also matches two major risk factors: (1) She has an absent father and a seriously ill mother. (2) She's a girl (and thus four times as likely as a boy to be depressed). If Geraldine were diagnosed with major depression, she could be treated with therapy and drugs. The passage of time might lead to resolution of some problems and allow her to move on to a happier life. AS

Objectives
- Visualize
- Respond to literature
- Use context clues
- Monitor comprehension

Teach

R1 **Reading Skill**

Responding **Ask:** What do you think of Mrs. Scott? Would you like to have her as a teacher? Why or why not? *(Possible response: She seems like a kind teacher who loves poetry and encourages her students. I would like to have her as a teacher because she is very sincere.)* **AS**

Viewing the Art

Say: Who do you think the illustration might represent? *(Students will probably say Geraldine.)* Explain your answer. *(Possible responses: The painting makes the girl look confused or distant. She looks like she has a lot on her mind like Geraldine does in the story.)* **AS**

"So for those who haven't done their homework, try it now," Mrs. Scott said. "Try **expressing** what it is like to be . . . to be alive in this . . . this glorious world."

"Oh, brother," Geraldine muttered to herself as Mrs. Scott moved up and down the **aisles** again, waving her hands and leaning over the students' shoulders and saying, "That's nice," or "Keep trying." Finally she came to Geraldine's desk and stopped, looking down at her.

"I can't write a poem," Geraldine said flatly, before she even realized she was going to speak at all. She said it very loudly, and the whole class looked up.

"And why not?" Mrs. Scott asked, looking hurt.

"I can't write a poem, Mrs. Scott, because nothing lovely's been happening in my life. I haven't seen a flower since Mother's Day, and the sun don't even shine on my side of the street. No robins come sing on my window sill."

Geraldine swallowed hard. She thought about saying that her father doesn't even come to visit any more, but changed her mind. "Just the rain comes," she went on, "and the bills come, and the men to move out our furniture. I'm sorry, but I can't write no pretty poem."

Teddy Johnson leaned over and was about to giggle and crack the whole class up, but Mrs. Scott looked so serious that he changed his mind.

"You have just said the most . . . the most poetic thing, Geraldine Moore," said Mrs. Scott. Her hands flew up to touch the silk scarf around her neck. "'Nothing lovely's been happening in my life.'" She repeated it so quietly that everyone had to lean forward to hear. **7**

"Class," Mrs. Scott said very sadly, clearing her throat, "you have just heard the best poem you will ever hear." She went

Portrait in Orange, Diana Ong

Analyzing the Art You can *respond* to art as well as to a story or poem you read. How do you respond to this picture? Explain.

Practice the Skills

7 **Key Reading Skill**

Responding How does Mrs. Scott react to Geraldine's outburst? How did you react?

R2

Vocabulary

expressing (eks PRES ing) *n.* the act of making feelings or opinions known

Additional Support

Reading Fluency

Reading Dialogue Have student pairs practice reading aloud the dialogue between Mrs. Scott and Geraldine (beginning with "So for those. . ."). Tell students to read only the parts in quotation marks out loud. While practicing, they should use information the narrator provides ("loudly," "hurt," "sadly," and so on) as a guide to the emotional content of the dialogue. Also suggest that they try varying the tone, speed, and volume of their voices. To avoid embarrassment, boys could read "Mr. Scott" and "Gerald." Ask volunteers to read the dialogue aloud for the class. **EL** **BL**

to the board and stood there for a long time staring at the chalk in her hand.

"I'd like you to copy it down," she said. She wrote it just as Geraldine had said it, bad grammar and all.

> Nothing lovely's been happening in my life.
> I haven't seen a flower since Mother's Day,
> And the sun don't even shine on my side of the street.
> No robins come sing on my window sill.
> Just the rain comes, and the bills come,
> And the men to move out our furniture.
> I'm sorry, but I can't write no pretty poem. **8**

Mrs. Scott stopped writing, but she kept her back to the class for a long time—long after Geraldine had closed her notebook.

And even when the bell rang, and everyone came over to smile at Geraldine or to tap her on the shoulder or to kid her about being the school poet, Geraldine waited for Mrs. Scott to put the chalk down and turn around. Finally Geraldine stacked up her books and started to leave. Then she thought she heard a **whimper**—the way Mrs. Watson's dog whimpered sometimes—and she saw Mrs. Scott's shoulders shake a little. **9** ○

Vocabulary

whimper (WHIM pur) *n.* a soft cry

Practice the Skills

8 💬 **BIG Question**

Geraldine's poem is very different from the kind of poem Mrs. Scott asked students to write. What does Geraldine's poem say about what has made her the person she is? Explain your answer on the "Geraldine Moore" page of Foldable 4. Your response will help you complete the Unit Challenge later. **BQ**

9 **Key Reading Skill**

Responding How do you feel about Mrs. Scott after the way she acts at the end of the story?

Geraldine Moore the Poet **417**

Teach

R₂ Reading Skill

Review Drawing Conclusions Say: Mrs. Scott tells the class "you have just heard the best poem you will ever hear." What conclusions about what makes a good poem can you draw from her statement? *(Possible response: Good poetry is about sharing honest feelings, not about describing pretty things.)* **AL**

BQ 💬 **BIG Question**

Say: Geraldine writes about her life in her poem. What influence have life events had on her? *(Possible response: She's had a hard time since her mother got sick, which has made her sad, angry, and frustrated.)* **OL**

Assess

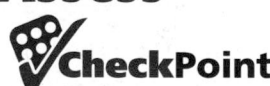 **CheckPoint**

Use the CheckPoint questions provided on Presentation Plus! to check for comprehension of the selection. These questions can be used with interactive response keypads for immediate student feedback.

Literature Focus Lesson

Theme Remind students that theme is the message about life the author tries to convey in a story. It is usually expressed as a sentence, such as "Bad things happen to good people." Have students state possible themes for "Geraldine Moore the Poet." Possible responses include "Good poetry comes from the heart" or "Sometimes life can be very unfair." **AL**

Objectives
- Respond to literature
- Draw conclusions from text and experience
- Identify literary elements: theme
- Find meaning in art

Assess

Resources for page 418

📁 Selection Quick Check, p. 34

📁 Selection and Unit Assessment, p. 40

💿 ExamView Assessment Suite

💿 Interactive Tutor: Self-Assessment

Students can respond to the *After You Read* items in their Learner's Notebooks or on a separate sheet of paper.

Answering the BIG Question

1. Possible response: Her mother's absence because of illness made Geraldine sad and concerned.

2. her sister Anita

3. Possible responses: They are poor. They care about each other.

Critical Thinking

4. Possible response: She might be saying that life is difficult.

5. Possible response: She has a right to be angry; she has to worry about adult concerns when she should be enjoying her youth.

6. Responses will vary. Students might mention grandparents, other relatives, or family friends.

7. Possible response: The poem Geraldine creates grabbed my attention. It is really beautiful.

After You Read

Geraldine Moore the Poet

Answering the BIG Question

1. Describe one experience in Geraldine's life that helped make her the person she was.

2. **Recall** Who is taking care of Geraldine at the time she writes her poem?
   Tip Right There

3. **Infer** From Geraldine's comments about other people who live in her neighborhood, what can you guess about them?
   Tip Think and Search

Critical Thinking

4. **Interpret** What might the author be using Geraldine's story to say about people and problems in the world in general?
   Tip Author and Me

5. **Evaluate** Geraldine is sometimes angry about what her life has become. Does she have a right to be angry? Give reasons for your answer.
   Tip Author and Me

6. **Connect** Who would you depend on if your parents or guardians could not take care of you?
   Tip On My Own

7. **Respond** What event or detail in this story grabbed your attention the most? Why?
   Tip On My Own

Objectives (pp. 418–419)
Reading Respond to literature
Literature Identify point of view
Vocabulary Use context clues to understand idioms
Writing Respond to literature: journal
Grammar Identify sentence fragments
• Fix sentence fragments

Write About Your Reading

Write a journal entry as if you are Geraldine and it is a year after the events in this story took place.

• What has changed in your life?
• Where are you living?
• How are your mother and your sister?
• How do you feel about the world now?

Write About Your Reading

Sample Response:
It's been a year since Anita and I got kicked out of our apartment. We stayed in a shelter for a while, and then Anita's husband sent us enough money to move into a new place. Mom passed away six months ago. I am still angry at the world sometimes, but I have faith that things will work out for the best. I joined a poetry club and love writing about my experiences and sharing them with other kids.
Until next time,
Geraldine

Skills Review

Key Reading Skill: Responding

8. Authors and poets hope that people will respond to what they read. Imagine talking with the author of "Geraldine Moore the Poet." What would you tell her about how you felt when you read her story?

Literary Element: Point of View

9. This story was written from a third-person limited point of view. Only Geraldine's thoughts were revealed. If you were to rewrite this story from another character's point of view, which character would you choose? Why?

Reviewing Skills: Drawing Conclusions

10. From what you know about Geraldine Moore, why do you think she didn't try to make up a pretty poem about flowers or raindrops?

Vocabulary Check

11. Match each word with its synonym, or word that means almost the same thing.

whine   grumbled   damp

a. muttered ___

b. moist ___

c. whimper ___

12. For each of these words, write a sentence that includes a definition or restatement.

manufacturing   shrugged   expressing

Web Activities For eFlashcards, Selection Quick Checks, and other Web activities, go to www.glencoe.com.

Grammar Link: Fixing Fragments

Do not use sentence fragments when you write for school or business. Remember, a fragment is a group of words that's missing one or more of the requirements for a sentence. Those requirements are a subject, a verb, and a complete thought.

- The blue shirt with long sleeves. (What about the shirt? This fragment needs a verb.)
- Ran like crazy toward home plate. (Who or what ran? This fragment needs a subject.)
- If Nina makes dinner. (What if she does? There's a subject and a verb, but the thought isn't complete.)

Fragments can result from ending a sentence before you've ended your thought. The whole thought may be there, but it's in two different sentence fragments instead of one complete sentence.

Incorrect: The boy next to me. Was snoring.
Correct: The boy next to me was snoring.

Sometimes only one sentence ends too soon, which also creates a fragment.

Incorrect: Mr. Reed taught English. Last year.
Correct: Mr. Reed taught English last year.

Grammar Practice

13. In the following paragraph, there are three sentence fragments. On a separate sheet of paper, fix the fragments in the way that seems best to you.

Haley and Jeff were best friends. They were in the same grade. In school. When Haley had to move. Geoff was unhappy. Walked around the neighborhood sadly.

Writing Application Look back at the journal entry you wrote. Make sure every sentence has both a subject and a verb.

Skills Review

Key Reading Skill: Responding

8. Possible response: I felt sad because Geraldine had so many problems, but I was impressed because she handled them without getting into trouble.

Literary Element: Point of View

9. Possible response: I would write it from Mrs. Scott's point of view. I would tell how strong and sad Geraldine is.

Reviewing Skills: Drawing Conclusions

10. Possible response: Her life wasn't pretty for Geraldine, and she couldn't pretend it was.

Vocabulary Check

11. a. grumbled
    b. damp
    c. whine

English Language Coach

12. Possible responses:

- The factory has started manufacturing, which means "making," cheap clothing.

- Sal shrugged, or raised his shoulders, to show he didn't care about dinner.

- Some people have a hard time expressing, or telling, their feelings.

Grammar Link: Fixing Fragments

Grammar Practice

13. Haley and Jeff were best friends. They were in the same grade in school. When Haley had to move, Geoff was unhappy and walked around the neighborhood sadly.

Close

Ask students to tell how very difficult events such as the ones Geraldine experiences can help make us who we are.

**Objective covered in this
workshop:**
• Interpret text

Teaching Students How to Interpret

Why Is It Important

• Every reader constructs meaning on the basis of what he or she understands about the world. Students will learn how to use their own experience and knowledge to decide what the events or ideas in a selection mean.

• Finding meanings as students read requires interaction with the text. Interpreting text will allow students to become more active readers.

• Students will learn how to determine what an author is *really* saying in his or her work.

How to Help Students Get It

• Have students think about what they already know about themselves and the world, and how it relates to the topic of each selection.

• Tell students to ask themselves questions as they read, such as: What is the author really trying to say here? What larger idea might these events be about?

• Remind students that interpreting is more than just remembering and understanding facts—it's creating meaning in text by using what they know about the world around them.

Reading to Answer the Big Question

Same Song by Pat Mora
In this poem, a mom describes the very different ways her daughter and her son work to look like the people they want to be.

Flowers and Freckle Cream by Elizabeth Ellis
A twelve-year-old girl is unhappy with her appearance, particularly her freckles. She becomes more distraught after she uses a mail order freckle-remover cream that makes the freckles even darker. Her grandfather gives her a special gift to help her understand that every person is uniquely beautiful.

Workshop Resources

PACING (DAYS)		LESSON	STUDENT MATERIALS	TEACHER RESOURCES
STANDARD	BLOCK			
1	½	Key Skill Lesson: Interpreting	🐾 Key Reading Skills Practice, p. 21 🐾 English Language Coach Review, p. 41	♨ Bellringer Options Transparencies – Daily Language Practice 36 ♨ Read Aloud, Think Aloud Transparencies – Key Reading Skills 14 💿 Presentation Plus!
1	1	"Same Song"	💻 Glencoe Online 🐾 Unit Vocabulary Review, p. 39 🐾 Academic Vocabulary Review, p. 42 📁 English Language Coach 🐾 Active Reading Graphic Organizer, p. 23 🐾 Literary Analysis, p. 22 💿 StudentWorks Plus™ 💻 Online Student Edition 💿 Literature Classics 📁 Selection and Unit Assessments, p. 41	♨ Literary and Text Analysis Transparencies 47 💻 Puzzlemaker 💿 Skill Level Up!™ A Language Arts Game 💻 BookLink 3 📓 Assessment by Learning Objective (Diagnostic and Formative) 💿 Interactive Tutor: Self-Assessment 💿 TeacherWorks Plus™
1		"Flowers and Freckle Cream"	💻 Glencoe Online 🐾 Unit Vocabulary Review, p. 39 🐾 Academic Vocabulary Review, p. 42 📁 English Language Coach 🐾 Active Reading Graphic Organizer, p. 25 💿 StudentWorks Plus™ 💻 Online Student Edition 💿 Literature Classics 📁 Selection and Unit Assessments, p. 42	♨ Literary and Text Analysis Transparencies 39 💻 Puzzlemaker 💿 Skill Level Up!™ A Language Arts Game 💻 BookLink 3 📓 Assessment by Learning Objective (Diagnostic and Formative) 💿 Interactive Tutor: Self-Assessment 💿 TeacherWorks Plus™

Keys for Unit Resource

📁 Blackline Master		🔲 DVD	
📓 Workbook		♨ Transparency	
📖 Supplemental Text		💻 Web-based	
💿 CD-ROM		🐾 Fast File	

Level Appropriate Code

AS = Activities for all students

AL = Activities for students working above grade level

OL = Activities for students working at grade level

BL = Activities for students working below grade level

EL = Activities for English language learners

Focus

BELLRINGER Options

- **Daily Language Practice Transparency 36**
Focus Activity Ask: Why do you think young people are often concerned with their looks? *(Possible response: TV and movies often present attractive people as "normal," so kids think they have to look like them to be normal.)* **AS**

Teach

Analyzing the Cartoon

Ask: What does *bilingual* mean? *(able to speak, read, and understand two languages)* **AL** **Ask:** Why might boys think girls speak a different language? *(Possible response: Boys often don't understand how girls think and feel.)* **Ask:** Do you think girls might feel the same way about boys? *(Responses will vary.)* **OL**

C Critical Thinking

Comprehension Say: Reread the paragraph about interpreting. What must readers use besides text to interpret what authors write? *(their own experiences)* **BL**

Skills Focus

You will practice using these skills when you read the following selections:

- "Same Song," p. 424
- "Flowers and Freckle Cream," p. 430

Reading

- Interpreting what you read

Literature

- Understanding sound devices: Alliteration

Vocabulary

- Using context clues that involve comparison and contrast
- Academic vocabulary: *interpret*

Writing/Grammar

- Identifying complete and simple subjects and predicates
- Identifying compound subjects and predicates

Objectives (pp. 420–421)
Reading Interpret text

Skill Lesson

Interpreting

Learn It!

What Is It? You say hello to a friend, but she only says, "Can't talk!" How do you **interpret** this? Is she angry with you or is she just late for her next class?

C

You interpret other people's words and actions all the time. You decide what certain statements or behaviors mean. In reading, you often need to interpret what a story or poem or essay means. You can do this by using information the writer provides and your own experience to form an opinion about the real meaning of a writer's words. Two people might have two different interpretations about the same selection. That's okay! It's possible for more than one interpretation to be reasonable.

BALDO © 2004 Partnership. Dist. By UNIVERSAL PRESS SYNDICATE. Reprinted with permission. All right reserved.

Analyzing Cartoons
These boys are busy interpreting certain statements. Do you think they're interpreting correctly?

Academic Vocabulary . . . .

interpret (in TUR prit) *v.* to explain the meaning of; make understandable

---

Additional Support

English Language Coach

Slang Tell students that girls and boys aren't the only ones who sometimes speak different languages, as implied in the cartoon. Kids often create and use slang, or nonstandard language made up of invented words and old words with new meanings. Have students create a Slang Dictionary for classroom-appropriate slang that kids today use. Tell students to write each word, its meaning, and a sample sentence showing how it is used. **EL BL OL** Have students share slang words their parents or grandparents used when they were kids, along with each word's meaning and a sample sentence. **AL**

Why Is It Important? Interpreting while you read lets you get a deeper understanding of what you are reading. It's especially important when you read poetry. That's because many poets don't come right out and declare their ideas. They often use images, sound, or something else to help get their ideas across.

How Do I Do It? Ask yourself, what is the author trying to say here? What larger idea might these events be about? What exact words did the writer use? What details stir up strong feelings in me and lead me to form opinions? Here is how one student interpreted "My Father Is a Simple Man."

Study Central Visit www.glencoe.com and click on Study Central to review interpreting.

> *He has taken me on this journey / and it's been lifelong. / He's sure I'll be healthy / so long as I eat more oranges, / and tells me the orange / has seeds and so is perpetual; / and we too will come back / like the orange trees.*

I think the part about the seeds in the orange means that the fruit will grow into a tree and the tree will make more oranges. Kind of like the relationship the father has with his son. Maybe one day the son will grow wise like the father and tell his kids the same story about the oranges.

Practice It!

In your Learner's Notebook, practice interpreting the lines from "My Father Is a Simple Man." There are three questions you can ask yourself to help with interpretation. First answer the question, "What does the selection say?" Next, ask, "What do I know about myself and the world as it relates to this topic?" Finally, ask yourself, "What is the author really saying; is there a larger idea?"

I ask him what he thinks / about death and he says / he will gladly face it when / it comes but won't jump / out in front of a car.

Use It!

As you read "Same Song" and "Flowers and Freckle Cream," remember to use these three questions to help you interpret. Write the questions out in your Learner's Notebook ahead of time, and answer them whenever you need help interpreting.

Teach

R Reading Skill

Interpreting Say: There are several ways of interpreting the phrase *simple man*. If you know the speaker admires his father, how might you interpret *simple man*? *(Possible response: It might mean not talking or acting in a fancy way.)* **Ask:** If you think the speaker does not respect his father, how might you interpret *simple man*? *(Possible response: It might mean he looks only at the surface of things.)* **OL AL**

BQ BIG Question

Ask: Why might your interpretation of a selection be different from your classmate's? *(Possible response: Our different experiences affect how we see things.)* **AL**

Resources for page 421

📖 Use Key Reading Skills Transparency 14 in *Read Aloud, Think Aloud* to help students practice interpreting.

Differentiated Instruction

Using a Graphic Organizer Some students may benefit from using a graphic organizer to interpret literature. Have students draw and complete this organizer to interpret the selections in this workshop. Discuss how students' prior knowledge and experiences influence their interpretations. **AS**

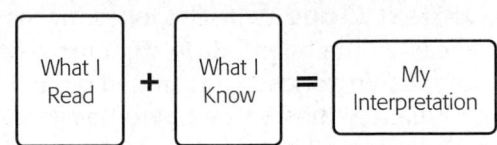

Objectives
• Interpret text
• Monitor comprehension

Teach

More About the Author

Because of the influence of her grandparents, who moved from Mexico to Texas in the early 1900s, Pat Mora spoke mainly Spanish at home. This former radio talk show host and teacher often includes Spanish phrases and Southwest culture in her books to preserve her Hispanic heritage.

V Vocabulary

Remembering Vocabulary

Say: How might sketching and labeling a simple drawing of a human figure help you remember some of the vocabulary words? *(Three of the words—biceps, triceps, and pectorals—are parts of the upper body; drawing and labeling them will help me visualize the body parts better when I read the vocabulary words.)* **OL**

Objectives (pp. 422–425)
Reading Interpret text • Make connections from text to self
Literature Identify sound devices: alliteration
Vocabulary Use context clues: comparison, contrast

Before You Read · Same Song

Meet the Author

Pat Mora grew up in El Paso, Texas, in a bilingual home. She spends most of her time writing and traveling to schools and other events to teach young writers. See page R4 of the Author Files for more on Pat Mora.

Author Search For more about Pat Mora, go to www.glencoe.com.

Vocabulary Preview

mauve (mohv) *adj.* a light purple or violet **(p. 424)** *She likes make-up with mauve colors in it.*

peers (peerz) *v.* looks closely at something **(p. 424)** *Her daughter peers at her face in the mirror.*

biceps (BY seps) *n.* a large muscle that runs down the front of the arm from the shoulder to the elbow **(p. 425)** *Her son was doing arm-curls with heavy weights because he wanted large biceps.*

triceps (TRY seps) *n.* a large muscle at the back of the upper arm **(p. 425)** *The triceps on his arms were not as big as he wanted them to be.*

pectorals (pek TOR ulz) *n.* muscles connecting the chest walls to the bones of the upper arm and shoulder **(p. 425)** *He was trying to strengthen his pectorals, but the exercises were hard.*

Partner Talk On a separate note card, write each vocabulary word one time. Turn the note card over and write the definition and part of speech on the back. Take turns testing each other by flashing the cards.

English Language Coach

Context Clues Sometimes a word's meaning is revealed by context clues that make a comparison to something familiar.

Eating Aunt Lucy's cooking is as **perilous** as riding a bike blindfolded.

Like and *as* are often used to make comparisons, so they're useful signals. Since you know that riding a bike blindfolded would be dangerous, you can figure out that *perilous* probably means something like "dangerous."

Sometimes a word's meaning is revealed by context clues that contrast it with a familiar word or phrase.

Instead of being late for class, try to be more **punctual.**

Contrast clues are often signaled by words such as *although, but, however, in contrast to,* or *instead of.* The sentence tells you that being punctual means the opposite of being late.

On Your Own Use context clues to define each word in dark type. Then tell if the context clues provided a *comparison* or a *contrast*.

1. The mat was **resilient**, like rubber.

2. Chaz is warm and friendly, but his brother is **aloof**.

422 UNIT 4 What Makes You Who You Are?

Additional Support

Author Search To expand students' appreciation of Pat Mora, have them access the Web site for additional information and resources.

English Language Coach

Context Clues Write the following sentences on the board. Have students give the meaning of each underlined word and identify the context clue(s) as comparison or contrast.

1. I thought the speaker was <u>charismatic</u>, but my friends found her unappealing. *(appealing or charming; contrast)*

2. Joe said the food was so <u>vile</u> that it was like eating boiled newspapers. *(boiled newspapers; comparison)*

3. Kids felt thankful for the snow day; their parents were <u>unappreciative</u>. *(ungrateful, unthankful; contrast)* **OL**

Skills Preview

Key Reading Skill: Interpreting

To interpret "Same Song," think about what the speaker says about the son and daughter. Think about what each might be trying to accomplish. Also, think about your own definition of *beauty*.

Partner Talk The poet Emily Dickinson wrote, "*Beauty—be not caused—It is.*" With a partner, interpret possible meanings of that statement. Keep your interpretation in mind when you read "Same Song."

Key Literary Element: Sound Devices: Alliteration

In Reading Workshop 2, you learned about rhyme, rhythm, and meter. These are three important "sound devices," or ways to use sound effectively in writing. Another sound device is **alliteration**, which is the repetition of consonant sounds at the beginnings of words. "Peter Piper picked a peck of pickled peppers" is a famous example. Usually, though, alliteration is used for only a few words. *Seeking the man in the moon* repeats the *m* sound only once, but the alliteration is effective.

It is the *sound* not the *letter* that creates alliteration.

• *A circle of sad psychiatrists* contains three alliterative words.

• *Gigantic goats gnawed the fence* contains no alliterative words.

Alliteration is often used in poetry to call attention to certain words and to add interest to the sound of the poem. It is also used in other writing.

Write to Learn In your Learner's Notebook, write a list of five phrases that use alliteration.

Interactive Literary Elements Handbook To review or learn more about the literary elements, go to www.glencoe.com.

Get Ready to Read

Connect to the Reading

Are you a hustle-out-the door person in the morning, taking little time to check your clothes and appearance? Or do you worry about a bad hair day? As you read "Same Song," think about how the way you *see* yourself shapes the way you experience life.

Class Discussion What do you think is more important: who you are on the inside or who you appear to be? Talk about why you think we focus so much on outward appearances. What influences how we want to appear on the outside?

Build Background

The poem you are about to read is one of Pat Mora's most popular poems. She often writes poems that celebrate her Mexican American heritage and the joy of accepting the things that make people different.

• She has often said, "I take pride in being a Hispanic writer."

• Mora says that a big reason for writing poetry "is to help people feel less lonely."

• Because she recognizes that Mexican Americans are well aware of the borders in their lives, she also likes to write about borders as places to bridge differences.

Set Purposes for Reading

BIG Question Read "Same Song" to explore whether appearances make us who we are.

Set Your Own Purpose What else would you like to learn from the reading to help you answer the Big Question? Write your purpose on the "Same Song" page of Foldable 4.

Keep Moving

Use these skills as you read the following selection.

Same Song **423**

Teach

L Literary Element

Alliteration Ask: What creates alliteration, the letter or the sound the letters make? (*The sound the letters make.*) **OL**

R Reading Skill

Review Connecting Say: What part of your appearance do you think says most about who you are? (*Responses will vary.*) **AS** Encourage students to remember their thoughts as they read "Same Song."

Interactive Literary Elements Handbook Have students access the Web site to improve their understanding of sound devices.

Literature Focus Lesson

Alliteration Discuss with students how a thesaurus can help them find words that both express their idea *and* begin with the same letter. On the board write *friends*, *gift*, and *pup*. Have student partners write alliterative phrases by adding at least one adjective to each noun.

Suggest that the partners first jot down ideas without worrying about alliteration. Then, for each noun and adjective, they can find synonyms that begin with the same letter or sound. Have students present their finished phrases to the class. **OL**

Objectives

• Identify literary devices
• Monitor comprehension
• Use context clues
• Make connections from text to self
• Learn and use new vocabulary

Teach

R1 Reading Skill

Interpreting Say: In "Snow White" the queen asks, "Mirror, mirror on the wall, who is the fairest of them all?" How does knowing the fairy tale help you interpret the poem? *(Possible response: It helps me guess that the girl peers into the mirror, wanting to know if she is beautiful.)* **AL**

R2 Reading Skill

Interpreting Ask: Why do you think the daughter frowns at herself when she looks in the mirror? *(Possible response: She is unhappy with her appearance.)* **OL**

L Literary Element

Sound Devices: Alliteration

Ask: What alliteration can you find in lines 11–12? *(frowns, face, fair)* **BL**

by Pat Mora

Practice the Skills

While my sixteen-year-old son sleeps,
my twelve-year-old daughter
stumbles into the bathroom at six a.m.
plugs in the curling iron
5 squeezes into faded jeans
curls her hair carefully
strokes Aztec Blue* shadow on her eyelids
smooths Frosted **Mauve** blusher* on her cheeks
outlines her mouth in Neon Pink*
10 **peers** into the mirror, mirror on the wall **R1**
frowns at her face, her eyes, her skin,
not fair. **L** **R2**

1 Key Literary Element

Sound Devices: Alliteration
Reread the first three lines.
What example of alliteration
do you find? **L**

---

7 ***Aztec Blue*** is just a fancy name for a shade of blue.

8 ***Frosted Mauve*** is a silvery or icy mauve color. ***Blusher*** is a kind of make-up that women use to add color to their cheeks.

9 ***Neon*** is a kind of light that results in very bright colors. So, ***Neon Pink*** is a bright pink lipstick.

Vocabulary

mauve (mohv) *adj.* a light purple or violet

peers (peerz) *v.* looks closely at something

424 **UNIT 4**   What Makes You Who You Are?

Additional Support

Differentiated Instruction

Rewriting Verbs Discuss how the poem's verbs *stumbles* and *peers* paint more vivid pictures than *walks* and *looks.* Write the following paragraph on the board. Have students work with partners to write more vivid verbs for underlined verbs.

Walking our dog is a pain! First, I have to <u>get</u> him to stand still for his leash. Then I <u>pull</u> him toward the door. He steps outside but <u>tries</u> to turn around and <u>go</u> back in. We finally <u>walk</u> to the corner. By that time, we are both ready to <u>go</u> home. **OL AL**

At night this daughter
stumbles off to bed at nine
15 eyes half-shut while my son
jogs a mile in the cold dark
then lifts weights in the garage
curls and bench presses*
expanding **biceps**, **triceps**, **pectorals**,
20 one-handed push-ups, one hundred sit-ups
peers into that mirror, mirror and frowns too. **2** **3** **4** ○

---

18. *Curls and bench presses* are two weight-lifting exercises for building muscles.

Vocabulary

biceps (BY seps) *n.* a large muscle that runs down the front of the arm from the shoulder to the elbow

triceps (TRY seps) *n.* a large muscle at the back of the upper arm

pectorals (pek TOR ulz) *n.* muscles connecting the chest walls to the bones of the upper arm and shoulder

Nancy's Sink, 2003. Pam Ingalls.

Analyzing the Art Can you visualize the speaker's daughter putting on her make-up in front of the mirror? Can you visualize the speaker's son peering into the mirror and frowning? Explain your answers.

Practice the Skills

2 **Key Reading Skill**

Interpreting Now that you have read the entire poem, think about the first stanza. How can you use the first stanza to help you interpret the second stanza? What do you think the poet is saying about the son and daughter? What is the poet saying about our views of beauty and strength? **R**

3 **English Language Coach**

Context Clues Read this interpretation: "The daughter thinks that make-up enhances her appearance, like gift wrap and ribbons do to a package." What might the word *enhances* mean?

4 **BIG Question**

What does this poem suggest about the importance of appearance in making us who we are? Write your answer on the "Same Song" page of Foldable 4. Your response will help you complete the Unit Challenge later. **BQ**

Same Song **425**

Teach

R Reading Skill

Interpreting Say: Both the daughter and the son frown during their activities. What do you think the poet is saying about being young by describing the son and daughter frowning? *(Possible response: They frown because they feel they must look a certain way.)* **AL**

BQ BIG Question

Ask: How important is your appearance to who you are as a person? *(Responses will vary.)*

Assess

✓CheckPoint

Use the CheckPoint questions provided on Presentation Plus! to check for comprehension of the selection. These questions can be used with interactive response keypads for immediate student feedback.

Reading in the Real World

Careers Students who are interested in physical fitness may like to learn more about personal trainers. Have students research this career on the Internet or at the library, focusing on job descriptions, education and training requirements, and job opportunities. Invite a personal trainer from a local gym, YMCA/YWCA, or university to talk to the class about physical fitness and the career of personal trainer. Ask students to write a paragraph on the benefits of physical fitness. **AS**

Objectives
• Interpret text
• Identify literary devices: sound devices
• Make connections from text to self

Assess

Resources for page 426

- 📁 Selection Quick Check, p. 35
- 📁 Selection and Unit Assessment, p. 41
- 💿 ExamView Assessment Suite
- 💿 Interactive Tutor: Self-Assessment

Students can respond to the *After You Read* items in their Learner's Notebooks or on a separate sheet of paper.

Answering the

BIG Question

1. Possible response: Looks are a big part of who they are. They'd probably be more confident if they thought they looked good.
2. The son's strong body is most important. The girl's face, hair, and clothes are most important.
3. She plugs in the curler, puts on jeans, curls her hair, applies makeup, and checks the mirror.

Critical Thinking

4. Possible response: Both care about and seem dissatisfied with how they look.
5. Possible response: The speaker wants to contrast how the son and daughter work on their appearance.
6. Possible response: Repeating the phrase suggests that both son and daughter want a fairy-tale mirror to tell them they're beautiful.

After You Read   **Same Song**

Answering the 🗨 BIG Question

1. How do you think the son and the daughter feel about appearances? How do you think their appearance affects who they are and what they do?

2. **Recall** What part of the son's and the daughter's appearance is most important to each?
   Tip Think and Search

3. **Summarize** What steps does the daughter take to get ready in the morning?
   Tip Think and Search

Critical Thinking

4. **Infer** What do the son and daughter have in common?
   Tip Think and Search

5. **Interpret** Why do you think the speaker starts each stanza, or section of the poem, by explaining who is sleeping, who is awake, what time it is, and what each person is doing?
   Tip Author and Me

6. **Analyze** Why do you think the author repeats the phrase "mirror, mirror"? Explain the importance of the mirror.
   Tip Author and Me

Write About Your Reading

Imagine you could write a letter to make the son and the daughter in the poem feel better about themselves. What would you tell them? What questions would you ask? Write a letter to either the boy or the girl in this poem. Think about these points as you write.

- What makes the body or face so important to the son and daughter?
- Does makeup and muscle add to who they really are?
- What might happen if all the mirrors in their home or school were covered?

Use examples from the poem in your letter. Be specific about what you have to say.

Objectives (pp. 426–427)
Reading Interpret text • Make connections from text to self
Literature Identify sound devices: alliteration
Vocabulary Use context clues: comparison, contrast
Writing Respond to literature: personal letter
Grammar Identify complete and simple subjects and predicates

426 UNIT 4   What Makes You Who You Are?

Write About Your Reading

Dear friend,

Do you remember lunchtime when you were worried your eye shadow didn't match your outfit? I said it didn't matter, but I could tell you didn't understand what I meant. I know you care a lot about how you look. Hey, I'm a 12-year-old girl, too! We *all* think about our looks. The difference is that I think you believe no one will like you unless you look good all the time. This is not true! You're thoughtful, kind, and never stuck-up. *That's* why people like you.

Skills Review

Key Reading Skill: Interpreting

7. How do you interpret the title of the poem? Explain your answer.

8. Look at how all the lines in the poem begin. What part of speech is used most often as the first word in a line? Why do you think so many lines begin with this type of word?

Key Literary Element: Sound Devices: Alliteration

9. What example of alliteration can you find in lines 11 and 12?

Vocabulary Check

Rewrite each sentence. Write *True* or *False* after each statement.

10. If you do chin-ups, you can build up your *biceps*.

11. *Mauve* is pale green.

12. Your *triceps* are muscles in your legs.

13. *Peers* means "glances quickly."

14. Body armor that covers your chest will protect your *pectorals*.

15. **Academic Vocabulary** What does it mean to *interpret* a poem? Explain your answer.

English Language Coach Write a definition for the underlined word in each sentence below.

16. Don't excite the fans; try to <u>subdue</u> them instead.

17. He <u>admonished</u> me as if he were a parent talking to a naughty child.

18. This machine will <u>hoist</u> the supplies like an elevator would.

Literature Online

Web Activities For eFlashcards, Selection Quick Checks, and other Web activities, go to www.glencoe.com.

Grammar Link: Subjects and Predicates

Every sentence is made up of two parts: a subject and a predicate. The subject is the part that is doing or being something. The predicate is the part that tells what the subject is doing or being.

- The **complete subject** contains all the words in the subject.
- The **complete predicate** contains all the words in the predicate.

Complete Subject	Complete Predicate
Most of Kevin's friends	usually wear similar clothes.
My friendly, smart cousin	is here.
Bees	try to protect their hives.

The **simple subject** is *just* the verb or verbs in the predicate. The **simple subject** is the word or the fewest words that can answer a "who or what?" question about the verb. (When a whole name is used, the whole name is the simple subject.) In the following sentences, the simple subject is underlined once. The simple predicate is underlined twice.

A huge, gentle <u>dog</u> with floppy ears <u>jumped</u> on me.

My team's <u>coach</u> rarely <u>sits</u> down during a game.

<u>Everyone</u> in the entire school <u>is</u> here today.

Grammar Practice

Copy each sentence. Underline the simple subject once and the simple predicate twice.

19. Good musicians play many songs by memory.

20. Some trees in the forest grow taller than others.

21. Nasty, rotten fruit of all different colors flew through the air.

22. The entire baseball team from Madison Middle School is on that bus.

Writing Application Look back at your writing assignment. Choose a sentence in which you can find the simple subject and the simple predicate. Underline the simple subject once and the simple predicate twice.

Skills Review

Key Reading Skill: Interpreting

7. Possible response: Both kids in the poem sing the "same song" because they think appearance makes them who they are.

8. verbs. Responses will vary.

Key Literary Element: Alliteration

9. frowns, face, fair

Vocabulary Check

10. true

11. false

12. false

13. true

14. true

15. **Academic Vocabulary** Possible response: to use what you read and what you already know to figure out what a poem means

English Language Coach

16. quiet

17. scolded

18. lift

Grammar Link: Complete Subjects and Predicates

Grammar Practice

19. <u>Good musicians play many songs by memory.</u>

20. <u>Some trees in the forest grow taller than others.</u>

21. <u>Nasty, rotten fruit of all different colors flew through the air.</u>

22. <u>The entire baseball team from Madison Middle School is on that bus.</u>

Close

Ask students to summarize what they learned from the selection to answer the Big Question.

Teach

More About the Author

Beginning her storytelling as a children's librarian at the Dallas Public Library, Elizabeth Ellis has continued to have fun with stories for more than 25 years. She has won the Circle of Excellence Award and the John Henry Faulk award from two storytelling associations.

V Vocabulary

Prefixes Say: The prefix *in–* in the word *inadequate* means *not.* You can predict that the definition of this word might begin with the word *not.* What do you think the word *inaccurate* means? *(Possible responses: not accurate; not correct; wrong)* **OL**

Before You Read Flowers and Freckle Cream

Meet the Author

Elizabeth Ellis learned to tell stories from her grandfather while she was growing up in the Appalachian Mountains. She has traveled all over the country and even to New Zealand, reading her stories to over 250,000 children and adults. Ellis says she loves making a living this way because she has so much fun.

Literature Online

Author Search For more about Elizabeth Ellis, go to www .glencoe.com.

Objectives (pp. 428–433)
Reading Interpret text • Make connections from text to self
Literature Identify and analyze point of view
Vocabulary Use context clues: examples

Vocabulary Preview

inadequate (in AD ih kwit) *adj.* not good enough **(p. 432)** *My teacher said that a one-paragraph book report was inadequate.*

Write to Learn Use the vocabulary word in a sentence.

English Language Coach

Context Clues You know that you can use context clues to figure out the meaning of an unfamiliar word. The context may define it, restate it, or compare or contrast it to something that you are familiar with. Unfamiliar words are sometimes made clear by a familiar **example.** The clue words *such as, for instance,* and *for example* are often used to point out examples.

We must respond quickly to **catastrophes** such as tornadoes, floods, and large forest fires.

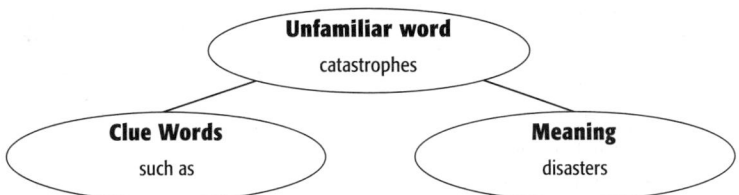

The words *such as* introduce examples of catastrophes. From the examples you can guess that *catastrophes* means "kinds of disasters."

On Your Own Use context clues to figure out the meaning of the word in dark type in the sentence below. Write the meaning of the word and the context clues that helped you figure out the word's meaning. Think about what all the animals have in common.

Domesticated animals like cows, pigs, and puppies can be found on many farms.

428 UNIT 4 What Makes You Who You Are?

Additional Support

Literature Online

Author Search To expand student's appreciation of Elizabeth Ellis, have them access the Web site for more information and resources.

English Language Coach

Context Clues: Signal Words Tell students that signal words can help them identify certain types of context clues. Give students the following signal words and have them use them to look for context clues as they read.

• Comparison signal words: *like, same as, similar to, and, just like*

• Contrast signal words: *however, while, although, different from, unlike, opposed to*

• Restatement signal words: *or, that is, which means, in other words* **EL BL**

Skills Preview

Key Reading Skill: Interpreting

As you read, think about what you already know combined with what the author is really saying. Ask yourself these questions:

- What is the selection about?
- What do you already know about this topic?
- What is the author's larger idea?

Write to Learn In your Learner's Notebook, answer these questions as you read the story.

Literary Element: Point of View

You have already learned about first-person and third-person point of view. You also know that a story is written from a first-person point of view if the narrator is a character in the story. In such a story, the narrator refers to himself or herself as *I*.

Stories with first-person narration can be quite different from each other. Think about "Eleven" in the last unit. The narrator seemed to be eleven years old, didn't she? The author didn't use a narrator who was remembering the experience. She used a narrator who was *in* the experience—a child.

Keep these questions in mind as you read "Flowers and Freckle Cream":

* Does the narrator know more than you'd think she'd really know at that moment?

* Does the narrator ever comment on her own actions, as if from a distance?

Write to Learn Write a short paragraph using first-person point of view. Use a narrator that is *not you*. Write as if you are older or younger than you are or as if you are a very different kind of person.

Interactive Literary Elements Handbook
To review or learn more about the literary elements, go to www.glencoe.com.

Get Ready to Read

Connect to the Reading

Most people have moments when they envy someone else for their looks, their brains, or their sense of humor. "Flowers and Freckle Cream" makes you think about times when you wanted to be like someone else and—perhaps—went about it the wrong way.

Write to Learn Think about a time that you learned from a mistake. What was the mistake? How does learning from a mistake help make you who you are? Write about that mistake and how you learned from it.

Build Background

This story is about wishing you were like someone else. It's also about being able to tell about it, learn from it, and laugh about it later.

- Elizabeth Ellis is an award-winning storyteller. She travels to storytelling festivals across the country, so when she *writes* a story she makes it sound as if she is *telling* it.
- The author says she learned to tell stories from her grandfather. Notice the important role he plays in this story.
- A tiger lily is a beautiful, speckled flower.

Set Purposes for Reading

BIG Question Read the selection "Flowers and Freckle Cream" to learn about how looking back on your misfortunes and learning from them is part of what makes you who you are.

Set Your Own Purpose What else would you like to learn from the selection to help you answer the Big Question? Write your own purpose on the "Flowers and Freckle Cream" page of Foldable 4.

Keep Moving

Use these skills as you read the following selection.

Teach

L Literary Element

Point of View Say: Tell the point of view of the following sentences.

- He walked aimlessly across the playground, and the children watched him curiously. *(third-person narration)*
- Every birthday, I wished for a new bike, but every year, my parents bought me two dresses and a pair of sneakers. *(first-person narrator)* **AS**

R Reading Skill

Review Connecting Say: Think of a time when you felt envious of someone else. What did you envy? How did it feel to be envious? *(Responses will vary.)* **AS**

Interactive Literary Elements Handbook Have students access the Web site to improve their understanding of point of view.

Literature Focus Lesson

Narrator Remind students that the narrator is the person telling the story. It might be the author, as in "Flowers and Freckle Cream," or a made-up character. Help students understand that the narrator in this story is remembering a time from her youth. **BL** Discuss with students how looking back on the story as an adult might affect the narrator's point of view. Talk about how she might be able to see things more clearly now that she's had a chance to reflect on the situation. **OL**

Objectives

- Make connections from text to self
- Interpret text
- Use context clues to determine word meaning
- Learn and use new vocabulary

429

Teach

R Reading Skill

Interpreting Ask: What are some things or people that cause the narrator to be concerned about her looks? *(her freckles, her mother's comments, her comparison of herself to her cousin)* **BL Ask:** How might the narrator's opinion of her looks have been different if her mother had behaved differently? *(Possible response: The narrator might have had more confidence if her mother had told her she was lovely.)* **AL**

EL Language Coach

Context Clues Say: The narrator uses a restatement clue to give her definition of "beautiful skin." How does she define beautiful skin? *(as skin that was all one color)* **EL BL** How can you tell this is an opinion, not a fact? *(Possible response: The adjective* beautiful *indicates this is the narrator's opinion. What is beautiful is a matter of opinion.)* **OL**

Readability Scores
Dale-Chall: 6.4
DRP: 54
Lexile: 1020

Flowers *and* Freckle Cream

by Elizabeth Ellis

When I was a kid about twelve years old, I was already as tall as I am now, and I had a lot of freckles. I had reached the age when I had begun to really look at myself in the mirror, and I was underwhelmed.[1] Apparently my mother was too, because sometimes she'd look at me and shake her head and say, "You can't make a silk purse out of a sow's ear."[2] **1 2**

I had a cousin whose name was Janette Elizabeth, and Janette Elizabeth looked exactly like her name sounds. She had a waist so small that men could put their hands around it . . . and they did. She had waist-length naturally curly blond hair too, but to me her unforgivable sin was that she had a flawless peaches-and-cream **complexion**. I couldn't help comparing myself with her and thinking that my life would be a lot different if I had beautiful skin too—skin that was all one color. **3**

---

1. **Underwhelmed** is a joke used to mean the opposite of *overwhelmed*, so it means "not at all impressed."

2. The phrase, *a silk purse out of a sow's ear*, means that you cannot make something beautiful from something ugly.

430 UNIT 4   What Makes You Who You Are?

Practice the Skills

1 Literary Element

Point of View Can you tell from this paragraph whether the narrator is a child or an adult who is remembering her childhood?

2 Reviewing Skills

Connecting A part of coming to terms with who you are is being able to accept who you are. Have you ever been embarrassed about something that you had no control over?

3 English Language Coach

Context Clues What context clue tells you what the word complexion means, and how the author defines a "flawless" *complexion*?

Additional Support

Differentiated Instruction

Conducting Research Freckles are skin cells that contain color. They are very small and light brown. When they overlap, they look larger and are more easily noticed. People with freckles tend to have light skin, eyes, and hair. Ultraviolet (UV) rays from the sun make freckles darker. These rays can damage any type of skin, so people with and without freckles should be exposed to only moderate amounts of sun and should use sun block to protect themselves from damage. Have students work with partners to research the topic of sun safety. **OL**

And then, in the back pages of Janette Elizabeth's *True Confessions* magazine, I found the answer: an advertisement for freckle-remover cream. I knew that I could afford it if I saved my money, and I did. The ad assured me that the product would arrive in a "plain brown wrapper."[3] Plain brown freckle color. For three weeks I went to the mailbox every day precisely at the time the mail was delivered. I knew that if someone else in my family got the mail, I would never hear the end of it. There was no way that they would let me open the box in private. Finally, after three weeks of scheduling my entire day around the mail truck's arrival, my package came. **4**

I went to my room with it, sat on the edge of my bed, and opened it. I was sure that I was looking at a miracle. But I had gotten so worked up about the magical package that I couldn't bring myself to put the cream on. What if it didn't work? What would I do then?

I fell asleep that night without even trying the stuff. And when I got up the next morning and looked at my freckles in the mirror, I said, "Elizabeth, this is silly. You have to do it now!" I smeared the cream all over my body. There wasn't

---

3. People ask for things to be delivered in a ***plain brown wrapper*** when they don't want anyone to know what the contents are.

Practice the Skills

R

EL

4 Key Reading Skill

Interpreting Think about the name of the magazine. Why do you think she chose that name? What do you think *True Confessions* means as it relates to the story?

A tobacco farm.

Flowers and Freckle Cream **431**

Teach

R Reading Skill

Interpreting Ask: What actions tell you that keeping her freckle-remover cream a secret is very important to the narrator? *(Possible response: She schedules her time every day for three weeks so she can get her package without her family knowing.)* **OL**

EL Language Coach

Context Clues Ask: What restatement context clue does the author provide for the word *miracle* in the first full paragraph? *(magical)* What does the word *miracle* tell readers about how strongly the girl feels about her freckles? *(Possible response: The girl thinks her freckles are so awful that anything that could remove them is a miracle.)* **OL**

Reading in the Real World

Citizenship Have students learn more about the Appalachian Mountains region of the United States. Have students form groups and use the library to research one of the following topics regarding Appalachia: living conditions, ethnic groups, folklore, crafts, music, and foods. Have students present their findings to the class in the form of an oral presentation, a poster, or a Web site. **OL AL**

Objectives
• Interpret text
• Use context clues to determine word meaning

Teach

EL Language Coach

Context Clues Ask: What contrast context clue explains what a "peaches-and-cream" complexion is? ("Instead of developing a peaches-and-cream complexion, you just get more and darker freckles" suggests that peaches-and-cream means skin without freckles.) **EL**

L Literary Element

Point of View Say:
Remember, when the story is told by a character who is referred to as "I," that story is told from the **first-person point of view**. Do you think it would have been more effective if this story were told from the **third-person point of view**? Why or why not? (Possible response: The first-person point of view is very effective because the narrator is within the story telling about her personal feelings and events. She also seems to be confiding in me, the reader.) **AL**

R Reading Skill

Review Responding Ask:
Why do you think Grandpa didn't laugh at the narrator? (Possible response: He is kind and doesn't want to hurt her feelings.) **BL**

---

as much of it as I had thought there would be, and I could see that I was going to need a part-time job to keep me in freckle remover.

Later that day I took my hoe and went with my brother and cousins to the head of the holler[4] to hoe tobacco, as we did nearly every day in the summer. Of course, when you stay out hoeing tobacco all day, you're not working in the shade. And there was something important I hadn't realized about freckle remover: if you wear it in the sun, it seems to have a reverse effect. Instead of developing a peaches-and-cream complexion, you just get more and darker freckles. **EL**

By the end of the day I looked as though I had leopard blood in my veins, although I didn't realize it yet. When I came back to the house, my family, knowing nothing about the freckle-remover cream, began to say things like, "I've never seen you with that many freckles before." When I saw myself in the mirror, I dissolved into tears and hid in the bathroom. **5**

My mother called me to the dinner table, but I ignored her. When she came to the bathroom door and demanded that I come out and eat, I burst out the door and ran by her, crying. I ran out to the well house[5] and threw myself down, and I was still sobbing when my grandfather came out to see what was wrong with me. I told him about how I'd sent for the freckle remover, and he didn't laugh—though he did suggest that one might get equally good results from burying a dead black cat when the moon was full.[6] **R**

It was clear that Grandpa didn't understand, so I tried to explain why I didn't want to have freckles and why I felt so **inadequate** when I compared my appearance with Janette Elizabeth's. He looked at me in stunned surprise, shook his

---

4. The **head of the holler** is a phrase in Appalachian dialect. It is the opening of a small valley.
5. A **well house** is a shed that covers the deep hole that people used to get their fresh drinking water from.
6. **Burying a dead black cat when the moon was full** refers to a superstitious practice. The grandfather suggests that using freckle cream has about as much chance of working as a superstitious practice.

Vocabulary

inadequate (in AD ih kwit) *adj.* not good enough

432 UNIT 4 What Makes You Who You Are?

5 Reviewing Skills

Connecting Have you ever been this disappointed? Can you remember how you felt?

Additional Support

Reading Fluency

Build Fluency To help students build fluency, have them form groups and take turns reading aloud, a paragraph at a time. Encourage group members to provide each other with positive, constructive feedback about their readings. Have students give suggestions about how other students might improve their tone, rate, and smoothness on their next try. Once students read the first paragraph without any difficulty, have them start the process with the next paragraph. **BL EL**

head, and said, "But child, there are all kinds of flowers, and they are all beautiful." I said, "I've never seen a flower with freckles!" and ran back to my room, slamming the door. |

When my mother came and knocked, I told her to go away. She started to say the kinds of things that parents say at times like that, but my grandfather said, "Nancy, leave the child alone." She was a grown-up, but he was her father. So she left me alone.

I don't know where Grandpa found it. It isn't at all common in the mountains where we lived then. But I know he put it in my room because my mother told me later. I had cried myself to sleep that night, and when I opened my swollen, sticky eyes the next morning, the first thing I saw, lying on the pillow next to my head, was a tiger lily. **6 7** ○

Practice the Skills

6 Key Reading Skill

Interpreting Consider the flower her grandfather put on her pillow. What do you think the tiger lily means to the story and to the author?

7 BIG Question

Do you think the grandfather's action at the end of the story makes Elizabeth feel differently about who she is on the outside *and* on the inside? Explain your answer on the "Flowers and Freckle Cream" page of Foldable 4. Your response will help you complete the Unit Challenge later.

Analyzing the Photo Why did the tiger lily (like the ones in this photo) in her room make the narrator feel better about her freckles?

Flowers and Freckle Cream **433**

Teach

R Reading Skill

Interpreting Ask: Why is it important that the narrator explains that she doesn't know where Grandpa found the flowers? *(Possible response: to suggest that Grandpa went to great effort to show her that beauty can mean many things)* **AL**

Viewing the Photo
Say: Why does Grandpa put a tiger lily in the narrator's room? *(Possible responses: to prove that some flowers do have "freckles"; to show that beauty comes in many forms)* **OL**

Assess

CheckPoint

Use the CheckPoint questions provided on Presentation Plus! to check for comprehension of the selection. These questions can be used with interactive response keypads for immediate student feedback

English Language Coach

Idioms In this story, Grandpa explains that all kinds of flowers are beautiful. Explain to students that the term "beauty is in the eyes of the beholder" means that everyone has a different idea of what is beautiful. To help students recognize the subjective nature of beauty, have them find something they think is beautiful, such as a rock, a painting, a song, a photograph. Ask them to bring it to class and explain why they find it beautiful. **EL**

Objectives
• Interpret text
• Use context clues to determine word meaning
• Use text features: photographs
• Understand idioms

433

Assess

Resources for page 434

- 📁 Selection Quick Check, p. 36
- 📁 Selection and Unit Assessment, p. 42
- 💿 ExamView Assessment Suite
- 💿 Interactive Tutor: Self-Assessment

Students can respond to the *After You Read* items in their Learner's Notebooks or on a separate sheet of paper.

Answering the

1. Possible response: They're very important to the author because she believes they make her who she is.

2. 12

3. a peaches-and-cream complexion, a small waist, and curly blond hair

Critical Thinking

4. Possible response: on a family tobacco farm in Appalachia

5. Possible response: He knows the narrator is beautiful.

6. Possible response: The author's mother doesn't understand her daughter. The author gets comfort from Grandpa, not her mother.

After You Read

Flowers and Freckle Cream

Answering the BIG Question

1. How important are the author's freckles to making her who she is?

2. **Recall** How old was the author when this story took place?
   Tip Right There

3. **Summarize** What qualities did Elizabeth's cousin have that made Elizabeth feel bad about herself?
   Tip Think and Search

Critical Thinking

4. **Infer** Where do you think the story takes place?
   Tip Author and Me

5. **Draw Conclusions** What does the narrator's grandfather know about her that she does not yet know?
   Tip On My Own

6. **Infer** When the author's mother says "You can't make a silk purse out of a sow's ear," what does this say about their relationship? Use other examples from the story to help you explain.
   Tip Author and Me

Talk About Your Reading

Beauty is Skin Deep The author measured her looks against her cousin Janette Elizabeth. How do you and the people you know measure the way you look? Sure, the way you look is a big part of what makes you who you are. But it's only *one part* of who you are. Think about your definition of *beauty*.

With a partner, or with the entire class, talk about the things that make you think someone or something is beautiful. Do your emotions affect judgments you make about beauty?

Objectives (pp. 434–435)
Reading Interpret text • Make connections from text to self
Literature Analyze point of view
Vocabulary Use context clues: examples
Grammar: Identify compound subjects and predicates

Talk About Your Reading

Encourage students to describe the things that influence their ideas of beauty. To add to the discussion, you might bring in illustrations showing vastly different beauty ideals from different times in the past (for example, men and women from the Elizabethan era, the nineteenth century, the 1920s, the 1940s, and the 1960s). Have students compare these ideals with the ideals of beauty today. Encourage students to note that ideals of beauty change.

Skills Review

Key Reading Skill: Interpreting

7. Do you think this story has a message? If not, why don't you think so? If so, what is the message?

Literary Element: Point of View

8. Imagine that the story was a series of diary entries, written as the story was taking place. Would the narrator's understanding of the situations be different?

9. Is the first-person point of view effective for this story? Why or why not?

Vocabulary Check

10. In your own words, write a definition for *inadequate* and use it in a sentence.

11. **Academic Vocabulary** Write a sentence using the word *interpret*.

English Language Coach Using the context clues in each sentence, match the underlined word in the sentences below with its synonym.

12. A carpenter needs such <u>implements</u> as a hammer and screwdriver, but an artist needs different ones, such as brushes.

13. Will your <u>vocation</u> be doctor, teacher, firefighter, auto mechanic, or something else?

14. Bill is so <u>affluent</u>. He has a swimming pool, tennis courts, and a gym in his house.

a. occupation

b. tools

c. wealthy

Web Activities For eFlashcards, Selection Quick Checks, and other Web activities, go to www.glencoe.com.

Grammar Link: Compound Subjects and Predicates

As you know, every complete sentence has a subject (*who* or *what*) and a predicate (what the subject *is* or *does*). You also know that complete subjects and predicates consist of more than one word. Now, learn about compound subjects and predicates.

• A **compound subject** has two or more simple subjects that have the same predicate. The subjects are most often joined by *and* or *or*.

The <u>girl</u> and her <u>grandfather</u> walked in the woods.

• A **compound predicate** has two or more simple predicates, or verbs, that have the same subject. The simple predicates are most often connected by *and* or *or*.

She <u>cried</u> and <u>slammed</u> the door.

• A sentence can have both a compound subject and a compound predicate.

The <u>boy</u> and his <u>father</u> often <u>cook</u> and <u>talk</u> in the kitchen.

Grammar Practice

Write whether each sentence has a *compound subject* or a *compound predicate* or both.

15. Daydreams and fantasies are a normal part of growing up.

16. Some people make decisions and plan their futures very early.

17. My dog and cat play and nap together.

Rewrite each sentence; add a word that completes the sentence and makes a compound subject or compound predicate. Write whether the sentence has a compound subject or a compound predicate.

18. The girls wash and ___ their hair.

19. Basil and ___ read a book for class.

20. To stay in shape we jog and ___ after school.

Skills Review

Key Reading Skill: Interpreting

7. Responses will vary.

Literary Element: Point of View

8. Responses will vary.

9. Possible response: First-person point of view lets the narrator describe her embarrassment, envy, and disappointment in great detail.

Vocabulary Check

10. The coach thought she was an inadequate player and would not let her play in the championship game.

11. We tried to interpret what the babies wanted by watching their eyes and listening to their cries.

English Language Coach

12. b

13. a

14. c

Close

Have students write a few sentences in their Learner's Notebooks about how the selection helped them answer the Big Question.

Grammar Link: Compound Subjects and Predicates

Grammar Practice

15. compound subject

16. compound predicate

17. compound subject and compound predicate

Possible responses and compound type:

18. <u>dry</u>; predicate

19. <u>Chuck</u>; subject

20. <u>swim</u>; predicate

Focus

BELLRINGER Options

✍ **Daily Language Practice Transparency 37**
Focus Activity Say: It's time to revisit your poem. Ask yourself whether readers will be able to picture the images in your poem. Can they connect to who you are? What changes do you need to make to give readers a clearer picture of you? *(Responses will vary.)* **AS**

Teach

W Writing

Figurative Language Say:
Make a figurative language chart. Choose objects, people, or animals in your poem that you can describe using a figure of speech. Think of things you can compare them to.

Object, person, animal	Things I could compare it to

Now write two similes or metaphors. Share them with a partner and decide if you'll include them in your poem. **OL**

Poetry
Revising, Editing, Presenting

ASSIGNMENT Write a poem
Purpose: To write a poem about what makes you who you are
Audience: You, your teacher, classmates, family, and friends

Revising Rubric

Your revised poem should have

• word choice that expresses your thoughts and emotions
• figurative language, such as similes and metaphors
• sensory details
• sound patterns

Objectives (pp. 436–439)
Writing Revise writing for poetic features, including sound devices, figurative language, word choice, and sensory imagery • Edit writing for: spelling, punctuation
Listening, Speaking, and Viewing Present poem • Use appropriate expressions and gestures • Listen for elements of poetry

In Writing Workshop Part 1, you wrote about personal traits and interests that make you who you are. You also learned that poems are usually written in lines and stanzas instead of in paragraphs. In Writing Workshop Part 2, you will learn more poetic elements such as figurative language, sensory details, and sound patterns.

Revising
Make It Better

Revising is your chance to reread your work and make any changes that you think would make your writing better.

Many poets use figurative language in their poems to help describe objects, feelings, and emotions. Figurative language consists of many different **figures of speech** such as *simile*, *metaphor*, and *personification*. These figures of speech make comparisons between things that seem unrelated. The chart below provides definitions and examples of figures of speech that you may want to use in your poem.

Figure of Speech	Definition	Example
Simile	Compares two unlike things using the words *like* or *as*.	• He rushed at me like a freight train. • Her hair was as dark as night.
Metaphor	Compares two unlike things without using the words *like* or *as*.	• His heart was a stone. • Her mind slammed shut.
Personification	Describes things as if they had human abilities, emotions, or characteristics.	• Wind kissed my hair. • The mountains stood guard over the town.

Figurative language creates images in your reader's imagination. Reread your poem and look for places where you can turn a description into a figure of speech.

Additional Support

English Language Coach

Sensory Language Tell students to help their readers really experience their poems by including sensory language, words that appeal to the five senses. Suggest that students practice using sensory language as a class by coming up with a description of the school cafeteria. Have student volunteers give five descriptions, one related to each sense. **OL**

Sound Patterns

Poetry often has a rhythm, or pattern of regular beats. Poetry also may include rhyme. Rhyme is the repetition of similar sounds at the end of words, such as those in Shel Silverstein's poem "Whatif." Notice how the repetition of the word *Whatif* creates a steady rhythm in this poem.

from **Whatif**

Whatif I'm dumb in school?
Whatif they've closed the swimming pool?
Whatif I get beat up?
Whatif there's poison in my cup?
Whatif I start to cry?
Whatif I get sick and die?

Silverstein's poem has a regular pattern of rhyme. The first two lines rhyme, then the next two, and so on. A regular pattern is called a "rhyme scheme." A rhyme scheme can help a poem flow and add interest to the sound of it.

Sensory Details

Descriptions that appeal to your five senses—hearing, sight, touch, smell, and taste—are called sensory details. Writers use sensory details to describe sounds, smells, feelings, sights, or tastes so that their readers can easily imagine them. Read the lines below and write in your Learner's Notebook which one of your senses the writer is appealing to.

1. Rotten eggs stunk up the refrigerator.
2. The sweet flavor of watermelon swirled in my mouth.
3. The wind roared, and tree branches crashed to the ground.

Now, try writing your own lines in your Learner's Notebook that appeal to each of your five senses. Look over your poem to see if you can add a sensory detail to help describe sights, sounds, smells, tastes, or feelings.

Editing

Finish It Up

After you have revised your poem, edit your writing for grammar, usage, mechanics, and spelling. Use the **Editing Checklist** to help you spot your mistakes.

- ☑ The poem is written in lines and stanzas.
- ☑ Words are spelled correctly.
- ☑ Punctuation tells the reader when to pause.

W1

> **Writing Tip**
>
> Poetic lines become more important when they are repeated. Experiment by repeating the same word or phrase in several lines of your poem.
> *My friends want to fight,*
> *But I keep walking.*
> *My family likes to argue,*
> *But I keep walking.*
> *My heart is racing,*
> *But I keep walking*
> How does repeating different lines change your poem?

> **Writing Tip**
>
> Alliteration is the repetition of a sound at the beginnings of words. Try writing a line of poetry with several words beginning with the same letter. Alliteration gives emphasis to words as their sounds are repeated. *The driver dreamt of Dublin* is an example of alliteration.

W2

WRITING WORKSHOP PART 2

Teach

W1 Writing

Rhythm Say: Read your poem aloud and have a partner tap along as you read. Does your poem have a smooth rhythm? Are there places that sound awkward? Have your partner help you make suggestions for revising. **OL**

W2 Writing

Editing Say: When you edit your poem, look for one kind of mistake at a time. This way, you'll be sure to focus your attention and not miss any errors. **OL**

Resources for page 437

📁 Use the Writing Workshop Graphic Organizer BLM in the Unit 4 Resource Booklet, pp. 27–28.

✒ Use the Grammar and Writing Workshop Transparencies 23–24.

Differentiated Instruction

Sound Devices Copy "Color Me Shy" on the board. Have students identify the two main sound devices and how the poet achieved them. *(Repetition and alliteration. Each line begins with two words and a dash; the two words are alliterative.)*

Color Me Shy
Quiet questions—I cannot raise my hand
Noiseless nods—I know the answers too
Soundless slipping—into a back-row desk
Silent suffering—no one talks to me
Have students use this formula to write a short poem about a topic of their choosing. **OL AL**

Objectives

- Revise writing for word choice and correct grammar
- Use literary techniques: repetition and alliteration
- Edit for use of Standard English grammar

437

Teach

L Literary Element

Figurative Language Write these words in a column on the board: *tomato, race car, squirrel.* **Say:** Sometimes it's hard to think of a simile or metaphor. With a partner, brainstorm words that come to mind for each word on the board. To help you focus on the senses, ask these questions:

- Sight: How does it look?
- Sound: How does it sound?
- Touch: How would it feel if I touched it?
- Smell: What smells do I connect with it?
- Taste: What tastes do I connect with it, even if it's not something to eat?

Then write a simile or metaphor for each word on the board, using the sensory words you wrote. **OL AL**

Presenting
Show It Off

- Read your poem one last time. The figurative language and sensory details should paint a picture in your head.
- On a fresh sheet of paper, draw the images that appear in your poem.
- Include the same details in your drawing that you included in your poem.
- When you finish drawing, write your poem on the back of your drawing.
- With a partner, take turns reading your poems to each other. Hold the paper so that your partner can look at your drawing as you read.
- Discuss how the words in your poem are different from or similar to what you drew.

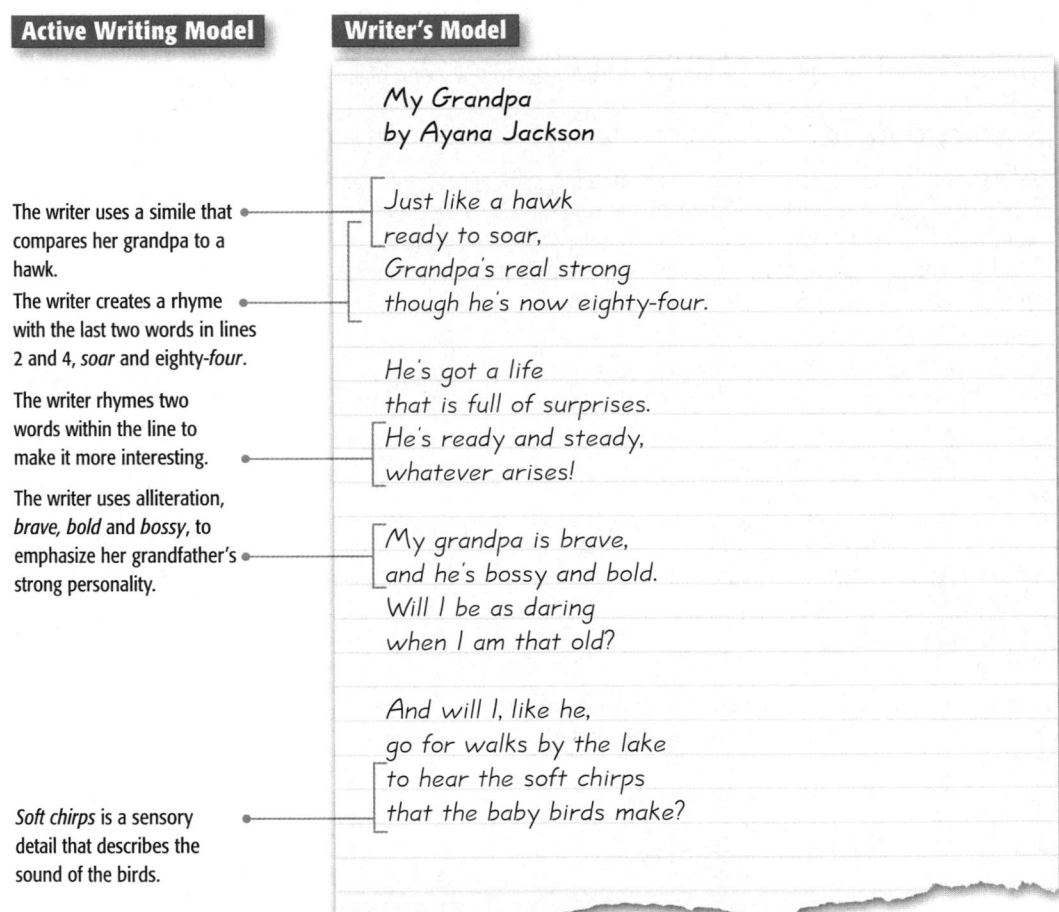

Active Writing Model

The writer uses a simile that compares her grandpa to a hawk.

The writer creates a rhyme with the last two words in lines 2 and 4, *soar* and eighty-*four.*

The writer rhymes two words within the line to make it more interesting.

The writer uses alliteration, *brave, bold* and *bossy,* to emphasize her grandfather's strong personality.

Soft chirps is a sensory detail that describes the sound of the birds.

Writer's Model

My Grandpa
by Ayana Jackson

Just like a hawk
ready to soar,
Grandpa's real strong
though he's now eighty-four.

He's got a life
that is full of surprises.
He's ready and steady,
whatever arises!

My grandpa is brave,
and he's bossy and bold.
Will I be as daring
when I am that old?

And will I, like he,
go for walks by the lake
to hear the soft chirps
that the baby birds make?

Additional Support

Literature Focus Lesson

Supporting Details Point out that in the last stanza of "Grandpa Joe," the poet used supporting details to describe the grandfather's personality. Work with a partner to write another stanza for "Grandpa Joe." Provide supporting details that show Grandpa Joe has a great sense of humor. Try to use a similar rhythm and similar rhymes. **AL**

Listening, Speaking, and Viewing

Reading Poetry Aloud

What Is It?

Think of your favorite songs. How many of them say something about the Big Question: What Makes You Who You Are? Many times, songwriters write about their own lives—their problems, their dreams, who they are, and what makes them who they are. Poets share these same ideas in their poetry, and just like musicians, poets like to share their work with an audience.

Why Is It Important?

Most poetry has musical qualities, such as rhythm, rhyme, and interesting word choice. Just like music, these qualities are best expressed when a poem is performed aloud.

How Do I Do It?

Follow these tips for reading poetry aloud.

1. Read with emotion and understanding

Audiences want to hear readers who understand the words and messages of the poems they are reading. Before you read, ask yourself:

- Are there words I don't know or can't pronounce? (If there are, ask someone for help or check a dictionary.)

- Do I understand what the poet is saying? (If you don't, discuss it with friends, classmates, or family. Discussing poetry helps everyone understand it better.)

2. Listen for good examples

- Listen to other people read poetry—your teacher or a recording of a poet. What makes their reading good? Do they pause to give you time to understand what they read? Do they change the volume or pitch of their voices as they read?

- Organize a poetry reading with students in your class. As your classmates read their poems, watch other people in the audience. How does the reader keep the audience's attention? Write down what you notice in your Learner's Workbook.

- Practice reading your own poetry. Ask your friends and family to listen to you read and give you feedback that will help you improve reading aloud. Write their tips in your Learner's Notebook. **LSV**

Writing Models For models and other writing activities, go to www.glencoe.com.

Teach

LSV Listening, Speaking, and Viewing

Reading Poetry Aloud Say: Use one of these tips to help you get better at reading poetry aloud:

- Practice in front of a mirror. Know your poem well enough to look up frequently. Notice how you stand and what facial expressions you use. Does your body language match your poem?

- Tape your reading. Listen to how you sound. Do you grab your audience's attention by speaking loudly, clearly, and with emotion? What changes should you make? **AS**

Literature Online

Writing Models Have students access the Web site for an additional and interactive Writing Workshop-based student model.

Assess

Have students share their revised poems with a partner. Ask partners to read the poem aloud and then comment on the writer's revisions.

Objectives
- Use literary techniques: figurative language
- Revise writing for word choice
- Use context clues: determine word meaning
- Listen for elements of poetry
- Read aloud

439

Reading in the Real World

Careers Many songwriters express personal feelings and opinions in lyrics. Have students form four groups and think of a classroom-appropriate song that they could study. Have students find a copy of the lyrics and identify poetic devices, such as repetition, alliteration, figurative language, or rhythm and meter in the song. If time permits, play each song for the class. Ask groups to present their comments. **AS**

Objective covered in this workshop:
• Use a variety of reading strategies to monitor comprehension

Teaching Students to Monitor Comprehension

Why Is It Important

• When students don't understand a selection, they're not reading it successfully.

• By monitoring their comprehension of a selection, students will learn to think about whether they understand what they're reading.

• Asking questions while reading helps build overall reading skills.

How to Help Students Get It

• Tell students to keep asking themselves questions about main ideas, characters, and events as they read.

• Remind students that to *monitor* something is to pay attention to it and that *comprehension* is understanding.

• When students can't answer a question about what they've read, have them review, read more slowly, or ask someone to help them.

• Briefly review reading skills such as activating prior knowledge, questioning, and predicting. Students may find those helpful ways to "check in" with their comprehension.

Reading to Answer the Big Question

The March of the Dead by Robert Service
The speaker of this poem describes a victory parade at the end of a war. In the midst of the celebration, he dreams of an army of the gaunt and bloody corpses of thousands of soldiers who died in battle. Readers are reminded to remember those who gave their lives for the lives and freedom that they enjoy.

Gene Scene by Jordan Brown
An *InTIME* article presents interesting and entertaining information about genetics through a mini-questionnaire, poetry, and graphics. Students will learn that both nature and nurture make them who they are.

Workshop Resources

Pacing (Days) Standard	Block	Lesson	Student Materials	Teacher Resources
1	½	Key Skill Lesson: Monitoring	🐾 Key Reading Skills Practice, p. 29 🐾 English Language Coach Review, p. 41	✋ Bellringer Options Transparencies – Daily Language Practice 38 ✋ Read Aloud, Think Aloud Transparencies – Key Reading Skills 15 ⚫ Presentation Plus!
1	1	"The March of the Dead"	💻 Glencoe Online 🐾 Unit Vocabulary Review, p. 39 🐾 Academic Vocabulary Review, p. 42 📁 English Language Coach 🐾 Active Reading Graphic Organizer, p. 31 🐾 Literary Analysis, p. 30 ⚫ StudentWorks Plus™ 💻 Online Student Edition ⚫ Literature Classics 📁 Selection and Unit Assessments, p. 43	✋ Literary and Text Analysis Transparencies 35 and 46 💻 Puzzlemaker ⚫ Skill Level Up!™ A Language Arts Game 💻 BookLink 3 📒 Assessment by Learning Objective (Diagnostic and Formative) ⚫ Interactive Tutor: Self-Assessment ⚫ TeacherWorks Plus™
1		"The Gene Scene"	💻 Glencoe Online 🐾 Unit Vocabulary Review p. 39 🐾 Academic Vocabulary Review, p. 42 📁 English Language Coach 🐾 Active Reading Graphic Organizer, p. 33 🐾 Literary Analysis, p. 30 ⚫ StudentWorks Plus™ 💻 Online Student Edition ⚫ Literature Classics 📁 Selection and Unit Assessments, p. 44	✋ Literary and Text Analysis Transparencies 35 and 46 💻 Puzzlemaker ⚫ Skill Level Up!™ A Language Arts Game 💻 BookLink 3 📒 Assessment by Learning Objective (Diagnostic and Formative) ⚫ Interactive Tutor: Self-Assessment ⚫ TeacherWorks Plus™

Keys for Unit Resource

📁 Blackline Master
📒 Workbook
📖 Supplemental Text
⚫ CD-ROM
📀 DVD
✋ Transparency
💻 Web-based
🐾 Fast File

Level Appropriate Code

AS = Activities for all students
AL = Activities for students working above grade level
OL = Activities for students working at grade level
BL = Activities for students working below grade level
EL = Activities for English language learners

Focus

✎ **Daily Language Practice Transparency 38**
Focus Activity Say: If you watch or read the news, you know that both good and bad things happen in the world. Why might it be useful for us to remember the bad things as well as the good? *(Possible response: It's useful to remember the bad things that have happened to help make sure they won't happen again.)* **AS**

Teach

R **Reading Skill**

Monitoring Comprehension

Ask: What does it mean to monitor something? *(Possible response: to keep track of something or check it.)*

READING WORKSHOP 4

Skills Focus

You will practice these skills when you read the following selections:
• "The March of the Dead," p. 444
• "The Gene Scene," p. 452

Reading

• Monitoring comprehension

Literature

• Understanding figurative language: simile, metaphor, and personification

Vocabulary

• Reviewing context clues

Writing/Grammar

• Identifying direct and indirect objects

Objectives (pp. 440–441)
Reading Monitor comprehension

Skill Lesson

Monitoring Comprehension

Learn It!

What Is It? Have you ever read a homework assignment and then found out the next day that you couldn't answer any of the teacher's questions about it? Having done your homework doesn't help much then, does it? If this has ever happened to you, maybe you should be monitoring your comprehension.

• To *monitor* is to keep track of it or check it.

• *Comprehension* is another word for "understanding."

NON-SEQUITUR © 2001 Wiley Miller. Dist by UNIVERSAL PRESS SYNDICATE. Reprinted with permission. All rights reserved.

Analyzing Cartoons
Why do you think the cartoonist calls this "the real-life reading and comprehension test"? How should the man in the cartoon monitor his comprehension?

Additional Support

Differentiated Instruction

Using Reference Sources Discuss with students what types of information they could find in the following reference sources:

• dictionaries *(word meanings, word histories, synonyms, antonyms, pronunciation)*

• glossaries *(definitions of new or unusual words used in a book)*

• thesauruses *(synonyms and antonyms)*

• encyclopedias *(information on events, people, places, and things)* **BL**

Why Is It Important? It's possible to read too quickly or not pay enough attention while reading. If that happens, it's like not having read at all. No matter what your purpose is for reading, your most important task is to understand what you have read.

How Do I Do It? Pause while you are reading and think about what you just read. Ask yourself if it makes sense to you. If it doesn't, use these tips:

- **Reread** the passage more slowly and carefully.
- **Ask yourself questions** about ideas, characters, and events.
- **Look for context clues** for words you don't understand.
- **Read on a little further,** which will sometimes clear up a confusing issue.
- **Use reference sources** such as dictionaries and encyclopedias to find information on words or topics you don't understand. **EL**

Here's how one student monitored her comprehension to understand a tough passage in "Geraldine Moore the Poet." **R**

Study Central Visit www.glencoe .com and click on Study Central to review monitoring comprehension.

> *Nothing lovely's been happening in my life. / I haven't seen a flower since Mother's Day, / And the sun don't even shine on my side of the street. / No robins come sing on my window sill.*

> *What? I think I'll read that again. Why did Geraldine say she hasn't seen a flower since Mother's Day? I remember reading something about her mother earlier. If I go back and reread that part, it might make more sense.*

Practice It!

Practice monitoring your comprehension by reading these lines from "The March of the Dead." Write down one question you have about this section. *And then there came a shadow, swift and sudden, dark and drear; / The bells were silent, not an echo stirred. / The flags were drooping sullenly, the men forgot to cheer; / We waited, and we never spoke a word*

Use It!

Use the tips below to monitor your comprehension as you read "The March of the Dead" and "The Gene Scene."

- Read hard parts slowly, write down any words you don't understand, and use footnotes or a dictionary.
- Write down a question you have about what you've read.

Teach

Study Central Have students access the Web site to review monitoring comprehension and to complete a related activity.

EL Language Coach

Context Clues Ask: What context clue helps you figure out what *reference sources* are? *(the words* dictionaries, glossaries, thesauruses, *and* encyclopedias) **Ask:** Why are examples good context clues? *(Possible response: They give real-life clues that most people can recognize.)* **EL**

R Reading Skill

Review Interpreting Ask: What does the phrase "a tough passage" mean? *(a part or section of text that is difficult to understand or interpret)* **BL**

Resources for page 441

 Use Key Reading Skills Transparency 15 in *Read Aloud, Think Aloud* to help students practice monitoring comprehension.

Reading Fluency

Monitoring Comprehension Have students write these sample questions in their Learner's Notebooks. Students can refer to the questions as they read the poem and article in this workshop.

- Who are the characters or people in the selection?

- What happens in the selection?
- Where does it happen?
- When do the events take place?
- Why do they happen?
- How does this selection affect me?
EL BL OL

Objectives
- Interpret text
- Use context clues to determine word meaning
- Monitor comprehension

Teach

More About the Author

Novelist and poet Robert Service also served as a war correspondent during the Balkan War and, later, in France during World War I. One of his best known books of poetry, *Rhymes of a Red Cross Man,* shows Service's feelings of patriotism and his admiration for soldiers.

V Vocabulary

Word Categories Say:

Sometimes putting words into categories helps you remember their definitions. Which of the vocabulary words do you associate with unhappiness? *(sullenly, ghastly, woe, writing)* Which do you associate with happiness? *(mirth)* **OL**

Before You Read : The March of the Dead

Robert Service

Meet the Author

Robert Service was born in 1874 in England. As a young man he worked as a logger, dishwasher, teacher, bank clerk, ranch hand, and fruit picker before turning to writing. He explained that, in his writing, he was after "something the man in the street would take notice of and the sweet old lady would paste in her album." See page R6 of the Author Files for more on Robert Service.

Author Search For more about Robert Service, go to www .glencoe.com.

Objectives (pp. 442–447)
Reading Monitor comprehension
• Make connections from text to self
Literature Identify and interpret figurative language • Identify literary elements: simile, metaphor, personification
Vocabulary Use context clues: definition, restatement, comparison, contrast, and examples

Vocabulary Preview

sullenly (SUL un lee) *adv.* gloomily and silently **(p. 445)** *The sky grew dark and the flags drooped sullenly.*

ghastly (GAST lee) *adj.* terrible, horrible **(p. 445)** *The Army of the Dead appeared frightening and ghastly as they crept out of the darkness.*

woe (woh) *n.* great sadness or suffering **(p. 445)** *The fallen soldiers had misery and woe in their eyes.*

writhing (RY thing) *adj.* twitching, twisting **(p. 446)** *Their writhing lips showed their pain as the wounded trudged through the streets.*

mirth (murth) *n.* joy, happiness **(p. 447)** *The parade of living soldiers was cause for mirth, but many were saddened by those who had fallen.*

Partner Talk Write each vocabulary word on a separate note card. Write the definition on the back. Take turns testing each other by flashing the cards.

English Language Coach

You have learned about several kinds of **context clues**.

Definition: When he got a scholarship, Bryant was <u>elated</u>—filled with joy.
• The writer gives a definition. *Elated* means "filled with joy."

Restatement: He was <u>elated</u> and this intense happiness lasted for hours.
• The writer has restated the idea. Someone who is *elated* is intensely happy.

Comparison: She was as <u>elated</u> as a fan whose team has just won the World Series.
• The writer has compared the feeling of being elated to a feeling everyone knows is a very happy one.

Contrast: Unlike his miserable friend, Norm was <u>elated</u>.
• The opposite of *elated* is "miserable," so elated must mean "very happy."

Example: There are many types of <u>precipitation</u>, including rain, sleet, hail, and snow.
• Rain, sleet, hail, and snow are examples of water that fall to earth, so that's what *precipitation* must mean.

Write to Learn Use *ravenous*, which means "extremely hungry," in a sentence using context clues. Use a type of clue mentioned above.

Additional Support

Author Search To expand students' appreciation of Robert Service, have them access the Web site for more information and resources.

English Language Coach

Context Clues Write the following sentences on the board. For each sentence, have students tell the definition of the underlined word and which type of context clue the sentence gives:

1. I was always <u>reckless</u>; he was the careful one. *(careless; contrast)*

2. Her coat was <u>scarlet</u>; her shoes were a brighter red. *(red; comparison)*

3. Kris adopted a <u>labradoodle</u>, a dog that's part Labrador retriever and part French poodle. *(a dog that's. . . French poodle; definition)* **EL** **OL**

Skills Preview

Key Reading Skill: Monitoring Comprehension

Use these tips to monitor your comprehension.

- Pause in your reading.
- Ask yourself what just happened.
- Try to summarize what has happened.
- Read on to see if later information helps.

Key Literary Element: Figurative Language

Someone who says, "That apple is red," just means that the apple is red. This is **literal language.** Literal language means exactly what it says. It is language without exaggeration. Language that suggests something beyond the exact meaning of the words is called **figurative language.** Someone who says, "She was so mad, she was burning up" is speaking figuratively, or using figurative language. No one was really "burning up." But it helps to create an image or feeling of just how angry the person was. Two kinds of figurative language often used to make comparisons are **similes** and **metaphors.**

- A *simile* uses the words *like* or *as* to compare two unlike things.

  Her diamond sparkled like a star.
- A *metaphor* compares two unlike things without using *like* or *as*.

  Her eyes were emeralds.

Personification is figurative language in which an animal, idea, or object is given human qualities. It is described as if it were human. In "The moon danced across the midnight sky," the moon is personified, or given a human quality—the ability to dance.

Write to Learn In your Learner's Notebook, write three sentences using figurative language.

Interactive Literary Elements Handbook
To review or learn more about the literary elements, go to www.glencoe.com.

Get Ready to Read

Connect to the Reading

"The more things change, the more they stay the same." Have you ever heard this expression? This saying applies to many things—including war. No matter how wars change, soldiers returning home from war always stir up people's feelings.

Write to Learn In your Learner's Notebook, write your feelings about war. Think about what you already know about war. Is there ever a good reason for war? Explain.

Build Background

"The March of the Dead" is a poem about a parade of British soldiers returning home from the Boer War.

- From 1899 to 1902, the British fought the Dutch for control of South Africa. The Dutch were known as the Boers, and the conflict was called the Boer War.
- The British suffered many defeats in the Boer War, and soldiers were killed on both sides.
- Robert Service, the author of the poem, saw war firsthand. He served as an ambulance driver during World War I.

Set Purposes for Reading

BIG Question Read the selection "The March of the Dead" to learn about how the wars in our time make us who we are.

Set Your Own Purpose What else would you like to learn from the reading to help you answer the Big Question? Write your purpose on "The March of the Dead" page of Foldable 4.

Keep Moving

Use these skills as you read the following selection.

The March of the Dead **443**

Teach

L Literary Element

Figurative Language Say: Identify each sentence as a simile, a metaphor, or personification:

- The sky wept all through the funeral. *(personification)*
- I'm like a coiled spring, ready to go to work. *(simile)*
- She's a freshly baked cookie, sparkly outside, soft and warm inside. *(metaphor)* **OL** **AL**

Interactive Literary Elements Handbook Have students access the Web site to improve their understanding of figurative language.

Reading in the Real World

Careers Students who are interested in world events may benefit from researching a career in journalism. Have students work in groups to research this career, including education requirements, job description, travel requirements, compensation, and types of employers, such as radio, TV, newspapers, and magazine publications. Tape a television correspondent's report. Have students study the tape and prepare a similar TV report for a fictitious event. **OL** **AL**

Objectives
- Use context clues to clarify word meaning
- Identify literary devices: figurative language
- Learn and use new vocabulary

Teach

Viewing the Photo
Ask: How does this photograph fit the mood, or atmosphere, of a poem about war? *(Possible response: Both are dark and serious.)* **OL**

R Reading Skill

Review Visualizing **Say:** You know from the Build Background section that this poem is about a parade of British soldiers. What images come to mind as you read the title "The March of the Dead"? *(Sample response: I see dead soldiers, all pale and ghostly in their uniforms, marching down an empty street. They are see-through, not really like people at all.)* **OL**

The March of the Dead

by Robert Service

444 UNIT 4 What Makes You Who You Are?

Additional Support

Literature Focus Lesson

Theme Remind students that the theme of a work of fiction is the message about life the writer conveys through the words, actions, and characters in the work. Explain that sometimes writers use works of fiction to comment on or make persuasive statements about important social issues, such as war, poverty, or crime. Have students tell why writing a poem, story, or song about a social issue might be an effective way to spread an important social message. For example, poems, songs, and stories often include descriptions that can be very persuasive ways to spread a message. **AL**

The cruel war was over—oh, the triumph was so sweet! **1**
We watched the troops returning, through our tears;
There was triumph, triumph, triumph down the scarlet
glittering street.
And you scarce could hear the music for the cheers.
5 And you scarce could see the house-tops for the flags that
flew between;
The bells were pealing* madly to the sky;
And everyone was shouting for the Soldiers of the Queen,
And the glory of an age was passing by. **2**

And then there came a shadow, swift and sudden, dark
and drear;
10   The bells were silent, not an echo stirred.
The flags were drooping **sullenly**, the men forgot to cheer;
We waited, and we never spoke a word.
The sky grew darker, darker, till from out the gloomy rack
There came a voice that checked the heart with dread:
15 "Tear down, tear down your bunting now, and hang up
sable black;*
They are coming—it's the Army of the Dead."

They were coming, they were coming, gaunt* and **ghastly**,
sad and slow;
They were coming, all the crimson* wrecks of pride;
With faces seared,* and cheeks red smeared, and haunting
eyes of **woe**,

---

6 Here *pealing* means ringing loudly.

15 *Rack* is a mass of high clouds broken by the wind. *Checked*, as it is used here, means
"stopped." *Bunting* is another word for flags and colorful banners. *Sable black* means
dark cloths hung in mourning.

17 *Gaunt* means extremely thin.

18 *Crimson* is a dark red color.

19 If something is *seared*, it is burnt.

Vocabulary

sullenly (SUL un lee) *adv.* gloomily and silently

ghastly (GAST lee) *adj.* terrible, horrible

woe (woh) *n.* great sadness or suffering

Practice the Skills

1 **Key Literary Element**

Figurative Language Find
the example of personification
in the first line. What is being
personified? Think about the fact
that cruelty is a human quality.

2 **Key Reading Skill**

Monitoring Comprehension
Each section of a poem is
known as a stanza; this poem
has six stanzas. Monitor your
comprehension after each
stanza. If you are unsure about
any part, go back and reread
the stanza. Look at the footnotes. Write any questions
you have in your Learner's
Notebook.

The March of the Dead **445**

Teach

R1 **Reading Skill**

Monitoring Comprehension Ask: What
is happening in the first stanza?
*(The war is over, and soldiers
are marching in a victory
parade.)* **BL** How would you
describe the scene in your own
words? *(There are many people
cheering, music is playing, flags
are flying, bells are ringing, and
soldiers are marching through
the streets.)* **OL**

L **Literary Element**

**Review Sound Devices:
Alliteration Ask:** What sound
devices do you see in the second stanza? *(alliteration, rhyme,
rhythm)* What alliteration is
there in line 9? *(then, there;
swift, sudden; dark, drear)* What
are the rhyming words in lines
13–16? *(rack, black; dread,
dead)* **OL**

R2 **Reading Skill**

Review Visualizing Say:
Describe how you see the
Army of the Dead in your own
words. *(They are skinny, pale,
walking slowly with their heads
down. They are bloody and
burned.)* **BL** **OL**

English Language Coach

Sensory Language Explain to students that language that appeals to the
senses helps readers "experience" an
event. Write the names of the five senses
on the board: sight, hearing, touch,
taste, smell. Have students find words
in the poem that appeal to the senses.
Volunteers should share their responses
with the class. Then have students tell
which sensory description they thought
was the most striking and why. **EL** **BL**

Objectives
• Monitor comprehension
• Visualize
• Identify literary devices: allitera-
  tion, rhyme
• Use text features: photographs
• Visualize
• Identify literary elements: theme

445

Teach

R₁ Reading Skill

Monitoring

Comprehension Ask: What do the dead soldiers want from the crowd? *(They want to be cheered; they want their glory and their pain to be remembered.)* **OL AL**

L Literary Element

Figurative Language Ask: What does the phrase "each tongue seemed weighted with lead" mean? *(Possible response: It means people were unable to talk.)* **AL**

R₂ Reading Skill

Monitoring

Comprehension Ask: How do you know that in line 41, the speaker will return to describing the "real" parade with the live soldiers? *(In line 40 he says the other scene "was a dream.)"* **OL**

Practice the Skills

20 And clotted holes the khaki couldn't hide.
Oh, the clammy brow of anguish! the livid, foam-
flecked lips!*
    The reeling ranks of ruin swept along!
The limb that trailed, the hand that failed, the bloody
finger tips!*
    And oh, the dreary rhythm of their song!

25 "They left us on the veldt-side, but we felt we couldn't stop
    On this, our England's crowning festal day;
We're the men of Magersfontein, we're the men of
Spion Kop,
    Colenso—we're the men who had to pay.*
We're the men who paid the **blood-price**. Shall the grave be
all our gain?
30   You owe us. Long and heavy is the score. **3**
Then cheer us for our glory now, and cheer us for our pain,
    And cheer us as ye never cheered before."

The folks were white and stricken, and each tongue seemed
weighted with lead;
    Each heart was clutched in hollow hand of ice; **4**
35 And every eye was staring at the horror of the dead,
    The pity of the men who paid the price.
They were come, were come to mock us, in the first flush of
our peace;
    Through **writhing** lips their teeth were all agleam;
They were coming in their thousands—oh, would they
never cease!
40   I closed my eyes, and then—it was a dream. **R₂**

3 **English Language Coach**

Context Clues Reread this entire stanza. What does the author mean by the expression **blood-price** in line 29? What context clue helped you under-stand the meaning of *blood-price*?

4 **Key Literary Element**

Figurative Language What makes line 34 an example of figurative language? What does this description mean?

---

21 **Anguish** means great pain, and **livid** means pale.

23 **Reeling** means "staggering" or "thrown off balance." A **limb** refers to an arm or leg.

28 **Veldt** is a Dutch word for an open grazing area or field. **Festal** means festive or happy. **Magersfontein, Spion Kop,** and **Colenso** are the names of extremely bloody battles in the Boer War.

Vocabulary

writhing (RY thing) *adj.* twitching, twisting

446 UNIT 4 What Makes You Who You Are?

Additional Support

Reading in the Real World

Citizenship Both men and women serve in the U.S. armed forces today. Have students find resources on the Internet or at the library about all the branches of the armed forces to put in a class resource list. Then have students work with partners to research the following elements of one branch of the armed services: recruitment and enlistment, jobs, training and education, uniforms, and length of service. Have students prepare a presentation to share their findings with the class. **OL**

Analyzing the Photo What is this a photo of? What line from the poem does it illustrate?

There was triumph, triumph, triumph down the scarlet gleaming street;

    The town was mad; a man was like a boy. **R1**

A thousand flags were flaming where the sky and city meet;

    A thousand bells were thundering the joy.

45 There was music, **mirth** and sunshine; but some eyes shone with regret;

    And while we stun with cheers our homing braves,*

O God, in Thy great mercy, let us nevermore forget

    The graves they left behind, the bitter graves. **5** ○ **R2**

---

46 *Homing braves* refers to the brave soldiers who are returning home.

Vocabulary

mirth (murth) *n.* joy, happiness

Practice the Skills

5

In what ways does this poem show how major events like war make us who we are? Write your answer on "The March of the Dead" page of Foldable 4. Your response will help you complete the Unit Challenge later.

The March of the Dead **447**

Teach

R1 **Reading Skill**

Monitoring Comprehension Ask: What does line 42 mean? In what ways was the town "mad"? *(Possible responses: The town is filled with the noisy, confused excitement of the crowd. The people are so wildly enthusiastic that they seem insane.)* **Ask: In what ways would a man of this town be "like a boy"?** *(Possible response: The men are like young boys caught up in the thrill and excitement of a circus or a sports event.)* **OL**

R2 **Reading Skill**

Monitoring Comprehension Ask: What theme, or message, might the poet be trying to deliver in the last lines of the poem? *(Possible response: People should never forget the soldiers who gave their lives for their country.)* **OL**

Assess

CheckPoint

Use the CheckPoint questions provided on Presentation Plus! to check for comprehension of the selection. These questions can be used with interactive response keypads for immediate student feedback.

Reading Fluency

Build Fluency Because this poem uses nonstandard word order, as well as names and words many students will be unfamiliar with, you may want to read it aloud as students read along silently. Use expression and repeat any lines students might find confusing. Then have students read the poem aloud with partners, taking turns reading each line and echoing. Students should continue until they can read the poem with fluency and understanding. **EL BL**

Objectives
• Monitor comprehension
• Identify literary device: figurative language

447

Assess

After You Read — The March of the Dead

Resources for page 448

📁 Selection Quick Check, p. 37

📁 Selection and Unit Assessment, p. 43

💿 ExamView Assessment Suite

💿 Interactive Tutor: Self-Assessment

Students can respond to the *After You Read* items in their Learner's Notebooks or on a separate sheet of paper.

Answering the BIG Question

1. Possible response: My feelings can affect what I do with my life; for example, I could enlist for military service or work for the Peace Corps.

2. People were cheering and flying flags.

3. The scene becomes quiet and dark.

Critical Thinking

4. **a.)** Possible response: Repeating the word *triumph* emphasizes the importance people place on winning victories.

   b.) The street was gleaming with blood and tears.

5. Responses will vary.

6. Possible response: because they served their country and deserve honor and gratitude

Objectives (pp. 448–449)
Reading Monitor comprehension
Literature Identify and interpret figurative language
Vocabulary Use context clues: definition, restatement, comparison, contrast, and examples
Writing Respond to literature: poetry review
Grammar Identify direct objects

Answering the BIG Question

1. Are your feelings about war part of what makes you who you are? Explain.

2. **Recall** In the first stanza of the poem, why could people scarcely hear the music or see the house-tops?
   Tip Right There

3. **Summarize** In the second stanza, how does the scene change when the Army of the Dead begins to arrive?
   Tip Think and Search

Critical Thinking

4. **Interpret a)** Why do you think the poet uses repetition in the line "There was triumph, triumph, triumph down the scarlet glittering street"? **b)** Why does he change the phrase to "gleaming street" at the end of the poem?
   Tip On My Own

5. **Infer** What does the speaker mean when he calls the soldiers "crimson wrecks of pride"?
   Tip Author and Me

6. **Analyze** Why do you think the dead feel they must march along with the living?
   Tip Author and Me

Write About Your Reading

Review Write a short review of the poem. (A review contains personal reactions as well as facts.) Your review could answer some of the following questions:
- Did it make sense?
- What did it mean to you?
- Did an image from the poem really stay in your head?
- How would you summarize the poem?
- What is the poet's message?
- Did you think it was a good poem or not? Why?

Write About Your Reading

Reviews will vary. Sample response:
The poem is somewhat complex. At first, the speaker is watching a parade of British soldiers who had been killed in battle—"the Army of the Dead." The mood is very dark and grim as the soldiers march by. But the speaker realizes that it's just a dream. The triumphant soldiers then march by and the mood becomes joyful and full of "music, mirth, and sunshine." However, during this jubilant celebration, the poet urges us to never forget the soldiers who gave their lives for their country.

Skills Review

Key Reading Skill: Monitoring Comprehension

7. Did you understand the poem? Without looking at the poem again, describe one image you remember from the poem.

Key Literary Element: Figurative Language

8. The speaker says "and each tongue seemed weighted with lead." What does this figurative description mean?

Vocabulary Check

Write a paragraph using each vocabulary word correctly.

9. sullenly
10. ghastly
11. woe
12. writhing
13. mirth

English Language Coach Use context clues to figure out the meaning of each underlined word. Write a synonym or short definition for each.

14. Her eyesight is as <u>keen</u> as a hawk's.
15. I move quickly in the morning, but my brother is <u>sluggish</u> when he wakes up.
16. I like their <u>abode</u>. That is, I like the place where they live.

Web Activities For eFlashcards, Selection Quick Checks, and other Web activities, go to www.glencoe.com.

Grammar Link: Direct Objects

You have learned that every sentence has a subject and a predicate. In some sentences, the predicate consists of only an action verb.

*The punter **kicks**.*

Usually sentences give more information. The predicate often says who or what received the action of the verb.

*The punter **kicks** the **football**.*

In the sentence above, *football* receives the action of the verb *kicks*. It answers the question *kicked what?* In this sentence, the word *football* is called a "direct object."

- A **direct object** receives the action of a verb. It answers the question *whom?* or *what?* after an action verb.
- A verb can have more than one direct object.
  *The team carried **gloves** and **bats** into the stadium.*
- Sometimes an action verb does not have a direct object.
  The team played well.

In the sentence above, *well* does not answer the question *whom?* or *what?* after the verb *played*. It is not a direct object.

Grammar Practice

Rewrite each sentence. Draw two lines under the action verb in each sentence. If the action verb has a direct object, circle the direct object.

17. The Statue of Liberty attracts many visitors.
18. Some people ride bikes.
19. They noticed fossils in the cave walls.
20. They play football and baseball after school.

Writing Application Look back at the letter you wrote. Find three sentences with action verbs. Underline the action verbs. If they have direct objects, circle them.

The March of the Dead **449**

Skills Review

Key Reading Skill: Monitoring Comprehension

7. **a.)** Responses will vary.

Key Literary Element: Figurative Language

8. No one could talk.

Vocabulary Check

9.–13. Sample response: The <u>ghastly</u> painting showed people's great <u>woe</u>. I <u>sullenly</u> walked through the museum and saw people <u>writhing</u> in pain. Leaving the horror museum was cause for <u>mirth</u>!

English Language Coach

14. sharp; having a strong sense
15. slothful; slow-moving
16. house; a place to live

Close

Ask students to summarize what they learned from the selection to help them answer the Big Question.

Grammar Link: Direct Objects

Grammar Practice

17. The Statue of Liberty <u>attracts</u> (millions) of visitors each year.
18. Some people <u>ride</u> (bikes) instead of walking.
19. They <u>noticed</u> (fossils) in the cave walls.
20. They <u>play</u> (football) and (baseball) after school.

Teach

More About *Time for Kids* Reporters

In addition to experienced adult reporters like Jordan Brown, *Time for Kids* uses teen reporters. The magazine runs a competition for teens to become part of its Kid Reporter Team. Sixteen lucky teens are chosen from around the country. These junior reporters, who must be good at writing and enjoy interviewing, get to write local news stories and interview politicians and celebrities.

V Vocabulary

Say: According to this definition of *generation*, you all belong to the same generation because you're all nearly the same age. But here's another way of looking at generations: Your grandparents are one, your parents are another, and you are still another. Each level of the family is a separate generation. How many generations of your family are alive now? How many generations of your family have you been in a room with at one time? *(Responses will vary.)* **AS**

Before You Read · The Gene Scene

Meet the Writer
Jordan Brown wrote this article "The Gene Scene" for *TIME* magazine.

Vocabulary Preview

generation (jen uh RAY shun) *n.* a group of persons born around the same time **(p. 452)** *Some features, like eye color, are passed on by parents to the next generation—their children.*

heredity (huh RED uh tee) *n.* the passing on of characteristics from an animal or plant to its offspring **(p. 454)** *Many of his facial features are due to heredity—he looks just like his father.*

chromosomes (KROH muh sohmz) *n.* parts of a cell in a plant or animal that carry the genes controlling features such as the color of hair and eyes **(p. 454)** *Your chromosomes are so small they are invisible to the human eye.*

Write to Learn Write a paragraph using all three vocabulary words correctly.

English Language Coach

Context Clues Getting comfortable with context clues will make reading so much easier! You will be able to read more quickly and understand more of what you read. Remember a context clue might be in a sentence before or after the difficult word. So pay close attention.

Write to Learn Copy the chart below. For each word in dark type, write the word, its meaning, and the context clues that helped you figure out the word's meaning.

1. *Janet put the wet clay pot in the **kiln**, or oven, to harden.*
2. *The new program has been **beneficial** for the school; for example, test scores are up and absences are down.*
3. *Maria thought the dress was **gaudy**. The colors were loud and they clashed.*
4. *Robins are **migratory** birds, unlike sparrows, which live in the same place year-round.*

Objectives (pp. 450–455)
Reading Monitor comprehension
• Make connections from text to self
Literature Identify literary elements: simile, metaphor
Vocabulary Use context clues

Word	Meaning	Context Clues

450 UNIT 4   What Makes You Who You Are?

Additional Support

Literature Focus Lesson

Informative Nonfiction Tell students that science writers, like other writers of specialized subjects, must be careful to define technical terms for their readers. Scientists have their own jargon, or specialized vocabulary. Science writers and other writers introducing their readers to new subjects must be careful to explain any terms or concepts that readers might not know. As students read "The Gene Scene," have them watch for times when the writer defines science terms or concepts for readers. **OL**

Skills Preview

Key Reading Skill: Monitoring Comprehension

Active readers monitor their understanding as they read. They have a few good strategies for monitoring their comprehension.

R

- Read the passage again—one sentence at a time.
- Question important ideas, characters, and events.
- Look for context clues in the surrounding sentences.
- Use reference sources and footnotes.

Write to Learn Look at the *Build Background* section on this page. Write down one question you have about the *Build Background*.

Key Literary Element: Figurative Language

Figurative language is often used for descriptive effect. Figures of speech like **similes** and **metaphors** are a part of figurative language.

L

- Writers sometimes compare unlike things by using similes and metaphors.
- A simile uses the words *like* or *as* to compare two unlike things.
- A metaphor compares two unlike things without using *like* or *as*.

Write to Learn Think of two metaphors and two similes and write them in your Learner's Notebook.

Interactive Literary Elements Handbook
To review or learn more about the literary elements, go to www.glencoe.com.

Get Ready to Read

Connect to the Reading

Can you wiggle your ears or raise one eyebrow? Do you have curly hair? All of those qualities were either passed on to you or not. Think about the things that make you who you are. Chances are some of them were passed on to you from your relatives.

Self-Portrait with Genes Make a list of ten things about yourself, such as eye color, that were probably passed on to you in your genes.

Build Background

The selection you are about to read tells what makes us who we are—scientifically speaking.

- Some things, like the color of your eyes, are determined before you are born. Other qualities, like the music you listen to, have a lot to do with the person you are.
- "Nature versus nurture" is shorthand for the argument about traits you were born with (nature) versus personal experiences (nurture) in determining the way you look and act.
- Most scientists agree that both nature and nurture make you who you are.

Set Purposes for Reading

BIG Question Read "The Gene Scene" to find out how genes help to make you who you are.

Set Your Own Purpose What else would you like to learn from the reading to help you answer the Big Question? Write your purpose on the "Gene Scene" page of Foldable 4.

Keep Moving

Use these skills as you read the following selection.

Teach

R Reading Skill

Monitoring Comprehension Ask: Which of the four monitoring comprehension strategies might be most helpful when reading about science? *(Possible response: Looking for context clues might be important to help define new words.)* **OL**

L Literary Element

Figurative Language Ask: Why might similes and metaphors be helpful for science writers who are trying to help readers understand difficult concepts? *(Possible response: Similes and metaphors compare two things; science writers could make comparisons to things readers already know to help them understand new information.)* **AL**

Interactive Literary Elements Handbook Have students access the Web site to improve their understanding of figurative language.

Reading in the Real World

Career Students who are interested in studying heredity may wish to learn more about genetics career people, such as medical geneticists and genetic counselors. Have students work in small groups to research the job description and education requirements for one of these careers. Then ask groups to research a genetic disorder and prepare a presentation on the disorder, including the role of the geneticist in diagnosing, treating, and/or preventing the disorder. **AL**

Objectives

- Monitor comprehension:
- Identify literary devices: figurative language
- Learn and use new vocabulary
- Identify elements of nonfiction

451

Teach

Viewing the Photo

Ask: How does the picture on this page connect to the topic of genetics? *(The photo illustrates traits that can be inherited.)* **BL**

EL₁ Language Coach

Context Clues Ask: In paragraph 1, what example does the writer use to help you understand inherited *traits?* *(eye color)* In paragraph 2, what context clue does the writer provide to help you understand the word *traits?* *(special features)* **EL**

EL₂ Language Coach

Context Clues Ask: What is a hitchhiker? *(someone who gets free rides from passing drivers)* Are there any context clues in the selection? *(no)* How do you find what a word means if there are no context clues? *(Possible responses: Look in a dictionary. Ask another person.)* **EL**

Readability Scores
Dale-Chall: 8.9
DRP: 59
Lexile: 790

TIME
THE GENE SCENE

What makes you <u>you</u>?

By JORDAN BROWN

Genetics is the study of how special features, such as eye color, are passed on from one **generation** to another. **1**
    To find out more about special features, called **EL₁** traits, find a friend and grab some paper and a pencil. Ask each other these questions. Then write your answers on the paper.

1. Can you curl your tongue?
You: YES   NO
Your Friend: YES   NO

2. Can you wiggle your ears?
You: YES   NO
Your Friend: YES   NO

3. Can you raise just one of your eyebrows?
You: YES   NO
Your Friend: YES   NO

4. Do you have a "hitchhiker's thumb"?[1] **EL₂**
You: YES   NO
Your Friend: YES   NO

---

1. A **hitchhiker's thumb** is a rare trait in humans where the end joint of the thumb can be bent at an angle of at least 45 degrees.

Vocabulary

generation (jen uh RAY shun) *n.* a group of persons born around the same time

452 UNIT 4   What Makes You Who You Are?

1 Reviewing Skills

Questioning Think about the title and the opening paragraph. Why do you think the idea of genetics might be important to the article? Does this paragraph help you understand what genetics is? What more do you want to know?

Additional Support

Differentiated Instruction

Using Math Skills On the board, write the "genetics investigation" questions (or key words from them). One question at a time, ask students to show a "yes" response by raising their hands. Record the hand count on the board after each question. Then work with students to convert each number to a percentage by dividing the hand count by the total number of students. Just for fun, ask for volunteers to demonstrate (or try to demonstrate) each trait for the class. **AS**

Congratulations!

You just did a genetics investigation.

Traits are a person's special features. Some traits are more common than others. Many people can curl their tongues. But eyebrow raisers, ear-wigglers, and people with a hitchhiker's thumb are harder to find. **2**

Traits, such as the ability to roll your tongue, are passed on through genes. You get your genes from your parents. Genes are inside every living cell. They are made of a chemical called DNA.**2** Genes are tiny, but they carry tons of information. **3**

Here are some amazing things scientists have discovered so far:

- All living things have DNA. So you have something in common with zebras, trees, mushrooms, and even bacteria. **R**
- There are about 30,000 genes in every cell of your body.
- Unless you are an identical twin, there is no one exactly like you. You are genetically unique. **EL**

Scientists are discovering many new secrets about life, such as what role genes play in determining what makes you you, whether people are healthy or sick, and how you grow. What they learn will greatly affect our future, from the medicine we take to the food we eat.

Denis Finnin/American Museum of Natural History (4)

---

2. **DNA** is a substance that is found in the genes of cells and that stores a person's unique patterns of traits.

The Gene Scene **453**

2 | **English Language Coach**

Context Clues In this paragraph, what kind of context clue does the writer give you to help you understand the meaning of the word **traits**?

3 | **Key Reading Skill**

Monitoring Comprehension Stop and check your reading comprehension so far. Is there anything you need to go back and reread? Any words you don't understand? Write down a question you have at this point.

Teach

R Reading Skill

Monitoring Comprehension Ask: What do people have in common with zebras, trees, mushrooms, and bacteria? *(We all have DNA.)* **BL**

EL Language Coach

Context Clues Ask: For which word in the bulleted list on this page did the writer include the context clue "there is no one exactly like you"? *(unique)* **OL**

Reading in the Real World

Citizenship Tell students that some of the foods we eat have been genetically modified. The genes of some foods, such as soybeans, corn, and canola, are altered to make them resistant to insecticides (sprays used to kill insects). The genes of other foods are altered to make them resistant to viruses or to increase their nutritional value. This process is very controversial. No one yet knows the effect it will have on the environment and on other organisms. The U.S. does not require food producers to label foods as being genetically modified. Ask, "Do you think these labels should be required? Why or why not?" **OL AL**

Objectives
- Use context clues to determine word meaning
- Monitor comprehension
- Use text features: photographs

453

Teach

L1 Literary Element

Review Meter, Rhythm, and Rhyme **Ask:** Do the stanzas in this poem have a set meter or are they free verse? *(They have a set meter.)* What are some words that rhyme in the first stanza? *(learn, concern; genes, beans)* **BL**

L2 Literary Element

Figurative Language **Ask:** What metaphor does the poet use for cells in the third stanza? *(teeny-tiny building blocks)* **OL** **AL**

R Reading Skill

Monitoring Comprehension **Ask:** What do you learn about chromosomes from the poem? *(There are 46 of them. We get half from each of our parents.)* **BL** **OL**

What Makes YOU YOU?
What Makes ME ME?

Genetics is fun!
So much to learn!
Oooh! But I have one concern.
I've searched and searched.
Where ARE my genes?
You've got to help me!
Spill the beans!

What makes you you?
What makes me me?
A lot is due to **heredity**.
Your genes control
What makes you you,
From the color of your hair
To the size of your shoe.

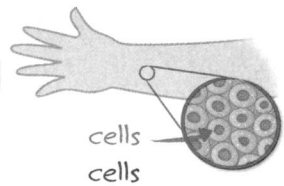

Dogs and frogs are made of cells.
Bananas have them, too!
These teeny-tiny building blocks
Even make up YOU!

cells
cells

This thing here's the **nucleus**.
It's small, but even so:
It tells the cell just what to do,
It really runs the show. 4

Then, there are your **chromosomes**,
They're 46 in all!
Half from mom, and half from dad,
They're really, really small.

Chromosome
Chromosome

4 | English Language Coach

Context Clues In this part of the poem, what kind of context clue does the writer give you to help you understand the meaning of the word **nucleus**?

Vocabulary

heredity (huh RED uh tee) *n.* the passing on of characteristics from an animal or plant to its offspring

chromosomes (KROH muh sohmz) *n.* parts of a cell in a plant or animal that carry the genes controlling features such as the color of hair and eyes

454 UNIT 4 What Makes You Who You Are?

Additional Support

Differentiated Instruction

Critical Thinking U.S. courts allow juries to consider DNA evidence in deciding a person's innocence or guilt. Explain that a DNA test can *only* show whether a DNA sample matches a suspect's DNA, and it cannot tell *why* that person's DNA was at a crime scene or *when* it came to be there. Invite students to discuss this case: Hairs found at a crime scene do not belong to the victim. A DNA test matches the hairs to a suspect. Ask whether the DNA test proves the suspect's guilt, and why or why not. **AL**

Your chromosomes are shaped like coils.
They always come in pairs.
They're made of stuff called DNA,
That's shaped like spiral stairs. **5**

L

Chromosomes
(made of coiled DNA)

Genes are the sections of DNA,
Where many traits are placed.
Learning what each gene controls
Is the puzzle experts face.

Gene
(section of DNA)

DNA is made of four bases
We call them G, C, A, and T.
These bases are in every plant
And animal you see!
[end poem]

DNA
(closer)

A —— C
G —— T
C —— T
A —— G

I GET IT NOW!
WHAT MAKES YOU <u>YOU</u>,
WHAT MAKES ME <u>ME</u>,
SHAPES EVERY LIVING THING YOU SEE.
WE'RE ALL RELATED IN A WAY
BECAUSE WE ALL HAVE DNA!

—Updated 2005, FROM *TIME FOR KIDS*, May 2001

5 ▐ **Key Literary Element**

Figurative Language Reread the lines "They're made of stuff called DNA / That's shaped like spiral stairs." Look at the "closer" view of DNA. It really is shaped exactly like spiral stairs, isn't it? Does this make the comparison "literal" or "figurative"?

Time & Life Pictures/Getty Images

Gregor Mendel, a scientist who lived in the 1800s, discovered the rules of genetics. By experimenting with pea plants, Mendel figured out how traits are passed from one generation to the next.

Thousands of different traits make you who you are. Some traits, such as eye color, are determined mostly or entirely by genes. These kind of traits are decided by nature.

Most traits, however, are due to a combination of nature (your genes) and nurture (everything in your life—where you live, the people you know, everything you experience). Scientists agree that both nature and nurture play important roles in making you who you are. **6**

EL

6 ◢**BIG Question**

How does this article add to your understanding of what makes you who you are? Write your answer on the "Gene Scene" page of Foldable 4. Your response will help you complete the Unit Challenge later.

The Gene Scene **455**

Teach

L **Literary Element**

Figurative Language Say: The author makes two comparisons in the first stanza on this page. What does he compare chromosomes to? *(coils)* What does he compare DNA to? *(stairs)* **OL** Why might the author compare chromosomes and DNA to familiar things like coils and stairs? *(Possible response: to help readers visualize them)* **AL**

EL **Language Coach**

Context Clues Ask: What type of context clues does the author use to explain how he uses the words *nature* and *nurture*? *(He uses definition context clues, putting the definition in parentheses after each word.)* **EL**

Assess

CheckPoint

Use the CheckPoint questions provided on Presentation Plus! to check for comprehension of the selection. These questions can be used with interactive response keypads for immediate student feedback.

Reading in the Real World

Career Explain that Gregor Mendel was an avid gardener who wondered how some plants maintained unusual (atypical) characteristics from one generation to the next. He decided to plant the seeds of the unusual plants next to the seeds of the normal plants to determine if they would be affected by each other. They were not. Instead, their traits were determined solely by their parents. Mendel's curiosity led him to study other subjects related to heredity and to learn how traits were passed from parents to their children. Have students discuss what traits besides curiosity a scientist might need. **AS**

Objectives
• Identify and analyze literary devices: figurative language, meter, rhythm, rhyme
• Monitor comprehension
• Use context clues to determine word meaning

Assess

Resources for page 456

📁 Selection Quick Check, p. 38

📁 Selection and Unit Assessment, p. 44

💿 ExamView Assessment Suite

💿 Interactive Tutor: Self-Assessment

Students can respond to the *After You Read* items in their Learner's Notebooks or on a separate sheet of paper.

Answering the BIG Question

1. Possible response: All living things have genes, which carry the traits that make me who I am.
2. genetics
3. We all have DNA.

Critical Thinking

4. Possible response: Identical twins are genetically identical. Non-identical twins do not have the same DNA.
5. Possible response: to show that genetics can be fun and easy to understand
6. Possible response: "Nature" refers to genetics; "nurture" refers to environment.

After You Read The Gene Scene

Denis Finnin/American Museum of Natural History (4)

Answering the BIG Question

1. In what ways does nature determine who you are?

2. **Recall** What is the name given to the study of how special features are passed from one generation to another?
   Tip Right There

3. **Recall** According to this selection, what do you have in common with a zebra, a tree, a mushroom, and even bacteria?
   Tip Right There

Critical Thinking

4. **Infer** What do you think is the difference, genetically speaking, between identical twins and fraternal, or nonidentical, twins?
   Tip On My Own

5. **Evaluate** Why do you think the author starts his article by making you do a genetics investigation?
   Tip On My Own

6. **Analyze** What is the difference between "nature" and "nurture"?
   Tip Author and Me

Talk About Your Reading

With a partner, talk about what makes you who you are. Discuss the things that are hereditary and the things that aren't. Talk about:

- the traits that you have likely inherited from your parents (such as eye and hair color).
- the traits that you have developed, such as your style, your likes and dislikes, or your favorite hobbies or subjects in school.
- the traits that might be partly inherited but also partly developed, such as your talents and abilities.

Objectives (pp. 456–457)
Reading Monitor comprehension • Make connections from text to self
Informational Text Identify literary elements: simile, metaphor
Vocabulary Use context clues
Grammar Identify indirect objects

456 UNIT 4 What Makes You Who You Are?

Talk About Your Reading

Encourage students to use the partner discussion to help them determine which traits are hereditary and which are not.

Skills Review

Key Reading Skill: Monitoring Comprehension

7. How did the footnotes and vocabulary definitions help you as you monitored your comprehension?

Key Literary Element: Figurative Language

8. Think about both selections you read—a poem and an article. In which type of text do you think you'd be more likely to see similes and metaphors? Explain.

9. Rewrite the following sentences. If they are similes, turn them into metaphors. If they are metaphors, turn them into similes.
   - His feet were ice cubes.
   - Yesterday was like a nightmare.
   - Her hair was a shining helmet.

Reviewing Skills: Questioning

10. List two questions you could have asked yourself to help you think about what information was important as you read.

Vocabulary Check

Write the vocabulary word that each clue describes.

generation   heredity   chromosome

11. how traits get passed on to offspring
12. people who were born around the same time
13. the part of a cell that carries the genes

English Language Coach   Use context clues to figure out the meaning of each underlined word. Write a synonym or short definition for each.

14. There was only a <u>scant</u> amount of food left, a piece of bread and one apple.
15. Hector can <u>disregard</u> the announcement, but Wally should pay attention to it.
16. That store carries <u>garments</u>, such as jeans, dresses, shirts, and coats.

Grammar Link: Indirect Objects

An **indirect object** tells *to whom* or *for whom* an action is done.
*Calvin **shows** his **teammates** new shots.*

The direct object in the sentence above is *shots*. The indirect object is *teammates*. *Teammates* answers the question *to whom?* after the action verb *shows*.

An indirect object appears only in a sentence that has a direct object. Two easy clues will help you find indirect objects.

- First, the indirect object always comes before a direct object.
- Second, you can add *to* or *for* before the indirect object and change its position. The sentence will still make sense, although it will no longer have an indirect object.

   *The helper gives the **players** towels.*

   *The helper gives the towels **to the players**.*

In the first sentence, *players* is the indirect object. Notice that *players* comes before the direct object (towels). In the second, the position of *players* in the sentence is changed to follow the word *to*.

Grammar Practice

Copy each sentence. Underline each direct object once. Underline each indirect object twice.

17. The girls gave Martha her present.
18. Randy handed the lifeguard a whistle.
19. The zookeepers gave the lion his dinner.

Literature Online

Web Activities For eFlashcards, Selection Quick Checks, and other Web activities, go to www.glencoe.com.

Skills Review

Key Reading Skill: Monitoring Comprehension

7. Responses will vary.

Key Literary Element: Figurative Language

8. Possible response: Poems use more similes and metaphors because they are more descriptive with fewer words.

9. Her feet were ice cubes. Yesterday was a nightmare. Her hair was like a shining helmet.

Reviewing Skills: Questioning

10. Possible responses: What are genes? What is heredity?

Vocabulary Check

11. heredity
12. generation
13. chromosome
14. Slight/ a small amount
15. ignore/ to pay no attention to
16. clothes/ article of clothing

Grammar Link: Indirect Objects

Grammar Practice

17. The girls gave <u>Martha</u> her <u>present</u>.
18. Randy handed the <u>lifeguard</u> a <u>whistle</u>.
19. The zookeepers gave the <u>lion</u> his <u>dinner</u>.

Assess/Close

Have students tell whether they think nature or nurture had the most influence in making them who they are.

Comparing Settings

**Objectives covered in
this workshop:**
• Understand and evaluate
authors' use of figurative
language
• Connect, compare, and
contrast figurative language
across texts

Teaching Student to Compare Figurative Language

Why Is It Important

• Comparing figurative language helps students generate a better picture of the characters and events in a selection.

• Comparing figurative language also helps students pay more attention to specific details.

• Looking at the figurative language from different selections within a genre helps students make connections from text to text.

How to Help Students Get It

• Have students keep track of the figurative language as they read. You may choose to have them create a chart for each selection.

• Tell students to think about how the figurative language helps them better understand the similarities and differences between the characters, settings, and events in each selection.

• Remind students to look for the language that includes similes, metaphors, and sensory images in the selections.

Reading to Answer the Big Question

maggie and milly and mollie and may by e.e. cummings
Maggie, Milly, Mollie, and May each find something special during a day at the beach. e.e. cummings closes this poem with the observation that we find ourselves in the sea.

Daydreamers by Eloise Greenfield
In this poem, Greenfield paints a vivid word picture of daydreams as active entities passing through the minds of children and helping them grow toward adulthood.

Workshop Resources

Pacing (Days) Standard	Block	Lesson	Student Materials	Teacher Resources
1	1	Comparing Literature: Comparing Figurative Language	📖 English Language Coach Review, p. 41	🖐 Bellringer Options Transparencies – Selection Focus Transparency 11 – Daily Language Focus 39 🖐 Read Aloud, Think Aloud Transparencies – Read Aloud, Think Aloud 35–38 💿 Presentation Plus!
1	1	"maggie and milly and mollie and may"	💻 Glencoe Online 📖 Unit Vocabulary Review, p. 39 📖 Academic Vocabulary Review, p. 42 📁 English Language Coach 📖 Comparing Literature Graphic Organizer, p. 34 💿 StudentWorks Plus™ 💻 Online Student Edition 💿 Literature Classics	💻 Puzzlemaker 💿 Skill Level Up!™ A Language Arts Game 💻 BookLink 3 📓 Assessment by Learning Objective (Diagnostic and Formative) 💿 Interactive Tutor: Self-Assessment 💿 TeacherWorks Plus™ 💿 ExamView Assessment Suite
1		"Daydreamers"	💻 Glencoe Online 📖 Unit Vocabulary Review, p. 39 📖 Academic Vocabulary Review, p. 42 📁 English Language Coach 📖 Comparing Literature Graphic Organizer, p. 34 💿 StudentWorks Plus™ 💻 Online Student Edition 💿 Literature Classics	💻 Puzzlemaker 💿 Skill Level Up!™ A Language Arts Game 💻 BookLink 3 📓 Assessment by Learning Objective (Diagnostic and Formative) 💿 Interactive Tutor: Self-Assessment 💿 TeacherWorks Plus™ 💿 ExamView Assessment Suite

Keys for Unit Resource

📁 Blackline Master 📀 DVD

📓 Workbook 🖐 Transparency

📖 Supplemental Text 💻 Web-based

💿 CD-ROM 📖 Fast File

Level Appropriate Code

AS = Activities for all students

AL = Activities for students working above grade level

OL = Activities for students working at grade level

BL = Activities for students working below grade level

EL = Activities for English language learners

Focus

Teach

🄛 Literary Element

Figurative Language Say:
Tell whether the following sentences include figurative or literal language.

- My little brother is a bull-dozer. *(figurative)*
- My little sister is friendly to most people. *(literal)*
- The yellow daisies look delightful. *(literal)*
- The yellow daisies are like a sunny day. *(figurative)* **OL**

"maggie and milly and molly and may" & "Daydreamers"

by e. e. cummings · by Eloise Greenfield

What You'll Learn

- How to compare two pieces of literature
- How to analyze figurative language

What You'll Read

- "maggie and milly and molly and may," p. 461
- "Daydreamers," p. 463

Point of Comparison

- Figurative language

Purpose

- To compare figurative language in two literary selections

Objectives (pp. 458–459)
Reading Compare and contrast: figurative language

458 UNIT 4

Do you think comparing things is hard? It's not. Really, it's easy as pie! As a matter of fact, the sentence you just read made a comparison. It compared *making a comparison* to *eating a piece of pie*. People use comparisons all the time to make what they're saying more powerful and interesting. For example, you might say, "This test is very difficult." But that's pretty dull. Instead, you could say, "This test is a nightmare." The test isn't *really* a nightmare, but by *comparing* it to a bad dream, your point comes across more powerfully.

How to Compare Literature: Figurative Language

When you say something like *"Mason was good at basketball yesterday,"* you're using *literal* language. *Literal* language means exactly what it says.

When you say, *"Mason was a ball of fire on the court,"* though, you're using *figurative* language. *Figurative* language isn't meant to be taken as the simple, exact truth. Figurative language usually does one of these things:

- compares things that aren't really alike
- describes something as though it were something else
- exaggerates something to an impossible degree to create a more powerful image than you could with literal language

L

Additional Support

Literature Focus Lesson

Imagery Remind students that images are the pictures that poets create through descriptive language. Many poets use just a few carefully chosen words to construct stunning images in their work. Have students skim through the unit for memorable images. Have them read aloud the lines describing the images. Tell students to look for images as they read the two poems in this workshop. You may wish to have students illustrate their favorite imagery from these poems. **AS**

Figurative language lets you be creative in describing things. In this workshop, you'll be comparing figurative language in two poems.

Get Ready to Compare

A **figure of speech** is often a comparison made using figurative language. Three of the most common types of figures of speech are *personification*, *similes*, and *metaphors*.

- **Personification** gives human characteristics to an object, animal, or idea.

  My bike hates me.

- **Similes** use the words *like* or *as* to compare two things that aren't really alike.

  She was quiet as a mouse during the lesson.

- **Metaphors** compare two unlike things without using the words *like* or *as*. A metaphor can say one thing is something else, or it can describe something as if it were something else.

  Allison was an angel while I was sick.

  (Allison is compared to an angel.)

  When Ms. Lowe called on her, Felicia's blood turned to ice water.

  (Felicia's blood is compared to ice water.)

Figurative Language

The clouds looked angry.

Meaning

The clouds are dark and scary. It looks like it's going to storm.

Effect

It makes the scene scarier. Something bad is going to happen.

Use Your Comparison

When you read a poem or other work of literature, take notes about the figures of speech (figurative language) that you find. A chart like this one can help you understand what the author is trying to say:

In the left circle, write down the figurative language that you found. In the center circle, write down what the author means. Then, in the right circle, write down the effect the figurative language has on the poem or the reader. Try to think of the image that it brings to mind or how it makes you feel.

In this workshop, you'll read two poems that use figurative language. For each selection, *read the poem all the way through first to get an idea of what the poem's about.* Then go back and make diagrams like the one above for each example of figurative language you find.

Teach

L Literary Element

Figurative Language Say: Describe the possible meaning and effect of each of these sentences.

- The puppy was a tornado. *(Possible meaning: The puppy ran around, making a mess. Possible effect: It makes the puppy seem like a tiny destructive force.)*

- The man was drowning in his grief. *(Possible meaning: The man was overcome by grief and sadness. Possible effect: The idea of drowning makes the man's grief seem greater and more terrible.)* **OL** **AL**

Assess/Close

Say: Write a simile or metaphor about your favorite hobby. Share your sentence with the class and explain why you chose to compare the two things. *(Responses will vary.)* **OL**

Resources for page 459

 Use the Comparing Literature Graphic Organizer BLM in the Unit 4 Resource Booklet, p. 34.

Differentiated Instruction

Personification To help students understand personification, ask them to work with partners to list things people can do that animals and nonliving things cannot, such as get angry, whisper, and make friends. Ask partners to share their responses with the class while you record them on the board. Then have partners use those traits to write expressions that personify the following: an animal of their choice, the ocean, pizza, music, and sports. Have them share two of their responses with the class. **EL** **BL**

Objectives

- Identify literary devices: figurative language, imagery, personification
- Compare and contrast literature

459

Teach

More About the Author

Because of his mother's encouragement, Edward Estlin Cummings kept a journal and wrote verse as a child. As a student at Harvard, he began writing free verse and became a self-taught painter. Shortly after finishing the only regular job of his life-time—working for a mail-order company—Cummings volunteered to work on an ambulance during World War I. While in France, he was unfairly accused of spying and imprisoned in a camp. From that experi-ence came his novel *The Enormous Room.*

V Vocabulary

Word Associations Say:

Sometimes a word imitates the idea it represents. Say the word *languid.* Doesn't it sound slow and relaxed? As you learn new vocabulary words, look for words like *languid* that imitate the ideas they represent. **AS**

Before You Read

maggie *and* milly *and* molly *and* may

e. e. cummings

Meet the Author

Edward Estlin Cummings (e. e. cummings) is famous for his experiments with poetry. Cummings rarely obeyed standard rules of grammar and capitalization in his poems. He didn't even capitalize his name when he signed his work. He felt that breaking accepted rules of grammar and usage helped him to express his ideas in a more original way. Cummings was born in 1894. He died in 1962. For more about e. e. cummings, see page R2 of the Author Files.

Author Search For more about e. e. cummings, go to www. glencoe.com.

Objectives (pp. 460–461)
Reading Compare and contrast across texts: figurative language

Vocabulary Preview

befriended (bih FREN dud) *v.* made friends with someone; form of the verb *befriend* **(p. 461)** *John befriended the boy he met in the park.*

stranded (STRAN did) *adj.* left helpless in a difficult place **(p. 461)** *When she missed the bus, the stranded girl was worried.*

rays (rayz) *n.* beams of light or energy **(p. 461)** *The sun's rays warmed my back.*

languid (LANG gwid) *adj.* slow-moving; without energy **(p. 461)** *The sound of the waves and the heat of the sun made me feel lazy and languid.*

Get Ready to Read

Connect to the Reading

Are you a worrier, a carefree type, a dreamer, or a deep thinker? Does your personality affect the way you see things and feel about them? In the poem you are about to read, four girls respond in different ways to a day at the beach. As you read "maggie and milly and molly and may," think about how who you are shapes the way you experience life.

Build Background

There is a sense of joy and fun in many of e. e. cummings's poems that makes them very popular. The poem you are about to read is one of his most widely read works.

- Cummings often wrote poems that celebrate nature and childhood.
- Sometimes, when you hold certain seashells to your ear, you can hear a noise that sounds like waves.
- Most common crabs walk sideways.
- Starfish dry out and die if they are left on the beach away from water.

Set Purposes for Reading

BIG Question Read the selection to explore how "maggie and milly and molly and may," who we are shapes the way we see the world.

Set Your Own Purpose What else would you like to learn from the poem to help you answer the Big Question? Write your own purpose on the "maggie and milly and molly and may" page of Foldable 4.

Additional Support

Author Search To expand students' appreciation of e. e. cummings, have them access the Web site for additional information and resources.

Literature Focus Lesson

Meter To help students identify meter, or regular rhythm, have them tap along lightly on their desks as you read aloud the first stanza of Robert Louis Stevenson's "The Swing." Then write the stanza on the board, and ask partners to copy the poem and take turns reading it aloud. When it's their turn to listen, partners should underline the stressed syllables they hear.

The Swing

How do you like to go up in a swing,
Up in the air so blue?
Oh, I do think it the pleasantest thing
Ever a child can do! **AS**

maggie
and milly *and*
molly *and* may

by e. e. cummings

maggie and milly and molly and may
went down to the beach(to play one day)

and maggie discovered a shell that sang **1**
so sweetly she couldn't remember her troubles,and

milly **befriended** a **stranded** star
whose **rays** five **languid** fingers were;

and molly was chased by a horrible thing
which raced sideways while blowing bubbles:and

may came home with a smooth round stone
as small as a world and as large as alone.

For whatever we lose(like a you or a me)
it's always ourselves we find in the sea **2** ○

L

R

Vocabulary

befriended (bih FREN dud) *v.* made friends with someone

stranded (STRAN did) *adj.* left helpless in a difficult place

rays (rayz) *n.* beams of light or energy

languid (LANG gwid) *adj.* slow-moving; without energy

Practice the Skills

1 ▌**Comparing Literature**

Figurative Language
Cummings says that the shell "sang." Singing is normally something that people do, not objects. What kind of figurative language assigns human characteristics to objects? Why do you think cummings said the shell "sang"?

2 **BIG Question**

What do you think e. e. cummings means in the last two lines? Write your answer on the "maggie and milly and molly and may" page of your Foldable 4. Your response will help you complete the Unit Challenge later.

maggie and milly and molly and may **461**

Teach

L **Literary Element**

Rhythm, Rhyme, and Meter Say: Words that come close to rhyming, such as *care* and *far*, are called "near rhyme." Give an example of an exact rhyme in this poem and an example of a near rhyme. *(Possible responses: exact— may and day; near—star and were)* **EL** **BL**

R **Reading Skill**

Visualizing Ask: What do you think the "horrible thing" might be? *(Sample response: I know that crabs live in sand on beaches and they move sideways. I think the horrible thing is a crab that blows bubbles.)* **OL**

Assess

CheckPoint

Use the CheckPoint questions provided on Presentation Plus! to check for comprehension of the selection. These questions can be used with interactive response keypads for immediate student feedback.

Reading Fluency

Build Fluency The rhythm in cummings's poem makes it tempting to stop at the end of each line when reading it. Model the appropriate way to read the poem by reading it aloud twice. The first time, stop at the end of each line. The next time, use punctuation to guide pauses and create a more lively reading. Encourage students to note how different the poem sounds when it is read correctly. Have students take turns reading the poem aloud, using pauses and tone effectively. **EL** **BL**

Objectives
• Identify literary devices: figurative language, rhyme, rhythm, meter
• Visualize
• Learn and use new vocabulary

Teach

More About the Author

Eloise Greenfield loves writing for children. Words make her laugh, she says, and even though it can sometimes be difficult to find the right ones, she keeps writing because she wants children to have the best. Greenfield grew up in a loving African American family with a strong sense of community. Her 38 children's books show how such strong, loving communities and families can help make people who they are.

R Reading Skill

Review Connecting Ask:

Why and when do you day-dream? *(Responses will vary.)* When might it not be appropriate to daydream? *(Possible responses: in class; during an exam; while playing a game)* **AS**

Before You Read · *Daydreamers*

Eloise Greenfield

Meet the Author

"I believe everyone spends time daydreaming," says Eloise Greenfield. "With writing, sometimes an idea will come, or an opening sentence, or an image, and then it may be months or years later before it really develops into a story." An award-winning author of books and poems for young people, Greenfield grew up in Washington, D.C.

Literature Online

Author Search For more about Eloise Greenfield, go to www. glencoe.com.

Objectives (pp. 462–463)
Reading Compare and contrast across texts: figurative language

Vocabulary Preview

promenade (PROM uh nayd) *v.* to walk or stroll in a slow, relaxed manner **(p. 464)** *We watched the tourists promenade down the boardwalk.*

Get Ready to Read

Connect to the Reading

We've all been there. You're supposed to be concentrating on something, but instead you find yourself staring out the window, lost in a daydream. As you read this selection, connect with the daydreamers and their dreams.

Build Background

The poem you will read is about daydreaming.
- Daydreams can be a way of dealing with fears of the unknown.
- By daydreaming, people sometimes find solutions to problems or get ideas about how to do something.
- Some artists and writers are daydreamers who turned their dreams into art.
- *Hopscotch* is a children's game. To play it, children hop into squares drawn on the ground, while trying to pick up a pebble they have thrown into one of the squares.
- *Doubledutch* is a fast-paced jump-rope game in which two ropes are swung at the same time.

Set Purposes for Reading

BIG Question Read the selection "Daydreamers" to find out how daydreaming is connected to growing up and changing—becoming a person who will shape his or her own future.

Set Your Own Purpose What else would you like to learn from the story to help you answer the Big Question? Write your own purpose on the "Daydreamers" page of Foldable 4.

Additional Support

Literature Online

Author Search To expand students' appreciation of Eloise Greenfield, have them access the Web site for more information and resources.

Literature Focus Lesson

Cultural References Tell students that writers often make cultural references to ideas, places, or activities most readers know about. Readers can use their prior knowledge to make inferences based on these references. In "Daydreamers," the poet makes references to hopscotch, doubledutch, and rollerskating. What do these three things have in common? *(They're all children's activities.)* **OL** What do they tell you about the daydreamers? *(They're probably children.)* **AL**

by Eloise Greenfield

Daydreamers . . .

holding their bodies still
for a time
letting the world turn around them **1**

5 while their dreams hopscotch,
doubledutch, dance, **2**

thoughts rollerskate,
crisscross,
bump into hopes and wishes.

10 Dreamers
thinking up new ways,
looking toward new days,

planning new tries,
asking new whys. **L**

15 Before long,
hands will start to move again,
eyes turn outward,
bodies shift for action,
but for this moment they are still, **R**

Practice the Skills

1 | **Comparing Literature**

Figurative Language What does the poet mean when she says the daydreamers let the world "turn around them"?

2 | **Comparing Literature**

Figurative Language While the daydreamers stand still, their dreams "hopscotch, doubledutch, dance." Is this an example of metaphor, simile, or personification? What does this suggest about the daydreams?

Daydreamers **463**

Teach

L Literary Element

Rhyme, Rhythm, and Meter Ask: What sound device does the poet use in lines 11–14? *(rhyme)* **BL** Why might the poet have used rhyme in these lines? *(Possible response: These lines are important because they describe what the kids are dreaming about. The poet may have used rhyme to emphasize the daydreams as being different from the physical activities.)* **AL**

R Reading Skill

Monitoring Comprehension Ask: What does the poet say will happen "before long"? *(The kids will return to their activities.)* **BL** What does this suggest about the time the kids spend daydreaming? *(Possible response: They do not daydream for long.)* **OL**

Reading in the Real World

Citizenship Many "daydreams" have become inventions that have helped the world. Have students learn about an inventor and his or her famous invention(s). Some choices are Thomas Edison, Eli Whitney, Alexander Graham Bell, Marie Curie, George Washington Carver, Thomas Adams, and Virginia Apgar. Ask students to write a description of one of the person's inventions. Have them share it with the class. **OL** **AL**

Objectives
• Identify literary devices: rhyme, rhythm, meter
• Make connections from text to self
• Monitor comprehension
• Recognize cultural references

Teach

L₁ Literary Element

Figurative Language Ask:
What type of figurative language does the poet use in lines 20–23? *(personification)* **OL**
What do these lines mean? *(Possible response: Daydreamers ignore the crazy, mixed-up world to concentrate on their own thoughts and ideas.)* **AL**

L₂ Literary Element

Figurative Language Ask:
What type of figurative language is the poet using in lines 24–28? *(personification)* **OL**
Does this language help you imagine the kids' daydreams? Why or why not? *(Sample response: This language does help me imagine the kids' daydreams. I can see the images passing quietly through the kids' minds.)* **AL**

Lilith, 1996. Diane Griffiths. Watercolor and crayon.
Analyzing the Art Which lines from the poem would make a good caption for this painting? Explain why.

²⁰ they are
   the daydreamers,
   letting the world dizzy itself
   without them. **3**   **L₁**

   Scenes passing through their minds
²⁵ make no sound
   glide from hiding places   **L₂**
   promenade and return
   silently

Vocabulary

promenade (PROM uh nayd) *v.* to walk or stroll in a slow, relaxed manner

464 UNIT 4 What Makes You Who You Are?

3 Comparing Literature

Figurative Language Can a nonliving object become dizzy? What kind of figurative language is the poet using in the line "letting the world dizzy itself"? What do you think this means?

Additional Support

Differentiated Instruction

Writing a Poem Have students write five-line poems about their dreams for the future. Students should call their poems "I Dream," and each of the five lines in the poems should begin "I dream that . . ." or "I dream of . . ." Tell students their poems can focus on personal dreams or their hopes for the entire world. Encourage students to use at least one example of figurative language in their poems. Have volunteers share their dream poems with the class. **OL AL**

the children watch their memories
30 with spirit-eyes
seeing more than they saw before

feeling more
or maybe less
than they felt the time before
35 reaching with spirit-hands
to touch the dreams
drawn from their yesterdays **4**
They will not be the same
after this growing time,
40 this dreaming.
In their stillness they have moved
forward   **EL**

toward womanhood
toward manhood.
45 This dreaming has made them
new. **5** ○

Practice the Skills

4 Comparing Literature

Figurative Language What do you think the author means when she says children use *spirit-eyes* and *spirit-hands* to look back on their memories and touch their dreams?

5 BIG Question

What do you think the poet is saying about daydreaming and the part it plays in becoming who you are? Write your answer on the "Daydreamers" page of Foldable 4. Your response will help you complete the Unit Challenge later.   **BQ**

Daydreamers **465**

Teach

EL Language Coach

Context Clues Help students understand the sentence "In their stillness they have moved forward." Tell students the words *moved forward* are being used figuratively here. **Ask:** What context clues suggest the meaning of *moved forward* as it is used here? *(The phrases* growing time, toward woman-hood, *and* toward manhood *suggest that moving forward means "getting older" or "growing up.")* **EL**

BQ BIG Question

Say: Think of two things you used to daydream about when you were in elementary school. In your Learner's Notebooks, write how these dreams might have helped make you who you are now. *(Responses will vary.)* **AS**

Assess

✔CheckPoint

Use the CheckPoint questions provided on Presentation Plus! to check for comprehension of the selection. These questions can be used with interactive response keypads for immediate student feedback.

Reading in the Real World

Career Tell students some of their daydreams may never come true but, with hard work and commitment, others can be possible. Have students think of one daydream they have that could become a reality. Tell students to write step-by-step instructions explaining how to make the daydream come true. For example,

students who daydream about being a composer might begin their list like this:

1. Study music in school.
2. Practice four hours per day.
3. Apply to music colleges.
4. Study under top composer.
AS

Objectives
• Identify literary devices: figurative language
• Use context clues to determine word meaning

Assess

Vocabulary Check

maggie and milly and molly and may

1. languid
2. rays
3. stranded
4. befriended

Daydreamers

5. false

Reading/Critical Thinking

maggie and milly and molly and may

6. Molly is chased by a crab.

7. Possible response: Maggie forgot her troubles, Milly found something to help, Molly became afraid, and May found a small treasure. This tells me that that the girls were different kinds of people. Maggie wanted to escape her troubles, Milly wanted to rescue, Molly worried a lot, and May appreciated small things.

After You Read

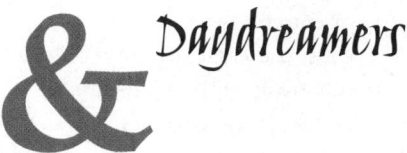

maggie and milly and molly and may **&** *Daydreamers*

Vocabulary Check

Look at the words listed below. Write the vocabulary word that each clue describes:

maggie and milly and molly and may

befriended   languid   stranded   rays

1. Someone who is lazy might look this way.
2. These are beams of light from a star.
3. When the tide goes out at the beach, some creatures find themselves in this situation.
4. Milly did this to the little animal when she helped it on the beach.

Daydreamers

Answer *true* or *false* to this statement:

5. When people *promenade*, they walk as fast as they can.

Reading/Critical Thinking

On a separate sheet of paper, answer the following questions.

maggie and milly and molly and may

6. **Recall** Which girl has a frightening experience at the beach?
   Tip Right There

7. **Compare and Contrast** How did the girls' experiences at the beach differ from one another? What does this tell you about each of the girls?
   Tip Author and Me

Objectives (pp. 466–467)
Reading Compare and contrast across texts: figurative language
Writing Write to compare and contrast literature

---

12. **maggie and milly and molly and may**

Sample responses:

Figurative Language	Meaning	Effect
a shell that sang so sweetly (P)	With the shell at her ear, Maggie hears the "waves."	It makes the shell seem sweet and healing.
a stranded star (M)	a starfish	It suggests that Milly helps a sad, lonely creature.
stone as small as a world and as large as alone (S)	Only May sees countless possibilities in the stone.	It suggests May has a good imagination.

8. **Compare and Contrast** Do the girls' experiences at the beach support the last line of the poem, "it's always ourselves we find in the sea"?

Tip Author and Me

Daydreamers

9. **Recall** What are the children doing while dreams go through their minds?

Tip Right There

10. **Interpret** Why does the poet say the daydreamers "will not be the same after this growing time, this dreaming"?

Tip Author and Me

11. **Evaluate** How well does the writer capture the thoughts and feelings of children in this poem? Why do you think this?

Tip On My Own

Writing: Compare the Literature

Use Your Notes

12. Follow these steps to use your notes to compare the author's use of figurative language in "maggie and milly and molly and may" and "Daydreamers."

Step 1: Look over the Figurative Language diagrams you created for both poems. Put a **P** by each example of personification, an **M** by each metaphor, and an **S** by each simile. If you found some examples of figurative language that don't seem to fit within those three categories, don't label them.

Step 2: For each example of figurative language you found in both poems, look at the note you made in the *Effects* oval. Pick one example from each poem that you think had a strong effect.

Step 3: With a partner, discuss the examples that the two of you selected. Do you agree about the effect that the use of figurative language has in these examples? Did either of you notice something that the other missed?

Step 4: Look at the other examples of figurative language you identified. Think about which ones you enjoyed the most and which ones you thought were most descriptive.

Get It on Paper

Answer the following questions on a separate sheet of paper.

13. In "maggie and milly and molly and may," which example of figurative language did you enjoy the most? Explain what the effect of this example was and why you enjoyed it.

14. In "Daydreamers," which example of figurative language did you enjoy the most? Explain what the effect of this example was and why you enjoyed it.

15. Now write a paragraph that compares the two examples that you chose. For each example, write down the figure of speech you found, what it meant, and how it affected the poem or the reader. At the end of your paragraph, explain which example of figurative language you think was more effective.

BIG Question

16. After reading these poems, how do you think e. e. cummings would answer the question, "What makes you who you are?" How do you think Greenfield would answer the same question? Write your answers in your Learner's Notebook.

8. The girls' experiences reflect who they are.

Daydreamers

9. being still

10. Possible response: The things people daydream about influence how they think and act.

11. Possible response: She captures them very well. She describes how children use their vivid imaginations to create many different scenes in their heads.

Writing: Compare the Literature

Use Your Notes

12. Completed diagrams will differ. Look below for sample responses.

Get It On Paper

13–15. Responses will vary.

BIG Question

16. Possible responses: Cummings might say your experiences and how you react to them make you who you are. Greenfield might say your hopes, thoughts, and memories make you who you are.

12. Daydreamers

Sample responses:

Figurative Language	Meaning	Effect
dreams hopscotch, / doubledutch, dance / thoughts rollerskate, / crisscross, / bump into hopes (P)	Dreams and thoughts change quickly and in complicated ways and become mixed up with hopes.	It suggests complex activity that's sometimes organized and intentional, sometimes chaotic and accidental.
scenes passing through their minds / make no sound / glide from hiding places (P)	Memories float up from deep in the mind.	It suggests a peaceful process that happens to the dreamers.

The Unit Challenge

Focus

Teach

Group Activity: Play a Game: Who Am I?

- Assign students to teams or let them select their own.
- Provide an index card for each student, and be sure to collect a card from every student.
- Limit the time students have to write their cards so that every team has an opportunity to play the guessing game.
- Intermingle the cards before they go into the bags to try to ensure a good mix.

Assess/Close

Ask: What have you learned from this activity about what makes people who they are? *(Suggest that students write responses in their Learner's Notebooks.)* **AS**

Answering The BIG Question — What Makes You Who You Are?

You've just read about people's responses to the Big Question: What makes you who you are? Now use what you've learned to do the Unit Challenge.

The Unit Challenge

Choose Activity A or Activity B and follow the directions for that activity.

A. Play a Game: Who Am I?

Let's see if the members of your class can figure out what makes you who you are by playing this game.

1. **Get Started** Form teams of about five or six members. Each team member should get an index card. On the card, write the following:
   Likes:
   Dislikes:
   Hobbies/Interests:
   Personality:
   Something special about me:
   Each member should jot down some information about himself or herself next to each entry on the index card. Use your Foldable notes to give you some ideas. This is what makes you who you are. Here are some examples to get you started. If you have other entries you wish to use, you may use those.

> Likes: watching scary movies
> Dislikes: getting up early on Saturday morning
> Hobbies: collecting comic books
> Personality: usually in a good mood
> Something special about me: can wiggle my ears

2. **Put It in the Bags** Divide cards into equal batches. Each team receives a bag with the same amount of cards. Shake the bag up and begin the game.

3. **Take a Guess**
   - Decide which team goes first.
   - One member from that team takes a card from the bag and reads only the first entry aloud.
   - After the entry is read, your team will be given ten seconds to decide which person from the class the first entry describes. If you cannot agree, take a vote. If you get the person's name right, the team gets five points.
   - If you don't get the name correct, read the second entry and guess again. Each entry after the first one is worth 1 less point.
   - If all the entries on a card are read and the team has not correctly identified the person, the team loses two points. The team with the most points wins.
   - Keep playing until all teams get a turn.

Literature Online

Big Question Link to Web resources to further explore the Big Question at www.glencoe.com.

Literature Online

Big Question Have students access the Web site for English and Spanish summaries and annotated links to related Web resources.

B. Self-Portrait Collage

It is your turn to share what you think helps to make you who you are. Use what you know about yourself to create a self-portrait collage.

1. **Get Started** Gather information about yourself. In your Learner's Notebook, list all of the things that you want to include about yourself. Here are some ideas to get you started.

   - List all your hobbies, interests, and activities.
   - Describe your likes and dislikes.
   - Include information from your Foldable notes.
   - Use this information to write a short essay about what makes you who you are.
   - Use a chart like the one below.

2. **Put It Together** Reread your essay and correct grammar or spelling errors.

   - Gather photos or drawings of you, your family, and friends. You're going to put them on a sheet of heavy paper or poster board, along with the essay that you wrote about yourself.
   - Decide how you want to arrange things before you glue them down.

3. **Show It** Present your collage to your class. Discuss the similarities and differences that you and your classmates have. Talk about what you and your classmates can do to understand and appreciate your differences.

ME		
My hobbies and interests	My likes and dislikes	Other information about me

Teach

Solo Activity: Self-Portrait Collage

- Have students complete the organizer with information about themselves.
- To help students think of "other information about me," have them consider how different areas of their lives—school, family, friends, community—influence who they are.
- Help students think of adjectives by listing a few on the board.
- If students are concerned about using prized photos on their posters, explain that they can keep their posters after the class has viewed them.

Assess/Close

Solo Activity
Encourage students to use this activity to think about all of the influences in their lives that make them who they are. Ask students to identify one influence they feel is most significant.

Objectives
- Participate in a group discussion
- Create a graphic organizer
- Write a short essay

469

Focus

Vocabulary Preview

Before students read, review these words as they're used in the poem.

 2 *might:* power; strength

54 *scrambling:* running, crawl-ing, or climbing quickly

58 *conveniently:* in a way that's easy to use; comfortably

82 *dismal:* very bad; terrible

98 *sympathize:* feel badly about another's sorrow or trouble.

Build Background

This poem tells a story about a walrus and a (human) carpenter on a beach at night.

- A walrus moves slowly and clumsily on land but swims and dives well. It can eat 4,000 clams as one meal.

- A carpenter can move fairly fast on land but not as well in water. No one knows for sure how many clams a carpenter could eat at one meal.

Teach

L Literary Element

Figurative Language Ask:
What figurative language does the poet use in the first two stanzas? *(personification)* **OL**

Your Turn: Read and Apply Skills

Lewis Carroll

Meet the Author
Lewis Carroll was the pen name of Charles Lutwidge Dodgson. Carroll was the third child of eleven brothers and sisters. Carroll taught mathematics and logic. He often used puzzles and games in his teaching. Many of his stories and poems reflect his logical mind, a joy in working through puzzling events. Carroll wrote comic fantasies and humorous verse that was often childlike. His novel *Alice's Adventures in Wonderland* was pub-lished in 1865, followed by *Through the Looking-Glass* in 1871. See page R1 of the Author Files for more about Lewis Carroll.

Author Search For more about Lewis Carroll, go to www.glencoe.com.

The Walrus and the Carpenter

by Lewis Carroll

The sun was shining on the sea,
　　Shining with all his might:
He did his very best to make
　　The billows* smooth and bright—
5 And this was odd, because it was
　　The middle of the night.

The moon was shining sulkily,*
　　Because she thought the sun
Had got no business to be there
10 　　After the day was done—
"It's very rude of him," she said,
　　"To come and spoil the fun!"

The sea was wet as wet could be,
　　The sands were dry as dry.
15 You could not see a cloud, because
　　No cloud was in the sky:
No birds were flying overhead—
　　There were no birds to fly.

L

---

4 *Billows* means big waves.

7 *Sulkily* means in a gloomy, pouting way.

Additional Support

Author Search To expand students' appreciation of Lewis Carroll, have them access the Web site for more information and resources.

Literature Focus Lesson

Summary In this poem, two friends stroll the beach at night, crying at the amount of sand they see. They invite oysters to join them on their walk and in a discussion of this, that, and the other thing. The older oysters are too wise to join in, but the younger oysters rush to accept. When the oysters realize they're to be a snack, they beg the friends to reconsider. The Walrus expresses regrets but joins the Carpenter in eating all of the oysters. **OL**

The walrus and the carpenter on the shore, from *Through the Looking Glass and What Alice Found There,* by Lewis Carroll, 1872.

The Walrus and the Carpenter
20   Were walking close at hand;
They wept like anything to see
   Such quantities of sand:
"If this were only cleared away,"
   They said, "it *would* be grand!"

25 "If seven maids with seven mops
   Swept it for half a year,
Do you suppose," the Walrus said,
   "That they could get it clear?"
"I doubt it," said the Carpenter,
30   And shed a bitter tear.

   "O Oysters, come and walk with us!"
     The Walrus did beseech.*
"A pleasant walk, a pleasant talk,
   Along the briny* beach:
35 We cannot do with more than four,
   To give a hand to each."

The eldest Oyster looked at him,
   But never a word he said:
The eldest Oyster winked his eye,
40   And shook his heavy head—
Meaning to say he did not choose
   To leave the oyster-bed.

But four young Oysters hurried up,
   All eager for the treat:
45 Their coats were brushed, their faces washed,
   Their shoes were clean and neat—
And this was odd, because, you know,
   They hadn't any feet.

Four other Oysters followed them,
50   And yet another four;
And thick and fast they came at last,
   And more, and more, and more—
All hopping through the frothy* waves,

---

32 *Beseech* means to beg or ask for in a serious way.
34 *Briny water* is salty.

53 *Frothy* water is foamy and bubbly.

Teach

Viewing the Art
Ask: What impression do you get of the beach from the illustration on this page? *(wavy sand with rocks, shells, and driftwood)* **Ask:** What impressions do you get of the Walrus and the Carpenter? *(Responses will vary. Many students probably will have had very different expectations.)* **AS**

L Literary Element

Sound Devices **Say:** Reread lines 25–27 of the poem. What three sound devices did the poet use in these lines? *(repetition of* seven; *alliteration in* seven, swept, suppose, said; *rhyme of* year, clear*)* **OL** **AL**

R Reading Skill

Interpreting **Ask:** How do you know in lines 37–42 that the eldest Oyster understands what the friends are up to? *(He winked and shook his head.)* **AL**

Differentiated Instruction

Characterization Have students do a little basic research on real-life oysters (so they can better appreciate the fun Carroll has with the Oysters). Then ask students to list things the poem's Oysters do that real ones could not possibly do. Point out, if students don't, some of Carroll's jokes, such as the "oyster-bed" in line 42. Explain that the place where real oysters live is called a bed, but the poem makes it seem as if the eldest Oyster has a comfy human-style mattress and box springs. Humorous details abound right through the Oysters' final words. **AS**

Objectives
• Identify literary devices: figurative language, sound devices
• Interpret text
• Find meaning in art

471

Teach

L1 Literary Element

Rhyme, Rhythm, and Meter **Ask:** Which lines in each stanza rhyme? *(the second, fourth, and sixth)* **BL** Does this poem have a set meter, or is it free verse? *(It has a set meter.)* How can you tell? *(Sample response: Meter is a rhythm I can tap with my fingers. Free verse is poetry without a set meter.)* **OL**

L2 Literary Element

Figurative Language **Say:** Line 66 comes from an old figure of speech: "when pigs have wings." What do you think this expression means? *(never)* **AL**

The walrus and the carpenter with oysters wearing tiny shoes, from *Through the Looking Glass and What Alice Found There*, by Lewis Carroll, 1872.

And scrambling to the shore.

55 The Walrus and the Carpenter
   Walked on a mile or so,
And then they rested on a rock
   Conveniently low: **L1**
And all the little Oysters stood
60   And waited in a row.

"The time has come," the Walrus said,
   "To talk of many things:
Of shoes—and ships—and sealing-wax—
   Of cabbages—and kings—
65 And why the sea is boiling hot—
   And whether pigs have wings." **L2**

"But wait a bit," the Oysters cried,
   "Before we have our chat;
For some of us are out of breath,
70   And all of us are fat!"
"No hurry!" said the Carpenter.
   They thanked him much for that.

"A loaf of bread," the Walrus said,
   "Is what we chiefly need:
75 Pepper and vinegar besides
   Are very good indeed—
Now if you're ready, Oysters dear,
   We can begin to feed."

"But not on us!" the Oysters cried,
80   Turning a little blue.
"After such kindness, that would be
   A dismal thing to do!"
"The night is fine," the Walrus said.
   "Do you admire the view?

85 "It was so kind of you to come!
   And you are very nice!"
The Carpenter said nothing but
   "Cut us another slice:
I wish you were not quite so deaf—
90   I've had to ask you twice!"

"It seems a shame," the Walrus said,

Additional Support

Literature Focus Lesson

Nonsense Verse Lewis Carroll was famous for writing nonsense verse, a form of poetry that is entertaining because of its rhythm and silly subject matter. Have students tell what elements of "The Walrus and the Carpenter" make it nonsense verse. *(Possible responses: its interesting rhythm, the talking animals, the silly subject)* **BL OL** Lines 61–66 are the best known lines from this poem. Why do you think this is so? *(Possible responses: The sound devices make the lines fun to say out loud. The listed items would make for a silly conversation. The images in 65–66 are funny.)* **AL**

"To play them such a trick,
After we've brought them out so far,
And made them trot so quick!"
95 The Carpenter said nothing but
"The butter's spread too thick!" **R1**

"I weep for you," the Walrus said:
"I deeply sympathize."
With sobs and tears he sorted out
100   Those of the largest size,
Holding his pocket-handkerchief
Before his streaming eyes. **R2**

"O Oysters," said the Carpenter,
"You've had a pleasant run!
105Shall we be trotting home again?"
But answer came there none—
And this was scarcely odd, because
They'd eaten every one. ○

The walrus and the carpenter have eaten all the oysters, from *Through the Looking Glass and What Alice Found There*, by Lewis Carroll, 1872.

Teach

R1 Reading Skill

Interpreting Ask: What does the Carpenter's reply in line 96 say about his feelings toward the Oysters? *(Possible response: He doesn't feel guilty for tricking the Oysters; he's just interested in eating.)* **AS**

R2 Reading Skill

Responding Ask: How do you feel about the Walrus's character? Explain your response. *(Sample response: I think he's heartless because he continues sorting the oysters, finding the biggest ones to eat, even though he claims he feels bad about playing a trick on them.)* **BL**

Differentiated Instruction

Illustrations Have students look carefully at the pictures used to illustrate this poem. Ask students to identify elements of the pictures that make them suitable for a poem with this tone and subject matter. Students should note that the images are unrealistic (*the man looks particularly odd*) and cartoonlike. Have students evaluate how well the images illustrate the art. If students feel they do a poor job, ask them what kinds of pictures they think would better illustrate the poem. **EL BL**

Objectives
• Identify literary devices: rhyme, rhythm, meter
• Interpret text
• Use text features: illustrations

473

Stress the importance of reading different literary genres that model what makes people who they are.

Fiction

Explain to students that reading fictional accounts of characters' experiences can help readers better understand what makes people who they are.

Ask students to tell about a fictional poem, story, or book they've read that shows how environment and experience shape who the characters are.

UNIT 4
Reading on Your Own

To read more about the Big Question, choose one of these books from your school or local library. Work on your reading skills by choosing books that are challenging to you.

Fiction

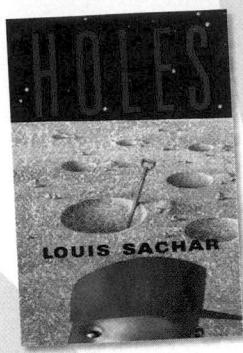

Dragon's Gate
by Laurence Yep

Fantastic characters on thrilling adventures—what more could a reader want? This tale has it all and then some! Read to find out what happens to Otter and Foxfire on "Snow Tiger," a mountain in the Sierra Nevadas, and about the many struggles they face.

Holes
by Louis Sachar

Funny, crazy, and full of Texas-sized characters, this strange story will leave you cheering for the underdog—whose name is Stanley Yelnats. Read about Stanley's adventures at Camp Green Lake and about the unlikely friends he makes there.

The Winter People
by Joseph Bruchac

When fourteen-year-old Saxo's village is attacked, he must track the raiders and bring his family back home. This book is a story of family, culture, courage, and survival.

The Wanderer
by Sharon Creech

Thirteen-year-old Sophie enjoys the ride of a lifetime when she sets out on a trans-Atlantic boat ride with her family. Read this tale of globetrotting adventure to find out what Sophie learns, and where she goes, while crossing the stormy sea.

Additional Support

Differentiated Instruction

 Use the Glencoe BookLink CD-ROM to create customized reading lists to help students answer the Big Question. Suggestions for Unit 4:
Grade 4: *The Barn*
by Avi
Grade 5: *As Long as There Are*

Mountains
by Natalie Kinsey-Warnock
Grade 6: *An Actor's Life for Me*
by Lillian Gish
Grade 7: *Amos Fortune: Free Man*
by Elizabeth Yates
Grade 8: *American Indian Women*
by Marion E. Gridley

Nonfiction

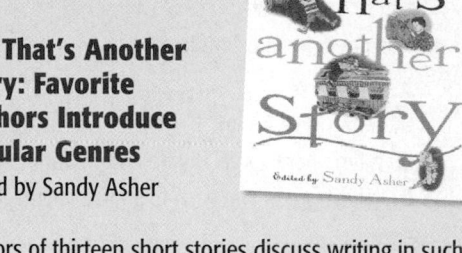

But That's Another Story: Favorite Authors Introduce Popular Genres
edited by Sandy Asher

Authors of thirteen short stories discuss writing in such genres as science fiction, fantasy, horror, and realistic fiction. Learn what makes a story from the author who wrote it.

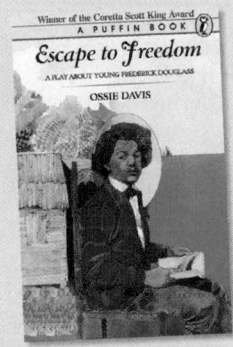

Escape to Freedom: A Play About Young Frederick Douglass
by Ossie Davis

Born a slave, future statesman Douglass endures cruelty and injustice before escaping to freedom. This play brings to life the hardships and triumphs that shaped Frederick Douglass.

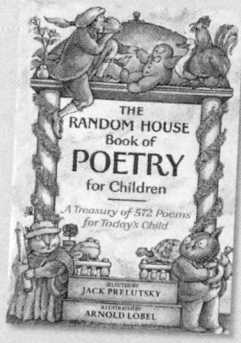

The Random House Book of Poetry for Children
by Jack Prelutsky

This collection of poems is divided into sections covering a wide variety of themes—such as seasons, nature, animals, children, and the city. Enjoy this collection of quick and engaging reads!

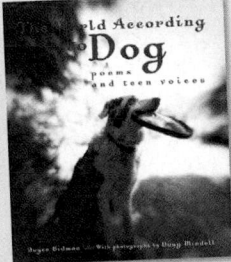

The World According to Dog: Poems and Teen Voices
by Joyce Sidman

This insightful collection of essays and poems explores the bond between teens and the dogs in their lives. The selections offer a look at how dogs accept us, love us, and help make us who we are.

Nonfiction

Tell students that all books on this page are nonfiction. The authors of the books tell about themselves or others and what makes them who they are.

BQ **BIG Question**

Ask: Why might reading one or more of these books help you understand what makes you who you are? *(The books are about real people with experiences, families, and communities that influence who they are. Students may identify with one or more of the real-life people in these books as they learn about what makes them who they are.)* **OL**

About the Subjects

Invite students to share what they know about the subjects on this page and which of the four books most intrigues them.

Test-Taking Tips

Tip Tell students they should read the poem, read the questions, and then read the poem again before they answer the questions. Because poems are generally shorter than prose pieces, they should have time to read a poem several times during a test. Each time, they will likely see a new element they did not notice before.

Tip Point out that students can use the process of elimination to guess the answer to difficult multiple-choice questions. Have the students read the question, and then read each possible answer to see if it could be correct. Tell students to eliminate any answers that are obviously incorrect. If students are left with two possible choices, tell them to make an educated guess.

Test Practice

Part 1: Literary Elements

1. C
2. D
3. B
4. D
5. A

Test Practice

Part 1: Literary Elements

On a separate sheet of paper, write the numbers 1–5. Next to each number, write the letter of the right answer for that question.

Use the following poem to answer questions 1 and 2.

Afternoon on a Hill

by Edna St. Vincent Millay

I will be the gladdest thing
    Under the sun!
I will touch a hundred flowers
    And not pick one.

5 I will look at cliffs and clouds
    With quiet eyes,
Watch the wind bow down the grass,
    And the grass rise.

And when the lights begin to show
10   Up from the town,
I will mark which must be mine,
    And then start down.

1. This poem is an example of

   A. free verse.
   B. a narrative poem.
   C. a lyric poem with rhyme and rhythm.
   D. a lyric poem with rich figurative language.

2. Which one of the following lines of the poem contains alliteration?

   A. line 1   C. line 9
   B. line 3   D. line 11

Use the following sentences to answer questions 3–5.

   1. Angry thunder rumbled in the sky.
   2. The wind cut into me like a knife.
   3. Steam rose from the still city streets.
   4. My fear was a prison, and I could not break out.

3. Which sentence contains a simile?

   A. Sentence 1   C. Sentence 3
   B. Sentence 2   D. Sentence 4

4. Which sentence contains a metaphor?

   A. Sentence 1   C. Sentence 3
   B. Sentence 2   D. Sentence 4

5. Which sentence contains personification?

   A. Sentence 1   C. Sentence 3
   B. Sentence 2   D. Sentence 4

Objectives (pp. 476–477)
Literature Identify poetic features • Identify sound devices: alliteration • Identify literary elements: simile, metaphor, personification
Reading Understand purpose of monitoring comprehension • Interpret text • Respond to poetry • Visualize

Part 2: Reading Skills

On a separate sheet of paper, write the numbers 1–5. Next to numbers 1–3, write the letter of the right answer for that question. Next to numbers 4 and 5, write your answers to these questions.

1. If you are having trouble understanding a poem, which part or parts are the best ones to reread?

   A. The first and last lines

   B. The parts you *do* understand

   C. The parts you find most difficult

   D. The parts with the strongest rhythm

Read the following poem and use it to answer questions 2–5.

XXXVIII

by A. E. Housman

Oh stay at home, my lad, and plough*
The land and not the sea,
And leave the soldiers at their drill
And all about the idle hill
Shepherd your sheep with me.

Oh stay with company and mirth*
And daylight and the air;
Too full already is the grave
Of fellows that were good and brave
And died because they were.

---

1. *Plough* is the British spelling of *plow*.

6. *Mirth* means "laughing gladness."

2. What is the main reason the speaker wants the listener to stay at home?

   A. The speaker needs his help with the sheep.

   B. The speaker wants him to remain safe and happy.

   C. The speaker fears that no work will get done if he leaves.

   D. The speaker knows he would do badly at another way of life.

3. All of the definitions shown below are correct meanings of *drill*. What would you interpret to be the meaning this word has in line 3?

   A. "A tool with a pointed end"

   B. "A mental exercise used to improve skill"

   C. "Military marching and practice exercises"

   D. "An approved way to accomplish something"

4. Respond briefly to this poem by telling whether you like it or not and why you feel as you do.

5. Describe one thing you visualize as you read this poem.

Test-Taking Tips

TIP Tell the students that even though the test directions begin with "Read the poem," it is often a better idea to begin by reading the questions that they will have to answer. It isn't necessary to read the question choices, but by reading the questions, they will be able to focus their reading on finding the answers that they will have to give later.

TIP Remind students to read each question carefully and to make sure they understand what the question is asking before looking for the answer.

Part 2: Reading Skills

1. C

2. B

3. C

4. *Sample Response:* I like the poem. It reminds me of something my father might say, telling his son to stay home where it's safe and happy.

5. *Sample Response:* I visualize an overflowing grave, full of soldiers in uniform, when I read the last three lines.

 Resources for page 476–479

 Use these resources to review, assess, or reteach the Unit: Active Learning, Note Taking Guide, Selection and Unit Assessments, ExamView Assessment Suite, and Skill Level Up!™ A Language Arts Game.

Part 3: Vocabulary Skills

1. C
2. B
3. C
4. D
5. B
6. B
7. C
8. A
9. A
10. D

Part 3: Vocabulary Skills

On a separate sheet of paper, write the numbers 1–10. Next to each number, write the letter of the right answer for that question.

Write the letter of the word or phrase that means about the same as the underlined word.

1. a perpetual problem

   A. unusual   **C.** everlasting

   B. important   **D.** complicated

2. to be stranded

   A. surprised   **C.** wounded

   B. abandoned   **D.** overly excited

3. inadequate clothing

   A. cheap   **C.** not enough

   B. unattractive   **D.** not suitable

4. an expression of woe

   A. pride   **C.** confusion

   B. excitement   **D.** deep sadness

5. to react sullenly

   A. quickly   **C.** with surprise

   B. in a gloomy way   **D.** loudly and angrily

Use context clues to figure out the meaning of each underlined word.

6. Unlike her **voluble** friend, Chrissie rarely said a word to anyone.

   A. rude   **C.** smart

   B. talkative   **D.** attractive

7. The damage to the vase was **irreparable**; it simply couldn't be mended.

   A. invisible   **C.** not fixable

   B. accidental   **D.** done on purpose

8. Marcy **loathed** olives, and I couldn't stand them either.

   A. hated   **C.** served

   B. bought   **D.** greedily ate

9. One can find spiders in every **abode**, from inexpensive apartments to huge mansions.

   A. home   **C.** jungle

   B. classroom   **D.** container

10. Canes, crutches, and wheelchairs can improve people's **mobility**.

   A. memory   **C.** general health

   B. understanding   **D.** ability to move

Objectives (pp. 478–479)
Vocabulary Learn and use new vocabulary • Use context clues
Writing/Grammar Identify sentence types • Use end punctuation correctly • Identify sentence fragments • Identify sentence elements: subject, predicate, direct object

Part 4: Writing Skills

On a separate sheet of paper, write the numbers 1–7. Next to each number, write the letter of the right answer for that question.

1. Which of the following is an exclamatory sentence?
   A. The game was exciting!
   B. Does anyone know this song?
   C. "Just go away," exclaimed Bo.
   D. A patient brother and loyal friend.

2. Which of the following is an imperative sentence?
   A. I didn't mean it!
   B. Open the window.
   C. What a crazy idea.
   D. No one came to the door.

3. Which of the following is a sentence fragment?
   A. The glass is full.
   B. Was the book good?
   C. I broke the window.
   D. Running happily in the yard.

4. Which sentence below has incorrect end punctuation?
   A. That's a surprise!
   B. Did you really say that.
   C. Nobody knew he could sing.
   D. If I asked, would you help me?

5. Which sentence below has a compound predicate?
   A. I took an apple and ate it.
   B. We saw Harry and his brother.
   C. Arabian horses are small but fast.
   D. Reba and Luanne are both runners.

6. What is the complete subject of the sentence below?

   Chickens do not deserve their reputation for stupidity.
   A. Chickens
   B. Chickens do not
   C. Chickens do not deserve
   D. Chickens do not deserve their reputation

7. Which sentence below contains a direct object?
   A. You must be crazy!
   B. She pointed to the sign.
   C. Read the story more slowly.
   D. My dog smells bad when he's wet.

Part 4: Writing Skills
1. A
2. B
3. D
4. B
5. A
6. A
7. C

Readability Scores Key
Dale-Chall/DRP/Lexile

PACING (DAYS)		INSTRUCTIONAL SEGMENT LITERATURE	READING SKILLS	LITERARY ELEMENTS
STANDARD	BLOCK			
1	1	**Unit Warm-Up, pp. 482–483** Genre Focus: "The Fan Club" by Rona Maynard **6.4/52/670**, p. 485	Fluency, TWE p. 481, 486 Drawing Conclusions, SE pp. 485, 489, 490, TWE pp. 486, 493 Understanding Cause and Effect, SE pp. 487, 489 Identifying Sequence, SE p. 489 Paraphrasing and Summarizing, SE p. 491, TWE p. 488 Connecting, TWE p. 482	Conflict, SE pp. 485, 493, TWE pp. 484, 492 Characterization, SE p. 486, 493, TWE pp. 484, 487, 488, 492 Dialogue, SE pp. 486, 492, TWE p. 484 Plot, SE pp. 488, 493, TWE p. 484
3	2	**Reading Workshop 1, pp. 494–515** "Street Magic" by Will Eisner **7.4/NA/180**, p. 498 "What Kids Say About Bullying" from KidsHealth.org **6.8/56/910**, p. 510	Drawing Conclusions, SE pp. 498, 499, 502, 504, 505, 510, 511, TWE pp. 494, 495, 501, 503 Connecting, TWE pp. 497, 509 Fluency, TWE p. 500	Dialogue, SE pp. 497, 499, 500, 504, 505 Review Stereotype, SE pp. 503, 511 Author's Purpose, SE pp. 509, 513, TWE p. 510
1		**Writing Workshop, Part 1, pp. 516–519** Writing Product: Short Story		Character, TWE p. 516
3	1	**Reading Workshop 2, pp. 520–543** "Tuesday of the Other June" by Norma Fox Mazer **4.9/47/780**, p. 524 "My Parents" by Sir Stephen Spender p. 540	Understanding Cause and Effect, SE pp. 520, 524, 525, 526, 528, 530, 531, 541, TWE pp. 521, 523, 540 Drawing Conclusions, TWE p. 524 Connecting, TWE p. 539 Fluency, TWE p. 539	Conflict, SE pp. 523, 528, 532, 533, 534, 539, 541, TWE p. 530, 531, 535

Unit 5 Big Question

The question, "How should you deal with bullies?" is designed to help students learn useful strategies for dealing with bullies.

Unit 5 Genre

Many of the selections in this unit are short stories. These selections will also help students answer the big question: "How should you deal with bullies?" Use these stories to help students recognize bullying behavior, and ways to prevent or stop it.

CRITICAL THINKING	VOCABULARY	WRITING AND GRAMMAR	LISTENING, SPEAKING, AND VIEWING

Evaluation, TWE p. 489
Analysis, TWE p. 491
			Analyzing the Photo,
			    SE pp. 488, 490
			Viewing the Illustration,
			    TWE p. 480

Evaluate, SE pp. 506, 514
Infer, SE pp. 506, 514
Apply, SE p. 506
Analysis, TWE p. 502
	Academic Vocabulary, SE p. 494
	Base Words, SE pp. 496, 498,
	    508, 511, TWE p. 502
	Context clues, TWE p. 496
	Idioms, TWE p. 499
	Vocabulary, TWE p. 508
		Write about your Reading, SE p. 506, 514
		Independent and Dependent Clauses,
		    SE p. 507
		Phrases and Clauses, SE p. 515
			Viewing the Illustration,
			    TWE p. 500

	Latin Words, TWE p. 516	Applying Good Writing Traits:
		    Organization, SE p. 517
		Independent and Dependent Clauses,
		    SE p. 519
		Theme, TWE p. 518	

Comprehension, TWE
    p. 526, 527, 534
Infer, SE pp. 529, 536, 542
Analyze, SE p. 536, TWE p. 525,
    528
Evaluate, SE pp. 536, 552
Synthesize, SE pp. 542, 552
	Academic Vocabulary, SE p. 520
	Suffixes, SE pp. 522, 524, 527,
	    532, 538, 541
	Substitution, TWE p. 538
		Write About Your Reading, SE p. 536
		Parts of Speech, SE p. 537
		Clauses, SE p. 543
			Analyzing the Photo,
			    SE pp. 526, 534, TWE p. 527
			Viewing the Art, TWE p. 540
			Talk About Your Reading,
			    SE p. 542

Readability Scores Key
Dale-Chall/DRP/Lexile

PACING (DAYS)		INSTRUCTIONAL SEGMENT LITERATURE	READING SKILLS	LITERARY ELEMENTS
STANDARD	BLOCK			
	3	**Reading Workshop 3, pp. 544–561** "Priscilla and the Wimps" by Richard Peck **5.6/55/810**, p. 548 "Let the Bullies Beware" by Rita Upadhyay and Andrea DeSimone **5.9/63/1000**, p. 556	Identifying Sequence, SE pp. 544, 547, 550, 551, 555, 559, TWE p. 545 Predicting, SE p. 549 Drawing Conclusions, TWE p. 548 Fluency, TWE p. 558	Plot, SE pp. 547, 548, 550, 551 Character, TWE p. 546 Titles and Subheads, SE pp. 555, 556, 557 Dialogue, TWE p. 555
		Writing Workshop, Part 2, pp. 562-565 **Writing Product: Short Story**		Dialogue, SE p. 562, TWE p. 563
3	1	**Reading Workshop 4, pp. 566–585** "Don't Let the Bedbugs Bite" by Ellen Conford **4.7/51/710**, p. 570 "The New Kid on the Block" by Jack Prelutsky p. 583	Paraphrasing and Summarizing, SE pp. 566, 569, 571, 575, 578, 582, 583, TWE p. 567 Visualizing, SE p. 574 Connecting, TWE p. 569 Fluency, TWE p. 571, 578	Characterization, SE pp. 569, 571, 572, 573, 579, 583, TWE pp. 574, 575, 576, 582 Point of View, TWE p. 572
3	2	**Reading Across Texts Workshop, pp. 586–597** "Bullies in the Park" by **7.3/62/930**, p. 589 "The Bully Battle" by Elizabeth Siris **6.3/61/1050**, p. 593	Comparing, SE p. 587 Identifying Problem and Solution, SE pp. 589, 590, 591, 593, 594, 595, TWE p. 586 Paraphrasing and Summarizing, TWE pp. 589, 595 Drawing Conclusions, TWE p. 590 Understanding Cause and Effect, TWE p. 593 Fluency, TWE p. 593	Author's Purpose, TWE p. 590
4	2	**Unit Wrap-Up, pp. 598–599** "El Enano" by Charles J. Finger **5.0/57/1190**, p. 600	Paraphrasing and Summarizing, TWE pp. 601, 605, 606 Understanding Cause and Effect, TWE pp. 601, 607 Identifying Sequence, TWE pp. 602, 606 Drawing Conclusions, TWE pp. 603, 605	Plot, TWE pp. 600, 603, 606 Characterization, TWE p. 601 Dialogue, TWE pp. 602, 604, 605 Conflict, TWE p. 603

CRITICAL THINKING	VOCABULARY	WRITING AND GRAMMAR	LISTENING, SPEAKING, AND VIEWING
Connect, SE p. 552 Infer, SE p. 560 Analyze, SE p. 560 Evaluate, SE p. 560, TWE p. 558 Synthesize, SE p. 560	Academic Vocabulary, SE p. 544 Prefixes, SE pp. 546, 549, 554, 556 Vocabulary, TWE p. 554	Write About Your Reading, SE pp. 552, 560 Commas, SE pp. 553, 561	
		Editing, SE p. 563 Revision, SE p. 562 Lead, TWE pp. 563, 564 Theme, TWE p. 564	Presenting, SE p. 563 Reading Aloud, SE p. 565 Visual Aids, TWE p. 565
Comprehension, TWE p. 575 Evaluate, SE pp. 580, 584, TWE p. 577 Compare, SE p. 580 Synthesize, SE p. 580 Infer, SE p. 584 Analyze, SE p. 584, TWE p. 577	Academic Vocabulary, SE p. 566 Roots, SE pp. 568, 574, 577, 578, TWE pp. 573, 576 Vocabulary, TWE p. 568 Context Clues, TWE p. 578	Commas, SE pp. 581, 585 Write About Your Reading, SE p. 584	Analyzing the Photo, SE pp. 572, 575, 579, TWE p. 570 Talk About Your Reading, SE p. 580
Analysis, TWE p. 587 Infer, SE p. 597 Synthesize, SE p. 597 Evaluate, SE p. 597, TWE p. 594 Comprehension, TWE pp. 591, 593	Parts of Speech, TWE p. 588 Word Parts, TWE p. 592 Prefixes, SE pp. 592, 594	Writing: Reading Across Texts, SE p. 597	Viewing the Illustration, TWE p. 589 Analyzing the Photo, SE p. 594
			Analyzing the Art, SE pp. 601, 602, 604 Analyzing the Photo, SE p. 605, 606, 607

Reading with Purpose offers a comprehensive package of tools to optimize student learning and the teaching experience. Each resource has been designed to assist students in specific areas and to offer instructional support for teachers. While all of these areas are covered in the core textbook, some students may need extra practice or additional help in specific areas. The resource package is designed so that you, the teacher, can choose which items will best assist your students. You may also use these resources as homework assignments and for assessment purposes. The following are resources recommended for use with Unit 5.

Keys for Unit Resources

- 📁 Blackline Master
- 📘 Workbook
- 📖 Supplemental Text
- 💿 CD-ROM
- 💾 DVD
- 📷 Transparency
- 💻 Web-based
- 📠 Fast File

Essential Instructional Support

FAST FILE UNIT 5 RESOURCES

Reading and Literature
- Academic Vocabulary Review
- Big Question: School to Home
- The Big Question Foldable
- Unit Challenge: Planner and Rubrics
- Comparing Literature Graphic Organizer
- Key Reading Skills
- Active Reading Graphic Organizers
- Literary Analysis
- Unit Vocabulary Review

Writing, Grammar, and Spelling
- Spelling and Handwriting Practice
- Grammar Practice
- Writing Workshop Graphic Organizer

Listening, Speaking, and Viewing
- Viewing and Representing
- Listening and Speaking

English Language Learners
- English Language Coach Review

DIFFERENTIATED INSTRUCTION

- 📁 Leveled Vocabulary Development
- 💿 Skill Level Up!™ A Language Arts Game
- 💿 Listening Library CD
- 💿 BookLink 3
- 💿 Literature Library Vocabulary Puzzlemaker
- 💿 Vocabulary Puzzlemaker

ASSESSMENT

GLENCOE'S ASSESSMENT ADVANTAGE

- 📁 Selection and Unit Assessments
- 📁 Selection Quick Checks
- 📁 Assessment by Learning Objectives
- 📁 Rubrics for Assessing Student Writing, Listening, and Speaking
- 💻 Glencoe Online Essay Grader
- 💿 Interactive Tutor: Self-Assessment
- 💿 ExamView Assessment Suite
- 💿 Literature Library ExamView Assessment Suite

Additional Instructional Support

WRITING, GRAMMAR, AND SPELLING

- Real Success in Writing: Research and Reports
- Writing Constructed Responses
- Spelling Power eWorkbook
- Grammar & Composition Handbook
- Grammar and Language Workbook
- Revising with Style eWorkbook

READING AND LITERATURE

- Active Learning and Note Taking Guide
- inTime Magazines
- Backpack Reader Volume 1
- Literature Library
- Literature Launchers Pre-Reading Videos DVD
- Literature Classics

TRANSPARENCIES

- Read Aloud, Think Aloud Transparencies
- Literary and Text Analysis Transparencies
- Bellringer Options Transparencies
- Grammar and Writing Workshop Transparencies
- Fine Art Transparencies

TECHNOLOGY

- TeacherWorks Plus™
- StudentWorks Plus™
- BookLink 3
- Skill Level Up!™ A Language Arts Game
- ExamView Assessment Suite
- Interactive Tutor: Self-Assessment
- Listening Library CD
- Spanish Listening Library CD
- Literature Classics
- Literature Launchers Pre-Reading Videos DVD
- Literature Library ExamView Assessment Suite
- Vocabulary Puzzlemaker
- Literature Library Vocabulary Puzzlemaker
- glencoe.com
- Online Student Edition
- Presentation Plus!
- Glencoe Online Essay Grader

ENGLISH LANGUAGE LEARNER

- English Language Coach
- Fluency Practice and Assessment
- inTime Magazines (Spanish)
- Spanish Listening Library CD

PROFESSIONAL DEVELOPMENT

- Professional Development Package

Additional Glencoe Resources

Dinah Zike's Foldables

Foldables are three-dimensional, interactive graphic organizers that help students practice basic writing skills, review key vocabulary terms, and answer Big Questions. Every unit contains a foldable activity. You can find the pattern and directions for the Unit 5 Foldable in the Unit 5 Resources Fast Files booklet. You can use the foldables as they are presented or modify them to suit the needs of your students. More information about foldables for Unit 5 can be found on pages R8–R9.

Unit
Big Question

Glencoe Literature Library

The collection of hardcover books includes full-length novels, novellas, plays, and works of nonfiction. Each volume consists of at least one complete extended-length reading accompanied by several related readings from a broad range of genres. A separate Study Guide for each Glencoe Literature Library book provides teaching notes and reproducible activity pages for students.

Glencoe Literature Library titles that complement this unit include:
> ***The Slave Dancer,*** by Paula Fox
> ***Taking Sides,*** by Gary Soto
> ***The True Confessions of Charlotte Boyle,*** by Avi

For a wealth of online resources that support the instruction in Unit 5 of *Glencoe Literature: Reading with Purpose,* students and teachers can visit our Web site at www.glencoe.com. Students will find additional learning, practice, and assessment opportunities such as these, which are noted in the student text:

- **Big Question Overview**
- **Study Central**
- **Author Search**
- **Writing Models**
- **Interactive Literary Elements Handbook**
- **Web Activities**

Teachers will find planning and instructional tools that include the following:

- **Book Lesson Plans**
- **Teacher Forum**
- **Professional Development**
- **Web Activities Lesson Plans (with answers to student activities)**

Go to www.glencoe.com to see the entire selection of Reading with Purpose online resources.

Reading List Generator CD-ROM

BOOKLINK

Use the Glencoe BookLink 3 CD-ROM, a database of more than 26,700 titles, to *create customized reading lists* for your students.

- Search for award-winning titles, (e.g., Newbery Award winners, Coretta Scott King Award winners, and Caldecott Medal winners) and for books on several state-recommended reading lists.
- Find Degrees of Reading Power™ (DRP) and Lexile™ readability scores for all selections.
- Organize reading lists by students' reading level, author, genre, theme, or area of interest.
- Get a brief summary of each selection.

You can find recommended leveled readings for this unit with Reading on Your Own (see page 608).

Glencoe's **Presentation Plus!**, a multimedia teaching tool, lets you present dynamic lessons that will engage your students. Using Microsoft PowerPoint,® you can customize the presentations to create your own personalized lessons. Use **CheckPoint** questions with interactive response keypads to get immediate student feedback during lessons, to increase student participation, and to assess student comprehension.

A lively collection of articles drawn from issues of the TIME family of magazines helps students develop the skills they need to interact with informational text in a meaningful way. Each of the news stories, feature articles, reviews, profiles, and essays in the magazine connect to an author, work, or theme in *Glencoe Literature: Reading with Purpose.* Articles for Unit 5 are found in Volume B. See the *inTIME* Teacher's Guide for specific connections to each unit and for reproducible student worksheets designed to develop students' reading and critical thinking skills.

Literature Launchers

Set the scene with Glencoe's Literature Launchers, engaging video segments that introduce each unit's genre focus. Each video brings the genre to life, relating it to your students' worlds.

Insert the Glencoe Literature Launchers Pre-Reading Videos DVD into your DVD player. Select the Unit 5 Launcher from the menu to introduce the genre and Big Question for this unit.

Online Essay Grader

Use Glencoe's Online Essay Grader to score your students' writing and to provide individualized feedback to each student automatically.

You and your students can visit www.glencoe.com to link to the essay grader. *Students* can enter their essays and receive feedback on demand. *You* can manage demographic data, assign tests and generate individual student and aggregated reports. The essay grader can help you

- Save time with automatic scoring and individualized feedback.
- Supplement in-class writing instruction using guided writing practice.
- Get reports for individual students or for special populations.
- Track student improvement over time.

REAL Success: Reading Excellence at All Levels

Glencoe now provides all of your students with the tools they need to become better, more enthusiastic readers. The REAL Success suite of reading and language arts products encourages reading excellence by meeting the needs of students at all levels. Glencoe products that can be used in conjunction with Unit 5 include the following:

- Jamestown Literature: An Adapted Reader
- Jamestown *Reading Fluency*
- Jamestown *Critical Reading Series, In the Line of Duty*
- *Vocabulary Builder*
- *The Glencoe Reader, Course 1*

To order these products, call Glencoe at 1-800-USA-READ.

Teacher Wraparound Edition Key

Level Appropriate Code

AS = Activities for all students

AL = Activities for students working above grade level

OL = Activities for students working at grade level

BL = Activities for students working below grade level

EL = Activities for English language learners

Teacher Wraparound Prompts

R **Reading Skill** These activities help you teach reading comprehension skills.

V **Vocabulary** These activities help students comprehend words and incorporate them into their reading and writing.

C **Critical Thinking** These strategies help students apply and extend what they have learned.

BQ **BIG Question** These activities and questions prompt students to prepare to answer the Big Question.

W **Writing** These activities provide writing opportunities to help students practice writing and comprehend text.

L **Literary Element** These activities and questions help students comprehend selections and learn more about each genre.

E **Text Element** These activities help students comprehend text elements.

LSV **Listening, Speaking, Viewing** These activities help students practice listening, speaking, and viewing skills.

EL **English Language Coach** These skills help English language learners as well as students who need additional reading support.

Doug Fisher

From an Author

Preparing Students to Read Short Stories

Set a purpose. In Unit 1, students learned about the importance of setting a purpose for reading. In Unit 3, they learned about previewing. This unit on the short story provides an excellent opportunity to review these skills. Remind students that they should preview a text before reading it. For the short story, this means spending fewer than 3 minutes figuring out who the characters are and what might be happening, the plot. In previewing a short story, students should focus on the beginning and end of the story, as these are important parts in short stories. Illustrations can also give students clues to what the story is about. Finally, students should generate questions based on their preview that they will answer during their reading.

Engage students with the text. Reading Workshop 3 in this unit teaches students about predicting. As students preview the short stories and other selections in this unit, you may help them learn to make simple predictions to pique their interest. Predictions also help students remain engaged with the text and comprehend the story. Start with the title. Ask students to speculate what the main idea of the short story will be based on the title the author gave to the piece. While predicting is important, and is a skill that students can learn to use, it is even more important that students learn from their predictions. Returning to predictions, verifying the guesses, and looking for missed clues when predictions are not quite accurate are also skills that students must develop. These same skills will help them as they analyze, question, and make inferences, which are the other skills taught in this unit.

Dianne Konkel
Cypress Lake Middle School
Fort Myers, FL

Teacher to Teacher

When I'm teaching the Big Question, "How should you deal with bullies?" I feel it's important to encourage discussion by drawing on the students' personal stories. I have students compile their own lists of suggestions of "How to Deal with Bullies" and "Why People Act Like Bullies." I tell them real-life stories of children whose lives were miserable because they were victims of bullies. One such story is about Jim, a boy who was so tormented by bullies at school, he felt he didn't want to live. On his way home from school one day, a group of boys deliberately bumped into him and knocked him down, scattering his books all over the street. Another classmate came along, helped him gather his things, and walked him home. The two became good friends through the rest of their school years, and on graduation day, Jim, who had become one of the top-ranked students in his graduating class, thanked his friend for having saved his life. My students usually connect very well to this real-life story.

Teacher Chat Room

Using Short Stories

 Why teach short stories?

 Short stories often contain structural and character elements that are familiar to students. These can be used as guides to help students think about the actions, themes, and contexts of the plot. For students who are not familiar with story grammar, short stories provide an excellent opportunity to develop or extend this knowledge base. Like longer pieces of fiction, short stories often contain characters, plot, setting, conflicts, imagery, and points of view. Each of these components can be analyzed in the short story so that students develop a stronger sense of these devices.

 What are the teaching points for short stories?

 As noted above, short stories can provide students and teachers an opportunity to develop an enhanced understanding of story grammar and literary devices. For example, students might focus on the role of characters while reading a particular short story and use the following questions to guide their reading:

- Which, if any, characters are flat or stereotypical?
- What motivates characters to behave as they do?

- How does the use of dialogue facilitate our understanding of the character?

In another short story, students might focus on point of view, using the following questions to guide their inquiry:

- Whose voice tells the story or provides the information readers need to understand what is happening?
- Does one character control the understanding of events, or do readers have an "omniscient" narrator who provides facts and insights that the characters themselves do not have?
- How does the point of view shape our understanding of the events and actions of the characters?
- What might happen if another point of view took charge?

 How can students be motivated to read short stories?

 To motivate students, remind them that short stories are a way that writers convey life lessons quickly. Ask them what they'd like to learn about life and tell them that they just might find this out in one of the short stories they'll read.

Key Unit Objectives

- Answer the Big Question
- Apply literary elements for analyzing short stories
- Apply strategies for reading short stories
- Write a short story

BIG Question

Why Is It Important?

Addressing this big question helps students learn useful strategies for dealing with bullies.

Viewing the Illustration

This illustration shows Doctor Octopus *(also known as "Doc Ock")* from the Marvel comic *Spiderman.* Born Otto Octavius, the esteemed atomic scientist became a criminal after a freak accident bonded a harness and four mechanical arms to his skin. The accident also changed Doc Ock, making him one of Spiderman's archenemies.
Ask: What does the illustration tell you about Doc Ock? How would you deal with Doc Ock if he bullied you? *(Possible response: The illustration tells me that Doc Ock is a frightening character with superhuman powers. I would probably have to have superhuman powers to deal with someone like Doc Ock.)* **AS**

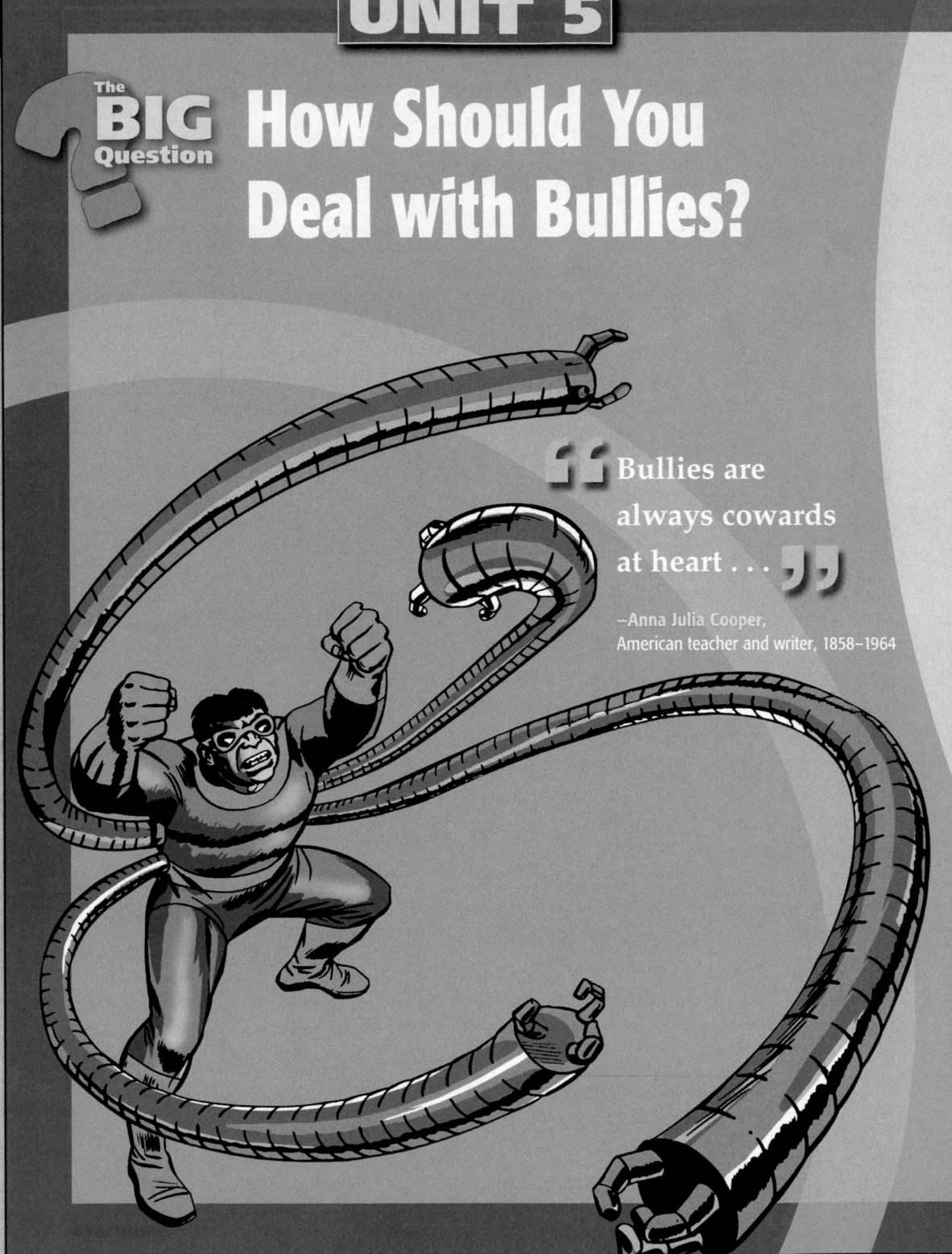

UNIT 5

The BIG Question — How Should You Deal with Bullies?

" Bullies are always cowards at heart . . . "

–Anna Julia Cooper,
American teacher and writer, 1858–1964

Unit Skills

Reading Skills

- Drawing Conclusions, p. 494
- Understanding Cause and Effect, p. 520
- Identifying Sequence, p. 544
- Paraphrasing and Summarizing, p. 566

Vocabulary

- Suffixes, p. 522
- Prefixes, p. 546

BIG Question — How should you deal with bullies?

Genre Focus: Short Stories

Literary Elements

- Dialogue, p. 497
- Conflict, p. 523
- Plot, p. 547
- Characterization, p. 569

Writing Skills/Grammar

- Short Story, pp. 516, 562
- Organization, p. 517

480

LOOKING AHEAD

The skill lessons and readings in this unit will help you develop your own answer to the Big Question.

481

About the Reading

Each selection in this unit provides insights that can help students address the Big Question, "How should you deal with bullies?" Students will assess how others cope with being bullied while analyzing and improving their own coping strategies.

About the Skills

The skills taught in this unit have been selected because they are particularly helpful when reading the featured genre—short story. Each reading selection provides students with opportunities to practice and develop these skills.

NO CHILD LEFT BEHIND

The goals of the NCLB Act include a strong emphasis on developing reading skills. One of the five areas in which systematic instruction must be applied is comprehension, or "the ability to understand and gain meaning from what has been read." Modeling the skills covered in this unit will help students improve in this area. For example, read a short passage from a unit selection aloud to your class and illustrate how to summarize it on the board.

Reading Fluency

Build Fluency One of the best ways for students to build reading fluency is to listen and follow along with a model. Because reading aloud to students should consume only a small percentage of your class time, try to obtain audiotapes of the unit selections with which students can work independently. If necessary, you may wish to contact community service organizations to have volunteers record selections onto cassette, or you may want to record them yourself. Encourage students to take the tapes home and practice reading with them on their own. Students should listen and follow along repeatedly until their fluency improves. **EL** **BL**

Focus

BELLRINGER Options

- 🔒 **Literature Launcher: Prereading DVD**
- 🖥 **Daily Language Practice Transparency 41**
  Focus Activity Write on the board: Have you ever been bullied or seen someone else being bullied? Write down a short description of the way a bully behaves. (*Responses will vary.*)

Teach

R Reading Skill

Review Connecting Ask students to write in their Learner's Notebooks about a time they were bullied or saw another person being bullied. Provide the following prompts:

- Who was involved?
- How did you or the person being bullied react?
- How would you handle the situation differently? **OL**

BQ BIG Question

- Have students work in groups to discuss the advantages and disadvantages of each of the three strategies mentioned in Lily's profile. **AS**

Connecting to The BIG Question — How Should You Deal with Bullies?

R No one likes bullies. Bullies tease people and call them names. Some bullies hit, kick, or shove people. Dealing with bullies isn't easy. They can make you feel afraid or uncomfortable. In this unit, you'll read about different kinds of bullies and how kids like you handled them.

Real Kids and the Big Question

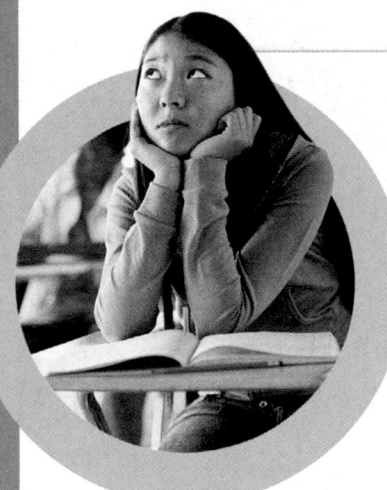

Lily is having a rough time at school. She has just moved to the neighborhood, and the classroom bully has started to pick on her. The bully likes to grab her backpack and push her around. Lily doesn't know what to do: tell the teacher, tell her parents, or fight back. What advice would you give Lily?

DENNIS is Eric's best friend. But this friendship doesn't seem to mean much to Eric. Eric does everything he can to make Dennis feel small. He makes fun of what Dennis wears and what he says. He's always telling Dennis what to do. When Eric's around other friends, he won't talk to Dennis. Dennis feels confused and hurt. What should he do?

BQ

Warm-Up Activity

Make a list of ways you think people can deal with bullies. Write a *L* next to ideas that you think would work best for Lily and a *D* next to ideas that would work best for Dennis. Compare your ideas with a partner's.

Additional Support

Differentiated Instruction

Book Search Have students search school and local libraries for nonfiction books that deal with bullying. If possible, have students check out several of the books. Students should then work in small groups to read the summaries on the back covers or inside jackets of the books and present the main idea of each book in a class booklist entitled "Library Resources for Dealing with Bullies." For a long-term project, assign each group a different book to read and have each group write a book report and give a group presentation about its assigned book. **OL AL**

You and the Big Question

People deal with bullies in different ways. As you read the selections in this unit, think about how you would answer the Big Question.

Plan for the Unit Challenge

At the end of the unit, you'll use notes from all your reading to complete the Unit Challenge.

You'll choose one of the following activities:

A. Brochure You'll work in a group to create a brochure about ways to deal with bullies.

B. Short Story You'll write a short story that shows how a character deals with a bully in a particular situation. To organize your story, you'll use a story map like the one below.

- Start thinking about which activity you'd like to do so that you can narrow your focus as you read each selection.
- In your Learner's Notebook, write your thoughts about which activity you'd like to do.
- Each time you make notes about the Big Question, think about how your ideas will help you with the Unit Challenge.

Keep Track of Your Ideas

FOLDABLES™
Study Organizer

As you read, you'll make notes about the Big Question. Later, you'll use these notes to complete the Unit Challenge. See pages R8–R9 for help with making Foldable 5. This diagram shows how it should look.

1. Use this Foldable for the selections in this unit. Label each page with a selection title. (See page 481 for titles.) You should be able to see all the titles without opening the Foldable.

2. Open each tab. Below the title, write **My Purpose for Reading.** You'll write your purpose for reading below this label.

3. A third of the way down on the page, write the label **The Big Question.** You'll write your thoughts about the Big Question below this label.

> Priscilla and the Wimps
> My Parents
> Tuesday of the Other June
> What Kids Say
> Street Magic
>
> Unit 5
> How Should You Deal
> with Bullies?

Reading in the Real World

Career Students may be interested in how beginning writers get their first stories published. Explain that writers must first choose a market and send their story to publications that are likely to publish it. Writers must then familiarize themselves with the styles and guidelines of the publications. This step is usually followed by writing a cover letter that includes a brief but catchy synopsis of the story. If the publication accepts the story, it may sell first serial rights, which entitles the publication to publish the story once, after which the writer still owns the story and may sell it to other publications. Have students research places on the Internet that accept student work for publication. **AL**

Teach

Big Question Have students access the Web site for English and Spanish summaries and annotated links to related Web resources.

BQ **BIG Question**

Have students write their initial response to the Big Question in their Learner's Notebooks. **OL**

FOLDABLES™
Study Organizer

For each selection they read, students will enter notes about how that selection applies to the Big Question. For details about using Dinah Zike's Foldables, see pages R8-R9.

Assess/Close

Ask students to share their thoughts about why looking for an answer to the Big Question might be important.

  Resources for page 483

📁 Use the Unit Challenge Planner BLM in the Unit 5 Resource Booklet, p. 35.

📁 Use the Foldable BLM in the Unit 5 Resource Booklet, p. 7.

Objectives
- Make connections from text to self
- Use text features: photographs

483

Focus

BELLRINGER Options

✏ **Daily Language Practice Transparency 42**
Focus Activity Ask: Aside from the amount of time it takes to read them, how does reading a short story differ from reading a full-length novel? Explain. *(Responses will vary.)* **OL**

Teach

L Literary Element

Dialogue, Conflict, Plot, and Characterization Say:
Explain how each literary element—dialogue, conflict, plot, and characterization—may be different in a short story than it is in a novel. *(Possible responses: **Dialogue:** Sometimes there is less dialogue in a short story, so readers must rely more on what the narrator tells them. **Conflict:** Conflict in a short story must be developed and resolved in a limited amount of space. **Plot:** The plot in a short story may be simpler than in a novel. **Characterization:** The characters in a short story may not be as fully developed as those in a novel.)* **OL AL**

A **short story** is a short piece of fictional, or made-up, writing about people, places, and events. You should be able to read a short story in one sitting. A short story shares all the elements of a novel, which includes setting, characters, point of view, plot, and theme.

Why Read Short Stories?

A good short story might teach you something about yourself or others. It might take you away from everything you know. Or it might remind you of people and places you know well. When you read short stories, you'll
• travel to new lands and meet new characters
• learn how characters deal with problems similar to yours

How to Read Short Stories

Key Reading Skills

These reading skills are especially useful tools for reading and understanding short stories. You'll see these skills modeled in the Active Reading Model on pages 485–493, and you'll learn more about them later in this unit.

■ **Drawing conclusions** Use the information from your reading to make a general statement about people, places, events, or ideas. (See Reading Workshop 1.)

■ **Understanding cause and effect** Look for the causes, or the reasons actions or events happen. Also look for effects—the results of the actions or events. (See Reading Workshop 2.)

■ **Identifying sequence** Look for clues or signal words that reveal the order in which events in the story happened. (See Reading Workshop 3.)

■ **Paraphrasing and summarizing** Paraphrase what you read by retelling it in your own words. Summarize by retelling the main points and important details in a logical order and in your own words. (See Reading Workshop 4.)

Key Literary Elements

Recognizing and thinking about the following literary elements will help you understand more fully what the writer is telling you.

■ **Dialogue:** conversation between characters in the story (See "Street Magic.")

■ **Conflict:** the struggle between people, ideas, or forces in the story (See "Tuesday of the Other June.")

■ **Plot:** a series of related events in which a problem is explored and then solved (See "Priscilla and the Wimps.")

■ **Characterization:** methods a writer uses to develop the personality of a character (See "Don't Let the Bedbugs Bite.")

L

Skills Focus

• Key skills for reading short stories
• Key literary elements of short stories

Skills Model

You will see how to use the key reading skills and literary elements as you read
• **"The Fan Club,"** p. 485

Objectives (pp. 484–493)
Reading Draw conclusions from text and experience • Understand cause and effect • Identify text structure: sequence • Paraphrase and summarize
Literature Identify literary elements: plot, conflict, dialogue, character

---

Additional Support

Literature Focus Lesson

Short Story Explain to students that because a short story is meant to be read in one sitting, an author faces certain challenges in writing one. For example, it may be harder to elicit sympathy for characters in a short story because the writer has less space to develop those characters. Similarly, a short story writer must not include more dialogue than is necessary, a limitation that may make the development of complex, realistic characters more difficult. **AS** To reinforce this concept, have students write a brief dialogue between two made-up characters. The goal of the dialogue should be to convey an important piece of information about each character in a limited amount of space. **AL**

THE Fan CLUB

by Rona Maynard

The notes in the side columns model how to use the skills and elements you read about on page 484.

Short Story

ACTIVE READING MODEL

It was Monday again. It was Monday and the day was damp and cold. Rain splattered the cover of *Algebra I* as Laura heaved her books higher on her arm and sighed. School was such a bore.

School. It loomed before her now, massive and dark against the sky. In a few minutes, she would have to face them again—Diane Goddard with her sleek blond hair and Terri Pierce in her candy-pink sweater. And Carol and Steve and Bill and Nancy. . . . There were so many of them, so exclusive as they stood in their tight little groups laughing and joking.

Why were they so cold and unkind? Was it because her long stringy hair hung in her eyes instead of dipping in graceful curls? Was it because she wrote poetry in algebra class and got A's in Latin without really trying? Shivering, Laura remembered how they would sit at the back of English class, passing notes and whispering. She thought of their identical brown loafers, their plastic purses, their hostile stares as they passed her in the corridors. She didn't care. They were clods, the whole lot of them. **1** **2**

She shoved her way through the door and there they were. They thronged[1] the hall, streamed in and out of doors, clustered under red and yellow posters advertising the latest dance. Mohair sweaters, madras shirts, pea-green raincoats. They were all alike, all the same. And in the

1 **Key Literary Element**

Conflict *I can see the conflict already. There's a conflict between Laura and all the cool, snooty kids in her school.* **L**

2 **Key Reading Skill**

Drawing Conclusions *I can tell that Laura is not a part of their group, because she calls them "clods." I think she wishes they were nicer.* **R**

---

1. **Thronged** means "crowded" or "pressed together in large numbers."

485

Teach

L Literary Element

Conflict Ask: What words or phrases give you clues that there is a conflict between Laura and the other students? *(Possible response: The narrator says that Laura has to "face them again"; Laura regards some of the students as "exclusive" as they stand in their "tight little groups.")* **OL**

R Reading Skill

Drawing Conclusions Ask: What conclusion can you draw about how Laura feels about her classmates? *(Possible response: She's irritated by the way they act, but she seems to want them to like her.)* **Ask:** What evidence is there to support your conclusion? *(Possible response: The author uses the word "hostile" to describe how they behave, but she also shows that Laura is bothered by how they exclude her from their daily activities.)* **OL**

Readability Scores
Dale-Chall: 6.4
DRP: 52
Lexile: 670

Differentiated Instruction

Build Background Some students—especially English language learners—may be unfamiliar with the types of clothing and fabric mentioned in the story. Cut out pictures from catalogs or print out images from the Internet to show examples of loafers, plastic purses, mohair sweaters, madras shirts, and pea-green raincoats. You may want to point out the following:

- A mohair sweater is made from the wool of an Angora goat.

- A madras shirt is a lightweight, often plaid, woven cotton shirt, named for the area in India from which it is imported. **AS**

Objectives
- Identify literary elements: dialogue, conflict, plot
- Draw conclusions from text and experience
- Interpret and analyze character

485

Teach

R Reading Skill

Drawing Conclusions Ask:
On the basis of the writer's description, what conclusion can you draw about Rachel's popularity? *(Possible response: She has very few, if any, friends in school.)* **Ask:** Which words in the text support your conclusion? *(Possible response: the words "alone as always")* **OL**

L Literary Element

Dialogue Ask: On the basis of the dialogue on this page, what do you think Rachel's attitude is toward Laura? Support your answer with examples. *(Possible response: Rachel respects Laura and considers her a friend. Rachel says that she liked hearing Laura's poem and wishes that she could write as well as Laura does.)* **Ask:** What is Laura's attitude toward Rachel? *(Possible response: She seems to tolerate Rachel, but she does not match Rachel's enthusiasm.)* **OL**

---

center of the group, as usual, Diane Goddard was saying, "It'll be a riot! I just can't wait to see her face when she finds out."

Laura flushed painfully. Were they talking about her?

"What a scream! Can't wait to hear what she says!"

Silently she hurried past and submerged[2] herself in the stream of students heading for the lockers. It was then that she saw Rachel Horton—alone as always, her too-long skirt billowing[3] over the white, heavy columns of her legs, her freckled face ringed with shapeless black curls. She called herself Horton, but everyone knew her father was Jacob Hortensky, the tailor. He ran that greasy little shop where you could always smell the cooked cabbage from the back rooms where the family lived. **R**

"Oh, Laura!" Rachel was calling her. Laura turned, startled.

"Hi, Rachel."

"Laura, did you watch *World of Nature* last night? On Channel 11?"

"No—no, I didn't." Laura hesitated. "I almost never watch that kind of program."

"Well, gee, you missed something—last night, I mean. It was a real good show. Laura, it showed this fly being born!" Rachel was smiling now; she waved her hands as she talked.

"First the feelers and then the wings. And they're sort of wet at first, the wings are. Gosh, it was a good show."

"I bet it was." Laura tried to sound interested. She turned to go, but Rachel still stood there, her mouth half open, her pale, moon-like face strangely urgent. It was as if an invisible hand tugged at Laura's sleeve. **3 4**

"And Laura," Rachel continued, "that was an awful good poem you read yesterday in English."

Laura remembered how Terri and Diane had laughed and whispered. "You really think so? Well, thanks, Rachel. I mean, not too many people care about poetry."

"Yours was real nice though. I wish I could write like you. I always like those things you write."

Laura blushed. "I'm glad you do."

---

2. ***Submerged*** (sub MURJD) means "put or went under, as in water."
3. A ***billowing*** skirt swells out.

3 Key Literary Element
Characterization *Interesting—a new character appears. The narrator describes Rachel as someone who is not very cool or popular.*

4 Key Literary Element
Dialogue *The way Rachel speaks shows a lot about her character.* **L**

Additional Support

Reading Fluency

Reading with Cues Very often, writers include cues—similar to stage directions—that indicate the way in which a character delivers a piece of dialogue. For example, on this page, Maynard writes, "Laura turned, startled. 'Hi, Rachel.'" Ask students to demonstrate how a character who is *startled* might deliver this line. Other cues in this scene include "Laura hesitated," "Laura tried to sound interested," and "Laura blushed." Have student pairs use the cues provided to practice reciting the dialogue between Laura and Rachel. Encourage students to switch roles after several minutes. Walk around the room and listen to each pair, offering suggestions when appropriate. **BL OL**

ACTIVE READING MODEL

"Laura, can you come over sometime after school? Tomorrow maybe? It's not very far and you can stay for dinner. I told my parents all about you."

Laura thought of the narrow, dirty street and the tattered awning in front of the tailor shop. An awful district, the kids said. But she couldn't let that matter. "Okay," she said. And then, faking enthusiasm, "I'd be glad to come." 🗐

Visual Vocabulary
An *awning* (AW ning) is a cloth or metal cover that acts as a small roof over a door or a window.

She turned into the algebra room, sniffing at the smell of chalk and dusty erasers. In the back row, she saw the "in" group, laughing and joking and whispering.

"What a panic!"

"Here, you make the first one."

Diane and Terri had their heads together over a lot of little cards. You could see they were cooking up something.

Fumbling through the pages of her book, she tried to memorize the theorems[4] she hadn't looked at the night before. The laughter at the back of the room rang in her ears. Also those smiles—those heartless smiles. . . .

A bell buzzed in the corridors; students scrambled to their places. "We will now have the national anthem," said the voice on the loudspeaker. Laura shifted her weight from one foot to the other. It was so false, so pointless. How could they sing of the land of the free, when there was still discrimination. Smothered laughter behind her. Were they all looking at her?

And then it was over. Slumping in her seat, she shuffled through last week's half-finished homework papers and scribbled flowers in the margins.

"Now this one is just a direct application of the equation." The voice was hollow, distant, an echo beyond the sound of rustling papers and hushed whispers. Laura sketched a guitar on the cover of her notebook. Someday she would live in the Village[5] and there would be no more algebra classes and people would accept her.

🗐 **Key Reading Skill**

Understanding Cause and Effect *Maybe Laura feels sorry for Rachel and that causes her to accept Rachel's invitation.*

R

L

---

4. *Theorems* (THEER umz) are basic math rules or ideas that can be shown to be true.
5. When Laura talks about the *Village,* she means Greenwich Village in New York City.

Teach

R Reading Skill

Understanding Cause and Effect **Ask:** What effect do the whisperings and laughter in the back of the classroom have on Laura? *(Possible response: Laura assumes that the students are plotting to do something against her and it makes her feel uncomfortable and rejected.)* **OL**

L Literary Element

Characterization **Ask:** Why does Laura think that singing the national anthem is "so false, so pointless"? *(Possible response: She thinks that people should not be celebrating freedom because so many people are still victims of discrimination.)* **OL** **Ask:** What does this show about her character? *(Possible response: It shows that Laura is a considerate person with strong values. It also shows that she feels oppressed herself and empathizes with others who are discriminated against.)* **AL**

Reading in the Real World

Citizenship Greenwich Village, the area in New York City south of 14th Street and west of Broadway, has long been a gathering place for poets, musicians, artists, and creative people who embrace alternative culture. In the story, Laura dreams of living in "the Village" because of its reputation for being a diverse, accepting place.

If your students are interested in learning more, have them work in groups to research places of interest and important figures from bohemian culture and the Beat era. Possible subjects for research include Caffe Reggio and Café Figaro, Washington Square Park, Bob Dylan, and Jack Kerouac. **OL**

Objectives
- Draw conclusions from text and experience
- Understand cause and effect
- Identify literary elements: dialogue
- Interpret and analyze character

487

Teach

Viewing the Photo

Ask: What scene from the story does this photo illustrate? *(Responses will vary. Students should support their answers with details from the text.)* **AS**

R Reading Skill

Paraphrasing and Summarizing **Say:** Summarize what you know so far about the cards that Diane and Terri are making. *(Possible responses: Diane and Terri have been laughing, joking, and whispering about making some sort of cards. Because of the comments she overhears, Laura thinks that they have something to do with making fun of her.)* **OL**

L Literary Element

Characterization **Ask:** How does the description of Rachel add to your understanding of her character? *(Possible response: The description shows that she does not fit in. She is somewhat messy and disorganized, and she does not appear to spend time thinking about her clothes or how she looks, which is very different from the other students.)* **AS**

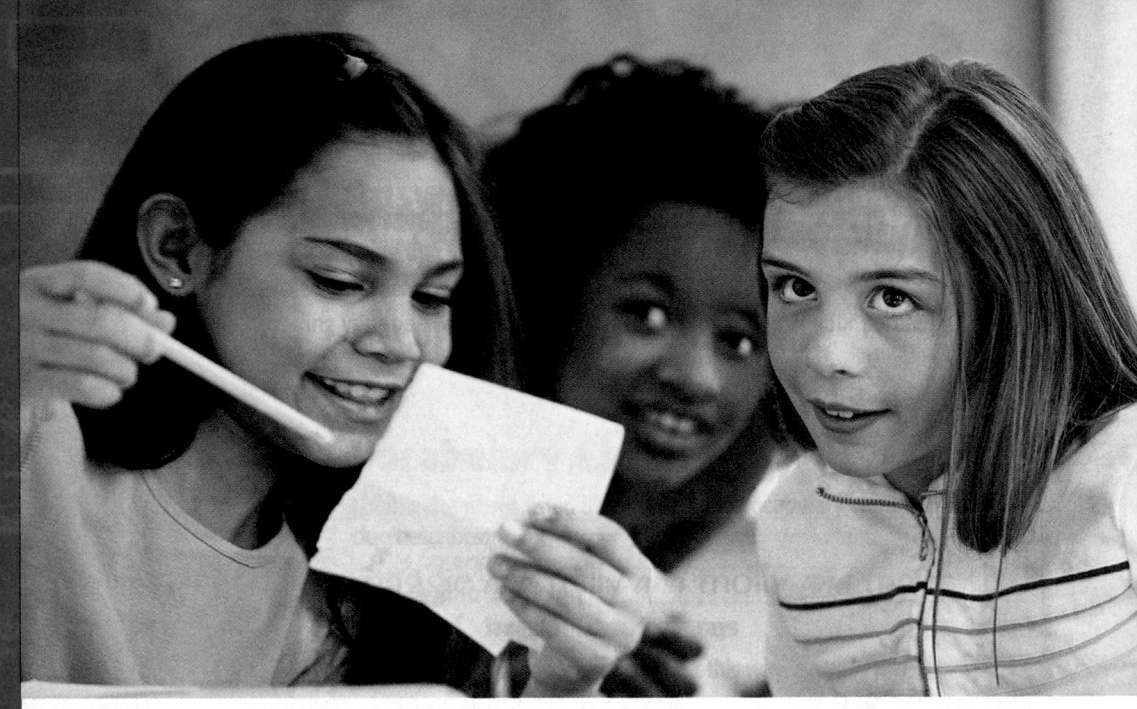

Analyzing the Photo Which characters from the story might these girls be acting like? Explain your answer with details from the story.

She turned towards the back row. Diane was passing around one of her cards. Terri leaned over, smiling. "Hey, can I do the next one?" **6**

". . . by using the distributive law." Would the class never end? Math was so dull, so painfully dull. They made you multiply and cancel and factor, multiply, cancel, and factor. Just like a machine. The steel sound of the bell shattered the silence. Scraping chairs, cries of "Hey, wait!" The crowd moved into the hallway now, a thronging, jostling[6] mass.

Alone in the tide of faces, Laura felt someone nudge her. It was Ellen. "Hey, how's that for a smart outfit?" She pointed to the other side of the hall.

The gaudy[7] flowers of Rachel Horton's blouse stood out among the fluffy sweaters and pleated skirts. What a

6. **Jostling** (JAW sling) means "pushing roughly."
7. **Gaudy** (GAW dee) means "too bright or showy."

ACTIVE READING MODEL

6 Key Literary Element
Plot *Those cards they're making must be important to the story. They might have something to do with the plot. I'll keep reading to see how they figure into the story.* **R**

L

Additional Support

Literature Focus Lesson

Narrator Without explaining specific types of narrators, prompt students to identify how the story is narrated. For example, ask, "Is this story told by one of the characters or by an outside person?" *(an outside person)* "Can the outside person read all of the characters' thoughts or just one character's thoughts?" *(just one character's*

thoughts) "Which character?" *(Laura)* Point out how, at times, the narrator's voice becomes the voice of Laura's thoughts, as in the following sentences: "What a lumpish, awkward creature Rachel was. Did she have to dress like that?" Have students find other examples in the story in which the narrator tells what Laura is thinking. **OL**

ACTIVE READING MODEL

lumpish, awkward creature Rachel was. Did she have to dress like that? Her socks had fallen untidily around her heavy ankles, and her slip showed a raggedy edge of lace. As she moved into the English room, shoelaces trailing, her books tumbled to the floor.

"Isn't that something?" Terri said. Little waves of mocking laughter swept through the crowd.

The bell rang; the laughter died away. As they hurried to their seats, Diane and Terri exchanged last-minute whispers. "Make one for Steve. He wants one too!" **7**

Then Miss Merrill pushed aside the book she was holding, folded her hands, and beamed. "All right, people, that will be enough. Now, today we have our speeches. Laura, would you begin please?"

So it was her turn. Her throat tightened as she thought of Diane and Carol and Steve grinning and waiting for her to stumble. Perhaps if she was careful they'd never know she hadn't thought out everything beforehand. Careful, careful, she thought. Look confident. **8**

"Let's try to be prompt." Miss Merrill tapped the cover of her book with her fountain pen.

Laura pushed her way to the front of the class. Before her, the room was large and still. Twenty-five round, blurred faces stared blankly. Was that Diane's laughter? She folded her hands and looked at the wall, strangely distant now, its brown paint cracked and peeling. A dusty portrait of Robert Frost, a card with the seven rules for better paragraphs, last year's calendar, and the steady, hollow ticking of the clock.

Laura cleared her throat. "Well," she began, "my speech is on civil rights." A chorus of snickers from the back of the room.

"Most people," Laura continued, "most people don't care enough about others. Here in New England, they think they're pretty far removed from discrimination and violence. Lots of people sit back and fold their hands and wait for somebody else to do the work. But I think we're all responsible for people that haven't had some of the advantages. . . ." **9**

7 Key Reading Skill
Understanding Cause and Effect *The bell ringing causes the students to quiet down.*

8 Key Reading Skill
Identifying Sequence *Okay, let me recall what's happened so far in the story. It's Monday, and Laura's at school. She thinks the "in" group is laughing at her. Rachel invites her for dinner. She accepts. And now she has to give a speech.*

9 Key Reading Skill
Drawing Conclusions *I think Laura is really talking about the "in" group and the advantages that they seem to have. The "in" group takes advantage of people's weaknesses and no one does anything about it.* **C**

Teach

R Reading Skill

Understanding Cause and Effect Say: You know that Rachel's appearance causes the other students to laugh and make fun of her. What effect does Rachel's appearance have on Laura? *(Possible response: Laura wonders why Rachel dresses the way she does. Also, Laura probably feels uncomfortable about being seen talking to Rachel in the hallway.)* **OL**

C Critical Thinking

Evaluation Say: Name another time in the story when Laura is concerned about discrimination. *(during the national anthem)* **BL Ask:** Why do you think that taking a stand against discrimination is so important to Laura? *(Possible response: Laura wants people to realize that discrimination takes place every day when people make unfair judgments about others.)* **OL**

Reading Fluency

Read Aloud The short paragraphs on this page are conducive to being read aloud by several students. Organize students into groups of three or four, and have group members take turns reading aloud, one paragraph at a time. You may want to walk around the room as students read to encourage good habits. Remind students to be courteous and to respect the fact that some students will read at slower speeds. Ask students to make a list of words that they have trouble pronouncing, and review these words with the entire class when the exercise is over. To shift the focus to comprehension, have each group write a short summary of the selected text. **EL BL**

Objectives

- Understand cause and effect
- Interpret and analyze character
- Evaluate text
- Draw conclusions from text and experience
- Identify literary elements: dialogue
- Paraphrase and summarize
- Use text features: photographs
- Identify and analyze narrator

Teach

R Reading Skill

Drawing Conclusions Ask:
What are the "narrow opinions" that Laura is talking about? *(Possible answer: She is talking about the judgments that students make about one another, such as regarding some of their classmates as not being cool.)* **OL Ask:** Do you think that the other students appreciate the point that Laura is making? Why or why not? *(Possible response: No; their faces are "empty" and "bored." The students in the "in" crowd are too caught up in whatever they are doing to understand that Laura is talking about them.)* **AL**

ACTIVE READING MODEL

Diane was giggling and gesturing[8] at Steve Becker. All she ever thought about was parties and dates—and such dates! Always the president of the student council or the captain of the football team.

"A lot of people think that race prejudice is limited to the South. But most of us are prejudiced—whether we know it or not. It's not just that we don't give other people a chance; we don't give ourselves a chance either. We form narrow opinions and then we don't see the truth. We keep right on believing that we're open-minded liberals when all we're doing is deceiving[9] ourselves." **10**

How many of them cared about truth? Laura looked past the rows of blank, empty faces, past the bored stares and cynical[10] grins.

---

8. **Gesturing** (JES chur ing) is using your hands, head, or other part of the body to show your thoughts or feelings.
9. If you are **deceiving** yourself, you are accepting something as true when you know it is false.
10. **Cynical** (SIN uh kul) means "mocking" here.

10 Key Reading Skill
Drawing Conclusions *Laura thinks that the "in" group doesn't give other students a chance and they form opinions about other students without knowing them.* **R**

Analyzing the Photo Does this girl look relaxed and comfortable about giving her report in class? What advice might you give her?

Additional Support

Differentiated Instruction

Making a Speech Have each student write a short speech like the one Laura makes about discrimination. Tell students to choose a topic or an issue that affects your school. Begin by brainstorming a list of possible topics, such as joining a team or club, or being bullied, and write these on the board. Then have students use Laura's speech as a model. For example, students may begin their speeches with the following sentences: "Most people (fill in the blank). Here in (your area), they (fill in the blank). Lots of people think that (fill in the blank)." Have student partners proofread each other's papers for spelling, grammar, and punctuation. Then invite students to deliver their speeches to the class. **OL**

ACTIVE READING MODEL

"But I think we should try to forget our prejudices. We must realize now that we've done too little for too long. We must accept the fact that one person's misfortune is everyone's responsibility. We must defend the natural dignity of people—a dignity that thousands are denied." **C**

None of them knew what it was like to be unwanted, unaccepted. Did Steve know? Did Diane?

"Most of us are proud to say that we live in a free country. But is this really true? Can we call the United States a free country when millions of people face prejudice and discrimination? As long as one person is forbidden to share the basic rights we take for granted, as long as we are still the victims of irrational[11] hatreds, there can be no freedom. Only when every American learns to respect the dignity of every other American can we truly call our country free."

The class was silent. "Very nice, Laura." Things remained quiet as other students droned[12] through their speeches. Then Miss Merrill looked briskly around the room. "Now, Rachel, I believe you're next." **11**

There was a ripple of dry, humorless laughter—almost, Laura thought, like the sound of a rattlesnake. Rachel stood before the class now, her face red, her heavy arms piled with boxes.

Diane Goddard tossed back her head and winked at Steve. **L**

"Well, well, don't we have lots of things to show," said Miss Merrill. "But aren't you going to put those boxes down, Rachel? No, no, not there!"

"Man, that kid's dumb," Steve muttered, and his voice could be clearly heard all through the room.

With a brisk rattle, Miss Merrill's pen tapped the desk for silence.

Rachel's slow smile twitched at the corners. She looked frightened. There was a crash and a clatter as the tower of boxes slid to the floor. Now everyone was giggling.

"Hurry and pick them up," said Miss Merrill sharply.

---

11. Something *irrational* (ih RA shuh nul) is not based on reason.
12. *Droned* (drohnd) means "spoke in a dull, boring way."

11 Key Reading Skill
Paraphrasing and Summarizing *The main idea of Laura's speech is that the United States isn't really a free country because many people are treated unfairly. She says that everyone needs to care about how people are treated.* **R**

Teach

C Critical Thinking

Analysis Ask: Do you agree that "one person's misfortune is everyone's responsibility"? Explain. *(Responses will vary.)* **AL**

R Reading Skill

Paraphrasing and Summarizing Say: Paraphrase what Laura means by "the basic rights we take for granted." What rights is she talking about? *(Responses will vary. Students may say that Laura is talking about the right to be treated fairly, without prejudice, as a citizen of the United States.)* **AS**

L Literary Element

Characterization Ask: Do you think that Steve's character is realistic? Do people really act this way? Explain. *(Responses will vary. Some students may say that it is unrealistic to think that a person would make such an offensive comment after hearing Laura's speech. Others may say that it is realistic because some people are cruel and unfeeling.)* **OL**

English Language Coach

Vocabulary Focus Because some students may have difficulty understanding the vocabulary words in Laura's speech, provide them with simple definitions or synonyms. For example, define *prejudice* and *discrimination* as "being unfair to other people," define *dignity* as "respect for yourself," and define *forbidden* as "not allowed." When students are comfortable with the definitions, have them go back and reread the speech, substituting these phrases for the original words. **EL BL**

Objectives
• Draw conclusions from text and experience
• Paraphrase and summarize
• Interpret and analyze character
• Analyze text
• Learn and use new vocabulary

Teach

L1 Literary Element

Characterization Say: Rachel's speech is about shells. What does this tell you about her character? *(Responses will vary. Students may say that Rachel appreciates beauty and that she is interested in life's simple things.)* **OL**

L2 Literary Element

Conflict Say: A conflict is a struggle between people, ideas, or forces. What is one conflict in the classroom? *(Possible response: Some of the students are making fun of Rachel as she gives her speech.)* **BL**
Ask: What conflict does Rachel probably have in her mind? *(Possible response: Rachel feels self-conscious and alone and wishes that more students liked her, or at least left her alone.)* **OL Ask:** What conflict does Laura probably have in her mind? *(Possible response: Laura feels bad for Rachel but is afraid to stand up to the other students because despite the fact that she thinks discrimination is wrong, she ultimately wants to fit in.)* **AL**

ACTIVE READING MODEL

Rachel crouched on her knees and began very clumsily to gather her scattered treasures. Papers and boxes lay all about, and some of the boxes had been broken open, spilling their contents in wild confusion. No one went to help. At last she scrambled to her feet and began fumbling with her notes. **L1**

"My—my speech is on shells."

A cold and stormy silence had settled upon the room.

"Lots of people collect shells, because they're kind of pretty—sort of, and you just find them on the beach."

"Well, whaddaya know!" It was Steve's voice, softer this time, but all mock amazement. Laura jabbed her notebook with her pencil. Why were they so cruel, so thoughtless? Why did they have to laugh?

"This one," Rachel was saying as she opened one of the boxes, "it's one of the best." Off came the layers of paper and there, at last, smooth and pearly and shimmering, was the shell. Rachel turned it over lovingly in her hands. White, fluted sides, like the closecurled petals of a flower; a scrolled coral back. Laura held her breath. It was beautiful. At the back of the room snickers had begun again.

"Bet she got it at Woolworth's,"[13] somebody whispered.

"Or in a trash dump." That was Diane.

Rachel pretended not to hear, but her face was getting very red and Laura could see she was flustered. **12**

"Here's another that's kind of pretty. I found it last summer at Ogunquit."[14] In her outstretched hand there was a small, drab, brownish object. A common snail shell. "It's called a . . . It's called. . . ."

Rachel rustled through her notes. "I—I can't find it. But it was here. It was in here somewhere. I know it was." Her broad face had turned bright pink again. "Just can't find it. . . ." Miss Merrill stood up and strode toward her. "Rachel," she said sharply, "we are supposed to be prepared when we make a speech. Now, I'm sure you remember those rules on page twenty-one. I expect you to know these things. Next time you must have your material organized."

12 Key Literary Element
Dialogue *The other kids are making fun of Rachel as she gives her speech. The dialogue shows that they are mean and spiteful. They enjoy making Rachel feel small and unwanted.* **L2**

---

13. **Woolworth's** was a chain of stores at which people could buy things for low prices.
14. **Ogunquit** (oh GUN kwit) is a seaside town in Maine where people like to vacation.

Additional Support

Literature Focus Lesson

Dialogue One element that contributes to the success of this scene is the rapid but smooth transitioning between narration and dialogue. To illustrate this point, distribute a copy of the page to each student, along with two different colored pens, pencils, crayons, or markers. Have students underline all of the narrator's words in one color and all of the dialogue in another color. You may also choose to do this on an overhead projector. When the activity is complete, ask for two volunteers to read the page aloud. Discuss how the constant color changes show rapid switches between narration and dialogue and how these "switches" add to the mounting tension in the scene. **AS**

ACTIVE READING MODEL

The bell sounded, ending the period. Miss Merrill collected her books.

Then, suddenly, chairs were shoved aside at the back of the room and there was the sound of many voices whispering. They were standing now, whole rows of them, their faces grinning with delight. Choked giggles, shuffling feet—and then applause—wild, sarcastic, malicious[15] applause. That was when Laura saw that they were all wearing little white cards with a fat, frizzy-haired figure drawn on the front. What did it mean? She looked more closely. "HORTENSKY FAN CLUB," said the bright-red letters. **13**

So that was what the whispering had been about all morning. She'd been wrong. They weren't out to get her after all. It was only Rachel.

Diane was nudging her and holding out a card. "Hey, Laura, here's one for you to wear."

For a moment Laura stared at the card. She looked from Rachel's red, frightened face to Diane's mocking smile, and she heard the pulsing, frenzied rhythm of the claps and the stamping, faster and faster. Her hands trembled as she picked up the card and pinned it to her sweater. And as she turned, she saw Rachel's stricken look. **14**

"She's a creep, isn't she?" Diane's voice was soft and intimate.

And Laura began to clap. **15** ○

---

15. Anything that is ***sarcastic*** (sar KAS tik) and ***malicious*** (muh LISH us) is meant to hurt or make fun of someone or something.

Think-Pair-Share Think about where and when you might use these skills outside of school: draw conclusions, understand cause and effect, identify sequence, and paraphrase and summarize. Share ideas with a partner. Then gather in a larger group to discuss how you might use these skills in everyday life.

 Literature Online

Study Central Visit www.glencoe.com and click on Study Central to review short stories.

13 Key Literary Element
Plot *Now I understand what the kids were doing earlier in the story. They were planning to humiliate Rachel all along.*

14 Key Literary Element
Characterization *The way Laura acts here tells me a lot about her. She's not as strong as I thought. She goes against her ideas about treating people fairly when she joins the others in making fun of Rachel.* **L**

15 Key Literary Element
Conflict *Laura is torn. She thinks that the group is mean, but she wants its members to like her. In the end, she gives in to the group to be accepted, even though her choice means turning against Rachel.* **R**

Teach

L Literary Element

Characterization Say: Think about what you know about Laura and what she says in her speech. How do you think she feels when she realizes that Rachel is the one being teased? *(Responses will vary. Some students may say that Laura is angry at the other students for being prejudiced. Others may say that Laura is probably just relieved that she isn't the one being humiliated.)* **OL**

R Reading Skill

Drawing Conclusions Ask: What conclusion can you draw from the last sentence of the story? What does Laura consider most important? Explain. *(Possible response: I can conclude that Laura would rather gang up on Rachel than feel like an outsider. Fitting in is ultimately more important to her than standing up for her beliefs about discrimination.)* **OL**

 Literature Online

Study Central Have students access the Web site to review short stories and to complete a related activity.

Reading in the Real World

College College admission essays often ask students to write about a time when they faced a challenge or hardship. Have students write an essay from Laura's perspective in which they reflect on the incident related in the story. Students should explain how they felt at the time the incident occurred and why they decided to act as they did, as well as how they feel about their actions now and whether they would act differently if given the chance to go through it again. **OL** As an alternate activity, have students rewrite the last three paragraphs of the story with a different ending. **AL**

Objectives
• Draw conclusions from text and experience
• Interpret and analyze character
• Identify literary elements: dialogue and conflict

Drawing Conclusions

**Objectives covered in
this workshop:**
• Draw conclusions about
events, characters, and settings
• Support conclusions with
text evidence and experi-
ence

Drawing Conclusions

Why Is It Important?

• Frequently in literature, conclusions are left to the reader. Authors are
often not explicit, preferring to let the reader draw his or her own
conclusions.

• Drawing conclusions allows students to consider the author's point of
view and how that relates to their comprehension and background
knowledge.

• Students can create new meaning by applying sound reasoning.

How to Help Students Get It

• Introduce the *if . . . then* clause. Ask students to consider different ideas
that can be added to this clause such as "If I miss breakfast, then I could
get hungry before lunch." Ask them how they knew what to add to the
"then" part. Tell students that these are conclusions–something known or
assumed based on the available information.

• In preparation for teaching students about drawing conclusions, list several questions that can be used to guide their thinking. These questions
should allow students to think about the information, but not give them
the information. The following sample questions might be helpful: What
conclusions can be made based on the details and facts? Do the facts add
up? How do you know the facts are accurate? What evidence does the
author provide? What facts/details support the author's conclusions? What
clues led to your conclusion?

• To cement students' knowledge of drawing conclusions, they should
regularly be asked to identify the evidence from the text that they used to
draw the conclusion. The key to drawing conclusions is to use what the
author provided, not to simply make up information or ideas.

Reading to Answer the Big Question

An amusing graphic story and an informational article in Unit 5, Reading
Workshop 1, will provide your students with ideas and information to help
them answer the Big Question: **How should we deal with bullies?**

Street Magic by Will Eisner
In this humorous graphic story, an immigrant named Mersh demonstrates
street smarts to his young cousin. Mersh knows when to keep quiet, when
to speak up, and how to outwit the bullies in their neighborhood.

What Kids Say About Bullying
An article from *KidsHealth* provides statistics to show the extent of bullying
in schools and informs students of some ways to deal with it.

Workshop Resources

Pacing (Days)		Lesson	Student Materials	Teacher Resources
Standard	**Block**			
1	½	Key Skill Lesson: Drawing Conclusions	🔖 Key Reading Skills Practice, p. 9 🔖 English Language Coach Review, p. 41	🖐 Bellringer Options Transparencies – Daily Language Practice 43 🖐 Read Aloud, Think Aloud Transparencies – Key Reading Skills 8 💿 Presentation Plus!
1	1	"Street Magic"	💻 Glencoe Online 🔖 Unit Vocabulary Review, p. 39 🔖 Academic Vocabulary Review, p. 42 📁 English Language Coach 🔖 Active Reading Graphic Organizer, p. 11 🔖 Literary Analysis, p. 10 💿 StudentWorks Plus™ 💻 Online Student Edition 💿 Literature Classics 📁 Selection and Unit Assessments, p. 49	🖐 Literary and Text Analysis Transparencies 13 💻 Puzzlemaker 💿 Skill Level Up!™ A Language Arts Game 💻 BookLink 3 📖 Assessment by Learning Objective (Diagnostic and Formative) 💿 Interactive Tutor: Self-Assessment 💿 TeacherWorks Plus
1		"What Kids Say About Bullying"	💻 Glencoe Online 🔖 Unit Vocabulary Review, p. 39 🔖 Academic Vocabulary Review, p. 42 📁 English Language Coach 🔖 Active Reading Graphic Organizer, p. 13 💿 StudentWorks Plus™ 💻 Online Student Edition 💿 Literature Classics 📁 Selection and Unit Assessments, p. 50	🖐 Literary and Text Analysis Transparencies 3 💻 Puzzlemaker 💿 Skill Level Up!™ A Language Arts Game 💻 BookLink 3 📖 Assessment by Learning Objective (Diagnostic and Formative) 💿 Interactive Tutor: Self-Assessment 💿 TeacherWorks Plus™

Keys for Unit Resource

📁 Blackline Master   🔒 DVD

📖 Workbook   🖐 Transparency

📖 Supplemental Text   💻 Web-based

💿 CD-ROM   🔖 Fast File

Level Appropriate Code

AS = Activities for all students

AL = Activities for students working above grade level

OL = Activities for students working at grade level

BL = Activities for students working below grade level

EL = Activities for English language learners

Focus

- **Daily Language Practice Transparency 43**
Focus Activity Ask: Has a bully ever bothered you or someone you know? How did you deal with the situation? What would you do if it happened again? *(Responses will vary.)* **AS**

Teach

R Reading Skill

Drawing Conclusions Say:
To help you draw conclusions as you read, write down the following steps in your Learner's Notebooks:

- First, gather information or evidence.
- Next, use what you know to make connections between pieces of information.
- Finally, make a judgment based on the information. **AS**

V Vocabulary

Academic Vocabulary Say:
Read the definition of *conclusion* on the bottom of page 494. In your Learner's Notebooks, make a word web showing synonyms for *conclusion.* *(Students' word webs will vary.)* **OL** **AL**

Skills Focus

You will practice using these skills when you read the following selections:
- "Street Magic," p. 498
- "What Kids Say About Bullying," p. 510

Reading
- Drawing conclusions

Literature
- Identifying dialogue in a short story
- Recognizing how dialogue helps develop plot, or a story's events
- Identifying author's purpose

Vocabulary
- Using base words to figure out word meanings
- Academic Vocabulary: *conclusions*

Writing/Grammar
- Identifying clauses
- Differentiating between independent clauses and dependent clauses
- Distinguishing between clauses and phrases

Objectives (pp. 494–495)
Reading Draw conclusions from text and experience

494 UNIT 5

Skill Lesson

Drawing Conclusions

Learn It!

R **What Is It?** Don't jump to conclusions! That means don't make a decision without all the facts. When you **draw conclusions**, however, you look at the facts before you make a judgment or decision. When you draw conclusions about your reading, you combine several pieces of information from the reading and your own experience. What you come up with is a conclusion about the people, events, or ideas in that selection.

- A *conclusion* is a judgment you make based on what you know.
- *Drawing conclusions* means creating bigger ideas from the information you read.

BALDO © 2004 Baldo Partnership. Distributed by UNIVERSAL PRESS SYNDICATE. Reprinted with permission. All rights reserved.

Analyzing Cartoons
What conclusion does the girl in the cartoon draw? What has she done to draw that conclusion?

V **Academic Vocabulary**

conclusions (kun KLOO zhunz) *n.* judgments or general statements based on information, experience, and observation

---

Additional Support

Differentiated Instruction

Building Background Hector Cantú and Carlos Castellanos began producing the comic strip *Baldo* in 2000. Its main character is a teenager named Baldo Bermudez. It is the first comic strip featuring a Hispanic family to appear in papers across the United States. The creators base their strip on their own experiences.

Castellanos says, "What we try to do is depict Hispanics in a very real way. . . ." Ask students why it is important that newspapers, magazines, television, and films portray people of different cultures in realistic ways. **AS** Then invite students to discuss portrayals of international cultures in the American media. **AL**

Teach

Why Is It Important? Drawing conclusions helps you find connections among characters, events, and ideas. It helps you see the bigger picture and understand what you read.

How Do I Do It? To draw conclusions, pay attention to details about characters, events, and ideas. Think about your own knowledge and background. Then combine the story details with your own experience to make general statements about people or events in the story.

Here's how one student used story details and her own experience to draw conclusions while reading the story "The Fan Club."

Study Central Visit www.glencoe.com and click on Study Central to review drawing conclusions.

> School. It loomed before her now, massive and dark against the sky. In a few minutes, she would have to face them again—Diane Goddard with her sleek blond hair and Terri Pierce in her candy-pink sweater. And Carol and Steve and Bill and Nancy. . . . There were so many of them, so exclusive as they stood in their tight little groups laughing and joking.

> *The speaker uses the words massive and dark to describe her school. She talks about having to face a group she describes as exclusive and tight. I conclude that she feels rejected by the "cool group" and that the situation makes her dread going to school.*

Practice It!

Write a conclusion you can draw from these facts.

1. Margo returns a library book by Will Eisner.
2. Margo checks out three new books by Will Eisner.
3. Margo asks a librarian whether she can place another book by Will Eisner on hold.

Use It!

As you read "Street Magic" and "What Kids Say About Bullying," try to draw at least one conclusion about the characters, events, or ideas in each selection.

Study Central Have students access the Web site to review drawing conclusions and to complete a related activity.

R Reading Skill

Drawing Conclusions Draw the graphic organizer below on the board. **Say:** Copy this graphic organizer in your Learner's Notebooks. Practice drawing conclusions by filling in the graphic organizer with details from the passage in the *How Do I Do It?* section.

Story Details	+	Reader's Experience	=	Conclusion

*(Possible response: **Story Details:** School is massive and dark, Group is exclusive and tight; **Reader's Experience:** Big, dark places are intimidating, Exclusive groups make others feel left out; **Conclusion:** The girl in the passage feels rejected and dreads going to school.)* **OL**

Resources for page 495

✎ Use Key Reading Skills Transparency 8 in *Read Aloud, Think Aloud* to help students practice drawing conclusions.

Reading in the Real World

Citizenship Share with students that the term *clique* refers to a close, exclusive group of friends. Explain that the term usually has a negative connotation because a clique often actively leaves out or rejects others. Ask students whether they have had any experience with cliques. As a class, discuss whether students think cliques are good or bad and how cliques are the same and different from bullies. **BL** Brainstorm ideas for ways that students can deal with cliques. If students feel comfortable doing so, ask them to role-play different scenarios in which students deal with members of a clique. **AS**

Objectives

• Draw conclusions from text and experience
• Learn and use new vocabulary

Teach

More About the Author

Will Eisner became interested in art during high school. Eisner's work was first published in his school newspaper. In the 1930s, Eisner and a partner established a drawing studio to produce comic strips. Eisner later created a comic section that appeared in newspapers across the United States. His adventure strip about a masked detective, *The Spirit,* was especially popular.

V Vocabulary

Context Clues Challenge students to write a sentence for each vocabulary word. Each sentence should include context clues that help convey the word's meaning. Point out that synonyms, antonyms, examples, related ideas, and definitions can all be used as context clues. **AS**

Before You Read | Street Magic

Will Eisner

Meet the Author

Will Eisner was born in Brooklyn, New York, in 1917. He died in 2005. Eisner was a great storyteller. Many of his stories come from his own experiences growing up in an immigrant neighborhood. Eisner chose to tell his stories with words and pictures in comics and graphic novels. See page R2 of the Author Files for more on Will Eisner.

Author Search For more about Will Eisner, go to www.glencoe.com.

Objectives (pp. 496–505)
Reading Draw conclusions from text and experience • Make connections from text to self
Literature Identify literary elements: dialogue
Vocabulary Identify word structure: base words

Vocabulary Preview

immigrant (IM ih grunt) *n.* a person who comes to live in a country in which he or she was not born **(p. 498)** *Mr. Toledo is an immigrant from Spain.*

hostile (HOS tul) *adj.* unfriendly **(p. 498)** *For your safety, it's best to avoid hostile areas.*

outrages (OUT ray jiz) *n.* violent or cruel acts **(p. 498)** *Bullies were responsible for outrages in the neighborhood.*

authority (uh THOR ih tee) *n.* a good source of information or advice **(p. 498)** *Mersh was an authority on bullies.*

application (ap lih KAY shun) *n.* the act of putting something to use **(p. 498)** *Mersh's kid cousin watched his application of survival skills on the street.*

Write to Learn Write sentences using three of the words correctly.

English Language Coach

Base Words Sometimes you will see a word that you don't recognize. Fortunately, you may know the **base word** in that unfamiliar word. A base word serves as the main part of a word, and it can stand on its own as a complete word. It carries the word's basic meaning. If you know the base word, you can often figure out the meaning of the word you don't know. Look at the word *survival,* for example. It contains the base word *survive.* If you know that *survive* means "to continue to live," you can guess at the meaning of *survival.*

Word	Base Word	Base Word Meaning	Word Meaning
survival	survive	to continue to live	having to do with continuing to live

What Do You Know? Write the base words contained in the following words:

1. odorous
2. magically
3. territorial

496 UNIT 5 How Should You Deal with Bullies?

Additional Support

Author Search To expand students' appreciation of Will Eisner, have them access the Web site for additional information and resources.

English Language Coach

Base Words Explain that a base word is a whole word that forms the "base" of a new word. Familiar base words can help unlock the meanings of unfamiliar words. For example, the base word *rage* is a good clue to the meaning of *outrages.* List the following words on the board and have students identify the base word in each:

- majority
- habitual
- magnetic
- informative

Then have students use what they know about the base words to write definitions for the words listed on the board in their Learner's Notebooks. **OL**

Skills Preview

Key Reading Skill: Drawing Conclusions

Skillful readers are always drawing conclusions, or figuring out more than what the author says directly. As you read the next selection, follow these steps to help you draw conclusions:

- First, look at details the author gives.
- Next, combine story details with your own knowledge and experience.
- Then, come up with a general statement about a character, an event, or something else in the story.

What's the Story? Write down an example of a time you have drawn a conclusion when you did one of the following: met a new student at your school; went to the first meeting of a new club; discovered a food you had never tasted; traveled to a new city.

List the reasons that caused you to reach your conclusion.

Key Literary Element: Dialogue

Dialogue is conversation between characters in a story. Writers use dialogue to move a story's plot forward. Most of the writing in a graphic novel is dialogue. The dialogue appears in balloons above or beside the characters' heads.

As you read, use these tips to think about dialogue in the selection:

- Identify the characters who take part in dialogue. *Which characters speak to one another?*

- Think about what you learn from the dialogue. The dialogue may show something about the character's personality, for instance. *What do the character's words tell you about him or her? Is the character funny, threatening, smart?*

Write to Learn Imagine that you and a friend are together in a leaky boat in the middle of a pond. In your Learner's Notebook, write a short dialogue that might take place between you and the friend.

Get Ready to Read

Connect to the Reading

Dealing with a bully is like solving a problem. Have you ever been in a situation when you were babysitting, cooking, or doing a homework project and had a problem? What was the problem? What did you do?

Think-Pair-Share Think about a time when you saw or experienced a situation involving a bully. Share the story with a partner.

Build Background

This selection is from Will Eisner's graphic novel *Minor Miracles.*

- Eisner was one of the first people to use the term *graphic novel* for a longer story told through dialogue and drawings.
- The story he had written was serious, and he didn't want to call it a *comic book.*
- *Minor Miracles* and many of Eisner's other graphic novels tell about the tough situations many kids deal with every day in their neighborhoods.

Set Purposes for Reading

BIG Question Read the selection "Street Magic" to find out how Mersh deals with bullies in his neighborhood.

Set Your Own Purpose What else would you like to learn from the selection to help you answer the Big Question? Write your own purpose on the "Street Magic" page of Foldable 5.

Interactive Literary Elements Handbook
To review or learn more about the literary elements, go to www.glencoe.com.

Keep Moving

Use these skills as you read the following selection.

Street Magic **497**

Teach

L Literary Element

Dialogue Ask: *What is dialogue? (Possible response: when characters in a story talk with one another)* **BL Ask:** *How does dialogue in a graphic novel differ from most pieces of writing? (Possible response: In most pieces of writing, quotation marks show when a character starts and stops talking. In a graphic novel, a character's words appear in a balloon.)* **OL**

R Reading Skill

Review Connecting Ask: *How were your own and your partner's experiences with bullies similar? (Students should utilize details from the Think-Pair-Share activity.)* **AS**

Literature Focus Lesson

Graphic Novel A graphic novel is a lengthy original story presented in a visual format. Will Eisner's *A Contract with God,* published in 1978, is often cited as one of the first graphic novels. Graphic novels cover many subjects and themes and are written for people of all ages. Have students do research on the Internet and at the library about the wide variety of graphic novels. Ask students to write a brief summary of a graphic novel discovered through their research and to share it with the rest of the class. These summaries may be put together in a class graphic novel book list, categorized by different types of graphic novels. **OL**

Objectives
- Identify literary elements: dialogue
- Make connections from text to self
- Identify word structure: base words
- Use context clues
- Analyze features of genres: graphic novels

Teach

EL Language Coach

Base Words **Say:** Understanding the meanings of suffixes will help you determine the meaning of unfamiliar words. Adding the suffix *-able* to a base word forms an adjective that means "capable of or fit for doing or being" whatever action the base word suggests. Use this knowledge to help you determine the meaning of *predictable*. *(Possible response: able to be predicted; happening or turning out as expected)* **EL** **BL**

R Reading Skill

Drawing Conclusions **Ask:** What does it mean to say that someone is an authority on something? *(Possible response: An authority has extensive knowledge about a particular subject.)* **OL** **Say:** The introduction says that survival skills were "not formally taught" and were "learned by emulating." How do you think Cousin Mersh became an authority on street magic? *(Possible response: Cousin Mersh may have learned street magic by watching his older relatives, and he may have learned through his own experience on the street.)* **AL**

Practice the Skills

1 English Language Coach

EL
Base Words What does **predictable** mean? The base word *predict* is a clue. If you know that *predict* means "to tell ahead of time," you can guess the meaning of *predictable*.

Street Magic

by Will Eisner

R **1** *Immigrant families on our block believed they were in hostile territory. Survival skills were brought from the old country. They were kept as magic spells the family used when dealing with the predictable outrages of neighborhood life. They were not formally taught. They were learned by emulating older and more experienced family members.*

Cousin Mersh, for instance, was an authority on the application of street magic.

KEEP YOUR MOUTH SHUT AND STAY CLOSE BY ME... THIS IS A ENEMY BLOCK!

YES, COUSIN MERSH!

Vocabulary

immigrant (IM ih grunt) *n.* a person who comes to live in a country in which he or she was not born

hostile (HOS tul) *adj.* unfriendly

outrages (OUT ray jiz) *n.* violent or cruel acts

authority (uh THOR ih tee) *n.* a good source of information or advice

application (ap lih KAY shun) *n.* the act of putting something to use

498 UNIT 5 How Should You Deal with Bullies?

Additional Support

498

Differentiated Instruction

Building Characters Through Dialogue Remind students that dialogue is one way for an author to develop characters. Therefore, dialogue helps show the traits of a character. A character who is thirteen years old and likes skateboarding would speak very differently than would a middle-aged businessperson. Often, dialogue does not follow standard grammar or spelling conventions. Point out that Mersh says "a enemy" rather than "an enemy." Discuss with students what they learn about Mersh from the dialogue on this page. **EL** **OL**

Practice the Skills

2 Key Literary Element

Dialogue What can you tell about the men so far based on their conversation?

Teach

L Literary Element

Dialogue Say: The dialogue in this story contains a great deal of slang, or informal language. Why do you think the author has the characters use slang? *(Possible response: Slang is part of everyday speech or conversation, and it makes the characters and dialogue seem more realistic.)* **OL**

R Reading Skill

Drawing Conclusions Say: Mersh walks down a street on which he has already been beaten up. Why do you think Mersh goes down that street again? *(Responses will vary. Students may suggest that Mersh does not want the bullies to feel that they have succeeded in scaring him off, or that he wants his young cousin to learn from direct experience.)* **OL**

English Language Coach

Idiomatic Expressions To enhance students' comprehension of the story, have them compile glossaries that explain the meaning of idioms and informal words and expressions in the story. Help students get started with these words and phrases:

Li'l: short way of saying "little"
Sheesh: interjection that expresses surprise

Gonna: short form of "going to"
Gimme: short form of "give me"
Yer: "your"
Whatchoo: short form of "What are you?"

Students may add to their glossaries as they continue to read. **AS**

Objectives
• Draw conclusions from text and experience
• Identify literary elements: dialogue
• Identify word structure: base words
• Understand idioms

499

Teach

Viewing the Illustration

Ask: What elements of the illustrations show that the three men are bullies? *(Possible response: They are much bigger than Mersh and his young cousin and they have mean expressions on their faces.)* **OL**

L Literary Element

Dialogue Ask: After reading the dialogue on this page, who do you think is the leader among the bullies? Explain your answer. *(Possible response: The man holding the hat is the leader because he thinks of the plan for tricking Mersh.)* **OL**

Ask: What do the bullies intend to do so that they can beat up Mersh "fairly"? *(Possible response: The bullies will put two pieces of paper in a hat. Both pieces of paper have the word* guilty *written on them. Mersh will have to draw one, and if it says* guilty, *the bullies will beat him up. Because* guilty *appears on both pieces of paper, Mersh will be beaten no matter which piece of paper he selects.)* **AS**

Practice the Skills

3 **Key Literary Element**

Dialogue In a short story, there are usually quotation marks and words that show who is speaking, such as *said John.* Why aren't there quotation marks in this story? How can you tell who is speaking?

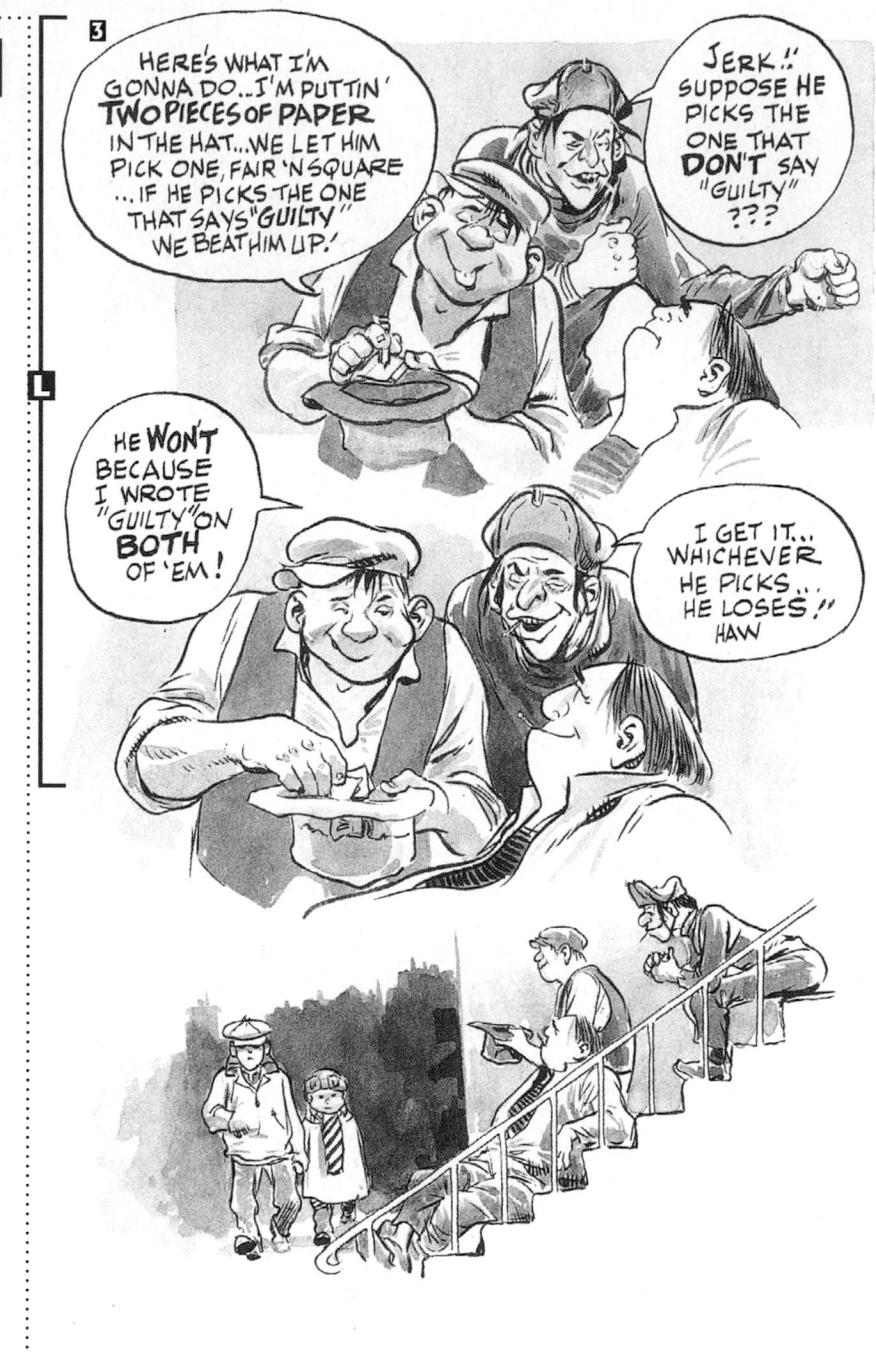

Additional Support

Reading Fluency

Build Fluency Have students form groups of three and take the parts of the three bullies. Have students practice reading aloud the dialogue between the bullies on pages 499 and 500. Circulate among the groups as they practice, checking students' pronunciation of slang in the dialogue. Correct students' delivery as necessary. On the second and third readings, remind students to pay close attention to punctuation and to read their parts with expression. When students can read with both understanding and expression, they should change parts and repeat the exercise. **EL** **BL**

Practice the Skills

4 **BIG Question**

How does Mersh respond to the bullies' warning that they don't want him and his cousin on their block? (Hint: What doesn't Mersh do?) Write your answer on the "Street Magic" page of Foldable 5. Your response will help you answer the Unit Challenge later.

BQ

Street Magic **501**

Teach

R Reading Skill

Drawing Conclusions Say: From what you have read so far, you know that the bullies intend to beat up Mersh. Why, then, do they tell him, "We're gonna give you a break"? *(Responses will vary. Students should conclude that the bullies are trying to trick Mersh because they don't want him to suspect anything. The bullies probably tell Mersh that he's getting a break so that he will let down his guard.)* **OL**

BQ **BIG Question**

Ask: From what you know of the bullies' plan, what advice would you give Mersh and his cousin about dealing with the bullies? *(Responses will vary. Students may say that they would tell Mersh and his cousin to ignore the bullies and keep walking.)* **OL**

Differentiated Instruction

Drawing a Character Ask students to close their eyes and listen closely as you read aloud the bullies' dialogue on pages 500–501. Then ask students to draw a picture of a person or people who would say what the bullies say. Remind students that in a graphic novel, illustrations replace description by a narrator.

Creators of graphic novels must develop their characters through illustrations as well as through dialogue. Tell students that someone looking at their illustrations should be able to tell that the characters are bullies. Encourage students to be creative and draw without thinking about Eisner's depictions of the bullies. **AS**

Objectives
• Draw conclusions from text and experience
• Identify literary elements: dialogue
• Use text features: illustrations

501

Teach

C Critical Thinking

Analysis Ask: If Mersh has had trouble with these bullies before, why do you think he goes along with drawing a piece of paper from the hat? *(Possible response: Mersh knows that the bullies are probably trying to trick him, and he thinks that if he plays along, he can out-smart them instead.)* **OL AL**

R Reading Skill

Drawing Conclusions Say: Look at the bullies' faces in the frame where Mersh draws a piece of paper from the hat. What do their faces tell you about how the bullies feel? *(Possible response: Their grins show that they think they have tricked Mersh.)* **Ask:** What does Mersh's cousin's expression and posture tell you about how he feels? Explain. *(Possible response: The cousin stands behind Mersh for protection. His eyes are wide as he watches what is happening, and he is probably nervous or frightened.)* **OL**

Practice the Skills

5 Key Reading Skill

Drawing Conclusions
Can you draw any conclusions about what the bullies might be expecting? What facts have you learned so far? What do you know about bullies?

5

C

R

502 UNIT 5 How Should You Deal with Bullies?

Additional Support

English Language Coach

Base Words Write the word *guilty* on the board, and ask students what base word it contains. *(guilt)* Tell students that adding a prefix or suffix to a base word changes the meaning of the word. Sometimes the change is small. A *guilty* look is one that shows *guilt*. However, sometimes the change is major. Someone who is *guiltless* has no guilt, or is innocent. As a class, make a chart of words containing the base word *guilt*. Then discuss the words' meanings. Caution students to watch for spelling changes when adding suffixes. Have them use a dictionary for help with finding words and with spelling. **EL OL**

Practice the Skills

6 **Key Reading Skill**

Drawing Conclusions Look closely at the drawings and think about what you've learned about these bullies. What do you think their attitude is toward Mersh?

OKAY, WHAT DOES IT SAY?

OPEN IT!! OPEN IT!!

Teach

L Literary Element

Review Stereotyping

Ask: How do you know right away that the characters waiting to beat up Mersh are bullies? *(Possible response: The characters talk about beating up Mersh. They look big and mean—the way bullies usually look in cartoons.)* **OL** Do you think the author also creates a stereotype of people bullies pick on? Explain your answer. *(Possible response: By making Cousin Mersh much smaller than the bullies and showing him with a child, the author suggests that small people and children are targets for bullies.)* **AL**

R Reading Skill

Drawing Conclusions **Ask:**

What can you conclude about the way the bullies feel as they wait for Mersh to read the piece of paper? Explain. *(Possible response: The bullies are confident that their trick is working, a conclusion that you can draw from their smiles. Their actions—making fists and rolling up their sleeves—show that they are getting ready to attack Mersh.)* **OL**

Differentiated Instruction

Thought Balloons On the board, draw a typical thought balloon, with a cloudlike border and a chain of smaller balloons that connect the larger balloon to the character. Explain that this type of balloon is known as a "thought" balloon and that it is often used in graphic novels or comic strips to show what a character is thinking. Have students draw and fill in a thought balloon for each character in the top frame of page 503 to show what Mersh, his kid cousin, and the bullies may be thinking. Invite students to share their thought balloons with the rest of the class. **AS**

Objectives
• Draw conclusions from text and experience
• Identify literary elements: dialogue and stereotype
• Identify word structure: base words

503

Teach

L Literary Element

Dialogue Ask: Why do you think the writer put a word of dialogue in bold print in the middle picture? *(Possible response: The bold print emphasizes the word, showing the bully's disbelief that Mersh would do something as crazy as swallowing a piece of paper.)* **OL Ask:** What does the bold print tell you about how the word would sound if read aloud? *(Possible response: The word would be read with extra stress and expression.)* **BL**

R Reading Skill

Drawing Conclusions Ask: Do you think that Mersh had a plan or strategy for dealing with the bullies? Why or why not? *(Responses will vary. Students may say that Mersh probably intended to let the bullies make the first move and then try to outsmart them.)* **OL**

Practice the Skills

7 Key Literary Element

L
Dialogue The bully says "Er...guilty." How does this piece of dialogue help you learn more about the bully and how he feels now?

8 Key Reading Skill

R
Drawing Conclusions At the beginning of the story, you learn that Mersh is an authority on using street magic. Now you have seen how he responds to the bullies. What conclusions can you draw about Mersh? How did he become an authority?

504 UNIT 5 How Should You Deal with Bullies?

Additional Support

Reading in the Real World

Career The U.S. market for graphic novels is one of the fastest growing in publishing, with annual sales topping $100 million. Readers of graphic novels find the visual format and extensive range of themes and subject matter appealing. Graphic novels today focus not only on superheroes but also on everyday people and their struggles. Encourage students interested in the genre to learn about the skills and education needed to create or publish graphic novels. Ask students to take notes in these areas: Job Description, Career Outlook, Skills, and Education. **AL**

Practice the Skills

9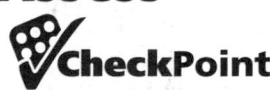

9 **Key Literary Element**

Dialogue What do you learn from the dialogue between Mersh and his cousin?

10 **BIG Question**

How does Mersh deal with the bullies in this story? Write your answer on the "Street Magic" page of Foldable 5. Your response will help you answer the Unit Challenge later.

BQ

Street Magic **505**

Teach

R **Reading Skill**

Drawing Conclusions **Ask:** What conclusion does Mersh draw about the piece of paper that he swallowed? *(He says it was the blank piece.)* **AS**
Ask: What reason does Mersh give for swallowing the paper? *(Mersh says that he swallowed the paper just in case the bullies were cheating.)* **BL**

BQ **BIG Question**

Ask: What do you think Mersh's cousin would say he learned from Mersh about dealing with bullies? *(Possible response: If you let the bullies make the first move, you may be able to outsmart them.)* **OL**

Assess

CheckPoint

Use the CheckPoint questions provided on Presentation Plus! to check for comprehension of the selection. These questions can be used with interactive response keypads for immediate student feedback.

Differentiated Instruction

Story Map On the board, draw a story map like the one shown below. To check comprehension, have students copy the story map in their Learner's Notebooks. Ask students to fill in key story elements and events. Then have students use their story maps as a reference as they retell the story. **EL** **BL**

Setting and Characters
↓
Beginning Events
↓
Middle Events
↓
Ending

Objectives
• Draw conclusions from text and experience
• Identify literary elements: dialogue

505

Assess

Resources for page 506

- Selection Quick Check, p. 41
- Selection and Unit Assessments, p. 49
- ExamView Assessment Suite
- Interactive Tutor: Self-Assessment

Students can respond to the *After You Read* items in their Learner's Notebooks or on a separate sheet of paper.

Answering the

1. Responses will vary.
2. He knows what to do in situations on the street.
3. He tells his cousin to keep his mouth shut, to stay close to him, to keep walking, and to avoid looking back.

Critical Thinking

4. Possible response: The bullies do not treat Mersh fairly. They act as though they are offering him a chance to go unharmed if he draws the right piece of paper from the hat, but both pieces of paper say the same thing: guilty.

5. Responses will vary. Students may observe that the immigrants' survival skills seem to help them get out of difficult situations magically or that the survival skills seem to have a magical effect on bullies.

6. Responses will vary. Students should cite specific techniques that Mersh uses.

After You Read Street Magic

Answering the BIG Question

1. What ideas for dealing with bullies did this selection give you?
2. **Recall** What is Cousin Mersh's special area of knowledge or experience?
   Tip Right There
3. **Recall** What instructions does Mersh give his young cousin while they are out walking?
   Tip Right There

Critical Thinking

4. **Evaluate** Do the bullies treat Mersh "fair and square"? Explain.
   Tip Author and Me

5. **Interpret** Why does the author call the immigrants' survival skills magic spells or street magic?
   Tip Author and Me

6. **Apply** Which of Mersh's ways of dealing with bullies do you think would work best for you?
   Tip On My Own

Write About Your Reading

Pretend you are Mersh. Make a list for the young kids in your neighborhood about ways to deal with the local bullies. To get started with your list, think about
- the advice that Mersh gives his cousin as they enter the "enemy block."
- Mersh's body language as the bullies approach him and talk to him.
- what Mersh says (or doesn't say) to the bullies.
- how Mersh outsmarts the bullies.
- the advice that Mersh gives his cousin as they walk away from the bullies.

Objectives (pp. 506–507)
Reading Draw conclusions from text and experience • Make connections from text to self
Literature Identify literary elements: dialogue
Vocabulary Identify word structure: base words
Writing Respond to literature: list
Grammar Identify sentence elements: independent and dependent clauses

506 UNIT 5 How Should You Deal with Bullies?

Write About Your Reading

Possible response:
Here are three tips for dealing with bullies: If a bully says something to you, don't say anything back. Never let a bully know what you're thinking or feeling. Keep walking when you see a bully. Follow these tips, and bullies won't have a chance to get their way.

Skills Review

Key Reading Skill: Drawing Conclusions

When you draw a conclusion about something in a story, you combine story details with your own knowledge and experience to make a general statement.

7. How do the bullies feel about Mersh's response to their trick? How can you tell?

8. After reading this story, what conclusion can you draw about what bullies are like? Support your conclusion with details from the story.

Key Literary Element: Dialogue

9. Which characters use the most dialogue in this story?

10. What does Mersh's lack of dialogue tell you about him as a character?

11. What can you tell about Mersh's cousin from what he says?

Vocabulary Check

Match each vocabulary word with the clue that best describes the word.

immigrant   outrages   hostile
authority   application

12. actions meant to hurt someone

13. a person born in Germany who lives in Canada

14. rude and unkind

15. the use of something for a certain purpose

16. an expert

17. **Academic Vocabulary** If you saw people outside wearing heavy jackets and ski hats, what *conclusion* might you draw?

18. **English Language Coach** Rewrite the words listed below and underline the base words in them.

formation   formal   formula
personify   personal   personality

Grammar Link: Clauses

- A clause (klawz) is a group of words that has a subject and a verb.
- An independent clause expresses a complete thought and can stand alone as a simple sentence.
- A dependent clause expresses an incomplete thought and cannot stand alone as a sentence. A dependent clause doesn't make sense by itself and needs an independent clause to complete its meaning.

Independent clause
The bullies made a plan.

Dependent clause
when they saw Mersh

Independent and dependent clause
The bullies made a plan when they saw Mersh.

Grammar Practice

Decide whether each clause below is dependent or independent. Write D for dependent and I for independent.

19. when they were on an enemy block.

20. because Mersh had a lot of experience on the street.

21. the bullies spoke rudely to Mersh.

22. if the paper had nothing written on it.

23. Mersh swallowed the paper.

Writing Application Look back at the list you wrote. Find or add a sentence that has both an independent clause and a dependent clause. Underline the independent clause once and the dependent clause twice.

Web Activities For eFlashcards, Selection Quick Checks, and other Web activities, go to www.glencoe.com.

Skills Review

Key Reading Skill: Drawing Conclusions

7. Possible response: The bullies were surprised by Mersh's response and didn't know what to do when Mersh swallowed the paper.

8. Responses will vary.

Key Literary Element: Dialogue

9. The bullies, especially the biggest one, have most of the dialogue.

10. Possible response: He is quiet and thoughtful.

11. Possible response: Mersh's cousin respects him and wants to learn from him.

Vocabulary Check

12. hostile

13. immigrant

14. outrages

15. application

16. authority

17. **Academic Vocabulary**
It is very cold outside.

18. **English Language Coach**

formation   formal   formula
personify   personal   personality

Grammar Link: Clauses

Grammar Practice

19. dependent

20. dependent

21. independent

22. dependent

23. independent

Close

Ask students to summarize what they learned about the Big Question from reading "Street Magic."

Teach

More About the Web Site

- KidsHealth has been on the Web since 1995. Millions of people have visited the site.

- KidsHealth was created by the Nemours Center for Children's Health Media, which also publishes printed text, videos, and CD-ROMs about children's health.

- The amount of information on the KidsHealth Web site would fill an 80-volume encyclopedia.

V Vocabulary

Using Vocabulary Words

Say: A word becomes a permanent part of your vocabulary when you understand how it is used and start using it yourself. In your Learner's Notebooks, write a sentence for each of the vocabulary words in this selection. **OL**

Before You Read : What Kids Say About Bullying

- More than 250,000 people a day visit KidsHealth on the Web. It's a great place to learn about health issues affecting children and teens.

- Doctors have approved every piece of information on the site, and it's all up-to-date and easy to understand.

- KidsHealth is divided into separate areas for kids, teens, and parents.

- In addition to articles such as "What Kids Say About Bullying," the kids' area has games and animations.

Vocabulary Preview

subjected (sub JEK tid) *v.* caused to experience; form of the verb *subject* (p. 511) *Bullies sometimes subjected others to violence.*

discipline (DIS uh plin) *v.* to punish (p. 512) *If no one will discipline bullies, they will keep hurting others.*

surveyed (sur VAYD) *adj.* polled; questioned (p. 512) *The kids surveyed said they were scared of bullies.*

Sentence Revision Find the sentences in which the vocabulary words appear in the selection. Then rewrite the sentences, replacing the vocabulary words with a synonym or phrase that has the same meaning. Underline the new words in the sentences.

English Language Coach

Base Words What can you do to unlock the meaning of new words? Be on the lookout for base words. Here's an example. *Operator* includes the base word *operate.* If you know that *operate* is a verb meaning "to perform a task or function," you can guess that the noun *operator* means "one who performs a task or function."

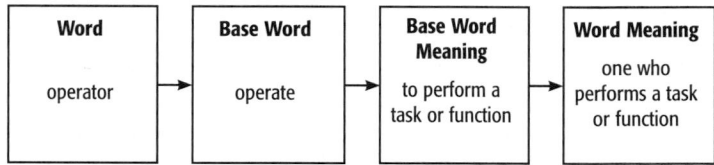

Word	Base Word	Base Word Meaning	Word Meaning
operator	operate	to perform a task or function	one who performs a task or function

Match Up Use what you know about base words to match each word on the left to its meaning.

1. topical   **a.** difficult to solve or deal with
2. repeatedly   **b.** having to do with a particular subject
3. problematic   **c.** the act of injuring or cheating someone
4. victimization   **d.** over and over again

Objectives (pp. 508–513)
Reading Draw conclusions from text and experience • Make connections from text to self
Literature Identify literary elements: author's purpose
Vocabulary Identify word structure: base words

Additional Support

English Language Coach

Base Words Using a graphic organizer such as the one shown on page 508 of the student edition may help students understand the relationship between base words and their longer counterparts.

Have students use a similar chart to find the definitions of the words listed for the *Match Up* activity. Encourage students to use this type of graphic organizer when they encounter other unfamiliar words in the text. **EL BL**

Skills Preview

Key Reading Skill: Drawing Conclusions

You can draw conclusions while reading any kind of text. The following selection is an example of informational text. As you read, you'll use the information from the selection and your own reasoning to form opinions and draw conclusions.

Quickwrite In your Learner's Notebook, explain why you think some people bully others. With your teacher, make a list of the top three reasons given by the students in your class.

Literary Element: Author's Purpose

What's an author's purpose for writing informational text? One purpose is to inform readers about a topic, of course! To find the topic of this selection, just take a look at its title. This selection is about what kids know and think about bullies.

Use these tips to help you think about the author's purpose in writing "What Kids Say About Bullying."

- Look for clues to the author's purpose.
  Does the author state his or her purpose in a sentence or paragraph, or do you have to draw conclusions from what and how he or she writes?

- Identify the audience of the selection.
  Who is the author speaking to? How can you tell this is the audience of the selection?

- Notice the text structure, or pattern of organization.
  How is the text organized? Why has the author organized the text this way?

Write to Learn Write a few sentences about the last thing you read outside of school. Was it an advertisement, an article, a Web site? Think about what the author's purpose might have been for writing about the topic. Was it to inform, persuade, or entertain you?

Get Ready to Read

Connect to the Reading

What kinds of experiences with bullies have you had? Have any of your friends or family members been bullied? Have you ever bullied others? Explain.

Class Poll Take a poll to see how many people in your class have ever been bullied. Write yes or no on a piece of paper, fold it up, and give it to your teacher to count and announce the result.

Build Background

This selection shows that the best way to find out about kids and bullying is to ask kids themselves.

- KidsPoll gathered information about bullying from kids between the ages of 9 and 13.
- The group of kids included an almost equal number of boys and girls.
- About 86 percent of the kids said that they'd seen someone else being bullied.
- Kids said they bully others to be popular, to get their way, or just to push others around.

Set Purposes for Reading

BIG Question Read the selection "What Kids Say About Bullying" to learn about good and bad ways to deal with bullies.

Set Your Own Purpose What else would you like to learn from the selection to help you answer the Big Question? Write your own purpose on the "What Kids Say" page of Foldable 5.

Literature Online

Interactive Literary Elements Handbook
To review or learn more about the literary elements, go to www.glencoe.com.

Keep Moving

Use these skills as you read the following selection.

What Kids Say About Bullying **509**

Teach

L Literary Element

Author's Purpose Ask: Who is the intended audience for this selection? Explain. *(Possible response: Because students are the subject of the article and many students have to deal with bullies, the intended readers are probably other students.)* **OL**

R Reading Skill

Review Connecting Say: Raise your hand if you think that more than half the class say they have been bullied. Raise your hand if you think that fewer than half have been bullied.

- Count hands, and write the numbers on the board.
- Announce the class poll results, and compare them with class predictions. **AS**

Literature Focus Lesson

Informational Text Explain that this selection is informational text, a type of nonfiction text. This text conveys facts and information.

- Have students brainstorm sources where they might find examples of informa-

tional text. *(Possible responses: newspapers, magazines, textbooks, the Internet)*

- Ask students to give specific examples of informational texts that they have read. Students should give the subject of each text and explain why they read it. **OL**

Objectives

- Identify author's purpose
- Make connections from text to self
- Identify word structure: base words
- Learn and use new vocabulary
- Analyze features of genres: informational text

INFORMATIONAL TEXT
WEB SITE
KidsHealth.org

Teach

L Literary Element

Author's Purpose Ask: What does the title of the article tell you about the author's purpose? *(Possible response: The title tells you that the author's purpose is to inform people about kids' opinions about bullying.)* **BL**

R Reading Skill

Drawing Conclusions To help students understand the magnitude of the bullying problem, ask every other student in the class to stand up. **Say:** Almost half of the students surveyed said that they had been bullied at least once. Half of this class is standing up. What does this tell you about the size of the bullying problem? *(Possible response: Bullying is a big problem if one out of two students has experienced it.)* **OL**

Readability Scores
Dale-Chall: 6.8
DRP: 56
Lexile: 910

What Kids Say ABOUT BULLYING

If you have been bullied, you know how bad it feels. But you might not know how many other kids have felt exactly the same way. We were wondering what kids thought about this tough topic so we asked 1,229 boys and girls to answer some questions about bullying. Nearly **half** of them said they had been bullied before. Some said it was happening every day. Others said it only happened once in a while. Here's how the group answered:

How often have you been bullied?
every day (8%[1])
every week, but not every day (7%)
once in a while, but not every week (33%)
never (52%) **1**

---

1. The symbol **%** stands for "percent." See page 513 for more information about percents.

510 UNIT 5 How Should You Deal with Bullies?

Practice the Skills

1 Key Reading Skill

Drawing Conclusions Look at the results of the question that asks how often students have been bullied. What conclusion can you draw from this information? **R**

Additional Support

Differentiated Instruction

Understanding Percentages Explain to students that a number stated as a percentage represents that number out of a group of one hundred. On page 510 of "What Kids Say About Bullying," percentages are given regarding students who have or have not been bullied. Tell students that 100 percent represents all the members of a group and that 50 percent represents half the members of a group. When a group is surveyed, all of the resulting percentages must add up to 100. Ask students to consider the percentages given on page 510 to determine why the article states that "nearly half" of the students surveyed said that they had been bullied. **AL**

The KidsPoll[2] also asked how many of these kids were bullies themselves. Most of them (58%) said they never bullied others, but the rest said that they did.

22% said they bullied others once in a while

5% said they bullied others every week

15% said they bullied others every day

As you have probably guessed, some kids said they were both bullies and the victims of bullies. Why is that? D'Arcy Lyness, a child psychologist,[3] explains it this way:

"Some kids learn to bully because they have been **subjected** to mean, unfair treatment themselves—by others or by their families. That's sad, but it's no excuse," Dr. Lyness **L** says. "Everyone can choose to act in new and better ways. It's never too late."

Most kids know what bullying is. It's when a person is repeatedly mean and hurtful toward someone else, often when that person has trouble defending himself or herself. The bully gets satisfaction (feels good) when he or she gets a **reaction** out of the person being bullied. Like if a bully tells a kid, "You're ugly!" and the kid cries and runs away, that's satisfaction for the bully. **2 3**

It can be hard for kids to know what to do if a bully bothers them. About half of the kids said they fight back. There are a lot of problems with this solution. First, one or both of the kids could get hurt. Unlike on TV, where actors are just pretending to fight, when kids punch, kick, and push each other, they can get real injuries, like bruises and cuts and broken bones.

Fighting is also against the rules (both in and out of school), so the two kids could get in trouble even if the bully started the whole thing by bullying. Another reason not to fight is that doesn't really solve the problem. The bully still gets the satisfaction of seeing the picked-on kid get really upset.

---

2. **KidsPoll** gets information about what kids think about a topic by asking certain questions.
3. A **child psychologist** (sy KAWL uh jist) is someone who studies how children think and behave.

Vocabulary

subjected (sub JEK tid) v. caused to experience

Practice the Skills

2 English Language Coach

Base Words The base word of **reaction** is *act*. How does the meaning of the base word help you understand what a *reaction* is? Use a dictionary if you need help. **EL**

3 Key Reading Skill

Drawing Conclusions Why do some people get satisfaction from bullying others? Combine what you've read so far with your own experiences to draw a conclusion. **R**

Teach

L Literary Element

Review Stereotyping Ask: When you hear the word *bully*, what images and phrases come to mind? How do these images and words differ from the characteristics of the bully described in the third paragraph on this page? *(Responses will vary. Students may note that while they think of bullies as mean and insensitive, some bullies may pick on others not out of meanness, but because they themselves have been victims of bullying.)* **OL**

EL Language Coach

Base Words Ask: How is *action* part of a *reaction*? *(Possible response:* Action *is something that somebody does. A* reaction *is defined as action taken in response to a particular action.)* **EL BL**

R Reading Skill

Drawing Conclusions Say: Put yourself in a bully's shoes. Why might seeing a victim cry make you feel satisfied? *(Responses will vary. Students may say that the bully feels satisfied because he or she has provoked a reaction. Students may note that making others feel bad about themselves might make a bully feel better about himself or herself.)* **OL**

Objectives

- Identify author's purpose
- Draw conclusions from text and experience
- Identify literary elements: stereotype
- Identify word structure: base words
- Analyze features of genres: narratives

Literature Focus Lesson

Writing a Narrative Tell students to use what they have read so far as a prompt to write a one-page narrative, or story, about dealing with bullies. Encourage students to be creative. Students may write a story about a victim of bullying, or they may write from the point of view of the person doing the bullying. Emphasize that whatever students choose to write, their stories should describe believable incidents. Suggest that students base their stories, even if only in part, on real experience. Have students share their stories in small groups. **OL**

Teach

READING WORKSHOP 1

BQ **BIG Question**

Say: You've learned some effective ways of dealing with bullies. Name three things you should NOT do. *(Responses will vary. Possible responses: fight back, talk back, join in bullying others)* **AS**

C Critical Thinking

Evaluation Say: Evaluate the findings of the survey. Do you agree that most kids do something when they see bullying? Explain. *(Responses will vary.)* **AS**

But the good news is that more than half of the kids said they did something other than fight. Here's what they said they do:

> talk to an adult (25%)
> just walk away and do nothing (20%)
> try to talk to the bully (8%)

There are two keys to solving bullying, Dr. Lyness says. They are:

1. Kids should tell adults when bullying is happening to them, a friend, or a classmate.
2. Adults should take action to prevent bullying and discipline kids who are bullies.

C Grown-ups are important because they can **discipline** kids who are bullies, help kids who have been bullied to build their confidence and strength, and help kids who witness bullying to use their power to change things for the better.

Without cooperation between kids and grown-ups, bullying can be a big problem that doesn't get better. And when no one does anything, the bullied kid can feel worse and worse. In fact, 14% of the kids **surveyed** said being bullied can make them afraid to go to school. **4**

So what do kids do when they see someone being bullied? Well, too many of them do nothing (16%) or join in (20%). But the rest of the kids are on the right track. They said they would say or do something to try and stop it (41%) or tell someone who could help (23%).

When kids tell an adult about a bully, it's a way of saying that bullying is **not** cool. Most kids (72%) already know this and said bullies are usually sort of un-cool or very un-cool. But 28% of kids said bullies are either sort of cool or very cool. Don't let bullies get this idea at your school, Dr. Lyness says.

"Kids can support each other by letting a bully know that treating others this way isn't cool or popular," she says.

Vocabulary

discipline (DIS uh plin) *v.* to punish

surveyed (sur VAYD) *adj.* polled; questioned

---

512 UNIT 5 How Should You Deal with Bullies?

Practice the Skills

4 **BIG Question**

What can adults do to help kids deal with bullies? Write your answer on the "What Kids Say" page of Foldable 5. Your response will help you answer the Unit Challenge later. **BQ**

Additional Support

Reading in the Real World

Citizenship Bullying is a problem that affects many young people, but, fortunately, there are solutions to the fear and hurt that bullies cause. Have students work in small groups to develop skits about dealing with bullies. In each skit, students should role-play a good way and a bad way to handle bullying.

Suggest that students look for their skit ideas in the selection or in other books and resources from the Internet or library. Have students perform their skits for the rest of the class. If students are interested, they might develop their skits further for a performance before another class as a school community service project. **AS**

What's a percentage?

The results of a poll like this one are usually expressed in percentages. A **percentage** is another way of expressing a fraction, **or a part of a whole,** like one slice of a pizza. In this case, the "whole" is all 1,229 kids who participated in the KidsPoll. If 25% (one-fourth) of them said the answer was "talk to an adult" that means about 308 kids answered that way. If 33% (one-third) said "they were bullied once in a while," about 406 kids chose that answer. For each question, all the **percentages** should add up to 100% to reflect the answers from the entire group of 1,229 kids. **5** ○

The bully in this photo may have himself been a victim of bullying.

Practice the Skills

5 ▌ Literary Element

Author's Purpose The author of this article wants to inform readers about bullying. What else do you think the author wants to do?

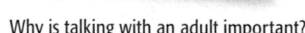

Why is talking with an adult important?

What Kids Say About Bullying **513**

Teach

L Literary Element

Author's Purpose Say:
Often, an author may hope that his or her work will move readers to do something. What might the author of this article want readers to do? *(Possible response: The author wants readers to take action against bullies by informing adults about bullying problems and by spreading the word that bullying is not "cool.")* **BL**

Assess

CheckPoint

Use the CheckPoint questions provided on Presentation Plus! to check for comprehension of the selection. These questions can be used with interactive response keypads for immediate student feedback.

Differentiated Instruction

Converting Percentages Have students convert the percentages listed in the article to actual numbers of survey respondents. Instruct students to multiply the total number of kids surveyed by the percentage in question. Remind students that a percentage can be stated as a decimal: 33% is the same as .33. For example, if 33% of the surveyed kids answered a question a certain way, the number of respondents can be expressed as 1,229 × .33, or 406. Students may use these numbers to show the survey results in the form of a bar graph or a table. Ask students to use the graphics they have created to present their converted findings to the class. **AL**

Objectives
• Identify author's purpose
• Draw conclusions from text and experience

513

Assess

Resources for page 514

📁 Selection QuickCheck, p. 42

📁 Selection and Unit Assessment, p. 50

🌐 ExamView Assessment Suite

🌐 Interactive Tutor: Self-Assessment

Students can respond to the *After You Read* items in their Learner's Notebooks or on a separate sheet of paper.

Answering the
BIG Question

1. Responses will vary. Students should support their responses with information from the selection.

2. Bullying is being repeatedly mean and hurtful toward someone else.

3. talk to an adult, walk away, or try to talk to the bully

4. Kids should tell adults when bullying is happening. Adults should discipline bullies.

Critical Thinking

5. Responses will vary. Students may suggest that victims believe that violence is the only effective solution.

6. Possible response: If bullies find out that people don't think bullying is cool, bullies may stop threatening and harming others.

7. Possible response: Bullies want a reaction, and if they don't get one, they may leave you alone.

514

After You Read

What Kids Say About Bullying

Answering the BIG Question

1. Did this selection change your ideas about how to deal with bullies? Explain.

2. **Recall** What is bullying?
   Tip Right There

3. **Recall** Besides fighting, name three other ways that kids deal with bullies.
   Tip Right There

4. **Recall** According to Dr. Lyness, what are the two keys to solving the problem of bullying?
   Tip Right There

Critical Thinking

5. **Synthesize** Why do you think fighting is the way many kids deal with bullies?
   Tip Author and Me

6. **Draw Conclusions** How does letting bullies know that they are not cool help stop them from bullying?
   Tip Author and Me

7. **Evaluate** Which way of dealing with bullies do you think works best? Why?
   Tip On My Own

Objectives (pp. 514–515)
Reading Draw conclusions from text and experience
Literature Identify literary elements: dialogue
Vocabulary Identify word structure: base words
Writing Prepare an interview
Grammar Identify sentence elements: clauses, phrases

Write About Your Reading

Suppose that you are going to interview one of the kids who took part in the poll. It could be one of the bullies or one of the students who was bullied. Write a list of five questions to ask him or her about bullying. Your questions might start with the words *who, what, where, when, how,* or *why.*

Write About Your Reading

Possible questions for a bully:
When did you start bullying people?
What kinds of people do you bully?
Where do you usually bully people?
How do you bully them?
Why do you bully others?
Who bullies you?

Skills Review

Key Reading Skill: Drawing Conclusions

8. In your Learner's Notebook, write a paragraph about what you've learned from this selection. Start it with one conclusion that you have drawn about bullying. Support your conclusion with information from the text.

Literary Element: Author's Purpose

9. Which sentence or sentences in the selection hint that the author's purpose is to inform?

10. Who is the article's audience? How do you know?

11. How does using a survey serve the author's purpose?

Vocabulary Check

Choose the best word from the list to complete each sentence below. Rewrite each sentence with the correct word.

subjected   discipline   surveyed

12. The boys ____ were of different ages, so the researchers got mixed results.

13. Would a bully have ____ his friend to mean treatment?

14. Only an adult can ____ a bully.

15. **Academic Vocabulary** What *conclusion* have psychologists drawn about why some kids bully other kids?

16. **English Language Coach** Use what you know about the base word in *disciplinary* to explain the word's meaning in this sentence: *Disciplinary actions help stop kids from bullying others.*

Web Activities For eFlashcards, Selection Quick Checks, and other Web activities, go to www.glencoe.com.

Grammar Link: Clauses and Phrases

You have already learned what a **clause** is. It is a group of words that has a subject and a verb. A **phrase**

• does **not** contain both a subject and a verb
• does the job of a single part of speech

Look at this sentence:
The kid in the red baseball cap waited at the corner.

The basic sentence is *The kid waited.* All of the other words in the sentence work to describe or add information to the basic sentence.

The kid **in the red baseball cap** (The phrase in bold does the job of an adjective, describing the kid.)
waited **at the corner** (The phrase in bold does the job of an adverb, describing how the kid waited.)

Phrases can also act as nouns. To identify a phrase, look at the group of words. If it does the job of an adjective, adverb, or noun and it doesn't have a subject *and* a verb, then it is a phrase.

Grammar Practice

Decide whether each group of words below is a clause or phrase. Write a **C** or a **P** next to each.

17. While I was going

18. to the store

19. Benito ran home

20. to do his homework

Writing Application Circle three phrases you used in the writing assignment. Underline the subjects and verbs in three clauses you used.

Skills Review

Key Reading Skill: Drawing Conclusions

8. Responses will vary. Students should support their responses with information from the text.

Literary Element: Author's Purpose

9. Responses will vary.

10. Possible response: The article is aimed at kids. In the first two sentences, the author talks directly to the reader and then refers to "many other kids."

11. Possible response: A survey is a good way to gather information.

Vocabulary Check

12. The boys <u>surveyed</u> were of different ages, so the researchers got mixed results.

13. Would a bully have <u>subjected</u> his friend to mean treatment?

14. Only an adult can <u>discipline</u> a bully.

15. **Academic Vocabulary** Possible response: Bullies may have been subjected to unfair treatment by others.

16. **English Language Coach** Possible response: *Disciplinary* means "relating to the enforcing of rules and the punishing of those who break them."

Grammar Link: Clauses and Phrases

Grammar Practice

17. clause

18. phrase

19. clause

20. phrase

Close

Ask students to summarize what "What Kids Say About Bullying" taught them about the Big Question.

Short Fictional Story

**Objectives covered in
this workshop:**
• **Writing** Write to entertain;
use a range of strategies
including dialogue and concrete language to develop
plot, setting, and character
• **Grammar** Identify dependent and independent
clauses

Teaching Students to Write a Short Fictional Story

Why Is It Important?
• Writing a short story will help students recognize literary elements such as plot, character, setting, and dialogue when they read.
• Becoming authors of short fiction will help students practice writing on non-academic subjects.
• Revising will help students add material to sections of the story that need detail, or don't make sense.
• Students will gain a deeper understanding of different organizational structures by practicing this form of narrative.

How to Help Students Get It
• The short story selections in this unit can serve as mentor texts for stu-dents. As they read, remind students that they will be writing their own short stories. They should notice elements and ideas that authors use and borrow those structures for their own creations.
• To begin writing, students may need to review "Broken Chain" (p. 255) or "Amigo Brothers" (p. 278) and pay attention to the structure of the plot. Both are written in sequential order, which serves as a good model for beginning writers.
• Encourage students to think about what will happen first in their stories, what will happen to develop the conflict, and what will happen to resolve the conflict. They may want to use a graphic organizer to compile their thoughts.
• Contrast "fictional short story" with "autobiographical narrative." Remind students that while autobiography is about something that happened to the author, fiction is about made-up events.
• Fiction can be fun! Remind students that in fiction, unlikely or impossible things can be part of the plot.
• Make sure students can identify the climax of their story, and the actions that lead up to it.
• Discuss the different ways point of view can impact the telling of a story: Has each writer chosen to tell the story from the most logical point of view?
• Highlight the importance of conflict and resolution. If nothing happens, there's no story. On the other hand, the reader will feel unsatisfied if the main problem goes unsolved.

Traits of Good Writing

Ideas	the message or the theme and the details that develop it
Voice	a writer's unique way of using tone and style
Organization: the arrangement of main points and supporting details	Have students use the following checklist when checking their compositions: • Are the beginning, middle, and end clearly linked? • Is the order of ideas easy to follow? • Does the introduction capture your readers' attention? • Do sentences and paragraphs flow from one to the next in a way that makes sense? • Does the conclusion wrap up the composition?
Word Choice: the vocabulary a writer uses to convey meaning	• Does the writer use lively verbs to show action? • Does the writer use vivid words to create word pictures in the readers' minds? • Does the writer use precise words to explain his or her ideas simply and clearly?
Sentence Fluency	the smooth rhythm and flow of sentences that vary in length and style
Conventions	correct spelling, grammar, usage, and mechanics
Presentation	the way words and design elements look on a page

Unit Focus

Workshop Resources

PACING (DAYS)		LESSON	STUDENT MATERIALS	TEACHER RESOURCES
STANDARD	BLOCK			
1	½	Writing Workshop Part 1: Prewriting and Drafting	• Writing Workshop Graphic Organizer, p. 14 • Grammar Practice, p. 15 • Spelling and Handwriting Practice, p. 44 • Spelling Power eWorkbook • Interactive Grammar and Language Workbook • Grammar and Composition Handbook, p. 192 • Real Success in Writing: Research and Reports • Writing Constructed Responses	• TeacherWorks Plus™ • Presentation Plus! • Rubrics for Assessing Student Writing, Listening, and Speaking, p. 25 • Grammar and Writing Workshop Transparencies 1–2
2	1	Writing Workshop Part 2: Editing, Revising, and Presenting	• Interactive Grammar and Language Workbook • Grammar and Composition Handbook, p. 192 • Real Success in Writing: Research and Reports • Writing Constructed Responses • Listening and Speaking, p. 27 • Viewing and Representing, p. 28	• Grammar and Writing Workshop Transparencies 25–26 • Interactive Grammar and Language Workbook • Rubrics for Assessing Student Writing, Listening, and Speaking, p. 25

Focus

BELLRINGER Options

- **Daily Language Practice Transparency 44 Focus Activity Say:** Describe an experience that involves bullying. *(Responses will vary.)* **AS**

Teach

L Literary Element

Character Say: In your Learner's Notebooks, write the following ways writers provide character information to readers: 1) through what a character says about himself or herself; 2) through a character's actions; 3) through what other characters say about a character; 4) through what the narrator says about a character. **OL**

Resources for page 516

- 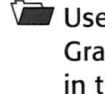 Use the Writing Workshop Graphic Organizer BLM in the Unit 5 Resource Booklet, p. 14.

- Use the Grammar and Writing Workshop Transparencies 1–2.

Short Story
Prewriting and Drafting

ASSIGNMENT Write a fictional short story about a bully

Purpose To tell a story about dealing with bullies

Audience You, your teacher, and possibly some classmates

Writing Rubric

As you work through this assignment, you should

- make a story guide
- organize a plot
- establish a setting
- create characters and conflict
- correctly use dependent and independent clauses

See page 564 in Part 2 for a model of a short story.

Objectives (pp. 516–519)
Writing Use the writing process: prewrite, draft • Use story elements: plot, setting, main character, conflict
Grammar Use sentence elements: independent and dependent clauses

In this Workshop, you will write a short story about a bully. As you write, you will think about the Unit 5 Big Question: How Should You Deal with Bullies?

A short story is a piece of short fiction. This means that the characters and events in the story are not real. Sometimes fiction writers get their ideas from real life, but they also use their imaginations to come up with the following story elements.

Main Character is the person that the story is about.

Setting is where the story takes place.

Conflict is a problem that the main character must overcome.

Plot is the series of events that happen throughout the story.

Prewriting
Get Ready to Write

Your short story should be about someone who deals with a bully. Follow the directions below to make a short story writing plan. This plan will help you organize your ideas. It will also help you start writing.

Gather Ideas

Character In your Learner's Notebook, write the name of your main character. List some traits or descriptions of your character such as:

- age
- physical description
- grade
- personality
- hobbies
- hopes and fears

L

Theo
- 11 years old
- 6th grade
- Listening to music
- Brown hair, wears glasses, shortest kid in his class
- Quiet, shy, and smart
- Wants to play the saxophone in a real band

Additional Support

English Language Coach

Latin Words Explain to students that the word *conflict* comes from the Latin word *confligere*, which means "to strike together." *Confligere* comes from the roots *com*, meaning "together," and *fligere*, meaning "to strike." **Ask:** How does the Latin meaning relate to the English meaning? *(The interests of two opposing characters conflict, or* strike together, creating a problem in a story.) Direct students to use a dictionary to locate the origin of the word *inflict*. (Inflict *comes from the Latin word* infligere, *meaning "to strike or beat against." Infligere comes from the roots* in, *meaning "on or against," and* fligere, *meaning "to strike or beat.")* **EL**

Setting Decide on a location where your story will take place. Here are some examples of setting:

- house
- neighborhood park
- classroom
- airport
- shopping mall
- community center

Conflict Remember that your story must be about someone who is being bullied. Ask yourself:

- How would a bully treat my main character?
- How could my main character deal with a bully?

Literature Online

Writing Models For models and other writing activities, go to www.glencoe.com.

Applying Good Writing Traits

Organization

Most short stories are made up of five parts called *exposition, rising action, climax, falling action,* and *resolution.* Put together, these parts make a story's **plot.** A **conflict,** or struggle between people, ideas, or forces, is what drives the plot.

What Is Organization?

Organization is the arrangement of events and ideas in a story.

Why Is Organization Important in My Writing?

Organization helps you write your story in an order that will make sense to your readers.

How Do I Organize My Writing?

Use the five stages of plot to organize your story:

Exposition is the beginning of the story. The writer describes the main character and setting and tells the reader about the situation causing the conflict.

Theo Thomas is an eleven year old boy who attends La Hoya Middle School in Coral Springs, Florida. Theo is learning how to play the saxophone and dreams of becoming a professional jazz player. Lately, he has been picked on by a bully named Eric.

Rising Action is a series of two or three events that relate to the conflict and lead to the climax. It is usually the longest part of the story.

1st Event
Theo's MP3 player is stolen at the bus stop by a bigger student named Eric.

2nd Event
The next day at the bus stop, Eric takes Theo's lunch money.

3rd Event
Theo goes to the bus stop. He has his saxophone with him because he has a lesson at school that day.

Climax
Theo refuses to give Eric his saxophone.

Falling Action is what happens to the main character after the conflict is resolved.
Eric leaves Theo alone and goes to talk with some his friends.

Resolution is the end of the story.
Eric doesn't bother Theo at the bus stop any more.

Write to Learn Activity In your Learner's Notebook, write down the five parts of plot and ideas you have for each part in your own story.

Teach

Literature Online

Writing Models Have students access the Web site for an additional and interactive Writing Workshop-based student model.

W Writing

Organization Students with visual learning styles may benefit from using a plot chart when planning their stories. On the board, draw a plot chart such as the one shown. Help students understand how the events in the *Writing Traits* box would translate to this graphic organizer. Then, suggest that students repeat the process with their own plot lines. **OL**

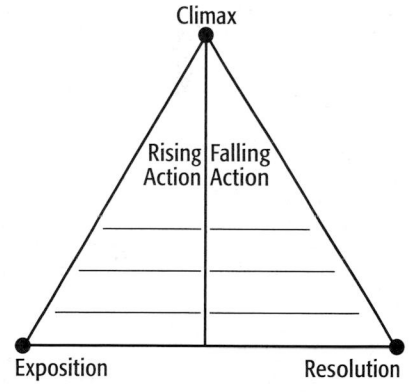

Differentiated Instruction

Descriptive Writing Encourage students to use sensory language to describe their settings. Provide students with the following sentences. Tell students to select one sentence with which to work. Then, instruct students to describe their settings by appealing to the senses. **Ask:** What sights, smells, sounds, tastes, and textures are present?

- The house looks old.
- The classroom smells musty.
- The airport is loud.
- The mall seems crowded.
- The community center is empty. **OL**

Objectives
- Interpret and analyze character
- Identify word structure: Latin roots and word origins
- Write a short story
- Use the writing process

WRITING WORKSHOP PART 1

Teach

W Writing

Theme Say: Another element of fiction is theme, or the main idea. When making your story plan, think about the main idea you want to express to your readers about bullies. Build this theme into your plot. **OL**

Assess

Have student partners exchange drafts and critique each other's work. Ask each student to determine whether his or her partner included all the elements of a short story. After a few minutes, tell each student to assess his or her partner's feedback, make any needed revisions, and save the revised draft for later use.

Make a Plan

After you decide on a main character, setting, and conflict, there are a few more details you should plan before you start writing.

Secondary Characters are other characters that appear in your story. These characters may be friends, family, or the source of the conflict.

Point of View describes the way a narrator "sees" or remembers the events. You may decide to write in first-person point of view, in which case the narrator is a character. Or, you may choose to have a narrator that is not a character. This is called third-person point of view.

To organize your ideas, make a Story Plan like the one below. Fill out the plan and use it to help you write your draft.

Writing Tip ▶

If you are having trouble planning your story, talk to a friend. Ask which ideas sound most like a story your friend would want to read.

Writing Tip ▶

Remember that stories written in the first-person point of view are narrated by a character in the story, usually the main character. "I plugged my nose as I toured the farm," is an example of first-person narration.

Writing Tip ▶

Stories that are written in the third-person point of view are narrated by an outside speaker, who tells the events of the story. "Mark plugged his nose as he toured the farm," is an example of third-person narration.

> STORY PLAN
>
> Main Character: Theo
> Point of View: Third person
> Secondary Characters: Eric
> Setting: The bus stop
> Conflict: Theo keeps getting his belongings stolen at the bus stop by a bully named Eric.
>
> Rising Action
> Event 1: Eric takes Theo's walkman.
> Event 2: Eric takes Theo's lunch money.
> Event 3: Eric tries to take Theo's saxophone.
> Climax: Theo refuses to give Eric his saxophone.
>
> Resolution: Eric stops bullying Theo at the bus stop.

Drafting

Start Writing!

Now that you have your story plan filled out, it's time to start writing your draft! Begin by introducing your main character and the setting, then go from there—follow your story plan if you don't know what to write next.

Additional Support

Literature Focus Lesson

Short Stories Have students gather examples of short stories at the library. Tell them to photocopy excerpts or bring books to class. Invite students to read their selections aloud in class. Then, ask the class to identify elements of character, setting, conflict, plot, and point of view. **OL** Ask students to identify elements of theme. **AL**

Grammar Link

Independent and Dependent Clauses

What Are They?

An **independent clause** is a group of words that states a complete thought. This group of words contains a subject and predicate. Independent clauses can stand alone as a sentence, or they can be part of a longer sentence.

Independent Clause: Holly was hungry.

Independent Clause: Holly was hungry after basketball practice.

Independent Clauses: Holly was hungry, so **she ate an orange.**

A **dependent clause** is a group of words that has a subject and a predicate, but it cannot stand alone as a sentence. A dependent clause is introduced by one of the words from the chart below.

after	even though	when
although	if	whenever
as	since	where
as if	than	whereas
as though	though	whatever
because	unless	whether
before	until	while

She returned the book **although she hadn't finished it (dependent clause).**

- To tell the difference between an independent clause and a dependent clause, ask yourself whether the clause makes sense by itself.

Independent clauses make sense by themselves; dependent clauses do not.

Complete sentence:
She returned the book. → independent clause
Not a complete sentence:
Although she hadn't finished it. → dependent clause

Why Are They Important?

When you add dependent clauses to independent clauses, your sentences become more interesting.

How Do I Use Them?

Remember that dependent clauses cannot stand alone—they must be linked to an independent clause. Use the words and phrases from the chart to link dependent clauses to independent clauses.

Grammar Practice

Underline the independent clauses and circle the dependent clauses in the following sentences.
1. I don't enjoy roller coasters because they make me dizzy.
2. Maria likes taking long walks before the sun rises.
3. When Ernie's flowers begin growing in July, he spends most of his time in the garden.
4. The teacher watched the children while they were at recess.
5. Since Mona finished first, she won the medal.

Writing Application Review your draft to make sure that all dependent clauses are attached to independent clauses.

Looking Ahead

Part 2 of the Writing Workshop is coming up later. Keep the writing you did here, and in Part 2 you'll learn how to turn your draft into a final product.

Teach

Grammar Link
Independent and
Dependent Clauses Say:

The words in the chart on page 519 are called *subordinating conjunctions* because they join a subordinate idea, or dependent clause, to a main clause. *A relative pronoun* may also be used to begin a dependent clause. **OL** Copy the chart below on the board for students.

who	what	whatever
whose	whom	
whomever	whoever	
that	whomever	

Grammar Practice

Independent and Dependent Clauses

1. I don't enjoy roller coasters (because) (they make me dizzy.)
2. Maria likes taking long walks (before) (the sun rises.)
3. (When Ernie's flowers begin growing in July,) he spends most of his time in the garden.
4. The teacher watched the children (while they were at recess.)
5. (Since Mona finished first,) she won the medal.

Encourage students to use the vocabulary words to develop original sentences with independent and dependent clauses. *(Responses will vary.)* **OL**

Objectives
- Write a short story
- Use the writing process
- Identify literary elements: theme

519

**Objectives covered in
this workshop:**
• Analyze texts by identifying
cause-and-effect relationships
• Use cause-and-effect to
locate, recall, and comprehend information

Teaching Students to Understand Cause and Effect

Why Is It Important?

• Causal relationships are central to narrative and informational text.

• Students who understand cause and effect structure will connect it to life actions and their consequences.

• Understanding cause and effect can provide a way to understand motivations and reactions in stories and in the real world.

How To Help Students Get It

• Emphasize that causal relationships are present at many levels in narratives: at the story level, in individual events, and in characters' behavior over time.

• Have students examine causal relationships within short stories, then apply the concept to a science experiment and an historical event, to ensure that they understand the general concept and how it crosses texts and literature.

• Use graphic organizers to help students map out causal relationships at each level.

Reading to Answer the Big Question

The main character of a short story and the speaker of a poem share their experiences in dealing with bullies. Their thoughts and actions will provide your students with food for thought as they answer the Big Question: **How should we deal with bullies?**

Tuesday of the Other June by Norma Fox Mazer
June lives in dread of Tuesdays because another girl named June bullies her every Tuesday at their swimming lesson. When the lessons end and June and her mother move to a different neighborhood, she is relieved—until she learns that the other June lives on their new block and is in her class at school. When June realizes that life could become miserable every day of the week, she finally confronts her bully.

My Parents by Stephen Spender
The speaker of this poem describes encounters he has with kids who are poorer and tougher than him. He admires their strength, but fears their bullying. He wants them to know he would forgive them, but is not able to make a connection.

Workshop Resources

PACING (DAYS)		LESSON	STUDENT MATERIALS	TEACHER RESOURCES
STANDARD	BLOCK			
1	½	Key Skill Lesson: Understanding Cause and Effect	👤 Key Reading Skills Practice, p. 16 👤 English Language Coach Review, p. 41	📖 Bellringer Options Transparencies – Daily Language Practice 45 📖 Read Aloud, Think Aloud Transparencies – Key Reading Skills 26 💿 Presentation Plus!
1	1	"Tuesday of the Other June"	💻 Glencoe Online 👤 Unit Vocabulary Review, p. 39 👤 Academic Vocabulary Review, p. 42 📁 English Language Coach 👤 Active Reading Graphic Organizer, p. 18 👤 Literary Analysis, p. 17 💿 StudentWorks Plus™ 💻 Online Student Edition 💿 Literature Classics 📁 Selection and Unit Assessments, p. 51	📖 Literary and Text Analysis Transparencies 9 💻 Puzzlemaker 💿 Skill Level Up!™ A Language Arts Game 💻 BookLink 3 📔 Assessment by Learning Objective (Diagnostic and Formative) 💿 Interactive Tutor: Self-Assessment 💿 TeacherWorks Plus™
1		"My Parents"	💻 Glencoe Online 👤 Unit Vocabulary Review, p. 39 👤 Academic Vocabulary Review, p. 42 📁 English Language Coach 👤 Active Reading Graphic Organizer, p. 20 👤 Literary Analysis, p. 17 💿 StudentWorks Plus™ 💻 Online Student Edition 💿 Literature Classics 📁 Selection and Unit Assessments, p. 52	📖 Literary and Text Analysis Transparencies 9 💻 Puzzlemaker 💿 Skill Level Up!™ A Language Arts Game 💻 BookLink 3 📔 Assessment by Learning Objective (Diagnostic and Formative) 💿 Interactive Tutor: Self-Assessment 💿 TeacherWorks Plus™

Keys for Unit Resource

📁	Blackline Master	🔒	DVD
📔	Workbook	📖	Transparency
📖	Supplemental Text	💻	Web-based
💿	CD-ROM	👤	Fast File

Level Appropriate Code

AS = Activities for all students

AL = Activities for students working above grade level

OL = Activities for students working at grade level

BL = Activities for students working below grade level

EL = Activities for English language learners

Focus

🖐 **Daily Language Practice Transparency 45**
Focus Activity Ask: Why do you think bullies act the way that they do? *(Responses will vary. Some students may say that bullies act the way they do in order to get attention. Others may suggest that bullies feel insecure and that they act the way they do in order to feel superior.)* **AS**

Teach

R **Reading Skill**

Understanding Cause and Effect Say: Listen to the following statement: "The weather broadcast said it was going to rain, so I took my umbrella to school." What is the effect? *(taking the umbrella to school)* And why did it happen? *(because it was going to rain)* **OL**

What You'll Read
You will practice using these skills when you read the following selections:
• "Tuesday of the Other June," p. 524
• "My Parents," p. 540

Reading
• Understanding cause and effect

Literature
• Identifying and analyzing conflict

Vocabulary
• Identifying suffixes
• Academic Vocabulary: *conflict*

Writing/Grammar
• Identifying parts of speech
• Understanding clauses as parts of speech

Objectives (pp. 520–521)
Reading Understand cause and effect

Skill Lesson

Understanding Cause and Effect

Learn It!

R **What Is It?** Think about this sentence: *A river overflows its banks, and the nearby town floods.* What caused the town to flood? If you answer *a river overflowing its banks,* you're right!

• A **cause** is a person, condition, or event that makes something happen.
• What happens as a result of the cause is the **effect.**

In "The Fan Club," some students put on "HORTENSKY FAN CLUB" signs as Rachel Hortensky finishes her speech. This is a cause. The effect is that Rachel is laughed at by the entire class.

"I wish you hadn't named me Snowball. I'm freezing!"
© 2003 Randy Glasbergen

Analyzing Cartoons
The cat thinks that its name, "Snowball," is a **cause** for its being cold. What do you think is the real cause-and-effect relationship here?

Additional Support

Reading in the Real World

Career Tell students that understanding cause-and-effect relationships is an important skill in many careers. Specifically, people often analyze certain effects to determine the cause of a problem accurately. Brainstorm with students a list of professions that involve analyzing effects to determine causes. To model students' thinking, explain how an auto mechanic analyzes effects, such as a shuddering steering wheel, to determine causes, such as an uneven brake rotor, or how physicians examine their patients' symptoms to determine the causes of their illnesses. **OL**

Teach

Why Is It Important? Seeing cause and effect relationships in stories will help you to understand why a character is in a certain situation and the events that led up to that situation. For example, Character A is afraid (cause) so she avoids the source of her fear (effect). Character B senses Character A's fear and seeks her out (cause). Eventually there will be a face-to-face meeting (effect).

R

How Do I Do It? You think about cause and effect all the time in every-day life. Why did your friend say that to you? What will happen if you don't do all your chores? Use the same skills as you read a story or poem. Two key questions to keep in mind are

• What is the cause of the action or event?

• What are the possible results, or effects, of the action or event?

Here's how one student thought about cause and effect in "The Fan Club."

> She turned into the algebra room, sniffing at the smell of chalk and dusty erasers. . . . Fumbling through the pages of her book, she tried to memorize the theorems she hadn't looked at the night before.

I bet I know why she's fumbling through her book. It's because she didn't study the night before. If she has a test or quiz, she could get a bad grade because she didn't memorize the theorems.

Practice It!

Think of possible causes and effects for the examples below.

Causes		**Effects**
You ate too much for dinner.	→	_____
_____	→	Your bike got a flat tire.
We fed the stray dog.	→	_____
_____	→	You got a good grade on the test.

Use It!

As you read "Tuesday of the Other June" and "My Parents," take notes in your Learner's Notebook about the cause and effect relationships.

Literature**Online**

Study Central Have students access the Web site to review cause and effect and to complete a related activity.

R **Reading Skill**

Understanding Cause and Effect Say: Look at the *How Do I Do It?* section. Another way to think about cause and effect is to use the words *if* and *then*. For example, *if* you eat healthy foods and exercise, *then* you will feel good. Reread the excerpt from "The Fan Club" and make a statement about it using *if* and *then*. *(Possible response: If you don't study for a test, then you will be nervous.)* **OL**

Resources for page 521

Use Key Reading Skills Transparency 26 in *Read Aloud, Think Aloud* to help students practice cause and effect.

Differentiated Instruction

Cause and Effect Chart Encourage students to keep track of cause-and-effect relationships in a two-column chart labeled "Causes" and "Effects." Students should match each cause with an effect. Prompt students to fill in their charts whenever they notice a cause or an effect. For example, in "Tuesday of the Other June," students may note that June does not want to go to swimming class. Have students write this in the column labeled "Effects." Then ask students to consider *why* she does not want to go. In this case, the cause is that she is afraid of being bullied by another girl. This should then be written in the column labeled "Causes." **BL** **OL**

Objectives
• Understand cause and effect
• Learn and use new vocabulary

Teach

More About the Author

Norma Fox Mazer has considered herself a writer since the age of 12. She frequently calls on her own early memories in her writing, and she is constantly drawn to the young person's point of view. Mazer believes that teenagers need books that "treat them with the respect and seriousness they deserve."

EL Language Coach

Suffix Contest One way to encourage students to explore words with the suffixes *-er, -or, -ful, -less,* and *-able* is to have a contest. Organize the class into groups of five or six students, and give each group a dictionary. Tell each group they will have ten minutes to list and define as many words as they can that contain the suffixes listed in the chart on this page. At the end of ten minutes, give each group one point for every word that is spelled and defined correctly. **EL BL OL**

Meet the Author

Norma Fox Mazer has written dozens of novels and short story collections for children and young adults. When talking about her books, Mazer says, "I write and my readers read to find out the answers to questions, secrets, problems, to be drawn into the deepest mystery of all—someone else's life." See page R4 of the Author Files for more on Norma Fox Mazer.

Author Search For more about Norma Fox Mazer, go to www.glencoe.com.

Objectives (pp. 522–535)
Reading Understand cause and effect • Make connections from text to self
Literature Identify literary elements: external and internal conflict
Vocabulary Identify word structure: suffixes

Before You Read — Tuesday of the Other June

Vocabulary Preview

recited (rih SY tid) *v.* repeated from memory; form of the verb *recite* **(p. 525)** *June recited her mother's advice for dealing with bullies.*

rigid (RIJ id) *adj.* stiff **(p. 525)** *When June felt afraid of the dark, she would lie under the covers with her body rigid.*

bureau (BYUR oh) *n.* a low chest of drawers **(p. 529)** *June kept winter sweaters in a bureau by her bed.*

Partner Talk With a partner, take turns calling out a vocabulary word and having your partner give the definition, or call out the definition and have the partner give the word. Next, trade off using the words correctly in sentences.

English Language Coach

Suffixes A suffix is a word part added to the end of a word. Sometimes adding a suffix greatly changes the meaning of a word. For example, adding the suffix *-less* to the word *joy* makes *joyless,* which describes a person without joy. Often, though, a suffix changes the meaning just a little. Many suffixes just change words from one part of speech to another.

Suffixes	Words	Meanings
-er means "one who," "that which," or "more"	runner	one who runs
	toaster	that which makes toast
	weaker	more weak
-or means "one who"	actor	one who acts
	conductor	one who conducts
-ful means "full of"	graceful	full of grace
	youthful	full of youth
-less means "without"	hairless	without hair
	spineless	without a spine
-able means "can be" or "having quality of"	believable	can be believed
	washable	can be washed
	valuable	having value

EL

Partner Talk With a partner, take turns identifying the part of speech of each example word above with and without its suffix.

Additional Support

Author Search To expand students' appreciation of Norma Fox Mazer, have them access the Web site for additional information and resources.

English Language Coach

Suffixes One common mistake among English language learners—as well as among English-proficient students—is the confusion of the suffixes *-er* and *-or.* Suggest that students make two piles of flashcards: one for words that end in *-er* (such as *banker* and *singer*) and one for words that end in *-or* (such as *actor* and *mayor*). Encourage students to review one pile at a time, slowly eliminating words from the pile until they are familiar with all of the words. **BL EL** More advanced students may create flashcards that contain the root word (such as *invent*) on the front and the suffix (such as *-or*) on the back. You may choose to mention that the suffixes *-ar, -eer,* and *-ist* also mean "one who." **OL**

Skills Preview

Key Reading Skill: Understanding Cause and Effect

In "Tuesday of the Other June," Norma Fox Mazer uses **cause** and **effect** by describing how characters deal with situations and how they cope with the effects of those events. The way characters relate to each other has a lot to do with the outcome of each new situation. As you read, ask yourself these questions:

- Why do the characters behave the way they do?
- What are the effects of their actions?

Write to Learn Write down a possible cause and effect for *each* of these situations: 1. Someone picks on you at school; 2. You move and have to go to a new school.

Key Literary Element: Conflict

Conflict is an important part of a story. Conflicts often create the events that characters must deal with.

When characters have **external conflicts,** they struggle with something outside themselves, such as another character, nature, the community, or even fate.

When characters have **internal conflicts,** they struggle against something inside themselves. Characters might have internal conflicts about how they act or feel.

As you read, use these tips to understand the conflicts in "Tuesday of the Other June":

- Look for external conflicts between characters.
  How does the "Other June" treat the narrator?
- Look for the characters' internal conflicts.
  What actions or feelings does the narrator struggle with in her mind?

Write to Learn Copy the questions above in your Learner's Notebook and answer them as you read.

Academic Vocabulary

V **conflict** (KAHN flikt) *n.* a struggle between opposing forces

Get Ready to Read

Connect to the Reading

Have you ever had a problem with a bully that you just couldn't get rid of? Maybe you saw the bully just about everywhere, and even the advice of a parent or teacher just didn't work. How did you deal with the bully?

Write to Learn Write about what you should do if the advice that a parent, teacher, or friend gives you about dealing with a bully just doesn't work. Think about reasons the advice might not work. What should you do? Who could you go to?

Build Background

You will see the names April, May, and June in the story. Our months get their names from the calendar used by the ancient Romans.

Set Purposes for Reading

BIG Question Read "Tuesday of the Other June" to find out how the narrator deals with a bully who won't go away.

Set Your Own Purpose What would you like to learn from the story to help you answer the Big Question? Write your own purpose on the "Tuesday of the Other June" page of Foldable 5.

Literature Online

Interactive Literary Elements Handbook
To review or learn more about the literary elements, go to www.glencoe.com.

Keep Moving

Use these skills as you read the following selection.

Tuesday of the Other June **523**

Teach

R Reading Skill

Understanding Cause and Effect Say: Certain words or phrases, such as *because, therefore,* and *as a result of,* are helpful in making cause-and-effect statements because they show the relationship between two events. As you complete the *Write to Learn* section, use these words or phrases to write your cause-and-effect statements. **OL**

L Literary Element

Conflict Say: Determine whether each statement below describes an external or an internal conflict.

- June's mother works hard and earns little money. *(external)*
- June doesn't want to make her mother's life any more difficult. *(internal)* **OL**

V Vocabulary

Academic Vocabulary Ask: What are some conflicts that you might encounter at school? *(Possible responses: being teased by a bully; taking a difficult math test)* **OL**

Literature Focus Lesson

Conflict Explain that simply being sad or angry is not a conflict. A conflict must involve two opposing forces. This concept may be confusing when a character has an internal conflict. Make sure that students understand the distinction between emotions and conflict, and discuss examples to reinforce the idea. **BL OL** Then explain to students that the plot of a story is built around a central conflict that must be resolved. The turning point of the plot is called the climax, the point of highest interest. This is the point where the outcome of the conflict is determined. **AS**

Objectives

- Understand cause and effect
- Identify literary elements: conflict
- Identify word structure: suffixes

523

Teach

R Reading Skill

Cause and Effect Ask: What effect do you think that June's mother's advice will have on her behavior? Explain. *(Possible response: June will become more mature and independent because she'll want to follow her mother's advice and won't want to bother her mother with any problems.)* **OL**

EL Language Coach

Suffixes Say: The suffix *-ed* forms the past tense of verbs such as *laugh*, *comb*, and *brush*. **BL EL** Which past-tense verbs in this paragraph do *not* have the suffix *-ed*? *(stood, came, grew)* **OL**

Readability Scores
Dale-Chall: 4.9
DRP: 47
Lexile: 790

READING WORKSHOP 2

Tuesday of the Other June

by Norma Fox Mazer

"**B**e good, be good, be good, be good, my Junie," my mother sang as she combed my hair; a song, a story, a croon, a plea. "It's just you and me, two women alone in the world, June darling of my heart; we have enough troubles getting by, we surely don't need a single one more, so you keep your sweet self out of fighting and all that bad stuff. People can be little-hearted, but turn the other cheek, smile at the world, and the world'll surely smile back." **1**

We stood in front of the mirror as she combed my hair, combed and brushed and smoothed. Her head came just above mine; she said when I grew another inch, she'd stand on a stool to brush my hair. "I'm not giving up this pleasure!" And she laughed her long honey laugh.

524 UNIT 5 How Should You Deal with Bullies?

Practice the Skills

1 Key Reading Skill

Understanding Cause and Effect June's mother says that they have troubles just getting by and they don't need any more. What might be one effect of having so many troubles? Think about what June's mother asks her not to do. **R**

Additional Support

Differentiated Instruction

Drawing Conclusions The first two paragraphs of the story provide students with an excellent opportunity to practice drawing conclusions, a reading skill taught in Reading Workshop 1. Prompt students to use clues from the text to draw conclusions about the relationship between June and her mother. The following clues are useful: June's mother calls her "Junie," her mother sings to her, her mother brushes her hair and calls it a "pleasure," and the narrator recalls her mother's "long honey laugh." From these clues, students may conclude that June and her mother are very close. **AS**

My mother was April, my grandmother had been May, I was June. "And someday," said my mother, "you'll have a daughter of your own. What will you name her?"

"January!" I'd yell when I was little. "February! No, November!" My mother laughed her honey laugh. She had little emerald[1] eyes that warmed me like the sun.

Every day when I went to school, she went to work. "Sometimes I stop what I'm doing," she said, "lay down my tools, and stop everything, because all I can think about is you. Wondering what you're doing and if you need me. Now, Junie, if anyone ever bothers you—"

"—I walk away, run away, come on home as fast as my feet will take me," I **recited.**

"Yes. You come to me. You just bring me your trouble, because I'm here on this earth to love you and take care of you."

I was safe with her. Still, sometimes I woke up at night and heard footsteps slowly creeping up the stairs. It wasn't my mother, she was asleep in the bed across the room, so it was robbers, thieves, and murderers, creeping slowly . . . slowly . . . slowly toward my bed.

I stuffed my hand into my mouth. If I screamed and woke her, she'd be tired at work tomorrow. The robbers and thieves filled the warm darkness and slipped across the floor more quietly than cats. **Rigid** under the covers, I stared at the shifting dark and bit my knuckles and never knew when I fell asleep again. **2**

In the morning we sang in the kitchen. "Bill Grogan's goat! Was feelin' fine! Ate three red shirts, right off the line!" I made sandwiches for our lunches, she made pancakes for breakfast, but all she ate was one pancake and a cup of coffee. "Gotta fly, can't be late."

---

1. _Emerald_ is a deep green color.

Vocabulary

recited (rih SY tid) _v._ repeated from memory

rigid (RIJ id) _adj._ stiff

Practice the Skills

2 | Key Reading Skill

Understanding Cause and Effect June stuffs her hand into her mouth instead of screaming. She says she does this so she won't wake her mother. If June's mother were awakened in the middle of the night, what would be the effect the next day?

"Be good, be good, be good, be good, my Junie," my mother sang . . .

Tuesday of the Other June **525**

Teach

C Critical Thinking

Analysis Ask: How would you characterize June's mother's attitude toward her daughter? Explain. _(Possible response: June's mother is very protective. She loves her daughter very much, and she wants to make sure that she always feels safe and loved.)_ **OL**

R Reading Skill

Understanding Cause and Effect Ask: How is June's behavior a result of what her mother tells her at the beginning of the story? _(Possible response: June's mother told her that they have enough problems and that they don't need any more. Because she doesn't want to worry her mother, June stuffs her hand in her mouth instead of screaming.)_ **AL**

English Language Coach

Build Background The song that June and her mother sing is "Bill Grogan's Goat," a traditional American folk song. Explain to students that such folk songs often contain silly lyrics that are written more for their rhythmic and humorous qualities and less for their content. Obtain the lyrics to "Bill Grogan's Goat" from the Internet or, if possible, obtain an audio recording from the library. Invite students to analyze the lyrics and guess why this song may be included in the story. **AS**

Objectives
• Understand cause and effect
• Identify word structure: suffixes
• Analyze text
• Draw conclusions from text and experience

Teach

Viewing the Photo

Ask: How does this photo illustrate how June feels about her current situation? *(Possible responses: It shows a young girl who looks serious or as though she's thinking about something important. June seems to think a lot about her mother's feelings and tries to come up with ways to make life easier for her.)* **OL**

C Critical Thinking

Comprehension Ask: What does June's mother mean when she calls herself a "worrywart"? *(Possible response: June's mother is finding a funny way to say that she worries often.)* **OL**

Analyzing the Photo
Look closely at this girl's face. What do you think she is feeling? Explain.

I wanted to be rich and take care of her. She worked too hard; her pretty hair had gray in it that she joked about. "Someday," I said, "I'll buy you a real house, and you'll never work in a pot factory again."

"Such delicious plans," she said. She checked the windows to see if they were locked. "Do you have your key?"

I lifted it from the chain around my neck.

"And you'll come right home from school and—"

"—I won't light fires or let strangers into the house, and I won't tell anyone on the phone that I'm here alone," I finished for her. **3**

"I know, I'm just your old worrywart mother." She kissed me twice, once on each cheek. "But you are my June, my only June, the only June."

She was wrong; there was another June. I met her when we stood next to each other at the edge of the pool the first day of swimming class in the Community Center.

526 UNIT 5 How Should You Deal with Bullies?

Practice the Skills

3 Key Reading Skill

Understanding Cause and Effect June's mother makes sure the windows are locked and makes sure June will come right home after school. What effect does she want to happen?

Additional Support

Differentiated Instruction

Responding to Quotations

Nineteenth-century British statesman Benjamin Disraeli once said, "Courage is fire, and bullying is smoke." Have students spend a few moments responding to Disraeli's statement, and then invite students to share their interpretations. Prompt students to identify Disraeli's distinction between fire and smoke *(fire is more powerful and substantial)* and how he connects that distinction with the concepts of courage and bullying. **OL** Invite students to write their own short quotations about the nature of bullying. **AL**

"What's your name?" She had a deep growly voice.

"June. What's yours?"

She stared at me. "June."

"We have the same name."

"No we don't. June is my name, and I don't give you permission to use it. Your name is Fish Eyes." She pinched me hard. "Got it, Fish Eyes?"

The next Tuesday, the Other June again stood next to me at the edge of the pool. "What's your name?"

"June."

"Wrong. Your—name—is—Fish—Eyes."

"June."

"Fish Eyes, you are really stupid." She shoved me into the pool.

The swimming **teacher** looked up, frowning, from her chart. "No one in the water yet." **4**

Practice the Skills

4 | **English Language Coach**

Suffixes The suffix *-er* is added to *teach* to make the word **teacher.** How does the suffix change the meaning of *teach*?

Tuesday of the Other June **527**

Reading in the Real World

Citizenship Many community centers, such as pools and play areas, post their rules on signs. In community centers where classes are held, these signs may also have information about whom to contact in case of a problem. Ask students to locate signs that are posted in public places in your community and to jot down the information that they offer. As a class, discuss whether any of the signs might help people facing problems like the ones June faces in the story. Ask students if they have ever been in a situation like the one June is in and how it was resolved. **OL**

Teach

C Critical Thinking

Comprehension Ask: What clues tell you that the nickname "Fish Eyes" is meant to be hurtful? *(Possible response: The other girl has a "deep growly voice," and she pinches June and calls her "really stupid.")* **OL**

Viewing the Photo

Ask: What does this photo show? *(A young girl in a pool.)* **BL** How does the photo help illustrate the story? *(Possible response: It illustrates the swimming lesson scenes.)* **OL**

Objectives
- Use text features: photograph
- Use comprehension skills

527

Teach

L Literary Element

Conflict Ask: How might June's external conflict result in an internal conflict? Explain. *(Possible response: June may have an internal conflict about how to handle being teased. She probably wants to fight back, but her mother told her to turn the other cheek and smile. She also probably wants to tell her mother about being teased but doesn't want to upset her mother or cause more trouble.)* **OL**

R Reading Skill

Understanding Cause and Effect Ask: What effect does being bullied have on the way June names the days of the week? *(Possible response: She has renamed the days according to how close they are to the day on which she is bullied.)* **BL Ask: What does this mean about the effect bullying has on June's life?** *(Possible response: The fact that June has renamed all of the days shows that being bullied has taken over her life. She can't escape thinking about it for even a day.)* **OL**

Later, in the locker room, I dressed quickly and wrapped my wet suit in the towel. The Other June pulled on her jeans. "You guys see that bathing suit Fish Eyes was wearing? Her mother found it in a trash can."

"She did not!"

The Other June grabbed my fingers and twisted. "Where'd she find your bathing suit?"

"She bought it, let me go."

"Poor little stupid Fish Eyes is crying. Oh, boo hoo hoo, poor little Fish Eyes."

After that, everyone called me Fish Eyes. And every Tuesday, wherever I was, there was also the Other June—at the edge of the pool, in the pool, in the locker room. In the water, she swam alongside me, blowing and huffing, knocking into me. In the locker room, she stepped on my feet, pinched my arms, hid my blouse, and knotted my braids together. She had large square teeth; she was shorter than I was, but heavier, with bigger bones and square hands. If I met her outside on the street, carrying her bathing suit and towel, she'd walk toward me, smiling a square, friendly smile. "Oh well, if it isn't Fish Eyes." Then she'd punch me, blam! her whole solid weight hitting me. **5**

I didn't know what to do about her. She was training me like a dog. After a few weeks of this, she only had to look at me, only had to growl, "I'm going to get you, Fish Eyes," for my heart to slink like a whipped dog down into my stomach. My arms were covered with bruises. When my mother noticed, I made up a story about tripping on the sidewalk.

My weeks were no longer Tuesday, Wednesday, Thursday, and so on. Tuesday was Awfulday. Wednesday was Badday. (The Tuesday bad feelings were still there.) Thursday was Betterday, and Friday was Safeday. Saturday was Goodday, but Sunday was Toosoonday, and Monday—Monday was nothing but the day before Awfulday. **6**

I tried to slow down time. Especially on the weekends, I stayed close by my mother, doing everything with her, shopping, cooking, cleaning, going to the Laundromat. "Aw, sweetie, go play with your friends."

"No, I'd rather be with you." I wouldn't look at the clock or listen to the radio (they were always telling you the date and the time). I did special magic things to keep the day from

Practice the Skills

5 ▌Key Literary Element

Conflict Remember that an external conflict is a struggle against something outside of oneself. What external conflict does June deal with? **L**

6 ▌Key Reading Skill

Understanding Cause and Effect The narrator says that she has renamed the days of the week. This is an effect. What do you think causes her to rename the days? **R**

Additional Support

Differentiated Instruction

Diary Entry June renames the days of the week, which revolve around her encounters with the Other June. Have students choose one of the days—Awfulday, Badday, Betterday, Safeday, Goodday, Toosoonday, or the day before Awfulday—and write a diary entry from June's perspective. Encourage students to imagine what June would do on that day and how she might feel about the rest of the week. If possible, make sure that at least one student writes an entry for each of the seven days. Ask for volunteers to share their entries, and then assemble an entire week of diary entries to read aloud to the class. **OL**

going away, rapping my knuckles six times on the bathroom door six times a day and never, ever touching the chipped place on my **bureau**. But always I woke up to the day before Tuesday, and always, no matter how many times I circled the worn spot in the living-room rug or counted twenty-five cracks in the ceiling, Monday disappeared and once again it was Tuesday.

The Other June got bored with calling me Fish Eyes. Buffalo Brain came next, but as soon as everyone knew that, she renamed me Turkey Nose.

Now at night it wasn't robbers creeping up the stairs, but the Other June, coming to torment me. When I finally fell asleep, I dreamed of kicking her, punching, biting, pinching. In the morning I remembered my dreams and felt brave and strong. And then I remembered all the things my mother had taught me and told me.

Be good, be good, be good; it's just us two women alone in the world. . . . Oh, but if it weren't, if my father wasn't long gone, if we'd had someone else to fall back on, if my mother's mother and daddy weren't dead all these years, if my father's daddy wanted to know us instead of being glad to forget us—oh, then I would have punched the Other June with a frisky heart, I would have grabbed her arm at poolside and bitten her like the dog she had made of me. **7**

One night, when my mother came home from work, she said, "Junie, listen to this. We're moving!"

Alaska, I thought. Florida. Arizona. Someplace far away and wonderful, someplace without the Other June.

"Wait till you hear this deal. We are going to be caretakers, trouble-shooters for an eight-family apartment building. Fifty-six Blue Hill Street. Not janitors; we don't do any of the heavy work. April and June, Trouble-shooters, Incorporated. If a tenant has a complaint or a problem, she comes to us and we either take care of it or call the janitor for service. And for that little bit of work, we get to live rent free!" She swept me around in a dance. "Okay? You like it? I do!"

Vocabulary

bureau (BYUR oh) *n.* a low chest of drawers

Practice the Skills

7 **Reviewing Skills**

Inferring It's just June and her mother; her grandparents are not a part of her life and her father is "long gone." How do you think this makes June feel? How do you think it affects her view of the world?

Tuesday of the Other June **529**

Teach

C Critical Thinking

Analysis Ask: Why do you think June starts circling, counting, and engaging in other strange behaviors? *(Responses will vary. Students may say that through the repetitive actions and routines, June comforts herself and avoids confronting her problem.)* **AL**

Reading Fluency

Build Fluency Have students use the text on this page to practice reading aloud with feeling. Provide a model for students by reading aloud the paragraphs in which June's mother explains that they are moving. Discuss as a class how to read lines such as "Junie, listen to this. We're moving!" and "Okay? You like it? I do!" Then have students find a quiet place to practice reading aloud, softly and on their own. **EL BL** Invite volunteers to read certain paragraphs aloud to the class. After students read these paragraphs aloud, ask them if they think it's ironic that June and her mother are going to be "trouble-shooters" for an apartment building but June can't bring herself to tell anyone that a bully is giving *her* trouble. **OL AL**

Objectives
• Understand cause and effect
• Identify literary elements: conflict
• Analyze text

529

Teach

R1 Reading Skill

Understanding Cause and Effect **Ask:** What effect does her mother's news about moving have on June? *(Possible response: June is not as happy as she thought she would be because she and her mother are not moving far enough away to be safe from the Other June.)* **OL**

L Literary Element

Conflict **Ask:** What is June's conflict at this point in the story? *(Possible response: June wants to be free from her tormentor immediately, but she has to wait six weeks.)* **OL** **Ask:** Is this conflict internal or external? *(Responses will vary. Some students may say that it is internal because June is making herself feel awful by not telling her mother or another adult about her situation.)* **AL**

R2 Reading Skill

Understanding Cause and Effect **Ask:** What effect do June's feelings have on the way she feels about the passage of time? *(Possible response: Time seems to move too fast toward Tuesday, the day of swim class.)* **OL**

R1 So. Not anywhere else, really. All the same, maybe too far to go to swimming class? "Can we move right away? Today?"

L "Gimme a break, sweetie. We've got to pack, do a thousand things. I've got to line up someone with a truck to help us. Six weeks, Saturday the fifteenth." She circled it on the calendar. It was the Saturday after the last day of swimming class.

Soon, we had boxes lying everywhere, filled with clothes and towels and glasses wrapped in newspaper. Bit by bit, we cleared the rooms, leaving only what we needed right now. The dining-room table staggered on a bunched-up rug, our bureaus inched toward the front door like patient cows. On the calendar in the kitchen, my mother marked off the days until we moved, but the only days I thought about were Tuesdays—Awfuldays. Nothing else was real except the too fast passing of time, moving toward each Tuesday . . . away from Tuesday . . . toward Tuesday . . .

And it seemed to me that this would go on forever, that Tuesdays would come forever and I would be forever trapped by the side of the pool, the Other June whispering Buffalo Brain Fish Eyes Turkey Nose into my ear, while she ground her elbow into my side and smiled her square smile at the swimming teacher. **8**

And then it ended. It was the last day of swimming class. The last Tuesday. We had all passed our tests, and, as if in celebration, the Other June only pinched me twice. "And now," our swimming teacher said, "all of you are ready for the Advanced Class, which starts in just one month. I have a sign-up slip here. Please put your name down before you leave." Everyone but me crowded around. I went to the locker room and pulled on my clothes as fast as possible. The Other June burst through the door just as I was leaving. "Goodbye," I yelled, "good riddance to bad trash!" Before she could pinch me again, I ran past her and then ran all the way home, singing, "Goodbye . . . goodbye . . . goodbye, good riddance to bad trash!" **9**

Later, my mother carefully untied the blue ribbon around my swimming class diploma.[2] "Look at this! Well, isn't this wonderful! You are on your way, you might turn into an Olympic swimmer, you never know what life will bring."

---

2. A *diploma* is a document that shows the completion of a course of study.

Practice the Skills

8 **Key Reading Skill**

Understanding Cause and Effect Think about how June is feeling. What is the main cause of her feelings? **R2**

9 **Key Reading Skill**

Understanding Cause and Effect June's decision to not sign up for swimming lessons is an effect. What causes June to decide she does not want to sign up for more swimming lessons?

Additional Support

Reading in the Real World

Citizenship Many states have a "Good Samaritan Law," which protects people who help a victim in an emergency from liability. In some states, individuals who witness emergencies are obligated to give "reasonable assistance," and the failure to do so is considered a misdemeanor. If your state has a Good Samaritan Law, encourage students to research it. Prompt students to discuss whether a person who witnesses an emergency should be required to act. **OL**

"I don't want to take more lessons."

"Oh, sweetie, it's great to be a good swimmer." But then, looking into my face, she said, "No, no, no, don't worry, you don't have to."

The next morning, I woke up hungry for the first time in weeks. No more swimming class. No more Baddays and Awfuldays. No more Tuesdays of the Other June. In the kitchen, I made hot cocoa to go with my mother's corn muffins. "It's Wednesday, Mom," I said, stirring the cocoa. "My favorite day."

"Since when?"

"Since this morning." I turned on the radio so I could hear the announcer tell the time, the temperature, and the day.

Thursday for breakfast I made cinnamon toast, Friday my mother made pancakes, and on Saturday, before we moved, we ate the last slices of bread and cleaned out the peanut butter jar.

"Some breakfast," Tilly said. "Hello, you must be June." She shook my hand. She was a friend of my mother's from work; she wore big hoop earrings, sandals, and a skirt as dazzling as a rainbow. She came in a truck with John to help us move our things. **10**

John shouted cheerfully at me, "So you're moving." An enormous man with a face covered with little brown bumps. Was he afraid his voice wouldn't travel the distance from his mouth to my ear? "You looking at my moles?" he shouted, and he heaved our big green flowered chair down the stairs. "Don't worry, they don't bite. Ha, ha, ha!" Behind him came my mother and Tilly balancing a bureau between them, and behind them I carried a lamp and the round, flowered Mexican tray that was my mother's favorite. She had found it at a garage sale and said it was as close to foreign travel as we would ever get.

The night before, we had loaded our car, stuffing in bags and boxes until there was barely room for the two of us. But it was only when we were in the car, when we drove past Abdo's Grocery, where they always gave us credit, when I turned for a last look at our street—it was only then that I understood we

Practice the Skills

10 | **Key Reading Skill**

Understanding Cause and Effect Moving can have many different effects. June thinks the effects will be good. What are some negative effects of moving to another place?

Teach

R Reading Skill

Understanding Cause and Effect Say: The Other June's bullying causes several changes in June's behavior. Name some of these changes. *(She stays close to her mother, she doesn't look at clocks or listen to the radio, and she develops rituals such as walking in circles and counting cracks.)* **Ask:** How does June's behavior change after her swim classes are over? *(Possible response: She wakes up hungry for the first time in weeks; she listens to the time, temperature, and date on the radio; she tells her mother that Wednesday is her favorite day)* **OL**

L Literary Element

Conflict Say: Moving is often a stressful activity. Does moving present a conflict for June and her mother? Give examples to support your response. *(Possible response: No; the move does not seem stressful for June and her mother. They have friends who joke with them and who help them with the work. June is looking forward to moving away from the Other June, and her mother is excited and happy.)* **OL**

Differentiated Instruction

Additional Reading Have students read other fictional books about bullies to explore how characters cope with being bullied. In addition to the books listed in the "Reading On Your Own" section of this unit, you may want to assign *Bad Girls,* by Cynthia Voigt. Appropriate for below-level sixth-grade readers, Voigt's novel is about two fifth-grade girls who earn a reputation for being troublemakers. Assign students books to read outside class, and encourage them to compare and contrast the ways in which different characters cope with being bullied. Provide comparison charts for students to use as they read. Have students present their comparisons to the class. **AS**

Objectives

• Understand cause and effect
• Identify conflict
• Understand idioms

Teach

L Literary Element

Conflict Ask: What does June realize about her new home? *(The Other June lives near her now.)* **BL Ask: Why does this create a conflict for June?** *(Possible response: June's mother is excited about living in the new apartment. June feels awful again but does not want to disappoint her mother by telling her about the Other June.)* **OL**

EL Language Coach

Suffixes Say: The verb *adjust* **can be made into an adjective by adding the suffix** *-able.* **What are some other verbs that you can make into adjectives by adding the suffix** *-able?* *(Possible responses: perish—perishable, wear—wearable, teach—teachable, read—readable)* **EL BL**

were truly going to live somewhere else, in another apartment, in another place mysteriously called Blue Hill Street.

Tilly's truck followed our car.

"Oh, I'm so excited," my mother said. She laughed. "You'd think we were going across the country."

Our old car wheezed up a long, steep hill. Blue Hill Street. I looked from one side to the other, trying to see everything.

My mother drove over the crest of the hill. "And now—ta da!—our new home!"

"Which house? Which one?" I looked out the window and what I saw was the Other June. She was sprawled on the stoop of a pink house, lounging back on her elbows, legs outspread, her jaws working on a wad of gum. I slid down into the seat, but it was too late. I was sure she had seen me.

My mother turned into a driveway next to a big white building with a tiny porch. She leaned on the steering wheel. "See that window there, that's our living-room window . . . and that one over there, that's your bedroom . . ."

We went into the house, down a dim, cool hall. In our new apartment, the wooden floors clicked under our shoes, and my mother showed me everything. Her voice echoed in the empty rooms. I followed her around in a daze. Had I imagined seeing the Other June? Maybe I'd seen another girl who looked like her. A double. That could happen.

"Ho yo, where do you want this chair?" John appeared in the doorway. We brought in boxes and bags and beds and stopped only to eat pizza and drink orange juice from the carton.

"June's so quiet, do you think she'll adjust all right?" I heard Tilly say to my mother.

"Oh, definitely. She'll make a wonderful **adjustment**. She's just getting used to things."

But I thought that if the Other June lived on the same street as I did, I would never get used to things. **11 12**

That night I slept in my own bed, with my own pillow and blanket, but with floors that creaked in strange voices and walls with cracks I didn't recognize. I didn't feel either happy or unhappy. It was as if I were waiting for something.

Practice the Skills

11 Key Reading Skill

Understanding Cause and Effect June has been looking forward to moving, but now something has changed her mind. What causes her to change her mind? What effect does it have on her? **L**

12 English Language Coach

Suffixes June's mother adds the suffix *-ment* to the verb *adjust* in order to form the noun **adjustment.** When you attach *-ment* to a verb, you make a noun. Think of two other examples of words formed by adding *-ment* to a verb. Write them in your Learner's Notebook. **EL**

Additional Support

English Language Coach

Breaking the Rules Explain to students that writers often break the rules of grammar to produce a desired style or effect. For example, in this story, Mazer often writes sentences that do not include a subject and main verb; the effect is that such sentences more closely resemble the way that June thinks. Ask students to locate examples in the text. *("An enormous man with a face covered with little brown bumps." "Blue Hill Street." "A double.")* Next, prompt students to add words to form complete sentences. *(Sentence 1: Add "He was"; Sentence 2: Add "It was called"; Sentence 3: Add "She could be")* **EL BL**

Monday, when the principal of Blue Hill Street School left me in Mr. Morrisey's classroom, I knew what I'd been waiting for. In that room full of strange kids, there was one person I knew. She smiled her square smile, raised her hand, and said, "She can sit next to me, Mr. Morrisey."

"Very nice of you, June M. OK, June T., take your seat. I'll try not to get you two Junes mixed up."

I sat down next to her. She pinched my arm. "Good riddance to bad trash," she mocked.

I was back in the Tuesday swimming class, only now it was worse, because every day would be Awfulday. The pinching had already started. Soon, I knew, on the playground and in the halls, kids would pass me, grinning. "Hiya, Fish Eyes."

The Other June followed me around during recess that day, droning in my ear, "You are my slave, you must do everything I say, I am your master, say it, say, 'Yes, master, you are my master.'"

I pressed my lips together, clapped my hands over my ears, but without hope. Wasn't it only a matter of time before I said the hateful words?

"How was school?" my mother said that night.

"OK."

R She put a pile of towels in a bureau drawer. "Try not to be sad about missing your old friends, sweetie; there'll be new ones."

L The next morning, the Other June was waiting for me when I left the house. "Did your mother get you that blouse in the garbage dump?" She butted me, shoving me against a tree. "Don't you speak anymore, Fish Eyes?" Grabbing my chin in her hands, she pried open my mouth. "Oh, ha ha, I thought you lost your tongue." **13**

W e went on to school. I sank down into my seat, my head on my arms. "June T., are you all right?" Mr. Morrisey asked. I nodded. My head was almost too heavy to lift.

The Other June went to the pencil sharpener. Round and round she whirled the handle. Walking back, looking at me, she held the three sharp pencils like three little knives.

Practice the Skills

13 🔵**BIG** Question

The conflict between June and the "Other June" gets worse every day. Do you think June should confront her bully now? Or should she wait? Write your answer on your Foldable.

Tuesday of the Other June **533**

Teach

R Reading Skill

Understanding Cause and Effect Ask: What cause-and-effect relationship does June's mother think she has discovered? *(Possible response: June's mother thinks that June is unhappy because she misses her friends.)* **Ask:** Is June's mother correct? Explain. *(Possible response: No; June is upset because she is still being bullied by the Other June, not because she misses her old friends.)* **AS**

L Literary Element

Conflict Ask: Could June avoid this situation without fighting? Explain your response. *(Possible response: Some students may say that June would have to fight in order to protect herself. Others may say that June could change her schedule to avoid leaving the house when the Other June is nearby or finally tell an adult about the situation.)* **AS**

Literature Focus Lesson

Dramatic Irony The incident in which the Other June invites June to sit next to her is an excellent example of dramatic irony. Explain to students that dramatic irony occurs when the audience or reader is aware of something that at least one character is not. In this case, Mr. Morrisey and the rest of the class

think that the Other June is being polite when she says, "She can sit next to me." However, readers know that the Other June will be able to bully June more easily, which she proves by pinching June's arm when she sits down. Have students research other stories that use this literary element for dramatic effect. **AL**

Objectives
- Understand cause and effect
- Identify literary elements: conflicts
- Identify word structure: suffixes

533

Teach

C Critical Thinking

Comprehension Ask: What advice does June's mother give her daughter about dealing with conflicts? *(She tells her not to fight back, to turn the other cheek, and to smile.)* **Ask:** What happens when June follows her mother's advice? *(The Other June's bullying only gets worse.)* **BL Ask:** How do you think June will resolve her conflict? *(Possible response: June will finally stand up for herself.)* **OL**

L Literary Element

Conflict Ask: What does June's dream tell you about how she would like to deal with the Other June? *(Possible response: She wants to fight her.)* **Ask:** Why do you think that June resists the urge to fight back? *(Possible response: Her mother told her not to fight and to turn the other cheek.)* **AS**

Analyzing the Photo Which character in the story might this man look like? How do you know?

Someone knocked on the door. Mr. Morrisey went out into the hall. Paper planes burst into the air, flying from desk to desk. Someone turned on a transistor radio. And the Other June, coming closer, smiled and licked her lips like a cat sleepily preparing to gulp down a mouse.

I remembered my dream of kicking her, punching, biting her like a dog.

C Then my mother spoke quickly in my ear: Turn the other cheek, my Junie; smile at the world, and the world'll surely smile back.

But I had turned the other cheek and it was slapped. I had smiled and the world hadn't smiled back. I couldn't run home as fast as my feet would take me. I had to stay in school—and in school there was the Other June. Every morning, there would be the Other June, and every afternoon, and every day, all day, there would be the Other June. **14**

534 UNIT 5 How Should You Deal with Bullies?

Practice the Skills

14 Key Literary Element

Conflict This paragraph lists many conflicts. What is the main reason for all of them? Is the main reason an internal conflict, an external conflict, or both? **L**

Additional Support

English Language Coach

Tone Encourage students to search for words or phrases in the final pages of the story that show that a change has taken place. Draw two columns on the board. In the first column, write down words from the beginning and middle of the story that show June's frustration. Examples include "hateful words," "sank down," and "throbbed." In the second column, write down words or phrases from the end of the story that show a switch to a more positive tone. Examples include "popped wide," "made me laugh," "it felt so good to say it," "twirling my braids." **EL BL**

Practice the Skills

She frisked down the aisle, stabbing the pencils in the air toward me. A boy stood up on his desk and bowed. "My fans," he said, "I greet you." My arm twitched and throbbed, as if the Other June's pencils had already poked through the skin. She came closer, smiling her Tuesday smile.

"No," I whispered, "no." The word took wings and flew me to my feet, in front of the Other June. "Noooooo." It flew out of my mouth into her surprised face.

The boy on the desk turned toward us. "You said something, my devoted fans?"

"No," I said to the Other June. "Oh, no! No. No. No. No more." I pushed away the hand that held the pencils.

The Other June's eyes opened, popped wide like the eyes of somebody in a cartoon. It made me laugh. The boy on the desk laughed, and then the other kids were laughing, too.

"No," I said again, because it felt so good to say it. "No, no, no, no." I leaned toward the Other June, put my finger against her chest. Her cheeks turned red, she squawked something— it sounded like "Eeeraaghyou!"—and she stepped back. She stepped away from me.

The door banged, the airplanes disappeared, and Mr. Morrisey walked to his desk. "OK. OK. Let's get back to work. Kevin Clark, how about it?" Kevin jumped off the desk, and Mr. Morrisey picked up a piece of chalk. "All right, class—" He stopped and looked at me and the Other June. "You two Junes, what's going on there?"

I tried it again. My finger against her chest. Then the words. "No—more." And she stepped back another step. I sat down at my desk. **L**

"June M.," Mr. Morrisey said.

She turned around, staring at him with that big-eyed cartoon look. After a moment she sat down at her desk with a loud slapping sound.

Even Mr. Morrisey laughed.

And sitting at my desk, twirling my braids, I knew this was the last Tuesday of the Other June. **15** ○

15 🔲**BIG** Question

How has June T. changed the way she deals with June M.'s bullying? How does June M. react? Write your answers in the "Tuesday of the Other June" page of Foldable 5. Your response will help you with the Unit Challenge later. **BQ**

Tuesday of the Other June **535**

Teach

L Literary Element

Conflict Ask: **What new conflict does the Other June face?** *(Possible responses: The Other June doesn't know what to do when June stands up to her.)* **OL Ask: What is shown about the situation when the Other June takes a step backward?** *(Possible response: This shows that the Other June does not have control over June anymore.)* **AL**

BQ **BIG** Question

Ask: Does June resolve her conflict by herself? Explain. *(Possible response: June relies on the help of her classmates and her teacher by confronting the Other June in class.)* **Ask: What is the advantage of standing up to the Other June in the classroom, as opposed to after school?** *(Possible response: By confronting the Other June in the classroom, June makes sure that they don't fight and that teachers are nearby.)* **OL**

Assess
✅CheckPoint

Use the CheckPoint questions provided on Presentation Plus! to check for comprehension of the selection. These questions can be used with interactive response keypads for immediate student feedback.

Objectives
• Identify literary elements: conflicts
• Use comprehension skills

Reading in the Real World

College University researchers from many different fields have conducted studies about the causes and effects of bullying. Have groups of students use library and Internet resources to research a university study about bullying. Ask students to note each researcher's field (such as psychology, child development, or education), and have each group identify the context and major conclusions of its study. Each group may present its findings to the class or write a brief report. **OL**

Assess

After You Read | Tuesday of the Other June

Resources for page 536

- 📁 Selection QuickCheck, p. 43
- 📁 Selection and Unit Assessment, p. 51
- 💿 ExamView Assessment Suite
- 💿 Interactive Tutor: Self-Assesement

Students can respond to the *After You Read* items in their Learner's Notebooks or on a separate sheet of paper.

Answering the BIG Question

1. Responses will vary. Students should support their answers with evidence from the text.
2. She meets the "Other June" on the first day of swimming class in the Community Center.
3. June's mother gets a new job as a caretaker or troubleshooter for an apartment building.

Critical Thinking

4. Possible response: June M. wants to have June T. next to her so that she can torment her.
5. Possible response: She is shocked that June T. has actually stood up for herself.
6. Possible response: June's mother cares deeply for June, but she isn't able to spend much time with her. June feels protective toward her mother and she doesn't want to make her worry.

Answering the BIG Question

1. What are your thoughts about dealing with bullies after reading "Tuesday of the Other June"? Explain.
2. **Recall** Where does the narrator first meet the "Other June"?
   Tip Right There
3. **Summarize** Why do June and her mother move to Blue Hill Street?
   Tip Think and Search

Critical Thinking

4. **Infer** Why does June M. volunteer to let June T. sit next to her in Mr. Morrisey's class?
   Tip Author and Me
5. **Analyze** June M. doesn't say anything when June T. tells her "No more" at the end of the story. Why doesn't June M. respond?
   Tip On My Own
6. **Evaluate** What kind of relationship does June have with her mother? Use details from the story to help you explain your answer.
   Tip Author and Me

Write About Your Reading

"Tuesday of the Other June" describes the conflict between the two Junes from June T.'s point of view. But you don't find out much about why the "Other June" acts the way she does. Use the questions below to help you write a diary entry from the point of view of the "Other June."

- How do you feel about June T.? What events made you feel this way?
- How have you acted toward June T.? How do you feel about your actions?
- Is June T. the only person you have treated this way? If not, who else have you bullied, and why?
- How do you feel now that June T. has stood up to you?

Objectives (pp. 536–537)
Reading Understand cause and effect • Make connections from text to self
Literature Identify literary elements: external and internal conflict
Vocabulary Identify word structure: suffixes
Writing Respond to literature: diary
Grammar Identify parts of speech: nouns, verbs, adjective, adverbs

536 UNIT 5 How Should You Deal with Bullies?

Write About Your Reading

Possible response:
Dear Diary,
Today in swim class I met a girl who has the same name as me—June! She's prettier than I am and a better swimmer. It made me so angry that people compare us because we have the same name. The last time I was this angry, I pushed around the kid who made me mad. That's what I did to this girl. I called her "Fish Eyes" because I couldn't bear to think that she was a June, too. I felt really good after I pushed her into the pool. I sort of wish I hadn't done it, though.

Skills Review

Key Reading Skill: Understanding Cause and Effect

7. What are the effects of June M.'s bullying? Explain.

Key Literary Element: Conflict

8. How does June T. first try to deal with the bullying? How successful is she?

9. How does June T. finally resolve her conflict with the "Other June"?

10. June T. experiences an internal conflict about disobeying her mother. Does she disobey her mother at the end of the story? Explain.

Reviewing Skills: Inferring

11. Why doesn't June tell her mother about being bullied?

Vocabulary Check

Choose the best word from the list to complete each sentence below. Rewrite each sentence with the correct word in place.

recited   rigid   bureau

12. He memorized the poem and _____ it to the teacher for a grade.

13. Oscar kept all of his winter sweaters in the _____ next to his bed.

14. As the lightning crackled, David's body became _____ with fear.

15. **Academic Vocabulary** Suppose you saw this headline: "Conflict at Westbridge High School." What do you expect the story will be about?

16. **English Language Coach** Add the suffix -er to the word *dance.* How does the suffix change the meaning of the word?

Grammar Link: Parts of Speech

A word's part of speech is determined by how the word is used in a sentence. Here are four parts of speech:

- **Nouns** are words that name a person, place, thing, or idea. Some examples are *hat, actor, country, sandwich,* and *peace.*

- **Verbs** are words that express action or a state of being. They are necessary to make a statement. Some action verbs are *run, persuade,* and *laugh.* Some verbs that express a state of being are *be, become,* and *appear.*

- **Adjectives** are words that describe nouns or pro-nouns. Some examples are *blue, flat,* and *three.*

- **Adverbs** describe verbs, adjectives, or other adverbs. Adverbs often end in *-ly.* Some examples are *quietly, sadly,* and *heavily.* Other examples are *very* and *only.*

Grammar Practice

Rewrite each sentence. Label the parts of speech of the underlined words.

17. Our old <u>car</u> <u>wheezed</u> up a long, <u>steep</u> hill.

18. The <u>singers</u> and dancers <u>moved</u> across the stage <u>gracefully</u>.

19. Madison <u>pounced</u> on the last cookie <u>hungrily</u>.

20. <u>Tito</u> made <u>extra</u> money by walking dogs and <u>eagerly</u> offering to mow lawns.

Writing Application Look back at the diary entry you wrote for the "Other June." Add two adjectives and two adverbs to help with details and descriptions.

Web Activities For eFlashcards, Selection Quick Checks, and other Web activities, go to www.glencoe.com.

Tuesday of the Other June **537**

Skills Review

Key Reading Skill: Understanding Cause and Effect

7. Possible response: June T. wants to move away, keeps secrets from her mother, and develops strange habits.

Key Literary Element: Conflict

8. Responses will vary.

9. Possible response: June T. stands up to June M.

10. Responses will vary.

Reviewing Skills: Inferring

11. Possible response: June doesn't want her mother to worry about her.

Vocabulary Check

12. He memorized the poem and <u>recited</u> it to the teacher for a grade.

13. Oscar kept all of his winter sweaters in the <u>bureau</u> next to his bed.

14. As the lightning crackled, David's body became <u>rigid</u> with fear.

15. **Academic Vocabulary** Possible response: It will describe some kind of argument or problem that takes place between two sides in a school.

16. **English Language Coach** Possible response: The suffix changes the verb to a noun that means "one who dances."

Grammar Link: Parts of Speech

17. car: noun; wheezed: verb; steep: adjective

18. singers: noun; moved: verb; gracefully: adverb

19. pounced: verb; hungrily: adverb

20. Tito: noun; extra: adjective; eagerly: adverb

Close

Ask students to discuss when it is appropriate to ignore a bully and when it is appropriate to take action.

Teach

More About the Author

Sir Stephen Spender's early life was shaped by conflict and loss. His father and mother both died during his adolescence, and he grew up during the Depression and the rise of Fascism. In his autobiography, *World Within Worlds*, Spender admits that he felt like an outsider during much of his life.

V Vocabulary

Substitution Encourage students to substitute other verbs for *employ* and to determine which of the suffixes in the web can be used to form words. **EL** Point out that verbs that do not take direct objects (such as *run*) will not work with the suffix *-ee*, which means "the object of." **AL**

Before You Read • My Parents

Sir Stephen Spender

Meet the Author

English writer Sir Stephen Spender was the son of a novelist and journalist. He was a poet, a literary critic, and an editor. Spender spoke about the value of friendship: "The friends of my lifetime whom I have most admired and loved, the books and paintings I love . . . exemplify for me what I most profoundly believe." See page R6 of the Author Files for more on Stephen Spender.

Literature Online

Author Search For more about Sir Stephen Spender, go to www.glencoe.com.

Objectives (pp. 538–541)
Reading Understand cause and effect • Make connections from text to self
Literature Identify literary elements: conflict
Vocabulary Identify word structure: suffixes

Vocabulary Preview

coarse (kors) *adj.* rough; lacking good manners **(p. 541)** *The boys behaved in a rude, coarse way in the restaurant.*

lisp (lisp) *n.* a speech problem affecting the *s* and *z* sounds **(p. 541)** *Other kids copied Javier's lisp, which made him afraid to speak.*

lithe (lyth) *adj.* flexible and moving easily **(p. 541)** *The bullies were lithe and quick as they sprang from behind the hedges.*

Partner Talk With a partner, copy the words onto one set of index cards and the definitions onto another set. Mix the cards up and place them face down on a desk or table. Take turns turning the cards over two at a time. When you match a word and its definition, you may take the pair. Write sentences with the words you have matched.

English Language Coach

Suffixes Learning the meanings and uses of suffixes can help you build your vocabulary. Sometimes you can add many suffixes to a word. Each one gives the word a slightly different meaning.

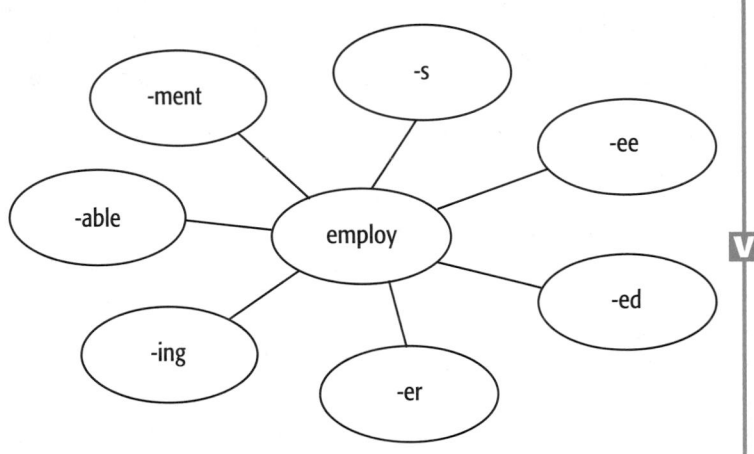

Write to Learn Write sentences using the word *employ* with each of the suffixes shown. If you are not sure what the word means when you add one of the suffixes, use a dictionary to look up the meaning. Be sure to include a sentence for the word *employ*.

538 UNIT 5   How Should You Deal with Bullies?

Additional Support

Author Search To expand students' appreciation of Sir Stephen Spender, have them access the Web site for additional information and resources.

Literature Focus Lesson

Poetry After writing about politics and current events in the 1930s, Stephen Spender began writing more about himself and about the human experience. Discuss with students what topics or themes might occur in poetry that is written by adults about their childhood.

Prompt students to take Spender's life into consideration when thinking about his approach to writing about childhood. You may also want to introduce poems by Robert Frost as a way to explore recollections of childhood. **AL**

Skills Preview

Key Reading Skill: Understanding Cause and Effect

Poems don't always show cause and effect as clearly as stories do. When you read a poem like "My Parents," ask yourself questions that help you to think about cause and effect:

- What sorts of activities do the speaker's parents keep him or her from? Why?
- What does the speaker do instead?
- How does this affect the speaker?

Write to Learn In your Learner's Notebook, answer the above questions as you read "My Parents."

Key Literary Element: Conflict

External and internal conflicts can make a story or poem more interesting. A writer can follow the course of a conflict from beginning to end. But sometimes the writer may give just a snapshot of a conflict and let you decide what came before or what will come later. When you think about conflict in a poem, keep in mind that:

- Authors don't always give you all the background information.

  Do you know the backgrounds of the speaker of the poem and the other children? Can you infer them?

- A conflict is not always cleared up by the end of a story or poem.

  Is the conflict between the speaker and the other boys cleared up at the end?

Partner Talk With a partner, talk about the conflicts below. First, decide if they are internal or external. Next, discuss what you should do in each of these situations.

- You're riding your bike home from school, the tire goes flat, and you get caught in a rain storm.
- Your parents told you to be home by 8:00 P.M., but your friends want you to stay out later.

Get Ready to Read

Connect to the Reading

Have you ever wanted to belong to a group of people who treated you badly? Have you ever done something to earn their respect or approval to fit in?

Write to Learn In your Learner's Notebook, quick-write about a time you did something to fit in. If you've never done something to fit in, write about someone you know who tried to fit in.

Build Background

Have you ever been told, "Sticks and stones will break your bones, but names will never hurt you." Often, we think of bullies as kids who hit or push other kids, but sometimes teasing can be just as bad.

- Often, kids who are bullied will feel bad about themselves.
- Sometimes, those kids are less likely to stand up for themselves if bullied again.

Set Purposes for Reading

BIG Question Read "My Parents" to see how one young person responds to bullying.

Set Your Own Purpose What else would you like to learn from the poem to help you answer the Big Question? Write your own purpose on the "My Parents" page of Foldable 5.

Interactive Literary Elements Handbook
To review or learn more about the literary elements, go to www.glencoe.com.

Keep Moving

Use these skills as you read the following selection.

Teach

L Literary Element

Conflict Say: You already know that an internal conflict occurs within a person's mind. Is it ever possible to tell when someone else has an internal conflict? Explain. *(Possible answer: Yes; Some people show physical signs of being upset. They might bite their fingernails or have a worried expression on their face.)* **OL**

R Reading Skill

Review Connecting Ask: Which is harder to put up with, being hit or being teased? Which is more hurtful? Explain. *(Responses will vary.)* **AS**

Reading Fluency

Build Fluency Short poems such as "My Parents" give students an excellent opportunity to build fluency. Note that unlike the lines in many poems, the majority of the lines in "My Parents" do not end with a comma or period. As students read the poem silently, encourage them to continue reading fluidly until they reach a punctuation mark, rather than pausing at the end of each line. Read the poem aloud once as a model, and then invite volunteers to practice reading it aloud, one stanza at a time. Note that some extra pauses will be necessary because of lengthy sentences. **EL BL**

Objectives

- Identify literary elements: conflict
- Identify word structure: suffixes
- Make connections from text to self

Teach

R **Reading Skill**

Understanding Cause and Effect **Ask:** As you scan the poem, what do you notice about its structure? *(the first word of each line is capitalized even though it is not the beginning of a sentence)* **BL** **Say:** In free verse poetry, this occurs less often. What effect does capitalization, or the lack of it, have on your reading of poems? *(Responses will vary.)* **OL** **AL**

Viewing the Art

Ask: What does this painting show? *(Possible response: It's an abstract-looking painting of two people.)* **BL** **Ask:** What do you learn about the figures in the painting from the painting's title? *(That one figure is male and the other is female.* **Ask:** How might this painting help illustrate the poem? Explain. *(Possible response: The poem is titled "My Parents." Maybe the painting is supposed to illustrate the speaker's parents. Or, because it's hard to see the figures clearly, maybe it represents the bullies mentioned in the poem.)* **OL**

My Parents

by Stephen Spender

Additional Support

Differentiated Instruction

Graphic Organizer Draw the cause and effect flowchart on the right on the board. Tell students that when they want to show a cause-and-effect relationship, they can use a flowchart like this. Have them arrange their ideas or the events in the selection in the boxes, putting them in logical order to show how one event flows into another. **OL**

Cause   Effect

Patrick Garland and Alexandra Bastedo, 1998. Stephen Finer. Oil on canvas, Private Collection.

My parents kept me from **children** who were rough
Who threw words like stones and wore torn clothes
Their thighs showed through rags they ran in the street
And climbed cliffs and stripped by the country streams. **1**

5 I feared more than tigers their muscles like iron
Their jerking hands and their knees tight on my arms
I feared the salt **coarse** pointing of those boys
Who copied my **lisp** behind me on the road. **2**

They were **lithe** they sprang out behind hedges
10 Like dogs to bark at my world. They threw mud
While I looked the other way, pretending to smile.
I longed to forgive them but they never smiled. **3** **4** ○

Vocabulary

coarse (kors) *adj.* rough; lacking good manners

lisp (lisp) *n.* a speech problem affecting the *s* and *z* sounds

lithe (lyth) *adj.* flexible and moving easily

Practice the Skills

1 **English Language Coach**

Suffixes The suffix *-ren* has been added to the word *child* to make **children.** The suffix makes the word plural, more than one child. Which of these three suffixes, *-or, -less,* or *-ness,* could also be added to the word *child*? How does the suffix change the meaning of the word?

2 **Key Literary Element**

Conflict The external conflict in "My Parents" is between the speaker and the other boys. Read the second stanza. What are two examples that give details of this conflict? **L**

3 **Key Reading Skill**

Understanding Cause and Effect Sometimes causes and effects aren't always directly stated, especially in a poem. What causes the speaker to look "the other way, pretending to smile"? What is the effect of this behavior?

4 **BIG Question**

How does the speaker deal with bullies? Write your answer on the "My Parents" page of Foldable 5. Your answer will help you complete the Unit Challenge later. **BQ**

My Parents **541**

Teach

L **Literary Element**

Conflict Ask: The narrator of the poem is tormented by a group of boys. Are there any reasons given for this conflict? If so, what are they? Why do the boys tease the narrator? *(Possible response: The bullies wear clothes that are torn and made of rags. These children seem to be poor and may be teasing the speaker out of jealousy.)* **OL**

BQ **BIG Question**

Say: The speaker is sorry that the bullies "never smiled." Why do you think he wishes to see this reaction from them? *(Possible response: If the bullies smiled, it would show that they were human and that they had feelings. The speaker would be able to forgive them if they showed emotion.)* **AL**

Assess

CheckPoint

Use the CheckPoint questions provided on Presentation Plus! to check for comprehension of the selection. These questions can be used with interactive response keypads for immediate student feedback.

Literature Focus Lesson

Dialogue Ask students to imagine that as an adult, the speaker meets the boys who bullied him when he was younger. Have students write a dialogue in which the speaker confronts the boys about their past behavior. Encourage students to consider what reasons the boys had for teasing the speaker, as well as how they probably feel about their actions as adults. In addition, have students consider what the speaker says in the final stanza of the poem and decide whether he can forgive the boys after the confrontation. **OL**

Objectives
• Identify literary elements: conflict
• Identify dialogue

541

Assess

After You Read My Parents

Resources for page 542

📁 Selection QuickCheck, p. 44

📁 Selection and Unit Assessment, p. 52

💿 ExamView Assessment Suite

💿 Interactive Tutor: Self-Assesesment

Students can respond to the *After You Read* items in their Learner's Notebooks or on a separate sheet of paper.

Answering the BIG Question

1. Responses will vary. Some students may say that the speaker believes in forgiving and forgetting.

2. The speaker compares the boys to tigers and dogs.

3. The other boys copy the speaker's lisp.

Critical Thinking

4. Possible response: The boys are pinning him down on the ground and kneeling on top of him.

5. Responses will vary. Students may suggest that the speaker blames his parents for his not belonging with the group of boys and that the speaker views his parents as the source of his problem.

6. Responses will vary. Some students may say that protecting children is a good idea. Others may say that protecting children too much will make them the victims of teasing.

542

Answering the BIG Question

1. How do you think the speaker in the poem would answer the Big Question? Explain your answer.

2. **Recall** To what animal does the speaker compare the boys?
   Tip Right There

3. **Recall** What characteristic of the speaker do the other boys copy?
   Tip Right There

Critical Thinking

4. **Infer** The speaker says that he feels the knees of the other boys "tight on my arms." What are the boys doing when he feels this?
   Tip Author and Me

5. **Interpret** Why do you think the speaker wants to forgive the boys for their cruel actions toward him?
   Tip Author and Me

6. **Synthesize** Do you think it's a good idea for parents to protect their children as the speaker's parents did? Explain.
   Tip On My Own

Talk About Your Reading

Imagine someone from a planet where there was no violence came to Earth and saw the events in the poem taking place. They have never seen anything like this before. Explain to them what is happening and why. Keep the poem in mind; be sure to use examples from the poem as you explain. Break into three groups and take these steps to get started:

• First, think about what kinds of questions someone who had *never* seen violence would ask. Write down at least three questions.

• Think about what you know from the poem and your own life to help answer those questions.

• Think about cause and effect, conflict, and the Big Question to help with your discussion.

Objectives (pp. 542–543)
Reading Understand cause and effect
• Make connections from text to self
Literature Identify literary elements: conflict
Vocabulary Identify word structure: suffixes
Grammar Use sentence elements: independent and dependent clauses

Talk About Your Reading

Responses will vary. Students should write questions indicating that violence seems unfamiliar and irrational. Responses should demonstrate comprehension of the poem and a firm grasp of conflict and cause and effect.

Skills Review

Key Reading Skill: Understanding Cause and Effect

7. What do the bullies do that causes the speaker to fear them?

Key Literary Element: Conflict

8. What are some of the reasons for the external conflict in the poem?

9. Do you think the speaker of the poem might have an internal conflict? Why or why not?

Vocabulary Check

10. Write a paragraph in which you use each vocabulary word correctly.

> coarse
> lisp
> lithe

11. **Academic Vocabulary** Write a sentence about why *conflict* is important in a story.

12. **English Language Coach** Add each of the suffixes below to the word *move.* Then explain how adding each suffix changes the meaning of the word.

> *-er*
> *-ment*
> *-able*

Grammar Link: Clauses

As you have learned, a **clause** is a group of words that has a subject and a verb or verb phrase known as a predicate. There are two types of clauses: **independent** and **dependent.** An independent clause has a subject and a predicate and can stand alone as a sentence. A dependent clause has a subject and a predicate, but it cannot stand alone as a sentence.

independent	dependent
She became a vegetarian	because she loves animals.

Dependent clauses do the job of different parts of speech. A dependent clause can do the job of a noun, an adjective, or an adverb.

- **Noun clauses** act like nouns. They name persons, places, ideas, or things. Noun clauses often begin with *whoever* or *whatever.*

  Whoever saw the car wreck *reported it to the police.*

- **Adjective clauses** describe nouns. You can spot an adjective clause by looking for words such as *who, whom, which,* or *that.*

  *The boys **who found the lost dog** received a reward.*

- **Adverb clauses** tell *how, when, where, why,* or *under what conditions* the action occurs. Words such as *after, when, where,* or *because* often start adverb clauses.

  *I was bored **because I broke my leg** and couldn't go out.*

Grammar Practice

Each of the sentences below contains a noun clause, an adjective clause, or an adverb clause. Identify the clauses and their parts of speech.

13. I went swimming with my friends after they played soccer.

14. She will buy whatever is on sale.

15. My cat sprang out from the blankets that covered our sofa.

16. Whoever played the drum solo was extremely good.

17. I was tired because I didn't sleep last night.

Literature Online

Web Activities For eFlashcards, Selection Quick Checks, and other Web activities, go to www.glencoe.com.

My Parents **543**

Skills Review

Key Reading Skill: Understanding Cause and Effect

7. Possible response: The bullies tease and harass the speaker.

Key Literary Element: Conflict

8. Students may suggest that the other children recognize that the speaker and his family are wealthy.

9. Responses will vary.

Vocabulary Check

10. Responses will vary.

11. **Academic Vocabulary** Responses will vary.

12. **English Language Coach** Mover Movement Movable Possible response: Adding suffixes changes the word's part of speech.

Close

Ask students to discuss what qualities allow some people to be bullied more easily than others. Have students debate whether people lose the urge to bully others as they grow up.

Grammar Link: Clauses

Grammar Practice

13. after they played soccer: adverb

14. whatever is on sale: noun

15. that covered our sofa: adjective

16. Whoever played the drum solo: noun

17. because I didn't sleep last night: adverb

Identifying Sequence

**Objective covered in this
workshop:**
• Use the story's structure to
locate, recall, and understand information

Teaching Students How to Identify Sequence

Why Is It Important?
• Readers need to keep track of the order of events in order to fully com-
prehend what they are reading.
• Writers use several types of order; students need to understand the rel-
evance of each form of sequencing.
• The form of sequencing a writer chooses to use can often point to the
author's main idea and theme.
• Understanding sequence can help students become better writers.

How to Help Students Get It
• Help students learn signal words such as first, then, next, and last. Once
students understand signal words, they will be able to quickly identify the
form of sequencing a writer uses.
• Remind them that they are simply finding the logical order of ideas and
events.
• Share different types of sequencing with students to help them understand their differences.

Reading to Answer the Big Question

Priscilla and the Wimps by Richard Peck
This short story is a comical spoof of bullies. Mighty Monk and his gang,
Klutter's Kobras, rule the halls and cafeteria of their school—until they
decide to pick on a little guy named Melvin. Melvin's best friend is Priscilla
Roseberry, a strong and assertive girl who has no problem dealing with
"The Head Honcho of the World."

Let the Bullies Beware by Ritu Upadhyay and Andrea DeSimone
This *InTIME* article describes programs and laws being established all
around the country to stop bullying in the schools.

Workshop Resources

PACING (DAYS)		LESSON	STUDENT MATERIALS	TEACHER RESOURCES
STANDARD	BLOCK			
1	½	Key Skill Lesson: Identifying Sequence	🪶 Key Reading Skills Practice, p. 22 🪶 English Language Coach Review, p. 41	🖐 Bellringer Options Transparencies – Daily Language Practice 46 – Selection Focus 13 🖐 Read Aloud, Think Aloud Transparencies – Key Readng Skills 12 💿 Presentation Plus!
1	1	"Priscilla and the Wimps"	💻 Glencoe Online 🪶 Unit Vocabulary Review, p. 39 🪶 Academic Vocabulary Review, p. 42 📁 English Language Coach 🪶 Active Reading Graphic Organizer, p. 24 🪶 Literary Analysis, p. 23 💿 StudentWorks Plus™ 💻 Online Student Edition 💿 Literature Classics 📁 Selection and Unit Assessments, p. 53	🖐 Literary and Text Analysis Transparencies 37 💻 Puzzlemaker 💿 Skill Level Up!™ A Language Arts Game 💻 BookLink 3 📕 Assessment by Learning Objective (Diagnostic and Formative) 💿 Interactive Tutor: Self-Assessment 💿 TeacherWorks Plus™
1		"Let the Bullies Beware"	💻 Glencoe Online 🪶 Unit Vocabulary Review, p. 39 🪶 Academic Vocabulary Review, p. 42 📁 English Language Coach 🪶 Active Reading Graphic Organizer, p. 26 💿 StudentWorks Plus™ 💻 Online Student Edition 💿 Literature Classics 📁 Selection and Unit Assessments, p. 54	🖐 Literary and Text Analysis Transparencies 55 💻 Puzzlemaker 💿 Skill Level Up!™ A Language Arts Game 💻 BookLink 3 📕 Assessment by Learning Objective (Diagnostic and Formative) 💿 Interactive Tutor: Self-Assessment 💿 TeacherWorks Plus™

Keys for Unit Resource

📁 Blackline Master   🔒 DVD
📕 Workbook   🖐 Transparency
📖 Supplemental Text   💻 Web-based
💿 CD-ROM   🪶 Fast File

Level Appropriate Code

AS = Activities for all students
AL = Activities for students working above grade level
OL = Activities for students working at grade level
BL = Activities for students working below grade level
EL = Activities for English language learners

Focus

BELLRINGER Options

✍ **Selection Focus Transparency 13**

✍ **Daily Language Practice Transparency 46**

Focus Activity Say: List four things that you do to prepare for a test, working from most important to least important. Then list them in the order in which you do them. *(Responses will vary.)* **BL**

Teach

R Reading Skill

Identifying Sequence Say: Suppose that the dog in the cartoon wanted to tell its owner about its three favorite activities. Write a brief description of these three activities from the dog's perspective in order of importance, from least favorite to most favorite. *(Responses will vary.)* **OL**

V Vocabulary

Academic Vocabulary Ask: Why is sequence important when explaining to someone how to bake a cake? *(The steps in the baking process must follow a certain order to produce a cake successfully.)* **BL**

Skills Focus

You will practice using these skills when you read the following selections:
- "Priscilla and the Wimps," p. 548
- "Let the Bullies Beware," p. 556

Reading

- Identifying and understanding sequence

Literature

- Explaining and analyzing plot structure, including rising action, climax, and resolution

Vocabulary

- Understanding word structure: prefixes
- Academic Vocabulary: *sequence*

Writing/Grammar

- Using commas in a series
- Using commas with direct address

Objectives (pp. 544–545)
Reading Identify text structure: sequence

544 UNIT 5

Skill Lesson

Identifying Sequence

Learn It!

What Is It? **Sequence** is the order in which thoughts or events are arranged. Here are three common forms of sequence:

- Authors often present events in a story in **chronological,** or time, order.

R - An author may present ideas in **spatial order**—or the order things are arranged in a certain space, such as a room or a playground.

- An author may present a range of ideas in their **order of importance,** either from most important to least important or from least to most.

© 1997 Randy Glasbergen.
www.glasbergen.com

"First my ball rolled under the sofa, then my water dish was too warm, then the squeaker broke on my squeaky rubber pork chop. I've had a horrible day and I'm completely stressed out!!!"

© 1997 Randy Glasbergen

Analyzing Cartoons
The dog lists the events of his day in chronological, or time, order. What order would you use to tell the sequence of events for a bad day in your life? Explain why.

Academic Vocabulary

V **sequence** (SEE kwens) *n.* the order of ideas or events; the arrangement of things in time, space, or importance

---

Additional Support

English Language Coach

Understanding Word Roots The dog in the cartoon says that it is "stressed out." Explain to students that this means that he is suffering from mental or emotional tension or strain. The word *stress* comes from the Latin word *stringere,* which means "to draw tight." These other English words have the same origin:

- distress
- restrain
- strict

Have students use dictionaries to define these three words. As a class, discuss how these definitions relate to the Latin root *stringere.* **EL**

Why Is It Important? Understanding the sequence of a selection helps you follow the writer's thinking. You'll understand and remember events and ideas better when you know the sequence the writer is using.

How Do I Do It? As you read, look at the order in which events occur or ideas are organized.

- If the author is telling a story, keep track of when events happen.
- Look for signal words that might point to either time order, spatial order, or order of importance. To learn when things happen, look for words like *first, then,* and *later.*
- Look for text features such as headings, sidebars, and lists that may give clues about the order of ideas.

Literature Online

Study Central Visit www.glencoe. com and click on Study Central to review identifying sequence.

Here's how one student noticed signal words to determine sequence in "The Fan Club."

> They were standing now, whole rows of them, their faces grinning with delight. Choked giggles, shuffling feet—and then applause—wild, sarcastic, malicious applause. That was when Laura saw that they were all wearing little white cards with a fat, frizzy-haired figure drawn on the front.

> *I see some signal words in this paragraph. It's easy to follow the events that the writer tells about. The students stood up. Laura heard giggling, shuffling, and then applause. That was when she realized what the kids were wearing.*

Practice It!

Copy the sentences below on a sheet of paper. Fill in the blanks with words that show sequence.

(1) The ___ thing I do when I wake up is put on my slippers. (2) ___ I feed the dog and make oatmeal for breakfast. (3) ___, I get dressed, brush my teeth, and run to catch the bus.

Use It!

In your Learner's Notebook, take notes about the sequence of events and ideas in "Priscilla and the Wimps" and "Let the Bullies Beware."

Teach

Literature Online

Study Central Have students access the Web site to review identifying sequence and to complete a related activity.

R Reading Skill

Identifying Sequence
Provide students with the following sequence signal words. Tell students to consult the list of time-order signal words for help with the *Practice It!* activity. **OL**

Time-Order Signal Words	Spatial-Order Signal Words
eventually	front/back
finally	here/there
first	high/low
second	in/out
third	left/right
last	near/far
later	over/under
next	above/below
then	beside

Resources for page 545

📖 Use Key Reading Skills Transparency 12 in *Read Aloud, Think Aloud* to help students practice identifying sequence.

Literature Focus Lesson

Sequence Identifying a sequence as chronological helps readers understand the order of events in complex works of literature. Understanding that a nonfiction essay presents ideas in order of importance will help readers identify the most important parts of an argument. Understanding spatial order will help readers better visualize settings and places described in pieces of writing. Suggest that students use their skimming and scanning skills to identify the sequence used in the selection before they begin reading. When they finish reading, ask students how identifying the sequence helped them better understand the selection. **AS**

Objectives
- Understand sequence
- Learn and use new vocabulary

545

Teach

More About the Author

For about ten years, Richard Peck worked as a middle- and high-school English teacher. During this time, Peck studied the problems, attitudes, and reading habits of his students. After leaving teaching, Peck began writing for adolescents. Peck says, "A young adult novel is the chronicle of one step in a young character's climb to maturity. It can be comic, tragic, and often faltering, but it is always a step up."

V Vocabulary

Prefix Game Pair students, and list the following prefixes on the board: *un-, mid-, dis-, inter-*. Tell one partner to write down as many words that contain these prefixes as he or she can in two minutes. Ask the other partner to act as the timer, calling the start and end of the two minutes. Then have partners switch roles. When each partner has had a turn making a list, determine which partner has generated more words. **OL**

Before You Read : Priscilla and the Wimps

Richard Peck

Meet the Author

"Priscilla and the Wimps" is Richard Peck's first short story. In the 1970s, an editor asked him to write a very short story about life in a junior high school. Peck had only thirty-six hours to write it. "But," says Peck, "I liked those characters so much, I wrote a novel for them called *Secrets of the Shopping Mall*. So now I very much believe in writing a short story first, to get me started in a certain direction." See page R5 of the Author Files for more on Richard Peck.

Author Search For more about Peck, go to www.glencoe.com.

Objectives (pp. 546–551)
Reading Identify text structure: sequence • Make connections from text to self
Literature Identify literary elements: plot
Vocabulary Identify word structure: prefixes

Vocabulary Preview

slithered (SLIH <u>thurd</u>) *v.* moved along with a sliding or gliding motion, as a snake; form of the verb *slither* **(p. 549)** *The students slithered like snakes down the hall.*

swaggers (SWAG urz) *v.* walks in a bold or proud way; from of the verb *swagger* **(p. 550)** *Full of confidence, Monk swaggers over to Priscilla.*

wittiness (WIT tee nes) *n.* ability to be smart and funny **(p. 550)** *He showed his wittiness when he described the scene to everyone.*

immense (ih MENS) *adj.* of great size; huge **(p. 551)** *Priscilla's hands and forearms seemed immense.*

stragglers (STRAG lurz) *n.* people who lag behind the main group **(p. 551)** *The last of the stragglers disappeared into their classroom.*

fate (fayt) *n.* a power that people believe determines events before they happen **(p. 551)** *It seemed like it was Priscilla's fate to become a legend in the school.*

Write to Learn Write a description of a day at school. Correctly use at least four vocabulary words. Share your story with the class.

English Language Coach

Prefixes A **prefix** is a word part added to the beginning of a word to form a new word. Look what happens when you add a prefix to the word *friendly*—it forms a new word that means its opposite.

$$\boxed{\text{un-}\ \text{(not)}} + \boxed{\text{friendly}} = \boxed{\text{unfriendly}}$$

Like *un-*, many other prefixes also reverse the meaning of a base word.

il-, in-, im- ("not")   *dis-* ("not," or "do the opposite of")
mis- ("bad" or "wrong")   *non-* ("not" or "without")
de- ("remove from" or "reduce")

Write to Learn In your Learner's Notebook, rewrite each sentence, adding one of the prefixes above to each word in dark type.

1. The student's argument was ___**logical.**
2. The warm sun made the snow ___**appear.**
3. If your homework is ___**complete,** you will get a zero.
4. When Julio visits his Grandma, he never ___**behaves.**

Additional Support

Author Search To expand students' appreciation of Richard Peck, have them access the Web site for additional information and resources.

Literature Focus Lesson

Character Tell students that taking notes in a character map is a helpful way to keep track of characters' traits. In the center circle, write the word *bully*. Ask students to think about someone they know or have read about who is a bully. Have students brainstorm traits of a bully, and record these traits in the outer circles. For example, students might suggest that a bully is superior, intimidating, or mean. Advise students to make character maps for the main characters in "Priscilla and the Wimps." **BL**

Skills Preview

Key Reading Skill: Identifying Sequence

Remember that sequence is the order in which a writer presents ideas or events. As you read "Priscilla and the Wimps," look for clues that tell you about sequence.

R • In a work of fiction, events usually happen in chronological, or time, order. Do events in "Priscilla and The Wimps" follow one another in chronological order? Do you see words such as *first, next, then, later,* and *eventually*?

Draw to Learn In your Learner's Notebook, make a cartoon strip with five boxes. As you read, draw a simple picture of an event from "Priscilla and the Wimps" in each box. Make sure that the events are in chronological order.

Key Literary Element: Plot

The **plot** of a story is all the events that happen. The plot is organized around the story's main conflict. A **conflict** is the struggle between opposing forces. Most plots develop in the following stages.

L • The plot of the story starts with the **exposition,** which introduces the characters, setting, and conflict of the story.

• The **rising action** is all of the events that lead to the **climax.**

• The **climax** is the point of most of the action, emotion, and suspense of the story.

• The **falling action** shows what happens to the characters after the climax.

• The **resolution** shows how the conflict is resolved or the problem solved. It is the final outcome of the story.

Interactive Literary Elements Handbook
To review or learn more about the literary elements, go to www.glencoe.com.

Get Ready to Read

Connect to the Reading

Why do people bully others? Why do some people get picked on more than others? What can you do if you are bullied? As you read "Priscilla and the Wimps," think about what bullying is and why it happens.

Mini-Questionnaire Agree or disagree with these statements. Discuss your answers with a partner.

____ Bullies make life miserable for many students.

____ Most people I know have the same feelings about bullies as I do.

____ I am sure that I could handle a bully.

____ Adults can help bullies and their victims.

____ At least one person thinks I'm a bully.

Build Background

A bully is someone who tries to tease or hurt someone. Bullies may pick on people to prove how powerful they are. Some do it because they feel that they are not as good as other people. Some do it for attention. Other bullies act tough so people will not bother them.

• Bullying may be obvious, such as pushing or hitting.

• Bullying can also be sneaky, such as spreading rumors or making cruel jokes.

• Some bullies say they are "just teasing" to try to excuse what they are doing.

Set Purposes for Reading

BIG Question Read "Priscilla and the Wimps" to find out how a fictional character deals with a bully.

Set Your Own Purpose What else would you like to learn from the story to help you answer the Big Question? Write your own purpose on the "Priscilla and the Wimps" page of Foldable 5.

Keep Moving

Use these skills as you read the following selection.

Priscilla and the Wimps **547**

Teach

R Reading Skill

Identifying Sequence Say: In your Learner's Notebooks, draw a time line to record the sequence of events in "Priscilla and the Wimps." Illustrate your time line and record any time-order signal words you find. **OL**

L Literary Element

Plot As students read the story, instruct them to record key details at the correct points on the plot chart below. **OL**

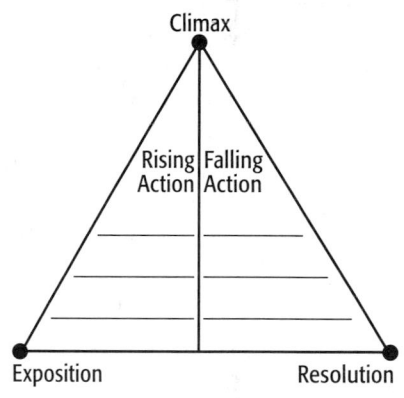

Reading in the Real World

Career Students might consult a school counselor for help dealing with bullies. Counselors work with young people in the areas of school and career planning. They also deal with social and developmental issues such as bullying. Students interested in working with others in these areas may consider careers as school counselors. Encourage such students to consult the Web site of the American School Counselor Association, in addition to other career sites, to find job descriptions and to learn about the preparation required for such a career. **OL**

Objectives

• Understand sequence
• Identify literary elements: plot
• Identify word structure: prefixes

547

Teach

L Literary Element

Plot Ask: At the beginning of the story, what information does the narrator share about Klutter's Kobras? *(Klutter's Kobras is a gang run by Monk Klutter. The gang takes money from students in exchange for privileges such as using the restroom.)* **OL Ask:** What do you learn about the narrator? Explain your answer. *(Possible response: The narrator finds Monk more intimidating than the teachers. The narrator also displays a sense of humor by sarcastically calling Monk "mighty Monk.")* **AL**

R Reading Skill

Review Drawing Conclusions Ask: What can you conclude about Monk from the information given in the exposition? *(Monk Klutter is a bully.)* **BL Ask:** How do you think students feel about Monk? Why? *(Possible response: The other students fear and dislike Monk because his gang takes money from them and controls the school.)* **OL**

Readability Scores
Dale-Chall: 5.6
DRP: 55
Lexile: 830

Priscilla and the Wimps

by Richard Peck

Listen, there was a time when you couldn't even go to the *rest room* around this school without a pass. And I'm not talking about those little pink tickets made out by some teacher. I'm talking about a pass that could cost anywhere up to a buck, sold by Monk Klutter.

Not that mighty Monk ever touched money, not in public. The gang he ran, which ran the school for him, was his collection agency.[1] They were Klutter's Kobras, a name spelled out in nailheads on six well-known black plastic windbreakers. **1**

Monk's threads were more . . . subtle.[2] A pile-lined suede battle jacket with lizard-skin flaps over tailored Levis and a pair of ostrich-skin boots, brassed-toed and suitable for kicking people around. One of his Kobras did nothing all day but walk a half step behind Monk, carrying a fitted bag with

---

1. A **collection agency** is a company that tries to force people to pay their debts.
2. **Threads** is a slang word for *clothes*. **Subtle** means "not very noticeable." In this case, the use of *subtle* is sarcastic because Monk's clothes are very noticeable.

548 UNIT 5 How Should You Deal with Bullies?

Practice the Skills

1 Key Literary Element

Plot The exposition sets the stage for the action and conflict. It also gives information about characters and setting. What do you learn about Monk Klutter in the first two paragraphs? **L**

Additional Support

Leveled Reading An adapted version of this selection (4th readability) is available on page 2 of **Jamestown Literature: An Adapted Reader** for grade 6.
548

Differentiated Instruction

Characterization The narrator gives a detailed description of Monk's clothes. Lead a discussion regarding what readers learn about Monk from the description of his clothing. To guide the discussion, ask students whether they think Monk wants to stand out or blend in with the crowd. Ask students whether they think Monk wants his clothes to have a particular effect on people. Provide students with fashion magazines that they can cut apart. Tell students to cut pictures of clothing from the magazines to create images of Monk. **BL**

Monk's gym shoes, a roll of restroom passes, a cashbox, and a switchblade that Monk gave himself manicures with at lunch over at the Kobras' table.

Speaking of lunch, there were a few cases of advanced **malnutrition** among the newer kids. The ones who were a little slow in handing over a cut of their lunch money and were therefore barred from the cafeteria. Monk ran a tight ship.[3] **2** **3**

I admit it. I'm five foot five, and when the Kobras **slithered** by, with or without Monk, I shrank. And I admit this, too: I paid up on a regular basis. And I might add: so would you.

This school was old Monk's Garden of Eden. **Unfortunately** for him, there was a serpent[4] in it. The reason Monk didn't recognize trouble when it was staring him in the face is that the serpent in the Kobras' Eden was a girl. **4**

Practically every guy in school could show you his scars. Fang marks from Kobras, you might say. And they were all highly visible in the shower room: lumps, lacerations,[5] blue bruises, you name it. But girls usually got off with a warning.

Except there was this one girl named Priscilla Roseberry. Picture a girl named Priscilla Roseberry, and you'll be light years off. Priscilla was, hands down, the largest student in our particular institution of learning. I'm not talking fat. I'm talking big. Even beautiful, in a bionic[6] way. Priscilla wasn't inclined toward organized crime. Otherwise, she could have put together a gang that would turn Klutter's Kobras into garter snakes.

Priscilla was basically a loner except she had one friend. A little guy named Melvin Detweiler. You talk about The Odd Couple. Melvin's one of the smallest guys above midget status ever seen. A really nice guy, but, you know—little. They even had lockers next to each other, in the same bank as mine. I

---

3. Running a **tight ship** means being strict.

4. In the Bible story, Adam and Eve live happily in the **Garden of Eden** until a **serpent** causes them to be sent away.

5. **Lacerations** are cuts or wounds.

6. **Bionic** refers to characters in science fiction stories who have artificial body parts that make them unusually fast and strong.

Vocabulary

slithered (SLIH thurd) v. moved along with a sliding or gliding motion, as a snake

Priscilla and the Wimps **549**

Practice the Skills

2 **English Language Coach**

Prefixes The prefix *mal-* means "bad," and it reverses the meaning of the base word. What does **malnutrition** mean? **EL**

3 **BIG Question**

What characteristics of a bully do you see in this description of Monk in the first four paragraphs? Write your answer on your Foldable. **BQ**

4 **English Language Coach**

Prefixes The prefix *un-* means "not, opposite of," or "lacking." What does **unfortunately** mean in this sentence? What other words can you think of with this prefix?

Teach

EL Language Coach

Prefixes **Ask:** If *nutrition* refers to the foods and vitamins the body needs, what do you think *malnutrition* means? *(Malnutrition means "a lack of healthful foods.")* **EL** **Say:** *Mal-* is a negative prefix because it adds "bad" or "badly" to the meaning of a base word. Some other common negative prefixes are *anti-*, which means "against"; *dis-*, which means "not, opposite"; *mis-*, which means "wrong, not"; and *un-*, which means "not." For each of these prefixes, list a word and its definition. *(Responses will vary.)* **EL** **OL**

BQ BIG Question

Say: Consider a bully whom you know, have read about, or have seen in a film. Compare and contrast this bully with Monk Klutter. What do you think are the most important characteristics that the bullies share? *(Responses will vary. Students should compare the two bullies and note the important characteristics that they share.)* **OL**

Literature Focus Lesson

Extended Metaphor Point out to students the many examples of snake imagery on this page: "Kobras," "slithered," "Garden of Eden," "serpent," "fang marks," and "garter snakes." Monk and his gang share certain characteristics with snakes. This type of figurative language is called *extended metaphor* because the author returns to the same comparison (between the gang and snakes) several times over the course of the story. As a class, discuss how the Kobras and snakes are alike. Ask students whether they think this extended metaphor is effective. **AL**

Objectives
• Understand sequence
• Identify literary elements: plot
• Identify word structure: prefixes

549

Teach

BQ BIG Question

Ask: In what two ways is Priscilla "above everything"? *(Priscilla is above the other students because of her height. In addition, she does not pay attention to the problems or dramas of the other students at school, which keeps her "above everything.")* **OL** **Ask:** How does being "above everything" affect the way Priscilla deals with Klutter's Kobras? *(Possible response: Priscilla is not afraid of Monk or his gang. The narrator notes that Priscilla probably does not notice them.)* **OL**

L Literary Element

Plot Ask: Who does the Kobra grab as the first event in the rising action? Why does the Kobra grab this student? *(The Kobra grabs Melvin by the neck because he wants to see Melvin's pass. However, the pass is just an excuse to steal money from Melvin.)* **BL** **Ask:** How do you think Priscilla will respond to the Kobra's actions? Why? *(Melvin is Priscilla's only friend, so she will probably do something to help him.)* **OL**

---

don't know what they had going. I'm not saying this was a romance. After all, people deserve their privacy.

Priscilla was sort of above everything, if you'll pardon a pun.[7] And very calm, as only the very big can be. If there was anybody who didn't notice Klutter's Kobras, it was Priscilla. **5**

Until one winter day after school when we were all grabbing our coats out of our lockers. And hurrying, since Klutter's Kobras made sweeps of the halls for after-school shakedowns.[8]

Anyway, up to Melvin's locker **swaggers** one of the Kobras. Never mind his name. Gang members don't need names. They've got group identity. He reaches down and grabs little Melvin by the neck and slams his head against his locker door. The sound of skull against steel rippled all the way down the locker row, speeding the crowds on their way.

"Okay, let's see your pass," snarls the Kobra.

"A pass for what this time?" Melvin asks, probably still dazed.

"Let's call it a pass for very short people," says the Kobra, "a dwarf tax." He wheezes a little Kobra chuckle at his own **wittiness.** And already he's reaching for Melvin's wallet with the hand that isn't circling Melvin's windpipe. All this time, of course, Melvin and the Kobra are standing in Priscilla's big shadow. **6 7**

She's taking her time shoving her books into her locker and pulling on a very large-size coat. Then, quicker than the eye, she brings the side of her enormous hand down in a chop that breaks the Kobra's hold on Melvin's throat. You could hear a pin drop in that hallway. Nobody'd ever laid a finger on a Kobra, let alone a hand the size of Priscilla's.

Then Priscilla, who hardly ever says anything to anybody except to Melvin, says to the Kobra, "Who's your leader, wimp?"

This practically blows the Kobra away. First he's chopped by a girl, and now she's acting like she doesn't know Monk Klutter, the Head Honcho of the World. He's so amazed, he tells her. "Monk Klutter." **8**

---

7. A **pun** is a joke in which a phrase has two meanings. Priscilla is "above everything" in two ways.

8. **Shakedowns** are threats that are used to demand money from victims.

Vocabulary

swaggers (SWAG urz) *v.* walks in a bold or proud way

wittiness (WIT tee nes) *n.* ability to be smart and funny

Practice the Skills

5 BIG Question

What does it mean when the narrator says, "Priscilla was sort of above everything"? Why might this be important to the story? Write your answers on your Foldable. **BQ**

6 Key Reading Skill

Identifying Sequence The Kobra walks up to Melvin's locker. What is the next thing that happens? Then what does the Kobra say after that? List two more events that happen next.

7 Key Literary Element

Plot The writer has introduced the setting and characters. Now he begins the rising action. The rising action is the series of plot events that build toward the climax. Which event starts the rising action? **L**

8 Key Reading Skill

Identifying Sequence The narrator tells this story in chronological order. Each event follows another event in time order. Scan this page and write down any signal words you see.

Additional Support

Differentiated Instruction

Role Playing Remind students that "Priscilla and the Wimps" is fiction. The writer creates a hero, Priscilla, to defend a weaker student from a bully. In real life, Priscilla is rarely around to save the day. To help students practice dealing with bullies in a more realistic context, have students role-play Melvin's encounter with the Kobra. Invite volunteers to play the two characters. First, ask "Melvin" what he might say when he sees a bully approaching threateningly. Ask "Melvin" what he might say if the bully continues to threaten and tease him. Let the rest of the class offer suggestions as well. **AS**

"Never heard of him," Priscilla mentions. "Send him to see me." The Kobra just backs away from her like the whole situation is too big for him, which it is.

Pretty soon Monk himself slides up. He jerks his head once, and his Kobras slither off down the hall. He's going to handle this interesting case personally. "Who is it around here doesn't know Monk Klutter?"

He's standing inches from Priscilla, but since he'd have to look up at her, he doesn't. "Never heard of him," says Priscilla.

Monk's not happy with this answer, but by now he's spotted Melvin, who's grown smaller in spite of himself. Monk breaks his own rule by reaching for Melvin with his own hands. "Kid," he says, "you're going to have to educate your girl friend."

Visual Vocabulary
In wrestling, a *hammerlock* is a hold in which one person twists the opponent's arm behind the opponent's back.

His hands never quite make it to Melvin. In a move of pure poetry Priscilla has Monk in a hammerlock. His neck's popping like gunfire, and his head's bowed under the **immense** weight of her forearm. His suede jacket's peeling back, showing pile.

Priscilla's behind him in another easy motion. And with a single mighty thrust forward, frog-marches[9] Monk into her own locker. It's incredible. His ostrich-skin boots click once in the air. And suddenly he's gone, neatly wedged into the locker, a perfect fit. Priscilla bangs the door shut, twirls the lock, and strolls out of school. Melvin goes with her, of course, trotting along below her shoulder. The last **stragglers** leave quietly. **9**

Well, this is where **fate**, an even bigger force than Priscilla, steps in. It snows all that night, a blizzard. The whole town ices up. And school closes for a week. **10 11** ○

---

9. When Priscilla *frog-marches* Monk, she holds him from behind and forces him to walk in front of her.

Vocabulary

immense (ih MENS) *adj.* of great size; huge

stragglers (STRAG lurz) *n.* people who lag behind the main group

fate (fayt) *n.* a power that people believe determines events before they happen

Practice the Skills

9 | **Key Literary Element**

Plot The climax is the high point of interest or suspense in a story. What is the climax of "Priscilla and the Wimps"? Why do you think so? **L**

10 | **Key Literary Element**

Plot The resolution of a story is the final outcome. What is the resolution of "Priscilla and the Wimps"?

11 |

Do you think Priscilla chose the best way to deal with a bully? Support your opinion with details from the text. Write your conclusions on the "Priscilla and the Wimps" page of Foldable 5. Your response will help you complete the Unit Challenge later.

Priscilla and the Wimps **551**

Teach

L **Literary Element**

Plot **Say:** Think of the climax as the turning point in a story. Everything will change after the climax, and the conflict will move toward resolution. What moment is a turning point in "Priscilla and the Wimps"? Explain. *(the confrontation between Priscilla and Monk.)* **OL**

R **Reading Skill**

Identifying Sequence
Say: Describe the sequence of events that happens after Priscilla says she has never heard of Monk Klutter. *(Monk tells Melvin to "educate" Priscilla; Monk tries to grab Melvin, but Priscilla steps in and locks him in her locker; the school is closed for a week.)* **Ask:** What signal words help you follow the sequence of this part of the story? *(Possible responses: by now, this is where)*

Assess

CheckPoint

Use the CheckPoint questions provided on Presentation Plus! to check for comprehension of the selection. These questions can be used with interactive response keypads for immediate student feedback.

Literature Focus Lesson

Resolution After students have read the ending of "Priscilla and the Wimps," discuss what happened to Monk. Was he in the locker the entire week that school was closed? Did the cleaning crew or a teacher release Monk from the locker before the blizzard struck? Was that punishment cruel, or did it fit Monk's actions? Have students write an explanation of what happened to Monk. **OL**

Objectives
• Understand sequence
• Identify literary elements: plot

Assess

Resources for page 552

📁 Selection QuickCheck, p. 45

📁 Selection and Unit Assessment, p. 53

💿 ExamView Assessment Suite

💿 Interactive Tutor: Self-Assessment

Students can respond to the *After You Read* items in their Learner's Notebooks or on a separate sheet of paper.

Answering the

1. Responses will vary. Students may say that the ending of the story is unrealistic. A bully isn't often bullied in real life.

2. Klutter's Kobras

3. Priscilla ignores Monk until he gets in her way. Then she uses her greater size to overpower him.

Critical Thinking

4. Responses will vary.

5. Responses will vary.

6. Students may say that refusing to be fearful of bullies and acting with integrity are two lessons they can learn from the story.

After You Read | Priscilla and the Wimps

Answering the BIG Question

1. How does the ending of the story compare with real-life situations involving bullies?

2. **Recall** What is the name of Monk's gang?
   Tip **Right There**

3. **Recall** What is the first technique Priscilla uses to handle Monk?
   Tip **Right There**

Critical Thinking

4. **Evaluate** Do you think Priscilla's methods of dealing with Monk are effective? Explain.
   Tip **Author and Me**

5. **Synthesize** Create another ending for the story in which there's no snowstorm.
   Tip **On My Own**

6. **Connect** What have you learned from the story that will help you deal with bullies?
   Tip **Author and Me**

Write About Your Reading

Make your own cartoon strip about a bully. Include a few lines of dialogue in caption bubbles. The plot should include rising action, climax, and resolution. Label at least three of the boxes to show the rising action, climax, and resolution.

Objectives (pp. 552–553)
Reading Identify text structure: sequence
Literature Identify literary elements: plot
Vocabulary Identify word structure: prefixes
Writing Respond to literature: cartoon
Grammar Use punctuation correctly: commas in a series

rising action   climax   resolution

552 UNIT 5 How Should You Deal with Bullies?

Write About Your Reading
Responses will vary.

Skills Review

Key Reading Skill: Identifying Sequence

7. List five examples of time order signal words.

8. Write a paragraph that tells the sequence of events from the time Priscilla meets Monk until she leaves school. Use at least four signal words.

Key Literary Element: Plot

9. What is a story's exposition?

10. How are climax and conflict related to each other?

11. Is the conflict solved in the resolution of "Priscilla and the Wimps"? Why or why not?

Vocabulary Check

Answer the questions about the following vocabulary words. If you answer a question with *no,* write the correct definition of the word.

12. Does *slithered* mean "expressed emotion in an exaggerated way"?

13. Are *stragglers* people who lag behind the rest of the group?

14. Do some bold and confident people *swagger*?

15. Would you need a microscope to find something *immense*?

16. Academic Vocabulary Give examples of two different kinds of sequence.

English Language Coach Below are more common prefixes. Rewrite each sentence below, adding a prefix to each word in dark type. Use context clues to choose the correct prefix.

> re- ("back" or "again")   sub- ("below")
> post- ("after")   pre- ("before")

17. I watched the ___ **game** show after the football game ended.

18. The community decided to ___ **build** after the hurricane.

19. People wear seat belts as a ___ **caution** against accidents.

20. The ___ **marine** went deep into the ocean.

Grammar Link: Commas in a Series

Commas help make writing easier to read. Without commas, much of what is written would be confusing and difficult to understand. One of the most common uses for commas is to separate items in a series.

- Use commas to separate three or more words, phrases, or clauses in a series.

  Jen, Mel, Jo, and Lucy like to water ski.

  My mom always wants to know where I'm going, how I'm getting there, and when I'll be home.

- Do not use a comma before the first item in a series or after the last item in a series.

  Wrong: We bought, shorts, tank tops, flip-flops, and suntan lotion at the store.

  Wrong: We bought shorts, tank tops, flip-flops, and suntan lotion, at the store.

- If *and* or *or* is used between words, phrases, or clauses, do not use commas.

  Our breakfast included eggs and bacon and orange juice.

  Do you know who she is or where she moved from or what class she's in?

Grammar Practice

Copy the sentences below and insert commas where they are needed.

21. Priscilla was tall calm strong and loyal.

22. Monk slides up jerks his head and asks a question.

23. Priscilla bangs the door shut twirls the lock and strolls out of school.

Writing Application Look back at your cartoon. Check to be sure that you used commas correctly in any series.

Web Activities For eFlashcards, Selection Quick Checks, and other Web activities, go to www.glencoe.com.

Priscilla and the Wimps **553**

Skills Review

Key Reading Skill: Identifying Sequence

7. Possible responses: now, then, later, first, afterward

8. Responses will vary.

Key Literary Element: Plot

9. Responses will vary.

10. Possible response: The climax is the high point of tension and suspense in the conflict.

11. Responses will vary.

Vocabulary Check

12. No, *slithered* means "moved slowly in a menacing, snakelike way."

13. Yes

14. Yes

15. No, *immense* means "huge or extremely large."

16. Academic Vocabulary Students should list two of the following: time order, spatial order, order of importance.

English Language Coach

17. pregame

18. rebuild

19. precaution

20. submarine

Close

Ask students to summarize what they learned about the Big Question from the story.

Grammar Link: Commas in a Series

Grammar Practice

21. Priscilla was tall, calm, strong, and loyal.

22. Monk slides up, jerks his head, and asks a question.

23. Priscilla bangs the door shut, twirls the lock, and strolls out of school.

Teach

More About the Writer

Ritu Upadhyay enjoys writing about people. She likes to "get inside someone else's mind and learn about how they see the world." Upadhyay experienced the other side of this reporting experience when she was chosen as Miss India Worldwide in 2000. As the winner of the pageant, Upadhyay had to meet with reporters who wanted to tell her story. In response, Upadhyay said, "I'm used to writing the news, not making it!"

V Vocabulary

Using Vocabulary

Words Say: To help cement new vocabulary words in your memory, use the words right away. Write a paragraph that includes each of the vocabulary words for this selection. The paragraph does not have to make perfect sense, but each word should be used correctly. *(Responses will vary.)* EL

Additional Support

Author Search To expand students' appreciation of Upadhyay and DeSimone, have them access the Web site for more information and resources.

Before You Read : Let the Bullies Beware

Meet the Authors

Ritu Upadhyay (oo POD e eye) wanted to be a journalist ever since she was the editor of her elementary school newspaper. She especially likes to write personality profiles for *TIME for Kids*. Andrea DeSimone writes for *Teen People* in addition to *TIME for Kids*.

Objectives (pp. 554–559)
Reading Identify text structure: sequence • Make connections from text to self
Informational Text Use text features: title, subheads
Vocabulary Identify word structure: prefixes

Vocabulary Preview

uproar (UP ror) *n.* noisy excitement and confusion **(p. 556)** *The surprise appearance of the movie star created an uproar in the restaurant.*

policies (POL uh seez) *n.* plans or rules **(p. 557)** *Many schools have introduced anti-violence policies.*

verbal (VUR bul) *adj.* expressed in spoken words **(p. 558)** *You can brainstorm clever verbal responses to bullies' comments.*

Write to Learn Make a poster with advice about how to deal with bullies. Use at least two of the vocabulary words in your suggestions. Display the posters in the classroom.

English Language Coach

Prefixes are word parts that are added to the beginning of a word to create a new word. The prefix *under-* means "below" or "too little." So if you add *under-* to the word *fed,* you get *underfed* which means "fed too little." Another prefix is *over-*, which means "too much." Something that is *overpriced* is "priced too much," or "too expensive."

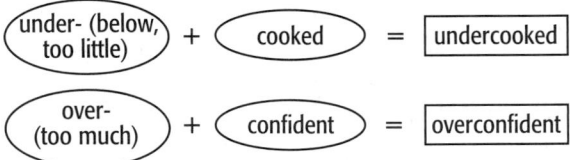

On Your Own Read these sentences. Complete each word with the correct prefix.

under-   over-

1. The sewer pipes lay deep ____ground.
2. We think that movie actors are ____paid.
3. Hugh will weed the garden before it gets ____grown.
4. The restaurant is ____staffed, so the service is slow.

Find six words that use the prefixes *under-* or *over-*. Write these words in your Learner's Notebook.

English Language Coach

Defining Words Students may have differing understandings of what constitutes bullying. For example, what one student considers gentle teasing, another may find extremely hurtful. Share with students the following definition of *bullying,* taken from the Colorado Bullying Prevention Program. "Bullying is repeated exposure, over time, to negative actions from one or more students. Negative actions can include physical, verbal or indirect actions that are intended to inflict injury or discomfort upon another." Analyze this definition with students, and then generate another definition in the students' own words. As a class, discuss activities that fall under the rubric of "bullying." EL BL

Skills Preview

Key Reading Skill: Identifying Sequence

Sequence is the order in which events occur or ideas are presented.

Common forms of sequence are:

- chronological order or time order–the order in which events happen
- order of importance–from the most to the least important
- spatial order–the order in which things are arranged. For example, you would use spatial order to describe where things in your school are located or what your bedroom looks like.

Write to Learn As you read "Let the Bullies Beware," write the three most important things you learned about dealing with bullies. Write them in order of importance–from the most to the least important. Write your list in your Learner's Notebook.

Text Element: Titles and Subheads

Titles and subheads tell or hint at what a selection is about. The title is at the very beginning of a selection. Subheads are located throughout a selection, and they are usually in bigger, darker type than regular text. These tips will help you use titles and subheads.

- Read the title of the article. Think about what it means.
  What hints does the title give you about what's in the article?
- Look at the subheads used to organize the text.
  What do the subheads tell you about the main ideas of the article?

Interactive Literary Elements Handbook
To review or learn more about the literary elements, go to www.glencoe.com.

Get Ready to Read

Connect to the Reading

What does it feel like to be bullied? Can bullies be stopped, or can they only be punished? What's the best way to handle bullying?

Partner Talk With a partner, act out a short talk-radio show discussion. One person should be the host who asks the questions. The other person should be the guest who is being interviewed on the subject of bullying. After two minutes, switch roles.

Build Background

Experts disagree about the need for anti-bullying laws. Some say bullying is a problem that should be handled by schools. Others say that laws would protect victims better. Here are some facts about bullying.

- Bullying generally takes place among kids in fourth through seventh grades.
- Anti-bullying programs run by schools reduce bullying behaviors by up to 50 percent.
- A study done by the FBI says that bullies are more likely to commit crimes as adults.

Set Purposes for Reading

BIG Question Read "Let the Bullies Beware" to find out how experts think kids should deal with bullies.

Set Your Own Purpose What else would you like to learn from the article to help you answer the Big Question? Write your own purpose on the "Let the Bullies Beware" page of Foldable 5.

Keep Moving

Use these skills as you read the following selection.

Teach

R Reading Skill

Identifying Sequence Say: After you have listed the bulleted points in order of importance, note the reasons that you ordered the points in this way. *(Responses will vary.)* **OL**

E Text Element

Titles and Subheads Have students read the title, subtitle, and subhead in "Let the Bullies Beware." Tell students to answer the Key Element questions that appear on page 555 in their Learner's Notebooks. *(The title suggests that the article will cover information about standing up to bullies. The subtitle suggests that schools are helping students stand up to bullies. The subhead suggests that state governments are involved in bullying prevention and that students can protect themselves from bullies.)* **OL**

Literature Focus Lesson

Dialogue Ask students to extend their talk radio shows to three minutes and to perform the shows for the class. Suggest that students draft scripts of their shows. Offer the following prompts:

- **Host:** What kind of radio show do you host? Why did you decide to do a show about bullying? Who is your audience? What questions will you ask your guest?
- **Guest:** What experience do you have in dealing with bullies? Are you a victim of bullying or an expert in human behavior? What message do you want to share with listeners? **AS**

Objectives

- Understand sequence
- Identify literary elements: titles and subheads
- Learn and use new vocabulary

555

Teach

E Text Element

Titles and Subheads Say: Does the information in the first three paragraphs match what you would expect to learn after reading the title and deck—the statement under the title? Explain. *(Possible response: The first paragraphs of the article fulfill expectations because this text contains information about bullying and an anti-bullying program, subjects mentioned or suggested by the title and deck.)* **AS**

EL Language Coach

Prefixes Say: Consider the meaning of the word *bullying,* and think about how the addition of the prefix *anti-* changes the meaning of a word. What might be a good name for an anti-bullying program? *(Responses will vary. Responses should reflect an understanding that anti-bullying means "against bullying.")* **EL**

Readability Scores
Dale-Chall: 5.9
DRP: 63
Lexile: 1000

TIME

Let the Bullies BEWARE [1]

Many schools are starting programs to help keep kids safe.

By RITU UPADHYAY and ANDREA DESIMONE

The school yard of Shawnee Elementary School in Grand Tower, Illinois, is usually in an **uproar** with kids playing. But every now and then some serious words can be heard: "I don't like it when you do that. Please stop."

Children in every grade at Shawnee Elementary were taught this response as part of an **anti-bullying** program that was introduced in the school. Principal Shelly Clover says students are using what they learned in the program all the time now. "It's nice to hear them taking care of things without an argument or fight." [2]

Five million elementary- and middle-school students in the United States are bullied each year. In some cases, bullying leads to a situation in which the kids who have been bullied become bullies themselves. Researchers[1] at the National Threat Center found that in more than 2/3 of 37 violent acts in schools, the kids who were the attackers had felt "bullied or threatened, attacked or injured" by other kids.

---

1. **Researchers** are people who study a topic and then give a report about their information.

Vocabulary ....

uproar (UP ror) *n.* noisy excitement and confusion

556 UNIT 5 How Should You Deal with Bullies?

[1] Text Element

Titles and Subheads
Remember that a title is the name of a selection. After reading the title, what do you think this selection will be about? **E**

[2] English Language Coach

Prefixes Sometimes the prefix *anti-* has a hyphen (-) to connect it to a base word. The prefix *anti-* means "against" or "opposite." What does **anti-bullying** mean? **EL**

Additional Support

Differentiated Instruction

Conducting Surveys Encourage small groups to create surveys in order to determine bullying statistics for your school. Help students brainstorm what information they would like to have. Then, help students formulate questions to obtain this information. Suggest that students ask questions that will provide them with information about both the victims of bullies and the bullies themselves. Provide students with guidance regarding how they should distribute and collect their surveys. When the completed surveys are returned to class, help students tally and analyze the results. **OL**

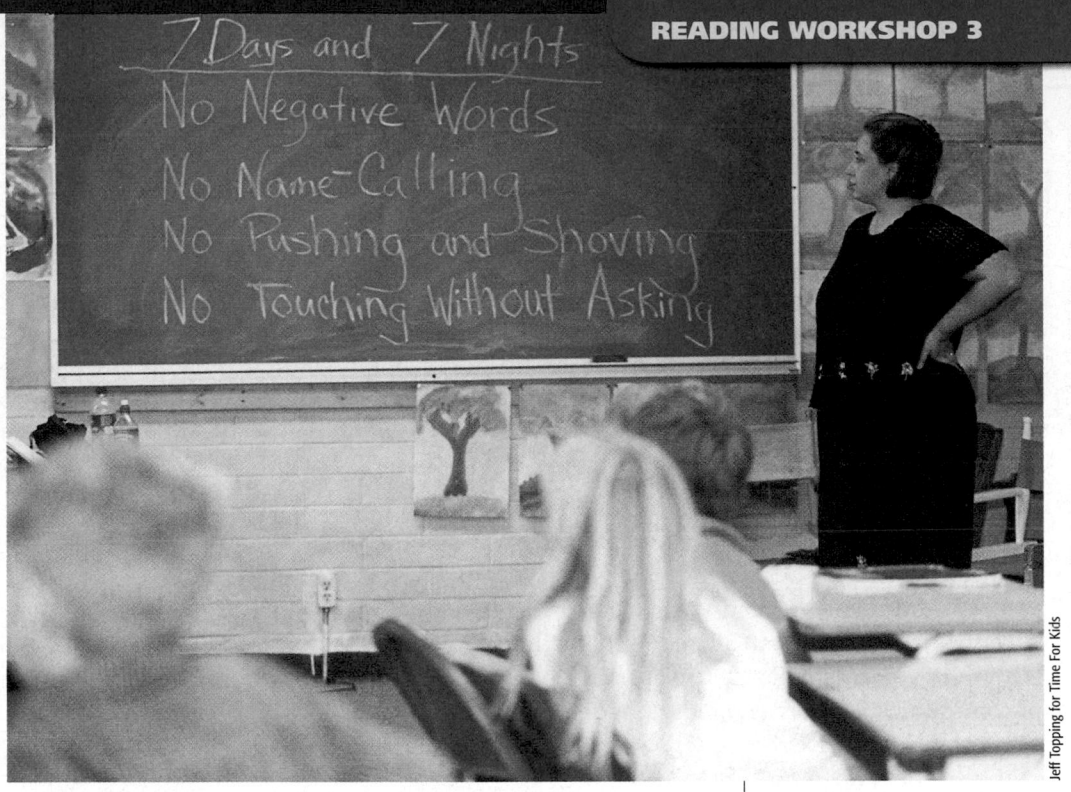

Jeff Topping for Time For Kids

A class at Mountain Oak Charter School in Arizona is challenged to stop bullying.

School officials, parents, and lawmakers are looking for ways to stop such acts and make schools safer. Many schools around the country have adopted anti-bullying **policies** to help stop school violence.

States Stopping the Bullies ₃

"Bullying isn't new, but it's causing children to take actions that we never dreamed of," says Colorado State Representative Don Lee. He worked to pass the Colorado Bullying Prevention Law. That state law, passed in 2001, says that all schools in Colorado must have an anti-bullying policy. Some states, including Georgia, Vermont, and New Hampshire, already have such plans.

Vocabulary

policies (POL uh seez) *n.* plans or rules

₃ Text Element

Titles and Subheads
What information would you expect to find under this subhead? Explain why.

Let the Bullies Beware **557**

Teach

E1 Text Element

Titles and Subheads Say: Consider what you have read so far. Think of a different title for the article based on your reading. *(Responses will vary. Responses should reflect an understanding that titles give readers hints about the content of articles.)* **OL**

E2 Text Element

Titles and Subheads Ask: Do you think "States Stopping the Bullies" is an appropriate subhead for this section of the article? Why or why not? *(Possible response: This is an appropriate subhead because this section discusses a state law aimed at bullying prevention.)* **AS**

Reading in the Real World

Career Some students may be interested in careers in state government. Encourage students to consult online references to learn about lawmakers in your state. Before they begin their research, make sure students understand the distinction between the state and the federal government. Provide students with the following research questions: Who are your state representatives? What are their educational and professional backgrounds? Does a bullying law exist in your state, or has one been proposed? If not, students may use their research to draft letters to state representatives regarding the issue of bullying. **AL**

Objectives
• Identify literary elements: titles and subheads
• Identify word structure: prefixes

Teach

BQ **BIG Question**

Ask: What evidence do the authors provide to show that anti-bullying plans are effective? *(The authors note that in Central York Middle School, the number of fights dropped from 17 to 4 after students signed anti-teasing promises.)* **BL**

C Critical Thinking

Evaluate Ask: Will anti-bullying programs stop all school violence? Explain. *(Responses will vary.)* **OL**

Ask: After reading the information in this article, what do you think are the most effective ways to prevent bullying? *(Responses will vary. Students may note that a combination of strategies both at home and at school are more effective than any single strategy.)* **AL**

Schools across the United States are seeing the benefits of bullying-prevention plans. At Central York Middle School in York, Pennsylvania, 700 students signed anti-teasing promises in 2001. The promises seemed to work. That year the number of fights at Central York dropped to **C** 4 from 17 the year before.

In some schools, classroom time is set aside to teach kids how to prevent and stop bullying. At McNair Elementary School in Hazelwood, Missouri, kids learn step-by-step **verbal** responses to bullying. At first they may respond by saying, "I'm going to ask you to stop," and finally by stating, "I'm going to get help."

Penfield Tate, a former Colorado senator, hopes that anti-bullying programs will stop violence by opening the lines of communication between kids. "Students don't feel comfortable talking to adults," he says. "School programs will help them open up." **4**

TFK Poll

Here's how kids answered a poll about bullying.

Has a bully ever picked on you in school?

Yes, I've been picked on	41%
No, I haven't been picked on	32%
No, I usually do the bullying	27%
Total responses: 4,019	

4 **BIG Question**

How do the programs and policies described in this selection help kids deal with bullies? Give examples from the text. Write your answer on the "Let the Bullies Beware" page of Foldable 5. **BQ**

Vocabulary

verbal (VUR bul) *adj.* expressed in spoken words

As part of an anti-bullying program, students role-play bullies and victims in class.

558 UNIT 5 How Should You Deal with Bullies?

Additional Support

Reading Fluency

Reading Surveys Explain that analyzing the results of surveys requires caution. Students should ask the following questions when considering survey data.

- Was the survey conducted by a trustworthy organization?
- When was the survey conducted? Could events at the time have

influenced people's responses?

- What questions were asked on the survey? Were the questions worded in a clear, unbiased way?

As a class, look over the *Time for Kids* Poll on page 558. Discuss possible sources of inaccuracies and unknowns in the survey results. **AL**

Bully Busters

Tips to help you deal with mean kids

Believe you're bully-proof. Keep bullies away by acting confident, says Carol Watkins, M.D., a psychiatrist[2] who gives talks and workshops on bullying. Stand up straight when walking through the halls, and look everyone in the eye when you talk to them.

Stay with your friends. There's safety in numbers, Watkins says, so surround yourself with friends—especially when entering places like the lunchroom or school yard where bullies hang out.

Speak up. Ignoring bullies doesn't always work. Watkins suggests that you respond to teasing with a funny comeback.[3] If that doesn't stop the teasing, just be honest and say, "What you're doing is wrong; stop it!"

Learn self-defense. Take up martial arts[4] to build your confidence and make yourself feel safer. If bullies turn violent, you will know how to stop them with very little physical contact.

Get help. Tell your parents and/or teachers about any bullying that goes on, Watkins says. Even if you think you can handle some teasing, you should never have to feel scared. Once bullies realize that bullying can bring them serious punishment—like suspension or worse—they will probably decide that bothering you is just not worth it. **5 6** ○

—Updated 2005, from *TIME FOR KIDS*, March 31, 2001, and *TEEN PEOPLE*, June/July 2004

---

2. A *psychiatrist* (sy KY uh trist) is a medical doctor who treats people with emotional problems and mental illness.

3. A *comeback* is a quick and witty reply.

4. *Martial* (MAR shul) *arts* are methods of self-defense, such as judo and karate, that originated in Asia.

5 **BIG Question**

Do you think these are helpful tips for someone who has to deal with a bully? Why or why not? Write your answers on the "Let the Bullies Beware" page of Foldable 5. Your response will help you complete the Unit Challenge later. **BQ**

6 **Key Reading Skill**

Identifying Sequence Reread the text box titled "Bully Busters." The writers have organized the information in a sequence of tips. What tip do the writers list last? Why do you think they made it the last tip? **R**

Teach

BQ **BIG Question**

Ask: Which tip do you think would be the least effective when dealing with a bully? Why? *(Responses will vary.)* **OL**

R Reading Skill

Identifying Sequence Say: Writers often list their most important idea either first or last. On this list, the most effective tip could be considered the writer's most important idea. Which tip do you think would be most effective? Where does it appear in the list? *(Possible response: The most effective tip is "Get help." This tip is listed last.)* **AS**

CheckPoint

Use the CheckPoint questions provided on Presentation Plus! to check for comprehension of the selection. These questions can be used with interactive response keypads for immediate student feedback.

Differentiated Instruction

Create a Poster Organize students into small groups of three or four. Ask each group to draft a new list of "Bully Busters." Tell students to follow the format of the existing tips in writing their suggestions, and suggest that students list their tips in order of importance. Have groups think of new titles for their lists of anti-bullying tips. Provide each group with paper and markers, and have students create posters of their lists. Encourage students to make the posters eye-catching in order to increase their effectiveness. Hang completed posters around the classroom and/or in the hallway. **OL**

Objectives
• Identify literary elements: titles and subheads
• Evaluate text
• Understand sequence

559

Assess

Resources for page 560

📁 Selection QuickCheck, p 46

📁 Selection and Unit Assessment, p. 54

💿 ExamView Assessment Suite

💿 Interactive Tutor: Self-Assesesment

Students can respond to the *After You Read* items in their Learner's Notebooks or on separate sheets of paper.

Answering the **BIG Question**

1. Research shows that anti-bullying programs reduce school violence.

2. Some states require that schools have anti-bullying policies.

3. Students may suggest any of the following strategies for handling bullies: believe that you're bully-proof, stay with friends, speak up, learn self-defense, get help.

4. Students may suggest any of the following verbal responses: "I don't like it when you do that. Please stop." "I'm going to ask you to stop." "I'm going to get help." "What you are doing is wrong; stop it!"

Critical Thinking

5. Responses will vary.
6. Responses will vary.
7. Responses will vary.
8. Responses will vary.

560

After You Read   Let the Bullies Beware

Answering the **BIG Question**

1. Why do experts say that anti-bullying programs are very important?

2. **Recall** What are states doing to prevent bullying?
   Tip Right There

3. **Recall** What are two ways that experts suggest for handling bullies?
   Tip Right There

4. **Recall** What are two verbal responses to bullying that students learn?
   Tip Right There

Critical Thinking

5. **Interpret** Why do you think the authors included the TFK poll results?
   Tip Author and Me

6. **Analyze** How do the authors try to convince you that anti-bullying programs work?
   Tip Author and Me

7. **Evaluate** Which do you think is the best piece of advice in the list of tips? Explain.
   Tip Author and Me

8. **Synthesize** Think about what you've read in this selection. Then review the unit opener quotation about bullies on page 480. Now make up a statement of your own about how to deal with bullies.
   Tip On My Own

Write About Your Reading

Write a letter to an advice column, describing a problem with a bully. Exchange letters with a partner. Write a response to your partner's letter as if you were the author of the advice column. You can use facts from the selection as well as your own opinions.

Objectives (pp. 560–561)
Reading Identify text structure: sequence • Make connections from text to self
Informational Text Use text features: title, subheads
Vocabulary Identify word structure: prefixes
Writing Respond to literature: letter
Grammar Use punctuation correctly: commas with direct address

Write About Your Reading

Responses will vary.

Dear Advising Anna,
I play for my school's basketball team. Every day at practice, one of the starting players pushes me around during the scrimmage. What should I do?

Sincerely,
Gina

Dear Gina,
I agree that your problem is tricky. I suggest that you talk privately with your coach about the problem. Perhaps your coach can pay attention to the shoving and begin calling legitimate fouls.

Best wishes,
Advising Anna

Skills Review

Key Reading Skill: Identifying Sequence

9. Name and describe two forms of sequence that writers use to organize information.

Text Element: Titles and Subheads

10. After reading the title, what did you predict the selection would be about? Were you correct?

11. Write a new title for this selection. Think about the information in the article, as well as words that will capture readers' attention.

Vocabulary Check

Write the word that best answers each question.

uproar   policies   verbal

12. If you answer a question by speaking, what kind of response are you giving?

13. If you don't obey these at school, you are likely to get in trouble.

14. If it is very loud and you can't understand what is going on, you might be in the middle of this.

15. **Academic Vocabulary** In this workshop, you learned three common types of sequence. Which type of sequence do you see most often in what you read every day? Give an example.
    • chronological order
    • spatial order
    • order of importance

16. **English Language Coach** Define each word below using the definition of its prefix.
    • *co-* ("with" or "together")
    • *inter-* ("existing between")
    • *trans-* ("across")
    • *super-* ("more than")

    cooperate   transatlantic

    superhero   intercompany

Grammar Link: Commas with Direct Address

You've used commas to separate items in a series. A comma is also used to separate the name of someone who is being talked to directly. This is called **direct address.** Look at the examples below.

Allison, please sit down.

Pardon me, Mr. Razer, when did you hurt your hand?

Can you see who's at the door, Derek?

Be careful to look at sentences closely, though. Commas are only used when someone is actually being addressed or spoken to, **not** when someone is being talked about.

Wrong: Latifah, is going to the store.
(Latifah is the subject of the sentence. She is not being addressed or spoken to.)

Right: Latifah, are you going to the store?
(Latifah is being directly addressed.)

Grammar Practice

Rewrite the following sentences, adding commas where needed.

17. Allen you have to read this article from *TIME* magazine about bullies.

18. Tanya was told that students should seek help when needed Mike.

19. Excuse me Jonathan there's a bully standing next to you.

Writing Application Review your advice column letters. Use at least one example of direct address.

Web Activities For eFlashcards, Selection Quick Checks, and other Web activities, go to www.glencoe.com.

Let the Bullies Beware **561**

Skills Review

Key Reading Skill: Identifying Sequence

9. Possible response: An author might present events in *chronological order,* or time order. An author might also present a range of ideas in their *order of importance.*

Text Element: Titles and Subheads

10. Responses will vary.

11. Responses will vary.

Vocabulary Check

12. verbal

13. policies

14. uproar

15. **Academic Vocabulary** Chronological order Sample response: First, I woke up very early. Then I washed and ate breakfast. Afterward, I went jogging.

16. **English Language Coach** cooperate: to do something together

    transatlantic: across the ocean

    superhero: being more than a hero

    intercompany: between companies

Grammar Link: Commas with Direct Address

Grammar Practice

17. Allen, you have to read this article from *Time* magazine about bullies.

18. Tanya was told that students should seek help when needed, Mike.

19. Excuse me, Jonathan, there's a bully standing next to you.

Close

Ask students to summarize what they learned about the Big Question from the article.

Focus

Daily Language Practice Transparency 47

Focus Activity Ask: Have you ever overheard a conversation between people whom you didn't know? On the basis of what you heard, what opinion did you form about the person? *(Responses will vary.)* **OL**

Teach

W Writing

Revision Say: To help you with revision, assign a color to each of the following elements in your story: main character, setting, conflict, and plot. The color-coding will help you see which elements are covered fully and which elements need additional support. **OL**

Resources for page 562

📁 Use the BLM in the Unit 5 Resource Booklet, pp. 27–28.

✎ Use the Grammar and Writing Workshop Transparencies 25–26.

WRITING WORKSHOP PART 2

Short Story
Revising, Editing, Presenting

ASSIGNMENT Write a fictional short story about a bully

Purpose: To tell a story about dealing with bullies

Audience: You, your teacher, and possibly some classmates

Revising Rubric

Your short story should have

• clear organization
• a developed plot line
• specific details that describe characters and setting
• descriptive dialogue

Objectives (pp. 562–565)
Writing Revise your writing for key elements, dialogue, and word choice
Grammar Use appropriate punctuation
Listening, Speaking, and Viewing Present short story • Use appropriate expressions and gestures • Maintain effective eye contact and posture

In Writing Workshop Part 1, you used a story plan to write the first draft of your short story. You decided on characters, a setting, conflict, and plot. Great job! In Writing Workshop Part 2, you will learn skills to make your work even better.

Revising

Make It Better

The first part of the revising process is to reread the draft you wrote. As you read, underline, circle, or cross out the parts of the story you want to change. Remember, your short story should have the following elements:

• a well-developed main character
• a clearly described setting
• a conflict that involves a bully
• a plot that includes exposition, rising action, climax, falling action, and resolution

If your story is missing any of these elements, now is the time to write them down and add them to the appropriate place in your draft.

Dialogue

Put the finishing touches on your story by adding dialogue. Dialogue is spoken conversations between characters in a written work. Dialogue is a helpful writing tool because readers "hear" how characters express themselves. You can tell a lot about a character by the way he or she speaks. Read the dialogue below to learn more about the characters Theo and Eric.

> "Hey, shrimp, what're you grooving to on those headphones?" asked Eric.
> "It's, um, it's jazz music," Theo said quietly.
> "Jazz music? What kind of dork listens to jazz music?" Eric said.
> "Well, I think it's all right," said Theo.
> "Let me see that MP3 player—now," demanded Eric.
> "Um, okay," said Theo.

This conversation tells the reader a lot about these two characters. Who is the bully? Who is being bullied? What words do the characters use that show their personalities?

Additional Support

Literature Focus Lesson

Dialogue Write a series of character traits on note cards, one trait per card and one card for each student. Place the cards in a bowl or box, and have each student draw a card. Next, ask pairs of students to write short dialogues between two characters. The dialogue of the first character must illustrate the trait on one partner's card without using the actual word on the card. The dialogue of the second character must illustrate the other trait. Then, have pairs of students read their dialogues aloud. Invite the class to guess the two character traits that partners have shown. **OL**

Try It!

Find a scene in your draft where two characters are speaking to each other. Write a dialogue between the two characters.

- Write dialogue the way you think your characters would talk.
- Keep each character's piece of dialogue short.
- Use dialogue to help describe the setting. For example, if a character says, "It's freezing out here!" that means the weather is cold outside.

Dialogue is punctuated in a certain way to tell readers that the characters are speaking. Follow the rules below to punctuate dialogue.

Place quotation marks before and after the spoken words.

"Hey, shrimp, what're you grooving to on those headphones?"

Periods and commas always go inside the quotation marks.

*"Jazz music isn't so bad. In fact, I think it's pretty cool,"
said Theo.*

Theo said, "Jazz music is really cool."

When an exclamation point or question mark punctuates the dialogue, it goes inside the quotation marks.

"That saxophone sounds amazing!" said Theo.

Editing
Finish It Up

When you finish revising, check for errors in grammar, spelling, and punctuation. Use the Editing Checklist to help you spot your mistakes.

Editing Checklist

☑ Spelling and capitalization are correct.
☑ All sentences have appropriate end punctuation.
☑ All dependent clauses are linked to independent clauses.
☑ Dialogue is correctly punctuated.

Presenting
Show It Off

By now you have made a lot of changes to your story and it might look messy. Using your best handwriting, copy the final version of your story onto a fresh sheet of paper. Or use a computer to type and print a final copy. Finally, read your story aloud to a partner or group of classmates.

Literature Online

Writing Models For models and other writing activities, go to www.glencoe.com.

◀ **Writing Tip**

Use precise verbs to describe dialogue. Instead of *said*, use *announced, observed, admitted, begged, explained, exclaimed, hinted, barked,* or *cried.*

◀ **Writing Tip**

Improve your handwriting by using two hands! Use one hand to hold the pencil and use your other hand to hold your paper steady on a flat surface.

Teach

W Writing

Lead Say: The lead is the beginning of a story. The lead grabs the reader's interest. A good lead often forces the reader to ask a question that will be answered only if the reader continues to read. A dialogue, or a conversation between characters, is one way to write a solid lead. Review the lead of your story. Does it grab the reader's attention by making the reader ask a question? If not, consider revising your lead by beginning your story with dialogue. **OL**

Differentiated Instruction

Punctuating Dialogue Invite students to punctuate the following dialogue correctly.

1. Curiouser and curiouser said Alice. *("Curiouser and curiouser," said Alice.)*

2. That gymnastics trick explained Amanda took me three months

to learn. *("That gymnastics trick," explained Amanda, "took me three months to learn.")*

3. I will be late said the senator's aide so don't wait for me. *("I will be late," said the senator's aide, "so don't wait for me.")* **OL**

Objectives
- Write to entertain
- Write short stories
- Communicate the significance of events in the plot
- Revise writing for key elements, style, and word choice
- Use punctuation: quotation marks

563

Teach

W Writing

Lead Ask: What question does the lead make the reader ask? *(The reader should wonder why Theo is tense.)* **Ask:** Is this question answered as the reader continues to read the story? *(Yes; Theo is being bullied at the bus stop.)* **OL**

Active Writer's Model	Writer's Model

Writer's Model

Bus Stop Blues
By Samuel Lewis

W The writer introduces the main character and describes the setting. This is the exposition of the story.

Theo Thomas ran a comb through his hair one last time and left the house. He was too tense to enjoy the Coral Springs, Florida, sunshine or notice the white seagulls flying through the blue sky. Theo was lost in thought. What would Eric do to him at the bus stop today? Slug him? Toss his sixth-grade science fair handbook into a mud puddle?

Eric wasn't at the bus stop when Theo got there. So Theo put on his MP3 player and let his ears feast on a banquet of jazz. He'd have to try playing some of those cool sounds on his saxophone.

This scene is part of the rising action. All of the events that lead up to the climax of the story are part of the rising action.

Suddenly, the jazz was gone. Eric was towering over Theo, holding Theo's MP3 player over his head. Give it back! Theo wanted to yell. But the words wouldn't come out.

The La Hoya Middle School bus screeched up to the curb. Theo considered telling the bus driver what had happened. No, he valued his life. Besides, he'd heard MP3 players weren't good for your hearing.

Descriptive dialogue helps the reader learn more about the characters and their personalities.

The next morning at the bus stop, Eric swaggered up to Theo and slapped him on the back. "Hey, Four Eyes, let me have some money," he said.

"I-I don't have any," Theo stammered.

"Sure you do. I see you buying lunch every day."

Theo wanted to say, You can't have my money. But he noticed that Eric's fists were clenched, so he handed over his lunch money.

He'd just have to skip lunch. Well, it was no big deal. Theo hated sitting by himself in the cafeteria, so he decided to spend lunch practicing his saxophone.

A couple of days later, Theo was standing at the bus stop, holding his saxophone. After his lesson was over, he was going to ask his music teacher, Ms. Robinson, if she thought he was good enough to play in a real band someday, and what he needed to do to become a professional jazz player.

This sentence begins with a dependent clause linked to an independent clause. *After his lesson was over* cannot stand alone as a sentence.

Suddenly, Eric strode up to him, saying, "Come on, let me have a look at your saxophone," in a fake-friendly voice.

Additional Support

Literature Focus Lesson

Figurative Language Point out to students some other elements of "Bus Stop Blues."

- **Reflection:** "Theo was lost in thought."
- **Figurative Language:** "let his ears feast on a banquet of jazz."

- **Active verbs:** "Theo stammered."
- **Body Language:** "Eric's fists were clenched."

Suggest that students incorporate some of these elements into their own stories. **OL**

This was too much. Taking Theo's saxophone wasn't like taking his lunch money, or even his MP3 player. His saxophone was his life. "You can't have my saxophone!" Theo yelled. "Leave me alone!"

"Temper, temper, temper," Eric teased. But he walked away to hang out with some other eighth-grade guys.

After that day, Eric never bothered Theo at the bus stop again.

Active Writing Model

This is the climax of the story because Theo faces his fears and finally stands up to Eric, the bully.

This sentence is the resolution of the story. It brings the story to an end. **W**

Listening, Speaking, and Viewing

Reading Aloud

Reading text aloud lets you share your story, or someone else's, with an audience.

What Is Reading Aloud?

When you read aloud, you use your speaking voice to say the words that you or someone else wrote.

Why Is Reading Aloud Important?

When you read your writing aloud, you
- read the words more carefully.
- notice mistakes that you might not catch during revision.
- find parts of the story you'd like to change.
- get to share your work with family and friends.

How Do I Do It?

First decide what to read. Choose a passage from the short story you wrote in the Writing Workshop or a passage from one of the stories in this unit. Then, follow these steps.

1. Copy or type the passage onto a fresh sheet of paper.
   - Make sure you are able to read your handwriting or see the typed words clearly.
2. Hold the paper in front of you and practice reading the passage.
   - In your head, imagine what is taking place and the mood of the characters or narrator.
   - Try to express these emotions in your voice.

3. Pause every time you see a
   - comma
   - dash
   - period
4. Change the sound of your voice to match the way characters speak by
   - creating different voices for each character.
   - raising your voice when characters ask questions.
   - sounding excited when you read a sentence that ends with an exclamation point!

Try It!

After you have practiced reading aloud to yourself several times, divide into small groups. Take turns reading your passages aloud to each other. Before you start to read, do the following: **LSV**
- Stand up straight and tall
- Take a deep breath
- Look at your audience

Class Reading

Choose one passage from your group to read aloud to the whole class. Divide the passage into parts and have each member of your group read a different part. Or, you may have one group member read the part of the narrator and other group members read the parts of different characters. Practice reading aloud as a group before you read to the class.

Reading Fluency

Read Aloud The ability to read aloud with feeling is an aspect of fluency. Take this opportunity to evaluate the reading fluency of all students. Those students who are unable to read aloud with feeling may need further assessment. The following checklist is a good evaluative tool:

√ able to read aloud with feeling

√ able to restate a story, including major details of character, setting, plot, conflict, and theme

√ able to comprehend a story whether it is read aloud or silently **BL**

Teach

W Writing

Theme Ask: What is the theme or main idea of this story? *(The main idea may be that you should stand up to bullies.)* **OL**

LSV Listening, Speaking, and Viewing

Visual Aids Say: Think about adding props to make your reading more dramatic. What props will help the audience follow the plot line, understand the characters, or grasp the theme? Consider adding hats, wigs, or accessories such as jewelry or clothing to your reading. Using such props may inspire you. **OL**

Assess

Lead students in a discussion about the effects of pauses and voice alteration on oral readings. How do these elements help the speaker communicate a message? How do these elements affect the audience?

Objectives
- Write to entertain
- Write short stories
- Analyze features of genres: short stories
- Read aloud

565

Paraphrasing and Summarizing

**Objectives covered in
this workshop:**
• Paraphrase and summarize
text to demonstrate understanding
• Paraphrase and summarize
text to recall and organize
ideas

Teaching Students to Paraphrase and Summarize

Why Is It Important?
• Research shows that summarization is one of the most effective
instructional approaches for fostering comprehension.
• The most effective form of summarization involves paraphrasing and
synthesis of an author's ideas.
• Paraphrasing can help students integrate critical information and
demonstrate comprehension in their writing process.

How to Help Students Get It
• Emphasize the importance of putting text into one's own words.
• Provide opportunities for guided practice in which you use think-alouds
to model summarizing as you and your students go through a text. Put up
a transparency of the text for use in showing how to indicate important
information through underlining.
• Have students work in pairs to practice summarizing orally, using longer
and longer pieces of text; partners can compare their summaries.
• After guided practice on how oral summarization works, have students
write summaries. Guide them by telling them to jot down main ideas,
then list important words or phrases that support those ideas, and finally,
ask them to rewrite the list into a short paragraph.

Reading to Answer the Big Question

Students will enjoy reading two humorous selections that portray bul-
lies as real and vulnerable people. The story and poem in Unit 5, Reading
Workshop 4, will give them a unique perspective as they think about the Big
Question: **How should we deal with bullies?**

Don't Let the Bedbugs Bite by Ellen Conford
Sally finds out that Tina, aka "Gruesome" Grossman, the bully who has
made her life miserable for the last three years, is going to be her new
stepsister. Students will be entertained by this amusing short story in which
Sally realizes that even the most intimidating bullies are vulnerable.

The New Kid on the Block by Jack Prelutsky
In this sixteen-line humorous poem, the speaker describes a big, strong,
muscular character who is picking on all the guys. Students will probably be
surprised when they read the last line of the poem: "I don't care for her
at all."

Workshop Resources

PACING (DAYS)		LESSON	STUDENT MATERIALS	TEACHER RESOURCES
STANDARD	BLOCK			
1	½	Key Skill Lesson: Paraphrasing and Summarizing	📖 Key Reading Skills Practice, p. 29 📖 English Language Coach Review, p. 41	📑 Bellringer Options Transparencies – Daily Language Practice 48 📑 Read Aloud, Think Aloud Transparencies – Key Reading Skills 16 – Read Aloud, Think Aloud 39–50 💿 Presentation Plus!
2	1	"Don't Let the Bedbugs Bite"	💻 Glencoe Online 📖 Unit Vocabulary Review, p, 39 📖 Academic Vocabulary Review, p. 42 📁 English Language Coach 📖 Active Reading Graphic Organizer, p. 31 📖 Literary Analysis, p. 30 💿 StudentWorks Plus™ 💻 Online Student Edition 💿 Literature Classics 📁 Selection and Unit Assessments, p. 55	📑 Literary and Text Analysis Transparencies 6 💻 Puzzlemaker 💿 Skill Level Up!™ A Language Arts Game 💻 BookLink 3 📘 Assessment by Learning Objective (Diagnostic and Formative) 💿 Interactive Tutor: Self-Assessment 💿 TeacherWorks Plus™
2		"The New Kid on the Block"	💻 Glencoe Online 📖 Unit Vocabulary Review, p. 39 📖 Academic Vocabulary Review, p. 42 📁 English Language Coach 📖 Active Reading Graphic Organizer, p. 33 📖 Literary Analysis, p. 30 💿 StudentWorks Plus™ 💻 Online Student Edition 💿 Literature Classics 📁 Selection and Unit Assessments, p. 56	📑 Literary and Text Analysis Transparencies 6 💻 Puzzlemaker 💿 Skill Level Up!™ A Language Arts Game 💻 BookLink 3 📘 Assessment by Learning Objective (Diagnostic and Formative) 💿 Interactive Tutor: Self-Assessment 💿 TeacherWorks Plus™

Keys for Unit Resource

- 📁 Blackline Master
- 📘 Workbook
- 📖 Supplemental Text
- 💿 CD-ROM
- 🔒 DVD
- 📑 Transparency
- 💻 Web-based
- 📖 Fast File

Level Appropriate Code

- **AS** = Activities for all students
- **AL** = Activities for students working above grade level
- **OL** = Activities for students working at grade level
- **BL** = Activities for students working below grade level
- **EL** = Activities for English language learners

Focus

BELLRINGER Options

✍ **Daily Language Practice Transparency 48**
Focus Activity Ask: Have you ever been forced to spend time with someone your age who seemed shy, unfriendly, or threatening? How did you feel about it before you spent time together? How did you feel afterward? *(Responses will vary.)* **AS**

Teach

R Reading Skill

Paraphrasing and Summarizing Ask: How would summarizing a speech be different from paraphrasing it? *(Possible response: A summary would focus on only the main ideas and the most important details. A paraphrased version of the speech would include smaller details.)* **OL**

V Vocabulary

Academic Vocabulary Point out that the word *summary* contains the root word *sum*.
Ask: What do you do when you find the sum of several numbers? *(You add them to find the total.)* **OL**

Skills Focus

You will practice using these skills when you read the following selections:
• "Don't Let the Bedbugs Bite," p. 570
• "The New Kid on the Block," p. 583

Reading
• Paraphrasing and summarizing

Literature
• Understanding characterization

Vocabulary
• Understanding word structure: roots
• Academic vocabulary: *summary*

Writing/Grammar
• Using commas with introductory words

Objectives (pp. 566–567)
Reading Paraphrase and summarize

Skill Lesson

Paraphrasing and Summarizing

Learn It!

R **What Are They?** Paraphrasing and summarizing are ways of retelling the author's ideas in your own words.

• **Paraphrasing** means restating someone else's ideas in your own words. You might paraphrase a sentence, or you might paraphrase a longer selection in your own words.

• **Summarizing** means briefly retelling the important events and ideas of a selection in your own words. When you summarize, you ask yourself, "What's important?" A good **summary** includes all the main ideas and the most important details. A summary should always be shorter than the original selection.

BALDO © 2005 Baldo Partnership. Distributed by UNIVERSAL PRESS SYNDICATE. Reprinted with permission. All rights reserved.

Analyzing Cartoons
What is the boy's summary of his chances of getting an "A" in English class? What makes his summary funny?

V **Academic Vocabulary**
summary (SUM ur ee) *n.* a brief statement of the main points of a piece of writing

566 UNIT 5

Additional Support

Reading in the Real World

Career Tell students that many professionals use summarizing and paraphrasing skills on a daily basis. For example, news reporters frequently summarize the main idea of a story in the first paragraph and then paraphrase what people have said about the topic in the following paragraphs. Nonfiction writers frequently paraphrase, or retell certain events in history, in their own words. Also point out that paraphrasing is an important part of being a good listener. For example, psychologists paraphrase what their patients tell them to show that they are listening and understanding. Encourage students to brainstorm other careers that involve summarizing and paraphrasing. **AS**

Why Are They Important? You use paraphrasing and summarizing to test whether you understand what you have read. Both skills teach you to rethink what you've read and to separate main ideas from details. Paraphrasing and summarizing help you remember and organize information, as well as explain a series of events.

How Do I Do Them? To paraphrase, restate the author's ideas in your own words. To summarize, ask yourself: What was that story about? Answer the questions *who, what, when, where, why,* and *how.* Use your own words. Decide what is most important. Then write the information in a logical order. Here's how one student summarized a paragraph of "What Kids Say About Bullying."

> It can be hard for kids to know what to do if a bully bothers them. About half of the kids said they fight back. There are a lot of problems with this solution. First, one or both of the kids could get hurt. Unlike on TV, where actors are just pretending to fight, when kids punch, kick, and push each other, they can get real injuries, like bruises and cuts and broken bones.

Now that I've read, I need to ask myself, "What is the most important idea?" The paragraph is about kids who fight back against bullies. When I think about the details that support that idea, I have to keep in mind that kids can get hurt. Here is my summary:

Half of the kids will fight back against a bully who bothers them. But those kids—or the bully—might get hurt.

Practice It!

Think about one of your favorite movies. How would you describe it to someone who has not seen it? In your Learner's Notebook, write a summary of the movie. Remember to include only the most important details.

Use It!

As you read "Don't Let the Bedbugs Bite" and "The New Kid on the Block," practice paraphrasing and summarizing the authors' ideas.

Literature Online

Study Central Visit www.glencoe.com and click on Study Central to review paraphrasing and summarizing.

Teach

Literature Online

Study Central Have students access the Web site to review paraphrasing and summarizing and to complete a related activity.

R **Reading Skill**

Paraphrasing and Summarizing Say: Paraphrase the *Why Is It Important?* section. *(Possible response: Paraphrasing and summarizing are ways of checking to make sure you've understood what you've read. Both skills help you remember and organize information and separate main ideas from details.)* Encourage students to pause, paraphrase, and summarize whenever they encounter a lengthy or complicated text. **OL**

Resources for page 567

📁 Use the Key Reading Skills Transparency 16 in *Read Aloud, Think Aloud* to help students practice paraphrasing and summarizing.

Differentiated Instruction

Learning to Summarize One of the best ways for students to develop the ability to summarize a text is to have the skill modeled for them. Use an overhead projector to display a selection of three or four short paragraphs so that all of your students can see it. Read the selection aloud, and underline key sentences, phrases, and words that are integral to the main idea. Then write your summary at the bottom, keeping the original text in view. **AS**

Objectives
• Paraphrase and summarize
• Learn and use new vocabulary

567

Teach

More About the Author

Ellen Conford has written more than thirty-five books for young people, including graphic novels and collections of short stories. She enjoys doing crossword puzzles and spending time with animals, especially dogs. Conford lives with her family in Great Neck, New York.

V Vocabulary

In Your Own Words Have students paraphrase the definition of each vocabulary word in their Learner's Notebooks. **Ask:** What is an example of something you might contemplate? *(Possible response: whether to try out for a team)* What is an example of a parody? *(Responses will vary.)* **AS**

Before You Read · Don't Let the Bedbugs Bite

Meet the Author

Ellen Conford began writing in third grade. She says, "I write the kinds of books for children and teenagers that I liked to read at their age, books meant purely to entertain, to amuse, to divert."

Author Search For more about Ellen Conford, go to www.glencoe.com.

Objectives (pp. 568–579)
Reading Paraphrase and summarize
• Make connections from text to self
Literature Identify literary elements: characterization
Vocabulary Identify word structure: roots

Vocabulary Preview

contemplate (KON tem playt) *v.* to have in mind as a possibility **(p. 571)** *Sally had to contemplate having a new sister.*

sordid (SOR did) *adj.* mean, rude **(p. 571)** *The teachers didn't want their students to spread sordid gossip.*

parody (PAIR uh dee) *n.* a piece of writing or musical work that imitates another by making fun of it **(p. 571)** *The marriage of two teachers from the same school seemed like a strange parody.*

potential (puh TEN shul) *adj.* capable of being **(p. 572)** *) Sally looked for potential husbands for her mother.*

aggression (uh GRESH un) *n.* angry and unfriendly action or behavior **(p. 573)** *Tina showed aggression when she bullied many students.*

Partner Talk On a separate note card, write each vocabulary word one time. Turn the note card over and write the definition and part of speech on the back. Take turns testing each other by flashing the cards. Take it a step further and say each word in a sentence when you give the definition.

English Language Coach

Roots The main part of a word is called its **root**. When a root is a complete word, it may be called a **base word**. But most roots are not whole words—they are parts of words.

Finding the root of an unfamiliar word can often help you understand what the word means. To find the root of a word, take away any prefixes or suffixes. Look at the roots, meanings, and example words below.

ROOT	MEANING	EXAMPLES
port	carry	**port**able, im**port**
div	divide	**div**ision, **div**orce
dict	speak	pre**dict**, **dict**ate

Write to Learn Use the list of roots above (and the prefixes and suffixes you've learned) to figure out the meaning of the underlined word.

1. The stream was <u>diverted</u> from its path.

2. Look up the word in a <u>dictionary</u>.

3. They had to <u>transport</u> the food across the country in trucks.

Additional Support

Author Search To expand students' appreciation of Ellen Conford, have them access the Web site for additional information and resources.

English Language Coach

Roots To explain roots more fully, write the words *microscope, periscope,* and *telescope* on the board, and ask students which letters all three words have in common *(scope)*. Then point out that *scope* comes from a Greek word meaning "see." Allowing students to first see words that contain the same root is frequently more effective than showing the roots first, followed by examples. Repeat this activity with more Greek and Latin roots. Examples of common roots include *act-* (do: actor, action, enact), *bio-* (life: biology, biography), *cycl-* (circle/ring: bicycle, cyclone), and *meter-* (measure: thermometer, centimeter, barometer). **AS**

Skills Preview

Key Reading Skill: Paraphrasing and Summarizing

As you read, think about the story and remember that paraphrasing and summarizing can help you

- organize main ideas and details
- explain a sequence of events
- remember what you have read

Write to Learn In your Learner's Notebook, list three times you need to paraphrase or summarize. Think about all your classes and after-school activities.

Key Literary Element: Characterization

Characterization is the way a writer develops the personality of a character. A writer bring a characters to life

- through the character's own words or actions
- by revealing the character's thoughts and feelings
- by revealing what others think about the character
- by stating directly what the character is like

As you read the story, think about the methods the author uses to make the characters in the story seem real. Ask:

- *What does the author want you to think about the character, based on his or her appearance?*
- *What does the character's speech and behavior show about the kind of person he or she is?*
- *What do the actions of others let you know about the character?*

Write to Learn Copy the list of questions above. Pick one character from the story, and, as you read, answer the questions with that character in mind.

Interactive Literary Elements Handbook
To review or learn more about the literary elements, go to www.glencoe.com.

Get Ready to Read

Connect to the Reading

Have you ever thought you knew all about someone and then discovered something new? Have you ever thought you wouldn't like someone and then made friends with him or her later?

Write to Learn Why might a bully tease and torment others? Why might someone want to scare other people? Copy the graphic organizer below. On the left side write the answers to these two questions *before* you read the story. *After* you've finished reading, answer the questions again on the right. Compare how your answers changed.

Before Reading	After Reading
1.	1.
2.	2.

Build Background

In this story, Sally is upset about living with someone who has bullied her. If her mother marries the bully's father, Sally will have a bully for a stepsister.

- A *stepfather* is a man who has married a person's mother after the death or divorce of the natural father. Don would become Sally's stepfather.
- A *stepmother* is a woman who has married a person's father after the death or divorce of the natural mother. Sally's mother would become Tina's stepmother.

Set Purposes for Reading

BIG Question Read "Don't Let the Bedbugs Bite" to see how getting to know a bully can surprise you.

Set Your Own Purpose What else would you like to learn from the story to help you answer the Big Question? Write your own purpose on the "Don't Let the Bedbugs Bite" page of your Foldable 5.

Keep Moving

Use these skills as you read the following selection.

Don't Let the Bedbugs Bite **569**

Teach

L Literary Element

Characterization Say:
Characterization is the way a writer reveals a character's personality. Give three words to describe your personality. *(Responses will vary.)* **OL** What does your physical appearance reveal about your personality? *(Responses will vary.)* **AL**

R Reading Skill

Review Connecting Ask:
What advice have parents or relatives given you about bullies? Do you agree with the advice that you have been given? Explain. *(Responses will vary.)* **AS**

Interactive Literary Elements Handbook Have students access the Web site to improve their understanding of characterization.

Literature Focus Lesson

Characterization Explain to students that there are two types of characterization: direct and indirect. In direct characterization, the writer says something about a character's personality. For instance, an author may write, "Vanessa was shy and had trouble making new friends." In indirect characterization, the writer reveals a character's personality through the character's own words, the character's thoughts and feelings, or what other characters think and say about that character. Challenge students to use indirect characterization in rewriting the above example about Vanessa. **AL**

Objectives

- Paraphrase and summarize
- Interpret and analyze character
- Identify word structure: roots
- Learn and use new vocabulary

569

Teach

Viewing the Photo

Say: Describe what you see in the photo. What can you tell about the person shown? What might she be doing? *(Possible responses: The photo shows a girl lying on her stomach with her feet in the air. She is wearing jeans. She might be reading a magazine or talking on the phone.)* **AS**

Readability Scores

Dale-Chall: 4.7
DRP: 51
Lexile: 720

Don't Let the Bedbugs Bite

by Ellen Conford

Additional Support

English Language Coach

Build Background Ask students to speculate about the origin of the expression "Don't let the bedbugs bite." Explain that bedbugs are small, wingless insects that feed on the blood of warm-blooded animals. When bedbugs bite (usually at night, when people are asleep), they inject a small amount of saliva into the skin, which may cause an allergic reaction. It is generally believed that the expression "Don't let the bedbugs bite" was originally meant in earnest because bedbugs were common in areas with poor hygiene. Challenge students to search library and Internet resources for the origin of the expression "sleep tight." **AS**

I admit that when my mother told me she was going to marry Tina Grossman's father, I did not take the news very well.

"You can't do this to me!"

"I'm not doing anything to you, Sally," my mother said. "I'm marrying a very nice man whom I love very much."

"And making Gruesome Grossman my sister! You know how many times she beat me up!"

"She never beat you up."

"Well, she threatened to. Twice a week. For three years."

"Sally, that was in fifth grade."

"And sixth grade," I said, "and seventh grade."

"She had problems," my mother admitted. "How would you feel if your mother left you to run off with a vacuum-cleaner salesman?"

"No worse than I feel now," I retorted. "At least I wouldn't have to worry about my stepsister murdering me in my sleep." **1**

Gruesome Grossman, my stepsister. The thought was too horrible to **contemplate.** Sure, I knew my mother had been going out with Tina's father for a year. But they'd been trying to keep it a secret because they both teach at Locksley Hall High. My school.

My mother had sworn me to secrecy, and even though I was dying to tell my friends that she was dating their German teacher, I didn't. Even when my best friend, Selena, got a massive crush on him and wrote him thirty-seven love notes that she (fortunately) never mailed. **2**

They didn't want to be teased and spied on. They didn't want to be the object of **sordid** teenage gossip and evil rumors. I could understand that. After all, I'm a teenager. I love sordid gossip and evil rumors.

But marriage? They were two middle-aged teachers with practically grown daughters. Why did they have to get married? Why couldn't they just go right on sneaking around, without forcing their children into this bizarre **parody** of a family?

Vocabulary

contemplate (KON tem playt) *v.* to have in mind as a possibility

sordid (SOR did) *adj.* mean, rude

parody (PAIR uh dee) *n.* a piece of writing or musical work that imitates another by making fun of it

Practice the Skills

1 **Key Literary Element**

Characterization A character's personality is sometimes shown through his or her words or actions. What does the conversation between Sally and her mother reveal about Sally? Does it reveal anything about Tina? **L**

2 **Key Reading Skill**

Paraphrasing and Summarizing Remember that paraphrasing means restating someone else's ideas in your own words. Practice paraphrasing this paragraph. **R**

Don't Let the Bedbugs Bite **571**

Teach

L Literary Element

Characterization Ask: How do you first learn about Tina Grossman? *(Sally and her mother talk about Tina.)* **Ask:** What does Sally say about Tina? *(Sally says that Tina used to bully her.)* **Ask:** What does Sally's mother say? *(Sally's mother says that Tina had problems and that Tina's mother ran off with a vacuum cleaner salesman.)* **BL OL Say:** Keep in mind that a long-term consequence of bullying is that the people they bully may still be uncomfortable around them years later. **AS**

R Reading Skill

Paraphrasing and Summarizing Say: To paraphrase, you must make sure that you understand the text. What thought is "too horrible" for Sally to contemplate? *(the thought of being Tina's stepsister)* **Ask:** What secret has Sally been keeping? *(Sally's mother has been dating Tina's father for the past year.)* **BL OL**

Reading Fluency

Reading Dialogue To help build fluency, have students work in groups of three to practice reading aloud the opening dialogue between Sally and her mother. Have one student read the narrative text, including the conversational tags such as "my mother said" and "I retorted," and have the other two students read and act out the actual dialogue. After students practice reading the text several times, encourage them to read with feeling, taking into account exclamation points and clues such as "retorted." When students are comfortable with the passage, have them present it to the entire class. **BL EL**

Objectives
• Paraphrase and summarize
• Interpret and analyze character
• Use text features: photograph

Teach

Viewing the Photo

Ask: How would you describe the reaction of the girl in the photo? *(Possible response: She does not believe what the woman is telling her.)* **BL**

Ask: How is Sally's reaction to her mother similar to the reaction of the girl in the photo? *(Possible response: Sally doesn't agree that her mother marrying Tina's father can work.)* **OL**

L Literary Element

Characterization Ask: Do you think that Sally is exaggerating her description of Tina? Explain. *(Some students may say that Sally is exaggerating in order to show how much she dislikes Tina. Other students may believe that Sally's descriptions are truthful.)* **OL**

I dropped into the nearest chair and glared at my mother. "Does Tina know about the impending nuptials?"[1] I said "nuptials" with such disgust that my mother winced.

"No. Remember, she was in my history class when I started seeing Don. And then, when I had to flunk her, we thought . . ."

"See! Even her father's afraid of her. And she must *hate* you. Can't you tell this is never going to work?"

"It will work," my mother said firmly, "if we work at making it work."

I scowled at her. "Nobody could work that hard."

It's not that I resented my mother remarrying. I wasn't jealous about "sharing" her with someone else. In fact, for years after my father died, I tried to fix her up with men so I could have a daddy again.

The man who came to service the oil burner, the shoe salesman who fitted me at Wee Walk Inn, even the UPS driver who occasionally delivered a package to our house—I considered all of them **potential** father material.

Of course, I was eight years old at the time, and kept seeing all these old movies on TV where a little kid brings two people together who never realize they love each other until they both realize they love *her*.

But the little kid never ended up with a stepsister. Let alone a stepsister like Tina Grossman. **3**

L ⌈ It was about this time that Tina—the Terror of Tyler Elementary School—began terrorizing me. Oh, she picked on other kids, too. I wasn't the only one who was afraid of her. But maybe I was the one who was most afraid of her. So ⌊ naturally I was the kid she most enjoyed bullying.

Analyzing the Photo Look at the expression on the young girl's face. Do you think Sally has a similar expression on her face as she argues with her mother?

Practice the Skills

3 | **Key Literary Element**

Characterization What have you learned about Sally's mother? Do you have an idea about what she is like? How does the author show you her personality?

---

1. ***Impending nuptials*** means that the wedding will take place very soon. ***Nuptials*** are the celebrations and ceremony that is part of marriage.

Vocabulary

potential (puh TEN shul) *adj.* capable of being

Additional Support

Literature Focus Lesson

Point of View Explain that point of view is the relationship of the narrator, or storyteller, to the story. "Don't Let the Bedbugs Bite" is told from a first-person point of view. In first-person point of view, one of the characters tells the story and refers to himself or herself as "I." Sally is the narrator in this story, and the events are seen through her eyes. Prompt students to discuss how the story would be different if it were told by a third-person narrator, or person outside the story. You may also want to ask whether the first-person point of view makes it easier or harder to identify with the narrator and have students explain their reasoning. **OL**

I handed over lunch money, granola bars, homework, snap bracelets—even pencils with my name printed on them that my grandmother had given me for Christmas.

All she had to do was stand over me with her fists on her hips and say, "Gimme that!" At first I'd say no. Then she'd say, "Gimme that or I'll break your arm."

EL I generally decided that I needed my arm more than the lunch money, granola bar, or whatever it was she was trying to extort from me that day.

Maybe that's why I longed for a father so much. Maybe I thought he'd protect me from Tina. But I'd gotten over it. And eventually, Tina got tired of terrorizing me, and channeled her **aggression** into school sports, where she became the captain of the softball team, the volleyball team, and the basketball team. Possibly by threatening to break all the other players' arms if they didn't elect her captain. **4**

Well, I was finally getting a father. Who was just as afraid of Tina as everyone else.

"When's the wedding?" I asked sourly. "And is there time to enroll me in boarding school before then?"

"July," my mother said.

"*July?*" I groaned. "That's only two months away. It's hardly enough time to write my will."

"I know it seems soon," my mother said. "That's why Don and I thought you girls ought to get better acquainted before then."

"We could hardly be worse acquainted," I said before I realized what she was getting at.

"So Saturday we're all going into the city together," she went on. "We have marvelous plans. First we'll go to a Yankee[2] game."

"I hate baseball," I said.

"Then on to a nice restaurant for dinner," she continued.

"I'm on a diet."

"And after dinner we have tickets for *Oui,[3] Oui, Odette.*"

---

2. *Yankee* refers to the New York Yankees baseball team.

3. *Oui* (wee) is the French word for *yes*.

Vocabulary

aggression (uh GRESH un) *n.* angry and unfriendly action or behavior

Practice the Skills

4 Key Literary Element

Characterization Think about what you already know about Tina's mother leaving the family and how that may have affected Tina. Why might she have "aggression"? How could sports have helped her? What does this paragraph tell you about both Tina and Sally?

Don't Let the Bedbugs Bite **573**

Teach

L Literary Element

Characterization Ask: What does Sally reveal about her own personality in her description of being bullied by Tina? *(Possible response: She is fearful, passive, and unsure of herself.)* **OL** Ask: Do you think that playing sports might help someone relieve aggression? Explain. *(Responses will vary.)* **AL**

EL Language Coach

Roots Say: The root *-tort* means "twist," and the prefix *ex-* means "out" or "from." Use this information to determine what *extort* means in this paragraph. *(to obtain by force)* **OL**

English Language Coach

Roots The words *impending* (p. 572) and *aggression* (p. 573) contain the Latin roots *-pend* and *-gress,* which are found in many English words. Have students form groups to determine the meaning of these roots and list examples of their use in English. Have each group use a dictionary to determine the meaning of each root (*-pend* means "hang," as in *pendulum* and *suspend; -gress* means "step" or "go," as in *progress* and *regress*) and to identify as many words as possible that contain these roots. Set a reasonable time limit for the activity. Then have the groups compete to list words that they have found. When a group can no longer provide a word, it must drop out. **OL** **AL**

Objectives
- Paraphrase and summarize
- Interpret and analyze: character
- Identify literary elements: point of view
- Use text features: photograph
- Identify word structure: roots

573

Teach

L Literary Element

Characterization Ask: How does Tina's physical appearance add to Sally's characterization of her? Explain. *(Possible response: Tina's sleeveless shirt emphasizes her "overdeveloped biceps"; even in a skirt, Tina looks like a bully. She still seems intimidating, especially to Sally.)* **OL**

EL Language Coach

Roots Ask: What does the word *entire* mean? *(complete; total)* How does the suffix *-ly* change a word? *(It usually forms an adverb.)* What does the suffix *-ly* mean? *("in a ___ way")* What does *entirely* mean? *(in a complete or total way)* **BL OL**

That shut me up. Momentarily. *Oui, Oui, Odette* was the hottest musical on Broadway.[4]

"And then Tina will come back here to sleep over." She said it rapidly, as if hoping she could slip it by me. Unfortunately, I heard it.

"It will be a wonderful day," she promised.

"It will be a day that will live in infamy,"[5] I replied.

When Mr. Grossman came to pick us up Saturday morning, Tina was sullen and withdrawn. Obviously her father had told her about the wedding plans. Obviously she was as thrilled as I was about the **prospect** of joining our families. [5]

She was wearing a white sleeveless T-shirt that displayed her overdeveloped biceps, and a denim skirt. For Tina this was practically formal wear. I couldn't remember ever seeing her in a skirt before. **L**

She'd even tried to tame her long, frizzy black hair with gel or something. It wasn't as wild as it usually looked. [6]

Tina and I immediately positioned ourselves as far apart as possible in the backseat of her father's car. She stared out the left window, silent. I stared out the right window. Silent.

My mother and Tina's father tried to get a conversation going. "Beautiful weather for the ball game, isn't it?" he said.

"If you like baseball," I said.

"Tina loves baseball, don't you, Tina?" my mother said. "Your dad says you're a real Yankee fan."

"Yeah," said Tina.

Things went on like this until I actually began to feel a little guilty about not trying to be nice. I liked Mr. Grossman— whom I'd been calling Don for three months. I supposed it wasn't entirely his fault that Tina was such a creep. **EL**

So as we approached the Midtown Tunnel I admired the city skyline. "There's the Chrysler Building," I said. Its golden roof and spire gleamed in the sun. "Isn't it beautiful?" Just trying to be pleasant.

"Yeah," said Tina.

"It's my favorite building in New York," I said. "What's your favorite building?"

---

4. ***Broadway*** in New York City is both the longest street in the world and the center of the theater district.

5. ***Infamy*** means "famous in a bad way."

Practice the Skills

5 English Language Coach

Roots The word **prospect** can be broken up into the prefix *pro-*, which here means "forward," and the root *spect*, which means "look." What do you think the word *prospect* means? What other words can you form with the root *spect*?

6 Reviewing Skills

Visualizing Read the descriptions of Tina in these two paragraphs. How do they help you to visualize what she looks like? What three details stand out the most in helping you picture her?

Additional Support

Differentiated Instruction

Build Background Ask students whether they recognize Sally's comment about "a day that will live in infamy." If they have not heard the phrase, have students perform an Internet search to find its source. Otherwise, explain that former President Franklin Delano Roosevelt used the phrase "a date which will live in infamy" to respond to the bombing of Pearl Harbor on December 7, 1941. Roosevelt called for the United States to declare war on Japan. Distribute a copy of Roosevelt's speech, and have students find and explain examples of persuasive language. **OL AL**

Finally she turned away from the window. She looked at me as if she thought I was nuts. "Favorite *building?*" She curled her lip in contempt.

I heard a sigh from the driver's seat.

We drove the rest of the way to Yankee Stadium without anybody trying to be nice to anybody else.

But once in our seats, Tina began to show signs of life. Too much life, if you ask me. She cheered or groaned with every pitch. She leaped up at every crack of the bat. She screamed extremely foul things to the umpires, to the Red Sox,[6] to the hot-dog vendor who blocked her view, and to the Yankee batter who failed to hit with three men on base in the bottom of the last inning. **7**

I was practically deaf by the time the game ended, and secretly thrilled that the Yankees had lost. Anything that made Tina so miserable made me happy.

Tina sulked all the way through dinner. We ate at a very classy, very expensive restaurant called Chez Philippe.[7] I loved my lobster bisque, my rack of lamb, and the three pastries I selected from the extravagant[8] dessert cart.

Our parents were really blowing a bundle on this stepsister-bonding business.

Tina had a hamburger. And ice cream.

---

6. The **Red Sox** are a major league baseball team that plays in Boston, Massachusetts.

7. *Chez Philippe* (shay fih LEEP) means "at the house of Philippe" or "at Philippe's" in French.

8. A **bisque** (bihsk) is a thick soup, and **extravagant** means fancy.

Practice the Skills

7 **Key Reading Skill**

Paraphrasing and Summarizing
The main idea of a paragraph can usually be found in either the first or the last sentence. What is the main idea of this paragraph? Summarize the paragraph in your own words.

R

Analyzing the Photo Based on what you've read, what baseball park is this? What details in the photo support your answer?

Don't Let the Bedbugs Bite **575**

Teach

R Reading Skill

Paraphrasing and Summarizing Ask: What does Sally mean when she says that Tina "began to show signs of life"? What "signs of life" does she show? *(Possible response: Tina is no longer quiet and cold, as she was during the car ride. When the game starts, she reacts to every pitch; stands up at every hit; and yells at the umpires, the Red Sox, the hot-dog vendor, and one of the Yankee batters.)* **OL**

C Critical Thinking

Comprehension Ask: What does Sally mean when she says that their parents were "blowing a bundle" on stepsister bonding? *(Possible response: She means that both parents spent a great deal of money to get the two girls to like each other.)* **EL** **BL**

Literature Focus Lesson

Characterization Ask students to use a Venn diagram to compare and contrast the characters of Sally and Tina. Have students search on pages 573–575 for details that characterize the two girls. Encourage students to include details about Sally and Tina's likes and dislikes about New York, baseball, and food. Then have students continue filling in their charts as they read. **OL**

Objectives
- Paraphrase and summarize
- Interpret and analyze character
- Identify word structure: roots
- Use comprehension skills

575

Teach

EL Language Coach

Roots **Say:** The prefix *im-* means "not," and the suffix *-ly* means "in a ____ way." Use this information to determine what *impatiently* means. *(in a way that is not patient)* **OL** When might you wait impatiently for something? *(Responses will vary.)* **AL**

L Literary Element

Characterization **Ask:** Are you surprised that Tina liked the musical? *(Responses will vary.)* Why is Sally surprised? *(Possible response: Sally can't imagine having anything in common with Tina. Tina does not seem to be a person who would enjoy musicals.)* **OL**

The only way the two of us would ever bond would be if someone Krazy-Glued our shoulders together.

I think we were all pretty tired when we headed for the theater. The strain of trying to act like one big happy family was wearing us down.

Although Tina couldn't have been particularly worn down, since she wasn't trying at all.

And much as I wanted to see *Oui, Oui, Odette,* I knew that the minute it ended, I'd have to go home with Tina. A grim, ugly prospect that took the edge off my anticipation of the show.

But once *Oui, Oui, Odette* started, I forgot everything—my wicked stepsister-to-be, Don, the boring ball game, all the French pastry I was digesting. The show was a takeoff on 1930s musicals. There was terrific tap-dancing, bouncy songs, and great costumes. I was so immersed in the whole experience that I didn't even move from my seat during intermission. I just waited impatiently for the next act to start, not wanting to break the mood the play had created.

At the curtain calls, I applauded so long and so hard that my hands began to sting. I glanced over at Tina. To my surprise, she was clapping as enthusiastically as I was.

"Wasn't that a great show?" I said as we walked to the parking garage.

"Yeah," Tina agreed. "It was." I was surprised that she added two more words than was absolutely necessary to reply.

I began to hum the tune to "Tap, *Tout le Monde,* Tap," the show's big production number.[9] I was even more surprised when Tina started humming along with me. **8**

But once in the car, she **reverted** to type. She sat all the way over on the other side of the seat again, and leaned her head against the window. **9**

Don and my mother kept up an enthusiastic stream of chatter about what a wonderful day it had been.

I still had to get through the night.

I tried to tell myself that it was, after all, only one night—eight hours. We were both tired and would probably go right to sleep.

But of course, it wasn't only one night. It was the first night of the rest of my life. Or at least until I went to college. And

---

9. In French, ***Tout la monde*** means "all the world." The French use it to mean "everyone." A ***production number*** is a song and dance performed by many members of the cast.

Practice the Skills

8 **Key Literary Element**

Characterization This is not the first time that Sally has been "surprised" by Tina. Maybe she doesn't know Tina as well as she thinks she does. What does this tell you about Sally? Think about her past interactions with Tina. Why might she have a hard time seeing the good things in Tina? **L**

9 **English Language Coach**

Roots You know that the prefix *re-* means "back" or "again." The root *vert* means "turn." What do you think the word **reverted** means?

Additional Support

English Language Coach

Cultural Literacy Some students may be unfamiliar with baseball terminology and references to American popular culture. Tell students to jot down questions in their Learner's Notebooks as they read. Have periodic question-and-answer sessions to encourage comprehension and build cultural literacy. Point out that when Sally calls Tina her "wicked stepsister-to-be," she is making a reference to a fairy tale character. **EL** **BL**

although it seemed unlikely now that she would murder me in my sleep, what about having to deal with her the rest of the time? What about breakfasts and dinners and summers and trips and—*everything?*|

C1 I felt a very unpleasant tightness in my stomach—and it wasn't because of the three desserts.

There was a soft rumble from Tina's direction. I looked over at her. She was slumped against the window, snoring. Even sound asleep she looked tough.

C2 When we got back to our house, Don declared that the day had been a rousing success.

"You girls ought to get right to bed," my mother urged. "Sally will show you where everything is, Tina."

Don hugged Tina and said he'd be back to pick her up in the morning. Tina got her sleeping bag and followed me up the stairs.

I felt like I was walking the Last Mile.

"The bathroom's there." I pointed. "You can use it first. My room's there." **10**

On Broadway you can see some of the most popular theatrical shows America has to offer. Broadway is bustling with activity; its dazzling lights have earned it the nickname, "The Great White Way."

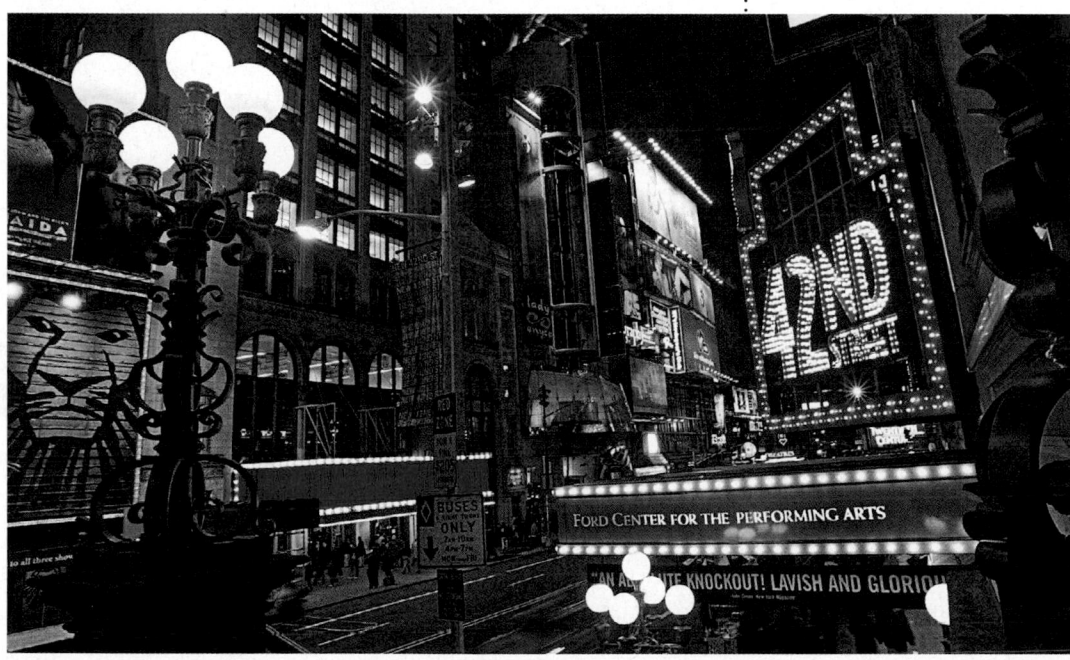

Practice the Skills

10 **Key Literary Element**

Characterization Earlier, Sally said that the day with Tina "will live in infamy." Now she talks about going upstairs as "walking the Last Mile." The "Last Mile" refers to the walk a prisoner takes to be executed. What do these two statements from Sally tell you about her character?

Teach

C1 Critical Thinking

Analysis **Ask:** What do you think causes Sally's stomach-ache? *(Possible response: Having Tina spend the night makes Sally think about how her life will change when her mother marries Tina's father.)* **OL**

C2 Critical Thinking

Evaluation **Ask:** Would Sally and Tina agree with Don that the day was a "rousing success"? Explain. *(Possible response: No; the girls would say that there were parts of the day they didn't enjoy at all.)* **Ask:** Why do you think Don says that the day was a success? *(Responses will vary. Students may say that Don is trying to be positive about the day because he wants the girls to get along.)* **OL**

Differentiated Instruction

Diary Entries Have students write two diary entries from the perspective of either Sally or Tina. In the first diary entry, students should describe their thoughts and feelings the night before the girls spend the day together in New York. In the second diary entry, students should discuss what the girls do together and how they feel about it afterward. You may also give students the option of writing diary entries from the perspective of Don or Tina's mother. In all cases, encourage students to empathize with the character they choose. Invite students to share their diary entries with the rest of the class. **OL** **AL**

Objectives
• Interpret and analyze character
• Identify word structure: roots
• Analyze text
• Evaluate text

Teach

R Reading Skill

Paraphrasing and Summarizing **Ask:** What two things do Sally and Tina agree about? *(They both liked the musical, and both would prefer not to sleep in the same room.)* **BL** **OL**

EL Language Coach

Context Clues Have students use context clues to determine the meaning of the word *tentative.* **Ask:** What words in the same sentence or surrounding sentences give clues about the definition of *tentative?* *(soft, childlike, meek)* Guide students in using these context clues to define tentative as "unsure, hesitant, or timid." **OL**

R "I don't see why we have to sleep in the same room," she said. Except for *Oui, Oui, Odette,* it was the only thing we agreed on all day. "I can put my sleeping bag anywhere."

"I don't see why, either," I said. "It's not like we're going to magically become friends overnight." Or ever. I was too tired to worry about insulting her. And she was probably too tired to punch me.

I got into my pajamas while she used the bathroom. She came back into my room wearing a green football jersey nightshirt, and unrolled her sleeping bag near my closet.

I spent a long time in the bathroom. I washed my face for five minutes and brushed my teeth till my gums nearly bled, hoping she'd be asleep by the time I got back to my room. **11**

But she wasn't. She was lying in her sleeping bag, arms behind her head, staring at the ceiling.

"Well, good night," I said.

I climbed into bed and switched off the lamp on my night table. I punched my pillow a few times, pulled the sheet halfway up over my head, and scrunched around under the covers until I was comfortable. Or as comfortable as I could get with Gruesome Grossman sharing my room.

"Uh—Sally?"

I was startled. It was the first time she'd called me by name all day.

I pulled the sheet down from my nose. "What is it?"

EL "Sometimes I don't sleep too well away from home." Her voice was soft, tentative—almost childlike.

I didn't know what to say. I didn't know what she was getting at. Was there something I was supposed to do to help her sleep? And why did she sound so meek?

"I sometimes have trouble sleeping in a strange bed, too," I said. "Not that you're in a bed, but—"

"Your room is so dark," she said.

"It's nighttime," I reminded her. "It's supposed to be dark."

"My room isn't this dark."

"What, you sleep with a nightlight or something?" I blurted it out without realizing how insulting it sounded.

There was a long silence. Long enough for me to figure out that I'd stumbled onto the truth. Gruesome Grossman slept with a nightlight. Gruesome Grossman was afraid of the dark. **12**

578 UNIT 5 How Should You Deal with Bullies?

Practice the Skills

11 **Key Reading Skill**

Paraphrasing and Summarizing Why does Sally spend so much time in the bathroom? Paraphrase what Sally is doing in this paragraph. Remember to retell what is happening in your own words.

12 **Key Literary Element**

Characterization A character's personality is often revealed through what he or she says and the *way* he or she speaks. What have you just learned about Tina? Has Tina changed, or has Sally's way of seeing her changed? Explain.

Additional Support

Reading Fluency

Using Clues Suggest that students use the text on this page to practice reading aloud. First have students find a quiet place to practice reading aloud for fluency. Then bring the class together and discuss how the writer includes clues about how Sally and Tina deliver their lines. For example, Conford writes that Sally is "startled" when she asks, "What is it?" In the following line, Tina speaks in a voice that is "soft, tentative—almost childlike." Encourage students to practice reading these and other lines aloud, paying special attention to the clues provided. **BL** **EL**

The shock was enough to get the adrenaline[10] pumping through my system. Suddenly I wasn't sleepy anymore. I sat up and flicked on the lamp.

Tina was hunched up like a snail in her sleeping bag. I looked at her for a long time before speaking.

"I didn't think," I said finally, "that you were afraid of *anything.*"

"I'm not afraid," she snapped. "I just don't like it too dark."

"Listen, everyone's afraid of *something,*" I said. I nearly added, "I'm afraid of you." But I didn't.

"I'm not afraid of the dark," she insisted. She sounded like herself again. Gruesome Grossman, spoiling for a fight, ready to deck anyone who disagreed with her.

"Okay, okay," I said. Not because I was afraid she'd deck me. But because I knew she must be feeling pretty embarrassed about this. And I found, to my surprise, that I had no desire to make her feel worse.

"Do you want me to leave the lamp on?" I asked.

She hesitated again. "But then you won't be able to sleep."

"Well," I agreed, "I do like it pretty dark." I thought for a moment. "I have an idea. There's a bulb in my closet."

I got out of bed and opened the closet door. The light came on. I closed the door halfway and got back into bed. I turned off the lamp.

"How's that?" I asked.

A narrow shaft of light illuminated the area around Tina's sleeping bag. If I turned toward the window and pulled the covers up to my nose again, it would hardly bother me.

"That's good," Tina said. She sounded relieved, as if she'd made it through a horror movie without having a heart attack.

"Thanks," she added.

"No problem," I said. "Good night."

She yawned deeply. "Good night," she said. "Sleep tight. Don't let the bedbugs bite." **13** ○

Analyzing the Photo Do you think this girl looks like Sally *before* or *after* she learns that Tina is afraid of the dark? Explain.

Visual Vocabulary
A *bedbug* is a small, wingless, bloodsucking insect. A bedbug's bite is red and itchy, like a mosquito's bite.

---

10. *Adrenaline* (uh DREHN uh lin) is a chemical in the body that increases heartbeat and blood pressure. It prepares the body to respond to danger or other stress.

Practice the Skills

13 **BIG Question**

What do you think Sally has learned about dealing with bullies? Do you think Sally has to worry about Tina bullying her in the future? Why or why not? Write your answer on the "Don't Let the Bedbugs Bite" page of Foldable 5. Your response will help you with the Unit Challenge later. **BQ**

Don't Let the Bedbugs Bite **579**

Teach

L Literary Element

Characterization Ask: How does Tina react when Sally suggests that Tina is afraid of the dark? *(Tina gets defensive and denies it.)* **OL**

BQ **BIG Question**

Ask: Do you think that Sally is still afraid of Tina? Why or why not? *(Possible response: No; Tina is not as tough as Sally once thought. Tina has fears and weaknesses, just as Sally does.)* **OL**

Assess

CheckPoint

Use the CheckPoint questions provided on Presentation Plus! to check for comprehension of the selection. These questions can be used with interactive response keypads for immediate student feedback.

Differentiated Instruction

Debate After reading the story, some students may think that Conford's characterization of Tina is unrealistic and that Tina is merely a stereotype of all bullies. Other students may find Tina's character more believable, claiming that all bullies have fears or weaknesses. Suggest that your class have a debate about whether Tina's character is realistic. Encourage students to use real-life examples to support their arguments. **AS**

Objectives
• Paraphrase and summarize
• Interpret and analyze character
• Use context clues
• Identify word structure: roots

579

Assess

Resources for page 580

📁 Selection QuickCheck, p. 47

📁 Selection and Unit Assessment, p. 55

💿 ExamView Assessment Suite

💿 Interactive Tutor: Self-Assesement

Answering the

1. Responses will vary. Possible responses may include that bullies have weaknesses too.

2. in elementary school

3. Tina is strong and athletic and used to threaten Sally in elementary school.

Critical Thinking

4. Possible response: They planned a day to do things that they knew the girls liked, such as going to a baseball game, having dinner, and seeing a musical. They also arranged to have Tina spend the night at Sally's house.

5. Possible response: Sally's attitude toward Tina softened when she realized that Tina had a weakness and was human.

6. Responses will vary.

580

After You Read

Don't Let the Bedbugs Bite

Answering the BIG Question

1. What have you learned about bullies in this story that will change the way you deal with them? Give examples from the story to support your thoughts.

2. **Recall** When did Tina bully Sally?
   Tip Right There

3. **Summarize** What reasons does Sally have for being afraid of Tina?
   Tip Author and Me

4. **Summarize** How do Sally's mother and Tina's dad try to bring their daughters together?
   Tip Think and Search

Critical Thinking

5. **Compare** How does Sally's attitude toward Tina change during the story?
   Tip Author and Me

6. **Synthesize** What effect do you think nicknames, such as "Gruesome Grossman" and "Tina, the Terror of Tyler Elementary School," have on bullies like Tina?
   Tip On My Own

Talk About Your Reading

Mohandas Gandhi led the struggle for India's freedom from British rule. He believed in nonviolent forms of dealing with an enemy. He once said, "An eye for an eye makes the whole world blind." With a partner, or in a group, talk about how the quote relates to the story. Some questions to discuss might be:

- What does the quote mean? Take turns paraphrasing the quote in your own words. How does the story relate to the quote?

- How did Tina treat Sally in elementary school, and how did Sally respond? What were the effects of this? What would you have done?

- Knowing their history, do you think it would have been easy for Sally to ignore Tina instead of getting to know her? What would you have done if you were Sally? How does this relate to the quote?

Objectives (pp. 580–581)
Reading Paraphrase and summarize • Make connections from text to self
Literature Identify literary elements: characterization
Vocabulary Identify word structure: roots
Grammar Use punctuation correctly: commas with introductory words

580 UNIT 5 How Should You Deal with Bullies?

Talk About Your Reading

Possible response:

- If people hurt others because others have hurt them, everyone will be hurt in the end. The story relates to the quote because Sally chooses to help Tina, even though Tina has hurt her in the past.

- Tina bullied Sally in elementary school; Sally was afraid of Tina and did what she said. Sally continued to be afraid of Tina. I would have tried to ignore Tina.

- Because their parents are getting married, Sally is forced to get to know Tina. I probably would have acted just as Sally did. This is the advice that Gandhi offers.

Skills Review

Key Reading Skill: Paraphrasing and Summarizing

7. Paraphrase this sentence: "Our parents were really blowing a bundle on this stepsister-bonding business."

8. Summarize Tina's reactions to the activities on the day in New York City.

Key Literary Element: Characterization

9. Sally's mom and Tina's dad are a big part of the story. What kind of people do they seem to be? How do you learn about them in the story?

10. Do Tina and Sally seem like people you know? Explain whether you found the two characters realistic, and why or why not.

Reviewing Skills: Visualizing

11. Which of the two characters can you picture more clearly in your head, Tina or Sally? Describe that character, using details from the story.

Vocabulary Check

Match the vocabulary words with the clues below.

> **parody   potential
> contemplate   aggression   sordid**

12. ____ mean and bad

13. ____ angry behavior

14. ____ something that copies and makes fun of something else

15. ____ to keep in mind

16. ____ capable of being

17. Academic Vocabulary How can writing a *summary* help you find the main idea when you read?

18. English Language Coach The root *tract* means "to pull or drag." In your Learner's Notebook, write at least two words that come from this root. Use a dictionary if needed.

Grammar Link: Commas with Introductory Words and Phrases

A comma can act the same way that a pause does when you are speaking, especially when you are using introductory words. An introductory word or phrase is at the beginning of a sentence and *introduces* an idea. Use a comma to show a pause after an introductory word or phrase.

- Use a comma after words such as *yes, no,* and *well* at the beginning of a sentence.

  <u>Yes,</u> I really enjoyed this short story.

  <u>No,</u> I hadn't read it before.

- Use a comma after one or more prepositional phrases at the beginning of a sentence.

  <u>At our first chess tournament this year,</u> I won first place.

  <u>By the end of the first paragraph,</u> I knew I liked the book.

- If the prepositional phrase is very short, you don't have to add a comma.

  <u>For many years</u> the Lakota hunted buffalo.

  (A comma could be used, but it is not needed.)

Grammar Practice

Insert commas where they are needed.

19. By the way this story comes from the book *I Love You, I Hate You, Get Lost.*

20. Well no one ever recommended those books to me.

21. No I didn't read that book.

22. On the second shelf in the last row you will find more books by that author.

Web Activities For eFlashcards, Selection Quick Checks, and other Web activities, go to www.glencoe.com.

Don't Let the Bedbugs Bite **581**

Skills Review

Key Reading Skill: Paraphrasing and Summarizing

7. Our parents were spending a lot of money trying to get us to bond.

8. Responses will vary.

Key Literary Element: Characterization

9. Responses will vary.

10. Responses will vary.

Reviewing Skills: Visualizing

11. Responses will vary.

Vocabulary Check

12. sordid

13. aggression

14. parody

15. contemplate

16. potential

17. Academic Vocabulary
Possible response: A summary focuses on the main points of a piece of writing.

18. English Language Coach
Possible responses: *extract, retract, tractor, traction, attractive*

Grammar Link: Commas with Introductory Words

Grammar Practice

19. By the way, this story comes from the book *I Love You, I Hate You, Get Lost.*

20. Well, no one ever recommended those books to me.

21. No, I didn't read that book.

22. On the second shelf in the last row, you will find more books by that author.

Close

Ask students to summarize what they learned about the Big Question from "Don't Let the Bedbugs Bite."

Teach

More About the Author

Jack Prelutsky was born in 1940 in Brooklyn, New York. Although he never liked poetry in school, he later decided to write poems about "things that kids really cared about." He gets ideas for poems everywhere. "Everything I see or hear can become a poem," he says.

R Reading Skill

Review Connecting Say:
Think about common stereotypes of bullies. Are bullies always big and strong? Explain. *(Possible response: Bullies can be male or female, big or small.)* **AS**

Interactive Literary Elements Handbook Have students access the Web site to improve their understanding of characterization.

Before You Read : The New Kid on the Block

Meet the Author
Jack Prelutsky has tried many occupations—singer, actor, photographer, carpenter, cab driver, artist. He wrote his first poems to go with some paintings he had done. Since then he has published several books of poetry for young people. "Poetry is as delightful and surprising as being tickled or catching a snowflake on a mitten," he claims.

Author Search For more about Jack Prelutsky, go to www.glencoe.com.

Objectives (pp. 582–583)
Reading Paraphrase and summarize
• Make connections from text to self
Literature Identify literary elements: characterization

Skills Preview

Key Reading Skill: Paraphrasing and Summarizing
When you read "The New Kid on the Block," think about the whole poem to help you paraphrase and summarize.

Key Literary Element: Characterization
Characterization is the way a writer brings a character to life. A writer may describe a character's actions or share what others think about the character to make the character seem real. Sometimes the writer will reveal a character's feelings or give you a glimpse of how he or she interacts with other characters.
• Look at the descriptions of the "new kid's" actions.
• How does the speaker describe the way the "new kid" looks?
• Does the speaker reveal how other kids feel about the "new kid"?
• How does the speaker feel about the "new kid"?

Get Ready to Read

Connect to the Reading
When you hear the word *bully*, what kind of person pops into your head?

Set Purposes for Reading
BIG Question Read "The New Kid on the Block" to find out how the speaker deals with a "new kid" who turns out to be a bully.

Set Your Own Purpose What else would like to learn from the poem to help you answer the Big Question? Write your own purpose on the "New Kid on the Block" page of Foldable 5.

Interactive Literary Elements Handbook
To review or learn more about the literary elements, go to www.glencoe.com.

Keep Moving
Use these skills as you read the following selection.

582 UNIT 5 How Should You Deal with Bullies?

Additional Support

Author Search To expand students' appreciation of Jack Prelutsky, have them access the Web site for additional information and resources.

Differentiated Instruction

Comparing Genres: Poems and Short Stories Remind students that most of the selections in this unit are short stories and that the selection they are about to read is a poem. Before they read the poem, ask students how a poem about bullying might differ from a short story about the same topic. For example, ask students whether they think a poem is likely to have characters, dialogue, a conflict, and a theme. You may also want to ask students whether they are more likely to remember details from a poem or from a short story. **OL**

The New Kid on the Block

by Jack Prelutsky

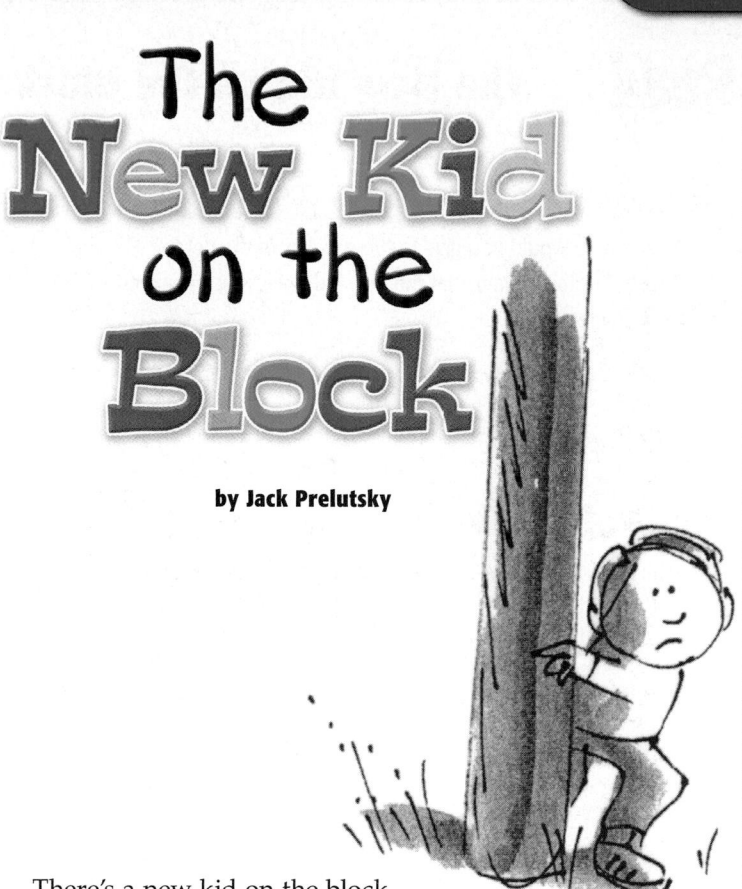

Practice the Skills

There's a new kid on the block,
and boy, that kid is tough,
that new kid punches hard,
that new kid plays real rough,
5 that new kid's big and strong,
with muscles everywhere,
that new kid tweaked my arm, **R**
that new kid pulled my hair. **1 2**

That new kid likes to fight,
10 and picks on all the guys,
that new kid scares me some,
(that new kid's twice my size),
that new kid stomped my toes,
that new kid swiped my ball,
15 that new kid's really bad,
I don't care for her at all. **3** ○

1 Key Reading Skill

Paraphrasing and Summarizing
How would you summarize the
first stanza of this poem? What is
its main idea?

2 Key Literary Element

Characterization The new kid
pulls the speaker's hair, plays
rough, and punches hard. What
do these actions tell you about
the new kid? What other descriptions help you imagine what the
new kid is like? **L**

3 BIG Question

How do you think the speaker
of the poem feels about bullies?
Write your answers in the "New
Kid on the Block" page of
Foldable 5. These notes will help
you with the Unit Challenge.

The New Kid on the Block **583**

Teach

R Reading Skill

**Paraphrasing and
Summarizing Ask:** How
would you paraphrase the
words "tweaked my arm"?
(pinched my arm) **BL**

L Literary Element

Characterization Ask: Does
the new kid fit the stereotype
of a bully? Explain. *(No. "Big"
and "muscular" are stereotypical characteristics of a bully, but
being a girl is not.)* **OL**

Literature Focus Lesson

Situational Irony In literature, situational irony exists when what actually
happens in a situation is the opposite
of what we expect. Ask students if they
think situational irony occurs in "The
New Kid on the Block." Most students
probably expected the bully to be a boy;
therefore, the fact that the bully is a girl
is situational irony. Have students find
descriptions in the poem that led them
to think that the bully was a boy. **OL AL**

Objectives
• Paraphrase and summarize
• Interpret and analyze character
• Recognize distinctive features of
  poetry

583

Assess

Resources for page 584

📁 Selection QuickCheck, p. 48

📁 Selection and Unit Assessment, p. 56

💿 ExamView Assessment Suite

💿 Interactive Tutor: Self-Assesesment

Students can respond to the *After You Read* items in their Learner's Notebooks or on a separate sheet of paper.

Answering the

BIG Question

1. Responses will vary. Students may suggest that the speaker ignore the bully, get help from an adult, or tell the bully to stop bothering him or her.

2. The bully tweaks the speaker's arm, pulls his or her hair, stomps on his or her toes, and swipes his or her ball.

3. The new kid bullies other children, especially guys.

Critical Thinking

4. Possible response: Calling the poem "The New Girl on the Block" would give away the surprise ending.

5. Possible response: No, I thought that the bully in the poem was male because the stereotypical bully is male.

6. Possible response: No, I wouldn't want to be friends with someone who picks on people, hurts them, and takes their things.

After You Read | The New Kid on the Block

Answering the ⭢BIG Question

1. What advice would you give to the speaker of the poem?

2. **Recall** List three ways that the new kid bullies the speaker.
   Tip Right There

3. **Recall** Does the new kid only bully the speaker, or other children as well?
   Tip Right There

Critical Thinking

4. **Interpret** Why do you think the writer chose to call the poem "The New Kid on the Block" instead of "The New Girl on the Block"? Explain.
   Tip Author and Me

5. **Evaluate** Were you surprised by the ending of the poem? Why or why not?
   Tip Author and Me

6. **Analyze** Would *you* want to be friends with the new kid? Explain.
   Tip Author and Me

Write About Your Reading

Use the RAFT system to write about "The New Kid on the Block." A RAFT assignment provides four details:

R is for your role as a writer—who or what you must pretend to be as you write.

A stands for your audience—the person or group who will read what you write.

F means format—the form for your writing, such as a letter or a speech.

T means topic—what your writing should be about.

Role: Write as the new kid.

Audience: Write to the speaker of the poem.

Format: A letter

Topic: Explain to the speaker why you are bullying him or her.

Objectives (pp. 584–585)
Reading Paraphrase and summarize
Literature Identify elements of poetry: characterization
Writing Use the RAFT system: respond to literature
Grammar Use punctuation correctly: commas with sentence interrupters

584 UNIT 5 How Should You Deal with Bullies?

Write About Your Reading

Possible response:

Dear John,

I've been so hurt since my parents said we were moving. I don't know why we had to move. I had lots of friends where we used to live, and we had family nearby, too. I feel lonely here. It doesn't help when other kids call me the new kid. I don't like the feeling that I don't fit in, so I just make other kids feel bad. That's not an excuse for being a bully, but I guess it helps explain why I act the way I do. Anyway, I'm sorry. Will you forgive me?

Skills Review

Key Reading Skill: Paraphrasing and Summarizing

7. Write a summary of the poem. Remember to use your own words and to only include the main idea and the important details.

Key Literary Element: Characterization

8. Use what you learned about characterization to describe what you think about the speaker of the poem.

9. Complete a web diagram like this one to tell everything the speaker reveals about the new kid on the block.

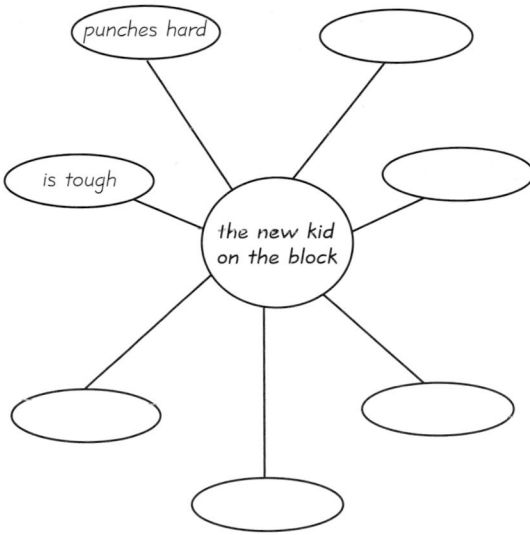

Vocabulary Check

10. **Academic Vocabulary** Suppose a friend asked you to give a *summary* of a movie you just watched. What would you tell him or her?

Grammar Link: Commas with Sentence Interrupters

Sometimes a group of words interrupts the flow of thought in a sentence. Use commas to separate these words from the rest of the sentence. Look at the examples below.

My dad, by the way, was born in Brooklyn, New York.

Nikki's poems, in my opinion, are terrific.

Ed, my neighbor, was teased by a bully.

Mr. Harris, our fifth grade teacher, helped him deal with the bully.

Grammar Practice

Insert commas where they are needed.

11. The story for example has an unexpected ending.

12. My teacher unlike my parents takes the train to work.

13. Snowy weather as you can imagine is more likely in New York than in Florida.

14. These poems as I was saying are fun to read aloud.

Writing Application

Look back at your letter. Add three sentences that use commas and sentence interrupters correctly.

Web Activities For eFlashcards, Selection Quick Checks, and other Web activities, go to www.glencoe.com.

Skills Review

Key Reading Skill: Paraphrasing and Summarizing

7. Possible response: The new kid on the block is a bully, and the speaker of the poem doesn't like her.

Key Literary Element: Characterization

8. Responses will vary. Possible response: The speaker of the poem doesn't stand up to the bully.

9. Responses will vary.

Vocabulary Check

10. **Academic Vocabulary** Students should respond with the main ideas of a movie, as well as with answers to the questions *who, what, when, where, why,* and *how.*

Close

Ask students to explain what they learned about the Big Question from the poem.

Web Activities Have students access the Web site for Interactive activities that will help them assess their understanding of the selection.

Grammar Link: Commas with Sentence Interrupters

Grammar Practice

11. The story, for example, has an unexpected ending.

12. My teacher, unlike my parents, takes the train to work.

13. Snowy weather, as you can imagine, is more likely in New York than in Florida.

14. These poems, as I was saying, are fun to read aloud.

Comparing Problem-Solution Texts

**Objectives covered in
this workshop:**
• Find similarities and differences across texts
• Understand and evaluate text by analyzing problem-solution text structure

Teaching Students to Compare Problem-Solution Texts

Why Is It Important

• Students often get more deeply involved in a selection when they identify a problem-solution structure, and the more deeply involved they get in the text, the higher the possibility that they will understand and be able to compare the selections they read.

• Different authors will not incorporate problem-solution text structure in exactly the same way or even use just one structure throughout their texts. The more experience students have in comparing problem-solution and other text structures in multiple selections, the more easily they will be able to shift from one structure to another and thus better understand what they read.

How to Help Students Get It

• Model identifying problem-solution in texts by doing a Think-Aloud with your students. As you read a selection, start by making comments such as: "I don't see a problem yet." "This is a problem, but I need to read on to see if this is the main problem in the story." "What this part of the article does is explain why this problem affects the community." "Why is this a problem?" "What caused it to happen?" "Is there a solution to the problem?" As you progress, shift the responsibility for identifying the problems and solutions to the students.

• Have students work in pairs to look for signal words that identify a problem-solution structure in a text. Some words they might list are *because, cause, effect, since, therefore, consequently, as a result, this led to, so, so that, nevertheless, accordingly, if . . . then,* and *thus.*

• Construct a graphic aid for students to use while reading and comparing selections. For instance, have them use a simple chart with three columns labeled *Problem, Reasons or Causes for Problem,* and *Solutions to Problem* for each story.

Reading to Answer the Big Question

Bullies in the Park: Elephants vs. Rhinos from *TIME for Kids*
There are bullies in the animal world. Zoologists believe that young male elephants that grow up without caring adult attention often become uncharacteristically violent. The article concludes that preserving families may be the key to preventing bullying even in the elephant community.

The Bully Battle from *TIME for Kids*
In this article, students will find first-hand anecdotes, factual information, and expert advice regarding the causes of and cures for bullying.

Workshop Resources

PACING (DAYS)		LESSON	STUDENT MATERIALS	TEACHER RESOURCES
STANDARD	BLOCK			
1	1	Key Skill Lesson: Reading for Author's Craft	🐜 English Language Coach Review, p. 41	📖 Bellringer Options Transparencies – Daily Language Practice 49 💿 Presentation Plus!
1	1	"Bullies in the Park"	💻 Glencoe Online 🐜 Unit Vocabulary Review, p. 39 🐜 Academic Vocabulary Review, p. 42 📁 English Language Coach 🐜 Reading Across Texts Graphic Organizer, p. 34 💿 StudentWorks Plus™ 💻 Online Student Edition 💿 Literature Classics	💻 Puzzlemaker 💿 Skill Level Up!™ A Language Arts Game 💻 BookLink 3 📕 Assessment by Learning Objective (Diagnostic and Formative) 💿 Interactive Tutor: Self-Assessment 💿 TeacherWorks Plus™ 💿 ExamView Assessment Suite
1		"The Bully Battle"	💻 Glencoe Online 🐜 Selection Vocabulary Development 🐜 Academic Vocabulary Development 📁 English Language Coach 🐜 Reading Across Texts Graphic Organizer, p. 34 💿 StudentWorks Plus™ 💻 Online Student Edition 💿 Literature Classics	💻 Puzzlemaker 💿 Skill Level Up!™ A Language Arts Game 💻 BookLink 3 📕 Assessment by Learning Objective (Diagnostic and Formative) 💿 Interactive Tutor: Self-Assessment 💿 TeacherWorks Plus™ 💿 ExamView Assessment Suite

Keys for Unit Resource

📁 Blackline Master   🔒 DVD

📕 Workbook   📖 Transparency

📖 Supplemental Text   💻 Web-based

💿 CD-ROM   🐜 Fast File

Level Appropriate Code

AS = Activities for all students

AL = Activities for students working above grade level

OL = Activities for students working at grade level

BL = Activities for students working below grade level

EL = Activities for English language learners

Focus

BELLRINGER Options

✊ **Daily Language Practice Transparency 49**
Focus Activity Copy the chart below onto the board. **Say:** Suppose that the school board is adding thirty minutes to the school day. The problem is that some people want that time added to the start of the day, but others want it added to the end. Use a chart like this to brainstorm the pros and cons of each possibility, and decide which option you support. **OL**

	Pros	Cons
Start of Day		
End of Day		

Teach

L **Literary Element**

Problem and Solution Ask:
What are some strategies an author might use to strengthen his or her argument? *(Possible responses: An author might include facts, examples, and opinions from experts to show the effectiveness of a solution.)* **OL**

BULLIES in the PARK & The Bully Battle

by Jon Swartz   *by Elizabeth Siris*

Skills Focus

You will use these skills as you read and compare the following selections:
• "Bullies in the Park," p. 589
• "The Bully Battle," p. 593

Reading

• Make connections across texts
• Compare and contrast information in different texts
• Analyze problem/solution text structure

Objectives (pp. 586–587)
Reading Analyze text • Identify problems and solutions • Compare and contrast: informational articles

586 UNIT 5

Have you ever listened to two or three people arguing about a problem? In most cases, each person has a different idea of what is causing the problem in the first place. And they all have different solutions.

To make sense of the problem, and to find a solution that works for you, you have to act like a detective. You need to sort out the facts from the opinions, and think about how each person's personal beliefs might slant what they are telling you. You also have to consider how strong their arguments are and whether their arguments support what they are saying. Then you form your own idea of what is causing the problem and how it can be solved. **L**

How to Read Across Texts

Comparing two informational articles about a topic is a little like listening to two people argue. You have to think like a detective to figure out what you believe and who you agree with. For both authors, you need to think about
• what problem they discuss
• what they think is causing the problem
• what solution they suggest
• what arguments they use to support their solutions
• how much you believe them

Additional Support

586

Literature Focus Lesson

Anecdote Authors of nonfiction texts often state the problem early in the text. Then they give solutions and offer supporting evidence for these solutions. Before introducing the problem, authors may include an anecdote—a short, interesting story—to capture readers' attention. This story usually turns out to be an example of the problem the text discusses. Point out to students that each selection in the workshop begins with an anecdote. After students have read the introductions, ask whether the anecdotes caught their attention. Encourage students to debate the effectiveness of these anecdotes in introducing the problem. **OL**

Get Ready to Compare

When you read two articles about similar problems, compare what the authors say, how they say it, and what solutions they offer. Sometimes two authors will agree completely. Often, though, writers will approach a problem from different angles. For example, one of these articles is about kids. The other is about elephants. What do they have in common? Both articles are also about bullies.

To help you compare the articles, ask questions like these as you read:

- What problem or issue is the author writing about?
- Does the author offer a solution? If so, what is it?
- What facts does the author give to support the cause of the problem or the best solution?
- What personal opinions or testimonials (experts' opinions) does the author use to support his or her argument?
- What is the author's purpose? What is he or she trying to convince you to do or believe?

C

Use Your Comparison

Before you begin to read these selections, copy this chart into your Learner's Notebook. Be sure to leave enough room to write comments in the empty boxes. Then, while you're reading, fill the chart in with comments and examples from your reading. Try to fill in as many boxes as you can for each selection.

	"Bullies in the Park"	"The Bully Battle"
Problem		
Solution		
Cause of Problem		
Facts		
Opinions		
Author's Purpose		

After you've finished, your chart will help you to compare the two articles and answer the Big Question.

Teach

C Critical Thinking

Analysis Say: One way to analyze a solution is to consider whether it solves all parts of a problem. Look at the chart you created. How did weighing the pros and cons of lengthening the school day help you determine a solution to the problem? *(Responses will vary. Students might say that charting the pros and cons helped them gather enough appropriate information to analyze the problem and choose the best solution.)* **OL**

Assess/Close

Say: Write about a problem that you recently had to solve. Try to persuade readers that your solution was effective. *(Reponses will vary.)* **AS**

Resources for page 587

Use the Reading Across Texts Graphic Organizer BLM in the Unit 5 Resource Booklet, p. 34.

Reading in the Real World

Career Emergency medical service providers, such as paramedics, emergency medical technicians (EMTs), and emergency room doctors, must constantly identify problems and come up with solutions. When treating a patient in need of urgent care, a doctor or other medical professional must quickly assess and evaluate the nature of the patient's illness or injury and determine an effective course of treatment. Encourage students to use library and school-approved Internet resources to learn more about the duties of emergency medical service professionals. **AS**

Objectives

- Identify problem and solution
- Analyze text
- Compare and contrast problem and solution across texts

587

Teach

More About the Topic

Elephants are often hunted for the ivory in their tusks. The hunting of elephants caused their population to drop from about 1.3 million in 1970 to half that number by 1989. Although a few African countries permit strictly regulated trade in elephant products, illegal killing of elephants continues. In some countries, it's on the rise.

V Vocabulary

Parts of Speech Say: For each vocabulary word in this selection, find a spelling that makes the word a different part of speech. Use this new form of the word in a sentence. *(Possible responses: endanger, v.: Don't endanger yourself by failing to buckle your seat belt. immunize, v.: This new vaccine will immunize you against the disease. stressful, adj.: I had a stressful day.)* **BL** **EL**

Readability Scores
Dale-Chall: 7.3
DRP: 62
Lexile: 930

Before You Read : Bullies in the Park

Animals of Africa

The animals of Africa face many problems. One of these problems is the loss of the land they live on. Only a small part of Africa is protected for game reserves and national parks. Because some African countries have large elephant populations, rangers sometimes have to reduce the herd sizes to keep the remaining elephants healthy.

Vocabulary Preview

endangered (en DAYN jurd) *adj.* in risk or danger of dying out completely **(p. 589)** *A lot of endangered animals have been hunted for many years.*

immune (ih MYOON) *adj.* not influenced or affected by **(p. 591)** *Even animals aren't immune to bullies.*

stress (stres) *n.* a harmful feeling of fear, worry, or strain **(p. 591)** *The young elephants felt the stress of living without parents.*

Get Ready to Read

Connect to the Reading

Have you ever solved one problem only to create another bigger problem? What did you do to solve the second problem? Were you able to figure out a way to solve both problems?

Build Background

This African elephant is ready for a battle with a rhino.

- African elephants are the largest land animals on Earth. Adults can reach a height of thirteen feet at the shoulder and a weight of 13,000 pounds.
- Young elephants are cared for by their mothers and aunts.
- When young male elephants are about fourteen years old, they leave the family to live by themselves or with groups of other males.
- When raising their young, elephant mothers stroke their babies lovingly. They also slap them with their trunks when they misbehave.

Set Purposes for Reading

BIG Question   Read to find out how animals can be bullies, too.

Set Your Own Purpose What else would you like to learn from the article to help you answer the Big Question? Write your own purpose in the "Bullies in the Park" page of Foldable 5.

Objectives (pp. 588–591)
Reading Analyze text • Identify problems and solutions • Compare and contrast: informational articles

Additional Support

Reading in the Real World

Citizenship Explain that wildlife parks and game reserves are areas in which the animals are protected by law. Within these reserves, animals cannot be hunted, and no human activity may take place without government approval. "Bullies in the Park" describes a problem that occurred in parks in South Africa. Challenge students to research the parks named in the article as well as other African parks, such as Kutse Game Reserve in Botswana. Ask students to create a profile of each park, including its location, size, permitted activities (such as camping), and any endangered species that inhabit the park. **OL**

INFORMATIONAL TEXT
MAGAZINE

TIME FOR KIDS

BULLIES in the PARK

Africa's orphan elephants turn against the rhinos.

By JON SWARTZ

The trouble started about three years ago. Nearly every month, rangers in Pilanesberg National Park in northwestern South Africa would find an **endangered** white rhinoceros that had been killed. Then the same thing started happening at Hluhluwe-Umfolozi (Slush-loo-ey Oom-fall-o-zee) Park, in southeastern South Africa. **1**

Rhinos are sometimes hunted for their valuable horns. But no one had touched the horns of these animals. Their wounds hadn't come from guns.

The rangers who solved the crime were surprised to learn what was to blame. Young male elephants, which usually leave rhinos alone, had attacked and killed them.

Vocabulary

endangered (en DAYN jurd) *adj.* in risk or danger of dying out completely

Practice the Skills

1 Reading Across Texts

Identifying Problem and Solution The writer begins this article almost like a mystery story. Why do you think the writer chose to start this way? **R**

Bullies in the Park **589**

Teach

Viewing the Illustration

Ask: Based on this photo, what do you think the article will be about? What details help you make your prediction? *(Possible response: There are elephants and a rhinoceros, so the article will probably be about how they live in the wild.)* **OL** **Say:** The article is called "Bullies in the Park" Judging from what you see in the photo, who do you think the bullies are? Why? *(Possible responses: The rhinoceros is outnumbered, and one elephant is crowding in on it; the elephants are the bullies; The elephants look like they're afraid the rhino will attack; the rhinoceros is the bully.)* **AL**

R Reading Skill

Paraphrasing and Summarizing Ask: What problem did the Pilanesberg park rangers find? What was mysterious about this problem? *(They kept finding dead rhinos that were not killed for their horns and not killed by guns.)* **OL** **Ask:** What did the rangers learn was the cause of the rhino deaths? *(Young male elephants were attacking and killing the rhinos.)* **BL**

Differentiated Instruction

Reenactment Write the following statements on the board under the heading "Known Information":

- White rhinos are sometimes killed for their horns.
- The dead rhinos still had their horns.
- The dead rhinos were not killed by guns.

Organize the class in small groups, and ask each group to imagine that they are the park rangers trying to solve the mystery using all the known pieces of information. Have each group present its reenactment to the class. After the presentations, discuss the steps that the rangers might take to find a solution to the problem. **AS**

Objectives
- Paraphrase and summarize
- Learn and use new vocabulary
- Use text features: photograph

589

Teach

L Literary Element

Author's Purpose Say: Look at the author's use of words and phrases such as "murder," "behaved badly," and "caring." Why do you think the author describes the elephants as if they were human? *(Possible responses: This description helps readers better understand and relate to the elephants' behavior.)* **OL**

R Reading Skill

Drawing Conclusions Ask: Why do animals kill other animals? What about the author's description suggests that the elephant killings were different? *(Possible response: Animals usually kill other animals out of necessity—for food or in self-defense. The author's use of the word* murder *suggests that the elephants did not kill the rhinos for food or in self-defense.)* **AL**

Angry Orphans

L Why would elephants murder rhinos? Experts guess the young elephants behaved badly because they had grown up without the attention of caring adults. **2**

Several years ago, the population of elephants in South Africa's Kruger National Park was growing too large. Rangers tried to control the growth by slaughtering older elephants and then moving the young elephants to other parks and reserves. Since 1978, almost 1,500 orphans—600 of them males, or bulls—have been moved to unfamiliar locations, where they grew up without older elephants around them.

Moving the orphans helped preserve an endangered species. But it changed the elephants' social order.

"The whole thing has much to do with the setup of elephant society," says South African zoologist[1] Marian Garai. Elephants normally live in tight-knit groups. Older males keep young bulls in line. But no such role models

---

1. A *zoologist* is a scientist who studies animals.

Practice the Skills

2 **Reading Across Texts**

Identifying Problem and Solution People don't usually say an animal "murders" another animal. Why do you think the writer uses this word here? Do you think the writer thinks this problem is similar to a human problem? What does this tell you about the writer's purpose? **R**

Even elephants need role models. Older bull elephants show the younger ones how to behave.

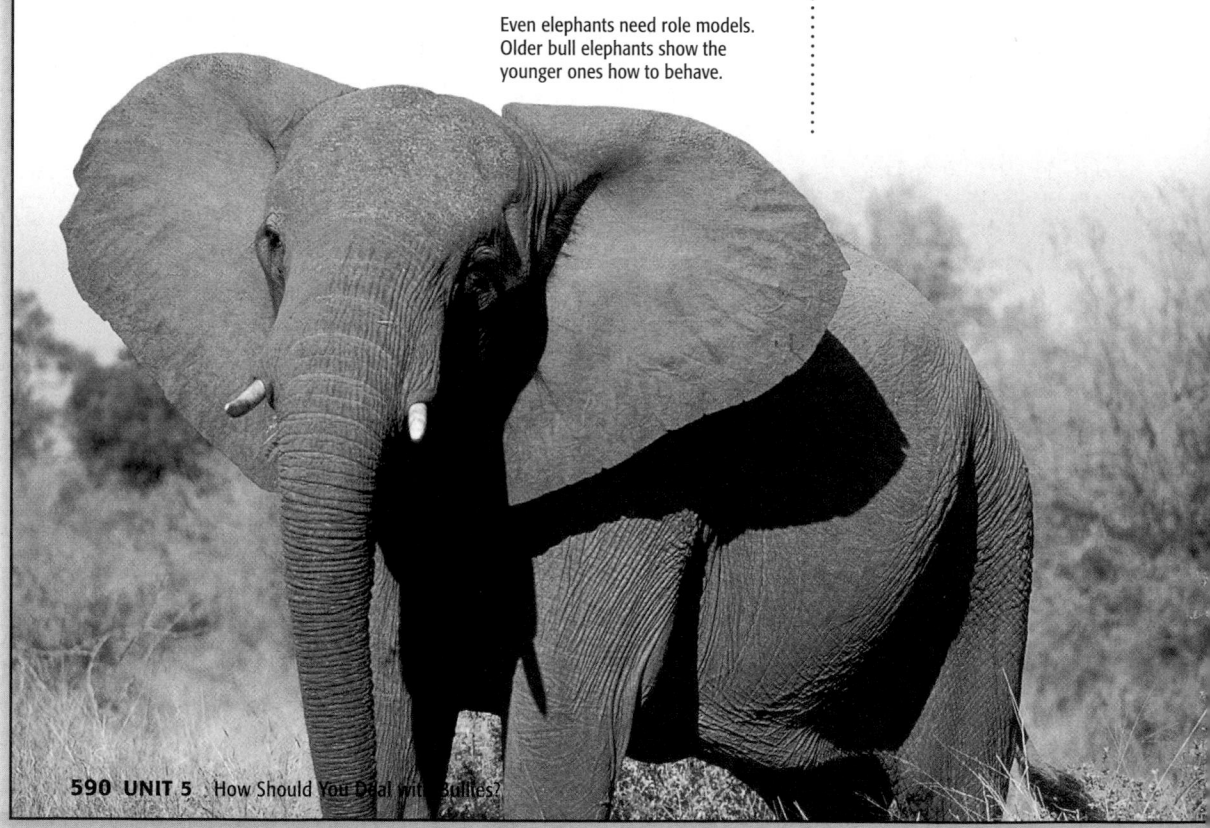

Additional Support

Literature Focus Lesson

Anthropomorphism Explain to students that authors often describe animals and objects in human terms. This descriptive technique, called *anthropomorphism*, can help readers understand and connect to the topic. It also makes writing more interesting. For example, an author might write, "The stars winked as she searched the sky." Saying that the stars did something that only humans can do is a way to capture readers' interest. Ask students to reread page 590 and then identify two instances in which the author uses human terms to describe the elephants. **BL OL**

were provided for the orphans from Kruger. Garai believes this upset the young elephants and led them to lash out at rhinos. **3**

"Elephants are complex and intelligent creatures," explains Garai. "They aren't **immune** to **stress.**"

What can be done? Some rangers believe the elephant bullies need foster parents. When two adult female circus elephants were returned to Pilanesberg in 1979, soon after the first orphans arrived, the nervous youngsters quickly settled down.

Now officials hope a similar plan will work for the rhino-bashing bulls. Two years ago, Kruger Park began to move entire families of elephants to new homes instead of killing the elders and hauling away their young. Early next year, a few 40-year-old male elephants will be moved to Pilanesberg.

Preserving families may be the key to raising well-behaved elephants. Meanwhile, South Africa's white rhinos had better watch out. **4 5** ○

—From *TIME FOR KIDS*

Vocabulary

immune (ih MYOON) *adj.* not influenced or affected by

stress (stres) *n.* a harmful feeling of fear, worry, or strain

Young orphan bull elephants are a danger to rhinos.

Practice the Skills

3 | **Reading Across Texts**

Identifying Problem and Solution The zoologist says the elephants attacked the rhinos because they didn't have good role models. Is her statement a fact or an opinion? Do you believe the zoologist? Why or why not?

4 | **Reading Across Texts**

Identifying Problem and Solution What problem is the article about? Do you think the writer has provided the facts and expert opinions about what is causing the problem? What solution is being tried? Do you think the solution is a good one? Why or why not? Add your answers to your chart.

C

5 | **BIG Question**

How did this article help you understand why some people (or animals) become bullies? Record your answer on the "Bullies in the Park" page of Foldable 5. Your response will help you with the Unit Challenge.

BQ

Bullies in the Park **591**

Teach

C Critical Thinking

Comprehension Ask: What does the author say appears to be the best solution for correcting the young elephants' bad behavior? *(Possible response: Keeping elephants in family groups may stop the bad behavior.)* **BL Ask:** What details does the author give to suggest that elephants are different from other animals? *(Possible response: The author quotes Garai as saying that elephants are "complex," "intelligent," and "not immune to stress." The descriptions of their social order support Garai's statement.)* **OL**

BQ

Ask: Do you think that a bullying animal is similar to a bullying person? Why or why not? *(Responses will vary. Students should support their opinions with information from the text and personal experience.)* **AS**

Assess

CheckPoint

Use the CheckPoint questions provided on Presentation Plus! to check for comprehension of the selection. These questions can be used with interactive response keypads for immediate student feedback.

Differentiated Instruction

Writing Realistic Fiction Some details in the article could spark engaging stories. Encourage students to use library and school-approved Internet resources to research the life cycles, habits, and behaviors of elephants. Encourage students to find true stories about these animals as well. Tell students to use this information to write realistic stories about the lives of elephants. Suggest that students focus on the journey of a single elephant or the challenges faced by an entire herd. Tell students that although they may make up the details of the events and characters (even elephant characters) in their stories, the information about elephants should be as accurate as possible. **AS**

Objectives
• Use comprehension skills
• Draw conclusions from text and experience
• Identify author's purpose

Teach

More About the Author

Elizabeth Siris Winchester has always had a strong interest in current events and world affairs. She has said that her favorite subject in school was social studies. During college, Winchester gained experience in journalism as an intern with news distributor CNN. When asked what she enjoys about her job, Winchester responded, "I'm always learning something new and sharing what I learn with kids and teachers."

V Vocabulary

Word Parts Say: Prefixes and suffixes can change the meanings or parts of speech of words. Adding the suffix *-ness* or *-ity* to a base word changes it into a noun. The vocabulary words *awareness* and *civility* have these suffixes. Find definitions, including parts of speech, for the base words of these nouns. **EL**

Readability Scores
Dale-Chall: 6.3
DRP: 61
Lexile: 1050

Before You Read : The Bully Battle

Meet the Author
When Elizabeth Siris was about eight years old, she started a neighborhood newspaper with her brother and two friends. Although her newspaper didn't last, her desire to be a writer did. She has written and edited articles for a variety of magazines and webzines including *inTime, TIME For Kids, Sports Illustrated for Women,* and *Parenting Magazine.*

Vocabulary Preview

ringleaders (RING leed urz) *n.* individuals who lead groups of people, especially those who cause trouble **(p. 594)** *She is one of the ringleaders of the kids who started a fight after school.*

promote (pruh MOT) *v.* to help something grow or prosper **(p. 595)** *Several students gave speeches to promote the program.*

civility (sih VIL uh tee) *n.* polite behavior **(p. 595)** *People should treat each other with courtesy and civility.* **V**

English Language Coach
You've learned that **prefixes** are syllables attached to the beginning of a root or base word. Prefixes change the meaning of a word. Some prefixes show *judgment.* In other words, they show if you are *for* or *against* something.

The prefix *anti-* means "against" or "not in favor of."
Example: An *anti*crime group would fight against crime.

You'll find these words in "The Bully Battle." Write them in your Learner's Notebook and try to write a definition of each before you read the article.
anti-bullying   antiviolence

Get Ready to Read

Connect to the Reading
Think of a time when you bullied someone else, were bullied yourself, or saw someone being bullied. How did you feel?

Set Purposes for Reading
BIG Question Read to learn how schools are dealing with bullies.

Set Your Own Purpose What else would you like to learn from the article to help you answer the Big Question? Write your own purpose on the "Bully Battle" page of Foldable 5.

Objectives (pp. 592–595)
Reading Analyze text • Identify problems and solutions • Compare and contrast: informational articles

---

Additional Support

Reading in the Real World

Citizenship This selection examines the problem of bullying in the United States. Ask students new to this country whether bullying is a problem in the cultures they came from. Encourage all students to use Internet resources to research problems with bullying in countries around the world. Assign individual students or student pairs a particular country to investigate. Students researching the United Kingdom, for example, might find that schools and organizations have started antibullying campaigns and have created resources for bullied students. Ask students to share their findings with the class. As a class, discuss some of the common solutions to bullying. **EL** **OL**

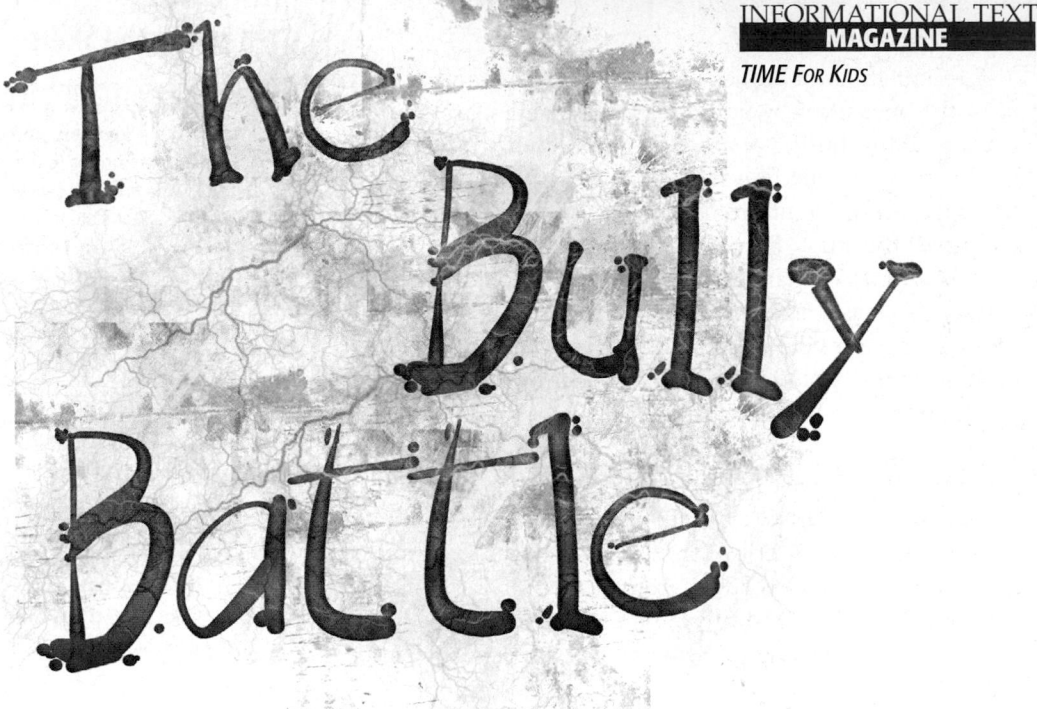

INFORMATIONAL TEXT
MAGAZINE

TIME FOR KIDS

The Bully Battle

Are nasty, mean kids making your life miserable? Take action!

By ELIZABETH SIRIS

R Christian Champ, 10, a fifth grader in Prescott, Arizona, got his first taste of bullying in kindergarten when a second grader pushed him off a swing. Since then, Christian has learned how to deal with bullies—people who tease, hurt, or threaten others. In fourth grade, when a bully cursed at him, tried to hit him, and started swinging a shoe, Christian followed his father's advice. "First I ignored the bully," he explains. "Then I told the teacher." **1**

C People don't like to be pushed or teased for getting good or bad grades or be made fun of for how they look. Sadly, about 1 in 7 schoolchildren is a bully or a victim of one. Five million elementary and middle school students in the U.S. are bullied each year, according to the National Association of School Psychologists. Each day, bullies' teasing leads some 160,000 fearful kids to skip school.

Practice the Skills

1 **Reading Across Texts**

Identifying Problem and Solution In this paragraph, the writer says, "Christian has learned how to deal with bullies." What does this tell you about the writer's purpose for this article? Fill in your chart.

The Bully Battle **593**

Teach

R **Reading Skill**

Understanding Cause and Effect **Ask:** What advice did Christian's father give him? *(Christian's father told him to ignore bullies and to tell a teacher if the bullying continued.)* **BL** **Ask:** What other solutions could Christian have tried when dealing with the bully? What do you think the best approach would have been? Why? *(Responses will vary. Some students may say that Christian could have confronted the bully. Students should recognize that a good approach to ending bullying would not involve violence.)* **OL**

C **Critical Thinking**

Comprehension **Say:** Reread the second paragraph. What broad statement can you make after reading these facts about bullying? *(Possible response: Bullying is a major problem in the United States, affecting millions of students.)* **OL**

Reading Fluency

Reading with a Partner Read aloud the two paragraphs on page 593, asking students to follow along silently as you do so. Then organize students in pairs. Ask each partner to choose one paragraph, and have students take turns reading their paragraphs aloud to each other. When students think that they can read their paragraphs smoothly and fluently, have them switch paragraphs and continue reading aloud. Remind students to observe punctuation, pausing at commas and periods. **EL** **BL**

Objectives
• Identify problem and solution
• Understand cause and effect
• Use comprehension skills
• Learn and use new vocabulary

Teach

C Critical Thinking

**Evaluation Ask: Whom does
the author quote to back up
statements about the study
on bullies?** *(The author quotes
Dorothy Espelage, an assistant
professor of psychology.)* **BL**
**Ask: What makes this person a
reliable source of information?**
*(As one of the study's authors,
she can speak reliably about
the study results. As a college
professor, she has probably had
a great deal of education.)* **OL**

EL Language Coach

**Prefixes Say: The author
notes that during Safe
Communities = Safe Schools
Awareness Week, "about 300
communities held antibullying and antiviolence activities." What might "antibullying
and antiviolence activities"
involve?** *(Responses will vary
but should reflect an awareness
that such activities would promote communication, respect
for others, and strategies for
nonviolent conflict resolution.)*
Have students identify other
frequently heard words having the prefix anti-. *(Possible
response: Students may mention antismoking, anti-inflation,
antiwar, antiterrorism, anti-
American.)* **AS**

The Big, Bad Bully

A recent study of bullies found that most often the popular
kids, the ones liked by both kids and teachers, are doing the
teasing. "Most bullies are the kids that other students look up
to, the ones everybody wants to hang out with," says Dorothy
Espelage, an assistant professor of psychology who co-
authored[1] the study. **2**

Psychologist William Pollack agrees that too often a bully's
behavior is encouraged and not stopped. Some bullies
become popular **ringleaders** with other kids, but not all
bullies are the cool kids, he says. Some are troubled students
who may have been bullied themselves.

Taking the Bully by the Horns

Schools across the U.S. are fighting back against bullying.
During one week in April, 36 states observed Safe Communities =
Safe Schools Awareness Week. From October 15 to 21, about 300
communities held **anti-bullying** and **antiviolence** activities[2]
for kids. The week was coordinated by Safe Schools, Safe
Students, an Arizona-based group founded by Rod Beaumont. **3**

---

1. Something that is *co-authored* is written by two or more people working together.
2. *Anti-bullying and antiviolence activities* give people a chance to speak out against those who
   tease or bully others.

Vocabulary

ringleaders (RING leed urz) *n.* individuals who lead groups of people, especially
those who cause trouble

594 UNIT 5 How Should You Deal with Bullies?

Practice the Skills

2 Reading Across Texts

**Identifying Problem and
Solution** According to the
article, who are most bullies?
Does the writer state this as a
fact or opinion? What evidence
does the writer give to back up
her statement about who the
bullies are? **C**

3 English Language Coach

Prefixes Look at the words
anti-bullying and **antiviolence**.
You wrote these words in your
Learner's Notebook and tried
to define them. Did you get the
definitions right? If not, correct
your definitions. **EL**

Analyzing the Photo Who do you
think the bullies might be in this photo?
Who is the victim? Support your
opinion with details from the photo.

Additional Support

Reading in the Real World

Citizenship This article discusses anti-
bullying programs in schools and communities. Give students the document
outlining your school's policy on bullying,
or explain the policy to them. (Or explain
what such a policy is for and what it
says.) As a class, discuss this policy and
its effectiveness. If students have
constructive suggestions for improving
the policy, invite them to write letters to
the principal outlining their ideas. If no
policy for dealing with bullying exists,
have students draft one as a class. Ask
students to create a document that they
can submit to the principal. **AS**

He says the purpose of the awareness week is to make people realize that bullying and other types of school violence are not something that can just be ignored.

The organization arranges bullying-prevention workshops.[3] Many of them are led by a huge, leather-wearing, tattoo-covered man called the Scary Guy. He challenges kids not to use mean words and not to push or shove others for at least seven days. "I was a bully my whole life," the Scary Guy admits, "but now I'm not." **4**

The workshops teach kids that words can hurt just as much as physical violence. Rebecca Sassoon of New York City, knows this well. When Rebecca was 7 years old, she was bullied by three boys in her class for being too smart. "I got things right on tests, and they didn't, so they teased me," she recalls. "I used to go home after school and cry."

Because bullying can start early, teachers in Massachusetts use bullying-prevention lessons with kids as young as age 5.

Suffern Middle School, about 40 miles north of New York City, is among many schools that have anti-bullying programs all year long. To kick off the program in September, the school held an assembly led by Show of Love, a group that teaches about respect. One week later, teachers, students, and parents discussed how to **promote** politeness and **civility** throughout the year. **5**

Bullies seem to have been around since school was invented! Can these new bully-busting programs really stop them? There may be hope. Spencer, a 10-year-old from Colorado, says bullies can change. "I teased people all the time when I was in second grade," he says, "but by third grade I got my act together. I didn't like making other people feel bad."

Some kids, like Jenna Gray of Prescott, Arizona, have their doubts. "Sometimes, the peer pressure can get to you," sighs Jenna, who has been both a bully and a victim. "It's hard to get away from it." **6** ○

—From *TIME FOR KIDS*

---

3. ***Bullying-prevention workshops*** teach student groups how to stop bullies and how to avoid being a bully.

Vocabulary

promote (pruh MOT) *v.* to help something grow or prosper

civility (sih VIL uh tee) *n.* polite behavior

Practice the Skills

4 🗨 **BIG Question**

The Scary Guy tells kids not to use mean words for at least seven days. Is that a good idea? Why or why not? Write your answer on the "Bully Battle" page of Foldable 5. **BQ1**

5 **Reading Across Texts**

Identifying Problem and Solution What problem is the article about? What is the cause of the problem? What solution is being tried? Do you think the solution is a good one? Why or why not?

6 🗨 **BIG Question**

Do you think programs like the ones described in this article can help to deal with the bully problem? Write your answer on the "Bully Battle" page of Foldable 5. Your response will help you complete the Unit Challenge later. **BQ2**

The Bully Battle **595**

Teach

BQ1 🗨 **BIG Question**

Ask: What do you think students would learn by going through an entire week without using any mean words? *(Responses will vary. Students may suggest that they would learn how to get along better with other students.)* **AS**

BQ2 🗨 **BIG Question**

Say: Imagine that you are working on an antibullying program. Write a slogan that states the most important part of your program's message. *(Responses will vary.)* **AS**

Assess

✓**CheckPoint**

Use the CheckPoint questions provided on Presentation Plus! to check for comprehension of the selection. These questions can be used with interactive response keypads for immediate student feedback.

Differentiated Instruction

Designing a Poster Remind students that an effective antibullying program addresses both bullies and their victims. Suggest that students use what they have learned from "The Bully Battle" to create posters that discourage bullying or offer advice to those who are bullied. Encourage students to invest time in making their posters colorful, interesting, and easy to understand. Display finished posters in the classroom and, if possible, throughout the school. **AS**

Objectives
• Paraphrase and summarize
• Evaluate text
• Identify word structure: prefixes

Assess

Resources for page 596

📁 Selection Quick Check, pp. 49–50

💿 ExamView Assessment Suite

💿 Interactive Tutor: Self-Assesesment

Vocabulary Check

Bullies in the Park

1. immune: a.
2. endangered: b.
3. stress: c.

The Bully Battle

4. ringleaders: e.
5. promote: d.
6. civility: f.

English Language Coach
Possible responses:

7. Responses will vary.
8. Possible responses: An alarm is an effective *antiburglary* device.

   Anticancer drugs have saved many lives.

   Animal rights activists support *anticruelty* laws.

   The *antiglare* glass made it much easier to see.

   The *antilitter* committee fines litterbugs.

   The *antinoise* headphones blocked out all sounds.

   Antislavery supporters were also called abolitionists.

   Antistress strategies can help people deal with tension and anxiety.

596

After You Read

BULLIES in the PARK & The Bully Battle

Vocabulary Check

On a separate piece of paper, write each of the six vocabulary words listed below. Then write the correct definition (a – f) after each vocabulary word.

BULLIES in the PARK

1. endangered
2. immune
3. stress

   a. *not influenced or affected by*
   b. *in risk or danger of dying out completely*
   c. *a harmful feeling of fear, worry, or strain*

The Bully Battle

4. ringleaders   5. promote   6. civility

   d. *to help something grow or prosper*
   e. *individuals who lead groups of people, especially those who cause trouble*
   f. *polite behavior*

Objectives (pp. 596–597)
Reading Analyze text • Identify problems and solutions • Compare and contrast: informational articles
Vocabulary Identify word structure: prefixes
Writing Write to compare and contrast: problems and solutions

English Language Coach

7. Write one sentence for each of the following words. Each sentence should tell something about one of the selections you just read.
   anti-bullying   antiviolence
8. Now add the prefix *anti-* to each of the following words. Write each new word in a sentence.

burglary	cruelty	litter	slavery
cancer	glare	noise	stress

596 UNIT 5 How Should You Deal with Bullies?

Writing: Reading Across Texts

Comparison Chart Sample Answers for "Bullies in the Park"
Problem: Bully elephants are killing white rhinos.
Author's Solution: Keep elephant family groups together and maintain older role models for young elephants.
Facts: Since 1978, almost 1,500 orphan elephants have been moved to unfamiliar locations. There, they grow up without older elephants.
Opinions: Providing elephants with role models and keeping family groups together may stop the bullying.
Author's Purpose: To inform

Reading/Critical Thinking

On a separate sheet of paper, answer the following questions.

BULLIES in the PARK

9. **Infer** How might rangers have prevented the conflict between the elephants and the rhinos?
   Tip Author and Me

10. **Synthesize** Based on the information in this article, describe one reason why human children might become bullies.
    Tip Author and Me

The Bully Battle

11. **Evaluate** Most of the quotations—things that people say—are from kids who were bullied. Should you believe what they are saying? Explain.
    Tip On My Own

12. **Evaluate** Do you think the "bully-busting" programs can really help stop bullying? Explain.
    Tip Author and Me

Writing: Reading Across Texts

13. Follow these steps to compare how the authors discussed the problems and solutions in "Bullies in the Park" and "The Bully Battle."

    Step 1: On the chart you completed, look at the problem you wrote down for each article. Write a sentence that explains how the problems are similar.

    Step 2: Look at what you wrote in the row that listed the cause of the problem. Did the authors have the same cause or causes of the problem?

    Step 3: Is the solution presented in each selection similar or different?

Step 4: On your chart, look at the rows that list the facts and opinions that you found in the two selections. Think about whether one author supported his or her argument better than the other.

Step 5: On your chart, look at the author's purpose for each article. Think about how the authors' purposes are similar and how they're different.

Get It on Paper

To compare how the authors discussed problems and solutions in "Bullies in the Park" and "The Bully Battle," answer these questions on a separate sheet of paper.

14. How is the problem described in "Bullies in the Park" similar to the one described in "The Bully Battle"? Did the authors deal with the cause of the problem in the same away? Give examples.

15. In "Bullies in the Park," does the author use facts to support the solution that the article describes? Does the author use opinions and testimonials to support the solution? Give examples to support your answers.

16. In "The Bully Battle," does the author use facts, opinions, or testimonials to support the solution that the article describes? Give examples.

17. Do you think the author of "Bullies in the Park" is trying to tell us something about why human children might become bullies? Explain.

18. What do you think the author of "The Bully Battle" is trying to convince us to do?

19. Do you think one article presents a better argument than the other? Explain.

BIG Question

20. Both "Bullies in the Park" and "The Bully Battle" discuss possible solutions to the problems they present. Which solution do you think is more likely to work? Explain why you picked that solution.

Reading/Critical Thinking

Bullies in the Park

9. Possible response: by keeping family groups together when moving elephants to other parks

10. Students may say that children who do not have good role models are more likely to become bullies.

The Bully Battle

11. Responses will vary.

12. Responses will vary.

Writing: Reading Across Texts

13. Responses will vary.

Get It on Paper

Possible responses:

14. both texts involve bullying

15. The author uses facts about elephant populations and studies.

16. The author quotes experts, for example, psychologist William Pollack.

17. The author describes the elephants in human terms. This suggests the author thinks humans and elephants may bully for some of the same reasons.

18. to take a more active role against bullying

19. Responses will vary.

BIG Question

20. Responses will vary.

Writing: Reading Across Texts

Comparison Chart Sample Answers for "The Bully Battle"
Problem: Bullies are a significant problem at schools across the United States.
Author's Solution: Start antibullying programs and raise community awareness.
Facts: One in seven schoolchildren is a bully or a bully's victim. Five million students are bullied each year. Each day, about 160,000 students skip school because of bullies.
Opinions: Some students are quoted as believing that antibullying programs will help stop bullies. Others fear that bullying will always be a problem.
Author's Purpose: To convince readers that awareness and action are necessary to stop bullying

The Unit Challenge

Focus

✍ **Daily Language Practice Transparency 50**
Focus Activity Ask: Of the stories we've read in this unit, which is the most realistic? Why? (*Responses will vary.*) **OL**

The discussion will remind students of the selections they've read, which will help them begin the group activity or the solo activity.

Teach

Group Activity: Brochure

- If students have difficulty delegating responsibility, select one student in each group to record ideas.

- Bring in a variety of brochures —particularly those that advertise events or services in your community—for students to use as models.

- Allow at least thirty minutes for students to make their own brochure.

- Encourage each member of the group to proofread the brochure for spelling and grammar mistakes before it is presented to the class.

Assess/Close

Group Activity Ask: What has creating a brochure taught you about how to deal with bullies? (*Suggest that students write their answers in their Learner's Notebooks.*) **AS**

598

UNIT 5 WRAP-UP

Answering How Should You Deal with Bullies?

You've just read different selections, and you thought about how to deal with bullies. Now use what you've learned to do the Unit Challenge.

The Unit Challenge

Choose Activity A or Activity B and follow the directions for that activity.

A. Group Activity: Brochure

You and three to five other students will create a brochure that explains how to deal with bullies.

1. **Discuss the Assignment** As a group, brainstorm ways to handle bullies. Look at the notes that you made on your Foldable. Think about what you learned from the selections. Also share ideas from your own experience. Choose a member of the group to write your ideas in a list.

2. **Make Choices** Brochures are short and to the point. They provide the basic information about a subject that people need. Choose two or three ideas from your list to present in your brochure.

3. **Plan Your Brochure** Think about brochures that you have seen. Maybe they're health-related or community-related. Or maybe they're advertising brochures. A brochure should have a strong, clear message and attract readers' attention. To do these things, a brochure often contains bright colors, bulleted lists, and pictures.
   - How will you organize your brochure?
   - What facts or tips will you include?
   - What pictures or graphics will you use?

4. **Create the Brochure** Work with other members of your group to plan your brochure. Take a sheet of paper and fold it into three vertical panels. Decide where you will put the information you want to include and where you will place any pictures or graphics. After you've made these decisions, put them into action and make your brochure. Divide your work among group members. Be sure to use bright colors and different text sizes to grab readers' attention.

5. **Present the Brochure** Present your brochure to the class. Then invite members of the audience to share what they learned from your brochure.

B. Solo Activity: Short Story

Write a short story—this time, from the point of view of a bully. Use "I" to refer to the bully.

1. **Choose Your Topic** In your Learner's Notebook, list any experiences you've had with bullies. Also skim your Foldable notes for any situations involving bullies that sound as though they really could happen. Add those situations to your list. Then choose the experience or situation that you think would make the best topic for your short story.

2. **Map Out the Story** Your story will have a beginning, a middle, and an ending. In your Learner's Notebook, copy the story map below. Then fill it in with details from the experience or situation you chose.

3. **Draft Your Short Story** Using your story map, make a rough draft of your short story.
   - Introduce the characters and setting.
   - Show the conflict between a character and the bully.
   - Tell how the character handles the bully.
   - Show how the bully reacts.

4. **Review Your Draft** Make sure the story you're telling is clear.
   - Are the setting and characters clearly described?
   - Do the dialogue and description explain the conflict with the bully?
   - Do you explain how the character resolves the conflict?

5. **Write Your Final Copy** Write your finished draft in your Learner's Notebook. Give your story a catchy title.

6. **Share Your Short Story** Read your short story to the class. Ask your classmates what they learned from your story about how to deal with bullies.

| Setting People | Beginning | Middle | End |

Teach

Solo Activity: Short Story

- Have each student submit a topic for your approval before mapping out a story. As you listen to or read each student's topic, make sure that no student is simply retelling a story from one of the selections.

- Make sure students do not spend too much time illustrating their story maps. The idea is to have a basic sequence of events, not a detailed illustration.

- Advise students to brainstorm story titles that are both creative and engaging.

- Encourage students to proofread their own stories before submitting them.

- Encourage students to read their stories aloud to the class.

Assess/Close

Solo Activity

Ask: Do you think that your short story is realistic? Could the events in your story ever take place in our school or anywhere else in your community? Explain. *(You may decide to have students answer the question as a class or individually in their Learner's Notebooks.)*

Objectives
- Write a brochure
- Write a short story
- Follow multi-step directions
- Make a presentation

Focus

Vocabulary Preview
Build Background
List the following words on the board:

- snag-toothed
- perish
- garment
- mischief

Review their definitions before students begin reading.

- "El Enano" was published in 1924 in *Tales from Silver Lands*, a collection of 19 folktales.
- The folktales included draw on elements of South American culture and provide explanations of phenomena such as how rabbits and rats got their tails.
- *Enano* is a Spanish word that means "dwarf."

Teach

L Literary Element

Plot Say: The exposition is background information about characters and setting. What do you learn about the character, El Enano, and the setting from the exposition? *(Possible response: El Enano lives in the forest. He is a short creature and he is cruel to people.)* **OL**

Readability Scores
Dale-Chall: 5.0
DRP: 57
Lexile: 1190

Charles J. Finger

Meet the Author
Charles J. Finger was born in Willesden, England, on December 25, 1867. His parents eventually moved to the United States, but Finger joined the crew of a ship that sailed to Chile. He worked at various odd jobs, including tour guide and sheepherder until 1895. He came to the United States that year and began writing newspaper articles. He settled in Texas and New Mexico and began writing stories for young adults. He wrote 36 books in the last 20 years of his life. "El Enano" is part of a book titled *Tales from Silver Lands*, which received a Newbery Medal in 1925.

Literature Online

Author Search For more about Charles J. Finger, go to www.glencoe.com.

EL ENANO

by Charles J. Finger

Everyone disliked El Enano who lived in the forest, because he always lay hidden in dark places, and when woodmen passed he jumped out on them and beat them and took their dinners from them. He was a squat[1] creature, yellow of skin and snag-toothed and his legs were crooked, his arms were crooked, and his face was crooked. There were times when he went about on all fours and then he looked like a great spider, for he had scraggy[2] whiskers that hung to the ground and looked like legs. At other times he had the mood to make himself very small like a little child, and then he was most horrible to see, for his skin was wrinkled and his whiskers hung about him like a ragged garment.

Yet all of that the people might have forgiven and he might have been put up with, were it not for some worse tricks. What was most disliked was his trick of walking softly about a house in the night-time while the people were inside, suspecting nothing, perhaps singing and talking. Seeing them thus, El Enano would hide in the shadows until someone went for water to the spring, then out he would leap, clinging fast to the hair of the boy or man and beating, hitting, scratching the while. Being released, the tortured one would of course run to reach the house, but El Enano would hop on one leg behind, terribly fast, and catch his victim again just as a hand was almost laid on the door latch. Nor could an alarm be raised, because El Enano cast a spell of silence, so that, try as one would, neither word nor shout would come.

---

1. A *squat* creature is short and solid.
2. *Scraggy* whiskers are ragged and uneven.

Additional Support

Literature Online

Author Search To expand students' appreciation of Charles J. Finger, have them access the Web site for additional information and resources.

Literature Focus Lesson

Summary In the beginning of this folktale, a troublesome dwarf named El Enano hides in the woods. A kindhearted old woman takes him back to the village, only to discover that he has an insatiable appetite. El Enano wreaks havoc and devours the village's food supply. The old woman seeks the advice of a fox. Under the fox's direction, the people of the village roast potatoes under hot coals. When El Enano demands to have potatoes, the fox allows him to overhear that there are more on the hearth. Pushing the villagers aside, El Enano reaches into the hearth and swallows a pile of hot coals. As he tries to cool himself by drinking water, the steam causes his stomach to expand, killing him. **OL**

Then there was his other evil trick of hiding close to the ground and reaching out a long and elastic arm to catch boy or girl by the ankle. But that was not worse than his habit of making a noise like hail or rain, hearing which the people in the house would get up to close a window, and there, looking at them from the dark but quite close to their faces, would be the grinning Enano holding in his hands his whiskers that looked like a frightening curtain, his eyes red and shining like rubies. That was very unpleasant indeed, especially when a person was alone in the house. Nor was it much better when he left the window, for he would hop and skip about the house yard for hours, screaming and howling and throwing sticks and stones. So, wherever he was there was chill horror.

One day, a good old woman who lived alone went with her basket to gather berries. El Enano saw her and at once made himself into a little creature no larger than a baby and stretched himself on a bed of bright moss between two trees leafless and ugly. He pretended to be asleep, though he whimpered[3] a little as a child does when it has a bad dream.

The good old woman was short-sighted but her ears were quick, and hearing the soft whimper she found the creature and took it in her arms. To do that bent her sadly, for Enano when small was the same weight as when his full size.

"Oh, poor thing," she said. "Someone has lost a baby. Or perhaps some wild creature has carried the tender thing from its home. So, lest it perish I will take care of it, though to be sure, a heavier baby I never held."

Analyzing the Art Does this look like an accurate picture of El Enano? Explain, using details from the story.

The dame[4] had no children of her own and, though poor, was both willing and glad to share what she had with any needy creature. Gently she took it home and having put dry sticks on the fire she made a bed of light twigs which she covered with a mat of feathers. Then she bustled about, getting bread and milk for supper for the little one, feeling happy at heart because she had rescued the unhappy creature from the dismal[5] forest.

At first she was glad to see the appetite of the homeless thing, for it soon finished the bread and milk and cried for more.

"Bless me! It must be half starved," she said. "It may have my supper." So she took the food she had set out for herself and El Enano swallowed it as quickly as he had swallowed the first bowl. Yet still he cried for more. Off then to the neighbors she went, borrowing milk from this one, bread from that, rice from another, until half the children of the village had to go on short commons that night. The creature

---

3. A **whimper** (WIM pur) is a weak, quiet cry.

4. **Dame** is an old word for "woman."
5. **Dismal** (DIZ mul) means "gloomy."

Teach

R₁ Reading Skill

Paraphrasing and Summarizing Say: Summarize the ways in which El Enano disturbs the people in the village. *(He hides and jumps out at them; he hits and scratches them; he catches boys and girls by the ankle; he fools people into thinking that it is raining or hailing; and he screams and throws sticks and stones.)* BL

L Literary Element

Characterization Ask: What do you learn about the old woman? What kind of person is she? *(The old woman has no children. Although she is poor, she is happy to share her food. She is a very caring person.)* OL

R₂ Reading Skill

Understanding Cause and Effect Ask: What does El Enano's crying cause the old woman to do? *(She gives El Enano her supper and then goes off to ask her neighbors for more food.)* OL

Differentiated Instruction

Visual Learning Visual learners may benefit from creating a graphic representation of the events on the page. Have students summarize the events in a comic strip with three frames. You may choose to guide students about which "snapshots" would best represent the action so far. For example, students may depict El Enano hiding in the woods in the first frame, the old woman carrying El Enano in the second frame, and El Enano crying for more food in the third frame. EL OL

Objectives
• Learn and use new vocabulary
• Identify literary elements: plot
• Paraphrase and summarize
• Interpret and analyze character
• Understand cause and effect

601

YOUR TURN

Teach

L Literary Element

Dialogue Say: Reread what the old woman says aloud. What do you think she is feeling? *(She is surprised and possibly even horrified.)* **OL** What does wonderful mean in this context? *(strange)* **AL**

R Reading Skill

Identifying Sequence Write the following events on the board. Say: Arrange the events in the order in which they happen in the story:

- A man tells El Enano that it is time for him to leave the village. *(4)*
- The old woman goes to her neighbors to borrow food to give to El Enano. *(2)*
- The old woman gives El Enano her supper. *(1)*
- El Enano grows to full size. *(3)* **AS**

A Lonely Life, c. 1873. Hugh Cameron. National Gallery of Scotland, Edinburgh.

Analyzing the Art Study the woman in this painting. What qualities does she seem to have in common with the "good old woman" in this story? Support your answer with details from the story.

devoured[6] all that was brought and still yelled for more and the noise it made was ear-splitting. But as it ate and felt the warmth, it grew and grew.

"Santa Maria!" said the dame. "What wonderful thing is this? Already it is no longer a baby, but a grown child. Almost it might be called ugly, but that, I suppose, is because it was motherless and lost. It is all very sad." Then, because she had thought it ugly she did the more for it, being sorry for her thoughts, though she could not help nor hinder them. As for the creature itself, having eaten all in the house, it gave a grunt or two, turned heavily on its side and went to sleep, snoring terribly.

Next morning matters were worse, for El Enano was stretched out on the floor before the fire, his full size, and seeing the dame he called for food, making so great a noise that the very windows shook and his cries were heard all over the village. So to still him, and there being nothing to eat in the house, the good old woman went out and told her tale to the neighbors, asking their help and advice, and to her house they all went flocking to look at the strange creature. One man, a stout-hearted[7] fellow, told El Enano that it was high time for him to be going, hearing which, the ugly thing shrieked with wicked laughter.

---

6. *Devoured* (dih VOWRD) means "ate up greedily."

7. A *stout-hearted* (stowt HART id) person is courageous.

Additional Support

English Language Coach

Cultural Literacy English language learners may be unfamiliar with some of the words and phrases on this page. For example, some students may not know that "ear-splitting" means deafening. A simple illustration or gesture can demonstrate this concept. Students may also misunderstand the meaning of *terribly* in the phrase "snoring terribly." Explain that El Enano is not doing a poor job of snoring; rather, *terribly* means "loudly" in this context, and refers to the effect that the snoring has on the listeners. Finally, explain that "high time" is a folk expression that means "about time." **EL BL**

"Well, bring me food," it said, looking at the man with red eyes. "Bring me food, I say, and when I have eaten enough I may leave you. But bring me no child's food, but rather food for six and twenty men. Bring an armadillo roasted and a pig and a large goose and many eggs and the milk of twenty cows. Nor be slow about it, for I must amuse myself while I wait and it may well be that you will not care for the manner of my amusement."

Indeed, there was small likelihood of any one there doing that, for his amusement was in breaking things about the house, the tables and benches, the pots and the ollas,[8] and when he had made sad havoc[9] of the woman's house he started on the house next door, smashing doors and windows, tearing up flowers by the roots, chasing the milk goats and the chickens, and setting dogs to fight. Nor did he cease in his mischief until the meal was set out for him, when he leaped upon it and crammed it down his throat with fearful haste, leaving neither bone nor crumb.

The people of the village stood watching, whispering one to another behind their hands, how they were shocked at all that sight, and when at last the meal was finished, the stout-hearted man who had spoken before stepped forward. "Now sir!" said he to El Enano, "seeing that you have eaten enough and more than enough, you will keep your word, going about your business and leaving this poor woman and us in peace. Will you?"

"No, *No* NO!" roared El Enano, each No being louder than the one before it.

8. *Ollas* (OY lus) are large containers used for storage, cooking, or holding water.

9. *Havoc* (HA vik) is widespread destruction.

"But you promised," said the man.

What the creature said when answering that made nearly everyone there faint with horror. It said:

"What I promised was that I would leave when I had eaten enough. I did not—"

The bold man interrupted then, saying, "Well, you have eaten enough."

"Ah yes, for one meal," answered the cruel Enano. "But I meant that I would leave when I have eaten enough for always. There is to-morrow and to-morrow night. There is the day after that and the next day and the next day. There are to be weeks of eating and months of eating and years of eating. You are stupid people if you think that I shall ever have eaten enough. So I shall not leave. No. *No.* NO!"

Having said that, the creature laughed in great glee and began to throw such things as he could reach against the walls, and so, many good things were shattered.

Now for three days that kind of thing went on, at the end of which time the men of the place were at their wits' ends to know what to do, for almost everything eatable in the village had gone down the creature's throat. Sad at heart, seeing what had come to pass, the good old woman went out and sat down to weep by the side of a quiet pool, for it seemed to her to be a hard thing that what she had done in kindness had ended thus, and that the house she had built and loved and kept clean and sweet should be so sadly wrecked and ruined. Her thoughts were broken by the sound of a voice, and turning she saw a silver-gray fox sitting on a rock and looking at her.

Teach

L1 Literary Element

Conflict Say: Describe the major conflict in the story so far. Is it external or internal conflict? Explain. *(Possible response: The major conflict occurs between El Enano and the people in the village. El Enano is eating all of their food and destroying their property. It is an external conflict because it takes place between two outside forces, not inside a character's mind.)* **AS**

R Reading Skill

Drawing Conclusions Ask: On the basis of what El Enano says, what conclusion can you draw about him? *(Responses will vary. Some students may conclude that he is cunning or smart. Others may conclude that he is evil and that his only desire is to terrorize the village.)* **OL**

L2 Literary Element

Plot Say: Conflict and suspense are building in the story. What stage of the plot does this represent? *(rising action)* **BL OL**

Objectives
• Identify literary elements: dialogue
• Understand sequence
• Identify literary elements: conflict and plot
• Draw conclusions from text and experience

Literature Focus Lesson

Epithets Ask students to make a list of the characters in the story. Then have students list the names by which they are called, such as "the cruel Enano," "the grinning Enano," "the stout-hearted fellow," "the dame," and "the good old woman." Explain that such phrases are called *epithets,* or terms used to characterize people or things. **OL** You may want to mention that this kind of epithet, known as the Homeric epithet, is positive. **AL** Have students create Homeric epithets for themselves, such as "the strong-willed Rebecca" or "the dark-haired Rashawn." **AS**

603

Teach

L Literary Element

Dialogue Ask: Are you surprised that the fox talks? Why or why not? *(Students may say that they are not surprised because animals frequently talk in folktales.)* **BL** **OL**

Still Life with Plums, Figs, and Bread, 18th century. Luis Melendez. Oil on canvas.

Analyzing the Art Do you think that this food would be enough to make El Enano go away? Why or why not?

L "It is well enough to have a good cry," he said, "but it is better to be gay[10] and have a good laugh."

"Ah! Good evening, Señor Zorro," answered the dame, drying her tears. "But who can be gay when a horrible creature is eating everything? Who can be otherwise than sad, seeing the trouble brought on friends?" The last she added, being one of those who are always saddened by the cheerlessness of others.

"You need not tell me," said the fox. "I know everything that has passed," and he put his head a little sideways like a wise young dog and seemed to smile.

"But what is there to do?" asked the dame. "I am in serious case indeed. This alocado[11] says that he will make no stir until he has had enough to eat for all his life, and certainly he makes no stir to go away."

"The trouble is that you give him enough and not too much," said the fox.

"Too much, you say? We have given him too much already, seeing that we have given him all that we have," said the old dame a little angrily.

"Well, what you must do is to give him something that he does not like. Then he will go away," said the fox.

---

10. **"It is better to be gay"** means "it is better to be happy."

11. **Alocado** means "thoughtless or crazy" in Spanish.

Additional Support

English Language Coach

Word Associations This part of the folktale introduces the character of the clever fox. Some English language learners may be unfamiliar with this idea of associating emotions or qualities with various animals. If students have limited proficiency, teach vocabulary words such as "clever," "strong," "brave," and "loyal," using students' primary language. When students are familiar with the words in English, use photographs or drawings to link them to animals that commonly depict these characteristics. For example, you may use a picture of a fox to teach "cunning," a picture of a bear to teach "strength," a picture of a lion to teach "courage," and a picture of a dog to teach "loyalty." **EL**

Teach

"Easier said than done," answered the old woman with spirit. "Did we but give him something of which he liked not the taste, then he would eat ten times more to take the bad taste away. Señor Zorro, with all your cleverness, you are but a poor adviser."

After that the fox thought a long while before saying anything, then coming close to the old woman and looking up into her face he said:

"Make your mind easy. He shall have enough to eat this very night and all that you have to do is to see that your neighbors do as I say, nor be full of doubt should I do anything that seems to be contrary."

So the good woman promised to warn her neighbors, knowing well the wisdom of the fox, and together they went to her house, where they found El Enano stretched out on the floor, looking like a great pig, and every minute he gave a great roar. The neighbors were both angry and afraid, for the creature had been very destructive that day. Indeed, he had taken delight in stripping the thatched roofs and had desisted[12] only when the men of the place had promised to double the amount of his meal.

Not five minutes had the fox and the dame been in the house when the men of the place came in with things—with berries and armadillos, eggs and partridges, turkeys and bread and much fish from the lake. At once they set about cooking, while the women commenced[13] to brew a great bowl of knot-grass tea. Soon the food was cooked and El Enano fell to as greedily as ever.

12. If something has ***desisted***, it has stopped.
13. ***Commenced*** (kuh MENST) means "started or began."

The fox looked at Enano for a while, then said:

"You have a fine appetite, my friend. What will there be for the men and the women and the children and for me to eat?"

"You may have what I leave, and eat it when I end," said El Enano.

"Let us hope then that our appetites will be light," said the fox.

A little later the fox began to act horribly, jumping about the room and whining, and calling the people lazy and inhospitable.[14]

14. An ***inhospitable*** (in haw SPIH tuh bul) person is unfriendly and not generous.

Analyzing the Photo Does the picture of a fox help you visualize the events on this page? Explain your answer.

R1 Reading Skill

Paraphrasing and Summarizing Say: Paraphrase what the old woman says to Señor Zorro when he suggests that the villagers give El Enano food he doesn't like. *(Possible response: The old woman says that if they gave El Enano food that he didn't like, he would eat ten times the amount to make the taste go away. Then she tells Señor Zorro that he does not give good advice.)* **BL OL**

R2 Reading Skill

Drawing Conclusions Ask: What is one conclusion that you can draw about Señor Zorro and his role in the village? *(Possible response: People often ask him for advice because he is very wise.)* **OL**

L Literary Element

Dialogue Say: Explain what the fox means when he says, "Let us hope then that our appetites will be light." Why does he say this? *(El Enano says that the people in the village can eat only what he leaves when he dies. Because El Enano is not likely to leave anything behind, the fox says that he hopes the villagers will not be very hungry.)* **BL OL**

Reading Fluency

Reading Aloud The text on this page lends itself well to being read aloud to a class. Choose several paragraphs to read aloud to your students while they follow along. If you wish, discuss how El Enano and the fox would sound and use students' suggestions when you read the dialogue. Be sure to model good inflection and intonation. Drop your voice for the words "he said" and raise the pitch of your voice at the end of a question. To reinforce these techniques, have students repeat the following sentence: "Think you," he said, "that this is the way to treat a visitor?" **EL BL**

Objectives
- Identify literary elements: dialogue
- Paraphrase and summarize
- Draw conclusions from text and experience

605

Teach

R1 Reading Skill

Paraphrasing and Summarizing Say: Reread what the fox says to the villagers when he starts acting strangely. Then paraphrase what he says in your own words. *(Possible response: Why haven't you offered me anything to eat? You should treat me with respect. Bring me some potatoes and roast them, or I will cause more damage than El Enano has done already.)* **AS**

R2 Reading Skill

Identifying Sequence Write the following events on the board. Say: Arrange the events in the order in which they happen in the story:

- The fox orders the people to bring him roasted potatoes. (2)
- The men begin eating the roasted potatoes. (3)
- El Enano asks for all the potatoes. (5)
- The fox tells the men to tell El Enano that there are no more potatoes. (4)
- The fox begins to jump around the room, whining and complaining. (1) **AS**

Analyzing the Photo How does this photo show what happens in the story? How is it different than what happens in the story?

R1 "Think you," he said, "that this is the way to treat a visitor? A pretty thing indeed to serve one and let the other go hungry. Do I get nothing at all to eat? Quick. Bring me potatoes and roast them, or it will be bad for all of you. The mischief I do shall be ten times worse than any done already."

Knowing that some plan was afoot the people ran out of the house and soon came back with potatoes, and the fox showed them how he wanted them roasted on the hearth. So they were placed in the ashes and covered with hot coals and when they were well done the fox told everyone to take a potato, saying that El Enano, who was crunching the bones of the animals he had eaten, would not like them. But all the while the men were eating, the fox ran from one to another whispering things but quite loud enough for Enano to hear. "Hush!" said he. "Say nothing. El Enano must not know how good they are and when he asks for some, tell him that they are all gone."

"Yes. Yes," said the people, keeping in with the plan. "Do not let Enano know."

By this time El Enano was suspicious and looked from one man to another. "Give me **R2** all the potatoes," he said.

"They are all eaten except mine," said the fox, "but you may taste that." So saying he

Additional Support

Reading in the Real World

Citizenship Students may benefit from learning about a piece of writing from the perspective of an author. If possible, contact local writers in your area and discuss having them come in to talk to your class about one of their stories. You may also want to research another writer who does not live nearby and compose a letter or an e-mail as a class. Encourage students to ask questions about the writing process and how writers develop material. **OL**

thrust the roasted potato into the hands of Enano and the creature crammed it down its throat at once.

"Ha! It is good," he roared. "Give me more. More. MORE."

"We have no more," said the fox very loud, then, quite softly to those who stood near him, he added, "Say nothing about the potatoes on the hearth,"[15] but loudly enough for El Enano to hear, though quite well he knew that there were none.

"Ah! I heard you," roared El Enano. "There are potatoes on the hearth. Give them to me."

"We must let him have them," said the fox, raking the red-hot coals to the front.

"Out of the way," cried El Enano, reaching over the fox and scooping up a double handful of hot coals, believing them to be potatoes. Red hot as they were he swallowed them and in another moment was rolling on the floor, howling with pain as the fire blazed in his stomach. Up he leaped again and dashed out of the house to fling himself by the side of the little river. The water was cool to his face and he drank deep, but the water in his stomach turned to steam, so that he swelled and swelled, and presently there was a loud explosion that shook the very hills, and El Enano burst into a thousand pieces. ○

---

15. A **hearth** (harth) is a brick, stone, or cement area that is the floor of a fireplace.

Analyzing the Photos Study the photos on pages 606 and 607. El Enano ate hot coals because he thought they were potatoes. Does that part of the story seem believable to you? Why or why not?

Teach

L1 Literary Element

Plot **Ask:** How would you describe this stage of the plot? Explain. *(Possible response: This seems to be the point of greatest interest or the turning point in the story, so it is probably the climax.)* BL What do you think will be the resolution? *(Responses will vary. Students may say that El Enano will eat the hot coals and die.)* OL

R Reading Skill

Understanding Cause and Effect **Ask:** Why does El Enano swell and eventually burst? *(The water from the river mixes with the coals in his stomach to make steam, which expands.)* OL

L2 Literary Element

Plot **Say:** Suppose that Charles Finger has asked you to write one more paragraph explaining what happens after El Enano's death. Write five or six sentences that complete the story's resolution. *(Responses will vary.)* BL OL AL

Differentiated Instruction

Reenactment Have students act out the climax and resolution of the story. Organize students into groups and assign the roles of El Enano, the good old woman, and the fox. Other students can stand in as residents of the village. Encourage students to think about more than just how they will read the lines. For instance, have students decide where

they will stand and where they will move as they act out the scene. To guide students, put tape on the floor to indicate the locations of the hearth, the edge of the house, and the river where El Enano drinks. Provide props, and have each group take a few minutes to practice walking through its presentation. OL

Objectives
• Paraphrase and summarize
• Understand sequence
• Identify literary elements: plot
• Understand cause and effect

607

Fiction

Tell students that these fictional accounts of people who encounter bullies can provide useful strategies for dealing with students' own conflicts.

Ask students to speculate on whether writers must have personal experience with bullies to write fictional accounts about them.

UNIT 5
Reading on Your Own

To read more about the Big Question, choose one of these books from your school or local library. Work on your reading skills by choosing books that are challenging to you.

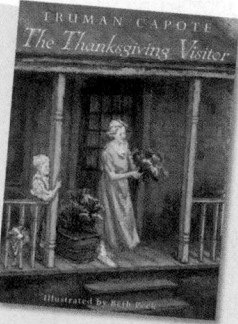

Fiction

The Thanksgiving Visitor
by Truman Capote

Buddy recalls a Thanksgiving in 1932 when he was a second grader in rural Alabama. His best friend was an aging spinster named Miss Sook. Read to discover what happens when Miss Sook invites Buddy's bully, Odd Henderson, to Thanksgiving dinner.

Blubber
by Judy Blume

Jill goes along with her classmates when they tease Linda. But Jill never expects that they might make fun of her next.

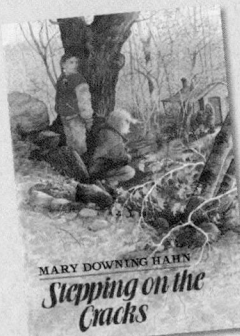

Stepping on the Cracks
by Mary Downing Hahn

While her brother is fighting Hitler overseas, eleven-year-old Margaret faces her own enemy at home. Margaret and her friend discover secrets about the bully, Gordy. Will they use this information to make Gordy treat them better, or will they have a change of heart? You'll have to read to find out!

The Bully of Barkham Street
by Mary Stolz

Martin's only friend is his dog, Rufus. Read to find out what happens when the eleven-year-old bully of Barkham Street begins to realize that it's time for him to make a change.

Additional Support

Differentiated Instruction

GLENCOE BOOKLINK Use the Glencoe BookLink CD-ROM to create customized reading lists to help students answer the Big Question. Suggestions for Unit 2:
Grade 4: *The Gooey Chewy Contest,* by Howard Goldsmith
Grade 5: *An Enchanted Hair Tale,* by Alexis De Veaux
Grade 6: *La Bamba,* by Gary Soto
Grade 7: *Raymond's Run,* by Toni Cade Bambara
Grade 8: *The Souls of Black Folk,* by W.E.B. Du Bois

Nonfiction

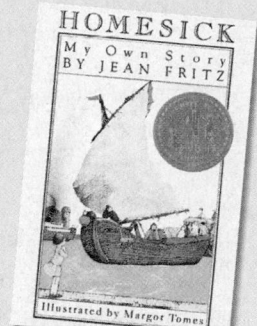

Homesick
by Jean Fritz

Jean Fritz is a member of an American family living in China, where Fritz attends a British elementary school. Fritz is uncomfortable singing the British national anthem, and she soon runs into trouble with her teacher and a bullying classmate.

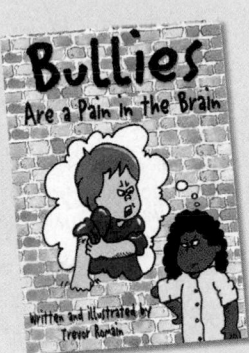

Bullies Are a Pain in the Brain
by Trevor Romain

This book discusses different kinds of bullying behavior and presents positive ways to deal with bullies. Use its resources—like lists of helpful books, Web sites, and organizations—to help you understand and deal with the bullies you know.

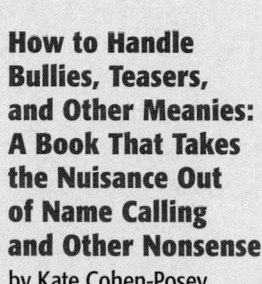

Little by Little
by Jean Little

Writer Jean Little recalls her childhood experience of entering a new class in Guelph, Ontario. Because she was visually impaired, her classmates teased her and chased her home after school. While Little's mother comforts her, she cannot solve the problem. Little discovers a place to belong when an older child takes her to the public library.

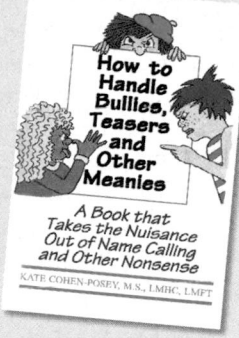

How to Handle Bullies, Teasers, and Other Meanies: A Book That Takes the Nuisance Out of Name Calling and Other Nonsense
by Kate Cohen-Posey

Sticks and stones can break your bones, but words can never hurt you. Only…they can. Sound familiar? If so, check out this guide to dealing with the verbal bully. Take the bite out of a bully's bark when you use these helpful tips.

Nonfiction

Explain to students that the books on this page are all nonfiction books. They will give factual information that is based on real-life occurrences or research.

Self-Help Books

Ask: If you were to group the books on this page into two categories by topic, how would you separate them? Explain. *(Possible response: Both* Homesick *and* Little by Little *are about a character who is teased. These are true stories.* Bullies Are a Pain in the Brain *and* Stick Up for Yourself! *give advice about how to deal with bullies. They are informational books.)* OL

About the subjects

Explain to students that the two books on the right-hand side of the page are self-help books. Self-help books, which are organized in one section of most bookstores, are usually written by qualified experts or by people who have done extensive research about a particular topic. These books are meant to help readers understand emotional issues, deal with internal conflicts, or improve their mental health. Invite students to brainstorm other topics for self-help books, aside from dealing with bullies.

Test Practice

Part 1: Literary Elements

On a separate sheet of paper, write the numbers 1–4. Next to each, write the letter of the correct answer for that question.

1. Think about the stories in this unit and other stories you have read. Which of the following stages of a plot is usually the longest and contains the most detail?

   A. exposition   **C.** climax

   B. rising action   **D.** falling action

Read the following passage and use it to answer questions 2–4.

> "It's time for you to give up," laughed Carly as the handle of Max's shovel broke in his hands.
>
> "No," replied Max, wiping the sweat from his forehead, "it's time for me to find another shovel."
>
> "The ground is as hard as a rock," said Carly, sympathetically. "Wouldn't you rather go swimming with me?"
>
> "Of course," said Max. "But then Dad would have to finish all the digging himself. No, I'm going to get this done, no matter how difficult it is."
>
> "Okay," sighed Carly. "Find a shovel for me, too."

2. What can you tell about Max from his dialogue?

   A. He's strong.

   B. He's determined.

   C. He's kindhearted.

   D. He's afraid of his father.

3. What can you tell about Carly from her dialogue?

   A. She's brave.

   B. She's helpful.

   C. She's confident.

   D. She's full of energy.

4. The main conflict in this passage is between

   A. Max and Carly.

   B. Max and his father.

   C. Max and the ground.

   D. Max's desire to dig and his desire to swim.

Objectives (pp. 610–611)
Reading Draw conclusions from text and experience • Paraphrase and summarize • Understand cause and effect • Identify text structure: sequence
Literature Identify literary elements: plot, conflict, dialogue, characterization

Test-Taking Tips

TIP Remind students that when they begin to answer the questions, they should refer back to the passage to find evidence for their answers.

TIP Occasionally students encounter questions that may seem extremely difficult. If that is the case, they should eliminate, guess, and then move on.

Part 1: Literary Elements

1. B
2. B
3. B
4. C

Part 2: Reading Skills

On a separate sheet of paper, write the numbers 1–4. Next to numbers 1–3, write the letter of the correct answer for that question. Next to number 4, write your answer for that question.

[1]Wendy didn't want to go to school. [2]There were many reasons, all of which swirled inside her head as soon as the alarm awakened her. [3]She didn't want to carry her heavy backpack. [4]Worse, the seven-block walk would be cold. [5]There was going to be a spelling quiz she didn't feel ready for. [6]But the worst thing, the thing that made her heart pound and her breath come fast in shaky gasps, was that Tamara would be waiting for her. [7]Just like all of last week and the week before, Tamara would be in the hallway or out on the playground, waiting. [8]Wendy didn't think she could face one more day of trying to be brave.

---

1. This sequence of this paragraph is arranged according to
   A. time order.
   B. spatial order.
   C. order of importance.
   D. both time and space.

2. Based on the information in this paragraph, you can conclude that
   A. Wendy is smaller than Tamara.
   B. Wendy often stays home from school.
   C. Tamara is a new student at Wendy's school.
   D. Tamara has been frightening Wendy for some time.

3. Which sentence in the paragraph states the effect of all the other sentences?
   A. sentence 1
   B. sentence 2
   C. sentence 6
   D. sentence 8

4. Write a one- or two-sentence summary of the paragraph.

UNIT 5 ASSESSMENT

Part 2: Reading Skills

1. C

2. D

3. A

4. *Possible response:* Tamara is frightening Wendy and that is one of many reasons Wendy doesn't want to go to school.

Resources for pages 610–613

Use these resources to review, assess, or reteach the Unit: Active Learning, Note Taking Guide, Selection and Unit Assessments, ExamView Assessment Suite, and Skill Level Up!™ A Language Arts Game.

Test-Taking Tips

TIP It can't be stressed often enough: Remind students to read the directions carefully and be sure that they answer the question they are asked.

TIP By reading the questions before they read the passage, students will know that they have to look for the sequence and choose details that support their answer.

Part 3: Vocabulary Skills

1. C
2. A
3. A
4. B
5. D
6. A
7. B
8. D
9. C
10. B

Part 3: Vocabulary Skills

On a separate sheet of paper, write the numbers 1–10. Next to each number, write the letter of the correct answer for that question.

Write the letter of the word or phrase that means about the same as the underlined word.

1. such <u>hostile</u> remarks
- **A.** funny
- **B.** confusing
- **C.** unfriendly
- **D.** welcoming

2. some <u>immense</u> animals
- **A.** huge
- **B.** wild
- **C.** strange
- **D.** dangerous

3. to <u>contemplate</u> an action
- **A.** think about
- **B.** recommend
- **C.** disapprove of
- **D.** successfully complete

4. with a <u>lithe</u> movement
- **A.** sudden
- **B.** flexible
- **C.** sneaky
- **D.** threatening

5. a <u>rigid</u> stem
- **A.** thin
- **B.** strong
- **C.** broken
- **D.** unbending

Choose the correct answer for each question.

6. Which of the following words has both a prefix and a suffix?
- **A.** unselfish
- **B.** friendliness
- **C.** disrespect
- **D.** handlebars

7. What is the base word in *dishonesty*?
- **A.** dish
- **B.** honest
- **C.** honesty
- **D.** dishonest

8. In which word are the letters *mis-* a prefix?
- **A.** misty
- **B.** mister
- **C.** missing
- **D.** misspell

9. Considering what you know about prefixes and base words, what does *disallow* mean?
- **A.** permit
- **B.** change
- **C.** forbid
- **D.** not pay for

10. Considering what you know about prefixes and base words, what does *overstate* mean?
- **A.** deny
- **B.** exaggerate
- **C.** say again
- **D.** apologize

Objectives (pp. 612–613)
Vocabulary Identify word structure
Grammar Identify sentence elements
• Use punctuation correctly

Part 4: Writing Skills

On a separate sheet of paper, write the numbers 1–7. Next to each number, write the letter of the correct answer for that question.

1. Which of the following is a phrase?

   A. if you understand

   B. shady places in the yard

   C. when my neighbors get home

   D. after the crowd leaves the stadium

2. An adjective clause is one that

   A. can be substituted for a noun or pronoun.

   B. modifies, or tells more about, an adjective.

   C. explains what an adjective in a sentence means.

   D. functions (works) in a sentence like an adjective does.

3. Which of the following is an independent clause?

   A. flowers are blooming

   B. the fish that live in the lake

   C. before they finished the book

   D. children who never want to nap

4. Which sentence is punctuated correctly?

   A. We bought apples carrots crackers and juice.

   B. We bought, apples carrots crackers, and juice.

   C. We bought apples, carrots, crackers, and juice.

   D. We bought, apples, carrots, crackers, and juice.

5. Where should a comma be inserted in the sentence below?

   If you want me to I'll go along.

   A. after *you*

   B. after *me*

   C. after *to*

   D. after *go*

6. Which of the following sentences is punctuated correctly?

   A. No I don't think so.

   B. Yes, I plan to be there.

   C. Please Mom, let me stay home.

   D. Well give me some help, Cherise.

7. Which of the following sentences is punctuated correctly?

   A. Rafael, unlike Billy cleaned his room.

   B. Don't point, at the tourists, like that.

   C. The bleachers as I said earlier, were full.

   D. I will, if you don't mind, have another helping.

Part 4: Writing Skills

1. A
2. D
3. A
4. C
5. C
6. B
7. D

Skills Scope and Sequence

Readability Scores Key
Dale-Chall/DRP/Lexile

PACING (DAYS) STANDARD	BLOCK	INSTRUCTIONAL SEGMENT LITERATURE	READING SKILLS	LITERARY ELEMENTS
1	1	**Unit Warm-Up, pp. 616–623** Genre Focus: "Persephone" by Alice Low **5.5/55/860**, p. 619	Activating Prior Knowledge, SE pp. 618, 619 Clarifying, SE pp. 618, 619 Comparing and Contrasting, SE pp. 618, 620, 621 Predicting, SE pp. 618, 622, TWE p. 621 Fluency, TWE pp. 615, 622 Connecting, TWE p. 616 How to Read Folktale, Fantasy and Myth, TWE p. 618	Hero, SE pp. 618, 623, TWE p. 622 Cultural Context, SE pp. 618, 623 Theme, SE pp. 618, 623 Setting, SE pp. 618, 621, TWE p. 620
3	2	**Reading Workshop 1, pp. 624–641** "Hurricane Heroes" by Thomas Fields Meye, Steve Helling and Long Rozsa, from *People* **4.9/57/910**, p. 626 "All Stories Are Anansi's" by Harold Courlander **5.2/47/610**, p. 634	Activating Prior Knowledge, SE pp. 624, 627, 628, 629, 630, 635, 636, TWE pp. 625, 630, 637 Questioning, SE p. 630 Identifying Problem and Solution, SE p. 639 Connecting, TWE pp. 627, 635, 638 Fluency, TWE p. 638	Hero, SE pp. 627, 629, 635, 636, 639
1		**Writing Workshop, Part 1, pp. 642–645** Writing Product: Fable	Fluency, TWE p. 645	Character, SE p. 642 Setting, SE p. 642 Plot, SE p. 642 Dialogue, SE p. 643 Hero, TWE p. 642
3	1	**Reading Workshop 2, pp. 646–669** "The Twelve Labors of Hercules" by Walker Brents **7.8/59/1030**, p. 648 "Pecos Bill" by Mary Pope Osbourne **6.4/52/950**, p. 658	Clarifying, SE pp. 646, 649, 651, 652, 659, 661, 662, 666, TWE p. 647 Evaluating, SE pp. 655, 664 Connecting, TWE pp. 649, 659 Drawing Conclusions, TWE p. 653 Identifying Cause and Effect, TWE p. 653 Activating Prior Knowledge, TWE p. 665	Cultural Context, SE pp. 649, 654, 659, 660, 664, 665, TWE p. 652 Setting, TWE p. 659

Unit 6 Big Question

Seeking answers to the question "What makes a hero?" will help students identify the qualities they admire in others and establish a course of action to attain those qualities themselves.

Unit 6 Genre

Many of the selections in this unit are folktales, fables, and myths, which familiarize students with cultures. These readings will also help students as they seek to answer the Big Question "What makes a hero?"

CRITICAL THINKING	VOCABULARY	WRITING AND GRAMMAR	LISTENING, SPEAKING, AND VIEWING
Comprehension, TWE p. 622			Analyzing the Art, SE pp. 619, 620, 622 Viewing the Photo, TWE p. 614
Synthesize, SE p. 632 Evaluate, SE pp. 632, 640, TWE pp. 630, 637 Analyze, SE pp. 632, 640, TWE p. 638 Identify, SE p. 640 Infer, SE p. 640	Compound Words, SE pp. 626, 629, 631 Etymology, TWE p. 626 Blended Words, SE p. 634	Capitalization of Sentences, SE p. 633 Write About Your Reading, SE p. 640 Simple Sentences, SE p. 641	Talk About Your Reading, SE p. 632 Viewing the Photo, TWE p. 631 Viewing the Art, TWE pp. 636, 637
Analysis, TWE p. 642		Applying Good Writing Traits: Voice, SE p. 644 Compound and Complex Sentences, SE p. 645 Dialogue, TWE p. 643	
Analyze, SE pp. 656, 668, TWE pp. 647, 663 Infer, SE p. 656 Compare, SE p. 656 Assess, SE p. 656 Evaluate, SE p. 668, TWE pp. 655, 664 Comprehension, TWE pp. 654, 661, 662 Application, TWE p. 667	Borrowed Words, SE pp. 648, 650, 651, 658, 663, TWE p. 666 Vocabulary File, TWE p. 658	Write About Your Reading, SE p. 656 Combine Sentences, SE p. 657 Combining Sentence Clauses, SE p. 669	Analyzing the Art, SE p. 646, 667 Viewing the Art, TWE p. 650 Viewing the Illustration, TWE p. 660

Skills Scope and Sequence *continued*

Readability Scores Key
Dale-Chall/DRP/Lexile

PACING (DAYS)		INSTRUCTIONAL SEGMENT LITERATURE	READING SKILLS	LITERARY ELEMENTS
STANDARD	BLOCK			
3	3	**Reading Workshop 3, pp. 670–701** "Dragon, Dragon" by John Gardner **6.5/54/1020**, p. 672 "The King of Mazy May" by Jack London **6.7/57/1220**, p. 686	Comparing and Contrasting, SE pp. 670, 671, 673, 675, 677, 680, 681, 682, 687, 689, 693, 696, TWE pp. 676, 693 Understanding Cause and Effect, SE pp. 683, 697, 699 Connecting, TWE pp. 673, 687, 696 Predicting, TWE pp. 678, 680 Inferring, TWE pp. 694, 698, 699	Theme, SE pp. 673, 679, 683, 687, 688, 693, 694, 699, TWE pp. 691, 698
2		**Writing Workshop, Part 2, pp. 702–705** Writing Product: Fable	Fluency, TWE p. 703	
3	1	**Reading Workshop 4, pp. 706–743** "Aunt Millicent" by Mary Steele **5.1/52/870**, p. 708 "A Mason-Dixon Memory" by Clifton Davis **6.7/59/880**, p. 732	Predicting, SE pp. 706, 707, 709, 710, 712, 713, 714, 718, 720, 725, 727, 733, 735, 738, 740, 741, TWE pp. 719, 722, 724, 726, 736 Connecting, TWE pp. 709, 712, 726, 726, 733, 735 Fluency, TWE pp. 724, 736	Setting, SE pp. 709, 712, 716, 717, 723, 733, 734, 736, 738, 741, TWE p. 715
3	2	**Comparing Literature Workshop, pp. 744–757** "The Toad and the Donkey" by Toni Cade Bambara **4.8/49/820**, p. 746 "Doc Rabbit, Bruh Fox, and Tar Baby" by Virginia Hamilton **5.2/45/600**, p. 750	Compare, SE p. 745 Activating Prior Knowledge, TWE pp. 744, 754 Predicting, TWE pp. 747, 748, 751 Connecting, TWE pp. 747, 749, 750 Fluency, TWE p. 751 Clarifying, TWE p. 752	Hero, SE pp. 744, 748, 749, 751, 753, 754, 755, TWE p. 745 Trickster tales, SE p. 747 Tone, TWE p. 751
4	2	**Unit Wrap-Up, pp. 758–765** Your Turn: "The Sand Castle" by Alma Luz Villanueva **5.9/55/850**, p. 760	Activating Prior Knowledge, TWE p. 761 Comparing and Contrasting, TWE pp. 761, 763 Clarifying, TWE p. 762 Predicting, TWE p. 762	Setting, TWE pp. 760, 764 Cultural Context, TWE p. 762 Theme, TWE pp. 763, 764

CRITICAL THINKING	VOCABULARY	WRITING AND GRAMMAR	LISTENING, SPEAKING, AND VIEWING
Analysis, TWE pp. 671, 692 Contrast, SE p. 684 Infer, SE pp. 684, 700 Interpret, SE p. 700 Explain, SE p. 700 Evaluation, TWE pp. 677, 679, 689, 690	Word Sources, SE pp. 672, 675, 678 Idioms, TWE p. 675 Word Histories, SE pp. 686, 691	Commas in Compound Sentences, SE p. 685 Write About Your Reading, SE pp. 684, 700 Commas in Complex Sentences, SE p. 701	Analyzing Cartoons, SE p. 670 Analyzing the Art, SE pp. 676, 689, 691, 696, TWE p. 681 Viewing the Illustration, TWE p. 674 Viewing the Image, TWE pp. 688, 696
Analysis, TWE p. 704		Voice, SE p. 702 Revising, TWE p. 702 Dialogue, TWE pp. 703, 704 Punctuation, TWE p. 703 Editing, SE p. 703 Revising, SE p. 703	Storytelling, SE p. 705 Active Listening, TWE p. 705
Identifying, TWE p. 723 Analyze, SE pp. 730, 742, TWE pp. 714, 719, 725, 727, 729 Evaluate, SE pp. 730, 742, TWE pp. 707, 715, 720, 736, 740 Synthesize, SE p. 730 Draw Conclusions, SE p. 742	Word History, SE pp. 708, 719, 720, 721, 732, 736, TWE p. 737	Run-on Sentences, SE pp. 731, 743	Analyzing Cartoons, SE p. 706 Analyzing the Photos, SE p. 725 Talk About Your Reading, SE p. 730 Viewing the Photo, TWE p. 710 Viewing the Image, TWE p. 734 Viewing the Photo, TWE p. 737
Analysis, TWE p. 748 Evaluation, TWE p. 752 Application, TWE p. 753	Concentration, TWE p. 746 Dialect, TWE pp. 747, 752	Compare the Literature, SE p. 757	Analyzing the Art, SE p. 754

Reading with Purpose offers a comprehensive package of tools to optimize student learning and the teaching experience. Each resource has been designed to assist students in specific areas and to offer instructional support for teachers. While all of these areas are covered in the core textbook, some students may need extra practice or additional help in specific areas. The resource package is designed so that you, the teacher, can choose which items will best assist your students. You may also use these resources as homework assignments and for assessment purposes. The following are resources recommended for use with Unit 6.

Keys for Unit Resources

- 🗀 Blackline Master
- 📕 Workbook
- 📖 Supplemental Text
- 💿 CD-ROM
- 💾 DVD
- 🔬 Transparency
- 💻 Web-based
- ⚙ Fast File

Essential Instructional Support

FAST FILE — UNIT 6 RESOURCES

Reading and Literature
- Academic Vocabulary Review
- Big Question: School to Home
- The Big Question Foldable
- Unit Challenge: Planner and Rubrics
- Comparing Literature Graphic Organizer
- Key Reading Skills
- Active Reading Graphic Organizers
- Literary Analysis
- Unit Vocabulary Review

Writing, Grammar, and Spelling
- Spelling and Handwriting Practice
- Grammar Practice
- Writing Workshop Graphic Organizer

Listening, Speaking, and Viewing
- Viewing and Representing
- Listening and Speaking

English Language Learners
- English Language Coach Review

DIFFERENTIATED INSTRUCTION

- 🗀 Leveled Vocabulary Development
- 💿 Skill Level Up!™ A Language Arts Game
- 💿 Listening Library CD
- 💿 BookLink 3
- 💿 Literature Library Vocabulary Puzzlemaker
- 💿 Vocabulary Puzzlemaker

ASSESSMENT — GLENCOE'S ASSESSMENT ADVANTAGE

- 🗀 Selection and Unit Assessments
- 🗀 Selection Quick Checks
- 🗀 Assessment by Learning Objectives
- 🗀 Rubrics for Assessing Student Writing, Listening, and Speaking
- 💻 Glencoe Online Essay Grader
- 💿 Interactive Tutor: Self-Assessment
- 💿 ExamView Assessment Suite
- 💿 Literature Library ExamView Assessment Suite

Additional Instructional Support

WRITING, GRAMMAR, AND SPELLING

- Real Success in Writing: Research and Reports
- Writing Constructed Responses
- Spelling Power eWorkbook
- Grammar & Composition Handbook
- Grammar and Language Workbook
- Revising with Style eWorkbook

READING AND LITERATURE

- Active Learning and Note Taking Guide
- inTime Magazines
- Backpack Reader Volume 2
- Literature Library
- Literature Launchers Pre-Reading Videos DVD
- Literature Classics

TRANSPARENCIES

- Read Aloud, Think Aloud Transparencies
- Literary and Text Analysis Transparencies
- Bellringer Options Transparencies
- Grammar and Writing Workshop Transparencies
- Fine Art Transparencies

TECHNOLOGY

- TeacherWorks Plus™
- StudentWorks Plus ™
- BookLink 3
- Skill Level Up!™ A Language Arts Game
- ExamView Assessment Suite
- Interactive Tutor: Self-Assessment
- Listening Library CD
- Spanish Listening Library CD
- Literature Classics
- Literature Launchers Pre-Reading Videos DVD
- Literature Library ExamView Assessment Suite
- Vocabulary Puzzlemaker
- Literature Library Vocabulary Puzzlemaker
- glencoe.com
- Online Student Edition
- Presentation Plus!
- Glencoe Online Essay Grader

ENGLISH LANGUAGE LEARNER

- English Language Coach
- Fluency Practice and Assessment
- inTime Magazines (Spanish)
- Spanish Listening Library CD

PROFESSIONAL DEVELOPMENT

- Professional Development Package

Additional Glencoe Resources

 Dinah Zike's Foldables

Foldables are three-dimensional, interactive graphic organizers that help students practice basic writing skills, review key vocabulary terms, and answer Big Questions. Every unit contains a foldable activity. You can find the pattern and directions for the Unit 6 Foldable in the Unit 6 Resources Fast Files booklet. You can use the foldables as they are presented or modify them to suit the needs of your students. More information about foldables for Unit 6 can be found on pages R8–R9.

 Glencoe Literature Library

This collection of hardcover books includes full-length novels, novellas, plays, and works of nonfiction. Each volume consists of at least one complete extended-length reading accompanied by several related readings from a broad range of genres. A separate Study Guide for each Glencoe Literature Library book provides teaching notes and reproducible activity pages for students.

Glencoe Literature Library titles that complement this unit include:
The Adventures of Tom Sawyer, by Mark Twain
Number the Stars, by Lois Lowry
Winter Thunder and The Christmas of the Phonograph Records, by Mari Sandoz

For a wealth of online resources that support the instruction in Unit 6 of *Glencoe Literature: Reading with Purpose,* students and teachers can visit our Web site at www.glencoe.com. Students will find additional learning, practice, and assessment opportunities such as these, which are noted in the student text:

- **Big Question Overview**
- **Study Central**
- **Author Search**
- **Writing Models**
- **Interactive Literary Elements Handbook**
- **Web Activities**

Teachers will find planning and instructional tools that include the following:

- **Book Lesson Plans**
- **Teacher Forum**
- **Professional Development**
- **Web Activities Lesson Plans (with answers to student activities)**

Go to www.glencoe.com to see the entire selection of Reading with Purpose online resources.

 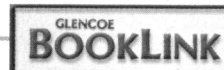

Use the Glencoe **Booklink 3** CD-ROM, a database of more than 26,700 titles, to *create customized reading lists* for your students.

- Search for award-winning titles (e.g., Newbery Award winners, Coretta Scott King Award winners, and Caldecott Medal winners) and for books on several state-recommended reading lists.
- Find Degrees of Reading Power™ (DRP) and Lexile™ readability scores for all selections.
- Organize reading lists by students' reading level, author, genre, theme, or area of interest.
- Get a brief summary of each selection.

You can find recommended leveled readings for this unit with Reading on Your Own (see page 766).

A lively collection of articles drawn from issues of the TIME family of magazines helps students develop the skills they need to interact with informational text in a meaningful way. Each of the news stories, feature articles, reviews, profiles, and essays in the magazine connect to an author, work, or theme in *Glencoe Literature: Reading with Purpose.* Articles for Unit 6 are found in Volume B. See the *inTIME* Teacher's Guide for specific connections to each unit and for reproducible student worksheets designed to develop students' reading and critical thinking skills.

Glencoe's **Presentation Plus!**, a multimedia teaching tool, lets you present dynamic lessons that will engage your students. Using Microsoft PowerPoint,® you can customize the presentations to create your own personalized lessons. Use **CheckPoint** questions with interactive response keypads to get immediate student feedback during lessons, to increase student participation, and to assess student comprehension.

Literature Launchers

Set the scene with Glencoe's Literature Launchers, engaging video segments that introduce each unit's genre focus. Each video brings the genre to life, relating it to your students' worlds.

Insert the Glencoe Literature Launchers Pre-Reading Videos DVD into your DVD player. Select the Unit 6 Launcher from the menu to introduce the genre and Big Question for this unit.

Online Essay Grader

Use Glencoe's Online Essay Grader to score your students' writing and to provide individualized feedback to each student automatically.

You and your students can visit www.glencoe.com to link to the essay grader. *Students* can enter their essays and receive feedback on demand. *You* can manage demographic data, assign tests and generate individual student and aggregated reports. The essay grader can help you

- Save time with automatic scoring and individualized feedback.
- Supplement in-class writing instruction using guided writing practice.
- Get reports for individual students or for special populations.
- Track student improvement over time.

REAL Success: Reading Excellence at All Levels

Glencoe now provides all of your students with the tools they need to become better, more enthusiastic readers. The REAL Success suite of reading and language arts products encourages reading excellence by meeting the needs of students at all levels. Glencoe products that can be used in conjunction with Unit 6 include the following:

- Jamestown Literature: An Adapted Reader
- Jamestown *Reading Fluency*
- Jamestown *Critical Reading Series, In the Line of Duty*
- *Vocabulary Builder*
- *The Glencoe Reader, Course 1*

To order these products, call Glencoe at 1-800-USA-READ.

Teacher Wraparound Edition Key

Level Appropriate Code

AS = Activities for all students

AL = Activities for students working above grade level

OL = Activities for students working at grade level

BL = Activities for students working below grade level

EL = Activities for English language learners

Teacher Wraparound Prompts

R **Reading Skill** These activities help you teach reading comprehension skills.

V **Vocabulary** These activities help students comprehend words and incorporate them into their reading and writing.

C **Critical Thinking** These strategies help students apply and extend what they have learned.

BQ **BIG Question** These activities and questions prompt students to prepare to answer the Big Question.

W **Writing** These activities provide writing opportunities to help students practice writing and comprehend text.

L **Literary Element** These activities and questions help students comprehend selections and learn more about each genre.

E **Text Element** These activities help students comprehend text elements.

LSV **Listening, Speaking, Viewing** These activities help students practice listening, speaking, and viewing skills.

EL **English Language Coach** These skills help English language learners as well as students who need additional reading support.

Taffy Raphael

From an Author

Preparing Students to Read Folktales and Myths

Make features visible Folktales are written versions of stories that historically were told orally, from generation to generation. Literary elements helped make the stories memorable so they could be retold over time in consistent ways. Explaining some of the traditional elements to students may help them better understand the genre. Some of those elements include the following characteristics: *Settings* are vague and in opposition (e.g., very rich or very poor, huge castles or tiny huts). *Characters* are clear cut (e.g., good or evil, smart or foolish), do not change, and readers are not told why they behave as they do. The *action* and *events* unfold with a basic pattern in which the victims obtain, through magical assistance, some sort of power over those who maligned them. This power provides status over those who had victimized them.

Introduce folktale categories There are different groups of folktales, including myths, cumulative tales, and *pourquoi* tales. Myths are what we call stories that explain beliefs of different cultures. For example, the "myths" we tell today of ancient Greeks were the "truths" of their belief systems. For example, myths often focus on explanations of how our world was created (e.g., stars, oceans). Myths must be shared with respect and caution since the ideas may be much more than simply a story to those within the culture from which the myth was taken.

Pourquoi tales also explain natural phenomena, like the bear's short tail or the mosquito's buzz. There are other forms of folktales that could be included such as fables, legends, and epics. The critical points are that folktales provide insights into cultures near and far, are based on the oral histories of peoples, and reflect a larger than life approach to narrative.

Teacher to Teacher

To teach this unit, I tie in the literature with current events and students' lives, backgrounds, and cultures. In cooperative learning group discussion, students may look at real-life stories of heroes in the media and compare them with the literature. In addition, I ask them to answer this question: What message or lesson about heroism does this selection have for readers today? After students have read and discussed all of the selections, I invite them to write their own imaginative tale with a well-developed hero. I encourage them to draw on the personalities of the characters in the literature, as well as their own knowledge and experiences, in shaping their stories. Then we hold a storytelling festival in which students perform the tales they have written for the class.

Jose Lopez
Eagle Pass High School
Eagle Pass, Texas

Teacher Chat Room

Teaching Folktales and Myths

 How do I make folktales and myths interesting to middle school students?

 Middle school students need to be able to get beyond the story since most of these are stories they will have heard in one form or another since they were very young. Unpacking how a folktale works and helping them connect this genre to their own storytelling is central to making the genre relevant to them. Help students substitute modern-day characters in folktales so they can apply the lessons better. This technique will also enhance their writing skills and nurture their creativity.

 How do I help them understand the importance of folktales to understanding different cultures, time periods, and beliefs?

 Middle school students are learning about gender stereotyping. Suggest they change the gender of characters and discuss how the story and moral would change. This practice will quite naturally lead to gender implications and beliefs prevalent during the origination of the folktale.

You may also want to change the location of some of the folktales or the nationality of some characters. How would "All Stories are Anansi's" be different if the main character were from a different culture? What values of West African culture are found in this folktale? What values might be highlighted if it were changed for another culture?

 How do I help middle schoolers understand the importance of oral traditions in storytelling?

 As much as possible allow students to read these folktales aloud. Tell them to try to find the rhythm or pattern that would have made this story easy to remember. Remind them that both the storyteller and his or her audience needed to remember the story.

If you can find recordings of folktales, play them for students. Encourage them to pay attention to the speaker's voice, rhythm, and word choice. Ask students to find other elements that may be missed in the reading of a folktale.

UNIT 6

What Makes a Hero?

Key Unit Objectives

- ● **Answer the Big Question**
- ● **Analyze the literary elements of folktale, fantasy, and myth**
- ● **Apply strategies for reading folktale, fantasy, and myth**
- ● **Write a fable**

BIG Question

Why Is It Important?
Searching for answers to this Big Question will help students identify the qualities they admire in others and establish a course of action to attain those qualities themselves.

BQ BIG Question
Say: Read the quote from Michael Jordan. In what ways are our parents or guardians heroes? Explain. *(Responses will vary.)* **AS**

Viewing the Photo
Ask: How does the photo on this page relate to the Big Question? *(Possible response: Rescue workers are oftentimes considered heroes because they risk their lives to help others.)* **AS** **OL**

> ❝ My heroes are and were my parents. I can't see having anyone else as my heroes. ❞
>
> —Michael Jordan
> Probably the greatest basketball player ever, five-time Most Valuable Player; led the Chicago Bulls to six championships

---

Unit Skills

Reading Skills
- Activating Prior Knowledge, p. 624
- Clarifying, p. 646
- Comparing and Contrasting, p. 670
- Predicting, p. 706

Vocabulary
- Compound Words, p. 626
- Words Borrowed from Names, p. 648

 BIG Question **What makes a hero?**

Genre Focus: Folktale, Fantasy, and Myth

Literary Elements
- Heroes, p. 627
- Cultural Context, p. 649
- Theme, p. 673
- Setting, p. 709

Writing Skills/Grammar
- Voice, p. 644
- Compound Sentences, p. 645

The skill lessons and readings in this unit will help you develop your own answer to the Big Question.

615

About the Reading

The selections in this unit provide a variety of models to help students answer the Big Question, "What makes a hero?" Students will examine the qualities they admire in others as well as the ways in which heroes solve problems and overcome obstacles.

About the Skills

The skills taught in this unit will help students get more out of reading the featured genres: folktale, fantasy, and myth. Each reading selection gives students a chance to practice and develop these skills.

NO CHILD LEFT BEHIND

The goals of the NCLB act include a strong emphasis on reading comprehension skills. Modeling the skills covered in this unit will help students develop them. For example, read aloud a passage and model clarifying as you read. Do the same with the other reading skills in this unit.

Reading Fluency

Reading Aloud Several of the reading selections in this unit lend themselves to dramatic reading. Help students develop reading fluency by assigning characters in the stories to students in the class. When a character speaks in a story, the designated student can read that character's lines aloud. Encourage the readers to adopt the characters' feelings and read with expression. When a selection is finished, have the class give constructive comments on the fluency of the reading. Allow all students the opportunity to read aloud from a selection. **AS**

Focus

BELLRINGER Options

- 🔒 **Literature Launchers: Pre-Reading Videos**
- 🖥 **Daily Language Practice Transparency 51**
  Focus Activity Ask: What qualities or achievements do you admire in others? Write down a list of these qualities and achievements. *(Responses will vary.)* **AS**

Teach

R Reading Skill

Review Connecting To help students connect their experiences to the Big Question, ask them to name people they have known, seen, or read about who have

- overcome a big obstacle
- solved a major problem
- survived a dangerous situation *(Responses will vary.)* **AS**

BQ BIG Question

- Have students read the profiles and look at the pictures of Jessica and Shea.
- Ask students to compare and contrast the heroic qualities of Jessica's cousin Sharon with those of Shea's father. **AL**

UNIT 6 WARM-UP

Connecting to The BIG Question — What Makes a Hero?

In real life, heroes are people admired for great qualities or achievements. Who are *your* heroes? What do your choices suggest about the qualities and achievements you admire? In literature, *hero* has a slightly different meaning. **BQ** In this unit, you'll read about some literary heroes and some real-life heroes. As you read, think about whether these heroes have qualities you admire.

Real Kids and the Big Question

JESSICA has always admired her cousin Luke. Luke is a wheelchair athlete who plays basketball. He is also an honor student. Whenever Jessica is feeling down about school, Luke always reminds her to keep a positive attitude. Luke helps Jessica with her Spanish class and acts as her big brother. If you asked Jessica what makes a hero, what do you think she might say? Why?

SHEA's father always takes time to help Shea with his homework. He drives him to baseball practice. They spend time together just talking. Shea's father tries to teach Shea those things that he feels are important in life. Shea looks up to his father. If you asked Shea what makes a hero, what do think he might say? Why?

Warm-Up Activity

In your Learner's Notebook, write the names of two people you admire and why you admire them.

Additional Support

Reading in the Real World

Career Both Jessica and Shea admire people in their families. Many young people can also find heroes in their schools and communities. Discuss with students jobs people have that are considered heroic. Have students choose a career to research or someone in that field to interview. Give them interview questions such as

- Why did you choose this career?
- What kind of training did you get?
- What is the most challenging part of your job?

Have students present their findings to the class. **OL AL**

You and the Big Question

Reading about heroes in different times and places may help you decide how you would answer the Big Question.

Plan for the Unit Challenge

At the end of the unit, you'll use notes from all your reading to complete the Unit Challenge.

You'll choose one of the following activities:

A. Wall of Heroes You and your classmates will interview people in your school about their heroes. You will create a Wall of Heroes in your classroom that has the pictures and stories of the heroes in your community.

B. A Hero for Today Choose one of the heroes in the stories you read, and write a story about what this hero would do today if he or she were a hero in your community.

- Start thinking about which activity you'd like to do so you can focus your thinking as you go through the unit.
- If you choose the first activity, decide who you will interview and the questions you will ask them about their heroes.
- If you choose the second activity, take notes as you read the selections so you can decide which hero you'd like to use as your "Hero for Today."

Keep Track of Your Ideas

As you read, you'll make notes about the Big Question. Later, you'll use these notes to complete the Unit Challenge. See pages R8–R9 for help with making Foldable 6. This diagram shows how it should look.

1. Make one Foldable page for each selection. At the end of the unit, you'll staple the pages together into one Foldable.

2. Label the front of the fold-over page with the selection title. (See page 615 for titles.)

3. Open the Foldable. Label the top of the inside page **My Purpose for Reading.** You will write your purpose for reading the selection below this label.

4. Halfway down the inside page, write the label **The Big Question.** You'll write your thoughts about the Big Question below this label.

Hurricane Heroes

Big Question Link to Web resources to further explore the Big Question at www.glencoe.com.

Teach

BQ **BIG Question**

Have students write their initial responses to the Big Question in their Learner's Notebooks. **OL**

FOLDABLES™
Study Organizer

For each selection they read, students will enter notes about how that selection applies to the Big Question. For details about using Dinah Zike's Foldables, see pages R8 and R9.

Assess/Close

Ask students to discuss how to decide what they admire in a hero.

Resources for page 617

📁 Use the Unit Challenge Planner BLM in the Unit 6 Resource Booklet, p. 37.

📁 Use the Foldable BLM in the Unit 6 Resource Booklet, p. 7.

Differentiated Instruction

Illustrations Hold a class discussion about what makes a hero. Have students list the qualities they admire and expect in a hero. Write the qualities on the board. Point out to students that other cultures may have different ideas about heroism. You may also wish to ask students whether they think male heroes and female heroes have similar qualities. Then ask students who enjoy drawing to create pictures of heroes, real or fictional, who have the qualities that were discussed in class. Some students may wish to find photos and images on the Internet or in old magazines to make into a "hero" collage instead. **AS**

Objectives
- Make connections from text to self
- Activate prior knowledge

617

UNIT 6 GENRE FOCUS: FOLKTALE, FANTASY, AND MYTH

Focus

BELLRINGER Options

- **Daily Language Practice Transparency 52**
  Focus Activity Say: In this unit, we will be reading three different types of stories: folktales, fantasies, and myths. What are some stories you've heard or read that could fit into these categories? *(Responses will vary.)* **OL**

Teach

R Reading Skill

How to Read Folktale, Fantasy, and Myth Ask: How will each reading skill help you understand folktales? *(Possible responses:* ***Activating prior knowledge:*** *It helps to rethink what you already know about the characters, topic, or setting before you start reading;* ***Clarifying:*** *Asking yourself questions as you read helps you make sure you understand the story;* ***Comparing and contrasting:*** *Thinking about how parts of the story are similar and different helps you understand the story;* ***Predicting:*** *Making guesses about what will happen next keeps you interested in what you're reading.)* **OL**

Skills Focus
- Key skills for reading folktales, fantasies, and myths
- Key literary elements of folktales, fantasies, and myths

Skills Model
You will see how to use the key reading skills and literary elements as you read
- "Persephone," p. 619

Objectives (pp. 618–623)
Reading • Activate prior knowledge • Clarify meaning • Compare and contrast • Make predictions
Literature Read folktales, fantasies, and myths • Identify key literary elements: hero, cultural context, theme, and setting

A **folktale** is a story that has been told by generations of storytellers before being written down. The story may be just fun, or it may teach a lesson about life. In this unit, you will also read fantasies and myths. A **fantasy** creates a new world very different from the world we live in today. A **myth** is usually about gods, goddesses, and large questions such as the origin of the earth, the sea, and the seasons.

Why Read Folktale, Fantasy, and Myth?

Folktales, fantasies, and myths take you to places, times, and people you never before imagined. They make you think about what's important to you and to all human beings. And they're fun to read!

How to Read Folktale, Fantasy, and Myth

Key Reading Skills

These skills are especially useful tools for reading folktales, fantasies, and myths. You'll learn more about these skills later in the unit.

- **Activating prior knowledge** Before you read, recall what you already know about the characters, topic, or the setting you'll read about. (See Reading Workshop 1.)
- **Clarifying** As you read, ask yourself questions about the plot, characters, setting, and point of view of the story to make sure you understand it. (See Reading Workshop 2.) **R**
- **Comparing and contrasting** As you read, compare and contrast within the story. Also compare and contrast different stories or styles to each other. (See Reading Workshop 3.)
- **Predicting** Make guesses about the characters and events in the story as you learn more about them. (See Reading Workshop 4.)

Key Literary Elements

Recognizing and thinking about the following literary elements will help you understand more fully what the writer is telling you.

- **Hero:** a literary work's main character, usually one with admirable qualities. A hero can be either male or female, but a female hero is sometimes called a *heroine* (HAIR oh un). (See "Hurricane Heroes.")
- **Cultural context:** shared qualities and beliefs of people living in a particular time and place (See "The Twelve Labors of Hercules.")
- **Theme:** the main idea of a story (See "Dragon, Dragon.")
- **Setting:** the time and place of a story (See "Aunt Millicent.")

Additional Support

Literature Focus Lesson

Folktale, Fantasy, and Myth The subtle differences in meaning between folktales, fantasies, and myths may be difficult for students to grasp. Explain that sometimes the characteristics of these forms of literature overlap. For example, a story could have the characteristics of both a myth and a fantasy.

Students may be familiar with creation myths or folktales from their cultures. Ask them to talk about and share these stories. If possible, bring in some picture books from your school library that illustrate folktales, fantasies, and myths from around the world. **AS**

PERSEPHONE

by Alice Low

Myth

> **ACTIVE READING MODEL**

Persephone[1] was a high-spirited, sunny girl who loved springtime and flowers and running outdoors with her friends. She was the daughter of Demeter,[2] goddess of the harvest, and she and her mother spent more time on earth than on Mount Olympus.[3]

One bright day on earth Persephone was picking lilies and violets with her friends. She could not gather enough of them, though her basket was overflowing. **1 2**

"Persephone, it is time to go home," called her friends.

"Just one minute longer," she called back. "I see the sweetest flower of all—a narcissus, I think. I must have one." She wandered into a far corner of the meadow, and just as she was about to pick the narcissus, she heard a deafening noise. Suddenly the earth split open at her feet. Out dashed a golden chariot pulled by black horses and driven by a stern-faced man in black armor.

Persephone dropped her basket and started to run, but the driver grabbed her by the wrist. He pulled her into

Four Seasons – Spring, (detail), 1896. Alphonse Mucha.
Analyzing the Art Do you think the young woman in this painting is a lot like Persephone? Why or why not?

---

1. **Persephone** (pur SEF uh nee)
2. **Demeter** (dih MEE tur)
3. **Mount Olympus** (oh LIM pus) is a tall mountain in Greece. People in ancient Greece believed the main gods and goddesses lived on top of this mountain.

1 Key Reading Skill
Activating Prior Knowledge *I know that things happen in myths that can't happen in real life. Gods and goddesses in myths had power over people's lives.*

2 Key Reading Skill
Clarifying *I have a feeling this story will mention several things that I don't understand very well. I'll take notes in my Learner's Notebook so I can find out about them and remember them. First, I'll write down Mount Olympus.*

619

Teach

R1 Reading Skill

Activating Prior Knowledge Say: Think about what you already know about Greek and Roman myths. At what point in time do they usually take place? *(Possible response: long ago; in ancient times)* **OL AL**

R2 Reading Skill

Clarifying Say: When you come across a word you don't know in a selection, you can stop and look for context clues to help you clarify its meaning. According to context clues, what is the meaning of *narcissus?* *(a sweet flower)* **Ask:** What is a *chariot?* *(a vehicle pulled by horses)* **EL BL**

Readability Scores
Dale-Chall: 5.5
DRP: 55
Lexile: 860

Differentiated Instruction

Spatial Learning Students with strong spatial abilities can use drawing to help themselves and other students visualize characters, setting, and key story events. As students read the story, have them stop and make drawings whenever they form strong visual impressions. They may also choose to add captions or labels to their drawings. Hades would be a good subject. Students could portray him as he appears to Persephone. Spatial learners may find these sketches very useful references for understanding the story. **AS**

Objectives

- Activate prior knowledge
- Clarify ideas and text
- Analyze features of genres: folk tales, fantasies, myths

619

Teach

L1 Literary Element

Setting Ask: What clues can you use to help you picture the time and the land of ancient Greece? *(Possible responses: The artwork shows people with long hair and flowing robes; the text describes chariots, gods, goddesses, and royalty; the text mentions Mount Olympus.)* **OL**

L2 Literary Element

Review Conflict Ask: At this point in the story, what seems to be the conflict? *(Hades takes Persephone away against her will.)* **OL**

L1

Pluto and Proserpine, 1914. Henry Bryson Burroughs. Oil on canvas, 24 x 36¼ in. National Academy Museum, New York.
Analyzing the Art Pluto and Proserpine are other names for Hades and Persephone.

his chariot, which descended back into the earth as quickly as it had risen. Then the earth closed up after it.

Persephone screamed and wept, but her friends could not hear her. Though they searched for her everywhere, all they found was her basket, with a few crushed flowers lying next to it.

Down into the earth the chariot sped, through dark caverns and underground tunnels, while Persephone **L1** cried, "Who are you? Where are you taking me?"

"I am Hades,[4] king of the underworld, and I am taking you there to be my bride."

"Take me back to my mother," screamed Persephone. "Take me back."

"Never!" said Hades. "For I have fallen in love with you. Your sunny face and golden hair will light up my dark palace." **3**

The chariot flew over the river Styx[5] where Charon,[6] the boatman, was ferrying ghostly souls across the water. "Now we are at the gate to my kingdom," said Hades, as they landed next to the huge three-headed dog who guarded it.

---

4. In Greek mythology, the god **Hades** (HAY deez) ruled the **underworld,** a place under the earth where the dead lived.
5. **Styx** (stiks)
6. **Charon** (KAR un)

ACTIVE READING MODEL

3 Key Reading Skill
Comparing and Contrasting
So far, I know that Persephone is a high-spirited and sunny girl. How is she different from Hades? Let's see, it says that Hades is stern-faced and wears black armor. How are they alike? Well, one is a goddess and the other is a god.

Additional Support

English Language Coach

Greek Mythology: Names This story includes many characters with Greek names. Some students may have trouble keeping track of who is who. On the board, create a list of the following names: Persephone, Demeter, Hades, Charon, Cerberus, Triptolemus, Helios, Zeus, and Hermes. As each character appears in the story, ask students to suggest key words that relate to the character. For example, a key word for Persephone could be *daughter* and for Demeter, *mother*. Add the key words to the list of characters. Use a similar strategy for the places mentioned: Mount Olympus, the river Styx, and Eleusis. **EL BL**

Persephone shivered, and Hades said, "Oh, that is Cerberus.[7] He guards the gate so that no live mortals enter and no souls of the dead escape. Nobody escapes from the underworld."

R1 Persephone became speechless. Never escape from this terrible place full of pale, shadowy ghosts, wandering through stony fields full of pale, ghostly flowers!

Beautiful Persephone, who loved sunshine, became Hades' queen and sat on a cold throne in his cold palace. Hades gave her a gold crown and bright jewels, but her heart was like ice and she neither talked nor ate nor drank.

R2 Persephone's mother, Demeter, knew that something terrible had happened to her daughter. She alone had heard Persephone's screams, which had echoed through the mountains and over the sea.

Demeter left Olympus, disguised as an old woman, and wandered the earth for nine days and nine nights, searching for her daughter. She called to the mountains and rivers and sea, "Persephone, where are you? Come back. Come back." But there was never an answer. She did not weep, for goddesses do not cry, but her heart was heavy. She could not eat or drink or rest, so deep was her grief. **4 5**

Finally she reached a placed called Eleusis, not far from the spot where Persephone had disappeared. There a prince named Triptolemus[8] recognized her and told her this story: "Over a week ago, my brother was taking care of the royal pigs. He heard a thundering noise, and the earth opened up. Out rushed a chariot, driven by a grim-faced man. He grabbed a beautiful young girl and down into the earth they went. They were swallowed up, along with the pigs."

"That man must have been Hades," cried Demeter. "I fear that he has kidnapped my daughter."

Demeter hurried to the sun, Helios,[9] who sees everything. And the sun confirmed Demeter's fears.

---

7. **Cerberus** (SUR buh rus)

8. **Triptolemus** (TRIP tuh lee mus)

9. **Helios** (HEE lee us)

4 Key Literary Element

Setting *The settings so far have been earth, the underworld, and Mount Olympus. There hasn't been much description of what Olympus is like, but the underworld seems really scary and creepy.*

5 Key Reading Skill

Comparing and Contrasting *Persephone and her mother react in similar ways when Persephone is first captured. Persephone is quiet and her heart is like ice. She doesn't eat or drink. Her mother Demeter can't eat or drink, and she becomes stony. But Persephone is helpless while Demeter has the power to help her daughter.*

Teach

R1 Reading Skill

Comparing and Contrasting

Ask: How is the underworld similar to the earth above? How is it different? *(Possible response: Both places have fields and flowers, but in the underworld, the fields are stony and the flowers are pale and ghostly.)* **BL OL**

R2 Reading Skill

Predicting Say: Demeter alone heard her daughter's cries for help. What do you think she will do, knowing that something terrible has happened to her daughter? *(Possible response: She may set out to search for her daughter herself or try to get help from the other gods and goddesses.)* **OL**

Literature Focus Lesson

Heroes Prompt students to begin thinking about who the hero may be in this story. Students are likely to be familiar with heroes from watching movies and TV, playing computer games, or reading comic books and magazines. Ask students to name fictional characters whom they think are heroic. Have students create lists of those characters in their Learner's Notebooks. Then have students choose one hero from the list and write a brief paragraph explaining how that character is a hero. **OL**

Objectives
• Identify literary elements: hero, setting
• Make predictions
• Compare and contrast

621

Teach

L Literary Element

Hero **Ask:** What qualities does Demeter have that make her heroic? *(Possible response: She is persistent; she does not give up.)* **Say:** Write an entry in your Learner's Notebooks that tells what you admire most about Demeter and her actions. *(Responses will vary.)* **OL**

C Critical Thinking

Comprehension **Ask:** Why does Zeus agree to help rescue Persephone? *(The earth is not bearing fruit, and Demeter says it won't unless her daughter returns.)* **BL** **Ask:** On what one condition does Zeus say he will be able to help Persephone? *(on the condition that she has not eaten the food of the dead)* **OL**

Demeter cried, "Persephone, my gay lovely daughter, is imprisoned in the underworld, never again to see the light of day or the flowers of spring."

Then Demeter became stony and angry, and she caused the earth to suffer with her. The earth became cold and barren. Trees did not bear fruit, the grass withered and did not grow again, and the cattle died from hunger. A few men succeeded in plowing the hard earth and sowing seeds, but no shoots sprouted from them. It was a cruel year for mankind. If Demeter continued to withhold her blessings from the earth, people would perish from hunger.

C Zeus begged Demeter to let the earth bear fruit again, but Demeter said, "The earth will never be green again. Not unless my daughter returns!"

Then Zeus knew that he must take action to save people from starvation. "I will see that Persephone returns," he told Demeter, "but only on one condition. She must not have eaten any of the food of the dead."

Zeus sent Hermes, messenger of the gods, down to the underworld to ask Hades for Persephone's release. When Persephone saw that Hermes had come to her home, she became lively and smiled and talked for the first time that year.

To her delight, Hades did not protest but said, "Go, my child. Although I love you, I cannot keep you here against Zeus's will. But you must eat a little something before you leave, to give you strength for your journey." Then he gave Persephone several seeds from a red pomegranate, which was the fruit eaten by the dead. He knew that if she ate even one, she would have to return to him. **6**

Persephone ate four seeds quickly. Then she climbed into the golden chariot and waved good-by. Hermes drove her to earth, to the temple where Demeter waited, and mother and daughter hugged and laughed and said they would never be parted again. Then Demeter remembered Zeus's warning and said,

The Return of Persephone, 1891. Frederic Leighton. Oil on canvas. Leeds Museums and Galleries, U.K.

Analyzing the Art This painting shows the return of Persephone to her mother. Who is each person in this painting? How do you know?

ACTIVE READING MODEL

6 Key Reading Skill
Predicting *Uh-oh. I think Zeus will make her go back to Hades because he said she can't eat any food of the dead.*

Additional Support

Reading Fluency

Building Fluency To develop fluency, students should hear good models, practice with properly leveled materials, and evaluate their own progress. One way to help students develop fluency is to pair them and have them read aloud to one another from different sections of the text. Ask each listener to keep a record of the other person's miscues and errors. Then have partners switch roles. After individual practice, they can repeat the activity until their fluency improves. **EL BL OL**

"I hope you did not eat anything while you were in the underworld."

"I was too sad to eat," said Persephone. "I didn't eat or drink all year."

"Not anything at all?" said Demeter.

"Oh, just a few little pomegranate seeds before I left," said Persephone. Why do you ask?"

"Because, my dearest," cried Demeter, "if you have eaten any of the food of the dead, you must return to Hades."

Zeus heard the loud wails of Demeter and her daughter, and he decided to compromise. Persephone must spend just four months of each year in the underworld, one for each of the seeds she had eaten. The rest of the year she could be with her mother on earth. **7**

That is why every year, for four months, the earth becomes cold and barren. Persephone is in the dark underworld and Demeter is overcome with grief. **8**

And every year, when Persephone returns to earth, she brings spring with her. The earth is filled with flowers and fruits and grasses. And summer and fall, the seasons of growth and harvest, follow in their natural order. Every year Demeter and the whole earth rejoice that Persephone has returned. **9** ○

Write to Learn Answer these questions in your Learner's Notebook.

1. Most ancient Greeks believed that their myths were true. Why do you think they believed the myth of Persephone?

2. What myths do people today believe in? What myths do you believe in?

ACTIVE READING MODEL

7 Key Literary Element
Hero *By the literary definition, Persephone is the hero of this story because she's the main character. But Demeter acts more like a* <u>real-life hero</u> *because she does all she can to save her daughter.*

8 Key Literary Element
Theme *I think the theme of the myth is that the gods control everything and even the other gods have to obey Zeus.*

9 Key Literary Element
Cultural Context *People in ancient Greece believed that gods and goddesses controlled everything, including the seasons.*

Study Central Visit www.glencoe.com and click on Study Central to review folktale, fantasy, myth.

Reading in the Real World

Career Myths helped people understand the forces of nature before there were scientific explanations. The story of Persephone explains why there are different seasons. Today, scientists study Earth to provide information about climate and weather and how they affect life. Ask your librarian to provide resource material on careers in meteorology, biology, ecology, and geography to share with the class or have students gather information from the Internet. Then have students work in groups to create posters that explain the change of seasons as scientists understand the process today. **OL AL**

UNIT 6 GENRE FOCUS

Teach

L Literary Element

Cultural Context **Say:** The times that people live in can affect their folktales and myths. Why were people in ancient Greece likely to believe this myth? *(Possible response: In those ancient times, people did not know the scientific reasons for the changing seasons.)* **Ask:** Why is it less likely that people of today would believe this myth? *(Possible response: Today, people know more about science. There are scientific facts that explain why the seasons change.)* **OL**

Study Central Have students access the Web site to review folktale, fantasy, and myth and to complete a related activity.

Objectives
• Identify literary elements: hero, cultural context
• Monitor comprehension

623

Activating Prior Knowledge

Objective covered in this workshop:
• Activate prior knowledge

Teaching Students to Activate Prior Knowledge

Why Is It Important?

• Teaching students to activate prior knowledge helps them use their experience and knowledge to better understand a selection.

• Research has proven that activating prior knowledge increases comprehension.

• Students who activate prior knowledge are better readers.

How to Help Students Get It

• Emphasize that reading is an interactive process—the author and the reader both participate.

• Reading is interactive when you combine your experiences and knowledge with the words in the text to produce meaning.

• Emphasizing that your students have unique experiences and knowledge helps them feel empowered when reading selections.

• Regardless of how foreign the subject may seem to students, helping them activate prior knowledge on even minor points in the selection can give them the confidence and interest they need to gain meaning from a selection.

Reading to Answer the Big Question

Hurricane Heroes by Thomas Fields-Meyer, Steve Helling, and Lori Rozsa
Three ordinary people are profiled in this *InTIME* article about heroic responses to the devastation on the Gulf Coast caused by hurricanes. The heroes' actions are recounted, and comments from the heroes themselves about how and why they acted as they did are included.

All Stories Are Anansi's by Harold Courlander
In this West-African folktale, Anansi the spider must perform three formidable tasks in order to buy all the stories of the world from the Sky God. Anansi uses his wits to defeat hornets, a python, and a leopard. As a result, Anansi's own heroic story has become a legend.

Workshop Resources

Pacing (days)		Lesson	Student Materials	Teacher Resources
Standard	Block			

1	½	Key Skill Lesson: Activating Prior Knowledge	⚒ Key Reading Skills Practice, p. 9
			⚒ English Language Coach Review, p. 43
				⚑ Bellringer Options Transparencies
				  – Selection Focus Transparency 14
				  – Daily Language Practice 53
				⚑ Read Aloud, Think Aloud Transparencies
				  – Key Reading Skills 1
				◉ Presentation Plus!

1	1	"Hurricane Heroes"	💻 Glencoe Online ⚒ Unit Vocabulary Review, p. 41 ⚒ Academic Vocabulary Review, p. 44 📁 English Language Coach ⚒ Active Reading Graphic Organizer, p. 11 ⚒ Literary Analysis, p. 10 ◉ StudentWorks Plus™ 💻 Online Student Edition ◉ Literature Classics 📁 Selection and Unit Assessments, p. 61	⚑ Literary and Text Analysis Transparencies 21 💻 Puzzlemaker ◉ Skill Level Up!™ A Language Arts Game 💻 BookLink 3 📘 Assessment by Learning Objective (Diagnostic and Formative) ◉ Interactive Tutor: Self-Assessment ◉ TeacherWorks Plus™
1		"All Stories Are Anansi's"	💻 Glencoe Online ⚒ Unit Vocabulary Review, p. 41 ⚒ Academic Vocabulary Review, p. 44 📁 English Language Coach ⚒ Active Reading Graphic Organizer, p. 13 ⚒ Literary Analysis, p. 10 ◉ StudentWorks Plus™ 💻 Online Student Edition ◉ Literature Classics 📁 Selection and Unit Assessments, p. 62	⚑ Read Aloud, Think Aloud Transparencies – Read Aloud, Think Aloud 51–54 ⚑ Literary and Text Analysis Transparencies 21 💻 Puzzlemaker ◉ Skill Level Up!™ A Language Arts Game 💻 BookLink 3 📘 Assessment by Learning Objective (Diagnostic and Formative) ◉ Interactive Tutor: Self-Assessment ◉ TeacherWorks Plus™

Keys for Unit Resource

- 📁 Blackline Master
- 📘 Workbook
- 📖 Supplemental Text
- ◉ CD-ROM
- 💾 DVD
- ⚑ Transparency
- 💻 Web-based
- ⚒ Fast File

Level Appropriate Code

- **AS** = Activities for all students
- **AL** = Activities for students working above grade level
- **OL** = Activities for students working at grade level
- **BL** = Activities for students working below grade level
- **EL** = Activities for English language learners

Focus

BELLRINGER Options

- **Selection Focus Transparencies 14**
- **Daily Language Practice Transparency 53**

Focus Activity Say: Think about what you already know about severe weather. Have you ever seen a big storm? How did it make you feel? *(Responses will vary.)* **AS**

Teach

R Reading Skill

Activating Prior Knowledge Say: When you think about things you know from past experience, you are activating prior knowledge. Describe an everyday situation in which you used prior knowledge. *(Possible responses: taking a test in school; answering questions for homework; dressing properly for the weather)* **OL**

Skills Focus

You will practice using these skills when you read the following selections:

- "Hurricane Heroes," p. 628
- "All Stories Are Anansi's," p. 636

Reading

- Activating prior knowledge

Literature

- Distinguishing real-life heroes from literary heroes
- Understanding the heroes of folktales

Vocabulary

- Understanding compound and blended words

Writing/Grammar

- Capitalizing sentences
- Identifying simple sentences

Objectives (pp. 624–625)
Reading Activate prior knowledge

624 UNIT 6

Skill Lesson

Activating Prior Knowledge

Learn It!

What Is It? Activating prior knowledge means using what you already know to understand what you are reading. This could be information you have already read or knowledge from your own experiences. Activating prior knowledge makes it easier to understand something new. For example, if you used what you already knew about Greek myths, it would be easier to understand "Persephone."

- To activate something is to make it active, to get it going so it can be useful.
- Prior knowledge is knowledge you already have—facts and experiences you remember or information you know.
- Activating prior knowledge is using what you know, or what you've already read to help clarify your understanding.

R

CALVIN AND HOBBES © 1995 Watterson. Dist. By UNIVERSAL PRESS SYNDICATE. Reprinted with permission. All rights reserved.

Analyzing Cartoons
Calvin didn't activate his prior knowledge in this cartoon. What should he have remembered about snowballs?

Additional Support

Reading in the Real World

Citizenship Be on the lookout for articles in your local newspaper about people in your community who are heroes. Have students read and listen to the news for stories of extraordinary citizenship. As you and your students find local examples, read them out loud to the class. You can post them on a bulletin board and encourage students to read from the board when they are between assignments. **BL OL AL**

Why Is It Important? Activating prior knowledge helps you understand what you read. It can help you guess about the meanings of related things. And it can help you predict what might happen.

How Do I Do It? Before you read, skim the text to see what it might be about. Then think about what you already know about that topic. Here's how one student used her prior knowledge of myths to understand the first paragraph of "Persephone."

Literature Online

Study Central Visit www.glencoe .com and click on Study Central to review activating prior knowledge.

> Persephone was a high-spirited, sunny girl who loved springtime and flowers and running outdoors with her friends. She was the daughter of Demeter, goddess of the harvest, and she and her mother spent more time on earth than on Mount Olympus.

> *I know myths usually have gods and goddesses. Since Persephone is the daughter of a goddess, this is probably a myth. I know that gods and goddesses in myths have supernatural powers. It sounds like Mount Olympus isn't on earth, so I bet that's where the gods and goddesses live.*

Practice It!

Below are some topics and genres related to the selections in this unit. What do you already know about each topic or genre? In your Learner's Notebook, write two things you know about each subject.

- folktales
- myths
- hurricanes
- heroes

Use It!

As you read from "Hurricane Heroes" and "All Stories Are Anansi's," remember what you wrote in your Learner's Notebook about hurricanes and folktales. Use this knowledge to help you understand what you read.

Teach

Literature Online

Study Central Have students access the Web site to review activating prior knowledge and to complete a related activity.

R   Reading Skill

Activating Prior Knowledge
Say: Look at the sections titled Why Is It Important? and How Do I Do It? How would you explain the skill of activating prior knowledge to someone who is unfamiliar with it? *(Possible response: Look quickly at your reading to see what you already know about the topic. Then use what you already know to help you understand what you read.)* **BL OL**

Resources for page 625

📖 Use Key Reading Skills Transparency 1 in *Read Aloud, Think Aloud* to help students practice activating prior knowledge.

Differentiated Instruction

Weather Research Have students do research on the weather in your area. Ask students to create a chart of the different kinds of weather from the mildest to the most severe. Have them use the following questions to guide their research: What seasons do we have?

What is the worst our weather ever gets? What do people in the area do in case of severe weather such as a hurricane or blizzard? How else does the weather affect us? Hold a class discussion on the impact of weather on your area and the people who live there. **OL**

Objective
• Activate prior knowledge

625

Teach

More About the Writers

- Thomas Fields-Meyer is no stranger to writing about real-life heroes. While working for *People* magazine, he contributed to a five-part series called "Heroes Among Us."

- Steve Helling has been a contributing writer for *People* magazine since 2000. He's covered stories in the U.S., the Caribbean, and South America.

- While reporting for the *Miami Herald* in the 1990s, Lori Rozsa became a hero herself by helping get an innocent man off death row.

EL Language Coach

Compound Words Have each student write a compound word on an index card (for example, *snowball*). Then have students cut the cards in half to separate the two words *(snow, ball).* Mix up all the card halves and work as a class to form as many different compound words as you can. **OL**

Before You Read : Hurricane Heroes

Meet the Authors

This selection is about actual events and was written by three authors: Thomas Fields-Meyer, Steve Helling, and Lori Rozsa. Each author reports on current events for news sources such as *People* magazine and the *Miami Herald*.

Literature Online
Author Search For more about the writers, go to www.glencoe.com.

Objectives (pp. 626–631)
Reading Activate prior knowledge
• Make connections from text to self
Literature Identify literary elements: hero
Vocabulary Explore word origins: compound words

Vocabulary Preview

makeshift (MAYK shift) *adj.* suitable as a temporary substitute **(p. 628)** *After a hurricane, makeshift hospitals need to be set up.*

anesthetist (uh NES thuh tist) *n.* the person who gives drugs to put a patient to sleep before surgery **(p. 629)** *It is important to have an anesthetist on an emergency medical team.*

Write to Learn Make a one-panel illustration for each word that shows the word's meaning. Add a caption explaining the illustration. Use the actual word in the caption.

English Language Coach

Compound Words Many words have interesting histories. Some come from the names of people or places. *Teddy bear,* a small stuffed bear, is named for President Teddy Roosevelt. *Hamburger,* a patty of ground meat, comes from Hamburg, Germany. Other words like *mailbox* and *riverbank* come from joining two existing words. *Mailbox* and *riverbank* are compound words. **Compound words** are made up of two or more words. One way that words enter the English language is by combining words to make new words.

You can often figure out the meaning of these compound words by thinking about the meanings of the words that make it up. For example, *mailbox* is a compound word made up of *mail* and *box.* It means "a box in which mail is deposited."

Compound words are hyphenated (like *well-known*), open (like *hot dog*), or closed (like *eggshell*). There's only one simple, clear rule to help you know which way to write a compound: Check a dictionary. **EL**

Partner Talk With a partner, talk about the individual words that form the compound words below. Then match each compound word with its definition below.

1. cry + baby
2. book + case
3. heart + ache

a. sorrow or grief
b. a person who often complains
c. shelves for books

Additional Support

Literature Online

Author Search To expand students' appreciation of the writers, have them access the Web site for additional information and resources.

English Language Coach

Etymology Explain to students that the etymology of a word is its history. The Mayan storm god is called Hunraken, and the Quiche god of thunder and lightning is known as Hurakan. As in the story of Persephone, severe weather was attributed to these gods. The Spanish word *huracan* and the English word *hurricane* evolved from these names. Other forms of severe weather include earthquakes, tsunamis, tornadoes, and cyclones. Have students conduct research on the Internet or in the library to find the etymology of these other storm-related words. **AL**

Skills Preview

Key Reading Skill: Activating Prior Knowledge

Before you read, think about the terrible hurricanes that have hit the U.S. and other places around the world. What do you remember from watching TV, reading, or hearing about hurricanes?

Class Talk With your class, discuss the responses to hurricanes that you remember.

Key Literary Element: Hero

There are three main definitions of the word **hero**.

- **Literary Hero** As you learned in the Genre Focus, the word *hero* has a specific meaning in literature. The hero of a story is the main character, who may or may not have admirable qualities. The most important character in the Genre Focus story is Persephone, and that makes her the hero. Once, most people would have called her the *heroine,* which was the term used for female main characters.

- **Mythic Hero** In mythology, the word *hero* can have another meaning. A *mythic hero* is usually a man who is superhuman and may even be half-god, half-human. This kind of hero has amazing courage and strength and the myths are about his adventures.

- **Real-Life Hero** The last definition of the word *hero* is the one we're all most familiar with: a person who acts bravely for the good of others, often putting his or her own life at risk.

Partner Talk Next you'll read about real-life heroes. With a partner, talk about what makes a real-life hero different from a literary or mythic hero.

Interactive Literary Elements Handbook
To review or learn more about the literary elements, go to www.glencoe.com.

Get Ready to Read

Connect to the Reading

Have you ever survived a difficult experience or a life-threatening situation? What was it? How did you get through? Imagine what it's like to survive something like a hurricane. What would it take for you to risk your life for someone else?

Write to Learn What kind of situation would it take for you to risk your life to try to save someone else's? In your Learner's Notebook, write for five minutes about the kind of situation that might cause you to take action.

Build Background

Hurricanes are large, severe storms with heavy rains and strong winds. You are about to read an article about a series of hurricanes that occurred in 2004 and did a great deal of damage to the southern part of the United States.

- Many hurricanes form over the Atlantic Ocean in the summer and then move west toward the U.S.
- Hurricanes are given names to help identify them and track their movements.
- The center of a hurricane is called "the eye." An eye is roughly circular, and the weather tends to be calm inside the eye.

Set Purposes for Reading

BIG Question Read "Hurricane Heroes" to find out how average people can become heroes when faced with an emergency.

Set Your Own Purpose What else would you like to learn about "Hurricane Heroes"? Write your own purpose on the "Hurricane Heroes" page of Foldable 6.

Keep Moving

Use these skills as you read the following selection.

Hurricane Heroes **627**

Teach

L Literary Element

Hero Say: Many movies tell stories about a hero's quest or the struggle between good and evil. What makes these movies exciting to watch? *(Possible response: They are suspenseful; we root for the "good guy.")*

R Reading Skill

Review Connecting Say: Think about a time when you or someone you know helped someone else stay safe or escape from danger. How did it make you feel to help someone else? *(Responses will vary.)* **OL**

Interactive Literary Elements Handbook Have students access the Web site to improve their understanding of heroes.

Literature Focus Lesson

Informative Nonfiction All types of writing have a main purpose, or an objective. The main purpose of most fiction is to entertain by telling a story. Nonfiction is about real people, events, and places. Informative nonfiction, one type of nonfiction, conveys facts and information. Its main purpose is to inform readers about a topic. However, few pieces of writing are confined to a single purpose. A single article may inform, persuade, and entertain all at the same time, but usually it will have one main purpose. Discuss with students what they think the writers' main purpose was in writing the article. **OL**

Objectives
- Identify literary element: hero
- Explore word origins
- Make connections from text to self
- Learn and use new vocabulary
- Analyze features of genres: nonfiction

Teach

R Reading Skill

Activating Prior Knowledge

Say: Think about a time when you were upset or your feelings were hurt. Now look at the first subhead. What do you think it means to have an invisible wound? *(Possible response: to be hurting emotionally, but not physically)* **OL** **Ask:** If you survived a hurricane without being hurt physically, what "invisible wounds" might you have? *(Possible responses: being scared; the loss of my home and my possessions; being worried that it might happen again)* **AL**

Readability Scores
Dale-Chall: 4.9
DRP: 57
Lexile: 910

TIME

HURRICANE HEROES

As storms slammed the South in 2004, some brave folks risked their lives to help others.

By **THOMAS FIELDS-MEYER, STEVE HELLING,** and **LORI ROZSA**

Charley, Frances, Ivan, Jeanne: four hurricanes in six weeks; more than 150 deaths and $44 billion in damage. Faced with wrecked bridges, shattered condos, floods, and mudslides, millions of people in Florida, Georgia, and Alabama had to decide when to flee, what to save, or whom to help. Meet three people who made it through and helped many others along the way. **1**

A Medical Marathon[1]

Ron Wegner treated wounds—some invisible

Wegner, 57, commander of Florida's 35-member Disaster Medical Assistance Team, spent several weeks living in Charley's and Ivan's disaster zones. He put in 20-hour shifts and helped treat everything from broken bones to heart attacks. Still, he says his most memorable patient was an 83-year-old woman. She came into the **makeshift** emergency

1. Originally, a ***marathon*** was a 26-mile foot race. Now the word is also used to refer to anything that lasts a long time and is difficult to bear.

Vocabulary

makeshift (MAYK shift) *adj.* suitable as a temporary substitute

628 UNIT 6 What Makes a Hero?

1 Key Reading Skill

Activating Prior Knowledge
Think about what you read in Build Background about hurricanes; add what you know about past hurricanes, like Hurricane Katrina. Activate that knowledge to help answer this question: Why does this paragraph begin with four names?

Additional Support

Reading Fluency

Teacher Read Aloud Read the introduction and the first profile aloud to the class. Instruct students to read silently to themselves as you read aloud. Suggest that students fold a piece of paper into a narrow strip and move it down the page line by line as an aid to keeping track of what is being read. Emphasize that students should keep up with your voice even if they don't know all of the words. **EL** **BL**

unit in the parking lot of a damaged Pensacola hospital where Wegner was stationed after Ivan. She showed him a bruise on her hand. "She admitted she hadn't really been injured, but her house was destroyed and she was alone, and she wanted to talk to somebody. So for 25 minutes I held her hand and we talked," he says. "Really, her problem was just as important as a chain-saw accident."

Wegner is an **anesthetist** who lives in Tampa. Like all of the disaster volunteers, Wegner was paid by the federal government what he would usually have earned in his regular job. Wegner is the nerve center of the medical team. "He's the ringmaster of the circus," says Butch Kinerney, a **spokesperson** for the Federal Emergency Management Agency.[2] In the first three days after Ivan, Wegner's team treated 460 people. Though he misses his girlfriend and 25-year-old daughter, there were no complaints from Wegner. "We've got our comfortable lives to go back to," he says. "A lot of these people have nothing." **2 3 4**

Karena Cawthorn/Silver Image

"You see so many people just wandering about stunned," says Ron Wegner (in Gulf Breeze, Florida).

He Came, He Saw, He Sawed

Jim Williams went out on many limbs

Driving to work the morning after Hurricane Charley ripped through Sanford, Florida, mail carrier Williams was so stunned by the number of fallen trees he saw that he had to pull over. The area "was just devastated," says Williams, 45, who grew up in the quiet community 25 miles north of Orlando. "I sat in my truck and cried."

---

2. The **Federal Emergency Management Agency** responds to natural and manmade disasters. It's often referred to by its initials, FEMA (FEE muh). The agency has helped many thousands of people recover from disasters; however, it was severely criticized for its slow, inadequate response after Hurricane Katrina hit Gulf Coast states in 2005.

Vocabulary

anesthetist (uh NES thuh tist) *n.* the person who gives drugs to put a patient to sleep before surgery

---

2 English Language Coach

Compound Words
Spokesperson is a compound word. It means "one who speaks on behalf of others."

3 Key Literary Element

Hero What differences do you notice between Wegner and a typical literary hero? Use evidence from this article to support your answer. **L**

4 Key Reading Skill

Activating Prior Knowledge
What do you think a "nerve center" is? Nerves send messages back and forth to the brain. What do you already know about a center? Combine those things with what you've already read to think about what a nerve center does.

Hurricane Heroes **629**

Teach

EL Language Coach

Compound Words Ask:
What other compound words can you identify in this paragraph? *(Possible responses: ringmaster; girlfriend)* **EL BL**

L Literary Element

Hero Ask: What are some characteristics of a literary hero? *(Possible response: He or she represents good; he or she must be strong to defeat the enemy; he or she might boast about his or her strength.)* Ask: How is real-life hero Wegner similar to a literary hero? How is he different? *(Possible responses: He is a good person; he does not boast about his physical strength.)* **OL**

Reading in the Real World

Career Paramedics, emergency room doctors and nurses, hospital administrators, electricians, phone technicians, truck drivers, firefighters, and police officers are necessary personnel in emergency situations. If possible, assign students to research what education and training is needed for each of these careers. Alternately, provide students with information on each career and ask them to read about it. Then have students use what they've learned about each career to answer the Big Question. Have them write their responses in their Learner's Notebooks. **OL**

Objectives
• Activate prior knowledge
• Identify compound words
• Identify literary element: hero

Teach

R Reading Skill

Activating Prior Knowledge
Ask: Is your neighborhood important to you? How would you feel if something bad happened to the place where you grew up? *(Responses will vary.)* **OL**

C Critical Thinking

Evaluation Ask: Why did Baldwin ask her fiancé to tell her parents that she loves them? *(Possible response: The hurricane was so frightening that Baldwin thought she might not survive. It was her way of saying goodbye in case she didn't live through it.)* **AL**

Then he took action. Returning home, Williams grabbed his chain saw and headed to the home of a friend's parents, where two huge oak trees had fallen. He sawed the rest of the day to clear the couple's driveway. Every day for the next three weeks, Williams delivered the mail through the cleanup from Charley and Frances. But he also spent hours after work using his chain saw wherever he could help—particularly outside the homes of retired people along his 18-mile mail route.

Williams spent nearly five hours clearing a 40-foot oak from atop the home of Ginny Taffer, 79, and husband Gene, 83. "He was my angel," says Ginny. What motivates Williams? He says that when his son James, 10 (with wife Gail, 47; he also has a daughter Leah, 16), was ill with lymphoma[3] at 6, he made a pledge to help people. Besides, he adds, "I was raised right and taught to do the right thing." **5**

Trapped in a Collapsing Hotel

Melissa Baldwin fought her fears and saved her guests

On August 13, 2004, the fierce winds of Charley ripped the roof off of a wing of the Best Western Waterfront in Punta Gorda, Florida. Fearing for her life, Melissa Baldwin, assistant manager of the motel, phoned her fiancé, Ted Barkenquast, from the front lobby. "Tell Mom and Dad I love them," she yelled as windows shattered around her. Then the phone went dead. Recalls Barkenquast: "All I could do was think the worst."

But the storm brought out the best in Baldwin, 33, who suffers from epileptic seizures[4] that can be brought on by

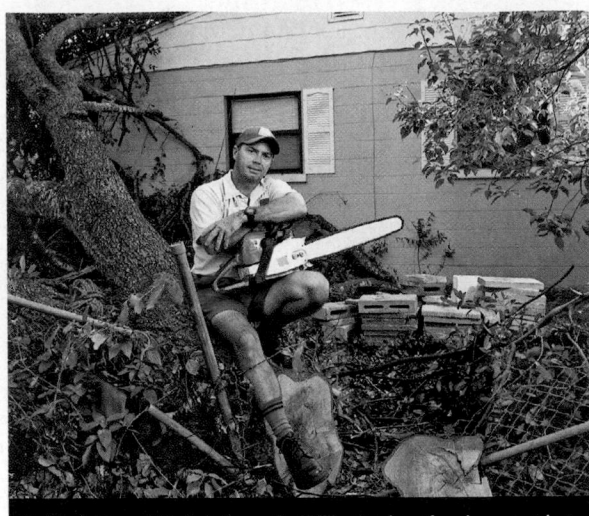
"I did what I could to help," says Jim Williams, who refused payment but did accept one offering: a pecan pie.

Ben Baker/Redux

5 Key Reading Skill

Hero Do you think Williams is a hero? Why or why not? Use details from this article to support your answers.

---

3. **Lymphoma** is a kind of tumor.

4. **Epilepsy** is a nervous-system disorder that causes attacks called **seizures**. A seizure may include loss of consciousness and violent shaking of the body.

Additional Support

Differentiated Instruction

Compare and Contrast Chart Three people are profiled in this article. On the board, create a chart that has three columns. Put the name of one of the three people profiled in the article at the top of each column. Ask students to list the details about each person in the column below his or her name. Have students compare and contrast the three people. Students can also draw a chart in their Learner's Notebooks and fill it in independently. **OL**

stress. "I figured if I was going to go down, I'd go down saving lives," she says. She raced upstairs to the fifth floor. Then working her way down, she moved 56 guests and employees to a windowless second-floor hall. Baldwin also ran outside and gathered people from a building next door. "It sounded like a freight train was going through the building. The wind was screaming, and people were screaming," she recalls. "I honestly thought, *So this is how I'm going to die.*"

Unable to move an elderly man in room 112, she helped him into a **bathtub** and cushioned his body with pillows. When one woman resisted, "I said, 'I'm not over-reacting. Just trust me,'" says Baldwin. The hurricane pounded the hotel so hard that walls collapsed and **air-conditioning** units were ripped away from the building. When the winds died down after midnight, Baldwin handed a list of the 56 guests—all breathing and unharmed—to a rescue worker. The worker marveled, "I can't believe you're all alive." **6 7**

Says Baldwin's coworker Lee Phillips, "Melissa was so comforting to the guests. If there were 15 of me, I don't think I could have been as comforting. She didn't crack." Baldwin is just happy everyone scraped through. "I don't know if I'll ever get over it," she says. "But the hurricane helped show me how strong I really am." **8**

—Updated 2005, from *PEOPLE*, October 4, 2004

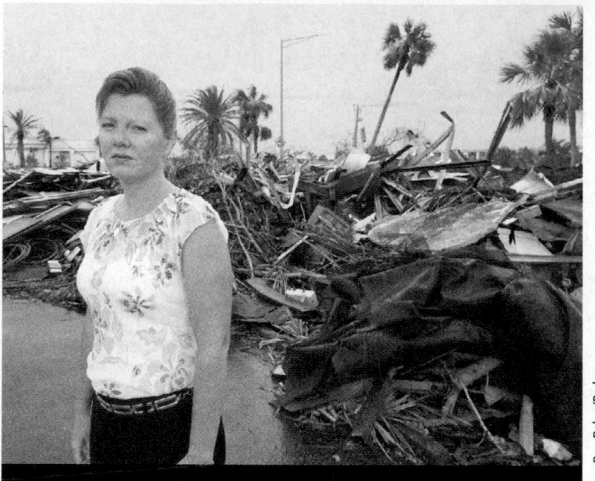

"I didn't have time to be scared," says Melissa Baldwin (at the hurricane-devastated Best Western).

Ben Baker/Redux

6 Key Literary Element

Hero Is Baldwin a hero? Why or why not? Use details from this article to support your answers.

7 English Language Coach

Compound Words **Bathtub** is always a closed compound. **Air-conditioning** is hyphenated when it's an adjective, but it can be either open or hyphenated when it's a noun.

8 BIG Question

Does this article change your idea about how a hero can find his or her strength? Write your answer on the "Hurricane Heroes" page of Foldable 6. Your response will help you complete the Unit Challenge later. **BQ**

Hurricane Heroes **631**

Teach

Viewing the Photos

Ask: How do the photos in this article help illustrate the stories? *(Possible response: The photos show the massive devastation caused by each of the hurricanes mentioned in the article. This illustrates the incredible power of the storms and the amazing courage that these heroes must have had to have been able to carry on in spite of the destruction.)* **AL**

BQ

Ask: How would you find your strength in a terrible situation? Choose one person from the article. If disaster struck, what advice do you think that person would give you? *(Responses will vary.)* **OL**

Assess

✔CheckPoint

Use the CheckPoint questions provided on Presentation Plus! to check for comprehension of the selection. These questions can be used with interactive response keypads for immediate student feedback.

Differentiated Instruction

Kinesthetic Activity Students with strong kinesthetic abilities may benefit from using movement to help themselves visualize key events and emotions. As students read the article, have them stop whenever they form a strong impression of motion and act out that impression. They may choose to swoop down like the hurricane-force winds, mimic the behavior of someone fleeing, or act out the toppling of a tree or building. Kinesthetic learners will find this experience very useful. **AS**

Objectives
• Activate prior knowledge
• Evaluate text
• Identify compound words

Assess

Resources for page 632

- 📁 Selection Quick Check, p. 51
- 📁 Selection and Unit Assessment, p. 61
- 💿 ExamView Assessment Suite
- 💿 Interactive Tutor: Self-Assessment

Students can respond to the *After You Read* items in their Learner's Notebooks or on a separate sheet of paper.

Answering the
BIG Question

1. Possible response: Sometimes people don't know how strong they are until extreme events put them to the test.

2. Ron Wegner: Charley and Ivan; Jim Williams: Charley and Frances; Melissa Baldwin: Charley

3. Possible response: He continued to deliver the mail and helped clear fallen trees.

Critical Thinking

4. Possible response: The heroes may not have reacted as strongly if they had not been in their hometowns.

5. Possible response: The writers presented facts about the hurricanes and the heroes' reactions to them. They presented opinions in quotes from the real-life heroes and those they helped.

6. Responses will vary.

After You Read | Hurricane Heroes

Answering the BIG Question

1. How might extreme events make heroes out of ordinary people?

2. **Recall** Name one real-life hero that you just read about, and give the name of the hurricane that he or she responded to.
   TIP Think and Search

3. **Summarize** What did Jim Williams do after the hurricane?
   TIP Think and Search

Critical Thinking

4. **Synthesize** Do you think the people in the article would have behaved similarly had these events unfolded before their eyes in another community? For example, if they were on vacation in another country and a hurricane struck, would they have reacted the same way? Explain.
   TIP On My Own

5. **Evaluate** Did the authors present facts, opinions, or both? Did the authors persuade you that the people in the article are real-life heroes? Explain.
   TIP Author and Me

6. **Analyze** Do you think the people described in this story always had heroic qualities or do you think they found special strength and courage when faced with an emergency? Explain.
   TIP On My Own

Talk About Your Reading

With a partner, talk about events or situations that would bring out the real-life hero in you. Would it be a natural disaster, or do you think you would be the kind of hero to stand up for a good cause? Consider the situations in "Hurricane Heroes." Think about what you already know about heroes. Use these questions to get started.

- Do you think you would be more likely to take action in an emergency, or would you be more likely to champion a cause?

- What kind of emergencies need heroes? What kind of causes need champions?

- In what ways can you start taking action to become a real-life hero right now?

Objectives (pp. 632–633)
Reading Activate prior knowledge • Make connections from text to self
Literature Identify literary elements: hero
Vocabulary Explore word origins

632 UNIT 6 What Makes a Hero?

Talk About Your Reading

Students should talk about circumstances that would bring out heroic qualities in them. Those circumstances could be an emergency situation or standing up for a good cause. Students may think of other kinds of circumstances that would make them react heroically. Students should mention the kinds of emergencies that require heroes and the kinds of causes that need champions.

Skills Review

Key Reading Skill: Activating Prior Knowledge

7. Did you activate knowledge about hurricanes beyond the facts presented in Build Background? If you hadn't known anything about hurricanes, would you still have been able to understand this article? Explain your answers.

8. Besides what you knew about hurricanes, did other prior knowledge help you to understand the article? For example, did knowing what a circus ringmaster (page 629) does help you see what Jim Wegner did on his medical team? Find two examples of words or ideas that made you activate prior knowledge to understand things in the article.

Key Literary Element: Hero

9. This article describes three different people that the writers consider heroes. Describe what made them heroes. Use details from the article.

10. Which person do you admire the most? Why?

11. Describe how this article might be different if it were a myth about hurricanes and the heroes were magical.

Vocabulary Check

Choose the best word from the list to complete each sentence below. Rewrite each sentence, with the correct word in place.

anesthetist   makeshift

12. Trailers are sometimes used as ___ housing after a hurricane.

13. The work of the ___ is to stop the feeling of pain.

English Language Coach Combine each word in the first column with a word in the second column. Each new word should be a compound word.

14. grand   port
15. news   board
16. down   father
17. card   paper
18. air   town

Grammar Link: Capitalization of Sentences

It's important to capitalize the first letter of each word at the beginning of a sentence so readers can tell where one sentence ends and the next sentence starts. All complete sentences start with a capital letter.

Grammar Practice

Copy these sentences, capitalizing the first word of every sentence.

19. my sister studies hard. she wants to go to college one day.

20. few people have a chance to be heroes. everyone can practice being kind.

21. hurricanes can be horrible. their effects can last for years.

22. our neighbor coaches soccer in his spare time. many of the kids see him as a hero.

Writing Application Write a short summary of the discussion you had with your partner for Talk About Your Reading on page 632. Be sure to capitalize the first letter of each word that begins a sentence.

Web Activities For eFlashcards, Selection Quick Checks, and other Web activities, go to www.glencoe.com.

Hurricane Heroes **633**

Skills Review

Key Reading Skill: Activating Prior Knowledge

7. Responses will vary.

8. Responses will vary.

Key Literary Element: Heroes

9. Responses will vary.

10. Responses will vary.

11. Responses will vary.

Vocabulary Check

12. makeshift

13. anesthetist

English Language Coach

14. grandfather

15. starlight

16. downtown

17. cardgame

18. airport

Close

Ask students to summarize what they learned about the Big Question from reading the article.

Web Activities Have students access the Web site for interactive activities that will help them assess their understanding of the selection.

Grammar Link: Capitalization of Sentences

Grammar Practice
The following words should be capitalized:

19. My; She

20. Few; Everyone

21. Hurricanes; Their

22. Our; Many

Teach

More About the Author

Harold Courlander was born in 1908 and died in 1996. He collected folktales from various parts of the world, especially Africa. Courlander was most interested in tales that showed the values of the people from whom the stories came. "All Stories Are Anansi's" was first published in 1957.

EL Language Coach

Borrowed Words Point out to students that many dictionary entries provide the name of the language from which a word comes. To demonstrate this, have students look up the two parts of the word *television*: *tele* and *vision*. **Ask:** From which languages do *tele* and *vision* come and what are their meanings? *(tele: Greek; "far off, afar"; vision: Latin; "sight")* **OL**

Before You Read : All Stories Are Anansi's

Harold Courlander

Meet the Author

Like all folktales, this story was passed around by word of mouth long before it was written. This version is a retelling by Harold Courlander. Courlander has always had a special interest in using narration to improve cross-cultural communication. See page R2 of the Author Files for more on Harold Courlander.

Author Search For more about Harold Courlander, go to www.glencoe.com.

Objectives (pp. 634–639)
Reading Activate prior knowledge
• Make connections from text to self
Literature Identify literary elements: hero
Vocabulary Explore word origins: borrowed words

Vocabulary Preview

yearned (yurnd) *v.* had a strong desire; form of the verb *yearn* **(p. 636)** *Anansi yearned to own all the stories in the world.*

dispute (dis PYOOT) *n.* a difference of opinion; argument or quarrel **(p. 637)** *Anansi had a dispute with his wife; they disagreed about the strength of the python.*

accustomed (uh KUS tumd) *adj.* used to; familiar with **(p. 638)** *The leopard didn't expect a trap because he was accustomed to walking in that area.*

merely (MEER lee) *adv.* just; only **(p. 639)** *Anansi wasn't merely confident, he was also very clever.*

acknowledge (ak NOL ij) *v.* to recognize the truth of something **(p. 639)** *According to this folktale, we must acknowledge that all stories belong to Anansi.*

Write to Learn Write a paragraph about something you want to do, using at least three of the vocabulary words above.

English Language Coach

Borrowed Words English has always been a mix of languages, especially Anglo-Saxon, Latin, and Greek. Modern English continues to change by adding new words from languages around the world. Such words are called **borrowed words.** The word *safari,* for example, came from Africa. *Coffee* came from Arabia, and *ketchup* from China! As you can see, many borrowed words are so familiar that we would never imagine they came from other languages. **EL**

Partner Talk Many of the foods we eat came from other countries and so did their names. *Pizza* is Italian, and *chili* is Mexican. With a partner, list as many borrowed food names as you can.

634 UNIT 6 What Makes a Hero?

Additional Support

Author Search To expand students' appreciation of Harold Courlander, have them access the Web site for additional information and resources.

English Language Coach

Borrowed Words Other examples of borrowed words include the following:

• From German: *kindergarten, schlep, nickel, quartz*
• From Swahili: *safari, Kwanza, jenga* (meaning to build, the name of a game)

• From French: *ballet, language, village*
• From Spanish: *canyon, rodeo, patio*

Talk with students about how words from other languages enter the English language. **AS**

Skills Preview

Key Reading Skill: Activating Prior Knowledge

Before you read the story, think about what you know about

- folktale heroes
- folktales about animals
- animals that live in Africa

Class Talk Think of other folktales that you have read. Have someone write the names of folktales on the board as class members think of them. Take turns naming the hero in each folktale. Then name a heroic action or characteristic of the hero.

Key Literary Element: Hero

Heroes in myths are often brave and strong and may even have supernatural powers. However, many cultures have folktales about a different kind of hero—a trickster. A trickster may be physically weak, but is able to use humor and cunning to get what he or she wants. As you read this story, use these tips to decide whether you admire the trickster hero, Anansi:

- Decide if he's physically strong compared to other characters. Decide if he's smart compared to other characters.
- Think about what he wants and how he gets it.
- Decide how the humor in the story affects the way you view Anansi.

Partner Talk With a partner, make a list of other trickster characters you know about. To help you remember more characters, look up the word *trickster* in an encyclopedia or on the Internet.

Literature Online

Interactive Literary Elements Handbook To review or learn more about the literary elements, go to www.glencoe.com.

Get Ready to Read

Connect to the Reading

Think of a time when you were tricked by someone or when you played a trick on someone else. As you read, pay attention to how Anansi uses trickery to become a hero.

Build Background

Anansi is a favorite character in many African and Caribbean folktales. A spider-man, he is shown as either a spider or as a man with spider characteristics. Anansi is a trickster who tries to make everything turn out the best way possible—for himself. His tricks are surprising, clever, and fun to read about.

- The trickster is usually a smaller, weaker character, who must use his or her brains to outsmart a larger and more powerful opponent.
- Clever tricksters get themselves out of trouble, but in many stories they get right back into it.
- Tricksters who try to take advantage of others and change the rules to favor themselves often end up caught in their own mischief.

Set Purposes for Reading

BIG Question Read "All Stories Are Anansi's" to find out if Anansi, the trickster, has the qualities of a real-life hero.

Set Your Own Purpose What else would you like to learn from "All Stories Are Anansi's"? Write your own purpose on the "All Stories Are Anansi's" page of Foldable 6.

Keep Moving

Use these skills as you read the following selection.

All Stories Are Anansi's **635**

Teach

L Literary Element

Hero Say: Think about stories you've read or movies you've seen in which a small or weak character triumphs over a large or strong character. How do stories like this make you feel? Do you admire characters who overcome their physical size to outsmart someone bigger or stronger? *(Responses will vary.)* **OL**

R Reading Skill

Review Connecting Ask: Do you think that it is ever okay to use a trick to help yourself out of a difficult situation? Why or why not? *(Responses will vary.)* **OL**

Interactive Literary Elements Handbook Have students access the Web site to improve their understanding of heroes.

Literature Focus Lesson

Origin Tales "All Stories Are Anansi's" is an African folktale about the origin of the world. Explain to students that the earliest people must have looked at the world around them and wondered how it came to be. Origin tales are folktales that answer questions about how things began. Often, the stories pass along a group's values and offer explanations of how things work. Have students conduct research in the library or on the Internet to find other origin tales from around the world. Have them work in small groups to put these stories together in a resource pamphlet titled "Origin Tales." **OL**

Objectives

- Form blended words
- Identify literary elements: hero
- Make connections from text to self
- Analyze features of genres: origin tales

635

Teach

Viewing the Art

Say: Look at the image of the African mask on this page. How might this mask reflect Anansi's attitude? *(Possible response: The mask reflects the trickster Anansi's self-confident and cunning nature.)* **AL**

L Literary Element

Hero Say: Think about how Anansi answers, "I can do it" before he hears what the price is. What heroic characteristic is Anansi showing here? *(Possible response: He is showing confidence in his own abilities.)* **OL**

Readability Scores
Dale-Chall: 5.2
DRP: 47
Lexile: 610

All Stories Are ANANSI'S

by Harold Courlander

Mask (Okorashi Oma). African Nigeria. Wood and pigment, 10½ x 6¾ x 4 in. Harn Museum of Art. University of Florida

IN THE BEGINNING, ALL TALES AND STORIES BELONGED TO Nyame,[1] the Sky God. But Kwaku Anansi, the spider, **yearned** to be the owner of all the stories known in the world, and he went to Nyame and offered to buy them. **1**

The Sky God said: "I am willing to sell the stories, but the price is high. Many people have come to me offering to buy, but the price was too high for them. Rich and powerful families have not been able to pay. Do you think you can do it?"

Anansi replied to the Sky God: "I can do it. What is the price?"

"My price is three things," the Sky God said. "I must first have Mmoboro, the hornets. I must then have Onini, the great **python**. I must then have Osebo, the leopard. For these things I will sell you the right to tell all stories." **2**

Anansi said: "I will bring them."

_____

1. **Nyame** is pronounced (en YAH may).

Vocabulary

yearned (yurnd) *v.* had a strong desire

636 UNIT 6 What Makes a Hero?

Practice the Skills

1 Key Reading Skill

Activating Prior Knowledge
What do you know about the importance of stories? Why would Anansi want to own all of the stories? What do you know about folktales that will help you understand this trickster tale? Think about what you learned in the Build Background.

2 English Language Coach

Borrowed Words The snake that we call the **python** got its name from a monstrous snake in mythology. Its Greek name was *Pythōn.*

Additional Support

Differentiated Instruction

Visual Vocabulary Familiarize students with the animals in the story: *spider, hornet, python,* and *leopard.* Show students pictures of these animals so that they can visualize them as they read. Talk with the class about how these animals are alike and how they are different in size, appearance, and tempera- ment. Then have students create a visual vocabulary dictionary in their Learner's Notebooks that includes the images and descriptions of the animals discussed above. Students can draw images by hand or search for images online or in old magazines. **EL BL**

Visual Vocabulary
A *calabash* (KAL uh bash) is a kind of gourd, or hard-shelled fruit.

He went home and made his plans. He first cut a gourd from a vine and made a small hole in it. He took a large calabash and filled it with water. He went to the tree where the hornets lived. He poured some of the water over himself, so that he was dripping. He threw some water over the hornets, so that they too were dripping. Then he put the calabash on his head, as though to protect himself from a storm, and called out to the hornets: "Are you foolish people? Why do you stay in the rain that is falling?"

The hornets answered: "Where shall we go?"

"Go here, in this dry gourd," Anansi told them.

C The hornets thanked him and flew into the gourd through the small hole. When the last of them had entered, Anansi plugged the hole with a ball of grass, saying: "Oh, yes, but you are really foolish people!"

He took his gourd full of hornets to Nyame, the Sky God. The Sky God accepted them. He said: "There are two more things."

Anansi returned to the forest and cut a long bamboo pole and some strong vines. Then he walked toward the house of Onini, the python, talking to himself. He said: "My wife is stupid. I say he is longer and stronger. My wife says he is shorter and weaker. I give him more respect. She gives him less respect. Is she right or am I right? I am right, he is longer. I am right, he is stronger."

When Onini, the python, heard Anansi talking to himself, he said: "Why are you arguing this way with yourself?"

R The spider replied: "Ah, I have had a **dispute** with my wife. She says you are shorter and weaker than this bamboo pole. I say you are longer and stronger." **3**

Onini said: "It's useless and silly to argue when you can find out the truth. Bring the pole and we will measure."

Vocabulary

dispute (dis PYOOT) *n.* a difference of opinion; argument or quarrel

Untitled, 1990. Twins Seven-Seven. African ink on plywood with plywood collage. The Pigozzi Collection, Geneva.

3 ▮ **English Language Coach**

Borrowed Words The word **bamboo** comes from an unusual source—Malay. That's one of the languages used by people in Southeast Asia. They spell it *bambu.*

All Stories Are Anansi's **637**

Teach

Viewing the Art
Ask: How does this image help illustrate the story? *(Students may say that the image seems to show a spider-like man who looks as though he is more powerful than the other figures.)* **OL**

C Critical Thinking

Evaluation Ask: What can you tell about Anansi from his interactions with the other animals? *(Possible responses: He is very clever, and he tricks the other animals easily; he is smarter than the other animals.)* **OL**

R Reading Skill

Activating Prior Knowledge
Say: Use your prior knowledge to predict how the python will react to this situation. *(Possible response: The python will be tricked by Anansi just as the hornets were.)* **OL**

Reading in the Real World

Citizenship Storytelling as an art form is alive and well in the world today. Some family stories, told orally from generation to generation, become more myth than fact because details are added every time the story is retold. Ask students to work in pairs or in small groups to tape-record stories told by someone they know. Suggest that before they go for the taped interview they prepare some questions: When did the event in the story take place? Who was there? What did they do? How was it done? Why did they do it? The tape-recorded stories can then be retold orally to the class by each student. **AS**

Objectives
• Activate prior knowledge
• Identify literary elements: hero
• Evaluate text
• Find meaning in art

Teach

R Reading Skill

Review Connecting Ask: Does Anansi remind you of anyone you know in real life? Do any parts of the story remind you of experiences you have had? *(Responses will vary. Students may say that they know someone who is good at outsmarting others.)* **AS**

C Critical Thinking

Analysis Ask: Why does Anansi tell Osebo that he is afraid of getting eaten? How will this benefit Anansi? *(Possible response: Anansi is reminding Osebo of how much smaller and weaker a spider is than a leopard. Osebo is more likely to trust Anansi if he thinks Anansi is afraid of him.)* **OL**

So Anansi laid the pole on the ground, and the python came and stretched himself out beside it.

"You seem a little short," Anansi said.

The python stretched further.

"A little more," Anansi said.

"I can stretch no more," Onini said.

"When you stretch at one end, you get shorter at the other end," Anansi said. "Let me tie you at the front so you don't slip."

He tied Onini's head to the pole. Then he went to the other end and tied the tail to the pole. He wrapped the vine all around Onini, until the python couldn't move.

"Onini," Anansi said, "it turns out that my wife was right and I was wrong. You are shorter than the pole and weaker. My opinion wasn't as good as my wife's. But you were even more foolish than I, and you are now my prisoner."

Anansi carried the python to Nyame, the Sky God, who said: "There is one thing more."

Osebo, the leopard, was next. Anansi went into the forest and dug a deep pit where the leopard was **accustomed** to walk. He covered it with small branches and leaves and put dust on it, so that it was impossible to tell where the pit was. Anansi went away and hid. When Osebo came prowling in the black of night, he stepped into the trap Anansi had prepared and fell to the bottom. Anansi heard the sound of the leopard falling, and he said: "Ah, Osebo, you are half-foolish!"

When morning came, Anansi went to the pit and saw the leopard there.

"Osebo," he asked, "what are you doing in this hole?"

"I have fallen into a trap," Osebo said. "Help me out."

C "I would gladly help you," Anansi said. "But I'm sure that if I bring you out, I will have no thanks for it. You will get hungry, and later on you will be wanting to eat me and my children." **4**

Relief from one of the chapels off the Hypostyle Hall, Great Temple of Seti (13th century B.C.), Abydos. Temple of Seti I, Abydos, Egypt.

Vocabulary

accustomed (uh KUS tumd) *adj.* used to; familiar with

4 | **Key Literary Element**

Hero How does Anansi's behavior with the hornets and the python show that he is a trickster hero?

Additional Support

Reading Fluency

Build Fluency Small groups of students can take turns reading the story aloud. Encourage students to read smoothly, with expression and understanding. As each student takes a turn, the other students can follow along in the book. When the story is finished, ask students to talk about words, sentences, or sections that they especially liked or that they found difficult. **BL OL**

"I swear it won't happen!" Osebo said.

"Very well. Since you swear it, I will take you out," Anansi said.

He bent a tall green tree toward the ground, so that its top was over the pit, and he tied it that way. Then he tied a rope to the top of the tree and dropped the other end of it into the pit.

"Tie this to your tail," he said.

Osebo tied the rope to his tail.

"Is it well tied?" Anansi asked.

"Yes, it is well tied," the leopard said.

"In that case," Anansi said, "you are not **merely** half-foolish, you are all-foolish."

And he took his knife and cut the other rope, the one that held the tree bowed to the ground. The tree straightened up with a snap, pulling Osebo out of the hole. He hung in the air head downward, twisting and turning. And while he hung this way, Anansi killed him with his weapons. **5 6**

Then he took the body of the leopard and carried it to Nyame, the Sky God, saying: "Here is the third thing. Now I have paid the price."

Nyame said to him: "Kwaku Anansi, great warriors and chiefs have tried, but they have been unable to do it. You have done it. Therefore, I will give you the stories. From this day onward, all stories belong to you. Whenever a man tells a story, he must **acknowledge** that it is Anansi's tale."

In this way Anansi, the spider, became the owner of all stories that are told. To Anansi all these tales belong. **7** ○

Practice the Skills

5 **Reviewing Skills**

Identifying Problem and Solution After Anansi caught the leopard in a pit, he had to solve the problem of how to get him out of the pit. What was his solution?

6 **Key Literary Element**

Hero In what way or ways is Anansi a typical literary hero?

7 **BIG Question**

Does Anansi have qualities you admire in real-life heroes? On the "Anansi" page of Foldable 6, write a short paragraph to support your answer. Use examples from the story. Your response will help you complete the Unit Challenge later.

All Stories Are Anansi's **639**

Teach

L Literary Element

Hero Say: Think about the kinds of "weapons" that literary heroes use to win their battles. List a few heroic traits that might be considered weapons. *(Possible responses: goodness; strength; courage)* **Say:** Now think about a trickster hero such as Anansi. He is not big or strong. What is his greatest weapon? *(Possible responses: his determination; his cleverness)* **OL**

BQ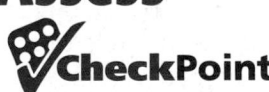

Ask: What qualities of Anansi's do you admire? What are some things you do not like about Anansi? *(Responses will vary. Students may say that they like his cleverness but do not admire his dishonesty.)* **OL**

Assess

CheckPoint

Use the CheckPoint questions provided on Presentation Plus! to check for comprehension of the selection. These questions can be used with interactive response keypads for immediate student feedback.

Differentiated Instruction

Drama After reading the story once, divide students into groups and assign each group a section of the story. Give each group time to plan a pantomime of its section. The pantomime does not have to be scripted, but the group could, for example, assign a character to each person. Then, have each group act out the action as you read the story aloud a second time. Watching and listening will reinforce the story for students who might have had trouble understanding it the first time it was read. **EL BL OL**

Objectives
• Make connections from text to self
• Identify literary elements: hero
• Analyze text

Assess

Resources for page 640

📁 Selection Quick Check, p. 52

📁 Selection and Unit Assessment, p. 62

🔘 ExamView Assessment Suite

🔘 Interactive Tutor: Self-Assessment

Students can respond to the *After You Read* items in their Learner's Notebooks or on a separate sheet of paper.

Answering the

1. Possible response: Yes. He is small and weak and must use his brains to outsmart the other characters.

2. Anansi said that he and his wife were having an argument about who was longer and stronger—the pole or the python. The python agreed to have himself measured.

3. He had to capture hornets, a python, and a leopard and bring them to the Sky God.

Critical Thinking

4. Possible response: The folktale is like a myth because things happen in it that could not happen in real life. Also, it includes gods.

5. Possible response: It shows that Anansi has pride and confidence.

6. Possible response: No, the folktale is being told as an amusing story that will entertain people.

7. Responses will vary.

640

After You Read | All Stories Are Anansi's

Answering the **BIG Question**

1. Do you think Anansi acts heroically?

2. **Recall** How did Anansi get the python to agree to be tied to a pole?
   Tip Right There

3. **Summarize** Summarize the three things Anansi had to do to pay for all the stories in the world.
   Tip Think and Search

Critical Thinking

4. **Identify** Name one way in which this folktale resembles a myth.
   Tip On My Own

5. **Infer** Anansi says he can pay Nyame's price before he knows what it is. What does that say about him?
   Tip Author and Me

6. **Analyze** Do you think the teller of this folktale expects the listener to believe that it really happened? Why or why not?
   Tip Author and Me

7. **Evaluate** Why do you think someone would want to own all the stories in the world?
   Tip On My Own

Write About Your Reading

Write a dialogue between Anansi and you. Anansi wants to take all of your stories about your life. You have to decide if you want to keep your stories or not.

- Start by having Anansi explain why he wants your stories. What will they give him? What is unique about your stories?

- Decide if you want to keep the stories about your life or if you will let them go so you can create new ones. Tell Anansi what you want to do. If you want to keep your stories, explain why. If you are willing to let him take your stories, tell him your price.

- Use words like "he said," "I asked," "he shouted," or "I whispered" to show who's talking and the emotions behind the words.

Objectives (pp. 640–641)
Reading Activate prior knowledge
• Make connections from text to self
Literature Identify literary elements: hero
Vocabulary Explore word origins: borrowed words
Writing Dialogue
Grammar Identify sentence types: simple; compound subject, compound predicate

640 UNIT 6 What Makes a Hero?

Write About Your Reading

Possible response:

Anansi said, "I want all the stories of your life. My life is boring and your stories will make mine more interesting."

"I will not give you my stories. Your life can be interesting only if you make it interesting. If you make your days fun and adventurous, you will have your own stories, and you will not need mine. Go and have fun for three days. Come back and tell me your stories. Then we will decide whether you still need mine," I said.

Anansi was afraid. "What if I get hurt?" he whispered.

"You will not get hurt," I said. "I will protect you for three days. Go. Have fun. Come back and we will talk again."

Skills Review

Key Reading Skill: Activating Prior Knowledge

8. In your Learner's Notebook, describe something you knew about folktales, trickster heroes, or Anansi before you read this story. Tell how the knowledge helped you understand or enjoy the story.

Key Literary Element: Hero

9. Name one thing that makes Anansi a literary hero.

10. Name one thing that makes Anansi a trickster hero.

11. Name one way in which Anansi is similar to a mythic hero.

Reviewing Skills: Identifying Problem and Solution

12. Anansi must convince the hornets that it is raining in order to get them to fly into his gourd. How does he solve that problem?

Vocabulary Check

Write your own fill-in-the-blank sentence for each vocabulary word below. Make sure you include enough clues for a classmate to fill in the correct word to complete the sentence. Exchange papers with a partner and fill in the blanks in each other's sentences.

13. yearned
14. dispute
15. accustomed
16. merely
17. acknowledge
18. **English Language Coach** Besides *pizza* and *chili,* list three foods Americans "borrowed" from other countries.

Grammar Link: Simple Sentences

A **simple sentence** has one complete subject and one complete predicate.

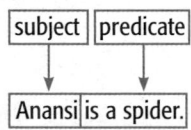

However, a simple sentence can have a compound subject, a compound predicate, or both.

Compound subject:
Lisa and Mike went to the store.

Compound predicate:
Many students read and enjoy novels.

Compound subject and predicate:
Lisa and Mike read and enjoy novels.

Grammar Practice

Decide whether each group of words below is a simple sentence. If it isn't a simple sentence, rewrite it in your Learner's Notebook as a complete simple sentence, adding the missing subject or predicate part.

19. Anansi was smart and cunning.   Yes   No
20. Anansi all the stories.   Yes   No
21. Anansi and Nyame made a deal.
    Yes   No

Writing Application Read the dialogue you wrote and underline the simple sentences. Sometimes it's okay to have sentence fragments in dialogue because people don't always talk in complete sentences.

Web Activities For eFlashcards, Selection Quick Checks, and other Web activities, go to www.glencoe.com.

All Stories Are Anansi's **641**

Skills Review

Key Reading Skill: Activating Prior Knowledge

8. Responses will vary.

Key Literary Element: Hero

9. Possible response: Anansi is the main character in the story.

10. Possible response: He devises clever ways to outsmart his enemies.

11. Possible response: He has great courage.

Reviewing Skills: Problem and Solution

12. Possible response: He pours water over himself and the hornets to trick them into thinking it was raining.

Vocabulary Check

Sample responses:

13. I ____ for a new bicycle.
14. I had a ____ with my friend.
15. I am ____ to getting up early every morning.
16. I thought a monster was in my closet, but it was ____ a shadow.
17. I ____ my mistake.
18. **English Language Coach** brunch

Close

Have students share their thoughts about how "All Stories Are Anansi's" helps them answer the Big Question.

Grammar Link: Simple Sentences

Grammar Practice

19. Yes
20. No; Anansi owns all the stories.
21. Yes

Web Activities Have students access the Web site for interactive activities that will help them assess their understanding of the selection.

Fable

Objectives covered in this workshop:
- **Writing** Create plot with characteristics of genre; develop appropriate voice
- **Grammar** Understand and use variety of sentence types; identify independent and dependent clauses

Teaching Students to Write a Fable

Why Is It Important?

- Fables are a traditional way of teaching lessons. Students who write their own fables will become more aware of the values of different times and cultures and of the shared values of their communities.

- The imaginative nature of the writing will encourage students to think outside the character roles that may initially come to them.

- Following the format of existing fables can give students the freedom or confidence to experiment with more complex sentence structure or vocabulary.

- Writing a fable will help students master the difference between a short fictional story and a fable.

- Creating a class binder of all the students' fables will foster a sense of involvement and community.

How to Help Students Get It

- Read and discuss two or three fables with the class.

- Give students examples of old sayings by writing some on the board and asking students to explain what each one means. Ask them to suggest old sayings that they have heard and tell whether or not they have seen them proven true. Then have the students choose or create an old saying or moral to use in their fable.

- Ask students to think about what characters, setting, and plot will best fit the theme of their fable.

- Fables are brief stories that usually get to the point quickly. Suggest that students consider describing who and where their characters are in their opening sentence of their story. For the sake of brevity, only necessary characters and plot details should be included in the fable.

- Suggest that students close their eyes and imagine themselves as characters stepping into their own fables. Have them imagine themselves walking around the scene, seeing the different elements they have described, such as setting, weather, characters, key objects, and so on. Then ask the students to "snap" mental photos of the events they visualized. Invite them to draw each "photo," including all the details they noticed.

- Suggest that students take a few minutes to think about an ideal audience. Will their audience be classmates, young children, or people the age of their parents? If a writer visualizes who the audience is and how he or she wants to affect that audience, the writer will use appropriate pacing and details, making the fable more effective.

- Have students use story maps to organize the elements of their fables.

- Remind students to maintain a consistent point of view in their fables. Most fables are told from the point of view of a third-person narrator.

- Remind students to include sensory details and dialogue in their fables.

Traits of Good Writing	
Ideas	the message or the theme and the details that develop it
Voice	Have students use the following checklist when checking their compositions: • Does your writing sound interesting when you read it? • Does your writing show what you think about your topic? • Does your writing sound like you—or does it sound like you're imitating someone else?
Organization	the arrangement of main points and supporting details
Word Choice	the vocabulary a writer uses to convey meaning
Sentence Fluency	the smooth rhythm and flow of sentences that vary in length and style
Conventions	correct spelling, grammar, usage, and mechanics
Presentation	the way words and design elements look on a page

Unit Focus

Workshop Resources

PACING (DAYS)		LESSON	STUDENT MATERIALS	TEACHER RESOURCES
STANDARD	BLOCK			
1	½	Writing Workshop Part 1: Prewriting and Drafting	👤 Writing Workshop Graphic Organizer, p. 15 👤 Grammar Practice, p. 16 👤 Spelling and Handwriting Practice, pp. 46–47 💻 Spelling Power eWorkbook 💿 Interactive Grammar and Language Workbook 📖 Grammar and Composition Handbook, p. 194 📁 Real Success in Writing: Research and Reports 📁 Writing Constructed Responses	💿 TeacherWorks Plus™ 💿 Presentation Plus! 📁 Rubrics for Assessing Student Writing, Listening, and Speaking, p. 23 ✎ Grammar and Writing Workshop Transparencies 11–12
2	1	Writing Workshop Part 2: Editing, Revising, and Presenting	💿 Interactive Grammar and Language Workbook 📖 Grammar and Composition Handbook, p. 194 📁 Real Success in Writing: Research and Reports 📁 Writing Constructed Responses 👤 Listening and Speaking, p. 29 👤 Viewing and Presenting, p. 30	✎ Grammar and Writing Workshop Transparencies 27–28 💿 Interactive Grammar and Language Workbook 📁 Rubrics for Assessing Student Writing, Listening, and Speaking, p. 23

Focus

Daily Language Practice Transparency 54
Focus Activity Say: Briefly summarize an experience you have had that taught you an important lesson. In this Writing Workshop you will write a fable that teaches a moral, or lesson about life. *(Responses will vary.)* **OL**

Teach

C Critical Thinking

Analysis Say: Your fable's theme will be the lesson it teaches about life. What lesson would you like your readers to learn from reading your fable? *(Responses will vary.)* **OL**

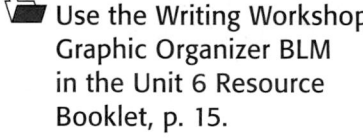

Resources for page 642

📁 Use the Writing Workshop Graphic Organizer BLM in the Unit 6 Resource Booklet, p. 15.

Use the Grammar and Writing Workshop Transparencies 11–12.

WRITING WORKSHOP PART 1

Fable
Prewriting and Drafting

ASSIGNMENT Write a fable

Purpose: To write a fable that teaches a moral

Audience: You, your teacher, and your classmates

Writing Rubric

As you work through this part of the workshop, you will

- describe a setting
- create characters
- develop a plot
- write dialogue
- develop voice

See page 703 in Part 2 for a model of a fable.

Objectives (642–645)
Writing Use the writing process: prewrite, draft • Write a fable • Use literary elements: setting, plot, dialogue, characterization, voice
Grammar Use compound and complex sentences

A fable is a folktale that's meant to teach a lesson about right and wrong. That lesson is called a *moral.* In "All Stories Are Anansi's," the moral is that brains are stronger than brawn (physical strength). Anansi is a small spider, but his cleverness tricks two larger animals and a swarm of hornets. In this workshop, you'll write your own fable.

Prewriting
Get Ready to Write

Before you start to write, you'll have to decide what moral you want your fable to teach. Think about phrases, sayings, or bits of wisdom that you have heard your parents or other family members say. Here are some suggestions:

- Honesty is the best policy.
- Big presents come in small packages.
- Slow and steady wins the race.

Write your moral in your Learner's Notebook.

Don't judge a book by its cover.

C

Create Your Characters

Characters in fables are often animals that behave like humans but still have animal qualities. Think about who your main and secondary characters will be. Write about them in your Learner's Notebook.

My main character is a beautiful peacock named Peter. He has long, beautiful feathers that magically change colors. My secondary character is a pig named Polly.

Create Your Setting and Plot

Fables often take place in the countryside. In your Learner's Notebook, write down where *your* fable will take place.

A forest

Additional Support

Differentiated Instruction

Partner Game If some students have trouble generating a moral, you can offer them a deck of index cards that has a moral written on each one. Pair the students and have them deal the cards between them and then take turns picking a card out of each other's hands.

They can keep morals that they like or agree with and discard ones they aren't interested in. As they play the card game, they will collect a group of morals from which they can choose one around which to build a fable. **BL OL**

Your fable should include a conflict, three main events, and a solution that tells the reader the moral of your story. In your Learner's Notebook write three main events.

> Peter and his friends are mean to Polly because Polly is not as beautiful as the peacocks. Polly makes herself look more attractive, but Peter and his friends laugh at Polly's efforts. Peter's feathers begin to fall out and his friends desert him.

Drafting

Start Writing

Tell Your Tale

This is the fun part—getting your fable on paper. Here are some tips to think about as you write:

- Start your story by describing the setting and the main character.

> Peter lived in the forest with the rest of his peacock friends. Peter was the most handsome peacock in the whole forest because his feathers magically changed from one magnificent color to another.

- Follow the order of your outline to write the rest of the fable.

> One day, Polly the pig walked by the pond where Peter and his friends were brushing their feathers . . .

Keep Going

- Don't worry about run-on sentences, spelling mistakes, or punctuation. You'll fix these things later in Writing Workshop Part 2.
- Write for ten minutes before taking a break.
- If you get stuck, look at the guide you made in your Learner's Notebook. That will tell you what to write next.

> ◄ **Writing Tip**
>
> The conflict in a fable is often connected to a contest, a race, or a challenge. Whatever you choose for a conflict, remember that it must make sense with the moral of your fable.

> ◄ **Writing Tip**
>
> The setting of a fable is usually not described in detail. This allows readers to use their imaginations.

> ◄ **Writing Tip**
>
> **Dialogue** Think about your character's voices. Who do they talk like? Your school principal? Your best friend? Do they use slang or big words? Pick a voice for each character and keep it the same throughout the fable. **W**

Teach

W **Writing**

Dialogue **Say:** The way a character speaks can tell a lot about him or her. Listen to these pieces of dialogue. After each one, list a few words that you think would describe the character who is speaking.

- "Pssst. Want to know a secret? But you can't tell anyone, 'cause it's about my best friend!" *(Possible responses: two-faced; gossipy)*

- "I am extremely well-educated and have advanced knowledge in calculus and chemistry." *(Possible responses: well-spoken; confident)*

- "Someone is hiding under my bed! I know it, I know it! Help me! Oops, it's just a shoe." *(Possible responses: cowardly; dramatic)* **OL**

Literature Focus Lesson

Fables Bring books of fables from the library into the classroom. Try to find books that include pictures. Allow students time to browse through the collection and talk about the fables they are familiar with. **AS** Assign several students to research Aesop's fables and present their findings to the class. They can use the following questions to guide their research:

- When did Aesop live?
- Where did Aesop live?
- Why did he love fables? **AL**

Objectives
- Write dialogue
- Use literary elements: plot, character, setting
- Write a fable
- Analyze text

Teach

W Writing

Voice Help students understand that they can change their writing voice when writing for different purposes and audiences. **Ask:** What kind of voice would you use to write

- a business letter asking for an after-school job? *(formal)*
- a letter to your cousin describing your new computer game? *(friendly)*
- a booklet of favorite jokes? *(humorous)*
- instructions for making a recipe? *(brief, direct)* **OL**

Assess

Have student partners exchange drafts and critique each other's work. Ask students to determine whether their partners included all the elements of a fable. After a few minutes, tell each student to assess his or her partner's feedback, make any needed revisions, and save the revised draft for later use.

Applying Good Writing Traits

Voice

People who know you well can probably identify you when you talk, even if they can't see you. You have a certain sound. You have a certain style of speaking. You choose certain words to express your thoughts and personality. All of these things are part of your *voice.*

What Is Voice?

Like your speaking voice, your writing voice reflects your thoughts and personality. Of course, readers don't hear you the way they do when you speak. However, they can "hear" you through the words you choose and how you put them together.

In some kinds of writing, like research reports and essays, your voice needs to be formal and proper. In creative writing, like a fable, you can be freer and less formal. You don't have to worry as much about grammar. You *do,* however, want your audience to be able to understand the story, so you can't ignore *all* the rules of grammar, spelling, punctuation, and capitalization.

Why Is Voice Important in My Writing?

- Writing in your own voice makes it easier to express your ideas, thoughts, and feelings.
- When you write in your own voice, your readers can tell that you care about the topic.
- Writing in your own voice makes your writing more interesting to read.
- Your writing voice is your "personality" on paper. When you write in your own voice, readers get to know the real you.

Analyzing Cartoons
What does the boy mean when he says "I've gotta be me . . . "? Is he trying to find his *voice?* Explain.

© 2000 Randy Glasbergen.

"I'VE GOTTA BE ME . . . BUT I CAN'T HELP THINKING SOMEONE ELSE WOULD BE MORE QUALIFIED!"

How Do I Do It?

To write in your voice try these suggestions:
- Write the kind of words that you use when talking.
- Write sentences the way you would say them.
- Share your thoughts and opinions about the topic.
- Make sure your writing sounds like you!

Write to Learn Activity In your Learner's Notebook, write a short paragraph about the folktale "All Stories Are Anansi's." Use your own voice to answer these questions in your paragraph:
- How did Anansi buy the stories from the Sky God?
- Do you think the way Anansi captured the other animals was fair? Why or why not?
- Would you want to be friends with a character like Anansi?

When you are finished, trade paragraphs with a partner. Underline words or phrases that you can tell are written in your partner's voice.

Additional Support

Differentiated Instruction

Role-Play To demonstrate voice, ask two students to role-play the following scenarios:

- A sixth grader telling her friend about a new video game she just bought
- A sixth grader telling his parents about a new video game he just bought

- A sixth grader talking to her teacher about a new video game she just bought

Ask listening students to discuss the changes in the students' voices in different scenes. **OL**

Grammar Link: Compound and Complex Sentences

Sentences are made up of independent clauses (which can stand alone as sentences) and dependent clauses (which cannot stand alone).

What Are Compound and Complex Sentences?

A **compound sentence** is made up of two or more independent clauses. (An **independent clause** can stand alone as a complete sentence.)

The clauses in a compound sentence can be joined together by a comma and a coordinating conjunction, such as *and*, *but*, or *or*.

Deeana likes to sing, and Johnny plays piano.
  independent   *independent*

A **complex sentence** has one main clause and one or more dependent clauses. (A **dependent clause** has a subject and a predicate, but it doesn't express a complete thought. It can't stand alone as a sentence.)

When Jai moved to Iowa, he made many friends.
  dependent   *independent*

Why Are Compound and Complex Sentences Important?

The best writing is made up of sentences that flow smoothly from one to another. Read your own writing aloud sometime. Does it have a smooth flow and rhythm? Or is it choppy and made up of lots of short sentences?

When you use compound and complex sentences along with simple sentences, your sentences will vary in length and structure. That helps them have a rhythm and a smooth flow.

How Do I Use Compound and Complex Sentences?

1. Use compound sentences to combine two sentences that are equally important.
   The bear was big.
   The turtle was slow.
   The bear was big, and the turtle was slow.

2. Use complex sentences to combine an important idea (independent clause) and a less important idea (dependent clause).
   Main Idea: The rabbit will win the race.
   Less Important Idea: The rabbit might trip and lose the race.
   Complex Sentence: The rabbit will win the race, unless he trips.

Practice It

The following paragraph uses only simple sentences. On a separate sheet of paper, rewrite the paragraph, changing simple sentences to compound or complex.

Last summer I went to the lake. I went swimming every day. My brother went swimming too. One day I caught a big fish. We built a fire. We cooked the fish. We slept in a cabin. We got up early every morning. We could catch a lot of fish early in the morning.

Looking Ahead

Continue writing the first draft of your fable. In Writing Workshop Part 2 you will revise and edit your draft.

Teach

Grammar Link

Compound and Complex Sentences Say: Listen to each pair of sentences. How can you combine each pair to make a compound or complex sentence?

- I was cold. I put on a sweater. *(Possible response: I was cold, so I put on a sweater.)*
- I like spinach. I don't like broccoli. *(Possible response: I like spinach, but I don't like broccoli.)*
- I have a dog. I have a cat. *(Possible response: I have a dog and a cat.)*
- My teacher needed a vacation. He was tired. *(Possible response: My teacher needed a vacation because he was tired.)*

Reading Fluency

Build Fluency Put students in pairs and do your best to place each pair in a quiet working space. Tell partners to work on their fables individually for 10 to 15 minutes and then take a break and read to each other what they have written. Encourage them to read their fables using a unique voice for each character. As students read to build fluency, they will also hear the voices they are creating. **AS**

Objectives
- Develop voice
- Use compound and complex sentences

Objective covered in this workshop:
• Clarify ideas and text

How to Help Students Clarify

Why Is It Important?

• Clarifying helps students clear up difficult portions of text.

• Students often need to clarify one idea before they can grasp another idea in a selection.

• When students develop clarifying skills, they become better readers and have more confidence in reading new passages.

How to Help Students Get It

• Tell students to reread sections that are not clear.

• Advise them to stop to clarify ideas before they get too far into a confusing text.

• Encourage students to use dictionaries to look up unfamiliar words and to enter the definitions in their Learner's Notebooks so they can review them.

• Emphasize the importance of context clues. What else is being said in the paragraph? Can this information help clarify the confusing part?

• Encourage students to practice several of the other reading strategies they have learned to clarify information. Questioning, responding, connecting, and activating prior knowledge can be particularly helpful when clarifying.

Reading to Answer the Big Question

The Twelve Labors of Hercules by Walker Brents
Hercules undertakes twelve heroic labors, each designed to be impossible. Students will read about many characters and settings from Greek mythology as Hercules travels far and wide to complete his quest.

Pecos Bill by Mary Pope Osborne
This tall tale is an amusing account of Pecos Bill's amazing adventures. The toughest cowboy who ever lived rides a mountain lion, carries a horse, and lassoes a cyclone. In the end, the hero meets and marries a heroic woman whose steel-spring bustle sends them to the moon.

Workshop Resources

PACING (DAYS) STANDARD	BLOCK	LESSON	STUDENT MATERIALS	TEACHER RESOURCES
1	½	Key Skill Lesson: Clarifying	🧸 Key Reading Skills Practice, p. 17 🧸 English Language Coach Review, p. 43	👆 Bellringer Options Transparencies – Selection Focus Transparency 15 – Daily Language Practice 55 👆 Read Aloud, Think Aloud Transparencies – Key Reading Skills 3 ⊙ Presentation Plus!
1	1	"The Twelve Labors of Hercules"	💻 Glencoe Online 🧸 Unit Vocabulary Review, p. 41 🧸 Academic Vocabulary Review, p. 44 📁 English Language Coach 🧸 Active Reading Graphic Organizer, p. 19 🧸 Literary Analysis, p. 18 ⊙ StudentWorks Plus™ 💻 Online Student Edition ⊙ Literature Classics 📁 Selection and Unit Assessments, p. 63	👆 Literary and Text Analysis Transparencies 10 💻 Puzzlemaker ⊙ Skill Level Up!™ A Language Arts Game 💻 BookLink 3 📋 Assessment by Learning Objective (Diagnostic and Formative) ⊙ Interactive Tutor: Self-Assessment ⊙ TeacherWorks Plus™
1		"Pecos Bill"	💻 Glencoe Online 🧸 Unit Vocabulary Review, p. 41 🧸 Academic Vocabulary Review, p. 44 📁 English Language Coach 🧸 Active Reading Graphic Organizer, p. 21 🧸 Literary Analysis, p. 18 ⊙ StudentWorks Plus™ 💻 Online Student Edition ⊙ Literature Classics 📁 Selection and Unit Assessments, p. 64	👆 Literary and Text Analysis Transparencies 10 💻 Puzzlemaker ⊙ Skill Level Up!™ A Language Arts Game 💻 BookLink 3 📋 Assessment by Learning Objective (Diagnostic and Formative) ⊙ Interactive Tutor: Self-Assessment ⊙ TeacherWorks Plus™

Keys for Unit Resource

📁 Blackline Master   🖴 DVD

📋 Workbook   👆 Transparency

📖 Supplemental Text   💻 Web-based

⊙ CD-ROM   🧸 Fast File

Level Appropriate Code

AS = Activities for all students

AL = Activities for students working above grade level

UL = Activities for students working at grade level

BL = Activities for students working below grade level

EL = Activities for English language learners

Focus

BELLRINGER Options

- ✎ **Selection Focus Transparency 15**
- ✎ **Daily Language Practice Transparency 55**
  Focus Activity Ask: Have you ever accomplished something that you thought you would not be able to do or that others told you was impossible? How did it make you feel? *(Responses will vary.)* `OL`

Teach

R Reading Skill

Clarifying Say: When you have a conversation with someone, there are times when you don't quite understand what that person is saying. You may want to ask the other person to stop and explain it to you. Reading is like having a conversation with the author. When you feel confused, you can stop to clarify the author's meaning. What are some ways to clarify meaning as you read? *(Possible responses: reread; look up a word; ask another reader or a teacher for help)* `OL`

READING WORKSHOP 2

Skills Focus

You will practice using these skills when you read the following selections:
- "The Twelve Labors of Hercules," p. 650
- "Pecos Bill," p. 660

Reading
- Clarifying meaning while reading

Literature
- Recognizing the cultural contexts of Greek mythology
- Recognizing the cultural contexts of the Wild West

Vocabulary
- Recognizing borrowed words

Writing/Grammar
- Correcting run-on sentences

Objectives (pp. 646–647)
Reading Clarify ideas and text

Skill Lesson

Clarifying

Learn It!

What Is It? Have you ever read something and then realized you didn't understand it very well? If you didn't monitor your comprehension and kept reading, you probably understood less and less. By the time you finished, you may have felt clueless.

Clarifying means clearing up whatever you don't understand. As you're reading, stop when something confuses you. Take the time to find out what's going on.

Analyzing the Art
Why is a magnifying glass often a symbol for clarifying, or trying to understand something more clearly?

Additional Support

Reading in the Real World

Career Asking and answering questions is a part of most jobs. For example, managers in offices, stores, warehouses, and restaurants need to create a working environment that encourages employees to ask questions. Managers also need to be able to do research to find answers they don't know and explain those answers clearly to their employees. All workers need to be able to read and understand processes, instructions, changes, and new policies. Ask students to talk with people in their family about how they ask questions and clarify ideas where they work. `AS`

Why Is It Important? Clarifying what you don't understand pays off! It helps you understand and enjoy the text you're reading. It also gives you more information to use in your life.

How Do I Do It? When you realize you don't understand something while you're reading, try these techniques:

- Read confusing parts slowly and carefully.
- Look up unfamiliar words.
- Use resources like dictionaries, encyclopedias, the Internet, and your teacher to figure out the things you don't understand.
- With your new information, reread the confusing parts of the text.

Here's how Dan clarified as he read about the Greeks:

C

> "When the great city of Troy was taken, all the chiefs who had fought against it set sail for their homes. But there was wrath in heaven against them, for indeed they had borne themselves haughtily and cruelly in the day of their victory. Therefore they did not all find a safe and happy return."

I don't get the second sentence. I need to look up <u>wrath</u>. Wrath means anger. "Wrath in heaven" must mean the gods were "angry." I also need to look up <u>haughtily</u>. Haughtily means "too proudly." The gods were angry when the Greeks behaved badly in their victory. Now I get why the Greeks didn't have a safe return!

Practice It!

Choose a paragraph in one of your textbooks. Make a list of any words or ideas that need clarification. Decide which sources to use to clarify what you don't understand.

Use It!

As you read about Hercules and Pecos Bill, write a list in your Learner's Notebook of things you don't understand. Clarify as you read to get the most out of each selection.

Reading Workshop 2 Clarifying **647**

Teach

Study Central Have students access the Web site to review clarifying and to complete a related activity.

C Critical Thinking

Analysis Say: Look at the model showing how Dan clarified the reading passage about the Greeks. What clarifying tip did he use from the How Do I Do It? section? *(Possible response: He looked up the words he didn't know.)* **OL**

R Reading Skill

Clarifying Have students look through the book to find a heading or selection title that they don't understand at first glance. Discuss as a group what students might do to clarify its meaning. **OL**

Resources for page 647

✎ Use Key Reading Skills Transparency 3 in *Read Aloud, Think Aloud* to help students practice clarifying.

Differentiated Instruction

Class Discussion Hold a class discussion on clarification techniques. Ask students to share the techniques they use to clarify what they don't understand as they read. Also have them think about other situations in which they use clarification techniques to get more information. Ask students to explain what they do when they don't understand something or they become confused. Remind students to ask questions whenever they need more information. **AS**

Objectives
- Clarify ideas and text
- Analyze text

647

Teach

More About the Author

Author Walker Brents majored in English and philosophy at Drury College in Springfield, Missouri. While working at a refugee center, he was able to listen to many stories told by refugees from around the world. Brents tells myths and folktales at the Asian Art Museum in San Francisco, teaches high school, and has published a number of poems and articles in literary magazines.

EL Language Coach

Words from Names Say:

Listen to this sentence. *Lifting the fallen tree off the house was a herculean task.* From the context of the sentence, what do you think *herculean* means? *(requiring great strength)* **EL BL** Have students look up the word *herculean*. **Ask:** What does the dictionary say the word means and from what was it borrowed? *("requiring great strength or effort" or "like Hercules in strength or courage"; from the name of Hercules, the son of Zeus)* **OL**

Before You Read : The Twelve Labors of Hercules

Walker Brents

Meet the Author

This myth about Hercules is a retelling by Walker Brents, a poet and storyteller. Born in 1958, Brents has loved myths since his father read to him about the Greek gods when he was five years old. Brents says, "The feeling the myths gave me was mysterious and yet somehow strangely familiar."

Author Search For more about Brents, go to www.glencoe.com.

Objectives (pp. 648–655)
Reading Clarify ideas and text
• Make connections from text to self
Literature Identify key literary elements: cultural context
Vocabulary Explore word origins: words from names

Vocabulary Preview

consciousness (KON shus nus) *n.* thoughts; awareness; the mind **(p. 650)** *The gods and goddesses had the power to control the consciousness of humans.*

delusion (dih LOO zhun) *n.* a false belief **(p. 650)** *Hercules had the delusion that he was at war and had to kill his enemies.*

remorse (rih MORS) *n.* a feeling of guilt and regret **(p. 651)** *Hercules felt remorse for killing his nephews and nieces.*

diverted (dih VUR tud) *v.* turned from one course to another; form of the verb *divert* **(p. 652)** *Hercules diverted two rivers to wash through an area that needed to be cleaned.*

grotesque (groh TESK) *adj.* very strange and unexpected in appearance **(p. 653)** *The slimy three-headed monster was grotesque.*

devoured (dih VOW urd) *v.* ate greedily; form of the verb *devour* **(p. 653)** *The birds killed their prey before they devoured it.*

foliage (FOH lee ij) *n.* plant and tree leaves **(p. 653)** *The foliage in the marsh was so thick that Hercules couldn't cut through it.*

iridescent (ir ih DES unt) *adj.* showing shimmering colors that look like a rainbow **(p. 654)** *The colors in the iridescent glass were beautiful.*

Partner Talk Play six rounds of "Twenty Questions" using the vocabulary words. One partner chooses one of the words. The other partner may ask up to twenty yes-or-no questions to guess the word.

English Language Coach

Words Borrowed from Names Some names become words. That's what happened with several names in the next selection. Atlas belonged to a family of giants called the Titans. They were so powerful that they rebelled against the gods and, for a time, ruled the earth. To punish Atlas for rebelling, the gods forced him to support the sky on his shoulders. From the names Atlas and Titan, we got these words:

- **atlas** (AT lus) *n.* a book of maps
- **titan** (TY tun) *n.* one who has great size or power
- **titanic** (ty TAN ik) *adj.* having great size or power

EL

Write to Learn Look up *Helios* in a dictionary or encyclopedia. In your Learner's Notebook, note who he is in Greek mythology and find one English word that came from his name.

Additional Support

Author Search To expand students' appreciation of Walker Brents, have them access the Web site for additional information and resources.

Differentiated Instruction

Group Discussion Arrange students in small groups. Have each group come up with a word for "personal flying device." Ask each group to share their word with the class, and have the class vote on the best one. Then have students imagine other future inventions that will need names. See which group can come up with the best new name for each invention. Challenge students to make up words borrowed from names for the inventions. **OL**

Skills Preview

Key Reading Skill: Clarifying

While you read about Hercules, use your Learner's Notebook to write down anything you don't understand in this myth. Include words you don't know.

Write to Learn Write this sentence from "The Twelve Labors of Hercules" in your Learner's Notebook: "Terrible remorse drove him to the oracle of the god Apollo at Delphi, and he asked the priestesses there what he could do to expiate his terrible deed." Circle every word or phrase that you don't understand.

Key Literary Element: Cultural Context

The **cultural context** is the culture that a story comes from when it was first told or written. The culture includes the time and place as well as the beliefs and practices of the people living in that time and place.

Hercules is part of Greek mythology, which was the religion of ancient Greece. In these myths, twelve gods and goddesses, living on Mount Olympus, interacted with humans and had power over all of Nature and human lives. As you read about Hercules, use these questions to help you think about the cultural context:

- Who are the gods and goddesses in this story? How do they hurt or help Hercules?
- In what ways are they powerful? In what ways are their powers limited?
- In what ways was Hercules like a god and in what ways was he human?

Class Talk The ancient Greek stories taught that there was a god or goddess for almost every element of nature (such as the sky, sea, earth, and the weather) and every major human activity (such as home, marriage, the hunt, and war). Discuss with your classmates why you think the Greeks might have written these stories.

Get Ready to Read

Connect to the Reading

Do you ever watch action or horror movies? Well, the myth of Hercules has the same sorts of things those movies do: an impossible mission, scary creatures, and bloody battles.

Build Background

The myth of Hercules includes references to these characters of Greek mythology:

- The **Oracle at Delphi** was a shrine to Apollo, the god of the sun. Apollo spoke through the priestesses who lived at Delphi. If asked, they could tell people's future.
- The **Amazons** were a tribe of warrior women.
- **Atlas** led the Titans, a race of giants, in a war against the gods of Mount Olympus. Zeus punished him by making him carry the sky on his shoulders.

Set Purposes for Reading

Read "The Twelve Labors of Hercules" to learn what made Hercules such an important hero to the ancient Greeks.

Set Your Own Purpose What else would you like to learn from this story about Hercules and his labors? Write your own purpose on "The Twelve Labors of Hercules" page of Foldable 6.

Interactive Literary Elements Handbook To review or learn more about the literary elements, go to www.glencoe.com.

Keep Moving

Use these skills as you read the following selection.

Teach

L Literary Element

Cultural Context **Say:** Many families have stories that are passed down from one generation to the next. Think of a story *(true or fictional)* that you've heard from an older relative. Then think about your family's culture. How does the story connect with your family's ideas and beliefs? *(Responses will vary.)* **AL**

R Reading Skill

Review Connecting **Say:** Think about a time when you had to do something that required a lot of strength. What did you do to prepare for the task? Did you succeed? *(Responses will vary.)* **OL**

Interactive Literary Elements Handbook Have students access the Web site to improve their understanding of cultural context.

Literature Focus Lesson

Heroes Review with students what they have learned about literary heroes. Ask what they already know about Hercules. Discuss why Hercules might be considered a hero. Then explain to students that other cultures might view heroes differently. As the class explores the cultural context of the story of Hercules, have them compare it to current American culture. Would Hercules be a hero in our culture? What were the values of Greek culture when the myth of Hercules was written? How are they different from or similar to the values in our culture? **AL**

Objectives

- Clarify ideas and text
- Identify literary elements: cultural context
- Identify borrowed words
- Make connections from text to self

649

Teach

Viewing the Art

Say: Look at the statue of Hercules. What can you tell about him from this image? What do you think Hercules is like? *(Possible responses: strong; serious; determined)* **OL**

EL Language Coach

Borrowed Words Say: Many English words have been borrowed from other languages. For instance, the word *foliage*, which means "the leaves on trees or other plants," was borrowed from the French word *feuillage*. Earlier this word had developed in French from the Latin word for leaves, *folia*. Look up the words *nephew* and *niece*. From which languages have they been borrowed? *(nephew: from the Old French* neveu *that came from the Latin* nepos*; niece: from the Old French* nece *that came from Latin* neptis*)* Help students pronounce each English word and the foreign words from which the words came so that students can hear the similarities. **EL OL**

Readability Scores

Dale-Chall: 7.8
DRP: 59
Lexile: 1030

The TWELVE LABORS of HERCULES

by Walker Brents

The goddess Hera[1] hated Hercules from the moment of his birth. In his infancy she sent two giant serpents to kill him as he slept, but **Hercules** strangled them instead. His parents rushed into the room to find the baby shaking the dead bodies of the snakes as if they were rattles. This was an early indication of his great strength, but this strength was not always used well. **1**

Once Hera sent madness and insanity into the **consciousness** of Hercules. His thoughts became scrambled. Under the **delusion** that he was at war, he mistook his nephews and nieces for enemies, and killed them. When the madness passed and he saw what he had done he was

---

1. *Hera* (HAIR uh) is the Queen of the Greek deities (gods and goddesses). She is the goddess of marriage and birth. Zeus (zoos) is her husband.

Vocabulary

consciousness (KON shus nus) *n.* thoughts; awareness; the mind

delusion (dih LOO zhun) *n.* a false belief

650 UNIT 6 What Makes a Hero?

Practice the Skills

1 **English Language Coach**

Words from Names The name **Hercules** became the English word *herculean* (hur kyuh LEE un). It can mean either "having great strength" or "having great difficulty."

Additional Support

Differentiated Instruction

Character Chart This story contains many Greek names of characters and places. Draw a chart like this one on the board and direct students to copy it into their Learner's Notebooks. As they read, students can fill in the chart to create their own reference guide. **BL OL**

Word	Character	Place	Memory Note
Hera	✓		cruel queen of the gods and goddesses
Hercules	✓		had great strength

R overwhelmed with grief and guilt. Terrible **remorse** drove him to the oracle of the god Apollo at Delphi, and he asked the priestesses there what he could do to expiate[2] his terrible deed. They told him, "Go to King Eurystheus,[3] and undertake the labors he will put upon you." **2 3**

Hercules went to Tiryns, the land ruled by King Eurystheus. He stood before the throne. Eurystheus said to him, "Go to Nemea, where a fierce lion terrorizes the people. No weapon can pierce through its terrible skin. Kill this lion, remove its skin, carry it here and show it to me." Eurystheus was shrewd, calculating, cunning, and cowardly. Each task he was to set before Hercules was designed to be impossible, but the determination of Hercules was to overcome the impossible. He followed the lion's tracks to a deep dark cave EL hidden in a hillside. He saw the bones strewn at the cave's entrance, and entered in. In such a darkness he could not see his hand before his face, the dank[4] air was filled with the smell of blood. The lion had just killed, and had carried its prey to this place which was its very den. Hercules leapt upon the lion and wrestled with it. His tremendous club and sharp knife were of no use, for the lion's hide was too thick. Hercules grasped the lion's neck with his hands and held it against the cave wall until the lion's thrashings ceased and it was dead. Then he dragged the lion into the light of day, skinning it with one of its own claws. He draped the skin over his shoulders, its head over his head like a helmet, and hurried back to the palace of King Eurystheus, who saw him approach from a distance and was so frightened at the sight that he hid in a giant olive jar. He sent his servants to Hercules to tell him of the next task. "Go to the swamp of Lerna and defeat the hydra, who lives at the confluence of the three springs."

Visual Vocabulary
A **hydra** (HY druh) is a serpent monster with nine heads that can regrow.

2. To **expiate** (EX pee ate) is to try and make up for having done something bad.
3. **Eurystheus** (yoo RIS thee us)
4. Air that is **dank** is damp and uncomfortable.

Vocabulary

remorse (rih MORS), *n.* a feeling of guilt and regret

Practice the Skills

2 | **Key Reading Skill**

Clarifying The twelve great labors of Hercules are amazing and exciting, but they might be hard to keep track of! Clarify by writing in your Learner's Notebook each time Hercules begins a new task.

3 | **Key Literary Element**

Cultural Context The goddess Hera made Hercules crazy. Because of this, he killed his relatives. Even though he didn't know what he was doing, Hercules wants to make up for the terrible crime. What does this say about what the ancient Greeks thought of personal responsibility?

Teach

R Reading Skill

Clarifying Say: To help clarify the paragraph, you can reread it, putting definitions in place of the vocabulary words. **BL** How would you explain this paragraph to a friend in your own words? *(Possible response: Hercules goes crazy and kills his relatives. He feels so guilty that he goes to a god to ask how he can make up for what he has done.)* **OL**

EL Language Coach

Borrowed Words Say: The word *cave* was borrowed from another language. Look up *cave* to find its etymology, or history. *(It comes from the Old French* cave, *which means "a den," going back to the Latin* cavus, *which means "a hollow.")* **Ask:** How is a cave a hollow? *(It is solid outside and empty inside.)* **EL OL**

Reading in the Real World

Citizenship Students are likely to have strong opinions about whether or not Hercules is responsible for murdering his nieces and nephews while under the influence of madness. Before reading about King Eurystheus, have students debate Hercules's position. Use the questions below as a framework.

- Does Hercules have reason to feel remorse?
- Should Hercules be punished?
- What does the fact that Hercules seeks to make amends show about him? **OL**

Objectives
- Clarify ideas and text
- Analyze borrowed words
- Find meaning in art

651

Teach

R Reading Skill

Clarifying Ask: What animal did Hercules have to kill first? How did he do it? *(a lion; held it against a cave wall)* What animal came next? How did he defeat this animal? *(a hydra; knocked off its heads, had someone burn its neck-stubs, and buried its central head)* **BL**

L Literary Element

Cultural Context Ask: What are Hercules's most outstanding qualities? Why did the Greeks admire him? *(Possible response: Hercules is strong and resourceful, and he conquers many enemies.)* **OL**

Hercules and one of his surviving nephews, Iolaus, found the monster in the depths of the swamp, at the confluence of three springs. Hercules shot his arrows at the monster so as to anger it enough to attack and come close enough for him to fight it with his oaken club. The monster had nine heads and came toward them screaming with rage, belching great gouts of poison bloody mud. Hercules began to knock off the creature's heads, but saw that three heads grew back from where one was knocked off! Iolaus lit the branch of a tree with fire, and held his torch against the neck-stubs where Hercules knocked the heads off. The burnt blood prevented the heads from growing back. With this the tide of the battle turned. The creature was weakening. Finally, Hercules tore off the central head, the primary one. He carried it away and buried it in the ground with a great rock over it, so that it could not rejoin the body and come alive again. Then Hercules dipped his arrow points in the poison blood of the hydra, which lay in pools all around, so as to make them deadly. **4**

Other labors followed, and they took Hercules far and wide. In the forest of Ceryneia he chased a deer with golden antlers for an entire year, caught it and carried it alive to King Eurystheus, then returned to Ceryneia and let the deer go. Earlier, he had gone to the land of King Augeias, who kept a stable filled with thousands upon thousands of cattle, which had never been cleaned. Eurystheus, gleefully imagining Hercules carrying baskets and baskets of dung, had ordered him to clean those stables. But Hercules **diverted** the course of two rivers and sent them through the stables so that they were entirely cleaned in one day. **5**

On Mount Erymanthus there lived a great boar. Searching amid the lower slopes of this mountain Hercules met an old friend of his, Pholos the centaur, who lived in a village of centaurs. Hercules shared a meal with his friend, but accidentally spilled a drop or two of wine upon the ground. The

Visual Vocabulary
A *centaur* (SEN tawr) is a creature that is half man and half horse.

Vocabulary

diverted (dih VUR tud) *v.* turned from one course to another

652 UNIT 6 What Makes a Hero?

Practice the Skills

4 Key Reading Skill

Clarifying One way to clarify a difficult sentence is to break it into parts. For example, look at the last sentence in this paragraph. It might be easier to understand if you turn it into three simple sentences: "Hercules dipped his arrows in the poison blood of hydra. The poison blood lay in pools all around. The poison blood made the arrows deadly."

5 Key Literary Element

Cultural Context Hercules was a hero to the Greeks. What does that tell you about the Greeks? What qualities did they admire? Write your answer in your Learner's Notebook.

Additional Support

Differentiated Instruction

Illustrations Students who like to draw can be encouraged to create images of the creatures from Greek mythology that appear in this selection. Ask students to draw images of the creatures that are described in the text but are not pictured. Provide picture books of Greek gods and goddesses or find images on the Internet that students can use as models. Have students write a caption for each of the images they draw to go with the story. Display students' pictures on a bulletin board or have students present them to the class. **AS**

smell of the wine drove the centaurs insane, and they attacked Hercules, who responded with a volley of arrows tipped with the hydra's poison blood. Many were killed. Pholos was burying their bodies when an arrow came loose from one of them, fell down and pierced the flesh near his hoof. The poison entered his veins and killed him. By this time, Hercules was on the upper part of the mountain hunting for the boar, but when he heard of his friend's death he returned to the centaur village and in great sadness helped with the funeral. But he had made enemies with some of the centaurs, and one of them, Nessus, swore revenge. Hercules returned to the hunt for the boar and chased it into deep snowdrifts, where he caught it. After that he went to the land of Thrace and fought against Diomedes, killing him and his man-eating horses. **6**

Another labor brought Hercules to the marshes of Stymphalus. Somewhere in these vast marshes there lived **grotesque** vicious birds that shot their feathers like arrows into people. Then they tore the people into pieces and carried their chunks of flesh away into the marshes where they **devoured** them. No one could get to the place from which they came. Hercules came very close to their lair, but not close enough. The **foliage** was so thick not even he could hack through it with his sword, so that his forward motion was stopped, and he sat upon the ground in despair. Here an ally came to him, the goddess Athena. She helped him. She caused a set of brazen cymbals to appear upon the ground next to his feet, and spoke these words into his consciousness:

Wild Boar, 1999. Mark Adlington. Graphite, conte, and charcoal on paper. Private collection.

6 Key Reading Skill

Clarifying How many tasks has Hercules completed? Is fighting the centaurs one of the tasks he was sent to accomplish?

Vocabulary

grotesque (groh TESK) *adj.* very strange and unexpected in appearance

devoured (dih VOW urd) *v.* ate greedily

foliage (FOH lee ij) *n.* plant and tree leaves

The Twelve Labors of Hercules **653**

Teach

R1 Reading Skill

Review Drawing Conclusions Ask: What can you tell about Hercules from the fact that he stops his labors to help with his friend's funeral? *(Possible response: Hercules is not only strong and fierce but also a loyal friend.)* **OL**

R2 Reading Skill

Review Identifying Cause and Effect Ask: What does Hercules do with the cymbals? *(He bangs them together.)* What effect does his action have? *(The loud noise makes the birds fly out so that he can shoot them.)* **BL**

Literature Focus Lesson

Theme Begin discussing the theme of the story with students. Talk about Hercules as a character who is undefeatable. Use the following questions as a guide:

• What are you learning about Hercules?
• What are you learning from Hercules?

• What is the nature of the relationship between Hercules and Eurystheus?

Have students discuss whether Hercules is a good model of what it means to be a hero. **OL**

Objectives
• Clarify ideas and text
• Identify literary elements: cultural context
• Draw conclusions
• Understand cause and effect

Teach

L Literary Element

Cultural Context Ask: What qualities do we value in our heroes today? How are these qualities different from what the Greeks valued? *(Responses will vary.)* OL

C Critical Thinking

Comprehension Ask: Do you think Hercules will continue to hold up the sky for Atlas, or do you think he will get out of the situation? What makes you think so? *(Responses will vary. Possible response: Hercules is clever as well as strong, and so he will probably figure out a way to get out of the situation.)* OL

"Strike the cymbals together. The sound of their brassy clashing will startle the birds from their branches and nests. They will fly into the air and become targets for your arrows." Hercules followed her instructions. As fast as the birds flew up his arrows pierced them. Most were killed and those who lived flew away and never returned.

He came to Themiscyra, where the river Thermodon flowed into the sea, in a place of many cliffs and rocky hiding places. This was the land of the Amazons, woman-warriors, whose queen, Hippolyte, had a sword-belt made of bronze and **iridescent** glass, given to her by the god of war, Ares. Hercules was to take this belt from her. Expecting a battle, he was surprised when Hippolyte gave it to him freely, but outside their meeting place, the goddess Hera filled the minds of the Amazons with rumors of war, so that as Hercules left he was suddenly attacked by battalions of Amazons. Once more his poison arrows did their deadly work, and, with the belt, he made his escape.

In Crete, he carried away the bull Poseidon gave to King Minos. On the island of Erytheia, he killed Geyron, a giant man-monster with one head and three bodies, and his two-headed dog, Orthrus. He took the herd of cattle they guarded—cattle whose hides were red as the rays of the setting sun. **Helios** the sun-god caused a floating golden cup to appear in the sea, and Hercules drove the bull of Crete and the red cattle onto this cup and floated back to Tiryns. **7**

"Your next to last task requires that you find the garden beyond the world. There, in the Garden of the Hesperides, grow the golden apples upon the branches of a tree guarded by the serpent that never sleeps. Bring back those apples." Hercules had no sooner heard these orders than he was off.

Garden of the Hesperides, 1869–73. Sir Edward Burne-Jones. Tempera, gouache, and oil on card and canvas. Hamburger Kunsthalle, Hamburg, Germany.

Practice the Skills

7 English Language Coach

Words from Names The name **Helios** gave us *helium* (the lighter-than-air gas used in balloons) and *heliotrope* (a plant whose flowers turn toward the sun).

Vocabulary

iridescent (ir ih DES unt) *adj.* showing shimmering colors that look like a rainbow

654 UNIT 6 What Makes a Hero?

Additional Support

English Language Coach

English as a Changing Language
The expression *a Herculean task* is used to describe a task that seems impossible. Give examples of what might be considered a Herculean task, such as preparing for a big test, recovering from an injury, or rescuing someone in need. Ask students to give examples of times they have felt that they faced a Herculean task. Have students use the expression *Herculean task* to write about the experiences in their Learner's Notebooks. OL

EL At the world's edge he met Atlas, the giant who holds up the sky. "The three sisters who live there are my own daughters. Let me bring back the apples. I am the only one they will let have them. But you must hold up the sky while I am gone." So Atlas said as he waited for Hercules to climb atop the high mountain preparatory to taking upon himself the burden of the sky. Once the load was transferred, Hercules stood with the sky upon his back, watching Atlas stride away, already waist-deep in the ocean that encircles the world. Some few moments, hours, days,

Heracles leading Cerberus to Eurystheus. Black figure hydria. 530–525 BCE, Roman. Louvre, Paris, France.

or months later Atlas returned, holding a branch with three golden apples. "Let me take the apples back to Eurystheus. You go on holding up the sky, for I am tired of it." Atlas was getting ready to go when Hercules said, "Friend, let me do just one thing before you're off. That lion's skin lying there—I carry it with me wherever I go. It would make a good pad to cushion my shoulders against this mighty burden. Kindly take up the sky again for a moment as I gather it up. Then you can return the load to me." Atlas agreed to do so, but once the sky was returned to his keeping Hercules took the branch and walked away, ignoring Atlas's angry cries for him to return. **8**

C The final labor required Hercules to go down to the world of the dead and bring back Cerberus, the fierce three-headed dog. The gods Hermes[5] and Athena[6] met him at the river between the two worlds and helped him. He carried Cerberus back to Tiryns and showed it to King Eurystheus. The three heads barked at him and bared their teeth, and Eurystheus died of fright. **9** ○

---

5. *Hermes* (HUR meez) is the messenger god.
6. *Athena* (uh THEE nuh) is the goddess of wisdom.

Practice the Skills

8 English Language Coach

Words from Names The name **Atlas** also gave us another proper name—*Atlantic* Ocean.

8 BIG Question

Does Hercules have the qualities of a real-life hero? Find a partner and discuss. Write your conclusions on the "Twelve Labors of Hercules" page of Foldable 6. Your response will help you complete the Unit Challenge later.

The Twelve Labors of Hercules **655**

Teach

EL Language Coach

Words from Names **Say:** Geographers in the sixteenth century used pictures of Atlas supporting the heavens to illustrate their collections of maps. Today, what is the relationship between Atlas and maps? *(Possible response: Today we call a book of maps an atlas.)* **EL** **OL**

C Critical Thinking

Evaluation **Ask:** What kinds of things can people do to make up for doing something wrong? In your opinion, does showing you are sorry make up for wrongdoing? *(Responses will vary.)* **AS**

BQ BIG Question

Say: Write a list of qualities you admire about Hercules. Then make a list of any qualities you do not like about him. Can a person have faults and still be a hero? Why or why not? *(Responses will vary.)* **OL**

Assess

CheckPoint

Use the CheckPoint questions provided on Presentation Plus! to check for comprehension of the selection. These questions can be used with interactive response keypads for immediate student feedback.

Objectives
- Identify literary elements: cultural context
- Monitor comprehension
- Evaluate text
- Identify English language changes

Differentiated Instruction

Writing from Reading Have students work in groups or with partners to write a modern day version of one of Hercules's labors. Encourage students to be creative and make Hercules someone such as an athlete, a student, or a computer programmer. The King could be a boss, a teacher, or a parent. Remind students that Hercules's tasks were often dangerous and appeared impossible. When students finish writing, have them read their stories to the class. **OL** **AL**

Assess

Resources for page 656

📁 Selection Quick Check, p. 53

📁 Selection and Unit Assessment, p. 63

💿 ExamView Assessment Suite

💿 Interactive Tutor: Self-Assessment

Students can respond to the *After You Read* items in their Learner's Notebooks or on a separate sheet of paper.

Answering the

BIG Question

1. Possible response: Hercules has great strength and is a tough warrior, but he also has human flaws that people can relate to.

2. Possible responses: He hid in a giant olive jar; he died of fright when he saw Cerberus.

Critical Thinking

3. Possible responses: Hercules made a mistake by killing his nephews and nieces; he accidentally dropped wine on the ground, causing the centaurs to attack.

4. Possible response: He was trying to make up for killing his nieces and nephews.

5. Possible response: Similarity: Anansi and Hercules are both clever. Difference: Anansi is small and weak; Hercules is big and strong.

6. Responses will vary.

After You Read

The Twelve Labors of Hercules

Answering the BIG Question

1. Why do you think Hercules has been such a popular hero since ancient times?

2. **Demonstrate** Give two examples that show that King Eurystheus was a coward.
   Tip Author and Me

Critical Thinking

3. **Analyze** Hercules had the traits of a hero, but he wasn't perfect. Give at least two examples from the story that show the human side of Hercules.
   Tip Author and Me

4. **Infer** Why did Hercules undertake the twelve labors?
   Tip Author and Me

5. **Compare** Name one major similarity and one major difference between Hercules and Anansi.
   Tip Author and Me

6. **Assess** What powers did the gods and goddesses in this story have? How do you know that there were limits to their powers?
   Tip Author and Me

Write About Your Reading

Pretend that you are writing a movie script for a modern version of this myth. In your version, Hercules is a hero enlisted by the President of the United States to solve twelve problems. Plan and organize the plot for your script.

• List the twelve problems you want Hercules to solve.
• List the difficulties he will encounter.
• List the skills he will use to solve each problem.

Objectives (pp. 656–657)
Reading Clarify ideas and text
Literature Identify key literary elements: cultural context
Vocabulary Explore word origins: words from names
Writing Plan and organize a movie script
Grammar Write compound sentences

656 UNIT 6 What Makes a Hero?

Write About Your Reading

Sample response:

Problems	Difficulties	Skills
Global Warming	affects entire globe, globe is large	has magical travel powers, can travel around globe and patch ozone layer
World Hunger	there are billions of people in the world; hard to get food to everyone in all locations	has great strength, can shop for and carry and distribute large amounts of food

Skills Review

Key Reading Skill: Clarifying

7. Look at the list of tasks you wrote in your Learner's Notebook. Do you have twelve listed? If not, go back and find the tasks you're missing.

Key Literary Element: Cultural Context

8. What beliefs of ancient Greeks do you see in this myth?

9. What weaknesses in the gods and goddesses do you see in this myth?

10. Why do you think the Greeks created imperfect heroes?

Vocabulary Check

Choose the *best* word from the list to complete each sentence below. Rewrite each sentence with the correct word in place.

consciousness   foliage   delusion   remorse

11. When Hercules thought that he was at war and had to kill his enemies, he was under a ____.

12. The gods sometimes interfered with humans by getting into their ____.

13. The ____ was so thick around the birds that even Hercules couldn't cut through it.

14. When Hercules killed his relatives, he was overcome with ____.

English Language Coach

15. If you are given a *herculean* task to do, is it an easy one or a difficult one?

16. What does *heliocentric* mean? (Hint: Our solar system is this.)

Grammar Link: Combine Sentences

Too many short sentences can make writing sound choppy or boring. One way to make your writing more interesting is to combine sentences that have closely related ideas into one longer sentence.

One way to combine sentences is to use coordinating conjunctions like *and, but, so,* and *or.* Place a comma before the conjunction.

> Hercules was strong. He liked challenges.
> Hercules was strong, and he liked challenges.

Grammar Practice

Combine each pair of sentences below using *and, but, so,* and *or.* Place a comma before the conjuction.

17. Hercules was courageous. He was smart.

18. Hera wanted to hurt Hercules. She made him temporarily insane.

19. Hercules killed Pholos. It was an accident.

20. Sam has three sisters. Matt has only one.

21. The hurricane season has begun. Fewer people are visiting Florida.

22. I might have spaghetti for dinner. My mom might order pizza.

Literature Online

Web Activities For eFlashcards, Selection Quick Checks, and other Web activities, go to www.glencoe.com.

The Twelve Labors of Hercules **657**

Skills Review

Key Reading Skill: Clarifying

7. Responses will vary.

Key Literary Element: Cultural Context

8. Possible response: They valued strong warriors and determination.

9. Possible response: Gods and goddesses do not always do good. Hera, for example, makes Hercules go mad.

10. Responses will vary. Students may say that imperfect heroes are easier for real people to relate to.

Vocabulary Check

11. delusion

12. consciousness

13. foliage

14. remorse

English Language Coach

15. Possible response: a job that requires great strength and determination; a job that seems impossible

16. Possible response: having the sun as the center.

Close

Ask students to summarize what they learned about the Big Question from reading the story of Hercules.

Grammar Link: Combine Sentences

Grammar Practice

17. Hercules was courageous, and he was smart.

18. Hera wanted to hurt Hercules, so she made him temporarily insane.

19. Hercules killed Pholos, but it was an accident.

20. Sam has three sisters, but Matt has only one.

21. The hurricane season has begun, so fewer people are visiting Florida.

22. I might have spaghetti for dinner, or my mom might order pizza.

Teach

More About the Author

Mary Pope Osborne's childhood was spent on Army posts with her parents, two brothers, and sister. As the daughter of a United States Army colonel, moving and traveling were part of her life. Osborne lived mostly in the southern United States and, for three years, in Austria. She says, "I feel that the years I spent traveling . . . the different jobs I've held . . . and my interests in philosophy and mythology have all informed and shaped my work."

Vocabulary

Vocabulary File Say: A good way to remember vocabulary words is to keep a vocabulary file. Write each word on a 3" × 5" index card, including the pronunciation if you need it. Include the meaning of the word and an example sentence using the word. **BL** **EL**

Before You Read : Pecos Bill

Meet the Author

Mary Pope Osborne has written more than fifty books. She is best known for her Magic Tree House books. Born in Oklahoma in 1949, Osborne feels lucky to have explored exciting topics through her books. As she puts it, "I've taken journeys to the times of dinosaurs, knights, mummies, pirates, and ninjas." See page R5 of the Author Files for more on Mary Pope Osborne.

Literature Online

Author Search For more about Mary Pope Osborne, go to www .glencoe.com.

Objectives (pp. 658–659)
Reading Clarify ideas and text
Literature Identify key literary elements: cultural context
Vocabulary Explore word origins: borrowed words

Vocabulary Preview

desolate (DES uh lut) *adj.* deserted or uninhabited **(p. 660)** *Much of the land was desolate at that time.*

spunk (spunk) *n.* courage, spirit, and determination **(p. 663)** *Cowboys needed a lot of spunk to survive in the Wild West.*

drought (drowt) *n.* a long period of very dry weather **(p. 664)** *Because of the drought, there was no water to drink.*

barren (BAIR un) *adj.* having little or no plant life; empty **(p. 666)** *The land was so barren that the cattle had no grass to eat.*

Write to Learn For each vocabulary word, write a sentence using it correctly.

English Language Coach

Borrowed Words The English language has borrowed words for just about everything—clothing, colors, weather, animals, cars, and sports. *Tulip* and *peach* are Persian. *Tea* and *typhoon* are Chinese. *Banana* and *okra* come from Africa.

Partner Talk With a partner, match the lists of words below with the languages they were borrowed from. Use a dictionary, an encyclopedia, or the Internet to help you.

1. tornado, coyote, rodeo
2. karate, tycoon, haiku
3. balcony, macaroni
4. chimpanzee, zebra, jumbo
5. jungle, shampoo, bandana
6. boomerang, kangaroo, koala

a. Italian
b. Spanish
c. Japanese
d. languages of Australia and New Zealand
e. languages of India
c. languages of Africa

Then, with your partner, look up each of the following words in a dictionary to learn what language it was borrowed from.

1. barbecue   4. canoe
2. hurricane   5. yak
3. spaghetti   6. bungalow

Additional Support

Author Search To expand students' appreciation of Mary Pope Osborne, have them access the Web site for more information and resources.

Differentiated Instruction

Building Background Students may be familiar with author Mary Pope Osborne from her Magic Tree House books. Explain to them that sometimes authors create stories from scratch, but much more often, authors use research and experience to supplement their imaginations. The original Pecos Bill stories were made up and told around campfires by cowboys. In the 1920s, a writer published "The Saga of Pecos Bill" in a magazine and since then, many different writers, including Mary Pope Osborne, have written and published their versions of Pecos Bill. **AS**

Skills Preview

Key Reading Skill: Clarifying

While you read about Pecos Bill, write down anything you don't understand. Also write down any words you don't know. Look up the answers in a dictionary, an encyclopedia, or on the Internet.

Partner Talk On the left are some words used in movies and books about the Wild West. With a partner, see how many you can match with words that have the same meaning in Standard American English.

Wild West Slang	Standard American English
1. howdy	a. get
2. pardner	b. jail
3. yonder	c. over there
4. chow	d. hello
5. fetch	e. food
6. pokey	f. partner

Key Literary Element: Cultural Context

The cultural context of a story has a lot to do with who tells the story. Each time and place in history has a different culture filled with people who have different beliefs and practices. Each person might tell the same story from a different cultural context. For example, "Pecos Bill" is a story about the American West. A story about the West could be told by

- a Native American
- a cowboy
- a Chinese immigrant

Depending on who is telling the story, the cultural context may change and a very different story will be told about the same time and place in history.

Literature Online

Interactive Literary Elements Handbook
To review or learn more about the literary elements, go to www.glencoe.com.

Get Ready to Read

Connect to the Reading

This folktale is about a hero who is "larger than life." You've probably read about larger-than-life heroes—comic-book superheroes, for example.

Class Talk Discuss who are today's most popular larger-than-life heroes.

Build Background

Folktales about the American West started being created almost as soon as the first European settlers arrived there. Books, stories, movies, and TV shows have all added to this folklore over the years. These tales often exaggerate the danger, excitement, and wildness of the area, which is why it became known as the Wild West.

The folktale you are about to read is a "tall tale." In a tall tale, things are exaggerated to be bigger and more amazing than they could possibly be in real life. A character in a tall tale might, for example, bite a nail in two or tame a tornado!

Set Purposes for Reading

BIG Question As you read, think about why settlers in the American West created heroes such as Pecos Bill.

Set Your Own Purpose What else would you like to learn about heroes in folktales? Write your own purpose on the "Pecos Bill" page of Foldable 6.

Keep Moving

Use these skills as you read the following selection.

Teach

L Literary Element

Cultural Context Say: Some stories are so popular that they are told again and again in many different cultures. Have you ever read another culture's version of a popular folktale or fairy tale, such as Cinderella? How was it different from the version you're used to? *(Responses will vary.)* **OL**

R Reading Skill

Review Connecting Ask: Have you ever used exaggeration when telling a story to make the story more entertaining? Did it improve the story? Why or why not? *(Responses will vary.)* **OL**

Literature Online

Interactive Literary Elements Handbook Have students access the Web site to improve their understanding of cultural context.

Literature Focus Lesson

Setting To help students understand the setting of the story, share pictures of the Old West with them. Help them identify coyotes, grizzly bears, broncos, cyclones, and other story references with which they may not be familiar. You may also wish to have students create a list of categories and examples in their Learner's Notebooks as they read the story and find visual representations. Categories could include *People, Animals, Weather,* and *The Land,* and examples of each could be *cowboy, coyote, cyclone,* and *desert.* **AS**

Objectives

- Clarify ideas and text
- Identify literary elements: setting, cultural context
- Make connections from text to self
- Learn and use new vocabulary

Teach

Viewing the Illustration

Ask: Which of the men in the picture is Pecos Bill? How can you tell? *(Possible response: The man riding the horse is Pecos Bill, because he is a cowboy and the main character of the story.)* What do you think Pecos Bill is like? *(Possible response: He is tough.)* **OL**

L Literary Element

Cultural Context Ask: In what way is the Wild West different from the area you live in today? Do you think you would have enjoyed living in the Wild West? Why or why not? *(Responses will vary.)* **OL**

Readability Scores
Dale-Chall: 6.4
DRP: 52
Lexile: 950

Pecos Bill

by Mary Pope Osborne

Bill riding his horse "Widow Maker".
Illustration from *American Tall Tales.*

Ask any **coyote** near the Pecos River in western Texas who was the best cowboy who ever lived, and he'll throw back his head and howl, "Ah-hooo!" If you didn't know already, that's coyote language for *Pecos Bill.* **1**

When Pecos Bill was a little baby, he was as tough as a pine knot. He teethed on horseshoes instead of teething rings and played with grizzly bears instead of teddy bears. He could have grown up just fine in the untamed land of eastern Texas. But one day his pappy[1] ran in from the fields, hollering, "Pack up, Ma! Neighbors movin' in fifty miles away! It's gettin' too crowded!" **2**

Before sundown Bill's folks loaded their fifteen kids and all their belongings into their covered wagon and started west.

As they clattered across the **desolate** land of western Texas, the crushing heat nearly drove them all crazy. Baby Bill got so hot and cross that he began to wallop his big brothers. Pretty soon all fifteen kids were going at one another tooth and nail. Before they turned each other into catfish bait, Bill fell out of the wagon and landed *kerplop* on the sun-scorched desert.

---

1. The word *pappy* is a changed form of papa, so it refers to a person's father.

Vocabulary

desolate (DES uh lut) *adj.* deserted or uninhabited

660 UNIT 6 What Makes a Hero?

Practice the Skills

1 **English Language Coach**
Borrowed Words What language was **coyote** borrowed from? Write your answer in your Learner's Notebook.

2 **Key Literary Element**
Cultural Context Think of the culture of American settlers in the Wild West. How does the description of Bill show what is important to that culture?

Additional Support

English Language Coach

Dialect Wild West dialect and drawl may not be familiar to some students. Bring in books that contain pictures of the Wild West or show a film or play a recording about the Wild West so that students can hear a cowboy's voice or a coyote's wail. As students read, encourage them to keep a list of words they don't understand in their Learner's Notebooks. Also have them write down any questions they have about Pecos Bill or the Wild West. Encourage them to use resources such as dictionaries and the Internet to learn the meanings of the words on their lists and to answer their questions. **EL BL**

The others were so busy fighting that they didn't even notice the baby was missing until it was too late to do anything about it.

Well, tough little Bill just sat there in the dirt, watching his family rattle off in a cloud of dust, until an old coyote walked over and sniffed him. **3**

"Goo-goo!" Bill said.

Now it's an amazing coincidence, but "Goo-goo" happens to mean something similar to "Glad to meet you" in coyote language. Naturally the old coyote figured he'd come across one of his own kind. He gave Bill a big lick and picked him up by the scruff of the neck and carried him home to his den.

Bill soon discovered the coyote's kinfolk[2] were about the wildest, roughest bunch you could imagine. Before he knew it, he was roaming the prairies with the pack. He howled at the moon, sniffed the brush, and chased lizards across the sand. He was having such a good time, scuttling about naked and dirty on all fours, that he completely forgot what it was like to be a human.

Pecos Bill's coyote days came to an end about seventeen years later. One evening as he was sniffing the sagebrush, a cowpoke came loping by on a big horse. "Hey, you!" he shouted. "What in the world are you?"

Bill sat on his haunches[3] and stared at the feller.[4]

"What *are* you?" asked the cowpoke[5] again.

"Varmint,"[6] said Bill hoarsely, for he hadn't used his human voice in seventeen years.

"No, you ain't!"

"Yeah, I am. I got fleas, don't I?"

"Well, that don't mean nothing. A lot of Texans got fleas. The thing varmints got that you ain't got is a tail."

"Oh, yes, I do have a tail," said Pecos Bill.

"Lemme see it then," said the cowpoke.

Bill turned around to look at his rear end, and for the first time in his life he realized he didn't have a tail.

"Dang," he said. "But if I'm not a varmint, what am I?"

---

2. **Kinfolk** is another word for relatives.

3. To sit on your **haunches** is to squat.

4. **Feller** means a boy or man.

5. **Cowpoke** is cowboy slang for a cowboy.

6. A **varmint** is a pesky, annoying animal or person.

Practice the Skills

3 | **Key Reading Skill**

Clarifying Be sure to read the footnotes for the meanings of words you don't understand and then reread the sentence or paragraph. That way, you won't miss any of the humor. **R**

Pecos Bill **661**

Teach

R Reading Skill

Clarifying Say: After reading the definitions of the footnoted words, paraphrase the text in which they appear. *(Responses will vary.)* How does the language used in the story help make it more humorous? *(Possible response: The Wild West dialect contributes to the story's tone.)* **AL**

C Critical Thinking

Comprehension Say: Bill's "human" voice is hoarse because he hasn't used it in seventeen years. How long has Bill been living as a coyote? About how old is he at this point in the story? How do you know? *(Possible response: He's been living as a coyote for seventeen years; he must be about seventeen years old, because he met the coyotes when he was a baby.)* **OL**

English Language Coach

Word Origins Understanding the origin of the word *varmint* can help students make sense of it. Point out that it evolved from *vermin*, which originally meant pests like rats and mice. Explain that its meaning has broadened to include any animal or any type of pest, including a human one. Have students work in small groups or with partners and use reference materials to do their own research on the origins of *varmint* and other unfamiliar words on this page. Then have students present their findings to the rest of the class. **EL OL**

Objectives

- Analyze cultural context
- Clarify ideas and text
- Monitor comprehension
- Use text features: illustration
- Understand word origins
- Understand dialect

Teach

C Critical Thinking

Comprehension Say: The expression "with a heavy heart" is a colorful way of describing a common emotion. What do you think it feels like to have a "heavy heart"? *(Possible responses: sad; tired; hurting)* **OL**

R Reading Skill

Clarifying Say: Putting a price on something helps tell what it's worth. Which is worth more, ten dollars or five cents? What does this say about Bill's hat in relation to his head? *(Possible response: Ten dollars is worth more than five cents. This means that people think Bill's hat is worth more than his head, which implies that he is not smart.)* **OL**

Pecos Bill and the Hell's Gate Gang. Illustration from *American Tall Tales.*

Analyzing the Art Pecos Bill stories are filled with exaggerated adventures and impossible happenings. What animal is Bill riding? What animals are on his shoulder and arm? How do the other cowboys seem to be reacting? Read on to learn what this picture is all about.

"You're a cowboy! So start acting like one!"

Bill just growled at the feller like any coyote worth his salt would. But deep down in his heart of hearts he knew the cowpoke was right. For the last seventeen years he'd had a sneaking suspicion that he was different from that pack of coyotes. For one thing, none of them seemed to smell quite as bad as he did.

C So with a heavy heart he said good-bye to his four-legged friends and took off with the cowpoke for the nearest ranch.

Acting like a human wasn't all that easy for Pecos Bill. Even though he soon started dressing right, he never bothered to shave or comb his hair. He'd just throw some water on his face in the morning and go around the rest of the day looking like a wet dog. Ignorant cowpokes claimed Bill wasn't too **R** smart. Some of the meaner ones liked to joke that he wore a ten-dollar hat on a five-cent head. **4**

The truth was Pecos Bill would soon prove to be one of the greatest cowboys who ever lived. He just needed to find the kind of folks who'd appreciate him. One night when he was licking his dinner plate, his ears perked up. A couple of ranch hands were going on about a gang of wild cowboys.

662 UNIT 6 What Makes a Hero?

Practice the Skills

4 **Key Reading Skill**

Clarifying What does "he wore a ten-dollar hat on a five-cent head" mean?

Additional Support

Literature Focus Lesson

Hero Begin talking about Pecos Bill as a hero. Make a list on the board of Bill's positive and negative qualities. Note that the author says Bill would become a great cowboy: "He just needed to find the kind of folks who'd appreciate him." Ask students to discuss how feeling appreciated influences greatness. Encourage students to share personal experiences with people who have been able to see beyond the surface to appreciate the positive qualities of another person. Ask students how they can help people feel that they are appreciated. **AS**

"Yep. Those fellas are more animal than human," one ranch hand was saying. **5**

"Yep. Them's the toughest bunch I ever come across. Heck, they're so tough, they can kick fire out of flint rock with their bare toes!"

"Yep. 'N' they like to bite nails in half for fun!"

"Who are these fellers?" asked Bill.

"The Hell's Gate Gang," said the ranch hand. "The mangiest,[7] meanest, most low-down bunch of low-life varmints that ever grew hair."

"Sounds like my kind of folks," said Bill, and before anyone could holler whoa, he jumped on his horse and took off for Hell's Gate Canyon.

Bill hadn't gone far when disaster struck. His horse stepped in a hole and broke its ankle.

"Dang!" said Bill as he stumbled up from the spill. He draped the lame critter around his neck and hurried on.

After he'd walked about a hundred more miles, Bill heard some mean rattling. Then a fifty-foot rattlesnake reared up its ugly head and stuck out its long, forked tongue, ready to fight.

"Knock it off, you scaly-hided fool. I'm in a hurry," Bill said.

The snake didn't give a spit for Bill's plans. He just rattled on.

Before the cussed[8] varmint could strike, Bill had no choice but to knock him cross-eyed. "Hey, feller," he said, holding up the dazed snake. "I like your **spunk**. Come go with us." Then he wrapped the rattler around his arm and continued on his way.

After Bill had hiked another hundred miles with his horse around his neck and his snake around his arm, he heard a terrible growl. A huge mountain lion was crouching on a cliff, getting ready to leap on top of him.

---

7. The word **mangiest** comes from *mange*, a skin disease of animals that causes loss of hair in spots. So "the mangiest" means "the most shabby or worn out in appearance."

8. The word **cussed** (KUS ud) means stubborn and difficult to deal with.

Vocabulary

spunk (spunk) *n.* courage, spirit, and determination

Practice the Skills

5 **English Language Coach**

Borrowed Words The word **ranch** was borrowed from the Spanish word *rancho*. Do you know what a *ranch hand* is? If not, look up *hand* in a dictionary and find a meaning that makes helps you define *ranch hand*.

Pecos Bill **663**

Teach

EL Language Coach

Borrowed Words Say: Now that you know that the word *ranch* comes from Spanish, think about the different ways the English word *hand* can be used. What does it mean to "lend a hand"? *(to help out)* From this expression, what do you think a ranch hand does? *(helps out or does chores on a ranch)* **EL** **BL**

C Critical Thinking

Analysis Ask: What does Bill admire about the rattlesnake? Why do you think he likes it and decides to take it along? *(Possible response: He admires the rattlesnake for putting up a fight. He values toughness in himself and others, so he takes the rattlesnake on the journey.)* **OL**

Differentiated Instruction

Music Discuss with students what makes Pecos Bill so popular. Pecos Bill has been the subject of films, stories, plays, and songs. In cowboy music, there are references to Pecos Bill as well as whole songs written about him. Bring one or two songs to class to play for students. Then have students work in small groups or with partners to write their own lyrics for a song about Pecos Bill. Ask for volunteers to sing and play these songs for the class. **OL**

Objectives
- Make inferences
- Clarify ideas and text
- Analyze borrowed words
- Monitor comprehension
- Identify literary elements: hero

Teach

L Literary Element

Cultural Context Ask: How is the dialogue in "Pecos Bill" different from the dialogue in "Hercules"? *(Possible response: The dialogue in "Pecos Bill" is more casual and contains more slang.)* What does this tell you about each culture? *(Possible response: This tells me that ancient Greek culture was formal, and Wild West culture was informal.)* **OL**

C Critical Thinking

Evaluation Say: Imagine that someone you admire at school starts spending a great deal of time with a tough crowd. What would you think of this choice? What advice might you give this person? *(Responses will vary. Possible response: It is an unwise choice; stop hanging out with tough kids.)* **OL**

"Don't jump, you mangy bobtailed fleabag!" Bill said.

Well, call any mountain lion a mangy bobtailed fleabag, and he'll jump on your back for sure. After this one leaped onto Bill, so much fur began to fly that it darkened the sky. Bill wrestled that mountain lion into a headlock, then squeezed him so tight that the big cat had to cry uncle. **6**

L When the embarrassed old critter started to slink off, Bill felt sorry for him. "Aw, c'mon, you big silly," he said. "You're more like me than most humans I meet."

He saddled up the cat, jumped on his back, and the four of them headed for the canyon, with the mountain lion screeching, the horse neighing, the rattler rattling, and Pecos Bill hollering a wild war whoop.

When the Hell's Gate Gang heard those noises coming from the prairie, they nearly fainted. They dropped their dinner plates, and their faces turned as white as bleached desert bones. Their knees knocked and their six-guns shook.

"Hey, there!" Bill said as he sidled up to their campfire, grinning. "Who's the boss around here?"

A nine-foot feller with ten pistols at his sides stepped forward and in a shaky voice said, "Stranger, I was. But from now on, it'll be you."

"Well, thanky, pardner," said Bill. "Get on with your dinner, boys. Don't let me interrupt."

Once Bill settled down with the Hell's Gate Gang, his true genius revealed itself. With his gang's help, he put together the biggest ranch in the southwest. He used New Mexico as a **corral** and Arizona as a pasture. **7**

Visual Vocabulary
A *tarantula* is a large, hairy spider. Its sting can be painful, but it is not usually dangerous to humans.

He invented tarantulas and scorpions as practical jokes. He also invented roping. Some say his rope was exactly as long as the equator; others argue it was two feet shorter.

Things were going fine for Bill until Texas began to suffer the worst **drought** in its history. It was so dry that all the rivers turned as powdery as biscuit flour.

Vocabulary

drought (drowt) *n.* a long period of very dry weather

664 UNIT 6 What Makes a Hero?

Practice the Skills

6 **Key Literary Element**

Cultural Context Is this story beginning to remind you of the Hercules myth you read? How are the stories similar so far? How do their cultural contexts make them different?

7 **English Language Coach**

Borrowed Words What language does **corral** come from? Look it up.

Additional Support

Literature Focus Lesson

Humor The author presents many exaggerated and humorous descriptions in the story. Invite students to list on the board exaggerated descriptions, such as "as tough as a pine knot" and "knock him cross-eyed." Invite students to describe the images that these exaggerations help them visualize. As they continue to read the story, have students create a chart in their Learner's Notebooks that lists dialogue, expressions, and comparisons that they find humorous. Then have students rewrite the items in their lists in their own words. **OL**

The parched[9] grass was catching fire everywhere. For a while Bill and his gang managed to lasso water from the Rio Grande.[10] When that river dried up, they lassoed water from the Gulf of Mexico.

No matter what he did, though, Bill couldn't get enough water to stay ahead of the drought. All his horses and cows were starting to dry up and blow away like balls of tumbleweed. It was horrible.

Just when the end seemed near, the sky turned a deep shade of purple. From the distant mountains came a terrible roar. The cattle began to **stampede,** and a huge black funnel of a cyclone appeared, heading straight for Bill's ranch.

The rest of the Hell's Gate Gang shouted, "Help!" and ran.

But Pecos Bill wasn't scared in the least. "Yahoo!" he hollered, and he swung his **lariat** and lassoed that cyclone around its neck.

Bill held on tight as he got sucked up into the middle of the swirling cloud. He grabbed the cyclone by the ears and pulled himself onto her back. Then he let out a whoop and headed that twister across Texas.

The mighty cyclone bucked, arched, and screamed like a wild **bronco.** But Pecos Bill just held on with his legs and used his strong hands to wring the rain out of her wind. He wrung out rain that flooded Texas, New Mexico, and Arizona, until finally he slid off the shriveled-up funnel and fell into California. The earth sank about two hundred feet below sea level in the spot where Bill landed, creating the area known today as Death Valley. **8**

"There. That little waterin' should hold things for a while," he said, brushing himself off.

After his cyclone ride, no horse was too wild for Pecos Bill. He soon found a young colt that was as tough as a tiger and as crazy as a streak of lightning. He named the colt Widow Maker and raised him on barbed wire[11] and dynamite. Whenever the two rode together, they back-flipped and somersaulted all over Texas, loving every minute of it. **9**

---

9. Something that is **parched** is dried out.

10. The **Rio Grande** is a large river that forms part of the border between Texas and Mexico. The words mean "large river" in Spanish.

11. **Barbed wire** has sharp points. On the plains, fences were made from barbed wire to keep cattle in and cattle thieves out.

Practice the Skills

8 English Language Coach

Borrowed Words The words **lariat** and **bronco** come from the same language. What is that language? What does each word mean?

9 Key Reading Skill

Clarifying Why does Pecos Bill name his horse Widow Maker? What do you think the name means?

Pecos Bill **665**

Teach

R Reading Skill

Review Activating Prior Knowledge Say: Bill "wrung the rain" out of the cyclone's wind and then fell into California. What do you know about Death Valley? How does this help you understand what happened in the story? *(Possible response: Death Valley is well below sea level and is very hot and dry. This helps explain how Bill "created" this place after wringing the water out of the wind and then landing in California.)* **AL**

L Literary Element

Cultural Context Ask: How does Bill show that he is big, wild, and tough? *(Possible responses: He is larger than life; he is able to manage wild animals; he is amazingly strong.)* **OL**

News Report Assign students to groups of three or four. Tell them to imagine that they are covering Bill's encounter with the cyclone for the evening news. Have them use the following guidelines:

• Include all the facts.
• Get a quote from Bill.

• Use expressive voice and body language.
• Interview bystanders.

Give students time to plan and rehearse their reports and then have each group perform for the class. **OL**

Objectives
• Identify literary elements: humor, cultural context
• Evaluate text
• Activate prior knowledge

Teach

R Reading Skill

Clarifying **Say:** Read the definition of *reverted* at the bottom of the page. What is Bill doing that shows he is reverting to his old ways? *(Possible response: He is howling at the moon like a coyote. This is reverting to his old ways because he left the coyotes a long time ago.)* **OL**

EL Language Coach

Borrowed Words **Say:** You know that *catastrophe* comes from the Greek language. Greeks often told tragic stories. Use context clues along with what you know about Greek culture to figure out what the word means. *(Possible response: a terrible or tragic event.)* **EL BL**

One day when Bill and Widow Maker were bouncing around the Pecos River, they came across an awesome sight: a wild-looking, red-haired woman riding on the back of the biggest catfish Bill had ever seen. The woman looked like she was having a ball, screeching, "Ride 'em, cowgirl!" as the catfish whipped her around in the air.

"What's your name?" Bill shouted.

"Slue-foot Sue! What's it to you?" she said. Then she war-whooped away over the windy water.

Thereafter all Pecos Bill could think of was Slue-foot Sue. He spent more and more time away from the Hell's Gate Gang as he wandered the **barren** cattle-lands, looking for her. When he finally found her lonely little cabin, he was so love-struck he reverted[12] to some of his old coyote ways. He sat on his haunches in the moonlight and began a-howling and ah-hooing.

Well, the good news was that Sue had a bit of coyote in her too, so she completely understood Bill's language. She stuck her head out her window and ah-hooed back to him that she loved him, too. Consequently Bill and Sue decided to get married. **10**

On the day of the wedding Sue wore a beautiful white dress with a steel-spring bustle,[13] and Bill appeared in an elegant buckskin suit.

But after a lovely ceremony, a terrible catastrophe occurred. Slue-foot Sue got it into her head that she just had to have a ride on Bill's wild bronco, Widow Maker.

"You can't do that, honey," Bill said. "He won't let any human toss a leg over him but me."

"Don't worry," said Sue. "You know I can ride anything on four legs, not to mention what flies or swims."

Bill tried his best to talk Sue out of it, but she wouldn't listen. She was dying to buck on the back of that bronco. Wearing her white wedding dress with the bustle, she jumped on Widow Maker and kicked him with her spurs.

---

12. The word ***reverted*** here means "returned to an earlier behavior."
13. A ***bustle*** is a pad or frame once worn by women under their skirts.

Vocabulary

barren (BAIR un) *adj.* having little or no plant life; empty

666 UNIT 6 What Makes a Hero?

Practice the Skills

10 **Key Reading Skill**

Clarifying Have you understood the last two paragraphs? Were any parts confusing? Were any words unfamiliar? Reread the two paragraphs carefully. Look up any words you don't know. Then, in your own words, tell what happens in the paragraphs.

Additional Support

Reading in the Real World

Career Pecos Bill is a thrill seeker. Nothing scares him. To be happy, he needs to face bigger and bigger challenges. Discuss with students what kinds of careers are best suited to Bill's personality. First, brainstorm together to list possible careers. For example, Bill could be a police officer, an astronaut, an athlete, or a mountain climber. Then have students work in pairs or small groups to research one of these careers. After students have conducted their research, ask them to share their findings with the class. **OL**

Well, that bronco didn't need any thorns in his side to start bucking to beat the band. He bounded up in the air with such amazing force that suddenly Sue was flying high into the Texas sky. She flew over plains and mesas, over canyons, deserts, and prairies. She flew so high that she looped over the new moon and fell back to earth.

But when Sue landed on her steel-spring bustle, she rebounded right back into the heavens! As she bounced back and forth between heaven and earth, Bill whirled his lariat above his head, then lassoed her. But instead of bringing Sue back down to earth, he got yanked into the night sky alongside her!

Together Pecos Bill and Slue-foot Sue bounced off the earth and went flying to the moon. And at that point Bill must have gotten some sort of foothold in a moon crater—because neither he nor Sue returned to earth. Not ever.

Folks figure those two must have dug their boot heels into some moon cheese and raised a pack of wild coyotes just like themselves. Texans'll tell you that every time you hear thunder rolling over the desolate land near the Pecos River, it's just Bill's family having a good laugh upstairs. When you hear a strange ah-hooing in the dark night, don't be fooled—that's the sound of Bill howling *on* the moon instead of *at* it. And when lights flash across the midnight sky, you can bet it's Bill and Sue riding the backs of some white-hot shooting stars. **11** ○

Practice the Skills

11 **BIG Question**

Was Pecos Bill a hero? On the "Pecos Bill" page of Foldable 6, write at least two reasons to support your answer. Your response will help you complete the Unit Challenge later.

Pecos Bill and Slue-foot Sue bouncing over the moon. Illustration from American Tall Tales.

Analyzing the Art Which sentence from the story tells what's happening in this picture?

Pecos Bill **667**

Teach

C Critical Thinking

Application Ask: What elements of exaggeration are used at the end of the story? How does the exaggeration build to a climax? *(Possible response: The ending of the story describes Sue's bouncing from the earth to the moon and back. The exaggeration builds to a climax when Bill and Sue land in outer space and stay there.)* **OL**

BQ **BIG Question**

Ask: What do you admire about Pecos Bill? What are some things you do not like about him? *(Possible response: He is strong, but he is very reckless.)* **AS**

Assess

CheckPoint

Use the CheckPoint questions provided on Presentation Plus! to check for comprehension of the selection. These questions can be used with interactive response keypads for immediate student feedback.

Literature Focus Lesson

Tall Tale Explain to students that a tall tale is a humorous, highly exaggerated story, often about a legendary hero. Many American tall tales were created during the 1800s as the United States expanded westward. People made up stories about heroes who handled the same problems they faced. People added their own exaggerations to the stories, making them more humorous, more impossible to believe, and more fun to listen to with each retelling. Have students think about some of the hardships in the Wild West that are included in this story. Talk with students about what kind of audience might be most interested in tall tales and why. **OL**

Objectives
• Clarify ideas and text
• Analyze borrowed words
• Apply information
• Find meaning in art

667

Assess

Resources for page 668

📁 Selection Quick Check, p. 54

📁 Selection and Unit Assessment, p. 64

⊙ ExamView Assessment Suite

⊙ Interactive Tutor: Self-Assessment

Students can respond to the *After You Read* items in their Learner's Notebooks or on a separate sheet of paper.

Answering the

1. Possible response: Bill is strong like Hercules but not clever like Anansi.

2. Three: a horse, a rattlesnake, and a mountain lion.

3. Bill started life with a human family. He became different because he fell out of the wagon and was raised by coyotes.

4. In the first subplot, Bill needs to solve a drought problem. In the second subplot, he meets Slue-foot Sue and wants to marry her.

Critical Thinking

5. Possible response: The fact that Bill and Sue landed on the moon and still live there.

6. Responses will vary.

668

After You Read Pecos Bill

Answering the **BIG Question**

1. Do you think Pecos Bill, as a hero, is more like Anansi or Hercules? Compare his qualities with those of Anansi and Hercules.

2. **Recall** When Pecos Bill met the Hell's Gate Gang, how many animals did he have with him and what were they?
   Tip Right There

3. **Recall** How did Pecos Bill start out in life? What event caused his life to be different from that of his brothers and sisters?
   Tip Right There

4. **Identify** After Pecos Bill defeats the Hell's Gate Gang, there are two more small plots, or subplots, to the story. In the first subplot, he faces a new problem. In the second subplot, he has a new goal. Identify these two subplots.
   Tip Think and Search

Critical Thinking

5. **Analyze** What do you think is the biggest exaggeration in this story?
   Tip Author and Me

6. **Evaluate** What personality traits of Pecos Bill do you admire?
   Tip On Your Own

Talk About Your Reading

Work with a partner to create a tall tale about an imaginary hero in your school. First think of a problem that needs to be solved. Then create a hero with exaggerated traits who will tackle the problem. How can you make your school, the problem, and your hero larger than life?

Objectives (pp. 668–669)
Reading Clarify ideas and text
Literature Identify key literary elements: cultural context
Vocabulary Explore word origins: borrowed words
Grammar Write complex sentences

Parts of my tall tale	Exaggerated descriptions
my school	
the problem	
the hero	

Talk About Your Reading

Possible response:

	large, beautiful building with spiral staircases, fancy windows, magnificent woodwork, marble floors
	Cafeteria Food: the cafeteria, spilled food, overflowing garbage cans, mushy shapeless food on plastic trays, students talking with mouths full of food, food dripping down onto students' clothes, everybody talking, nobody listening
	The Perfect Student: popular with both students and teachers, neatly dressed and fashionable, able to slide through nastiness without being affected

Skills Review

Key Reading Skill: Clarifying

7. In your Learner's Notebook, read the list of things you needed to clarify in this folktale. If you haven't looked them all up, do it now.

8. Give one example of how the skill of clarifying helped you understand this story. Write your answer in your Learner's Notebook.

Key Literary Element: Cultural Context

9. Think about the character of Pecos Bill. What do his special qualities tell you about the culture of the American West?

10. Is Pecos Bill mean or violent? Why or why not? What does that tell you about the culture in the American West?

11. How does Pecos Bill interact with nature? What does that tell you about the culture of the American West?

Vocabulary Check

Write your own fill-in-the-blank sentences for the vocabulary words below. Include enough context clues for a classmate to complete each sentence correctly. Then exchange papers and fill in your classmate's exercise.

12. drought

13. spunk

14. desolate

15. barren

16. **English Language Coach** Many of the words in this story were borrowed from Spanish. What does this tell you about the American West and who lived there?

Grammar Link: Combining Sentence Clauses

A **complex sentence** has one independent clause and one or more dependent clauses. A complex sentence can sometimes make your meaning more clear than two or more simple sentences. When you write two or more sentences that are closely related in meaning, try combining them to form a complex sentence.

A **dependent clause** has a subject and a predicate, but it does not express a complete thought. A dependent clause is always used with an independent clause.

Realizing that he was not a coyote,	→	Pecos Bill went to live with people.
dependent clause		*independent clause*

Before the cussed varmint could strike,	→	Bill had no choice but to knock him cross-eyed.
dependent clause		*independent clause*

Grammar Practice

Write each sentence. Underline each dependent clause.

17. When Pecos Bill got thirsty, he squeezed a cloud to drink.

18. Pecos Bill became the leader of the Hell's Gate Gang because he was so tough.

19. Slue-foot Sue rode a huge catfish on the Pecos River, which ran through the Wild West.

Literature Online

Web Activities For eFlashcards, Selection Quick Checks, and other Web activities, go to www.glencoe.com.

Skills Review

Key Reading Skill: Clarifying

7. Responses will vary.

8. Responses will vary.

Key Literary Element: Cultural Context

9. Possible response: Things in the West were big, wild, and tough.

10. Possible response: Bill isn't mean; he is rough, not violent; he often befriends the varmints he has fought; he is a match for the problems and dangers people faced in the West.

11. Responses will vary.

Vocabulary Check

Sample responses:

12. The _____ was so bad that no one had any water to drink.

13. My little sister showed _____ when she stood up to the class bully.

14. After everyone moved out, the town was _____.

15. Death Valley is a _____ place.

16. **English Language Coach** Answers will vary.

Close

Ask students to summarize how reading "Pecos Bill" helps them answer the Big Question.

Grammar Link: Combining Sentence Clauses

Grammar Practice

17. When Pecos Bill got thirsty, he squeezed a cloud to drink.

18. Pecos Bill became the leader of the Hell's Gate Gang because he was so tough.

19. Slue-foot Sue rode a huge catfish on the Pecos River, which ran through the Wild West.

Comparing and Contrasting

Objective covered in this workshop:
• Compare and contrast

Teaching Students to Compare and Contrast

Why Is It Important?

• Comparing and contrasting helps writers relate to and influence readers.

• Comparing and contrasting helps readers find and understand the argument in a selection.

• Students who are able to see similarities and differences in events, people, and ideas in a text are better able to construct meaning from a selection.

How to Help Students Get It

• Ask students to look carefully at the descriptions and other details an author includes in a selection.

• Have students look for clue words—*both, same, alike, also,* and *similarly,* or *unlike, but, although, yet,* and *instead*—that signal that the author is comparing or contrasting items.

• Invite students to think about why a writer might compare or contrast things or people. Is there a larger purpose or idea the author may wish to convey?

• Tell students that sometimes there are no signal words to indicate comparison or contrast. In those instances, students must infer similarities or differences between items from descriptive details.

Reading to Answer the Big Question

Dragon, Dragon by John Gardner
When a mischievous dragon threatens a kingdom, the king offers his daughter's hand in marriage to anyone who will slay the dragon. The only son of a cobbler follows his father's advice and turns out to be the hero. A forgetful wizard who accidentally turns the queen into a rosebush is just one of the other unique characters in this humorous fairy tale.

The King of Mazy May by Jack London
Walt's father has left him alone in the Klondike to look after their land and a neighbor's claim. He is put to the test when he learns that claim-jumpers plan to steal the neighbor's land. Walt becomes a hero when he protects the claim by undertaking a dangerous journey with the claim-jumpers' own sled and dogs.

Workshop Resources

PACING (DAYS)		LESSON	STUDENT MATERIALS	TEACHER RESOURCES
STANDARD	BLOCK			
1	½	Key Skill Lesson: Comparing and Contrasting	🐾 Key Reading Skills Practice, p. 23 🐾 English Language Coach Review, p. 43	🖋 Bellringer Options Transparencies –Selection Focus Transparencies 16–17 –Daily Language Practice 56 🖋 Read Aloud, Think Aloud Transparencies –Key Reading Skills 4 💿 Presentation Plus!
1	1	"Dragon, Dragon"	💻 Glencoe Online 🐾 Unit Vocabulary Review, p. 41 🐾 Academic Vocabulary Review, p. 44 📁 English Language Coach 🐾 Active Reading Graphic Organizer, p. 25 🐾 Literary Analysis, p. 24 💿 StudentWorks Plus™ 💻 Online Student Edition 💿 Literature Classics 📁 Selection and Unit Assessments, p. 65	🖋 Literary and Text Analysis Transparencies 54 💻 Puzzlemaker 💿 Skill Level Up!™ A Language Arts Game 💻 BookLink 3 📔 Assessment by Learning Objective (Diagnostic and Formative) 💿 Interactive Tutor: Self-Assessment 💿 TeacherWorks Plus™
1		"The King of Mazy May"	💻 Glencoe Online 🐾 Unit Vocabulary Review, p. 41 🐾 Academic Vocabulary Review, p. 44 📁 English Language Coach 🐾 Active Reading Graphic Organizer, p. 27 🐾 Literary Analysis, p. 24 💿 StudentWorks Plus™ 💻 Online Student Edition 💿 Literature Classics 📁 Selection and Unit Assessments, p. 66	🖋 Literary and Text Analysis Transparencies 54 💻 Puzzlemaker 💿 Skill Level Up!™ A Language Arts Game 💻 BookLink 3 📔 Assessment by Learning Objective (Diagnostic and Formative) 💿 Interactive Tutor: Self-Assessment 💿 TeacherWorks Plus™

Keys for Unit Resource

📁 Blackline Master   🔒 DVD

📔 Workbook   🖋 Transparency

📖 Supplemental Text   💻 Web-based

💿 CD-ROM   🐾 Fast File

Level Appropriate Code

AS = Activities for all students

AL = Activities for students working above grade level

OL = Activities for students working at grade level

BL = Activities for students working below grade level

EL = Activities for English language learners

Focus

BELLRINGER Options

- **Selection Focus Transparencies 16–17**
- **Daily Language Practice Transparency 56**

Focus Activity Say: Think about fairy tales that you know well. Which one is your favorite, and who are your favorite characters in it? Why? *(Responses will vary.)* **OL**

Teach

R Reading Skill

Comparing and Contrasting

Help students practice the skill by holding up two different but related items, such as a pen and a pencil. **Ask:** How are these two things alike? *(They are both writing instruments; they have a similar shape.)* How are they different? *(One uses ink; the other, graphite.)* When you tell how things are alike and different, you are comparing and contrasting. You can compare and contrast characters, settings, and plots in your reading as well. **AS**

Skills Focus

You will practice using these skills when you read the following selections:
- "Dragon, Dragon," p. 674
- "The King of Mazy May," p. 688

Reading

- Comparing and contrasting

Literature

- Recognizing and analyzing theme

Vocabulary

- Understanding word sources and histories

Writing/Grammar

- Using commas in compound and complex sentences

Objectives (pp. 670–671)
Reading Compare and contrast

670 UNIT 6

Skill Lesson

Comparing and Contrasting

Learn It!

What Is It? Comparing and contrasting means looking for similarities and differences. We do this all the time. You compare your teachers to one another and your classmates to one another, don't you? You also compare foods, the weather, cars, TV shows, and music.

Sometimes an author wants you to compare and contrast two or more characters, settings, or ideas to help you understand or feel parts of a story. For example, if one character is a coward, you may have a better appreciation of how brave another character is.

R

Copyright 1997 Randy Glasbergen.
www.glasbergen.com

GLASBERGEN

"No dolphin ever spent $2,000 just to play silly games on a computer that will be obsolete in six months. That *proves* we're smarter than humans!"

© 1995 Randy Glasbergen.

Analyzing Cartoons
The dolphins contrast themselves to humans. Why is their comparison funny?

Additional Support

Differentiated Instruction

Analyzing Cartoons As you discuss the cartoon at the beginning of the workshop, invite students to bring in cartoons from newspapers or magazines they read. Instruct them to look for cartoons that involve comparison. When students find a cartoon or comic to share, give them a few minutes to present it to the class. If several students read the same newspaper, they may bring in the same comic. The class can make its own comic book by collecting cartoons in a three-ring binder. **AS**

Why Is It Important? When you pay attention to similarities and differences, you understand things better. For example, if you are a football player and you want to understand soccer, it helps to find out how it's both similar to and different from the game of football.

How Do I Do It? As you read, be alert for things to compare. You will read a folktale about three brothers seeking their fortune. Compare and contrast everything the brothers do and say. Sometimes it's a good idea to compare and contrast something you read about to something or someone you already know—like yourself!

Here's how one student compared two characters in "Persephone."

> Persephone was a high-spirited, sunny girl who loved springtime and flowers and running outdoors with her friends . . . Suddenly the earth split open at her feet. Out dashed a golden chariot pulled by black horses and driven by a stern-faced man in black armor.

> *Persephone's bright and loves running in the sunlight. The man is wearing black armor and his chariot is pulled from underground by black horses. She's happy, and he's stern. I have a feeling that these differences between the characters are going to be an important part of the story.*

Study Central Visit www.glencoe.com and click on Study Central to review comparing and contrasting.

Practice It!

Make a list of similarities between four of the characters you've read about in Unit 6: Persephone, Hades, Pecos Bill, and Hercules. Then make a list of their differences. You can compare and contrast their strengths, weaknesses, physical traits, character traits, their actions, or ideas about why they are heroes.

Use It!

As you read "Dragon, Dragon," compare and contrast the three brothers to each other. When you begin "The King of Mazy May," notice how the author compares and contrasts the main character to other boys.

Teach

Study Central Have students access the Web site to review comparing and contrasting and to complete a related activity.

C Critical Thinking

Analysis Say: Read the selection paragraph in the How Do I Do It? section. Sometimes it's a good idea to compare and contrast what's in a story to what you know from your own life. When you do this, what other reading skills are you using? *(activating prior knowledge and connecting)* **OL**

R Reading Skill

Comparing and Contrasting Have students look through the book to find two photos or images that they can compare and contrast. Have them share their observations with the class. **AS**

Resources for page 671

Use Key Reading Skills Transparency 4 in *Read Aloud, Think Aloud* to help students practice comparing and contrasting.

Reading in the Real World

Citizenship Ask students to interview someone who contributes to their community. It might be a teacher, a coach, a religious leader, or someone in their family. Guide students to identify what they admire about the person and then have them ask the person the following questions:

- What motivates you to help others?
- What people have been influential in your life?
- What advice do you have for young people? **OL**

Objectives
- Compare and contrast
- Analyze text

671

Teach

More About the Author

"The house was full of books," John Gardner remembered of his childhood home. His mother, a former English teacher, and father, a farmer, loved to read aloud at home and at community gatherings. Gardner credited the Bible, Charles Dickens, and Walt Disney as important influences on his taste in literature as he grew up. As an adult, he became an expert on literature from the Middle Ages, and he used this knowledge in his fairy tales. Gardner was born in 1933 and died in 1982. This story was first published in 1975.

EL Language Coach

Word Histories You may wish to introduce students to a few more words that come from myths. For example, we say someone is *narcissistic* if he or she is self-centered; this word comes from the myth of Narcissus, a boy who fell in love with his own reflection. **EL**

Before You Read : Dragon, Dragon

John Gardner

Meet the Author

John Gardner wrote novels, short stories and other selections for young readers, books on how to write, and more. Gardner was also a teacher and studied classic literature. Gardner wanted his books to deliver a moral message. "True art is moral," he said. "It seeks to improve life." See page R3 of the Author Files for more on John Gardner.

Author Search For more about John Gardner, go to www .glencoe.com.

Objectives (pp. 672–683)
Reading Compare and contrast • Make connections from text to self
Literature Identify key literary elements: theme
Vocabulary Explore word histories

Vocabulary Preview

plagued (playgd) *v.* was greatly troubled or distressed; form of the verb *plague* **(p. 675)** *The kingdom was plagued by a dragon.*

ravaged (RAV ijd) *v.* destroyed violently; ruined; form of the verb *ravage* **(p. 675)** *The dragon ravaged villages and farms.*

tyrant (TY runt) *n.* a cruel, unjust ruler **(p. 676)** *The king was no tyrant; he loved his people and treated them well.*

quest (kwest) *n.* a search for a particular object or goal **(p. 679)** *The cobbler's son went on a quest to kill the dragon.*

meekly (MEEK lee) *adv.* in a timid and mild manner; gently **(p. 769)** *After hearing the dragon's roar, the boy responded meekly.*

lunged (lunjd) *v.* made a sudden forward movement; charged; form of the verb *lunge* **(p. 679)** *The dragon lunged before the boy had time to think or run.*

Write to Learn In your Learner's Notebook, write at least one synonym for each vocabulary word.

English Language Coach

Word Histories So far in this book, you've learned that many English words are based on words from other languages. You've learned to recognize roots, base words, prefixes, and suffixes. You've learned about compound words, borrowed words, and words from names. All these things are part of etymology (et uh MOL uh jee), the study of words and their histories.

People who study words enjoy discovering interesting and unusual word origins. For example, in "Dragon, Dragon," the king's magician says a *spell*. This word first meant simply "a talk" or "to talk." In the 1500s, when many people believed in magic, an additional meaning came into use—"words thought to have magical power." **EL**

Write to Learn *Abracadabra* is a well-known "magic" word (and a fun one to spell out too). What language did it come from? Write your guess in your Learner's Notebook, and then look it up.

Additional Support

Author Search To expand students' appreciation of John Gardner, have them access the Web site for additional information and resources.

Differentiated Instruction

Vocabulary Game Reinforce vocabulary words from the previous stories in this unit by incorporating them into a vocabulary concentration game. Choose a few words from each story, including the words on this page. Make a pair of cards for each word. Put the words on only one side. Place the cards face down in a square. Divide students into teams that will take turns turning over two cards and then turning them face down again as they try to find matches. When a match is found, the team has to define the word or use it in a sentence to earn a point. If they are unable to do so, the cards go back and the next team gets a chance. **OL**

Skills Preview

Key Reading Skill: Comparing and Contrasting

To compare and contrast means to look for similarities and differences between characters, settings, events, and ideas. To compare characters, look for the words the author uses to describe them. Notice the similarities and differences in different *kinds* of characters. For example, do all the female characters act in one way? Do all the elderly characters do the same thing? You can also compare and contrast details and ideas in the story.

Partner Talk With a partner, choose two stories you've read in this unit. Make a list of the differences between the stories in genre, setting, and heroes. Then list their similarities.

Key Literary Element: Theme

The theme is the main idea or meaning behind a story. It may be the moral of the story or simply an idea to think about, such as:

- Hard work pays off, or
- How can a member of society still be an individual?

It can be difficult to find the theme of a story. Often the author doesn't state it directly, so you must figure it out for yourself.

Write to Learn Think of a theme you might like to express in a short story. Write your theme in your Learner's Notebook.

Interactive Literary Elements Handbook
To review or learn more about the literary elements, go to www.glencoe.com.

Get Ready to Read

Connect to the Reading

What do you think it would be like to live in the time of castles, kings, queens, knights, wizards, and dragons? What fairy-tale character would you like to be? Why?

Class Talk Brainstorm a list of characters that often appear in fairy tales. Then brainstorm a list of events that usually happen. Write these lists on the board.

Build Background

This story seems to be a typical fairy tale or folktale at first. There are all the usual characters doing the usual things. But you'll notice one difference very soon—the humor. Here are some places to look for humor:

- the dragon—the ways it troubles the kingdom
- the queen—what she's turned into and how she's taken care of
- the cobbler—the advice he gives his sons

Read carefully to be sure you understand all of the jokes.

Set Purposes for Reading

BIG Question Read "Dragon, Dragon" to meet a different sort of hero.

Set Your Own Purpose What else would you like to learn from the story to help you answer the Big Question? Write your own purpose on the "Dragon, Dragon" page of Foldable 6.

Keep Moving

Use these skills as you read the following selection.

Dragon, Dragon **673**

Teach

L Literary Element

Theme Ask: What book or story have you read, or what movie have you seen that made you think about an important question or life lesson? Describe the book, story, or movie and state its theme. *(Responses will vary.)* **OL**

R Reading Skill

Review Connecting Say: Imagine meeting up with a dangerous dragon in real life. What would you do? *(Responses will vary.)* **OL**

Interactive Literary Elements Handbook Have students access the Web site to improve their understanding of theme.

Literature Focus Lesson

Moral Remind students of the morals they developed when they began writing their fable. Explain that in a fable, the theme is stated at the end of the story but that in other stories, themes are less obvious. Choose a fable to read to the class. Give students the title and ask them to guess the moral. Ask for volunteers to explain their thinking. If there are several ideas about what the moral is, emphasize that readers can have different ideas about the moral or theme of a story but that those ideas must be supported by details from the story. **OL**

Objectives

- Identify literary elements: theme, moral
- Understand word histories
- Make connections from text to self

Teach

Viewing the Illustration

Say: Look at the picture. What mood does it set? *(Possible response: a mood of foreboding.)* What does it tell you about the story? *(Possible responses: that castles and royalty will be part of the story; that it is set in a time long ago)* **OL**

Readability Scores
Dale-Chall: 6.5
DRP: 54
Lexile: 1020

Dragon, Dragon

by John Gardner

674 UNIT 6   What Makes A Hero?

Additional Support

Differentiated Instruction

Building Background A castle is an image associated with fairy tales. Bring books of fairy tales to class. Have students look through the books and write down the main people, places, and objects that they find in the fairy tales. Have students share their lists with the class. Make a list on the board of the most common people, places, and things found in the fairytales. Have students talk about the ideas that they associate with each of the people, places, and things on the list. **AS**

674

There was once a king whose kingdom was plagued by a dragon. The king did not know which way to turn. The king's knights were all cowards who hid under their beds whenever the dragon came in sight, so they were of no use to the king at all. And the king's **wizard**[1] could not help either because, being old, he had forgotten his magic spells. Nor could the wizard look up the spells that had slipped his mind, for he had unfortunately misplaced his wizard's book many years before. The king was at his wit's end. **1 2**

Every time there was a full moon the dragon came out of his lair and **ravaged** the countryside. He frightened maidens and stopped up chimneys and broke store windows and set people's clocks back and made dogs bark until no one could hear himself think.

He tipped over fences and robbed graves and put frogs in people's drinking water and tore the last chapters out of novels and changed house numbers around so that people crawled into bed with their neighbors' wives.

He stole spark plugs out of people's cars and put firecrackers in people's cigars and stole the clappers from all the church bells and sprung every bear trap for miles around so the bears could wander wherever they pleased.

And to top it all off, he changed around all the roads in the kingdom so that people could not get anywhere except by starting out in the wrong direction. **3**

"That," said the king in a fury, "is enough!" And he called a meeting of everyone in the kingdom.

Now it happened that there lived in the kingdom a wise old cobbler[2] who had a wife and three sons. The cobbler and his family came to the king's meeting and stood way in back by the door, for the cobbler had a feeling that since he was nobody important there had probably been some mistake, and no doubt the king had intended the meeting for everyone in the kingdom except his family and him.

---

1. A **wizard** is a magician or sorcerer.
2. A **cobbler** is a person who makes or mends shoes.

Vocabulary

plagued (playgd) *v.* was greatly troubled or distressed

ravaged (RAV ijd) *v.* destroyed violently; ruined

Practice the Skills

1 Key Reading Skill

Comparing and Contrasting
So far, does this fairy tale seem like most others you know? As you read, compare and contrast how this tale is the same as and different from what you might expect.

2 English Language Coach

Word Histories **Wizard** comes from a Middle English word (*wys*), meaning "wise." Another word near the end of this paragraph also comes from *wys*. Can you find it?

3 Key Reading Skill

Comparing and Contrasting
Think of a monster from a movie and compare and contrast it to this dragon. First describe two or more qualities or actions that are similar about the two beasts. Then describe two or more qualities or actions that are different between the two beasts.

Dragon, Dragon **675**

Teach

EL Language Coach

Idioms Say: When a problem we face is very difficult to solve, we say that we are at our *wit's end.* Using what you just learned about the source of the word *wit,* what do you think the phrase means? *(Possible response: We have used up all our ideas and haven't found a solution.)* **OL**

R Reading Skill

Comparing and Contrasting
Say: Think about a time when you may have played a practical joke on someone—or had one played on you. How were those practical jokes the same as or different from the ones the dragon played? *(Possible responses: They are similar because they make people feel foolish and they are amusing. They are different because some of them could cause real danger.)* **OL**

Reading Fluency

Sentence Fluency Point out the long sentences on this page that list the dragon's evil deeds. These are sentences in which fluency is intentionally difficult. Ask proficient readers to read these sentences out loud. Discuss with students why the author repeats the word *and* between each item and doesn't use any commas. Point out that making the lists long and overwhelming makes the problem with the dragon seem overwhelming, too. **AS**

Objectives
• Identify idioms
• Use text features: illustration
• Compare and contrast

Teach

R Reading Skill

Comparing and Contrasting

Ask: How is the tone of this fairy tale different from the tone of other fairy tales you've read? *(Possible response: The tone here is very modern and casual.)* **Ask:** How does the language used add humor? *(Possible response: The tale is funny because outrageous things are described in a matter-of-fact way.)* **OL**

BQ BIG Question

Ask: Who is usually the hero in other fairy tales you've read? Do rich and powerful people usually win the battles, or do meek and poor people rise to a challenge? *(Possible response: The meek and poor people usually end up being the quiet heroes.)* **OL**

"Ladies and gentlemen," said the king when everyone was present. "I've put up with that dragon as long as I can. He has got to be stopped."

All the people whispered amongst themselves, and the king smiled, pleased with the impression he had made.

But the wise cobbler said gloomily, "It's all very well to talk about it—but how are you going to do it?"

R And now all the people smiled and winked as if to say, "Well, King, he's got you there!"

The king frowned.

"It's not that His Majesty hasn't tried," the queen spoke up loyally.

"Yes," said the king, "I've told my knights again and again that they ought to slay that dragon. But I can't *force* them to go. I'm not a **tyrant**." **4**

"Why doesn't the wizard say a magic spell?" asked the cobbler.

"He's done the best he can," said the king.

Vocabulary

tyrant (TY runt) *n.* a cruel, unjust ruler

Practice the Skills

4 **BIG Question**

At this point in the story, who do you think will be a hero—the king, the wizard, one of the knights, or the cobbler? Explain your answer. **BQ**

Analyzing the Art Make a list of words that you would use to describe the dragon in this illustration.

Additional Support

Literature Focus Lesson

Character Begin looking at the characters in terms of which one might be a hero. Make two columns on the board labeled "King" and "Cobbler." Direct students to copy the columns into their Learner's Notebooks and to write in the columns words from the story that describe each character. For the king, sample responses might include *pleased with the impression he made* and *not a tyrant.* For the cobbler, sample responses might be *wise* and *gloomily.* Add columns to the chart as the story unfolds and more characters are introduced. **OL**

The wizard blushed and everyone looked embarrassed. "I used to do all sorts of spells and chants when I was younger," the wizard explained. "But I've lost my spell book, and I begin to fear I'm losing my memory too. For instance, I've been trying for days to recall one spell I used to do. I forget, just now, what the **deuce** it was for. It went something like— 5

> Bimble
> Wimble
> Cha, Cha
> CHOOMPF!

Suddenly, to everyone's surprise, the queen turned into a rosebush.

"Oh dear," said the wizard.

"Now you've done it," groaned the king.

"Poor Mother," said the princess.

"I don't know what can have happened," the wizard said nervously, "but don't worry, I'll have her changed back in a jiffy." He shut his eyes and racked his brain for a spell that would change her back.

But the king said quickly, "You'd better leave well enough alone. If you change her into a rattlesnake we'll have to chop off her head."

Meanwhile the cobbler stood with his hands in his pockets, sighing at the waste of time. "About the dragon . . ." he began.

"Oh yes," said the king. "I'll tell you what I'll do. I'll give the princess' hand in marriage to anyone who can make the dragon stop."

"It's not enough," said the cobbler. "She's a nice enough girl, you understand. But how would an ordinary person support her? Also, what about those of us that are already married?" 6

"In that case," said the king, "I'll offer the princess' hand or half the kingdom or both—whichever is most convenient."

The cobbler scratched his chin and considered it. "It's not enough," he said at last. "It's a good enough kingdom, you understand, but it's too much responsibility."

Practice the Skills

5 English Language Coach

Word Histories The Latin word for "two" came into French and English as **deuce** (doos). It normally refers to two of something. However, in the expression "what the deuce," *deuce* is a polite substitution for the word *devil*.

6 Key Reading Skill

Comparing and Constrasting At this point in the story, how would you describe the cobbler's behavior? How is the cobbler different from the king? How is he different from the wizard?

Dragon, Dragon **677**

Teach

C Critical Thinking

Evaluation Ask: What can you conclude about the cobbler from what he has said and done so far? *(Possible responses: He seems wise; he shows his wisdom when he questions the king's offer; he has courage; he is not afraid to speak up.)* **OL**

English Language Coach

Idioms Write these phrases on the board: *slipped his mind, to top it all off,* and *leave well enough alone.* Explain to English language learners that these are all examples of idioms. Have students look through the selection for other idioms. Ask them to make one list of idioms that they understand and another of those that they have trouble with. Then pair English language learners with English-proficient students to discuss the meanings of the terms. Suggest that partners take turns reading aloud to each other the passages in which they found idioms. **EL**

Objectives

- Evaluate text
- Compare and contrast
- Identify idioms
- Identify literary elements: character

Teach

EL Language Coach

Word Histories **Say:** There is another word for "old" that comes from the Latin word *antiquus.* Can you guess what the word is in English? *(antique)* **EL** **BL**

R Reading Skill

Review Predicting **Ask:** Do you think that the eldest son will succeed or fail in slaying the dragon? What makes you think so? *(Possible response: The eldest son will fail because he is proud and does not want to follow his father's advice.)* **OL**

"Take it or leave it," the king said.

"I'll leave it," said the cobbler. And he shrugged and went home.

But the cobbler's **eldest** son thought the bargain was a good one, for the princess was very beautiful and he liked the idea of having half the kingdom to run as he pleased. So he said to the king, "I'll accept those terms, Your Majesty. By tomorrow morning the dragon will be slain." **7**

"Bless you!" cried the king.

"Hooray, hooray, hooray!" cried all the people, throwing their hats in the air.

The cobbler's eldest son beamed with pride, and the second eldest son looked at him enviously. The youngest son said timidly, "Excuse me, Your Majesty, but don't you think the queen looks a little unwell? If I were you I think I'd water her."

"Good heavens," cried the king, glancing at the queen who had been changed into a rosebush, "I'm glad you mentioned it!"

Now the cobbler's eldest son was very clever and was known far and wide for how quickly he could multiply fractions in his head. He was perfectly sure he could slay the dragon by somehow or other playing a trick on him, and he didn't feel that he needed his wise old father's advice. But he thought it was only polite to ask, and so he went to his father, who was working as usual at his cobbler's bench, and said, "Well, Father, I'm off to slay the dragon. Have you any advice to give me?"

The cobbler thought a moment and replied, "When and if you come to the dragon's lair, recite the following poem.

Dragon, dragon, how do you do?
I've come from the king to murder you.

Say it very loudly and firmly and the dragon will fall, God willing, at your feet."

"How curious!" said the eldest son. And he thought to himself, "The old man is not as wise as I thought. If I say something like that to the dragon, he will eat me up in an instant. The way to kill a dragon is to outfox³ him." And

---

3. To *outfox* means to outsmart.

Practice the Skills

7 ► **English Language Coach**

Word Histories In Old English, *eld* meant "old." The word changed over time to *old*, but the **EL** original word left us the words *elder, elderly,* and **eldest**.

Additional Support

Differentiated Instruction

Graphic Organizer Have students create a graphic organizer like this one to help them understand the cause-and-effect connections that move the plot along. After filling in two or three rows, have students continue the chart on their own as they read. **BL** **OL**

Cause	Effect
A dragon threatens the kingdom.	The king calls a meeting and offers a reward to anyone who can stop the dragon.
The cobbler's eldest son decides to go after the dragon.	The cobbler gives him a poem to recite to the dragon.

keeping his opinion to himself, the eldest son set forth on his **quest**.

When he came at last to the dragon's lair, which was a cave, the eldest son slyly disguised himself as a peddler and knocked on the door and called out, "Hello there!"

"There's nobody home!" roared a voice.

The voice was as loud as an earthquake, and the eldest son's knees knocked together in terror.

"I don't come to trouble you," the eldest son said **meekly**. "I merely thought you might be interested in looking at some of our brushes. Or if you'd prefer," he added quickly, "I could leave our catalog with you and I could drop by again, say, early next week."

"I don't want any brushes," the voice roared, "and I especially don't want any brushes next week."

"Oh," said the eldest son. By now his knees were knocking together so badly that he had to sit down.

Suddenly a great shadow fell over him, and the eldest son looked up. It was the dragon. The eldest son drew his sword, but the dragon **lunged** and swallowed him in a single gulp, sword and all, and the eldest son found himself in the dark of the dragon's belly. "What a fool I was not to listen to my wise old father!" thought the eldest son. And he began to weep bitterly.

"Well," sighed the king the next morning, "I see the dragon has not been slain yet."

"I'm just as glad, personally," said the princess, sprinkling the queen. "I would have had to marry that eldest son, and he had warts." **8**

Now the cobbler's middle son decided it was his turn to try. The middle son was very strong and was known far and wide for being able to lift up the corner of a church. He felt perfectly sure he could slay the dragon by simply laying into him, but he thought it would be only polite to ask his father's advice. So he went to his father and said to him, "Well,

Practice the Skills

8 Key Literary Element

Theme What could the main idea or the meaning behind the story be? Do you expect there to be a moral or an important idea to think about? Write down one or more possible themes in your Learner's Notebook.

Vocabulary

quest (kwest) *n.* a search for a particular object or goal

meekly (MEEK lee) *adv.* in a timid and mild manner; gently

lunged (lunjd) *v.* made a sudden forward movement; charged

Dragon, Dragon **679**

Teach

C Critical Thinking

Evaluation Ask: Do you think that the eldest son's strategy is a good one? *(Possible response: His strategy is bad because he assumes that he doesn't need his father's advice.)* **Ask:** Is this son as clever as he thinks he is? *(Possible response: The son is not as smart as he thinks he is because his strategy fails.)* **OL**

L Literary Element

Theme Say: Sometimes characters' behavior—and especially the mistakes they make—can help you identify the theme of a story. What is the eldest son's biggest mistake? *(Possible response: His biggest mistake is not taking his father's advice.)* **Ask:** What might that tell you about the theme? *(Possible response: The theme might be about respecting your elders.)* **OL**

Reading Fluency

Dialogue Help less-proficient readers connect with the story by helping them speak the dialogue. Have students act out a scene from the story. Encourage them to rehearse the scene until they know the dialogue by heart. Help each performer get inside his or her charac- ter's head by asking questions about that character's motivation—what the character wants, knows, and feels. Remind students to say the words as though they are really conversing. You may wish to have these students perform the scene for the rest of the class. **BL OL**

Objectives
• Analyze word histories
• Make predictions
• Evaluate text
• Identify literary elements: theme

Teach

R1 Reading Skill

Review Predicting Ask: Do you think that the middle son will succeed or fail in slaying the dragon? What makes you think so? *(Possible response: The middle son will fail because, like the eldest son, he is proud and doesn't listen to his father.)* OL

R2 Reading Skill

Comparing and Contrasting

Ask: What goes wrong with each son's plan to slay the dragon? What does each son do that is the same? *(Possible response: The first son uses his wits; the second uses his strength. Each plan fails because the sons overestimate their talents. Neither son listens to his father.)* OL

Father, I'm off to slay the dragon. Have you any advice for me?"

The cobbler told the middle son exactly what he'd told the eldest.

"When and if you come to the dragon's lair, recite the following poem.

Dragon, dragon, how do you do?
I've come from the king to murder you.

Say it very loudly and firmly, and the dragon will fall, God willing, at your feet."

R1 "What an odd thing to say," thought the middle son. "The old man is not as wise as I thought. You have to take these dragons by surprise." But he kept his opinion to himself and set forth.

When he came in sight of the dragon's lair, the middle son spurred his horse to a gallop and thundered into the entrance swinging his sword with all his might.

But the dragon had seen him while he was still a long way off, and being very clever, the dragon had crawled up on top of the door so that when the son came charging in he went under the dragon and on to the back of the cave and slammed into the wall. Then the dragon chuckled and got down off the door, taking his time, and strolled back to where the man and the horse lay unconscious from the terrific blow. Opening his mouth as if for a yawn, the dragon swallowed the middle son in a single gulp and put the horse in the freezer to eat another day.

R2 "What a fool I was not to listen to my wise old father," thought the middle son when he came to in the dragon's belly. And he too began to weep bitterly. **9**

That night there was a full moon, and the dragon ravaged the countryside so terribly that several families moved to another kingdom.

"Well," sighed the king in the morning, "still no luck in this dragon business, I see."

"I'm just as glad, myself," said the princess, moving her mother, pot and all, to the window where the sun could get at her. "The cobbler's middle son was a kind of humpback."

Practice the Skills

9 Key Reading Skill

Comparing and Contrasting Name at least three ways the eldest two brothers are alike and at least three ways their characters and actions are different.

Additional Support

English Language Coach

Metaphor Ask students to think about a time when they or someone they know succeeded at something that seemed extraordinarily difficult or impossible. For example, conquering a bad habit, such as sleeping through the alarm or forgetting to bring books back to the library.

As students begin to relate stories of overcoming hardship, explain that the phrase "slaying a dragon" is a metaphorical way of expressing the overcoming of hardship. **EL** Have students work in small groups to create other metaphorical phrases. **OL**

Now the cobbler's youngest son saw that his turn had come. He was very upset and nervous, and he wished he had never been born. He was not clever, like his eldest brother, and he was not strong, like his second-eldest brother. He was a decent, honest boy who always minded his elders. **10**

He borrowed a suit of armor from a friend of his who was a knight, and when the youngest son put the armor on it was so heavy he could hardly walk. From another knight he borrowed a sword, and that was so heavy that the only way the youngest son could get it to the dragon's lair was to drag it along behind his horse like a plow.

When everything was in readiness, the youngest son went for a last conversation with his father.

"Father, have you any advice to give me?" he asked.

"Only this," said the cobbler. "When and if you come to the dragon's lair, recite the following poem.

> *Dragon, dragon, how do you do?*
> *I've come from the king to murder you.*

Say it very loudly and firmly, and the dragon will fall, God willing, at your feet."

"Are you certain?" asked the youngest son uneasily.

"As certain as one can ever be in these matters," said the wise old cobbler.

And so the youngest son set forth on his quest. He traveled over hill and dale and at last came to the dragon's cave. The dragon, who had seen the cobbler's youngest son while he

The cobbler's youngest son came to the dragon's cave with heavy armor and a huge sword.

Practice the Skills

10 | **Key Reading Skill**

Comparing and Contrasting
How is the youngest son different from his two brothers?

Dragon, Dragon **681**

Teach

Viewing the Art
Ask: What does this image tell you about the cobbler's youngest son? *(Possible response: He looks very weak and tiny.)* **BL**
Do you think he will succeed in slaying the dragon? *(Possible response: He looks far too weak to defeat the dragon.)* **OL**

R Reading Skill

Comparing and Contrasting
Say: Compare the cobbler's youngest son's response to his father's advice to that of his older brothers. Do you think he will defeat the dragon? Explain. *(Possible response: Because the youngest son minds his elders, unlike his brothers, he will defeat the dragon.)* **OL**

Literature Focus Lesson

Fairy Tales For centuries, fairy tales were told, not written down. Even today, many children first meet these tales as bedtime stories. Have students make up fairy tales of their own that are inspired by the events in this selection. Encourage them to focus first on their characters and then on their audience. Whom do they want to make the story's hero? What will their classmates find entertaining? Then have volunteers tell their tales to the class. Suggest that they use a tape recorder or a partner with which to practice the presentation. **OL**

Objectives
- Make predictions
- Compare and contrast
- Find meaning in art
- Analyze metaphor
- Analyze features of genre: fairy tales

681

Teach

C Critical Thinking

Comprehension Ask: When you think of a knight, do you usually think of someone strong and brave? What makes the image of the youngest son in "a suit of armor twice his size" so humorous? *(Possible response: Knights are usually big and strong, and the youngest son seems weak and small. Picturing him in the armor is funny because it contradicts one's idea of a knight.)* **OL**

was still a long way off, was seated up above the door, inside the cave, waiting and smiling to himself. But minutes passed and no one came thundering in. The dragon frowned, puzzled, and was tempted to peek out. However, reflecting that patience seldom goes unrewarded, the dragon kept his head up out of sight and went on waiting. At last, when he could stand it no longer, the dragon craned his neck and looked. There at the entrance of the cave stood a trembling young man in a suit of armor twice his size, struggling with a sword so heavy he could lift only one end of it at a time.

At sight of the dragon, the cobbler's youngest son began to tremble so violently that his armor rattled like a house caving in. He heaved[4] with all his might at the sword and got the handle up level with his chest, but even now the point was down in the dirt. As loudly and firmly as he could manage, the youngest son cried—

Dragon, dragon, how do you do?
I've come from the king to murder you.

"What?" cried the dragon, flabbergasted.[5] "You? *You?* Murder *Me???*" All at once he began to laugh, pointing at the little cobbler's son. *"He he he ho ha!"* he roared, shaking all over, and tears filled his eyes. *"He he he ho ho ho ha ha!"* laughed the dragon. He was laughing so hard he had to hang onto his sides, and he fell off the door and landed on his back, still laughing, kicking his legs helplessly, rolling from side to side, laughing and laughing and laughing.

The cobbler's son was annoyed. "I *do* come from the king to murder you," he said. "A person doesn't like to be laughed at for a thing like that."

"He he he!" wailed the dragon, almost sobbing, gasping for breath. "Of course not, poor dear boy! But really, *he he*, the *idea* of it, *ha ha ha!* And that simply rid*i*culous *poem!*" Tears streamed from the dragon's eyes and he lay on his back perfectly helpless with laughter. **11**

"It's a good poem," said the cobbler's youngest son loyally. "My father made it up." And growing angrier he shouted,

---

4. Here ***heaved*** means "lifted an object with force."

5. To be ***flabbergasted*** is to be astonished.

Practice the Skills

11 Key Reading Skill

Comparing and Contrasting List some ways the cobbler's youngest son and the dragon are different from each other.

Additional Support

Differentiated Instruction

Plot Diagram This fairy tale has a lot of ups and downs. Have students diagram the plot. Draw a traditional diagram of a story on the board with the following labels: *exposition*, *rising action*, *conflict*, *climax*, *falling action*, and *resolution*. Explain this diagram to students and then have them design plot diagrams for "Dragon, Dragon." When students finish reading the fairy tale and designing their diagrams, discuss how "Dragon, Dragon" does and does not conform to a traditional story plot. **OL**

R "I want you to stop that laughing, or I'll—I'll—" But the dragon could not stop for the life of him. And suddenly, in a terrific rage, the cobbler's son began flopping the sword end over end in the direction of the dragon. Sweat ran off the youngest son's forehead, but he labored on, blistering mad, and at last, with one supreme heave, he had the sword standing on its handle a foot from the dragon's throat. Of its own weight the sword fell, slicing the dragon's head off.

"He he ho huk," went the dragon—and then he lay dead. **12**

The two older brothers crawled out and thanked their younger brother for saving their lives. "We have learned our lesson," they said.

Then the three brothers gathered all the treasures from the dragon's cave and tied them to the back end of the youngest brother's horse, and tied the dragon's head on behind the treasures, and started home.

"I'm glad I listened to my father," the youngest son thought. "Now I'll be the richest man in the kingdom." **13**

There were hand-carved picture frames and silver spoons and boxes of jewels and chests of money and silver compasses and maps telling where there were more treasures buried when these ran out. There was also a curious old book with a picture of an owl on the cover, and inside, poems and odd sentences and recipes that seemed to make no sense.

When they reached the king's castle the people all leaped for joy to see that the dragon was dead, and the princess ran out and kissed the youngest brother on the forehead, for secretly she had hoped it would be him.

"Well," said the king, "which half of the kingdom do you want?"

"My wizard's book!" exclaimed the wizard. "He's found my wizard's book!" He opened the book and ran his finger under the words and then said in a loud voice, "Glmuzk, shkzmlp, blam!"

Instantly the queen stood before them in her natural shape, except she was soaking wet from being sprinkled too often. She glared at the king.

"Oh dear," said the king, hurrying toward the door. **14** ○

Practice the Skills

12 **Reviewing Skill**

Understanding Cause and Effect Name two different causes that led to the death of the dragon.

13 **BIG Question**

Do you think that the youngest son is the hero of the story? Why or why not? Write your answers on the "Dragon, Dragon" page of Foldable 6. Your response will help you complete the Unit Challenge later.

14 **Key Literary Element**

Theme Spend a minute or two thinking about the whole story. Then write a sentence or a phrase in your Learner's Notebook stating the story's theme.

Dragon, Dragon **683**

Teach

R **Reading Skill**

Review Understanding Cause and Effect Say: Briefly summarize the effect that the poem has on the dragon. What problem does this cause for the dragon? *(Possible response: The poem makes the dragon laugh hysterically. This causes him to be distracted, so he doesn't see the sword coming.)* **OL**

BQ **BIG Question**

Say: List some of the youngest son's traits that you admire. Then list traits that you do not admire. *(Responses will vary.)* **OL**

Assess

CheckPoint

Use the CheckPoint questions provided on Presentation Plus! to check for comprehension of the selection. These questions can be used with interactive response keypads for immediate student feedback.

Literature Focus Lesson

Moral The ending of a story tells a lot about the story's moral. Discuss this story's conclusion with students. Ask them what they think the moral is. Then have them talk about different ways in which the story could have ended and how those endings would have changed the moral. **OL** Have students write a new ending that indicates a different moral. Ask volunteers to read their new endings. Then ask students to guess the moral of each new ending. **AL**

Objectives
• Monitor comprehension
• Compare and contrast
• Understand cause and effect
• Identify literary elements: moral

Assess

Resources for page 684

📁 Selection Quick Check, p. 55

📁 Selection and Unit Assessment, p. 65

💿 ExamView Assessment Suite

💿 Interactive Tutor: Self-Assessment

Students can respond to the *After You Read* items in their Learner's Notebooks or on a separate sheet of paper.

Answering the

BIG Question

1. Possible response: Heroes do not have to be strong or clever. The youngest son slayed the dragon by being decent and honest.

2. The eldest son was known for being smart; he could multiply fractions in his head. The middle son was known for being strong; he could lift up the corner of a church.

3. Possible response: The dragon confused townspeople by changing roads and house numbers. He put frogs in their drinks and played other annoying tricks on them.

Critical Thinking

4. Possible response: This fairy tale ends humorously. Typical fairy tales, such as "Cinderella," end "happily ever after."

5. Possible responses: The owl stands for wisdom; the author implies that the wizard is not really very wise.

684

After You Read Dragon, Dragon

Answering the BIG Question

1. What ideas does this tale offer about what makes a hero—or what does *not* make a hero? Explain your answer, using information from the story.

2. **Recall** What trait was the eldest son known for and what example showed that trait? What trait was the middle son known for and what example showed *his* trait?

    Tip Right There

3. **Summarize** Briefly describe the damage the dragon caused throughout the kingdom.

    Tip Author and Me

Critical Thinking

4. **Contrast** In what way is the ending of this tale different from the typical ending of a fairy tale or folktale? Give an example of a typical ending to help support your answer.

    Tip Author and Me

5. **Infer** The author describes the wizard's book as having an owl on the cover. What do you think the owl stands for? The inside of the book contains "poems and odd sentences and recipes that seemed to make no sense." What do you think the author is implying with this description?

    Tip Author and Me

Write About Your Reading

Most of the characters in fairy tales play traditional roles. The men are strong and hunt and kill monsters. The women stay home waiting to be rescued and get married. Poor people work for rich people and risk their lives to save others. And all monsters are bad.

Imagine what this fairy tale would be like if the characters played different roles. In your Learner's Notebook, write about how you would change the characters and events in this fairy tale and why you would make those changes.

Objectives (pp. 684–685)
Reading Compare and contrast
Literature Identify key literary elements: theme
Vocabulary Explore word histories
Writing Respond to literature
Grammar Use punctuation: commas in compound sentences

684 UNIT 6 What Makes a Hero?

Write About Your Reading

Possible response:

I would change it so that women in the story do more. I would have the princess go out and meet with the dragon. Maybe she would reason with him so he wouldn't have to die. I would make the queen stronger, and I would change her relationship with the king so they like each other more. I would have the riches from the dragon's lair given to all the poor people so that they would have more power in the kingdom. I think this would make the story more interesting. I would change the moral to something like, "You have to fight for yourself and for the changes that you want."

Skills Review

Key Reading Skill: Comparing and Contrasting

6. What did you learn about the brothers by comparing and contrasting them? How did this help you to understand and enjoy the fairy tale?

7. How is this tale similar to a typical fairy tale? How is it different? Do the similarities and differences make the story funnier? Why or why not?

Key Literary Element: Theme

8. Why do you think stories have themes? What purpose do they serve?

9. Does the author directly state the tale's theme or let readers figure it out? Explain your answer.

10. If you wrote a story about your life, what would be the theme?

Reviewing Skills: Understanding Cause and Effect

11. What did the wizard do to cause the queen to turn into a rosebush?

12. What did the youngest son do to make the dragon laugh?

Vocabulary Check

Rewrite each sentence, filling in the blank with the correct word from the list.

quest   tyrant   plagued   lunged

13. The king claimed that he was not a ___.

14. The kingdom was ___ with problems caused by a dragon.

15. The three brothers all went on a ___ to slay the dragon.

16. The dragon ___ at the eldest son and swallowed him in a gulp.

17. **English Language Coach** Remember that *wizard* came from *wys* ("wise"). Which of the following words does *not* come from *wys*?

wish   wit   witch

Grammar Link: Commas in Compound Sentences

A **compound sentence** contains two or more simple sentences. When you combine the simple sentences with a coordinating conjunction like *and* or *but*, you must place a comma before the conjunction.

The people all leaped for joy to see that the dragon was dead. The princess ran out and kissed the youngest brother.

The people all leaped for joy to see that the dragon was dead, and the princess ran out and kissed the youngest brother.

Grammar Practice

Copy each sentence below, adding a comma where it belongs.

18. The wizard didn't know what happened but he said he'd change the queen back into a woman.

19. The dragon robbed graves and he put frogs in people's drinking water.

20. The eldest son didn't think he needed his father's advice but he thought it was only polite to ask.

Writing Application Read the ideas you wrote in your Learner's Notebook about making changes to "Dragon, Dragon." Make sure you have commas before coordinating conjunctions in your compound sentences.

Web Activities For eFlashcards, Selection Quick Checks, and other Web activities, go to www.glencoe.com.

Dragon, Dragon **685**

Skills Review

Key Reading Skill: Comparing and Contrasting

6. Responses will vary.

7. Possible response: It has the same kinds of characters that are found in a fairy tale, but they do not behave the way we expect them to. That makes the tale humorous.

Key Literary Element: Theme

8. Possible response: Themes make readers think about important ideas and life lessons.

9. Possible response: The author states the theme indirectly through the two older sons when each says, "What a fool I was not to listen to my wise old father!" and the youngest son when he says, "I'm glad I listened to my father."

10. Responses will vary.

Reviewing Skills: Understanding Cause and Effect

11. The wizard recited a spell that he did not know.

12. He recited his father's poem.

Vocabulary Check

13. tyrant

14. plagued

15. quest

16. lunged

17. **English Language Coach** witch

Grammar Link: Commas in Compound Sentences

Grammar Practice

18. The wizard didn't know what happened, but he said he'd change the queen back into a woman.

19. The dragon robbed graves, and he put frogs in people's drinking water.

20. The eldest son didn't think he needed his father's advice, but he thought it was only polite to ask.

Teach

More About the Author

Like his character Walt Masters, Jack London had "seen the sun at midnight, watched the ice-jams on one of the mightiest of rivers, and played beneath the northern lights. . . " At age twenty-one, London was living the rough life of a gold prospector in Canada's Klondike territory. Although he did not find gold, his experiences gave him a "gold mine" of ideas for stories. London was born in San Francisco in 1876 and died in 1916. This story was published in 1899.

EL Language Coach

Word Histories Invite students to create a timeline in their Learner's Notebooks, spanning from 500 AD to 1897. At appropriate points along the line, have them write the dates and origins of the word *stampeder*. **EL BL**

Before You Read : The King of Mazy May

Meet the Author

Jack London is considered one of the greatest adventure writers of all time. He drew on his life as a pirate, sailor, and Alaskan gold prospector for locations, events, and characters in his novels and stories. "The proper function of man is to live, not exist," he once declared. See page R4 of the Author Files for more on Jack London.

Author Search For more about Jack London, go to www.glencoe .com.

Objectives (p. 686–699)
Reading Compare and contrast • Make connections from text to self
Literature Identify key literary elements: theme
Vocabulary Explore word histories

Vocabulary Preview

endured (en DURD) *v.* held up under pain or hardship; form of the verb *endure* **(p. 689)** *Walt and his father endured many troubles.*

industrious (in DUS tree us) *adj.* hard-working **(p. 690)** *Finding and mining gold required people who were industrious.*

prospectors (PRAH spek turz) *n.* people who explore an area for mineral or oil deposits **(p. 690)** *Prospectors discovered gold in the Yukon and Klondike territories.*

perilously (PAIR uh lus lee) *adv.* dangerously; at risk of injury **(p. 694)** *The sled went perilously near the edge of the cliff.*

floundering (FLOUN dur ing) *v.* struggling to move or gain balance; form of the verb *flounder* **(p. 696)** *The dogs were floundering in the deep snow.*

Partner Talk With your partner, use each vocabulary word in a different question about life in the Klondike territory of northwestern Canada in the 1890s.

English Language Coach

Word Histories It isn't surprising that cowboys invented the word *stampede* to describe cattle running wild. Mexican cowboys brought *estampida* to the United States in the 1820s. American cowboys knew a good word when they heard it, and they just changed the pronunciation and spelling a little.

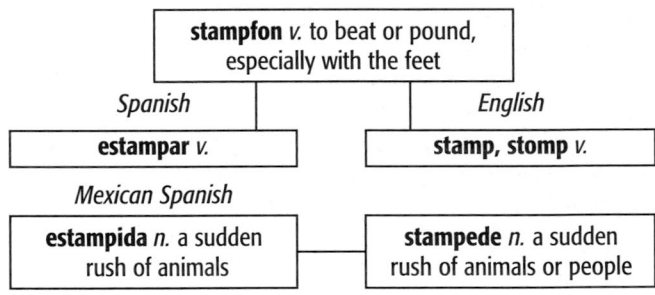

Old German

stampfon *v.* to beat or pound, especially with the feet

Spanish — **estampar** *v.* | *English* — **stamp, stomp** *v.*

Mexican Spanish — **estampida** *n.* a sudden rush of animals | **stampede** *n.* a sudden rush of animals or people

Partner Talk What do you suppose a stampede was called before the word *stampede* existed? With a partner, invent a new word that has the same meaning. You can use *stamp* or *stomp* as part of your word or, if you prefer, think up a whole new word.

Additional Support

Author Search To expand students' appreciation of Jack London, have them access the Web site for additional information and resources.

Reading Fluency

Build Fluency As a way to help students build reading fluency and learn vocabulary words, assign them to groups of four for "echo reading." Have two students read the vocabulary word, say its definition, and then read the sentence in *Vocabulary Check.* Then have the second two students echo the exercise. When the echo exercise is complete, have students write definitions for the vocabulary words in their own words in their Learner's Notebooks. **AS**

Skills Preview

Key Reading Skill: Comparing and Contrasting

Sometimes when people read, they compare and contrast what they read with what they know. They think about how characters are like themselves or other people in their lives. Or they compare and contrast the events in the text with events they have lived or read about. This kind of comparing and contrasting can help bring a text alive with meaning.

Write to Learn Draw a two-column chart in your Learner's Notebook. Label one column *Similarities* and one column *Differences*. While you read, fill in the chart by comparing and contrasting yourself with the King of Mazy May.

Key Literary Element: Theme

The theme of a story is the central idea the author wants you to understand or think about. It's what makes a story mean something to you. Sometimes it's a challenge to find the theme, but the challenge makes it more worthwhile.

Use these tips to find the theme:

- Stories usually have a conflict between two characters or forces.

  What people or forces are in conflict in "The King of Mazy May"?

- Often the good character or the good force wins the conflict.

  Who wins the conflict in this story? How does he win the conflict?

- The ending of the conflict shows readers what the theme of the story is.

  What do you think the author wants you to learn from this story?

Partner Talk With a partner, select one of the stories that you read in this unit. Work together to apply the above tips and find the theme.

Get Ready to Read

Connect to the Reading

The boy in "The King of Mazy May" knows what to do when he sees an injustice. Have you ever stood up for someone who was being treated badly?

Class Talk Have a discussion about movies, books, and stories you know that involve injustice. What was the injustice? Did someone do something to make things right? What risks were involved? Do you know anyone personally who's stood up for something that was right?

Build Background

In 1896 gold was discovered in the Klondike of Canada. Thousands set out to strike it rich. Perhaps they'd have stayed home if they'd known the following:

- They'd risk their lives to carry tons of needed equipment across steep, frozen mountain passes.
- Local people had already claimed most of the gold.
- The gold that remained was ten feet below permanently frozen ground.

Most fortune-seekers found only hardship—if they were lucky enough to survive!

Set Purposes for Reading

BIG Question The hero of this story is only fourteen. How could a boy that age be a hero? Read "The King of Mazy May" to find out.

Set Your Own Purpose What else would you like to learn from the story to help you answer the Big Question? Write your own purpose on the "King of Mazy May" page of Foldable 6.

Keep Moving

Use these skills as you read the following selection.

The King of Mazy May **687**

Teach

L Literary Element

Theme Say: Think about a conflict you've seen in a story or movie. How is the conflict resolved? *(Responses will vary.)* **Ask:** What does the conflict's resolution tell you about the theme of the story or movie? Share your observations with the class. *(Possible response: The conflict's resolution reveals the story or movie's theme.)* **OL**

R Reading Skill

Review Connecting Ask: If you saw a friend being treated unfairly, what would you do? Would you stand up for your friend? Why or why not? *(Responses will vary.)* **OL**

Reading in the Real World

Citizenship Bring in or have students find a newspaper article about someone in your community who stood up against an injustice. Read the article with the class prior to reading "The King of Mazy May." Then, after students have read the story, have them compare your local hero to the boy in the story. **OL** Invite students to write their own stories about standing up against an injustice or have them do research to find more information about local heroes that can be presented to the class. **AL**

Objectives

- Compare and contrast
- Identify literary elements: theme
- Understand word histories
- Make connections from text to self

687

Teach

Viewing the Photo

Ask: Have you ever seen this kind of dog before? How might a dog like this help people who live in the frozen mountains? *(Possible response: a sled dog that can help people get through the snow)* **OL**

L Literary Element

Theme Say: The way that authors describe their characters can help you figure out whether they will be "good guys" or "bad guys." What does the author say about Walt Masters? Does he seem to admire him? What makes you think so? *(Possible response: The author seems to admire Walt's brave and adventurous spirit.)* **OL**

Readability Scores
Dale-Chall: 6.7
DRP: 57
Lexile: 1020

The King of Mazy May

by Jack London

alt Masters is not a very large boy, but there is manliness in his make-up, and he himself, although he does not know a great deal that most boys know, knows much that other boys do not know. **1**

He has never seen a train of cars or an elevator in his life, and for that matter, he has never once looked upon a cornfield, a plow, a cow, or even a chicken. He has never had a pair of shoes on his feet, or gone to a picnic or a party, or talked to a girl. But he has seen the sun at midnight, watched the ice-jams on one of the mightiest of rivers, and played beneath the northern lights,[1] the one white child in thousands of square miles of frozen wilderness.

---

1. The **northern lights** are beautiful streams and arches of moving colored light. They're seen at times in the night sky over northern regions of Earth. The light comes from atoms speeding through Earth's magnetic field. When such lights appear in the southern hemisphere, they're called the "southern lights."

688 UNIT 6 What Makes a Hero?

Practice the Skills

1 Key Reading Skill

Comparing and Contrasting
How does the author use comparing and contrasting to help you get to know the character of Walt?

Additional Support

Leveled Reading
An adapted version of this selection (4th grade readability) is available on page 14 of **Jamestown Literature: An Adapted Reader** for Grade 6.
688

English Language Coach

Building Background Some students may not be familiar with the gold rush fever of the Klondike and the rigors of life in the far north of Alaska and Canada. Preview the photos and illustrations to help students visualize the story's setting. Ask your librarian for additional picture books about the gold rush, dog sledding, and the far North or search for them on the Internet. **AS** Interested students can do additional research on these topics and share what they learn with the class. **AL**

Visual Vocabulary
Moccasins are soft leather shoes with the sole and sides made of one piece.

R

Walt has walked all the fourteen years of his life in sun-tanned, moose-hide moccasins, and he can go to the Indian camps and "talk big" with the men, and trade calico[2] and beads with them for their precious furs. He can make bread without baking-powder, yeast or hops, shoot a moose at three hundred yards, and drive the wild wolf-dogs fifty miles a day on the packed trail.

Last of all, he has a good heart, and is not afraid of the darkness and loneliness, of man or beast or thing. His father is a good man, strong and brave, and Walt is growing up like him. **2**

Walt was born a thousand miles or so down the Yukon, in a trading-post below the Ramparts. After his mother died, his father and he came on up the river, step by step, from camp to camp, till now they are settled down on the Mazy May Creek in the Klondike[3] country. Last year they and several others had spent much toil and time on the Mazy May, and **endured** great hardships; the creek, in turn, was just beginning to show up its richness and to reward them for their heavy labor. But with the news of their discoveries, strange men began to come and go through the short days and long nights, and many unjust things they did to the men who had worked so long upon the creek.

C

2. **Calico** is a type of cotton cloth with a pattern on it. The word comes from Calicut, the town in India where the cloth was made.

3. The **Yukon** River flows from Canada's Yukon Territory through Alaska to the Bering Sea. It was a major route to the Klondike during the gold rush of 1897–1898. The **Klondike** is the name of both a river and a gold-mining region in the Yukon Territory of Canada near the Alaskan border.

Vocabulary

endured (en DURD) *v.* held up under pain or hardship

Practice the Skills

2 | **Key Reading Skill**

Comparing and Contrasting
In the table you prepared in your Learner's Notebook, use the information in the first four paragraphs to fill in differences and similarities between yourself and Walt Masters.

Klondike Gold Rush, Summer 1898, Julius Price in the Illustrated London News 20 August 1898.

Analyzing the Art Which characters mentioned on this page might this art show? Explain your answer.

The King of Mazy May **689**

Teach

R Reading Skill

Comparing and Contrasting
After students have read the first two paragraphs on this page, ask them to paraphrase the descriptions and list Walt's traits and abilities. Have them make a similar list of their own traits and abilities. Once students have compared and contrasted Walt's character with their own, have them share their thoughts with the class. **OL**

C Critical Thinking

Evaluation **Ask:** What were the "discoveries" of those who settled on the Mazy May Creek? How do you know? *(Possible response: The discoveries were gold; I know this from reading the background information and from the descriptions in the story so far.)* **OL**

Differentiated Instruction

Character Illustration The story begins with a rich description of Walt, where he lives, and how he lives. Ask students to sketch a picture of Walt in his daily life. After they're done, have students compare and contrast their drawings of Walt with those of their classmates. Then discuss the author's statement, "Last of all, he has a good heart, and is not afraid of the darkness and loneliness, of man or beast or thing." Ask students to consider what experience they have of being "not afraid of darkness or loneliness." Have them write a brief summary of their experience in their Learner's Notebooks. **OL**

Objectives
• Use text features: photographs
• Identify literary elements: theme
• Compare and contrast
• Evaluate text

Teach

C1 Critical Thinking

Evaluation Say: Walt looks after not only his father's claim, but also that of a neighbor. What conclusions can you draw about Walt's character from these actions? *(Possible response: He is responsible, caring, and loyal; he goes out of his way to help others.)* **OL**

C2 Critical Thinking

Synthesis Say: Loren Hall had no dogs. Ask: How does this slow him down? *(Possible response: Dog sleds are the only means of transportation. Loren Hall has to walk instead of ride a dog sled.)*

Si Hartman had gone away on a moose-hunt, to return and find new stakes driven and his claim jumped.[4] George Lukens and his brother had lost their claims in a like manner, having delayed too long on the way to Dawson to record them. In short, it was an old story, and quite a number of the earnest, **industrious prospectors** had suffered similar losses.

C1 But Walt Masters's father had recorded his claim at the start, so Walt had nothing to fear, now that his father had gone on a short trip up the White River prospecting for quartz. Walt was well able to stay by himself in the cabin, cook his three meals a day, and look after things. Not only did he look after his father's claim, but he had agreed to keep an eye on the adjoining[5] one of Loren Hall, who had started for Dawson to record it. **3**

C2 Loren Hall was an old man, and he had no dogs, so he had to travel very slowly. After he had been gone some time, word came up the river that he had broken through the ice at Rosebud Creek, and frozen his feet so badly that he would not be able to travel for a couple of weeks. Then Walt Masters received the news that old Loren was nearly all right again, and about to move on afoot for Dawson, as fast as a weakened man could.

Walt was worried, however; the claim was liable to be jumped at any moment because of this delay, and a fresh stampede[6] had started in on the Mazy May. He did not like the looks of the newcomers, and one day, when five of them came by with crack[7] dog-teams and the lightest of camping

Shooting the white-horse rapids en route to the Klondike gold fields, 1898. Hand-colored halftone.

3 Key Literary Element

Theme Do you see the beginning of a conflict here? Who do you think the "good" character will be? Write your thoughts in your Learner's Notebook.

---

4. A *claim* was a piece of land that a prospector claimed to be his or her own. The prospector drove wooden *stakes* into the ground to mark its boundaries, and then recorded the claim with the gold commissioner in the city of *Dawson.* Someone who *jumped a claim* took over and recorded a claim for land that had been staked out, but not yet recorded, by someone else.

5. *Adjoining* means "located next to."

6. Usually a *stampede* is a sudden rush of animals. In this story, the word refers to the rush of people searching for gold in the Klondike.

7. Here *crack* means "excellent, first-rate."

Vocabulary

industrious (in DUS tree us) *adj.* hard-working

prospectors (PRAH spek turz) *n.* people who explore an area for mineral or oil deposits

690 **UNIT 6** What Makes a Hero?

Additional Support

Literature Focus Lesson

Sequence of Events Such words as *when, then, meanwhile, since, while, later, until, earlier, finally,* and *during* signal time order. The order in which events occur may be presented in a straight time sequence or in another order. Ask students to close their books and listen as you read page 690 aloud. Have students jot down any signal words they hear. Then have students work in small groups to review the next two pages, locating and listing the words that signal the order of events.

The result of the year's "wash up": A sketch in the Bank of British North America, Dawson City, 1898. Jules M. Price. Illustration from *From Euston to Klondike*.

Analyzing the Art: What do you think the man is weighing? How important is the measurement?

outfits, he could see that they were prepared to make speed, and resolved to keep an eye on them. So he locked up the cabin and followed them, being at the same time careful to remain hidden. **4**

He had not watched them long before he was sure that they were professional stampeders, bent[8] on jumping all the claims in sight. Walt crept along the snow at the rim of the creek and saw them change many stakes, destroy old ones, and set up new ones.

In the afternoon, with Walt always trailing on their heels, they came back down the creek, unharnessed their dogs, and went into camp within two claims of his cabin. When he saw them make preparations to cook, he hurried home to get something to eat himself, and then hurried back. He crept so

---

8. Here ***bent*** means "determined" or "intending."

Practice the Skills

4 | **Key Reading Skill**

Comparing and Contrasting
Walt is given a lot of freedom but also many responsibilities. Compare and contrast this with the freedom and responsibilities in your own life.

The King of Mazy May **691**

Teach

EL Language Coach

Word Histories Say: Read the footnote to find the meaning of *stampede* as it is used in this story. How is a stampede of people similar to a stampede of animals? *(Possible responses: A stampede of people is a crowd that moves quickly toward a goal.)* **EL** **BL**

L Literary Element

Theme Ask: If people try to take something that is not rightfully theirs, what does that say about them? *(Possible response: They are thoughtless and self-centered. It's not right to take something that belongs to someone else.)* **BL** **Ask:** How do you feel about the claim-jumpers in this story? What part do they play in the conflict between good and evil? *(Possible response: The claim-jumpers are the evil force in the story.)* **OL**

Reading in the Real World

Career Students may be interested in researching modern-day mining for gold and other resources. For example, students can discover in which parts of the world gold is found today, how much it is worth, and what its uses are. Have students work in small groups to locate information about mining. Then have students report their findings to the class. **OL** As an extension, have students create charts, graphs, or other visual aids to help their classmates understand their findings. **AL**

Objectives
• Synthesize information
• Understand word histories
• Identify literary elements: theme, sequence
• Evaluate text

Teach

C Critical Thinking

Analysis What does an Irishman suggest the stampeders do to stay warm? *(run after the dogs)* **Ask:** For what other reason does the Irishman say the stampeders should run? *(to make sure they get to record the land as theirs first)* **OL**

close that he could hear them talking quite plainly, and by pushing the underbrush aside he could catch occasional glimpses of them. They had finished eating and were smoking around the fire.

"The creek is all right, boys," a large, black-bearded man, evidently the leader said, "and I think the best thing we can do is to pull out tonight. The dogs can follow the trail; besides, it's going to be moonlight. What say you?"

"But it's going to be beastly cold," objected one of the party. "It's forty below zero now."

C "An' sure, can't ye keep warm by jumpin' off the sleds an' runnin' after the dogs?" cried an Irishman. "An' who wouldn't? The creek as rich as a United States mint! Faith, it's an ilegant chanst[9] to be gettin' a run fer yer money! An' if ye don't run, it's mebbe you'll not get the money at all, at all."

"That's it," said the leader. "If we can get to Dawson and record, we're rich men; and there is no telling who's been sneaking along in our tracks, watching us, and perhaps now off to give the alarm. The thing for us to do is to rest the dogs a bit, and then hit the trail as hard as we can. What do you say?"

Evidently the men had agreed with their leader, for Walt Masters could hear nothing but the rattle of the tin dishes which were being washed. Peering out cautiously, he could see the leader studying a piece of paper. Walt knew what it was at a glance—a list of all the unrecorded claims on Mazy May. Any man could get these lists by applying to the gold commissioner at Dawson. **5**

---

9. ***Ilegant chanst*** is the character's way of saying "elegant chance," meaning "excellent opportunity."

692 UNIT 6 What Makes a Hero?

Klondike Gold Rush, 1904, artist unknown.

5 Reviewing Skills

Understanding Cause and Effect Walt followed the claim-jumpers. What was the effect of his actions?

Additional Support

Differentiated Instruction

Tactile Learning Tactile learners may appreciate some experiments with cold. Point out the description on this page of "beastly cold" at forty below zero. Remind students that water freezes at 32 degrees and bring in ice for them to touch. Talk about the different ways that people stay warm, from wearing special clothing to using heaters and electric blankets. Have students write descriptions or draw pictures of how they imagine it would feel to be outside in forty below zero weather. Ask for volunteers to share what they wrote or drew. **AS**

"Thirty-two," the leader said, lifting his face to the men. "Thirty-two isn't recorded, and this is thirty-three. Come on; let's take a look at it. I saw somebody had been working on it when we came up this morning."

Three of the men went with him, leaving one man to remain in camp. Walt crept carefully after them till they came to Loren Hall's shaft. One of the men went down and built a fire on the bottom to thaw out the frozen gravel, while the others built another fire on the dump and melted water in a couple of gold-pans. This they poured into a piece of canvas stretched between two logs, used by Loren Hall in which to wash his gold.

In a short time a couple of buckets of dirt were sent up by the man in the shaft, and Walt could see the others grouped anxiously about their leader as he proceeded to wash it. When this was finished, they stared at the broad streak of black sand and yellow gold-grains on the bottom of the pan, and one of them called excitedly for the man who had remained in camp to come. Loren Hall had struck it rich, and his claim was not yet recorded. It was plain that they were going to jump it.

Walt lay in the snow, thinking rapidly. He was only a boy, but in the face of the threatened injustice against old lame Loren Hall he felt that he must do something. He waited and watched, with his mind made up, till he saw the men begin to square up new stakes. Then he crawled away till out of hearing, and broke into a run for the camp of the stampeders. Walt's father had taken their own dogs with him prospecting, and the boy knew how impossible it was him to undertake the seventy miles to Dawson without the aid of dogs. **6**

Gaining the camp, he picked out, with an experienced eye, the easiest running sled and started to harness up the stampeders' dogs. There were three teams of six each, and from these he chose ten of the best. Realizing how necessary it was to have a good head-dog, he strove to discover a leader amongst them; but he had little time in which to do it, for he could hear the voices of the returning men. By the time the team was in shape and everything ready, the claim-jumpers came into sight in an open place not more than a hundred yards from the trail, which ran down the bed of the creek. They cried out to him, but he gave no heed, grabbing up one

Practice the Skills

6 **Key Reading Skill**

Comparing and Contrasting
Add entries to your table to contrast how Walt travels to where he needs to go and how you get around.

The King of Mazy May **693**

Teach

L Literary Element

Theme Say: Think of the chase as a race between good and evil. Who is ahead at this point in the story? Which force do you think will win out? *(Possible response: "Good" is ahead and will eventually win out.)* **OL**

R Reading Skill

Comparing and Contrasting
Say: Look at the description of the men as they discover the "yellow gold-grains on the bottom of the pan." Then look at the description of Walt as he lies in the snow close by. How are Walt's feelings different from the men's feelings at this point in the story? *(Possible response: The men are excited, but Walt is depressed and frightened.)* **OL**

Literature Focus Lesson

Heroes Talk about the similarities and the differences between heroes such as Hercules and heroes such as Walt. Have students discuss which heroes they like better and why. Then have students discuss what they can learn from these different kinds of heroes. Ask groups of students to create a hero who has the characteristics they most admire in heroes. Be sure to introduce examples of female heroes into the discussion. **OL**

Objectives
• Compare and contrast
• Analyze text
• Identify literary elements: theme, hero

693

Teach

BQ BIG Question

Ask: How has Walt shown bravery so far in the story? What other qualities of a hero does he possess? *(Possible response: Although he is just a boy, he is bravely escaping a group of angry men and traveling a dangerous route by himself. He is also showing loyalty to his neighbors and determination to save their land.)* **OL**

of their fur sleeping-robes which lay loosely in the snow, and leaping upon the sled.

"<u>Mush</u>! Hi! <u>Mush on</u>!" he cried to the animals, snapping the keen-lashed whip among them. **7**

BQ The dogs sprang against the yoke-straps,[10] and the sled jerked under way so suddenly as to almost throw him off. Then it curved into the creek, poising **perilously** on one runner. He was almost breathless with suspense, when it finally righted with a bound and sprang ahead again. The creek bank was high and he could not see, although he could hear the cries of the men and knew they were running to cut him off. He did not dare to think what would happen if they caught him; he only clung to the sled, his heart beating wildly, and watched the snow-rim of the bank above him.

Suddenly, over this snow-rim came the flying body of the Irishman, who had leaped straight for the sled in a desperate attempt to capture it; but he was an instant too late. Striking on the very rear of it, he was thrown from his feet, backward, into the snow. Yet, with the quickness of a cat, he had clutched the end of the sled with one hand, turned over, and was dragging behind on his breast, swearing at the boy and threatening all kinds of terrible things if he did not stop the dogs; but Walt cracked him sharply across the knuckles with the butt of the dog-whip till he let go.

It was eight miles from Walt's claim to the Yukon—eight very crooked miles, for the creek wound back and forth like a snake, "tying knots in itself," as George Lukens said. And because it was so crooked, the dogs could not get up their best speed, while the sled ground heavily on its side against the curves, now to the right, now to the left.

Travelers who had come up and down the Mazy May on foot, with packs on their backs, had declined to go around all the bends, and instead had made short cuts across the narrow necks of creek bottom. Two of his pursuers had gone back to

---

10. A *yoke-strap* is part of the dog's harness.

Vocabulary

perilously (PAIR uh lus lee) *adv.* dangerously; at risk of injury

Practice the Skills

7 **English Language Coach**

Word Histories The word <u>mush</u> as a command to dogs was first recorded in 1862. In French, *marche* means "go" or "march." French-Canadian dog-sledders got their dogs to move by shouting "*Marchon!*" (mar SHAWN), meaning "Let's go!" English-speaking dogsledders mispronounced the command, saying "Mush on!"

Additional Support

Literature Focus Lesson

Heroes Discuss what risks Walt is taking to protect Loren Hall and his land. Discuss his motivation: Is he more moved to help Loren or to defeat the wrongdoers? Ask students to recall other kinds of heroes who sacrificed their lives for a cause. Ask students whether there are causes for which they would be willing to sacrifice everything. Have students discuss this question: Will Walt be a hero only if he succeeds or is he a hero just for trying? **AS**

harness the remaining dogs, but the others took advantage of these short cuts, running on foot, and before he knew it they had almost overtaken him.

"Halt!" they cried after him. "Stop, or we'll shoot!"

But Walt only yelled the harder at the dogs, and dashed round the bend with a couple of revolver bullets singing after him. At the next bend they had drawn up closer still, and the bullets struck uncomfortably near to him; but at this point the Mazy May straightened out and ran for half a mile as the crow flies. Here the dogs stretched out in their long wolf-swing, and the stampeders, quickly winded, slowed down and waited for their own sled to come up. 8

Looking over his shoulder, Walt reasoned that they had not given up the chase for good, and that they would soon be after him again. So he wrapped the fur robe about him to shut out the stinging air, and lay flat on the empty sled, encouraging the dogs, as he well knew how.

At last, twisting abruptly between two river islands, he came upon the mighty Yukon sweeping grandly to the north. He could not see from bank to bank, and in the quick-falling twilight it loomed[11] a great white sea of frozen stillness. There was not a sound, save the breathing of the dogs, and the churn of the steel-shod sled.

No snow had fallen for several weeks, and the traffic had packed the main-river trail till it was hard and glassy as glare ice. Over this the sled flew along, and the dogs kept the trail fairly well, although Walt quickly discovered that he had made a mistake in choosing the leader. As they were driven in single file, without reins, he had to guide them by his voice, and it was evident the head-dog had never learned the meaning of "gee" and "haw."[12] He hugged the inside of the curves too closely, often forcing his comrades behind him into the soft snow, while several times he thus capsized the sled.

---

11. Something that *loomed*, came into view in a way that seemed large and threatening.

12. These are commands used to direct the dogs. *Gee* means "to the right" and *haw* means "to the left."

How to reach the KLONDIKE.

COLUMBIA NAVIGATION
AND TRADING COMPANY.

S. S. City of Columbia (1900 tons) will depart from the Old Dominion Line Pier 26, North River.

Wednesday, Dec. 1st, for

ST. MICHAEL,

connecting with Company's river steamers for

DAWSON CITY.

Fare to Dawson City, including 1000 pounds of baggage, $680.00 up, according to accommodation. Passengers desiring to meet the ship at San Francisco or Seattle will be provided with transportation by rail to either point at same rate.

For passage tickets and further information apply to the agents,

RAYMOND & WHITCOMB,
31 East Fourteenth Street, New York.
296 Washington St., Boston, Mass.
1005 Chestnut St., Philadelphia, Pa.
95 Adams St., Chicago, Ill.

Ad for the S. S. City of Columbia to Klondike Country.

Practice the Skills

8 **BIG Question**

Do you think Walt has the qualities of a real-life hero? Support your answer with details from the story.

The King of Mazy May **695**

R Reading Skill

Review Inferring Say: Walt is able to lie down in the sled and still encourage the dogs, "as he well knew how." What does this part of the story say about Walt and his chances of winning? *(Possible response: Walt has a lot of experience in this environment, so he has a good chance of winning.)* **OL**

English Language Coach

Idiom *As the crow flies* is an expression that students may not understand. Explain that it means "the most direct distance between two places." A road between two places may need to twist and turn around the geographic obstacles that a flying crow would not have to avoid. Ask students to share idioms they know in other languages. **AS**

Objectives
- Make inferences
- Understand idioms
- Identify literary elements: hero

Teach

Viewing the Art

Ask: What kind of weather is shown in this painting? *(cold, windy, snowy weather)* **BL** **Ask:** Do you think that it would be difficult to survive in this environment? *(Possible response: Yes. The environment looks barren and frightening.)* **OL**

R1 Reading Skill

Comparing and Contrasting

Ask: When does it get cool in your area? What is the lowest temperature you can remember? Do you think the weather where Walt lives is harsher than the weather where you live? *(Responses will vary.)* **OL**

R2 Reading Skill

Review Connecting **Say:**

Imagine how you would feel once night fell and you had to continue the chase in the "blackness." What would you be thinking and feeling in this situation? *(Possible response: that I could be thrown from the sled and die in cold)* **OL**

On the Klondike. 1890s. Roper.

Analyzing the Art Compare the men in this painting with the stampeders.

R1 There was no wind, but the speed at which he traveled created a bitter blast, and with the thermometer down to forty below, this bit through fur and flesh to the very bones. Aware that if he remained constantly upon the sled he would freeze to death, and knowing the practice of Arctic travelers, Walt shortened up one of the lashing-thongs, and whenever he felt chilled, seized hold of it, jumped off, and ran behind till warmth was restored. Then he would climb on and rest till the process had to be repeated. **9**

Looking back he could see the sled of his pursuers, drawn by eight dogs, rising and falling over the ice hummocks[13] like a boat in a seaway. The Irishman and the black-bearded leader were with it, taking turns in running and riding.

R2 Night fell, and in the blackness of the first hour or so, Walt toiled desperately with his dogs. On account of the poor lead-dog, they were constantly **floundering** off the beaten track

---

13. **Hummocks** are ridges or hills on the ice.

Vocabulary

floundering (FLOUN dur ing) *v.* struggling to move or gain balance

696 UNIT 6 What Makes a Hero?

Practice the Skills

9 **Key Reading Skill**

Comparing and Contrasting
Add a final row to your table comparing the weather where Walt lived and the weather where you live.

Additional Support

Differentiated Instruction

Visual Learning Show students a chase scene from a movie. After watching the film, talk about what made the chase suspenseful. Write a few of the following words and phrases on the board: *like a flash, glanced back, he cried, dashed, turned fiercely.* Ask students to find these words in the text, along with other words and phrases that build suspense. **BL** Add the students' words to the list on the board. Then assign pairs of students to write a short chase scene between two kids on bikes. **OL AL**

into the soft snow, and the sled was as often riding on its side or top as it was in the proper way. This work and strain tried his strength sorely. Had he not been in such haste he could have avoided much of it, but he feared the stampeders would creep up in the darkness and overtake him. However, he could hear them occasionally yelling to their dogs, and knew from the sounds that they were coming up very slowly.

When the moon rose he was off Sixty Mile, and Dawson was only fifty miles away. He was almost exhausted, and breathed a sigh of relief as he climbed on the sled again. Looking back, he saw his enemies had crawled up within four hundred yards. At this space they remained, a black speck of motion on the white river-breast. Strive as they would, they could not shorten this distance, and strive as he would he could not increase it.

He had now discovered the proper lead-dog, and he knew he could easily run away from them if he could only change the bad leader for the good one. But this was impossible, for a moment's delay, at the speed they were running, would bring the men behind upon him.

When he got off the mouth of Rosebud Creek, just as he was topping a rise, the ping of a bullet on the ice beside him, and the report[14] of a gun, told him that they were this time shooting at him with a rifle. And from then on, as he cleared the summit of each ice-jam, he stretched flat on the leaping sled till the rifle-shot from the rear warned him that he was safe till the next ice-jam.

Now it is very hard to lie on a moving sled, jumping and plunging and yawing[15] like a boat before the wind, and to shoot through the deceiving moonlight at an object four hundred yards away on another moving sled performing equally wild antics.[16] So it is not to be wondered at that the black-bearded leader did not hit him. **10**

After several hours of this, during which, perhaps, a score[17] of bullets had struck about him, their ammunition began to give out and their fire slackened. They took greater care, and

---

14. A gun's **report** is the sound it makes when fired.
15. When a sled is **yawing,** it is turning from side to side and going off the course.
16. **Antics** are odd, silly, or comical actions.
17. A **score** is twenty.

Practice the Skills

R

10 | **Reviewing Skills**

Understanding Cause and Effect The claim-jumper could not hit Walt no matter how many times he shot at the boy. What was the cause of this effect?

The King of Mazy May **697**

R **Reading Skill**

Review Understanding Cause and Effect Ask: Do you think Walt made the right decision? Why or why not? *(Responses will vary.)* **Ask:** What effect would his changing the lead dog possibly have on the chase? *(Possible response: He could get farther ahead or he could get caught when he stops to change the dog.)* **Ask:** What effect could Walt's not changing the lead dog have on the chase? *(Possible response: The men could catch up with him.)*

C **Critical Thinking**

Comprehension According to the narrator, why isn't the black-haired leader able to hit Walt? *(Possible response: The sled from which he is shooting is moving, the moonlight is deceiving, Walt is 400 yards away, and Walt's sled is also moving.)* **OL**

Reading in the Real World

Careers Humans and animals co-exist in many ways. Humans have used horses, camels, and mules for transportation throughout history. They have also used oxen and mules for farming. Have students brainstorm to list and then research careers in which animals and humans work together. Suggest anthropologist Margaret Mead and horse jockey Red Pollard as examples of people in such careers. **OL**

Objectives
• Understand cause and effect
• Find meaning in art
• Make connections from self to text
• Compare and contrast
• Monitor comprehension

Teach

R **Reading Skill**

Review Inferring Ask: Why do the men begin to shoot at Walt only at "the most favorable opportunities"? *(Possible response: They are running out of bullets and don't want to waste any.)* **OL**

L **Literary Element**

Theme Say: Walt is a young boy, yet he defeats a group of larger, older, and stronger men. What theme might this point to? *(Possible answer: Bravery and goodness will always win out over evil, no matter what the size of the fighters.)* **OL**

Klondike Gold Rush. Edward Roper. *The Illustrated London News* 30 October 1897, page 618.

R only whipped a shot at him at the most favorable opportunities. He was also beginning to leave them behind, the distance slowly increasing to six hundred yards.

Lifting clear on the crest of a great jam off Indian River, Walt Masters met his first accident. A bullet sang past his ears, and struck the bad lead-dog.

The poor brute plunged in a heap, with the rest of the team on top of him.

Like a flash, Walt was by the leader. Cutting the traces with his hunting knife, he dragged the dying animal to one side and straightened out the team. **11**

He glanced back. The other sled was coming up like an express-train. With half the dogs still over their traces, he cried, "Mush on!" and leaped upon the sled just as the pursuing team dashed abreast of him.

The Irishman was just preparing to spring for him,—they were so sure they had him that they did not shoot,—when Walt turned fiercely upon them with his whip.

11 **English Language Coach**

Word Histories Traces are leather straps that connect a dog's yoke-strap to the sled. The word came from the French *traiz* ("to pull"), which came from a much older Latin word.

698 UNIT 6   What Makes a Hero?

Additional Support

Differentiated Instruction

Map Making Have students work with a partner to make a map of Walt's journey that can be displayed at a monument in honor of Walt. Students should add markers to the map to show the highlights of Walt's journey. **BL OL** Next, have students devise a board game to be played on the map. They should create two dog sleds that will race each other. Have them use events from the story and imagination as they create a deck of cards that will advance the sleds on the race to Dawson. **AL**

R He struck at their faces, and men must save their faces with their hands. So there was no shooting just then. Before they could recover from the hot rain of blows, Walt reached out from his sled, catching their wheel-dog[18] by the fore legs in mid-spring, and throwing him heavily. This brought the whole team into a snarl, capsizing the sled and tangling his enemies up beautifully.

Away Walt flew, the runners of his sled fairly screaming as they bounded over the frozen surface. And what had seemed an accident proved to be a blessing in disguise. The proper lead-dog was now to the fore, and he stretched low to the trail and whined with joy as he jerked his comrades along.

By the time he reached Ainslie's Creek, seventeen miles from Dawson, Walt had left his pursuers, a tiny speck, far behind. At Monte Cristo Island he could no longer see them. And at Swede Creek, just as daylight was silvering the pines, he ran plump into the camp of old Loren Hall.

Almost as quick as it takes to tell it, Loren had his sleeping-furs rolled up, and had joined Walt on the sled. They permitted the dogs to travel more slowly, as there was no sign of the chase in the rear, and just as they pulled up at the gold commissioner's office in Dawson, Walt, who had kept his eyes open to the last, fell asleep.

BQ And because of what Walt Masters did on this night, the men of the Yukon have become very proud of him, and always speak of him now as the King of Mazy May. **12** **13** ○

---

18. The **wheel-dog** is the dog nearest the front end of the sled. The term was borrowed from horse teams in which the wheel horse is the horse nearest the front wheels of a wagon or carriage.

Practice the Skills

12 🔵**BIG Question**

What qualities make Walt a hero to the people of the Mazy May Creek? How do you think he developed those qualities at such a young age? On the "King of Mazy May" page of your Foldable, write a short paragraph to support your answers. Your response will help you complete the Unit Challenge later.

13 **Key Literary Element**

Theme What is the theme of this story? Write a statement of the theme in your Learner's Notebook using one or two sentences.

The King of Mazy May **699**

Teach

R **Reading Skill**

Review Understanding Cause and Effect Ask: Why must men "save their faces with their hands"? How does this affect the men's ability to fight back? *(Possible response: It is a natural instinct to block your face with your hands when someone is striking you. Because their hands are busy, the men are unable to use their guns.)* **OL**

BQ 🔵**BIG Question**

Ask: What do you admire about Walt? What qualities does he have that you would like to have yourself? *(Possible response: his bravery and determination)* **AS**

Assess

☑**CheckPoint**

Use the CheckPoint questions provided on Presentation Plus! to check for comprehension of the selection. These questions can be used with interactive response keypads for immediate student feedback.

Differentiated Instruction

Create a Play Students could present several scenes as skits. Possible scenes include the men panning for gold as Walt watches, the men witnessing Walt stealing the sled and dogs, and the men shooting at and chasing Walt. Have students work in small groups to prepare brief skits. Because many of the scenes include only Walt, suggest that students either write monologues that express Walt's feelings or provide a third-person narrator who tells Walt's thoughts. Encourage students to be creative in their presentations. **AS**

Objectives
• Understand cause and effect
• Make inferences
• Identify literary elements: theme

Assess

Resources for page 700

📁 Selection Quick Check, p. 56

📁 Selection and Unit Assessment, p. 66

💿 ExamView Assessment Suite

💿 Interactive Tutor: Self-Assessment

Students can respond to the *After You Read* items in their Learner's Notebooks or on a separate sheet of paper.

Answering the

1. Possible response: Yes, Walt was trying to protect his neighbor's land.

2. He saw them find gold on the land and study the list of unrecorded claims. He also overheard their conversation about their plans to jump the claim.

3. Possible answer: He struck at the men's faces so that they would have to protect themselves and be unable to use their hands.

Critical Thinking

4. Possible response: Walt will be treated with great respect.

5. Possible response: Walt took tremendous risks in fighting for what he believed in.

6. Possible response: Walt knew that lists of unrecorded claims were easily available. He was probably right to be sure.

700

After You Read   The King of Mazy May

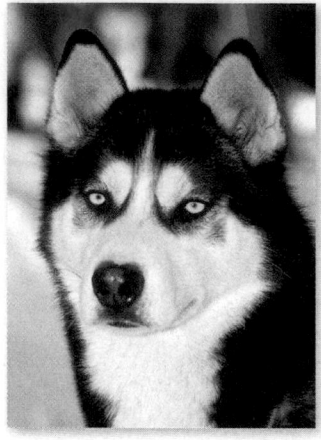

Answering the BIG Question

1. Walt's life and property were not in danger, yet he stole the stampeders' dogs and sled. Can someone steal and still be a hero? Explain.

2. **Recall** What evidence did Walt have that the newcomers were going to "jump" Loren Hall's claim?
   Tip Right There

3. **Support** Give an example of a time when Walt used his brains rather than his physical strength and endurance to help him come out ahead in the race.
   Tip Author and Me

Critical Thinking

4. **Interpret** At the end of the story, the men of the Yukon call Walt "the King of Mazy May." What might the word "king" suggest about the way Walt will be treated after this incident?
   Tip On My Own

5. **Explain** Jack London once declared, "The proper function of man is to live, not exist." Explain how Walt carried out the author's idea of the "proper function" even before he became a man.
   Tip Author and Me

6. **Infer** Walt saw the leader of the newcomers studying a piece of paper and "knew at a glance" what it was. Why did Walt think he knew what the paper was? Do you think Walt was right to be so sure?
   Tip Author and Me

Objectives (700–701)
Reading Compare and contrast • Make connections from text to self
Literature Identify key literary elements: theme
Vocabulary Explore word histories
Writing Respond to literature: personal letter
Grammar Use punctuation: commas in complex sentences

Write About Your Reading

Imagine that it's 1898, and you've gone to the Klondike to search for gold. You're about to write a letter to a family member back home.

- Decide who you are. You can be any kind of character you want. Use a "voice" that sounds natural for that character.
- Plan what you'll write. To make your letter believable, you'll need plenty of details. What's the weather like? What hardships did you suffer to get here? What are you going through now? What adventures have you had?
- Now write your letter.

Write About Your Reading

Possible response:

Dear Mom and Dad,

I have arrived safely in the Klondike after a difficult journey. You would not believe the barrenness of the land and how cold it is here! I feel at times like I am on the moon, except that there are many other travelers here seeking their fortunes. Who can be trusted? All of my food was stolen the second night of the trip, but I have been able to share with a family I met. So many men I see have a hungry look in their eyes. I keep mostly to myself. I hope to find gold and make us all rich. I will write again when I can.

Your loving son,
Lucky

Skills Review

Key Reading Skill: Comparing and Contrasting

7. While you read, you used a chart to compare and contrast your life to Walt's. Write three or four sentences to summarize the major similarities and differences.

Key Literary Element: Theme

8. Can you connect the theme of this story to your life? Explain why or why not.

9. Did thinking about the story's theme make the story more meaningful to you? Why or why not?

Reviewing Skills: Understanding Cause and Effect

10. What do you think caused the Gold Rush in the United States and Canada?

Vocabulary Check

Rewrite each sentence, filling in the blank with the correct word from the list.

industrious   floundering
perilously   prospectors   endured

11. All of the ___ wanted to find lots of gold.

12. It was not easy to find gold, and miners had to be ___ to succeed.

13. The dogs were ___ without a good leader.

14. The bullets came ___ close to hitting Walt.

15. Walt ___ in spite of all the difficulties.

16. **English Language Coach** What is the most common meaning of the word *stampede*? What does *stampede* mean in this story?

Web Activities For eFlashcards, Selection Quick Checks, and other Web activities, go to www.glencoe.com.

Grammar Link: Commas in Complex Sentences

A **complex sentence** has one independent clause and one or more dependent clauses. An independent clause has a subject and a predicate and can stand alone as a sentence. A dependent clause has a subject and a predicate but cannot stand alone.

A dependent clause that comes *before* an independent clause *should be* followed by a comma.

• **Since the dragon moved to the kingdom,** he has lived on the outside of town.

A dependent clause that comes *after* an independent clause should *not* be followed by a comma if the dependent clause is necessary to understand the independent clause.

• Everyone says **that the dragon eats the people who live in the town**.

If the dependent clause is not necessary to understand the independent clause, it should be set apart with commas.

• The dragon, **who lived on the outside of town,** scared the people in the kingdom.

Grammar Practice

Put commas in the complex sentences below to separate the dependent clauses from the independent clauses.

17. When you work hard you deserve what you get.

18. Susan the captain of the cheerleading team had the highest score on the math test.

19. Although the city fixed all the roads they still hadn't repaired the sidewalks.

Writing Application Read the letter you wrote about your trip to the Klondike. Make sure you used commas to set apart any dependent clauses in your complex sentences.

The King of Mazy May **701**

Skills Review

Key Reading Skill: Comparing and Contrasting

7. Responses will vary.

Key Literary Element: Theme

8. Responses will vary.

9. Responses will vary.

Reviewing Skills: Understanding Cause and Effect

10. Possible response: Someone found gold in these areas, and people rushed there to find gold of their own and get rich.

Vocabulary Check

11. prospectors

12. industrious

13. floundering

14. perilously

15. endured

16. **English Language Coach** a rush of animals; a rush of fortune hunters looking for gold

Close

Ask students to summarize their thoughts about the Big Question in relation to "The King of Mazy May."

Grammar Link: Commas in Complex Sentences

Grammar Practice

17. When you work hard, you deserve what you get.

18. Susan, the captain of the cheerleading team, had the highest score on the math test.

19. Although the city fixed all the roads, they still hadn't repaired the sidewalks.

Focus

BELLRINGER Options

  Daily Language Practice Transparency 57
Focus Activity Say: Now that you've gotten your fable's plot and characters down on paper, the next stop is to revise. How can you make your first draft better? *(Possible response: improve the characters' personalities or make the fable's lesson clearer.)* **OL**

Teach

W Writing

Revising Say: Look at the Revising Rubric. A good way to revise is to read your story several times, each time looking for a different element. Refer to this rubric as you make your revisions. **OL**

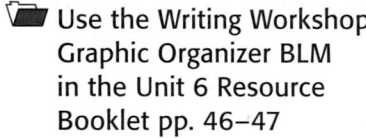

Resources for page 702

📁 Use the Writing Workshop Graphic Organizer BLM in the Unit 6 Resource Booklet pp. 46–47

 Use the Grammar and Writing Workshop Transparencies 27–28

Fable
Revising, Editing, and Presenting

ASSIGNMENT Write a fable

Purpose: To write a fable that teaches a moral

Audience: You, your teacher, and your classmates

Revising Rubric

Your revised folktale should have

W
- well-developed characters
- a conflict
- three main events
- a moral
- dialogue
- correct spelling and grammar

Objectives (pp. 702–705)
Writing Revise writing for key elements, style, voice, and dialogue
Grammar Write compound and complex sentences
Listening, Speaking, and Viewing Present fable • Use appropriate expressions and gestures • Maintain effective eye contact and posture • Ask for feedback

You started planning your fable and writing your first draft in Part 1 of this Writing Workshop. If you didn't finish your first draft, do that now. Use the story guide you created earlier to finish writing your draft.

Revising
Make It Better

Read your draft and answer the following questions:
- Does the story have a moral?
- Is there a main character?
- Does the story include three main events and a conflict?

How Do I Create Characters?

You are special and different from anyone else. Each character you create should be special and different too. Write such characters by giving them their own personalities.

The easiest way to express a character's personality is through dialogue. The way a character speaks and responds to other characters tells the reader about his or her personality. Read this example from "The Tortoise and the Hare."

> A conceited Hare boasted about her speed to everyone who would listen. "Not even the North Wind is as fast as I am!" she declared. "No animal in the forest can beat me in a race!"

What can you tell about the Hare's personality by the way she talks?

Try It

Add dialogue to your story to express your characters' personalities. Start a new line of text every time a different character speaks.

> "Without my feathers, I don't have any friends!" cried Peter.
> "Sure you do. I'm still your friend," said Polly.
> "You really want to be my friend even though I don't have any feathers?" asked Peter.
> "Of course I do!"

Additional Support

Literature Focus Lesson

Dialogue Practice writing dialogue a few times as a class. Give each student blank index cards. Direct students to write down the name of one character in the story, along with a brief description. Next, collect the cards and randomly choose two from the deck. Ask for two volunteers to act out each of the characters. Give one character a starting line and ask students to improvise a dialogue. Repeat the exercise with two more characters and two more students, this time pausing along the way to record the dialogue on the board. **OL**

Editing
Finish It Up

Use the editing checklist to find and correct errors in your fable.
- ☑ Sentences are complete.
- ☑ Compound and complex sentences are correctly punctuated.
- ☑ Dialogue includes quotation marks and correct punctuation.
- ☑ Spelling is correct.

Presenting
Show It Off

Print out your final draft or use your best handwriting to copy it onto a fresh sheet of paper.

Writing Tip

Read your dialogue aloud to make sure your characters have their own ways of speaking.

Writer's Model

Fair-Feathered Friends
By Laticia Arnold

Peter the Peacock lived in the forest with his peacock friends. Peter was the most handsome peacock in the forest because his feathers magically changed from one magnificent color to another.

One day, Polly the Pig walked by the pond where Peter and his friends were brushing their feathers. "Stay away from me," warned Peter. "You'll get mud on my feathers."

"Get lost, you ugly pig!" said Peter's friend Pierre.

"You don't belong with us," said Peter. "You're fat and filthy and you don't even have any feathers!" While Peter spoke, his own feathers changed from light purple to dark red, and the other peacocks cheered.

Active Writing Model

The writer introduces the main character and setting in the first paragraph.

The writer does a good job of creating Peter; the way he speaks shows the reader that Peter is proud and thoughtless and says mean things. **W1**

Reading Fluency

Reading to Revise Put as much space as possible between students. Then have each student read his or her fable out loud two times, trying each time to read with expression and understanding. Tell students to make a small pencil mark near parts of the text that they cannot read smoothly. If those places are still troublesome after the second reading, they may need revising. Have students take time to revise their fables so that they can read them more fluently. **OL**

Teach

W1 Writing

Dialogue Say: Sometimes the best way to move action along in a story is through dialogue. Which sentence sounds more exciting?

- Letitia was frightened and called out to Anna for help.
- "Anna! Anna! Please! Help me!" Letitia cried.

(Possible response: The second sentence is more exciting because it sounds like a real person calling for help.) **OL**

W2 Writing

Punctuation Say: If you're not sure where to place a comma in a compound or complex sentence, it may help to read it aloud. The place where you pause naturally is probably where the comma should be. **AS**

Assess

Have student partners exchange papers and use the checklist to proofread each other's work. Have them make any final changes before adding their final drafts to the class collection.

Objectives
- Write a fable
- Use literary elements: voice, point of view, dialogue
- Edit for spelling, punctuation
- Use compound and complex sentences

703

Teach

W Writing

Dialogue Invite students to analyze the personalities of the characters in the model through their dialogue.

- Divide the class into partners. Have them discuss what Peter is like and what Polly is like.

- Have each student take on a role, inventing a special voice that expresses their character's personality.

- Have students read the dialogue together, using their special voices. **OL**

C Critical Thinking

Analysis Ask: How strong do you think the conflict is in this model? Why do you think so? *(Responses will vary.)* **OL Ask:** How would you rewrite the dialogue to make the conflict even stronger? *(Responses will vary.)* **AL**

Active Writing Model

Writer's Model

Polly slunk away, hid under a tree, and cried. When she had no more tears to shed, she decided to improve her appearance. She washed herself in a pond on the other side of the forest. After she finished her bath, she rolled around in the grass to cover her body with daisies, violets, and bright green leaves. Then she admired her reflection in the pond and said, "How beautiful I look!" She hurried back to the pond, certain that now the peacocks would be her friends.

Polly couldn't have been more wrong. The peacocks took one look at her and burst out laughing. "She thinks that trash from the forest floor is as beautiful as our feathers!" jeered Peter.

"And she's got grass and soil stains on her back," another peacock said.

"Will you be my friend?" Polly asked Peter. "Your feathers change colors, so it won't matter if I stain them a little."

"Me be friends with you?" Peter laughed. "Why should I spend time with a fat, ugly, old pig when I have the loveliest feathers in the forest?" Peter puffed up his feathers so hard that two of them fell out.

For the next few days, Peter's feathers continued to fall out. As he lost his feathers, he also lost his friends.

"You look like a plucked chicken!" the other peacocks told him. "You don't belong with us anymore."

Peter slunk away, hid under a tree, and cried. Polly came along and asked, "What's wrong?"

"Without my feathers, I don't have any friends," Peter sobbed.

"Sure you do. I still want to be your friend," said Polly.

"You still want to be my friend even though I don't have any feathers?" asked Peter.

"Of course I do!"

"You forgive me for being mean to you?"

"I'm sure you'll be nicer now that you know how it feels to be hurt."

This is a complex sentence that begins with a dependent clause, so the word *bath* is followed by a comma.

The writer uses dialogue to express the characters' personalities.

The conflict is between appearance and behavior. Here, Peter faces the same problem Polly faced earlier.

W

C

Additional Support

Differentiated Instruction

Listening Skills Bring in a tape of a storyteller from your school or town library. Play a few stories for the class and discuss the ways in which the artist's voice makes the story fun. Have students notice the following:

- pace of voice

- volume of voice
- pitch of voice
- use of slang or funny words

Have students keep these things in mind as they prepare to tell a story to their classmates. **OL**

Active Writing Model

Polly taught Peter how to have fun splashing in the pond, rolling in the grass, and decorating himself with flowers and leaves. Before long, his feathers grew back. They even changed colors.

But Peter didn't change his colors toward Polly. When Peter's peacock friends wanted him back, he said, "I'm sticking with Polly. She stuck by me when I lost my good looks. I don't need fair-feathered friends!"

Moral: Don't judge others based on appearances.

This is the resolution of the conflict.

The fable ends with the moral. Peter learns that a beautiful appearance doesn't guarantee true friendship.

Listening, Speaking, and Viewing

Storytelling

Whenever you get together with your friends, stories are told—about sport events, dances, trips, or what happened in yesterday's math class. Stories are an easy way to share information about events at school and in your community.

What Is Storytelling?

Storytelling is a very old art form. Before people invented newspapers, television, or the Internet, storytelling was the only way to share information. History, legends, and myths were passed from generation to generation by professional storytellers who memorized important information and turned it into stories.

Why Is Storytelling Important?

Storytelling is fun and entertaining. It is also a good way to share a lesson or a moral. Before writing was invented, folktales were shared through storytelling. The tales were often rhymed or put to music to make them even more enjoyable.

How Do I Do It?

The main purpose of telling a story is to make the story as memorable as possible for the audience. In this workshop you will tell your fable to your classmates. The following tips will help you prepare to tell your fable:

1. Read your fable silently to yourself.
2. Read your fable aloud to a partner.
3. Start at the beginning of your fable; underline all of the important events that lead to the conclusion.
4. Consider the characters in your fable. What do their voices sound like? Use different voices when different characters speak.
5. Practice telling your fable aloud. Memorize it.
6. Keep your eyes on the audience instead of your script.

Gather Round Tell your fable to a small group of listeners. Make your fable as entertaining as possible by changing your voice for different characters, moving your body, or using props.

Teach

LSV Listening, Speaking, and Viewing

Active Listening Say: As you listen to other group members' stories, briefly note questions that come up. For instance, you may have questions about a conflict, a character's motivation, or a tricky twist in the plot. After each reading, ask your questions so that the author can answer them and improve your understanding of the story. **OL**

BQ BIG Question

Ask: What have you learned from your classmates' fables that can help you answer the Big Question? Write a brief summary in your Learner's Notebooks. *(Responses will vary.)* **OL**

Reading in the Real World

Career Have students research the storytelling profession. How do professional storytellers get their training? Do colleges offer degrees in storytelling? Do storytellers even *need* training? Through the Internet, find profiles of professional storytellers in your area and see whether they would be available for an interview or a classroom visit. **OL**

Objectives
• Evaluate a fable
• Practice dialogue
• Listen actively

Objective covered in this workshop:
• Make predictions

Teaching Students How to Predict

Why Is It Important?

• Predicting helps readers monitor comprehension when they compare what they had expected to read with what they have actually read.

• Predicting engages students more actively with the texts they are reading.

• Predicting is a familiar skill that serves as a good model of the way reading strategies enhance comprehension.

How to Help Students Get It

• Point out that reading is an interactive process involving both the reader and the author.

• Emphasize that using background knowledge (including what they have already read in the text) to make a prediction is one way to become more engaged with what they are reading

• Predicting is one way to make inferences. To make a prediction, readers have to think about what they have read, recall what they know about the relevant events or information, and compose an idea of what will happen next.

Reading to Answer the Big Question

Aunt Millicent by Mary Steele
Jamie invents an Aunt Millicent in response to a classmate's bragging about her relatives. Aunt Millicent is a heroic adventurer exploring the Cameroons. When Jamie's real-life family members get involved in the tales of Aunt Millicent's exploits, they are inspired to become more adventurous.

A Mason-Dixon Memory by Clifton Davis
An award-winning actor and musician intertwines two true stories about teenage boys who stand up for their friends in the face of racial discrimination. One account is a personal experience Davis had in 1959; the other is a more recent incident. In both cases, when an African American teen is denied acceptance to an important event, his friends reject their privileged status to show solidarity with the excluded person.

Workshop Resources

Pacing (Days) Standard	Block	Lesson	Student Materials	Teacher Resources
1	½	Key Skill Lesson: Predicting	🐟 Key Reading Skills Practice, p. 31 🐟 English Language Coach Review, p. 43	🖐 Bellringer Options Transparencies –Selection Focus Transparency 18 –Daily Language Practice 58 🖐 Read Aloud, Think Aloud Transparencies –Key Reading Skills 17 💿 Presentation Plus!
1	1	"Aunt Millicent"	💻 Glencoe Online 🐟 Unit Vocabulary Review, p. 41 🐟 Academic Vocabulary Review, p. 44 📁 English Language Coach 🐟 Active Reading Graphic Organizer, p. 33 🐟 Literary Analysis, p. 32 💿 StudentWorks Plus™ 💻 Online Student Edition 💿 Literature Classics 📁 Selection and Unit Assessments, p. 67	🖐 Literary and Text Analysis Transparencies 45 💻 Puzzlemaker 💿 Skill Level Up!™ A Language Arts Game 💻 BookLink 3 📰 Assessment by Learning Objective (Diagnostic and Formative) 💿 Interactive Tutor: Self-Assessment 💿 TeacherWorks Plus™
1		"A Mason-Dixon Memory"	💻 Glencoe Online 🐟 Unit Vocabulary Review, p. 41 🐟 Academic Vocabulary Review p. 44 📁 English Language Coach 🐟 Active Reading Graphic Organizer, p. 35 🐟 Literary Analysis, p. 32 💿 StudentWorks Plus™ 💻 Online Student Edition 💿 Literature Classics 📁 Selection and Unit Assessments, p. 68	🖐 Literary and Text Analysis Transparencies 45 💻 Puzzlemaker 💿 Skill Level Up!™ A Language Arts Game 💻 BookLink 3 📰 Assessment by Learning Objective (Diagnostic and Formative) 💿 Interactive Tutor: Self-Assessment 💿 TeacherWorks Plus™

Keys for Unit Resource

📁 Blackline Master   🔒 DVD

📰 Workbook   🖐 Transparency

📖 Supplemental Text   💻 Web-based

💿 CD-ROM   🐟 Fast File

Level Appropriate Code

AS = Activities for all students

AL = Activities for students working above grade level

OL = Activities for students working at grade level

BL = Activities for students working below grade level

EL = Activities for English language learners

706B

Focus

BELLRINGER Options

📖 **Selection Focus Transparency 18**
📖 **Daily Language Practice Transparency 58**
Focus Activity Ask: Is there a member of your family whom you greatly admire? Who is he or she, and what do you admire about him or her? *(Responses will vary.)* **OL**

Teach

R Reading Skill

Predicting Say: Think about real-life situations in which you can use clues to make predictions. For example, if the sky gets dark and the wind begins blowing strongly, what can you predict will happen? *(There will be a big storm.)* **BL** What other predictions do you make in everyday life? *(Responses will vary.)* **OL**

READING WORKSHOP 4

Skills Focus

You will practice using these skills when you read the following selections:
• "Aunt Millicent," p. 710
• "A Mason-Dixon Memory," p. 734

Reading

• Predicting

Literature

• Analyzing the setting

Vocabulary

• Understanding English word histories

Writing/Grammar

• Identifying and correcting run-on sentences

Objectives (pp. 706–707)
Reading Make predictions

Skill Lesson

Predicting

Learn It!

What Is It? Have you ever said to yourself while watching a movie, "I know what's going to happen!"? If so, you were making a prediction. You thought about what was going on in the movie, you picked up clues, and then you made an educated guess about what would happen. Whether they turn out to be right or wrong, it's always fun to make predictions.

The skill of predicting is just as useful, satisfying, and fun when you read as when you watch a movie.

Why Is It Important? Predicting gives you another good reason to read. You want to find out if your prediction matches the events, don't you? If your prediction doesn't look like it's working out, don't worry, you can always make new predictions as the text changes. As you read, adjust or change your prediction if it doesn't fit what you learn.

© Patrick McDonnell. Reprinted with permission of King Features Syndicate.

Analyzing Cartoons
Based on this cartoon, how would you rate these two "mutts" on their skill of making predictions?

Additional Support

Differentiated Instruction

Reading Strategies Some students may feel overwhelmed or intimidated by a long story. If so, suggest that they use the following reading strategies:

• Preview the story to see whether there are any natural breaks in it.
• Pause after each two-page spread to make a few notes in your Learner's Notebook.

• Close the book every few pages, shut your eyes, and visualize what you have just read.
• Read half the story, take a break and, for the second half, change the place where you are sitting. **BL**

How Do I Do It? Combine what you already know about an author or subject with what you learn as you read to guess what will happen next. Do these things as you read:

- Pay attention to details. Be on the hunt for clues.
- Stop occasionally and think about what you know.
- Ask yourself questions about what might happen.
- As the story unfolds, adjust your predictions and make new ones.

Here's how one student made a prediction while reading "The King of Mazy May."

> Looking back he could see the sled of his pursuers, drawn by eight dogs, rising and falling over the ice hummocks like a boat in a seaway. The Irishman and the black-bearded leader were with it, taking turns in running and riding.
> Night fell, and in the blackness of the first hour or so, Walt toiled desperately with his dogs . . .

C *I don't know if Walt is going to escape, I think he will get away because of the title of the story. Also, since the story's about Walt I think he is going to be the King of Mazy May. They can't catch up with him now! He can only be the King if he escapes. I'll have to keep reading to see if I'm right.*

Practice It!

Below are two events in "Aunt Millicent." Write at least one prediction for each situation. You might have more than one prediction; if you think of other predictions write them down too.

- The teacher assigns a report about an aunt or uncle, but Jamie doesn't have any aunts or uncles.
- Angelica has nineteen aunts and uncles and can't decide which one to write her report about.

Use It!

As you read "Aunt Millicent," remember the predictions you made. If you make other predictions, add them to your notes.

Literature Online

Study Central Visit www.glencoe .com and click on Study Central to review predicting.

Teach

Literature Online

Study Central Have students access the Web site to review predicting and to complete a related activity.

C Critical Thinking

Evaluation Say: Reread the student prediction about "The King of Mazy May." Do you think this was a good prediction? Why or why not? *(Responses will vary.)* **OL**

R Reading Skill

Predicting Have students look ahead through the book to find a story title that interests them. Have them read the first paragraph and predict what the story will be about. Let students share their predictions with the class. **OL**

Resources for page 707

📖 Use Key Reading Skills Transparency 17 in *Read Aloud, Think Aloud* to help students practice predicting.

Reading in the Real World

Career Tell students that Aunt Millicent is an explorer. She is much admired in her town for living an exciting and unconventional life. Talk about historical examples of women who broke barriers, such as aviator Amelia Earhart and mountaineer Annie Smith Peck. Ask students whether they know people whose jobs involve foreign travel or danger. You may wish to have students research or even interview people in your area who have adventurous careers. **OL AL**

Objectives
- Make predictions
- Evaluate text

707

Teach

More About the Author

"I had my own collection of books, which I read over and over again," Mary Steele recalls of her childhood, "and in them I could lose myself in another world." She says, "One need never be bored or lonely in the company of a good book." Mary Steele was born in 1930. This story is from a book of Australian short stories called *Dream Time*, published in 1991.

EL Language Coach

Word Histories On the board, make a chart that has three columns labeled "Root," "Meaning," and "Example." List these roots: *sphere, ject, duct, auto.* Then list their meanings: *ball, throw, lead, self.* Ask students to name words that have these roots. List the words in the third column. (*Possible responses:* atmosphere, eject, abduct, automatic) Then have students use a dictionary to see from which language each root came. (sphere: *Greek;* ject: *Latin;* duct: *Latin;* auto: *Latin*) EL BL OL

Before You Read | Aunt Millicent

Meet the Author

Mary Steele is one of Australia's best-loved writers for children. She writes in a humorous, light-hearted, and optimistic way. She says, "I believe that most children are born with a natural tendency toward fun and laughter."

Literature Online

Author Search For more about Mary Steele, go to www.glencoe.com.

Objectives (pp. 708–729)
Reading Make predictions • Make connections from text to self
Literature Identify key literary elements: setting
Vocabulary Explore word histories

Vocabulary Preview

tedious (TEE dee us) *adj.* boring; tiresome **(p. 711)** *The teacher found Angelica's bragging tedious.*

drab (drab) *adj.* lacking brightness; dull **(p. 714)** *Most people felt drab in comparison to Jamie's exciting aunt.*

expedition (ek spuh DISH un) *n.* a journey taken for a special purpose, such as exploration **(p. 716)** *Aunt Millicent was on an expedition to map the Cameroons.*

exotic (eg ZOT ik) *adj.* excitingly different; unusual; foreign **(p. 720)** *Jamie's mother brought home exotic hunting spears from Kenya.*

encounter (en KOUN tur) *n.* an unexpected or unpleasant meeting **(p. 723)** *Dr. Nutbeam did not enjoy his encounter with Mrs. Tonks.*

hoax (hohks) *n.* an act meant to fool or trick **(p. 727)** *Some people might say that Aunt Millicent was part of a hoax.*

Partner Talk Write each vocabulary word on a separate note card. Turn the note card over and write the word's definition and part of speech on the back. Take turns testing a partner by flashing each other the cards. Say each word in a sentence when you give the definition.

English Language Coach

Word Histories Another way that words come into English is, well, sort of mysterious. Some words just don't have clear histories. Take *hoax,* for example. The experts say that *hoax* is "probably" a shortened version of *hocus pocus.* Look that up, and you see that it is (again) "probably" a form of a Latin phrase.

Write to Learn The three words listed below are also related to *hocus pocus.* Copy each word into your Learner's Notebook, and tell what you know it means or might mean. Then look up the words in a good dictionary and copy one meaning for each word.

hokey

hokeypokey

hokum

EL

Additional Support

Literature Online

Author Search To expand students' appreciation of Mary Steele, have them access the Web site for additional information and resources.

English Language Coach

Word Parts Students have already studied prefixes and suffixes. Use the word *expedition* to introduce the exercise on roots. First, write the word on the board. Then, break it into parts as follows:

Ex ped i tion

Ask students to name other words that contain the same prefix, suffix, or root. Possible responses include *example, extra, pedestrian, pedestal, motion, communication.* Explain that the root *ped* means *foot* and discuss how that relates to the meaning of *expedition.* EL BL

Skills Preview

Key Reading Skill: Predicting

When you make predictions, you use your prior knowledge and the information you gather from reading to guess what will happen next. As you gather more information you might want to change your predictions. Sometimes you'll find that your guesses are right. A couple of things to ask yourself as you predict are:

• *What* will happen next?

• *Why* do I think that will happen next?

Write to Learn Read the first five paragraphs of "Aunt Millicent" and write a prediction.

Key Literary Element: Setting

Setting is the time and place in which a story's events occur. Sometimes authors give the time and place at the beginning of the story. The author may tell the setting later or gradually reveal it with clues. In "Aunt Millicent," you won't learn about the setting right away, but it is revealed eventually.

There can be more than one setting; for example, Aunt Millicent's travels call to mind other, more mysterious places. Remember the following as you think about the setting:

L

• You might not learn about the setting right away.
  When is the setting revealed?

• A story can have more than one setting. If the story moves to another place or time, that's a new setting.
  Do you notice more than one setting? If so, what events occur in each setting? Is there a reason events occur in different settings?

• Descriptions of characters and places, the way characters speak, and the time in which the story occurs can help show the setting.
  What details help you picture the setting?

What's *Your* Setting? Write a few sentences to describe one important setting in your life.

Get Ready to Read

Connect to the Reading

R Think about what it would be like to travel all over the world and live the life of an explorer. Where would you go? What places have you always wanted to visit?

Write to Learn Make a list of the top three places you would travel to if you could go anywhere. Pick one of those places and write a paragraph explaining why you picked that place above all the others on your list.

Build Background

Jamie's exciting Aunt Millicent is rumored to be in Cameroon at one point and climbing a peak in the Peruvian Andes at another. That's the life of an explorer!

• Cameroon, officially called Republic of Cameroon, is in West Africa.

• Lima is the capital of Peru; the Andes Mountains run through Peru along the western part of South America.

Set Purposes for Reading

BIG Question Read "Aunt Millicent" to learn about a family's new—and suprising—hero.

Set Your Own Purpose What else would you like to learn from the story to help you answer the Big Question? Write your purpose on the "Aunt Millicent" page of Foldable 6.

Interactive Literary Elements Handbook
To review or learn more about the literary elements, go to www.glencoe.com.

Keep Moving

Use these skills as you read the following selection.

Aunt Millicent **709**

Teach

L Literary Element

Setting **Ask:** What have been some of your favorite settings in books you have read or movies you have seen? Would you rather read an adventure that takes place in a wild jungle or a story set in a big, bustling city? *(Responses will vary.)* **OL**

R Reading Skill

Review Connecting **Ask:** Has anyone ever brought you a souvenir from an interesting or faraway place? Where did they go, and what did they bring you? Did it make you want to visit the place? Why or why not? *(Responses will vary.)* **OL**

Interactive Literary Elements Handbook Have students access the Web site to improve their understanding of setting.

Literature Focus Lesson

Heroes Discuss with students that the title character in the story, Aunt Millicent, is an imaginary person. Prepare them to begin thinking about how this might make her like a mythological hero. Give students some of the following questions to think about as they read:

• Can animals be literary heroes? Can animals be real heroes?

• Can objects be literary heroes? Can objects be real heroes?

• What are the limits to being a literary hero?

Objectives

• Make predictions
• Analyze settings
• Understand word histories
• Make connections to the text
• Identify literary elements: setting
• Analyze word parts

709

Teach

Viewing the Photo

Ask: Where do you think this photograph was taken? (*somewhere in Africa*) **Ask:** Why do you think so? (*There is a rhinoceros in the picture as well as an acacia tree, both of which are found in Africa.*) **EL** **BL** Is that somewhere you would like to visit? Why or why not? (*Responses will vary.*) **AS**

R Reading Skill

Predicting Say: Reread the paragraph describing Angelica Tonks. What problems and conflicts do you predict a character like Angelica might cause? (*Possible response: Angelica is self-centered, so other characters may become annoyed with her persistent bragging.*) **OL**

Readability Scores
Dale-Chall: 5.1
DRP: 52
Lexile: 870

Additional Support

Aunt Millicent

by Mary Steele

"I," said Angelica Tonks, grandly, "have eight uncles and eleven aunts."

Angelica Tonks had more of most things than anyone else. She held the class record for pairs of fashion sneakers and Derwent pencil sets, and her pocket-money supply was endless. Now, it seemed, she also had the largest uncle-and-aunt collection in town. Her classmates squirmed and made faces at each other. *Awful* Angelica Tonks.

Mr. Wilfred Starling dusted the chalk from his bony hands and sighed. "Well, Angelica, aren't you a lucky one to have nineteen uncles and aunts. You'll just have to choose the most interesting one to write about, won't you?"

"But they're *all* interesting," objected Angelica. "The Tonks family is a wonderfully interesting family, you know. It will be terribly hard to choose just one." **1**

There were more squirms. The class was fed up with the wonderfully interesting Tonks family. In fact, Mr. Wilfred Starling nearly screamed. He just managed to swallow his exasperation, which sank down to form a hard bubble in his stomach. Straightening his thin shoulders, he said, "Right, everyone, copy down this week's homework assignment from

710 UNIT 6 What Makes a Hero?

Practice the Skills

1 Key Reading Skill

Predicting What do you know about Angelica Tonks at this point? Do you predict that she will be a character that you like? Why or why not? **R**

Reading Fluency

Build Fluency This story, which has lots of characters and dialogue, provides excellent opportunities for students to practice fluency. Choose a section of the story and have students take turns reading aloud in small groups. Alternately, have groups read out loud in choral fashion. Whenever you are reading aloud, remind the students to follow along and listen to the way that your voice reflects the content of the text and emotion of the story. **AS**

the board. And remember, Angelica, a pen-portrait[1] of just *one* aunt or uncle is all I want. Just *one*." *Please not a whole gallery of **tedious** and terrible Tonkses, he thought to himself.*

The class began to write. Jamie Nutbeam, sitting behind Angelica, leaned forward and hissed, "If the rest of your family is so *wonderfully interesting*, they must be a big improvement on you, Honky![2] And, anyway, I bet the aunt I write about will beat any of yours!"

"I bet she won't," Angelica hissed back. "She'll be so *boring*. What's her name, this boring aunt?"

Jamie finished copying and put down his pen. "Aunt Millicent, and she's pretty special."

"Millicent!" scoffed Angelica. "What a name! No one's called Millicent these days!"

"QUIET, you two!" barked Mr. Starling, massaging his stomach, "and start tidying up, everyone—it's time for the bell." *Oh bliss,* he thought.

As the classroom emptied, Jamie lingered behind.

"What is it, Jamie?" asked Mr. Starling wearily, piling his books and papers together and trying not to burp.

"Well, the trouble is I haven't any aunts or uncles to do a portrait of," said Jamie, turning rather red, "so is it all right if I make one up? An aunt?"

"Oh, I see! Well, in that case . . . yes, perfectly all right," replied Mr. Starling. He gazed rather sadly out the window. "The most interesting characters in the world are usually the made-up ones, you know, Jamie. Think of Sherlock Holmes and Alice and Dr. Who and Indiana Jones . . ."

Jamie interrupted. "Does anyone need to know I've made her up? This aunt?"

"Well, *I* won't say anything," promised Mr. Starling. "It's for you to make her seem real so we all believe in her. You go home and see what you can dream up." **2**

---

1. The **pen-portrait** is an assignment to write a descriptive report about someone or something.
2. Adding this nickname to Angelica's last name makes her **Honky Tonks,** and honky-tonks just happens to be a term for cheap, noisy nightclubs.

Vocabulary

tedious (TEE dee us) *adj.* boring; tiresome

Practice the Skills

R

BQ

2 ███ **Key Literary Element** ███

Setting What would you say is the main setting of the story so far? What clues tell you that? Has the author described it in great detail?

Aunt Millicent **711**

Teach

R Reading Skill

Review Inferring Say: Think about how Mr. Starling acts. What can you tell about him from this behavior? How do you think he is feeling? *(Possible responses: He is tired of his job; he doesn't like dealing with obnoxious students.)* **BL AL**

BQ BIG Question

Ask: If you were to make up a relative who was a hero, what traits would you give him or her? How would you make this person seem impressive? *(Responses will vary.)* **OL**

Differentiated Instruction

Building Background Some students may not be familiar with the references to Sherlock Holmes, Alice, Dr. Who, and Indiana Jones. You can place students in small groups to discuss these characters or provide an opportunity for students to research them in the library or on the Internet. Ask students to think about what traits make these characters heroic. You may also wish to invite students from other cultures to share information about famous literary characters in their cultures. Have groups present their findings to the class. **OL**

Objectives
• Make predictions
• Make inferences
• Use text features: photographs

Teach

L Literary Element

Setting Ask: If you were to write a story that takes place in a classroom, what clues would you give the reader about the setting? *(Possible responses: desks; papers; pencils; a teacher; a chalkboard)* OL

R Reading Skill

Review Connecting Say: You can use another reading skill—connecting—to help you make predictions. If you were in Jamie's position, what would you do at this point in the story? Do you think Jamie will do the same thing? *(Possible response: I would make up an outrageous aunt or uncle who would impress Angelica and put her in her place.)* OL

"She has a name already," Jamie called back as he left the room. "She's Aunt Millicent."

Aunt Millicent Nutbeam! The hard bubble in Mr. Starling's stomach began to melt away. **3**

That evening, Jamie Nutbeam said to his family at large, "Did you know that awful Angelica Tonks has eight uncles and eleven aunts?"

"Well, everybody knows that they're a big family," replied his mother. "Prolific,³ I'd call it," grunted Jamie's father from behind his newspaper.

"Yes, dear—prolific. Now, Mrs. Tonks was a Miss Blizzard," continued Mrs. Nutbeam, "and there are lots of Blizzards around here as well as Tonkses, all related, no doubt. But fancy⁴ nineteen! Who told you there were nineteen, Jamie?"

"She did—old Honky Tonks herself. She told the whole class *and* Mr. Starling—boasting away as usual. She's a *pill*." Jamie was jotting things on paper as he talked. "We have to write a pen-portrait of an aunt or uncle for homework, and Honky can't decide which one to do because they're all so *wonderfully interesting*, she says. Urk!" He paused and then added, "I'm doing Aunt Millicent."

Jamie's father peered over the top of his newspaper. **R** "Aunt who?"

"Who's Aunt Millicent?" demanded Jamie's sister, Nerissa.

"You haven't got an Aunt Millicent," said his mother. "You haven't any aunts at all, or uncles, for that matter."

"I *know* I haven't," Jamie snapped. "It's *hopeless* belonging to a **nuclear** family!⁵ It's unfair—I mean, awful Honky has nineteen aunts and uncles and Nerissa and I haven't got any, not one." Jamie ground the pencil between his teeth. **4**

"You won't have any teeth either, if you munch pencils like that," remarked his father, who was a dentist.

Jamie glowered, spitting out wet splinters.

"Anyway, he's right," announced Nerissa. "It would be

---

3. Here **prolific** refers to having many children.

4. Here **fancy** means "imagine," said with surprise.

5. Parents and their children make up a **nuclear family.** Angelica has an extended family, which includes aunts, uncles, cousins, and other close relatives.

Practice the Skills

3 Key Reading Skills

Predicting What do you predict will happen next, and why? What details have already happened to make you think that? Write your prediction in your Learner's Notebook.

4 English Language Coach

Word Histories The word **nuclear** was first used in English in 1833, but it wasn't used to refer to a family until 1949! It comes from the Latin *nucleus,* meaning "inner part." An atom's nucleus is its center, and the nucleus of a family is the parents and their children.

Additional Support

Differentiated Instruction

Character Sketch Ask students to write sketches of real relatives. Have them begin by completing an information web similar to the one shown here. Students can include the information in their character sketches. OL

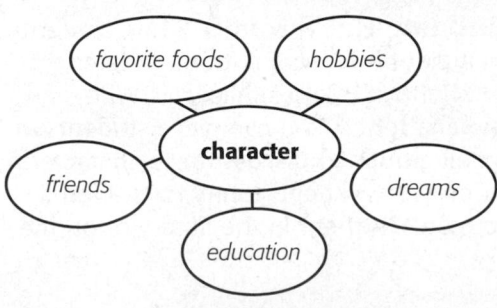

great to have even one aunt or uncle. Then we might have some cousins, too. Everyone else has cousins. Angelica Tonks probably has about a hundred-and-twenty-seven."

"Well, I'm sorry," sighed Mrs. Nutbeam, "but your father and I are both 'onlys' and there's nothing we can do about that, is there? Not a thing! Now, what's all this about an Aunt Millicent?"

"Oh, it's okay," grumbled her son. "Mr. Starling said to write about *an* aunt or uncle, not exactly *my* aunt or uncle. He says I can invent one."

"Will you explain that she's not real?" asked Nerissa, doubtfully.

"Mr. Starling says I don't have to, and he's not going to tell. He says I have to make people believe that she *is* real. Anyway, I don't want Honky Tonks to know that she's made up, because Aunt Millicent is going to be amazing—much better than any of those boring Tonkses. It's time Honky was taken down a peg or two."[6] **5**

Dr. Nutbeam quite understood how Jamie felt. From time to time Angelica Tonks visited his dentist's chair. She would brag about her "perfect" teeth if there was nothing to be fixed, but if she needed a filling her shrieks of "agony" would upset everyone in the waiting room and Mrs. Tonks would call Dr. Nutbeam a *brute*. He was often tempted to give Angelica a general anesthetic and post her home in a large jiffy bag.

Now he folded his newspaper; Jamie's project sounded rather fun. "Right, Jamie," he said, "tell us about Aunt Millicent and let us get some facts straight. Is she my sister, or Mum's? We must get that settled to start with."

"I can't decide," frowned Jamie. "What do you think?" **6**

"She'd better be your sister, dear," said Mrs. Nutbeam calmly to her husband. "I grew up here and everyone knows I was an only child, but you came from another town. You're more mysterious."

Dr. Nutbeam looked pleased. "Mm . . . mm. That's nice . . . having a sister, I mean. Is she younger than me?"

"No, older," said Jamie.

---

6. The expression **taken down a peg** means "made less proud and more humble."

Practice the Skills

5 | **Reviewing Skills**

Responding It might seem surprising that Mr. Starling agrees to let Jamie invent an aunt. How does that make you feel about Mr. Starling? Do you like him? Explain. How do you feel about Jamie, and what do you think of his plan? **R1**

6 | **Key Reading Skill**

Predicting Now Jamie's entire family is interested in his project. The project even sounds "rather fun" to his father. What do you think will happen? What clues affect your decision? **R2**

Aunt Millicent **713**

Teach

R1 Reading Skill

Review Responding Ask: Do you think fictional stories can be just as valuable as nonfictional stories? How does this affect the way you feel about Mr. Starling, Jamie, and Jamie's plan to make up a relative to write about? *(Responses will vary.)* **OL**

R2 Reading Skill

Predicting Ask: How do you think Jamie's family will feel about having a new "relative" to think and talk about? *(Possible response: Jamie's family seems excited about his project. They will probably enjoy making the relative into whoever they want her to be.)* **OL**

English Language Coach

Colloquialisms Point out to students that the author of this story is Australian. Just as the English that is spoken in various regions of the United States differs, Australian English sometimes differs from American English. On this page, the mother is called *Mum*, and Dr. Nutbeam sometimes wants to *post her* (Angelica) *home in a jiffy bag*. Ask students to keep a list in their Learner's Notebooks of other colloquialisms and discuss them periodically as a class. You may wish to have students do research to find colloquialisms from other cultures or share those with which they are familiar. **AS**

Objectives
• Identify literary elements: setting
• Respond to literature
• Make predictions
• Make connections from self to text

713

Teach

R Reading Skill

Predicting Say: Aunt Millicent is turning into quite an unusual person. Do you predict that her character will make the story more believable or less believable to Jamie's classmates? *(Responses will vary.)* **OL**

C Critical Thinking

Analysis Say: Mrs. Nutbeam wonders how Aunt Millicent got started in a career as an explorer. Do you think Mrs. Nutbeam is just going along with the fun, or is she starting to believe the story? *(Possible response: Mrs. Nutbeam seems to be having fun going along with the story, but she may be getting involved and thinking about the possible careers for a woman.)* **OL**

"Where does she live?" asked Nerissa. "Has she a family of her own? Lots of cousins for us?"

"No way—she hasn't time for all that sort of thing. And she doesn't live anywhere in particular."

Mrs. Nutbeam looked puzzled. "What *do* you mean, dear? What does Auntie Millicent do, exactly?"

"She's an explorer," said Jamie, proudly. "She works for foreign governments, and she's terribly busy—flat out."

There was something of a pause. Then Dr. Nutbeam said, "Ah," and stroked his bald patch. "That explains why we haven't seen her for so long."

"What does she explore?" demanded Nerissa. "Is there anything left in the world to look for?"

Jamie was beginning to feel a bit rushed. "Well, I'm not sure yet, but foreign governments need people like her to search for water in deserts and rich mineral deposits and endangered species and things . . . you know." **7**

Visual Vocabulary
A *machete* (muh SHET ee) is a wide, heavy knife that can be used as a weapon and a tool.

Nerissa lay on the floor with her eyes closed and began to imagine her new aunt slashing a path through tangled jungle vines, searching for a rare species of dark blue frog. The mosquitoes were savage. The leeches were huge and bloated. Aunt Millicent's machete was razor sharp . . .

"This is all very unexpected," murmured Mrs. Nutbeam, "to have a sister-in-law who is an explorer, I mean. I wonder how you get started in that sort of career?" Her own job as an assistant in an antique and curio shop[7] suddenly seemed rather **drab**.

Dr. Nutbeam was staring at the wall. In his mind's eye he clearly saw his sister on a swaying rope suspension bridge above a terrifying ravine.[8] She was leading a band of native bearers to the other side. How much more adventurous, he

---

7. A *curio shop* sells rare or unusual objects.

8. In this case, the *suspension bridge* hangs from ropes attached to posts at each end of the *ravine*, which is a narrow steep-sided valley.

Vocabulary

drab (drab) *adj.* lacking brightness; dull

Practice the Skills

7 **Key Reading Skill**

Predicting Do you predict that Jamie will fool everyone at school into believing that Aunt Millicent is a real person? Explain. **R**

Additional Support

Literature Focus Lesson

Character Some of the humor in this story comes from the unexpected interest of adults in an exciting but make-believe character. Point out that Mrs. Nutbeam calls her Auntie Millicent on this page. On the next page, Dr. Nutbeam calls her Millie. Ask students whether they can think of other stories in which adults, such as Willie Wonka in *Charlie and the Chocolate Factory*, conspire with children rather than take on a traditional role. **OL** Ask students to write a description of a fictional adult character who has as much fun as children typically do. **AL**

thought, than drilling little holes in people's teeth. He wrenched his gaze back to Jamie and asked,

C "Do we know what Millie is actually exploring at present?" **8**

Jamie munched his pencil for a moment and then said, "She's in Africa, somewhere near the middle, but I'm not sure where, exactly."

"In the middle of Africa, is she?" echoed Dr. Nutbeam. "Mm . . . then it wouldn't surprise me if she were in the Cameroons. There's a lot of dense forest in the Cameroons, you know."

"I thought Cameroons were things to eat," frowned Nerissa. "Sort of coconut biscuits."

"No, no, dear, those are macaroons," said her mother.

"They're bad for your teeth, too," remarked her father, absently, "like eating pencils."

Jamie fetched the atlas and found a map of Africa. His father stood behind him, peering at it. "There it is, in the middle on the left-hand side, just under the bump."

"It's called Cameroon here," Jamie said. "Just one of them."

"Well, there's East Cameroon and West Cameroon, see," pointed his father, "and sometimes you lump them together and call them Cameroons. Look—here's the equator just to the south, so it must be pretty hot and steamy at sea-level."

L "Poor Millicent," sighed Mrs. Nutbeam. "I do hope her feet don't swell in the heat, with all that walking."

Jamie examined the map closely. "That's peculiar—the north border of the Cameroons seems to be floating in a big lake . . . um, Lake Chad[9] . . . it looks all swampy, with funny

Aunt Millicent might have sent back a picture like this one from her travels in Africa.

8 | **Key Literary Element**

Setting A few different settings have just been described, including Nerissa's image of the jungle and Dr. Nutbeam's image of the suspension bridge. How are these settings different from the story's "real" setting?

---

9. *Lake Chad,* in the nation of Chad, is on the northeastern border of Cameroon.

Aunt Millicent **715**

Teach

C Critical Thinking

Evaluation Say: Jamie's family has gone from calling their imaginary relative "Aunt Millicent" to calling her "Auntie Millicent" to calling her "Millie." What conclusions can you draw about the family's feelings? *(Possible response: As they talk more about her, the family is starting to feel the kind of affection for her that they would feel for a real person. That's why they are starting to give her nicknames.)* **OL**

L Literary Element

Setting Ask: In general, do details about setting make stories seem more believable? *(Responses will vary.)* **Ask:** Do you think Aunt Millicent will seem more realistic if Jamie continues to do research about the settings he puts her in? *(Possible response: The more well-researched details Jamie includes, the more realistic his stories will be.)* **OL**

Differentiated Instruction

Geography Show a map of Cameroon and explain that East Cameroon and West Cameroon merged in 1961 to become a unified country. Students who enjoy art or geography might like to color a map and add details about the country's people, economy, and history. **OL**

You can ask some students to do research about what could be explored in Cameroon today. They could then present their findings to the class. **AL**

Objectives
- Make predictions
- Analyze text
- Draw conclusions
- Evaluate text
- Identify literary elements: character, setting

715

Teach

R Reading Skill

Review Understanding Cause and Effect **Ask:** Why is Jamie afraid to tell Grandma about Aunt Millicent? How does he think his creation might affect her? *(Possible response: Jamie is afraid because he has invented a daughter for Grandma without asking. He may be concerned that she will not appreciate the lie.)* **OL**

C Critical Thinking

Analysis **Ask:** Why is the family so interested in Jamie's new relative? *(Possible response: They want to help him write a good report.)* What do their reactions tell you about them? *(Possible response: They are helpful; they are creative.)* **OL**

dotted lines and things. I bet that bit needs exploring. They've probably lost their border in the mud and Aunt Millicent could be on an **expedition** to find it." **9**

"Is she all by herself?" asked Nerissa. "I'd be scared in a place like that."

"Of course she's not by herself," snorted Jamie. "She works for a foreign government, don't forget, and she'd have a whole support team of porters and cooks and scientists and things."

"She must be an expert at something herself, don't you think?" suggested Mrs. Nutbeam. "I would imagine that she's a surveyor."**10**

"Yes, she'd use one of those instruments you look through, on legs," added Nerissa.

"You mean a theodolite, dimwit," answered her brother.

"She'd certainly need one of those, if she's measuring angles and distances and drawing maps," agreed Dr. Nutbeam.

"My word, what a clever old sister I have!"

"I wonder if she was good at geography at school?" said Nerissa.

"Well, you'll be able to ask Grandma tomorrow. She's coming for her winter visit, remember?"

"Oh help! What'll Grandma *say*?" gasped Jamie. "Do you think she'll mind? I mean—we've invented a daughter for her without asking!"

"I shouldn't think she'd mind," said his mother. "We'll break the news to her carefully and see how she takes it."

Grandma Nutbeam, as it turned out, was delighted.

"How exciting!" she exclaimed. "I always wanted a daughter, and it's been very lonely since Grandpa died. Now I'll have a new interest! Just show me on the map where Millicent is at the moment, please dear."

Visual Vocabulary A *theodolite* (thee OH duh lite) is used by surveyors to measure angles.

R

---

10. A *surveyor* is a person who measures angles and distances of land to determine its boundaries, area, or elevations.

Vocabulary

expedition (ek spuh DISH un) *n.* a journey taken for a special purpose, such as exploration

Practice the Skills

9 Key Literary Element

Setting Jamie has thought of a setting for his story about Aunt Millicent. He has put her in a *time* and *place*. Pay close attention to how the settings help to make Aunt Millicent both real and mysterious.

Additional Support

Reading in the Real World

Career Have students interested in careers that involve expeditions and exploration do library or Internet research. You may wish to find out whether there is a surveyor in your town government. If you find one, invite the surveyor to speak to your class. Ask him or her to bring some instruments, particularly a theodolite, and show the class how they are used. Help students prepare questions in advance about the training, education, risks, and benefits of being a surveyor. **AS**

Jamie pointed to the dotted lines in swampy Lake Chad near the top end of the Cameroons, and Grandma stared in astonishment. **10**

"Gracious heaven! What an extraordinary place to go to, the silly girl! I hope she's remembered her quinine[11] tablets. Millicent was never very good at looking after herself, you know. Let me see—I think I'll get some wool tomorrow and knit her some good stout hiking socks."

Jamie blinked. "There's no need to do that, Grandma. She's not really real, you know."

"Well, she'll be more real to me if I make her some socks," Grandma declared.

"Wouldn't they be rather hot in the Cameroons?" objected Nerissa. "It's awfully near the equator, don't forget."

"Woollen socks are best in any climate," said Grandma firmly. "They breathe."

"Now, Mother," interrupted Dr. Nutbeam, "you can tell us what Millicent was like as a girl. I can't remember her very well, as she was so much older than me, but I have a feeling that she ran away from home a lot."

Grandma pondered a moment. "Now that you mention it, she did. She did indeed. I thought we'd have to chain her up sometimes! We lived near the edge of town, you'll remember, and Millie would look out towards the paddocks[12] and hills and say that she wanted to know what was over the horizon, or where the birds were flying to, or where the clouds came from behind the hills. We never knew where she'd be off to next—but she certainly ended up in the right job! I'm so glad she became an explorer. If I were a bit younger and had better feet, I might even go and join

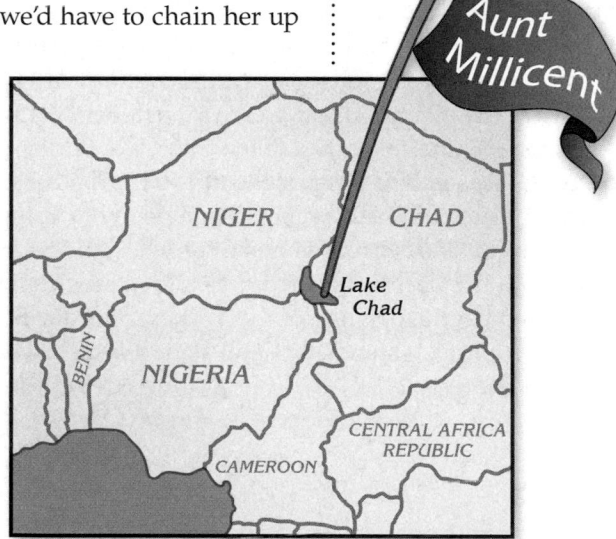

Aunt Millicent

NIGER   CHAD

Lake
Chad

BENIN

NIGERIA

CENTRAL AFRICA
REPUBLIC

CAMEROON

---

11. **Quinine** (QWY nine) is a drug made from the bark of a tree, used to treat malaria and other diseases.

12. **Paddocks** are small, fenced fields in which animals can graze and exercise.

Aunt Millicent **717**

Practice the Skills

10 Key Reading Skill

Predicting What do you think Aunt Millicent will be like? Will she be kind, brave, stubborn, angry, mean, or something else entirely?

Teach

L Literary Element

Setting Ask: How does Grandma react to the setting in which she finds Aunt Millicent? Why do you think she reacts this way? *(Possible response: Grandma is astonished but fascinated. She probably reacts this way because the setting is exotic and foreign.)* **OL**

C Critical Thinking

Comprehension Say: Think about the way Grandma talks about Aunt Millicent's childhood. Does Grandma sound like a typical mother? *(Possible response: Grandma speaks in a loving way, as any mother would, about her child. She sounds accepting and proud of her fictional daughter's adventurous spirit.)* **OL**

English Language Coach

Prefixes and Suffixes Review the meanings of the following prefixes and suffixes with students:

- *un-*: not
- *en-*: to put into or on
- *-ous*: having; full of; like
- *-ist*: a person who

Then have students define each of the following words and use each word in a sentence.

1. mysterious *(full of mystery)*
2. scientist *(a person who is skilled in science)*
3. enfold *(to cover or hold)*
4. unexpected *(not expected)* **EL BL**

Objectives
- Understand cause and effect
- Analyze text
- Monitor comprehension
- Identify prefixes and suffixes
- Identify literary elements: setting

717

Teach

Ask: What heroic qualities have the Nutbeams given to Aunt Millicent so far? *(Possible responses: adventurousness; cleverness; independence)* **OL**

R Reading Skill

Predicting Say: Sometimes you can use what you know about the characters in a story to predict what will happen. Think about what you know about Angelica's character and about Jamie's character. Which character do you predict will write a better pen-portrait? *(Possible response: Angelica is conceited and boastful; Jamie is creative and funny. Characters like Jamie usually come out on top.)* **OL**

her. It would be most interesting to see the Cameroons. It's full of monkeys, I believe."

"Was Aunt Millicent good at geography at school?" Nerissa remembered to ask.

"Let me think—yes, she must have been because one year she won a prize for it, and the prize was a book called *Lives of the Great Explorers*."

"Well, there you are," remarked Mrs. Nutbeam. "That's probably how it all started."

Next day, Grandma Nutbeam began to knit a pair of explorer's socks. She decided on khaki with dark blue stripes round the top.

Angelica Tonks had found it so difficult to select one of the nineteen aunts and uncles, that her pen-portrait was left until the very last minute and then scrawled out in a great hurry. She had finally chosen Aunt Daisy Blizzard, Mrs. Tonks's eldest sister. **11**

Mr. Wilfred Starling asked Angelica to read her portrait to the class first, to get it over with. As he had expected and as Jamie Nutbeam had hoped, Angelica's aunt sounded anything but wonderfully interesting. She had always lived in the same street, her favorite color was deep purple and she grew African violets on the bathroom shelf, but that was about all.

Many of the other portraits weren't much better, although there was one uncle who had fallen into Lake Burley Griffin and been rescued by a passing Member of Parliament.[13] Someone else's aunt had competed in a penny-farthing bicycle race in Northern Tasmania,[14] only to capsize and sprain both her knees; and there was a great-uncle who had been present at the opening of the Sydney Harbour Bridge in 1932, but couldn't remember it at all as he'd been asleep in his pram[15] at the time.

---

13. **Lake Burley Griffin** is a man-made lake near the **Parliament** buildings in Canberra, the capital of Australia.

14. **Tasmania** is an island off the southeastern coast of Australia. The **penny-farthing** is a type of bicycle that has a very large front wheel and a very small back wheel.

15. **Sydney Harbour Bridge** is in the city of Sydney in southern Australia. A **pram** is what Australians call a baby carriage.

718 UNIT 6 What Makes a Hero?

Practice the Skills

11 **Key Reading Skill**

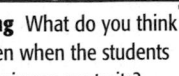

Predicting What do you think will happen when the students present their pen-portraits? **R**

Additional Support

Reading in the Real World

Career The selection underscores the fact that women can be involved in just as many adventurous activities as men. Have students work in small groups to discuss women they know or have read about who have adventurous hobbies or careers, such as archaeologist, police officer, rock-climber, or pilot. Have each group choose one woman and list the challenges of her activity or occupation, the character traits that helped her achieve her goal, and the training and education required for her position. **OL**

Mr. Starling saved Jamie's portrait until last, hoping for the best. Jamie cleared his throat nervously and began:

"I have never met Aunt Millicent and no one in my family knows her very well, as she hasn't been in Australia for a long time. This is because Aunt Millicent is an explorer . . ."

Mr. Wilfred Starling had been hoping for a bright spot in his day, and Aunt Millicent Nutbeam was it. He smiled happily when Jamie explained how Millicent had gained her early training as an explorer by regularly running away from home. He sighed with pleasure as Jamie described the swampy region of Lake Chad, where Millicent was searching through the mud and papyrus[16] for the northern border of the Cameroons. He positively beamed when he heard that Grandma Nutbeam was knitting explorer's socks for her daughter.

The rest of the class sat spellbound as Jamie read on, except for Angelica Tonks, whose scowl grew darker by the minute. Jamie had barely finished his portrait when her hand was waving furiously.

Mr. Starling's beam faded. "What is it, Angelica?"

"I don't believe it. Women don't go exploring! I think Jamie's made it all up! He's a cheat!"

Mr. Starling's stomach lurched, but before he had time to say anything the other girls in the class rose up in a passion and rounded on Angelica.

"Who *says* women don't go exploring?"

"Women can do anything they want to these days, Angelica Tonks! Don't you know that?"

"*I'd* really like to be an explorer or something—maybe a test-pilot."

"Well, *I'd* like to be a diver and explore the ocean floor and have a good look at the Titanic."[17]

"What does your aunt wear when she's at work?"

"What color are her new socks?"

The boys began to join in.

"Can your aunt really use a **machete**?" **12**

"How many languages can she speak?"

---

16. Surrounded by swamps, Lake Chad is the sort of place where *papyrus,* a tall grassy plant, grows well.

17. The *Titanic* was an ocean liner that sank in the North Atlantic in 1912 after hitting an iceberg.

Practice the Skills

12 English Language Coach

Word Histories Like *hoax,* **machete** is a word whose origin is not certain. American natives had invented the knife long before Europeans came to the New World. Spanish explorers probably adapted their noun *macho* ("big hammer"). Though we usually think of a machete as a cutting tool, its wide, flat side is good for pounding.

Aunt Millicent **719**

Teach

C Critical Thinking

Analysis Ask: Why is Mr. Starling so delighted with Jamie's story? *(Possible response: Mr. Starling mentioned earlier that some of the most interesting characters are made-up ones. A creative, exciting story seems to brighten his usually dull and stressful day.)* OL AL

R Reading Skill

Predicting Say: Your knowledge of how plots work can help you make predictions. Now that Jamie has introduced Aunt Millicent, the rising action will probably start. What complications do you think there could be? *(Possible response: Everyone is so curious about Aunt Millicent that more questions will probably arise, and Jamie will have to make up more information. He might end up getting caught in his "lie" after all.)* OL

Differentiated Instruction

Illustrations Discuss with students their thoughts about Aunt Millicent. What does she look like? What does she like to do between expeditions? What kind of music does she listen to? What's her favorite card game or sport? Have students draw an illustration of Aunt Millicent in Cameroon or write an entry for her diary. Have volunteers share their work with the class. **AS**

Objectives
• Make predictions
• Analyze text

Teach

C Critical Thinking

Evaluation Ask: How is the creation of Aunt Millicent affecting the members of the Nutbeam family? Explain. *(Possible response: Aunt Millicent, although imaginary, is inspiring the Nutbeams to learn more about the world around them.)* **OL**

EL Language Coach

Word Histories You may wish to mention that the word *souvenir* also comes from the French word meaning "remember." **AS**

"Does she always carry a gun? I bet she's a crack shot!"

"How does a theodolite work?"

The clamor[18] was so great that hardly anyone heard the bell. Angelica Tonks heard it and vanished in a sulk. Mr. Starling heard it and happily gathered up his books. He gave Jamie a secret wink as he left the room. **13**

The end of the assignment was not the end of Aunt Millicent. At school, the careers teacher ran some special sessions on "Challenging Occupations for Women" after he had been stormed by the girls from Jamie's class for information about becoming test-pilots, mobile-crane drivers, buffalo hunters and ocean-floor mappers. The science teacher was asked to explain the workings of a theodolite to the class.

At home, Aunt Millicent settled happily into the Nutbeam family, who all followed her adventures with great interest. Dr. Nutbeam brought home library books about the Cameroons and Central Africa. Jamie roared his way through one called *The Bafut Beagles*. Mrs. Nutbeam rummaged through an old storeroom at the curio shop and began to collect **exotic** objects. She brought home a brace[19] of hunting spears from Kenya, which she hung on the family-room wall. **C**

Visual Vocabulary
A *mongoose* is a small mammal native to parts of Asia, Africa, and Europe. It has a pointy face and shaggy fur and is two to three feet long.

"Just the sort of **souvenir** Millicent could have sent us," she explained. "See—those marks on the blades are very probably dried bloodstains." **14**

Another time she unwrapped a stuffed mongoose, announcing that Auntie had sent this from India on one of her earlier trips.

Jamie and Nerissa stroked it. "What a funny animal," said Nerissa. "Like a weasel."

---

18. A *clamor* is a loud noise.

19. Here a *brace* is a pair.

Vocabulary

exotic (eg ZOT ik) *adj.* excitingly different; unusual; foreign

720 UNIT 6 What Makes a Hero?

Practice the Skills

13 Key Reading Skill

Predicting Aunt Millicent is very popular with all of the students, and even Mr. Starling is pleased with her. Angelica, on the other hand, thinks that Jamie "made it all up." Now that Aunt Millicent is such a hit, what do you think will happen to her? What clues help with your prediction?

14 English Language Coach

Word Histories The word **souvenir** comes from the Latin word *subvenire. Sub* means "up," and *venire* means "to come." So *subvenire* meant "to come up" or "to come to mind." In English, the word became *souvenir,* or something that reminds us of where we've been. **EL**

Additional Support

Reading Fluency

Using Graphic Organizers Remind students that a cause is that which makes something happen. An effect is the result of a cause. Have students work in small groups to create a two-column chart like the one here and jot down cause-and-effect examples from the story. **BL OL**

Cause	Effect
Jamie writes about Aunt Millicent.	Angelica becomes jealous; she accuses him of making it up.
Students like Jamie's story about a woman explorer.	Students want to learn more about adventurous careers for women.

Grandma was knitting her way down the second sock leg. "That funny animal is a very brave creature," she admonished,[20] tapping the mongoose with her knitting needle. "I'll always remember Kipling's story of Rikki-Tikki-Tavi and how he fought that dreadful king cobra. Brrr!"

"Who won?" asked Jamie.

"You could read it yourself and find out, young man," said Grandma, starting to knit a new row. "I expect Millicent has met a few cobras in her time."

Nerissa had splendid dreams nearly every night. Aunt Millicent strode through most of them, wielding her machete or shouldering her theodolite. Sometimes Nerissa found herself wading through swirling rivers or swinging on jungle vines like a gibbon. Jamie was often there, too, or some of her school friends, or Grandma followed by a mongoose on a lead.[21] Once, Mrs. Nutbeam speared a giant toad, which exploded and woke Nerissa up. In another dream, Nerissa's father was polishing the fangs of a grinning crocodile, which lay back in the dentist's chair with its long tail tucked neatly under the sterilizer. It looked slightly like Mrs. Tonks.

Visual Vocabulary
A *gibbon* is a type of small ape.

Mrs. Nutbeam brought home still more **curios**: a bamboo flute and a small tom-tom which Jamie and Nerissa soon learnt to play. Mysterious drumbeats and thin flutey tunes drifted along the street from the Nutbeams' house. School friends came to beat the tom-tom and to stroke the mongoose and to see how the explorer's socks were growing. **15**

Visual Vocabulary
The *bamboo flute* is a woodwind instrument. It has an airy sound and is usually hand carved. A *tom-tom* is a long narrow drum that is typically beaten with the hands.

"Will you be sending them off soon, to the Cameroons?" they asked Grandma, who was turning the heel of the second sock.

"I think I'll make another pair, perhaps even three pairs," replied Grandma. "I might just as well send a large parcel as a small one."

---

20. *Admonished* means "scolded mildly."
21. The mongoose is on a leash, or *lead.*

Practice the Skills

R

15 | **English Language Coach**

Word Histories Curios are objects that are considered rare or strange. *Curio* is a shortened form of *curiosity.*

Aunt Millicent **721**

Teach

R **Reading**

Review Understanding Cause and Effect **Ask:** What effect has all of the talk about Aunt Millicent had on Nerissa? *(Possible response: The family's new interest is causing Nerissa to have splendid dreams.)* **Ask:** Do you think this is helpful or harmful? Explain your answer. *(Responses will vary.)* **OL**

Literature Focus Lesson

Characterization Explain to English language learners that characterization is the way in which a writer develops the personality of a character. In this story the writer reveals the characters' personalities indirectly, through their own words and actions and others' responses to them. Have these students work with English-speaking partners to reread the story and jot down phrases or words that describe each character. **EL OL**

Objectives
• Understand word histories
• Evaluate text
• Understand cause and effect
• Identify literary elements: character

Teach

Ask: Have you ever had as a hero a fictional person, such as someone from a book or a movie? Who was the hero and how did he or she inspire you? Did it matter to you that this hero was not a real person? *(Responses will vary.)* **OL**

R Reading Skill

Predicting Ask: What do you think Angelica's mother will say in her interaction with Dr. Nutbeam? What makes you think so? *(Possible responses: Angelica's mother will probably try to expose Aunt Millicent as a fraud. She will do this because she wants her daughter to be the "star.")* **OL**

"Yes, and then Aunt Millie will have spare pairs of socks she can wash," said Nerissa. "Socks must get very smelly near the equator."

Word of Millicent Nutbeam, intrepid[22] explorer, began to spread through the town. Children told their families about the spears, the tom-tom, the mongoose and the khaki socks. Not every small town could claim to be connected to a famous international explorer—it was exciting news. **16**

Angelica Tonks, however, told her mother that she didn't believe Jamie's aunt was an explorer at all. "I bet he just invented that to make his aunt seem more interesting than all the rest," she scoffed.

Mrs. Tonks sniffed a good deal and then decided it was time to have a dental check-up. "I'll get to the bottom of that Millicent Nutbeam, you mark my words," she told Angelica, as she telephoned Dr. Nutbeam's surgery[23] for an appointment.

Well, well—good morning Mrs. Tonks," said Dr. Nutbeam, a few days later. "We haven't seen you for a while! Just lie right back in the chair please, and relax!"

Mrs. Tonks lay back, but she didn't relax one bit. Her eyes were sharp and suspicious. "Good morning, Dr. Nutbeam. How is the family?" she enquired. "And how is your sister?"

Dr. Nutbeam pulled on his rubber gloves. "My sister? Which one? . . . Er, probe, please nurse."

Before he could say "Open wide," Mrs. Tonks snapped, "Your sister the so-called explorer. Huh! The one in the Cameroons."

"Ah, *that* sister. You mean Millicent . . . now, just open wider and turn this way a little. Yes, our Millie, she does work so hard . . . oops, there's a beaut cavity! A real crater!" He crammed six plugs of cotton wool around

---

22. Someone who is **intrepid** is very brave.
23. In Australia a doctor's or dentist's office is called a **surgery**.

Practice the Skills

How and why has Aunt Millicent become a hero for the town? Does a hero have to be real? Think about how the girls in Jamie's class view her. Think about how the town views her. **BQ**

Here's another picture that Aunt Millicent might have sent from her travels in Africa.

Additional Support

Reading in the Real World

Citizenship From the first page of this story, the Tonkses are portrayed as difficult and unpleasant people. Although reading about Mrs. Tonks's experience in the dentist chair is humorous, dealing with difficult people is often a serious real-life problem. Ask students to write in their Learner's Notebooks about an experience they have had with a difficult person. Ask a few volunteers to share kind and effective ways to deal with difficult people as you list the ways on the board. **OL**

Mrs. Tonks's gums. "My word, what a lot of saliva! We'll have some suction please nurse, and just wipe that dribble from the patient's chin." He continued to poke and scrape Mrs. Tonks's molars, none too gently. "Ah, here's another trouble spot. Mm . . . have you ever been to the Cameroons, Mrs. Tonks?"

Mrs. Tonks's eyes glared. She tried to shake her head, but could only gurgle, "Arggg . . ." **17**

"No, I didn't think you had. Such a fascinating place!" Dr. Nutbeam turned on the squealing high-speed drill and bored into her decaying tooth, spraying water all over her chin.

When he had told his family about this **encounter** with Mrs. Tonks, his wife complained, "It's all very well for you. You can just cram people's mouths full of wadding and metal contraptions and suction tubes if they start asking awkward questions, but what am I supposed to do?"

The truth was that increasing numbers of townsfolk were calling at the antique shop where Mrs. Nutbeam worked. They were eager to know more about Millicent Nutbeam and her adventurous life. They felt proud of her.

"It's getting quite tricky," Mrs. Nutbeam explained. "People are asking to see photos of Millicent and wanting us to talk at the elderly citizens' club about her. This aunt is becoming an embarrassment. I wish people weren't so curious. Sometimes I don't know what to say!"

Grandma found herself on slippery ground, too, when she met the postman at the gate.

"Morning," he said, sorting through his mailbag. "You must be Jamie's grandmother, then."

"Yes, I am," Grandma replied, rather surprised.

"Mother of the explorer, eh?"

"Gracious!" exclaimed Grandma. "Fancy you knowing about that!"

"Oh, my girl Julie has told us all about it. She's in Jamie's class at school. Funny thing—Julie's gone round the twist since she heard about all that exploring business. Says she

Vocabulary

encounter (en KOUN tur) *n.* an unexpected or unpleasant meeting

Aunt Millicent **723**

Practice the Skills

17 | **Key Literary Element**

Setting So far the story has more than one setting. What is the setting for this encounter? Can you think of two other settings you have noticed besides this one? What clues give the setting away? Think about Dr. Nutbeam's job. **L**

Teach

L Literary Element

Setting Ask: What other clues could you use to make this setting apparent? (*Possible responses: bright light; x-ray machine; dental mirror*) **OL**

C Critical Thinking

Comprehension Ask: What conflict has Aunt Millicent created for the Nutbeam family? (*Possible response: They can no longer handle making up enough stories to keep the character of Aunt Millicent alive.*) **OL**

Differentiated Instruction

Drama Have students work in pairs to act out the dialogue between Grandma and the postman. Encourage students to embellish the scene with facial expressions, hand movements, and their own humor. Instruct them to portray the postman as increasingly suspicious and Grandma as increasingly flustered at having to improvise her role as mother of the explorer. Ask volunteers to present the scene to the class. **OL**

Objectives
• Make predictions
• Monitor comprehension
• Identify literary elements: setting

Teach

BQ **BIG Question**

Ask: When you think of a famous explorer, do you imagine a man or a woman? Why did the author chose to write about an aunt rather than an uncle? How does this affect the girls at school? *(Possible response: It sometimes surprises people that women are adventurous. The girls at school are inspired by the idea of a woman explorer.)* **OL**

R Reading Skill

Predicting Ask: Do you think that the letter from Peru could cause problems for the Nutbeams? Why do you think so? *(Possible response: It could cause problems because they will have to invent more stories about Aunt Millicent.)* **OL**

---

wants to buy a camel and ride it round Australia, and one of her friends is going to apply for a job on an oil rig. I ask you!"

"Well, that's nice," said Grandma, soothingly. "Girls are so enterprising[24] these days."

"Huh! Mad, I call it." The postman held out a bundle of letters. "Here you are. Now, that's *another* funny thing—the Nutbeams don't get much foreign mail, come to think of it. You'd think the explorer would write to them more often, her being in the traveling line."

Grandma breathed deeply. "Oh, it's not easy, you know, writing letters when you're exploring. For one thing, there's never a decent light in the tent at night—and besides, there's hardly ever a post office to hand when you need it. She glanced through the letters. "Goodness! There's one from South America . . . Peru." **18**

"That's what made me wonder. Is it from her?" asked the postman, eagerly.

"Her? Ah . . . Millicent. I don't know. It's for Dr. Nutbeam, my son, and it's typed. Anyway, as far as we know, Millicent is still in the Cameroons, although we've not had word for some time."

"She could have moved on, couldn't she?" suggested the postman, "Peru, eh?

Oh well, I'd better move on, too. G'day to you!"

---

24. Someone who is **enterprising** is ready and willing to undertake new projects.

Practice the Skills

R

18 **Key Reading Skill**

Predicting Who do you think wrote the letter from Peru?

Additional Support

Reading Fluency

Build Reading Fluency Pair students and assign them to read out loud to each other. At this point in the story, they have a good grasp of the characters and the plot. Instruct them to concentrate on reading with expression and understanding. At the end of reading a page or two, have each student in the pair offer feedback to the other on where his or her reading was the most fluent. **AS**

Teach

At school, Julie the postman's daughter said to Jamie, "Why has your auntie gone to South America? What's she exploring now?"

"Who said she's gone to South America?" demanded Jamie. He felt he was losing control of Aunt Millicent.

"My dad said there was a letter from her in Peru," replied Julie.

"Well, no one told *me*," growled Jamie.

At home he announced, "Julie is telling everybody that our Aunt Millicent is in Peru! What's she talking about? What's happening?"

Grandma stopped knitting. "Julie. Is that the name of the postman's girl?"

"Yes—her dad said there was a letter for us from Auntie in Peru, or somewhere mad."

"Oh, I remember—he asked me about it," said Grandma.

"Well . . . what did you *say*?" wailed Jamie.

"I just said I didn't know who the letter was from and that I thought Millicent was still in the Cameroons, but that we hadn't heard for a while where she was. That's all."

"The letter from Peru," chuckled Dr. Nutbeam, "is about the World Dental Conference on plaque, which is being held next year in Lima.[25] It has nothing to do with Millicent."

"Well of *course* it hasn't," spluttered Jamie. "She doesn't exist!"

"But Jamie, in a funny sort of way she *does* exist," said Mrs. Nutbeam.

His father grinned. "My sister is quite a girl! She's begun to live a life of her own!"

"That's the trouble," said Jamie. "She seems to be doing things we don't know about." [19]

Practice the Skills

[19] Key Reading Skill

Predicting Did you predict earlier that the Nutbeams would fool the town into thinking that Aunt Millicent was a real person? Is your prediction the same now? Explain.

---

25. This kind of **plaque** (plak) is film that forms on teeth if not removed by cleaning. The conference is in **Lima** (LEE muh), the capital of Peru.

Analyzing the Photos Describe what you see in these pictures from the Andes.

Aunt Millicent **725**

C1 Critical Thinking

Analysis Ask: How does the letter from Peru introduce more complications? What is the central conflict in the story at this point? *(Possible response: The story is being spread by other people and is getting out of control. The Nutbeams are also experiencing conflict as they wonder whether they can keep up with the story.)* **OL**

C2 Critical Thinking

Comprehension Who is the letter from Peru really from? *(the World Dental Conference)* **BL** **Ask:** Why did people think Millicent was in Peru? *(Possible response: The postman told his daughter that the Nutbeams had received a letter from Peru.)* **OL**

R Reading Skill

Predicting Ask: What could happen if new stories continue to pop up about Aunt Millicent? Do you think that the Nutbeams will be exposed? Why or why not? *(Responses will vary.)* **OL**

Reading in the Real World

Citizenship Although this selection is a humorous fictional story, it brings up the serious issue of gossip and its consequences. Discuss the spreading of stories and the kinds of problems it creates for the person who tells the stories as well as for others. Have students work in small groups. Invite them to think of an experience or a story involving gossip. Have each group choose one student's experience and use it as the basis for a skit. Tell students to first decide on a theme or moral and then work together to write, practice, and perform a short skit that illustrates the experience and its moral. **OL**

Objectives
• Analyze text
• Make predictions
• Monitor comprehension

Teach

R1 Reading Skill

Review Connecting Ask:
Why is the family upset by the idea of telling the truth about Aunt Millicent? How would you feel if you lost such an aunt, even if she were imaginary? *(Possible response: Aunt Millicent has given the family a lot of fun. It would be sad to lose such an entertaining character.)* OL

R2 Reading Skill

Predicting Say: Think about how Mr. Starling feels about Aunt Millicent. Do you think he will help Jamie find a way out of the mess? *(Possible response: Mr. Starling loves the idea of Aunt Millicent. He will probably help Jamie find a good solution.)* OL

While they were talking, the telephone rang. Dr. Nutbeam was no longer grinning when he came back from answering it. "That was Frank Figgis from the local paper."

"Frank, the editor?" asked Mrs. Nutbeam. "What did he want?"

"He wants to do a full-page feature on our Millicent," groaned her husband. "He's heard that she's about to set out on a climbing expedition in the Andes! Up some peak that has never yet been conquered!"

"What nonsense!" snapped Grandma. "She's too old for that sort of thing."

"It's just a rumor!" shouted Jamie. "Who said she's going to the Andes? *I* didn't say she was going there. She's still in the Cameroons!"

"Calm down, dear," said his mother, "and let's hear what Dad said to Frank Figgis."

Dr. Nutbeam was rubbing his head. "I stalled for time—I said we'd not heard she was in the Andes, but that we'd make enquiries[26] and let him know. Whatever happens, Millicent mustn't get into print. We'll all be up on a charge of false pretenses[27] or something!"

Jamie snorted. "Well, if she's climbing an Ande, it might be best if she fell off and was never seen again."

Nerissa shrieked, "*No!* She mustn't—she's our only aunt and we've only just got her!"

Mrs. Nutbeam sighed. "Listen, Jamie, perhaps the time has come to own up[28] that Aunt Millicent is not real."

"We can't do that!" wailed Jamie. "Everyone would think we're loony . . . and that Grandma's absolutely bonkers, knitting socks for an aunt who isn't there. And what about the mongoose? Anyway, I *can't* let Honky Tonks find out now—she'd never stop crowing and she'd be more awful than ever." **20**

Jamie decided to lay the whole problem of Aunt Millicent Nutbeam before Mr. Starling, right up to her unexpected expedition to the Andes and Mr. Figgis's plan to write a full-page feature about her for the local paper. He finished by saying, "I think I might have to kill her off."

R1

R2

20 Key Reading Skill

Predicting What do you think will happen to Aunt Millicent?

---

26. To **make enquiries** is to ask questions.

27. The term **false pretenses** refers to acts of lying or misleading.

28. The expression **own up** means to "confess fully."

726 UNIT 6 What Makes a Hero?

Additional Support

Differentiated Instruction

Spatial Learning Students who learn best through spatial perception will benefit from an additional mapping activity. Begin by showing students a map of Cameroon and asking them to note Cameroon's borders and landforms and the location of Lake Chad. Provide art materials and invite students to imagine the region around Millicent's camp and draw a map of it. Remind them that she would probably be surveying Cameroon's borders and that their maps should include appropriate landmarks, vegetation keys, and the placement of the camp, trails, and roads. **AS**

"That'd be a shame," sighed Mr. Starling. "She's quite a lady, your aunt!"

"It would be pretty easy to get rid of her," Jamie went on. "In her sort of job she could sink into a quicksand, or be trampled by a herd of elephants, or something."

Mr. Starling shook his head violently. "No, no—it would only make things worse if she died a bloodcurdling death like that. No one would be likely to forget her if she was squashed flat by a stampeding elephant. She'd become more interesting than ever!"

"Well, she could die of something boring, like pneumonia," said Jamie. "Or . . . will I have to own up that she isn't real?"

"Do you want to own up?"

"Not really. I'd feel stupid, and I specially don't want Angelica Tonks to know I invented an aunt."

Mr. Starling quite understood. "I see! Anyway, a lot of people would be sad to discover that Millicent Nutbeam was a **hoax**. The girls in your class, for example—she means a lot to them."

"What'll I do then?"

"If you want people to lose interest in her, you'll just have to make her less interesting. I think she should retire from exploring, for a start."

"Aw, gee!" Jamie felt very disappointed. "I suppose so. I'll see what they think at home." **21**

"**W**hat he means," said Dr. Nutbeam, when Jamie had repeated Mr. Starling's advice, "is that it's time my dear sister Millicent settled down."

"I quite agree with that," remarked Grandma, who was up to the sixth sock foot. "She's not as young as she was, and it's high time she had some normal home life. I think she should get married, even though she's getting on a bit. Perhaps to a widower."

"That sounds terribly boring," yawned Nerissa.

"Well, that's what we need," said Jamie, "something terribly boring to make people lose interest."

Practice the Skills

21 **Key Reading Skill**

Predicting Now that rumors about Aunt Millicent are out of control, Jamie doesn't know what to do with her. She has taken on a life of her own! What do you think will become of Aunt Millicent?

Vocabulary

hoax (hohks) *n.* an act meant to fool or trick

Aunt Millicent **727**

Teach

C Critical Thinking

Analysis Ask: Do you agree with Mr. Starling that Aunt Millicent would become more interesting if she died a violent death? Why or why not? *(Possible response: Yes, people are always interested in grisly details.)* **OL**

R Reading Skill

Predicting Ask: How will the Nutbeams react to Mr. Starling's suggestion? Will they be disappointed, as Jamie seems to be? Explain. *(Possible response: The Nutbeams will be disappointed at the idea of "toning down" Aunt Millicent after she has provided so much excitement for them.)* **OL**

Differentiated Instruction

Writing Activity The characters in "Aunt Millicent" are looking for a way to end the questions about her. Have each student write an ending to the story that they think would best conclude Aunt Millicent's adventures. Ask volunteers to share their conclusions with the class. Finish reading the story and talk about whether students find the conclusion satisfying and why or why not. **OL**

Objectives
• Analyze text
• Make predictions
• Make connections from text to self

Teach

BQ

Ask: Do you think that someone becomes less of a hero when he or she gets older and begins to have a quieter life? Why or why not? *(Responses will vary.)* **OL**

Grandma sniffed. "In my day it would have been called a happy ending."

"Well, I suppose it's a happier ending than being squashed by an elephant," conceded Jamie.

"How about marrying her to a retired accountant who used to work for a cardboard box company?" suggested his father. "That sounds pretty dull."

"Good heavens, it's all rather sudden!" said Mrs. Nutbeam. "Last time we heard of her she was climbing the Andes!"

"No, she wasn't." At last Jamie felt he had hold of Aunt Millicent again. "That South American stuff was just a rumor. The postman started it because of the letter from Peru, and then the story just grew!"

Dr. Nutbeam nodded. "Stories seem to have a habit of doing that, and so do rumors! But we can easily squash this one about the Andes. I'll just explain about the World Dental Conference on plaque. I even have the letter to prove it."

Dr. Nutbeam called Frank Figgis on the phone. He explained about the letter from Peru and about the ridiculous rumor which the postman had started. "In your profession Frank," he added sternly, "you should be much more careful than to listen to baseless rumor.[29] It could get you into all sorts of trouble! In any case, Millicent is giving up exploring to marry a retired accountant. She's had enough."

Frank Figgis was fast losing interest. "I see—well, sometime when she's in Australia we could do an interview about her former life . . . maybe."

"Maybe, although she has no immediate plans to return here. I believe she and her husband are going to settle down in England—somewhere on the seafront, like Bognor." **22**

Jamie passed on the same information to his classmates. The girls were shocked.

"She's what?"

"Getting married to an *accountant?*"

"She can't be!"

"How boring for her!"

---

29. A **baseless rumor** is a rumor that cannot be supported by facts.

728 UNIT 6   What Makes a Hero?

22 | **Key Literary Element**

Setting Compared to other places mentioned in the story, what do you imagine Bognor, England, would be like? What was the most detailed setting in the entire story? How did that affect the story?

Additional Support

Reading in the Real World

Career Angelica Tonks says, "See! Your Aunt Millicent is just like any other old aunt, after all!" Have students discuss the meaning of these words. What are the gender expectations for men and women in American culture? What are they in other cultures? What role did Aunt Millicent play in expanding these expectations for the boys and girls in Jamie's town? Have students work in small groups to gather research in the library or on the Internet about changing gender roles. Ask volunteers to present their findings to the class. **OL**

"Where in the world is Bognor? Is there really such a place?"

Angelica Tonks smiled like a smug pussycat. "See! Your Aunt Millicent is just like any other old aunt, after all!"

Jamie caught Mr. Starling's eye. It winked.

C Aunt Millicent Nutbeam retired, not to Bognor but to live quietly with her family. Nerissa still had wonderful dreams. Dr. Nutbeam still brought home books about far-off places. The blood-stained spears remained on the wall and the mongoose on the shelf. Jamie and Nerissa still played the tom-tom and the bamboo flute.

Grandma Nutbeam's holiday came to an end and she packed up to return home. She left a parcel for Jamie. When he opened it, he found three pairs of khaki socks with dark blue stripes, and a card which said:

Dear Jamie,

Aunt Millicent won't have any use for these now that she has settled down, so you might as well have them for school camps. Isn't it lucky that they are just your size!

With love from Grandma **23**

Practice the Skills

23 🔖 **BIG Question**

Who do you think is most like a real-life hero in this story? Explain. Write your conclusions on the "Aunt Millicent" page of Foldable 6. Your responses to all of the Big Question sidenotes will help you complete the Unit Challenge later.

BQ

Aunt Millicent **729**

Teach

C Critical Thinking

Analysis Ask: What does the author really mean when she says that Aunt Millicent retired, not to Bognor but to live with her family? *(Possible response: That the experience of making up Aunt Millicent stayed with the Nutbeams forever.)* **OL**

BQ 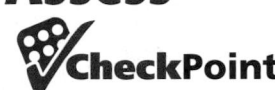 **BIG Question**

Say: List some traits for each main character. Which traits do you admire most? Who is the main hero? *(Responses will vary.)* **OL**

Assess

🍕 **CheckPoint**

Use the CheckPoint questions provided on Presentation Plus! to check for comprehension of the selection. These questions can be used with interactive response keypads for immediate student feedback.

Differentiated Instruction

Write a Letter Have students imagine being Aunt Millicent or Jamie. Ask them to write a letter that comes one year after the ending of the story. Where are they and what are they doing? Is Aunt Millicent still retired? Does Jamie wear the socks for an adventure? Encourage students to use their imaginations to take the story to a new place. **OL**

Objective
• Make predictions

Assess

Resources for page 730

📁 Selection Quick Check, p. 57

📁 Selection and Unit Assessment, p. 67

⊙ ExamView Assessment Suite

⊙ Interactive Tutor: Self-Assesesment

Students can respond to the *After You Read* items in their Learner's Notebooks or on a separate sheet of paper.

Answering the

1. Responses will vary.
2. She left the assignment until the last minute.

Critical Thinking

3. Possible response: The Nutbeams are more interested in learning about new things. The kids at school have new ambitions.

4. Possible response: Considering her adventurous life, it does not sound like something Aunt Millicent would do.

5. Possible response: No. A woman meant more to the girls in the class because she inspired them. She gave the boys new ideas about what women are capable of doing.

6. Possible response: Grandma was knitting the socks for Jamie all along.

730

After You Read | Aunt Millicent

Answering the **BIG** Question

1. Does Aunt Millicent have qualities of a real-life hero? Explain.
2. **Recall** Why wasn't Angelica's pen-portrait as good as she said it would be?
   Tip Right There

Critical Thinking

3. **Analyze** What lasting effect has the story of Aunt Millicent had on the Nutbeam family? What lasting effect has the story had on the students at the school? Give evidence from the story to support your answer.
   Tip Author and Me

4. **Evaluate** Does marrying an accountant and retiring sound like something Aunt Millicent would really do? Explain.
   Tip On My Own

5. **Synthesize** Imagine that Jamie created an Uncle Milton rather than Aunt Millicent. Do you think the story would have been as meaningful to Jamie's classmates? Why or why not?
   Tip On My Own

6. **Interpret** At the end of the story, Grandma sends Jamie three pairs of socks with a card that says, "Isn't it lucky that they are just your size." What do you think that message means?
   Tip On My Own

Talk About Your Reading

With a partner, or in a small group, think up an imaginary person with an interesting life. Decide on the age, gender, appearance, and past history of your imaginary person. Then introduce your imaginary person to the class, telling a bit about him or her. Think about these questions to get started, but don't stop there. Let the person take on a life of his or her own, like Jamie's Aunt Millicent.

- How would you describe this person?
- What job qualities, hobbies, or traits does this person have that make him or her interesting?
- What adventures has this person had?
- Where does this person live?

Objectives (pp. 730–731)
Reading Make predictions
Literature Identify key literary elements: setting
Vocabulary Explore word histories
Grammar Identify run-ons

730 UNIT 6 What Makes a Hero?

Talk About Your Reading

Possible response:
Carla Burton is thirteen years old. She's the smartest person in her school. The teachers let her off the hook on all her homework. One day the principal asks her to help solve a problem. The school football team needs to go to the state championship, but the school bus is too old and rickety to get to the other side of the state. Carla will either invent ways to repair the bus so it can do the job, quickly learn to fly a plane, or talk a rich local woman into lending the school her private jet to get the team to the game.

Skills Review

Key Reading Skill: Predicting

7. At what point in the story did you have to change one of your predictions? Explain why you changed it and what your new prediction was.

Key Literary Element: Setting

8. Describe the main setting of this story in one or two sentences. Pick another setting and describe it in one or two sentences.

9. How did Jamie's use of setting help to make Aunt Millicent's travels seem real to other characters in the story?

Reviewing Skills: Responding

10. Would you want a relative like Aunt Millicent? Why or why not?

Vocabulary Check

Rewrite this postcard from an explorer and put the vocabulary words in the correct spaces.

**tedious   drab   expedition   exotic
encounter   hoax**

Life seemed **11.** ___ after our exciting **12.** ___ to an island that wasn't on the map. We had hoped for an **13.** ___ with an **14.** ___ bird believed to be extinct. Rumor had it that the bird could still be found on the island. We never saw the bird, so the tales could have been a **15.** ___, but who knows! Its feathers are **16.** ___ in color and it blends in with tree bark (making it hard to spot).

17. **English Language Coach** Why are word histories important?

Web Activities For eFlashcards, Selection Quick Checks, and other Web activities, go to www.glencoe.com.

Grammar Link: Recognizing Run-on Sentences

Remember, an independent clause has a subject and a predicate. It can stand alone as a complete sentence. Sometimes, though, a writer puts together two independent clauses, or sentences, without the correct punctuation.

A **run-on sentence** is two or more sentences incorrectly written as one sentence.

> **Example:** *Tonight we are going to a skating competition I hope it is like the Olympics.*

Now study these three ways to correct a run-on sentence.

A. Separate the two independent clauses with a period. Begin the second sentence with a capital letter.

> **Example:** Tonight we are going to a skating competition. I hope it is like the Olympics.

B. Place a comma and a coordinating conjunction between two independent clauses.

> **Example:** Tonight we are going to a skating competition, and I hope it is like the Olympics.

C. Place a semicolon between to two independent clauses.

> **Example:** Tonight we are going to a skating competition; I hope it is like the Olympics.

Grammar Practice

On a separate sheet of paper, write a correct version of each run-on sentence.

18. Yori took an aspirin there was only one left.

19. Of all the birds at the pet store, we liked the parrots best.

20. Look at all the people at the parade I wonder where we can sit.

21. The actors are sewing their own costumes it is quite a challenge.

Skills Review

Key Reading Skill: Predicting

7. Responses will vary.

Key Literary Element: Setting

8. Possible response: The main setting is Jamie's classroom. In it are desks, a teacher, and students. Another setting is Dr. Nutbeam's office. It contains dental equipment and a patient.

9. Possible response: He did lots of research and included many details that made the places seem real.

Reviewing Skills: Responding

10. Responses will vary.

Vocabulary Check

11. tedious
12. expedition
13. encounter
14. exotic
15. hoax
16. drab
17. **English Language Coach** Sample response: They help you understand the meanings of words.

Close

Ask students to summarize what they learned to answer the Big Question from reading "Aunt Millicent."

Grammar Link: Recognizing Run-On Sentences

Grammar Practice

18. Yori took an aspirin, but there was only one left.

19. no

20. Look at all the people at the parade! I wonder where we can sit.

21. The actors are sewing their own costumes; it is quite a challenge.

Teach

More About the Author

Clifton Davis was born in Chicago, Illinois, in 1945. In addition to being an actor and songwriter, he is also an ordained Seventh Day Adventist minister. After acting in many venues, he went to school to get his divinity degree. He later played a minister on the television series "Amen." Davis has a wife, Ann, a daughter, Holly, and a son, Noel.

EL Language Coach

Word Histories Invite students to use a dictionary to find the etymology of a vocabulary word of their choice. *(Responses will vary.)* **EL BL**

Before You Read : A Mason-Dixon Memory

Meet the Author

Clifton Davis is an actor, singer, and songwriter. One of his songs, "Never Can Say Goodbye," sold two million records. He has acted in several movies, Broadway plays, and TV shows. Davis told his "Mason-Dixon Memory" story to Mel White, who wrote it in Davis's voice.

Author Search For more about Clifton Davis, go to www.glencoe.com.

Objectives (pp. 732–741)
Reading Make predictions • Make connections from text to self
Literature Identify key literary elements: setting
Vocabulary Explore word histories

Vocabulary Preview

civic (SIV ik) *adj.* having to do with a city or the duties of a citizen **(p. 734)** *Civic leaders from around the country came to hear Dondré Green speak.*

predominantly (prih DOM uh nunt lee) *adv.* mainly; mostly **(p. 734)** *Dondré attended a predominantly white school in Louisiana.*

resolve (rih ZOLV) *v.* to make a firm decision **(p. 737)** *The boys could give up, or they could resolve to stand up for Dondré.*

ominous (OM ih nus) *adj.* threatening **(p. 738)** *The woman explained the Mason-Dixon line in ominous tones.*

bigotry (BIG uh tree) *n.* unfair and unreasonable opinions or treatment of a person or group **(p. 740)** *Dondré learned that love can overcome hatred and bigotry.*

Vocabulary Concentration With a partner, copy the words onto one set of note cards and the definitions onto another set. Mix the cards up and place them face down on a desk or table. Take turns turning the cards over two at a time. When you match a word and its definition take the pair; use the word in a sentence once you make a match.

English Language Coach

Word Histories Sometimes it's difficult to figure out how a modern word came from a very different older word. For example, look at these words from the selection you're about to read:

- **banquet** (BANK wut) *n.* a large meal celebrating a special event [Middle French, from Old Italian *banchetto,* from *banca* "bench"] **EL**
- **chaperone** (SHAP uh rohn) *n.* a person who goes with and is responsible for a group of young people [French *chaperon,* from earlier French *chape,* from Latin *cappa* "head covering; cloak"]

Class Discussion Using your imagination and logic, discuss how
- *banquet* could come from a word meaning "bench."
- *chaperone* could come from a word meaning "head covering; cloak."

Additional Support

Author Search To expand students' appreciation of Clifton Davis, have them access the Web site for additional information and resources.

English Language Coach

Names To illustrate the concept of word histories, ask students to discuss the stories behind their names. Say that often people are named after an admired family member or historical figure. Some people have names related to an event or a quality. Nicknames usually have good stories behind them. Assign students to talk with their parents or guardians about how and why they were named and then report to the class the next day. You may also ask students to learn the history behind their last name or family name. **AS**

Skills Preview

Key Reading Skill: Predicting

"A Mason-Dixon Memory" is told in three parts. There are many places you could pause and make a prediction. Whenever you notice a break in the story, ask yourself what you think will happen in the next part. As you read, adjust or change your predictions if you notice the story isn't turning out as you first predicted.

Partner Talk With a partner, discuss the passage below and make predictions about what you think might happen next.

Although most of his friends and classmates were white, Dondré's race was never an issue. Then, on April 17, 1991, Dondré's black skin provoked an incident that made nationwide news.

Key Literary Element: Setting

The setting often helps to create an atmosphere, or mood. Knowing the setting will help you to understand a story by "placing" the events—connecting them to other things you know about that time and place. "A Mason-Dixon Memory" brings together two incidents that happened in different places and times. The two settings are thirty-two years and almost a thousand miles apart.

As you think about the setting notice

- the different times and places in the story
  Do the differences in time and place affect each situation?
- descriptions of places and the way characters speak
  What details help you picture the setting?

Partner Talk After you read the selection, discuss the questions above with a partner.

Interactive Literary Elements Handbook
To review or learn more about the literary elements, go to www.glencoe.com.

Get Ready to Read

Connect to the Reading

What would you do if someone you know was experiencing discrimination? What if you had to make the decision to defend them or do nothing?

Write to Learn Write about a time you made the right decision while others pressured you to do something that would affect another person in a negative way. Answer these questions as you write:

- What was the situation (bullying, discriminating, lying) and what decision did you make?
- How did you know what the *right* decision was?
- Why did you decide as you did?

Build Background

In the story you are about to read, the Mason-Dixon line is described as "a kind of invisible border between the North and the South."

- Originally, the Mason-Dixon line was the boundary between Maryland and Pennsylvania.
- It was a 233-mile-long invisible line determined by Charles Mason and Jeremiah Dixon in 1765–68 to settle a land dispute between the Penn family of Pennsylvania and the Calvert family of Maryland.
- By 1820 the Mason-Dixon line was used to show the dividing line between the slave states to the south and the free states to the north.

Set Purposes for Reading

BIG Question Read to find out how real boys fought against racism and became heroes.

Set Your Own Purpose What else would you like to learn from the story to help you answer the Big Question? Write your own purpose on the "A Mason-Dixon Memory" page of Foldable 6.

Keep Moving

Use these skills as you read the following selection.

A Mason-Dixon Memory **733**

Teach

L Literary Element

Setting Say: Remember that setting is not only where a story takes place but also when it takes place. Imagine that someone wrote a story about your life. How would the setting change if you lived in another time period, such as the Colonial era? *(Possible response: Clothing would be different, as well as neighborhood, styles of homes, and so on.)* **OL**

R Reading Skill

Review Connecting Ask: Have you or someone you know ever been treated unfairly or differently in some way? How did it make you feel? *(Responses will vary.)* **OL**

Interactive Literary Elements Handbook Have students access the Web site to improve their understanding of setting.

Differentiated Instruction

Predictions Ask students to review their predictions from the last story. How often were they right? How often wrong? Discuss the difference between predictions that are founded on information versus those that are just guesses.

Encourage students to use reason in making predictions. If possible, offer a prize for the next group of students that makes a correct prediction in "A Mason-Dixon Memory." **AS**

Objectives

- Identify literary elements: setting
- Understand word histories
- Make connections from text to self

Teach

Viewing the Photo

Ask: Have you ever seen a road sign like this before? What does it illustrate about the Mason-Dixon line? *(Possible response: It is on the border between Maryland and another state, probably Pennsylvania.)* **OL**

L Literary Element

Setting Say: When you try to figure out when a story takes place, look for clues that indicate the time period. If you have trouble finding clues, read further. Read to the end of this page. What clue do you find? *(the date: 1991)* **BL**

Readability Scores
Dale-Chall: 6.7
DRP: 59
Lexile: 880

A MASON-DIXON Memory

by Clifton Davis

Dondré Green glanced uneasily at the **civic** leaders and sports figures filling the hotel ballroom in Cleveland. They had come from across the nation to attend a fund-raiser for the National Minority College Golf Scholarship Foundation. I was the banquet's featured entertainer. Dondre, an 18-year-old high school senior from Monroe, Louisiana, was the evening's honored guest.

"Nervous?" I asked the handsome young man in his starched white shirt and rented tuxedo.

"A little," he whispered, grinning.

One month earlier, Dondré had been just one more black student attending a **predominately** white school. Although most of his friends and classmates were white, Dondré's race was never an issue. Then, on April 17, 1991, Dondré's black skin provoked[1] an incident that made nationwide news. **1**

---

1. *Provoked* means "caused to feel or act."

Vocabulary

civic (SIV ik) *adj.* having to do with a city or the duties of a citizen

predominantly (prih DOM uh nunt lee) *adv.* mainly; mostly

734 UNIT 6 What Makes a Hero?

Practice the Skills

1 Key Literary Element

Setting In what time and place does the story begin? Although the author hasn't mentioned the exact year, does it seem to be taking place recently or long ago? Explain.

Additional Support

Reading in the Real World

Citizenship This story tells about ordinary kids who stood up against bigotry. Discuss the word *activist* and explain that it applies to people who fight injustice in many different ways. Many people, even if they don't consider themselves activists, have moments of activism in their lives. Brainstorm social issues that are important today, and assign students to research how kids can become involved. Ask volunteers to share their findings with the class. **OL**

"Ladies and gentlemen," the emcee said, "our special guest, Dondré Green."

As the audience stood applauding, Dondré walked to the microphone and began his story. "I love golf," he said quietly. "For the past two years, I've been a member of the St. Frederick High School golf team. And though I was the only black member, I've always felt at home playing at mostly white country clubs across Louisiana."

The audience leaned forward; even the waiters and busboys stopped to listen. As I listened, a memory buried in my heart since childhood fought its way to life.

"Our team had driven from Monroe," Dondré continued. "When we arrived at the Caldwell Parish Country Club in Columbia, we walked to the putting green."

R1 Dondré and his teammates were too absorbed to notice the conversation between a man and St. Frederick athletic director James Murphy. After disappearing into the clubhouse, Murphy returned to his players. **2**

"I want to see the seniors," he said. "On the double!" His face seemed strained as he gathered the four students, including Dondré.

R2 "I don't know how to tell you this," he said, "but the Caldwell Parish Country Club is reserved for whites only." Murphy paused and looked at Dondré. His teammates glanced at each other in disbelief.

"I want you seniors to decide what our response should be," Murphy continued. "If we leave, we forfeit this tournament. If we stay, Dondré can't play."

As I listened, my own childhood memory from 32 years ago broke free. **3**

Dondré Green (top row, 2nd from left) poses for the yearbook with his golf team.

Practice the Skills

2 **Key Reading Skill**

Predicting What do you think Coach Murphy is going to talk to his players about? How do you know?

3 **Key Reading Skill**

Predicting Now that you've come to the first break, think about what you know. The narrator has begun to tell you a story about someone else, Dondré Green. What do you think the narrator will tell you about in the next section? Find two clues that lead you to your prediction.

A Mason-Dixon Memory **735**

Teach

R1 **Reading Skill**

Review Drawing Conclusions
Ask: What clues from earlier in the story help you know what conversation took place between the coach and the other man? *(Possible response: On the previous page, the author mentions that a national news incident occurred because of Dondré's skin color; the conversation probably had something to do with discrimination.)* **OL**

R2 **Reading Skill**

Review Connecting Say: Think about your favorite sport or activity. How would you feel if you were the only player or member who was not allowed to play in a tournament? *(Possible responses: uncomfortable; left out)* **OL**

Differentiated Instruction

Hearing the Author's Voice Bring in an audio or video recording of Clifton Davis and play it for the class. Remind them that in this story, Davis worked closely with another writer. As they read, suggest that they assess whether the written voice and the spoken voice sound similar. Ask students how hearing the author's real voice in advance affects their reading of the story. **OL**

Objectives
• Identify literary elements: setting
• Make connections from text to self
• Draw conclusions
• Use text features: photographs

Teach

R Reading Skill

Predicting Ask: What will the theme of this story be? Why? (Possible response: that prejudice is wrong and can be conquered.) **OL**

C Critical Thinking

Evaluation Ask: What can you tell about the author from the fact that he felt sad "for about ten seconds" before deciding to earn the money himself? (Possible responses: He is optimistic and resourceful; he doesn't give up easily.) **OL**

R In 1959 I was thirteen years old, a poor black kid living with my mother and stepfather in a small black ghetto on Long Island, New York. My mother worked nights in a hospital, and my stepfather drove a coal truck. Needless to say, our standard of living was somewhat short of the American dream. **4**

Nevertheless, when my eighth-grade teacher announced a graduation trip to Washington, D.C., it never crossed my mind that I would be left behind. Besides a complete tour of the nation's capital, we would visit Glen Echo Amusement Park in Maryland. In my imagination, Glen Echo was Disneyland, Knott's Berry Farm, and Magic Mountain rolled into one.

My heart beating wildly, I raced home to deliver the mimeographed³ letter describing the journey. But when my mother saw how much the trip cost, she just shook her head. We couldn't afford it.

C After feeling sad for ten seconds, I decided to try to fund the trip myself. For the next eight weeks, I sold candy bars door-to-door, delivered newspapers, and mowed lawns. Three days before the deadline, I'd made just barely enough. I was going!

The day of the trip, trembling with excitement, I climbed onto the train. I was the only nonwhite in our section.

Our hotel was not far from the White House. My roommate was Frank Miller, the son of a businessman. Leaning together out of our window and dropping water balloons on tourists quickly cemented our new friendship.

The White House

Practice the Skills

4 Key Literary Element

Setting The author introduces a new setting in this paragraph. Use at least three details from the paragraph to describe the setting.

---

3. If a letter was **mimeographed,** many copies were made.

736 UNIT 6 What Makes a Hero?

Additional Support

Reading Fluency

Build Fluency As the story switches from Dondré's experience to Clifton's, use a choral reading format. Begin by reading a paragraph, modeling the rhythm and tone of the text. Then have the students, as a group, read a paragraph. Alternate in this fashion to build fluency. **AS**

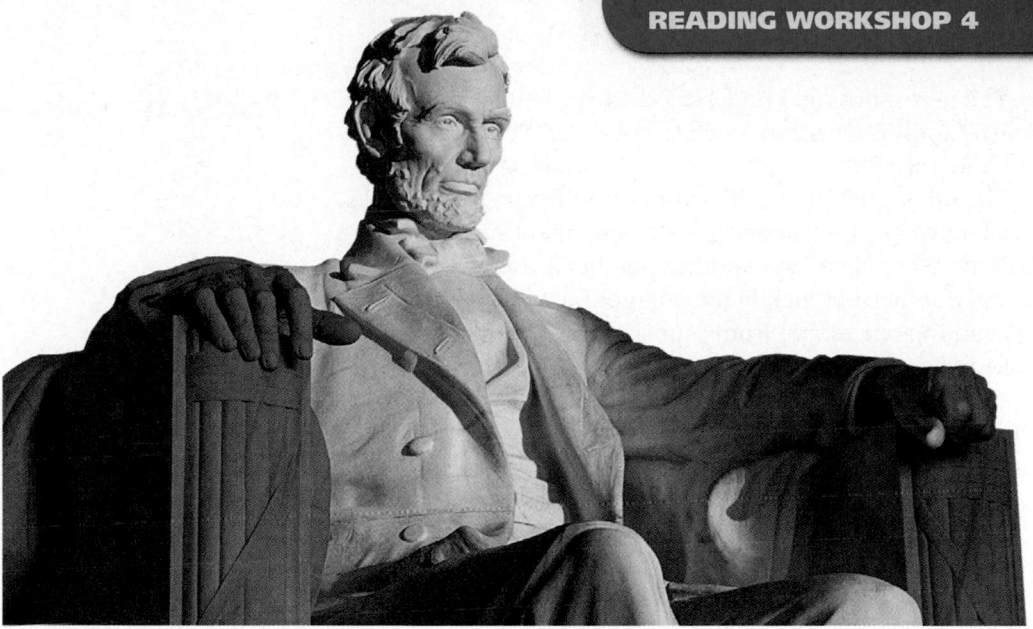

The Lincoln Memorial in Washington, D.C., is a tribute to the 16th President of the United States, Abraham Lincoln. It is a symbol of freedom and the sacrifices of the Civil War.

Every morning, almost a hundred of us loaded noisily onto our bus for another adventure. We sang our **school** fight song dozens of times–en route[4] to Arlington National Cemetery and even on an afternoon cruise down the Potomac River. **5**

We visited the Lincoln Memorial twice, once in daylight, the second time at dusk. My classmates and I fell silent as we walked in the shadows of those thirty–six marble columns, one for every state in the Union that Lincoln labored to preserve. I stood next to Frank at the base of the nineteen-foot seated statue. Spotlights made the white Georgian marble seem to glow. Together, we read those famous words from Lincoln's speech at Gettysburg, remembering the most bloody battle in the War Between the States: ". . . we here highly **resolve** that these dead shall not have died in vain — that this nation, under God, shall have a new birth of freedom . . ."

As Frank motioned me into place to take my picture, I took one last look at Lincoln's face. He seemed alive and so terribly sad.

---

4. **En route** (awn ROOT) means "on the way."

Vocabulary

resolve (rih ZOLV) *v.* to make a firm decision

5 █ **English Language Coach**

Word Histories Some word histories reveal how people's thinking changes over time. **School** came from the Latin word *schola* and meant "school." But the original Greek word meant "spare time." Thousands of years ago in Greece, only rich people had time to study at what we now call school.

A Mason-Dixon Memory **737**

Teach

Viewing the Photo

Ask: How does this image of the Lincoln Memorial make you feel? What does it symbolize to you? *(Possible response: Lincoln stands for freedom and justice, and looking at this image of him makes me proud.)* **OL**

EL Language Coach

Word Histories Say: The word *love* is also related to the Latin *libet*, which means "it is pleasing." What is pleasing about friendship and love? *(Responses will vary.)* **EL** **BL**

Differentiated Instruction

Research Report Students with an interest in history may want to provide the rest of the class with background material on Abraham Lincoln, the Civil War, the Lincoln Monument, or the civil rights movement of the 1960s. Encourage students to search for books, films, music, or photographs to include in their reports. Allow students to share their findings with the class. Set up a classroom display of the books and other resource materials that the students might have found. Have the class refer to these resources throughout the time they are working with this story. **OL**

Objectives
• Make predictions
• Evaluate text
• Use text features: photographs

Teach

R Reading Skill

Predicting Ask: When an author leads you to make a certain prediction, and something quite different happens in the story, what is your reaction as a reader? Do you like stories to be unpredictable or not? Explain. *(Possible response: It surprises me and makes what really happened in the story have more of an impact.)* **OL**

L Literary Element

Setting Say: Clifton Davis's story takes place in a different time and place from Dondré's story. What do the two settings have in common? *(Possible response: There is discrimination in both times and places.)* **OL**

The next morning, I understood a little better why he wasn't smiling. "Clifton," a chaperone said, "could I see you for a moment?"

The other guys at my table, especially Frank, turned pale. We had been joking about the previous night's direct water-balloon hit on a fat lady and her poodle. It was a stupid, dangerous act, but luckily nobody got hurt. We were celebrating our escape from punishment when the chaperone asked to see me.

"Clifton," she began, "do you know about the Mason-Dixon line?"

"No," I said, wondering what this had to do with drenching fat ladies.

"Before the Civil War," she explained, "the Mason-Dixon line was originally the boundary between Maryland and Pennsylvania — the dividing line between the slave and free states." Having escaped one disaster, I could feel another brewing. I noticed that her eyes were damp and her hands were shaking.

"Today," she continued, "the Mason-Dixon line is a kind of invisible border between the North and the South. When you cross that invisible line out of Washington, D.C., into Maryland, things change."

There was an **ominous** drift to this conversation, but I wasn't following it. Why did she look and sound so nervous?

"Glen Echo Amusement Park is in Maryland," she said at last, "and the management doesn't allow Negroes inside." She stared at me in silence. **6 7**

I was still grinning and nodding when the meaning finally sank in.

"You mean I can't go to the park," I stuttered, "because I'm a Negro?"

She nodded slowly. "I'm sorry, Clifton," she said, taking my hand.

"You'll have to stay in the hotel tonight. Why don't you and I watch a movie on television?"

I walked to the elevators feeling confusion, disbelief, anger,

Vocabulary

ominous (OM ih nus) *adj.* threatening

738 UNIT 6 What Makes a Hero?

Practice the Skills

6 Key Reading Skill

Predicting Did you predict what the chaperone would say? Were you right? Sometimes an author will lead you to make a certain prediction, but what you thought would happen turns out to be wrong. Why would an author do this? **R**

7 Key Literary Element

Setting The chaperone talks about a difference in the settings between North and South. How is the Mason-Dixon line an important part of the setting, even though it is an "invisible border"? Think about what you learned in the Build Background, and add that to what the chaperone tells Clifton. **L**

Additional Support

Literature Focus Lesson

Theme Discuss the theme of this selection with students. Encourage students to think about a time they had to make a difficult decision or a time they decided to make a personal sacrifice for another person. How do they remember those times? What did they learn from them? Their personal experiences will help them to understand the theme of the selection. Have students write about their experiences in their Learner's Notebooks. **OL**

and a deep sadness. "What happened, Clifton?" Frank said when I got back to the room. "Did the fat lady tell on us?"

Without saying a word, I walked over to my bed, lay down, and began to cry. Frank was stunned into silence. Junior-high boys didn't cry, at least not in front of each other.

It wasn't just missing the class adventure that made me feel so sad. For the first time in my life, I was learning what it felt like to be a "nigger." Of course there was discrimination in the North, but the color of my skin had never officially kept me out of a coffee shop, a church — or an amusement park.

"Clifton," Frank whispered, "what is the matter?"

"They won't let me go to Glen Echo Park tonight," I sobbed.

"Because of the water balloon?" he asked.

"No," I answered, "because I'm a Negro."

"Well, that's a relief!" Frank said, and then he laughed, obviously relieved to have escaped punishment for our caper with the balloons. "I thought it was serious!"

Wiping away the tears with my sleeve, I stared at him. "It *is* serious. They don't let Negroes into the park. I can't go with you!" I shouted. "That's pretty damn serious to me."

I was about to wipe the silly grin off Frank's face with a blow to his jaw when I heard him say, "Then I won't go either."

For an instant we just froze. Then Frank grinned. I will never forget that moment. Frank was just a kid. He wanted to go to that amusement park as much as I did, but there was something even more important than the class night out. Still, he didn't explain or expand. **8**

The next thing I knew, the room was filled with kids listening to Frank. "They don't allow Negroes in the park," he said, "so I'm staying with Clifton."

Practice the Skills

R1

8 Reviewing Skills

Interpreting The author points out that Frank didn't "explain or expand" about why he decided to stay behind. He also mentions that it was because "there was something more important than the class night out." What is the author *really* saying? What do you already know that can help you interpret those sentences?

R2

A Mason-Dixon Memory **739**

Teach

R1 Reading Skill

Review Responding Ask: What do you think of the rule at the amusement park? Do you think Davis's chaperone handled the situation well? *(Possible response: The rule is extremely unjust and unfair. The chaperone did the best she could in a terrible situation.)* **OL**

R2 Reading Skill

Interpreting Say: Interpreting involves reading between the lines. From what has happened in the story so far, what would you say that Clifton and Frank think is more important than the night out? *(Possible responses: justice; fairness)* **OL**

Differentiated Instruction

Role-Play Assign two students to act out this scene between Frank and Clifton before the class reads what happens. Then, read the text. Ask students some of the following questions.

• Do Frank's actions surprise you?

• What do you think Clifton would have done had Frank continued insisting that it wasn't serious?

• What would you have done if you were Frank? If you were Clifton? If you were the teacher? **OL**

Objectives
• Make predictions
• Identify literary elements: setting, theme
• Respond to text
• Interpret text

Teach

C Critical Thinking

Evaluation Ask: What can you tell about Dondré's teammates, friends, and the people of Louisiana from the fact that they passed anti-discrimination legislation and proclaimed a Dondré Green Day? *(Possible response: They were appalled by the discrimination and wanted to make up for it in every way possible.)* **OL**

"Me, too," a second boy said.

"Those jerks," a third muttered. "I'm with you, Clifton." My heart raced. Suddenly, I was not alone. A pint-size revolution had been born. The "water-balloon brigade,"[5] eleven white boys from Long Island, had made its decision: "We won't go." And as I sat on my bed in the center of it all, I felt grateful. But, above all, I was filled with pride. **9**

Dondré Green's story brought that childhood memory back to life. His golfing teammates, like my childhood friends, faced an important decision. If they stood by their friend it would cost them dearly. But when it came time to decide, no one hesitated.

"Let's get out of here," one of them whispered.

"They just turned and walked toward the van," Dondré told us. "They didn't debate it. And the younger players joined us without looking back."

Dondré was astounded by the response of his friends — and the people of Louisiana. The whole state was outraged and tried to make it right. The Louisiana House of Representatives proclaimed a Dondré Green Day and passed legislation permitting lawsuits for damages, attorneys' fees and court costs against any private facility that invites a team, then bars any member because of race.

As Dondré concluded, his eyes glistened with tears. "I love my coach and my teammates for sticking by me," he said. "It goes to show that there are always good people who will not give in to **bigotry**. The kind of love they showed me that day will conquer hatred every time."

My friends, too, had shown that kind of love. As we sat in the hotel, a chaperone came in waving an envelope. "Boys!" he shouted. "I've just bought thirteen tickets to the Senators-Tigers game. Anybody want to go?"

---

5. A **brigade** (brih GAYD) is a group of people organized for a specific purpose.

Vocabulary

bigotry (BIG uh tree) *n.* unfair and unreasonable opinions or treatment of a person or group

Practice the Skills

9 | **Key Reading Skill**

Predicting A break in the text is a good time to predict. What do you think will happen next? Keep in mind that there are really two stories: Clifton's and Dondré Green's. Have you heard the rest of Dondré's story yet? How do you think it will relate to Clifton's story?

Additional Support

Reading in the Real World

Citizenship There have been many changes in anti-discrimination laws in this country. Arrange students in small groups and have each group research federal and state laws against discrimination. Create a bulletin board that shows a time line of the progress in anti-discrimination legislation in the United States. **OL**

The room erupted[6] in cheers. Not one of us had ever been to a professional baseball game in a real baseball park.

On the way to the stadium, we grew silent as our driver paused before the Lincoln Memorial. For one long moment, I stared through the marble pillars at Mr. Lincoln, bathed in that warm, yellow light. There was still no smile and no sign of hope in his sad and tired eyes.

". . . We here highly resolve . . . that this nation, under God, shall have a new birth of freedom . . ." **10**

In his words and in his life, Lincoln made it clear, that freedom is not free. Every time the color of a person's skin keeps him out of an amusement park or off a country-club fairway, the war for freedom begins again. Sometimes the battle is fought with fists and guns, but more often the most effective weapon is a simple act of love and courage.

Whenever I hear those words from Lincoln's speech at Gettysburg, I remember my eleven white friends, and I feel hope once again. I like to imagine that when we paused that night at the foot of his great monument, Mr. Lincoln smiled at last.

As Dondré said, "The kind of love they showed me that day will conquer hatred every time." **11** ○ **R**

6. **Erupted** means exploded or burst forth.

Practice the Skills

10 | Key Literary Element

Setting Thinking of all the different settings in this story, why do you suppose the author chose to end at the Lincoln Memorial? What happened when he was there earlier? How did he feel? How does a return to this setting add to the story's meaning?

11 | BIG Question

How many heroes did you read about in "A Mason-Dixon Memory?" On the "Mason-Dixon Memory" page of Foldable 6, list and write about the heroes in this selection. Explain what each one of them did to become a hero. Your response will help you complete the Unit Challenge later. **BQ**

A Mason-Dixon Memory **741**

Teach

R Reading Skill

Predicting Say: Dondré made a prediction. He said, "The kind of love they showed me that day will conquer hatred every time." Do you agree with him? *(Possible answer: Yes; it seems that people are standing up against racism and using love to fight hatred more and more.)* **OL**

BQ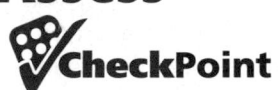

Ask: What do you admire about Clifton's friends and Dondré's teammates? What makes them heroes? *(Possible response: They are heroes because they stood up against injustice.)* **OL**

Assess

CheckPoint

Use the CheckPoint questions provided on Presentation Plus! to check for comprehension of the selection. These questions can be used with interactive response keypads for immediate student feedback.

Differentiated Instruction

Debate Write Dondré's statement on the board: *The kind of love they showed me that day will conquer hatred every time.* Take an informal poll of students to see how many agree with this sentiment. Divide students into groups and have them develop points to support their agreement or disagreement with Dondré. Tell them to pretend that they will be appearing on a Sunday morning talk show. Assign a talk show host and have students debate Dondré's statement. **OL**

Objectives
• Make predictions
• Evaluate text

Assess

Resources for page 742

📁 Selection Quick Check, p. 58

📁 Selection and Unit Assessment, p. 68

💿 ExamView Assessment Suite

💿 Interactive Tutor: Self-Assesesment

Students can respond to the *After You Read* items in their Learner's Notebooks or on a separate sheet of paper.

Answering the
BIG Question

1. Possible response: They had to confront racism head-on and give up what they wanted for the cause of justice.

2. Possible responses: They passed new anti-discrimination legislation and proclaimed a special day for Dondré.

3. Glen Echo Amusement Park, Maryland

Critical Thinking

4. Possible response: They were ordinary people who did the right thing. A hero is anyone who stands up against injustice.

5. Possible response: They may have acted in the same way even if they hadn't known them. They seem to be good, caring people.

6. Possible response: the line between racism and freedom

742

After You Read A Mason-Dixon Memory

Answering the BIG Question

1. The author states that "freedom is not free." In what ways did the heroes in this story have to pay for freedom?

2. **Summarize** In what ways did Dondré's experience prompt the state of Louisiana to make changes? Give two examples of those changes.
   Tip Think and Search

3. **Recall** Where did the author, Clifton Davis, have his experience with racism? Name the state and place.
   Tip Right There

Critical Thinking

4. **Evaluate** Were the heroes in the story born heroes or just ordinary people who did the right thing? Support your answer by explaining your definition of a hero.
   Tip On My Own

5. **Draw Conclusions** In both cases, do you think the other boys would have defended Dondré or the narrator if they had not known them? Explain.
   Tip Author and Me

6. **Analyze** What is the Mason-Dixon line a symbol of in this story?
   Tip Author and Me

Write About Your Reading

Answer the questions to trace the similarities and differences between the two experiences—Dondré's and Clifton's. Use your answers to write a paragraph that compares and contrasts the two experiences.

- In what year did each experience take place?
- How old was the narrator? Dondré?
- In what state did the narrator grow up? Dondré?
- Where did they experience racism? Write the state and setting.
- Who stood up for the narrator? Dondré?
- List the heroes in each case. Why are they heroes?

Objectives (pp. 742–743)
Reading Make predictions • Make connections from text to self
Literature Identify key literary elements: setting
Vocabulary Explore word histories
Writing Write a paragraph: compare and contrast
Grammar Correct run-ons

Write About Your Reading

Possible responses:
- The narrator's experience took place in 1959. Dondré's experience took place in 1991.
- The narrator was 13. Dondré was 18.
- The narrator grew up in New York City. Dondré grew up in Louisiana.
- The narrator experienced racism in Maryland from an amusement park. Dondré experienced racism in Louisiana from a golf club.
- Classmates and a teacher stood up for the narrator. Teammates stood up for Dondré.
- The heroes in Dondré's story are the members of the golf team. The heroes in the narrator's story are his classmates and his teacher.

Skills Review

Key Reading Skill: Predicting

7. Did anything happen in this story that you did not predict? Explain.

8. How did predicting help you to understand the story better?

Key Literary Element: Setting

9. How were the settings important to both Dondré's and the narrator's experiences?

10. What does the title of the story have to do with setting?

11. How does the difference in time play a part in the outcomes of both experiences?

Reviewing Skills: Interpreting

12. What does the Lincoln Memorial mean to the author? What does it come to stand for by the end of the story? Explain.

Vocabulary Check

Choose the best word from the list to complete each sentence below. Rewrite each sentence with the correct word in place.

ominous bigotry civic resolve predominantly

13. The goldfish were ___ orange, but a few were white.

14. To have a world free of ___ you must learn to understand people who are different from you.

15. You should write your ___ leaders if you want to influence their decisions.

16. Every New Year's Eve, we ___ to watch less television.

17. We came in after the sky turned to a scary, ___ gray and the thunder began to boom.

18. **English Language Coach** In a sentence or two, tell how the modern meaning of the noun *banquet* relates to the Old Italian word that meant "bench."

Grammar Link: Correcting Run-on Sentences

A **run-on sentence** is two or more sentences incorrectly written as one sentence.
   Example: *Jordon won the race the crowd cheered.*

Correct a run-on sentence by

- writing separate sentences

   Jordon won the race. The crowd cheered.

- combining the sentences with a semicolon (;)

   Jordon won the race; the crowd cheered.

- combining the sentences with a comma and *and, or,* or *but.*

   Jordon won the race, and the crowd cheered.

Grammar Practice

Rewrite this paragraph, correcting the run-on sentences.

   If you're looking for something to do with your free time, start a collection. Collecting is fun, collecting can be profitable. The items you collect can increase in value over the years, stamps, and coins are a good example. Some people collect baseball cards, some people collect the autographs of famous people, did you know there are even some people who collect shopping bags from different stores?

Writing Application Read the comparison and contrast you wrote about Dondré and the narrator's experiences. Correct any run-on sentences in your paragraph.

Web Activities For eFlashcards, Selection Quick Checks, and other Web activities, go to www.glencoe.com.

A Mason-Dixon Memory **743**

Skills Review

Key Reading Skill: Predicting

7. Responses will vary.

8. Responses will vary.

Key Literary Element: Setting

9. Possible response: In each case, the settings were places where racism was still widely practiced.

10. Davis's experience took place below the Mason-Dixon line.

11. Possible response: In Davis's time, there was a small "brigade of heroes." In Dondré's time, everyone got involved.

Reviewing Skills: Interpreting

12. Possible response: The Lincoln Memorial symbolizes freedom and the fight against racism.

Vocabulary Check

13. predominantly

14. bigotry

15. civic

16. resolve

17. ominous

18. **English Language Coach** Possible response: The Italian word *banchetto* meant "little bench," the kind that was used at a feast table.

Grammar Link: Correcting Run-On Sentences

Grammar Practice

Corrected sentences: Collecting is fun, and collecting can be profitable. The items you collect can increase in value over the years; stamps and coins are a good example of this.

Some people collect baseball cards; some collect the autographs of famous people. Did you know there are even some people who collect colorful shopping bags from different stores?

Comparing Heroes

Objective covered in this workshop:
• Compare and contrast heroes

Teaching Students to Compare Heroes

Why Is It Important?

• Understanding heroes is integral to comprehending text, especially in fictional stories, folktales, fairy tales, and myths.

• Students will gain insight into the qualities valued in the hero's time and culture. Understanding and comparing characters in texts will also help students learn how to understand and compare contemporary heroes in the media and in their lives.

• Students can be inspired by and learn lessons from heroes' words and actions when they perceive and compare them.

How to Help Students Get It

• Read one or more selections with rich compelling heroic characters. Choose two or three heroes to compare. Together with your students, create a Venn diagram which compares several relevant characteristics such as wisdom, power, kindness, courage, and strength.

• Model identifying and comparing heroes in texts by doing a Think Aloud with your students. Choose two selections. As you read the first selection, comment on them when you come across significant descriptions, actions, thoughts, words, interactions, and responses to a hero. Discuss what those elements reveal about the hero. As you progress, shift the responsibility for recognizing attributes of the heroes to the students. When you read the second selection, ask students to help you compare the hero in that selection to the hero in the first selection.

Reading to Answer the Big Question

The Toad and the Donkey by Toni Cade Bambara
In this African American trickster tale, Donkey, who boasts that he is the fastest animal, consents to race Toad. Toad has his relatives hop into the road ahead of Donkey, tricking him into thinking he's lost the race and causing Donkey to give up.

Doc Rabbit, Bruh Fox, and Tar Baby by Virginia Hamilton
In this African American trickster tale, Doc Rabbit and Bruh Fox take turns tricking each other until Doc finally wins out.

Workshop Resources

Pacing (days) Standard	Pacing (days) Block	Lesson	Student Materials	Teacher Resources
1	1	Key Skill Lesson: Comparing Cultural Context	🐟 English Language Coach Review, p. 43	🔖 Bellringer Options Transparencies –Selection Focus Transparency 19 –Daily Language Practice 59 ⊙ Presentation Plus!
1	1	"The Toad and the Donkey"	💻 Glencoe Online 🐟 Unit Vocabulary Review, p. 41 🐟 Academic Vocabulary Review, p. 44 📁 English Language Coach 🐟 Comparing Literature Graphic Organizer, p. 36 ⊙ StudentWorks Plus™ 💻 Online Student Edition ⊙ Literature Classics	💻 Puzzlemaker ⊙ Skill Level Up!™ A Language Arts Game 💻 BookLink 3 📓 Assessment by Learning Objective (Diagnostic and Formative) ⊙ Interactive Tutor: Self-Assessment ⊙ TeacherWorks Plus™ 📁 ExamView Assessment Suite
1		"Doc Rabbit, Bruh Fox, and Tar Baby"	💻 Glencoe Online 🐟 Unit Vocabulary Review, p. 41 🐟 Academic Vocabulary Review, p. 44 📁 English Language Coach 🐟 Comparing Literature Graphic Organizer, p. 36 ⊙ StudentWorks Plus™ 💻 Online Student Edition ⊙ Literature Classics	💻 Puzzlemaker ⊙ Skill Level Up!™ A Language Arts Game 💻 BookLink 3 📓 Assessment by Learning Objective (Diagnostic and Formative) ⊙ Interactive Tutor: Self-Assessment ⊙ TeacherWorks Plus™ 📁 ExamView Assessment Suite

Keys for Unit Resource

📁 Blackline Master   💾 DVD

📓 Workbook   🔖 Transparency

📖 Supplemental Text   💻 Web-based

⊙ CD-ROM   🐟 Fast File

Level Appropriate Code

AS = Activities for all students

AL = Activities for students working above grade level

OL = Activities for students working at grade level

BL = Activities for students working below grade level

EL = Activities for English language learners

Focus

BELLRINGER Options

- **Selection Focus Transparency 19**
- **Daily Language Practice Transparency 59**

Focus Activity Draw a Venn diagram on the board. **Say:** Think of two people or characters whom you consider heroes. They can be people you know, celebrities, or characters from stories. Use a Venn diagram to compare these two heroes. In each hero's circle, list character traits and achievements. In the center section, list the traits and achievements that both heroes share. *(Responses will vary.)* **OL**

Teach

R Reading Skill

Review Activating Prior Knowledge Say: In this unit, you have already read a story about one trickster hero: Anansi. From that story, what do you already know about trickster characters? *(Possible responses: They often use brains rather than physical strength to defeat an opponent; they play clever tricks on the other characters in the story.)* **OL**

The Toad and the Donkey
by Toni Cade Bambara

& Doc Rabbit, Bruh Fox, and Tar Baby
by Virginia Hamilton

Skills Focus

You will use these skills as you read and compare the following selections:

- "The Toad and the Donkey," p. 748
- "Doc Rabbit, Bruh Fox, and Tar Baby," p. 757

Reading

- Making connections across texts
- Comparing and contrasting myths, fables, and their heroes

Literature

- Recognizing and analyzing heroes

Objectives (pp. 744–745)
Reading Compare and contrast heroes

744 UNIT 6

A real-life hero overcomes hardship or danger to do something generous for someone else. So are all heroes equal? No. You learned in this unit that a hero in literature can be very different from a real-life hero. In fact, one kind of literary hero—the trickster—often does not seem like a hero at all.

How to Compare Literature: Heroes

Trickster tales are found all around the world. In fact, they're especially common on cartoon shows you might have watched. Bugs Bunny, for example, is a trickster hero. In a trickster tale, the *trickster hero* uses clever tricks to defeat an opponent who's usually bigger, stronger, or faster than he is.

Some trickster heroes have good reasons for playing tricks. Other tricksters might just want to cheat someone or steal something. When you compare trickster tales, think about who the trickster hero is and why he's tricking his opponent.

R

Additional Support

Reading in the Real World

Careers Ask students whether there is a career especially suited to people who like comparing things. Talk about comparing as a kind of analysis. Then, talk about appraisers. Property appraisers are important in local governments and in the real estate market. Jewelry appraisers play an important role in the insur-ance industry and in estate settlement. Consumer reviewers in electronics and many other product markets are increasingly powerful on Internet Web sites. Assign interested students to research one of these careers and to share their findings with the class. **AL**

Get Ready to Compare

In a trickster tale, the trickster's opponent usually has some weakness that allows him or her to be tricked. The opponent may not be as smart as the trickster, or he may be greedy or self-centered. The trickster then takes advantage of this weakness to defeat his opponent. To understand the trickster tales "The Toad and the Donkey" and "Doc Rabbit, Bruh Fox, and Tar Baby," keep track of the tricks that are played in a chart like the one below. For each trick:

- describe the trick
- identify the trickster and opponent
- briefly describe the strengths and weaknesses of the trickster and opponent.

You'll find that in some tales several tricks are played. And more than one character in a single tale might be a trickster!

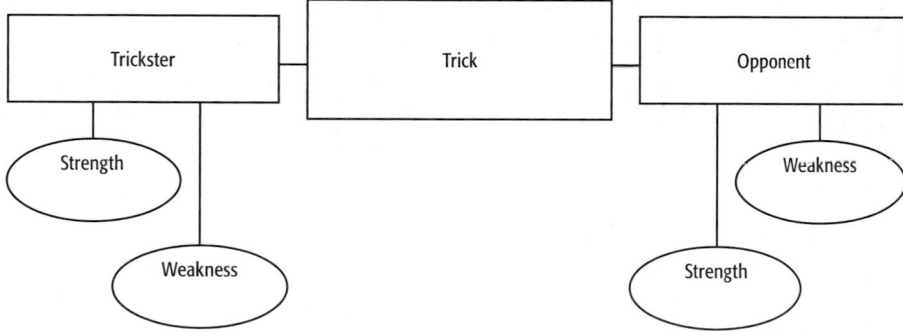

Here's a hint to help you with your charts: in "The Toad and the Donkey," only one trick is played, though it is repeated several times. You only have to make one chart for that selection. In "Doc Rabbit, Bruh Fox, and Tar Baby," though, several tricks are played, so you'll need several charts.

Use Your Comparison

After you have filled out your *Tricks* charts, think about why the trickster played the tricks in both selections. Did the trickster have a good reason for playing the trick or was he just taking advantage of the other character?

Teach

L Literary Element

Hero Say: A hero does not have to be perfect. In real life and in stories, a hero has many strengths and weaknesses.

- Have students form small groups. Assign each group one hero from the selections in this unit.
- Have each group draw a line down the middle of a sheet of paper. They should write *Strengths* on one side and *Weaknesses* on the other.
- After students complete their lists, have them share their notes with the class. (*Responses will vary.*) **OL**

Assess/Close

Ask: What are the characteristics of a trickster hero? (*Trickster heroes win their battles through intelligence and deception.*) **Say:** Now describe the characteristics of a literary hero. (*Literary heroes are often strong and honest.*) **Ask:** How are they alike? (*Possible response: They both overcome obstacles.*) **OL**

Resources for page 745

 Use the Comparing Literature Graphic Organizer BLM in the Unit 6 Resource Booklet, p. 36.

Reading Fluency

Setting a Purpose for Reading Remind students that they should have a clear purpose in mind when they begin to read a selection. Discuss various purposes that students may have for reading folktales—to be entertained, to learn about the folktale's culture of origin, or to learn a lesson about human behavior, even from animal characters. Encourage students to set a purpose for reading each of the two folktales. As they read and the action unfolds, suggest that students reevaluate why they are reading the selection, perhaps adding a second or third purpose for reading. **OL**

Objectives

- Compare and contrast
- Identify literary elements: heroes
- Activate prior knowledge

Teach

More About the Author

Toni Cade Bambara said that the Harlem community she grew up in had a great influence on her writing. There was a place called Speakers' Corner in her neighborhood, where she heard people speak and learned the power of language. She also said that the music of the 1940s and 1950s helped her find her writing voice. Although the cultural diversity of her neighborhood was important to her, Bambara said that her mother was her greatest inspiration because her mother had "great respect for the life of the mind."

V Vocabulary

Vocabulary Game:

Concentration Have pairs of students play Concentration with the vocabulary words. Have one partner write the words on index cards. The other partner should write the definitions. Players should then place all of the cards face down and turn over two at a time until all the pairs have been matched. **OL**

Before You Read : The **Toad** and the **Donkey**

Toni Cade Bambara

Meet the Author

Toni Cade added "Bambara" to her name after she found the name on a sketchbook in her great-grandmother's trunk. Born in the Harlem community of New York, she became a college professor, a writer, and an activist for African American women.

Bambara was born in 1939 and died in 1995. This story was published in 1971. See page R1 of the Author Files for more about Toni Cade Bambara.

Author Search For more about Toni Cade Bambara, go to www.glencoe.com.

Objectives (pp. 746–749)
Reading Compare and contrast heroes

Vocabulary Preview

reputation (rep yuh TAY shun) *n.* what other people think of someone (p. 748) *The donkey had a reputation for being a very fast runner.*

milepost (MYL pohst) *n.* one of a number of posts placed one mile apart (p. 748) *Toad's relatives hid in wait at each milepost.*

well (wel) *n.* a hole dug in the ground to get water (p. 749) *Donkey paused at the well for a drink.*

slashed (slasht) *v.* hit sharply enough to cause a cut; form of the verb *slash* (p. 749) *He slashed his back with his own tail.*

horsewhip (HORS whip) *n.* a whip or stick used to make a horse go faster (p. 749) *He used his tail like a horsewhip.*

Get Ready to Read

Connect to the Reading

Think about a time when you got mad at someone who bragged too much. Did you want to teach that person a lesson? How do you think you would have felt if someone had fooled that person by playing a trick on him or her?

Build Background

Trickster tales were common among enslaved African Americans during the 1800s. Many trickster tales have been handed down and rewritten by famous writers.

- In this tale Brother Spider proposes that Toad and Donkey race.
- In Africa the spider Anansi is an important figure in trickster tales and mythology.
- Donkeys have a reputation for being slow and stubborn.

One of the most popular types of folktales in cultures around the world is the trickster tale. In a trickster tale, the trickster hero is usually a smaller weaker character, while the opponent is larger and more powerful. But the opponent has some weakness or flaw that allows him to be tricked. The trickster takes advantage of the opponent's weakness to defeat him.

Additional Support

Author Search To expand students' appreciation of Toni Cade Bambara, have them access the Web site for more information and resources

Literature Focus Lesson

Folktales Students in your class may discover that they each know a version of the same story from their countries of origin. If possible, invite adults from your students' families to visit your class and tell some folktales from their cultures. Also, find books of folktales from the countries represented in your classroom and make them available for the students to read. **AS**

What Are Trickster Tales?

In many Native American, African American, and African folktales, the trickster is a rabbit. The rabbit seems small and helpless, but it wins by being quick and smart. In other cultures, foxes, turtles, spiders, ravens, badgers, and many other animals are the heroes of trickster tales.

Clever tricksters use their wits to get themselves out of trouble or to win a contest. But in many stories, the trickster gets right back into trouble. Tricksters who try to take advantage of others or cheat their opponents often get caught up in their own mischief. Sometimes they even become the victims of other tricksters.

Same Story, Different Culture

Some folktales are told in slightly different versions in different cultures. In *The People Could Fly: American Black Folktales,* Virginia Hamilton writes, "There are some three hundred versions of the Tar Baby tale. . . . In the Bahamas the elephant creates the tar baby; in Brazil an old woman or man traps a monkey in a sticky wax (doll). There is a version from India, and there are African versions among the Ewes and Yorubas [people of Western Africa], all showing the great . . . universality of this tale."

Set Purposes for Reading

BIG Question   Read to find out if anyone in this tale has the qualities of a real-life hero.

Set Your Own Purpose What other purpose might you have for reading this tale? Write your own purpose on the "Toad and the Donkey" page of Foldable 6.

Teach

R1 Reading Skill

Review Predicting Say: Think about what you know about toads and donkeys. Which animal is bigger? Which animal do you think is smarter? Who do you predict will be the trickster in this tale, and who will be the opponent? *(Possible response: the smaller animal, the toad, will be the trickster.)* **OL**

R2 Reading Skill

Review Connecting Say: Think about a time when you challenged someone who thought too much of themselves. What did you challenge this person to do? Did he or she succeed? How did it make you feel to see them succeed or fail? *(Responses will vary.)* **OL**

The Toad and the Donkey **747**

English Language Coach

Dialect These stories use dialect, or variations in a language as it is spoken in different regions. Dialects in the U.S. differ from Standard English in spelling, word use, and pronunciation. In these stories, for example, characters use words and expressions such as *dude, yer,* and *can't tell nothing.* Have students work with partners and read the sentences that are in dialect aloud. Have partners listen closely to try to identify the Standard English meaning and pronunciation. Allow students to use a dictionary or other reference aids if necessary. **AS**

Objectives
• Make predictions
• Make connections from text to self
• Understand dialect
• Learn and use new vocabulary
• Analyze features of genres: folktales

Teach

C Critical Thinking

Analysis **Ask:** What effect did Donkey's bragging have on Toad? *(Donkey's bragging made Toad want to race.)* **Ask:** What causes Donkey to agree to the race even though he thinks it's "ridiculous"? *(Possible response: Donkey agrees to the race because he thinks Spider will give him a great prize.)* **OL**

R Reading Skill

Review Predicting **Say:** Think about what Toad says to his family. Briefly summarize the plan. *(Possible response: When Donkey howls, different toads along the trail will howl back.)* **Ask:** How do you think this plan will work? What will it make Donkey do? *(Possible response: Donkey will be confused by the toads and think he is losing the race.)* **OL**

Readability Scores
Dale-Chall: 4.8
DRP: 49
Lexile: 820

The Toad and the Donkey

by Toni Cade Bambara

One day Brother Spider didn't have nothing better to do so he asked ole Toad and ole Donkey to have a race across the island.

C The donkey said, "What? You want me, the fastest dude around here, to race that little old hop frog. I've got a **reputation**, you know." **1**

And the toad said, "Never mind all that, Big Mouth—let's race." **2**

The donkey thought to himself, this is ridiculous. But since Brother Spider always had good prizes (Brother Spider was a terrific thief), he agreed.

"O.K.," said Spider. "The only rule is that Brother Donkey has to howl every mile so we can know where you all are."

Toad says, "Fine with me. Let's set the race for Saturday."

"Oh no," says Donkey, for he suspected something trickified. "Tomorrow morning."

R So Toad went home for dinner and put it to the family like so: "Listen here, we spread out along the path in the bushes, then at every **milepost** when Mr. Donkey howls out, one of you steps out and howls too." So they each packed a little breakfast of gungo peas and sweet potato bread and bakes all wrapped up in tanya leaves and took up their positions along the road.

Vocabulary

reputation (rep yuh TAY shun) *n.* what other people think of someone

milepost (MYL pohst) *n.* one of a number of posts placed one mile apart

Practice the Skills

1 **Comparing Literature**

Heroes What do you think Donkey's *strength* will be in this tale? Who do you think the trickster will be in this tale?

2 **Comparing Literature**

Heroes How does Toad feel about what Donkey has just said? What do you think Donkey's weakness will be?

Additional Support

Differentiated Instruction

Illustration Tell students to imagine that they work for the book publisher who is preparing this story for publication. Their job will be to design the book cover. As they read, students must generate ideas for a book cover that will be attractive enough to get readers' attention and, at the same time, provide information about the story. When the story is finished, give students art supplies to draw their covers. Put the covers on display around the classroom. **OL**

So the race began. And Spider lit a cigar and lay back.

Brother Donkey took off at a light trot, his tail stuck up in the air to match his nose, stopping every now and then to stick his face through somebody's fence to munch on some grass. And when he got to the first milepost, he sang out, "La, la, la. Here I am. Where are you? Ha ha." **3**

And way in front of him Uncle Julius Toad sang back, "Up here. La, la, la," and licked his fingers.

Which really surprised Donkey. So he cut out the grass eating and got a move on. But then he passed a **well** and decided he had time for a drink, for how much hopping can a toad do. And at the next post he sang out, "Tra, la, la. Here I am. Where are you?"

And way up ahead Aunt Minnie Toad sang back, "Up here. Ha, ha."

By the fifth post, Donkey started getting a little worried so he **slashed** himself with his tail like a **horsewhip** and started galloping. But Cousins Emery, Walter and Cecil Toad were on the case. And it's the same story each time. "Tra la la, I'm up the road ahead of you, Donkey."

And Donkey began to get sad in his mind when he realized he was not going to beat Toad. And he decided before he even got to the finish line that he would never race again. And donkeys have been kind of stubborn about running ever since. **4 5** ○

Illustration for *Public and Private Animals*. 1877. by J Granville.

Practice the Skills

3 **Comparing Literature**

Heroes Does Donkey seem to be taking the race seriously? How does Donkey's attitude help to excuse Toad for playing a trick on him?

4 **Comparing Literature**

Heroes In some trickster tales, like myths, the trickster hero's actions explain why something happens in nature. What does this tale explain about donkeys?

5 **BIG Question**

Toad was a trickster hero in this tale. If something like this happened in real life, would you call him a hero?

Vocabulary

well (wel) *n.* a hole dug in the ground to get water

slashed (slasht) *v.* hit sharply enough to cause a cut

horsewhip (HORS wip) *n.* a whip or stick used to make a horse go faster

The Toad and the Donkey **749**

Teach

R **Reading Skill**

Review Connecting Say: Imagine you are Brother Spider, lying back and watching the race. Who would you want to win? Why? Would you enjoy watching this trick? Why or why not? *(Possible response: It would be enjoyable to see Toad win, because Donkey is proud and boastful.)* **OL**

BQ

Ask: Do you respect Toad's decision to play a trick? Why or why not? *(Responses will vary.)* **Ask:** If you were to meet someone who brags a great deal, how important would it be to you to teach that person a lesson? *(Responses will vary.)* **OL**

Assess

CheckPoint

Use the CheckPoint questions provided on Presentation Plus! to check for comprehension of the selection. These questions can be used with interactive response keypads for immediate student feedback.

Literature Focus Lesson

Trickster Tale This story explains why donkeys are thought to be stubborn. Have students brainstorm with a partner to list other animal behaviors that could be explained by a short trickster story. Why do pigs roll in mud, for example? Why does a rooster crow? How did the giraffe get such a long neck? In their Learner's Notebooks, have students draft a short story or create an outline for a folktale that explains an animal characteristic or behavior. Give them time to share the draft or outline in pairs or in small groups. **OL**

Objectives
- Make predictions
- Analyze text
- Make connections from text to self
- Analyze features of genres: trickster tales

749

Teach

More About the Author

Because Hamilton grew up with such gifted storytellers, she likes to use traditional oral storytelling methods in her writing. For example, Hamilton enjoys writing as if she were telling the story out loud. She says, "I rarely think about writing until I sit down to write. I know that sounds strange, but all the 'magic stuff' is kept way deep inside and all comes out when I'm ready to write."

R Reading Skill

Review Connecting Ask:
Have you ever been tricked or fooled by someone and wanted to "get back" at that person? What did you do? Do you think it's better to "even the score" or better to "keep the peace"? *(Responses will vary.)* **OL**

Before You Read

Doc Rabbit, Bruh Fox, and Tar Baby

Virginia Hamilton

Meet the Author

"I grew up within the warmth of loving aunts and uncles, all reluctant farmers but great story-tellers," says Virginia Hamilton. She is proud to be descended from Levi Perry, who escaped from slavery and settled in Ohio.

Virginia Hamilton was born in 1936. This story was published in 1985.

Literature Online

Author Search For more about Virginia Hamilton, go to www.glencoe.com.

Objectives (pp. 750–755)
Reading Compare and contrast heroes
Literature Recognize and analyze heroes

Vocabulary Preview

crock (krok) *n.* a large clay or ceramic pot (p. 751) *The boys kept their apple cider in a crock.*

toiled (toyld) *v.* worked hard; form of the verb *toil* (p. 752) *Raphael toiled all day weeding the garden.*

scurried (SKUR eed) *v.* ran quickly; form of the verb *scurry* (p. 752) *The mouse scurried across the floor to escape.*

Get Ready to Read

Connect to the Reading

Have you ever enjoyed a television program, movie, or story in which the characters kept playing tricks on each other? Which character did you like the best? Who did you want to "win"?

Build Background

This is one of many different stories from around the world that feature a rabbit or hare as a trickster.

- A hare is a larger relative of a rabbit, although people often use the words "hare" and "rabbit" to mean the same thing. A hare can grow to be the size of a large cat.
- There are many different trickster tales about a rabbit and a tar baby.
- Tar is the thick, sticky black substance that is often used to pave blacktop roads.

Set Purposes for Reading

BIG Question Read to find out whether any of the characters in this tale are like real-life heroes.

Set Your Own Purpose What else would you like to learn from this tale? Write your own purpose on the "Doc Rabbit, Bruh Fox, and Tar Baby" page of Foldable 6.

Additional Support

Literature Online

Author Search To expand students' appreciation of Virginia Hamilton, have them access the Web site for additional information and resources.

Differentiated Instruction

Building Background Bugs Bunny is one of the most well-known trickster rabbits. If possible, show a Bugs Bunny cartoon and ask students to try to understand how the humor works as they watch. **BL OL** Interested students can research the creation of Bugs Bunny and the ways in which the character has evolved over time. **AL**

Doc Rabbit, Bruh Fox, and Tar Baby

by Virginia Hamilton

Heard tell about Doctor Rabbit and Brother Fox. They were buildin a house. And they kept a **crock** of cream in the bubbly brook down below the house they were buildin. Every once in a while, Doc Rabbit got thirsty. And he hollered aside so Bruh Fox wouldn't know who it was, "Whooo-hooo, whooo-hooo, whooo-hooo," like that. Scared Bruh Fox to death. **1**

"Who is it there?" Bruh Fox say.

"Sounds like somebody callin bad," said Doc Rabbit.

"Well, can you tell what they want?" Bruh Fox say.

"Can't tell nothin and I'm not lookin to see," said Doc.

"Oh, but yer the doctor. Yer the doctor, you'd better go see," says Bruh Fox. **2**

So Doc Rabbit went off down to the bubbly brook where the water ribbled, keepin the cream cold. He drank a long drink of sweet cream. Then he went back to help Bruh Fox with the house.

"Who was it callin?" asks Bruh Fox.

"Just started callin me, was all it was," said Doc Rabbit.

So Doc Rabbit got down to work. But the sun was hot and he came thirsty again. He went about callin out the side of his mouth:

"Whoo-ahhh, whooo-ahhh, whoo-ahhh!"

Vocabulary

crock (krok) *n.* a large clay or ceramic pot

Practice the Skills

1 **Comparing Literature**

Heroes Who do you think is going to be the trickster? What do you think Bruh Fox's weakness is?

2 **Comparing Literature**

Heroes Why do you think Doc Rabbit tells Bruh Fox that he doesn't want to go see who is calling?

Doc Rabbit, Bruh Fox, and Tar Baby **751**

Teach

L Literary Element

Review Tone Ask: How is language used in this story? What makes it unusual? What effect does this have on the story's tone or mood? *(Possible response: The story is written in dialect, and the language is very casual. The writer uses interesting spellings and expressions. This sets a whimsical tone for the story.)* **OL**

R Reading Skill

Review Predicting Ask: When Doc Rabbit gets thirsty a second time, do you think Bruh Fox will fall for the same trick again? Why or why not? *(Possible response: Bruh Fox will fall for the trick because he does not seem very bright.)* **OL**

Readability Scores
Dale-Chall: 5.2
DRP: 45
Lexile: 600

Reading Fluency

Developing Fluency To establish the voices of these characters, read the first paragraph out loud to the class. Then ask the class to join you by reading the part of Bruh Fox or Doc Rabbit while you continue reading the other parts out loud. Continue in this way for another page or two and then have students continue reading on their own. **AS**

Objectives
• Make connections from text to self
• Make predictions
• Identify literary elements: tone

Teach

Review Clarifying Say:
Think about what Doc Rabbit says when Bruh Fox asks who is calling. He replies, "Name of about half done callin'." How much cream did Doc Rabbit just drink? What do you think he means by his answer? *(Possible response: Doc Rabbit is making a joke to himself. He says that the person calling is named "about half done." He is referring to the cream.)* **OL**

C **Critical Thinking**

Evaluation Say: The author never tells us how Bruh Fox feels when he sees that the cream is all gone. What can you infer from his actions? *(Possible response: He has been working very hard and is probably thirsty too. He is probably very angry and wants to get back at Doc Rabbit.)* **OL**

"Who is callin so scared?" says Bruh Fox, trembly all over.

"Somebody callin me for help, I expect," Doc Rabbit said. "But I am sure not goin this time, me."

"You have to go. You have to, yer the only doctor. Go ahead on, you," Bruh Fox say.

Big Doc Rabbit went down to the brook again. The water was so cool and ribbly and it kept the crock of cream so fresh and cold. Doc Rabbit drank about half of the cream this time. Then he went back up to help Brother Fox with the hard labor of raisin the roof.

Bruh Fox says, "What was the name of the one callin you this time?"

R "Name of about half done callin," mumbled Doc Rabbit. "Whew! This work is hard labor."

The rabbit **toiled** and sweated until his fur was wringin wet. He took off his fur coat, too. He wrung it dry and put it back on. But that didn't even cool him any. He says over his shoulder, says, "Whooo-wheee, whooo-wheee!" like that. **3**

The fox says, lookin all around, "Somebody else callin you, Rabbit."

"I sure am not goin this time," Doc Rabbit said. "I'll just stay right here this time."

"You go on," says Bruh Fox. "Go ahead on, folks needin you today."

So Doc Rabbit **scurried** down to the ribblin brook. It was nice by the water. He sat himself down, took up the crock of cream. He drank it all down. Then he ran off.

C Fox feel a suspicion. He went down there, saw the cream was all gone. He filled up the crock with some lemon and sugar water he had. He knew Rabbit was after anything cold and sweet.

"Who are you, I say" Harrison Candy. Engraving.

Practice the Skills

3 **BIG Question**

How do you feel about the trick Doc Rabbit is playing on Bruh Fox? If something like this happened in real life, would you call Doc Rabbit a hero?

> **Vocabulary**
>
> **toiled** (toyld) v. worked hard
> **scurried** (SKUR eed) v. ran quickly

Additional Support

English Language Coach

Dialect The dialect in this story may be difficult for non-native speakers to understand. Write the following sentence on the board and discuss its meaning: *"Sounds like somebody callin bad,"* *said Doc Rabbit.* Have students rework the sentence into Standard English. For example, *"It sounds like someone who needs help badly is calling," said Doc Rabbit.* Pair language learners with proficient readers and ask them to work together to select passages that are in dialect and use conventional spelling and grammar as they rewrite them. **EL** **OL**

"Think I'll catch me a doctor and a hare together," Fox says to himself. **4**

Next, he made a little baby out of the tar there. The baby lookin just like a baby rabbit. He named it Tar Baby and sat it right there on the waterside. Bruh Fox went back up the hill and he worked on his house. He thought he might keep the house to himself. Doc Rabbit was bein bad so and not workin at all. **5**

Doc Rabbit came back for a drink. He spied the new crock full. And he spied Tar Baby just sittin, gazin out on the water.

"What you doin here, baby rabbit?" Rabbit asked Tar Baby. Tar Baby wouldn't say. Too stuck up.

"You better speak to me," Doc Rabbit said, "or I'll have to hurt you."

But the Tar Baby wasn't gone speak to a stranger.

So Doc Rabbit kicked Tar Baby with his left hind foot. Foot got stuck, it did.

"Whoa, turn me loose!" the rabbit cried. "Turn me loose!" **6**

Tar Baby stayed still. Gazin at the water. Lookin out over the ribbly water.

So Doc Rabbit kicked hard with his right hind foot. "Oh, oh, I'm stuck again. You'd better let me loose, baby," Doc Rabbit said. "I got another good foot to hit you with."

Tar Baby said nothin. Gazin at the water. Lookin far on by the waterside.

Doc Rabbit kicked Tar Baby with another foot, and that foot got stuck way deep. "Better turn me loose," Rabbit hollered, gettin scared now. Shakin now. Says, "I got one foot left and here it comes!" **7**

He kicked that tar baby with the one foot left, and that got stuck just like the other three.

"Well, well, well," said Doc Rabbit, shakin his head and lookin at Tar Baby.

Tar Baby gazin on the water. Watchin out for the pretty birds.

"Well, I still got my head," Doc Rabbit said. "I'm mad, now! I'm agone use my head, too."

He used his head on the little tar baby. Butted his head in the tar baby's stomach as hard as he could. Doc Rabbit's head got stuck clear up to his eyes. His big rabbit ears went whole in the tar of Tar Baby.

Practice the Skills

4 **Comparing Literature**

Heroes Who do you think is going to be the trickster now? What weakness of Doc Rabbit does Bruh Fox take advantage of?

5 **Comparing Literature**

Heroes Do you think Bruh Fox was right in feeling that he should keep the house for himself? Explain.

6 **Comparing Literature**

Heroes How did Bruh Fox know that Doc Rabbit would kick or hit Tar Baby? What strength does Bruh Fox have now?

7 **Comparing Literature**

Heroes Doc Rabbit keeps kicking Tar Baby, even though he keeps getting more and more stuck. What is Doc Rabbit's weakness in this part of the story?

Doc Rabbit, Bruh Fox, and Tar Baby **753**

Teach

C Critical Thinking

Application Say: Look at the author's descriptions of Doc Rabbit's interactions with Tar Baby. What is one way that the author uses the element of humor? *(Possible response: She describes Tar Baby from Doc Rabbit's point of view. The reader knows Tar Baby is not real, but she describes how it gazes at the water and is too "stuck up" to answer Doc Rabbit.)* **OL**

R Reading Skill

Review Predicting Ask: Now that Bruh Fox has tricked Doc Rabbit into getting stuck, what do you think he will do next? What do you think will happen when Bruh Fox lets Doc Rabbit loose? *(Possible response: Doc Rabbit will trick Bruh Fox again.)* **OL**

Literature Focus Lesson

Humor Ask students what they think of Doc Rabbit's work ethic. How do they feel about Bruh Fox's being tricked? Explain that most humor is based on a change in somebody's status. In this case, Bruh Fox changes from a trusting friend to a dupe. Then Doc Rabbit changes from crafty trickster to a stuck bunny. Ask whether any of the students feel compassion or sympathy for those who are tricked. **OL**

Objectives
• Clarify ideas and text
• Make predictions
• Apply information
• Evaluate text
• Identify literary elements: humor
• Understand dialect

Teach

Viewing the Art

Ask: How does this picture illustrate the events in this story? *(Doc Rabbit is stuck to Tar Baby, and Bruh Fox is rolling about with laughter.)* **EL** **BL** **Ask:** Who seems to be having the last laugh now? *(Bruh Fox)* **OL**

R Reading Skill

Review Activating Prior Knowledge **Say:** Think about what you know about the places in which rabbits can live. Do you think a rabbit would be comfortable in a briar patch? What is Doc Rabbit doing? *(Possible response: Rabbits can live comfortably in briar patches; Doc Rabbit is tricking Bruh Fox yet again.)* **OL**

Brer Rabbit stuck on the Tar Baby. Engraving.

Analyzing the Art Who seems to be having the last laugh? What might Doc Rabbit do next?

That was the way Bruh Fox found him. Doc Rabbit was stuck in Tar Baby. Bruh Fox got him loose.

"What must I do with you?" Bruh Fox said. He led Rabbit along to the house they were buildin. "You the one drank up my crock of cream. I didn't get one taste. Have a mind to burn you in a fire, too."

"Oh, I like fires," Doc Rabbit said. "Do go on burn me up, Bruh Fox, for it's my pleasure to have my coat on fire."

"Well, then, I won't burn you," said the fox. "Burnin up is too good for you." **8**

"Huh," grunted Doc Rabbit. He said no more. Bruh Fox had him in his mouth, a-danglin down his back. Then he laid the rabbit under his paws so he could speak.

"Well, I think I'll throw you in that thorny briar patch," Bruh Fox said. "How do you like that?"

754 UNIT 6 What Makes a Hero?

Practice the Skills

8 **Comparing Literature**

Heroes Why does Doc Rabbit tell Bruh Fox to burn him in the fire? Who is being the trickster now?

Additional Support

Differentiated Instruction

Role-Play Some students may need help understanding the way that Doc Rabbit manipulates Bruh Fox into throwing him into the briar patch. Call on volunteers to role-play the final scene. Give them some time to practice the lines with exaggerated expressions. Hearing the words and seeing facial expressions will help all students understand Doc Rabbit's ultimate trickery. **AS**

Hare, William De Morgan (1839–1917) Watercolor on paper. Private collection.

"Oh, mercy, don't do that!" cried Doc Rabbit. "Whatever you do with me, don't dare throw me in those thorny briars!"

"That's what I'll do, then," Bruh Fox said.

And that's what Brother Fox did. He sure did. Took Doc Rabbit by the short hair and threw him—*Whippit! Whappit!*—right in the briar patch.

"Hot lettuce pie! This is where I want to be," Doc Rabbit hollered for happiness. He was square in the middle of the briar patch. "Here is where my mama and papa had me born and raised. Safe at last!" **9**

"Didn't know rabbits have they homes in the briars," Bruh Fox said, scratching his tail.

He knows it now. **10** ○

Practice the Skills

9 Comparing Literature

Heroes What is the final trick played in this tale? Who is the trickster?

10 **BIG Question**

Which character in this tale would you rather have as a friend? Would either of these characters be a hero in real life? Explain your answer on the "Doc Rabbit, Bruh Fox, and Tar Baby" page of Foldable 6. Your response will help you complete the Unit Challenge later. **BQ**

Doc Rabbit, Bruh Fox, and Tar Baby **755**

Teach

BQ

Ask: What qualities of Bruh Fox do you admire? What are some things you do not like about him? What are some qualities of Doc Rabbit you admire? What don't you like about him? *(Possible response: Bruh Fox is hardworking, but he lacks intelligence. Doc Rabbit is clever, but he is lazy.)* **OL**

Assess

✓CheckPoint

Use the CheckPoint questions provided on Presentation Plus! to check for comprehension of the selection. These questions can be used with interactive response keypads for immediate student feedback.

Literature Focus Lesson

Folktales Remind students that the folktales that endure over time are the ones that communicate some wisdom about life. Many folktales incorporate lessons about how to behave or how to solve problems. Ask students to discuss in small groups the lessons they have learned from each of the folktales in this workshop. Then have each group write a sentence that sums up the moral or lesson from one of the stories. Have them work together to write an original folktale that teaches a similar lesson. **OL**

Objectives
• Activate prior knowledge
• Find meaning in art
• Analyze features of genre: folktales

Assess

Resources for page 756

📁 Selection Quick Check, pp. 59–60

💿 ExamView Assessment Suite

💿 Interactive Tutor: Self-Assessment

Vocabulary Check

"The Toad and the Donkey"

1. well
2. reputation
3. horsewhip
4. slashed
5. milepost

"Doc Rabbit, Bruh Fox, and Tar Baby"

6. toiled
7. crock
8. scurried

After You Read

Objectives (pp. 756–757)
Reading Compare and contrast: heroes
Writing Create a chart: compare and contrast

The Toad and the Donkey & Doc Rabbit, Bruh Fox, and Tar Baby

Vocabulary Check

Copy each sentence, filling in the blank with the best word from the list.

The Toad and the Donkey

reputation   milepost   well   slashed   horsewhip

1. Angelina went to the ___ to get some water.

2. The toad had a ___ for being a trickster.

3. The cowboy used a ___ to make his horse go faster.

4. The thorny weeds ___ at his ankles.

5. Tony could tell by the ___ how far he had traveled.

Doc Rabbit, Bruh Fox, and Tar Baby

crock   toiled   scurried

6. Jasmine ___ all day to get the house cleaned up.

7. People sometimes used to keep milk in a ___ .

8. When we heard the thunder, we ___ home.

756 UNIT 6 What Makes a Hero?

13. Sample Chart

Trickster:	Toad
Strength:	intelligence, cunning
Weakness:	small size, can only hop
Trick:	Had family members pretend to be him along the trail so donkey always thought he was behind
Opponent:	Donkey
Strength:	speed, size, four legs
Weakness:	arrogance, stubbornness

756

Reading/Critical Thinking

On a sheet of paper, answer the following questions.

The **Toad** and the **Donkey**

9. **Recall** Why does Donkey agree to race against Toad?

   Tip Right There

10. **Evaluate** Was Toad justified in tricking Donkey? Explain.

    Tip On My Own

Doc Rabbit, Bruh Fox, and Tar Baby

11. **Recall** What does Bruh Fox do right after he creates the tar baby?

    Tip Right There

12. **Evaluate** Who do you think would be a better friend—Doc Rabbit or Bruh Fox? Explain why you picked that character.

    Tip On My Own

Writing: Compare the Literature

Use Your Notes

13. Follow these steps to compare the trickster heroes.

Step 1: Look over the charts you made. For each trick that you listed, think about the weakness in the trickster's opponent that allowed the trickster to fool him. Then look at the strengths you listed for each trickster on your charts.

Step 2: Now think about why the trickster played each trick. Did the trickster's opponent deserve to be tricked?

Step 3: Which two tricksters do you think were most alike? Write a short paragraph that explains why you feel those two tricksters were most alike. Consider their strengths, weaknesses, the kind of tricks they played, and why they played the trick.

Get It on Paper

To compare the trickster heroes in "The Toad and the Donkey" and "Doc Rabbit, Bruh Fox, and Tar Baby," answer the following questions on a separate sheet of paper.

14. Which trickster do you think is the cleverest? Explain why you chose this answer.

15. Which opponent do you think most deserves to be fooled by the trickster? Explain your answer.

16. Which opponent do you think least deserves to be fooled by the trickster? Explain.

BIG Question

17. Would you consider any of these tricksters real heroes, not just literary heroes? Explain why or why not.

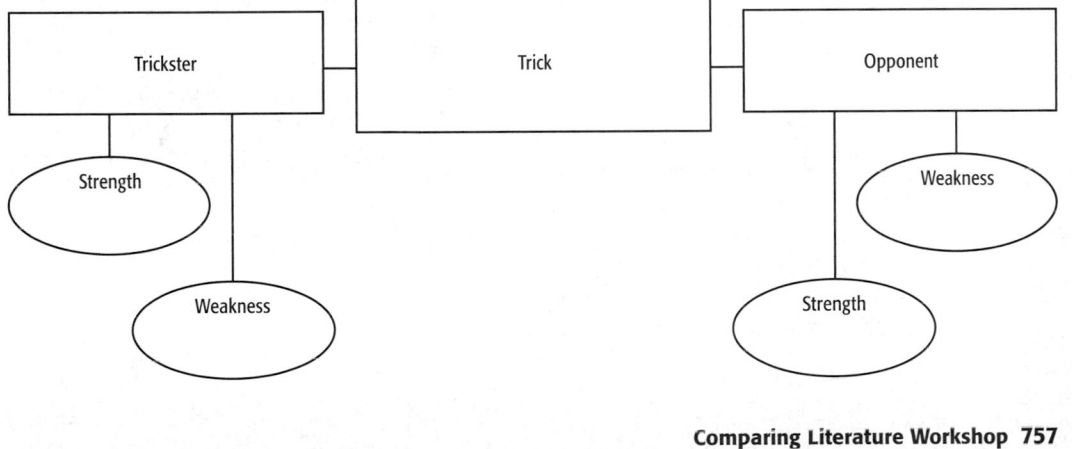

Reading/Critical Thinking

"The Toad and the Donkey"

9. Possible response: He thinks Spider will give him a great prize.

10. Possible response: Yes; Donkey was too proud and boastful.

"Doc Rabbit, Bruh Fox, and Tar Baby"

11. Possible response: He goes back up the hill to keep working on the house.

12. Responses will vary.

Writing: Compare the Literature

13. Completed charts will differ. Students may say that Toad and Doc Rabbit are most alike, because both use their brains to win in the end.

Get It On Paper

14. Possible response: Toad is the cleverest because he does all the tricking and never gets tricked.

15. Possible response: Donkey most deserves to be fooled because he thinks too much of himself.

16. Possible response: Bruh Fox least deserves to be fooled because he is working hard on the house.

17. Possible response: Toad might be a real hero because he gathers a team together to help stand up to a conceited opponent.

Close

Hold a class discussion that is based on student responses to question 17.

The Unit Challenge

Focus

BELLRINGER Options

✎ **Daily Language Practice Transparency 60**
Focus Activity Say: Think about the stories in this unit. Which hero overcame the biggest obstacles? Which hero do you admire most? Why? *(Responses will vary.)* **OL**

Teach

Group Activity: A Wall of Heroes

• Have one student in the group take notes during the group discussion and write down the finalized interview questions.

• Set aside a quiet corner in the classroom in which students can conduct interviews. Create a time limit for each interview to allow groups time to rotate.

• Have each student proofread the paragraphs. Provide art supplies students can use to design the Wall of Heroes.

• Set aside a day on which visitors can view the Wall. You may wish to send invitations and provide refreshments for a hero celebration.

Assess/Close

Group Activity

Say: Use the information on the wall to decide what makes a hero. Which hero would you most want to be like? **AS**

UNIT 6 WRAP-UP

Answering ? **The BIG Question** What Makes a Hero?

You've learned about many different types of heroes—heroes of folktale, fantasy, and myth as well as heroes in real life. Now apply what you've learned to do the Unit Challenge.

The Unit Challenge

Choose Activity A or Activity B and follow the directions for that activity.

A. Group Activity: A Wall of Heroes

With three other students, imagine that you have been hired by your school to discover the local heroes in your community. Your school has asked you to interview people about their heroes and create a wall so that everyone can learn about them.

1. **Design Interviews** Make a list of three or four people in your class that you want to interview about their heroes. Decide if you will interview each person together or if each member of your group will interview one person. Using the notes from your Foldables, write three or four questions you will ask each person about their heroes. What do you want to know aboutthe heroes?

2. **Interviews** Once you have a list of people to interview and a list of questions, it's time to do the interviews. Find a quiet place in the classroom and start your interviews. Ask your questions slowly and give people time to talk while you listen. Write down their answers. Ask people if they have pictures of their heroes they would like to put on the wall.

3. **Put the Results Together** After your interviews, put together a list of local heroes. Write a paragraph describing each hero and

attach a picture of the hero to each paragraph if you have one.

4. **Create a Wall of Heroes** Find a place in your classroom like a wall or a bulletin board to put up the paragraphs and pictures about local heroes. Design your wall so people can learn about the heroes and their accomplishments. Use markers, paints, and colored paper to make the wall look good. Invite people from your school to come and look at the Wall of Heroes.

Fruits of Expression mural inspired by American Bill of Rights, Albuquerque, New Mexico.

B. Solo Activity: A Hero for Today

The world can always use another hero. You've just read about many heroes from the past and some heroes from the present. What kind of hero do you think the world needs today?

1. **Choose a Hero** Look over your notes on the heroes you read about in this unit. Which one do you like the best? What skills did he or she use? Choose a hero for today.

2. **Bring Your Hero Alive** Think of the problems of today. Which ones would you like to solve? How could a hero help do this? Write a list of traits you want to give to your hero to help solve problems of today. Your hero can have all the traits you read about, but he or she may need new ones for today's problems. Use a web like the one below to think

of powers and skills that would help your hero solve the problem you chose.

3. **Write a Story** Write a story about how your hero helps solve the type of problems people face today. What adventures does he or she have? What powers does your hero use? How does your hero make the world a better place? Draw a picture of your hero to go with your story.

4. **Tell Your Story** Once you finish writing your story, it's time to tell it to the class. Use your best storytelling skills and bring your hero alive for your classmates by telling them about the adventures of your hero and why your hero is a hero for today.

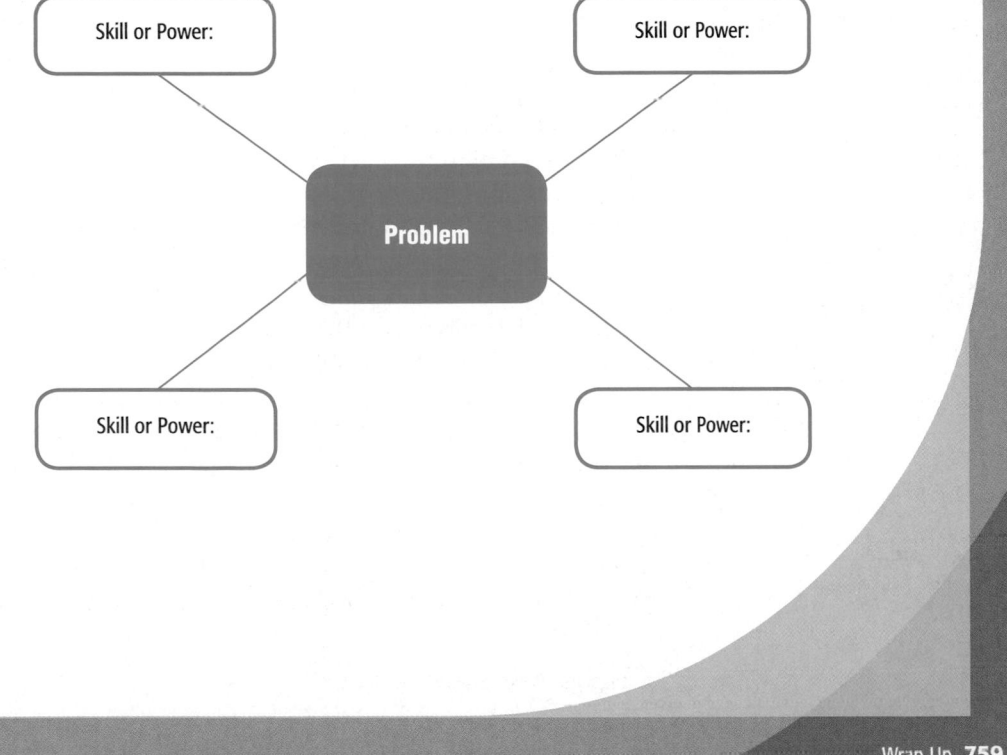

Teach

Solo Activity: A Hero Today

- Have students pick their favorite hero from the unit. Then have them decide on a name for their own hero character.

- Have students write a current problem in the center of a web. They can then write the skills and the strengths that their hero will need to solve the problem on the spokes of the web. If necessary, suggest that students make a separate web for each problem they would like their hero to solve.

- Have students use their webs as they begin writing their stories. Be sure that they proofread and edit the first draft before creating the final draft.

- Set aside a special time when students can present their stories. After the reading, authors can hold a question-and-answer session with the audience.

Assess/Close

Solo Activity

Have students turn in their webs and stories for your review. If you like, you can hold individual conferences with students to discuss what they have learned in this unit.

Objectives
- Conduct interviews
- Create a class display
- Organize information graphically
- Write and present stories

759

Focus

Vocabulary Preview
List the following words on the board:

- banned
- cumbersome
- listlessly
- trudged
- incredulously

Review their definitions before students begin reading.

Build Background
This story takes place in an imagined future world where the sun is dangerous.

- Some environmentalists say that people's lifestyles are causing *global warming.*
- This theory, called the *greenhouse effect,* says that gases released into the atmosphere are causing Earth's temperature to rise and will deplete the ozone layer, exposing the earth and its people to the sun's radiation.

Teach

L Literary Element

Setting Say: This story has two different settings. Describe them. *(Responses will vary.)* **OL**

Readability Scores
Dale-Chall: 5.9
DRP: 55
Lexile: 850

Your Turn: Read and Apply Skills

Alma Luz Villanueva

Meet the Author
Alma Luz Villanueva is a poet and novelist. She uses themes from her Mexican American and Yaqui Indian heritage, such as the Native American sense of oneness with nature. She says that the inspiration for her writing is mysterious because "when we touch the most personal, the most hidden within ourselves, we touch the universal." See page R7 of the Author Files for more about Alma Luz Villanueva.

Author Search For more about Alma Luz Villanueva, go to www.glencoe.com.

The Sand Castle

by Alma Luz Villanueva

"**H**AVE YOU DRESSED YET?" their grandmother called. "Once a month in the sun and they must almost be forced," she muttered. "Well, poor things, they've forgotten the warmth of the sun on their little bodies, what it is to play in the sea, yes. . . ." Mrs. Pavloff reached for her protective sun goggles that covered most of her face.

It screened all ultraviolet light[1] from the once life-giving sun; now, it, the sun, scorched the Earth, killing whatever it touched. The sea, the continents, had changed. The weather, as they'd called it in the last century, was entirely predictable now: warming.

Mrs. Pavloff slipped on the thick, metallic gloves, listening to her grandchildren squabble and she heard her mother's voice calling her, "Masha, put your bathing suit under your clothes. It's so much easier that way without having to go to the bathhouse first. Hurry! Father's waiting!" She remembered the ride to the sea, the silence when the first shimmers of water became visible. Her father had always been first into the chilly water. "Good for the health!" he'd yell as he dove into it, swimming as far as he could, then

L

---

1. The sun's **ultraviolet light** is invisible, and it can be harmful.

Literature Focus Lesson

Summary This story takes place in the future when Earth's ozone layer has been depleted and the sun has become a dangerous force. Whenever people go outdoors, they must wear layers of protective clothing that cover their bodies entirely. In this story, a grandmother wants her grandchildren to share some of her memories of the sea, so she takes them on an outing to build a sand castle. The story moves between the grandmother's memories of her childhood on Earth as we know it and her observations of the way her grandchildren live in the new world. **AS**

back. Then he'd lie exhausted on the sand, stretched to the sun. Such happiness to be warmed by the sun.

Then the picnic. She could hear her mother's voice, "Stay to your knees, Masha! Only to your knees!" To herself: "She'd be a mermaid if I didn't watch," and she'd laugh. Masha would lie belly down, facing the sea and let the last of the waves roll over her. She hadn't even been aware of the sun, only that she'd been warm or, if a cloud covered it, cold. It was always there, the sun: its light, its warmth. But the sea—they traveled to it. So, she'd given all of her attention to the beautiful sea.

She saw her father kneeling next to her, building the sand castle they always built when they went to the sea. Her job was to find seashells, bird feathers, and strips of seaweed to decorate it. How proud she'd felt as she placed her seashells where she chose, where they seemed most beautiful. Only then was the sand castle complete. She heard her father's voice, "The Princess's castle is ready, now, for her Prince! Come and look, Anna! What do you think?" She saw herself beaming with pride, and she heard her mother's laugh. "Fit for a queen, I'd say! Can I live in your castle, too, Masha? Please, Princess Masha?"

Analyzing the Art Does this sand castle look like the one Masha and her father built? Why or why not?

Teach

R1 Reading Skill

Activating Prior Knowledge
Ask: What do you know about mermaids? *(Possible response: mermaids live in the ocean.)* **BL Ask:** What does Masha's mother mean when she says, "She'd be a mermaid if I didn't watch."? *(Possible responses: She means that Masha might swim out too far if she didn't keep an eye on her; she might never come out of the water on her own.)* **OL**

R2 Reading Skill

Comparing and Contrasting
Ask: How was Masha's attitude toward the sun as a child different from her attitude as an adult? *(Possible response: She enjoyed the light and warmth from the sun, but she hardly paid attention to it when she was a child; now it is an overpowering and dangerous force.)* **OL**

Differentiated Instruction

Tactile Learning Some students may not be familiar with the beach and building sand castles. Invite students who are familiar with the beach to explain what it feels like to walk on sand and build shapes from wet sand. Have students work in small groups to look for pictures of sand castle designs in books, magazines, or on the Internet. Then supply groups with wet sand in large baking pans, cups, jars, pans, and other implements and have them create their own sand castles. Take pictures of the finished castles to display in the classroom. **AS**

Objectives
• Identify literary elements: setting
• Activate prior knowledge
• Compare and contrast

761

Teach

R1 Reading Skill

Clarifying Ask: What is the state of the ozone layer at the time this story takes place? What do scientists in the story predict will happen someday? *(Possible responses: The ozone layer is too thin. Scientists are predicting that banning chemicals and ending nuclear testing will help to repair it.)* **OL**

L Literary Element

Cultural Context Ask: What modern cultural phenomena do you think led the author to write this story? *(Possible responses: global warming; pollution)* **OL**

R2 Reading Skill

Predicting Ask: Do you think Masha's grandchildren will enjoy the beach as much as she did when she was a child? *(Responses will vary. Students may predict that they won't enjoy the beach quite as much because of the restrictions, but that they will probably end up enjoying building the sand castle.)* **OL**

"Of course, Mother! You can live with me always. . . . " She remembered her mother's laughing face, her auburn hair lit up by the sun, making her look bright and beautiful.

R1 The sun, the sun, the sun. The scientists were saying that with the remedies they were employing now and the remedies begun twenty years ago—they'd stopped all nuclear testing and all manufacturing of ozone-depleting² chemicals was banned³ worldwide—the scientists were saying that the sun, the global problem, would begin to get better. Perhaps for her grandchildren's children. Perhaps they would feel the sun on their unprotected bodies. Perhaps they would feel the delicious warmth of the sun.

All vehicles were solar powered. The populations took buses when they needed transportation and people emerged mainly at night. So, most human activity was conducted after the sun was gone from the sky. Those who emerged during the day wore protective clothing. Everything was built to screen the sun's light. Sometimes she missed the natural light of her childhood streaming through the windows so intensely the urge to just run outside would overtake her. She missed the birds, the wild birds.

R2 But today they were going out, outside in the daytime, when the sun was still in the sky. Masha knew they were squabbling because they hated to dress up to go outside. The clothing, the gloves, the goggles, were uncomfortable and cumbersome.⁴ She sighed, tears coming to her eyes. Well, they're coming, Masha decided. They can remove their goggles and gloves on the bus.

The sea was closer now and the bus ride was comfortable within the temperature controlled interior. Those with memories of the sea signed up, bringing grandchildren, children, friends, or just went alone. Masha had taken her grandchildren before, but they'd sat on the sand, listlessly,⁵ sifting it through their gloved hands with bored little faces. She'd tried to interest them in the sea with stories of her father swimming in it as far as he could. But they couldn't touch it, so it, the sea, didn't seem real to them. What was it: a mass of undrinkable, hostile water. Hostile like the sun. They'd taken no delight, no pleasure, in their journey to the sea.

But today, yes, today we will build a sand castle. Masha smiled at her secret. She'd packed everything late last night to surprise them at the sea.

Why haven't I thought of it before? Masha asked herself, and then she remembered the dream, months ago, of building a sand castle with her father at the sea. It made her want to weep because she'd forgotten. She'd actually forgotten one of the most joyful times of her girlhood. When the sea was still alive with life.

Today we will build a sand castle.

---

2. ***Ozone-depleting chemicals*** reduce (or "deplete") the ozone layer. This upper layer of the atmosphere protects life on earth by blocking certain kinds of harmful radiation.

3. ***Banned*** means "forbidden" or "outlawed."

4. Something that is ***cumbersome*** is hard to handle or carry because of size or weight.

5. ***Listlessly*** means "with little energy, interest, or concern."

Additional Support

Reading in the Real World

Citizenship Explain that global warming is a real problem, not something that the author made up for the story. Direct students to learn about organizations and people who are trying to save Earth's already depleted ozone layer.

While reading about global warming, students will find various opinions about the scope of the problem and how to fix it. Have students present persuasive speeches about what they think should be done about global warming. **AL**

Beach Scene. Charles-Garabed Atamian (1913–1942). Private collection.

They trudged[6] on the thick, dense sand toward the hiss of pale blue. Only the older people picked up their step, excited by the smell of salt in the air. Masha's grandchildren knew they'd be here for two hours and then trudge all the way back to the bus. The darkened goggles made the sunlight bearable. They hated this forlorn place where the sun had obviously drained the life out of everything. They were too young to express it, but they felt it as they walked, with bored effort, beside their grandmother.

"We're going to build a sand castle today—what do you think of that?" Masha beamed, squinting to see their faces.

"What's a sand castle?" the boy mumbled.

"You'll see, I'll show you. . . ."

"Is it fun, Grandmama?" the girl smiled, taking her grandmother's hand.

"Yes, it's so much fun. I've brought different sized containers to mold the sand, and, oh, you'll see!"

The boy gave an awkward skip and nearly shouted, "Show us, Grandmama, show us what you mean!"

---

6. *Trudged* means "walked steadily but with great effort."

Teach

L Literary Element

Theme Ask: What is the theme, or message, of the story so far? *(Possible responses: The future world is harsh because people have destroyed the planet; Masha misses the old world and wants her grandchildren to experience at least some of its pleasures.)* **OL**

R Reading Skill

Comparing and Contrasting
Say: Think about the grandchildren's attitudes at the beginning of the story. How have they changed? Compare the grandchildren's feelings about the sand castle to Masha's. *(Possible responses: At first, they do not want to go to the beach; now that they are building the sand castle, they are excited to be there. The grandchildren are beginning to see, like Masha, how special a sand castle can be.)* **OL**

Differentiated Instruction

Illustration As students gather details about the story, have them draw pictures of the way they imagine each character and the setting. **AS** Or, have students create a brochure with pictures and text that explains the safety precautions one would have to take in a world without an ozone layer. Have them work in small groups or pairs, using the library or Internet to gather information on protection from the sun's harmful rays and contaminated water. When students are finished creating their pictures or brochures, arrange the work in a classroom display. **AL**

Objectives
• Identify literary elements: cultural context, theme
• Make predictions
• Compare and contrast
• Clarify ideas and text

763

Teach

L Literary Element

Setting Ask: What clues does the author use to indicate the futuristic setting of the story? *(Possible responses: People can't have picnics; there are no wild birds and no eagles; the water is dangerous.)* **OL**

Masha laughed, sounding almost like a girl. "We're almost there, yes, we're almost there!"

The first circle of sandy shapes was complete, and the children were so excited by what they were building they forgot about their protective gloves.

"Now, we'll put a pile of wet sand in the middle and build it up with our hands and then we'll do another circle, yes, children?"

The children rushed back and forth from the tide line carrying the dark, wet sand. They only had an hour left. Their eyes, beneath the goggles, darted with excitement.

"Just don't get your gloves in the water, a little wet sand won't hurt, don't worry, children. When I was a girl there were so many birds at the sea we'd scare them off because they'd try to steal our food.

Seagulls, they were, big white birds that liked to scream at the sea, they sounded like eagles to me. . . ."

"You used to eat at the sea, Grandmama?" the girl asked incredulously.[7]

"We used to call them picnics. . . ."

"What are eagles, Grandmama?" the boy wanted to know, shaping the dark sand with his gloved hands.

"They used to be one of the largest, most beautiful wild birds in the world. My grandfather pointed them out to me once. . . ." Until that moment, she'd forgotten that memory of nearly sixty years ago. They'd gone on a train, then a bus, to the village where he'd been born. She remembered her grandfather looking up toward a shrill, piercing cry that seemed to come from the sky. She'd seen the tears in

---

7. *Incredulously* (in KREJ uh lus lee) means "having a hard time believing."

Additional Support

English Language Coach

Context Clues Write the following sentences on the board:

1. They trudged on the thick, <u>dense</u> sand.
2. They hated this <u>forlorn</u> place where the sun had obviously drained the life out of everything.
3. Their eyes <u>darted</u> with excitement.
4. She remembered her grandfather

looking up to a shrill, <u>piercing</u> cry that seemed to come from the sky.

Have students copy these sentences. Ask them to circle any words that give them clues to the meanings of the underlined words and to use those clues to write brief definitions of the underlined words. **EL**

Teach

L Literary Element

Theme Ask: What is the main message at the end of the story? *(Possible response: People may have almost destroyed the planet, but there is hope for the future.)* **OL**

BQ BIG Question

Ask: What qualities does Masha have that make her character heroic? *(Possible responses: She is optimistic and loving; she cares about the earth; she wants her grandchildren to be happy; she believes in a bright future.)* **OL**

her grandfather's eyes and on his cheeks. He'd pointed up to a large, dark flying-thing in the summer blue sky: "That's an eagle, my girl, the spirit of the people."

Sadness overtook Masha, but she refused to acknowledge its presence. The sand castle, Masha told herself sternly—the sand castle is what is important now. "I've brought a wonderful surprise, something to decorate the sand castle with when we're through building it."

"Show us, Grandmama, please?"

"Yes, please, please show us now!"

Masha sighed with a terrible, sudden happiness as she brought out the plastic bag. Quickly, she removed each precious shell from its protective cotton: eight perfect shells from all over the world.

"But Grandmama, theses are your special shells! You said the sea doesn't make them **BQ** anymore. . . ."

"It will, Anna, it will." Masha hugged her granddaughter and made her voice brighten with laughter. "Today we will decorate our sand castle with the most beautiful shells in the world, yes!" ○

Literature Focus Lesson

Science Fiction Remind students that a story's theme is its main idea, or the message the author wants to communicate to the readers. Science fiction themes often show the outcome, for a person or for humankind, of right and wrong decisions. For example, a story might show a world without fresh water and tell about a time when governments wouldn't pass laws to protect the rivers. Seeing the author's view of the future sometimes causes readers to look differently at today's world. Discuss the selection's message with students. Have them work in small groups to write their own science fiction stories. Ask volunteers to present their stories to the class. **OL**

Objectives
- Identify literary elements: setting, theme
- Analyze features of genres: science fiction
- Understand context clues

765

Suggest to students that they choose a special place and time each day to do their independent reading. It may be under a tree in the afternoon, in a corner of the library, or in bed at night before going to sleep, but it should be a quiet place with few distractions.

Fiction

Tell students that reading fictional stories can teach them as much about what makes a hero as reading nonfiction can. A fictional character can become a hero by standing up to a bully, overcoming an obstacle, or simply working to improve his or her own character.

Invite students to share an example of a fictional story they have read that made them think about what it takes to be a hero.

UNIT 6
Reading on Your Own

To read more about the Big Question, choose one of these books from your school or local library. Work on your reading skills by choosing books that are challenging to you.

Fiction

Aesop's Fables
Aesop, adapted by Jerry Pinkney

This collection includes brief retellings of more than sixty of Aesop's fables. Read this entertaining batch of retellings to find human flaws in animal forms and to learn the source of sayings like, "Don't count your chickens before they hatch."

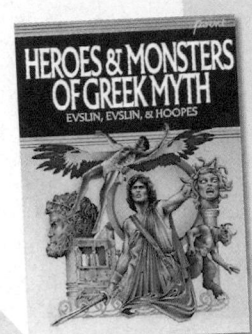

Heroes & Monsters of Greek Myth
by Bernard Evslin

Want to know how Perseus slays the Medusa, or how the Minotaur devours its victims? Ever wonder how the very-married Zeus juggles so many girlfriends? If so, check out this classic collection of great Greek myths.

Anansi the Spider: A Tale from the Ashanti
by Gerald McDermott

Anansi the Spider, the wise and mischievous hero of traditional folktales of Ghana, got into all sorts of trouble but was saved by his six sons. Read to find out how Anansi decides which son to reward with a very special gift.

The Call of the Wild
by Jack London

This classic book relates the adventures of a dog named Buck. When Buck is kidnapped from his comfortable California home—and forced to work as a sled dog in the Yukon gold rush of the late 1800s—he doesn't know what lies ahead. Follow Buck as he fights to survive out in the big, wide world.

Additional Support

Differentiated Instruction

 Use the Glencoe BookLink CD-ROM to create customized reading lists to help students answer the Big Question. Suggestions for Unit 6:
Grade 4: *The People Could Fly* by Virginia Hamilton
Grade 5: *The Greek Gods* by Bernard and Dorothy Evslin

Grade 6: *The Hero and the Crown* by Robin McKinley
Grade 7: *Dragondrums* by Anne McCaffrey
Grade 8: *Una Linda Raza: Cultural and Artistic Traditions of the Hispanic Southwest* by Angel Vigil

Nonfiction

Old Hickory: Andrew Jackson and the American People
by Albert Marrin

Andrew Jackson lacked formal schooling, but that didn't stand between him and success. Known for his fierce intelligence and stubborn disposition, Jackson excelled as a solider, a lawyer, a judge, and a president. Read to learn more about the man history calls "Old Hickory."

The Civil Rights Movement for Kids
by Mary Turck

This is a complete history of the civil rights movement in the United States in the twentieth century. Read to learn what it was like to live under discrimination laws and how the struggle for freedom and equality changed the country.

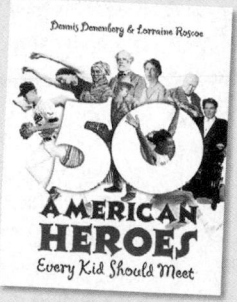

50 American Heroes Every Kid Should Meet
by Dennis Denenberg and Lorraine Roscoe

This book contains short biographies of famous people from various eras and fields of accomplishment. Read to learn about such heroes as Susan B. Anthony, Frederick Douglass, Cesar Chavez, Dolores Huerta, Bill Cosby, John Glenn, and Harriet Tubman.

Martin Luther King, Jr.
by Amy Pastan

This biography tells the story of the man who was at the forefront of the fight for racial justice in the United States during the 1950s and 1960s. Read to understand the nonviolent methods that Dr. King used to fight oppression and inequality.

Nonfiction
Tell students that all of the books on this page are nonfiction. The authors of the books tell about the lives of American heroes and the people and events that influenced them.

Biography
Ask: Why might reading one or more of these biographies help you find out more about what it means to be a hero? *(Possible response: The books are about real people who have real problems.)* Students may identify with one or more of the subjects as they tell how their lives have been shaped by people, experiences, and events around them. **AS**

About the subjects
Real-life civil rights leader Martin Luther King Jr. and former President Andrew Jackson model the way that challenge and adversity can shape people and make them stronger. Students will also learn about other American figures who emerged from adversity stronger and wiser. The folktales and fables on the preceding page will allow students to see how other cultures identify heroes.

Test-Taking Tips

TIP Remind students to read all directions carefully. Understanding the directions can prevent making mistakes. Encourage students to ask for help if they have questions about the directions.

TIP Tell students to answer the easier items first. By skipping the hard items, they will have time to answer all of the easy ones first. Then, in the time that is left, they can return to the items they skipped.

Test Practice

Part 1: Literary Elements

1. A
2. C
3. C
4. D

Test Practice

Part 1: Literary Elements

On a separate sheet of paper, write the numbers 1–4. Next to each, write the letter of the correct answer for that question.

Read the following passage and use it to answer questions 1 and 2.

When Hank rode into town, the streets were empty, but a group of men had gathered outside the sheriff's office. Hank tied his horse to a hitching post and stepped up onto the wooden sidewalk.

"Howdy," he said, nodding at the men, none of whom wore the star-shaped badge he was looking for. "Is the sheriff inside?"

"We don't have a sheriff these days," replied one man. "Vic Morrison ran him right out of town."

Hank hooked his thumbs in his belt and looked out at the deserted street. "Is Morrison still around?"

"Sure is," said the tallest of the group. "He's over at the café with some of his men. They've pretty much taken over the town. With no sheriff, the law-abiding folks around here don't have much of a chance."

"We'll see about that," said Hank softly. He took off his hat, smoothed his hair, and replaced the hat firmly. "We'll just see."

---

1. Which of the following is a clue to what the setting of this story is?
   A. "The streets were empty . . ."
   B. "Hank tied his horse to a hitching post . . ."
   C. "Hank hooked his thumbs in his belt . . ."
   D. "He took off his hat, smoothed his hair . . ."

2. If Hank turns out to be the hero of this story, that will be because he
   A. is a stranger in town.
   B. is friendly and polite.
   C. has confidence in himself.
   D. demonstrates strength and bravery.

3. The theme of this story is **most** likely to have something to do with the importance of
   A. love.
   B. patience.
   C. courage.
   D. hard work.

4. It be most important for you to learn about the cultural context of
   A. a short story written in the 1960s.
   B. a poem written last year by someone you know.
   C. a news article about jazz, written ten years ago.
   D. a Native American myth from hundreds of years ago.

Objectives (pp. 768–769)
Reading Activate prior knowledge • Make predictions • Compare and contrast
Literature Identify key literary elements: setting, hero, cultural context, theme

Part 2: Reading Skills

On a separate sheet of paper, write the numbers 1–4. Next to each number, write the letter of the correct answer for that question.

Story 1: A crow who was dying of thirst saw a pitcher and flew to it, hoping to get a drink. He found only a few inches of water at the bottom. Because the pitcher was tall and narrow, the crow could not get to the water. He was desperate, but nothing he tried was successful. Finally, he collected stones and dropped them, one by one, into the pitcher. This caused the water to rise until it was at a height he could reach, thus saving his life.

Story 2: A fox saw a crow steal a bit of cheese and settle in a tree with the cheese in his beak. The fox walked up to the tree and said, "How handsome you look, Crow! Your feathers are so glossy and your eyes so bright. If your voice were also beautiful, you would surely be considered the King of Birds." Then the crow opened his beak to let out his best "Caw, caw, caw," which is as close as any crow can come to singing. The cheese dropped to the ground, and the fox quickly snapped it up.

1. Imagine that while you were reading Story 2, you didn't understand why the crow tried to sing. In this case, it would be most helpful to activate your prior knowledge about
   A. how animals react to cheese.
   B. common reactions to flattery.
   C. what a beautiful bird song sounds like.
   D. what glossy feathers and bright eyes look like.

2. In which story does the crow get what he wants?
   A. Story 1
   B. Story 2
   C. Both stories
   D. Neither story

3. In which story does an animal behave cleverly?
   A. Story 1
   B. Story 2
   C. Both stories
   D. Neither story

4. Imagine that Story 2 went on to say: "A few weeks later, the crow met the same fox again. But, this time, the crow was ready for him." What would be *most* likely to happen next?
   A. The fox would trick the crow again.
   B. The fox would be unable to trick the crow.
   C. The fox would give some cheese to the crow.
   D. The fox and the crow would become friends.

Part 2: Reading Skills
1. B
2. A
3. C
4. B

Resources for pages 768–771

Use these resources to review, assess, or reteach the Unit: Active Learning and Note Taking Guide, Selection and Unit Assessments, ExamView Assessment Suite, and Skill Level Up!™ A Language Arts Game

Test-Taking Tips

TIP Tell students to read the first question carefully and make sure they understand it. Then have them read all of the responses before selecting one. That way they can eliminate the responses that are clearly incorrect and focus on only those that might be correct.

TIP If students run into an unfamiliar word on a test, sometimes they will be able to get an idea of its meaning if they focus on its parts.

Part 3: Vocabulary Skills

1. B
2. D
3. C
4. A
5. C
6. C
7. A
8. A
9. B

Part 3: Vocabulary Skills

On a separate sheet of paper, write the numbers 1–9. Next to each number, write the letter of the correct answer for that question.

For questions 1–5, write the letter of the word or phrase that means about the same as the underlined word.

1. to acknowledge a fact

   A. hide   **C.** understand
   B. admit   **D.** worry about

2. the ominous sounds

   A. loud   **C.** interesting
   B. funny   **D.** threatening

3. to be a tyrant

   A. hero   **C.** cruel ruler
   B. winner   **D.** spoiled child

4. such tedious work

   A. boring   **C.** difficult
   B. important   **D.** dangerous

5. to express remorse

   A. excitement   **C.** guilty regret
   B. deep anger   **D.** determination

Choose the correct answer for each question.

6. What do the following words have in common?

   banana macaroni karate rodeo

   A. They come from names.
   B. They are very new words.
   C. They are borrowed words.
   D. They can be used as nouns or verbs.

7. Which of the following words is a compound word?

   A. shoelace   **C.** moustache
   B. preschool   **D.** subscription

8. What is the "etymology" of a word?

   A. its history
   B. its spelling
   C. its pronunciation
   D. its part of speech

9. Which of the following is most likely a true statement about the word e-mail?

   A. It comes from a person's name.
   B. It is a recent addition to the language.
   C. It was borrowed from another language.
   D. It came into the language during the Civil War.

Objectives (pp. 770–771)
Vocabulary Explore word histories • Identify word origins • Identify borrowed words
Grammar Identify sentence types • Use correct punctuation
Writing Use key elements: voice

Part 4: Writing Skills

On a separate sheet of paper, write the numbers 1–7. Next to each number, write the letter of the correct answer for that question.

1. Which of the following is a simple sentence?
   - **A.** A long walk on the beach.
   - **B.** Rabbits ate all the petunias.
   - **C.** Max got there early, but Lucy was late.
   - **D.** When Jessie and Max arrive with food.

2. Which of the following is a compound sentence?
   - **A.** Delia and Jeremy argued for hours.
   - **B.** When I was younger, I didn't like swimming.
   - **C.** They were late, and the train left without them.
   - **D.** I threw a stick for my dog to catch and bring back.

3. Which of the following is a complex sentence?
   - **A.** Tigers live in India, not Africa.
   - **B.** If you feel sick, you should stay home.
   - **C.** She dropped off the book and came home.
   - **D.** Rita hit a fly ball, and Rafael scored from third.

4. Which sentence is punctuated correctly?
   - **A.** We had sandwiches, and some fruit.
   - **B.** If there's enough food, I'd like another helping.
   - **C.** I don't enjoy being outdoors, when it's really cold.
   - **D.** Nobody knew what to do, before the ambulance arrived.

5. Which sentence is punctuated correctly?
   - **A.** That's the man, that I saw before.
   - **B.** If Sam helps me I'll get my work done faster.
   - **C.** When people tell lies, life can be very confusing!
   - **D.** The movie had already started, when we got there.

6. Which of the following is a run-on sentence?
   - **A.** Cheri walks to school so does Marcella.
   - **B.** Nobody is sure about what the answer is.
   - **C.** I wish I knew what to do, but I'm just not sure.
   - **D.** Don't be rude, but do try to keep the conversation short.

7. What does it mean to describe a piece of writing as having "a clear voice"?
   - **A.** A reader can tell what the writer is like.
   - **B.** A reader can easily understand the writing.
   - **C.** The writer has included a great deal of dialogue.
   - **D.** The writer has used correct spelling and punctuation.

Part 4: Writing Skills

1. B
2. C
3. B
4. B
5. C
6. A
7. B

Skills Scope and Sequence

Readability Scores Key
Dale-Chall/DRP/Lexile

PACING (DAYS)		INSTRUCTIONAL SEGMENT LITERATURE	READING SKILLS	LITERARY ELEMENTS
STANDARD	BLOCK			
1	1	**Unit Warm-Up, pp. 774–781** Genre Focus: Historical Fiction and Nonfiction "The Great Radio Scare" **6.7/67/1200**, SE p. 776	Synthesizing, SE pp. 776, 777 Determining Main Idea and Supporting Details, SE pp. 776, 778 Evaluating, SE pp. 776, 779, TWE p. 778 Taking and Reviewing Notes, SE pp. 776, 780 Connecting, TWE p. 774 How to Read Historical Fiction and Nonfiction, TWE p. 776 Fluency, TWE p. 779	Symbol, SE pp. 776, 777 Narrator, SE pp. 776, 780 Description, SE pp. 776, 781 Time Order/Sequence, SE pp. 776, 781
3	2	**Reading Workshop 1, pp. 782–813** "The Gold Cadillac" by Mildred D. Taylor **3.9/47/780**, SE p. 784 "Nadia the Willful" by Sue Alexander **7.6/54/900**, SE p. 804	Synthesizing, SE pp. 782, 785, 788, 793, 796, 797, 798, 801, 805, 807, TWE pp. 783, 791 Drawing Conclusions, SE pp. 794, 795, 800, 809, 811 Connecting, TWE pp. 785, 805 Fluency, TWE pp. 788, 793, 806	Symbol, SE pp. 785, 786, 787, 788, 790, 793, 794, 796, TWE pp. 791, 798, 799, 800 Plot, SE pp. 805, 806, 807, 808, 810, 811
1		**Writing Workshop, Part 1, pp. 814–817** Writing Product: Personal Narrative	Fluency, TWE p. 816	Narrator, TWE p. 814
3	1	**Reading Workshop 2, pp. 818–839** "The Bracelet" by Yoshiko Uchida **4.7/51/830**, SE p. 820	Determining Main Idea and Supporting Details, SE pp. 818, 821, 823, 825, 827, 831, 833, 834, TWE pp. 819, 822, 836	Narrator, SE pp. 821, 822, 823, 824, 826, 831, 832, 834, 836 Review Plot, TWE p. 832

Unit 7 Big Question

Addressing the Big Question "What can we learn from our mistakes?" will help students learn how to handle their mistakes, and also how to learn lessons from them.

Unit 7 Genre

Historical fiction uses imagination to create realistic depictions of true time periods, and historical nonfiction tells true stories of people and events in real places and times. These historical selections will help your students answer the Big Question: "What can we learn from our mistakes?"

CRITICAL THINKING	VOCABULARY	WRITING AND GRAMMAR	LISTENING, SPEAKING, AND VIEWING
	English Language Coach, TWE p. 777		Viewing the Photo, TWE pp. 772, 778
Infer, SE pp. 802, 812 Conclude, SE p. 802 Visualize, SE p. 812 Respond, SE p. 812 Compare and Contrast, SE p. 812 Evaluation, SE p. 812, TWE p. 797 Analysis, TWE pp. 789, 792, 799, 808 Comprehension, TWE pp. 795, 798	Academic Vocabulary, SE p. 782 Base Words and Roots, SE pp. 784, 790, 794, 804, 806, 809, TWE pp. 786, 787 Word Map, TWE p. 784 English Language Coach, TWE p. 797 Parts of Speech, TWE p. 804	Write About Your Reading, SE pp. 802, 812 Finding the Verb, SE pp. 803, 813	Analyzing the Painting, SE pp. 789, 792 Analyzing the Photo, SE pp. 796, 799
		Prewriting, SE p. 815 Drafting, SE p. 815 Applying Good Writing Traits: Voice, SE p. 816 Subject-Verb Agreement, SE p. 817 Organization, TWE p. 815	
Infer, SE pp. 828, 838 Interpret, SE pp. 828, 838 Evaluation, SE p. 828, TWE p. 836	Academic Vocabulary, SE p. 818 Latin Roots, SE pp. 820, 823, 826, 830, 833 Vocabulary File Quiz, TWE p. 820	Subjects Separated from Verbs, SE p. 829 Writing About Your Reading, SE p. 838 Agreements with Compounds, SE p. 839	Analyzing the Photo, SE pp. 824, 826 Talk About Your Reading, SE p. 828

Readability Scores Key
Dale-Chall/DRP/Lexile

PACING (DAYS)		INSTRUCTIONAL SEGMENT LITERATURE	READING SKILLS	LITERARY ELEMENTS
STANDARD	BLOCK			
	cont'd.	**"Too Soon a Woman"** by Dorothy M. Johnson **5.0/50/730**, SE p. 830	Clarifying, SE p. 825 Interpreting, SE pp. 833, 834, TWE p. 835 Fluency, TWE pp. 821, 827, 834	
3	2	**Reading Workshop 3, pp. 840–865** "President Cleveland, Where Are You?" by Robert Cormier **6.4/59/1040**, SE p. 842 "Nobody's Perfect" by David Fischer from Sports Illustrated for Kids **5.2/53/790**, SE p. 858	Evaluating, SE pp. 840, 843, 845, 846, 848, 851, 855, 859, 861, 862, TWE pp. 841, 847, 852, 853, 860 Monitoring Comprehension, SE pp. 850, 855 Questioning, SE p. 852 Predicting, SE pp. 853, 854 Fluency, TWE pp. 853, 861	Description, SE pp. 843, 844, 847, 848, 851, 859, 860, 863, TWE pp. 845, 853
1		**Writing Workshop, Part 2, pp. 866–869** Writing Product: Personal Narrative	Fluency, TWE p. 867	
2	1	**Reading Workshop 4, pp. 870–893** "The Shutout" by Patricia C. McKissack & Frederick McKissack, Jr. **9.3/67/1270**, SE p. 872 "The Talking Skull" by Donna L. Washington **4.8/50/700**, SE p. 882	Inferring, SE pp. 870, 873, 874, 877, 884, 886, 889, TWE p. 871 Evaluating, SE pp. 879, 890 Activating Prior Knowledge, TWE pp. 874, 884	Sequence of Events/Time Order, SE pp. 873, 875, 876, 877, 878, 883, 886, TWE p. 888
2	2	**Reading Across Texts Workshop, pp. 894–909** from The Great Fire by Jim Murphy **7.4/63/1150**, p. 896 "Letters About the Fire" by Justin, and Fannie Belle Becker **5.9/54/1520**, SE p. 904	Identifying Main Idea and Supporting Details, TWE pp. 897, 899 Fluency, TWE pp. 897, 900, 907 Evaluating, TWE pp. 900, 901, 903 Synthesizing, TWE p. 907	Author's Credibility, SE pp. 894, 897, 899, 901, 903, 905, 906, TWE p. 907 Description, TWE pp. 897, 898, 906 Sequence of Events / Time Order, TWE p. 902
2	1	**Unit Wrap-Up, pp. 910-919** **Your Turn:** "A Lesson in Courtesy" by Stan Sakai SE p. 912	Evaluating, TWE pp. 913, 915, 918 Identifying Main Idea and Supporting Details, TWE pp. 916, 919	Description, TWE pp. 914, 918 Sequence of Events, TWE p. 915 Symbol, TWE p. 919

CRITICAL THINKING	VOCABULARY	WRITING AND GRAMMAR	LISTENING, SPEAKING, AND VIEWING
Analysis, SE p. 838, TWE pp. 822, 824 Synthesis, TWE p. 837	English Language Coach, TWE pp. 823, 833 Vocabulary, TWE p. 830		Analyzing the Art, SE p. 835 Viewing the Art, TWE p. 825
Recall, SE p. 856 Infer, SE pp. 856, 864 Interpret, SE p. 856 Evaluate, SE pp. 856, 864 Draw Conclusions, SE p. 864 Comprehension, TWE pp. 848, 854, 860, 862 Analysis, TWE p. 852	Academic Vocabulary, SE p. 840 Greek Roots, SE pp. 842, 846, 849, 854, 858, 860, TWE pp. 843, 859	Write About Your Reading, SE pp. 856, 864 Subject-Verb Agreement with Here and There Sentence Beginnings, SE p. 857 Subject-Verb Agreement in Inverted Sentences, SE p. 865	Analyzing the Photo, SE pp. 847, 848 Viewing the Photo, TWE p. 844
Analysis, TWE p. 868 Evaluation, TWE p. 868		Revision, TWE p. 866 Dialogue, TWE p. 867 Voice, TWE p. 868	News Report, SE p. 869 Listening, Speaking and Viewing, TWE p. 869
Infer, SE pp. 880, 892 Connect, SE pp. 880, 892 Synthesize, SE p. 880 Comprehension, TWE pp. 876, 879, 886, 888 Analysis, TWE pp. 877, 884, 889, 890	Academic Vocabulary, SE p. 870 Anglo-Saxon Origins, SE p. 872 Anglo-Saxon Roots, SE pp. 882, 891, TWE pp. 883, 886, 888 Unlock Meaning, TWE p. 872 Connotations, TWE p. 882 Suffixes, TWE p. 890	Write About Your Reading, SE pp. 880, 892 Subject-Verb Agreement with Special Nouns, SE p. 881 Subject-Verb Agreement with Indefinite Pronouns, SE p. 893	Analyzing the Art, SE p. 876 Viewing the Photo, TWE p. 878 Viewing the Illustration, TWE pp. 885, 887
Recall, SE p. 909 Evaluate, SE p. 909 Infer, SE p. 909 Draw Conclusion, SE p. 909 Comprehension, TWE p. 901	Vocabulary Connections, TWE p. 896 English Language Coach, TWE p. 903 Verb Tenses, TWE p. 904		Analyzing the Art, SE pp. 898, 907 Viewing the Art, TWE p. 901
Comprehension, TWE p. 913	English Language Coach, TWE p. 913		

Reading with Purpose offers a comprehensive package of tools to optimize student learning and the teaching experience. Each resource has been designed to assist students in specific areas and to offer instructional support for teachers. While all of these areas are covered in the core textbook, some students may need extra practice or additional help in specific areas. The resource package is designed so that you, the teacher, can choose which items will best assist your students. You may also use these resources as homework assignments and for assessment purposes. The following are resources recommended for use with Unit 7.

Keys for Unit Resources

- Blackline Master
- Workbook
- Supplemental Text
- CD-ROM
- DVD
- Transparency
- Web-based
- Fast File

Essential Instructional Support

FAST FILE UNIT 7 RESOURCES

Reading and Literature
- Academic Vocabulary Review
- Big Question: School to Home
- The Big Question Foldable
- Unit Challenge: Planner and Rubrics
- Reading Across Texts Graphic Organizer
- Key Reading Skills
- Active Reading Graphic Organizers
- Literary Analysis
- Unit Vocabulary Review

Writing, Grammar, and Spelling
- Spelling and Handwriting Practice
- Grammar Practice
- Writing Workshop Graphic Organizer

Listening, Speaking, and Viewing
- Viewing and Representing
- Listening and Speaking

English Language Learners
- English Language Coach Review

DIFFERENTIATED INSTRUCTION

- Leveled Vocabulary Development
- Skill Level Up!™ A Language Arts Game
- Listening Library CD
- BookLink 3
- Literature Library Vocabulary Puzzlemaker
- Vocabulary Puzzlemaker

ASSESSMENT

GLENCOE'S ASSESSMENT ADVANTAGE

- Selection and Unit Assessments
- Selection Quick Checks
- Assessment by Learning Objectives
- Rubrics for Assessing Student Writing, Listening, and Speaking
- Glencoe Online Essay Grader
- Interactive Tutor: Self-Assessment
- ExamView Assessment Suite
- Literature Library ExamView Assessment Suite

Additional Instructional Support

WRITING, GRAMMAR, AND SPELLING

- Real Success in Writing: Research and Reports
- Writing Constructed Responses
- Spelling Power eWorkbook
- Grammar & Composition Handbook
- Grammar and Language Workbook
- Revising with Style eWorkbook

READING AND LITERATURE

- Active Learning and Note Taking Guide
- inTime Magazines
- Backpack Reader Volume 1
- Literature Library
- Literature Launchers Pre-Reading Videos DVD
- Literature Classics

TRANSPARENCIES

- Read Aloud, Think Aloud Transparencies
- Literary and Text Analysis Transparencies
- Bellringer Options Transparencies
- Grammar and Writing Workshop Transparencies
- Fine Art Transparencies

TECHNOLOGY

- TeacherWorks Plus™
- StudentWorks Plus™
- BookLink 3
- Skill Level Up!™ A Language Arts Game
- ExamView Assessment Suite
- Interactive Tutor: Self-Assessment
- Listening Library CD
- Spanish Listening Library CD
- Literature Classics
- Literature Launchers Pre-Reading Videos DVD
- Literature Library ExamView Assessment Suite
- Vocabulary Puzzlemaker
- Literature Library Vocabulary Puzzlemaker
- glencoe.com
- Online Student Edition
- Presentation Plus!
- Glencoe Online Essay Grader

ENGLISH LANGUAGE LEARNER

- English Language Coach
- Fluency Practice and Assessment
- inTime Magazines (Spanish)
- Spanish Listening Library CD

PROFESSIONAL DEVELOPMENT

- Professional Development Package

Additional Glencoe Resources

Dinah Zike's Foldables

Foldables are three-dimensional, interactive graphic organizers that help students practice basic writing skills, review key vocabulary terms, and answer Big Questions. Every unit contains a foldable activity. You can find the pattern and directions for the Unit 7 Foldable in the Unit 7 Resources Fast Files booklet. You can use the foldables as they are presented or modify them to suit the needs of your students. More information about foldables for Unit 7 can be found on pages R8–R9.

Glencoe Literature Library

This collection of hardcover books includes full-length novels, novellas, plays, and works of nonfiction. Each volume consists of at least one complete extended-length reading accompanied by several related readings from a broad range of genres. A separate Study Guide for each Glencoe Literature Library book provides teaching notes and reproducible activity pages for students.

Glencoe Literature Library titles that complement this unit include:

The Summer of the Swans, by Betsy Byars
Tuck Everlasting, by Natalie Babbitt
The View from Saturday, E. L. Konigsburg

For a wealth of online resources that support the instruction in Unit 7 of *Glencoe Literature: Reading with Purpose,* students and teachers can visit our Web site at www.glencoe.com. Students will find additional learning, practice, and assessment opportunities such as these, which are noted in the student text:

- **Big Question Overview**
- **Study Central**
- **Author Search**
- **Writing Models**
- **Interactive Literary Elements Handbook**
- **Web Activities**

Teachers will find planning and instructional tools that include the following:

- **Book Lesson Plans**
- **Teacher Forum**
- **Professional Development**
- **Web Activities Lesson Plans (with answers to student activities)**

Go to www.glencoe.com to see the entire selection of Reading with Purpose online resources.

Use the Glencoe **BookLink 3** CD-ROM, a database of more than 26,700 titles, to *create customized reading lists* for your students.

- Search for award-winning titles, (e.g., Newbery Award winners, Coretta Scott King Award winners, and Caldecott Medal winners) and for books on several state-recommended reading lists.
- Find Degrees of Reading Power™ (DRP) and Lexile™ readability scores for all selections.
- Organize reading lists by students' reading level, author, genre, theme, or area of interest.
- Get a brief summary of each selection.

You can find recommended leveled readings for this unit with Reading on Your Own (see page 920).

Glencoe's **Presentation Plus!**, a multimedia teaching tool, lets you present dynamic lessons that will engage your students. Using Microsoft PowerPoint,® you can customize the presentations to create your own personalized lessons. Use **CheckPoint** questions with interactive response keypads to get immediate student feedback during lessons, to increase student participation, and to assess student comprehension.

A lively collection of articles drawn from issues of the TIME family of magazines helps students develop the skills they need to interact with informational text in a meaningful way. Each of the news stories, feature articles, reviews, profiles, and essays in the magazine connect to an author, work, or theme in *Glencoe Literature: Reading with Purpose.* Articles for Unit 7 are found in Volume B. See the *inTIME* Teacher's Guide for specific connections to each unit and for reproducible student worksheets designed to develop students' reading and critical thinking skills.

Literature Launchers

Set the scene with Glencoe's Literature Launchers, engaging video segments that introduce each unit's genre focus. Each video brings the genre to life, relating it to your students' worlds.

Insert the Glencoe Literature Launchers Pre-Reading Videos DVD into your DVD player. Select the Unit 7 Launcher from the menu to introduce the genre and Big Question for this unit.

Online Essay Grader

Use Glencoe's Online Essay Grader to score your students' writing and to provide individualized feedback to each student automatically.

You and your students can visit www.glencoe.com to link to the essay grader. *Students* can enter their essays and receive feedback on demand. *You* can manage demographic data, assign tests and generate individual student and aggregated reports. The essay grader can help you

- Save time with automatic scoring and individualized feedback.
- Supplement in-class writing instruction using guided writing practice.
- Get reports for individual students or for special populations.
- Track student improvement over time.

REAL Success: Reading Excellence at All Levels

Glencoe now provides all of your students with the tools they need to become better, more enthusiastic readers. The REAL Success suite of reading and language arts products encourages reading excellence by meeting the needs of students at all levels. Glencoe products that can be used in conjunction with Unit 7 include the following:

- Jamestown Literature: An Adapted Reader
- Jamestown *Reading Fluency*
- Jamestown *Critical Reading Series, In the Line of Duty*
- *Vocabulary Builder*
- *The Glencoe Reader, Course 1*

To order these products, call Glencoe at 1-800-USA-READ.

Teacher Wraparound Edition Key

Level Appropriate Code

AS = Activities for all students

AL = Activities for students working above grade level

OL = Activities for students working at grade level

BL = Activities for students working below grade level

EL = Activities for English language learners

Teacher Wraparound Prompts

R Reading Skill These activities help you teach reading comprehension skills.

V Vocabulary These activities help students comprehend words and incorporate them into their reading and writing.

C Critical Thinking These strategies help students apply and extend what they have learned.

BQ BIG Question These activities and questions prompt students to prepare to answer the Big Question.

W Writing These activities provide writing opportunities to help students practice writing and comprehend text.

L Literary Element These activities and questions help students comprehend selections and learn more about each genre.

E Text Element These activities help students comprehend text elements.

LSV Listening, Speaking, Viewing These activities help students practice listening, speaking, and viewing skills.

EL English Language Coach These skills help English language learners as well as students who need additional reading support.

From an Author

Preparing Students to Read Historical Fiction

Build background knowledge in historical contexts. Before getting into the specific problem of the story and introducing students to the characters, discuss the setting using pictures of people, places, and artifacts of the time period. For example, you might show historically accurate pictures of fictionalized characters and have students talk about what they think the characters are like from the pictures. You might also show primary historical documents with pictures of houses, towns, or settlements and forms of transportation and ask students what it must have been like to live during the time period. It is now possible via the Internet to find many primary historical documents, like pictures and newspaper stories, to show and discuss.

Compare and contrast fiction and nonfiction. A key prerequisite for understanding historical fiction is to understand the difference between fact and fiction and to know when authors are fictionalizing facts and characters to make historical fiction more interesting. Another critical reading skill is to understand point of view. One way to teach these critical reading skills is to put pieces of text from historical fiction alongside primary historical texts so that students can compare them. Using transparencies or computer slides with two-column tables is a good way to display these. Then students can compare them on various issues like who was there in the event, what they said, and what happened. You can ask if the time orders of the document and the story mesh, and if the main themes are the same or different.

David O'Brien

Teacher to Teacher

When opening the Big Question "What can we learn from our mistakes?" I have students write "Live and Learn" sentences. I say, "From birth to death, our entire lives are journeys on which we live and learn. Along the way, we make mistakes. What have you lived and learned?" I give a few examples: "I've learned that going out with pretty girls isn't all it's cracked up to be. I've learned that two heads are better than one, provided one of those heads isn't two-faced. I've learned that the best way to shut out trouble is to have an open mind, open heart, and open arms." First, each student writes ten sentences, and then in groups they decide on the ten best sentences and refine them. We pick the best thirty or forty as a class and display them in the hall.

Dave Barclay
Harwood Middle School
Evansville, Indiana

Teacher Chat Room

Using Historical Fiction and Nonfiction

 Why is historical fiction an important genre?

 Historical fiction allows students to engage with both interesting stories and important content from social studies. At the same time that they hone important reading skills, they learn content that is integrated with other parts of the curriculum. Historical fiction also provides students with a way to deal with contemporary issues and problems by looking back and seeing that these issues and problems span decades and centuries.

 How do you interest students in historical fiction when they seem disinterested because stories don't seem immediately relevant?

 Whereas nonfiction historical texts focus in depth on key time periods or events, a fictionalized story allows readers to live vicariously during a particular time period, to "be there" and to experience how characters face and solve problems through their choices and actions. One creative approach can be to dramatize a story by having students assume the roles of historical characters and assigning other students to interview them. Students can also engage in media writing activities such as creating Weblogs (blogs, for short) in which they write from the point of view of a character in the story and take his or her approach to solving problems.

 What are some issues to consider when selecting historical fiction?

 If your purpose is primarily to teach about a historical period, make sure that the pieces you select are historically accurate and present characters that are believable within the time period. On the other hand, if your purpose is to have students experience an engaging text that is more fictionalized and would serve as a good example for critical comparisons with historical fact, you might select texts that take some liberties with historical fact in order to teach the critical reading skills of distinguishing fact from fiction and comparing differing points of view. Since students enjoy dramatizing, you may want to consider selecting pieces that are written as dramas or are easily adaptable and include plenty of parts for students to perform. Of course, it also makes sense to select pieces that include characters of the same age as your students, who face contemporary problems at an earlier point in history. Another practical issue is to select stories about time periods and important events that are widely documented in order to be able to use primary documents, photos, and other artifacts from the time period.

UNIT 7

The BIG Question

What Can We Learn from Our Mistakes?

Key Unit Objectives

- Answer the Big Question
- Apply the unit's key reading strategies to historical fiction and nonfiction
- Analyze the literary elements of historical fiction and nonfiction
- Write a personal narrative

BIG Question

Why Is It Important?
Addressing this big question helps students learn not only how to handle their mistakes but also how to learn lessons from them.

Viewing the Photo
Say: Making mistakes is a valuable part of every new experience. No one learns how to ride a skateboard without getting a few scrapes along the way. The girl in the photo looks like she wants to give up skateboarding because she thinks she's not good at it. What advice would you give her to help her learn from her mistakes? *(Responses will vary.)* **AS**

Unit Skills

Reading Skills

- Synthesizing, p. 782
- Identifying Main Idea and Supporting Details, p. 818
- Evaluating, p. 840
- Inferring, p. 870

Vocabulary

- Base Words and Roots, p. 784
- Latin Roots, p. 820
- Greek Roots, p. 842
- Anglo-Saxon Origins, p. 872

BIG Question What can we learn from our mistakes?

Genre Focus: Historical fiction and nonfiction

Literary Elements

- Symbol, p. 785
- Plot, p. 805
- Narrator, pp. 821, 831
- Description, pp. 843, 859
- Sequence of Events/ Time Order, pp. 873, 883

Writing Skills/Grammar

- Personal Narrative, pp. 814, 866
- Voice, p. 816
- Subject-Verb Agreement, p. 817

772

LOOKING AHEAD

The skill lessons and readings in this unit will help you develop your own answer to the Big Question.

773

About the Reading

Each selection in this unit provides insights that can help students address the question "What can we learn from our mistakes?" Students will read about how people have dealt with their mistakes and what they managed to learn from them.

About the Skills

The skills taught in this unit have been selected because they are particularly helpful when reading the featured genres: historical fiction and nonfiction. Each reading selection provides students with opportunities to practice and develop these skills.

NO CHILD LEFT BEHIND

Research has shown that explicit and systematic instruction must be provided in a number of areas of reading, including fluency, or the capacity to read text accurately and quickly. To help students build fluency, model good reading habits and allow students the opportunity to practice at their own pace.

Differentiated Instruction

Class Discussion Many students will be quite familiar with the concept of learning from one's mistakes. Therefore, students may be eager to answer the unit's big question by restating the idea that "it is important to learn from your mistakes." Remind students that the big question in this unit focuses on *what* people can learn from their mistakes. In other words, the emphasis will be not on the importance of learning from one's mistakes but rather on concrete, practical strategies for doing so. Discuss with students the quote from Albert Einstein on the facing page. Ask students whether or not they agree with Einstein and what role they think making mistakes might play in learning something new. **AS**

Focus

- 🔒 **Literature Launcher**
- ✍ **Daily Language Practice Transparency 61**
- **Focus Activity Write on the board:** In your Learner's Notebooks, write about a time when you learned from a mistake. *(Responses will vary.)* **AS**

Teach

R Reading Skill

Review Connecting To help students connect their experiences to the Big Question, ask them to write several sentences in their Learner's Notebooks about a time when they made a poor decision. Provide the following as prompts:

- What decision did you make?
- How did you feel afterward?
- What did you learn? **OL**

BQ 🗨**BIG** Question

- Have students read the profiles and look at the pictures of Ramón and Carolyn.
- Have students work in groups to write a skit about one of the profiles that includes what might be learned from the situation.

UNIT 7 WARM-UP

Connecting to ❓The **BIG** Question — What Can We Learn from Our Mistakes?

R Everyone makes mistakes. And that's a good thing. Why? Making mistakes is part of being human. Mistakes teach you a lot about yourself and others. Mistakes help you grow and change. In this unit, you'll read about mistakes different people made and what they learned from them.

Real Kids and the Big Question

RAMÓN and Jaime were friends. Ramón knew what people were saying about Jaime wasn't true, but Ramón told the story to some other kids anyway. He wanted the other kids to notice him. He wasn't thinking of Jaime. What's worse, Jaime heard that Ramón was helping to spread the story. Jaime told Ramón they weren't friends anymore. What do you think Ramón will learn from his mistake? **BQ**

CAROLYN didn't even think of calling home. When the other girls said they were going to Katara's and asked her to come along, she just went. Most afternoons Carolyn went straight home. When Carolyn didn't come home, her mother began to worry. She had no idea where Carolyn was. What will Carolyn learn from her mistake?

Warm-Up Activity

With a small group, act out two short skits that show what Ramón and Carolyn should have done in each situation.

Additional Support

Reading in the Real World

Career Ramón and Jaime may seek the help of a mediator to resolve their dispute. Students may be interested to know that professional mediators work in many different contexts, including schools, businesses, and family counseling centers. Those who are interested in becoming mediators may pursue degrees in conflict management or dispute resolution and can apply their skills in a variety of different environments. Successful mediators must have good listening skills and believe in the importance of fairness and equality. Have students conduct additional research about this career and present their findings to the class. **AS**

You and the Big Question

BQ You can turn a mistake into a learning experience. As you read the selections in this unit, think about how you would answer the Big Question.

Literature Online

Big Question Link to Web resources to further explore the Big Question at www.glencoe.com.

Plan for the Unit Challenge

At the end of the unit, you'll use notes from all your reading to complete the Unit Challenge.

You'll choose one of the following activities:

A. Chart You'll work in a group to create a chart about making mistakes and learning from them.

B. Bumper Sticker You'll create slogans for several bumper stickers about learning from mistakes. A slogan (SLOH gun) is a phrase or saying that expresses an idea.

- Start thinking about the activity you'd like to do. Make the activity the focus of your thinking as you work through the unit.

- In your Learner's Notebook, quickwrite about why you chose the activity. Tell how it will help you answer the Big Question and learn from your mistakes.

- When you take notes about the Big Question, think about how those ideas will help you complete the Unit Challenge activity.

Keep Track of Your Ideas

FOLDABLES™
Study Organizer

As you read, you'll make notes about the Big Question. Later, you'll use these notes to complete the Unit Challenge. See pages R8–R9 for help with making each Unit 7 Foldable. This diagram shows how each should look.

1. Make one Foldable for each workshop. Keep all of your Foldables for the unit in your Foldables folder.

2. On the bottom fold of your Foldable, write the workshop number and the Big Question.

3. Write the titles of the selections in the workshop on the front of the flaps—one title on each flap. (See page 773 for the titles.)

4. Open the flaps. At the very top of each flap,

write **My Purpose for Reading**. Below each crease, write **The Big Question**.

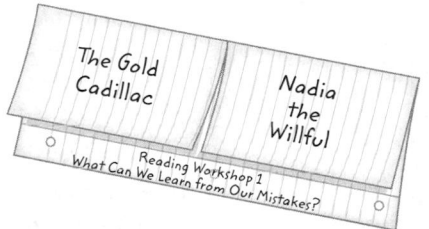

The Gold Cadillac

Nadia the Willful

Reading Workshop 1
What Can We Learn from Our Mistakes?

Teach

BQ **BIG Question**

Have students brainstorm several brief answers to the Big Question and write them in their Learner's Notebooks. **OL**

FOLDABLES™
Study Organizer

For each selection they read, students will enter notes about how that selection applies to the Big Question. For details about using Dinah Zike's Foldables, see page R8–R9.

Assess/Close

Ask students to discuss why learning from one's mistakes might be more beneficial than trying never to make mistakes.

Resources for page 775

📁 Use the Unit Challenge Planner BLM in the Unit 7 Resource Booklet, p. 36.

📁 Use the Foldable BLM in the Unit 7 Resource Booklet, p. 7.

Differentiated Instruction

Drawing a Comic Strip Have students reread the profiles of Ramón and Carolyn and choose one to illustrate in the form of a comic strip. Tell students to illustrate the series of events described in the profile and then continue the comic strip by writing an ending, or resolution. Suggest that students end by having the main character reflect on the experience and what he or she has learned. Encourage students who are artistically inclined to use detail in their drawings, but remind other students not to focus too much on the illustration portion. You may choose to have students work in pairs to complete the project. **AS**

Objectives

- Make connections from text to self
- Use text features: photographs
- Participate in a group discussion

775

Focus

Daily Language Practice Transparency 62 Focus Activity Say:

Suppose that you are writing about the life of a sixth-grader in the early twenty-first century. What events or information would you include?

(Responses will vary but should reflect details about life in the early twenty-first century.) **OL**

Teach

R Reading Skill

How to Read Historical Fiction and Nonfiction Ask:

How might each of the following skills help you read historical fiction and nonfiction? *(Possible responses: Synthesizing—Pulling together new ideas helps you draw conclusions about what you read; determining main idea and supporting details— You can focus on the most important information in the selection; evaluating can help you distinguish fact from opinion; inferring can help you fill in the holes in the story by figuring out what the author doesn't say directly.)* **OL**

UNIT 7 GENRE FOCUS: HISTORICAL FICTION AND NONFICTION

In **historical fiction** the characters, plot, and setting are fictional, or imaginary, but the time period is true. **Historical nonfiction** is writing that tells about real people, real places, and real events in the past. Biographies, autobiographies, essays, letters, and documents are some examples of historical nonfiction.

Why Read Historical Fiction and Nonfiction?

Historical writing takes readers to different places and times in history. It introduces readers to people and ways of life from the past. You'll read historical fiction and nonfiction to
• gain an understanding of past events
• learn how people lived, how they dressed, and how they spoke

How to Read Historical Fiction and Nonfiction

Key Reading Skills

These key reading skills are especially useful tools for reading and understanding historical fiction and nonfiction. You'll learn more about these skills later in the unit.

■ **Synthesizing** As you read, bring together information and ideas from the text to make new ideas of your own. (See Reading Workshop 1.)

■ **Identifying main idea and supporting details** Find the most important idea in a paragraph or in a selection. Look for examples, reasons, or details that explain it. (See Reading Workshop 2.)

R ■ **Evaluating** Make judgments and form opinions as you read. Decide whether characters are interesting, events are believable, or information is one-sided, for example. (See Reading Workshop 3.)

■ **Inferring** Use clues from the text to figure out what the author isn't directly telling you.

Key Literary Elements

Recognizing and thinking about the following literary elements will help you understand more fully what the author is telling you.

■ **Symbol:** any object, person, place, or experience that stands for something else (See "The Gold Cadillac.")

■ **Narrator:** the person who tells a story or relates an experience (See "The Bracelet.")

■ **Description:** a detailed explanation of a person, a place, a thing, or an event (See "President Cleveland, Where Are You?")

■ **Sequence of events/Time order:** the order in which events take place, the steps in a process, or the order of importance (See "The Shutout.")

Skills Focus
• Key skills for reading historical fiction and nonfiction
• Key literary elements of historical fiction and nonfiction

Skills Model
You will see how to use the key reading skills and literary elements as you read
• "The Great Radio Scare," p. 777

Objectives (pp. 776–781)
Reading Synthesize information • Identify main ideas and supporting details • Evaluate text • Make inferences
Literature Identify literary devices: symbolism • Identify literary elements: narrator, description • Identify text structure: sequence, time order

---

Additional Support

Differentiated Instruction

Build Background Tell students that the period from the 1920s to the late 1950s is generally considered the "Golden Age of Radio." At this time, radio became the most popular form of home entertainment in the United States, with radio shows airing as regularly as television shows do now. Anthologies, such as *The Mercury Theater on the Air,* were radio shows that featured a new set of characters and a new plot with each broadcast. With the spread of television after World War II, the popularity of radio programs declined. **AS**

The Great Radio Scare

U.S. Terrorized by Radio's 'Men From Mars'

The notes in the side columns model how to use the skills and elements you read about on page 776.

Historical Fiction and Nonfiction

ACTIVE READING MODEL

NEW YORK, Oct 30, 1938 (AP)—Hysteria[1] among radio listeners throughout the nation and actual panicky evacuations from sections of the metropolitan area resulted from a too-realistic radio broadcast tonight describing a fictitious and devastating visitation of strange men from Mars.

Excited and weeping persons all over the country swamped newspaper and police switchboards with the question:

"It is true?"

FALLING METEORS

It was purely a figment of H.G. Wells's imagination[2] with some extra flourishes of radio dramatization by Orson Welles. It was broadcast by the Columbia Broadcasting System.

The broadcast was an adaptation of Wells's "War of the Worlds" in which meteors[3] and gas from Mars menace the Earth. **1 2**

New York police were unable to contact the CBS studios by telephone so swamped was its switchboard and a radio car was sent there for information.

A woman ran into a church in Indianapolis screaming: "New York destroyed. It's the end of the world. You might as well go home to die. I just heard it on the radio." Services were dismissed immediately.

---

1. **Hysteria** is behavior that shows uncontrolled panic or fear.
2. When you say that something is a **figment of someone's imagination,** you mean that that person made it up.
3. A **meteor** (MEE tee ur) is a piece of rocky material from space that falls to Earth at a high speed. It becomes very hot and glows as it enters Earth's atmosphere.

1 Key Reading Skill
Synthesizing *The broadcast happened in the 1930s. That was a long time ago. I know from science class that we have sent machines to Mars since then. People must not have known much about Mars back then.*

2 Key Literary Element
Symbol *Meteors and gas from Mars may have been symbols of the end of the world to some people. Maybe that's why they were so scared.*

Actor Orson Welles broadcast *War of the Worlds* on his radio show, *The Mercury Theater on the Air*

777

Teach

R Reading Skill

Synthesizing Ask: Which details in the first paragraph help you understand that the radio broadcast led to wide-spread panic? *(Possible response: The paragraph mentions "hysteria" and "panicky evacuations." The writer notes that these types of reactions occurred "throughout the nation" and "all over the country.")* **OL**

L Literary Element

Symbol Ask: In times of chaos and uncertainty, such as during the panic described in the article, who or what may serve as a symbol of safety, aid, and public order? *(Possible response: Police officers, firefighters, government officials, clergy, and Red Cross workers symbolize safety and order.)* **AL**

Readability Scores
Dale-Chall: 6.7
DRP: 67
Lexile: 1200

English Language Coach

Base Words and Roots Write the words *metropolitan, police,* and *Indianapolis* on the board. Underline the root *pol* in *metropolitan, police,* and *Indianapolis.* Explain that *pol* comes from *polis,* a Greek root meaning "city or state." Have students use dictionaries to find the definitions of these words. Ask students to connect the definitions with the meaning of the Greek root. (metropolitan: *having to do with a large city;* police: *people who keep order in a city;* Indianapolis: *capital city of Indiana)* Ask students to list additional words that share the root *pol* or *polis.* **EL OL**

Objectives
- Synthesize information
- Analyze features of genres: historical fiction and nonfiction
- Identify literary elements: symbol
- Identify word structure: base words

Teach

Viewing the Photo

Ask: How do this photo and caption help you read the article? *(Possible response: The photo shows the live radio broadcast as well as details from the time period. It also indicates that the broadcast was just a play by showing people reading scripts during a rehearsal.)* **AS**

R1 Reading Skill

Identifying Main Idea and Supporting Details **Say:** In this article, the writer describes people's reactions to the radio broadcast. Write a paragraph that states these details and the main idea of the first two pages. *(Responses will vary, but should contain a statement that people across the country reacted to the broadcast with fear and confusion and include details to support that idea.)* **AS**

R2 Reading Skill

Evaluating **Ask:** Do you think that people's reactions to the broadcast were understandable? Explain. *(Possible response: Yes, because information spread more slowly in 1938 than it does now and people did not have the information they needed.)* **OL**

Five boys at Brevard (N.C.) college fainted and panic gripped the campus for a half hour with many students fighting for telephones to inform their parents to come and get them.

PLEA FOR REASSURANCE

At Fayette, N.C., people with relatives in the section of New Jersey where the mythical visitation had its locale,[4] went to a newspaper office in tears, seeking information.

Many New Yorkers seized personal effects and raced out of their apartments, some jumping into their automobiles and heading for the wide open spaces.

A message from Providence, R.I., said:

"Weeping and hysterical women swamped the switchboard of the Providence Journal for details of the massacre[5] and destruction at New York and officials of the electric company received scores of calls urging them to turn off all lights so that the city would be safe from the enemy."

At Concrete, Wash., women fainted and men prepared to take their families into the mountains for safe-keeping when electric power failed during the radio dramatization.

At a highly effective dramatic high in the radio program when all sorts of monsters were flocking down on New Jersey from the planet Mars, lights went out in most of the homes of the town of 1000. For a time the village verged on[6] mass hysteria. **3**

Because of the power failure, many persons actually thought the invasion had reached Washington State.

Elsewhere in the Northwest calls poured into newspaper and press association offices by the thousands.

The Boston Globe told of one woman who "claimed she could 'see the fire' and said she and many others in her neighborhood were 'getting out of here.'"

---

4. A *locale* (loh KAL) is the place of an event.
5. A *massacre* (MAS uh kur) is a bloody killing of many people or animals.
6. *Verged* (vurjd) *on* means "was close to or on the border of."

In this picture, Orson Welles and others are getting ready for the *War of the Worlds* broadcast.

ACTIVE READING MODEL

3 Key Reading Skill
Identifying Main Idea and Supporting Details *This section gives examples of what people did when they heard the broadcast. Those details tell me that the main idea of the section is that people all across the country were scared and wanted to know what was happening.*
R1 **R2**

Additional Support

Literature Focus Lesson

Author's Purpose Explain that the author's purpose in this article is both to inform and to entertain, and the writer's word choice reflects these two purposes. For example, the writer states, "Many New Yorkers seized personal effects and raced out of their apartments." The words *seized* and *raced* not only tell readers what people were doing but also give a sense of the urgency and fear with which people acted. Ask students to point out other strong word choices that fulfill the author's purposes. **AS**

PHONE BOARDS DELUGED

Minneapolis and St. Paul police switchboards were deluged[7] with calls from frightened people.

In Atlanta there was worry in some quarters[8] that "the end of the world" had arrived.

It finally got so bad in New Jersey that the State police put reassuring messages on the state teletype[9] instructing their officers what it was all about.

R1 And all this despite the fact that the radio play was interrupted four times by the announcement: "This is purely a fictional play."

The Times-Dispatch of Richmond, Va., reported some of their telephone calls came from people who said they were "praying." **4**

The Kansas City bureau of the Associated Press received queries[10] on the "meteors" from Los Angeles, Salt Lake City, Beaumont, Texas, and St. Joseph, Mo.

One telephone informant said he had loaded all his children into his car, had filled it with gasoline and was **R2** going somewhere.

"Where is safe?" he wanted to know.

Residents of Jersey City, N.J., telephoned their police frantically, asking where they could get gas masks. In both Jersey City and Newark hundreds of citizens ran out into the streets. . . .

In Birmingham, Ala., people gathered in groups and prayed, and Memphis had its full quota[11] of weeping women calling in to learn the facts. **5**

SYSTEM'S STATEMENT

In later broadcasts tonight the Columbia system announced:

"For the listeners who tuned to Orson Welles's Mercury Theater of the Air, broadcast from 8 to 9 p.m. Eastern standard time, tonight and did not realize that the program was merely a radio adaptation of H.G. Wells's famous novel

---

7. **Deluged** (DEL yoojd) is another way of saying overwhelmed or swamped.
8. Here, **quarters** means "areas."
9. A **teletype** was a machine used to send and receive messages from far away before the Internet and e-mail existed.
10. **Queries** (KWEER eez) are questions.
11. A **quota** (KWOH tuh) is the part of a total amount that is expected from a group.

ACTIVE READING MODEL

4 **Key Reading Skill**
Evaluating *Wait a minute! The radio play was interrupted four times by an announcement that it was all made up. People couldn't have been paying much attention. I'm sure that I would have noticed and understood what was going on.*

5 **Key Literary Element**
Narrator *This is a newspaper article. The author of the article is the person telling the story to the reader.*

Teach

R1 Reading Skill

Evaluating Ask: Which organizations seemed to receive the greatest number of phone calls from panicked citizens? *(police departments and newspapers)* **BL Ask:** Why do you think these particular organizations received so many phone calls? *(Possible response: People turned to these organizations for reassurance and advice in a time of fear and uncertainty.)* **AL**

R2 Reading Skill

Evaluating Ask: What happens when panic-stricken people form a group? *(Possible response: A panic-stricken person is anxious, and his or her actions reflect that tension and anxiety. People in a group feed off one another's emotions, so feelings of anxiety and panic would be multiplied in a group.)* **OL Ask:** What do you think contributed to the great number of people missing the message that the broadcast's report was fictional? *(Possible response: As panic spread, people stopped listening to the broadcast and joined in the chaos.)* **AS**

Reading Fluency

Script Reading Students may be interested in presenting a portion of the script of the "War of the Worlds" broadcast in readers' theater format. Locate the script of the broadcast at the library or online. Organize students into small groups, and allow each group to choose a selection from the script. Assign roles within each group. Tell group members to practice reading aloud from the script until they can do so smoothly and with expression. When students present their readings, you may wish to have them sit on stools or chairs in a semicircle, with music stands or sturdy binders available to hold their scripts. **AS**

Objectives
- Evaluate text
- Identify main ideas and supporting details
- Use text features: photographs
- Analyze features of genres: historical fiction and nonfiction

Teach

L Literary Element

Narrator Say: The narrator in a newspaper article is the writer reporting the story. Writers of news articles often include quotations in their reports. Who or what does the writer quote in this article? *(The writer quotes the Columbia System and* The Mercury Theater on the Air.*)* **AS**

Ask: How do the quotations add to the reader's understanding? *(Possible response: The writer wants readers to understand that the events reported actually happened. Also, these quotations give readers, especially those who did not hear the original broadcast, a better understanding of how the performance could have led to panic.)* **OL**

R Reading Skill

Inferring Ask: What do you think listeners who didn't hear that this was a fictional story thought was happening when they heard this report? *(Possible response: They thought the Earth was being invaded.)* **OL**

'The War of the Worlds,' we are repeating the fact, made four times on the program that the entire content of the play was entirely fictitious."

The Columbia System also issued a formal statement which said in part:

L "Naturally it was neither Columbia nor the Mercury Theater's intent to mislead anyone, and when it became evident that part of the audience has been disturbed by the performance five announcements were made over the network later in the evening to reassure those listeners." . . . **6**

The program which brought such unexpected developments opened with a regular announcement that another of the Mercury Theater of the Air's radio dramatizations—H.G. Wells's novel—was about to be presented.

The drama began with dance music, which was interrupted after a few seconds with a breath-taking announcement in news broadcast tempo.

"We interrupt our program of dance music to bring you a special bulletin from the Intercontinental Radio News," it said. "Twenty minutes before 8, Professor Farrell of the Mt. Jennings Observatory, Chicago, Ill., reports observing several explosions of incandescent[12] gas occurring at regular intervals on the planet Mars."

R An object was reported "moving toward the Earth with enormous velocity,[13] like a jet of blue gas shot from a gun.

"We return you now to our New York studios," the drama continued.

After a few more bars of music, the scene shifted to an observatory at Princeton, N.J., for an interview with an astronomer about the phenomenon[14] just reported.

Illustration of a Man Encountering a Martian by Alvim Correa, 1906

Analyzing the Art Study this illustration from the H.G. Wells novel *War of the Worlds*. Based on the selection you are reading, what do you think is happening here? Explain.

ACTIVE READING MODEL

6 Key Reading Skill
Inferring *Even though the author doesn't say it, I think the company does not want people to blame them.*

---

12. *Incandescent* (in kun DES unt) means "glowing with great heat."
13. *Velocity* (vuh LOS uh tee) is speed or rate of motion.
14. A *phenomenon* (fuh NOM uh nun) is an unusual event.

Additional Support

Literature Focus Lesson

Sequence Explain that the article begins by relating details about the panic that occurred on October 30, 1938. The article then reveals the details of the cause of the panic: a fictitious radio broadcast that reported an alien invasion. This article is set up in reverse cause-and-effect order—the effects are listed, and then the cause is given. Discuss with students possible reasons for the reporter's choosing to present information in this way. For example, the writer may think that details about the panic would grab readers' attention more quickly than details about the broadcast itself. Ask students whether this sequence is effective. **AS**

After some routine astronomical questions, the "announcer" in the drama asked the scientist about the possibility of life on Mars. The actor replied the chances were a thousand to one against it, noting that Mars was 40,000,000 miles away.

INTENSE SHOCK

. . . The scene shifted back to the New York studios; whereupon there was an announcement that a meteorite had struck at "Grovers Mill, New Jersey," and that a mobile broadcasting unit was being rushed there for a description.

There was 30 seconds more of music, and the broadcast from the supposed scene started. The announcer described huge men, like octopuses, emerging from the meteorite. Just as they were starting to wield[15] a death-dealing "heat ray," his description broke off. **7**

The program returned to New York "because of circumstances beyond our control" and a few seconds later there came a "telephone bulletin" from the scene reporting that the bodies of more than 40 people had been found there. This program ended a few seconds later. **8** ○

15. To **wield** (weeld) means to hold or use a weapon or tool.

Illustration of a Martian Fighting Machine Attacking Humans by Alvim Correa, 1906.
Analyzing the Art What do you think is happening in *this* picture from the H.G. Wells novel?

Partner Talk You read how the *War of the Worlds* radio program created a great scare. With a partner, talk about what you might have done if you thought Martians had really come to this planet.

Study Central Visit www.glencoe.com and click on Study Central to review historical fiction and nonfiction.

ACTIVE READING MODEL

7 Key Literary Element
Description *The announcer described giant men that looked like octopuses coming out of the meteorite. That description must have terrified the people who were listening.* **L1**

8 Key Literary Element
Sequence of Events/Time Order *Let's see. What was the order of the program? It began with dance music that was interrupted by a special bulletin. After that, there was more music. Then more announcements interrupted the music until the program finally ended.* **L2**

Teach

L1 Literary Element

Description Say: Adjectives are words that describe nouns. Use your imagination to picture the aliens in this description: "The announcer described huge men, like octopuses, emerging from the meteorite." What other adjectives could you use to describe the aliens? (*Responses will vary. Encourage students to be creative in their responses, and record students' answers on the board.*) **AS**

L2 Literary Element

Sequence of Events/Time Order Say: Words such as *first, next, then, later, before, after,* and *finally* signal time order. When a writer uses time order, he or she tells the events of a story according to the order in which they took place. What words signal the order of events in the radio program? (*opened, began, after, whereupon, started, just as, later*) **OL**

Study Central Have students access the Web site to review historical fiction and nonfiction and to complete a related workshop.

Differentiated Instruction

Writing a Radio Play Organize students into small groups. Ask students to use details and information from the article to write radio broadcasts about an alien invasion. Encourage students to model the language and tone of their dialogue on that of the *Mercury Theater* broadcast. Remind students that because the audience does not see the actors or set in a radio play, the dialogue must contain all of the information in order to allow the listeners to understand what is happening. Have each group practice reading its radio play aloud before sharing it with the class. **AS**

Objectives
- Understand sequence: time order words
- Identify literary elements: description
- Take notes
- Identify and analyze narrator
- Analyze features of genres: historical fiction and nonfiction

Synthesizing

**Objectives covered in
this workshop:**
• Synthesize to demonstrate comprehension of text
• Compare text events and passages with own experience by synthesizing main ideas and supporting details

Teaching Students to Synthesize

Why Is It Important?

• Synthesizing helps readers move to a higher level of thinking; it extends the literal meaning of a text to an inferential level.

• Synthesizing helps students think of new ideas. They use what they have read and what they already know to come up with a new idea or a new understanding.

• Readers who synthesize remember more and tend to perform better on assessments, tests, and in life.

How to Help Students Get It

• Tell students that they have probably been synthesizing when answering the Big Questions. Each time they use a theme, character, or idea from a selection they have read to help them think of a new idea, or a new way of answering the Big Question, they are synthesizing.

• Model synthesizing for students by reading aloud a newspaper or other article. Identify the key points and focus on the ideas you come up with as a result of your reading. Remember that synthesizing is not simply summarizing; it extends into an understanding of the implications from the text and helps you to apply them to form a new idea.

Reading to Answer the Big Question

The Gold Cadillac by Mildred D. Taylor
Two sisters are excited when their father buys a new Cadillac. Their mother is unhappy about the purchase and refuses to ride in the car until the father decides to take it on a trip through the segregated South. There the father is arrested for supposedly stealing the Cadillac. After returning home, the father decides to sell the car of his dreams because he realizes that it's more important to have family unity and to put the money toward buying a house.

Nadia the Willful by Sue Alexander
This short story takes place in the desert where Tarik, sheik of a Bedouin tribe, lives with his wife and two children. Overcome with grief when his son Hamed is lost, Tarik decrees that no one is ever to speak Hamed's name again. After his daughter Nadia refuses to obey his edict, Tarik comes to realize that it is good to keep Hamed alive in their memories by talking about him.

Workshop Resources

PACING (DAYS)		LESSON	STUDENT MATERIALS	TEACHER RESOURCES
STANDARD	BLOCK			
1	1/2	Key Skill Lesson: Synthesizing	🐾 Key Reading Skills Practice, p. 9 🐾 English Language Coach Review, p. 42	🖐 Bellringer Options Transparencies –Daily Language Practice 63 –Selection Focus 21 🖐 Read Aloud, Think Aloud Transparencies –Key Reading Skills 24 💿 Presentation Plus!
1	1	"The Gold Cadillac"	💻 Glencoe Online 🐾 Unit Vocabulary Review, p. 40 🐾 Academic Vocabulary Review, p. 43 📂 English Language Coach 🐾 Active Reading Graphic Organizer, p. 11 🐾 Literary Analysis, p. 10 💿 StudentWorks Plus™ 💻 Online Student Edition 💿 Literature Classics 📂 Selection and Unit Assessments, p. 73	🖐 Literary and Text Analysis Transparencies, 51 💻 Puzzlemaker 💿 Skill Level Up!™ A Language Arts Game 💻 BookLink 3 📘 Assessment by Learning Objective (Diagnostic and Formative) 💿 Interactive Tutor: Self-Assessment 💿 TeacherWorks Plus™
1		"Nadia the Willful"	💻 Glencoe Online 🐾 Unit Vocabulary Review, p. 40 🐾 Academic Vocabulary Review, p. 43 📂 English Language Coach 🐾 Active Reading Graphic Organizer, p. 13 💿 StudentWorks Plus™ 💻 Online Student Edition 💿 Literature Classics 📂 Selection and Unit Assessments, p. 74	🖐 Literary and Text Analysis Transparencies 37 💻 Puzzlemaker 💿 Skill Level Up!™ A Language Arts Game 💻 BookLink 3 📘 Assessment by Learning Objective (Diagnostic and Formative) 💿 Interactive Tutor: Self-Assessment 💿 TeacherWorks Plus™

Keys for Unit Resource

📂 Blackline Master	🔒 DVD
📘 Workbook	🖐 Transparency
📖 Supplemental Text	💻 Web-based
💿 CD-ROM	🐾 Fast File

Level Appropriate Code

AS = Activities for all students
AL = Activities for students working above grade level
OL = Activities for students working at grade level
BL = Activities for students working below grade level
EL = Activities for English language learners

Focus

BELLRINGER Options

- **Selection Focus Transparencies 21**
- **Daily Language Practice Transparency 63**
  Focus Activity Say: Think about items that people buy to show their wealth or status, such as cars, clothing, and jewelry. Why might these items be important to some people? *(Possible response: People might buy these items to show their success.)* **AS**

Teach

R Reading Skill

Synthesizing Say: When you synthesize, you put together information from different places. Give an example of a time when you synthesized information from more than one source. *(Responses will vary.)* **AS**

V Vocabulary

Academic Vocabulary Say: Use a dictionary to find and define other words that are related to *synthesize*. *(Possible response: synthesis: the combination of parts to make a whole)* **OL**

Skills Focus

You will practice using these skills when you read the following selections:
- "The Gold Cadillac," p. 786
- "Nadia the Willful," p. 806

Reading

- Synthesizing

Literature

- Identifying symbols and analyzing their use in texts
- Explaining and analyzing plot sequence (exposition, rising action, climax, falling action, resolution)

Vocabulary

- Using base words and roots to understand word meanings
- Academic Vocabulary: *synthesize*

Writing/Grammar

- Identifying verbs

Objectives (pp. 782–783)
Reading Synthesize information

782 UNIT 7

Skill Lesson

Synthesizing

Learn It!

What Is It? When you **synthesize**, you combine ideas to come up with something new. It may be a new understanding of an important idea or a new way of presenting information.

R The ideas you bring together may come from different places. Many readers take ideas from their reading and combine them with what they already know to come to new understandings. For example, you might combine information from an article like "What Kids Say About Bullying" with your own experiences in order to come up with a plan for dealing with bullies.

CALVIN AND HOBBES © 1995 Watterson. Dist. By UNIVERSAL PRESS SYNDICATE. Reprinted with permission. All rights reserved.

Analyzing Cartoons
Calvin has read the library book. He has thought about a lot of the ideas in the book. What new idea does he come up with?

V Academic Vocabulary ....
synthesize (SIN thuh syz) *v.* to bring together to create something new

---

Additional Support

Reading in the Real World

College Many music schools offer a degree program in music synthesis. This field explores the use of synthesizers, or electronic instruments that generate and combine simple waveforms to produce sounds. Students of music synthesis study performance, computer programming, and acoustics. They frequently go on to pursue careers as sound designers, digital audio editors, and musical arrangers. Have interested students research information on what courses are required for pursuing this field of study. Ask volunteers to present their findings to the class. **AS**

Why Is It Important? Synthesizing helps you move to a higher level of thinking. You go beyond remembering what you've learned from someone else to creating something new of your own. You might create your own ending to a story. You might develop your own position on an issue. You might think of a new way you can use information or a new idea.

How Do I Do It? Start by thinking about the ideas or events in a selection. Then, take a step beyond what you've learned. Ask yourself:

- Do I see something more than the main ideas here? Do I imagine the events developing in a different way?
- What can I create with what I know? How can I use this information?

Here's what Michelle thought about while reading "Aunt Millicent." She combined ideas from the story with her own experience.

> Mrs. Nutbeam sighed. "Listen, Jamie, perhaps the time has come to own up that Aunt Millicent is not real."
>
> "We can't do that!" wailed Jamie. "Everyone would think we're looney . . . and that Grandma's absolutely bonkers, knitting socks for an aunt who isn't there."

I thought about Jamie's problem. He had a lot of fun making up stories about an imaginary Aunt Millicent, but the situation got out of hand when the whole town got involved. I also thought about "The Great Radio Scare," the account of another made-up story that caused problems when people believed it was real. After thinking about these stories and my own experiences, I decided that I don't want to ever let a story or joke go too far.

Practice It!

In your Learner's Notebook, write a paragraph about what you learned from "Aunt Millicent" and "The Great Radio Scare" that you can use in your everyday life.

Use It!

As you read "The Gold Cadillac" and "Nadia the Willful," look for ideas from the selections to combine with your own thoughts to create and reach new understandings.

Study Central Visit www.glencoe. com and click on Study Central to review synthesizing.

Teach

Study Central Have students access the Web site to review synthesizing and to complete a related activity.

R Reading Skill

Synthesizing Point out that the student in the example interprets Jamie's problem, draws a conclusion about it, and connects the problem to her own life.
Ask: How is synthesizing related to interpreting, drawing conclusions, and connecting? *(Possible response: Synthesizing involves doing all of these things. To synthesize, you must understand what you read, connect with it, and draw a new idea from it.)* **OL** **AL**

Resources for page 783

📁 Use Key Reading Skills Transparency 24 in *Read Aloud, Think Aloud* to help students practice synthesizing.

Differentiated Instruction

Write an Alternate Ending One way that students can practice synthesizing is by creating their own endings to a story. Have students select a story from a previous unit and use the existing characters and themes to write an alternate ending. Suggest that students reflect on what they learned from the story and what new thoughts the story inspired them to have. Encourage students to develop outlines before they write. Invite volunteers to share their alternate endings with the class. **OL**

Objectives
- Synthesize information
- Learn and use new vocabulary

Teach

More About the Author

Mildred D. Taylor was born in 1943 in Jackson, Mississippi, and grew up in Toledo, Ohio. After college, she joined the Peace Corps and spent two years in Africa teaching English and history. She later earned a master's degree in journalism at the University of Colorado, where she helped start a black studies program. Taylor is perhaps best known for her book *Roll of Thunder, Hear My Cry,* but she also wrote *Song of the Trees* and *Let the Circle Be Unbroken.*

V Vocabulary

Word Map Say: Answer the following questions about the word *caravan:*

- What is its definition? *(a group of people or vehicles traveling together)*
- What is a description of it? *(a long, often slow-moving line)*
- What are some examples of it? *(Possible responses: camels crossing the desert; cars following one another in a procession; covered wagons heading west)* **AS**

Additional Support

Author Search To expand students' appreciation of Mildred D. Taylor, have them access the Web site for additional information and resources.

Before You Read The Gold Cadillac

Mildred D. Taylor

Meet the Author

Mildred D. Taylor was born in Mississippi in 1943. When she was very young, her family moved to Ohio, where she went to public school and to college. Taylor grew up to become a well-known writer. She won the Newbery Medal for *Roll of Thunder, Hear My Cry.* See page R6 of the Author Files for more on Mildred D. Taylor.

Author Search For more about Mildred D. Taylor, go to www.glencoe.com.

Objectives (pp. 784–801)
Reading Synthesize information
• Make connections from text to self
Literature Identify literary devices: symbolism
Vocabulary Identify word structure: roots and bases

Vocabulary Preview

features (FEE churz) *n.* parts or qualities **(p. 787)** *The dashboard in the new car had many special features.*

practical (PRAK tih kul) *adj.* having or showing good sense about everyday activities **(p. 787)** *The mother was practical, so she wanted to save money.* **V**

caravan (KAIR uh van) *n.* a group of people or vehicles traveling together **(p. 791)** *The relatives got into their cars and set out for Mississippi in a caravan.*

Choose a Synonym Choose the best example for the word in **dark** type. Write your answer in your Learner's Notebook.

1. Which of the following is an example of a **caravan**?
   a. wagon train **b.** foot race **c.** cruise ship
2. Which of the following is an example of a car's **features**?
   a. road **b.** driver **c.** air bags
3. Which of the following is a **practical** place to save money?
   a. mall **b.** museum **c.** bank

English Language Coach

Base Words and Roots You run across a word you don't know, but you don't have a dictionary handy. And there aren't enough context clues to help you with the word's meaning. You're not clueless! Many words themselves contain clues to their meanings. A familiar base word or root can give information about the meaning of a word.

Take the word *drowsiness,* for example. *Drowsiness* contains the base word *drowsy.* If you know that *drowsy* means "sleepy," you might guess that *drowsiness* means "a sleepy feeling."

Word	Base Word	Meaning
drowsiness →	drowsy = sleepy →	a sleepy feeling

Take a Guess Find the base word you see in each word, and then use it to guess the word's meaning.

1. heroism
2. unnatural
3. irregularity

English Language Coach

Base Words and Roots Point out to students that the spelling of a base word often changes when a suffix is added. For example, when the suffix *-ness* is added to a base word ending in *y,* the *y* usually changes to *i.* For example, *drowsy* becomes *drowsiness.* However, this is not true of the suffix *-ing.* The word *study* keeps its final *y* to form *studying.* Also point out that when the suffix *-able* is added to a base word that ends in a silent *e,* the *e* is usually dropped. For example, *love* becomes *lovable.* However, when the suffix begins with a consonant, the silent *e* of the base word is usually kept, as in *loveless.* **EL** **OL**

Skills Preview

Key Reading Skill: Synthesizing

"That's it! Now I get it!" It's like a light bulb goes on in your head. Suddenly everything comes together, and you understand. You're synthesizing. Here's how it happens.

- You identify the most important ideas.
- You see connections among the ideas.
- You come up with new ideas or understandings of your own.

Think-Pair-Share "Aha!" moments often happen while you're reading. Think of a time when you got a new idea from something you read. Share the experience with a partner.

Key Literary Element: Symbol

A **symbol** is an object, person, place, or experience that stands for something else. Symbols usually represent something abstract—that is, an idea or thought. For example, a dove is a symbol for peace. Writers use symbols in stories to add meaning. In "The Gold Cadillac," cars have special meanings.

Write to Learn Write the following questions in your Learner's Notebook. As you read, use them to think about the meaning of symbols in the selection.

- What does the gold Cadillac stand for?
- What do the Mercury cars represent?

Interactive Literary Elements Handbook
To review or learn more about the literary elements, go to www.glencoe.com.

Get Ready to Read

Connect to the Reading

When people go through something together, they often grow closer to one another. Think of an experience, such as a trip, school project, party, or crisis, that you've shared with your family or another group. Did the experience help you become closer? Explain.

Write to Learn In your Learner's Notebook, write a short description of your experience and how it helped you become closer to members of your family or another group.

Build Background

This story takes place in 1950. At that time, segregation was allowed in many Southern states.

- Segregation is the separation of groups of people according to some characteristic, such as race.
- In some cities, schools, hospitals, hotels, trains, buses, restaurants, and theaters were segregated.
- Some drinking fountains were labeled "White Only" or "Colored." Some city parks had signs reading "Whites Only."

Mildred Taylor's family moved north from Mississippi when she was just a baby. Every year they visited their relatives in the South. The family had to pack food for the trip, because as African Americans, they were not welcome in many Southern restaurants in those days.

Set Purposes for Reading

BIG Question Read the selection "The Gold Cadillac" to find out how a father and his family learn from their mistakes about what's really important.

Set Your Own Purpose What else would you like to learn from the selection to help you answer the Big Question? Write your own purpose on the "Gold Cadillac" part of the Workshop 1 Foldable.

> ### Keep Moving
>
> Use these skills as you read the following selection.

The Gold Cadillac **785**

Teach

L Literary Element

Symbol Say: The verb form of *symbol* is *symbolize.* What do the following items symbolize?

- an olive branch *(peace)*
- a four-leafed clover *(good luck)*
- a light bulb *(idea)* **AS**

R Reading Skill

Review Connecting Ask: Why do people often grow closer to one another when they face a challenge or hardship? *(Responses will vary. Students may suggest that facing challenges or hardships forces people to cooperate.)* **AS**

Interactive Literary Elements Handbook Have students access the Web site to improve their understanding of symbol.

Literature Focus Lesson

Symbol Discuss with students whether all symbols are universal—that is, whether each symbol means the same thing to people around the world. For example, ask students to consider whether a person from another country would understand the concept behind a drawing of a person with a light bulb above his or her head. Have students research symbols in other cultures and present their findings to the class. **OL** You may also wish to challenge students to think about whether hand signals and gestures that are used for communication, such as those used in sign language, are common across languages and cultures. **AL**

Objectives

- Learn and use new vocabulary
- Make connections from text to self
- Identify literary elements: symbol

Teach

L Literary Element

Symbol Ask: What does the color gold usually symbolize? *(Possible responses: wealth; newness or shininess)* **Ask:** What might a new Cadillac symbolize? *(Possible responses: luxury; success; top of the line product)* **OL**

EL Language Coach

Base Words and

Roots Say: The base word *plex* means "a building that is divided into a number of spaces." Use this information to define the following words:

- cineplex *(a building with several movie theaters)*
- multiplex *(a building with many sections, such as a movie theater)*
- complex *(having many parts; a building divided into several parts)*

Use reference resources to verify your responses. **EL BL OL**

Readability Scores
Dale-Chall: 3.9
DRP: 47
Lexile: 780

The Gold Cadillac

by Mildred D. Taylor

My sister and I were playing out on the front lawn when the gold Cadillac rolled up and my father stepped from behind the wheel. We ran to him, our eyes filled with wonder. "Daddy, whose Cadillac?" I asked.

And Wilma demanded, "Where's our Mercury?"

My father grinned. "Go get your mother and I'll tell you all about it."

"Is it ours?" I cried. "Daddy, is it ours?"

"Get your mother!" he laughed. "And tell her to hurry!" Wilma and I ran off to obey as Mr. Pondexter next door came from his house to see what this new Cadillac was all about. We threw open the front door, ran through the downstairs front parlor[1] and straight through the house to the kitchen where my mother was cooking and one of my aunts was helping her. "Come on, Mother-Dear!" we cried together. "Daddy say come on out and see this new car!"

"What?" said my mother, her face showing her surprise. "What're you talking about?"

"A Cadillac!" I cried. **1**

"He said hurry up!" relayed Wilma.

And then we took off again, up the back stairs to the second floor of the duplex.[2] Running down the hall, we

---

1. A *parlor* (PAR lur) is a room used for entertaining guests.

EL 2. *Duplex* (DOO pleks) means "double." A duplex apartment building has rooms on two floors, and a duplex house has two separate living spaces for two families.

786 UNIT 7 What Can We Learn from Our Mistakes?

Practice the Skills

1 Key Reading Skill

Synthesizing Why is the Cadillac so important? Think about what you've read and combine it with your knowledge of vocabulary and punctuation. Why did the sisters' eyes *fill with wonder*? Why did the author use an exclamation point after "A Cadillac"? Now, can you understand what a Cadillac means to them?

Additional Support

English Language Coach

Word Meanings Readers who pause to look up every new vocabulary word in context may lose continuity and overall comprehension. Suggest that students keep a log of new vocabulary words as they read the selection. Tell students to look up the words in their log after they read, unless understanding a given word is necessary for comprehension. After students read the selection and look up the definitions of the words in their lists, have them exchange and study one another's logs. Collect students' logs and use them for a vocabulary quiz. **EL BL**

banged on all the apartment doors. My uncles and their wives stepped to the doors. It was good it was a Saturday morning. Everybody was home.

"We got us a Cadillac! We got us a Cadillac!" Wilma and I proclaimed in unison.[3] We had decided that the Cadillac had to be ours if our father was driving it and holding on to the keys. "Come on see!" Then we raced on, through the upstairs sunroom, down the front steps, through the downstairs sunroom, and out to the Cadillac. Mr. Pondexter was still there. Mr. LeRoy and Mr. Courtland from down the street were there too and all were admiring the Cadillac as my father stood proudly by, pointing out the various **features.**

"Brand-new 1950 Coupe deVille!"[4] I heard one of the men saying.

"Just off the showroom floor!" my father said. "I just couldn't resist it."

My sister and I eased up[5] to the car and peeked in. It was all gold inside. Gold leather seats. Gold carpeting. Gold dashboard. It was like no car we had owned before. It looked like a car for rich folks.

"Daddy, are we rich?" I asked. My father laughed. **2**

"Daddy, it's ours, isn't it?" asked Wilma, who was older and more **practical** than I. She didn't intend to give her heart too quickly to something that wasn't hers.

"You like it?"

"Oh, Daddy, yes!"

He looked at me. "What 'bout you, 'lois?"[6]

"Yes, sir!"

My father laughed again. "Then I expect I can't much disappoint my girls, can I? It's ours all right!"

Wilma and I hugged our father with our joy. My uncles came from the house and my aunts, carrying their babies,

---

3. **Proclaimed** means "announced publicly", and **in unison** means "speaking the same words at the same time."

4. **Coupe deVille** (koop duh VIL) is a style of car.

5. When you **ease up to** something, you move slowly or carefully toward it.

6. Daddy is referring to Eloise by her nickname, **'lois.**

Vocabulary

features (FEE churz) *n.* parts or qualities

practical (PRAK tih kul) *adj.* having or showing good sense about everyday activities

Practice the Skills

2 ┃ **Key Literary Element**

Symbol Symbols take many forms. They can be objects, people, places, or experiences. In this story, the gold Cadillac symbolizes, or stands for, different things to different people in the story. What do you think the Cadillac symbolizes to 'lois?

The Gold Cadillac **787**

Teach

EL Language Coach

Base Words and Roots Say: The word *resist* contains the root *sist*, which means "withstand." What other words contain the root *sist*? (Possible responses: insist, persist, assist) **OL**

L Literary Element

Symbol Ask: What does the gold Cadillac seem to symbolize for 'lois? (wealth) Say: Support your answer with details from the text. (Possible response: She wants the neighbors to see the Cadillac; she describes it as "a car for rich folks" and asks her father if they are rich.) **OL**

Differentiated Instruction

Graphic Organizer To help students keep track of what the Cadillac symbolizes for each character, suggest that they create a three-column chart in their Learner's Notebooks. In the first column, have students list the names of the characters in the story. In the second column, have students list quotations that reveal what each character thinks and says about the Cadillac. Students should fill in this column as they read. When students have finished reading the selection, have them write in the third column a brief conclusion about what the car symbolizes for each character. **AS**

Objectives

- Identify word structure: base words
- Identify literary elements: symbol
- Learn and use new vocabulary

Teach

L Literary Element

Symbol Ask: Have you ever been proud of an accomplishment? How did you show your pride? *(Responses will vary.)*
Ask: Why do you think 'lois's father is proud as he shows off the gold Cadillac? *(Possible response: He probably worked hard to earn the money to buy it.)* **OL**

R Reading Skill

Synthesizing Ask: Has there ever been a time when you weren't as excited about something as your friends or family? Explain. *(Responses will vary.)*
Ask: What reasons might 'lois's mother have for not being excited about the Cadillac? *(Responses will vary. Students may say that 'lois's mother doesn't think their previous car was old enough to need replacing. Other students may say that she resents not being asked about purchasing a new car.)* **AS**

---

came out too. Everybody surrounded the car and owwed and ahhed. Nobody could believe it.

Then my mother came out.

Everybody stood back grinning as she approached the car. There was no smile on her face. We all waited for her to speak. She stared at the car, then looked at my father, standing there as proud as he could be. Finally she said, "You didn't buy this car, did you, Wilbert?" **3**

"Gotta admit I did. Couldn't resist it."

"But . . . but what about our Mercury? It was perfectly good!"

"Don't you like the Cadillac, Dee?"

"That Mercury wasn't even a year old!"

My father nodded. "And I'm sure whoever buys it is going to get themselves a good car. But we've got ourselves a better one. Now stop frowning, honey, and let's take ourselves a ride in our brand-new Cadillac!"

My mother shook her head. "I've got food on the stove," she said and turning away walked back to the house.

There was an awkward silence and then my father said, "You know Dee never did much like surprises. Guess this here Cadillac was a bit too much for her. I best go smooth things out with her."

Everybody watched as he went after my mother. But when he came back, he was alone.

"Well, what she say?" asked one of my uncles.

My father shrugged and smiled. "Told me I bought this Cadillac alone, I could just ride in it alone."

Another uncle laughed. "Uh-oh! Guess she told you!"

"Oh, she'll come around," said one of my aunts. "Any woman would be proud to ride in this car."

"That's what I'm banking on,"**7** said my father as he went around to the street side of the car and opened the door. "All right! Who's for a ride?"

"We are!" Wilma and I cried.

All three of my uncles and one of my aunts, still holding her baby, and Mr. Pondexter climbed in with us and we took off for the first ride in the gold Cadillac. It was a glorious ride and we drove all through the city of Toledo.**8** We rode past

---

7. If someone is **banking on** something, he or she is depending on it.

8. **Toledo** (tuh LEE doh) is a city in northwestern Ohio, near the state's border with Michigan. **Detroit** (dih TROYT) is north of Toledo, in Michigan.

788 UNIT 7 What Can We Learn from Our Mistakes?

Practice the Skills

3 Key Literary Element

Symbol Remember that the way characters feel about an object can hint at what it symbolizes for them. The writer uses the words *proudly* and *proud* to describe how 'lois's father acts as he shows off the gold Cadillac. What do you think the Cadillac symbolizes to him? **L**

Additional Support

Reading Fluency

Reading Dialogue Have students work in pairs to practice reading the dialogue between the narrator's mother and father, beginning with the question "You didn't buy this car, did you, Wilbert?" and ending with the statement "I best go smooth things out with her." Review with students how to adjust intonation for exclamation points and question marks. Tell students to read only the dialogue, using the nonverbal text such as "My father nodded" as a guide for gestures that they may wish to add to their reading. When student pairs have had ample time to practice, have them present oral readings to the class. **BL EL**

Dolly and Rach, 1930. John Wesley Hardrick. Oil on board, 38 x 33 in. Collection of Georgia A. Hardrick Rhea.

Analyzing the Painting In what ways does the relationship between the girls in the painting reflect the relationship between Wilma and 'lois?

Teach

BQ **BIG Question**

Ask: Why might it be a mistake for someone to make a large purchase, such as buying a brand new car? *(Possible responses: The purchase might be more expensive than the person can really afford; the purchase might not be practical for the buyer's needs.)* **OL**

C Critical Thinking

Analysis Ask: Do you agree with 'lois's family that the mother will finally give in and ride in the Cadillac? Why or why not? *(Responses will vary. Some students may say that the mother will not give in because of how serious she seemed when she discovered that her husband had bought the car. Others may suggest that she will give in when she learns what her husband's motives actually were for buying the car.)* **OL**

the church and past the school. We rode through Ottawa Hills where the rich folks lived and on into Walbridge Park and past the zoo, then along the Maumee River. But none us had had enough of the car so my father put the car on the road and we drove all the way to Detroit. We had plenty of family there and everybody was just as pleased as could be about the Cadillac. My father told our Detroit relatives that he was in the doghouse[9] with my mother about buying the Cadillac. My uncles told them she wouldn't ride in the car. All the Detroit family thought that was funny and everybody, including my father, laughed about it and said my mother would come around.[10] **4**

9. When you're *in the doghouse,* you're in trouble with someone.
10. *Come around* is a way of saying "give in to a point of view or action."

Practice the Skills

4 **Key Literary Element**

Symbol From reading the footnote, you know that *in the doghouse* means "being in trouble." Why do you think being sent to a doghouse symbolizes being in trouble?

The Gold Cadillac **789**

Differentiated Instruction

Write a Letter Have students work in pairs. One student in each group should write a letter to 'lois's father from her mother's perspective, explaining why she is so reluctant to ride in the car. Tell students to explain why the Cadillac upsets her and what she wants him to do about the car. Then tell students to

exchange letters and write a response from 'lois's father's perspective. Students should respond to the mother's concerns, explain the father's motivation for purchasing the car, and describe what the car symbolizes for the father. Invite student pairs to share their letters with the class. **AS**

Objectives
• Identify literary elements: symbol
• Synthesize information
• Analyze text

Teach

EL Language Coach

Base Words and

Roots Ask: What other words can you form by using the root *agree*? *(Possible responses: agreeable, agreeing, disagreeing, agreement, disagreement, agreed, disagreed, agreeably, disagreeably)* **AS**

BQ BIG Question

Ask: What do you learn about the mother's priorities? *(Possible response: She cares more about moving into a better house than about driving a nicer car.)* **Ask:** Do you agree with her that buying the Cadillac is a mistake? Explain. *(Responses will vary.)* **OL**

L Literary Element

Symbol Ask: How has buying the gold Cadillac affected the family? *(Possible response: The Cadillac has made the father and his family proud, but it has also made it more difficult for the family to save for a new house.)* **OL Ask:** Given your response, discuss all of the things that the car symbolizes. *(Possible response: It symbolizes hard work and pride, but it also symbolizes a broken promise.)* **AL**

It was early evening by the time we got back home, and I could see from my mother's face she had not come around. She was angry now not only about the car, but that we had been gone so long. I didn't understand that, since my father had called her as soon as we reached Detroit to let her know where we were. I had heard him myself. I didn't understand either why she did not like that fine Cadillac and thought she was being terribly **disagreeable** with my father. That night as she tucked Wilma and me in bed I told her that too. **5**

"Is this your business?" she asked.

"Well, I just think you ought to be nice to Daddy. I think you ought to ride in that car with him! It'd sure make him happy."

"I think you ought to go to sleep," she said and turned out the light.

Later I heard her arguing with my father. "We're supposed to be saving for a house!" she said.

"We've already got a house!" said my father.

"But you said you wanted a house in a better neighborhood. I thought that's what we both said!"

"I haven't changed my mind."

BQ "Well, you have a mighty funny way of saving for it, then. Your brothers are saving for houses of their own and you don't see them out buying new cars every year!"

"We'll still get the house, Dee. That's a promise!"

"Not with new Cadillacs we won't!" said my mother and then she said a very loud good night and all was quiet. **6 7**

The next day was Sunday and everybody figured that my mother would be sure to give in and ride in the Cadillac. After all, the family always went to church together on Sunday. But she didn't give in. What was worse she wouldn't let Wilma and me ride in the Cadillac either. She took us each by the hand, walked past the Cadillac where my father stood waiting and headed on toward the church, three blocks away. I was really mad at her now. I had been looking forward to driving up to the church in that gold Cadillac and having everybody see.

On most Sunday afternoons during the summertime, my mother, my father, Wilma, and I would go for a ride. Sometimes we just rode around the city and visited friends

790 UNIT 7 What Can We Learn from Our Mistakes?

Practice the Skills

5 English Language Coach

Base Words and Roots Look at the word **disagreeable**. You probably know the meaning of the base word *agree*. The prefix *dis-* means "not" or "the opposite of." Take a guess about what *disagreeable* means. **EL**

6 Key Reading Skill

Synthesizing You have now read why the mother doesn't like the Cadillac. Combine it with your own experience or with other things you have read about wanting a better life for yourself or your family. Has your understanding of the mother changed? Why or why not?

7 Key Literary Element

Symbol The gold Cadillac symbolizes one thing for the father and something very different for the mother. What does the new car represent for the mother? What statement explains the symbolism, or meaning, of the gold Cadillac for the mother? **L**

Additional Support

Literature Focus Lesson

Narrator Point out to students that the story is told by a first-person narrator who uses the personal pronouns *I, me, my,* and *we.* Because the story has a first-person narrator, readers learn only 'lois's thoughts and feelings. This limited point of view enables the author to build up the reader's curiosity about why the mother is upset about the Cadillac. To demonstrate this concept, have students write several paragraphs in which they retell the story from an omniscient point of view, one in which the narrator knows the thoughts and feelings of all of the characters. **OL**

and family. Sometimes we made short trips over to Chicago or Peoria or Detroit to see relatives there or to Cleveland where we had relatives too, but we could also see the Cleveland Indians play. Sometimes we joined our aunts and uncles and drove in a **caravan** out to the park or to the beach. At the park or the beach Wilma and I would run and play. My mother and my aunts would spread a picnic and my father and my uncles would shine their cars. **L**

But on this Sunday afternoon my mother refused to ride anywhere. She told Wilma and me that we could go. So we left her alone in the big, empty house, and the family cars, led by the gold Cadillac, headed for the park. For a while I played and had a good time, but then I stopped playing and went to sit with my father. Despite his laughter he seemed sad to me. I think he was missing my mother as much as I was. **8**

Vocabulary

caravan (KAIR uh van) *n.* a group of people or vehicles traveling together

Toledo, Ohio, in the 1950s

Practice the Skills

8 BIG Question

The gold Cadillac continues to create problems in 'lois's family. How has it changed the family's Sunday afternoons? What signs are there that 'lois's father has begun to think that buying the gold Cadillac was a mistake? Write your answers on your Foldable. Your response will help you complete the Unit Challenge later. **R**

The Gold Cadillac **791**

Teach

L Literary Element

Symbol Say: Reread the narrator's description of how her family likes to spend Sunday afternoons. What do cars in general seem to symbolize for the family? *(Possible response: Because the family likes to go on trips, cars seem to symbolize family time and togetherness.)* **OL**

R Reading Skill

Synthesizing Ask: Why is it significant that the mother is left alone "in the big, empty house"? *(Possible response: The empty house symbolizes that the family is no longer together. Also, it is ironic that the mother is left in the house because the Cadillac has ruined her dream of moving into a nicer house.)* **OL**

English Language Coach

Imperfect Tense Write the following sentences on the board: *Wilma and I would run and play. My mother and my aunts would spread a picnic and my father and my uncles would shine their cars.* One use of the imperfect tense is to describe a past habit. In English,

past habits are frequently described with the words *used to* and *would.* In the sentences on this page, the speaker describes past habits on Sunday afternoons in the summertime. Have students write three original sentences in the imperfect tense. **OL**

Objectives
- Identify literary elements: symbol
- Identify word structure: base words
- Identify and analyze narrator
- Synthesize information

791

Teach

Viewing the Art

Ask: How would you describe the woman in the painting? What might she be thinking? *(Responses will vary.)* **AS**

C Critical Thinking

Analysis **Ask:** Why do you think 'lois's father takes his wife out to dinner? *(Possible responses: He wants to talk to her about the Cadillac and the problems it has caused; he wants to do something nice for her because she is upset about the Cadillac.)* **Ask:** What is ironic about how they get there? *(Possible response: It is ironic that they walk because they own a new car.)* **OL**

Springtime (Portrait of Ella Mae Moore), 1933. John Wesley Hardrick. Oil on board, 48 x 32 in. Private Collection.

Analyzing the Painting Does this woman remind you of 'lois's mother? Why or why not?

That evening my father took my mother to dinner down at the corner café. They walked. Wilma and I stayed at the house chasing fireflies in the backyard. My aunts and uncles sat in the yard and on the porch, talking and laughing about the day and watching us. It was a soft summer's evening, the kind that came every day and was expected. The smell of charcoal and of barbecue drifting from up the block, the sound of laughter and music and talk drifting from yard to yard were all a part of it. Soon one of my uncles joined Wilma and me in our chase of fireflies and when my mother and father came home we were at it still. My mother and father

792 UNIT 7 What Can We Learn from Our Mistakes?

Additional Support

Differentiated Instruction

Visual Representation Visual learners may benefit from demonstrating comprehension through illustration. Have students illustrate the scene that is narrated on this page. Some students may wish to draw a direct representation of the characters and their surroundings, and others may wish to draw a more abstract version that is suggestive of the scene's theme. Have students present their illustrations to the class, identifying various aspects of their work and explaining how they chose to capture such details as "It was a soft summer's evening." **AS**

watched us for awhile, while everybody else watched them to see if my father would take out the Cadillac and if my mother would slide in beside him to take a ride. But it soon became evident that the dinner had not changed my mother's mind. She still refused to ride in the Cadillac. I just couldn't understand her objection to it. **R**

Though my mother didn't like the Cadillac, everybody else in the neighborhood certainly did. That meant quite a few folks too, since we lived on a very busy block. On one corner was a grocery store, a cleaner's, and a gas station. Across the street was a beauty shop and a fish market, and down the street was a bar, another grocery store, the Dixie Theater, the café, and a drugstore. There were always people strolling to or from one of these places and because our house was right in the middle of the block just about everybody had to pass our house and the gold Cadillac. Sometimes people took in[11] the Cadillac as they walked, their heads turning for a longer look as they passed. Then there were people who just outright[12] stopped and took a good look before continuing on their way. I was proud to say that car belonged to my family. I felt mighty important as people called to me as I ran down the street. "'Ey, 'lois! How's that Cadillac, girl? Riding fine?" I told my mother how much everybody liked that car. She was not impressed and made no comment. **L**

Since just about everybody on the block knew everybody else, most folks knew that my mother wouldn't ride in the Cadillac. Because of that, my father took a lot of good-natured kidding from the men. My mother got kidded too as the women said if she didn't ride in that car, maybe some other woman would. And everybody laughed about it and began to bet on who would give in first, my mother or my father. But then my father said he was going to drive the car south into Mississippi to visit my grandparents and everybody stopped laughing.

My uncles stopped.
So did my aunts.
Everybody. **9**

---

11. *Took in* is another way of saying "became aware of" or "noticed."
12. *Outright* means "suddenly" or "completely."

Practice the Skills

9 Reviewing Skills

Activating Prior Knowledge
Think about what you learned in the Build Background section. Why do you think everyone stops laughing when the father says that he is driving the Cadillac to Mississippi?

The Gold Cadillac **793**

Teach

R Reading Skill

Synthesizing Ask: What is 'lois's reaction to her mother's disapproval? *(Possible response: 'lois is bewildered by her mother's disapproval of the Cadillac. At times, 'lois seems upset by her mother's disapproval, especially because the car is causing a rift in the family.)* **OL**

L Literary Element

Symbol Ask: Why do you think the people on the block enjoy stopping by and admiring the Cadillac? How does it make them feel? *(Responses will vary. Students may suggest that the people on the block are proud that one of their neighbors owns a gold Cadillac or that the neighbors experience a vicarious thrill from looking at the car.)* **AS**

Reading Fluency

Build Fluency Review the following tips with students.

• **Don't rush.** Read aloud at a pace that feels comfortable.

• **Pronounce each word clearly and confidently.**

• **Pay attention to punctuation.** Use a short pause for a comma, a slightly longer pause for a period, and an even longer pause for a new paragraph.

• **Read with feeling.** Vary the pitch, tone, and volume of your voice when appropriate.

Have students practice reading this page aloud. Invite volunteers to read aloud to the class. **EL BL**

Objectives
• Synthesize information
• Identify literary elements: symbol
• Analyze text
• Find meaning in art

Teach

R Reading Skill

Review Drawing Conclusions Ask: Based on what you've read, how do you think people in the 1950s would have reacted to an African American man driving an expensive car in the rural South? Why? *(Students may mention that because racial prejudice was still prevalent, some people might assume that the car was stolen or that the driver was boasting about his wealth. Some people were not yet comfortable with the idea that African Americans were entitled to the same rights and privileges as whites.)* **AS**

EL Language Coach

Base Words and Roots Ask: Is it always a bad thing to be *heedful* of what others say? Explain. *(Possible response: No; Young children should be heedful of what their parents tell them.)* **OL**

Ask: Why is 'lois's father tired of being heedful? *(Possible response: He believes that he has the right to act as he pleases and not as other people want him to act.)* **AL**

"Look here, Wilbert," said one of my uncles, "it's too dangerous. It's like putting a loaded gun to your head."[13]

"I paid good money for that car," said my father. "That gives me a right to drive it where I please. Even down to Mississippi."

My uncles argued with him and tried to talk him out of driving the car south. So did my aunts and so did the neighbors, Mr. LeRoy, Mr. Courtland, and Mr. Pondexter. They said it was a dangerous thing, a mighty dangerous thing, for a black man to drive an expensive car into the rural[14] South.

"Not much those folks hate more'n to see a northern Negro coming down there in a fine car," said Mr. Pondexter. "They see those Ohio license plates, they'll figure you coming down uppity, trying to lord[15] your fine car over them!"

I listened, but I didn't understand. I didn't understand why they didn't want my father to drive that car south. It was his.

"Listen to Pondexter, Wilbert!" cried another uncle. "We might've fought a war to free people overseas, but we're not free here! Man, those white folks down south'll lynch[16] you soon's look at you. You know that!"

Wilma and I looked at each other. Neither one of us knew what *lynch* meant, but the word sent a shiver through us. We held each other's hand.

My father was silent, then he said: "All my life I've had to be **heedful** of what white folks thought. Well, I'm tired of that. I worked hard for everything I got. Got it honest, too. Now I got that Cadillac because I liked it and because it meant something to me that somebody like me from Mississippi could go and buy it. It's my car, I paid for it, and I'm driving it south." **10 11**

My mother, who had said nothing through all this, now stood. "Then the girls and I'll be going too," she said.

---

13. *It's like putting a loaded gun to your head* is a way of saying that you risk being killed.

14. *Rural* (RER ul) means "in the country, away from cities or towns."

15. When someone *lords* something over someone else, he or she behaves in a grand, overly proud way.

16. *Lynch* (linch) means "to murder, usually by hanging, through the action of a mob." Someone who is lynched does not get a lawful trial and often is put to death because of racial hatred.

794 UNIT 7 What Can We Learn from Our Mistakes?

Practice the Skills

10 English Language Coach

Base Words and Roots What does **heedful** mean? You can figure that out if you know that *heed* means "pay attention." Now explain what 'lois's father means when he says that all his life he's had to be heedful of what white people thought. **EL**

11 Key Literary Element

Symbol Has the information on this page changed what you think the Cadillac symbolizes for the father? Explain.

Additional Support

English Language Coach

Suffixes: -ive and -ous Tell students that studying common suffixes will help them make educated guesses about the meanings of new vocabulary words. Point out that the word *expensive* contains the suffix *-ive*, which means "having the quality of." Explain that this suffix also appears as *-ative* and *-itive.* Have students brainstorm examples of words that contain these variations. Common examples include *sensitive, competitive,* and *talkative.* Perform this exercise with the suffix *-ous* (also *-eous, -ose,* and *-ious*), which means the same or nearly the same as *-ive.* **EL BL**

"No!" said my father.

My mother only looked at him and went off to the kitchen. **12**

My father shook his head. It seemed he didn't want us to go. My uncles looked at each other, then at my father. "You set on doing this, we'll all go," they said. "That way we can watch out for each other." My father took a moment and nodded. Then my aunts got up and went off to their kitchens too.

All the next day my aunts and my mother cooked and the house was filled with delicious smells. They fried chicken and baked hams and cakes and sweet potato pies and mixed potato salad. They filled jugs with water and punch and coffee. Then they packed everything in huge picnic baskets along with bread and boiled eggs, oranges and apples, plates and napkins, spoons and forks and cups. They placed all that food on the back seats of the cars. It was like a grand, grand picnic we were going on, and Wilma and I were mighty excited. We could hardly wait to start.

My father, my mother, Wilma, and I got into the Cadillac. My uncles, my aunts, my cousins got into the Ford, the Buick, and the Chevrolet, and we rolled off in our caravan headed south. Though my mother was finally riding in the Cadillac, she had no praise for it. In fact, she said nothing about it at all. She still seemed upset and since she still seemed to feel the same about the car, I wondered why she had insisted upon making this trip with my father.

We left the city of Toledo behind, drove through Bowling Green and down through the Ohio countryside of farms and small towns, through Dayton and Cincinnati, and across the Ohio River into Kentucky. On the other side of the river my father stopped the car and looked back at Wilma and me and said, "Now from here on, whenever we stop and there're white people around, I don't want either one of you to say a word. *Not one word!* Your mother and I'll do all the talking. That understood?"

"Yes, sir," Wilma and I both said, though we didn't truly understand why.

My father nodded, looked at my mother and started the car again. We rolled on, down Highway 25 and through the bluegrass hills of Kentucky. Soon we began to see signs.

Practice the Skills

12 Reviewing Skills

Interpreting The mother has been unwilling to ride in the Cadillac, but now she decides that she and the girls will go on the trip to Mississippi. Up to this point, the father has wanted them all to ride in the car, but now he says, "No." What reasons do you think they might have for changing their minds?

The Gold Cadillac **795**

Teach

R Reading Skill

Review Interpreting Ask: What do you know about the trip the father plans to take? (*It will be dangerous.*) How might this influence his refusal to bring his wife and daughters? (*Possible response: He does not want to put his family in danger.*) **OL**

C Critical Thinking

Comprehension Ask: Why does the father insist that Wilma and her sister not say a word when there are white people around? (*Possible response: He does not want his family to attract any more attention. Speaking out of turn could result in trouble in the region they will be traveling through.*) **OL**

Differentiated Instruction

Map It Students with spatial or visual learning styles may benefit from charting the family's journey from Toledo to Mississippi on a map. Have students produce basic maps of Ohio, Kentucky, Tennessee, and Mississippi. Tell students to fill in state capitals, major cities, and other geographical features, being sure to include those cities mentioned in the story. Then have students use a colored pencil or marker to draw the family's route from Toledo to Mississippi by way of Dayton, Cincinnati, and Memphis. Have students keep their maps on hand so that they can refer to them as they read the rest of the selection. **AS**

Objectives
- Draw conclusions from text and experience
- Identify word structure: base words
- Monitor comprehension

795

Teach

R Reading Skill

Synthesizing Say: Describe 'lois's experience with segregation in the South. Why does she no longer think that the picnic her family packed is "grand"? *(Possible response: 'lois sees signs that prevent black people from drinking from water fountains, eating in restaurants, sleeping in motels, and using restrooms. She realizes that the family has packed food because segregation prevents them from ordering food in restaurants.)* **OL**

L Literary Element

Symbol Ask: Do you think that 'lois's father is still proud of his Cadillac and what it symbolizes at this point? Explain. *(Responses will vary. Students may say that he is still proud of it, even though it brings him trouble when he drives it in the South.)* **AL**

Viewing the Photo

Ask: What evidence of segregation do you notice in the photo? *(The drinking fountain is for black people only.)* What evidence of integration do you notice? *(The restroom is for both blacks and whites.)* **OL**

Signs that read: WHITE ONLY, COLORED NOT ALLOWED. Hours later, we left the Bluegrass State and crossed into Tennessee. Now we saw even more of the signs saying: WHITE ONLY, COLORED NOT ALLOWED. We saw the signs above water fountains and in restaurant windows. We saw them in ice cream parlors and at hamburger stands. We saw them in front of hotels and motels, and on the restroom doors of filling stations. I didn't like the signs. I felt as if I were in a foreign land.

I couldn't understand why the signs were there and I asked my father what the signs meant. He said they meant we couldn't drink from the water fountains. He said they meant we couldn't stop to sleep in the motels. He said they meant we couldn't stop to eat in the restaurants. I looked at the grand picnic basket I had been enjoying so much. Now I understood why my mother had packed it. Suddenly the picnic did not seem so grand. **13**

Finally we reached Memphis. We got there at a bad time. Traffic was heavy and we got separated from the rest of the family. We tried to find them but it was no use. We had to go on alone. We reached the Mississippi state line and soon after we heard a police siren. A police car came up behind us. My father slowed the Cadillac, then stopped. Two white policemen got out of their car. They eyeballed[17] the Cadillac and told my father to get out.

---

17. When you *eyeball* something, you look at it closely in order to evaluate it.

Analyzing the Photo What did 'lois do when she saw signs like the ones in this photo? How did she feel?

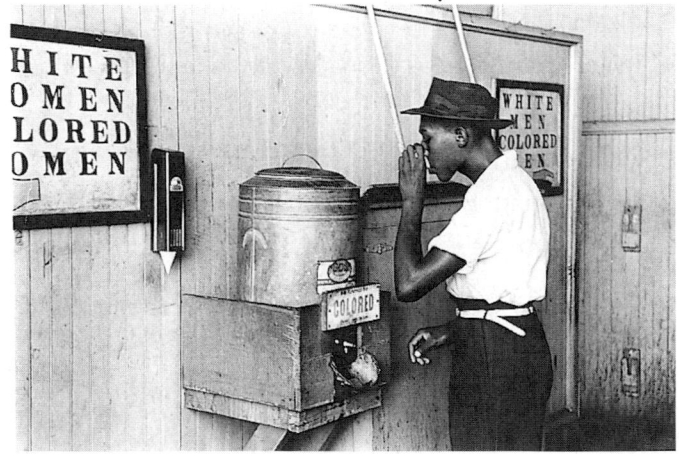

Practice the Skills

13 Key Reading Skill

Synthesizing Think about the preparations 'lois's family made for their trip south. Combine that information with what 'lois and her sister see as they travel into the South. What new understanding do you and 'lois have of the grand picnic basket the family packed? **R**

Additional Support

Reading in the Real World

Citizenship Have students work in small groups to research segregation in the South, from the years immediately after the Civil War through the end of the Civil Rights Movement. Assign each group one of the following topics: *Brown v. Board of Education, Plessy v. Ferguson,* Booker T. Washington, forced busing, Little Rock Central High School, and Jim Crow laws. Have each group give a brief presentation about its findings. Then have groups compile their research to create a time line of major laws, court cases, and events related to segregation in the United States. **AL**

"Whose car is this, boy?"[18] they asked.

I saw anger in my father's eyes. "It's mine," he said.

"You're a liar," said one of the policemen. "You stole this car."

"Turn around, put your hands on top of that car and spread eagle,"[19] said the other policeman.

My father did as he was told. They searched him and I didn't understand why. I didn't understand either why they had called my father a liar and didn't believe that the Cadillac was his. I wanted to ask but I remembered my father's warning not to say a word and I obeyed that warning. **14**

The policemen told my father to get in the back of the police car. My father did. One policeman got back into the police car. The other policeman slid behind the wheel of our Cadillac. The police car started off. The Cadillac followed. Wilma and I looked at each other and at our mother. We didn't know what to think. We were scared.

The Cadillac followed the police car into a small town and stopped in front of the police station. The policeman stepped out of our Cadillac and took the keys. The other policeman took my father into the police station.

"Mother-Dear!" Wilma and I cried. "What're they going to do to our daddy? They going to hurt him?"

"He'll be all right," said my mother. "He'll be all right." But she didn't sound so sure of that. She seemed worried.

We waited. More than three hours we waited. Finally my father came out of the police station. We had lots of questions to ask him. He said the police had given him a ticket for speeding and locked him up. But then the judge had come. My father had paid the ticket and they had let him go. **15**

He started the Cadillac and drove slowly out of the town, below the speed limit. The police car followed us. People standing on steps and sitting on porches and in front of stores stared at us as we passed. Finally we were out of the town. The police car still followed. Dusk was falling. The night grew black and finally the police car turned around and left us.

---

18. The policeman calls 'lois's father **boy** to put him down.

19. To stand **spread eagle** is to stand with arms and legs spread wide. In this position, a person cannot surprise a police officer by pulling out a hidden weapon.

Practice the Skills

C

14 **Key Reading Skill**

Synthesizing Sometimes grown-up black men were called "boy" by white people. Use all the information you have learned in the story to answer these questions: Why would calling a grown man "boy" be insulting? Why might some white people have used this term? Why might the policeman have used it with the father?

15 **Key Reading Skill**

Synthesizing In your Learner's Notebook, write a description of what the father might have been thinking while he was locked up. Keep in mind everything you've learned about the South and the treatment that the father received from the policemen. **R**

The Gold Cadillac **797**

Teach

C Critical Thinking

Evaluation Ask: Is 'lois right to follow her father's warning and not speak to the police officers? Explain. *(Possible response: Yes; By speaking up, 'lois could make the police officers angry and get her father into even more trouble.)* **OL**

R Reading Skill

Synthesizing Ask: Do you think that 'lois's father deserved the speeding ticket? How do you think he felt about being locked up and fined? *(Responses will vary. Students may say that 'lois's father didn't deserve to go to jail, even if he had been speeding. Students may speculate that 'lois's father felt outraged that he was assumed to be a thief.)* **AS**

BQ 🏈 **BIG Question**

Ask: Do you think that 'lois's father regrets his decision to drive the Cadillac to Mississippi? Explain your answer. *(Responses will vary. Some students may say that he realizes his mistake in driving the car to Mississippi because of the danger involved. Others may say that he does not regret his decision because he does not want to be heedful of what white people tell him.)* **OL**

English Language Coach

Irregular Verbs Point out examples of verbs on this page that form the past tense regularly by adding -d or -ed. Examples include *searched, called, wanted, remembered, obeyed,* and *followed.* Then point out examples of verbs that form the past tense irregularly. Examples include *stole, did, told, got,* and *took.* Have students make a list of verbs from the text with irregular past-tense forms. Then have students use their lists to create flashcards. Students should write the present-tense form of each verb (for example, *steal*) on the front of a card and the irregular past tense (for example, *stole*) on the back. Have students quiz each other with the flashcards. **EL**

Objectives
• Synthesize information
• Evaluate text
• Identify literary elements: symbol
• Use text features: photographs
• Use irregular verbs

797

Teach

C Critical Thinking

Comprehension Ask: Why is 'lois upset when her father goes to sleep? *(Possible response: In addition to being scared by the events of the day, she is anxious about the dark, unknown woods. She wants her father to be awake to protect her.)* **OL**

L Literary Element

Symbol Ask: What does the knife symbolize for 'lois? *(Responses will vary. Students may suggest that the knife represents security, safety, or protection.)* **AS**

BQ BIG Question

Ask: Does the father admit that driving the Cadillac to Mississippi was a mistake? *(Yes; he says that driving farther south is "not worth the risk.")*
Ask: What does he plan to do now? *(Possible response: He plans to drive the car to his cousin's in Memphis, leave it there, and borrow his cousin's car to continue the trip.)* **OL**

We drove and drove. But my father was tired now and my grandparents' farm was still far away. My father said he had to get some sleep and since my mother didn't drive, he pulled into a grove of trees at the side of the road and stopped.

"I'll keep watch," said my mother.

"Wake me if you see anybody," said my father.

"Just rest," said my mother.

C So my father slept. But that bothered me. I needed him awake. I was afraid of the dark and of the woods and of whatever lurked there. My father was the one who kept us safe, he and my uncles. But already the police had taken my father away from us once today and my uncles were lost.

"Go to sleep, baby," said my mother. "Go to sleep."

L But I was afraid to sleep until my father woke. I had to help my mother keep watch. I figured I had to help protect us too, in case the police came back and tried to take my father away again. There was a long, sharp knife in the picnic basket and I took hold of it, clutching it tightly in my hand. Ready to strike, I sat there in the back of the car, eyes wide, searching the **blackness** outside the Cadillac. Wilma, for a while, searched the night too, then she fell asleep. I didn't want to sleep, but soon I found I couldn't help myself as an unwelcome drowsiness came over me. I had an **uneasy** sleep and when I woke it was dawn and my father was gently shaking me. I woke with a start[20] and my hand went up, but the knife wasn't there. My mother had it. **16**

My father took my hand. "Why were you holding the knife, 'lois?" he asked.

I looked at him and at my mother. "I—I was scared," I said.

My father was thoughtful. "No need to be scared now, sugar," he said. "Daddy's here and so is Mother-Dear." Then after a glance at my mother, he got out of the car, walked to the road, looked down it one way, then the other. When he came back and started the motor, he turned the Cadillac north, not south.

"What're you doing?" asked my mother.

BQ "Heading back to Memphis," said my father. "Cousin Halton's there. We'll leave the Cadillac and get his car. Driving this car any farther south with you and the girls in the car, it's just not worth the risk."

---

20. **With a start** is another way of saying "with a sudden movement that can't be controlled."

Practice the Skills

16 English Language Coach

Base Words and Roots Look at the underlined words in this paragraph. Write down the base words and their definitions. Then explain how the prefix and the suffix change the meaning of each base word.

Additional Support

Literature Focus Lesson

Readers Theater This story lends itself to a Readers Theater production. Assign students the roles of the father, Wilma, 'lois, the mother, and others. Assign the role of 'lois to a skilled reader, since the majority of the story will be read by that student. Then have all the students read their characters' dialogue. Make sure students have time to practice so that the reading sounds like a dramatic production. Emphasize the importance of using inflection and tone to convey meaning in reading. Have students present their production to the rest of the class. **OL AL**

And so that's what we did. Instead of driving through Mississippi in golden splendor,[21] we traveled its streets and roads and highways in Cousin Halton's solid, yet not so splendid, four-year-old Chevy. When we reached my grandparents' farm, my uncles and aunts were already there. Everybody was glad to see us. They had been worried. They asked about the Cadillac. My father told them what had happened, and they nodded and said he had done the best thing.

We stayed one week in Mississippi. During that week I often saw my father, looking deep in thought, walk off alone across the family land. I saw my mother watching him. One day I ran after my father, took his hand, and walked the land with him. I asked him all the questions that were on my mind. I asked him why the policemen had treated him the way they had and why people didn't want us to eat in the restaurants or drink from the water fountains or sleep in the hotels. I told him I just didn't understand all that.

21. **Splendor** (SPLEN dur) is great brightness or beauty.

Analyzing the Photo Use this photo to help you visualize the family's land in Mississippi. If you had serious things to think about, would this be a good place to walk and think? Explain.

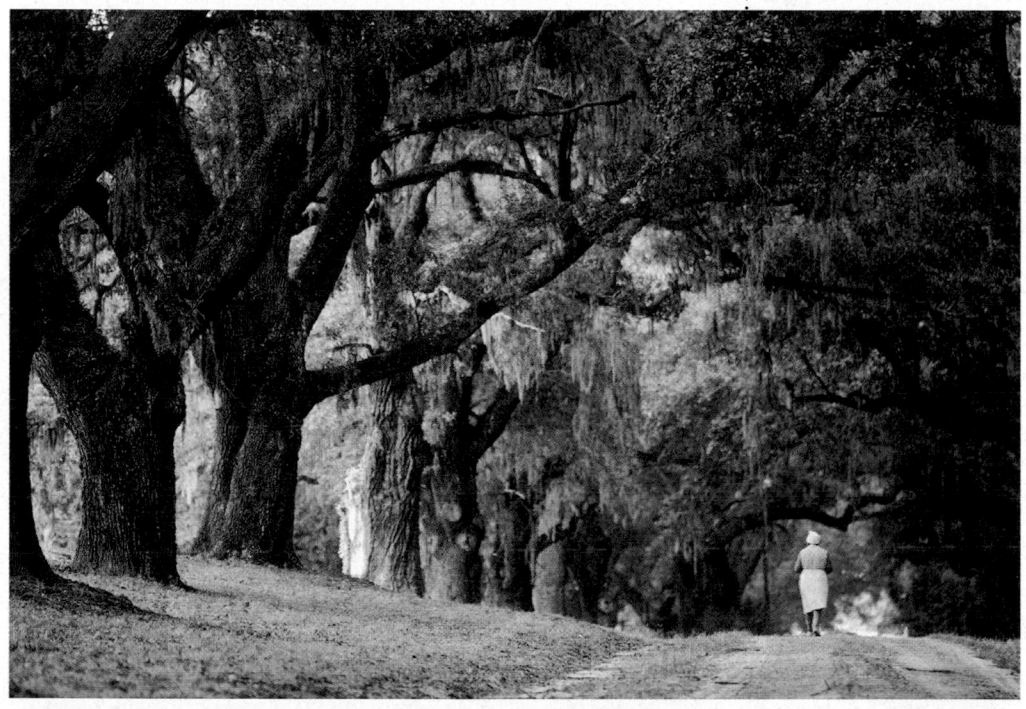

The Gold Cadillac **799**

Teach

L Literary Element

Symbol Say: At one point, the gold Cadillac symbolized success and pride. What does it symbolize for the family now? *(Responses will vary. Students may say that it symbolizes segregation or the unfairness with which blacks in the South are treated.)* **OL**

C Critical Thinking

Analysis Say: 'lois's father spends much of the time in Mississippi walking by himself and thinking. What do you think is on his mind? *(Possible responses: regrets about buying the gold Cadillac and driving it to Mississippi; the situation of his family and of other blacks in the South)* **OL**

Differentiated Instruction

Freewriting Have students spend ten or fifteen minutes writing their response to the picture on this page. Do not give students guidelines about what to write; instead, have them write whatever comes to mind from looking at the picture. If students have difficulty beginning the exer- cise, have them start by describing what they see. Tell students not to worry about spelling or organization during the free- writing. Invite students to share excerpts from their freewriting. Then have students select a passage from their freewriting and revise it to form a finished piece. **AS**

Objectives

• Identify literary elements: symbol
• Analyze text
• Monitor comprehension

Teach

R Reading Skill

Review Drawing Conclusions Ask: What must change before the family can drive down the road without being bothered by police and without seeing any signs of segregation? *(Possible response: Ignorance and prejudice must end, and segregation laws must change.)* **OL**

L Literary Element

Symbol Ask: Why does 'lois's mother tell her husband to keep the Cadillac? Why have her views changed? What does the Cadillac now symbolize for her? *(Responses will vary. Students may say that the trip to Mississippi has reminded 'lois's mother to be proud of her racial identity, and therefore to be proud of the car that her husband earned. The Cadillac may now symbolize her identity as a proud, successful African American.)* **AS**

My father looked at me and said that it all was a difficult thing to understand and he didn't really understand it himself. He said it all had to do with the fact that black people had once been forced to be slaves. He said it had to do with our skins being colored. He said it had to do with stupidity and ignorance. He said it had to do with the law, the law that said we could be treated like this here in the South. And for that matter, he added, any other place in these United States where folks thought the same as so many folks did here in the South. But he also said, "I'm hoping one day though we can drive that long road down here and there won't be any signs. I'm hoping one day the police won't stop us just because of the color of our skins and we're riding in a gold Cadillac with northern plates." **17**

When the week ended, we said a sad good-bye to my grandparents and all the Mississippi family and headed in a caravan back toward Memphis. In Memphis we returned Cousin Halton's car and got our Cadillac. Once we were home my father put the Cadillac in the garage and didn't drive it. I didn't hear my mother say any more about the Cadillac. I didn't hear my father speak of it either.

Some days passed and then on a bright Saturday afternoon while Wilma and I were playing in the backyard, I saw my father go into the garage. He opened the garage doors wide so the sunshine streamed in, and began to shine the Cadillac. I saw my mother at the kitchen window staring out across the yard at my father. For a long time, she stood there watching my father shine his car. Then she came out and crossed the yard to the garage and I heard her say, "Wilbert, you keep the car."

He looked at her as if he had not heard.

"You keep it," she repeated and turned and walked back to the house.

My father watched her until the back door had shut behind her. Then he went on shining the car and soon began to sing. About an hour later he got into the car and drove away. That evening when he came back he was walking. The Cadillac was nowhere in sight.

"Daddy, where's our new Cadillac?" I demanded to know. So did Wilma.

He smiled and put his hand on my head. "Sold it," he said as my mother came into the room.

"But how come?" I asked. "We poor now?"

800 UNIT 7 What Can We Learn from Our Mistakes?

Practice the Skills

17 Reviewing Skills

Drawing Conclusions What general statement can you make about African Americans in the United States in the 1950s, given what 'lois's father says in this paragraph? **R**

Additional Support

Literature Focus Lesson

Character Development Point out to students that although authors have limited space in short stories, they frequently have characters develop and change over time. These changes may be physical or psychological. In this story, 'lois's mother's character develops as her views about the Cadillac change. Have students revisit the charts in which they listed what each character said or thought about the Cadillac. Tell students to add another column to explain how each character has changed throughout the story, if at all. **OL**

"No, sugar. We've got more money towards our new house now and we're all together. I figure that makes us about the richest folks in the world." He smiled at my mother and she smiled too and came into his arms.

After that we drove around in an old 1930s Model A Ford my father had. He said he'd factory ordered us another Mercury, this time with my mother's approval. Despite that, most folks on the block figured we had fallen on[22] hard times after such a splashy showing of good times and some folks even laughed at us as the Ford rattled around the city. I must admit that at first I was pretty much embarrassed to be riding around in that old Ford after the splendor of the Cadillac. But my father said to hold my head high. We and the family knew the truth. As fine as the Cadillac had been, he said, it had pulled us apart for awhile. Now, as ragged and noisy as that old Ford was, we all rode in it together and we were a family again. So I held my head high. **18**

Still though, I thought often of that Cadillac. We had had the Cadillac only a little more than a month, but I wouldn't soon forget its splendor or how I'd felt riding around inside it. I wouldn't soon forget either the ride we had taken south in it. I wouldn't soon forget the signs, the policemen, or my fear. I would remember that ride and the gold Cadillac all my life. ○

R

22. *Fallen on* means "met with."

African American family, Detroit, Michigan, 1942.

The Gold Cadillac **801**

Practice the Skills

18 BIG Question

At the end of the story, does 'lois's mother think that she has made a mistake about the Cadillac? Does 'lois's father think that he made a mistake? Write your answers on your Foldable. Your response will help you complete the Unit Challenge later. **BQ**

Teach

BQ **BIG Question**

Say: At the beginning of the story, Wilbert does not share his wife's opinion of the Cadillac. What does he learn from his experience? *(Possible response: Wilbert realizes that his family's togetherness, as well as saving for a better house, is far more important than owning an expensive car.)* **AS**

R Reading Skill

Synthesizing Ask: Is 'lois's memory of the Cadillac positive or negative? Explain. *(Responses will vary. Some students may suggest that 'lois's memory of the Cadillac is negative because it reminds her of the segregation and discrimination that her family encountered. Others may suggest that her memory of the Cadillac is more positive because it brought her family closer together in the end.)* **AS**

Assess

CheckPoint

Use the CheckPoint questions provided on Presentation Plus! to check for comprehension of the selection. These questions can be used with interactive response keypads for immediate student feedback.

Differentiated Instruction

Write an Epilogue 'lois mentions briefly that some people in the neighborhood laugh as she and her family drive around in the old Ford. Have students write an epilogue, or follow-up to the story, in which they describe a specific encounter with someone from the neighborhood. In their epilogues, students should address the neighbor's assumption that the family has fallen on hard times. Tell students to continue the story in 'lois's voice, using a combination of narration and dialogue to illustrate what 'lois has learned from her experience and what she values most. **OL AL**

Objectives
• Synthesize information
• Draw conclusions from text and experience
• Identify literary elements: symbol

801

Assess

 Resources for page 802

📁 Selection Quick Check, p. 61

📁 Selection and Unit Assessment, p. 73

💿 ExamView Assessment Suite

💿 Interactive Tutor: Self-Assessment

Students can respond to the *After You Read* items in their Learner's Notebooks or on a separate sheet of paper.

Answering the
 BIG Question

1. Responses will vary.

2. 'lois's mother is angry because the family is supposed to be saving money for a better house.

3. They think it will be very dangerous.

4. Possible response: Police officers stop the car and accuse 'lois's father of having stolen it.

Critical Thinking

5. Possible response: 'lois's mother decides to ride in the car when the father says that he is going to drive it to Mississippi. She knows it will be a dangerous trip and she does not want her husband to go on it alone.

6. Students may say that 'lois's father realizes that the family should be saving for a new home.

7. Responses will vary.

8. Responses will vary.

802

After You Read | The Gold Cadillac

Answering the BIG Question

1. Why does 'lois's mother change her mind about the Cadillac? What does she learn through the family's experience with the Cadillac?

2. **Recall** Why is 'lois's mother angry about the gold Cadillac?
   TIP Think and Search

3. **Recall** What do 'lois's uncles, aunts, and neighbors think about driving the Cadillac to the South?
   TIP Think and Search

4. **Summarize** What happens when the family takes the Cadillac to Mississippi?
   TIP Think and Search

Critical Thinking

5. **Infer** When does 'lois's mother decide to ride in the car after all? Why does she make this decision?
   TIP Author and Me

6. **Infer** Why do you think 'lois's father sells the Cadillac?
   TIP Author and Me

7. **Interpret** How do you think the trip to Mississippi changes 'lois? How does it change her father?
   TIP Author and Me

8. **Evaluate** Would you have sold the Cadillac? Why or why not?
   TIP On My Own

Objectives (pp. 802–803)
Reading Synthesize information
Literature Identify literary devices: symbolism
Vocabulary Identify word structure: roots and bases
Writing Compare and contrast
Grammar Identify parts of speech: verbs

Write About Your Reading

The girls' parents have different feelings about the Cadillac. Write two paragraphs, one for each parent, describing their different views of the car. Include the following in each paragraph:

• Tell how the parent feels about the car at the beginning of the story.

• Describe how the parent shows his or her feelings about the car.

• Explain how and why the parent's view changes after the trip to Mississippi.

Write About Your Reading

Possible responses:
Father:
'lois's father is extremely proud of the Cadillac. He always assumes that his wife will come around, so he doesn't take her disapproval too seriously. After the trip to Mississippi, he realizes that keeping his family together is more important than having a status symbol.

Mother:
'lois's mother is upset about the Cadillac because the family has been saving for a new house and because she disapproves of having an unnecessary display of wealth. At first, she refuses to ride in the Cadillac. After the trip, she admires her husband for buying the car to take a stand against racial prejudice. However, she is still happy when he sells it so the family can continue saving for a new home.

Skills Review

Key Reading Skill: Synthesizing

9. When you synthesize, you combine ideas to create something new. What new understanding did you gain about why people might take risks? Explain.

Key Literary Element: Symbol

10. Before the trip to Mississippi, 'lois's father says: "I got that Cadillac because I liked it and because it meant something to me that somebody like me from Mississippi could go and buy it. It's my car, I paid for it, and I'm driving it south." What does this say about what the car symbolizes for him?

11. At the beginning of the story, do you think 'lois's mother understands what the car symbolizes to 'lois's father? Explain.

12. Remember that the Cadillac is gold. What does this add to its symbolism? Explain.

Reviewing Skills: Drawing Conclusions

13. After reading this story, what conclusions can you draw about life in the South for African Americans in the 1950s?

Vocabulary Check

Write the vocabulary word that each clue describes.

features   practical   caravan

14. Driving in one might keep you from getting lost.
15. A new computer has many of these.
16. It means "realistic and sensible."
17. **Academic Vocabulary** Write a sentence using the word *synthesize* correctly.
18. **English Language Coach** The word *unison* contains the root *uni.* The root means *one* or *single.* Use the root to explain the meaning of *unison.* Use a dictionary if you need help.

Grammar Link: Finding the Verb

- Every sentence has a subject and a verb.
- Some verbs show action, or what the subject *does.*
    Their father *stepped* out of the new car.
    Wilma and 'lois *ran* to him.
- Other verbs tell what the subject *is* or *is like.*
    The new car *was* a gold Cadillac.
    The girls' mother *seemed* angry.
- The verb often directly follows the subject.
    The old Ford *rattled*.

Grammar Practice

Copy the sentences below. Circle the verb in each sentence.

19. Wilma and 'lois rode in the Cadillac with their father.
20. The girls went for a ride with their father.
21. Their other car was less than a year old.
22. At two o'clock, the caravan of cars rolled across the Ohio River.
23. The whole family drove south.
24. Two policemen stopped them in Mississippi.
25. Their mother looked worried.
26. People who were not white were not allowed in hotels in Mississippi.

Writing Application List the verbs in the paragraphs you wrote. Put a checkmark next to the verbs that directly follow their subjects.

Literature Online

Web Activities For eFlashcards, Selection Quick Checks, and other Web activities, go to www.glencoe.com.

The Gold Cadillac **803**

Skills Review

Key Reading Skill: Synthesizing

9. Responses will vary.

Key Literary Element: Symbol

10. Possible response: The Cadillac symbolizes hard work, entitlement, and pride.

11. Possible response: No, she doesn't even want to ride in the car at first.

12. Possible response: Gold symbolizes wealth and royalty so the gold Cadillac shows wealth and special status.

Reviewing Skills: Drawing Conclusions

13. Possible response: Life was hard and unfair.

Vocabulary Check

14. caravan
15. features
16. practical
17. **Academic Vocabulary** I am trying to synthesize all of the new information.
18. **English Language Coach** *Unison* means "performed together at the same time."

Close

Ask students to summarize what they learned about the Big Question from reading this selection.

Grammar Link: Finding the Verb

Grammar Practice

19. Wilma and 'lois rode in the Cadillac with their father.
20. The girls went for a ride with their father.
21. Their other car was less than a year old.
22. At two o'clock, the caravan of cars rolled across the Ohio River.
23. The whole family drove south.
24. Two policemen stopped them in Mississippi.
25. Their mother looked worried.
26. People who were not white were not allowed in hotels in Mississippi.

Teach

More About the Author

Sue Alexander has written more than twenty books. Her stories, poems, plays, and puzzles for children have also been published in magazines and newspapers. In addition to writing, Alexander enjoys reading books of all kinds, but she especially likes picture books. As a child, Alexander was greatly inspired by Phyllis Whitney's *The Silver Inkwell.*

Vocabulary

Parts of Speech Ask: What part of speech are the vocabulary words for this selection? *(verbs)* What do verbs do? *(Verbs express action or a state of being.)* **BL** Have students use each verb orally in a sentence. **EL OL** Challenge students to use all four vocabulary words in a single coherent paragraph. **AL**

Before You Read : Nadia the Willful

Sue Alexander

Meet the Author

Sue Alexander based the story "Nadia the Willful" on a problem in her own life. When her own brother died, her father did not want anyone to talk about him. Alexander says, "I knew my father was wrong, but I didn't know how to tell him so. So I did what I've always done when I've had a problem—I wrote a story." Alexander said she chose a different setting and characters for the story to make telling it less painful.

Author Search For more information about Sue Alexander, go to www.glencoe.com.

Objectives (pp. 804–811)
Reading Synthesize information
• Make connections from text to self
Literature Identify literary elements: plot
Vocabulary Identify word structure: roots and bases

Vocabulary Preview

utter (UT ur) *v.* to speak or say aloud **(p. 807)** *No one was allowed to utter Hamed's name.*

cease (sees) *v.* to stop **(p. 809)** *Nadia would not stop saying Hamed's name even after her mother told her to cease.*

banished (BAN isht) *v.* sent away, forced to be separate from a place or group **(p. 810)** *Tarik banished whoever said his son's name.*

pondered (PON durd) *v.* thought about **(p. 811)** *Nadia pondered what to say to her father.*

Choose a Synonym For each word in the **bold** type, choose the word that has nearly the same meaning.
utter talk total sing write
cease buy begin fold halt
banished welcomed expend separated questioned
pondered stomped ignored considered took

English Language Coach

Base Words and Roots Sometimes the best clue to a word's meaning is in the word itself. Look closely at a new word, and you might see a familiar base word. Or you might find a root whose meaning you know. A *root* is a **word part** that forms the base of a word. A *base word* is a **whole word** that is part of a larger word.

Table It Copy the table below into your Learner's Notebook. Put each word listed below next to its root and root meaning or next to its base word. The first two are done for you.

survive   illogical
telescope   replace
interrupt   nonexistent
variety   misbehave
spectator   distrust

Root	Base
viv = *live* survive	logic illogical
var = *different*	trust
spec = *to look at*	exist
rupt = *break*	behave
tele = *distant*	place

Additional Support

Author Search To expand students' appreciation of Sue Alexander, have them access the Web site for additional information and resources.

English Language Coach

Base Words and Roots List these common roots and their meanings on the board: *dic, dict:* say; *fac, fact:* make, do; *mort:* die; *port:* carry; *sol:* alone; *terr:* land; *tort:* twist, turn; *trans:* across, through. Have students record these roots and their meanings in their Learner's Notebooks. Then have students form small groups, and give each group a root from the list. Allow students five minutes to list as many words as they can that contain the assigned root. Encourage students to consult a dictionary for help. Tell students that they must be able to define each word that they list. **EL OL**

Skills Preview

Key Reading Skill: Synthesizing

When you synthesize information, you use many of the skills you have already learned. You connect, use your prior knowledge, clarify, and draw conclusions. The result is a new understanding about what you read and about life. It might sound hard, but don't worry! If you are an active reader and thinker, then you synthesize all the time when you read.

Literary Element: Plot

Plot is a story's events. Most plots center on a conflict, or problem, for one or more of the characters. Most plots also develop in five stages: exposition, rising action, climax, falling action, and resolution. The diagram shows the five stages in the plot, or story line.

Use these tips to understand and identify the stages in the plot.

- The exposition introduces the characters, setting, and conflict of the story.
  Who are the main characters? Where and when does the story take place? What is the conflict?

- The rising action adds complications to the conflict.
  How does the conflict develop?

- The climax is the point of greatest interest or suspense.
  What is the highest point of the story?

- The falling action is the logical result of the climax.
  What happens after the climax?

- The resolution presents the final outcome.
  How is the conflict resolved? How does the story end?

What's the Plot? Copy the diagram into your Learner's Notebook. Use two side-by-side pages to make it as large as possible. Write your answers to the questions about stages in the plot on the diagram as you read.

Get Ready to Read

Connect to the Reading

People—even friends and family members—disagree at times. Have you ever had a conflict with a friend or family member? What was it about? How did it end?

Write to Learn In your Learner's Notebook, write about a time you came into conflict with someone else. Describe what you both said and how the conflict was resolved.

Build Background

Sue Alexander chose the Bedouin and the desert to be the characters and setting for this story.

- The Bedouin are people of the Middle East. They speak Arabic.

- The Bedouins used to be nomads, which means they moved from place to place in the deserts of Saudi Arabia, Iraq, Syria, Jordan, and Sudan. They traveled by camel and were sheep and goat herders. Today, most Bedouins live in settlements.

Set Purposes for Reading

BIG Question Read the selection "Nadia the Willful" to learn what a father and his family learned from a mistake.

Set Your Own Purpose What else would you like to learn from the selection to help you answer the Big Question? Write your own purpose on the "Nadia the Willful" part of the Workshop 1 Foldable.

Interactive Literary Elements Handbook
To review or learn more about the literary elements, go to www.glencoe.com.

Keep Moving

Use these skills as you read the following selection.

Teach

L Literary Element

Plot Say: Recall a movie or book that you enjoyed. Using the diagram on this page, connect the events from the movie or book with the stages in the story line. Write your responses in your Learner's Notebooks. *(Responses will vary. Students should be able to identify important points in the plot.)* **OL**

R Reading Skill

Review Connecting Say: As you think about a conflict you have had with a friend or family member, consider how the conflict was resolved. Do you believe that it was resolved fairly? What did you learn from this conflict? Explain. *(Responses will vary.)* **OL**

Interactive Literary Elements Handbook Have students access the Web site to improve their understanding of plot.

Literature Focus Lesson

Plot Provide students with the following exposition:

Carlos had never walked to school by himself before. His older sister, Mirella, had always made the walk with him, saying good-bye at the playground before joining her older friends. This year, however, Mirella was at the high school on the other side of town, and Carlos had to face his first day of fifth grade alone. He squared his shoulders and set off down the street.

Tell students to use information from the exposition to outline the possible plot of a story about Carlos. **OL**

Objectives

- Identify literary elements: plot
- Make connections from text to self
- Learn and use new vocabulary
- Identify word structure: base words

Teach

EL Language Coach

Base Words and

Roots Emphasize that the base word in *willful* is a noun meaning "a determination to make things happen in a certain way." **Ask:** How do you think a willful person acts? *(Possible responses: A willful person may be bossy and do things their own way; a willful person probably does not pay much attention to what others say or want.)* **AS**

L Literary Element

Plot Say: Identify some important traits of each of the three main characters. *(Possible response: Nadia is willful, stubborn, and quick-tempered. Sheik Tarik is kind and gracious. Hamed is playful and loving.)* **AS Ask:** How do these traits cause conflict between Nadia and Tarik? What role does Hamed play in this ongoing conflict? *(Possible response: Tarik does not know how to calm his willful daughter. Hamed teases Nadia to calm her temper.)* **OL**

Readability Scores
Dale-Chall: 7.6
DRP: 54
Lexile: 900

Nadia the Willful

by Sue Alexander

In the land of the drifting sands where the Bedouin move their tents to follow the fertile grasses, there lived a girl whose stubbornness and flashing temper caused her to be known throughout the desert as Nadia the <u>Willful</u>. **1**

Nadia's father, the sheik[1] Tarik, whose kindness and graciousness caused his name to be praised in every tent, did not know what to do with his willful daughter.

Only Hamed, the eldest of Nadia's six brothers and Tarik's favorite son, could calm Nadia's temper when it flashed. "Oh, angry one," he would say, "shall we see how long you can stay that way?" And he would laugh and tease and pull at her dark hair until she laughed back. Then she would follow Hamed wherever he led. **2**

One day before dawn, Hamed mounted his father's great white stallion and rode to the west to seek new grazing ground for the sheep. Nadia stood with her father at the edge of the oasis and watched him go.

Hamed did not return.

Nadia rode behind her father as he traveled across the desert from oasis to oasis, seeking Hamed.

---

1. The head of a family and of tribes and other groups among the Bedouin is called a *sheik* (sheek).

Practice the Skills

1 English Language Coach

Base Words and Roots Willful is going to be an important word in the story. It contains the base word *will*, which means "determination" or "firmness of purpose." Think about what it means to say that someone is "full" of will. Then use your own words to tell what *willful* means. **EL**

2 Literary Element

Plot The exposition, or first stage in the plot, gives the reader important background information. It tells the setting and main characters. Add the setting and character information to the exposition part of your plot chart. **L**

Additional Support

Reading Fluency

Storytelling Read aloud the first paragraph of the selection. Point out that the words sound as though they could have been spoken aloud by a storyteller. The descriptions of the setting are quite detailed—someone hearing the story could easily visualize the setting. In addition, the words and the sentence structure are interesting to the ear. Organize students into small groups, assigning each student one of the first three paragraphs. Have students in the groups take turns reading their paragraphs aloud as though the readers were storytellers. Encourage students to ask one another for help when they encounter unfamiliar words. **EL BL**

Shepherds told them of seeing a great white stallion fleeing before the pillars of wind that stirred the sand. And they said that the horse carried no rider.

Passing merchants, their camels laden[2] with spices and sweets for the bazaar,[3] told of the emptiness of the desert they had crossed.

Tribesmen, strangers, everyone whom Tarik asked, sighed and gazed into the desert, saying, "Such is the will of Allah." **3**

At last Tarik knew in his heart that his favorite son, Hamed, had been claimed, as other Bedouin before him, by the drifting sands. And he told Nadia what he knew—that Hamed was dead.

Nadia screamed and wept and stamped the sand, crying, "Not even Allah[4] will take Hamed from me!" until her father could bear no more and sternly bade her to silence.[5]

Nadia's grief knew no bounds.[6] She walked blindly through the oasis, neither seeing nor hearing those who would console[7] her. And Tarik was silent. For days he sat inside his tent, speaking not at all and barely tasting the meals set before him.

Then, on the seventh day, Tarik came out of his tent. He called all his people to him, and when they were assembled, he spoke. "From this day forward," he said, "let no one **utter** Hamed's name. Punishment shall be swift for those who would remind me of what I have lost."

Hamed's mother wept at the decree.[8] The people of the clan[9] looked at one another uneasily. All could see the hardness that had settled on the sheik's face and the coldness in his eyes, and so they said nothing. But they obeyed. **4**

---

2. *Laden* (LAY dun) means "loaded down."
3. A *bazaar* (buh ZAR) is an outdoor market of small shops.
4. *Allah* (AW luh) is the name for God in the Islamic religion.
5. *Bade her to silence* is another way of saying "ordered her to keep quiet."
6. The expression *knew no bounds* means "had no limits."
7. *Console* (kun SOHL) means "to comfort."
8. A *decree* (dih KREE) is an official order or decision.
9. A *clan* is a group of related families.

Vocabulary

utter (UT ur) *v.* to speak or say aloud

Practice the Skills

3 Key Reading Skill

Synthesizing Try connecting the pieces of information in the story to explain what you think happened to Hamed. **R**

4 Key Literary Element

Plot The exposition part of the plot is finished, a conflict has been introduced, and the rising action has begun. What event do you think started the rising action? What do you think will be the main conflict in the story? Add these notes to the rising action part of your plot chart. **L**

Teach

R Reading Skill

Synthesizing Ask: What do the shepherds and merchants tell Nadia and her father? *(They mention seeing a horse with no rider, and they say that the desert is empty.)* **Ask:** What does this information suggest? *(that Hamed has disappeared)* **AS**
Ask: How do tribesmen and others respond when Tarik asks about his son? What do you think this response means? *(Possible response: They say it is Allah's, or God's, will. Their response suggests that nothing can be done if Hamed is dead. Tarik and his family must learn to accept the death.)* **OL**

L Literary Element

Plot Say: Recall the description of the characters given in the exposition. How has Hamed's death caused Tarik to change? *(Possible response: In the exposition, Tarik was described as kind and gracious. After Hamed's death, all of the people can see hardness and coldness in Tarik.)* **Ask:** How do you think Tarik's decree will affect Nadia? *(Possible response: Because Nadia is willful, she probably will not obey her father's decree, and her behavior will increase the conflict between them.)* **OL**

Differentiated Instruction

Comparison-Contrast Chart Have students create a two-column chart in their Learner's Notebooks to compare and contrast Nadia's reaction to the death of Hamed with Tarik's. Students should label the columns "Nadia" and "Tarik," and they should list details from the text that describe each character's reaction. Ask students how these differing reactions could contribute to the conflict, and have students write their predictions as to what might happen at the climax of the story. Have volunteers explain their predictions to the class. **AS**

Objectives

- Synthesize information
- Identify literary elements: plot
- Identify word structure: base words

Teach

C Critical Thinking

Analysis **Ask:** How does remaining silent about Hamed isolate Nadia from others in her tribe? *(Possible response: Her sadness makes her angry, so people stay away from her. This makes her lonelier than she has ever been.)* **AS** **Ask:** Why do you think Nadia reacts so strongly to having to keep silent about Hamed? *(Possible response: Nadia is passionate and strong-willed. It is difficult for her to bottle up her emotions.)* **OL**

L Literary Element

Plot **Say:** The story has not yet built to the climax. The rising action continues with another complication. Describe this new complication in the plot. *(Nadia disobeys her father's decree when she says Hamed's name by accident.)* **OL** **Ask:** Do you think this development will add to the conflict between Nadia and her father even though Tarik does not hear Nadia say Hamed's name? Explain. *(Possible response: This development will eventually add to the conflict. Tarik will probably find out that Nadia has mentioned Hamed, and he will have to take action in accordance with his decree.)* **AL**

Additional Support

Nadia, too, did as her father decreed, though each day held something to remind her of Hamed. As she passed her brothers at play, she remembered games Hamed had taught her. As she walked by the women weaving patches for the tents and heard them talking and laughing, she remembered tales Hamed had told her and how they had made her laugh. And as she watched the shepherds with their flock, she remembered the little black lamb Hamed had loved.

C Each memory brought Hamed's name to Nadia's lips, but she stilled the sound. And each time that she did so, her unhappiness grew until, finally, she could no longer contain it. She wept and raged at anyone and anything that crossed her path. Soon everyone at the oasis fled at her approach. And she was more lonely than she had ever been before.

One day, as Nadia passed the place where her brothers were playing, she stopped to watch them. They were playing one of the games that Hamed had taught her. But they were playing it wrong.

Without thinking, Nadia called out to them. "That is not the way! Hamed said that first you jump this way and then you jump back!"

Her brothers stopped their game and looked around in fear. Had Tarik heard Nadia say Hamed's name? But the sheik was nowhere to be seen. **5**

Practice the Skills

5 **Literary Element**

Plot During the *rising action*, new complications are added to the plot. What new complication has just happened?

Bedouins live in the deserts of the Middle East and North Africa.

808 UNIT 7 What Can We Learn from Our Mistakes?

Literature Focus Lesson

Setting Point out that although time and place are the main elements of setting, the concept also includes the customs, values, and beliefs of a culture or people. Use the photograph on this page as a springboard to a discussion of the story's setting. Ask students to scan what they have read for details that are specific not only to the desert locale of the story but also to Bedouin culture. Have students use library resources to research Bedouin culture further. Ask students to connect their findings to specific details in the text and to share these connections with the class. **OL**

"Teach us, Nadia, as our brother taught you," said her smallest brother.

And so she did. Then she told them of other games and how Hamed had taught her to play them. And as she spoke of Hamed, she felt an easing of the hurt within her. **R** **6**

So she went on speaking of him.

She went to where the women sat at their loom and spoke of Hamed. She told them tales that Hamed had told her. And she told how he had made her laugh as he was telling them.

At first the women were afraid to listen to the willful girl and covered their ears, but after a time, they listened and laughed with her.

"Remember your father's promise of punishment!" Nadia's mother warned when she heard Nadia speaking of Hamed. "**Cease,** I implore you!" **7**

Nadia knew that her mother had reason to be afraid, for Tarik, in his grief and bitterness, had grown quick-tempered and sharp of tongue. But she did not know how to tell her mother that speaking of Hamed eased the pain she felt, and so she said only, "I will speak of my brother! I will!" And she ran away from the sound of her mother's voice.

She went to where the **shepherds** tended the flock and spoke of Hamed. The shepherds ran from her in fear and hid behind the sheep. But Nadia went on speaking. She told of Hamed's love for the little black lamb and how he had taught it to leap at his whistle. Soon the shepherds left off their hiding and came to listen. Then they told their own stories of Hamed and the little black lamb. **8**

The more Nadia spoke of Hamed, the clearer his face became in her mind. She could see his smile and the light in his eyes. She could hear his voice. And the clearer Hamed's voice and face became, the less Nadia hurt inside and the less her temper flashed. At last, she was filled with peace.

But her mother was still afraid for her willful daughter. Again and again she sought to quiet Nadia so that Tarik's bitterness

Vocabulary

cease (sees) *v.* to stop

Practice the Skills

6 **Key Reading Skill**

Synthesizing Nadia was in great pain when she could not talk about Hamed. She feels better when she does talk about him. Combine this information with anything else you have read or know from your own experience. Why does Nadia need to talk about Hamed?

7 **BIG Question**

Do you think Nadia's father made a mistake in not allowing anyone to talk about Hamed? Why or why not? Write your response on your Foldable. Your response will help you complete the Unit Challenge later. **BQ**

8 **English Language Coach**

Base Words and Roots What is a **shepherd**? The word *shepherd* comes from a root word that means *sheep*, and from the base word *herd*, which means *gather*. Use that information to figure out the meaning of the word.

Nadia the Willful **809**

Teach

R Reading Skill

Review Drawing Conclusions
Ask: How does talking about Hamed help Nadia deal with his death? *(Possible response: Talking about Hamed helps her remember the good times she had with him.)* **Ask:** How does hearing about Hamed affect others in the story? Use details from the text to support your answer. *(Possible response: The women of the tribe enjoy laughing at Hamed's stories. The shepherds also like talking about Hamed and sharing their own stories.)* **AS**

BQ BIG Question

Ask: How does Tarik's decision to not talk about Hamed affect him? *(Possible response: Tarik has done nothing to ease his grief. This makes him quick-tempered and mean.)* **AS** **Ask:** What has Nadia learned from making the "mistake" of talking about Hamed? What do you think she might tell her father to do? *(Possible response: Nadia has learned that talking about Hamed helps her remember the good things about him. She might tell her father that he, too, would feel better if he talked about Hamed.)* **OL**

Differentiated Instruction

Illustrations Tell students that visualizing, or creating pictures in your mind as you read, makes the material more vivid and easier to recall. Read aloud the passage in which Nadia talks to the shepherds about Hamed. Have students sketch what they hear as you read the passage. Tell students to draw the image or images that best capture the scene for them. After they have finished their sketches, have students compare their drawings with partners, discussing similarities and differences in the images. Ask volunteers to explain their sketches to the entire class. **AS**

Objectives
• Analyze text
• Draw conclusions from text and experience
• Identify literary elements: plot and setting

809

Teach

L₁ Literary Element

Plot Say: Suspense is a feeling of uncertainty or dread about what is going to happen next. What do you fear may happen when Nadia continues to talk about Hamed? *(Possible response: Tarik may hear Nadia using Hamed's name and banish her from the tribe.)* **AS**

Ask: How does Nadia's mother add to the suspense? *(Possible response: She reminds Nadia that her father promised to punish anyone who spoke of Hamed, and she begs Nadia to stop talking about him. Her warnings remind readers of the possible consequences of Nadia's actions.)* **OL**

L₂ Literary Element

Plot Ask: What event is the climax of this story? *(when Nadia goes to talk to her father about Hamed)* **Ask:** What are two possible outcomes of the climax? *(Possible response: Nadia could persuade the sheik to abandon his decree. The sheik could banish Nadia along with the shepherd.)* **OL**

---

would not be turned against her. And again and again Nadia tossed her head and went on speaking of Hamed.

Soon, all who listened could see Hamed's face clearly before them.

One day, the youngest shepherd came to Nadia's tent, calling, "Come, Nadia! See Hamed's black lamb; it has grown so big and strong!"

But it was not Nadia who came out of the tent.

It was Tarik.

Visual Vocabulary
A *scimitar* (SIM uh tur) is a curved sword.

On the sheik's face was a look more fierce than that of a desert hawk, and when he spoke, his words were as sharp as a scimitar.

"I have forbidden my son's name to be said. And I promised punishment to whoever disobeyed my command. So shall it be. Before the sun sets and the moon casts its first shadow on the sand, you will be gone from this oasis—never to return."

"No!" cried Nadia, hearing her father's words.

"I have spoken!" roared the sheik. "It shall be done!"

Trembling, the shepherd went to gather his possessions.

And the rest of the clan looked at one another uneasily and muttered among themselves.

In the hours that followed, fear of being **banished** to the desert made everyone turn away from Nadia as she tried to tell them of Hamed and the things he had done and said.

And the less she was listened to, the less she was able to recall Hamed's face and voice. And the less she recalled, the more her temper raged within her, destroying the peace she had found. **9**

L₂ **B**y evening, she could stand it no longer. She went to where her father sat, staring into the desert, and stood before him.

"You will not rob me of my brother Hamed!" she cried, stamping her foot. "I will not let you!"

Tarik looked at her, his eyes colder than the desert night. **10**

Vocabulary

banished (BAN isht) *v.* sent away, forced to be separate from a place or group

Practice the Skills

9 Literary Element

Plot Suspense builds as the conflict in the story continues to develop. How does the conflict become more complicated after the young shepherd is banished?

10 Key Literary Element

Plot The climax is the point of highest conflict in the story. Describe the climax of this story. **L₁**

Additional Support

Literature Focus Lesson

Figurative Language Figurative language is imaginative language used for descriptive effect. The author uses figurative language to describe the sheik's reaction to hearing the shepherd say Hamed's name. First the author compares the look on the sheik's face to that of a desert hawk. Then she uses a simile to describe the sheik's words. A simile is a figure of speech that uses the word *like* or *as* to compare two things. The author says the sheik's words were "as sharp as a scimitar." Discuss what these images suggest about the sheik. Have students write their own similes to describe Nadia's feelings when people again refuse to listen to her stories of Hamed. **OL**

But before he could utter a word, Nadia spoke again. "Can you recall Hamed's face? Can you still hear his voice?"

Tarik started in surprise, and his answer seemed to come unbidden[10] to his lips. "No, I cannot! Day after day I have sat in this spot where I last saw Hamed, trying to remember the look, the sound, the happiness that was my beloved son—but I cannot."

And he wept.

Nadia's tone became gentle. "There is a way, honored father," she said. "Listen."

And she began to speak of Hamed. She told of walks she and Hamed had taken and of talks they had had. She told how he had taught her games, told her tales, and calmed her when she was angry. She told many things that she remembered, some happy and some sad.

And when she was done with the telling, she said gently, "Can you not recall him now, Father? Can you not see his face? Can you not hear his voice?"

Tarik nodded through his tears, and for the first time since Hamed had been gone, he smiled.

"Now you see," Nadia said, her tone more gentle than the softest of the desert breezes, "there is a way that Hamed can be with us still."

The sheik **pondered** what Nadia had said. After a long time, he spoke, and the sharpness was gone from his voice.

"Tell my people to come before me, Nadia," he said. "I have something to say to them."

When all were assembled, Tarik said, "From this day forward, let my daughter Nadia be known not as willful but as wise. And let her name be praised in every tent, for she has given me back my beloved son." **11**

And so it was. The shepherd returned to his flock, kindness and graciousness returned to the oasis, and Nadia's name was praised in every tent. And Hamed lived again—in the hearts of all who remembered him. **12** ○

---

10. **Unbidden** means "without being asked."

Practice the Skills

11 Literary Element

Plot The falling action is what happens after the climax. The resolution is the final outcome. In this story, what are the falling action and the resolution? Add these details to your plot chart.

12 BIG Question

What does Nadia's father learn from his mistake? Write your answer on your Foldable. Your **BQ** response will help you complete the Unit Challenge later.

Bedouin clothing protects wearers from intense sunlight and heat.

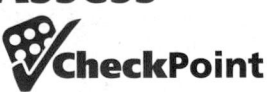
Nadia the Willful **811**

Teach

L Literary Element

Plot **Ask:** Is the last line of the story the falling action or the resolution. Why? *(It is the resolution because it is the final outcome of the story.)* **BL**

BQ BIG Question

Say: Nadia helps her father realize that he made a mistake. What traits does Nadia show when talking to her father? *(Possible responses: Nadia's refusal to give up shows that she is still willful. However, she is also more considerate of others' feelings.)* **OL** **Ask:** What do you think Nadia learns from Hamed's death and talking to her father? *(Possible response: Nadia learns that you have to deal with grief. She also learns that she must combine her willfulness with understanding. These lessons make her a wiser character.)* **AL**

Assess

CheckPoint

Use the CheckPoint questions provided on Presentation Plus! to check for comprehension of the selection. These questions can be used with interactive response keypads for immediate student feedback.

Differentiated Instruction

Poetry Tell students that poetry is an important art form in the culture of the Bedouin people. In ancient times, poets were held in high esteem because they served as both entertainers and historians for their tribes. The history of a tribe was preserved through poems that had been memorized and passed down orally from previous poets. Heroes of a tribe were often celebrated through verse. Tell students to assume the role of the poet for Tarik's tribe. Ask students to write poems of at least six lines in which they tell the story of Nadia the Wise. Ask volunteers to share their poems with the class. **OL**

Objectives
• Identify literary elements: plot
• Identify literary devices: figurative language

Assess

Resources for page 812

📁 Selection Quick Check, p. 62

📁 Selection and Unit Assessment, p. 74

💿 ExamView Assessment Suite

💿 Interactive Tutor: Self-Assessment

Students can respond to the *After You Read* items in their Learner's Notebooks or on a separate sheet of paper.

Answering the

1. Responses will vary.

2. Hamed was the only person who could calm Nadia's temper.

3. Possible response: Nadia feels angry when she cannot speak of Hamed. When she does speak of him, she feels happy and at peace.

Critical Thinking

4. Responses will vary.

5. Possible response: Because of his grief, Tarik was probably not thinking clearly.

6. Possible response: Nadia was known for her stubbornness and temper; Tarik was known for his kindness and graciousness. Both love Hamed and miss him terribly after his death.

7. Possible response: Like Nadia, people miss Hamed.

8. Responses will vary. Students should draw on the story and their own experience to respond.

812

After You Read : Nadia the Willful

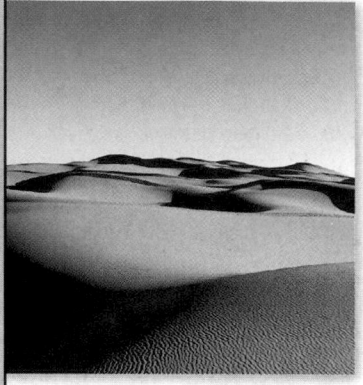

Answering the **BIG Question**

1. What new ideas did this selection give you about learning from mistakes?

2. **Recall** Why were Nadia and Hamed so close?
   Tip Right There

3. **Summarize** How does Nadia feel when she can't speak of Hamed after he is gone? How does she feel when she does speak of him?
   Tip Think and Search

Critical Thinking

4. **Visualize** Can you picture a scene in the desert from this story? What details help you visualize it?
   Tip Author and Me

5. **Respond** How did you feel toward Tarik when he said that Hamed's name could not be uttered?
   Tip Author and Me

6. **Compare and Contrast** How are Tarik and Nadia alike? How do they differ?
   Tip Author and Me

7. **Infer** Why do people break Tarik's rule against talking about Hamed?
   Tip Author and Me

8. **Evaluate** What is the best way to deal with losing someone you love?
   Tip On My Own

Objectives (pp. 812–813)
Reading Synthesize information
Literature Identify literary elements: plot
Vocabulary Identify word structure: roots and bases
Grammar Identify parts of speech: verbs

Talk About Your Reading

In the story, Nadia talks about Hamed to various people. One person Nadia doesn't talk to is her mother. With a partner, role play a dialogue between Nadia and her mother. Have Nadia describe how talking about Hamed helps her deal with her loss. Have Nadia's mother tell her how she feels.

Talk About Your Reading
Students' dialogues should not only reflect story details but also exhibit creative thinking.

Skills Review

Key Reading Skill: Synthesizing

9. Answer the following questions:
   - What is the most important event or idea to understand in this selection?
   - How does it relate to your own life?

Literary Element: Plot

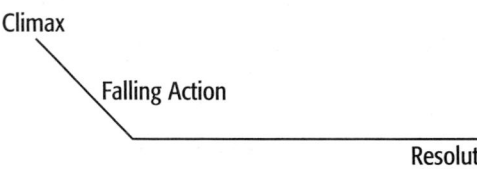

Climax

Falling Action

Resolution

10. The falling action shows what happens to characters after the climax. What happens as a result of the climax in this story?

11. How is the conflict between Nadia and her father resolved?

Vocabulary Check

Choose the correct word to fill the blank in each sentence.

12. It was forbidden to ___ Hamed's name.

    utter
    cease

13. When Nadia spoke of Hamed, her mother told her to ___.

    utter
    cease

14. Anyone who mentioned Hamid would be ___.

    banished
    pondered

15. Tarik ___ Nadia's words.

    banished
    pondered

16. **Academic Vocabulary** In which of the following sentences is the word *synthesize* used correctly?
    - When I write an essay, I *synthesize* all that I read on the subject and draw my own conclusions.
    - When I go shopping, I *synthesize* all the groceries into the shopping cart.

17. **English Language Coach** *Willpower* and *willingness* both contain the base word *will*. Use the words *willpower* and *willingness* correctly in sentences.

Grammar Link: Finding the Verb

- Words sometimes come between the subject and the verb.

  | Subject | Verb |

  Nadia's *memories* of Hamed *were* strong.
  The *merchants* in the bazaar *knew* nothing.

- The verb sometimes comes before its subject.
  There *was* a girl with a flashing temper.
  Out of the tent *came* Tarik.
  Try to recall Hamed's face.

- Sometimes the verb or verb phrase stands alone. The word *you* is understood to be the subject.
  (You) *Tell* us about Hamed.
  (You) *Do* not *say* his name.

Grammar Practice

Copy the sentences below. Circle the verb or verb phrase in each sentence.

18. Across the sands galloped a white stallion.
19. Here is the sheik.
20. Speak of Hamed.
21. Do you miss him?

Literature Online

Web Activities For eFlashcards, Selection Quick Checks, and other Web activities, go to www.glencoe.com.

Nadia the Willful **813**

Skills Review

Key Reading Skill: Synthesizing

9. Students should note that the most important idea in the story is that one cannot hide from one's emotions.

Key Literary Element: Plot

10. Possible response: Nadia convinces her father that speaking of Hamed is the way to keep him alive in their hearts, and her father tells the people that Nadia should be known as wise, not willful.

11. Possible response: Nadia and her father share their feelings about their loss.

Vocabulary Check

12. utter
13. cease
14. banished
15. pondered
16. **Academic Vocabulary** When I write an essay, I synthesize all that I read on the subject and draw my own conclusions.
17. **English Language Coach** Possible response: It took *willpower* not to talk about Hamed. Tarik's *willingness* to listen to Nadia helped him see his mistake.

Grammar Link: Finding the Verb

Grammar Practice

18. Across the sands (galloped) a white stallion.
19. Here (is) the sheik.
20. (Speak) of Hamed.
21. (Do) you (miss) him?

Close

Ask students to describe new ideas they had about the Big Question after reading this selection.

**Objectives covered in
this workshop:**
- **Writing** Write a personal
narrative using the writing
process
- **Grammar** Use proper grammar, usage, and mechanics

Teaching Students to Write a Personal Narrative

Why Is It Important?

- Personal narrative provides students with practice writing from the first-person point of view.

- Students will be more engaged in writing about something they have personally experienced. Writing personal narratives empowers students to learn about themselves and tell their stories to others.

- Writing in their own voices will help students hone their understanding of tone and word choice.

- Setting a purpose for their personal narrative will help students think about the significance and impact of their experiences.

How to Help Students Get It

- Have your students read several different kinds of personal narratives before they start to write their own. Magazines such as *Reader's Digest* include many personal narrative essays.

- Tell students that we all engage in personal narratives every day. Whenever someone asks "What did you do this weekend?" you answer by telling them a story about yourself.

- Model writing your own narrative. Start with showing students a concept map, then write the narrative as a Talk-Aloud. As you write, point out that you are using the first-person point of view throughout, that you have a beginning, middle, and end, and that you are including vivid details.

- Give students ideas for topics. Some ideas are achievement of a personal goal, the overcoming of an obstacle, a family ritual or tradition, a well-known place, a childhood event, or a life-changing experience.

- Remind students to use the language that comes naturally to them. This will help them develop their writing "voice."

- Encourage students to use different kinds of sense words to engage the reader and provide detail: "smelled like . . ." "saw . . ." "I could taste . . ." "I could hear . . ."

Traits of Good Writing	
Ideas	the message or the theme and the details that develop it
Voice: a writer's unique way of using tone and style	Have students use the following checklist when checking their compositions: • Does your writing sound interesting when you read it aloud? • Does your writing show what you think about your topic? • Does your writing sound like you—or does it sound like you're imitating someone else?
Organization	the arrangement of main points and supporting details
Word Choice	the vocabulary a writer uses to convey meaning
Sentence Fluency	the smooth rhythm and flow of sentences that vary in length and style
Conventions	correct spelling, grammar, usage, and mechanics
Presentation	the way words and design elements look on a page

Unit Focus (arrow pointing to Voice row)

Workshop Resources

PACING (DAYS)		LESSON	STUDENT MATERIALS	TEACHER RESOURCES
STANDARD	BLOCK			
1	1/2	Writing Workshop Part 1: Prewriting and Drafting	📖 Writing Workshop Graphic Organizer, p. 15 📖 Grammar Practice, p. 14 📖 Spelling and Handwriting Practice, p. 45 💻 Spelling Power eWorkbook 💿 Interactive Grammar and Language Workbook 📖 Grammar and Composition Handbook, p. 206	💿 TeacherWorks Plus™ 💿 Presentation Plus! 📁 Rubrics for Assessing Student Writing, Listening, and Speaking, p. 14
			📁 Real Success in Writing: Research and Reports 📁 Writing Constructed Responses	📑 Grammar and Writing Workshop Transparencies 5–6
2	1	Writing Workshop Part 2: Editing, Revising, and Presenting	💿 Interactive Grammar and Language Workbook 📖 Grammar and Composition Handbook, p. 206	📑 Grammar and Writing Workshop Transparencies 29–30
			📁 Real Success in Writing: Research and Reports 📁 Writing Constructed Responses	💿 Interactive Grammar and Language Workbook
			📖 Listening and Speaking, p. 28 📖 Viewing and Representing, p. 29	📁 Rubrics for Assessing Student Writing, Listening, and Speaking, p. 14

Focus

- **Daily Language Practice Transparency 64**
  Focus Activity Ask: What are some characteristics that make a story interesting or entertaining? *(Possible responses may include an interesting conflict and well-developed characters.)* **OL**

Teach

L Literary Element

Narrator Say: Because this narrative is about an event in your life, you will be the first-person narrator. What pronouns will you use to tell about your own thoughts, feelings, and actions? *(first-person pronouns such as* I, my, *and* me*)* **OL**

Resources for page 814

Use the Writing Workshop Graphic Organizer BLM in the Unit 7 Resource Booklet, p. 14.

Use the Grammar and Writing Workshop Transparencies 5–6.

WRITING WORKSHOP PART 1

Personal Narrative
Prewriting and Drafting

ASSIGNMENT Write a personal narrative

Purpose: Write a narrative about a time you made a mistake

Audience: You, your teacher, and classmates

Writing Rubric

As you work through this assignment, you should

- share a personal experience
- include important details
- write an essay that has a beginning, middle, and end
- use chronological time order
- use correct subject-verb agreement

See page 868 in Part 2 for a model of a personal narrative.

Objectives (pp. 814–817)
Writing Use the writing process: personal narrative, prewrite, draft • Use text structure: chronological order • Use elements of writing: voice
Grammar Use correct subject and verb agreement

In this Writing Workshop, you will write a personal narrative to help you answer the Unit 7 Big Question: What can we learn from our mistakes?

What Is It?

A personal narrative is a true story about a memorable event in your life. The event may be really big (traveling to a foreign country, meeting the president) or fairly ordinary (dinner at your grandparents' house, going to the mall). The most important thing about this personal narrative is that the writer (you) learned a lesson worth sharing.

Your assignment is to write a personal narrative about a time you made a mistake.

Prewriting
Get Ready to Write

Everybody makes mistakes now and then. Mistakes are important because they teach lessons that you can't learn in a book or a classroom. When you make a mistake, it is up to you to fix it, or else you have to live with the consequences.

Gather Ideas

Have you ever said something that you wish you could take back?
Have you ever made a decision that turned out to be a bad one?
Have you ever accidentally hurt someone's feelings?
Have you ever done something wrong that wasn't on purpose?

If you answered yes to any of these questions, then you have a topic for your personal narrative. In small groups, discuss the mistake that you are going to write about. Tell your group members:

- The mistake you made
- Who was involved
- The result of your mistake
- What you learned from your mistake

Tell your group members what you like about their stories. Tell them what parts you think they can leave out. Ask your group if your story is interesting and what details they want to hear more about. Write down the suggestions and points of your story that interested your group members. Make sure you include these points when you start your draft.

Additional Support

Differentiated Instruction

Prewriting Some students may benefit from writing notes about their mistakes before being asked to share their stories aloud in a group setting. Such prewriting allows students to gather their ideas and helps guide smooth storytelling. Tell students to use web diagrams to brainstorm details about their stories, including people's names, locations, main events, and lessons learned. If students recall additional details while sharing their stories orally, encourage them to add those details to their diagrams. **BL**

Make a Plan

Your narrative should be written in chronological order. That means you should write the events in the order they happened. Before you start writing, make a time line that includes the important events that led to your mistake and the events that resulted from the mistake. You can use the time line to help you write your draft.

```
EVENT 1  →  EVENT 2  →  EVENT 3  →
```

Drafting
Start Writing!

Your narrative should be divided into three sections: beginning, middle, and end.

Beginning The beginning of your narrative should describe the setting and introduce the people involved in your story.

It was my eleventh birthday, and I was sitting at the dining room table with all my friends. Well, actually, I was sitting there with all my friends and Jerry. Last June, Jerry showed he <u>wasn't</u> my friend when he had our whole class over to his swimming pool in the middle of the school day. He knew I couldn't swim . . .

Middle The middle of your narrative is when the main action happens.

Al started laughing about Jerry's silly new haircut. This was my party, and I knew that if I joined in, everybody else would too. So I shouted out, "Who cut your hair, Jerry, your baby sister?"

End The ending of your narrative brings the story to a close. You tell how the experience was resolved and what you learned from it.

Jerry said he was sorry and that he had forgotten that I couldn't swim. Then we both went back to my party. Next time one of my friends upsets me, I'll tell him why I'm angry instead of trying to get even.

Literature Online

Writing Models For models and other writing activities, go to www.glencoe.com.

> **Writing Tip**
>
> **Prewriting** When you make your time line, only include the events that are important to the story you are telling.

> **Writing Tip**
>
> **Drafting** Start new paragraphs by skipping a line and indenting a space before you write more. Start a new paragraph when you get to the middle and end of your story or when a new character speaks.

Teach

W Writing

Organization Students with visual learning styles may benefit from completing a plot chart instead of a time line. Using a story of your own, show students how to complete a plot chart by filling in the exposition, rising action, climax, falling action, and resolution. **OL**

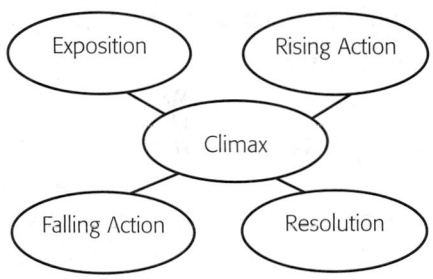

Literature Focus Lesson

Descriptive Language Encourage students to use descriptive language as they write their narratives. In the beginning of their narratives, students should use sensory language—language that appeals to the senses of sight, smell, sound, touch, and taste—to describe setting and to introduce characters. In the middle and end of their narratives, students should use adjectives and adverbs to add detail to nouns and verbs, respectively. Review with students different types of figurative language, including simile, metaphor, and personification. **OL AL**

Objectives
- Identify and analyze narrator
- Identify literary elements: symbol and descriptive language
- Write a personal narrative
- Gather and organize information
- Use the writing process

815

Teach

W Writing

Voice **Say:** Notice that in the sample letters about wooden and aluminum bats, the writer uses two different voices. The voice in each example depends on the audience. In the first letter, the writer uses an informal, conversational voice. In the second letter, the writer uses a formal, official voice. To determine the voice you will use in your narrative, first decide what audience will be reading your story. **AS**

Assess

Have pairs of students exchange drafts and critique each other's work. Ask each student to determine whether his or her partner included a beginning, a middle, and an end to their narrative, as well as whether the writing seems to have a natural voice. After a few minutes, tell each student to assess his or her partner's feedback, make any needed revisions, and save the revised draft for later use.

Applying Good Writing Traits

Voice

Reading a personal narrative or autobiography is a good way to find out what a person is like. You can discover a writer's personality from the way he or she "talks" on paper.

What Is Voice?

Just as each person has his or her own unique speaking voice, a writer has a particular writing voice. It is a voice that clearly shows a writer's personality. The writer's personality comes through in word choices, tone, and sentence patterns he or she uses. Here's how two different people might write about the same subject.

Trees and Cans

Yowza!! Who would have thought the same stuff that we drink our sodas out of might change the game of baseball? But it's true! Aluminum bats send the old hardball at least twelve feet farther than the old wooden ones. Look out, outfield!

Ash versus Aluminum

The game of baseball is about to change. It looks as though the day of aluminum has arrived. Bats of that metal send the ball twelve feet farther than their more natural ancestors. All those who want the day of the Louisville Slugger to remain, say your prayers. There is little hope left for you now.

Why Is Voice Important in My Writing?

- Writing in your own voice helps you express your real thoughts, ideas, and feelings.
- Writing in your own voice is easier than trying to sound like someone else.
- Reading something written in your voice is more interesting to your audience. It shows there's a real person behind the writing.

How Do I Do It?

- Write words that you might use when you're talking.
- Don't try to write like someone else. Find your own voice.
- Think about what you're trying to say. Say it aloud. Then write it down.
- Let your feelings guide what you're trying to say about your topic.

Write to Learn Pick a subject that you feel strongly about and write a paragraph about it. Let your words flow. Don't worry about making mistakes; you can fix those later. With a partner, read aloud what you wrote and feel the rhythm of your words as you read. This is your voice. Your writing should show the "real" you. Then rewrite or change any words or sentences so that your voice is heard in your writing.

Additional Support

Reading Fluency

Reading and Writing Some students may find that they can better analyze their drafts by reading them aloud. Reading aloud is especially helpful for determining whether each student's voice is present in his or her writing. Allow these students to select partners for oral reading. Students should take turns reading their own drafts to their partners and then discuss the content, including voice. Encourage students to use the bulleted list on page 814 as a guideline for discussing their drafts. **OL**

Grammar Link

Subject-Verb Agreement

What Are Subjects and Verbs?

The **subject** is the part of a sentence that is doing something or about which something is said. The **verb** is the part of a sentence that tells what the subject is doing.

- The subject and verb must agree in person and number.

  With a singular subject (**fire**), use the singular form of the verb (**burns**). With a plural, or more than one, subject (**fires**), use the plural form of the verb (**burn**).

  A **fire burns** in Chicago.

  Fire is the singular subject, so the singular form of the verb *burn* is used.

  Fires burn in different parts of the city.

  The word *fires* is the plural subject. Since there is more than one fire, the plural form of the verb *burn* is used.

Why Is Subject and Verb Agreement Important?

When the subject and verb of a sentence do not agree in person and number, a major rule of English grammar is broken. This confuses readers and distracts them from what they are reading.

How Do I Make Subjects and Verbs Agree?

- Find the subject and verb in a sentence.

  <u>Joshua</u> *eats* pizza for dinner.

- Make sure that the verb agrees with the subject in person and number.

  <u>Joshua</u> (singular) *eats* (singular) pizza for dinner.

  <u>Joshua and Sadie</u> (plural) *eat* (plural) pizza for dinner.

Grammar Practice

For each sentence, underline the subject. Circle the correct form of the verb so that the subject and verb agree.

1. Mr. Gray (write, writes) to Mr. Holden.
2. His arguments (is, are) persuasive.
3. The journalist (has, have) done his research.
4. He (hope, hopes) the Council will be persuaded.
5. The Council members must (build, builds) a bridge between Chicago's past and future.

Writing Application Review your draft. Make sure that all your subjects and verbs agree.

Looking Ahead

Part 2 of this Writing Workshop is coming up later. Save the writing you did so far, you'll need it to complete your final draft.

Teach

Grammar Link

Subject-Verb Agreement Share the following subject-verb agreement problems and solutions with students:

1. Subject and verb are separated: Make sure that the verb agrees with the subject of the sentence rather than with the object of the intervening phrase.

   Example: The members of my babysitting club are saving money.

2. Subject comes after verb: Make sure that the verb agrees with the subject.

   Example: Where are my aunt and uncle?

3. Indefinite pronoun is the subject: Determine whether the pronoun is singular or plural.

   Example: Each of the candidates is qualified. All of the problems on the test were hard.

4. Compound subject joined by *and:* Different things take a plural verb; a singular unit takes a singular verb.

   Example: Fishing tackle and a life jacket were stowed on the boat.

   Example: Peanut butter and jelly is delicious.

5. Compound subject joined by *or* or *nor:* Make the verb agree with the subject closest to it.

   Example: Neither onions nor pepper improves the taste of this sauce.

Objectives

- Write a personal narrative
- Develop voice
- Use the writing process
- Use correct subject-verb agreement

Differentiated Instruction

Grammar Practice

1. subject: Mr. Gray; verb: writes
2. subject: arguments; verb: are
3. subject: journalist; verb: has
4. subject: He; verb: hopes
5. subject: members; verb: build

As students review their drafts to check subject and verb agreement, encourage them to make sure that they can correctly identify the complete subject in each sentence. Students will frequently isolate a singular part of a plural subject by accident, resulting in disagreement between subject and verb. **AS**

Identifying the Main Idea and Supporting Details

**Objective covered in
this workshop:**
• Determine the main idea
  and support details

Teaching Students to Identify the Main Idea and Supporting Details

Why Is It Important?

• Understanding the main ideas in a selection helps students comprehend the material better.

• Supporting details help point readers to the main ideas.

• Readers can use the details they identify to visualize what is happening in the story, which will improve comprehension.

• When students can clearly distinguish main ideas from supporting details, they will also become better writers. They will better understand the need to add ideas that explain, collaborate, and enhance their main ideas.

How to Help Students Get It

• Ask students where they think they might find the key idea of a selection. The main idea is often presented as the topic sentence in informational text, but it's usually not included in a creative attention-getting introduction. It's also rare to have the main idea clearly stated in fiction.

• Ask students to review a text from a previous unit, focusing on the author's use of details. They should make a list of the words the author uses to convey his or her ideas. Remembering to notice details will help students to learn to incorporate them into their own writing.

• Discuss the types of details that an author can use, including facts, statistics, anecdotes, adjectives, dialogue, and rich descriptions.

Reading to Answer the Big Question

The Bracelet by Yoshiko Uchida
When Ruri's Japanese-American family is sent to an internment camp during World War II, her best friend Laurie gives her the gift of a bracelet. Ruri promises that she'll always wear it, so when the bracelet gets lost in the confusion of the move, she becomes very upset. Her mother reminds Ruri that she doesn't need a bracelet to remember Laurie and others left behind.

Too Soon a Woman by Dorothy M. Johnson
The narrator, an eleven-year-old boy, tells of going West in a Conestoga wagon with his Pa and two sisters. On the way, his Pa reluctantly agrees to allow a young woman named Mary to travel with them. When Pa is forced to leave in search of food, it is Mary's resourcefulness and courage that save the children. In the end, the narrator states that his stepmother Mary was a wonderful woman.

Workshop Resources

PACING (DAYS) STANDARD	BLOCK	LESSON	STUDENT MATERIALS	TEACHER RESOURCES
1	1/2	Key Skill Lesson: Identifying the Main Idea and Supporting Details	🦶 Key Reading Skills Practice, p. 16 🦶 English Language Coach Review, p. 42	🖐 Bellringer Options Transparencies –Daily Language Practice 65 🖐 Read Aloud, Think Aloud Transparencies –Key Reading Skills 6 💿 Presentation Plus!
1	1	"The Bracelet"	💻 Glencoe Online 🦶 Unit Vocabulary Review, p. 40 🦶 Academic Vocabulary Review, p. 43 📁 English Language Coach 🦶 Active Reading Graphic Organizer, p. 18 🦶 Literary Analysis, p. 17 💿 StudentWorks Plus™ 💻 Online Student Edition 💿 Literature Classics 📁 Selection and Unit Assessments, p. 75	🖐 Literary and Text Analysis Transparencies 32 💻 Puzzlemaker 💿 Skill Level Up!™ A Language Arts Game 💻 BookLink 3 📘 Assessment by Learning Objective (Diagnostic and Formative) 💿 Interactive Tutor: Self-Assessment 💿 TeacherWorks Plus™
1		"Too Soon a Woman"	💻 Glencoe Online 🦶 Unit Vocabulary Review, p. 40 🦶 Academic Vocabulary Review, p. 43 📁 English Language Coach 🦶 Active Reading Graphic Organizer, p. 20 🦶 Literary Analysis, p. 17 💿 StudentWorks Plus™ 💻 Online Student Edition 💿 Literature Classics 📁 Selection and Unit Assessments, p. 76	🖐 Bellringer Options Transparencies –Selection Focus 22 🖐 Literary and Text Analysis Transparencies 32 💻 Puzzlemaker 💿 Skill Level Up!™ A Language Arts Game 💻 BookLink 3 📘 Assessment by Learning Objective (Diagnostic and Formative) 💿 Interactive Tutor: Self-Assessment 💿 TeacherWorks Plus™

Keys for Unit Resource

📁 Blackline Master
📘 Workbook
📖 Supplemental Text
💿 CD-ROM

📀 DVD
🖐 Transparency
💻 Web-based
🦶 Fast File

Level Appropriate Code

AS = Activities for all students

AL = Activities for students working above grade level

OL = Activities for students working at grade level

BL = Activities for students working below grade level

EL = Activities for English language learners

Focus

BELLRINGER Options

- 📖 **Selection Focus 22**
- 📖 **Daily Language Practice Transparency 65**
  Focus Activity Ask: Have you ever felt singled-out because of how you look? How did that make you feel? *(Possible responses: upset; confused; angry; lonely)* **AS**

Teach

R Reading Skill

Identifying Main Idea and Supporting Details Ask: What is one way to determine the main idea of a nonfiction selection? *(Possible response: skim the introductory or concluding paragraphs)* **Ask:** How might you determine the main idea of a work of fiction? *(Possible response: by reading the entire selection)* **AL**

V Vocabulary

Academic Vocabulary Ask: How might a person's *perspective* affect how he or she would draw the objects in a still-life? *(Possible response: The drawing would look different depending on the person's position relative to the objects.)* **AL**

Skills Focus

You will practice using these skills when you read the following selections:
- "The Bracelet," p. 822
- "Too Soon a Woman," p. 832

Reading
- Identifying main idea and supporting details

Literature
- Explaining how the narrator affects a story

Vocabulary
- Understanding word structure: Latin roots

Writing/Grammar
- Identifying subject-verb agreement

Objectives (pp. 818–819)
Reading Identify main ideas and supporting details

Skill Lesson

Identifying Main Idea and Supporting Details

Learn It!

What Is It? The most important idea in a selection, passage, or paragraph is the **main idea**. The examples or details that support the main idea are called **supporting details**.

- Sometimes an author states the main idea. Other times, readers must figure out the main idea.
- The main idea often will be the first sentence of a paragraph. But a main idea may be anywhere, even in the last sentence.
- You can find main ideas and supporting details in almost any paragraph. However, a selection may also have one central main idea.

© Patrick McDonnell. Reprinted with permission of King Features Syndicate.

Analyzing Cartoons
What main idea is the cat trying to express? What details support that main idea?

Additional Support

Differentiated Instruction

Small Group Activity Write the following paragraph on the board. Have students work together in small groups, completing a graphic organizer on the board that identifies the main idea and supporting details of the paragraph. **AS**
Making a peanut butter and jelly sandwich is easy for me. First, I put two slices of bread on a plate. Then, I spread about a half inch of extra-creamy peanut butter on one slice. Next, I scoop out a heaping teaspoon of jelly and slather it on top of the other slice. Finally, I put the two slices together.

R₁ **Why Is It Important?** Finding main ideas and details helps you understand what the author is writing about and why it is important. Details will also help you form your own opinions and decide whether you agree with the author.

How Do I Do It? Consider what you know about the author and the topic. Notice how the author organizes ideas. Then look for the one idea that all of the sentences in the paragraph, or all of the paragraphs in a selection, are about. To find the main idea, ask yourself:

- What is each sentence about?
- Is there one sentence that explains the whole passage or is more important than the others?
- If the main idea is not directly stated, what main idea do the supporting details point out?

Here's how one student found the main idea and supporting details in a paragraph from "Nadia the Willful."

Literature Online

Study Central Visit www.glencoe.com and click on Study Central to review identifying main idea and supporting details.

R₂

Nadia, too, did as her father decreed, though each day held something to remind her of Hamed. As she passed her brothers at play, she remembered games Hamed had taught her. As she walked by the women weaving patches for the tents and heard them talking and laughing, she remembered tales Hamed had told her and how they had made her laugh.

This paragraph is about things that remind Nadia of Hamed. The first sentence says that Nadia saw things that made her think about Hamed. That must be the main idea. The other sentences give details of what she saw and how they remind her of him.

Practice It!

Choose a paragraph from "The Gold Cadillac" on p. 786. Find and write the main idea. List at least two supporting details.

Use It!

Copy the questions from "How Do I Do It?" Answer the questions at the end of the selections you read to help you figure out what the main idea and supporting details are.

Teach

R₁ **Reading Skill**

Identifying Main Idea and Supporting Details Say: In your own words, explain the relationship between summarizing and finding the main idea. *(Possible response: Finding the main idea allows you to isolate the most important piece or pieces of information that are necessary for summarizing a piece of writing.)* **AL**

R₂ **Reading Skill**

Identifying Main Idea and Supporting Details Say: In this example, the student identifies one main idea that is stated directly. What is another main idea from the paragraph? *(Possible response: Nadia misses Hamed.)* **OL**

Resources for page 819

📁 Use Key Reading Skills Transparency 6 in *Read Aloud, Think Aloud* to help students practice determining the main idea and supporting details.

Reading in the Real World

College Tell students that determining main ideas and supporting details is an essential skill for success in college. Explain that some courses may require students to read large volumes of text each week and that students must use note-taking strategies to help them record main ideas and supporting details. Also explain that some professors give lectures without handouts, making students responsible for keeping track of the lecture's main ideas. Discuss with students the strategies they might use to help them keep track of the main ideas and supporting details when taking notes. **AL**

Objectives
- Identify main ideas and supporting details
- Learn and use new vocabulary

819

Teach

More About the Author

Yoshiko Uchida writes about life in Japanese internment camps during World War II because she experienced that life first-hand. After spending more than a year in the camp with her family, Uchida went on to earn a graduate degree from Smith College and become a teacher. She then began writing children's stories about Japanese American culture and continued doing so until her death in 1992.

V Vocabulary

Vocabulary File Quiz Say: One way to build vocabulary is to practice definitions with a quiz. On the front of an index card, write one of the Latin roots on page 820. On the back of the card, write as many words as you can that contain the root. Use reference resources if necessary. Include a brief definition for each word, and quiz yourself by looking at the front of each card and trying to recall the contents on the back. **AS**

Before You Read   The Bracelet

Yoshiko Uchida

Meet the Author

Yoshiko Uchida was born in Alameda, California. Her parents came from Japan. She says of her writing, "I feel it's so important for Japanese American . . . children to be aware of their history and culture. . . . At the same time, I write for *all* children, and I try to write about values and feelings that are universal." See page R7 of the Author Files for more on Yoshiko Uchida.

Literature Online

Author Search For more about Yoshiko Uchida, go to www.glencoe.com.

Objectives (pp. 820–827)
Reading Identify main ideas and supporting details • Make connections from text to self
Literature Identify literary elements: narrator
Vocabulary Identify word structure: Latin roots

Vocabulary Preview

evacuated (ih VAK yoo ay tid) *v.* removed; moved out of; form of the verb *evacuate* **(p. 822)** *The government evacuated Japanese Americans from their homes on the West Coast.*

forsaken (for SAY kun) *adj.* abandoned **(p. 824)** *The town looked run down and forsaken.*

looming (LOO ming) *adj.* appearing in the distance **(p. 826)** *The girls saw the camp looming ahead as they drove down the highway.*

Write to Learn Answer each question about the vocabulary words.
1. What does a building look like after it has been **evacuated**?
2. What happens when a town looks **forsaken**?
3. What do mountains **looming** in the distance look like?

English Language Coach

Latin Roots A root carries the basic meaning of a word. Most roots are not complete words on their own—they need other word parts to form complete words. Many words in English come from Latin roots. One Latin root is *ject*, which means "to throw." Look at the following English words formed from the root *ject*.

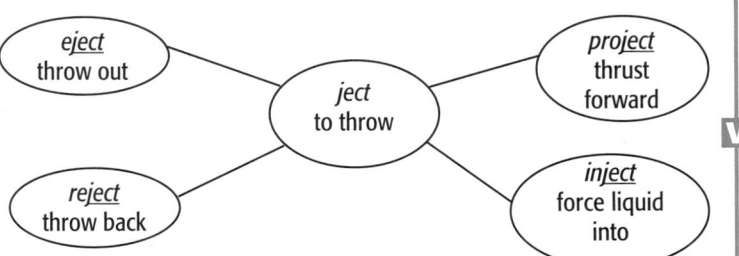

eject throw out — *ject* to throw — *project* thrust forward
reject throw back — *ject* to throw — *inject* force liquid into

On Your Own List two examples each of words that use the following roots. Give a brief definition for each word, showing how it is related to the meaning of the root. Use a dictionary if you need help.
1. *port,* meaning "to carry"
2. *dict,* meaning "to say"

820 UNIT 7 What Can We Learn from Our Mistakes?

Additional Support

Literature Online

Author Search To expand students' appreciation of Yoshiko Uchida, have them access the Web site for additional information and resources.

English Language Coach

Latin Roots English language learners might understand the roots of English words if they work with related roots from their own languages. Have students work in small groups that include English speakers. Ask the groups to add as many words as possible to the word webs they made on this page. Assist students with spelling or allow them to use dictionaries. Later, ask the groups to share their words with the class. Keep a list of the words posted on the board for students to refer to as they continue with this workshop. **EL OL**

Skills Preview

Key Reading Skill: Identifying Main Idea and Supporting Details

The main idea is the most important idea in a paragraph or a selection. Other sentences in the paragraph or selection add information to or support the main idea.

R Often a writer will directly state the main idea. Sometimes, though, a writer will not state the main idea, and it's up to you (the reader) to figure it out. To find the main idea, ask yourself: "What is the one idea that all of the sentences in the paragraph are about? What is the one idea that all of the paragraphs in the selection are about?"

Write to Learn Turn to the first page of "The Bracelet." Read the first five paragraphs. In one sentence, write the main idea. Next, list three supporting details.

Key Literary Element: Narrator

A **narrator** is the person or "voice" that tells a story. When a story uses words like *I* and *my,* the story is told from the **first-person point of view.** Readers see and experience what happens in the story through that first-person **narrator.**

L As you read, ask yourself these questions to help you think about the narrator:

- *Who is telling the story?*
- *How would this story change if it were told from a different point of view?*
- *How does knowing the narrator's thoughts and feelings affect you as you read the story?*

Interactive Literary Elements Handbook
To review or learn more about the literary elements, go to www.glencoe.com.

Get Ready to Read

Connect to the Reading

Suppose that you have brown hair, and a new law states that all brown-haired people must go to special jails. How would you feel if this happened to you? How would you feel if your hair were a different color? As you read "The Bracelet," think about what it was like for the characters who were forced to leave home for reasons that made no sense to them.

Partner Talk With your partner, discuss your answers to the questions above.

Build Background

During World War II the United States was at war with Japan. "The Bracelet" is an account of how Japanese people living on the West Coast at that time were sent to live in internment camps, or relocation centers.

- Some U.S. leaders feared that Japanese Americans might spy on or damage military bases.
- In 1942 President Franklin D. Roosevelt gave the U.S. War Department the authority to take Japanese Americans from their homes and send them to internment (in TURN ment) camps. An *internment camp* is a place where people are forced to stay.
- About 110,000 Japanese Americans were forced to live in internment camps. Two-thirds of them were U.S. citizens.
- Years later, in 1988, the U.S. Congress apologized to all the Japanese Americans who had been interned in these camps.

Set Purposes for Reading

BIG Question As you read "The Bracelet," think about what we can learn from mistakes.

Set Your Own Purpose What else would you like to learn from the story to help you answer the Big Question? Write your own purpose on "The Bracelet" part of the Workshop 2 Foldable.

Keep Moving

Use these skills as you read the following selection.

The Bracelet **821**

Teach

R Reading Skill

Identifying Main Idea and Supporting Details Ask: For what event is the family preparing? *(The family is packing for relocation to a Japanese internment camp.)* **Ask:** How do they feel about it? *(Possible response: They are upset.)* **BL OL**

L Literary Element

Narrator Ask: Why might readers be likely to sympathize with a first-person narrator? *(Possible response: Readers may identify with what the narrator is thinking or feeling.)* **OL**

Interactive Literary Elements Handbook Have students access the Web site to improve their understanding of narrator.

Reading Fluency

Citizenship Explain to students that following the bombing of Pearl Harbor, many Japanese Americans were sent to internment camps. Have students work in groups to find answers to the following questions.

- What was Executive Order 9066? Who signed it? When?

- How many internment camps were established? What were conditions like in the camps? When did the camps close?

- What actions did the United States take as an apology to Japanese Americans? **OL AL**

Objectives

- Identify main ideas and supporting details
- Identify and analyze narrator
- Learn and use new vocabulary

Teach

C Critical Thinking

Analysis Ask: Why doesn't Ruri want her older sister to see her crying? *(Students may say that Ruri doesn't want her older sister to think of her as a baby, or that she doesn't want to make her sister sad by crying in front of her.)* **OL**

R Reading Skill

Identifying Main Idea and Supporting Details Ask: What is the main idea in the fourth paragraph? *(The house is empty.)* **Ask:** What details in the fourth paragraph support its main idea? *(Possible response: The clothes, junk, and rag doll are gone; the rugs and furniture are gone; the pictures and drapes are down; the closets and cupboards are empty.)* **OL**

L Literary Element

Narrator Ask: What words give clues about the narrator's point of view? *(I, me, my)* Who is telling the story? *(Ruri)* **OL**

Readability Scores
Dale-Chall: 4.7
DRP: 51
Lexile: 830

The Bracelet

by Yoshiko Uchida

C "**M**ama, is it time to go?"

I hadn't planned to cry, but the tears came suddenly, and I wiped them away with the back of my hand. I didn't want my older sister to see me crying.

"It's almost time, Ruri," my mother said gently. Her face was filled with a kind of sadness I had never seen before.

R I looked around at my empty room. The clothes that Mama always told me to hang up in the closet, the junk piled on my dresser, the old rag doll I could never bear to part with—they were all gone. There was nothing left in my room, and there was nothing left in the rest of the house. The rugs and furniture were gone, the pictures and drapes were down, and the closets and cupboards were empty. The house was like a gift box after the nice thing inside was gone: just a lot of nothingness. **L**

It was almost time to leave our home, but we weren't moving to a nicer house or to a new town. It was April 12, 1942. The United States and Japan were at war, and every Japanese person on the West Coast was being **evacuated** by the government to a concentration camp.[1] Mama, my sister Keiko, and I were being sent from our home, and out of Berkeley, and eventually out of California.

The doorbell rang, and I ran to answer it before my sister could. I thought maybe by some miracle a messenger from the government might be standing there, tall and proper and

---

1. A **concentration camp** is a place where political prisoners and prisoners of war are confined.

Vocabulary

evacuated (ih VAK yoo ay tid) *v.* removed; moved out of

Practice the Skills

L Key Literary Element

Narrator The narrator is the person who "speaks," or tells the story. This narrator has a certain point of view. What is the narrator's point of view? How do you know? **L**

Additional Support

Differentiated Instruction

Diary Entry Tell students to imagine that the government is forcing them to leave their homes and relocate to an internment camp. They have been told that they can pack only what they can carry. In their Learner's Notebooks, have students write a short diary entry explaining how they feel about what is happening. Suggest that students discuss specific items that they will bring, how their family members are responding to the situation, and what they will miss most about the homes they are leaving. Remind students to write in the first person, using the pronouns *I, me,* and *my.* **OL**

buttoned into a uniform, come to tell us it was all a terrible mistake, that we wouldn't have to leave after all. Or maybe the messenger would have a **telegram** from Papa, who was interned[2] in a prisoner-of-war camp in Montana because he had worked for a Japanese business firm. **2 3**

The FBI had come to pick up Papa and hundreds of other Japanese community leaders on the very day that Japanese planes had bombed Pearl Harbor.[3] The government thought they were dangerous enemy aliens.[4] If it weren't so sad, it would have been funny. Papa could no more be dangerous than the mayor of our city, and he was every bit as loyal to the United States. He had lived here since 1917.

When I opened the door, it wasn't a messenger from anywhere. It was my best friend, Laurie Madison, from next door. She was holding a package wrapped up like a birthday present, but she wasn't wearing her party dress, and her face drooped like a wilted tulip.

"Hi," she said. "I came to say goodbye."

She thrust the present at me and told me it was something to take to camp. "It's a bracelet," she said before I could open the package. "Put it on so you won't have to pack it." She knew I didn't have one inch of space left in my suitcase. We had been instructed to take only what we could carry into camp, and Mama had told us that we could each take only two suitcases.

"Then how are we ever going to pack the dishes and blankets and sheets they've told us to bring with us?" Keiko worried.

"I don't really know," Mama said, and she simply began packing those big impossible things into an enormous duffel bag—along with umbrellas, boots, a kettle, hot plate, and flashlight.

"Who's going to carry that huge sack?" I asked.

But Mama didn't worry about things like that. "Someone will help us," she said. "Don't worry." So I didn't.

Laurie wanted me to open her package and put on the bracelet before she left. It was a thin gold chain with a heart dangling on it. She helped me put it on, and I told her I'd never take it off, ever. **4**

---

2. Someone who is *interned* is detained, confined, or imprisoned.

3. The Japanese bombed the U.S. naval base at *Pearl Harbor,* Hawaii, on December 7, 1941. This attack brought the United States into World War II.

4. *Aliens* are people who are not citizens of the country in which they live.

Practice the Skills

2 English Language Coach

Latin Roots **Telegram** is formed by combining the Latin root *gram*, which means "write," with *tele*, which means "far off." How are these meanings combined in the meaning of *telegram*?

3 Key Literary Element

Narrator How does the narrator's point-of-view make you feel about what is happening?

4 Key Reading Skill

Identifying Main Idea and Supporting Details What is the main idea of this paragraph? What details support that main idea?

The Bracelet **823**

Teach

L Literary Element

Narrator Ask: Do you think that it is easier to identify with a first-person narrator? Why or why not? *(Responses will vary. Students may say that it is easier to identify with a first-person narrator because the reader views events through the narrator's eyes.)* **OL**

R Reading Skill

Identifying Main Idea and Supporting Details Say: Write a sentence that you could add to this paragraph—either at the beginning or at the end—that states the main idea directly. *(Possible response: The FBI was wrong to think that Papa and other Japanese community leaders were dangerous.)* **OL**

English Language Coach

Building Background Ruri hopes that a messenger has brought a telegram from Papa. A telegram is a message sent by a telegraph, or system of transmitting information by code. In 1835, Samuel F. B. Morse invented a system of dots and dashes known as Morse code, and in 1837 he was granted a patent on an electromagnetic telegraph that transferred the dots and dashes to paper. The first message was transmitted on May 24, 1844, and the telegraph, to which many improvements were later made, became the primary means of transmitting print messages for the next 100 years. **AS**

Objectives
• Identify main ideas and supporting details
• Identify and analyze narrator
• Analyze text

Teach

L Literary Element

Narrator Ask: What does Ruri reveal about her feelings when she describes saying goodbye to Laurie? Explain. *(Possible response: By saying that she slammed the door shut and that she didn't want to watch Laurie anymore, Ruri reveals that she is upset about saying goodbye.)* **OL**

C Critical Thinking

Analysis Ask: Why do you think Ruri's mother goes from room to room, as if she is taking a mental picture of the house? *(Responses will vary. Students may say that Ruri's mother wants to memorize the images so that she can think of home when she is in the camp.)* **OL**

"Well, goodbye, then," Laurie said awkwardly. "Come home soon."

"I will," I said, although I didn't know if I would ever get back to Berkeley again.

I watched Laurie go down the block, her long blond pigtails bouncing as she walked. I wondered who would be sitting in my desk at Lincoln Junior High now that I was gone. Laurie kept turning and waving, even walking backward for a while, until she got to the corner. I didn't want to watch anymore, and I slammed the door shut. **5**

The next time the doorbell rang, it was Mrs. Simpson, our other neighbor. She was going to drive us to the Congregational Church, which was the Civil Control Station where all the Japanese of Berkeley were supposed to report.

It was time to go. "Come on, Ruri. Get your things," my sister called to me.

It was a warm day, but I put on a sweater and my coat so I wouldn't have to carry them, and I picked up my two suitcases. Each one had a tag with my name and our family number on it. Every Japanese family had to register and get a number. We were Family Number 13453.

Mama was taking one last look around our house. She was going from room to room, as though she were trying to take a mental picture of the house she had lived in for fifteen years, so she would never forget it.

I saw her take a long last look at the garden that Papa loved. The irises beside the fish pond were just beginning to bloom. If Papa had been home, he would have cut the first iris blossom and brought it inside to Mama. "This one is for you," he would have said. And Mama would have smiled and said, "Thank you, Papa San"[5] and put it in her favorite cut-glass vase.

But the garden looked shabby and **forsaken** now that Papa was gone and Mama was too busy to take care of it. It looked the way I felt, sort of empty and lonely and abandoned.

Practice the Skills

5 Key Literary Element

Narrator Think about the narrator's descriptions of Laurie. The narrator's point of view does not allow you to read Laurie's mind, but you still get a feel for her thoughts and feelings. How do you think Laurie feels? How can you tell? **L**

---

5. *San* is a term of respect added to Japanese names.

Vocabulary

forsaken (for SAY kun) *adj.* abandoned

824 UNIT 7 What Can We Learn from Our Mistakes?

Additional Support

Reading in the Real World

Citizenship Discuss with students the effects of having one's name replaced with a number or code. Ask students to consider why the U.S. government would have assigned each Japanese family a number and how those families must have felt under the circumstances. Discuss the following questions: What is the value of having a name? What is lost when that name is replaced by a number? Was this system put in place for convenience or for other reasons? Have students do additional research about personal stories of people who were forced to live in concentration and internment camps during WWII. **AL**

When Mrs. Simpson took us to the Civil Control Station, I felt even worse. I was scared, and for a minute I thought I was going to lose my breakfast right in front of everybody. There must have been over a thousand Japanese people gathered at the church. Some were old and some were young. Some were talking and laughing, and some were crying. I guess everybody else was scared too. No one knew exactly what was going to happen to us. We just knew we were being taken to the Tanforan Racetracks,[6] which the army had turned into a camp for the Japanese. There were fourteen other camps like ours along the West Coast. **6**

What scared me most were the soldiers standing at the doorway of the church hall. They were carrying guns with mounted bayonets.[7] I wondered if they thought we would try to run away and whether they'd shoot us or come after us with their bayonets if we did.

A long line of buses waited to take us to camp. There were trucks, too, for our baggage. And Mama was right; some men were there to help us load our duffel bag. When it was time to board the buses, I sat with Keiko, and Mama sat behind us. The bus went down Grove Street and passed the small Japanese food store where Mama used to order her bean-curd cakes and pickled radish. The windows were all boarded up, but there was a sign still hanging on the door that read, "We are loyal Americans." **7**

---

6. **Tanforan Racetrack** was a famous racetrack near San Francisco. It opened in 1899 and burned down in 1964. People came to Tanforan to see horse races and car races.

7. **Bayonets** are long knives on the end of rifles.

Practice the Skills

6 ▌ **Reviewing Skills**

Clarifying Think about the things you might need to clarify in this paragraph: How can you find out what the Civil Control Station is? What is happening at the Tanforan Racetracks? If you're not sure about the answers, go back and read or look at the footnotes.

R1

7 ▌ **Key Reading Skill**

Identifying Main Idea and Supporting Details Is the description of the Japanese food store a main idea or a minor detail? Explain.

R2

Irises (detail), Edo Period. Ogata Korin. Colour on gilded paper, 150.9 x 338 cm. Nezu Museum, Tokyo, Japan.

The Bracelet **825**

Teach

R1 **Reading Skill**

Review Clarifying Ask: Other than footnotes, what are some resources that you can use to clarify this kind of information? *(Possible responses: encyclopedia; Internet search)* **BL** **OL**

R2 **Reading Skill**

Identifying Main Idea and Supporting Details Ask: How is the message on the sign similar to Ruri's previous comment about her father? *(Possible response: Just as the message on the sign claims that the store's owners are loyal Americans, Ruri claims that her father is loyal and does not pose a threat.)* **OL** **AL**

Viewing the Art

Ask: What does this image represent in the story? *(Possible response: The image represents what the family will be leaving behind – their home, their friends, and their normal lives – as they are forced to move to the camps with next to nothing.)* **AL**

English Language Coach

Cultural Background Students may be unfamiliar with *bean-curd cakes* and *pickled radish,* items that Ruri's mother used to purchase at the Japanese food store. Explain that the Japanese diet is rich in whole grains, beans, and vegetables. Traditional Japanese foods include many variations on the soybean, including miso, tofu (bean curd), natto, and soy sauce. The Japanese frequently pickle seaweed, plums, and radishes. You may wish to provide examples of these foods for students to taste or ask students of Japanese heritage if they would like to bring samples of the foods to class. **AS**

Objectives
- Identify main ideas and supporting details
- Identify and analyze narrator
- Analyze text
- Clarify ideas and text

825

Teach

EL Language Coach

Latin Roots Ask: What word that contains this root means "the power to get things done"? *(leverage)* What word that contains this root means "altitude"? *(elevation)* **OL**

L Literary Element

Narrator Ask: What do the narrator's expectations tell us about her? *(Possible response: We see that she is young and innocent.)* **Ask:** A narrator who is outside the story would know something about the apartment that Ruri doesn't know. What would this knowledge be? *(Possible response: An outside narrator would know that the apartment will not be luxurious.)* **OL**

The crazy thing about the whole evacuation was that we were all loyal Americans. Most of us were citizens because we had been born here. But our parents, who had come from Japan, couldn't become citizens because there was a law that prevented any Asian from becoming a citizen. Now everybody with a Japanese face was being shipped off to concentration camps.

"It's stupid," Keiko muttered as we saw the racetrack **looming** up beside the highway. "If there were any Japanese spies around, they'd have gone back to Japan long ago."

"I'll say," I agreed. My sister was in high school and she ought to know, I thought.

When the bus turned onto Tanforan, there were more and more armed guards at the gate, and I saw barbed wire strung around the entire grounds. I felt as though I were going into a prison, but I hadn't done anything wrong.

We streamed off the buses and poured into a huge room, where doctors looked down our throats and peeled back our eyelids to see if we had any diseases. Then we were given our housing assignments. The man in charge gave Mama a slip of paper. We were in Barrack 16, Apartment 40.

"Mama!" I said. "We're going to live in an apartment!" The only apartment I had ever seen was the one my piano teacher lived in. It was in an enormous building in San Francisco, with an **elevator** and thick-carpeted hallways. I thought how wonderful it would be to have our own elevator. A house was all right, but an apartment seemed elegant and special. **8 9**

We walked down the racetrack, looking for Barrack 16. Mr. Noma, a friend of Papa's, helped us carry our bags. I was so busy looking around I slipped and almost fell on the muddy track. Army barracks had been built everywhere, all around the racetrack and even in the center oval.

Mr. Noma pointed beyond the track toward the horse stables. "I think your barrack is out there."

He was right. We came to a long stable that had once housed the horses of Tanforan, and we climbed up the wide ramp. Each stall had a number painted on it, and when we got to 40, Mr. Noma pushed open the door.

"Well, here it is," he said, "Apartment 40."

Vocabulary

looming (LOO ming) *adj.* appearing in the distance

Practice the Skills

8 English Language Coach

Latin Roots The word **elevator** comes from the Latin root *levare,* meaning "to raise." Think about how the root's meaning relates to an *elevator.* **EL**

9 Key Literary Element

Narrator When the narrator is a character in the story, readers see the action through that character's eyes. Do you think Ruri is right that her new home will be elegant and special? Explain. **L**

Analyzing the Photo Based on what you've read, what do you think is happening in this photo?

Additional Support

Reading in the Real World

Citizenship Have students use library and school-approved Internet resources to research laws in the United States that have restricted immigration and citizenship. Tell students to list the conditions of the Immigration Act of 1924, also known as the National Origins Act or Johnson-Reed Act. Tell students to note the number of immigrants permitted to enter the United States and the countries from which people were prohibited from emigrating to the United States. Suggest that students find out the origins of restrictive immigration and citizenship laws involving Asians, beginning with the Chinese Exclusion Act of 1882. **AL**

The stall was narrow and empty and dark. There were two small windows on each side of the door. Three folded army cots were on the dust-covered floor, and one light-bulb dangled from the ceiling. That was all. This was our apartment, and it still smelled of horses.

Mama looked at my sister and then at me. "It won't be so bad when we fix it up," she began. "I'll ask Mrs. Simpson to send me some material for curtains. I could make some cushions too, and . . . well . . ." She stopped. She couldn't think of anything more to say.

Mr. Noma said he'd go get some mattresses for us. "I'd better hurry before they're all gone." He rushed off. I think he wanted to leave so that he wouldn't have to see Mama cry. But he needn't have run off, because Mama didn't cry. She just went out to borrow a broom and began sweeping out the dust and dirt. "Will you girls set up the cots?" she asked.

It was only after we'd put up the last cot that I noticed my bracelet was gone. "I've lost Laurie's bracelet!" I screamed. "My bracelet's gone!"

We looked all over the stall and even down the ramp. I wanted to run back down the track and go over every inch of ground we'd walked on, but it was getting dark and Mama wouldn't let me.

I thought of what I'd promised Laurie. I wasn't ever going to take the bracelet off, not even when I went to take a shower. And now I had lost it on my very first day in camp. I wanted to cry. **10**

I kept looking for it all the time we were in Tanforan. I didn't stop looking until the day we were sent to another camp, called Topaz, in the middle of a desert in Utah. And then I gave up.

But Mama told me never mind. She said I didn't need a bracelet to remember Laurie, just as I didn't need anything to remember Pap or our home in Berkeley or all the people and things we loved and had left behind.

"Those are things we can carry in our hearts and take with us no matter where we are sent," she said.

And I guess she was right. I've never forgotten Laurie, even now. **11** ○

Analyzing the Photo How does this picture help you understand the author's description of Tanforan? Explain, using details from the text.

Practice the Skills

10 | **Key Reading Skill**

Identifying Main Idea and Supporting Details What did the bracelet mean to Ruri when Laurie gave it to her? What details support your answer? How is the loss of the bracelet important in the story? **R**

11 | **BIG Question**

Does Ruri think that losing the bracelet means losing her friend? What does her mother's advice teach Ruri? Write your answers on your Foldable. Your response will help you complete the Unit Challenge later. **BQ**

The Bracelet **827**

Teach

R **Reading Skill**

Identifying Main Idea and Supporting Details Ask: Why does Laurie give Ruri the bracelet? *(Possible response: so that Ruri will remember their friendship)* **BL** Does the bracelet still serve its purpose even though Ruri loses it? *(Responses will vary. Students may say that even though Ruri lost the bracelet long ago, she still remembers her friendship with Laurie.)* **OL**

BQ **BIG Question**

Ask: Does Ruri make a mistake in this story? If so, what is it? Who else makes a mistake? *(Possible response: Ruri mistakenly assumes that one needs physical objects or reminders in order to have memories. The United States government mistakenly assumes that Japanese Americans are disloyal.)* **OL** **AL**

CheckPoint

Use the CheckPoint questions provided on Presentation Plus! to check for comprehension of the selection. These questions can be used with interactive response keypads for immediate student feedback.

Reading Fluency

Build Fluency One way to help students build fluency is to have them read aloud in pairs. Both students in each pair should read each paragraph aloud so that they can hear the words pronounced by a partner. As one student reads, the other should keep track of errors and miscues. Have students perform this activity after they have read the story once so that they will already be familiar with the text. This will allow students to focus on reading fluently and avoid being bogged down by problems with comprehension. Encourage struggling readers to practice reading the same paragraph three or four times, if necessary. **EL** **BL**

Objectives
- Identify main ideas and supporting details
- Identify and analyze narrator
- Identify word structure: Latin roots

827

Assess

Resources for page 828

📁 Selection Quick Check, p. 63

📁 Selection and Unit Assessment, p. 75

⊙ ExamView Assessment Suite

⊙ Interactive Tutor: Self-Assessment

Students can respond to the *After You Read* items in their Learner's Notebooks or on a separate sheet of paper.

Answering the

1. Responses will vary. Students may say that it is wrong to judge people on the basis of ethnicity.
2. Ruri's father had already been sent to a different internment camp.
3. Ruri loses the bracelet that Laurie gave her.

Critical Thinking

4. Responses will vary. Students may say that the people were outnumbered or that they didn't want to make matters worse by protesting.
5. Students may say that the bracelet is Ruri's connection to her life before the war, especially her friendship with Laurie.
6. Responses will vary. Students may say that they agree with Ruri's mother because Ruri still remembers Laurie, even without the bracelet.

After You Read | The Bracelet

Answering the **BIG Question**

1. Name one mistake in "The Bracelet" that the world can learn from. Explain your answer.
2. **Summarize** Why was Ruri's father not with the family?
   Tip Think and Search
3. **Recall** What makes Ruri want to cry the first day she is in her new "apartment" at Tanforan?
   Tip Right There

Critical Thinking

4. **Interpret** Why do you think the people in the story went to the camps without a fight?
   Tip Author and Me
5. **Interpret** Why is the bracelet so important to Ruri?
   Tip Think and Search
6. **Evaluate** Do you agree or disagree with Ruri's mother that Ruri doesn't need the bracelet to help her remember Laurie? Explain.
   Tip On Your Own

Talk About Your Reading

This story takes place in 1942 when Franklin D. Roosevelt was president of the United States. What if Ruri had the chance to talk to President Roosevelt and share her story about the internment camp? With a partner, take turns role-playing Ruri's argument. Try to imagine how it would feel to lose your freedom. Use these questions to get started.

If you could talk to the president about the internment camps, what would you say to persuade him to shut down the camps?

• Think about ways the situation affected your community, your family, and your life; what should you tell him?
• How did you feel about leaving the life you knew?
• What examples from the story will you use to support your point-of-view?

Objectives (pp. 828–829)
Reading Identify main ideas and supporting details • Make connections from text to self
Literature Identify literary elements: narrator
Vocabulary Identify word structure: Latin roots
Grammar Identify parts of speech: subjects and verbs

828 UNIT 7 What Can We Learn from Our Mistakes?

Talk About Your Reading

Responses will vary. Students should include details from the story as well as personal opinions to offer a persuasive argument.

Skills Review

Key Reading Skill: Identifying Main Idea and Supporting Details

7. What is the main idea in "The Bracelet?"

Key Literary Element: Narrator

8. **a)** Describe Ruri as a narrator. **b)** Is she believable? Explain. **c)** Can you relate to her? Explain.

9. How did the narrator's descriptions cause you to feel or respond to events in the story? What part of those descriptions made the biggest impression on you?

Reviewing Skills: Clarifying

10. Name a part of the story that you clarified. How did you do it?

Vocabulary Check

Write *True* or *False* for each sentence. If the answer is false, rewrite the statement to make it true. Be sure to use the vocabulary word.

11. If you have **evacuated**, you have stayed in place.

12. If you followed through with something, you have **forsaken** your goals.

13. A storm **looming** in the distance might mean a dark sky on the horizon.

14. **English Language Coach** The Latin root *vers* means "turn." How does this root relate to the words below? Write a definition for each word, showing how it is related to the meaning of the root. Use a dictionary if you need help.

    universe

    version

    conversation

Grammar Link: Subjects Separated from Verbs

When a prepositional phrase comes between a subject and the verb, the verb must agree with the subject, not the object of the preposition.

- Mentally remove the word or phrase from the sentence. Read the sentence without the prepositional phrase.

  Thousands of Italian Americans were arrested.

  Think: *Thousands were arrested.*

- Make sure that the verb agrees with the subject, not the noun closest to the verb.

  Incorrect: *A park on the islands contain a volcano.*

    The subject is *park*. *Islands* is the object of the preposition *on.*

  Correct: *A park on the islands contains a volcano.*

Grammar Practice

For each of the following sentences, write the verb that agrees with the subject.

15. Relocation camps in Arizona (was/were) in terrible condition.

16. The duffel bag with a kettle, a hot plate, and boots (was/were) heavy.

17. A friend of her parents (helps/help) them move into the horse stall.

18. The guard next to the towers (look/looks) angry

19. The flowers in the garden (is/are) blooming.

20. The stable with the cots (is/are) where we will live.

Web Activities For eFlashcards, Selection Quick Checks, and other Web activities, go to www.glencoe.com.

The Bracelet **829**

Skills Review

Key Reading Skill: Identifying Main Idea and Supporting Details

7. Possible responses: Ruri and her family are forced to live in a Japanese internment camp.

Key Literary Element: Narrator

8. Possible responses: **a)** Ruri is an honest and observant narrator. **b)** Ruri is believable because her comments and concerns are age appropriate. **c)** I can relate to Ruri's sadness about moving away and losing the bracelet.

9. Responses will vary.

Reviewing Skill: Clarifying

10. Responses will vary.

Vocabulary Check

11. False; If you have *evacuated,* you had to move somewhere else.

12. False; If you have given up on something, you have *forsaken* your goals.

13. True

14. universe: the earth, the galaxies; things that turn in space

    version: altered form of something; to turn one thing into something else

    conversation: talk between two or more people; to take turns talking

---

Grammar Link: Subjects Separated from Verbs

Grammar Practice

15. were
16. was
17. helps
18. looks
19. are
20. is

Close

Ask students to summarize what they learned about the Big Question from the story.

Teach

More About the Author

Three of Dorothy M. Johnson's short stories—"The Hanging Tree," "The Man Who Shot Liberty Valance," and "A Man Called Horse"—were made into popular movies. John Wayne and Jimmy Stewart are two actors who brought Johnson's characters to life for movie audiences. As Johnson's biographer said of her, "she described the Western frontier for later generations of Americans . . . She was a guide and an interpreter for the average person."

V Vocabulary

Vocabulary Ask: Would a person offering hospitality act in a *grudging* manner? *(no)* Would a tired person act *sedately? (yes)* **OL**

Before You Read : Too Soon a Woman

Dorothy M. Johnson

Meet the Author

Dorothy M. Johnson moved to Montana from Iowa when she was a child. The beautiful scenery and the exciting history of the Old West inspired her stories for both children and adults. An honorary member of the Blackfoot tribe, Johnson wrote vividly about Native Americans, cowboys, and outlaws.

Author Search For more information about Dorothy M. Johnson, go to www.glencoe.com.

Objectives (pp. 830–837)
Reading Identify main ideas and supporting details • Make connections from text to self
Literature Identify literary elements: narrator
Vocabulary Identify word structure: Latin roots

Vocabulary Preview

skimpy (SKIM pee) *adj.* lacking in quantity; barely or not quite enough **(p. 832)** *The family's load was skimpy because they were almost out of food.*

hospitality (hos pih TAL uh tee) *n.* friendly treatment of guests **(p. 833)** *They showed hospitality toward the strangers and gave them food.*

grudging (GRUJ ing) *adj.* given resentfully or without wanting to **(p. 833)** *The father finally gives Mary a grudging nod hello.*

sedately (sih DAYT lee) *adv.* in a quiet, calm manner **(p. 837)** *Mary sedately accepted the father's thanks.*

V

Partner Talk Discuss the pronunciation and definition of each vocabulary word with a partner. Then use each word in a sentence to be sure you understand its definition.

English Language Coach

Latin Roots Look at this family of words based on the Latin root *flect* or *flex*, which means "to bend."

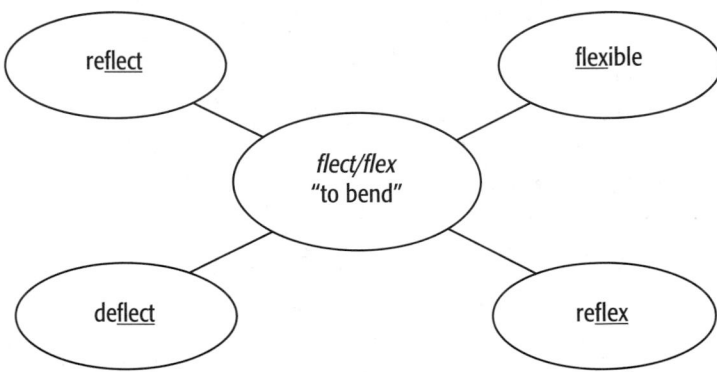

reflect — flexible — flect/flex "to bend" — deflect — reflex

On Your Own Copy the words in the circles in your Learner's Notebook. Think about how the root relates to each word and write the meaning of each word. Use a dictionary if you need help.

Additional Support

Author Search To expand students' appreciation of Dorothy M. Johnson, have them access the Web site for additional information and resources.

Differentiated Instruction

Free Writing Ask students if they have ever been told that they are "growing up quickly," and have them discuss what responsibilities accompany adulthood. Prompt students to think about certain milestones in society that indicate that a child has "grown up." Then have students think about the title of this short story—"Too Soon a Woman"—and write several sentences about what they think the story will be about. Encourage students to use clues on this page, such as facts from Johnson's life and vocabulary words that appear in the story, to make guesses about the meaning of the title and the topic of the story. **OL**

Skills Preview

Key Reading Skill: Identifying Main Idea and Supporting Details

Use these questions to help you find the **main idea** and **supporting details** in "Too Soon a Woman."

R
- What **main idea** do you get from each section of this story?
- What **details** support each main idea?
- What overall main idea do you get from the whole story?
- What are two details that support that main idea?

Write to Learn In your Learner's Notebook, draw a box, leaving room to write the main idea in it. Draw smaller boxes under the main idea box to be filled with supporting details. As you read "Too Soon a Woman," fill in this diagram with possible main ideas and supporting details.

Key Literary Element: Narrator

The narrator is the one telling the story. The narrator explains what happens from his or her point of view. Here are three points of view.
- **First-person:** The narrator is a character in the story.
- **Third-person:** The narrator is outside the story.
- **Omniscient:** The narrator is not in the story but knows all of the characters' thoughts and actions.

L
As you read, use these tips to help you learn about the story through the narrator.
- Identify the narrator.
  Does a character tell the story? If so, who is it?
- Think about why the author chose this character to tell the story.
  How would the story change if it were told from another point of view?
- Consider what the narrator tells you about events and other characters.
  How does knowing the narrator's thoughts and feelings affect you as you read the story?

Get Ready to Read

Connect to the Reading

What if you were starving in a life-and-death situation? You might eat things you wouldn't usually consider eating. Bugs? Strange plants? What risks would you be willing to take to survive?

Write to Learn In your Learner's Notebook, write what you would do to survive if you were starving in the wilderness.

Build Background

During the 1800s many families moved west. These trips were never easy, and settlers could expect to face many trials along the way.
- Pioneers, or settlers, traveled west on overland routes such as the Oregon Trail.
- Pioneers began traveling the Oregon Trail in the 1840s.
- Beginning in 1843, and for the next twenty-five years, more than half a million people traveled the Oregon Trail to the West Coast.

Set Purposes for Reading

BIG Question Read "Too Soon a Woman" to find out why it may never be too late to learn from your mistake in time to correct it.

Set Your Own Purpose What else would you like to learn from the short story to help you answer the Big Question? Write your own purpose on the "Too Soon a Woman" part of the Workshop 2 Foldable.

Interactive Literary Elements Handbook
To review or learn more about the literary elements, go to www.glencoe.com.

Keep Moving

Use these skills as you read the following selection.

Too Soon a Woman **831**

Teach

R **Reading Skill**

Identifying Main Idea and Supporting Details Say: The following is a fictional short story. Do you expect to learn the main idea at the beginning of the story or toward the end? Explain. *(Possible response: toward the end; nonfiction pieces usually give the main idea first, but fictional stories often reveal the main idea toward the end.)* **OL**

L **Literary Element**

Narrator Ask: Would a third-person narrator usually reveal his or her name? Explain. *(Possible response: probably not; a third-person narrator is outside the story.)* **AS**

English Language Coach

Building Background Point out to students that "the great migration" on the Oregon Trail demonstrates the westward, expansionist mentality known as Manifest Destiny. Explain that the term originated in the 1840s to describe the ideal of an America that extended from the Atlantic Ocean in the East to the Pacific Ocean in the West. Supporters believed that expansion was obvious (manifest) and inevitable (destiny). Part of this idea of westward expansion also included the notion that it was America's duty to spread democracy. Also mention the negative aspects of Manifest Destiny, including the displacement of Native Americans that resulted from westward expansion. **AS**

Objectives
- Identify main ideas and supporting details
- Identify and analyze narrator
- Learn and use new vocabulary

Teach

L1 Literary Element

Narrator Ask: On the basis of what you know about the narrator, will he be able to say what other characters think and feel? Explain. *(Possible response: No, only omniscient narrators can tell about other characters' thoughts and feelings. This story has a first-person narrator.)* **OL**

L2 Literary Element

Review Plot Ask: Which part of the plot do the opening paragraphs represent? *(the exposition)* What information is revealed? *(Possible response: The opening paragraphs introduce the characters, setting, and conflict.)* **OL**

Readability Scores
Dale-Chall: 5.0
DRP: 50
Lexile: 730

Too Soon a Woman

by Dorothy M. Johnson

L2

We left the home place behind, mile by slow mile, heading for the mountains, across the prairie where the wind blew forever.

At first there were four of us with the one-horse wagon and its **skimpy** load. Pa and I walked, because I was a big boy of eleven. My two little sisters romped and trotted until they got tired and had to be boosted up into the wagon bed. **1**

That was no covered Conestoga,[1] like Pa's folks came west in, but just an old farm wagon, drawn by one weary horse, creaking and rumbling westward to the mountains, toward the little woods town where Pa thought he had an old uncle who owned a little two-bit[2] sawmill.

Two weeks we had been moving when we picked up Mary, who had run away from somewhere that she wouldn't tell. Pa didn't want her along, but she stood up to him with no fear in her voice.

"I'd rather go with a family and look after the kids," she said, "but I ain't going back. If you won't take me, I'll travel with any wagon that will."

Pa scowled at her, and her wide blue eyes stared back.

"How old are you?" he demanded.

"Eighteen," she said. "There's teamsters[3] come this way sometimes. I'd rather go with you folks. But I won't go back."

"We're prid'near out of grub," my father told her. "We're clean out of money. I got all I can handle without taking

---

1. A **Conestoga** (kahn ih STOW gah) is a covered wagon with a canvas top and large, wood wheels.
2. The expression **two-bit** means "practically worthless."
3. **Teamsters** are people who drove teams, or groups, of horses or oxen.

Vocabulary

skimpy (SKIM pee) *adj.* lacking in quantity; barely or not quite enough

Practice the Skills

1 Key Literary Element

Narrator The narrator is the one who tells the story. A narrator may or may not be a character in the story. What do you know about the narrator so far? From what point of view is this story told? **L1**

Additional Support

Differentiated Instruction

Research Skills The Conestoga was a large wagon typically drawn by six horses. A smaller version of the Conestoga, known as the Prairie Schooner, was typically drawn by two to four horses or oxen. The narrator says that his family's wagon is old and drawn by a single horse. Have students gather information in encyclopedias and other resources about travel on the Oregon Trail. Have students who like to draw create illustrations of the types of transportation used by those who traveled to the West. **OL**

anybody else." He turned away as if he hated the sight of her. "You'll have to walk," he said.

So she went along with us and looked after the little girls, but Pa wouldn't talk to her. **2**

On the prairie, the wind blew. But in the mountains, there was rain. When we stopped at little timber claims along the way, the homesteaders[4] said it had rained all summer. Crops among the blackened stumps were rotted and spoiled. There was no cheer anywhere and little **hospitality**. The people we talked to were past worrying. They were scared and desperate. **3 4**

So was Pa. He traveled twice as far each day as the wagon. He ranged through the woods with his rifle, but he never saw game. He had been depending on venison,[5] but we never got any except as a **grudging** gift from the homesteaders.

He brought in a porcupine once; that was fat meat and good. Mary roasted it in chunks over the fire, half crying with the smoke. Pa and I rigged up the tarp sheet for a shelter to keep the rain from putting the fire clean out.

The porcupine was long gone, except for some of the tried-out[6] fat that Mary had saved, when we came to an old, empty cabin. Pa said we'd have to stop. The horse was wore out, couldn't pull anymore up those grades on the deep-rutted roads in the mountains.

At the cabin, at least there was shelter.

We had a few potatoes left and some corn meal. There was a creek that probably had fish in it, if a person could catch them. Pa tried it for half a day before he gave up. To this day I don't care for fishing. I remember my father's sunken eyes in his gaunt, grim face.

He took Mary and me outside the cabin to talk. Rain dripped on us from branches overhead.

---

4. **Homesteaders** are people who claimed and settled land.

5. **Venison** is deer meat.

6. **Tried-out** refers to the melted and hardened fat from the roasted porcupine.

Vocabulary

hospitality (hos pih TAL uh tee) *n.* friendly treatment of guests

grudging (GRUJ ing) *adj.* given resentfully or without wanting to

Practice the Skills

2 Reviewing Skills

Interpreting When you interpret, you use your own understanding of the world and what you've read in the text to decide what the events or ideas in a selection mean. Why do you think Pa decided to let Mary go with the family?

3 Key Reading Skill

Identifying Main Idea and Supporting Details What is the main idea of this paragraph? Is the main idea directly stated or do you have to think about it? Find two details that support the main idea.

4 English Language Coach

Latin Roots The word **hospitality** comes from the Latin root *hospes*, meaning "guest." The word *hospice* (a lodge for travelers) and the word *hospital* both have the same root. What might those words have in common with *hospitality*?

Too Soon a Woman **833**

Teach

R Reading Skill

Review Interpreting Ask: What does Mary say or do that convinces Pa to let her go along? *(Mary stands up to Pa without fear and she offers to take care of the children.)* If you were Pa, would you allow her to travel with you? Explain. *(Responses will vary about whether students would let Mary travel with them.)* **OL**

EL Language Coach

Latin Roots Ask: What does it mean if a person is hospitable? *(He or she is kind and generous.)* **EL OL**

English Language Coach

Dialect Explain to students that dialect is the form or variety of a spoken language that is particular to a region, community, social group, or occupational group. Such varieties may deviate from standard language in terms of pronunciation, syntax, and so on. English language learners and low-level readers are especially likely to have trouble comprehending written dialect. Help students understand the dialect in the story by first sounding it out and then translating it into Standard English. Then lead students in a discussion about why an author might choose to write in dialect. **EL BL OL**

Objectives

- Identify main ideas and supporting details
- Identify and analyze narrator
- Identify word structure: Latin roots
- Interpret text
- Understand dialect

Teach

L Literary Element

Narrator Say: Remember that the narrator is eleven years old when the story takes place. How do you think he feels about Pa's comment? *(Responses will vary. Students may say that the narrator is probably pleased to be considered Pa's "pardner." Students may also suggest that Pa recognizes and even praises Mary, which pleases the narrator.)* **OL**

R Reading Skill

Identifying Main Idea and Supporting Details Ask: In what ways is life difficult for the narrator and his family when Pa is gone? Give examples to support your answer. *(Possible response: The cabin is full of blinding smoke; they lose the horse; the narrator gets lost a few times; the sisters are scared and hungry.)* **OL**

"I think I know where we are," he said. "I calculate[7] to get to old John's and back in about four days. There'll be grub in the town, and they'll let me have some whether old John's still there or not."

He looked at me. "You do like she tells you," he warned. It was the first time he had admitted Mary was on earth since we picked her up two weeks before.

"You're my pardner," he said to me, "but it might be she's got more brains. You mind what she says." **5**

He burst out with bitterness, "There ain't anything good left in the world, or people to care if you live or die. But I'll get grub in the town and come back with it." **6**

He took a deep breath and added, "If you get too all-fired hungry, butcher the horse. It'll be better than starvin'."

He kissed the little girls good-bye and plodded off through the woods with one blanket and the rifle.

The cabin was moldy and had no floor. We kept a fire going under a hole in the roof, so it was full of blinding smoke, but we had to keep the fire so as to dry out the wood.

The third night, we lost the horse. A bear scared him. We heard the racket, and Mary and I ran out, but we couldn't see anything in the pitch dark.

In gray daylight I went looking for him, and I must have walked fifteen miles. It seemed like I had to have that horse at the cabin when Pa came or he'd whip me. I got plumb[8] lost two or three times and thought maybe I was going to die there alone and nobody would ever know it, but I found the way back to the clearing.

That was the fourth day, and Pa didn't come. That was the day we ate up the last of the grub.

The fifth day, Mary went looking for the horse. My sisters whimpered, huddled in a quilt by the fire, because they were scared and hungry.

I never did get dried out, always having to bring in more damp wood and going out to yell to see if Mary would hear me and not get lost. But I couldn't cry like the little girls did, because I was a big boy, eleven years old.

It was near dark when there was an answer to my yelling, and Mary came into the clearing.

---

7. To **calculate** means to "figure out" or "estimate."
8. **Plumb** means "completely."

834 UNIT 7 What Can We Learn from Our Mistakes?

Practice the Skills

5 Key Literary Element

Narrator Think about what Pa tells Mary and the narrator. Think about the way the narrator shares conversations and events. What do you learn about the other characters through the narrator? How would the story be different if Pa or Mary were telling the story? **L**

6 Reviewing Skills

Interpreting Think about what Pa means when he says, "There ain't anything good left in the world, or people to care if you live or die." Why do you think he says this? How do you feel about this statement?

Additional Support

Reading Fluency

Build Fluency Have students use the text on this page to practice building fluency, first reading silently and then aloud in pairs. Begin by having students preread the selected passage. Students should scan the text and list words or phrases with which they are unfamiliar. Have students submit their lists to you and discuss the meaning and pronunciation of these words as a class. Then have students go back and reread the passage. Students should work in pairs, alternating reading aloud to each other. As one student reads aloud, the other student should follow along. **EL BL**

Mary didn't have the horse—we never saw hide nor hair of that old horse again—but she was carrying something big and white that looked like a pumpkin with no color to it.

She didn't say anything, just looked around and saw Pa wasn't there yet, at the end of the fifth day.

"What's that thing?" my sister Elizabeth demanded.

"Mushroom," Mary answered. "I bet it hefts[9] ten pounds."

R "What are you going to do with it now?" I sneered. "Play football here?"

"Eat it—maybe," she said, putting it in a corner. Her wet hair hung over her shoulders. She huddled by the fire.

My sister Sarah began to whimper again. "I'm hungry!" she kept saying.

"Mushrooms ain't good eating," I said. "They can kill you."

"Maybe," Mary answered. "Maybe they can. I don't set up to know all about everything, like some people."

"What's that mark on your shoulder?" I asked her. "You tore your dress on the brush."

"What do you think it is?" she said, her head bowed in the smoke.

"Looks like scars," I guessed.

" 'Tis scars. They whipped me. Now mind your own business. I want to think." **7**

Elizabeth whimpered, "Why don't Pa come back?"

"He's coming," Mary promised. "Can't come in the dark. Your pa'll take care of you soon's he can."

She got up and rummaged around in the grub box.

"Nothing there but empty dishes," I growled. "If there was anything, we'd know it."

Mary stood up. She was holding the can with the porcupine grease.

"I'm going to have something to eat," she said coolly. "You kids can't have any yet. And I don't want any squalling,[10] mind."

---

9. In this sentence, something that **hefts** ten pounds weighs ten pounds. *Hefts* actually means "lifts up."

10. **Squalling** is the screaming cries of complaint Mary expects from the hungry little girls.

Analyzing the Art Describe what you see in this picture. Do you think this cabin is similar to the one the family is in? Explain.

Practice the Skills

7 **BIG Question**

Do you think that making the trip was a mistake for Mary? What must her choices have been? Keep in mind that she said she was "whipped." At this point does the trip seem like a mistake for the entire family? Write your answer on your Foldable. **BQ**

Too Soon a Woman **835**

Teach

R Reading Skill

Review Interpreting Ask: Why does the narrator sneer? What is the meaning of his question? *(Possible response: The narrator does not realize that Mary intends to use the mushroom to feed the family.)* **OL**

BQ BIG Question

Ask: What reasons did families like this one have for making the trip west? *(Responses will vary. Students may suggest that poverty spurred pioneers to look for land and wealth elsewhere.)* **OL** **Ask:** Were the pioneers justified in taking such a large risk by leaving home? *(Responses will vary. Some students may say that the families faced almost certain starvation if they stayed home.)* **AL**

Reading in the Real World

Citizenship Explain to students that even today people must be very careful when choosing wild mushrooms to eat. Students may better understand Mary's sacrifice if they do some research on poisonous mushrooms. Have students use the library or the Internet to research mushrooms. Ask them to gather information about how many types of poisonous mushrooms there are, what some of their names are, what they look like, and where they grow. You may wish to have students compile their findings into an informational pamphlet that includes illustrations and resources for additional information. **OL** **AL**

Objectives
- Identify main ideas and supporting details
- Identify and analyze narrator
- Interpret text

835

Teach

C Critical Thinking

Evaluation Ask: Is Mary being cruel or kind? Explain. *(Responses will vary. Some students may say that Mary is being kind because she is protecting the family from possible harm. Others may say that it is cruel to eat the mushroom in front of the hungry children.)* **OL**

R Reading Skill

Identifying Main Idea and Supporting Details Ask: What is the first half of this page about? State the main idea of this section. *(Possible response: Mary cooks part of the mushroom so that she can determine whether it is safe to eat. The narrator thinks Mary is cruel for eating in front of the children and tempting them.)* **OL**

L Literary Element

Narrator Ask: What would an omniscient narrator be able to explain that this narrator cannot? *(Possible response: An omniscient narrator would be able to tell what Mary is thinking as she eats the mushroom.)* **OL**

It was a cruel thing, what she did then. She sliced that big, solid mushroom and heated grease in a pan.

The smell of it brought the little girls out of their quilt, but she told them to go back in so fierce a voice that they obeyed. They cried to break your heart.

I didn't cry. I watched, hating her.

I endured the smell of the mushroom frying as long as I could. Then I said, "Give me some."

"Tomorrow," Mary answered. "Tomorrow, maybe. But not tonight." She turned to me with a sharp command: "Don't bother me! Just leave me be."

She knelt there by the fire and finished frying the slice of mushroom.

If I'd had Pa's rifle, I'd have been willing to kill her right then and there.

She didn't eat right away. She looked at the brown, fried slice for a while and said, "By tomorrow morning, I guess you can tell whether you want any."

The little girls stared at her as she ate. Sarah was chewing an old leather glove. **8**

When Mary crawled into the quilts with them, they moved away as far as they could get.

I was so scared that my stomach heaved, empty as it was.

Mary didn't stay in the quilts long. She took a drink out of the water bucket and sat down by the fire and looked through the smoke at me.

She said in a low voice, "I don't know how it will be if it's poison. Just do the best you can with the girls. Because your pa will come back, you know. . . . You better go to bed, I'm going to sit up."

And so would you sit up. If it might be your last night on earth and the pain of death might seize you at any moment, you would sit up by the smoky fire, wide-awake, remembering whatever you had to remember, savoring life.

Practice the Skills

8 Key Literary Element

Narrator Think about the different points of view a narrator might have. Which type of narrator would know Mary's thoughts as she eats the mushroom? Explain.

Additional Support

Differentiated Instruction

Journal Entry Because this story is written in the first person, readers are told the incident involving the mushroom from the perspective of the narrator, an eleven-year-old boy. His thoughts are mainly about how difficult it is to watch Mary eat the mushroom and not be able to eat any himself. Ask students to consider what the experience must be like for Mary, and tell students to write a journal entry from her perspective. Encourage students to think about what is going through Mary's mind when she eats the mushroom. Is she afraid about what will happen? Is she conflicted about letting the children eat it? **AS**

We sat in silence after the girls had gone to sleep. Once I asked, "How long does it take?"

"I never heard," she answered. "Don't think about it."

I slept after a while, with my chin on my chest. Maybe Peter dozed that way at Gethsemane[11] as the Lord knelt praying.

Mary's moving around brought me wide-awake. The black of night was fading.

"I guess it's all right," Mary said. "I'd be able to tell by now, wouldn't I?"

I answered gruffly, "I don't know."

Mary stood in the doorway for a while, looking out at the dripping world as if she found it beautiful. Then she fried slices of the mushroom while the little girls danced with anxiety.

We feasted, we three, my sisters and I, until Mary ruled, "That'll hold you," and would not cook any more. She didn't touch any of the mushroom herself.

That was a strange day in the moldy cabin. Mary laughed and was gay; she told stories, and we played "Who's Got the Thimble?" with a pine cone.

In the afternoon we heard a shout, and my sisters screamed, and I ran ahead of them across the clearing.

The rain had stopped. My father came plunging out of the woods leading a packhorse—and well I remember the treasures of food in that pack.

He glanced at us anxiously as he tore at the ropes that bound the pack.

"Where's the other one?" he demanded.

Mary came out of the cabin then, walking **sedately**. As she came toward us, the sun began to shine.

C My stepmother was a wonderful woman. **9** ○

---

11. The New Testament of the Christian Bible says that Jesus, knowing his death was near, went to the Garden of **Gethsemane** (geth SE muh nee) to pray. Although **Peter** and the other disciples had come to pray with him, they all fell asleep.

Vocabulary

sedately (sih DAYT lee) *adv.* in a quiet, calm manner

Practice the Skills

9 **BIG Question**

The characters have learned from the challenges in this story. Choose one character, and explain what he or she has learned. Write your answer on your Foldable. Your response will help you complete the Unit Challenge later. **BQ**

Too Soon a Woman **837**

Teach

C Critical Thinking

Synthesis Ask: What happens between Pa and Mary after Pa returns from his trip? *(They get married.)* **OL**

BQ **BIG Question**

Ask: Which character in the story makes the greatest mistake? Explain. *(Responses will vary. Some students may suggest that Pa makes the greatest mistake by bringing his family on a trip without adequate supplies; others may say the children make the mistake of not trusting Mary's actions with the mushroom.)* **AS**

Assess

✓ CheckPoint

Use the CheckPoint questions provided on Presentation Plus! to check for comprehension of the selection. These questions can be used with interactive response keypads for immediate student feedback.

Literature Focus Lesson

Theme Remind students that the theme of a story is its underlying message or idea. Have students revisit their predictions about the meaning of the title "Too Soon a Woman" and discuss how their thoughts have changed after reading the story. Invite students to explain their interpretation of the story's theme. Some students may suggest that the theme of the story is that Mary becomes a woman at an early age by taking on the responsibility of the children. Others may suggest that the theme has to do with Pa's initial distrust of Mary and his subsequent reversal of opinion. **OL AL**

Objectives
• Identify and analyze narrator
• Synthesize text
• Evaluate text
• Identify main ideas and supporting details

Assess

Resources for page 838

📁 Selection Quick Check, p. 64

📁 Selection and Unit Assessment, p. 76

💿 ExamView Assessment Suite

💿 Interactive Tutor: Self-Assessment

Students can respond to the *After You Read* items in their Learner's Notebooks or on a separate sheet of paper.

Answering the
 BIG Question

1. Responses will vary. Students may say that Pa makes a mistake when he brings the family on a trip without adequate supplies, that Pa makes a mistake when he at first distrusts Mary, or that the narrator makes a mistake when he lets the horse run away.

2. The family and Mary have to solve the problem of how to survive with so little food.

3. Mary marries Pa. She becomes the narrator's step-mother.

Critical Thinking

4. Possible response: The mother of the family is probably dead.

5. Possible response: Mary wants to make sure that the mushroom is not poisonous before she shares it with the children.

6. Students may say that the circumstances force Mary to grow up too quickly.

838

After You Read Too Soon a Woman

Answering the BIG Question

1. Who makes a mistake in "Too Soon a Woman"? Support your opinion with details from the story.

2. **Recall** What is the biggest problem that the family and Mary have to solve?
   Tip Think and Search

3. **Recall** What do you find out about Mary from the last sentence of the story?
   Tip Right There

Critical Thinking

4. **Infer** What can you infer about the mother of the family?
   Tip Author and Me

5. **Draw Conclusions** Why does Mary refuse to share the mushroom at first?
   Tip Author and Me

6. **Analyze** Why do think the author chose "Too Soon a Woman" for the title?
   Tip Author and Me

Write About Your Reading

Write a journal entry about the trip from Pa or Mary's point of view. In addition to telling about the experience, explain your feelings at the end of the story. Answer these questions as you write your entry:

• How did you feel throughout the ordeal?

• Why might you have made some of the decisions you made, and did you learn from any mistakes?

• What would you do differently? Why?

Objectives (pp. 838–839)
Reading Identify main ideas and supporting details • Make connections from text to self
Literature Identify literary elements: narrator
Vocabulary Identify word structure: Latin roots
Writing Respond to literature: journal entry
Grammar Use correct subject and verb agreement: compound subjects

Write About Your Reading

Possible response:

I got away today. They were out milking the cows, and I sneaked out the back door. I joined up with a father and his three children. The father doesn't talk much, but that's okay. We're hungry, but that ain't new either. I can't remember the last time my belly was full. The father is going for supplies. I'm supposed to watch the children while he's gone. I found a giant mushroom in the woods, but I'm going to try it before I let the children touch it. I may die, but I won't be responsible for sending those kids to their graves. I survived eating the mushroom, and I fed the children. Now their father is back with supplies. The sun is out today, and hope has returned. Maybe things are going to be okay after all.

Skills Review

Key Reading Skill: Identifying Main Idea and Supporting Details

7. Does the title of the story support the main idea, or is it the main idea? Explain, and give examples from the story.

Key Literary Element: Narrator

8. List three things you learn about the narrator from what he says about himself.

9. What else might readers learn from this story if it were told by an omniscient narrator?

Reviewing Skills: Interpreting

10. Interpret the title of the story. What does it mean? Give examples from the story to support your interpretation.

Vocabulary Check

In each blank, write the vocabulary word that has the opposite meaning of the underlined word.

skimpy hospitality grudging sedately

11. We expected <u>stinginess</u>, but everyone showed their ___.

12. Some people react ___ to good news, while others jump up and down <u>excitedly</u>.

13. The portions that were served weren't <u>generous</u> at all; they were actually ___.

14. People want <u>willing</u> help when someone volunteers for a task, not ___ participation.

15. **English Language Coach** The Latin root *terra* means "land." How does this root relate to the words below? Write a definition for each word, showing how it is related to the meaning of the root. Use a dictionary if you need help.

   territory

   terrain

   terrestrial

Grammar Link: Agreement with Compounds

- A **compound subject** contains two or more subjects that have the same verb. Compound subjects may require a plural or singular verb, depending on how the subjects are joined.

- When *and* joins compound subjects, use the plural form of the verb.

   A <u>horse</u> and a <u>mule</u> <u>cross</u> the path in front of us.
   Horse and *mule* are the subjects; *cross* is the verb.

- When *or* or *nor* joins compound subjects, the verb should agree with the subject that is closest to the verb.

   Two <u>cars</u> or a <u>van</u> is needed.
   The verb *is* agrees with *van*, which is the subject closest to it.

Grammar Practice

Rewrite each sentence using the correct verb. Underline the compound subject in each sentence.

16. The bears and the raccoons (raid, raids) our campsite.

17. A boat or a canoe (work, works) well enough.

18. The experienced campers or the ranger (lead, leads) the hikes.

19. Neither the trees nor the building (block, blocks) our view.

Writing Application Look back at the journal entry you wrote. Make sure that your subjects and verbs agree in sentences with compound subjects.

Literature Online

Web Activities For eFlashcards, Selection Quick Checks, and other Web activities, go to www.glencoe.com.

Too Soon a Woman **839**

Skills Review

Key Reading Skill: Identifying Main Idea and Supporting Details

7. Students may say when children are left to fend for themselves, they are forced to grow up too quickly.

Key Literary Element: Narrator

8. Possible responses: he's a big 11-year-old; he doesn't like to fish; he felt like he couldn't cry like his sisters.

9. Responses will vary.

Reviewing Skill: Interpreting

10. Students may say Mary endures hardships that cause her to assume adult responsibilities.

Vocabulary Check

11. hospitality

12. sedately

13. skimpy

14. grudging

15. territory: any large area of land

   terrain: region of land, esp. with regard to its natural features, i.e. hilly terrain

   terrestrial: of, relating to, or representing the earth

Close

Ask students to summarize what they learned about the Big Question from the story.

Grammar Link: Agreement with Compounds

Grammar Practice

16. <u>The bears or the raccoons</u> raid our campsite.

17. <u>A boat or a canoe</u> works well enough.

18. <u>The experienced campers</u> or <u>the ranger</u> leads the hikes.

19. <u>Neither the trees nor the building</u> blocks our view.

Skill Lesson: Evaluating

**Objectives covered in
this workshop:**
• Evaluate literature and
historical context
• Evaluate texts

Helping Students Evaluate Texts

Why Is It Important?

• Evaluating is making a judgment or forming an opinion about a text.
Students will learn that they can evaluate a character, the author's craft, or
the value of the information in a text.

• Evaluating helps students become wise readers. For example, they can
judge whether an author is qualified to speak about a topic or whether
the author's points make sense. They can also avoid being misled by what
they read.

• Evaluating will also help them make good decisions about situations in
their daily lives, such as what to listen to or watch next.

How to Help Students Get It

As students read, they should ask themselves questions such as the
following:

• Is this character realistic and believable? Are the feelings and events in the
story or poem realistic and believable?

• Does the author use language, tone, and style that keep you interested in
the characters and plot?

• Is this author qualified to write about this subject? Is this author biased?
Does this author present opinions as facts?

Reading to Answer the Big Question

President Cleveland, Where Are You? by Robert Cormier
During the Great Depression, Jerry and his friends collect trading cards.
When Jerry's brother asks him to help pay for a birthday gift for his dad,
Jerry contributes only a small amount because he wants to keep enough
to get a popular trading card. He later regrets his selfishness. When he has
another opportunity to choose between doing something good for a family
member and getting another important card, he makes a better choice.

Nobody's Perfect by David Fischer
This *InTime* article recounts eight stories of mistakes by great athletes,
including NFL quarterback Brett Favre, NBA forward Kevin Garnett, and
Olympic softball player Dani Tyler. In each case, the athlete figures out his
or her error and gets back into the game.

Workshop Resources

PACING (DAYS)		LESSON	STUDENT MATERIALS	TEACHER RESOURCES
STANDARD	BLOCK			
1	1/2	Key Skill Lesson: Evaluating	🏃 Key Reading Skills Practice, p. 22 🏃 English Language Coach Review, p. 42	📖 Bellringer Options Transparencies –Daily Language Practice 66 –Selection Focus 23 📖 Read Aloud, Think Aloud Transparencies –Key Reading Skills 9 💿 Presentation Plus!
1	1	"President Cleveland, Where Are You?"	💻 Glencoe Online 🏃 Unit Vocabulary Review, p. 40 🏃 Academic Vocabulary Review, p. 43 📁 English Language Coach 🏃 Active Reading Graphic Organizer, p. 24 🏃 Literary Analysis, p. 23 💿 StudentWorks Plus™ 💻 Online Student Edition 💿 Literature Classics 📁 Selection and Unit Assessments, p. 77	📖 Literary and Text Analysis Transparencies 11 💻 Puzzlemaker 💿 Skill Level Up!™ A Language Arts Game 💻 BookLink 3 📗 Assessment by Learning Objective (Diagnostic and Formative) 💿 Interactive Tutor: Self-Assessment 💿 TeacherWorks Plus™
1		"Nobody's Perfect"	💻 Glencoe Online 🏃 Unit Vocabulary Review, p. 40 🏃 Academic Vocabulary Review, p. 43 📁 English Language Coach 🏃 Active Reading Graphic Organizer, p. 26 🏃 Literary Analysis, p. 23 💿 StudentWorks Plus™ 💻 Online Student Edition 💿 Literature Classics 📁 Selection and Unit Assessments, p. 78	📖 Literary and Text Analysis Transparencies 11 💻 Puzzlemaker 💿 Skill Level Up!™ A Language Arts Game 💻 BookLink 3 📗 Assessment by Learning Objective (Diagnostic and Formative) 💿 Interactive Tutor: Self-Assessment 💿 TeacherWorks Plus™

Keys for Unit Resource

📁 Blackline Master   💿 DVD

📗 Workbook   📖 Transparency

📙 Supplemental Text   💻 Web-based

💿 CD-ROM   🏃 Fast File

Level Appropriate Code

AS = Activities for all students

AL = Activities for students working above grade level

OL = Activities for students working at grade level

BL = Activities for students working below grade level

EL = Activities for English language learners

Focus

BELLRINGER Options

- **Selection Focus Transparency 23**
- **Daily Language Practice Transparency 66**
  Focus Activity Say: Think about a mistake that you or someone you know made in front of other people. How did it make you feel? *(Possible responses: embarrassed; upset; uncomfortable)* **AS**

Teach

R Reading Skill

Evaluating Ask: How do you judge, or evaluate, the food that you like? List some words that describe good food. *(Possible response: Food can be judged, or evaluated, by how it looks and tastes.* Tasty, delicious, *and* flavorful *are words that describe good food.)* **AS**

V Vocabulary

Academic Vocabulary Say: What criteria, or standards, would you use to evaluate a movie? *(Possible response: Some criteria for evaluating a movie include its script, acting, camera work, costumes, lighting, and music.)* **OL**

Skills Focus

You will practice using these skills when you read the following selections:
- "President Cleveland, Where Are You?," p. 844
- "Nobody's Perfect," p. 860

Reading
- Evaluating

Literature
- Describing characters, images, and ideas

Vocabulary
- Understanding word meanings, using Greek roots
- Academic Vocabulary: *evaluate*

Writing/Grammar
- Identifying subjects and verbs
- Using correct subject-verb agreement

Objectives (pp. 840–841)
Reading Evaluate text

Skill Lesson

Evaluating

Learn It!

What Is It? When you **evaluate**, you make a judgment or form an opinion. If you've attended a movie, play, or concert, you've probably heard people comment on the performance. They're evaluating what they saw when they say, "The story was silly, but the special effects were awesome!"

R • When you evaluate something, you make judgments about its strengths and weaknesses.
- An evaluation has to be supported with facts and examples to be convincing.
- As you read, you might evaluate a character, an author's style, or the value of the information in the text.

© 1998 John McPherson/Dist. by Universal Press Syndicate
At the Slinky Quality Control Center.
© 1998 John McPherson/Dist. by Universal Press Syndicate

Analyzing Cartoons
The workers in this cartoon are trying to evaluate, or make a judgment about, the slinky's quality. When you evaluate something, you form an opinion about it. What judgments do you make when you read? What kinds of things influence your opinions?

V Academic Vocabulary

evaluate (ih VAL yoo ayt) *v.* to find value; to judge or determine worth

---

Additional Support

Reading in the Real World

Career Many businesses and organizations that produce products—from food products to small appliances to computer programs—employ quality control specialists. Tell students that these people evaluate products to ensure that they meet quality and safety standards set out by the company. Organize students into small groups, and give each group a classroom "product," such as a pencil or a calculator. Have group members generate a list of standards that their product must meet, and ask each group to write a brief evaluation of a sample product. Have groups share their evaluations with the class. **OL**

Why Is It Important? **Evaluating** helps you become a smart reader. For example, when you judge whether an author is qualified to write about a topic or whether the author's points make sense, you can avoid being misled by what you read. It will also help you decide what you like or don't like, and why.

How Do I Do It? As you read, ask yourself these questions:

- Do I understand this? Has the author been clear?
- Is this believable? Am I convinced?
- Is this information presented completely and accurately?
- What are the strengths and weaknesses?

Here's how one student evaluated a short passage from "The Gold Cadillac."

> The next day was Sunday and everybody figured that my mother would be sure to give in and ride in the Cadillac. . . . But she didn't give in. What was worse she wouldn't let Wilma and me ride in the Cadillac either. She took us each by the hand, walked past the Cadillac where my father stood waiting and headed on toward the church, three blocks away.

I think the mother is a really stubborn person. But at least she stands up for herself. She's a strong person, too. And she doesn't yell or scream at the dad. So it seems like she's not really a mean person either.

Practice It!

You can do more than just evaluate characters when you read. Use the tips from **How Do I Do It?** to evaluate the following description from "The Gold Cadillac." What do you think of this description? Did the author do a good job describing the Cadillac?

My sister and I eased up to the car and peeked in. It was all gold inside. Gold leather seats. Gold carpeting. Gold dashboard. It was like no car we had owned before. It looked like a car for rich folks.

Use It!

In your Learner's Notebook, write questions you can ask yourself to evaluate fiction. Consider questions about plot, conflict, and theme.

Reading Workshop 3 Evaluating **841**

Study Central Visit www.glencoe.com and click on Study Central to review evaluating.

Teach

Study Central Have students access the Web site to review evaluating and to complete a related activity.

R Reading Skill

Evaluating **Say:** Read the passage from "The Gold Cadillac" in the *How Do I Do It?* section. What clues in the passage tell you that there is tension between the characters? *(Possible responses: The narrator notes that the mother does not "give in" and ride in the Cadillac, nor does she let her children ride in it.)* **Ask:** What information in the passage indicates that the mother is not happy about the Cadillac? *(Possible response: The mother walks past the father, who expects her to ride in the Cadillac to church. The mother and children walk to church instead.)* **OL**

Resources for page 841

✎ Use Key Reading Skills Transparency 9 in *Read Aloud, Think Aloud* to help students practice evaluating.

Objectives
- Learn and use new vocabulary
- Evaluate text

Differentiated Instruction

Using Rubrics Show students the sample rubric below, which offers a method of evaluating pizza. Tell students that they will need to develop criteria that determine what makes a pizza "excellent," "above average," and so on. Encourage students to make their criteria as specific as possible. **OL**

Evaluating Pizza				
	Crust	Toppings	Sauce	Overall
Excellent				
Good				
Fair				
Poor				

Teach

More About the Author

Writing "President Cleveland, Where Are You?" was an important step in Robert Cormier's path to becoming a writer. Cormier describes a house in the story as "a big white birthday cake of a house." He says that finding this metaphor taught him that "words were truly tools, that figures of speech were not just something fancy to dress up a piece of prose but words that could evoke scene and event and emotion."

EL Language Coach

Greek Roots Say: In many dictionaries, word entries include notes about the origin of the entry word or its root. Often, an abbreviation that comes before the definition indicates the origin of the word. For example, words that have Greek roots often have the abbreviation *Gk.* Use dictionaries to identify three words of Greek origin other than those listed in the chart on page 842. *(Possible responses: millimeter, geometry, biodegradable)* **AS**

Additional Support

Author Search To expand students' appreciation of Robert Cormier, have them access the Web site for additional information and resources.

Before You Read

Robert Cormier

Meet the Author

Like the main character in this story, Robert Cormier (kor MEER) was a boy during the 1930s. Cormier started writing in the seventh grade. But he was never published until his college art teacher sent one of his stories to a magazine. The $75 he was paid for that story started his professional career. See page R2 of the Author Files for more on Robert Cormier.

Author Search For more information about Robert Cormier, go to www.glencoe.com.

Objectives (pp. 842–855)
Reading Evaluate text • Make connections from text to self
Literature Identify literary elements: description, sensory details
Vocabulary Identify word structure: Greek roots

President Cleveland, Where Are You?

Vocabulary Preview

splurge (splurj) *v.* to spend more money than usual **(p. 847)** *It was only occasionally that the boys could splurge on extra cards.*

obsessed (ub SEST) *adj.* concentrating completely **(p. 850)** *The boys were obsessed with collecting the president cards.*

dismal (DIZ mul) *adj.* gloomy; miserable; cheerless **(p. 850)** *Life seemed dismal to the boys when cowboy cards were gone.*

dominant (DOM ih nunt) *adj.* having the greatest power or force; controlling **(p. 852)** *Card collecting was the dominant activity that summer.*

dejection (dih JEK shun) *n.* sadness; low spirits **(p. 853)** *Armand's face showed dejection, not hope, as he sat on the steps.*

blissfully (BLIS fuh lee) *adv.* in an extremely happy way; joyfully **(p. 854)** *Jerry went off blissfully to find the Grover Cleveland card.*

Write to Learn Write a brief paragraph about something you collect or would like to collect, such as trading cards or coins. Use at least three of the vocabulary words in your paragraph.

English Language Coach

Greek Roots The **root** of a word is its main part. Knowing the meaning of a word's root can help you figure out the meaning of the whole word. English contains many Greek roots, prefixes, and suffixes. Some of these word parts are called "combining forms" because they are so often used with other Greek parts. For example, any word with the root *meter* (which means "measure") has something to do with measurement. A *thermometer* measures your body temperature, for example.

This chart shows some common Greek roots or combining forms. **EL**

Root	Meaning	Example
bio	life	biography
geo	earth	geography
meter	measure	centimeter
graph	write/record	graphic
log/logy	word/study/speak	dialogue, biology

Partner Talk With a partner discuss what you think **geology** means. When you have decided upon a definition, check the meaning in a dictionary. Then write the word's meaning in your Learner's Notebook.

Differentiated Instruction

Build Background "President Cleveland, Where Are You?" is set during the Great Depression, a time of great economic hardship in the 1930s. Students may want to learn more about the Great Depression and how people coped with economic difficulties. Suggest that students ask older people in their own families and community to share memories of this time. Have students use library materials or school-approved online resources to find more information about the Great Depression. Ask volunteers to share their findings with the class. **OL**

Skills Preview

Key Reading Skill: Evaluating

R As you read, think about the story and what makes it interesting. These questions will help you to evaluate what you read. Don't forget to support your opinions.
- What makes the plot believable or unbelievable?
- How does the setting add to the story?
- Which characters do you like or dislike?

Write to Learn In your Learner's Notebook, write an evaluation of a movie you've seen recently. You might evaluate the plot, setting, characters, or theme. Or you might evaluate how well the actors played the parts. You might even evaluate how well the camera person shot the movie. It's up to you! Whichever elements you choose to evaluate, be sure to back up your judgments with details from the movie.

Key Literary Element: Description

L Descriptive writing brings experiences and events to life. Good descriptive writing helps readers see, hear, smell, taste, and feel details from the story. As you read, pay attention to the kinds of descriptive details the writer provides.
- Sensory details: *Which senses does the writer appeal to? What colors, shapes, sizes, and textures can you picture or feel?*
- Word choice: *What nouns, verbs, adjectives, and adverbs are especially lively?*
- Comparisons: *Which comparisons does the author make? Are the comparisons new and fresh, or have you heard them many times before?*

Interactive Literary Elements Handbook
To review or learn more about the literary elements, go to www.glencoe.com.

Get Ready to Read

Connect to the Reading

Have you ever tried to collect something such as model cars, dolls, or some other toy? What was the hardest part of completing your collection? In this story, you'll read about Jerry. He makes a choice to collect trading cards.

Partner Talk Think of a mistake you've made in the past that involved a family member or close friend. Share your experience with your partner.

Build Background

- This story takes place during the Great Depression, which began in late 1929 and lasted through the 1930s. It was a time of hardship for many people. Banks closed and so did many other businesses. Thousands of people lost their savings. Millions of people lost their jobs.

Set Purposes for Reading

BIG Question Read the selection to find out if someone learns from a mistake.

Set Your Own Purpose What would you like to learn from the selection to help you answer the Big Question? Write your own purpose on the "President Cleveland" part of the Workshop 3 Foldable.

> **Keep Moving**
>
> Use these skills as you read the following selection.

President Cleveland, Where Are You? **843**

Teach

R Reading Skill

Evaluating Say: You can evaluate developments in a movie in much the same way that you evaluate a book. What characteristics are most important for your enjoyment of a movie? *(Responses will vary. Students may say that an interesting plot is important.)* **AS**

L Literary Element

Description Say: Imagine that you are writing a short story about sixth-graders. What details might you include to describe what these students like to do or how they talk or act? *(Possible response: information about the computer games or movies that kids like today and descriptions of the clothes that young people wear.)* **AS Say:** "President Cleveland, Where Are You?" is set during the Great Depression. What details might it include to describe this time period? *(Possible response: details about people's clothing, appliances, or popular activities of the time)* **OL**

English Language Coach

Greek Roots Write the following Greek roots and their definitions on the board. Challenge students to write as many words as they can that contain each of these roots. Have students use reference resources if necessary. **EL OL**

1. photo: light *(photograph, photosynthesis)*
2. graphein: to write *(autograph, biography, graphic)*
3. chron: time *(chronology, chronicle)*
4. polis: city *(metropolis, police, political)*
5. therm: heat *(thermometer, thermal, thermostat)*

Objectives
- Evaluate text
- Identify literary elements: description
- Identify word structure: Greek roots
- Learn and use new vocabulary

843

Teach

Viewing the Photo

Ask: What does the photo tell you about the boy's interest in baseball? *(Possible response: The number of cards in the box and in the boy's hands indicates that he probably enjoys collecting baseball cards. The baseball and the glove indicate that the boy is interested in baseball.)* **AS**

L Literary Element

Description Ask: What words does the narrator use to describe the cowboys that appear on the cards? *(The cowboys are described as "rock-faced men with eyes of blue steel.")* **BL Say:** Restate this description in your own words. *(Possible response: The cowboys had strong features and serious-looking blue eyes.)* **OL**

Readability Scores

Dale-Chall: 6.4
DRP: 59
Lexile: 1040

PRESIDENT CLEVELAND,
Where Are You?

by Robert Cormier

That was the autumn of the cowboy cards—Buck Jones and Tom Tyler and Hoot Gibson and especially Ken Maynard.[1] The cards were available in those five-cent packages of gum: pink sticks, three together, covered with a sweet white powder. You couldn't blow bubbles with that particular gum, but it couldn't have mattered less. The cowboy cards were important—the pictures of those rock-faced men with eyes of blue steel. **1**

On those wind-swept, leaf-tumbling afternoons we gathered after school on the sidewalk in front of Lemire's Drugstore, across from St. Jude's Parochial School,[2] and we swapped and bargained and matched for the cards. Because a Ken Maynard serial[3] was playing at the Globe every Saturday afternoon, he was the most popular cowboy of all, and one of his cards was worth at least ten of any other kind.

Rollie Tremaine had a treasure of thirty or so, and he guarded them jealously. He'd match you for the other cards, but he risked his Ken Maynards only when the other kids threatened to leave him out of the competition altogether.

You could almost hate Rollie Tremaine. In the first place, he was the only son of Auguste Tremaine, who operated the Uptown Dry Goods Store, and he did not live in a tenement[4] but in a big white birthday cake of a house on Laurel Street.

---

1. **Buck Jones, Tom Tyler, Hoot Gibson, and Ken Maynard** were all popular stars of cowboy movies in the 1930s.
2. A **parochial** (puh ROH kee ul) **school** is run by a church or another religious organization rather than by a city or state government.
3. In the 1930s, moviegoers watched **serials**, long stories that were shown in individual episodes.
4. Here, **tenement** means "apartment building."

844 UNIT 7 What Can We Learn from Our Mistakes?

Practice the Skills

1 Key Literary Element

Description Good descriptive writing helps you experience details from the story. What details are used to describe the gum? What details are used to describe the cowboys? **L**

Additional Support

Differentiated Instruction

Build Background "Western" movies are films set in the American West. Their subjects are most often cowboys who participate in bank robberies, cattle drives, and confrontations with Native Americans. In the 1930s, actors such as Ken Maynard starred in films called "B-films" because they were inexpensive to make. These popular, action-packed films provided Depression-era audiences with a way to escape daily problems and enter an exciting world of heroes and villains. **AS** Have interested students do additional research to find out more about the themes of popular Westerns throughout the history of film. **OL**

He was too fat to be effective in the football games between the Frenchtown Tigers and the North Side Knights, and he made us constantly aware of the jingle of coins in his pockets. He was able to stroll into Lemire's and casually select a quarter's worth of cowboy cards while the rest of us watched, aching with envy. **L**

Once in a while I earned a nickel or dime by running errands or washing windows for blind old Mrs. Belander, or by finding pieces of copper, brass, and other valuable metals at the dump and selling them to the junkman. The coins clutched in my hand, I would race to Lemire's to buy a cowboy card or two, hoping that Ken Maynard would stare boldly out at me as I opened the pack. At one time, before a disastrous matching session with Roger Lussier (my best friend, except where the cards were involved), I owned five Ken Maynards and considered myself a millionaire, of sorts.

One week I was particularly lucky; I had spent two afternoons washing floors for Mrs. Belander and received a quarter. Because my father had worked a full week at the shop, where a rush order for fancy combs had been received, he allotted my brothers and sisters and me an extra dime along with the usual ten cents for the Saturday-afternoon movie. Setting aside the movie fare, I found myself with a bonus of thirty-five cents, and I then planned to put Rollie Tremaine to shame the following Monday afternoon. **2**

Monday was the best day to buy the cards because the candy man stopped at Lemire's every Monday morning to deliver the new assortments. There was nothing more exciting in the world than a fresh batch of card boxes. I rushed home from school that day and hurriedly changed my clothes, eager to set off for the store. As I burst through the doorway, letting the screen door slam behind me, my brother Armand blocked my way.

He was fourteen, three years older than I, and a freshman at Monument High School. He had recently become a stranger to me in many ways—indifferent to such matters as cowboy cards and the Frenchtown Tigers—and he carried himself with a mysterious dignity that was fractured now and then when his voice began shooting off in all directions like some kind of vocal fireworks.

Practice the Skills

2 Key Reading Skill

Evaluating You can evaluate or judge characters by what they say and do. What kind of person do you think the narrator is, based on what he says about earning money and buying cards? **R**

Collector's cards of Presidents Benjamin Harrison and Warren Harding.

President Cleveland, Where Are You? **845**

Teach

L Literary Element

Description Ask: Which words tell you that Rollie Tremaine has more money than the narrator? *(Possible response: "jingle of coins in his pockets," "able to . . . casually select a quarter's worth of cowboy cards.")* **OL Ask:** Judging from the details the narrator gives, what kind of person is Rollie Tremaine? *(Possible response: He seems spoiled. He is also a bit of a show-off.)* **AS**

R Reading Skill

Evaluating Ask: What do you think is the most important part of card collecting for the narrator? Explain. *(Possible response: Although the narrator likes having the cards, what he likes most about collecting is having more valuable cards than the other kids, especially Rollie Tremaine.)* **AL**

Reading in the Real World

Citizenship Although he is only eleven, the narrator earns money by running errands and doing household chores. Discuss with students whether they earn an allowance and how they earn it. **AS** Have students find more information about state and national child labor laws.

Ask students to find out how old young people must be to work in their state and how many hours each week they are allowed to work. Challenge students to list local businesses at which young people often work in after-school jobs. **AL**

Objectives
- Evaluate text
- Identify literary elements: description
- Identify word structure: Greek roots
- Use text features: photographs

Teach

R Reading Skill

Evaluating Ask: Why might Jerry be impatient with his older brother? *(Possible responses: Jerry has plans to buy more cards. He becomes impatient because he does not want to waste any time; Jerry doesn't like it when his older brother bosses him around.)* **OL**

EL Language Coach

Greek Roots Say: A form of the Greek root *mnen* is found in the word remember. Mnem means memory. A mnemonic *(neh MAW nik)* device is a trick that helps you memorize something. For example, the sentence "My very energetic mom just sliced up nine pizzas" may help you remember the nine planets of the solar system: Mercury, Venus, Earth, Mars, Jupiter, Saturn, Uranus, Neptune, Pluto. How does the Greek root *mnemon* fit in the definition of mnemonic device? *(The root mnemon means "mindful," and a mnemonic device is a trick or an aid that helps you remember something.)* **AL**

"Wait a minute, Jerry," he said. "I want to talk to you." He motioned me out of earshot of my mother, who was busy supervising the usual after-school skirmish[5] in the kitchen.

I sighed with impatience. In recent months Armand had become a figure of authority, siding with my father and mother occasionally. As the oldest son he sometimes took advantage of his age and experience to issue rules and regulations. **3**

"How much money have you got?" he whispered.

"You in some kind of trouble?" I asked, excitement rising in me as I remembered the blackmail plot of a movie at the Globe a month before.

He shook his head in annoyance. "Look," he said, "it's Pa's birthday tomorrow. I think we ought to chip in and buy him something . . ."

I reached into my pocket and caressed the coins. "Here," I said carefully, pulling out a nickel. "If we all give a nickel we should have enough to buy him something pretty nice."

He regarded me with contempt. "Rita already gave me fifteen cents, and I'm throwing in a quarter. Albert handed over a dime—all that's left of his birthday money. Is that all you can do—a nickel?"

"Aw, come on," I protested. "I haven't got a single Ken Maynard left, and I was going to buy some cards this afternoon."

"Ken Maynard!" he snorted. "Who's more important—him or your father?"

His question was unfair because he knew that there was no possible choice—"my father" had to be the only answer. My father was a huge man who believed in the things of the spirit, although my mother often maintained that the spirits[6] he believed in came in bottles. He had worked at the Monument Comb Shop since the age of fourteen; his booming laugh—or grumble—greeted us each night when he returned from the factory. A steady worker when the shop had enough work, he quickened with gaiety on Friday nights and weekends, a bottle of beer at his elbow, and he was fond of making long speeches about the good things in life. In the middle of the Depression, for instance, he paid cash for a

---

5. A **skirmish** is a brief or minor disagreement.

6. Spiritual matters are often called **things of the spirit**, but bottled **spirits** are alcoholic beverages.

Practice the Skills

3 Key Literary Element

Description How does the author bring Armand to life? Are any of the author's word choices especially interesting or lively? Does he use comparisons (figurative language)?

Additional Support

Literature Focus Lesson

First-Person Narration Point out that the narrator of "President Cleveland, Where Are You?" uses the pronoun *I* when telling the story. He narrates from his own point of view. Explain that this is called first-person narration. To help students gain a better understanding of first-person narration, ask them to write a journal entry from the perspective of the narrator. Suggest that students reflect on the incident with Armand in their journal entries. Have volunteers share their entries with the class. **OL**

Analyzing the Photo What attitudes toward winning do you see on these boys' faces?

Teach

R1 Reading Skill

Evaluating Say: Jerry's father buys a piano during the Depression. What does this information tell you about what Jerry's father values? *(Possible response: Even though the family might not have much money, he thinks it is important to have the "good things in life," such as music lessons.)* **OL Ask:** What message do you think the purchase of a piano might send to Jerry and his siblings? *(Possible response: By buying the family a piano, Jerry's father lets them feel that they deserve to have some luxury in their lives, even during difficult economic times.)* **AL**

R2 Reading Skill

Evaluating Say: Consider the amount of money Jerry contributes to the purchase of his father's birthday present. Do you think Jerry gives his brother Armand an appropriate amount? Should Jerry give more or less? Explain. *(Responses will vary. Students may say that Jerry could give more money because he has more. Others may say that Jerry gives appropriately.)* **AS**

R1 piano, of all things, and insisted that my twin sisters, Yolande and Yvette, take lessons once a week.

R2 I took a dime from my pocket and handed it to Armand.

"Thanks, Jerry," he said. "I hate to take your last cent."

"That's all right," I replied, turning away and consoling myself with the thought that twenty cents was better than nothing at all.

When I arrived at Lemire's I sensed disaster in the air. Roger Lussier was kicking disconsolately[7] at a tin can in the gutter, and Rollie Tremaine sat sullenly on the steps in front of the store.

"Save your money," Roger said. He had known about my plans to **splurge** on the cards.

"What's the matter?" I asked.

"There's no more cowboy cards," Rollie Tremaine said. "The company's not making any more."

"They're going to have President cards," Roger said, his face twisting with disgust. He pointed to the store window. "Look!" **4**

---

7. **Disconsolately** means "hopelessly unhappy" or "cheerless."

Vocabulary .....

splurge (splurj) v. to spend more money than usual

Practice the Skills

....

4 **Key Literary Element**

Description The details in the description of the boys' actions and facial expressions tell how the boys felt. Point out one detail that shows how the boys felt.

President Cleveland, Where Are You? **847**

Differentiated Instruction

Illustrating The boys in this story enjoy collecting cards with information and pictures of cowboy heroes whom they admire. Provide students with blank paper and white index cards. Have students design trading cards that feature their heroes. Explain that the front of each card should have a picture of a hero and that the back of the card should provide more information about that hero. Allow students time to conduct research about their heroes and find or draw pictures of them. Tell students to use the blank paper as scrap for planning the cards before they create the final version. **AS**

Objectives
- Evaluate text
- Identify literary elements: description and point of view
- Identify word structure: Greek roots

847

Teach

C Critical Thinking

Comprehension Ask: What are the makers of Caramel Chew doing to encourage children to buy their candy? *(Possible response: The candy makers are including president cards with their candy and promising a baseball glove to the person who collects a complete set of cards.)* **OL Ask:** Do you think this is an effective way to sell candy? Why or why not? *(Some students may say this might not be an effective way to sell candy because the boys don't seem excited about the president cards. Others may say that the baseball glove might make them more eager to collect the cards.)* **AL**

BQ BIG Question

Say: Jerry feels guilty for the way he acted when Armand asked him to contribute money for their father's birthday present. How does Jerry try to fix his mistake? *(Possible response: Jerry tries to reach Armand and his sisters before they can buy a present. He wants to give them the money he had intended to spend on cowboy cards.)* **AS**

A placard in the window announced: "Attention, Boys. Watch for the New Series. Presidents of the United States. Free in Each 5-Cent Package of Caramel Chew."

"President cards?" I asked, dismayed.

I read on: "Collect a Complete Set and Receive an Official Imitation Major League Baseball Glove, Embossed with Lefty Grove's Autograph."[8]

Glove or no glove, who could become excited about Presidents, of all things?

Rollie Tremaine stared at the sign. "Benjamin Harrison, for crying out loud," he said. "Why would I want Benjamin Harrison when I've got twenty-two Ken Maynards?"

I felt the warmth of guilt creep over me. I jingled the coins in my pocket, but the sound was hollow. No more Ken Maynards to buy.

"I'm going to buy a Mr. Goodbar," Rollie Tremaine decided.

I was without appetite, indifferent even to a Baby Ruth, which was my favorite. I thought of how I had betrayed Armand and, worst of all, my father. [5]

"I'll see you after supper," I called over my shoulder to Roger as I hurried away toward home. I took the shortcut behind the church, although it involved leaping over a tall wooden fence, and I zigzagged recklessly through Mr. Thibodeau's garden, trying to outrace my guilt. I pounded up the steps and into the house, only to learn that Armand had already taken Yolande and Yvette uptown to shop for the birthday present.

I pedaled my bike furiously through the streets, ignoring the indignant[9] horns of automobiles as I sliced through the traffic. Finally I saw Armand and my sisters emerge from the Monument Men's Shop. My heart sank when I spied the long, slim package that Armand was holding. [6]

"Did you buy the present yet?" I asked, although I knew it was too late.

---

8. **Robert Grove** (1900–1970) was an outstanding pitcher for the Philadelphia Athletics and the Boston Red Sox between 1925 and 1941. A machine carved his *embossed* autograph by making shallow cuts in the glove's leather.

9. If the car horns sound *indignant,* the drivers are beeping because they're angry and annoyed.

Practice the Skills

5 BIG Question

Jerry thinks that he betrayed his father and Armand. What was Jerry's mistake? Write your answer on your Foldable.

BQ

6 Key Literary Element

Description The author uses vivid verbs and adverbs to describe how Jerry raced through the town. On a piece of paper, write three verbs and two adverbs that tell about his journey.

Analyzing the Photo How are these young people like Jerry and his friends at Lemire's Drugstore?

Additional Support

English Language Coach

Building Background Baseball's popularity grew despite the Great Depression, in part because of the rise of radio broadcasting. Radio generated many new fans of the game. Left-handed pitcher Robert "Lefty" Grove was named the American Baseball League's Most Valuable Player in 1931. During his career, he led the league seven times in strikeouts and nine times in earned-run averages. He was elected to the Baseball Hall of Fame in 1947. Have interested students do additional research on "Lefty" and other popular Depression-era baseball players and present their findings to the class. **OL**

"Just now. A blue tie," Armand said. "What's the matter?"

"Nothing," I replied, my chest hurting.

He looked at me for a long moment. At first his eyes were hard, but then they softened. He smiled at me, almost sadly, and touched my arm. I turned away from him because I felt naked and exposed.

"It's all right," he said gently. "Maybe you've learned something." The words were gentle, but they held a curious dignity, the dignity remaining even when his voice suddenly cracked on the last syllable.

I wondered what was happening to me, because I did not know whether to laugh or cry. **7**

Sister Angela was amazed when, a week before Christmas vacation, everybody in the class submitted a history essay worthy of a high mark—in some cases as high as A-minus. (Sister Angela did not believe that anyone in the world ever deserved an A.) She never learned—or at least she never let on that she knew—we all had become experts on the Presidents because of the cards we purchased at Lemire's. Each card contained a picture of a President, and on the reverse side, a summary of his career. We looked at those cards so often that the <u>biographies</u> imprinted themselves on our minds without effort. Even our street-corner conversations were filled with such information as the fact that James Madison was called "The Father of the Constitution," or that John Adams had intended to become a minister. **8**

The President cards were a roaring success and the cowboy cards were quickly forgotten. In the first place we did not receive gum with the cards, but a kind of chewy caramel. The caramel could be tucked into a corner of your mouth, bulging your cheek in much the same manner as wads of tobacco bulged the mouths of baseball stars. In the second place the competition for collecting the cards was fierce and frustrating—fierce because everyone was intent on being the first to send away for a baseball glove and frustrating because although there were only thirty-two Presidents, including Franklin Delano Roosevelt, the variety at Lemire's was at a minimum. When the deliveryman left the boxes of cards at the store each Monday, we often discovered that one entire box was devoted to a single President—two weeks in a row

Practice the Skills

7 **BIG Question**

What lesson does Armand think Jerry may have learned? Write your answer on your Foldable. **BQ**

8 **English Language Coach**

Greek Roots The word <u>biographies</u> comes from two Greek roots, *bio* meaning "life" and *graph* meaning "write" or "describe." Define *biography* using the meanings of these Greek roots. **EL**

President Cleveland, Where Are You? **849**

Teach

BQ **BIG Question**

Ask: Do you think that the lesson Jerry learns is important? Explain. *(Responses will vary. Students may say that the lesson is important because people should value their families above material possessions.)* **OL** **Ask:** How do you think this lesson will change Jerry's behavior? *(Responses will vary. Students may say that from now on they expect Jerry to consider his family's needs before he spends money on something for himself.)* **AL**

EL Language Coach

Greek Roots **Say:** The Greek root *auto* means "same" or "self." Explain how this root fits in the definition of *autobiography*. *(Students should note that an autobiography is a biography of a person written by that person. It is a "self biography.")* **EL** **BL**

Differentiated Instruction

Talk Show Interview Some students may benefit from script writing and role-playing. First briefly review with students how Jerry betrays his father and Armand. Then put students in pairs. Tell each pair to write a script for an interview between Jerry and a talk show host. The host should ask Jerry questions about the mistake he made and how he feels about it. Jerry should then explain whether he has learned from his mistake. Have students present their interviews to the class. **OL**

Objectives
- Monitor comprehension
- Identify word structure: Greek roots

849

Teach

C Critical Thinking

Comprehension Ask: Why would the boys rather have the sample glove than a new glove from the card company? *(Possible response: They want to get a glove without having to wait for it to arrive in the mail.)* **BL Ask:** Why does Rollie Tremaine say that he is going to buy a glove? *(Possible response: He spends fifty cents on cards, all of which feature the same president. Rollie decides that the wait isn't worth the frustration when he can just buy a glove himself.)* **OL**

the boxes contained nothing but Abraham Lincoln. One week Roger Lussier and I were the heroes of Frenchtown. We journeyed on our bicycles to the North Side, engaged three boys in a matching bout and returned with five new Presidents, including Chester Alan Arthur, who up to that time had been missing.

Perhaps to sharpen our desire, the card company sent a sample glove to Mr. Lemire, and it dangled, orange and sleek, in the window. I was half sick with longing, thinking of my old glove at home, which I had inherited from Armand. But Rollie Tremaine's desire for the glove outdistanced my own. He even got Mr. Lemire to agree to give the glove in the window to the first person to get a complete set of cards, so that precious time wouldn't be wasted waiting for the postman.

We were delighted at Rollie Tremaine's frustration, especially since he was only a substitute player for the Tigers. Once after spending fifty cents on cards—all of which turned out to be Calvin Coolidge—he threw them to the ground, pulled some dollar bills out of his pocket and said, "The heck with it. I'm going to buy a glove!"

"Not that glove," Roger Lussier said. "Not a glove with Lefty Grove's autograph. Look what it says at the bottom of the sign."

We all looked, although we knew the words by heart: "This Glove Is Not For Sale Anywhere."

Rollie Tremaine scrambled to pick up the cards from the sidewalk, pouting more than ever. After that he was quietly **obsessed** with the Presidents, hugging the cards close to his chest and refusing to tell us how many more he needed to complete his set. **9**

I too was obsessed with the cards, because they had become things of comfort in a world that had suddenly grown **dismal**. After Christmas a layoff at the shop had thrown my father out of work. He received no paycheck for four weeks, and the only income we had was from Armand's after school job at the Blue and White Grocery Store—a job he lost finally when business dwindled as the layoff continued.

Vocabulary

obsessed (ub SEST) *adj.* concentrating completely

dismal (DIZ mul) *adj.* gloomy; miserable; cheerless

850 UNIT 7 What Can We Learn from Our Mistakes?

Practice the Skills

9 Key Reading Skill

Evaluating Think about the description of Rollie Tremaine at the beginning of the story. Add that information to the description of Rollie on this page. What do you think of Rollie? Evaluate him as a person. What are his strengths and weaknesses? Use details from the selection in your answer.

Additional Support

Reading in the Real World

Citizenship Employers may lay off workers when business is poor or slow. Often, these workers are rehired when business picks up again. Nevertheless, widespread layoffs can be devastating for a community. Many workers were laid off during the Great Depression, and some people claim that at times more than twenty percent of the population was unemployed. As a class, discuss the problems that could result from large-scale unemployment. Have students brainstorm possible ways of dealing with these problems. **OL**

Although we had enough food and clothing—my father's credit had always been good, a matter of pride with him—the inactivity made my father restless and irritable. He did not drink any beer at all, and laughed loudly, but not convincingly, after gulping down a glass of water and saying, "Lent[10] came early this year." The twins fell sick and went to the hospital to have their tonsils removed. My father was confident that he would return to work eventually and pay off his debts, but he seemed to age before our eyes. **10**

When orders again were received at the comb shop and he returned to work, another disaster occurred, although I was the only one aware of it. Armand fell in love.

I discovered his situation by accident, when I happened to pick up a piece of paper that had fallen to the floor in the bedroom he and I shared. I frowned at the paper, puzzled.

"Dear Sally, When I look into your eyes the world stands still . . ."

The letter was snatched from my hands before I finished reading it.

"What's the big idea, snooping around?" Armand asked, his face crimson. "Can't a guy have any privacy?"

He had never mentioned privacy before. "It was on the floor," I said. "I didn't know it was a letter. Who's Sally?"

He flung himself across the bed. "You tell anybody and I'll muckalize[11] you," he threatened. "Sally Knowlton."

Nobody in Frenchtown had a name like Knowlton.

"A girl from the North Side?" I asked, incredulous.[12]

He rolled over and faced me, anger in his eyes, and a kind of despair too. **11**

"What's the matter with that? Think she's too good for me?" he asked. "I'm warning you, Jerry, if you tell anybody . . ."

"Don't worry," I said. Love had no particular place in my life; it seemed an unnecessary waste of time. And a girl from the North Side was so remote that for all practical purposes she did not exist. But I was curious. "What are you writing her a letter for? Did she leave town, or something?"

---

10. **Lent** is the forty-day period before Easter. During Lent some Christians show sorrow for their sins by giving up something they enjoy.

11. **Muckalize** is a made-up word. Muck is dirty, sticky, slimy mud, or anything that's messy and disgusting. The suffix *-ize* means "cause to be or become."

12. To be **incredulous** (in KREH joo lus) is to be unwilling or unable to believe something.

Practice the Skills

10 Key Reading Skill

Evaluating Evaluating how a character is described is different than evaluating the character as a person. Look back at the description of Jerry's father on page 846. Combine it with the description of him on this page. Is he a believable character? Is the author making him come alive for you? Use details from the story to explain your answers. **R**

11 Key Literary Element

Description What vivid words does the author use to describe Armand's reaction to Jerry reading the letter? **L**

Teach

R Reading Skill

Evaluating Ask: Judging from the information given about Jerry's father, what do you think are the strengths of this character? *(Possible response: Jerry's father takes pride in paying his bills and taking care of his family. He tries to remain positive despite the difficult times.)* **OL Ask:** Do you think that Jerry's father responds to the Depression and unemployment in realistic ways? Explain. *(Possible response: Jerry's father responds realistically because he gets restless and irritable, a reasonable reaction to difficulty, but he also tries to remain a good father.)* **AL**

L Literary Element

Description Ask: What details in the story tell you about the differences between Frenchtown and the North Side? *(Possible response: Jerry says nobody in Frenchtown has a name like "Knowlton," and Armand accuses Jerry of thinking that Sally is "too good" for him.)* **OL**

Differentiated Instruction

Neighborhood Maps Help students understand the character of different parts of a city by having them draw maps of the neighborhoods around their school or home. These maps should include stores, parks, and other important areas or landmarks. Maps may indicate general neighborhood boundaries. After students have completed their maps, ask them to answer these questions: "What qualities are important in a neighborhood?" and "What elements give each neighborhood its own personality and character?" Invite students to share their neighborhood maps with the class. **AS**

Objectives
• Monitor comprehension
• Identify literary elements: description
• Evaluate text

851

Teach

R Reading Skill

Evaluating Ask: Why is Armand's behavior so puzzling to Jerry? *(Possible response: Armand is older and has feelings for a girl. Jerry has not experienced these feelings yet.)*
Ask: Why does Jerry's baseball glove seem more important to Jerry than Armand's situation does? *(Possible response: Armand's behavior does not make sense to Jerry. Jerry's baseball glove, however, is worn out and will affect his ability to play baseball.)* **OL**

C Critical Thinking

Analysis Ask: What causes Jerry to feel sympathy for Armand? *(Possible response: Armand is not behaving as he normally does. He seems frustrated, writes a letter that he won't send, and leaves his pie untouched.)* **OL Ask:** Does the story make you think that Jerry's problems are more important than Armand's? Explain your response. *(Possible response: The story indicates that both Armand's and Jerry's problems are important. It indicates, though, that Armand is more mature and that the president cards seem childish to him.)* **AL**

"She hasn't left town," he answered. "I wasn't going to send it. I just felt like writing to her."

R I was glad that I had never become involved with love—love that brought desperation[13] to your eyes, that caused you to write letters you did not plan to send. Shrugging with indifference, I began to search in the closet for the old baseball glove. I found it on the shelf, under some old sneakers. The webbing was torn and the padding gone. I thought of the sting I would feel when a sharp grounder slapped into the glove, and I winced.

"You tell anybody about me and Sally and I'll—"

"I know. You'll muckalize me."

C I did not divulge[14] his secret and often shared his **agony**, particularly when he sat at the supper table and left my mother's special butterscotch pie untouched. I had never realized before how terrible love could be. But my compassion was short-lived because I had other things to worry about: report cards due at Eastertime; the loss of income from old Mrs. Belander, who had gone to live with a daughter in Boston; and, of course, the Presidents. **12**

Because a stalemate[15] had been reached, the President cards were the **dominant** force in our lives—mine, Roger Lussier's and Rollie Tremaine's. For three weeks, as the baseball season approached, each of us had a complete set—complete except for one President, Grover Cleveland. Each time a box of cards arrived at the store we hurriedly bought them (as hurriedly

Analyzing the Photo What does this photograph tell you about the 1930s?

Practice the Skills

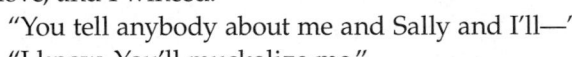

12 English Language Coach

Greek Roots The word **agony** comes from the Greek root *agon*, which means "struggle" or "anguish." Can you see how *agony* came to mean "great suffering of the mind or body"?

---

13. **Desperation** means "distress caused by great need or loss of hope."
14. To **divulge** a secret is to reveal it or make it known.
15. A **stalemate** refers to a situation in which no further action is possible.

Vocabulary

dominant (DOM ih nunt) *adj.* having the greatest power or force; controlling

---

Additional Support

Literature Focus Lesson

Identifying Conflicts and Resolutions Several of the characters in the story cope with conflicts. Help students create a conflict chart like the one below. Tell them that each of the characters listed may cope with more than one conflict. A sample entry has been done. **AS**

Character	Conflict	Resolution
Jerry	He can't find the last president card.	He helps Armand instead of buying the card.
Armand		
Jerry's father		

as our funds allowed) and tore off the wrappers, only to be confronted by James Monroe or Martin Van Buren or someone else. But never Grover Cleveland, never the man who had been the twenty-second and the twenty-fourth President of the United States. We argued about Grover Cleveland. Should he be placed between Chester Alan Arthur and Benjamin Harrison as the twenty-second President or did he belong between Benjamin Harrison and William McKinley as the twenty-fourth President? Was the card company playing fair? Roger Lussier brought up a horrifying possibility—did we need *two* Grover Clevelands to complete the set?

Indignant, we stormed Lemire's and protested to the harassed[16] storeowner, who had long since vowed never to stock a new series. Muttering angrily, he searched his bills and receipts for a list of rules.

"All right," he announced. "Says here you only need one Grover Cleveland to finish the set. Now get out, all of you, unless you've got money to spend."

Visual Vocabulary
A *piazza* (pee AHT zuh) is a large covered porch.

Outside the store, Rollie Tremaine picked up an empty tobacco tin and scaled it across the street. "Boy," he said. "I'd give five dollars for a Grover Cleveland." **13**

When I returned home I found Armand sitting on the piazza steps, his chin in his hands. His mood of **dejection** mirrored my own, and I sat down beside him. We did not say anything for a while.

"Want to throw the ball around?" I asked.

He sighed, not bothering to answer.

"You sick?" I asked.

He stood up and hitched up his trousers, pulled at his ear and finally told me what the matter was—there was a big dance next week at the high school, the Spring Promenade,[17] and Sally had asked him to be her escort.

I shook my head at the folly of love. "Well, what's so bad about that?"

---

16. Someone who is *harassed* (huh RAST) is repeatedly bothered or annoyed by someone else.

17. A formal dance or ball was once called a *promenade*. Today, the term is shortened to *prom*.

Vocabulary

dejection (dih JEK shun) *n.* sadness; low spirits

Practice the Skills

R

13 Key Reading Skill

Evaluating What do you think about this part of the story? What do you think about the boys collecting president cards? Is it believable? Has the author described it well? Explain your answer using details from the story.

L

President Cleveland, Where Are You? **853**

Teach

R Reading Skill

Evaluating Ask: Would Rollie be able to pay five dollars for a card, or is his statement an exaggeration? Explain. *(Possible response: People often exaggerate when they say how much they'd give to have something. But the story has shown that Rollie is a show-off, has more money than all the other boys, and is willing to spend it.)* **OL**

Ask: Does Jerry need the baseball glove or the five dollars? Explain. *(Possible response: It is likely that Jerry needs money to help his family more than he needs a glove.)* **AS**

L Literary Element

Description Say: Jerry knows that something is wrong with his brother before Armand opens his mouth. What details let Jerry know that Armand has a problem? *(Possible response: Armand is sitting with "his chin in his hands." He doesn't talk even when Jerry asks him a question, and he sighs.)* **OL**

Ask: What does Armand's posture tell you about the importance of noticing a character's body language? *(Possible response: A character's body language can tell you about his or her emotions. Readers should pay attention to how characters stand and sit.)* **AL**

Reading Fluency

Dialogue Help students develop fluency by having them practice reading dialogue from the story. First put students in pairs, and have each pair read a short section of dialogue silently, identifying difficult words and determining the main emotions expressed. Then have partners discuss the passage, determining words they want to emphasize and strategies they can use to convey the primary emotion. Finally, have partners practice reading aloud to each other. After they have polished their presentation, have them present it to another pair for feedback. **EL BL**

Objectives
• Evaluate text
• Identify literary elements: description and conflict
• Analyze text

Teach

C Critical Thinking

Comprehension Ask: What does Armand need in order to go to the dance? *(He needs a corsage and new shoes.)* **BL** Does he get what he wants? Explain. *(Possible response: He does get the corsage and shoes because the narrator describes him as all dressed up with the corsage in a box under his arm.)* **OL Say:** The story indicates that Jerry is going to get a Grover Cleveland card. What is the connection between Jerry's card and Armand's needs? *(Possible response: Jerry went to get the Grover Cleveland card—he must have been successful. Then he must have sold the card and given the money to Armand.)* **AL**

EL Language Coach

Greek Roots Say: The ancient Greeks believed that if people drank from the river Lethe, a body of water in Hades, they would forget their past. The Greek word *lethargia* takes its root from the name of this river. How might people with *lethargy* show that they are drowsy or forgetful? *(Possible response: People with lethargy might move slowly, showing that they have no energy or purpose.)* **AL**

Visual Vocabulary
A *corsage* (kor SAZH) is a flower or small bunch of flowers worn by a woman, usually at the shoulder or on the waist.

"How can I take Sally to a fancy dance?" he asked desperately. "I'd have to buy her a corsage . . . And my shoes are practically falling apart. Pa's got too many worries now to buy me new shoes or give me money for flowers for a girl."

I nodded in sympathy. "Yeah," I said. "Look at me. Baseball time is almost here, and all I've got is that old glove. And no Grover Cleveland card yet . . ." **14**

"Grover Cleveland?" he asked. "They've got some of those up on the North Side. Some kid was telling me there's a store that's got them. He says they're looking for Warren G. Harding."

"Holy Smoke!" I said. "I've got an extra Warren G. Harding!" Pure joy sang in my veins. I ran to my bicycle, swung into the seat—and found that the front tire was flat.

"I'll help you fix it," Armand said.

Within half an hour I was at the North Side Drugstore, where several boys were matching cards on the sidewalk. Silently but **blissfully** I shouted: President Grover Cleveland, here I come!

After Armand had left for the dance, all dressed up as if it were Sunday, the small green box containing the corsage under his arm, I sat on the railing of the piazza, letting my feet dangle. The neighborhood was quiet because the Frenchtown Tigers were at Daggett's Field, practicing for the first baseball game of the season.

I thought of Armand and the ridiculous expression on his face when he'd stood before the mirror in the bedroom. I'd avoided looking at his new black shoes. "Love," I muttered.

Spring had arrived in a sudden stampede of apple blossoms and fragrant breezes. Windows had been thrown open and dust mops had banged on the sills all day long as the women busied themselves with housecleaning. I was puzzled by my lethargy.[18] Wasn't spring supposed to make everything bright and gay?

---

18. *Lethargy* (LETH er jee) is a feeling or condition of laziness or drowsiness.

Vocabulary

blissfully (BLIS fuh lee) *adv.* in an extremely happy way; joyfully

854 UNIT 7 What Can We Learn from Our Mistakes?

Practice the Skills

14 English Language Coach

Greek Roots The Greek root *path* means "disease" or "feeling." Find a word on in this paragraph that contains *path* and means "the ability to feel and understand other people's sorrow."

Additional Support

Differentiated Instruction

Series of Events Chain A precise series of events allows Jerry to get his final president card and Armand to go to the dance. Have students create a series of events chain like the one shown here. Tell students that they may add additional events if necessary. **AS**

SERIES OF EVENTS

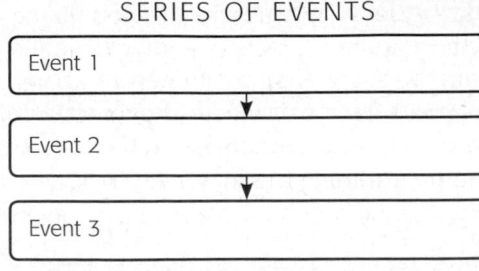

Event 1

Event 2

Event 3

I turned at the sound of footsteps on the stairs. Roger Lussier greeted me with a sour face.

"I thought you were practicing with the Tigers," I said.

"Rollie Tremaine," he said. "I just couldn't stand him." He slammed his fist against the railing. "Jeez, why did he have to be the one to get a Grover Cleveland? You should see him showing off. He won't let anybody even touch that glove . . ."

I felt like Benedict Arnold[19] and knew that I had to confess what I had done.

"Roger," I said, "I got a Grover Cleveland card up on the North Side. I sold it to Rollie Tremaine for five dollars."

"Are you crazy?" he asked.

"I needed that five dollars. It was an—an emergency."

"Boy!" he said, looking down at the ground and shaking his head. "What did you have to do a thing like that for?"

I watched him as he turned away and began walking down the stairs.

"Hey, Roger!" I called.

He squinted up at me as if I were a stranger, someone he'd never seen before.

"What?" he asked, his voice flat.

"I had to do it," I said. "Honest." **15**

He didn't answer. He headed toward the fence, searching for the board we had loosened to give us a secret passage.

I thought of my father and Armand and Rollie Tremaine and Grover Cleveland and wished that I could go away someplace far away. But there was no place to go.

Roger found the loose slat in the fence and slipped through. I felt betrayed: weren't you supposed to feel good when you did something fine and noble?

A moment later two hands gripped the top of the fence and Roger's face appeared. "Was it a real emergency?" he yelled.

"A real one!" I called. "Something important!"

His face dropped from sight and his voice reached me across the yard: "All right."

"See you tomorrow!" I yelled.

I swung my legs over the railing again. The gathering dusk began to soften the sharp edges of the fence, the rooftops, the distant church steeple. I sat there a long time, waiting for the good feeling to come. **16** ○

---

19. **Benedict Arnold** was an American general who became a traitor during the Revolutionary War.

Practice the Skills

C

15 🗨 BIG Question

Does Jerry make a mistake by selling the card to Rollie Tremaine? Explain. Write your answer on your Foldable. Your response will help you complete the Unit Challenge later. **BQ**

16 Key Reading Skill

Evaluating How would you evaluate Jerry's actions? Do you think he did a good thing? Explain.

President Cleveland, Where Are You? **855**

Teach

C Critical Thinking

Comprehension **Ask:** Why is Roger angry with Jerry? *(Roger is angry because Jerry has let Rollie win the new glove.)* **OL**

BQ 🗨 BIG Question

Ask: How do you know that Jerry has learned from his earlier mistake? Explain. *(Responses will vary. Students may say that selling the card to Rollie and giving the money to Armand shows that Jerry realizes that it's important to help family members and show your appreciation for them, especially during difficult times.)* **OL**

Assess

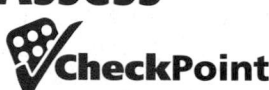
CheckPoint

Use the CheckPoint questions provided on Presentation Plus! to check for comprehension of the selection. These questions can be used with interactive response keypads for immediate student feedback.

Reading in the Real World

Citizenship In "President Cleveland, Where Are You?" Jerry performs an act of heroism, giving up something he wants to help his family. Challenge students to find "local heroes," volunteers in their community who give their time to help others.

Have students contact libraries, parks, or community centers to learn about the work of volunteers there. Ask students to record three facts that they learn about volunteers and post their facts on a "Local Hero" wall in the classroom. **OL**

Objectives
• Monitor comprehension
• Identify word structure: Greek roots

Assess

Resources for page 856

📁 Selection QuickCheck, p. 65

📁 Selection and Unit Assessment, p. 77

⚪ ExamView Assessment Suite

⚪ Interactive Tutor: Self-Assessment

Students can respond to the *After You Read* items in their Learner's Notebooks or on a separate sheet of paper.

Answering the BIG Question

1. Possible response: Jerry gives his brother only fifteen cents for their father's present. In the end, he gives money to his brother for the dance.
2. Responses will vary.
3. Jerry rides to the North Side and trades a Warren G. Harding card for it.

Critical Thinking

4. Possible response: Rollie is ungracious.
5. Jerry sells his card and gives Armand the money.
6. They're inexpensive.
7. Possible response: He selflessly helped out his brother.
8. Responses will vary.

856

After You Read

President Cleveland, Where Are You?

Answering the BIG Question

1. What mistake does Jerry make early in the story? Does he correct this mistake? Explain.
2. **Connect** From this story, what have you learned about making and correcting mistakes?
   TIP Author and Me
3. **Recall** How does Jerry get the Grover Cleveland card?
   TIP Right There

Critical Thinking

4. **Infer** Why don't the boys like Rollie Tremaine?
   TIP Think and Search

5. **Draw Conclusions** How does Armand get the shoes and corsage?
   TIP Author and Me

6. **Interpret** At the beginning of the story, why do the boys enjoy collecting cards?
   TIP Author and Me

7. **Interpret** Why doesn't Jerry feel good at the end of the story?
   TIP Author and Me

8. **Draw Conclusions** What values does Jerry learn from Armand throughout the story?
   TIP Author and Me

Objectives (pp. 856–857)
Reading Evaluate text • Make connections from text to self
Literature Identify literary elements: description, sensory details
Vocabulary Identify word structure: Greek roots
Writing Respond to literature: personal e-mail
Grammar Use correct subject and verb agreement: *here* and *there*

Write About Your Reading

Write an e-mail to a friend. In your e-mail, tell your friend what you thought about "President Cleveland, Where Are You?" Evaluate the characters and the plot, and explain how well the author entertained you through his story. End your e-mail by telling your friend why he or she should or should not read the story.

Write About Your Reading

Possible response:
Dear Kim,
I just read a short story called "President Cleveland, Where Are You?" I hope you'll read it so that we can talk about it together. I think the story does a great job of showing how brothers care about each other, even if they don't always get along. In the story, the main character actually gives up a new baseball glove so that his older brother can have money to go to a dance! I also like the story's historical setting—it takes place during the Great Depression. Please hurry and read this story. I want to know what you think!
—Tamika

Skills Review

Key Reading Skill: Evaluating

9. Does the setting (the Depression) make the story better? Does it not affect the story? Or does it hurt the story? Explain your answer.

10. A great piece of literature has a timeless message that remains true for many generations of readers. Do you consider "President Cleveland, Where Are You?" a great short story? Explain.

Key Literary Element: Description

11. Does the author devote more description to setting or to characterization? Explain your answer using details from the story.

Vocabulary Check

Rewrite the following sentences, inserting the correct vocabulary word in each.

obsessed   splurge   dismal   dominant

12. After winning the lottery, Gladys plans to ___ on vacations and cars.

13. That black Labrador puppy is the strongest and most ___ in the litter.

14. November is a ___ month, filled with gray skies, dead leaves, and cold winds.

15. Many young children are ___ with dinosaurs when they are young.

16. **Academic Vocabulary** How does evaluating make you more aware as a reader?

17. **English Language Coach** The Greek root *phon* or *phone* means "sound." It is often used at the end of a word. How many words can you think of that end in the word *phone*? (Hint: Some are musical instruments.) How do their definitions relate to sound?

Grammar Link: Subject-Verb Agreement with *Here* and *There* Sentence Beginnings

Some sentences begin with *here* or *there*. But *here* or *there* is never the subject of the sentence. Follow these tips for identifying the subject and verb in sentences beginning with *here* or *there*.

- In sentences that begin with *here* or *there*, the verb will appear before the subject. Example: There **were** too many **people** in line. The *verb* **were** comes before the *subject* **people**.

- In sentences that begin with *here* or *there*, choose the verb that agrees with the subject. Example: Here **is** a great **poem**. The *verb* **is** agrees with the *subject* **poem**.

Grammar Practice

Choose the verb that agrees with the subject.

18. Here (comes, come) my very favorite car.

19. There (seem, seems) to be several spelling mistakes in this paragraph.

20. Here (lie, lies) the greatest baseball player who ever lived.

21. There (is, are) only twelve letters in the Hawaiian alphabet.

Writing Application Look back at your e-mail from the **Write About Your Reading** exercise. Check to be sure that your subjects and verbs agree in sentences that begin with *here* or *there*.

Literature Online

Web Activities For eFlashcards, Selection Quick Checks, and other Web activities, go to www.glencoe.com.

Skills Review

Key Reading Skill: Evaluating

9. Responses will vary.

10. Responses will vary. Students should use examples from the story in their responses.

Key Literary Element: Description

11. Possible response: The characterization is better defined because of the vivid descriptions of Armand, the father, Jerry, and Jerry's friends.

Vocabulary Check

12. splurge

13. dominant

14. dismal

15. obsessed

16. **Academic Vocabulary** Responses will vary.

17. **English Language Coach** Possible responses: Megaphone: a device used to amplify sound Xylophone: an instrument that sounds by striking the bars with mallets. Telephone: an instrument that transmits sound

Grammar Link: Subject-Verb Agreement with *Here* and *There* Sentence Beginnings

Grammar Practice

18. comes

19. seem

20. lies

21. are

Close

Ask students to tell what Jerry's example taught them about mistakes that can hurt the feelings of friends or family members.

Teach

More About the Author

David Fischer has written about sports for adults and children. His books include *The 50 Coolest Jobs in Sports, A Thing or Two About Baseball,* and *The Encyclopedia of the Summer Olympics.*

EL Language Coach

Greek Roots Say: The Greek root *aero* means "air." Name some words that contain this root. *(Possible responses: aerobics, aerodynamic)* **Say:** The Greek root *pod* means "foot." Find the word *podium* in the dictionary. What connection does the meaning of the root *pod* have to the word *podium*? *(A podium is a small raised platform that someone giving a speech can stand on.)* **OL**

Meet the Author

David Fischer is a feature writer for a magazine. His goal is to entertain and to inform. Feature articles deal with interesting subjects that grab a reader's attention.

Author Search For more about David Fischer, go to www.glencoe.com.

Objectives (pp. 858–863)
Reading Evaluate text • Make connections from text to self
Informational text Identify literary elements: description, sensory details
Vocabulary Identify word structure: Greek roots

Before You Read Nobody's Perfect

Vocabulary Preview

competing (kum PEET ing) *v.* taking part in a contest; form of the verb *compete* **(p. 860)** *The runner was competing in the race.*

barrier (BAIR ee ur) *n.* something that prevents passage; an obstacle **(p. 862)** *The skater accidentally flew over the barrier.*

fumbled (FUM buld) *v.* lost one's grasp on something; form of the verb *fumble* **(p. 862)** *The football player fumbled the ball.*

referee (ref uh REE) *n.* a sports official who makes sure rules are followed in a game **(p. 862)** *The referee called the player out.*

Partner Activity With a partner, write a sports article about a recent game or competitive event. Use the vocabulary words above to write your article.

English Language Coach

Greek Roots You learned that the **root** of a word is its main part. Knowing the meaning of a word's root can help you figure out the meaning of the whole word. The English language borrowed many roots, prefixes, and suffixes from Greek. These word parts are called "combining forms" because they are often used with other Greek parts. The word part *mono* means "one" or "alone." A *monologue* is a long speech given by one person. Here are some other examples of Greek roots.

Root	Meaning	Example
auto	self	automatic, automobile
cycle	circle, ring	recycle
gram	write/draw	diagram, telegram
graph	write	autograph
mono	one/alone/single	monogram, monorail
scope	see	telescope
tele	far	telegraph, telephone

EL

On Your Own Make flash cards for Greek roots. Use the list above to help you. On the front of the card, write the Greek root. On the back of the card, write the root's meaning and three words that contain the root. Review your flash cards with a partner.

Additional Support

Author Search To expand students' appreciation of David Fischer, have them access the Web site for additional information and resources.

Literature Focus Lesson

Sports Writing Sports writing can serve a number of purposes. Some articles entertain readers by recreating the excitement of a sporting event. Other articles provide biographical information about athletes or give general facts about past, ongoing, or upcoming sporting events. Still others express the writer's opinion about an issue surrounding a particular athlete or event. The best sports writing gives readers a new understanding of or appreciation for an aspect of a sport. Have students follow a particular sportswriter's column in a newspaper, magazine, or blog, and invite them to bring in examples of interesting stories. **OL**

Skills Preview

Key Reading Skill: Evaluating

Good readers do more than just understand what they read. They also evaluate the writer's ideas. When you evaluate, you judge the value of what you have read. In the last selection, you evaluated a fictional, or made up, story. In the next selection, you will be evaluating a news article that is nonfiction. Evaluating nonfiction is a lot like evaluating fiction, but you ask some different questions.

- Does the author make his or her purpose clear?
- Does the information make sense?
- Does the author present information in such a way that allows me to form my own opinion?
- Does the author present facts or only opinions?
- Does the author's style match the article's subject?

Write to Learn Write the questions listed above in your Learner's Notebook. Use them as a checklist. Answer the questions as you read the selection.

Key Literary Element: Description

Writers use descriptions to engage readers in the text. Descriptions help you understand a text better. An effective description presents a clear picture to the reader. As you read the article, ask yourself these questions:

- What words does the writer use to describe the athletes and their mistakes?
- How do the words make the article more exciting or humorous?

Interactive Literary Elements Handbook
To review or learn more about the literary elements, go to www.glencoe.com.

Get Ready to Read

Connect to the Reading

Everyone makes mistakes. It's how people react to their mistakes that really matters. How do you react **R** when you make a mistake?

Partner Talk With a classmate, discuss a mistake that you have made. Explain what happened and how you reacted. Then, discuss what you learned from the mistake and how you've avoided similar blunders since then.

Build Background

Everyone makes mistakes—even professional athletes. It's bad enough to do something embarrassing in front of your friends or teammates, but imagine making a big mistake in front of millions of people watching TV. This selection is about famous athletes who made mistakes and learned from them. Some of the athletes you'll read about are

- Brett Favre, a record-holding NFL football player who started a foundation that provides aid to disadvantaged and disabled children.
- Kevin Garnett, who achieved the honor of being the NBA's Most Valuable Player in his ninth NBA season.
- Midori Ito, an Olympic silver medalist who has been ice skating since she was four years old.

Set Purposes for Reading

BIG Question As you read "Nobody's Perfect," think about why athletes have to bounce back from their mistakes.

Set Your Own Purpose What else would you like to learn from the article to help you answer the Big Question? Write your own purpose on the "Nobody's Perfect" part of the Workshop 3 Foldable.

Keep Moving

Use these skills as you read the following selection.

Teach

L Literary Element

Description Say: The famous baseball player Babe Ruth once said, "I swing big, with everything I've got. I hit big or I miss big. I like to live as big as I can." How might this quotation make an article more engaging? Explain. *(Possible response: The quotation reveals something about Babe Ruth as a person and the way his personality influenced his style of playing.)* OL AL

R Reading Skill

Review Connecting Say: Think of mistakes that you have seen people make in public. Which strategies seem to be most effective for coping with such mistakes? *(Responses will vary. Students may suggest that having a sense of humor usually helps people cope.)* Tell students to use their experiences to connect to the people in the article. AS

English Language Coach

Greek Roots Prepare a set of five index cards for each student. On each index card, write a root from the chart on page 858. Give each student a set of cards. Then think of several words that contain the roots that you wrote on the cards. Write these words on the board.

Point to a word, and then have students identify its root by holding up the card that contains the correct root. Repeat this process with all the words. Then have students work in pairs to quiz each other. EL BL

Objectives

- Make connections from text to self
- Identify word structure: Greek roots
- Learn and use new vocabulary
- Identify literary elements: description

Teach

C Critical Thinking

Comprehension Ask: What purpose does the author state in the first paragraph? *(The author is going to discuss bloopers.)* **BL Ask:** Do you agree with the author's advice about dealing with mistakes? Explain. *(Responses will vary. Most students will agree that laughing is the best way to handle a blooper.)* **OL**

R Reading Skill

Evaluating Ask: How do you think Suzy Favor Hamilton felt when she realized that she had stopped running too soon? *(Possible responses: She was embarrassed; she was disappointed.)* **OL Ask:** Would this description be as effective if the writer had paraphrased Hamilton's words? Explain. *(Possible answer: No; the quotation is more effective because it shows Hamilton's feelings about the experience.)* **AL**

Readability Scores
Dale-Chall: 5.2
DRP: 53
Lexile: 790

Additional Support

TIME

Nobody's Perfect

By DAVID FISCHER

Making a mistake is not the end of the world. It can be pretty funny!

C Everyone makes mistakes, even great **athletes**. In sports, mistakes are called bloopers. The best way to get over a mistake is to figure out what you did wrong, correct it, and then laugh about it. Here are some of our favorite bloopers. **1**

It's Not Over?

Suzy Favor Hamilton is one of the best distance runners in the United States, but in 1994 she lost a race because she lost count.

R Suzy was **competing** in the mile event at a track meet in Fairfax, Virginia. The runners had to complete eight laps. Near the end of lap 7, Suzy sprinted into the lead. As soon as she crossed the finish line, she stopped running. Suzy thought that the race was over and that she had won! As she watched the other racers run past, she realized her mistake.

"I wanted to tell everybody to stop so that I could jump back in the race," says Hamilton.

Suzy Hamilton stopped running one lap before the race was over.

Keith Locke

Vocabulary

competing (kum PEET ing) *v.* taking part in a contest

1 English Language Coach

Greek Roots The word **athlete** comes from the Greek root *athlon,* meaning "contest." In your own words, explain how the root helps to show the meaning of *athlete.*

Differentiated Instruction

Using an Organizational Chart Tell students to choose three bloopers from the article and describe what happens in each situation. Tell students to create a chart like this to keep track of their ideas. Have students include an explanation of each athlete's reaction to his or her blooper. **AS**

	What happened?	What was the reaction?
Blooper 1		
Blooper 2		
Blooper 3		

Somebody Get Brett!

Quarterback Brett Favre[1] of the Green Bay Packers is cool under pressure. He proved how cool he can be when he led the Packers to victory in Super Bowl XXXI in 1997. But Brett wasn't always so calm.

In 1992, Brett was the Packers' second-string[2] quarterback. In the third game of the season, he went into **R1** action against the Cincinnati Bengals. In the fourth quarter, Green Bay trailed Cincinnati by 13 points. But in the last eight minutes of the game, Brett led Green Bay to two touchdowns.

After the second touchdown, he ran off the field. He started jumping and screaming. Brett was so busy celebrating that he forgot an important part of his job. To win the game, Green Bay needed to kick the extra point. Brett was supposed to be on the field, holding the ball for the kick! **2**

Green Bay kicker Chris Jacke ran to the sideline and dragged Brett back onto the field. Chris then kicked the extra point, and the Packers won the game, 24–23.

Where's My Jersey?

Basketball forward Kevin Garnett of the Minnesota Timberwolves joined the NBA in 1995. He was 19 years old and straight out of high school.

During a game in the early days of his career, Kevin found **R2** that he had left something important behind in the locker room. Near the end of the first quarter, Minnesota's coach told Kevin to enter the game. Kevin ran to the scorer's table and pulled off his warm-up top. Then he looked down. Surprise! He was wearing only a T-shirt from practice. Kevin had to race back to the locker room to get the official game jersey that was part of his uniform.

Even though he's older now, Kevin sometimes still acts like a kid. **3**

---

1. *Favre* (farv)
2. A player who is *second-string* substitutes for a starting player.

Keith Locke

Hey, Brett: Get in the game!

2 **Key Literary Element**

Description Look at the verbs the author uses in this paragraph to describe what happened. Does he use active verbs that bring the scene to life, or not? Write your answers in your Learner's Notebook and include examples from the selection.

3 **Key Reading Skill**

Evaluating What do you think of this part of the article? Has the author given you the facts you need to understand his point? Does the author prove his last statement? Explain.

Nobody's Perfect **861**

Teach

R1 Reading Skill

Evaluating Ask: Does the writer tell the story about Brett Favre's blooper effectively? Explain. *(Possible response: Yes; the writer explains the actions in a clear sequence.)* **OL**

Ask: What is the writer's attitude toward Brett Favre? How do you know? *(Possible response: The writer thinks that the incident is humorous and does not blame Favre for making a mistake. The tone of the story is lighthearted.)* **AL**

R2 Reading Skill

Review Identifying Main Idea and Supporting Details Ask: What mistake did Kevin Garnett make? *(When he entered the game, he realized that he had forgotten to put on his team jersey.)* **AS**

Reading Fluency

Build Fluency The anecdotes on this page will provide students with an excellent opportunity to practice reading aloud. Have students find a quiet place to read silently. As students become more familiar with the text, encourage them to read aloud and to pay careful attention to punctuation marks as they do so. Remind students that exclamation points indicate that text should be read with emphasis, and model the sentences "Brett was supposed to be on the field, holding the ball for the kick!" and "Surprise!" **EL** **BL**

Objectives
• Evaluate text
• Identify main ideas and supporting details
• Monitor comprehension

Teach

R Reading Skill

Evaluating Ask: Does Jim Marshall's error show that he is not a good football player? Explain. *(Possible response: No; his error seems to have been an isolated mistake. He must have been talented to have a twenty-year career in football.)* **OL**

C Critical Thinking

Comprehension Ask: What makes Marshall realize that he has done something wrong? Explain why this event makes him realize that he has made an error. *(Possible response: Marshall knows that he has made an error when a player from the opposing team gives him a hug. The player from the 49ers does this because Marshall scored two points for the 49ers.)* **AL**

Look Out Below!

Midori Ito[3] of Japan is one of the best jumpers in figure skating. But during the 1991 World Championships, Midori jumped right out of the skating rink!

During the short program of the women's singles event, Midori was performing a jump. She started the jump too close to the edge of the rink. She flew over a 12-inch wooden barrier at the edge of the ice and landed on a cameraman!

Midori got up, hopped back over the **barrier,** and completed her routine. She finished in fourth place. **4**

Which Way Do I Go?

Jim Marshall was a star defensive end for the Minnesota Vikings from 1960 to 1979. He is best remembered for getting lost on the football field.

It happened in a 1964 game when the Vikings were playing the San Francisco 49ers. In the third quarter, a 49er running back **fumbled** the football. Jim scooped up the loose ball and ran 66 yards to the end zone.

Jim was pumped.[4] He thought he had scored a touchdown. "A 49ers player ran up and gave me a hug," says Jim. "That's when I knew something was wrong." He had run to the wrong end zone!

The **referee** ruled that Jim had scored a safety (2 points) for San Francisco. Even so, the Vikings won the game, 27–22. "I still feel embarrassed about that play," says Jim. "But I don't see any reason to hide. I know I was hustling. If people want to laugh, I'll go along with it." **5**

Out By a Foot

Third baseman Dani Tyler of the United States women's softball team learned a lesson at the 1996 Summer Olympics: Always watch your step.

---

3. **Midori Ito** (meh DOOR ee EE toh)

4. **Pumped** is a shortened slang expression for **pumped up,** which means filled with excitement, strength, and energy.

Vocabulary

barrier (BAIR ee ur) *n.* something that prevents passage; an obstacle

fumbled (FUM buld) *v.* lost one's grasp on something

referee (ref uh REE) *n.* a sports official who makes sure rules are followed in a game

862 UNIT 7 What Can We Learn from Our Mistakes?

4 Key Literary Element

Description What words help you visualize what happened to Midori Ito?

5 Key Reading Skill

Evaluating The writer says that Jim Marshall is best remembered for getting lost on the football field. Does the writer prove this? Explain. **R**

Additional Support

Reading in the Real World

Career Ask students to name people who have sports-related careers. Examples include athletes, agents, team owners, coaches, referees, personal trainers, announcers, and writers. Tell students to choose one career, such as coaching, and find out more about it. Then have students create a list of qualifications necessary for the selected career. For example, suggest that students start by reading biographies of famous coaches. Encourage students to find out how many coaches were professional athletes, what degrees they earned in college, and at what age they began coaching. **OL**

In the fifth inning of a scoreless game against Australia, Dani hit a home run. When she reached home plate, she leaped to high-five[5] a teammate and jumped right over the plate! The umpire called her out because she never touched home. The United States lost the game in extra innings. It was the U.S. team's second international loss in 10 years.

After the game, Dani said, "From now on, I'm going to paint a big X on home plate and step on it with both feet." The United States went on to win the gold medal. **6**

Wrong Target

At the 2004 Summer Olympic Games in Athens, Greece, Matthew Emmons of the United States was in first place before his final shot in the 50-meter rifle three-position[6] competition.

Matthew was one easy shot away from his second gold medal of the Olympics. All he needed to do was hit the target. So how did Matthew end up in eighth place? He shot at an Austrian competitor's target in the next lane. This Austrian competitor ended up winning the bronze medal.[7] **7**

—Updated 2005, from *Sports Illustrated for Kids*, April 1997

---

5. A **high-five** is a gesture of greeting or victory in which two people slap each other's upraised hands.

6. A **three-position competition** includes firing from a standing position, a seated position, and a prone (lying on the stomach) position.

7. A **bronze medal** is awarded to an athlete for winning third place.

Dani danced over the plate.

Keith Locke

6 **Key Literary Element**

Description How does the description of the event help you visualize what's happening? Write your answer in your Learner's Notebook. Remember to select examples from the text to support your answer. **L**

7 **BIG Question**

What do you think the athletes mentioned in this article would say about what a person can learn from his or her mistakes? Record your answer on your Foldable. This response will help you complete the Unit Challenge. **BQ**

Teach

L Literary Element

Description **Say:** Dani Tyler said that she would "paint a big X on home plate." How does this quotation add to the description of the incident? *(Possible responses: It emphasizes the fact that Tyler overlooked something very obvious.)* **OL** **Ask:** What does the quotation tell you about Tyler? *(Possible response: She has a sense of humor.)* **AL**

BQ BIG Question

Ask: Is it ever all right for athletes to be angry with themselves for making mistakes? Explain. *(Possible response: It's normal to feel disappointed, but athletes should never be angry with themselves because everyone makes mistakes.)* **OL** **Ask:** How can making a mistake be a positive experience? *(Possible response: Mistakes teach people how they can improve.)* **AS**

Assess

CheckPoint

Use the CheckPoint questions provided on Presentation Plus! to check for comprehension of the selection. These questions can be used with interactive response keypads for immediate student feedback.

Differentiated Instruction

Illustration Students may benefit from drawing what happened in one of the blooper anecdotes that is not illustrated in the article. First tell students to choose an unillustrated anecdote from the article. Then tell them to write a brief description of what happened. Remind students to put the actions in sequential order. When students have their ideas in order, have them create a cartoon illustrating the events in the anecdote. Encourage students to share their cartoons with the class. **OL**

Objectives
• Evaluate text
• Identify literary elements: description
• Monitor comprehension

863

Assess

Resources for page 864

📁 Selection Quick Check, p. 66

📁 Selection and Unit Assessment, p. 78

💿 ExamView Assessment Suite

💿 Interactive Tutor: Self-Assessment

Students can respond to the *After You Read* items in their Learner's Notebooks or on a separate sheet of paper.

Answering the
BIG Question

1. Possible response: Mistakes make a person better appreciate the times when he or she is successful.

2. Ito got up and finished her routine.

3. Kevin Garnett ran back to the locker room and put on his jersey.

4. Possible response: Hamilton may have learned to focus more closely on counting the laps.

Critical Thinking

5. Possible response: Favre felt embarrassed but still very excited.

6. Possible response: The athletes were careless, forgetful, or distracted.

7. Possible response: The stories are appropriate because none had truly serious consequences.

8. Possible response: Laugh about it.

864

After You Read   Nobody's Perfect

Keith Locke

Answering the BIG Question

1. After reading this article, what are your thoughts about what you can learn from your mistakes?

2. **Recall** What did Midori Ito do after she fell over the barrier of the rink?
   Tip Right There

3. **Recall** What did Kevin Garnett do when he realized that he had forgotten his jersey?
   Tip Right There

4. **Summarize** What happened to Dani Tyler at the softball game?
   Tip Right There

Critical Thinking

5. **Draw Conclusions** What do you think Suzy Favor Hamilton learned from her mistake?
   Tip Author and Me

6. **Draw Conclusions** Overall, what do you think caused most of the mistakes described in the article?
   Tip Author and Me

7. **Evaluate** The deck at the beginning of the article says that mistakes can be funny. Do you think the writer proved this point?
   Tip Author and Me

8. **Draw Conclusions** What is the best way to get over a mistake?
   Tip On My Own

Objectives (pp. 864–865)
Reading Evaluate text • Make connections from text to self
Informational text Identify literary elements: description, sensory details
Vocabulary Identify word structure: Greek roots
Writing Respond to literature: interview
Grammar Use correct subject-verb agreement: inverted sentences

Write About Your Reading

Write an interview between a news reporter and one of the athletes in the article. First, come up with questions that a reporter would ask about the mistakes the athlete made. Then, imagine that you are the athlete and write responses to the questions. When you are done, proofread your interview to correct any errors in grammar, punctuation, and spelling.

864 UNIT 7   What Can We Learn from Our Mistakes?

Write About Your Reading

Possible response:

Interviewer: So, Brett, what was going through your mind when you realized you'd forgotten about the field goal kick?
BF: I completely panicked because I was so focused on winning the game.
Interviewer: Did your teammates make fun of your "forgetfulness"?
BF: Yeah. Luckily we won so we were all able to laugh about it.
Interviewer: What did you learn from it?
BF: I need to focus on the game until it's completely over.

Skills Review

Key Reading Skill: Evaluating

9. Does the writer present the information in a way that allows you to understand and enjoy the article? Explain.

10. What was the writer's purpose? Was he successful in achieving that purpose? Why or why not?

Key Literary Element: Description

11. Reread the third paragraph under the subhead "Somebody Get Brett!" To what senses does the writer appeal in this paragraph?

12. Of all the events described in the story, which do you think was the most interesting and vivid? Why?

Vocabulary Check

Match each definition with the correct vocabulary word.

13. competing ____
14. barrier ____
15. fumbled ____
16. referee ____

   a. something that prevents passage; an obstacle
   b. a sports official who makes sure rules are followed in a game
   c. taking part in a contest
   d. lost one's grasp on something

17. **Academic Vocabulary** In which of the following sentences is the word *evaluate* used correctly?

   The judges will **evaluate** the dancers' performances before they announce the winner.

   Marco will **evaluate** the clock when he arrives late for class.

18. **English Language Coach** The words *democracy, demography,* and *pandemic* all share the same Greek root. What is that root, what does it mean, and how does it relate to the definitions of the three words? Use a dictionary.

Grammar Link: Subject-Verb Agreement in Inverted Sentences

In most sentences, the subject comes before the verb.

Example: Subject   Verb
Langston Hughes   wrote stories about living in Harlem.

Other kinds of sentences, such as questions, begin with part or all of the predicate. This type of sentence is an inverted sentence. The subject comes after the verb.

Example: Verb   Subject   Predicate
Are   you   still reading that short story?

The best way to find the subject and verb is to rephrase the sentence so that the subject comes before the verb.

Example 1: Where (is/are) the instructions for the game? (Rephrased: The instructions for the game are where? *Instructions* is the subject. *Are* is the verb.)

Example 2: Under the shelves (was/were) a frightened mouse. (Rephrased: A frightened mouse was under the shelves. *Mouse* is the subject. *Was* is the verb.)

Choose the verb that agrees with the subject.

19. On his feet (was/were) brand new shoes.
20. When (are/is) your parents coming?
21. (Doesn't/Don't) Amy know the way to the mall?
22. In the back of the closet (was/were) Alan's birthday presents.

Writing Application Look back at your interview from **Write About Your Reading.** Check to be sure that your subjects and verbs agree, particularly those in inverted sentences.

Web Activities For eFlashcards, Selection Quick Checks, and other Web activities, go to www.glencoe.com.

Nobody's Perfect **865**

Skills Review

Key Reading Skill: Evaluating

9. Possible response: Yes; by showing what happened in a humorous way, the writer reminds readers that even skilled professionals make mistakes and learn from them.

10. Possible response: The writer's purpose is to entertain. He achieves it because he tells funny stories about famous athletes.

Key Literary Element: Description

11. Possible response: The writer appeals to the senses of sight and sound.

12. Responses will vary.

Vocabulary Check

13. c
14. a
15. d
16. b

17. **Academic Vocabulary** The judges will evaluate the dancers' performances before they announce the winner.

18. **English Language Coach** Demos means people.

Grammar Link: Subject-Verb Agreement in Inverted Sentences

Grammar Practice

19. were
20. Are
21. Doesn't
22. were

Close

Ask students to consider why sports mistakes, or bloopers, can be humorous.

Focus

BELLRINGER Options

 Daily Language Practice Transparency 67
Focus Activity Ask: What are some benefits of having other people read your writing? *(Responses will vary.)* **OL**

Teach

W Writing

Revision Before students engage in peer conferences, review the following guidelines.

1. Say something positive about your partner's work before giving any criticism.

2. For each comment you give, include a specific example and, whenever possible, suggest an improvement.

3. Be respectful of your partner's feelings, and refrain from saying anything that you wouldn't want said to you. **AS**

Resources for page 866

📁 Use the BLM in the Unit 7 Resource Booklet, pp. 28–29.

📁 Use the Grammar and Writing Workshop Transparencies, pp. 29–30.

ASSIGNMENT Write a personal narrative

Purpose: Write a narrative about a time you made a mistake

Audience: You, your teacher, and classmates

Revising Rubric

As you revise your draft, you should

• write in your own voice

• use a tone appropriate to purpose and audience

• revise your draft for word choice

• use suggestions from other students to improve your narrative

Objectives (pp. 866–869)
Writing Use the writing process: personal narrative • Use literary elements: voice • Revise a draft to include: main ideas and supporting details, description • Edit writing for: grammar, spelling, punctuation • Present writing
Listening, Speaking, and Viewing Present a news report • Listen actively

---

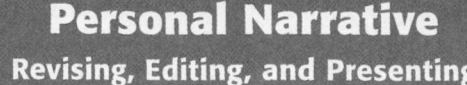

WRITING WORKSHOP PART 2

Personal Narrative
Revising, Editing, and Presenting

In Writing Workshop Part 1, you drafted a personal narrative about a mistake you once made. In this workshop, you will share your work with classmates to improve your writing.

Revising

Make It Better

Sharing your writing with other people may seem scary, but it is actually a great way to find the parts of your work that need to be revised. Sometimes writers get so involved in the piece they are working on that they forget about the audience who will someday read their work.

Start by trading drafts with a partner. As you read your partner's work, underline the parts of the draft that you find confusing. Circle the parts that you especially like. Then answer the Writing Response Sheet questions on a blank piece of paper.

> **Writing Response Sheet**
>
> Writer's Name:
> Reader's Name:
> What mistake was this narrative about?
> What did the writer learn from his or her mistake?
> Did the narrative have a beginning, a middle, and an end?
> What words, descriptions, or sentences did you most enjoy?
> What part(s) did you find confusing? Why?
> What suggestions do you have for the writer?

Return the completed Writing Response Sheet to your partner along with the marked up draft. With your partner, talk about the strengths and weaknesses of each other's writing. Here are some example topics to get your discussion started:

• It isn't clear to me why this event is a mistake.

• The image of "broken piñatas" really struck my mind.

• I'd like to know more about what you learned from this experience.

Additional Support

Differentiated Instruction

Tips for Peer Revision Suggest that students read each other's personal narratives at least twice during the revision process. Students should read the narrative once for a "gut," or initial, reaction and then write a few thoughts about how the piece struck them. Students should then read the narrative a second time, reading more slowly and carefully to note confusing sentences, weak or awkward constructions, and insufficient descriptions. When offering feedback, students should draw from their responses to both readings. **AS**

Make Adjustments

Focus on revising the parts of your narrative that your partner found most confusing. You may need to:

- Add details and description to make your writing more interesting.

  When I got home, **a half-eaten birthday cake, broken piñatas, and melted ice cream** *were all that remained of my sister's birthday party.*

- Delete repeated information.

  I felt so guilty for skipping the party. I didn't want to face my family ~~because I felt so guilty~~.

Raise Your Voice

Check your narrative style by reviewing voice and word choice. A personal narrative is about something that happened to *you;* make your writing sound as much like *you* as possible. Ask yourself:

☑ Does the narrative voice sound like me?

☑ Do I use these words and expressions when I talk?

☑ Have I used words that reflect my emotions about the topic?

Editing

Finish It Up

After you revise your personal narrative, edit your work by following the checklist below.

Proofreading Checklist

☑ Thoughts and feelings are clearly expressed.

☑ Subjects and verbs agree in person and number.

☑ Sentences have proper end punctuation.

☑ Names and places are capitalized.

☑ All words are spelled correctly.

Presenting

Show It Off

Copy your narrative neatly and read it aloud to your classmates. Be sure to read your narrative slowly enough that people can understand you.

Literature Online

Writing Models For models and other writing activities, go to www.glencoe.com.

◀ **Writing Tip**

Writing Tip Make certain that your narrative includes your thoughts and opinions about the topic you chose. **W₁**

◀ **Writing Tip**

Writing Tip Check your narrative for mistakes in verb forms. Remember, most past tense verbs end in *-ed*. Past tense forms of irregular verbs, though, do not end in *-ed*. **W₂**

Teach

W₁ Writing

Thoughts and Opinions Remind students that the writer's thoughts and opinions about the topic should be apparent from reading the selection. Encourage students to ask themselves, *How did the writer feel when that happened?* If students cannot answer this question right away, the writer should add words or sentences that describe how he or she felt about the mistake. **AS**

W₂ Writing

Dialogue Remind students that although most verbs should appear in the past tense, dialogue should be written as it was spoken, which may have been in the present tense. Use the following sample sentence as an example: *I shouted, "You know that I can't swim!"* **OL**

Reading Fluency

Pace Tell students that they should read aloud at a pace that feels comfortable. Ideally, students should aim to read fluently, but slowly enough so that each word can be heard and understood. As students prepare to read their narratives aloud to the class, have them practice reading aloud to partners at several different speeds. Encourage students to try reading more slowly and more quickly than usual to assess their range of comfort. Students should help one another determine an appropriate pace for the class presentation. **EL BL**

Objectives

- Write a personal narrative
- Revise writing for key elements, style, and word choice
- Use the writing process: draft, edit, rewrite, and present

867

Teach

C1 Critical Thinking

Analysis Ask: How does Wallace feel about the mistake he made? Are you able to answer this question without rereading? Explain. *(Possible response: Wallace regrets his comment when Jerry runs out of the house. Students should recognize that the writer makes this clear.)* **BL** **OL**

W Writing

Voice Ask: How would you describe Wallace's voice? Did it feel natural to read his story, as though Wallace were talking to you? Explain. *(Responses will vary. Students may say that Wallace's voice is simple and conversational.)* **AS**

C2 Critical Thinking

Evaluation Ask: What letter grade would you give Wallace's personal narrative? Why? What else can Wallace do to improve his story? *(Responses will vary. Students may suggest that Wallace can include more descriptive detail about the setting or about the main characters in the story.)* **OL** **AL**

Active Writing Model | **Writer's Model**

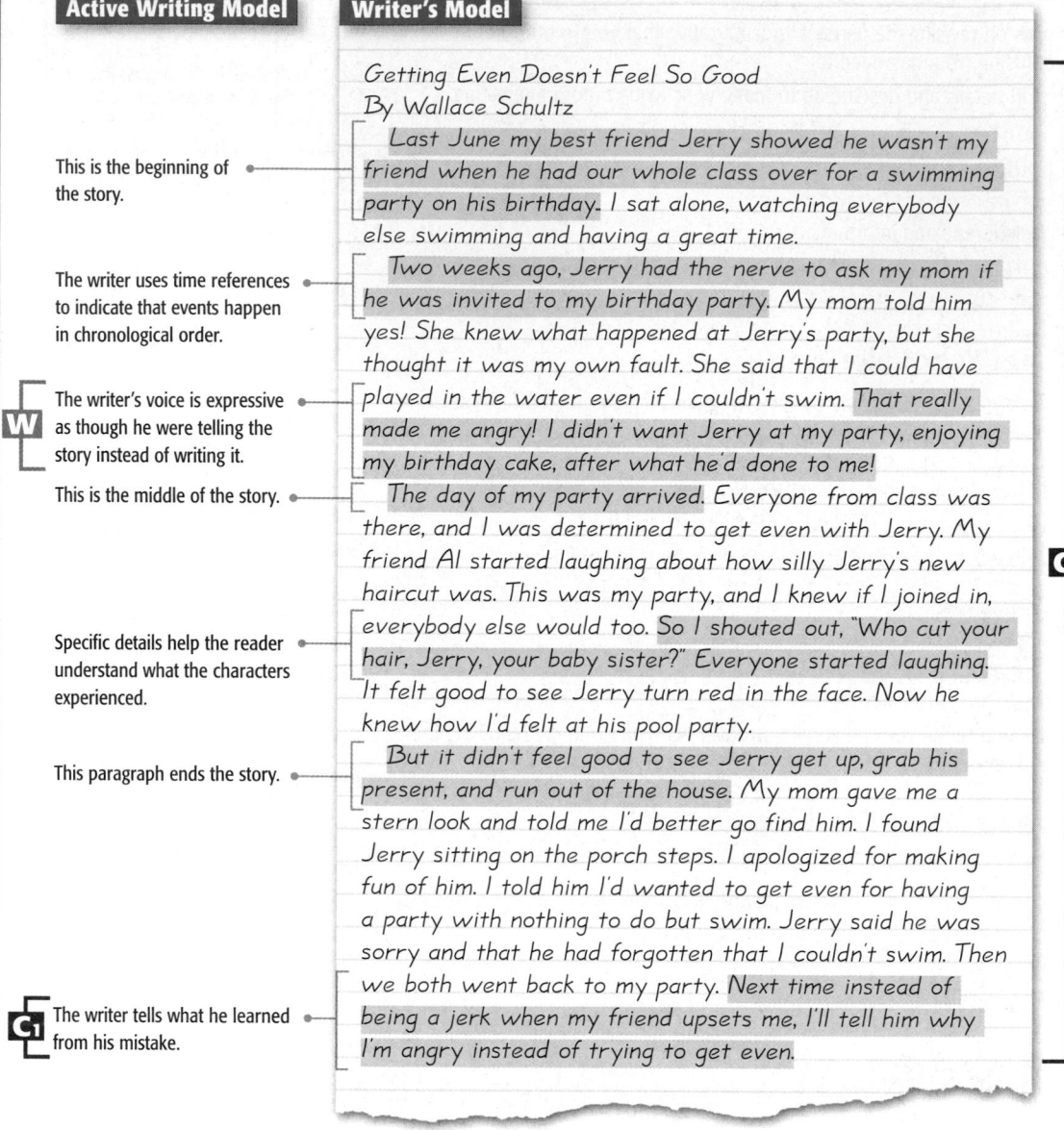

This is the beginning of the story.

The writer uses time references to indicate that events happen in chronological order.

W The writer's voice is expressive as though he were telling the story instead of writing it.

This is the middle of the story.

Specific details help the reader understand what the characters experienced.

This paragraph ends the story.

C1 The writer tells what he learned from his mistake.

Getting Even Doesn't Feel So Good
By Wallace Schultz

Last June my best friend Jerry showed he wasn't my friend when he had our whole class over for a swimming party on his birthday. I sat alone, watching everybody else swimming and having a great time.

Two weeks ago, Jerry had the nerve to ask my mom if he was invited to my birthday party. My mom told him yes! She knew what happened at Jerry's party, but she thought it was my own fault. She said that I could have played in the water even if I couldn't swim. That really made me angry! I didn't want Jerry at my party, enjoying my birthday cake, after what he'd done to me!

The day of my party arrived. Everyone from class was there, and I was determined to get even with Jerry. My friend Al started laughing about how silly Jerry's new haircut was. This was my party, and I knew if I joined in, everybody else would too. So I shouted out, "Who cut your hair, Jerry, your baby sister?" Everyone started laughing. It felt good to see Jerry turn red in the face. Now he knew how I'd felt at his pool party.

But it didn't feel good to see Jerry get up, grab his present, and run out of the house. My mom gave me a stern look and told me I'd better go find him. I found Jerry sitting on the porch steps. I apologized for making fun of him. I told him I'd wanted to get even for having a party with nothing to do but swim. Jerry said he was sorry and that he had forgotten that I couldn't swim. Then we both went back to my party. Next time instead of being a jerk when my friend upsets me, I'll tell him why I'm angry instead of trying to get even.

C2

Additional Support

Literature Focus Lesson

Transitions To help students use clear, logical transitions in their personal narratives, have them examine and evaluate the transitions in the writer's model. For instance, Wallace begins several paragraphs with time order words, such as "Last June" and "Two weeks ago." Ask students what words they might add to smooth the transition into the sentence *The day of my party arrived.* One possibility is to insert the words *before long* at the beginning of the sentence. Have students reread the last paragraph of the narrative and suggest a better transition to avoid beginning the first sentence with the word *but.* **OL**

Listening, Speaking, and Viewing

News Report

Many of the reading selections in this unit are about topics and events that happened in the past. When you read about the past, you read about events that have already happened. One of the first sources to report events that have already happened is nightly news broadcasts.

What Is It?

A news broadcast is a program on television or radio that reports the most important news stories from that day. Each story is told by a reporter or a news anchor. A reporter is someone who goes out and researches a story. A news anchor reads the news from the radio or television station.

Why Is It Important?

People depend on news broadcasts to learn about events that happen in their neighborhood, in other parts of the country, and around the world.

How Do I Do It?

LSV

The most important rule in news reporting is to write only the facts. This means that everything you include in your report must be true and have really happened. The best way to report a news story is to find out the 5 W's of the story; *who, what, when, where,* and *why.*

- Choose a historical event that interests you or a historical topic that you have read about in this unit. Examples from the unit include desegregation, internment camps, the great radio scare, and westward migration.

- Answer the 5 W's about your topic. You may have to use the Internet, encyclopedias, or textbooks to find your answers.
- Make a chart like the one below to organize your research.

Japanese Internment

Who	Japanese Americans
What	Much of the Japanese population in the United States was forced to leave their homes and live together in large camps.
When	beginning in 1942
Where	in the western part of the United States
Why	because the United States and Japan were fighting against each other during World War II

- Once you have researched your topic and identified the 5 W's, turn your notes into a short paragraph about your topic. Remember to include only facts, not your own opinions, about the topic.

Speak to Learn Imagine you are a news reporter assigned to broadcast a story about your topic. Use the information you collected to present a short news report about your chosen historical event. Practice reading your paragraph aloud. Speak slowly and clearly, making certain that your broadcast includes the 5 W's. Practice reporting your story to a partner before sharing it with the class.

Differentiated Instruction

TV Segment Have students work in groups to produce a ten-minute television segment. Create a "set" in your classroom and have students act out the segment live. The theme of the segment should be a news story, and the segment should include factual reports, interviews, editorial commentary, traffic and weather updates, and even brief commercial breaks. Help students choose a current event that is appropriate to the unit and that can be researched relatively easily. Provide time for planning and rehearsal, and encourage students to design costumes that are appropriate for the "set." **AS**

Teach

LSV Listening, Speaking and Viewing

Say: Reporters frequently reference their source or sources of information in their news stories. For example, a reporter might begin a sentence by saying, "According to the Associated Press . . ." If certain information is likely to be true but has not yet been proved, a reporter might use words such as *reportedly* or *allegedly.* Use reference sources of information whenever possible, and use language that indicates whether your information has been proven. **OL AL**

Assess/Close

Explain that although news reports contain only factual information, editorials contain the writer's opinions. Lead students in a discussion about the value of having both news and editorial coverage of a given event.

Objectives
- Evaluate text
- Analyze text
- Present a news report
- Use appropriate expressions and gestures

869

Inferring

**Objectives covered in
this workshop:**
• Taking notes
• Reviewing notes to understand and recall ideas from
texts

Teaching Students to Infer

Why Is It important?

• Inferences depend on seeing connections that are not articulated.

• Most writers do not come out and say everything a character thinks;
readers need to make inferences to fully comprehend what is being
communicated.

• Students who make inferences successfully understand characters better
and are better able to identify themes.

How to Help Students Get It

• Tell students to always pay attention to everything a writer tells them
through a character's actions as well as words.

• Help students notice descriptions, dialogue, events, and relationships.

• Encourage students to ask themselves: "Why does the author tell me this?
What does this suggest about this character or situation?"

• To build their confidence in making inferences while reading, remind
students that they already make many inferences in everyday life.

Reading to Answer the Big Question

The Shutout by Patricia C. McKissack and Frederick McKissack, Jr.
The history of baseball is traced from its inception to the establishment of
professional leagues. The authors focus on how and why African American
players were excluded from most of organized baseball. Students will learn
that historians now recognize the significant accomplishments of African
American players who played and excelled in the game despite discourage-
ment and discrimination.

The Talking Skull by Donna L. Washington
This African fable illustrates the importance of listening and thinking before
opening one's mouth. A man, well known for wasting people's time with
useless conversation, finds a talking skull. The skull tells him that talking led
to his bad end. When the man tries to show off the talking skull, the skull
refuses to speak and the man is branded a liar and banished from his village. Unfortunately, the man hasn't learned from the skull's mistake.

Workshop Resources

PACING (DAYS) STANDARD	BLOCK	LESSON	STUDENT MATERIALS	TEACHER RESOURCES
1	1/2	Key Skill Lesson: Inferring	Key Reading Skills Practice, p. 30 English Language Coach Review, p. 42	Bellringer Options Transparencies –Daily Language Practice 68 Read Aloud, Think Aloud Transparencies –Key Reading Skills 13 Presentation Plus!
1	1	"The Shutout"	Glencoe Online Unit Vocabulary Review, p. 40 Academic Vocabulary Review, p. 43 English Language Coach Active Reading Graphic Organizer, p. 32 Literary Analysis, p. 31 StudentWorks Plus™ Online Student Edition Literature Classics Selection and Unit Assessments, p. 79	Literary and Text Analysis Transparencies 44 Puzzlemaker Skill Level Up!™ A Language Arts Game BookLink 3 Assessment by Learning Objective (Diagnostic and Formative) Interactive Tutor: Self-Assessment TeacherWorks Plus™
1		"The Talking Skull"	Glencoe Online Unit Vocabulary Review, p. 40 Academic Vocabulary Review, p. 43 English Language Coach Active Reading Graphic Organizer, p. 34 Literary Analysis, p. 31 StudentWorks Plus™ Online Student Edition Literature Classics Selection and Unit Assessments, p. 80	Literary and Text Analysis Transparencies 44 Puzzlemaker Skill Level Up!™ A Language Arts Game BookLink 3 Assessment by Learning Objective (Diagnostic and Formative) Interactive Tutor: Self-Assessment TeacherWorks Plus™

Keys for Unit Resource

- Blackline Master
- Workbook
- Supplemental Text
- CD-ROM
- DVD
- Transparency
- Web-based
- Fast File

Level Appropriate Code

- **AS** = Activities for all students
- **AL** = Activities for students working above grade level
- **OL** = Activities for students working at grade level
- **BL** = Activities for students working below grade level
- **EL** = Activities for English language learners

Focus

BELLRINGER Options

✍ **Daily Language Practice
Transparency 68
Focus Activity Say:**
Suppose that a friend is giving you very detailed information about how to get to the library, including landmarks, billboards, and other buildings. How much information should you write down to find the library? *(Responses will vary.)* **AS**

Teach

R Reading Skill

Inferring Say: An inference involves using your reason and experience to come up with an idea based on what the author implies or suggests. How could your experiences help you make inferences? *(Possible response: If I read about a situation that is similar to one I've experienced, I could look at the outcome of that situation to infer about the outcome of the situation I'm reading about.)* **OL** **AS**

Skills Focus

You will practice using these skills when you read the following selections:
- "The Shutout," p. 874
- "The Talking Skull," p. 884

Reading
- Making inferences

Literature
- Identifying, analyzing, and evaluating sequence of events/time order

Vocabulary
- Using Anglo-Saxon roots to determine the meanings of unfamiliar words

Writing/Grammar
- Determining subject-verb agreement for special noun subjects

Objectives (pp. 870–871)
Reading Make inferences

Skill Lesson

Inferring

Learn It!

What Is It? You already learned about making inferences in Unit 3, but let's go back over the basics. You **infer** when you figure out information the author doesn't give you directly. You "read between the R lines." **Inferring** uses many of the skills you have learned in the previous units, such as activating your prior knowledge, connecting, asking questions, and predicting. Reading would not be much fun if the author didn't give you a chance to infer!

Analyzing Cartoons
What can you infer from this cartoon? Does the boy like to do homework?

© 2002 Bill Amend/Distributed by Universal Press Syndicate

Additional Support

Differentiated Instruction

Building Background *Foxtrot* cartoonist Bill Amend majored in physics in college. As a result, his comic strip often includes humorous references to mathematics. He thinks that cartoons are more than just funny pictures; indeed, he thinks that they are evidence of a brain at work. "Too many young cartoonists forget that what makes a comic strip work is much more than the ability to draw funny pictures. What sustains a strip, what makes it worth reading day after day, is the mind behind it." If possible, provide students with other *Foxtrot* cartoons and have them discuss the elements of the cartoons' humor. **AS**

Why Is It Important? If you infer as you read, reading is more fun, and you understand more of what you read. It helps you understand characters, identify main ideas and themes, and connect to what you are reading.

How Do I Do It? As you read, follow these steps:
- Ask "I wonder" questions as you read.
- Look at the text for important clues.
- Think about what you already know that connects to information in the text.
- See if you can now answer your "I wonder" questions.

Here is how one student made an inference while reading "The Gold Cadillac."

Study Central Visit www.glencoe.com and click on Study Central to review inferring.

> The policeman told my father to get in the back of the police car. My father did. One policeman got back into the police car. The other policeman slid behind the wheel of our Cadillac. The police car started off. The Cadillac followed. Wilma and I looked at each other and at our mother. We didn't know what to think. We were scared.

> *Wait a minute. I can't quite picture this scene. Who is driving the Cadillac? The text tells me that the policeman slid behind the wheel of the Cadillac. I know that whoever is driving is behind the wheel. Even though the author doesn't come right out and say it, I know that the policeman must be driving the Cadillac. Now the picture is clearer.*

Practice It!

In your Learner's Notebook, copy the steps listed in "How Do I Do It?"

Use It!

As you read the selections, ask and try to answer your "I Wonder" questions.

Teach

Study Central Have students access the Web site to review taking and reviewing notes and to complete a related activity.

R Reading Skill

Inferring Ask: What is the student's reasoning that leads her to infer the policeman is driving the car? *(Possible response: She reasons that the person sitting behind the wheel of the car must be the one driving it.)* **AL**

Resources for page 871

📁 Use Key Reading Skills Transparency 13 in *Read Aloud, Think Aloud* to help students practice inferring.

Reading in the Real World

College Tell students that taking notes and reviewing them will be even more important in college, when instructors may give a great deal of information in a short amount of time. Work with students to practice writing shortcuts, such as abbreviations, that may be used in taking notes. If possible, have an instructor from a higher grade visit the class and talk about his or her expectations for note taking. Encourage students to ask questions that will help them determine what lecture material should be written down and what material may be omitted. **OL**

Objectives
- Take and review notes
- Learn and use new vocabulary

Teach

More About the Authors

Before he became interested in writing, Fred McKissack owned a construction company. After he sold his business, he expected to help his wife, Patricia, for a short time. Instead, the two have continued to write. What motivated him, McKissack says, is "the importance of a story and what it meant to a child's development." As his wife, Patricia, explains, the couple works to "enlighten, to change attitudes," and "to build bridges with books."

V Vocabulary

Unlock Meaning Say:

Sometimes when you know the meaning of one word, you can use it to learn the meaning of another word. Look at the word *documentation*. It contains the word *document*. You know what a *document* is and you know that *to document* means "to record information." You can use what you already know to figure out that documentation means "something recorded." Use this strategy when you see other unfamiliar words. **AS**

Before You Read | The Shutout

Meet the Authors

The McKissacks are a husband-and-wife writing team. Since 1984, they have written more than 100 books. Fred does the research, and Patricia does the writing. Fred McKissack says, "One of the reasons we write for children is to introduce them to African and African American history and historical figures and to get them to internalize the information not just academically, but also emotionally. We want them to feel the tremendous amount of hurt and sadness that racism and discrimination cause all people, regardless of race."

Literature Online

Author Search For more about the McKissacks, go to www.glencoe.com.

Objectives (pp. 872–879)
Reading Make inferences • Make connections from text to self
Literature Identify text structure: sequence, time order
Vocabulary Explore word origins: Anglo-Saxon

Vocabulary Preview

rivaling (RY vul ing) *v.* being equal to or matching; form of the verb *rival* **(p. 875)** *Baseball is rivaling basketball in popularity.*

privileged (PRIH vih lijd) adj. having or enjoying one or more advantages **(p. 878)** *Horse racing was a sport enjoyed only by privileged people.*

composed (kum POHZD) *v.* formed by putting together; form of the verb *compose* **(p. 878)** *The Negro Leagues were composed of the best players.*

documentation (dok yuh men TAY shun) *n.* something recorded that serves as proof **(p. 879)** *Players needed documentation to be included in the Hall of Fame.*

V

Write to Learn In your Learner's Notebook, write a sentence for each vocabulary word that fits its meaning.

English Language Coach

Anglo-Saxon Origins Anglo-Saxon is the name of a language also known as Old English. It developed when the Angles and the Saxons conquered England in the fifth century.

Many English base words and roots come from Anglo-Saxon, or Old English. Most of the basic, simple words that we use generally come from Old English. Look at the words *silly* and *ridiculous.* Which word do you think comes from Old English? That's right, *silly* comes from Old English. *Ridiculous* comes from Latin.

Guess the Roots Guess which word in each pair is the one that came from Old English. Then check your guesses in a dictionary. (The history of a word is given inside [] marks at the beginning of the dictionary entry. "OE" means "Old English.")

1. forward/advance
2. like/admire
3. fear/panic
4. revolve/spin

Additional Support

Author Resources To expand students' appreciation of Patricia and Fred McKissack, have them access the Web site for additional information and resources.

Differentiated Instruction

Historical Research Students interested in historical research may want to learn more about baseball history and the role that African Americans have played in it. Possibilities for further research topics include Moses Fleetwood Walker, the Kansas City Monarchs, Satchel Paige, and Jackie Robinson.

Suggest that students search for other books and articles about African Americans in baseball. Have students share their findings with the class. You may wish to have students compile their findings in a pamphlet or a classroom display. **OL**

Skills Preview

Key Reading Skill: Inferring

Before you read, look at the steps for inferring you wrote in your Learner's Notebook.

Remember that inferring is not making wild guesses! Your answer to your "I wonder" questions must be backed up by clues from the text.

Key Literary Element: Sequence of Events/Time Order

Sequence of events is the order in which events take place. Often the sequence of events organizes a written work. But sometimes writers will go back and forth in time. To understand the sequence of events, it is important to keep track of when things happen.

As you read, use these tips to understand the order in which things happen.

- Pay attention to dates and times.
- Make a list of important dates and events.

Date	Event
1820	Baseball was played in Mr. Mumford's pasture.
1834	Carver wrote about American version of rounders.

Write to Learn Use a chart like the one above to help you organize dates and events as you read "The Shutout." Label the left-hand column *Date.* Label the other column *Event.*

- Read a few paragraphs at a time before filling in the chart because events may not be mentioned in chronological order.
- Enter your notes in pencil. As you read, you may find information that needs to be inserted before something you have already written.
- In the *Date* column, it may not always be possible to list an exact year; for example, you may have to list a period of time such as *Before the Civil War.*

Get Ready to Read

Connect to the Reading

Have you ever been excluded, or kept out, of a team, a club, or a group of friends? Why were you excluded? How did being excluded make you feel? How did you react? How was the problem solved?

Write to Learn In your Learner's Notebook, write about this experience. If you wish, volunteer to read your entry aloud to the class.

Build Background

The title "The Shutout" is a pun—a play on words in which a double meaning is given to the same word. In baseball, the word *shutout* means "a game in which one team doesn't score any runs." Shut out also means "to exclude" or "to not allow to join or participate." In this article, it refers to African American players' being kept from joining all-white baseball teams.

Set Purposes for Reading

BIG Question Read "The Shutout" to find out what kinds of mistakes were made as the game of baseball developed and what lessons were learned from them.

Set Your Own Purpose What else would you like to learn from the selection to help you answer the Big Question? Write your own purpose for reading this selection on "The Shutout" part of the Workshop 4 Foldable.

Interactive Literary Elements Handbook
To review or learn more about the literary elements, go to www.glencoe.com.

Keep Moving

Use the skills above as you read the following selection.

Teach

R Reading Skill

Review Connecting Ask: Have you ever excluded someone from a group activity? Why? How do you think it made that person feel? (*Responses will vary.*) **AL Say:** Use these feelings to connect to the people in "The Shutout."

L Literary Element

Sequence of Events/Time Order Say: Information in a nonfiction article is often presented in chronological order. Why would a graphic organizer be helpful when information in a selection is not presented chronologically? (*Possible responses: A graphic organizer can help readers keep track of the order of events.*) **OL**

Interactive Literary Elements Handbook Have students access the Web site to improve their understanding of sequence of events.

English Language Coach

Build Background Baseball terms have made their way into everyday language. For example, if someone "hits a home run," he or she performs successfully. On the other hand, if a person "strikes out," he or she fails. Some English language learners may not be familiar with these terms and phrases. Review the terms and phrases with students. Write them on the board and provide definitions. You may also wish to have students share common sports-related terms from their primary languages. **EL**

Objectives

- Take and review notes
- Understand sequence of events: time order
- Learn and use new vocabulary

Teach

R Reading Skill

Review Activating Prior Knowledge Say: Many sports teams have long histories. Think of baseball teams in your school, city, or state. What do you know about these teams, and how long have they have played in your area? *(Responses will vary.)* **AS**

C Critical Thinking

Comprehension Ask: Why might it not be a fact that baseball was invented in 1839? *(Possible response: Records show that people were playing stick-and ball games long before 1839.)* **AS**

Readability Scores
Dale-Chall: 9.3
DRP: 67
Lexile: 1270

The Shutout

by Patricia C. McKissack and Frederick McKissack, Jr.

R The history of baseball is difficult to trace because it is embroidered with wonderful anecdotes[1] that are fun but not necessarily supported by fact. There are a lot of myths that persist about baseball—the games, the players, the owners, and the fans—in spite of contemporary research that disproves most of them. For example, the story that West Point cadet[2] Abner Doubleday "invented" baseball in 1839 while at Cooperstown, New York, continues to be widely accepted, even though, according to his diaries, Doubleday never visited Cooperstown. A number of records and **C** documents show that people were playing stick-and-ball games long before the 1839 date. **1**

---

1. **Anecdotes** (AN ik dohts) are short, entertaining tales.
2. **West Point** in New York is the location of the United States Military Academy. A **cadet** (kuh DET) is a student at the academy.

Practice the Skills

1 Key Reading Skill

Inferring You have to make an inference to understand what the authors are saying in this paragraph. Ask yourself this question: "I wonder, did Abner Doubleday invent baseball?" Look for clues in the paragraph.

874 UNIT 7 What Can We Learn from Our Mistakes?

Additional Support

Differentiated Instruction

Acrostic Puzzle Students may benefit from doing a puzzle to help them think about the topic and write what they know about it. On the board, write the title of the selection vertically. Tell students to do the same on a sheet of paper. Explain that they will complete an acrostic puzzle. Tell students that for each letter in the title, they must write a sentence that begins with that letter and tells something about baseball or another sport. Encourage volunteers to complete the acrostic on the board. **OL**

Albigence Waldo, a surgeon with George Washington's troops at Valley Forge,[3] wrote in his diary that soldiers were "batting balls and running bases" in their free time. Samuel Hopkins Adams (1871–1958), an American historical novelist, stated that his grandfather "played baseball on Mr. Mumford's pasture" in the 1820's.

Although baseball is a uniquely American sport, it was not invented by a single person. Probably the **game** evolved[4] from a variety of stick-and-ball games that were played in Europe, Asia, Africa, and the Americas for centuries and brought to the colonies by the most diverse[5] group of people ever to populate a continent. More specifically, some historians believe baseball is an outgrowth of its first cousin, *rounders,* an English game. Robin Carver wrote in his *Book of Sports* (1834) that "an American version of rounders called *goal ball* was **rivaling** cricket[6] in popularity." **2**

It is generally accepted that by 1845, baseball, as it is recognized today, was becoming popular, especially in New York. In that year a group of baseball enthusiasts organized the New York Knickerbocker Club. They tried to standardize the game by establishing guidelines for "proper play." **3**

The Knickerbockers' rules set the playing field—a diamond-shaped infield with four bases (first, second, third, and home) placed ninety feet apart. At that time, the pitching distance was forty-five feet from home base and the "pitch" was thrown underhanded. The three-strikes-out rule, the three-out inning, and the ways in which a player could be called out were also specified. However, the nine-man team and nine-inning game were not established until later. Over the years, the Knickerbockers' basic rules of play haven't changed much.

---

3. **Valley Forge,** Pennsylvania, was the site of the 1777–1778 winter quarters of George Washington and his Continental Army during the Revolutionary War.
4. Something that has **evolved** (ih VOLVD) has developed slowly.
5. A **diverse** (dih VURS) group is made up of members from different races or backgrounds.
6. **Cricket** (KRIK uht) is an English ball game played by two sides of 11 players each on a field with two wickets, or sets of stumps, set 66 feet apart. The ball is bowled at the wickets, each of which is defended by a batsman.

Vocabulary

rivaling (RY vul ing) *v.* being equal to or matching

Practice the Skills

L1

2 **English Language Coach**

Anglo-Saxon Origins Look up the word **game** in a dictionary. What is the Old English word for *game*?

3 **Key Literary Element**

Sequence of Events/Time Order What date did the writers include in this paragraph? Why? What else happened that year? Record the date and the two events on your chart. **L2**

The Shutout **875**

Teach

L1 Literary Element

Sequence of Events/Time Order **Ask:** In what year was Samuel Hopkins Adams born? *(Adams was born in 1871.)* **BL** **Ask:** Was he already born when his grandfather played baseball in Mr. Mumford's pasture? *(He was not yet born when his grandfather played baseball in the pasture in the 1820s.)* **OL**

L2 Literary Element

Sequence of Events/Time Order **Say:** The selection gives specific dates for some events but only approximate dates for others. Using the footnotes, determine dates when troops might have played baseball at Valley Forge. *(1777–1778)* **Ask:** How many years after the *Book of Sports* appeared was the New York Knickerbocker Club formed? Explain how you found your answer. *(Eleven years later; I counted the years between the dates 1834 and 1845.)* **OL**

English Language Coach

Baseball Terms Have students review terms that describe baseball rules and playing. Encourage students familiar with the terms to act out or draw the terms below. Ask students to compare these responses with explanations found in an encyclopedia or another reference source. **AS**

- infield
- bases
- pitch
- three-strikes-out rule
- inning
- three-out inning

Objectives

- Understand sequence of events: time order
- Activate prior knowledge
- Take and review notes

875

Teach

C Critical Thinking

Comprehension Ask: In what region of the United States did baseball develop? *(It developed in the East.)* **OL**

Ask: Why do you think that the twenty-five clubs formed by the National Association of Base Ball Players were mostly from eastern states? *(Possible response: Limited transportation and communication at the time may have made it difficult for the game to spread to the West and South.)* **AL**

Viewing the Art

Say: This illustration represents an early baseball game, but similarities to a modern baseball game are shown, too. Look at the man wearing a coat and hat and standing near the players at the bottom right. What job does he have in this game? *(Possible response: He is an umpire or possibly a coach.)* **OL**

In 1857–1858, the newly organized National Association of Base Ball Players was formed, and baseball became a business. Twenty-five clubs—mostly from eastern states—formed the Association for the purpose of setting rules and guidelines for club and team competition. The Association defined a professional player as a person who played for money, place, or emolument (profit)." The Association also authorized an admission fee for one of the first "all-star" games between Brooklyn and New York. Fifteen hundred people paid fifty cents to see that game. Baseball was on its way to becoming the nation's number-one sport. **5**

Grand match for the championship at the Elysian Fields, Hoboken, New Jersey. Currier and Ives, 1865

Analyzing the Art Study this picture of a baseball game of the late 1800s. Based on the picture, in what ways was baseball different than it is today? In what ways was it similar to baseball today?

876 UNIT 7   What Can We Learn From Our Mistakes?

Practice the Skills

5 Key Literary Element

Sequence of Events/Time Order What year did baseball become a business? Record this on your chart. What year is the date of one of the earliest mentions of baseball? (Make sure this date is on your chart.)

Additional Support

Reading in the Real World

Citizenship Different civic groups often support sports teams as a way to encourage a community's young people. Instruct students to find out about the civic sports sponsors in their area and the ways in which these groups help provide uniforms and equipment to local teams. If possible, have a representative of a civic organization speak to students about the sports opportunities available to youth in the area. Have the class collect information about community sports in a directory that interested students may use as a reference. **OL**

Monte Irvin, Willie Mays, and Henry Thompson played in the 1951 World Series for the New York Giants. It was the first time in World Series history that a team had an all African American outfield.

By 1860, the same year South Carolina seceded[7] from the Union, there were about sixty teams in the Association. For obvious reasons none of them were from the South. Baseball's development was slow during the Civil War years, but teams continued to compete, and military records show that, sometimes between battles, Union soldiers chose up teams and played baseball games. It was during this time that records began mentioning African-American players. One war journalist noted that black players were "sought after as teammates because of their skill as ball handlers." **6 7**

Information about the role of African Americans in the early stages of baseball development is slight. Several West African cultures had stick-and-ball and running games, so at least some blacks were familiar with the concept of baseball. Baseball, however, was not a popular southern sport, never

---

7. After South Carolina **seceded** (sih SEE dud) from the Union in 1860, ten other states also withdrew and formed the Confederate States of America during the Civil War (1861–1865).

R

L

Practice the Skills

6 Key Literary Element

Sequence of Events/Time Order Record the date 1860 on your chart. What happened in that year? Enter the event in the Event column.

7 Key Reading Skill

Inferring "I wonder why none of the teams were from the South?" What clue do the writers give you to answer this question? (Hint: Would two groups at war with each other play in the same association?)

The Shutout **877**

Teach

R Reading Skill

Inferring Ask: In 1858, the Association included twenty-five baseball clubs, and by 1860, that number had increased to sixty. Given these numbers, what can you infer about the game of baseball? *(Possible response: Baseball was popular, profitable, and well organized.)* **OL Ask:** Why is it "obvious" that the teams in the National Association of Base Ball Players were not from the South? *(Possible response: When the North and South were at war, teams in southern states would not join an organization located in the Union.)* **AL**

L Literary Element

Sequence of Events/Time Order Say: The selection includes information about baseball during the Civil War. Who began playing baseball during these war years? *(Records show that African Americans began playing baseball.)* **OL**

Differentiated Instruction

Mapping Activity Students can trace the development of baseball by marking sites important to the sport on a map. Distribute copies of a world map. Have students mark each site mentioned in the selection. Then tell them to annotate each site with information that explains why that site is important to baseball history. Important sites should include New York, Cooperstown, Valley Forge, and Great Britain. Have students create a classroom display of their maps. **OL**

Objectives
- Monitor comprehension
- Understand sequence of events: time order
- Find meaning in art
- Analyze text

877

Teach

C Critical Thinking

Comprehension Ask: How did the Civil War affect baseball? *(Possible response: During the war, former slaves learned about baseball. After the war, interest in baseball spread to the North and Midwest, but by December 1867, teams with black players could no longer join the Association.)* `OL` `AL`

Viewing the Photo

Ask: How would you describe the expression of the African American batter pictured at the plate? *(Possible response: He looks confident and professional.)* `OL`

---

equal to boxing, wrestling, footracing, or horse racing among the **privileged** landowners.

Slave **owners** preferred these individual sports because they could enter their slaves in competitions, watch the event from a safe distance, pocket the winnings, and personally never raise a sweat. There are documents to show that slave masters made a great deal of money from the athletic skills of their slaves. **8**

Free blacks, on the other hand, played on and against integrated[8] teams in large eastern cities and in small midwestern hamlets.[9] It is believed that some of the emancipated[10] slaves and runaways who served in the Union Army learned how to play baseball from northern blacks and whites who had been playing together for years.

After the Civil War, returning soldiers helped to inspire a new interest in baseball all over the country. Teams sprung up in northern and Midwestern cities, and naturally African Americans were interested in joining some of these clubs. But the National Association of Base Ball Players had other ideas. They voted in December 1867 not to admit any team for membership that "may be **composed** of one or more colored persons." Their reasoning was as irrational[11] as the racism that shaped it: "If colored clubs were admitted,"

Practice the Skills

8 English Language Coach

Anglo-Saxon Origins Look up the word **owner** in a dictionary. What was the Old English word it came from?

A batter for the New York Black Yankees stands at home plate with Newark Eagles' catcher and the umpire waiting for a pitch.

---

8. *Integrated* (IN tuh gray tid) teams were open to both African American and white players.

9. *Hamlets* (HAM luhts) are small villages.

10. *Emancipated* (ih MAN suh pay tid) slaves had been freed from slavery.

11. Reasoning that is *irrational* (ih RASH uh nul) is unreasonable or lacking sense.

Vocabulary

privileged (PRIH vih lijd) *adj.* having or enjoying one or more advantages

composed (kum POHZD) *v.* formed by putting together

Additional Support

Differentiated Instruction

Ideas in Verse Students may benefit from writing a poem or song to help them organize ideas from the selection. Tell students to choose powerful or interesting ideas from the selection. They may also choose to write about a person. Encourage students to use the selected information to write a poem or a song. Students can write music to accompany the poem or song lyrics, or they may choose sounds or styles of music to accompany their verse. Ask volunteers to share their poems and songs with the class. `OL` the Association stated, "there would be in all probability some division of feeling whereas, by excluding them no injury could result to anyone . . . and [we wish] to keep out of the convention the discussion of any subjects having a political bearing as this [admission of blacks on the Association teams] undoubtedly would." **9**

So, from the start, organized baseball tried to limit or exclude African-American participation. In the early days a few black ball players managed to play on integrated minor league teams. A few even made it to the majors, but by the turn of the century, black players were shut out of the major leagues until after World War II. That doesn't mean African Americans didn't play the game. They did. **10**

Black people organized their own teams, formed leagues, and competed for championships. The history of the old "Negro Leagues" and the players who barnstormed[12] on black diamonds is one of baseball's most interesting chapters, but the story is a researcher's nightmare. Black baseball was outside the mainstream of the major leagues, so team and player records weren't well kept, and for the most part, the white press ignored black clubs or portrayed them as clowns. And for a long time the Baseball Hall of Fame didn't recognize any of the Negro League players. Because of the lack of **documentation,** many people thought the Negro Leagues' stories were nothing more than myths and yarns, but that is not the case. The history of the Negro Leagues is a patchwork of human drama and comedy, filled with legendary heroes, infamous owners, triple-headers, low pay, and long bus rides home—not unlike the majors. **11** ○

C

---

12. Players who **barnstormed** (BARN stormd) toured rural areas, stopping briefly to take part in baseball games.

Vocabulary

documentation (dok yuh men TAY shun) *n.* something recorded that serves as proof

---

Practice the Skills

9 | **Key Literary Element**

Sequence of Events/Time Order Two events in this paragraph belong on your chart. The first event does not have an exact date. How will you list it in the Date column?

10 | **Key Literary Element**

Sequence of Events/Time Order After baseball became a business, what year were African American players shut out of the major leagues? Record the event and the year it happened on your chart.

11 | **BIG Question**

Did anyone make a mistake in this selection? What was the mistake? Was the mistake corrected? Did anyone learn from the mistake? Write your answers on your Foldable. Your response will help you complete the Unit Challenge.

BQ

The Shutout **879**

Teach

C Critical Thinking

Comprehension Ask: Why is it difficult to collect information about the old Negro Leagues? *(Possible response: Most sports writers did not write about black players.)* **OL Ask:** What might be a good source of information about African Americans who played baseball before World War II? *(Possible response: Interviews with former players or fans might be a good source of information. Articles that were printed in black newspapers may also provide information.)* **AL**

Say: Organized baseball teams made a mistake by excluding black players. What was the cost of this mistake to organized baseball? *(Possible response: Baseball teams missed out on some talented baseball players.)* **OL**

Assess

✓CheckPoint

Use the CheckPoint questions provided on Presentation Plus! to check for comprehension of the selection. These questions can be used with interactive response keypads for immediate student feedback.

Reading in the Real World

Citizenship On the board, post a large baseball diamond with each of the positions marked. Then challenge the class to research the Negro Leagues and find a player for each of the positions. Encourage students to consult the Baseball Hall of Fame as they look for players. Ask students to find information about the players' teams, the years they played, and any interesting facts about their careers. Tell students to post their findings on the baseball diamond, putting each player's information near the position at which he played. **AS**

Objectives
- Understand sequence of events: time order
- Use text features: photographs
- Monitor comprehension

Assess

Resources for page 880

📁 Selection Quick Check, p. 67

📁 Selection and Unit Assessment, p. 79

💿 ExamView Assessment Suite

💿 Interactive Tutor: Self-Assessment

Students can respond to the *After You Read* items in their Learner's Notebooks or on a separate sheet of paper.

Answering the

1. Possible response: Although progress has been made, it is not clear that Americans have learned all the lessons that their history of racism has to teach.

2. The New York Knickerbocker Club

3. Responses will vary.

Critical Thinking

4. Possible response: Soldiers who returned from the Civil War created enthusiasm for the game.

5. Responses will vary. Students may say that as equally talented players, they would have felt angry and frustrated.

6. Responses will vary. Students may note that sports are segregated by gender and social class.

7. Responses will vary.

880

After You Read   The Shutout

Answering the Big Question

1. After reading this selection, what are your thoughts about learning from mistakes?

2. **Recall** Who created the playing rules for baseball?
   Tip **Right There**

3. **Summarize** What do historians know about the origins of the game of baseball?
   Tip **Think and Search**

Critical Thinking

4. **Infer** In what way did the end of the Civil War help baseball grow in popularity?
   Tip **Author and Me**

5. **Connect** How might you have felt as an African American baseball player who was not allowed to play in the major leagues?
   Tip **On My Own**

6. **Synthesize** Do you think that there is segregation in sports today? Explain.
   Tip **On My Own**

7. **Evaluate** The National Association of Base Ball Players argued that they were keeping African Americans out of the Association so that "no injury could result to anyone." Do you agree with that argument? Explain.
   Tip **On My Own**

Objectives (pp. 880–881)
Reading Make inferences
Literature Identify text structure: sequence, time order
Vocabulary Explore word origins: Anglo-Saxon
Writing Use the RAFT system: respond to literature
Grammar Use correct subject-verb agreement: special nouns

Write About Your Reading

Use the RAFT system to write about "The Shutout."
Role: A Union Army soldier
Audience: Your family
Format: A letter
Topic: The new game you just learned about (baseball)

880 UNIT 7   What Can We Learn from Our Mistakes?

Write About Your Reading

Dear Family:

I've learned a new game while away at war. You probably have never heard about this game called baseball. Well, there are two teams of fifteen men. One team stands in the "field" while the other team takes turns batting. The field consists of a diamond-shape infield with four bases, which are placed ninety feet apart, and an outfield. A man standing in the middle of the diamond pitches the ball to a man, the batter, from the other team. The batter hits the ball and then runs the bases. There are many rules to the game that I hope to teach you all when I return home.

Love,

Your son, Paul

Skills Review

Key Reading Skill: Inferring

8. When the authors write that slave owners could "watch the event from a safe distance, pocket the winnings, and personally never raise a sweat," what are they inferring about slave owners?

Key Literary Element: Sequence of Events/Time Order

Use your chart to answer the following questions.

9. When did Albigence Waldo see a game of "batting balls and running bases"?
10. When did Robin Carver write about *goal ball*?
11. When was the Knickerbocker Club organized?
12. When were African Americans allowed into the major leagues?

Vocabulary Check

Match the following vocabulary words with their definitions.

13. **rivaling**
14. **documentation**
15. **privileged**
16. **composed**

a. formed by putting together
b. having or enjoying one or more advantages
c. being equal to
d. something recorded that serves as proof

17. **English Language Coach** The Anglo-Saxon root and prefix *fore* has two meanings. One is "before" and the other is "in front of."

Look at the words below and define four of them using your knowledge of *fore*.

foretell	forewarn	foresee
foreleg	forehead	forefather
forecast	foremost	foreclose

Grammar Link: Subject-Verb Agreement with Special Nouns

Subject-verb agreement can be a problem when nouns such as *glasses, pants, pliers,* and *scissors* are used as the subject of a sentence.

- Even if they stand for only one item, some words that end in *s* (such as *pants*) are considered plural. Because they are plural, they need plural verbs.

  My **pants are** in the closet.

- It is a different story when *pair of* comes before those same words *(pair of pants)*. The words then take a singular verb. This is because the word *pair* becomes the subject, and *of pants* becomes a prepositional phrase. The word *pair* is singular.

  A **pair of pants is** hanging in the closet.

Watch Out! There are words that don't follow this rule. Even though *news* ends in an *s*, it is a singular noun. The same goes for the word *measles*.

Grammar Practice

On a separate sheet of paper, write the correct verb for each sentence.

18. The scissors (is, are) in the art box.
19. The pliers (is, are) in the drawer.
20. That pair of scissors (need, needs) to be sharpened.
21. The news (is, are) on at ten o'clock.
22. Where (is, are) your glasses?
23. Those pants (is, are) too tight.

Writing Application Look back at the RAFT assignment you wrote. Make sure that all of the subjects and the verbs agree.

Literature Online

Web Activities For eFlashcards, Selection Quick Checks, and other Web activities, go to www.glencoe.com.

The Shutout **881**

Skills Review

Key Reading Skill: Inferring

8. Responses will vary.

Key Literary Element: Sequence of Events/Time Order

9. 1777–1778
10. 1843
11. 1845
12. after World War II

Vocabulary Check

13. c
14. d
15. b
16. a
17. **English Language Coach**
    forecast: to predict the future (before)
    forewarn: to warn in advance (before)
    forehead: the front of the head (front)
    forefather: ancestor, or a person of an earlier period (before)

Grammar Link: Subject-Verb Agreement with Special Nouns

Grammar Practice

18. are
19. are
20. needs
21. is
22. are
23. are

Close

Ask students to think of examples from history in which people were excluded because of race, gender, religion, or disability. Ask students to think about how and what people have learned from those examples.

Teach

More About the Author

As a child, Donna L. Washington and her siblings listened as their father told stories at the dinner table. Now Washington writes and performs her own stories and has adapted folktales for stage production.

Vocabulary

Connotations Ask: When are people *smart* and when are they *intellectual?* Do you ever see *commotion* at a party, or do you see only *festivity?* Think about the connotations that are associated with the vocabulary words. List the vocabulary words and as many synonyms as you can find for each one. Next to the vocabulary words and synonyms, jot down notes that describe the words' connotations, such as "formal," "informal," "positive," or "negative."*(Responses will vary.)* **AS**

Before You Read : The Talking Skull

Donna L. Washington

Meet the Author
Donna L. Washington is a writer, storyteller, and actress. "The Talking Skull" is from Washington's book *A Pride of African Tales.*

Literature Online

Author Search For more about Donna L. Washington, go to www.glencoe.com.

Objectives (pp. 882–891)
Reading Make inferences • Make connections from text to self
Literature Identify text structure: sequence, time order
Vocabulary Explore word origins: Anglo-Saxon • Identify compound words

Vocabulary Preview

stammer (STAM mur) *v.* to speak with difficulty; to repeat the same sound several times when trying to say a word **(p. 886)** *Eventually, the man was able to stammer some words.*

spout (spowt) *v.* to speak rapidly; to say something in a loud, boastful manner **(p. 886)** *The man was amazed that the skull was able to spout words of wisdom.*

commotion (kuh MOH shun) *n.* noisy rushing about; confusion **(p. 889)** *There was so much commotion, the chief came to see what was going on.*

intellectual (in tuh LEK choo ul) *adj.* requiring thought and understanding **(p. 890)** *The scholar was sure the chief would understand an intellectual matter.*

Write to Learn Be creative. Write one or two paragraphs about a strange walk in the woods. Use as many vocabulary words as you can.

English Language Coach

Anglo-Saxon Origins and Compound Words Many basic English words come from Anglo-Saxon, or Old English. These basic words can often be combined to form compound words. A compound word combines two words. The meaning of a compound word combines the meanings of the individual words in some way.

Here are some compounds formed from words with Anglo-Saxon origins.

Compound Word	Definition
homemade	made in the home
rowboat	a small boat designed to be rowed
horseshoe	iron put on a horse's hoof to protect it

Write to Learn How many compound words can you create by combining the words below? What are their definitions?

day	night	time	play
home	one	every	some
body	to	thing	no

Additional Support

Literature Online

Author Resources To expand students' appreciation of Donna L. Washington, have them access the Web site for additional information and resources.

Literature Focus Lesson

Fable A fable is a short, simple tale that teaches a moral, or a universal truth—one that is known everywhere. The author adapted this fable from a story that is told in Cameroon, a country near the equator in western Africa. Challenge students to find fables or moral tales from countries around the world. Some possibilities include Aesop's fables, the Jatakas, or ancient Indian folktales, and the French tales of Jean de La Fontaine. Have students compile their findings in a resource pamphlet entitled "Fables of the World." **OL**

Skills Preview

Key Reading Skill: Inferring

Because they are not stated directly in the text, inferences can be easy to miss. Fiction writers can ask you to infer a lot more than nonfiction writers.

Use these tips to help you infer as you read:

- Monitor your comprehension. Stop when you get confused.
- Ask yourself "I wonder" questions.
- Look for clues in the text.
- Hint: Writers sometimes use punctuation, style, or word choice to give you clues about what they are inferring.
- Use your own experience and knowledge to help you figure out what the writer isn't saying directly.

Write to Learn In your Learner's Notebook, make a list of points to remember so that you can infer as you read.

Key Literary Element: Sequence of Events/Time Order

In fiction, the sequence of events is the plot, or action, of the story. In the plot, a problem is explored and then usually solved. The sequence of events can move the plot forward in two ways: by relating to past or present action or by suggesting future action.

As you read, ask yourself the following questions about each event in the plot:

- What does this event tell me about past action?
- What does this event tell me about present action?
- What does this event tell me about future action?

Write to Learn In your Learner's Notebook, write each important event in the story's plot. For each entry, write whether the event relates to a past action, a present action, or a future action.

Get Ready to Read

Connect to the Reading

Has someone you know ever made the same mistake over and over? What was the mistake? Why did the person continue to make it? Why didn't the person learn his or her lesson after making the mistake the first or second time? What finally helped the person not to make the mistake again?

Partner Talk With a partner, discuss your answers to the questions above.

Build Background

This fable is from Cameroon, a country in western Africa. Here are some facts about the people of Cameroon:

- Most of the people live in small towns or villages.
- Most of the people are farmers of cacao, coffee, tobacco, cotton, or bananas. Others are herders of cattle, goats, sheep, or pigs.
- The people belong to more than 200 ethnic groups. Each group speaks its own language.

Set Purposes for Reading

BIG Question Read the selection "The Talking Skull" to find out about learning from mistakes.

Set Your Own Purpose What else would you like to learn from the article to help you answer the Big Question? Write your own purpose on "The Talking Skull" part of the Workshop 4 Foldable.

Interactive Literary Elements Handbook
To review or learn more about the literary elements, go to www.glencoe.com.

Keep Moving

Use these skills as you read the following selection.

The Talking Skull **883**

Teach

R Reading Skill

L Literary Element

English Language Coach

Anglo-Saxon Roots Words with Anglo-Saxon roots are often shorter than synonyms with roots in other languages, such as Latin or French. For example, the word *ask* has an Anglo-Saxon root. Its longer synonym, *interrogate*, comes from Latin, and its synonym *question* has a French root. Have students look at the words below which have Anglo-Saxon roots. Then tell students to use a dictionary to compare these words and their roots with their French- and Latin-based synonyms. **EL**

- fear *(terror; horror)*
- holy *(sacred; pious)*
- rise *(mount; ascend)*

Objectives

- Learn and use new vocabulary
- Take and review notes
- Understand sequence of events: time order
- Understand word structure: Anglo-Saxon roots

Teach

R Reading Skill

Review Activating Prior Knowledge Ask: What fables have you read? *(Responses will vary.)* **BL Say:** Fables often contain characters that are animals or unusual creatures. What might you expect to happen in a tale about a talking skull? *(Possible response: Because a skull cannot really talk, the fable will probably describe magical events.)* **OL**

C Critical Thinking

Analysis Ask: What are some "ordinary problems" that you deal with each day? *(Possible responses: solving homework problems, writing essays, dealing with bullies, understanding new lessons in class)* **OL**
Ask: How would you describe a person who couldn't be bothered with "ordinary problems"? *(Possible response: That person isn't very practical. Such a person may have too high an opinion of himself or herself.)* **AL**

Readability Scores
Dale-Chall: 4.8
DRP: 50
Lexile: 700

The Talking Skull

A Fable from Cameroon from *A Pride of African Tales*

by Donna L. Washington

R "The Talking Skull" is an African fable about the importance of listening and thinking before opening one's mouth.

Once a man was walking down the road toward his village. He was not paying attention to anything around him. This man considered himself a scholar[1] of life. He was always deep in thought. He liked to think about important things. He did not put his mind to ordinary problems. If it wasn't impossible, or at least very complicated, he didn't care about it at all.

This man spent all day looking out over the ocean, and he only noticed things he thought were useful. He didn't notice the beauty of the ocean. The only things he considered were sharks and **shipwrecks**. **1** He didn't notice the clear blue sky. He was

---

1. A *scholar* is a person who has knowledge in a certain area.

Practice the Skills

1 English Language Coach

Anglo-Saxon Origins and Compound Words What two basic words make up the compound word **shipwrecks**? What are *shipwrecks*?

Additional Support

English Language Coach

Building Background The country of Cameroon is culturally and linguistically diverse. It is home to more than two-hundred ethnic groups. Native languages from three language families are spoken in Cameroon. Bantu speakers live in the southern part of the country, Sudanic-speaking peoples live in the north, and people speaking Semi-Bantu languages live in the west. In addition, Europeans brought German, English, and French to Cameroon during the country's colonial periods. If possible, provide students with images that illustrate some of the many cultures of Cameroon's people. **AS**

The Talking Skull **885**

Teach

Viewing the Illustration

Ask: What does this illustration show? *(a man with a walking stick in a forest)* **EL BL Ask:** What information does this illustration provide about the story? *(Possible response: It seems to illustrate the main character of the story as he walks, deep in thought, toward his village.)* **OL**

Differentiated Instruction

Character Interaction Help students create the graphic organizer here, and tell them to chart the interactions that the man has with different people in the village. After students have completed the graphic organizer, ask them to compare the main character's intended goal with the final outcome. **OL**

```
┌──────────────────────┐   ┌──────────────────────┐
│ Main character's goals│   │ Villagers' goals:    │
│ ─────────────────────│   │ ─────────────────────│
└──────────┬───────────┘   └──────────┬───────────┘
           ▼                          ▼
┌──────────────────────────────────────────────────┐
│ Action          Interaction         Reaction      │
│ ─────────   ─────────────────▶   ─────────        │
│ Action                              Reaction      │
│ ─────────   ◀─────────────────   ─────────        │
└──────────┬───────────────────────────┬───────────┘
           ▼                           ▼
┌──────────────────┐        ┌──────────────────┐
│ Outcome: _____│        │ Outcome: _____│
└──────────────────┘        └──────────────────┘
```

Objectives

• Activate prior knowledge
• Analyze text
• Use text features: illustrations

885

Teach

L Literary Element

Sequence of Events/Time Order **Say:** The man in the story finds a talking skull. What do the skull's words tell you about what happened to him? *(Possible response: Talking created problems for him and may have caused his death.)* **OL**

Ask: What might the skull's words tell you about future events in the story? *(Possible response: Some form of magic is at work here. The man in the story may suffer a fate like that of the dead person he finds, or some other misfortune may strike him.)* **AL**

C Critical Thinking

Comprehension **Ask:** Why are people alarmed when the man enters the village? *(Possible response: The villagers fear being trapped in a pointless conversation with him.)* **AS**

---

thinking about all the storms that must have been churning far away. He did not notice the wonderful songs of the birds. He only thought about how many of their nests had been robbed. He didn't notice the playful animals swinging through branches or rustling in the grass. He only wondered whether or not the great cats were on the prowl. That was the kind of man he was. **2**

As he walked back toward the village that day, he happened to pass a pile of bones. They were bleached white and they gleamed in the bright sun. He stopped and stared down at them. He was the sort of man who would stop to stare down at a pile of bones. The skull on the pile was resting above all the other bones, and it seemed to be watching the man just as intently as he was watching it. **3**

The man reached out and picked up the skull. He held it one way and then another. He looked gravely into the empty eye sockets and said, "What brought you here, brother?"

"Talking," the skull replied without much interest.

The man was so shocked, he dropped the skull and jumped back. He watched the skull for a few minutes before he managed to **stammer** out, "You can talk!"

"Yes," said the skull. "Talking is very easy. All you have to do is open up your mouth and out it comes. Talking is easy. Finding something worthwhile to say is not."

The man was amazed. He had never seen a talking skull before, let alone one that could **spout** such wisdom. "I must take you to the village!" the man exclaimed.

He scooped up the skull and ran as fast as he could. The villagers saw him coming, and a great many of them ran for their homes. You see, he was the kind of man who was always getting busy people into useless conversations when there was work to be done. He never seemed to be quiet, and he never spoke about anything anyone ever wanted to hear.

Vocabulary

stammer (STAM mur) *v.* to speak with difficulty; to repeat the same sound several times when trying to say a word

spout (spowt) *v.* to speak rapidly; to say something in a loud, boastful manner

Practice the Skills

2 **Key Reading Skill**

Inferring What is the author inferring about the man?

3 **Key Literary Element**

Sequence of Events/Time Order What events have taken place so far in the plot? Has anything in the story so far told you about past action? **L**

Additional Support

English Language Coach

Compounds with Anglo-Saxon Roots Point out the word *something* on page 886. Tell students that *some*, which means "an unknown unit or amount," comes from the Anglo-Saxon word *sum*. Then explain that *something* means "a thing whose identity is uncertain or unknown." Help students find definitions

for each of the following compound words that have the root *some*. **AS**

1. Someone *(a person of uncertain or unknown identity)*

2. Somehow *(in a way that is uncertain or unknown)*

3. Sometime *(at an unknown point in time)*

The Talking Skull **887**

Teach

Viewing the Illustration

Ask: How do illustrations help you understand a story? *(Possible response: If there is an illustration of a character, I can focus on that person and what he or she is doing. Illustrations make it easier to visualize actions.)* **BL Say:** Look at the expression on the man's face. What does his expression tell you about what he is doing? Does this illustration show the man before or after the skull speaks to him? Explain. *(Possible response: He is studying the skull closely. This must be happening before the skull speaks because the man looks calm and curious. After the skull speaks, the man is shocked and startled.)* **OL**

Differentiated Instruction

Chat Room Conversation Remind students that the man in the story has a reputation for being a talker. People run from him because they don't want to get trapped in a useless conversation. Tell students to imagine that the man in this story finds people to talk to in an Internet chat room. Encourage students to think about what the man might say about what he has found and what others might say to him. Put students in pairs, and have each pair write a conversation that the man might have while visiting a chat room. Ask volunteers to share their work. **OL**

Objectives
• Understand word structure: Anglo-Saxon roots
• Use text features: illustration
• Monitor comprehension
• Understand sequence of events: time order

887

C Critical Thinking

Comprehension Ask: How do the villagers react when the man says that he has "a marvelous mystery"? *(Possible response: Some of them suddenly seem interested and stop what they are doing.)* **AS**

L Literary Element

Sequence of Events/Time Order Say: Several events have happened so far in this story. Record the following events in your Learner's Notebooks, and place them in the order in which they happen.

- The man sees a pile of bones. *(2)*
- The man walks down a road, thinking about things, such as storms at sea. *(1)*
- The villagers run from the man. *(6)*
- The man picks up a skull. *(3)*
- The man tells the villagers that he has a mystery. *(7)*
- The skull talks to the man. *(4)*
- The man takes the skull to the village. *(5)* **OL**

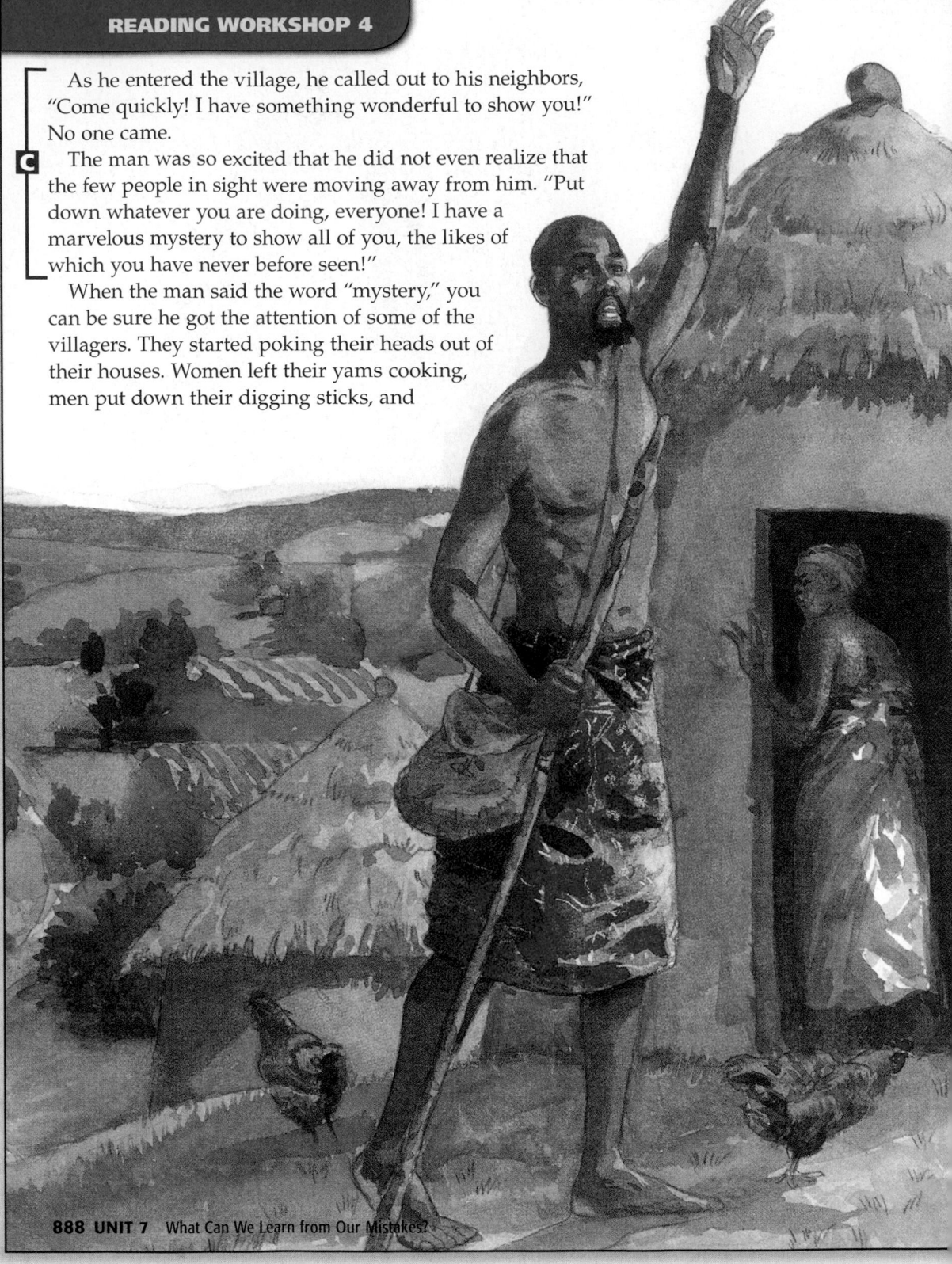

As he entered the village, he called out to his neighbors, "Come quickly! I have something wonderful to show you!" No one came.

C The man was so excited that he did not even realize that the few people in sight were moving away from him. "Put down whatever you are doing, everyone! I have a marvelous mystery to show all of you, the likes of which you have never before seen!"

When the man said the word "mystery," you can be sure he got the attention of some of the villagers. They started poking their heads out of their houses. Women left their yams cooking, men put down their digging sticks, and

888 UNIT 7 What Can We Learn from Our Mistakes?

Additional Support

English Language Coach

Anglo-Saxon Roots The word *talk* comes from an Old English word that means "to tell or relate." Have students look up the roots of the following synonyms for *talk*, and ask them to identify the language from which each synonym developed. Challenge students to compare the connotations of the different synonyms and form generalizations about the different languages. **BL OL**

- speak (Old English)
- converse (Latin)
- discuss (Latin)
- utter (middle low German)
- voice (Latin)

children stopped their playing. They all began to gather around the man. **4**

When he saw that he had everyone's attention, he drew out the skull. He could not have prepared himself for what happened next.

Everyone stared at the skull for a moment. Then they all started yelling.

"Mama! What is he doing?" cried a little boy.

"How dare you bring that thing here!" his mother howled, waving a spoon.

"Somebody do something!" said another, clutching her child.

"Send him away!" demanded a third mother.

The men who still had gardening tools in their hands started waving them.

"Move out of the way!" yelled a man with a digging stick.

"Somebody get the chief!" said an old man holding his grandson's hand. **5**

There was so much **commotion**, the chief came to see what was happening.

"What is going on?" the chief roared. He was a very orderly chief, and he did not like all this yelling and brandishing² of gardening tools in the middle of the village.

---

2. *Brandishing* something means waving or shaking it in a challenging way.

Vocabulary

commotion (kuh MOH shun) *n.* noisy rushing about; confusion

Practice the Skills

4 **Key Reading Skill**

Inferring What is the author inferring when she says that the word *mystery* got some people's attention?

5 **Key Literar Element**

Sequence of Events/Time Order A new event has taken place in the plot. What is it? Has this event happened in time order? What does this event tell you about present action?

The Talking Skull **889**

Teach

C Critical Thinking

Comprehension Ask: What causes the commotion in the village? *(Possible response: The villagers become very upset when the man reveals the skull.)* **OL**

R Reading Skill

Inferring Say: Judging from the reaction of the villagers, what can you infer about their culture's attitude toward the presence of a skull? *(Possible response: The villagers seem very upset. A skull must have a negative meaning in their culture.)* **OL**

Reading in the Real World

Citizenship In the fable, the village chief comes to settle a dispute. Ask students to find out how disputes are settled in their own community. Students may write letters to the mayor, city manager, or another official, asking how the community settles disputes between neighbors or local businesses. You may wish to lead a discussion about whether or not the same procedures could be applied in the classroom. If possible, have a town official visit the class and explain the town's policy for resolving problems, such as preventing conflict when a person complains about a noisy neighbor or wants to cut down a tree on a property line. **OL**

Objectives
- Take and review notes
- Analyze text
- Monitor comprehension
- Understand sequence of events: time order
- Understand word structure: Anglo-Saxon roots

889

Teach

R Reading Skill

Inferring **Ask:** What do the people of the village infer when the man takes out the skull? *(Possible response: They think he is trying to call the Dark Spirits of the village.)* **OL**

C Critical Thinking

Analysis **Ask:** Why do you think the villagers and the chief are angry? *(Possible response: They may think that the man is making fun of them by showing them the skull. They may believe that he is wasting their time.)* **OL** **Ask:** Do you think the skull is not talking because it can't or because it is choosing not to talk? Explain. *(Possible response: The text says that "the skull remained silent" and that it "said nothing." I think these words suggest that the skull is not talking for a particular reason.)* **AS**

All the people were silent except for one villager. He stood up and pointed to the man with the skull.

R "This man told us he had something to show us. Then he pulled out that awful skull. We thought he was trying to call the Dark Spirits to the village, and we were trying to stop him."

"Oh," said the chief, eyeing the man with the skull. "And were you going to call Dark Spirits to my village?"

"Certainly not!" the scholar declared, glad that the chief was there. He was sure the chief would understand this **intellectual** matter.

"Then what were you doing?" the chief asked with curiosity.

"Well," the man said in a pompous[3] voice, "I was on my way home from the ocean when I came across a pile of bones. On top of the heap was this skull. It spoke to me! I brought it here to share this wonder with the village." **6**

The chief did not look convinced.

C "I'll show you," the man said, raising the skull so that it looked at the chief. "Say something to the chief," he commanded.

The skull said nothing. The chief frowned.

"Speak!" the man said. "I command you!"

The skull remained silent. One of the children laughed.

"Speak!" he said. "You must speak!" The man started getting nervous.

The skull said nothing. The man begged and pleaded with the skull. The skull remained silent. The people began to get angry again, and the chief got angry right along with them.

"You are always a troublemaker in my village, and now you come here with this nonsense!" The chief and the people had had enough. They took the skull from the man, found the mound of bones he had taken it from, and put it back there.

That very day the villagers held a meeting with the chief and decided to throw the man out of their village. They watched him collect his few belongings and said to him, "Since you found that skull so much company, why don't you go live with it!" **7**

---

3. A **pompous** voice is one that sounds self-important.

Vocabulary

intellectual (in tuh LEK choo ul) *adj.* requiring thought and understanding

890 UNIT 7 What Can We Learn from Our Mistakes?

Practice the Skills

6 Reviewing Skills

Evaluating The man says that he has brought the skull to the village because he wants to share it. Do you believe him? Explain.

7 Key Literary Element

Sequence of Events/Time Order A new event has taken place in the plot. What is it? Has this event happened in time order? What does the event tell you about future action?

Additional Support

English Language Coach

Suffixes: -ous Draw students' attention to the -ous ending in the word *pompous.* Tell them that the -ous ending is used to form adjectives meaning "full of." The word *pomp* means "an overly fancy or showy display." When -ous is added to *pomp*, the resulting adjective, *pompous*, means "full of an overly fancy or showy display." Have students form adjectives from these nouns by applying the -ous ending. **EL**

- curiosity (*curious*)
- virtue (*virtuous*)
- wonder (*wondrous*)
- joy (*joyous*)
- fury (*furious*)

The man stormed out of the village and down the road to the pile of bones. He picked up the skull. Before he could get one word out of his mouth, the skull said, "Sorry about that."

"What? Now you talk! That is not going to do me much good! Why didn't you say something back in the village?"

"I told you," the skull replied. "It is easy to talk. It is not always easy to find something **worthwhile** to say." **8**

"You are absolutely unpleasant!" the man screamed. "I don't know what trouble you caused that brought you to this sorry state, but you deserve everything you got!"

"I already told you what got me into trouble," the skull replied. "Talking. Same as you." **9** ○

Practice the Skills

8 **English Language Coach**

Anglo-Saxon Origins and Compound Words What are the origins and meanings of the words *worth* and *while*? What does **worthwhile** mean?

9 **BIG Question**

What mistake do you think the skull made in the past? What lesson is he trying to teach the man? Record your response on your Foldable. Your response will help you complete the Unit Challenge later. **BQ**

The Talking Skull **891**

Teach

EL English Language Coach

Anglo-Saxon Roots This is the second time the skull has mentioned finding "something *worthwhile* to say." The compound word *worthwhile* is made up of two Anglo-Saxon roots or base words. What are the origins and meanings of *worth* and *while*? What does *worthwhile* mean? *(Possible response: worth means "value," and while means "a period of time." So, the word," worthwhile" means being worth the time.)*

BQ BIG Question

Say: U.S. President Abraham Lincoln once said that it is "better to remain silent and be thought a fool than to speak out and remove all doubt." How does this quotation relate to the main character's mistake? *(Possible response: The speaker could have kept the information about the skull to himself. Instead, he talked too much and got himself into trouble by alarming the villagers.)* **OL AL**

Differentiated Instruction

Using a Graphic Organizer Tell students that many of the characters in fables are animals or unusual figures. Have students use the evidence found in the story to analyze the character of the skull. Tell them to examine the character by filling out this chart and drawing conclusions about their findings. **OL**

Evaluating the Skull	
When does the skull talk?	
What does the skull talk about?	
When does the skull not talk?	
What does the skull think of the main character?	

Objectives
• Make connections from text to self
• Analyze text
• Take and review notes

891

Assess

Resources for page 892

- Selection Quick Check, p. 68
- Selection and Unit Assessment, p. 80
- ExamView Assessment Suite
- Interactive Tutor: Self-Assessment

Students can respond to the *After You Read* items in their Learner's Notebooks or on a separate sheet of paper.

Answering the BIG Question

1. Responses will vary. Students may say that repeating a mistake leads to more and more severe consequences.

2. The villagers panic because they think that the man is trying to call Dark Spirits to the village.

3. The skull does not talk for the villagers.

Critical Thinking

4. Responses will vary.

5. Responses will vary.

6. Responses will vary. Students may agree with the skull, saying that most of what people say is not especially important.

After You Read   The Talking Skull

Answering the BIG Question

1. After reading this fable, what are your thoughts about learning from your mistakes?

2. **Recall** Why do the villagers panic when they see the skull?
   TIP Right There

3. **Recall** What does the skull do when the man asks it to speak to the villagers?
   TIP Right There

Critical Thinking

4. **Evaluate** Do you think the chief is a good leader? Explain.
   TIP Author and Me

5. **Predict** What do you think will happen to the man now? Explain.
   TIP On Your Own

6. **Connect** Do you agree with the skull's opinion that talking is easy but finding something worthwhile to say is not? Explain.
   TIP On Your Own

Write About Your Reading

Use the RAFT system to write about "The Talking Skull."
Role: The talking skull
Audience: The main character
Format: A letter
Topic: Your story of how you made your mistake and what happened after you made it

Objectives (pp. 892–893)
Reading Make inferences • Make connections from text to self
Literature Identify text structure: sequence, time order
Vocabulary Explore word origins: Anglo-Saxon • Identify compound words
Writing Use the RAFT system: respond to literature
Grammar Use correct subject-verb agreement: indefinite pronouns

892 UNIT 7 What Can We Learn from Our Mistakes?

Write About Your Reading
Possible response:
Dear Man,

Like you, I tried to engage the people of my village in useless conversation. I did no work; I only talked.
One day, while I was out wandering in the woods, the villagers decided to move. When I returned the next day, everyone and everything was gone. Because I never did any work, I had no survival skills; I starved and died in the place where you found my bones.

Sincerely, The Talking Skull

Skills Review

Key Reading Skill: Inferring

7. How do you think the man feels about himself? What clues in the text help you answer this question?

8. Did the skull learn from its mistake? Explain.

Key Literary Element: Sequence of Events/Time Order

Use your notes from your reading to answer the following questions.

9. What was one event in the plot that told you about past action?

10. What was one event in the plot that told you about present action?

11. What was one event in the plot that told you about future action?

Vocabulary Check

Match each vocabulary word with its definition.

12. spout   **a.** to speak with difficulty

13. intellectual   **b.** to say something in a loud, boastful manner

14. stammer   **c.** noisy rushing about; confusion

15. commotion   **d.** requiring thought

16. English Language Coach Use the words *ship, wreck, wind, break, worth, while,* or compound words that contain them as you write a diary entry about a trip to the beach in winter.

Web Activities For eFlashcards, Selection Quick Checks, and other Web activities, go to www.glencoe.com.

Grammar Link: Subject-Verb Agreement with Indefinite Pronouns

An indefinite pronoun is a pronoun that does not stand for a particular person, place, or thing. The chart shows which indefinite subject pronouns use singular verbs, which use plural verbs, and which use singular or plural verbs, depending on the words to which they refer.

Indefinite Pronouns – Singular Verbs
another, anybody, anyone, anything, each, either, everybody, everyone, everything, much, neither, nobody, no one, nothing, one, somebody, someone, something
Examples
<u>Another</u> bus was coming.   <u>Anybody</u> is welcome here. <u>Either</u> hat will be warm.   <u>Everyone</u> was invited.

Indefinite Pronouns – Plural Verbs
both, few, many, others, several
Examples
<u>Many</u> are asked to dance.   <u>Few</u> were chosen to sing.

Indefinite Pronouns – Singular or Plural Verbs
all, any, enough, most, some, none
Tip: When you can count the thing to which a pronoun refers, the pronoun uses a plural verb. Otherwise it uses a singluar verb.
Examples
<u>All</u> of the ants <u>were</u> here.   <u>All</u> of the pie <u>was</u> here. <u>Some</u> of the pens <u>are</u> red.   <u>Some</u> of the water <u>is</u> red.

Grammar Practice

Complete the following sentences with the correct verb.

17. Someone (need, needs) to wash the clothes.

18. Several (come, comes) to the show every day.

19. All of the sky (is, are) blue.

Writing Application Look back at the RAFT assignment you wrote. Make sure that all of the subjects and the verbs agree. Pay close attention to subject-verb agreement with indefinite pronouns.

Skills Review

Key Reading Skill: Inferring

7. Responses will vary.

8. Responses will vary.

Key Literary Element: Sequence of Events/Time Order

9. Responses will vary.

10. Responses will vary.

11. Responses will vary.

Vocabulary Check

12. b

13. d

14. a

15. c

16. English Language Coach Paragraphs will vary. Students should use words correctly in their diary entries.

Grammar Link: Subject-Verb Agreement with Indefinite Pronouns

Grammar Practice

17. Someone <u>needs</u> to wash the clothes.

18. Several <u>come</u> to the show every day.

19. All of the sky <u>is</u> blue.

Close

Ask students to think about times when they have made the same mistake more than once. Ask them to suggest what needs to happen for people to learn from their mistakes and avoid repeating them.

Author's Credibility

How to Help Students Read for Author's Credibility

Why Is It Important?
- Students need to be able to differentiate between credible statements and information and questionable information.
- Knowing when an author is credible will help students choose helpful sources when creating their own documents.

How to Help Students Get It
- Have students look for author's bias.
- Have students look at the writer's sources—those cited and implied.
- Have students think about the author's background and why this writer would be writing about the particular subject.

Reading to Answer the Big Question

The Great Fire by Jim Murphy
This historical account of the Great Fire that burned through the city of Chicago in 1871 shows that devastation of the city was due in part to mistakes on the part of city officials and firefighters. Detailed anecdotes demonstrate how many individuals made what proved to be disastrous errors in judgment.

Letters About the Fire (Primary Document)
Actual letters written by two children describe their families' struggles to survive the Great Chicago Fire. The letters retain their original spelling and grammar. Students will perceive the disaster from a child's point of view.

Objectives covered in this workshop:
- Find similarities and differences across texts
- Compare and contrast authors' credibility across texts

Workshop Resources

PACING (DAYS) STANDARD	BLOCK	LESSON	STUDENT MATERIALS	TEACHER RESOURCES
1	1	Key Skill Lesson: Reading for Author's Credibility	📖 English Language Coach Review, p. 42	✦ Bellringer Options Transparencies –Daily Language Practice 69 ✦ Read Aloud, Think Aloud Transparencies –Read Aloud, Think Aloud 55–66 💿 Presentation Plus!
1	1	"The Great Fire"	💻 Glencoe Online 📖 Unit Vocabulary Review, p. 40 📖 Academic Vocabulary Review, p. 43 📁 English Language Coach 📖 Reading Across Texts Graphic Organizer, p. 35 💿 StudentWorks Plus™ 💻 Online Student Edition 💿 Literature Classics	💻 Puzzlemaker 💿 Skill Level Up!™ A Language Arts Game 💻 BookLink 3 📘 Assessment by Learning Objective (Diagnostic and Formative) 💿 Interactive Tutor: Self-Assessment 💿 TeacherWorks Plus™ 💿 ExamView Assessment Suite
1		"Letters About the Fire"	💻 Glencoe Online 📖 Unit Vocabulary Review, p. 40 📖 Academic Vocabulary Review, p. 43 📁 English Language Coach 📖 Reading Across Texts Graphic Organizer, p. 35 💿 StudentWorks Plus™ 💻 Online Student Edition 💿 Literature Classics	💻 Puzzlemaker 💿 Skill Level Up!™ A Language Arts Game 💻 BookLink 3 📘 Assessment by Learning Objective (Diagnostic and Formative) 💿 Interactive Tutor: Self-Assessment 💿 TeacherWorks Plus™ 💿 ExamView Assessment Suite

Keys for Unit Resource

📁 Blackline Master 　　🔒 DVD

📘 Workbook 　　✦ Transparency

📖 Supplemental Text 　　💻 Web-based

💿 CD-ROM 　　📖 Fast File

Level Appropriate Code

AS = Activities for all students

AL = Activities for students working above grade level

OL = Activities for students working at grade level

BL = Activities for students working below grade level

EL = Activities for English language learners

Focus

 Daily Language Practice Transparency 69
Focus Activity Say:
Suppose that two people witnessed the same event. Why might their accounts of that event be different? *(Responses will vary. Some students may say that no two people view an event in the same way. Others may say that memories fade with the passage of time.)* **OL**

Teach

L **Literary Element**

Author's Credibility Say:
Suppose you are going to read an account of tryouts for the school band. Name several people who would be credible authors for such an account. *(Possible responses: the band teacher; students who auditioned for the band)* **Say:** Name a person who would *not* be a credible author for such an account. *(Possible response: a student or parent who heard about the tryouts from someone else)* **AS**

READING ACROSS TEXTS WORKSHOP

from **The Great Fire**
by Jim Murphy

&

Letters About the Fire
by Justin and Fannie Belle Becker

Skills Focus

You will use these skills as you read and compare the following selections:
• from *The Great Fire,* p. 897
• "Letters About the Fire," p. 905

Reading

• Making connections across texts
• Comparing/contrasting information in different texts

Literature

• Reading and understanding informative text
• Evaluating author's credibility

Objectives (pp. 894–895)
Reading Compare and contrast: author's credibility across texts

894 UNIT 7

Do you believe everything you hear? Probably not. If two people tell you about something, their stories will hardly ever be exactly the same. You use your intelligence and experience to figure out who and what you want to believe. When you figure out who to believe and how much to believe, you're evaluating the speaker's **credibility.**

How to Read Across Texts: Author's Credibility

Credibility is believability. If you think that someone knows a topic well and you don't think he or she is lying, you consider him or her to be *credible.* If you don't think that person is biased, or influenced by someone or something, you **L** think he or she is *credible.* You believe the speaker or writer.

You evaluate speakers' and writers' credibility everyday. When you read or hear something, you should think about
• who said or wrote it
• whether they know about the topic
• why they said or wrote what they did
• whether you believe it

Additional Support

Literature Focus Lesson

Evaluating Author Credibility Tell students that evaluating an author's credibility is an important part of using the Internet to conduct research. Reputable Web sites typically have credible authors who check the validity of facts. However, Web sites created by individuals should be checked for accuracy and credibility. When students use a Web site, they should determine whether the author is an expert in his or her field, whether he or she has an underlying motive, and how recently he or she has posted the available information. **AS**

Get Ready to Compare

When you want to learn about something, it's a good idea to get different points of view on the subject. You can do that by asking different people, or by reading articles, stories, and letters by different people. Then you decide which information and which people are most credible.

When you're reading about an event, ask yourself questions like these to determine which information is credible:

- **Knowledge** Does the author seem to know a lot about the event or one small part of the event?
- **Firsthand Experience** Did the author experience the event himself or herself (firsthand experience), or did the author get information from reading or speaking to other people?
- **Time** How long after the event did the author write the article or letter?
- **Details** Does the author give you many details? Are the details believable?
- **Purpose and Bias** What is the author's purpose for writing? Does the author seem to be trying to get you to believe his or her opinion? Does the author seem to be biased toward one opinion?
- **Fact and Opinion** Does the author present facts, opinions, or a combination of both?

Use Your Comparison

The three selections in this workshop are about the Great Chicago Fire. To help you evaluate the credibility of the authors and information in these selections, create a chart like the one pictured below in your Learner's Notebook. As you read, use the questions listed above to help you fill in this chart. You'll use the notes you enter in this chart to compare the selections later.

	from *The Great Fire*	Letter–Justin	Letter–Fannie Belle Becker
Knowledge			
Firsthand Experience			
Time			
Details			
Purpose and Bias			
Fact and Opinion			

Reading Across Texts Workshop **895**

Teach

L Literary Element

Review Author's Purpose
Say: Some authors may skew, misrepresent, or withhold facts in an effort to persuade audiences to adopt a particular point of view. In what kind of writing would an author try to persuade an audience this way? *(Possible response: an advertisement; an editorial)* **OL**

Assess/Close

Have students identify other examples of how an author's purpose may cause him or her to misrepresent facts. Have students share their examples with the class.

Resources for page 895

Use the Reading Across Texts Graphic Organizer BLM in the Unit 7 Resource Booklet, p. 35.

Reading in the Real World

Career Tell students that the skewing, misrepresenting, and withholding of facts occurs frequently in the field of advertising. For example, an Internet provider may advertise that it provides high-speed Internet access for only $15 per month. However, the advertiser may not mention that this rate is available only if consumers sign up for a one-year plan or that users will be charged an additional set-up fee. Ask students to bring in examples of advertisements that skew or misrepresent facts. For each example, have students identify the advertiser's credibility, the advertiser's purpose or bias, and the facts that are skewed or misrepresented. **AS**

Objectives
- Identify author's purpose
- Evaluate author's credibility

Teach

More About the Author

Jim Murphy has always had a vivid imagination. Growing up in New Jersey, Murphy and his friends loved to create adventures, pretending to be explorers on a jungle river or soldiers checking for the enemy in an abandoned factory. After graduating from college, Murphy took a job in juvenile publishing and eventually became managing editor. He published his first book, *Weird and Wacky Inventions,* in 1978. Since then, he has written many award-winning books.

V Vocabulary

Vocabulary Connections
Say: One way to remember new vocabulary words is to write their definitions in your own words. In your Learner's Notebooks, write a definition for each word and use each word correctly in a sentence. *(Responses will vary. Students should demonstrate an understanding of each vocabulary word.)* **AS**

Before You Read from *The Great Fire*

Meet the Author

Jim Murphy writes books about everything from lonely dinosaurs to weird inventions. He often writes about young people involved in historic events. According to Murphy, ". . . children weren't just observers of our history. They were actual participants and sometimes did amazing and heroic things."

To find out about the Great Chicago Fire, Murphy read letters and articles by people who were caught in the fire.

The Great Fire was published in 1995.

Literature Online

Author Search For more about Jim Murphy, go to www.glencoe.com.

Objectives (pp. 896–903)
Reading Compare and contrast: author's credibility across texts • Make connections from text to self

Vocabulary Preview

remnants (REM nunts) *n.* what is left over; small remaining parts **(p. 897)** *Remnants of the burned house continued to glow.*

consequences (KON suh kwen suz) *n.* results of an action; outcomes **(p. 899)** *Poor communication led to tragic consequences.*

phantom (FAN tum) *adj.* looking or seeming real but is not **(p. 899)** *Firefighters wasted time looking for a phantom fire.*

vapor (VAY pur) *n.* small particles of mist, steam, or smoke that can be seen **(p. 899)** *When you breathe through your mouth in the winter, your breath turns to vapor.*

singe (sinj) *v.* to burn slightly **(p. 900)** *Flames began to singe the hair on the firefighters' heads and arms.*

velocity (vuh LOS uh tee) *n.* speed **(p. 902)** *The velocity of the wind helped spread the fire.*

Get Ready to Read

Connect to the Reading

What would you do if you saw a blazing fire in your neighborhood? Discuss your answer with a partner.

Build Background

On a fall evening in 1871, a fire broke out near the barn of Katherine O'Leary at 137 DeKoven Street in Chicago. By the time the fire was under control, a day and a half later, it had destroyed much of one of America's largest cities and left 90,000 people homeless. One-third of Chicago was destroyed in the Great Fire. The Great Chicago Fire is one of the most famous disasters in United States history.

Set Purposes for Reading

BIG Question Read to find out what mistakes allowed the Great Chicago Fire to spread so quickly.

Set Your Own Purpose What would you like to learn from *The Great Fire* that could help you to answer the Big Question? Write your own purpose on "The Great Fire" part of the Reading Across Texts Foldable.

Additional Support

Literature Online

Author Search To expand students' appreciation of Jim Murphy, have them access the Web site for additional information and resources.

Differentiated Instruction

Using an Evaluation Chart To practice evaluating author credibility, students can use the criteria on page 895 to evaluate the information in the Build Background section on this page. Tell students to reproduce the chart shown on page 895 and complete it by using the text in the Build Background paragraph.

Ask students to consider how the author obtained information about the subject, what the author's purpose was, how long after the event the paragraph was written, and whether the author states any opinions as facts. As a class, discuss the results of this exercise. **AS**

The Great Fire

by Jim Murphy

Courthouse Square becoming engulfed in flames during the Chicago Fire, 1871. Hand-colored woodcut.

The fire that swept through the heart of Chicago began on Sunday night, October 8, 1871. The Great Fire would burn for the rest of Sunday, all of Monday, and into the early hours of Tuesday with little real opposition. **1**

On duty at the Courthouse[1] that night was forty-year-old Mathias Schaffer. Schaffer was showing some visitors around the tower when one of them pointed to smoke in the distance. Schaffer glanced at the smoke, but dismissed the sighting. It was just the smoldering embers from the previous night's fire, he assured them. Nothing to worry about.

Several minutes passed before Schaffer looked up from what he was doing and saw flames leaping wildly into the black sky. The light *was* from a different fire after all; he'd been fooled because this new blaze was almost directly behind the still-flickering **remnants** of the Saturday October 7 fire.

---

1. The ***Courthouse*** was a building with a high tower that was used to watch for fires. When a fire was sighted, a watchman in the tower sent an alarm to a firehouse near the blaze.

Vocabulary

remnants (REM nunts) *n.* what is left over; small remaining parts

Practice the Skills

1 | **Reading Across Texts**

R **Author's Credibility** Reread **Meet the Author** and answer these questions: Do you think the author knows a lot about this subject? Is this firsthand experience? How much time passed between when the event happened and when the author wrote the story? Fill in your chart.

L

from *The Great Fire* **897**

Teach

R **Reading Skill**

Identifying Main Idea and Supporting Details **Ask:** What is the main idea of the first paragraph? *(Possible response: The night of the Great Fire, a guard named Mathias Schaffer ignored smoke in the distance because he thought it was just smoldering embers from the previous night's fire.)* **BL OL**

L **Literary Element**

Description **Ask:** Judging from what you have read so far, does the author use many details in his description? Give examples to support your answer. *(Possible response: Yes; the author includes the name and age of the guard, and he describes the flames as "leaping wildly into the black sky.")* **OL**

Reading Fluency

Sentence Structure Write the first sentence in the selection on the board and ask students to identify the subject. Remind them that the subject is *who* or *what* the sentence is about. In this sentence, the subject is *Mathias Schaffer,* which is modified by the adjective *forty-year-old.* Next, ask students to identify the main verb. In this case, it is the linking verb *was.* Finally, ask students to identify what purpose is served by the phrase *on duty at the Courthouse that night.* This series of adverb phrases answers the questions *where* and *when.* Schaffer was *on duty at the Courthouse* (where) *that night* (when). **AS**

Objectives

- Identify literary elements: description
- Identify main ideas and supporting details
- Learn and use new vocabulary

Teach

L Literary Element

Description Ask: What does the use of phrases such as "moonless sky" and "swirling, smoky haze" tell you about the author's purpose? *(Students may point out that the author's purpose might be to describe and entertain as well as to inform.)* **OL**

BQ **BIG Question**

Ask: What is the immediate effect of Schaffer's mistake? *(Possible response: The firefighters are sent to the wrong location.)* **OL**

Flaming buildings and boats along the Chicago River during the Great Fire, 1871. Hand-colored woodcut.

Analyzing the Art How do you think people in Chicago felt as they saw buildings and boats aflame along the Chicago River?

L He studied the flames, trying to determine their exact location. This wasn't easy because of the distance and tall buildings between him and the flames. In addition, the moonless sky was made even murkier[2] by the swirling, smoky haze. Schaffer signaled down the speaking tube[3] and had his assistant strike Box 342.[4] This sent engines rumbling through the streets—to a location almost a mile away from the O'Leary's barn. **2**

Schaffer's first signal went out at 9:30. Several minutes later, Schaffer realized his mistake and ordered Box 319 struck. This was still seven blocks away from the O'Learys', but close enough that firefighters could see the flames and alter their course. Unfortunately, Schaffer's young assistant, William J. Brown, stubbornly refused to strike Box 319, saying he was afraid it would confuse the situation. Brown was so stubborn about his decision that even after the fire he was able to write

---

2. *Murky* means "hazy" or "hard to see through." It was hard for the watchman to see because the smoke from earlier fires made the sky *murkier.*

3. A *speaking tube* was a pipe made to carry a voice from one part of a building to another.

4. Watchmen at the courthouse sent alarms to local fire stations by hitting numbered boxes that were linked to the local stations. The station linked to *Box 342* was a mile from the fire.

898 UNIT 7 What Can We Learn from Our Mistakes?

Practice the Skills

2 **BIG Question**

Murphy describes the first mistake that fire officials made in responding to the fire. What was it? Start a list titled "Mistakes Made" on "The Great Fire" part of your Foldable. Write your answer as the first item on this list. Add to your list as your read further. **BQ**

Additional Support

Reading in the Real World

College Tell students that college-level writing assignments often require documentation of source material in the form of a bibliography or works cited page. In addition, some professors require students to provide an annotated bibliography, which contains several evaluative sentences about each source. The purpose of the annotation is to inform readers of the relevance, accuracy, and quality of the sources cited. In particular, annotations should include an evaluation of each author's credibility, based on criteria such as first-hand experience, degree of expertise, and personal bias. **AS**

arrogantly[5] in a letter that "I am still standing the watch[6] that burned Chicago." **3**

These errors had two fatal **consequences.** The most obvious was that a number of engines and dozens of firefighters were sent on a wild-goose chase[7] and did not get to the fire for many minutes. More critical is that it kept fire companies located near De Koven Street[8] in their stations. Several had seen the eerie, dancing glow beyond the rooftops near them and, even without official notice from Schaffer, prepared to respond. When they heard Box 342 rung, however, they assumed the fire was out of their territory and unhitched the horses. Only two fire companies were not fooled by the misleading alarm. **4**

The clang of bells and the sound of pounding hooves could be heard above the roar of the fire. *America* arrived on the scene first, closely followed by *Little Giant*. Hoses were rolled out, attached to water outlets, and the water turned on. Unfortunately, *America* was a hose cart and could not throw water any great distance, while *Little Giant* was eleven years old (the oldest engine in service). Their limited range forced firefighters to stand very close to the flames. The newer, more powerful pumping engines were either a mile away searching for a **phantom** fire, or still in their stations. **5**

The fire had begun near the corner of De Koven and Jefferson and quickly fanned out thanks to increasingly gusty winds. One tongue traveled north up Jefferson, while the other headed east toward Lake Michigan. There was no way firefighters from two engines could contain a wind-driven fire with such a wide front. Still, they did their best.

Two men hauled the cumbersome canvas hose as close to the flames as possible and aimed a stream of water at the burning building. The water hissed and boiled when it struck the burning wood, sending up a **vapor** of white steam. The

---

5. When you act ***arrogantly***, you act like you think you're smarter or more important than other people.
6. ***Standing the watch*** means "being on guard duty."
7. A ***wild-goose chase*** is a search that has no chance of success.
8. The fire started near 137 **DeKoven** Street.

Vocabulary

consequences (KON si kwen siz) *n.* results of an action; outcomes

phantom (FAN tum) *adj.* looking or seeming real but is not

vapor (VAY pur) *n.* small particles of mist, steam, or smoke that can be seen

from *The Great Fire* **899**

Practice the Skills

3 Reading Across Texts

Author's Credibility The author describes Brown's attitude as "stubborn" and says that Brown wrote "arrogantly" about his decision. Are the author's statements facts or opinions? Where do you think the author got this information? Fill in your chart. **L**

4 BIG Question

What mistakes resulted from Brown's actions? Write your answer on your Foldable. **BQ**

5 Reading Across Texts

Author's Credibility The main idea of this article is that the Great Chicago Fire would not have been so bad if it weren't for a series of mistakes and some bad luck. What does this tell you about the author's purpose? Is he biased? What details support the author's main idea? Continue filling in your chart. **R**

Teach

L Literary Element

Author's Credibility Say: Suppose that the information about Brown was obtained from a witness's account of the fire. How might a news reporter use language to indicate this? *(Possible response: A news reporter might say "According to eyewitness accounts . . .")* **AL**

BQ BIG Question

Ask: Did Brown learn from his mistake? Explain. *(Responses will vary. The quotation from Brown's letter suggests that he did not learn from his mistake.)* **OL**

R Reading Skill

Identifying Main Idea and Supporting Details Ask: Which problems with the fire engines were due to bad luck? Which problems were due to human error? *(Possible response: The fact that America and Little Giant were not able to handle the fire was bad luck. The fact that other engines were far from the fire was due to human error.)* **AS Ask:** What natural condition made matters even worse for the firefighters? *(The strong winds caused the fire to spread rapidly in two directions.)* **OL**

Objectives
- Evaluate author's credibility
- Identify literary elements: description
- Identify main ideas and supporting details

Differentiated Instruction

Research Report Have students consult encyclopedias, nonfiction books, and Internet articles to compare firefighting techniques and equipment used at the time of the Chicago Fire with those used today. Suggest that students research response systems, truck and hose equipment, and firefighter uniforms, including the material used in helmets, boots, gloves, and jackets. Tell students to use their research to write one or two paragraphs describing how the events described in the selection would have been different had the firefighters in 1871 had access to today's equipment. **OL**

Teach

R Reading Skill

Evaluating Ask: How would you describe the way Marshal Williams handles the fire and his crew? Give examples to support your answer. *(Possible response: He seems to handle the situation well. He acts quickly and delegates responsibility.)* **AS Ask:** What does Marshal Williams's composure during the fire suggest about him? *(Possible response: It suggests that he is a competent leader and that he is good at keeping a level head.)* **OL**

L Literary Element

Narrator Ask: What happens to the narration after the paragraph break? Does the narrator continue to tell the story chronologically? Explain. *(Possible response: The narrator moves back in time and retells the story of the fire as it happened to twelve-year-old Claire Innes.)* **OL**

---

firefighters held their position until the fierce heat began to **singe** the hair on their heads and arms, and their clothes began to smolder. When the pain became unbearable, they staggered back from the flames for a moment's relief, then lunged forward again.

More engines began arriving at the scene, as did the department's Chief Marshal Robert A. Williams. A common fire-fighting technique of the time was to surround a blaze with engines and use a flood of water to stop it from spreading. Williams immediately set about repositioning engines, hoping to halt the fire's advance until all the missing equipment could get to the scene.

The firefighters were already engulfed in a wave of withering heat, and the flames were reaching out toward them. "Marshal," one of the men yelled, "I don't believe we can stand it here!"

"Stand it as long as you can," Williams told them, before hurrying to another engine. Along the way he noticed that several houses were smoking and on the verge of igniting.

He came upon the driver of *America* and its foreman, John Dorsey. "Turn in a second alarm!" Williams ordered Dorsey. "This is going to spread!" A second alarm would bring in additional engines and men. **6**

Meanwhile, Chamberlin[9] had retreated several blocks in the face of the advancing flames. "I stepped in among some sheds south of Ewing Street; a fence by my side began to blaze; I beat a hasty retreat, and in five minutes the place where I had stood was all ablaze. Nothing could stop that conflagration there. It must sweep on until it reached a broad street, and then, everybody said, it would burn itself out."

The heat and dry air had left twelve-year-old Claire Innes tired and listless all day. She went to bed sometime between eight and eight-thirty only to be startled awake later when a horse-and-wagon clattered past her window at high speed. This was followed by loud voices from the street below her window.

"I was only half awake and not inclined to get up when I heard a man outside say that a fire was burning in the West

---

9. One of the first people to reach the fire was Joseph E. **Chamberlin**, a reporter for the *Chicago Evening Post.*

Vocabulary

singe (sinj) *v.* to burn slightly

Practice the Skills

6 Reading Across Texts

Author's Credibility Look at the quotations in this paragraph. Do you think the author knew exactly what Williams and the firefighter said in those moments? Where do you think the author got this information? Continue filling in your chart.

Additional Support

Reading Fluency

Build Fluency The text that describes the mounting tension as the fire spread through the city is an excellent excerpt for students to use to improve fluency. First have students read the selected text silently, and tell them to note any words with which they are unfamiliar. Discuss these unfamiliar words as a class, and have students repeat the pronunciations aloud. Then have students work in pairs, reading aloud to each other. Encourage students to read with inflection, particularly as they read the dialogue between firefighters. Invite volunteers to read aloud in front of the class. **EL**

The Great Fire in Chicago, October 8–10, 1871. Currier & Ives. Contemporary lithograph.

Sailboats and steamboats fled to the safety of Lake Michigan, as flames destroyed the city.

Division. Father went to the door and asked about the fire and the man repeated what he had told his companions, but this time he added that the fire was a big one and that they were going to have a look at it. Father came inside and said something to Mother. . . . His voice did not sound unusual, [so] I turned over and closed my eyes again."

Claire and her family were staying in the South Division of the city, many blocks from the fire. There really was no reason for them to become alarmed. In fact, most citizens would see the glowing nighttime sky and dismiss it as nothing important. Not even the warning words in that day's *Chicago Tribune* drew much attention: "For dayspast alarm has followed alarm, but the comparatively trifling losses have familiarized us to the pealing of the Courthouse bell, and we [have] forgotten that the absence of rain for three weeks [has] left everything in so dry and inflammable a condition that a spark might set a fire which would sweep from end to end of the city." **7**

But no one seemed very concerned. This was evident by what Alfred L. Sewell observed while strolling through the city at around 9:30 that night. "Many people were just returning from the Sunday evening services at the various churches when the general alarm was given, but, beyond the immediate vicinity of the beginning of the conflagration, no unusual fear or solicitude

Practice the Skills

7 **Reading Across Texts**

Author's Credibility The author gives us quotations from Claire Innes and the *Chicago Tribune* newspaper to support his point that people weren't worried about the fire even though they were warned. Does the author's use of quotations add to his credibility? Fill in your chart. **C**

from *The Great Fire* **901**

Teach

Viewing the Art
Ask: What does this illustration tell you about the fire? *(Possible response: The fire looks so intense and out of control that even the ships in the harbors do not seem safe.)* **OL**

C Critical Thinking

Comprehension Ask: What is the main idea expressed in the quotation from the *Chicago Tribune*? *(Possible response: People have become desensitized to the fire alarms because so little damage has actually occurred. But the absence of rain has made everything dry, which means that a fire has the potential to be very destructive.)* **OL**

R Reading Skill

Evaluating Ask: How could the citizens of Chicago be so unconcerned with fire raging through the city? Explain your answer. *(Responses will vary. Some students may say that the citizens might not have been worried because the fire was far away, or that there had been so many false alarms and other smaller fires recently that they were no longer concerned about them.)* **AS**

Differentiated Instruction

News Story Have students expand the quotation from the *Chicago Tribune* into a one-page news story about the Chicago Fire. Tell students to write the story from the perspective of a reporter who has witnessed the fire and interviewed citizens of Chicago. Students should use details from the text as well as their own creativity to write the article. Suggest that they elaborate on the "trifling losses" mentioned in the quotation, as well as the "absence of rain" that has made everything dry and extremely flammable. Invite volunteers to read their news stories aloud in front of the class. **OL**

Objectives
- Identify and analyze narrator
- Evaluate text
- Find meaning in art
- Monitor comprehension

Teach

BQ **BIG Question**

Ask: What do you think caused firefighter Dorsey to make this mistake? *(Responses will vary. Students may suggest that Dorsey's anxiety about the spreading fire caused him to forget to pull the lever the correct number of times.)* **AS**

L Literary Element

Sequence of Events/Time Order Say: Use the information in the selection to construct a time line of events that occurred between Saturday evening and Sunday night. *(Possible response: A fire began in Chicago on Saturday night. On Sunday night, a new fire started. An alarm signal was sent, but to the wrong box, sending firefighters to the wrong location. Some trucks eventually arrived, but they were unprepared to fight the fire. Firefighters worked through Sunday night to put out the fire, but without success.)* **OL**

was felt by the citizens. The German beerhouses were filled with merry crowds, and as it was a warm evening, the streets all over the city were filled with joyful idlers and promenaders, in their Sunday apparel. A pleasanter, quieter, or a happier evening than was that one is seldom known in a great city."

And despite his own paper's editorial, not even the editor in chief of the *Chicago Tribune*, Horace White, smelled a good story in the smoke that was blowing into his neighborhood. "I had retired to rest, though not to sleep [that night], when the great bell struck the alarm; but fires had been so frequent of late, and had been so speedily extinguished, that I did not deem it worthwhile to get up and look at it, or even to count the strokes of the bell to learn where it was."

As the rest of the city went about its business, fireman Dorsey was racing through the streets to the closest signal box, which happened to be at Goll's drugstore. He opened the small door on the box and used his thumb to pull down the lever. Dorsey then headed back to the scene of the fire, not realizing that he'd made a mistake—he had forgotten to pull down the lever four times, a special signal that would have made it a true second alarm. At the Courthouse, Schaffer and Brown would hear Dorsey's alarm, but, assuming it was simply another signal telling them about the original fire, they failed to call out more engines. The fire had now been burning for over an hour, and the wind was increasing in **velocity.** 🖼

Despite this, Chief Marshal Williams had managed to get a thin circle of engines around the fire. He had five steamers at the scene now, plus three hose carts and a hook-and-ladder wagon, all of them pumping water into the fire at various locations. Spectators were asked to help and many responded by chopping up fences and sidewalks, hoping to deprive the fire of fuel.

Meanwhile the heat was beginning to wear down some of the firemen. Charles Anderson remembered when his friend Charles McConners came by and said, "Charley, this is hot!"

"It is, Mac," Anderson replied.

His friend disappeared for a few moments, then returned carrying a wooden door, which he positioned like a warrior's

Chicago Fire victims' camp on Lake Michigan shore near Lincoln Park, 1871. Hand-colored woodcut.

Some Chicagoans lived in tents on the shore of Lake Michigan after the Great Fire destroyed much of their city.

Practice the Skills

8 **BIG Question**

What mistake did Dorsey make? At the Courthouse, do you think Schaffer and Brown should have called out more engines even though they hadn't received a true second alarm signal? Explain. **BQ**

Vocabulary

velocity (vuh LOS uh tee) *n.* speed

Additional Support

Literature Focus Lesson

Sequence of Events Point out to students that the events described on this page—Dorsey's pulling the alarm, Marshal Williams's circling the fire with engines, McConners's using a door as a shield—occur simultaneously. The author uses words such as *meanwhile* to show that the events are taking place in different locations at the same time. Ask students to consider how they would convey this idea if they were to adapt the selection into a short film. If students need prompting, discuss techniques such as voice-over narration and split-screen images. **AL**

shield between Anderson and the fire.

I have it now, Anderson thought. I can stand it a considerable time.

Anderson no sooner thought this when the door caught fire and burned McConners' hand. McConners flung the door down and then Anderson's clothes began to smoke. The heat was so intense that his leather hat began to twist out of shape.

Williams came by and issued new orders. "Charley, come out as fast as possible. Wet the other side of the street or it will burn!"

With the help of onlookers, Anderson began to reposition his hose. He hadn't gotten it very far when water pressure suddenly dropped and only a trickle of liquid came from the hose. A powerful steam engine had arrived at the fire and had simply removed Anderson's hose from its water plug. This was routine procedure, done under the assumption that a steamer would always be more effective than a simple hose cart. Sadly, the steamer did not drag its hose to Anderson's position and he had to watch as four or five houses across the street caught fire.

At the same moment that Anderson's hose stopped, another steamer malfunctioned and its water also gave out. A well-aimed rap of a hammer got the engine working again, but then, at about 10:30, an old section of hose burst and the flow of water stopped again. Two valuable links in the chain of defense were gone, and there was nothing to stop the fire in these locations. **9**

Williams rushed to get the water going and to reposition his engines, but it was too late. The wind had pushed the fire past his circle, a wind that was blowing directly toward the heart of the city.

Later at the official inquiry, all of the mistakes and missed chances that occurred in the opening minutes of the fire would be discussed in great detail. As one firefighter put it, "From the beginning of that fatal fire, everything went wrong!" **10** ○

Practice the Skills

R
L

9 ▸ Reading Across Texts

Author's Credibility The author gives you a lot of details about what happened to the firefighters. Based on what you know about the author and what you have read so far, do you believe these details? Explain why or why not in your chart.

10 ▸ BIG Question

What mistakes turned the fire into a major disaster? What can you learn from those mistakes? Write your answer on your Foldable. Your response will help you complete the Unit Challenge later.

BQ

from *The Great Fire* **903**

Teach

R Reading Skill

Evaluating Ask: Is it a good idea to use a wooden door for protection from a fire? Explain. *(Possible response: No; wood is extremely flammable.)* **AS**

L Literary Element

Author's Credibility Say: Notice that the author describes the exchange between Anderson and McConners in his own words. Why do you think he does this? How does this affect his credibility? *(Responses will vary. Students may suggest that Murphy was not able to find out exactly what Anderson and McConners said to each other.)* **AS**

BQ BIG Question

Ask: What might some of the people mentioned in this selection have learned from their mistakes? *(Possible responses: Schaffer might have learned to be careful to strike the correct box; Dorsey might have learned to be sure to pull the lever four times when calling in a second alarm; McConners might have learned not to use a wooden door as a shield from fire; and the steam engine operators might have learned to pay attention before removing other hoses from a water plug.)* **AS**

English Language Coach

Conjunctions Point out to students that the author uses three types of conjunctions: coordinating, correlative, and subordinating. Coordinating conjunctions such as *and, but, for, nor, or, so*, and *yet* join words, phrases, and clauses. For example, in the sentence *Williams came by and issued new orders*, the coordinating conjunction *and* joins the verbs *came by* and *issued*. Correlative conjunctions such as *both . . . and, either . . . or, neither . . . nor*, and *not only . . . but also* appear in pairs. Subordinating conjunctions such as *after, although, because, before*, and *that* introduce a dependent clause. **EL**

Objectives
• Evaluate author's credibility
• Understand sequence of events: time order
• Evaluate text

Teach

More About the Author

The Chicago Historical Society's library of eyewitness accounts includes the *Chicago Tribune's* original report of the fire. As a result of damage to its building, the *Tribune* was forced to suspend publication for two days. A full account of the fire appeared in the issue published on Wednesday, October 11.

V Vocabulary

Verb Tenses Ask: What is the present-tense verb form of *stifled? (stifle)* **Say:** Use the present-tense verb form in a sentence. *(Possible response: Please don't stifle my creativity.)* **AS**

Before You Read | Letters About the Fire

Meet the Authors

A boy named Justin (we don't know his last name for sure) and a girl named Fannie Belle lived through the Great Chicago Fire of 1871. Like other people who lived through that disaster, they wrote what they saw, heard, and felt on those October days. Justin wrote his letter eleven days after the fire broke out. Fannie wrote hers about two years after the fire. These and other eyewitness accounts are kept by the Chicago Historical Society and can be found online at www .chicagohs.org/fire.

Objectives (pp. 904–907)
Reading Compare and contrast: author's credibility across texts • Make connections from text to self

Vocabulary Preview

cinders (SIN durz) *n.* hot ashes **(p. 906)** *Cinders from the fire filled the air.*
stifled (STY fuld) *v.* choked; smothered **(p. 906)** *The heat of the fire stifled everyone's breathing.*

Get Ready to Read

Connect to the Reading

The families in these letters rescue items from the fire that are important to them. What would you rescue? What things have special memories for you?

Build Background

- By the 1870s, Chicago was already an important city. It connected businesses in the East with the farms in the West.
- Before the fire, Chicago had 57 miles of wood-paved streets and more than 500 miles of wooden sidewalks.
- Justin's house burned during the Great Chicago Fire. He and his family were in their house when it started to burn. His family and the family goat escaped without harm.
- Fannie Belle and her mother left their home as the fire approached them. Fannie Belle rescued her doll named Jennie. Fannie Belle kept Jennie as a reminder of the Great Fire.
- Hundreds of survivors of the fire wrote letters and articles about their experiences in the fire.

Set Purposes for Reading

BIG Question Read to find out how two families dealt with a dangerous situation and what mistakes they made.

Set Your Own Purpose What can you learn from these accounts of escaping the Great Chicago Fire? Write your purpose for reading on the "Letters About the Fire" part of the Reading Across Texts Foldable.

904 UNIT 7 What Can We Learn from Our Mistakes?

Additional Support

Literature Focus Lesson

Eyewitness Accounts Tell students that an eyewitness account is a version of an event that is given by someone who saw or experienced it. Have students brainstorm a list of eyewitness accounts that they have read or heard. Be sure to explain that although eyewitness accounts are excellent sources of information, they may still contain opinions and inconsistencies. A person may write an eyewitness account several days, weeks, or even months after an event occurs, in which case the witness may have difficulty remembering events exactly as they happened. **AS**

Letters About the Fire

Justin

Justin sent this letter about his family fleeing to his "chum" Philip Prescott on October 19, 1871. **1**

Dear Chum,

We are burnt out of house and home and so we had to come up here.[1] I suppose you would like to hear about the fire and how we escaped from it. Half past one Monday morning we were awakened by a loud knocking at the front door we were awake in an instant and dressing ourselves we looked about and saw a perfect shower of sparks flying over our house. I got some water and went out in the yard while my brother went up on the roof we worked for one or two hours at the end of that time we had to give up. We tried to get a wagon but could not so we put two trunks on a wheelbarrow and each of us shouldered a bundle and we marched for the old skating park I leading my goat. We got along very well until the Pes[h]tigo Lumber yard[2] caught on fire then it was all we could do to breathe. Mother caught on fire once but we put it out at last we heard that there was a little shanty that hadn't burnt down so we marched there but had to leave our trunks and everything else but Charlie and father went back and got one but could not get the other as the sand was blowing in their faces and cut like glass at last a wagon drove up and we all piled in and escaped so good by **2**

yours Justin

---

1. **Justin** wrote his letter from Lake Forest, Illinois, a town about thirty miles north of Chicago, where his family had found shelter.

2. The **Peshtigo Lumber Yard,** a large lumberyard in Chicago, burned during the Great Fire.

Practice the Skills

1 **Reading Across Texts**

Author's Credibility Reread **Meet the Authors.** Do you think Justin knows a lot about this subject? Does he have firsthand experience? How much time passed between when the event happened and when he wrote the letter? Fill in your chart. **L**

2 **Reading Across Texts**

Author's Credibility What do you think was Justin's purpose for writing this letter? Does he have bias? If so, what is it? Does the author include many details? Is the letter mostly fact or opinion? Continue filling in your chart.

Letters About the Fire **905**

Teach

L Literary Element

Author's Credibility Ask: Do spelling, grammar, and punctuation errors detract from an author's credibility? Explain. *(Responses will vary. Some students may say that what an author says is more important than how he or she says it. Others may suggest that poor writing may make an author seem careless and therefore less credible.)* **AS**

English Language Coach

Make Corrections Many students, especially English language learners, may have trouble reading Justin's account because of its many errors. As an incentive, hold a contest to see which student can find and correct the most errors. If necessary, review rules regarding run-on sentences, spelling, punctuation, and capitalization. Create an overhead projector transparency of the text, and make a "key" that contains all of the errors and their corrections. Tell students to exchange papers. Then reveal the transparency and have students count the number of errors they were able to correct. **AS**

Objectives
• Learn and use new vocabulary
• Evaluate author's credibility

Teach

L1 Literary Element

Author's Credibility Say:
Think about something that happened to you two years ago. How well do you remember it? Could you write a detailed account of it? Explain. *(Responses will vary.)* **AS**

Say: Use your answer to fill in your comparison chart.

L2 Literary Element

Description Ask: Why does Fannie Belle list the items that she and her mother were able to save? *(Possible response: The list of items that they were able to save helps the reader understand the experience of being driven out of one's home by a fire.)* **OL**

Fannie Belle Becker

Fannie Belle Becker (later Fanny Dement), ten at the time of the fire, wrote "My Experience of the Chicago Fire" almost exactly two years later. **3**

Saturday evening Oct the 8th 1871 there was a large Fire in Chicago it was probably the largest Fire ever in that city then it was the lumberyard burning there was a great many people out to see it. They stayed untill a late hour and so were very tired but did not get much rest for Monday morning at three o'clock I was awakened and told to Dress for the Fire was all around us and we would soon be burnt out. My ma put all her valubals[3] into her sewing machine and locked it up and threw some things in to her trunk. I carried ma's fur box (with furs in it), and, account book,[4] and a parasol,[5] and, a little lady called Jennie. And perhaps some of my little friends in Fruit-Port have made her [acquaintance] but some of you may not know who little Jennie is so I will say that she is a little China doll[6] a Christmas present when I was Five years old and I will always keep her as a Relic[7] of the Chicago Fire. We could not save the Sewing Machine but did save the trunk. We had a gentleman friend who helped us; we all went down right away but ma stayed, she said that she would stay as long as she could. So we went around the corner to monroe street and waited and when she came she brought a large hair[8] Matrass. The air was so full of **cinders** and was so hot that it almost **stifled** her. We could not get an express man to carry the things for there were none to be had. So our friend drew[9] our trunk and a trunk that belonged to a friend of his who

Analyzing the Art How does this image of the Great Chicago Fire show the confusion and fear that Fannie and her family experienced?

Practice the Skills

3 Reading Across Texts

Author's Credibility Do you think Fannie Belle Becker knows a lot about her subject? Does she have firsthand experience? How much time passed between when the event happened and when she wrote her story? Fill in your chart. **L1**

---

3. **Valubals** is an incorrect spelling of the word *valuables*.
4. An **account book** is a notebook in which records about money are kept.
5. A **parasol** (PAIR uh sawl) is a light umbrella that protects a person (usually a woman) from the sun.
6. A **China doll** is a doll with a head made of porcelain, a breakable material.
7. A **relic** is a thing from the past.
8. A **hair Matrass (mattress)** is a mattress filled with animal hair. Hair mattresses can catch fire.
9. In this letter, **drew** means "pulled."

Vocabulary

cinders (SIN durs) *n.* hot ashes

stifled (STY fuld) *v.* choked; smothered

906 UNIT 7 What Can We Learn from Our Mistakes?

Additional Support

Reading in the Real World

Career Some photographers earn a living by working for one or more than one newspaper or magazine. Photographers who cover news stories are assigned to attend newsworthy events and take photographs that are then edited and incorporated with the text before the story goes to print. If a publication runs a story about a person whose picture has already been taken, it may choose to run a *stock image* or *photo*. Publicity agents, particularly those who represent performing artists, will often send *press photos* to a variety of publications, thereby eliminating the publication's need to hire a photographer. **AS**

was out of the city. He lashed the two together and lashed the Matrass on top of the trunks, and then drew them along. The trunks both has castors[10] on. When we got to the corners of Dearborn street ma told me to go Down on Jackson st. a few blocks away to the house of a friend and see if they thought the fire would come there and if not we would go there and stay. And Just as I was about to start a man who had been standing near and heard what ma said told her that he would see me safe there. Ma thanked him and said we would not trouble him but he said it was no trouble and walked along beside me. He said he would take my account book I did not like his looks and so told him that I could carry it myself, and, as we went through a crowd just then I dodged away from him and ran and I have not seen anything of him since. When I got to the house they had all their things packed and out on the side walk and, in a little while ma came and then we went back to monroe st and then as the Fire came on we went on toward Lake Michigan as we went on we came to our friends brothers house we stayed here until the fire drove us out then the heat was so intense that it drove us down to the waters Edge and then my uncle who was with us (and, had arrived Saturday) took his hat and poured water on the things to keep them from burning but thousands and thousands of dollar's worth of goods were burned right there on the waters Edge. Although our things were saved we sat there until I was almost blind with the dirt and cinders that filled the air I could not open my eyes, so that when I walked ma had to lead me. I did not have anything to eat from Sunday afternoon until Monday afternoon at about four o'clock. Then we went out to the City limits on the South side to the house of a friend I stayed there two days and then I went out in the country with my cousins, and stayed there one week and then I came to Fruit-Port [Michigan]. I shall ever remember with thankfulness my reception by my little friends in Fruit-Port. I almost went barefoot and without any good clothes. I was well treated and one of them even took off her over shoes and let me wear them that I might go out in the cold weather and play. Never while I live will I forget my friends in Fruit Port. **4 5** ○

---

10. **Castors** is a misspelling of the word *casters*. Casters are small wheels attached to the bottom of heavy objects. These wheels make objects easy to move by rolling.

Practice the Skills

4 ▶ **Reading Across Texts**

Author's Credibility What do you think was the author's purpose for writing this story? Does she have bias? Does she include details? Is the letter fact or opinion?

5 🖋 **BIG Question**

Did Fannie Belle or her mother make any mistakes? If so, do you think they learned from them? Write your answers on your Foldable.

Analyzing the Art List some ways that these boys from the 1800s seem different from kids today.

Letters About the Fire **907**

Teach

L Literary Element

Author's Credibility Ask: Which of the details that Fannie Belle mentions could you check today? *(the names of the streets—Dearborn, Jackson, and Monroe)* **BL Ask:** Does the fact that you can check these details make Fannie's account more credible? *(yes, slightly)* **OL Say:** Use your answers to fill in your comparison chart.

R Reading Skill

Synthesizing Ask: What does Fannie mean when she says that she didn't like the looks of the man who offered to take her account book? *(Possible response: She means that she suspected the man to be a thief. She didn't trust him to return her money.)* **OL**

BQ 🖋 BIG Question

Ask: What lesson can you learn from the mistakes that Fannie Belle and her mother made? *(Responses will vary. Students may say that they will take only what they truly need in the event of an emergency.)* **AS**

Reading Fluency

Read Fluently Follow up on the previous activity, in which students made corrections to the text. Have students correct Fannie Belle's account to practice reading and improve fluency. Tell students to list any words with which they are unfamiliar, and discuss these words as a class. Then have student pairs read aloud to each other, reading at a pace that is comfortable and fluid. Encourage students to keep their eyes slightly ahead of the word being read, both when they are following along and when they are reading aloud. Invite volunteers to read selections aloud in front of the class. **EL BL**

Objectives
• Evaluate author's credibility
• Synthesize text
• Identify literary elements: description

Assess

Resources for page 908

📁 Selection Quick Check, pp. 69–70

💿 ExamView Assessment Suite

💿 Interactive Tutor: Self-Assessment

Vocabulary Check

1. stifled
2. consequences
3. velocity
4. phantom
5. cinders
6. remnants
7. vapor
8. singe

After You Read

from *The Great Fire* & *Letters About the Fire*

Vocabulary Check

For items 1–8, choose the best words from the lists to fill in each blank. Then write the complete sentences on a separate sheet of paper.

consequences phantom remnants singe vapor velocity cinders stifled

1. The heat and smoke from the fire nearly ___ Fannie Belle and her mother.

2. One of the ___ of sending the wrong signal was that the firemen went to the wrong part of the city.

3. The ___ of the wind increased, causing the fire to spread.

4. The more powerful engines were on a wild-goose chase, looking for a ___ fire.

5. Fannie Belle described the burning ___ that filled the hot air.

6. The new blaze could have been started by the ___ of a fire from the previous day.

7. The water hissed when it hit the burning wood, sending up a cloud of ___.

8. The heat from the fire began to ___ the firefighters' hair.

Objectives (pp. 908–909)
Reading Compare and contrast: author's credibility across texts • Make connections from text to self
Writing Respond to informational text: author's credibility

Writing: Reading Across Texts

13. Possible responses:
Step 1: Murphy seems to know the most about how the fire started and why firefighters couldn't put it out. He knows this from researching other accounts.
Step 2: Murphy attempts to convince the reader that the fire got out of control because of a series of mistakes and unfortunate events.
Step 3: Murphy depends on other accounts of the fire; Justin and Fannie Belle experienced it firsthand.
Step 4: Murphy states his opinion about the firefighters as a fact.
Step 5: Responses will vary.

Reading/Critical Thinking

On a separate sheet of paper, answer the following questions.

from *The Great Fire*

9. **Recall** When the fire first started, what mistakes kept fire trucks from going to the right location?

   Tip Right There

10. **Evaluate** Murphy describes events from the points of view of many people at the Great Fire. Does this technique of using several points of view make his narrative more or less believable? Explain.

    Tip Author and Me

Letters About the Fire

11. **Infer** Why do you think Justin sounds both excited and relieved?

    Tip Author and Me

12. **Draw a Conclusion** Do you think Fannie did the right thing when the man offered to carry the account book? Explain why or why not.

    Tip Author and Me

Writing: Reading Across Texts

Use Your Notes

13. Follow these steps to compare the credibility of the authors of "The Great Fire" and "Letters About the Fire."

    Step 1: Review the chart you've completed. Which author seems to know the most about how the fire started and why the firemen couldn't put it out? How does that author know those details? Do you believe the author?

Step 2: Which author or authors depend on what other people say for their information? Which author or authors actually saw and experienced the fire?

Step 3: Did the authors have different purposes for writing? What were they? Were any of the authors biased? If so, did that affect whether you believed them?

Step 4: Do any of these writers present opinions as if they were facts? Explain.

Step 5: Think about what persuades you to believe a writer. Is it the writer's knowledge, firsthand experience, supporting details, or what?

Get It on Paper

To show what you think about the credibility of these authors and selections, answer the following questions on a separate sheet of paper.

14. Which writer, do you think, had the best knowledge of how it felt to be caught in the fire *at the time that he or she wrote the selection*? Explain why you chose this writer over the other writers.

15. Which writer seemed to give you the most opinions about why and how things happened? Did that writer back up those opinions with enough details to be credible?

16. If you wanted to know exactly how the fire spread through Chicago, which writer would you ask? Explain why you chose that writer.

17. Explain why you feel Murphy's use of quotations to describe the fire scenes is or is not effective.

BIG Question

18. After reading both selections, do you believe that the mistakes made in the Great Chicago Fire could be repeated today? Explain the reasons for your answer.

17. Responses will vary. Students may say that Murphy's use of quotations shows readers how the fire affected different people.

BIG Question

18. Responses will vary. Students should recognize that modern technology would prevent many errors made in 1871 from being made today.

Reading/Critical Thinking

The Great Fire

9. Schaffer told his assistant to strike Box 342 instead of Box 319. Brown then refused to correct the error.

10. Possible response: The multiple perspectives give a more comprehensive account of the event, which in turn makes the narrative more believable.

Letters About the Fire

11. Possible response: Justin is excited because the fire had taken place only 11 days before he wrote the letter. He is relieved because he and his family escaped unharmed.

12. Possible response: Fannie did the right thing because she suspected that the man planned to steal her money.

Writing: Reading Across Texts

13. See bottom channel.

Get It On Paper

14. Possible response: Justin had the best sense of what it was like to be caught in the fire because his account was written the soonest after the event.

15. Possible response: Murphy gave the most opinions but he also provided enough details and source information to make his opinions credible.

16. Possible response: Murphy would be the best resource because he has the most comprehensive understanding of how the fire spread.

The Unit Challenge

Focus

Teach

Group Activity: Create a Chart

- Remind students to focus on something that they learned from each mistake, even if they haven't learned it until now.
- Make sure that students are contributing equally to the unit challenge.
- You may want to have students make their charts on poster board so that they can be displayed in your classroom and read from a distance.

Assess/Close

Group Activity Ask: How have you used what you learned from your mistakes? *(Suggest that students write their answers in their Learner's Notebooks.)* **AS**

UNIT 7 WRAP-UP

Answering What Can We Learn from Our Mistakes?

While reading the selections, you've been thinking about what people can learn from their mistakes. Now use what you've learned to complete the Unit Challenge.

The Unit Challenge

Choose Activity A or Activity B and follow the directions for that activity.

A. Group Activity: Chart

- You know that everyone makes mistakes and that mistakes have consequences. With group of classmates make a chart of mistakes and what can be learned as a result of the mistakes.
- Your chart can help you think about your decisions and learn from your mistakes.

1. Discuss the Assignment

- Choose one group member to be the note-taker for the discussion.
- Review the notes you wrote in your Learner's Notebook and on your Foldables for the selections you read in this unit.
- Discuss the mistakes you think the characters made. Then discuss what you can learn, or what the characters learned, from their mistakes. For example, in "Nadia the Willful," Nadia's father learned that it's a mistake to not remember someone you love. He corrected his mistake by letting Nadia and the rest of the people remember what her brother meant to them.
- Think about people you know who have made mistakes. Then discuss what happened as the result of their mistakes, and what can be learned from the mistakes. Make a list of those mistakes.

2. Create a Chart Draw a chart like the one below. Use your list to fill in the Mistake column. Brainstorm with the classmates about lessons learned from the mistakes.

Now fill in the "What I Learned" column. If you can't think of something that was learned, leave it blank. You can fill it in later.

3. Present Your Chart Have a group member read the chart to the class. Discuss any mistakes that they think could be added to the chart. Add any ideas about mistakes they have. Discuss the most common mistakes that people make. What do you think can prevent these kinds of mistakes?

Mistake	What I Learned
I forgot my homework.	I should put my homework in my book bag.
I stayed out past curfew.	I should call if I'm going to be late.

B. Solo Activity: Bumper Sticker

Bumper stickers are a form of advertising. They advertise, or make public, ideas and beliefs. You'll use words and pictures to create several bumper stickers about learning from mistakes.

1. **Consider the Topic** Review your Foldable notes to recall what people in the selections learned from their mistakes. In your Learner's Notebook, make notes about what you've learned from mistakes. Describe two or three mistakes you've made, tell what you learned from them, and how they helped you grow or change.

2. **Diagram Ideas** In your Learner's Notebook, draw a web like the one below. Write the Big Question in the center box. In the outside boxes, write lessons you or characters from the selections learned from mistakes. You don't have to include a lesson for every selection or from every experience of your own. Just include those you think might suggest good slogans for bumper stickers.

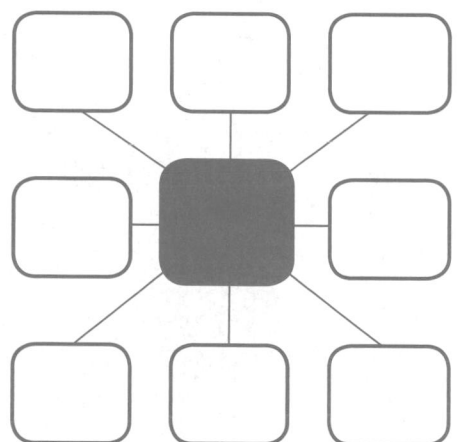

3. **Brainstorm Slogans** Which four boxes in the web do you think show the most important lessons about learning from mistakes? From each of these boxes draw a line and box. In each new box write a slogan that summarizes the idea. Here are some tips.

   - A slogan should be *concise* (kun SYS), or short. Use no more than ten or fifteen words for each slogan.
   - A slogan should be *catchy.* Choose words that will grab people's interest.
   - A slogan should be *clear.* Test out each slogan. Say it to a classmate, friend, or family member and ask him or her to explain what it means.
   - Rewrite each slogan until it's just right—that is, concise, catchy, and clear.
   - Here are some examples of slogans.
     The only really bad mistake is the one you make more than once.
     Those who don't learn from their mistakes are sure to repeat them again.
     No child is mistake proof.
     Show me a mistake, and I made it.
     For every mistake, there is a lesson to be learned.

4. **Design Bumper Stickers** Draw four rectangles in your Learner's Notebook. Write one slogan in each rectangle. Then decorate each with a border, drawings, photos, or symbols that have to do with the idea expressed in the slogan.

5. **Create a Bumper Sticker** Which of your four bumper sticker ideas do you find most inspiring? Use paper or cardboard to create that bumper sticker for yourself. Post it by your bed or desk or tape it on your notebook or backpack.

Teach

Solo Activity: Bumper Sticker

- Before the beginning of this activity, have students spend some time recording slogans on bumper stickers that they notice on cars in your community.

- If there are billboards in your city or town, have students list the more memorable advertising slogans displayed on them.

- When students are creating their webs, allow them to look back through the unit to recall specific information.

- As students design their bumper stickers, encourage them to consider how they will lay out the text. If you have access to computers, have students experiment with font, color, size, and formatting.

Assess/Close

Solo Activity

Ask: Does your slogan sound like something that you would see on a real bumper sticker? Why or why not? *(If students answer yes, suggest that they research ways of getting their bumper stickers printed professionally.)* **AS**

Objectives
- Create a chart
- Participate in a group activity
- Create a bumper sticker
- Follow multi-step directions

Focus

Vocabulary Preview

List the following words on the board:

- arrogant
- fetch
- conquest
- courtesy

Review their definitions before students begin reading.

Build Background

This comic strip is about a samurai who learns a lesson about the code of conduct known as Bushido.

- Samurai were members of the Japanese military class.
- The Japanese word *bushido* translates to "way of the warrior."

Teach

R Reading Skill

Identifying Main Idea and Supporting Details Say: Reread what the sensei says about Usagi. What do you think will be the main idea or lesson of this comic strip? *(Possible response: The main idea will be that a strong person must learn to be humble and respectful, not overconfident and arrogant.)* **OL**

UNIT 7

Your Turn: Read and Apply Skills

by Stan Sakai

Meet the Author
Stan Sakai was born in Japan and grew up in Hawaii. He lives in California with his wife and children. His character Usagi Yojimbo first appeared in comics in 1984. Stan received the National Cartoonists Society Comic Book Division Award for his work.

Literature Online

Author Search For more about Stan Sakai, go to www.glencoe.com.

A LESSON IN COURTESY

Additional Support

Author Search To expand students' appreciation of Stan Sakai, have them access the Web site for additional information and resources.

Literature Focus Lesson

Summary In this comic strip, a young and arrogant student named Usagi is training to become a samurai. While fetching water for his master, Usagi finds a traveler who has stopped to rest and demands to know his business. The traveler, who identifies himself as Tsukahara, advises Usagi to learn some courtesy. When Usagi attacks, Tsukahara throws him into the water and leaves. Years later, Usagi travels to Yamashita village to seek Tsukahara. Instead of resuming the fight, Usagi bows deferentially and thanks Tsukahara for the lesson. **OL**

Teach

R Reading Skill

Evaluating Ask: Does the sensei give Usagi good advice? Is his advice good only for samurai? Explain. *(Possible response: Yes; the sensei's advice is good because being a samurai is also about being honest, loyal, and respectful. The advice can be useful to all people who focus too much on one thing.)* **OL**

C Critical Thinking

Comprehension Say: Review what has happened between Usagi and his sensei. How does Usagi feel at this point? *(Usagi is angry because he is impatient and wants to be a great warrior.)* **OL**

English Language Coach

Identify Proverbs The sensei speaks to Usagi in sentences that resemble proverbs. Because students may be unfamiliar with proverbs, explain that these are short sayings or expressions that make observations or teach lessons. Use the following as an example: "It is better to be safe than sorry." Invite students to discuss the meaning of this proverb and reasons for its existence. Invite students to share other proverbs with which they are familiar. **BL EL** Organize students into groups, and have each group research proverbs from a particular culture, such as Chinese, Japanese, and Hindu. **OL**

Objectives
- Learn and use new vocabulary
- Identify main ideas and supporting details
- Evaluate text
- Take and review notes

913

Teach

R Reading Skill

Synthesizing Say: You already know that Usagi wants very badly to defeat his sensei. In this frame, Usagi is angry that he has to fetch water for his sensei. What can you determine about how Usagi feels about the samurai code? (*Possible response: Usagi does not honor and respect his master, which is part of the samurai code. He is too impatient and arrogant to follow the code.*) **OL**

L Literary Element

Description Say: Look closely at the third frame. Describe the scene. (*The traveler is resting on a rock by the water; Usagi, however, is standing aggressively and drawing his sword.*) **EL BL Ask:** What does this description show you about the differences between the two characters? (*Possible response: The sensei has said that Usagi is too focused on conquest, so it's not surprising that Usagi looks aggressive. The traveler says he is just there to rest, and his actions show he means no harm—he's more peaceful than Usagi.*) **OL**

Additional Support

Literature Focus Lesson

Narrator Explain to students that this comic strip has neither a first-person nor a third-person narrator. Then point out that in this comic strip, no single person or voice is responsible for telling the story. Instead, readers understand the events of the story by viewing the images and reading the dialogue, just as they would by watching an animated TV show. Point out that some comic strips do have narrators, and that such strips contain boxes of text that narrate events. Bring in the comics section of a newspaper and have students identify those strips that have narrators. **AS**

Teach

L Literary Element

Sequence of Events/Time Order Say: Use the words *first, next, then,* and *finally* to describe the events in these four frames. *(Possible response: First, Usagi warns the traveler not to tell him what to do. Next, Usagi charges at the traveler. Then, the traveler throws a stick at Usagi, stopping his attack. Finally, Usagi lands in the water.)* **BL**

R Reading Skill

Evaluating Ask: Given what you know about Usagi, do his actions seem believable? Explain. *(Possible response: Yes; his actions seem believable because he is overconfident and focused on proving that he is a good warrior.)* **OL**

Reading in the Real World

Career Many people who are interested in storytelling have become successful cartoonists or graphic novelists. Professions within this field include writing, editing, penciling, inking, coloring, and lettering. Writers and editors typically create something similar to a screenplay, which includes the story's plot and ideas for artistic layout. Pencilers then sketch the story in individual panels, which are embellished by inkers and colorists. Captions and dialogue are added by letterers, who use style to suggest tone and volume. Aspiring writers generally break into the field by preparing portfolios and attending conventions. **AS**

Objectives
• Synthesize text
• Evaluate text
• Identify literary elements: description
• Understand sequence: time order

915

Teach

R Reading Skill

Identifying Main Idea and Supporting Details Ask:

Why might the incident between Usagi and the traveler be important to the story's plot? *(Possible responses: Usagi will make it his goal to find the traveler and finish the fight; Usagi may learn a lesson from the traveler about being humble and respectful.)*
Ask: What do you think will be the outcome of the story? *(Responses will vary.)* **OL**

R

Additional Support

Reading Fluency

Reading Comic Strips Point out that the same rules apply to reading both ordinary text and comic strips—that is, one reads from left to right and from top to bottom. For example, in the frame in which Usagi yells to Tsukahara, students should read the word bubbles from left to right. In the bottom frame, students should read Tsukahara's reply (top), and then Usagi's retort (bottom). Have students find a quiet place to practice reading aloud fluently and with expression. **EL BL**

Teach

L Literary Element

Narrator Say: Although this comic strip does not have a narrator, the box that says "Years later . . ." indicates that time has passed since the last frame. **EL BL** Look at the next frame. How else might you know that time has passed? *(Usagi looks older.)* **OL**

R Reading Skill

Synthesizing Say: In this strip, Usagi asks where he can find Yamashita village. Synthesize this information with what you learned earlier in the strip. What do you think Usagi intends to do? *(Possible response: Usagi intends to settle the fight that began when Tsukahara threw him into the water.)* **OL**

Literature Focus Lesson

Time Order Authors, cartoonists, and filmmakers have various ways of showing audiences that time has elapsed. In this comic strip, the cartoonist draws a box that says "Years later . . ." Explain that authors and filmmakers also compress time, and ask students to think about how they accomplish this. For example, to show that one night has passed, a filmmaker may have light fade out to suggest night and fade in to suggest a sunny day. To compress a longer period of time, filmmakers frequently use a montage, or progression of shots. Bring in examples of montages to share with students. **AS**

Objectives
- Identify main idea and supporting details
- Synthesize text
- Identify and analyze narrator
- Understand sequence: time order

917

Teach

L Literary Element

Description **Say:** Look at the way the cartoonist has drawn Usagi's face in these frames. On the basis of these drawings, can you guess how Usagi feels at this moment? *(Responses will vary. Some students may say that Usagi is angry or vengeful. Other students may suspect that Usagi has come to thank Tsukahara and that he is serious but grateful.)* **AS**

R Reading Skill

Evaluating **Ask:** Is it realistic that Tsukahara does not recognize Usagi? Explain. *(Some students may say that although Usagi obviously remembers their earlier meeting, Tsukahara probably forgot about it soon after it happened. Other students may point out that Usagi has matured and has become a dignified samurai.)* **OL**

Additional Support

English Language Coach

Build Background Explain to students that in Japan, people often refer to one another by last name and a title, which varies with rank. *Sensei,* for example, is used for educated people and for those who give instruction. *San,* as in "Tsukahara-*san,*" is the most common title and is used in most situations. *Sama* is a more polite form of san and is commonly used in formal situations and letters. *Kun* is an informal title used to address boys and girls who are younger than the speaker. *Chan* is an informal title that is used for young children and for very close friends or relatives. **AS**

Teach

L Literary Element

Symbol **Say:** Remember that the comic strip begins with the sound of Usagi's sword. As a young student, Usagi was very eager to use his sword. Now that he has found Tsukahara, he draws his sword again. How might Usagi's sword be a symbol in the story? What do you think it represents? Explain. *(Possible response: The sword represents Usagi's arrogance and eagerness to fight. It is also a common symbol of the samurai in general.)* **AL**

R Reading Skill

Identifying Main Idea and Supporting Details **Ask:** What lesson does Usagi learn from Tsukahara? *(Possible response: Usagi learns to behave more like a samurai. He learns to be humble and to show respect to others.)* **Ask:** How does learning this lesson relate to the Big Question? *(Possible response: Usagi has learned from the mistakes he made as a young, arrogant student. Now that he has matured, he appreciates the importance of being humble and courteous.)* **OL**

Differentiated Instruction

Draw a Comic Strip Have students work together to create comic strips about a character who learns from his or her mistakes. Encourage students to begin by developing a limited number of characters and a plot. Students should then create a dialogue, at which point they may begin laying out the story in frames. If students work in large groups, assign each student a different task, such as sketching, inking, coloring, and lettering. When all the strips have been completed, arrange them on a large poster board for display in your classroom. **AS**

Objectives
- Evaluate text
- Identify main idea and supporting details
- Identify literary elements: description
- Identify literary devices: symbols

919

Point out to students that independent reading can improve their vocabularies. Have them make lists of unfamiliar words that they encounter in their reading. Encourage them to figure out word meanings by using context clues. Students can check their guesses in a dictionary.

Fiction

Point out to students that mistakes people make and the lessons they learn from their mistakes are often central to works of fiction. Ask students for examples of stories they've read which feature examples of people learning from their mistakes. They can name fictional stories from this unit or stories they've read elsewhere. Discuss with students what they discovered about how to learn from their own mistakes from reading these stories.

UNIT 7
Reading on Your Own

To read more about the Big Question, choose one of these books from your school or local library. Work on your reading skills by choosing books that are challenging to you.

Fiction

The Secret Garden
by Frances H. Burnett

Lonely and bad tempered, Mary is an orphan who lives in an empty mansion on the Yorkshire moors. She begins to change when she discovers a secret walled garden and meets a boy named Dickon. Read to find out what Mary learns from her secret garden.

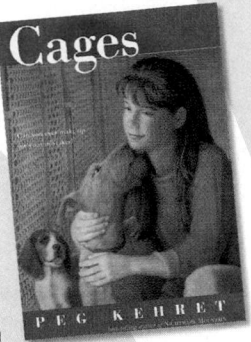

Cages
by Peg Kehret

It was the most terrible day of Kit's life—the day she tried shoplifting and got caught. Sentenced to twenty hours of volunteer work at the Humane Society, Kit ends up with some time to think. Read to find out what she learns from her mistake.

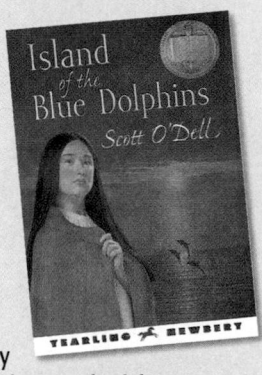

Island of the Blue Dolphins
by Scott O'Dell

When Karana is accidentally abandoned by her people, she spends eighteen years on a lonely island by herself. Read to find out more about what she discovered on that island—strength, serenity, and an amazing will to survive.

A Christmas Carol
by Charles Dickens

Ebenezer Scrooge is so obsessed with business and money that he has isolated himself from others. On Christmas Eve, several spirits visit Scrooge. The spirits take Scrooge to revisit scenes from his own life in an effort to reawaken the humanity within him. Read to find out what Scrooge learns from his mistakes.

Additional Support

Differentiated Instruction

 Use the Glencoe BookLink CD-ROM to create customized reading lists to help students answer the Big Question. Suggestions for Unit 7:

Grade 4: *Animals in Danger*
by Gare Thompson
Grade 5: *Behind the Bedroom Wall*
by Laura E. Williams

Grade 6: *The Medicine Bag*
by Virginia Driving Hawk Sneve
Grade 7: *Sojourner Truth and the Struggle for Freedom*
by Edward Beecher Calflin
Grade 8: *My Antonia*
by Willa Cather

Nonfiction

Malcolm X: By Any Means Necessary
by Walter Dean Myers

By age twenty, Malcolm Little was in prison. There he discovered Islam as a way to recover his dignity and set his life straight. Later, he became a revered leader of the Nation of Islam. Read to find out what Malcolm believed and how he changed the world.

The Story of Thomas Alva Edison
by Margaret Cousins

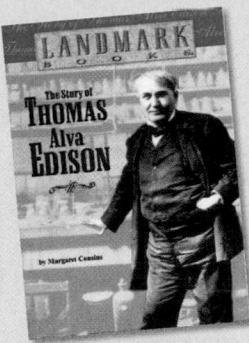

Thomas Edison made many mistakes before he invented a successful light bulb. Read to find out how his curiosity about how things work lasted a lifetime—and made the world a brighter place.

Knots in My Yo-yo String: The Autobiography of a Kid
by Jerry Spinelli

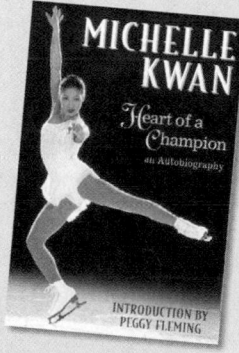

The creator of *Maniac Magee* recalls his childhood from six to sixteen like this: " ten years of . . . salamanders and snakes and candy cigarettes, coal dust on the clothesline, baseball cleats swinging from my handlebars, Ovaltine in my milk, knots in my yo-yo string." Read to find out more about Spinelli's exciting adventures.

Michelle Kwan: Heart of a Champion
by Michelle Kwan

Ever wondered what it's like to be a figure skating champion at the age of twelve? If so, check out this book. Read to find out more about Michelle Kwan's triumphs, her disasters, and her incredible love of skating.

Nonfiction
Tell students that the books on this page are all nonfiction books. They tell true stories about real people. These books give detailed accounts of the lives of their subjects.

Autobiographies and Biographies
Remind students that an autobiography is the story of a person's life told by that person. A biography is a story of a person's life told by a different person. Ask students what they can learn from reading biographies and autobiographies. *(Possible response: Reading autobiographies and biographies can provide new insights into people's lives and show additional examples of how real people have learned from their mistakes.)* **OL**

About the Subjects
Invite students to evaluate any of the subjects of the books listed in the student edition. Then ask students to share why they may or may not want to read one of these books.

Test-Taking Tips

TIP Remind students that when they begin to answer passage-based questions, they should refer to the passage to find evidence for their answers. Students are never asked to speculate without adequate evidence; they need only refer to the passage and find clues in the text.

TIP Tell students that tests will often contain constructed-response questions. Before they start writing, students should make sure that they understand the question. Suggest that students reread the question to make sure that they know exactly what information their responses should include.

Test Practice

Part 1: Literary Elements

1. A
2. B
3. A
4. Responses will vary.

Test Practice

Part 1: Literary Elements

Read the passage. On a separate sheet of paper, write the numbers 1–4. Next to numbers 1–3, write the letter of the correct answer. Next to number 4, write your answer to the question.

When my mother left North Carolina, she couldn't bring her sisters or the deep feather bed she'd slept in or the thick forests of her childhood. She couldn't bring the splashing mountain streams. So she brought what she could, a lilac bush.

On the prairie where my parents settled, a bitter wind blew endlessly. My mother built a small stone wall to protect her lilac until our small house went up and could take over that job. I remember finding her on cold, damp, spring mornings, crouched by the bush, studying its glossy green leaves. She was waiting, waiting. And soon, a softly warm afternoon would come. The first purple-blue blossoms would appear on delicate branches. For the next three weeks, a sweet and spicy fragrance filled our yard.

During this time every spring, my mother was different. Her usual happiness was deeper. Her eyes were filled with memory. She would spend too much money on a ham and bake the fluffy biscuits her own mother had taught her, years ago, to make. Over dinner, she would tell stories about relatives I had never met and descriptions of birds and forest animals I had never seen. And then the lilac's flowers would fade, and my mother would turn her attention back to our everyday life.

Objectives (pp. 922–923)
Reading Identify main ideas and supporting details • Synthesize information • Make inferences • Evaluate text
Literature Identify literary elements: point of view, narrator, symbolism, description, sensory details

1. Which of the following sentences reveals that the narrator is using a first-person point of view?
   A. "On the prairie where my parents settled, a bitter wind blew endlessly."
   B. "So she brought what she could, a lilac bush."
   C. "And soon, a softly warm afternoon would come."
   D. "The first purple-blue blossoms would appear on delicate branches."

2. What does the lilac bush symbolize for the narrator's mother?
   A. loss, sadness, and pain
   B. the life she left behind
   C. the importance of change
   D. the hardships of everyday life

3. Which of the following events actually occurs *first*?
   A. The mother moves to the prairie.
   B. The narrator's house is built.
   C. The narrator hears stories.
   D. The mother learns to make biscuits.

4. Explain how the author's use of description in this passage can help a reader experience the story. Give at least two examples.

Part 2: Reading Skills

On a separate sheet of paper, write the numbers 1–4. Next to each number, write the letter of the right answer.

Read the following passages and use them to answer questions 1 and 2.

Passage 1. In December of 1777, the American army set up camp at Valley Forge, Pennsylvania, where they would remain all winter. The location kept the soldiers safe from attack. They were not safe from nature. Many of the soldiers had no shoes. Most were dressed in rags. They huddled together in small crowded wooden huts. The army's commander, George Washington, did what he could to obtain supplies. On most days, however, their only food was flat pancakes made of flour and water. Their rag-wrapped feet left blood on the snow as they marched and trained. Disease was common, frostbite more so. By spring, thousands had died.

Passage 2. It was miserably hot in New Jersey on June 28, 1778. The men tramping down the road had once been farmers and shopkeepers in America's countryside and towns. Now they were soldiers fighting to be free. Their respect for their leader, George Washington, meant they would obey any command he gave. Soon he would be giving the command to fight. The Battle of Monmouth was only hours away.

1. What is the main idea of Passage 1?
   - **A.** The winter at Valley Forge was a very difficult one.
   - **B.** The housing at Valley Forge was crowded and cold.
   - **C.** The American army was led by George Washington.
   - **D.** Those who survive hardship are stronger because of it.

2. Synthesize information in Passage 2 to decide which of the following statements is true.
   - **A.** Farmers and shopkeepers make poor soldiers.
   - **B.** The Battle of Monmouth took place on June 28, 1778.
   - **C.** George Washington became the army's commander in 1778.
   - **D.** More soldiers died in the Battle of Monmouth than in any other battle.

3. What can you infer from Passage 1?
   - **A.** George Washington was a bad commander.
   - **B.** The year 1777 was the coldest on record.
   - **C.** The soldiers were not well supplied.
   - **D.** The soldiers did not know how to march.

4. Which of the following is always involved in evaluating a story or other text?
   - **A.** making inferences
   - **B.** synthesizing information
   - **C.** combining ideas to create new ones
   - **D.** coming up with opinions about the text

Test-Taking Tips

TIP Encourage students to take notes about the main idea and supporting details while and immediately after reading a selection. Such notes will be helpful when students are later asked to answer questions. Point out that in a real test situation, students should feel free to underline words and write in the margins.

TIP Remind students to always read questions and answer choices slowly and carefully. Certain words will often change the focus or scope of a question, and some phrases may relate to a key word in the passage that gives a clue to the correct answer.

Test Practice

Part 2: Reading Skills

1. A
2. B
3. C
4. D

Resources for page 922–925

Use these resources to review, assess, or reteach the Unit: Active Learning, Note Taking Guide, Selection and Unit Assessments, ExamView Assessment Suite, and Skill Level Up!™ A Language Arts Game.

Test-Taking Tips

Tip When asked about the meaning of a particular word, students should consider whether they have seen, heard, or written the word anywhere else. If they have, students should try to remember the context in which the word appeared and use that context to help eliminate incorrect choices and make an educated guess about the word's meaning.

Tip Remind students that when answering multiple-choice questions, they should begin by eliminating answer choices that they know are incorrect. Stress the idea that students who make a best guess from only the remaining choices have a higher likelihood of answering the question correctly.

Test Practice

Part 3: Vocabulary Skills

1. A
2. B
3. C
4. D
5. D
6. B
7. A
8. D
9. B
10. B

Part 3: Vocabulary Skills

On a separate sheet of paper, write the numbers 1–10. Next to each number, write the letter of the correct answer for that question.

Write the letter of the word or phrase that means about the same as the underlined word.

1. told her to cease
   - **A.** stop
   - **B.** stand
   - **C.** watch
   - **D.** speak

2. a forsaken town
   - **A.** busy
   - **B.** abandoned
   - **C.** large
   - **D.** successful

3. their dismal life
   - **A.** active
   - **B.** complicated
   - **C.** miserable
   - **D.** peaceful

4. too much commotion
   - **A.** violence
   - **B.** difficulty
   - **C.** reckless speed
   - **D.** noise and disorder

5. a grudging welcome
   - **A.** loud
   - **B.** joyful
   - **C.** shy
   - **D.** unwilling

Objectives (pp. 924–925)
Vocabulary Identify word structure: bases, roots • Identify compound words
Grammar Identify parts of speech: verbs, nouns • Use correct subject-verb agreement

Write the letter of the best answer.

6. Use what you know about base words to complete the sentence below.

   A person who is *desirous* of water is
   - **A.** wet.
   - **B.** thirsty.
   - **C.** busily swimming.
   - **D.** afraid of drowning.

7. The Latin root *aud* means "hear," as in *audience.* What part of your body would a doctor who's an audiologist need to examine?
   - **A.** ears
   - **B.** eyes
   - **C.** nose
   - **D.** throat

8. The Latin root *brev* means "short," as in *abbreviation.* If someone complains about the brevity of a movie, that person is saying it was
   - **A.** boring.
   - **B.** too violent.
   - **C.** poorly acted.
   - **D.** not long enough.

9. The Greek root *astr* or *aster* means "star," as in *astronomy* and *astrology.* Which of the following symbols is an asterisk?
   - **A.** &
   - **B.** *
   - **C.** #
   - **D.** $

10. The Latin root *mono* means "one" and the Greek root *chrome* means "color." Which of the following is most likely to be monochromatic?
    - **A.** a rainbow
    - **B.** a snowy field
    - **C.** a nation's flag
    - **D.** a flower garden

Part 4: Writing Skills

On a separate sheet of paper, write the numbers 1–8. For the first 7 questions write the letter of the correct answer for that question. Next to number 8, write your answer to that question.

---

1. What is the verb in the following sentence?

The players on the team rarely arrived on time for the game.

- **A.** players
- **B.** rarely
- **C.** arrived
- **D.** on

2. What is the subject in the following sentence?

The people in the park were walking dogs, playing catch, and having fun.

- **A.** The
- **B.** people
- **C.** park
- **D.** dogs

3. Which of the following sentences has a compound subject?

- **A.** My favorite animals are dogs.
- **B.** A sandwich and an apple will be enough.
- **C.** Did Sayid call, or was that Nathaniel?
- **D.** Grown-ups who are mean to kids make me mad.

4. Which forms of the verbs belong in the following sentence?

The bikes in the garage (needs, need) new tires, but nobody (has, have) money to buy them.

- **A.** needs, has
- **B.** need, has
- **C.** needs, have
- **D.** need, have

5. Which forms of the verbs belong in the following sentence?

Inside the box (was, were) a tie and a pair of pants, and the pants (was, were) just my size.

- **A.** was, was
- **B.** was, were
- **C.** were, was
- **D.** were, were

6. Which forms of the verbs belong in the following sentence?

Everybody (knows, know) the best running shoes in the whole store (is, are) the ones over there.

- **A.** knows, is
- **B.** knows, are
- **C.** know, is
- **D.** know, are

7. Which forms of the verbs belong in the following sentence?

How (do, does) Luke know which of the scissors (is, are) his?

- **A.** do, is
- **B.** do, are
- **C.** does, is
- **D.** does, are

8. What can you do to make sure your writing (especially in a personal narrative) reflects your voice?

Test-Taking Tips

TIP When students must select the proper word for a sentence, encourage them to use their "ears" as well as their knowledge of grammar. In some instances, students may choose the correct word by reading the sentence aloud. Remind students that this is a preliminary tactic and that the rules of grammar should always take precedence over intuition.

TIP Remind students to review all written work for correct spelling, capitalization, and punctuation. When answering a constructed-response question in a real test situation, students should develop a brief outline and then write the response as clearly and concisely as possible. If time permits, students may also choose to write a final draft.

Test Practice

Part 4: Writing Skills

1. C
2. B
3. B
4. B
5. D
6. B
7. C
8. Responses will vary.

UNIT 8
Skills Scope and Sequence

Readability Scores Key
Dale-Chall/DRP/Lexile

PACING (DAYS)		INSTRUCTIONAL SEGMENT LITERATURE	READING SKILLS	LITERARY ELEMENTS
STANDARD	BLOCK			
1	1	**Unit Warm-Up, pp. 928–937** Genre Focus: Drama from *Novio Boy* by Gary Soto **3.6/NA/NA**, SE p. 931	Visualizing, SE pp. 930, 932, TWE p. 937 Clarifying, SE pp. 930, 936, TWE pp. 928, 934 Skimming and Scanning, SE pp. 930, 931, TWE p. 933 Predicting, SE pp. 930, 935, 936 Fluency, TWE pp. 927, 937 How to Read Drama, TWE p. 930	Act and Scene, SE pp. 930, 931, TWE p. 937 Characterization, SE pp. 930, 933, 934, 937, TWE p. 932 Stage directions, SE pp. 930, 931, TWE pp. 932, 933, 934, 935 Sensory Image, SE pp. 930, 937, TWE p. 932
3	2	**Reading Workshop 1, pp. 938–965** "The Reluctant Dragon" Scene 1, by Kenneth Grahame **4.3/NA/NA**, SE p. 940 "The Reluctant Dragon" Scene 2, by Kenneth Grahame **4.3/NA/NA**, SE p. 953	Visualizing, SE pp. 938, 941, 942, 943, 946, 947, 948, 950, 953, 956, 957, 958, 959, 961, TWE pp. 939, 944, 945, 962 Predicting, SE pp. 944, 957, TWE pp. 955, 956, 961, 963 Clarifying, TWE pp. 943, 956, 957, 961	Scene, SE pp. 941, 942, 953, 954, TWE pp. 946, 950, 951, 961 Characterization, TWE p. 948 Conflict, TWE p. 954 Stage Directions, TWE pp. 956, 959
1		**Writing Workshop, Part 1, pp. 966–969** Writing Product: Speech	Fluency, TWE p. 968	Speech, TWE p. 966
3	1	**Reading Workshop 2, pp. 970–995** "Damon and Pythias" by Fan Kissen **4.4/NA/NA**, SE p. 974 "Charlie Johnson" by Joe Smith **4.0/48/780**, SE p. 988	Clarifying, SE pp. 970, 973, 975, 978, 987, 990, 992, 993, TWE pp. 971, 972, 976, 982 Predicting, SE pp. 979, 993, TWE p. 978 Fluency, TWE pp. 970, 976, 979, 990 Visualizing, TWE pp. 975, 980, 988 Connecting, TWE p. 988	Characterization, SE pp. 973, 977, 980, 981, 983, 987, 988, 991, 992, 993, TWE pp. 975, 976, 979, 982, 989, 990 Dialogue, TWE pp. 978, 989

Unit 8 Big Question

Addressing the Big Question "What makes a friend?" helps students to consider how important friends are in helping us to set goals, pursue our dreams, and make life richer.

Unit 8 Genre

Reading drama will give your students another way to understand stories. Accessing this form, and thinking about the stories told in this unit, will help your students answer the Big Question: "What makes a friend?"

CRITICAL THINKING	VOCABULARY	WRITING AND GRAMMAR	LISTENING, SPEAKING, AND VIEWING
Comprehension, TWE p. 934 Analysis, TWE p. 936	Synonyms, TWE p. 928 Slang, TWE pp. 931, 933, 934, 935 Idioms, TWE p. 936		Viewing the Photo, TWE p. 926
Analyze, SE pp. 952, 964, TWE pp. 944, 945, 949, 957, 960, 962 Infer, SE p. 964 Synthesize, SE p. 964, TWE p. 958 Application, TWE pp. 947, 959 Evaluation, TWE p. 947	Slang, SE pp. 940, 945, TWE p. 950 Dialect, SE pp. 953, 958, 960, 962 Word Meanings, TWE p. 940 Synonyms and Antonyms, TWE p. 942 Idioms, TWE pp. 948, 949, 950, 954	Hypens, SE p. 965 Write About Your Reading, SE p. 964	Analyzing the Art, SE pp. 946, 951, 960, 963 Talk About Your Reading, SE p. 952 Analyzing the Illustration, SE p. 955 Viewing the Art, TWE pp. 942, 955, 960
		Beginning, SE p. 967 Middle, SE p. 967 End, SE p. 967 Applying Good Writing Traits: Presentation, SE p. 968 Apostrophes, SE p. 969 Organization Skills, TWE p. 967	
Interpret, SE p. 984 Visualize, SE p. 984 Evaluate, SE pp. 984, 994 Analyze, SE p. 994, TWE pp. 979, 991 Infer, SE p. 994 Comprehension, TWE p. 978	Academic Vocabulary, SE p. 970 Idioms, SE pp. 972, 976, 986, 988, 989, TWE pp. 977, 991, 992 Multiple-Meaning Words, TWE p. 980	Semicolons with Main Clauses, SE p. 985 Write About Your Reading, SE p. 994 Semicolons with Long Clauses that Include Commas, SE p. 995	Analyzing the Art, SE pp. 976, 983, 990, 992 Viewing the Photo, TWE pp. 974, 993 Viewing the Art, TWE p. 979 Talk About Your Reading, SE p. 984

Readability Scores Key
Dale-Chall/DRP/Lexile

PACING (DAYS)		INSTRUCTIONAL SEGMENT LITERATURE	READING SKILLS	LITERARY ELEMENTS
STANDARD	BLOCK			
3	3	**Reading Workshop 3, pp. 996–1031** "The Bully of Barksdale Street" by Eric Alter **5.4/NA/NA**, SE p. 998 "Tales of the Tangled Tresses" by Christina Hamlett **5.0/NA/NA**, SE p. 1014	Skimming and Scanning, SE pp. 996, 999, 1001, 1015, 1016, 1025, 1028, TWE pp. 1000, 1018, 1021, 1026 Visualizing, SE p. 1009 Predicting, SE p. 1018 Evaluating, SE pp. 1027, 1028 Fluency, TWE pp. 997, 1006, 1023, 1026, 1029	Stage Directions, SE pp. 999, 1000, 1002, 1003, 1004, 1005, 1007, 1010, 1015, 1016, 1017, 1019, 1021, 1025, 1026, 1027, TWE pp. 997, 1022
2		**Writing Workshop, Part 2, pp. 1032–1035** Writing Product: Speech	Fluency, TWE p. 1032	
3	1	**Reading Workshop 4, pp. 1036–1055** "Zlateh the Goat" by Isaac Bashevis Singer **5.5/51/810**, SE p. 1038 "Best of Buddies" by Kevin Gray and Cindy Damper **7.6/60/930**, SE p. 1050	Predicting, SE pp. 1036, 1039, 1040, 1041, 1042, 1045, 1046, 1051, 1053 Connecting, SE p. 1039, TWE p. 1057	Sensory Imagery, SE pp. 1039, 1044, 1045, 1047 Problem and Solution, SE pp. 1051, 1052, 1053
3	2	**Reading Across Texts Workshop, pp. 1056–1071** "Baby Hippo Orphan Finds a Friend" by Catherine Clarke Fox **5.9/58/1020**, p. 1058 from *The Caretaker's Diary* by Stephen Tuei **5.2/54/990**, SE p. 1062	Comparing Sources of Information, SE pp. 1056, 1059, 1060, 1061, 1063, 1064, 1066, 1067 Drawing Conclusions, TWE p. 1058 Clarifying, TWE p. 1062 Fluency, TWE p. 1063	Point of View, SE p. 1069, TWE p. 1056 Primary and secondary Sources, SE p. 1060 Chronological Order, TWE p. 1064
4	2	**Unit Wrap-Up, pp. 1072–1077** **Your Turn**: "A Time to Talk" by Robert Frost SE p. 1074	Fluency, TWE p. 1075 Drawing Conclusions, TWE p. 1075	

CRITICAL THINKING	VOCABULARY	WRITING AND GRAMMAR	LISTENING, SPEAKING, AND VIEWING
Interpret, SE p. 1012 Evaluate, SE pp. 1012, 1030, TWE pp. 1001, 1004, 1006, 1008, 1009, 1019 Synthesize, SE p. 1012 Infer, SE p. 1030 Comprehension, TWE pp. 999, 1000, 1010, 1017 Analysis, TWE p. 1002 Comprehension, TWE pp. 1015, 1016, 1024, 1029	Clipped Words, SE pp. 998, 1003, 1009 Jargon, SE pp. 1014, 1017, 1023, 1024, TWE p. 1020 Dialect and Slang, TWE pp. 1001, 1009 Connotation, TWE p. 1011 Plurals, TWE p. 1014	Using Colons in Time Notations and After Salutations, SE p. 1013 Write About Your Reading, SE p. 1012, 1030 Using a Colon to Introduce a List, SE p. 1031	Analyzing the Art, SE pp. 1018, 1021 Viewing the Illustration, TWE pp. 1006, 1009, 1011 Viewing the Art, TWE pp. 1021, 1027
		Presenting, SE p. 1033 Revising, SE p. 1032 Editing, SE p. 1033	Oral Presentation, SE p. 1035 Diction, TWE p. 1033
Compare, SE p. 1048 Analyze, SE p. 1048, TWE pp. 1044, 1045 Evaluate, SE p. 1048, TWE p. 1047 Connect, SE p. 1048 Infer, SE p. 1054 Conclude, SE p. 1054 Assess, SE p. 1054 Comprehension, TWE p. 1041	Academic Vocabulary, SE p. 1036 Literal and Figurative Meanings, SE pp. 1038, 1043, TWE p. 1046 Idioms, SE pp. 1050, 1053	Quotation Marks, SE pp. 1049, 1055 Write About Your Reading, SE p. 1048	Viewing the Illustration, TWE p. 1042 Viewing the Photo, TWE p. 1052
Recall, SE p. 1071 Draw Conclusions, SE p. 1071 Interpret, SE p. 1071 Analyze, SE p. 1071 Application, TWE p. 1057 Comprehension, TWE pp. 1063, 1064 Evalution, TWE p. 1065		Write About Your Reading, SE p. 1071	Analyzing the Map, SE p. 1059 Analyzing the Photo, SE pp. 1061, 1065, 1068
	Connotation, TWE p. 1074		Group Activity, SE p. 1072 Viewing the Photo, TWE p. 1075

Reading with Purpose offers a comprehensive package of tools to optimize student learning and the teaching experience. Each resource has been designed to assist students in specific areas and to offer instructional support for teachers. While all of these areas are covered in the core textbook, some students may need extra practice or additional help in specific areas. The resource package is designed so that you, the teacher, can choose which items will best assist your students. You may also use these resources as homework assignments and for assessment purposes. The following are resources recommended for use with Unit 8.

Keys for Unit Resources

- 📁 Blackline Master
- 📓 Workbook
- 📖 Supplemental Text
- 💿 CD-ROM
- 💾 DVD
- 🖼 Transparency
- 💻 Web-based
- 🔨 Fast File

Essential Instructional Support

FAST FILE UNIT 8 RESOURCES

Reading and Literature

- Academic Vocabulary Review
- Big Question: School to Home
- The Big Question Foldable
- Unit Challenge: Planner and Rubrics
- Reading Across Texts Graphic Organizer
- Key Reading Skills
- Active Reading Graphic Organizers
- Literary Analysis
- Unit Vocabulary Review

Writing, Grammar, and Spelling

- Spelling and Handwriting Practice
- Grammar Practice
- Writing Workshop Graphic Organizer

Listening, Speaking, and Viewing

- Viewing and Representing
- Listening and Speaking

English Language Learners

- English Language Coach Review

DIFFERENTIATED INSTRUCTION

- 📁 Leveled Vocabulary Development
- 💿 Skill Level Up!™ A Language Arts Game
- 💿 Listening Library CD
- 💿 BookLink 3
- 💿 Literature Library Vocabulary Puzzlemaker
- 💿 Vocabulary Puzzlemaker

ASSESSMENT

GLENCOE'S ASSESSMENT ADVANTAGE

- 📁 Selection and Unit Assessments
- 📁 Selection Quick Checks
- 📁 Assessment by Learning Objectives
- 📁 Rubrics for Assessing Student Writing, Listening, and Speaking
- 💻 Glencoe Online Essay Grader
- 💿 Interactive Tutor: Self-Assessment
- 💿 ExamView Assessment Suite
- 💿 Literature Library ExamView Assessment Suite

Additional Instructional Support

WRITING, GRAMMAR, AND SPELLING

- Real Success in Writing: Research and Reports
- Writing Constructed Responses
- Spelling Power eWorkbook
- Grammar & Composition Handbook
- Grammar and Language Workbook
- Revising with Style eWorkbook

READING AND LITERATURE

- Active Learning and Note Taking Guide
- inTime Magazines
- Backpack Reader Volume 1
- Literature Library
- Literature Launchers Pre-Reading Videos DVD
- Literature Classics

TRANSPARENCIES

- Read Aloud, Think Aloud Transparencies
- Literary and Text Analysis Transparencies
- Bellringer Options Transparencies
- Grammar and Writing Workshop Transparencies
- Fine Art Transparencies

TECHNOLOGY

- TeacherWorks Plus™
- StudentWorks Plus™
- BookLink 3
- Skill Level Up!™ A Language Arts Game
- ExamView Assessment Suite
- Interactive Tutor: Self-Assessment
- Listening Library CD
- Spanish Listening Library CD
- Literature Classics
- Literature Launchers Pre-Reading Videos DVD
- Literature Library ExamView Assessment Suite
- Vocabulary Puzzlemaker
- Literature Library Vocabulary Puzzlemaker
- glencoe.com
- Online Student Edition
- Presentation Plus!
- Glencoe Online Essay Grader

ENGLISH LANGUAGE LEARNER

- English Language Coach
- Fluency Practice and Assessment
- inTime Magazines (Spanish)
- Spanish Listening Library CD

PROFESSIONAL DEVELOPMENT

- Professional Development Package

Additional Glencoe Resources

Dinah Zike's Foldables

Foldables are three-dimensional, interactive graphic organizers that help students practice basic writing skills, review key vocabulary terms, and answer Big Questions. Every unit contains a foldable activity. You can find the pattern and directions for the Unit 8 Foldable in the Unit 8 Resources Fast Files booklet. You can use the foldables as they are presented or modify them to suit the needs of your students. More information about foldables for Unit 8 can be found on pages R8–R9.

Unit
Big Question

Glencoe Literature Library

This collection of hardcover books includes full-length novels, novellas, plays, and works of nonfiction. Each volume consists of at least one complete extended-length reading accompanied by several related readings from a broad range of genres. A separate Study Guide for each Glencoe Literature Library book provides teaching notes and reproducible activity pages for students.

Glencoe Literature Library titles that complement this unit include:
The Cay, by Theodore Taylor
I, Juan de Pareja, by Elizabeth Borton de Trevino
Mrs. Frisby and the Rats of NIMH, by Robert C. O'Brien

For a wealth of online resources that support the instruction in Unit 8 of *Glencoe Literature: Reading with Purpose,* students and teachers can visit our Web site at www.glencoe.com. Students will find additional learning, practice, and assessment opportunities such as these, which are noted in the student text:

- **Big Question Overview**
- **Study Central**
- **Author Search**
- **Writing Models**
- **Interactive Literary Elements Handbook**
- **Web Activities**

Teachers will find planning and instructional tools that include the following:

- **Book Lesson Plans**
- **Teacher Forum**
- **Professional Development**
- **Web Activities Lesson Plans (with answers to student activities)**

Go to www.glencoe.com to see the entire selection of Reading with Purpose online resources.

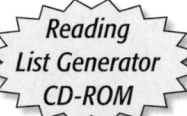

Use the Glencoe **BookLink 3** CD-ROM, a database of more than 26,700 titles, to *create customized reading lists* for your students.

- Search for award-winning titles, (e.g., Newbery Award winners, Coretta Scott King Award winners, and Caldecott Medal winners) and for books on several state-recommended reading lists.
- Find Degrees of Reading Power™ (DRP) and Lexile™ readability scores for all selections.
- Organize reading lists by students' reading level, author, genre, theme, or area of interest.
- Get a brief summary of each selection.

You can find recommended leveled readings for this unit with Reading on Your Own (see page 1076).

Glencoe's **Presentation Plus!**, a multimedia teaching tool, lets you present dynamic lessons that will engage your students. Using Microsoft PowerPoint,® you can customize the presentations to create your own personalized lessons. Use **CheckPoint** questions with interactive response keypads to get immediate student feedback during lessons, to increase student participation, and to assess student comprehension.

A lively collection of articles drawn from issues of the TIME family of magazines helps students develop the skills they need to interact with informational text in a meaningful way. Each of the news stories, feature articles, reviews, profiles, and essays in the magazine connect to an author, work, or theme in *Glencoe Literature: Reading with Purpose.* Articles for Unit 8 are found in Volume B. See the *inTIME* Teacher's Guide for specific connections to each unit and for reproducible student worksheets designed to develop students' reading and critical thinking skills.

Literature Launchers

Set the scene with Glencoe's Literature Launchers, engaging video segments that introduce each unit's genre focus. Each video brings the genre to life, relating it to your students' worlds.

Insert the Glencoe Literature Launchers Pre-Reading Videos DVD into your DVD player. Select the Unit 8 Launcher from the menu to introduce the genre and Big Question for this unit.

Online Essay Grader

Use Glencoe's Online Essay Grader to score your students' writing and to provide individualized feedback to each student automatically.

You and your students can visit www.glencoe.com to link to the essay grader. *Students* can enter their essays and receive feedback on demand. *You* can manage demographic data, assign tests and generate individual student and aggregated reports. The essay grader can help you

- Save time with automatic scoring and individualized feedback.
- Supplement in-class writing instruction using guided writing practice.
- Get reports for individual students or for special populations.
- Track student improvement over time.

REAL Success: Reading Excellence at All Levels

Glencoe now provides all of your students with the tools they need to become better, more enthusiastic readers. The REAL Success suite of reading and language arts products encourages reading excellence by meeting the needs of students at all levels. Glencoe products that can be used in conjunction with Unit 8 include the following:

- Jamestown Literature: An Adapted Reader
- Jamestown *Reading Fluency*
- Jamestown *Critical Reading Series, In the Line of Duty*
- *Vocabulary Builder*
- *The Glencoe Reader, Course 1*

To order these products, call Glencoe at 1-800-USA-READ.

Teacher Wraparound Edition Key

Level Appropriate Code

AS = Activities for all students
AL = Activities for students working above grade level
OL = Activities for students working at grade level
BL = Activities for students working below grade level
EL = Activities for English language learners

Teacher Wraparound Prompts

R **Reading Skill** These activities help you teach reading comprehension skills.

V **Vocabulary** These activities help students comprehend words and incorporate them into their reading and writing.

C **Critical Thinking** These strategies help students apply and extend what they have learned.

BQ **BIG Question** These activities and questions prompt students to prepare to answer the Big Question.

W **Writing** These activities provide writing opportunities to help students practice writing and comprehend text.

L **Literary Element** These activities and questions help students comprehend selections and learn more about each genre.

E **Text Element** These activities help students comprehend text elements.

LSV **Listening, Speaking, Viewing** These activities help students practice listening, speaking, and viewing skills.

EL **English Language Coach** These skills help English language learners as well as students who need additional reading support.

Professional Development Center

From an Author

Jeff Wilhelm

Helping Students Review the Writing Conventions of Drama

There are several conventional features of scripts that students should understand before they read drama. Understanding these features facilitates comprehension.

Pre-reading/Framing Systems

- Titles (topics)
- Media (TV, stage, cinema, etc.)
- Cast (order, names, titles, class designations, physical descriptions)
- Genre tips (adventure, horror, documentary, etc.)

Setting Descriptions

- Settings (where the action takes place, the constraints that the setting and situation place on characters)
- Type of people living in this environment
- Social and historical situation and perspectives
- Cues of emotional mood and tone
- Description embedded in dialogue

Technical Stage Directions

- Aural and visual cues: sounds, lighting, properties
- Description and movement of properties
- Cues for mood, tone, expectations, symbolic meanings

Character Cues from Dialogue

- Characters portrayed through dialogue (own and that of others)
- Character cues from tone, style, word choice, individual language, and voice
- Cues from subtext, purpose and effect of language

Stage Directions/Descriptions of Characters

- Character portrayal from appearance
- Character portrayal from movements, gestures, body language, reactions of other characters
- Character portrayal from symbolic implications

Watch performances Dramatic scripts are not written to be read—except by producers, directors, and actors. They are written to be performed and experienced. Therefore it is important to watch versions of a script. You don't have to watch a whole performance but can select important and powerful scenes that can help students experience the script or consider important issues or ideas.

Teacher to Teacher

Emma Clowers
Brinkley Middle School
Jackson, Mississippi

When opening the Big Question "What makes a friend?" I give my class the following writing prompt: "You are a passenger on the Titanic along with all of your friends. As the ship sinks, you are seated in a lifeboat. You must choose five of your friends to be in the lifeboat. Who will you choose and why? What factors will you consider in the decision?" Sometimes I assign vocabulary words to be used in their responses, such as nouns ending in *–ty—loyalty, responsibility, longevity,* and *honesty,* for example. This activity makes students reflect on the deeper meanings of life, and at the same time sharpens their writing and vocabulary skills. After volunteers read their responses aloud, there is a class discussion. As students challenge one another on the choices they have made or the reasons they present, the disagreements sharpen their critical thinking skills.

Teacher Chat Room

Using Dramatic Scripts

 How can I help students learn to imagine a staged performance in their head as they read?

 As always, the most important time to teach is **before** students undertake a challenge. One frontloading activity I use is designed to help students understand how the conventions of scripts help readers stage a play in their mind. Before reading a play, I have students translate cartoons into scripts for another group to perform. They quickly learn that many things that are obvious in a visual text must be described through various kinds of stage directions in a script. Through such activities, I can fairly quickly help students identify, read, and write the cuing systems of scripts.

I also have students watch performances. When I teach plays, I always watch video segments of one or even multiple versions of performances with my students. I also always watch major scenes in a play before we read the scene since this provides background knowledge and frontloading that assists in the reading. After reading the scene, we can discuss how the director used or ignored particular stage directions and cues in the script.

 How can putting on a production help students?

 It is powerful to place students in the position of being producers, directors, actors, or critics. This gets them into the flow, and makes them active participants using scripts. Get them to interpret, adapt, and perform scenes; make videos of scenes, ads, or promotions for a play; review and critique scripts and various professional interpretations. I especially like to bring in scripts of TV shows or popular movies (these are widely available on the Internet) to help students explore how their favorite shows or movies are scripted.

Students can also be asked to perform their own version of a scene or event. The performance could be set in our own school, or another historical situation or setting. These can be contrasted with the video versions already viewed. Students can also be helped to compose and perform their own super-short plays or scenes that explore a major theme or issue from the reading in their own way, or through their own experience.

UNIT 8

The BIG Question: What Makes a Friend?

Key Unit Objectives

- Analyze the Big Question
- Apply strategies for reading dramas
- Analyze the literary elements of dramas
- Write a speech

BIG Question

Why Is It Important?
Addressing this big question helps students to consider how important friends are in helping us to set goals, pursue our dreams, and make life richer.

Viewing the Photo
Invite students to describe what the photo says about friendship. Ask how the quotation connects to the comfortable appearance of the women in the photo. (*Responses will vary.*) **AS**

Unit Skills

Reading Skills
- Visualizing, p. 938
- Clarifying, p. 970
- Skimming and Scanning, p. 996
- Predicting, p. 1036

Vocabulary
- Dialect and Slang, p. 940
- Idioms, p. 972
- Clipped Words, p. 998
- Jargon, p. 1014

BIG Question What makes a friend?
Genre Focus: Drama

- Literal and Figurative Meanings, p. 1038

Literary Elements
- Act and Scene, p. 941
- Characterization, p. 973
- Stage directions, p. 999
- Sensory Imagery, p. 1039

Writing Skills/Grammar
- Speech, p. 966
- Presentation, p. 968
- Apostrophes, p. 969

LOOKING AHEAD

The skill lessons and readings in this unit will help you develop your own answer to the Big Question.

927

INTRODUCING UNIT 8

About the Reading
Each selection in this unit provides insights that can help students address the question, "What makes a friend?" Students will consider aspects of friendship, while questions invite them to explore friendships in their own lives.

About the Skills
The skills taught in this unit have been selected because they are particularly helpful when reading drama. Each reading selection provides students with opportunities to practice and develop these skills.

NO CHILD LEFT BEHIND

The goals of the NCLB Act include a strong emphasis on teaching reading skills. You can help students develop the skills covered in this unit by, for example, reading a passage aloud and modeling how to identify the main idea and supporting details. See www.ed.gov/nclb/landing. jhtml for more information.

Reading Fluency

Build Fluency Dramas are perfect texts for students to build fluency. A simple and useful alternative to fully staging a play is to present it as readers theater. The plays in this unit allow students a variety of ways to read aloud dialogue and stage directions. Readers theater requires that students practice, usually with a partner or in an echo situation, in order to build reading skills and be able to read their parts fluently. **EL BL**

927

Focus

BELLRINGER Options

 Daily Language Practice Transparency 71 Focus Activity Ask: What is the main quality you look for in a friend? *(Responses will vary.)* **AS**

Teach

BQ **BIG Question**

Have students read the profiles and look at the pictures of Rebecca and Sammy. Discuss each situation and ask students to decide how they would advise each person. **AS**

R Reading Skill

Clarifying Say: Read Sammy's profile. What "stupid stuff" might Sammy's friend Keith be doing? *(Responses will vary. Students should support their responses with details from the text.)* **AS**

Connecting to The BIG Question — What Makes a Friend?

How do you know who's a real friend—and who isn't? Sometimes it's hard to know. Of course, a friend is someone you like to hang out with, someone who makes you laugh. A friend is someone you can talk to and trust. In this unit, you'll read about different people and how they figured out who their real friends were.

Real Kids and the Big Question

REBECCA and Alexandra have been best friends since third grade. But suddenly, things are changing. Alexandra is hanging out with a new crowd, and Rebecca feels left out. On the one hand, she's jealous, but on the other hand, she doesn't really like the kids in that group. She wishes things could be the way they used to be. What would you tell Rebecca?

B

R

SAMMY is really angry. His best friend, Keith, is doing stupid stuff. Sammy tried talking to Keith, but Keith told him to mind his own business. Sammy could keep his mouth shut, but he doesn't want to abandon his friend. What do you think Sammy should do?

Warm-Up Activity

In a small group, talk about the advice you would give Rebecca and Sammy. Explain to each other why you would give that advice.

928 UNIT 8 What Makes a Friend?

Additional Support

English Language Coach

Synonyms There are many words for different kinds of friendships. Have students list all the synonyms for friendship they can think of without using a dictionary or thesaurus. Have students tell the sort of friendship each of these *friend* synonyms suggests to them—very close, close, not close, and so on. **OL AL**

Possible responses:

• acquaintance	• homie
• buddy	• pal
• companion	• sidekick

You and the Big Question

Reading about how other people decided who their real friends were will help you think about how you would answer the Big Question. **BQ**

Big Question Link to Web resources to further explore the Big Question at www.glencoe.com.

Plan for the Unit Challenge

At the end of the unit, you'll use notes from all your reading to complete the Unit Challenge.

You'll choose one of the following activities:

A. The Friendship Play Work with a group to write, rehearse, and perform a play about friendship.

B. Create a Friendship Story Create your own graphic story about friendship that illustrates the dos and don'ts of being a good friend.

- Start thinking about which activity you'd like to do so that you can focus your thinking as you go through the unit.
- In your Learner's Notebook, write which activity you'd like to do.
- Each time you make notes about the Big Question, think about how your ideas will help you with the Unit Challenge activity you chose.

Keep Track of Your Ideas

As you read, you'll make notes about the Big Question. Later, you'll use these notes to complete the Unit Challenge. See pages R8–R9 for help with making Foldable 8. This diagram shows how it should look.

1. Use this Foldable for all selections in this unit.

2. On the front, write **Unit 8** and **What Makes a Friend?** Leave the other half of that folded page blank.

3. Across the top of each of the next folded pages, write a selection title. (See page 927 for titles.)

4. To the left of each crease, write **My Purpose for Reading.** Below this heading, you will write your purpose for reading each selection.

5. To the right of each crease, write **The Big Question.** Below this, you will write your thoughts about the Big Question.

Warm-Up **929**

Big Question Have students access the Web site for English and Spanish summaries and annotated links to related Web resources.

BQ 🔖**BIG Question**

Have students write their initial response to the Big Question in their Learner's Notebooks. *(Responses will vary.)* **AS**

FOLDABLES™
Study Organizer

For each selection they read, students will enter notes about how that selection applies to the Big Question. For details about using Dinah Zike's Foldables, see pages R8–R9.

Assess/Close

Ask students to share their ideas on why thinking about the Big Question might help them become a better friend to others.

Resources for page 929

📁 Use the Unit Challenge Planner BLM in the Unit 8 Resource Booklet, p. 36

📁 Use the Foldable BLM in the Unit 8 Resource Booklet, p. 7

Differentiated Instruction

Visual Clues Draw students' attention to the photos of Rebecca and Sammy. Explain that photographs and other illustrations can add meaning and understanding to a text. Ask students what visual clues in Rebecca's and Sammy's pictures suggest something about who they are and how they feel. Such clues can provide a way for students to connect their own feelings and experiences to a selection. Suggest that, in their Learner's Notebooks, students illustrate their Big Question entries by including art and photos cut from magazines, as well as their own drawings. **AS**

Objectives
- Clarify ideas and text
- Use synonyms
- Use text features: photographs

929

Focus

BELLRINGER Options

✏ **Daily Language Practice Transparency 72**
Focus Activity Ask: Have you ever seen a play? What was it? What did you like about it? *(Responses will vary.)* **AS**

Teach

R Reading Skill

How to Read Drama Ask:

Have you ever *read* a play? A play is just another way of telling a story, but a printed play looks different than a printed story. First, a printed play is called a script, and the writer is a playwright. Most of the script is what the characters say. Their words are not in quotation marks like in a short story, and there's no narrator saying "she said." Instead, the character's name appears at the beginning of his or her speech. A script also has stage directions. The playwright writes these to help the actors, director, and set designers. Finally, plays are often divided into acts and scenes, which are similar to divisions in a book. **AS**

Skills Focus
• Key skills for reading drama
• Key literary elements of drama

Skills Model
You will see how to use the key reading skills and literary elements as you read
• from *Novio Boy,* p. 931

Objectives (pp. 930–937)
Reading Read drama • Visualize • Clarify ideas and text • Skim and scan text • Make predictions
Literature Understand elements of drama: act and scene • Understand literary elements: characterization • Understand elements of drama: stage directions • Identify sensory imagery

Drama is a work of literature that is performed for an audience. Since ancient times, people have been acting out exciting stories of heroes and their deeds. In modern times, writers have written plays to be performed for the stage, the movies, on the radio, or on television. Elements of drama, like fiction, include character, setting, theme, and plot. **R**

Why Read Drama?

Plays are performed in front of audiences, but they can also be read. Reading a play can be a very different experience from reading a story or a poem. You'll find out that you identify with some of the characters and their problems. You're about to read part of a play called *Novio Boy*, by Gary Soto. In this excerpt, two friends discuss a problem that is typical for boys their age.

How to Read Drama?

Key Reading Skills

These key reading skills are especially useful tools for reading and understanding drama. You'll learn more about these skills later in the unit.

■ **Visualizing** is picturing a writer's ideas or descriptions in your mind's eye. (See Reading Workshop 1.)

■ **Clarifying** is looking at difficult sections of text in order to clear up what is confusing. (See Reading Workshop 2.)

■ **Skimming and scanning** is looking over an entire selection quickly to get a general idea of what the piece is about (skimming) and glancing quickly over a selection in order to find specific information (scanning). (See Reading Workshop 3.)

■ **Predicting** is taking a reasonable guess about what will happen in a selection. (See Reading Workshop 4.)

Key Literary Elements

Recognizing and thinking about the following literary elements will help you understand what you read more fully.

■ **Act and scene:** the section into which plays are divided. Each scene usually takes place in a different setting or time and may have different scenery. (See "The Reluctant Dragon, Scene 1.")

■ **Characterization:** the way a writer shows the personality of a character (See "Damon and Pythias.")

■ **Stage directions:** instructions that have to do with actors' movements, sound effects, and other details of a play. (See "The Bully of Barksdale Street.")

■ **Sensory imagery:** language that appeals to any of the reader's five senses (See "Zlateh the Goat.")

Additional Support

Literature Focus Lesson

Characterization People often judge a play or movie by how well they liked or connected to its characters. Ask students questions such as these: How important are the characters in a play or movie? Who is your favorite character in a play or movie? Is this character like you or someone you know? Tell students to draw a picture or write a short paragraph about their favorite character from a play or movie. Then invite volunteers to read their paragraphs or show their drawings to the class. **AS**

from **NOVIO BOY**

by Gary Soto

SCENE ONE ❶ ❷

The scene begins in a backyard where two boys, both Mexican American, are philosophizing[1] about girls. They are sloppy-looking, with holes in the knees of their pants. Stage right, two girls are silhouetted on a couch in a living room. The room is dim. Lights come up on RUDY and ALEX. RUDY paces back and forth and ALEX tries to keep up with him. RUDY throws himself down on a lawn chair. ALEX keeps pacing for a moment and then, noticing that his friend has sat down, joins him. ❸

RUDY: What am I gonna talk about? She's older than me and good-looking.

ALEX: Just level with her. Tell her you're sorry you look like you do.

RUDY: Sorry? You mean I should be sorry that I look like Tom Cruise? *(pause)* You're cold, homes.[2] You're no help at all.

ALEX: *(giggling)* Just joking, Rudy. Listen man, you got to start simple. Break the ice. Ask her . . . what her favorite color is or something.

RUDY: Color?

ALEX: Yeah, color. Like, red or white.

---

1. To *philosophize* means "to talk about life, love, and other basic questions."
2. *Cold* is slang for cold-hearted, or unfeeling. *Homes* as used here is slang for "friend."

Drama

ACTIVE READING MODEL

❶ **Key Literary Element**
Act and Scene *I see that this is Scene One. I wonder if this excerpt includes other scenes.*

❷ **Key Reading Skill**
Skimming and Scanning *Before I start reading, I'll skim the selection. I see the excerpt is dialogue between two characters, Alex and Rudy. It looks easy to read. I wonder what they're talking about.* **R1**

❸ **Key Literary Element**
Stage Directions *I can see that these are stage directions because there's no name in front of them, and the kind of type looks different. Stage directions tell where the play takes place, who's onstage, and what they are doing.*

931

Teach

R1 Reading Skill

Skimming and Scanning
Say: Look over this page. Who are the characters? *(boys named Alex and Rudy)* **EL BL**

R2 Reading Skill

Visualizing Say: Rudy is pacing as the scene opens. What does this visual clue tell you about his feelings? *(Possible response: He's nervous or upset.)* **OL**

BQ BIG Question

Ask: How is Alex helping his friend? *(Possible response: by giving advice)* **AS**

English Language Coach

Slang The boys use both Spanish and English slang to express their ideas. Tell students to list, as they read, the words and expressions that are not Standard English and look up any terms they don't know. (Pronunciations for Spanish terms in the play follow.) **OL AL**

boca (BOH kuh) p. 932
pleitos (PLAY tohs) p. 934
y Más (ee mahs) p. 934
pues (pways) p. 934
huevos con (WAY vohs kohn) p. 935
huango (WAYNG goh) p. 935
cállate (KY uh tay) p. 936
mi abuelita (mee ah bway LEE tuh) p. 936
telenovelas (tay luh noh VAY lus), p. 936
ese (AY say) p. 936
carnal (kar NAHL) p. 937

Objectives
• Analyze features of genres: drama
• Interpret and analyze character
• Visualize
• Skim and scan text
• Understand slang

Teach

L1 Literary Element

Sensory Imagery Say: Color can be an important part of a description. At the top of this page, the boys simply list a few colors that don't describe anything. However, even the names of colors can call up certain ideas and feelings. What does "green" suggest to you? *(Responses will vary.)* **Ask:** Does "grass green" suggest something? *(Responses will vary.)* **Ask:** What does "forest green" bring to mind, and how is this green different from "grass green"? *(Responses will vary.)* **AS**

L2 Literary Element

Characterization Ask: What do you learn about Alex that might cause you to doubt his advice? *(Possible responses: His advice doesn't come from personal experience. He's repeating what he's heard on a talk show.)* **OL** **AL**

L3 Literary Element

Stage Directions Ask: What does the stage direction near the bottom of the page tell you about Rudy? *(Possible response: He's seriously considering Alex's advice.)* **OL**

ACTIVE READING MODEL

RUDY: You mean, like, blue or yellow?

ALEX: Lavender!

RUDY: Purple!

ALEX: Forest green!

RUDY: Chevy chrome!

ALEX: That's it, man.

(RUDY gets up and starts to pace. ALEX gets up, too.) **4**

RUDY: *(incredulous[3])* Colors?

ALEX: Colors. I picked up this little *secreto* from Mama Rosa on the Spanish station.

RUDY: Mama Rosa! You get your advice from her?

ALEX: She's for real. She's an expert about love and things. She says you got to get your *boca*[4] rattling. One thing leads to the next, you know.

RUDY: No, I don't know.

ALEX: Listen, man. Sometimes I'm talking about nothing and the next thing I know people are listening. Like I'm the president or something.

RUDY: You're not the president.

ALEX: I know that. What I'm saying is that you got to just talk stuff—anything!

(Pause. RUDY reflects.) **L3**

RUDY: I just start talking?

ALEX: That's right.

RUDY: Just . . . say things?

ALEX: Colors, start with colors. Just ask, "Patricia, what's your favorite color?"

---

3. *Incredulous* means "with disbelief."
4. *Boca* means "mouth" in Spanish.

4 Key Reading Skill
Visualizing *The stage directions help me visualize the two boys and what they are doing.*

Additional Support

Reading in the Real World

Career Explain to students that advice columnists have been popular for many years. Newspaper columns such as *Dear Abby* and *Ann Landers* have been joined by TV and radio experts Dr. Joyce Brothers, Dr. Phil McGraw, and others. Brainstorm with students the educational qualifications an advice columnist should have and why many advice personalities are psychologists. Also discuss the responsibilities of someone who gives advice for a living. Have students work with a partner to write their idea of a good advice column about friendship. **AL**

RUDY: She won't think I'm weird? **5**

ALEX: No. She'll know immediately you're trying to start something, so she'll play along. She'll say something like "Green" or "Pink."

RUDY: And I'll tell her that my favorite color is dark blue.

ALEX: There you go, homes. (*pause*) So guess mine.

RUDY: Your what?

ALEX: My favorite color!

RUDY: Black and silver, like the Raiders?

ALEX: Nope.

RUDY: Blue and gold, like the Chargers?

ALEX: Nah. It's red, like my tongue.

(*ALEX wiggles tongue at RUDY.*)

RUDY: (*punching ALEX*) That's asco!

ALEX: (*chuckling*) Don't worry, homes. Just be cool. **EL**

RUDY: Cool.

ALEX: Like an iceberg.

(*The boys pace around the stage. They stop.*)

RUDY: Man, I can't believe I'm going out with a girl in the eleventh grade. And yesterday, guess what I was doing. **R2**

ALEX: Helping your dad pour cement at a job site?

(*RUDY shakes his head.*)

ALEX: Lifting weights?

RUDY: You won't laugh if I tell you?

ALEX: Laugh at my best friend?

ACTIVE READING MODEL

5 Key Literary Element
Characterization *Rudy doesn't seem very sure of himself. I bet that's why he's getting advice from his friend.*

Teach

R1 Reading Skill

Skimming and Scanning
Say: Scan the page to find Alex's interests. What words hint that he likes sports? *(Raiders, Chargers, lifting weights)* **OL**

EL Language Coach

Slang Ask: What expression does Alex use to tell Rudy to relax? *(Just be cool.)* **OL**

R2 Reading Skill

Predicting Ask: What did Rudy do yesterday, and why do you think so? *(Possible responses: He did something silly or childish; he's embarrassed about it. He did what a little kid would do; he brings it up in contrast to dating an older girl.)* **OL AL**

Literature Focus Lesson

Stage Directions Stage directions give many kinds of information. Explain to students that stage directions usually describe:

- sets, lighting, and sound effects
- costumes and props
- characters' gestures and actions
- characters' thoughts and feelings
- how characters say lines **AS**

With students, work through the first three pages of the scene to identify what each direction says, how it might help the actors, and what it tells readers.

Objectives
- Interpret and analyze characters
- Make predictions
- Skim and scan text
- Identify literary elements: stage direction
- Understand slang

Teach

C Critical Thinking

Comprehension Ask: Who are GI Joe, Ken, and Barbie? *(Possible responses: dolls; action figures)* **BL**

R Reading Skill

Clarifying Ask: What does Alex mean by "fifteen bones," and how do you know? *(Fifteen dollars. Rudy says it in the next line.)* **AS**

L Literary Element

Stage Directions Ask: Who can demonstrate what the last stage direction on the page means? *(Responses will vary. Students may respond by pointing one thumb to their chests.)* **AS**

ACTIVE READING MODEL

RUDY: (*hesitates; long pause*) I was playing G.I. Joes with my cousin Isaac. Man, it was fun. G.I. Joe was beating up Ken, and Barbie was kicking back watching the *pleitos*.[5] **C**

(*ALEX laughs.*)

RUDY: I got another problem. I told Patricia I was taking her to grub at Steaks, Steaks, y Más Steaks.[6]

ALEX: You told her you were taking her there? What's wrong with you, homes? Those hamburgers cost twice as much as McDonald's. And you got to tip, too.

(*RUDY reflects on his error.*)

ALEX: You got enough money?

RUDY: How much do you think I'll need?

ALEX: At least fifteen bones. **R**

RUDY: Fifteen dollars!

(*RUDY shakes his head and shrugs his shoulders. ALEX starts to go through his pockets.*)

ALEX: (*teasing*) Here, this should help.

(*RUDY takes ALEX's quarter and looks at it.*)

RUDY: (*sarcastically*) You're cool, Alex. This quarter might get me a piece of gum.

(*They sit and reflect on the dilemma.*)

ALEX: (*perks up*) Let me give you some advice. You got to talk intelligent, like you know something.

RUDY: Like I know something?

ALEX: Remember, she's two years ahead of you and in eleventh grade. You got to be *suave*, kind of like—*pues*,[7] like me. (*hooks a thumb at himself*) **6 L**

---

5. *Pleitos* means "fights" in Spanish.
6. *Steaks, Steaks, y Más Steaks* means "Steaks, Steaks, and More Steaks."
7. *Suave* means "smooth and confident." *Pues* is a Spanish expression for "y'know."

6 Key Literary Element
Characterization *Alex is the cool one with all the answers. He says what he thinks. He tries to give Rudy some good advice so he won't look bad on his date. He's being a good friend.*

Additional Support

English Language Coach

Slang Americans have many words for money, and many of them are slang terms. Have students name a few money words they know. Then ask them to work in pairs or small groups to identify all the English terms for money they can find, along with any foreign terms that Americans sometimes use (such as *dinero*). Tell them to use a thesaurus (and a dictionary) and to note which terms are slang. **AS**

RUDY: Help me then, Alex.

ALEX: (*thinking about it*) It so happens I got this love letter from Sylvia Hernandez. Remember her?

RUDY: No.

ALEX: Yeah, you do. She threw up *huevos con* weenies[8] in fifth grade. (*imitates someone vomiting*) It was all over the classroom and down the hall. It was like that old movie The Blob after she was all done.

RUDY: (*reflecting*) Yeah, I remember that girl now. She got some on my shoes. (*pause*) So what did the letter say?

ALEX: (*reaches into his pocket*) Got it right here. **7**

(*ALEX sniffs the letter for perfume, and RUDY sniffs it as well. ALEX starts to read letter.*)

ALEX: "Alex, I think you have the coolest eyes. And the cutest nose."

RUDY: You got a fat *huango*[9] nose.

ALEX: Hey, dude, you want me to help you or not? **EL BQ**

RUDY: I take that back. You got a real cute nose. (*pulls up his own nose into the shape of a pig's snout*)

ALEX: That's better. (*continues reading*) "I really care about you a lot, Alex. I really don't know how to say this, but here goes. I think that you like me but don't want to tell me because of what your friends might say. Forget them. They don't have to live your life. You do! Last year I fell totally in love with this guy Kendall—"

RUDY: What kind of name is Kendall?

(*ALEX gives RUDY a look.*)

ALEX: (*continues reading*) "At first Kendall was nice to me. Then he started being mean to me and talking behind my back. It hurt me when he told this girl from Selma that I

---

8. *Huevos con weenies* is eggs with hot dogs.
9. *Huango* is Spanish slang. Here it means something like "big and floppy."

ACTIVE READING MODEL

7 Key Reading Skill
Predicting *This letter that Alex is reading to Rudy must be important, or else he wouldn't share it. Let's see if I am right.*

Teach

L1 Literary Element

Sensory Imagery Say: Sensory details are not always pretty or peaceful or pleasant. What senses are involved in Alex's second speech on this page and in Rudy's response? *(Students might list any or all of the five senses.)* **EL BL OL**

L2 Literary Element

Stage Directions Ask: What details about the boys' behavior are in the stage directions on this page but not in the dialogue? *(Possible responses: They sniff the perfumed letter. Rudy kids Alex by making a face.)* **AS**

EL Language Coach

Slang Ask: What slang word for *friend* does Alex use on this page? *(dude)* **AS**

BQ BIG Question

Say: Alex doesn't seem to care that Rudy makes fun of his nose. What does this say about friendship? *(Possible response: Alex knows Rudy is kidding, and good friends often kid each other this way.)* **AS**

Differentiated Instruction

Visualizing Discuss with students the mental picture of Rudy, Alex, and Sylvia Hernandez that they may have formed by this point in the play. Have students use details from the scene to make a sketch of one of the characters or write a brief paragraph describing his or her appearance and personality. Then ask volunteers to compare their impressions with another student who selected the same character. Remind students that when talking about their ideas, they should note details from the play that support their visualization of the character. **OL**

Objectives
- Clarify ideas and text
- Identify literary elements: stage directions, dialogue
- Understand slang
- Monitor comprehension

Teach

C Critical Thinking

Analysis Ask: What is Rudy saying about Sylvia's letter when he compares it to his grandmother's soap operas? *(Possible response: The letter is very mushy or romantic like the soap operas.)* **OL**

R Reading Skill

Clarifying Ask: What is a "floor plan"? *(Possible response: a drawing that shows how furniture should be arranged in a room)* **Ask:** What does Alex mean by "floor plan for your love life"? *(Possible response: Rudy should use Sylvia's letter as a guide for what to do on a date.)* **AS**

EL Language Coach

Idioms Ask: What does "lay it on thick" mean? *(Possible responses: Say nice, romantic things. Use compliments or flattery.)* **OL** **AL**

---

was stuck-up. I guess it was to get me to stop liking him. But I didn't stop liking him for a long time. Now I like you, Alex. I dream about—"

RUDY: Man, she knows how to talk.

ALEX: ¡*Cállate!*[10] You're interrupting the flow of my love letter. (*pause*) Here's a good part. "Alex, you're nicer than Kendall. You're cute, too. All the boys from Roosevelt are cute, but you're the cutest. Please don't be like Kendall. I will shower you with kisses forever and ever."

RUDY: (*takes the letter and examines it*) Sounds like poetry. No, like *mi abuelita's telenovelas.*[11] **C**

ALEX: This letter should be the floor plan for your love life. You got to lay it on thick. Be romantic, ese. Suave.[12] **R**

RUDY: (*reflecting*) Suave. (*pulls out a small notepad*) I better write some of this stuff down so I don't forget: "Be romantic." "Lay it on thick." **8** **EL**

ALEX: I went on a date once.

RUDY: You're lying.

ALEX: No, I did. (*pause*) It wasn't exactly a date. Me and this girl went to the playground. **9**

RUDY: Get serious.

ALEX: Yeah, I picked her up on my bike and . . . don't laugh.

RUDY: Why would I laugh at my best friend?

ALEX: I can see it. You're gonna laugh!

RUDY: No, I promise.

(*RUDY and ALEX trade glances.*)

---

10. ¡*Cállate!* means "shut up" in Spanish.
11. *Mi abuelitas's telenovelas* means "my grandmother's soap operas."
12. *Ese* is Spanish slang with a meaning similar to *dude* or *man* or *homie*.

8 Key Reading Skill
Clarifying *So I get the picture now. Alex read the letter to show Rudy techniques for breaking the ice and starting a conversation when he goes on his date. He wants Rudy to be suave.*

9 Key Reading Skill
Predicting *Now the tables are turned and Alex is going to make a confession. Just like Rudy did before. But now it's Alex who is afraid that Rudy is going to laugh. I predict he's going to reveal something about himself that shows he isn't as cool as he pretends to be.*

Additional Support

English Language Coach

Building Background Soap operas began as radio programs in the 1930s but soon switched to TV. No one sings and they're not about soap, so why are they called "soap operas"? The stories center around the characters' love lives, so they were compared to the dramatic romances of characters in operas. The audience was mainly housewives, so the most common ads were for personal and household products, such as bath soaps and laundry detergents. Putting "soap" and "opera" together gave this kind of show its name. (In a similar way, shows about cowboys were called "horse operas.") **EL**

ACTIVE READING MODEL

ALEX: She had to pedal the bike because I didn't have enough leg strength. It's hard with two people!

(*RUDY chokes, muffling his laugh.*)

ALEX: (*continuing*) It was a lot of fun. We spent a couple hours on the monkey bars. Then we played tetherball, and then a game of chess. Yeah, it was going pretty good—until Frankie Torres came by and started teasing me.

RUDY: Frankie did that?

ALEX: Yeah. Because I was all dressed up. (*laughs*) I had on this pink shirt, and a bow tie, and buckets of my dad's Aqua Velva.[13] **10**

RUDY: Dressed up at the playground?

ALEX: Yeah, plus . . .

RUDY: What?

(*ALEX kicks at the ground, embarrassed.*)

RUDY: Hey, I'm your *carnal*.[14]

ALEX: She was getting a drink of water, so I was holding her purse.

RUDY: And that's when Frankie saw you.

ALEX: (*nodding his head*) He called me a girl because I had her purse on my shoulder. (*Pause. ALEX stands up.*) That was my first date. Age nine.

(*RUDY shakes his head sympathetically. He takes the letter from ALEX and reads it silently. Lights fade.*) **11** ○

---

13. ***Aqua Velva*** is a brand of aftershave for men.

14. In Mexican slang, ***"I'm your carnal"*** means "I'm your brother" in the way that a friend is like a brother. It is similar to "bro" in English.

Partner Talk Discuss how the boys in the play react to each other's embarrassing stories. Do the boys have a healthy sense of humor about themselves? Explain your answers.

 Literature Online **Study Central** Visit www.glencoe.com and click on Study Central to review drama.

R
C

10 Key Literary Element
Sensory Imagery *This description appeals to the senses of sight and smell. I can see Alex in my mind, and I can almost smell him drenched in aftershave.*

11 Key Literary Element
Characterization *Even though Alex revealed an embarrassing story to Rudy, Rudy did not laugh. I can tell that these boys are very good friends.*

L

Genre Focus: Drama **937**

Teach

R Reading Skill

Visualizing Ask: Does Alex's description of what he wore on his date help you form a good mental picture of him? (*Responses will vary.*) **AS**

C Critical Thinking

Analysis Ask: What does Alex's date outfit suggest about his knowledge of dating? (*Possible responses: He didn't know much about dating. He was trying to look grown up.*) **AS**

L Literary Element

Act and Scene Ask: Do you think this scene would make a good play all by itself? (*Possible response: No, it doesn't tell a complete story.*) **AS**

 Literature Online

Study Central Have students access the Web site to review drama and to complete a related activity.

Reading Fluency

Build Fluency To help students build fluency, have them follow along as they listen to an audiotape (or two of your best readers reading) part of the scene aloud. Have students pay attention to the flow of the dialogue and how closely it resembles conversation in both wording and timing. Then have students work with a partner to read the scene aloud. Tell students not to do the movements indicated in the stage directions so that they can focus on the dialogue. They should reread the play until they're able to read with fluency, expression, and comprehension. **EL BL**

Objectives
• Clarify ideas and text
• Analyze text
• Understand idioms
• Visualize
• Identify literary elements: act and scene

937

Objectives covered in this workshop:
• Visualize author's ideas or descriptions

Teaching Students to Visualize

What Is It?
• Visualizing is picturing a writer's ideas or descriptions.
• Visualizing helps students better understand what the author is saying.
• Visualizing helps students remember what they have read.

How to Help Students Get It
• Remind students to pay attention to each detail the writer uses to describe a character, the setting, or the action on stage.
• Tell students to constantly ask themselves as they read: What would this look like? How would this work?
• Some students may benefit from actually illustrating their visualizations. Encourage students to keep unlined paper near by when they are reading selections in this unit. When they feel the need to see a description more vividly, invite them to draw what they visualize.

Reading to Answer the Big Question

The Reluctant Dragon Scene 1 by Kenneth Grahame
This play is an adaptation of Grahame's book by the same title. Once upon a time in England, some children find a dragon. Only Edward is brave enough to talk with him. When he and the dragon, whose name is Horace, become friends, Edward realizes that he will have to save Horace from destruction by the villagers.

The Reluctant Dragon Scene 2 by Kenneth Grahame
In Scene II of the play, the villagers have recruited the noble St. George to slay the dragon. When Edward persuades St. George to meet Horace, the dragon is able to convince St. George that he is harmless. They stage a mock fight to satisfy the villagers, after which Horace is allowed to write poetry and live with them in peace.

Workshop Resources

PACING (DAYS)		LESSON	STUDENT MATERIALS	TEACHER RESOURCES
STANDARD	BLOCK			
1	1/2	Key Skill Lesson: Visualizing	🐾 Key Reading Skills Practice, p. 9 🐾 English Language Coach Review, p. 42	👆 Bellringer Options Transparencies –Daily Language Practice 73 👆 Read Aloud, Think Aloud Transparencies –Key Reading Skills 30 💿 Presentation Plus!
1	1	"The Reluctant Dragon" Scene 1	💻 Glencoe Online 🐾 Unit Vocabulary Review, p. 40 🐾 Academic Vocabulary Review, p. 43 📁 English Language Coach 🐾 Active Reading Graphic Organizer, p. 11 🐾 Literary Analysis, p. 10 💿 StudentWorks Plus™ 💻 Online Student Edition 💿 Literature Classics 📁 Selection and Unit Assessments, p. 85	💻 Puzzlemaker 💿 Skill Level Up!™ A Language Arts Game 💻 BookLink 3 📘 Assessment by Learning Objective (Diagnostic and Formative) 💿 Interactive Tutor: Self-Assessment 💿 TeacherWorks Plus™
1		"The Reluctant Dragon" Scene 2	💻 Glencoe Online 🐾 Unit Vocabulary Review, p. 40 🐾 Academic Vocabulary Review, p. 43 📁 English Language Coach 🐾 Active Reading Graphic Organizer, p. 12 🐾 Literary Analysis, p. 10 💿 StudentWorks Plus™ 💻 Online Student Edition 💿 Literature Classics 📁 Selection and Unit Assessments, p. 86	💻 Puzzlemaker 💿 Skill Level Up!™ A Language Arts Game 💻 BookLink 3 📘 Assessment by Learning Objective (Diagnostic and Formative) 💿 Interactive Tutor: Self-Assessment 💿 TeacherWorks Plus™

Keys for Unit Resource

📁 Blackline Master   🔒 DVD

📘 Workbook   👆 Transparency

📖 Supplemental Text   💻 Web-based

💿 CD-ROM   🐾 Fast File

Level Appropriate Code

AS = Activities for all students

AL = Activities for students working above grade level

OL = Activities for students working at grade level

BL = Activities for students working below grade level

EL = Activities for English language learners

Focus

✏ **Daily Language Practice Transparency 73**
Focus Activity Ask: Did you ever make a friend unexpectedly? Why was it surprising that this person became a friend? *(Responses will vary.)* **AS**

Teach

R **Reading Skill**

Visualizing Say: The words *visualize, vision, visible,* and *visit* come from a Latin word that means "to see." How is visualizing people similar to or different from visiting them? *(Possible response: Visualizing people is seeing them in your mind. Visiting them is going to see them in person.)* **AS**

Analyzing the Cartoon

Say: Traction is a way of keeping people with broken bones or other injuries from moving so that they can heal. What is Calvin hinting? *(Possible response: that he'll hurt Hobbes if Hobbes doesn't help him)* **OL**

READING WORKSHOP 1

Skills Focus

You will practice these skills when you read the following selections:
• "The Reluctant Dragon," Scene 1, p. 942
• "The Reluctant Dragon," Scene 2, p. 954

Reading
• Visualizing

Literature
• Understanding act and scene

Vocabulary
• Slang and dialect

Writing/Grammar
• Using hyphens in compound words
• Using hyphens to divide words

Objective (pp. 938–939)
Reading Visualize

Visualizing

Learn It!

What Is It? You learned about **visualizing** in Unit 4, so you remember that visualizing is "seeing" what is being described in words. In *Novio Boy,* both the dialogue and the stage directions provided information you needed to visualize what was happening.

• To visualize something is to form a picture of it in your mind. The writer chooses words to help you "see" a person, place, or thing.

R

Why Is It Important? Visualizing helps you understand anything you read. It's especially important while reading a play. All plays except radio plays are meant to be seen. So, you need to visualize what's happening in order to understand the play.

CALVIN AND HOBBES © 1990 Watterson. Distributed By UNIVERSAL PRESS SYNDICATE. Reprinted with permission. All rights reserved.

Analyzing Cartoons
What does Calvin visualize in the third frame of this cartoon? How does what he "sees" change his mind about doing his math homework?

Additional Support

English Language Coach

Build Background Bill Watterson's comic strip presents the adventures of six-year-old Calvin, who is an expert visualizer. He sees great adventures in life's boring, everyday ordinary events. Calvin battles pirates; his mom tells him to stop splashing the bath water. Calvin builds a skyscraper; his dad yells about stepping on toy blocks. Calvin shares his adventures with a live, full-sized tiger named Hobbes; to everyone else Hobbes is a small, stuffed toy. Now that's visualizing! Provide samples of Calvin comics or invite students to bring some from newspapers. Have them describe other events and situations that Calvin uses his imagination to visualize. **AS**

How Do I Do It? Understanding stage directions will help you visualize. The most important thing to know is that stage directions are written for the people in the play. So, start by imagining that you are an actor on a stage.

- *Stage left* and *stage right* are left and right for an actor on the stage who is looking at the audience. For someone in the audience looking at the stage, stage left is to the right. So, these directions are the opposite of what you might expect.

- *Upstage* is toward the back of the stage (away from the audience). *Downstage* is toward the front (close to the audience). *Center stage* is in the middle of the stage.

- *Off* means "off the stage," where the audience can't see.

Sometimes, playwrights use shorthand. So, *right, left, up, down,* and *center* all have an invisible *stage* in them.

Here is how Kezia used information from the stage directions at the beginning of *Novio Boy.*

The scene begins in a backyard where two boys, both Mexican-American, are philosophizing about girls. They are sloppy-looking, with holes in the knees of their pants. . . . RUDY paces back and forth and ALEX tries to keep up with him.

> The stage directions really help me imagine the boys—what they're wearing and doing. People often pace when they're worried, so I'll bet Rudy is worried.

Study Central Visit www.glencoe .com and click on Study Central to review visualizing.

Practice It!

Below is an image related to a selection in this workshop. In your Learner's Notebook, write or sketch what you "see" in your mind's eye when you think about:

- a knight fighting a bright green dragon

Use It!

As you read remember the notes or sketches you made to practice visualizing. When you find a detail that you can picture clearly, add it to your notes and sketches.

Differentiated Instruction

Visualizing To help students practice visualizing, ask them to imagine their bedroom as the setting of a play. Draw this organizer to help students move from large to small details. Have students include sensory details, such as color, texture, and so on. **AS**

Teach

Literature Online

Study Central Have students access the Web site to review visualizing and to complete a related activity.

R Reading Skill

Visualizing Say: It's often one of our five senses that triggers a mental picture. The smell of fresh cookies might make you visualize your grandma. A few notes of a favorite song might bring you an image of the performer. Do you have a particular "sense memory"—something that calls to mind a person or experience? *(Responses will vary.)* **OL AL**

Resources for page 939

🖎 Use Key Reading Skills Transparency 30 in *Read Aloud, Think Aloud* to help students practice visualizing.

Objectives
- Analyze text
- Analyze text features: cartoon
- Visualize

939

Teach

More About the Author

Amazingly, Kenneth Grahame's *The Wind in the Willows* was rejected by an American publisher. When it was published in Great Britain, it had a lukewarm greeting until the animal characters, and E.H. Shephard's illustrations, gained popularity. A. A. Milne, who had created Winnie the Pooh, dramatized the book in 1929 as *Toad of Toad Hall.* Much of Grahame's fantasy was removed, and Milne focused mainly on the animal characters. William Horwood created a sequel trilogy—a series of three books—to follow *The Wind in the Willows,* imitating Grahame's style and phrasing.

Vocabulary

Word Meanings Ask: Which word does the writer clarify by giving its definition within the same sentence? *(slang)* **OL**

Before You Read

Meet the Author

Kenneth Grahame was born in Edinburgh, Scotland, on March 8, 1859, and died in 1932. As a student he did well in school and sports, but didn't have enough money to attend college. He became a banker and, in his spare time, wrote children's stories. When his son Alastair went on a vacation he asked his father to send him bedtime stories by mail. Grahame's best-known book, "The Wind in the Willows," started out in these letters. Grahame mailed the letters to his son every day. For more about Kenneth Grahame, see page R3 of the Author Files.

Author Search For more about Kenneth Grahame, go to www.glencoe.com.

Objectives (pp. 940–951)
Reading Visualize • Make connections from text to self
Literature Understand elements of drama: act and scene
Vocabulary Identify and understand slang

The Reluctant Dragon
Scene 1

Vocabulary Preview

scourge (skurj) *n.* cause of widespread hardship or suffering **(p. 947)** *The grasshoppers were a scourge that ate most of our crops.*

solemnly (SOL um lee) *adv.* seriously; without joy or humor **(p. 947)** *He spoke so solemnly that we knew he wasn't kidding.*

lavishly (LAV ish lee) *adv.* plentifully; with more than is usual or needed **(p. 947)** *The table was lavishly heaped with gifts.*

elaborately (ih LAB ur it lee) *adv.* in a fancy way that involves many details or complicated parts **(p. 948)** *Their handshake was done so elaborately that I knew I couldn't copy it.*

exasperated (eg ZAS pur ay tid) *adj.* angered or greatly irritated **(p. 949)** *Ruth yelled in an exasperated way when the dog knocked over her bucket of water.*

Partner Talk On a separate note card write each vocabulary word one time. Turn the note card over and write the definition and part of speech on the back. Take turns testing each other by flashing the cards.

English Language Coach

Slang Informal language that is appropriate for casual conversation but not for formal speech or writing is **slang.** It is language in which made-up words and ordinary words are used to mean something different than in formal English. Some slang is widely understood. Some slang, however, is only understood by people within a certain social group. Each new generation creates its own original words and expressions for describing things.

Here are some examples of slang:

Slang	Slang Meaning	Example
cool	very nice, excellent	That's a cool hat you're wearing.
ride	automobile, such as a car, truck, or SUV	Wow, that's a nice ride.
chill	to relax	You need to chill.

Partner Talk Now brainstorm six other slang sayings with a partner. Make sure the slang is appropriate for use in school.

Additional Support

Author Search To expand students' appreciation of Kenneth Grahame, have them access the Web site for more information and resources.

Literature Focus Lesson

Script Scripts often begin with a list of characters in the order they first appear in the play or in some other logical order. In addition to the names, playwrights often provide brief descriptions to help actors see who the characters are or how they're related to one another. Stage directions often include special words used and understood by people who work in theater. For example, the first words on page 942 are "at rise." Ask students if they know what this phrase means. *(It refers to the moment when the stage curtains rise and/or when the lights come up on the stage.)* **AS**

Skills Preview

Key Reading Skill: Visualizing

Before you read the selection, visualize

- a shepherd boy
- dragons you've seen in books or movies
- places where dragons live

Write to Learn In your Learner's Notebook, jot down a few notes about the pictures that came to mind when you thought about the topics above. After you read, check to see if what you visualized from the text matches your notes.

Key Literary Element: Act and Scene

Books (except for very short ones) are divided into sections called chapters. Plays are also divided into sections. A short play is often called a "one-act play" because it has only one main part, that is, one **act.** Longer plays may have two or even three acts.

Each act in a play is divided into scenes. A **scene** is the section of a play that presents events in a single setting. A new scene begins whenever there is a change in the place where events are taking place or in the time.

"The Reluctant Dragon" is a one-act play that has two scenes.

- Each scene takes place at a particular place and time.
  Ask yourself: When and where does this scene take place?

- Each scene adds to the plot, or storyline, of the drama.
  Ask yourself: What happens in this scene and how does it move the plot forward?

Interactive Literary Elements Handbook
To review or learn more about the literary elements, go to www.glencoe.com.

Get Ready to Read

Connect to the Reading

How would you feel if you saw something that wasn't *supposed* to exist, like a sea monster or a dragon? What if—instead of being ferocious—it turned out to be friendly?

Write to Learn Write about a fictional creature you'd like to meet. Why would you want to meet that creature? What would it look like? What questions would you ask it?

Build Background

Dragons are legendary creatures often pictured with wings and claws. Usually, dragons are shown as giant fire-breathing lizards. Dragons have symbolized different things in different cultures throughout history.

- In China, dragons are a sign of happiness and success.

- Ancient Greeks and Romans sometimes saw dragons as symbols of good related to the secrets of the earth and sometimes as symbols of evil.

- The image of a dragon was seen as a warlike sign in Norse cultures and medieval England.

Set Purposes for Reading

BIG Question Read Scene 1 of "The Reluctant Dragon" to discover how getting to know an enemy may help to teach you the true meaning of friendship.

Set Your Own Purpose What else would you like to learn from the selection to help you answer the Big Question? Write your purpose on the "Reluctant Dragon" page of Foldable 8.

Keep Moving

Use these skills as you read the following selection.

The Reluctant Dragon **941**

Teach

R Reading Skill

Visualizing Say: Describe a dragon as you visualize it. *(Possible responses: big, with wings, sharp claws, green scales, and breathing fire)* **AS**

L Literary Element

Act and Scene Say: A playwright usually describes the time and place of each new scene. The audience doesn't read a script, so why does the writer include these descriptions? *(Possible response: People working on the play need these descriptions.)* **OL AL**

Interactive Literary Elements Handbook Have students access the Web site to improve their understanding of scene.

Differentiated Instruction

Using a Graphic Organizer To help students sequence events in the storyline, draw this organizer on the board. Have students copy and use the organizer to sequence the events in Scene 1. Encourage students to add boxes as necessary. **AS**

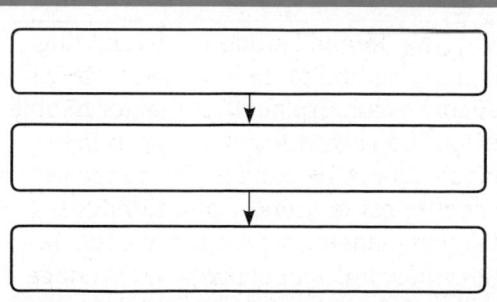

Objectives

- Learn and use new vocabulary
- Analyze features of genres: drama
- Visualize
- Identify literary elements: scene

Teach

Viewing the Illustration

Say: Look at the list of characters and then at the illustration. Which boy is Edward, and why do you think so? (*Possible responses: Edward is holding the long stick, or walking stick, or staff. A shepherd carries this kind of stick. Edward is the first character listed, so he might be the main character; plus, all the children in the drawing are looking at and listening to him.*) **BL** **OL**

EL Language Coach

Synonyms and Antonyms

Ask: What does *reluctant* mean? Look it up and find two synonyms and two antonyms for the word. (*Possible responses: Synonyms—hesitant, shy, unenthusiastic, unwilling; antonyms—eager, enthusiastic, willing*) **AS**

Readability Scores
Dale-Chall: 4.3
DRP: N/A
Lexile: N/A

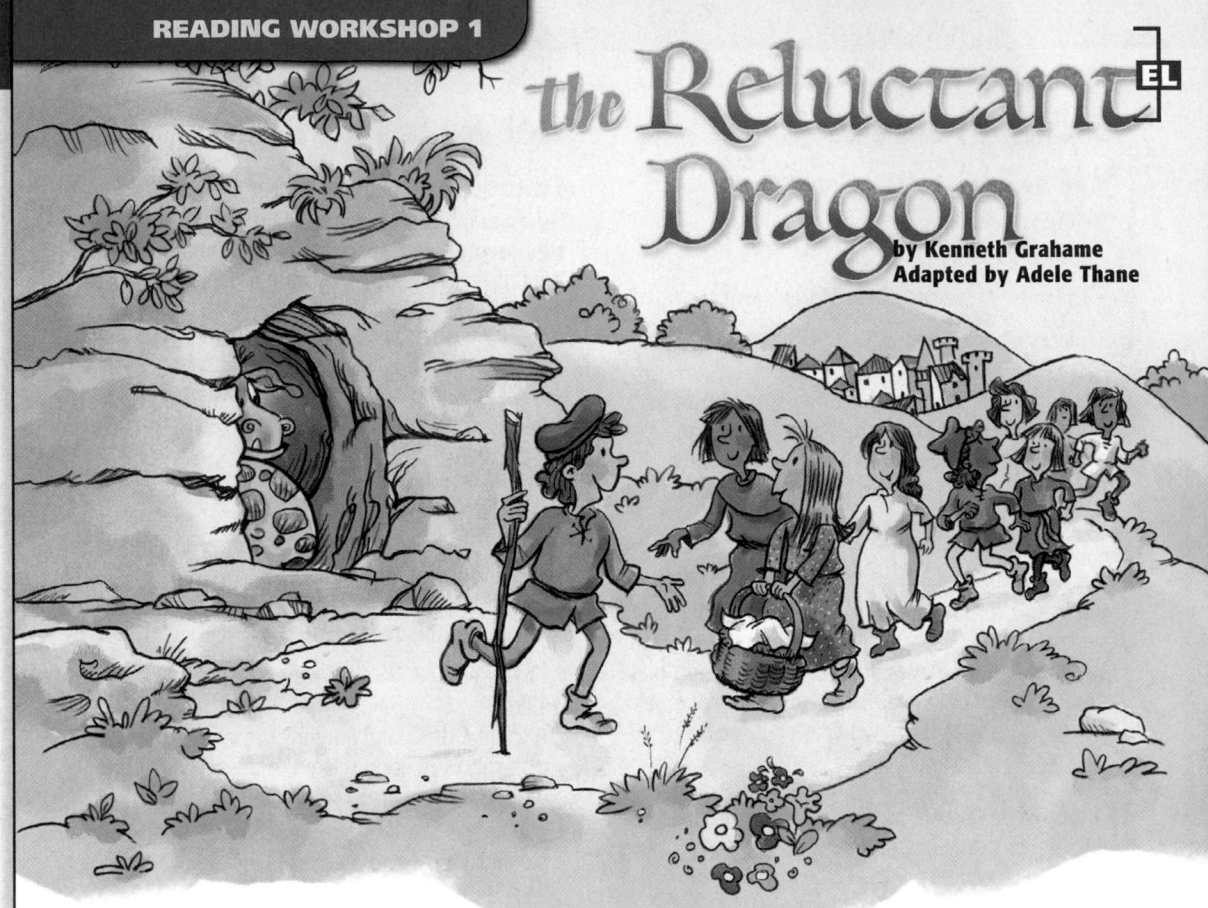

the Reluctant Dragon

by Kenneth Grahame
Adapted by Adele Thane

Characters
EDWARD, *a shepherd boy*
SELINA, *his sister*
HORACE, *the dragon*
ST. GEORGE
CHILDREN
VILLAGERS

SCENE 1 **1**

TIME: *Once upon a time. A summer day.*

SETTING: *A hillside in England. The green rolling countryside can be seen in the distance, with a hint of old gray cities on the horizon. The opening to Horace's cave is left; the path to the village is at right.* **2**

942 UNIT 8 What Makes a Friend?

Practice the Skills

1 **Key Literary Element**

Act and Scene The beginning of a new scene usually includes an explanation of the time and setting. Think about how the time and setting will affect the action.

2 **Key Reading Skill**

Visualizing Can you picture the scene?

Additional Support

942

Literature Focus Lesson

Setting Remind students that setting is the time and place in which a story's events occur. Explain that theater people often use *setting* to refer only to the place. When the word is shortened to *set*, it refers to scenery and furniture. Early in planning a play, a designer creates drawings that show how the stage will look from the front (an audience view) and how it would look from above (a floor plan). These drawings range from simple pencil sketches to detailed computer graphics. (They don't typically show characters.) Have students work alone or in pairs to design a set for "Reluctant Dragon." Advise them to use the playwright's descriptions as their starting point. **AS**

AT RISE: *Inside the cave, but visible to audience, is what appears to be a large green rock. Actually, this is* HORACE, *the dragon, curled up asleep.* EDWARD *runs in, stops, and looks around curiously.*

R1

EDWARD: (*Shouting and beckoning off right*): Come on, hurry up! This is the place. (SELINA *and* CHILDREN *enter, carrying picnic baskets.*)

SELINA: Oh, Edward, it's a lovely place for a picnic!

1ST GIRL (*Standing on a rock at back*): Look at the view! I can see the spire of the cathedral a hundred miles away.

1ST BOY (*Standing on another rock*): There's the village. I can see my house. **3**

2ND BOY (*Glancing about*): How did you know about this place, Edward?

EDWARD: I bring the sheep up here.

3RD BOY (*Peering into cave*): What's this cave?

EDWARD: Oh, just a cave.

3RD BOY: Let's explore it.

EL

2ND GIRL: No, let's eat first. I'm starved.

3RD GIRL: So am I.

1ST BOY (*As he joins* 3RD BOY *in front of cave*): You girls unpack the baskets while we boys explore the cave.

1ST GIRL (*Coming over*): No, we want to go with you.

2ND BOY (*Catching sight of* HORACE *inside cave*): Hey! Look at that rock all covered with emeralds![1]

R2

EDWARD: Where?

2ND BOY (*Pointing*): There.

EDWARD: That's funny. I never saw that rock before.

3RD BOY: I'll bet this cave is full of treasures. Come on!

---

1. **Emeralds** are very valuable green stones.

Practice the Skills

3 Key Reading Skill

Visualizing Reread the description of the view from the rock. Then close your eyes. Can you picture the village and the spire of the cathedral?

The Reluctant Dragon **943**

Teach

R1 Reading Skill

Review Clarifying Ask: What is the "large green rock" inside the cave? *(Horace, the dragon)* **EL BL OL**

EL Language Coach

Figurative Meaning
Ask: Are the girls really starved? Explain. *(Possible response: No, they're exaggerating to emphasize that they're very hungry.)* **AS**

R2 Reading Skill

Visualizing Ask: How do you picture the expression on the 2nd boy's face? *(Possible response: eyes and mouth open in surprise or greed)* **AS**

Reading in the Real World

Career Students who enjoy working with animals may wish to learn more about careers in veterinarian sciences. Have students work with a partner to research the care requirements of sheep. Then have each pair of students write an advertisement that seeks applications from veterinarians. The advertisement should list the duties of a veterinarian. Invite volunteers to share their advertisements in a classroom display. **AS**

Objectives
• Use text features: illustration
• Clarify ideas and text
• Use synonyms and antonyms
• Identify literary elements: setting
• Visualize
• Distinguish literal from figurative meanings

Teach

R Reading Skill

Visualizing Ask: How do you picture the expression on the 2nd boy's face now? *(Possible response: eyes and mouth open in fear, surprise, or amazement)* **AS**

C1 Critical Thinking

Comprehension Say: Horace does what people and animals sometimes do when they wake up—stretch, yawn, and sneeze. Why are the children so frightened by this ordinary behavior? *(Possible response: They thought he was a rock, and rocks don't do these things.)* **AS**

C2 Critical Thinking

Analysis Ask: How can you tell that Edward is different from the other children? *(Possible response: He wants to stay at the cave and doesn't seem to be afraid of dragons.)* **AS**

R (*As* CHILDREN *are about to enter cave,* 2ND BOY, *who is in the lead, suddenly stops short, frightened.*)

2ND BOY: Wait!

3RD BOY: What's the matter?

2ND BOY: That rock just moved!

1ST BOY: You're crazy!

2ND BOY: I'm not! It did! (CHILDREN *stare at* HORACE *in amazement as he slowly gets to his feet, stretches, yawns, then sneezes.* CHILDREN *scream and scatter, hiding behind the rocks upstage-all except* EDWARD, *who stands at center.*) **C1**

EDWARD: Don't be afraid. It's only a dragon.

1ST GIRL: Only a *dragon!*

3RD GIRL: *Only* a dragon! (HORACE *peeks out of cave.*)

EDWARD: I've always said this cave was a dragon cave and ought to have a dragon in it.

3RD BOY: Well, it has a dragon in it, and I'm going home!

1ST BOY: Let's clear out of here! (CHILDREN *run toward exit, but* EDWARD *bars the way.*)

C2 **EDWARD:** Why? He's not **ramping** or **carrying on** or doing anything wrong, is he? **4**

2ND BOY: Look here, Edward, dragons may be your line, but they're not mine. Let me by! (*He pushes* EDWARD *out of the way.*)

1ST BOY: Come on, everybody, or the dragon will eat you!

3RD BOY: I'll beat you to the village and be the first to tell! (*He runs off, and the other* CHILDREN *race after him.* EDWARD *catches hold of* SELINA's *arm.*)

EDWARD: Selina, you will stay, won't you?

SELINA (*Glancing toward the cave*): I—I'll come back later—maybe. (*She hands* EDWARD *picnic basket and runs off right.* EDWARD *looks after her and sighs, then turns to* HORACE, *who has come out of cave, and is walking upright.*)

944 UNIT 8 What Makes a Friend?

Practice the Skills

4 ■ **English Language Coach**

Slang Carrying on is slang for making a fuss or making trouble. **Ramping** is not slang. It's an unusual word that means "to stand up on the back legs and raise the forelegs in a threatening way."

Additional Support

Differentiated Instruction

Visualizing Word Meanings The verb *ramp* is rarely used now the way Edward uses it. Ask students which of these definitions he means: (1) to stand up and move threateningly with arms or forelegs raised; (2) to act furiously or move about wildly; (3) to creep up. **AL** Either 1 or 2 could be correct. To help students understand how frightening a ramping animal could be, ask them to visualize the attack of a wild grizzly bear. It's more usual for words to be shortened over time, but *ramp* was stretched to *rampage* during the 1700s. Today it means "to act furiously or move about wildly." (Horace uses *rampaging* on page 945.) **AS**

EDWARD (*Cheerfully*): Hello, dragon!

HORACE (*Cowering*): Now don't you hit me, or throw stones, or squirt water at me. I won't have it! (*He sneezes.*) Atchoo!

EDWARD: I'm not going to hit you. I just want to ask you how you are, but if I'm in the way, I'll go.

HORACE (*Hastily*): No, no, don't go! I'm sorry I misjudged you. (*He bows apologetically.*) Permit me to introduce myself. My name is Horace. (*He holds out his paw, and EDWARD shakes it.*)

EDWARD: <u>Howdy do</u>, Horace. I'm Edward. Are you hungry? **5**

HORACE: Terribly!

EDWARD (*In a matter-of-fact tone*): You don't eat children, do you?

HORACE (*Revolted*): Oh, no! Or grown-ups, either.

EDWARD (*Digging into picnic basket*): That's good, because there are only egg and cheese sandwiches in here. Shall we sit down?

HORACE: By all means. (*He sneezes.*) Atchoo!

EDWARD: Do you have a cold?

HORACE (*Sniffling and wiping his eyes*): No—hay fever. (*They sit on a rock and eat sandwiches as they talk.*)

EDWARD: Are you planning to stay here long?

HORACE: I think I will. It seems a nice enough place—and besides, I'm such a lazy fellow! I'm not much for moving around.

EDWARD (*Politely*): Is that so?

HORACE: All the other dragons I knew were so active and earnest—always rampaging, and chasing knights, and devouring damsels.

EDWARD: And you didn't?

Practice the Skills

5 | **English Language Coach**

Slang When Edward says, "**Howdy do**, Horace," this is slang. He really means, *How do you do?* Can you see how Edward turned a phrase like *How do you do?* into *Howdy Do?* What kind of phrases do you shorten or change to make slang when you talk with your friends?

The Reluctant Dragon **945**

Teach

R1 Reading Skill

Visualizing Ask: What does *cowering* mean? *(showing fear)* Why is Horace cowering? *(He's afraid Edward will hurt him.)* **Ask:** Does this fit your idea of a dragon? *(Possible response: Dragons are supposed to be mean and fierce, and people are afraid of them.)* **OL**

C Critical Thinking

Analysis Ask: What human traits and qualities does Horace show? *(Possible responses: the ability to talk, think, and feel; logic; emotions; manners; hay fever)* **AS**

R2 Reading Skill

Visualizing Ask: How would Horace's face look now? *(Possible response: red, watery nose and eyes)* **OL**

English Language Coach

Slang Many slang words are shortened forms of Standard English words or phrases. "How do you do" became "Howdy do" and then "Howdy." A word is usually shortened only once and keeps the same meaning, like *refrigerator* and *fridge.* However, we have some shortened words that came from two different words and have two different meanings. For example, *con* is short for both *convict,* meaning "prisoner," and *contra,* meaning "against." Ask students to tell what *temp* means in "temp worker" *(temporary)* and "time and temp" *(temperature)* by using the context clue in each phrase. **AS**

Objectives
• Visualize
• Monitor comprehension
• Analyze text
• Understand slang

945

Teach

L Literary Element

Act and Scene Ask: What big event took place in the storyline sometime before this scene? *(an earthquake)* **AS**

BQ [BIG Question]

Ask: What surprising thing do you learn about Horace? *(He writes poetry.)* Ask: How might the fact that both Horace and Edward write poetry affect their friendship? *(Possible response: Friends usually have common interests, so this might lead to a good friendship.)* **OL**

HORACE: No, I liked to get my meals regularly and then snooze a bit. So when it happened, I really got caught!

EDWARD: When what happened, Horace?

HORACE: The earthquake. The bottom dropped right out from under me, and I found myself miles underground, wedged in as tight as tight. After a while, I began to work my way upstairs, and I came out through this cave. (*HORACE rises and looks about with satisfaction.*) Hm-m. This is the place for me, Edward. Nice view—nice country. Quiet, too. And no ragweed.[2] (*He sneezes.*) Atchoo! Well, maybe some. **6**

EDWARD (*Getting up*): What will you do up here all day long?

HORACE (*Looking away bashfully*): Uh—did you ever—just for fun—try to make up—well—poetry?

EDWARD: Of course I have, heaps of it, and some of it is quite good, too.

HORACE: Now you have culture,[3] you have! I hope my other neighbors are as cultured as you are.

---

2. A *ragweed* is a weedy herb that produces allergy-causing pollen.
3. Here *culture* means knowledge of the fine arts.

6 Key Reading Skill

Visualizing Can you visualize what Horace just described? How would a dragon like Horace get out of that kind of situation? Would his way be different from another dragon's?

Analyzing the Art Does Horace look like a fearsome, dangerous dragon? Does he look like "an enemy of the human race"? Explain your answer.

Additional Support

Differentiated Instruction

Build Background When Horace uses the words *culture* and *cultured*, he's talking about knowing and enjoying the arts, including literature, music, and theater. Cultured people have "good taste" and are well educated (which does not necessarily mean formally educated). Another meaning of *culture* has to do with a certain group's arts, customs, beliefs, foods, and so on. We talk about the culture of nations and ethnic groups (American, Polish, Mexican); the culture of religious groups (Amish, Mormon, Buddhist); and the culture of economic classes, corporations, and even governments. **AS**

EDWARD (*Trying to break it gently*): Horace, I'm afraid there won't be any other neighbors.

HORACE: How's that?

EDWARD: Well, you are a dragon, aren't you?

HORACE (*Throwing out his chest*): Yes, and I'm mighty proud of it!

EDWARD: But being a dragon makes you an enemy of the human race.

BQ **HORACE** (*Happily*): Don't have an enemy in the world! Too lazy to make them. And what if I do read other fellows my poetry? I'm always ready to listen to theirs!

EDWARD: Oh, dear, don't you understand? When the other people find you out, they'll come after you with shovels and pitchforks and all sorts of things.

HORACE (*Innocently*): Why? I'm not doing anything to them.

C1 **EDWARD:** That's not the point. The way they see it, you are a **scourge** and a pest, and they will have to get rid of you.

C2 **HORACE** (*Shaking his head* **solemnly**): There's not a word of truth in that. Couldn't I read them my poetry? That ought to convince them I'm harmless. Now, here's a little verse I was working on this morning. (*He removes a piece of bark from under a scale of his costume and reads from it.*) Summer.
By Horace Dragon.
Atchoo! Atchoo! The ragweed is in bloom.
Sowing far and wide allergic gloom.
How **lavishly** it pollinates the breeze,
And, oh! how lavishly it makes me sneeze. Atchoo!
(HORACE *pauses to blow his nose.*) Well, Edward, what do you think of it? **7**

Vocabulary

scourge (skurj) *n.* cause of widespread hardship or suffering

solemnly (SOL um lee) *adv.* seriously; without joy or humor

lavishly (LAV ish lee) *adv.* plentifully; with more than is usual or needed

Practice the Skills

7 **Key Reading Skill**

Visualizing Review all the stage directions for Horace on this page. Tell how they help you visualize this conversation.

The Reluctant Dragon **947**

Teach

BQ **BIG Question**

Ask: What do Horace's ideas about enemies suggest about his idea of friends? (*Possible response: He thinks enemies are people you've harmed; he hasn't harmed anyone, so everyone is a friend.*) **AL**

C1 Critical Thinking

Evaluation Ask: Considering how most dragons in stories behave, do the people have good reason to want to harm Horace? Why or why not? (*Responses will vary.*) **AS**

C2 Critical Thinking

Application Ask: What kind of poem is Horace's "little verse"—narrative, lyric, or free verse? (*lyric*) **Ask:** If you ignore the last "Atchoo," is there a rhyme pattern? (*yes*) **Ask:** Is there a regular rhythm? (*yes, sort of*) **Ask:** All in all, what do you think of the poem? (*Responses will vary.*) **AS**

Reading in the Real World

Citizenship Ask students what makes a "good neighbor," and list their ideas on the board. Have students write a speech, letter, or editorial asking the villagers to accept Horace as a friend and neighbor. Students should use the "good neighbor" traits to support their argument. **OL** If Edward is correct, the villagers will see Horace as a stereotype—someone with all the traits supposedly shared by all the members of a group. When we stereotype others, we don't see them as individuals with good and bad qualities; we lump them unfairly into a group. **AS**

Objectives
• Identify literary elements: scene
• Evaluate text
• Apply information

Teach

EL Language Coach

Idioms **Ask:** What does the expression "feather in our cap" mean? *(Possible responses: an honor; something that sets one apart as special)* **AL**

C Critical Thinking

Synthesis **Ask:** When would it make sense *not* to follow a custom? *(Possible responses: when it no longer makes sense; when you no longer enjoy it; when it hurts others)* **AS**

R Reading Skill

Visualizing **Ask:** How do you picture Horace's expression during this conversation? *(Possible responses: forehead wrinkled; a small frown; a look of confusion or frustration)* **OL**

EDWARD (*Hesitating*): Well—it's certainly—unusual.

HORACE (*Beaming*): Yes, isn't it! (SELINA *has entered from right during these speeches.* HORACE *sees her and bows* **elaborately**.) Welcome, fair damsel!

EDWARD (Pleased): Selina! You did come back!

SELINA (Bursting out excitedly): Oh, Edward, the village is in an uproar!

EDWARD: I thought it would be.

HORACE: What about?

SELINA: About you, sir. They say you are a pest and a scourge and must be destroyed.

EDWARD (*To* HORACE): Didn't I tell you?

HORACE: But I haven't disturbed even a hen roost!

SELINA: That has nothing to do with it. You are a dragon, and they are afraid of you. The funny part of it is, they are proud of you, too.

HORACE: Why, my dear?

SELINA (*Smiling*): It's not every village that has a dragon of its own, you know. You are quite a feather in our cap.[4]

HORACE (*More confused than ever*): Then why do they want to destroy me?

EDWARD (*Breaking in*): Because dragons have been destroyed since the beginning of time. It's the custom.

HORACE: But I don't behave like a dragon. **8**

EDWARD: It doesn't make sense, does it, Horace? But our village is famous for not making sense.

---

4. A ***feather in our cap*** means "a success or achievement that others will see as a credit to us."

Vocabulary

elaborately (ih LAB ur it lee) *adv.* in a fancy way that involves many details or complicated parts

Practice the Skills

8 **Key Reading Skill**

Visualizing What details from the play help you to imagine Horace? Even though he doesn't act like a dragon, how must the way he looks affect the way people feel? Make a list of the things people find frightening about his appearance. **R**

Additional Support

Literature Focus Lesson

Characterization Authors and playwrights use narration, dialogue, and actions to develop characters. Have students work in pairs to describe Horace by choosing three adjectives. Students can chart their responses, supporting their choices with details from the script. **OL**

Horace is . . .	I know because the script says . . .

SELINA: That's not all, Edward. They are going to send for St. George![5]

HORACE: St. George! (*He sneezes.*) Atchoo!

EDWARD (*Shaking* HORACE *by the tail for emphasis*): Now you will have to pull yourself together and do something!

HORACE (*Pulling his tail out of* EDWARD's *hand*): Don't be so violent, Edward! Sit down and listen to another poem.

EDWARD (**Exasperated**): That's right, take it calmly. I hope you'll be half as calm when St. George gets here. Of course you can lick him—a great big fellow like you!

HORACE: Oh, dearie me, this is too awful! I won't see him, and that's that! When he comes, you must tell him to go away at once. Say he can write if he likes, but I can't give him an interview.

EDWARD: Oh, Horace, don't be so pigheaded! You have to fight him some time or other.

HORACE: I don't see why.

EDWARD: Because he is St. George and you are a dragon.

HORACE (*Gravely*): My dear boy, please understand, once and for all, that I can't fight and I won't fight. I've never fought in my life, and I'm not going to begin now, just to give your village a Roman holiday.[6]

EDWARD (*Miserably*): But if you don't fight, St. George will cut off your head!

HORACE: Oh, I don't think so. You will be able to arrange something, Edward—you are such a good manager. I leave it entirely up to you. And now, if you will excuse me, I should get back to my writing. Thank you for the sandwiches. (*He goes into the cave.*) **9**

---

5. **St. George** is a legendary figure and patron saint of England. He is often seen as an example of bravery and defender of the poor and helpless. Although he was a real person, writers and artists have shown him as a dragon-slayer.

6. By **Roman holiday**, Horace means he doesn't want to be a source of amusement.

Vocabulary . . . .

exasperated (eg ZAS pur ay tid) *adj.* angered or greatly irritated

Practice the Skills

9 ▶ **Reviewing Skills**

Comparing and Contrasting Think about what you know or have read about dragons. How is Horace similar to or different from those dragons?

The Reluctant Dragon **949**

Teach

C Critical Thinking

Analysis Ask: How can you tell that Horace doesn't believe he's in danger? *(Possible responses: he wants to recite a poem; he thinks he can choose not to meet or fight St. George; He goes off to write.)* **AS**

EL Language Coach

Idioms Say: A Roman holiday is not a trip to the beach. It refers to the Roman Empire, when gladiators were forced to fight as a form of public entertainment. Sometimes their opponents were wild beasts. Why would Horace say his fighting St. George would be a Roman holiday? *(Possible response: Villagers would be entertained by Horace's suffering and death.)* **AL**

BQ BIG Question

Ask: How do you know that Horace considers Edward a friend? *(Possible response: He trusts Edward to keep him safe.)* **AS**

Differentiated Instruction

Build Background Explain to students that most British knights began as pages around age seven. They were sent from their homes to a lord's castle, where they served as pages—basically waiters and personal servants. At age 14, a page could become a squire, serving one particular knight. Squires learned the art of battle by watching the knights they served. If squires performed an act of bravery on the battlefield, or when they completed their training, they were knighted. Before becoming a knight, men swore to follow the code of chivalry, which required them to be honorable, respectful, brave, and protective of women. **AS**

Objectives
- Understand idioms
- Analyze text
- Synthesize text
- Visualize
- Interpret and analyze character

Teach

L Literary Element

Act and Scene **Say:** It might seem as if a new scene begins when Horace and Selina return to the stage. What would be required to call this a new scene? *(a change in the setting or time)* **OL**

EL Language Coach

Slang **Ask:** What does Selina mean when she says "set the cave to rights"? *(Possible responses: clean up; put things in order; straighten the mess)* **AS**

BQ BIG Question

Ask: How does Selina show what makes a friend? *(by volunteering to do things for or help Horace)* **AS**

Visual Vocabulary
Croquet is a game in which players use mallets (which resemble wooden golf clubs) to drive wooden balls through a series of small arches on a lawn.

EDWARD (*To* SELINA): Arrange something indeed! Horace treats the whole affair as if it were an invitation to play croquet! Come on, let's go home. (*He picks up picnic basket and exits right, followed by* SELINA. *After a moment,* HORACE *appears in entrance to cave, carrying a stool and several pieces of bark. He places stool just outside cave, sits down and begins to scribble on a piece of bark with a lump of charcoal. He ponders over words, rhyming them out loud, and sneezes once or twice. Presently,* SELINA *enters from right and speaks to* HORACE *softly.*) **10**

SELINA: Mr. Horace—

HORACE (*Looking up with a start*): Oh! My dear! (*He rises and bows.*) I didn't expect you back so soon.

SELINA (*Crossing to him*): Mr. Horace, if there's anything I can do for you—like mend things, or set the cave to rights, or cook a little something when you're writing poetry and forget about meals, I—I'd be glad to do it.

HORACE: Thank you, Selina. I'd appreciate that.

SELINA: I'll start tomorrow. Is there anything in particular you'd like?

HORACE: I wonder if you'd bring me a bit of flannel to polish my scales with. (*He sneezes.*) Atchoo!

SELINA: Bless you! I'll bring the flannel and some smelling salts[7] for that hay fever, too. Goodbye!

HORACE: Goodbye, my dear. (SELINA *skips away, singing.*) What a nice child. I'll write a sonnet[8] to her. (*He sits down again, selects a clean piece of bark, and inscribes the title with a flourish.*) To Selina. By Horace Dragon. Now, let me think—how shall I begin it? (*He speaks the lines as he slowly sets them down.*)

---

7. ***Smelling salts*** are a strong-scented mixture used for waking up someone who has fainted. They used to be used for hay fever.

8. A ***sonnet*** is a fourteen line rhyming poem.

Practice the Skills

10 Key Reading Skill

Visualizing Pay close attention to the stage directions. How do they help you visualize what Horace does? **L**

Additional Support

English Language Coach

Idioms Explain to students that hay fever causes itchy skin, sneezing, and red, puffy, watery eyes. But *hay fever* isn't a real medical term; it's just what ordinary people call the symptoms of an allergy to pollen. Pollen is the fine dust that acts as the male seed of flowering plants. Farmers allergic to hay pollen called the condition "hay fever," but anyone can have it. Horace blames his condition on ragweed. When pollen is breathed in, the body fights it with chemicals called histamines. Some people have a bad reaction to the histamines, and that bad reaction is what we call hay fever. Maybe it should be "histamine fever!" **AS**

Analyzing the Art What is Horace writing in this picture? How do you know?

Selina in her braids and calico
Is fairer far than any flower I know.
So sweet is she, this dainty shepherd's daughter,
I blush to say she makes my big mouth water. (HORACE
writes on the bark, then holds up his poem and regards it with
C *delight. Suddenly he jumps to his feet with a cry of horror.*) Oh!
What am I thinking of? Is it possible that I am a damsel-
devouring dragon after all? Oh, dearie, dearie me! (*He reaches*
L *behind for his tail and, using it as an eraser, he frantically rubs out*
what he has written, as curtain falls.) **11** ○

Practice the Skills

11 🔵 **BIG Question**

Would you make friends with a dragon like Edward and Selina do, or would you run away like the other children? What about Horace might make him a good friend? Write your answer on the "Reluctant Dragon, Scene 1" page of Foldable 8. Your answer will help you complete the Unit Challenge later.

The Reluctant Dragon **951**

Teach

Viewing the Illustration

Ask: How does Horace here compare with dragons you've seen in books, movies, or on TV? (*Responses will vary.*) **AS**

C Critical Thinking

Comprehension Ask: Why does Horace jump up in horror? (*Possible response: He realizes that Selina makes his mouth water, which is what often happens as you think of eating something tasty.*) **AS**

L Literary Element

Act and Scene Say: "Curtain falls" indicates the end of the scene. This expression goes back to when most stages had curtains that came down, or "fell," from above the stage. Today some stages have curtains that close from the sides, and some don't have curtains at all. **AS** Is this a good spot to end the scene? Why or why not? (*Responses will vary.*) **OL**

Reading Fluency

Build Fluency Form groups of eight to read the scene, with one student in each group reading the main stage directions and the others assuming the speaking parts. First review the pronunciations and meanings of words that might present difficulties. Then discuss other aspects of the scene, including emotions, actions, and cultural references. Make suggestions as needed with regard to reading smoothly, with expression, and for understandability. Have the groups practice and then present the scene for the class. **AS**

Objectives
• Identify literary elements: scene
• Use text features: illustration
• Understand slang and idioms
• Monitor comprehension

Assess

Resources for page 952

📁 Selection Quick Check, p. 71

📁 Selection and Unit Assessment, p. 85

💿 ExamView Assessment Suite

💿 Interactive Tutor: Self-Assessment

Students can respond to the *After You Read* items in their Learner's Notebooks or on a separate sheet of paper.

Answering the BIG Question

1. Responses will vary, but should include an explanation.

Critical Thinking

2. Possible response: Horace is proud to be a dragon, but he's reluctant to behave as a dragon is expected to.

Talk About Your Reading

Students may say that Horace is not a "damsel-devouring dragon" and will never become one.

Skills Review

Key Reading Skill: Visualizing

3. Sketches will vary.

Key Literary Element: Act and Scene

4. Possible response: They help me understand when and where things take place.

After You Read

The Reluctant Dragon Scene 1

Answering the BIG Question

1. Would you want to be friends with Horace? Explain your answer.

Critical Thinking

2. **Analyze** Think about Horace's personality. What makes him a *reluctant* dragon?

Tip Author and Me

Talk About Your Reading

Scene 1 ends with Horace concerned that he might *really* be a "damsel-devouring dragon after all." What do you think? With a partner, talk about what might happen in the next scene, and why it might happen.

Skills Review

Key Reading Skill: Visualizing

3. Find all the descriptions of what Horace looks like. (Hint: They're all on the first few pages.) Now use your imagination to make a sketch of him.

Key Literary Element: Scene

4. How do details like *time* and *setting* at the beginning of a new scene help you to understand what is happening in the play?

Vocabulary Check

Rewrite the sentences using four of the words that fit best.

scourge solemnly lavishly elaborately exasperated

The invaders were a **5.** ___ throughout the kingdom. The king spent money **6.** ___ to make sure the castle was protected. However, with a sad face, he **7.** ___ announced he could not protect the people. The knights were so **8.** ___ by this that they decided to fight on their own.

9. **Academic Vocabulary** What does it mean to visualize as you read?

10. **English Language Coach** What is another slang term for *carrying on*?

Objectives (p. 952)
Reading Visualize
Literature Understand elements of drama: act and scene
Vocabulary Identify and understand slang

Vocabulary Check

5. scourge
6. lavishly
7. solemnly
8. exasperated
9. **Academic Vocabulary** Possible response: to form mental pictures of what is described
10. **English Language Coach** Possible response: pitching a fit

Before You Read

The Reluctant Dragon
Scene 2

Vocabulary Preview

contemplation (kon tem PLAY shun) *n.* a state of deep thought **(p. 954)**
The knight was lost in contemplation.

R **crevice** (KREV is) *n.* narrow opening; split or crack **(p. 954)** *His spear was wedged in the crevice of a rock.*

conceited (kun SEE tid) *adj.* having a high opinion of oneself **(p. 961)** *The dragon became proud and conceited when the crowd cheered for him.*

warily (WAIR uh lee) *adv.* cautiously **(p. 961)** *The knight warily circled the dragon.*

spar (spar) *v.* to move around as if fighting without landing a blow **(p. 961)** *A crowd gathered when the knight and the dragon began to spar.*

English Language Coach

EL **Dialect** The way a language is spoken in one area or by a group of people is called **dialect**. Some dialects might look like Standard English but use a different vocabulary or word order. At other times, written dialect can look very different. For example, "Twarn't no good a-tall" in Standard English would be: "It wasn't any good at all."

Skills Preview

Key Reading Skill: Visualizing
As you read the next scene, use what you already know about the characters to visualize them.

Key Literary Element: Act and Scene
Directions at the beginning of a new scene will help you to understand actions and learn about characters.

Get Ready to Read

Objectives (pp. 953–963)
Reading Visualize
Literature Understand elements of drama: scene
Vocabulary Identify and understand dialect

Partner Talk With a partner, discuss what you think will happen between Horace and St. George.

Keep Moving ➡

Use these skills as you read the following selection.

The Reluctant Dragon **953**

Teach

R Reading Skill

Visualizing Ask: What do you see when you visualize the sample sentence for the vocabulary word *crevice*? *(Responses will vary.)* **EL BL OL**

EL Language Coach

Dialect Ask: Do you think the characters in "The Reluctant Dragon" are speaking a dialect? *(Responses will vary.)* **AL**
Say: The dialogue is written with proper grammar, and most of the words are Standard English. Often it's hard to recognize dialect just from looking at printed text. Sometimes you have to hear people talking to know that they're using a dialect. Remember that "The Reluctant Dragon" is set in England, so actors performing the play would use a British accent. **AS**

Differentiated Instruction

Writing Activity Write these lines of dialogue on the board:
Jarom: I do believe that I should like to see a dragon some day.
Micah: Indeed! It would be a simply lovely sight, would it not?
Jarom: Yes, although I fear that I might be overcome with fright.

Micah: Do not fret, my kind friend. I would endeavor to defeat the beast before it could devour you.
Jarom: My thanks, good companion.

Have students work with a partner, to rewrite the lines on the board so that they sound the way kids talk today. **OL**

Objectives
• Understand dialect
• Visualize
• Identify literary elements: dialogue

Teach

L Literary Element

Act and Scene Ask: What has changed since the end of Scene 1? *(Possible responses: Three days have passed. A new character, St. George, is onstage.)* OL

EL Language Coach

Idioms Ask: What does it mean to "get the lay of the land"? *(Possible responses: check things out; look things over; prepare)* AL

the Reluctant Dragon

by Kenneth Grahame
Adapted by Adele Thane

SCENE 2

TIME: Three days later.

SETTING: The same as Scene 1.

AT RISE: ST. GEORGE *is standing on a rock upstage, leaning on his sword, lost in* **contemplation** *of distant hills. His red-plumed[1] helmet is resting on the rock beside him. His spear is stuck upright in a* **crevice**. *HORACE is nowhere to be seen. After a moment,* EDWARD *enters from right.* **1**

EDWARD (*Politely*): St. George, sir!

ST. GEORGE (*Turning, startled*): Yes?

EDWARD: I hope I'm not intruding, sir.

ST. GEORGE: Not at all, boy. I'm just getting the lay of the land. Magnificent view up here. What can I do for you? (*He comes down from rock.*)

EDWARD: If you please, sir, I'd like to talk to you about the dragon.

ST. GEORGE (*Sighing*): Alas! Is it another tale of misery and wrong?

---

1. A **red-plumed** helmet has a cluster of red feathers on it.

> **Vocabulary**
>
> **contemplation** (kon tem PLAY shun) *n.* a state of deep thought
>
> **crevice** (KREV is) *n.* narrow opening; split or crack

Practice the Skills

1 **Key Literary Element**

Act and Scene This is Scene 2. From details about the *time* and *setting*, what do you notice about this new scene? **L**

Additional Support

Literature Focus Lesson

Conflict There are many kinds of conflict in life. In literature, an internal conflict is a struggle within the character. An external conflict is a struggle between characters, between a character and society, or between a character and nature. Ask students to identify internal and external conflicts in "The Reluctant Dragon." *(Possible responses: Horace the poet vs. Horace the dragon, Horace vs. St. George, Horace vs. the villagers)* Ask students to write a brief paragraph beginning, "The most important conflict in this play is ____." Tell them to support their idea with details from what they've read so far. OL AL

EDWARD: Nothing of the sort! There's a misunderstanding somewhere, and I want to put it right. The fact is, sir, this is a *good* dragon.

ST. GEORGE (*Smiling*): Exactly. A good dragon—a worthy foe of my steel (*He lifts his sword high*), and no feeble specimen of his noxious tribe.[2]

EDWARD: He's not noxious! I tell you, he's a *good* dragon, and a friend of mine. Why, he has been so kind to my sister, she'd do anything for him.

ST. GEORGE (*Clapping EDWARD on shoulder*): I like a fellow who sticks up for his friends! What is your name, boy?

EDWARD: Edward, sir.

ST. GEORGE: Now, Edward, I'm sure the dragon has his good points, but that's not the question. He has been stealing and killing—

EDWARD (*Shocked*): Horace? Stealing and killing? (*Impatiently*) Oh, you've been listening to all those **yarns** the villagers have been telling. Why, our villagers are the biggest story-tellers in the country.

ST. GEORGE (*Amazed*): Do you mean that the dragon hasn't molested[3] anybody?

EDWARD: That's right. Horace is a real gentleman, every inch of him. All the villagers want is to see a fight.

ST. GEORGE: But what are we to do? (*Pointing to cave.*) In there is the dragon and out here am I, and we're supposed to be thirsting for each other's blood. What do you suggest? Can't you arrange things, somehow? **2**

R

---

2. ***Noxious*** means "harmful" and a ***specimen*** is an example of something. When St. George says, ***"no feeble specimen of his noxious tribe,"*** he means that Horace would be a worthy opponent, not a weak dragon.

3. Here, ***molested*** means "injured or bothered."

Analyzing the Illustration Does this picture match the way you visualize St. George? Why or why not?

Practice the Skills

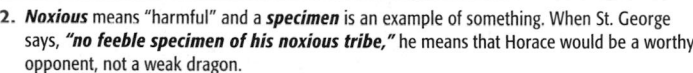

2 **English Language Coach**

Dialect **Yarn**, which means "exaggerated story," is an example of dialect in this story. It's common in old-fashioned ways of speaking. Also, in a dialect, words may be arranged differently than you'd expect. Find an example near the end of this page where that occurs.

The Reluctant Dragon **955**

Teach

Viewing the Illustration

Ask: In what way does St. George look like your mental picture of a knight? *(Possible response: He's wearing armor and carrying a sword.)* **Ask:** How is he different? *(Possible response: He looks scrawny and cartoonish—not like he could defeat a dragon.)* **OL**

R Reading Skill

Review Predicting Ask: What do you think Edward will do? *(Possible response: figure out a way to keep St. George from killing Horace)* **AS**

Reading in the Real World

Career Edward is performing the duties of a friend, but he's also behaving like an ambassador trying to prevent a conflict between nations. Some students may be interested in learning about careers in diplomacy. Have them research the duties of a U.S. ambassador or secretary of state. Students could choose an area of the world in which there's ongoing conflict and propose a resolution. Have them write a paper presenting both the problem and how they would try to solve it. **AL**

Objectives
- Use text features: illustration
- Make predictions
- Identify literary elements: scene, conflict
- Understand idioms

Teach

C Critical Thinking

Comprehension Ask: Why won't St. George leave? *(Possible response: The "rules" of knighthood require him to fight a dragon.)* **AS**

R1 Reading Skill

Review Clarifying Ask: Why does Edward explain Selina's presence at the cave? *(Possible response: So St. George won't think Horace is harming Selina.)* **AS**

R2 Reading Skill

Review Predicting Ask: What might Edward think will happen unless he tells Horace to use common sense? *(Possible response: He thinks Horace might refuse to talk to St. George.)* **OL**

EDWARD: That's just what Horace said! Really, the way you two seem to leave everything to me! (*Coaxing*) I suppose, sir, you couldn't be persuaded to go away quietly, could you?

ST. GEORGE (*Loftily*): Impossible! It's quite against the rules.

EDWARD: Then would you please see the dragon and talk it over?

ST. GEORGE: We-e-ell, it's irregular, but I guess it's the most sensible thing to do.

EDWARD: I'm glad you feel that way, St. George. (*He goes to entrance of cave and calls out loudly.*) Horace! I've brought a friend to see you! (*There is a sneeze inside cave, and SELINA comes running out, holding a bottle of smelling salts.*)

SELINA: He'll be right out.

ST. GEORGE: What ho! A damsel in distress! (*He draws his sword.*)

EDWARD: Hold on! That's my sister, Selina. She looks after him.

ST. GEORGE (*With a sheepish grin*): Oh. (*He puts his sword away.* HORACE *appears, rubbing his scales with a square of flannel. He gives the flannel to* SELINA *and extends his paw to* ST. GEORGE.)

HORACE: Pleased to make your acquaintance, sir.

EDWARD: This is St. George.

HORACE (*Frightened*): St. George?

ST. GEORGE (*Shaking* HORACE's *paw*): How do you do, Horace.

HORACE: So—so glad to meet you. (SELINA *hovers over* HORACE *during the following scene, polishing his scales and giving him smelling salts whenever he shows signs of sneezing.*) **3**

EDWARD: We've come to talk things over quietly, Horace, so for goodness' sake, do let us have a little straight common sense.

956 UNIT 8 What Makes a Friend?

Practice the Skills

3 Key Reading Skill

Visualizing Reread the stage directions describing Selina and Horace. How do you visualize Horace and Selina's actions?

Additional Support

Literature Focus Lesson

Stage Directions Explain that stage directions often tell readers and actors what emotions a character feels at a certain time. Have students work with a partner to identify three emotions characters feel in this scene. Ask students to write a brief paragraph, explaining how actors could use body language and facial expression to convey one of the three emotions they listed. If time permits, allow volunteers to act out their chosen emotion. Have other students volunteer the emotion the actor is portraying. **OL**

ST. GEORGE (*Pleasantly*): Now, don't you think that the simplest plan would be just to fight it out and let the best man win?

EDWARD: Oh, yes, do, Horace! It will save such a lot of bother.

ST. GEORGE: They are betting on you down in the village, Horace, but I don't mind.

HORACE: Believe me, George, there's nobody in the world I'd sooner oblige than you and Edward, but the whole thing is nonsense. There's absolutely nothing to fight about. Anyhow, I'm not going to fight, so that settles it. **4**

ST. GEORGE (*Slightly angry*): Suppose I make you fight?

HORACE: You can't. I should only go into my cave and stay there. You'd soon get sick of sitting outside and waiting for me to come out and fight.

ST. GEORGE (*As he gazes about*): But Horace, this would be a beautiful place for a fight. What a picture we would make!—I in my golden armor showing up against your big green scaly coils. **5**

HORACE (*Wavering*): Now you're trying to get at me through my poetic sense,⁴ but it won't work.

EDWARD: Don't you see, Horace, that there *has* to be a fight of some sort, even if it's only "pretend"?

HORACE: You mean, a mock fight?

ST. GEORGE (*Eagerly*): Yes! I'm sure we can manage it. (*He studies his sword.*) I would have to touch you somewhere, but I won't hurt you very much. How about here? (*He places the tip of his sword behind* HORACE's *knee.*)

HORACE (*Giggling*): You're tickling me, George! (*He sneezes.*) That place won't do. I'd only laugh and spoil everything. (*He sniffs the smelling salts that* SELINA *holds under his nose.*)

---

4. By ***poetic sense***, Horace means his appreciation of beauty. He realizes that the image of a bright green dragon fighting a knight in golden armor would be a poetic moment.

Practice the Skills

4 Reviewing Skills

Predicting Do you think that Horace will fight or not? Explain your prediction.

5 Key Reading Skill

Visualizing Even St. George is visualizing. Do his descriptions fit the way *you* visualize St. George and Horace?

The Reluctant Dragon **957**

Teach

R Reading Skill

Review Clarifying Ask: How does Horace explain why he thinks the whole thing is nonsense? (*Possible response: He says there's nothing to fight about, which makes fighting pointless.*) **OL**

C Critical Thinking

Analysis Ask: Do you think the conversation on this page makes sense? Why or why not? (*Possible response: I think the conversation is silly. No one wants to fight so why are they talking about it?*) **OL**

Reading Fluency

Reading Dialogue To help students appreciate humorous dialogue, play a tape of Abbott and Costello's "Who's on first?" routine. Have them compare the lack of communication between Abbott and Costello to the communication among Horace, Edward, and St. George. Ask students to work with a partner to create several lines of nonsense dialogue in which two students argue over a school issue. Students who choose to use the "Who's on first?" model should show how people fail to understand each other's points. Students who choose the play model should demonstrate how both sides actually agree but keep arguing. **AL**

Objectives
• Analyze text
• Clarify ideas and text
• Make predictions
• Monitor comprehension

Teach

C1 Critical Thinking

Synthesis Ask: Why is the first stage direction on this page necessary? *(Possible response: To let the actors and readers know where St. George should nick Horace.)* **OL**

BQ BIG Question

Ask: How do Edward's questions show that he is Horace's friend? *(Possible response: He wants to make sure that Horace will benefit from the mock fight.)* **AS**

C2 Critical Thinking

Comprehension Ask: What does St. George mean about Horace's being "converted"? *(Possible response: Horace will change from a mean dragon to a friendly one or from a monster to a poet.)* **OL**

C1 **ST. GEORGE:** Well, here, then. (*He flicks his sword at the nape of* HORACE's *neck.*) If I nicked you here, you'd never know I'd done it.

HORACE (*Anxiously*): Are you sure you can hit the right place?

ST. GEORGE: Now, don't you fret. Of course you will have to do your share of the fighting, too, Horace. Can you **ramp** and breathe fire? **6**

HORACE (*Confidently*): Oh, I can ramp all right. I'm a little out of practice breathing fire, but I'll do my best. **7**

BQ **EDWARD** (*Concerned*): Look here, St. George, if there's to be a fight and Horace is to be licked, what is he going to get out of it?

HORACE: That's right, George. What will I get out of it?

ST. GEORGE: Well, you will be led in triumph down to the market place—

EDWARD: Exactly—led in triumph by you!

C2 **ST. GEORGE:** Then there will be toasts and speeches, and I shall explain that Horace has converted.

EDWARD: And then?

ST. GEORGE: Why, then there will be a big banquet, and that is where Horace will come in.

HORACE: What do you mean?

ST. GEORGE: I mean, you will read some of your poetry with the dessert, and everyone will know how clever you are!

HORACE: Splendid! I might even go into society and read my poems at garden parties and teas.

ST. GEORGE (*Picking up his helmet from the rock*): There ought to be a princess chained to this rock. Edward, can't you arrange a princess?

EDWARD (*Firmly*): No, I can't arrange a princess, and anyway, here come the villagers to see the fight. (*Noise of a crowd is heard from off right.*)

958 UNIT 8 What Makes a Friend?

Practice the Skills

6 **English Language Coach**

Dialect You learned what *ramping* means on page 944, so you can figure out what *ramp* means here. This is another old-fashioned word.

7 **Key Reading Skill**

Visualizing Is it easy to visualize Horace breathing fire? Why or why not?

Additional Support

Differentiated Instruction

Sequencing St. George, Edward, and Horace work out a step-by-step plan for the mock fight and the celebration that will follow. Have students work with a partner to make a "recipe" for Horace's mock fight. Draw the following "recipe card" on the board for students to complete. **AS**

> **DRAGON–KNIGHT STEW**
> **Ingredients (Participants):** ____ and ____
> **Kitchen Location (Setting):** ____ **Tools (Weapons):** St. George's ____ and Horace's ____
> **Baking (Fighting) Time:** 10 minutes **Directions:**
> 1. Horace and St. George will ____ .
> 2. St. George will ____ .
> 3. Horace will ____ .
> 4. The villagers will ____ .
> **Serves:** one dragon and one entire village

ST. GEORGE: Horace, get into your cave and don't come out until I call you. (HORACE *trots into cave.*) Come, Edward, you will be my squire[5] and carry my spear. (*He loosens spear from crevice and gives it to* EDWARD; *then he strides off left of cave.*)

EDWARD (*To* SELINA, *as he follows*
ST. GEORGE *off*): Act as if you'd just arrived! (SELINA *hastily tosses flannel cloth into cave and sits on a rock, assuming a casual pose.* VILLAGERS *and* CHILDREN *enter, dressed in their Sunday best, laughing and chattering gaily. They group themselves, sitting and standing, on the rocks,* CHILDREN *in the foreground and* VILLAGERS *behind.*)

1ST BOY: Who do you think will win?

2ND BOY: The dragon.

3RD BOY: St. George.

1ST BOY (*To* 2ND BOY): Hey, don't sit so close to the cave!

2ND BOY: Why not?

1ST BOY: If the dragon wins, he'll bite off your head! (BOYS *cuff at*[6] *each other. Then* VILLAGERS *on higher portions of the rocks begin to cheer and wave their handkerchiefs as they look off left.*)

VILLAGERS: St. George! Here comes St. George! (ST. GEORGE *enters, followed by* EDWARD, *who carries spear.* ST. GEORGE *takes up a position downstage in front of cave, with* EDWARD *beside him.*) 🎦

EDWARD (*In a low tone, to* ST. GEORGE): Do you think Horace can be depended on, sir?

ST. GEORGE: Oh, I think so.

EDWARD: He might consider the whole thing a lot of bosh[7] and change his mind.

ST. GEORGE: Haven't you more faith in your friend than that? (EDWARD *sits cross-legged, with his back to audience.*

---

5. Here, *squire* means someone who carries a knight's shield, armor, or weapon.

6. To *cuff at* each other is to slap at each other with open hands.

7. *Bosh* means nonsense.

Practice the Skills

🎦 **Key Reading Skill**

Visualizing How do you visualize the villagers? Think about the villagers you have already met, like Edward and Selina. What details in the script help you to picture the villagers in your imagination?

The Reluctant Dragon **959**

Teach

C Critical Thinking

Application Ask: What feature on this page is there to help you understand *squire?* *(Visual Vocabulary)*

BQ BIG Question

Ask: What do you learn about friendship from St. George's comments on this page? *(Possible response: Friends trust each other.)* **OL**

Literature Focus Lesson

Stage Directions Get all students "in the act" by having students act out the play from the villagers' entrance to the end. Ask for volunteers to play the roles of Edward, St. George, Horace, Selina, and the three village boys. Have other students speak in unison as the villagers. If possible, use a large area or stage. Review stage directions with students to help them understand positions and movements. If time permits, repeat the performance allowing other students to play the principal roles. **OL**

Objectives
- Apply information
- Synthesize text
- Monitor comprehension
- Identify literary elements: stage directions

959

Teach

Viewing the Illustration

Say: Use the illustration to describe the mood of the villagers. *(Possible responses: happy, excited, thrilled)* **AS**

C Critical Thinking

Analysis Ask: Why do you think St. George misses on his first charge? *(Possible response: He purposely misses to build the crowd's excitement and put on a good show.)* **AS**

ST. GEORGE *faces opening of cave, and talks loudly to* HORACE.) Dragon, come forth! *(Inside cave, there is low muttering, mingled with snorts and sneezes, which rises to a bellowing roar. Then a cloud of smoke rolls out of the cave, and* HORACE *prances magnificently forth, lashing his long tail from side to side.)*

VILLAGERS: Ooh! Ooh!

EDWARD *(Applauding wildly)*: Bully for you, Horace! I didn't think you had it in you! *(ST. GEORGE draws his sword and charges at HORACE, who rears back with a loud roar.)* **9**

VILLAGERS: Missed! *(ST. GEORGE retreats and swings his sword high in the air, then charges again. HORACE sits down and roars viciously.)*

EDWARD *(Shouting, as he stands up and waves the spear)*: End of Round One! *(SELINA runs to his side and whispers to him uneasily.)*

SELINA: I hope St. George won't get excited and hurt Horace.

Analyzing the Art Study this picture. Do Horace and St. George seem to be putting on a good show? Do you think the villagers are enjoying the battle? Support your answers with details from the picture.

Practice the Skills

9 English Language Coach

Dialect To understand dialect in what you read, it is extremely helpful to use your context clues skills. Look at what Edward is doing and what he says after he says, "Bully for you, Horace!" What do you think "Bully for you" means?

Additional Support

Differentiated Instruction

Analyzing Characters Write the following questions on the board: Why does Edward first speak with St. George? Why do the villagers want a fight? Why does Selina help Horace? Why does Horace finally agree to the mock fight? Explain to students that motivation is someone's reason for doing something.

For example, hunger is a motivation for eating. Knowing a character's motivation helps an actor better understand and portray the character. Have students work with a partner to decide each character's motivation in acting as he or she did. **AS**

EDWARD: I don't think he will. What a regular play-actor that Horace is! (ST. GEORGE *looks toward them as he wipes his brow. He smiles and nods and holds up three fingers.*) That means he will finish off Horace in Round Three. Whatever is that old fool of a dragon up to now? (HORACE *is giving a ramping performance for* VILLAGERS. *He swaggers around and around in a wide circle.* EDWARD *raps on ground with the spear.*) Time! (HORACE *begins to leap from side to side with ungainly bounds, whooping like an Indian.* ST. GEORGE *dances about, thrusting his sword at* HORACE, *but is unable to make contact.* VILLAGERS *cheer.* HORACE *struts to and fro, his tail in the air.* ST. GEORGE *comes toward* EDWARD *and* SELINA, *tightening his armor.*) It's a grand fight, St. George. Can't you let it last a bit longer?

ST. GEORGE: No, I'd better not. Horace is getting **conceited** now that they've started to cheer him. He'll forget all about the agreement and play the fool. There's no telling how far he might go. I'll just finish him off this round.

SELINA: Oh, *do* be careful, sir—of Horace, I mean.

ST. GEORGE (*Kindly*): Now don't you worry. I've marked the exact spot. (ST. GEORGE *turns upstage and cautiously approaches* HORACE, *who crouches, flicking his tail so that it cracks like a whip.* ST. GEORGE *circles* **warily** *around him.* HORACE *paces guardedly around the same circle, occasionally feinting[8] with his head. They* **spar** *for an opening, while the spectators maintain a breathless silence. Then suddenly there is a lightning movement of* ST. GEORGE's *arm, a whirl and a confusion of scales, claws, tail and flying bits of turf.* VILLAGERS *cheer as* ST. GEORGE *stands astride* HORACE. ST. GEORGE *holds his sword over* HORACE, *menacingly.* EDWARD *and* SELINA *run to* ST. GEORGE.) **10**

EDWARD: Oh, sir, he isn't really hurt, is he? (HORACE *lifts his head slightly, looks at* EDWARD, *then collapses again.*)

---

8. By *feinting* Horace is making a false move, or "faking out" his opponent.

Vocabulary

conceited (kun SEE tid) *adj.* having a high opinion of oneself

warily (WAIR uh lee) *adv.* cautiously

spar (spar) *v.* to move around as if fighting without landing a blow

Practice the Skills

10 | Key Reading Skill

Visualizing How do you visualize the fight between Horace and St. George? Imagine Horace cracking his tail *"like a whip,"* as the two pace in a circle. Imagine St. George's *"lightning movement,"* and a whirl of *"scales, claws, tail and . . . flying bits of turf."* What other details from the play help you to visualize the fight?

The Reluctant Dragon **961**

Teach

R1 Reading Skill

Review Clarifying Ask: What does Edward mean when he calls Horace a "play-actor"? *(Possible response: He says Horace is "hamming it up" by putting on a big show for the audience.)* **OL**

L Literary Element

Act and Scene Ask: What is the main action of this scene? *(the mock fight)* **AS**

R2 Reading Skill

Review Predicting Ask: What does St. George predict? *(that Horace is going to forget about the agreement)* **Ask:** Do you agree? *(Responses will vary.)* **AS**

English Language Coach

Building Background Edward serves as a "referee" for the mock fight, in much the same way as a boxing referee monitors the progress of a boxing match. Explain to students that the mock fight is staged in *rounds*—set times, or intervals. In boxing, for example, a round is anywhere from one to three minutes.

Between rounds, the opponents rest. As in boxing, both fighters obey the referee when a round ends. At the end of a boxing match, it is traditional for the referee to raise the arm of the winning fighter. In the case of Horace and St. George, the winner—St. George—assumes a victor's stance astride the dragon. **AS**

Objectives
- Use text features: illustration
- Analyze text
- Clarify ideas and text
- Identify literary elements: scene
- Make predictions
- Interpret and analyze character

Teach

C Critical Thinking

Analysis Ask: Why do you think the villagers cheered both St. George and Horace? *(Possible response: They wanted to thank both for the fine show.)* **OL**

R Reading Skill

Visualizing Say: Picture St. George wagging his finger at Horace. What does this mental picture remind you of? *(Possible response: a parent scolding a naughty child)* **AS** **Ask:** How does this mental picture affect your mood? *(Possible response: It makes me laugh because I know St. George really likes Horace.)* **OL**

1ST VILLAGER (*An old man in the crowd*): Aren't you goin' to cut 'is 'ead off, master? **11**

ST. GEORGE (*Affably*): Not today, grandfather. I'll give him a good talking-to, and you'll find he will be a very different dragon.

VILLAGERS: Three cheers for St. George! Three cheers for the dragon! (*While the crowd is cheering,* ST. GEORGE *pretends to scold* HORACE, *wagging his finger at him with a stern expression.* VILLAGERS *start to form for the march to the village, and* ST. GEORGE *raises his hand to get their attention.*)

ST. GEORGE: Just a moment! I have something to say to all of you. The dragon has been thinking things over, and he says he's not going to rampage any more. He would like to settle down here and write poetry. So you must make friends with him and admit him into society.[9] (VILLAGERS *cheer again.*)

HORACE (*To* ST. GEORGE): I couldn't have done it better myself. Jolly fight, wasn't it? I didn't sneeze once. (*He sneezes, and* SELINA *whips out the smelling salts.*) Thank you, my dear.

ST. GEORGE: Well, shall we start down to the village?

HORACE: Wait! My poems!

SELINA: I'll get them for you! (*She rushes into the cave;* CHILDREN *and* VILLAGERS *joyfully march offstage and down through the audience, singing to the tune of "The Campbells Are Coming."*[10])

---

9. To ***admit him into society*** means "let him be a part of the community."
10. ***"The Campbells Are Coming"*** is a traditional Scottish bagpipe tune.

962 UNIT 8 What Makes a Friend?

11 **English Language Coach**

Dialect A new dialect has just been introduced—one that is very common in London, England. (It's called "cockney.") How does the old man pronounce *his* and *head*?

Additional Support

Differentiated Instruction

Using a Graphic Organizer To help students identify the mood of this scene, ask them to pay close attention to the sights and sounds of the mock fight. Draw this organizer for students to complete. **OL**

First, . . .
Then, . . .
Next, . . .
Finally, . . .

Sounds
Sights

ALL (*Singing*):
St. George caught a dragon,
    Hooray! Hooray!
A strange sort of dragon,
    Hooray! Hooray!
He sits in his cave
    Writing poems all day!
A strange sort of dragon,
    Hooray! Hooray!

(EDWARD, ST. GEORGE, SELINA, *and* HORACE, *with his poems tucked under his scales, bring up the rear,* HORACE *singing loudest of all, as curtain falls.*)

THE END 🔢 ⚪

Practice the Skills

🔢 BIG Question

Even though dragons and people are supposed to be enemies, Edward and Selina befriend Horace. What does this tell you about friendship? Write your answer on the "Reluctant Dragon, Scene 2" page of Foldable 8. Your answer will help you complete the Unit Challenge later.

Analyzing the Art Review the end of the play, beginning with Selina's final line. Then answer the question: What is happening in this picture? Support your answer with details from the play and from the picture.

The Reluctant Dragon **963**

Teach

R Reading Skill

Review Predicting Ask:
What do you think Horace's life will be like in the future? *(Possible response: He'll become an accepted member of the village and will make friends.)* **AS**

CheckPoint

Use the CheckPoint questions provided on Presentation Plus! to check for comprehension of the selection. These questions can be used with interactive response keypads for immediate student feedback.

Literature Focus Lesson

Resolution Ask students whether or not they think the ending fits the tone of the play. Ask them to explain their responses. Tell students that a good ending is one that is a logical conclusion to the events in the storyline. With a partner, have students write a new ending for this play. Ask them to list events and character traits that may need to be changed in order to make their new ending logical. When students have completed the assignment, ask volunteers to share their new ending with the class. **OL**

Objectives
• Analyze text
• Make predictions
• Visualize
• Identify literary elements: resolution

963

Assess

Resources for page 964

📁 Selection Quick Check, p. 72

📁 Selection and Unit Assessment, p. 86

💿 ExamView Assessment Suite

💿 Interactive Tutor: Self-Assessment

Students can respond to the *After You Read* items in their Learner's Notebooks or on a separate sheet of paper.

Answering the BIG Question

1. Responses will vary, but should include an explanation of the traits that make the selected character a friend.

2. He is polite but frightened.

3. They appeal to Horace's "common sense," "poetic sense," and pride in his poetry.

Critical Thinking

4. Horace appears to enjoy being a "play-actor" and participating fully in the mock fight. He roars, ramps, struts, submits to defeat, allows St. George to scold him, and doesn't sneeze once.

5. Possible response: The most unexpected people can become friends.

6. Most students will say that the villagers have already accepted Horace, since they cheered for him and seemed to respect St. George's opinion of him.

964

After You Read

The Reluctant Dragon Scene 2

Answering the BIG Question

1. If you could pick one of the characters as a friend, whom would you pick and why do you think the character would make a good friend? Support your answer with details from the story.

2. **Recall** How does Horace first react when he meets St. George?
   Tip Right There

3. **Summarize** How did Edward and St. George persuade Horace to fight?
   Tip Think and Search

Critical Thinking

4. **Infer** What is Horace's attitude toward the fight with St. George while the battle is going on? How can you tell?
   Tip Author and Me

5. **Analyze** What is the message about friendship in "The Reluctant Dragon"?
   Tip Author and Me

6. **Synthesize** Do you think the rest of the village will make friends with Horace "and admit him into society" as St. George instructs? Support your answer with details from the story.
   Tip On Your Own

Write About Your Reading

Part of making a great play is designing the costumes. What kind of costumes would you design for Horace and St. George?

- Skim through the play and make a list of any details you find that will help you to visualize the way Horace and St. George look.
- Using those descriptions, draw the costumes.
- Write a paragraph about why you designed the costumes as you did. Be sure to include the details from the play that you put on your list.

Objectives (pp. 964–965)
Reading Visualize
Literature Understand elements of drama: scene
Vocabulary Understand dialect
Writing Design and write about costumes
Grammar Use punctuation correctly: hyphens

964 UNIT 8 What Makes a Friend?

Write About Your Reading

Possible response:

I made Horace's costume shiny and pretty, because I wanted him to look friendly and appealing, not gross and scary. His scales are polished to a high gloss. His eyes and nose are a little pink because of his allergies. St. George's costume is shiny, too, but it is softer looking than regular metal. I wanted to show that he wasn't the typical knight who enjoyed battle and killing. I made the red plume bright and long so it looked cheerful and pretty.

Skills Review

Key Reading Skill: Visualizing

7. Was it easier for you to visualize the scenery, the characters, or the action? Explain.

8. Make a sketch of the stage, showing the cave, the path to the village, and whatever else you want to add.

9. The author writes, "ST. GEORGE *takes up a position downstage in front of the cave, with* EDWARD *beside him*." Where are Edward and St. George? Add them to your sketch.

Key Literary Element: Act and Scene

10. Why do you think it's important to change scenes in a play?

Reviewing Skills: Predicting

11. What part of the play turned out differently from one of your predictions? What did *you* predict would happen instead of what did happen?

Vocabulary Check

Answer each statement *true* or *false*. If the statement is false, rewrite it to make it true.

12. A person in the act of **contemplation** is sleeping.

13. A surface with a **crevice** is perfectly smooth.

14. A **conceited** person doesn't have much confidence.

15. A spy would never behave **warily**.

16. If you **spar** with a friend you don't actually touch him or her.

17. **English Language Coach** Rewrite, "Ain't you fightin' dat dragon?" in Standard English.

Literature Online

Web Activities For eFlashcards, Selection Quick Checks, and other Web activities, go to www.glencoe.com.

Grammar Link: Hyphens

- A **hyphen** (-) is a punctuation mark that's used to show that words or parts of words belong together.
  He is a well-known artist. (The hyphen shows that *well* and *known* go together as a compound adjective.)

- Use a hyphen in compound numbers.
  My coat cost sixty-five dollars.

- Use a hyphen or hyphens in certain compound words. Use a dictionary if you aren't sure how to write a compound word.
  bull's-eye   brother-in-law   wide-awake

- Use a hyphen to show the division of a word at the end of a line. Always divide the word between syllables.
  Last term my social studies grade was a disappoint-ment.

Grammar Practice

Match up the words from Column A and Column B to form compound words. Then write each compound word in your Learner's Notebook. Add a hyphen if you think it is needed. Then check your answers in a dictionary to see if you have used hyphens correctly.

	Column A	Column B
18.	narrow	size
19.	life	spoken
20.	soft	minded

Writing Application Circle any hyphens you used in the Write About Your Reading activity you completed. Fix any mistakes you made.

Skills Review

Key Reading Skill: Visualizing

7. Responses will vary.

8. Sketches will vary.

9. Sketches will vary.

Key Literary Element: Act and Scene

10. Possible response: Life events don't happen in the same place at the same time. Changing scenes makes places more realistic.

Reviewing Skills: Predicting

11. Responses will vary.

Vocabulary Check

12. false

13. false

14. false

15. false

16. false

17. **English Language Coach** Possible response: Aren't you going to fight that dragon?

Close

Ask students to describe what they learned about what it means to be a good friend from the selection.

Grammar Link: Hyphens

Grammar Practice

18. narrow-minded

19. life-size

20. soft-spoken

A Speech

Objectives covered in this workshop:
• **Writing** Write expository paragraphs to explain and inform; gather information from a variety of sources; maintain clear purpose and focus
• **Grammar** Identify and correctly use apostrophes

Teaching Students to Write and Present a Speech

Why Is It Important?

• When students listen to each other speak, they will become better listeners. When listening to and observing their peers, they will be particularly attuned to verbal and nonverbal clues.

• Students will be engaged when they speak about something they believe or have personally experienced. Giving speeches empowers students to learn about themselves and tell their stories to others.

• Giving speeches will help students build confidence in their ability to communicate.

• Speaking in their own voices will help students hone their understanding of tone and word choice.

• Setting a purpose for their speech will help students think about the significance and impact of their experiences.

• Writing a speech will help students organize their thoughts in a logical way.

How to Help Students Get It

• Read at least one speech to your students. If possible, watch a video version of a speech being delivered. Give students a checklist of items to evaluate as they listen to or watch the presentation, then discuss both the content and the delivery with the class.

• Tell students that we all give informal speeches every day. Whenever someone asks your opinion on a topic or about an experience, you are giving a short speech.

• Model writing and delivering your own short speech. Start with showing students a concept map, then write the speech as a Talk-Aloud. As you write, point out that you have decided on a purpose; you have created a strong introduction; you have a beginning, middle, and end; you have included supporting facts; and you have created a powerful ending. When you give the speech, remind students of the goals you plan to achieve in your delivery.

• Give students ideas for topics. Some ideas are: the achievement of a personal goal, a family ritual or tradition, a life-changing experience, an issue related to their school or community, or a commentary on something in the media.

• Remind students to use the language that comes naturally to them; this will help them develop their "voice."

Traits of Good Writing	Student Checklist
Ideas	the message or the theme and the details that develop it
Organization	the arrangement of main points and supporting details
Voice	a writer's unique way of using tone and style
Word Choice	the vocabulary a writer uses to convey meaning
Sentence Fluency	the smooth rhythm and flow of sentences that vary in length and style
Conventions	correct spelling, grammar, usage, and mechanics
Presentation: the way words and design elements look on a page	• Handwritten papers should be neat and legible. • If a word processor is used, the text should be double spaced and the font should be readable. • Use design elements—such as bold faced headings, bulleted lists, pictures, and charts—to make papers attractive and inviting.

Unit Focus ➤

Workshop Resources

PACING (DAYS)		LESSON	STUDENT MATERIALS	TEACHER RESOURCES
STANDARD	**BLOCK**			
1	1/2	Writing Workshop Part 1: Prewriting and Drafting	🖉 Writing Workshop Graphic Organizer, p. 14 🖉 Grammar Practice, p. 15 🖉 Spelling and Handwriting Practice, p. 45 💻 Spelling Power eWorkbook 🌐 Interactive Grammar and Language Workbook 📖 Grammar and Composition Handbook, p. 261 📁 Real Success in Writing: Research and Reports 📁 Writing Constructed Responses	💿 TeacherWorks Plus™ 💿 Presentation Plus! 📁 Rubrics for Assessing Student Writing, Listening, and Speaking, p. 18 ✍ Grammar and Writing Workshop Transparencies 1–2
2	1	Writing Workshop Part 2: Editing, Revising, and Presenting	🌐 Interactive Grammar and Language Workbook 📖 Grammar and Composition Handbook, p. 261 🖉 Listening and Speaking, p. 27 🖉 Viewing and Representing, p. 28 📁 Real Success in Writing: Research and Reports 📁 Writing Constructed Responses	✍ Grammar and Writing Workshop Transparencies 31–32 💿 Interactive Grammar and Language Workbook 📁 Rubrics for Assessing Student Writing, Listening, and Speaking, p. 18

Focus

 Daily Language Practice Transparency 74

Focus Activity Say:
Briefly tell the class about a friendship that has meant a lot to you. You will describe both the friend and experiences you have shared. You will write about this friend as a speech for this Writing Workshop. **AS**

Teach

C Critical Thinking

Analysis Ask: What is the difference between writing an essay about a friendship and writing a speech about the friend? *(Responses will vary but should relate to how a speech uses more dramatic elements than the essay does.)* **AS**

Resources for page 966

📁 Use the Writing Workshop Graphic Organizer BLM in the Unit 8 Resource Booklet, p. 14.

📁 Use the Grammar and Writing Workshop Transparencies 1-2.

WRITING WORKSHOP PART 1

Speech
Prewriting and Drafting

ASSIGNMENT Write a speech and present it in front of an audience

Purpose: To write a speech about a friend and why your friendship is special

Audience: You, your teacher, and classmates

Writing Rubric

As you work through this writing assignment, you should

• describe an important friendship
• gather interesting details
• organize your speech into three main parts: the beginning, the middle, and the end
• include visual aids

See page 1034 in Part 2 for a model of a speech.

Objectives (pp. 966–969)
Writing Use the writing process: prewrite, draft • Write a speech • Use text structure: beginning, middle, end • Write with fluency and clarity • Practice presentation
Grammar Use punctuation correctly: apostrophes

A speech is great way to share what you know and what you believe in. There are three types of speeches. They are explained below:

Speech	Purpose
Informative	Share information and your knowledge about a topic to educate the audience
Persuasive	Persuade the audience to agree with your views and opinions about a topic
Demonstrative	Show the audience how to do something or how something works

Prewriting
Get Ready to Write

Making friends isn't always easy. Keeping those friends takes work, too. In this workshop, you will write an informative speech about an important friend in your life and what makes your friendship work.

Choose a Topic

Think about the friendships you have read about in this unit. In *Novio Boy*, Rudy and Alex share secrets and advice. Who is one friend you talk to when you have a problem? This person will be the topic of your speech.

Gather Ideas

Now that you have chosen a topic, follow the steps below to gather ideas.

1. Freewrite about your friend for five minutes. Write descriptions, experiences, feelings, or memories about that person.

2. Talk to other people who know your friend. What do they have to say? Write their responses in your Learner's Notebook.

3. Choose the main reason why this person is your friend. Write that reason as a phrase or sentence.

Christine is my friend because we both like karate.

Additional Support

English Language Coach

Idioms and Slang English language learners will find it helpful to brainstorm with a partner good ways for describing friends or an incident. Many speeches, just like everyday conversation, can be full of idiomatic phrases. Help students to know that idioms should not be taken literally. For instance, when you see a friend whom you haven't seen for a long time, you might say, "Long time no see." Or you've come in from getting caught in a big rain storm and say, "It's raining cats and dogs." In pairs, have students discuss what the literal meaning of some idiomatic examples are and the real meaning of them. **EL OL**

Drafting
Start Writing!

Literature Online

Writing Models For models and other writing activities, go to www.glencoe.com.

A speech has three main parts: a beginning, middle, and end. Speeches are different from most writing because they are heard by an audience, not read. As you begin to write, remember that your audience will be listening to what you write. To make your speech interesting:

- include descriptions that help the audience picture in their minds what you are saying.
- write in a way that will sound natural when you speak.

Get It on Paper

Use these tips as you write each part of your draft.

Strong Beginning

The introduction of your speech must grab your listeners' attention. Here are some suggestions for a great opening.

- Ask a question: *How many of your friends do you fight with just for fun?*
- Share a surprising story: *Even though Christine is my best friend, we fight nearly every day. Luckily, the fights take place at Kick Start, a martial arts studio in Mayfield.*
- Read a quote: *"Christine is full of promise and strength," says May Lee, one of Christine's karate instructors at Kick Start.*
- Report a fact: *Christine was the first student in the class to pass the examination on her first try.*

Informative Middle

Now that you have your audience's attention, get to the main point of your speech.

- Describe your friend, using interesting descriptions.
- Explain how you keep your friendship strong.
- Use quotes from other people to support your claims about your friend.

Powerful Ending

Your ending should retell the main reason for your speech and bring your speech to a natural sounding close. Here are some suggestions for ending.

- Share a joke or short story about your friendship.
- Use a quote about the importance of friendship.
- Repeat a part of the introduction.

◄ Writing Tip

Beginning Get your audience's attention by asking them to imagine a scenario or incident that relates to your speech.
Imagine it's your first day at a new school . . .
Try to imagine your best friend in a karate tournament.

◄ Writing Tip

Middle Organize the body of your speech by using the cause-and-effect structure. Describe a quality about your friend. Then tell what effect that quality has on your friendship.

◄ Writing Tip

End If your speech topic is complex, allow audience members to ask questions at the end of the speech.

Teach

W Writing

Organization Skills Say: Start organizing your speech by taking that list of ideas you've been preparing and see which ideas jump out at you as the most workable. Imagine actually telling one other person about the situation or friend. Think of the details you would say. Keep that picture in your head of talking through the event so that you can hear your own voice as you write your speech.

Steps to a satisfying presentation:

1. **Follow the tips:** Know what you're doing and where you're going at the beginning, middle, and end of your speech.

2. **Outline the path.** What do you want to say at each of these benchmark points?

3. **Remember that speaking is usually less formal than writing.** So listen for your own voice as you write, and make the writing match how you speak.

4. **Think and write in pictures.** Colorful descriptions of events and characteristics will make your speech on a friend vivid in the minds of your audience.

5. **Keep your audience in mind throughout the speech.** **AS**

Differentiated Instruction

Auditory Learners Encourage auditory learners to use quotations or dialogue from conversations with friends. Remind them that their ear for hearing details in conversations can help them in this project. You might suggest that they begin their speech with something funny or strong that a friend said. They can make it all the richer by mimicking tone or accent to emphasize the meaning or purpose of the friend's words. Auditory learners benefit from opportunities to give answers orally and in their own words. Finally, ask auditory learners to be consultants to other students, giving tips for presenting their written speeches with a flair. **AS**

Objectives
- Write a speech
- Identify literary elements: scene
- Understand idioms and slang
- Use organizational skills

Teach

W Writing

Presentation **Ask:** How is writing a speech different from writing an essay? Could it be more embarrassing? *(Possible responses may include that saying something in front of the class that is poorly organized will be much more embarrassing than turning in a poorly organized written essay.)* **AS**

Applying Good Writing Traits

Analyzing Cartoons
List three details from the cartoon that show how important *presentation* is to the girl—even at lunch.

Heart of the City © 1998 Mark Tatulli. Distributed by Universal Press Syndicate.

W Presentation

The way you present, or share, your speech is just as important as the words you wrote. If your presentation is sloppy, your audience will not be interested in what you have to say.

What Is Presentation?

Presentation is a combination of the spoken message, voice, gesture, and overall appearance.

Why Is Presentation Important?

• A thoughtful presentation makes your speech easy to understand and is more likely to interest your audience.

• The audience will take your speech more seriously if you have a polished presentation.

How Do I Do It?

Each person who presents a speech is different. Most likely, everyone in your class will have a different presentation style. The most important part of presenting a speech is that you be your-self. Your personality makes you special, so let it shine!

1. Do not start your speech until everyone in the audience is focused on you, the speaker. If you don't have the full attention of your audience from the start, your speech will likely be forgotten or ignored.

2. Make sure that all audience members can see you and your visual aids clearly.

3. Stand up straight and tall. Good posture tells your audience that you are comfortable and confident.

4. Speak loudly enough to be heard in the back of the room. If audience members can't hear you, they will lose interest in your speech.

5. Relax! Audiences respond better to a speaker who is relaxed and conversational, not one who is stiff and formal.

Write to Learn Enhance your presentation by adding graphics. Find photos, maps, or illustrations that relate to your speech. Use a projector or computer, or make multiple copies to display the graphic.

Additional Support

Reading Fluency

Reading and Writing Encourage students to work with a partner to say aloud the general sequence of events that they want to relate. Then they can hone the words and phrases to make it an interesting and engaging speech. Partners should listen for how clearly one another express his or her ideas. Help students to critique each other's details for interest, humor, or depth. Make a short checklist of these points for partners to use in their critiques. **EL BL OL**

Grammar Link

Apostrophes

Apostrophes are small marks of punctuation (') that have several different uses. This Grammar Link will show when to use apostrophes.

What Are Apostrophes?

Apostrophes are used to show possession and to form contractions.

Why Are Apostrophes Important?

An apostrophe is a big tool in a little package. This small mark of punctuation (') can combine words and replace letters.

How Do I Use Apostrophes?

1. Use an apostrophe to show that letters have been left out of a word or phrase. This is called a contraction.
- **can't** (the *n* and *o* of *cannot* is replaced by an apostrophe)
- *We're* (an apostrophe replaces the *a* of the phrase *we are*)
2. Use an apostrophe followed by the letter *s* to form the possessive of a singular noun.
- Chad**'s** bike is green with black stripes.
- The band**'s** song hit the top of the charts.
3. To show the possessive form of a plural noun, just add an apostrophe after the *s*.
- My parents**'** car is blue.
- The two schools**'** principals discussed the game.

Watch Out!

Not all plural nouns end in *s* (*women, children, mice*). Use an apostrophe and an *s* to form the possessive of a plural noun that does not end in *s*.
- *women's, children's, mice's*

Grammar Practice

Try rewriting each sentence below to include an apostrophe.

1. She is going to Florida for vacation.
2. These chips do not taste good.
3. It is going to rain.

Each sentence below has a misplaced apostrophe. Rewrite the sentence putting the apostrophe in the right place.

1. Leroys' kick is strong.
2. All of my sibling's eyes are green.
3. The cars' engine is hot.

Looking Ahead

Keep all of the writing you've done so far. You will finish your speech in Writing Workshop Part 2.

Grammar Practice

1. She's going to Florida for vacation.
2. These chips don't taste good.
3. It's going to rain.

1. Leroy's kick is strong.
2. All of my siblings' eyes are green.
3. The car's engine is hot.

Grammar Link

Write the following sentences on the board. In their Learner's Notebooks, have students change each phrase to show possession in a shorter way or change the sentences by using a contraction. **AS**

1. the frog that the child has; the ____ frog (*child's*)
2. the hat of my mother; my ____ hat (*mother's*)
3. the question of Nancy; ____ question (*Nancy's*)
4. She did not sleep. She ____ sleep. (*didn't*)
5. We were not allowed inside. We ____ allowed inside. (*weren't*)

Assess

Have students read aloud the first drafts of their speeches to a partner. Ask partners to critique each other's writing and oral reading. After a few minutes, have students assess their own speeches, make revisions, and save their revised speeches for later use.

Objectives
- Use punctuation: apostrophes
- Practice and use effective speaking techniques

969

Clarifying

Objectives covered in this workshop:
• Connect and clarify main ideas and concepts
• Clarify meaning by questioning and rereading
• Predict what will happen in the selection

How to Help Students Clarify

Why Is It Important?

• Clarifying helps students clear up difficult portions of text.
• Students often need to clarify one idea before they can grasp another idea in a selection.
• When students gain clarifying skills, they become better readers and have more confidence in reading new passages.

How to Help Students Get It

• Tell students to reread sections that are not clear.
• Advise them to stop to clarify ideas before they get too far into a confusing text.
• Encourage students to use dictionaries to look up unfamiliar words and to enter the definitions in their Learner's Notebooks so they can review them.
• Emphasize the importance of context clues. What else is being said in the paragraph? Can this information help clarify the confusing part?
• Encourage students to practice several of the other reading strategies they have learned to clarify information. Questioning, responding, connecting, and activating prior knowledge can be particularly helpful when clarifying.

Reading to Answer the Big Question

Damon and Pythias by Fan Kissen
In this ancient Greek tale, Pythias speaks out against a cruel king and is sentenced to death. His friend Damon offers to take his place in prison so that Pythias can visit his mother and sister before his execution. When Damon returns in time to save Pythias, the king is so impressed with the loyalty shown by the friends that he frees them both.

Charlie Johnson by Joe Smith
Old Charlie Johnson befriends young Ben Evans after he tries to steal a Christmas tree from Charlie's field. Charlie's son Dave refuses to accept Ben until after Charlie dies, when Ben's actions finally convince him that Charlie's faith in Ben was justified.

Workshop Resources

PACING (DAYS) STANDARD	BLOCK	LESSON	STUDENT MATERIALS	TEACHER RESOURCES
1	1/2	Key Skill Lesson: Clarifying	🔸 Key Reading Skills Practice, p. 16 🔸 English Language Coach Review, p. 42	🔸 Bellringer Options Transparencies –Daily Language Practice 75 –Selection Focus 24 🔸 Read Aloud, Think Aloud Transparencies –Key Reading Skills 2 ⬤ Presentation Plus!
1	1	"Damon and Pythias"	💻 Glencoe Online 🔸 Unit Vocabulary Review, p. 40 🔸 Academic Vocabulary Review, p. 43 📁 English Language Coach 🔸 Active Reading Graphic Organizer, p. 18 🔸 Literary Analysis, p. 17 ⬤ StudentWorks Plus™ 💻 Online Student Edition ⬤ Literature Classics 📁 Selection and Unit Assessments, p. 87	🔸 Literary and Text Analysis Transparencies 6 💻 Puzzlemaker ⬤ Skill Level Up!™ A Language Arts Game 💻 BookLink 3 ▪ Assessment by Learning Objective (Diagnostic and Formative) ⬤ Interactive Tutor: Self-Assessment ⬤ TeacherWorks Plus™
1		"Charlie Johnson"	💻 Glencoe Online 🔸 Unit Vocabulary Review, p. 40 🔸 Academic Vocabulary Review, p. 43 📁 English Language Coach 🔸 Active Reading Graphic Organizer, p. 20 🔸 Literary Analysis, p. 17 ⬤ StudentWorks Plus™ 💻 Online Student Edition ⬤ Literature Classics 📁 Selection and Unit Assessments, p. 88	🔸 Literary and Text Analysis Transparencies 6 💻 Puzzlemaker ⬤ Skill Level Up!™ A Language Arts Game 💻 BookLink 3 ▪ Assessment by Learning Objective (Diagnostic and Formative) ⬤ Interactive Tutor: Self-Assessment ⬤ TeacherWorks Plus™

Keys for Unit Resource

📁 Blackline Master   🔒 DVD

▪ Workbook   🔸 Transparency

📖 Supplemental Text   💻 Web-based

⬤ CD-ROM   🔸 Fast File

Level Appropriate Code

AS = Activities for all students

AL = Activities for students working above grade level

OL = Activities for students working at grade level

BL = Activities for students working below grade level

EL = Activities for English language learners

Focus

BELLRINGER Options

- **Selection Focus Transparency 24**
- **Daily Language Practice Transparency 75**
Focus Activity Say: Think of a time a friend was in a difficult situation. Did you try to help him or her? How far would you be willing to go to help a friend? *(Responses will vary.)* **AS**

Teach

Analyzing the Cartoon

Say: The cat replies that he can't clarify what caused him to complain. Based on this, what do you predict might cause him to complain in the future? *(Possible response: The cat will most likely complain without any particular reason to complain.)* **OL** **AL**

V Vocabulary

Academic Vocabulary Say: Look at the definition for *clarify* at the bottom of page 970. What are some synonyms for *clarify*? *(Possible responses: explain, simplify, shed light on)* **OL**

Skills Focus

You will practice these skills when you read the following selections:
- "Damon and Pythias," p. 974
- "Charlie Johnson," p. 988

Reading
- Clarifying

Literature
- Understanding characterization

Vocabulary
- Understanding idioms
- Academic Vocabulary: *clarify*

Writing/Grammar
- Using semicolons to separate independent clauses
- Using semicolons with conjunctive adverbs

Objectives (pp. 970–971)
Reading Clarify ideas and text

Skill Lesson

Clarifying

Learn It!

What Is It? **Clarifying** is one way to understand the hardest parts of a text. When you pause in your reading to really think about and clear up a confusing section, you are clarifying. To **clarify**, stop reading to make sure you understand what you've read. Read slowly, reread, and ask questions. Good readers clarify information as they read.

Analyzing Cartoons
The characters in the cartoon ask a question to *clarify* the cat's complaint. What is the question they ask? What is the cat's answer?

Mutts © 2005 Patrick McDonnell. Distributed by King Features.

V **Academic Vocabulary**

clarify (KLAR uh fy) *v.* to make clear

Additional Support

Reading Fluency

Analyzing Cartoons Patrick McDonnell, author/cartoonist of the *Mutts* comic strip, was born in New Jersey and graduated from the School of Fine Arts in New York City in 1978. His famous *Mutts* cartoon strip began in 1994 and features the friendship between the dog Earl and the cat Mooch.

In many cartoons, cats and dogs are portrayed as enemies. Gather additional copies of McDonnell's cartoon strips for students to read. Ask students to describe the relationship between Earl and Mooch as it is portrayed in *Mutts* and to tell what makes them such good friends. **AS**

Why Is It Important? In a text, the information you *have read* is as important as the information you *will read.* Authors often build ideas one on another. It's important to clear up confusing passages as you go so you will understand main ideas and the information that comes later.

How Do I Do It? If something you are reading becomes unclear, slow down. Go back and read that section again. Look up words you don't know, and read any footnotes. Ask questions about what you don't understand. Sometimes you may want to read on to see if further information helps. Start with these questions as you clarify:

• Do characters in the play or story make their thoughts and ideas clear?
• Do examples and descriptions make sense?
• Do I understand the main points the author is trying to make?

Here's how a student clarified some lines from "The Reluctant Dragon."

St. George: Exactly. A good dragon—a worthy foe of my steel (*He lifts his sword high*), and no feeble specimen of his noxious tribe.

> That was so confusing I slowed down and read it twice. I understood that his *steel* was his sword, but at first I forgot to look at the footnote. When I did, I understood most of it, but I need to look up the word *foe.*

Literature Online

Study Central Visit www.glencoe.com and click on Study Central to review clarifying.

Practice It!

With a partner, practice clarifying this poem by Horace Dragon.

Atchoo! Atchoo! The ragweed is in bloom,
Sowing far and wide allergic gloom.
How lavishly it pollinates the breeze,
And, oh! how lavishly it makes me sneeze! Atchoo!

Use It!

Copy this list of questions in your Learner's Notebook. As you read, write answers to the questions to help you clarify.
• Are thoughts and ideas clear?
• Do examples and descriptions make sense?
• Can I state the main points in my own words?

Teach

Literature Online

Study Central Have students access the Web site to review clarifying and to complete a related activity.

R Reading Skill

Clarifying Ask: In the quotation from "The Reluctant Dragon," what words clarify the word "steel"? (*"He lifts his sword high"*) **Ask:** How would you clarify other words in the text you may not understand? (*Possible response: look them up on the Internet or in references such as a dictionary or thesaurus*) **AS**

Resources for page 971

Use Key Reading Skills Transparency 2 in *Read Aloud, Think Aloud* to help students practice Clarifying.

Differentiated Instruction

Cartoon Illustration Some students may benefit from creating illustrations. Have students use the poem by Horace Dragon to create a cartoon in which each cartoon frame illustrates a corresponding line of the poem. Have students continue drawing the cartoon strip until all the lines of the poem are illustrated. Then ask volunteers to share their cartoons with class members. Discuss how illustration can help clarify text. **AS**

Objectives
• Clarify ideas and text
• Analyze text features: cartoons
• Learn and use new vocabulary

Teach

More About the Author

Author Fan (or Fanny) Kissen taught elementary school in New York City. Soon she transferred her love of folktales to writing radio scripts, or plays including instructions for music and sound effects. Her radio series, *Tales from the Four Winds,* was broadcast for 17 years. She traveled widely in Europe, the Near East, and South America. She spoke French, German, and "tourist" Italian.

R Reading Skill

Clarifying Ask: Why is it important to clarify idiomatic phrases? *(Possible response: In idiomatic phrases, common words are used to mean something else, so clarifying them helps readers understand exactly what's being said.)* **AS**

Before You Read · Damon and Pythias

Meet the Author

Fan Kissen was born in 1893 and died in 1978. Kissen spent most of her writing career turning folktales and legends into plays for young people. The plays were first performed on radio on Kissen's series, *Tales from the Four Winds.* Before writing radio plays, Kissen taught elementary school in New York City.

Author Search For more about Fan Kissen, go to www.glencoe.com.

Objectives (pp. 972–983)
Reading Clarify ideas and text • Make connections from text to self
Literature Understand literary elements: characterization
Vocabulary Identify and understand idioms

Vocabulary Preview

proclaimed (pruh KLAYMD) *v.* declared publicly, announced; form of the verb *proclaim* **(p. 975)** *The king proclaimed that no one could speak against him.*

champion (CHAM pyun) *n.* one who fights for or speaks for another person; one who defends a cause; hero **(p. 976)** *The poor citizens needed a champion to stand up for them.*

Write to Learn Below each vocabulary word in dark type, there are four words. Three of them are synonyms. One is not. Which one is not?

proclaimed

told   asked   stated   declared

champion

assistant   defender   hero   protector

English Language Coach

Idiom An **idiom** (ID ee um) is an expression that has a different idea than the literal (actual and ordinary) meaning of the words. Different languages and regions sometimes have their own idioms. Some idioms can be found in a dictionary, but many cannot. Luckily, you can figure out the meanings of many of them. Look at these examples:

Idiom	Meaning
Zip your lip	Be quiet
Turn a blind eye	Ignore it
Call it a day	Quit working for the day
Spitting image	Exact likeness

Partner Talk Copy the graphic organizer below into your Learner's Notebook. Read each idiom and talk with a partner about what it means. If it's unfamiliar, try to figure it out. Write the meaning in the right column of the graphic organizer.

Idiom	Meaning
Keep an eye on your little brother.	
Let's *step on it* so we're not late.	
It's late; I need to *hit the sack.*	
I would never *bad-mouth* a friend.	

Additional Support

Author Search To expand students' appreciation of Fan Kissen, have them access the Web site for additional information and resources.

Literature Focus Lesson

Script Explain to students that a script is the written form of a play. It includes exactly what the characters say and gives suggestions for presenting the story. In a script, the cast, or set of characters, is listed and an actor is assigned to play each cast member. Using the well-known nursery rhyme, *Jack and Jill,* have students work in pairs to write a short script for this poem. They should use Jack and Jill as characters who are telling about their experience in climbing the hill. Ask volunteers to present their scripts to the class. **OL**

Skills Preview

Key Reading Skill: Clarifying

If you read something that doesn't make sense, take a minute and clarify. To clarify hard sections in "Damon and Pythias," look for footnotes; make sure you understand the words. Slow down and read the confusing sections again. Ask these questions:

- Are the characters' thoughts and ideas clear?
- Do examples and descriptions make sense?
- Do I understand the main points the author is trying to make, and can I state them in my own words?

If you are unsure about the answers, clarify.

Write to Learn Before you read, look over the passage and list words you aren't sure you know. Try to write definitions for the words on your list. (Hint: Do you recognize parts of these words? Are any words similar to ones you know?) After you read, use a dictionary to check your definitions.

Key Literary Element: Characterization

Characterization is the way an author presents details that give you clues to a character's personality. Writers develop a character

- by describing what the character looks like
- by revealing the character's thoughts, feelings, words, and actions
- by revealing what other characters think or say about the character and how they behave toward him or her
- by stating directly what a character is like

Write to Learn Write a few lines presenting details about a character. Your character can be from real life, a TV show, a movie, or from something you've read.

Interactive Literary Elements Handbook
To review or learn more about the literary elements, go to www.glencoe.com.

Get Ready to Read

Connect to the Reading

In these scenes you'll read about two friends, Damon and Pythias, who are legendary for their loyalty to each other. As you read the story, think about your friends and what you would have done in Damon's place.

Partner Talk With a partner, talk about a time when a friend stood up for you or you showed loyalty to one of your friends. Discuss what happened and how it affected the friendship.

Build Background

Two thousand years ago, a Roman statesman and author named Cicero wrote about the ancient Greek story of Damon and Pythias.

- According to Cicero, Damon and Pythias lived in the fourth century B.C.
- Cicero identified the tyrant in this story as Dionysius, King of Syracuse.
- There are many versions of the Damon and Pythias story.
- The play you are about to read was first published in 1964.
- This play is a radio play. That means it was not written to be *seen*; it was written to be *heard*. Keep that in mind as you read.

Set Purposes for Reading

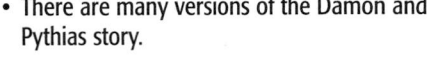 Read "Damon and Pythias" and think about what makes a friend.

Set Your Own Purpose What else would you like to learn from the selection to help you answer the Big Question? Write your purpose on the "Damon and Pythias" page of Foldable 8.

Keep Moving

Use these skills as you read the following selection.

Damon and Pythias **973**

Teach

L Literary Element

Characterization Ask:
How does the writer characterize Dionysius, King of Syracuse, in the Build Background section? *(Dionysius is described as a tyrant.)* **Ask:** What does the word *tyrant* mean? Use reference resources if necessary. *(Possible response: a harsh, cruel ruler)* **AS**

Interactive Literary Elements Handbook Have students access the Web site to improve their understanding of characterization.

Reading in the Real World

Citizenship There are many forms of government. A number of countries still have monarchies ruled by a king or queen like the country in this story. The United States has a representative democracy. Ask English language learners about the types of governments in their families' homelands. Do they know anyone who left because of problems with the government? What do they think is the best form of government and why? **EL** Have interested students do additional research on the systems of government in ancient Greece. **AL**

Objectives
- Interpret and analyze character
- Clarify ideas and text
- Analyze features of genres: drama

Teach

Ask: What do you think is the basis for true friendship? *(Responses will vary.)* **AS**

Viewing the Photo

Ask: Why is this image of ancient ruins appropriate for the setting of this play? *(Possible response: The play takes place a long time ago. It is an appropriate representation of the play's setting.)* **AS**

Damon AND Pythias

by Fan Kissen

Cast
DAMON
FIRST ROBBER
FIRST VOICE
PYTHIAS
SECOND ROBBER
SECOND VOICE
KING
MOTHER
THIRD VOICE
SOLDIER
NARRATOR

[*Sound: Iron door opens and shuts. Key in lock.*]
[*Music: Up full and out.*]

BQ

NARRATOR. Long, long ago there lived on the island of Sicily two young men named Damon and Pythias. They were known far and wide for the strong friendship each had for the other. Their names have come down to our own times to mean true friendship. You may hear it said of two persons:

FIRST VOICE. Those two? Why, they're like Damon and Pythias!

NARRATOR. The king of that country was a cruel tyrant. He made cruel laws, and he showed no

Additional Support

Literature Focus Lesson

Drama Literature is classified into groups that have common features. The story of Damon and Pythias belongs to a classification of literature called drama. Have students work in small groups using graphic organizers to answer this question: What features make drama different from fiction or poetry? Have students list features under each genre.

mercy toward anyone who broke his laws. Now, you might very well wonder:

SECOND VOICE. Why didn't the people rebel? **1**

NARRATOR. Well, the people didn't dare rebel because they feared the king's great and powerful army. No one dared say a word against the king or his laws—except Damon and Pythias speaking against a new law the king had **proclaimed**.

SOLDIER. Ho, there! Who are you that dares to speak so about our king?

PYTHIAS. [*Unafraid.*] I am called Pythias.

Vocabulary

proclaimed (pruh KLAYMD) *v.* declared publicly, announced

Practice the Skills

1 **Key Reading Skill**

Clarifying Remember, this is a radio play. Many of the "stage directions" are sounds. Imagine hearing the sound of an iron door locking. What do you imagine when you hear that? Now, think about the Voices. Why do you think they are named that?

This ancient Greek-Roman theater is on the island of Sicily—the same island where "Damon and Pythias" takes place.

Damon and Pythias **975**

Teach

L Literary Element

Characterization Ask:
What do you learn about Damon and Pythias? *(Possible responses: They care about the people and are brave enough to express their feelings.)* **AS**

R Reading Skill

Review Visualizing Ask:
What expression do you think you would see on the soldier's face as he questions Pythias? *(Possible response: anger, rage, annoyance)* **AS**

Differential Instruction

Build Background The play is set in Syracuse, a city on the island of Sicily. In the fourth century B.C., Syracuse was a powerful city in the ancient world and was ruled by King Dionysius. Have students research King Dionysius, his gov- ernment, and the time in which he lived. Then have the students research the government in Sicily today and the city of Syracuse today. Have students create displays comparing the Syracuse during these two different time periods. **AL**

Objectives
• Visualize
• Use text features: photographs
• Interpret and analyze character
• Analyze features of genres: drama

Teach

R Reading Skill

Clarifying Say: Pythias tells the king that "the people are suffering . . . [t]hey want to have a voice . . ." What does he mean? *(They want to be heard.)* **Ask:** What sentence explains or restates the term "voice"? *("You do not allow them to speak up for themselves.")* **OL**

L Literary Element

Characterization Ask: What does Pythias's behavior as he confronts the king show about his character? *(Possible response: It shows that he is brave enough to speak up and risk angering the king and being imprisoned.)* **Ask:** What does the king's response to Pythias show about him? *(Possible response: that he really is a cruel and intolerant tyrant)* **OL**

SOLDIER. Don't you know it is a crime to speak against the king or his laws? You are under arrest! Come and tell this opinion of yours to the king's face!

[*Music: A few short bars in and out.*]

NARRATOR. When Pythias was brought before the king, he showed no fear. He stood straight and quiet before the throne.

KING. [*Hard, cruel.*] So, Pythias! They tell me you do not approve of the laws I make.

PYTHIAS. I am not alone, your Majesty, in thinking your laws are cruel. But you rule the people with such an iron hand that they dare not complain. **2**

KING. [*Angry.*] But you have the daring to complain for them! Have they appointed you their **champion**?

PYTHIAS. No, your Majesty. I speak for myself alone. I have no wish to make trouble for anyone. But I am not afraid to tell you that the people are suffering under your rule. They want to have a voice in making the laws for themselves. You do not allow them to speak up for themselves.

KING. In other words, you are calling me a tyrant! Well, you shall learn for yourself how a tyrant treats a rebel! Soldier! Throw this man into prison!

Street Musicians, before a.d. 79. Dioscurides of Samos. Mosaic from the Villa of Cicero, Pompeii. Musea Archeologico Nazionale, Naples, Italy.

Analyzing the Art List some ways that these street musicians are different from street musicians today.

Practice the Skills

2 English Language Coach

Idiom Pythias tells the king that he rules with "an iron hand." What does Pythias mean? What are some characteristics of iron? How are those characteristics like the way the king rules?

Vocabulary

champion (CHAM pyun) *n.* one who fights for or speaks for another person; one who defends a cause; hero

Additional Support

Reading Fluency

Reading Scripts Help English language learners grasp the differences between the dialogue and the stage directions. Make three copies of the script on this page. Assign four volunteers to these parts: Pythias, solider, narrator, and King. Have each participant highlight his or her part. Remind each student to read aloud only his or her part, or highlighted words, to the class. Then add a director to coach the reader on the characters' facial expressions and on the background directions on this page. Have students rehearse this scene and present it to the class. **EL BL OL**

SOLDIER. At once, your Majesty! Don't try to resist, Pythias!

PYTHIAS. I know better than to try to resist a soldier of the king! and for how long am I to remain in prison, your Majesty, merely for speaking out for the people?

KING. [*Cruel.*] Not for very long, Pythias. Two weeks from today at noon, you shall be put to death in the public square as an example to anyone else who may dare to question my laws or acts. Off to prison with him, soldier! **3**

[*Music: In briefly and out.*] **4**

NARRATOR. When Damon heard that his friend Pythias had been thrown into prison, and about the severe punishment that was to follow, he was heartbroken. He rushed to the prison and persuaded the guard to let him speak to his friend.

DAMON. Oh, Pythias! How terrible to find you here! I wish I could do something to save you!

PYTHIAS. Nothing can save me, Damon, my dear friend. I am prepared to die. But there is one thought that troubles me greatly.

DAMON. What is it? I will do anything to help you.

PYTHIAS. I'm worried about what will happen to my mother and my sister when I'm gone.

DAMON. I'll take care of them, Pythias, as if they were my own mother and sister.

PYTHIAS. Thank you, Damon. I have money to leave them. But there are other things I must arrange. If only I could go see them before I die! But they live two days' journey from here, you know.

DAMON. I'll go to the king and beg him to give you your freedom for a few days. You'll give your word to return at the end of that time. Everyone in Sicily knows you for a man who has never broken his word.

Practice the Skills

3 Key Literary Element

Characterization What can you tell about Pythias from his behavior when he challenges the king?

4 Key Reading Skill

Clarifying Plays are usually divided into acts and scenes, which often are signaled by a stage curtain opening and closing. A radio play does not have the same cues. What signals a change of setting here?

Damon and Pythias **977**

Teach

EL Language Coach

Idioms Say: The narrator states that Damon was heartbroken. What does this mean? (*Possible response: deeply saddened*) **OL**

L Literary Element

Characterization Ask: What can you tell about Damon from his reaction to hearing that Pythias is in prison? (*Possible response: He is upset and promises Pythias that he will take care of his relatives – he even offers to take his place in prison. He, too, is very caring.*) **AS**

Reading in the Real World

Citizenship In the fourth century B.C., no one in Syracuse could risk speaking up to defend someone like Pythias. Today a ruler might release someone like Pythias because of world protest. Have students write a speech in support of Pythias. Remind students that their goal is to make the king take action by stirring up public opinion. Post these guidelines for speaking persuasively:
- State your subject and your position on it.
- Give reasons for your position.
- Use words that appeal to listeners' emotions.

Ask volunteers to share their speeches with the class. **OL**

Objectives
- Clarify ideas and text
- Interpret and analyze character
- Understand idioms

Teach

C1 Critical Thinking

Evaluation Ask: Is the dialogue between Damon and Pythias written the way people might actually speak? *(Responses will vary, but may include that most of the dialogue sounds formal and that modern American English speakers would probably not talk to each other this way.)* **OL**

C2 Critical Thinking

Comprehension Ask: In your own words, tell what has happened to Pythias and Damon by the end of the third scene. *(Possible response: Pythias has argued with the king and has been imprisoned, but Damon has persuaded the king to let him take Pythias's place in prison until Pythias returns from his mother's.)* **AS**

R Reading Skill

Review Predicting Ask: Do you think the king will show mercy if Pythias fails? Why or why not? *(Possible response: No, because the king is a tyrant.)* **AS**

PYTHIAS. Do you believe for one moment that the king would let me leave this prison, no matter how good my word may have been all my life?

DAMON. I'll tell him that I shall take your place in the prison cell. I'll tell him that if you do not return by the appointed day, he may kill *me* in your place!

PYTHIAS. No, no, Damon! You must not do such a foolish thing! I cannot—I will not—let you do this! Damon! Damon! Don't go! [*To himself.*] Damon, my friend! You may find yourself in a cell beside me! **5**

[*Music: In briefly and out.*]

DAMON. [*Begging.*] Your Majesty! I beg of you! Let Pythias go home for a few days to bid farewell to his mother and sister. He gives his word that he will return at your appointed time. Everyone knows that his word can be trusted.

KING. In ordinary business affairs—perhaps. But he is now a man under sentence of death. To free him even for a few days would strain his honesty—*any* man's honesty—too far. Pythias would never return here! I consider him a traitor, but I'm certain he's no fool.

DAMON. Your Majesty! I will take his place in the prison until he comes back. If he does not return, then you may take *my* life in his place.

KING. [*Astonished.*] What did you say, Damon?

DAMON. I'm so certain of Pythias that I am offering to die in his place if he fails to return on time.

KING. I can't believe you mean it!

DAMON. I do mean it, your Majesty.

KING. You make me very curious, Damon, so curious that I'm willing to put you and Pythias to the test. This exchange of prisoners will be made. But Pythias must be back two weeks from today, at noon.

DAMON. Thank you, your Majesty!

Practice the Skills

Additional Support

Differentiated Instruction

Using a Graphic Organizer Sometimes it is helpful to visualize what happens from scene to scene. Cartoonists help readers do this by illustrating one scene per frame. Have students create a visual or graphic organizer of the events that have occurred in the first three scenes, using these prompts.

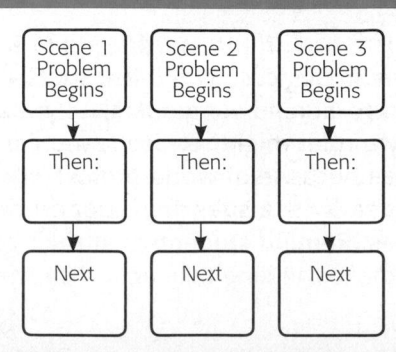

KING. The order with my official seal shall go by your own hand,[1] Damon. But I warn you, if your friend does not return on time, you shall surely die in his place! I shall show no mercy.

[*Music: In briefly and out.*]

NARRATOR. Pythias did not like the king's bargain with Damon. He did not like to leave his friend in prison with the chance that he might lose his life if something went wrong. But at last Damon persuaded him to leave and Pythias set out for his home. More than a week went by. The day set for the death sentence drew near. Pythias did not return. Everyone in the city knew of the condition on which the king had permitted Pythias to go home. Everywhere people met, the talk was sure to turn to the two friends.

FIRST VOICE. Do you suppose Pythias will come back?

SECOND VOICE. Why should he stick his head under the king's ax once he has escaped?

THIRD VOICE. Still would an honorable man like Pythias let such a good friend die for him?

FIRST VOICE. There's no telling what a man will do when it's a question of his own life against another's.

SECOND VOICE. But if Pythias doesn't come back before the time is up, he will be killing his friend.

Practice the Skills

6 English Language Coach

Idiom Do you know what the idiom "there's no telling" means? Can you figure it out from the context?

Tragic and Comic Masks (detail). before A.D. 79. Mosaics from the House of the Faun, Pompeii. Museo Archeologico Nazionale, Naples, Italy.

---

1. In asking Damon to carry the order in his **own hand,** the king means that Damon should carry the order himself.

Damon and Pythias **979**

Reading Fluency

Reading Aloud One way to clarify scenes in a play is to have students read the parts aloud. In this scene, the narrator speaks and then a dialogue takes place between the three voices. Make a copy of this page for the following: narrator, first voice, second voice, and third voice. Have the narrator stand to one side while the three voices stand near one another. Ask the audience to describe the difference between the role of the narrator and the roles of the voices. **AS**

Teach

C Critical Thinking

Analysis Ask: What is the purpose of the narrator in this play? *(Possible response: The narrator lets the reader know what every character thinks and does, and at times provides background information.)* **OL**

L Literary Element

Characterization Ask: How would you characterize the voices in this scene? *(Possible response: They are not actually individual characters. They seem to instead represent three views regarding Pythias's return: faith, lack of faith, and confusion.)* **AL**

Viewing the Art

Ask: What is the expression on the mask pictured here? Why is this an appropriate image to place on this page? *(Possible response: The mask looks sad and scared, which is how Damon, or even the townspeople, might be feeling.)* **OL**

Objectives
• Interpret and analyze character
• Identify literary elements: dialogue
• Analyze text
• Monitor comprehension
• Make predictions
• Find meaning in art

Teach

Ask: Do you agree with the Second Voice's statement that an individual's own life is more important than friendship? Why or why not? *(Responses will vary.)* **AS**

R Reading Skill

Review Visualizing Ask: How do the stage directions given here help you visualize the scene? *(Possible response: You can see the iron door and feel the loneliness and confinement of the prison when the door locks.)* **AS**

THIRD VOICE. Well, there's still a few days' time. I, for one, am certain that Pythias *will* return in time.

SECOND VOICE. And *I am* just as certain that he will *not.* Friendship is friendship, but a man's own life is something stronger, *I* say! **7**

NARRATOR. Two days before the time was up, the king himself visited Damon in his prison cell.

[*Sound: Iron door unlocked and opened.*]

KING. [*Mocking.*] You see now, Damon, that you were a fool to make this bargain. Your friend has tricked you! He will not come back here to be killed! He has deserted you.

R DAMON. [*Calm and firm.*] I have faith in my friend. I know he will return.

KING. [*Mocking.*] We shall see! **8**

[*Sound: Iron door shut and locked.*]

NARRATOR. Meanwhile, when Pythias reached the home of his family, he arranged his business affairs so that his mother and sister would be able to live comfortably for the rest of their years. Then he said a last farewell to them before starting back to the city.

MOTHER. [*In tears.*] Pythias, it will take you two days to get back. Stay another day, I beg you!

PYTHIAS. I dare not stay longer, Mother. Remember, Damon is locked up in my prison cell while I'm gone. Please don't weep for me. My death may help bring better days for all our people. **9**

NARRATOR. So Pythias began his journey in plenty of time. But bad luck struck him on the very first day. At twilight, as he walked along a lonely stretch of woodland, a rough voice called:

FIRST ROBBER. Not so fast there, young man! Stop!

PYTHIAS. [*Startled.*] Oh! What is it? What do you want?

980 UNIT 8 What Makes a Friend?

Practice the Skills

7 **BIG Question**
How do the Voices help you think about friendship? Write your answer on the "Damon and Pythias" page of Foldable 8.

8 **Key Literary Element**
Characterization What kind of person is the king? In what ways has the author let you know what he is like?

9 **Key Literary Element**
Characterization Review what Pythias has just said. Based on his words, what kind of person is he? Do you think he really means what he says? Explain.

Additional Support

English Language Coach

Multiple-Meaning Words Many words have more than one meaning and readers have to decide which meaning is correct based on how it is used in a sentence. One way to determine a word's meaning is to replace it with another word. Have students practice this in the following sentences. Ask them to replace each of the underlined words with another word.

1. Damon is locked up in my prison <u>cell</u>.
2. He walked along a lonely <u>stretch</u> of woodland.

Discuss with students the choices they made and the similarities between their choices and the underlined words. **EL OL**

SECOND ROBBER. Your money bags.

PYTHIAS. My money bags? I have only this small bag of coins. I shall need them for some favors, perhaps, before I die.

FIRST ROBBER. What do you mean, before you die? We don't mean to kill you, only take your money.

PYTHIAS. I'll give you my money, only don't delay me any longer. I am to die by the king's order three days from now. If I don't return on time, my friend must die in my place.

FIRST ROBBER. A likely story! What man would be fool enough to go back to prison ready to die?

SECOND ROBBER. And what man would be fool enough to die *for* you?

FIRST ROBBER. We'll take your money, all right. And we'll tie you up while we get away.

PYTHIAS. [*Begging.*] No! No! I must get back to free my friend! [*Fade.*] I must go back!

NARRATOR. But the two robbers took Pythias's money, tied him to a tree, and went off as fast as they could. Pythias struggled to free himself. He cried out for a long time. But no one traveled through that lonesome woodland after dark. The sun had been up for many hours before he finally managed to free himself from the ropes that had tied him to the tree. He lay on the ground, hardly able to breathe. **10**

[*Music: In briefly and out.*]

NARRATOR. After a while Pythias got to his feet. Weak and dizzy from hunger and thirst and his struggle to free himself, he set off again. Day and night he traveled without stopping, desperately trying to reach the city in time to save Damon's life.

[*Music: Up and out.*]

NARRATOR. On the last day, half an hour before noon, Damon's hands were tied behind his back, and he was taken into the public square. The people muttered angrily as

---

Practice the Skills

10 Key Literary Element

Characterization Think about the conversation between the robbers. What can you learn about them from their discussion?

Damon and Pythias **981**

Teach

L1 Literary Element

Characterization Ask: What do the robbers think about Pythias and his promise to return to prison? *(They think he's lying.)* **AS Ask:** How are they similar to or different from the "voices" in the previous scene? *(Possible response: Like some of the voices, they doubt Pythias will return.)* **OL**

L2 Literary Element

Characterization Ask: What do you learn about Pythias's character from his behavior in this scene? *(Possible responses: He is so determined to return to his friend that he travels day and night without stopping even though he is weak and dizzy from hunger and thirst.)* **OL**

Reading in the Real World

Career People who make their living by making sound effects are called Foley artists. When a play calls for a certain sound, Foley artists recreate the sound. Discuss ways in which Foley artists might create sounds, such as crinkling cellophane to create the sound of flames.

Divide the class into groups. Have each group choose a scene from the play and create two or more sound effects to present to the other groups. Have the other groups try to guess which scene the sound effects represent. **OL**

Objectives
• Interpret and analyze character
• Visualize
• Use context clues: multiple-meaning words

Teach

R Reading Skill

Clarifying Ask: How does the image of the Visual Vocabulary word help you clarify the meaning of *noon mark*? *(Responses will vary.)* **AS**

L Literary Element

Characterization Ask: What words in the dialogue tell you about Damon's feelings about his friendship for Pythias? *("I would have died for you gladly, my friend.")* **AS**

Damon was led in by the jailer. Then the king entered and seated himself on a high platform.

[*Sound: Crowd voices in and hold under single voices.*] **11**

SOLDIER. [*Loud.*] Long live the king!

FIRST VOICE. [*Low.*] The longer he lives, the more miserable our lives will be!

Visual Vocabulary
R The **noon mark** appears on a sundial, a device that indicates the time of day by the position and length of a shadow cast on a surface marked with numerals.

KING. [*Loud, mocking.*] Well, Damon, your lifetime is nearly up. Where is your good friend Pythias now?

DAMON. [*Firm.*] I have faith in my friend. If he has not returned, I'm certain it is through no fault of his own.

KING. [*Mocking.*] The sun is almost overhead. The shadow is almost at the noon mark. And still your friend has not returned to give back your life!

DAMON. [*Quiet.*] I am ready and happy to die in his place.

KING. [*Harsh.*] And you shall, Damon! Jailer, lead the prisoner to the—

[*Sound: Crowd voices up to a roar, then under.*]

FIRST VOICE. [*Over noise.*] Look! It's Pythias!

SECOND VOICE. [*Over noise.*] Pythias has come back!

PYTHIAS. [*Breathless.*] Let me through! Damon!

DAMON. Pythias!

PYTHIAS. Thank the gods I'm not too late!

L DAMON. [*Quiet, sincere.*] I would have died for you gladly, my friend.

CROWD VOICES. [*Loud, demanding.*] Set them free! Set them both free!

11 Key Reading Skill

Clarifying Do you understand this stage direction? (Think about the meanings of *in* and *hold*.) It means that crowd noises come into the scene and remain there under the sounds of Damon's discussion with the king. How does that sound help create the scene?

Additional Support

Reading in the Real World

Citizenship The people ask the king to free Damon and Pythias when Pythias returns. Although the king is considered a tyrant, he complies with the people's wishes. When a government is influenced by the will of the people, we call it a democracy. Divide students into two groups and have one research monarchy and the other research democracy. Then have the two groups report on the differences between the two forms of government. **OL AL**

KING. [*Loud.*] People of the city! [*Crowd voices out.*] Never in all my life have I seen such faith and friendship, such loyalty between men. There are many among you who call me harsh and cruel. But I cannot kill *any* man who proves such strong and true friendship for another. Damon and Pythias, I set you both free. [*Roar of approval from crowd.*] I am king. I command a great army. I have stores of gold and precious jewels. But I would give all my money and power for one friend like Damon or Pythias. **12**

[*Sound: Roar of approval from crowd up briefly and out.*]
[*Music: Up and out.*] ○

Practice the Skills

12 **BIG Question**
Do you agree with what the king says about friendship? Explain your answer and write it on the "Damon and Pythias" page of Foldable 8. Your response will help you complete the Unit Challenge later. **BQ**

Tragic and Comic Masks (detail). before A.D. 79. Mosaics from the House of the Faun, Pompeii. Museo Archeologico Nazionale, Naples, Italy.

Damon and Pythias **983**

Teach

BQ **BIG Question**

Ask: What message about friendship is found in this play? *(Possible response: The message is that loyalty and friendship are more valuable than power or money.)* **OL**

Viewing the Art
Ask: In what way is this mask different from the one that is shown earlier in the story? *(This mask is smiling and the other is frowning.)* **BL**
Ask: What relation does it have to the play's conclusion? *(Possible response: It reflects the ending's happy mood.)* **OL**

 CheckPoint

Use the CheckPoint questions provided on Presentation Plus! to check for comprehension of the selection. These questions can be used with interactive response keypads for immediate student feedback.

Differentiated Instruction

Art Activity The comedy and drama masks originated in Greece and have been around for 2500 years. Masks challenged the actors to portray characters' feelings in subtle ways with voice and body language. These two masks have come to represent theatre. The play Damon and Pythias is indeed a drama. Have students create a drama mask for a character in this play. Display the masks in the classroom, labeling the character for which each mask is intended. **AS**

Objectives
• Find meaning in art
• Clarify ideas and text
• Interpret and analyze character

983

Assess

Resources for page 984

📁 Selection Quick Check, p. 73

📁 Selection and Unit Assessment, p. 87

💿 ExamView Assessment Suite

💿 Interactive Tutor: Self-Assessment

Students can respond to the *After You Read* items in their Learner's Notebooks or on a separate sheet of paper.

Answering the

1. Responses may vary. Responses could include that they were willing to die for one another.

2. Two weeks

3. They didn't believe that he would return to die or that a friend would die in his place.

Critical Thinking

4. Possible response: The king was known as a tyrant and harsh ruler.

5. Responses will vary. Students should use details from the selection.

6. Responses will vary, but may include that he knew friendship and family were worth more to Pythias than his life.

984

After You Read | Damon and Pythias

Answering the 〈BIG Question〉

1. Why did Damon and Pythias become known for their friendship? How does their story help you answer the question "What makes a friend?"

2. **Recall** How much time did Pythias have to return to the prison before Damon would be put to death in his place?
   Tip Right There

3. **Summarize** Why didn't the robbers believe Pythias?
   Tip Think and Search

Critical Thinking

4. **Interpret** Why did the First Voice say that the longer the king lived, the more miserable his people's lives would be?
   Tip On My Own

5. **Visualize** Try to picture Damon standing tall and brave in a dark, damp, stone prison cell. Write down the scene you picture.
   Tip On My Own

6. **Evaluate** Was Damon foolish to risk his life on the faithfulness of his friend Pythias?
   Tip On My Own

Talk About Your Reading

With a partner, debate this issue:
Would the king really give up all of his power and money for one friend like Damon or Pythias?
Consider these questions:

• If the king doesn't mean what he said, why did he release Damon and Pythias?

• If the king does mean what he said, why does he treat people so cruelly?

Objectives (pp. 984–985)
Reading Clarify ideas and text • Make connections from text to self
Literature Understand literary elements: characterization
Vocabulary Identify and understand idioms
Grammar Use punctuation correctly: semicolons with independent clauses

Talk About Your Reading

Possible responses:

• The king had never experienced true friendship and had been a tyrant for a long time—he probably would never really give up his money and power.

• The king was impressed that two commoners had such a rich level of friendship although neither had riches or gold.

• Riches meant more to the king, never having experienced friendship—his priority is wealth, not people.

Skills Review

Key Reading Skill: Clarifying

7. After Pythias asks the king how long he will have to remain in prison, the king says, "Not for very long, Pythias." What does he mean by this?

8. On page 981, the author includes the stage direction "[*Fade*.]" in the middle of Pythias's line. What do you think this means? What might Pythias's voice sound like after this direction? What effect was the author trying to create?

Key Literary Element: Characterization

9. How would you describe the character of Pythias? Use examples from the play.

10. How would you describe the king? Use examples from the play.

Vocabulary Check

Below each vocabulary word in dark type, there are three words. Which one is a synonym of the vocabulary word?

11. proclaimed

silenced   announced   denied

12. champion

defender   coward   opponent

13. Academic Vocabulary When you *clarify* a section of text, what are you doing?

In the sentences below, the idioms are underlined. Copy each idiom and write down what it means. If you don't know, make a reasonable guess.

14. That's my book; hand it over.

15. The future is in your hands.

16. Could you give me a hand with this box?

17. The band was great, so let's give them a hand.

Web Activities For eFlashcards, Selection Quick Checks, and other Web activities, go to www.glencoe.com.

Grammar Link: Semicolons with Independent Clauses

A semicolon is used in only a few situations. One of those uses is to join two independent clauses when they are not joined with a conjunction. (You learned about independent clauses in Unit 5.)

Once in a while, you might write two sentences that are very closely related to each other. A period between them provides a strong separation. If you want to let one thought flow right into the next, you could use a semicolon instead of a period. That emphasizes how closely related the statements are.

Example: Simon couldn't stand his cousin; he disliked every single thing she did.

The two clauses must be closely related. If they are not, do not join them!

Correct: Americans eat far too much junk food; they should eat almost none at all.
Incorrect: Josie really likes dogs; she is eleven years old.

Grammar Practice

Read each sentence and determine if the semicolons are used correctly. On a separate sheet of paper, write a "C" if the sentence correct and an "I" if it is incorrect.

18. The main characters of the play are Damon, Pythias, and the king; some theaters have over two hundred seats.

19. Pythias arranged his business affairs to provide for his mother and sister; they would be able to live comfortably for the rest of their lives.

20. The king said he would give up all of his money and power for a true friend like Damon or Pythias; they lived on the island of Sicily.

Damon and Pythias **985**

Skills Review

Key Reading Skill: Clarifying

7. Possible response: He meant that he would die by execution.

8. Responses will vary.

Key Literary Element: Characterization

9. Possible response: He is determined, for he struggled to free himself and traveled though thirsty, hungry, and penniless.

10. Responses will vary.

Vocabulary Check

11. announced

12. defender

13. Academic Vocabulary Possible response: clearing up confusing things in the text

14. give it to me

15. is up to you to decide

16. help me

17. clap for them

Close

Ask students what they learned from the selection about what it means to make sacrifices for a friend.

Grammar Link: Semicolons with Independent Clauses

Grammar Practice

18. I

19. C

20. I

Teach

More About the Author

Cricket Magazine, which published Joe Smith's story, is a magazine directed toward students between the ages of nine and fourteen. For thirty years, this magazine has entertained students with fiction, fantasy, folktales, adventures, poems, history, and biography. Its stories are written by top-notch writers and illustrated by award-winning artists.

EL Language Coach

Idioms Say: Using what you've learned about the vocabulary words and about idioms, tell what the expression "hick town" means. *(Possible response: It's an unsophisticated town.)* **EL BL**

Before You Read Charlie Johnson

Meet the Author

Joe Smith's story, "Charlie Johnson," was published in *Cricket* magazine in December 1998. *Cricket* has been in publication for over thirty years. During that time, it has won virtually every award given to kids' literary magazines.

Author Search For more about Joe Smith, go to www.glencoe.com.

Objectives (pp. 986–993)
Reading Clarify ideas and text • Make connections from text to self
Literature Understand literary elements: characterization
Vocabulary Identify and understand idioms

Vocabulary Preview

hick (hik) *adj.* small, rural, unexciting **(p. 988)** *Ben moved from the city of Boston to a place he thought of as a hick town.*

obituaries (oh BIH choo air eez) *n.* notices of deaths, usually in newspapers **(p. 992)** *Ben found out about the man's death when he read the obituaries in the local newspaper.*

Partner Talk With a partner, make a list of the things you might find—or *not* find—in a **hick** town. Then make a list of the kinds of information you might find in **obituaries.**

English Language Coach

Idioms Some phrases have a literal meaning and an idiomatic meaning. Your mother might really *put her foot down*—on the floor, the ground, or the gas pedal. However, if you say that your mother *put her foot down* about the mess in your room, you are using the phrase as an idiom. It means "to tell someone in a strong way that something must be done or must not be done." This is why you might hear someone say something like "He was *literally* all tied up." This makes it clear that the person was actually restrained by a rope rather than simply being very busy with something.

Other idioms make no sense at all with their literal meaning. It never actually *rains cats and dogs* (rains hard). No one is ever actually *on cloud nine* (very happy).

Even if an idiom is unfamiliar, you can often figure out what it means if you think about the literal meaning and use context clues.

Write to Learn The idioms in the sentences below are underlined. Combine your prior knowledge, literal meanings, and context clues to figure out what they mean. Write each idiom and your definition in your Learner's Notebook.

- After I realized my mistake, I had to <u>go back to square one</u>.
- Brad had the latest news, and Jacinta was <u>all ears</u>.
- My boss hates to fire people, so she makes her assistant <u>do her dirty work</u> for her.
- Rafi was feeling <u>under the weather</u> today, so he didn't come to school.
- When Amy saw someone bullying a smaller child, it <u>made her blood boil</u>.

Additional Support

Author Search To expand students' appreciation of Joe Smith, have them access the Web site for additional information and resources.

English Language Coach

Idioms Informal dialogue frequently uses idiomatic phrases. Besides writing out what a phrase means, it is sometimes helpful to draw a picture of the phrase as a way of explaining it. Ask English language learners to work with a native English speaker to draw pictures that represent the meanings of the following idioms:
- It's a piece of cake.
- They're selling like hot cakes.
- That takes the cake!

Or, have students draw pictures of the three idioms they listed in the *Write to Learn* activity. **EL OL**

Skills Preview

Key Reading Skill: Clarifying

If you become confused while reading a piece of non-fiction, you might go to another source of information for help. You might use an encyclopedia or the Internet to help you clarify. When you're reading fiction, you *usually* use another source only to find word definitions. There are, however, other steps to take that are just as useful with fiction as with nonfiction.

- Reread the confusing part more slowly.
- Read on further to see if later information helps.
- Ask yourself questions about what you don't understand.

Partner Talk With a partner, look through a magazine, newspaper, library book, or one of your textbooks. Find a section that you don't fully understand. It can be a sentence, paragraph, idea, or instruction. Work together to make a plan for clarifying that section. First, write down the steps you took to clarify. Next, discuss the meaning of the section.

Key Literary Element: Characterization

Characterization, revealing the personality of a character, is a big part of most stories. Characters are usually developed by their words, their actions, and the way others relate and respond to them. Think about these questions as you read:

- What do the characters' words and actions tell you about their personalities?
- What information about the characters does the narrator reveal?
- What do the characters think of each other?

Interactive Literary Elements Handbook
To review or learn more about the literary elements, go to www.glencoe.com.

Get Ready to Read

Connect to the Reading

In the story "Charlie Johnson," you will read about a friendship between a teenage boy and an elderly man. Do you have any friends who are much older than you? What are the benefits to you of a friendship with an older person?

Write to Learn If you could have a friendship with any adult in the world, who would you choose? Why would you choose that person? Write a short note to that person explaining why you would like to have him or her as a friend.

Build Background

Charlie Johnson is a Christmas tree farmer. Growing trees is a full-time, year-round job. Of course the busiest time of year for Christmas tree farmers is in November and December when trees are cut down and sold. However, during the rest of the year they must

- plant new seedlings—very young trees
- protect the trees from insects, disease, and bad weather
- constantly remove weeds and other plants that could crowd out the trees
- prune the trees to give them their traditional shape

Set Purposes for Reading

BIG Question As you read this story, notice what Ben Evans says, does, and thinks about his friendship with Charlie Johnson.

Set Your Own Purpose What would you like to learn from the selection to help you answer the Big Question? Write your purpose on the "Charlie Johnson" page of Foldable 8.

Keep Moving

Use these skills as you read the following selection.

Teach

R Reading Skill

Clarifying Ask: What are some things you can do to clarify something you don't understand at school? *(Possible responses: Ask the teacher questions; use references to look for the answer; ask a friend; restate the confusing passage in my own words.)* **AS**

L Literary Elements

Characterization Say: Think about Damon offering to take Pythias's place. What does this behavior tell you about Damon's character? *(Possible response: Damon took Pythias's place in jail and never doubted Pythias would return. That showed Damon was a true and loyal friend.)* **AS**

LiteratureOnline

Interactive Literary Elements Handbook Have students access the Web site to improve their understanding of characterization.

Literature Focus Lesson

Narrator Remind students that an author may use a narrator who participates in the story. This is called a first-person point of view. A story with a narrator who tells the story but does not participate in it is a story told from a third-person point of view. In the play *Damon and Pythias,* the narrator speaks from the third-person point of view. In the story *Charlie Johnson,* Ben Evans is the narrator and a main character. Discuss with students why an author may or may not choose to have the narrator be a character in the story. **AS**

Objectives
- Clarify ideas and text
- Understand idioms
- Identify and analyze narrator
- Interpret and analyze character

987

Teach

L Literary Element

Characterization Ask: What words does the author use to describe Dave Johnson? *(big dumb farmer; temper to match his size)* **AS** Ask: What does it tell you about the narrator's view of Dave Johnson? *(Possible response: He thought Dave was big, stupid, and quick-tempered.)* **OL**

R₁ Reading Skill

Connecting Ask: Have you ever evaluated someone based only on what you heard about him or her? What did you hear and how did it shape your impressions of that person? Explain. *(Responses will vary.)* **AS**

R₂ Reading Skill

Review Visualizing Ask: If you were writing a play about this, what items would you have to include in this first scene of your play? *(Responses should include a saw, a stone wall, and Christmas trees.)* **BL**

Readability Scores
Dale-Chall: 4.0
DRP: 48
Lexile: 780

Charlie Johnson

by Joe Smith

Practice the Skills

It was almost four months since we had moved from Boston to this stupid little **hick** town, and the aura[1] of being the new kid was wearing thin. I had to do something soon to make my reputation. **1**

L R₁ Dave Johnson was the perfect target. He was a big dumb farmer whose place was just down the road from our house. The kids said that he had a temper to match his size, and they were all scared stiff of him. I figured that if I pulled one over on Johnson, I'd really be somebody. **2**

R₂ I put my plan into effect one December afternoon after school. Mom and Dad weren't home, as usual, so I grabbed a saw out of the cellar and headed down the path behind our house. A short distance through the woods there was a stone wall, then a field full of Christmas trees. Johnson's Christmas trees.

It was almost too easy. I jumped over the wall into the rows of trees and chose a likely victim. As I sawed, I thought about what I was going to tell the kids at school the next day. But as

1 English Language Coach

Idioms When the narrator says the aura of being the new kid is "wearing thin," he does not mean that something is literally wearing out. He means that he is getting tired of being seen that way. Look for another idiom in the last sentence of the following paragraph.

2 Key Literary Element

Characterization Consider the narrator's plan to make a reputation for himself. What does it tell you about his character?

1. An *aura* is a quality that seems to surround a person or thing.

Vocabulary

hick (hik) *adj.* small, rural, unexciting

Additional Support

Reading in the Real World

Career Many people make a living by planting and selling trees. Some sell trees to add shade to lawns and to protect houses from direct sunlight. Others plant only specific types of trees to sell once a year at Christmas. These people are called Christmas tree farmers. Invite a local businessperson from a tree farm or a nursery to talk about different types of trees and how to care for them. **AS** Some students may be interested in doing additional research to find out about other careers related to raising and caring for trees. Have volunteers share their findings with the class. **OL AL**

soon as I had the tree cut, a shadow fell over me. I looked up to find the giant farmer standing there. Without a word he hauled me off to his truck and drove me to the farm. "Wait here," he grunted, then disappeared into the barn.

A moment later a figure emerged, but it wasn't the big farmer. It was an old man, wearing a red-checkered coat and big boots.

He shuffled up to my side of the truck and stared at me with watery eyes that were almost hidden by bushy eyebrows. Then he smiled.

"So you're the tree rustler," he said in a gravelly voice. "Come out here where I can get a good look at you."

I glanced nervously toward the barn, and the man chuckled. "I see you've met my son. Don't worry about him. He gets upset easy, but he'll calm down."

"Why, you're barely thirteen or fourteen," he said as he looked me up and down. "The way Dave was talking, I thought we had a hardened criminal on our hands!"

Then he shoved a huge hand toward me. "My name's Charlie Johnson," he said. "You must be the Evans kid that just moved in down the road."

"Yeah, Ben Evans," I said. His grip was surprisingly strong.

"Well, listen, Ben. We're kind of busy right now. Maybe you could lend me a hand for a few minutes."

I had been ready for a lecture, even for some yelling and screaming, but this caught me off balance. **3**

I followed the old man around to the back of the truck and accepted the trees he handed to me. Then I followed him to the row of empty stands, where we leaned each of the trees in place.

He talked as we worked. I had never met him before, but somehow he seemed to know all about me, my parents, and my friends.

We soon had the stands full of trees. He grabbed one and shoved it toward me.

"Throw it on the back of the truck and get in. I'll give you a ride home. I figure I almost worked the price of that tree out of you by now."

I had to laugh. Until that moment I hadn't realized what the old man was doing.

Practice the Skills

3 | **English Language Coach**

Idioms What do you think Ben means when he says that Charlie's response "caught me off balance"?

Charlie Johnson **989**

Teach

L Literary Element

Characterization Ask: What words does Ben use to characterize Charlie Johnson? *(Responses should include the following: old man, bushy eyebrows, smiled, gravelly voice, chuckled, surprisingly strong grip)* **BL Ask:** What conclusion can you draw about Ben's first impression of Charlie? *(Possible response: He is surprised by Charlie's friendly behavior, but also relieved.)* **OL**

R Reading Skill

Review Inferring Say: Charlie has most of the dialogue on this page. Why do you think Ben says so little in return? *(Possible response: Ben's a little caught off-guard. Based on what he thought about Dave, he's not sure what to think of Charlie. Instead of talking, Ben is trying to form opinions about Charlie.)* **OL AL**

Differentiated Instruction

Illustration Some students may benefit from creating illustrations of the characters. There is quite a difference in age between Ben and Charlie, and yet they seem to be able to work together quite well. Have students use the narrator's description of Charlie and their own impressions of Ben to draw a picture of the two of them working side by side to place the trees by the stand. Display the pictures around the room. Discuss any similarities and differences between students' drawings of the two characters. **AS**

Objectives
• Identify literary elements: dialogue
• Visualize
• Make connections from text to self
• Interpret and analyze character

Teach

L1 Literary Element

Characterization Ask: How would you describe Ben's parents? What words lead you to your description? *(Possible response: Ben and his parents aren't close. He says that he doubts they'll care and that he barely sees them.)* **OL**

L2 Literary Element

Characterization Ask: What is Charlie's reaction to hearing about Ben's parents? What have you learned about Charlie from his response? *(Possible response: Charlie frowns when he hears Ben's reply. He also smiles and waves as he leaves. Charlie seems to care about Ben.)* **OL**

"Almost, but not quite," he continued. "If you come back about the middle of April when the new trees come in, I'll get another hour of work out of you, and then we'll call it even. How does that sound?"

What could I say? I agreed, and he drove me home.

"What are you going to tell your parents about the tree?" he asked as we pulled into the driveway.

L1 "I doubt they'll even care. I barely see them anyway," I said as I hopped out and grabbed the tree. He frowned when

L2 I said that, but he gave me a big smile and a wave as he drove away.

My parents didn't ask, but I told everyone at school that I stole the tree, figuring I might as well get something out of the mess. I think some of the kids even believed me. **4**

Winter passed slowly. I had forgotten all about the old man and his trees. He hadn't forgotten about me, though. One spring day I came home to find him sitting in his truck in my driveway.

Practice the Skills

4 Key Reading Skill

Clarifying Ben says he told everyone he stole the tree so he'd "get something out of the mess." What do you think he hopes to get?

Field of Dreams, Cindy Coakley
Analyzing the Art Do you think Charlie Johnson's truck looked like this one? Explain your answer.

990 UNIT 8 What Makes a Friend?

Additional Support

Reading Fluency

Reading Aloud Reading aloud helps readers understand an author's characterization. Help students notice that after some time, Ben is talking directly to Charlie and is sharing things about his home life. Have students get into pairs and read this page aloud, with one partner as Charlie and the other as Ben.

Explain to students that Ben is revealing things about himself through his dialogue with Charlie and as the narrator. Discuss with students some of the thoughts that Ben shares with the reader as a narrator and what these thoughts show about his character. **AS**

He brought me to the barn, where there were several long boxes full of seedlings. He showed me the different kinds of trees, and I helped to count and separate them.

L

C When we were done, Charlie told me that if I came back Saturday, he'd pay me to help him plant the trees. I'd never planted a tree in my life and I had better things to do with my Saturday, but a little money would sure impress the other kids, so I said yes.

I showed up early on Saturday. He took me out to the field and showed me what to do. It was hard going, but Charlie kept up a steady stream of talk the whole time.

He had come here when he was younger, too. "Bought this farm and thought I was gonna show the locals how it should be done," he said.

But the '38 hurricane came and blew down his barn and most of the trees on the property. "I would've packed it in right there, but the whole town came together and helped me rebuild the barn and get started again. I wasn't such a hotshot after that." He started planting trees to replace what was lost and he'd been at it ever since. **5**

By the end of the day, I was sore all over. The worst part of it was that Charlie had planted twice as many trees as I had and was as fit at the end as when we started.

I spent a lot of time at the farm that summer and earned a bit of money, too. Most times I'd see the younger Johnson, but he'd just scowl and turn away when he saw me. Charlie kept me busy, shearing the trees or mowing the grass between the rows.

I kind of felt sorry for the old man. His son took care of the milk cows and the hayfields, so it seemed as if all he had left were his trees. And the way he bent my ear, I figured I must be the only one he had to talk to.

I didn't mind listening, though. I guess I even learned something, and it was funny how he always knew what I'd been up to. I figured that perhaps I was such a celebrity the whole town was talking about me. **6**

That Christmas I bought a tree with my own money. Charlie just laughed, winked, and pocketed the bills. It felt good.

It was a pretty bad winter, and I didn't get over to see him for a couple of months. Then, one gray March morning, my

Practice the Skills

5 | **English Language Coach**

Idioms Charlie says, "I would've packed it in right there . . ." What does he mean? **EL**

6 | **Key Literary Element**

Characterization Sometimes we learn about a character from what he or she says or thinks. What do you learn about Ben from what he reveals about himself?

Charlie Johnson **991**

Teach

L **Literary Element**

Characterization Ask: *What do you learn about Ben based on his reason for accepting work from Charlie? (Possible response: He doesn't really want to work. He seems more concerned about impressing his friends.)* **AS**

C **Critical Thinking**

Analysis Ask: *Why do you think it is so important to Ben that his friends notice him? (Possible response: He's still the new kid. Also, his parents don't notice if he's home or not or what he does.)* **OL AL**

EL **Language Coach**

Idiom Say: *Charlie says he wasn't such a "hotshot" after the hurricane destroyed his barn. What does he mean by this term? (Possible response: He means that he didn't know everything like he thought he did and that he needed help from others just like anyone else.)* **OL**

Literature Focus Lesson

Point of View Remind students that in the third-person point of view, the narrator is not part of the story but knows everything about the characters. In the first-person point of view, the narrator is a character and the reader is limited to knowing only what the character/ narrator knows, thinks, or feels. Discuss with students how Charlie's and Ben's points of view might be different. Have students write a paragraph as it might be written if Charlie were the narrator of this story. Ask volunteers to share their work with the class. **OL AL**

Objectives
• Analyze text
• Understand idioms
• Interpret and analyze character
• Indentify and analyze narrator

Teach

R **Reading Skill**

Clarifying Ask: What does Ben learn about himself when he attends Charlie's funeral? *(Possible response: He learns that he hadn't realized how important Charlie was to so many people and that he had been mistaken to pity Charlie.)* **AS**

EL **Language Coach**

Idioms Ask: What does the phrase "big shot" mean? *(Possible response: It means someone who acts like he or she knows everything.)* **Ask:** What other idiom from the story is this similar to? *(hotshot)* **BL OL**

L **Literary Element**

Characterization Say: When Dave Johnson sees Ben approach the farm, he snarls at him. What does he think about Ben? *(Possible response: He doesn't seem to like Ben.)* **BL** **Ask:** Do you think he will accept Ben's help with the trees? *(Reponses will vary. Some students may say that Dave doesn't seem to want Ben around, while others may say that Dave may let Ben help because that's what his father would have wanted.)* **OL**

father shoved the morning paper under my nose. There was Charlie's picture on the page. It was a few moments before I figured out that I was looking at the **obituaries**.

The funeral was a couple of days later. Since I knew he didn't have too many friends, I decided to go so at least someone was there.

The service was held in the church at the center of town. As I walked down the main street I was surprised to see so many cars go by. As I got closer I could see parked cars lining both sides of the street and a policeman directing traffic, but it wasn't until I saw the line before the church door that I realized they were all going the same place I was.

Somewhat in shock, I joined the crowd. When I finally made it inside, all the seats were taken, and I had to stand up against the wall behind the last pew.

I listened as, one after another, people got up to speak. They talked about all Charlie had done for the town and the people in it, how he was always ready to help, but most of all, they talked about how he was their friend. **7**

The minister said a few more words, then the people started rising and filing out of the church. I slipped out and stood looking at the crowd as it grew on the lawn. About an hour before, I was a big shot, going to an old man's funeral out of pity; now I was just a jerk. Embarrassed by my own stupidity, I turned and hurried home. **8**

It was in early April that I found my feet leading me back to the farm. Dave Johnson was in the empty farm stand. He looked up as I approached, that old familiar scowl on his face. "What do you want?" he snarled.

"I thought I could help. With the trees."

Analyzing the Art Does this picture help you understand how Ben felt at Charlie Johnson's funeral service? Explain.

Practice the Skills

7 **Key Literary Element**

Characterization Sometimes we learn about a character from what others say or do. What does the information about the people at Charlie's funeral reveal about him?

8 **Key Reading Skill**

Clarifying Ben felt stupid when he saw a crowd of people at Charlie's funeral. Do you understand why Ben had not known that Charlie had many other friends? If not, go back and reread. **R**

Vocabulary

obituaries (oh BIH choo air eez) *n.* notices of deaths, usually in newspapers

Additional Support

Differentiated Instruction

Writing a Letter Some students might benefit from a writing activity. Have students think about what Ben might want to tell Charlie now that he has found out what an important member of the community he was. Ask students to write a letter to Charlie as if they were Ben. Have them tell Charlie what they learned about him and what they learned about friendship through him. Ask volunteers to share their letters with the class. **AS**

He looked annoyed. "Come with me," he said.

He led me into the barn. Three big boxes full of seedlings were on the floor. "It's kind of funny you should show up; they just came this morning." Then he turned and sat on one of them and looked at me.

"I never understood why my father wanted to bother with you," he said, "but I guess he saw something there that I couldn't see. You'd come strutting around here like you were doing him a favor, and I felt like thrashing you. He'd just laugh, though, and he'd say, 'Don't worry, he'll be all right.' I thought he was nuts."

I could have told him to stick it. Maybe a little while ago I would have, but now all I could say was "I'm sorry."

His face softened at that, and I think for a moment he was at a loss for words. "You didn't have to come here," he finally said, "but you did. Maybe Charlie was right after all." **9 10**

Then he put out his hand, and in the darkness of the barn, I shook it, not because I had anything to prove or because I wanted to impress anyone, but because I just wanted to be his friend. **11** ○

Analyzing the Photo
Do you think Ben might see a tree decorated like this one on the Johnsons' land? Why or why not?

Practice the Skills

9 ▐ Key Literary Element

Characterization Now you see a different side of Dave Johnson's character. Do you think this is the *real* Dave?

10 ▐ Key Reading Skill

Clarifying What was Charlie right about? Think about the entire story. Can you clarify the author's main idea about friendship?

11 ◀ BIG Question

Why do you think Dave is willing to reach out to Ben? Why do you think Ben wants to become friends with Dave? Write your answers on the "Charlie Johnson" page of Foldable 8. Your response will help you complete the Unit Challenge later.

R

Charlie Johnson **993**

Teach

R Reading Skill

Review Predicting Ask: Based on what Ben has learned about himself, what do you predict about his relationship with Dave? *(Possible response: He will be a good friend to Dave because of what he has learned about friendship from Charlie.)* **Ask:** What lines in the text support this? ("... I shook it, not because I had anything to prove or because I wanted to impress anyone, but because I just wanted to be his friend.") **OL**

Viewing the Photo

Ask: What relationship do you think this image has to the ending of the story? *(Responses will vary. Some students may say that it represents the memory of Charlie or what Ben has learned about the meaning of friendship from his experiences with Charlie and the tree farm.)* **AS**

✓ CheckPoint

Use the CheckPoint questions provided on Presentation Plus! to check for comprehension of the selection. These questions can be used with interactive response keypads for immediate student feedback.

Literature Focus Lesson

Imagery Explain to students how authors use imagery to convey meanings or to set tone. On this page, the author describes the boxes on the barn floor as three big boxes full of seedlings. The image of a seedling can also represent the new relationship that Ben is forming with Dave. Discuss with students how a seedling is like a new relationship. Include how the care of a seedling could be like caring for a new friend. Challenge students to think of other images that might represent a budding friendship. **AS**

Objectives
• Make predictions
• Understand idioms
• Clarify ideas and text
• Use text features: photographs
• Interpret and analyze character
• Identify literary elements: imagery

993

Assess

Resources for page 994

📁 Selection Quick Check, p. 74

📁 Selection and Unit Assessment, p. 88

💿 ExamView Assessment Suite

💿 Interactive Tutor: Self-Assessment

Students can respond to the *After You Read* items in their Learner's Notebooks or on a separate sheet of paper.

Answering the
BIG Question

1. Possible response: Charlie talks to Ben, gives him work to do and pays him for it, and shares examples from his own life with Ben.

2. He stacks trees by the stand, he counts and separates seedlings, and he plants trees.

3. Possible response: Ben says he is sorry for acting the way he did.

Critical Thinking

4. Possible response: He helps Charlie with his work, and he lets Charlie teach him about trees.

5. Possible response: Now he understands what it means to do something *for* a friend.

6. Possible response: He probably recalls how he felt when he was Ben's age, and since he needs help anyway, this is a better way to work it out.

994

After You Read — Charlie Johnson

Answering the BIG Question

1. How is Charlie a good friend to Ben?
2. **Recall** Name three jobs Ben did for Charlie.
   Tip Think and Search

3. **Summarize** In the end, what changes Dave's opinion of Ben?
   Tip Think and Search

Critical Thinking

4. **Evaluate** Is Ben a good friend to Charlie?
   Tip Author and Me

5. **Analyze** How does Ben's friendship with Charlie change his character?
   Tip Author and Me

6. **Infer** When Ben tried to steal the tree, why do you think Charlie made him work on the farm instead of calling the police or Ben's parents?
   Tip On My Own

Write About Your Reading

Which character in "Charlie Johnson" would you the most want to be friends with—Charlie, Dave, or Ben? Why? Write a letter to that character introducing yourself and explaining why you would like to become friends.

• Describe your personality and interests.
• State what interests you about Charlie, Dave, or Ben.
• If there is something you have in common, mention it.
• End with a statement about the kind of friendship you hope will develop.

Objectives (pp. 994–995)
Reading Clarify ideas and text • Make connections from text to self
Literature Understand literary elements: characterization
Vocabulary Identify and understand idioms
Writing Respond to literature: letter
Grammar Use punctuation correctly: semicolons with conjunctive adverbs

994 UNIT 8 What Makes a Friend?

Write About Your Reading

Possible response:
Dear Charlie,
I have always loved trees, but no one ever taught me about the different kinds of trees or how to care for them. I like learning and I am very responsible. After all your experience with trees, I know you could teach me a lot about them. I think you must be patient because it takes a while to watch trees grow. I'm patient, too. I hope you can be my teacher and I can be your helper. That way we will both give something to each other.
–Yearning to Learn

Skills Review

Key Reading Skill: Clarifying

7. Why did Dave always scowl (frown in an unfriendly way) at Ben?

8. Did Charlie talk to Ben because he was lonely or for some other reason? Explain.

Key Literary Element: Characterization

9. Did you learn more about Charlie from Charlie's own words and actions or through the way other characters reacted to him? Give examples to support your answer.

10. Do the characters in "Charlie Johnson" seem true to life? Why or why not? Support your answer with examples of their behavior or conversation.

11. Which character do you think the author characterized as changing the most, Ben or Dave? Explain your answer.

Vocabulary Check

12. What information would you find by reading the **obituaries** in a newspaper?

13. Would most people consider Chicago to be a **hick** town?

14. **Academic Vocabulary** List three ways to *clarify* a text.

15. **English Language Coach:** Charlie and Ben use two very similar idioms to describe themselves. Charlie says he was a *hotshot* when he was younger. Ben thought he was a *big shot* before he went to Charlie's funeral. What do those two idioms mean?

Web Activities For eFlashcards, Selection Quick Checks, and other Web activities, go to www.glencoe.com.

Grammar Link: Semicolons with Conjunctive Adverbs

You've learned about using a semicolon to connect two related independent clauses if the clauses are not connected by a conjunction.

Correct: Erika plays the drums; she is really good.
Incorrect: Erika plays the drums; and she is really good.

Here is another common use for semicolons. There are certain words that aren't conjunctions but that do connect parts of a sentence. They include *however* and *therefore*. These special words, called "conjunctive adverbs," require a semicolon before them and a comma after them.

- The cat was small; however, he was brave.
- I overslept; therefore, I missed the bus.

Grammar Practice

Read each sentence and decide if it is correct or incorrect. On a separate sheet of paper, write a "C" if the sentence is correct and an "I" if it is incorrect. (Think about both uses of semicolons taught in this workshop.)

16. Ben was new in town; therefore, he didn't know many people.

17. Dave Johnson had a temper; he grew Christmas trees.

18. Ben made a plan; he intended to steal a tree.

19. At first, Dave scared Ben, however, he didn't hurt him.

20. Ben didn't want to work on Saturdays; but he wanted to earn some money.

21. Charlie Johnson's barn was destroyed; however, the town helped him rebuild it.

22. Charlie was respected in the town; many people admired his hard work and helpfulness.

Writing Application Review your Write About Your Reading activity. Check to see if you have two closely related sentences that can be connected using a semicolon.

Charlie Johnson **995**

Skills Review

Key Reading Skill: Clarifying

7. Responses will vary.

8. Responses will vary.

Key Literary Element: Characterization

9. Possible response: I learned more about him from his actions, such as not calling the police on Ben, and teaching Ben about caring for trees.

10. Possible response: I think they're realistic because Charlie's like a grandfather teaching his grandson about farming and life.

11. Possible response: I think Ben changed the most because at first he always did things just to impress other people, but now he knows the true meaning of friendship.

Vocabulary Check

12. Information about peoples' deaths

13. No

14. **Academic Vocabulary** Possible response: reread confusing parts; look for footnotes; ask yourself questions

15. **English Language Coach** Possible response: A *hotshot* is someone who is extremely talented at something. A *big shot* is someone who is extremely popular.

Grammar Link: Semicolons with Conjunctive Adverbs

Grammar Practice

16. C

17. I

18. C

19. I

20. I

21. C

22. C

Close

Ask students to discuss what they learned about unexpected friendships from reading the selection.

Skimming and Scanning

Objectives covered in this workshop:
• Skim to get an overview of a selection
• Scan to find specific information styles

Teaching Students to Skim and Scan

Why Is It Important?
• Skimming and scanning are very useful tools when readers need to find information quickly.
• Skimming includes previewing the selection to get an idea of what it is about.
• Skimming is helpful when students need to find out whether or not a document contains the information they are searching for.
• Scanning is glancing over a selection to find specific information, such as the time a bus leaves from a certain station.

How to Help Students Get It
• Tell students that they already use these skills.
• While skimming, students should read headlines, headings, captions, and part of the first paragraph to get an overview of the piece.
• While scanning, students should look for key words that would help them.
• Before skimming and scanning, make sure students know what they are looking for.

Reading to Answer the Big Question

The Bully of Barksdale Street by Eric Alter
In this three-character play, Josh and his friend Bill outsmart a seventh grade bully named Blane. Since Billy's transfer to a new school, Blane has been victimizing him and taking his baseball cards. Josh threatens Blane and tells him to stay away from Billy. Blane runs away, after agreeing to give the stolen baseball cards to Josh.

The Tangled Tresses by Christina Hamlett
The setting of this humorous one-act play is a beauty shop where fairy tale characters get makeovers. The owners of the Fabulous Frills Salon befriend Goldilocks, Rapunzel, Cinderella, Sleeping Beauty, and Alice in Wonderland. Students will also read about Helen of Troy, King Midas, Little Miss Muffet, and Medusa.

Workshop Resources

Pacing (days) Standard	Block	Lesson	Student Materials	Teacher Resources
1	1/2	Key Skill Lesson: Skimming and Scanning	🐾 Key Reading Skills Practice, p. 21 🐾 English Language Coach Review, p. 42	🔖 Bellringer Options Transparencies –Daily Language Practice 76 🔖 Read Aloud Think Aloud Transparencies –Key Reading Skills 8 –Read Aloud, Think Aloud 67-81 💿 Presentation Plus!
1	1	"The Bully of Barksdale Street"	💻 Glencoe Online 🐾 Unit Vocabulary Review, p. 40 🐾 Academic Vocabulary Review, p. 43 📁 English Language Coach 🐾 Active Reading Graphic Organizer, p. 23 🐾 Literary Analysis, p. 22 💿 StudentWorks Plus™ 💻 Online Student Edition 💿 Literature Classics 📁 Selection and Unit Assessments, p. 89	🔖 Literary and Text Analysis Transparencies 49 💻 Puzzlemaker 💿 Skill Level Up!™ A Language Arts Game 💻 BookLink 3 📔 Assessment by Learning Objective (Diagnostic and Formative) 💿 Interactive Tutor: Self-Assessment 💿 TeacherWorks Plus™
1		"The Tangled Tresses"	💻 Glencoe Online 🐾 Unit Vocabulary Review, p. 40 🐾 Academic Vocabulary Review, p. 43 📁 English Language Coach 🐾 Active Reading Graphic Organizer, p. 25 🐾 Literary Analysis, p. 22 💿 StudentWorks Plus™ 💻 Online Student Edition 💿 Literature Classics 📁 Selection and Unit Assessments, p. 90	🔖 Literary and Text Analysis Transparencies 49 💻 Puzzlemaker 💿 Skill Level Up!™ A Language Arts Game 💻 BookLink 3 📔 Assessment by Learning Objective (Diagnostic and Formative) 💿 Interactive Tutor: Self-Assessment 💿 TeacherWorks Plus™

Keys for Unit Resource

- 📁 Blackline Master
- 📔 Workbook
- 📖 Supplemental Text
- 💿 CD-ROM
- 💾 DVD
- 🔖 Transparency
- 💻 Web-based
- 🐾 Fast File

Level Appropriate Code

- **AS** = Activities for all students
- **AL** = Activities for students working above grade level
- **OL** = Activities for students working at grade level
- **BL** = Activities for students working below grade level
- **EL** = Activities for English language learners

Focus

BELLRINGER Options

🖐 **Daily Language Practice Transparency 76**
Focus Activity Ask: What are some characteristics of a bully? Describe. *(Responses will vary.)* **AS**

Teach

R Reading Skill

Skimming and Scanning

Ask: When do you skim or scan something in daily life? *(Possible response: when I quickly read newspaper headlines, the cafeteria menu, a movie review, or the home page of a Web site)* **AS**

Analyzing the Cartoon

Say: The cartoon character Calvin flips through a book without really reading it. How is what he does different from skimming and scanning? *(When you skim, you quickly read through something to get a general idea of what it is about. When you scan, you look for headings, and key words and phrases to get you to specific information. Calvin didn't do either of these.)* **OL AL**

READING WORKSHOP 3

Skills Focus
You will practice these skills when you read the following selections:
- "The Bully of Barksdale Street," p. 1000
- "Tales of the Tangled Tresses," p. 1016

Reading
- Skimming and scanning

Literature
- Understanding stage directions in a play

Vocabulary
- Understanding jargon and clipped words

Writing/Grammar
- Using a colon to introduce a list
- Using a colon in a time notation and after a salutation

Objectives (pp. 996–997)
Reading Skim and scan text

Skill Lesson

Skimming and Scanning

Learn It!

What Is It? Skimming and scanning are reading strategies that you can use to get the general idea of a text or to answer specific questions you might have.

R
- **Skimming** is reading rapidly through a piece of writing. You skim a text to get a general idea of what it is about or to refresh your memory of it.
- **Scanning** is running your eyes quickly over a piece of writing. You scan to look at section headings, words in boldfaced type, and key words or phrases to find specific information.

CALVIN AND HOBBES © 1987 Watterson. Distributed By UNIVERSAL PRESS SYNDICATE. Reprinted with permission. All rights reserved.

Analyzing Cartoons
Would you ever skim or scan the way that Calvin does? Why or why not?

Additional Support

Reading in the Real World

Career Some students may be interested in careers as psychologists. Explain that there are many kinds of psychologists. Those who work with young people can help them with issues like bullying. Invite your students to research the field of psychology to find out how a person becomes a psychologist, what kind of education they need, and what kinds of jobs they do. Have students write up their findings and make a short report to the class. **AS**

Why Is It Important? Skimming a piece of writing gives you an idea of what to expect when you read it carefully later. If the piece of writing isn't what you are looking for, you don't need to read all of it. Scanning helps you find information quickly. Instead of reading an entire piece of writing, you can scan it for the particular fact or idea that you need.

How Do I Do It? To skim a piece of writing, read its title and then look quickly through the whole piece. Read headings, captions, and maybe the beginning of several paragraphs to get the main idea. For a play, read the first page to find out where and when the play takes place and who the main characters are. Then read a few lines from each page to get a general idea of what's happening.

To scan a piece of writing, move your eyes quickly over the lines until they fall on headings, words in boldfaced type, or key words or phrases that are about the information you are looking for. Here is what one student said as he skimmed and scanned "Damon and Pythias."

Study Central Visit www.glencoe.com and click on Study Central to review skimming and scanning

> When I skimmed the play, I found out it takes place long ago in Sicily. The main characters are friends named Damon and Pythias. The play has a king, soldiers, a narrator, and "Voices."
>
> I never heard of "Voices" in a play, so I scanned to find out what kind of things they said. Sometimes they seemed like part of the audience, and sometimes they seemed like regular characters in the play.

Practice It!

When you're getting ready to read a play, you might skim over it to get an idea of what it's like. You can also scan for anything that you're curious about. In your Learner's Notebook, jot down these four questions:

1. What does the play seem to be about?
2. Does the play seem to be serious or funny?
3. Have I ever heard of any of the characters in the play before?

Use It!

Before you read this play, skim over it to answer the first two questions you wrote down. Then scan the play until you find the answer to question 3. Write all your answers in your Learner's notebook.

Teach

Study Central Have students access the Web site to review skimming and scanning and to complete a related activity.

L Literary Element

Stage Directions Say: When you read a play, most of what you read is dialogue, or what characters say to each other. Sometimes you see instructions to the actors written in parentheses. These words are not meant to be spoken aloud by the actors. What are these lines for? *(They are stage directions, telling actors where to go and what to do.)* **OL**

Resources for page 997

Use Key Reading Skills Transparency 8 in *Read Aloud, Think Aloud* to help students practice skimming and scanning.

Reading Fluency

Build Fluency Building reading fluency with drama is fun, especially when reading realistic, conversational sentences like those in Eric Alter's play. Invite students to choose one part of the play that they particularly like. Explain that reading a play aloud includes reading the names of characters and the stage instructions.

Have students find a quiet place to practice reading aloud the passage. Tell them to reread it several times until they can read all the sentences with expression and understanding. They should try to make the dialog sound like natural speech. **EL BL**

Objectives
• Skim and scan text
• Identify literary elements: stage direction
• Analyze text features: cartoons

997

Teach

More About the Author

In addition to writing plays and screenplays, Eric Alter has founded a production company called Apricot Sky Productions. Its purpose is to create new projects for film, TV, and theater, and help foster the careers of new actors, writers, directors, and technical people. Apricot Sky is located in New York City.

EL Language Coach

Clipped Words Ask: What kinds of words do you think tend to get clipped, or shortened? *(Response: words that are familiar and used a lot)* **AS**

Before You Read : The Bully of Barksdale Street

Eric Alter

Meet the Author

Eric Alter has written more than 40 plays and screenplays for a wide variety of audiences. He also directs plays and writes novels.

Author Search For more about Eric Alter, go to www.glencoe.com.

Objectives (pp. 998–1011)
Reading Skim and scan text • Make connections from text to self
Literature Understand elements of drama: stage directions
Vocabulary Identify clipped words

Vocabulary Preview

tribute (TRIB yoot) *n.* something done to show respect **(p. 1000)** *In his speech, Joe made a tribute to his best friend.*

backdrop (BAK drop) *n.* a curtain or temporary wall that covers the back of a stage **(p. 1000)** *We painted a picture of a desert on the backdrop.*

fencing (FEN sing) *n.* the sport of fighting with swords **(p. 1003)** *The swords used in fencing have a dull protective tip on the end so people won't get hurt.*

rambling (RAM bling) *v.* talking in a disorganized manner **(p. 1005)** *I had trouble understanding Jason because he was rambling so much.*

pummel (PUM ul) *v.* to hit or beat someone **(p. 1006)** *The bully tried to pummel Antoine, but he failed.*

mocking (MOK ing) *v.* making fun of someone by imitating the person in a ridiculous manner **(p. 1007)** *When Jennifer started mocking John, he got very angry.*

menacingly (MEN uh sing lee) *adv.* in a threatening manner **(p. 1007)** *The dark clouds hung menacingly over the city.*

English Language Coach

Clipped Words A **clipped word** is a word that has been shortened. In a clipped word, the beginning, the end, or both the beginning and the end of the word have been cut off. People use clipped words every day. Look at these examples, and think about clipped words you use.

Clipped Word	Full Word
bike	bicycle
flu	influenza
fridge	refrigerator
ump	umpire

EL

Write to Learn In your Learner's Notebook, write the clipped word you would use instead of each of the following words: *teenager, telephone, mathematics, photograph, referee.*

998 UNIT 8 What Makes a Friend?

Additional Support

Author Search To expand students' appreciation of Eric Alter, have them access the Web site for more information and resources.

Literature Focus Lesson

Stage Directions Invite students to use the following chart to write an original one-page play. Remind them that stage directions are always put in parentheses to indicate that they are instructions for the actors, not words to be spoken aloud. **AL**

Character's Name	Stage Directions	Dialogue

Skills Preview

Key Reading Skill: Skimming and Scanning

Before you read the selection, skim it to get a general idea of what it is about and how it is structured. Then scan the selection quickly to find out the answers to the questions below. Write the answers in your Learner's Notebook.

- Where does the play take place?
- Which characters are talking when the play begins?
- Who is the character who appears later in the play?

Key Literary Element: Stage Directions

Stage directions are written in italics and are often enclosed in brackets or parentheses. They are a playwright's instructions to the actors, the director, and the stage crew. When a play is performed, the stage directions are not spoken. Instead, the actors or others involved with the play *do* what the stage directions indicate.

In Reading Workshop 1, you learned some of the terms playwrights use to refer to parts of the stage and actors' movements on the stage. Now, look for stage directions that have to do with:

- scenery and props—objects and furniture onstage
- lighting—which parts of the stage are lit
- movement of actors onstage
- action by an actor—anything that an actor does
- emotions that the actor should show
- how the actor should say the lines
- music and sound effects

Interactive Literary Elements Handbook
To review or learn more about the literary elements, go to www.glencoe.com.

Get Ready to Read

Connect to the Reading

Have you ever needed someone's help when you had a serious problem? Were you able to get help from a friend? Do you think a person has a right to ask his or her friend to do something difficult in order to help solve a problem?

Group Talk If your friend has a problem, is it your problem too? In a small group, talk about this question.

Build Background

Millions of people around the world collect some type of item. Some people collect things because they believe the items will increase in value as time passes. Other people collect things simply because they like them.

Collecting baseball cards has been a popular hobby in the United States for more than 75 years. Some baseball cards from the early days of professional baseball are worth more than $100,000. The value of a baseball card depends on several things:

- the condition of the card
- how rare the card is
- the company that made the card
- the year that the card was issued
- how popular the player is or was

Set Purposes for Reading

BIG Question Read "The Bully of Barksdale Street" to find out how one boy helped his friend out of a difficult situation.

Set Your Own Purpose What else would you like to learn from the selection that will help you answer the Big Question? Write your own purpose for reading this selection on the "Bully of Barksdale Street" page of Foldable 8.

Keep Moving

Use these skills as you read the following selection.

Teach

C Critical Thinking

Comprehension Say: Bullies are often people who are very insecure. That is why they pick on people who are weaker than they are. Often bullies are people who have themselves been bullied. How do you think this cycle of bullying might be ended? *(Responses will vary.)* OL AL

Interactive Literary Elements Handbook Have students access the Web site to improve their understanding of stage directions.

Reading in the Real World

Citizenship Explain to students that bullying is a real problem and should not be handled alone. If students are aware of a bullying problem, they should inform a teacher or a parent. It's important to let people in the community know about bullying problems and get some help before someone really gets hurt. Tell students if they know about a bullying problem, they shouldn't be silent or look the other way. We all have a responsibility to look out for each other. Ask students to give suggestions about how to deal with bullies. **AS**

Objectives
- Monitor comprehension
- Identify literary elements: stage direction
- Understand clipped words

Teach

C Critical Thinking

Comprehension **Ask:** How do you know if someone is really your friend? *(Responses will vary.)* **Say:** In the play you are about to read, Josh helps his friend Billy deal with a bully. Make a prediction in your Learner's Notebooks about how Josh might do this. *(Responses will vary.)* **AS**

R Reading Skill

Skimming and Scanning

Say: What do you notice about the words in bold typeface on this page of the play? *(The time, setting, and character names are set in boldface.)* **Ask:** How does this help you scan the play? *(Possible response: You can easily pick out the bold-faced words on the page.)* **AS**

Readability Scores
Dale-Chall: 5.4
DRP: N/A
Lexile: N/A

The Bully of Barksdale Street

by Eric Alter

C Josh outsmarts the neighborhood tough guy—a **tribute** to best friends and baseball-card collectors everywhere. . . .

Characters
BILLY WINSTON, 11
JOSH, 11
BLANE

TIME: *The present.*

SETTING: *A street in a typical American suburb.* **Backdrop** *may show houses if desired. There is a street sign up left that reads,* BARKSDALE STREET. **1**

AT RISE: *Standing underneath the street sign is* BILLY WINSTON. *He wears backpack, holds baseball cards, and looks around nervously. After a moment, he waves to* JOSH, *who enters.* JOSH *also wears backpack.* **2**

JOSH: Hey!

BILLY: Hey!

Vocabulary

tribute (TRIB yoot) *n.* something done to show respect

backdrop (BAK drop) *n.* a curtain or temporary wall that covers the back of a stage

Practice the Skills

1 **Key Literary Element**

Stage Directions Remember that *left* and *right* are from the actor's point of view, and *up* is short for *upstage* which means "toward the back of the stage area, away from the audience." What do you think "up left" means?

2 **Key Literary Element**

Stage Directions "AT RISE" means when the play begins. Where do you think that term came from? (Think about curtains and lights.)

Additional Support

Differentiated Instruction

Design a Graphic Novel To better follow the action of the play, invite students with strong visual comprehension to create a graphic novel version of the play. Have them use what they visualize about each character and their actions in the play to create illustrations. Have students put the character's words in balloons and suggest they explain stage directions at the bottom of each frame. Have volunteers share their work with the class. **AS**

JOSH: You got some new ones, huh?

BILLY (*Looking at his cards*): Yep.

JOSH: Sweet! **3**

BILLY: Thanks for meeting me over here.

JOSH: No problem.

BILLY: Your mom is so nice.

JOSH: How do you know?

BILLY: When I called you last night, she was really nice. Nobody else's mom asks me how I'm doing when I call.

JOSH: Yeah. She's cool. Lets me stay up late, too. (*After a pause*) Hey, get this—I made the baseball team at my school.

BILLY (*Impressed*): No way!

EL JOSH: Yeah! (*They high-five one another.*)

BILLY: Maybe I could come and watch some games.

Practice the Skills

3 | **Key Reading Skill**

Skimming and Scanning
Scan the stage directions for the next two pages to find where Billy "holds up a card proudly." What card does he hold up?

Teach

EL Language Coach

Dialect and Slang Ask: What does the expression "to high-five someone" mean? *(to slap each other's hands in greeting)* **Ask:** What are some other slang or dialect expressions for greeting someone? *(Responses will vary.)* **OL**

The Bully of Barksdale Street **1001**

Literature Focus Lesson

Stage Directions To help students understand the function of stage directions, have groups of three read this page together. Have two students read the lines of dialog, and one student read the stage directions. Afterwards, students can discuss the different kinds of instructions that stage directions can include such as directions for actions and directions for emotions. You may then wish to have students reread the page and utilize the stage directions as they read. **EL** **BL**

Objectives
- Monitor comprehension
- Skim and scan text
- Identify literary elements: stage directions
- Understand dialect and slang
- Evaluate text

Teach

C Critical Thinking

Analysis Ask: How are Billy and Josh similar? *(same age; both are into baseball cards)* **Ask:** How are they different? *(Josh goes to private school, Billy to public school; Billy has a dad, Josh doesn't.)* **BL** **OL**

L Literary Element

Stage Directions Ask: How many times are stage directions given on this page? *(five)* How do you know which words are stage directions? *(Possible response: The stage directions are in italics and between parentheses.)* **BL**

JOSH: I dunno . . . it's far.

BILLY: Yeah. (*After a pause*) I really wish I could go to your school.

JOSH: Yeah, me, too.

BILLY: I don't like school.

JOSH: How come?

BILLY: Just because.

JOSH: You'd like my school. We get to eat lunch outside when it's nice.

BILLY: No way!

JOSH: Yeah. But we start school earlier.

BILLY: Yeah, that's not a good thing.

JOSH: You wanna come over?

BILLY: I can't. I only have like fifteen minutes. I have to go to the hardware store with my dad. He's working on some project for the house this weekend, and he wants me to help.

JOSH: Cool!

BILLY: Not really.

JOSH: Yeah, well, just remember . . . you have a dad.

BILLY: Yeah. Sorry. You know I didn't mean—

JOSH: I know. It's O.K. (*After a pause*) So, what have you got?

BILLY (*Holding a card up proudly*): The Topps Ken Griffey[1]—in mint condition,[2] of course.

JOSH: No way! Lemme see. (JOSH *begins examining the card carefully.*)

BILLY: What have you got to trade? (JOSH *pulls out a huge wad of cards from backpack.*) **4**

---

1. **Ken Griffey** is a famous baseball player.
2. **Mint condition** means that something looks like it is brand new.

Practice the Skills

4 **Key Literary Element**

Stage Directions List three things you learn from the stage directions on this page. **L**

Additional Support

Differentiated Instruction

Build Background Bring in some baseball cards to show to students who may not be familiar with this aspect of American culture. Or, look for a Web site with pictures of baseball cards. Invite knowledgeable students to explain the meaning of the different statistics on the backs of the cards. Then have interested students create their own baseball cards of their favorite ball players. Display their work in the classroom. **EL** **BL** **OL**

JOSH: I got a Kerry Wood . . .

BILLY: Fleer or Topps?[3]

JOSH: Fleer, of course.

BILLY: No way! Lemme see. (*Now* BILLY *examines the card carefully.*)

JOSH: Trade?

L **BILLY** (*Smiling*): Trade! (*They high-five one another.*)

JOSH: O.K. . . . let's see what else I've got.

BILLY: O.K. (JOSH *begins pulling out cards from everywhere. Some fall on the ground.*) **5**

JOSH: They don't let us have baseball cards in school, so I had to sneak them in. I kept a few of them in the back of my math book.

BILLY: Wow. Private school is strict.

JOSH: Not really . . . we can chew gum during lunch.

BILLY: Wow. Is there anything you can't do during lunch?

JOSH: Yeah. (*Smiles*) Trade baseball cards. Do you know how much my collection would grow if I could trade?

BILLY: Yeah. So . . . you guys have gym three times a week? **6**

JOSH: We have it twice a week.

BILLY: We're playing softball now.

JOSH: We're doing **fencing**.

BILLY: Fencing?

JOSH: Yeah, you know . . . swords and stuff.

BILLY: Wow. Man, you private school kids are smart.

---

3. **Kerry Wood** is a famous baseball player. **Topps** and **Fleer** are brands of baseball cards.

Vocabulary . . . .

fencing (FEN sing) *n.* the sport of fighting with swords

Practice the Skills

5 **Key Literary Element**

Stage Directions Using these stage directions, how could the actor who plays Josh make this a funny moment in the play?

6 **English Language Coach**

Clipped Words There is a clipped word in this line. In your Learner's Notebook write the clipped word and the whole word that it comes from.

The Bully of Barksdale Street **1003**

Teach

L Literary Element

Stage Direction **Ask:** What stage direction does the author give after Billy says "Trade!"? (*They high-five one another.*) **BL** **Ask:** Why do you think the author chose to include this direction in the script? (*Possible response: to indicate to the actors that they should show enthusiasm and agreement for the trade*) **OL** **AL**

Literature Focus Lesson

Stage Directions Point out to students that many lines contain no stage directions. Ask: What do you think the characters are doing in these places? (*Responses will vary.*) Why do you think the author often leaves out stage directions? (*Possible response: to allow actors to find their own actions and movements*) Discuss how stage directions can be used either sparingly or extensively. In their Learner's Notebooks, have students write additional stage directions that they think could be included on this page of the play. **AS**

Objectives
- Analyze text
- Identify literary elements: stage direction

1003

Teach

C1 Critical Thinking

Application Say: The author includes many ellipses in Billy's lines of dialogue. What do ellipses indicate in dialogue? *(a pause)* Why might the author have included so many ellipses here? *(Possible response: to show that Billy feels embarrassed and slightly uncomfortable about having lost cards he promised to trade with Josh)* **OL**

C2 Critical Thinking

Evaluation Ask: Do you think the author succeeds in realistically portraying Billy? Explain your response. *(Responses will vary.)* **BL OL**

JOSH (*Laughing*): What else you got?

BILLY (*Shrugging*): Um . . . not much.

JOSH: What do you mean?

BILLY: Well, I uh . . . kinda lost some.

JOSH: Lost some? What do you mean?

C1 **BILLY:** Nothing. I just . . . well . . . (*Shrugs*) lost some of 'em.

JOSH: Baseball cards are like—candy. You don't lose them!

BILLY: Yeah . . . well, I did.

JOSH: How many did you lose? (BILLY *doesn't answer.*) You still have my Sammy Sosa[4] you promised me, right?

BILLY: Um . . . well . . . **7**

JOSH: Billy! You promised me. I had to trade some serious players for that!

BILLY: I know, I know. I'm sorry, Josh.

JOSH: Well, what about Clemens? I know you have Roger Clemens,[5] right?

BILLY (*Shaking his head quickly no*): Lost it.

JOSH: Where?!

C2 **BILLY:** On my way home from school.

JOSH: Are you kidding me?

BILLY: No.

JOSH: How long ago?

BILLY: Last week sometime.

JOSH: Well, let's go and see if we can find them! Maybe no one picked them up yet. It hasn't rained in a week. They could be—

BILLY (*Interrupting*): Nah . . . they're probably just gone.

---

4. **Sammy Sosa** is a famous baseball player.
5. **Roger Clemens** is a famous baseball player.

Practice the Skills

7 **Key Literary Element**

Stage Directions In your Learner's Notebook, write stage directions for this short line so that the audience can see how Billy feels. Write one stage direction that tells how the lines should be delivered (tone of voice, emotion) and one stage direction that tells what Billy should be doing while he says his line.

Additional Support

Reading in the Real World

Career Some students may be interested in careers in baseball. Have interested students conduct Internet or library research to learn more about the skills and training needed to pursue this kind of career. You may also wish to have students read short biographies of well-known players such as Sammy Sosa and Roger Clemens and report on how these two famous stars got their start in baseball. **BL OL**

JOSH: I don't understand. . . . (*Suddenly* BILLY *notices someone behind* JOSH. *He squints to make the person out while* JOSH *just keeps* **rambling** *on.*) Roger Clemens . . . (*Shakes head*) Man, how does someone lose Roger Clemens?

BILLY: Oh, no. Not here.

JOSH: What?

BILLY: No!

JOSH: What's the matter?

BILLY (*Quickly*): Look . . . I lied, O.K.?

JOSH: About what? You still have Roger Clemens?

BILLY: No, I lied about losing them. I didn't exactly lose them.

JOSH: What's wrong with you? What? (JOSH *begins to look behind him.*)

BILLY: No, don't look behind you!

JOSH: Why? What's going on?

BILLY: O.K., I gotta go. (*Bends down and begins packing up his books*)

JOSH: Billy, what's wrong?

BILLY: I didn't lose them. This kid, Blane Davenport . . . he took them.

JOSH: Huh?

BILLY: Look, this kid's been bothering me, and he's about— please don't turn around . . . he's about a hundred yards from us. He never comes this way! I thought I'd be safe.

JOSH: Wait a sec . . . this kid Blane has been bothering you? 8

BILLY: Yeah. I try and race home every day, but he always catches up with me.

Practice the Skills

8 **English Language Coach**

Clipped Words What is the clipped word in this line? Write it and the word it comes from in your Learner's Notebook.

Vocabulary

rambling (RAM bling) *v.* talking in a disorganized manner

The Bully of Barksdale Street **1005**

Teach

R Reading Skill

Skimming and Scanning

Say: Quickly skim this page and say what happens in the plot. What new twist in the story is introduced? *(Possible response: It's clear that Billy didn't just lose the cards, and that he appears to be afraid of someone coming up behind them.)*
Ask: What do you think will happen next? *(Responses will vary.)* **AS**

Literature Focus Lesson

Stage Directions Discuss the role that the stage directions play on this page. Have students try reading the page while leaving out the stage directions. Discuss how stage directions are sometimes critical to understanding what is going on in a play. Ask volunteers to act out this scene from the play first without using the stage directions, then have them act it out again including the directions. Discuss with students how including the stage directions made the scene different. **BL OL**

Objectives
• Identify literary elements: stage directions, dialogue
• Skim and scan text
• Evaluate text

Teach

Viewing the Illustration

Ask: What does this illustration show? *(It shows the three characters: Josh, Billy, and Blane.)* How does this illustration help you visualize the action in the play? *(Responses will vary. Students may say the image helps them visualize how much bigger Blane the bully is compared to Billy and Josh.)* **AS**

C Critical Thinking

Evaluation Ask: What do you think of the way Billy has been dealing with the bully up until this point? *(Responses will vary.)* **OL AL**

JOSH: What grade is he in?

BILLY: Seventh. He's huge.

JOSH: And lemme guess . . . he likes baseball cards?

BILLY: If I give him cards, he doesn't rearrange my face. It's a nice agreement. I gotta run. . . .

JOSH: Wait a second. Just wait a second.

BILLY: I really don't want to stick around. . . .

JOSH: How far is he?

BILLY: Thirty yards.

JOSH: Stand up. **9**

BILLY (*Confused*): What are you—

JOSH: Stand up! I want you to do exactly what I tell you to do.

BILLY: What're you talking about? He'll **pummel** us both!

JOSH: Just do what I tell you to do, O.K.?

Vocabulary

pummel (PUM ul) *v.* to hit or beat someone

1006 UNIT 8 What Makes a Friend?

Practice the Skills

9 **◄BIG Question**

Billy "lost" the baseball cards that Josh was expecting. Is Josh mad at Billy for not having the cards? What does Josh's reaction tell you about their friendship?

Additional Support

Reading Fluency

Build Fluency Invite students to work in pairs to read the dialog on this page. Point out the ellipses on the page. Remind students that the ellipses represent sentences that trail off, expressing incomplete thoughts and representing short pauses. Have students find a quiet place to practice reading aloud the passage. Have them reread the passage several times with a partner until they can both smoothly read all the sentences, pausing to allow space for ellipses. **EL BL**

Practice the Skills

BILLY: No, I don't want—(BLANE DAVENPORT *enters.*)

JOSH (*Firmly*): Billy, just do what I tell you to do . . . understand?

BLANE (*Calling out*): Hey, Winston!

JOSH (*After a pause, in a loud voice, to* BILLY): I said . . . I want to see all your cards!

BILLY: Huh?

JOSH (*Whispering*): Do what I say. (*After a pause, again in a loud voice*) I said I want to see your cards! Now! Open your bag and let me see!

BLANE (*Calling out,* **mocking**): Oh, Winston! (*Crosses to join* JOSH *and* BILLY)

JOSH (*To* BILLY; *loudly*): Forget about him. Do what I tell you. (BILLY *grabs some cards and hands them to* JOSH.) This is it? This is all you've got?

BLANE: Hey, what's—(JOSH *turns to face* BLANE; *gives him an up-and-down stare.*) **10**

JOSH (*To* BLANE): Hey, pal, beat it, would ya? I'm working over here. (*After a pause; to* BILLY) I asked you a question! I said is this all you have?!

BLANE: Hey—

JOSH (*Slowly turning to* BLANE): Hey, maybe you didn't hear me. I said I'm working over here.

BLANE (*Puzzled*): What do you mean?

JOSH: I mean I'm taking this kid's baseball cards. It's what I do around here. I take all the cards that I want.

BLANE (*Laughing*): Are you kidding me? You? How about I take your cards and his cards. (*He looks down* **menacingly** *at* JOSH. JOSH *doesn't flinch.*)

Vocabulary

mocking (MOK ing) *v.* making fun of someone by imitating the person in a ridiculous manner

menacingly (MEN uh sing lee) *adv.* in a threatening manner

10 | **Key Literary Element**

Stage Directions Josh gives Blane an "up-and-down stare." What do you think that kind of stare means? **L**

The Bully of Barksdale Street **1007**

Teach

L Literary Element

Stage Directions Say: The author includes a lot of stage direction on this page. Why might he have included so many directions? *(Possible response: The addition of the stage direction helps readers feel the tension that is building in this scene. Also, the direction helps readers recognize the deception that Josh is trying to create to fool Blane.)* **AL**

Literature Focus Lesson

Stereotypes Review the meaning of the term "stereotype" with students: an oversimplified idea about a group of people. Invite students to say whether they think the character of Blane is a stereotype of a bully. Have students explain their answers. Discuss how this portrait of a bully is perhaps a stereotype, but also contains some truth. Ask students if they think there are other stereotypical characters in the play. **AS**

Objectives
- Evaluate text
- Identify literary elements: stage directions, stereotype
- Use text features: illustrations

1007

Teach

C Critical Thinking

Evaluation Ask: How would you describe Josh's strategy towards Blane? *(Responses will vary.)* Do you think his strategy will be effective? Explain your answers. *(Responses will vary.)* **AS**

BILLY: I could just give both you guys my cards—

JOSH (*Breaking from* BLANE's *stare*): I said be quiet. I will deal with you in a minute. (*Goes back to staring at* BLANE) You could try—and I do mean try. But you see, you're wearing white. **11**

BLANE: Yeah, so?

JOSH: You ever see blood get on a white shirt?

BLANE: Huh?

JOSH: Doesn't come out. Trust me. Three days ago, I knocked a kid's front teeth out, blood got all on my good white shirt—had to throw it out. (*After a long pause*) But if you'd like to give it a go, we could. (*Quick pause*) But lemme just warn you . . . well, I am supposed to warn you—that's what my karate instructor tells me. He says with my talent and speed, I should warn someone before I fight him . . . and if I do, and they choose to continue to fight me, the police won't press charges.

BLANE: Huh?

JOSH: Enough of this talk. (*After a beat, turns to* BILLY, *then checks his watch*) This is only gonna take about two minutes, and when I'm done, I'm gonna deal with you. So don't run off, or else I'm gonna have to chase you down. (*Turns to* BLANE) You ready?

BLANE: What was that you said about karate?

JOSH: What about it? Been doing it since I was five. Black belt. Why?

BLANE: Well, I . . . uh . . .

JOSH: You—uh—nothing. You mean you never heard of me?

BLANE (*Shaking his head*): No. You don't go to our school.

JOSH: 'Course I don't. I go to reform school. They wouldn't let me in that public school.

BLANE: How come?

Practice the Skills

11 **BIG** Question
Why does Josh tell Billy to be quiet? Is Josh really being rude to Billy?

Additional Support

Differentiated Instruction

Stage Directions In the middle of the page, the stage directions state, *(After a beat, turns to BILLY, then checks his watch.)* Discuss the meaning of this stage direction with students. Then invite volunteers to read Josh's line and demonstrate how they would interpret that stage direction. **EL BL**

JOSH: How come? (*Snorts in laughter*) 'Cause in fourth grade I was shaking down kids for lunch money every day. One of the kids happened to be the nephew of the principal. Bad scene. **12**

BLANE: Wow.

JOSH: This is my area. I deal with all the kids from South Orange Middle School.

BLANE: Yeah, but—

JOSH: That is . . . until this kid here tells me he doesn't have the Roger Clemens that I want, or the Sammy Sosa, and a bunch of other cards, and that gets me mad. (*After a pause*) Wait a second . . . are you really telling me you never heard of me?

BLANE (*After a long pause*): Not really. (JOSH *begins looking around; the street sign catches his attention.*)

JOSH: I'm the bully of Barksdale Street.

BLANE (*Slowly nodding*): Yeah. (*Smiling*) Oh, yeah . . . I think I have heard of you.

JOSH: You think?

BLANE (*Nodding*): I remember it now.

JOSH (*Slowly nodding*): You're interfering with my territory, Blane.

BLANE: How'd you know my name?

JOSH: You don't think I do my homework? Billy here tells me you've been shaking him down for the past few weeks.

BLANE: Yeah, but I—

JOSH (*Smiling calmly*): Look, I can somewhat appreciate what you do. (*Looks at* BILLY, *then winks at him*) I mean, he's a weakling, but he's my weakling, you understand?

BLANE: I . . . uh . . . guess.

Practice the Skills

12 English Language Coach

Clipped Words There's a clipped word in this speech. Find the clipped word, and write it and the word it comes from in your Learner's Notebook.

The Bully of Barksdale Street **1009**

Teach

C Critical Thinking

Evaluation Ask: How does Josh manage to convince Blane that Josh is also a bully? *(Responses will vary.)* By referring to Billy as a weakling, does Josh gain Blane's trust? Explain. *(Responses will vary.)* **OL AS**

Viewing the Illustration
Say: What character in the play does this illustration represent *(Blane)* Does he look different than he did earlier in the selection? *(Possible response: He still looks big, but now he also looks confused and a little afraid.)* **EL BL**

English Language Coach

Dialect and Slang There are several slang expressions on this page: *shaking down kids for lunch money, interfering with my territory, do my homework.* Discuss the figurative meaning of these expressions in terms of the context of this scene. Discuss the connotations of these expressions, i.e., illegal activities, gangsters, etc. Discuss with students how a playwright needs to have what is called a "good ear" for dialogue and the way different characters speak. **OL**

Objectives
• Evaluate text
• Use text features: illustrations
• Identify literary elements: stage direction
• Understand dialect and slang

1009

Teach

C Critical Thinking

Comprehension Ask: Do you think Josh's strategy towards Blane would work in real life? Explain your answer. (*Responses will vary.*) **AS**

JOSH: You see, Blane, I don't think it's such a good idea for you to be bullying people. Not around here, anyway . . . not anyone at South Orange Middle School. That's my neck of the woods. (*Loudly*) Understand?!

BLANE (*Slowly nodding*): Uh-huh.

JOSH: Now, before you go, I want you to understand: I don't want Billy touched. That's my job. Get it?

BLANE: Uh-huh.

JOSH: Good. And before I let you go . . . I think there's something you have that belongs to me.

BLANE: Huh?

JOSH: Roger Clemens, Sammy Sosa, and a bunch of other cards you took from my kid over here.

BLANE (*Stalling*): I—uh—I don't have them on me.

JOSH: Oh, boy.

BLANE (*Quickly***):** But I can get them to you. I'll give them to Billy first thing tomorrow. Then he can give them to you. (*After a pause*) You'd make sure he gets them, right, Billy?

BILLY (*To* JOSH): You're gonna want all the cards, right? (*Winks at* JOSH)

JOSH: Yeah, Blane . . . all of 'em. (*After a beat*) So, we have an understanding, right? **13**

BLANE: Yeah, we do.

JOSH: Good. Now, if you'll excuse me, I've got some pummeling of my own to do.

BLANE: Oh, yeah . . . sure.

JOSH: In other words . . . BEAT IT.

BLANE: Good luck, Billy. (BLANE *runs off.*)

JOSH (*Calling out*): Don't forget the cards!

BILLY (*Shaking his head*): That was amazing.

Practice the Skills

13 **Key Literary Element**

Stage Directions A *beat* is a pause. Why do you think the playwright indicated a "beat" here?

Additional Support

Literature Focus Lesson

Character Have students describe what is really at the heart of the character of a bully according to this portrait of a bully. Responses will vary, but students should understand that at heart, bullies are themselves cowardly. Discuss how drama can reveal character, and how that is similar to or different from the way character is revealed in fiction. **OL**

JOSH: Is he gone?

BILLY: Long gone. (*JOSH lets out the longest sigh.*) Josh, I don't know what to say. That was . . . incredible!

JOSH (*Relieved*): Whew . . . he bought it.

BILLY: I am amazed! How did you—

JOSH (*Shrugging*):Bullies . . . they're not used to anyone standing up to them. That's why they're bullies. They pick on people smaller, people they think won't give them any problems. (*After a pause*) But the moment you stand up to one, that can all change.

BILLY (*Smiling*): The Bully of Barksdale Street?

JOSH: Has a nice ring to it, huh? (*They laugh.*)

BILLY: I don't know how to say thanks.

JOSH: Don't worry about it . . . you'd do the same for me.

BILLY: What would you have done if it didn't work?

JOSH: Run. Fast. Very fast.

BILLY: Yeah.

JOSH: He could only get one of us then, right? (Laughing)

BILLY (*Laughing*): Man . . . you're smart, Josh . . . really smart. (*They high-five one another as curtain falls.*) **14**

THE END

Practice the Skills

14 **BIG Question**
How would you describe the friendship between Josh and Billy? What makes them such good friends? Write your answers on the "Bully of Barksdale Street" page of Foldable 8. Your response will help you complete the Unit Challenge later.

The Bully of Barksdale Street **1011**

Teach

Viewing the Illustration
Say: Describe the illustration. (*It shows the characters Josh and Billy high-fiving each other.*) **BL**
Ask: What does this illustration indicate about the characters? (*Possible response: that Josh and Billy are proud of themselves for out-smarting the bully together*) **OL**

EL Language Coach
Connotation Ask: Why do you think the playwright created the street name *Barksdale*, which he then uses in the title? (*Responses will vary. Help students understand that* Barksdale *includes the word* bark, *which makes you think of a barking dog. The connotation makes you think of the expression. A dog's bark is often worse than his bite. In other words, tough guys aren't always as tough as they appear.*) **AS**

Differentiated Instruction

Sequencing To help students understand the concept of dramatic development, have them review the sequence of events in the play. Introduce the terms *rising action* (circumstances of the main conflict), *climax* (moment when the climax comes to a peak), and *falling action* (what happens after the climax, or the winding down of the plot, the after-effects). Invite students to use these terms to plot the play's structure with a line graph. **AS**

Objectives
• Monitor comprehension
• Interpret and analyze character
• Understand word connotation
• Use text features: illustrations

Assess

Resources for page 1012

📁 Selection Quick Check. p. 75

📁 Selection and Unit Assessment, p. 89

💿 ExamView Assessment Suite

💿 Interactive Tutor: Self-Assessment

Students can respond to the *After You Read* items in their Learner's Notebooks or on a separate sheet of paper.

Answering the

BIG Question

1. Responses will vary. Students should explain their answer by drawing on events from the selection.

2. Josh

3. In their own words, students should summarize how Josh helps Billy get his baseball cards back.

Critical Thinking

4. Responses will vary. Students should say whether or not they think Billy would still like to go to Josh's school at the end of the story, and support their responses with details from the selection.

5. Students should give reasons for their answers, based on clues in the story, and on what they know from their own experience.

6. Students should give reasons for their answers based on clues in the story and on their own experience.

1012

After You Read

The Bully of Barksdale Street

Answering the **BIG Question**

1. In your opinion, what kind of help should you be able to expect from a friend when you are in trouble? Explain your answer by drawing on events from the selection.

2. **Recall** Which of the boys made the baseball team at school?
   Tip Right There

3. **Summarize** In your own words, summarize how Josh helps Billy get his baseball cards back.
   Tip Think and Search

Critical Thinking

4. **Interpret** Why did Billy wish that he could go to Josh's school at the beginning of the story? Do you think he would still like to go to Josh's school at the end of the story? Refer to specific places in the text that support your answer.
   Tip Author and Me

5. **Evaluate** Do you think that the trick Josh plays on Blane is a realistic solution to Billy's problem? Explain the reasons for your answer.
   Tip Author and Me

6. **Synthesize** At the end of the play, what do you think Billy has learned about dealing with bullies? If another bully tried to take away his baseball cards, do you think he would do anything differently? Explain your answer.
   Tip Author and Me

Objectives (pp. 1012–1013)
Reading Skim and scan text • Make connections from text to self
Literature Understand elements of drama: stage directions
Vocabulary Identify clipped words
Writing Use the RAFT system: letter to the editor
Grammar Use punctuation correctly: colons in time notations, in salutations

Write About Your Reading

Use the RAFT system to write about "The Bully of Barksdale Street."

Role: Josh

Audience: Middle school students who are having trouble with bullies

Format: Letter to be published in the school newspaper

Topic: How to deal with a bully

Write a letter to the editor that could be published in a school newspaper, telling students how they can deal with a bully.

Write About Your Reading

Sample response:
Dear Editor:
    One big problem that many kids have is dealing with bullies. It can be dangerous, and every kid should know what to do if confronted with a bully. Most importantly, let other people, especially adults, know about the person who is threatening you. Avoid confronting the person alone. Also, don't act frightened or intimidated. Remember that often bullies are people who have been bullied themselves. In fact, bullying is a sign of cowardliness. If we stick together, we can deal with bullies, and maybe even help them change their ways.
Sincerely, Josh

Skills Review

Key Reading Skill: Skimming and Scanning

7. After you have read a text, if there's a particular fact from the text that you can't remember, would you skim the text or scan the text to find the answer?

Key Literary Element: Stage Directions

8. What is the setting for "The Bully of Barksdale Street"?

9. Besides describing the setting, list at least three things that stage directions can do.

Vocabulary Check

For each sentence, choose the word in boldface type that best fits in the blank.

**pummel   tribute   fencing   menacingly
rambling   mocking   backdrop**

10. In Elise's speech, she was ___ so much that we couldn't tell what she was trying to say.

11. The honors ceremony was a ___ to the students who had worked so hard.

12. The ___ hangs at the back of the stage.

13. Craig was ___ the girls when he talked with an exaggerated version of their accent.

14. Jeremy was afraid the bully would ___ him.

15. Ike looked ___ at his enemy before he attacked.

16. Lauren doesn't like swords, so I don't think she would like ___ .

17. **English Language Coach** In your Learner's Notebook, write the clipped word that would come from each of these words: gasoline, hamburger, airplane.

Grammar Link: Using Colons in Time Notations and After Salutations

• Use a colon to separate the hour and the minutes when you write the time of day.

Mr. Jordon announced that Violet Haskins would arrive at the gymnasium at exactly 12:14 P.M.

• Also use a colon after the salutation, or greeting, of a business letter.

Dear Mr. Spencer:

Grammar Practice

Add a colon wherever one is necessary.

18. Dear Mr. Greenberg

19. The parade will start at exactly 11 00 a.m.

20. At about 11 30 a.m. the parade will turn right on Valen Street.

Writing Application Review the Write About Your Reading activity. Make sure that you used colons correctly after the salutation of the letter and in any time notations.

Web Activities For eFlashcards, Selection Quick Checks, and other Web activities, go to www.glencoe.com.

The Bully of Barksdale Street **1013**

Skills Review

Key Reading Skill: Skimming and Scanning

7. Responses will vary.

Key Literary Element: Stage Directions

8. A suburban street not far from a middle school

9. Possible response: what action an actor should take, what emotion an actor should express, and when an actor should pause

Vocabulary Check

10. rambling
11. tribute
12. backdrop
13. mocking
14. pummel
15. menacingly
16. fencing

English Language Coach: Clipped Words

17. gas, burger, airplane

Close

Ask students to summarize what they learned from the selection to help them answer the Big Question.

Grammar Link: Using Colons in Time Notations and After Salutations

Grammar Practice

18. Dear Mr. Greenberg:
19. 11:00
20. 11:30

Teach

More About the Author

Christina Hamlett's book "ScreenTEENwriters" is full of idea-starter exercises for would-be screenwriters and playwrights. Some of the areas of scriptwriting that she addresses include: dialogue, character development, structure, pacing, originality, marketability and recommendations for direct submission, film festivals, and scriptwriting competitions. Plus, she offers plenty of "been there/done that" advice from industry pros.

V Vocabulary

Plurals Say: Notice that *tresses* and *frills* are both plurals. When do you add -*es* as a plural ending and when do you add just -*s*? *(For most nouns, simply add* -*s. For words ending in* ch, s, sh, ss, x, *and* z, *add* -*es.)* **OL** Review with students the other rules for making singular words plural: y to i and add -*es;* f or *fe* to v and add -*es;* most words ending in o, add -*es;* musical words ending in o, just add -*s*.

Before You Read : Tales of the Tangled Tresses

Christina Hamlett

Meet the Author

A former actress and theater director, Christina Hamlett has written more than 20 books and 110 plays and musicals. One of her books is designed to help teenagers write their own plays. Hamlett has also written hundreds of articles on topics ranging from the performing arts to travel. She lives in California.

Literature Online

Author Search For more about Christina Hamlett, go to www.glencoe.com.

Objectives (pp. 1014–1029)
Reading Skim and scan text • Make connections from text to self
Literature Understand elements of drama: stage directions
Vocabulary Identify jargon

Vocabulary Preview

tresses (TRES uz) *n.* long hair **(p. 1016)** *She combed her lovely dark tresses.*

frills (frilz) *n.* things that are added on for decoration but are not really necessary **(p. 1016)** *Jack bought a basic CD player with no frills or added features.*

brunette (broo NET) *n.* a person with black or brown hair **(p. 1020)** *The brunette next to Ahmed dropped her soda.*

widower (WID oh ur) *n.* a man whose wife has died **(p. 1021)** *My uncle has been a widower for four years.*

fiasco (fee AS koh) *n.* something that has failed completely, possibly in a ridiculous way **(p. 1022)** *When Edith tried to paint her room, it turned into a real fiasco.*

Write to Learn Using at least three of the vocabulary words, write a one-paragraph story about getting a haircut. Find a partner and read each other's stories.

English Language Coach

Jargon There is a special kind of slang called **jargon.** (It's also called "lingo.") Jargon is easily understood by members of a group but often unknown to other people. The group may be people who do the same kind of work or who share a particular interest.

In almost any job, there are words or terms that are known to people who do that kind of work. Doctors, computer programmers, cooks, and hairdressers have their own jargon. Activities other than work also have their own jargon. In baseball jargon, a *can of corn* is a fly ball that's easy to catch. In rock-and-roll jargon, an *axe* is a guitar.

As you read, look for examples of jargon. Use context clues to figure out what the term might mean. If context doesn't provide a good idea, look in a dictionary. Like any slang, if jargon is used for long enough, it becomes part of the language and enters the dictionary.

Group Talk In a small group, try to list several examples of jargon that your parents, grandparents, or some other people in your class might not understand. Then write down who might use those terms and the meaning of each term. Compare your lists with other groups.

Additional Support

Literature Online

Author Search To expand students' appreciation of Christina Hamlett, have them access the Web site for more information and resources.

English Language Coach

Jargon Invite students to report back to the class on the examples of jargon that they brainstormed in small groups. Discuss the difference between jargon and slang and idioms. Explain that jargon is usually related to a particular profession or area of expertise. Slang is used commonly in daily life. In their Learner's Notebooks, have students keep a list of jargon that they come across in the selection. **AS**

Skills Preview

Key Reading Skill: Skimming and Scanning

When you skim and scan a piece of literature, you can get an idea of when and where it takes place, whether it is realistic or not, and whether it is serious or funny.

Write to Learn Before you read "Tales of the Tangled Tresses" carefully, skim and scan it to find out the answers to the questions from page 997 that you wrote in your Learner's Notebook. Answer them.

Key Literary Element: Stage Directions

Stage directions tell the actors what to do while the play is going on. For example, if a stage direction says *[picks up telephone]*, then the actor pauses and picks up the telephone.

Stage directions also tell the director of the play when to use sound, lighting, and other special effects on stage. For example, a stage direction might say *[The painting on the wall suddenly crashes to the floor]*.

Stage directions are
- printed in *italics* and are often set in *brackets* [ ] or *parentheses*.
- not spoken aloud when the play is performed

Literature Online

Interactive Literary Elements Handbook
To review or learn more about the literary elements, go to www.glencoe.com.

Get Ready to Read

Connect to the Reading

Does anyone you know go to a particular store, shop, or restaurant to find out the neighborhood news or hang out with friends? As you read this play, imagine what you would think if you were sitting in the Fabulous Frills Salon while all these unusual people came in and told their stories.

Partner Talk With your partner, discuss places in your neighborhood where people go to hang out with friends.

Build Background

A beauty salon is a shop where people can have their hair cut, colored, and styled and makeup applied. Many people make close friendships with the people they meet at beauty salons or barber shops.

In this play, some of the characters who are mentioned are from famous myths.
- In ancient Greek mythology, King Menelaus's wife, Helen, was kidnapped by a man named Paris and taken off to the city of Troy. The Trojan War was fought to get Helen back from Troy.
- Midas was a king who wished that everything he touched would turn to gold. His wish was granted.
- Medusa had snakes on her head instead of hair. Anyone who looked at her turned to stone.

Set Purposes for Reading

BIG Question Read "Tales of the Tangled Tresses" to see how two friends who work together deal with some unusual customers.

Set Your Own Purpose What else would you like to learn from the selection that might help you answer the Big Question? Write your own purpose for reading on the "Tales of the Tangled Tresses" page of Foldable 8.

Keep Moving

Use these skills as you read the following selection.

Tales of the Tangled Tresses **1015**

Teach

C Critical Thinking

Comprehension Ask: What makes a story or play fantastical as opposed to realistic? *(Possible response: Fantasies contain people, places, or events that do not or could not exist in real life.)* As students scan the selection, have them jot down things they notice that are elements of a fantasy. **AS**

Literature Online

Interactive Literary Elements Handbook Have students access the Web site to improve their understanding of stage directions.

Literature Focus Lesson

Plot Review the terms *rising action* (circumstances of the main conflict), *climax* (moment when the climax comes to a peak), and *falling action* and *resolution* (what happens after the climax, and the after-effects or results). Invite students to track events from the play on this chart: **OL**

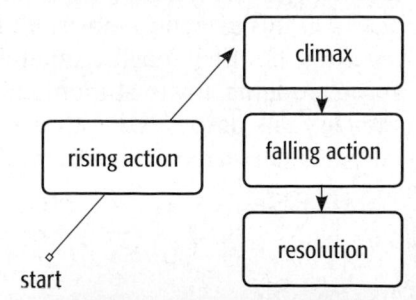

Objectives
- Learn and use new vocabulary
- Understand jargon
- Identify literary elements: plot

1015

Teach

C Critical Thinking

Comprehension Say: Imagine this group of fairy tale characters altogether in one room. How do you think they would get along? *(Answers will vary.)* **OL**

L Literary Element

Stage Directions Ask: When does this play take place? *(the present)* **BL** How might this add humor to the play? *(Possible response: Most of the characters are from tales set in times past. Setting them in the present gives them a "fish-out-of-water" quality, which adds humor.)* **AL**

Readability Scores
Dale-Chall: 5.0
DRP: N/A
Lexile: N/A

Tales of the Tangled Tresses [1]

by Christina Hamlett

Fairy tale characters get major makeovers at Fabulous Frills Salon. . . .

Characters
OLIVIA, owner of the Fabulous Frills Salon
HILDA, her assistant
GOLDILOCKS
RAPUNZEL
C CINDERELLA
BRIAR ROSE
ALICE

SCENE 1

[**TIME:** The present.]

[**SETTING:** *Reception area of Fabulous* **Frills** *Salon; color scheme is pink and white. Receptionist table with a phone on it is down left. Three archways leading to "styling booths" are upstage. Main entrance to salon is right. Photos of different hairstyles adorn walls, and wig heads, hair spray cans, magazines, etc., round out the salon décor.*] **2**

Vocabulary

tresses (TRES uz) *n.* long hair

frills (frilz) *n.* things that are added on for decoration but are not really necessary

1016 UNIT 8 What Makes a Friend?

Practice the Skills

1 Key Literary Skill

Skimming and Scanning
Skim the play before you read it to answer these two questions.
• Where and when does the play take place?
• Is the play real-life or fantasy?

2 Key Literary Element

Stage Directions Notice that the scene begins with stage directions that tell the reader where and when the action is taking place. Can you picture this scene in your head? Review the definitions on page 939. Then, in your Learner's Notebook, make a rough drawing of what you think the set would look like. **L**

Additional Support

Differentiated Instruction

Reading Fairy Tales Five of the characters in this selection are fairy tale favorites, but they may be unfamiliar to some students. Invite students to read the fairy tale associated with each of the fairy tale characters. Have them discuss the tales and the role of each main character. Invite students to take notes about the characters and the events in each tale, and refer back to them as they read the selection. **AS**

AT RISE: *OLIVIA is sitting at table doing her nails. HILDA enters from one of the arches and crosses to her. Both women have extreme hairstyles.*

HILDA (*Sighing heavily*): This has to be the slowest day we've ever had!

OLIVIA: You can say that again. I'm almost tempted to close up shop and call it a day.

HILDA: That's pretty bad, considering it's not even lunchtime yet.

OLIVIA: Well, we've styled and restyled each other's hair so much already that—(*Phone rings.*)

HILDA: Hey! Things could be looking up!

OLIVIA (*Answering phone*): Fabulous Frills Salon. Olivia speaking. . . . This afternoon? (*Smiles at HILDA*) Yes, I'm pretty sure we can fit you in. (*Reaches for the calendar*) Name, please? . . . Helen. . . . Yes, two-o'clock would be fine. . . . A special occasion? (*Nods*) Your face is going to launch a thousand ships so you want to look your best for the press? Well, don't worry, Helen. My assistant Hilda will send you out in style. See you at two. (*Hangs up*) **3**

HILDA: A new client? Where's she from?

OLIVIA: She says she's from Sparta[1] and her last name is Menelaus.

HILDA: Wow! You think she's any relation to the king?

OLIVIA: It sure wouldn't hurt our business if she was. Can you imagine the publicity that would generate? Anyway, she says she wants to look special for Paris.

HILDA: Sounds like there's going to be a big tip in it if she's pleased.

OLIVIA: In your capable hands, Hilda, how could she be anything else?

---

1. *Sparta* was a city in ancient Greece. The caller, *Helen,* is Helen of Troy.

Practice the Skills

3 | **Key Literary Element**

Stage Directions Look over the stage directions during this speech. Can you visualize what Olivia is doing as she's talking on the phone? Why do you think Olivia smiles at Hilda?

Tales of the Tangled Tresses **1017**

Teach

BQ **BIG Question**

Say: Hilda is Olivia's employee and they work together every day. Do you think they are also friends? Explain. (*Responses will vary.*) **AS**

C Critical Thinking

Analysis Say: Reread Olivia's phone conversation. What do the ellipses indicate? (*pauses*) **Ask:** Why did the author include ellipses here? (*Possible response: Olivia's character is talking on the phone. The ellipses show the reader when the caller is speaking.*) **OL**

English Language Coach

Idioms Students whose first language is not English may have trouble understanding the following expressions or idioms: *close up shop, call it a day, things could be looking up.* Have students create a three-column chart with the following headings: Idiom, Literal Meaning, and Figurative Meaning. Have students work in pairs with students whose first language is English to fill in the chart. Encourage students to add other unfamiliar expressions to the list as they read. **EL** **BL** **OL**

Objectives
• Monitor comprehension
• Understand idioms
• Identify literary elements: dialogue, stage directions

1017

Teach

R1 Reading Skill

Skimming and Scanning Say: Quickly scan this page. Which new character is introduced? *(Goldilocks)* Skim the page. Why did she go to the Fabulous Frills Salon? *(Possible response: She's being pursued by three bears and wants Olivia and Hilda to help her out.)* **AS**

R2 Reading Skill

Review Predicting Ask: Do you think that Hilda and Olivia will be able to help Goldilocks get "out of a lot of hot water"? Explain your prediction. *(Responses will vary.)* **OL**

HILDA: Well, as you always say, don't count your curlers until they're in! (*A breathless GOLDILOCKS suddenly rushes in, looking behind her as if she's being pursued.*)

OLIVIA: Can I help you?

GOLDILOCKS: Is this the Fabulous Frills Salon?

HILDA: At your service. I'm Hilda and this is my boss, Olivia.

GOLDILOCKS: And is it true what your sign says: "Curl Up to a New You"?

OLIVIA (*Pleased*): I thought of that slogan[2] myself.

HILDA: What can we do for you, Miss . . . ?

GOLDILOCKS: Locks. Goldi Locks. And what you can do is get me out of a lot of hot water!

OLIVIA: What seems to be the problem?

R1 GOLDILOCKS: Well, it all started with these three bears—

OLIVIA and HILDA (*In unison; startled*): Bears?! **4**

GOLDILOCKS: Yeah, there's a father bear, a mother bear, and a little kid bear who's really a whiner.

OLIVIA: And you say you know these bears personally, dear?

GOLDILOCKS: Oh, I've seen 'em wandering around the neighborhood, but we've never been formally introduced. Anyway, it seems they've got a warrant out for my arrest.

HILDA: Why would a bunch of bears want to arrest someone they don't even know?

---

2. A *slogan* is a short, catchy phrase that is used to advertise a product or store.

Practice the Skills

4 BIG Question
Do you have a friend so close that you finish each other's sentences or say the same things at the same time? Do you think Olivia and Hilda have this kind of friendship?

"Goldilocks" is the next customer at Fabulous Frills.

Analyzing the Art What is Goldilocks doing in this picture? Whose house is she in? How do you know?

Additional Support

Literature Focus Lesson

Characterization The art on this page shows Goldilocks eating from the smallest bowl of the Three Bears. Discuss this image and the kinds of associations it conveys about the story of Goldilocks. (*a basically harmless but overly curious girl,* *dangerously hot soup, a beautiful rustic setting outside*) Invite students to give their interpretation of the "lesson" of the Goldilocks story. Have them explain their interpretations. **AS**

GOLDILOCKS: Listen, it's nothing serious, really. I wandered into their house by mistake and they got in a big huff about it. I tried to explain, but would they listen? Of course not! In fact, they were downright grizzly about it.

OLIVIA: I don't think I like the sound of this. **5**

HILDA: Why didn't you just tell them you were in the wrong house? That kind of thing could happen to anyone.

OLIVIA: Especially if it was late at night and out in those confusing suburbs.

GOLDILOCKS: Actually it was the middle of the morning and—(*She hesitates.*)

HILDA: And what?

GOLDILOCKS: And I kinda sorta broke some furniture while I was there. Oh, and they'd left their breakfast out and I was sorta hungry so I helped myself.

OLIVIA: Didn't you have breakfast at home before you went out?

HILDA: It is the most important meal of the day.

GOLDILOCKS (*With a shrug*): I was in a hurry. What can I say? Anyway, I really need your help.

HILDA: Doing what?

GOLDILOCKS (*Pointing to her head*): Well, you see this hair?

OLIVIA: It's very pretty.

HILDA: Quite lovely, yes.

GOLDILOCKS: It's also a dead giveaway to the police.

OLIVIA and HILDA (*In unison*): The police?

GOLDILOCKS: Based on what those stupid bears told 'em, they've got an APB out on a girl with golden locks. Until I can get a good attorney to defend me, I need a disguise. **6**

Practice the Skills

5 ▎ **Key Literary Element**

Stage Directions How does Olivia react to Goldilocks's story here? What could Olivia do onstage that would make her reaction even clearer to the audience? In your Learner's Notebook, write at least one stage direction that tells Olivia what to do while she's listening to Goldilocks. Use the author's stage directions as a model for your writing.

6 ▎ **English Language Coach**

Jargon An APB is an All Points Bulletin. It is a message that police stations send out to local police officers to let them know to look for someone

Tales of the Tangled Tresses **1019**

Teach

C Critical Thinking

Evaluation **Ask:** What kind of impression does Goldilocks make so far? *(Responses will vary but may include the following: not entirely truthful; self-justifying; liar; reckless; lawbreaker)* **Ask:** How are these characteristics similar to or different from the characteristics of the Goldilocks from the original story? *(Responses will vary.)* **AS**

Differentiated Instruction

Partner Activity Students whose first language is not English may have trouble understanding the following expressions: *get me out of a lot of hot water, big huff, downright grizzly, kinda sorta, dead giveaway.* Have students add to the three-column chart which they started on page 1017. Have students work in pairs with students whose first language is English to fill in the chart. Encourage students to add these and other unfamiliar expressions to their list as they read. **EL** **BL** **OL**

Objectives
- Evaluate text
- Make predictions
- Understand idioms
- Skim and scan text
- Interpret and analyze character

1019

Teach

Say: Reread the dialogue between Olivia and Hilda on this page. What do you learn about both characters from how they interact with one another? *(Possible response: Olivia seems practical and concerned about assisting a possible fugitive, while Hilda seems more forgiving and willing to assist Goldilocks.)* **Ask:** What does this interaction tell you about their friendship? *(Possible response: They seem to have a healthy friendship, discussing situations instead of one telling the other what to do and vice versa.)* **AL**

HILDA: What sort of disguise?

OLIVIA: We're hairdressers, dear, not wizards.

HILDA: Although we have been known to work magic with split ends and cowlicks.

GOLDILOCKS: I was thinking of something **brunette**. Maybe super-straight with feathered bangs. **7**

OLIVIA: Well . . .

HILDA: She really does seem like a nice girl, Olivia.

OLIVIA: But what about the bears? Breaking and entering is a crime, you know.

HILDA: Yes, but you know how grumpy bears can be when they get up on the wrong side of the bed. She said herself that they wouldn't even let her apologize.

GOLDILOCKS: Will you do it, please? (*Looks at her watch*) They could be here any second!

OLIVIA: Oh, all right. (*To HILDA*) Take her back to Gladys.

HILDA: Will do.

OLIVIA (*To GOLDILOCKS*): You'll be a different person in no time flat!

GOLDILOCKS (*Thankfully*): Thanks! You won't regret it! (*Phone rings.*)

OLIVIA (*Answering phone*): Good morning, Fabulous Frills Salon. (*Responds in amazement*) What? Could you say that again, please? . . . No, I have to admit I've never heard anything like that before. How exactly did it happen? . . . (HILDA *returns.*) I'm at a loss on what to tell you to do, sir. Are you sure it turned completely gold and not just dishwater blond? . . . Even the hairbrush? Well, you might try a good conditioner first and, if that doesn't work, we can schedule an emergency appointment for you. . . . O.K., good luck. (*Hangs up, shaking head*)

Vocabulary

brunette (broo NET) *n.* a person with black or brown hair

1020 UNIT 8 What Makes a Friend?

Practice the Skills

7 **English Language Coach**

Jargon Some words and phrases that are familiar to everyone started out as jargon. What word in this line was probably first used by hairdressers?

Additional Support

English Language Coach

Jargon Invite students to list the jargon the hairdressers used on this page: *split ends, cowlicks, feathered bangs, dishwater blond.* Discuss their meanings with students. You may wish to have students look for images of these words and phrases in age-appropriate books, magazines, or on Internet sites. Have students continue to work in pairs to add this jargon to the lists that they began on p. 1014 as they continue to read the selection. **AS**

HILDA: What was that all about?

OLIVIA: Remember the Midas family? They moved here a year or so ago?

R **HILDA:** A **widower**, wasn't he? With a little girl, I seem to recall.

OLIVIA: The apple of his eye. Yes, that's the one. Well, apparently he's come down with this very peculiar condition.

HILDA: What kind of condition?

OLIVIA: Whenever he touches things, they turn to gold.

HILDA: Hm-m . . . that could come in pretty handy between paydays.

OLIVIA: Not if it happens to everything. This morning, for instance, he offered to brush his daughter's hair, and as soon as he touched it—zap! Fourteen carat and the brush along with it!

HILDA: That's the weirdest thing I've ever heard in my life!

RAPUNZEL (*Offstage*): Yoo-hoo! Are you open? **8**

HILDA (*Waving a welcome*): Sure! Come on in! (*RAPUNZEL enters with hair so long that it drags on the floor.*)

RAPUNZEL: Thank goodness! (*She trips over her tresses.*) I've been tripping all over the street looking for a good salon.

OLIVIA (*In disbelief*): My goodness, Hilda, just look at her hair!

HILDA: It's absolutely gorgeous!

OLIVIA: Have you ever seen hair that long?

Vocabulary

widower (WID oh ur) *n.* a man whose wife has died

Practice the Skills

8 **Key Literary Element**

Stage Directions The stage direction (*Offstage*) means that the audience can't see the actor when he or she is delivering the lines. Usually the actor stands to the side of the set behind the curtain and yells or speaks loudly so that the audience can hear him or her.

Grimm's Fairy Tales Book Illustration with Rapunzel in Her Tower, 19th Century

Analyzing the Art Do you think that Rapunzel should get her hair cut at Fabulous Frills? Why or why not?

Teach

R **Reading Skill**

Skimming and Scanning
Say: This is the second time in the play that Olivia speaks with someone unseen on the telephone. Who was the first phone conversation with? *(Helen of Troy)* **Ask:** What do Helen of Troy and King Midas have in common? *(Both are figures from Greek mythology.)* Scan the rest of the play to see if either of these characters appears on stage in person. *(No.)* **OL**

Viewing the Art
Ask: What words would you use to describe the mood that the painting creates? *(Possible responses: romantic, beautiful, rustic)* **Ask:** Is this mood similar to or different from the mood created in the selection? Explain. *(Possible response: The mood is different. The painting is romantic and beautiful, while the selection is humorous and even satirical.)* **OL** **AL**

Literature Focus Lesson

Stage Directions Discuss the role that offstage characters play. How can they influence the action? Why would an author choose to leave some characters offstage? Responses will vary, but might include that having a character speak offstage could create suspense about who that person is, or that it might be too difficult to show some of the characters in person and how they affect their surroundings, such as King Midas turning everything to gold. Have students discuss how the play would be different if all of the characters made an on-stage appearance. **OL**

Objectives
- Skim and scan text
- Understand jargon
- Identify literary elements: stage direction
- Find meaning in art

1021

Teach

L Literary Element

Stage Directions Ask: What does the stage direction "In unison" mean? *(together; at the same time)* **BL Ask:** Why would the author choose to have the characters speak in unison here? *(Possible response: Hilda and Olivia are hairdressers who love hair and are both surprised that anyone would want to cut all their hair off. It also shows that they are such good friends that they sometimes think and respond alike.)* **OL**

RAPUNZEL: That's exactly why I'm here. I want you to cut it.

L **OLIVIA and HILDA** (*In unison*): Cut it?!

HILDA: Are you sure that's what you want, dear?

OLIVIA: We have clients who would give their eye teeth to be able to grow tresses that tremendous! 9

RAPUNZEL: Yeah, well, they'd shear their chignons, too, if they knew how much trouble this hair is worth.

HILDA: Like what?

RAPUNZEL: Like having a witch keep me locked up in a huge tower with no elevator or stairs.

OLIVIA: But if it doesn't have an elevator or stairs, how does a person—

RAPUNZEL (*Pointing to her hair*): Three guesses and the first two don't count.

OLIVIA: By climbing up your hair?

RAPUNZEL: Bingo.

HILDA (*Rubbing her head in sympathy*): Ouch! That's gotta hurt.

RAPUNZEL: Talk about a major headache, too.

OLIVIA: Not to mention a follicle[4] **fiasco**.

RAPUNZEL: It's also inconvenient. I mean, there I am, just doing my nails or watching the soaps, and I have to listen to "Rapunzel, Rapunzel, let down your hair" day in and day out. I'm sick of it.

HILDA: You're really sure you want to do this?

---

4. A **follicle** is the root of a hair.

Vocabulary

fiasco (fee AS koh) *n.* something that has failed completely, possibly in a ridiculous way

Practice the Skills

9 **BIG Question**

When Rapunzel wants to cut her hair, Hilda and Olivia try to talk her out of it. Do they do that because cutting her hair will be too difficult, or because they're trying to stop her from doing something she might regret later? When should a person try to stop a friend from doing something he or she might regret?

Additional Support

English Language Coach

Idioms English language learners may have trouble understanding the following expressions: *give their eye teeth, shear their chignons, bingo, follicle fiasco, watching the soaps.* Have students continue to work in pairs with students whose first language is English to fill in their charts started on p. 1017. Encourage students to continue to add other unfamiliar expressions to the list as they read. **EL BL OL**

OLIVIA: It could take quite awhile to grow it back that long again.

HILDA: Not to mention how long it will take to sweep out the salon afterwards.

OLIVIA: Are you positive you've given this enough thought?

RAPUNZEL: Absolutely! And besides the sign out front says your prices are a steal.

OLIVIA (*Contemplating RAPUNZEL's features*): Something short and perky, maybe?

HILDA: She'd look awfully cute in a "Winona," don't you think? **10**

OLIVIA (To HILDA): Take her back to Loretta. She loves to chop locks.

RAPUNZEL: That's great she can take me on short notice. If she does a good job, I'll be grateful all the way to my roots! (*She and HILDA exit upstage. Phone rings. OLIVIA answers it.*)

OLIVIA: Good morning, Fabulous Frills Salon. . . . Uh-huh. . . . Uh-huh. . . . Uh-huh. Yes, that sounds horribly messy. . . . Well, of course, I'd be startled if that happened, too. (*HILDA returns as she's talking.*) This was a big spider, you say? . . . Oh dear! Well, you might try a good shampoo and give us a call if it doesn't come out. . . . Certainly, any time. (*She hangs up.*)

HILDA: Who was that?

OLIVIA: One of Esther's regulars—that Muffet girl who's into health foods?

HILDA: I remember that stuff she was eating under the dryer last week. Curds and whey—ick!⁵ **11**

OLIVIA: Well, it seems that she was eating a big bowl of it outside and a spider came along and scared her so much that she jumped and the entire bowl of it ended up on her head.

HILDA: Serves her right for eating it in the first place.

---

5. Cottage cheese is a common form of **curds and whey.** The curds are the solid clumps, while the whey is the liquid.

Practice the Skills

10 | **English Language Coach**

Jargon Barbers and hair stylists often invent names for new hairstyles. In this hair salon, "Winona" is jargon for a particular style of haircut. **EL**

11 | **Key Literary Element**

Stage Directions Write a stage direction that tells Hilda how she should react to curds and whey.

Tales of the Tangled Tresses **1023**

Teach

EL Language Coach

Jargon Ask: What kind of haircut is a "Winona"? (*Possible response: hair that is short and perky*) **OL Ask:** Why might a haircut have a woman's name? (*Possible response: Possibly because a famous person with that name received a lot of attention for wearing her hair in that style.*) **AL**

Reading Fluency

Build Fluency Have students work in groups of four to develop fluency in reading this page. Have one person read the stage directions, and the other three the parts of Hilda, Olivia, and Rapunzel. Point out the use of ellipses on the page and review the purpose of ellipses (*indicate pause*). Tell students to find a quiet place to practice reading aloud. Ask them to read the page several times until they can read smoothly and with expression, pausing for stage directions. **EL BL**

Objectives
• Identify literary elements: stage directions
• Understand jargon
• Understand idioms

Teach

C Critical Thinking

Comprehension Say: On this page, Hilda tells Cinderella to take her time and tell her story. "That's what hairdressers are here for," she says. What does this suggest about the relationship between hairdressers and their customers? *(Possible response: Hairdressers serve a social as well as a styling function.)* **AL**

(*CINDERELLA limps in, wearing ragged clothes and one shoe which appears to be made of glass.*)

CINDERELLA: Excuse me, but do you take walk-ins? **12**

OLIVIA: It looks more like "limp-ins" to me. What happened to you?

HILDA: Why are you walking around with only one shoe?

OLIVIA: And a glass shoe at that!

CINDERELLA: It's a long story. I really don't want to bother you.

C HILDA: Take your time, sweetie. That's what hairdressers are here for.

CINDERELLA: Well, it all began after I got to the dance club last night. I wasn't really supposed to go at all, you see. My stepmother and stepsisters had this long list of horrible chores for me to do instead. Anyway, I managed to sneak out of the house with the help of my fairy godmother and I met this wonderful guy who turned out to be a prince.

OLIVIA: How romantic!

HILDA: And was it love at first sight?

CINDERELLA: Well, I think it could have been if I hadn't kept watching the clock.

HILDA: Why were you watching the clock?

CINDERELLA: Because if I didn't get out by midnight, I'd be stuck with a bunch of mice and a double-parked pumpkin and I'd have no way to get home. Anyway, I want to look really fantastic this afternoon because this guy is going to be paying me a visit.

HILDA: How nice!

CINDERELLA: Yes, especially if it fits.

OLIVIA (*Puzzled*): If what fits?

Practice the Skills

12   English Language Coach

Jargon "Walk-in" is a term commonly used in hair salons, doctors' offices, and other businesses that people go to. It refers to a person who comes in without an appointment.

Cinderella, ca. 1905, Hans Printz (1865–1925)

Additional Support

Literature Focus Lesson

Plot As a character in this selection, Cinderella enters in a bedraggled state, limping, with one (glass) shoe. Invite students to say at which point of the original story this Cinderella is entering from. *(after the climax, which was midnight at the ball).* Ask: What is the literary term for the part of the story that comes just after the climax? *(falling action)* Ask: At what point are we at in terms of dramatic development in the selection right now? *(Responses will vary.)* Invite students to predict what they think might happen next. *(Responses will vary.)* **OL AL**

CINDERELLA: The shoe he found in the parking lot—the mate to this one. If it does, I can leave this life of drudgery and despair behind and waltz off in grand style.

OLIVIA (*Checking the calendar*): Francine just happens to have an opening. Hilda will show you the way.

CINDERELLA: Thanks, guys! By the way, if the shoe fits, I'll see that you get an invitation to the wedding. **13**

HILDA (*As she walks her back*): So this friend of yours—the prince?—does he happen to have a brother? (*BRIAR ROSE enters wearing a long princess-style dress covered with cobwebs. Her hair is a tangled mess with curls tied in different color ribbons.*) **14**

BRIAR ROSE: Hi there. **15**

OLIVIA (*Gasping*): Oh, no! (*Calling out*) Hilda, come quick! You have to see this! (*HILDA rushes back.*)

HILDA: What's wrong? (*She sees BRIAR ROSE and gasps in shock.*) Oh, my! I haven't seen hair like that since—goodness, but I can't even remember!

OLIVIA: You're here for an appointment . . . I hope?

BRIAR ROSE: Do you have one available on short notice?

HILDA: Forgive us for appearing rude, but where have you been for the last hundred years?

BRIAR ROSE: Actually, I've been asleep.

HILDA (*Suddenly remembering*): So you must be that girl I read about in the Gazette, the one named—

OLIVIA: Sleeping Beauty, isn't it?

BRIAR ROSE: That's me.

HILDA: Well, I'm as much in favor of a good nap as the next person, but honestly—a hundred years?! Isn't that a little excessive?

BRIAR ROSE: Unfortunately, I didn't have much say-so about it. You see, I pricked my finger on a magic spinning wheel and fell into a really deep sleep. The next thing I knew,

Practice the Skills

13 **Key Reading Skill**

Skimming and Scanning Before you read about Briar Rose, scan the names of the characters who speak in the remainder of the play. What other new characters will come into the salon before the end of the play?

14 **Key Literary Element**

Stage Directions Read the stage directions that describe what Briar Rose is wearing and how she looks. Can you guess who she is?

15 **Key Reading Skill**

Skimming and Scanning Scan the next page to see where Alice appears. What does she look like? What does she ask?

Tales of the Tangled Tresses **1025**

Teach

L **Literary Element**

Stage Directions Say: Hilda's job seems to include walking customers to the "back" of the salon, to one of the unseen hairdressers. Here, she walks Cinderella to the back of the salon. What does she use this occasion to do? *(to ask if the prince has a brother)* **Ask:** What does this show about the relationship between Hilda and the customers? *(She is very friendly with the customers.)* **EL** **BL**

Differentiated Instruction

Build Background Discuss with students the Sleeping Beauty and Briar Rose stories. For those who are not familiar with the stories, provide copies for students to read or read them aloud to the class. Ask students how they think the stories are similar and how are they different. Explain that there are many different versions of fairy tales and other folk tales. Invite interested students to do further research into the variety of versions of each fairy tale and present their findings to the class. **AS**

Objectives
- Monitor comprehension
- Identify literary elements: stage directions, plot

Teach

R Reading Skill

Skimming and Scanning

Say: Scan the page. Which new character enters? *(Alice)*

Say: Now scan back to the list of characters at the beginning of the selection. Have all the characters now entered? *(Yes)*

Ask: Are the characters listed at the beginning in the order of their appearance? *(Yes)* **AS**

---

this strange man I had never seen before was giving me a kiss and I woke up.

HILDA: That explains the hairstyle.

BRIAR ROSE: Does it also explain why he fainted?

OLIVIA: Well, it is rather alarming, dear. No one has worn that style for decades. Or, in your case, centuries. Not to worry, though. Hilda's going to take you back to Martha. She's a whiz with the latest styles. *(She and HILDA exit upstage just as a frantic ALICE enters. Her long blond hair is quite disheveled and, in fact, has a bunch of leaves and a couple of playing cards in it.)*

ALICE: Am I late?

OLIVIA: Late for what?

ALICE: For a very important date.

OLIVIA *(Reaching in confusion for the calendar)*: Did you have an appointment?

ALICE: Oh dear, I just can't seem to recall. My life has been rather turbulent lately. And it's all because of that silly hare.

OLIVIA: Whose hair?

ALICE: Hare as in rabbit. The one with the waistcoat and pocketwatch that I followed down the rabbit hole? It was infinitely more interesting, you see, than being read to by my sister from a book without any pictures. Books without pictures are so boring! **16**

OLIVIA: I suppose. But what about the rabbit?

ALICE: Well, he led me on a wild goose chase. Or rather, a wild rabbit chase all over the countryside. That's the last time I'll ever do that, that's for sure!

OLIVIA: Excuse me, but your hair—

Sleeping Beauty, Roland Risse (b. 1835)

Practice the Skills

16 **Key Literary Element**

Stage Directions Write a stage direction giving Alice an action to do while she says this line.

Additional Support

Reading Fluency

Build Comprehension Students unfamiliar with Lewis Carroll's *Alice in Wonderland* will not understand the references on this page. Show students a copy of the book and let them look at the illustrations (the original illustrations, if possible). Invite them to read the first chapter, which sets Alice off on her adventures following the rabbit. Or, invite them to read the tea party chapter. After students have familiarized themselves with *Alice*, discuss the references to her story on this page. **EL BL**

ALICE: It's a mess, isn't it? Tell me about it! The way my afternoon went yesterday, I'm lucky I still have a head on my shoulders. It was bad enough eating those mushrooms and playing Trivial Pursuit about ravens and writing desks at the tea party, but when the Red Queen started shouting, "Off with her head!"—well, I had quite a busy day, as you can imagine. **17**

OLIVIA: Then you've come to the right place for relaxation. Can I set you up with an appointment?

ALICE: Sure, that would be—(*Something offstage suddenly catches her eye.*) Oh! There he goes again!

OLIVIA (Puzzled): Who?

ALICE: That stupid rabbit. (*As she runs out*) He's got a lot of explaining to do! (*Phone rings. OLIVIA answers it.*) **18**

BQ **OLIVIA:** Fabulous Frills Salon. . . . What's that you say? . . . (*HILDA returns.*) . . . No, I'm afraid none of us here have any experience with managing snakes.

Alice in Wonderland is the next customer in the "Fabulous Frills Salon."

Tales of the Tangled Tresses **1027**

Practice the Skills

17 **Key Literary Element**

Stage Directions Pick two sentences in the speech that could use stage directions. Then, in your Learner's Notebook, write each of those sentences followed by a stage direction that you create for Alice.

18 **Reviewing Skills**

Evaluating You've probably seen a movie or cartoon of "Alice in Wonderland" or read the story. How does this Alice compare to the one you're familiar with? Does this Alice act the way you would expect? Explain your answer.

Teach

Viewing the Art

Ask: What part of the original Alice in Wonderland story does this picture show? *(when Alice meets the Cheshire Cat)* **Ask:** Is this the animal that Alice has been complaining about? *(Possible response: No, she's angry with the rabbit, not the cat.)* **AS**

BQ **BIG Question**

Ask: What role does the Fabulous Frills Salon play in the lives of its clients? *(Responses will vary.)* **Ask:** Would you say that the salon functions as a sort of friend to the clients? Explain your answer. *(Responses will vary.* **AS**

Reading in the Real World

Career Some students may be interested in careers in make-up and hair styling. Point out that this career is very important in theater and film. Have students research the educational requirements for this field. Have them also research employment opportunities for make-up artists and hair stylists in theater and film. Ask volunteers to present their findings to the class. **AS**

Objectives
• Skim and scan text
• Find meaning in art

Teach

R Reading Skill

Skimming and Scanning

Say: Now all the characters listed in the beginning have been introduced. Scan the next two pages to see which characters are reintroduced. *(Goldilocks, Rapunzel, Briar Rose)* **AS**

HILDA (*Puzzled*): Snakes?

OLIVIA (*Into phone*): Well, I'd recommend you look in the phone book under snake charmers. Maybe you can find someone to get them to settle down and behave themselves. (*Hangs up*)

HILDA: What was that all about?

OLIVIA: Mrs. Medusa. She said she woke up this morning with a head full of snakes.

HILDA (*Laughing*): More "coils" than she knew what to do with?

OLIVIA: She said her neighbors were so scared at the sight of her that they all turned to stone.

HILDA: Well, that's just "asping" for trouble.

OLIVIA: Not to mention "adderly"[6] ridiculous! (*They chuckle as GOLDILOCKS emerges from upstage wearing a wig of long, straight, black hair.*) **19**

GOLDILOCKS: You guys are just fantastic! Look at this! I love it! (*She starts to exit.*)

HILDA: Going so soon?

GOLDILOCKS: The porridge has probably cooled down by now. And in all that excitement of being chased by bears, I totally forgot about lunch! (*She exits. RAPUNZEL comes out next, sporting a sleek, modern style.*)

RAPUNZEL: Wow! I feel 50 pounds lighter already! Not to mention how much I'm going to save on shampoo.

HILDA: Can I offer you some coffee before you leave? You don't have to rush off so soon.

RAPUNZEL: Thanks, but no. I've got a date with this dreamy guy I met the other day while I was hanging my hair out the window to dry. Bye! (*She exits. CINDERELLA emerges next. She has her hair piled on top of her head in a very elegant style. In fact, she looks like she's ready to go to a ball.*) **20**

---

6. *Asps* and *adders* are types of poisonous snakes.

1028 UNIT 8 What Makes a Friend?

Practice the Skills

19 **Reviewing Skills**

Evaluating Several times during this play, Olivia has spoken to people (like Little Miss Muffet) on the phone. Although we never actually see or hear those people, we learn their stories through Olivia's half of the phone conversation. Do you like the way the author uses the telephone to introduce additional characters' stories? Why do you think the author doesn't have those characters come into the salon?

20 **Key Reading Skill**

Skimming and Scanning
Will Briar Rose be happy with her haircut? Skim the next page to find out.

Additional Support

Differentiated Instruction

Build Background Some students may be unfamiliar with the myth of Medusa and her head of snakes. Provide them with copies of a version of this myth to read, or read aloud the myth to the class. Discuss with students the differences between the mood and tone in the original story of Medusa and how her story is referenced in this selection.

Talk about how that adds to the humor of the selection. **AS** You may wish to have interested students write a brief addition to the selection that includes other notorious figures from Greek mythology that could have hair-related problems. Ask volunteers to share their work with the class. **AL**

CINDERELLA: My fairy godmother was right. You two really do work miracles around here! (*She proceeds to exit, with both women calling after her.*)

OLIVIA: Don't forget about that wedding invitation!

HILDA: Don't forget to ask the prince if he has a brother! (*The last one to come out now is BRIAR ROSE, whose hairstyle is multi-color, spikey and really huge.*)

BRIAR ROSE: Well! What do you think of the new and improved me?

OLIVIA: Briar Rose! For a second I didn't even recognize you!

BRIAR ROSE: Pretty chic, huh?

OLIVIA: Think you'll become one of our regulars?

BRIAR ROSE: Sure, why not!

HILDA: Just don't wait another hundred years! (*Laughing, BRIAR ROSE exits.*)

OLIVIA: I can't believe they all left so fast.

HILDA: I guess they were just in a hurry to turn people's heads.

OLIVIA (*Contemplating the empty salon*): It sure got quiet all of a sudden.

HILDA: Maybe that's why they say what they do.

OLIVIA: And what's that?

HILDA: Hair today and gone tomorrow! (*They laugh; quick curtain*) **21**

THE END ○

Practice the Skills

R

C

21 **BIG Question**

Think about how Olivia and Hilda talk to each other and how they work together. Do you think they're close friends? Give two or three examples from the play to explain your answer. Write your answer on the "Tales of the Tangled Tresses" page of Foldable 8. Your response will help you complete the Unit Challenge later.

Teach

C Critical Thinking

Comprehension Say: The title of this play is *Tales of the Tangled Tresses.* Now that you have read the play, what do you think the title means? (*Possible response: The tales of these fairy tale characters are indeed tangled up; by placing these characters in a modern setting, the author can mix the characters and give us a new look at them through a modern lens.*) **AL**

Assess

CheckPoint

Use the CheckPoint questions provided on Presentation Plus! to check for comprehension of the selection. These questions can be used with interactive response keypads for immediate student feedback.

Reading Fluency

Build Fluency Have groups of students build fluency by reading aloud the last page of the play. Point out the "jokes" or puns on the page (*fairy godmother saying the hair stylists work miracles, don't wait another hundred years, hair today* *gone tomorrow*) and discuss their meanings with students. Then have students find a quiet place to practice reading aloud the passage. Remind them to read and follow stage directions. **EL** **BL**

Objectives
• Skim and scan text
• Monitor comprehension

Assess

Resources for page 1030

📁 Selection Quick Check, p. 76

📁 Selection and Unit Assessment, p. 90

💿 ExamView Assessment Suite

💿 Interactive Tutor: Self-Assessment

Students can respond to the *After You Read* items in their Learner's Notebooks or on a separate sheet of paper.

Answering the

1. Possible response: learn to get along, have a good sense of humor, enjoy each other's company, and be friendly

2. Students should list two of the following: Medusa, King Midas, Miss Muffet, Helen of Troy.

3. Possible response: Goldilocks wanted Hilda and Olivia to change her look/disguise her so she wouldn't be recognized by the police. The Three Bears had reported her for breaking and entering their house, destroying their furniture, and eating their porridge.

Critical Thinking

4. Responses will vary. Students should give reasons for their responses.

5. Possible response: Hilda is hoping to find a date for herself.

6. Responses will vary. Students should explain their responses.

Write About Your Reading

Make sure students' dialogue follows the instructions above.

1030

After You Read | Tales of the Tangled Tresses

Answering the BIG Question

1. Hilda and Olivia work together every day in a small shop. What do you think two people have to do to build and keep a friendship when they're working closely together?

2. **Recall** Name two of the people who called Olivia on the telephone.
   Tip Right There

3. **Summarize** Summarize what Goldilocks wanted Hilda and Olivia to do and why she wanted them to do it.
   Tip Right There

Critical Thinking

4. **Evaluate** Do you think Hilda and Olivia should have helped Goldilocks to change her appearance? Give reasons to back up your answer.
   Tip On Your Own

5. **Infer** Why does Hilda say to Cinderella, "So this friend of yours—does he happen to have a brother?"
   Tip Author and Me

6. **Evaluate** Do Hilda and Olivia treat their customers better, as well as, or worse than most shopkeepers, barbers, and hairdressers? Explain your answer.
   Tip Author and Me

Write About Your Reading

Imagine that your favorite superhero or a character from a movie walks into the Fabulous Frills Salon with a big problem that only Hilda and Olivia can solve. Write some additional lines of dialogue for "Tales of the Tangled Tresses" that tell what happens.

For your dialogue:

- Make sure you identify who is speaking at the beginning of each speech.
- Make sure to have the characters explain the problem and how to solve it.
- Include at least one stage direction.

Objectives (pp. 1030–1031)
Reading Skim and scan text
Literature Understand elements of drama: stage directions
Vocabulary Identify jargon
Writing Write dialogue
Grammar Use punctuation correctly: colons with a list

Skills Review

Key Reading Skill: Skimming and Scanning

7. If you were asked to find and highlight all of the stage directions in this play, how would scanning help you?

Key Literary Element: Stage Directions

8. How does a playwright indicate which parts of a play are the stage directions?

9. Why are stage directions included in a play?

Vocabulary Check

For each sentence, choose the word that best fits in the blank.

tresses   frills   brunette   widower   fiasco

10. The ___ asked the hairdressers if they could lighten her hair enough to make it blond.

11. Joel's attempt to cut Martin's hair with nail scissors turned into a real ___.

12. Her long ___ were so beautiful that nobody could understand why she wanted to cut them.

13. He was a ___ for seven years before he decided to marry again.

14. My uncle saved a lot of money by buying a car that had now power windows or other ___.

English Language Coach Answer the questions below. Use a dictionary if necessary. (Some of the terms will be there.)

15. With what activity or profession is this jargon associated?

air ball   fake   pick   box out

16. With what activity or profession is this jargon associated?

virus   boot   laptop   crash

Grammar Link: Using a Colon to Introduce a List

A punctuation mark called a colon (:) is sometimes used to introduce a list of items that ends a sentence.

- Use a word or a phrase such as *these, the following,* or *as follows* somewhere in the sentence to introduce the list.

  The following five people came into the Fabulous Frills Salon: Goldilocks, Rapunzel, Cinderella, Briar Rose, and Alice.

- Do not use a colon immediately after a verb or preposition. Either leave the colon out or reword the sentence.

  Hilda enjoyed talking **to** *Alice, Rapunzel, and Briar Rose.*

  Goldilocks **made** *Papa Bear, Mama Bear, and Baby Bear very angry.*

Grammar Practice

Write each of the following sentences in your Learner's Notebook. Place a colon in a sentence if you think it is needed. Remove a colon from a sentence if it is used incorrectly. Write *correct* if the sentence does not need to be changed.

17. Please obey the following rules stay with your group, follow your guide, and take notes.

18. We saw the machines that manufactured: barbers' chairs, barber poles, and hair-cutting tools.

19. For his birthday, Jesse received these gifts: a football, a backpack, three books, and a shirt.

20. The shelves were full of: scissors, brushes, combs, and hair spray.

Literature Online

Web Activities For eFlashcards, Selection Quick Checks, and other Web activities, go to www.glencoe.com.

Tales of the Tangled Tresses **1031**

Skills Review

Key Reading Skill: Skimming and Scanning

7. Possible response: Scanning; when you scan you look for specific information.

Key Literary Element: Stage Directions

8. Possible response: Stage directions are put in parentheses or brackets.

9. Possible response: to indicate to the actors or to the director what should happen at that moment, what emotions should be expressed, or when there should be pauses

Vocabulary Check

10. brunette

11. fiasco

12. tresses

13. widower

14. frills

English Language Coach: Jargon

15. playing basketball

16. operating a computer

Close

Ask students to describe what they learned about friendship from reading the selection.

Grammar Link: Using a Colon to Introduce a List

Grammar Practice

17. Please obey the following rules: stay with your group, follow your guide, and take notes.

18. We saw the machines that manufactured barbers' chairs, barber poles, and hair-cutting tools.

19. Correct

20. The shelves were full of scissors, brushes, combs, and hair spray.

Focus

BELLRINGER Options

 Daily Language Practice Transparency 77
Focus Activity Say: Now reread your speech. How clearly have you described your friend? Use this time to make revisions to your speech. **AS**

Teach

W Writing

Explain and Inform Say:
When you read over your writing, ask these questions:

- Will I be comfortable saying this out loud? What will make it sound more like me?
- Have I made funny stories funny? Sad anecdotes sad?
- Have I painted vivid word pictures of situations?

Begin revising wherever problems occurred in answering the questions above. **BL OL**

Resources for page 1032

📁 Use the Writing Workshop Graphic Organizer BLM in the Unit 8 Resource Booklet.

 Use the Grammar and Writing Workshop Transparencies, Unit 8.

ASSIGNMENT Write a speech and present it in front of an audience

Purpose: To write a speech about a friend and why your friendship is special

Audience: You, your teacher, and classmates

Revising Rubric

Your revised speech should have

- clear description
- relevant stories or anecdotes
- three main parts: the beginning, the middle, and the end
- a presentation outline or note cards
- visual aids

Objectives (pp. 1032–1035)
Writing Revise for key elements, style, and word choice • Use transitions
Listening, Speaking, and Viewing Give a speech • Use visuals in presentation • Use appropriate expressions and gestures • Utilize note cards

In Writing Workshop Part 1, you drafted a speech about an important friendship. Now you will revise your work and prepare to present your speech in front of an audience.

Revising

Make It Better

Reread your draft. Keep in mind that everything you wrote you will have to say in front of an audience. You may need to rewrite some parts of your speech to make it easier for you to present and your audience to understand.

Try It Out

Quietly read your speech aloud. Underline sentences that you have difficulty reading. These are the parts you need to focus on revising. Consider the following tips:

- Use words and phrases that you feel comfortable saying.
- Delete extra sentences that do not apply to the topic of your speech.
- Use transition phrases when you move to a new thought. For example, "*Another* reason Christine is a good friend . . ."

Add a Visual

Visual aids are useful tools when giving a speech because they focus the audience's attention. Choose your visuals carefully. Too many visuals may confuse your audience or cause the audience to ignore your actual speech. Some visuals that can support your speech are

- photographs
- posters
- slides
- artwork
- handouts
- short videos

If you use a visual, it should support and add to your speech. Read over your draft. Try to think of pictures or objects that would help the audience visualize the things you describe in your speech.

Additional Support

Reading Fluency

Build Fluency Invite students to build fluency by reading aloud to a partner or giving their speeches to one another. Have the listener of the pair mark places on the writer's paper to "chunk" phrases. The writer can then read it again, stopping at the phrase marks. Afterward, have the listener critique the speech again. Explain that this technique may also help the students notice where they have used awkward expressions or need to make their meaning clearer. **EL BL OL**

Editing
Finish It Up

Read your speech again and use the Editing Checklist to help you spot errors. Use the proofreading symbols on page R19 to mark your corrections.

Editing Checklist

- ☑ Verbs and subjects agree and all verb tenses are correct.
- ☑ Pronouns refer clearly to their antecedents and agree with them in person, number, and gender.
- ☑ Punctuation is correct. (Especially apostrophes.)
- ☑ Capitalization and spelling are correct.

Presenting
Show It Off

Instead of turning a final draft in to your teacher, you will present your speech in front of an audience. Unless you choose to memorize your speech, you will probably need your written work in front of you when you present your speech. From the choices below, pick the format you feel most comfortable using. Rewrite your speech in the format you choose.

1. Full Text

Type, or neatly write, your entire speech on fresh paper. This format allows you to say everything that you planned to say because your whole speech will be right in front of you.

2. Partial Text

Type, or neatly write, the introduction and conclusion of your speech and type, or neatly write, only notes for the middle part. The notes should remind you of key points you want to cover. Using notes instead of a full text allows you more eye contact with the audience.

3. Note Cards

This format involves using index cards for notes. They are small and easy to organize and hold during a speech. You can easily write only the main points on the cards. Using only note cards allows for a great deal of eye contact with the audience. It also, often, results in a natural-sounding speech.

Literature Online

Writing Models For models and other writing activities, go to www.glencoe.com.

◀ **Writing Tip**

Presenting The main advantage of using the full text is that all of your words are right in front of you. But don't read your speech word-for-word and forget about the audience! Practice pausing and making eye contact with audience members every few sentences. **W**

◀ **Writing Tip**

Presenting Number your note cards in the order they will be presented. If you happen to drop the cards during your speech, the numbers will help you to quickly put them back in order. **LSV**

Teach

W Writing

Writing Expository Paragraphs **Say:** Your focus will be on using your voice to tell an audience something interesting about a friend. You will have an easier time doing this if your organization is clear to you. If you are describing a situation, your images should be clear and vivid. If you are telling about an event, you need to be sure your sequence is easily followed. **AS**

LSV Listening, Speaking, and Viewing

Diction **Say:** Reading aloud a speech that requires the same good diction that a character in a play needs. What is diction? *(Possible response: Diction refers to good word choice in writing and clearly pronounced words in speaking.)* **OL**

Literature Online

Writing Models Have students access the Web site for an additional and interactive Writing Workshop-based student model.

Differentiated Instruction

Speech-Giving Techniques Make a graphic organizer of these techniques so that students can use them as checklist reminders while they practice their speeches.

- If you're speaking about a story you know well, memorize the main points.
- If you have a complicated speech that needed a lot of organization, use

notes, or type up the whole speech.
- Practice, practice, practice. The more you practice, the more you sound spontaneous.
- Try to memorize your introduction.
- Don't be afraid to add some style and polish—something to spice up your words. Audiences like that. **AS**

Objectives
- Practice and use effective speaking techniques
- Write a speech
- Use the writing process
- Edit for use of Standard English grammar, spelling, and punctuation

1033

Teach

C Critical Thinking

Analysis Say: Use these questions to analyze the writer's model:

1. Why does the first sentence work? *(Possible response: It surprises the audience by contrasting good friends with fighting every day.)*

2. What ideas support the main idea stated in the first sentence? *(Possible responses may include: examples of Christine being a fair fighter, fair in her dealings with the writer, a good listener, and a supporter when the writer was injured)*

3. What purpose does the ending serve? *(Possible responses may include: This friendship could be competitive, but instead it seems to be a cooperative friendship.)* **OL**

Writer's Model

The surprising opening sentence grabs the audience's attention.

Even though Christine is my best friend, we fight nearly every day. Luckily, most of our fights take place at Kick Start, a martial arts studio in Mayfield. We've been taking karate lessons there since we were seven.

The writer includes outside opinions to strengthen her main idea.

The writer supports a main idea with an anecdote.

Miko Sadako, one of our instructors at Kick Start, is always saying Christine is a fair fighter because she follows all the rules. Christine is a fair fighter in our friendship too. Even though she's a little taller and stronger than I am, she always flips a coin to see who throws the first punch when we practice together. We have most of our Friday night karate practice sleepovers at my house because I have my own room, and Christine has to share a room with her little sister. But she invites me to sleep over at her house whenever her sister goes to a slumber

The beginning phrase of this sentence, *I also*, creates a smooth transition from one topic to another.

party. I also have loads of fun chatting with Christine on the phone every night. I can talk to her about anything because I know that if she disagrees with me, she'll explain her point of view without putting me down. If I do something that upsets Christine, she doesn't act cold or insult me or try to get even. Instead, she tells me exactly why she's angry and listens to what I have to say in my defense.

Last year, when I hurt my right wrist in a tournament, Christine showed me she was always there for me, even when I wished she'd go away. I didn't want to do anything except sit around watching TV and feeling sorry for myself. But Christine came over every day and made sure I got my homework done. As soon as I was strong enough, she made me practice karate, too, using just my legs and left arm.

The writer includes one more example of Christine's fairness.

She didn't take any advantage of the fact that I could strike and block with only one arm. And when I got overconfident and wanted to try blocking with my right arm too soon, she told me I'd better wait until my doctor said I was ready.

The writer ends the speech with a strong sentence that restates her purpose for speaking.

When things go wrong, and when they go right, I can always count on Christine to be a fair fighter and a true friend.

Additional Support

Reading in the Real World

Career Giving a good speech is no small skill. Some students may find this writing and speaking task difficult but exhilarating. It's also an achievement to overcome stage fright. With so many careers in film and video, many students may be interested in finding out more about how TV and film personnel handle the high stress of performing. Encourage students to look up the many Web sites on giving speeches, on effectively "talking" with one's body, and handling difficult audiences. Many sites will also show beginners how to add humor and make a speech sparkle. **AS**

Listening, Speaking, and Viewing

Oral Presentation

The final step of writing a speech is presenting it before an audience.

What Is an Oral Presentation?

An oral presentation is a speech, or report, that is usually presented by a single speaker. The speaker's main tool for sharing information is the spoken word.

Why Is It Important?

- Oral presentations allow speakers to share important information with many people, all at the same time.
- Oral presentations are a great way for listeners to learn about a new topic without having to do any research.

How Do I Give an Oral Presentation?

Once you write your speech, practice it as much as possible.

- Read the speech to yourself several times.
- Practice in front of a mirror. Pause between sentences and check for unnatural facial expressions or gestures.
- Record yourself reading the speech. As you listen to yourself, notice the parts where you sound awkward or dull. Work on these spots.
- Rehearse in front of your family and friends.

Before the Presentation

You've prepared and practiced; now you just need to relax. Take deep breaths and think about all the hard work you have put into your presentation. After all your hard work, you know more about your topic than anyone else in the room. Take deep breaths and remain confident!

Scan the Audience

Before you begin, take a moment to look at the audience. You created your presentation just for them. Keeping this in mind will help you stay confident.

During the Presentation

- Pause a moment after making an important point. This allows the audience to think about what you've said.
- Look around the room as you speak, and try to make eye contact with members of the audience.
- Speak loud enough to be heard in the last row of the audience.
- After you finish your prepared speech, thank the audience for their attention. You may also choose to ask the audience if there are any questions about the presentation.

LSV

Listen and Speak to Learn Use the guidelines above to present the speech you wrote in this workshop. As you listen to others' speeches, take notes about what makes a good friend.

Teach

LSV Listening, Speaking, and Viewing

Oral Presentation Say:
Presentations give everyone a chance to practice a little of each of these three important skills—*listen* to speeches, *present* a speech, and use *visuals* to make a speech more memorable. As you read over the points on this page for giving a speech, keep in mind that all speakers need every single step. No one, no matter how practiced, can afford to skip a step. As classmates give their presentations, give your complete attention to each speaker and show interest and encouragement in any discussion time after the speeches. **AS**

Assess

Give students an abbreviated version of the speech-giving techniques and ask them to keep this list. As students give their speeches, they can use the techniques list as a rubric to critique the speeches. Suggest that each student complete a written critique of one of the speeches.

Reading Fluency

Public Speaking Students will build fluency by using the skills gained in this activity and engaging in other speaking situations. Suggest other situations in which students may find themselves relying on this public speaking skill:

- As a member of a concerned citizen group speaking before school boards, city councils, neighborhood

organizations

- Impromptu speeches—where you're asked to say a few words—when receiving an award or explaining steps in a process
- Joining the debate team, or speaking on a school council panel
- Introducing other speakers **AS**

Objectives
- Write a speech
- Analyze text
- Practice and use effective speaking techniques

1035

Predicting

Objectives covered in this workshop:
• Predict what will happen in a story

Teaching Students How to Predict

Why Is It Important?

• Predicting helps readers monitor comprehension when they compare what they had expected to read to what they have actually read.

• Predicting engages students more actively with the texts they are reading.

• Predicting is a familiar skill that serves as a good model of a reading strategy that enhances comprehension.

How to Help Students Get It

• Point out that reading is an interactive process involving both the reader and the author.

• Emphasize that using background knowledge (including what they have already read in the text) to make a prediction is one way to become more engaged with what they are reading.

• Predicting is one way to make inferences. To make a prediction, readers have to think about what is already read, recall what they know about the relevant events or information, and compose an idea of what will happen next.

Reading to Answer the Big Question

Zlateh the Goat by Isaac Bashevis Singer
When twelve-year-old Aaron takes his family's goat Zlateh into town to be sold, he and Zlateh are caught in a terrible blizzard. They take shelter under a haystack which provides food for Zlateh, who in turn provides milk and companionship for Aaron. When the storm ends and Aaron and the goat return home, the family welcomes Zlateh back as a friend and never again speaks of selling her.

Best of Buddies
Best Buddies is a program designed to enrich the lives of people with mental disabilities. This *InTime* article describes how thousands of volunteers are matched up with people from group homes and special schools. The founder of this successful organization expresses his dream that someday such friendships will come naturally.

Workshop Resources

Pacing (days) Standard	Block	Lesson	Student Materials	Teacher Resources
1	1/2	Key Skill Lesson: Predicting	🐾 Key Reading Skills Practice, p. 29 🐾 English Language Coach Review, p. 42	🖐 Bellringer Options Transparencies –Daily Language Practice 78 –Selection Focus 25 🖐 Read Aloud, Think Aloud Transparencies –Key Reading Skills 17 💿 Presentation Plus!
1	1	"Zlateh the Goat"	💻 Glencoe Online 🐾 Unit Vocabulary Review, p. 40 🐾 Academic Vocabulary Review, p. 43 📁 English Language Coach 🐾 Active Reading Graphic Organizer, p. 31 🐾 Literary Analysis, p. 30 💿 StudentWorks Plus™ 💻 Online Student Edition 💿 Literature Classics 📁 Selection and Unit Assessments, p. 91	🖐 Literary and Text Analysis Transparencies 25 💻 Puzzlemaker 💿 Skill Level Up!™ A Language Arts Game 💻 BookLink 3 📘 Assessment by Learning Objective (Diagnostic and Formative) 💿 Interactive Tutor: Self-Assessment 💿 TeacherWorks Plus™
1		"Best of Buddies"	💻 Glencoe Online 🐾 Unit Vocabulary Review, p. 40 🐾 Academic Vocabulary Review, p. 43 📁 English Language Coach 🐾 Active Reading Graphic Organizer, p. 33 💿 StudentWorks Plus™ 💻 Online Student Edition 💿 Literature Classics 📁 Selection and Unit Assessments, p. 92	💻 Puzzlemaker 💿 Skill Level Up!™ A Language Arts Game 💻 BookLink 3 📘 Assessment by Learning Objective (Diagnostic and Formative) 💿 Interactive Tutor: Self-Assessment 💿 TeacherWorks Plus™

Keys for Unit Resource

- 📁 Blackline Master
- 📘 Workbook
- 📖 Supplemental Text
- 💿 CD-ROM
- 💾 DVD
- 🖐 Transparency
- 💻 Web-based
- 🐾 Fast File

Level Appropriate Code

- **AS** = Activities for all students
- **AL** = Activities for students working above grade level
- **OL** = Activities for students working at grade level
- **BL** = Activities for students working below grade level
- **EL** = Activities for English language learners

Focus

BELLRINGER Options

- **Selection Focus Transparency 25**
- **Daily Language Practice Transparency 78**
  Focus Activity Ask: Have you ever relied on a friend to help you get through a difficult situation? How did he or she help you? *(Responses will vary.)* **AS**

Teach

R Reading Skill

Predicting Ask: What are some things you make predictions about in daily life? *(Possible responses: the outcome of a sporting event, novel or movie, or a situation at school)* **Ask:** When you read a selection, what kinds of things help you predict what is going to happen? *(Possible responses: dialogue between characters; narrator's observations; drawing on your own experience in similar situations)* **AS**

READING WORKSHOP 4

Skills Focus

You will practice using these skills when you read the following selections:
- "Zlateh the Goat" p. 1040
- "Best of Buddies" p. 1052

Reading

- Predicting what will happen in a selection

Literature

- Understanding sensory imagery
- Understanding problem and solution

Vocabulary

- Understanding figurative meanings of words
- Identifying and understanding idioms

Writing/Grammar

- Using quotation marks

Objectives (pp. 1036–1037)
Reading Make predictions

Skill Lesson

Predicting

Learn It!

What Is It? As you learned in Unit 2, whenever you make a guess about what someone you know (or a character in a story or TV show or movie) will do next, you are **predicting**. When you predict, you make a good guess about what will happen next. Your guess is called a prediction.

- Predicting is a useful reading skill that helps you understand ideas as you read.
- When you predict, you think about what you already know about the topic, author, or characters. Then you use that information to help you guess what will happen later.

R

Analyzing Cartoons
What prediction does the boy's mom make? Do you think her prediction will be correct? Explain your answer.

Additional Support

Reading in the Real World

Citizenship Have students discuss problems that they feel need some immediate attention in your school or community. Have students predict what the outcome will be if these problems are not addressed. Challenge them to brainstorm ways of addressing these problems. Have small groups of students write a letter together to an adult who is in a position to address these problems. In the letter, students should address the problem, its possible outcome if not addressed, and some possible solutions. Tell students to ask for a reply. **OL**

Why Is It Important? Predicting helps you remember important ideas. Predicting also gives you a reason to read, and it makes reading more interesting.

How Do I Do It? As you read, use what you already know about the author or story to guess what you will learn or what might happen next. Make guesses about story events, characters, and outcomes. Make guesses before and during your reading. Don't worry about whether your original guess is accurate. In fact, many authors will lead you into making the wrong prediction on purpose! They do this because they want the story to contain a series of surprises. This makes the story more interesting and fun to read. So as you read, just change your predictions if they don't match the events. Here's one student's prediction after reading part of "The Bully of Barksdale Street." Is her prediction correct? Was yours when you read it?

JOSH: How far is he?

BILLY: Thirty yards.

JOSH: Stand up.

BILLY (*Confused*): What are you—

JOSH: Stand up. I want you to do exactly what I tell you to do.

> *I think Josh has got a plan to distract the bully. Then he and Billy will be able to run away.*

Practice It!

Read the paragraph below and make a prediction. What do you think will happen next? Write your prediction in your Learner's Notebook.

> "Get in there, Chacha! You know you can make the team. I'll try out, too, but you know I don't have a shot. We've been playin' ball together for nine years, and I gotta tell you *this is your chance.* Someday I'll be sayin', 'I knew him when!'"

Use It!

As you read "Best of Buddies" and "Zlateh the Goat," predict what will happen next in the story. Record your predictions in your Learner's Notebook. Use the suggestions under **How Do I Do It?** to help you. After you have read the story, review your notes and see if your predictions were correct.

Reading Workshop 4   Predicting   **1037**

Teach

R Reading Skill

Predicting Say: When you read a short story, the author often uses foreshadowing to give the reader hints about what will happen. Foreshadowing is a literary device that allows a writer to present a suggestion of what is going to happen beforehand. As you read the next selection, take notes on words, phrases, or details that you think might contain foreshadowing. **AS**

Resources for page 1037

📁 Use Key Reading Skills Transparency 17 in *Read Aloud, Think Aloud* to help students practice predicting.

Differentiated Instruction

Questionnaire Predicting is an important skill in many careers. Polltakers make predictions about voters. Marketing analysts collect information about consumer likes and dislikes, and use it to predict consumer preferences. Have students create a student profile questionnaire. Questions can address consumer preferences or opinions about local issues. Students should distribute and answer the questionnaires (anonymously), then collect and analyze them. Then students should present their predictions about students' likes, dislikes, or opinions, based on the information they collected. **AL**

Objectives
• Make predictions
• Learn and use new vocabulary

1037

Teach

More About the Author

Isaac Bashevis Singer came from a long line of Jewish rabbis, or religious leaders. His parents wanted him to become a rabbi, too, but Singer wanted to become a writer. Singer won the Nobel Prize for Literature in 1978.

V Vocabulary

Vocabulary File Say: One way to learn and remember the vocabulary words is to keep a vocabulary file. Write each word on a 3-by-5 index card. Include the pronunciation, the definition, and a sentence that gives you an example of how to use the word. This is a good way to file any information that you want to learn and keep. **EL BL**

Before You Read : Zlateh the Goat

Isaac Bashevis Singer

Meet the Author

Isaac Bashevis Singer was born in Poland in 1904. As a boy, he visited his grandfather's *shtetl,* or rural Jewish village. Village life later inspired much of his writing. Singer left Poland for New York City in 1935. There he began a long career as a journalist and writer.

Literature Online

Author Search For more about Isaac Bashevis Singer, go to www.glencoe.com

Objectives (pp. 1038–1047)
Reading Make predictions • Make connections from text to self
Literature Identify literary elements: sensory imagery • Understand problem and solution
Vocabulary Understand figurative meanings of words

Vocabulary Preview

dense (dens) *adj.* thick **(p. 1041)** *The snow was so dense that Aaron couldn't see where he was going.*

penetrated (PEN uh tray tid) *v.* passed into or through; form of the verb *penetrate* **(p. 1041)** *The icy cold wind penetrated Aaron's jacket.*

astray (uh STRAY) *adv.* off the right path or route **(p. 1043)** *Aaron realized that they'd gone astray when his boots touched the soft, plowed field.*

eddies (ED eez) *n.* circling currents of air, water, or snow **(p. 1043)** *The wind caused snow eddies in the fields where Aaron and Zlateh walked.*

contented (kun TEN tid) *adj.* happy, pleased, or satisfied with one's situation **(p. 1044)** *Zlateh was contented when she had hay to eat.*

chaos (KAY ahs) *n.* total confusion **(p. 1044)** *The blowing snow had created chaos outside the haystack.*

Partner Talk With a partner, take turns calling out a vocabulary word and having your partner give the definition.

English Language Coach

Literal and Figurative Meanings
You have already learned about figurative language, such as metaphors and similes. Single words can also have both **literal** and **figurative** meanings. If a figurative meaning is used often enough, it becomes part of the dictionary definition of a word.

> Days of hard rain **flooded** the town. (Here, *flooded* means "covered with water.")

> The new style of pants **flooded** the stores. (Here, *flooded* means "plentifully filled," like a flood of water would fill an area.)

If a word is used in a way that is unfamiliar to you, it often helps to think of its familiar meaning. That can be a clue to a figurative meaning.

Group Discussion With your group, discuss the meaning of each underlined word below. Remember, think about the word's most literal meaning and go from there.

1. Latreece tries to <u>mirror</u> Simone's behavior.
2. Their bad acting <u>butchered</u> the play.
3. Success on the track team helped Seth <u>bloom</u> in other areas.
4. Barry spent the whole day spreading the <u>poisonous</u> gossip.

Additional Support

Literature Online

Author Search To expand students' appreciation of Isaac Bashevis Singer, have them access the Web site for more information and resources.

Literature Focus Lesson

Dialogue Writers often use dialogue to establish the personalities of characters, or the problems they face. Ask students to think of one of their favorite TV programs. Then give them an assignment to jot down notes about the first few minutes of dialogue of an episode. Then have them explain what is established by the dialogue, such as the characters' personalities, relationships, conflicts, or problems. Have students share their results with the class. **OL**

Skills Preview

Key Reading Skill: Predicting

When you make a prediction, you use story clues and the knowledge you already have to guess what might happen next. As you read "Zlateh the Goat," pay attention to what the characters say and do. Use that information to help you make predictions. Record your predictions in your Learner's Notebook.

- What do you think will happen next?
- What will happen to Aaron and Zlateh?
- How do you think the story will end?
- After you have finished reading the story, go back and see if your predictions were correct.

Key Literary Element: Sensory Imagery

Sensory imagery is language that appeals to any of the reader's five senses. Authors use sensory imagery to bring a scene in a story to life. Good sensory imagery can help you see, hear, smell, feel, and even taste what is being described.

As you read, keep in mind your five senses. Pay attention to descriptions that help you understand

- how something *looks*
- how something *sounds*
- how something *smells*
- how something *feels*
- how something *tastes*

Example: The wind whipped Lara's hair across her face, and salty seawater stung her eyes. She gasped and flung out a hand to grip the railing of the wildly rocking boat.

This description provides a pretty good idea of what the scene looks like and what Lara is feeling.

Interactive Literary Elements Handbook
To review or learn more about literary elements, go to www.glencoe.com.

Get Ready to Read

Connect to the Reading

Have you ever felt alone and scared? Would it have helped if you'd had a friend to talk to? Read about how an unusual friendship helps Aaron through a bad time.

Partner Talk Share with a partner how an animal or favorite pet befriended you in a time of need.

Build Background

Hanukkah (or Chanukah) is an eight-day Jewish holiday that celebrates an event that took place thousands of years ago.

- Greeks had captured Palestine, where many Jews lived. They didn't let the Jewish people practice their religion. Instead the Greeks used the temple for worshipping Greek gods and goddesses.
- The Jews overthrew the Greeks and became independent once again. To rededicate their temple, they burned a *menorah*, or holder of oil-filled candles.
- They had enough oil for only one night, yet the candles burned for eight nights, long enough for them to prepare more oil.
- Today, the lighting of the candles is an important part of Hanukkah.

Set Purposes for Reading

BIG Question Read "Zlateh the Goat" to find out what makes a friend for Aaron and Zlateh.

Set Your Own Purpose What else would you like to learn from the story to help you answer the Big Question? Write your answer on the "Zlateh the Goat" page of Foldable 8.

Keep Moving

Use these skills as you read the following selection.

Zlateh the Goat **1039**

Teach

L Literary Element

Sensory Imagery Ask: In the example paragraph, what words or phrases appeal to hearing, smell, and taste? *(Possible responses: hearing–* wind, gasped; *smell–*wind, seawater; *taste–*salty seawater*)* **AS**

R Reading Skill

Review Connecting Ask: Have you ever been lost? Do you remember that helpless feeling of thinking you may not be able to figure out the right way? Describe the thoughts that race through your head when you've been lost. *(Responses will vary.)* **AS**

Interactive Literary Elements Handbook Have students access the Web site to improve their understanding of dialogue.

Differentiated Instruction

Art Project Weather is an important factor in Singer's story. Suggest that students work in pairs to discuss other weather-related stories they know and, in particular, if weather has affected a holiday or family celebration of their own. Then as a class, discuss how weather affects mood and activity. As students read the story have them make a drawing or poster of the weather scene. Challenge them to come up with a caption to their artwork that briefly describes Aaron and Zlateh's dilemma. **EL BL**

Objectives

- Learn and use new vocabulary
- Identify literary elements: dialogue
- Make connections from text to self

Teach

R Reading Skill

Predicting Ask: What can you tell about this family from their circumstances? *(They are poor.)* **BL Say:** Make a prediction about whether or not they will change by the end of the story. *(Responses will vary.)* **OL AL**

Readability Scores

Dale-Chall: 5.5
DRP: 51
Lexile: 810

Zlateh the Goat

by Isaac Bashevis Singer
Translated by the author and Elizabeth Shuh

At Hanukkah time the road from the village to the town is usually covered with snow, but this year the winter had been a mild one. Hanukkah had almost come, yet little snow had fallen. The sun shone most of the time. The peasants complained that because of the dry weather there would be a poor harvest of winter grain. New grass sprouted, and the peasants[1] sent their cattle out to pasture.

For Reuven the furrier[2] it was a bad year, and after long hesitation he decided to sell Zlateh the goat. She was old and gave little milk. Feivel the town butcher had offered eight gulden[3] for her. Such a sum would buy Hanukkah candles, potatoes and oil for pancakes, gifts for the children, and other holiday necessaries for the house. Reuven told his oldest boy Aaron to take the goat to town. **1**

Aaron understood what taking the goat to Feivel meant, but had to obey his father. Leah, his mother, wiped the tears from her eyes when she heard the news. Aaron's younger sisters, Anna and Miriam, cried loudly. Aaron put on his quilted jacket and a cap with earmuffs, bound a rope around Zlateh's neck, and took along two slices of bread with cheese to eat on the road. Aaron was supposed to deliver the goat by evening, spend the night at the butcher's, and return the next day with the money. **2**

---

1. **Peasants** were poor farmers.
2. A **furrier** is someone who makes or sells fur clothing.
3. **Gulden** (GOOL den) is the name of gold or silver coins once used in many European countries.

1040 UNIT 8 What Makes a Friend?

Practice the Skills

1 Key Reading Skill

Predicting What do you think Feivel will do with Zlateh?

2 BIG Question

The author provides clues about how the family feels about Zlateh. In your Foldable, write how each family member reacts to Zlateh's leaving.

Additional Support

Literature Focus Lesson

Folktales Singer's story begins similar to many folktales. Have students read *Jack and the Beanstalk* and jot down notes about the sequence of events in this folktale. Then, as they read Singer's story, have them jot down notes about the sequence of events in "Zlateh the Goat." After they finish reading "Zlateh," have them discuss how the two stories are similar and how they are different. **EL BL**

C While the family said goodbye to the goat, and Aaron placed the rope around her neck, Zlateh stood as patiently and good-naturedly as ever. She licked Reuven's hand. She shook her small white beard. Zlateh trusted human beings. She knew that they always fed her and never did her any harm.

When Aaron brought her out on the road to town, she seemed somewhat astonished. She'd never been led in that direction before. She looked back at him questioningly, as if to say, "Where are you taking me?" But after a while she seemed to come to the conclusion that a goat shouldn't ask questions. Still, the road was different. They passed new fields, pastures, and huts with thatched[4] roofs. Here and there a dog barked and came running after them, but Aaron chased it away with his stick.

The sun was shining when Aaron left the village. Suddenly the weather changed. A large black cloud with a bluish center appeared in the east and spread itself rapidly over the sky. A cold wind blew in with it. The crows flew low, croaking. At first it looked as if it would rain, but instead it began to hail as in summer. It was early in the day, but it became dark as dusk. After a while the hail turned to snow.

In his twelve years Aaron had seen all kinds of weather, but he had never experienced a snow like this one. It was so **dense** it shut out the light of the day. In a short time their path was completely covered. The wind became as cold as ice. The road to town was narrow and winding. Aaron no longer knew where he was. He could not see through the snow. The cold soon **penetrated** his quilted jacket. **3**

---

4. A *thatched* roof is made of thick grass or straw.

Vocabulary

dense (dens) *adj.* thick

penetrated (PEN uh tray tid) *v.* passed into or through

When the family said goodbye to the goat, and Aaron placed the rope around her neck, Zlateh stood as patiently and good-naturedly as ever.

Practice the Skills

3 | Key Literary Element

Sensory Imagery In the last two paragraphs, which of your senses have been used? Do you *feel* the cold? Do you *hear* the crows? Do you *see* the clouds and snow?

Zlateh the Goat **1041**

Teach

C Critical Thinking

Comprehension Ask: Why does Zlateh trust human beings? *(Possible response: Because they always fed her and never did her any harm.)* **AS**

R Reading Skill

Predicting Say: Make a prediction about what will happen to the friendship between Zlateh and Aaron. *(Responses will vary.)* **Ask:** What did you base your prediction on? *(Responses will vary. Students should use evidence from the text.)* **AS**

Differentiated Instruction

Visualize Students with strong visual comprehension can benefit from a discussion about the art on the page. Invite students to describe the mood that the art conveys. Ask them to say what feelings the picture evokes. Ask students if they think the picture captures the events described on this page. Students may want to draw their own picture of this scene. **EL BL**

Objectives
• Make predictions
• Monitor comprehension
• Analyze features of genres: folktales

Teach

Viewing the Illustration

Say: From the look of Zlateh and Aaron in this illustration, predict what you think might happen next. *(Responses will vary, but should indicate reasonable predictions.)* **AS**

When Aaron saw the huge haystack, he realized that he and Zlateh were saved from the blizzard. **4**

reprinted from Harper-Collins, Illustration by Maurice Sendak. (r) Doug Martin

1042 UNIT 8 What Makes a Friend?

Practice the Skills

4 **Key Reading Skill**

Predicting Do you think the huge haystack will save Aaron and Zlateh from the blizzard? Why or why not?

Additional Support

Reading Fluency

Echo Reading Read an entire paragraph aloud to pairs of students. Then have them go back to the beginning and practice echo reading: one pair reads a sentence, and then the second pair echoes or reads it aloud. The first time through, students should mark sentences for words they have difficulty pronouncing and places to pause. Then they should echo read the paragraph again, with the second pair leading and the first pair echoing. Students should continue practicing reading aloud the paragraph in this way until they can read the entire passage smoothly, with expression and understanding. **EL** **BL**

At first Zlateh didn't seem to mind the change in weather. She, too, was twelve years old and knew what winter meant. But when her legs sank deeper and deeper into the snow, she began to turn her head and look at Aaron in wonderment. Her mild eyes seemed to ask, "Why are we out in such a storm?" Aaron hoped that a peasant would come along with his cart, but no one passed by.

The snow grew thicker, falling to the ground in large, whirling flakes. Beneath it Aaron's boots touched the softness of a plowed field. He realized that he was no longer on the road. He had gone **astray**. He could no longer figure out which was east or west, which way was the village, the town. The wind whistled, howled, whirled the snow about in **eddies**. It looked as if white imps[5] were playing tag on the fields. A white dust rose above the ground. Zlateh stopped. She could walk no longer. Stubbornly she **anchored** her cleft hooves[6] in the earth and bleated as if pleading to be taken home. Icicles hung from her white beard, and her horns were glazed with frost. **5**

Aaron did not want to admit the danger, but he knew just the same that if they did not find shelter they would freeze to death. This was no ordinary storm. It was a mighty blizzard. The snowfall had reached his knees. His hands were numb, and he could no longer feel his toes. He choked when he breathed. His nose felt like wood, and he rubbed it with snow. Zlateh's bleating began to sound like crying. Those humans in whom she had so much confidence had dragged her into a trap. Aaron began to pray to God for himself and for the innocent animal.

Suddenly he made out the shape of a hill. He wondered what it could be. Who had piled snow into such a huge heap? He moved toward it, dragging Zlateh after him. When he came near it, he realized that it was a large haystack which the snow had blanketed. **6**

---

5. Here, **imps** are playful, fairylike spirits.
6. A **cleft** is a space or opening. Goats, sheep, cattle, and pigs all have **cleft** (split) hooves.

Vocabulary

astray (uh STRAY) *adv.* off the right path or route

eddies (ED eez) *n.* circling currents of air, water, or snow

Practice the Skills

5 ▌**English Language Coach**

Literal and Figurative Meanings An *anchor* is a heavy metal object. Sailors throw it off a boat with a rope. Its weight keeps the boat in place. But what does the word **anchored** mean in this story? How does Zlateh *anchor* her hooves into the earth? Use the literal meaning of *anchor* as a clue.

6 ▌**English Language Coach**

Literal and Figurative Meanings What does the word *blanket* mean to you? Is there a real blanket in this passage? How did the snow blanket the haystack?

Zlateh the Goat **1043**

Teach

EL Language Coach

Literal and Figurative Meanings **Say:** Figurative language includes many different kinds of figures of speech. One kind is called *personification.* In personification, a writer gives human characteristics to things, ideas, or animals. For example, look at the sentence, "The wind whistled, howled, and whirled the snow . . . " Can wind really whistle and howl the way people can? *(Responses will vary.)* **Say:** Look for other examples of personification as you continue to read the selections in this unit. **AS**

Differentiated Instruction

Build Background The *shtetl* life that Singer describes is basically a very rural existence, where children grew up doing chores such as taking care of barnyard animals. Some students may come from rural backgrounds and have considerable experience with and knowledge about animals. Others may come from urban backgrounds and have little to no experience with or knowledge of farm animals. Initiate a discussion comparing the knowledge of rural and urban kids. How would a 12-year-old from a city survive under the circumstances of the story? How does Aaron's knowledge serve him well? Ask volunteers to give their responses. **AS**

Objectives
• Distinguish literal from figurative meanings
• Use text features: illustrations

Teach

C Critical Thinking

Analysis Say: The author writes that Zlateh's confidence in man is restored after Aaron finds shelter for them in the haystack. What is the irony, or seeming contradiction, in this statement? *(Possible response: Her confidence in man is restored, although she is on her way to be slaughtered.)* **OL**

Aaron realized immediately that they were saved. With great effort he dug his way through the snow. He was a village boy and knew what to do. When he reached the hay, he hollowed out a nest for himself and the goat. No matter how cold it may be outside, in the hay it is always warm. And hay was food for Zlateh. The moment she smelled it she became **contented** and began to eat. Outside, the snow continued to fall. It quickly covered the passageway Aaron had dug. But a boy and an animal need to breathe, and there was hardly any air in their hideout. Aaron bored a kind of a window through the hay and snow and carefully kept the passage clear.

C Zlateh, having eaten her fill, sat down on her hind legs and seemed to have regained her confidence in man. Aaron ate his two slices of bread and cheese, but after the difficult journey he was still hungry. He looked at Zlateh and noticed her udders were full. He lay down next to her, placing himself so that when he milked her he could squirt the milk into his mouth. It was rich and sweet. Zlateh was not accustomed to being milked that way, but she did not resist. On the contrary, she seemed eager to reward Aaron for bringing her to a shelter whose very walls, floor, and ceiling were made of food.

Through the window Aaron could catch a glimpse of the **chaos** outside. The wind carried before it whole drifts of snow. It was completely dark, and he did not know whether night had already come or whether it was the darkness of the storm. Thank God that in the hay it was not cold. The dried hay, grass, and field flowers exuded[7] the warmth of the summer sun. Zlateh ate frequently; she nibbled from above, below, from the left and right. Her body gave forth an animal warmth, and Aaron cuddled up to her. He had always loved Zlateh, but now she was like a sister. He was alone, cut off from his family, and wanted to talk. He began to talk to Zlateh. "Zlateh, what do you think about what has happened to us?" he asked. **7**

---

7. **Exuded** (ig ZOOD id) means gave off or oozed forth.

Vocabulary

contented (kun TEN tid) *adj.* happy, pleased, or satisfied with one's situation

chaos (KAY ahs) *n.* total confusion

1044 UNIT 8 What Makes a Friend?

7 Key Literary Element

Sensory Imagery In the last two paragraphs, the author has provided descriptions that appeal to all five senses. In your Learner's Notebook, write down the five senses and give an example of sensory imagery from the text for each.

Additional Support

Literature Focus Lesson

Dialogue In many older cultures, there was a common belief that people could communicate with animals. In fact, many folktales are based on this idea. Often, the animals communicate important information to the people and even help them survive. Have students research folktales in which people communicate with animals. In particular, they may wish to look at Native American folktales. Students can share their research about the dialogue between people and animals in folktales with the class. **AS**

"Maaaa," Zlateh answered.

"If we hadn't found this stack of hay, we would both be frozen stiff by now," Aaron said.

"Maaaa," was the goat's reply.

"If the snow keeps on falling like this, we may have to stay here for days," Aaron explained.

"Maaaa," Zlateh bleated.

"What does 'maaaa' mean?" Aaron asked. "You'd better speak up clearly."

"Maaaa, maaaa," Zlateh tried.

"Well, let it be 'maaaa' then," Aaron said patiently. "You can't speak, but I know you understand. I need you and you need me. Isn't that right?"

"Maaaa."

Aaron became sleepy. He made a pillow out of some hay, leaned his head on it, and dozed off. Zlateh, too, fell asleep.

When Aaron opened his eyes, he didn't know whether it was morning or night. The snow had blocked up his window. He tried to clear it, but when he had bored through to the length of his arm, he still hadn't reached the outside. Luckily he had his stick with him and was able to break through to the open air. It was still dark outside. The snow continued to fall and the wind wailed, first with one voice and then with many. Sometimes it had the sound of devilish laughter. Zlateh, too, awoke, and when Aaron greeted her, she answered, "Maaaa." Yes, Zlateh's language consisted of only one word, but it meant many things. Now she was saying, **C** "We must accept all that God gives us —heat, cold, hunger, satisfaction, light, and darkness."

Aaron had awakened hungry. He had eaten up his food, but Zlateh had plenty of milk.

For three days Aaron and Zlateh stayed in the haystack. Aaron had always loved Zlateh, but in these three days he loved her more and more. She fed him with her milk and helped him keep warm. She comforted him with her patience. He told her many stories, and she always cocked her ears and listened. When he patted her, she licked his hand and his face. Then she said, "Maaaa," and he knew it meant, I love you, too. **8**

The snow fell for three days, though after the first day it was not as thick and the wind quieted down. Sometimes

Practice the Skills

8 Key Reading Skill

Predicting Reread this paragraph. What can you predict about the goat's fate?

Zlateh the Goat **1045**

Teach

C **Critical Thinking**

Analysis Say: Sometimes authors use a vehicle, or a gimmick, through which they want to carry an idea. When Singer writes that the goat tells Aaron "to accept all . . . —the heat, cold, hunger, satisfaction, light, and darkness," why do you think he wrote those words as if they came from the goat? *(Possible response: When words like those are from a goat they don't sound so pious. They sound like words to help get Aaron through a very hard time.)* **AL**

Differentiated Instruction

Research Activity A parable is a kind of story that, like a fable, has a moral. More often, fables involve animals while parables are about human characters. Invite students who enjoy reading and telling stories to look up other differences between fables and parables. Have them collect examples of each and prepare to describe these differences to the class. Challenge students to show how Singer's story may seem to show aspects of both kinds of stories, in that he uses an animal *and* a person. **AL**

Objectives
• Identify literary elements: dialogue
• Analyze text

Teach

EL Language Coach

Literal and Figurative Meanings **Ask:** On this page, can you find any examples of personification, where the author gives human characteristics to non-human things? *(the moon casts silvery nets, the world ... dreaming dreams of heavenly splendor; the moon swam in the sky)* **Ask:** What kind of effect does the author create with his use of personification? *(Responses will vary, but might include a poetic, magical effect.)* OL AL

Viewing the Illustration

Say: Look at the picture of Zlateh on this page. What words would you use to describe her? *(Responses will vary.)* **Ask:** Do you agree with the artist's interpretation of how Zlateh looks? Explain. *(Responses will vary.)* BL OL AL

Aaron felt that there could never have been a summer, that the snow had always fallen, ever since he could remember. He, Aaron, never had a father or mother or sisters. He was a snow child, born of the snow, and so was Zlateh. It was so quiet in the hay that his ears rang in the stillness. Aaron and Zlateh slept all night and a good part of the day. As for Aaron's dreams, they were all about warm weather. He dreamed of green fields, trees covered with blossoms, clear brooks, and singing birds. By the third night the snow had stopped, but Aaron did not dare to find his way home in the darkness.

EL The sky became clear and the moon shone, casting silvery nets on the snow. Aaron dug his way out and looked at the world. It was all white, quiet, dreaming dreams of heavenly splendor. The stars were large and close. The moon swam in the sky as in a sea.

On the morning of the fourth day Aaron heard the ringing of sleigh bells. The haystack was not far from the road. The peasant who drove the sleigh pointed out the way to him—not to the town and Feivel the butcher, but home to the village. Aaron had decided in the haystack that he would never part with Zlateh. **9**

Aaron's family and their neighbors had searched for the boy and the goat but had found no trace of them during the storm. They feared they were lost. Aaron's mother and sisters cried for him; his father remained silent and gloomy. Suddenly one of the neighbors came running to their house with the news that Aaron and Zlateh were coming up the road.

For three days Aaron and Zlateh stayed in the haystack.

Practice the Skills

9 **Key Reading Skill**

Predicting How do you think Aaron's father will react when he finds out about Aaron's decision to never leave Zlateh?

1046 UNIT 8 What Makes a Friend?

Additional Support

Reading in the Real World

Careers Some students may be interested in careers as short story writers. Have them brainstorm ideas for a short story of their own, based on an experience they have had. They may wish to choose a theme similar to that of *Zlateh*, about the relationship between a person and an animal. Have them jot down their ideas and the sequence of events for their story. Then have them write their stories, including dialogue between people and animals. Have interested students research the Web to find places that publish student writing. OL

There was great joy in the family. Aaron told them how he had found the stack of hay and how Zlateh had fed him with her milk. Aaron's sisters kissed and hugged Zlateh and gave her a special treat of chopped carrots and potato peels, which Zlateh gobbled up hungrily.

Visual Vocabulary
Similar to spinning a top, the **dreidel** is a toy used in a game played during Hanukkah.

Nobody ever again thought of selling Zlateh, and now that the cold weather had finally set in, the villagers needed the services of Reuven the furrier once more. When Hanukkah came, Aaron's mother was able to fry pancakes every evening, and Zlatch got her portion, too. Even though Zlateh had her own pen, she often came to the kitchen, knocking on the door with her horns to indicate that she was ready to visit, and she was always admitted. In the evening Aaron, Miriam, and Anna played dreidel. Zlateh sat near the stove watching the children and the flickering of the Hanukkah candles.

Once in a while Aaron would ask her, "Zlateh, do you remember the three days we spent together?"

And Zlateh would scratch her neck with a horn, shake her white bearded head, and come out with the single sound which expressed all her thoughts, and all her love. **10** ◯

Practice the Skills

10 ✓ **BIG** Question **BQ**
In the last paragraphs of the story, what do you learn about what makes a friend? Write your answer on the "Zlateh the Goat" page of Foldable 8. Your answer will help you complete the Unit Challenge later.

Teach

C Critical Thinking

Evaluation Ask: Was the author's style effective in getting the reader to believe in the human characteristics he gave Zlateh? *(Possible responses should show the students' understanding of how the author's style makes a plot believable or not.)* **AL**

BQ

Ask: If Zlateh could really talk, what do you think the goat would say about what makes a friend? *(Students should interpret what the goat means by her bleats and actions. Then they should describe the actions that are most friend-like.)* **AS**

Assess

✓CheckPoint

Use the CheckPoint questions provided on Presentation Plus! to check for comprehension of the selection. These questions can be used with interactive response keypads for immediate student feedback.

Differentiated Instruction

Auditory Learners Ask students with a good ear to look up and tell the story of Hanukkah with descriptions of the sounds children make playing dreidel and the sounds of adults celebrating at dinner. Encourage the students to listen to the students' way of telling the story. Then ask for reactions to how the sounds Zlateh made must have helped to keep Aaron alive and hopeful during the storm. Discuss what people's voices mean to us—especially those voices of the people close to us. **AS**

Objectives
• Evaluate text
• Distinguish literal from figurative meanings
• Use text features: illustrations

1047

Assess

Resources for page 1048

📁 Selection Quick Check, p. 77

📁 Selection and Unit Assessment, p. 91

💿 ExamView Assessment Suite

💿 Interactive Tutor: Self-Assessment

Students can respond to the *After You Read* items in their Learner's Notebooks or on a separate sheet of paper.

Answering the
〈 **BIG** Question 〉

1. Possible responses: loyalty, understanding, comforting

2. They are very sad to see the goat go.

3. They are caught in a snow storm, lose their way off the road, and have to seek shelter. They find it in a snow-covered haystack where they stay for three days.

Critical Thinking

4. Possible response: Aaron knew he had to obey his father and does not put up any argument.

5. Responses will vary.

6. Possible response: Yes. The family realizes that what Zlateh provides is much more important.

7. Responses will vary.

After You Read Zlateh the Goat

Answering the 〈 **BIG** Question 〉

1. What qualities of friendship are present in Aaron and Zlateh's relationship?

2. **Recall** How do Aaron's mother and sister react when his father tells him to take the goat to Feivel?
   Tip Right There

3. **Summarize** What happens to Aaron and Zlateh on their way to town?
   Tip Think and Search

Critical Thinking

4. **Compare** When he hears that he must take Zlateh to Feivel, how does Aaron's reaction differ from that of his sisters and mother? Why do you think he reacts this way?
   Tip Think and Search

5. **Analyze** Do you think Zlateh is really thinking or saying all the things the author says she is? Why or why not?
   Tip Author and Me

6. **Evaluate** In the beginning of the story, the family needs to sell Zlateh for money. In the end, do you think the family's decision to keep Zlateh instead is a wise one? Why or why not?
   Tip On My Own

7. **Connect** Which person or animal can you count on as a friend if you need help?
   Tip On My Own

Write About Your Reading

Pretend that you are Aaron. A week after your return, your father has decided, once again, to sell Zlateh to Feivel the butcher. Write a letter to your father asking him to keep Zlateh. Explain why the goat should not be sold. Use events from the story to help support your argument.

When you have finished, proofread your letter. Try to examine your writing as though you were reading it for the first time. Check for errors in spelling, grammar, and punctuation.

Objectives (pp. 1048–1049)
Reading Make predictions • Make connections from text to self
Literature Understand sensory imagery
Vocabulary Understand figurative meanings of words
Writing Respond to literature: letter
Grammar Use punctuation correctly: quotation marks

Write About Your Reading

Sample response:
Dear Father,
    I would never go against your wishes. You know I have always obeyed you. When you asked me to take Zlateh to the butcher, I led her by the rope and headed off. You know what happened to us. But maybe you don't know how frightened I was. Without Zlateh, I wouldn't have found us shelter, and I would not have had her milk to keep me going. Most of all, she seemed to share her confidence that we would be all right. And we were.
    Please let Zlateh stay.
    Your son,
        Aaron

Skills Review

Key Reading Skill: Predicting

8. What change in the setting helps the reader to predict that Aaron and Zlateh will find themselves in trouble?

Key Literary Element: Sensory Imagery

9. What sensory imagery in the story affected you the most? Explain your answer.

10. To which sense does this description appeal?

   "His hands were numb, and he could no longer feel his toes. He choked when he breathed. His nose felt like wood, and he rubbed it with snow."

Vocabulary Check

Choose the best answer for each question.

11. A **contented** person would be most likely to
   a. whine.   **b.** smile.   **c.** yell.

12. To keep from going **astray**, people use
   a. maps.   **b.** diets.   **c.** medicine.

13. There is most likely to be **chaos** during a
   a. play.   **b.** riot .   **c.** funeral.

14. Water moves in **eddies** when it is
   a. falling as rain.
   b. shooting up in fountains.
   c. being drained out of tubs and sinks.

English Language Coach

In each sentence below, decide whether the underlined word is used figuratively or literally.

15. **a.** The <u>dense</u> cloud of smoke drove the firefighters out of the building.
   b. Habib is so <u>dense</u> that he can't even answer a simple question.

16. **a.** His words <u>penetrated</u> me deeply.
   b. The smell <u>penetrated</u> the room.

Grammar Link: Quotation Marks

When an author provides the exact words of a speaker, he or she is using a **quotation.** Quotations are easy to spot because **quotation marks** appear at the beginning and end of the speaker's statement.

There are rules for quotations—for both punctuation and capitalization. The following tips will be helpful as you write quotations.

• Use quotation marks before and after the speaker's exact words. Example: **"**I feel fine,**"** said Joshua.

• When the quotation is a complete sentence, always capitalize the first letter of the first word. Example: "**H**e's my friend," she said.

• If a quoted sentence is interrupted to identify the speaker, do *not* capitalize the first word of the second part of the sentence. Example: "She was," explained Kathy, "**a** great teacher."

Grammar Practice

Read each pair of sentences. Write the letter of the one that uses quotation marks correctly and has correct punctuation and capitalization.

17. **a.** Aaron would ask her, Zlateh, do you remember the three days we spent together?"
   b. Aaron would ask her, "Zlateh, do you remember the three days we spent together?"

18. **a.** "Take Zlateh to Feivel the butcher," said Reuven.
   b. "take Zlateh to Feivel the butcher," said Reuven.

19. **a.** "If we hadn't found this stack of hay," Aaron said, "We would be frozen stiff by now."
   b. "If we hadn't found this stack of hay," Aaron said, "we would be frozen stiff by now."

Writing Application Look back at your Write About Your Reading assignment for this selection. Add two quotations to your letter. Follow the rules above to help you.

Zlateh the Goat **1049**

Skills Review

Key Reading Skill: Predicting

8. Possible response: Once the snow was so dense that Aaron could not see, you knew there would be trouble.

Key Literary Element: Sensory Imagery

9. Responses will vary.

10. touch

Vocabulary Check

11. b
12. a
13. b
14. c

English Language Coach

15. literally/figuratively
16. figuratively/literally

Close

Ask students to predict how Aaron will treat Zlateh after they have returned home. Discuss how their responses help them answer the Big Question.

Literature Online

Web Activities Have students access the Web site for interactive activities that will help them assess their understanding of the selection.

Grammar Link: Quotation Marks

Grammar Practice

17. b.
18. a.
19. b.

Teach

More About Best Buddies

Founder Anthony Shriver started Best Buddies in 1989 with just one chapter. Now there are more than 1,200 chapters spread across middle schools, high schools, college campuses and in other countries. This is how it works in middle school: the organization matches one student with intellectual disabilities with other middle school students. The connection allows a one-to-one friendship to develop. Often, students with disabilities are able to share the same classroom but they are often left out of social activities. When friendships can grow, students with disabilities have many new opportunities.

V Vocabulary

Vocabulary File Say: One way to learn and remember the vocabulary words is to keep a vocabulary file. Write each word on a 3-by-5 index card. This is a good way to file and keep words you want to learn. **EL** **BL**

Before You Read : Best of Buddies

Author Search For information about Kevin Gray and Cindy Dampier, go to www.glencoe.com.

Vocabulary Preview

integrate (IN tuh grayt) *v.* to bring together or make something part of a whole **(p. 1052)** *Anthony was able to integrate his friend into his life.*

routine (roo TEEN) *n.* a regular way of doing something **(p. 1052)** *Shriver hoped that people could add new friends without a big change in their routine.*

professional (proh FESH uh nul) *adj.* relating to a lifelong occupation or career **(p. 1053)** *Shriver's organization trains people for professional jobs.*

develop (dih VEL up) *v.* to get or bring about little by little over a period of time **(p. 1053)** *People need to develop skills before they can get good jobs.*

isolated (EYE suh lay tid) *v.* to be set or kept away from others **(p. 1053)** *Mentally challenged people are often isolated.*

addresses (uh DRES uz) *v.* deals with or pays attention to; form of the verb *address* **(p. 1053)** *Shriver has made sure that his organization addresses many needs of people with mental disabilities.*

Partner Talk With a partner, take turns calling out a vocabulary word and having your partner give the definition.

English Language Coach

Idioms When people talk with each other, they often use **idioms.** An idiom is a phrase that has a special meaning that is different from the actual meaning of the phrase. For example, if something is very easy, we often say it's "a piece of cake." Of course, the task itself is not really a slice of cake. The saying is just used to express that something is simple to do. Take a look at the following idiom and its actual meanings.

Idiom	Actual meaning	Special meaning of idiom
spill the beans	to drop beans on the floor	to reveal a secret

Group Talk With a small group, think of three more idioms. Discuss what each idiom means. Record the idiom, the actual meaning, and the special meaning of each idiom in your Learner's Notebook.

Objectives (pp. 1050–1053)
Reading Make predictions • Make connections from text to self
Informational text Identify problem and solution
Vocabulary Identify and understand idioms

Additional Support

Author Search To expand students' appreciation of Kevin Gray and Cindy Dampier, have them access the Web site for additional information and resources.

Differentiated Instruction

Research Activity Reading about nonfiction topics often piques students' interests. Suggest that interested students look up more information on Best Buddies and other programs like it that serve people with disabilities. Besides the Internet, students can find information at the library and at a local chapter of a county or municipal disability office. Ask students to share their findings with the rest of the students. **OL**

Skills Preview

Key Reading Skill: Predicting

As you read "Best of Buddies," look for clues that will help you predict, or figure out, what may happen next. As you gather more information you might want to change your predictions, and that's a big part of predicting. As you read, ask yourself:

- *What* will I learn from this article?
- *What* will happen next?
- *Why* do I think that will happen next?

Write to Learn Use your Learner's Notebook to record your predictions.

Literary Element: Problem and Solution

Many informational texts are about **problems and solutions**. It is important to be able to recognize them when you read. In order to do so, ask yourself the following questions:

Find the Problem

- Is something going wrong?
- Is something bad happening?
- Is there a conflict?

Find the Solution

- Who cares about the problem?
- Are they taking action?
- What action are they taking?
- Is it working?

Literature Online

Interactive Literary Elements Handbook To review or learn more about literary elements, go to www.glencoe.com.

Get Ready to Read

Connect to the Reading

How do you choose a friend? Have any of your friendships started with an offer of help? Read about someone who values friendships so much that he started an entire organization to arrange them!

Think-Pair-Share With a partner, make a list of qualities you look for in a friend. Then answer the following question: How can you tell if a person is a true friend? Discuss your answer with your partner.

Build Background

The Americans with Disabilities Act of 1990 (ADA) made it illegal for employers to discriminate against people with mental disabilities.

- According to the ADA, a mental disability is one that keeps someone from taking part in one or more of the main activities of life.
- Some learning disabilities—for example, those that keep someone from being able to read and understand—are also covered by the ADA.

Set Purposes for Reading

BIG Question Read "Best of Buddies." When you are finished, use the selection to help you think about what makes a friend.

Set Your Own Purpose What else would you like to learn from the selection to help you answer the Big Question? Write your own purpose on the "Best of Buddies" page of Foldable 8.

Keep Moving

Use these skills as you read the following selections.

Best of Buddies **1051**

Teach

R Reading Skill

Review Connecting Ask: How do you know if an offer of help is sincerely intended? *(Responses will vary.)* **Ask:** Why must you learn to evaluate people's motivations? *(Possible response: to be able to tell who is a real friend and who is not)* **AS**

Literature Online

Interactive Literary Elements Handbook Have students access the Web site to improve their understanding of dialogue.

Reading in the Real World

Citizenship The Americans with Disabilities Act (ADA) was passed by Congress in 1990. This legislation is intended to protect the civil rights of citizens with a wide variety of physical and mental disabilities. Some of the changes that came about because of the ADA include the following: most emergency services now include TDD (telephone device for the deaf) and ramp access added to public buildings for wheelchair users. Have students research these and other ways that the ADA improved the lives of Americans with disabilities. Have students brainstorm ways they can help people with disabilities. **AS**

Objectives
- Learn and use new vocabulary
- Make connections from text to self

Teach

Viewing the Photo

Say: Look at the photo on this page. Where are the people and what are they doing? *(They are on an athletic field and they seem to be setting up equipment.)* **Ask:** What does the boy's t-shirt say? *(The next friend you make could be your best friend.)* **Ask:** What does this photo tell you about what it means to be a friend? *(Responses will vary.)* **AS**

L Literary Element

Problem and Solution Ask: Shriver identified a problem involving people with mental disabilities. While looking for a solution, he recognized a second problem. What was that second problem, and who did it involve? *(Possible responses: Shriver saw that his college buddies were not doing things to help the community.)* **AL**

Readability Scores
Dale-Chall: 7.6
DRP: 60
Lexile: 930

TIME

Best of BUDDIES

Anthony Shriver's program for the mentally disabled encourages people to stop staring and start sharing.

By KEVIN GRAY and CINDY DAMPIER

Shriver teams up with buddy Jorge Mentado (left).

Anthony Kennedy Shriver[1] is thinking about the day in 1994 when he and Jorge Mentado,[2] 39, went shopping together. Shriver and Mentado, who is mentally challenged, are good friends. "You'd think World War III[3] had broken out," says Shriver, with a chuckle. "Jorge is very hard to understand. He had on big boots with the laces untied. In [one shop], he'd say hello to every pretty girl and talk to the salespeople. One woman came in with a little dog, and Jorge started petting it. It was like a movie. People need to see that sort of thing."

Shriver is founder and president of Best Buddies. The main goal of Best Buddies is to better the lives of people with mental disabilities. The program helps them to make new friends and to find jobs. Another goal "is to make it so people won't stare," says Shriver. "So, when you go downtown or into a church, they're used to having people with mental disabilities in there." **1**

Shriver came up with the idea in 1987 while he was a student at Georgetown University. "I saw a lot of my buddies not doing a whole heck of a lot in the community," he says. "I figured it wouldn't take a huge effort for them to **integrate** someone into their daily **routine**." Fifty volunteers came to Shriver's first Best

1 Literary Element

Problem and Solution What is one problem identified so far in this article? What is the solution?

---

1. **Shriver** (SHREYE vur)
2. **Jorge Mentado** (HOHR hay mayn TAH doh)
3. **World War III** is a name people use for the next global war. World Wars I and II took place in the twentieth century.

Vocabulary

integrate (IN tuh grayt) *v.* to bring together or make something part of a whole

routine (roo TEEN) *n.* a regular way of doing something

1052 UNIT 8 What Makes a Friend?

Additional Support

Literature Focus Lesson

Informational Text Reporters often conduct interviews with experts or people knowledgeable about their subject. Before conducting an interview, reporters prepare their questions. Suggest that students prepare to write an article about what it is like to have a disability. Have them prepare questions for an interview with a disabled person. Remind them that their questions should be respectful. They should keep in mind the kinds of information they want to put into their article, and the kinds of things that readers might want to know. Students may then conduct an interview and write an article, or keep this work as an exercise in how to prepare for an interview. **AS**

Buddies meeting. He paired them with people from group homes[4] and special schools. After Shriver graduated, interest in the project continued. He received calls from students who wanted to start branches of Best Buddies at other colleges.

"I thought I'd just take a couple of months to get this going at a couple of other colleges. I never stopped," recalls Shriver. **2**

Since then, Best Buddies has grown to include more than 6,500 "buddies." Today, Best Buddies International Inc. has branches in all 50 states and in more than 12 countries. There are even branches in middle schools and high schools and in corporations and churches. Best Buddies Jobs trains the mentally challenged so they can get **professional** jobs, not just jobs bagging groceries. Shriver believes everyone has a special talent. "It's up to us," he says, "to create opportunities for these individuals to **develop** and share their skills."

Best Buddies helps people to realize what they have in common, instead of focusing on differences. In schools, students are paired with kids in special education. These friends meet weekly to have lunch, shop, go to an event, or just hang out and talk. **3**

Judy Hales of Miami, whose mentally challenged son David, 12, has a buddy, calls the program a roaring success. "The first time David went out," she says, "our family all said, 'Where's David?' because he never got to go out without one of us." George Zitnay, an expert on mental disabilities, says getting people like David into the community is a great idea. "People with mental disabilities have been **isolated** for too long," says Zitnay. "Best Buddies **addresses** the need for valued friendship." **L**

Shriver's hope is that one day Best Buddies will no longer be needed. "Hopefully, people will just start having these friendships naturally," he says. Until then, Best Buddies will continue educating students, employers, and communities about the needs and abilities of people with mental disabilities. **4** **R**

—Updated 2005, from *PEOPLE*, February 27, 1995

---

4. **Group homes** give mentally disabled people an opportunity to live away from family and still be within a group setting. Many times, group homes help people learn life skills, such as cooking and cleaning.

Vocabulary

professional (proh FESH uh nul) *adj.* relating to a lifelong occupation or career

develop (dih VEL up) *v.* to get or bring about little by little over a period of time

isolated (EYE suh lay tid) *v.* to be set or kept away from others

addresses (uh DRES uz) *v.* deals with or pays attention to

---

2 Key Reading Skill

Predicting Do you think the Best Buddies program will start branches in places other than colleges? Explain why. Write your prediction and your explanation in your Learner's Notebook.

3 English Language Coach

Idioms People in the Best Buddies program sometimes "hang out." What is the actual meaning of *hang out*? What is the special meaning of the idiom? Record your answer in your Learner's Notebook.

4 BIG Question

What can people learn about being a friend from the Best Buddies program? Write your answer on the "Best of Buddies" page of Foldable 8. Your answer will help you complete the Unit Challenge later.

Best of Buddies **1053**

Teach

L Literary Element

Problem and Solution

Ask: How does George Zitnay define the problem that Shriver saw? *("People with mental disabilities have been isolated for too long.")* **EL** **BL**

Ask: What does Zitner mean? In what ways have people with mental disabilities been "isolated"? **OL** **AL**

R Reading Skill

Predicting Say: I want you to predict something, even though you won't know for many years whether you predicted correctly. Think about the hopes Shriver expresses in the article's last paragraph. Will those hopes ever be fulfilled? Will people with mental disabilities ever fit in naturally in schools, workplaces, and communities? *(Responses will vary.)* **AS**

CheckPoint

Use the CheckPoint questions provided on Presentation Plus! to check for comprehension of the selection. These questions can be used with interactive response keypads for immediate student feedback.

Reading Fluency

Build Fluency Have students choose a paragraph from this page that includes some dialogue. Have them practice reading the paragraph aloud by themselves or with a partner. Suggest they develop two distinct "voices": one for the informational sentences and one for the quotations. Have them reread the passage several times until they can read it smoothly and with expression and understanding. They should try to make their reading sound like natural speech. **EL** **BL**

Objectives
- Identify literary elements: dialogue
- Use text features: photographs
- Analyze features of genres: informational text

Assess

Resources for page 1054

📁 Selection Quick Check, p. 78

📁 Selection and Unit Assessment, p. 92

💿 ExamView Assessment Suite

💿 Interactive Tutor: Self-Assessment

Students can respond to the *After You Read* items in their Learner's Notebooks or on a separate sheet of paper.

Answering the

1. Students should support their responses with information from the selection.

2. 1987

3. It tries to improve the lives of people with mental disabilities by helping them get out into their communities, make new friends, and find jobs.

Critical Thinking

4. Possible response: It might make him feel really good about himself, and useful.

5. Possible response: Shriver is a caring person who feels that community involvement is a very important thing for college students.

6. Responses will vary. Students should support their responses with details from the article.

1054

After You Read | Best of Buddies

Answering the BIG Question

1. Who does Anthony Kennedy Shriver consider a good friend? What makes this person a good friend?

2. **Recall** When did Shriver start Best Buddies?
   Tip Right There

3. **Summarize** What does Best Buddies do?
   Tip Think and Search

Critical Thinking

4. **Infer** How might Shriver's friendship with Mentado make him feel? How might the friendship make Mentado feel?
   Tip Think and Search

5. **Draw Conclusions** What can you tell about Shriver from his words?
   Tip Think and Search

6. **Evaluate** Is the Best Buddies program a good idea? Support your opinion with details from the article.
   Tip Author and Me

Talk About Your Reading

Discuss the article with a partner. Share your thoughts about Best Buddies and Shriver's efforts. What do you think about the program? What are some of the advantages of being a "buddy?" Tell why you think you and your partner should or should not participate in the program. Use a chart like the one below to help organize your thoughts.

Objectives (pp. 1054–1055)
Reading Make predictions • Make connections from text to self
Informational text Identify problem and solution
Vocabulary Identify and understand idioms
Grammar Use punctuation correctly: quotation marks

Best Buddies	
What I think about the program	
Advantages of being a "buddy"	
Why we should (or shouldn't) participate in Best Buddies	

Talk About Your Reading

Responses will vary. Students should fill in the chart based on their conversations with their partners.

Skills Review

Key Reading Skill: Predicting

Authors give clues to help readers guess what will happen next in a selection. Answer the following to see how Kevin Gray and Cindy Dampier provided information to help you make predictions.

7. Which words help you predict that Shriver's friends will get involved?

8. In paragraph 3, what information helps you predict the growth of Best Buddies International Inc.?

Literary Element: Problem and Solution

9. Summarize the problem introduced in this article.

10. Summarize Shriver's solution.

Vocabulary Check

11. Which word means *to get or bring about little by little*?

  integrate   routine   develop

12. Which word means *to bring together or make something part of a whole*?

  develop   integrate   isolated

13. Which word completes this sentence? *Going to the gym every day is a part of my dad's daily ___.*

  professional   routine   addresses

14. Answer *true* or *false* to this statement: To **isolate** a person is to keep the person far away from others.

15. **English Language Coach** Using idioms can be fun. What are some other reasons why people use idioms?

Grammar Link: Quotation Marks

Quotation marks are used around a speaker's exact words. These tips will help you use them correctly.

- Use quotation marks before and after a direct quotation. Example: "I'm hungry," said Ed.
- Use quotation marks only if the speaker's exact words are used. Example: Ed said he was hungry.
- If the speaker is identified at the beginning, put a comma after the identification. Put a period at the very end, inside the end quotation mark. Example: Lena said, "I'm not going."
- If the speaker is identified at the end, put a comma after what was said and put the period after the identification. Example: "Sure," replied Tom.
- When a quoted sentence is interrupted to identify the speaker, place quotation marks around both parts. Place a comma directly after the last word in the first part. Also place a comma at the end of the interruption. Example: "Well," said Murray, "I don't think that's a good idea."
- When a quotation ends with a question mark or exclamation point, place the question mark or exclamation point inside the end quotation mark. Examples: "What do you want for breakfast?" asked Dad. "Pancakes!" replied Susan.

Grammar Practice

Rewrite each of the following sentences. Add quotation marks and the correct punctuation.

16. Tito shouted Look out

17. I don't think said Ana that we should go.

18. Is that your bike asked Wesley.

Literature Online

Web Activities For eFlashcards, Selection Quick Checks, and other Web activities, go to www.glencoe.com.

Best of Buddies **1055**

Skills Review

Key Reading Skill: Predicting

7. Possible response: "I figured it wouldn't take a huge effort for them to integrate someone into their daily routine."

8. Possible response: After Shriver graduated, interest in the project continued. He received calls from students who wanted to start branches of Best Buddies at other colleges.

Key Literary Element: Problem and Solution

9. Possible response: People with mental disabilities have been left out of school and community life and stuck in low-paying, unskilled jobs.

10. Possible response: Shriver founded an organization that brings people with disabilities into the community and trains them for professional jobs.

Vocabulary Check

11. develop

12. integrate

13. routine

14. true

15. **English Language Coach** Possible responses: habit, creativity, slang

Grammar Link: Quotation Marks

Grammar Practice

16. Tito shouted, "Look out!"

17. "I don't think," said Ana, "that we should go."

18. "Is that your bike?" asked Wesley.

Close

Ask students to explain what they learned about the Big Question from reading the selection.

Primary & Secondary Sources

Objectives covered in this workshop:
• Find similarities and differences across texts
• Compare information from several sources

Teaching Students to Compare Primary and Secondary Sources

Why Is It Important?

• When students compare selections about an issue or event written from primary sources with selections written from secondary sources, they learn to understand how the source of the writing affects the content. By comparing primary and secondary sources, students will gain in their understanding of the strengths and weaknesses of each, and of the relationship between them.

• Distinctions between primary and secondary sources can be ambiguous. A particular document might be a primary source in one context and a secondary source in another. For example, a newspaper article from 1800 might be a primary source for research about an event from that year, whereas an article from a recent edition of a newspaper might be a secondary source.

How to Help Students Get It

• With your students, read two short selections on the same topic, one written from a primary source and one from a secondary source. On an overhead or chalkboard, provide a chart with columns for each selection. The columns should be labeled with the words "Primary" and "Secondary." The rows should be labeled: "Who?" "What?" "Why?" "Strengths" and "Weaknesses." For the "Who?" "What?" and "Why" columns, discuss with the students how well the writers answered those questions and write the comments in the columns. Then discuss and list the "Strengths" and "Weaknesses" of the sources.

• Divide your class into groups. Give each group a copy of a Venn diagram, labeled as follows: "Primary Sources" (left circle), "Secondary Sources" (right circle), and "Either" (center circle). Each group should also have a list of diverse kinds of texts such as autobiographies, directories, almanacs and fact books, speeches, science articles, diaries, interviews, letters, and textbooks. Ask them to place the name of each text category in one of the diagram circles. Display the diagrams and discuss the reasons students chose the categories for each of the kinds of text.

Reading to Answer the Big Question

Baby Hippo Orphan Finds a Friend by Catherine Clarke Fox
A National Geographic Kids News article describes the unusual friendship between an abandoned hippopotamus and a giant gray tortoise living together in Haller Park, a wild animal sanctuary in Mombassa, Kenya.

from **The Caretaker's Diary** by Stephen Tuei
In a diary, a Haller Park Sanctuary caretaker chronicles the daily activities of Owen the hippo and Mzee the tortoise. The entries reveal the development of the amazing friendship between the two animals.

Workshop Resources

PACING (DAYS)		LESSON	STUDENT MATERIALS	TEACHER RESOURCES
STANDARD	BLOCK			
1	1	Reading Across Texts: Primary and Secondary Sources	🦶 English Language Coach Review, p. 42	🖐 Bellringer Options Transparencies –Daily Language Practice 79 💿 Presentation Plus!
2	2–3	"Baby Hippo Orphan Finds a Friend"	💻 Glencoe Online 🦶 Unit Vocabulary Review, p. 40 🦶 Academic Vocabulary Review, p. 43 📁 English Language Coach 🦶 Reading Across Texts Graphic Organizer, p. 33 💿 StudentWorks Plus™ 💻 Online Student Edition 💿 Literature Classics	💻 Puzzlemaker 💿 Skill Level Up!™ A Language Arts Game 💻 BookLink 3 📗 Assessment by Learning Objective (Diagnostic and Formative) 💿 Interactive Tutor: Self-Assessment 💿 TeacherWorks Plus™ 💿 ExamView Assessment Suite
2		from "The Caretaker's Diary"	💻 Glencoe Online 🦶 Unit Vocabulary Review, p. 40 🦶 Academic Vocabulary Review, p. 43 📁 English Language Coach 🦶 Reading Across Texts Graphic Organizer, p. 33 💿 StudentWorks Plus™ 💻 Online Student Edition 💿 Literature Classics	💻 Puzzlemaker 💿 Skill Level Up!™ A Language Arts Game 💻 BookLink 3 📗 Assessment by Learning Objective (Diagnostic and Formative) 💿 Interactive Tutor: Self-Assessment 💿 TeacherWorks Plus™ 💿 ExamView Assessment Suite

Keys for Unit Resource

📁 Blackline Master
📗 Workbook
📖 Supplemental Text
💿 CD-ROM

🔒 DVD
🖐 Transparency
💻 Web-based
🦶 Fast File

Level Appropriate Code

AS = Activities for all students
AL = Activities for students working above grade level
OL = Activities for students working at grade level
BL = Activities for students working below grade level
EL = Activities for English language learners

Focus

- **Daily Language Practice Transparency 79**

Focus Activity Copy the following chart on the board. **Say:** Comparing primary and secondary sources can be easy if you use a chart. You might start thinking about this comparison with a chart like this:

Compare	Primary	Secondary
Point of View		
Main Idea		
Details		

Teach

L Literary Element

Review Point of View Ask: How can you recognize first-person point of view? *(selection is written from the point of view of a speaker who refers to him or herself as "I")* How can you recognize third-person point of view in nonfiction writing? *(selection is written from an "objective" point of view, by someone who collected the information but does not refer to him or herself)* **OL**

Additional Support

Baby Hippo Orphan Finds a Friend
by Catherine Clarke Fox

& from The Caretaker's DIARY
by Stephen Tuei

Skill Focus

You will use these skills as you read and compare the following selections:
- "Baby Hippo Orphan Finds a Friend," p. 1059
- from *The Caretaker's Diary*, p. 1063

Reading

- Making connections across texts
- Comparing/contrasting information in different texts
- Analyzing multiple points of view of a real-world situation

Literature

- Reading and understanding informative text
- Reading primary source documents

Objectives (pp. 1056–1057)
Reading Compare and contrast: primary and secondary sources

1056 UNIT 8

Suppose you wanted to find out whether your favorite team won a championship game. Would you check the news or would you try to find one of the player's diaries? Well, if you're like most people, you'd probably check the news. But what if you wanted to know how it felt to be part of the team? You'd get a clearer picture by reading the journal or diary of one of the team members.

How to Read Across Texts

A **primary source** is a piece of writing by a person who took part in an event or witnessed it. Letters, diaries, speeches, interviews, and autobiographies are all primary sources. Primary sources are most often written from the first-person point of view.

A **secondary source** is written after the events it describes. History books, biographies, and many magazine articles are secondary sources. The writer may *use* primary sources (such as interviews) to get information, but the writer didn't take part in the events being described. He or she didn't experience the events or witness them. Secondary sources are most often written from the third-person point of view.

In this workshop, you'll read a diary (primary source) and a Web site article (secondary source) about an unlikely friendship. As you read, think about what information you get from each selection and how it fits together to give you a complete picture.

Literature Focus Lesson

Author's Purpose The way students read can influence how they judge the author's credibility. Here are four tips to remember:

- Preview the essay by skimming and scanning to identify the author's tone. Do you expect to laugh or cry?
- Clarify and ask yourself if the writer makes the ideas and events clear. Can

you understand the main idea?
- Visualize as you read so that you can picture the events, people, and animals being described.
- Analyze the multiple points of view as you read. Which selection touches you more? Which presents more facts? How do the selections complement each other? **OL**

Get Ready to Compare

Diaries, letters, and other primary sources are often written from the first-person point of view. They include words like "I and "we" because the writers are talking about their own experiences and feelings. A diary tells you what a person did and experienced and how he or she felt.

Secondary sources are generally written from the third-person point of view. They include words like "he," "she," and "they" instead of "I" or "we" because the writers didn't experience the events. Secondary sources gather information from primary sources and then summarize the most important points.

Sometimes it's interesting to read both a primary source and a secondary source to find out about a topic. From the primary source, you can find out how it felt to be a person involved in a news story. You can also get a detailed personal description of what happened. From the secondary source, you can find out background information, and sometimes you can get information that was collected from a lot of different people.

As you read each of these selections, use a chart like the one below to keep track of the types of information you get from each source. In the left column, list each major event in the selection. Next, list a few facts the writer gives (if any). Does the writer include his or her feelings and opinions about the event? If so, fill those in under "Feelings and Opinions." Does the writer include details? Give a few examples of those details. (Remember, details can be facts, feelings, or opinions, so you can repeat those on your chart.)

Selection: *(put the title here)*
Point of View: *(put the point of view here)*

Events and Facts	Feelings & Opinions	Details

Use Your Comparison

After you have read the selections and completed your charts, look back over them to see what types of information came from each type of selection.

Teach

C Critical Thinking

Application Say: Look at the chart on this page and decide if it will fit your purposes. As you read, you may alter it to fit the way you want to take notes. Remember that you are not just comparing which selection you *like* the best. You want to be able to judge *how* the writer presented the material. Ask students to look for

- where the authors' information comes from; and

- whether the authors show bias. **AS**

Resources for page 1057

 Use the Reading Across Texts Graphic Organizer BLM in the Unit 8 Resource Booklet, p. 33.

Reading in the Real World

Career The first selection in this workshop is a piece of journalistic reportage from *National Geographic Kids News.* Some students may be interested in careers as journalists. Have students research the profession of journalists, including what educational requirements are needed and what journalism students study. Journalists with different areas of expertise cover different fields, such as finance, medicine, and the environment. Students may want to consider how they might combine an interest in a particular field with a desire to write. Invite students to share the results of their research with the class. **AS**

Objectives

- Compare and contrast informational texts
- Identify author's purpose
- Identify literary elements: point of view
- Apply information

READING ACROSS TEXTS

Build Background

A tsunami is a series of giant waves that occur after an undersea disturbance. There are many causes of tsunamis—such as earthquakes, volcanic eruptions, and landslides. Since science cannot predict earthquakes, it is not possible to predict tsunamis either. Tsunami warning centers monitor undersea disturbances that might cause tsunamis. These centers broadcast warnings through several channels: radio and television, the Coast Guard, and channels for reaching local authorities.

R Reading Skill

Review Drawing Conclusions Ask: How might a tsunami affect both animals and people? (Possible responses: Animals and people might drown, or they might be left stranded and separated from their families.) BL

Before You Read

Baby Hippo Orphan
Finds a Friend

Catherine Clarke Fox

Meet the Author

"Writing is like getting paid to learn about the world. The sky's the limit," says author Catherine Clarke Fox. Fox launched her career in publishing when she joined the staff of *National Geographic* magazine. Since then, she's written for newspapers, magazines, webzines, atlases, and encyclopedias. The mother of an eleven-year-old son and a fourteen-year-old daughter, Fox balances her love of gardening, cycling, hiking, and fishing with her passion for writing.

Literature Online

Author Search For more about Catherine Clarke Fox, go to www.glencoe.com.

Objectives (pp. 1058–1061)
Reading Compare and contrast: primary and secondary sources

Vocabulary Preview

tsunami (tsoo NAH mee) *n.* a huge ocean wave that is caused by an underwater earthquake, volcano, or landslide **(p. 1060)** *The tsunami caused flooding and destruction in Asia and East Africa.*

surf (surf) *n.* breaking waves and foam near the shore of an ocean, lake, or river **(p. 1060)** *Trees and litter floated in the surf by the beach.*

sanctuary (SANK choo wair ee) *n.* a safe and protected place **(p. 1060)** *Since the park is a sanctuary for animals, it forbids hunting.*

tortoise (TOR tus) *n.* a large turtle that lives on land **(p. 1060)** *A tortoise can live to be more than 100 years old.*

Get Ready to Read

Connect to the Reading

Have you ever seen two different kinds of pets become friends? Does it surprise you that animals of two different kinds can become friends and help each other? What do you think can cause two animals of different species to become friends?

Build Background

On December 26, 2004, an undersea earthquake caused an enormous tsunami to strike parts of Asia and Africa. The earthquake and tsunami killed more than 250,000 people and countless animals. Many people and animals were left homeless.

- Hippopotamuses are social animals by nature and like to stay with their mothers for the first four years of their lives.
- Tortoises can live to be well over 100 years old.
- Mombasa, Kenya, is a large city on the coast of the Indian Ocean. Almost 2,000 years old, it is Kenya's only large port.

R

Set Purposes for Reading

BIG Question Read "Baby Hippo Orphan Finds a Friend" to find out about an unusual friendship between a hippopotamus and a tortoise.

Set Your Own Purpose What else would you like to find out about the unusual friendship between these two animals? Write your own purpose on the "Baby Hippo" page of Foldable 8.

Additional Support

Literature Online

Author Search To expand students' appreciation of Catherine Clarke Fox, have them access the Web site for more information and resources.

Reading in the Real World

Citizenship Although the tsunami struck Asia and Africa in 2004, many people are still recovering. Take students to the library to investigate the lives of these survivors and what they and other people are doing to help them recover. Talk about:

- Organizations that come to the help of people when natural disasters strike. AS

- Architectural, engineering, and design advances that have been made to provide low-cost, easily-assembled, emergency housing. AL

Suggest that students try to find a resource telling about a particular village or area and how it is coping with the aftermath of the tsunami. AS

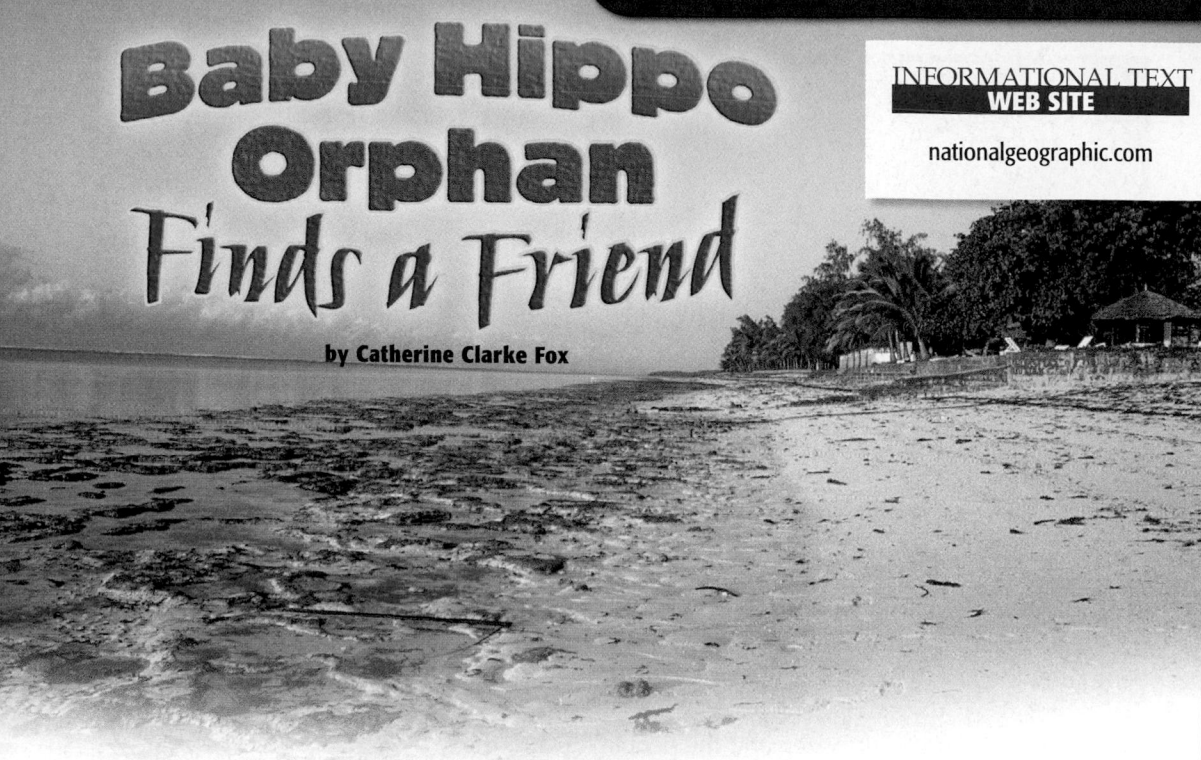

Baby Hippo Orphan Finds a Friend

by Catherine Clarke Fox

INFORMATIONAL TEXT
WEB SITE

nationalgeographic.com

Teach

Viewing the Map

Say: How does the map support the information in the first paragraph? *(It shows the area in question.)* **Ask:** Does the map make it easier to visualize the area in question? Explain. *(Responses will vary.)* **AL**

Have you noticed that sometimes the most unlikely pairs form the best friendships? Late last December [2004], flood waters in the East African country of Kenya swept a herd of hippopotamuses down the Sabaki River[1] and into the Indian Ocean (see map). After a few days, most of them struggled to shore and returned inland. **1**

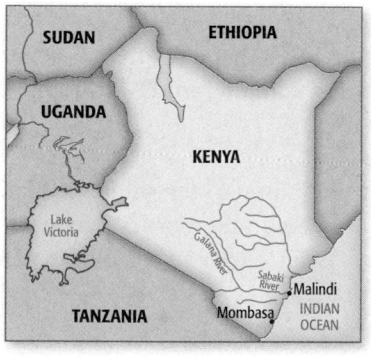

Analyzing the Map Find the place where the Sabaki River meets the Indian Ocean. What city name do you see there?

---

1. The **Sabaki River** is the second largest river in Kenya.

Practice the Skills

1 | **Reading Across Texts**

Primary and Secondary Sources What events and facts does the writer provide? (Graphics, such as maps, count!) Fill these in on your chart.

Baby Hippo Orphan Finds a Friend **1059**

Readability Scores
Dale-Chall: 5.9
DRP: 58
Lexile: 1020

Differentiated Instruction

Using a Map Many students may have only a vague idea of the geography of the continent of Africa. Explain that the map on this page shows only a small portion of Africa's Eastern coast. Have students use an atlas to look at the entire continent. Have them locate the area shown in the inset map and conduct the following research:

- Identify the location of the underground earthquake that caused the tsunami.
- Calculate the distance the tsunami covered to reach the coast of Kenya.
- Find out about the history of Mombassa, the 2,000-year-old trading center on the coast of the Indian Ocean. **OL AL**

Objectives
- Compare and contrast informational texts
- Draw conclusions
- Use text features: maps

Teach

L Literary Element

Primary and Secondary Sources Spend some time discussing the idea of sources.
Ask: Where do you think this journalist got her information? *(Possible responses: by doing research; by interviewing the people involved; by visiting the place after the fact)*
Ask: How do you think she checked her sources to make sure the information was correct? *(Possible response: she checked the information against other sources, talked to other people)* **AS**

Hippos live in and around fresh water.

Then, right after the Asian **tsunami** hit on December 26, local people spotted a baby hippo in the rough **surf**, apparently left behind by the herd. They were worried. **2**

Hippos live around fresh water, and the people figured the salt water wasn't good for the little fellow. Besides, he had no mother to look out for him.

After hours of effort, they caught the big baby (about 600 pounds, or 270 kilograms). They named him Owen after one of his rescuers. **3**

Wildlife officials took Owen the hippo to the safety of Haller Park, a **sanctuary** for wild animals in the port city of Mombasa. To their surprise, Owen, about a year old, trotted right up to a giant gray **tortoise**. **3**

Vocabulary

tsunami (tsoo NAH mee) *n.* a huge ocean wave that is caused by an underwater earthquake, volcano, or landslide

surf (surf) *n.* breaking waves and foam near the shore of an ocean, lake, or river

sanctuary (SANK choo wair ee) *n.* a safe and protected place

tortoise (TOR tus) *n.* a large turtle that lives on land

1060 UNIT 8 What Makes a Friend?

Practice the Skills

2 Reading Across Texts

Primary and Secondary Sources How can you tell that the writer did not participate in the events she is describing? (That means the article must be a secondary source.) This clue also tells you the point of view of the article. Fill in the "Point of View" above your chart. **L**

3 Reading Across Texts

Primary and Secondary Sources What new event(s) have occurred? What facts, feelings, opinions, and details (if any) has the writer included? Use your answers to fill in your chart.

Additional Support

Reading in the Real World

College Call students' attention to the two references to Owen's weight, in pounds and in kilograms (on this page and the page before). In the United States, we use what is called the standard system of weights and measurements, based on pounds and inches.

Most of the rest of the world uses the metric system of weights and measurements, based on grams and meters. Have students use a conversion table to figure out their own height and weight in both systems. **AL**

Tortoises are among the longest-living creatures on Earth. This one's name is Mzee, which means "old man" in the Swahili language. He is more than a hundred years old.

"Mzee hissed, lifted himself up off the ground, and tried to run," reported Paula Kahumbu, an ecologist in charge of Haller Park. (Ecologists study how living things relate to their surroundings.) "But by the next morning, they were together!"

They have been together ever since, even staying close and touching when they sleep.

Owen could weigh more than 6,000 pounds (2,700 kilograms) when he is grown—heavier than a minivan. Eventually he will be introduced to Cleo, an adult hippo, so he can be with his own kind.

But Kahumbu said Owen and Mzee will still spend time together if they wish. To find out what happens next, check out the caretaker's diary at the Lafarge Eco Systems Web site. **4 5** ○

Analyzing the Photo Would you say that Owen and Mzee seem to be friends in this picture? Explain your answer.

Practice the Skills

4 **Reading Across Texts**

Primary and Secondary Sources Add to your chart all the events included in the last few paragraphs. Add any facts, opinions, or details the author includes.

5 **BIG Question**

Why do you think Owen befriended Mzee so quickly? What makes Owen and Mzee such good friends? Write your answer on the "Baby Hippo" page of Foldable 8. Your response will help you complete the Unit Challenge later. **BQ**

Teach

BQ **BIG Question**

Ask: What do you think made Mzee accept Owen? *(Responses will vary.)* **Ask:** Do you think it is possible for people who don't speak the same language, and who are different ages, to become friends? Explain. *(Responses will vary.)* **AS**

Viewing the Photo

Ask: What information about Owen and Mzee can you learn from this photograph? *(Possible response: I can see what they both really look like.)* **BL**
Ask: Do you think the way they look has anything to do with their friendship? *(Responses may vary. Some students may say that Owen identified with Mzee because of the general similarity in their appearances.)* **AS**

Baby Hippo Orphan Finds a Friend **1061**

English Language Coach

Word Origins Swahili is a language that originated on the Eastern coast of Africa. It is a mixture of Bantu (an African language) and other languages including Arabic and Persian. This mix came about as a result of the lively trading culture that developed in early times across the Indian Ocean between eastern Africa and the Asian continent. Discuss how languages change and evolve as a result of trade and migration. Students may wish to list new words and expressions entering the English language from other languages and cultures through immigration. **AL**

Objectives
- Compare and contrast informational text
- Explore word origins
- Identify literary elements: primary and secondary sources
- Use text features: photographs

Build Background

Share the following background information on tortoises with your students:

Did you know that tortoises of the desert kind usually do not spend much time around water? They only go to the water to bathe or drink. Unlike the turtle, tortoises do not usually go swimming; their elephant-shaped legs and high domes make them unlike the turtle. So, most hippos would probably not run into tortoises, making Owen all the luckier to find a friend in Mzee.

R Reading Skill

Review Clarifying Say: In this selection, you will read about Owen the hippo from the point of view of someone who helped rescue him. As you read, clarify facts and details that were unclear to you from the first selection. Take notes about new things you learn. **AS**

Before You Read

from The Caretaker's DIARY

Meet the Author

As caretaker of animals at Haller Park in Kenya, Stephen Tuei makes sure that all animals are fed and cared for properly. He has raised and bottle-fed many different kinds of animals from infancy, including antelopes and hippopotamuses. His day begins by 7:00 A.M., when he takes the antelope out to grazing areas and continues past 8:00 P.M., when he feeds the owls and other night-loving animals. Tuei is often accompanied on his rounds by his eleven-year-old son Kibet.

Literature Online

Author Search For more about Stephen Tuei, go to www.glencoe.com.

Vocabulary Preview

convoy (KON voy) *n.* a group of cars, trucks, or other vehicles traveling together **(p. 1063)** *I saw a convoy of trucks traveling down the road.*

subdued (sub DOOD) *adj.* quiet, weak, under control **(p. 1064)** *The cat looked subdued after it came back into the house.*

traumatized (TROM uh tyzd) *adj.* upset or injured as a result of a frightening event **(p. 1064)** *Fireworks made the puppy feel traumatized.*

enclosure (en KLOH zhur) *n.* a fenced-in or walled-in place **(p. 1065)** *We built an enclosure in the yard for the dogs.*

hissed (hisd) *v.* made a sound like air escaping from a balloon; form of the verb *hiss* **(p. 1066)** *Her cat hissed when the dog walked by.*

Get Ready to Read

Connect to the Reading

Have you ever become friends with someone who is very different from you? What caused you to become friends?

Build Background

- This selection includes parts of a diary that has been kept since Owen and Mzee were first brought together.
- The diary was originally published on a Web site. New entries were put on the Web site as they were written. Thousands of people have read the diary since it was first published. **R**
- There have been many instances of unusual animal friendships. In 2002, a lioness in Samburu National Park in Africa tried to adopt and care for several baby antelopes. Lions normally hunt antelope for food.

Set Purposes for Reading

BIG Question Read from "The Caretaker's Diary" to find out how the friendship between Owen and Mzee developed and changed.

Set Your Own Purpose What else would you like to find about the friendship of these unlikely buddies? Write your own purpose on the "Caretaker's Diary" page of Foldable 8.

Objectives (pp. 1062–1069)
Reading Compare and contrast: primary and secondary sources
Writing Compare and contrast: sources of information

Additional Support

Literature Online

Author Search To expand students' appreciation of Stephen Tuei, have them access the Web site for more information and resources.

Reading in the Real World

Career Some students may be interested in careers as animal caretakers—in zoos, wildlife preserves, and other contexts (pet daycare centers). Tell them there are many opportunities for students with interests in this area. Have students choose and research one career in the field of animal caretaking, and ask them to explore educational requirements and employment opportunities. Have students take notes on their findings and present them to the class. **AS**

from **The Caretaker's DIARY**

by Stephen Tuei

INFORMATIONAL TEXT
WEB SITE

lafargeecosystems.com

27th December, 2004

C Today is a day that I will never forget. I was at the hospital getting treatment when my phone rang. Only my boss Sabine Baer would call me during the holiday. I knew it must be important.

"Stephen, we have to rescue a baby hippo, can you come?"

I didn't hesitate "Yes" I said. "It will take me twenty minutes to get to the office from the hospital." **1**

"But you have malaria,¹ perhaps you should rest?"

"No, the malaria has gone." It was a half lie, my head was sore but I would not give up on a baby hippo for anything. **2**

I rode my motorbike back as fast as I possibly could safely. Paula, the General Manager, she was waiting with two other people who would also help with bringing the baby back. Sabine would work as fast as possible with another team to prepare the baby's home.

We contacted Dr. Kashmiri, a local wildlife veterinarian who joined us and we drove in **convoy**. It took us two long hours to drive to Malindi, a small coastal town north of Mombasa.

---

1. *Malaria* is a serious disease caused by the bite by an infected mosquito.

Vocabulary

convoy (KON voy) *n.* a group of cars, trucks, or other vehicles traveling together

Practice the Skills

1 **Reading Across Texts**

Primary and Secondary Sources What clues indicate that this is a diary? Write the point of view above your chart. **R**

2 **BIG Question**

Most people believe that a good friend is someone you can rely on when you need help. What does the caretaker say that shows that he is a good friend to animals? Write your answer on your Foldable.

The Caretaker's Diary **1063**

Teach

C **Critical Thinking**

Comprehension Ask: Where was Stephen when he got the call to go rescue the baby hippo, and why was he there? *(He was in the hospital because he had malaria.)* **AS**

R **Reading Skill**

Comparing and Contrasting Ask: In what ways does this diary contain the literary elements of a short story? *(Possible response: There is an unfolding story whose outcome is not yet known, suspense, dialogue, [real-life] characters, and a setting [time and place].)* **Say:** Look for other similarities and differences between these two genres *(diary and short story)* as you read. **AL**

Readability Scores
Dale-Chall: 5.2
DRP: 54
Lexile: 990

Reading Fluency

Build Fluency Although this is a nonfiction selection, it is a diary and it has a very personal tone and voice. Tell students to find a quiet place to practice reading aloud the first diary entry.

Students should reread it several times until they can smoothly read all the sentences with expression and understanding. They should try to make the reading sound like natural speech. **EL BL**

Objectives
• Compare and contrast informational text
• Clarify text
• Monitor comprehension

Teach

L Literary Element

Review Chronological Order Remind students that when something is told in chronological order, it is told in the order in which the events happened. Tell students to look at the first two paragraphs. **Ask:** What do Stephen, Dr. Kashmiri, and the helpers do after they arrive at Marine Park and introduce themselves? *(They examine the hippo.)* **AS**

C Critical Thinking

Comprehension Ask: Why was it shocking for the hippo when the blanket fell off his face? *(Possible response: He saw many strangers around him, and many people started taking pictures of him.)* **Ask:** What was the hippo's reaction? *(He started trying to jump out of the truck while snapping at everyone.)* **AS**

We drove straight to the Malindi Marine Park[2] where a small crowd surrounded a green pickup truck. Inside lay something tightly wrapped in fishing nets. The crowd had been here for hours and seemed relieved that we had arrived.

We introduced ourselves and got to work. Dr. Kashmiri examined the hippo which looked very **subdued**, quiet and tired. He had small wounds all over his legs, his color was a dull dark gray, and he lay silently. His head was covered and my job was to keep him constantly wet to keep his body cool.[3] We decided on a plan to unwrap him from the fishing net, and all hands were at work trying to get him out of the tangle. Suddenly he stood up and some people backed off in fear, then Kashmiri gave the order to remove the net quickly. Everyone was busy but the tangle was a mess. It seemed impossible and the hippo was getting upset, standing up and lying down every few minutes.

Then the worst thing happened, the blanket fell off his face and for the first time he saw all of us around him. That must have given him a huge shock. There were cameras flashing everywhere and the excited voices of the helpers probably scared him even more. He started trying desperately to jump out of the truck while snapping at everyone around.

Most people fled, but Dr. Kashmiri and I have handled many wild animals before. We held onto him as others struggled to put the blanket over his eyes again. It was a scary few minutes—if he had jumped out of the car he would have suffered serious injuries. **3**

After that the unwrapping became much easier, and before long the net was returned to its owner and the hippo was safely tied to prevent him from biting or seeing anyone. He was moved by many hands to Paula's car which was quickly closed. We did not waste time saying goodbye, we knew the hippo was **traumatized** and needed to get to a safe place

---

2. **Malindi Marine Park** is a park on the north coast of Kenya where people observe wildlife and plants and go swimming, diving, and snorkeling.

3. Scientists covered the head of the baby hippo to keep him from being frightened by the crowd surrounding him.

Vocabulary

subdued (sub DOOD) *adj.* quiet, weak, under control

traumatized (TROM uh tyzd) *adj.* upset or injured as a result of a frightening event

Practice the Skills

3 **Reading Across Texts**

Primary and Secondary Sources Does this selection provide more information about the rescue of the hippo than the first one did? What facts, feelings, opinions, and details are included in this diary? Put this information in your chart.

Additional Support

Differentiated Instruction

Creating a Storyboard Students who are visually oriented may benefit from creating a storyboard detailing the sequence of events described on this page. They may wish to include sentences from the selection under some of the boxes. Encourage them to draw pictures that show what is happening to the hippo. Ask volunteers to present their completed storyboards in a classroom display. **EL OL**

quickly. But before we left, we asked the crowd what name they wanted to give him. At first the name Mark rang out. Mark Easterbrook is an honorary game warden[4] who lives in Malindi and who helped coordinate the rescue. But Mark would not take the honor, he suggested Owen, and a young French man looked up in surprise. "What?" "Yes," Mark said, "You are the person with the greatest courage for the final rugby[5] tackle that brought Owen down." The crowd agreed and laughed as they practiced the name "Owen the hippo." **4**

We drove back to Mombasa at a slow pace, baby Owen just slept. We stopped twice and I poured cold water over him.

By the time we arrived in Haller Park,[6] it was getting dark. A small team of our staff led by Sabine were here to meet us and help. Their expressions of joy were unmistakable.

It didn't take long for us to get Owen out of the vehicle, and he seemed more than eager to get away from us. It took ten of us to lift him out of the car, then I helped Dr. Kashmiri remove all the ties and let him go. Owen hardly glanced at us then trotted off away into the **enclosure** that Sabine and her

---

4. A *game warden* is a person in charge of managing animals and wildlife.
5. *Rugby* is a game similar to football that is popular in Europe, Africa, and India.
6. *Haller Park* is an environmental park in Mombasa.

Vocabulary

enclosure (en KLOH zhur) *n.* a fenced-in or walled-in place

Practice the Skills

4 **BIG Question**

Mark Easterbrook—the honorary game warden—could have had the baby hippo named after him. But he suggested that it be named after the man who tackled the hippo. What does this tell you about Mark Easterbrook? Do you think he might make a good friend? Why? Write your answers on your Foldable.

Analyzing the Photo What seems to be happening in this picture? Explain your answer.

The Caretaker's Diary **1065**

Teach

C Critical Thinking

Evaluation Ask: Do you think it was a good idea to ask the crowd to name the hippo? Why? (*Possible responses: Yes, it was a good idea because the people in the crowd seemed very interested in the welfare of the hippo; that's probably why they had stayed for hours waiting for the rescuers and seemed relieved when they got there. They also probably felt connected to him after waiting with him for so long.*) **AS**

Viewing the Photo

Say: Write an informational caption for this photo. (*Responses will vary.*) **Say:** Now write a second caption for this photo. This time, make up words to express what you imagine the animals might be feeling. (*Responses will vary.*) **AS**

Reading in the Real World

Citizenship Explain that different cultures have different attitudes toward animals and nature. Some cultures believe animals exist to provide humans with what we need—food, clothing, and sport—and others respect animals and appreciate their gifts to humans. Have English language learners discuss their cultures' attitudes toward animals and nature. Ask them to work together to create a word web with "Animals" in the center and different cultures' attitudes around it. **AL**

Objectives
- Compare and contrast informational texts
- Monitor comprehension
- Understand sequence: chronological order
- Evaluate text
- Use text features: photographs

Teach

Skimming and Scanning Say: To find out how much time has elapsed between the entry dated 2nd January and the entry before, scan backwards in the selection. About how long has it taken Mzee to show some interest in Owen? *(about a week)* **AS**

R2 **Reading Skill**

Review Paraphrasing and Summarizing Say: Summarize the information from the January 2nd, 2005 entry. *(Possible response: Owen seems very interested in Mzee. He follows him, sleeps beside him, and even copies him in eating and drinking.)* **AS**

---

team had prepared. They had piled up lots of freshly cut grass and even brought bottles of milk in case he needed it. We stood and watched him as the light faded. He didn't explore his new home, but went straight up to one of our oldest giant tortoises named Mzee and stood with him.

To be honest, Mzee does not appreciate his new roommate and at first **hissed** angrily at Owen, then lifted himself up and tried to run. Imagine a 100 year old giant tortoise trying to run! It was not hard for Owen to keep up.

Once darkness had fallen everyone left, except Sabine and I. I am responsible for making sure that Owen is alright all night long. It was such an exciting day, I am exhausted, but I am so happy, all of this and I've got malaria too. **5**

2nd January, 2005

Today I noticed that Mzee is beginning to show some interest in Owen. He does not seem to mind Owen following him. In the heat of the day Owen was sleeping beside him, some part of his body always touches Mzee, just like a human child reaching out for some security.

Owen has started following Mzee to the pond to swim, and then back out again to the food, and the most extraordinary thing happened today. I noticed Owen copying Mzee in eating dairy cubes (concentrated food that we give the other hippos) and drinking water. I wonder if my eyes are deceiving me, but Owen seemed to be copying Mzee. **6**

5th January, 2005

Owen is much stronger now and his attachment to Mzee is greater now than ever. Most of the time they are just together, but now Owen is trying to get Mzee to

Practice the Skills

5 **Reading Across Texts**

Primary and Secondary Sources What major event(s) has the author described in the last two pages? Were they included in the previous selection? Add the major event(s) to your chart and fill in the other columns.

6 **BIG Question**

Mzee didn't seem to like Owen at first. But now he seems to be more interested in Owen. Why do you think he changed his mind? Write your answer on your Foldable.

Vocabulary ....

hissed (hisd) *v.* made a sound like air escaping from a balloon

---

Additional Support

Differentiated Instruction

Kinesthetic and Literary Activities Students with strong kinesthetic skills may benefit from acting out the encounter between Owen and Mzee. Challenge them to create a silent scene showing the different stages of the evolving relationship between the two animals. **EL** **BL** Students with strong verbal-linguistic skills may benefit from writing a "diary" from the point of view of either Owen or Mzee. Challenge them to tell in their own words what either animal might have been thinking or feeling. **OL** **AL**

respond. This evening he licked Mzee on the face several times and I am sure that Mzee liked it! But as affectionate as Owen is I have to remember that he is still a hippo and hippos are territorial and strong. Especially males. Today he charged me and I discovered just how fast he really is! I had to dash behind a big old fig tree. I'm nearby all the time but Owen does not take his eyes off me. Does he think I am going to hurt Mzee? **7**

11th January, 2005

The story of Owen's amazing relationship with Mzee has gone all around the world. Everyone is interested and fascinated in this strange behavior and I have to admit, in all my 20 years of working with wild animals, I have never seen anything like it.

I suppose it is unique because the story has had such an impact all over the world—we have appeared on CNN, German TV, and people have contacted us from so many countries including Australia, India, France, USA, Germany, and South Africa. We actually captured a scene where Mzee put his head into Owen's mouth as if they are playing. I really wish I could understand what these two are saying to each other. **8**

15th January, 2005

It has been almost three weeks since we rescued Owen and he is doing so much better. He has regained his beautiful pink color, and is looking really fat and healthy. The media are still really excited about his relationship with Mzee.

30th January, 2005

During the day, when Mzee the tortoise is feeding on the grass, Owen follows him around and they feed together.

Practice the Skills

7 **BIG Question**
Sometimes two people just seem to like each other the first time they meet. But sometimes, one person has to "win" the other person's friendship. What is Owen doing to win Mzee's friendship? Have you ever seen or been involved in a relationship in which one person had to win the other person's friendship? Explain on your Foldable.

8 **Reading Across Texts**
Primary and Secondary Sources The author is giving you some details of life with Owen. Add any important events and information to your chart.

The Caretaker's Diary **1067**

Teach

R Reading Skill

Review Distinguishing Fact from Opinion Say: Territorial animals become attached to a particular area and are likely to fight to defend it. When Stephen states that "hippos are territorial," is he stating a fact or an opinion? *(fact)*

Literature Focus Lesson

Diary Entry A diarist usually records things that happen in his or her daily life, including sights, sounds, and thoughts. Have each student write two short diary entries about the past weekend. They should write about experiences that they participated in or witnessed on both Saturday and Sunday. Prompt students to describe the experience using sensory details. **AS**

Objectives
- Compare and contrast informational text
- Skim and scan text
- Paraphrase and summarize
- Distinguish fact from opinion

Teach

Viewing the Photo

Say: Write an informational caption for this photo. *(Responses will vary.)* **Say:** Now write a second caption for this photo. This time, make up words to express what you imagine the animals might be feeling. *(Responses will vary.)* **BL**

C Critical Thinking

Synthesis Ask: How do you know that Mzee and Owen are bonding? *(Possible response: They seem to wait for each other before they make a move. Owen seemed to help Mzee climb over a log. And, sometimes Owen licks Mzee's face and neck.)* **AS**

Owen also spends a lot of time trying to cool himself in the small pond while Mzee walks around often away from Owen. Even though they are inseparable, they are giving each other some space. **9**

7th February, 2005

Owen spent most of his time resting in the water with the tortoises. There are two tortoises in the enclosure, he shares his attention between the two. Owen's now changed his feeding habits as after feeding, he has started to feed on carrots and he also wanders freely around the enclosure, feeding on fallen leaves, fallen branches from trees around.

From about 6:45 P.M., he loves walking around alone at night. Visitors now enjoy watching him during his and Mzee's feeding time (which is daily at 4:30 P.M.). I think he has settled very, very well into his new home and he is finally at ease.

22nd April, 2005

Sometimes I think that Owen and Mzee are communicating, they often look as if they are deep in conversation. When they move Mzee sometimes waits for Owen to get up before he moves on. Owen always looks for Mzee before he goes exploring. At one point Owen looked as if he was helping Mzee to climb over a fallen log by nudging the back of his shell when he **C** seemed stuck with all four legs off the ground! The bond between them is stronger than ever. Owen can sometimes be seen licking Mzee's wrinkled face and neck as the old tortoise stretches his neck out, or nudging Mzee's shell with his fat foot when he wants to go for a walk.

Analyzing the Photo From viewing this photo, what can you say about the friendship between Owen and Mzee? Explain your answer.

1068 UNIT 8 What Makes a Friend?

Practice the Skills

9 BIG Question
What do you think the author means when he says, "They are giving each other some space"? Do you think that friends need to "give each other some space"? Why or why not? Write your answer on your Foldable.

Additional Support

Differentiated Instruction

Research Activity Ask students to research the phenomenon of animal communication. For instance:
• Many animals release a smell that sends a message.
• Chimpanzees touch hands to say hello.

• Elephants wrap their trunks around other elephants they like.
Ask students to choose an animal and research how it communicates. Have them draw a picture of the animal communicating and present it to the class. **AS**

He still sleeps with his head nestled comfortably on Mzee's enormous scaly arm. Mzee reciprocates[7] and has been filmed putting his head trustingly into Owen's mouth during a yawn.

When they fell asleep Mzee looked as if he was watching over Owen and only put his head down after Owen had closed his eyes. **10**

10th November, 2005

When Owen wants to go somewhere, he bites Mzee's foot. That's what happened when I brought their dinner today. Mzee wasn't interested, he had filled up on leaves. But Owen wanted the carrots and dairy cubes but didn't want to go to the feeding site alone. He could hear me whistling to call him and got up first but Mzee was busy eating leaves. He nudged Mzee and then mouthed his foot and kept doing it until Mzee moved to the food. Every now and again Mzee grumbled but he didn't sound too angry. When the crowds have left Haller Park and Mzee is settled Owen gets to lie down against him. He looks like he is in Hippo heaven.

28th November, 2005

R It is so enjoyable updating this diary because I enjoy reading all your comments. I must thank you all for caring so much about Owen and Mzee. I hope you will come and visit Owen and Mzee here in Mombasa. They have pleased thousands of visitors already this year. Please keep checking the Diary and let us know what you would like to read about. **11** ○

---

7. When someone **reciprocates,** he or she gives something back of equal value to what he or she received.

Practice the Skills

10 🗨 **BIG** Question
How do Owen and Mzee help and take care of each other? How do human friends help and take care of each other? Write your answers on the "Caretaker's Diary" page of Foldable 8. Your response will help you complete the Unit Challenge later.

11 **Reading Across Texts**
Primary and Secondary Sources Look over the last few paragraphs and add to your Comparison Chart any facts or events that you think are important.

The Caretaker's Diary **1069**

Assess

Resources for page 1070

📁 Selection Quick Check, pp. 79–80

⦿ ExamView Assessment Suite

⦿ Interactive Tutor: Self-Assessment

Vocabulary Check

Baby Hippo Orphan Finds a Friend

1. T
2. F
3. T
4. F
5. Responses will vary.

from The Caretaker's Diary

6. e
7. d
8. a
9. c
10. b

After You Read

Baby Hippo Orphan Finds a Friend & from The Caretaker's DIARY

Vocabulary Check

On a separate sheet of paper, write the numbers 1–4. Next to each number, write *T* or *F* to show whether the statement is true or false. Then write your answer to item 5.

Baby Hippo Orphan *Finds a Friend*

tsunami
surf
sanctuary
tortoise

1. A tsunami can cause flooding and destruction.
2. A tortoise usually has fur and loves to run quickly.
3. A wildlife sanctuary is a place where animals are safe from hunters.
4. The ocean's surf is found between deep water and dry land.
5. Now, on your sheet of paper, write a paragraph that uses all four of the vocabulary words correctly.

from The Caretaker's DIARY

For items 6–10, choose the letter of the definition that best matches each word. Write your answers on a separate sheet of paper.

6. ___ convoy
7. ___ subdued
8. ___ traumatized
9. ___ enclosure
10. ___ hissed

a. very upset
b. made a sound like air escaping
c. fenced-off place
d. quiet and weak
e. a group of cars traveling together

Objectives (pp. 1070–1071)
Reading Compare and contrast: primary and secondary sources
Writing Compare and contrast: sources of information

Reading/Critical Thinking

On a separate sheet of paper, answer the following questions.

Baby Hippo Orphan *Finds a Friend*

11. **Recall** How did the baby hippo end up in the Indian Ocean?
    Tip Right There

12. **Draw Conclusions** As an ecologist, why would Paula Kahumbu not expect the tortoise to become a friend of Owen's?
    Tip Author and Me

from The Caretaker's DIARY

13. **Interpret** At the beginning of the journal, how do you think the caretaker felt when he learned he was needed to rescue a baby hippopotamus?
    Tip Author and Me

14. **Analyze** Why do you think Owen first selected Mzee as his friend?
    Tip Author and Me

15. **Analyze** Why do you think so many people came to see Owen and Mzee in the park?
    Tip On My Own

Writing: Reading Across Texts

Use Your Notes

16. Follow these steps to find out what types of information come from primary sources and secondary sources.

    Step 1: Look over the charts you made for these two selections. As you compare the charts, remember that "The Caretaker's Diary" was much longer than "Baby Hippo Orphan Finds a Friend," so you will probably have more entries on that chart.

    Step 2: Look over your charts carefully. What is the point of view in each selection? Which chart has more feelings and opinions? Which chart has more details?

    Step 3: Think about the facts, details, feelings, and opinions in each selection.

Get It on Paper

To compare the secondary source article and the primary source, answer the following questions on a separate sheet of paper.

17. Which selection gives you a shorter overview of what happened? Explain your answer.

18. Which selection gives you more details about how the friendship between Owen and Mzee developed?

19. Which selection gives you a better idea of what it would be like to work with Owen and Mzee? Explain why you chose that selection.

20. If you wanted to get general information about a topic quickly, would you go to a primary source or a secondary source? Explain your choice.

21. If you wanted to find out what a particular kind of job was like, would you go to a news article about that job or the diary of someone who held that job? Explain your choice.

BIG Question

22. These selections are about how two very different animals became close friends. How can people make friends with others who are very different from themselves?

Reading/Critical Thinking

Baby Hippo Orphan Finds a Friend

11. The other hippos got separated from the baby hippo.

12. Possible response: They live in different environments.

from The Caretaker's Diary

13. Possible response: excited and ready to help

14. Possible response: Mzee showed interest in Owen.

15. Possible response: They had an unusual friendship.

Write About Your Reading

Use Your Notes

16. Responses will vary.

Get It On Paper

17. Possible response: Baby Hippo Orphan Finds a Friend—it is presented as a news story with highlights.

18. Possible response: from The Caretaker's Diary

19. Possible response: from The Caretaker's Diary—the diary spells out the day-in and day-out activities.

20. Possible response: Go to a secondary source because its purpose is to summarize and present only the high points.

21. Possible response: Go to the diary because you would read about the person's activities and responsibilities on the job.

 BQ **BIG Question**

22. Responses will vary.

Close

Ask students to discuss what makes animals interesting and why people would want to study their behaviors.

The Unit Challenge

Focus

BELLRINGER Options

✍ **Daily Language Practice Transparency 80 Focus Activity Ask:** Of the selections you read in this unit, which do you think best tells what makes a friend? Why? *(Responses will vary.)* **AS** The discussion will remind students of the selections they've read, which will help them begin the group or the solo activity.

Teach

Group Activity: The Friendship Play

Make sure each group member has a task. Here are some plot ideas to share with the groups:

- The day the wall of cliques fell down
- Our team needed only one point to win when (some-thing) happened.
- My mom finally accepts my friends.
- The Homework Club takes on (subject).

Assess/Close

Group Activity

Ask: How does your play address some of the important parts of what makes a friend? *(Suggest that students write responses in their Learner's Notebooks.)* **AS**

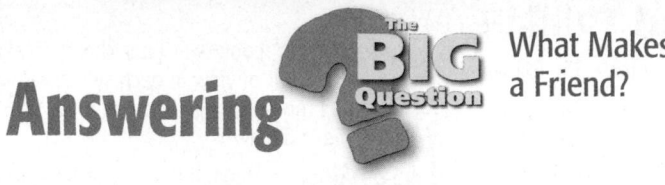

UNIT 8 WRAP-UP

Answering The BIG Question — What Makes a Friend?

You've just read about people who faced the Big Question: What makes a friend? Now use what you've learned to do the Unit Challenge.

The Unit Challenge

Choose Activity A or Activity B and follow the directions for that activity.

A. Group Activity: The Friendship Play

A play has many different elements, including acts and scenes, dialogue, characterization, and stage directions. Now get ready to write your own play.

1. **Think About Your Scene** Divide into groups of four or five. Each group will write a scene based on the Big Question: What makes a friend? As a group, use the notes you each made in your Foldables to help you decide how you want your scene to answer the Big Question.

2. **Script Development** To write your script:
   - Decide what problem (or conflict) the scene is about. Then decide on the solution.
   - Choose one student to play the Narrator. Discuss what you think the Narrator should say to introduce the scene.
   - Discuss the types of characters you want in the scene.
   - Start by role-playing. As you role-play, make up what characters will say and do. Have one or two group members take notes.
   - Choose group members to create the setting, props, and costumes, as needed.

3. **Theater Artists at Work** When you have all the elements of the scene worked out, do the following:
   - Writers: Create the final draft of the script and give everyone a copy. Remember to include stage directions that tell when and where the scene is set.
   - Set designers: Create the scenery and props.
   - Actors: Practice your lines.

4. **Dress Rehearsal** Now it's time to rehearse:
   - Set up the scenery, put the props in place, have actors get into costumes (if necessary), and rehearse the scene.
   - If actors have trouble remembering the lines, allow them to make up their own lines.
   - Be sure to work toward having a scene that is lively and explores the Big Question in some way. The Narrator can comment on the action or address the Big Question directly.

5. **Perform and Present** Each group should perform its scene for the class.

Literature Online

Big Question Have students access the Web site for English and Spanish summaries and annotated links to related Web resources.

B. Solo Activity: Create a Friendship Comic Book

Today, the comic book (or graphic novel) is considered an art form. It's a visual way to explore important themes. You'll create a comic book that answers the Big Question: What makes a friend?

1. Create a Storyboard Review your Foldable notes.

- Think about a situation that shows what you think makes a friend. Use that situation as the story for your comic book.

- Create your storyboards—rough sketches and descriptions of what you think each page of your comic book will look like.

2. Design Your Panels, Plan Your Story

- Begin to sketch the different scenes, write dialogue, and write descriptions that go with your sketches. Plan as you go. Make more storyboards if necessary.

- In a comic book, as in a play, there is often a Narrator. Who will be the Narrator in your comic? It might be one of the characters. It could be you, commenting on the action. Either way, the Narrator should introduce and directly address the Big Question: What makes a friend?

3. Pen and Ink

In the comic book industry, the author "pens" the story and the illustrator "inks" the pictures. In this case, you do both.

- Add the dialogue to your panels.
- Add color to your story.
- Don't forget the cover and title.

4. Publish

Present your book to the class. Leave it on permanent display somewhere in the classroom where your classmates can read it.

Teach

Solo Activity: Create a Friendship Comic Book

- Have on hand some appropriate comic books or graphic novels. Invite students to browse and notice how simple or detailed a comic book presentation can be.

- Some students may benefit from brainstorming with a partner or a small group to come up with story ideas about the big question.

- While students will have a narrative, you may need to help them with the dialogue. Show students how to move a story along by the words characters say rather than by *telling* a story.

- If helpful, students can seek the help of fellow students adept at art to consult or help with their drawings.

- As a last step, students may wish to photocopy their comic book and distribute it to classmates.

Assess/Close

Solo Activity

Ask students to identify how their story line and drawings develop the question—what makes a friend? Further, what were they able to show about a friend because they could use both words and drawings? **AS**

Objectives
- Brainstorm ideas
- Establish a writing plan
- Write dialogue

1073

Focus

Vocabulary Preview

List the following words on the board:

- "meaning walk"
- plod
- mellow
- "blade-end up"

Review their definitions before students begin reading.

Teach

EL Language Coach

Connotation Say: The words in poems, especially short poems, are chosen very carefully—not just for their correct definition or denotation. They are also chosen for their connotation. For instance, the ground isn't just *soft* ground—it's *mellow.* That means it's more than soft, it's *comfortingly soft,* so you get the feeling the poet wants to work it, not stop and talk. Instead, he turns the hoe "blade-end up" so that it is not ready for work. Keep this in mind as you read the following selection. **AS**

Robert Frost

Meet the Author

Robert Frost was born in 1874 and died in 1963. A farmer for part of his life, he often wrote about our relationship to nature. He used the harsh New England countryside as a backdrop for his thoughts and observations. In 1961, he read a poem for the inauguration of President John F. Kennedy. After Frost's death, President Kennedy remembered the poet in this way: "Our national strength matters; but the spirit which informs and controls our strength matters just as much. This was the special significance of Robert Frost." See page R3 of the Author Files for more on Robert Frost.

Literature Online

Author Search For more about Robert Frost, go to www.glencoe.com.

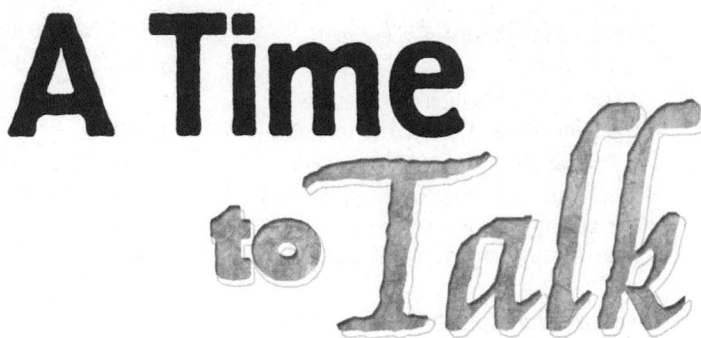

A Time to Talk

by Robert Frost

When a friend calls to me from the road
And slows his horse to a meaning walk,[1]
I don't stand still and look around
On all the hills I haven't hoed,
5 And shout from where I am, What is it?

EL

---

1. Here, the ***meaning walk*** is a "meaningful or purposeful pace," with the friend slowing down to show that he wishes to talk with the speaker of the poem.

Additional Support

Literature Online

Author Search To expand students' appreciation of Robert Frost, have them access the Web site for additional information and resources.

Literature Focus Lesson

Summary Students can easily summarize the surface events in this Frost poem. After students have written a short summary, ask them to describe how Frost has captured in ten short lines some very complex feelings. Frost must have struggled to find just the right words, for he has here transformed a simple exchange with a neighbor into a picture of self-sacrifice. The man turns away from his job with a hoe—not in a begrudging way, though he feels ungiving of time. Instead, he only shows, in his slow walk to meet the neighbor, some resistance. The poem is as rich in feelings as the earth he's turning over with his hoe. **AS**

No, not as there is a time to talk.
I thrust my hoe in the mellow ground,
Blade-end up and five feet tall,
And plod:[2] I go up to the stone wall
10 For a friendly visit.

R

2. To **plod** is to walk along slowly and heavily.

Teach

Viewing the Photo

Say: In your own words, describe the photo. What mood does it convey? *(Possible response: It's a country scene from a beautiful angle. It makes the country look peaceful and rich and comforting.)* **Ask:** How does it add or detract from the poem? If you could choose another kind of visual, what would it be? Why? **OL**

R Reading Skill

Review Drawing Conclusions Ask: Why do you think the speaker is so reluctant to go talk with his neighbor?*(Possible response: He's busy; he wants to get his work done.)* **Ask:** Does the poem show him staying aloof or giving in and talking? *(He goes for a friendly visit.)* **AS**

Reading Fluency

Choral Reading Break the class into two groups for a choral reading of the poem. During rehearsal, encourage students to work on such vocal traits as musicality, dynamics, enunciation, and expressiveness to communicate meaning and engage listeners. Encourage them to use appropriate intonations (clued by punctuation) and reflect Frost's tone (clued by Frost's word choice and sentence construction). As one group performs, invite the other group to listen and enjoy the reading. **AS**

Objectives:
• Draw conclusions
• Learn and use new vocabulary
• Analyze features of genres: poetry
• Understand connotation

1075

Stress the importance of reading a variety of selections that present different types of communities. Suggest the books listed here that are related to the Big Question.

Fiction

Explain to students how reading fictional stories about how friends survive tough times together is an excellent way to see what makes a friend. Ask students to give examples from their own reading—or from watching a TV program or news report—that clearly shows what makes a friend.

UNIT 8

Reading on Your Own

To read more about the Big Question, choose one of these books from your school or local library. Work on your reading skills by choosing books that are challenging to you.

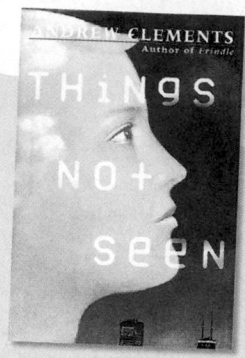

Fiction

Things Not Seen
by Andrew Clements

Bobby's new friend, Alicia, is blind, but that doesn't stop her from helping Bobby solve a problem. When Bobby wakes up invisible one morning, he relies on Alicia—and her special sight—to help him tackle his biggest challenge ever.

Bronx Masquerade
by Nikki Grimes

The students at a Bronx high school gain a new respect for their own inner lives—and for the lives of their classmates—when they begin to read their own poems aloud. Read to find out how language and performance changed these students' lives.

The Princess Diaries
by Meg Cabot

Mia is fourteen and lives in New York when she discovers that her father is the Prince of Genovia. With the help of a good friend and a caring grandmother, Mia survives (and thrives!) during this unexpected life change.

Buddha Boy
By Kathe Koja

Justin is just trying to get through high school unnoticed when he meets Jinsen, an artistic and soft-spoken Buddhist whose religious devotion sets him apart from his schoolmates. Read to find out what Justin learns from his unlikely friendship with the young man the others call "Buddha Boy."

Additional Support

Differentiated Instruction

 Use the Glencoe BookLink CD-ROM to create customized reading lists to help students answer the Big Question. Suggestions for Unit 8:
Grade 5: *The View from Saturday* by E.L. Konigsburg
Grade 6: *The Kid Nobody Could Handle* by Kurt Vonnegut

Grade 6: *Sound-Shadows of the New World* by Ved Mehta
Grade 7: *All Things Bright and Beautiful* by James Herriot
Grade 8: *Winter Thunder and the Christmas of the Phonograph Records* by Mari Sandoz

Nonfiction

The Story of My Life
by Helen Keller

Everything changed for Helen Keller when she met Anne Sullivan. Deaf, blind, and unable to speak, Keller was virtually cut off from the world. Then Anne broke through and helped Helen unlock her powers of communication. Read to learn more about the lifelong friendship these women shared.

Path of Hunters
by Robert Newton Peck

Robert Newton Peck grew up on a farm in Vermont where he learned to respect even the smallest of animals. Check out this book to learn more about nature and the survival of meadow animals.

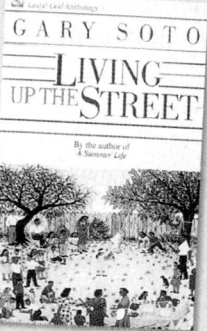

Through a Window
by Jane Goodall

Ever wonder how chimpanzees talk to each other, or what they do all day? This book answers those questions and many more. Read to meet chimps Gigi, Goblin, and Passion and to find out why protecting them—and their environment—is more important now than ever.

Living Up the Street
by Gary Soto

This powerful collection of coming-of-age stories peels back the curtain of time on Gary Soto's childhood. Read to learn more about his growing-up experiences on the industrial side of Fresno, California.

Nonfiction

Explain to students that the books featured on this page are all nonfiction. In them, the authors tell about the extraordinary friendships that had big effects upon the persons (or chimp).

Autobiographies

Ask: How can you tell if these are biographies or autobiographies? *(Possible response: The author's name with the title, as in "The Story of My Life" by Helen Keller. The blurb also tells the reader who it is about.)* **OL**

About the Subjects

Nikki Grimes allows the voices of 18 students to show the richness of their views and tentativeness of their reaching out to belong. In Gary Soto's book of recollections, the award-winning author gives glimpses of his life in an ethnically mixed neighborhood in Fresno, California, as a Mexican American. He shows the big gap between the lives of white kids and Chicanos.

Test-Taking Tips

Tip Remind students to read each question carefully and be sure they understand what the question is asking before looking for the answer.

Tip Remind students that the plot is carried along by dialogue in a drama, so they should read the dialogue carefully.

Tip Remind students that, sometimes, the main idea of a passage is not explicitly stated. The reader must infer the main idea from the passage.

Test Practice

Part 1: Literary Elements

1. D
2. D
3. In act one

Unit Assessment Have students access the Web site to prepare for the Unit 8 test.

Test Practice

Part 1: Literary Elements

Read the following play excerpt and use it to answer the questions. On a separate sheet of paper, write the numbers 1–4. Next to numbers 1–3, write the letter of the correct answer. Next to number 4, write your answer to the question.

Act One
Scene One

The lights come up on the tidy bedroom of Lily, who is working at a computer. The walls are covered with posters of women's basketball. A wastebasket has a hoop (with net) above it. Another teenage girl, Sasha, *enters hurriedly.*

Sasha. (*Frantic*) Lily, you've got to help me!

Lily. (*Reading from a spiral notebook as she types*) George Washington lived on a plantation named Mount Vernon . . .

Sasha. Lily! Listen to me!

Lily. (*Tearing herself away from the screen*) What? I'm in the middle of—

Sasha. Let it wait, Lily! I'm in terrible trouble! Can't you help your own sister when she's in terrible trouble?

Lily. Again? Oh, Sasha, you're always in trouble, and it's always terrible trouble, and you always get into it without my help. And then I have to drop what I'm doing and rescue you. Why should I keep getting you out of trouble I didn't get you into?

---

1. Sasha's character is revealed **mainly** by
   A. stage directions.
   B. what she does.
   C. what she says about herself.
   D. what Lily says about her.

2. Which of the following do the stage directions reveal?
   A. what Lily is writing
   B. Sasha's attitude toward Lily
   C. what the relationship is between Lily and Sasha
   D. some clues about Lily's personality and interests

3. To which sense does the description of the set appeal?
   A. sight   B. hearing
   C. smell   D. taste

4. When in the play does this scene occur?

Objectives (pp. 1078–1079)
Reading Skim and scan text • Visualize • Make predictions • Clarify text and ideas
Literature Understand literary elements: characterization • Understand elements of drama: act and scene, stage directions • Identify sensory imagery

Part 2: Reading Skills

On a separate sheet of paper, write the numbers 1–4. Next to each number, write the letter of the correct answer. Read the following play excerpt and use it to answer the questions.

Scene Two

The lights come up on a backyard. A five-foot, solid fence extends across the back of the stage. Lily and Sasha are gazing over the fence.

Lily. Good grief! What did you do? It used to be so beautiful! How'd you get it home?

Sasha. Oh, it drives all right. It just looks sort of . . . bad.

Lily. Sort of? This morning, that was a shiny, racy, dazzling little sports car . . . and now it's a crumpled, smashed, twisted *mess.* Dad's going to have a fit!

Sasha. But see, that's why I need your help! OK, I did kind of mess up the car. And Dad will be unhappy. But think how much more unhappy he'd be if he knew his own daughter did it. Think how much better it would be for him if he thought a stranger took it and crashed it and . . . left it somewhere.

Lily. (*Backing away from Sasha*) Stop right there! I do not like the direction you're headed.

---

1. Imagine that a reader is confused about what Lily is referring to as *it* in her first few lines. What would be the best way to clarify the situation?

   A. Reread Lily's first few lines.

   B. Look up words in a dictionary.

   C. Ask questions of another reader.

   D. Read on to see if further information helps.

2. What is the most likely reason that this section of the play has details about the car's appearance?

   A. to show that Lily is an expert on cars

   B. to help the audience or reader visualize the car

   C. to make the reader feel sorry for Sasha

   D. to show how Sasha looks at the problem

3. If the rest of this scene were printed here, which of the following could you tell if you **only** scanned it?

   A. whether Lily agrees to help Sasha

   B. exactly what Sasha's plan involves

   C. if any new characters are in the scene

   D. how Sasha got into a wreck involving the car

4. Which of the following is the most logical prediction of what will happen next?

   A. Lily and Sasha will argue.

   B. Lily will take the blame for Sasha.

   C. Sasha will decide the problem isn't serious.

   D. The car will get fixed before the father comes home.

Resources for pages 1078–1081

Use these resources to review, assess, or reteach the Unit: Active Learning and Note Taking Guide, Selection and Unit Assessment, ExamView Assessment Suite, and Skill Level Up!™ A Language Arts Game.

Part 2: Reading Skills

1. D
2. B
3. B
4. A

Part 3: Vocabulary

1. B
2. B
3. B
4. C
5. D
6. B
7. D
8. D
9. C
10. C

Part 3: Vocabulary

On a separate sheet of paper, write the numbers 1–10. Next to each number, write the letter of the correct answer for that question.

Write the letter of the word or phrase that means about the same as the underlined word.

1. to move warily
   - **A.** quickly
   - **B.** very carefully
   - **C.** unexpectedly
   - **D.** in a clumsy way

2. to be a fiasco
   - **A.** problem
   - **B.** total flop
   - **C.** courage
   - **D.** amusing event

3. penetrated her coat
   - **A.** ruined
   - **B.** went through
   - **C.** decorated
   - **D.** made a mess of

4. to be conceited
   - **A.** hidden
   - **B.** worried
   - **C.** stuck up
   - **D.** dishonest

5. to integrate them
   - **A.** notice
   - **B.** choose
   - **C.** favor
   - **D.** combine

Objectives (pp. 1080–1081)
Vocabulary Identify slang, idioms, clipped words, figurative meanings of words
Grammar Use punctuation correctly: hyphens, apostrophes, semicolons, colons, quotation marks

Write the letter of the best answer.

6. Which sentence contains slang?
   - **A.** That was a good game.
   - **B.** That boy's sure got game.
   - **C.** Do you want to play a game?
   - **D.** I don't know the rules of the game.

7. What does the underlined idiom mean in the sentence below?

   I don't have time to hear all the details, so cut to the chase.
   - **A.** Go away.
   - **B.** Tell me later.
   - **C.** Come with me.
   - **D.** Get to the point.

8. Use logic to choose the word that the clipped word *ad* comes from.
   - **A.** advice
   - **B.** admission
   - **C.** adjustment
   - **D.** advertisement

9. In which sentence is the word *swims* used figuratively?
   - **A.** Jose swims every day.
   - **B.** The trout swims upstream.
   - **C.** The moon swims in the inky sky.
   - **D.** The otter swims playfully in the lake.

10. Use what you know about *mob* to figure out what *mob* means in the sentence below?

    Let's mob to the party, okay?
    - **A.** hurry
    - **B.** be late
    - **C.** go as a group
    - **D.** take a short cut

Part 4: Writing Skills

On a separate sheet of paper, write the numbers 1–7. Next to each number, write the letter of the correct answer for that question.

1. Which phrase uses an apostrophe correctly?

   A. a horses' head

   B. the childrens' bikes

   C. both teachers' ideas

   D. my grandparents's house

2. Which of the following could be divided with a hypen if it appeared at the end of a line?

   A. mouse

   B. branch

   C. maybe

   D. straight

3. Which of the following sentences uses apostrophes correctly?

   A. Im sure thats something we shouldn't do.

   B. I'm sure that's something we should'nt do.

   C. I'm sure thats something we shouldn't do.

   D. I'm sure that's something we shouldn't do.

4. Which of the following sentences is written correctly?

   A. I wish I had pets I really like them.

   B. I wish I had pets; I really like them.

   C. I wish I had pets, I really like them.

   D. I wish I had pets; because I really like them.

5. Which of the following is written correctly?

   A. The time is now 4:30.

   B. I want: a big house and a car.

   C. So I said: "Give me that, now!"

   D. I think we deserve: a second chance.

6. What sentence is written correctly?

   A. "Don't be so sure Pete said, angrily."

   B. "If you help," said Teresa, "we'll soon be done."

   C. "I wonder," said Barbra, "About what you mean."

   D. "Really"? asked Paul. "Are you serious about that?"

7. Which correction should be made to the sentence below?

   Kelly said "that she liked your gift."

   A. Capitalize *that*.

   B. Remove the quotation marks.

   C. Start the quotation before *said*.

   D. Add a comma after *said*.

Part 4: Writing Skills

1. C
2. C
3. D
4. B
5. A
6. B
7. B

REFERENCE SECTION

AUTHOR FILES

Maya Angelou (1928–)

- was originally named Marguerite; Maya is the name her brother called her as a child
- at the age of three, was sent to live with her grandmother who ran the only black-owned general store in the town of Stamps, Arkansas
- has been a professor at Wake Forest University for more than twenty years
- speaks French, Spanish, Italian, Arabic, and Fanti (a language of southern Ghana) fluently

Avi (1937–)

- his grandmother, an aunt, and his parents were writers; two uncles were painters and another a composer
- late in his school career, it was discovered that he has dysgraphia, an impairment that causes him to reverse letters or misspell words
- his twin sister gave him the name "Avi" when they were both about a year old

Quote: *"Everybody has ideas. The vital question is, what do you do with them?"*

Toni Cade Bambara (1939–1995)

- studied acting and mime in Italy and France
- worked as an investigator for the New York State Department of Welfare for two years
- was encouraged by her mother to be creative
- contributed to several films as a writer and commentator

Quote: *"She gave me permission to wonder, to dawdle, to daydream."*

Ray Bradbury (1920–)

- does not like technology even though he writes about it; he doesn't drive a car, use a computer, or fly in airplanes
- feels that much of his work is too fantastic to be considered science fiction, which he said he felt had to be based on possibilities for the future
- has written more than 30 books and 600 short stories

Quote: *"The great fun in my life has been getting up every morning and rushing to the typewriter…"*

Gwendolyn Brooks (1917–2000)

- was born in Topeka, Kansas, but lived most of her life in Chicago
- was the first black writer to win the Pulitzer Prize (1950) and the first black woman appointed poetry consultant to the Library of Congress
- followed Carl Sandburg as Poet Laureate of Illinois in 1968; served until her death in 2000

Quote: *"I am interested in telling my particular truth as I have seen it."*

Lewis Carroll (1832–1898)

- Charles Lutwidge Dodson, the third of eleven children, took the pen name Lewis Carroll in his twenties
- wanted to be a clergyman like his father, but a severe stutter prevented him from most public speaking
- in addition to the children's books for which he is best known, he published more than ten books on mathematics

Sandra Cisneros (1954–)

- was the only girl in a family of seven children
- was in the news in Texas for two years because of the color of her house
- has been a National Endowment for the Arts fellow and was awarded the American Book Award from the Before Columbus Foundation

Quote: *"I feel like a cartographer. I'm determined to fill a literary void."*

Judith Ortiz Cofer (1952–)

- grew up speaking Spanish at home but learned English well enough to become a writer and college professor
- lives in Georgia on a farm that has been in her husband's family for generations
- believes that immigrants do not have to choose one identity over another and says she uses her art "as a bridge between [her] cultures…traveling back and forth without fear and confusion"

Robert Cormier (1925–2000)

- in eighth grade, saw through his classroom window that his house was on fire; was not allowed to check on his family until he had recited the rosary
- his book for young adults, *The Chocolate War,* was banned in many cities

Quote: *"I was a skinny kid living in a ghetto-type neighborhood wanting the world to know that I existed."*

Harold Courlander (1908–1996)

- was a farmer, a historian, an editor, a press officer, and a writer
- won a copyright infringement suit against *Roots* author Alex Haley
- worked "in the field" studying and recording the folktales of people in Haiti, Cuba, Ethiopia, Nigeria, Ghana, the Pacific Islands, and the American Southwest

E. E. Cummings (1894–1962)

- joined the ambulance service in World War I because he believed that violence was wrong
- published over forty texts, including books of poetry, artwork, and plays
- once characterized himself as "an author of pictures"
- changed modern poetry by bending or breaking rules of grammar, punctuation, and even the placement of words on a page

Will Eisner (1917–2005)

- is credited with a leading role in creating the graphic novel form
- helped the careers of many other famous comic artists, such as Jack Kirby and Bob Kane
- used his drawing abilities in the service of his country when he was drafted into the Army
- co-founded the famous Eisner-Iger studio

Robert Frost (1874–1963)

- lived during times of great change; was born less than ten years after the Civil War and died less than ten years before a man walked on the moon
- decided to be a poet when he was sixteen
- married Elinor White and had six children; Elinor and four of the children died during his lifetime
- was very shy but developed a style of quoting poetry that made him one of the most popular performers in America and overseas

John Gardner (1933–1982)

- when he was eleven, a tractor he was riding ran over his seven-year-old brother
- wrote thirty-five books in twenty-five years
- died in a motorcycle accident
- was the son of an English-teacher mother and a preacher/ dairy farmer father

Quote: *"True art is moral; it seeks to improve life, not debase it."*

Nikki Giovanni (1943–)

- her real first name is Yolande, the same as her mother's
- during the 1960s she was known as the "Princess of Black Poetry"
- named "Woman of the Year" three times by well-known publications
- appeared on *The Tonight Show* in 1972

Quote: *"Everything will change. The only question is growing up or decaying."*

Kenneth Grahame (1859–1932)

- became the Secretary of the Bank of England
- was born blind in one eye, with a severe squint in the other
- created his most famous character, Toad, to amuse and educate his young son Alastair
- he and his two siblings were brought up by elderly relatives, after the illness of their father and death of their mother
- his cousin, Sir Anthony Hope Hawkins, wrote *The Prisoner of Zenda*

Jim Haskins (1941–2005)

- in college, was arrested for marching on Montgomery, Alabama, as part of the Civil Rights movement
- started his writing career by keeping a diary of his thoughts when he was teaching public school in Harlem
- wrote the book *The Cotton Club,* which was made into a movie
- published more than 100 books
- read the encyclopedia as a child, because he could not use the segregated town library

Kristin Hunter (1931–)

- her novel *The Landlord* was made into a movie
- was awarded both the 1968 Council on Interracial Books for Children Award and the 1971 Lewis Carroll Shelf Award
- landed her first writing job as a teenager; for six years, as a high school and college student, wrote a column for a newspaper

Quote: *"Every one of us is a wonder. Every one of us has a story."*

Francisco Jiménez (1943–)

- is a former illegal immigrant migrant worker; went on to earn advanced college degrees
- has taught in universities in the United States and in Mexico
- won awards for his children's books, his nonfiction, and his teaching
- his collection of autobiographical short stories has been translated into Spanish, Chinese, Japanese, and Korean

Bill Littlefield (1948–)

- in addition to writing books and essays, frequently contributes to newspapers
- has been a National Public Radio commentator since 1984
- has won six Associated Press Awards
- taught writing courses at the Harvard University Summer School and the John F. Kennedy School Summer Program for Masters Candidates

Jack London (1876–1919)

- was a coal shoveler, a sailor, a hobo, and a convict all before he entered high school; he then went to the Yukon in search of gold
- wrote nearly two dozen novels, as well as hundreds of short stories
- was raised by his "Aunt Jennie" after mental illness made his mother too weak to care for him
- in 1894, marched on Washington, D.C., to protest mass unemployment
- ran for mayor of Oakland, California, in 1901

Norma Fox Mazer (1931–)

- to support their family, she and her husband wrote fiction for the women's romance and confession market
- as a teenager, her nickname was "the Cold One"
- has published 31 books
- decided to become a writer when she was thirteen

Quote: *"I write and my readers read to find out the answers to questions, secrets, problems, to be drawn into the deepest mystery of all—someone else's life."*

Patricia C. & Frederick McKissack, Jr. (1944–), (1939–)

- husband and wife team have worked together on more than fifty books
- best known for their biographies of important African Americans, written for younger readers
- were jointly awarded the Coretta Scott King Award twice

Quote: *on marching in the Civil Rights Movement, "In a sense we marched from the Old South to a new America."*

Pat Mora (1942–)

- has written picture books, a biography, a board book, a counting book, and two retellings of Mayan folktales
- her grandparents left Mexico during the revolution to escape the violent raids of Pancho Villa
- winner of more than twenty major awards

Quote: *"Writing is a way of finding out how I feel about anything and everything."*

Lensey Namioka (1929–)

- says she is the only person in the world named Lensey; her father made up the name
- is the daughter of a linguist (an expert in languages) and a doctor/writer
- was encouraged by her parents to love music, which became a subject for many of her books
- is from China and her husband is from Japan, so she is interested in writing about both places
- has been writing books for more than thirty years and has won numerous awards

Mary Pope Osborne (1949–)

- lived in a cave in Crete for six weeks
- grew up in a military family and had lived on two continents and more than six army posts before she was fifteen
- loves the theater and has worked as a drama teacher
- survived an earthquake in northern Afghanistan and a riot in Kabul

Quote: *"Our imaginations plus our reading and writing skills … take us wherever we want to go."*

Richard Peck (1934–)

- his book *Amanda/Miranda* was a bestseller and has been translated into nine languages
- three of his young adult novels have been made into TV movies
- started writing books for young people after being a high school teacher

Quote: *"You and I, we people of the word, spend our lives hollering across the famous generation gap, hoping to hear an answering echo."*

Cynthia Rylant (1954–)

- wrote her first children's book in one hour; drew on her own life as a child in the Appalachian Mountains for that book and many others
- has written novels, stories, and poems for young children, teenagers, and young adults
- has written more than 60 books and won the Newbery Medal in 1993

Quote: *"I love being a writer because I want to leave something here on earth to make it better, prettier, stronger."*

Stan Sakai (1953–)

- grew up reading the work of Stan Ditko, and Marvel and DC comics
- is the Chief Executive Officer of *Usagi Studios,* which has one employee–himself
- was born in Kyoto; moved with his family to Hawaii at the age of two
- winner of the Eisner Award several times
- does his own historical research for his comic set in Japan's past

Luis Omar Salinas (1937–)

- orphaned at the age of four; lived with his aunt and uncle and considered them his parents
- particularly enjoys reaching audiences by reading his poetry aloud
- attended Fresno State University and also became a creative writing instructor there

Quote: *"Sometimes life is harsh, and the poet has to find a way to escape."*

Robert Service (1874–1958)
- lived and traveled in many different countries
- was an instant success after his first book was published
- worked during World War I as a correspondent and an ambulance driver
- had several of his books made into movies
- has three schools named after him in Alaska and Canada and was honored on a Canadian stamp
- was the most popular poet in America but called himself "only a 'rhymer' and an 'inkslinger'"

Shel Silverstein (1930–1999)
- played guitar, piano, saxophone, and trombone
- was first published in *Playboy* magazine
- wrote and recorded "A Boy Named Sue," a song made famous by Johnny Cash
- worked as a writer, cartoonist, lyricist, musician, composer, and even an actor
- his first book for children was made into an animated movie

Isaac Bashevis Singer (1904–1991)
- won the 1978 Nobel Prize in Literature
- wrote almost all his works in Yiddish and sometimes re-wrote them in English
- son of a Hassidic rabbi; both his grandfathers were also rabbis
- published hundreds of short stories, volumes of autobiography, a dozen novels, and even more children's books

Quote: *"A writer has to write in his own language or not at all."*

Gary Soto (1952–)
- is a third-generation Mexican American
- has edited story collections and written poetry, essays, novels, young adult and children's books, and made movies
- taught English and Chicano Studies at the University of California, Berkeley
- enjoys theater, tennis, basketball, traveling, and working in the garden

Quote: *"I discovered that reading builds a life inside the mind."*

Stephen Spender (1909–1995)
- primarily known as one of the "Oxford poets;" his name was frequently linked with W. H. Auden
- served on the UN Economic and Scientific Committee (UNESCO)
- in 1993, filed a lawsuit claiming that the novel *While England Sleeps* was taken from his own autobiography
- received the knighthood in 1983
- much of his early poetry was political and social protest

Mildred D. Taylor (1943–)
- as part of the Peace Corps in Ethiopia, she taught English and history for two years
- helped create a Black Studies program at the University of Colorado
- was born in Mississippi; her family moved to newly-integrated Toledo, Ohio, when she was only three months old
- won the Coretta Scott King Award for three of her books

Yoshiko Uchida (1921–1992)

- graduated from high school in just two and a half years
- during World War II, lived in a Japanese-American internment camp for about a year
- received a Ford Foundation fellowship in 1952
- is known primarily for her children's books; has also written fiction and nonfiction for adults

Quote: *"I write to celebrate our common humanity, for the basic elements of humanity are present in all our strivings."*

Alma Luiz Villanueva (1944–)

- lived in the Mission district of San Francisco until she was eleven years old
- served on the National Endowment for the Arts fiction panel
- was raised by her Yaqui Indian grandmother and Mexican-American aunt
- began publishing poetry in her early thirties

Quote: *"Poetry for me is the source, the mother tongue, the sun, moon, and stars."*

Judith Viorst (1931–)

- her first break as a writer came when she was hired to write a book for NASA
- her credits include a magazine column, nonfiction works, collections of poetry, and picture books
- she and her husband, writer and political analyst Milton Viorst, have three sons
- her most famous children's book is *Alexander and the Terrible, Horrible, No Good, Very Bad Day*

Mary Whitebird

- is the pen name of a writer/filmmaker who is neither an Indian nor a woman
- once received a letter from a Cherokee reader who said about Whitebird's work, "Only an Indian could have written this."
- another correspondent wrote: "It's obvious that, as a woman, you are concerned with feminist issues."

Jane Yolen (1939–)

- is the daughter of two authors; her father also popularized kite flying, and her mother created crossword puzzles for magazines
- studied music and ballet
- has written more than 250 books, which have been translated into 22 languages
- ran a workshop for new authors for twenty years

Quote: *"My advice for young people interested in writing: read and write. Read and read and read."*

Paul Zindel (1936–2003)

- had a troubled childhood—said in an interview, "I felt worthless as a kid, and dared to speak and act my feelings only in fantasy and secret"
- wrote stories that involve the gap between teens and the adults who don't understand them
- wrote a memoir, *The Pigman and Me*, and the novel *The Pigman*

Quote: *"I know it's a continuing battle to get through the years between twelve and twenty … so I write always from their point of view."*

by Dinah Zike, M.Ed., Creator of Foldables™

Reading and Thinking with Foldables™

As you read the selections in each unit, the following Foldables will help you keep track of your ideas about the Big Questions. Follow these directions to make your Foldable, and then use the directions in the Unit Warm Up for labeling your unit Foldable.

Foldable 1 and Foldable 5—For Units 1 and 5

Step 1 Stack three sheets of paper with their top edges about a half-inch apart. These top edges will be tabs, so be sure to keep them straight.

Step 2 Fold up the bottom edges of the papers to form six tabs. Align the edges so that all of the layers or tabs are the same distance apart. Crease the bottom tightly.

Step 3 Follow steps 1 and 2 again to make a second set of tabbed pages. Then place the two sets of tabbed pages back-to-back and staple them together at the bottom.

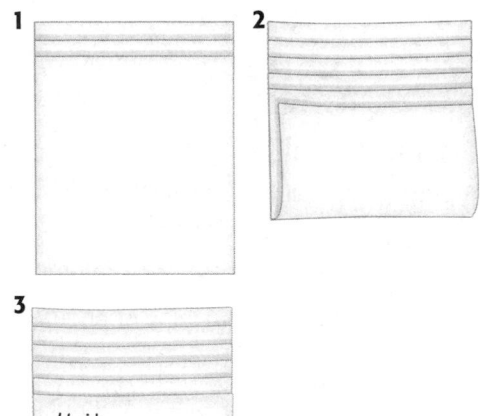

Step 4 On the top page of one side of the tabbed pages, write the unit number and the big question. Then, working your way up, label the tabs in order with the titles of the reading selections in the Reading Workshops and the Comparing Literature or Reading Across Texts Workshop. Use both tabbed sides.

Step 5 Below each title, write **My Purpose for Reading.** A third of the way down from that, write the label **The Big Question.**

Foldable 2 and Foldable 7—For Units 2 and 7

Step 1 Fold a sheet of paper in half so that one side is one inch longer than the other side. Fold the one-inch tab over the short side to form a fold. On the fold, write the workshop number and the Big Question for that unit.

Step 2 Cut the front flap in half toward the top crease to create two flaps. Write the title of the first selection in Reading Workshop 1 on the left flap and the title of the second selection on the right flap.

Step 3 Open the flaps. At the very top of each flap, write **My Purpose for Reading.** Below each crease, write **The Big Question.**

Step 4 Repeat these steps for each remaining Reading Workshop and the

Continued on page R9

Continued from page R8

Reading Across Texts or Comparing Literature Workshop.

Step 5 Fold a 11 x 14 sheet of paper in half. Open the paper and fold up one of the long sides two inches to form a pocket. Glue the outer edges of the pocket. Refold the paper so that the pockets are on the inside. Keep your Foldables for the unit inside.

Foldable 3 and Foldable 6–For Units 3 and 6

Step 1 Fold ten sheets of paper in half.

Step 2 On the top flap of each folded paper, make a cut one inch from the side (top flap only).

Step 3 Stack the folded papers on top of one another. Staple the ten sections together. Write the unit number and Big Question on the stapled edge.

Step 4 On the top flap, write the first selection title from Reading Workshop 1. Open the flap. Near the top of the page, write **My Purpose for Reading.** Below the crease, write **The Big Question.**

Step 5 Repeat these steps for each remaining selection in the Reading Workshops and the Comparing Literature Workshop.

Foldable 4 and Foldable 8–For Units 4 and 8

Step 1 Fold six sheets of paper in half and cut the sheets in half along the fold line.

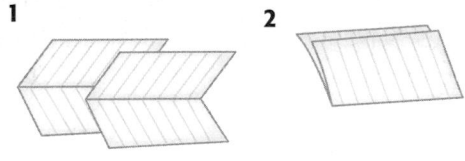

Step 2 Fold each section of paper in half, but fold one side one-half inch shorter than the other side. This will form a tab that is one-half inch long.

Step 3 Fold each tab over the shorter side and then fold it back the opposite way.

Step 4 Glue the straight edge of one section into the tab valley of another section. Glue all the sections together to form an accordion.

Step 5 On the front cover, write the unit number and the Big Question. Turn the page. Across the top, write the selection title. To the left of the crease, write **My Purpose for Reading.** To the right of the crease, write **The Big Question.** Repeat until you have all the titles from the Reading Workshops and the Comparing Literature or Reading Across Texts Workshop in your Foldable.

LITERARY TERMS HANDBOOK

A

Act A major unit of a drama. A play may be subdivided into several acts. Many modern plays have two or three acts. A short play can be composed of one or more scenes but only one act.

See also SCENE.

Alliteration The repetition of consonant sounds, usually at the beginnings of words or syllables. Alliteration gives emphasis to words. For example,

> Over the cobbles he clattered and clashed

Allusion A reference in a work of literature to a well-known character, place, or situation in history, politics, or science or from another work of literature, music, or art.

Analogy A comparison between two things, based on one or more elements that they share. Analogies can help the reader visualize an idea. In informational text, analogies are often used to explain something unfamiliar in terms of something known. For example, a science book might compare the flow of electricity to water moving through a hose. In literature, most analogies are expressed in metaphors or similes.

See also METAPHOR, SIMILE.

Anecdote A brief, entertaining story based on a single interesting or humorous incident or event. Anecdotes are frequently biographical and reveal some aspect of a person's character.

Antagonist A person or force that opposes the protagonist, or central character, in a story or a drama. The reader is generally meant not to sympathize with the antagonist.

See also CONFLICT, PROTAGONIST.

Anthropomorphism Representing animals as if they had human emotions and intelligence. Fables and fairy tales often contain anthropomorphism.

Aside In a play, a comment made by a character that is heard by the audience but not by the other characters onstage. The speaker turns to one side, or "aside," away from the other characters onstage. Asides are common in older plays—you will find many in Shakespeare's plays—but are infrequent in modern drama.

Assonance The repetition of vowel sounds, especially in a line of poetry.

See also RHYME, SOUND DEVICES.

Author's purpose The intention of the writer. For example, the purpose of a story may be to entertain, to describe, to explain, to persuade, or a combination of these purposes.

Autobiography The story of a person's life written by that person. *I know Why the Caged Bird Sings* by Maya Angelou, is an example of autobiography.

See also BIOGRAPHY, MEMOIR.

B

Ballad A short musical narrative song or poem. Folk ballads, which usually tell of an exciting or dramatic episode, were passed on by word of mouth for generations before being written down. Literary ballads are written in imitation of folk ballads.

See also NARRATIVE POETRY.

Biography The account of a person's life written by someone other than the subject. Biographies can be short or book-length.

See also AUTOBIOGRAPHY, MEMOIR.

C

Character A person in a literary work. (If a character is an animal, it displays human traits.) Characters who show varied and sometimes contradictory traits are called **round.** Characters who reveal only one personality trait are called **flat.** A **stereotype** is a flat character of a familiar and often-repeated type. A **dynamic** character changes during the story. A **static** character remains primarily the same throughout the story.

Characterization The methods a writer uses to develop the personality of the character. In **direct characterization,** the writer makes direct statements about a character's personality. In **indirect characterization,** the writer reveals a character's personality through the character's words and actions and through what other characters think and say about the character.

Climax The point of greatest emotional intensity, interest, or suspense in a narrative. Usually the climax comes at the turning point in a story or drama, the point at which the resolution of the conflict becomes clear. The climax in "Icarus and Daedelus" occurs when Icarus forgets his father's warning and flies too high.

Comedy A type of drama that is humorous and has a happy ending. A heroic comedy focuses on the exploits of a larger-than-life hero. In American popular culture, comedy can take the form of a scripted performance involving one or more performers—either as a skit that is part of a variety show, as in vaudeville, or as a stand-up monologue.
See also HUMOR.

Conflict The central struggle between opposing forces in a story or drama. An **external conflict** exists when a character struggles against some outside force, such as nature, society, fate, or another person. An **internal conflict** exists within the mind of a character who is torn between opposing feelings or goals.
See also ANTAGONIST, PLOT, PROTAGONIST.

Consonance A pleasing combination of sounds, especially in poetry. Consonance usually refers to the repetition of consonant sounds in stressed syllables.
See also SOUND DEVICES.

Couplet Two successive lines of verse that form a unit and usually rhyme.

D

Description Writing that seeks to convey the impression of a setting, a person, an animal, an object, or an event by appealing to the senses. Almost all writing, fiction and nonfiction, contains elements of description.

Details Particular features of things used to make descriptions more accurate and vivid. Authors use details to help readers imagine the characters, scenes, and actions they describe.

Dialect A variation of language spoken by a particular group, often within a particular region. Dialects differ from standard language because they may contain different pronunciations, forms, and meanings.

Dialogue Conversation between characters in a literary work.
See also MONOLOGUE.

Drama A story intended to be performed by actors on a stage or before movie or TV cameras. Most dramas before the modern period can be divided into two basic types: tragedy and comedy. The script of a drama includes dialogue (the words the actors speak) and stage directions (descriptions of the action and scenery).
See also COMEDY, TRAGEDY.

E

Elegy A mournful or melancholy poem that honors someone who is dead. Some elegies are written in rhyming couplets that follow a strict metric pattern.

Epic A long narrative poem, written in a dignified style, that celebrates the adventures and achievements of one or more heroic figures of legend, history, or religion.
See also NARRATIVE POETRY.

Essay A short piece of nonfiction writing on a single topic. The purpose of the essay is to communicate an idea or opinion. A **formal essay** is serious and impersonal. An **informal essay** entertains while it informs, usually in a light conversational style.

Exposition The part of the plot of a short story, novel, novella, or play in which the characters, setting, and situation are introduced.

Extended metaphor An implied comparison that continues through an entire poem.
See also METAPHOR.

F

Fable A short, simple tale that teaches a moral. The characters in a fable are often animals who speak and act like people. The moral, or lesson, of the fable is usually stated outright.

Falling action In a play or story, the action that follows the climax.

See also PLOT.

Fantasy A form of literature that explores unreal worlds of the past, the present, or the future.

Fiction A prose narrative in which situations and characters are invented by the writer. Some aspects of a fictional work may be based on fact or experience. Fiction includes short stories, novellas, and novels.

See also NOVEL, NOVELLA, SHORT STORY.

Figurative language Language used for descriptive effect, often to imply ideas indirectly. Expressions of figurative language are not literally true but express some truth beyond the literal level. Although it appears in all kinds of writing, figurative language is especially prominent in poetry.

See also ANALOGY, FIGURE OF SPEECH, METAPHOR, PERSONIFICATION, SIMILE, SYMBOL.

Figure of speech Figurative language of a specific kind, such as **analogy, metaphor, simile,** or **personification.**

First-person narrative. *See POINT OF VIEW.*

Flashback An interruption in a chronological narrative that tells about something that happened before that point in the story or before the story began. A flashback gives readers information that helps to explain the main events of the story.

Folklore The traditional beliefs, customs, stories, songs, and dances of the ordinary people (the "folk") of a culture. Folklore is passed on by word of mouth and performance rather than in writing.

See also FOLKTALE, LEGEND, MYTH, ORAL TRADITION.

Folktale A traditional story passed down orally long before being written down. Generally the author of a folktale is anonymous. Folktales include animal stories, trickster stories, fairy tales, myths, legends, and tall tales.

See also LEGEND, MYTH, ORAL TRADITION, TALL TALE.

Foreshadowing The use of clues by an author to prepare readers for events that will happen in a story.

Free verse Poetry that has no fixed pattern of meter, rhyme, line length, or stanza arrangement.

See also RHYTHM.

G

Genre A literary or artistic category. The main literary genres are prose, poetry, and drama. Each of these is divided into smaller genres. For example: **Prose** includes fiction (such as novels, novellas, short stories, and folktales) and nonfiction (such as biography, autobiography, and essays). **Poetry** includes lyric poetry, dramatic poetry, and narrative poetry. **Drama** includes tragedy, comedy, historical drama, melodrama, and farce.

H

Haiku Originally a Japanese form of poetry that has three lines and seventeen syllables. The first and third lines have five syllables each; the middle line has seven syllables.

Hero A literary work's main character, usually one with admirable qualities. Although the word *hero* is applied only to males in traditional usage (the female form is *heroine*), the term now applies to both sexes.

See also LEGEND, MYTH, PROTAGONIST, TALL TALE.

Historical fiction A novel, novella, play, short story, or narrative poem that sets fictional characters against a historical backdrop and contains many details about the period in which it is set.

See also GENRE.

Humor The quality of a literary work that makes the characters and their situations seem funny, amusing, or ludicrous. Humorous writing can be as effective in nonfiction as in fiction.

See also COMEDY.

I

Idiom A figure of speech that belongs to a particular language, people, or region and whose meaning cannot be obtained, and might even appear ridiculous, by joining the meanings of the words composing it. You would be using an idiom if you said you *caught* a cold.

Imagery Language that emphasizes sensory impressions to help the reader of a literary work see, hear, feel, smell, and taste the scenes described in the work.

See also FIGURATIVE LANGUAGE.

Informational text One kind of nonfiction. This kind of writing conveys facts and information without introducing personal opinion.

Irony A form of expression in which the intended meaning of the words used is the opposite of their literal meaning. *Verbal irony* occurs when a person says one thing and means another—for example, saying "Nice guy!" about someone you dislike. *Situational irony* occurs when the outcome of a situation is the opposite of what was expected.

J

Journal An account of day-to-day events or a record of experiences, ideas, or thoughts. A journal may also be called a diary.

L

Legend A traditional story, based on history or an actual hero, that is passed down orally. A legend is usually exaggerated and gains elements of fantasy over the years. Stories about Daniel Boone and Davy Crockett are American legends.

Limerick A light humorous poem with a regular metrical scheme and a rhyme scheme of *aabba*.

See also HUMOR, RHYME SCHEME.

Local color The fictional portrayal of a region's features or peculiarities and its inhabitants' distinctive ways of talking and behaving, usually as a way of adding a realistic flavor to a story.

Lyric The words of a song, usually with a regular rhyme scheme.

See also RHYME SCHEME.

Lyric poetry Poems, usually short, that express strong personal feelings about a subject or an event.

M

Main idea The most important idea expressed in a paragraph or an essay. It may or may not be directly stated.

Memoir A biographical or autobiographical narrative emphasizing the narrator's personal experience during a period or at an event.

See also AUTOBIOGRAPHY, BIOGRAPHY.

Metaphor A figure of speech that compares or equates seemingly unlike things. In contrast to a simile, a metaphor implies the comparison instead of stating it directly; hence, there is no use of connectives such as *like* or *as*.

See also FIGURE OF SPEECH, IMAGERY, SIMILE.

Meter A regular pattern of stressed and unstressed syllables that gives a line of poetry a predictable rhythm.

See also RHYTHM.

Monologue A long speech by a single character in a play or a solo performance.

Mood The emotional quality or atmosphere of a story or poem.

See also SETTING.

Myth A traditional story of unknown authorship, often involving goddesses, gods, and heroes, that attempts to explain a natural phenomenon, a historic event, or the origin of a belief or custom.

N

Narration Writing or speech that tells a story. Narration is used in prose fiction and narrative poetry. Narration can also be an important element in biographies, autobiographies, and essays.

Narrative poetry Verse that tells a story.

Narrator The person who tells a story. In some cases the narrator is a character in the story.

See also POINT OF VIEW.

Nonfiction Factual prose writing. Nonfiction deals with real people and experiences. Among the categories of nonfiction are biographies, autobiographies, and essays.

See also AUTOBIOGRAPHY, BIOGRAPHY, ESSAY, FICTION.

Novel A book-length fictional prose narrative. The novel has more scope than a short story in its presentation of plot, character, setting, and theme. Because novels are not subject to any limits in their presentation of these elements, they encompass a wide range of narratives.

See also FICTION.

Novella A work of fiction shorter than a novel but longer than a short story. A novella usually has more characters, settings, and events and a more complex plot than a short story.

O

Ode A lyric poem, usually rhymed, often in the form of an address and usually dignified or lofty in subject.

See also LYRIC POETRY.

Onomatopoeia The use of a word or a phrase that actually imitates or suggests the sound of what it describes.

See also SOUND DEVICES.

Oral tradition Stories, knowledge, customs, and beliefs passed by word of mouth from one generation to the next.

See also FOLKLORE, FOLKTALE, LEGEND, MYTH.

P

Parallelism The use of a series of words, phrases, or sentences that have similar grammatical form. Parallelism emphasizes the items that are arranged in the similar structures.

See also REPETITION.

Personification A figure of speech in which an animal, object, or idea is given human form or characteristics.

See also FIGURATIVE LANGUAGE, FIGURE OF SPEECH, METAPHOR.

Plot The sequence of events in a story, novel, or play. The plot begins with **exposition,** which introduces the story's characters, setting, and situation. The plot catches the reader's attention with a **narrative hook.** The **rising action** adds complications to the story's conflict, or problem, leading to the **climax,** or point of highest

emotional pitch. The **falling action** is the logical result of the climax, and the **resolution** presents the final outcome.

Plot twist An unexpected turn of events in a plot. A surprise ending is an example of a plot twist.

Poetry A form of literary expression that differs from prose in emphasizing the line as the unit of composition. Many other traditional characteristics of poetry—emotional, imaginative language; use of metaphor and simile; division into stanzas; rhyme; regular pattern of stress, or meter—apply to some poems.

Point of view The relationship of the narrator, or storyteller, to the story. In a story with **first-person point of view,** the story is told by one of the characters, referred to as "I." The reader generally sees everything through that character's eyes. In a story with a **limited third-person point of view,** the narrator reveals the thoughts of only one character, but refers to that character as "he" or "she." In a story with an **omniscient point of view,** the narrator reveals the thoughts of several characters.

Props Theater slang (a shortened form of *properties*) for objects and elements of the scenery of a stage play or movie set.

Propaganda Speech, writing, or other attempts to influence ideas or opinions, often through the use of stereotypes, faulty generalizations, logical fallacies, and/or emotional language.

Prose Writing that is similar to everyday speech and language, as opposed to poetry. Its form is based on sentences and paragraphs without the patterns of rhyme, controlled line length, or meter found in much poetry. Fiction and nonfiction are the major categories of prose. Most modern drama is also written in prose.

See also DRAMA, ESSAY, FICTION, NONFICTION.

Protagonist The central character in a story, drama, or dramatic poem. Usually the action revolves around the protagonist, who is involved in the main conflict.

See ANTAGONIST, CONFLICT.

Pun A humorous play on two or more meanings of the same word or on two words with the same sound. Today puns often appear in advertising headlines and slogans—for example, "Our hotel rooms give you suite feelings."

See also HUMOR.

R

Refrain A line or lines repeated regularly, usually in a poem or song.

Repetition The recurrence of sounds, words, phrases, lines, or stanzas in a speech or piece of writing. Repetition increases the feeling of unity in a work. When a line or stanza is repeated in a poem or song, it is called a refrain.

See also PARALLELISM, REFRAIN.

Resolution The part of a plot that concludes the falling action by revealing or suggesting the outcome of the conflict.

Rhyme The repetition of sounds at the ends of words that appear close to each other in a poem. **End rhyme** occurs at the ends of lines. **Internal rhyme** occurs within a single line. **Slant rhyme** occurs when words include sounds that are similar but not identical. Slant rhyme usually involves some variation of **consonance** (the repetition of consonant sounds) or **assonance** (the repetition of vowel sounds).

Rhyme scheme The pattern of rhyme formed by the end rhyme in a poem. The rhyme scheme is designated by the assignment of a different letter of the alphabet to each new rhyme. For example, one common rhyme scheme is *ababcb.*

Rhythm The pattern created by the arrangement of stressed and unstressed syllables, especially in poetry. Rhythm gives poetry a musical quality that helps convey its meaning. Rhythm can be regular (with a predictable pattern or meter) or irregular, (as in free verse).

See also METER.

Rising action The part of a plot that adds complications to the problems in the story and increases reader interest.

See also FALLING ACTION, PLOT.

S

Scene A subdivision of an act in a play. Each scene takes place in a specific setting and time. An act may have one or more scenes.

See also ACT.

Science fiction Fiction dealing with the impact of real science or imaginary superscience on human or alien societies of the past, present, or future. Although science fiction is mainly a product of the twentieth century, nineteenth-century authors such as Mary Shelley, Jules Verne, and Robert Louis Stevenson were pioneers of the genre.

Screenplay The script of a film, usually containing detailed instructions about camera shots and angles in addition to dialogue and stage directions. A screenplay for an original television show is called a teleplay.

See also DRAMA.

Sensory imagery Language that appeals to a reader's five senses: hearing, sight, touch, taste, and smell.

See also VISUAL IMAGERY.

Sequence of events The order in which the events in a story take place.

Setting The time and place in which the events of a short story, novel, novella, or play occur. The setting often helps create the atmosphere or mood of the story.

Short story A brief fictional narrative in prose. Elements of the short story include **plot, character, setting, point of view, theme,** and sometimes symbol and irony.

Simile A figure of speech using *like* or *as* to compare seemingly unlike things.

Sonnet A poem containing fourteen lines, usually written in iambic pentameter. Sonnets have strict patterns of rhyme and usually deal with a single theme, idea, or sentiment.

Sound devices Techniques used to create a sense of rhythm or to emphasize particular sounds in writing. For example, sound can be controlled through the use of **onomatopoeia, alliteration, consonance, assonance,** and **rhyme.**

See also RHYTHM.

Speaker The voice of a poem–sometimes that of the poet, sometimes that of a fictional person or even a thing. The speaker's words communicate a particular tone or attitude toward the subject of the poem.

Stage directions Instructions written by the dramatist to describe the appearance and actions of characters, as well as sets, costumes, and lighting.

Stanza A group of lines forming a unit in a poem. Stanzas are, in effect, the paragraphs of a poem.

Stereotype A character who is not developed as an individual but as a collection of traits and mannerisms supposedly shared by all members of a group.

Style The author's choice and arrangement of words and sentences in a literary work. Style can reveal an author's purpose in writing and attitude toward his or her subject and audience.

Suspense A feeling of curiosity, uncertainty, or even dread about what is going to happen next. Writers increase the level of suspense in a story by giving readers clues to what may happen.

See also FORESHADOWING, RISING ACTION.

Symbol Any object, person, place, or experience that means more than what it is. **Symbolism** is the use of images to represent internal realities.

T

Tall tale A wildly imaginative story, usually passed down orally, about the fantastic adventures or amazing feats of folk heroes in realistic local settings.

See also FOLKLORE, ORAL TRADITION.

Teleplay A play written or adapted for television.

Theme The main idea of a story, poem, novel, or play, usually expressed as a general statement. Some works have a **stated theme,** which is expressed directly. More frequently works have an **implied theme,** which is revealed gradually through other elements such as plot, character, setting, point of view, symbol, and irony.

Third-person narrative. *See POINT OF VIEW.*

Title The name of a literary work.

Tone The attitude of the narrator toward the subject, ideas, theme, or characters. A factual article would most likely have an objective tone, while an editorial on the same topic could be argumentative or satiric.

Tragedy A play in which the main character suffers a downfall. That character often is a person of dignified or heroic stature. The downfall may result from outside forces or from a weakness within the character, which is known as a tragic flaw.

V

Visual imagery Details that appeal to the sense of sight.

Voice An author's distinctive style or the particular speech patterns of a character in a story.

See also STYLE, TONE.

The Writing Process

The writing process consists of five stages: prewriting, drafting, revising, editing/proofreading, and publishing/presenting. By following the stages in order, you can turn your ideas into polished pieces of writing. Most writers take their writing through all five stages, and repeat stages when necessary.

The Writing Process 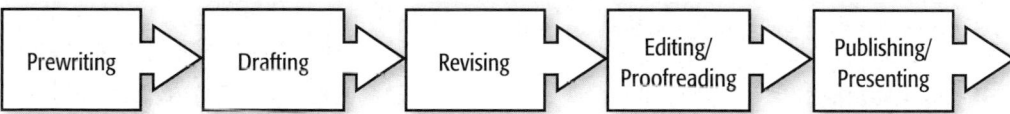 Prewriting → Drafting → Revising → Editing/Proofreading → Publishing/Presenting

Prewriting

Prewriting is the process of gathering and organizing your ideas. It begins whenever you start to consider what you will write about or what will interest your readers. Try keeping a small notebook with you for several days and using it to jot down possible topics. Consult the chart below for tips on using the prewriting techniques known as listing, questioning, and clustering.

Listing, Questioning, and Clustering

LISTING List as many ideas as you can—whatever comes into your head on a particular subject. This is called brainstorming. Then go back over the list and circle the ideas you like best. Eventually you'll hit on an idea you can use.

QUESTIONING If your audience is your class-mates, ask yourself questions such as the following:
- *What do my friends like to learn about?*
- *What do my friends like to read about?*
- *What have I done that my friends might like to hear about?*

CLUSTERING Write your topic in the middle of a piece of paper. Organize related ideas around the topic in a cluster of circles, with lines showing how the ideas are related. Clustering can help you decide which part of a topic to write about.

When you have selected your topic, organize your ideas around the topic. Identify your main ideas and support-ing ideas. Each main idea needs examples or facts to support it. Then write a plan for what you want to say.

The plan might be an organized list or outline. It does not have to use complete sentences.

Drafting

Drafting is the stage that turns your list into sentences and paragraphs. Use your prewriting notes to remember what you want to say. Begin by writing an introduction that gets the reader's attention. Move ahead through the topic, paragraph by paragraph. Let your words flow. This is the time to express yourself or try out a new idea. Don't worry about mistakes in spelling and grammar; you can correct them later. If you get stuck, try one of the tricks below.

Tips for drafting
- Work on the easiest part first. You don't have to begin at the beginning.
- Make a diagram, sketch, or drawing of the topic.
- Focus on just one sentence or paragraph at a time.
- Freewrite your thoughts and images. You can organize them later.
- Pretend that you are writing to a friend.
- Ask more questions about your topic.
- Speak your ideas into a tape recorder.
- Take a break. Take a walk or listen to music. Return to your writing later.

Revising

The goal of revising is to make your writing clearer and more interesting. When you revise, look at the whole piece of writing. Ask whether the parts go together smoothly and whether anything should be added or deleted. You may decide to organize the draft in a different way. Some writers make several revisions before they are satisfied. Ask yourself these questions:

- ☑ Did I stick to my topic?
- ☑ Did I accomplish my purpose?
- ☑ Did I keep my audience in mind?
- ☑ Does my main idea come across clearly?
- ☑ Do all the details support the main idea?
- ☑ Did I give enough information? too much?
- ☑ Did I use transition words such as *first, then* and *next* to make my sentences flow smoothly?

Tips for revising

- Step back. If you have the time, set your draft aside for a while. When you look at it again, you may see it from a new point of view. You may notice that some information is missing or that part of the paper is disorganized.
- Read your paper aloud. Listen carefully as you read your paper aloud. How does it sound?
- Have a writing conference with a peer reviewer, one of your friends or classmates. A second opinion helps. Your reader can offer a fresh point of view.

Peer review

You can direct peer responses in one or more of the following ways.

- Ask readers to tell you what they have read in their own words. If you do not hear your ideas restated, revise your writing for clarity.
- Ask readers to tell you the part they liked best and why. You may want to expand those parts.
- Repeat what the readers have told you in your own words. Ask the readers if you have understood their suggestions.
- Discuss your writing with your readers. Listen to their suggestions carefully.

As you confer, make notes of your reviewers' comments. Then revise your draft, using your own judgment and including what is helpful from your reviewers' comments.

Editing/Proofreading

When you are satisfied with the changes you've made, edit your revised draft. Replace dull, vague words with lively verbs and precise adjectives. Vary the length of your sentences. Take time to correct errors in spelling, grammar, capitalization, and punctuation. Refer to the Proofreading Checklist on page R19 and on the inside back cover of this book.

Editing for style

Use the following checklist:

- ☑ Have I avoided clichés?
- ☑ Have I avoided wordiness?
- ☑ Is the tone of my writing appropriate to my purpose?
- ☑ Have I made clear connections between ideas?
- ☑ Do my sentences and paragraphs flow smoothly?

Publishing/Presenting

Now your writing is ready for an audience. Make a clean, neat copy, and add your name and date. Check that the paper has a title. If you wish, enclose the paper in a folder or binder to give it a professional look. Hand it in to your teacher, or share it in one of the ways described below. When the paper is returned, keep it in your writing portfolio.

Ideas for presenting

- **Illustrations** A photograph, diagram, or drawing can convey helpful information.
- **Oral presentation** Almost any writing can be shared aloud. Try including music, slides, or a group oral reading.
- **Class book** A collection of class writing is a nice contribution to the school library.
- **Newspaper** Some schools have a school newspaper. Local newspapers often publish student writing, especially if it is about local people and events.
- **Literary magazine** Magazines such as *Cricket* and *MidLink* publish student writing. Some schools have a literary magazine that publishes student writing once or twice a year.
- **Bulletin board** A rotating display of student writing is an effective way to see what your classmates have written. Illustrations and photographs add interest.

Some writing, such as journal writing, is private and not intended for an audience. However, even if you don't share your paper, don't throw it away. It might contain ideas that you can use later.

Proofreading Help

Use this proofreading checklist to help you check for errors in your writing, and use the proofreading symbols in the chart below to mark places that need corrections.

☑ Have I avoided run-on sentences and sentence fragments and punctuated sentences correctly?

☑ Have I used every word correctly, including plurals, possessives, and frequently confused words?

☑ Do verbs and subjects agree? Are verb tenses correct?

☑ Do pronouns refer clearly to their antecedents and agree with them in person, number, and gender?

☑ Have I used adverb and adjective forms and modifying phrases correctly?

☑ Have I spelled every word correctly, and checked the unfamiliar ones in a dictionary?

Proofreading Symbols		
⊙	Lieut Brown	Insert a period.
∧	No one came the party.	Insert a letter or a word.
≡	I enjoyed paris.	Capitalize a letter.
/	The Class ran a bake sale.	Make a capital letter lowercase.
⌒	The campers are home sick.	Close up a space.
⊕	They visited N.Y. ⊕	Spell out.
∧ ∧	Sue please come I need your help.	Insert a comma or a semicolon.
∩	He enjoyed feild day.	Transpose the position of letters or words.
#	alltogether	Insert a space.
℈	We went to to Boston.	Delete letters or words.
⌄ ⌄ ⌄	She asked, Who's coming?	Insert quotation marks or an apostrophe.
/ = /	mid January	Insert a hyphen.
¶	"Where?" asked Karl. "Over there," said Ray.	Begin a new paragraph.

Writing Modes

There are four main types, or modes, of writing—expository, descriptive, narrative, and persuasive. Each mode has its own purpose and characteristics.

Expository Writing

Expository writing communicates knowledge. It provides and explains information; it may also give general directions or step-by-step instructions for an activity.

Use this checklist as you write.

- ☑ Is the opening paragraph interesting?
- ☑ Are my explanations accurate and complete? Is information clear and easy to read?
- ☑ Is information presented in a logical order?
- ☑ Does each paragraph have a main idea? Does all the information support the main idea?
- ☑ Does my essay have an introduction, a body, and a conclusion?
- ☑ Have I defined any unfamiliar terms?
- ☑ Are my comparisons clear and logical?

Kinds of expository writing

Expository writing covers a wide range of styles. The chart below describes some of the possibilities.

Descriptive Writing

Descriptive writing can make a person, place, or thing come to life. The scene described may be as unfamiliar and far away as the bottom of the sea or as familiar and close as the gym locker room. By presenting details that awaken the reader's senses, descriptive writing can help your readers see the world more clearly.

Use this checklist to help you revise your description.

- ☑ Does my introduction identify the person or place that will be described?
- ☑ Are my details vivid? Are nouns and adjectives precise?
- ☑ Do all the details contribute to the same impression?
- ☑ Is it clear why this place or person is special?
- ☑ Are transitions clear? Do the paragraphs follow a logical order?
- ☑ Does each paragraph contain a main idea?
- ☑ Have I communicated a definite impression or mood?

Kinds of Expository Writing	Examples
Instructional writing	Explain how to train for a cross-country race, how to arrange a surprise party, or how to avoid cleaning up your room.
Compare-and-contrast essay	Compare two athletes or two sports, two fictional characters, two books or movies, two places, or two kinds of vacations.
Step-by-step directions	Give directions for building a model plane, making apple pie, or drawing on a computer screen.
Information and explanation	Explain what causes sunspots, how plants grow in the desert, or why camels have a hump.
Report or essay	Write a book report, a report on the Buddhist religion, or a report on a new wildlife center.

Narrative Writing

Narrative writing tells a story, either real or fictional. It answers the question *What happened?*

A well-written narrative holds the reader's attention by presenting interesting characters in a carefully ordered series of events.

This checklist will help you improve your narrative.

- ☑ Does my first sentence get the reader's attention?
- ☑ Are the characters and setting introduced with enough detail?
- ☑ Do the characters speak and behave realistically?
- ☑ Are the events narrated in an order clear enough for the reader to follow?
- ☑ Are there places where dialogue should be added?
- ☑ Is my ending satisfying to the reader?

Persuasive Writing

Persuasive writing presents an opinion. Its goal is to make readers feel or think a certain way about a situation or an idea. The writer includes facts and opinions often designed to urge readers to take action. Good persuasive writing can sometimes be hard to resist.

As you revise your persuasive writing, use this checklist as a guide.

- ☑ Is my main idea expressed in a clear statement?
- ☑ Have I presented good reasons to support my point of view?
- ☑ Have I supported my reasons with facts and opinions?
- ☑ Have I taken account of the opposing points of view?
- ☑ Have I addressed the interests of my audience?
- ☑ Have I ended with a strong closing statement?

Research Report Writing

When you write a research report, you explore a topic by gathering factual information from several different resources. Through your research, you develop a point of view or draw a conclusion. This point of view or conclusion becomes the main idea, or thesis, of your report.

Select a Topic

Because a research report usually takes time to prepare and write, your choice of topic is especially important. Follow these guidelines.

- Brainstorm a list of questions about a subject you would like to explore. Choose one that is neither too narrow nor too broad for the length of paper you will write. Use that question as your topic.
- Select a topic that genuinely interests you.
- Be sure you can find information on your topic from several different sources.

Do Research

Start by looking up your topic in an encyclopedia to find general information. Then find specific information in books, magazines, and newspapers, on CD-ROMs and the Internet, and from personal interviews when this seems appropriate. Use the computerized or card catalog in the library to locate books on your topic. Then search for up-to-date information in periodicals (magazines) or newspapers and from electronic sources, such as CD-ROMs or the Internet. If you need help in finding or using any of these resources, ask the librarian.

As you gather information, make sure each source you use relates closely to your topic. Also be sure that your source is reliable. Be extra careful if you are using information from the Internet. If you are not sure about the reliability of a source, consult the librarian or your teacher.

Make Source Cards

In a research report, you must document the source of your information. To keep track of your sources, write the author, title, publication information, and location of each source on a separate index card. Give each source card a number and write it in the upper right-hand corner. These cards will be useful for preparing a bibliography.

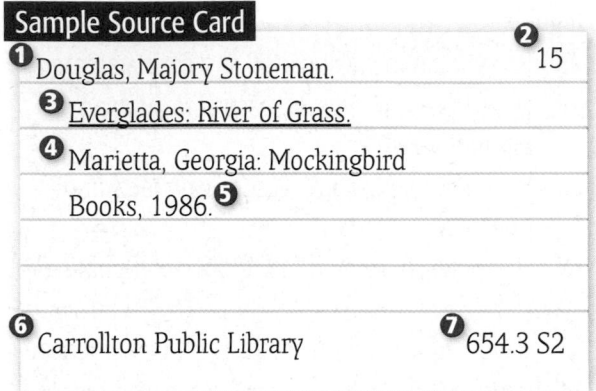

Sample Source Card

❶ Douglas, Majory Stoneman. ❷15
❸ Everglades: River of Grass.
❹ Marietta, Georgia: Mockingbird
Books, 1986. ❺

❻ Carrollton Public Library ❼654.3 S2

❶ Author
❷ Source number
❸ Title
❹ City of publication/Publisher
❺ Date of publication
❻ Location of source
❼ Library call number

Take Notes

As you read, you encounter many new facts and ideas. Taking notes will help you keep track of information and focus on the topic. Here are some helpful suggestions:

- Use a new card for each important piece of information. Separate cards will help you to organize your notes.
- At the top of each card, write a key word or phrase that tells you about the information. Also, write the number of the source you used.
- Write only details and ideas that relate to your topic.
- Summarize information in your own words.
- Write down a phrase or a quote only when the words are especially interesting or come from an important source. Enclose all quotes in quotation marks to make clear that the ideas belong to someone else.

This sample note card shows information to include.

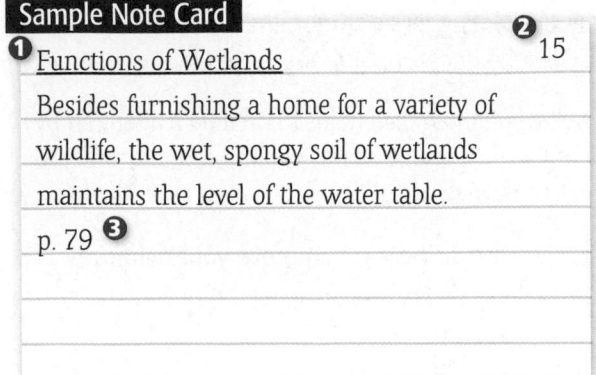

Sample Note Card

❶ Functions of Wetlands ❷15
Besides furnishing a home for a variety of
wildlife, the wet, spongy soil of wetlands
maintains the level of the water table.
p. 79 ❸

❶ Write a key word or phrase that tells you what the information is about.
❷ Write the source number from your source card.
❸ Write the number of the page or pages on which you found the information.

Develop Your Thesis

As you begin researching and learning about your topic, think about the overall point you want to make. Write one sentence, your *thesis statement,* that says exactly what you plan to report on.

Sample Thesis Statement

Everglades National Park is a beautiful but endangered animal habitat.

Keep your thesis in mind as you continue to do research and think about your topic. The thesis will help you determine what information is important. However, be prepared to change your thesis if the information you find does not support it.

Write an Outline

When you finish taking notes, organize the information in an outline. Write down the main ideas that you want to cover. Write your thesis statement at the beginning of your outline. Then list the supporting details. Follow an outline form like the one on the next page.

❶ Everglades National Park is a beautiful but endangered animal habitat.

    I.   Special aspects of the Everglades

    ❷ A.   Characteristics of wetlands

        B.   Endangered birds and animals

    II. Pressures on the Everglades

        A.   Florida agriculture

        B.   Carelessness of visitors

    III. How to protect the Everglades

        A.   Change agricultural practices

        B.   Educate park visitors

            1.   Mandatory video on safety for

       ❸   individuals and environment

            2.   Instructional reminders posted

                throughout the park

❶ The thesis statement identifies your topic and the overall point you will make.

❷ If you have subtopics under a main topic, there must be at least two. They must relate directly to your main topic.

❸ If you wish to divide a subtopic, you must have at least two divisions. Each must relate to the subtopic above it.

Document Your Information

You must document, or credit, the sources of all the information you use in your report. There are two common ways to document information.

Footnotes

To document with footnotes, place a number at the end of the information you are documenting. Number your notes consecutively, beginning with number 1. These numbers should be slightly raised and should come after any punctuation. The documentation information itself goes at the bottom of the page, with a matching number.

In-text number for note:
The Declaration of Independence was read in public for the first time on July 6, 1776.[3]
Footnote at bottom of page:
      [3] John Smith, The Declaration of Independence (New York: DI, 2001) 221.

Parenthetical Documentation

In this method, you give the source for your information in parentheses at the end of the sentence where the information appears. You do not need to give all the details of the source. Just provide enough information for your readers to identify it. Here are the basic rules to follow.

- Usually it is enough to give the author's last name and the number of the page where you found the information.

  The declaration was first read in public by militia colonel John Nixon (Smith 222).

- If you mention the author's name in the sentence, you do not need to repeat it in the parentheses.

  According to Smith, the reading was greeted with wild applause (224).

- If your source does not identify a particular author, as in a newspaper or encyclopedia article, give the first word or two of the title of the piece.

  The anniversary of the reading was commemorated by a parade and fireworks ("Reading Celebrated").

Full information on your sources goes in a list at the end of your paper.

Bibliography or Works Cited

At the end of your paper, list all the sources of information that you used in preparing your report. Arrange them alphabetically by the author's last name (or by the first word in the title if no author is mentioned) as shown below. Title this list *Works Cited.* (Use the term *bibliography* if all your sources are printed media, such as books, magazines, or newspapers.)

Works Cited ❶

❷ Bertram, Jeffrey. "African Bees: Fact or Myth?" *Orlando Sentinel* 18 Aug. 1999: D2.

❸ Gore, Rick. "Neanderthals." <u>National Geographic.</u> January 1996: 2–35. ❽

❹ Gould, Stephen J. <u>The Panda's Thumb.</u> New York: W. W. Norton & Co., 1982.

❺ "Governor Chiles Vetoes Anti-Everglades ❾ Bills–5/13/98." <u>Friends of the Everglades.</u> May 1998. 26 Aug 1998 <http://www.everglades. org/pressrel_may28.htm>.

❻ "Neanderthal man." <u>The Columbia Encyclopedia.</u> 5th Edition. New York: Columbia University Press, 1993.

❼ Pabst, Laura (Curator of Natural History Museum), Interview. March 11, 1998.

❶ Indent all but the first line of each item.

❷ Newspaper article

❸ Magazine article

❹ Book with one author

❺ On-line article

❻ Encyclopedia

❼ Interview

❽ Include page numbers for a magazine article but not for a book, unless the book is a collection of essays by different authors.

❾ Include database (underlined), publication medium (online), computer service, and date of access.

Business Writing

Two standard formats for business letters are block style and modified block style. In block style all the parts of the letter begin at the left-hand margin.

Business Letter

The following business letter uses modified block style

❶ 10 Pullman Lane
Cromwell, CT 06416
January 16, 2006

❷ Mr. Philip Fornaro
Principal
Cromwell School
179 West Maple St.
Cromwell, CT 06416

❸ Dear Mr. Fornaro:

❹ My friends and I in the seventh grade at Brimmer Middle School feel that there is not enough to do in Cromwell during the winter vacation week. Some students can afford to go away for vacation. Many families, however, cannot afford to go away, or the parents have to work.

❺ I would like to suggest that you keep the Brimmer Middle School gym open during the vacation week. If the gym were open, the basketball teams could practice. The fencing club could meet. We could meet our friends there instead of going to the mall.

❻ Thanks for listening to my request. I hope you will think it over.

❼ Sincerely,

Kim Goodwin

Kim Goodwin

❶ In the heading, write your address and the date on separate lines.

❷ In the inside address, write the name and address of the person to whom you are sending the letter.

❸ Use a colon after the greeting.

❹ In your introduction, say who you are and why you are writing.

❺ In the body of your letter, provide details concerning your request.

❻ Conclude by restating your purpose and thanking the person you are writing to.

❼ In the closing, use *Sincerely, Sincerely yours,* or *Yours truly* followed by a comma. Include both your signature and your printed or typed name.

General guidelines

Follow these guidelines when writing a business letter.

- Use correct business-letter form. Whether you write by hand, or use a computer, use 8 1/2-by-11-inch white or off white paper. Be sure your letter is neat and clean.
- Use Standard English. Check your spelling carefully.
- Be polite, even if you are making a complaint or expressing a negative opinion.
- Be brief and to the point. State your reason for writing within the first two or three sentences.
- Include all necessary information.
- If you are making a request, be specific. Make sure what you are asking is reasonable. Express your appreciation at the end of the letter.
- Be considerate. Request only information you cannot get another way.
- When expressing an opinion or a complaint, state your reasons clearly and logically. Avoid emotional language.
- When requesting an interview, make it easy for the interviewee to meet with you. Suggest a few dates.

Writing a Memo

A memo, or memorandum, is a brief, efficient way of communicating information to another person or group of people. It begins with a header that provides basic information. A memo does not have a formal closing.

TO: *Brimmer Banner* newspaper staff
FROM: Terry Glinski
SUBJECT: Winter issue
DATE: January 18, 2006

Articles for the winter issue of the *Brimmer Banner* are due by February 1. Please see Terry about your assignment as soon as possible! The following articles or features have not yet been assigned:

Cafeteria Mess: Who Is Responsible?
Teacher Profile: Mr. Jinks, Ms. Magee
Sports roundup

Using a Computer for Writing

Using a computer offers advantages at every stage of the writing process.

Prewriting

A computer can help you gather and organize ideas and information.

Brainstorming
While brainstorming for topics or details, you can dim the computer screen and do "invisible writing." Some writers find that this technique allows their ideas to flow more freely.

Researching
Use the Internet or a CD-ROM encyclopedia to find not only text and pictures, but also sound, animated cartoons or graphics, and live-action video clips.

Outlining
Some word-processing programs offer an outlining feature that automatically indents headings and uses different type styles for main headings and subheadings.

Drafting/Revising

Most word-processing programs make it easy to do the following.

- *insert* new text at any point in your document
- *delete* or *copy* text
- *move* text from one position to another
- *undo* a change you just made
- *save* each draft or revision of your document
- *print* copies of your work-in-progress for others to read

Editing/Proofreading

You can edit and proofread directly on the computer, or you can mark your changes on a printout, or hard copy, and then input the changes on screen. The following word-processing features are helpful.

- **Grammar checker** The computer finds possible errors in grammar and suggests revisions.
- **Spelling checker** The computer finds misspellings and suggests corrections.

- **Thesaurus** If you want to replace an inappropriate or overused word, you can highlight the word and the computer will suggest synonyms.
- **Search and replace** If you want to change or correct something that occurs several times in your document, the computer can quickly make the change throughout the document.

TIP

The grammar checker, spelling checker, and thesaurus cannot replace your own careful reading and judgment. Because English grammar is so complex, the suggestions that the grammar checker makes may not be appropriate. Also, the spelling checker will not tell you that you have typed *brake* when you meant *break,* for example, because both are valid words. The thesaurus may offer you several synonyms for a word, but you need to consider the connotations of each before deciding which, if any, fits your context.

Presenting

The computer allows you to enhance the readability, attractiveness, and visual interest of your document in many ways.

Formatting your text
The computer gives you a variety of options for the layout and appearance of your text. You can easily add or change the following elements.

- margin width
- number of columns
- type size and style
- page numbering
- header or footer (information such as a title that appears at the top or bottom of every page)

Visual aids
Some word-processing programs have graphic functions that allow you to create graphs, charts, and diagrams. Collections of *clip art,* pictures you can copy and paste into your document, are also available.

Troubleshooter

Use the Troubleshooter to recognize and correct common writing errors.

Sentence Fragment

A sentence fragment does not express a complete thought. It may lack a subject or verb or both.

- **Problem: Fragment that lacks a subject**

  The lion paced the floor of the cage. Looked hungry. *frag*

  Solution: Add a subject to the fragment to make a complete sentence.

  The lion paced the floor of the cage. He looked hungry.

- **Problem: Fragment that lacks a predicate**

  I'm painting my room. The walls yellow. *frag*

  Solution: Add a predicate to make the sentence complete.

  I'm painting my room. The walls are going to be yellow.

- **Problem: Fragment that lacks both a subject and a predicate**

  We walked around the reservoir. Near the parkway. *frag*

  Solution: Combine the fragment with another sentence.

  We walked around the reservoir near the parkway.

- **TIP**

  You can use fragments when talking with friends or writing personal letters. Some writers use fragments to produce a special effect. Use complete sentences, however, for school or business writing.

Run-on Sentence

A run-on sentence is two or more sentences written incorrectly as one sentence.

- **Problem: Two main clauses separated only by a comma**

  Roller coasters make me dizzy, I don't enjoy them. *run-on*

  Solution A: Replace the comma with a period or other end mark. Start the second sentence with a capital letter.

  Roller coasters make me dizzy. I don't enjoy them.

  Solution B: Replace the comma with a semicolon.

  Roller coasters make me dizzy; I don't enjoy them.

- **Problem: Two main clauses with no punctuation between them**

  Acid rain is a worldwide problem there are no solutions in sight. *run-on*

  Solution A: Separate the main clauses with a period or other end mark. Begin the second sentence with a capital letter.

  Acid rain is a worldwide problem. There are no solutions in sight.

  Solution B: Add a comma and a coordinating conjunction between the main clauses.

  Acid rain is a worldwide problem, but there are no solutions in sight.

- **Problem: Two main clauses with no comma before the coordinating conjunction**

  Our chorus has been practicing all month but we still need another rehearsal. *run-on*

Solution: Add a comma before the coordinating conjunction.

Our chorus has been practicing all month, but we still need another rehearsal.

Lack of Subject-Verb Agreement

A singular subject calls for a singular form of the verb. A plural subject calls for a plural form of the verb.

- **Problem: A subject that is separated from the verb by an intervening prepositional phrase**

The two policemen at the construction site looks bored. *agr*

The members of my baby-sitting club is saving money. *agr*

Solution: Make sure that the verb agrees with the subject of the sentence, not with the object of the preposition. The object of a preposition is never the subject.

The two policemen at the construction site look bored.

The members of my baby-sitting club are saving money.

TIP

When subject and verb are separated by a prepositional phrase, check for agreement by reading the sentence without the prepositional phrase.

- **Problem: A sentence that begins with *here* or *there***

Here come the last bus to Pelham Heights. *agr*

There is my aunt and uncle. *agr*

Solution: In sentences that begin with *here* or *there*, look for the subject after the verb. Make sure that the verb agrees with the subject.

Here comes the last bus to Pelham Heights.

There are my aunt and uncle.

- **Problem: An indefinite pronoun as the subject**

Each of the candidates are qualified. *agr*

All of the problems on the test was hard. *agr*

Solution: Some indefinite pronouns are singular; some are plural; and some can be either singular or plural, depending on the noun they refer to. Determine whether the indefinite pronoun is singular or plural, and make sure the verb agrees with it.

Each of the candidates is qualified.

All of the problems on the test were hard.

- **Problem: A compound subject that is joined by *and***

Fishing tackle and a life jacket was stowed in the boat. *agr*

Peanut butter and jelly are delicious. *agr*

Solution A: If the compound subjects refer to different people or things, use a plural verb.

Fishing tackle and a life jacket were stowed in the boat.

Solution B: If the parts of a compound subject name one unit or if they refer to the same person or thing, use a singular verb.

Peanut butter and jelly is delicious.

- **Problem: A compound subject that is joined by *or* or *nor***

Either my aunt or my parents plans to attend parents' night. *agr*

Neither onions nor pepper improve the taste of this meatloaf. *agr*

Solution: Make the verb agree with the subject that is closer to it.

Either my aunt or my parents plan to attend parents' night.

Neither onions nor pepper improves the taste of this meatloaf.

Incorrect Verb Tense or Form

Verbs have different tenses to show when the action takes place.

- **Problem: An incorrect or missing verb ending**

    The Parks Department install a new water fountain last week. *tense*

    They have also plant flowers in all the flower beds. *tense*

    Solution: To form the past tense and the part participle, add -*ed* to a regular verb.

    The Parks Department installed a new water fountain last week.

    They have also planted flowers in all the flower beds.

- **Problem: An improperly formed irregular verb**

    Wendell has standed in line for two hours. *tense*

    I catched the fly ball and throwed it to first base. *tense*

    Solution: Irregular verbs vary in their past and past participle forms. Look up the ones you are not sure of.

    Wendell has stood in line for two hours.

    I caught the fly ball and threw it to first base.

- **Problem: Confusion between the past form and the past participle**

    The cast for *The Music Man* has began rehearsals. *tense*

    Solution: Use the past participle form of an irregular verb, not its past form, when you use the auxiliary verb *have*.

    The cast for *The Music Man* has begun rehearsals.

- **Problem: Improper use of the past participle**

    Our seventh grade drawn a mural for the wall of the cafeteria. *tense*

    Solution: Add the auxiliary verb *have* to the past participle of an irregular verb to form a complete verb.

    Our seventh grade has drawn a mural for the wall of the cafeteria.

> **TIP**
>
> Because irregular verbs vary, it is useful to memorize the verbs that you use most often.

Incorrect Use of Pronouns

The noun that a pronoun refers to is called its antecedent. A pronoun must refer to its **antecedent** clearly. Subject pronouns refer to subjects in a sentence. Object pronouns refer to objects in a sentence.

- **Problem: A pronoun that could refer to more than one antecedent**

    Gary and Mike are coming, but he doesn't know the other kids. *ant*

    Solution: Substitute a noun for the pronoun to make your sentence clearer.

    Gary and Mike are coming, but Gary doesn't know the other kids.

- **Problem: Personal pronouns as subjects**

    Him and John were freezing after skating for three hours. *pro*

    Lori and me decided not to audition for the musical. *pro*

    Solution: Use a subject pronoun as the subject part of a sentence.

    He and John were freezing after skating for three hours.

    Lori and I decided not to audition for the musical.

- **Problem: Personal pronouns as objects**

    Ms. Wang asked Reggie and I to enter the science fair *pro*

    Ms. Wang helped he and I with the project. *pro*

    Solution: Use an object pronoun as the object of a verb or a preposition.

    Ms. Wang asked Reggie and me to enter the science fair.

    Ms. Wang helped him and me with the project.

Incorrect Use of Adjectives

Some adjectives have irregular forms: comparative forms for comparing two things and superlative forms for comparing more than two things.

Problem: Incorrect use of *good, better, best*

Their team is more good at softball than ours. *adj*

They have more better equipment too. *adj*

Solution: The comparative and superlative forms of *good* are *better* and *best*. Do not use *more* or *most* before irregular forms of comparative and superlative adjectives.

Their team is better at softball than ours.

They have better equipment too.

Problem: Incorrect use of *bad, worse, worst*

The flooding on East Street was the baddest I've seen. *adj*

Mike's basement was in badder shape than his garage. *adj*

Solution: The comparative and superlative forms of *bad* are *worse* and *worst*. Do not use *more* or *most* or the endings -*er* or -*est* with *bad*.

The flooding on East Street was the worst I've seen.

Mike's basement was in worse shape than his garage.

Problem: Incorrect use of comparative and superlative adjectives

The Appalachian Mountains are more older than the Rockies. *adj*

Mount Washington is the most highest of the Appalachians. *adj*

Solution: Do not use both -*er* and *more* or -*est* and *most* at the same time.

The Appalachian Mountains are older than the Rockies.

Mount Washington is the highest of the Appalachians.

Incorrect Use of Commas

Commas signal a pause between parts of a sentence and help to clarify meaning.

Problem: Missing commas in a series of three or more items

Sergio put mustard catsup and bean sprouts on his hot dog. *com*

Solution: If there are three or more items in a series, use a comma after each one, including the item preceding the conjunction.

Sergio put mustard, catsup, and bean sprouts on his hot dog.

Problem: Missing commas with direct quotations

"A little cold water" the swim coach said "won't hurt you." *com*

Solution: The first part of an interrupted quotation ends with a comma followed by quotation marks. The interrupting words are also followed by a comma.

"A little cold water," the swim coach said, "won't hurt you."

Problem: Missing commas with nonessential appositives

My sneakers a new pair are covered with mud. *com*

Solution: Determine whether the appositive is important to the meaning of the sentence. If it is not essential, set off the appositive with commas.

My sneakers, a new pair, are covered with mud.

Incorrect Use of Apostrophes

An apostrophe shows possession. It can also indicate missing letters in a contraction.

Problem: Singular possessive nouns

A parrots toes are used for gripping. *poss*

The bus color was bright yellow. *poss*

Solution: Use an apostrophe and an *s* to form the possessive of a singular noun, even one that ends in *s*.

A parrot's toes are used for gripping.

The bus's color was bright yellow.

Problem: Plural possessive nouns ending in -s

The visitors center closes at five o'clock. *poss*

The guide put several tourists luggage in one compartment. *poss*

Solution: Use an apostrophe alone to form the possessive of a plural noun that ends in *s*.

The visitors' center closes at five o'clock.

The guide put several tourists' luggage in one compartment.

Problem: Plural possessive nouns not ending in -s

The peoples applause gave courage to the young gymnast. *poss*

Solution: Use an apostrophe and an *s* to form the possessive of a plural noun that does not end in *s*.

The people's applause gave courage to the young gymnast.

Problem: Possessive personal pronouns

Jenny found the locker that was her's; she waited while her friends found their's. *poss*

Solution: Do not use apostrophes with possessive personal pronouns.

Jenny found the locker that was hers; she waited while her friends found theirs.

Incorrect Capitalization

Proper nouns, proper adjectives, and the first words of sentences always begin with a capital letter.

Problem: Words referring to ethnic groups, nationalities, and languages

Many canadians in the province of quebec speak french. *cap*

Solution: Capitalize proper nouns and adjectives that refer to ethnic groups, nationalities, and languages.

Many Canadians in the province of Quebec speak French.

Problem: Words that refer to a family member

Yesterday aunt Doreen asked me to baby-sit. *cap*

Don't forget to give dad a call. *cap*

Solution: Capitalize words that are used as part of or in place of a family member's name.

Yesterday Aunt Doreen asked me to baby-sit.

Don't forget to give Dad a call.

> **TIP**
>
> Do not capitalize a word that identifies a family member when it is preceded by a possessive adjective: *My father bought a new car.*

Problem: The first word of a direct quotation

The judge declared, "the court is now in session." *cap*

Solution: Capitalize the first word in a direct quotation.

The judge declared, "The court is now in session."

> **TIP**
>
> If you have difficulty with a rule of usage, try rewriting the rule in your own words. Check with your teacher to be sure you understand the rule.

Troublesome Words

This section will help you choose between words and expressions that are often confusing or misused.

accept, except

Accept means "to receive." *Except* means "other than."

> Phillip walked proudly to the stage to accept the award.

> Everything fits in my suitcase except my sleeping bag.

affect, effect

Affect is a verb meaning "to cause a change in" or "to influence." *Effect* as a verb means "to bring about or accomplish." As a noun, *effect* means "result."

> Bad weather will affect our plans for the weekend.

> The new medicine effected an improvement in the patient's condition.

> The gloomy weather had a bad effect on my mood.

ain't

Ain't is never used in formal speaking or writing unless you are quoting the exact words of a character or a real person. Instead of using *ain't,* say or write *am not, is not, are not;* or use contractions such as *I'm not, she isn't.*

> The pizza is not going to arrive for another half hour.

> The pizza isn't going to arrive for another half hour.

a lot

The expression *a lot* means "much" or "many" and should always be written as two words. Some authorities discourage its use in formal writing.

> A lot of my friends are learning Spanish.

> Many of my friends are learning Spanish.

all ready, already

All ready, written as two words, is a phrase that means "completely ready." *Already,* written as one word, is an adverb that means "before" or "by this time."

> By the time the fireworks display was all ready, we had already arrived.

all right, alright

The expression *all right* should be written as two words. Some dictionaries do list the single word *alright* but usually not as a preferred spelling.

> Tom hurt his ankle, but he will be all right.

all together, altogether

All together means "in a group." *Altogether* means "completely."

> The Minutemen stood all together at the end of Lexington Green.

> The rebel farmers were not altogether sure that they could fight the British soldiers.

among, between

Use *among* for three or more people, things, or groups. Use *between* for two people, things, or groups.

> Mr. Kendall divided the jobs for the car wash among the team members.

> Our soccer field lies between the gym and Main Street.

amount, number

Use *amount* with nouns that cannot be counted. Use *number* with nouns that can be counted.

> This recipe calls for an unusual amount of pepper.

> A record number of students attended last Saturday's book fair.

bad, badly

Bad is an adjective; it modifies a noun.
Badly is an adverb; it modifies a verb, an adjective, or another adverb.

> The badly burnt cookies left a bad smell in the kitchen.

> Joseph badly wants to be on the track team.

beside, besides

Beside means "next to." *Besides* means "in addition to."

> The zebra is grazing beside a wildebeest.

> Besides the zoo, I like to visit the aquarium.

bring, take

Bring means "to carry from a distant place to a closer one." *Take* means "to carry from a nearby place to a more distant one."

> Please bring a bag lunch and subway money to school tomorrow.

> Don't forget to take your art projects home this afternoon.

can, may

Can implies the ability to do something. *May* implies permission to do something.

> You may take a later bus home if you can remember which bus to get on.

TIP

Although *can* is sometimes used in place of *may* in informal speech, a distinction should be made when speaking and writing formally.

choose, chose

Choose means "to select." *Chose,* the past tense of *choose,* means "selected."

> Dad helped me choose a birthday card for my grandmother.

> Dad chose a card with a funny joke inside.

doesn't, don't

The subject of the contraction **doesn't** (*does not*) is the third-person singular (*he* or *she*). The subject of the contraction **don't** (*do not*) is *I, you, we,* or *they.*

> Tanya doesn't have any tickets for the concert.

> We don't need tickets if we stand in the back row.

farther, further

Farther refers to physical distance. *Further* refers to time or degree.

> Our new apartment is farther away from the school.

> I will not continue this argument further.

fewer, less

Fewer is used to refer to things or qualities that can be counted. *Less* is used to refer to things or qualities that cannot be counted. In addition, *less* is used with figures that are regarded as single amounts.

> Fewer people were waiting in line after lunch.

> There is less fat in this kind of peanut butter.

> Try to spend less than ten dollars on a present. [The money is treated as a single sum, not as individual dollars.]

good, well

Good is often used as an adjective meaning "pleasing" or "able." *Well* may be used as an adverb of manner telling how ably something is done or as an adjective meaning "in good health."

> That is a good haircut.

> Marco writes well.

> Because Ms. Rodriguez had a headache, she was not well enough to correct our tests.

in, into

In means "inside." *Into* indicates a movement from outside toward the inside.

> Refreshments will be sold in the lobby of the auditorium.

> The doors opened, and the eager crowd rushed into the auditorium.

it's, its

Use an apostrophe to form the contraction of *it is.* The possessive of the personal pronoun *it* does not take an apostrophe.

> It's hard to keep up with computer technology.

> The computer industry seems to change its products daily.

lay, lie

Lay means "to place." *Lie* means "to recline."

I will lay my beach towel here on the warm sand.

Help! I don't want to lie next to a hill of red ants!

learn, teach

Learn means "to gain knowledge." *Teach* means "to give knowledge."

I don't learn very quickly.

My uncle is teaching me how to juggle.

leave, let

Leave means "to go away." *Let* means "to allow." With the word *alone,* you may use either *let* or *leave.*

Huang has to leave at eight o'clock.

Mr. Davio lets the band practice in his basement.

Leave me alone. Let me alone.

like, as

Use *like,* a preposition, to introduce a prepositional phrase. Use *as,* a subordinating conjunction, to introduce a subordinate clause. Many authorities believe that *like* should not be used before a clause in formal English.

Andy sometimes acts like a clown.

The detective looked carefully at the empty suitcase as she examined the room.

> **TIP**
>
> *As* can be a preposition in cases like the following: *Jack went to the costume party as a giant pumpkin.*

loose, lose

Loose means "not firmly attached." *Lose* means "to misplace" or "to fail to win."

If you keep wiggling that loose tooth, you might lose it.

raise, rise

Raise means to "cause to move up." *Rise* means "to move upward."

Farmers in this part of Florida raise sugarcane.

The hot air balloon began to rise slowly in the morning sky.

set, sit

Set means "to place" or "to put." *Sit* means "to place oneself in a seated position."

I set the tips of my running shoes against the starting line.

After running the fifty-yard dash, I had to sit down and catch my breath.

than, then

Than introduces the second part of a comparison. *Then* means "at that time" or "after that."

I'd rather go to Disney World in the winter than in the summer.

The park is too crowded and hot then.

their, they're

Their is the possessive form of they. *They're* is the contraction of *they are.*

They're visiting Plymouth Plantation during their vacation.

to, too, two

To means "in the direction of." *Too* means "also" or "to an excessive degree." *Two* is the number after one.

I bought two tickets to the concert.

The music was too loud.

It's my favorite group too.

who, whom

Who is a subject pronoun. *Whom* is an object pronoun.

Who has finished the test already?

Mr. Russo is the man to whom we owe our thanks.

who's, whose

Who's is the contraction of *who is. Whose* is the possessive form of *who.*

Who's going to wake me up in the morning?

The policeman discovered whose car alarm was making so much noise.

Mechanics

This section will help you use correct capitalization, punctuation, and abbreviations in your writing.

Capitalization

Capitalizing Sentences, Quotations, and Salutations

Rule: A capital letter appears at the beginning of a sentence.

Example: Another gust of wind shook the house.

Rule: A capital letter marks the beginning of a direct quotation that is a complete sentence.

Example: Sabrina said, "The lights might go out."

Rule: When a quoted sentence is interrupted by explanatory words, such as she said, do not begin the second part of the sentence with a capital letter.

Example: "There's a rainbow," exclaimed Jeffrey, "over the whole beach."

Rule: When the second part of a quotation is a new sentence, put a period after the explanatory words; begin the new part with a capital letter.

Example: "Please come inside," Justin said. "Wipe your feet."

Rule: Do not capitalize an indirect quotation.

Example: Jo said that the storm was getting worse.

Rule: Capitalize the first word in the salutation and closing of a letter. Capitalize the title and name of the person addressed.

Example: Dear Dr. Menino
Dear Editor
Sincerely

Capitalizing Names and Titles of People

Rule: Capitalize the names of people and the initials that stand for their names.

Example: Malcolm X   J. F. K.
Robert E. Lee   Queen Elizabeth I

Rule: Capitalize a title or an abbreviation of a title when it comes before a person's name or when it is used in direct address.

Example: Dr. Salinas
"Your patient, Doctor, is waiting."

Rule: Do not capitalize a title that follows or is a substitute for a person's name.

Example: Marcia Salinas is a good doctor.
He asked to speak to the doctor.

Rule: Capitalize the names and abbreviations of academic degrees that follow a person's name. Capitalize Jr. and Sr.

Example: Marcia Salinas, M.D.
Raoul Tobias, Attorney
Donald Bruns Sr.
Ann Lee, Ph.D.

Rule: Capitalize words that show family relationships when used as titles or as substitutes for a person's name.

Example: We saw Uncle Carlos.
She read a book about Mother Teresa.

Rule: Do not capitalize words that show family relationships when they follow a possessive noun or pronoun.

Example: Your brother will give us a ride.
I forgot my mother's phone number.

Rule: Always capitalize the pronoun I.

Example: After I clean my room, I'm going swimming.

Capitalizing Names of Places

TIP

Do not capitalize articles and prepositions in proper nouns: *the Rock of Gibraltar, the Statue of Liberty.*

Rule: Capitalize the names of cities, counties, states, countries, and continents.

> **Example:** St. Louis, Missouri
> Marin County
> Australia
> South America

Rule: Capitalize the names of bodies of water and other geographical features.

> **Example:** the Great Lakes   Cape Cod
> the Dust Bowl

Rule: Capitalize the names of sections of a country and regions of the world.

> **Example:** East Asia
> New England
> the Pacific Rim
> the Midwest

Rule: Capitalize compass points when they refer to a specific section of a country.

> **Example:** the Northwest   the South

Rule: Do not capitalize compass points when they indicate direction.

> **Example:** Canada is north of the United States.

Rule: Do not capitalize adjectives indicating direction.

> **Example:** western Utah

Rule: Capitalize the names of streets and highways.

> **Example:** Dorchester Avenue   Route 22

Rule: Capitalize the names of buildings, bridges, monuments, and other structures.

> **Example:** World Trade Center
> Chesapeake Bay Bridge

Capitalizing Other Proper Nouns and Adjectives

Rule: Capitalize the names of clubs, organizations, businesses, institutions, and political parties.

> **Example:** Houston Oilers
> the Food and Drug Administration
> Boys and Girls Club

Rule: Capitalize brand names but not the nouns following them.

> **Example:** Zippo brand energy bar

Rule: Capitalize the names of days of the week, months, and holidays.

> **Example:** Saturday   June
> Thanksgiving Day

Rule: Do not capitalize the names of seasons.

> **Example:** winter, spring, summer, fall

Rule: Capitalize the first word, the last word, and all important words in the title of a book, play, short story, poem, essay, article, film, television series, song, magazine, newspaper, and chapter of a book.

> **Example:** *Not Without Laughter*
> *World Book Encyclopedia*
> "Jingle Bells"
> Star Wars
> Chapter 12

Rule: Capitalize the names of ethnic groups, nationalities, and languages.

> **Example:** Latino   Japanese
> European   Spanish

Rule: Capitalize proper adjectives that are formed from the names of ethnic groups and nationalities.

> **Example:** Shetland pony
> Jewish holiday

Punctuation

Using the Period and Other End Marks

Rule: Use a period at the end of a declarative sentence.

My great-grandfather fought in the Mexican Revolution.

Rule: Use a period at the end of an imperative sentence that does not express strong feeling.

Please set the table.

Rule: Use a question mark at the end of an interrogative sentence.

How did your sneakers get so muddy?

Rule: Use an exclamation point at the end of an exclamatory sentence or a strong imperative.

How exciting the play was!

Watch out!

Using Commas

Rule: Use commas to separate three or more items in a series.

The canary eats bird seed, fruit, and suet.

Rule: Use commas to show a pause after an introductory word and to set off names used in direct address.

Yes, I offered to take care of her canary this weekend.

Please, Stella, can I borrow your nail polish?

Rule: Use a comma after two or more introductory prepositional phrases or when the comma is needed to make the meaning clear. A comma is not needed after a single short prepositional phrase, but it is acceptable to use one.

From the back of the balcony, we had a lousy view of the stage.

After the movie we walked home. (no comma needed)

Rule: Use a comma after an introductory participle and an introductory participial phrase.

Whistling and moaning, the wind shook the little house.

Rule: Use commas to set off words that interrupt the flow of thought in a sentence.

Tomorrow, I think, our projects are due.

Rule: Use a comma after conjunctive adverbs such as *however, moreover, furthermore, nevertheless,* and *therefore.*

The skating rink is crowded on Saturday; however, it's the only time I can go.

Rule: Use commas to set off an appositive if it is not essential to the meaning of a sentence.

Ben Wagner, a resident of Pittsfield, won the first round in the golf tournament.

Rule: Use a comma before a conjunction (*and, or, but, nor, so, yet*) that joins main clauses.

We can buy our tickets now, or we can take a chance on buying them just before the show.

Rule: Use a comma after an introductory adverb clause.

Because I stayed up so late, I'm sleepy this morning.

Rule: In most cases, do not use a comma with an adverb clause that comes at the end of a sentence.

The picnic will be canceled unless the weather clears.

Rule: Use a comma or a pair of commas to set off an adjective clause that is not essential to the meaning of a sentence.

Tracy, who just moved here from Florida, has never seen snow before.

Rule: Do not use a comma or pair of commas to set off an essential clause from the rest of the sentence.

Anyone who signs up this month will get a discount.

Rule: Use commas before and after the year when it is used with both the month and the day. If only the month and the year are given, do not use a comma.

On January 2, 1985, my parents moved to Dallas, Texas.

I was born in May 1985.

Rule: Use commas before and after the name of a state or a country when it is used with the name of a city. Do not use a comma after the state if it is used with a ZIP code.

The area code for Concord, New Hampshire, is 603.

Please forward my mail to 6 Madison Lane, Topsham, ME 04086

Rule: Use commas or a pair of commas to set off an abbreviated title or degree following a person's name.

The infirmary was founded by Elizabeth Blackwell, M.D., the first woman in the United States to earn a medical degree.

Rule: Use a comma or commas to set off *too* when *too* means "also."

We, too, bought groceries, from the new online supermarket.

Rule: Use a comma or commas to set off a direct quotation.

"My nose," exclaimed Pinocchio, "is growing longer!"

Rule: Use a comma after the salutation of a friendly letter and after the closing of both a friendly letter and a business letter.

Dear Gary,

Sincerely,

Best regards,

Rule: Use a comma when necessary to prevent misreading of a sentence.

In math, solutions always elude me.

Using Semicolons and Colons

Rule: Use a semicolon to join the parts of a compound sentence when a coordinating conjunction, such as *and, or, nor,* or *but,* is not used.

Don't be late for the dress rehearsal; it begins at 7 o'clock sharp.

Rule: Use a semicolon to join parts of a compound sentence when the main clauses are long and are subdivided by commas. Use a semicolon even if these clauses are already joined by a coordinating conjunction.

In the gray light of early morning, on a remote airstrip in the desert, two pilots prepared to fly on a dangerous mission; but accompanying them were a television camera crew, three newspaper reporters, and a congressman from their home state of Nebraska.

Rule: Use a semicolon to separate main clauses joined by a conjunctive adverb. Be sure to use a comma after the conjunctive adverb.

We've been climbing all morning; therefore, we need a rest.

Rule: Use a colon to introduce a list of items that ends a sentence. Use words such as *these, the following,* or *as follows* to signal that a list is coming.

Remember to bring the following items: a backpack, a bag lunch, sunscreen, and insect repellent.

Rule: Do not use a colon to introduce a list preceded by a verb or preposition.

Remember to bring a backpack, a bag lunch, sunscreen, and insect repellent. (No colon is used after *bring.*)

Rule: Use a colon to separate the hour and the minutes when you write the time of day.

My Spanish class starts at 9:15.

Rule: Use a colon after the salutation of a business letter.

Dear Dr. Coulombe:
Director of the Personnel Dept.:

Using Quotation Marks and Italics

Rule: Use quotation marks before and after a direct quotation.

"Curiouser and curiouser," said Alice.

Rule: Use quotation marks with both parts of a divided quotation.

"This gymnastics trick," explained Amanda, "took me three months to learn."

Rule: Use a comma or commas to separate a phrase such as *she said* from the quotation itself. Place the comma that precedes the phrase inside the closing quotation marks.

"I will be late," said the cable technician, "for my appointment."

Rule: Place a period that ends a quotation inside the closing quotation marks.

Scott said, "Thanks for letting me borrow your camping tent."

Rule: Place a question mark or an exclamation point inside the quotation marks when it is part of the quotation.

"Why is the door of your snake's cage open?" asked my mother.

Rule: Place a question mark or an exclamation point outside the quotation marks when it is part of the entire sentence.

How I love "The Pit and the Pendulum"!

Rule: Use quotation marks for the title of a short story, essay, poem, song, magazine or newspaper article, or book chapter.

short story: "The Necklace"
poem: "The Fish"
article: "Fifty Things to Make from Bottlecaps"

Rule: Use italics or underlining for the title of a book, play, film, television series, magazine, newspaper, or work of art.

book: *To Kill a Mockingbird*
magazine: *The New Republic*
painting: *Sunflowers*

Rule: Use italics or underlining for the names of ships, trains, airplanes, and spacecraft.

ship: *Mayflower*
airplane: *Air Force One*

Using Apostrophes

Rule: Use an apostrophe and an *s* (*'s*) to form the possessive of a singular noun.

my brother's rock collection
Chris's hat

Rule: Use an apostrophe and an *s* (*'s*) to form the possessive of a plural noun that does not end in *s*.

the geese's feathers
the oxen's domestication

TIP

If a thing is owned jointly by two or more individuals, only the last name should show possession: *Mom and Dad's car.* If the ownership is not joint, each name should show possession: *Mom and Dad's parents are coming for Thanksgiving.*

Rule: Use an apostrophe alone to form the possessive of a plural noun that ends in *s*.

the animals' habitat
the instruments' sound

Rule: Use an apostrophe and an *s* (*'s*) to form the possessive of an indefinite pronoun.

everyone's homework
someone's homework

Rule: Do not use an apostrophe in a possessive pronoun.

The dog knocked over its dish.
Yours is the best entry in the contest.
One of these drawings must be hers.

Rule: Use an apostrophe to replace letters that have been omitted in a contraction.

it + is = it's
can + not = can't
I + have = I've

Rule: Use an apostrophe to form the plural of a letter, a figure, or a word that is used as itself.

Write three 7's.
The word is spelled with two m's.
The sentence contains three and's.

Rule: Use an apostrophe to show missing numbers in a year.

the class of '02

Using Hyphens, Dashes, and Parentheses

Rule: Use a hyphen to show the division of a word at the end of a line. Always divide the word between its syllables.

With the new recycling program, more residents are recycling
their trash.

> **TIP**
>
> One-letter divisions (for example, *e-lectric*) are not per-missible. Avoid dividing personal names, if possible.

Rule: Use a hyphen in a number written as a compound word.

He sold forty-six ice creams in one hour.

Rule: Use a hyphen in a fraction.

We won the vote by a two-thirds majority.

Two-thirds of the votes have been counted.

Rule: Use a hyphen or hyphens in certain compound nouns.

great-grandmother

merry-go-round

Rule: Hyphenate a compound modifier only when it precedes the word it modifies.

A well-known musician visited our school.

The story was well written.

Rule: Use a hyphen after the prefixes *all-, ex-,* and *self-* when they are joined to any noun or adjective.

all-star

ex-president

self-conscious

Rule: Use a hyphen to separate any prefix from a word that begins with a capital letter.

un-American

mid-January

Rule: Use a dash or dashes to show a sudden break or change in thought or speech.

Daniel—he's kind of a pest—is my youngest cousin.

Rule: Use parentheses to set off words that define or helpfully explain a word in the sentence.

The transverse flute (*transverse* means "sideways") is a wind instrument.

Abbreviations

Rule: Abbreviate the titles *Mr., Mrs., Ms.,* and *Dr.* before a person's name. Also abbreviate any professional or academic degree that follows a name. The titles *Jr.* and *Sr.* are *not* preceded by a comma.

Dr. Stanley Livingston (doctor)

Luisa Mendez, M.A. (Master of Arts)

Martin Luther King Jr.

Rule: Use capital letters and no periods with abbreviations that are pronounced letter by letter or as words. Exceptions are *U.S.* and *Washington, D.C.,* which do use periods.

NAACP	National Association for the Advancement of Colored People
UFO	unidentified flying object
MADD	Mothers Against Driving Drunk

Rule: With exact times use A.M. (*ante meridiem,* "before noon") and P.M. (*post meridiem,* "after noon"). For years use B.C. (before Christ) and, sometimes, A.D. (*anno Domini,* "in the year of the lord," after Christ).

8:15 A.M.	6:55 P.M.
5000 B.C.	A.D. 235

Rule: Abbreviate days and months only in charts and lists.

School will be closed on

Mon., Sept. 3

Wed., Nov. 11

Thurs., Nov. 27

Rule: In scientific writing abbreviate units of measure. Use periods with English units but not with metric units.

inch(es) in.	yard(s) yd.
meter(s) m	milliliter(s) ml

Rule: On envelopes only, abbreviate street names and state names. In general text, spell out street names and state names.

Ms. Karen Holmes

347 Grandville St.

Tilton, NH 03276

Karen lives on Grandville Street in Tilton, New Hampshire.

Writing Numbers

Rule: In charts and tables, always write numbers as numerals. Other rules apply to numbers not in charts or tables.

Student Test Scores

Student	Test 1	Test 2	Test 3
Lai, W.	82	89	94
Ostos, A.	78	90	86

Rule: Spell out a number that is expressed in one or two words.

We carried enough supplies for twenty-three days.

Rule: Use a numeral for a number of more than two words.

The tallest mountain in Mexico rises 17,520 feet.

Rule: Spell out a number that begins a sentence, or reword the sentence so that it does not begin with a number.

One hundred forty-three days later the baby elephant was born.

The baby elephant was born 143 days later.

Rule: Write a very large number as a numeral followed by the word *million* or *billion*.

There are 15 million people living in or near Mexico City.

Rule: Related numbers should be written in the same way. If one number must be written as a numeral, use numerals for all the numbers.

There are 365 days in the year, but only 52 weekends.

Rule: Spell out an ordinal number (*first, second*).

Welcome to our fifteenth annual convention.

Rule: Use words to express the time of day unless you are writing the exact time or using the abbreviation A.M. or P.M.

My guitar lesson is at five o'clock. It ends by 5:45 P.M.

Rule: Use numerals to express dates, house and street numbers, apartment and room numbers, telephone numbers, page numbers, amounts of money of more than two words, and percentages. Write out the word *percent*.

August 5, 1999

9 Davio Dr.

Apartment 9F

24 percent

Spelling

The following rules, examples, and exceptions can help you master the spelling of many words.

Spelling *ie* and *ei*

Put *i* before *e* except when both letters follow *c* or when both letters are pronounced together as an **a** sound.

believe	sieve	weight
receive	relieve	neighborhood

It is helpful to memorize exceptions to this rule. Exceptions include the following words: *species, science, weird, either, seize, leisure,* and *protein*.

Spelling unstressed vowels

Notice the vowel sound in the second syllable of the word *won-d_r-ful*. This is the unstressed vowel sound; dictionary respellings use the schwa symbol (ə) to indicate it. Because any of several vowels can be used to spell this sound, you might find yourself uncertain about which vowel to use. To spell words with unstressed vowels, try thinking of a related word in which the syllable containing the vowel sound is stressed.

Unknown Spelling	Related Word	Word Spelled Correctly
wond_rful	wonder	wonderful
fort_fications	fortify	fortifications
res_dent	reside	resident

Suffixes and the silent *e*

For most words with silent *e*, keep the e when adding a suffix. When you add the suffix -*ly* to a word that ends in *l* plus silent *e*, drop the -*le*. Also drop the silent *e* when you add a suffix beginning with a vowel or a *y*.

wise + ly = wisely
peaceful + ly = peacefully
skate + ing = skating
gentle + ly = gently

There are exceptions to the rule, including the following:

awe + ful = awful
judge + ment = judgment

true + ly = truly
noise + y = noisy
dye + ing = dyeing
mile + age = mileage

Suffixes and the final *y*

When you are adding a suffix to words ending with a vowel + *y*, keep the *y*. For words ending with a consonant + *y*, change the *y* to *i* unless the suffix begins with *i*. To avoid having two *i*'s together, keep the *y*.

enjoy + ment = enjoyment
merry + ment = merriment
display + ed = displayed
lazy + ness = laziness
play + ful = playful
worry + ing = worrying

Note: For some words, there are alternate spellings:

sly + er = slyer or slier
shy + est = shyest or shiest

Adding prefixes

When you add a prefix to a word, do not change the spelling of the word.

un + done = undone
re + schedule = reschedule
il + legible = illegible
semi + sweet = semisweet

Doubling the final consonant

Double the final consonant when a word ends with a single consonant following one vowel and the word is one syllable, or when the last syllable of the word is accented both before and after adding the suffix.

sit + ing = sitting
rub + ing = rubbing
commit + ed = committed
confer + ed = conferred

Do not double the final consonant if the suffix begins with a consonant, if the accent is not on the last syllable, or if the accent moves when the suffix is added.

cancel + ing = canceling
commit + ment = commitment
travel + ed = traveled
defer + ence = deference

Do not double the final consonant if the word ends in two consonants or if the suffix begins with a consonant.

climb + er = climber
nervous + ness = nervousness

import + ance = importance
star + dom = stardom

When adding -ly to a word that ends in ll, drop one l.

hill + ly = hilly   full + ly = fully

Forming compound words

When forming compound words, keep the original spelling of both words.

home + work = homework
scare + crow = scarecrow
pea + nut = peanut

Forming Plurals

General Rules for Plurals		
If the noun ends in	**Rule**	**Example**
s, ch, sh, x, or z	add -es	loss→losses, latch→latches, box→boxes, bush→bushes, quiz→quizzes
a consonant + y	change y to i and add -es	ferry→ferries, baby→babies, worry→worries
a vowel + y	add -s	chimney→chimneys, monkey→monkeys, toy→toys
a vowel + o	add -s	cameo→cameos, radio→radios, rodeo→rodeos
a consonant + o	add -es but sometimes add -s	potato→potatoes, echo→echoes photo→photos, solo→solos
f or ff	add -s but sometimes change f to v and add -es	proof→proofs, bluff→bluffs sheaf→sheaves, thief→thieves, hoof→hooves
lf	change f to v and add -es	calf→calves, half→halves, loaf→loaves
fe	change f to v and add -s	knife→knives, life→lives

Special Rules for Plurals	
Rule	**Example**
To form the plural of most proper names and one-word compound nouns, follow the general rules for plurals.	Jones→Joneses, Thomas→Thomases, Hatch→Hatches
To form the plural of hyphenated compound nouns or compound nouns of more than one word, make the most important word plural.	credit card→credit cards mother-in-law→mothers-in-law district attorney→district attorneys
Some nouns have irregular plural forms and do not follow any rules.	man→men, foot→feet, tooth→teeth
Some nouns have the same singular and plural forms	deer→deer, species→species, sheep→sheep

Listening Effectively

A large part of the school day is spent either listening or speaking to others. By becoming a better listener and speaker, you will know more about what is expected of you, and understand more about your audience.

Listening to instructions in class

Some of the most important listening in the school day involves listening to instructions. Use the following tips to help you.

- First, make sure you understand what you are listening for. Are you receiving instructions for homework or for a test? What you listen for depends upon the type of instructions being given.
- Think about what you are hearing, and keep your eyes on the speaker. This will help you stay focused on the important points.
- Listen for keywords, or word clues. Examples of word clues are phrases such as *above all, most important,* or *the three basic parts.* These clues help you identify important points that you should remember.
- Take notes on what you hear. Write down only the most important parts of the instructions.
- If you don't understand something, ask questions. Then if you're still unsure about the instructions, repeat them aloud to your teacher to receive correction on any key points that you may have missed.

Interpreting nonverbal clues

Understanding nonverbal clues is part of effective listening. Nonverbal clues are everything you notice about a speaker *except* what the speaker says. As you listen, ask yourself these questions:

- Where and how is the speaker standing?
- Are some words spoken more loudly than others?
- Does the speaker make eye contact?
- Does he or she smile or look angry?
- What message is sent by the speaker's gestures and facial expression?

PRACTICE

Work with a partner to practice listening to instructions. Each of you should find a set of directions for using a simple device–for example, a mechanical tool, a telephone answering machine, or a VCR. Study the instructions carefully. If you can bring the device to class, ask your partner to try to use it by following your step-by-step instructions. If you cannot have the device in class, ask your partner to explain the directions back to you. Then change roles and listen as your partner gives you a set of directions.

Speaking Effectively

- Speak slowly, clearly, and in a normal tone of voice. Raise your voice a bit, or use gestures to stress important points.
- Pause a few seconds after making an important point.
- Use words that help your audience picture what you're talking about. Visual aids such as pictures, graphs, charts, and maps can also help make your information clear.
- Stay in contact with your audience. Make sure your eyes move from person to person in the group you're addressing.

Speaking informally

Most oral communication is informal. When you speak casually with your friends, family, and neighbors, you use informal speech. Human relationships depend on this form of communication.

- Be courteous. Listen until the other person has finished speaking.
- Speak in a relaxed and spontaneous manner.
- Make eye contact with your listeners.
- Do not monopolize a conversation.
- When telling a story, show enthusiasm.
- When giving an announcement or directions, speak clearly and slowly. Check that your listeners understand the information.

Presenting an oral report

The steps in preparing an oral report are similar to the steps in the writing process. Complete each step carefully and you can be confident of presenting an effective oral report.

Steps in Preparing an Oral Report	
Prewriting	Determine your purpose and audience. Decide on a topic and narrow it.
Drafting	Make an outline. Fill in the supporting details. Write the report.
Revising and editing	Review your draft. Check the organization of ideas and details. Reword unclear statements.
Practicing	Practice the report aloud in front of a family member. Time the report. Ask for and accept advice.
Presenting	Relax in front of your audience. Make eye contact with your audience. Speak slowly and clearly.

PRACTICE

Pretend that you have been invited to give an oral report to a group of fifth graders. Your report will tell them what to expect and how to adjust to new conditions when they enter middle school. As you plan your report, keep your purpose and your audience in mind. Include lively descriptions and examples to back up your suggestions and hold your audience's attention. As you practice giving your report, be sure to give attention to your body language as well as your vocal projection. Ask a partner to listen to your report to give you feedback on how to improve your performance. Do the same for your partner after listening to his or her report.

Viewing Effectively

Critical viewing means thinking about what you see while watching a TV program, newscast, film, or video. It requires paying attention to what you hear and see and deciding whether information is true, false, or exaggerated. If the information seems to be true, try to determine whether it is based on a fact or an opinion.

Fact versus opinion

A **fact** is something that can be proved. An opinion is what someone believes is true. **Opinions** are based on feelings and experiences and cannot be proved.

Television commercials, political speeches, and even the evening news contain both facts and opinions. They use emotional words and actions to persuade the viewer to agree with a particular point of view. They may also use faulty reasoning, such as linking an effect with the wrong cause. Think through what is being said. The speaker may seem sincere, but do his or her reasons make sense? Are the reasons based on facts or on unfair generalizations?

Commercials contain both obvious and hidden messages. Just as you need to discover the author's purpose when you read a writer's words, you must be aware of the purpose of nonverbal attempts to persuade you.

What does the message sender want, and how is the sender trying to influence you?

For example, a magazine or TV ad picturing a group of happy teenagers playing volleyball on a sunny beach expresses a positive feeling. The advertiser hopes viewers will transfer that positive feeling to the product being advertised—perhaps a soft drink or a brand of beachwear. This technique, called **transfer,** is one of several propaganda techniques regularly used by advertisers to influence consumers.

Following are a few other common techniques.

Testimonial—Famous and admired people recommend or praise a product, a policy, or a course of action even though they probably have no professional knowledge or expertise to back up their opinion.

Bandwagon—People are urged to follow the crowd ("get on the bandwagon") by buying a product, voting for a candidate, or whatever else the advertiser wants them to do.

Glittering generalities—The advertiser uses positive, good-sounding words (for example, *all-American* or *medically proven*) to impress people.

PRACTICE

Think of a television commercial that you have seen often or watch a new one and take notes as you watch it. Then analyze the commercial.

- What is the purpose behind the ad?
- What is expressed in written or spoken words?
- What is expressed nonverbally (in music or sound effects as well as in pictures and actions)?
- What methods does the advertiser use to persuade viewers?
- What questions would you ask the advertiser if you could?
- How effective is the commercial? Why?

Working in Groups

Working in a group is an opportunity to learn from others. Whether you are planning a group project (such as a class trip) or solving a math problem, each person in a group brings specific strengths and interests to the task. When a task is large, such as planting a garden, a group provides the necessary energy and talent to get the job done.

Small groups vary in size according to the nature of the task. Three to five students is a good size for most small-group tasks. Your teacher may assign you to a group, or you may be asked to form your own group. Don't work with your best friend if you are likely to chat too much. Successful groups often have a mix of student abilities and interests.

Individual role assignments give everyone in a group something to do. One student, the group recorder, may take notes. Another may lead the discussion, and another report the results to the rest of the class.

Roles for a Small Group

Reviewer	Reads or reviews the assignment and makes sure everyone understands it
Recorder 1 (of the process)	Takes notes on the discussion
Recorder 2 (of the results)	Takes notes on the final results
Reporter	Reports results to the rest of the class
Discussion leader	Asks questions to get the discussion going; keeps the group focused
Facilitator	Helps the group resolve disagreements and reach a compromise

For a small group of three or four students, some of these roles can be combined. Your teacher may assign a role to each student in your group. Or you may be asked to choose your own role.

Tips for working in groups

- Review the group assignment and goal. Be sure that everyone in the group understands the assignment.
- Review the amount of time allotted for the task. Decide how your group will organize its time.
- Check that all the group members understand their roles in the group.
- When a question arises, try to solve it as a group before asking a teacher for help.
- Listen to other points of view. Take turns during a discussion.
- When it is your turn to talk, address the subject and help the project move forward.

Study Skills

Studying for school and doing your homework are like any other tasks—if you understand your assignment, set a goal, and make a plan, you'll save time and do great work. The tips that follow will teach you the skills you need to make schoolwork easier and more enjoyable.

Get Organized

- Keep an assignment notebook. Keep it up to date.
- Keep your notes for each course together in one place.
- Find a good place to study. Choose a place that has as few distractions as possible. Try to study in the same place each day.
- Try to study at the same time each day.
- Don't study one subject too long. If you haven't finished after thirty minutes, switch to another subject.
- Take notes on your reading. Keep your notes in one place.

Understand Your Purpose

The purpose is the reason you have been given a particular assignment. If you understand the purpose, you should be able to set a goal to work toward. With schoolwork, this means making sure you understand your assignment and you know how long you have to do it.

Set goals

These steps will help you set study goals for an assignment.

1. Listen as the teacher explains the assignment. Find out everything you need to do to finish the assignment.
2. Understand the quality of work your teacher expects from you. Are you supposed to turn in a finished paper or a rough draft?
3. Find out how much time you have. Ask: Is everything due on the same day, or are some parts due earlier?
4. In your assignment notebook, write down the assignment details and the dates when your work is due.

Homework Checklist

Goal: To understand and finish my homework assignment.

Plan: Follow these steps to reach my goal:

- ☑ Bring home the all the materials I need, including this textbook, and my notebook.
- ☑ Find a quiet space where I can concentrate. Also, make sure I have a table or other hard, flat surface to write on.
- ☑ Keep my notebook out and take notes as I read.
- ☑ Write down questions about the parts of the assignment that I don't understand. Ask my teacher or an adult at home to help me understand.
- ☑ Check this plan from time to time to make sure I stay on task.
- ☑ Take my completed homework back to school and hand it in.

Make a Plan

Making a plan is the best way to reach your goals. Try to make plans that include the work you have finish and the time you have until the assignment is due. Think about how you study best, when you might need help, and what gets in your way.

You can use a **task, obstacle, and solution chart** to show

1. what you need to do (task)
2. what might get in your way (obstacle)
3. how you can get around an obstacle (solution)

Karen's goal is to read a chapter of science before school tomorrow. Check out the chart she made which includes **task, obstacle, and solution.**

1. (task)	I have to…	read chapter 4 tonight
2. (obstacle)	But…	after dinner I have basketball practice
3. (solution)	So I need to…	read before practice

Try it! In your **Learner's Notebook,** make your own **task, obstacle, and solution chart** for an assignment from this book. You can use Karen's plan as a model.

Take Notes

Writing notes about what you read or what you hear in a presentation will help you remember information you're expected to learn. The Cornell Note-Taking System is a way to organize the notes you take in class or the notes you take as you read. Use this system to organize your note-taking and make sense of the notes you take.

Cornell Notes

Divide the pages that you're using for notes into two sections or columns as shown below. As you read or listen, write notes in Section B. In Section A, write the highlights (main ideas and vocabulary) from Section B.

Section A [highlights]	Section B [notes]
Use this section SECOND. Review the notes you took in Section B and write in this section: • Vocabulary words to remember • Main idea statements • Questions and other hints that will help you remember the information	Use this section FIRST. As you read or listen, take notes in this section: • When you're taking notes on your reading, write down the subtitles that break the text into different section. In most cases, subtitles form an outline of the information in a chapter. • Write down the most important information: main ideas and concepts. Don't write every word or take time to write complete sentences. (Hint: if the teacher writes something on the board, it's probably important.) • Use abbreviations and shortened word forms to get the ideas on paper quickly. (For example, POV is a good abbreviation for Point of View.) • Define new terms and concepts in your own words so that you'll be able to understand them later.

Model These are some notes one student made as she read about biographies and autobiographies.

| A.
biography

autobiography

Major elements of biography | B. Looking at the Genre: Biography
What is it?
    real people, real life
    Autobiography is about yourself
Why is it important?
    many reasons (interest, learn, entertain, etc.)
What are the important elements?
    Narrator: who tells the story
    Point of view: from who's telling the story
    Setting: time and place of a story |

Try It! Divide a sheet of paper into two columns as shown above. Practice taking notes using the Cornell system as you read your homework assignment.

Test-Taking Skills

How well you perform on a test is not a matter of chance. Some specific strategies can help you answer test questions. This section of the handbook will show how to improve your test-taking skills.

Tips for preparing for tests

Here are some useful suggestions for preparing to take a test.

- Gather information about the test. When will it be given? How long will it take? Exactly what material will it cover?

- Review material from your textbook, class notes, homework, quizzes, and handouts. Review the study questions at the end of each section of a textbook. Try to define terms in boldface type.

- Make up some sample questions and answer them. As you skim selections, try to predict what may be asked.

- Draw charts and cluster or Venn diagrams to help you remember information and to picture how one piece of information relates to another.

- Give yourself plenty of time to study. Avoid cramming for a test. Several short review sessions are more effective than one long one.

- In addition to studying alone, study with a partner or small group. Quiz one another on topics you think the test will cover.

Plan your strategy

Try following these steps:

- Read all directions carefully. Understanding the directions can prevent mistakes.

- Ask for help if you have a question.

- Answer the easier items first. By skipping the hard items, you will have time to answer all the easy ones.

- In the time that is left, return to the items you skipped. Answer them as best you can. If you won't be penalized for doing so, guess at an answer.

- If possible, save some time at the end to check your answers.

Objective Tests

An objective test is a test of factual information. The questions are usually either right or wrong; there is no difference of opinion. On an objective test, you are asked to recall information, not to present your ideas. Objective test questions include true-or-false items, multiple-choice items, fill-in-the-blanks statements, short-answer items, and matching items. At the beginning of an objective test, scan the number of items. Then budget your time.

Multiple-choice items Multiple-choice questions ask you to answer a question or complete a sentence. They are the kind of question you will encounter most often on objective tests. Read all the choices before answering. Pick the best response.

What is a peninsula?

(a) a range of mountains

(b) a circle around the moon

(c) a body of land surrounded by water on three sides

Correct answer: (c)

- Read the question carefully. Be sure that you understand it.

- Read all the answers before selecting one. Reading all of the responses is especially important when one of the choices is "all of the above" or "none of the above."

- Eliminate responses that are clearly incorrect. Focus on the responses that might be correct.

- Look for absolute words, such as *never, always, all, none.* Most generalizations have exceptions. Absolute statements are often incorrect. (Note: This tip applies to true/false items also.)

Answering essay questions

Essay questions ask you to think about what you have learned and to write about it in one or more paragraphs. Some tests present a choice of essay questions. If a test has both an objective part and an essay part, answer the objective questions first, but leave yourself enough time to work on the essay.

Read the essay question carefully. What does it ask you to do? Discuss? Explain? Define? Summarize? Compare and contrast? These key words tell what kind of information you must give in your answer.

Key Verbs in Essay Questions	
Argue	Give your opinion and supporting reasons.
Compare and contrast	Discuss likenesses and differences.
Define	Give details that show exactly what something is like.
Demonstrate	Give examples to support a point.
Describe	Present a picture with words.
Discuss	Show detailed information on a particular subject.
Explain	Give reasons.
Identify	Give specific characteristics.
List (also outline, trace)	Give details, give steps in order, give a time sequence.
Summarize	Give a short overview of the most important ideas or events.

Tips for answering essay questions

You might wish to consider the following suggestions:

- Read the question or questions carefully. Determine the kind of information required by the question.
- Plan your time. Do not spend too much time on one part of the essay.
- Make a list of what you want to cover.
- If you have time, make revisions and proofreading corrections.

Taking standardized tests

Standardized tests are taken by students all over the country. Your performance on the test is compared with the performance of other students at your grade level. There are many different kinds of standardized tests. Some measure your progress in such subjects as English, math, and science, while others measure how well you think. Standardized tests can show how you learn and what you do best.

Preparing for standardized tests

There is no way to know exactly what information will be on a standardized test, or even what topics will be covered. The best preparation is to do the best you can in your daily schoolwork. However, you can learn the *kinds* of questions that will appear on a standardized test. Some general tips will also help.

Tips for taking standardized tests

You might find the following suggestions helpful.

- Get enough sleep the night before the test. Eat a healthful breakfast.
- Arrive early for the test. Try to relax.
- Listen carefully to all test directions. Ask questions if you don't understand the directions.
- Complete easy questions first. Leave harder items for the end.
- Be sure your answers are in the right place on the answer sheet.
- If points are not subtracted for wrong answers, guess at questions that you aren't sure of.

Analogies Analogy items test your understanding of the relationships between things or ideas. On standardized tests, analogies are written in an abbreviated format, as shown below.

man : woman :: buck : doe

The symbol : means "is to"; the symbol :: means "as."

This chart shows some word relationships you might find in analogy tests.

Relationship	Definition	Example
Synonyms	Two words have a similar meaning.	huge : gigantic :: scared : afraid
Antonyms	Two words have opposite meanings.	bright : dull :: far : near
Use	Words name a user and something used.	farmer : tractor :: writer : computer
Cause-Effect	Words name a cause and its effect.	tickle : laugh :: polish : shine
Category	Words name a category and an item in it.	fish : tuna :: building : house
Description	Words name an item and a characteristic of it.	knife : sharp :: joke : funny

GLOSSARY/GLOSARIO
Academic and Selection Vocabulary

|

A

abandoned (uh BAN dund) *v.* given up or left behind **(p. 292)**

accustomed (uh KUS tumd) *adj.* used to; familiar with **(p. 638)**

acknowledge (ak NOL ij) *v.* to recognize the truth of something **(p. 639)**

acquired (uh KWY urd) *v.* obtained, got, received **(p. 349)**

addresses (uh DRESS uz) *v.* deals with or pays attention to **(p. 1053)**

administrator (ad MIN uh stray tur) *n.* person who manages or directs **(p. 21)**

adopt (uh DOPT) *v.* to accept and put into effect **(p. 303)**

advisory (ad VY zuh ree) *adj.* having the power to give advice **(p. 21)**

aggression (uh GRESH un) *n.* angry and unfriendly action or behavior **(p. 573)**

amassed (uh MAST) *v.* piled up, collected, or gathered a great quantity of something **(p. 93)**

ambitions (am BISH unz) *n.* strong desires to succeed **(p. 193)**

anesthetist (uh NES thuh tist) *n.* the person who gives drugs to put a patient to sleep before surgery **(p. 629)**

application (ap lih KAY shun) *n.* the act of putting something to use **(p. 498)**

appointed (uh POIN tid) *v.* selected or named for an office or position **(p. 180)**

architect (AR kuh tekt) *n.* a person who designs buildings **(p. 271)**

astray (uh STRAY) *adv.* off the right path or route **(p. 1043)**

authority (uh THOR ih tee) *n.* a good source of information or advice **(p. 498)**

abandonado(a) *adj.* que se renunció a algo; que fue dejado sin amparo **(p. 292)**

acostumbrado(a) *adj.* habituado; usual **(p. 638)**

reconocer *v.* admitir o aceptar un hecho real **(p. 639)**

adquirió *v.* obtuvo, consiguió, compró; forma del verbo *adquirir* **(p. 349)**

trata *v.* que habla de algo o lo estudia; forma del verbo *tratar* **(p. 1053)**

administrador(a) *s.* persona que dirige o dispone **(p. 21)**

adoptar *v.* tomar resoluciones y hacerlas propias **(p. 303)**

consultivo(a) *adj.* junta establecida para ser consultada y brindar opiniones **(p. 21)**

agresión *s.* ataque violento **(p. 573)**

acumuló *v.* juntó, recolectó o amontonó en grandes cantidades; forma del verbo *acumular* **(p. 93)**

aspiraciones *s.* objetivos pretendidos o deseados **(p. 193)**

anestesista *s.* especialista en aplicar una sustancia que produce la pérdida de la sensibilidad de los pacientes durante una cirugía **(p. 629)**

aplicación *s.* puesta en práctica de algo con un uso determinado **(p. 498)**

designó *v.* que eligió o nombró a alguien para un cargo público o puesto; forma del verbo *designar* **(p. 180)**

arquitecto(a) *s.* persona que proyecta y construye edificios **(p. 271)**

extraviado(a) *adj.* que se desvió del camino o lo perdió **(p. 1034)**

autoridad *s.* que tiene crédito o prestigio en su conocimiento y competencia en una materia **(p. 498)**

B

backdrop (BAK drop) *n.* a curtain or temporary wall that covers the back of a stage (p. 1000)

banished (BAN isht) *v.* sent away; forced to be separate from a place or group (p. 810)

barren (BAIR un) *adj.* having little or no plant life; empty (p. 666)

barrier (BAIR ee ur) *n.* something that prevents passage; an obstacle (p. 862)

beckoned (BECK und) *v.* moved the head or a hand to make a sign to approach or come nearer (p. 272)

befriended (bih FREN dud) *v.* made friends with someone (p. 461)

biceps (BY seps) *n.* a large muscle that runs down the front of the arm from the shoulder to the elbow (p. 425)

bigotry (BIG uh tree) *n.* unfair and unreasonable opinions or treatment of a person or group (p. 740)

blissfully (BLIS fuh lee) *adv.* in an extremely happy way; joyfully (p. 854)

brilliant (BRIL yunt) *adj.* having or showing ability or talent (p. 43)

brunette (broo NET) *n.* a person with black or brown hair (p. 1020)

buffet (BUF it) *v.* to strike with force (p. 275)

bureau (BYUR oh) *n.* a low chest of drawers (p. 529)

telón de fondo *frase nom.* cortina que cierra la escena y forma la decoración (p. 996)

desterró *v.* abandonó un lugar o fue expulsado de la patria; forma del verbo *desterrar* (p. 810)

yermo(a) *adj.* terreno estéril o sin cultivo; despoblado (p. 666)

barrera *s.* valla o impedimento que cierra el paso; obstáculo (p. 862)

hizo una seña *frase verbal* dio indicios; realizó gestos o para dar algo a entender; forma del verbo *hacer* (p. 272)

fraternizó *v.* se hizo amigo de alguien; forma del verbo *fraternizar* (p. 461)

bíceps *s.* músculo de dos orígenes o cabezas que se extiende por el antebrazo desde el hombro hasta el codo (p. 425)

fanatismo *s.* intolerancia (p. 740)

dichosamente *adv.* con gran felicidad; con regocijo (p. 854)

brillante *adj.* admirable o sobresaliente por sus cualidades (p. 43)

morena *s.* mujer de cabello negro o castaño (p. 1020)

golpear *v.* pegar con fuerza (p. 275)

cómoda *s.* mueble con cajones que se usa para guardar ropa (p. 529)

C

calories (KAL uh reez) *n.* units used to measure the energy supplied by food (p. 22)

caravan (KAIR uh van) *n.* a group of people or vehicles traveling together (p. 791)

cavities (KAV ih teez) *n.* hollow spaces in a tooth caused by decay (p. 88)

cease (sees) *v.* to stop (p. 809)

champion (CHAM pyun) *n.* one who fights for or speaks for another person; one who defends a cause; hero (p. 974)

chaos (KAY ahs) *n.* total confusion and disorder (p. 198, 1044)

calorías *s.* unidad de medida que determina el valor energético de los alimentos (p. 22)

caravana *s.* grupo de personas o vehículos que viajan juntos (p. 791)

caries *s.* erosión del esmalte dental causada por bacterias (p. 88)

dejar (de) *v.* cesar, detenerse (p. 809)

campeón(ona) *s.* persona que defiende con esfuerzo una causa o doctrina; héroe (p. 974)

caos *s.* gran confusión y desorden (p. 198, 1044)

chromosomes (KROH muh sohmz) *n.* parts of a cell in a plant or animal that carry the genes controlling features such as the color of hair and eyes **(p. 454)**

cicadas (sih KAY duz) *n.* large insects also called locusts; males make a buzzing sound **(p. 271)**

cinders (SIN durz) *n.* hot ashes **(p. 906)**

civic (SIV ik) *adj.* having to do with a city or the duties of a citizen **(p. 734)**

civility (sih VIL uh tee) *n.* polite behavior **(p. 595)**

clarify (KLAIR uh fy) *v.* to make clear **(p. 970)**

coarse (kors) *adj.* rough; lacking good manners **(p. 541)**

coincidence (koh IN sih dens) *n.* a situation in which two events that seem unrelated accidentally occur at the same time **(p. 341)**

commotion (kuh MOH shun) *n.* noisy rushing about; confusion **(p. 889)**

competing (kum PEET ing) *v.* taking part in a contest **(p. 860)**

composed (kum POHZD) *v.* formed by putting together **(p. 878)**

conceited (kun SEE tid) *adj.* having a high opinion of oneself **(p. 960)**

conclusions (kun KLOO zhuns) *n.* judgments or general statements based on information, experience, and observation **(p. 494)**

condemn (kun DEM) *v.* to express a strong feeling against something **(p. 264)**

confiscated (KON fis kay tid) *v.* took someone's property by authority **(p. 79)**

conflict (KON flikt) *n.* struggle between opposing forces **(p. 523)**

confrontations (kON frun TAY shunz) *n.* unpleasant face-to-face meetings **(p. 154)**

Congress (KONG gris) *n.* the part of the United States government that makes laws **(p. 180)**

consciousness (KON shus ness), *n.* thoughts; awareness; the mind **(p. 650)**

consequences (KON suh kwen suz) *n.* results of an action; outcome **(p. 899)**

consumption (kun SUMP shun) *n.* the act of eating, drinking, or using up **(p. 392)**

contemplate (KON tem playt) *v.* to have in mind as a possibility **(p. 571)**

cromosomas *s.* parte del núcleo de las células de animales y plantas que transmiten información genética tal como el color del cabello y los ojos **(p. 454)**

cigarras *s.* insectos de cabeza y abdomen gruesos con alas transparentes; los machos hacen un zumbido estridente y monótono **(p. 271)**

ceniza *s.* polvo residual de una combustión **(p. 906)**

cívico(a) *adj.* que pertenece a la ciudad o al comportamiento de los ciudadanos **(p. 734)**

civilidad *s.* educación, urbanidad **(p. 595)**

aclarar *v.* poner en claro; explicar **(p. 970)**

tosco(a) *adj.* sin delicadeza; sin educación **(p. 541)**

coincidencia *s.* sucesos que ocurren en forma casual, en el mismo lugar y al mismo tiempo **(p. 341)**

conmoción *s.* tumulto; confusión **(p. 889)**

compitiendo *v.* luchar o rivalizar con otros para obtener un objetivo **(p. 860)**

compuesto(a) *v.* formado con varias cosas juntas **(p. 878)**

engreído(a) *adj.* persona demasiado convencida de su propio valor **(p. 960)**

conclusión *s.* deducción o resolución basada en la información, la experiencia y la observación **(p. 494)**

condenar *v.* reprobar o desaprobar algo **(p. 264)**

decomisó *v.* se apoderó por la fuerza de la propiedad ajena; forma del verbo *decomisar* **(p. 79)**

nudo *s.* enlace o complicación de la acción en una obra literaria **(p. 523)**

encaramientos *s.* colocarse frente a otro en una actitud violenta **(p. 154)**

Congreso *s.* organismo gubernamental de los Estados Unidos que elabora las leyes **(p. 180)**

conciencia *s.* noción del mundo y de uno mismo **(p. 650)**

consecuencias *s.* hechos que resultan de otros; resultado **(p. 899)**

consumo *s.* utilización de comestibles o elementos que se extinguen **(p. 392)**

contemplar *v.* considerar con atención y cuidado **(p. 571)**

contemplation (kon tem PLAY shun) *n.* a state of deep thought (p. 949)

contented (kun TEN tid) *adj.* happy, pleased, or satisfied with one's situation (p. 1044)

convoy (KON voy) *n.* a group of cars, trucks, or other vehicles traveling together (p. 1063)

coping (KOHP ing) *v.* successfully dealing with something difficult (p. 395)

crevice (KREV is) *n.* narrow opening; split or crack (p. 949)

crock (krok) *n.* a large clay or ceramic pot used to hold liquid (p.751)

contemplación *s.* estado de meditación profunda (p. 949)

satisfecho(a) *adj.* contento, complacido, conforme (p. 1044)

convoy *s.* grupo de vehículos o barcos que viajan juntos (p. 1063)

sobrellevando *v.* afrontar un problema o situación, forma del verbo *sobrellevar* (p. 395)

grieta *s.* abertura estrecha; hendidura (p. 949)

vasija *s.* recipiente de barro o cerámica que se usa para contener líquidos (p.751)

D

dazed (dayzd) *adj.* stunned or confused as a result of a blow or a surprise (p. 550)

decent (DEE sunt) *adj.* kind or thoughtful (p. 219)

defiance (dih FY uns) *n.* bold resistance to authority (p. 199)

dejection (dih JEK shun) *n.* sadness; low spirits (p. 853)

delusion (dih LOO zhun), *n.* a false belief (p. 650)

dense (dens) *adj.* thick (p. 1041)

desolate (DES uh lit) *adj.* deserted or uninhabited (p. 660)

develop (dih VEL up) *v.* to get or bring about little by little over a period of time (p. 1053)

devoured (dih VOWrd) *v.* ate up greedily (p. 655)

discipline (DIS uh plin) *v.* to punish (p. 512)

discipline (DIS uh plin) *n.* self-control; the obeying of rules (p. 303)

disgraced (dis GRAYSD) *v.* brought shame or dishonor upon (p. 386)

dismal (DIZ mul) *adj.* gloomy; miserable; cheerless (p. 850)

dismay (dis MAY) *n.* a sudden feeling of disappointment or unpleasant surprise (p. 341)

dispute (dis PYOOT) *n.* a difference of opinion; argument or quarrel (p. 637)

distinguish (dis TING gwish) *v.* to know the difference between, tell apart (p. 260)

distress (dis TRES) *n.* pain or suffering (p. 294)

aturdido(a) *adj.* perturbado o confundido por un golpe, un ruido o una mala noticia (p. 550)

decente *adj.* amable o respetuoso (p. 219)

desafío *s.* oposición o contradicción a la autoridad (p. 199)

abatimiento *s.* desaliento; pérdida del ánimo (p. 853)

engaño *s.* equivocación, falsa impresión (p. 650)

denso(a) *adj.* espeso (p. 1041)

desolado(a) *adj.* despoblado, desierto (p. 660)

desarrollar *v.* acrecentar, aumentar, crecer en lo físico, intelectual o moral (p. 1053)

devoraron *v.* comieron con ansia; forma del verbo *devorar* (p. 655)

sancionar *v.* castigar (p. 512)

disciplina *s.* acatamiento de una persona a las normas que desarrollan autocontrol y orden (p. 303)

avergonzó *v.* causar humillación y deshonra; forma del verbo *avergonzar* (p. 386)

deprimente *adj.* sombrío; taciturno; triste (p. 850)

consternación *s.* alteración del ánimo y pérdida de la tranquilidad (p. 341)

polémica *s.* diferencia de opinión; altercado o discusión (p. 637)

distinguir *v.* ser capaz de diferenciar (p. 260)

aflicción *s.* dolor o sufrimiento (p. 294)

diverted (dih VUR tud) *v.* turned from one course to another (p. 652)

documentation (dok yuh men TAY shun) *n.* something recorded that serves as proof (p. 879)

dominant (DOM ih nunt) *adj.* having the greatest power or force; controlling (p. 852)

drab (drab) *adj.* lacking brightness; dull (p. 714)

drone (drohn) *n.* steady, low, humming sound (p. 351)

drought (drowt) *n.* a long period of very dry weather (p. 664)

desvió *v.* cambió la dirección o el curso; forma del verbo *desviar* (p. 652)

documentación *s.* conjunto de registros que sirven de evidencia de algo (p. 879)

dominante *adj.* que prevalece o es superior a algo; controlador (p. 852)

soso(a) *adj.* sin gracia; apagado (p. 714)

zumbido *s.* ruido sordo y continuado (p. 351)

sequía *s.* período largo de tiempo seco (p. 664)

E

eddies (ED eez) *n.* circling currents of air, water, or snow (p. 1043)

elaborately (ih LAB ur it lee) *adv.* in a fancy way that involves many details or complicated parts (p. 946)

emerald (EM ur uld) *adj.* brightly or richly green (p. 161)

emerged (ih MERJD) *v.* came out (p. 198)

enclosure (en KLOH zhur) *n.* a fenced-in or walled-in place (p. 1065)

encounter (en KOWN ter) *n.* an unexpected or unpleasant meeting (p. 723)

endangered (en DAYN jurd) *adj.* at risk or in danger of dyiing out completely (p. 589)

endure (en DOOR) *v.* to put up with (p. 264)

endured (en DURD) *v.* held up under pain or hardship (p. 690)

envy (EN vee) *n.* jealousy; desire to have something that someone else has (p. 286)

evacuated (ih VAK yoo ay tid) *v.* removed; moved out of area (p. 822)

evaluate (ih VAL yoo ayt) *v.* to find value; to judge or determine worth (p. 840)

exasperated (eg ZAS pur ay tid) *v.* greatly angered or irritated (p. 947)

exotic (eg ZOT ik) *adj.* excitingly different; unusual; foreign (p. 720)

expedition (ek spuh DISH un) *n.* a journey taken for a special purpose, such as exploration (p. 716)

exploits (EK sploytz) *n.* brave acts or deeds (p. 156)

remolinos *s.* movimiento circular rápido del aire, agua o nieve (p. 1043)

detalladamente *adv.* minuciosamente (p. 946)

esmeralda *adj.* de color verde azulado brillante (p. 161)

aparecieron *v.* salieron; pretérito del verbo *aparecer* (p. 198)

cerca *s.* vallado o muro que protege o divide algo (p. 1057)

encuentro *s.* discusión, pelea (p. 723)

en vías de extinción *frase idiomática* en peligro de desaparecer; cuando la existencia de una especie animal o vegetal está comprometida debido a que solo queda un reducido número de miembros (p. 589)

soportar *v.* tolerar o aguantar (p. 264)

soportaron *v.* resistieron al dolor y a las dificultades; forma del verbo *soportar* (p. 690)

envidia *s.* celos; deseo de lo que no se posee o es un bien ajeno (p. 286)

evacuó *v.* desocupar o desalojar; forma del verbo evacuar (p. 822)

evaluar *v.* examinar detalladamente; estimar (p. 840)

(se) exasperó *v.* se irritó o se enfureció; forma del verbo *exasperar(se)* (p. 947)

exótico(a) *adj.* extraño; raro; extranjero (p. 720)

expedición *s.* viaje de exploración (p. 716)

hazañas *s.* acciones valerosas, proezas (p. 156)

expressing (eks PRES ing) *n.* the act of making feelings or opinions known **(p. 416)**

expresar *v.* manifestar sentimientos y opiniones **(p. 416)**

F

familiar (FUH mil yur) *adj.* commonly seen, heard or experienced; well-known **(p. 43)**

familiar *adj.* que resulta conocido; que se tiene por sabido **(p. 43)**

fanfare (FAN fair) *n.* a very noticeable public display **(p. 381)**

fanfarria *s.* música interpretada por un conjunto de instrumentos, gen. en actos públicos **(p. 381)**

fate (fayt) *n.* a power that people believe determines events before they happen **(p. 551)**

destino *s.* fuerza que actúa inevitablemente sobre sucesos y personas **(p. 551)**

feat (feet) *n.* an act that shows skill, strength, or courage **(p. 96)**

proeza *s.* hazaña que muestra gran fuerza y valentía **(p. 96)**

features (FEE churz) *n.* parts or qualities **(p. 787)**

características *s.* cualidades propias de algo **(p. 787)**

fencing (FEN sing) *n.* the sport of fighting with swords **(p. 1003)**

esgrima *s.* deporte en el que se combate con espadas **(p. 1003)**

fiasco (fee AS koh) *n.* something that has failed completely, possibly in a ridiculous way **(p. 1022)**

fiasco *s.* fracaso, decepción, chasco **(p. 1022)**

floundering (FLOUN dur ing) *v.* struggling to move or gain balance **(p. 695)**

(se) resbalaban *v.* desplazarse o deslizarse involuntariamente perdiendo el equilibrio; forma del verbo *resbalar(se)* **(p. 695)**

foliage (FOH lee ij) *n.* plant and tree leaves **(p. 653)**

follaje *s.* ramas y hojas de árboles y plantas **(p. 653)**

formal (FOR mul) *adj.* proper, following rules **(p. 34)**

formal *adj.* conforme a las reglas o requisitos **(p. 34)**

former (FOR mur) *adj.* earlier; coming before in time **(p. 88)**

antiguo(a) *adj.* que fue hace mucho tiempo **(p. 88)**

forsake (for SAYK) *v.* to give up someone or something **(p. 265)**

renunciar *v.* dejar o abandonar algo **(p. 265)**

forsaken (for SAY kun) *adj.* given up or abandoned **(p. 824)**

abandonado(a) *adj.* descuidado o dejado **(p. 824)**

fragments (FRAG munts) *n.* small pieces that are broken off **(p. 81)**

fragmento(s) *s.* trozo separado de un todo **(p. 81)**

frills (frilz) *n.* things that are added on for decoration but are not really necessary **(p. 1010)**

adornos *s.* detalles agregados para embellecer algo pero que no son necesarios **(p. 1010)**

fumbled (FUM buld) *v.* lost one's grasp on something **(p. 862)**

dejó caer *frase verbal* perdió el control de la pelota, esp. en fútbol americano **(p. 862)**

G

generation (jen uh RAY shun) *n.* a group of persons born around the same time **(p. 452)**

generación *s.* conjunto de personas nacidas alrededor de la misma fecha **(p. 452)**

ghastly (GAST lee) *adj.* terrible, horrible **(p. 445)**

espantoso(a) *adj.* terrible, horrible **(p. 445)**

gloomy (GLOO mee) *adj.* dull, dark, and depressing **(p. 226)**

sombrío(a) *adj.* lúgubre, oscuro y deprimente **(p. 226)**

goal (gohl) *n.* something that you aim for **(p. 192)**

grief (greef) *n.* unhappiness or suffering, often about the loss of something **(p. 329)**

grotesque (groh TESK) *adj.* very strange and unexpected **(p. 653)**

grudging (GRUJ ing) *adj.* resentfully or without wanting to **(p. 833)**

grudgingly (GRUJ ing lee) *adv.* unhappily, unwillingly **(p. 293)**

meta *s.* fin u objetivo personal que se desea alcanzar **(p. 192)**

dolor *s.* sentimiento de gran pena o sufrimiento **(p. 329)**

grotesco(a) *adj.* ridículo, de mal gusto **(p. 653)**

hecho(a) de mala gana *frase adj.* realizado a regañadientes; sin voluntad **(p. 833)**

de mala gana *frase adv.* a regañadientes, sin voluntad **(p. 293)**

H

heredity (huh RED uh tee) *n.* the passing on of characteristics from an animal or plant to its off-spring **(p. 454)**

hesitantly (HEZ uh tunt lee) *adv.* in a way that shows uncertainty or fear **(p. 353)**

hick (hik) *adj.* small, rural, unexciting **(p. 985)**

hissed (hisd) *v.* made a sound like air escaping from a balloon **(p. 1058)**

hoax (hohks) *n.* an act meant to fool or trick **(p. 727)**

horsewhip (HORS wip) *n.* a whip or stick used to make a horse go faster **(p. 749)**

hospitality (hos pih TAL uh tee) *n.* friendly treatment of guests **(p. 833)**

hostile (HOS tul) *adj.* unfriendly **(p. 498)**

herencia *s.* transmisión de los caracteres genéticos de los seres vivos a su descendencia **(p. 454)**

con titubeos frase *adv.* que muestra indecisión o perplejidad **(p. 353)**

campesino(a) *adj. peyor.* pequeño, rural, apegado a costumbres lugareñas **(p. 985)**

silbó *v.* hacer sonidos dejando escapar el aire; pretérito del verbo *silbar*; para sonidos de animales: *bufar* o *resoplar* **(p. 1058)**

broma *s.* chiste o truco **(p. 727)**

fusta *s.* látigo o vara usada para estimular o castigar a los caballos **(p. 749)**

hospitalidad *s.* recibimiento acogedor que se da a invitados **(p. 833)**

hostil *adj.* que muestra enemistad **(p. 498)**

I

immense (ih MENS) *adj.* of great size; huge **(p. 551)**

immigrant (IM ih grunt) *n.* a person who comes to live in a country in which he or she was not born **(p. 498)**

immune (ih MYOON) *adj.* not influenced or affected by **(p. 591)**

inadequate (ih AD ih kwit) *adj.* not good enough **(p. 432)**

incident (IN suh dunt) *n.* an event or situation **(p. 97)**

indifference (in DIF fur uns) *n.* a lack of feeling or concern **(p. 200)**

indignities (in DIG nuh teez) *n.* insulting treatment **(p. 264)**

inmenso(a) *adj.* muy grande; enorme **(p. 551)**

inmigrante *s.* persona que llega a un lugar, distinto del que nació, para establecerse en él **(p. 498)**

inmune *adj.* que está exento de peligros o de enfermedades **(p. 591)**

impropio(a) *adj.* sin las cualidades convenientes **(p. 432)**

incidente *s.* suceso o episodio **(p. 97)**

indiferencia *s.* falta de sentimientos o de interés **(p. 200)**

indignidades *s.* humillaciones, falta de mérito **(p. 264)**

individuality (in duh vij oo AL uh tee) *n.* the combined qualities or characteristics that make one person or thing different from another (**p. 303**)

individualidad *s.* propiedad de alguien o algo por lo que se lo distingue de lo demás (**p. 303**)

industrious (in DUS tree us) *adj.* hardworking (**p. 690**)

laborioso(a) *adj.* muy trabajador (**p. 690**)

infer (in FUR) *v.* to use reason and experience to figure out what an author does not say directly (**p. 298**)

inferir *v.* deducir conclusiones de un texto usando la experiencia o el razonamiento (**p. 298**)

instinctively (in STINK tiv lee) *adv.* in a way that comes naturally, without thinking (**p. 351**)

instintivamente *adv.* que proviene de un impulso natural (**p. 351**)

integrate (IN tuh grayt) *v.* to bring together or make something part of a whole (**p. 1052**)

integrar *v.* incorporar o unir a un todo (**p. 1052**)

intellectual (in tuh LEK choo ul) *adj.* requiring thought and understanding (**p. 890**)

intelectual *adj.* relacionado con la facultad de razonar y comprender (**p. 890**)

interpret (in TUR prit) *v.* to explain the meaning of; make understandable (**p. 420**)

interpretar *v.* explicar el significado de algo; hacer comprensible (**p. 420**)

interrogated (in TAIR uh gay tid) *v.* asked questions harshly or in great detail (**p. 79**)

interrogó *v.* hacerle preguntas a alguien para aclarar un asunto; forma del verbo *interrogar* (**p. 79**)

iridescent (ir ih DES unt) *adj.* showing shimmering colors that look like a rainbow (**p. 654**)

iridiscente *adj.* que muestra o destella los colores del arco iris (**p. 654**)

isolated (EYE suh lay tid) *v.* to be set or kept away from others (**p. 1053**)

aislado(a) *v.* apartado o separado del trato con los demás (**p. 1053**)

K

kin (kin) *n.* family or relatives (**p. 329**)

familia *s.* congéneres o parientes (**p. 329**)

L

languid (LANG gwid) *adj.* slow-moving; without energy (**p. 461**)

lánguido(a) *adj.* débil; falto de ánimo; sin energía (**p. 461**)

laughingstock (LAF ing STOK) *n.* a person or thing that is made fun of (**p. 89**)

hazmerreír *s.* personas que por su aspecto o comportamiento sirven de diversión a los demás (**p. 89**)

lavishly (LAV ish lee) *adv.* in a way that provides much more than is needed (**p. 387, 946**)

espléndidamente *adv.* hecho con generosidad y desprendimiento (**p. 387, 946**)

lisp (lisp) *n.* a speech problem affecting the *s* and *z* sounds (**p. 541**)

ceceo *s.* problema de pronunciación que afecta a los sonidos *s* y *z* (**p. 541**)

lithe (lyth) *adj.* flexible and moving easily (**p. 541**)

ágil *adj.* que se mueve con agilidad y soltura (**p. 541**)

looming (LOO ming) *adj.* appearing in the distance (**p. 826**)

(se) levantaba *v.* que sobresale en altura, que se yergue y separa; forma de verbo *levantar(se)* (**p. 826**)

lunged (lunjd) *v.* made a sudden forward movement; charged (**p. 679**)

arremetió *v.* atacó con ímpetu; embistió; forma del verbo *arremeter* (**p. 679**)

M

makeshift (MAKE shift) *adj.* suitable as a temporary substitute (p. 628)

mane (mayn) *n.* the long, thick hair on an animal's neck or head (p. 161)

manufacturing (man yuh FAK chur ing) *v.* making out of raw materials (p. 415)

mauve (mohv) *adj.* a light purple or violet (p. 424)

meekly (MEEK lee) *adv.* in a timid and mild manner; gently (p. 679)

menacingly (MEN uh seen lee) *adv.* in a threatening manner (p. 1007)

merely (MEER lee) *adv.* just, only (p. 639)

migrant (MY grunt) *adj.* moving from place-to-place (p. 173)

milepost (MYL pohst) *n.* one of a number of signs placed one mile apart (p. 748)

minded (MYN did) *v.* took charge of (p. 412)

mirth (murth) *n.* joy, happiness (p. 447)

mocking (MOK ing) *v.* making fun of someone by imitating them in a ridiculous manner (p. 1007)

moist (moyst) *adj.* just wet enough to notice (p. 415)

monitor (MON ih tur) *v.* to check or watch (p. 36)

mope (mohp) *v.* to be gloomy or in low spirits (p. 134)

morale (muh RAL) *n.* the state of a person's mind and spirit (p. 181)

muster (MUS tur) *v.* to find and gather together; collect (p. 342)

muttered (MUT urd) *v.* spoke quietly to complain or express anger (p. 412)

N

nourished (NUR ishd) *v.* provided with food or other substances necessary for life (p. 72)

nutrition (noo TRI shun) *n.* the process by which living things use food (p. 72, 287)

O

obesity (oh BEE sih tee) *n.* condition of being extremely overweight (p. 20)

provisorio(a) *adj.* temporal, no permanente (p. 628)

crin *s.* conjunto de cerdas o pelos gruesos que crece en el cuello de algunos animales, por ej., el caballo (p. 161)

fabricar *v.* producir o elaborar objetos mecánicamente; forma del verbo *fabricar* (p. 415)

malva *adj.* de color violeta pálido (p. 424)

dócilmente *adv.* de modo apacible y obediente; sumisamente (p. 679)

amenazante *adv.* de modo intimidante o peligrosamente (p. 1007)

simplemente *adv.* solamente, sólo (p. 639)

itinerante *adj.* que va de un lugar a otro (p. 173)

mojón *s.* poste usado para señalar la distancia y la posición en un camino (p. 748)

cuidé *v.* se ocupó de algo; pretérito del verbo *cuidar* (p. 412)

regocijo *s.* alborozo, felicidad (p. 447)

burlarse *v.* hacer bromas o ridiculizar a alguien (p. 1007)

húmedo(a) *adj.* ligeramente mojado (p. 415)

controlar *v.* vigilar o verificar (p. 36)

andar deprimido(a) *frase verbal* que tiene el ánimo decaído o con la moral baja (p. 134)

moral *s.* estado de ánimo o de confianza en uno mismo (p. 181)

juntar *v.* reunir o agrupar; acumular (p. 342)

refunfuñó *v.* habló expresando enojo o enfado; pretérito del verbo *refunfuñar* (p. 412)

nutrido(a) *v.* que recibe las sustancias necesarias para crecer y desarrollarse (p. 72)

nutrición *s.* función por la cual los seres vivos se alimentan (p. 72, 287)

obesidad *s.* gordura en exceso (p. 20)

obituaries (oh BIH chuh wair eez) *n.* notices of deaths, usually in newspapers **(p. 988)**

observant (ub ZER vunt) *adj.* good at noticing details **(p. 216)**

obsessed (ub SEST) *adj.* concentrating completely **(p. 850)**

ominous (OM ih nus) *adj.* threatening **(p. 738)**

outrages (OUT ray jiz) *n.* violent or cruel acts **(p. 498)**

obituario *s.* sección de noticias necrológicas de un periódico o revista **(p. 988)**

observador(a) *adj.* que advierte y nota con mucho **(p. 216)**

obsesivo(a) *adj.* que tiene fijación con ciertas ideas que no puede quitar de su mente **(p. 850)**

ominoso(a) *adj.* alarmante, de mal agüero **(p. 738)**

atrocidades *s.* crueldades muy grandes **(p. 498)**

P

paranoid (PAIR uh noyd) *adj.* feeling like everyone is against you **(p. 211)**

parody (PAIR uh dee) *n.* a piece of writing or musical work that imitates another by making fun of it **(p. 571)**

pectorals (pek TOR ulz) *n.* muscles connecting the chest walls to the bones of the upper arm and shoulder **(p. 425)**

peers (peerz) *v.* looks closely at something **(p. 424)**

pelted (PEL tid) *v.* struck over and over again **(p. 94)**

penetrated (PEN uh tray tid) *v.* passed into or through **(p. 1041)**

perilously (PAIR uh lus lee) *adv.* dangerously, at risk of injury **(p. 694)**

perpetual (pur PEH choo ul) *adj.* continuing forever **(p. 380)**

phantom (FAN tum) *adj.* looking or seeming real although unreal **(p. 899)**

plagued (playgd) *v.* was greatly troubled or distressed **(p. 675)**

policies (POL uh seez) *n.* plans or rules **(p. 557)**

pondered (PON durd) *v.* thought about **(p. 811)**

potential (puh TEN shuhl) *adj.* capable of being or becoming something possible **(p. 152, 572)**

practical (PRAK tih kul) *adj.* having or showing good sense about everyday activities **(p. 787)**

predominantly (prih DOM ih nunt lee) *adv.* mainly; mostly **(p. 734)**

prejudice (PREJ uh dis) *n.* an opinion that is formed unfairly **(p. 154)**

paranoico(a) *adj.* obsesionado con una idea fija, por ej., que todos están en su contra **(p. 211)**

parodia *s.* imitación burlesca y exagerada de algo **(p. 571)**

pectorales *s.* músculos del pecho conectados a los huesos de los hombros y los antebrazos **(p. 425)**

(se) escruta *v.* explora y examina cuidadosa y atentamente; forma del verbo *escrutar(se)* **(p. 424)**

(se) acribillaban *v.* causar muchas heridas o picaduras repetidamente; forma del verbo *acribillar(se)* **(p. 94)**

penetró *v.* se introdujo o se infiltró; forma del verbo *penetrar* **(p. 1041)**

peligrosamente *adv.* que puede causar un daño o riesgo **(p. 693)**

perpetuo(a) *adj.* que dura para siempre **(p. 380)**

fantasma *adj.* sentimiento o visión de algo imaginario o irreal **(p. 899)**

atormentado *v.* que causa disgusto o aflicción; forma del verbo *atormentar* **(p. 675)**

políticas *s.* métodos y orientaciones designadas para un fin **(p. 557)**

caviló *v.* pensó profundamente; forma del verbo *cavilar* **(p. 811)**

potencial *adj.* que puede ser **(p. 152, 572)**

práctico(a) *adj.* que tiene buen juicio para captar la realidad y actúa de acuerdo a ella **(p. 787)**

predominantemente *adv.* que prevalece en cantidad numérica **(p. 734)**

prejuicio *s.* opinión o juicio desfavorable formado de antemano **(p. 154)**

pretense (PREE tens) *n.* a false show or appearance; pretending **(p. 381)**

prior (PRY ur) *adj.* earlier; coming before **(p. 126)**

privileged (PRIH vih lijd) *adj.* having or enjoying one or more advantages **(p. 878)**

process (PRAH ses) *n.* a series of steps to follow in making or doing something **(p. 51)**

proclaimed (pruh KLAYMD) *v.* declared publicly, announced **(p. 973)**

professional (pruh FESH uh nul) *adj.* relating to a life-long occupation or career **(p. 1053)**

profile (PROH fyl) *n.* a side view **(p. 131)**

promenade (PROM uh nayd) *v.* to walk or stroll in a slow, relaxed manner **(p. 464)**

prominent (PROM uh nunt) *adj.* well-known **(p. 171)**

promote (pruh MOT) *v.* to help grow or prosper **(p. 595)**

pronunciation (pro nun see AY shun) *n.* how a word is said **(p. 000)**

prospectors (PRAH spek turs) *n.* people who explore an area for mineral or oil deposits **(p. 690)**

pummel (PUM ul) *v.* to hit or beat someone **(p. 1006)**

apariencia *s.* falso, que parece algo que no es **(p. 381)**

previo(a) *adj.* anterior; que viene primero **(p. 126)**

privilegiado(a) *adj.* que tiene ventajas o beneficios especiales **(p. 878)**

proceso *s.* conjunto de pasos sucesivos en la producción de un fenómeno u operación **(p. 51)**

proclamó *v.* anunciar o declarar públicamente y en voz alta, forma del verbo *proclamar* **(p. 973)**

profesional *adj.* personas que ejercen un trabajo con relevante capacidad y aplicación **(p. 1053)**

perfil *s.* contorno de la vista lateral de algo **(p. 131)**

pasear(se) *v.* andar o desplazarse de un lugar a otro por ejercicio o distracción **(p. 464)**

prominente *adj.* ilustre, famoso, destacado **(p. 171)**

promocionar *v.* dar a conocer algo para mejorarlo en reputación y apreciación **(p. 595)**

pronunciación *s.* forma en que se emite y articula un sonido para hablar **(p. 000)**

explorador(a) *s.* persona que investiga una cosa o lugar para hacer descubrimientos **(p. 690)**

golpear con los puños frase *v.* pegar con los puños **(p. 1006)**

Q

quest (kwest) *n.* a search for a particular object or goal **(p. 679)**

quivers (KWIV urz) *v.* shakes or moves with a slight trembling motion **(p. 161)**

búsqueda *s.* indagación que se hace para conseguir algo **(p. 679)**

vibrar *v.* temblar o estremecerse con movimientos pequeños y rápidos **(p. 161)**

R

rambling (RAM bling) *v.* talking in a disorganized manner **(p. 1005)**

ravaged (RAV ijd) *v.* destroyed violently; ruined **(p. 675)**

rays (rayz) *n.* beams of light or energy **(p. 461)**

recited (rih SY tid) *v.* repeated from memory **(p. 525)**

referee (ref uh REE) *n.* a sports official who makes sure rules are followed in a game **(p. 862)**

relish (REL ish) *v.* to enjoy **(p. 204)**

divagando *v.* hablando o escribiendo separándose del tema principal; forma del verbo *divagar* **(p. 1005)**

devastado(a) *v.* destruido, arrasado; forma del verbo *devastar* **(p. 675)**

rayos *s.* haces de luz o energía **(p. 461)**

recitado(a) *v.* repetido de memoria y en voz alta; forma del verbo *recitar* **(p. 525)**

árbitro(a) *s.* persona que hace que se cumpla el reglamento en competencias deportivas **(p. 862)**

saborear *v.* disfrutar el sabor de algo que se come o se bebe **(p. 204)**

remnants (REM nunts) *n.* what is left over; small remaining parts **(p. 897)**

remorse (rih MORS), *n.* feeling of guilt and regret **(p. 651)**

reputation (rep yuh TAY shun) *n.* what other people think about someone **(p. 230, 748)**

resolve (rih ZOLV) *v.* to make a firm decision **(p. 738)**

resourceful (rih SORS ful) *adj.* able to deal with new or difficult situations **(p. 44)**

retreat (rih TREET) *v.* to move backward, away from a situation **(p. 225)**

rigid (RIJ id) *adj.* stiff **(p. 525)**

ringleaders (RING leed urz) *n.* individuals who lead groups of people, expecially those who cause trouble **(p. 594)**

rivaling (RY vul ing) *v.* being equal to or matching **(p. 875)**

routine (roo TEEN) *n.* a regular way of doing something **(p. 1052)**

S

sanctuary (SANK choo wair ee) *n.* a safe and protective place **(p. 1060)**

sarcastic (sar KAS tik) *adj.* describes sharp or bitter words that are meant to hurt or make fun of someone **(p. 81)**

savoring (SAY vur ing) *v.* taking great delight in **(p. 352)**

scholar (SKOL ur) *n.* a person of great learning **(p. 381)**

scourge (skurj) *n.* cause of widespread hardship or suffering **(p. 946)**

scurried (SKUR eed) *v.* ran quickly **(p. 752)**

sedately (sih DAYT lee) *adv.* in a quiet, calm manner **(p. 837)**

self-discipline (self DIS uh plin) *n.* control over your behavior in order to improve yourself **(p. 170)**

seminary (SEM ih nair ee) *n.* a school for advanced education **(p. 180)**

sequence (SEE kwens) *n.* the order of ideas or events; the arrangement of things in time, space, or importance **(p. 544)**

remanente *s.* aquello que queda de algo **(p. 897)**

remordimiento *s.* inquietud o culpa que queda después de una mala acción **(p. 651)**

reputación *s.* fama o prestigio ante las personas **(p. 230, 748)**

resolver *v.* tomar una determinación decisiva **(p. 738)**

con recursos *frase prep.* que tiene los medios para conseguir lo deseado en caso de necesidad **(p. 44)**

retirar(se) *v.* apartarse de algo, irse **(p. 225)**

rígido(a) *adj.* tieso; que no se puede doblar **(p. 525)**

cabecilla *s.* jefe de un grupo de rebeldes **(p. 594)**

rivalizaba *v.* que estaba en competencia con otro **(p. 875)**

rutina *s.* costumbre de hacer algo repetidamente de la misma manera **(p. 1052)**

santuario *s.* lugar que se considera valioso por alguna razón **(p. 1060)**

sarcástico(a) *adj.* que expresa burlas o ironías crueles para ofender o humillar a alguien **(p. 81)**

saborear *v.* percibir con deleite el sabor de lo que se come o bebe **(p. 352)**

erudito(a) *s.* persona con conocimientos profundos adquiridos mediante el estudio **(p. 381)**

azote *s.* instrumento de castigo **(p. 946)**

se escabulló *v.* escapó a toda prisa; forma del verbo *escabullir(se)* **(p. 752)**

tranquilamente *adv.* de manera calmada **(p. 837)**

autodisciplina *s.* capacidad de control sobre uno mismo en la conducta **(p. 170)**

instituto educativo *frase nom.* centro de enseñanza de educación superior **(p. 180)**

secuencia *s.* sucesión de elementos relacionados entre sí **(p. 544)**

sharecropper (SHAIR krop ur) *n.* a farmer who works land owned by someone else and shares the crop or the money from its sale with the landowner **(p. 347)**

sheared (sheerd) *v.* cut off sharply **(p. 329)**

shrugged (shrugd) *v.* raised the shoulders to show doubt, lack of interest, or uncertainty **(p. 412)**

singe (sinj) *v.* to burn slightly **(p. 900)**

skimpy (SKIM pee) *adj.* lacking in quantity; barely or not quite enough **(p. 832)**

slashed (slasht) *v.* hit sharply enough to cause a cut **(p. 749)**

slithered (SLITH urd) *v.* moved along with a sliding or gliding motion, as a snake **(p. 549)**

slums (slumz) *n.* parts of cities where poor people live in crowded, run-down buildings **(p. 173)**

solemnly (SOL um lee) *adv.* seriously; without joy or humor **(p. 946)**

sordid (SOR did) *adj.* mean; rude of human nature **(p. 571)**

spar (spar) *v.* to move around as if fighting without landing a blow **(p. 960)**

spectacle (SPEK tik ul) *n.* something that attracts too much of the wrong kind of attention **(p. 388)**

splurge (splurj) *v.* to spend more money than usual **(p. 847)**

spout (spowt) *v.* to speak rapidly; to say something in a loud, boastful manner **(p. 886)**

spunk (spunk) *n.* courage, spirit, and determination **(p. 663)**

stammer (STAM mur) *v.* to speak with difficulty; to repeat the same sound several times when trying to say a word. **(p. 886)**

stifled (STY fuld) *v.* choked; smothered **(p. 906)**

stragglers (STRAG lurz) *n.* people who lag behind the main group **(p. 551)**

stranded (STRAND id) *adj.* left helpless in a difficult place **(p. 329, 461)**

stress (stres) *n.* a harmful feeling of fear, worry, or strain **(p. 591)**

subdued (sub DOOD) *adj.* quiet, weak, under control **(p. 1064)**

aparcero *s.* persona que trabaja unas tierras bajo contrato a cambio de dar al propietario de las tierras una parte de los beneficios que de ellas obtenga **(p. 347)**

(se) recortaba *v.* perfilar, forma del verbo *recortar* **(p. 329)**

encogió los hombros *frase v.* elevar los hombros de manera simultánea para mostrar falta de interés o conocimiento; expresión *encogerse de hombros* **(p. 412)**

chamuscar *v.* quemar la parte exterior o superficialmente **(p. 900)**

escaso(a) *adj.* limitado, corto, insuficiente **(p. 832)**

acuchilló *v.* hirió o cortó con un arma afilada; forma del verbo *acuchillar* **(p. 749)**

reptaron *v.* se arrastraron o deslizaron como una serpiente, forma del verbo *reptar* **(p. 549)**

barrios bajos *frase nom.* zona poblada por las clases sociales más pobres **(p. 173)**

solemnemente *adv.* con mucha seriedad o gravedad **(p. 946)**

sórdido(a) *adj.* sucio, escandaloso, indecente **(p. 571)**

entrenar *v.* simular una pelea sin llegar a golpear **(p. 960)**

espectáculo *s.* acción que causa extrañeza o escándalo **(p. 388)**

derrochar *v.* gastar demasiado sin pensar **(p. 847)**

hablar a borbotones *frase v.* expresar una idea aceleradamente, queriendo decirlo todo de una sola vez **(p. 886)**

arrojo *s.* osadía, coraje, atrevimiento **(p. 663)**

tartamudear *v.* hablar entrecortadamente y con repetición **(p. 886)**

sofocar *v.* ahogar; impedir la respiración **(p. 906)**

rezagados(as) *s.* personas que se quedan atrás separándose del resto del grupo **(p. 551)**

varado(a) *adj.* quedarse detenido imprevistamente en un lugar **(p. 329, 461)**

estrés *s.* tensión nerviosa provocada por situaciones agobiantes **(p. 591)**

subyugado *adj.* dominado, bajo el control de algo o alguien **(p. 1064)**

subjected (sub JEKT id) *v.* caused to experience (p. 511)

sullenly (SUL un lee) *adj.* gloomily and silently (p. 445)

summary (SUM uh ree) *n.* a brief statement of the main points of a piece of writing (p. 566)

surf (surf) *n.* breaking waves and foam near the shore of an ocean, lake, or river (p. 1060)

surveyed (sur VAYD *or* SUR vayd) *adj.* polled; questioned (p. 512)

swaggers (SWAG urz) *v.* walks in a bold or proud way (p. 550)

synthesize (SIN thuh syz) *v.* to bring together to create something new (p. 782)

sometido(a) *v.* dominio impuesto sobre alguien por la fuerza, forma del verbo *someter* (p. 511)

sombríamente *adj.* triste, melancólico (p. 445)

resumen *s.* reducción de un escrito a sus puntos básicos (p. 566)

oleaje *s.* sucesión de olas en el mar, lago o río (p. 1060)

encuestaron *v.* preguntaron a un número de personas sobre un tema determinado para conocer el estado de opinión general; forma del verbo *encuestar* (p. 512)

(se) pavonea *v.* hacer ostentación de algo, presumir con exageración; forma del verbo *pavonear(se)* (p. 550)

sintetizar *v.* componer algo a través de la suma de sus partes (p. 782)

T

taunt (tawnt) *v.* to try to anger someone by teasing him or her (p. 222)

tedious (TEE dee us) *adj.* boring; tiresome (p. 711)

tended (TEN did) *v.* cared for; kept in working order (p. 330)

text (tekst) *n.* the printed or written words of a page, book, or another form of communication (p. 8)

timidly (TIM ud lee) *adv.* fearfully (p. 292)

toiled (toyld) *v.* worked hard (p. 752)

tortoise (TOR tus) *n.* a large turtle that lives on land (p. 1060)

traumatized (TROM uh tyzd) *adj.* upset or injured as a result of a frightening event (p. 1064)

treacherous (TRECH ur us) *adj.* dangerous and unpredictable (p. 95)

tresses (TRES uz) *n.* long hair (p. 1016)

tribute (TRIB yoot) *n.* something done to show respect (p. 1000)

triceps (TRY seps) *n.* a large muscle at the back of the upper arm (p. 425)

tsunami (tsoo NAH mee) *n.* a huge ocean wave that is caused by an underwater earthquake, volcano, or landslide (p. 1060)

fastidiar *v.* molestar a alguien provocando su enfado o disgusto (p. 222)

tedioso(a) *adj.* aburrido, molesto (p. 711)

atendía *v.* se ocupaba o cuidaba de algo o alguien, forma del verbo *atender* (p. 330)

texto *s.* grupo de palabras que forman un documento escrito (p. 8)

tímidamente *adv.* con temor (p. 292)

(se) afanó *v.* trabajó duro, forma del verbo *afanar(se)* (p. 752)

tortuga *s.* reptil del orden de los Quelonios, los hay de tipo terrestre y de tipo marino; tienen el cuerpo cubierto por un caparazón del que salen las extremidades (p. 1060)

traumatizado(a) *adj.* que ha sufrido una impresión fuerte, negativa y duradera (p. 1064)

traicionero(a) *adj.* que es astuto e imprevisible (p. 95)

mechones *s.* porciones de pelo (p. 1016)

tributo *s.* manifestación de admiración y respeto; reconocimiento (p. 1000)

tríceps *s.* músculo de tres porciones que se extiende al antebrazo (p. 425)

tsunami *s.* ola de gran tamaño causada por un terremoto o una erupción volcánica en el fondo del mar (p. 1060)

tyrant (TY runt) *n.* a cruel, unjust ruler (p. 676)

tirano(a) *s.* gobernante cruel que abusa de su poder y que es injusto (p. 676)

U

ultimate (UL tih mut) *adj.* greatest; most important (p. 22)

principal *adj.* fundamental; más importante (p. 22)

unique (yoo NEEK) *adj.* having no like or equal (p. 287)

único(a) *adj.* solo, sin otro de su misma especie (p. 287)

unmindful (un MYND ful) *adj.* not aware (p. 204)

ignorante *adj.* que desconoce un asunto; carente de información (p. 204)

uproar (UP ror) *n.* noisy excitement and confusion (p. 556)

alboroto *s.* desorden, tumulto (p. 556)

ushers (USH urz) *n.* people who help others find their seats in a theater or stadium (p. 15)

acomodadores(as) *s.* persona que indica a los asistentes de un teatro o estadio los asientos que ocuparán (p. 15)

utter (UT ur) *v.* to speak or say aloud (p. 807)

pronunciar *v.* emitir o articular sonidos al hablar; decir en voz alta (p. 807)

V

vapor (VAY pur) *n.* small particles of mist, steam, or smoke that can be seen (p. 899)

vapor *s.* gas que se forma cuando un líquido es transformado por la acción del calor (p. 899)

velocity (vuh LOS uh tee) *n.* speed; swiftness (p. 902)

velocidad *s.* rapidez de movimiento (p. 902)

vendors (VEN durz) *n.* people who sell products or services (p. 14)

vendedores(as) *s.* personas que venden productos o servicios (p. 14)

verbal (VUR bul) *adj.* expressed in spoken words (p. 558)

verbal *adj.* que se sirve de la palabra hablada (p. 558)

vicious (VISH us) *adj.* mean and cruel (p. 216)

fiero(a) *adj.* cruel y de trato difícil (p. 216)

victory (VIK tur ee) *n.* the win in a contest or battle (p. 193)

victoria *s.* triunfo; éxito en un enfrentamiento (p. 193)

vile (vyl) *adj.* very bad; unpleasant; foul (p. 344)

repugnante *adj.* asqueroso; aversivo; horrible (p. 344)

vinyl (VY nul) *adj.* made of vinyl, which is a tough, shiny plastic (p. 130)

vinilo *adj.* resina dura plastificable (p. 130)

visualize (VIZH wul ize) *v.* to form a mental image or picture of (p. 376)

visualizar *v.* formar una imagen mental de algo (p. 376)

W

warily (WAIR uh lee) *adv.* cautiously (p. 960)

cautelosamente *adv.* con cuidado y recelo (p. 960)

well (WEL) *n.* a hole dug in the ground to get water (p. 749)

pozo *s.* hoyo profundo en la tierra que, por lo general, se hace para sacar agua (p. 749)

well-being (wel BEE ing) *n.* good physical and mental condition (p. 286)

bienestar *s.* en buen estado físico y mental (p. 286)

whimper (WIM pur) *n.* a soft cry (p. 417)

widower (WID oh ur) *n.* a man whose wife has died (p. 1021)

withdrawn (with DRAWN) *adj.* shy, reserved, or unsociable (p. 344)

wittiness (WIT tee nes) *n.* ability to be smart and funny (p. 550)

woe (woh) *n.* great sadness or suffering (p. 445)

writhing (RY thing) *adj.* twitching, twisting (p. 446)

Y

yearned (yurnd) *v.* had a strong desire (p. 636)

yearning (YUR ning) *n.* wanting something badly (p. 201)

quejido *s.* llanto suave y corto; voz lastimosa de dolor o pesar (p. 417)

viudo *s.* hombre cuya esposa ha muerto (p. 1021)

retraído(a) *adj.* tímido, reservado, apartado (p. 344)

agudeza *s.* perspicacia o viveza de ingenio; facultad *mental para crear con rapidez* (p. 550)

infortunio *s.* desdicha, fortuna adversa (p. 445)

retorcido(a) *adj.* doblado, contorsionado (p. 446)

anhelaba *v.* tenía un deseo vehemente por conseguir algo, forma del verbo *anhelar* (p. 636)

anhelo *s.* deseo intenso (p. 201)

INDEX OF SKILLS

Grammar and Language

Research and Study Skills

INDEX OF AUTHORS AND TITLES

INDEX OF ART AND ARTISTS

INDEX OF ART AND ARTISTS

ACKNOWLEDGMENTS

Unit 1

"Ballpark Foods" by Consumer Reports 4 Kids. From zillions.org.

"How He Did It: Health Advice, Kid-to Kid" by Amy Bertrand. *St. Louis Post-Dispatch*, May 2, 2005. Reprinted with permission of the St. Louis Post-Dispatch, copyright © 2005.

"Messaging Mania" by Kathryn R. Hoffman. Updated 2005, from *TIME for Kids*, May 2, 2003.

"Make Your Own Kite." From sears.com.

"To Young Readers" by Gwendolyn Brooks. Reprinted by consent of Brooks Permissions.

"Why Books Are Dangerous" by Neil Gaiman, copyright © 2005, from *Guys Write for Guys Who Read*, ed. by Jon Scieszka. Published by Viking, a division of Penguin Young Readers Group.

"The South Paw" by Judith Viorst. Copyright © 1974 by Judith Viorst. From *Free to Be . . . You and Me.* This usage granted by permission. All rights reserved.

"Concha" by Mary Helen Ponce. Reprinted by permission of the author.

"The Scribe" from *Guests in the Promised Land* by Kristin Hunter. Copyright © 1968 by Kristin E. Lattany. Reprinted by permission of Dystel & Goderich Literary Management.

Unit 2

"Madam C. J. Walker" from *One More River to Cross: The Story of Twelve Black Americans* by Jim Haskins. Copyright © 1992 by James Haskins.

"The Jacket" by Gary Soto appears in *The Effects of Knut Hamsun on a Fresno Boy: Recollections and Short Essays* by Gary Soto. Copyright © 1983, 2000 by Gary Soto. Reprinted by permission of Book Stop Literary Agency and Persea Books, Inc. (New York).

"The World Is Not a Pleasant Place to Be" from *My House* by Nikki Giovanni. Copyright © 1972 by Nikki Giovanni. Reprinted by permission of HarperCollins Publishers.

"Satchel Paige" from *Champions: Stories of Ten Remarkable Athletes* by Bill Littlefield. Copyright © 1993 by Bill Littlefield (text); copyright © 1993 by Bernie Fuchs (illustrations). By permission of Little, Brown and Co., Inc. and Mews Books.

"Song for a Surf-Rider" by Sara Van Alstyne. Copyright © 1966 by Scholastic, Inc.

"Eleanor Roosevelt" reprinted with the permission of Atheneum Books for Young Readers, an imprint of Simon & Schuster Children's Publishing Division from *Great Lives: Human Rights* by William Jay Jacobs. Copyright © 1990 William Jay Jacobs.

"Primary Lessons" is reprinted with permission from the publisher of *Silent Dancing* by Judith Ortiz Cofer (Houston: Arte Publico Press–University of Houston, copyright © 1990).

From "Pigman & Me" by Paul Zindel. Copyright © 1990 by Paul Zindel. First appeared in *The Pigman & Me*, published by HarperCollins. Reprinted by permission of Curtis Brown, Ltd.

"The Goodness of Matt Kaizer" copyright © 1994 by Avi. From his book *What Do Fish Have To Do With Anything?* (Candlewick Press). Reprinted by permission.

"Ta-Na-E-Ka," by Mary Whitebird. Copyright © 1973 by Scholastic, Inc.

Unit 3

"Perserving a Great American Symbol," by Richard Durbin.

"Looking for America" by Elizabeth Partridge, copyright © 2003, from *Open Your Eyes*, ed. by Jill Davis. Reprinted by permission of Elizabeth Partridge. All rights are reserved by the author.

"Stray" reprinted with permission of Atheneum Books for Young Readers, an imprint of Simon & Schuster Children's Publishing Division from *Every Living Thing* by Cynthia Rylant. Copyright © 1985 Cynthia Rylant.

"Eleven" from *Woman Hollering Creek.* Copyright © 1991 by Sandra Cisneros. Published by Vintage Books, a division of Random House, Inc., and originally in hardcover by Random House, Inc. Reprinted by permission of Sandra Bergholz Literary Services, New York. All rights reserved.

From *50 Simple Things Kids Can Do To Save the Earth* © 1990 EarthWorks press. Reprinted with permission of Andrews McMeel Publishing. All rights reserved.

"Greyling," copyright © 1968 by Jane Yolen. First appeared in *Greyling*, published by Penguin Putnam, Inc. Reprinted by permission of Curtis Brown Ltd.

"The Circuit" by Franciso Jimenez. Reprinted by permission of the author.

"All Summer in a Day" by Ray Bradbury. Copyright © 1954, renewed 1982 by Ray Bradbury. Reprinted by permission of Don Congdon Associates, Inc.

Unit 4

"Whatif" from *A Light in the Attic* by Shel Silverstein. Copyright © 1981 by Evil Eye Music, Inc. Used by permission of HarperCollins Publishers.

"My Father Is a Simple Man" is reprinted with permission from the publisher of *The Sadness of Days* by Luis Omar Salinas (Houston: Arte Publico Press–University of Houston, © 1987).

"The All-American Slurp" by Lensey Namioka, copyright © 1987, from *Visions*, ed. by Donald R. Gallo. Reprinted by permission of Lensey Namioka. All rights are reserved by the author.

"A Minor Bird" from *The Poetry of Robert Frost* edited by Edward Connery Lathem. Copyright © 1928, 1969 by Henry Holt and Company. Copyright © 1956 by Robert Frost. Reprinted by permission of Henry Holt and Company LLC.

"Life Doesn't Frighten Me" copyright © 1978 by Maya Angelou, from *And Still I Rise* by Maya Angelou. Used by permission of Random House, Inc.

"Geraldine Moore the Poet" by Toni Cade Bambara. Reprinted by permission of Karma Bambara.

"Same Song" is reprinted with permission from the publisher of *Borders* by Pat Mora (Houston: Arte Publico Press–University of Houston, © 1986).

"Flowers and Freckle Cream" by Elizabeth Ellis. Reprinted by permission of the author.

"maggie and milly and molly and may," copyright © 1956, 1984, 1991 by the Trustees for the E.E. Cummings Trust, from *Complete Poems: 1904–1962* by E.E. Cummings, edited by George J. Firmage. Used by permission of Liveright Publishing Corporation.

From *Daydreamers* by Eloise Greenfield, copyright © 1981 by Eloise Greenfield. Used by permission of Dial Books for Young Readers, a division of Penguin Young Readers Group, a member of Penguin Group (USA) Inc., 345 Hudson Street, New York, NY 10014. All rights reserved.

Unit 5

"The Fan Club" by Rona Maynard. Reprinted by permission of the author.

"What Kids Say About: Bullying." This information was provided by KidsHealth, one of the largest resources online for medically reviewed health information written for parents, kids and teens. For more articles like this one, visit www.KidsHealth.org or www.TeensHealth.org.

"Tuesday of the Other June" by Norma Fox Mazer. Copyright ©1986 by Norma Fox Mazer.

"My Parents" from *Collected Poems: 1928–1985* by Stephen Spender. Copyright ©1934 and renewed ©1962 by Stephen Spender.

"Priscilla and the Wimps" by Richard Peck, from *Sixteen: Short Stories* ed. by Donald R. Gallo. Copyright ©1984 by Richard Peck.

"Don't Let the Bed Bugs Bite" from *I Love You, I Hate You, Get Lost*, by Ellen Conford. Copyright ©1995 by Scholastic, Inc.

From *The New Kid on the Block* by Jack Prelutsky. Copyright © 1984 by Jack Prelutsky. Used by permission of HarperCollins Publishers.

"Bullies in the Park: Elephants vs. Rhinos" by Jon Swartz, from *TIME for Kids*.

"The Bully Battle" by Elizabeth Siris, from *TIME for Kids*.

"El Enano" from *Tales From Silver Lands*, by Charles J. Finger.

Unit 6

"Persephone" reprinted with the permission of Simon & Schuster Books for Young Readers, an imprint of Simon & Schuster's Children's Publishing division from *The Macmillan Book of Greek Gods and Heroes* by Alice Low. Copyright © 1985 Macmillan Publishing Company.

"All Stories Are Anansi's" from *The Hat-Shaking Dance and Other Ashanti Tales from Ghana* by Harold Courlander with Albert Kofi Prempeh, copyright © 1957, 1985 by Harold Courlander. Reprinted by permission of Michael Courlander.

From "The Twelve Labors of Hercules" by Walker Brents. Reprinted by permission of the author.

"Pecos Bill" from *American Tall Tales* by Mary Pope Osborne, copyright © 1991 by Mary Pope Osborne. Illustrations copyright © 1991 by Michael McCurdy. Used by permission of Alfred A. Knopf, an imprint of Random House Children's Books, a division of Random House, Inc. [**For electronic/ digital uses:** Used by permission of Brandt & Hochman Literary Agents, Inc. Any electronic copying or distribution of this text is expressly forbidden.]

"Dragon, Dragon" from *Dragon, Dragon and Other Tales* by John Gardner. Copyright © 1975 by Boskydell Artists, Ltd. Reprinted by permission of Georges Borchardt, Inc., for the Estate of John Gardner.

"Aunt Millicent" by Mary Steele, from *Dream Time*, edited by Toss Gascoigne, Jo Goodman and Margot Tyrell. Copyright © 1989 by Mary Steele. Collection copyright © 1989 by the Children's Book Council of Australia. Reprinted by permission of Houghton Mifflin Co. All rights reserved.

"A Mason-Dixon Memory" by Clifton Davis, adapted from *Reader's Digest*, March 1993. Copyright ©1993 by Mel White.

"The Toad and the Donkey," by Toni Cade Bambara.

"Doc Rabbit, Bruh Fox and Tar Baby" from *The People Could Fly: American Black Folktales* by Virginia Hamilton, illustrated by Leo and Diane Dillon, copyright © 1985 by Virginia Hamilton. Illustrations copyright © 1985 by Leo and Diane Dillon. Used by permission of Alfred A. Knopf, an imprint of Random House Children's Books, a division of Random House, Inc.

"The Sand Castle" by Alma Luz Villanueva. Reprinted by permission of the author.

Unit 7

"US terrorized by radio's 'Men from Mars'" Reprinted with permission of the Associated Press, copyright © 1938. All rights reserved.

From *The Gold Cadillac* by Mildred D. Taylor, copyright © 1987 by Mildred D. Taylor, text. Used by permission of Dial Books for Young Readers, a division of Penguin Young Readers Group, a member of Penguin Group (USA) Inc., 345 Hudson St., New York, NY 10014. All rights reserved.

"Nadia the Willful," copyright © 1983 by Sue Alexander. First appeared in *Nadia the Willful*, published by Alfred A. Knopf. Reprinted by permission of Curtis Brown, Ltd.

"The Bracelet" by Yoshiko Uchida, from *Desert Exile*, copyright © 1982 by Yoshiko Uchida, courtesy of the Bancroft Library, University of California, Berkeley.

"Too Soon a Woman" by Dorothy M. Johnson. Copyright ©1953 and renewed ©1981 by Dorothy M. Johnson.

"President Cleveland, Where Are You?" copyright © 1965 by Robert Cormier, from *Eight Plus One: Stories* by Robert Cormier. Used by permission of Random House Children's Books, a division of Random House, Inc.

"The Shut Out" from *Black Diamond: The Story of the Negro Baseball Leagues* by Patricia C. and Frederick McKissack, Jr. Copyright © 1994 by Patricia C. and Frederick McKissack, Jr.

"The Talking Skull" from *A Pride of African Tales* by Donna Washington, illustrated by James Ransome. Text copyright © 2004 by Donna Washington. Used by permission of HarperCollins Publishers.

From "The Great Fire" by Jim Murphy. Copyright © 1995 by Jim Murphy.

"Letter About the Fire" from The Chicago Historical Society.

Unit 8

From *Novio Boy*, copyright © 1997 by Gary Soto, reprinted by permission of Harcourt, Inc.

"The Reluctant Dragon" by Kenneth Grahame as adapted by Adele Thane from March 1963 © *Plays, the Drama Magazine for Young People and Plays from Famous Stories and Fairy Tales*, copyright © 1967 and © 1997, reprinted with the permission of the publisher Plays/Sterling Partners, Inc., PO Box 600160, Newton, MA 02460.

"The Legend of Damon and Pythias" from *The Bag of Fire and Other Plays* by Fan Kissen. Copyright © 1964 by Houghton Mifflin Company, renewed © 1993 by John Kissen Heaslip. Reprinted by permission of Houghton Mifflin Company. All rights reserved.

"Charlie Johnson" by Joseph K. Smith, reprinted by permission of *Cricket* magazine, December 1998, Vol. 26, No. 4, text © 1998 by Joseph K. Smith.

"The Bully of Barksdale Street" by Eric Alter, January/February *Plays, the Drama Magazine for Young People,* copyright © January 2006, is reprinted with the permission of the publisher Plays/Sterling Partners, Inc., PO Box 600160, Newton, MA 02460.

"Tales of the Tangled Tresses" by Christina Hamlett, January/February *Plays, the Drama Magazine for Young People,* copyright © January 2006, is reprinted with the permission of the publisher Plays/Sterling Partners, Inc., PO Box 600160, Newton, MA 02460.

"Zlateh the Goat" from *Zlateh the Goat and Other Stories* by Isaac Bashevis Singer. Text copyright 1966 © by Isacc Bashevis Singer.

"Baby Hippo Orphan Finds a Friend" by Catherine Fox. *National Geographic Kids News,* March 4, 2004. Reprinted by permission of the National Geographic Society.

From "The Caretaker's Diary" by Stephen Tuei. From lafargeecosystems.com, 2005.

Photography

Cover Imtek Imagineering/Masterfile; 0 Getty Images, 2 (l)Jose Luis Pelaez/CORBIS, (r)Mary Kate Denny/PhotoEdit; 7 Edwin Fotheringham; 8 HEART OF THE CITY © 2004 Mark Tatulli. Dist. By UNIVERSAL PRESS SYNDICATE. Reprinted with permission. All rights reserved; 9 John Evans; 12 CORBIS; 13 (b)Associated Press, OLATHE DAILY NEWS, (t)Paul A. Sauders/CORBIS; 15 (l)Spot Jason Hosking/Zefa/CORBIS, (r)Icon SMI/CORBIS; 16 (l)CORBIS, (r)Images.com/CORBIS; 20 John Paterson/Getty Images; 21 Tom Stewart/CORBIS; 23 Rolf Bruderer; 24 John Paterson/Getty Images; 27 Images.com/CORBIS; 30 Randy Glasbergen; 30 Getty Images; 31 (r)John Evans, (l)PhotoObjects.net; 35 37 38 Dean MacAdam; 42 Glynis Sweeny Time for Kids; 43 (br)Gottfried Stoppel Time for Kids; 44 (tr)Murdo Macleod/CORBIS/Sygma Time for Kids; 45 (tr)Pitchal Frederic/CORBIS/Sygma Time for Kids; 46 (tl)Glynis Sweeny Time for Kids; 48 (c)CLOSE TO HOME 2005 John McPherson. Reprinted with permission of UNIVERSAL PRESS SYNDICATE. All rights reserved; 49 Getty Images; 52 54 Don Smetzer/Stone/Getty Images; 58 59 60 61 62 From BONE ®: THE GREAT COW RACE by Jeff Smith. Copyright © 2005, 1993, 1992 by Jeff Smith. Published by Graphix, an imprint of Scholastic Inc. Reprinted by permission. Scholastic; 68 Images.com/CORBIS; 69 Getty Images; 70 Bettmann/CORBIS; 73 Smithsonian American Art Museum, Washington, DC/Art Resource, NY National Museum of American Art; 74 Smithsonian American Art Museum, Washington, DC/Art Resource, NY National Museum of American Art; 76 Neville Elder/CORBIS; 78 Stockbyte/Creatas; 79 Janine Wiedel Photolibrary/Alamy; 80 Getty Images; 81 Printed by permission by the Norman Rockwell Family Agency. 1926. The Norman Rockwell Family Entities. John Rockwell; 82 Stockbyte/Creatas; 86 AP/Wide World Photos; 88 Getty Images; 89 Gary Stretar, courtesy www.skylinepictures.com. AIM Enterprises; 90 Mark C. Burnett; 91 Ken Chernus/Taxi/Getty Images; 92 Courtesy of Mary Helen Ponce; 93 Brand X Pictures/Creatas; 94 Tim Flach/Getty Images; 95 Zurbaran Galeria/SuperStock; 96 With respect to 1983.208, Rufino Tamayo (Mexican, 1899-1991), Children's Games, 1959, Oil on Canvas; 51 1/4 x 76 3/4 in., The Metropolitan Museum of Art, Gift of Mr. and Mrs. Ralph E. Colin, 1983 (1983.208) Photograph 1984; 97 Getty Images; 98 (l)Getty Images, (r)Tim Flach/Getty Images; 102 Mitch Kezar/Stone/Getty Images; 103 Marc Asnin/CORBIS; 104 The Arab Scribe, Cairo, John Frederick Lewis (1805-76)/Private Collection, Christie's Images/Bridgeman Art Library; 107 CORBIS; 108 109 Eclipse Studios; 114 Taxi/Getty Images; 116 (l)Taxi/Getty Images, (r)WireImageStock/Masterfile; 119 121 122 123 A.Lelia Bundles/Walker Family Collection; 124 (tr)Underwood & Underwood/CORBIS; 125 (bl)A. Lelia Bundles/Walker Family Collection;

126 CALVIN AND HOBBES, Watterson. Dist. By UNIVERSAL PRESS SYNDICATE. Reprinted with permission; 128 Courtesy of Gary Soto; 130–135 Chris Vallo; 138 Courtesy of Nikki Giovanni; 139 140 Images.com/CORBIS; 144 HOME by UNIVERSAL PRESS SYNDICATE. Reprinted with permission. All rights reserved.; 146 CORBIS; 148 L. Barry Hetherington; 150 Associated Press; 151 PhotoObjects.net/Jupiter Images, (b)National Baseball Hall of Fame Library, Cooperstown, NY; 153 The Granger Collection, NY; 154 Bettmann/CORBIS; 155 Bettmann/CORBIS; 157 158 AP/Wide World; 161 Peter Griffith/Masterfile; 162 Peter Griffith/Masterfile; 164 CLEATS Bill Hinds. Dist. by UNIVERSAL PRESS SYNDICATE. Reprinted with permission. All rights reserved; 168 Bettmann/CORBIS; 169 CORBIS; 170 Bettmann/CORBIS; 171 Bachrach/Keystone/Getty Images; 172 (t)Courtesy of the Franklin D. Roosevelt Presidential Library, (b)The Art Archive/Culver Pictures; 173 Thomas D. Mcavoy/Time Magazine, Copyright Time Inc./Time Life Pictures/Getty Images; 174 Topham/The Image Works; 175 Leo Rosenthal/Time Life Pictures/Getty Images; 176 180 Bettmann/CORBIS; 181 (t)CORBIS, (b)Andre Jenny/The Image Works; 182 Bettmann/CORBIS; 188 Patrick McDonnell. Reprinted with permission of King Features Syndicate.; 189 RIchard Hutchings/Photo Researchers; 192 194 Mike Blake/Reuters/NewsCom; 196 (tl)Miriam Berkley; 198 CORBIS; 199 courtesy Judith Ortiz Cofer; 200 Rafael Ferrer; 203 Charles E. Rotkin/CORBIS; 205 Ira Nowinski/CORBIS; 206 UPI/CORBIS; 210 Roger Ressmeyer/CORBIS; 211 Dirk Anschutz/The Image Bank/Getty Images; 212 Erich Lessing/Art Resource, NY; 214 Matthias Kulka/CORBIS; 216 Peter Scoones/Photo Researchers; 217 Images.com/CORBIS; 218 Purestock/SuperStock; 221 Kurt Stier/CORBIS; 222 Rubberball/SuperStock; 226 PhotoAlto/Getty Images; 229 Images.com/CORBIS; 230 Edimedia/CORBIS; 233 Scala/Art Resource, NY.; 234 Dirk Anschutz/The Image Bank/Getty Images, (b)Kurt Stier/CORBIS; 238 Frank Krahmer/Zefa/CORBIS; 240 H. Reinhard/Zefa/CORBIS; 242 Getty Images; 243 Tipp Howell/Taxi/Getty Images; 246 247 Eclipse Studios; 252 Dave Bartruff/CORBIS; 257 Hulton Archive; 258 Hampton University Museum, Hampton, VA/ Elizabeth Catlett/Licensed by VAGA, New York, NY; 259 file photo 260 POOCH CAFE 2005 Dist. by UNIVERSAL PRESS SYNDICATE. Reprinted with permission; 261 John Evans; 262 Courtesy of Richard Durban; 264 Taxi/Getty Images; 266 Taxi/Getty Images; 270 Getty Images; 271 Stone/Getty; 272 Michael Alberstat/Masterfile; 275 Digital Image The Museum of Modern Art/Licensed by SCALA / Art Resource, NY; 276 Getty Images; 283 Getty Images; 286 288 Gaslight Advertising Archives; 290 courtesy Blue Sky Press; 292 Rommel/Masterfile; 293 Pat Doyle/CORBIS; 295 Getty Images; 296 Rommel/Masterfile; 298 Calvin & Hobbes Watterson. Dist. By UNIVERSAL PRESS SYNDICATE; 299 John Evans; 303 (t)Courtesy of Long Beach Unified School District, (b)Courtesy of Allen Lichtenstein; 306 M. Toussant/Liaison/Getty Images; 308 file photo; 310 Dave Robertson/Masterfile; 311 Andrew Judd/Masterfile; 312 file photo; 318 CALVIN & HOBBES Watterson. Dist. By UNIVERSAL PRESS SYNDICATE. Reprinted with permission. All rights reserved.; 319 Rubberball/SuperStock; 323 324 Jose Luis Pelaez/CORBIS; 326 Jason Stemple; 328 The Image Bank/Getty Images; 331 Brooklyn Museum of Art/CORBIS; 332 David Job/Getty Images; 334 The Image Bank/Getty Images; 339 Masterfile; 340 Mark Burnett; 342 Walter H. Hodge/Peter Arnold, Inc.; 343 Gerald Peters Gallery, Santa Fe, NM; 345 Tom Stewart/CORBIS; 346 San Jose Mercury News photographer: Eugene Louie; 347 Ed and Chris Kumler; 348 Trabajadores, 1950. Castera Bazile. Oil on canvas, 27 x 19Z\x in. Private collection.; 349 Despedida, 1941. Hector Poleo. Oil on linen, 60 x 50 cm. Private collection.; 350 Index Stock Imagery; 354 Masterfile; 354 Eising Food Photography/Stockfood America; 358 (l)Satelight/Gamma Liaison, (r)Michael Prince/CORBIS; 359 Freeman Patterson/Masterfile; 360 Trinette Reed/CORBIS; 362 file photo; 363 Brooklyn Museum of Art/CORBIS; 370 Catherine Karnow/CORBIS; 372 (l) NOVASTOCK/PhotoEdit, (r)Stone/Getty Images; 375 Shel Silverstein; 376 (c)CALVIN AND HOBBES, Watterson. Dist. By UNIVERSAL PRESS SYNDICATE. Reprinted with permission. All rights reserved.; 377 CORBIS; 380 382 Jose Luis Pelaez/CORBIS; 384 Courtesy Lensey Namioka-photo by Don Perkins; 386 CORBIS; 388 Mary Kate Denny/Getty Images; 391 (l)JupiterImages/Comstock, (r)Dale Kennington/SuperStock; 392 Images.com/CORBIS; 394 (l)Arthur Beck/CORBIS